TOTAL METS

David Ferry

Total Mets

The Definitive Encyclopedia of the New York Mets' First Half-Century

Foreword by Ed Kranepool

TRIUMPH
BOOKS

This book is available in quantity at special discounts for your group or organization. For further information, contact:

Triumph Books LLC
814 North Franklin Street
Chicago, Illinois 60610
(312) 939-3330 I Fax (312) 663-3557
www.triumphbooks.com

Printed in U.S.A.
ISBN: 978-1-60078-661-7
Editorial production by Prologue Publishing Services, LLC
All photos courtesy of AP Images unless otherwise noted

To my wife, Jacki, for her unwavering patience as I wrote this book. She has dealt with my mood swings that are often the byproduct of the team's success, and has coped with my obsession with a ballclub I have followed for over 40 years.

And to my daughter, Janie, who learned to recognize the Mets logo and interlocking "NY" before her second birthday. May she root for the Mets with the same passion I did as a kid.

Contents

Foreword

October 16, 1969. I'm in the dugout as Orioles second baseman Davey Johnson steps to the plate with the Mets just one out away from their first championship. For me, after so many years of finishing on the bottom, you're now on top of the world. You expect to win at this point.

Jerry Koosman is the pitcher, and a fly ball goes into left field, and it's like the end of a dream. That's the culmination of your whole career. When you start out in baseball, your one goal in life is to be in a World Series. With the early Mets, when you finish with 100 games in the loss column for seven or eight years, you think you're never going to get an opportunity. It was a miracle year for us.

Flip the calendar back seven years. I had no young players around me when I signed in 1962. My roommate that year was Frank Thomas. He was 35 years of age, a great guy with a family of five. But I was 17 years old and had nothing in common with him. I couldn't even go out and drink with the guys, so it was a lonely existence on the road until we started bringing up our own players, the Swobodas, the McGraws, guys that I could pal around with.

Meanwhile, the fans were tremendous. In the beginning years, they were there to have fun. The Mets were a comedy act to them. These were the Dodgers and Giants fans who loved National League baseball. They forgave all the mistakes that were being made. But as a player, winning is the most important thing. This is what the culmination of your career is all about: championships. When you lose a game, you miss a popup or make an error, there's nothing funny about that.

Casey Stengel was a good manager for the early years because he took the pressure off the players through his theatrics with the press. But you were still the one who was looking like a fool out there.

Casey was a bright guy. I loved playing for him because he wasn't there to ridicule players. He wasn't there to maliciously point out mistakes. He'd point out what you were doing wrong so you would benefit from it, and he loved the young players. He loved developing those guys.

At the All-Star break, when you were 30 games out and should be working out for three days, he'd come up with a line like, "Fellas, I'm giving you three days off. Take your records with you!" Once you analyzed it, he was saying, "Take your records. You're in last place." That was great.

Casey was perfect for the Mets. He was part of an era, but I'm glad we moved forward to the championship years. Unfortunately, we lost Gil Hodges two years after we won the World Series. We might have won another couple of World Series with Gil because we had the best pitching in baseball. We should have won more pennants but didn't, and then we started to go in the opposite direction.

The ballclub was sold in 1980, and the owners have had a little bit of a good time since. They won the World Series in 1986 and the pennant in 2000, but now they're almost back where they started. They're struggling now, but let's hope they find some magic somewhere. I don't know if you can ever rekindle '69 because that's a once-in-a-lifetime happening, but we'll see.

The '69 Mets were a very close ballclub. We traveled together, we played together, and we socialized together. We still do the same thing today, although not in the abundance in which we did. In '69, we'd go out after a game and there might be 15 or 18 guys in the same place, so if they threw a grenade in there, they'd kill the ballclub! When we were out, we were out together. We had a good time together, and that carried forward.

To this day I still see Art Shamsky, Bud Harrelson, Ed Charles, and Joe Pignatano quite often. The New York guys are still here, and we still see each other. This little core of five or six guys still do some things socially together, and when the team has a reunion, then we get the whole ballclub from around the country. And it's good to see them. You rehash the old war stories—you become a better player the longer you're out of the game! You remember all the positive things.

Unfortunately, we've lost some guys. I was close to Tug McGraw, who was my roommate. I was close to Donn Clendenon. These were guys with whom we really had some things in common. We weren't just a ballclub. We weren't just a group of guys who played together during the season and then disappeared, which was the case with some of the other clubs I played on.

I was there for the good, the bad, and the ugly of the Mets, and we went from the outhouse to the penthouse overnight in '69. Being young, you always have dreams, and they kept you in a positive frame. Obviously, winning is contagious, and so is losing.

Before 1969, after a while you're getting beaten down. Every day you have a negative statistic. The press doesn't write about the positive things. You might get two or three hits, and the next thing you know you still lose the ballgame, so there's really nothing to write about in a positive vein. After a while, the press just starts browbeating you. It affects you, and I think by the end of 1967 we had to have a change and acquire a new manager. Gil came back to New York and was a different type of personality; very strong, a very good leader, a military guy from the Marines who wouldn't stand for any negativity.

Gil set the tone in spring training of 1968 as he weeded out some people and molded the club around pitching and defense. The next thing you know we started to believe in his theory, and he didn't play games. He had one set of rules for 25 players, and you either played it his way or you hit the highway. With him, this was the way it had to be played, kind of like: "You're going to play under my managing and you have no choice. If you don't like it, we're going to get rid of you."

I wonder how my career might have turned out had I played for another team. Quite honestly, I think it might have been easier for me in the major leagues. When you start out your career on a bad ballclub, everything is centered around yourself. I was a young bonus player, and the anticipation of me coming in and leading the ballclub to the Promised Land doesn't happen. One player is not enough. Baseball is a team game, and they pitch around you and put tremendous pressure on you.

I did well at the beginning, then I struggled, and I think it took its toll. I think if you put yourself in a better lineup, you develop faster, you become a better player for it, your career is greater, and it's more fun.

However, I was fortunate enough to have played in my hometown: New York. It's the greatest sports town around. If you can play in New York and have a career here, they remember you for life. They still talk 40 years after the fact about our winning in '69 as if it were yesterday. I can't remember what I did three weeks ago! People still want to relate to me how the '69 Mets were the highlight of all of their lives. That season was followed by millions and millions of people across the country, and it's something that they'll never forget.

There are other World Series teams that you forget three years later, but people just remember the '69 Mets. It was a happening. The world was in turmoil, and the country had problems, but we won the pennant and everyone was there to enjoy it. Everyone was following us. Everyone knew about it.

It's great to walk around Manhattan these days. I have so many people who still recognize me, which is surprising since I'm a little grayer now. They still remember you. They yell at you: doormen, bus drivers. It's crazy. It's the common guy who's a Mets fan. The executives watch the Yankees. The common guy watches the Mets.

And when you're in Manhattan, people still love you. It's a good feeling.

—Ed Kranepool

Introduction

Before you read any further, I must provide full disclosure and admit to being a Mets fan since 1971, which means I have followed both the greatness and the nonsense this franchise has bestowed upon its fan base for more than 40 of the team's 50-season history. Is it a proud, rich heritage that's on par with the Cardinals, Dodgers, Red Sox, or Yankees? Not even close, and that doesn't matter to Mets fans.

The Mets' tradition is one of quirkiness, and all aspects of the club's history were proudly acknowledged as we bid farewell to Shea Stadium on September 28, 2008. The team asked Tom Seaver and Mike Piazza to serve as batterymates for the final pitch at the ballpark, recognizing two windows of greatness in Mets history. The Mets trotted out Jerry Koosman, Dwight Gooden, Darryl Strawberry, Keith Hernandez, Willie Mays, Rusty Staub, and Al Leiter among dozens of former players to take their final bows in the Stadium. But they also brought back George Theodore, a man who hit .219 while appearing in only 105 games over two seasons with the Mets. Theodore—and the numerous former Mets of his ilk—is just as important to the fabric of the team's history as any of the Mets' two Cy Young recipients, five 20-game winners, or three home run champions. The "Theodore Factor" is what sets Mets fans apart from the rest of baseball's ardent supporters, and I hope to have captured such spirit in this book.

The fan base has the ability to appreciate the team's entire history, warts and all. I endured seven consecutive horrible seasons as a Mets fan from 1977 to 1983, yet still look back with fondness on a 1980 campaign in which the team, bereft of starting pitching and lacking any semblance of power hitting, managed to stay in contention through mid-August. This was a ballclub that eventually lost 95 frigging games, yet one of my biggest thrills as a Mets fan occurred at Shea on June 14 of that season, when Steve Henderson belted a walk-off, three-run homer to cap a five-run ninth in a 7–6 thriller against the Giants. As a Mets fan, you learned early to appreciate the little victories as much as the big ones.

The 1980 season means almost as much to me as 1986, and I have attempted to write this book with that in mind. Every Mets fan has his or her list of special moments in club history, and I have tried to balance the good and the bad. If you peruse chapter one, Year-by-Year Recaps, you will notice I have written of the 1979 season (99 losses) with the same detail in which I have chronicled the 1985 campaign (98 wins). Again, Mets fans take the good with the bad.

The player biography section features 50 different Mets. Many of these players granted interviews for the book, while other bios were written with help from the vast archives of *The New York Times* and Google books. My policy with player interviews was to allow each subject to make his own "final edit" of his biography to ensure accuracy and provide a comfort level that allowed him to speak freely without the possibility of seeing his quotes "taken out of context." Biographies of all 917 Mets players were completed last October, but the vast word count made it impossible to include each one in this book. There are plans to publish each of these bios in a separate book in the future.

I set out to produce the type of Mets book that I would want to read, one that featured a good mix of biographies, year-by-year accounts, playoff recaps, and statistics.

The Shea Stadium scoreboard

I began the project in July 2007, when the Mets enjoyed a four-game lead in the National League East and appeared on their way to winning a second straight division crown for the first time in team history. Four years later, the team was in rebuilding mode.

But Mets fans are used to the ebbs and flows of the franchise. We may curse the present, but we look forward to the future while embracing our past. Hopefully, this encyclopedia will allow fans to recollect and appreciate past achievements as the team strives toward greater accomplishments.

Dave Ferry
2012

TOTAL METS

Year-by-Year Recaps

1962

NATIONAL LEAGUE

Team	W	L	PCT	GB	AVG	ERA
Giants	103	62	.624	—	.278	3.79
Dodgers	102	63	.618	1.0	.268	3.62
Reds	98	64	.605	3.5	.270	3.65
Pirates	93	68	.578	8.0	.268	3.37
Braves	86	76	.531	15.5	.252	3.68
Cardinals	84	78	.519	17.5	.271	3.55
Phillies	81	80	.503	20.0	.260	4.28
Colt 45s	64	96	.400	36.5	.246	3.83
Cubs	59	103	.364	42.5	.253	4.54
Mets	40	120	.250	60.5	.240	5.04

Mets president George Weiss built an Opening Day roster full of names familiar to New York National League fans. The ballclub included former Dodgers Gil Hodges, Don Zimmer, Charlie Neal, Roger Craig, and Clem Labine. Hodges, Zimmer, and Neal were former National League All-Stars, as were original Mets Frank Thomas, Richie Ashburn, and Gus Bell. Ed Bouchee finished second in the NL Rookie of the Year voting just five years earlier. This would have been a formidable lineup—in 1957. But most of these former All-Stars were at or near the end of their careers.

The pitching was threadbare. Roger Craig was one of the Mets' top two pitchers that season despite being miscast as a starter. Craig had been a spot-starter and long reliever before 1962, and received MVP consideration after going 11–5 with a 2.06 ERA for the champion Dodgers in 1959.

Al Jackson proved to be the ace of the staff after failing to catch on with the Pirates. Jackson tossed the Mets' only complete-game shutouts in 1962 (4) and led the team with a 4.40 ERA.

No fewer than 14 pitchers started games for the '62 Amazin's, a team that ended the season with 24-game, 20-game, 19-game, and 17-game losers.

"We had absolutely no pitching," remembered Mets supersub Rod Kanehl, who developed a fan following almost immediately. "And we had no bullpen. We had one of the finest relief pitchers in the National League, Roger Craig, as a starter. He would have set all kinds of relief records had he been able to be used as a reliever. Roger was a good five-inning pitcher, had a good pickoff move, and he had a good sinker/slider. He could come in and get a ground ball, and, boom, it was over. He was perfect for relief. But we had to use him as a starter."[1]

Although the pitching was unable to keep up with the mediocre hitting, the fielding was even worse. The Mets committed 210 errors, 17 more than the NL's second-worst collection of fielders. The glove work contributed to 147 unearned runs, nearly one per game.

The poor play made manager Casey Stengel even more valuable from a PR standpoint, and he played the media like Isaac Stern played the fiddle. The 72-year-old former Yankees skipper knew he had a bad team and would put the focus on himself when things went poorly. Which meant the focus was often on him.

Casey had little problem promoting his players, even when the player's name would escape him.

"And in right field we have this here fellow who can hit with power and played at Cincinnati and you know he does good with his arm and has eight children. And he hits the ball off the wall and rings the bell—and that's his name, Gus Bell."[2]

Stengel had two Bob Millers on the team and kept their names straight by calling one of them "Nelson." One time, Stengel told pitching coach Red Ruffing to warm up Nelson. Ruffing knew there was no Nelson on the roster, but yelled for Nelson to warm up. Sure enough, the right Bob Miller got off the bench and began his warm-up tosses.

There actually was one Nelson on the team, Mets broadcaster Lindsey Nelson. Stengel would call him "Lindsey Miller," according to catcher Joe Pignatano.

Stengel would throw "my writers," as he called them, a good line that might prevent a player from absorbing heaps of abuse in the papers. He dubbed them "The Amazin' Mets," a moniker that has stuck to this day. Put him on the rubber chicken circuit and he was pure gold, pitching his Mets without shame.

"If you want rapid advancement, go play for the Mets," Stengel told a gathering at a 1962 luncheon honoring Pirates skipper Danny Murtaugh. "We've got the bonus money. We'll even buy you a glove. So join us, take the bonus money. Play a year or two. Then you can go back to school."[3]

One player willing to take the Mets' bonus money was Ed Kranepool, then a 17-year-old slugger out of James Monroe High School in the Bronx. He signed his first pro contract in the spring of 1962 and was playing for the Mets by September 22. That will tell you what kind of talent the Mets had in the farm system and at the major league level.

Karl Ehrhardt, the Mets fan known as the "Sign Man," holds up a "Met Power" sign during the eighth inning of Game 3 of the 1969 World Series.

A vendor serves the Mets' newest fans at the Polo Grounds as the team faces the San Francisco Giants on June 1, 1962.

Before Kranepool tried his hand at first base, the Mets had Marv Throneberry, who quickly became a cult hero and the darling of Mets fans seeking a poster boy for this bumbling ballclub. Throneberry needed just 97 games at first base to pile up 17 errors, many coming in untimely situations. He was one of the few legitimate power threats in the lineup, finishing second on the team with 16 homers and fourth with 49 RBIs. But he usually altered a game's outcome with his glove rather than his bat.

Throneberry didn't even need a glove to make a memorable miscue. He laced a would-be two-run triple that sparked a Mets rally in an eventual one-run loss. However, he was called out for missing first base while rounding the bag. When Stengel went out to argue the call, he was intercepted as he neared the first-base foul line. "Forget it, Case," he was told. "He missed second, too."

Throneberry wasn't the only Met ready to provide comic relief, or disbelief, on the field. There had been times during the season when center fielder Richie Ashburn and shortstop Elio Chacon would collide while running down popups. Ashburn finally asked someone how to say "I got it" in Spanish as a way to avoid another mishap with the Spanish-speaking Chacon.

Eventually, Ashburn had a chance to show off his new language skills, yelling, "Yo lo tengo," loud enough for Chacon to avoid a collision. Problem was, left fielder Frank Thomas didn't understand Spanish and slammed into Ashburn.

After Thomas muffed another play in left, Throneberry was said to have asked him, "What are you trying to do, steal my fans?"

There were three early signs that this wouldn't be an easy season. First, 16 Mets were stuck in an elevator at the Chase Hotel in St. Louis a day before the scheduled season opener with the Cardinals. Second, the season opener was postponed by rain. Third, the home opener would be played on Friday the 13th.

The Mets wasted no time showing their new fans what would come, allowing 16 hits and committing three errors that led to four unearned runs in a season-opening 11–4 loss to the Cardinals. They dropped the home opener as well—and the seven games that followed—before Jay Hook and the Mets rolled to a 9–1 win at Pittsburgh.

Stengel was elated following the victory. "Hook's going to pitch every day," he said. "He will pitch the next hundred games so I can win the pennant. That damn [losing] streak cost us the pennant. We might win the next 20 in a row."[4]

The Mets actually had extended success near the end of April and early May, going 12–10 following their season-opening nine-game losing streak. They traveled to Houston following a doubleheader sweep that left them 12–19. But the Mets' charter plane was delayed by several hours before fog rolled into Houston, forcing the team to land in Dallas. The Mets finally arrived at their intended destination and crept into their hotel around 8:30 AM. Stengel, who usually could—and would—stay up later than most of his ballplayers, was more than ready for some shuteye.

"If anyone wants me, tell 'em I'm being embalmed," Casey told traveling secretary Lou Niss.

Little did Stengel know the team would immediately embark on a 17-game losing streak that night, a skid that remains a team record. Thirteen of those losses came against the Dodgers and Giants, whose departure from New York made the Mets possible.

Hook again would serve as the "stopper," ending the streak with a 4–3 win over the Cubs on June 6. Losing skids of 13 and 11 games would follow before the Mets eventually chalked up their 120th setback in the season finale, setting a modern major league record.

Weiss couldn't find a way to stop the losing while his veteran ballclub continued to break down. Hodges appeared in just 54 games due to a bad knee. Bell, Zimmer, Jim Marshall, and Hobie Landrith started the Mets' first-ever game but were all traded by May 20. There were no prospects in the minors and little help coming from major league general managers.

Harry Chiti was one of Weiss' most memorable transactions that season. Chiti was acquired by Cleveland for a player to be named on April 26. The "player to be named" became Chiti himself after he batted .195 during his 50 days as a Met.

Ashburn would be named the Mets' Most Valuable Player. "MVP on the worst team ever? Just how did they mean that?" asked Ashburn.

Throneberry earned the Mets' Good Guy Award from the media, an honor that prompted another great Stengel quip: "I don't know if you should hand it to him or mail it to him. If you hand it to him, he's liable to drop it."

Craig summed up his Mets career best. "The losses don't bother me," he said. "It's the non-winning that kills you."[5]

Craig's misery would continue in 1963.

1962 Mets Statistics

Hitting	G	AB	R	H	2B	3B	HR	RBI	BB	SO	BA	OBP	SLG	SB	CS	GDP	HP	SH	SF	IBB
Richie Ashburn	135	389	60	119	7	3	7	28	81	39	.306	.424	.393	12	7	4	0	1	2	2
Gus Bell	30	101	8	15	2	0	1	6	10	7	.149	.221	.198	0	1	2	0	2	2	0
Ed Bouchee	50	87	7	14	2	0	3	10	18	17	.161	.302	.287	0	0	2	0	0	1	2
Chris Cannizzaro	59	133	9	32	2	1	0	9	19	26	.241	.335	.271	1	1	5	1	1	2	1
Elio Chacon	118	368	49	87	10	3	2	27	76	64	.236	.368	.296	12	7	13	1	3	1	3
Harry Chiti	15	41	2	8	1	0	0	0	1	8	.195	.233	.220	0	0	2	1	0	0	0
Joe Christopher	119	271	36	66	10	2	6	32	35	42	.244	.338	.362	11	3	4	4	3	1	0
Choo Choo Coleman	55	152	24	38	7	2	6	17	11	24	.250	.303	.441	2	4	1	1	1	1	2
Cliff Cook	40	112	12	26	6	1	2	9	4	34	.232	.275	.357	1	0	0	3	0	1	0
John DeMerit	14	16	3	3	0	0	1	1	2	4	.188	.278	.375	0	0	0	0	0	0	0
Sammy Drake	25	52	2	10	0	0	0	7	6	12	.192	.276	.192	0	0	0	0	1	0	1
Joe Ginsberg	2	5	0	0	0	0	0	0	0	1	.000	.000	.000	0	0	0	0	0	0	0
Rick Herrscher	35	50	5	11	3	0	1	6	5	11	.220	.291	.340	0	0	0	0	0	0	0
Jm Hickman	140	392	54	96	18	2	13	46	47	96	.245	.328	.401	4	4	9	3	7	3	2
Gil Hodges	54	127	15	32	1	0	9	17	15	27	.252	.331	.472	0	0	4	0	0	0	1
Rod Kanehl	133	351	52	87	10	2	4	27	23	36	.248	.296	.322	8	6	7	1	3	0	2
Ed Kranepool	3	6	0	1	1	0	0	0	0	1	.167	.167	.333	0	0	0	0	0	0	0
Hobie Landrith	23	45	6	13	3	0	1	7	8	3	.289	.389	.422	0	0	0	0	0	1	0
Felix Mantilla	141	466	54	128	17	4	11	59	37	51	.275	.330	.399	3	1	11	5	3	7	0
Jim Marshall	17	32	6	11	1	0	3	4	3	6	.344	.400	.656	0	0	0	0	0	0	0
Charlie Neal	136	508	59	132	14	9	11	58	56	90	.260	.330	.388	2	8	17	0	9	6	1
Joe Pignatano	27	56	2	13	2	0	0	2	2	11	.232	.259	.268	0	0	3	0	0	0	0
Bobby Gene Smith	8	22	1	3	0	1	0	2	3	2	.136	.240	.227	0	1	1	0	0	0	0
Sammy Taylor	68	158	12	35	4	2	3	20	23	17	.222	.323	.329	0	0	4	2	0	3	1
Frank Thomas	156	571	69	152	23	3	34	94	48	95	.266	.329	.496	2	1	15	8	0	6	4
Marv Throneberry	116	357	29	87	11	3	16	49	34	83	.244	.306	.426	1	3	7	0	1	4	4
Gene Woodling	81	190	18	52	8	1	5	24	24	22	.274	.353	.405	1	0	5	1	0	3	3
Don Zimmer	14	52	3	4	1	0	0	1	3	10	.077	.127	.096	0	1	1	0	0	0	0
Pitchers																				
Craig Anderson	50	32	2	3	0	0	0	0	1	12	.094	.121	.094	0	0	0	0	3	0	0
Galen Cisco	4	7	0	0	0	0	0	0	0	1	.000	.000	.000	0	0	1	0	0	0	0
Roger Craig	42	76	1	4	0	0	0	2	4	33	.053	.111	.053	0	0	1	1	4	0	0
Ray Daviault	36	15	0	1	0	0	0	0	1	8	.067	.125	.067	0	0	0	0	0	0	0
Larry Foss	5	1	0	0	0	0	0	0	0	0	.000	.000	.000	0	0	0	0	0	0	0
Dave Hillman	13	1	0	0	0	0	0	0	0	1	.000	.000	.000	0	0	0	0	0	0	0
Jay Hook	41	69	6	14	0	0	0	5	8	24	.203	.286	.203	0	0	0	0	6	0	0
Willard Hunter	27	13	1	3	0	0	0	0	0	7	.231	.231	.231	0	0	0	0	0	0	0
Al Jackson	44	73	5	5	2	0	0	2	2	27	.068	.093	.096	0	0	3	0	6	0	0
Sherman Jones	8	7	0	3	0	0	0	1	0	2	.429	.429	.429	0	0	0	0	0	0	0
Ken Mackenzie	42	12	0	1	0	0	0	1	0	6	.083	.083	.083	0	0	0	0	1	0	0
Bob G. Miller	17	1	0	0	0	0	0	0	0	0	.000	.000	.000	0	0	0	0	0	0	0
Bob L. Miller	40	41	2	5	0	1	0	0	1	17	.122	.143	.171	0	0	0	0	2	0	0
Vinegar Bend Mizell	17	8	1	2	0	0	0	0	0	2	.250	.250	.250	0	0	0	0	0	0	0
Herb Moford	7	4	0	1	0	0	0	0	0	1	.250	.250	.250	0	0	0	0	0	0	0
Bob Moorhead	38	22	2	1	0	0	0	0	5	11	.045	.222	.045	0	0	0	0	1	0	0
TOTAL	161	5492	617	1318	166	40	139	573	616	991	.240	.317	.361	59	48	122	32	58	44	29

Pitching	G	ERA	W–L	SV	GS	GF	CG	SHO	IP	H	R	ER	HR	BB	SO	BFP	WP	HBP	BK	IBB
Craig Anderson	50	5.35	3–17	4	14	20	2	0	131.1	150	108	78	18	63	62	617	8	5	0	2
Galen Cisco	4	3.26	1–1	0	2	0	1	0	19.1	15	7	7	0	11	13	87	1	3	0	2
Roger Craig	42	4.51	10–24	3	33	8	13	0	233.1	261	133	117	35	70	118	998	7	7	2	3
Ray Daviault	36	6.22	1–5	0	3	14	0	0	81.0	92	64	56	14	48	51	377	6	4	1	1
Larry Foss	5	4.63	0–1	0	1	2	0	0	11.2	17	6	6	2	7	3	57	0	1	0	0
Dave Hillman	13	6.32	0–0	1	1	4	0	0	15.2	21	12	11	5	8	8	76	0	1	0	0
Jay Hook	37	4.84	8–19	0	34	2	13	0	213.2	230	137	115	31	71	113	938	9	8	0	4
Willard Hunter	27	5.57	1–6	0	6	6	1	0	63.0	67	41	39	9	34	40	287	3	1	0	0
Al Jackson	36	4.40	8–20	0	33	2	12	4	231.1	244	132	113	16	78	118	997	9	5	0	5
Sherman Jones	8	7.71	0–4	0	3	1	0	0	23.1	31	22	20	3	8	11	110	3	2	1	2
Clem Labine	3	11.25	0–0	0	0	3	0	0	4.0	5	6	5	1	1	2	19	0	0	0	0
Ken Mackenzie	42	4.95	5–4	1	1	16	0	0	80.0	87	47	44	10	34	51	355	0	3	0	3
Bob G. Miller	17	7.08	2–2	1	0	12	0	0	20.1	24	16	16	2	8	8	88	1	1	0	0
Bob L. Miller	33	4.89	1–12	0	21	7	1	0	143.2	146	98	78	20	62	91	646	12	6	1	2
Vinegar Bend Mizell	17	7.34	0–2	0	2	9	0	0	38.0	48	35	31	10	25	15	182	3	1	0	0
Herb Moford	7	7.20	0–1	0	0	1	0	0	15.0	21	15	12	3	1	5	69	2	0	0	0
Bob Moorhead	38	4.53	0–2	0	7	11	0	0	105.1	118	69	53	13	42	63	462	7	4	0	4
TOTAL	161	5.04	40–120	10	161	118	43	4	1430.0	1577	948	801	192	571	772	6365	71	52	5	28

1963

Team	W	L	PCT	GB	BA	ERA
Dodgers	99	63	.611	–	.251	2.85
Cardinals	93	69	.574	6.0	.271	3.32
Giants	88	74	.543	11.0	.258	3.35
Phillies	87	75	.537	12.0	.252	3.09
Reds	86	76	.531	13.0	.246	3.29
Braves	84	78	.519	15.0	.244	3.27
Cubs	82	80	.506	17.0	.238	3.08
Pirates	74	88	.457	25.0	.250	3.10
Colt 45s	66	96	.407	33.0	.220	3.44
Mets	51	111	.315	48.0	.219	4.12

It isn't often a team finishes 60 games under .500 and actually shows improvement over the previous season. There were signs of progress, although it was provided by one rookie and an otherwise different group of aging veterans and discard pitchers.

The Mets shaved a game off their 1962 season-opening nine-game losing streak, beginning the season 0–8 before beating the Braves. They won 11 more games than in the previous year and lowered their ERA by nearly a run a game (5.04 to 4.12), all while committing the same 210 errors they racked up in '62.

George Weiss once again grabbed a piece of New York baseball nostalgia, buying outfielder Duke Snider from the Dodgers a week before the season opener. Snider hit his 400th career homer in '63 and committed just two errors in 106 games in the outfield. He would be the Mets' lone All-Star representative.

Weiss may have made his best acquisition right after the 1962 season, sending cash to the Milwaukee Braves for Ron Hunt. Hunt finished second to Pete Rose in 1963 NL Rookie of the Year voting after batting .272 with 10 homers and 42 RBIs. Hunt committed 26 errors at second base but already was showing a willingness to sacrifice his body to get on base. He was hit by 13 pitches in 1963 on his way to what would be a major league–record 243.

Eighteen-year-old Ed Kranepool also got a chance to show his stuff, although he often looked overmatched while hitting .209.

The starting rotation was deeper than the 1962 staff with the addition of Tracy Stallard and Carl Willey. Galen Cisco made 17 starts in '63 after being acquired from the Red Sox in September 1962.

But the hitting, which provided several highlights during an otherwise bleak and comical 1962 season, was futile. Marv Throneberry hit just .143 in 14 at-bats after batting .244 with 16 homers the previous year. Throneberry was shipped to the minors in May and never played in the majors again.

Gil Hodges was traded to Washington in May and became the Senators' manager until the end of the 1967 season, when he would return to the Mets as their skipper. Richie Ashburn retired following the '62 season, leaving the Mets without his .300 average, decent wheels, and solid glove in center.

The Mets finished the '63 season among the bottom three in every major offensive category except walks, hitting .219 with 96 homers and just 501 runs scored.

Acquired in the Hodges deal, Jim Piersall showed up one homer shy of 100 for his major league career. It took 30 games as a Met, but he finally smacked his milestone homer and made it memorable, circling the bases backward after hitting a shot off future Mets pitcher and manager Dallas Green on June 23. He had three hits that game but was batting only .194 as a Met when he was released a month later.

The Mets played decent baseball for about three weeks following their 0–8 start, going 13–7 during a stretch that began with a four-game sweep of the Braves at the Polo Grounds. They also swept a two-game set at Wrigley and won three of three versus the Phillies.

A 14-inning win over the Cubs put the Mets' record 29–45 on June 26, 1½ games ahead of the cellar-dwelling Colt 45s. Two days later New York began a 15-game losing streak that would put them in last place for good. The Mets were able to redecorate the basement while going 4–25 in July.

It was a very tough season for Roger Craig, who went the distance on a seven-hitter to beat the Dodgers 4–2 on April 29. He lost his next 18 decisions until August 9, when Jim Hickman hit a grand slam in the bottom of the ninth to give Craig and the Mets a 7–3 win over the Cubs.

Another bright spot in the season came in a game that didn't count. The Mets played their first-ever Mayor's Trophy game against the Yankees, drawing over 50,000 in the Bronx. The Yankees had just completed a game that afternoon, and manager Ralph Houk put his bench players in the lineup while Mets skipper Casey Stengel used his best players, along with Jay Hook and Willey on the mound. Tim Harkness delivered a two-run single in a five-run fifth that sent the Mets to a 6–2 win over the Bombers.

One of the goofier losses came August 27 at Pittsburgh after the Mets carried a 1–0 lead into the bottom of the ninth. Grover Powell and Galen Cisco had combined to three-hit the Pirates until Cisco issued a one-out walk to Ducky Schofield. Manny Mota stepped to the plate and hit a bouncer that eluded Cisco's glove—and the middle-infielders—for a single. Center fielder Duke Carmel charged the ball and let it glance off his glove for an error. Right fielder Joe Christopher grabbed the carom and tried to nail Schofield at the plate, but the ball went somewhere between home and third for the second throwing error on the play. Mota continued to third base and ignored a stop sign from the third-base coach. Cisco fired the ball to the plate, in plenty of time to get Mota. But in the confusion, catcher Jesse Gonder had wandered into foul territory as he awaited the throw. He made a swipe tag but was nowhere near the plate, allowing Mota to score the winning run in a 2–1 Pirates victory.

The Mets finally said good-bye to the Polo Grounds, one year behind schedule. Shea Stadium originally was supposed to open in 1963, but construction problems kept the Mets in the Giants' old ballpark another season. On September 18, just 1,752 fans paid to see the Mets lose to the Phillies 5–1 in the final game at the Polo Grounds. Despite their record, the Mets finished fourth in the National League in home attendance, drawing 1,080,108, nearly 400,000 more than the Giants drew in their final season at the Horseshoe.

1963 Mets Statistics

Hitting	G	AB	R	H	2B	3B	HR	RBI	BB	SO	BA	OBP	SLG	SB	CS	GDP	HP	SH	SF	IBB
Larry Burright	41	100	9	22	2	1	0	3	8	25	.220	.291	.260	1	0	0	2	0	0	1
Chris Cannizzaro	16	33	4	8	1	0	0	4	1	8	.242	.257	.273	0	0	0	0	0	1	0
Duke Carmel	47	149	11	35	5	3	3	18	16	37	.235	.307	.369	2	2	0	0	1	1	2
Joe Christopher	64	149	19	33	5	1	1	8	13	21	.221	.295	.289	1	3	2	3	2	1	0
Choo Choo Coleman	106	247	22	44	0	0	3	9	24	49	.178	.264	.215	5	5	4	5	1	0	3
Cliff Cook	50	106	9	15	2	1	2	8	12	37	.142	.229	.236	0	1	1	0	2	0	4
Chico Fernandez	58	145	12	29	6	0	1	9	9	30	.200	.244	.262	3	0	0	0	1	2	2
Jesse Gonder	42	126	12	38	4	0	3	15	6	25	.302	.328	.405	1	2	3	0	0	2	0
Pumpsie Green	17	54	8	15	1	2	1	5	12	13	.278	.409	.426	0	2	1	0	0	0	0
Tim Harkness	123	375	35	79	12	3	10	41	36	79	.211	.290	.339	4	3	5	7	0	2	5
Jim Hickman	146	494	53	113	21	6	17	51	44	120	.229	.291	.399	0	5	8	1	3	4	1
Joe Hicks	56	159	16	36	6	1	5	22	7	31	.226	.272	.371	0	2	1	3	0	0	0
Gil Hodges	11	22	2	5	0	0	0	3	3	2	.227	.320	.227	0	0	0	0	0	0	0
Ron Hunt	143	533	64	145	28	4	10	42	40	50	.272	.334	.396	5	4	13	13	8	6	0
Cleon Jones	6	15	1	2	0	0	0	1	0	4	.133	.133	.133	0	0	0	0	0	0	0
Rod Kanehl	109	191	26	46	6	0	1	9	5	26	.241	.268	.288	6	3	7	2	3	0	0
Ed Kranepool	86	273	22	57	12	2	2	14	18	50	.209	.256	.289	4	2	10	0	1	2	0
Al Moran	119	331	26	64	5	2	1	23	36	60	.193	.274	.230	3	7	6	1	1	1	1
Charlie Neal	72	253	26	57	12	1	3	18	27	49	.225	.302	.316	1	2	1	1	1	0	3
Jim Piersall	40	124	13	24	4	1	1	10	10	14	.194	.250	.266	1	2	3	0	4	2	1
Ted Schreiber	39	50	1	8	0	0	0	2	4	14	.160	.236	.160	0	1	1	1	0	0	0
Norm Sherry	63	147	6	20	1	0	2	11	10	26	.136	.205	.184	1	0	6	3	0	1	1
Dick Smith	20	42	4	10	0	1	0	3	5	10	.238	.319	.286	3	2	0	0	0	0	2
Duke Snider	129	354	44	86	8	3	14	45	56	74	.243	.345	.401	0	1	2	1	0	4	9
Sammy Taylor	22	35	3	9	0	1	0	6	5	7	.257	.341	.314	0	0	3	0	0	1	1
Frank Thomas	126	420	34	109	9	1	15	60	33	48	.260	.317	.393	0	0	23	3	0	2	5
Marv Throneberry	14	14	0	2	1	0	0	1	1	5	.143	.200	.214	0	0	0	0	0	0	0
Pitchers																				
Craig Anderson	3	3	0	1	0	0	0	0	0	0	.333	.333	.333	0	0	0	0	0	0	0
Ed Bauta	9	3	0	0	0	0	0	0	0	2	.000	.000	.000	0	0	0	0	0	0	0
Larry Bearnarth	58	30	2	6	1	1	0	3	0	12	.200	.226	.300	0	0	0	1	0	0	0
Galen Cisco	51	38	0	5	1	0	0	3	4	9	.132	.209	.158	0	0	0	0	2	1	0
Roger Craig	46	69	0	6	0	0	0	0	5	39	.087	.149	.087	0	2	2	0	3	0	0
Jay Hook	41	38	4	9	1	0	0	1	2	13	.237	.268	.263	0	0	1	0	2	1	0
Al Jackson	49	79	8	16	2	0	0	4	1	23	.203	.210	.228	0	1	1	0	3	1	0
Ken Mackenzie	34	10	0	0	0	0	0	0	0	5	.000	.000	.000	0	0	0	0	0	0	0
Grover Powell	20	10	1	2	0	0	0	0	2	3	.200	.333	.200	0	0	0	0	0	0	0
Don Rowe	26	13	0	3	0	0	0	1	0	5	.231	.231	.231	0	0	0	0	0	0	0
Tracy Stallard	39	48	1	3	0	0	0	1	0	21	.063	.063	.063	0	0	1	0	2	0	0
Carl Willey	30	54	3	6	0	0	1	5	2	32	.111	.143	.167	0	0	1	0	6	0	0
TOTAL	162	5336	501	1168	156	35	96	459	457	1078	.219	.281	.315	41	52	106	47	46	35	41

Pitching	G	ERA	W–L	SV	GS	GF	CG	SHO	IP	H	R	ER	HR	BB	SO	BFP	WP	HBP	BK	IBB
Craig Anderson	3	8.68	0–2	0	2	0	0	0	9.1	17	15	9	0	3	6	51	1	0	0	0
Ed Bauta	9	5.21	0–0	0	0	1	0	0	19.0	22	11	11	0	9	13	86	0	0	0	0
Larry Bearnarth	58	3.42	3–8	4	2	34	0	0	126.1	127	61	48	7	47	48	544	4	5	0	9
Galen Cisco	51	4.34	7–15	0	17	15	1	0	155.2	165	88	75	15	64	81	688	10	7	2	1
Roger Craig	46	3.78	5–22	2	31	9	14	0	236.0	249	117	99	28	58	108	1014	4	6	6	2
Steve Dillon	1	10.80	0–0	0	0	0	0	0	1.2	3	2	2	0	1	7	10	0	0	0	0
Jay Hook	41	5.48	4–14	1	20	13	3	0	152.1	168	104	93	21	53	89	672	6	9	0	2
Al Jackson	37	3.96	13–17	1	34	1	11	0	227.0	237	128	100	25	84	142	1000	9	12	2	2
Ken Mackenzie	34	4.97	3–1	3	0	17	0	0	58.0	63	35	32	11	12	41	252	0	2	0	2
Grover Powell	20	2.72	1–1	0	4	10	1	1	49.2	37	23	15	2	32	39	218	9	1	0	0
Don Rowe	26	4.28	0–0	0	1	12	0	0	54.2	59	27	26	6	21	27	237	1	1	5	0
Tracy Stallard	39	4.71	6–17	1	23	7	5	0	154.2	156	89	81	23	77	110	684	6	1	4	6
Carl Willey	30	3.10	9–14	0	28	1	7	4	183.0	149	74	63	24	69	101	755	7	4	1	2
TOTAL	162	4.12	51–111	12	162	120	42	5	1427.0	1452	774	653	162	529	806	6208	57	48	20	26

1964

NATIONAL LEAGUE

Team	W	L	PCT	GB	BA	ERA
Cardinals	93	69	.574	—	.272	3.43
Reds	92	70	.568	1.0	.249	3.07
Phillies	92	70	.568	1.0	.258	3.36
Giants	90	72	.556	3.0	.246	3.19
Braves	88	74	.543	5.0	.272	4.12
Dodgers	80	82	.494	13.0	.250	2.95
Pirates	80	82	.494	13.0	.264	3.52
Cubs	76	86	.469	17.0	.251	4.08
Colt 45s	66	96	.407	27.0	.229	3.41
Mets	53	109	.327	40.0	.246	4.25

It was a very eventful year for the Mets, who finally moved into Shea Stadium after a one-year delay. The stadium itself was a work in progress right up until opening pitch, as workers painted the outfield fences while the Mets and Pirates took batting practice prior to the April 17 opener.

The city chose the Flushing Meadows site for the ballpark so fans would have an easier time getting there, be it by train or car. The facility was accessible from numerous major highways in Queens and Long Island, and straphangers could get to Shea by taking the No. 7 train or the Long Island Railroad.

The stadium had many one-of-a-kind features, including escalators and an immense scoreboard that featured a front-projection screen that was designed to show headshots of each player as he took his turn at bat. The Mets also boasted the Diamond Club restaurant for fans who wanted a decent meal before or after games. The escalators were terrific for those holding upper-deck tickets, the restaurant received raves, and the scoreboard was state-of-the-art. But the front-projection slideshow was scrapped when it was quickly determined fans couldn't see the headshots during day games. The projection setup was replaced by a Mets logo that would highlight the top of the scoreboard for years to come.

The World's Fair was in progress across the street from the stadium, giving New York residents and tourists another reason to visit Shea Stadium. The season was a success at the turnstiles, as the Mets drew more than 1.7 million fans, an increase of nearly 700,000 from 1963. Accessibility proved to be a drawing card with more than 20,000 parking spaces available.

There were three very memorable games at Shea during the team's first season, all coming within a 38-day span.

The first was a doubleheader against the Giants that drew 57,037, the largest gathering at Shea that season. Game 1 was a pedestrian 5–3 win for the Giants, but the nightcap became a classic after Joe Christopher hit a game-tying three-run homer in the seventh inning. They played into the 10th, and the 15th, and the 20th, with the score still 6–6. The Mets even turned the second triple play in team history when Roy McMillan speared a liner to start the triple-killing in the 14th inning. Giants pitcher Gaylord Perry, with his roster spot tenuous at best, scattered seven hits and struck out nine over 10 shutout innings of relief. Reliever Larry Bearnarth held the Giants to just three hits in seven frames, and Galen Cisco limited San Francisco to two hits over his first eight innings. But with Cisco still on the mound in the 23rd, Jim Davenport hit a two-out triple and scored on pinch-hitter Del Crandell's double before Jesus Alou added an RBI single to make it 8–6. Before Crandell's hit, manager Casey Stengel elected to walk Cap Peterson intentionally, even after Peterson went 0-for-4 in the game and was a lifetime .228 hitter in 79 at-bats at that point.

Three weeks later Philadelphia's Jim Bunning celebrated Father's Day by throwing a perfect game at Shea, beating the Mets 6–0 in the first game of a twinbill. Eight days earlier Bunning allowed a pair of homers and three other hits while going the distance in an 8–2 win over the Mets. This time, he struck out 10, including a game-ending whiff of pinch-hitter Johnny Stephenson.

The All-Star game was performed at Shea on July 7, the only Midsummer Classic to be played there. The American League entered the bottom of the ninth holding a 4–3 lead, and they had Boston's Dick Radatz on the mound. But Willie Mays walked, stole second, and scored when Joe Pepitone mishandled Orlando Cepeda's game-tying single. Johnny Callison ended it with a three-run homer, allowing Met-killer Juan Marichal to pick up yet another victory at Shea.

Although the Mets were enjoying their new digs, fans were witnessing what was becoming a tired act on the field. The team had begun to stockpile talented prospects like Ron Swoboda, Tug McGraw, and Dick Selma, who were assembled along with other young players for an early training camp at St. Petersburg. But the kids were a year away.

And so it was another year of castoffs and has-beens as the Mets made only a two-game improvement from the previous year. George Altman was acquired from the Cardinals with Bill Wakefield for Roger Craig. Altman was an All-Star in 1961 and '62, hitting over .300 each season while averaging 25 homers for the Cubs. But his power numbers dropped to nine homers and 34 extra-base hits for the Cardinals in 1963, and his average would fall to .230 during his lone season as a Met.

Wakefield was a workhorse, setting a team record with 62 appearances, including four starts. Wakefield also compiled a 3.61 ERA, the lowest on the team for anyone with more than 100 innings. But it would be his only major league season.

The rotation took a big hit when Carl Willey was slammed in the face by a line drive during spring training, causing him to miss most of the season. Willey pitched four of the Mets' five shutouts while compiling a team-best 3.10 ERA in 1963.

Newcomer Jack Fisher led the Mets with 227⅔ innings pitched in '64, and Al Jackson topped the team in wins (11) for the second straight year. But Fisher, Jackson, Tracy Stallard, and Galen Cisco combined for a 37–72 record as the Mets continued to display an underwhelming rotation.

The hitting showed improvement at times as the club batted .246, a 27-point increase from 1963. The team also had a pair of .300 hitters in Ron Hunt (.303) and Joe Christopher (.300), but Charley Smith was the lone Met to reach the 20-home run mark. Frank Thomas was most affected by the move to Shea, although injuries played a part in his power-outage. He belted just three homers in 197 at-bats before he was traded to the Phillies in August.

New names, new ballpark, same result. The role of "lovable losers" was starting to wear thin on fans and the media. The 1962 Mets found unique, torturous ways to lose ballgames, particularly in late innings. That team kept fans in the seats and created good copy for sportswriters employed to cover the worst ballclub in modern major league baseball.

But the 1964 team was just bad. The starting rotation often deserved a better fate, but it's tough to garner much sympathy when the top four starters allow 880 hits in 856⅓ innings. The defense was a little tighter, making just 167 errors after amassing 210 in each of the first two seasons. But the 1964 Mets didn't play a decent stretch of games until mid-August after the team already had dropped 82 of its first 117 games. They never escaped the cellar after April 28.

The Mets had now averaged 113 losses in their first three seasons. Meanwhile, their expansion brothers, the Houston Colts, had yet to lose 100 games in a season while showing some potential in their farm system. Joe Morgan, Rusty Staub, John Bateman, Jimmy Wynn, and Jerry Grote were starting to contribute at the major league level. And the Colts starting pitching was better than New York's rotation. Led by Bob Bruce (15–9, 2.76 ERA), each of Houston's top-five starters owned ERAs under four.

The Mets didn't appear ready to close the gap on the Colts anytime soon, leaving team president George Weiss and manager Casey Stengel open to criticism. Weiss selected "name" players in the expansion draft while Colts GM Paul Richards went with youth. Stengel continued to be a quote machine, but the beat writers were looking for positive results. Howard Cosell was often critical of Stengel and began to use his radio show to call for "the Ol' Perfessor's" dismissal. Members of the Fourth Estate followed suit, and the Mets had internal discussions regarding a successor to the now 74-year-old Stengel.

1964 Mets Statistics

Hitting	G	AB	R	H	2B	3B	HR	RBI	BB	SO	BA	OBP	SLG	SB	CS	GDP	HP	SH	SF	IBB
George Altman	124	422	48	97	14	1	9	47	18	70	.230	.262	.332	4	2	8	1	2	2	4
Larry Burright	3	7	0	0	0	0	0	0	0	0	.000	.000	.000	0	0	0	0	0	0	0
Chris Cannizzaro	60	164	11	51	10	0	0	10	14	28	.311	.367	.372	0	5	3	1	2	1	2
Joe Christopher	154	543	78	163	26	8	16	76	48	92	.300	.360	.466	6	5	18	6	1	6	5
Larry Elliot	80	224	27	51	8	0	9	22	28	55	.228	.320	.384	1	2	6	3	0	1	2
Jesse Gonder	131	341	28	92	11	1	7	35	29	65	.270	.329	.370	0	0	16	2	0	2	5
Wayne Graham	20	33	1	3	1	0	0	0	0	5	.091	.091	.121	0	0	0	0	0	0	0
Tim Harkness	39	117	11	33	2	1	2	13	9	18	.282	.336	.368	1	1	5	1	0	1	1
Jim Hickman	139	409	48	105	14	1	11	57	36	90	.257	.319	.377	0	1	11	2	0	1	4
Ron Hunt	127	475	59	144	19	6	6	42	29	30	.303	.357	.406	6	2	16	11	5	1	4
Rod Kanehl	98	254	25	59	7	1	1	11	7	18	.232	.256	.280	3	1	1	1	2	0	0
Bobby Klaus	56	209	25	51	8	3	2	11	25	30	.244	.325	.340	3	4	2	0	2	0	0
Ed Kranepool	119	420	47	108	19	4	10	45	32	50	.257	.310	.393	0	1	9	2	3	4	2
Roy McMillan	113	379	30	80	8	2	1	25	14	16	.211	.246	.251	3	1	18	4	6	2	2
Al Moran	16	22	2	5	0	0	0	4	2	2	.227	.280	.227	0	0	1	0	0	1	0
Amado Samuel	53	142	7	33	7	0	0	5	4	24	.232	.264	.282	0	1	2	2	3	0	0
Charley Smith	127	443	44	106	12	0	20	58	19	101	.239	.275	.402	2	2	8	3	5	1	1
Dick Smith	46	94	14	21	6	1	0	3	1	29	.223	.247	.309	6	2	2	2	0	0	0
John Stephenson	37	57	2	9	0	0	1	2	4	18	.158	.226	.211	0	0	0	1	0	0	0
Hawk Taylor	92	225	20	54	8	0	4	23	8	33	.240	.272	.329	0	0	7	2	0	0	1
Frank Thomas	60	197	19	50	6	1	3	19	10	29	.254	.295	.340	1	1	4	2	0	1	1
Pitchers																				
Craig Anderson	4	3	0	0	0	0	0	0	0	1	.000	.000	.000	0	0	0	0	0	0	0
Larry Bearnarth	44	14	0	2	0	0	0	0	0	6	.143	.143	.143	0	0	0	0	0	0	0
Galen Cisco	36	54	2	6	1	0	0	4	4	19	.111	.186	.130	0	0	3	1	6	0	0
Jack Fisher	40	76	5	12	1	0	0	8	5	24	.158	.205	.171	0	0	2	0	2	2	0
Jerry Hinsley	9	1	0	0	0	0	0	0	0	1	.000	.000	.000	0	0	0	0	0	0	0
Jay Hook	3	3	0	0	0	0	0	0	0	1	.000	.000	.000	0	0	0	0	0	0	0
Willard Hunter	41	1	0	1	0	0	0	0	0	0	1.000	1.000	1.000	0	0	0	0	2	0	0
Al Jackson	50	72	6	11	3	1	1	4	2	26	.153	.176	.264	0	0	1	0	2	0	0
Gary Kroll	8	3	0	1	0	0	0	0	0	1	.333	.333	.333	0	0	1	0	0	0	0
Frank Lary	13	17	1	2	0	0	0	1	4	5	.118	.286	.118	0	0	1	0	1	0	0
Ron Locke	25	5	1	0	0	0	0	0	0	3	.000	.000	.000	0	0	0	0	3	0	0
Tom Parsons	4	7	1	0	0	0	0	0	0	5	.000	.000	.000	0	0	0	0	0	0	0
Dennis Ribant	17	20	2	2	1	0	0	1	1	2	.100	.143	.150	0	0	0	0	0	0	0
Tracy Stallard	36	79	5	15	3	0	0	1	0	22	.190	.200	.228	0	0	2	1	1	0	0
Tom Sturdivant	16	1	0	0	0	0	0	0	0	0	.000	.000	.000	0	0	0	0	0	0	0
Darrell Sutherland	10	5	0	1	0	0	0	0	0	4	.200	.200	.200	0	0	0	0	0	0	0
Bill Wakefield	62	24	0	4	0	0	0	0	0	8	.167	.167	.167	0	0	0	0	3	0	0
Carl Willey	14	4	0	0	0	0	0	0	0	1	.000	.000	.000	0	0	0	0	1	0	0
TOTAL	163	5566	569	1372	195	31	103	527	353	932	.246	.291	.348	36	31	147	48	52	26	34

Pitching	G	ERA	W–L	SV	GS	GF	CG	SHO	IP	H	R	ER	HR	BB	SO	BFP	WP	HBP	BK	IBB
Craig Anderson	4	5.54	0–1	0	1	1	0	0	13.0	21	9	8	0	3	5	61	0	0	0	0
Ed Bauta	8	5.40	0–2	1	0	3	0	0	10.0	17	6	6	1	3	3	47	0	0	0	1
Larry Bearnarth	44	4.15	5–5	3	1	20	0	0	78.0	79	38	36	6	38	31	343	3	2	0	1
Galen Cisco	36	3.62	6–19	0	25	5	5	2	191.2	182	85	77	17	54	78	787	5	6	0	4
Steve Dillon	2	9.00	0–0	0	0	2	0	0	3.0	4	3	3	1	2	2	15	0	0	0	0
Jack Fisher	40	4.23	10–17	0	34	3	8	1	227.2	256	124	107	23	56	115	985	5	10	0	0
Jerry Hinsley	9	8.22	0–2	0	2	2	0	0	15.1	21	17	14	0	7	11	76	1	0	0	0
Jay Hook	3	9.31	0–1	0	2	0	0	0	9.2	17	10	10	2	7	5	51	2	0	0	0
Willard Hunter	41	4.41	3–3	5	0	26	0	0	49.0	54	25	24	4	9	22	204	2	2	0	1
Al Jackson	40	4.26	11–16	1	31	2	11	3	213.1	229	115	101	18	60	112	916	4	4	0	3
Gary Kroll	8	4.15	0–1	0	2	4	0	0	21.2	19	11	10	1	15	24	97	2	1	4	0
Frank Lary	13	4.55	2–3	1	8	3	3	1	57.1	62	33	29	7	14	27	243	2	4	0	2
Ron Locke	25	3.48	1–2	0	3	13	0	0	41.1	46	23	16	3	22	17	188	2	1	0	0
Tom Parsons	4	4.19	1–2	0	2	2	1	0	19.1	20	9	9	1	6	10	81	0	0	0	0
Dennis Ribant	14	5.15	1–5	1	7	3	1	1	57.2	65	35	33	8	9	35	242	4	0	0	1
Tracy Stallard	36	3.79	10–20	0	34	1	11	2	225.2	213	111	95	20	73	118	945	12	6	0	3
Tom Sturdivant	16	5.97	0–0	1	0	5	0	0	28.2	34	20	19	2	7	18	125	3	2	0	0
Darrell Sutherland	10	7.76	0–3	0	4	3	0	0	26.2	32	26	23	1	12	9	127	0	2	0	0
Bill Wakefield	62	3.61	3–5	2	4	18	0	0	119.2	103	57	48	10	61	61	521	4	9	1	6
Carl Willey	14	3.60	0–2	0	3	7	0	0	30.0	37	19	12	5	8	14	136	2	1	0	2
TOTAL	**163**	**4.25**	**53–109**	**15**	**163**	**123**	**40**	**10**	**1438.0**	**1511**	**776**	**679**	**130**	**466**	**717**	**6190**	**53**	**50**	**5**	**24**

1965

NATIONAL LEAGUE

Team	W	L	PCT	GB	BA	ERA
Dodgers	97	65	.599	—	.245	2.81
Giants	95	67	.586	2.0	.252	3.20
Pirates	90	72	.556	7.0	.265	3.01
Reds	89	73	.549	8.0	.273	3.88
Braves	86	76	.531	11.0	.256	3.52
Phillies	85	76	.528	11.5	.250	3.53
Cardinals	80	81	.497	16.5	.254	3.77
Cubs	72	90	.444	25.0	.238	3.78
Astros	65	97	.401	32.0	.237	3.84
Mets	50	112	.309	47.0	.211	4.06

On the surface, the Mets appeared to regress by compiling 112 losses in 1965, still the second-most in team history. The Mets also made their first managerial change when Wes Westrum replaced Casey Stengel, who retired after breaking a hip in a fall. But the Mets took a step forward by looking at their farm system, which had shown little during the first three seasons.

The Mets changed their philosophy and put some of their minor league talent into serious game situations following an administrative gaffe that caused them to lose prospect Paul Blair to the Orioles in the first-year draft. The first-year draft was supposed to help some of the lesser teams pluck talent from the better clubs, although the chosen players had to spend the following season with the major league team. After losing Blair, the Mets protected Tug McGraw, Ron Swoboda, Jim Bethke, and Danny Napoleon and put them on the major league roster.

McGraw enjoyed a very productive major league career, and Ron Swoboda spent nine seasons in the majors. But Swoboda didn't think he was ready for the majors after just one year of pro ball.

Mets fans also got glimpses of Cleon Jones, Bud Harrelson, and Kevin Collins, all of whom would play for the 1969 Mets. Ed Kranepool represented the Mets in the 1965 All-Star Game and finished the season with a career-high 133 hits.

Youth was served on August 26 as McGraw became the first Met to beat Sandy Koufax. McGraw pitched into the eighth, holding the Dodgers to two runs and eight hits. The rookie lefty compiled a 3.32 ERA but went just 2–7 with the Mets that season.

Dick Selma emerged as a legitimate prospect following his late-season callup. Selma became the first Met to win his major league debut when he allowed three runs in five innings against the Cardinals on September 3. Selma was even better in his second start, scattering four hits while setting a team record with 13 strikeouts in a 1–0, 10-inning win over the Braves on September 12.

But the Mets also continued to acquire "name" players who were past their prime. The organization bought Warren Spahn from the Braves to serve as a pitcher and pitching coach and activated Yogi Berra briefly in May after signing him as a coach.

Spahn was 4–4 with a 3.97 ERA before he lost his last eight decisions. The Hall of Famer appeared more interested in continuing his own career than helping the rest of the staff, often keeping himself in games longer than he should. The experiment ended when he was released and signed by the Giants in July.

Berra knew better. He made two starts for the Mets in May before realizing his bat speed was better suited for long fungos, and B.P. Berra became a permanent coach later that month and stayed with the organization another 10 years.

The Mets might have fared better in 1965 had Ron Hunt and Joe Christopher been able to duplicate their 1964 seasons. Hunt was the National League starting second baseman in the 1964 All-Star game before ending that season with a .303 average. But he missed almost three months of the 1965 campaign after separating a shoulder during a game in May. Hunt hit just .240 in 196 at-bats. Christopher hit only .249 with five homers and 40 RBIs in '65, one season after he batted .300 with 16 homers and a team-high 76 RBIs.

Most of the Mets' pitching staff struggled to find an identity. Jack Fisher and Al Jackson were the only hurlers to make more than 19 starts. Sixteen different pitchers started at least one game for the Mets, and 10 had at least one save. It was a patchwork staff of over-the-hill veterans and prospects, almost none of whom were in their prime.

Kranepool and Swoboda got off to terrific starts. Kranepool was batting .287 with seven homers and 37 RBIs heading into his All-Star game appearance. He hit just .216 with three homers and 16 RBIs the rest of the season to finish the year with a .253 average. Swoboda belted 15 homers in his first 71 games, covering 209 at-bats. But he developed a longer swing and hit only four homers while batting .200 in his final 64 games. Both players might have benefited from better coaching.

The Mets were 6–7 after 13 games, the closest the team had been to the .500 mark that late in a season. But that was followed by a six-game losing streak that had members of the media joining Howard Cosell in suggesting a managerial change. Stengel broke his wrist during a trip to West Point for an exhibition game in May. The Mets were 9–15 at that point when several writers called for his dismissal. Stengel looked at the busted wrist as an asset.

"If I wanna take a pitcher out, I can hit him over the head with my cast to convince him. I didn't fall on my head, so I don't think I'll handicap the club if I manage with one arm."[6]

The Mets dropped 20 of 23 at the beginning of June, fueling further speculation that Stengel was on his way out. He had the media thinking he was set to quit after the season when he said during a ceremony at City Hall on Casey Stengel Day that, "When I go home this fall, I hope to leave a young team." The young team would be in place, but Stengel wouldn't be around to manage it.

A day after the ceremony, the Mets held Old Timers Day at Shea to honor members of the Brooklyn Dodgers and New York Giants, two of Stengel's former teams. The night was capped by a party at Toots Shor's restaurant with Stengel in attendance. He walked into the men's room and slipped on a wet floor before returning to the revelry. Stengel had broken his left hip and would require surgery hours later.

The Mets would get a new manager. Stengel called team president George Weiss to say Westrum should get the job over Yogi Berra, to whom he had referred as his assistant manager during their days with the Yankees. Stengel initially thought he'd be back on the bench, but the 75-year-old skipper realized five weeks later that he had managed his final game. The Mets retired his jersey No. 37 in September hours before a game against the Astros. The team could have given Stengel a wonderful send-off to honor a man who gave them free publicity through miles of newspaper copy. Instead, the public was shut out, and just more than 11,000 attended the game.

The Mets actually played worse for Westrum, going 19–48 to finish in 10th place for the fourth straight year. At this point, they had won 194 games during their four-year history. Meanwhile, the Houston Astros, their expansion brothers, had won 261 games. It would be another three seasons before the Mets finished a year with more wins than Houston.

1965 Mets Statistics

Hitting	G	AB	R	H	2B	3B	HR	RBI	BB	SO	BA	OBP	SLG	SB	CS	GDP	HP	SH	SF	IBB
Yogi Berra	4	9	1	2	0	0	0	0	0	3	.222	.222	.222	0	0	0	0	0	0	0
Chris Cannizzaro	114	251	17	46	8	2	0	7	28	60	.183	.270	.231	0	2	5	2	3	0	4
Joe Christopher	148	437	38	109	18	3	5	40	35	82	.249	.311	.339	4	4	10	6	4	4	3
Kevin Collins	11	23	3	4	1	0	0	0	1	9	.174	.208	.217	0	1	0	0	0	0	0
Billy Cowan	82	156	16	28	8	2	3	9	4	45	.179	.205	.314	3	2	2	1	1	0	1
Jesse Gonder	53	105	6	25	4	0	4	9	11	20	.238	.308	.390	0	0	6	0	0	1	4
Greg Goossen	11	31	2	9	0	0	1	2	1	5	.290	.313	.387	0	0	0	0	0	0	0
Bud Harrelson	19	37	3	4	1	1	0	0	2	11	.108	.154	.189	0	0	0	0	0	0	0
Jim Hickman	141	369	32	87	18	0	15	40	27	76	.236	.291	.407	3	1	9	2	1	1	3
Chuck Hiller	100	286	24	68	11	1	5	21	14	24	.238	.275	.336	1	1	6	1	1	1	2
Ron Hunt	57	196	21	47	12	1	1	10	14	19	.240	.309	.327	2	7	5	6	6	1	2
Cleon Jones	30	74	2	11	1	0	1	9	2	23	.149	.171	.203	1	0	0	0	0	0	0
Bobby Klaus	119	288	30	55	12	0	2	12	45	49	.191	.302	.253	1	6	4	1	3	0	0
Gary Kolb	40	90	8	15	2	0	1	7	3	28	.167	.191	.222	3	0	2	0	0	1	0
Ed Kranepool	153	525	44	133	24	4	10	53	39	71	.253	.303	.371	1	4	13	2	1	8	7
Johnny Lewis	148	477	64	117	15	3	15	45	59	117	.245	.331	.384	4	7	8	3	4	1	4
Roy McMillan	157	528	44	128	19	2	1	42	24	60	.242	.280	.292	1	0	7	4	16	2	1
Danny Napoleon	68	97	5	14	1	1	0	7	8	23	.144	.222	.175	0	0	4	2	0	1	1
Jimmie Schaffer	24	37	0	5	2	0	0	0	1	15	.135	.158	.189	0	0	2	0	0	0	0
Charley Smith	135	499	49	122	20	3	16	62	17	123	.244	.273	.393	2	1	13	4	7	4	3
John Stephenson	62	121	9	26	5	0	4	15	8	19	.215	.264	.355	0	1	7	0	2	0	2
Ron Swoboda	135	399	52	91	15	3	19	50	33	102	.228	.291	.424	2	3	10	3	1	2	3
Hawk Taylor	25	46	5	7	0	0	4	10	1	8	.152	.167	.413	0	0	2	0	0	1	0
Pitchers																				
Larry Bearnarth	40	9	1	1	1	0	0	0	1	4	.111	.200	.222	0	0	0	0	0	0	0
Jim Bethke	25	4	0	0	0	0	0	0	0	2	.000	.000	.000	0	0	0	0	0	0	0
Galen Cisco	35	27	5	7	0	0	0	4	2	9	.259	.310	.259	0	0	0	0	4	0	0
Dave Eilers	11	1	0	1	0	0	0	0	0	0	1.000	1.000	1.000	0	0	0	0	0	0	0
Jack Fisher	43	78	2	12	2	0	0	2	2	22	.154	.185	.179	0	1	3	1	4	0	0
Rob Gardner	5	7	0	0	0	0	0	0	0	4	.000	.000	.000	0	0	0	0	1	0	0

Gary Kroll	32	26	3	3	1	0	0	0	0	9	.115	.115	.154	0	0	0	0	3	0	0
Al Jackson	56	60	5	7	1	0	0	2	2	23	.117	.145	.133	0	0	1	0	8	0	0
Frank Lary	14	19	3	4	0	0	0	0	0	4	.211	.211	.211	0	0	0	0	0	0	0
Tug McGraw	38	23	0	3	0	0	0	0	0	10	.130	.130	.130	0	0	1	0	0	0	0
Larry Miller	28	11	0	2	0	0	0	0	0	5	.182	.182	.182	0	0	0	0	0	0	0
Dennis Musgraves	5	2	0	0	0	0	0	0	0	0	.000	.000	.000	0	0	0	0	0	0	0
Tom Parsons	35	18	0	1	0	0	0	0	1	14	.056	.105	.056	0	0	0	0	1	0	0
Dennis Ribant	19	6	0	0	0	0	0	0	0	1	.000	.000	.000	0	0	0	0	0	0	0
Gordie Richardson	35	7	0	0	0	0	0	0	0	7	.000	.000	.000	0	0	0	0	1	0	0
Dick Selma	7	9	1	2	0	0	0	0	0	4	.222	.222	.222	0	0	1	0	0	0	0
Warren Spahn	21	35	0	4	1	0	0	2	7	12	.114	.279	.143	0	1	0	1	2	0	0
Darrell Sutherland	18	13	0	2	0	1	0	0	0	4	.154	.154	.308	0	0	0	0	0	0	0
Carl Willey	13	5	0	0	0	0	0	0	0	3	.000	.000	.000	0	0	0	0	2	0	0
TOTAL	164	5441	495	1202	203	27	107	460	392	1129	.221	.273	.327	28	42	121	39	76	28	40

Pitching	G	ERA	W–L	SV	GS	GF	CG	SH	IP	H	R	ER	HR	BB	SO	BFP	WP	HBP	BK	IBB
Larry Bearnarth	40	4.60	3–5	1	3	17	0	0	60.2	75	43	31	6	28	16	286	4	4	0	2
Jim Bethke	25	4.28	2–0	0	0	12	0	0	40.0	41	24	19	3	22	19	184	3	6	0	2
Galen Cisco	35	4.49	4–8	0	17	8	1	1	112.1	119	63	56	12	51	58	499	3	1	2	2
Dave Eilers	11	4.00	1–1	2	0	8	0	0	18.0	20	11	8	2	4	9	80	0	2	0	3
Jack Fisher	43	3.94	8–24	1	36	4	10	0	253.2	252	121	111	22	68	116	1054	6	4	1	6
Rob Gardner	5	3.21	0–2	0	4	0	0	0	28.0	23	13	10	4	7	19	115	0	0	0	0
Al Jackson	37	4.34	8–20	1	31	2	7	3	205.1	217	111	99	17	61	120	884	6	8	2	4
Gary Kroll	32	4.45	6–6	1	11	11	1	0	87.0	83	48	43	12	41	62	391	1	6	1	0
Frank Lary	14	2.98	1–3	1	7	3	0	0	57.1	48	24	19	2	16	23	230	4	1	1	0
Tug McGraw	37	3.32	2–7	1	9	17	2	0	97.2	88	47	36	8	48	57	416	7	3	0	2
Larry Miller	28	5.02	1–4	0	5	7	0	0	57.1	66	32	32	6	25	36	260	2	1	0	0
Bob Moorhead	9	4.40	0–1	0	0	3	0	0	14.1	16	7	7	0	5	5	64	3	0	0	0
Dennis Musgraves	5	0.56	0–0	0	1	0	0	0	16.0	11	2	1	0	7	11	65	2	2	0	0
Tom Parsons	35	4.67	1–10	1	11	6	1	1	90.2	108	53	47	17	17	58	391	2	0	0	2
Dennis Ribant	19	3.82	1–3	3	1	11	0	0	35.1	29	16	15	5	6	13	136	1	0	0	0
Gord Richardson	35	3.78	2–2	2	0	14	0	0	52.1	41	27	22	5	16	43	206	2	2	0	2
Dick Selma	4	3.71	2–1	0	4	0	1	1	26.2	22	11	11	2	9	26	108	0	1	0	0
Warren Spahn	20	4.36	4–12	0	19	1	5	0	126.0	140	70	61	18	35	56	543	1	2	0	1
Darrell Sutherland	18	2.81	3–1	0	2	6	0	0	48.0	33	16	15	4	17	16	191	1	4	0	2
Carl Willey	13	4.18	1–2	0	3	5	1	0	28.0	30	13	13	2	15	13	129	5	2	0	1
TOTAL	164	4.06	50–112	14	164	135	29	11	1454.0	1462	752	656	147	498	776	6232	53	49	7	29

1966

NATIONAL LEAGUE

Team	W	L	PCT	GB	BA	ERA
Dodgers	95	67	.586	—	.256	2.62
Giants	93	68	.578	1.5	.248	3.24
Pirates	92	70	.568	3.0	.279	3.52
Phillies	87	75	.537	8.0	.258	3.57
Braves	85	77	.525	10.0	.263	3.68
Cardinals	83	79	.512	12.0	.251	3.11
Reds	76	84	.475	18.0	.260	4.08
Astros	72	90	.444	23.0	.255	3.76
Mets	66	95	.410	28.5	.239	4.17
Cubs	59	103	.364	36.0	.254	4.33

"Nice guys finish last."
—*Leo Durocher*

There were two significant changes to the National League standings between the 1965 and 1966 seasons. The Mets made a league-best 16-win improvement over the '65 season, winning a team-record 66 games under Wes Westrum, who was in his first full season as manager. Meanwhile, the Cubs slid from 72–90 to 59–103 in their first year under skipper Leo Durocher, allowing the Mets to finish out of the cellar for the first time in their five-year history.

Only a late swoon prevented the Mets from challenging the Reds for seventh place. New York never reached the .500 mark after the fourth game of the season, but the team was only eight games off the break-even point after going 18–14 in July, the first winning month in team history.

The Mets continued to funnel prospects into a starting lineup that already featured home-grown players Ed Kranepool and Ron Swoboda. Cleon Jones played his first full season in the majors, finishing second on the team with a .275 average and tying for second with 57 RBIs. Bud Harrelson became the Mets' everyday shortstop after being recalled in mid-August.

Run Hunt bounced back from his injury-plagued 1965 season to lead the team in hitting at .288. Kranepool paced the team with 16 homers and finished tied for second with 57 ribbies, but his batting average was just .254.

One of the bigger offensive disappointments was Swoboda, who batted just .222 and hit eight homers after clubbing 19 his rookie season. But Swoboda's defense improved greatly as he committed just two errors and had seven assists in 97 games in the outfield after making 11 errors and throwing out nine runners in 112 games the previous season.

George Weiss stayed on as team president after many expected him to retire following the 1965 season. The move was a long-term blessing as it gave GM-in-waiting Bing Devine another year to assess the farm system, which would factor into the Mets' later success.

Weiss didn't shy away from acquiring over-the-hill talent. Ken Boyer had slumped to .260 with 75 RBIs for the Cardinals in 1965, just a year after winning the National League MVP with a .295 average, 24 homers, and 119 RBIs for the World Series champs. Weiss sent original Met Al Jackson and Charley Smith to the Cards for Boyer, who got off to a great start and led the team with 61 RBIs.

Perhaps the best deal Weiss made after the 1965 season involved a red-ass catcher who spent the 1965 season in the minors after batting .181 for the Colts in '64. Houston already had Ron Brand and John Bateman behind the plate, making Jerry Grote expendable at the end of the '65 season. The Mets made their first true "steal" by getting Grote for pitcher Tom Parsons. Grote would play for the Mets deep into the 1977 season. Parsons never appeared in the majors again.

The 1966 season also gave Mets fans their first glimpse of Nolan Ryan, who struck out three over two innings in his major league debut on September 11 against Atlanta. But the pitching staff continued to be comprised of journeymen hurlers or prospects not quite ready to face major league batters.

Dick Rusteck was outstanding in his major league debut, tossing a four-hit shutout before finishing the year 1–2 with a 3.00 ERA. Dick Selma showed flashes while going 4–6 with a 4.24 ERA. But Tug McGraw was pounded during many of his 12 starts, going 2–9 with a 5.34 ERA. McGraw was just 4–16 as a major leaguer following the 1966 season.

Dennis Ribant and Bob Shaw became the first pitchers in Mets history to win more than 10 games in a season while compiling a winning record. Ribant was 9–3 during one stretch before finishing 11–9. Shaw won 11 games after being acquired from the Giants early in the season.

Jack Fisher continued to anchor the rotation, leading the team with 33 starts and tying for the team lead with 11 wins. Fisher also paced the team with 230 innings pitched and 127 strikeouts.

Although Rusteck and Selma were impressive in spots, Mets fans were still awaiting that "Oh-My-God-This Guy-Is-The-Real-Deal" prospect. They didn't know it at the time, but that prospect was in Jacksonville going 12–12 with a 3.13 ERA.

There was still plenty of promise at the major league level as the Mets stayed out of last place the entire season, thanks in part to the Cubs' 33–71 start. The Mets showed spunk by immediately following their season-worst seven-game losing streak in July with a team-record seven-game winning streak. They were only 2½ games behind the sixth-place Reds on the morning of August 1, but the Mets finished 19–40 the rest of the way.

The team looked a lot better than the 1965 squad, which made Westrum appear like a genius at times. For the first time in their history, the Mets were trying to balance prospects with veterans at the major league level. By September, a typical Mets lineup would include Grote, Swoboda, Kranepool, Jones, and Harrelson, with Boyer, Hunt, and Al Luplow usually filling out the squad. The team continued to stumble over the final month and finished behind Houston for the sixth straight year, but at least there was productivity coming out of the farm system.

Grote, Swoboda, Kranepool, Jones, and Harrelson would become mainstays in 1967. They would be joined by a right-hander from Fresno, California, who would embark on a Hall-of-Fame career.

1966 Mets Statistics

Hitting	G	AB	R	H	2B	3B	HR	RBI	BB	SO	BA	OBP	SLG	SB	CS	GDP	HP	SH	SF	IBB
Ken Boyer	136	496	62	132	28	2	14	61	30	64	.266	.304	.415	4	3	15	0	1	7	5
Eddie Bressoud	133	405	48	91	15	5	10	49	47	107	.225	.304	.360	2	2	11	1	7	4	4
Choo Choo Coleman	6	16	2	3	0	0	0	0	0	4	.188	.188	.188	0	0	0	0	0	0	0
Larry Elliot	65	199	24	49	14	2	5	32	17	46	.246	.306	.412	0	1	3	0	0	0	1
Shaun Fitzmaurice	9	13	2	2	0	0	0	0	2	6	.154	.267	.154	1	0	0	0	0	0	0
Greg Goossen	13	32	1	6	2	0	1	5	1	11	.188	.235	.344	1	0	0	1	0	0	0
Jerry Grote	120	317	26	75	12	2	3	31	40	81	.237	.327	.315	4	3	9	3	3	1	8
Bud Harrelson	33	99	20	22	2	4	0	4	13	23	.222	.313	.323	7	3	1	0	1	0	1
Jim Hickman	58	160	15	38	7	0	4	16	13	34	.238	.299	.356	2	1	4	1	0	0	0
Chuck Hiller	108	254	25	71	8	2	2	14	15	22	.280	.332	.350	0	0	2	5	1	0	0
Ron Hunt	132	479	63	138	19	2	3	33	41	34	.288	.356	.355	8	10	10	11	10	2	2
Cleon Jones	139	495	74	136	16	4	8	57	30	62	.275	.318	.372	16	8	13	3	5	4	2
Lou Klimchock	5	5	0	0	0	0	0	0	0	3	.000	.000	.000	0	0	1	0	0	0	0
Ed Kranepool	146	464	51	118	15	2	16	57	41	66	.254	.316	.399	1	1	5	3	0	4	9
Johnny Lewis	65	166	21	32	6	1	5	20	21	43	.193	.282	.331	2	0	1	0	0	1	0
Al Luplow	111	334	31	84	9	1	7	31	38	46	.251	.331	.347	2	6	10	2	2	1	3
Roy McMillan	76	220	24	47	9	1	1	12	20	25	.214	.284	.277	1	1	4	2	3	1	3
Billy Murphy	84	135	15	31	4	1	3	13	7	34	.230	.271	.341	1	2	3	1	2	1	0
Danny Napoleon	12	33	2	7	2	0	0	0	1	10	.212	.235	.273	0	1	1	0	0	0	0
John Stephenson	63	143	17	28	1	1	1	11	8	28	.196	.248	.238	0	0	7	2	0	0	0
Dick Stuart	31	87	7	19	0	0	4	13	9	26	.218	.292	.356	0	1	5	0	0	0	2
Ron Swoboda	112	342	34	76	9	4	8	50	31	76	.222	.296	.342	4	2	9	5	2	1	4
Hawk Taylor	53	109	5	19	2	0	3	12	3	19	.174	.204	.275	0	1	6	1	0	0	0

Hitting (continued) Pitchers	G	AB	R	H	2B	3B	HR	RBI	BB	SO	BA	OBP	SLG	SB	CS	GDP	HP	SH	SF	IBB
Gerry Arrigo	17	10	2	5	2	0	0	3	2	1	.500	.583	.700	0	0	0	0	0	0	0
Larry Bearnarth	29	9	1	1	1	0	0	0	0	3	.111	.111	.222	0	0	1	0	0	0	0
Dave Eilers	23	1	0	0	0	0	0	0	0	0	.000	.000	.000	0	0	0	0	0	0	0
Jack Fisher	38	67	2	6	2	0	0	0	7	26	.090	.176	.119	0	0	0	0	6	0	0
Bob Friend	22	29	1	1	0	0	0	1	0	17	.034	.034	.034	0	0	0	0	5	0	0
Rob Gardner	43	41	1	7	1	0	0	1	0	12	.171	.171	.195	0	0	0	0	1	0	0
Jack Hamilton	57	38	2	5	0	0	0	0	1	13	.132	.154	.132	0	0	1	0	1	0	0
Bill Hepler	37	14	0	3	0	0	0	0	0	7	.214	.214	.214	0	0	0	0	1	0	0
Tug McGraw	15	17	3	4	0	0	0	0	1	1	.235	.278	.235	0	0	1	0	2	0	0
Larry Miller	4	2	0	1	0	0	0	0	0	1	.500	.500	.500	0	0	0	0	0	0	0
Dennis Ribant	40	61	3	12	1	0	0	5	1	11	.197	.210	.213	0	0	1	0	4	0	0
Gordie Richardson	15	1	0	0	0	0	0	0	0	1	.000	.000	.000	0	0	0	0	0	0	0
Dick Rusteck	8	5	0	0	0	0	0	0	0	3	.000	.000	.000	0	0	0	0	0	0	0
Dick Selma	31	14	1	1	0	1	0	1	2	7	.071	.222	.214	0	0	0	1	1	1	0
Bob Shaw	26	50	1	13	0	0	0	2	4	15	.260	.309	.260	0	0	0	0	5	1	0
Darrell Sutherland	31	3	1	2	0	0	0	0	0	1	.667	.667	.667	0	0	0	0	0	0	0
Ralph Terry	11	6	0	1	0	0	0	0	0	3	.167	.167	.167	0	0	0	0	0	0	0
TOTAL	161	5371	587	1286	187	35	98	534	446	992	.239	.298	.342	55	46	127	42	63	29	44

Pitching	G	ERA	W–L	SV	GS	GF	CG	SHO	IP	H	R	ER	HR	BB	SO	BFP	WP	HBP	BK	IBB
Gerry Arrigo	17	3.74	3–3	0	5	5	0	0	43.1	47	20	18	5	16	28	194	1	0	0	2
Larry Bearnarth	29	4.45	2–3	0	1	12	0	0	54.2	59	31	27	11	20	27	238	2	1	0	6
Dave Eilers	23	4.67	1–1	0	0	12	0	0	34.2	39	18	18	7	7	14	147	0	1	0	2
Jack Fisher	38	3.68	11–14	0	33	4	10	2	230.0	229	108	94	26	54	127	960	12	8	0	2
Bob Friend	22	4.40	5–8	1	12	8	2	1	86.0	101	52	42	11	16	30	373	0	1	1	6
Rob Gardner	41	5.12	4–8	1	17	5	3	0	133.2	147	82	76	15	64	74	597	8	3	0	4
Dallas Green	4	5.40	0–0	0	0	2	0	0	5.0	6	3	3	2	2	1	21	0	0	0	1
Jack Hamilton	57	3.93	6–13	13	13	29	3	1	148.2	138	89	65	13	88	93	662	18	5	0	4
Bill Hepler	37	3.52	3–3	0	3	13	0	0	69.0	71	30	27	3	51	25	318	9	3	0	6
Tug McGraw	15	5.34	2–9	0	12	0	1	0	62.1	72	38	37	11	25	34	276	4	0	0	2
Larry Miller	4	7.56	0–2	0	1	1	0	0	8.1	9	7	7	3	4	7	37	0	0	0	0
Dennis Ribant	39	3.20	11–9	3	26	6	10	1	188.1	184	78	67	20	40	84	779	6	1	0	5
Gord Richardson	15	9.16	0–2	1	1	2	0	0	18.2	24	19	19	7	6	15	86	2	0	0	1
DickRusteck	8	3.00	1–2	0	3	3	1	1	24.0	24	10	8	1	8	9	96	0	0	0	0
Nolan Ryan	2	15.00	0–1	0	1	0	0	0	3.0	5	5	5	1	3	6	17	1	0	0	1
Dick Selma	30	4.24	4–6	1	7	7	0	0	80.2	84	47	38	11	39	58	355	4	3	0	5
Bob Shaw	26	3.92	11–10	0	25	0	7	2	167.2	171	85	73	12	42	104	710	8	7	2	1
Darrell Sutherland	31	4.87	2–0	1	0	9	0	0	44.1	60	25	24	6	25	23	207	1	2	0	8
Ralph Terry	11	4.74	0–1	1	1	6	0	0	24.2	27	14	13	1	11	14	104	0	0	0	1
TOTAL	161	4.17	66–95	22	161	124	37	9	1427.0	1497	761	661	166	521	773	6177	76	35	3	57

1967

NATIONAL LEAGUE

Team	W	L	PCT	GB	BA	ERA
Cardinals	101	60	.627	—	.263	3.05
Giants	91	71	.562	10.5	.245	2.92
Cubs	87	74	.540	14.0	.251	3.48
Reds	87	75	.537	14.5	.248	3.05
Phillies	82	80	.506	19.5	.242	3.10
Pirates	81	81	.500	20.5	.277	3.74
Braves	77	85	.475	24.5	.240	3.47
Dodgers	73	89	.451	28.5	.236	3.21
Astros	69	93	.426	32.5	.249	4.03
Mets	61	101	.377	40.5	.238	3.73

A new era was dawning at Shea Stadium, although you couldn't tell by the team's record. The Mets claimed the National League cellar again following a one-year respite, losing more than 100 games for the fifth time in their six-season existence. But there were several reasons to believe the Mets were headed in the right direction.

Tom Seaver became the club's ace after just one year in the minors. Seaver was the first Met to win a postseason honor, capturing the NL Rookie of the Year Award after going 16–13 with 170 strikeouts and a 2.76 ERA. He set team records for wins, strikeouts, and ERA while displaying a hate-to-lose mentality that contrasted the team's early history.

Ron Taylor and Seaver were among 13 Mets from the 1967 team who would be on the postseason roster two years later. Taylor was the team's top reliever after signing a minor league deal prior to the '67 season. He stabilized a shaky bullpen, appearing in a team-high 50 games and posting a 2.34 ERA, the lowest of any Mets pitcher with more than 17 innings.

The starting lineup usually included Jerry Grote, Ed Kranepool, Bud Harrelson, Ed Charles, Cleon Jones, and Ron Swoboda, all of whom would play a significant role in the Mets' miracle 1969 season. Swoboda arguably had his best season in the majors, hitting a career-best .281 with 13 homers and 53 RBIs. Harrelson was second to Tommy Davis with 151 games played, and Kranepool's .269 average was a career-high at that point.

Davis was the team's top hitter in his only season as a Met, pacing the team with a .302 average, 174 hits, 16 homers, and 73 RBIs. He would be the key player in a deal that sent Tommie Agee and Al Weis to the Mets following the 1967 season.

Bob Johnson also would become a one-year Met despite hitting .348 in 230 at-bats. Johnson had the highest slugging percentage (.474) of any Met with at least 200 at-bats that season.

Charles played well enough to unseat Ken Boyer at third base, three years after Boyer won the NL MVP Award. Boyer, who led the Mets with 61 RBIs the previous season, was shipped to the White Sox in July.

The Mets thought they had their center fielder of the future when they landed Don Bosch from the Pirates in a December 1966 deal that also brought Don Cardwell to New York. But Bosch was an absolute bust, batting .140 in 93 at-bats while displaying no power and only a decent glove.

Bosch was one of 54 players used by the Mets in 1967, as Bing Devine did everything in his power to turn around the team. Devine had just been elevated to team president in the fall of 1966, following the retirement of George Weiss. Devine worked in the Mets' scouting department after being fired as the Cardinals' general manager in August 1964. The Mets promised him the team presidency upon Weiss' expected retirement after the 1965 season, but Weiss decided to stay on an extra year, allowing Devine to play a major role in the development of the Mets' talent pool.

The Mets had a steady shuttle of players throughout the 1967 season as Devine tinkered with the roster. The team set a major league record by using 27 pitchers, eight of whom would play for the 1969 squad. But of those eight pitchers, only Seaver, Cardwell, and Cal Koonce had established themselves in the majors by the end of the 1967 season.

The losing started to affect the team's profit margin. Although the Mets finished third in the league in attendance at 1,565,492, that figure represented a drop of nearly 400,000 from 1966. In their sixth year of existence, the 1967 Mets had made just a 10-win improvement over the '63 squad. Jones had yet to swing a consistent bat, hitting only .249 with five homers and 30 RBIs after producing a

.275 average with 57 ribbies the previous season. Harrelson showed great range at shortstop, but his 32 errors were a bit alarming if you didn't notice that two-thirds of those miscues came by the All-Star break. Grote batted just .195, and Kranepool was proving to be a middle-of-the-road outfielder/first baseman after gaining notoriety by breaking many of Hank Greenberg's records at James Monroe High in the Bronx. For the second straight season, Kranepool carried a .300+ average into mid-July before fading.

Although Seaver's emergence generated excitement, the Mets had become an otherwise boring team. They finished ninth in the league with a .238 team average and just 83 homers, and were dead last in runs scored, doubles, and triples. Jack Fisher was the only pitcher other than Seaver to win more than five games, going 9–18 in his final season with the Mets.

The Mets never got in a groove during the season. Thanks in part to Seaver, the team's longest losing streak was "only" eight games. But the Mets never won more than five straight, and they occupied the basement from August 22 through the end of the season.

Manager Wes Westrum tried to maintain a positive attitude in the clubhouse, but he was a beat writer's worst nightmare after games. Westrum would speak in clichés and malapropism ("that game was a real cliff-dweller"), giving the media very little to work with after they watched the team muddle through nine innings. He also was wearing out his welcome among the Mets hierarchy who expected the team to build on its 1966 season.

Westrum was signed through the end of the season and had hoped to hear about an extension before the final game. The Mets finally told Westrum in September that his services would not be retained, prompting him to resign with 11 games left in the season. Salty Parker led the Mets to a 4–7 mark the rest of the way.

Looking at the glass half-full, the Mets only finished 12 games behind the defending NL champion Dodgers. But the Mets also wound up 26 games behind the Cubs, the team that finished in the NL cellar a year ago. The Astros ended up eight games ahead of the Mets, who now had 81 fewer wins than its expansion brothers.

1967 Mets Statistics

Hitting	G	AB	R	H	2B	3B	HR	RBI	BB	SO	BA	OBP	SLG	SB	CS	GDP	HP	SH	SF	IBB
Sandy Alomar	15	22	1	0	0	0	0	0	0	6	.000	.000	.000	0	0	1	0	0	0	0
Don Bosch	44	93	7	13	0	1	0	2	5	24	.140	.184	.161	3	1	3	0	3	0	0
Ken Boswell	11	40	2	9	3	0	1	4	1	5	.225	.233	.375	0	0	3	0	0	2	0
Ken Boyer	56	166	17	39	7	2	3	13	26	22	.235	.335	.355	2	1	6	0	0	2	3
Jerry Buchek	124	411	35	97	11	2	14	41	26	101	.236	.283	.375	3	5	10	2	3	2	5
Ed Charles	101	323	32	77	13	2	3	31	24	58	.238	.300	.319	4	1	5	7	5	6	1
Kevin Collins	4	10	1	1	0	0	0	0	0	3	.100	.100	.100	0	0	1	0	0	0	0
Tommy Davis	154	577	72	174	32	0	16	73	31	71	.302	.342	.440	9	3	16	7	1	5	10
Greg Goossen	37	69	2	11	1	0	0	3	4	26	.159	.216	.174	0	0	1	1	0	0	0
Jerry Grote	120	344	25	67	8	0	4	23	14	65	.195	.226	.253	2	2	5	1	4	4	8
Bud Harrelson	151	540	59	137	16	4	1	28	48	64	.254	.317	.304	12	13	5	4	7	4	0
Bob Heise	16	62	7	20	4	0	0	3	3	1	.323	.354	.387	0	1	2	0	0	0	0
Chuck Hiller	25	54	0	5	3	0	0	3	2	11	.093	.125	.148	0	0	1	0	1	0	0
Bob Johnson	90	230	26	80	8	3	5	27	12	29	.348	.377	.474	1	1	8	0	2	2	0
Cleon Jones	129	411	46	101	10	5	5	30	19	57	.246	.282	.331	12	2	8	4	7	5	6
Ed Kranepool	141	469	37	126	17	1	10	54	37	51	.269	.321	.373	0	4	13	1	5	4	15
Johnny Lewis	13	34	2	4	1	0	0	2	2	11	.118	.167	.147	0	0	0	0	0	0	0

Hitting	G	AB	R	H	2B	3B	HR	RBI	BB	SO	BA	OBP	SLG	SB	CS	GDP	HP	SH	SF	IBB
Phil Linz	24	58	8	12	2	0	0	1	4	10	.207	.270	.241	0	0	2	1	2	0	0
Al Luplow	41	112	11	23	1	0	3	9	8	19	.205	.260	.295	0	0	3	1	0	2	1
Joe Moock	13	40	2	9	2	0	0	5	0	7	.225	.225	.275	0	0	1	0	0	0	0
Amos Otis	19	59	6	13	2	0	0	1	5	13	.220	.292	.254	0	4	0	1	1	0	0
Tommie Reynolds	101	136	16	28	1	0	2	9	11	26	.206	.278	.257	1	1	3	3	1	1	3
Bart Shirley	6	12	1	0	0	0	0	0	0	5	.000	.000	.000	0	0	0	0	0	0	0
Larry Stahl	71	155	9	37	5	0	1	18	8	25	.239	.283	.290	2	2	3	2	0	1	0
John Sullivan	65	147	4	32	5	0	0	6	6	26	.218	.248	.252	0	2	2	0	2	0	3
Ron Swoboda	134	449	47	126	17	3	13	53	41	96	.281	.340	.419	3	1	7	1	0	3	4
Hawk Taylor	13	37	3	9	3	0	0	4	2	8	.243	.282	.324	0	0	0	0	0	0	1
Pitchers																				
Dennis Bennett	8	8	1	2	0	0	0	0	0	3	.250	.250	.250	0	0	0	0	0	0	0
Don Cardwell	27	38	1	6	1	0	1	3	3	15	.158	.220	.263	0	0	1	0	0	0	0
Bill Connors	6	1	0	0	0	0	0	0	0	0	.000	.000	.000	0	0	0	0	0	0	0
Bill Denehy	15	9	1	0	0	0	0	0	1	5	.000	.100	.000	0	0	0	0	2	0	0
Chuck Estrada	9	5	0	0	0	0	0	0	0	3	.000	.000	.000	0	0	0	0	0	0	0
Jack Fisher	39	70	3	7	1	0	0	3	3	23	.100	.137	.114	0	0	0	0	6	0	0
Danny Frisella	14	23	1	2	1	0	0	1	1	8	.087	.125	.130	1	0	1	0	0	0	0
Bill Graham	5	8	0	1	0	0	0	1	0	2	.125	.125	.125	0	0	0	0	0	0	0
Joe Grzenda	11	1	0	0	0	0	0	0	0	0	.000	.000	.000	0	0	0	0	0	0	0
Jack Hamilton	17	5	2	1	0	0	1	4	0	1	.200	.200	.800	0	0	0	0	0	0	0
Bob Hendley	15	18	1	2	0	0	0	1	2	15	.111	.200	.111	0	0	0	0	4	0	0
Cal Koonce	13	13	1	2	0	0	0	0	0	4	.154	.154	.154	0	0	0	0	1	0	0
Jerry Koosman	9	2	0	0	0	0	0	0	1	1	.000	.333	.000	0	0	0	0	0	0	0
Jack Lamabe	16	5	0	0	0	0	0	0	1	3	.000	.167	.000	0	0	0	0	0	0	0
Tug McGraw	4	4	1	1	1	0	0	0	0	1	.250	.250	.500	0	0	0	0	0	0	0
Hal Reniff	29	4	0	0	0	0	0	0	0	4	.000	.000	.000	0	0	0	0	0	0	0
Les Rohr	3	6	0	0	0	0	0	0	0	3	.000	.000	.000	0	0	0	0	0	0	0
Tom Seaver	36	77	5	11	2	0	0	5	8	24	.143	.230	.169	2	0	0	1	6	1	0
Dick Selma	43	22	2	2	0	0	0	0	0	10	.091	.091	.091	0	0	0	0	1	0	0
Bob Shaw	23	25	0	1	0	0	0	0	1	10	.040	.077	.040	0	0	1	0	1	0	0
Don Shaw	40	3	1	0	0	0	0	0	2	1	.000	.400	.000	0	0	0	0	1	0	0
Ron Taylor	50	7	0	0	0	0	0	0	0	5	.000	.000	.000	0	0	0	0	1	0	0
Nick Willhite	4	2	0	0	0	0	0	0	0	0	.000	.000	.000	0	0	1	0	0	0	0
Billy Wynne	6	1	0	0	0	0	0	0	0	0	.000	.000	.000	0	0	0	0	0	0	0
TOTAL	162	5417	498	1288	178	23	83	461	362	981	.238	.286	.325	58	44	113	37	68	44	60

Pitching	G	ERA	W:–L	SV	GS	GF	CG	SHO	IP	H	R	ER	HR	BB	SO	BFP	WP	HBP	BK	IBB
Dennis Bennett	8	5.13	1–1	0	6	1	0	0	26.1	37	15	15	4	7	14	121	1	1	0	1
Don Cardwell	26	3.57	5–9	0	16	3	3	3	118.1	112	55	47	8	39	71	498	5	7	1	8
Bill Connors	6	6.23	0–0	0	1	3	0	0	13.0	9	9	9	3	5	13	54	0	1	0	0
Bill Denehy	15	4.70	1–7	0	8	1	0	0	53.2	51	38	28	8	29	35	240	6	0	0	2
Chuck Estrada	9	9.41	1–2	0	2	0	0	0	22.0	28	24	23	5	17	15	106	4	1	0	1
Jack Fisher	39	4.70	9–18	0	30	3	7	1	220.1	251	121	115	21	64	117	958	5	4	1	10
Danny Frisella	14	3.41	1–6	0	11	1	0	0	74.0	68	32	28	6	33	51	316	1	0	0	1
Bill Graham	5	2.63	1–2	0	3	0	1	0	27.1	20	10	8	3	11	14	111	0	0	0	0
Joe Grzenda	11	2.16	0–0	0	0	3	0	0	16.2	14	4	4	0	8	9	70	1	1	0	4
Jack Hamilton	17	3.73	2–0	1	1	9	0	0	31.1	24	15	13	2	16	22	135	3	1	0	5
Bob Hendley	15	3.44	3–3	0	13	2	2	0	70.2	65	35	27	11	28	36	304	1	1	0	4
Jerry Hinsley	2	3.60	0–0	0	0	1	0	0	5.0	6	2	2	0	4	3	23	0	0	0	0
Cal Koonce	11	2.80	3–3	0	6	1	2	1	45.0	45	16	14	2	7	24	183	0	0	0	1
Jerry Koosman	9	6.04	0–2	0	3	1	0	0	22.1	22	17	15	3	19	11	105	0	0	1	4
Jack Lamabe	16	3.98	0–3	1	2	8	0	0	31.2	24	15	14	4	8	23	129	2	0	0	1
Tug McGraw	4	7.79	0–3	0	4	0	0	0	17.1	13	16	15	3	13	18	78	4	0	0	2
Hal Reniff	29	3.35	3–3	4	0	16	0	0	43.0	42	20	16	1	23	21	191	4	1	0	4
Les Rohr	3	2.12	2–1	0	3	0	0	0	17.0	13	7	4	1	9	15	71	0	0	0	0
Al Schmelz	2	3.00	0–0	0	0	2	0	0	3.0	4	1	1	1	1	2	12	0	0	0	0
Tom Seaver	35	2.76	16–13	0	34	1	18	2	251.0	224	85	77	19	78	170	1029	5	5	0	6
Dick Selma	38	2.77	2–4	2	4	12	0	0	81.1	71	29	25	3	36	52	341	5	2	0	6
Bob Shaw	23	4.29	3–9	0	13	5	3	1	98.2	105	54	47	9	28	49	420	4	2	0	9
Don Shaw	40	2.98	4–5	3	0	18	0	0	51.1	40	19	17	5	23	44	216	0	0	0	5
Ron Taylor	50	2.34	4–6	8	0	31	0	0	73.0	60	21	19	1	23	46	297	1	1	2	14
Ralph Terry	2	0.00	0–0	0	0	1	0	0	3.1	1	0	0	0	0	5	11	0	0	0	0
Nick Willhite	4	8.64	0–1	0	1	0	0	0	8.1	9	8	8	1	5	9	40	2	0	1	0
Billy Wynne	6	3.12	0–0	0	1	3	0	0	8.2	12	4	3	0	2	4	41	0	0	0	0
TOTAL	162	3.73	61–101	19	162	126	36	10	1433.0	1369	672	594	124	536	893	6100	54	28	6	88

1968

NATIONAL LEAGUE						
Team	W	L	PCT	GB	BA	ERA
Cardinals	97	65	.599	—	.249	2.49
Giants	88	74	.543	9.0	.239	2.71
Cubs	84	78	.519	13.0	.242	3.41
Reds	83	79	.512	14.0	.273	3.56
Braves	81	81	.500	16.0	.252	2.92
Pirates	80	82	.494	17.0	.252	2.74
Dodgers	76	86	.469	21.0	.230	2.69
Phillies	76	86	.469	21.0	.233	3.36
Mets	73	89	.451	24.0	.228	2.72
Astros	72	90	.444	25.0	.231	3.26

The philosophy started to change at Shea Stadium months before the start of the 1968 season, beginning with the hiring of a no-nonsense manager who would serve as a surrogate father to some and a Catholic school nun to others. The Mets improved their future by dipping into their past, acquiring manager Gil Hodges from the Senators for pitcher Bill Denehy and a reported $100,000 cash on October 11, 1967. Hodges was an original Met who had been one of the most respected players among the Brooklyn Dodgers in the 1950s.

The Indiana-born Hodges was Brooklyn's own following 11 seasons at Ebbets Field. Jackie Robinson revitalized the Dodgers in 1947, and Roy Campanella won NL MVP awards three times in five years, but Hodges provided the consistency that helped the Dodgers win one World Series and five pennants between 1949 and 1956. He hit at least 22 homers each year between 1949 and 1959, and drove in more than 100 runs in seven straight seasons. He also retired as the all-time National League leader with 14 grand slams and was the Senior Circuit's all-time leader among right-handed batters with 370 homers.

Hodges retired in 1963 upon taking over as manager of the Senators. His teams improved each year under his watch, topping out with a franchise-record 76 wins in 1967, the best season for Washington baseball since 1953.

Hodges would take over a Mets team that regressed in '67, losing 101 games after going 66–95 the previous season. But the days of acquiring over-the-hill veterans were over, thanks in part to a now-productive farm system that was built by Johnny Murphy, Whitey Herzog, and Bing Devine. The Mets would sink or swim with prospects culled by scouts who had a keen eye for pitching. Tom Seaver, Jerry Koosman, Dick Selma, and Nolan Ryan were part of the rotation at the start of the season. The Mets later added home-grown right-hander Jim McAndrew, who was victimized by poor run support but showed he belonged in the majors.

Most of the Mets' everyday lineup came through the farm system. Cleon Jones and Ron Swoboda were the corner outfielders, although ex-Red Art Shamsky split time with Swoboda in right field. Former Mets farmhands Bud Harrelson and Ken Boswell comprised the middle of the infield, and Ed Kranepool was back at first base.

Hodges had been impressed by a White Sox center-fielder who was the AL Rookie of the Year in 1966 but had slumped to .234 a year later. The skipper had suggested to Murphy, the Mets' new general manager, that they acquire Tommie Agee despite his sub-par season. In a break from tradition, the Mets dealt experience for youth when they picked up Agee and Al Weis from the Chisox for veterans Jack Fisher and Tommy Davis, along with Billy Wynne. The trade demonstrated the Mets would be a younger team that relied on fundamentals, a little speed, and plenty of pitching.

The Mets were well-armed in the Year of the Pitcher. Seaver followed his Rookie-of-the-Year season by going 16–12 with a 2.20 ERA, five shutout,s and a team-record 205 strikeouts. Selma was brilliant through mid-July, going 8–3 with a 2.01 ERA before tailing off in the second half. Ryan began the season 3–2 with a 1.02 ERA while striking out 44 over his first 35⅓ innings, covering five starts. But a blister problem would cause him to miss the entire month of August. McAndrew was the tough-luck pitcher of the group as the Mets were shut out in each of his first four decisions. He ended the season with three straight wins.

The real revelation was Koosman, who went 0–2 with a 6.04 ERA in nine games a year earlier. The lefty from Minnesota opened the '68 season with back-to-back shutouts and was 12–4 with a 1.82 ERA by the All-Star break. Koosman's ERA didn't rise above 2.00 until September 24, and he finished the year with the most shutouts for an NL rookie in 57 years. He set team records with 19 wins, seven shutouts, and a 2.08 ERA.

The four veterans on the staff were Don Cardwell, Ron Taylor, Cal Koonce, and Al Jackson, who was reacquired by the Mets before the season. Cardwell led the team with 13 losses despite a 2.96 ERA, and Taylor set a club record with 14 saves. Koonce had a 1.98 ERA until he was hammered in his last outing. And Jackson recorded a 3.69 ERA, his best as a Met.

The Mets allowed just 499 runs and pitched to a 2.72 ERA, fourth-best in the National League. Although the team finished fifth in the league with 81 homers, the Mets scored just 473 runs and were last in the NL with a .228 average.

Much of the Mets' offensive woes centered around Agee, whose average stayed under .200 for more than five months. Agee's Mets career began when he was drilled on the helmet by Bob Gibson's first pitch of spring training. The Mobile, Alabama, native went 5-for-16 (.312) in his first four regular season games, but he began his tailspin by going 0-for-10 in the Mets' 24-inning loss to the Astros. Things got so bad that Don Bosch received ample playing time in center for a while after batting a robust .140 the previous season.

Swoboda, Grote, Jones, and Ed Charles provided much of the Mets' offense. Swoboda got off to a fantastic start, hitting eight homers and driving in 22 runs in the Mets' first 25 games. Grote was named to the NL All-Star team and batted a career-best .282. Jones flirted with .300 for most of the season, and Charles led the team with 15 homers while batting .276 after winning a roster spot in spring training.

There were signs the Mets could compete in the National League. They stood in sixth place at 35–36 on June 27, just nine games off the lead. The ridiculous losses that plagued previous Mets teams were minimized. Any Met will tell you things began to jell under Murphy and Hodges, who were hell-bent on shedding the team of its laughingstock image. The improvement showed up

at the gate as the Mets drew a team-record 1,781,657 to Shea.

But the Mets absorbed a shocking blow on September 24 in Atlanta when Hodges suffered what was called a "mild" heart attack. He threw batting practice as usual that day but was in the trainer's room by the end of the first inning. He was hospitalized for nearly a month before spending the winter recuperating in St. Petersburg. Some didn't expect Hodges to return to the dugout, but the "Quiet Man" would be with the team for the start of spring training 1969.

1968 Mets Statistics

Hitting	G	AB	R	H	2B	3B	HR	RBI	BB	SO	BA	OBP	SLG	SB	CS	GDP	HP	SH	SF	IBB
Tommie Agee	132	368	30	80	12	3	5	17	15	103	.217	.255	.307	13	8	8	4	3	1	3
Don Bosch	50	111	14	19	1	0	3	7	9	33	.171	.231	.261	0	2	2	0	1	1	1
Ken Boswell	75	284	37	74	7	2	4	11	16	27	.261	.300	.342	7	2	6	1	3	2	0
Jerry Buchek	73	192	8	35	4	0	1	11	10	53	.182	.234	.219	1	1	8	3	2	0	5
Ed Charles	117	369	41	102	11	1	15	53	28	57	.276	.328	.434	5	4	7	2	6	4	4
Kevin Collins	58	154	12	31	5	2	1	13	7	37	.201	.233	.279	0	1	2	0	5	2	2
Duffy Dyer	1	3	0	1	0	0	0	0	1	1	.333	.500	.333	0	0	0	0	0	0	0
Greg Goossen	38	106	4	22	7	0	0	6	10	21	.208	.288	.274	0	0	4	2	1	0	0
Jerry Grote	124	404	29	114	18	0	3	31	44	81	.282	.357	.349	1	5	6	3	3	0	11
Bud Harrelson	111	402	38	88	7	3	0	14	29	68	.219	.273	.251	4	5	3	1	4	1	2
Bob Heise	6	23	3	5	0	0	0	1	1	1	.217	.250	.217	0	0	1	0	1	0	0
Cleon Jones	147	509	63	151	29	4	14	55	31	98	.297	.341	.452	23	12	8	5	4	3	3
Mike Jorgensen	8	14	0	2	1	0	0	0	0	4	.143	.143	.214	0	0	0	0	0	0	0
Ed Kranepool	127	373	29	86	13	1	3	20	19	39	.231	.271	.295	0	3	6	2	10	1	5
Phil Linz	78	258	19	54	7	0	0	17	10	41	.209	.243	.236	1	0	7	2	3	2	0
J.C. Martin	78	244	20	55	9	2	3	31	21	31	.225	.298	.316	0	0	4	5	3	2	3
Art Shamsky	116	345	30	82	14	4	12	48	21	58	.238	.292	.406	1	0	6	7	4	4	6
Larry Stahl	53	183	15	43	7	2	3	10	21	38	.235	.314	.344	3	0	1	0	1	0	1
Ron Swoboda	132	450	46	109	14	6	11	59	52	113	.242	.325	.373	8	1	14	4	1	1	1
Al Weis	90	274	15	47	6	0	1	14	21	63	.172	.234	.204	3	1	3	2	2	2	3
Pitchers																				
Don Cardwell	30	61	3	3	0	0	1	4	0	34	.049	.049	.098	0	0	3	0	3	0	0
Bill Connors	9	1	0	1	0	0	0	0	1	0	1.000	1.000	1.000	0	0	0	0	1	0	0
Danny Frisella	19	12	0	1	0	0	0	0	0	7	.083	.083	.083	1	0	1	0	0	0	0
Al Jackson	27	28	2	7	1	0	0	2	0	9	.250	.241	.286	0	0	1	0	1	1	0
Cal Koonce	55	14	0	0	0	0	0	0	2	8	.000	.125	.000	0	0	1	0	0	0	0
Jerry Koosman	35	91	3	7	1	0	1	4	3	62	.077	.106	.121	0	0	1	0	3	0	0
Jim McAndrew	12	22	1	1	0	0	0	0	1	15	.045	.087	.045	0	0	0	0	2	0	0
Les Rohr	2	0	0	0	0	0	0	0	1	0	1.000			0	0	0	0	0	0	0
Nolan Ryan	21	44	2	5	0	0	0	2	2	29	.114	.152	.114	0	0	0	0	1	0	0
Tom Seaver	38	95	5	15	2	0	0	3	3	44	.158	.184	.179	0	0	0	0	3	0	0
Dick Selma	39	58	4	12	2	0	0	1	0	20	.207	.207	.241	1	0	1	0	4	0	0
Bill Short	34	2	0	0	0	0	0	0	0	2	.000	.000	.000	0	0	0	0	0	0	0
Ron Taylor	58	9	0	0	0	0	0	0	0	6	.000	.000	.000	0	0	0	0	0	0	0
TOTAL	163	5503	473	1252	178	30	81	434	379	1203	.228	.277	.315	72	45	104	43	75	27	50

Pitching	G	ERA	W-L	SV	GS	GF	CG	SHO	IP	H	R	ER	HR	BB	SO	BFP	WP	HBP	BK	IBB
Don Cardwell	29	2.96	7–13	1	25	1	5	1	179.2	156	69	59	9	50	82	747	7	10	1	11
Bill Connors	9	9.00	0–1	0	0	3	0	0	14.0	21	14	14	0	7	8	72	1	1	0	1
Danny Frisella	19	3.91	2–4	2	4	10	0	0	50.2	53	23	22	5	17	47	216	4	0	0	6
Al Jackson	25	3.69	3–7	3	9	7	0	0	92.2	88	42	38	5	17	59	376	0	2	0	6
Cal Koonce	55	2.41	6–4	11	2	31	0	0	97.0	80	27	26	4	32	50	385	4	1	0	11
Jerry Koosman	35	2.08	19–12	0	34	0	17	7	263.2	221	72	61	16	69	178	1058	8	8	0	7
Jim McAndrew	12	2.28	4–7	0	12	0	2	1	79.0	66	20	20	5	17	46	314	4	4	0	4
Les Rohr	2	4.50	0–2	0	1	1	0	0	6.0	9	4	3	0	7	5	34	1	0	1	3
Nolan Ryan	21	3.09	6–9	0	18	1	3	0	134.0	93	50	46	12	75	133	559	7	4	0	4
Tom Seaver	36	2.20	16–12	1	35	1	14	5	277.2	224	73	68	15	48	205	1088	8	8	1	5
Dick Selma	33	2.76	9–10	0	23	3	4	3	169.2	148	63	52	11	54	117	703	7	5	0	5
Don Shaw	7	0.73	0–0	0	0	3	0	0	12.1	3	1	1	1	5	11	41	3	0	0	0
Bill Short	34	4.75	0–3	1	0	13	0	0	30.1	24	17	16	0	14	24	128	5	1	0	1
Ron Taylor	58	2.70	1–5	14	0	44	0	0	76.2	64	24	23	4	18	49	307	0	1	0	9
TOTAL	163	2.72	73–89	33	163	118	45	25	1483.0	1250	499	448	87	430	1014	6028	59	45	3	67

1969

NL EAST

Team	W	L	PCT	GB	BA	ERA
Mets	100	62	.617	—	.242	2.99
Cubs	92	70	.568	8.0	.253	3.34
Pirates	88	74	.543	12.0	.277	3.61
Cardinals	87	75	.537	13.0	.253	2.94
Phillies	63	99	.389	37.0	.241	4.14
Expos	52	110	.321	48.0	.240	4.33

Mets Beat Braves in NLCS 3–0
Mets Beat Orioles in World Series 4–1

Sure, the Mets had shown improvement during the 1968 season. They had young arms in Tom Seaver, Jerry Koosman, and Nolan Ryan, with another fireballer, Gary Gentry, on the way. Jerry Grote had learned to handle a pitching staff, Bud Harrelson was emerging as a vacuum at short, and Cleon Jones had become the most talented hitter produced through the Mets farm system. But 100 wins and a World Series title a year later? C'mon. Even manager Gil Hodges was met with skeptical glances from the media when he told them in February 1969 he thought the team could win 85 games.

Several Mets thought their pitching could carry them a long way, although Koosman wasn't so sure.

"If that was, it was the older guys because the young guys…Hell, none of us had been there before," Koosman said. "We finished ninth the year before, and we didn't know what it would take to win. The ones who felt we had a shot would have been the older, experienced guys."

The pitching staff in 1968 was either first or second in the league in shutouts, hits, runs, and strikeouts while posting the NL's fourth-best ERA (2.72). But the offense was dead last in hitting (.228) and first in strikeouts, putting the burden on a pitching staff that would be downright giddy if given a two-run lead.

Runs continued to be scarce in 1969 as the Mets finished ninth in the NL with 632, averaging 3.90 per game. But timely hitting backed up a solid staff that had the talent and confidence to protect 2–1 or 3–2 leads.

The '69 Mets didn't get off to a rousing start, losing to the Expos in the expansion team's first-ever game. New York reached the .500 mark in Game 36, a lofty goal for the National League misfits. But a loss to the expansion Padres on May 27 dropped the Mets to 18–23, nine games behind the first-place Cubs. The Mets wouldn't lose again until June 11, reeling off a team-record 11 straight wins that showed Hodges' 85-win prediction wasn't off-base. Although the Mets were able to shave just two games off the Cubs' lead during the winning streak, it was down to 4.5 games after New York took two of three from the Cubbies at Shea in early July, including Tom Seaver's one-hitter.

The Cubs appeared destined to make their first post-season appearance since 1945, winning 40 of their first 58 games to take an 8½-game lead in the NL East. The front end of the rotation—Ferguson Jenkins and Ken Holtzman—was a combined 18–4 by June 14, while Bill Hands was 5–6 despite a 2.94 ERA. The lineup consisted of All-Star-caliber performers everywhere except in center and right. Left-fielder Billy Williams and basemen Ernie Banks and Ron Santo would become Hall of Famers.

Santo and the Cubs drew the ire of at least one Met.

"When they'd win a game," Koosman remembered some four decades later, "Ron Santo would jump up in the air and click his heels, which was kind of rubbing it in our face. They were certainly cocky playing against us.

"The fans are involved and the writers help create the storm, too, so there was a big rivalry. Leo Durocher would always say something in the paper that would get our blood flowing. They knew they were better than us and they'd say so."

But the Mets had it all over the Cubs in two areas: deep pitching and a solid bench. Hodges used his depth to his advantage. Cubs manager Leo Durocher cracked the whip and got burned.

Durocher could call on veterans Phil Regan (12–6, 17 saves) and Hank Aguirre (2.60 ERA in 41 games) to spell the starters. The rest of the bullpen was ineffective, and the role players were unproductive when Durocher gave them a rare chance to play.

The Cubs had five players appear in at least 151 games. Meanwhile, Tommie Agee and Cleon Jones were the lone Mets to play more than 124 games. Hodges platooned at first, second, third, and right field while keeping Grote fresh behind the plate. The days off would make a difference down the stretch.

"Leo had stuck with his horses, and maybe that hurt us the last month of the season," said Glenn Beckert in Peter Golenbock's book *Wrigleyville*. "That's second-guessing now. But there was no platooning with Leo. I knew I was tired, and I knew I had an injury before that [Beckert missed 26 games in June]. Kess [Don Kessinger] was getting a little weary, not only physically but mentally. Ron [Santo] and Randy [Hundley] were hurting.

"We were playing banged up, and maybe that was the time we could have used a couple days' rest."

Hodges wasn't afraid to rest his regulars, even for disciplinary reasons. Cleon Jones was challenging for the batting title and was the offensive catalyst in the lineup. But Jones appeared to loaf on a hit by Astros catcher Johnny Edwards in late July, playing it into a double. Hodges stepped out of the dugout as if to make a pitching change. But his stroll continued past the mound, beyond the lip of the infield, and out to left field, where he took Jones out of the game. Hodges was miffed at his best offensive weapon and was prepared to show the ballclub he'd bench anyone who didn't hustle. It would be five days before Jones started another game.

The Mets run onto the field to celebrate their World Series win over the Orioles at Shea Stadium, October 16, 1969.

The benching came at a key time for the team, which was in the process of losing a doubleheader to Houston by a combined 27–8 score.

"You don't slough off when you play for Gil Hodges," said Koosman. "You give him 100 percent all the time. It sends a message to the rest of the club."[7]

The Mets were 9½ games out of first on August 13 after getting swept in a three-game series at Houston. The team would go 38–11 the rest of the way, winning 18 of 24 heading into a huge series against the Cubs at Shea Stadium.

The Cubs were clinging to a 2½-game lead when they arrived at Shea on September 8. They were a half-game ahead when they left. Chicago tried to intimidate the Mets from the start of the series opener in an attempt to end a four-game losing streak. Bill Hands threw at Tommie Agee's head on his very first pitch in the bottom of the first. Agee eventually grounded out but was a contributor to all the Mets runs in a 3–2 win. The center fielder gave the Mets an early lead with a two-run homer in the third before scoring the tiebreaking run on Wayne Garrett's single, eluding Hundley's tag at the plate.

Jerry Koosman knew what to do after Agee was thrown at. With Ron Santo leading off the top of the second, Koos-

man immediately plunked him on the forearm. Touche.

"Nobody told me to throw at Santo," recalled Koosman. "My feeling was I wasn't going to let Bill Hands intimidate my hitters. And the best way to prove it was, I had the clean-up hitter, so let's stop [the brushbacks] right now."[8]

Game 2 of the series featured a battle of aces, Seaver against Jenkins. Art Shamsky and Donn Clendenon homered to support Seaver's five-hitter as the Mets whipped the Cubbies 7–1.

Clendenon's contributions to the season can't be overstated. He gave the Mets a much-needed power threat in the lineup after being acquired from the Expos in mid-June. Clendenon belted 12 homers and drove in 37 runs in just 202 at-bats for the team that season.

The Mets had a chance to finally move into first place when they hosted a doubleheader against the Expos on September 10. Even if the Cubs won that day, New York would be percentage points ahead with a sweep of the Expos. The Mets took the opener 3–2 in 12 innings, then completed a 7–1 rout of the Expos after the Cubs lost 6–2 at Philadelphia. The lead was a game.

The Mets were 2½ games ahead two days later after sweeping a doubleheader in Pittsburgh.

"I think we believed in ourselves," Jim McAndrew said. But just like everybody says, the doubleheader in Pittsburgh has to be the one where we looked around as if to say we're a team of fate.

"They had murderer's row as far as hitters were concerned. We went in there for the double-dip and we won both games 1–0. Koosman and Cardwell shut them out, they both went nine innings and drove in the only runs."

Koosman batted just .048 (4-for-84) the entire season.

"He swung hard but had trouble with contact. He became a better hitter as he got older."

The Mets won their tenth in a row a day later to stretch the gap to 3 ½ games. But they would drop the first three games of a five-game set against the Pirates at Shea on the next-to-last weekend of the season, capping the skid with Bob Moose's no-hitter. But the Cubs were able to shave just a game off their deficit, putting them four behind with eight to play.

The Mets wrapped up the division title by winning their final regular season home game, dominating the Cardinals 6–0 on September 24. Clendenon hit a three-run homer and Ed Charles added a two-run blast in a five-run first that chased Steve Carlton from the mound. Just nine days earlier, Carlton set a major league record by striking out 19 Mets, only to lose 4–3 on a pair of two-run homers by Ron Swoboda.

Clendenon would homer again in the fifth inning to make it 6–0. Gentry did the rest, throwing a four-hitter that ended when Joe Torre hit into a 6–4–3 double play.

Having dispatched the Cubs, the Mets prepared for the NL West–champion Braves in the first-ever National League Championship Series. The Mets' starting pitchers struggled mightily in the series, but the team batted .327 with six homers in a three-game sweep of the Braves.

Next up were the Orioles, who won 108 games during the regular season before sweeping the Twins in the ALCS. The Birds took the World Series opener 4–1 but scored just five runs over the next four contests as the Mets took the Fall Classic in five games. The Orioles hit a meager .146 with three homers, none in Games 2, 3, or 4.

Seaver won the NL Cy Young Award after going 25–7 with a 2.21 ERA. Al Weis was given the Babe Ruth Award as the World Series MVP, batting .455 with a rare homer and three RBIs against the Orioles. Clendenon was *Sport Magazine*'s World Series MVP, hitting three homers, including a two-run shot that started the Mets' comeback in Game 5.

1969 Mets Statistics

Hitting	G	AB	R	H	2B	3B	HR	RBI	BB	SO	BA	OBP	SLG	SB	CS	GDP	HP	SH	SF	IBB
Tommie Agee	149	565	97	153	23	4	26	76	59	137	.271	.342	.464	12	9	5	3	6	2	2
Ken Boswell	102	362	48	101	14	7	3	32	36	47	.279	.347	.381	7	3	13	2	4	1	3
Ed Charles	61	169	21	35	8	1	3	18	18	31	.207	.286	.320	4	2	6	1	0	1	3
Donn Clendenon	72	202	31	51	5	0	12	37	19	62	.252	.321	.455	3	2	3	2	2	1	4
Kevin Collins	16	40	1	6	3	0	1	2	3	10	.150	.209	.300	0	0	0	0	0	0	1
Duffy Dyer	29	74	5	19	3	1	3	12	4	22	.257	.295	.446	0	0	3	0	1	0	0
Wayne Garrett	124	400	38	87	11	3	1	39	40	75	.218	.290	.268	4	2	5	3	6	5	3
Rod Gaspar	118	215	26	49	6	1	1	14	25	19	.228	.313	.279	7	3	1	2	7	1	2
Jim Gosger	10	15	0	2	2	0	0	1	1	6	.133	.188	.267	0	0	0	0	0	0	1
Jerry Grote	113	365	38	92	12	3	6	40	32	59	.252	.313	.351	2	1	10	1	6	2	5
Bud Harrelson	123	395	42	98	11	6	0	24	54	54	.248	.341	.306	1	3	5	2	5	1	7
Bob Heise	4	10	1	3	1	0	0	0	3	2	.300	.462	.400	0	0	1	0	0	0	1
Cleon Jones	137	483	92	164	25	4	12	75	64	60	.340	.422	.482	16	8	11	7	1	3	10
Ed Kranepool	112	353	36	84	9	2	11	49	37	32	.238	.307	.368	3	2	10	0	2	4	7
J.C. Martin	66	177	12	37	5	1	4	21	12	32	.209	.257	.316	0	0	6	0	1	2	1
Amos Otis	48	93	6	14	3	1	0	4	6	27	.151	.202	.204	1	0	0	0	3	0	1
Bobby Pfeil	62	211	20	49	9	0	0	10	7	27	.232	.260	.275	1	4	5	1	4	0	0
Art Shamsky	100	303	42	91	9	3	14	47	36	32	.300	.375	.488	1	2	5	3	2	5	2
Ron Swoboda	109	327	38	77	10	2	9	52	43	90	.235	.326	.361	1	1	10	2	1	2	4
Al Weis	103	247	20	53	9	2	2	23	15	51	.215	.259	.291	3	3	3	0	6	1	1
Pitchers																				
Don Cardwell	30	47	3	8	0	0	1	5	0	26	.170	.184	.234	0	0	0	1	2	1	0
Jack Dilauro	23	12	0	0	0	0	0	0	0	9	.000	.000	.000	0	0	0	0	0	0	0
Danny Frisella	3	1	0	0	0	0	0	0	0	0	.000	.000	.000	0	0	0	0	0	0	0
Gary Gentry	35	74	2	6	1	0	0	1	1	52	.081	.104	.095	0	0	0	1	7	1	0
Al Jackson	9	1	0	0	0	0	0	0	0	0	.000	.000	.000	0	0	0	0	0	0	0
Cal Koonce	40	17	1	4	0	0	0	1	0	7	.235	.235	.235	0	0	0	0	0	0	0
Jerry Koosman	32	84	1	4	0	0	0	1	1	46	.048	.059	.048	0	0	2	0	4	0	0
Jim McAndrew	27	37	0	5	1	0	0	3	3	18	.135	.200	.162	0	1	0	0	5	0	0
Tug McGraw	43	24	1	4	1	0	0	3	1	6	.167	.200	.208	0	0	0	0	0	0	0
Nolan Ryan	25	29	3	3	0	0	0	2	0	14	.103	.103	.103	0	0	1	0	3	0	0
Tom Seaver	39	91	7	11	3	0	0	6	7	34	.121	.200	.154	1	0	0	2	4	0	0
Ron Taylor	59	4	0	1	0	0	0	0	0	2	.250	.250	.250	0	0	0	0	0	0	0
TOTAL	162	5427	632	1311	184	41	109	598	527	1089	.242	.309	.351	66	43	105	33	82	33	58

Pitching	G	ERA	W–L	SV	GS	GF	CG	SHO	IP	H	R	ER	HR	BB	SO	WP	HP	BK	IBB
Don Cardwell	30	3.01	8–10	0	21	2	4	0	152.1	145	63	51	15	47	60	8	5	0	10
Jack Dilauro	23	2.40	1–4	1	4	8	0	0	63.2	50	19	17	4	18	27	2	0	0	5
Danny Frisella	3	7.71	0–0	0	0	0	0	0	4.2	8	4	4	1	3	5	1	0	0	0
Gary Gentry	35	3.43	13–12	0	35	0	6	3	233.2	192	94	89	24	81	154	9	5	0	5
Jesse Hudson	1	4.50	0–0	0	0	1	0	0	2.0	2	1	1	0	2	3	0	0	0	0

Pitching (continued)	G	ERA	W–L	SV	GS	GF	CG	SHO	IP	H	R	ER	HR	BB	SO	WP	HP	BK	IBB
Al Jackson	9	10.64	0–0	0	0	1	0	0	11.0	18	13	13	1	4	10	0	1	0	0
Bob Johnson	2	0.00	0–0	1	0	2	0	0	1.2	1	0	0	0	1	1	0	0	0	0
Cal Koonce	40	4.99	6–3	7	0	19	0	0	83.0	85	53	46	8	42	48	4	3	1	8
Jerry Koosman	32	2.28	17–9	0	32	0	16	6	241.0	187	66	61	14	68	180	7	4	2	11
Jim McAndrew	27	3.47	6–7	0	21	3	4	2	135.0	112	57	52	12	44	90	7	2	0	6
Tug McGraw	42	2.24	9–3	12	4	26	1	0	100.1	89	31	25	6	47	92	8	0	0	7
Les Rohr	1	20.25	0–0	0	0	0	0	0	1.1	5	4	3	0	1	0	0	0	1	0
Nolan Ryan	25	3.53	6–3	1	10	4	2	0	89.1	60	38	35	3	53	92	1	1	3	3
Tom Seaver	36	2.21	25–7	0	35	1	18	5	273.1	202	75	67	24	82	208	8	7	1	9
Ron Taylor	59	2.72	9–4	13	0	44	0	0	76.0	61	23	23	7	24	42	1	1	0	6
TOTAL	162	2.99	100–62	35	162	111	51	28	1468.0	1217	541	488	119	517	1012	56	29	8	70

1970

NL EAST						
TEAM	W	L	PCT	GB	BA	ERA
Pirates	89	73	.549	–	.270	4.10
Cubs	84	78	.519	5.0	.259	3.76
Mets	83	79	.512	6.0	.249	3.45
Cardinals	76	86	.469	13.0	.263	4.06
Phillies	73	88	.453	15.5	.238	4.17
Expos	73	89	.451	16.0	.237	4.50

The Mets' faithful would have killed for an 83-win season just two years earlier, but a World Series title in 1969 created high hopes for the team and erased its "lovable-loser" image. There were several highlights during a year in which a team-record 2,697,479 fans paid their way into Shea Stadium to see the Mets lose what was a very winnable division title.

The Mets reported to camp just a month after general manager Johnny Murphy died following his second heart attack in 15 days. Murphy had been in charge of a farm system that produced most of the Mets' current pitching staff and more than half the team's starting lineup.

What transpired afterward shaped the franchise for the next two decades. With his front office experience productive yet minimal, the Mets could have promoted Whitey Herzog from director of player development to GM, which might have saved the team from agonizing losses to the Cardinals during the 1985 and '87 division races. Herzog, Murphy, Joe McDonald, and Bing Devine were the people most responsible for the Mets' flourishing farm system. But Herzog also would stand up to team president M. Donald Grant when Grant tried to meddle in roster decisions. Instead of handing the GM duties to Herzog, the Mets elevated special assignment scout Bob Scheffing to general manager and put him on the hot seat for five seasons as the team tried to replicate its 1969 season.

There were numerous signs of a post-World Series hangover.

"Oh, absolutely," said Jerry Koosman in a 2008 interview. "We called it the 'Rubber Chicken Circuit.' You'd go to a lot of sports dinners. There's a photographers' dinner. There's a writers' dinner. There are sports banquets in Chicago and all over.

"I think I was home alone with my family for about two days all winter. You're traveling, you're seeing the guys all the time, and it wasn't like you'd go to spring training and you were glad to see everybody. You'd seen everybody all winter long.

"You're still kind of hung over from a tough winter on the 'circuit.'

"We went to spring training not feeling as hungry and rested [as we might have] had we not won the World Series."

Tom Seaver set a National League record with 283 strikeouts, led the circuit with a 2.82 ERA, and tied Steve Carlton's major league mark with 19 strikeouts against the Padres on April 22, including a record-breaking 10 in a row to end the game. However, Seaver took much of the blame for the Mets' finish after winning just one of his last 10 starts, posting a 4.14 ERA during that span. Many forgot that the Mets scored just twice in Seaver's first five losses of the season.

What stymied the Mets was the rest of the starting rotation. Jerry Koosman was limited to 29 starts because of arm troubles that cut his strikeouts down to 118 in 212 innings. Koosman finished 12–7 and saw his ERA rise by almost one run over '69. Gary Gentry had shoulder issues while going 9–9 with a 3.68 ERA, just a year after he earned 13 wins as a rookie.

Nolan Ryan continued to tease the Mets, going 2–1 with a 0.69 ERA in his first three starts, including a one-hit, 15-strikeout game in his first outing. Ryan fanned 13 or more three times during the season, but he also walked 97 in 131⅓ innings.

Don Cardwell struggled before the Mets sold him to the Braves in mid-July. Jim McAndrew posted a 2.60 ERA in the second half of the season but went just 6–7 during that span. And newcomer Ray Sadecki was 6–2 with a 3.24 ERA by July 3 before winning just two games the rest of the way.

If you want to pin the blame on Seaver for the Mets' inability to win the division, consider this: Gary Gentry went 0–3 with a 5.82 ERA after August 18. Nolan Ryan was 1–5 with a 4.12 ERA following his 13-strikeout, three-hit shutout versus the Cubs August 4. Ray Sadecki won just once after July 8 while compiling a 4.67 ERA.

Pitching created "miracles" in 1969, but the Mets' offense in 1970 wasn't good enough to overcome the downslide on the mound. Donn Clendenon and Tommie Agee carried the offense as the Mets set a team record with 640 RBIs. Clendenon drove in 97 to break Frank Thomas' team mark of 94 set in 1962. Clendenon batted .285 with

16 homers and 76 RBIs in the Mets' final 98 games of the year. Agee's 24 homers were two more than Clendenon's total.

Cleon Jones set a team record by hitting safely in 23 straight games between August 25 and September 15. He batted .408 during the streak while driving in 16 runs. But he ended the year hitting .277, 63 points lower than his team-record mark of 1969.

The most disappointing Met was Joe Foy, who was supposed to be the team's third baseman of the future after being acquired from Kansas City for Amos Otis. Foy had 22 stolen bases but hit only .236 with six homers and 37 RBIs in 99 games. Otis was dispatched after refusing to play third base in 1969. As a center fielder for the Royals, he hit .285 and made the first of his five All-Star game appearances.

Wayne Garrett and Ken Boswell emerged as two of the team's nicer surprises in 1970. Garrett batted .254 with 12 homers after hitting only .218 with one home run as a rookie the previous season. Boswell, whose glovework was often criticized before the season, set a major league record for second basemen by playing 85 games without an error.

The glue of the infield was Bud Harrelson, who earned a trip to the All-Star Game and tied a major league mark for shortstops with 54 straight errorless games. Harrelson sat out just five games and set a team record with 95 walks.

Harrelson seemed to produce his best offense when his buddy, Seaver, was on the mound. Harrelson hit .331 in games started by Seaver.

But the Mets hugged the .500 mark like they were cradling a newborn. They were never more than seven games over or three games under .500 until July, when they embarked on a seven-game winning streak that was immediately followed by a five-game skid.

There were two "crucial" series during the season, but one proved to be a mirage. The Mets were 2½ games off the lead until they swept a five-game series from the first-place Cubs at Wrigley Field in June. However, New York's lead was just 1½ after the Pirate overtook the Cubbies for second place during the series.

The Mets were 2½ games off the pace when they began a four-game set with the first-place Pirates at Shea on September 18. Manager Gil Hodges didn't have the services of Seaver, who lost to the Expos the game before the Pittsburgh series began. The Mets could have pulled within a half-game of the division lead by taking three of four. But New York won just once in the series as the Pirates pulled out back-to-back one-run games before taking the series finale in extra innings. Pittsburgh put the Mets out of contention by sweeping a three-game set in Pittsburgh during the final weekend of the season.

Hodges and Scheffing tried all season to find the right formula. First baseman Ed Kranepool was hitting only .118 when he was banished to Triple A Tidewater from June 24 until mid-August. Art Shamsky saw plenty of time at first base as the lefty-righty platoon with Clendenon. Ron Swoboda was given the right field job with Shamsky playing first, but newcomer Dave Marshall took playing time from Swoboda.

The Mets entered September 1½ games behind the first-place Pirates and were tied for the lead as late as September 14. Scheffing tried to solidify the staff by acquiring Ron Herbel and former AL Cy Young Award winner Dean Chance in September, but they didn't stop the Mets from dropping 10 of their final 15 games. The Mets were eliminated when the Pirates beat New York 2–1 on September 27 after Chance and Herbel were the losers in the first two games of the series.

A few of the Mets' losses were right out of the 1962 playbook, including a pair of eye-covering setbacks on consecutive Saturdays in August. New York was holding a 2–1 lead in the ninth inning against the Braves on August 15 when Seaver struck out Bob Tillman with the bases loaded for the second out. However, Grote couldn't glove the wild pitch, allowing Tony Gonzalez to head home. Grote tried to throw to Seaver covering near the plate for what would have been the game-ending out, but Grote's errant toss allowed by Gonzalez and Rico Carty to score, giving the Braves a 3–2 win.

A week later, same score, same inning, the Reds had runners on first and second with nobody out after Joe Foy couldn't come up with Pete Rose's grounder. Tug McGraw and Ryan got the next two outs before Johnny Bench hit a go-ahead, two-run double to put the Reds up 3–2.

There also was an excruciating loss at Montreal, where Bob Bailey belted a grand slam in the bottom of the ninth on May 18 after the Mets carried a 4–3 lead into the inning. And there was an August 26 loss to the Braves in which the Mets led 7–1 in the seventh.

One reason for the 17-win drop-off was the Mets' record against the NL's latest expansion teams. New York combined to go 24–6 against the Padres and Expos in 1969, but Montreal took the season series in 1970 10–8 while San Diego split its 12 games with the Mets. That represented a 10-win difference that would have slid the Mets back into the playoffs.

New York also went 6–12 against the Pirates when a 9–9 mark would have created a tie for the division lead at season's end.

Another factor was the team's inability to win tight games with the same regularity as it did in 1969. The Mets went 10–6 in extra-inning games and were 41–23 in one-run contests in '69. New York finished under .500 in both categories a year later, dropping 11 of 20 extra-inning games and playing to a 24–27 mark in one-run affairs.

1970 Mets Statistics

Hitting	G	AB	R	H	2B	3B	HR	RBI	BB	SO	BA	OBP	SLG	SB	CS	GCP	HP	SH	SF	IBB
Tommie Agee	153	636	107	182	30	7	24	75	55	156	.286	.344	.469	31	15	11	2	1	2	3
Ken Boswell	105	351	32	89	13	2	5	44	41	32	.254	.331	.345	5	4	13	2	3	5	8
Donn Clendenon	121	396	65	114	18	3	22	97	39	91	.288	.348	.515	4	1	15	1	0	7	4
Duffy Dyer	59	148	8	31	1	0	2	12	21	32	.209	.308	.257	1	1	5	0	1	0	4
Tim Foli	5	11	0	4	0	0	0	1	0	2	.364	.364	.364	0	0	0	0	0	0	0
Joe Foy	99	322	39	76	12	0	6	37	68	58	.236	.373	.329	22	13	4	4	2	3	5
Wayne Garrett	114	366	74	93	17	4	12	45	81	60	.254	.390	.421	5	1	4	2	3	2	6
Rod Gaspar	11	14	4	0	0	0	0	0	1	4	.000	.067	.000	1	0	0	0	0	0	0
Jerry Grote	126	415	38	106	14	1	2	34	36	39	.255	.313	.308	2	1	14	1	6	5	8
Bud Harrelson	157	564	72	137	18	8	1	42	95	74	.243	.351	.309	23	4	9	3	12	8	4
Cleon Jones	134	506	71	140	25	8	10	63	57	87	.277	.352	.417	12	3	26	5	0	6	2
Mike Jorgensen	76	87	15	17	3	1	3	4	10	23	.195	.278	.356	2	2	0	0	1	0	1
Ed Kranepool	43	47	2	8	0	0	0	3	5	2	.170	.250	.170	0	0	0	0	0	0	0
Dave Marshall	92	189	21	46	10	1	6	29	17	43	.243	.304	.402	4	1	0	0	0	1	0
Ted Martinez	4	16	0	1	0	0	0	0	0	3	.063	.063	.063	0	0	0	0	0	0	0
Art Shamsky	122	403	48	118	19	2	11	49	49	33	.293	.371	.432	1	1	11	3	0	3	13
Ken Singleton	69	198	22	52	8	0	5	26	30	48	.263	.361	.379	1	1	5	1	4	1	1
Leroy Stanton	4	4	0	1	0	1	0	0	0	0	.250	.250	.750	0	0	1	0	0	0	0
Ron Swoboda	115	245	29	57	8	2	9	40	40	72	.233	.340	.392	2	4	7	1	1	2	0
Al Weis	75	121	20	25	7	1	1	11	7	21	.207	.254	.306	1	1	5	1	0	1	1
Pitchers																				
Don Cardwell	16	5	0	0	0	0	0	1	0	3	.000	.000	.000	0	0	0	0	1	0
Rich Folkers	16	6	1	2	0	0	0	0	0	4	.333	.333	.333	0	0	0	0	0	0	0
Danny Frisella	30	13	0	4	0	0	0	1	1	4	.308	.357	.308	0	0	0	0	1	0	0
Gary Gentry	32	59	2	4	2	0	0	2	5	39	.068	.141	.102	0	1	0	0	5	0	0
Cal Koonce	13	1	0	0	0	0	0	0	0	1	.000	.000	.000	0	0	0	0	0	0	0
Jerry Koosman	30	70	5	6	1	0	0	4	8	46	.086	.179	.100	0	0	2	0	8	0	0
Jim McAndrew	32	54	6	8	3	0	0	2	5	17	.148	.220.	204	0	0	1	0	8	0	0
Tug McGraw	57	13	1	4	1	0	0	5	0	2	.308	.286	.385	0	0	0	0	0	1	0
Nolan Ryan	27	45	2	8	0	0	0	0	0	21	.178	.178	.178	1	0	0	0	2	0	0
Ray Sadecki	28	39	2	8	0	0	0	3	2	10	.205	.244	.205	0	0	1	0	8	0	0
Tom Seaver	42	95	9	17	1	1	1	10	10	31	.179	.257	.242	0	0	1	0	7	0	0
Ron Taylor	57	4	0	0	0	0	0	0	1	4	.000	.200	.000	0	0	0	0	1	0	0
TOTAL	162	5443	695	1358	211	42	120	640	684	1062	.249	.333	.370	118	54	139	26	74	48	60

Pitching	G	ERA	W–L	SV	GS	GF	CG	SHO	IP	H	R	ER	HR	BB	SO	BFP	WP	HBP	BK	IBB
Don Cardwell	16	6.48	0–2	0	1	2	0	0	25.0	31	19	18	3	6	8	112	1	3	0	1
Dean Chance	3	13.50	0–1	1	0	2	0	0	2.0	3	3	3	0	2	0	10	1	0	0	1
Rich Folkers	16	6.44	0–2	2	1	5	0	0	29.1	36	21	21	6	25	15	145	2	0	1	4
Danny Frisella	30	3.02	8–3	1	1	8	0	0	65.2	49	23	22	4	34	54	279	3	0	0	11
Gary Gentry	32	3.68	9–9	1	29	1	5	2	188.1	155	88	77	19	86	134	798	6	9	1	7
Ron Herbel	12	1.38	2–2	1	0	7	0	0	13.0	14	3	2	1	2	8	54	0	0	0	1
Cal Koonce	13	3.27	0–2	0	0	8	0	0	22.0	25	9	8	2	14	10	99	0	1	0	5
Jerry Koosman	30	3.14	12–7	0	29	0	5	1	212.0	189	87	74	22	71	118	884	7	2	3	14
Jim McAndrew	32	3.56	10–14	2	27	3	9	3	184.1	166	77	73	18	38	111	745	6	2	0	6
Tug McGraw	57	3.28	4–6	10	0	32	0	0	90.2	77	40	33	6	49	81	398	2	1	2	17
Nolan Ryan	27	3.42	7–11	1	19	4	5	2	131.2	86	59	50	10	97	125	570	8	4	0	2
Ray Sadecki	28	3.89	8–4	0	19	2	4	0	138.2	134	67	60	18	52	89	592	5	0	0	9
Tom Seaver	37	2.82	18–12	0	36	1	19	2	290.2	230	103	91	21	83	283	1173	6	4	0	8
Ron Taylor	57	3.93	5–4	13	0	40	0	0	66.1	65	31	29	5	16	28	275	1	0	0	10
TOTAL	162	3.45	83–79	32	162	115	47	10	1459.0	1260	630	559	135	575	1064	6134	48	26	7	96

1971

NL EAST

Team	W	L	PCT	GB	BA	ERA
Pirates	97	65	.599	—	.274	3.31
Cardinals	90	72	.556	7.0	.275	3.85
Mets	83	79	.512	14.0	.249	2.99
Cubs	83	79	.512	14.0	.258	3.61
Expos	71	90	.441	25.5	.246	4.12
Phillies	67	95	.414	30.0	.233	3.71

The Mets decided to stand pat despite a disappointing finish to the 1970 season. The Joe Foy experiment went awry almost from the start, prompting the Mets to acquire another third baseman, Bob Aspromonte, from the Braves for reliever Ron Herbel during the winter of 1971. Fan fa-

vorite Ron Swoboda was jettisoned just before the start of the season, going to Montreal for Don Hahn.

Other than that, general manager Bob Scheffing made no significant moves over the winter. The lineup would still include Grote behind the plate, Ed Kranepool and Donn Clendenon platooning at first, Ken Boswell at second, Bud Harrelson at shortstop, Cleon Jones and Tommie Agee patrolling the left side of the outfield, and Art Shamsky sharing right field with Ken Singleton and others.

Scheffing's strategy was working in the first half of the season, but what looked so promising in June turned to rubble in July. The Mets got off to the best start in team history to date and stayed in first place between April 28 and May 18, doing it with outstanding pitching and timely hitting. They owned a share of the division lead as late as

June 9 and were 45–29 heading into July, just two games behind the Pirates. The 1969 Mets were just 40–34 through 74 games and entered July 7½ games out of first.

Nolan Ryan had emerged as the Mets' No. 2 starter, going 8–4 with a 2.08 ERA, 93 strikeouts, and 54 walks in 92⅓ innings. Ryan walked at least six batters in five of his first 12 starts, but he allowed more than four hits just once in those five outings.

Tom Seaver was even better, starting off 10–3 with a 2.03 ERA and 138 strikeouts in 137⅓ innings. Seaver's WHIP was 0.99 during that span, and there was only one occasion in which he didn't go at least seven innings.

Gary Gentry was pitching at his usual .500 pace by July 1, never winning or losing more than two in a row. Gentry's mark stood at 7–5 with a 2.74 ERA, although his record might have been better with more bullpen help.

Jerry Koosman was 4–5 heading into July despite a 2.97 ERA. But Koosman failed to display the overpowering stuff that made him an All-Star in 1968 and '69, averaging just 4.2 strikeouts per nine innings.

Ron Taylor had taken a step back after leading the staff with 13 saves while tying Tug McGraw for the team lead with 57 appearances in 1970. But McGraw and Danny Frisella were forming a tremendous lefty-right duo, landing them on the cover of *The Sporting News*. McGraw and Frisella, along with Seaver, were the most consistent Mets pitchers during the season. Both relievers posted ERA's under 2.00 and combined for 23 percent of the Mets' wins.

The hitting was unspectacular yet solid over the first three months. Jones was back in 1969 form, batting .306 with six homers and 25 RBI in his first 59 games. Agee was flirting with the .300 mark while contributing seven homers and 22 ribbies. Grote was just as productive at the plate as he was behind it, hitting .304 with 21 RBI by the end of June. And Kranepool had become a tough out after spending nearly two months of the 1970 season in the minors. Kranepool had emerged as the everyday first baseman, providing seven homers and 25 RBI while hitting .307 in the Mets' first 74 games.

Shamsky and Singleton combined for 10 homers and 34 RBIs through June 30. Aspromonte collected 22 of his 33 RBIs by May 25. Tim Foli and Mike Jorgensen were providing sparks off the bench. And Duffy Dyer was hitting .294 in his first 20 games.

By all indications, the Mets were poised for a fine stretch run that would erase the stench of 1970. And then the bottom fell out.

The Mets opened July by dropping 14 of their first 16 games, which put them 13½ games behind the first-place Pirates, an 11-game difference from the start of the month. New York had to win five of its last eight just to finish the month 9–20.

Ryan had suddenly stopped winning, walking 62 while striking out just 44 in his final 59⅔ innings. Ryan's WHIP was an unsightly 2.06 as he went 2–10 during the second half.

Gentry never displayed consistency as manager Gil Hodges continued to show little confidence in the hurler in the late innings.

Koosman battled arm troubles for the second straight year, and tightness in his left side kept him inactive for more than a month. The Mets recalled Jon Matlack in July, but he was a work in progress who flashed serious potential when he wasn't getting roughed up.

The Mets' offense also went south with the pitching as the team batted just .242 with only 47 homers and 149 extra-base hits in the final 88 games. The bats sprung to life August 7 in Atlanta, where the Mets scored a team-record 20 runs on 21 hits in a rout of the Braves. New York hit .232 the rest of the season.

Aspromonte stopped hitting altogether, prompting the Mets to recall Wayne Garrett in late-July. Garrett and Tim Foli shared third-base duties through the final two months, but they combined for only one homer.

Grote couldn't sustain his great start and batted just .232 over the second half, leaving him with a .270 mark. And a knee injury limited Agee's power production following a home-plate collision in June, although he still finished the season hitting .285.

Shamsky and Clendenon were non-factors by season's end, just two years after they contributed mightily to the World Series club.

The Mets' home run totals were embarrassing. Agee, Jones, and Kranepool tied for the club lead with just 14, one more than Singleton. Clendenon was the only other Met to finish the season in double-digits in homers, hitting 11 in 263 at-bats.

The season wasn't a total bust.

The Mets led the league with a 2.99 ERA and had 243 more strikeouts than the NL's second-best team. Seaver arguably had his finest year in the majors, leading the league with 289 strikeouts and a 1.76 ERA, both career bests. Seaver also became a 20-game winner for the second time while serving as the only consistent hurler in the rotation.

Jones challenged for the NL batting title before finishing sixth with a .319 average. Singleton looked like a keeper, especially if he could improve on his .245 average. Foli, Jorgensen, and Ted Martinez (.288 average) seemed like solid backups.

Rookie pitcher Charlie Williams looked terrific at times, awful in others. And Koosman seemed to pitch better in September, giving hope he would contribute in 1972.

But it was evident the Mets needed more pop in their lineup. New York also had to spend the winter searching for another starting third baseman and hope their pitching prospects could contribute in 1972.

1971 Mets Statistics

Hitting	G	AB	R	H	2B	3B	HR	RBI	BB	SO	BA	OBP	SLG	SB	CS	GDP	HP	SH	SF	IBB
Tommie Agee	113	425	58	121	19	0	14	50	50	84	.285	.362	.428	28	6	12	2	4	1	2
Bob Aspromonte	104	342	21	77	9	1	5	33	29	25	.225	.285	.301	0	2	15	0	5	1	4
Ken Boswell	116	392	46	107	20	1	5	40	36	31	.273	.334	.367	5	2	11	2	2	4	4
Donn Clendenon	88	263	29	65	10	0	11	37	21	78	.247	.302	.411	1	2	12	1	0	3	3
Duffy Dyer	59	169	13	39	7	1	2	18	14	45	.231	.292	.320	1	0	4	1	0	1	4
Francisco Estrada	1	2	0	1	0	0	0	0	0	0	.500	.500	.500	0	0	0	0	0	0	0
Tim Foli	97	288	32	65	12	2	0	24	18	50	.226	.272	.281	5	0	7	1	3	2	4
Wayne Garrett	56	202	20	43	2	0	1	11	28	31	.213	.310	.238	1	3	6	1	3	1	2
Jerry Grote	125	403	35	109	25	0	2	35	40	47	.270	.339	.347	1	4	19	2	4	1	4
Don Hahn	98	178	16	42	5	1	1	11	21	32	.236	.317	.292	2	3	4	1	1	2	1
Bud Harrelson	142	547	55	138	16	6	0	32	53	59	.252	.319	.303	28	7	6	2	13	3	0
Cleon Jones	136	505	63	161	24	6	14	69	53	87	.319	.382	.473	6	5	9	2	3	5	6
Mike Jorgensen	45	118	16	26	1	1	5	11	11	24	.220	.303	.373	1	2	4	3	0	0	1
Ed Kranepool	122	421	61	118	20	4	14	58	38	33	.280	.340	.447	0	4	7	1	5	2	6
Dave Marshall	100	214	28	51	9	1	3	21	26	54	.238	.322	.332	3	1	6	2	5	3	3
Ted Martinez	38	125	16	36	5	2	1	10	4	22	.288	.323	.384	6	0	1	3	2	1	2
John Milner	9	18	1	3	1	0	0	1	0	3	.167	.167	.222	0	0	0	0	0	0	0
Ken Singleton	115	298	34	73	5	0	13	46	61	64	.245	.374	.393	0	1	12	2	2	3	9
Art Shamsky	68	135	13	25	6	2	5	18	21	18	.185	.299	.370	1	1	6	1	0	0	2
Leroy Stanton	5	21	2	4	1	0	0	2	2	4	.190	.261	.238	0	0	1	0	0	0	1
Al Weis	11	11	3	0	0	0	0	1	2	4	.000	.143	.000	0	0	0	0	0	1	1
Pitchers																				
Buzz Capra	3	1	0	0	0	0	0	0	0	0	.000	.000	.000	0	0	0	0	0	0	0
Danny Frisella	53	13	1	3	0	0	0	1	1	2	.231	.286	.231	0	0	0	0	1	0	0
Gary Gentry	32	68	2	5	0	0	0	3	0	36	.074	.072	.074	0	0	1	0	6	1	0
Jerry Koosman	26	50	3	8	0	0	0	0	3	25	.160	.222	.160	0	0	1	1	6	0	0
Jon Matlack	7	11	1	3	0	0	0	0	1	6	.273	.333	.273	0	0	0	0	0	0	0
Jim McAndrew	24	23	0	1	1	0	0	1	1	11	.043	.083	.087	0	0	0	0	1	0	0
Tug McGraw	51	18	3	4	2	0	1	2	0	5	.222	.222	.500	0	0	2	0	0	0	0
Nolan Ryan	30	47	4	6	0	1	0	1	3	21	.128	.180	.170	0	0	1	0	3	0	0
Ray Sadecki	34	50	2	10	0	0	0	2	2	12	.200	.231	.200	0	0	0	0	5	0	0
Tom Seaver	39	92	8	18	3	0	1	7	6	31	.196	.245	.261	0	0	1	0	11	0	0
Ron Taylor	45	4	1	1	0	0	0	0	0	3	.250	.250	.250	0	0	0	0	0	0	0
Charlie Williams	31	23	1	2	0	0	0	1	2	11	.087	.160	.087	0	0	0	0	4	0	0
TOTAL	162	5477	588	1365	203	29	98	546	547	958	.249	.317	.351	89	43	147	28	91	35	59

Pitching	G	ERA	W–L	SV	GS	GF	CG	SHO	IP	H	R	ER	HR	BB	SO	BFP	WP	HBP	BK	IBB
Buzz Capra	3	8.44	0–1	0	0	1	0	0	5.1	3	6	5	0	5	6	24	0	0	0	1
Danny Frisella	53	1.99	8–5	12	0	42	0	0	90.2	76	28	20	6	30	93	376	5	3	1	9
Gary Gentry	32	3.23	12–11	0	31	0	8	3	203.1	167	84	73	16	82	155	850	2	6	0	8
Jerry Koosman	26	3.04	6–11	0	24	0	4	0	165.2	160	66	56	12	51	96	694	7	1	0	4
Jon Matlack	7	4.14	0–3	0	6	1	0	0	37.0	31	18	17	2	15	24	153	3	0	0	0
Jim McAndrew	24	4.38	2–5	0	10	4	0	0	90.1	78	50	44	10	32	42	382	6	1	0	5
Tug McGraw	51	1.70	11–4	8	1	34	0	0	111.0	73	22	21	4	41	109	441	6	3	0	11
Don Rose	1	0.00	0–0	0	0	0	0	0	2.0	2	0	0	0	0	1	7	0	0	0	0
Nolan Ryan	30	3.97	10–14	0	26	1	3	0	152.0	125	78	67	8	116	137	705	6	15	1	4
Ray Sadecki	34	2.92	7–7	0	20	3	5	2	163.1	139	56	53	10	44	120	664	0	4	0	5
Tom Seaver	36	1.76	20–10	0	35	1	21	4	286.1	210	61	56	18	61	289	1103	5	4	1	2
Ron Taylor	45	3.65	2–2	2	0	25	0	0	69.0	71	28	28	7	11	32	281	0	1	0	6
Charlie Williams	31	4.78	5–6	0	9	8	1	0	90.1	92	53	48	7	41	53	398	1	2	0	8
TOTAL	162	2.99	83–79	22	162	120	42	13	1466.0	1227	550	487	100	529	1157	6078	41	40	3	63

1972

NL EAST

Team	W	L	PCT	GB	BA	ERA
Pirates	96	59	.619	–	.274	3.31
Cubs	85	70	.548	11.0	.258	2.81
Mets	83	73	.532	13.5	.225	3.26
Cardinals	75	81	.481	21.5	.260	3.42
Expos	70	86	.449	26.5	.234	3.59
Phillies	59	97	.378	37.5	.236	3.66

The 1972 season is etched in the memory of longtime Mets fans despite a rather pedestrian 83–73 record. If you count the off-season, it included one of the worst trades in team history, the death of a manager, a players strike, the arrival of a popular Met, the return of a baseball icon, a tremendous start, and a summer swoon. And, oh yes, injuries, injuries, injuries.

The Mets came away from the 1971 winter meetings with nada, bupkis, zilch, despite an 83–79 season that screamed for improvements. Less than a week later the front office eventually awoke from its collective slumber to acquire the Mets' latest third baseman of the future. Joe Foy and Bob Aspromonte had played themselves out of the position the previous two years; why not get a player who would be playing *out* of position. Thus, the Mets were able to pry six-time All-Star shortstop Jim Fregosi from the California Angels. All it took were prospects Leroy Stanton, Don Rose, Francisco Estrada, and...*Nolan Ryan!*

To be fair, Ryan had been given two seasons to show what he could do in the starting rotation. The Alvin, Texas, native could overpower and intimidate hitters with his blazing fastball, striking out 13 batters in a game five times between 1968 and 1971. But he also walked six or more batters 14 times during that span and had experienced second-half swoons after getting off to great starts in 1970 and '71.

Besides, the Mets had Jon Matlack waiting in the wings, along with prospects Buzz Capra, Charlie Williams, and Tommy Moore. Ryan was deemed expendable and would have to earn the remainder of his 295 career victories and 5,221 strikeouts somewhere else.

Fregosi was named to the AL All-Star team each season between 1966 and '70, but he slumped to .233 with five homers and 33 RBIs in 1971. He would practically match those numbers in 1972 while Ryan was earning the first of his eight All-Star nods.

Even Stanton outproduced Fregosi in 1972, hitting .251 with 12 homers and 39 RBIs.

Opening Day was scheduled for April 6 at Pittsburgh, but a 10-day strike delayed the season and shaved six games off the Mets' docket. Despite the work stoppage, the Mets sent shockwaves through the baseball world on two occasions.

On April 2, manager Gil Hodges had just completed a round of golf with coaches Rube Walker, Joe Pignatano, and Eddie Yost when the four arranged dinner plans. Hodges took a few steps away from his staff before collapsing, falling backward onto the walkway. He had suffered his second heart attack in 3½ years, this one fatal.

The Mets had lost the person who had molded a group of prospects and aging veterans into a champion three years earlier. Hodges continued to be held in high esteem despite the team's disappointing showing the previous two years. The "Quiet Man" would be very hard to replace, but the Mets callously upstaged the funeral by making two major announcements.

The first was that first base coach Yogi Berra would become the new skipper, seven years after he was bypassed for the job in favor of Wes Westrum. Berra was the lone holdover from the group of coaches who were with the team prior to Hodges' arrival. He also got the job three months after being elected to the Baseball Hall of Fame.

The Mets dropped another bombshell at the news conference by announcing a trade that was in the works prior to Hodges' passing. Rusty Staub, "Le Grande Orange" to his Expos fans, was coming to New York for Ken Singleton, Tim Foli, and Mike Jorgensen. The Mets were sacrificing their surplus of talent for the hitter they so desired.

Staub looked like the final piece in a lineup that seemed vastly improved over 1971. The Mets now had seven past and present All-Stars in their projected starting lineup. Like Fregosi, Jerry Grote, Ed Kranepool, Bud Harrelson, Cleon Jones, and Tommie Agee had been selected to the Midsummer Classic. Staub had been chosen to the last five All-Star Games and was coming off a 19-homer, 97-RBI season that would have led the Mets by a wide margin in both categories the previous year.

The Mets finally played ball on Saturday, April 15 at Shea Stadium, shutting out the defending-champion Pirates behind Tom Seaver and Tug McGraw. New York dropped its next two games before reeling off winning streaks of seven and 11 games to surge to the front of the pack at 25–7, the best start in team history at that point.

Seaver's seventh win of the year gave the Mets a six-game lead by May 21. Matlack was living up to his potential by starting the season 5–0. Even Jim McAndrew was winning ballgames after waiting until Labor Day weekend to pick up his first victory in 1971. Gary Gentry posted a 2.13 ERA in his first eight starts to help the Mets overcome a slow start by Jerry Koosman. Ryan be damned; the Mets were going to steamroll over the rest of the NL East.

Along the way, the Mets were able to acquire a future Hall of Famer. Willie Mays slumped during the second half of 1971 and opened the '72 season batting just .184 with no homers and three RBI in the Giants' first 23 games. Mets owner Joan Payson had long coveted her favorite player from her days as a New York Giants stockholder, once offering Giants owner Horace Stoneham a reported $500,000 for Mays' services. By 1972, Stoneham was ready to deal the outfielder for Williams and $100,000. Days after the trade, Mays snapped a 4–4 tie with a homer in his Mets debut, sending them to a Mother's Day win over his former team.

The Mets headed into June with a five-game lead over the second-place Pirates. New York was 31–12 on June 3 following a win over the Braves, a game in which George Stone plunked Staub on the right hand by a pitch. Staub continued to play every game until June 18, when the pain became excruciating. The Mets went 5–8 during that span, leaving them with a half-game lead.

Staub sat out the next month before playing again July 18. A day later, the Mets finally diagnosed the "bone bruise" as a broken hamate bone. By then, the Pirates were five games in front of the Mets.

Staub spent the next two months on the disabled list, and he had plenty of company in the Mets' infirmary. The number of significant injuries bordered on the ridiculous as half the Mets' opening-day lineup missed huge chunks of the summer schedule. Bud Harrelson landed on the disabled list with a strained back. Tommie Agee battled hamstring problems that limited him to 114 games played. Jerry Grote appeared in only 64 games due to elbow chips that eventually required surgery. Cleon Jones damaged his elbow while playing first base, keeping him out of the lineup for 20 games during a 25-game stretch. John Milner pulled a groin muscle in late June before suffering a neck injury in a collision with Harrelson. By the end of the season, Ed Kranepool was leading the team with just 122 games played.

The injuries forced the 41-year-old Mays to play hurt, and to also play first base for 11 games. Mays received a cortisone shot on three occasions and was annoyed that Berra continued to play him.

The banged up bodies forced the Mets to dip into their farm system, which had been left shallow by the recent departures of Amos Otis, Singleton, Foli, Jorgensen, and Stanton. Dave Schneck and Lute Barnes made their major league debuts and enjoyed success immediately after their recall. But they weren't the answer.

Teddy Martinez appeared in 103 games while playing second, third, and short. Fregosi played six games at his natural shortstop position and also saw time at first base. Things got so desperate that Grote and Duffy Dyer each played a game in right field. Grote also appeared in three games at third base.

One of the more puzzling problems was Gary Gentry's performance. The right-hander went 2–7 with a 4.94 ERA in 13 starts between May 28 and August 3, earning him a demotion to the bullpen. Gentry had continued to pitch with a very sore shoulder that was eventually diagnosed as a torn rotator cuff. But the diagnosis came months after he left the Mets following the season.

It didn't take the Mets long to fade out of the playoff picture. Armed with a five-game lead at the start of June, the Mets were 10 games off the pace by August 13. The last few weeks were reserved for personal achievement, mainly reserved for the pitching staff.

Tom Seaver finished fifth in the Cy Young voting after reaching the 20-win mark for the third time in four years despite a career-worst 2.92 ERA. Seaver made it to the All-Star Game for the sixth time in as many major league seasons, and he paced the league in strikeouts for the third consecutive year.

Matlack became the second Met to win the NL Rookie of the Year Award, five years after Seaver did it. Matlack kept the rotation afloat while Koosman struggled during the first five weeks of the year. The lefty finished fourth in the league in ERA, 10th in strikeouts, and sixth in shutouts.

Tug McGraw obliterated the team record for saves in a season, finishing with 27 while compiling a 1.70 ERA for the second straight year. McGraw made it to the All-Star Game for the first time, getting the victory in Atlanta.

Jim McAndrew had by far the best season of his major league career, just a year after going 2–5 with a 4.40 ERA. McAndrew won nine of his first 12 decisions and posted the league's 11th-best ERA.

The nicest surprise at the plate was Milner, who set a team record for home runs by a left-handed hitter. Milner paced the team in round-trippers, hitting seven of them while collecting 13 RBIs during a 19-game stretch late in the season.

The year ended with plenty of "what ifs," most of them regarding the health of the team. Ryan did have a breakthrough season with the Angels, but he wouldn't have been much of a factor for the depleted Mets.

1972 Mets Statistics

Hitting	G	AB	R	H	2B	3B	HR	RBI	BB	SO	BA	OBP	SLG	SB	CS	GDP	HP	SH	SF	IBB
Tommie Agee	114	422	52	96	23	0	13	47	53	92	.227	.317	.374	8	9	18	4	1	3	6
Lute Barnes	24	72	5	17	2	2	0	6	6	4	.236	.291	.319	0	1	2	0	0	1	1
Jim Beauchamp	58	120	10	29	1	0	5	19	7	33	.242	.282	.375	0	0	2	1	0	3	1
Ken Boswell	100	355	35	75	9	1	9	33	32	35	.211	.274	.318	2	2	15	0	9	4	1
Duffy Dyer	94	325	33	75	17	3	8	36	28	71	.231	.299	.375	0	1	8	5	2	3	9
Jim Fregosi	101	340	31	79	15	4	5	32	38	71	.232	.311	.344	0	1	6	1	2	1	2
Wayne Garrett	111	298	41	69	13	3	2	29	70	58	.232	.374	.315	3	2	5	0	5	4	3
Jerry Grote	64	205	15	43	5	1	3	21	26	27	.210	.304	.288	1	0	5	3	4	3	8
Don Hahn	17	37	0	6	0	0	0	1	4	12	.162	.244	.162	0	0	1	0	0	0	0
Bud Harrelson	115	418	54	90	10	4	1	24	58	57	.215	.313	.266	12	4	6	3	7	4	4
Cleon Jones	106	375	39	92	15	1	5	52	30	83	.245	.305	.331	1	6	10	4	2	4	4
Ed Kranepool	122	327	28	88	15	1	8	34	34	35	.269	.336	.394	1	0	11	1	2	4	13
Ted Martinez	103	330	22	74	5	5	1	19	12	49	.224	.254	.279	7	4	10	1	4	0	2
Dave Marshall	72	156	21	39	5	0	4	11	22	28	.250	.346	.359	3	3	4	1	1	0	1
Willie Mays	69	195	27	52	9	1	8	19	43	43	.267	.402	.446	1	5	5	1	3	0	5
John Milner	117	362	52	86	12	2	17	38	51	74	.238	.340	.423	2	1	8	5	5	0	1
Joe Nolan	4	10	0	0	0	0	0	0	1	3	.000	.091	.000	0	0	0	0	0	0	0
Dave Schneck	37	123	7	23	3	2	3	10	10	26	.187	.254	.317	0	1	2	1	0	0	2
Rusty Staub	66	239	32	70	11	0	9	38	31	13	.293	.372	.452	0	1	5	2	1	5	7
Bill Sudakis	18	49	3	7	0	0	1	7	6	14	.143	.236	.204	0	0	1	0	1	0	0
Pitchers																				
Buzz Capra	14	12	1	3	0	0	0	1	3	3	.250	.400	.250	0	0	0	0	0	0	0
Danny Frisella	39	7	0	2	0	0	0	1	0	1	.286	.286	.286	0	0	0	0	0	0	0
Gary Gentry	32	48	2	5	1	0	0	3	4	28	.104	.173	.125	0	0	0	0	3	0	0
Jerry Koosman	34	47	1	4	0	0	0	1	0	18	.085	.085	.085	0	0	1	0	9	0	0
Jon Matlack	34	78	6	10	1	0	0	2	10	44	.128	.227	.141	0	0	1	0	5	0	0
Jim McAndrew	28	43	2	2	0	0	0	1	3	14	.047	.128	.047	0	0	0	1	10	0	0
Tug McGraw	54	20	1	2	0	0	0	0	2	4	.100	.182	.100	0	0	0	0	2	0	0
Tommy Moore	3	3	1	1	0	0	0	0	0	1	.333	.333	.333	0	0	0	0	0	0	0
Bob Rauch	19	3	0	0	0	0	0	0	0	2	.000	.000	.000	0	0	0	0	0	0	0
Ray Sadecki	34	13	1	2	0	0	0	1	0	5	.154	.154	.154	0	0	0	1	0	0	0
Tom Seaver	36	89	5	13	3	1	3	4	5	41	.146	.191	.303	0	0	1	0	6	0	0
Brent Strom	11	6	0	0	0	0	0	0	0	0	.000	.000	.000	0	0	0	1	1	0	0
Chuck Taylor	20	3	0	0	0	0	0	0	0	1	.000	.000	.000	0	0	0	0	0	0	0

Hitting (continued)	G	AB	R	H	2B	3B	HR	RBI	BB	SO	BA	OBP	SLG	SB	CS	GDP	HP	SH	SF	IBB
Hank Webb	6	5	1	0	0	0	0	0	0	0	.000	.000	.000	0	0	0	0	0	0	0
TOTAL	156	5135	528	1154	175	31	105	490	589	990	.225	.305	.332	41	41	127	34	86	39	70

Pitching	G	ERA	W–L	SV	GS	GF	CG	SHO	IP	H	R	ER	HR	BB	SO	BFP	WP	HBP	BK	IBB
Buzz Capra	14	4.58	3–2	0	6	2	0	0	53.0	50	27	27	7	27	45	227	1	0	0	1
Danny Frisella	39	3.34	5–8	9	0	31	0	0	67.1	63	31	25	8	20	46	284	6	0	0	5
Gary Gentry	32	4.01	7–10	0	26	3	3	0	164.0	153	82	73	20	75	120	712	6	6	0	5
Jerry Koosman	34	4.14	11–12	1	24	5	4	1	163.0	155	81	75	14	52	147	692	9	6	0	7
Jon Matlack	34	2.32	15–10	0	32	1	8	4	244.0	215	79	63	14	71	169	1003	7	2	1	14
Jim McAndrew	28	2.80	11–8	1	23	3	4	0	160.2	133	54	50	12	38	81	643	6	5	0	5
Tug McGraw	54	1.70	8–6	27	0	47	0	0	106.0	71	26	20	3	40	92	419	2	3	0	11
Tommy Moore	3	2.92	0–0	0	1	0	0	0	12.1	12	4	4	1	1	5	47	1	0	0	0
Bob Rauch	19	5.00	0–1	1	0	7	0	0	27.0	27	16	15	3	21	23	126	4	0	0	2
Ray Sadecki	34	3.09	2–1	0	2	13	0	0	75.2	73	33	26	3	31	38	328	2	2	0	6
Tom Seaver	35	2.92	21–12	0	35	0	13	3	262.0	215	92	85	23	77	249	1060	8	5	0	2
Brent Strom	11	6.82	0–3	0	5	3	0	0	30.1	34	25	23	7	15	20	134	1	0	1	1
Chuck Taylor	20	5.52	0–0	2	0	8	0	0	31.0	44	19	19	2	9	9	143	0	1	0	3
Hank Webb	6	4.42	0–0	0	2	1	0	0	18.1	18	9	9	1	9	15	79	0	0	0	1
TOTAL	156	3.26	83–73	41	156	124	32	12	1414.0	1263	578	512	118	486	1059	5897	53	30	2	63

1973

NL EAST						
Team	W	L	PCT	GB	BA	ERA
Mets	82	79	.509	—	.246	3.26
Cardinals	81	81	.500	1.5	.259	3.25
Pirates	80	82	.494	2.5	.261	3.73
Expos	79	83	.488	3.5	.251	3.71
Cubs	77	84	.478	5.0	.247	3.66
Phillies	71	91	.438	11.5	.249	3.99

Mets beat Reds in NLCS, 3–2
Mets lost to Athletics in World Series, 4–3

The Mets were the worst team in the National League East for 58 days in 1973. By season's end, they were the worst team ever to win a major league pennant. The Mets followed three straight 83-win seasons with an 82-victory campaign, but it was good enough to finish first in an underwhelming division. The Cardinals and Cubs were the only teams in the East to climb more than 10 games over .500 at any point in the season. The Cards were 11 games over by August despite an 8–23 start, and the Cubs enjoyed a 47–31 record before going 30–53 the rest of the way.

It seemed no team was particularly interested in playing October baseball, which was a bonus for the Mets, who were turning injuries into a true art form. John Milner, Jerry Grote, and Willie Mays were on the disabled list simultaneously by mid-May. The Mets also lost Bud Harrelson and Cleon Jones to injury during the first week of June, while Grote was transferred to the 60-day DL. Even third-string catcher Jerry May landed on the DL, which turned into a positive as it forced the Mets to recall Ron Hodges from Double A Memphis.

Jones spent 36 days on the disabled list before he was activated July 7, one day before fellow outfielder George Theodore dislocated his right hip in a horrible collision with center fielder Don Hahn. Harrelson reappeared on the DL on August 3 and wouldn't play again for another 15 days.

Tug McGraw pitches against the Chicago Cubs at Shea Stadium, September 17, 1973. The Mets knocked the Cubs out of playoff contention two weeks later, on the final day of the regular season.

Any doubt of Harrelson's value to the team was dismissed during the season. The Mets went 18–29 during the shortstop's two stints on the disabled list while the Mets tried Ted Martinez, Wayne Garrett, and rookie Brian Ostrosser. Even third baseman Jim Fregosi played 17 games at his natural shortstop position before the Mets finally sold him to Texas in July.

Ironically, one of the two healthiest Mets in the everyday lineup was the biggest injury concern in 1972.

Rusty Staub appeared in 152 games after a broken hamate bone caused him to miss most of the previous campaign.

The other healthy Met was newcomer Felix Millan, acquired from Atlanta in one of the biggest swindles in team history. The former Gold Glove–winning second baseman stabilized the middle of the infield while serving as the contact hitter the Mets had sorely lacked between 1970 and 1972. Millan played a team-high 153 games, posted a .989 fielding percentage, and struck out just 22 times in 638 at-bats. Of the Mets' starting eight, only Millan, Staub, and Hahn played the entire season without at least one trip to the disabled list.

The Mets didn't get off to the blazing start they crafted the previous two years, but they were just 2½ games off the pace with a 20–17 record following a 19-inning win over the Dodgers on May 24. That's when the bottom fell out.

It took the Mets just 30 days to plummet from second to last place despite a five-game winning streak in mid-June. New York went 24–40 between May 25 and July 31, putting them 10½ games behind the division-leading Cardinals. Along the way, Tug McGraw was blowing leads at a rapid rate while newly acquired reliever Phil Hennigan was playing himself off the team.

McGraw was coming off his finest season, 8–6 with a team-record 27 saves and a 1.70 ERA. The lefty from California got off to a good start, collecting five saves and compiling a 1.32 ERA in his first nine appearances. But he was the National League's piñata between May 6 and July 7, going 0–4 with six saves and a ridiculous 8.07 ERA in 23 games. McGraw gave up at least three runs six times in that stretch, including a whopping seven during 1⅓ innings against the Expos on July 3. He blew leads in six of those games before manager Yogi Berra gave him two starts in late July.

It seemed the Mets were screwing up an otherwise outstanding season by Tom Seaver, who was fresh off back-to-back 20-win seasons. Seaver put together winning streaks of five and four games, and his ERA got as low as 1.69 when he struck out 13 in a five-hitter against the Phillies September 4. Nine of Seaver's 19 wins came after Mets losses as he dutifully served the role of stopper.

Jerry Koosman was pitching injury-free for the first time since 1969. He opened the season with five straight wins and closed it by winning six of seven decisions. But he went 3–14 in between, posting a 4.09 ERA while the Mets were scoring more than three runs just five times in his 19 starts.

Reigning NL Rookie of the Year Jon Matlack was pitching just well enough to lose, dropping 14 of his first 21 decisions despite a 3.51 ERA. Matlack avoided the disabled list after Braves infielder Marty Perez drilled him in the face with a line drive during a game May 8. The lefty was back on the mound 11 days later, but the losing continued.

The Mets got nothing from Jim McAndrew and Buzz

Capra, who were a combined 5–15. Their ineffectiveness prompted Berra to put George Stone into the rotation.

Stone was part of the trade that brought Millan to New York for pitchers Gary Gentry and Danny Frisella. All Stone did was lead the league in winning percentage, finishing 12–3 following a season-ending eight-game winning streak. Gentry and Frisella won a total of five games for the Braves in 1973.

The Mets were 53–66 when Harrelson came off the disabled list August 18, giving New York its Opening Day starting lineup for the first time since late-April. Two days later, McGraw was hammered for five runs over 3⅓ innings of a 16-inning loss to the Reds, lifting his ERA to 5.45. But McGraw had been visiting a close friend who was a practitioner of self-actualization. He told McGraw that he could succeed if he started believing in himself. A lightbulb turned on, and "Ya Gotta Believe" became his rallying cry.

Around this time, Mets chairman M. Donald Grant decided it was time to give the team a pep talk. Grant assured the ballclub the front office still had faith in the players and felt the Mets would come around if they only believed in themselves. Those words were seconded by an overenthusiastic McGraw, who interrupted the speech by screaming, "Yeah, that's right, YA GOTTA BEEELIEEEEEEEVE." Ed Kranepool pulled his teammate aside and told him Grant might have thought McGraw was mocking him. The reliever was relieved after speaking to Grant, who told him he felt no disrespect.

Grant had enough on his plate. The *New York Post* had run a survey asking fans who should be fired: Grant, general manager Bob Scheffing, or Berra. An overwhelming minority placed the blame on Berra, leaving Grant and Scheffing to endure the wrath of the Mets faithful.

Fortunately, no one had run away with the division. The Cardinals were cooling off, the Cubs were plummeting, and the Pirates were struggling to stay around .500. For a while, the fifth-year Expos, with rookie Steve Rogers anchoring the rotation, were looking like a team ready to challenge for the division crown.

And then it was the Mets' turn to get hot.

New York climbed out of the cellar for good on August 31, thanks to a sizzling 4–4 stretch. Fourth place was theirs after Ray Sadecki and Tug McGraw combined to blank the Phillies on September 5. McGraw had already embarked on a season-ending stretch in which he factored in 17 Mets victories in 19 outings, going 5–0 with 12 saves and a 0.88 ERA.

Koosman set a team record by going 31⅔ innings without allowing a run between August 19 and September 7. Matlack went 3–2 with a 2.43 ERA in six September starts. Stone's 4–0 mark in the final month included a 2.15 ERA. Sadecki made two starts in seven September appearances while going 2–1 with a 2.25 ERA. Seaver went 4–2 with a 3.94 ERA during the final month, making him the "weak link" of the staff.

The Mets didn't exactly tear the cover off the ball in September, hitting .256 with 19 homers while averaging 4.04 runs in 27 games. But they constantly got timely hits when needed.

Jones drove in 21 runs in his final 26 games despite a .244 average, and Grote batted .276 in the final month. Garrett concluded his best offensive season to date by hitting .323 with six homers and 17 RBIs in September. Staub hit .307 with four homers and 16 ribbies over the final 4½ weeks.

But it was the way they were winning that showed Mets fans they had to believe. McGraw hit a two-run single in the 15th inning of a victory September 7. Nine days later, Grote's bunt single in the eighth put the Mets ahead to stay against the Cubs. New York scored fives times in the ninth to erase a 5–1 deficit in a win at Pittsburgh on September 18. The "Ball off the Wall" play led to a 13-inning win over the Pirates, capped by Hodge's RBI single on September 20.

The pitching was spectacular as the Mets held opponents to two runs or less 18 times in their final 31 games, including six shutouts.

Willie Mays added to the drama by announcing he would retire after the season. Mays gave his "Say Goodbye to America" speech September 25 before Jerry Koosman and Tug McGraw pitched the Mets to a 2–1 victory over the Expos.

Five teams were still alive in the division race on the final scheduled day of the season. The Mets split a pair with the Cubs, knocking Chicago and the Expos out of contention. Three teams remained alive when the Mets took the field for a makeup doubleheader at Wrigley Field. All they had to do is win once and they were headed to Cincinnati for the NLCS. New York ended the suspense by taking the opener before the second game was rained out.

"We end up winning because it seemed like nobody wanted to win," said Koosman.

What followed was a memorable five-game series with the Reds. Tom Seaver and Jon Matlack pitch superbly as the Mets split the first two games in Cincinnati. Game 3 featured the Pete Rose–Harrelson fight after the Mets jumped out to a huge lead. Rose got his revenge the next day by hitting the game-winning homer in extra innings, but the Mets finally clinched the pennant before an overly raucous —and downright scary —crowd at Shea.

The World Series seemed anticlimactic, considering what the Mets already had gone through. Still, the Mets took a 3–2 lead in the series before the A's prevailed.

1973 Mets Statistics

Hitting	G	AB	R	H	2B	3B	HR	RBI	BB	SO	BA	OBP	SLG	SB	CS	GDP	HBP	SH	SF	IBB
Lute Barnes	3	2	2	1	0	0	0	1	0	1	.500	.500	.500	0	0	0	0	0	0	0
Jim Beauchamp	50	61	5	17	1	1	0	14	7	11	.279	.343	.328	1	0	1	0	0	2	1
Ken Boswell	76	110	12	25	2	1	2	14	12	11	.227	.303	.318	0	0	1	0	1	0	2
Rich Chiles	8	25	2	3	2	0	0	1	0	2	.120	.120	.200	0	0	2	0	0	0	0
Duffy Dyer	70	189	9	35	6	1	1	9	13	40	.185	.245	.243	2	0	5	2	0	0	1
Jim Fregosi	45	124	7	29	4	1	0	11	20	25	.234	.340	.282	1	2	2	0	0	0	3
Wayne Garrett	140	504	76	129	20	3	16	58	72	74	.256	.348	.403	6	5	8	1	9	3	4
Jim Gosger	38	92	9	22	2	0	0	10	9	16	.239	.304	.261	0	1	1	0	0	1	2
Jerry Grote	84	285	17	73	10	2	1	32	13	23	.256	.290	.316	0	0	11	1	5	1	1
Don Hahn	93	262	22	60	10	0	2	21	22	43	.229	.285	.290	2	1	7	0	4	4	2
Bud Harrelson	106	356	35	92	12	3	0	20	48	49	.258	.348	.309	5	1	4	1	3	0	4
Greg Harts	3	2	0	1	0	0	0	0	0	0	.500	.500	.500	0	0	0	0	0	0	0
Ron Hodges	45	127	5	33	2	0	1	18	11	19	.260	.314	.299	0	1	6	0	2	2	2
Cleon Jones	92	339	48	88	13	0	11	48	28	51	.260	.315	.395	1	1	11	3	1	8	6
Ed Kranepool	100	284	28	68	12	2	1	35	30	28	.239	.310	.306	1	0	7	0	4	2	4
Ted Martinez	92	263	34	67	11	0	1	14	13	38	.255	.294	.308	3	5	6	2	1	1	2
Jerry May	4	8	0	2	0	0	0	0	1	1	.250	.333	.250	0	0	0	0	0	0	0
Willie Mays	66	209	24	44	10	0	6	25	27	47	.211	.303	.344	1	0	7	1	1	1	0
Felix Millan	153	638	82	185	23	4	3	37	35	22	.290	.332	.353	2	2	20	6	18	2	3
John Milner	129	451	69	108	12	3	23	72	62	84	.239	.329	.432	1	1	15	1	0	5	6
Brian Ostrosser	4	5	0	0	0	0	0	0	0	2	.000	.000	.000	0	0	0	0	0	0	0
Dave Schneck	13	36	2	7	0	1	0	0	1	4	.194	.216	.250	0	0	2	0	0	0	1
Rusty Staub	152	585	77	163	36	1	15	76	74	52	.279	.361	.421	1	1	16	3	1	3	10
George Theodore	45	116	14	30	4	0	1	15	10	13	.259	.320	.319	1	0	7	1	6	1	0
Pitchers																				
Buzz Capra	24	2	1	0	0	0	0	0	2	0	.000	.500	.000	0	0	1	0	1	0	0
Phil Hennigan	30	3	0	1	0	0	0	0	0	1	.333	.333	.333	0	0	0	0	0	0	0
Jerry Koosman	35	78	3	8	1	0	0	3	2	37	.103	.125	.115	0	0	2	0	15	0	0
Jon Matlack	35	65	5	9	0	0	0	2	13	38	.138	.282	.138	0	0	0	0	12	0	0
Jim McAndrew	24	15	3	2	1	0	0	2	6	7	.133	.381	.200	0	0	0	0	2	0	0
Tug McGraw	60	24	0	4	0	0	0	2	2	9	.167	.259	.167	0	0	0	1	3	0	0
Tommy Moore	4	0	1	0	0	0	0	0	0	0	.000	.000	.000	0	0	0	0	0	0	0
Harry Parker	38	23	0	4	0	0	0	2	0	8	.174	.174	.174	0	0	1	0	5	0	0
Ray Sadecki	31	31	3	7	2	0	0	1	0	5	.226	.226	.290	0	0	0	0	2	0	0
Tom Seaver	39	93	9	15	2	1	1	5	7	34	.161	.220	.237	1	0	3	0	9	0	0
George Stone	28	48	4	13	0	0	0	5	0	8	.271	.271	.271	0	0	1	0	3	0	0
Craig Swan	3	2	0	0	0	0	0	0	0	2	.000	.000	.000	0	0	0	0	0	0	0
TOTALS	**161**	**5457**	**608**	**1345**	**198**	**24**	**85**	**553**	**540**	**805**	**.246**	**.314**	**.338**	**27**	**22**	**147**	**23**	**108**	**36**	**54**

Pitching	G	ERA	W:L	SV	GS	GF	CG	SHO	IP	H	R	ER	HR	BB	SO	BFP	WP	HBP	BK	IBB
Bob Apodaca	1	INF	0–0	0	0	0	0	0	0.0	0	1	0	0	2	0	2	0	0	0	0
Buzz Capra	24	3.86	2–7	4	0	10	0	0	42.0	35	18	18	4	28	35	188	3	2	0	9
Phil Hennigan	30	6.23	0–4	3	0	17	0	0	43.1	50	30	30	6	16	22	195	3	1	0	6
Jerry Koosman	35	2.84	14–15	0	35	0	12	3	263.0	234	93	83	18	76	156	1071	3	4	0	6
Jon Matlack	34	3.20	14–16	0	34	0	14	3	242.0	210	93	86	16	99	205	1011	6	2	0	14
Jim McAndrew	23	5.38	3–8	1	12	8	0	0	80.1	109	60	48	9	31	38	372	5	3	0	8
Tug McGraw	60	3.87	5–6	25	2	46	0	0	118.2	106	53	51	11	55	81	503	7	3	0	9
Bob Miller	1	0.00	0–0	0	0	0	0	0	1.0	0	0	0	0	0	1	3	0	0	0	0
Tommy Moore	3	10.80	0–1	0	1	2	0	0	3.1	6	5	4	1	3	1	18	0	0	0	0
Harry Parker	38	3.35	8–4	5	9	16	0	0	96.2	79	40	36	7	36	63	410	2	3	0	3
Ray Sadecki	31	3.39	5–4	1	11	7	1	0	116.2	109	47	44	11	41	87	489	3	1	0	3
Tom Seaver	36	2.08	19–10	0	36	0	18	3	290.0	219	74	67	23	64	251	1147	5	4	0	5
George Stone	27	2.80	12- 3	1	20	5	2	0	148.0	157	53	46	16	31	77	621	0	0	1	3
John Strohmayer	7	8.10	0–0	0	0	3	0	0	10.0	13	10	9	2	4	5	46	1	0	0	1
Craig Swan	3	8.64	0–1	0	1	0	0	0	8.1	16	9	8	2	2	4	42	0	0	0	0
Hank Webb	2	10.80	0–0	0	0	0	0	0	1.2	2	2	2	1	2	1	9	1	0	0	0
TOTAL	161	3.26	82–79	40	161	114	47	15	1465.0	1345	588	531	127	490	1027	6127	39	23	1	67

1974

NL EAST

TEAM	W	L	PCT	GB	BA	ERA
Pirates	88	74	.543	—	.274	3.49
Cardinals	86	75	.534	1.5	.265	3.48
Phillies	80	82	.494	8.0	.261	3.91
Expos	79	82	.491	8.5	.254	3.60
Mets	71	91	.438	17.0	.235	3.42
Cubs	66	96	.407	22.0	.251	4.28

The 1974 season was eerily similar to the previous year, at least until July 21. The Mets were in last place at 40–51, but just 6½ games out of first. The Phillies, the only team eliminated from the NL East race heading into the final weekend of the 1973 season, were leading the division with a 48–46 mark at that point. A year earlier, the Mets also were 40–51 after 91 games, but they were 9½ off the pace.

Once again the Mets were dealing with another lousy start by Tug McGraw, who helped the team rally to a National League pennant just months earlier. But there was a new wrinkle to the Mets' problems. Tom Seaver was experiencing a sciatic nerve problem that severely hampered his effectiveness at times. Seaver allowed four or more runs in eight of his first 20 starts, including four appearances in which he surrendered at least six earned runs.

With the Cardinals and Pirates both under .500 midway through the '74 campaign, there was hope the Mets could get back in the race if Seaver and McGraw would revert to form. Jerry Koosman and Jon Matlack were a combined 19–13 by July 20, displaying the performances that helped the Mets surge from last to first in the final 30 games of 1973. Harry Parker gave the Mets several quality starts, although the offense and bullpen often abandoned him. Ray Sadecki was very effective after May 15, and Bob Apodaca was giving the Mets quality innings after he was lit up early in the season.

The comeback never materialized, thanks in part to a patchwork offense necessitated by another rash of injuries. Wayne Garrett and Rusty Staub were the only players from the Opening Day lineup to appear in more than 137 games. Catcher Jerry Grote was constantly nicked up and played just 97 games, which actually surpassed his 1972 and '73 totals. Bud Harrelson suffered, in order, a groin strain, a bruised finger, a broken hand, and a sprained right knee before another groin injury took him out of the lineup for good on September 11. Cleon Jones made just nine starts after August 26 because of a knee injury that would require surgery. Even durable Felix Millan was limited to 136 games because of a bone chip in his hand and a nose infection.

The injuries allowed the Mets to display a depleted farm system that featured the likes of Rich Puig, Brock Pemberton, Benny Ayala, and Ike Hampton. Of the four, only Ayala would have a major league career that consisted of more than 135 major league at-bats. Ayala also provided one of the few season highlights when he became the 40th player in major league history—and the first Met—to homer in his first big league at-bat.

But the paucity of hitting wasted many a good outing by the Mets' starters when the bullpen wasn't blowing leads. New York was dead last in the league in slugging percentage, doubles, triples, and stolen bases while finishing next-to-last in batting average, on base percentage, hits, and runs. The Mets were held to five hits or fewer 31 times, going 5–26 in those games.

The bullpen was absolutely horrible early in the season, and it didn't get much better after that. Bob Apodaca was 1–3 with a 7.32 ERA over 19⅔ innings in his first nine games, and he was one of the most effective pitchers out of the pen. Sadecki had a 10.64 ERA in his first eight appearances. McGraw was 0–3 with a 9.00 ERA and two blown saves in three chances by May 15, when he was placed on the disabled list with a strained back. Original Met Bob Miller was the best reliever in the first two months, and Jack Aker provided bullpen help after being purchased from the Braves a day before the June 15 trade deadline.

The Aker acquisition was the only deal the Mets made at the deadline despite a 24–35 record. The back end of the starting rotation was in shambles because of George Stone's shoulder woes. The injury problems created a need for a solid backup middle infielder and a veteran outfielder. God forbid general manager Bob Scheffing and chairman M. Donald Grant pulled the trigger on a big

Bake McBride of the St. Louis Cardinals comes in with the winning run in the 25th inning as Mets catcher Ron Hodges looks for the ball at Shea Stadium in the early morning hours of September 12, 1974. The Mets and Cardinals set a National League record in the marathon night game that took 7 hours, 4 minutes, and 25 innings for a 4–3 Cardinals victory. Fans went home at 3:10 AM.

trade that would bring them a solid bat or a fourth starter. Then again, they had little to offer.

And so the Mets trudged on through the rest of the season, hoping lightning would strike twice in consecutive seasons. Koosman and Matlack, the glue to the rotation in the early going, went 9–13 after mid-July. McGraw pitched well after August 1, going 5–5 with a 2.11 ERA in 11 games before imploding in his final appearance as a Met. But Tug did his best pitching as a starter during that span, going 2–1 with a 1.96 ERA in 23 innings.

The most depressing part of the season was seeing the Mets become inconsequential to the media. Only a year ago, the Mets' slow start prompted the *New York Post* to run a fan poll asking who should be fired for the team's poor start. This year, the Mets were being upstaged by their temporary co-tenants as the Yankees challenged for the AL East crown while calling Shea Stadium home. The Mets drew a fairly solid 1,722,209 fans, fifth-best in the National League. The Yankees drew 500,000 fewer fans but finished second in the AL in attendance. They were playing meaningful games in September.

Seaver continued to be an enigma through late September, looking like the old Tom Terrific in several starts

but leaving early in others. He appeared ready to pack it in after limping off the mound following a six-inning stint on September 25. But he felt pain-free in his final start, striking out 14 to become the first National League hurler to fan 200 batters in seven consecutive seasons.

Ironically, the Mets' 1975 media guide gives credit to Grant for helping Seaver get over his injury. The guide says Grant suggested to team doctor James Parkes that Seaver see a noted osteopath, who gave the Franchise two treatments over a five-day period. Seaver felt good enough to make one more start, and it allowed him to set a league strikeout record.

One of the few bright spots to the season was Ed Kranepool, who hit only .239 with one homer in 285 at-bats during 1973. Kranepool was the Mets' lone .300 hitter in 1974 as he became the team's best hitter off the bench. He batted .486 as a pinch-hitter, going 14–29 with one homer and four RBIs, numbers that helped him extend his major league career another four years.

But Kranepool went 0-for–1 off the bench in one of the longest games in major league history. The Cardinals were challenging for the division title when they won a 25-inning affair with the Mets on September 11. Jerry Koosman was one out away from a regulation 3–1 victory when Ken Reitz belted a two-run homer. The Mets put the potential winning run on third in the 10th, 23rd, and 24th, as they eclipsed team records for longest game in terms of time and innings. Finally, Bake McBride scored the winning run on a botched pickoff and an error at the plate. Much like the season, an occasionally exciting game was made excruciating by its outcome.

Changes were made at the end of the season. Scheffing was dismissed and replaced by Joe McDonald, who had helped develop the Mets' farm system during its heyday. Grant said at McDonald's introductory news conference that he never considered another candidate outside the organization. It would be up to McDonald to return the team to its past glory, although Grant's fingerprints would show up on many transactions, most notably on June 15, 1977.

1974 Mets Statistics

Hitting	G	AB	R	H	2B	3B	HR	RBI	BB	SO	BA	OBP	SLG	SB	CS	GDP	HP	SH	SF	IBB
Benny Ayala	23	68	9	16	1	0	2	8	7	17	.235	.308	.338	0	0	3	1	0	2	0
Bruce Boisclair	7	12	0	3	1	0	0	1	1	4	.250	.308	.333	0	0	1	0	0	0	0
Ken Boswell	96	222	19	48	6	1	2	15	18	19	.216	.277	.279	0	1	8	1	2	1	1
Duffy Dyer	63	142	14	30	1	1	0	10	18	15	.211	.302	.232	0	0	6	1	0	1	2
Wayne Garrett	151	522	55	117	14	3	13	53	89	96	.224	.337	.337	4	6	6	2	2	4	7
Jim Gosger	26	33	3	3	0	0	0	0	3	2	.091	.167	.091	0	0	2	0	1	0	1
Jerry Grote	97	319	25	82	8	1	5	36	33	33	.257	.326	.335	0	1	11	2	4	5	4
Don Hahn	110	323	34	81	14	1	4	28	37	34	.251	.328	.337	2	0	10	1	3	2	5
Ike Hampton	4	4	0	0	0	0	0	1	0	1	.000	.000	.000	0	0	0	0	0	1	0
Bud Harrelson	106	331	48	75	10	0	1	13	71	39	.227	.366	.266	9	4	5	2	8	0	1
Ron Hodges	59	136	16	30	4	0	4	14	19	11	.221	.310	.338	0	0	2	0	0	3	3
Cleon Jones	124	461	62	130	23	1	13	60	38	79	.282	.343	.421	3	3	11	6	2	3	3
Ed Kranepool	94	217	20	65	11	1	4	24	18	14	.300	.350	.415	1	0	5	0	0	2	0
Ted Martinez	116	334	32	73	15	7	2	43	14	40	.219	.247	.323	3	2	13	0	3	4	4
Felix Millan	136	518	50	139	15	2	1	33	31	14	.268	.317	.311	5	1	12	8	24	4	2
John Milner	137	507	70	128	19	0	20	63	66	77	.252	.337	.408	10	2	18	0	0	3	9
Brock Pemberton	11	22	0	4	0	0	0	1	0	3	.182	.182	.182	0	1	0	0	0	0	0
Rich Puig	4	10	0	0	0	0	0	0	1	2	.000	.091	.000	0	0	0	0	0	0	0
Dave Schneck	93	254	23	52	11	1	5	25	16	43	.205	.254	.315	4	1	1	1	0	1	2
Rusty Staub	151	561	65	145	22	2	19	78	77	39	.258	.347	.406	2	1	21	3	1	7	12
George Theodore	60	76	7	12	1	0	1	1	8	14	.158	.247	.211	0	0	7	1	4	0	0
Pitchers																				
Jack Aker	24	2	1	1	1	0	0	0	0	0	.500	.500	1.000	0	0	0	0	0	0	0
Bob Apodaca	35	25	2	3	2	0	0	2	3	6	.120	.207	.200	0	0	0	0	1	1	0
Jerry Cram	10	3	0	1	0	0	0	0	0	1	.333	.333	.333	0	0	0	0	0	0	0
Nino Espinosa	2	2	0	1	0	0	0	0	0	0	.500	.500	.500	0	0	0	0	0	0	0
Jerry Koosman	35	86	5	16	2	1	0	5	7	29	.186	.247	.233	0	0	2	0	10	0	0
Jon Matlack	34	79	3	8	0	0	0	8	5	34	.101	.153	.101	0	0	1	0	11	1	0
Tug McGraw	41	14	2	1	1	0	0	3	2	5	.071	.188	.143	0	0	0	0	1	0	0
Bob Miller	58	9	0	1	1	0	0	0	0	4	.111	.111	.222	0	0	0	0	0	0	0
Harry Parker	40	36	1	0	0	0	0	1	2	20	.000	.053	.000	0	0	0	0	3	0	0
Ray Sadecki	34	27	1	7	0	0	0	2	1	1	.259	.286	.259	0	0	0	0	0	0	0
Tom Seaver	32	71	3	7	0	0	0	4	9	28	.099	.200	.099	0	0	3	0	7	0	0
Randy Sterling	3	2	0	0	0	0	0	0	1	2	.000	.333	.000	0	0	0	0	0	0	0
George Stone	15	26	0	3	0	0	0	4	1	5	.115	.148	.115	0	0	0	0	0	0	0
Craig Swan	7	11	2	4	0	0	0	1	1	2	.364	.417	.364	0	0	0	0	0	0	0
Hank Webb	3	3	0	0	0	0	0	1	0	2	.000	.000	.000	0	0	0	0	0	0	0
TOTAL	162	5468	572	1286	183	22	96	538	597	735	.235	.310	.329	43	23	148	29	87	45	56

Pitching	G	ERA	W–L	SV	GS	GF	CG	SHO	IP	H	R	ER	HR	BB	SO	BFP	WP	HBP	BK	IBB
Jack Aker	24	3.48	2–1	2	0	16	0	0	41.1	33	18	16	4	14	18	173	1	2	0	1
Bob Apodaca	35	3.50	6–6	3	8	15	1	0	103.0	92	47	40	7	42	54	434	3	2	3	9
Jerry Cram	10	1.61	0–1	0	0	2	0	0	22.1	22	4	4	1	4	8	84	1	0	0	3
Nino Espinosa	2	5.00	0–0	0	1	0	0	0	9.0	12	5	5	1	0	2	39	0	0	2	0
Jerry Koosman	35	3.36	15–11	0	35	0	13	0	265.0	258	113	99	16	85	188	1118	8	7	1	7
Jon Matlack	34	2.41	13–15	0	34	0	14	7	265.1	221	82	71	8	76	195	1076	4	5	1	11
Tug McGraw	41	4.16	6–11	3	4	26	1	1	88.2	96	43	41	12	32	54	390	4	0	0	6
Bob Miller	58	3.58	2–2	2	0	30	0	0	78.0	89	39	31	2	39	35	353	2	1	0	13
Harry Parker	40	3.92	4–12	4	16	14	1	0	131.0	145	64	57	10	46	58	575	6	3	0	5
Ray Sadecki	34	3.41	8–8	0	10	8	3	1	103.0	107	49	39	7	35	46	440	5	2	0	6
Tom Seaver	32	3.20	11–11	0	32	0	12	5	236.0	199	89	84	19	75	201	956	4	3	2	10
Randy Sterling	3	4.82	1–1	0	2	1	0	0	9.1	13	8	5	0	3	2	44	1	1	0	0
George Stone	15	5.03	2–7	0	13	2	1	0	77.0	103	57	43	10	21	29	349	0	0	1	4
John Strohmayer	1	0.00	0–0	0	0	1	0	0	1.0	0	0	0	0	1	0	4	0	0	0	0
Craig Swan	7	4.45	1–3	0	5	0	0	0	30.1	28	19	15	1	21	10	138	1	0	0	3
Hank Webb	3	7.20	0–2	0	2	1	0	0	10.0	15	9	8	1	10	8	55	0	1	1	0

1975

NL EAST						
TEAM	W	L	PCT	GB	BA	ERA
Pirates	92	69	.571	—	.263	3.01
Phillies	86	76	.531	6.5	.269	3.02
Mets	82	80	.506	10.5	.256	3.39
Cardinals	82	80	.506	10.5	.259	3.57
Cubs	75	87	.463	17.5	.259	4.49
Expos	75	87	.463	17.5	.244	3.72

The 1975 Mets season was a substantial upgrade over the previous year. Tom Seaver posted the second-highest win total of his career, going 22–9 with a 2.38 ERA en route to his third NL Cy Young Award. Dave Kingman smacked 36 homers in his first year with the team, breaking the team record of 34 home runs set by Frank Thomas in the Mets' first season. Rusty Staub drove in 105 runs to top the previous team mark of 97 RBIs set by Donn Clendenon. Jon Matlack earned his 16th victory by August 29, surpassing his previous career-high win total. And rookie Mike Vail put some interest into the end of the season by embarking on a 23-game hitting streak, tying the Mets' record set by Cleon Jones in 1970.

But it was still another disappointing year as the core Mets got another year older. John Milner played just 91 games and hit .191 in 220 at-bats, missing a large chunk of the season due to a pulled leg muscle. Milner was an ironman compared to Bud Harrelson, who had just 73 at-bats due to a damaged right knee that eventually required surgery and rehab. Wayne Garrett batted a career-high .266 while platooning with newcomer Joe Torre at third base. The two combined for only 12 homers and 69 RBIs, one reason why many great pitching performances were wasted.

Mets mainstay Cleon Jones was gone by the end of July following two incidents that embarrassed the team. The outfielder stayed behind in Florida to rehab his surgically repaired knee when the Mets broke camp in April. Police found Jones in van with a woman who wasn't his wife, leading to his arrest for indecent exposure.

The Mets forced Jones to make a public apology to his teammates and fans, further humiliating the veteran. Jones wasn't a very good public speaker at the time and looked uncomfortable at the news conference.

Jones eventually returned to the active roster but was playing sparingly in part because of Ed Kranepool's production at first base, which kept Kingman firmly entrenched in left. Kranepool was hitting .342 by the end of June, and Kingman was providing the power bat the Mets had been seeking since, well, forever. That left no room for Jones, who had played a vital role in the Mets' runs to the 1969 and 1973 World Series.

Jones hadn't had so much as an at-bat in a few straight games when manager Yogi Berra asked him to pinch-hit for Kranepool against lefty Tom House in the seventh inning of a game against the Braves at Shea Stadium July 18. Berra had planned to put Jones in left field to start the eighth while moving Kingman from left to first base. Instead, Garrett came in to play third in place of Torre, who was shuttled over to first. Jones had refused Berra's request to play left field, touching off a dugout squabble that ended with Berra telling Jones to take off his uniform.

The Mets held a news conference the next day without diffusing the situation. Jones wasn't actually suspended, but he wouldn't play for the Mets again. Berra didn't get his wish to have Jones immediately suspended or released, leaving both to twist in the wind for a while in yet another Mets PR disaster.

Jones went just 2-for-24 in his final 11 games as a Met. His knee was shot, robbing him of his ability to cover ground in the outfield and show some power at the plate. The Mets were ready to toss their former postseason hero to the curb.

It took a while for the team to throw its full support toward Berra. Jones wasn't released until July 27, nine days after his argument with Berra. The Mets won eight of 11 following the incident, which helped justify Jones' departure. But it was obvious that Berra had lost control of the clubhouse.

Team discipline wasn't Berra's chief problem at the start of the season. The bullpen was horrible and the rotation lacked a serious No. 4 and 5 starter. The Mets received little pitching help in return for popular closer Tug McGraw, who was shipped to the Phillies with outfielders Don Hahn and Dave Schneck for reliever Mac Scarce, catcher John Stearns, and outfielder Del Unser. The deal gave the Mets a significant upgrade in center as Unser finished the season batting .294 with 53 RBIs in 147 games.

But Scarce's career as a Met lasted all of one batter. He gave up a game-winning single to Richie Hebner in the bottom of the ninth on April 11 in Pittsburgh. Four days later, Scarce was sent to the Reds for reliever Tom Hall, who was outstanding in his first seven appearances for the Mets before posting a 5.47 ERA in 51 innings the rest of the season.

Bob Apodaca became the closer following McGraw's departure, converting 13 of his 14 save opportunities while serving as the team's only dependable reliever until help arrived later in the season.

Rookie Rick Baldwin led the team with 54 appearances, but he also topped the ballclub with seven blown leads. Harry Parker and Jerry Cram also came out of the bullpen with mixed success, prompting Berra to use his starters a little longer than he would have liked.

The pen got much better with the arrivals of Skip Lockwood and Ken Sanders. With Apodaca pitching the ninth inning, the three formed a trio that suddenly gave the Mets one of the better bullpens. But the season might have been more successful if new general manager Joe McDonald had realized the team's bullpen deficiencies sooner.

McDonald was a busy man upon his promotion from farm director to GM on October 1, 1974. He acquired Joe Torre from the Cardinals 12 days later before trading Mc-Graw to the Phillies in December. Kingman was purchased by the Mets from the Giants in late February.

McDonald would role the dice with his rotation hoping Randy Tate, Hank Webb, and/or Craig Swan would show they were ready to pitch in the majors. Tate and Webb looked terrific at times, while Swan spent most of the year at Triple A Tidewater.

Webb went 5–3 with a 2.54 ERA, one shutout, and three complete games between June 23 and August 25. But he posted a 10.67 over his final 14⅓ innings.

Tate saved some of his more overpowering performances for losses. He took a no-hitter and a 3–0 lead into the eighth inning of a start against the Expos August 4. He opened the eighth with a strikeout but was trailing 4–3 just four batters later following a walk, two singles, and a three-run homer.

Swan was overpowering for the Tides after recovering from a stress fracture in his pitching elbow. He made his season debut for the Mets August 16, pitching into the ninth inning of a 4–2 win over the Giants. But he went 0–3 with a 7.94 ERA in his final five starts to help the Mets fade out of the playoff picture.

Torre struggled in his first season with the Mets, four years after winning the NL MVP Award. He hit a career-worst .247 and produced his lowest RBI total since 1962. Torre also set a team mark by hitting into four double plays during a loss to the Astros July 21.

The Mets climbed back into the NL East race after Mc-Donald reconstructed the bullpen. They were within six games of the lead at the beginning of August after winning three straight in Pittsburgh. But the first-place Pirates bounced back by sweeping a doubleheader that started the Mets on an ugly five-game skid that cost Berra his job. First base coach Roy McMillan was promoted to interim manager following a doubleheader in which New York lost both games by 7–0 scores.

The Mets opened 4–5 under McMillan before going on an 11–4 run that pushed them within four games of the division lead. Seaver picked up his 20th victory with a 3–0 shutout of the Pirates on Labor Day. But it took the Mets just nine days following Seaver's gem to fall 10 games off the pace with 17 games to play. There would be no miracle this year.

The Mets' problems were evident by the end of the season. They needed two starting pitchers and another power bat in the lineup. McDonald landed another pitcher by dealing his top run-producer in the process.

The Mets sent Staub to the Tigers for Mickey Lolich in a deal that almost made sense at the time. Mike Vail appeared to be the right fielder of the future following his team record–tying hitting streak, which made Staub appear expendable. But Vail wrecked those plans by tearing ligaments in his ankle while playing basketball over the winter.

McDonald never got another hitter during the off-season, and once again the core Mets got another year older without many reinforcements coming in the foreseeable future.

1975 Mets Statistics

Hitting	G	AB	R	H	2B	3B	HR	RBI	BB	SO	BA	OBP	SLG	SB	CS	GDP	HP	SH	SF	IBB
Jesus Alou	62	102	8	27	3	0	0	11	4	5	.265	.299	.294	0	1	4	1	1	0	2
Gene Clines	82	203	25	46	6	3	0	10	11	21	.227	.269	.286	4	4	4	1	0	1	1
Bob Gallagher	33	15	5	2	1	0	0	0	1	3	.133	.188	.200	0	0	1	0	0	0	0
Wayne Garrett	107	274	49	73	8	3	6	34	50	45	.266	.379	.383	3	2	3	1	1	2	4
Jerry Grote	119	386	28	114	14	5	2	39	38	23	.295	.357	.373	0	1	11	1	0	3	8
Bud Harrelson	34	73	5	16	2	0	0	3	12	13	.219	.329	.247	0	0	1	0	2	0	2
Jack Heidemann	61	145	12	31	4	2	1	16	17	28	.214	.291	.290	1	0	2	0	2	3	3
Ron Hodges	9	34	3	7	1	0	2	4	1	6	.206	.229	.412	0	0	1	0	2	0	0
Cleon Jones	21	50	2	12	1	0	0	2	3	6	.240	.283	.260	0	0	0	0	0	0	0
Dave Kingman	134	502	65	116	22	1	36	88	34	153	.231	.284	.494	7	5	13	4	1	2	5
Ed Kranepool	106	325	42	105	16	0	4	43	27	21	.323	.370	.409	1	1	12	0	0	5	6
Felix Millan	162	676	81	191	37	2	1	56	36	28	.283	.329	.348	1	6	17	12	17	2	2
John Milner	91	220	24	42	11	0	7	29	33	22	.191	.302	.336	1	1	5	2	0	0	4
Brock Pemberton	2	2	0	0	0	0	0	0	0	1	.000	.000	.000	0	0	0	0	0	0	0
Mike Phillips	116	383	31	98	10	7	1	28	25	47	.256	.300	.326	3	0	8	1	2	4	5
Roy Staiger	13	19	2	3	1	0	0	0	0	4	.158	.158	.211	0	0	2	0	0	0	0
Rusty Staub	155	574	93	162	30	4	19	105	77	55	.282	.371	.448	2	0	18	9	1	9	14
John Stearns	59	169	25	32	5	1	3	10	17	15	.189	.268	.284	4	1	6	2	3	2	4
Joe Torre	114	361	33	89	16	3	6	35	35	55	.247	.317	.357	0	2	22	2	2	0	3
Del Unser	147	531	65	156	18	2	10	53	37	76	.294	.337	.392	4	3	8	0	8	4	6
Mike Vail	38	162	17	49	8	1	3	17	9	37	.302	.339	.420	0	0	3	0	0	0	1
Pitchers																				
Bob Apodaca	46	11	2	4	0	0	0	0	1	5	.364	.417	.364	0	0	0	0	0	0	0
Rick Baldwin	54	15	1	3	0	0	0	0	0	5	.200	.200	.200	0	0	0	0	2	0	0
Tom Hall	35	5	2	2	0	0	0	0	0	1	.400	.400	.400	0	0	0	0	1	0	0
Jerry Koosman	36	78	4	14	2	0	0	6	4	31	.179	.220	.205	1	0	0	0	7	0	0
Skip Lockwood	24	6	0	1	0	0	0	1	0	0	.167	.167	.167	0	0	0	0	1	0	0
Jon Matlack	33	70	6	7	0	0	0	2	13	33	.100	.241	.100	0	0	0	0	5	0	0
Harry Parker	18	2	0	0	0	0	0	1	4	2	.000	.667	.000	0	0	0	0	1	0	0
Ken Sanders	30	2	0	0	0	0	0	0	0	1	.000	.000	.000	0	0	0	0	0	0	0

Hitting (continued)	G	AB	R	H	2B	3B	HR	RBI	BB	SO	BA	OBP	SLG	SB	CS	GDP	HP	SH	SF	IBB
Tom Seaver	37	95	7	17	1	0	0	5	8	24	.179	.250	.189	0	0	2	1	7	0	0
George Stone	13	18	2	3	0	0	0	2	1	5	.167	.211	.167	0	0	0	0	2	0	0
Craig Swan	6	7	0	0	0	0	0	1	0	5	.000	.000	.000	0	0	0	0	2	0	0
Randy Tate	26	41	2	0	0	0	0	0	1	22	.000	.024	.000	0	1	0	0	5	0	0
Hank Webb	31	31	5	8	0	0	0	3	2	7	.258	.303	.258	0	0	0	0	0	0	0
TOTAL	162	5587	646	1430	217	34	101	604	501	805	.256	.317	.361	32	26	143	37	75	37	70

Pitching	G	ERA	W:-L	SV	GS	GF	CG	SHO	IP	H	R	ER	HR	BB	SO	BFP	WP	HBP	BK	IBB
Bob Apodaca	46	1.49	3–4	13	0	36	0	0	84.2	66	18	14	4	28	45	338	2	0	0	9
Rick Baldwin	54	3.33	3–5	6	0	29	0	0	97.1	97	39	36	4	34	54	418	5	4	2	4
Jerry Cram	4	5.40	0–1	0	0	2	0	0	5.0	7	3	3	2	2	2	23	0	0	0	0
Nino Espinosa	2	18.00	0–1	0	0	0	0	0	3.0	8	6	6	0	1	2	18	0	0	0	0
Tom Hall	34	4.75	4–3	1	4	15	0	0	60.2	58	39	32	10	31	48	272	2	3	0	3
Jerry Koosman	36	3.42	14–13	2	34	2	11	4	239.2	234	106	91	19	98	173	1018	7	4	7	6
Skip Lockwood	24	1.49	1–3	2	0	8	0	0	48.1	28	9	8	3	25	61	192	5	1	0	6
Jon Matlack	33	3.38	16–12	0	32	0	8	3	228.2	224	105	86	15	58	154	954	7	1	1	6
Harry Parker	18	4.41	2–3	2	1	5	0	0	34.2	37	17	17	2	19	22	159	4	0	0	5
Ken Sanders	29	2.30	1–1	5	0	18	0	0	43.0	31	11	11	2	14	8	172	0	0	0	7
Mac Scarce	1	INF.	0–0	0	0	1	0	0	0.0	1	0	0	0	0	0	1	0	0	0	0
Tom Seaver	36	2.38	22- 9	0	36	0	15	5	280.1	217	81	74	11	88	243	1115	7	4	1	6
George Stone	13	5.05	3–3	0	11	0	1	0	57.0	75	38	32	3	21	21	261	4	0	1	3
Craig Swan	6	6.39	1–3	0	6	0	0	0	31.0	38	22	22	4	13	19	142	0	1	2	2
Randy Tate	26	4.45	5–13	0	23	1	2	0	137.2	121	73	68	8	86	99	605	1	5	2	3
Hank Webb	29	4.07	7–6	0	15	5	3	1	115.0	102	58	52	12	62	38	502	4	1	4	4
TOTAL	162	3.39	82–80	31	162	122	40	14	1466.0	1344	625	552	99	580	989	6190	48	24	20	64

1976

NL EAST

TEAM	W	L	PCT	GB	BA	ERA
Phillies	101	61	.623	—	.272	3.08
Pirates	92	70	.568	9.0	.267	3.36
Mets	86	76	.531	15.0	.246	2.94
Cubs	75	87	.463	26.0	.251	3.93
Cardinals	72	90	.444	29.0	.260	3.60
Expos	55	107	.340	46.0	.235	3.99

How does a team fail to contend for a division title when the pitching staff leads the league in ERA, strikeouts, complete games, shutouts, fewest hits allowed, and fewest runs allowed? It's easy when the offense ranks in the bottom half of every major category except home runs (5th) and slugging percentage (6th).

New manager Joe Frazier had been successful at the minor league level, winning four championships from 1971 to 1975. He was promoted to the Mets about a month after guiding the Tidewater Tides to the International League title. But few prospects accompanied Frazier to the majors, a warning sign for a ballclub about to take a nosedive. Unheralded rookie Bruce Boisclair didn't disappoint after winning a roster spot out of spring training. Craig Swan compiled a 2.73 ERA in his last 79 innings while showing major league ability. But Roy Staiger was (over)hyped as the third baseman of the future and was practically force-fed 304 at-bats while hitting .220 with two homers. Catching prospect John Stearns spent most of the season in the minors, and the rest of the talent in the farm system seemed to rest in the switch-hitting bat of Brooklyn native Lee Mazzilli, who spent the year with Double A Jackson before he was recalled in September.

The Mets easily had the best starting four in the National League, if not the majors. Jerry Koosman and Jon

Matlack set career-highs for victories while finishing with ERAs below 3.00. Tom Seaver led the team in strikeouts and innings pitched as usual but received little support, both on and off the field. Newcomer Mickey Lolich threw over 190 innings as the fourth starter while pitching in tough luck, some of it his own doing.

Seaver almost was dealt before the season began. He had wanted a multiyear contract in the six-figure range after earning his third Cy Young Award. General manager Joe McDonald and Mets chairman M. Donald Grant dragged their feet and threatened to trade their top player. Jack Lang reported in the *Long Island Press* late in spring training that the team was close to sending Seaver to the Dodgers for fellow pitcher Don Sutton. Mets fans reacted angrily following the report, and the deal was killed before Seaver and the team finally worked out a three-year package worth nearly $700,000.

The Mets scored three runs or fewer in 10 of Seaver's 11 losses, including five shutouts. He also left the game with a lead in three of his 10 no-decisions and also pitched 10 shutout innings in a game the Mets would eventually lose 1–0.

Matlack was well on his way to a 20-win season, picking up his 10th victory on July 1. Win No. 11 didn't come until August 5 as the Mets scored a total of two runs during a three-start stretch with Matlack on the mound. He tossed nine shutout innings in one no-decision after pitching 9⅔ innings of shutout ball in another no-decision.

Koosman might have been the worst of the Mets' "Big Three" in the first half of the season. He was 9–6 with a 4.00 ERA at the All-Star break before posting a 1.64 ERA the rest of the way. Koosman threw 14 complete games and three shutouts in his last 16 starts, allowing more than two earned runs just three times. Seven of his 12 post-All-Star break victories were decided by one run.

Lolich's numbers looked good on paper, but he always seemed to pitch well enough to lose. He went 0–5 during a six-start stretch in which the Mets scored a total of six runs. New York gave him two runs or fewer in 15 of his 30 starts. He also had trouble fielding his position, especially bunts. He was responsible for six of the team's 13 errors among starting pitchers, which in part led to his team-high 14 unearned runs.

McDonald was able to solidify the rotation by acquiring Lolich from the Tigers in December 1975. The team was sorely lacking a legitimate No. 4 starter in '75, causing the Mets to fade out of the postseason picture in early September. But the Lolich deal cost the Mets Rusty Staub, who was the team's most polished hitter at the time of the trade. Staub was made expendable by his ability to make more money than Mike Vail, who became the heir apparent in right field. Vail batted .302 in '75 and tied Cleon Jones' team record by putting together a 23-game hitting streak a few games after his recall from Triple A Tidewater in August. But the Mets weren't expecting Vail to dislocate his right foot while playing basketball a few weeks before the start of spring training, causing him to miss the first 2½ months of the season and leading Frazier to play Dave Kingman in right for 104 games.

Kingman carried the Mets' offense through the middle of July while challenging Roger Maris' single-season record of 61 home runs. "Kong" had nine homers and 20 RBIs in April and tied a team record with three homers while setting a franchise mark with eight RBIs in a game at Los Angeles. He had 32 homers and 72 ribbies when he tried to make a diving catch against Atlanta pitcher Phil Niekro July 19. Niekro wound up with a double, and Kingman came away with a dislocated thumb that caused him to miss the next 33 games. The Mets hit just six home runs during Kingman's absence.

The Mets' offense was paltry at best without Kingman, who finished second to Mike Schmidt in the NL home run race despite playing in only 123 games. John Milner was the team's next-best offensive weapon, hitting 15 homers and driving in 78 while batting .278. Ed Kranepool was the only other Met with more than 10 home runs or 49 RBIs. Felix Millan finished fourth on the team with only 35 RBIs while serving as the No. 2 hitter in the lineup.

Millan had an up-and-down season. He batted .346 in April before posting a .151 average over the next seven weeks. He salvaged his season by hitting .349 in his last 47 games, when the Mets already had thrown up the white flag.

Harrelson played just 113 games at shortstop, leaving the position in the hands of the decent-hitting, shaky-gloved Mike Phillips. Joe Torre hit .306 to make up for his .247 average in his first season as a Met the previous year. But Torre delivered just 31 RBIs and played only 30 innings at third base after losing the job to Wayne Garrett and Staiger.

Del Unser, who batted .294 in 1975, was hit on the helmet by a pitch early in the season. He hit only .213 in his final 239 at-bats as a Met before he was dealt to the Expos with Garrett for outfielders Pepe Mangual and Jim Dwyer in late July. Mangual and Dwyer were a pair of Punch-and-Judy hitters put in a lineup that already was scaring small children.

Kranepool put together another strong season and was difficult to keep out of the lineup when healthy. He started 78 games at first base and another 28 at the corner outfield spots. He injured an elbow crashing into the outfield fence, causing him to miss 3½ weeks in August.

The only problem with having Kranepool in the starting lineup was that the Mets didn't have their top pinch-hitter. Kranepool went 4-for-10 with three RBIs as a pinch-hitter after going a combined 25-for-55 (.455) with one homer and seven RBIs the previous two seasons.

With Kranepool playing every day, Boisclair was the Mets' top hitter off the bench, collecting 12 hits in 21 at-bats. Boisclair was the most pleasant surprise on an offense that didn't have many others, compiling a .287 average that included a 12-for-21 mark as a pinch-hitter.

The bullpen wasn't bad, but it wasn't as strong as it appeared during stretches in the second half of 1975. Bob Apodaca's ERA almost doubled to 2.81 from 1.49. Skip Lockwood paced the team with 19 saves, although his ERA grew by more than a run from '75. Ken Sanders also had a spike in his earned run average as the pen was constantly asked to protect tiny leads.

The bench was ineffective and the farm system was barren. That didn't stop the Mets from posting the second-best regular season record in team history to date. By late September, they moved 15 games over .500 for the first time in over four years, but the Mets were long out of the NL East race by then.

The fans understood the team's days as a championship contender were in the past. New York finished fifth in the league in attendance at more than 1.4 million, which represented a drop of almost 50 percent from the team's high-water mark in 1970. The Mets opened the schedule with a three-game home series that was seen by just more than 41,000. They didn't draw more than 18,000 fans until their 10th home game and didn't handle a crowd of over 30,000 until their 18th game at Shea. Unfortunately for the franchise, the fans knew the jig was up before management took notice.

Grant had taken over control of the team following the death of owner Joan Payson in the fall of 1975. Payson had always relied on her front office to develop the farm system and mold the big-league roster. Grant wanted to be more hands-on and show he could run the franchise with little help outside of McDonald. Any deals negotiated by McDonald had to be approved by Grant, who was about to take a declining franchise and turn it into rubble.

1976 Mets Statistics

Hitting	G	AB	R	H	2B	3B	HR	RBI	BB	SO	BA	OBP	SLG	SB	CS	GDP	HP	SH	SF	IBB
Benny Ayala	22	26	2	3	0	0	1	2	2	6	.115	.179	.231	0	1	0	0	0	0	0
Billy Baldwin	9	22	4	6	1	1	1	5	1	2	.273	.292	.545	0	0	0	0	0	1	0
Bruce Boisclair	110	286	42	82	13	3	2	13	28	55	.287	.350	.374	9	5	3	0	0	0	5
Leon Brown	64	70	11	15	3	0	0	2	4	4	.214	.257	.257	2	4	3	0	0	0	0
Jim Dwyer	11	13	2	2	0	0	0	0	2	1	.154	.267	.154	0	0	0	0	0	0	1
Leo Foster	24	59	11	12	2	0	1	15	8	5	.203	.299	.288	3	0	0	0	0	0	1
Wayne Garrett	80	251	36	56	8	1	4	26	52	26	.223	.359	.311	7	5	5	1	1	0	5
Jerry Grote	101	323	30	88	14	2	4	28	38	19	.272	.350	.365	1	2	15	1	3	1	4
Bud Harrelson	118	359	34	84	12	4	1	26	63	56	.234	.351	.298	9	3	1	2	8	0	5
Jack Heidemann	5	12	0	1	0	0	0	0	0	0	.083	.083	.083	0	0	0	0	0	0	0
Ron Hodges	56	155	21	35	6	0	4	24	27	16	.226	.339	.342	2	0	4	0	1	1	2
Dave Kingman	123	474	70	113	14	1	37	86	28	135	.238	.286	.506	7	4	11	5	0	3	4
Jay Kleven	2	5	0	1	0	0	0	2	0	1	.200	.200	.200	0	0	1	0	0	0	0
Ed Kranepool	123	415	47	121	17	1	10	49	35	38	.292	.344	.410	1	0	10	0	2	3	4
Pepe Mangual	41	102	15	19	5	2	1	9	10	32	.186	.259	.304	7	3	0	0	3	0	0
Lee Mazzilli	24	77	9	15	2	0	2	7	14	10	.195	.323	.299	5	4	0	1	0	1	0
Felix Millan	139	531	55	150	25	2	1	35	41	19	.282	.341	.343	2	4	15	7	6	2	5
John Milner	127	443	56	120	25	4	15	78	65	53	.271	.362	.447	0	7	12	0	0	3	1
Mike Phillips	87	262	30	67	4	6	4	29	25	29	.256	.315	.363	2	2	2	0	3	5	8
Roy Staiger	95	304	23	67	8	1	2	26	25	35	.220	.278	.273	3	3	8	1	1	4	6
John Stearns	32	103	13	27	6	0	2	10	16	11	.262	.364	.379	1	2	4	1	0	1	0
Joe Torre	114	310	36	95	10	3	5	31	21	35	.306	.358	.406	1	3	16	5	2	2	1
Del Unser	77	276	28	63	13	2	5	25	18	40	.228	.275	.344	4	4	4	1	5	3	1
Mike Vail	53	143	8	31	5	1	0	9	6	19	.217	.243	.266	0	1	4	0	0	3	0
Pitchers																				
Bob Apodaca	43	16	0	2	1	0	0	0	1	3	.125	.176	.188	0	0	2	0	1	0	0
Rick Baldwin	11	3	0	1	0	0	0	0	0	2	.333	.333	.333	0	0	0	0	0	0	0
Nino Espinosa	12	9	1	0	0	0	0	0	1	3	.000	.100	.000	0	0	0	0	1	0	0
Jerry Koosman	34	79	5	17	2	0	0	6	2	34	.215	.235	.241	0	0	1	0	13	0	0
Skip Lockwood	56	18	2	6	1	0	0	2	2	3	.333	.400	.389	0	1	0	0	3	0	0
Mickey Lolich	31	54	5	7	0	0	0	1	5	25	.130	.217	.130	0	0	2	1	11	0	0
Jon Matlack	35	88	10	17	1	0	0	9	8	35	.193	.268	.205	0	0	3	1	7	0	0
Bob Myrick	21	3	0	0	0	0	0	1	0	2	.000	.000	.000	0	0	0	0	0	0	0
Ken Sanders	31	2	0	0	0	0	0	0	0	0	.000	.000	.000	0	0	0	0	0	0	0
Tom Seaver	35	82	5	7	0	0	0	3	9	26	.085	.176	.085	0	0	1	0	9	0	0
Craig Swan	23	39	3	4	0	0	0	1	3	17	.103	.186	.103	0	0	0	1	6	0	0
Hank Webb	8	1	1	0	0	0	0	0	1	0	.000	.500	.000	0	0	0	0	0	0	0
TOTAL	162	5415	615	1334	198	34	102	560	561	797	.246	.317	.352	66	58	127	28	92	33	53

Pitching	G	ERA	W–L	SV	GS	GF	CG	SHO	IP	H	R	ER	HR	BB	SO	BFP	WP	HBP	BK	IBB
Bob Apodaca	43	2.81	3–7	5	3	30	0	0	89.2	71	34	28	4	29	45	364	0	3	0	12
Rick Baldwin	11	2.38	0–0	0	0	4	0	0	22.2	14	6	6	0	10	9	89	0	2	0	1
Nino Espinosa	12	3.67	4–4	0	5	0	0	0	41.2	41	21	17	3	13	30	175	1	0	0	3
Tom Hall	5	5.79	1–1	0	0	2	0	0	4.2	5	3	3	0	5	2	25	0	0	0	2
Jerry Koosman	34	2.69	21–10	0	32	0	17	3	247.1	205	81	74	19	66	200	994	3	1	1	7
Skip Lockwood	56	2.67	10–7	19	0	44	0	0	94.1	62	31	28	6	34	108	375	3	2	1	8
Mickey Lolich	31	3.22	8–13	0	30	1	5	2	192.2	184	83	69	14	52	120	797	11	0	2	1
Jon Matlack	35	2.95	17–10	0	35	0	16	6	262.0	236	94	86	18	57	153	1054	13	3	3	5
Bob Myrick	21	3.25	1–1	0	1	8	0	0	27.2	34	13	10	2	13	11	126	0	0	0	1
Ken Sanders	31	2.87	1–2	1	0	18	0	0	47.0	39	16	15	4	12	16	188	0	1	1	4
Tom Seaver	35	2.59	14–11	0	34	0	13	5	271.0	211	83	78	14	77	235	1079	12	4	0	9
Craig Swan	23	3.54	6–9	0	22	1	2	1	132.1	129	64	52	11	44	89	568	0	5	3	3
Hank Webb	8	4.50	0–1	0	0	1	0	0	16.0	17	9	8	2	7	7	74	0	2	1	0
TOTAL	162	2.94	86–76	25	162	109	53	18	1449.0	1248	538	473	97	419	1025	5908	43	23	12	56

1977

NL EAST

TEAM	W	L	PCT	GB	AVG	ERA
Phillies	101	61	.623	—	.279	3.71
Pirates	96	66	.593	5.0	.274	3.61
Cardinals	83	79	.512	18.0	.270	3.81
Cubs	81	81	.500	20.0	.266	4.01
Expos	75	87	.463	26.0	.260	4.01
Mets	64	98	.395	37.0	.244	3.77

A new era in Major League Baseball had been ushered in during the winter of 1977. A few months later, Tom Seaver and Dave Kingman were ushered out of Shea as the Mets, under the leadership of chairman M. Donald Grant, showed absolutely no interest in improving the ballclub through baseball's new rules.

The end of the 1976 season marked the first true free-agent signing period as teams willing to fork over a few extra bucks were able to make immediate improvements. Reggie Jackson, Don Baylor, Bobby Grich, Gary Matthews, Joe Rudi, Don Gullett, and Rollie Fingers were among the All-Stars and high-profile players who left their teams for bigger contracts with new ballclubs.

The Mets went through the motions of "drafting" free agents as teams could negotiate only with players on their free-agent draft list. The Mets gave lip service to Matthews

Tom Seaver shows off his Cy Young Awards after winning his third in 1975. By the end of the 1977 season, he had been traded.

and a few available players, making lowball offers that weren't even close to the new market value. Grant was still living in the days when a GM and player would squabble over $5,000.

Besides, the Mets had come off an 86-win season in which attendance dropped by only 262,000 fans. They were just 10½ games out of first place by June 1, 1976, and a 10-game winning streak put them within 12½ games on July 4. Certainly, there was no urgent need to improve the team through free agency. Jerry Grote, Felix Millan, and Bud Harrelson had aged by just one year. The Mets already had two players on their roster who hit more than 10 homers in '76. And why spend money on Reggie Jackson when you had Mike Vail in right field. Plus, the Mets had Lee Mazzilli waiting in the wings to take over center field and make fans forget about Willie, Mickey, and the Duke.

"Grant was not willing to pay anyone," said Lenny Randle, who joined the Mets a month into the '77 campaign. "He still had a 1918 mentality about the game."[9]

The Mets did make a huge free-agent move before the start of the '77 season. They dipped into their past by inking Ray Sadecki to bolster the bullpen and serve as a spot starter. Sadecki spent 33 wondrous days with the Mets before he was released in May.

There was little hope the Mets were going to contend for a division title heading into 1977, but a total collapse wasn't expected this soon. The front of the rotation still featured Tom Seaver, Jerry Koosman, and Jon Matlack,

but the lineup was lacking any semblance of power after Dave Kingman and John Milner. Ed Kranepool was considered the team's No. 3 power threat when the Mets broke camp.

Seaver posted a 2.59 ERA in 1976 but went only 14–11 as the Mets simply refused to score runs for him. Koosman won a career-high 21 games, and Matlack topped a personal best with 17 victories in '76. But the back end of the rotation was questionable as Grant and McDonald hoped Craig Swan and Nino Espinosa could handle major league batters. By the end of the '77 season, Swan and Espinosa were two of their three best pitchers. Koosman was losing, Matlack was hurting, and Seaver was gone.

The free-agent period had an adverse effect on Seaver's relationship with the Mets. He was almost dealt to the Dodgers the previous spring before accepting a multiyear contract. But Seaver's current $225,000 annual salary had been dwarfed by those signed by the new free agents. Gullett accepted a six-year, $2 million contract from the Yankees, and the Padres were paying Fingers $267,000 a season to close ballgames for the next five years. Seaver was being grossly underpaid, but Grant believed a contract was a contract.

The Mets opened their second season under manager Joe Frazier by taking the first two games at Wrigley Field. The Mets had Seaver pitching the home opener, but fewer than 24,000 fans paid their way into Shea to see him throw a five-hitter in a 4–0 victory. The Mets averaged 8,546 patrons at their next four ballgames before Seaver improved to 3–0 while pitching in front of over 35,000. It was evident Seaver remained the team's real drawing card, but Grant was more interested in honoring the contract.

Let's say for argument's sake that an average ticket to a Mets game in 1977 was $3. The team had grossed $177,732 in Seaver's first two home starts, an average of $88,866. The Mets had totaled $102,552 in the four other home games, an average of $25,638. Seaver was worth more than three times the rest of the pitchers at the gate.

But even with Seaver on the mound, the Mets weren't filling up the stadium like they used to. They had done little to improve the ballclub since the 1973 pennant, and the same veterans were playing fewer games due to injury. The starting middle infielders, Millan and Harrelson, were 33, one year younger than Grote and three years younger than Joe Torre. Management was hoping Harrelson and Grote could each play 100 games, something they had done just once in the same season since 1971. Instead, fans were seeing more of Mike Phillips at short and Ron Hodges behind the plate than they would have liked. To the paying public, that wasn't worth three bucks.

The Mets got off to their expected mediocre start in 1977, splitting their first 18 games while Seaver was opening 4–0. They fell into the basement two games later, a spot they would relinquish for just one day the rest of the season. The Mets followed their 9–9 start by going 6–21, costing Frazier his job as manager. At first glance the team appeared listless, but upon further review it was evident the talent just wasn't there.

Mazzilli struggled mightily while starting 156 of his 159 games in center field. The Brooklyn native was making female fans swoon, but his offensive numbers hardly took one's breath away. He hit just six homers, displayed a below-average arm in center and struggled to get his batting average to .250.

Roy Staiger started 19 of the Mets' first 24 games before the team decided it needed another third baseman. The Mets came up with Randle, who became the team's everyday third baseman once Torre became manager on May 31.

Randle had been with the Rangers in spring training but was sold to the Mets about a month after he punched Texas manager Frank Lucchesi in the face, leaving Lucchesi with a fractured cheek. Randle hit .426 in 59 at-bats during his first 17 games with New York.

Randle gave the Mets a productive bat, but the rest of the lineup was dormant. Millan and Mazzilli were hitting .217 when Torre took over, Harrelson was batting .138, Torre was at .180 and Kingman had slumped to .213 with eight homers and 24 RBIs in 42 games. Besides Randle, John Milner was the only Mets starter with an average above .246.

The Mets showed signs of life by going 7–1 in their first eight games under Torre after dropping nine of their last 10 for Frazier. Meanwhile, Seaver reportedly was in the process of negotiating a new contract with team owner Lorinda de Roulet. Tom Terrific had bypassed both McDonald and Grant to reopen talks, and things were going smoothly until Grant planted a ridiculous story through *Daily News* columnist Dick Young, who had been getting Mets gossip spoon-fed to him by the highest-ranking source. Young wrote that Seaver only wanted a bigger contract because Seaver's wife, Nancy, was jealous of Ruth Ryan, whose husband, Nolan, was making more money than Seaver. Seaver and de Roulet had worked out a package that was worth a total of $700,000 for the 1978 and '79 seasons, a hometown discount compared to what Seaver could have made on the open market.

Once Young's column was published on June 15, Seaver phoned Mets PR director Arthur Richman, telling him to "get me out of here." Hours later, the "Midnight Massacre" was completed. Seaver was shipped to the Reds for reigning NL Rookie of the Year Pat Zachry, utility infielder Doug Flynn, and outfield prospects Steve Henderson and Dan Norman. In addition to the Seaver deal, the Mets also sent Kingman to the Padres for utilityman Bobby Valentine and reliever Paul Siebert. Phillips was jettisoned to the Cardinals for Joel Youngblood in a swap that would benefit the Mets during their lean years.

The Mets continued to play hard for Torre, a team trademark during his four-plus seasons on their bench. They won four of six after learning the Seaver trade was a done deal. The Mets followed that by dropping six straight and 15 of 17, with all but four of the losses decided by two runs or fewer. That ugly stretch was followed by a 15–8 record as Zachry and Henderson began to contribute to victories. But the Mets went 18–38 the rest of the way to finish with 98 losses, the team's worst record in 10 years.

Koosman and Matlack were pitching in bad luck, and Matlack was pitching with a sore arm. Koosman tossed a beautiful 4–1 win over the Padres on July 29 to improve to 8–11. He went 0–9 the rest of the season to finish with 20 losses, one year after winning 21 games. Two days before Koosman's final victory, Matlack picked up his sixth win of the year by combining with three relievers on a three-hitter in a 7–4 triumph over the Giants. Matlack won just one more the rest of the season.

Henderson spent much of the season batting over .300 before settling at .297 with 12 homers and 65 RBIs. He finished one vote behind outfielder Andre Dawson for the NL Rookie of the Year Award. Zachry wasn't Seaver, but he was good enough to go 7–4 with a 3.53 ERA in his last 15 starts. Espinosa and Swan combined for 19 of the Mets' 64 victories while showing they belonged in the majors.

Bruce Boisclair continued to hit, be it off the bench or as a starter. He had batted .289 over 605 at-bats in his first two major league seasons, but that included only six homers for a team that lacked power. The Mets belted just one home run in their last 17 games and hit only 48 after Kingman was traded.

Shea Stadium had turned into Grant's tomb. The team drew more than 25,000 just three times following the Seaver trade, all during a series against Seaver's Reds. Over 46,000 dropped in to Shea to see Seaver beat Koosman 5–1 on August 21, proving once again that the best pitcher in team history could still line the coffers of Mets ownership.

The Mets veterans were disappearing as the season wore on. Millan suffered a separated shoulder when he was thrown to the turf by burly Pirates catcher Ed Ott August 12, causing him to miss the rest of the season. Millan left the Mets to sign a deal with the Taiyo Whales after the season. Grote was mercifully dealt to the Dodgers August 31 for two players who never made it to the majors. Matlack and Milner were part of a four-team, 11-player deal in December, three months before Harrelson was shipped to the Phillies for Fred Andrews, who never played another major league game after the trade.

Grant had purged the team of its veterans—and its fan base. The Mets would draw 2.86 million at Shea between 1977 and 1979. They drew nearly 2.7 million in 1970 alone.

1977 Mets Statistics

Hitting	G	AB	R	H	2B	3B	HR	RBI	BB	SO	BA	OBP	SLG	SB	CS	GDP	HP	SH	SF	IBB
Luis Alvarado	1	2	0	0	0	0	0	0	0	0	.000	.000	.000	0	0	0	0	0	0	0
Bruce Boisclair	127	307	41	90	21	1	4	44	31	57	.293	.359	.407	6	4	5	1	7	1	0
Doug Flynn	90	282	14	54	6	1	0	14	11	23	.191	.220	.220	1	3	4	0	5	2	2
Leo Foster	36	75	6	17	3	0	0	6	5	14	.227	.284	.267	3	1	2	1	0	0	0
Jerry Grote	42	115	8	31	3	1	0	7	9	12	.270	.333	.313	0	0	5	2	2	0	1
Bud Harrelson	107	269	25	48	6	2	1	12	27	28	.178	.255	.227	5	4	3	1	7	1	1
Steve Henderson	99	350	67	104	16	6	12	65	43	79	.297	.372	.480	6	3	13	1	0	4	2
Ron Hodges	66	117	6	31	4	0	1	5	9	17	.265	.317	.325	0	2	0	0	0	0	1
Dave Kingman	58	211	22	44	7	0	9	28	13	66	.209	.263	.370	3	2	3	3	0	1	3
Ed Kranepool	108	281	28	79	17	0	10	40	23	20	.281	.330	.448	1	4	10	0	0	5	7
Pepe Mangual	8	7	1	1	0	0	0	2	1	4	.143	.250	.143	0	0	0	0	0	0	0
Lee Mazzilli	159	537	66	134	24	3	6	46	72	72	.250	.340	.339	22	15	4	3	4	2	6
Felix Millan	91	314	40	78	11	2	2	21	18	9	.248	.294	.315	1	1	8	3	3	2	3
John Milner	131	388	43	99	20	3	12	57	61	55	.255	.353	.415	6	2	9	0	0	4	7
Dan Norman	7	16	2	4	1	0	0	0	4	2	.250	.400	.313	0	0	1	0	0	0	0
Mike Phillips	38	86	5	18	2	1	1	3	2	15	.209	.244	.291	0	1	1	2	0	0	0
Len Randle	136	513	78	156	22	7	5	27	65	70	.304	.383	.404	33	21	15	2	3	2	3
Luis Rosado	9	24	1	5	1	0	0	3	1	3	.208	.250	.250	0	0	1	1	0	2	0
Roy Staiger	40	123	16	31	9	0	2	11	4	20	.252	.276	.374	1	0	2	0	2	0	0
John Stearns	139	431	52	108	25	1	12	55	77	76	.251	.370	.397	9	8	15	7	1	4	7
Joe Torre	26	51	2	9	3	0	1	9	2	10	.176	.204	.294	0	0	3	0	0	1	1
Mike Vail	108	279	29	73	12	1	8	35	19	58	.262	.310	.398	0	7	9	2	0	3	0
Bobby Valentine	42	83	8	11	1	0	1	3	6	9	.133	.191	.181	0	0	4	0	1	0	0
Joel Youngblood	70	182	16	46	11	1	0	11	13	40	.253	.301	.324	1	3	6	0	1	1	1
Pitchers																				
Bob Apodaca	59	6	0	1	0	0	0	1	0	3	.167	.167	.167	0	0	0	0	1	0	0
Rick Baldwin	40	4	1	2	0	0	0	0	0	2	.500	.500	.500	0	0	0	0	0	0	0
Nino Espinosa	32	62	1	8	1	0	0	5	3	15	.129	.169	.145	0	0	3	0	7	0	0
Roy Lee Jackson	4	6	0	0	0	0	0	0	0	1	.000	.000	.000	0	0	0	0	1	0	0
Jerry Koosman	32	72	2	8	0	0	1	7	0	30	.111	.122	.153	0	0	2	1	5	1	0
Skip Lockwood	63	15	1	3	0	0	0	1	0	1	.200	.200	.200	0	0	1	0	3	0	0
Jon Matlack	26	50	1	3	1	0	0	0	7	27	.060	.175	.080	0	0	2	0	1	0	0
Doc Medich	1	2	0	0	0	0	0	0	0	1	.000	.000	.000	0	0	0	0	0	0	0
Bob Myrick	44	11	0	2	0	0	0	2	0	3	.182	.182	.182	0	0	0	0	0	0	0
Tom Seaver	13	31	1	5	0	0	0	4	2	12	.161	.206	.161	0	0	0	0	2	1	0
Paul Siebert	25	1	1	0	0	0	0	0	0	0	.000	.000	.000	0	0	0	0	0	0	0
Craig Swan	26	48	3	9	0	0	0	0	0	12	.188	.188	.188	0	0	0	0	6	0	0
Jackson Todd	19	17	0	1	0	0	0	0	1	8	.059	.111	.059	0	0	1	0	0	0	0
Pat Zachry	19	42	0	6	0	0	0	1	0	13	.143	.143	.143	0	0	4	0	1	0	0
TOTAL	162	5410	587	1319	227	30	88	525	529	887	.244	.311	.346	98	81	136	30	63	37	45

Pitching	G	ERA	W:–L	SV	GS	GF	CG	SHO	IP	H	R	ER	HR	BB	SO	BFP	WP	HBP	BK	IBB
Bob Apodaca	59	3.43	4–8	5	0	27	0	0	84.0	89	38	32	7	30	53	367	2	1	1	11
Rick Baldwin	40	4.45	1–2	1	0	13	0	0	62.2	62	32	31	6	31	23	274	2	5	1	9
Nino Espinosa	32	3.42	10–13	0	29	2	7	1	200.0	188	82	76	17	55	105	825	2	5	2	5
Roy Lee Jackson	4	6.00	0–2	0	4	0	0	0	24.0	25	16	16	2	15	13	116	2	3	0	1
Jerry Koosman	32	3.49	8–20	0	32	0	6	1	226.2	195	102	88	17	81	192	940	2	4	4	8
Skip Lockwood	63	3.38	4–8	20	0	50	0	0	104.0	87	40	39	5	31	84	427	3	4	1	11
Jon Matlack	26	4.21	7–15	0	26	0	5	3	169.0	175	86	79	19	43	123	702	2	2	2	7
Doc Medich	1	3.86	0–1	0	1	0	0	0	7.0	6	3	3	0	1	3	25	0	0	0	0
Bob Myrick	44	3.61	2–2	2	4	19	0	0	87.1	86	39	35	5	33	49	367	2	1	0	5
John Pacella	3	0.00	0–0	0	0	3	0	0	4.0	2	2	0	0	2	1	17	1	0	0	0
Ray Sadecki	4	6.00	0–1	0	0	2	0	0	3.0	3	2	2	1	3	0	14	0	0	0	0
Tom Seaver	13	3.00	7–3	0	13	0	5	3	96.0	79	33	32	7	28	72	390	3	0	1	3
Paul Siebert	25	3.86	2–1	0	0	14	0	0	28.0	27	12	12	0	13	20	123	1	1	0	4
Craig Swan	26	4.23	9–10	0	24	2	2	1	146.2	153	76	69	10	56	71	638	1	1	2	3
Jackson Todd	19	4.77	3–6	0	10	3	0	0	71.2	78	41	38	8	20	39	312	2	2	1	5
Pat Zachry	19	3.76	7–6	0	19	0	2	1	119.2	129	59	50	14	48	63	524	0	3	1	4
TOTAL	162	3.77	64–98	28	162	135	27	12	1433.0	1378	663	600	118	490	911	6061	25	32 16	76	98

1978

NL EAST

TEAM	W	L	PCT	GB	AVG	ERA
Phillies	90	72	.556	—	.258	3.33
Pirates	88	73	.547	1.5	.257	3.41
Cubs	79	83	.488	11.0	.264	4.05
Expos	76	86	.469	14.0	.254	3.42
Cardinals	69	93	.426	21.0	.249	3.58
Mets	66	96	.407	24.0	.245	3.87

The Mets won 66 games in their final year before Tom Seaver's arrival, and they managed to win 66 games in their first full season after Seaver was shipped to the Reds. The '78 version of the Mets hit only 86 homers, posted the National League's second-worst team batting average and compiled the NL's third-worst ERA. The team was so bad that a true Mets fans almost wished Jerry Koosman had been traded after the 1977 season, if only to spare him the misery of a 3–15 season. Koosman spent his final days as

Outfielder Lee Mazzilli and manager Joe Torre talk shop with coach Willie Mays during spring training in 1978.

a Met pitching out of the bullpen after recording several agonizing no-decisions. He went 1–7 through a stretch of 17 games (16 starts) in which he posted a 3.22 ERA over 117.1 innings.

Koosman and Ed Kranepool were the lone Mets remaining from the 1973 pennant winners. The team had shipped Bud Harrelson to the Phillies prior to the season opener after sending Jon Matlack to Texas in a December deal that brought first baseman Willie Montanez to Shea Stadium.

Lenny Randle was back at third after leading the Mets in hitting the previous year. But Randle got off to a slow start following a contract squabble and batted .233, the lowest average of any Met with more than 214 at-bats.

Aside from Randle, Montanez, and Tim Foli, manager Joe Torre stuck with the kids and saw his team hover near the .500 mark for the first two months of the season. It was a pattern that would stay with Torre during his Mets career: little talent, big effort, little hope.

The starting lineup also featured John Stearns, Doug Flynn, Steve Henderson, and Lee Mazzilli, none of whom had been a starter for more than one year heading into 1978. But all four played at least 143 games while preventing a bad season from becoming worse. Stearns set a modern National League record for catchers with 25 stolen bases. Flynn showed Gold Glove capability at second base

and finished tied for second on the team with eight triples. Henderson matched a single-season club record with nine triples and tied for the team lead with 156 hits, but he also paced the squad in strikeouts and double-play grounders.

Mazzilli showed the most promise of the young Mets, finishing second on the team with 20 steals and belting 16 homers after managing just six round-trippers in his rookie season a year earlier. "Maz" also was the biggest reason why female baseball fans would go to Shea, although his arm was the biggest reason why runners would go from second to home on a base hit to center. But Mazzilli was emerging as the Mets' best home-grown offensive talent since Ken Singleton.

The Mets got off to a decent start despite Montanez, who hit just .232 with two homers and 20 RBIs in his first 41 games. Montanez followed his slow start by batting .365 with seven home runs and 22 RBIs in his next 20 games, but he appeared to lose interest as the Mets sunk into oblivion, hitting .233 with no homers and five RBIs in his final 20 games.

Kranepool had perhaps the most disappointing season among the hitters, although he was 15-for-50 (.300) with three homers and 17 RBIs as a pinch-hitter. Kranepool had just 81 at-bats and made only nine starts with Montanez entrenched at first base. Steady Eddie also went 0-for-16 as a pinch-hitter between July 5 and September 13.

Joel Youngblood became the Mets' top utility player, seeing time at six different positions. Elliott Maddox also pushed himself into the starting lineup in his return to the ballpark that derailed what was becoming a productive career. Maddox hit .303 and .307 in 1974 and '75 as a Yankee while the team was serving as co-tenants at Shea Stadium. But he injured his knee while playing outfield at Shea June 13, 1975, causing him to miss the rest of the season and undergo two operations.

Pat Zachry got off to the best start among the Mets' starting hurlers and was the team's lone representative at the All-Star Game. The pitcher acquired in the Seaver deal was 10–3 with a 2.90 ERA after a two-hit shutout of the Phillies July 4. Just 20 days later, Zachry broke his foot during a fit of anger after surrendering a base hit to Pete Rose, which allowed the Red menace to tie the National League's consecutive game hitting streak. Zachry was done for the season, leaving the Mets extremely short-handed in the rotation the rest of the year.

Craig Swan was the team's unluckiest pitcher during the first half of the season. He tossed a five-hit shutout in his first start April 10 against the Cubs before going 0–5 despite a 2.82 ERA in his next 16 games. But Swan was terrific after that, winning seven straight decisions and going 8–1 with a 2.22 ERA in his final 13 starts. He became the second Met to win the National League ERA title.

Nino Espinosa had a lousy second half, going 2–7 with a 6.35 ERA in his last 11 starts. But Espinosa still finished with a team-high 11 wins despite a 4.73 ERA, which was nearly a full run higher than Koosman's.

Koosman followed his 20-loss season with a 3–15 mark that included no wins after July 13. Koosman had no-de-cisions in seven games when allowing two runs or fewer, and he went 0–2 with a 2.76 ERA in his final eight starts as a Met.

Skip Lockwood went through a second-half swoon and missed the last four weeks with a sore shoulder. Lockwood was 7–4 with a 2.88 ERA on June 16 before losing his final nine decisions. He finished with 15 saves and closed out 12 of the Mets' 27 one-run victories, but Lockwood was a prime contributor to blown leads in the late innings.

The rest of the Mets' bullpen consisted of castoffs and has-beens. Bob Apodaca had to miss the entire season with a torn elbow ligament, leaving the middle innings to the likes of Dale Murray, Kevin Kobel, Dwight Bernard, and Paul Siebert. Kobel posted a 1.82 ERA in 21 games out of the pen.

But at least one positive came out of the season. M. Donald Grant was relieved of his duties as chairman of the team by the end of the year, replaced by owner Lorinda de Roulet. Grant had been primarily responsible for the condition of the Mets, who now had a weak team and a weaker farm system. Bernard, Mike Bruhert, Roy Jackson, Juan Berenguer, Sergio Ferrer, and Gil Flores had been disguised as minor leaguers ready to make the next step. General manager Joe McDonald had begun to replenish the farm a year earlier by drafting Wally Backman and Mookie Wilson, and took Hubie Brooks and Brian Giles with the Mets' first two picks of the 1978 draft. But it would be years before McDonald's selections would make an impact on the team.

In the meantime, Mets fans continued to stay away from Shea while McDonald attempted to fortify his roster with Ken Hendersons and Tom Grieves.

1978 Mets Statistics

Hitting	G	AB	R	H	2B	3B	HR	RBI	BB	SO	BA	OBP	SLG	SB	CS	GDP	HP	SH	SF	IBB
Butch Benton	4	4	1	2	0	0	0	2	0	0	.500	.600	.500	0	0	0	1	0	0	0
Bruce Boisclair	107	214	24	48	7	1	4	15	23	43	.224	.293	.322	3	3	4	0	2	5	3
Sergio Ferrer	37	33	8	7	0	1	0	1	4	7	.212	.316	.273	1	0	2	1	2	0	0
Gil Flores	11	29	8	8	1	0	0	1	3	5	.276	.344	.345	1	0	0	0	1	0	0
Doug Flynn	156	532	37	126	12	8	0	36	30	50	.237	.277	.289	3	5	14	1	6	3	10
Tim Foli	113	413	37	106	21	1	1	27	14	30	.257	.283	.320	2	5	10	2	12	2	1
Tom Grieve	54	101	5	21	3	0	2	8	9	23	.208	.273	.297	0	1	3	0	0	0	0
Ken Henderson	7	22	2	5	2	0	1	4	4	4	.227	.346	.455	0	1	0	0	0	0	1
Steve Henderson	157	587	83	156	30	9	10	65	60	109	.266	.333	.399	13	7	24	2	0	5	3
Ron Hodges	47	102	4	26	4	1	0	7	10	11	.255	.322	.314	1	2	4	1	0	2	0
Ed Kranepool	66	81	7	17	2	0	3	19	8	12	.210	.280	.346	0	0	4	1	0	3	2
Elliott Maddox	119	389	43	100	18	2	2	39	71	38	.257	.370	.329	2	11	8	2	2	5	1
Lee Mazzilli	148	542	78	148	28	5	16	61	69	82	.273	.353	.432	20	13	7	1	2	5	6
Willie Montanez	159	609	66	156	32	0	17	96	60	92	.256	.320	.392	9	4	13	1	0	9	19
Dan Norman	19	64	7	17	0	1	4	10	2	14	.266	.284	.484	1	0	0	0	0	1	0
Len Randle	132	437	53	102	16	8	2	35	64	57	.233	.330	.320	14	11	7	1	2	4	7
John Stearns	143	477	65	126	24	1	15	73	70	57	.264	.364	.413	25	13	11	8	2	6	4
Alex Trevino	6	12	3	3	0	0	0	0	1	2	.250	.308	.250	0	0	1	0	0	0	0
Bobby Valentine	69	160	17	43	7	0	1	18	19	18	.269	.346	.331	1	1	7	1	6	2	1
Joel Youngblood	113	266	40	67	12	8	7	30	16	39	.252	.294	.436	4	0	4	1	1	3	1
Pitchers																				
Juan Berenguer	5	3	0	0	0	0	0	0	0	2	.000	.000	.000	0	0	0	0	0	0	0
Dwight Bernard	30	5	0	1	0	0	0	0	1	2	.200	.333	.200	0	0	0	0	0	0	0
Mike Bruhert	27	40	0	3	0	0	0	0	0	21	.075	.075	.075	0	0	0	0	1	0	0
Nino Espinosa	32	67	6	14	3	0	0	4	1	28	.209	.221	.254	0	0	0	0	7	0	0
Tom Hausman	10	17	1	3	1	0	0	2	1	5	.176	.222	.235	0	0	0	0	1	0	0
Roy Lee Jackson	4	3	0	2	0	0	0	0	0	0	.667	.667	.667	0	0	0	0	0	0	0
Kevin Kobel	32	25	3	4	1	0	0	2	1	8	.160	.192	.200	0	0	0	0	4	0	0
Jerry Koosman	38	70	1	6	3	0	0	2	0	27	.086	.086	.129	0	0	0	0	5	0	0

Hitting (continued)	G	AB	R	H	2B	3B	HR	RBI	BB	SO	BA	OBP	SLG	SB	CS	GDP	HP	SH	SF	IBB
Skip Lockwood	57	11	1	2	1	0	1	1	0	5	.182	.182	.545	0	0	0	0	2	0	0
Dale Murray	53	7	1	0	0	0	0	0	1	4	.000	.125	.000	0	0	0	0	0	0	0
Bob Myrick	17	2	0	0	0	0	0	0	0	0	.000	.000	.000	0	0	0	0	0	0	0
Paul Siebert	27	1	0	0	0	0	0	0	0	0	.000	.000	.000	0	0	0	0	0	0	0
Craig Swan	29	65	2	10	0	0	0	3	3	15	.154	.191	.154	0	0	1	0	8	0	0
Pat Zachry	21	43	4	3	0	0	0	0	4	19	.070	.149	.070	0	0	2	0	5	0	0
TOTAL	162	5433	607	1332	227	47	86	561	549	829	.245	.314	.352	100	77	126	24	71	55	59

Pitching	G	ERA	W–L	SV	GS	GF	CG	SHO	IP	H	R	ER	HR	BB	SO	BFP	WP	HBP	BK	IBB
Juan Berenguer	5	8.31	0–2	0	3	1	0	0	13.0	17	12	12	1	11	8	65	0	1	0	0
Dwight Bernard	30	4.31	1–4	0	1	10	0	0	48.0	54	25	23	4	27	26	213	2	0	0	3
Mike Bruhert	27	4.78	4–11	0	22	1	1	1	133.2	171	83	71	6	34	56	585	10	1	2	5
Mardie Cornejo	25	2.45	4–2	3	0	10	0	0	36.2	37	12	10	1	14	17	155	1	3	1	5
Nino Espinosa	32	4.73	11–15	0	32	0	6	1	203.2	230	117	107	24	75	76	888	0	3	3	10
Tom Hausman	10	4.70	3–3	0	10	0	0	0	51.2	58	28	27	6	9	16	216	0	1	2	1
Roy Lee Jackson	4	9.24	0–0	0	2	0	0	0	12.2	21	13	13	2	6	6	61	0	2	0	0
Kevin Kobel	32	2.91	5–6	0	11	12	1	0	108.1	95	42	35	9	30	51	442	1	2	0	9
Jerry Koosman	38	3.75	3–15	2	32	6	3	0	235.1	221	110	98	17	84	160	986	5	8	1	11
Skip Lockwood	57	3.57	7–13	15	0	40	0	0	90.2	78	36	36	10	31	73	371	3	0	1	5
Butch Metzger	25	6.51	1–3	0	0	11	0	0	37.1	48	28	27	4	22	21	180	0	1	1	7
Dale Murray	53	3.65	8–5	5	0	38	0	0	86.1	85	39	35	4	36	37	373	5	2	1	19
Bob Myrick	17	3.28	0–3	0	0	7	0	0	24.2	18	10	9	3	13	13	102	0	0	0	2
Craig Swan	29	2.43	9–6	0	28	0	5	1	207.1	164	62	56	12	58	125	819	1	2	0	8
Paul Siebert	27	5.14	0–2	1	0	5	0	0	28.0	30	16	16	2	21	12	130	2	1	1	5
Pat Zachry	21	3.33	10–6	0	21	0	5	2	138.0	120	57	51	9	60	78	579	3	1	2	4
TOTAL	162	3.87	66–96	26	162	141	21	7	1455.0	1447	690	626	114	531	775	6165	33	28	15	94

1979

NL EAST

TEAM	W	L	PCT	GB	AVG	ERA
Pirates	98	64	.605	—	.272	3.41
Expos	95	65	.594	2.0	.264	3.14
Cardinals	86	76	.531	12.0	.278	3.72
Phillies	84	78	.519	14.0	.266	4.16
Cubs	80	82	.494	18.0	.269	3.88
Mets	63	99	.389	35.0	.250	3.84

By 1979 the Mets had a third baseman who didn't want to play for the team, a fan base that didn't want to watch the team and an owner who just didn't want the team.

The franchise had hit rock bottom, although owner Lorinda de Roulet made a significant change by naming herself board chaiman, unseating M. Donald Grant at the helm. The Mets' 1979 information guide calls de Roulet "a baseball fan for many years." But she lacked the baseball passion and front office savvy possessed by her mother, original Mets owner Joan Payson.

The franchise became even more laughable by mid-season despite manager Joe Torre's ability to get maximum effort from his players. Mrs. de Roulet put two of her daughters on front office payroll, one of whom suggested the team could save money by washing and reusing batting practice balls. The team also came up with the bright idea of bringing in a live mascot, a mule named Mettle, who would graze beyond the outfield fence and leave his "calling card" without becoming a drawing card.

The Mets didn't need a mule to stink up Shea Stadium. With a paucity of quality pitching and little power at the plate, the Mets were creating their own stench. The only significant addition to the lineup was third baseman Richie Hebner, who came to the team kicking and screaming but managed to put up decent numbers after replacing Lenny Randle.

The Mets also swapped shortstops early in the season, sending Tim Foli to the Pirates for Frank Taveras. Foli helped the Bucs win the 1979 World Series while solidifying their infield. Taveras set a team record with 42 stolen bases but was erratic in the field and at the plate.

The biggest upgrade to the lineup was provided by Joel Youngblood, whose ability to play several positions made him a valuable player. He paced the team in homers, doubles, and runs scored while batting .275 in 158 games.

Otherwise, there were no changes to a lineup that had finished near the bottom of the league in every major offensive category in 1978. John Stearns, Willie Montanez, Doug Flynn, Steve Henderson, and Lee Mazzilli represented the rest of the lineup but combined for only 38 homers in 1979. Of the eight regulars, only Hebner and Montanez were seasoned veterans, keeping team payroll low.

Mazzilli led the Mets with a .303 average and was the team's lone All-Star representative. He became the first Met to homer in the Midsummer Classic, but he belted just 15 round-trippers in the regular season.

It was becoming apparent that Henderson wasn't going to be a power hitter, batting .306 but smacking just five homers and 29 extra-base hits in 393 plate appearances. Any help from the minors wouldn't come until late in the 1980 season.

Jerry Koosman was shipped to the Twins the previous December, leaving Ed Kranepool as the only player left from the 1973 World Series roster. Hebner was acquired from the Phillies for Nino Espinosa, which sent the Mets into the season with little starting pitching after Craig Swan and Pat Zachry.

Swan paced the team in wins, strikeouts, ERA, and innings pitched. But Zachry made only seven starts due to irritation of the ulna nerve in his throwing elbow.

Pete Falcone was a bust after being acquired the previous December. Falcone owned a heavy fastball but no command as he led the team in walks and wild pitches.

The Mets were relegated to in-season tryouts for starting pitchers. Dock Ellis was acquired during the year but failed to give the Mets a boost at the mound. He was shipped to the Pirates in September before retiring.

The conga line of starting pitchers included Andy Hassler, Kevin Kobel, Tom Hausman, Ray Burris, Wayne Twitchell, and youngsters Dwight Bernard and Mike Scott. The Mets opened the season with rookie Neil Allen in the starting rotation, but he was wisely sent to the bullpen after posing a 7.65 ERA.

Allen and Jeff Reardon were two of the bright spots on the staff. Reardon spent the previous year as a starter in the minors before he was converted to the bullpen in spring training. Reardon performed well out of the Mets' pen, giving fans hope that things were improving in the minors.

Allen and Reardon were among five Mets who made their major league debut in 1979, a relatively low number considering the ballclub's six-year spiral down the standings. One such player was Kelvin Chapman, an undrafted player who suddenly emerged as the team's top prospect. He batted .333 in spring training and was given the starting second base job as the Mets hoped Chapman would allow second sacker Doug Flynn to replace the more expensive Foli, who wasn't exactly making Reggie Jackson–type money.

Chapman was great on Opening Day but was back in Tidewater by mid May. He returned to Shea in September and wasn't seen in the majors again until 1984. So much for the team's top prospect of 1979.

Future All-Star pitchers Jesse Orosco and Mike Scott also made their big-league debuts but weren't close to being ready.

The relief corps was thinned by injuries to Skip Lockwood and Bob Apodaca. Lockwood didn't pitch after June 6 because of a shoulder injury that was originally diagnosed as "soreness." An elbow injury caused Apodaca to miss his second straight season and led to his premature retirement.

The Mets overachived in the first half of the season and were 38–48 following a five-game winning streak. But overall the team remained a farce at the major league level. They needed a season-ending six-game winning streak just to avoid their first 100-loss season since 1967. Attendance had dropped by more than 200,000, to a franchise-low 788,905. The financial condition of the team was such that de Roulet finally began negotiations to sell.

The Mets also decided after the season not to re-sign Kranepool, who was the team's eldest statesman and their top pinch-hitter. The Krane hit .308 in 74 plate appearances between July 8 and August 29. But a .200 average in September left him at .232, the second straight year in which he hit under .240.

The 1979 draft wasn't a big help to the Mets. They took phenom Tim Leary with the second overall pick and put him on the 1981 opening-day roster before an injury hampered the Mets portion of his career.

Others taken by the Mets in the draft were Ron Gardenhire and Walt Terrell, who declined to sign with the team. Gardenhire, Terrell, and Leary were the only 1979 Mets draft picks to appear in at least 25 major league games during their careers.

1979 Mets Statistics

Hitting	G	AB	R	H	2B	3B	HR	RBI	BB	SO	BA	OBP	SLG	SB	CS	GDP	HP	SH	SF	IBB
Bruce Boisclair	59	98	7	18	5	1	0	4	3	24	.184	.210	.255	0	2	2	1	1	3	0
Jose Cardenal	11	37	8	11	4	0	2	4	6	3	.297	.409	.568	1	0	0	1	0	0	0
Kelvin Chapman	35	80	7	12	1	2	0	4	5	15	.150	.198	.213	0	0	1	0	1	1	0
Sergio Ferrer	32	7	7	0	0	0	0	0	2	3	.000	.222	.000	0	2	0	0	0	0	0
Gil Flores	70	93	9	18	1	1	1	10	8	17	.194	.262	.258	2	0	1	1	3	1	0
Doug Flynn	157	555	35	135	19	5	4	61	17	46	.243	.265	.317	0	3	15	0	6	2	7
Tim Foli	3	7	0	0	0	0	0	0	0	0	.000	.000	.000	0	0	1	0	0	0	0
Richie Hebner	136	473	54	127	25	2	10	79	59	59	.268	.354	.393	3	1	7	8	1	8	6
Steve Henderson	98	350	42	107	16	8	5	39	38	58	.306	.380	.440	13	5	7	4	1	0	6
Ron Hodges	59	86	4	14	4	0	0	5	19	16	.163	.311	.209	0	0	0	0	0	1	3
Ed Kranepool	82	155	7	36	5	0	2	17	13	18	.232	.287	.303	0	1	6	1	0	5	2
Elliott Maddox	86	224	21	60	13	0	1	12	20	27	.268	.335	.339	3	2	3	3	1	1	0
Lee Mazzilli	158	597	78	181	34	4	15	79	93	74	.303	.395	.449	34	12	6	0	0	3	5
Willie Montanez	109	410	36	96	19	0	5	47	25	48	.234	.277	.317	0	1	15	1	1	5	7
Dan Norman	44	110	9	27	3	1	3	11	10	26	.245	.311	.373	2	0	1	1	0	1	2
John Stearns	155	538	58	131	29	2	9	66	52	57	.243	.312	.355	15	15	21	4	3	5	5
Frank Taveras	153	635	89	167	26	9	1	33	33	72	.263	.301	.337	42	19	11	2	10	0	1
Alex Trevino	79	207	24	56	11	1	0	20	20	27	.271	.338	.333	2	2	8	1	4	0	2
Joel Youngblood	158	590	90	162	37	5	16	60	60	84	.275	.346	.436	18	13	7	7	4	4	7
Pitchers																				
Neil Allen	50	14	0	0	0	0	0	0	0	6	.000	.000	.000	0	0	0	0	0	0	0
Juan Berenguer	5	7	0	1	0	0	0	0	2	2	.143	.333	.143	0	0	0	0	1	0	0
Dwight Bernard	32	0	0	0	0	0	0	0	1	0	.000	1.000	.000	0	0	0	0	2	0	0
Ray Burris	4	6	0	1	0	0	0	0	0	2	.167	.167	.167	0	0	0	0	1	0	0
Dock Ellis	17	26	2	2	0	0	0	1	1	7	.077	.111	.077	0	0	0	0	1	0	0
Pete Falcone	33	52	1	9	0	0	0	2	2	19	.173	.204	.173	0	0	2	0	5	0	0
Hitting (continued)	G	AB	R	H	2B	3B	HR	RBI	BB	SO	BA	OBP	SLG	SB	CS	GDP	HP	SH	SF	IBB
Ed Glynn	46	4	0	0	0	0	0	0	0	1	.000	.000	.000	0	0	0	0	0	0	0
Andy Hassler	29	22	0	0	0	0	0	0	1	17	.000	.043	.000	0	0	1	0	0	0	0
Tom Hausman	19	26	0	3	0	0	0	0	0	4	.115	.115	.115	0	0	1	0	1	0	0

Roy Lee Jackson	8	1	0	1	0	0	0	0	0	0	1.000	1.000	1.000	0	0	0	0	0	0	0
Kevin Kobel	30	46	1	9	1	0	0	2	0	18	.196	.196	.217	0	0	1	0	9	0	0
Skip Lockwood	28	2	0	0	0	0	0	0	0	1	.000	.000	.000	0	0	0	0	1	0	0
Dale Murray	58	6	0	0	0	0	0	0	1	3	.000	.143	.000	0	0	0	0	2	0	0
Jesse Orosco	18	6	0	0	0	0	0	0	0	4	.000	.000	.000	0	0	0	0	1	0	0
John Pacella	4	4	0	0	0	0	0	0	0	1	.000	.000	.000	0	0	0	0	0	0	0
Mike Scott	18	12	1	0	0	0	0	0	1	8	.000	.077	.000	0	0	0	0	1	0	0
Craig Swan	35	81	3	10	2	0	0	2	6	38	.123	.184	.148	0	1	0	0	4	0	0
Wayne Twitchell	33	8	0	3	0	0	0	0	0	5	.375	.375	.375	0	0	0	0	1	0	0
Pat Zachry	7	16	0	2	0	0	0	0	0	7	.125	.125	.125	0	0	0	0	0	0	0
TOTAL	163	5591	593	1399	255	41	74	558	498	817	.250	.312	.350	135	79	117	35	66	40	53

Pitching	G	ERA	W:–L	SV	GS	GF	CG	SHO	IP	H	R	ER	HR	BB	SO	BFP	WP	HBP	BK	IBB
Neil Allen	50	3.55	6–10	8	5	27	0	0	99.0	100	46	39	4	47	65	431	6	0	0	13
Juan Berenguer	5	2.93	1–1	0	5	0	0	0	30.2	28	13	10	2	12	25	126	0	1	2	0
Dwight Bernard	32	4.70	0–3	0	1	6	0	0	44.0	59	26	23	2	26	20	208	1	0	0	4
Ray Burris	4	3.32	0–2	0	4	0	0	0	21.2	21	10	8	2	6	10	93	1	1	0	3
Dock Ellis	17	6.04	3–7	0	14	3	1	0	85.0	110	60	57	9	34	41	391	2	1	0	10
Pete Falcone	33	4.16	6–14	0	31	1	1	1	184.0	194	91	85	24	76	113	797	10	1	1	10
Ed Glynn	46	3.00	1–4	7	0	20	0	0	60.0	57	22	20	3	40	32	269	1	2	0	10
Andy Hassler	29	3.70	4–5	4	8	11	1	0	80.1	74	35	33	5	42	53	343	7	0	2	8
Tom Hausman	19	2.75	2–6	2	10	7	1	0	78.2	65	25	24	6	19	33	315	2	4	0	1
Roy Lee Jackson	8	2.20	1–0	0	0	0	0	0	16.1	11	4	4	1	5	10	61	1	1	0	0
Kevin Kobel	30	3.51	6–8	0	27	1	1	1	161.2	169	74	63	14	46	67	683	2	3	2	4
Skip Lockwood	27	1.49	2–5	9	0	22	0	0	42.1	33	7	7	3	14	42	164	2	0	0	5
Dale Murray	58	4.82	4–8	4	0	24	0	0	97.0	105	58	52	6	52	37	428	3	0	0	14
Jesse Orosco	18	4.89	1–2	0	2	6	0	0	35.0	33	20	19	4	22	22	154	0	2	0	0
John Pacella	4	4.41	0–2	0	3	0	0	0	16.1	16	8	8	0	4	12	69	0	0	0	0
Jeff Reardon	18	1.74	1–2	2	0	10	0	0	20.2	12	7	4	2	9	10	81	2	0	0	3
Mike Scott	18	5.33	1–3	0	9	0	0	0	52.1	59	35	31	4	20	21	229	1	0	1	3
Craig Swan	35	3.29	14–13	0	35	0	10	3	251.1	241	102	92	20	57	145	1027	2	2	1	9
Wayne Twitchell	33	5.23	5–3	0	2	9	0	0	63.2	55	44	37	6	55	44	294	1	4	1	8
Pat Zachry	7	3.59	5–1	0	7	0	1	0	42.2	44	19	17	3	21	17	194	1	2	1	2
TOTAL	163	3.84	63–99	36	163	147	16	10	1482.0	1486	706	632	120	607	819	6357	45	24	11	107

1980

NL EAST

TEAM	W	L	PCT	GB	AVG	ERA
Phillies	91	71	.562	—	.270	3.43
Expos	90	72	.556	1.0	.257	3.48
Pirates	83	79	.512	8.0	.266	3.58
Cardinals	74	88	.457	17.0	.275	3.93
Mets	67	95	.414	24.0	.257	3.85
Cubs	64	98	.395	27.0	.251	3.89

It had been three seasons since the Mets were anything close to being competitive, but a new regime was in place, and there was hope in the farm system. The team made only a four-win improvement over 1979, but there were many signs that the stinkfest was about to end.

On January 24 the de Roulet family had completed the sale of the team to Doubleday & Co. Inc. for $21,100,000, a record amount for a major league team at the time. The ballclub was now in the hands of book publishing magnate Nelson Doubleday and Fred Wilpon, chairman of the board of Sterling Equities Inc. and City Investing Co. Doubleday would serve as board chairman of the Mets, with Wilpon installed as president. Both were in their forties and appeared more than willing to pump a little life—and a few bucks—into the franchise.

"People would like to go back to Shea," said Doubleday. "New York is a National League town. It's a wonderful opportunity for us."[10]

Both owners were native New Yorkers. Wilpon's previous claim in baseball was being the No. 1 pitcher for a Lafayette High School team that had Sandy Koufax as its first baseman.

Doubleday and Wilpon quickly reorganized the top of the Mets' staff, demoting hard-working but budget-strapped Joe McDonald from general manager to vice president of baseball operations. The new owners went to the commissioner's office for help as they sought a replacement for McDonald, whose farm system would finally bear fruit at the end of 1980.

Commissioner Bowie Kuhn suggested Frank Cashen would be a great choice as the new GM. Cashen had been the Orioles' executive vice president for 10 years, winning two World Series, four AL pennants, and four AL East titles before stepping down in 1975. A former sportswriter and columnist, Cashen was VP of sales and marketing for Carling National Breweries Inc. between 1975 and 1978 before joining Kuhn in the commissioner's office as administrator of baseball in January 1979.

Fortunately for the Mets, Cashen got the itch to return to a major league front office, but it would be a year before he would make major changes to the ballclub.

Cashen wanted to use 1980 as an evaluation period before making significant changes. The decision included keeping McDonald on staff and retaining manager Joe Torre, who continued to get maximum effort out of minimal talent.

There was absolutely no reason to think the Mets were

going to become contenders overnight. They went 5–11 in spring training and opened the regular season 9–18 while the roster was full of untested rookies and marginal veterans. Elliott Maddox replaced Richie Hebner at third base, and Torre converted center fielder Lee Mazzilli into a first baseman to make room for Joel Youngblood and Jerry Morales in center. Otherwise, the lineup was very similar to the 1979 version that finished 10th in batting and 11th in homers and runs scored.

The pitching was full of question marks. Craig Swan was coming off his first injury-free season in the majors, but Pat Zachry was recovering from elbow surgery and was unable to make his season debut until May 5. Ray Burris led the team with 29 starts and 170⅓ innings, and Pete Falcone served as the No. 4 starter and a long reliever once Zachry returned. Filling out the rotation was Mark Bomback, a Brewers castoff who didn't pitch in the majors in 1979 and had worked just 1⅔ big league innings before 1980.

The staff also included unproven John Pacella, Roy Lee Jackson, Tom Hausman, and Mike Scott. But the team's mound strength was its bullpen as Jeff Reardon and Neil Allen provided a nice one-two punch if the Mets had a lead by the seventh inning. Along with Hausman, the bullpen also featured Dyar Miller and Ed Glynn as middle relievers. Allen, Reardon, Hausman, Miller, and Glynn were responsible for 424 of the team's 1451 innings pitched.

The Mets were 8½ games out of first and nine games under .500 following a 15–4 debacle at Cincinnati May 13. They blew a 6–2 lead in the ninth inning the next day before pulling out an 11-inning victory. That's when the team started to gel and excitement returned to Shea.

Mets fans who actually showed up between 1977 and 1979 were treated to some putrid baseball at times. But there was something a little different about this team, which was beginning to show some determination. The Mets' starting lineup for the May 13 massacre included Doug Flynn (.186), Frank Taveras (.223), Lee Mazzilli (.253, 5 RBIs), and Steve Henderson (0 HR, 7 RBIs). Two months later, Flynn was batting .245, Taveras was at .279, Mazzilli had a .284 average with 36 RBIs, and Henderson boasted a .315 average. The Mets were now in fourth place and within 4½ games of the division lead.

And that's all Mets fans were asking at the time: improvement and competent play. The team went 10–4 immediately after May 13 and enjoyed a 15–7 stretch that put the team at the .500 mark at 42–42 on July 15. They were pulling out games they had no business winning, like the night they trailed 6–2 in the ninth before Steve Henderson crushed a walk-off, three-run homer to beat the Giants 7–6 on June 14. Or the twi-nighter at Philadelphia in which Neil Allen picked up a win and a save in the Mets' first doubleheader sweep at Veterans Stadium in eight years.

Cashen fortified the lineup by acquiring free-agent-to-be Claudell Washington from the White Sox for a minor league pitcher June 7. One week later, Washington crushed three homers in a win at Los Angeles after entering the game with just one home run the entire season.

John Stearns spent much of the year hitting over .300, and Joel Youngblood batted .362 with 23 RBIs in 163 at-bats between June 25 and August 13. The team lacked power, but the players were getting on base and delivering timely hits.

Such a thought might have been delusional, but the Mets were challenging for the NL East title when they opened a five-game series against the Phillies at Shea on August 14. A sweep—ridiculous as it seemed—would put the Mets no worse than third place and 6½ games out of first. Mazzilli, Taveras, Henderson, and Youngblood were hitting .290 or better at that point, and even Doug Flynn was contributing with a .260 mark. But the Mets had started to break down in July. Stearns needed season-ending surgery after breaking his right index finger July 26, and Swan was on the disabled list with a sore shoulder. But their presence probably wouldn't have mattered while the Phillies demolished the Mets in sweeping the series by a combined 40–12. It dropped the Mets 11 games off the pace with 42 games remaining, but a .500 mark didn't seem out of the question.

The Mets continued to lose games and players. Flynn broke his right wrist in a game against the Giants immediately following the Phillies' sweep. The injury cost Flynn the rest of the season and left the Mets without a middle-infielder who would receive his first Gold Glove after the season. Flynn tied a modern major league mark by hitting three triples August 5 against the Expos.

The Mets were 58–64 following a win over the Dodgers August 22, but they would drop 18 of their next 19 to kill any chance of a .500 season. However, the swoon allowed the Mets to take a look at their future as Mookie Wilson, Wally Backman, Hubie Brooks, and Ed Lynch received significant playing time in September. Backman and Brooks hit over .300, and Wilson batted .248 with seven steals. Mets fans were getting a glimpse at a productive farm system that now included Darryl Strawberry, who had been taken with the first pick in the draft three months earlier.

The Mets' summer flirtation with respectability had caused a spike at the gate and helped the team avoid the cellar for the first time since 1976. Team attendance rose by more than 400,000 in the first year under new ownership. The ballclub and the city had begun to replace the original wooden seats at Shea with plastic ones while refurbishing the exterior of the ballpark. The Mets were taking on a new look, and the 1981 roster would feature additional power after the Amazin's hit only 61 homers in 1980.

1980 Mets Statistics

Hitting	G	AB	R	H	2B	3B	HR	RBI	BB	SO	BA	OBP	SLG	SB	CS	GDP	HP	SH	SF	IBB
Bill Almon	48	112	13	19	3	2	0	4	8	27	.170	.225	.232	2	0	0	0	0	0	1
Wally Backman	27	93	12	30	1	1	0	9	11	14	.323	.396	.355	2	3	3	1	4	1	1
Butch Benton	12	21	0	1	0	0	0	0	2	4	.048	.167	.048	0	0	1	1	0	0	0
Hubie Brooks	24	81	8	25	2	1	1	10	5	9	.309	.364	.395	1	1	1	2	1	0	0
Jose Cardenal	26	42	4	7	1	0	0	4	6	4	.167	.265	.190	0	1	3	0	0	1	0
Doug Flynn	128	443	46	113	9	8	0	24	22	20	.255	.288	.312	2	2	15	0	6	3	14
Steve Henderson	143	513	75	149	17	8	8	58	62	90	.290	.368	.402	23	12	17	3	3	3	3
Ron Hodges	36	42	4	10	2	0	0	5	10	13	.238	.377	.286	1	1	1	0	1	1	1
Mike Jorgensen	119	321	43	82	11	0	7	43	46	55	.255	.349	.355	0	3	10	0	1	0	6
Elliott Maddox	130	411	35	101	16	1	4	34	52	44	.246	.336	.319	1	9	9	6	5	4	5
Phil Mankowski	8	12	1	2	1	0	0	1	2	4	.167	.286	.250	0	0	0	0	0	0	0
Lee Mazzilli	152	578	82	162	31	4	16	76	82	92	.280	.370	.431	41	15	8	3	0	5	11
Jerry Morales	94	193	19	49	7	1	3	30	13	31	.254	.293	.347	2	3	2	1	1	8	2
Jose Moreno	37	46	6	9	2	1	2	9	3	12	.196	.240	.413	1	0	1	0	1	1	2
Dan Norman	69	92	5	17	1	1	2	9	6	14	.185	.235	.283	5	0	1	0	0	0	0
Mario Ramirez	18	24	2	5	0	0	0	0	1	7	.208	.240	.208	0	0	1	0	1	0	0
Luis Rosado	2	4	0	0	0	0	0	0	0	1	.000	.000	.000	0	0	1	0	0	0	0
John Stearns	91	319	42	91	25	1	0	45	33	24	.285	.346	.370	7	3	5	1	2	8	1
Frank Taveras	141	562	65	157	27	0	0	25	23	64	.279	.308	.327	32	18	15	1	10	2	0
Alex Trevino	106	355	26	91	11	2	0	37	13	41	.256	.281	.299	0	3	11	1	2	5	1
Claudell Washington	79	284	38	78	16	4	10	42	20	63	.275	.324	.465	17	5	5	1	0	1	5
Mookie Wilson	27	105	16	26	5	3	0	4	12	19	.248	.325	.352	7	7	0	0	2	0	0
Joel Youngblood	146	514	58	142	26	2	8	69	52	69	.276	.340	.381	14	11	10	2	0	9	10
Pitchers																				
Neil Allen	59	14	0	2	0	0	0	0	1	7	.143	.200	.143	0	0	0	0	1	0	0
Mark Bomback	36	43	5	10	3	0	0	5	3	15	.233	.313	.302	0	0	0	2	5	0	0
Ray Burris	29	51	1	5	0	0	0	0	2	18	.098	.132	.098	0	1	0	0	3	0	0
Pete Falcone	37	41	2	6	0	0	0	3	2	12	.146	.186	.146	0	0	0	0	6	0	0
Ed Glynn	38	6	0	0	0	0	0	0	0	2	.000	.000	.000	0	0	0	0	2	0	0
Tom Hausman	55	16	0	1	0	0	0	0	0	7	.063	.063	.063	0	0	1	0	1	0	0
Roy Lee Jackson	26	16	2	3	0	1	0	0	0	4	.188	.188	.313	0	1	0	0	0	0	0
Kevin Kobel	14	2	0	0	0	0	0	0	0	0	.000	.000	.000	0	0	0	0	0	0	0
Ed Lynch	5	6	0	2	0	0	0	0	0	2	.333	.333	.333	0	0	0	0	0	0	0
Dyar Miller	31	1	0	0	0	0	0	0	0	0	.000	.000	.000	0	0	0	0	1	0	0
John Pacella	32	20	0	2	1	0	0	1	0	7	.100	.100	.150	0	0	0	0	2	0	0
Jeff Reardon	61	8	0	0	0	0	0	0	1	6	.000	.111	.000	0	0	0	0	0	0	0
Mike Scott	6	9	0	1	0	0	0	1	2	5	.111	.273	.111	0	0	0	0	0	0	0
Craig Swan	21	32	1	7	0	0	0	5	4	13	.219	.306	.219	0	0	2	0	7	0	0
Pat Zachry	28	46	0	2	0	0	0	1	2	21	.043	.082	.043	0	0	3	0	5	1	0
TOTAL	162	5478	611	1407	218	41	61	554	501	840	.257	.319	.345	158	99	126	25	73	53	63

Pitching	G	ERA	W–L	SV	GS	GF	CG	SHO	IP	H	R	ER	HR	BB	SO	BFP	WP	HBP	BK	IBB
Neil Allen	59	3.70	7–10	22	0	47	0	0	97.1	87	43	40	7	40	79	407	2	0	1	9
Juan Berenguer	6	5.79	0–1	0	0	4	0	0	9.1	9	9	6	1	10	7	46	0	0	0	2
Mark Bomback	36	4.09	10–8	0	25	2	2	1	162.2	191	80	74	17	49	68	710	4	4	0	3
Ray Burris	29	4.02	7–13	0	29	0	1	0	170.1	181	86	76	20	54	83	726	5	4	2	5
Pete Falcone	37	4.52	7–10	1	23	5	1	0	157.1	163	89	79	16	58	109	684	9	2	1	9
Ed Glynn	38	4.13	3–3	1	0	11	0	0	52.1	49	26	24	5	23	32	228	1	0	0	4
Tom Hausman	55	3.98	6–5	1	4	14	0	0	122.0	125	63	54	12	26	53	513	2	3	0	8
Scott Holman	4	1.29	0–0	0	0	1	0	0	7.0	6	2	1	0	1	3	26	1	0	1	1
Roy Lee Jackson	24	4.20	1–7	1	8	4	1	0	70.2	78	37	33	4	20	58	299	4	0	1	4
Kevin Kobel	14	7.03	1–4	0	1	3	0	0	24.1	36	21	19	5	11	8	114	0	0	0	3
Ed Lynch	5	5.12	1–1	0	4	0	0	0	19.1	24	12	11	0	5	9	86	0	1	0	0
Dyar Miller	31	1.93	1–2	1	0	12	0	0	42.0	37	9	9	1	11	28	170	0	0	1	3
John Pacella	32	5.14	3–4	0	15	6	0	0	84.0	89	51	48	5	59	68	388	5	2	3	2
Jeff Reardon	61	2.61	8–7	6	0	35	0	0	110.1	96	36	32	10	47	101	475	2	0	0	15
Mike Scott	6	4.30	1–1	0	6	0	1	1	29.1	40	14	14	1	8	13	132	1	0	0	1
Craig Swan	21	3.58	5–9	0	21	0	4	1	128.1	117	59	51	20	30	79	520	0	0	1	3
Pat Zachry	28	3.01	6–10	0	26	1	7	3	164.2	145	65	55	16	58	88	680	2	5	2	5
TOTAL	162	3.85	67–95	33	162	145	17	9	1451.0	1473	702	621	140	510	886	6204	38	21	13	77

1981

NL EAST						
TEAM	**W**	**L**	**PCT**	**GB**	**AVG**	**ERA**
Cardinals	59	43	.578	—	.265	3.63
Expos**	60	48	.556	2.0	.246	3.30
Phillies*	59	48	.551	2.5	.273	4.05
Pirates	46	56	.451	13.0	.257	3.56
Mets	41	62	.398	18.5	.248	3.55
Cubs	38	65	.369	21.5	.236	4.01

* = Won 1st Half of Split Season, 1.5 games ahead of Cardinals
** = Won 2nd Half of Split Season, .5 games ahead of Cardinals
Cardinals did not make postseason despite owning best record
Mets 1ST half: 17–34, 15 behind Phillies
Mets 2ND half: 24–28, 5.5 behind Expos

Frank Cashen was a widely respected talent evaluator during his successful run with the Orioles and was entering his first full off-season as the Mets' general manager. He knew what he had after assessing the organization over the past 10 months: no power hitting and little pitching depth. He set out to address both issues by reacquiring Dave Kingman and Rusty Staub, and sending John Pacella and Jose Moreno to the Padres for former Cy Young Award winner Randy Jones. Kingman remained an everyday player, but Staub had become a part-timer and Jones was coming off four straight losing seasons since posting back-to-back 20-win campaigns.

Cashen had hoped to re-sign outfielder Claudell Washington, who had provided an offensive spark and a solid glove. But the Braves, looking for instant credibility, overpaid for Washington through free agency. Cashen, sticking to his "Rome wasn't built in a day" formula, continued to make small moves to restructure the roster. Bob Bailor and Mike Cubbage were added to provide bench depth, and Dave Roberts was brought in to lend experience.

However, some of the best changes to the roster were made through the farm system. Rookies Mookie Wilson and Hubie Brooks became everyday players after showing during their September 1980 call-ups that they could thrive at the major league level. Brooks became the team's top hitter among the regulars, becoming only the seventh Met to bat .300 or better in a full season. Wilson got off to a sluggish start, hitting only .203 in his first 29 games. But he was the Mets' top hitter for average from May 25 to August 25, batting .372 with 15 stolen bases in 135 plate appearances.

Brooks and Wilson joined fellow homegrown talent Lee Mazzilli in the starting lineup. Mazzilli played in 95 of the Mets' 105 games, but a nagging back injury caused him to endure a season-long slump in which his batting average never climbed above .237 after Opening Day. Kingman finished tied for third in the National League with 22 home runs, but his .221 average was a drag on the lineup.

The Mets were hitting .264 as a team through their first 41 games. Joel Youngblood was batting .361 in part-time duty, Brooks was at .340 and Kingman—barring a strike—

was on pace for a 40-homer season. Even light-hitting Doug Flynn was hitting .279 as the No. 8 batter in the lineup.

The pitching wasn't bad at that point, either, compiling a 3.65 ERA in that 41-game span despite the loss of Craig Swan, who spent a month on the disabled list with a fractured rib.

The Mets also were playing without rookie Tim Leary, the 1979 first-round pick who was expected to be one of the team's top hurlers after going 15–8 with a 2.76 ERA for Double A in 1980. Leary started the Mets' third game of the season, taking the mound on a raw day at Wrigley Field. He lasted just two innings before leaving the game with a tender elbow. He didn't pitch again for the Mets in 1981, making six starts for Tidewater after coming off the disabled list in August.

Although the Mets had a decent batting average and ERA by the end of May, their record stood at just 14–26 when Cashen decided to make a big move, sending reliever Jeff Reardon to the Expos for Ellis Valentine. It became one of Cashen's worst trades as a Mets executive.

Valentine batted .315 for the 1980 Expos despite getting hit in the face by a pitch in May, leaving him with a fractured cheekbone that caused him to miss 39 games. Valentine batted .331 with 39 RBIs in 47 games after returning from the injury, but he got off to a poor start in '81, hitting .208 at the time of the trade.

Valentine never got back on track and was out of the majors four years later. Reardon became one of the NL's top closers and was a four-time All-Star before retiring in 1994.

The Mets were just 17–34 when the players began their two-month-long strike June 12. Fortunately for them, the Cubs were even worse as the Mets headed into the strike in fifth place.

The Mets got off to a terrific start after the strike, winning six of eight and nine of 15 to put them in a tie for the second-half division lead. The strike actually had given the Mets a shot at an improbable playoff berth. But unlike previous seasons, pennant fever never fully arrived at Shea.

"The caliber of the club we had at the time in '81 was nowhere near the caliber of the clubs we had in '84, '85, '86," recalled Ed Lynch, who pitched very well in the second half. "I think we somewhat believed [we could make the playoffs]. It was post-strike, the fans were thinking, 'Wait, they're going to have a first-half champion and a second-half champion?' The baseball purists hated the whole concept. We were kind of just working our way through it day-by-day, and I was just a young kid happy to be there. I didn't really get caught up in the emotion of what was happening in the standings because I was just trying to survive.

"I don't really remember us coming to the park late in '81 in a pennant-race atmosphere. But I do remember the day that Montreal clinched it in Shea Stadium. Gary Carter was the catcher, and I remember sitting in the dugout watching them jumping up and down. I think Jeff Reardon, my former teammate, was on the mound, and my future teammate was catching, so it was kind of an ironic day."

A four-game winning streak put them within 2 ½ games of first place on September 21, but they played themselves out of the race by winning just three of their next dozen contests.

The Mets' second-half turnaround was accomplished without Swan or Jones in the rotation. Both pitchers were inured while the Mets were playing a two-game exhibition series with the Blue Jays as a tuneup for the second half. The rotation was anchored by the likes of Pat Zachry, Mike Scott, Greg Harris, and Lynch by the end of the season.

The Mets went 24–28 after the strike, but the team's flirtation with a playoff berth couldn't save manager Joe Torre. The Mets announced during their season finale that Torre would not return in 1982.

The team was taking baby steps toward respectability. Brooks and Wilson looked like solid major leaguers, and the Mets hit 57 homers in 105 games after managing just 61 during a full 1980 schedule. Lynch and Scott appeared to be talented enough to become mainstays in the rotation. But, overall, the pitching was no better in 1981 than it was in 1977.

1981 Mets Statistics

Hitting	G	AB	R	H	2B	3B	HR	RBI	BB	SO	BA	OBP	SLG	SB	CS	GDP	HP	SH	SF	IB
Wally Backman	26	36	5	10	2	0	0	0	4	7	.278	.350	.333	1	0	0	0	2	0	0
Bob Bailor	51	81	11	23	3	1	0	8	8	11	.284	.352	.346	2	0	3	1	4	1	0
Hubie Brooks	98	358	34	110	21	2	4	38	23	65	.307	.345	.411	9	5	9	1	1	6	2
Mike Cubbage	67	80	9	17	2	2	1	4	9	15	.213	.289	.325	0	0	2	0	0	1	1
Doug Flynn	105	325	24	72	12	4	1	20	11	19	.222	.247	.292	1	2	12	0	7	0	8
Ron Hodges	35	43	5	13	2	0	1	6	5	8	.302	.375	.419	1	0	0	0	0	0	2
Ron Gardenhire	27	48	2	13	1	0	0	3	5	9	.271	.340	.292	2	2	0	0	0	0	2
Brian Giles	9	7	0	0	0	0	0	0	0	3	.000	.000	.000	0	0	0	0	1	0	0
Mike Howard	14	24	4	4	1	0	0	3	4	6	.167	.276	.208	2	0	0	0	0	1	0
Mike Jorgensen	86	122	8	25	5	2	3	15	12	24	.205	.270	.352	4	0	2	0	2	3	1
Dave Kingman	100	353	40	78	11	3	22	59	55	105	.221	.326	.456	6	0	9	1	1	2	7
Lee Mazzilli	95	324	36	74	14	5	6	34	46	53	.228	.324	.358	17	7	5	2	0	4	3
Rusty Staub	70	161	9	51	9	0	5	21	22	12	.317	.398	.466	1	0	6	1	0	2	3
John Stearns	80	273	25	74	12	1	1	24	24	17	.271	.329	.333	12	2	10	0	7	1	2
Frank Taveras	84	283	30	65	11	3	0	11	12	36	.230	.263	.290	16	4	3	2	5	3	0
Alex Trevino	56	149	17	39	2	0	0	10	13	19	.262	.323	.275	3	0	4	1	1	1	0
Ellis Valentine	48	169	15	35	8	1	5	21	5	38	.207	.227	.355	0	3	2	0	0	2	0
Mookie Wilson	92	328	49	89	8	8	3	14	20	59	.271	.317	.372	24	12	3	2	0	0	3
Joel Youngblood	43	143	16	50	10	2	4	25	12	19	.350	.398	.531	2	5	4	2	0	4	1
Pitchers																				
Neil Allen	43	5	0	1	0	1	0	0	0	4	.200	.200	.600	0	0	0	0	2	0	0
Pete Falcone	35	22	1	4	0	0	1	5	0	4	.182	.182	.318	0	0	1	0	0	0	0
Greg Harris	17	22	1	4	1	0	0	0	0	13	.182	.182	.227	0	0	0	0	0	0	0
Tom Hausman	20	2	0	0	0	0	0	0	1	1	.000	.333	.000	0	0	0	0	0	0	0
Randy Jones	13	17	0	2	0	0	0	0	0	9	.118	.118	.118	0	0	0	0	1	0	0
Terry Leach	21	1	1	0	0	0	0	0	2	0	.000	.667	.000	0	0	0	0	0	0	0
Tim Leary	1	1	0	0	0	0	0	0	0	0	.000	.000	.000	0	0	0	0	0	0	0
Ed Lynch	17	21	0	3	1	0	0	1	4	10	.143	.269	.190	0	0	0	0	2	1	0
Mike Marshall	20	0	0	0	0	0	0	0	1	0	.000	1.000	.000	0	0	0	0	0	0	0
Dyar Miller	23	3	0	1	0	0	0	0	0	0	.333	.333	.333	0	0	0	0	0	0	0
Jesse Orosco	8	2	0	0	0	0	0	0	0	2	.000	.000	.000	0	0	0	0	0	0	0
Charlie Puleo	4	2	0	0	0	0	0	0	0	2	.000	.000	.000	0	0	0	0	0	0	0
Jeff Reardon	18	1	0	0	0	0	0	0	0	0	.000	.000	.000	0	0	0	0	0	0	0
Dave Roberts	7	4	1	1	0	0	0	0	0	2	.250	.250	.250	0	0	0	0	0	0	0
Mike Scott	23	41	4	3	0	0	0	1	3	18	.073	.133	.073	0	0	2	0	1	1	0
Ray Searage	26	1	0	1	0	0	0	0	0	0	1.000	1.000	1.000	0	0	0	0	0	0	0
Craig Swan	5	3	0	0	0	0	0	0	0	1	.000	.000	.000	0	0	0	0	0	0	0
Pat Zachry	24	38	1	6	0	0	0	2	3	12	.158	.214	.158	0	0	1	0	4	1	0
TOTAL	105	3493	348	868	136	35	57	325	304	603	.248	.309	.356	103	42	78	13	41	34	35

Pitching	G	ERA	W:–L	SV	GS	GF	CG	SHO	IP	H	R	ER	HR	BB	SO	BFP	WP	HBP	BK	IBB
Neil Allen	43	2.97	7–6	18	0	35	0	0	66.2	64	26	22	4	26	50	286	3	0	0	8
Dan Boitano	15	5.51	2–1	0	0	4	0	0	16.1	21	10	10	2	5	8	76	0	2	0	0
Pete Falcone	35	2.55	5–3	1	9	5	3	1	95.1	84	32	27	3	36	56	397	2	0	1	4
Greg Harris	16	4.46	3–5	1	14	2	0	0	68.2	65	36	34	8	28	54	300	3	2	2	2
Tom Hausman	20	2.18	0–1	0	0	5	0	0	33.0	28	8	8	2	7	13	130	2	0	1	1
Randy Jones	13	4.85	1–8	0	12	0	0	0	59.1	65	48	32	8	38	14	284	2	1	0	1
Terry Leach	21	2.55	1–1	0	1	3	0	0	35.1	26	11	10	2	12	16	139	0	0	0	1
Tim Leary	1	0.00	0–0	0	1	0	0	0	2.0	0	0	0	0	1	3	7	1	0	0	0
Ed Lynch	17	2.91	4–5	0	13	0	0	0	80.1	79	32	26	6	21	27	336	3	1	1	2
Mike Marshall	20	2.61	3–2	0	0	9	0	0	31.0	26	10	9	2	8	8	127	2	0	0	1
Dyar Miller	23	3.29	1–0	0	0	8	0	0	38.1	49	20	14	2	15	22	174	2	1	1	2
Jesse Orosco	8	1.56	0–1	1	0	4	0	0	17.1	13	4	3	2	6	18	69	0	0	1	2
Charlie Puleo	4	0.00	0–0	0	1	2	0	0	13.1	8	1	0	0	8	8	53	1	0	0	2
Jeff Reardon	18	3.45	1–0	2	0	14	0	0	28.2	27	11	11	2	12	28	124	0	1	0	4
Dave Roberts	7	9.39	0–3	0	4	0	0	0	15.1	26	18	16	5	5	10	76	0	0	0	0
Mike Scott	23	3.90	5–10	0	23	0	1	0	136.0	130	65	59	11	34	54	551	1	1	2	1

Pitching	G	ERA	W: L	SV	GS	GF	CG	SHO	IP	H	R	ER	HR	BB	SO	BFP	WP	HBP	BK	IBB
Ray Searage	26	3.68	1–0	1	0	7	0	0	36.2	34	16	15	2	17	16	156	3	0	0	3
Craig Swan	5	3.29	0–2	0	3	0	0	0	13.2	10	6	5	0	1	9	50	0	0	0	0
Pat Zachry	24	4.14	7–14	0	24	0	3	0	139.0	151	78	64	13	56	76	616	1	4	1	1
TOTAL	105	3.55	41–62	24	105	98	7	3	926.0	906	432	365	74	336	490	3951	26	13	10	35

1982

NL EAST

TEAM	W	L	PCT	GB	AVG	ERA
Cardinals	92	70	.568	—	.264	3.37
Phillies	89	73	.549	3.0	.260	3.61
Expos	86	76	.531	6.0	.262	3.31
Pirates	84	78	.519	8.0	.273	3.81
Cubs	73	89	.451	19.0	.260	3.92
Mets	65	97	.401	27.0	.247	3.88

The Mets made several significant moves as they headed into year three of general manager Frank Cashen's five-year plan. Joe Torre was replaced as manager by George Bamberger in the hope he could turn a staff full of prospects, suspects, and rejects into serviceable major league pitchers. Bamberger had a tremendous reputation as a pitching coach with the Orioles, and he certainly appeared to be a good motivator while managing the Brewers. Like Cashen, Bamberger was thinking about taking baby steps while the team tried to emerge from its five-season funk. He told his ballclub at spring training he thought the Mets could finish .500, a goal that seemed optimistic by the media and insulting by several players. Judging by the spring training roster, 81–81 would have been a miracle.

Cashen's second big move of the off-season was landing outfielder and former two-time MVP George Foster from the Reds just prior to spring training. Foster had belted 52 homers for the 1977 Reds, but his power numbers steadily fell to 22 by 1981. But the acquisition of Foster gave the appearance that Cashen was ready to take a serious charge at respectability.

The final major change was the biggest, but it wouldn't make a real difference until the end of 1983. The Mets shipped popular outfielder and first baseman Lee Mazzilli to the Rangers for a couple of pitching prospects, Walt Terrell and Ron Darling. Mazzilli split the '82 season with the Rangers and Yankees while Terrell and Darling spent the bulk of the year in the minors.

New faces on the Mets included pitchers Brent Gaff, Tom Gorman, Charlie Puleo, Rick Ownbey, and Scott Holman. Ownbey and Holman were considered the Mets' top pitching prospects, although a 17-year-old fireballer named Dwight Gooden would be drafted in June.

Jesse Orosco was given a full season to show his stuff, giving the Mets a huge boost to a bullpen that included Gaff, Gorman, Carlos Diaz, and Terry Leach by the end of the year. Neil Allen was back for his fourth season as the team's closer.

But the rotation lacked a top-of-the-line pitcher, and the everyday lineup was only slightly better than it was in 1981. Foster was the only impact player added to the batting order, joining Dave Kingman, Hubie Brooks, John Stearns, and Mookie Wilson. Ron Gardenhire was the closest thing the Mets had to a regular shortstop, and second base was patrolled by Bob Bailor, Brian Giles, and Wally Backman, depending on which one was Bamberger's Flavor of the Week.

Things seemed to click during the first 64 games of the season. Kingman was on his way to a second NL home run crown despite his alarming number of strikeouts. Wilson (.293), Stearns (.316), Bailor (.304), and Brooks (.269) were getting on base and driving in runs to help the Mets open the year a surprising 34–30, their best 64-game start in 10 years. They were winning despite a pitching staff that had a 3.71 ERA and just 296 strikeouts in its first 580⅓ innings. Charlie Puleo was the Mets' winningest starter at that point in the season. Craig Swan was making a strong comeback following an injury-plagued season. Randy Jones got off to a nice start, opening 4–1 with a 2.60 ERA before fading. Pat Zachry also started 4–1 but kept his ERA near 5.00 before landing in the bullpen.

But the final 98 games were a replay of the previous five seasons as the Mets failed to display consistency in any facet of the game. Great pitching performances were wasted by muted bats or leaky gloves. When the Mets scored runs, it was time for the pitchers to blow up, making for a very long final three months of the season. The Mets followed their 34–30 start by dropping 16 of their next 20 to end any talk of a possible playoff berth. And that wasn't the team's worst part of the season.

The Mets were 50–65 after beating the Cubs in the first game of a doubleheader August 15. They didn't win again the rest of the month, dropping 15 straight to come within two of the club record for consecutive losses. It didn't help that Allen missed most of the final two months due to a sore elbow, leaving the closer's role to Mike Scott and Jesse Orosco.

Orosco proved he belonged in the majors, but Scott had another adventurous year before the Mets finally shipped him to the Astros for Danny Heep after the season.

Kingman banged out 37 homers but batted just .204 while striking out a career-high 156 times. The Mets also didn't get much bang for their buck from Foster or Ellis Valentine, who were supposed to provide some power while anchoring the corner outfield positions. Foster experienced his worst major league season since 1971, hitting only 13 homers and batting just .247. Valentine's average climbed from .207 to .288, but he hit only eight homers and drove in a measly 38 runs.

The Mets returned to the cellar following a two-year absence, and Bamberger failed to be the miracle worker the team needed. But at least the farm system appeared to have a few legitimate pitching prospects

One of the young pitching talents was Ed Lynch, who went just 4–8 but compiled a 3.55 ERA in 139⅓ innings. Terrell didn't look bad in his three-start trial with the Mets, going 0–3 but doing it with a 3.43 ERA. Darling pitched well for Triple A Tidewater, and Gooden averaged a strikeout per inning while going 6–6 with a 2.47 ERA in rookie ball.

And, oh, 1980 first-round pick Darryl Strawberry wore out Texas League pitching, hitting .283 with 34 homers, 97 RBIs, and 45 stolen bases. The Mets finally had a productive farm system, but the talent remained thin at the Triple A level, giving New York little chance to make any progress in 1982.

1982 Mets Statistics

Hitting	G	AB	R	H	2B	3B	HR	RBI	BB	SO	BA	OBP	SLG	SB	CS	GDP	HP	SH	SF	IBB
Wally Backman	96	261	37	71	13	2	3	22	49	47	.272	.387	.372	8	7	6	0	2	0	1
Bob Bailor	110	376	44	104	14	1	0	31	20	17	.277	.313	.319	20	3	5	2	2	4	0
Bruce Bochy	17	49	4	15	4	0	2	8	4	6	.306	.358	.510	0	0	1	0	0	0	0
Hubie Brooks	126	457	40	114	21	2	2	40	28	76	.249	.297	.317	6	3	11	5	3	5	5
George Foster	151	550	64	136	23	2	13	70	50	123	.247	.309	.367	1	1	13	2	0	6	9
Ron Gardenhire	141	384	29	92	17	1	3	33	23	55	.240	.279	.313	5	6	11	0	12	5	2
Brian Giles	45	138	14	29	5	0	3	10	12	29	.210	.270	.312	6	1	0	0	0	2	1
Ron Hodges	80	228	26	56	12	1	5	27	41	40	.246	.358	.373	4	3	5	0	5	2	6
Mike Howard	33	39	5	7	0	0	1	3	6	7	.179	.298	.256	2	0	0	1	1	1	0
Mike Jorgensen	120	114	16	29	6	0	2	14	21	24	.254	.370	.360	2	0	2	0	1	0	3
Dave Kingman	149	535	80	109	9	1	37	99	59	156	.204	.285	.432	4	0	11	4	3	6	9
Phil Mankowski	13	35	2	8	1	0	0	4	1	6	.229	.237	.257	0	1	2	0	0	2	0
Gary Rajsich	80	162	17	42	8	3	2	12	17	40	.259	.333	.383	1	3	2	1	2	0	3
Ronn Reynolds	2	4	0	0	0	0	0	0	1	1	.000	.200	.000	0	0	0	0	0	0	0
Rusty Staub	112	219	11	53	9	0	3	27	24	10	.242	.309	.324	0	0	10	0	1	6	1
John Stearns	98	352	46	103	25	3	4	28	30	35	.293	.349	.415	17	7	8	2	5	3	2
Rick Sweet	3	3	0	1	0	0	0	0	0	1	.333	.333	.333	0	0	0	0	0	0	0
Rusty Tillman	12	13	4	2	1	0	0	0	0	4	.154	.154	.231	1	0	0	0	0	0	0
Ellis Valentine	111	337	33	97	14	1	8	48	5	38	.288	.294	.407	1	3	11	1	0	7	0
Tom Veryzer	40	54	6	18	2	0	0	4	3	4	.333	.362	.370	1	0	1	0	0	1	2
Mookie Wilson	159	639	90	178	25	9	5	55	32	102	.279	.314	.369	58	16	5	2	1	3	4
Joel Youngblood	80	202	21	52	12	0	3	21	8	37	.257	.302	.361	0	4	4	5	1	0	1
Pitchers																				
Neil Allen	50	6	1	1	0	0	0	0	2	2	.167	.375	.167	0	0	0	0	1	0	0
Pete Falcone	40	53	0	6	1	0	0	3	0	24	.113	.113	.132	0	0	1	0	2	0	0
Brent Gaff	7	8	0	0	0	0	0	0	2	3	.000	.200	.000	0	0	0	0	1	0	0
Tom Gorman	3	1	0	0	0	0	0	0	0	0	.000	.000	.000	0	0	0	0	1	0	0
Tom Hausman	21	2	0	0	0	0	0	0	0	1	.000	.000	.000	0	0	0	0	0	0	0
Scott Holman	4	9	1	2	0	0	0	1	0	3	.222	.222	.222	0	0	1	0	1	0	0
Randy Jones	28	27	1	4	0	0	0	0	3	10	.148	.233	.148	0	0	0	0	2	0	0
Terry Leach	21	8	0	1	0	0	0	0	0	5	.125	.125	.125	0	0	0	0	1	0	0
Ed Lynch	43	33	2	0	0	0	0	0	1	18	.000	.029	.000	0	0	0	0	3	0	0
Jesse Orosco	54	14	0	2	0	0	0	0	0	4	.143	.143	.143	0	0	1	0	0	0	0
Rick Ownbey	9	15	3	3	0	0	0	1	2	4	.200	.294	.200	0	0	0	0	1	0	0
Charlie Puleo	36	48	3	6	0	0	0	0	2	18	.125	.160	.125	0	0	0	0	6	0	0
Mike Scott	37	48	2	7	4	0	0	3	2	21	.146	.180	.229	0	0	0	0	0	0	0
Craig Swan	37	44	4	8	1	0	1	4	7	15	.182	.294	.273	0	0	1	0	3	0	0
Walt Terrell	3	5	0	2	0	0	0	0	0	2	.400	.400	.400	0	0	0	0	1	0	0
Pat Zachry	36	38	3	3	0	0	0	0	1	17	.079	.103	.079	0	0	0	0	2	0	0
TOTAL	162	5510	609	1361	227	26	97	568	456	1005	.247	.305	.350	137	58	112	25	64	53	49

Pitching	G	ERA	W–L	SV	GS	GF	CG	SHO	IP	H	R	ER	HR	BB	SO	BFP	WP	HBP	BK	IBB
Neil Allen	50	3.06	3–7	19	0	42	0	0	64.2	65	22	22	5	30	59	279	4	1	0	5
Carlos Diaz	4	0.00	0–0	0	0	3	0	0	3.1	6	2	0	0	4	0	21	0	0	0	1
Pete Falcone	40	3.84	8–10	2	23	6	3	0	171.0	159	82	73	24	71	101	718	10	1	0	4
Brent Gaff	7	4.55	0–3	0	5	1	0	0	31.2	41	22	16	3	10	14	142	2	1	0	0
Tom Hausman	21	4.42	1–2	0	0	12	0	0	36.2	44	26	18	4	6	16	162	1	2	0	1
Scott Holman	4	2.36	2–1	0	4	0	1	0	26.2	23	10	7	2	7	11	107	0	0	0	0
Tom Gorman	3	0.96	0–1	0	1	0	0	0	9.1	8	1	1	0	0	7	36	0	0	0	0
Randy Jones	28	4.60	7–10	0	20	4	2	1	107.2	130	68	55	11	51	44	493	1	4	0	3
Terry Leach	21	4.17	2–1	3	1	12	1	1	45.1	46	22	21	2	18	30	194	0	0	0	5
Ed Lynch	43	3.55	4–8	2	12	11	0	0	139.1	145	57	55	6	40	51	585	2	1	3	4
Jesse Orosco	54	2.72	4–10	4	2	22	0	0	109.1	92	37	33	7	40	89	451	3	2	2	2
Rick Ownbey	8	3.75	1–2	0	8	0	2	0	50.1	44	23	21	3	43	28	232	0	3	0	1
Charlie Puleo	36	4.47	9–9	1	24	8	1	1	171.0	179	99	85	13	90	98	759	3	2	2	7
Mike Scott	37	5.14	7–13	3	22	10	1	0	147.0	185	100	84	13	60	63	670	1	2	2	3
Doug Sisk	8	1.04	0–1	1	0	4	0	0	8.2	5	1	1	1	4	4	34	0	1	0	2
Craig Swan	37	3.35	11–7	1	21	6	2	0	166.1	165	70	62	13	37	67	691	0	0	0	4
Walt Terrell	3	3.43	0–3	0	3	0	0	0	21.0	22	12	8	2	14	8	97	1	0	1	2
Pat Zachry	36	4.05	6–9	1	16	6	2	0	137.2	149	69	62	10	57	69	600	4	0	0	5
TOTAL	162	3.88	65–97	37	162	147	15	5	1447.0	1508	723	624	119	582	759	6271	32	17	13	49

1983

NL EAST						
Team	W	L	PCT	GB	BA	ERA
Phillies	90	72	.556	—	.249	3.34
Pirates	84	78	.519	6.0	.264	3.55
Expos	82	80	.506	8.0	.264	3.58
Cardinals	79	83	.488	11.0	.270	3.79
Cubs	71	91	.438	19.0	.261	4.08
Mets	68	94	.420	22.0	.241	3.68

The Mets were finally about to turn the corner, but it would be a few weeks into the season before there was any noticeable improvement. Cashen had dipped into the team's past to improve the present, reacquiring Tom Seaver from the Reds for Charlie Puleo, Lloyd McClendon and Jason Felice. The Mets' GM also picked up Mike Torrez from the Boston Red Sox in another effort to give manager George Bamberger some much-needed pitching.

The pitching staff was very thin in 1982, and the prospects either weren't ready for the majors or were running out of time to prove they belonged. Adding Seaver and Torrez was a no-brainer if just for PR value after the team finished ninth in the NL in attendance with just over 1.3 million people in 1982.

It would be easy to dismiss the pitching staff as another collection of worn-out veterans and can't-do rookies. The team's ERA leader (Seaver) was 38 years old, and the wins leader was a relief pitcher (Jesse Orosco with 13). Torrez and Ed Lynch led the starting staff with 10 wins apiece, but Torrez also lost a team-high 17 games, and Lynch surrendered 208 hits in 174⅔ innings.

Craig Swan's effectiveness completely evaporated as he went 2–8 with a 5.51 ERA after topping the 1982 staff with 11 wins and a 3.55 ERA. But the real mystery was Neil Allen, who collected 19 saves in '82 before missing most of the final two months with a shoulder injury. Allen was 0–4 with two saves, one blown save and a 5.68 in his first 11 appearances of '83, prompting Bamberger to move him into the rotation in an effort to get Allen on track. Hey, it worked for Tug McGraw in 1973.

Seaver got off to a nice start and was 4–5 with a 2.54 ERA in his first 13 starts. But outside of Lynch, none of the Mets' "homegrown" talent was showing any ability to work deep into starts. The dearth of pitching was a contributing factor to Bamberger's decision to resign three times before Cashen finally allowed him to leave.

The bullpen would become a strong suit despite Allen's struggles. Orosco took over for Allen as the closer and became an immediate fan favorite. He won eight straight decisions while compiling six of his 17 saves between July 22 and September 5, when the Mets started to get solid contributions from their farm system. Orosco was selected to the All-Star Game before ending the season 13–7 with a 1.47 ERA. He also was the NL Pitcher of the Month for August.

Orosco also had help in the pen as rookies Doug Sisk and Carlos Diaz formed a successful setup tandem. Sisk was second on the team with 11 saves, and Diaz owned the second-lowest ERA among Mets relievers at 2.05.

The big question for the Mets at midseason was what to do with Allen. The former closer tossed a six-hit shutout against the Dodgers on May 20 before surrendering nine earned runs over 8⅔ innings in his next two starts. Allen also landed on the back page of the New York tabloids by going AWOL for about 48 hours. He blamed his disappearance on alcoholism and was welcomed back by his teammates, but his days as a Met were numbered.

Allen indirectly helped the Mets become contenders again. Cardinals manager Whitey Herzog was at odds with Keith Hernandez and was looking to ship him out of St. Louis before the June 15 trade deadline. Cashen made a call and asked what it would take to land the Gold Glove first baseman and former National League co-MVP, who had just helped the Redbirds win the World Series. You can picture Cashen coming close to swallowing his bow-tie when Herzog asked for Allen and pitching prospect Rick Ownbey. Cashen couldn't make the deal fast enough, and Hernandez found himself going from first to worst in a deal he originally hated.

Hernandez even considered retiring rather than accept a trade to the sad-sack Mets. However, he was in the walk year of his contract and could punch his own ticket after the season. Hernandez stuck it out and would become impressed by the Mets' young talent.

Hernandez supplanted Dave Kingman at first base and joined a lineup that now included George Foster, Hubie Brooks, Mookie Wilson, and a rookie named Darryl Strawberry. Kingman had hit 12 homers in 53 games at the time of the Hernandez trade, but he had driven in just 23 and was batting just .204 while continuing to display the same shaky fielding that aggravated Mets fans.

The Mets' faithful also had been waiting for Strawberry's arrival since the day he was taken first overall in the 1980 draft. He made his major league debut May 6 against the Reds, going 0-for-4 but walking twice and scoring on Foster's game-winning three-run homer in the 13th inning. Strawberry went hitless in his first 11 at-bats before delivering an RBI single in his third game on May 8 versus the Reds. He played his first seven games without a homer before belting three in a four-game span. But it would take another 24 games before he finally hit his fourth of the season.

Strawberry was batting .186 with three homers and 12 RBIs prior to Hernandez's arrival. Interim manager Frank Howard had tried numerous lineup combinations before Hernandez settled the batting order. Strawberry was one of the beneficiaries, batting .285 with 23 homers and 62 RBIs in his final 91 games while usually hitting behind

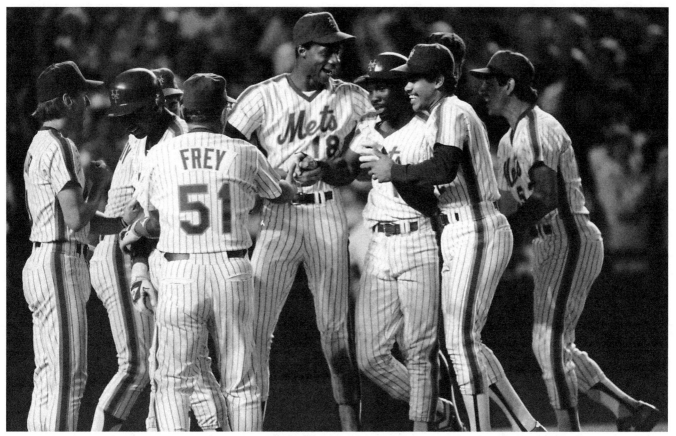

Mookie Wilson (center) is welcomed home by teammates at the plate in Shea Stadium, July 26, 1983, after Wilson hit a home run in the 10th inning to beat the Atlanta Braves 2–1.

Foster in the order. Strawberry's success in turn helped Foster see better pitches. Foster had just three homers and seven RBIs in 21 games when Strawberry was promoted to the majors. The former Red contributed 25 homers and 83 RBIs from the cleanup spot the rest of the year.

Wilson and Brooks usually formed the top of the lineup. Wilson set a team record with 54 stolen bases while hitting .276, but his .300 on-base percentage and 103 strikeouts didn't make him a quintessential leadoff hitter. Brooks spent his second consecutive season batting around the .250 mark after posting a .307 average in 1981.

There remained question marks behind the plate and through the middle of the infield. Veteran Ron Hodges did the bulk of the catching after spending most of his previous 10 major league seasons as the Mets' No. 3 backstop. Brian Giles started 120 games at second base, but his limited range and .245 average would soon make him a former Met. New York also had slick-fielding Jose Oquendo at shortstop, but that was before Oquendo learned how to hit major league pitching. His .213 batting average was the second-worst among National League hitters with at least 300 at-bats, and his .244 slugging percentage was dead last.

With the top six in the batting order firmly established, it was time for Cashen to call up his pitching prospects. Cashen had picked up right-handers Ron Darling and Walt

Terrell from Texas for Lee Mazzilli before the 1982 season, a deal that was extremely unpopular at the time. Terrell was the first to make an impact on the Mets, going 8–8 with a 3.57 ERA in 20 starts. His most memorable start of the season occurred on August 6 at Wrigley Field, when he belted a pair of two-run homers off Ferguson Jenkins while holding the Cubs to a run and seven hits in 7⅓ innings.

Darling was called up once the rosters expanded in September. He debuted on September 6 against the Phillies at Shea Stadium, giving up just one run and five hits in 6⅓ innings. His lone blemish came in the fourth inning, when he was called for two balks with Mike Schmidt at the plate, allowing Joe Morgan to score from second.

Darling ended the year 1–3 with a 2.80 ERA in five starts, lending hope that the Mets had solved their rotation problems.

The improvements were clearly evident by the end of the year, but so were the shortcomings. The Mets were outscored by 105 runs as they went 68–94 to finish last for the fifth time in seven years. The team was in need of a more productive middle-infield, and another stud pitcher wouldn't hurt. Fortunately, they had Dwight Gooden and Wally Backman waiting in the wings. They also had the reigning NL Rookie of the Year as Strawberry became the third Met to win the honor.

1983 Mets Statistics

Hitting	G	AB	R	H	2B	3B	HR	RBI	BB	SO	BA	OBP	SLG	SB	CS	GDP	HP	SH	SF	IBB
Tucker Ashford	35	56	3	10	0	1	0	2	7	4	.179	.270	.214	0	0	1	0	0	0	1
Wally Backman	26	42	6	7	0	1	0	3	2	8	.167	.205	.214	0	0	2	0	1	0	0
Bob Bailor	118	340	33	85	8	0	1	30	20	23	.250	.290	.282	18	3	11	1	3	4	2
Mike Bishop	3	8	2	1	1	0	0	0	3	4	.125	.364	.250	0	0	0	0	0	0	0
Mark Bradley	73	104	10	21	4	0	3	5	11	35	.202	.278	.327	4	2	2	0	0	0	1
Hubie Brooks	150	586	53	147	18	4	5	58	24	96	.251	.284	.321	6	4	14	4	7	3	2
Mike Fitzgerald	8	20	1	2	0	0	1	2	3	6	.100	.217	.250	0	0	0	0	0	0	1
George Foster	157	601	74	145	19	2	28	90	38	111	.241	.289	.419	1	1	19	4	0	4	5
Ron Gardenhire	17	32	1	2	0	0	0	1	1	4	.063	.091	.063	0	0	1	0	0	0	0
Brian Giles	145	400	39	98	15	0	2	27	36	77	.245	.308	.298	17	10	8	2	4	3	1
Danny Heep	115	253	30	64	12	0	8	21	29	40	.253	.326	.395	3	3	5	1	1	5	6
Keith Hernandez	95	320	43	98	8	3	9	37	64	42	.306	.424	.434	8	4	5	2	2	1	9
Ron Hodges	110	250	20	65	12	0	0	21	49	42	.260	.383	.308	0	3	8	2	2	2	6
Mike Howard	1	3	0	1	0	0	0	1	0	1	.333	.333	.333	0	0	0	0	0	0	0
Clint Hurdle	13	33	3	6	2	0	0	2	2	10	.182	.229	.242	0	0	1	0	0	0	0
Mike Jorgensen	38	24	5	6	3	0	1	3	2	4	.250	.333	.500	0	1	1	1	0	0	0
Dave Kingman	100	248	25	49	7	0	13	29	22	57	.198	.265	.383	2	1	2	1	1	1	1
Jose Oquendo	120	328	29	70	7	0	1	17	19	60	.213	.260	.244	8	9	10	2	3	1	2
Junior Ortiz	68	185	10	47	5	0	0	12	3	34	.254	.270	.281	1	0	1	1	1	0	0
Gary Rajsich	11	36	5	12	3	0	1	3	3	1	.333	.400	.500	0	0	1	1	0	0	1
Ronn Reynolds	24	66	4	13	1	0	0	2	8	12	.197	.280	.212	0	0	2	0	0	1	1
Rusty Staub	104	115	5	34	6	0	3	28	14	10	.296	.371	.426	0	0	4	1	0	2	3
John Stearns	4	0	2	0	0	0	0	0	0	0	.000	.000	.000	0	0	0	0	0	0	0
Darryl Strawberry	122	420	63	108	15	7	26	74	47	128	.257	.336	.512	19	6	5	4	0	2	9
Mookie Wilson	152	638	91	176	25	6	7	51	18	103	.276	.300	.367	54	16	6	4	2	1	3
Pitchers																				
Neil Allen	21	10	0	0	0	0	0	0	0	3	.000	.000	.000	0	0	0	0	1	0	0
Ron Darling	5	10	0	1	0	0	0	0	0	3	.100	.100	.100	0	0	0	0	1	0	0
Carlos Diaz	54	5	1	0	0	0	0	0	1	2	.000	.167	.000	0	0	0	0	1	0	0
Brent Gaff	4	3	0	0	0	0	0	0	0	1	.000	.000	.000	0	0	0	0	0	0	0
Tom Gorman	25	4	0	1	0	0	0	0	0	2	.250	.250	.250	0	1	0	0	1	0	0
Scott Holman	35	23	1	5	0	0	0	2	0	9	.217	.217	.217	0	0	0	0	2	0	0
Tim Leary	2	3	0	1	0	0	0	0	0	1	.333	.333	.333	0	0	0	0	0	0	0
Ed Lynch	30	52	3	8	0	0	0	4	1	17	.154	.170	.154	0	0	0	0	11	0	0
Jesse Orosco	62	12	0	4	0	0	0	2	1	3	.333	.357	.333	0	0	0	0	2	1	0
Rick Ownbey	12	9	2	1	0	0	0	0	0	2	.111	.111	.111	0	0	0	0	1	0	0
Tom Seaver	34	64	6	10	0	2	0	4	6	26	.156	.225	.219	0	0	2	0	6	1	0
Doug Sisk	67	6	0	3	0	0	0	0	0	2	.500	.500	.500	0	0	0	0	1	0	0
Craig Swan	27	26	0	2	0	0	0	1	0	11	.077	.077	.077	0	0	0	0	1	0	0
Walt Terrell	21	44	3	8	1	0	3	8	1	17	.182	.200	.409	0	0	1	0	3	0	0
Mike Torrez	39	65	2	3	0	0	0	2	1	20	.046	.061	.046	0	0	1	0	8	0	0
TOTAL	162	5444	575	1314	172	26	112	542	436	1031	.241	.298	.344	141	64	113	31	66	32	54

Pitching	G	ERA	W–L	SV	GS	GF	CG	SHO	IP	H	R	ER	HR	BB	SO	BF	WP	HP	BK	IBB
Neil Allen	21	4.50	2–7	2	4	9	1	1	54.0	57	29	27	6	36	32	246	2	0	0	5
Ron Darling	5	2.80	1–3	0	5	0	1	0	35.1	31	11	11	0	17	23	148	3	3	2	1
Carlos Diaz	54	2.05	3–1	2	0	20	0	0	83.1	62	22	19	1	35	64	339	2	1	0	13
Brent Gaff	4	6.10	1–0	0	0	2	0	0	10.1	18	9	7	0	1	4	53	1	0	0	1
Tom Gorman	25	4.93	1–4	0	4	9	0	0	49.1	45	29	27	3	15	30	204	2	0	1	4
Scott Holman	35	3.74	1–7	0	10	10	0	0	101.0	90	48	42	7	52	44	439	3	1	1	8
Tim Leary	2	3.38	1–1	0	2	0	1	0	10.2	15	10	4	0	4	9	53	0	0	1	0
Ed Lynch	30	4.28	10–10	0	27	1	1	0	174.2	208	94	83	17	41	44	749	3	3	2	10
Jesse Orosco	62	1.47	13–7	17	0	42	0	0	110.0	76	27	18	3	38	84	432	1	1	2	7
Rick Ownbey	10	4.67	1–3	0	4	3	0	0	34.2	31	19	18	4	21	19	152	1	1	2	0
Tom Seaver	34	3.55	9–14	0	34	0	5	2	231.0	201	104	91	18	86	135	962	10	4	0	5
Doug Sisk	67	2.24	5–4	11	0	39	0	0	104.1	88	38	26	1	59	33	447	5	4	1	7
Craig Swan	27	5.51	2–8	1	18	4	0	0	96.1	112	63	59	14	42	43	424	1	0	1	3
Walt Terrell	21	3.57	8–8	0	20	1	4	2	133.2	123	57	53	7	55	59	561	5	2	0	7
Mike Torrez	39	4.37	10–17	0	34	4	5	0	222.1	227	120	108	16	113	94	972	7	1	1	11
TOTAL	162	3.68	68–94	33	162	144	18	7	1451.0	1384	680	593	97	615	717	6181	46	21	14	82

1984

NL EAST

Team	W	L	PCT	GB	BA	ERA
Cubs	96	65	.596	—	.260	3.75
Mets	90	72	.556	6.5	.257	3.60
Cardinals	84	78	.519	12.5	.252	3.58
Phillies	81	81	.500	15.5	.266	3.62
Expos	78	83	.484	18.0	.251	3.31
Pirates	75	87	.463	21.5	.255	3.11

The Mets had shown some promise by the end of the 1983 season. Darryl Strawberry captured the NL Rookie of the Year award by hitting .257 with 26 homers and 74 RBIs. Keith Hernandez decided to stay in New York after hitting .306 for the Mets following his trade from St. Louis. George Foster bounced back in '83, belting 28 homers after managing just 13 in his first year as a Met. Ron Darling and Walt Terrell appeared more than ready to become contributing members of the Mets' rotation. And Jesse Orosco had emerged into one of the National League's top closers in the second half of '83.

But the Mets made a huge blunder before spring training even started. General manager Frank Cashen exposed Tom Seaver in the free agent compensation draft, expecting no team to pick up the 38-year-old's hefty contract. Cashen miscalculated as the White Sox snatched up the Franchise, sending Seaver away just a year after his return.

But losing Seaver actually might have been a plus for the '84 Mets as it created a huge hole in the rotation. Having failed to come up with a veteran hurler to replace Seaver, the Mets had to rely on their farm system to fill the void.

Enter Dwight Eugene Gooden, a 19-year-old flame-throwing Floridian with a wicked curve and poise to match. He blew away the Carolina League in 1983, striking out 300 in 191 innings while going 19–4 with a 2.50 ERA. Gooden also impressed Tidewater manager Davey Johnson by making two outstanding starts during the 1983 Triple A World Series.

As the team's new manager, Johnson was ready to bring Gooden north with him once the Mets broke camp in St. Petersburg. Cashen wasn't so sure, and Tim Leary was a big reason for his apprehension.

Leary had been a top-five draft pick before making a quick assent to the majors. But he injured his shoulder while pitching just two innings in major league debut at a very chilly Wrigley Field in Game 3 of the 1981 season. Leary pitched a grand total of 12⅔ innings for the Mets from 1981 through 1983. Cashen wasn't about to let anything happen to Gooden, his newest phenom.

Johnson was adamant that Gooden was ready for the majors, but it took most of spring training before he convinced Cashen. The GM finally relented, and the magic returned to Shea Stadium in 1984 as a great mix of young and veteran talent put the Mets back in serious playoff contention for the first time in a decade.

"I think the acquisition of Keith Hernandez really put it together," said Ed Lynch. "Darryl Strawberry was coming into his own. Some of the young guys that I came up with were starting to come into their own: Mookie, myself and Hubie Brooks, Wally Backman, Mike Fitzgerald. There was a good group of young players, and we had a veteran mix of veteran players: Rusty Staub, Keith Hernandez, people like that."

Despite Gooden, it took a while for Johnson and Cashen to mold a deep pitching staff. Mike Torrez opened the season as the No. 1 starter despite his 10–17 record in 1983. Craig Swan was in the bullpen, joined by newcomer/old-timer Dick Tidrow in a corps that included Orosco and Doug Sisk. Swan and Tidrow were released in May, and Torrez lasted another month before he was let go.

Johnson now had a much younger pitching staff that would take its lumps at times. The Mets surrendered an average of 9.17 runs in their first 12 losses as Torrez, Gooden, Darling, Terrell, and Leary were all pounded occasionally. But when the starting pitching was good, the Mets generally had enough offense to earn a victory. The combination had players thinking they could make a run at the division.

"I remember Opening Day we went into Cincinnati," recalled Lynch. "Mike Torrez was pitching, and I was the long reliever. I remember he got hit around pretty good, and I was on the mound around the sixth inning, trailing 8–0. Someone hit a popup directly over the mound, and Hubie Brooks ran over, Keith Hernandez ran over, I stood there, and the ball landed in the middle of the three of us. It was on the news that night. 'Same old Mets.' That kind of thing. 'Look at this, they stink.'

"Then we went out and won our next six. I started to see the rest of the league, and I think about three weeks of making our rounds around our division, I started to look around and saying to myself, *You know what? I don't see anybody here that's that much better than us.*"

It seemed like a statistical improbability for the Mets to be leading the NL East by two games on May 4. The offense was batting .245 with 16 homers and 86 runs scored in the first 23 games, and the pitchers allowed 100 runs while compiling a 3.71 ERA in that span. But the Mets were getting timely hitting and terrific pitching in their victories, allowing them to be in first place in May for the first time since 1972. Darryl Strawberry was wearing out NL hurlers with a .349 mark on May 4, and Keith Hernandez lifted his average to .327 by May 11. Even Foster was hitting consistently following two subpar seasons, batting .283 with four homers and 20 RBIs in the Mets' first 20 games.

Johnson also found a solution at second base by platooning Wally Backman and Kelvin Chapman. Neither player was highly regarded by the organization at the end of 1983, but Johnson liked Backman's grittiness and felt Chapman had been buried in the minors too long.

Gooden opened the season at the back-end of the rotation, and he often pitched like it during the first five weeks. He struck out 11 while tossing a four-hit shutout in a 2–0 win at Los Angeles May 11, but he was just 3–3 with a 4.15 ERA a week later before his career took off.

Gooden struck out 14 and scattered three hits May 25 against the Dodgers, beginning a season-ending streak in which he went 14–6 with a 2.22 ERA and a ridiculous 217 strikeouts in 174⅔ innings. He posted a 1.12 ERA in six starts from May 25 to June 22, and Darling won seven consecutive starts between June 4 and July 6.

Terrell also opened the season strong but often pitched well enough to lose. He had a 3.23 ERA in his first 15 starts, yet his record was only 5–7 as the Mets went six consecutive starts without furnishing Terrell with more than three runs.

The Mets remained shaky at the back end of the rotation. Torrez was a bust and Lynch struggled at times, forcing Cashen to make a move at the trade deadline. He sent Jay Tibbs to the Reds for Bruce Berenyi, who owned a heavy fastball and little control. Berenyi was 3–7 with a 6.00 ERA for Cincinnati, walking 42 in 51 innings. But Berenyi also had struck out 53 and was too young to write off. Cashen's deal paid off as Berenyi went 9–6 with a 3.76 ERA following the trade.

The Mets still needed another starter, but they needed to look no further than Tidewater. Cashen had pulled off an under-the-radar deal with the Dodgers that winter, sending reliever Carlos Diaz and utilityman Bob Bailor to L.A. for a Hawaiian lefty with a rather funky delivery. It was time for Sid Fernandez to make his Mets debut.

The Mets started to take off sometime between the arrivals of Berenyi and Fernandez. They were in third place, just two games back following a loss to the Braves on June 29. The team sizzled for the next four weeks, winning 21 of 25 to vault into first place by a comfortable 4½ games over the Cubs.

Chicago had its own pitching problems at the trade deadline. While the Mets were landing Berenyi, the Cubs were picking up Rick Sutcliffe from the Indians. Sutcliffe would be the difference between the Cubs and the Mets the rest of the season as he went 16–1 with a 2.69 ERA. He beat the Mets three times after August 1, including twice over a one-week span.

The Cubs won seven straight against the Mets from July 27 to August 8 before the two teams split six games in September. Gooden beat the Cubs 10–0 on a one-hitter to open a three-game series against Chicago on September 7. But Sutcliffe killed any momentum from that victory by blanking the Mets 6–0 to put Chicago seven games in front with 20 games remaining.

With the race seemingly over, it was time to watch Gooden wrap up the NL Rookie of the Year Award. Gooden was 9–8 with a 3.42 ERA before morphing into Dr. K, an unhittable strikeout machine who could buzz hitters with his rising fastball and freeze them with his curve, which would be dubbed "Lord Charles." Gooden went 8–1 with a 1.07 ERA and 105 strikeouts in 76 innings over his final nine starts. He struck out 16 in back-to-back outings to set a National League record for Ks in consecutive starts.

Gooden picked up 23 of 24 first-place votes in the rookie balloting.

Darling was a serious Rookie of the Year candidate as he went 10–3 with a 3.34 ERA in the first half. Darling faded in the second half to finish 12–9 with a 3.81 ERA.

Strawberry belted 26 homers and drove in 97 runs, but he hit only .232 after May 5. Strawberry got cold just as Hubie Brooks was heating up. Brooks broke a team record by hitting safely in 24 straight games from May 1 to June 1.

Brooks shattered career highs by smacking 16 homers and driving in 73 runs. He also became the Mets' starting shortstop after Ray Knight was acquired from Houston. But Brooks' position switch merely served as an audition that would allow the Mets to land another batter in the off-season.

Backman and Chapman were a nice combo at second base as both hit over .280 while combining for 32 doubles and 49 RBIs. Together, they compiled a .359 on-base percentage.

The Mets' most pressing need was at catcher following Brooks' move to short. Mike Fitzgerald did a nice job throwing out runners (40 of 128), but he was a young catcher handling a young pitching staff. Cashen hit the phone trying to land an experienced first-string catcher who might have some pop in his bat. He wound up getting the NL's best catcher, acquiring Gary Carter in a deal that sent Brooks to the Expos. It was another power-hitting bat in the lineup, moving the Mets another step closer to the playoffs.

1984 Mets Statistics

Hitting	G	AB	R	H	2B	3B	HR	RBI	BB	SO	BA	OBP	SLG	SB	CS	GDP	HP	SH	SF	IBB
Wally Backman	128	436	68	122	19	2	1	26	56	63	.280	.360	.339	32	9	13	0	5	2	2
Billy Beane	5	10	0	1	0	0	0	0	0	2	.100	.100	.100	0	1	0	0	0	0	0
Hubie Brooks	153	561	61	159	23	2	16	73	48	79	.283	.341	.417	6	5	17	2	0	2	15
Kelvin Chapman	75	197	27	57	13	0	3	23	19	30	.289	.356	.401	8	7	7	2	4	1	0
John Christensen	5	11	2	3	2	0	0	3	1	2	.273	.308	.455	0	1	0	0	0	1	0
Mike Fitzgerald	112	360	20	87	15	1	2	33	24	71	.242	.288	.306	1	0	17	1	5	4	7
George Foster	146	553	67	149	22	1	24	86	30	122	.269	.311	.443	2	2	14	6	0	6	9
Ron Gardenhire	74	207	20	51	7	1	1	10	9	43	.246	.276	.304	6	1	7	0	1	1	1
John Gibbons	10	31	1	2	0	0	0	1	3	11	.065	.065	.065	0	0	0	1	0	0	1
Danny Heep	99	199	36	46	9	2	1	12	27	22	.231	.319	.312	3	1	9	1	1	5	3
Keith Hernandez	154	550	83	171	31	0	15	94	97	89	.311	.409	.449	2	3	9	1	0	9	12
Ron Hodges	64	106	5	22	3	0	1	11	23	18	.208	.351	.264	1	1	3	1	1	1	0
Ross Jones	17	10	2	1	1	0	0	1	3	4	.100	.308	.200	0	0	0	0	0	0	0

Hitting (continued)	G	AB	R	H	2B	3B	HR	RBI	BB	SO	BA	OBP	SLG	SB	CS	GDP	HP	SH	SF	IBB
Ray Knight	27	93	13	26	4	0	1	6	7	13	.280	.337	.355	0	0	1	1	0	0	1
Jerry Martin	51	91	6	14	1	0	3	5	6	29	.154	.206	.264	0	0	5	0	0	0	0
Kevin Mitchell	7	14	0	3	0	0	0	1	0	3	.214	.214	.214	0	1	0	0	0	0	0
Jose Oquendo	81	189	23	42	5	0	0	10	15	26	.222	.284	.249	10	1	2	2	3	2	2
Junior Ortiz	40	91	6	18	3	0	0	11	5	15	.198	.235	.231	1	0	2	0	0	2	0
Rafael Santana	51	152	14	42	11	1	1	12	9	17	.276	.317	.382	0	3	3	0	1	0	0
Rusty Staub	78	72	2	19	4	0	1	18	4	9	.264	.291	.361	0	0	1	0	0	3	3
John Stearns	8	17	6	3	1	0	0	1	4	2	.176	.333	.235	1	0	0	0	0	0	0
Darryl Strawberry	147	522	75	131	27	4	26	97	75	131	.251	.343	.467	27	8	8	0	1	4	15
Mookie Wilson	154	587	88	162	28	10	10	54	26	90	.276	.308	.409	46	9	5	2	2	2	2
Herm Winningham	14	27	5	11	1	1	0	5	1	7	.407	.429	.519	2	1	0	0	0	0	0
Pitchers																				
Bruce Berenyi	19	37	3	9	1	0	0	3	0	5	.243	.237	.270	0	0	1	0	5	1	0
Ron Darling	39	67	7	10	1	0	0	3	1	19	.149	.159	.164	0	0	1	0	6	1	0
Sid Fernandez	15	28	0	5	0	0	0	1	0	9	.179	.179	.179	0	0	0	0	3	0	0
Brent Gaff	47	6	0	0	0	0	0	0	0	2	.000	.000	.000	0	0	0	0	0	0	0
Wes Gardner	21	1	1	0	0	0	0	0	0	0	.000	.000	.000	0	0	0	0	0	0	0
Dwight Gooden	31	70	5	14	0	0	0	3	1	14	.200	.205	.200	0	0	3	0	10	2	0
Tom Gorman	36	3	0	0	0	0	0	0	0	1	.000	.000	.000	0	0	0	0	0	0	0
Tim Leary	20	10	2	3	0	0	1	1	0	2	.300	.300	.600	1	0	0	0	3	0	0
Ed Lynch	40	27	0	6	1	0	0	1	0	9	.222	.222	.259	0	0	1	0	3	0	0
Jesse Orosco	60	4	1	1	0	0	0	1	3	2	.250	.571	.250	0	0	0	0	1	0	0
Calvin Schiraldi	5	3	0	0	0	0	0	0	0	0	.000	.000	.000	0	0	0	0	0	0	0
Doug Sisk	50	11	0	1	0	0	0	0	1	6	.091	.167	.091	0	0	1	0	2	0	0
Craig Swan	10	0	0	0	0	0	0	0	0	0				0	0	0	0	1	0	0
Walt Terrell	33	75	3	6	2	0	0	0	1	33	.080	.092	.107	0	0	1	0	1	0	0
Mike Torrez	9	10	0	3	0	0	0	1	1	1	.300	.364	.300	0	0	1	0	0	0	0
TOTAL	162	5438	652	1400	235	25	107	607	500	1001	.257	.320	.369	149	54	132	20	59	49	73

Pitching	G	ERA	W:–L	SV	GS	GF	CG	SHO	IP	H	R	ER	HR	BB	SO	BF	WP	HP	BK	IBB
Bruce Berenyi	19	3.76	9–6	0	19	0	0	0	115.0	100	58	48	6	53	81	486	7	1	0	2
Ron Darling	33	3.81	12–9	0	33	0	2	2	205.2	179	97	87	17	104	136	884	7	5	1	2
Sid Fernandez	15	3.50	6–6	0	15	0	0	0	90.0	74	40	35	8	34	62	371	1	0	4	3
Brent Gaff	47	3.63	3–2	1	0	18	0	0	84.1	77	39	34	4	36	42	358	5	1	2	11
Wes Gardner	21	6.39	1–1	1	0	12	0	0	25.1	34	19	18	0	8	19	116	1	0	0	2
Dwight Gooden	31	2.60	17–9	0	31	0	7	3	218.0	161	72	63	7	73	276	879	3	2	7	2
Tom Gorman	36	2.97	6–0	0	0	12	0	0	57.2	51	20	19	6	13	40	230	2	1	0	3
Tim Leary	20	4.02	3–3	0	7	3	0	0	53.2	61	28	24	2	18	29	237	2	2	3	3
Ed Lynch	40	4.50	9–8	2	13	14	0	0	124.0	169	77	62	14	24	62	556	1	4	0	3
Jesse Orosco	60	2.59	10–6	31	0	52	0	0	87.0	58	29	25	7	34	85	355	1	2	1	6
Calvin Schiraldi	5	5.71	0–2	0	3	0	0	0	17.1	20	13	11	3	10	16	80	0	0	0	0
Doug Sisk	50	2.09	1–3	15	0	31	0	0	77.2	57	24	18	1	54	32	329	1	3	0	5
Craig Swan	10	8.20	1–0	0	0	2	0	0	18.2	18	17	17	5	7	10	81	1	0	2	0
Walt Terrell	33	3.52	11–12	0	33	0	3	1	215.0	232	99	84	16	80	114	926	6	4	0	1
Dick Tidrow	11	9.19	0–0	0	0	5	0	0	15.2	25	19	16	5	7	8	78	1	0	0	0
Mike Torrez	9	5.02	1–5	0	8	1	0	0	37.2	55	25	21	3	18	16	175	2	2	0	0
TOTAL	162	3.60	90–72	50	162	150	12	15	1442.0	1371	676	577	104	573	1028	6141	41	27	20	43

1985

NL EAST						
Team	**W**	**L**	**PCT**	**GB**	**BA**	**ERA**
Cardinals	101	61	.623	—	.264	3.10
Mets	98	64	.605	3.0	.257	3.11
Expos	84	77	.522	16.5	.247	3.55
Cubs	77	84	.478	23.5	.254	4.16
Phillies	75	87	.463	26.0	.245	3.68
Pirates	57	104	.354	43.5	.247	3.97

An unusually high level of optimism permeated throughout Shea Stadium as the New York Mets played their season opener against the Cardinals. The Mets appeared to have made their roster more "Cub-proof" after finishing 6½ games behind the first-place Cubbies in 1984.

Not only did the '84 Mets post the second-best record in team history at that point, they also enjoyed a highly successful off-season. General manager Frank Cashen had acquired All-Star catcher Gary Carter from the Expos for Hubie Brooks, Mike Fitzgerald, Floyd Youmans, and Herm Winningham on December 10, three days after third baseman Howard Johnson came over from the Tigers for pitcher Walt Terrell. Terrell would be missed until Rick Aguilera emerged as the Mets' No. 4 starter by midseason.

Carter became an instant hero after torturing the Mets the previous decade. The Mets blew a 5–2 lead in the opener before Carter launched a homer in the bottom of the 10th to give New York a 6–5 win over the Cardinals.

The Mets also won their second game in extra innings and earned a pair of one-run victories before Dwight Gooden tossed a shutout against the Reds, giving the Mets a 5–0 record for the first time in team history.

The Mets continued to chew up opponents during the early portion of the schedule, opening 21–9 to climb into first place by 1½ games. But the lineup took a severe hit when Darryl Strawberry tore thumb ligaments while trying to make a diving catch in right field. Danny Heep played admirably in right during Strawberry's absence, but the team endured a 15–24 stretch that left them just 38–35 following a 1–0 loss to the Pirates on July 1.

The offense was wasting several outstanding pitching performances while the team slid into fourth place, five games behind the Cardinals. Carter was batting .268 with 11 homers by July 1, but he drove in just 33 runs in 70 games, putting him on pace for about 70 for the season. Keith Hernandez was in the midst of a two-month funk in which he batted .225 with 17 RBIs in 53 games. George Foster had just 31 RBIs and a .238 average during a 53-game stretch through July 1. Rookie Lenny Dykstra gave the Mets a brief spark as the leadoff hitter, hitting a homer in his second at-bat in his major league debut. Dykstra was hitting .267, and Wally Backman owned a .245 batting average heading into July.

The offense continued to sputter for a few games after Strawberry returned to the lineup in late June. But the bats came alive during one of the wildest nights in Mets history. An expected pitcher's duel between Gooden and Rick Mahler was short-circuited by a lengthy rain delay in the bottom of the third. Another rain delay halted play for about two more hours in the ninth inning.

It was well past midnight when Dykstra hit a game-tying single in the ninth to force extra innings and create a crazy morning in Atlanta. Howard Johnson belted a two-run homer in the 13th to put the Mets up 10–8, and Tom Gorman struck out a pair in the bottom of the inning before Terry Harper extended the game with a two-run blast off the lefty.

Neither team scored again until the 18th, when Dykstra came through again, this time with a sac-fly. Gorman retired the first two hitters in the last half of the inning and was facing pitcher Rick Camp, who entered the game a lifetime 10-for-167 hitter (.060) . Camp picked this moment to hit his only major league homer, tying the game 11–11.

The Mets scored five times in the 19th, but Harper laced a two-run single off reliever Ron Darling before Darling struck out Camp for the final out.

The Atlanta Marathon seemed to wake up the offense. Hernandez hit for the cycle to begin a season-ending run in which he batted .356 with 60 RBIs in 84 games. Backman also had four hits as part of a 10-game hitting streak that included a .388 average.

The Mets went 19–6 in July to climb back into the NL East race. They scored in double digits six times in those victories, reaching the 16-run plateau on three occasions.

The inconsistent hitting never stopped Gooden from winning. The second-year hurler and reigning Rookie of the Year didn't lose between May 30 and August 25, and he was even better in September.

Gooden put together a 14-game winning streak that included three shutouts and 10 complete games in 18 starts. He finally suffered a loss August 31 at San Francisco despite holding the Giants to two runs and six hits in six innings. However, he didn't lose the rest of the year, going 4–0 with a 0.34 ERA and two shutouts in his final six starts.

Gooden anchored a staff that finished third in the National League with a 3.11 ERA, 32 complete games, and 19 shutouts. The Mets also paced the league with 1,039 strikeouts, 268 provided by Gooden.

Sid Fernandez usually was the pitcher given the least offensive support. The Mets scored a measly 32 runs in his first 13 starts, leaving him just 3–6 despite a 2.74 ERA. El Sid also received 12 runs in a complete-game win over the Padres on September 2. But New York scored fewer than four runs in half of his 26 starts, leading to a 9–9 record.

Darling was superb in his second full season, starting the year 10–2 with a 2.62 ERA. He later won six consecutive starts from August 19 to September 15 to put him 16–5 with a 2.74 ERA. But the Hawaiian struggled in three of his final four starts as the Mets failed to catch the Cardinals.

The Mets likely wouldn't have been in contention without Aguilera, who was called up from Triple A Tidewater a day after New York absorbed a 26–7 loss at Philadelphia. The rookie won his major league debut and was 9–4 with a 2.88 ERA from July 5 to September 28. But with the Mets needing a victory to pull into a first-place tie heading into the final weekend of the season, Aguilera gave up four runs and nine hits in six innings of a 4–3 loss to the Cardinals on October 3, putting the Mets two games off the lead with three to play.

Aguilera wasn't the only rookie to have a hand in the Mets' success. Roger McDowell earned a spot on the major league roster in April before combining with Jesse Orosco to form a dynamic duo in the bullpen. McDowell became a mainstay in the pen after making back-to-back mediocre starts early in the season, recording 17 saves and posting a 4–4 record with a 2.29 ERA in his final 55 appearances. NL hitters batted just .215 against McDowell, who allowed only 117 base runners in 110 innings after May 4. He was fifth on the team with 127⅓ innings, eclipsing Orosco's total by 48.

Orosco had another solid year as he tied McDowell for the team lead with 17 saves while recording a 2.73 ERA. Orosco also kept the team's ERA down by stranding 37 of his 46 inherited runners in his third full season as the team's top reliever.

Carter was mentoring the young pitching staff, but the extra-base hits were sparse until mid August. He drove in 55 runs and had a .355 on-base percentage in his first 99 games before going on a late-season tear. Carter smacked 18 of his 32 homers after August 10, batting .309 with 45 RBIs in the process. He set a Mets record by homering five times in a two-game span in San Diego while the Mets were trying to set themselves up for a viable playoff push against the Cards.

The Redbirds immediately became the Mets' kryptonite after dropping their first three meetings with New York New York took four of six from the Cardinals in September, but St. Louis ran wild against Gary Carter while winning eight of nine from the Mets between April 22 and June 30.

The Mets and Cardinals were tied for the division lead when they opened a three-game series at Shea Stadium September 10. Hernandez delivered an RBI single in the bottom of the ninth to give the Mets a 7–6 win in the rubber match and a one-game lead in the NL East. But New York's reign atop the division was over just 48 hours later, and they would spend the rest of the season chasing St. Louis.

The Mets had one final chance to catch the Cardinals when they opened a three-game series at Busch Stadium. A sweep would leave the two teams in a tie for first with three games remaining.

Strawberry won the first game by crushing a long homer in the 11th inning of a 1–0 win over the Cardinals. Gooden picked up his 24th win while helping the Mets pull within a game of first. But the Cardinals salvaged the series finale and wrapped up the division title two days later.

The Mets had finished second for the second straight year despite 98 victories, just two off the team record. Gooden was the runaway winner of the NL Cy Young Award after going 24–4 with 268 strikeouts and a 1.53 ERA. Carter was the answer behind the plate, leading the team with 32 homers and 100 RBI. Hernandez ended the year hitting .309 despite a slow start and several personal problems. And Strawberry finished with 29 homers and 79 RBIs despite missing seven weeks with the thumb injury.

The Mets deficiencies were limited but glaring. Kelvin Chapman failed to match his 1984 offensive numbers, leaving the team without a legitimate right-handed hitter at second base. Backman batted a robust .324 as a lefty hitter, but he was just 16-for-131 (.122) from the other side of the plate. A right handed-hitting infielder would solve some of the Mets' problems against lefty hurlers.

The Mets also lacked depth at starting pitching by the end of the year. Bruce Berenyi missed most of the season due to a shoulder injury, and Ed Lynch developed an injury by the end of the season, leaving the team in the market for another starter.

Cashen would solve the second-base problem and pitching shortage during the winter, leaving the team virtually bullet-proof heading into 1986.

1985 Mets Statistics

Hitting	G	AB	R	H	2B	3B	HR	RBI	BB	SO	BA	OBP	SLG	SB	CS	GDP	HP	SH	SF	IBB
Wally Backman	145	520	77	142	24	5	1	38	36	72	.273	.320	.344	30	12	3	1	14	3	1
Billy Beane	8	8	0	2	1	0	0	1	0	3	.250	.250	.375	0	0	0	0	0	0	0
Terry Blocker	18	15	1	1	0	0	0	0	1	2	.067	.125	.067	0	0	0	0	0	0	0
Larry Bowa	14	19	2	2	1	0	0	2	2	2	.105	.190	.158	0	0	0	0	1	0	0
Gary Carter	149	555	83	156	17	1	32	100	69	46	.281	.365	.488	1	1	18	6	0	3	16
Kelvin Chapman	62	144	16	25	3	0	0	7	9	15	.174	.231	.194	5	4	2	2	3	1	0
John Christensen	51	113	10	21	4	1	3	13	19	23	.186	.303	.319	1	2	3	0	1	0	1
Lenny Dykstra	83	236	40	60	9	3	1	19	30	24	.254	.338	.331	15	2	4	1	4	2	0
George Foster	129	452	57	119	24	1	21	77	46	87	.263	.331	.460	0	1	8	2	0	4	5
Ron Gardenhire	26	39	5	7	2	1	0	2	8	11	.179	.319	.282	0	0	2	0	2	0	0
Danny Heep	95	271	26	76	17	0	7	42	27	27	.280	.341	.421	2	2	12	1	0	6	1
Keith Hernandez	158	593	87	183	34	4	10	91	77	59	.309	.384	.430	3	3	14	2	0	10	15
Clint Hurdle	43	82	7	16	4	0	3	7	13	20	.195	.313	.354	0	1	1	1	1	0	3
Howard Johnson	126	389	38	94	18	4	11	46	34	78	.242	.300	.393	6	4	6	0	1	4	10
Ray Knight	90	271	22	59	12	0	6	36	13	32	.218	.252	.328	1	1	17	1	0	5	1
Tom Paciorek	46	116	14	33	3	1	1	11	6	14	.284	.325	.353	1	0	2	1	1	0	1
Ronn Reynolds	28	43	4	9	2	0	0	1	0	18	.209	.227	.256	0	0	1	1	2	0	0
Rafael Santana	154	529	41	136	19	1	1	29	29	54	.257	.295	.302	1	0	14	0	4	2	12
Darryl Strawberry	111	393	78	109	15	4	29	79	73	96	.277	.389	.557	26	11	9	1	0	3	13
Rusty Staub	54	45	2	12	3	0	1	8	10	4	.267	.400	.400	0	0	1	0	0	0	3
Mookie Wilson	93	337	56	93	16	8	6	26	28	52	.276	.331	.424	24	9	9	0	1	1	6
Pitchers																				
Rick Aguilera	22	36	1	10	2	0	0	2	1	5	.278	.297	.333	0	0	1	0	7	0	0
Bruce Berenyi	3	4	1	1	1	0	0	1	0	2	.250	.250	.500	0	0	0	0	2	0	0
Ron Darling	42	76	9	13	4	0	0	0	4	25	.171	.213	.224	1	0	0	0	13	0	0
Sid Fernandez	26	52	2	11	0	1	0	1	0	26	.212	.212	.250	0	0	1	0	7	0	0
Dwight Gooden	35	93	11	21	2	0	1	9	5	15	.226	.265	.280	0	0	1	0	9	0	0
Tom Gorman	34	5	0	0	0	0	0	0	0	3	.000	.000	.000	0	0	0	0	1	0	0
Bill Latham	7	3	1	1	0	0	0	1	1	0	.333	.500	.333	0	0	0	0	1	0	0
Terry Leach	22	12	1	2	1	0	0	0	1	8	.167	.231	.250	0	0	0	0	1	0	0
Ed Lynch	31	52	1	4	0	0	0	0	3	30	.077	.127	.077	0	0	1	0	9	0	0
Roger McDowell	62	19	1	3	1	0	0	1	1	7	.158	.200	.211	0	0	0	0	2	0	0
Jesse Orosco	54	7	0	3	0	0	0	0	0	1	.429	.429	.429	0	0	0	0	2	0	0
Calvin Schiraldi	10	8	0	1	0	0	0	0	0	4	.125	.125	.125	0	0	1	0	0	0	0
Doug Sisk	42	12	1	0	0	0	0	1	0	7	.000	.000	.000	0	0	0	0	0	0	0
TOTAL	162	5549	695	1425	239	35	134	651	546	872	.257	.323	.385	117	53	131	20	89	44	88

Pitching	G	ERA	W–L	SV	GS	GF	CG	SHO	IP	H	R	ER	HR	BB	SO	WP	HP	BK	IBB
Rick Aguilera	21	3.24	10–7	0	19	1	2	0	122.1	118	49	44	8	37	74	507	5	2	2	2
Bruce Berenyi	3	2.63	1–0	0	3	0	0	0	13.2	8	6	4	0	10	10	58	3	1	0	0
Ron Darling	36	2.90	16–6	0	35	1	4	2	248.0	214	93	80	21	114	167	1043	7	3	1	1
Sid Fernandez	26	2.80	9–9	0	26	0	3	0	170.1	108	56	53	14	80	180	685	3	2	2	3
Wes Gardner	9	5.25	0–2	0	0	8	0	0	12.0	18	14	7	1	8	11	61	1	0	0	2
Dwight Gooden	35	1.53	24–4	0	35	0	16	8	276.2	198	51	47	13	69	268	1065	6	2	4	4
Tom Gorman	34	5.13	4–4	0	2	12	0	0	52.2	56	32	30	8	18	32	227	2	0	2	2
Bill Latham	7	3.97	1–3	0	3	1	0	0	22.2	21	10	10	1	7	10	93	1	0	1	1
Terry Leach	22	2.91	3–4	1	4	4	1	1	55.2	48	19	18	3	14	30	226	0	1	0	3
Ed Lynch	31	3.44	10–8	0	29	1	6	1	191.0	188	76	73	19	27	65	777	0	1	0	1
Roger McDowell	62	2.83	6–5	17	2	36	0	0	127.1	108	43	40	9	37	70	516	6	1	2	8
Randy Myers	1	0.00	0–0	0	0	1	0	0	2.0	0	0	0	0	1	2	7	0	0	0	0
Randy Niemann	4	0.00	0–0	0	0	0	0	0	4.7	5	0	0	0	0	2	18	0	0	0	0
Jesse Orosco	54	2.73	8–6	17	0	39	0	0	79.0	66	26	24	6	34	68	331	4	0	0	7
Joe Sambito	8	12.66	0–0	0	0	2	0	0	10.2	21	18	15	1	8	3	60	0	0	0	0
Calvin Schiraldi	10	8.89	2–1	0	4	2	0	0	26.1	43	27	26	4	11	21	131	2	3	1	0
Doug Sisk	42	5.30	4–5	2	0	22	0	0	73.0	86	48	43	3	40	26	341	1	2	1	2
TOTAL	162	3.11	98–64	37	162	130	32	19	1488.0	1306	568	514	111	515	1039	6146	41	18	14	36

1986

NL EAST

Team	W	L	PCT	GB	BA	ERA
Mets	108	54	.667	—	.263	3.11
Phillies	86	75	.534	21.5	.253	3.85
Cardinals	79	82	.491	28.5	.236	3.37
Expos	78	83	.484	29.5	.254	3.78
Cubs	70	90	.438	37.0	.256	4.49
Pirates	64	98	.395	44.0	.250	3.90

Mets win NLCS over Astros, 4–2
Mets win World Series over Red Sox, 4–3

There were three primary reasons why the Mets were unable to beat out the Cardinals for the NL East title in 1985.

One was the lack of a productive right-handed-hitting second baseman. General manager Frank Cashen solved that by acquiring Tim Teufel from the Twins after switching-hitting Wally Backman hit only .122 in 131 at-bats during 1985.

The Mets also lacked pitching depth down the stretch following injuries to Bruce Berenyi and Ed Lynch. Cashen settled that situation with another trade, stealing lefty Bob Ojeda from the Red Sox.

Another problem was the team's inability to stop the Cardinals' running game, but that was something the Mets could live with as long as catcher Gary Carter continued to produce. That situation was remedied by the pitching staff, which held the Redbirds to a .202 average in 1986.

Now armed with Teufel and Ojeda, the Mets were supremely confident they would win their first division title in 13 years following two near-misses. Manager Davey Johnson said during spring training that the Mets would dominate during the season, and the rest of the team echoed his confidence.

The Mets played the '86 regular season as if they were entitled to a playoff berth. They spent the season winning blowout games when they weren't pulling out several victories in dramatic fashion. The Mets never felt they were out of a game as long as they still had one more out, a trait best shown during Game 6 of the World Series.

Their supreme confidence was perceived as utter arrogance by the rest of the National League. Opposing players, especially the Phillies and Cardinals, grew to hate the Mets. The Mets didn't care.

The Mets further annoyed visiting players with their numerous curtain calls following home runs. The Mets didn't care.

Fans despised the Mets and saved some of their most vociferous jeering for the men in blue pinstripes. The Mets didn't care.

The Mets were labeled as bullies following altercations with the Dodgers, Braves, and Reds. The Mets didn't care. In fact, it was getting hard to spell "New York Mets" without an "F" and a "U."

The Mets didn't give a damn what you thought of them. They were the band of marauders who ransacked your village, stole your liquor, and took away your women. They also won a team-record 108 games and wrapped up the division with 17 games left in the season.

The Mets were even better than their spring training expectations. Third basemen Ray Knight and Howard Johnson had strong seasons after the two combined to hit a meager .229 with 17 homers and 82 RBIs in 669 at-bats the previous season. Knight hit .298, belted 11 home runs and drove in 76 runs in 137 games. Johnson showed improvement while playing third and shortstop, recording a .245 average with 11 homers and 39 ribbies.

Teufel's presence allowed Backman to relax at the plate. Backman hit .320 in 440 plate appearances and led the team with 14 sacrifice hits. Teufel was productive in his own right, accounting for 62 runs in just 279 at-bats. He won an early season game with a pinch-hit grand slam that ended an 8–4 win over the Phillies.

The Mets also had a two-headed monster in outfielders Lenny Dykstra and Mookie Wilson. They provided 56 of the team's 118 stolen bases and hit .282 with 17 home runs and 90 RBIs. Wilson was outstanding after missing the first month of the season with an eye injury suffered when he was hit in the glasses by a thrown ball during spring training. Wilson and Dykstra hit well enough for Cashen to release George Foster shortly after the All-Star break.

Foster was one of the few blemishes on a near-perfect season. He got off to a miserable start, causing Johnson to play Danny Heep and rookie Kevin Mitchell more and more in left field. Foster irritated his teammates by staying in the dugout during their fight with the Reds after the All-Star break. He sealed his doom by saying racism was a factor in his frequent benchings.

Wilson and Mitchell were the biggest contributing factors to Foster's departure. Mitchell earned a spot on the opening-day roster by leading the team in most offensive categories during the exhibition season. He was the Mets' most versatile player, appearing at a team-high six different positions and doing it by June 11. Mitchell carried a .368 average into July while contributing numerous go-ahead hits.

The Mets did dominate the season even without "career years" from Carter, Keith Hernandez, or Darryl Strawberry. However, all three were terrific in their own right.

Hernandez paced the team with a .310 average and captured his ninth consecutive Gold Glove while serving as the quarterback of the infield. Hernandez also mentored and encouraged the pitching staff when needed.

Carter hit only .259 but slugged 24 home runs and tied Rusty Staub's club record of 105 RBI. Carter did it on bad knees, appearing in 132 games despite missing two weeks with a thumb injury.

Strawberry was on cruise control the entire season, leading the club with 27 homers and a .507 slugging average. One of his more memorable games of the year occurred on Fireworks Night as he belted a pair of game-tying, two-run homers in a 6–5 win over the Astros on July 3. The second homer knotted the score in the 10th inning, three batters before Knight won it with a walk-off blast.

The Mets also didn't get a "career year" out of Dwight Gooden, although it was going to be difficult for him to match his sensational 1985 campaign. Gooden went 17–6 with 200 strikeouts and a 2.84 earned run average, one season after leading the league with 24 wins, 268 strikeouts, and a team-record 1.53 ERA.

Gooden remained the ace of a starting staff that tossed 27 complete games and went 78–33 with a 3.16 ERA. Sid Fernandez and Ron Darling remained a big part of a rotation that now featured four flame-throwers and Ojeda's "dead-fish" changeup.

Ojeda put together his finest season, setting career highs with 18 wins, a 2.57 ERA, 148 strikeouts, and a .783 winning percentage. He was 12–2 with a 2.28 ERA by July 28 following a season-best six-game winning streak.

Fernandez averaged one strikeout per inning and set career highs with 16 victories and 200 strikeouts. Like Ojeda, El Sid won 12 of his first 14 decisions and entered the All-Star break on a seven-game winning streak.

Darling's 2.81 earned run average would be the best of his career. He also went 15–6 and fanned 184 but led the team with 13 no-decisions. The Mets went 26–8 in his 34 starts, almost 25 percent of the team's victories.

Gary Carter is lifted in the air by pitcher Jesse Orosco following the Mets 8–5 victory over the Boston Red Sox in Game 7 of the World Series, October 27, 1986.

The four starters were at or near a 20-win pace by the All-Star break before settling for 66 wins. Rick Aguilera rounded out the rotation and went 5–0 with a 1.33 ERA over a five-start span beginning July 12.

Roger McDowell and Jesse Orosco finished what the starters couldn't. McDowell set a team record with 14 relief victories, topping the mark of 13 set by Orosco three years earlier. McDowell also finished with 22 saves, one more than Orosco.

Orosco had the team's best ERA among pitchers with at least 80 innings. The lefty saved some of his best pitching for the postseason, winning three games in the NLCS and limiting the Red Sox to no runs and two hits in 5⅔ innings during the World Series.

The Mets didn't look like world beaters during the first five games, playing sloppily in dropping three straight, including the home opener against the Cardinals. That was followed by a team record–tying 11-game winning streak that gave the Mets a five-game lead through 16 contests. They also proved they could beat the Cardinals by sweeping a four-game set at Busch Stadium in late April. The sweep put the Mets in first place to stay.

The lead grew into double digits by June 14 and became a 20-game bulge in late August. Things were going so well that the souvenir stands were selling "National League East Champions" T-shirts by mid-August.

The Mets had five winning streaks of at least six games and never lost more than four straight. Just as Johnson had predicted, the Mets dominated.

The playoffs were a different story. The Mets showed their tough side by capturing the NLCS and World Series by the thinnest of margins. New York batted only .189 in the championship series against the Astros and did little against former Met Mike Scott, who allowed only one run and eight hits in two complete-game victories. The Mets pulled out three of their four NLCS wins in their final at-bat, two coming in extra innings.

But that was nothing compared to the way they won the World Series. They dropped the first two games at Shea Stadium and were one out from falling to the Red Sox in six games before pulling out an improbable 6–5, 10-inning victory.

The Mets also tested their mettle by falling behind 3–0 in Game 7 before scoring eight runs over their final three at-bats to win their second World Series title.

1986 Mets Statistics

Hitting	G	AB	R	H	2B	3B	HR	RBI	BB	SO	BA	OBP	SLG	SB	CS	GDP	HP	SH	SF	IBB
Wally Backman	124	387	67	124	18	2	1	27	36	32	.320	.376	.385	13	7	3	0	14	3	1
Gary Carter	132	490	81	125	14	2	24	105	62	63	.255	.337	.439	1	0	21	6	0	15	9
Tim Corcoran	6	7	1	0	0	0	0	0	2	0	.000	.222	.000	0	0	0	0	0	0	1
Lenny Dykstra	147	431	77	127	27	7	8	45	58	55	.295	.377	.445	31	7	4	0	7	2	1
Kevin Elster	19	30	3	5	1	0	0	0	3	8	.167	.242	.200	0	0	0	0	0	0	1
George Foster	72	233	28	53	6	1	13	38	21	53	.227	.289	.429	1	1	7	0	0	2	1
John Gibbons	8	19	4	9	4	0	1	1	3	5	.474	.545	.842	0	0	1	0	0	0	1
Ed Hearn	49	136	16	36	5	0	4	10	12	19	.265	.322	.390	0	1	4	0	2	1	0
Danny Heep	86	195	24	55	8	2	5	33	30	31	.282	.379	.421	1	4	3	1	0	1	5
Keith Hernandez	149	551	94	171	34	1	13	83	94	69	.310	.413	.446	2	1	14	4	0	3	9
Stan Jefferson	14	24	6	5	1	0	1	3	2	8	.208	.296	.375	0	0	1	1	0	0	0
Howard Johnson	88	220	30	54	14	0	10	39	31	64	.245	.341	.445	8	1	2	1	1	0	8
Ray Knight	137	486	51	145	24	2	11	76	40	63	.298	.351	.424	2	1	19	4	3	8	2
Barry Lyons	6	9	1	0	0	0	0	2	1	2	.000	.100	.000	0	0	0	0	0	0	1
Dave Magadan	10	18	3	8	0	0	0	3	3	1	.444	.524	.444	0	0	1	0	0	0	0
Lee Mazzilli	39	58	10	16	3	0	2	7	12	11	.276	.417	.431	1	1	1	2	0	0	1
Kevin Mitchell	108	328	51	91	22	2	12	43	33	61	.277	.344	.466	3	3	6	1	1	1	0
Rafael Santana	139	394	38	86	11	0	1	28	36	43	.218	.285	.254	0	0	15	2	1	3	12
Darryl Strawberry	136	475	76	123	27	5	27	93	72	141	.259	.358	.507	28	12	4	6	0	9	9
Tim Teufel	93	279	35	69	20	1	4	31	32	42	.247	.324	.369	1	2	6	1	3	3	1
Mookie Wilson	123	381	61	110	17	5	9	45	32	72	.289	.345	.430	25	7	5	1	0	1	5
Pitchers																				
Rick Aguilera	32	51	4	8	0	0	2	6	3	12	.157	.204	.275	0	0	0	0	3	0	0
Rick Anderson	15	11	1	1	0	0	0	0	0	4	.091	.091	.091	0	0	0	0	1	0	0
Bruce Berenyi	14	11	0	0	0	0	0	0	0	3	.000	.000	.000	0	0	0	0	1	0	0
Ron Darling	34	81	4	8	2	0	0	0	3	29	.099	.131	.123	0	0	0	0	10	0	0
Sid Fernandez	32	68	6	11	3	0	0	4	3	23	.162	.197	.206	1	0	2	0	6	0	0
Dwight Gooden	33	81	5	7	0	1	0	4	2	16	.086	.119	.111	0	0	3	1	13	0	0
Roger McDowell	75	18	1	5	0	0	0	3	1	4	.278	.316	.278	0	0	0	0	1	0	0
John Mitchell	4	2	0	0	0	0	0	0	0	1	.000	.000	.000	0	0	0	0	0	0	0
Randy Niemann	31	6	1	2	0	0	0	0	1	1	.333	.429	.333	0	0	0	0	0	0	0
Bob Ojeda	32	71	3	8	0	0	0	0	1	30	.113	.125	.113	0	0	0	0	8	0	0
Jesse Orosco	58	3	1	0	0	0	0	1	2	0	.000	.333	.000	0	0	0	0	0	1	0
Doug Sisk	41	4	0	0	0	0	0	0	0	2	.000	.000	.000	0	0	0	0	0	0	0
Totals	162	5558	783	1462	261	31	148	730	631	968	.263	.338	.401	118	48	122	31	75	53	68

Pitching	G	ERA	W:–L	SV	GS	GF	CG	SHO	IP	H	R	ER	HR	BB	SO	WP	HBP	BK	IBB
Rick Aguilera	28	3.88	10–7	0	20	2	2	0	141.2	145	70	61	15	36	104	5	7	3	1
Rick Anderson	15	2.72	2–1	1	5	4	0	0	49.2	45	17	15	3	11	21	1	0	1	3
Bruce Berenyi	14	6.35	2–2	0	7	2	0	0	39.2	47	30	28	5	22	30	4	1	0	0
Ron Darling	34	2.81	15–6	0	34	0	4	2	237.0	203	84	74	21	81	184	7	3	3	2
Sid Fernandez	32	3.52	16–6	1	31	1	2	1	204.1	161	82	80	13	91	200	6	2	0	1
Dwight Gooden	33	2.84	17–6	0	33	0	12	2	250.0	197	92	79	17	80	200	4	4	4	3
Terry Leach	6	2.70	0–0	0	0	1	0	0	6.2	6	3	2	0	3	4	0	0	0	0
Ed Lynch	1	0.00	0–0	0	0	0	0	0	1.2	2	0	0	0	0	1	0	0	0	0
Roger McDowell	75	3.02	14–9	22	0	52	0	0	128.0	107	48	43	4	42	65	3	3	3	5
John Mitchell	4	3.60	0–1	0	1	1	0	0	10.0	10	4	4	1	4	2	2	0	0	0
Randy Myers	10	4.22	0–0	0	0	5	0	0	10.2	11	5	5	1	9	13	0	1	0	1
Randy Niemann	31	3.79	2–3	0	1	11	0	0	35.2	44	17	15	2	12	18	2	0	0	2
Bob Ojeda	32	2.57	18–5	0	30	1	7	2	217.1	185	72	62	15	52	148	2	1	3	3
Jesse Orosco	58	2.33	8–6	21	0	40	0	0	81.0	64	23	21	6	35	62	2	3	0	3
Doug Sisk	41	3.06	4–2	1	0	15	0	0	70.2	77	31	24	0	31	31	2	5	1	5
Totals	162	3.11	108–54	46	162	135	27	11	1484.0	1304	578	513	103	509	1083	40	31	16	29

1987

NL EAST

Team	W	L	PCT	GB	BA	ERA
Cardinals	95	67	.586	—	.263	3.91
Mets	92	70	.568	3.0	.268	3.84
Expos	91	71	.562	4.0	.265	3.92
Phillies	80	82	.494	15.0	.254	4.18
Pirates	80	82	.494	15.0	.264	4.20
Cubs	76	85	.472	18.5	.264	4.55

It has been labeled one of the most disappointing seasons in Mets history. Fresh off a 108-win regular season and their second World Series championship, the 1987 Mets spent the first 3½ months chasing their own tails before they finally began to resemble a playoff contender. They were in fifth place as late as May 26 and sat 10 games behind the division-leading Cardinals on July 22.

The Mets managed to shave 8½ games off their deficit within six weeks before heading into a season-turning three-game series against the Cards at Shea Stadium in early September. The Mets were one out from pulling within a half-game of St. Louis on September 11 until Terry Pendleton ruined the late-season surge with a blast that continues to gnaw at Mets fans the way Bucky Dent's playoff homer chafes Red Sox supporters. New York was eliminated from playoff contention before its final series of the season.

But in many respects it's a miracle the Mets ever put themselves back in the playoff picture. Six starting pitchers landed on the disabled list or supplemental disabled list at some point during the season, and a seventh suffered a season-ending injury in September. Jesse Orosco muddled through his worst year as a Met while co-closer Roger McDowell gave up more than one hit per inning. Darryl Strawberry was a clubhouse pariah for a few weeks, Gary Carter struggled at the plate, Keith Hernandez hit below .297 for the first time since 1978, and Wally Backman watched his average fall 70 points below his 1986 figure.

The first ominous sign happened in the fifth game of the season April 12 versus the Braves at Shea. The Mets trailed 2–1 when Dion James led off the third with a lazy fly ball to left field. It was going to be an easy catch for Kevin McReynolds until the ball hit a bird in mid-flight, causing the bird and the ball to land a few dozen feet in front of the Mets' new left fielder. Shortstop Rafael Santana grabbed the fallen bird by the wing while James stood on second with a double, three batters before Dale Murphy smashed a two-run homer. It was one of the oddest plays in the history of Shea Stadium and served as a harbinger for the rest of the season.

Team chemistry was compromised a few weeks after the Mets rode up the Canyon of Heroes. Free-agent third baseman Ray Knight was given what he considered an insulting contract offer to return to the Mets before he settled for even less money with the Orioles. Kevin Mitchell was

packaged in a trade that brought the quiet McReynolds to New York. Knight and Mitchell were two of the toughest individuals on the title team and would be sorely missed while the Mets were sleep-walking through the first half of the season.

Losing Knight and Mitchell meant having McReynolds and Howard Johnson in the everyday lineup. McReynolds played as advertised, flashing an outstanding glove and smart base-running while hitting .276 with 29 homers and 95 RBIs. Johnson had his breakout year as the starting third baseman, crushing 36 home runs and stealing 32 bases while hitting .265 with 99 RBIs.

But the team lacked the competitive edge it had demonstrated time and again in 1987. The Mets led the National League with a .268 average and set a club record with 192 home runs, but they also batted just .237 with two out and runners in scoring position.

The pitching was in big trouble even before the season began. Dwight Gooden rocked the Mets' world when he was given a 60-day suspension following a positive test for cocaine. He was ordered into rehab and didn't pitch until June 5. By the time Gooden made his season debut, starters Rick Aguilera, Bob Ojeda, and newcomer David Cone already had landed on the DL during the first two months. Sid Fernandez and Ron Darling would be sidelined later in the year, and McDowell opened the season on the disabled list.

Darling opened the season as the de facto staff ace, a position for which he soon learned he was unsuited. Darling was brutal during Gooden's absence, going 2–4 with a 5.58 ERA in 71 innings. New York won just five of his 12 starts before Gooden returned.

Things got so bad that general manager Frank Cashen coaxed Tom Seaver out of retirement. The 42-year-old Seaver had nothing left and abandoned his comeback attempt after 16 days, forcing Cashen and manager Davey Johnson to consider many, many other options.

The Mets went through 12 starting pitchers, including Terry Leach, John Mitchell, Jeff Innis, Don Schulze, Tom Edens, and late-season pickup John Candelaria. Only Leach came close to supplying what Mets fans had grown accustom to in 1986, and even he came down with an injury.

Leach became the first Met to open a season with 10 straight wins. He started the year at Tidewater and joined the Mets' bullpen before joining the rotation June 1. He was 8–0 with a 2.08 ERA by July 11 and likely would have been an All-Star if not for a cartilage tear in his right knee.

There were only 11 days during the season in which Gooden, Darling, Fernandez, Ojeda, and Aguilera were available at the same time—September 1 through September 11. The quintet combined to go 53–31, led by Gooden's 15–7 mark. But their collective ERA spiked to 3.77 after they compiled a 3.05 ERA in 1986. Four Mets worked over 200 innings in '86; Darling was the only Met to crack 200 innings in 1987.

The team also survived some midseason shenanigans by Strawberry, who still managed to accumulate what was one of his three best major league seasons. The right fielder was chronically late for batting practice and drew the ire of his teammates by begging out of the starting lineup one night due to illness. Strawberry claimed he was unable to play because of the flu, although he was healthy enough to cut a rap record earlier in the day. Mazzilli and Backman went public concerning their displeasure with Strawberry, and Darryl threatened to punch out the diminutive Backman.

Strawberry, who hit .370 with five homers and 15 RBIs in the Mets' first eight games, batted only .252 over the next 71 contests. But he was arguably the team's best performer after July 7, hitting .303 with 19 home runs, 56 RBIs, 24 stolen bases, and 60 runs scored in his 75 contests.

HoJo was a revelation, playing just the way the Mets envisioned when they acquired him from Detroit in the winter of 1984. Playing third on an everyday basis for the first time as a Met, Johnson batted .268 with 33 homers, 87 RBIs, and 27 steals in his final 131 games. He became the first Met to join the 30–30 club on September 11, 10 days before Strawberry earned membership.

The bullpen, often considered the backbone of the staff in 1986, was wildly inconsistent the following year and only got worse when Leach was forced to join the rotation.

Although it might be unfair, the season can be encapsulated by three huge gopher balls allowed by Orosco and McDowell, who went 10–14 with 41 saves and a 4.29 ERA

after going 22–15 with 43 saves and a 3.06 earned run average for the World Series champs.

Orosco blew leads in the ninth and 10th innings of a 12–8 loss in St. Louis on April 18, setting the tone for the season. The Mets had retaken the lead on a wild pitch in the top of the 10th, but Orosco gave it back when Tom Pagnozzi hit an RBI single. Orosco was one out from ending the threat until Tom Herr launched a walk-off grand slam that put the Cards in a first-place tie with the Mets at 6–4.

The most memorable blast came off Pendleton's bat against McDowell on September 11. Everything was going right for the Mets at that point. The Cardinals had managed just one hit through eight innings and trailed 4–1 after McDowell retired two of the first three hitters in the ninth. Willie McGee kept St. Louis alive with an RBI single, allowing Pendleton to force extra innings with a two-run drive that landed over the fence in dead center. The Redbirds won it by scoring twice off Orosco in the 10th after Hernandez stranded the bases loaded in the bottom of the ninth. Instead of being a half-game out, the Mets were 2½ down with 22 to play.

The coup de grace occurred in Philadelphia on September 26, just before the Mets were scheduled to fly to St. Louis for a season-ending three-game series. Orosco entered a 3–3 tie in the bottom of the 10th after Gooden had retired his final nine batters. Orosco got the leadoff hitter before serving up a game-winning homer by pinch-hitter Luis Aguayo. The devasting loss put the Mets 3½ games behind the Cardinals, who wrapped up the division the next night before facing New York.

1987 Mets Statistics

Hitting

	G	AB	R	H	2B	3B	HR	RBI	BB	SO	BA	OBP	SLG	SB	CS	GDP	HP	SH	SF	IBB
Bill Almon	49	54	8	13	3	0	0	4	8	16	.241	.339	.296	1	0	0	0	0	0	0
Wally Backman	94	300	43	75	6	1	1	23	25	43	.250	.307	.287	11	3	5	0	9	1	0
Mark Carreon	9	12	0	3	0	0	0	1	1	1	.250	.308	.250	0	1	0	0	0	0	0
Gary Carter	139	523	55	123	18	2	20	83	42	73	.235	.290	.392	0	0	14	1	1	6	1
Lenny Dykstra	132	431	86	123	37	3	10	43	40	67	.285	.352	.455	27	7	1	4	4	0	3
Kevin Elster	5	10	1	4	2	0	0	1	0	1	.400	.400	.600	0	0	1	0	0	0	0
Keith Hernandez	154	587	87	170	28	2	18	89	81	104	.290	.377	.436	0	2	15	4	0	4	8
Clint Hurdle	3	3	1	1	0	0	0	0	0	1	.333	.333	.333	0	0	0	0	0	0	0
Gregg Jefferies	6	6	0	3	1	0	0	2	0	0	.500	.500	.667	0	0	0	0	0	0	0
Howard Johnson	157	554	93	147	22	1	36	99	83	113	.265	.364	.504	32	10	8	5	0	3	18
Barry Lyons	53	130	15	33	4	1	4	24	8	24	.254	.301	.392	0	0	1	2	0	3	1
Dave Magadan	85	192	21	61	13	1	3	24	22	22	.318	.386	.443	0	0	5	0	1	1	2
Lee Mazzilli	88	124	26	38	8	1	3	24	21	14	.306	.399	.460	5	3	3	0	0	3	3
Kevin McReynolds	151	590	86	163	32	5	29	95	39	70	.276	.318	.495	14	1	13	1	1	8	5
Keith Miller	25	51	14	19	2	2	0	1	2	6	.373	.407	.490	8	1	1	1	3	0	0
Randy Milligan	3	1	0	0	0	0	0	0	1	1	.000	.500	.000	0	0	0	0	0	0	0
Al Pedrique	5	6	1	0	0	0	0	0	1	2	.000	.143	.000	0	0	0	0	0	0	0
Rafael Santana	139	439	41	112	21	2	5	44	29	57	.255	.302	.346	1	1	11	1	0	1	10
Darryl Strawberry	154	532	108	151	32	5	39	104	97	122	.284	.398	.583	36	12	4	7	0	4	13
Tim Teufel	97	299	55	92	29	0	14	61	44	53	.308	.398	.545	3	2	7	2	3	2	2
Mookie Wilson	124	385	58	115	19	7	9	34	35	85	.299	.359	.455	21	6	2	2	2	1	8

Pitchers

	G	AB	R	H	2B	3B	HR	RBI	BB	SO	BA	OBP	SLG	SB	CS	GDP	HP	SH	SF	IBB
Rick Aguilera	18	40	5	9	1	0	1	3	1	17	.225	.244	.325	0	0	0	0	6	0	0
John Candelaria	3	5	0	1	0	0	0	0	0	0	.200	.200	.200	0	0	0	0	0	0	0
David Cone	21	31	0	2	1	0	0	0	0	14	.065	.094	.097	0	0	0	1	3	0	0
Ron Darling	32	65	5	8	5	0	0	4	2	22	.123	.149	.200	0	0	0	0	10	0	0
Tom Edens	2	3	0	0	0	0	0	0	0	3	.000	.000	.000	0	0	0	0	0	0	0
Sid Fernandez	29	43	2	7	1	1	0	2	1	19	.163	.178	.233	0	0	2	0	10	1	0
Dwight Gooden	25	64	4	14	0	0	0	4	1	9	.219	.227	.219	0	0	1	0	5	1	0
Jeff Innis	17	3	0	0	0	0	0	0	0	1	.000	.000	.000	0	0	0	0	0	0	0
Terry Leach	44	33	1	2	0	0	0	0	2	14	.061	.114	.061	0	0	0	0	4	0	0

Hitting	G	AB	R	H	2B	3B	HR	RBI	BB	SO	BA	OBP	SLG	SB	CS	GDP	HP	SH	SF	IBB
Roger McDowell	56	13	1	3	1	0	0	0	1	5	.231	.286	.308	0	0	0	0	0	0	0
John Mitchell	20	35	1	4	1	0	0	1	0	14	.114	.114	.143	0	0	0	0	5	0	0
Randy Myers	54	7	1	2	0	0	0	0	0	3	.286	.286	.286	0	0	0	0	0	0	0
Bob Ojeda	10	14	3	1	0	0	0	0	2	4	.071	.188	.071	0	0	0	0	0	0	0
Jesse Orosco	58	8	0	0	0	0	0	0	0	7	.000	.000	.000	0	0	0	0	1	0	0
Don Schulze	5	2	1	0	0	0	0	1	2	2	.000	.500	.000	0	0	0	0	1	0	0
Doug Sisk	55	5	0	0	0	0	0	0	0	3	.000	.000	.000	0	0	0	0	0	0	0
Gene Walter	21	1	0	0	0	0	0	0	1	0	.000	.500	.000	0	0	0	0	1	0	0
TOTAL	162	5601	823	1499	287	34	192	771	592	1012	.268	.338	.434	159	49	94	31	70	39	74

Pitching	G	ERA	W–L	SV	GS	GF	CG	SHO	IP	H	R	ER	HR	BB	SO	BF	WP	HP	BK	IBB
Rick Aguilera	18	3.60	11–3	0	17	0	1	0	115.0	124	53	46	12	33	77	494	9	3	0	2
John Candelaria	3	5.84	2–0	0	3	0	0	0	12.1	17	8	8	1	3	10	57	0	0	1	0
David Cone	21	3.71	5–6	1	13	3	1	0	99.1	87	46	41	11	44	68	420	2	5	4	1
Ron Darling	32	4.29	12–8	0	32	0	2	0	207.2	183	111	99	24	96	167	891	6	3	3	3
Tom Edens	2	6.75	0–0	0	2	0	0	0	8.0	15	6	6	2	4	4	42	2	0	0	0
Sid Fernandez	28	3.81	12–8	0	27	0	3	1	156.0	130	75	66	16	67	134	665	2	8	0	8
Bob Gibson	1	0.00	0–0	0	0	0	0	0	1.0	0	0	0	0	1	2	4	0	0	0	0
Dwight Gooden	25	3.21	15–7	0	25	0	7	3	179.2	162	68	64	11	53	148	730	1	2	1	2
Jeff Innis	17	3.16	0–1	0	1	8	0	0	25.2	29	9	9	5	4	28	109	1	1	1	1
Terry Leach	44	3.22	11–1	0	12	7	1	1	131.1	132	54	47	14	29	61	542	0	1	1	5
Roger McDowell	56	4.16	7–5	25	0	45	0	0	88.2	95	41	41	7	28	32	384	3	2	1	4
John Mitchell	20	4.11	3–6	0	19	0	1	0	111.2	124	64	51	6	36	57	493	7	2	1	3
Randy Myers	54	3.96	3–6	6	0	18	0	0	75.0	61	36	33	6	30	92	314	3	0	0	5
Bob Ojeda	10	3.88	3–5	0	7	0	0	0	46.1	45	23	20	5	10	21	192	1	0	0	1
Jesse Orosco	58	4.44	3–9	16	0	41	0	0	77.0	78	41	38	5	31	78	335	2	2	0	9
Don Schulze	5	6.23	1–2	0	4	1	0	0	21.2	24	15	15	4	6	5	91	0	1	0	0
Doug Sisk	55	3.46	3–1	3	0	17	0	0	78.0	83	38	30	5	22	37	339	2	3	0	4
Gene Walter	21	3.20	1–2	0	0	6	0	0	19.2	18	10	7	1	13	11	89	1	1	0	3
TOTAL	162	3.84	92–70	51	162	146	16	7	1454.0	1407	698	620	135	510	1032	6191	42	34	13	51

1988

NL EAST

Team	W	L	PCT	GB	BA	ERA
Mets	100	60	.625	—	.256	2.91
Pirates	85	75	.531	15.0	.247	3.47
Expos	81	81	.500	20.0	.251	3.08
Cubs	77	85	.475	24.0	.261	3.84
Cardinals	76	86	.469	25.0	.249	3.47
Phillies	65	96	.404	35.5	.239	4.14

Mets lost to Dodgers in NLCS, 4–3

The Mets have been to only one postseason in which they failed to win a single playoff round. This was the year.

The seven-game loss to the Dodgers in the NLCS left the season every bit as unfulfilling as 1984, '85, and '87. The team was expected to roll into the World Series after going 10–1 against Los Angeles during the regular season. Instead, they dropped three of the last four games in the series after earning two victories in their final at-bat.

Although the Mets won the NL East by a whopping 15 games, they never gave you that feeling of invincibility until the final five weeks of the regular season. The only regulars to match their 1987 stats were outfielders Darryl Strawberry, Mookie Wilson, and Kevin McReynolds.

Keith Hernandez played just 95 games and hit .276, missing almost seven weeks with a torn hamstring. Gary Carter hit only .242 with 11 homers and 46 RBIs in 130 games. Carter belted his 299th career home run May 16 and didn't hit another until August 11, a span of 63 games and 225 at-bats. Howard Johnson hit .230 with 24 homers, 23 steals, and 68 RBIs a year after joining the 30–30 club.

Strawberry began the season hitting .361 with six homers and 18 runs scored in April. He had 21 go-ahead hits and finished with a career-high 39 home runs for the second straight year.

Wilson managed to hit .296 in 112 games without having a set position. He started just 81 games—62 in center—due to the presence of Strawberry, McReynolds, and Len Dykstra. Mookie also was growing frustrated about his playing time and finally began to go public with his displeasure after spending most of the previous two seasons sharing center with Dykstra.

Dykstra also continued to grouse loudly about playing time, but manager Davey Johnson was able to avert a mutiny while getting solid production from his two center fielders. The duo combined to bat .276 with 14 homers, 62 RBIs, 104 runs scored, and 33 stolen bases when playing center.

McReynolds continued to play with robotic precision, which some media members would say matched his clubhouse personality. McReynolds led all Mets who qualified for the batting title with a .288 average and was second to Strawberry in homers (27) and RBIs (99). McReynolds also paced the club with 30 doubles, led all Mets outfielders with 18 assists, and was 21-for-21 in stolen base attempts.

Wally Backman hit over .300 for the second time in three years while platooning at second with Tim Teufel. Backman also compiled a .388 on-base percentage, second only to Dave Magadan among Mets with at least 300 plate appearances. Unfortunately for Backman and Magadan, their slugging averages were lower than their on-base percentages.

The Mets did not provide the same composite offensive numbers as they had in 1987, when the baseball was believed to be juiced. The '88 Mets hit .256 with 152 home runs and 703 runs scored compared to a .268 average, 192 homers, and 823 runs the previous year. However, the Mets paced the NL in homers, runs on-base percentage (.325), and slugging (.396) while finishing second in hitting. That was more than enough support for a starting rotation that managed to stay relatively healthy until after the Mets clinched the division.

New York's top five starters combined for a 77–44 record and a dazzling 2.92 ERA in 1,097⅔ innings. Dwight Gooden won 18 games, his best total since 1985. Ron Darling earned a career-high 17 victories and averaged just one walk per four innings after issuing a league-high 114 free passes in 1985, Bob Ojeda recorded a 2.88 ERA and a sparkling 1.004 WHIP. Sid Fernandez was second on the team with 189 strikeouts and led the league in fewest hits per nine innings (6⅓).

Rick Aguilera opened the season as the No. 5 starter but missed most of the season with an elbow injury that eventually required surgery. He made his first two starts before the pain forced him out of action.

Johnson and pitching coach Mel Stottlemyre filled the rotation with a kid from Kansas City who pitched to a 5–6 record for the Mets in 1987. David Cone won his first five starts and owned a 0.76 ERA in his first six starts. He also closed the season by going 8–0 with three complete games and a 1.68 ERA in his final eight starts.

Cone did more than fill Aguilera's shoes, leading the Mets in wins (20), strikeouts (213), and ERA 2.22. His .970 winning percentage led the NL and set a still-standing Mets record for pitchers with more than 175 innings.

There were changes made to the bullpen as Randy Myers replaced the departed Jesse Orosco as the lefty closer. Myers became the third Met to go over the 25-save plateau, finishing with 26 while recording a 1.72 ERA. Roger McDowell bounced back from a rather mediocre 1987 campaign, finishing with 16 saves and a 2.63 earned run average.

The season itself could be broken down into three segments; two exceptional runs sandwiching a very unimpressive one. The Mets opened by slamming six homers—two each by Strawberry and McReynolds—in a 10–6 win at Montreal. But as they did in 1986, the Mets fell to 2–3 before getting white hot. They put together a seven-game winning streak, a six-game streak, and a pair of five-gamers en route to a 30–11 record, matching their 41-game start in '86.

The next 81 games could be best described as frustrating and almost coincided with Hernandez's absence and Carter's power drought. The pitching allowed only 665 hits and compiled a 3.10 ERA in 82 games from May 24 to August 21. But the offense provided just 66 homers and a .246 average while scoring just 3.9 runs per game. New York went just 41–41 during that span, prompting GM Frank Cashen to summon Tidewater for an infusion of young talent.

Gregg Jefferies was the most highly touted Mets prospect since Strawberry and was exactly what ailed the team's offense after the Pirates climbed within 3½ games of the NL East lead. The lead had grown to 6½ games when Jefferies made his Mets season debut August 28 in San Francisco, going 2-for-5 with a double and a run scored.

Jefferies had a .462 batting average, five homers, 10 RBIs, and 13 runs scored in his first 13 games while spending most of that time at second base. He ended the year as the Mets' starting third baseman, which forced Howard Johnson to play short and put Kevin Elster on the bench.

Wherever Davey Johnson played Jefferies, someone was going to be ticked off. Jefferies cut into Backman's playing time and weakened the infield defense when he forced Howard Johnson to shortstop. But he looked like a tremendous, natural hitter, particularly after he went 15-for-25 (.600) in six games from September 6 through September 12.

The problem was, few people on the team could stand him. That would become a major issue in 1989, when Jefferies brooded his way through a .258 season.

The Mets closed the season with a strong charge, winning 29 of their final 37 games to finish 15 games ahead of the Pirates. The A's were the only other team to play .700 during that stretch, and they were expected to face the Mets in the World Series.

But then Ojeda decided to do a little gardening. Ojeda had been the hard-luck starter on the staff, tying a career high with five shutouts but sporting a 10–13 record when he clipped his middle finger with hedge clippers on September 21.

The injury wasn't expected to be a deterrent in the championship series, but it was felt mightily during Game 5. Fellow lefty Sid Fernandez was pounded over four-plus innings of a 7–4 loss to the Dodgers at Shea, which gave Los Angeles a 3–2 lead in the series. Ojeda would have been the likely starter in that game and might have halted the Dodgers' momentum gathered from their Game 4 comeback against Gooden.

The Mets were within three outs of taking a 3–1 series lead when Gooden served up a game-tying, two-run homer to Mike Scioscia, altering the course of the series.

Orel Hershiser ended the Mets' season by tossing a five-hit shutout in Game 7. The Mets wouldn't return to the postseason again until Hershiser helped them win the 1999 wild-card.

1988 Mets Statistics

Hitting	G	AB	R	H	2B	3B	HR	RBI	BB	SO	BA	OBP	SLG	SB	CS	GDP	HP	SH	SF	IBB
Wally Backman	99	294	44	89	12	0	0	17	41	49	.303	.388	.344	9	5	6	1	9	2	1
Mark Carreon	7	9	5	5	2	0	1	1	2	1	.556	.636	1.111	0	0	0	0	0	0	0
Gary Carter	130	455	39	110	16	2	11	46	34	52	.242	.301	.358	0	2	8	7	1	6	1
Lenny Dykstra	126	429	57	116	19	3	8	33	30	43	.270	.321	.385	30	8	3	3	2	2	2
Kevin Elster	149	406	41	87	11	1	9	37	35	47	.214	.282	.313	2	0	5	3	6	0	12
Keith Hernandez	95	348	43	96	16	0	11	55	31	57	.276	.333	.417	2	1	11	1	0	4	3
Gregg Jefferies	29	109	19	35	8	2	6	17	8	10	.321	.364	.596	5	1	1	0	0	1	0
Howard Johnson	148	495	85	114	21	1	24	68	86	104	.230	.343	.422	23	7	6	3	2	8	25
Barry Lyons	50	91	5	21	7	1	0	11	3	12	.231	.253	.330	0	0	3	0	3	1	0
Dave Magadan	112	314	39	87	15	0	1	35	60	39	.277	.393	.334	0	1	9	2	1	3	4
Lee Mazzilli	68	116	9	17	2	0	0	12	12	16	.147	.227	.164	4	1	3	1	0	3	0
Kevin McReynolds	147	552	82	159	30	2	27	99	38	56	.288	.336	.496	21	0	6	4	1	5	3
Keith Miller	40	70	9	15	1	1	1	5	6	10	.214	.276	.300	0	5	1	0	3	0	0
Mackey Sasser	60	12	9	35	10	1	1	17	6	9	.285	.313	.407	0	0	4	0	0	2	4
Darryl Strawberry	153	543	101	146	27	3	39	101	85	127	.269	.366	.545	29	14	6	3	0	9	21
Tim Teufel	90	273	35	64	20	0	4	31	29	41	.234	.306	.352	0	1	6	1	2	4	1
Mookie Wilson	112	378	61	112	17	5	8	41	27	63	.296	.345	.431	15	4	12	2	1	2	2
Pitchers																				
Rick Aguilera	11	4	1	1	0	0	0	0	0	1	.250	.250	.250	0	0	0	0	0	0	0
David Cone	35	80	2	12	3	0	0	2	3	14	.150	.181	.188	0	1	0	0	5	0	0
Ron Darling	34	82	4	18	4	2	0	4	1	21	.220	.229	.317	0	0	1	0	9	0	0
Sid Fernandez	31	56	1	14	2	0	0	9	5	14	.250	.308	.286	0	0	2	1	7	3	0
Dwight Gooden	34	90	8	16	1	0	1	9	1	18	.178	.185	.222	0	0	1	0	9	1	0
Terry Leach	52	14	1	2	1	0	0	3	0	9	.143	.143	.214	0	0	0	0	0	0	0
Roger McDowell	63	9	1	3	3	0	0	2	0	5	.333	.333	.667	0	0	0	0	0	0	0
John Mitchell	1	1	0	0	0	0	0	0	0	0	.000	.000	.000	0	0	0	0 0	0	0	0
Randy Myers	55	4	1	1	1	0	0	1	0	2	.250	.250	.500	0	0	0	0	0	0	0
Bob Ojeda	30	61	0	10	1	0	0	3	1	22	.164	.177	.180	0	0	0	0	'4	0	0
David West	2	2	1	2	1	0	0	0	0	0	1.000	1.000	1.500	0	0	0	0	0	0	0
TOTALS	160	5408	703	1387	251	24	152	659	544	842	.256	.324	.396	140	51	94	32	65	56	79

Pitching	G	ERA	W:–L	SV	GS	GF	CG	SHO	IP	H	R	ER	HR	BB	SO	BFP	WP	HBP	BK	IBB
Rick Aguilera	11	6.93	0–4	0	3	2	0	0	24.2	29	20	19	2	10	16	111	1	1	1	2
David Cone	35	2.22	20–3	0	28	0	8	4	231.1	178	67	57	10	80	213	936	10	4	10	7
Ron Darling	34	3.25	17–9	0	34	0	7	4	240.2	218	97	87	24	60	161	971	7	5	2	2
Sid Fernandez	31	3.03	12–10	0	31	0	1	1	187.0	127	69	63	15	70	189	751	4	6	9	1
Dwight Gooden	34	3.19	18–9	0	34	0	10	3	248.1	242	98	88	8	57	175	1024	5	6	5	4
Jeff Innis	12	1.89	1–1	0	0	7	0	0	19.0	19	6	4	0	2	14	80	0	0	0	1
Terry Leach	52	2.54	7–2	3	0	21	0	0	92.0	95	32	26	5	24	51	392	0	3	0	4
Bob McClure	14	4.09	1–0	1	0	5	0	0	11.0	12	5	5	1	2	7	46	1	1	0	0
Roger McDowell	62	2.63	5–5	16	0	41	0	0	89.0	80	31	26	1	31	46	378	6	3	1	7
John Mitchell	1	0.00	0–0	0	0	0	0	0	1.0	2	0	0	0	1	1	5	0	0	0	0
Randy Myers	55	1.72	7–3	26	0	44	0	0	68.0	45	15	13	5	17	69	261	2	2	0	2
Edwin Nunez	10	4.50	1–0	0	0	4	0	0	14.0	21	7	7	1	3	8	65	1	0	0	0
Bob Ojeda	29	2.88	10–13	0	29	0	5	5	190.1	158	74	61	6	33	133	752	4	4	7	2
Gene Walter	19	3.78	0–1	0	0	5	0	0	16.2	21	9	7	0	11	14	80	0	0	3	1
David West	2	3.00	1–0	0	1	0	0	0	6.0	6	2	2	0	3	3	25	0	0	2	0
TOTALS	160	2.91	100–60	46	160	129	31	22	1439.0	1253	532	465	78	404	1100	5877	41	35	40	33

1989

NL EAST

Team	W	L	PCT	GB	BA	ERA
Cubs	93	69	.574	—	.261	3.43
Mets	87	75	.537	6.0	.246	3.29
Cardinals	86	76	.531	7.0	.258	3.36
Expos	81	81	.500	12.0	.247	3.48
Pirates	74	88	.457	19.0	.241	3.64
Phillies	67	95	.414	26.0	.243	4.04

The 1989 final standings show the Mets finished second for the fourth time in six seasons, just six games behind the Cubs. They never fell more than seven games back and were within 1½ games of the division lead as late as August 21.

But in many respects the Mets never truly seemed to be in the division race with the same zeal they showed in 1984, '85, and '87. Any time they came close to first place,

the Cubs would stage a winning streak to pull away. The Mets never held sole possession of the division lead after May 21 and spent almost as many days in fourth place as first.

There were numerous reasons for the air of vulnerability, beginning with three of their stars from 1986.

Knee injuries caught up to Gary Carter, who was finally unable to play through the searing pain and was on the disabled list from May 12 to July 25. Carter was batting .114 and hearing an inordinate amount of boos before he opted for surgery. He hit .290 in 22 games over the final two months to raise his average to a career-worst .183.

Keith Hernandez also spent nearly two months on the disabled list and appeared in just 75 games, his fewest since 1975. Hernandez batted only .233 with 19 RBIs in 215 at-bats after entering the season with a .300 career average. His hitting woes actually began in 1988, when he compiled a .234 average in his final 38 games.

Dwight Gooden was on the disabled list from July 2 to September 2 after getting off to an excellent start. He was 9–2 with a 2.56 ERA and 90 strikeouts in 105⅓ innings following a 5–3 win over the Expos on June 19. He lasted a total of six innings over his next two starts before he was diagnosed with a small tear in the back of his throwing shoulder.

The center field situation was a mess by the end of the season. Len Dykstra and Mookie Wilson weren't too happy about sharing the position, and hadn't been since 1985. Both players had legitimate reasons for believing they should start every game.

General manager Frank Cashen did Dykstra a favor by shipping him and reliever Roger McDowell to the Phillies for Juan Samuel on June 18. But Wilson still found himself on the bench after Samuel was anointed the new center fielder.

The deal was among the three worst in Cashen's tenure with the Mets. Samuel himself hated the trade, hated playing center field, and hated being in New York, where fans quickly got on his case. He stole 28 bases but otherwise played poorly as a Met, batting .228 with 28 RBIs in 86 games.

Wilson stuck around until July 31, when he and his .205 average were dealt to the Blue Jays for reliever Jeff Musselman and minor leaguer Mike Brady. Mookie hit .298 in 54 games the rest of the season, making his departure among Cashen's worst moves.

If center field was the Mets' most puzzling position, second base ran a close second. Gregg Jefferies was given the job when Wally Backman was traded to the Twins during the winter, a move that was very unpopular within the clubhouse. Backman—like Ray Knight and Kevin Mitchell before him—was a tough-minded player whose personality would be missed by the Mets.

Jefferies was the anti-Backman, a naturally gifted athlete who would brood during his extended batting slumps. Jefferies looked as uncomfortable on the field as he did at the plate, demonstrating an inability to turn a double play when he wasn't having trouble with popups and grounders.

Jefferies became a very unpopular player in the clubhouse. He insisted on having his bats packed separately from the rest of the team equipment, which led McDowell to saw off Jefferies bats early in the season. Players also were turned off by his helmet-throwing and relative immaturity.

Jefferies also didn't help his cause by carrying a puny .230 average into the All-Star break after being touted as the future of the Mets.

Jefferies wasn't the only player embroiled in clubhouse turmoil. Hernandez and Darryl Strawberry had a public fight during the team photo shoot in spring training. The two made up the following day, but the brawl signaled that Strawberry wasn't going to take any more of Hernandez's criticism distributed through the media.

Strawberry had his worst season as a Met, batting .225 with 29 homers and 77 RBIs in 134 games. He was no longer the Mets' most feared hitter by the end of the season. That distinction belonged to Howard Johnson, who was making a habit out of producing his best seasons in odd-numbered years.

Johnson was a 30–30 man for the second time in three seasons and fell just four homers shy of becoming a 40–40 player. HoJo led the Mets in batting (.287), hits (164), doubles (41), homers (36), RBIs (101), runs scored (104), walks (77), steals (41), on-base percentage (.369), and slugging (.559). He also tied for first with three triples and was the only Met with more than 245 total bases (319).

But there wasn't enough support around Johnson to compliment a pitching staff that finished second in the NL with a 3.30 ERA. McReynolds hit a respectable .272 with 22 homers and 85 RBIs, but all three figures were below his 1987 and '88 stats. Dave Magadan hit .286 and smacked just four homers in 127 games while playing the power positions in the infield. Kevin Elster was outstanding at shortstop but mediocre at the plate, hitting .231 with 55 RBIs.

The Mets got very good starting pitching, although no one had more than 14 victories. Sid Fernandez was the team's most successful starter, tying for the team lead in wins and finishing with a league-best .737 winning percentage at 14–5. El Sid also was ninth in the NL with a 2.83 ERA, third with 198 strikeouts and second with 6.52 hits allowed per nine innings.

David Cone and Ron Darling also finished with 14 victories, one more than Bob Ojeda. Ojeda managed to go 13–11 with two shutouts and a 3.47 ERA less than a year after nearly severing the tip of his left middle finger in a hedge-trimming accident at home.

The bullpen was a conundrum, recording a 2.96 earned run average but only 38 saves and an 18–25 record. Rick Aguilera became the right-handed closer to complement the lefty Randy Myers, who was 7–4 with 24 saves and a 2.35 ERA. Once McDowell was shipped to Philadelphia, the setup men consisted of journeyman Don Aase and rookie Jeff Innis until Musselman arrived in August.

The bullpen was sacrificed when Cashen tried to bolster the rotation at the trade deadline. Cashen acquired reigning AL Cy Young Award winner Frank Viola from the Twins on July 31, shortly after New York absorbed a three-game sweep at Wrigley Field to fall six games off the pace. But the trade cost the Mets Aguilera, who would become one of the American League's top closers.

The Mets took off immediately after acquiring Viola, winning 15 of 19 to pull within striking distance of Chicago. But New York never put together another winning streak longer than three games until they were eliminated from playoff contention.

The Mets finished 87–75, the first time since 1983 they had failed to win at least 90 games. Outside of Johnson, there was little personal achievement from the ballclub as it continued to find frustrating ways to fritter away a very winnable division.

Nearly every one of Cashen's roster moves seemed to backfire. Dykstra became a three-time All-Star with the Phillies and an MVP runner-up before a back injury caused him to retire prematurely. Aguilera went to consecutive All-Star Games and averaged 34 saves during his five full seasons in Minnesota. Wilson hit .267 in 287 games as a Blue Jay while the Mets were spending time and money seeking a permanent center fielder. And McDowell picked up 19 saves and compiled a 1.11 ERA in 56⅔ innings for the Phils in '89.

The front office also began to turn the screws on Davey Johnson, who by now was the winningest manager in team history. Johnson was being blamed for everything from Strawberry's season-long slump to Jefferies' poor rookie season. He also was accused of losing control of the team by treating his players in the same manner they were treated from 1984 through 1988.

But there were too many internal negatives for Johnson to guide the Mets to a playoff berth. Things would only get worse by the time Johnson was replaced just 42 games into the 1990 season.

1989 Mets Statistics

Hitting	G	AB	R	H	2B	3B	HR	RBI	BB	SO	BA	OBP	SLG	SB	CS	GDP	HP	SH	SF	IBB
Mark Carreon	68	133	20	41	6	0	6	16	12	17	.308	.370	.489	2	3	1	1	0	0	0
Gary Carter	50	153	14	28	8	0	2	15	12	15	.183	.241	.275	0	0	5	0	0	1	0
Lenny Dykstra	56	159	27	43	12	1	3	13	23	15	.270	.362	.415	13	1	2	2	4	4	0
Kevin Elster	151	458	52	106	25	2	10	55	34	77	.231	.283	.360	4	3	13	2	6	8	11
Keith Hernandez	75	215	18	50	8	0	4	19	27	39	.233	.324	.326	0	3	4	2	0	0	3
Gregg Jefferies	141	508	72	131	28	2	12	56	39	46	.258	.314	.392	21	6	16	5	2	5	8
Howard Johnson	153	571	104	164	41	3	36	101	77	126	.287	.369	.559	41	8	4	1	0	6	8
Phil Lombardi	18	48	4	11	1	0	1	3	5	8	.229	.302	.313	0	0	2	0	0	0	0
Barry Lyons	79	235	15	58	13	0	3	27	11	28	.247	.283	.340	0	1	7	2	1	3	1
Dave Magadan	127	374	47	107	22	3	4	41	49	37	.286	.367	.393	1	0	2	1	1	4	6
Lee Mazzilli	48	60	10	11	2	0	2	7	17	19	.183	.364	.317	3	0	1	0	0	0	0
Jeff McKnight	6	12	2	3	0	0	0	0	2	1	.250	.357	.250	0	0	1	0	0	0	0
Kevin McReynolds	148	545	74	148	25	3	22	85	46	74	.272	.326	.450	15	7	8	1	0	7	10
Keith Miller	57	143	15	33	7	0	1	7	5	27	.231	.262	.301	6	0	3	1	3	0	0
Tom O'Malley	9	11	2	6	2	0	0	8	0	2	.545	.545	.727	0	0	0	0	0	0	0
Juan Samuel	86	333	37	76	13	1	3	28	24	75	.228	.299	.300	31	9	5	10	2	1	1
Mackey Sasser	72	182	17	53	14	2	1	22	7	15	.291	.316	.407	0	1	3	0	1	1	4
Craig Shipley	4	7	3	1	0	0	0	0	0	1	.143	.143	.143	0	0	0	0	0	0	0
Darryl Strawberry	134	476	69	107	26	1	29	77	61	105	.225	.312	.466	11	4	4	1	0	3	13
Tim Teufel	83	219	27	56	7	2	2	15	32	50	.256	.350	.333	1	3	4	1	0	2	1
Lou Thornton	13	13	5	4	1	0	0	1	0	1	.308	.308	.385	2	0	0	0	0	0	0
Mookie Wilson	80	249	22	51	10	1	3	18	10	47	.205	.237	.289	7	4	0	1	0	2	3
Pitchers																				
Don Aase	49	5	0	0	0	0	0	0	0	3	.000	.000	.000	0	0	0	0	0	0	0
Rick Aguilera	36	7	1	0	0	0	0	0	1	2	.000	.125	.000	0	0	0	0	0	0	0
Blaine Beatty	2	2	0	1	0	0	0	0	0	0	.500	.500	.500	0	0	0	0	0	0	0
David Cone	34	77	9	18	2	0	0	4	2	13	.234	.253	.260	0	0	1	0	6	0	0
Ron Darling	35	73	8	9	1	0	2	5	1	28	.123	.147	.219	0	0	0	1	5	0	0
Sid Fernandez	35	71	2	15	3	0	1	8	1	25	.211	.233	.296	0	0	0	1	10	0	0
Dwight Gooden	19	40	1	8	3	0	0	1	0	7	.200	.195	.275	0	0	1	0	3	1	0
Jeff Innis	29	2	0	0	0	0	0	0	0	0	.000	.000	.000	0	0	0	0	0	0	0
Terry Leach	10	4	0	0	0	0	0	0	0	3	.000	.000	.000	0	0	0	0	0	0	0
Roger McDowell	25	2	0	1	0	0	0	0	0	0	.500	.500	.500	0	0	0	0	0	0	0
Jeff Musselman	20	0	0	0	0	0	0	0	1	0	1.000	1.000	1.000	0	0	0	0	0	0	0
Randy Myers	65	5	0	0	0	0	0	0	0	3	.000	.000	.000	0	0	0	0	0	0	0
Bob Ojeda	32	66	3	7	0	0	0	0	3	14	.106	.145	.106	0	0	0	0	6	0	0
Kevin Tapani	3	2	0	0	0	0	0	0	0	1	.000	.000	.000	0	0	0	0	0	0	0
Frank Viola	12	23	2	3	0	0	0	1	1	7	.130	.167	.130	0	0	0	0	5	0	0
David West	11	5	0	1	0	0	0	0	0	2	.200	.200	.200	0	0	0	0	0	0	0
Wally Whitehurst	9	1	1	0	0	0	0	0	1	1	.000	.500	.000	0	0	0	0	1	0	0
TOTAL	162	5489	683	1351	280	21	147	633	504	934	.246	.310	.385	158	53	87	33	56	48	69

Pitching	G	ERA	W–L	SV	GS	GF	CG	SHO	IP	H	R	ER	HR	BB	SO	BFP	WP	HBP	BK	IBB
Don Aase	49	3.94	1–5	2	0	22	0	0	59.1	56	27	26	5	26	34	261	0	1	1	3
Rick Aguilera	36	2.34	6–6	7	0	19	0	0	69.1	59	19	18	3	21	80	284	3	2	3	3
Blaine Beatty	2	1.50	0–0	0	1	0	0	0	6.0	5	1	1	1	2	3	25	0	0	0	0
David Cone	34	3.52	14–8	0	33	0	7	2	219.2	183	92	86	20	74	190	910	14	4	4	6
Ron Darling	33	3.52	14–14	0	33	0	4	0	217.1	214	100	85	19	70	153	922	12	3	4	7
Sid Fernandez	35	2.83	14–5	0	32	0	6	2	219.1	157	73	69	21	75	198	883	1	6	3	3
Dwight Gooden	19	2.89	9–4	1	17	1	0	0	118.1	93	42	38	9	47	101	497	7	2	5	2
Manny Hernandez	1	0.00	0–0	0	0	0	0	0	1.0	0	0	0	0	0	1	3	0	0	0	0
Jeff Innis	29	3.18	0–1	0	0	12	0	0	39.2	38	16	14	2	8	16	160	0	1	0	0
Terry Leach	10	4.22	0–0	0	0	4	0	0	21.1	19	11	10	1	4	2	85	0	1	0	0
Julio Machado	10	3.27	0–1	0	0	9	0	0	11.0	9	4	4	0	3	14	45	0	0	0	0
Roger McDowell	25	3.31	1–5	4	0	15	0	0	35.1	34	21	13	1	16	15	156	3	2	1	3
John Mitchell	2	6.00	0–1	0	0	0	0	0	3.0	3	7	2	0	4	4	17	1	0	0	1
Jeff Musselman	20	3.08	3–2	0	0	4	0	0	26.1	27	11	9	1	14	11	119	1	0	0	3
Randy Myers	65	2.35	7–4	24	0	47	0	0	84.1	62	23	22	4	40	88	349	3	0	0	4

Pitching (continued)	G	ERA	W: L	SV	GS	GF	CG	SHO	IP	H	R	ER	HR	BB	SO	BFP	WP	HBP	BK	IBB
Bob Ojeda	31	3.47	13–11	0	31	0	5	2	192.0	179	83	74	16	78	95	824	0	2	2	5
Kevin Tapani	3	3.68	0–0	0	0	1	0	0	7.1	5	3	3	1	4	2	31	0	0	1	0
Frank Viola	12	3.38	5–5	0	12	0	2	1	85.1	75	35	32	5	27	73	351	3	1	0	3
David West	11	7.40	0–2	0	2	0	0	0	24.1	25	20	20	4	14	19	112	1	1	0	2
Wally Whitehurst	9	4.50	0–1	0	1	4	0	0	14.0	17	7	7	2	5	9	64	1	0	0	0
TOTAL	162	3.29	87–75	38	162	138	24	12	1454.0	1260	595	532	115	532	1108	6098	50	26	24	45

1990

NL EAST

Team	W	L	PCT	GB	BA	ERA
Pirates	95	67	.586	---	.259	3.40
Mets	91	71	.562	4.0	.256	3.42
Expos	85	77	.525	10.0	.250	3.37
Cubs	77	85	.475	18.0	.263	4.34
Phillies	77	85	.475	18.0	.255	4.07
Cardinals	70	92	.432	25.0	.256	3.87

As the Mets gathered for 1990 spring training, no one could have envisioned that this would be their last serious run at a division title until the end of the decade.

The rotation still featured Dwight Gooden, Ron Darling, Sid Fernandez, David Cone, and Bob Ojeda. They also had Frank Viola, who was entering his first full season with the team after being acquired at the 1989 non-waiver trade deadline. No team had as deep a rotation, but the number of competent starters eventually became a problem.

The bullpen had a new closer. Randy Myers was traded to the Reds for fellow lefty John Franco, who averaged 34 saves from 1987 to 1989. No Met had ever had more than 31 saves in a season, and Myers topped out at 26.

The Mets allowed Keith Hernandez and Gary Carter to sign elsewhere after both veterans spent about two months on the disabled list in '89. Mike Marshall was picked up from the Dodgers to replace Hernandez, and Mackey Sasser eventually emerged as Carter's successor behind the plate.

In addition to Marshall, the Mets still had Darryl Strawberry, Howard Johnson, and Kevin McReynolds at the heart of the order. But the rest of the lineup was rather questionable heading into Opening Day. The Mets were banking on Gregg Jefferies hitting better than his .258 average from last season. Kevin Elster was back at shortstop, but his .223 lifetime average didn't exactly worry opposing pitchers.

The Mets also had to trade Juan Samuel after he asked to be dealt as per the parameters of his contract. That left the team without a bona fide center fielder after the team jettisoned Len Dykstra, Mookie Wilson, and Lee Mazzilli during the 1989 campaign.

Keith Miller was asked to take over at center, a position he had played just 10 times previously. Miller was the quintessential team player who would have sold hot dogs between innings if asked. He was more than willing to learn how to play center, especially if it meant more at-bats.

Although the lineup wasn't exactly what Mets fans had grown accustomed to in the 1980s, the pitching looked

good enough to spark a playoff run if the defense held up. The Cubs had come from nowhere to win the 1989 NL East crown, the Cardinals were coming off a down year, the Phillies had pitching questions, and the Expos were coming off a .500 season.

The Pirates were just lying in the weeds. They showed promise in 1988 by giving the Mets a scare during the summer months before falling well off the pace. The Bucs never contended in 1989 and were believed to be another year away from challenging for a playoff berth. That left many believing the Mets were the team to beat if everything fell into place. That never happened.

It took nine innings to realize the Mets could be in trouble. The Pirates hit three homers, three doubles, and a triple while pounding out a 12–3 rout in the season opener at Shea. The bullpen was hit hard after Gooden was reached for five runs in 4⅔ innings. The Mets homered twice but were held to just one hit over the final seven innings. The game also featured two errors by Jefferies and a misplayed fly ball by Miller. Like many fly balls hit to center, Miller was in over his head.

The Mets found a solution by acquiring Daryl Boston off the White Sox's waiver wire at the end of April. He was a sure-handed center fielder who had exceptional talent but fell into disfavor with manager Jeff Torborg. Boston hit .288 in his first 20 games with the Mets while solidifying the outfield.

Marshall quickly proved he wasn't the answer at first base. He homered and drove in six runs against the Dodgers May 22 but finished the month with a .227 average and was on pace for a 12-homer season. He started just three games for the Mets after lifting his average to .255 on June 11.

Marshall was replaced by Magadan, who was finally given a chance to play regularly after three seasons as a caddy for Hernandez and Howard Johnson. Magadan challenged for the NL batting title and recorded what was then the second-highest batting average in team history.

Jefferies looked liked the player the Mets expected he'd be when they gave him the starting second base job in 1989. He was hitting .302 by June 1 and showing some defensive improvement, although he couldn't pull the Mets out of their early season tailspin.

The noose was already hanging over manager Davey Johnson when he assembled his team in spring training. Johnson was the first manager to lead the Mets to multiple postseason berths, but he came under fire as the team played through a lackluster 87–75 season in 1989. The Mets opened the '90 season by losing six of nine and never climbed more than two games over .500 during the

Darryl Strawberry hits one of his eight September 1990 home runs to beat the St. Louis Cardinals 10–8.

first seven weeks of the season despite Viola, who won his first seven starts.

Gooden and Fernandez opened the year 3–4, Cone and Ojeda were 1–3, and Darling was 1–4 out of the bullpen before Johnson was dismissed May 29. Johnson left as the team's all-time winningest manager at 595–417.

Johnson was replaced by Bud Harrelson, a fan favorite during his playing career. Harrelson had been part of Johnson's coaching staff since 1985 but had never managed higher than the low minors before taking over the Mets.

New York dropped four of its first five games under Harrelson, putting the team 8½ games behind the first-place Pirates on June 4. The Mets were tied for first by June 28, thanks to a team record-tying 11-game winning streak that included a pair of series sweeps against the Cardinals. The streak was part of a 32-game stretch in which the Mets went 27–5. They hit .307 with 50 homers while averaging a whopping 6.7 runs, allowing the pitching staff to hide its mediocre 3.80 ERA.

Two of the offensive catalysts were a pair of unlikely suspects. Magadan batted .384 and recorded a .470 on-base percentage during the team's 32-game run, providing 22 RBIs and scoring 29 times. Mags posted a .512 average in 43 at-bats during his season-high 11-game hitting streak from June 10 through June 22, allowing the Mets to dump Marshall. Magadan carried a .355 average into the All-Star break and was making Mets fans miss Hernandez less and less.

Sasser was just as impressive, hitting .378 with 15 RBIs and 16 runs scored during the hot stretch while taking over the starting catching job from Barry Lyons. Sasser was batting .336 for the season and was touted as an All-Star candidate before he suffered a severe ankle sprain while tagging out Jim Presley in Atlanta on July 8. The ankle, along with an injured right elbow, limited him to just 31 starts in the Mets' final 84 games.

The true offensive star was Strawberry, who was in the final year of his contract and in somewhat contentious negotiations with the Mets. Strawberry opened the year with a .247 average before taking off, hitting .377 with 16 home runs, 39 RBIs, and 32 runs in 36 games from June 1 through July 13. He was on pace for a 46-homer season through 81 games before his average slowly drifted downward. But Darryl was one of the club's better hitters in September, belting eight homers and driving in 23 games while batting .278 before missing the final six games.

Gooden was winning games despite failing to display his overpowering form. "Doc" was just 3–5 with a 4.44 ERA in his first 12 starts before getting hot around the same time the Mets did. Gooden went 8–0 with a 2.96 in nine starts from June 12 through July 29 on his way to a 19-win season, the second-most in his career. However, his 3.83 ERA was more than a run per game higher than his career earned run average heading into the season.

Viola was the most consistent starter and the lone bright spot while the Mets were stinking up the joint during the first two months. He opened the season winning his first seven starts while recording a 0.87 ERA. His earned run average never rose above 2.79 as he became the fifth Met to win 20 games.

Cone was third on the team with 14 wins and led the Mets with 233 strikeouts, 10 more than Gooden. Cone also had the second-lowest ERA among starters at 3.23.

Fernandez was victimized by incredibly poor run support. The Mets averaged just 1.79 runs in his 14 team-high 14 losses and were held under four runs in four of his seven no-decisions. New York went just 11–19 in his 30 starts.

Darling and Ojeda were shuttled in and out of the bullpen while serving as a two-headed fifth starter. Johnson and Harrelson usually altered his rotation if Darling or Ojeda had consecutive bad starts.

Besides Franco, the bullpen was rather spotty. Franco set a club record with 33 saves and went 5–3 with a 2.53 ERA. Ojeda was outstanding in middle relief, recording a 2.19 ERA in 49⅓ innings. But it was hit or miss anytime Darling, Alejandro Pena, and Jeff Musselman came on to pitch.

The Mets were in first place by Labor Day following a seven-game winning streak that was prodded by several newcomers. Veterans Tom Herr, Charlie O'Brien, and Pat Tabler were contributors to the streak while adding bench depth after Mark Carreon went down with a season-ending knee injury on August 20. Carreon finished with 10 homers despite only 188 at-bats.

Things looked good until the offense completely shut down in a five-game losing streak that put them 3½ games behind Pittsburgh by September 7. The skid began with four consecutive losses to left-handed starters as Joe Magrane, Zane Smith, Neal Heaton, and Randy Tomlin held the Mets to a grand total of two runs.

The streak continued when right-handed Jose DeJesus beat Cone 4–1, one day after the Pirates completed a three-game sweep. But opposing managers took notice of the Mets' problems with lefty starters and began to show them a steady dose of southpaws, a major contributor to the team's downfall. Expos rookie lefty Chris Nabholz provided the best performance during the Mets' September swoon, tossing a one-hit shutout while Montreal was completing a three-game sweep at Shea.

The sweep left the rest of the season quite meaningless despite the Mets' 8–4 finish. Viola picked up his 20th victory in the season finale, one day after Gooden claimed his 19th.

1990 Mets Statistics

Hitting	G	AB	R	H	2B	3B	HR	RBI	BB	SO	BA	OBP	SLG	SB	CS	GDP	HP	SH	SF	IBB
Kevin Baez	5	12	0	2	1	0	0	0	0	0	.167	.167	.250	0	0	2	0	0	0	0
Daryl Boston	115	366	65	100	21	2	12	45	28	50	.273	.328	.440	18	7	7	2	0	0	2
Chuck Carr	4	2	0	0	0	0	0	0	0	2	.000	.000	.000	1	0	0	0	0	0	0
Mark Carreon	82	188	30	47	12	0	10	26	15	29	.250	.312	.473	1	0	1	2	0	0	0
Mario Diaz	16	22	0	3	1	0	0	1	0	3	.136	.130	.182	0	0	0	0	0	1	0
Kevin Elster	92	314	36	65	20	1	9	45	30	54	.207	.274	.363	2	0	4	1	1	6	2
Tom Herr	27	100	9	25	5	0	1	10	14	11	.250	.342	.330	0	0	1	0	0	0	0
Keith Hughes	8	9	0	0	0	0	0	0	0	4	.000	.000	.000	0	0	0	0	0	0	0
Todd Hundley	36	67	8	14	6	0	0	2	6	18	.209	.274	.299	0	0	1	0	1	0	0
Gregg Jefferies	153	604	96	171	40	3	15	68	46	40	.283	.337	.434	11	2	12	5	0	4	2
Chris Jelic	4	11	2	1	0	0	1	1	0	3	.091	.091	.364	0	0	0	0	0	0	0
Howard Johnson	154	590	89	144	37	3	23	90	69	100	.244	.319	.434	34	8	7	0	0	9	12
Dave Liddell	1	1	1	1	0	0	0	0	0	0	1.000	1.000	1.000	0	0	0	0	0	0	0
Barry Lyons	24	80	8	19	0	0	2	7	2	9	.238	.265	.313	0	0	2	1	0	0	0
Dave Magadan	144	451	74	148	28	6	6	72	74	55	.328	.417	.457	2	1	11	2	4	10	4
Mike Marshall	53	163	24	39	8	1	6	27	7	40	.239	.278	.411	0	2	2	3	0	3	0
Kevin McReynolds	147	521	75	140	23	1	24	82	71	61	.269	.353	.455	9	2	8	1	0	8	11
Orlando Mercado	42	90	10	19	1	0	3	7	8	11	.211	.290	.322	0	0	4	2	0	0	3
Keith Miller	88	233	42	60	8	0	1	12	23	46	.258	.327	.305	16	3	2	2	2	2	1
Charlie O'Brien	28	68	6	11	3	0	0	9	10	8	.162	.272	.206	0	0	1	1	2	2	2
Tom O'Malley	82	121	14	27	7	0	3	14	11	20	.223	.286	.355	0	0	1	0	0	1	1
Darren Reed	26	39	5	8	4	1	1	2	3	11	.205	.262	.436	1	0	0	0	0	0	0
Mackey Sasser	100	270	31	83	14	0	6	41	15	19	.307	.344	.426	0	0	7	1	0	2	9
Darryl Strawberry	152	542	92	150	18	1	37	108	70	110	.277	.361	.518	15	8	5	4	0	5	15
Pat Tabler	17	43	6	12	1	1	1	10	3	8	.279	.340	.419	0	0	0	1	0	0	0
Tim Teufel	80	175	28	43	11	0	10	24	15	33	.246	.304	.480	0	0	5	0	1	1	1
Lou Thornton	3	0	0	0	0	0	0	0	0	0				0	0	0	0	0	0	0
Kelvin Torve	20	38	0	11	4	0	0	2	4	9	.289	.386	.395	0	0	1	2	0	0	0
Alex Trevino	9	10	0	3	1	0	0	2	1	0	.300	.333	.400	0	0	0	0	0	1	0
Pitchers																				
David Cone	32	70	7	14	1	0	0	5	5	12	.200	.253	.214	0	0	2	0	9	0	0
Ron Darling	34	31	2	4	0	0	0	2	3	12	.129	.206	.129	0	0	0	0	5	0	0
Sid Fernandez	30	58	3	11	1	0	0	4	0	22	.190	.190	.207	0	0	2	0	5	0	0
John Franco	55	5	0	0	0	0	0	0	0	1	.000	.000	.000	0	0	0	0	0	0	0
Dwight Gooden	35	75	4	14	1	1	1	9	2	15	.187	.225	.267	0	0	0	2	14	1	0
Jeff Innis	18	0	0	0	0	0	0	0	0	0				0	0	0	0	1	0	0
Jeff Musselman	28	1	0	0	0	0	0	0	0	0	.000	.000	.000	0	0	0	0	0	0	0
Bob Ojeda	38	30	2	4	1	0	0	0	0	11	.133	.133	.167	0	0	0	0	0	0	0
Alejandro Pena	52	6	2	1	0	0	0	1	1	3	.167	.286	.167	0	0	0	0	0	0	0
Julio Valera	3	5	0	1	0	0	0	2	0	1	.200	.200	.200	0	0	0	0	0	0	0
Frank Viola	35	85	4	13	0	0	0	4	0	20	.153	.153	.153	0	0	1	0	7	0	0
Wally Whitehurst	38	8	0	2	0	0	0	0	0	0	.250	.250	.250	0	0	0	0	1	0	0
TOTAL	162	5504	775	1410	278	21	172	734	536	851	.256	.322	.408	110	33	89	32	54	56	65

Pitching	G	ERA	W–L	SV	GS	GF	CG	SHO	IP	H	R	ER	HR	BB	SO	BFP	WP	HBP	BK	IBB
Kevin Brown	2	0.00	0–0	0	0	1	0	0	2.0	2	0	0	0	1	0	9	0	0	0	0
David Cone	31	3.23	14–10	0	30	1	6	2	211.2	177	84	76	21	65	233	860	10	1	4	1
Ron Darling	33	4.50	7–9	0	18	3	1	0	126.0	135	73	63	20	44	99	554	5	5	1	4
Sid Fernandez	30	3.46	9–14	0	30	0	2	1	179.1	130	79	69	18	67	181	735	1	5	0	4
John Franco	55	2.53	5–3	33	0	48	0	0	67.2	66	22	19	4	21	56	287	7	0	2	2
Dwight Gooden	34	3.83	19–7	0	34	0	2	1	232.2	229	106	99	10	70	223	983	6	7	3	3
Jeff Innis	18	2.39	1–3	1	0	12	0	0	26.1	19	9	7	4	10	12	104	1	1	1	3
Julio Machado	27	3.15	4–1	0	0	14	0	0	34.1	32	13	12	4	17	27	151	3	2	0	4
Jeff Musselman	28	5.63	0–2	0	0	5	0	0	32.0	40	22	20	3	11	14	144	3	1	0	1
Bob Ojeda	38	3.66	7–6	0	12	9	0	0	118.0	123	53	48	10	40	62	500	2	2	3	4
Alejandro Pena	52	3.20	3–3	5	0	32	0	0	76.0	71	31	27	4	22	76	320	0	1	0	5
Dan Schatzeder	6	0.00	0–0	0	0	3	0	0	5.2	5	0	0	0	0	2	19	0	0	0	0
Julio Valera	3	6.92	1–1	0	3	0	0	0	13.0	20	11	10	1	7	4	64	0	0	0	0
Frank Viola	35	2.67	20–12	0	35	0	7	3	249.2	227	83	74	15	60	182	1016	11	2	0	2
Wally Whitehurst	38	3.29	1–0	2	0	16	0	0	65.2	63	27	24	5	9	46	263	2	0	2	2
TOTAL	162	3.42	91–71	41	162	144	18	14	1440.0	1339	613	547	119	444	1217	6009	51	27	14	35

1991

NL EAST

Team	W	L	PCT	GB	BA	ERA
Pirates	98	64	.605	—	.263	3.44
Cardinals	84	78	.519	14.0	.255	3.69
Phillies	78	84	.481	20.0	.241	3.86
Cubs	77	83	.481	20.0	.253	4.03
Mets	77	84	.478	20.5	.244	3.56
Expos	71	90	.441	26.5	.246	3.64

There was a front office shift at the end of the 1990 season. General manager Frank Cashen gave up some of his responsibilities to Al Harazin and Gerry Hunsicker, who was named director of baseball operations in October after serving two years as the director of minor league operations. Although he reported to Cashen, Harazin oversaw the entire operation and became the team's chief negotiator.

The front office allowed Darryl Strawberry to go to the Dodgers after breaking off negotiations with the seven-time All-Star during the summer of '90. Strawberry wanted a salary similar to Jose Canseco's, and the Mets countered with a contract that was designed to make him want to leave.

The Mets replaced Strawberry with speed merchant Vince Coleman, who had stolen 64 bases in 98 games lifetime against New York. Strawberry's departure meant Howard Johnson and Kevin McReynolds were the lone power threats heading into 1991. Disastrous results would soon follow.

The '91 Mets played some exceptional baseball for four weeks after plodding through the first 2½ months of the season. They stood at 31–29 on June 16 before winning 18 of 23, a streak capped by 10 straight victories. New York hit .264 during the hot stretch while the pitchers combined for a 3.16 ERA. The Mets were in second place following their 10th straight win July 13, 2½ games behind the Pirates.

And then the season went straight to hell. The Mets dropped 12 of 14 from July 23 through August 6, then won two straight before losing 11 in a row to fall to 57–61, 12½ games out of first on August 21.

One day later, Dwight Gooden tossed five innings of three-hit ball in what would be his final start of the season, a 6–0 shutout of the Cardinals. He landed on the disabled list with shoulder inflammation on September 3, four days before undergoing season-ending arthroscopic surgery. Dr. James Parkes removed loose fragments from his shoulder and repaired a slight tear to his rotation cuff. Gooden ended up being the only Mets starter with a winning record as Cone, Viola, Darling, Fernandez, and Wally Whitehurst combined to go 40–50.

The Gooden injury gave manager Bud Harrelson's detractors even more reason to call for his dismissal. Those critics believed Gooden's problems stemmed from his marathon performance against the Expos in April, when he threw 149 pitches and struck out 14 in a complete game. However, Gooden was 6–1 with a 2.28 ERA in his 10 starts prior to landing on the DL.

Gooden's absence left Cone and Viola as the team's only experienced starting pitchers over the final six weeks.

Harrelson had a dugout run-in with Cone early in the season, an altercation that was caught on television. Cone was complaining that bench coach Doc Edwards had too much influence on game strategy. By midseason, several other players felt Harrelson was delegating many baseball decisions to his staff and had become nothing more than a marionette for Harazin. Those sentiments grew stronger as the Mets played themselves out of the race.

In one of his last moves as GM, Cashen removed Harrelson with one week left in the season. It was a very disappointing end to what initially appeared to be a bright managerial future for the team's longtime shortstop.

Harrelson's dismissal was just the capper on what evolved into a truly hideous season. Fernandez missed four months of the year due to separate injuries, Darling was ineffective before he was dealt to the Expos, and the bullpen was a high-wire act much of the year.

But the biggest mound meltdown came from Frank Viola, a 20-game winner in 1990. The lefty was excellent through the first 3½ months of the '91 campaign, going 11–5 with a 2.78 ERA in his first 19 starts through July 12. Viola was pretty lousy after that, dropping 10 of 12 decisions while compiling a hefty 5.75 ERA. His problems coincided with the Mets' free fall and led to Viola's departure through free agency.

Coleman's first full season away from artificial turf was woeful by his lofty standards. He opened his career with three straight seasons of at least 100 stolen bases and had never swiped fewer than 65 in a single year before joining the Mets.

Coleman got off to a slow start in 1991, strained his hamstring June 14, and started just 14 games the rest of the year. He finished with a .255 average and just 37 stolen bases in only 72 games. Coleman complained the infield dirt at Shea Stadium slowed him down, but that couldn't be used as a reason for his range in center. A left fielder throughout the Cardinals portion of his career, Coleman had trouble adjusting to center field and was a bit tentative on balls hit behind him. As it was, Daryl Boston wound up appearing in more games in center.

Kevin McReynolds' stats also took a nosedive as the left fielder batted just .259 with 16 home runs and 74 RBIs, his second-worst full major league season to date. However, he was the only player other than Johnson to play more than 140 games.

Dave Magadan's batting average dropped 70 points after he finished third in the National League with a .328 average. He also finished with only four home runs, by far the fewest among major league first basemen with at least 40 games played.

Gregg Jefferies had a nice season at the plate, batting .272 and finishing second on the team with 62 RBIs. However he appeared to have plateaued as a hitter, failing to match the expectations thrust upon him by the front office.

Catcher Rick Cerone hit .273 but drove in just 16 runs in 227 at-bats and was unable to play every day at age 37. Mackey Sasser recorded a .272 average when he wasn't having a mental block making throws back to the mound. Sasser would double-, triple-, and quadruple-pump before tossing a ball to his batterymate. Moreover, he was able to throw out 29 percent of his 34 base runners.

Johnson managed to keep his head above the fray, leading the National League with 38 homers and a then team-record 117 RBIs while batting .259 with a .342 on-base average. He was a 30–30 member for the third time in five seasons and finished fifth in the MVP balloting for the second time in three years. HoJo also willingly played right field, a precursor to his often rocky experience as an outfielder in 1992.

Cone failed to post a winning record for the first time in four years but led the NL in strikeouts (241) for the second straight season. He capped the year by tossing a three-hitter and tying an NL record with 19 strikeouts in a 7–0 shutout at Philadelphia, shortly after he was accused by a couple of female fans of some tawdry conduct in the Mets bullpen earlier in the year. Cone's gem was an unlikely way for the Mets to complete an awful season.

It was the Mets' first losing season since 1983. They finished ninth in the 12-team NL with a .244 batting average, were eighth with 640 runs scored, and seventh in home runs despite Johnson's league-leading total.

The disappointing performance caused Harazin to revamp the lineup in 1992, bringing in veteran All-Stars Bobby Bonilla, Eddie Murray, Willie Randolph, and Bret Saberhagen. The moves were designed to put the Mets back on top without having to wait for the farm system to produce.

But by 1993, the '91 season was looking pretty darn good by comparison.

1991 Mets Statistics

Hitting	G	AB	R	H	2B	3B	HR	RBI	BB	SO	BA	OBP	SLG	SB	CS	GDP	HP	SH	SF	IBB
Daryl Boston	137	255	40	70	16	4	4	21	30	42	.275	.350	.416	15	8	2	0	0	1	0
Hubie Brooks	103	357	48	85	11	1	16	50	44	62	.238	.324	.409	3	1	7	3	0	3	8
Chuck Carr	12	11	1	2	0	0	0	1	0	2	.182	.182	.182	1	0	0	0	0	0	0
Mark Carreon	106	254	18	66	6	0	4	21	12	26	.260	.297	.331	2	1	13	2	1	1	2
Rick Cerone	90	227	18	62	13	0	2	16	30	24	.273	.360	.357	1	1	9	1	0	0	2
Vince Coleman	72	278	45	71	7	5	1	17	39	47	.255	.347	.327	37	14	3	0	1	0	0
Chris Donnels	37	89	7	20	2	0	0	5	14	19	.225	.330	.247	1	1	0	0	1	0	1
Kevin Elster	115	348	33	84	16	2	6	36	40	53	.241	.318	.351	2	3	4	1	1	4	6
Jeff Gardner	13	37	3	6	0	0	0	1	4	6	.162	.238	.162	0	0	0	0	0	1	0
Tom Herr	70	155	17	30	7	0	1	14	32	21	.194	.328	.258	7	2	1	0	2	2	4
Todd Hundley	21	60	5	8	0	1	1	7	6	14	.133	.221	.217	0	0	3	1	1	1	0
Gregg Jefferies	136	486	59	132	19	2	9	62	47	38	.272	.336	.374	26	5	12	2	1	3	2
Howard Johnson	156	564	108	146	34	4	38	117	78	120	.259	.342	.535	30	16	4	1	0	15	12
Dave Magadan	124	418	58	108	23	0	4	51	83	50	.258	.378	.342	1	1	5	2	7	7	3
Terry McDaniel	23	29	3	6	1	0	0	2	1	11	.207	.233	.241	2	0	0	0	0	0	0
Kevin McReynolds	143	522	65	135	32	1	16	74	49	46	.259	.322	.416	6	6	8	2	1	4	7
Keith Miller	98	275	41	77	22	1	4	23	23	44	.280	.345	.411	14	4	2	5	0	1	0
Charlie O'Brien	69	168	16	31	6	0	2	14	17	25	.185	.272	.256	0	2	5	4	0	2	1
Mackey Sasser	96	228	18	62	14	2	5	35	9	19	.272	.298	.417	0	2	6	1	1	4	2
Garry Templeton	80	219	20	50	9	1	2	20	9	29	.228	.257	.306	3	1	7	0	4	2	3
Tim Teufel	20	34	2	4	0	0	1	2	2	8	.118	.167	.206	1	1	0	0	0	0	0
Kelvin Torve	10	8	0	0	0	0	0	0	0	1	.000	.000	.000	0	0	1	0	0	0	0
Pitchers																				
Tim Burke	35	5	0	0	0	0	0	0	0	4	.000	.000	.000	0	0	0	0	0	0	0
Tony Castillo	10	4	0	0	0	0	0	0	0	0	.000	.000	.000	0	0	0	0	2	0	0
David Cone	34	72	3	9	0	0	0	5	3	14	.125	.179	.125	0	0	3	2	6	1	0
Ron Darling	17	34	0	4	3	0	0	1	0	14	.118	.118	.206	0	0	0	0	5	0	0
Sid Fernandez	8	13	1	2	1	0	0	0	0	7	.154	.154	.231	0	0	0	0	1	0	0
John Franco	52	1	0	0	0	0	0	0	0	1	.000	.000	.000	0	0	0	0	0	0	0
Dwight Gooden	27	63	7	15	3	0	1	6	0	9	.238	.238	.333	1	1	1	0	8	0	0
Jeff Innis	69	2	0	0	0	0	0	0	0	1	.000	.000	.000	0	0	0	0	0	0	0
Doug Simons	42	3	0	0	0	0	0	0	0	0	.000	.000	.000	0	0	0	0	1	0	0
Pete Schourek	35	22	0	3	1	0	0	3	2	9	.136	.208	.182	0	0	0	0	0	0	0
Frank Viola	35	71	2	9	2	0	0	1	2	13	.127	.151	.155	0	0	1	0	10	0	0
Wally Whitehurst	36	33	2	6	1	0	0	0	2	6	.182	.229	.212	0	0	0	0	5	0	0
Anthony Young	10	14	0	2	1	0	0	0	0	4	.143	.143	.214	0	0	0	0	1	0	0
TOTAL	161	5359	640	1305	250	24	117	605	578	789	.244	.317	.365	153	70	97	27	60	52	53

Pitching	G	ERA	W–L	SV	GS	GF	CG	SHO	IP	H	R	ER	HR	BB	SO	BFP	WP	HBP	BK	IBB
Blaine Beatty	5	2.79	0–0	0	0	1	0	0	9.2	9	3	3	0	4	7	42	1	0	0	1
Terry Bross	8	1.80	0–0	0	0	4	0	0	10.0	7	2	2	1	3	5	39	0	0	0	0
Tim Burke	35	2.75	3–3	1	0	15	0	0	55.2	55	22	17	5	12	34	231	2	0	0	2
Tony Castillo	10	1.90	1–0	0	3	1	0	0	23.2	27	7	5	1	6	10	104	0	0	0	1
David Cone	34	3.29	14–14	0	34	0	5	2	232.2	204	95	85	13	73	241	966	17	5	1	2
Ron Darling	17	3.87	5–6	0	17	0	0	0	102.1	96	50	44	9	28	58	427	9	6	4	1

Pitching (continued)	G	ERA	W–L	SV	GS	GF	CG	SHO	IP	H	R	ER	HR	BB	SO	BFP	WP	HBP	BK	IBB
Sid Fernandez	8	2.86	1–3	0	8	0	0	0	44.0	36	18	14	4	9	31	177	0	0	0	0
John Franco	52	2.93	5–9	30	0	48	0	0	55.1	61	27	18	2	18	45	247	6	1	0	4
Dwight Gooden	27	3.60	13–7	0	27	0	3	1	190.0	185	80	76	12	56	150	789	5	3	2	2
Jeff Innis	69	2.66	0–2	0	0	29	0	0	84.2	66	30	25	2	23	47	336	4	0	0	6
Alejandro Pena	44	2.71	6–1	4	0	24	0	0	63.0	63	20	19	5	19	49	261	1	0	2	4
Rich Sauveur	6	10.80	0–0	0	0	0	0	0	3.1	7	4	4	1	2	4	19	0	0	0	0
Pete Schourek	35	4.27	5–4	2	8	7	1	1	86.1	82	49	41	7	43	67	385	1	2	0	4
Doug Simons	42	5.19	2–3	1	1	11	0	0	60.2	55	40	35	5	19	38	258	3	2	0	5
Julio Valera	2	0.00	0–0	0	0	1	0	0	2.0	1	0	0	0	4	3	11	0	0	0	1
Frank Viola	35	3.97	13–15	0	35	0	3	0	231.1	259	112	102	25	54	132	980	6	1	1	4
Wally Whitehurst	36	4.19	7–12	1	20	6	0	0	133.1	142	67	62	12	25	87	556	3	4	4	3
Anthony Young	10	3.10	2–5	0	8	2	0	0	49.1	48	20	17	4	12	20	202	1	1	0	1
TOTAL	**161**	**3.56**	**77–84**	**39**	**161**	**149**	**12**	**11**	**1437.0**	**1403**	**646**	**568**	**108**	**410**	**1028**	**6030**	**59**	**25**	**14**	**41**

1992

NL EAST						
Team	W	L	PCT	GB	BA	ERA
Pirates	96	66	.593	—	.255	3.35
Expos	87	75	.537	9.0	.252	3.25
Cardinals	83	79	.512	13.0	.262	3.38
Cubs	78	84	.481	18.0	.254	3.39
Mets	72	90	.444	24.0	.235	3.66
Phillies	70	92	.432	26.0	.253	4.11

The Mets went on a spending spree in the months following a lousy 1991 campaign, signing free agents Bobby Bonilla and Eddie Murray during a one-week period to bolster an offense that had just finished ninth in batting, seventh in homers, and dead last in base hits. New York also picked up veteran second baseman Willie Randolph in December and engineered a blockbuster trade that sent Kevin McReynolds, Gregg Jefferies, and Keith Miller to the Royals for two-time AL Cy Young Award winner Bret Saberhagen later in the month.

Bonilla was the top prize on the free agent market after hitting .302 with 18 home runs, a league-best 44 doubles, and 100 RBIs. He earned an All-Star for the fourth consecutive season before helping the Pirates win their second straight division title.

The Mets went on an 11th-hour bidding war to get Bonilla for $29 million over five years, then the richest free-agent package in major league history. Not only was he going to the Mets, his departure from Pittsburgh was sure to weaken the Pirates.

Murray signed a few days before Bonilla following an off year with the 1991 Dodgers. He made the '91 All-Star team solely by virtue of his career-high .330 average and 96 RBIs for Los Angeles the previous season. He had lost a step at first base but still remained a defensive standout with a lethal bat, something the Mets lacked once Keith Hernandez began to break down in 1988.

Randolph was winding down a career that included six All-Star berths and the admiration of his teammates. He was the calm in the storm that was the Yankees clubhouse during the team's "Bronx Zoo" era.

New GM Al Harazin referred to Bonilla, Murray, and Randolph as "character guys." Mets fans believed the trio would fill the leadership vacuum created when Hernandez and Gary Carter left after 1989. All three were playoff tested and were perceived as outstanding clubhouse guys, although Murray had his problems with the media.

Saberhagen became the rotation replacement for Frank Viola, who was allowed to sign with the Red Sox after going 13–15. Saberhagen was 13–8 in 1991, two years after winning a career-high and league-best 23 games.

The Mets entered spring training with Saberhagen, David Cone, Sid Fernandez, and a surgically repaired Dwight Gooden, who had his shoulder cleaned out the previous September. It was the best front-four in the National League on paper, although the No. 5 spot would be determined during the exhibition season.

Finding a fifth starter was the least of the Mets' worries once they began to report to training camp February 21. Darryl Strawberry had written a book in which he claimed Gooden had started his cocaine addiction during the 1986 season, leading to speculation he might have been high when he pitched. No sooner had the "he said, he said" played out when Gooden was part of another bombshell. A woman accused him of luring her into his home and raping her with the help of teammates and outfielders Daryl Boston and Vince Coleman. News reporters began to filter down to St. Lucie as the tabloids continued to dig up any dirt they could on the social lives of the Mets. Stories began to depict the ballclub as a collection of sexually depraved men, reports that overshadowed the actual start of spring training.

The players finally had enough as reporters outnumbered the roster. The team eventually voted to boycott the media for a few days after a few reports, headlines, and even cartoons crossed the line. The team was a national joke…and they hadn't played their first exhibition game.

This was not the type of attention Harazin expected to receive after trying to fill the roster with vanilla personalities. It also made the spring difficult on first-year manager Jeff Torborg, who was trying to lay down his own rules without causing a player rift.

Torborg lived a clean life and was a no-nonsense skipper, something the Mets sought after Bud Harrelson seemed to lose the respect of the ballclub. He banned alcohol on team flights and became the latest manager to attempt to bar golf during spring training. That didn't exactly endear him to his new players.

The Mets managed to ride out the controversy and headed to St. Louis to start the season. The opener went according to script as Bonilla went 3-for-5 with two homers and three RBIs, including a tiebreaking, two-run blast in the 10th inning to beat the Cardinals 4–2. New York dropped six of its next seven before a 14–4 stretch left them 16–10 and two games out of first by May 4.

The Mets were within a half-game of the lead following a win over the Giants on June 2. But their record was just 27–24, hardly the juggernaut Harazin thought he had assembled. The team dropped under .500 for good just 10 days later, making for a long, ugly season.

It eventually became a team even Mets fans hated and led to a wonderful chronicle of the season by beat writers Bob Klapisch and John Harper in the book, *The Worst Team Money Could Buy*. Klapisch and Harper no longer were covering a baseball team. Every day seemed to have a new clubhouse soap opera involving many of Harazin's character guys.

Bonilla, who told the media they wouldn't be able to wipe the smile off his face, was the creator of more clubhouse lowlights than on-field homers. He called PR Director Jay Horwitz from the dugout during a game to complain about an official scorer's decision after being charged with an error. When pressed on the contents of the conversation, Bonilla made up a tale about wanting to call a flu-ridden Horwitz to see how he was feeling. The Mets' highest-paid player didn't want to face the music, and he allegedly didn't want to hear the boos later in the season.

Bonilla went to the outfield wearing earplugs during a game after becoming the target of Shea boo-birds. The company line was that Bonilla was using the earplugs to better concentrate at the plate and left them in because they were too hard to insert. Since he couldn't own up to the phone call to Horwitz, the writers weren't buying his excuse about the earplugs.

Bonilla also had several spats with umpires over balls and strikes. He was tossed from one game for taking too much time stepping back into the batter's box following a marginal strike call. Torborg came out of the dugout, but instead of taking up Bonilla's charge, he told his right fielder to get his head in the game.

Coleman also was ejected from a game, leading Torborg to attempt to separate his outfielder from the umpire. Torborg was pushing Coleman back to the dugout when Coleman pushed back. This prompted Bonilla to hustle his teammate back to the clubhouse before Coleman and Torborg had a very heated exchange. It was becoming evident that Torborg did not have the respect of his players.

By July, the only interesting sidebar to the Mets' season was whether they would retain Cone, who was slated for free agency in November after beating them in arbitration over the winter. Cone was leading the majors in strikeouts when the Mets decided to become sellers at the trade deadline. Cone was sent to the Blue Jays on August 27 for infielder Jeff Kent and a player to be named, which would become Ryan Thompson.

Kent looked good in his first two months as a Met, but even he added to the season of lowlights by refusing to go along with a rookie initiation. He had a fit when he went to his locker and noticed his clothes had been replaced by a pimp's outfit.

Once Kent refused to board a team bus for the airport, an already exasperated Torborg asked the veterans to give the kid his clothes back.

Saberhagen was among the many injured Mets in '92. He was roughed up in his first three starts before going 3–0 with a 0.69 ERA over his next five. He was working on a three-hitter in Los Angeles on May 15 when he was taken out with what the team called stiffness in his right index finger. The Mets described him as day-to-day after the game, but day-to-day became 9½ weeks. The Mets went from 26–21 to 45–48 before he threw another pitch.

The number of injuries was almost as ridiculous as the Mets' play on the field. Coleman sat out 90 games due to three stints on the disabled list due to a pulled rib cage and two strained left hamstring injuries. Dave Magadan played 99 games before breaking his right wrist on August 9, costing him the rest of the season. Willie Randolph's season ended after 90 games due to a broken bone in his left hand. Howard Johnson broke his left wrist on August 2, ending his season and leaving him with just seven homers, 43 RBIs, and a .223 batting average in 100 games. HoJo also played through shoulder and knee problems. And John Franco sat out the final month of the season after spending most of the summer pitching with a painful elbow.

Randolph retired after the season, and Magadan was allowed to sign with the expansion Marlins. Johnson muddled through another injury-filled season in 1993 and was never the same hitter after 1991. Coleman also returned in '93, playing 92 games before he was asked in August to stay away from the team.

The Mets opened spring training wishing the media would just go away. They got their wish by August as newspapers radio stations and television outlets began to ignore them. No need to cover a team with no place to go but down.

1992 Mets Statistics

Hitting	G	AB	R	H	2B	3B	HR	RBI	BB	SO	BA	OBP	SLG	SB	CS	GDP	HP	SH	SF	IBB
Kevin Baez	6	13	0	2	0	0	0	0	0	0	.154	.154	.154	0	0	1	0	0	0	0
Kevin Bass	46	137	15	37	12	2	2	9	7	17	.270	.303	.431	7	2	2	0	0	1	2
Bobby Bonilla	128	438	62	109	23	0	19	70	66	73	.249	.348	.432	4	3	11	1	0	1	10
Daryl Boston	130	289	37	72	14	2	11	35	38	60	.249	.338	.426	12	6	5	3	0	4	6
Vince Coleman	71	229	37	63	11	1	2	21	27	41	.275	.355	.358	24	9	1	2	2	1	3
Chris Donnels	45	121	8	21	4	0	0	6	17	25	.174	.275	.207	1	0	1	0	1	0	0
D.J. Dozier	25	47	4	9	2	0	0	2	4	19	.191	.264	.234	4	0	0	1	1	1	0

Hitting (continued)	G	AB	R	H	2B	3B	HR	RBI	BB	SO	BA	OBP	SLG	SB	CS	GDP	HP	SH	SF	IBB
Kevin Elster	6	18	0	4	0	0	0	0	0	2	.222	.222	.222	0	0	1	0	0	0	0
Dave Gallagher	98	175	20	42	11	1	1	21	19	16	.240	.307	.331	4	5	7	1	3	7	0
Pat Howell	31	75	9	14	1	0	0	1	2	15	.187	.218	.200	4	2	0	1	1	0	0
Todd Hundley	123	358	32	75	17	0	7	32	19	76	.209	.256	.316	3	0	8	4	7	2	4
Howard Johnson	100	350	48	78	19	0	7	43	55	79	.223	.329	.337	22	5	7	2	0	3	5
Jeff Kent	37	113	16	27	8	1	3	15	7	29	.239	.289	.407	0	2	2	1	0	0	0
Dave Magadan	99	321	33	91	9	1	3	28	56	44	.283	.390	.346	1	0	6	0	2	0	3
Rodney McCray	18	1	3	1	0	0	0	1	0	0	1.000	1.000	1.000	2	0	0	0	0	0	0
Jeff McKnight	31	85	10	23	3	1	2	13	2	8	.271	.287	.400	0	1	2	0	0	0	0
Eddie Murray	156	551	64	144	37	2	16	93	66	74	.261	.336	.423	4	2	15	0	0	8	8
Junior Noboa	46	47	7	7	0	0	0	3	3	8	.149	.212	.149	0	0	2	1	0	1	0
Charlie O'Brien	68	156	15	33	12	0	2	13	16	18	.212	.289	.327	0	1	4	1	4	0	1
Bill Pecota	117	269	28	61	13	0	2	26	25	40	.227	.293	.297	9	3	7	1	5	2	3
Willie Randolph	90	286	29	72	11	1	2	15	40	34	.252	.352	.318	1	3	6	4	6	0	1
Mackey Sasser	92	141	7	34	6	0	2	18	3	10	.241	.248	.326	0	0	4	0	0	5	0
Dick Schofield	142	420	52	86	18	2	4	36	60	82	.205	.309	.286	11	4	11	5	10	3	4
Steve Springer	4	5	0	2	1	0	0	0	0	1	.400	.400	.600	0	0	0	0	0	0	0
Ryan Thompson	30	108	15	24	7	1	3	10	8	24	.222	.274	.389	2	2	2	0	0	1	0
Chico Walker	107	227	24	70	12	1	4	36	24	46	.308	.369	.423	14	1	9	0	0	4	3
Pitchers																				
Mike Birkbeck	1	2	0	0	0	0	0	0	0	0	.000	.000	.000	0	0	0	0	0	0	0
David Cone	27	65	5	6	1	0	0	4	3	19	.092	.132	.108	0	0	1	0	7	0	0
Mark Dewey	20	1	0	0	0	0	0	0	0	1	.000	.000	.000	0	0	0	0	0	0	0
Sid Fernandez	32	74	8	15	3	0	0	0	0	25	.203	.203	.243	0	0	1	0	7	0	0
Tom Filer	9	3	0	0	0	0	0	0	0	1	.000	.000	.000	0	0	0	0	0	0	0
John Franco	31	1	0	0	0	0	0	0	0	1	.000	.000	.000	0	0	0	0	0	0	0
Paul Gibson	43	6	0	0	0	0	0	0	1	3	.000	.143	.000	0	0	0	0	1	0	0
Dwight Gooden	33	72	8	19	3	1	1	9	1	16	.264	.274	.375	0	0	1	0	4	0	0
Lee Guetterman	43	2	0	0	0	0	0	0	0	2	.000	.000	.000	0	0	0	0	0	0	0
Eric Hillman	11	13	0	1	0	0	0	0	0	7	.077	.077	.077	0	0	0	0	5	0	0
Jeff Innis	76	2	0	0	0	0	0	0	0	0	.000	.000	.000	0	0	0	0	0	0	0
Bret Saberhagen	17	28	0	3	0	0	0	0	1	9	.107	.138	.107	0	0	0	0	3	0	0
Pete Schourek	23	42	0	2	0	0	0	1	0	13	.048	.047	.048	0	0	0	0	2	1	0
Wally Whitehurst	44	22	1	4	1	0	0	3	1	5	.182	.217	.227	0	1	0	0	1	0	0
Anthony Young	52	27	2	3	0	0	0	0	1	13	.111	.143	.111	0	0	0	0	2	0	0
TOTAL	162	5340	599	1254	259	17	93	564	572	956	.235	.309	.342	129	52	117	28	74	45	53

Pitching	G	ERA	W–L	SV	GS	GF	CG	SHO	IP	H	R	ER	HR	BB	SO	BFP	WP	HBP	BK	IBB
Mike Birkbeck	1	9.00	0–1	0	1	0	0	0	7.0	12	7	7	3	1	2	33	1	0	0	1
Tim Burke	15	5.74	1–2	0	0	9	0	0	15.2	26	15	10	1	3	7	76	2	0	0	0
David Cone	27	2.88	13–7	0	27	0	7	5	196.2	162	75	63	12	82	214	831	9	9	1	5
Mark Dewey	20	4.32	1–0	0	0	6	0	0	33.1	37	16	16	2	10	24	143	0	0	1	2
Sid Fernandez	32	2.73	14–11	0	32	0	5	2	214.2	162	67	65	12	67	193	865	0	4	0	4
Tom Filer	9	2.05	0–1	0	1	1	0	0	22.0	18	8	5	2	6	9	88	1	0	0	2
John Franco	31	1.64	6–2	15	0	30	0	0	33.0	24	6	6	1	11	20	128	0	0	0	2
Paul Gibson	43	5.23	0–1	0	1	12	0	0	62.0	70	37	36	-7	25	49	273	1	0	0	0
Dwight Gooden	31	3.67	10–13	0	31	0	3	0	206.0	197	93	84	11	70	145	863	3	3	1	7
Lee Guetterman	43	5.82	3–4	2	0	15	0	0	43.1	57	28	28	5	14	15	196	3	1	0	5
Eric Hillman	11	5.33	2–2	0	8	2	0	0	52.1	67	31	31	9	10	16	227	1	2	0	2
Jeff Innis	76	2.86	6–9	1	0	28	0	0	88.0	85	32	28	4	36	39	373	1	6	0	4
Barry Jones	17	9.39	2–0	1	0	7	0	0	15.1	20	16	16	0	11	11	76	1	0	0	3
Bill Pecota	1	9.00	0–0	0	0	1	0	0	1.0	1	1	1	1	0	0	4	0	0	0	0
Bret Saberhagen	17	3.50	3–5	0	15	0	1	1	97.2	84	39	38	6	27	81	397	1	4	2	1
Pete Schourek	22	3.64	6–8	0	21	0	0	0	136.0	137	60	55	9	44	60	578	4	2	0	6
Joe Vitko	3	13.50	0–1	0	1	1	0	0	4.2	12	11	7	1	1	6	29	1	0	0	0
Wally Whitehurst	44	3.62	3–9	0	11	7	0	0	97.0	99	45	39	4	33	70	421	2	4	1	5
Anthony Young	52	4.17	2–14	15	13	26	1	0	121.0	134	66	56	8	31	64	517	3	1	1	5
TOTAL	162	3.66	72–90	34	162	145	17	13	1446.0	1404	653	588	98	482	1025	6118	34	36	9	54

1993

NL EAST

Team	W	L	PCT	GB	BA	ERA
Phillies	97	65	.599	—	.274	3.95
Expos	94	68	.580	3.0	.257	3.55
Cardinals	87	75	.537	10.0	.272	4.09
Cubs	84	78	.519	13.0	.270	4.18
Pirates	75	87	.463	22.0	.267	4.77
Marlins	64	98	.395	33.0	.248	4.13
Mets	59	103	.364	38.0	.248	4.05

You know you've had a horrible season when:

1. Your only on-field story to gain national attention is a pitcher's record-breaking losing streak.
2. Your center fielder throws firecrackers at fans seeking autographs in the stadium parking lot.
3. Your ace pitcher sprays bleach at media members who have pretty much given him a free ride despite winning a total of 10 games during a pair of injury-plagued seasons. The bleach incident comes the same month that pitcher tosses a firecracker at reporters.

4. Your two best pitchers combine to win only 19 games.

5. Your highest-paid player bats .265 in what is considered a "rebound year."

6. Your opening-day manager is fired 38 games into the season, one month before your general manager resigns.

7. Your team fails to compile a winning streak longer than three games until the final week of the season.

8. Your team fails to put together any sort of winning streak from April 18 through June 30.

9. Your team is 29 games out of first place by the All-Star break and is eliminated from postseason contention before the calendar is turned to September.

10. Two expansion teams post better records than you do.

11. David Letterman ridicules you in his monologue on a daily basis.

First, the highlights from 1993.

- Bobby Bonilla regained his hitting stroke, leading the Mets with a career-high 34 home runs after hitting just 19 in the first season of his five-year, $29 million contract. The power numbers hid his .265 average.

- Eddie Murray proved he could still produce at age 37, driving in 100 runs and collecting a team-best 177 hits while batting .285.

- Jeff Kent was steady in his first full season as a Met, hitting, 270 with 21 homers and 80 RBI in 140 games.

- Bobby Jones and Jeromy Burnitz showed promise in their first major league seasons. Jones recorded a 3.65 ERA in nine starts, and Burnitz smacked 13 homers in 263 at-bats while compiling a .475 slugging average.

- Dwight Gooden recorded a 3.45 earned run average and a 1.193 WHIP, his best numbers in both categories since 1989.

But the lowlights far exceeded the highlights as the Mets compiled their worst record since 1965. They needed a season-ending six-game winning streak to finish 59–103. The back end of the rotation was wildly inconsistent, the bullpen compiled a mere 22 saves, and the offense finished 13th in the 14-team National League with 672 runs and a .248 average.

The Mets did manage to begin the season 8–7, although six of those 15 games were against the first-year Rockies. The team ERA was a nifty 3.24 through that period while the offense averaged 4.4 runs.

But in between the first 15 games and the final six, the Mets went 45–96 and clinched the NL East cellar with nine games left in the season.

Manager Jeff Torborg was let go May 14 with the Mets already 14 games out of first at 13–25. As sorry as 1992 may have been, the Mets didn't fall 14 games off the division lead until August 19.

The Mets brought in veteran skipper Dallas Green, a field general in every definition. Green had a much stronger personality than Torborg and put a harness on the malcontents who had spread a virus throughout the organization. He had no trouble with Bonilla, who was occasionally at odds with Torborg in 1992. However, a pair of off-field incidents further damaged the Mets' reputation.

The Mets had just lost 5–4 to the Dodgers in Los Angeles on July 24 when a crowd gathered along a chain-link fence in the parking lot. Vince Coleman thought it would be a good idea to introduce himself to the fans by throwing a firecracker from the passenger seat of a parked car that belonged to Dodgers outfielder Eric Davis. According to *New York Times* accounts in the days following the incident, a spokesman for the arson division of the Los Angeles Fire department said a two-year-old girl, an 11-year-old boy, and a 33-year-old woman were hospitalized and treated for injuries. The toddler suffered second-degree burns to her cheek, an injured finger, and an eye injury.

Coleman eventually was arraigned August 12 on a felony charge of igniting an explosive. The charge was reduced to a misdemeanor in November, with Coleman receiving three years' probation in exchange for a $1,000 fine and 200 hours of community service. Coleman also agreed to make restitution to the three victims.

Just three days after Coleman's fireworks fiasco, Kent hit a three-run homer and a tiebreaking solo homer as the Mets turned a 3–0 deficit into a 4–3 win for Dwight Gooden over the Marlins. Reporters were circled around the winning pitcher when a liquid substance began to rain near Gooden's locker. The writers quickly deduced the substance was bleach sprayed by a player or a clubhouse attendant.

It was later revealed the culprit was Bret Saberhagen, who claimed his innocence for about two weeks before finally owning up to the incident. Saberhagen also had tossed fireworks at a group of reporters in the clubhouse July 7, one of the few opportunities he had to scare anyone with his arm. Again, it took him weeks to fess up.

"It was a practical joke," Saberhagen said during his confession. "If the reporters can't take it, forget them."[11]

It was interesting to see how the Mets handled Coleman and Saberhagen. Coleman was the oft-injured, speedster who didn't come close to meeting the Mets' expectations when they signed him as a free agent in the fall of 1990. He was placed on paid leave in early August before the Mets announced later that month that he had played his final game with the team.

In contrast, Saberhagen was excellent on the mound when he wasn't on the disabled list. He made only 34 starts from 1992 to 1993 but compiled a 3.38 ERA during that span. The Mets forgave his indiscretions and allowed him to remain with the team until the 1995 trade deadline, when they took his hefty contract off the books by sending him to Colorado.

Mets fans spent the year rallying around Anthony Young, who continued to find unfathomable ways to lose. He carried a 14-game losing streak into the season and proceeded to lose his first 13 decisions of 1993, shattering the previous record of 23 consecutive losses set by Cliff Curtis of the Braves from 1910 to 1911.

Young was on the brink of his 28th straight setback on July 28 after giving up a tiebreaking run on a bunt single in the ninth inning. He was bailed out in the bottom half as Ryan Thompson knotted the game with a single before scoring the walk-off run on Murray's double.

Thompson was among the few Mets rookies to show some promise in 1993, hitting .250 with 11 homers and 19 doubles in 288 at-bats. He put on awesome power displays in BP and during games, but his 81 strikeouts were Kingmanesque.

The Mets said good-bye to 1986 holdovers Howard Johnson and Sid Fernandez, who missed almost three months of the season following right knee surgery on May 11. It was the second time in three years El Sid had been held under 19 starts, although his ERA was under 3.00 each season.

Johnson appeared in a Mets career-low 72 games, and hit under .240 with seven home runs for the second straight year.

There was a fitting end to the season: a 75-minute rain delay with the Mets actually leading the Marlins 9–2 in the ninth. The game was called after Florida opened the bottom half of the inning with a single. Considering the team's fortunes in '93, who knows if the Mets would have held on to win?

1993 Mets Statistics

Hitting	G	AB	R	H	2B	3B	HR	RBI	BB	SO	BA	OBP	SLG	SB	CS	GDP	HP	SH	SF	IBB
Kevin Baez	52	126	10	23	9	0	0	7	13	17	.183	.259	.254	0	0	1	0	4	0	1
Tim Bogar	78	205	19	50	13	0	3	25	14	29	.244	.300	.351	0	1	2	3	1	1	2
Bobby Bonilla	139	502	81	133	21	3	34	87	72	96	.265	.352	.522	3	3	12	0	0	8	11
Jeromy Burnitz	86	263	49	64	10	6	13	38	38	66	.243	.339	.475	3	6	2	1	2	2	4
Vince Coleman	92	373	64	104	14	8	2	25	21	58	.279	.316	.375	38	13	2	0	3	2	1
Tony Fernandez	48	173	20	39	5	2	1	14	25	19	.225	.323	.295	6	2	3	1	3	2	0
Dave Gallagher	99	201	34	55	12	2	6	28	20	18	.274	.338	.443	1	1	7	0	7	1	1
Wayne Housie	18	16	2	3	1	0	0	1	1	1	.188	.235	.250	0	0	0	0	0	0	0
Todd Hundley	130	417	40	95	17	2	11	53	23	62	.228	.269	.357	1	1	10	2	2	4	7
Butch Huskey	13	41	2	6	1	0	0	3	1	13	.146	.159	.171	0	0	0	0	0	2	1
Darrin Jackson	31	87	4	17	1	0	1	7	2	22	.195	.211	.241	0	0	0	0	1	1	0
Howard Johnson	72	235	32	56	8	2	7	26	43	43	.238	.354	.379	6	4	3	0	0	2	3
Jeff Kent	140	496	65	134	24	0	21	80	30	88	.270	.320	.446	4	4	11	8	6	4	2
Ced Landrum	22	19	2	5	1	0	0	1	0	5	.263	.263	.316	0	0	0	0	1	0	0
Jeff McKnight	105	164	19	42	3	1	2	13	13	31	.256	.311	.323	0	0	3	1	3	2	0
Eddie Murray	154	610	77	174	28	1	27	100	40	61	.285	.325	.467	2	2	24	0	0	9	4
Tito Navarro	12	17	1	1	0	0	0	1	0	4	.059	.059	.059	0	0	1	0	1	0	0
Charlie O'Brien	67	188	15	48	11	0	4	23	14	14	.255	.312	.378	1	1	4	2	3	1	1
Joe Orsulak	134	409	59	116	15	4	8	35	28	25	.284	.331	.399	5	4	6	2	0	2	1
Doug Saunders	28	67	8	14	2	0	0	0	3	4	.209	.243	.239	0	0	2	0	3	0	0
Ryan Thompson	80	288	34	72	19	2	11	26	19	81	.250	.302	.444	2	7	5	3	5	1	4
Chico Walker	115	213	18	48	7	1	5	19	14	29	.225	.271	.338	7	0	3	0	0	2	0
Pitchers																				
Mike Draper	29	3	1	2	0	0	0	0	0	1	.667	.667	.667	0	0	0	0	0	0	0
Sid Fernandez	18	32	2	3	0	0	0	2	2	13	.094	.147	.094	0	0	2	0	8	0	0
John Franco	35	1	0	0	0	0	0	0	0	0	.000	.000	.000	0	0	0	0	0	0	0
Dwight Gooden	30	70	5	14	2	2	2	9	0	11	.200	.200	.371	0	0	1	0	6	0	0
Eric Hillman	27	44	2	7	1	0	0	0	0	14	.159	.178	.182	0	0	0	1	6	0	0
Jeff Innis	67	0	0	0	0	0	0	0	0	0				0	0	0	0	2	0	0
Bobby Jones	9	20	0	1	0	0	0	0	0	7	.050	.050	.050	0	0	0	0	2	0	0
Mike Maddux	58	3	0	0	0	0	0	0	0	3	.000	.000	.000	0	0	0	0	0	0	0
Josias Manzanillo	6	1	0	0	0	0	0	0	0	1	.000	.000	.000	0	0	0	0	0	0	0
Bret Saberhagen	19	45	2	5	1	0	0	0	5	10	.111	.200	.133	0	0	1	0	8	0	0
Pete Schourek	41	32	2	7	0	0	0	4	3	11	.219	.278	.219	0	0	2	0	3	1	0
Frank Tanana	29	58	3	9	1	1	0	5	2	11	.155	.183	.207	0	1	0	0	3	0	0
Dave Telgheder	24	15	0	1	1	0	0	0	1	8	.067	.125	.133	0	0	0	0	4	0	0
Anthony Young	39	14	0	2	0	0	0	0	1	3	.143	.200	.143	0	0	1	0	2	0	0
TOTAL	162	5448	672	1350	228	37	158	632	448	879	.248	.305	.390	79	50	108	24	89	47	43

Pitching	G	ERA	W–L	SV	GS	GF	CG	SHO	IP	H	R	ER	HR	BB	SO	BFP	WP	HBP	BK	IBB
Mike Draper	29	4.25	1–1	0	1	11	0	0	42.1	53	22	20	2	14	16	184	0	0	1	3
Sid Fernandez	18	2.93	5–6	0	18	0	1	1	119.2	82	42	39	17	36	81	469	2	3	0	0
John Franco	35	5.20	4–3	10	0	30	0	0	36.1	46	24	21	6	19	29	172	5	1	0	3
Paul Gibson	8	5.19	1–1	0	0	1	0	0	8.2	14	6	5	1	2	12	42	1	0	0	0
Dwight Gooden	29	3.45	12–15	0	29	0	7	2	208.2	188	89	80	16	61	149	866	5	9	2	1
Mauro Gozzo	10	2.57	0–1	1	0	5	0	0	14.0	11	5	4	1	5	6	57	0	0	0	1
Kenny Greer	1	0.00	1–0	0	0	1	0	0	1.0	0	0	0	0	0	2	3	0	0	0	0
Eric Hillman	27	3.97	2–9	0	22	1	3	1	145.0	173	83	64	12	24	60	627	0	4	1	2
Jeff Innis	67	4.11	2–3	3	0	30	0	0	76.2	81	39	35	5	38	36	345	3	6	1	12
Bobby Jones	9	3.65	2–4	0	9	0	0	0	61.2	61	35	25	6	22	35	265	1	2	0	3
Jeff Kaiser	6	11.57	0–0	0	0	2	0	0	4.2	6	6	6	1	3	5	21	0	0	0	0

Pitching	G	ERA	W–L	SV	GS	GF	CG	SHO	IP	H	R	ER	HR	BB	SO	BFP	WP	HBP	BK	IBB
Mike Maddux	58	3.60	3–8	5	0	31	0	0	75.0	67	34	30	3	27	57	320	4	4	1	7
Josias Manzanillo	6	3.00	0–0	0	0	2	0	0	12.0	8	7	4	1	9	11	54	0	0	0	0
Bret Saberhagen	19	3.29	7–7	0	19	0	4	1	139.1	131	55	51	11	17	93	556	2	3	2	4
Pete Schourek	41	5.96	5–12	0	18	6	0	0	128.1	168	90	85	13	45	72	586	1	3	2	7
Frank Tanana	29	4.48	7–15	0	29	0	0	0	183.0	198	100	91	26	48	104	784	7	9	2	7
Dave Telgheder	24	4.76	6–2	0	7	7	0	0	75.2	82	40	40	10	21	35	325	1	4	0	2
Mickey Weston	4	7.94	0–0	0	0	0	0	0	5.1	11	5	5	0	1	2	30	0	1	0	0
Anthony Young	39	3.77	1–16	3	10	19	1	0	100.1	103	62	42	8	42	62	445	0	1	2	9
TOTAL	162	4.05	59–103	22	162	146	16	8	1438.0	1483	744	647	139	434	867	6151	32	50	14	61

1994

NL EAST						
Team	W	L	PCT	GB	BA	ERA
Expos	74	40	.649	–	.278	3.56
Braves	68	46	.596	6.0	.267	3.57
Mets	55	58	.487	18.5	.250	4.13
Phillies	54	61	.470	20.5	.262	3.85
Marlins	51	64	.443	23.5	.266	4.50

No division winner due to players strike

Mets were 12.5 behind Braves for wild-card at time of strike

For just the fourth time in team history, the Mets played the final game of a major league season. However, the circumstances were much different this time.

Mauro Gozzo gave up a bases-loaded single with two out in the bottom of the 15th, allowing the Phillies to beat the Mets 2–1 at Veterans Stadium. The game ended in the wee hours of the morning of August 12, sometime after the major league players' strike went into effect. Once the remainder of the season was canceled, the Mets-Phillies game went in the books as the last completed game of the season.

The strike finished what had been an encouraging season for the Mets. Rookies Bobby Jones and Rico Brogna showed they belonged in the majors. Bret Saberhagen was outstanding while avoiding injuries for the first time in his three seasons as a Met. Bobby Bonilla lifted his batting average to the standards he set with the Pirates. John Franco had his best season in three years. And Todd Hundley began to display a power stroke.

Best of all, the season was free of sprayed bleach, tossed firecrackers, bitching players, and fired managers. With the exception of Dwight Gooden, players stayed on their best behavior and appeared to bust their butts for Dallas Green, who was in his first full season as Mets skipper.

However, the Mets played in relative anonymity in 1994, entering the year with no expectations following a 59–103 season. Although they showed improvement, the other team in New York was racking up the American League's best record and took over the town, a stranglehold they've enjoyed ever since. The Mets finished just 12th among the 14 NL teams in attendance with fewer than 1.2 million fans.

It was going to be hard to stink as much as the 1993 version. The Mets opened the '94 campaign with three straight wins and were 18–14 through 32 games compared to their 12–20 mark in 1993. A 17–31 skid soon followed,

putting the Mets a season-worst 10 games under .500 at 35–45. But a rookie began to infuse some enthusiasm and excitement into the team after being recalled from Triple A Norfolk in June.

First baseman Rico Brogna was acquired for Alan Zinter in one of those under-the-radar deals just before the season opener. Brogna spent his first six pro seasons with the Tigers but failed to impress management while hitting .257 with 69 home runs in the minors. He hit just .244 in 67 games for the Tides before an injury to David Segui left a void at first base on the Mets. Brogna was called up June 20 and went 0-for-5 over his first three games before becoming the Mets' top hitter the rest of the season. He compiled hitting streaks of six (.375, 24 AB) and eight games (.423, 26 AB) before hitting in 15 straight from July 22 through August 7. He went 25-for-56 (.446) with two home runs, 12 RBIs, and seven runs scored to lift his average from .308 to .372. Brogna's on-base percentage was .446 by August 7, and his slugging average stood at .661.

Brogna also was the defensive equal to the slick-fielding Segui, making things easier on fellow infielders Jeff Kent, Jose Vizcaino, and Bobby Bonilla. As a hitter, he was everything Jeromy Burnitz was not during his 45 games with the '94 Mets.

Burnitz took a step back following a good rookie season in 1993. He took a seat in Green's doghouse while hitting .238 with three homers, 15 RBIs, and 45 strikeouts in 143 at-bats. Burnitz spent two months in the minors after hitting only .192 with 15 hits and 26 strikeouts in 78 at-bats.

Hundley began to display the power that would make him one of the National League's most feared hitters within two years. Hundley smacked 16 home runs in only 291 at-bats after hitting only 19 in his first 902 big league at-bats. He also improved his throwing, nailing 22 of 65 base-runners (34 percent).

Bonilla was the team leader in games played (108), home runs (20), and RBIs (67) while continuing to settle in as a Met. The misery of 1992 were becoming a distant memory as he served as a very capable leader on a ballclub that had become markedly younger in his third season with the team.

One of those young players was Ryan Thompson, whom many in the front office believed had a bigger upside than Kent. Thompson easily had the greatest power among all Mets and was second on the team with 18 homers in just 334 at-bats. But his free swinging also led to 94 strikeouts, and his .225 average was the lowest among Mets with at least 60 at-bats.

Kent continued to put up nice numbers, pacing the club with a .292 average and 68 RBIs while tying Bonilla for the team lead with 24 doubles. Kent was settling in as a hitter and a fielder, although his 14 errors were second to Bonilla.

The Mets brought back Kevin McReynolds, who was re-acquired from the Royals for Vince Coleman. McReynolds was a shell of his former self at age 34, battling back and groin issues that landed him on the disabled list. McReynolds was able to play just 51 games while hitting .256 in his final major league season.

Another former Royal fared much better in 1994. Bret Saberhagen avoided injuries for the first time in three seasons as a Met, allowing him to enjoy his finest season in pinstripes. Saberhagen was second in the NL winning percentage (.778), third in wins (14), and fourth in strikeouts (143). He was named to the All-Star Game and finished third in the NL Cy Young balloting.

Saberhagen's control was unbelievable throughout the season. He led the majors in walks per nine innings (0.7), a modern major league record. He also was the fourth pitcher in major league history to have more wins than walks in at least 150 innings pitched. Saberhagen didn't allow a walk in a team-record 47⅓ innings from May 10 through June 13.

Bobby Jones became the No. 2 starter in his third major league season, finishing second on the team with 12 victories, 80 strikeouts, and a 3.15 ERA while rarely hitting higher than 90 on the radar. At 24, Jones had the guile of a 10-year veteran and would be the only member of the '94 squad to play for the Mets in the 2000 postseason.

Pete Smith was a bust after being acquired from the Braves, the first indication Atlanta GM John Schuerholz knew when to part with a pitcher. But the gravest disappointment was Gooden, who was suspended June 28 following a cocaine relapse. He immediately went into drug rehab, only to test positive on numerous occasions from August to November. Gooden was suspended for the entire 1995 season, putting his career in jeopardy before his 30th birthday.

Gooden was terrible when he was able to pitch in 1994, going 3–4 with a 6.31 ERA despite 40 strikeouts in 41 innings. He was on the disabled list from April 29 to June 9 with a broken toe and allowed eight earned runs over 5⅓ innings in his final start as a Met on June 24 against the Pirates.

Gooden aside, there was reason for optimism heading into 1995 if owners and players could hammer out a contract agreement after the strike canceled the last seven weeks of the regular season and the playoffs. Edgardo Alfonzo and Rey Ordonez had strong seasons for Double A Binghamton in '94, as did pitchers Bill Pulsipher and Jason Isringhausen. The Mets also parlayed the first overall pick in the 1994 draft to take Florida State hurler Paul Wilson. The minor league talent level was high for the first time in a decade, giving Mets fans some hope in 1995 following a season of low expectations.

1994 Mets Statistics

Hitting	G	AB	R	H	2B	3B	HR	RBI	BB	SO	BA	OBP	SLG	SB	CS	GDP	HP	SH	SF	IBB
Tim Bogar	50	52	5	8	0	0	2	5	4	11	.154	.211	.269	1	0	1	0	2	1	1
Bobby Bonilla	108	403	60	117	24	1	20	67	55	101	.290	.374	.504	1	3	10	0	0	2	9
Rico Brogna	39	131	16	46	11	2	7	20	6	29	.351	.380	.626	1	0	2	0	1	0	0
Jeromy Burnitz	45	143	26	34	4	0	3	15	23	45	.238	.347	.329	1	1	2	1	1	0	0
John Cangelosi	62	111	14	28	4	0	0	4	19	20	.252	.371	.288	5	1	1	2	3	0	1
Shawn Hare	22	40	7	9	1	1	0	2	4	11	.225	.295	.300	0	0	4	0	0	0	0
Todd Hundley	91	291	45	69	10	1	16	42	25	73	.237	.303	.443	2	1	3	3	3	1	4
Jeff Kent	107	415	53	121	24	5	14	68	23	84	.292	.341	.475	1	4	7	10	1	3	3
Jim Lindeman	52	137	18	37	8	1	7	20	6	35	.270	.303	.496	0	0	0	1	0	1	2
Jeff McKnight	31	27	1	4	1	0	0	2	4	12	.148	.250	.185	0	0	0	0	0	1	0
Kevin McReynolds	51	180	23	46	11	2	4	21	20	34	.256	.328	.406	2	0	2	0	0	1	1
Joe Orsulak	96	292	39	76	3	0	8	42	16	21	.260	.299	.353	4	2	11	3	0	7	2
Rick Parker	8	16	1	1	0	0	0	0	0	2	.063	.063	.063	0	0	0	0	2	0	0
Luis Rivera	32	43	11	12	2	1	3	5	4	14	.279	.367	.581	0	1	1	2	0	0	0
David Segui	92	336	46	81	17	1	10	43	33	43	.241	.308	.387	0	0	6	1	1	3	6
Kelly Stinnett	47	150	20	38	6	2	2	14	11	28	.253	.323	.360	2	0	3	5	0	1	1
Ryan Thompson	98	334	39	75	14	1	18	59	28	94	.225	.301	.434	1	1	8	10	3	4	7
Fernando Vina	79	124	20	31	6	0	0	6	12	11	.250	.372	.298	3	1	4	12	2	0	0
Jose Vizcaino	103	410	47	105	13	3	3	33	33	62	.256	.310	.324	1	11	5	2	5	6	3
Pitchers																				
Juan Castillo	2	5	0	1	0	0	0	1	0	1	.200	.200	.200	0	0	0	0	0	0	0
John Franco	47	3	0	0	0	0	0	0	0	3	.000	.000	.000	0	0	0	0	0	0	0
Dwight Gooden	7	12	1	2	0	0	0	2	0	1	.167	.167	.167	0	0	0	0	4	0	0
Mauro Gozzo	23	16	1	4	1	0	0	1	1	9	.250	.294	.313	0	0	0	0	1	0	0
Eric Hillman	11	8	0	0	0	0	0	0	0	4	.000	.000	.000	0	0	0	0	1	0	0
Jason Jacome	8	16	0	1	0	0	0	1	0	9	.063	.063	.063	0	0	0	0	1	0	0
Bobby Jones	24	46	3	5	1	0	0	1	0	19	.109	.109	.130	0	0	0	0	8	0	0
Doug Linton	32	7	0	0	0	0	0	0	0	3	.000	.000	.000	0	0	0	0	2	0	0
Mike Maddux	27	3	0	0	0	0	0	0	0	2	.000	.000	.000	0	0	0	0	0	0	0
Josias Manzanillo	37	4	0	0	0	0	0	0	0	2	.000	.000	.000	0	0	0	0	1	0	0
Mike Remlinger	10	16	1	0	0	0	0	1	1	6	.000	.059	.000	0	0	0	0	3	0	0
Bret Saberhagen	24	58	7	10	2	0	0	1	4	14	.172	.226	.207	0	0	0	0	8	0	0
Frank Seminara	10	3	0	0	0	0	0	0	0	0	.000	.000	.000	0	0	0	0	0	0	0
Pete Smith	21	37	2	5	1	0	0	1	4	9	.135	.220	.162	0	0	0	0	6	0	0
TOTAL	**113**	**3869**	**506**	**966**	**164**	**21**	**117**	**477**	**336**	**807**	**.250**	**.310**	**.394**	**25**	**26**	**70**	**52**	**59**	**31**	**40**

Pitching	G	ERA	W–L	SV	GS	GF	CG	SHO	IP	H	R	ER	HR	BB	SO	BFP	WP	HBP	BK	IBB
Juan Castillo	2	6.94	0–0	0	2	0	0	0	11.2	17	9	9	2	5	1	54	0	0	0	0
John Franco	47	2.70	1–4	30	0	43	0	0	50.0	47	20	15	2	19	42	216	1	1	0	0
Dwight Gooden	7	6.31	3–4	0	7	0	0	0	41.1	46	32	29	9	15	40	182	2	1	0	1
Mauro Gozzo	23	4.83	3–5	0	8	5	0	0	69.0	86	48	37	5	28	33	323	5	1	0	10
Eric Gunderson	14	0.00	0–0	0	0	3	0	0	9.0	5	0	0	0	4	4	31	0	0	0	0
Eric Hillman	11	7.79	0–3	0	6	0	0	0	34.2	45	30	30	9	11	20	156	1	2	1	3
Jonathan Hurst	7	12.60	0–1	0	0	5	0	0	10.0	15	14	14	5	5	6	50	1	0	0	0
Jason Jacome	8	2.67	4–3	0	8	0	1	1	54.0	54	17	16	3	17	30	222	2	0	0	2
Bobby Jones	24	3.15	12–7	0	24	0	1	1	160.0	157	75	56	10	56	80	685	1	4	3	9
Doug Linton	32	4.47	6–2	0	3	8	0	0	50.1	74	27	25	4	20	29	241	2	0	0	3
Mike Maddux	27	5.11	2–1	2	0	12	0	0	44.0	45	25	25	7	13	32	186	2	0	0	4
Josias Manzanillo	37	2.66	3–2	2	0	14	0	0	47.1	34	15	14	4	13	48	186	2	3	0	2
Roger Mason	41	3.51	2–4	1	0	11	0	0	51.1	44	23	20	6	20	26	215	0	2	0	4
Mike Remlinger	10	4.61	1–5	0	9	0	0	0	54.2	55	30	28	9	35	33	252	3	1	0	4
Bret Saberhagen	24	2.74	14–4	0	24	0	4	0	177.1	169	58	54	13	13	143	696	0	4	0	0
Frank Seminara	10	5.82	0–2	0	1	5	0	0	17.0	20	12	11	2	8	7	75	1	0	1	0
Pete Smith	21	5.55	4–10	0	21	0	1	0	131.1	145	83	81	25	42	62	565	3	2	1	4
Dave Telgheder	6	7.20	0–1	0	0	0	0	0	10.0	11	8	8	2	8	4	48	0	0	0	2
TOTAL	113	4.13	55–58	35	113	106	7	2	1023.0	1069	526	469	117	332	640	4383	26	21	6	48

1995

NL EAST						
Team	W	L	PCT	GB	BA	ERA
Braves	90	54	.625	—	.250	3.40
Mets	69	75	.479	21.0	.267	3.88
Phillies	69	75	.479	21.0	.262	4.21
Marlins	67	76	.469	22.5	.262	4.27
Expos	66	78	.458	24.0	.259	4.11

Mets finish eight games behind Rockies for wild-card

The major league players' strike spilled into March, prompting owners to start spring training with replacement players. It gave Mets fans another opportunity to learn a new set of names following the team's overhauls of 1992, '93, and '94. No fewer than 105 players had taken the field for the Mets since the 1991 season opener.

Owners finally hammered out a collective bargaining agreement in early April, just days before the regular season would have begun with rookies and retreads. Spring training was prolonged by three weeks for established players to prepare for the season. Due to the extension of the exhibition docket, the regular season was trimmed to 144 games, giving the Mets an opportunity to avoid 90 losses.

The Mets began the season with several new faces, including veteran outfielder Brett Butler and a rookie infielder named Edgardo Alonzo. The lineup still included Bobby Bonilla, Todd Hundley, Jeff Kent, Rico Brogna, Jose Vizcaino, Ryan Thompson, and Joe Orsulak, but many of the bench players from 1994 were replaced by youngsters, leaving Bonilla, Butler, and Orsulak as the only position players over age 30.

Bret Saberhagen and Bobby Jones again represented the top of a rotation that also had Pete Harnisch, Dave Mlicki, and a host of hurlers trying to earn the No. 5 spot. Mike Birkbeck briefly emerged as the best of the fifth-starter candidates before he asked for his release to sign with a Japanese team.

The Mets got off to a terrible start and seemed poised to lose 90 games despite the help of the reduced schedule.

They dropped 32 of 47 from May 20 to July 9 to fall 19 games out of first. The Mets hit well enough through the first week of July, posting a .262 average with 65 home runs and 168 extra-base hits in 69 games. Hundley continued to improve his power numbers, hitting .260 with 12 homers and 36 RBIs. Bonilla had a .315 average by July 9. Orsulak was hitting .291 and teamed with Chris Jones to form a very potent pinch-hitting duo. But Kent, Brogna, and Butler were hitting slightly below expectations, Alfonzo struggled at the plate, and Thompson didn't make his season debut until late May due to an elbow injury.

The pitching was a mess, surrendering 76 home runs and compiling a 4.19 ERA while striking out just 445 strikeouts in 627 innings through July 9. Saberhagen recorded a 2.91 ERA in 15 starts after being tagged for seven runs in five innings of his season debut. Jones also was rocked in his first start of the year before recording a 2.77 earned run average over his next 16 games. Harnisch pitched in tough luck, failing to earn a decision in his first four starts despite a 1.73 ERA in 26 innings. The Mets managed to win all of Harnisch's games.

Mlicki was a disappointment during the first four months, going 4–5 with a 5.07 ERA in 16 games, including 15 starts. Dave Telgheder and Jason Jacome each tried to earn the No. 5 slot but were a combined 1–6 with a 7.71 ERA.

Pitching reinforcements began to filter into Shea by mid-June. Reid Cornelius was acquired from the Expos for first baseman David Segui, who had lost the first base job to Brogna. The Mets also recalled a couple of pitching prospects who would breathe some fresh air into the franchise and make the second half of the 1995 season a lot of fun.

The first to emerge was Bill Pulsipher, a hard-throwing southpaw who already had pitched more than 90 innings for Triple A Norfolk in 1995. Pulsipher was brought up June 14, four weeks before the Mets dipped into the farm system to showcase another promising rookie.

The Mets were 25–44 when they recalled Jason Isringhausen from Norfolk. New York went 44–31 the rest of the season as "Izzy" and "Pulse" electrified Shea Stadium.

Pulsipher was knocked around a bit in his first eight starts, compiling a 4.42 ERA and allowing at least four runs on five occasions. But he also had two outings in which he held opponents to one run or fewer while tossing at least seven innings. It was obvious he had major league talent.

Like Pulspher, Isringhausen took his lumps early, going 1–1 with a 4.56 ERA in 23⅔ innings over his first four starts before looking like a Cy Young candidate. He tossed eight shutout innings in his fifth start, opening a season-ending stretch in which he was 8–1 with a 2.21 ERA. He gave up only three home runs and averaged just 2.46 walks per nine innings in his last 10 starts.

Everything began to fall into place for the Mets once Isringhausen and Pulsipher started to flourish. The Mets were confident in the rookie tandem even before they got hot, sending Saberhagen to the Rockies in a salary dump at the July 31 trade deadline.

Over the final two months, Mlicki compiled a 3.30 ERA in 73⅔ innings, rookie Carl Everett batted .277 with eight homers and 43 RBIs in 56 games, and Alfonzo hit .290 after recording a .221 average over the first two months.

The hitting was more timely than good in August and September as the Mets began to rely on their young stud hurlers. Bonilla was traded to the Orioles in late July, three weeks before Butler was jettisoned to the Dodgers. Losing the two veterans didn't stop the Mets from hitting .256 and averaging 4.6 runs the last two months. The offensive production complimented a pitching staff that compiled a 3.46 earned run average in that span.

The Mets owned the National League's worst record—and the second worst in the majors—at 32–52 after blowing a 9–7 lead in a 10–9 loss to the Pirates on July 28. They were the NL's best ballclub the rest of the way, posting a 37–23 record that allowed them to finish third in the East at 69–75.

Pulsipher wasn't around for the end of the season. He was ordered to rest after being diagnosed with sprained ligaments in his pitching elbow on September 13.

Pulsipher was showing signs of leaking oil by late August. He went 2–1 with a 2.20 ERA but only 19 strikeouts in 41 innings over five starts from July 31 to August 21. Pulsipher pitched to a 5.65 ERA in his last four starts before he was shut down. He went 8–12 with a 5.89 ERA in 200⅓ innings the rest of his career.

The lefty's elbow was destroyed in part by overwork. He tossed 201 innings for Binghamton in 1994 and a combined 218⅓ innings with Norfolk and the Mets in '95. The team hoped a few months of rest would be the right tonic for one of its three top young hurlers.

Another pitching prospect was looking good for the Mets in 1995. Paul Wilson was a combined 11–6 with a 2.41 ERA and 194 strikeouts in 186⅔ innings for Binghamton and Norfolk, just a year after the Mets took him with the first overall pick in the draft. Mets fans envisioned a 1996 rotation that featured Isringhausen, Pulsipher, Wilson, Jones, and either Mlicki or Harnisch.

The team also had a surplus of position players in the minors. Rey Ordonez was dazzling the International League with his glove at shortstop while Butch Huskey was hitting 28 home runs for the Tides. Jay Payton led Binghamton with a .345 average and hit 14 home runs despite playing just 85 games. They were three reasons why the Mets were named the 1995 Organization of the Year by Baseball America, *USA Today*, and Topps.

Hundley, Kent, Brogna, Vizcaino, and Alfonzo all hit .278 or better while appearing in at least 90 games. Everett seemed like a star on the rise in right field, and the Mets also had highly touted prospect Alex Ochoa ready to become an everyday player in the outfield. By the end of 1995 there was no reason to believe the Mets were going to finish below .500 for a sixth consecutive year.

But the Mets would learn two valuable lessens after 1995: 1) don't count on your minor leaguers until they produce in the majors, and 2) put your best pitching prospects on a pitch count.

1995 Mets Statistics

Hitting	G	AB	R	H	2B	3B	HR	RBI	BB	SO	BA	OBP	SLG	SB	CS	GDP	HP	SH	SF	IBB
Edgardo Alfonzo	101	335	26	93	13	5	4	41	12	37	.278	.301	.382	1	1	7	1	4	4	1
Jeff Barry	15	15	2	2	1	0	0	0	1	8	.133	.188	.200	0	0	0	0	0	0	0
Tim Bogar	78	145	17	42	7	0	1	21	9	25	.290	.329	.359	1	0	2	0	2	1	0
Bobby Bonilla	80	317	49	103	25	4	18	53	31	48	.325	.385	.599	0	3	11	1	0	2	10
Rico Brogna	134	495	72	143	27	2	22	76	39	111	.289	.342	.485	0	0	10	2	2	2	7
Damon Buford	44	136	24	32	5	0	4	12	19	28	.235	.346	.360	7	7	3	5	0	2	0
Brett Butler	90	367	54	114	13	7	1	25	43	42	.311	.381	.392	21	7	4	0	6	2	2
Alberto Castillo	13	29	2	3	0	0	0	0	3	9	.103	.212	.103	1	0	0	1	0	0	0
Carl Everett	79	289	48	75	13	1	12	54	39	67	.260	.352	.436	2	5	11	2	1	0	2
Brook Fordyce	4	2	1	1	1	0	0	0	1	0	.500	.667	1.000	0	0	0	0	0	0	0
Todd Hundley	90	275	39	77	11	0	15	51	42	64	.280	.382	.484	1	0	4	5	1	3	5
Butch Huskey	28	90	8	17	1	0	3	11	10	16	.189	.267	.300	1	0	3	0	1	1	0
Chris Jones	79	182	33	51	6	2	8	31	13	45	.280	.327	.467	2	1	2	1	2	3	1
Jeff Kent	125	472	65	131	22	3	20	65	29	89	.278	.327	.464	3	3	9	8	1	4	3
Aaron Ledesma	21	33	4	8	0	0	0	3	6	7	.242	.359	.242	0	0	2	0	0	0	1
Alex Ochoa	11	37	7	11	1	0	0	0	2	10	.297	.333	.324	1	0	1	0	0	0	0
Joe Orsulak	108	290	41	82	19	2	1	37	19	35	.283	.323	.372	1	3	3	1	1	6	2
Ricky Otero	35	51	5	7	2	0	0	1	3	10	.137	.185	.176	2	1	1	0	1	0	0
David Segui	33	73	9	24	3	1	2	11	12	9	.329	.420	.479	1	3	2	1	4	2	1
Bill Spiers	63	72	5	15	2	1	0	11	12	15	.208	.314	.264	0	1	0	0	1	2	1
Kelly Stinnett	77	196	23	43	8	1	4	18	29	65	.219	.338	.332	2	0	3	6	0	0	3
Ryan Thompson	75	267	39	67	13	0	7	31	19	77	.251	.306	.378	3	1	12	4	0	4	1

Hitting (continued)	G	AB	R	H	2B	3B	HR	RBI	BB	SO	BA	OBP	SLG	SB	CS	GDP	HP	SH	SF	IBB
Jose Vizcaino	135	509	66	146	21	5	3	56	35	76	.287	.332	.365	8	3	14	1	13	3	4
Pitchers																				
Mike Birkbeck	4	6	1	2	0	0	0	0	1	1	.333	.500	.333	0	0	0	1	1	0	0
Paul Byrd	17	1	0	1	0	0	0	0	0	0	1.000	1.000	1.000	0	0	0	0	0	0	0
Reid Cornelius	10	20	0	2	0	0	0	0	0	7	.100	.100	.100	0	0	0	0	0	0	0
Jerry Dipoto	58	5	0	0	0	0	0	0	0	3	.000	.000	.000	0	0	0	0	1	0	0
Don Florence	14	1	0	0	0	0	0	0	0	1	.000	.000	.000	0	0	0	0	0	0	0
Eric Gunderson	30	0	1	0	0	0	0	0	0	0		1.000		0	0	0	0	1	0	0
Pete Harnisch	18	33	0	3	0	0	0	0	0	6	.091	.091	.091	0	0	0	0	3	0	0
Doug Henry	51	1	1	1	0	0	0	0	0	0	1.000	1.000	1.000	0	0	0	0	1	0	0
Jason Isringhausen	14	27	2	4	1	0	0	0	2	10	.148	.233	.185	0	0	1	1	4	0	0
Jason Jacome	5	7	0	0	0	0	0	0	0	6	.000	.000	.000	0	0	0	0	1	0	0
Bobby Jones	30	56	3	9	0	0	0	2	1	25	.161	.175	.161	0	0	0	0	18	0	0
Kevin Lomon	6	0	0	0	0	0	0	0	0	0				0	0	0	0	1	0	0
Blas Minor	35	2	0	0	0	0	0	0	0	0	.000	.000	.000	0	0	0	0	0	0	0
Dave Mlicki	29	39	2	2	0	0	0	2	8	12	.051	.213	.051	0	0	0	0	12	0	0
Robert Person	3	3	1	2	0	0	0	0	0	0	.667	.667	.667	0	0	0	0	0	0	0
Bill Pulsipher	17	38	4	4	2	0	0	4	5	19	.105	.200	.158	0	0	0	0	4	2	0
Mike Remlinger	5	1	0	0	0	0	0	0	0	0	.000	.000	.000	0	0	0	0	0	0	0
Bret Saberhagen	16	35	2	4	1	0	0	0	1	8	.114	.139	.143	0	0	0	0	5	0	0
Dave Telgheder	7	6	1	2	0	0	0	1	0	3	.333	.333	.333	0	0	0	0	1	0	0
TOTAL	144	4958	657	1323	218	34	125	617	446	994	.267	.327	.400	58	39	105	42	92	43	44

Pitching	G	ERA	W–L	SV	GS	GF	CG	SHO	IP	H	R	ER	HR	BB	SO	BFP	WP	HBP	BK	IBB
Mike Birkbeck	4	1.63	0–1	0	4	0	0	0	27.2	22	5	5	2	2	14	104	3	0	1	0
Paul Byrd	17	2.05	2–0	0	0	6	0	0	22.0	18	6	5	1	7	26	91	1	1	2	1
Reid Cornelius	10	5.15	3–7	0	10	0	0	0	57.2	64	36	33	8	25	35	258	1	1	1	5
Jerry Dipoto	58	3.78	4–6	2	0	26	0	0	78.2	77	41	33	2	29	49	330	3	4	1	8
Don Florence	14	1.50	3–0	0	0	3	0	0	12.0	17	3	2	0	6	5	57	0	0	0	0
John Franco	48	2.44	5–3	29	0	41	0	0	51.2	48	17	14	4	17	41	213	0	0	0	2
Eric Gunderson	30	3.70	1–1	0	0	7	0	0	24.1	25	10	10	2	8	19	103	1	1	0	3
Pete Harnisch	18	3.68	2–8	0	18	0	0	0	110.0	111	55	45	13	24	82	462	0	3	1	4
Doug Henry	51	2.96	3–6	4	0	20	0	0	67.0	48	23	22	7	25	62	273	6	1	1	6
Jason Isringhausen	14	2.81	9–2	0	14	0	1	0	93.0	88	29	29	6	31	55	385	4	2	1	2
Jason Jacome	5	10.29	0–4	0	5	0	0	0	21.0	33	24	24	3	15	11	110	1	1	0	0
Bobby Jones	30	4.19	10–10	0	30	0	3	1	195.2	209	107	91	20	53	127	839	2	7	1	6
Kevin Lomon	6	6.75	0–1	0	0	1	0	0	9.3	17	8	7	0	5	6	47	0	0	0	1
Josias Manzanillo	12	7.88	1–2	0	0	4	0	0	16.0	18	15	14	3	6	14	73	5	0	0	2
Blas Minor	35	3.66	4–2	1	0	10	0	0	46.2	44	21	19	6	13	43	192	3	1	0	1
Dave Mlicki	29	4.26	9–7	0	25	1	0	0	160.2	160	82	76	23	54	123	696	5	4	1	2
Robert Person	3	0.75	1–0	0	1	0	0	0	12.0	5	1	1	1	2	10	44	0	0	0	0
Bill Pulsipher	17	3.98	5–7	0	17	0	2	0	126.2	122	58	56	11	45	81	530	2	4	1	0
Mike Remlinger	5	6.35	0–1	0	0	4	0	0	5.2	7	5	4	1	2	6	27	0	0	0	0
Bret Saberhagen	16	3.35	5–5	0	16	0	3	0	110.0	105	45	41	13	20	71	452	2	5	0	2
Dave Telgheder	7	5.61	1–2	0	4	2	0	0	25.2	34	18	16	4	7	16	118	0	0	1	3
Pete Walker	13	4.58	1–0	0	0	10	0	0	17.2	24	9	9	3	5	5	79	0	0	0	0
TOTAL	144	3.88	69–75	36	144	135	9	9	1291.0	1296	618	557	133	401	901	5483	39	35	12	48

1996

NL EAST

Team	W	L	PCT	GB	BA	ERA
Braves	96	66	.593	—	.270	3.54
Expos	88	74	.543	8.0	.262	3.78
Marlins	80	82	.494	16.0	.257	3.95
Mets	71	91	.438	25.0	.270	4.22
Phillies	67	95	.414	29.0	.256	4.49

Mets finish 19 games behind Dodgers for wild-card

Prior to 1996, the Mets had developed an order of progression when the team was in rebuilding mode. They showcased several talented rookie pitchers (Koosman, Boswell, McAndrew, and Ryan) in 1968, finished in ninth place, and captured a World Series the following year. The Mets later unveiled pitchers Ron Darling and Walt Terrell in 1983, finished last in the NL East, and won 90 games a year later with rookies Dwight Gooden and Sid Fernandez in the rotation.

A similar order of progression was anticipated in 1996. The top of the rotation was expected to include Jason Isringhausen, Bill Pulsipher, and rookie Paul Wilson, a highly touted trio of hurlers expected to eventually win 20 games apiece, lead the franchise to several World Series, marry supermodels, and rescue kittens from trees.

Isringhausen and Pulsipher were promoted to the Mets in the summer of '95 and were the primary reasons why the ballclub posted the National League's second-best record after the All-Star break. New York finished with an ordinary 69–75 record, but their 44–31 mark in the second half was cause for celebration.

Executive VP of Baseball Operations Joe McIlvaine fortified the 1996 lineup by acquiring Lance Johnson and Bernard Gilkey and promoting slick-fielding rookie Rey Ordonez to join a squad that included 20-somethings Todd Hundley, Butch Huskey, Jose Vizcaino, Jeff Kent, Edgardo Alfonzo, and Alex Ochoa.

The mix of arms and youth had giddy fans thinking about a 1969 repeat. By February, comparisons were being made between the '96 team and the Miracle Mets. The big difference was that this team had the potential to be a dangerous offensive juggernaut.

The offense more than lived up to expectations as Hundley, Johnson, and Gilkey set or tied several single-season team records and were at or near the top of the league in many offensive categories. But the "Big Three" of Pulsipher, Isringhausen, and Wilson quickly fell apart and led a very disappointing 71–91 finish. By season's end, journeyman Mark Clark was the ace of the staff, and Bobby Jones was the best of the Mets' homegrown starting pitchers.

Isringhausen stumbled through the season and finished 6–14 with a 4.77 ERA, making him the most successful of the "Big Three." Izzy was just 3–7 with a 3.58 earned run average after tossing a six-hit shutout against the Marlins on June 9. But he threw just one complete game the rest of the way while compiling a 6.02 ERA.

NL hitters were blasting Wilson on a regular basis. His best outing came in a no-decision as he pitched one-hit ball over eight innings of a 3–2 win against the Pirates on July 31. He also scattered three hits over eight innings in two other games and compiled a 1.91 ERA in his final six starts. But his 5–12 record and 5.38 ERA stopped any talk of Wilson being the next Tom Seaver.

Pulsipher didn't throw a single pitch. He underwent surgery on his left elbow in April after experiencing pain during spring training. Pulsipher had been shut down the previous September due to elbow pain after tossing 218⅓ innings for the Mets and Norfolk.

Manager Dallas Green grew frustrated with Isringhausen and Wilson, saying publicly that they didn't belong in the majors if they continued to pitch poorly. His two phenoms were being pounded almost daily, killing whatever chances the Mets had of earning a playoff berth.

Clark and Jones were nice surprises in a season of disappointments, combining for a 26–19 record, a 3.90 ERA and five of the Mets' 10 complete games. That compared very favorably with the 11–26 record and 5.05 earned run average compiled by the tandem of Isringhausen and Wilson.

Clark didn't join the Mets until March 31, when he was acquired from Cleveland for Reid Cornelius and Ryan Thompson in the team's best trade of the season. Clark was sensational from May 18 through July 16, going 9–1 with a 2.17 ERA. The Mets won 11 of his 12 starts during that span but were 12–20 in games started by Isringhausen, Jones, and Pete Harnisch during that same stretch.

Jones had mixed success during the season despite a 12–8 record. He tossed a four-hit shutout in his next-to-last start of the year and pitched at least 7⅓ innings of shutout ball in three other outings. However, he also allowed at least six runs in four starts and yielded five runs in three other appearances.

The hitters compiled nice statistics but not enough runs. The Mets finished second in the league with a .270 average and 1,515 hits, but they were dead last with 445 walks and 10th with 746 runs and a .324 on-base percentage. The Mets also were next-to-last with 97 stolen bases and averaged 6.9 runners left on base per game.

Mets fielders didn't help the pitchers, either. New York compiled a league-high 159 errors, the most by a Mets team since 1982. The miscues led to 104 unearned runs, second only to the Giants' 105.

Hundley, Gilkey, and Johnson salvaged what was an otherwise unwatchable season. All three had career years and combined to manufacture 528 of the Mets' 746 runs.

Hundley set a major league single-season record for catchers with 41 home runs and made the NL All-Star team for the first time. He was fourth in the NL in home runs and seventh with a .549 slugging percentage while compiling a career-best .992 field percentage.

Gilkey finished fourth in the league with 44 doubles and was among the top 10 in batting (.317), slugging (.562), and RBIs (117). He received MVP consideration after being snubbed for the All-Star Game.

All Johnson did was pace the NL with 21 triples and 227 hits while recording a .333 batting average, fourth best in the league. He shattered the team record for triples and finished with 61 extra-base hits and a team-high 50 stolen bases. His 117 runs scored represented a team record until Alfonzo scored 123 times in 1999.

McIlvaine tried to spark the team by getting three-time All-Star second baseman Carlos Baerga and utilityman Alvaro Espinoza from the Indians for Jeff Kent and Jose Vizcaino in late July. Unlike the Clark deal, McIlvaine was burned by Cleveland this time.

Kent and Vizcaino were batting a combined .297 in 698 at-bats as Mets prior to the trade. Baerga hit only .193 with two home runs and 11 RBIs in 26 games as a Met and would never come close to producing his Cleveland numbers.

Baerga wasn't the only new face by late August. Green was made the scapegoat for the team's underwhelming season and was fired after 39 months as manager. He was replaced by Bobby Valentine, the former Met utilityman and third base coach who enjoyed moderate success as manager of the Rangers from 1985 to 1992. The team didn't play any better under Bobby V., winning just 12 of 31 games. But they showed some enthusiasm that carried into 1997.

In many ways 1996 marked a turning point on the New York baseball landscape. Had Isringhausen, Wilson, and Pulsipher been able to make positive contributions, the Mets likely would have finished with a winning record and a possible wild-card berth. But on the 10-year anniversary of the 1986 championship team, the Mets had become an afterthought among city baseball fans following five straight losing seasons. The Yankees won the 1996 World Series a year after capturing the AL wild-card. They had taken over as the city's most important sports franchise and remain so to this day.

Pulsipher never pitched effectively again. Isringhausen found success as a closer for the A's and Cardinals, and Wilson never won more than 11 games in a single major league season. The trio combined to pitch in only 36 games as Mets after '96, going a combined 3–7 with a 7.30 ERA in 90 innings.

1996 Mets Statistics

Hitting	G	AB	R	H	2B	3B	HR	RBI	BB	SO	BA	OBP	SLG	SB	CS	GDP	HP	SH	SF	IBB
Edgardo Alfonzo	123	368	36	96	15	2	4	40	25	56	.261	.304	.345	2	0	8	0	9	5	2
Carlos Baerga	26	83	5	16	3	0	2	11	5	2	.193	.253	.301	0	0	8	2	0	1	0
Tim Bogar	91	89	17	19	4	0	0	6	8	20	.213	.287	.258	1	3	0	2	3	2	0
Rico Brogna	55	188	18	48	10	1	7	30	19	50	.255	.318	.431	0	0	4	0	0	4	1
Alberto Castillo	6	11	1	4	0	0	0	0	0	4	.364	.364	.364	0	0	0	0	0	0	0
Alvaro Espinoza	48	134	19	41	7	2	4	16	4	19	.306	.324	.478	0	2	4	0	5	1	0
Carl Everett	101	192	29	46	8	1	1	16	21	53	.240	.326	.307	6	0	4	4	1	1	2
Matt Franco	14	31	3	6	1	0	1	2	1	5	.194	.235	.323	0	0	1	1	0	1	0
Bernard Gilkey	153	571	108	181	44	3	30	117	73	125	.317	.393	.562	17	9	18	4	0	8	7
Charlie Greene	2	1	0	0	0	0	0	0	0	0	.000	.000	.000	0	0	0	0	0	0	0
Jason Hardtke	19	57	3	11	5	0	0	6	2	12	.193	.233	.281	0	0	1	1	0	0	0
Todd Hundley	153	540	85	140	32	1	41	112	79	146	.259	.356	.550	1	3	9	3	0	2	15
Butch Huskey	118	414	43	115	16	2	15	60	27	77	.278	.319	.435	1	2	10	0	0	4	3
Lance Johnson	160	682	117	227	31	21	9	69	33	40	.333	.362	.479	50	12	8	1	3	5	8
Chris Jones	89	149	22	36	7	0	4	18	12	42	.242	.307	.369	1	0	3	2	0	0	1
Jeff Kent	89	335	45	97	20	1	9	39	21	56	.290	.331	.436	4	3	7	1	1	3	1
Brent Mayne	70	99	9	26	6	0	1	6	12	22	.263	.342	.354	0	1	4	0	2	0	1
Alex Ochoa	82	282	37	83	19	3	4	33	17	30	.294	.336	.426	4	3	2	2	0	3	0
Rey Ordonez	151	502	51	129	12	4	1	30	22	53	.257	.289	.303	1	3	12	1	4	1	12
Roberto Petagine	50	99	10	23	3	0	4	17	9	27	.232	.313	.384	0	2	4	3	1	1	1
Kevin Roberson	27	36	8	8	1	0	3	9	7	17	.222	.348	.500	0	0	0	1	0	2	0
Andy Tomberlin	63	66	12	17	4	0	3	10	9	27	.258	.355	.455	0	0	0	1	0	0	0
Jose Vizcaino	96	363	47	110	12	6	1	32	28	58	.303	.356	.377	9	5	6	3	6	2	0
Pitchers																				
Paul Byrd	38	2	0	0	0	0	0	0	0	0	.000	.000	.000	0	0	0	0	0	0	0
Mark Clark	32	69	3	3	1	0	0	2	1	26	.043	.056	.058	0	0	0	0	10	1	0
Jerry Dipoto	57	1	0	0	0	0	0	0	0	1	.000	.000	.000	0	0	0	0	0	0	0
John Franco	51	1	0	0	0	0	0	0	0	1	.000	.000	.000	0	0	0	0	0	0	0
Pete Harnisch	32	55	3	5	1	0	0	1	2	18	.091	.121	.109	0	0	0	0	10	1	0
Doug Henry	58	5	0	0	0	0	0	0	0	0	.000	.000	.000	0	0	0	0	0	0	0
Jason Isringhausen	27	51	5	13	2	0	2	9	3	15	.255	.291	.412	0	0	0	0	2	1	0
Bobby Jones	31	60	6	7	2	0	0	2	3	20	.117	.159	.150	0	0	1	0	9	0	0
Blas Minor	17	1	0	0	0	0	0	0	0	0	.000	.000	.000	0	0	0	0	0	0	0
Dave Mlicki	51	10	0	1	0	0	0	0	1	3	.100	.182	.100	0	0	0	0	0	0	0
Robert Person	29	21	1	3	1	0	0	0	0	12	.143	.143	.190	0	0	0	0	5	0	0
Paul Wilson	26	50	3	4	0	0	1	4	1	32	.080	.115	.140	0	0	0	1	4	0	0
TOTAL	162	5618	746	1515	267	47	147	697	445	1069	.270	.323	.412	97	48	114	33	75	49	54

Pitching	G	ERA	W°–L	SV	GS	GF	CG	SHO	IP	H	R	ER	HR	BB	SO	BFP	WP	HBP	BK	IBB
Paul Byrd	38	4.24	1–2	0	0	14	0	0	46.2	48	22	22	7	21	31	204	3	0	0	4
Mark Clark	32	3.43	14–11	0	32	0	2	0	212.1	217	98	81	20	48	142	883	6	3	2	8
Jerry Dipoto	57	4.19	7–2	0	0	21	0	0	77.1	91	44	36	5	45	52	364	3	3	3	8
John Franco	51	1.83	4–3	28	0	44	0	0	54.0	54	15	11	2	21	48	235	2	0	0	0
Mike Fyhrie	2	15.43	0–1	0	0	0	0	0	2.1	4	4	4	0	3	0	14	0	0	0	0
Pete Harnisch	31	4.21	8–12	0	31	0	2	1	194.2	195	103	91	30	61	114	839	7	7	3	5
Doug Henry	58	4.68	2–8	9	0	33	0	0	75.0	82	48	39	7	36	58	343	6	1	1	6
Jason Isringhausen	27	4.77	6–14	0	27	0	2	1	171.2	190	103	91	13	73	114	766	14	8	0	5
Bobby Jones	31	4.42	12–8	0	31	0	3	1	195.2	219	102	96	26	46	116	826	2	3	0	6
Bob MacDonald	20	4.26	0–2	0	0	6	0	0	19.0	16	10	9	2	9	12	79	1	0	0	0
Pedro A. Martinez	5	6.43	0–0	0	0	0	0	0	7.0	8	7	5	1	7	6	36	0	0	0	4
Blas Minor	17	3.51	0–0	0	0	4	0	0	25.2	23	11	10	4	6	20	104	1	0	0	2
Dave Mlicki	51	3.30	6–7	1	2	16	0	0	90.0	95	46	33	9	33	83	393	7	6	0	8
Robert Person	27	4.52	4–5	0	13	1	0	0	89.2	86	50	45	16	35	76	390	3	2	0	3
Ricky Trlicek	5	3.38	0–1	0	0	2	0	0	5.1	3	2	2	0	3	3	20	0	1	0	1
Derek Wallace	19	4.01	2–3	3	0	11	0	0	24.2	29	12	11	2	14	15	115	2	0	0	2
Paul Wilson	26	5.38	5–12	0	26	0	1	0	149.0	157	102	89	15	71	109	677	3	10	3	11
TOTAL	162	4.22	71–91	41	162	152	10	10	1440.0	1517	779	675	159	532	999	6288	60	44	12	73

1997

NL EAST

TEAM	W	L	PCT	GB	BA	ERA
Braves	101	61	.623	—	.270	3.18
Marlins	92	70	.568	9.0	.259	3.83
Mets	88	74	.543	13.0	.262	3.95
Expos	78	84	.481	23.0	.258	4.14
Phillies	68	94	.420	33.0	.255	4.87

The 1996 season seemed to take the Mets a few steps back in their rebuilding process. The three pitchers expected to be the cornerstone of the franchise for the next decade—Jason Isringhausen, Paul Wilson, and Bill Pulsipher—were all recovering from shoulder and/or elbow surgeries by mid-November, leaving the Mets with a rotation of Pete Harnisch, Mark Clark, Bobby Jones, Armando Reynoso, and Rick Reed heading into the 1997 season.

Outfielders Lance Johnson and Bernard Gilkey and catcher Todd Hundley were fresh off career years as they reported to 1997 training camp. Mets VP of baseball operations Joe McIlvaine was banking on them to duplicate their 1996 statistics, but only Hundley came close before undergoing elbow surgery at the end of the year.

Carlos Baerga was beginning his first full spring training as a Met following consecutive subpar seasons. Baerga was putting up Hall-of-Fame numbers with the Indians until 1995 and was a tremendous disappointment after joining the Mets in July 1996.

McIlvaine picked up John Olerud, a Gold Glove–caliber first baseman who owned a sweet stroke before Blue Jays manager Cito Gaston tried to turn him into a power hitter. Gaston didn't appreciate Olerud's natural line-drive swing and was more than willing to part with the 1993 AL batting champ. McIlvaine fleeced the Blue Jays in December 1996, acquiring Olerud for Robert Person and getting Toronto to kick in a few bucks to cover Olerud's salary.

Otherwise, the Mets were going with the same lineup that helped them finish 71–91 in 1996. Butch Huskey, Edgardo Alfonzo, and Rey Ordonez joined fellow home-grown Met Hundley in a lineup that also included Gilkey, Johnson, Olerud, and Baerga. Carl Everett was slated to be the fourth outfielder, and prospect Alex Ochoa would be given a chance to fulfill his minor league potential.

The question entering the season was whether the offense could support a patchwork rotation. The pitching staff compiled a 3.63 ERA over the first 22 games, yet the Mets were just 8–14 through April 26.

Jones (4–2, 3.50), Reed (2–1, 1.03), and Clark (3–1, 3.43) pitched very well in April, and Mlicki had a 3.99 through the end of the month. Hundley delivered six home runs and 20 RBIs while Olerud recorded a .356 average and 19 RBIs during the first month. But the Mets had a .244 average through April, with Gilkey contributing a .209 average with two homers and 13 RBIs.

The season began to turn around at the end of April. The Mets salvaged the finale of a three-game set in Montreal on April 27 to start a 23–9 spurt that put them six games off the NL East lead at 31–23 by June 1. Jones was the staff ace in May, going 5–0 with a 1.15 ERA in 39 innings en route to his first and only All-Star appearance. Jones was the National League pitcher of the month in May and stretched an eight-start winning streak into June.

Armando Reynoso was giving the Mets solid innings. He was 4–0 with a 2.95 ERA in 58 innings through the end of May, with the Mets winning eight of his nine starts.

Olerud's level swing led to six home runs and 21 RBIs in May. Hundley hit .347 with six homers and 20 RBIs for the month, and even Baerga contributed a .368 average, 15 RBIs, and 13 runs scored in May.

The most memorable pitching performance of the first half belonged to Dave Mlicki, who had the honor of starting the Mets' first regular-season meeting ever against the Yankees. Mlicki was just 2–5 with a 4.70 ERA in 13 starts as he took the mound at Yankee Stadium June 16. He shaved a half-run off his earned run average by the end of the night, throwing 119 pitches in a nine-hitter as the Mets blanked the Yanks 6–0.

Alfonzo was one of the Mets' pleasant surprises at the plate in 1997 after entering the season with a lifetime .269 average in 703 at-bats. Alfonzo reeled off a 20-game hitting streak from June 20 to July 20 to lift his average to .322. He maintained a batting average of at least .315 the rest of the season while displaying exceptional defense at third base.

Hundley was still contributing despite a painful elbow, and Huskey had a .290 average with 10 home runs and 39 RBIs through June. Lance Johnson hit .289 through the first three months despite a seven-week stay on the disabled list.

The Mets also were getting contributions from Everett and backup Matt Franco. Everett batted .345 in 25 games during June after entering the month with a .212 average. Franco hit .356 in 45 at-bats in June and emerged as manager Bobby Valentine's favorite pinch-hitter.

Reserve catcher Todd Pratt was recalled in early July and batted .379 with two homers and eight RBIs in 29 at-bats the rest of the month. Pratt would garner significant at-bats the rest of the season and become a fixture on the ballclub the next four years.

If there was one glaring deficiency, it was the inconsistent bullpen. John Franco had a strong July following a mediocre June, and Greg McMichael was the team workhorse and top setup man. But the rest of the pen was spotty and in need of a shakeup if the Mets were going to make a serious charge toward a postseason berth.

New York was 65–49 and just 6 ½ games out of first when general manager Steve Phillips, in his first major trade since replacing McIlvaine on July 16, acquired relievers Mel Rojas and Turk Wendell from the Cubs. The Mets also received center fielder Brian McRae in the August 8 deal and shipped Johnson and two players to be named (Clark and shortstop Manny Alexander) to Chicago.

Edgardo Alfonzo slides under Tiger Damion Easley to steal second base in a June 1997 game in Detroit. Alfonzo became the 12th Met to hit .300 or better for a full season that year.

The Mets still managed to clinch their first winning season in seven years by September 15, improving to 82–67 and sitting six games behind the wild-card-leading Marlins in the loss column. New York finished four games off the wild-card at 88–74, their best season since 1990.

Alfonzo became the 12th Met to hit .300 or better for a full season, finishing at .315 with 10 homers, 27 doubles, and 72 RBIs as the No. 2 hitter. Olerud hit .294 and paced the team with 102 RBIs, 34 doubles, and 57 extra-base hits. Gilkey ended the year strong to finish with a .249 average, 18 homers, and 31 doubles. And Hundley became the third Met with two straight 30-homer seasons, joining Dave Kingman (1975–1976) and Darryl Strawberry (1987–1988).

The Mets had four players with at least 18 home runs, the first time that had happened since 1987. The Mets' .262 average ranked fifth-best in team history at the time, and their 777 runs scored was third-best up to that point.

Other than Reed, the rotation sputtered in the second half. Reed, a replacement player during the strike just two years earlier, went 8–5 over the final three months and was the staff ace by the end of the year. Reynoso failed to finish the season because of tendinitis in his pitching shoulder. And Jones struggled with a tired arm in the second half, going 3–4 with a 4.66 ERA after the All-Star break.

The Mets were able to revive local interest in the franchise without the services of Wilson and Pulsipher. Isringhausen returned in late August but was 2–2 with a 7.56 ERA in 29⅔ innings.

It was apparent the Mets needed a stud starting pitcher and a scary presence in the middle of the lineup to make the next step. Phillips solved the pitching problem by getting Al Leiter just before the start of 1998 spring training. The hitting help would come in the form of Mike Piazza, acquired from the Marlins in May.

The trade looked pretty good on paper but was horrible on the field. Rojas and Wendell were awful, combining for a 5.06 ERA over 42⅔ innings when the Mets needed a bridge between the starters and Franco. The Mets dropped 13 of their first 19 games following the trade to fall out of the division race.

1997 Mets Statistics

Hitting	G	AB	R	H	2B	3B	HR	RBI	BB	SO	BA	OBP	SLG	SB	CS	GDP	HP	SH	SF	IBB
Manny Alexander	54	149	26	37	9	3	2	15	9	38	.248	.294	.389	11	0	3	1	1	1	1
Edgardo Alfonzo	151	518	84	163	27	2	10	72	63	56	.315	.391	.432	11	6	4	5	8	5	0
Carlos Baerga	133	467	53	131	25	1	9	52	20	54	.281	.311	.396	2	6	13	3	3	5	1
Steve Bieser	47	69	16	17	3	0	0	4	7	20	.246	.346	.290	2	3	0	4	0	1	1
Alberto Castillo	35	59	3	12	1	0	0	7	9	16	.203	.304	.220	0	1	3	0	2	1	0
Carl Everett	142	443	58	110	28	3	14	57	32	102	.248	.308	.420	17	9	3	7	3	2	3
Matt Franco	112	163	21	45	5	0	5	21	13	23	.276	.330	.399	1	0	4	0	0	0	4
Shawn Gilbert	29	22	3	3	0	0	1	1	1	8	.136	.174	.273	1	0	0	0	0	0	0
Bernard Gilkey	145	518	85	129	31	1	18	78	70	111	.249	.338	.417	7	11	9	6	0	12	1
Jason Hardtke	30	56	9	15	2	0	2	8	4	6	.268	.323	.411	1	1	3	1	0	1	1
Todd Hundley	132	417	78	114	21	2	30	86	83	116	.273	.394	.549	2	3	10	3	0	5	16
Butch Huskey	142	471	61	135	26	2	24	81	25	84	.287	.319	.503	8	5	21	1	0	8	5
Lance Johnson	72	265	43	82	10	6	1	24	33	21	.309	.385	.404	15	10	6	0	0	1	2
Luis Lopez	78	178	19	48	12	1	1	19	12	42	.270	.330	.365	2	4	2	4	2	0	2
Brian McRae	45	145	23	36	5	2	5	15	13	22	.248	.317	.414	3	4	2	2	1	1	0
Carlos Mendoza	15	12	6	3	0	0	0	1	4	2	.250	.500	.250	0	0	0	2	0	0	0
Kevin Morgan	1	1	0	0	0	0	0	0	0	0	.000	.000	.000	0	0	0	0	0	0	0
Alex Ochoa	113	238	31	58	14	1	3	22	18	32	.244	.300	.349	3	4	7	2	2	2	0
John Olerud	154	524	90	154	34	1	22	102	85	67	.294	.400	.489	0	0	19	13	0	8	5
Rey Ordonez	120	356	35	77	5	3	1	33	18	36	.216	.255	.256	11	5	10	1	14	2	3
Roberto Petagine	12	15	2	1	0	0	0	2	3	6	.067	.222	.067	0	0	0	0	0	0	0
Todd Pratt	39	106	12	30	6	0	2	19	13	32	.283	.372	.396	0	1	1	2	0	0	0
Andy Tomberlin	6	7	0	2	0	0	0	0	1	3	.286	.375	.286	0	0	0	0	0	0	0
Gary Thurman	11	6	0	1	0	0	0	0	0	0	.167	.167	.167	0	1	1	0	0	0	0

Hitting (continued)	G	AB	R	H	2B	3B	HR	RBI	BB	SO	BA	OBP	SLG	SB	CS	GDP	HP	SH	SF	IBB
Pitchers																				
Juan Acevedo	22	6	0	0	0	0	0	0	0	5	.000	.000	.000	0	0	0	0	1	0	0
Brian Bohanon	20	33	0	6	0	0	0	4	0	15	.182	.176	.182	0	0	0	0	1	1	0
Toby Borland	13	0	0	0	0	0	0	0	0	0				0	0	0	0	1	0	0
Mark Clark	23	43	1	2	0	0	1	2	2	19	.047	.089	.116	0	0	0	0	4	0	0
Joe Crawford	18	11	0	0	0	0	0	0	0	5	.000	.000	.000	0	0	0	0	0	0	0
Pete Harnisch	6	8	0	0	0	0	0	0	0	3	.000	.000	.000	0	0	0	0	1	0	0
Bobby Jones	29	62	4	8	2	0	0	3	3	18	.129	.169	.161	0	0	0	0	4	0	0
Jason Isringhausen	6	7	1	1	0	0	0	1	0	4	.143	.125	.143	0	0	0	0	1	1	0
Ricardo Jordan	21	1	0	0	0	0	0	0	0	1	.000	.000	.000	0	0	0	0	0	0	0
Takashi Kashiwada	32	1	0	0	0	0	0	0	0	1	.000	.000	.000	0	0	0	0	0	0	0
Cory Lidle	51	5	1	0	0	0	0	0	1	4	.000	.167	.000	0	0	0	0	0	0	0
Barry Manuel	19	2	0	0	0	0	0	0	0	1	.000	.000	.000	0	0	0	0	0	0	0
Greg McMichael	70	3	0	2	0	0	0	0	0	1	.667	.667	.667	0	0	0	0	0	0	0
Dave Mlicki	30	48	3	9	3	0	0	3	3	22	.188	.231	.250	0	0	1	0	3	1	0
Yorkis Perez	9	1	0	0	0	0	0	0	0	0	.000	.000	.000	0	0	0	0	0	0	0
Rick Reed	31	57	6	10	5	0	1	5	3	18	.175	.217	.316	0	0	0	0	6	0	0
Armando Reynoso	15	29	3	7	0	0	1	3	2	15	.241	.281	.345	0	0	0	0	0	1	0
Turk Wendell	13	2	0	0	0	0	0	0	0	0	.000	.000	.000	0	0	0	0	0	0	0
TOTAL	**162**	**5524**	**777**	**1448**	**274**	**28**	**153**	**740**	**550**	**1029**	**.262**	**.329**	**.405**	**97**	**74**	**127**	**58**	**59**	**45**	**100**

Pitching	G	ERA	W–L	SV	GS	GF	CG	SHO	IP	H	R	ER	HR	BB	SO	BFP	WP	HBP	BK	IBB
Juan Acevedo	25	3.59	3–1	0	2	4	0	0	47.2	52	24	19	6	22	33	215	0	4	1	2
Brian Bohanon	19	3.82	6–4	0	14	0	0	0	94.1	95	49	40	9	34	66	412	3	4	1	2
Toby Borland	13	6.08	0–1	1	0	5	0	0	13.1	11	9	9	1	14	7	65	3	1	0	0
Mark Clark	23	4.25	8–7	0	22	0	1	0	142.0	158	74	67	18	47	72	608	4	3	0	2
Joe Crawford	19	3.30	4–3	0	2	9	0	0	46.1	36	18	17	7	13	25	182	0	0	1	1
John Franco	59	2.55	5–3	36	0	53	0	0	60.0	49	18	17	3	20	53	244	6	1	0	2
Pete Harnisch	6	8.06	0–1	0	5	0	0	0	25.2	35	24	23	5	11	12	121	1	1	0	1
Jason Isringhausen	6	7.58	2–2	0	6	0	0	0	29.2	40	27	25	3	22	25	145	3	1	0	0
Bobby Jones	30	3.63	15–9	0	30	0	2	1	193.1	177	88	78	24	63	125	806	3	2	1	3
Ricardo Jordan	22	5.33	1–2	0	0	4	0	0	27.0	31	17	16	1	15	19	123	0	2	0	2
Takashi Kashiwada	35	4.31	3–1	0	0	11	0	0	31.1	35	15	15	4	18	19	145	4	3	0	4
Cory Lidle	54	3.53	7–2	2	2	20	0	0	81.2	86	38	32	7	20	54	345	2	3	0	4
Barry Manuel	19	5.26	0–1	0	0	6	0	0	25.2	35	18	15	6	13	21	123	0	1	1	1
Greg McMichael	73	2.98	7–10	7	0	23	0	0	87.2	73	34	29	8	27	81	355	5	2	0	6
Dave Mlicki	32	4.00	8–12	0	32	0	1	1	193.2	194	89	86	21	76	157	838	5	5	1	7
Yorkis Perez	9	8.31	0–1	0	0	1	0	0	8.2	15	8	8	2	4	7	45	1	0	0	0
Rick Reed	33	2.89	13–9	0	31	0	2	0	208.1	186	76	67	19	31	113	824	0	5	0	4
Armando Reynoso	16	4.53	6–3	0	16	0	1	1	91.1	95	47	46	7	29	47	388	4	6	1	4
Mel Rojas	23	5.13	0–2	2	0	12	0	0	26.1	24	17	15	4	6	32	111	1	2	0	1
Ricky Trlicek	9	8.00	0–0	0	0	4	0	0	9.0	10	9	8	2	5	4	39	2	0	0	0
Turk Wendell	13	4.96	0–0	1	0	3	0	0	16.1	15	10	9	3	14	10	76	0	1	0	1
TOTAL	**162**	**3.95**	**88–74**	**49**	**162**	**155**	**7**	**8**	**1459.0**	**1452**	**709**	**640**	**160**	**504**	**982**	**6210**	**47**	**47**	**7**	**43**

1998

NL EAST						
TEAM	**W**	**L**	**PCT**	**GB**	**BA**	**ERA**
Braves	106	56	.654	—	.272	3.25
Mets	88	74	.543	18.0	.259	3.77
Phillies	75	87	.463	31.0	.264	4.64
Expos	65	97	.401	41.0	.249	4.39
Marlins	54	108	.333	52.0	.248	5.20

Mets fans entered the 1997–1998 off-season hoping the '97 campaign was not an aberration. They had just witnessed the ballclub post a 44–31 record after the 1995 All-Star break, only to see the Mets fall back into last place in '96.

The '97 Mets finished with a winning record for the first time in seven years, but new general manager Steve Phillips made few moves in the fall of 1997 to demonstrate the team was truly serious about reaching the postseason. Phillips acquired lefty reliever Dennis Cook a week before Christmas and signed Japanese pitcher Masato Yoshii in January, but he didn't gain the confidence of Mets fans until he engineered a trade that brought Al Leiter to New York two weeks before the start of spring training.

The Mets also entered training camp knowing catcher Todd Hundley was months away from returning from Tommy John surgery, leaving the Mets without their top home run hitter. Manager Bobby Valentine had hoped to find another power hitter in his clubhouse when he reported to Port St. Lucie in February 1998. He'd have to wait three more months before the front office found a solution to their catching problems.

Expectations rose dramatically when the Mets acquired catcher Mike Piazza from the Marlins on May 22. New York already was nine games off the NL East lead when Piazza donned the pinstripes for the first time, but the club was just 1½ games off the wild-card. With Piazza behind the plate and Leiter anchoring the rotation, the Mets led the wild-card race heading into the final week of the season. And then the bottom fell out.

The Mets put together the first true late-season collapse in team history. Had they won just two of their final five games, New York would have been in the postseason for the first time in a decade. One victory would have forced a three-way tie with the Cubs and Giants for the wild-card. Instead, they were shut out twice and scored just 10 runs in a season-ending five-game skid that cost them a playoff berth.

It was a shock to Mets fans. It marked the first time the Mets had failed to earn a postseason berth after leading a division or wild-card after September 13. The 1969 Cubs and 1973 Pirates put together tank jobs that allowed the Mets to win division titles after entering the month of September 4½ games or more out of first place each time. The 1998 collapse left fans devastated, particularly after New York's other team had set an American League record with 114 wins. In many ways the 1998 season changed the culture and mindset of Mets fans for years to come and prepared them for the abominable late-season finishes of 2007 and '08.

The Mets' lineup was full of question marks heading into 1998. Bernard Gilkey and Carlos Baerga were looking to bounce back from lackluster 1997 seasons. Hundley's injury left the team with a catching core of Todd Pratt, Alberto Castillo, Tim Spehr, and Rick Wilkins until Piazza arrived. Much was expected from Butch Huskey after he batted .287 with 24 homers in 1997, and Brian McRae was entering his first full season as the Mets' center fielder. But Gilkey and Baerga fell far short of expectations, Huskey failed to duplicate his 1997 numbers, and McRae hit .264 with 21 homers without providing any consistent production. With the bottom of the order struggling at times, opposing pitchers had little reason to challenge Piazza, who was the unfair target of boo-birds as the Mets struggled to score runs during his first three months with the team.

Edgardo Alfonzo improved on his power numbers in 1998 at the expense of his batting average. Alfonzo drove in 78 runs and scored 94 times while hitting 17 homers and 28 doubles, all career highs at that point. But he carried a .258 average into the second week of August before finishing at .278, nearly 40 points below his .315 mark of 1997.

John Olerud was by far the most consistent hitter in the Mets' lineup, setting team records with a .354 average and a .447 on-base percentage while driving in a team-high 93 runs. Take away his .222 average in June and Olerud batted .375 with 21 homers and 80 RBIs in 133 games. Oddly, Olerud's June slump came shortly after Piazza arrived at Shea.

The Piazza acquisition came as a total shock to the media—and Hundley. Phillips had insisted early in the season that Hundley would return as the starting catcher once he was healthy enough to make throws to second base. When Piazza was being shopped by the Marlins shortly after his acquisition from the Dodgers, Phillips said the Mets had no interest in acquiring a catcher that hit .331 for Los Angeles.

Hundley felt betrayed after Piazza came to the Mets. With Gilkey producing little offense, the Mets now planned to convert Hundley into a left fielder. Problem

was, Hundley hit poorly after his return and looked extremely uncomfortable in the outfield.

It took time for Piazza to adjust to his new surroundings. He produced an RBI double in his Mets debut against the Brewers and hit safely in his first nine games as a Met, but he had just 24 RBIs in his first 57 games with the team as pitchers gave him little to hit.

Leiter was superb despite a knee injury that landed him on the disabled list near the end of June. Leiter allowed three runs over six innings in his first start before going 9–2 with a 1.41 ERA in his next 12 outings. His cutter allowed him to finish the season with 17 wins and 174 strikeouts in the best season by a Mets pitcher since David Cone in 1992.

Rick Reed was almost as good as the No. 2 starter, compiling a 16–11 record and a 3.48 ERA. Reed and Leiter were the only Mets hurlers to win more than nine games in '98.

The Mets' bullpen became a team strength as Cook and Turk Wendell served as outstanding setup men for John Franco. Cook posted a 2.38 ERA in 73 games and Wendell crafted a 2.93 ERA and a 5–1 record in 66 games as the top right-hander in the bullpen. Wendell outpitched fellow righty Mel Rojas, who became a bullpen pariah in the eyes of Mets fans by going 5–2 with a 6.05 ERA in 50 outings.

Franco had a very uneven year in his ninth season as the Mets' closer. The lefty provided 38 of the Mets' 46 saves but went 0–8 in 61 games, becoming the first Met in team history to lose that many games without a victory in a single season.

The rotation was questionable after Leiter and Reed. Bobby Jones began the year 6–3 with a 3.61 ERA before recording just one won over the next two months. Newcomer Masato Yoshii allowed three hits over seven shutout innings in his major league debut but was just 2–7 with a 4.75 ERA over the final four months. Hideo Nomo, Armando Reynoso, Willie Blair, Brian Bohanon, and even Bill Pulsipher were give opportunities to secure the No. 5 starting job without much success.

Armed with an inconsistent lineup and a thin pitching staff, the Mets hovered around .500 until Piazza and Alfonzo started to click. The Mets were just 56–50 the morning of August 1, when Piazza began a season-ending stretch in which he batted .367 with 14 homers, 18 doubles, 52 RBIs, and 30 runs scored. Alfonzo dragged a .258 average into an August 6 game against the Giants before hitting .312 with 11 homers, 29 RBIs, and 41 runs scored in his final 51 games.

The Mets went 32–19 from August 1 to September 20 despite a 4.30 earned run average. The offense compiled a .262 average with 60 home runs, 97 doubles, and 236 runs scored during that period, putting the ballclub in the thick of the wild-card chase. The team won 12 of 18 from September 2 through September 20 to take over the lead for the wild-card, putting destiny in its own hands heading into the last week of the season. That's when the offense completely flat-lined.

The Mets hit only .202 with no home runs over the final five games while averaging one strikeout per 5.09 at-bats. Half of those runs came during an agonizing 6–5 loss to Atlanta in which September call-up and pinch-runner Jay Payton was thrown out at third on Olerud's RBI single to snuff out an eighth-inning rally, leaving Piazza on the on-deck circle. Payton wore the goat horns though the Mets left 12 men on base and went 4-for-19 with runners in scoring position. The record book shows the Mets were eliminated on the final day of the season, but this loss sealed their fate.

The Mets still had a chance to force a playoff for the wild-card before they took on the Braves in the season finale. Manager Bobby Valentine asked Nomo, a midseason pickup and former Rookie of the Year, to start the franchise's most important game in a decade, although Nomo hadn't pitched in almost three weeks and compiled an 8.28 ERA over his previous 29⅓ innings.

Valentine's options were down to Nomo and Reynoso after starting Jones, Leiter, and Reed in the three previous games. Nomo had more big-game experience of the two candidates, having thrown a no-hitter in the majors and making two postseason starts as a member of the Dodgers. Rather than embrace the honor of starting the pivotal contest, Nomo declined the assignment by saying he was not worthy of such a responsibility. Valentine had to go with Reynoso, who had begun the Mets' season-ending losing streak by allowing five runs in five innings of a 5–3 loss to the Expos five days earlier.

Nomo eventually appeared in the season-ender and produced one of his best outings as a Met, allowing three hits while striking out three in four shutout innings. But he entered the game with New York trailing 5–1 after

Reynoso surrendered five runs over the first 1⅔ innings. Nomo's outstanding relief effort only served to cause Mets fans to become further incensed by his request to beg out of the start. The Mets lost 7–2 to finish one game behind the Cubs and Giants, who squared off at Wrigley Field for a one-game playoff to decide the wild-card.

The five-game skid overshadowed some of the good things about the season. Leiter became the stud lefty the Mets had lacked since Frank Viola's 20-win season in 1990. Wendell and Cook gave the team hope that a lead would still be intact once Franco was asked to pitch. Rey Ordonez became the first Mets infielder to win two Gold Gloves. Piazza emerged as the Mets' most dangerous hitter since Darryl Strawberry, and Alfonzo's final two months set him apart from Huskey, Hundley, and the rest of the Mets' home-grown talent.

Steve Phillips and Mets owners Nelson Doubleday and Fred Wilpon kept Valentine's head off the chopping block and refrained from making any panic moves. Instead, Phillips spent the winter rebuilding the roster.

1998 Mets Statistics

Hitting	G	AB	R	H	2B	3B	HR	RBI	BB	SO	BA	OBP	SLG	SB	CS	GDP	HP	SH	SF	IBB
Benny Agbayani	11	15	1	2	0	0	0	0	1	5	.133	.188	.133	0	2	1	0	0	0	0
Edgardo Alfonzo	144	557	94	155	28	2	17	78	65	77	.278	.355	.427	8	3	11	3	2	3	1
Jermaine Allensworth	34	54	9	11	2	0	2	4	2	16	.204	.246	.352	0	2	0	1	0	0	0
Carlos Baerga	147	511	46	136	27	1	7	53	24	55	.266	.303	.364	0	1	21	6	3	7	6
Rich Becker	49	100	15	19	4	2	3	10	21	42	.190	.331	.360	3	1	1	0	0	0	2
Alberto Castillo	38	83	13	17	4	0	2	7	9	17	.205	.290	.325	0	2	1	1	6	0	0
Jorge Fabregas	20	32	3	6	0	0	1	5	1	6	.188	.212	.281	0	0	1	0	1	0	0
Matt Franco	103	161	20	44	7	2	1	13	23	26	.273	.366	.360	0	1	8	1	1	1	6
Shawn Gilbert	3	3	1	0	0	0	0	0	0	1	.000	.000	.000	0	0	0	0	0	0	0
Bernard Gilkey	82	264	33	60	15	0	4	28	32	66	.227	.317	.330	5	1	6	4	2	3	1
Todd Haney	3	3	0	0	0	0	0	0	1	0	.000	.250	.000	0	0	0	0	0	0	0
Lenny Harris	75	168	18	39	7	0	6	17	9	12	.232	.272	.381	5	2	5	1	4	2	1
Todd Hundley	53	124	8	20	4	0	3	12	16	55	.161	.261	.266	1	1	0	1	0	1	0
Butch Huskey	113	369	43	93	18	0	13	59	26	66	.252	.300	.407	7	6	13	1	2	4	3
Mike Kinkade	3	2	2	0	0	0	0	0	0	0	.000	.000	.000	0	0	0	0	0	0	0
Wayne Kirby	26	31	5	6	0	1	0	0	1	9	.194	.219	.258	1	1	0	0	1	0	0
Luis Lopez	117	266	37	67	13	2	2	22	20	60	.252	.312	.338	2	2	10	4	3	2	3
Brian McRae	159	552	79	146	36	5	21	79	80	90	.264	.360	.462	20	11	5	5	3	5	3
Ralph Milliard	10	1	3	0	0	0	0	0	0	1	.000	.000	.000	0	0	0	0	0	0	0
John Olerud	160	557	91	197	36	4	22	93	96	73	.354	.447	.551	2	2	15	4	1	7	11
Rey Ordonez	153	505	46	124	20	2	1	42	23	60	.246	.278	.299	3	6	11	1	15	4	7
Craig Paquette	7	19	3	5	2	0	0	0	0	6	.263	.263	.368	1	0	3	0	0	0	0
Jay Payton	15	22	2	7	1	0	0	0	1	4	.318	.348	.364	0	0	0	0	0	0	0
Tony Phillips	52	188	25	42	11	0	3	14	38	44	.223	.351	.330	1	1	1	0	1	2	0
Mike Piazza	109	394	67	137	33	0	23	76	47	53	.348	.417	.607	1	0	12	2	0	3	10
Todd Pratt	41	69	9	19	9	1	2	18	2	20	.275	.296	.522	0	0	0	0	0	0	1
Tim Spehr	21	51	3	7	1	0	0	3	7	16	.137	.267	.157	1	0	0	2	0	0	1

Hitting (continued)	G	AB	R	H	2B	3B	HR	RBI	BB	SO	BA	OBP	SLG	SB	CS	GDP	HP	SH	SF	IBB
Jim Tatum	35	50	4	9	1	2	2	13	3	19	.180	.211	.400	0	0	0	0	0	4	0
Rick Wilkins	5	15	3	2	0	0	0	1	2	2	.133	.235	.133	0	0	0	0	0	0	0
Preston Wilson	8	20	3	6	2	0	0	2	2	8	.300	.364	.400	1	1	0	0	0	0	0
Pitchers																				
Rigo Beltrán	7	1	0	0	0	0	0	0	0	0	.000	.000	.000	0	0	0	0	0	0	0
Willie Blair	11	4	0	1	0	0	0	0	2	1	.250	.500	.250	0	0	0	0	0	0	0
Brian Bohanon	23	14	1	6	1	0	0	3	0	4	.429	.429	.500	0	0	0	0	0	0	0
Dennis Cook	70	3	0	0	0	0	0	0	0	0	.000	.000	.000	0	0	0	0	0	0	0
John Franco	58	2	0	0	0	0	0	0	0	1	.000	.000	.000	0	0	0	0	0	0	0
Bobby Jones	27	48	1	9	1	0	0	4	2	21	.188	.220	.208	0	0	1	0	12	0	0
Al Leiter	27	57	1	6	3	0	0	4	7	32	.105	.203	.158	0	0	0	0	5	0	0
Greg McMichael	22	1	0	0	0	0	0	0	0	0	.000	.000	.000	0	0	0	0	0	0	0
Dave Mlicki	10	16	3	3	0	0	0	0	2	5	.188	.278	.188	0	0	0	0	3	0	0
Hideo Nomo	16	30	3	8	0	0	0	3	1	11	.267	.290	.267	0	0	0	0	2	0	0
Bill Pulsipher	13	1	0	0	0	0	0	0	0	0	.000	.000	.000	0	0	0	0	0	0	0
Rick Reed	30	64	6	8	0	0	1	5	3	21	.125	.164	.172	0	0	0	0	12	0	0
Armando Reynoso	11	30	2	5	2	0	0	0	0	15	.167	.167	.233	0	0	0	0	1	0	0
Jeff Tam	13	1	0	0	0	0	0	0	0	0	.000	.000	.000	0	0	0	0	0	0	0
Turk Wendell	62	4	0	0	0	0	0	0	0	2	.000	.000	.000	0	0	0	0	0	0	0
Masato Yoshii	27	48	3	3	1	0	0	3	3	27	.063	.118	.083	0	0	0	0	8	0	0
TOTAL	162	5510	706	1425	289	24	136	671	572	1049	.259	.328	.394	62	46	126	37	88	48	55

Pitching	G	ERA	W–L	SV	GS	GF	CG	SHO	IP	H	R	ER	HR	BB	SO	BFP	WP	HBP	BK	IBB
Rigo Beltrán	7	3.38	0–0	0	0	0	0	0	8.0	6	3	3	1	4	5	33	0	0	0	0
Willie Blair	11	3.14	1–1	0	2	2	0	0	28.2	23	10	10	4	10	21	116	1	1	0	0
Brian Bohanon	25	3.15	2–4	0	4	4	0	0	54.1	47	21	19	4	21	39	230	1	6	0	2
Brad Clontz	2	9.00	0–0	0	0	0	0	0	3.0	4	3	3	1	2	2	14	0	0	0	0
Dennis Cook	73	2.38	8–4	1	0	18	0	0	68.0	60	21	18	5	27	79	286	1	3	1	4
John Franco	61	3.62	0–8	38	0	54	0	0	64.2	66	28	26	4	29	59	289	2	4	0	7
John Hudek	28	4.00	1–4	0	0	15	0	0	27.0	23	13	12	2	19	28	123	0	2	0	3
Bobby Jones	30	4.05	9–9	0	30	0	0	0	195.1	192	88	88	23	53	115	804	2	8	2	2
Al Leiter	28	2.47	17–6	0	28	0	4	2	193.0	151	55	53	8	71	174	789	4	11	1	2
Greg McMichael	52	4.02	5–3	1	0	18	0	0	53.1	64	31	24	8	29	44	251	5	3	1	7
Dave Mlicki	10	5.68	1–4	0	10	0	1	0	57.0	68	38	36	8	25	39	264	4	5	0	4
Hideo Nomo	17	4.82	4–5	0	16	0	1	0	89.2	73	49	48	11	56	94	392	9	1	3	2
Bill Pulsipher	15	6.91	0–0	0	1	1	0	0	14.1	23	11	11	2	5	13	68	0	0	0	1
Rick Reed	31	3.48	16–11	0	31	0	2	1	212.1	208	84	82	30	29	153	845	1	6	0	2
Armando Reynoso	11	3.82	7–3	0	11	0	0	0	68.1	64	31	29	4	32	40	292	2	5	2	3
Mel Rojas	50	6.05	5–2	2	0	19	0	0	58.0	68	39	39	9	30	41	262	2	3	0	5
Jeff Tam	15	6.28	1–1	0	0	5	0	0	14.1	13	10	10	2	4	8	60	0	2	0	1
Turk Wendell	66	2.93	5–1	4	0	17	0	0	76.2	62	25	25	4	33	58	319	1	2	0	9
Masato Yoshii	29	3.93	6–8	0	29	0	1	0	171.2	166	79	75	22	53	117	724	5	6	1	5
TOTAL	162	3.77	88–74	46	162	153	9	16	1458.0	1381	645	611	152	532	1129	6161	40	68	11	59

1999

NL EAST

TEAM	W	L	PCT	GB	BA	ERA
Braves	103	59	.636	—	.266	3.63
Mets	97	66	.595	6.5	.279	4.27
Phillies	77	85	.475	26.0	.275	4.93
Expos	68	94	.420	35.0	.265	4.69
Marlins	64	98	.395	39.0	.263	4.90

Mets win NLDS over Diamondbacks 3–1

Mets lose NLCS to Braves 4–2

NLWILD-CARD

TEAM	W	L	PCT	GB
Mets	97	66	.595	—
Reds	96	67	.589	1.0
Giants	86	76	.531	10.5
Pirates	78	83	.484	18.0
Dodgers	77	85	.475	19.5
Phillies	77	85	.475	19.5

Mets beat Reds 5–0 in one-game playoff for wild-card

As good as the Mets were in 1998, general manager Steve Phillips shrewdly made sure this edition of the ballclub was much, much better.

The Mets finished dead last in the National League with 62 stolen bases in '98 before Phillips acquired outfielders Roger Cedeno and Rickey Henderson. The pair accounted for 103 of the Mets' 150 stolen bases in 1999 while scoring 179 runs.

Phillips inked free-agent Robin Ventura to solidify the infield, add power to the lineup and protect Mike Piazza. Ventura had his finest season as a major leaguer at the plate and captured another Gold Glove while sealing up a defensive infield that *Sports Illustrated* proclaimed the best of all time in a cover story.

Phillips fleeced the Orioles in December 1998 by getting reliever Armando Benitez for All-Star catcher Charles Johnson. Benitez took over as the team's closer when Franco went on the DL and kept the job through the rest of the season.

Phillips added another bat before the trade deadline, getting Darryl Hamilton from the Rockies. Hamilton hit .339 in 55 games for New York and displayed an excellent glove in right.

Phillips also signed free-agent Orel Hershiser, who gave the '99 Mets his last good season. Hershiser mentored young hurlers like Octavio Dotel, a rookie with a live fastball and an 8–3 record by the end of the season.

When Phillips realized the team needed another starting pitcher, he picked up Kenny Rogers from the Athletics and watched the Mets go 10–2 in his 12 starts. Phillips also crafted a terrific under-the-radar move by landing Pat Mahomes, who went 8–0 in 39 appearances and won a game with his bat at Wrigley Field.

The most important signing was Piazza, who accepted a seven-year, $105 million package after playing out his contract in 1998. Piazza was treated more harshly by Mets fans than he had in Los Angeles, but he still liked the idea of playing in New York for the remainder of his productive years.

The starting infielders—Ventura, Rey Ordonez, Edgardo Alfonzo, and John Olerud—committed a total of 27 errors and constantly bailed out a pitching staff that did not have a single starter with an ERA under 4.00. Ordonez recorded just four errors in 154 games while finishing fifth on the team with 60 RBI, a tremendous accomplishment for a No. 8 hitter. Olerud set a team record with 125 walks, posted a .425 on-base percentage for the second straight year and played the type of defense that would have made Keith Hernandez proud.

Alfonzo was deserving of the National League Gold Glove at second base after making a smooth transition from the hot corner following Ventura's arrival. Alfonzo made only five errors and participated in 98 double plays in 158 games while Gold Glove winner Pokey Reese of Cincinnati committed seven errors in 146 games. Alfonzo also established career highs with 27 homers, 41 doubles, 191 hits, and 108 RBIs while batting .304.

The Mets had five players hit .300 or better and qualify for the batting title, the first time that had happened in team history. Olerud finished two hits shy of becoming the sixth.

They had two players with at least 35 steals, three players drive in 100 runs, four players with at least 30 doubles, and four players with at least 55 extra-base hits, all single-season club records. The Mets had three players with at least 27 homers, only the second time that had happened in club history. And they still almost managed to blow a playoff berth in the same manner the '98 squad frittered away the wild-card.

Starting pitching was a problem at times during the season. Bobby Jones missed 3½ months of the season with bursitis and a right shoulder strain. A strained calf caused Rick Reed to sit out almost four weeks early in the season. Hershiser and Al Leiter were the only pitchers to make more than 29 starts, and Jason Isringhausen pitched his way off the rotation and out of New York in what would become Phillips' worst trade of the season. Eventually, manager Bobby Valentine had a reliable rotation down the stretch after utilizing a six-man starting staff in September 1998.

The Mets slugged their way to a 27–20 start, averaging 5.2 runs and recording a .280 average with an exceptional .374 on-base percentage and 57 home runs. The hitting and defense made up for a staff that compiled a 4.67 ERA and a 1.45 WHIP during that span.

The pitching woes were exposed during an eight-game losing streak that dropped the Mets to 27–28 and led to a coaching upheaval. The Mets hit .231 and scored just 25 during the skid while the staff carved out a gaudy 6.04 ERA.

The Mets were on the verge of being swept at Yankee Stadium in early June when Phillips fired pitching coach Bob Apodaca, bullpen coach Randy Niemann, and hitting coach Tom Robson. The bullpen had been pretty good through the first two months of the season, and the hitting was the only thing that kept them close to .500 through 55 games. But none of the starters had an ERA under five at that point, leading to a team earned run average of 4.84. The hitting slump dropped the Mets' average to .265, ranking them 10th in the league.

Apodaca was puzzled by the decision. "All I know is that over the past three years I have been prepared for every game and the pitchers have been prepared for every game," he said after his dismissal. "All I can say is if I'm responsible for Al Leiter's knee, for Bobby Jones' shoulder, for Rick Reed being on the DL, then I've got to go."[12]

Valentine was spared, although he knew he'd be the next to go if the team continued to struggle. He laid down a challenge to the front office and his players by saying if the Mets didn't show marked improvement over the next 55 games, he should be fired as well.

The Mets ended the eight-game skid by playing one of their best games of the year. They pummeled Roger Clemens, building a 7–0 lead by the third inning of a 7–2 win over the Yankees. Leiter allowed a run and four hits in seven innings of what was arguably his most important start as a Met to date. The victory sparked a 55-game stretch in which the Mets compiled a 3.98 ERA and averaged 5.7 runs. Leiter was the NL Pitcher of the Month for June after going 5–0 with a 2.62 ERA. The Mets went 40–15 to improve to 67–43, putting them 1½ games ahead of the second-place Braves by August 6. By then, the Mets had acquired Hamilton and Rogers while Benitez emerged as the new closer.

Benitez blew away opposing batters in June and July, fanning 38 in 22 innings. He converted 13 of his 15 save opportunities during those two months, with the Mets winning the two games he blew.

With Benitez serving as the closer, the Mets went 22–13 from August 7 through September 13 to improve to 89–56. The Braves went 24–10 during that span to take over the division lead, one game ahead of New York. But the Mets held a 2½-game lead over the Reds for the wild-card and had a magic number of 16 with 17 remaining. The wild-card lead grew to four games over Cincinnati after the Mets beat the Phillies September 19, giving New York a magic number of just nine with 12 games to play. New York also had a division title in its sights as the Mets were only one game behind the Braves heading into a three-game set in Atlanta. That was when the Mets stopped hitting for a week.

New York was outscored 32–12 during a six-game skid that included sweeps by the Braves and Phillies. The losing streak reached seven games with a 9–3 loss to the Braves at Shea Stadium before Leiter outpitched Greg Maddux in a 9–2 rout of Atlanta the following day. When late-season pickup Shawon Dunston misplayed a fly ball in the 11th inning of a 4–3 loss to the Braves, the Mets were two games behind the Astros and Reds for the wild-card with three games to play. Anything short of a sweep of the Pirates in the final regular season series would likely lead to Valentine's dismissal and cause Phillips to spend another year of answering questions about the team's wind passage. Worse, the Mets didn't have Leiter available for the Pirates series.

Rogers was terrific in the series opener as he carried a three-hitter and a 2–0 lead into the eighth inning before tiring. Warren Morris tied the game with a cheap infield single with the bases loaded in the eighth off John Franco. Franco got out of the jam by fanning Adrian Brown before Armando Benitez struck out the side in the ninth.

The Mets went three innings without a hit until Dunston atoned for his miscue the previous night by leading off the 11th with a single. The Mets eventually loaded the bases on a bunt and two intentional walks before Ventura ended the game with an RBI single. Thanks to losses by the Astros and Reds, the Mets were one game down with two to play.

Reed picked the next night to pitch his best game of the year. He struck out 12 in a three-hitter as the Mets blasted the Pirates 7–0. Reed also singled home a pair of runs in the eighth before Piazza capped the five-run rally with his 40th home run, a two-run blast that sealed the win. Coupled with the Reds' loss at Milwaukee, the Mets and Cincinnati were even for the wild-card heading into the final regular season game.

Orel Hershiser was asked to send the Mets to the promised land. The 41-year-old right-hander gave up a scratch run in the first inning before holding the Bucs to one hit over the next 4⅓ frames. He left with the game tied 1–1 and a runner in scoring position before Dennis Cook and Mahomes each struck out a batter to get out of the jam.

Cook and Mahomes were part of a bullpen that was 31–19 with a 3.67 ERA during the regular season. Cook was the top lefty out of the pen, leading all Mets relievers with 10 wins while appearing in 71 games.

Next out of the pen against the Pirates was Turk Wendell, who led the Mets with 80 appearances and posted a 3.05 ERA. Wendell retired his first five batters in order before allowing a single to Kevin Young, the Pirates' third hit of the game. In came Benitez, who fanned Aramis Ramirez with Young on second to end the threat and keep the game tied 1–1.

Bobby Bonilla was asked to pinch-hit in the bottom of the ninth. Bonilla spent most of the season with a sore knee and contributed little to the offense, hitting .160 in 119 at-bats. Bonilla received cheers from optimistic Mets fans as he stepped to the plate but was booed off the diamond after tapping out weakly to first base.

Melvin Mora had been equally inept at the plate for the Mets, going 4-for-30 before he stepped into the box against reliever Greg Hansell. Unlike Bonilla, Mora came through with a base hit before moving to third on Alfonzo's single.

Olerud was walked intentionally to set up a potential double play with the equally slow-footed Piazza due to bat next. Pirates manager Gene Lamont brought in Brad Clontz, a former Brave who was a washout during his short stay with the Mets.

The Mets won the game without Piazza taking the bat off his shoulder. Clontz uncorked a wild pitch to bring home Mora and spark a massive celebration at Shea. All the Mets needed now was for the Reds to lose to the Brewers.

But there was no scoreboard watching at Shea. The Reds-Brewers game was rain-delayed for several hours and didn't start until after the Mets began to filter out of their clubhouse. Several Mets left the ballpark not knowing whether they were heading to Cincinnati for a one-game playoff for the wild-card or leaving for Phoenix to face the Diamondbacks in the NLDS.

The Reds beat Milwaukee to put the Mets in the first one-game playoff in team history. This time, Valentine had Leiter at his disposal as the team traveled to enemy territory.

It took the Mets just six pitches to take the lead for good. Henderson led off with a single and scored on Alfonzo's two-run blast off Steve Parris. Henderson added a solo homer in the fifth, one inning before Alfonzo's RBI double put the Mets up 5–0.

Leiter did the rest, tossing a two-hitter and erasing doubts that he couldn't win a big game. The outcome game the Mets 97 victories, their highest total since 1988.

1999 Mets Statistics

Hitting	G	AB	R	H	2B	3B	HR	RBI	BB	SO	BA	OBP	SLG	SB	CS	GDP	HP	SH	SF	IBB
Benny Agbayani	101	276	42	79	18	3	14	42	32	60	.286	.363	.525	6	4	8	3	0	3	4
Edgardo Alfonzo	158	628	123	191	41	1	27	108	85	85	.304	.385	.502	9	2	14	3	1	9	2
Jermaine Allensworth	40	73	14	16	2	0	3	9	9	23	.219	.310	.370	2	1	1	1	2	1	0
Bobby Bonilla	60	119	12	19	5	0	4	18	19	16	.160	.277	.303	0	1	4	1	0	2	1
Roger Cedeno	155	453	90	142	23	4	4	36	60	100	.313	.396	.408	66	17	5	3	7	2	3
Shawon Dunston	42	93	12	32	6	1	0	16	0	16	.344	.354	.430	4	1	4	2	1	1	0
Matt Franco	122	132	18	31	5	0	4	21	28	21	.235	.366	.364	0	0	9	0	0	1	3
Shane Halter	7	0	0	0	0	0	0	0	0	0				0	0	0	0	0	0	0
Darryl Hamilton	55	168	19	57	8	1	5	21	19	18	.339	.410	.488	2	3	2	1	1	0	0
Rickey Henderson	121	438	89	138	30	0	12	42	82	82	.315	.423	.466	37	14	4	2	1	3	1
Mike Kinkade	28	46	3	9	2	1	2	6	3	9	.196	.275	.413	1	0	1	2	0	0	0
Terrence Long	3	3	0	0	0	0	0	0	0	2	.000	.000	.000	0	0	1	0	0	0	0
Luis Lopez	68	104	11	22	4	0	2	13	12	33	.212	.308	.308	1	1	1	3	1	1	0
Brian McRae	96	298	35	66	12	1	8	36	39	57	.221	.320	.349	2	6	6	5	0	2	1
Melvin Mora	66	31	6	5	0	0	0	1	4	7	.161	.278	.161	2	1	0	1	3	0	0
John Olerud	162	581	107	173	39	0	19	96	125	66	.298	.427	.463	3	0	22	11	0	6	5
Rey Ordonez	154	520	49	134	24	2	1	60	49	59	.258	.319	.317	8	4	16	1	11	7	12
Jay Payton	13	8	1	2	1	0	0	1	0	2	.250	.333	.375	1	2	0	1	0	0	0
Mike Piazza	141	534	100	162	25	0	40	124	51	70	.303	.361	.575	2	2	27	1	0	7	11
Todd Pratt	71	140	18	41	4	0	3	21	15	32	.293	.369	.386	2	0	1	3	0	2	0
Jorge Toca	4	3	0	1	0	0	0	0	0	2	.333	.333	.333	0	0	0	0	0	0	0
Robin Ventura	161	588	88	177	38	0	32	120	74	109	.301	.379	.529	1	1	14	3	1	5	10
Vance Wilson	1	0	0	0	0	0	0	0	0	0				0	0	0	0	0	0	0
Pitchers																				
Rigo Beltrán	20	1	0	0	0	0	0	0	0	0	.000	.000	.000	0	0	1	0	0	0	0
Armando Benitez	72	5	0	0	0	0	0	1	0	2	.000	.000	.000	0	0	0	0	0	0	0
Dennis Cook	66	1	0	0	0	0	0	0	0	1	.000	.000	.000	0	0	0	0	0	0	0
Octavio Dotel	18	24	2	3	0	0	0	1	4	17	.125	.276	.125	0	0	0	1	1	0	0
Orel Hershiser	31	62	3	9	1	0	0	3	1	18	.145	.154	.161	1	0	3	0	3	2	0
Jason Isringhausen	11	12	2	1	1	0	0	1	0	4	.083	.083	.167	0	0	0	0	1	0	0
Bobby Jones	12	16	1	5	0	0	1	1	0	4	.313	.313	.500	0	0	0	0	1	0	0
Al Leiter	29	57	1	6	2	0	0	5	2	29	.105	.136	.140	0	0	0	0	11	0	0
Pat Mahomes	40	16	2	5	3	0	0	3	0	6	.313	.313	.500	0	0	0	0	0	0	0
Josias Manzanillo	13	1	0	1	0	0	0	0	0	0	1.000	1.000	1.000	0	0	0	0	0	0	0
Rick Reed	25	45	2	11	2	0	0	5	1	14	.244	.261	.289	0	0	1	0	8	0	0
Kenny Rogers	12	25	2	3	0	0	0	1	2	10	.120	.185	.120	0	0	0	0	3	0	0
Allen Watson	13	10	0	3	1	0	0	0	0	1	.300	.300	.400	0	0	3	0	0	0	0
Turk Wendell	74	6	0	0	0	0	0	0	1	3	.000	.143	.000	0	0	0	0	0	0	0
Masato Yoshii	29	55	1	9	0	0	0	2	0	16	.164	.164	.164	0	1	3	0	6	0	0
TOTAL	163	5572	853	1553	297	14	181	814	717	994	.279	.361	.434	150	61	151	48	63	54	53

Pitching	G	ERA	W–L	SV	GS	GF	CG	SHO	IP	H	R	ER	HR	BB	SO	BFP	WP	HBP	BK	IBB
Rigo Beltrán	21	3.48	1–1	0	0	10	0	0	31.0	30	15	12	5	12	35	134	6	0	0	2
Armando Benitez	77	1.85	4–3	22	0	42	0	0	78.0	40	17	16	4	41	128	312	2	0	0	4
Dennis Cook	71	3.86	10–5	3	0	12	0	0	63.0	50	27	27	11	27	68	262	0	1	0	1
Octavio Dotel	19	5.38	8–3	0	14	1	0	0	85.1	69	52	51	12	49	85	368	3	6	2	1
John Franco	46	2.88	0–2	19	0	34	0	0	40.2	40	14	13	1	19	41	182	0	2	0	1
Matt Franco	2	13.50	0–0	0	0	2	0	0	1.1	3	2	2	1	3	2	10	0	0	0	0
Orel Hershiser	32	4.58	13–12	0	32	0	0	0	179.0	175	92	91	14	77	89	776	6	11	0	2
Jason Isringhausen	13	6.41	1–3	1	5	2	0	0	39.1	43	29	28	7	22	31	179	2	2	0	2
Bobby Jones	12	5.61	3–3	0	9	0	0	0	59.1	69	37	37	3	11	31	253	0	2	0	0
Al Leiter	32	4.23	13–12	0	32	0	1	1	213.0	209	107	100	19	93	162	923	4	9	1	8
Pat Mahomes	39	3.68	8–0	0	0	12	0	0	63.2	44	26	26	7	37	51	265	2	2	0	5
Josias Manzanillo	12	5.79	0–0	0	0	1	0	0	18.2	19	12	12	5	4	25	80	0	2	0	1
Chuck McElroy	15	3.38	0–0	0	0	7	0	0	13.1	12	5	5	0	8	7	59	1	1	0	1
Greg McMichael	19	4.82	1–1	0	0	4	0	0	18.2	20	10	10	3	8	18	84	4	0	0	3
Dan Murray	1	13.50	0–0	0	0	1	0	0	2.0	4	3	3	0	2	1	12	1	0	0	0
Rick Reed	26	4.58	11–5	0	26	0	1	1	149.1	163	77	76	23	47	104	637	1	1	0	2
Kenny Rogers	12	4.03	5–1	0	12	0	2	1	76.0	71	35	34	8	28	58	317	1	4	0	1
Glendon Rusch	1	0.00	0–0	0	0	1	0	0	1.0	1	0	0	0	0	0	3	0	0	0	0
Jeff Tam	9	3.18	0–0	0	0	3	0	0	11.1	6	4	4	3	3	8	43	0	0	0	0
Billy Taylor	18	8.10	0–1	0	0	5	0	0	13.1	20	12	12	2	9	14	68	0	0	0	5
Allen Watson	14	4.08	2–2	1	4	6	0	0	39.2	36	18	18	5	22	32	173	2	1	0	3
Turk Wendell	80	3.05	5–4	3	0	14	0	0	85.2	80	31	29	9	37	77	369	2	2	1	8
Masato Yoshii	31	4.40	12–8	0	29	1	1	0	174.0	168	86	85	25	58	105	723	1	6	0	3
TOTALS	163	4.27	97–66	49	163	158	5	7	1456.1	1372	711	691	167	617	1172	6232	38	52	4	53

2000

NL EAST							
TEAM	W	L	PCT	GB	BA	ERA
Braves	95	67	.586	—	.271	4.05
Mets	94	68	.580	1.0	.263	4.16
Marlins	79	82	.491	15.5	.262	4.59
Expos	67	95	.414	28.0	.266	5.13
Phillies	65	97	.401	30.0	.251	4.77

NL WILD-CARD				
TEAM	W	L	PCT	GB
Mets	94	68	.580	—
Dodgers	86	76	.531	8.0
Reds	85	77	.525	9.0
D'backs	85	77	.525	9.0
Rockies	82	80	.506	12.0

Mets beat Giants in NLDS 3–1
Mets beat Cardinals in NLCS 4–1
Mets lose to Yankees in World Series 4–1

A number of slumps and injuries could have derailed the Mets' charge toward a repeat appearance in the National League playoffs. But a deep bench, a strong bullpen, a solid lineup, and a new lefty starter made sure the ballclub played October baseball.

Left fielder Rickey Henderson opened the year in a deep funk that led to his departure in mid-May. Center fielder Darryl Hamilton appeared in the Mets' first five games before sitting out the next four months with a damaged left foot. The team didn't miss a beat as Jay Payton replaced Hamilton in center while Benny Agbayani took over for Henderson in left.

Robin Ventura wasn't the same hitter he was in 1999, when he hit a career-high .301 with 32 homers and 120 RBIs. Ventura's numbers in 2000 dropped to .232 with 24 round-trippers and 84 ribbies, but the lineup was more than capable of compensating for Ventura's lower production.

Three-time Gold Glove shortstop Rey Ordonez hit only .188 before breaking his left forearm during a May 29 game in Los Angeles, causing him to miss the rest of the season. Mets manager Bobby Valentine used 1999 playoff hero Melvin Mora at short for about two months before his defense prompted general manager Steve Phillips to send Mora to the Orioles for gold glover Mike Bordick.

The bench was far superior to the Mets' contingent of reserves in '99 as Bobby Valentine had eventual all-time pinch-hit king Lenny Harris at his disposal for the final four months of the regular season. Others occupying the Mets' bench at the start of games included Todd Pratt, Joe McEwing, Matt Franco, Kurt Abbott, and Bubba Trammell before a September call-up named Timo Perez played himself onto the postseason roster with his speed, defense, and potent bat.

The pitching was marginally better than in 1999, although the top two starters were a marked improvement. Al Leiter led the team with 200 strikeouts and was 16–8 with a 3.20 ERA, shaving one full run off his 1999 earned run average. Mike Hampton was the other part of the lefty tandem and was almost as effective as Leiter, producing 15 victories, 151 strikeouts, and a 3.14 earned run average.

Hampton came over from the Astros in a deal that also brought outfielder Derek Bell. In return, the Mets sent speedy outfielder Roger Cedeno and flame-thrower Octavio Dotel to the Astros in a swap that altered the team's on-field persona.

The Mets had an outstanding mix of speed and power in 1999 before sacrificing stolen bases for a deeper rotation. Without Cedeno, the Mets went from 150 steals to 66 in 2000, with Bell and Harris tying for the club lead with just eight.

The club also lost free agent first baseman John Olerud to the Mariners in the winter of 2000, depriving New York of a Gold Glove–caliber infielder and a hitter who had compiled .437 on-base percentage over the previous two seasons. Phillips replaced Olerud with Todd Zeile, who had played all of 2⅔ innings at first base from 1997 through 1999 but hit .293 with 24 homers and 98 RBIs in 1999 and proved to be a quick study at the position.

Mike Piazza and Edgardo Alfonzo remained the centerpieces of the Mets' lineup, tying for 10th among all National Leaguers in batting and combining for 63 homers, 66 doubles, and 207 RBIs. Piazza set a team record and fell two short of the major league mark by collecting at least one RBI in 15 straight games from June 14 to July 2, batting .349 with eight homers and 28 runs batted in. That was part of a 21-game hitting streak in which the Mets went 13–8 to find themselves in a tie for the wild-card and within two games of the NL East–leading Braves. Alfonzo owned a .350 average with 12 homers and 47 RBIs by June 9 before Piazza got hot.

Payton was a pleasant surprise in his first full season with the Mets, hitting .291 with 17 homers, 23 doubles, and 62 RBIs in 149 games to finish third in NL Rookie of the Year voting. Agbayani was just as solid, recording a .289 average with 15 home runs and 60 runs batted in.

Agbayani provided two of the season's highlights, beginning with a grand slam in the 10th inning of the Mets' victory over the Cubs in Game 2 at Tokyo. He also committed the funniest blunders of the year the night of August 12, when he lost track of the number of outs and handed a ball to a fan after making a catch in left. The gaffe allowed a run to score from second, but it didn't stop the Mets from winning.

Bell was the streakiest of Mets hitters. He opened the season in a 4-for-29 slump before hitting .538 with 10 RBIs and seven extra-base hits in his next 52 at-bats. Bell also produced an 11-game hitting streak that put his average at .360 through May 21. That was immediately followed by a 3-for-45 skid and a 12-game hitting streak before Bell hit a meager .157 in his final 39 games to end up with a .266 average.

The bullpen had terrific balance and was used to perfection by Valentine. Armando Benitez averaged 12.55

Joe McEwing (47) high-fives teammate Mike Bordick after scoring the go-ahead run during the eighth inning against the Los Angeles Dodgers in L.A. in an August 2000 game. The Mets won 9–6.

strikeouts per nine innings in his first full season as the Mets closer and set a club record with 41 saves. Fellow right-hander Turk Wendell and lefties John Franco and Dennis Cook were exceptional setup men for Benitez, combining for seven saves and a 19–13 record. Franco didn't blow a lead the entire regular season as he was used more as a situational lefty than ever before, tossing just 55⅔ innings in 64 appearances. Wendell was the workhorse, appearing in a team-high 77 games and retaining 17 leads in 21 tries.

It took a while for Valentine to find another reliable reliever. Pat Mahomes was not as effective as in 1999, and Bobby M. Jones, Rich Rodriguez, and Eric Cammack failed to earn Valentine's confidence. The pen finally gelled when Phillips picked up right-hander Rick White from the Rays at the July trade deadline, giving Bobby V. another option against lefty hitters.

Much was expected of Hampton after he led the National League with 22 wins and an .846 winning percentage while compiling a 2.90 ERA for the Astros in 1999. Named the Opening-Day starter against the Cubs in Tokyo, the lefty allowed two runs and four hits while walking nine in just five innings of a 5–3 loss. He also lost his next

two starts, beat up a plastic water cooler in Denver and was 2–4 with a 6.52 ERA through his first seven starts.

Hampton averaged almost one walk per inning and owned an unsightly 1.99 WHIP until May 9, when he took a shutout into the ninth inning of a 2–0 win over the Pirates. The victory began a season-ending stretch in which Hampton was 13–6 with a 2.41 ERA in 26 starts.

Leiter was named to the NL All-Star team after opening the year 10–1. He went 6–7 the rest of the season despite a 3.39 ERA and just 78 hits allowed in 95⅔ innings.

A third lefty became an effective part of the rotation as Glendon Rusch flourished in his first full season with the Mets, going 11–11 with a 4.01 ERA. Rusch posted a 1.99 ERA in 22⅔ innings over his first three starts and was 3–1 with a 2.57 ERA in his last seven appearances to help the Mets wrap up the wild-card.

The only disappointment among the starters was Bobby J. Jones, although he still managed to go 11–6 despite a 5.06 ERA and a 1.42 WHIP. Jones failed for the second straight year to throw enough innings to qualify for the ERA title, but he went 3–1 with a 3.54 ERA in his last four starts before pitching the game of his life in the NLDS against the Giants.

The season itself was without the agonizing drama that accompanied the 1999 campaign, particularly in the second half. The Mets split their first 40 games and were seven games off the division lead as late as May 31 before picking up steam at mid-summer. Sitting six games behind the Braves at 53–44 following a 1–0 loss in Atlanta on July 23, the Mets won 26 of their next 36 to move into a tie with Atlanta at 79–54 heading into September. Best of all, New York was 5½ games ahead of the Diamondbacks for the wild-card.

The Mets made things a little interesting by dropping seven of their first eight September games, scoring 25 runs while allowing 39. But the Mets still had a healthy 3½-game lead over the Diamondbacks and were within 3½ games of Atlanta for the NL East.

New York won 14 of its last 21 and secured a playoff berth during the final week before finishing one game behind the Braves. Atlanta actually clinched the division crown at Shea Stadium with five games remaining, but the Mets wrapped up the wild-card the following night with a 6–2 victory against the Braves to ignite a season-ending five-game winning streak, a complete reversal of their 1998 finish. Phillips deserved a lot of credit for molding the roster. He wasn't afraid to make a good team better, constantly scouring the majors for middle relievers and bench players that could fit into the Mets' scheme. He acquired six players—Perez, McEwing, Trammell, White, Bordick, and Harris—who were on the Mets' postseason roster after opening training camp with other teams or without a contract.

Phillips will forever be castigated for the Bordick trade,

acquiring a potential free agent who quickly went back to Baltimore. Mora eventually became a two-time All-Star with the Orioles.

The deal came a year after Phillips sent Jason Isringhausen to the Athletics for Kenny Rogers in another trade that backfired in the long term. But in both cases, it is doubtful the Mets would have appeared in the postseason unless those trades were made.

One of Valentine's assets was knowing early which players could help him over the long haul. Henderson was released after his poor start, Payton and Agbayani quickly became mainstays in the outfield, Rodriguez was deemed a bullpen bust by April, and Mora was given enough time to play himself out of the starting shortstop position. Bordick sparked the Mets immediately after joining the team, Rick White wasted little time becoming a workhorse in the bullpen and Jones was given enough time to right himself.

One of Valentine's best decisions was knowing Timo Perez should be part of the Mets' postseason roster. Perez was signed to a minor league contract on St. Patrick's Day and didn't play for the Mets until September 1. Perez hit just 6-for-27 (.222) in his first 18 games but displayed speed and strong defensive skills at all three outfield positions. The Mets won each of his last six starts as he recorded a .364 average in his final 22 at-bats to secure a spot on the NLDS roster. That decision allowed the Mets to beat the Giants and Cardinals to reach the World Series for the first time in 14 years.

Valentine became the first skipper in Mets history to lead the team to consecutive playoff berths. He would be fired just two years later.

2000 Mets Statistics

Hitting	G	AB	R	H	2B	3B	HR	RBI	BB	SO	BA	OBP	SLG	SB	CS	GDP	HP	SH	SF	IBB
Kurt Abbott	79	157	22	34	7	1	6	12	14	51	.217	.283	.389	1	1	2	1	0	1	2
Edgardo Alfonzo	150	544	109	176	40	2	25	94	95	70	.324	.425	.542	3	2	12	5	0	6	1
Benny Agbayani	119	350	59	101	20	1	15	60	54	68	.289	.391	.480	5	5	6	7	0	3	2
Derek Bell	144	546	87	145	31	1	18	69	65	125	.266	.348	.425	8	4	14	6	2	3	0
Mike Bordick	56	192	18	50	8	0	4	21	15	28	.260	.321	.365	3	1	4	2	2	0	0
Matt Franco	101	134	9	32	4	0	2	14	21	22	.239	.340	.313	0	0	3	0	1	1	3
Darryl Hamilton	43	105	20	29	4	1	1	6	14	20	.276	.358	.362	2	0	0	0	0	1	0
Lenny Harris	76	138	22	42	6	3	3	13	17	17	.304	.381	.457	8	1	4	0	2	0	1
Rickey Henderson	31	96	17	21	1	0	0	2	25	20	.219	.387	.229	5	2	2	2	0	1	1
Mark Johnson	21	22	2	4	0	0	1	6	5	9	.182	.333	.318	0	0	1	0	0	0	0
Mike Kinkade	2	2	0	0	0	0	0	0	0	1	.000	.000	.000	0	0	0	0	0	0	0
David Lamb	7	5	1	1	0	0	0	0	1	1	.200	.333	.200	0	0	0	0	0	0	0
Joe McEwing	87	153	20	34	14	1	2	19	5	29	.222	.248	.366	3	1	2	1	8	2	0
Ryan McGuire	1	2	0	0	0	0	0	0	1	0	.000	.333	.000	0	0	1	0	0	0	0
Melvin Mora	79	215	35	56	13	2	6	30	18	48	.260	.317	.423	7	3	3	2	2	5	3
Jon Nunnally	48	74	16	14	5	1	2	6	17	26	.189	.337	.365	3	1	1	0	0	1	0
Rey Ordonez	45	133	10	25	5	0	0	9	17	16	.188	.278	.226	0	4	4	0	4	1	2
Jay Payton	149	488	63	142	23	1	17	62	30	60	.291	.331	.447	5	11	9	3	0	8	0
Timo Perez	24	49	11	14	4	1	1	3	3	5	.286	.333	.469	1	1	0	1	0	1	0
Mike Piazza	136	482	90	156	26	0	38	113	58	69	.324	.398	.614	4	2	15	3	0	2	10
Todd Pratt	80	160	33	44	6	0	8	25	22	31	.275	.378	.463	0	0	5	5	2	1	1
Jorge Toca	8	7	1	3	1	0	0	4	0	1	.429	.429	.571	0	0	0	0	0	0	0
Bubba Trammell	36	56	9	13	2	0	3	12	8	19	.232	.323	.429	1	0	3	0	0	1	0
Jason Tyner	13	41	3	8	2	0	0	5	1	4	.195	.222	.244	1	1	0	1	3	2	0
Jorge Velandia	15	7	1	0	0	0	0	0	2	2	.000	.222	.000	0	0	0	0	0	0	0
Robin Ventura	141	469	61	109	23	1	24	84	75	91	.232	.338	.439	3	5	14	2	1	4	12
Vance Wilson	4	4	0	0	0	0	0	0	0	2	.000	.000	.000	0	0	0	0	0	0	0
Todd Zeile	153	544	67	146	36	3	22	79	74	85	.268	.356	.467	3	4	15	2	0	3	4

Hitting	G	AB	R	H	2B	3B	HR	RBI	BB	SO	BA	OBP	SLG	SB	CS	GDP	HP	SH	SF	IBB
Pitchers																				
Eric Cammack	8	1	0	1	0	1	0	1	0	0	1.000	1.000	3.000	0	0	0	0	0	0	0
Dennis Cook	63	0	0	0	0	0	0	0	0	0				0	0	0	0	1	0	0
John Franco	58	1	0	0	0	0	0	0	0	1	.000	.000	.000	0	0	0	0	0	0	0
Mike Hampton	34	73	7	20	0	0	0	8	5	20	.274	.313	.274	0	1	0	0	4	2	0
Bobby Jones	24	44	4	2	0	0	0	0	3	21	.045	.125	.045	0	0	0	1	7	0	0
Bobby Jones	10	2	0	1	0	0	0	0	1	1	.500	.667	.500	0	0	0	0	1	0	0
Al Leiter	29	58	1	3	0	0	0	0	4	33	.052	.113	.052	0	0	1	0	9	0	0
Pat Mahomes	49	17	1	4	1	0	0	1	1	5	.235	.278	.294	0	0	0	0	2	0	0
Bill Pulsipher	2	2	0	0	0	0	0	0	0	1	.000	.000	.000	0	0	0	0	0	0	0
Rick Reed	29	49	6	10	0	0	0	2	1	11	.204	.226	.204	0	0	0	1	14	2	0
Grant Roberts	4	0	0	0	0	0	0	0	0	0				0	0	0	0	1	0	0
Rich Rodriguez	28	1	0	0	0	0	0	0	0	1	.000	.000	.000	0	0	0	0	0	0	0
Glendon Rusch	29	50	2	3	0	0	0	1	3	19	.060	.113	.060	0	0	0	0	4	0	0
Dennis Springer	2	4	0	0	0	0	0	0	0	3	.000	.000	.000	0	0	0	0	0	0	0
Turk Wendell	74	4	0	1	0	0	0	0	0	0	.250	.250	.250	0	0	0	0	0	0	0
Rick White	24	5	0	1	0	0	0	0	0	1	.200	.200	.200	0	0	0	0	0	0	0
TOTAL	162	5486	807	1445	282	20	198	761	675	1037	.263	.346	.430	66	46	122	45	70	51	42

Pitching	G	ERA	W–L	SV	GS	GF	CG	SHO	IP	H	R	ER	HR	BB	SO	BFP	WP	HBP	BK	IBB
Derek Bell	1	36.00	0–0	0	0	1	0	0	1.0	3	5	4	0	3	0	10	0	0	0	0
Armando Benitez	76	2.61	4–4	41	0	68	0	0	76.0	39	24	22	10	38	106	304	0	0	0	2
Eric Cammack	8	6.30	0–0	0	0	2	0	0	10.0	7	7	7	1	10	9	48	0	1	0	1
Dennis Cook	68	5.34	6–3	2	0	15	0	0	59.0	63	35	35	8	31	53	269	3	5	2	4
John Franco	62	3.40	5–4	4	0	14	0	0	55.7	46	24	21	6	26	56	239	2	2	0	6
Mike Hampton	33	3.14	15–10	0	33	0	3	1	217.7	194	89	76	10	99	151	929	10	8	0	5
Bobby Jones	27	5.06	11–6	0	27	0	1	0	154.7	171	90	87	25	49	85	676	2	5	1	3
Bobby Jones	11	4.15	0–1	0	1	4	0	0	21.7	18	11	10	2	14	20	99	0	3	0	1
Al Leiter	31	3.20	16–8	0	31	0	2	1	208.0	176	84	74	19	76	200	874	4	11	1	1
Pat Mahomes	53	5.46	5–3	0	5	12	0	0	94.0	96	63	57	15	66	76	439	5	2	0	4
Jim Mann	2	10.13	0–0	0	0	2	0	0	2.7	6	3	3	1	1	0	15	0	0	0	0
Bill Pulsipher	2	12.15	0–2	0	2	0	0	0	6.7	9	9	9	1	6	7	39	0	1	0	0
Rick Reed	30	4.11	11–5	0	30	0	0	0	184.0	192	90	84	28	34	121	768	2	5	1	3
Jerrod Riggan	1	0.00	0–0	0	0	0	0	0	2.0	3	2	0	0	0	1	10	0	0	0	0
Grant Roberts	4	11.57	0–0	0	1	0	0	0	7.0	11	10	9	0	4	6	38	0	0	0	1
Rich Rodriguez	32	7.78	0–1	0	0	13	0	0	37.0	59	40	32	7	15	18	185	2	3	1	0
Glendon Rusch	31	4.01	11–11	0	30	0	2	0	190.7	196	91	85	18	44	157	802	2	6	0	2
Dennis Springer	2	8.74	0–1	0	2	0	0	0	11.3	20	11	11	2	5	5	59	2	1	0	0
Turk Wendell	77	3.59	8–6	1	0	17	0	0	82.7	60	36	33	9	41	73	346	0	5	1	7
Rick White	22	3.81	2–3	1	0	6	0	0	28.3	26	14	12	2	12	20	127	0	2	0	2
TOTAL	162	4.16	94–68	49	162	154	8	10	1450.0	1398	738	670	164	574	1164	6276	34	60	7	42

2001

NL EAST						
TEAM	W	L	PCT	GB	BA	ERA
Braves	88	74	.543	—	.260	3.59
Phillies	86	76	.531	2.0	.260	4.15
Mets	82	80	.506	6.0	.249	4.07
Marlins	76	86	.469	12.0	.264	4.32
Expos	68	94	.420	20.0	.253	4.68

Mets finished 11 games behind Astros for wild-card

They drove you nuts. They made you cheer. They got you angry. They made you proud. The 2001 Mets managed to evoke a plethora of emotions from the fan base as they turned 4½ months of missteps into one helluva late-season charge not seen from the team since the 1973 pennant winners. Unlike the '73 squad, management quit on this ballclub long before the players did, making the team's September charge as improbable as the late push forged by the "Ya Gotta Believe" Mets.

The Mets were 0–2 before they even played their first spring training game. General manager Steve Phillips had tried to re-sign free-agent lefty Mike Hampton after fail-ing to work out a contract with Mariners free agent Alex Rodriguez, leaving him scrambling for reinforcements by mid-November.

The Mets opened the free-agent market as the favorites to land Rodriguez, who was coming off his third straight season of at least 41 home runs and possessed an exceptional glove at shortstop. Although Rey Ordonez was Rodriguez's superior on defense, the Mets had grown tired of his anemic bat.

The Mets made a hard charge for A-Rod, whose agent, Scott Boras, was seeking a 10-year, $250 million package for his client. New York spent a week negotiating with Boras before they suddenly pulled out of the running. The Mets tried to paint a portrait of Rodriguez as a selfish player who would have been a bad fit in the clubhouse, although they blamed Boras for the aborted negotiations.

"I have serious reservations that a structure in which you have a 24-plus-one-man roster can really work," said Phillips.

"I think it'd be a bad thing if he got everything he's allegedly asking for," added pitcher Al Leiter.[13]

According to the *New York Times*, the Mets said Boras demanded a marketing staff and an office for Rodriguez at Shea. The paper added that Phillips intimated the demands included a private plane and a "billboard presence in the city."

Leiter spent the 2001 season hitting behind Ordonez after Rodriguez received his $250 million contract from the Rangers instead of the Mets. Losing Rodriguez eventually was a bad move for both A-Rod and the Mets.

Rodriguez went on to win three AL MVP awards from 2003 through 2007 and averaged 52 homers and 132 RBIs in his three years in Texas. He moved on to the Yankees in 2004 and was criticized for his inability to hit in the clutch during the postseason until his exceptional performance in 2009. After flaming out in the 2007 ALDS, he invoked a clause in his contract that allowed him to become a free agent after the season. Rodriguez re-upped with the Yankees and won a World Series with the Bombers in 2009, but he admitted in the spring of 2008 that he wished he and Boras had handled his 2000 negotiations differently.

"I went for the contract when my true desire was to go play for the Mets," Rodriguez told the *New York Daily News*, seven years after negotiations.[14]

From a Mets perspective, acquiring Rodriguez might have prevented them from making several personnel blunders from 2002 through 2004. There would have been no need to acquire Mo Vaughn and Roberto Alomar in the fall of 2001 unless the Mets were looking to build a super lineup of American League All-Stars. Jose Reyes would have been just fine at second base upon his recall in 2004, which might have dissuaded the Mets from going after Kaz Matsui in the winter of '04.

Then again, the Mets had painstakingly purged the clubhouse of questionable characters after the 1999 season, a move that helped the team succeed the following October. A-Rod's presence might have prompted the Mets to deal Reyes or David Wright before they reached the majors.

Once they lost out on Rodriguez, Hampton was the focus of the Mets' attention. Hampton entered the 2000 offseason as the best lefty on the free-agent market and was in terrific bargaining position with the Mets since the team had absolutely no starting pitching prospects in the minors. Hampton was the Mets' most effective starting pitcher over the final two months of 2000 before he was named the MVP of the National League Championship Series. The only other team willing to come close to the Mets' offer to Hampton was the Rockies, and who the heck would want to pitch at Coors Field in those days? Hampton opted for Colorado, citing Denver's school system and a chance to raise his children in a calmer environment.

Spurned by Hampton, the Mets inked free-agent right-hander Kevin Appier and kept Rick Reed, who earned a team-high 51 wins from 1997 to 2000. Bobby Jones was allowed to sign with the Padres, where he led the National League in losses in 2001 before retiring the following season. Jones was replaced by Steve Trachsel, another soft-tossing right-hander who won 15 games for the 1998 Cubs before going 16–33 over the next two seasons.

The Mets entered 2001 with a rotation consisting of Leiter, Appier, Reed, Trachsel, and Glendon Rusch, a lefty who appeared to have turned the corner in 2000 and was being counted on to take a stronger role in the rotation. The bullpen was virtually unchanged after Armando Benitez, John Franco, Turk Wendell, Dennis Cook, and Rick White comprised one of the league's best relief corps in 2000.

Phillips picked up veteran utilityman Desi Relaford off the Padres' waiver wire and signed flamboyant Japanese outfielder Tsuyoshi Shinjo, giving the Mets more depth while padding a bench that had been very successful in 2000. The core lineup was expected to remain the same, with Mike Piazza, Edgardo Alfonzo, Robin Ventura, Todd Zeile, and Jay Payton serving as featured players while Shinjo, Benny Agbayani, and 2000 postseason hero Timo Perez battled for playing time at the corner outfield spots.

The Mets entered 2001 as one of the favorites to reach the playoffs despite the loss of Hampton and their failure to land Rodriguez. Instead of challenging for the NL East lead, the Mets split their first four games and didn't reach the .500 mark again until September 18. They opened the year by taking two of three from the Braves in Atlanta before being swept at Montreal. They were also swept in three-game series by the Reds and Brewers before the calendar was flipped to May.

New York was 18–27 before posting its first three-game winning streak of the season. That was followed by a 1–5 stretch that put the Mets 22–32 and 13 games out of first place by June. They hit .243 while averaging 3.8 runs during the first two months despite Shinjo's .277 average and Relaford's .295 mark. Ventura had a .294 average and an .898 OPS through May 31, but the rest of the holdovers were struggling mightily to duplicate their 2000 seasons while the pitching staff posted a hefty 4.96 earned run average.

Alfonzo got off to a mystifying start as he played through back pain. He was on pace for 40 doubles and 25 homers through May, but his .250 batting average and .332 on-base percentage were far below his 2000 figures. Like Alfonzo, Piazza put up exceptional power numbers over the first two months (14 homers and 31 RBIs in 48 games), but his .262 average was about 40 points below his norm.

The bullpen was undependable and remained that way the rest of the season, a big reason why no Mets starter won more than 11 games for the first time since the strike-shortened 1995 season. Benitez experienced a horrible May, allowing five homers in 11 innings while recording a 7.36 ERA. Wendell had three holds, one save and two blown saves while allowing 37 percent of his 19 inherited runners to score through May 31. Cook stranded seven of his eight inherited runners in April, but he allowed 10 runs and 14 hits in nine innings the following month. Franco pitched scoreless ball for at least one inning in 16 of 22 appearances through May, but he was reached for at least two runs in five other outings while recording a 5.14 ERA during that span.

The biggest disappointment in the early going was Trachsel, who was 1–6 with an 8.24 ERA in seven starts after surrendering four home runs in the third inning of a 15–3 loss to the Padres May 17. His early season scuffles prompted the Mets to send him to the minors for two weeks to work out his problems.

June wasn't any kinder to the Mets, who fell to 35–47 while Phillips and manager Bobby Valentine tried everything to spark a winning streak. The month did include a nice comeback in which the Mets put together a six-run eighth to beat the Yankees 8–7, capped by Piazza's two-run blast. Shinjo kept the inning alive by beating out a potential inning-ending double play grounder, allowing the Mets to get within 7–6. But Shinjo jammed his ankle while stepping on first and spent the next month on the disabled list.

Shinjo was fast becoming a popular figure at Shea. Donned with oversized wristbands and a penchant for showmanship, the Osaka native had a .281 average before the injury and was playing center field well enough to lead Valentine to move Payton to right. Unfortunately for the Mets, the position switch was prompted in part by Timo Perez's inability to correct the hitting flaws exposed by the Yankees in the 2000 World Series.

June turned into July without the Mets looking like playoff contenders. The team promoted No. 1 prospect Alex Escobar, whom the Mets touted as a five-tool player and the future center fielder. Escobar hit .216 with three homers in his first 11 games, looking more like Don Bosch than Tommie Agee before he was returned to Norfolk at the end of June. Although he showed signs of potential, the Mets were still trying to move back into the playoff chase when he was demoted.

The white flag was raised the fourth week in July. The Mets were fourth in the NL East at 44–55, 12 games off the pace on July 23 when Todd Pratt was sent to the Phillies for fellow catcher Gary Bennett, who remained property of the Mets for exactly one month. Four days later, Phillips parted with Cook and Wendell by sending them to the Phillies for lefty starter Bruce Chen and prospect Adam Walker. Chen's arrival allowed the Mets to send Reed to the Twins for outfielder Matt Lawton on July 30. Within one week the team had purged itself of four vitally important members of the 2000 pennant winners.

The Mets won nine of 14 immediately after the Pratt deal before a seven-game losing streak dropped them to 54–68 by August 17, 13½ games behind the first-place Braves. Alfonzo (.226), Ventura (.230), Payton (.236), Piazza (.289), and Zeile (.263) were all hitting below their 2000 averages. Lawton gave the offense an instant spark upon his arrival, but that was short lived. Utilitymen Joe McEwing (.301) and Desi Relaford (.299) had become the team's most dependable hitters, and Shinjo's productivity allowed Phillips to demote the underperforming Perez to Norfolk for two weeks.

Only the most optimistic Mets fans were looking at 1973 and drawing positive comparisons to this club. Like the 2000 club, the '73 Mets spent the summer wasting good starting pitching by blowing late-inning leads or failing to generate timely hits. The '73 Mets were last in the NL East at 53–66 through August 17, only a half-game better than the 2001 contingent.

However, the 1973 Mets were just 7½ games out of first on August 17 and close to returning to full strength after injuries hampered the ballclub most of the summer. The 2001 Mets had no reinforcements in waiting, they were six games farther from the division lead than the '73 squad and were chasing a Braves team that was much better than the '73 Cardinals or Pirates. With the Yankees atop the AL East and the Jets and Giants preparing for their 2001 seasons, the Mets had become inconsequential in the eyes of the media and the New York sports fan.

The seven-game skid included an 0–4 start to a six-game swing through southern California before the Mets took the final two games at Los Angeles. The team returned to New York for a 13-game homestand and went 9–4 in winning all four series, but they were 8½ games behind the East-leading Braves and 11½ games behind the Cubs for the wild-card as of September 2.

New York opened a 10-game road trip by sweeping three in Philadelphia and taking three straight in Florida before falling to the Marlins in the series finale. The loss at Florida prevented the Mets from reaching the .500 mark and put them eight games behind Atlanta with 18 games remaining.

The Mets were in Pittsburgh the morning of September 11 when two commercial planes slammed into the World Trade Center. A third plane rammed through the Pentagon in Arlington, Virginia, and another crashed near Shanksville, Pennsylvania. Al Qaeda operatives hijacked each of the planes and flew them into three of their four intended targets. The attacks killed thousands and left the country in mourning for weeks.

Major League Baseball commissioner Bud Selig put a temporary halt to the pennant races as New Yorkers grieved the loss of Trade Center employees and the brave police, firefighters, EMTs, and Port Authority personnel who had tried to rescue workers in the Twin Towers before the buildings collapsed under extreme heat. Other professional and college sports also postponed their schedules through the weekend as the nation focused its attention on rescue efforts amid the rubble of the Trade Center.

Shea Stadium served as one of numerous staging areas for city rescue and recovery efforts. Truckloads of food and equipment funneled through the parking lot as drivers were met by a familiar Mets employee: Bobby Valentine. The man from nearby Stamford, Connecticut, served as a leader of the staging area, working 18-hour days handling supplies that would be shuttled to Ground Zero. Mets coaches and players also provided countless hours of time to help the city regain some sense of normalcy. As disappointing as the team had been, the Mets were making the city proud with their dedication to the relief effort.

Some said Valentine was a better manager in the Shea Stadium parking lot than in the Mets dugout. He took a lot of heat for the team's lethargic showing during the summer and was rumored to be on thin ice when the club headed into September. Under Valentine, the Mets gave New York a reason to smile after the 9-11 attacks.

The season resumed on Monday, September 17. The Mets had been scheduled to begin a three-game set at home that night, but the series was shifted to Pittsburgh to give New York City officials more time to secure Shea Stadium for another potential attack. Mets players donated their game salaries to the rescue efforts and were greeted to a standing ovation as they took the field in the bottom of the first at PNC Park. Players wore caps from the NYPD, NYFD, Port Authority, and EMT in appreciation for the rescue efforts and the lives lost at the Trade Center. However, it took the Mets a few innings to shake off the rust of an eight-day layoff.

Leiter was brilliant over seven innings, allowing a run and four hits but leaving the game tied 1–1. The Mets finally took the lead through the help of some unlikely sources as Ordonez lined a tiebreaking RBI single with two out in the ninth before scoring on pinch-hitter Mark Johnson's two-run double.

Piazza put the Mets ahead to stay the next night by ripping a two-run homer in the eighth. A 9–2 victory on Wednesday completed a three-game sweep and pushed the Mets over .500 for the first time since April 5. They were within 5½ games of Atlanta heading into a three-game series with the Braves at Shea.

The division race took a backseat during an emotionally-charged ceremony prior to the series opener on Friday, September 21. Bagpipers played "Amazing Grace" and several military songs as members of the New York City police, firefighters, EMT, and Port Authority marched into Shea from beyond the center-field fence. Marc Anthony solemnly sang "The Star Spangled Banner," and Diana Ross performed "God Bless America" while accompanied by two choirs. The Mets and Braves had lined up along the foul lines for the pregame festivities, which concluded with players from each side hugging each other as a form of national solidarity and support for New York.

Bobby Valentine hugging Tom Glavine? Bobby Cox embracing Jay Payton? The teams had been arch enemies for several years, but the circumstances allowed them to shed any animosity toward each other while uniting the country.

The Mets also received the go-ahead from the commissioner's office to continue to wear the hats of city rescue workers. It was supposed to be a one-time deal in Pittsburgh until the team insisted they play the rest of the season with the headwear. MLB was in no position to reject the Mets' demand.

The Mets and Braves plodded through the first 6½ innings as if baseball was secondary. Mets fans were uncharacteristically subdued in the team's first home game in 19 days, politely cheering the team while saving their usual venomous attacks on the Braves for another time.

Liza Minnelli loosened up the crowd during the seventh-inning stretch with a theatrical performance of "New York, New York," which featured a kick-line of Minnelli flanked by police and firemen. Minnelli concluded her high-energy performance by walking over to Payton on the on-deck circle and planting a big kiss on the outfielder. But the Mets were retired in order in the bottom of the seventh, putting fans on edge once again.

Chen was marvelous against his old team considering the circumstances, allowing a run and six hits in seven innings. He was followed Franco, the native New Yorker who had tears in his eyes during the pregame ceremony. Franco retired the first two hitters in the eighth before allowing a walk and a single, prompting Valentine to replace him with Benitez.

One pitch later, Benitez surrendered an RBI double to Brian Jordan to put Atlanta ahead 2–1. Benitez later walked the bases loaded before retiring Andruw Jones on a fly ball to center, giving the Mets six outs to muster a game-tying run.

It took the Mets just one out to take the lead, thanks to Piazza's titanic, two-run blast to center. All the pent-up energy from the crowd of 41,235 at Shea was let loose following the home run.

Benitez went out to pitch the ninth and promptly allowed a single to Javy Lopez. But the closer fanned B.J. Surhoff on a 1–2 pitch before Keith Lockhart hit into a game-ending double play, getting the Mets within 4½ games of first.

Trachsel beat the Braves 7–3 the next day to cut the deficit to 3½ games, allowing one run in seven innings. Trachsel was very effective following his minor league stint in May, going 10–6 with a 3.23 ERA in his final 19 starts.

The Braves took the series finale before the Mets headed to Montreal for a three-game set with the last-place Expos. New York had been 2–4 in Montreal and needed to sweep the Expos to have a realistic chance of catching Atlanta down the stretch.

Appier tossed a four-hitter, and Piazza homered as the Mets took the opener 2–0, putting New York four games behind the Braves. They remained four games back after Rusch combined with White and Benitez to beat the Expos 5–2. Benitez picked up his 42nd save to break his own club record.

Game 3 of the series started poorly as Montreal built a 6–2 lead against Chen by the third inning. The Mets chipped away until Relaford's two-run homer in the eighth put them ahead 7–6. Piazza followed with a three-run double in the ninth before the Mets concluded a 12–6 victory that put them within three games of the Braves heading into a three-game set in Atlanta. The Mets now had a chance to pull into a tie for first if they could somehow sweep the Braves in a ballpark where they were 7–20 since July 13, 1997, including a 1–10 mark in September.

The Mets dropped the opener 5–3 before building a 5–1 lead against John Burkett the following afternoon. Leiter was exceptional in Game 2, holding the Braves to a run and four hits in eight innings until he put the game in the capable hands of Benitez, who had been 17-for-17 in save situations since August 4 while compiling a 2.22 ERA. Benitez hadn't allowed a run in his previous 11 appearances and looked like money in the bank as he tried to close out the Braves in a non-save situation. Benitez never got the third out.

Andruw Jones led off the bottom of the ninth with a single and moved to second on defensive indifference before scoring on a single by Javy Lopez. The next batter was pinch-hitter Dave Martinez, who slapped a grounder to second to put the Mets within one out of a 5–2 win. But Lockhart walked before Marcus Giles laced a two-run double to get Atlanta within 5–4. Benitez walked the next hitter intentionally, setting up a force at second before Valentine brought in Franco to shut the door.

Franco was not pitching well prior to taking the mound, allowing four runs in 5⅓ innings while blowing two leads in seven games since August 21. He missed on a 3–2 pitch to Wes Helms to load the bases, bringing up the right-handed Jordan to face the lefty Franco.

Franco quickly got an 0–2 count on Jordan before the Braves outfielder sent his next pitch over the left-center wall for a grand slam, capping a seven-run rally that gave Atlanta an 8–5 win. The loss put New York five games back with seven to play, snuffing out any possibility of the team producing a "Ya Gotta Believe" repeat.

The Mets won the next day and lost four of their last six to finish six games off the pace. The team went 31–19 over the final 50 games, which almost mirrors the Mets' 30–19 finish in 1973. The late-season stretch allowed Phillips and Mets ownership to believe the team wasn't that far from a postseason berth despite spending much of the season in fourth place.

Phillips picked up All-Stars Roberto Alomar and Mo Vaughn in the off-season while losing only Appier, Escobar, and Lawton from the 25-man roster. The roster shuffle helped boost attendance by 150,000 in 2002, but it never paid off in the standings.

2001 Mets Statistics

Hitting	G	AB	R	H	2B	3B	HR	RBI	BB	SO	BA	OBP	SLG	SB	CS	GDP	HP	SH	SF	IBB
Benny Agbayani	91	296	28	82	14	2	6	27	36	73	.277	.364	.399	4	5	11	5	1	1	0
Edgardo Alfonzo	124	457	64	111	22	0	17	49	51	62	.243	.322	.403	5	0	7	5	1	5	0
Gary Bennett	1	1	0	1	0	0	0	0	0	0	1.000	1.000	1.000	0	0	0	0	0	0	0
Darren Bragg	18	57	4	15	6	0	0	5	4	23	.263	.323	.368	3	2	0	1	1	0	0
Alex Escobar	18	50	3	10	1	0	3	8	3	19	.200	.245	.400	1	0	1	0	0	0	0
Darryl Hamilton	52	126	15	27	7	1	1	5	19	20	.214	.322	.310	3	1	2	2	2	2	3
Lenny Harris	110	135	12	30	5	1	0	9	8	9	.222	.266	.274	3	2	3	0	0	0	0
Mark Johnson	71	118	17	30	6	1	6	23	16	31	.254	.338	.475	0	2	0	0	0	2	1
Matt Lawton	48	183	24	45	11	1	3	13	22	34	.246	.352	.366	10	2	2	8	0	0	0
Joe McEwing	116	283	41	80	17	3	8	30	17	57	.283	.342	.449	8	5	2	10	6	3	0
Rey Ordonez	149	461	31	114	24	4	3	44	34	43	.247	.299	.336	3	2	17	1	7	2	17
Jay Payton	104	361	44	92	16	1	8	34	18	52	.255	.298	.371	4	3	11	5	0	2	1
Timo Perez	85	239	26	59	9	1	5	22	12	25	.247	.287	.356	1	6	1	2	6	1	0
Jason Phillips	6	7	2	1	1	0	0	0	0	1	.143	.143	.286	0	0	0	0	0	0	0
Mike Piazza	141	503	81	151	29	0	36	94	67	87	.300	.384	.573	0	2	20	2	0	1	19
Todd Pratt	45	80	6	13	5	0	2	4	15	36	.163	.306	.300	1	0	4	2	0	1	1
Desi Relaford	120	301	43	91	27	0	8	36	27	65	.302	.364	.472	13	5	4	5	2	5	1
Tsuyoshi Shinjo	123	400	46	107	23	1	10	56	25	70	.268	.320	.405	4	5	8	7	4	2	3
Jorge Toca	13	17	3	3	0	0	0	1	0	8	.176	.176	.176	0	0	0	0	0	0	0
Jorge Velandia	9	9	1	0	0	0	0	0	2	1	.000	.182	.000	0	0	0	0	0	0	0
Robin Ventura	142	456	70	108	20	0	21	61	88	101	.237	.359	.419	2	5	13	1	0	4	10
Vance Wilson	32	57	3	17	3	0	0	6	2	16	.298	.339	.351	0	1	1	2	0	1	0
Todd Zeile	151	531	66	141	25	1	10	62	73	102	.266	.359	.373	1	0	15	6	0	2	3
Pitchers																				
Kevin Appier	31	62	4	7	0	0	0	4	1	24	.113	.141	.113	0	0	0	1	3	0	0
Armando Benitez	71	1	0	0	0	0	0	1	0	0	.000	.000	.000	0	0	0	0	0	0	0
Bruce Chen	11	19	0	3	0	0	0	0	0	9	.158	.158	.158	0	0	1	0	2	0	0
Dennis Cook	40	1	0	0	0	0	0	0	0	0	.000	.000	.000	0	0	0	0	0	0	0
Dicky Gonzalez	15	20	1	2	0	0	0	0	1	4	.100	.143	.100	0	0	0	0	1	0	0
Brett Hinchliffe	1	1	0	0	0	0	0	0	0	1	.000	.000	.000	0	0	0	0	0	0	0
Al Leiter	27	62	2	4	0	1	0	3	2	28	.065	.094	.097	0	0	0	0	0	0	0
Tom Martin	14	3	0	0	0	0	0	0	0	1	.000	.000	.000	0	0	0	0	0	0	0
Rick Reed	19	40	2	5	1	0	0	4	1	15	.125	.143	.150	0	0	0	0	4	1	0
Jerrod Riggan	35	2	0	0	0	0	0	0	0	2	.000	.000	.000	0	0	0	0	0	0	0
Grant Roberts	16	3	0	0	0	0	0	0	0	3	.000	.000	.000	0	0	0	0	0	0	0
Brian Rose	3	1	0	0	0	0	0	0	0	0	.000	.000	.000	0	0	0	0	0	0	0
Glendon Rusch	31	54	0	3	0	0	0	5	1	23	.056	.073	.056	0	0	1	0	6	0	0
Steve Trachsel	26	56	2	9	1	0	0	2	0	13	.161	.161	.179	0	0	0	0	5	0	0
Pete Walker	2	1	0	0	0	0	0	0	0	1	.000	.000	.000	0	0	0	0	1	0	0
Donne Wall	32	0	1	0	0	0	0	0	0	0				0	0	0	0	0	0	0
Turk Wendell	46	2	0	0	0	0	0	0	0	1	.000	.000	.000	0	0	0	0	0	0	0
Rick White	52	3	0	0	0	0	0	0	0	2	.000	.000	.000	0	0	0	0	0	0	0
TOTAL	162	5459	642	1361	273	18	147	608	545	1062	.249	.323	.387	66	48	124	65	52	35	59

Pitching	G	ERA	W–L	SV	GS	GF	CG	SHO	IP	H	R	ER	HR	BB	SO	BFP	WP	HBP	BK	IBB
Kevin Appier	33	3.57	11–10	0	33	0	1	1	206.2	181	89	82	22	64	172	856	12	15	0	4
Armando Benitez	73	3.77	6–4	43	0	64	0	0	76.1	59	32	32	12	40	93	320	5	1	0	6
Bruce Chen	11	4.68	3–2	0	11	0	0	0	59.2	56	37	31	10	28	47	253	3	0	0	0
Dennis Cook	43	4.25	1–1	0	0	11	0	0	36.0	28	18	17	6	10	34	148	3	1	1	1
Mark Corey	2	16.20	0–0	0	0	0	0	0	1.2	5	3	3	0	3	3	13	0	0	0	1
John Franco	58	4.05	6–2	2	0	16	0	0	53.1	55	25	24	8	19	50	232	4	2	1	2
Dicky Gonzalez	16	4.88	3–2	0	7	2	0	0	59.0	72	33	32	4	17	31	261	5	1	0	3
Brett Hinchliffe	1	36.00	0–1	0	1	0	0	0	2.0	9	8	8	2	1	2	17	0	1	0	0
Al Leiter	29	3.31	11–11	0	29	0	0	0	187.1	178	81	69	18	46	142	772	5	4	2	3
Tom Martin	14	10.06	1–0	0	0	2	0	0	17.0	23	22	19	4	10	12	85	0	1	0	2
C.J. Nitkowski	5	0.00	0–0	0	0	2	0	0	5.2	3	0	0	0	3	4	21	0	0	0	1
Rick Reed	20	3.48	8–6	0	20	0	3	1	134.2	119	53	52	16	17	99	531	2	1	0	3
Desi Relaford	1	0.00	0–0	0	0	1	0	0	1.0	0	0	0	0	0	1	3	0	0	0	0
Jerrod Riggan	35	3.40	3–3	0	0	12	0	0	47.2	42	19	18	5	24	41	202	4	0	0	7
Grant Roberts	16	3.81	1–0	0	0	2	0	0	26.0	24	11	11	2	8	29	110	0	0	1	1
Brian Rose	3	4.15	0–1	0	0	0	0	0	8.2	10	4	4	3	2	4	37	0	0	0	1
Glendon Rusch	33	4.63	8–12	0	33	0	1	0	179.0	216	101	92	23	43	156	785	3	7	2	2
Steve Trachsel	28	4.46	11–13	0	28	0	1	1	173.2	168	90	86	28	47	144	726	4	3	0	7
Pete Walker	2	2.70	0–0	0	0	1	0	0	6.2	6	2	2	0	0	4	25	0	0	0	0
Donne Wall	32	4.85	0–4	0	0	14	0	0	42.2	51	24	23	8	17	31	193	1	1	0	6
Turk Wendell	49	3.51	4–3	1	0	14	0	0	51.1	42	23	20	8	22	41	218	1	3	0	6
Rick White	55	3.88	4–5	2	0	15	0	0	69.2	71	38	30	7	17	51	299	1	2	0	4
TOTAL	**162**	**4.07**	**82–80**	**48**	**162**	**156**	**6**	**14**	**1445.2**	**1418**	**713**	**654**	**186**	**438**	**1191**	**6107**	**53**	**43**	**7**	**60**

2002

NL EAST

TEAM	W	L	PCT	GB	BA	ERA
Braves	101	59	.631	—	.260	3.13
Expos	83	79	.512	19.0	.261	3.97
Phillies	80	81	.497	21.5	.259	4.17
Marlins	79	83	.488	23.0	.261	4.36
Mets	75	86	.466	26.5	.256	3.89

Mets finish 20 games behind Giants for wild-card

Mets owners Nelson Doubleday and Fred Wilpon had no trouble taking on huge contracts as general manager Steve Phillips assembled the roster for the 2002 season. Phillips manufactured three blockbuster trades that brought All-Stars Roberto Alomar, Mo Vaughn, and Jeromy Burnitz to New York. He also picked up pitcher Jeff D'Amico in the Burnitz swap and acquired former 19-game winner Shawn Estes from the Rockies. Roger Cedeno returned to the Mets following a two-year absence, signing a free-agent contract the same day reliever Dave Weathers inked a package with New York. Free-agent right-hander Pedro Astacio joined the team in mid-January to round out manager Bobby Valentine's rotation.

Gone were Robin Ventura, Kevin Appier, Matt Lawton, Lenny Harris, Glendon Rusch, Benny Agbayani, Todd Zeile, Tsuyoshi Shinjo, and Desi Relaford, representing 36 percent of the Mets' 2001 season-opening roster. The Mets also parted with prospects Alex Escobar, Billy Traber, and Jerrod Riggan, completing a massive turnover for a team that finished only six games behind Atlanta and was nine games better than its projected Pythagorean record of 73–79 in '01.

Phillips seized the opportunity to turn the Mets into a powerhouse that appeared on paper to be the finest starting lineup in the National League. The team was a speed threat with the arrivals of Alomar and Cedeno, who com-

bined for 85 stolen bases in 2001 compared to the Mets' team total of 66.

Alomar was supposed to bolster a power attack that now featured Vaughn, Burnitz, Mike Piazza, and Edgardo Alfonzo. The quintet had combined to hit 580 home runs from 1997 through 2001, and that includes Vaughn's absence in 2001 due to a left arm injury that caused him to miss the entire season.

Of the new hitters, Vaughn's physical status was the only question mark heading into '02. Alomar hit .336 and drove in 100 runs for the 2001 Indians, Cedeno batted .293 and swiped 55 bases in Detroit, and Burnitz provided 34 homers, 32 doubles, and 100 RBIs for the Brewers.

The rotation was not as strong as the lineup heading into the season. After Al Leiter, the starters were all reclamation projects with large upsides but recent sub-par performances. Astacio was 8–14 with a 5.09 ERA in 2001 while Estes went 9–8 with a 4.02 ERA in just 27 starts. D'Amico was 12–7 with a 2.66 earned run average for Milwaukee in 2000, and was the team's starter in the first game at Miller Park before a nerve injury in his right arm limited him to 10 games and led to a 6.08 ERA in '01. The Mets were also banking on Steve Trachsel to open the year better than he did in 2001, when he was 1–6 with an 8.24 ERA in his first seven outings before correcting a few flaws during a minor league stint. Trachsel had a fine second half in '01 and was slated to be the No. 2 or No. 3 starter.

Weathers and Mark Guthrie joined a bullpen in which John Franco and closer Armando Benitez were the only holdovers among the late-inning relievers. Franco underwent Tommy John surgery in May and missed the entire season.

The offense was expected to compensate for any holes in the pitching staff. If pitching coach Charlie Hough could work wonders with the rag-tag rotation, and Weathers and Guthrie could provide capable relief, there was no reason the Mets shouldn't challenge the Braves for the NL East unless the offense grossly underachieved.

The power-hitting quintet finished with just 105 home runs while recording a .266 average. Alfonzo was the only one of the five to hit higher than .280, and Piazza was the lone Met with more than 26 homers. Piazza paced the club with 98 RBIs, 26 more than runner-up Vaughn.

Cedeno suddenly showed an aversion to running, stealing just 25 bases in 29 attempts and finishing with two triples. Burnitz homered just once per 25.2 at-bats and delivered only 54 RBIs and a .215 average in a team-high 154 games.

Vaughn opened the campaign by hitting .230 with five homers and 26 RBIs in 62 games. He went 17 straight games without a home run from April 4 to May 8, and failed to drive in a run during a 12-game stretch from August 12 to August 24.

But the biggest stiff in the lineup was Alomar, who experienced his worst major league season to date. Alomar hit just .204 against lefties, provided a disappointing 19 extra-base hits at home and mustered just 38 RBIs in 106 at-bats with runners in scoring position.

Alomar also failed to come close to resembling the second baseman that had won 10 Gold Gloves the previous 11 seasons, struggling with popups and demonstrating rather limited range while producing 11 errors in 147 games. Mets fans spent the year watching the career of a future Hall of Famer go dormant in the blink of an eye.

Trachsel was the lone Mets starting pitcher who performed above expectations, compiling a team-best 3.37 ERA while going 11–11 in 30 starts. He pitched shutout ball in two of his no-decisions and didn't allow an earned run in a third. Trachsel also suffered losses of 1–0, 2–1, and 2–0, thanks to the Mets' often impotent offense.

Leiter also pitched in bad luck while going 13–13 with a 3.48 earned run average in 33 starts. He gave up one earned run or fewer in five of his no-decisions and absorbed losses of 1–0 and 2–1.

Astacio led the Mets with three complete games and was second with 191⅔ innings pitched but faded badly in the second half while pitching through shoulder pain. He was 8–3 with a 3.17 ERA in his first 17 starts, including a 4–1 mark and a 2.50 earned run average in April. But he was brutal following the All-Star break, losing eight of his 12 decisions while posting a 7.00 ERA.

D'Amico and Estes weren't very good in either half, combining for a 10–19 record and a 4.75 ERA. D'Amico, Estes, and Astacio helped the Mets finish near the bottom of the NL in ERA among starters despite the efforts of Leiter and Trachsel.

Phillips continued to make an effort to improve the pitching, getting Scott Strickland during the first week of the season and picking up starter John Thomson and reliever Steve Reed in a July trade with the Rockies. Phillips also promoted Mike Bacsik, who went 3–2 with a 4.37 ERA in 11 games after being acquired with Alomar in December.

Guthrie was a capable lefty fill-in for Franco, going 33 straight games from May 25 through August 3 without allowing a run. Guthrie's ERA was 1.01 after the scoreless streak, but he finished the year yielding nine runs in 12⅓ innings to finish with a 2.44 ERA, tops among all relievers with at least 35 appearances.

Grant Roberts looked promising, compiling a 2.20 ERA while usually pitching in lost causes. Roberts allowed just two runs in his first 30⅔ innings over 23 games, but the Mets won just five of those contests.

Benitez opened the season by converting his first nine save opportunities, but it took him 17 appearances and seven weeks of the season to do it. He blew only four save chances the entire year but finished with 33 saves, 10 off his team-record total of 2001.

The Mets looked like a playoff shoe-in after winning 18 of their first 29 games. Astacio was responsible for five of those victories, and Benitez closed out seven of the wins. The team hit .256 while averaging 4.6 runs during the season-opening stretch despite sputtering production from Alomar, Vaughn, and Burnitz. The pitching was surprisingly good as the Mets posted a 2.68 ERA and allowed just 13 percent of their inherited runners to score.

The strong start was followed by a six-game losing streak, an indication Mets fans were in for a bumpy ride as the team fell from first place to third. The team recovered to win five straight in mid May, giving New York a two-game division lead through 43 games. The Mets were 13½ games back by July 13 as the Braves got extremely hot while New York went 20–27. The deficit grew to 20 games a month later as everything managed to fall apart at the same time. The position players couldn't run, couldn't field, and couldn't hit in the clutch. The back end of the rotation was being pummeled semi-regularly, often taking the Mets out of games long before the seventh-inning stretch.

The Mets already were under .500 and fading fast when Roger Clemens and the Yankees came to Shea in mid-June. Clemens started the second game of the series and was going to have to face Mets pitching for the first time since he beaned Mike Piazza two years earlier. The speculation wasn't whether Clemens would be dropped on his ass, but when.

Estes was given the task of evening the score for Piazza as he took the mound against Clemens. The lefty wasted no time throwing at Clemens, but the pitch went behind the Rocket before hitting the backstop. Both teams were warned after the pitch, denying Estes another chance to drill Clemens.

However, Estes got even at the plate, opening the scoring with a suicide squeeze in the bottom of the third before drilling a two-run homer off Clemens in his next at-bat. Piazza added a solo blast in the sixth off Clemens, who was tagged for four runs and six hits in 5⅔ innings.

Estes was outstanding in an 8–0 win over the Bombers, allowing five hits while striking out 11 in seven innings. It turned out to be one of his very few highlights as a Met, and one of the last bright spots in a season that was lost by August

Two weeks after beating Clemens, the Mets were trying to beat down their first off-field controversy. Pitcher Mark Corey suffered a seizure outside his hotel near Shea Stadium after being driven there by teammate Tony Tarasco. Both Corey and Tarasco later admitted to smoking marijuana shortly before Corey's seizure.

Three months and many losses later, the Mets were further embarrassed when a photo surfaced in *Newsday* showing Roberts smoking marijuana. Roberts said the photo was taken during the 1998 off-season and was given to the newspaper by a woman who was extorting him.

Newsday reported in mid-September that at least seven players were using marijuana, that one player smoked it regularly in the parking lot, that pot had been mailed to Shea, and that numerous Mets would travel to visiting stadiums via limo rather than the team bus so they could toke up before batting practice.

The allegations put the organization in spin control at the end of its worst season in six years. The team that craved equal media attention to the Yankees was now wishing the press would just let the players end the season anonymously.

Valentine's detractors used the marijuana allegations as another example of a manager that had lost control of the club. They also harped on an annoying habit picked up by Alomar, Cedeno, and Rey Ordonez of sliding into first base on close plays at the bag. Although the laws of physics suggest that sliding into first slows down the runner, Valentine publicly defended the players and spent too much time on his WFAN radio segments with Mike Francesa and Chris Russo trying to explain why he wasn't bothered by the maneuver.

But there was no defending the team's record in August. The Mets began the month 55–51 and within 4½ games of the wild-card lead despite a shaky rotation, poor defense on the right side of the infield, and inconsistent hitting, especially from Alomar, Vaughn, Burnitz, and Cedeno. Phillips tried to improve the pitching by getting Reed and Thomson from the Rockies for Jay Payton before the July trade deadline. The trade didn't stop the Mets from opening the month with five straight losses, a streak that was soon followed by a 12-game skid. New York went 6–21 for the month, including an 0–13 mark at home. The Mets also lost their last home game of July, and the 14-game skid broke a team record and tied a National League mark for futility at home.

A messy internal divorce played itself out in August. Doubleday sold his half of the Mets to Wilpon, ending their 22-year run as co-owners of the team. Doubleday agreed to sell earlier in the season but balked when a financial assessment of the team came in much lower than he expected. Wilpon sued Doubleday to force him to abide by their original agreement of setting the sale price according to a financial valuation of the team, which came in at $391 million. Doubleday countersued, claiming the valuation was a sham and that MLB had co-conspired with Wilpon to keep the sale price low.

Doubleday was out of the picture by the end of August, allowing Wilpon to give his son, Jeff, more power within the organization. The move has gone a long way toward molding the Mets into what they are today.

The Mets showed some life while winning seven straight and nine of 11 in early September. But they dropped 10 of their final 15 to finish 75–86, their worst full year under Valentine, who went into his season-ending front office meeting armed with a strategy to improve the ballclub. Valentine was allowed to speak for several minutes, not knowing that he was about to be told his services were no longer needed.

Valentine had cultivated plenty of enemies in opposing dugouts during his days with the Mets, including pending free agents Cliff Floyd and Tom Glavine. Phillips had hoped to sign both players, who entered the free-agent signing period as two of the most coveted players. The Mets had no hope of landing either if Valentine was still in the dugout.

The World Series was in full swing when news leaked that the Mets would hire Oakland skipper Art Howe as Valentine's replacement. Howe was a respected baseball man with a lower profile than Valentine and a string of success with the low-budget A's. Although Howe led Oakland to three straight playoff appearances, he went 0–3 in the ALDS while Valentine went 3–2 in postseason series from 1999 through 2000.

The Mets had no choice but to spend even more money in the off-season if they were going to contend in 2003. Vaughn, Alomar, Cedeno, Burnitz, and Piazza all had exorbitant contracts that prevented the Mets from unloading them on other teams. The top players in the farm system were years away from maturity. Ty Wigginton represented the best of the Mets' prospects, and he was not a polished defensive player. The Mets' only hope to compete in '03 would be to spend more money, a strategy that didn't work in 2002 and would burn them again in '03. Phillips picked up Glavine and Floyd but soon followed Valentine out the door.

2002 Mets Statistics

Hitting	G	AB	R	H	2B	3B	HR	RBI	BB	SO	BA	OBP	SLG	SB	CS	GDP	HP	SH	SF	IBB
Edgardo Alfonzo	135	490	78	151	26	0	16	56	62	55	.308	.391	.459	6	0	5	7	0	3	8
Roberto Alomar	149	590	73	157	24	4	11	53	57	83	.266	.331	.376	16	4	12	1	6	1	4
Jeromy Burnitz	154	479	65	103	15	0	19	54	58	135	.215	.311	.365	10	7	11	10	1	2	5
Roger Cedeno	149	511	65	133	19	2	7	41	42	92	.260	.318	.346	25	4	10	2	5	2	1
McKay Christensen	4	3	1	1	0	0	0	0	1	1	.333	.500	.333	0	0	0	0	0	0	0
Brady Clark	10	12	3	5	1	0	0	1	1	2	.417	.462	.500	0	0	0	0	0	0	0
Raul Gonzalez	30	81	9	21	2	0	3	11	4	17	.259	.291	.395	2	2	2	0	0	1	0
Mark Johnson	42	51	5	7	4	0	1	4	9	18	.137	.267	.275	0	0	0	0	1	0	0
Mark Little	3	3	0	0	0	0	0	0	0	1	.000	.000	.000	0	1	0	0	0	0	0
Gary Matthews Jr.	2	1	0	0	0	0	0	0	0	0	.000	.000	.000	0	0	0	0	0	0	0
Joe McEwing	105	196	22	39	8	1	3	26	9	50	.199	.242	.296	4	4	0	3	3	3	0
Rey Ordonez	144	460	53	117	25	2	1	42	24	46	.254	.292	.324	2	2	19	2	9	4	11
Jay Payton	87	275	33	78	6	3	8	31	21	34	.284	.336	.415	4	1	8	1	2	1	0
Timo Perez	136	444	52	131	27	6	8	47	23	36	.295	.331	.437	10	6	10	2	10	2	2
Jason Phillips	11	19	4	7	0	0	1	3	1	1	.368	.409	.526	0	0	1	1	0	1	0
Mike Piazza	135	478	69	134	23	2	33	98	57	82	.280	.359	.544	0	3	26	3	0	3	9
Marco Scutaro	27	36	2	8	0	1	1	6	0	11	.222	.216	.361	0	1	1	0	1	1	0
Esix Snead	17	13	3	4	0	0	1	3	1	4	.308	.357	.538	4	3	0	0	0	0	0
Tony Tarasco	60	96	15	24	5	0	6	15	8	13	.250	.305	.490	2	1	2	0	0	1	0
John Valentin	114	208	18	50	15	0	3	30	22	37	.240	.339	.356	0	0	6	10	0	2	0
Mo Vaughn	139	487	67	126	18	0	26	72	59	145	.259	.349	.456	0	1	15	10	0	2	6
Ty Wigginton	46	116	18	35	8	0	6	18	8	19	.302	.354	.526	2	1	4	2	0	1	0
Vance Wilson	74	163	19	40	7	0	5	26	5	32	.245	.301	.380	0	1	4	8	2	0	0
Pitchers																				
Pedro Astacio	30	62	3	10	2	0	0	1	0	31	.161	.175	.194	0	0	0	1	6	0	0
Mike Bacsik	11	18	0	2	1	0	0	2	0	3	.111	.111	.167	0	0	0	0	3	0	0
Jaime Cerda	29	1	0	0	0	0	0	0	0	0	.000	.000	.000	0	0	0	0	0	0	0
Mark Corey	13	1	0	0	0	0	0	0	0	1	.000	.000	.000	0	0	0	0	0	0	0
Jeff D'Amico	27	37	2	4	0	0	0	0	2	22	.108	.154	.108	0	0	1	0	5	0	0
Shawn Estes	23	35	1	3	1	0	1	3	0	14	.086	.086	.200	0	0	1	0	5	0	0
Mark Guthrie	65	2	0	0	0	0	0	0	0	0	.000	.000	.000	0	0	0	0	0	0	0
Satoru Komiyama	22	1	0	0	0	0	0	0	1	1	.000	.500	.000	0	0	0	0	1	0	0
Al Leiter	30	53	3	8	1	0	0	2	8	28	.151	.262	.170	0	0	2	0	3	0	0
Jason Middlebrook	3	5	0	0	0	0	0	0	1	2	.000	.167	.000	0	0	0	0	0	0	0
Steve Reed	24	1	0	0	0	0	0	0	0	1	.000	.000	.000	0	0	0	0	0	0	0
Grant Roberts	33	1	1	1	0	0	0	0	0	0	1.000	1.000	1.000	0	0	0	0	0	0	0
John Thomson	9	18	2	5	0	0	0	1	1	7	.278	.316	.278	0	0	0	0	3	0	0
Steve Trachsel	29	46	4	5	0	1	0	4	1	19	.109	.128	.152	0	0	2	0	9	0	0
Tyler Walker	5	2	0	0	0	0	0	0	0	1	.000	.000	.000	0	0	0	0	0	0	0
Dave Weathers	68	1	0	0	0	0	0	0	0	0	.000	.000	.000	0	0	0	0	0	0	0
TOTAL	161	5496	690	1409	238	22	160	650	486	1044	.256	.322	.395	87	42	142	63	75	30	46

Pitching	G	ERA	W–L	SV	GS	GF	CG	SHO	IP	H	R	ER	HR	BB	SO	BFP	WP	HBP	BK	IBB
Pedro Astacio	31	4.79	12–11	0	31	0	3	1	191.2	192	106	102	32	63	152	828	1	16	2	5
Mike Bacsik	11	4.37	3–2	0	9	1	1	0	55.2	63	29	27	8	19	30	247	0	4	0	3
Armando Benitez	62	2.27	1–0	33	0	52	0	0	67.1	46	20	17	8	25	79	275	1	3	0	0
Jaime Cerda	32	2.45	0–0	0	0	7	0	0	25.2	22	7	7	0	14	21	113	0	1	1	0
Bruce Chen	1	0.00	0–0	0	0	0	0	0	0.2	1	0	0	0	0	0	3	0	0	0	0
Mark Corey	12	4.50	0–3	0	0	5	0	0	10.0	10	7	5	2	8	9	49	1	1	0	1
Jeff D'Amico	29	4.94	6–10	0	22	1	1	1	145.2	152	84	80	20	37	101	621	0	8	0	8
Kane Davis	16	7.07	1–1	0	0	5	0	0	14.0	15	11	11	2	11	24	70	1	1	0	2
Shawn Estes	23	4.55	4–9	0	23	0	1	1	132.2	133	70	67	12	66	92	580	2	5	1	9
Pedro Feliciano	6	7.50	0–0	0	0	3	0	0	6.0	9	5	5	0	1	4	26	0	1	0	0
Mark Guthrie	68	2.44	5–3	1	0	13	0	0	48.0	35	13	13	3	19	44	190	4	1	0	3
Bobby Jones	12	5.29	0–0	0	0	1	0	0	17.0	20	11	10	3	11	11	81	0	1	0	2
Satoru Komiyama	25	5.61	0–3	0	0	13	0	0	43.1	53	29	27	7	12	33	194	1	3	0	4
Al Leiter	33	3.48	13–13	0	33	0	2	2	204.1	194	99	79	23	69	172	868	1	8	1	5
Jason Middlebrook	3	3.94	1–0	0	3	0	0	0	16.0	13	7	7	1	7	14	67	0	0	1	0
Steve Reed	24	2.08	0–1	0	0	4	0	0	26.0	23	6	6	0	4	14	103	1	2	0	1
Grant Roberts	34	2.20	3–1	0	0	6	0	0	45.0	43	12	11	3	16	31	192	0	1	0	7
Jae Weong Seo	1	0.00	0–0	0	0	1	0	0	1.0	0	0	0	0	0	1	3	0	0	0	0
Pat Strange	5	1.13	0–0	0	0	4	0	0	8.0	6	1	1	0	1	4	30	0	0	1	1
Scott Strickland	68	3.59	6–9	2	0	21	0	0	67.2	61	29	27	7	33	67	296	3	2	0	9
John Thomson	9	4.31	2–6	0	9	0	0	0	54.1	65	39	26	7	17	31	250	0	0	0	3
Steve Trachsel	30	3.37	11–11	0	30	0	1	1	173.2	170	80	65	16	69	105	741	4	0	4	4
Pete Walker	1	9.00	0–0	0	0	0	0	0	1.0	2	1	1	0	0	0	5	0	0	0	0
Tyler Walker	5	5.91	1–0	0	1	3	0	0	10.2	11	7	7	3	5	7	49	0	0	0	1
David Weathers	71	2.91	6–3	0	0	12	0	0	77.1	69	30	25	6	36	61	331	2	3	0	7
TOTAL	161	3.89	75–86	36	161	152	9	10	1442.2	1408	703	624	163	543	1107	6212	22	55	7	75

2003

NL EAST

TEAM	W	L	PCT	GB	BA	ERA
Braves	101	61	.623	—	.284	4.10
Marlins	91	71	.562	10.0	.266	4.04
Phillies	86	76	.531	15.0	.261	4.04
Expos	83	79	.512	18.0	.258	4.01
Mets	66	95	.410	34.5	.247	4.48

Mets finish 24½ games behind Marlins for wild-card

The Mets were an abject failure in 2002, finishing with a losing record for the first time in six years after turning over the right side of the infield to a pair of high-priced, highly decorated, underachieving veterans. The team's disappointing performance led to manager Bobby Valentine's dismissal after the season, giving general manager Steve Phillips his first—and last—opportunity to hire a skipper.

There would several interesting managerial candidates available, with Lou Piniella topping the list. "Sweet Lou" had just watched the Mariners lose Ken Griffey Jr. and Alex Rodriguez, killing any chance of the team building off its 116-win season of 2001. Piniella had just led Seattle to a 93-win campaign despite having six regulars aged 32 of older. That alone made him a great fit for the Mets, who were embarking on their first season with Fred Wilpon as majority owner and son Jeff Wilpon as chief operating officer.

Giants manager Dusty Baker publicly stated during the World Series that he wasn't sure he'd return to San Francisco in 2003, even if he led the Giants to their first championship since the franchise moved to California.

The Mets didn't wait for Baker to make his decision, and they passed on Piniella as well. Instead, the Mets hired mild-mannered Art Howe, who had just led Oakland to a third straight postseason berth.

Howe had averaged 99 wins over his last three seasons with the Athletics, losing the division series in five games each time.

A red flare should have gone up above Shea Stadium when the A's gleefully allowed the Mets to interview Howe for the job. Why would a team be so willing to replace a manager that had just won 296 games in a three-year span? Unfair or not, whispers grew louder in Oakland that the success of the A's was fueled by bench coach Ken Macha and pitching coach Rick Peterson.

Howe's hiring was leaked to the media while Baker's Giants were hosting the Angels in the Fall Classic. The Mets curiously showed only lukewarm interest in Piniella, although he made it appear from that start that he was planning to become the Devil Rays' manager with a chance to work a few miles from his Tampa home.

Guys seemed to play hard for Howe at Oakland. The question was whether he could get the full attention of several Mets who fell woefully short of expectations in 2002, particularly Roberto Alomar, Mo Vaughn, Jeromy Burnitz,

and Roger Cedeno. A good year out of that quartet could make the difference in the Mets contending in 2003. They were prime reasons why the ballclub fell into last place in the NL East in '02, and they helped Phillips get fired in June 2003.

Phillips was in a bad situation of his own doing. The farm system had been depleted since 2000 and wasn't getting any better, although there were players in the system who would play key roles on the 2006 team. Fortunately, when the Mets were dealing their prospects for veteran talent with huge price tags in an effort to build an instant pennant winner, the departed players never blossomed with their new teams. Conversely, Vaughn, Alomar, Cedeno, and Burnitz had little market value by the spring of 2003, making their hefty contracts impossible to move. The only thing Phillips could do at this stage was hope the veterans returned to peak form, because there was little help coming from the minors in 2003 other than a teenage shortstop named Jose Reyes.

Phillips went into the off-season confident enough to sign free-agent Tom Glavine to a multiyear contract, figuring the former Cy Young Award winner might be the final piece of a winning puzzle. Glavine won 18 games and posted a 2.96 ERA for the Braves in 2002, so the contract hardly looked like a risk. Then again, Alomar hit .336 the year before coming to the Mets.

Phillips also picked up free-agent left fielder Cliff Floyd, a 2001 All-Star who batted .288 with 28 homers in '02. The signing gave the Mets a lineup of All-Stars at catcher, first, second, left, and right.

The year included the return of David Cone, who was trying to squeeze out another season after going 13–21 with a 5.70 ERA in his previous two years. Cone won a roster spot out of spring training to join a rotation that included Glavine, Al Leiter, Steve Trachsel, and Jae Seo.

The team didn't look to bad on paper, especially if the underachievers from 2002 could step it up a notch. Phillips bolstered the bench by bringing in former All-Stars Tony Clark and Jay Bell. The bullpen looked solid enough with John Franco, Mike Stanton, David Weathers, Dan Wheeler, and Graeme Lloyd setting things up for Armando Benitez. But by the end of the season, and in stark contrast to the criticism levied on the farm system, three of the Mets' most exciting players were all home-grown products: Reyes, Ty Wigginton, and the slow-footed, bespectacled Jason Phillips.

The excitement of the season opener at Shea Stadium lasted about five minutes. Glavine received a thunderous ovation as he walked to the mound to toss his warm-up pitches. Floyd was also greeted warmly in his first at-bat, but the Mets already were trailing 4–0 in the bottom of the first when Cliff came to the plate.

Glavine was down 3–0 before he retired his first batter, surrendering two doubles, a single, and a walk. It was 5–2 Cubs when Glavine was lifted in the fourth, serenaded by a chorus of boos as he walked to the dugout.

The Mets dropped two of three to the Cubs before Cone was sent to the mound on a ridiculously chilly night at Shea to begin a three-game set with the Expos. With a game time temperature of 37 degrees and 14 mph gusts, Cone braved the elements and turned back the clock by holding Montreal to two hits in five laborious shutout innings. He threw 84 pitches and worked out of a base-loaded jam in the third by striking out Vladimir Guerrero.

The Mets took two of three from the Expos and opened their road schedule with a win at Florida, giving New York a 4 –3 record. It marked the last time the Mets were over .500 for the season.

Injuries destroyed the power portion of the Mets' lineup. Mo Vaughn went 0-for-3 on May 2 before sitting out the rest of the season with a knee injury that ended his career. Piazza left the lineup two weeks later, suffering a torn groin that kept him out of action for three months. Those injuries left Floyd with little protection at the plate since the rest of the lineup lacked power when Clark wasn't in the game. Clark ended the season ranked third with 16 homers despite starting just 50 games.

Alomar actually hit worse than he did in 2002. He had just two homers and 20 extra-base hits in 302 plate appearance before he was part of the Mets' midseason fire sale. His speed was even more limited than his power, and his range at second base continued to deteriorate.

Alomar's double play partner at the start of the year was Rey Sanchez, a more than capable shortstop with the Cubs and Royals, and a .286 hitter for the Red Sox in 2002. Sanchez hit .294 in 48 games for the Mariners over the final two months of 2003, but he carved out a meager .207 average as a Met when he wasn't on the disabled list.

The Sanchez injury forced the Mets to recall Reyes a lot sooner than they had hoped. Reyes was hitting a modest .269 with no homers and 13 RBIs for Triple A Tidewater when he was promoted, but he already possessed excellent defensive skills and stole 26 bases in 42 games for the Tides.

Reyes went 2-for-4 with two runs scored in his big league debut June 10, a day shy of his 20th birthday. He went 3-for-4 with a grand slam and five RBIs versus the Angels just five days later, and drove in four runs against the Marlins June 18, giving him 11 RBIs in his first nine games as a Met. But he was batting just .207 with one stolen base through July 11 before putting together a second half that turned him into a franchise building block.

Reyes reeled off a nine-game hitting streak in July and dwarfed that by hitting in 17 straight from July 30 through August 18, hiking his average to .316. He swiped 12 bases in his final 45 games while hitting .351 to end the year with a .307 mark. But Reyes missed the final month with an ankle sprain, taking him out of contention for NL Rookie of the Year honors.

Jason Phillips emerged as the Mets' top rookie after replacing Vaughn at first base. Phillips batted .379 in his first 12 games and compiled a 14-game hitting streak that put his average at .327 by July 26. The converted catcher ended the year with 34 multi-hit games and a .298 average while trying to learn a new position.

Wigginton played in a team-high 156 games and led the club with 36 doubles and 71 RBIs, but his .255 average and erratic glovework were slight disappointments. He had excellent range at third base and could smother a grounder with the best of them, but his throws could be difficult to handle, especially by an inexperienced first baseman. Wigginton was the least of the Mets' problems.

The biggest mystery on the team aside from Alomar was Cedeno, who seemed to lack any confidence as a base-stealer after setting a team record of 66 steals as a first-year Met in 1999. Cedeno swiped just 14 bags in 23 attempts and had only four triples among his 129 hits. His value to the team was limited as long as he kept his on-base percentage at the .320 range.

Burnitz bounced back nicely, hitting .274 with 18 homers and 45 RBIs in 69 games before he was placed on the front lawn as part of the Mets' July yard sale. Burnitz also had to endure impatient fans who were still ticked off by his .215 average and 54 RBIs in 154 games in 2002.

The one player who truly earned the appreciation of Mets fans in 2003 was Floyd, who continued to take his spot in left field despite a painful Achilles' injury that required surgery. Floyd started slowly but hit .332 with eight homers, 39 RBIs, and 37 runs scored in 61 games after May 26 before finally giving in to surgery with the team firmly in last place. He received a standing ovation at Shea as he walked off the field for a defensive replacement in the ninth inning of his last game August 19, one day after going 4-for-4 and two days after collecting four RBIs.

The starting rotation wasn't too bad after it was finally settled. Cone announced his retirement during the season and Pedro Astacio underwent surgery after pitching in pain for seven starts. Their departures allowed Seo to go 9–12 with a 3.82 ERA in 32 games, including 31 starts. Trachsel led the Mets with 16 of their 66 victories, and Leiter went 15–9 to post a team-high .625 winning percentage. Glavine had 12 starts in which he pitched at least six innings and game up two runs or fewer, but he finished 9–14 with a 4.52 ERA in his worst season since 1988.

The Mets also gave Aaron Heilman a chance to crack the rotation, but the rookie appeared overmatched just two years after being drafted in the first round. He made 13 starts and went 2–7 with a 6.75 ERA, an obvious rush job by a franchise desperate for any encouraging sign from its prospects.

Trachsel was the team ERA leader at 3.78, slightly better than Seo's 3.82 and Leiter's 3.99. The earned run averages were inflated by a bullpen that had trouble throwing quality pitches with inherited runners on base. The pen allowed 31 percent of its 193 inherited runners to score while going 9–30 with a 4.31 ERA.

Stanton was the most effective reliever on the team, although he was the target of boo-birds at Shea. Franco was still trying to round into shape after missing all of 2002 following Tommy John surgery. Lloyd emerged as a lefty specialist, giving Franco a chance to ease into the season without taxing his arm. Wheeler looked exceptional at times but was wildly inconsistent and prone to a big inning that would turn a small deficit into a rout. However, Wheeler wasn't the team's biggest enigma out of the pen.

Armando Benitez got off to a miserable start and owned an 0–3 record with eight saves in 11 chances and a 7.24 ERA by the end of April. He was terrific from May 1 through June 17, collecting nine straight saves and compiling a 0.38 earned run average with 23 strikeouts in 23 innings. But he blew three saves in seven chances during his final nine games as a Met before he was jettisoned to the Yankees right after the All-Star break. By then, the Mets had a new GM.

Jim Duquette was given the task of purging the roster in a long-awaited rebuilding effort. In addition to Benitez, Duquette dealt Alomar, Burnitz, Lloyd, and Sanchez. In return, the Mets received Victor Diaz, Royce Ring, Jason Anderson, Edwin Almonte, and six prospects who never played a game for the Mets. Diaz and Ring showed some potential upon their first stint in the majors before flaming out.

The Mets were 21 games out of first by the All-Star break and never pulled themselves out of the basement after June 18. They won just four of their final 23 games and finished 11th in the National League in attendance. It wasn't quite the season Fred Wilpon had envisioned when he wrestled controlling interest in the club from Nelson Doubleday the previous August.

2003 Mets Statistics

Hitting	G	AB	R	H	2B	3B	HR	RBI	BB	SO	BA	OBP	SLG	SB	CS	GDP	HP	SH	SF	IBB
Roberto Alomar	73	263	34	69	17	1	2	22	29	40	.262	.336	.357	6	0	8	2	4	4	2
Jay Bell	72	116	11	21	1	0	0	3	22	38	.181	.319	.190	0	0	4	2	1	1	1
Jeromy Burnitz	65	234	38	64	18	0	18	45	21	55	.274	.344	.581	1	4	4	4	0	0	6
Roger Cedeno	148	484	70	129	25	4	7	37	38	86	.267	.320	.378	14	9	8	1	2	2	3
Tony Clark	125	254	29	59	13	0	16	43	24	73	.232	.300	.472	0	0	8	1	0	1	2
Joe DePastino	2	2	0	0	0	0	0	0	0	1	.000	.000	.000	0	0	0	0	0	0	0
Jeff Duncan	56	139	13	27	0	2	1	10	17	41	.194	.291	.245	4	2	1	2	8	0	3
Cliff Floyd	108	365	57	106	25	2	18	68	51	66	.290	.376	.518	3	0	10	3	0	6	2
Danny Garcia	19	56	5	12	2	0	2	6	2	11	.214	.274	.357	0	0	2	3	1	1	0
Mike Glavine	6	7	0	1	0	0	0	0	0	2	.143	.143	.143	0	0	0	0	0	0	0
Raul Gonzalez	107	217	28	50	12	2	2	21	27	34	.230	.317	.332	3	0	8	1	0	1	1
Joe McEwing	119	278	31	67	11	0	1	16	25	57	.241	.309	.291	3	0	6	3	6	1	4
Timo Perez	127	346	32	93	21	0	4	42	18	29	.269	.301	.364	5	6	5	2	7	9	1
Jason Phillips	119	403	45	120	25	0	11	58	39	50	.298	.373	.442	0	1	21	10	0	1	3
Mike Piazza	68	234	37	67	13	0	11	34	35	40	.286	.377	.483	0	0	11	1	0	3	3
Prentice Redman	15	24	3	3	1	0	1	2	1	9	.125	.192	.292	2	0	1	1	1	0	0
Jose Reyes	69	274	47	84	12	4	5	32	13	36	.307	.334	.434	13	3	1	0	2	3	0
Rey Sanchez	56	174	11	36	3	1	0	12	8	18	.207	.240	.236	1	1	7	0	0	1	2
Marco Scutaro	48	75	10	16	4	0	2	6	13	14	.213	.333	.347	2	0	1	1	1	1	2
Tsuyoshi Shinjo	62	114	10	22	3	0	1	7	6	12	.193	.238	.246	0	1	0	1	2	1	1
Mo Vaughn	27	79	10	15	2	0	3	15	14	22	.190	.323	.329	0	0	2	2	0	1	2
Jorge Velandia	23	58	6	11	3	1	0	8	10	15	.190	.304	.276	0	0	1	0	3	1	1
Matt Watson	15	23	0	4	2	0	0	2	1	5	.174	.208	.261	0	0	1	0	1	0	0
Ty Wigginton	156	573	73	146	36	6	11	71	46	124	.255	.318	.396	12	2	15	9	1	4	2
Vance Wilson	96	268	28	65	9	1	8	39	15	56	.243	.293	.373	1	2	6	5	2	2	1
Pitchers																				
Edwin Almonte	12	1	0	0	0	0	0	0	0	0	.000	.000	.000	0	0	1	0	0	0	0
Pedro Astacio	7	11	1	1	0	0	0	0	0	2	.091	.091	.091	0	0	0	0	3	0	0
Mike Bacsik	4	3	0	0	0	0	0	0	0	1	.000	.000	.000	0	0	0	0	0	0	0
Armando Benitez	43	1	0	0	0	0	0	0	0	1	.000	.000	.000	0	0	0	0	0	0	0
Jaime Cerda	27	1	0	0	0	0	0	0	0	1	.000	.000	.000	0	0	0	0	0	0	0
David Cone	5	4	0	1	0	0	0	0	0	1	.250	.250	.250	0	0	0	0	0	0	0
Pedro Feliciano	21	3	0	0	0	0	0	0	1	1	.000	.250	.000	0	0	0	0	1	0	0
Tom Glavine	33	53	4	8	1	0	0	3	4	13	.151	.211	.170	0	0	0	0	10	0	0
Jeremy Griffiths	7	9	0	0	0	0	0	0	1	3	.000	.100	.000	0	0	0	0	1	0	0
Aaron Heilman	14	22	1	1	0	0	0	1	1	13	.045	.087	.045	0	0	0	0	0	0	0
Al Leiter	28	53	2	1	0	0	0	0	2	28	.019	.055	.019	0	0	2	0	5	0	0
Orber Moreno	7	1	0	0	0	0	0	0	0	1	.000	.000	.000	0	0	0	0	0	0	0
Jason Roach	1	2	0	2	0	0	0	0	0	0	1.000	1.000	1.000	0	0	0	0	0	0	0
Jae Weong Seo	33	51	3	5	1	0	0	0	3	19	.098	.148	.118	0	0	0	0	4	0	0
Mike Stanton	49	1	0	0	0	0	0	0	0	0	.000	.000	.000	0	0	1	0	0	0	0
Pat Strange	6	1	0	0	0	0	0	0	0	0	.000	.000	.000	0	0	0	0	0	0	0
Scott Strickland	19	1	0	0	0	0	0	0	0	0	.000	.000	.000	0	0	0	0	1	0	0
Steve Trachsel	34	58	3	11	2	0	0	4	2	16	.190	.213	.224	0	0	1	0	11	1	0
Dave Weathers	72	3	0	0	0	0	0	0	0	1	.000	.000	.000	0	0	0	0	0	0	0
Dan Wheeler	34	2	0	0	0	0	0	0	0	0	.000	.000	.000	0	0	0	0	0	0	0
TOTAL	161	5341	642	1317	262	24	124	607	489	1035	.247	.314	.374	70	31	136	54	78	45	42

Pitching	G	ERA	W–L	SV	GS	GF	CG	SHO	IP	H	R	ER	HR	BB	SO	BFP	WP	HBP	BK	IBB
Edwin Almonte	12	11.12	0–0	0	0	3	0	0	11.1	21	15	14	3	5	7	57	1	0	0	1
Jason Anderson	6	5.06	0–0	0	0	2	0	0	10.2	10	6	6	2	5	7	47	0	1	0	1
Pedro Astacio	7	7.36	3–2	0	7	0	0	0	36.2	47	30	30	8	18	20	174	4	3	0	1
Mike Bacsik	5	10.19	1–2	0	3	1	0	0	17.2	28	21	20	5	8	12	85	0	0	0	0
Armando Benitez	45	3.10	3–3	21	0	40	0	0	49.1	41	18	17	5	24	50	209	3	0	1	1
Jaime Cerda	27	5.85	1–1	0	0	9	0	0	32.1	32	21	21	4	20	19	144	3	0	1	1
David Cone	5	6.50	1–3	0	4	0	0	0	18.0	20	13	13	4	13	13	85	0	0	0	1
Pedro Feliciano	23	3.35	0–0	0	0	8	0	0	48.1	52	21	18	5	21	43	218	3	3	1	3
John Franco	38	2.62	0–3	2	0	13	0	0	34.1	35	11	10	5	13	16	148	2	1	0	2
Tom Glavine	32	4.52	9–14	0	32	0	0	0	183.1	205	94	92	21	66	82	791	2	2	0	7
Jeremy Griffiths	9	7.02	1–4	0	6	1	0	0	41.0	57	34	32	5	19	25	199	1	2	0	2
Aaron Heilman	14	6.75	2–7	0	13	0	0	0	65.1	79	53	49	13	41	51	315	5	3	0	2
Al Leiter	30	3.99	15–9	0	30	0	1	1	180.2	176	83	80	15	94	139	798	5	9	1	11
Graeme Lloyd	36	3.31	1–2	0	0	12	0	0	35.1	39	16	13	2	7	17	149	1	0	0	2
Jason Middlebrook	5	10.29	0–0	0	0	2	0	0	7.0	13	8	8	0	4	3	36	1	0	0	0
Orber Moreno	7	7.88	0–0	0	0	4	0	0	8.0	10	7	7	1	3	5	36	0	0	0	0
Jason Roach	2	12.00	0–2	0	2	0	0	0	9.0	14	12	12	3	4	2	46	2	1	0	0
Grant Roberts	18	3.79	0–3	1	0	5	0	0	19.0	19	9	8	0	3	10	79	0	1	0	1
Jae Weong Seo	32	3.82	9–12	0	31	0	0	0	188.1	193	94	80	18	46	110	806	2	6	0	11
Mike Stanton	50	4.57	2–7	5	0	24	0	0	45.1	37	25	23	6	19	34	194	2	2	1	4
Pat Strange	6	11.00	0–0	0	0	1	0	0	9.0	13	11	11	4	11	5	48	0	0	0	0
Scott Strickland	19	2.25	0–2	0	0	3	0	0	20.0	16	6	5	1	10	16	84	1	1	0	1
Steve Trachsel	33	3.78	16–10	0	33	0	2	2	204.2	204	90	86	26	65	111	857	5	3	2	9
Dave Weathers	77	3.08	1–6	7	0	20	0	0	87.2	87	33	30	6	40	75	384	1	6	0	6
Dan Wheeler	35	3.71	1–3	2	0	10	0	0	51.0	49	23	21	6	17	35	215	1	1	0	4
TOTAL	161	4.48	66–95	38	161	158	3	10	1413.1	1497	754	704	168	576	907	6204	45	45	7	71

2004

NL EAST

TEAM	W	L	PCT	GB	BA	ERA
Braves	96	66	.593	—	.270	3.74
Phillies	86	76	.531	10.0	.267	4.45
Marlins	83	79	.512	13.0	.264	4.10
Mets	71	91	.438	25.0	.249	4.09
Expos	67	95	.414	29.0	.249	4.33

Mets finish 21 games behind Astros for wild-card

The Mets spent the winter of 2004 continuing to look for quick fixes to a franchise that has seen its win total drop each season since 1999. The Mets had been burned by recent trades involving All-Stars Roberto Alomar and Mo Vaughn, two deals that led to Steve Phillips' removal as general manager. Interim GM Jim Duquette dealt Alomar and Armando Benitez the previous summer in an effort to restock the farm system and cut costs on what was becoming a very expensive last-place team. Duquette was named the team's permanent GM in October 2003 after showing a desire to build the team from within while stifling the Mets' reputation as a free-spending team.

But Duquette and the front office still felt this team could contend in 2004 with a little tweaking and a couple of free agents despite a 66–95 campaign under rookie manager Art Howe. Duquette signed outfielder Mike Cameron and closer Braden Looper before acquiring free-agent infielder Kazuo Matsui from Japan.

The Cameron signing made sense. The Mets were in need of a center fielder after using Timo Perez, Jeff Duncan, Tsuyoshi Shinjo, and five others at the position in 2003. Cameron also could provide some much-needed power to a lineup that included Mike Piazza and Cliff Floyd, who combined for only 599 at-bats in '03 because of injuries.

Getting Matsui made a nice splash on the back pages of the tabloids, but it made little sense on the roster. The Mets already had Jose Reyes, who hit .307 in 274 at-bats while showing great range at short as a rookie the previous year. The Mets were able to sign Matsui with the provision he become the everyday shortstop, which meant a position change for the 20-year-old Reyes. Matsui had been a Gold Glove–caliber shortstop in Japan, where most ballparks possessed artificial surfaces and all the charm of Montreal's Olympic Stadium. He was now thrust into a league where 15 of the 16 infields had natural grass and dirt infields, to which he was unaccustomed.

Reyes wasn't the only Mets regular learning a new position during spring training. Jason Phillips had hit .298 with 11 homers and 58 RBIs as the team's first baseman in 2003, but his natural position was catcher. Incumbent Mike Piazza was heading to the Hall of Fame with unprecedented power numbers as a catcher, but his throwing arm always left a lot to be desired. The Mets handed Piazza a first baseman's glove in 2004, figuring the move would keep his bat fresh while prolonging his career. Piazza gave it a try, but his footwork was awkward and his range made Mets fans miss the days when Dave Kingman was at first.

In theory, the position changes were made to bolster the lineup. Piazza would deliver more pop than did Phillips at first, and the Mets hoped Reyes and Matsui would give the Mets a one-two punch they hadn't had at the top of the lineup since the days of Lenny Dykstra and Wally Backman. But that theory blew up in the Mets' faces when Reyes was placed on the disabled list March 15 with a strained right hamstring. The injury appeared to be a minor problem in spring training, and it was expected to be a day-to-day or week-to-week problem. But Reyes didn't got off the DL until June 19.

Duquette also brought back Todd Zeile, a fan favorite who helped the Mets win the 2000 NL pennant. Zeile had become a role player in 2003, hitting .227 for the Yankees and Rockies. He would provide depth to a bench that lacked a proven hitter.

Adding outfield depth, Duquette also acquired Karim Garcia and Shane Spencer, each of whom hit well at the start of the 2004 season before fading.

The pitching staff seemed okay heading into 2004. Tom Glavine, the Mets' big free-agent pickup in 2003, was coming off his worst season in 15 years. Much of that was due to circumstance as he left the first-place Braves for a ballclub with a leaky bullpen and a sub-par offense.

Al Leiter and Steve Trachsel combined to earn 31 of the team's 66 victories in '03 and were healthy heading into 2004. Jae Seo would be the fourth starter, but the team never found a bonafide No. 5 guy until midseason.

Looper was signed as the closer following a rather tumultuous year with the Marlins. He saved 28 wins for the World Series champs in 2003 but finished the season 0–1 with two blown saves and a 21.50 ERA in his last five appearances. Ugueth Urbina emerged as Florida's top closer in the playoffs, making Looper available.

The middle relief corps included John Franco, Mike Stanton, and David Weathers, a trio that would hear a wrath of boos during 2004.

The pitching staff was now under the tutelage of Rick Peterson, Howe's pitching coach at Oakland. Peterson had mentored Tim Hudson, Barry Zito, and Eric Mulder, three Cy Young candidates who helped the A's reach the postseason the last four seasons. Peterson also had gained a reputation as a pitching guru who could find any hurler's flaw and turn him into a productive major leaguer. After all, he had been on board when the A's picked up Jason Isringhausen from the Mets, helping turn him into one of the game's top closers.

The Mets were more than competitive during the first half of the 2004 season. Matsui became the third Met to homer in his first major league at-bat, sending a Russ Ortiz pitch over the wall at Turner Field to ignite a 7–2 win on Opening Day. But the team desperately needed a productive right fielder as it opened the season 30–34. Duquette sent Dan Wheeler to the Astros for Richard Hidalgo in mid-June, a deal that brought the enigmatic outfielder to Shea Stadium. Hidalgo had gotten off to a slow start in 2004 after hitting 53 homers the previous two seasons. He went 0-for-7 in his first two games with the Mets before hitting .390 with eight homers and 15 RBIs in his next 15 contests. Hidalgo could carry the Mets on his back at times, as he did when he set a club record with homers in five straight games.

The Hidalgo trade seemed to spark the Mets, who went 13–6 immediately after the deal. New York was in the division race despite a 43–40 record, a half-game ahead of the Braves and just one game behind the first-place Phillies.

The Mets went 6–12 over the next 18 games, but they were within six games of the division lead and in the mix for the wild-card. That's when the Mets erroneously decided they were contenders for a playoff berth despite:

- Matsui, who was hitting .274 but rarely displaying his Gold Glove reputation at shortstop.
- Phillips, who was batting .207 with five homers and 25 RBIs as the heir apparent to Piazza behind the plate.
- Piazza, who played first base like a natural-born catcher.
- Cliff Floyd, who appeared in just 70 of the Mets' first 100 games due to nagging injuries.
- Reyes, who was still getting accustomed to making the pivot at second.

A rookie third baseman named David Wright already had supplanted Ty Wigginton, who was now seeing time at second and first base. Wigginton was arguably the team's most productive infielder heading into the stretch run, but Wright's presence made him expendable. The Mets were able to secure another starter by dealing Wigginton, getting former No. 1 draft pick Kris Benson from the Pirates.

A rotation of Glavine, Leiter, Trachsel, and Benson was nice, but a fifth starter would certainly get the Mets over the top, right? Seo wasn't winning his starts, and Aaron Heilman didn't appear ready to join the rotation on a permanent basis. So Duquette, who had worked so hard to replenish the Mets' farm system, jettisoned his top minor league prospect to the Devil Rays. Duquette came away with Victor Zambrano, another talented but enigmatic player who was dominant when throwing strikes. Zambrano never had command of the strike zone during his major league career, but Peterson was sure he could solve the right-hander's problems.

And all it took to acquire Zambrano was Scott Kazmir, the Mets' most prized possession in the farm system. Kazmir reminded many of Ron Guidry with his slight frame and blazing fastball, but the impatient Mets needed results right away. There was a wild-card berth to win.

There were reports the veteran pitchers really didn't take a liking to Kazmir in spring training. Part of it supposedly was the team's pampering of the lefty, although the older hurlers might have feared a successful Kazmir would mean their departure. The Mets already had experienced a similar problem 16 years ago when Gregg Jefferies irritated his teammates and made the very popular Wally Backman expendable. The ballclub may not have wanted a repeat of the Jefferies scenario.

The two trades seemed to help the Mets in the short term. New York lost three straight after the deals but was 10–10 in the first 20 games following the swaps, leaving them seven games off the wild-card lead by August 21.

Instead of a charge toward the wild-card, the Mets experienced a free-fall that had them scrambling to stay out of the NL East cellar. New York had just pulled out a 12-inning victory over the Giants before dropping 19 of their next 21. They ended the season going 7–18 in their last 25 home games, including series wins over the Braves and Cubs. Benson was a .500 pitcher for the Mets, and Zambrano pitched just 14 innings before he was sidelined by a shoulder injury.

By September, Mets fans were seeing a lot of prospects Jeff Keppinger, Victor Diaz, Wilson Delgado, and Craig Brazell. Wright appeared to be a star in the making at third base, and Reyes hit .275 after July 25. Piazza eventually became the starting catcher toward the end of the year, but his .266 average was by far his worst in a season with more than 400 at-bats at that point.

Phillips hit only .218, and Matsui committed 23 errors while batting .274. Cameron was the Mets' most productive hitter with 30 homers and 76 RBIs despite a team-high 143 strikeouts and a .231 batting average. Cameron also struggled in center during day games, finishing the season with eight errors.

Hidalgo had one of the streakiest half-seasons in team history. He was the backbone of the offense when he was going well, but his cold stretches were longer that his hot streaks.

He smacked seven homers and had 12 RBIs while batting .400 during a 13-game hitting streak that began in late-June. He also batted .110 with 23 strikeouts in his last 22 games.

Wright was everything Jefferies was not. Wright became a fan favorite almost instantly and was a very popular guy in the clubhouse. Just 21 at the time of his major league debut, Wright had a keen awareness of the game and an even better awareness of how a rookie should act. It also didn't hurt that he batted .304 with 13 homers and 39 RBIs in his final 62 games, numbers that would have projected to 34 homers and 102 RBIs for a full 162-game season.

The top of the rotation pitched effectively. Glavine, Leiter, and Trachsel combined to go 33–35 while the rest of the staff was 38–56. Looper saved 29 games but usually had little reason to take the mound in the ninth inning. His bullpen cotenants, Stanton and Bottalico, combined to blow nine leads in the seventh inning or later.

The August swoon led to Howe's departure in October. Howe protected his players and seemed to keep an upbeat attitude no matter what crisis bedeviled the Mets at any point in the season. But he was on thin ice after the Mets hired Omar Minaya as VP and general manager in September.

2004 Mets Statistics

Hitting	G	AB	R	H	2B	3B	HR	RBI	BB	SO	BA	OBP	SLG	SB	CS	GDP	HP	SH	SF	IBB
Craig Brazell	24	34	3	9	2	0	1	3	1	7	.265	.286	.412	0	0	1	0	0	0	0
Brian Buchanan	2	3	0	0	0	0	0	0	1	1	.000	.250	.000	0	0	0	0	0	0	0
Mike Cameron	140	493	76	114	30	1	30	76	57	143	.231	.319	.479	22	6	5	8	1	3	2
Wilson Delgado	42	130	11	38	4	1	2	13	15	29	.292	.366	.385	1	0	1	0	2	0	3
Victor Diaz	15	51	8	15	3	0	3	8	1	15	.294	.321	.529	0	0	3	1	0	0	0
Jeff Duncan	13	15	2	1	0	0	0	1	1	5	.067	.125	.067	3	0	0	0	1	0	0
Cliff Floyd	113	396	55	103	26	0	18	63	47	103	.260	.352	.462	11	4	8	11	0	3	6
Danny Garcia	58	138	23	32	7	1	3	17	22	34	.232	.371	.362	3	0	1	9	4	1	2
Karim Garcia	62	192	24	45	7	2	7	22	10	35	.234	.272	.401	3	0	6	0	0	0	0
Ricky Gutierrez	24	63	2	11	2	0	0	5	6	8	.175	.257	.206	0	0	3	1	0	0	0
Richard Hidalgo	86	324	46	74	11	1	21	52	27	76	.228	.296	.463	3	2	12	5	0	2	3
Joe Hietpas	1	0	0	0	0	0	0	0	0	0	----	----	----	0	0	0	0	0	0	0
Jeff Keppinger	33	116	9	33	2	0	3	9	6	7	.284	.317	.379	2	1	6	0	0	1	0
Kazuo Matsui	114	460	65	125	32	2	7	44	40	97	.272	.331	.396	14	3	3	2	5	2	4
Joe McEwing	75	138	17	35	3	1	1	16	9	32	.254	.297	.312	4	1	0	0	6	1	4
Jason Phillips	128	362	34	79	18	0	7	34	35	42	.218	.298	.326	0	1	11	8	2	5	4
Mike Piazza	129	455	47	121	21	0	20	54	68	78	.266	.362	.444	0	0	14	2	0	3	14
Jose Reyes	53	220	33	56	16	2	2	14	5	31	.255	.271	.373	19	2	1	0	4	0	0
Esix Snead	1	0	1	0	0	0	0	0	0	0	----	----	----	0	0	0	0	0	0	0
Shane Spencer	74	185	21	52	10	1	4	26	13	37	.281	.332	.411	6	0	1	2	2	2	0
Eric Valent	130	270	39	72	15	2	13	34	28	61	.267	.337	.481	0	1	10	1	0	1	4
Ty Wigginton	86	312	46	89	23	2	12	42	23	48	.285	.334	.487	6	1	11	1	1	2	4
Gerald Williams	57	129	17	30	8	2	4	11	8	26	.233	.277	.419	2	1	2	0	1	0	1
Tom Wilson	4	4	0	1	0	0	0	0	1	2	.250	.400	.250	0	0	0	0	0	0	0
Vance Wilson	79	157	18	43	10	1	4	21	11	24	.274	.335	.427	1	0	5	5	1	3	2
David Wright	69	263	41	77	17	1	14	40	14	40	.293	.332	.525	6	0	7	3	0	3	0
Todd Zeile	137	348	30	81	16	0	9	35	44	83	.233	.319	.356	0	0	13	1	1	2	1
Pitchers																				
James Baldwin	2	2	0	0	0	0	0	0	0	1	.000	.000	.000	0	0	0	0	0	0	0
Heath Bell	17	1	0	0	0	0	0	0	0	0	.000	.000	.000	0	0	0	0	0	0	0
Kris Benson	11	19	1	1	0	0	0	2	1	9	.053	.100	.053	0	0	0	0	5	0	0
Ricky Bottalico	57	2	0	0	0	0	0	0	0	0	.000	.000	.000	0	0	0	0	0	0	0
Scott Erickson	2	3	0	0	0	0	0	0	0	2	.000	.000	.000	0	0	0	0	0	0	0
Matt Ginter	13	14	1	3	1	0	0	1	2	5	.214	.313	.286	0	0	0	0	3	0	0
Tom Glavine	33	54	5	11	2	0	0	8	10	10	.204	.328	.241	0	0	2	0	8	0	0
Aaron Heilman	5	7	0	0	0	0	0	0	0	3	.000	.000	.000	0	0	0	0	3	0	0
Al Leiter	28	54	0	5	1	0	0	0	3	30	.093	.140	.111	0	0	1	0	2	0	0
Braden Looper	69	2	0	0	0	0	0	0	0	1	.000	.000	.000	0	0	0	0	0	0	0

Hitting (continued)	G	AB	R	H	2B	3B	HR	RBI	BB	SO	BA	OBP	SLG	SB	CS	GDP	HP	SH	SF	IBB
Orber Moreno	32	1	0	0	0	0	0	0	0	0	.000	.000	.000	0	0	0	0	0	0	0
Jae Weong Seo	25	32	2	5	1	0	0	1	2	9	.156	.229	.188	1	0	1	1	3	0	0
Mike Stanton	79	2	0	1	0	0	0	1	0	1	.500	.500	.500	0	0	0	0	0	0	0
Steve Trachsel	33	59	6	11	1	0	0	5	1	17	.186	.200	.203	0	0	1	0	11	0	0
Dan Wheeler	30	5	1	1	0	0	0	0	0	1	.200	.200	.200	0	0	0	1	1	0	0
Tyler Yates	21	11	0	1	0	0	0	0	0	5	.091	.091	.091	0	0	0	0	1	0	0
Victor Zambrano	3	6	0	1	0	0	0	0	0	1	.167	.167	.167	0	0	0	0	1	0	0
TOTAL	162	5532	684	1376	289	20	185	658	512	1159	.249	.317	.409	107	23	129	61	69	34	54

Pitching	G	ERA	W–L	SV	GS	GF	CG	SHO	IP	H	R	ER	HR	BB	SO	BFP	WP	HBP	BK	IBB
James Baldwin	2	15.00	0–2	0	2	0	0	0	6.0	13	10	10	3	5	1	36	0	1	0	1
Heath Bell	17	3.33	0–2	0	0	2	0	0	24.1	22	9	9	5	6	27	94	0	0	0	0
Kris Benson	11	4.50	4–4	0	11	0	1	1	68.0	65	37	34	8	17	51	290	3	4	0	3
Ricky Bottalico	60	3.38	3–2	0	0	8	0	0	69.1	54	30	26	3	34	61	296	3	4	0	7
Vic Darensbourg	5	7.94	0–1	0	0	2	0	0	5.2	10	5	5	1	2	1	28	0	0	0	0
Mike DeJean	17	1.69	0–0	0	0	8	0	0	21.1	21	5	4	0	5	24	91	2	2	0	2
Scott Erickson	2	7.88	0–1	0	2	0	0	0	8.0	15	9	7	1	4	3	42	1	0	0	0
Pedro Feliciano	22	5.40	1–1	0	0	3	0	0	18.1	14	12	11	2	12	14	82	1	1	0	0
Bartolome Fortunato	15	3.86	1–0	1	0	5	0	0	18.2	14	8	8	2	13	20	82	1	0	0	0
John Franco	52	5.28	2–7	0	0	16	0	0	46.0	46	28	27	6	24	36	207	2	1	0	2
Matt Ginter	15	4.54	1–3	0	14	0	0	0	69.1	82	41	35	8	20	38	313	1	5	0	5
Tom Glavine	33	3.60	11–14	0	33	0	1	1	212.1	204	94	85	20	70	109	904	0	0	0	10
Aaron Heilman	5	5.46	1–3	0	5	0	0	0	28.0	27	17	17	4	13	22	119	0	0	0	0
Al Leiter	30	3.21	10–8	0	30	0	0	0	173.2	138	65	62	16	97	117	750	1	11	1	8
Braden Looper	71	2.70	2–5	29	0	60	0	0	83.1	86	28	25	5	16	60	346	1	3	0	3
Orber Moreno	33	3.38	3–1	1	0	8	0	0	34.2	29	17	13	0	11	29	146	2	3	1	0
Jose Parra	13	3.21	1–0	0	0	7	0	0	14.0	14	6	5	2	6	14	61	0	0	0	1
Grant Roberts	4	17.36	0–0	0	0	1	0	0	4.2	9	9	9	2	6	1	29	0	0	0	1
JaeWeongSeo	24	4.90	5–10	0	21	1	0	0	117.2	133	67	64	17	50	54	512	0	2	1	7
MikeStanton	83	3.16	2–6	0	0	19	0	0	77.0	70	32	27	6	33	58	337	1	2	0	6
SteveTrachsel	33	4.00	12–13	0	33	0	0	0	202.2	203	104	90	25	83	117	881	4	5	2	9
DaveWeathers	32	4.28	5–3	0	0	10	0	0	33.2	41	19	16	5	15	25	156	1	2	1	0
DanWheeler	32	4.80	3–1	0	1	7	0	0	50.2	65	29	27	9	17	46	232	4	0	1	2
TylerYates	21	6.36	2–4	0	7	2	0	0	46.2	61	36	33	6	25	35	228	1	3	1	3
VictorZambrano	3	3.86	2–0	0	3	0	0	0	14.0	12	9	6	0	6	14	62	1	0	0	0
ToddZeile	1	45.00	0–0	0	0	1	0	0	1.0	4	5	5	0	2	0	9	0	0	0	0
TOTAL	162	4.09	71–91	31	162	160	2	6	1449.0	1452	731	658	156	592	977	6333	30	49	8	70

2005

NL EAST

TEAM	W	L	PCT	GB	BA	ERA
Braves	90	72	.556	–	.265	3.98
Phillies	88	74	.543	2.0	.270	4.21
Mets	83	79	.512	7.0	.258	3.76
Marlins	83	79	.512	7.0	.272	4.16
Nationals	81	81	.500	9.0	.252	3.87

Mets finish 6.0 games behind Astros for wild-card

Omar Minaya already had a reputation as a "go-for-it" general manager before he assumed the position with the Mets. As general manager of the Expos in 2003, he recognized Major League Baseball was ready to drop the franchise, so he did his best to create renewed fan interest in Montreal by acquiring several All-Stars in a bid to steal a wild-card berth. When MLB decided to move the franchise to Washington, D.C., in September 2004, Minaya opted to return to the Mets as executive vice president and general manager after previously serving as Mets assistant GM under Steve Phillips.

Minaya wasted little time making the Mets important again by signing free agents Pedro Martinez and Carlos Beltrán, acquiring veteran infielders Doug Mientkiewicz and Miguel Cairo, and landing valuable utilitymen Marlon Anderson and Chris Woodward.

What Minaya failed to do was improve the pitching staff underneath Martinez and Tom Glavine. Al Leiter was allowed to walk after Minaya offered him an incentive-laden, one-year offer. The rotation took another hit during spring training, when Steve Trachsel was diagnosed with a back injury that required surgery, keeping him out of action until late August.

Martinez and Glavine were viewed as an imposing front-end tandem in the rotation despite Glavine's 20–28 record in his first two seasons with the Mets. Glavine pitched to a very respectable 3.60 ERA in 2004 and could have won 17 games with a little more run support or a better bullpen.

The rest of the rotation was a patchwork assemblage of Kris Benson, Victor Zambrano, Jae Seo, Aaron Heilman, and Kaz Ishii, although Benson was injured late in spring training and was unable to make his season debut until May. Ishii was acquired from the Dodgers at the end of training camp following Benson's injury. Seo pitched himself off the season-opening roster, making the rotation all the more worrisome after Martinez and Glavine. Zambrano entered the regular season as the No. 3 starter, and Heilman was at the back end of the rotation by Opening Day despite going 3–10 with a 6.36 ERA in his first two seasons with the Mets.

The bullpen received a complete makeover, with 40-year-old Roberto Hernandez and 35-year-old rookie Dae-Sung Koo serving as the top newcomers. Heath Bell was given an opportunity as a middle-innings flame-thrower after looking impressive in spots for the Mets the previous year. Braden Looper was back for his second season as the Mets' closer and was coming off a solid yet unspectacular season.

Gone was John Franco, who was allowed to become a free agent at age 43. Mike Stanton also left after appearing in 83 games in 2004, traded for a very ineffective Felix Heredia.

Although the rotation and bullpen looked shaky heading into 2005, the offense appeared to be the best the Mets had assembled since 1999. Beltrán was coming off one of the greatest postseasons in major league history and possessed power and range, although he was replacing a center fielder who also had power and range.

Mike Cameron was shifted from center to right field after Beltrán was signed. Add Cliff Floyd to the mix, and the Mets had a starting outfield with the potential to hit more than 100 home runs. However, Cameron looked uncomfortable in right and missed the last weeks of the season following a violent outfield collision with Beltrán in San Diego, leaving Cameron with multiple facial fractures.

Mientkiewicz was signed to play first base after Minaya was unable to ink free agent Carlos Delgado. Mientkiewicz won a Gold Glove in 2001 and was expected to be a settling influence on a rather inexperienced infield.

Reyes was back at shortstop after spending almost all of 2004 either at second base or on the disabled list. Kaz Matsui was shifted from short to second following a very underwhelming first season on the field and at the plate. Third baseman David Wright was entering his first full season in the majors after an outstanding final two months at the plate in 2004, but his sometimes erratic throwing made Mientkiewicz a very valuable part of the infield.

Catcher Mike Piazza was completing the final year of a seven-year contract he signed after the 1998 season. Piazza remained the Mets' scariest presence at the plate by reputation, although his numbers had declined steadily each season since 2000. At age 36, he was the oldest position player when the Mets broke camp.

The revamped lineup was orchestrated by first-year skipper Willie Randolph, a longtime Yankees bench coach who had been interviewed about a dozen times for major league managerial positions before he was hired by the Mets. High on Randolph's list of responsibilities was teaching Matsui how to play second and instilling the winning attitude that permeated throughout the Yankees clubhouse during his days as a player and coach.

Martinez started the opener on an incredibly cold day in Cincinnati. The three-time Cy Young Award winner dominated at times, striking out 12 and allowing just three hits in six innings. He held the Reds hitless following Adam Dunn's three-run homer in the first inning and left with a 6–3 lead.

Beltrán belted a two-run homer in his second at-bat of the game after Kaz Matsui homered in his first plate appearance of the season for the second straight year. But the work of Martinez, Beltrán, and Matsui was wasted by Looper, who lost the game by serving up back-to-back homers to Dunn and Joe Randa in the bottom of the ninth.

The Reds swept the season-opening series before the Mets dropped two straight in Atlanta, leaving New York 0–5 for the first time since 1963, when Martinez made his second start in the series finale against the Braves. Martinez was brilliant in a 6–1 win, striking out nine in a complete-game two-hitter that triggered a six-game winning streak.

The best pitching gem of the winning streak belonged to Heilman, who had never tossed a complete game heading into the season and was tagged for two homers and five runs over five innings in his first start of 2005. Heilman fired a one-hitter against the Marlins April 15, allowing only three walks and a third-inning single to Luis Castillo to get the Mets back to .500.

The Mets hovered around .500 over the next four months despite constant alterations to the rotation and the bullpen. Ishii was wildly inconsistent, Zambrano continued to have trouble locating the strike zone, and the relievers—other than Hernandez—were hit or miss. New York finally moved four games over .500 for the first time all season following a June 7 victory, but they fell into last place three days later and remained there the rest of the month.

Wright and Floyd were the Mets' top run producers over the first three months. Wright hit .292 with 11 homers, 20 doubles, 41 RBIs, and 44 runs scored while starting 76 of the Mets' first 78 games. Floyd batted .366 in April and compiled a .289 average with 21 doubles, 53 RBIs, and 47 runs scored through his first 71 games.

Wright and Floyd made up for Piazza's slow start. Piazza continued to hit fourth or fifth in the lineup but had a meager .255 average with seven homers and 29 RBIs through June 18. His slugging average was an uncharacteristic .423 as pitchers beat him with a steady diet of high fastballs that he would have blasted out of the park five years earlier.

Beltrán hit .294 over the first two months, but his power and speed were hampered by nagging injuries. He had just six homers, one stolen base, and no triples heading into June after being hyped as the best five-tool player in team history. Things got worse in June, although he hit safely in seven of his first eight games that month to hike his average to .300. He hit .139 in 72 at-bats the rest of the month to drop his average to .258 and prompt the boobirds to fly over Shea with each strikeout or popup with runners in scoring position. Beltrán continued to play through pain, but his production wasn't winning over any fans in Queens.

The Mets' other high-profile free agent was doing quite nicely. Martinez earned the appreciation of the Shea faithful with his pitching and his showmanship. He was on the mound at Shea one afternoon when the infield sprinklers accidentally went off, causing a brief delay. Rather than run for cover, Pedro danced through the water to the delight of Mets fans.

Martinez also delighted fans by going 12–3 with a 2.79 ERA in his first 20 starts. The Mets scored a total of four runs in his three losses, and he left with the lead in three of his five no-decisions. Martinez could have been 15–0 with a little bit of luck.

The Mets were 62–62 as they approached the July 31 trade deadline, last in the NL East but just eight games out of first. They won 16 of their next 24 to pull within four games of the NL East lead and just 1½ games behind the Phillies for the wild-card. New York won six in a row at the end of that streak, capped by a 1–0 victory at San Francisco in Trachsel's season debut.

The Mets recorded a 3.24 ERA during their 16–8 run while the offense compiled a .285 average with a .353 on-base percentage, 29 home runs, and 48 doubles. Mike Jacobs was the catalyst of the six-game winning streak following his recall from Triple A. Jacobs hit a three-run homer in his first major league at-bat, went 2-for-3 with a homer two games later and was 4-for-5 with two homers and four RBIs the next game. He supplanted Mientkiewicz at first base in early September and hit .324 in his final 20 games.

Fans believed the Mets had a legitimate shot at a playoff berth as the team opened a three-game series against the visiting Phillies August 30. New York took the opener 6–4 to pull within a half-game of Philadelphia for the wild-card. A sweep would give them a chance to take over the wild-card lead heading into Labor Day weekend. Instead, the Mets dropped the last two games to open a torturous

stretch in which they dropped 10 of 11 to fall out of contention. The Mets scored 19 runs in the 10 losses and received poor contributions from Looper down the stretch. Looper hid a shoulder injury from the Mets as he tried unsuccessfully to close down games. He went 0-for-3 in save situations in September while compiling a 9.95 ERA in 6⅓ innings before he was shut down with 11 games remaining.

The Mets won 11 of their last 14 to finish 83–79, their best record since 2000. Wright became the first Met to collect 100 RBIs in his first full major league season. Reyes led the National League with 17 triples, 60 stolen bases, and 696 at-bats while batting .273. Floyd paced the team with a career-high 34 homers and finished with 98 RBIs to compensate for a lackluster offensive performance by Piazza, who batted a career-low .251 with 62 RBIs.

Matsui also had another mediocre year at the plate and played second base as well as he played shortstop in 2004, which wasn't great. Matsui likely would have followed Piazza out the door if he wasn't due $8 million on the final year of his contract.

2005 Mets Statistics

Hitting	G	AB	R	H	2B	3B	HR	RBI	BB	SO	BA	OBP	SLG	SB	CS	GDP	HP	SH	SF	IBB
Marlon Anderson	123	235	31	62	9	0	7	19	18	45	.264	.316	.391	6	1	2	1	4	2	0
Carlos Beltrán	151	582	83	155	34	2	16	78	56	96	.266	.330	.414	17	6	9	2	4	6	5
Miguel Cairo	100	327	31	82	18	0	2	19	19	31	.251	.296	.324	13	3	5	4	12	5	2
Mike Cameron	76	308	47	84	23	2	12	39	29	85	.273	.342	.477	13	1	5	4	1	1	0
Ramon Castro	99	209	26	51	16	0	8	41	25	58	.244	.321	.435	1	0	7	0	3	3	2
Brian Daubach	15	25	4	3	2	0	1	3	7	5	.120	.324	.320	0	0	2	1	0	1	1
Victor Diaz	89	280	41	72	17	3	12	38	30	82	.257	.329	.468	6	2	13	1	0	2	7
Mike Difelice	11	17	0	2	0	0	0	0	2	5	.118	.211	.118	0	0	1	0	0	0	0
Cliff Floyd	150	550	85	150	22	2	34	98	63	98	.273	.358	.505	12	2	5	11	0	2	13
Anderson Hernandez	6	18	1	1	0	0	0	0	1	4	.056	.105	.056	0	1	0	0	0	0	0
Mike Jacobs	30	100	19	31	7	0	11	23	10	22	.310	.375	.710	0	0	5	1	0	1	0
Kazuo Matsui	87	267	31	68	9	4	3	24	14	43	.255	.300	.352	6	1	2	5	5	4	1
Doug Mientkiewicz	87	275	36	66	13	0	11	29	32	39	.240	.322	.407	0	1	12	2	2	2	7
Jose Offerman	53	72	5	18	2	0	1	10	6	11	.250	.316	.319	0	0	3	1	1	0	0
Mike Piazza	113	398	41	100	23	0	19	62	41	67	.251	.326	.452	0	0	7	3	0	0	6
Jose Reyes	161	696	99	190	24	17	7	58	27	78	.273	.300	.386	60	15	7	2	4	4	0
Eric Valent	28	43	4	8	3	0	0	1	7	17	.186	.300	.256	0	0	0	0	0	0	3
Gerald Williams	39	30	9	7	2	0	1	3	1	7	.233	.258	.400	2	0	0	0	1	0	0
Chris Woodward	81	173	16	49	10	0	3	18	13	46	.283	.337	.393	0	0	2	2	2	2	0
David Wright	160	575	99	176	42	1	27	102	72	113	.306	.388	.523	17	7	16	7	0	3	2
Pitchers																				
Heath Bell	42	3	0	0	0	0	0	0	0	1	.000	.000	.000	0	0	0	0	0	0	0
Kris Benson	28	49	4	9	1	0	0	6	5	22	.184	.273	.204	0	0	0	1	6	0	0
Tom Glavine	33	64	2	13	0	0	0	3	2	13	.203	.227	.203	0	0	0	0	5	0	0
Aaron Heilman	53	14	0	0	0	0	0	0	1	7	.000	.067	.000	0	0	0	0	2	0	0
Kazuhisa Ishii	19	25	1	5	0	0	0	2	1	12	.200	.231	.200	0	0	0	0	4	0	0
Dae-Sung Koo	33	2	1	1	1	0	0	0	0	1	.500	.500	1.000	0	0	0	0	0	0	0
Pedro Martinez	31	69	2	6	0	0	0	1	1	26	.087	.100	.087	0	0	1	0	6	0	0
Juan Padilla	24	2	0	1	0	0	0	0	0	1	.500	.500	.500	0	0	0	0	0	0	0
Jae Weong Seo	14	29	2	3	1	0	0	4	3	11	.103	.188	.138	0	0	0	0	2	0	0
Steve Trachsel	6	15	0	1	0	0	0	0	0	7	.067	.067	.067	0	0	0	0	0	0	0
Victor Zambrano	31	53	2	7	0	1	0	2	0	22	.132	.132	.170	0	0	0	0	5	0	0
TOTALS	162	5505	722	1421	279	32	175	683	486	1075	.258	.322	.416	153	40	104	48	69	38	49

Pitching	G	ERA	W–L	SV	GS	GF	CG	SHO	IP	H	R	ER	HR	BB	SO	BFP	WP	HBP	BK	IBB
Manny Aybar	22	6.04	0–0	0	0	4	0	0	25.1	31	17	17	4	7	27	114	0	1	0	1
Heath Bell	42	5.59	1–3	0	0	12	0	0	46.2	56	30	29	3	13	43	206	0	1	1	3
Kris Benson	28	4.13	10–8	0	28	0	0	0	174.1	171	86	80	24	49	95	737	4	4	0	5
Mike DeJean	28	6.31	3–1	0	0	12	0	0	25.2	36	19	18	3	18	17	131	2	1	0	2
Tom Glavine	33	3.53	13–13	0	33	0	2	1	211.1	227	88	83	12	61	105	901	1	3	0	5
Danny Graves	20	5.75	0–0	0	0	11	0	0	20.1	29	17	13	5	8	12	98	0	3	0	1
Tim Hamulack	6	23.14	0–0	0	0	2	0	0	2.1	7	6	6	3	1	2	14	0	0	0	1
Aaron Heilman	53	3.17	5–3	5	7	20	1	1	108.0	87	40	38	6	37	106	439	1	6	1	4
Felix Heredia	3	0.00	0–0	0	0	1	0	0	2.2	1	0	0	0	1	2	10	0	1	0	0
Roberto Hernandez	67	2.58	8–6	4	0	20	0	0	69.2	57	20	20	5	28	61	291	4	2	0	4
Kazuhisa Ishii	19	5.14	3–9	0	16	0	0	0	91.0	87	59	52	13	49	53	399	2	3	0	3
Dae-Sung Koo	33	3.91	0–0	0	0	4	0	0	23.0	22	12	10	2	13	23	106	0	2	0	1
Braden Looper	60	3.94	4–7	28	0	54	0	0	59.1	65	31	26	7	22	27	271	1	5	0	3
Pedro Martinez	31	2.82	15–8	0	31	0	4	1	217.0	159	69	68	19	47	208	843	4	4	0	3
Mike Matthews	6	10.80	1–0	0	0	0	0	0	5.0	9	6	6	0	4	2	28	2	0	0	1
Juan Padilla	24	1.49	3–1	1	0	5	0	0	36.1	24	7	6	0	13	17	149	0	2	0	2
Royce Ring	15	5.06	0–2	0	0	2	0	0	10.2	10	6	6	0	10	8	51	0	0	0	1
Jose Santiago	4	3.18	0–0	0	0	1	0	0	5.2	10	2	2	0	2	3	27	0	1	0	0
Jae Weong Seo	14	2.59	8–2	0	14	0	1	0	90.1	84	26	26	9	16	59	363	2	1	0	0
Shingo Takatsu	9	2.35	1–0	0	0	4	0	0	7.2	11	2	2	2	3	6	38	0	0	0	1
Steve Trachsel	6	4.14	1–4	0	6	0	0	0	37.0	37	20	17	6	12	24	157	1	1	0	0
Victor Zambrano	31	4.17	7–12	0	27	2	0	0	166.1	170	85	77	12	77	112	748	8	15	2	2
TOTAL	**162**	**3.76**	**83–79**	**38**	**162**	**154**	**8**	**11**	**1435.2**	**1390**	**648**	**599**	**135**	**491**	**1012**	**6121**	**32**	**56**	**4**	**43**

2006

NL EAST

TEAM	W	L	PCT	GB	BA	ERA
Mets	97	65	.599	—	.264	4.14
Phillies	85	77	.525	12.0	.267	4.60
Braves	79	83	.488	18.0	.270	4.60
Marlins	78	84	.481	19.0	.264	4.37
Nationals	71	91	.438	26.0	.262	5.03

Mets beat Dodgers in NLDS 3–0
Cardinals beat Mets in NLCS 4–3

Omar Minaya already had gained a reputation as a baseball executive who wasn't afraid to make headlines in the off-season. Minaya spent his first winter as the Mets' general manager acquiring free agents Pedro Martinez and Carlos Beltrán as he sought quick improvement to a franchise that posted a losing record for the third consecutive season. The additions contributed to the Mets' 83–79 season in 2005, but the ballclub showed serious holes during an early September swoon that saw New York play itself out of the wild-card chase. More changes would be needed if the Mets were to reach the postseason in 2006.

Minaya made three huge moves during the fall of 2005, being with the acquisition of Carlos Delgado from the Marlins for fellow first baseman Mike Jacobs and two minor leaguers. Jacobs had hit well during his short stay with the 2005 Mets, but Delgado was able to give the team a huge presence in the middle of the lineup, thus protecting Beltrán.

Five days after the Delgado deal, Minaya won the bidding for free-agent closer Billy Wagner, who would be a significant upgrade over Braden Looper. Wagner had five seasons of at least 35 saves between 1999 and 2005, and he would give the Mets their first hard-throwing lefty closer since Randy Myers in the late '80s.

Minaya was back on the phone with the Marlins in December as he sought a catcher to replace free agent Mike Piazza, who had been battling injuries and Father Time during the back end of his stay with the Mets. The Mets came away with Paul Lo Duca, an All-Star in his previous three seasons. Lo Duca was a solid contact hitter and the perfect player to put in the two-hole behind Jose Reyes.

Minaya made a rather curious move in January 2006, sending Kris Benson to the Orioles for Jorge Julio and pitching prospect John Maine. Julio was expected to give the Mets a solid setup man behind Wagner, but the move took Benson out of a starting rotation that already appeared thin. Minaya was hoping Mets minor leaguers Mike Pelfrey, Alay Soler, and Brian Bannister could contribute in 2006, but he hedged that gamble by signing the likes of Jose Lima and Geremi Gonzalez.

Some of the Mets' best moves before the 2006 season flew under the radar. Duaner Sanchez was picked up from the Dodgers in a deal that sent Jae Seo to L.A. Pedro Feliciano accepted a minor league contract to return to the Mets after a year in Japan. Free agent reliever Chad Bradford accepted a one-year pact with the Mets, and Darren Oliver was coaxed out of retirement with a minor league invite. Sanchez, Feliciano, Bradford, and Oliver would join Aaron Heilman and Wagner to form one of the more formidable bullpens in the majors.

The Mets said good-bye to Mike Cameron, who was playing out of position following the signing of Beltrán. Cameron was sent to the Padres for Xavier Nady, who became the opening-day right fielder.

The Mets also grabbed one of the Braves' top pinch-hitters and platoon players when they inked 47-year-old Julio Franco. Minaya also gave veteran infielders Bret Boone and Jose Valentin invitations to spring training. Boone retired during the exhibition season, but Valentin stuck around long enough to supplant opening-day second baseman Anderson Hernandez.

Endy Chavez also earned a roster spot after inking a minor league deal, and he made major contributions

Victor Zambrano. Photo courtesy of Oscar W. Gabriel

through Game 7 of the NLCS. Chavez hit a career-high .306 in 353 at-bats while playing all three outfield positions.

The Mets entered the season with a more balanced lineup, a deeper bullpen, and a starting rotation full of question marks after Martinez and Tom Glavine. No. 3 starter Steve Trachsel missed most of the 2005 season due to back surgery. Victor Zambrano continued to be an enigma, displaying no-hit stuff during innings in which he wasn't walking the ballpark. And Bannister emerged as the No. 5 starter, 34 months after being taken in the seventh round of the major league draft.

The rotation didn't stop the Mets from bursting out of the gates, grabbing a seven-game lead by April 29. New York opened the season winning 10 of 12 and 21 of 30 despite injuries to the back end of the rotation and Jorge Julio's inability to put any movement on his 99 mph fastball.

Bannister started the Mets' second game of the season and showed an ability to work out of big jams during his first five starts. But a strained hamstring suffered on April 26 kept Bannister off a major league mound for four months.

Zambrano's season ended May 6, when he walked off the mound with a torn flexor tendon in his right elbow. The injury left the Mets without two-fifths of their starting rotation just five weeks into the season.

Not to worry. Soler was recalled from Norfolk and inserted into the rotation on May 24. Soler enjoyed a three-game stretch in which he went 2–1 with a 0.82 ERA, but he was dispatched to the minors after surrendering eight runs in back-to-back starts against the Red Sox and Yankees.

Minaya engineered a May 24 deal that added another arm to the rotation while ridding the team of a very ineffective Julio. The Mets picked up Orlando Hernandez from the Diamondbacks for Julio in one of the most important midseason deals of the year.

The evolution of the everyday lineup was a thing of beauty. Reyes and Lo Duca were serving as the best table-setters the Mets ever had at the top of the lineup, surpassing the duo of Lenny Dykstra and Wally Backman, both of whom didn't play much against left-handed starters.

Reyes put together his first full .300 season in the majors while setting career-highs with 19 homers, 81 RBIs, and 64 stolen bases. The Mets' shortstop also hit 17 triples for the second straight season, giving him a team-record 34 of a two-season stretch.

Lo Duca was the National League's third-hardest hitter to strike out in '06, fanning just once every 14½ plate appearances. The Brooklyn-born Lo Duca also finished sixth in the league with a .318 average, and was second among all major league receivers with 157 hits.

Beltrán bounced back from a disappointing first season with the Mets by setting career highs with 41 homers and 116 RBIs while batting .275. Beltrán tied the team's single-season record for homers while falling eight shy of the RBI mark.

Wright matched Beltrán with 116 RBIs while finishing ninth in the NL with a .311 average. Wright banged out 26 homers and became the fourth Met with consecutive 100-RBI seasons. He also finished second to Ryan Howard in the All-Star Home Run Derby before becoming the seventh-youngest player to homer in a Midsummer Classic.

Delgado was outstanding while hitting in between Beltrán and Wright, finishing second with 38 homers and third with 114 RBIs. Delgado socked nine homers and drove in 20 runs in the Mets' first 23 games while hitting .311. He endured a slump that saw him bat only .145 with two homers in 90 at-bats, but Delgado also ended the season by hitting .323 with 12 homers and 40 RBIs in his final 36 games.

Cliff Floyd made two trips to the disabled list and never got on track as the No. 6 hitter. He finished with 11 homers and 44 RBIs, a far cry from the 34 home runs and 98 RBIs he amassed a year earlier.

Valentin had Mets fans wondering why he was still on the team after opening the season hitting .095 in his first 21 at-bats as a utility outfielder. But a vacancy was created at second when Anderson Hernandez was placed on the disabled list with a bulging disk in his back. Valentin was batting just .167 until he went 2-for-4 with a homer and four RBIs in a win against the Brewers on May 13. That began a stretch in which he batted .280 with 18 homers and 60 RBIs in his final 110 games.

The offense allowed the Mets to muscle themselves to a sizeable lead as July came to a close. The Mets were 13½ games ahead following a 10–6 rout in Atlanta, and an off-day heading into a series in Florida allowed Sanchez to spend time with friends in the Miami area. The group had decided to head to a restaurant when he separated his pitching shoulder in a taxicab accident, causing him to miss the rest of the season.

Sanchez had been outstanding as the Mets' primary setup man, allowing no earned runs and getting credit for seven holds in 21 innings over his first 15 appearances. He had a 2.60 ERA in 49 games at the time of the injury.

Scrambling for another setup man, Minaya was able to acquire former Met Roberto Hernandez from the Pirates. But the Bucs came away with Nady in the deal, robbing the Mets of the lefty-righty balance they enjoyed in the lineup. Pittsburgh also parted with former phenom and current reclamation project Oliver Perez, who had lost about 10 miles off his fastball just two years after finishing sixth in the league with a 2.90 ERA.

Three weeks later, Minaya eventually filled the loss of Nady by getting Shawn Green from Arizona. Chavez and Lastings Milledge had been platooning in right field following the Nady trade, but neither seemed to be the answer in right.

The loss of Nady didn't stop Steve Trachsel from piling up wins despite a rather inflated ERA. Trachsel posted a 5.21 earned run average in 15 starts between June 9 and August 29, yet he went 12–1 in those games. The key to his success was that the Mets were averaging 6.73 runs a game during that span.

Even the loss of Pedro Martinez didn't stop the Mets' juggernaut from charging toward the team's first division title in 18 years. Martinez didn't pitch for a month after he surrendered six runs in one-plus innings against the Phillies on August 14. The three-time Cy Young Award winner was hampered by a strained calf that had raised his ERA to 3.84 by mid-August. The one-month layoff didn't help, as he went 0–3 with an 11.81 ERA in 10⅔ innings over his final three starts.

Martinez was diagnosed on September 29 with a torn muscle tendon in his left calf, which was going to cause him to miss the rest of the season. And, oh yeah, another MRI revealed a torn right rotator cuff, which would keep him off a major league mound for the next 11 months.

Leave it to the Mets to add drama to a runaway division title. Martinez had been asked to start the potential division-title clincher at Pittsburgh on September 15, the opener of a three-game series. With thousands of Mets fans at PNC Park, New York absorbed a three-game sweep by the Pirates in a series reminiscent of the team's inability to close out the NL East in Philadelphia 20 years earlier. The Phillies commuted their death sentence with a three-game sweep of the Mets in 1986 before New York eventually clinched.

The 2006 clincher came on September 18 as Steve Trachsel picked a great time to pitch one of his best games of the season. Trachsel worked 6⅓ shutout innings, and Jose Valentin hit a pair of homers as the Mets beat the Marlins 4–0 to wrap up the division.

The Mets proceeded to lose seven of nine after the clincher before winning their final four games of the year. New York capped the season with two convincing victories over the Nationals in Washington as they prepared for the NLDS against the Dodgers. What they weren't prepared for was losing Game 1 starter Orlando Hernandez to a right calf injury while running in the outfield on the eve of the series opener.

That left manager Willie Randolph to start Maine in the series opener. Glavine had pitched the penultimate game of the regular season, leaving Maine as the best example of starting pitching heading into the Dodgers series. Maine had a 3.40 ERA in 15 games following his July call up, and he gave the Mets 4⅓ solid innings in the opener against the Dodgers. Glavine was superb in Game 2, and the Mets' offensive clicked in Game 3 to wrap up a sweep in L.A.

The NLCS was a struggle. The Mets never led the series after Game 1 and needed an outstanding pitching performance from Maine to force a seventh game. Oliver Perez pitched almost as well as Maine in Game 7, although he got a little help from Endy Chavez in left field. Chavez made one of the greatest catches in team playoff history, reaching the fence on the dead run and extending his glove beyond the wall to rob Scott Rolen of a tiebreaking two-run homer.

But Chavez had no chance on Yadier Molina's drive off Aaron Heilman in the ninth inning. Molina's two-run homer put the Cardinals ahead 3–1 before the Mets loaded the bases with two out in the bottom half and their top run-producer at the plate against rookie Adam Wainwright. Three pitches later, Beltrán was looking at strike three, ending the series.

2006 Mets Statistics

Hitting	G	AB	R	H	2B	3B	HR	RBI	BB	SO	BA	OBP	SLG	SB	CS	GDP	HP	SH	SF	IBB
Carlos Beltrán	140	510	127	140	38	1	41	116	95	99	.275	.388	.594	18	3	6	4	1	7	6
Ramon Castro	40	126	13	30	7	0	4	12	15	40	.238	.322	.389	0	0	2	1	1	1	2
Endy Chavez	133	353	48	108	22	5	4	42	24	44	.306	.348	.431	12	3	7	0	11	2	3
Carlos Delgado	144	524	89	139	30	2	38	114	74	120	.265	.361	.548	0	0	12	10	0	10	11
Victor Diaz	6	11	0	2	1	0	0	2	0	5	.182	.182	.273	0	0	0	0	0	0	0
Mike Difelice	15	25	3	2	1	0	0	1	5	10	.080	.233	.120	0	0	0	0	0	0	0
Cliff Floyd	97	332	45	81	19	1	11	44	29	58	.244	.324	.407	6	0	5	12	0	3	3
Julio Franco	95	165	14	45	10	0	2	26	13	49	.273	.330	.370	6	1	11	1	0	0	2
Shawn Green	34	113	14	29	9	0	4	15	8	18	.257	.325	.442	0	0	8	4	0	1	1

Hitting (continued)

	G	AB	R	H	2B	3B	HR	RBI	BB	SO	BA	OBP	SLG	SB	CS	GDP	HP	SH	SF	IBB
Anderson Hernandez	25	66	4	10	1	1	1	3	1	12	.152	.164	.242	0	0	3	0	0	0	0
Ricky Ledee	27	32	4	3	1	0	1	1	4	6	.094	.194	.219	0	0	0	0	0	0	0
Pau ILoDuca	124	512	80	163	39	1	5	49	24	38	.318	.355	.428	3	0	15	6	7	2	0
Eli Marrero	25	33	4	6	1	0	2	5	4	15	.182	.282	.394	2	0	0	1	2	1	0
Kazuo Matsui	38	130	10	26	6	0	1	7	6	19	.200	.235	.269	2	0	1	0	3	0	1
Lastings Milledge	56	166	14	40	7	2	4	22	12	39	.241	.310	.380	1	2	4	5	1	1	4
Xavier Nady	75	265	37	70	15	1	14	40	19	51	.264	.326	.487	2	1	7	6	1	1	4
Jose Reyes	153	647	122	194	30	17	19	81	53	81	.300	.354	.487	64	17	6	1	2	0	6
Kelly Stinnett	7	12	0	1	0	0	0	0	0	4	.083	.083	.083	0	0	0	0	0	0	0
Michael Tucker	35	56	3	11	4	0	1	6	16	14	.196	.378	.321	2	0	2	1	0	1	0
Jose Valentin	137	384	56	104	24	3	18	62	37	71	.271	.330	.490	6	2	5	0	5	6	5
Chris Woodward	83	222	25	48	10	1	3	25	23	55	.216	.289	.311	1	1	2	1	4	3	2
David Wright	154	582	96	181	40	5	26	116	66	113	.311	.381	.531	20	5	15	5	0	8	13

Pitchers

	G	AB	R	H	2B	3B	HR	RBI	BB	SO	BA	OBP	SLG	SB	CS	GDP	HP	SH	SF	IBB
Brian Bannister	8	12	2	4	3	0	0	2	0	3	.333	.333	.583	0	0	0	0	1	0	0
Heath Bell	22	1	0	0	0	0	0	0	0	1	.000	.000	.000	0	0	0	0	0	0	0
Pedro Feliciano	64	3	0	0	0	0	0	0	0	1	.000	.000	.000	0	0	0	0	0	0	0
Tom Glavine	32	53	6	9	1	0	0	2	7	18	.170	.267	.189	0	0	2	0	10	0	0
Geremi Gonzalez	3	3	1	0	0	0	0	0	1	1	.000	.250	.000	0	0	0	0	2	0	0
Orlando Hernandez	20	35	4	5	0	1	0	2	0	10	.143	.143	.200	1	0	0	0	5	0	0
Jorge Julio	18	1	0	0	0	0	0	0	0	1	.000	.000	.000	0	0	0	0	0	0	0
Jose Lima	4	5	0	0	0	0	0	0	0	3	.000	.000	.000	0	0	0	0	1	0	0
John Maine	16	28	3	1	1	0	0	0	0	16	.036	.069	.071	0	0	0	1	3	0	0
Pedro Martinez	23	38	2	4	1	0	0	1	2	16	.105	.150	.132	0	0	0	0	9	0	0
Darren Oliver	45	15	2	2	1	0	0	2	1	7	.133	.188	.200	0	0	0	0	0	0	0
Mike Pelfrey	4	9	0	0	0	0	0	0	0	4	.000	.000	.000	0	0	0	0	0	0	0
Oliver Perez	7	13	0	1	0	0	0	0	2	4	.077	.200	.077	0	0	1	0	0	0	0
Duaner Sanchez	49	1	1	0	0	0	0	0	0	1	.000	.500	.000	0	0	0	1	0	0	0
Alay Soler	8	11	0	1	0	0	0	0	0	6	.091	.091	.091	0	0	0	0	4	0	0
Steve Trachsel	30	50	4	7	1	0	1	2	4	13	.140	.218	.220	0	0	0	1	4	0	0
Dave Williams	6	9	1	2	0	0	0	0	2	4	.222	.364	.222	0	0	0	0	0	0	0
Victor Zambrano	5	5	0	0	0	0	0	0	0	1	.000	.167	.000	0	0	0	1	0	0	0
TOTAL	162	5558	834	1469	323	41	200	800	547	1071	.264	.334	.445	146	35	114	62	77	47	63

Pitching

	G	ERA	W–L	SV	GS	GF	CG	SHO	IP	H	R	ER	HR	BB	SO	BFP	WP	HBP	BK	IBB
Brian Bannister	8	4.26	2–1	0	6	1	0	0	38.0	34	18	18	4	22	19	171	2	2	0	2
Heath Bell	22	5.11	0–0	0	0	6	0	0	37.0	51	25	21	6	11	35	166	1	0	0	2
Chad Bradford	70	2.90	4–2	2	0	15	0	0	62.0	59	22	20	1	13	45	252	0	0	0	4
Pedro Feliciano	64	2.09	7–2	0	0	10	0	0	60.1	56	15	14	4	20	54	256	1	3	0	1
Bartolome Fortunato	2	27.00	0–0	0	0	0	0	0	3.0	7	9	9	2	2	0	18	0	1	0	0
Tom Glavine	32	3.82	15–7	0	32	0	0	0	198.0	202	94	84	22	62	131	842	1	6	0	7
Geremi Gonzalez	3	7.71	0–0	0	3	0	0	0	14.0	21	12	12	4	6	8	67	0	0	0	1
Aaron Heilman	74	3.62	4–5	0	0	14	0	0	87.0	73	37	35	5	28	73	356	5	3	0	2
Orlando Hernandez	20	4.09	9–7	0	20	0	1	0	116.2	103	58	53	14	41	112	495	1	8	3	2
Roberto Hernandez	22	3.48	0–0	0	0	5	0	0	20.2	15	8	8	2	8	15	83	2	0	0	1
Philip Humber	2	0.00	0–0	0	0	1	0	0	2.0	0	0	0	0	1	2	7	0	0	0	0
Jorge Julio	18	5.06	1–2	1	0	12	0	0	21.1	21	15	12	4	10	33	96	2	1	0	1
Jose Lima	4	9.87	0–4	0	4	0	0	0	17.1	25	22	19	3	10	12	91	1	2	1	0
John Maine	16	3.60	6–5	0	15	1	1	1	90.0	69	40	36	15	33	71	365	3	2	0	1
Pedro Martinez	23	4.48	9–8	0	23	0	0	0	132.2	108	72	66	19	39	137	550	2	10	1	2
Guillermo Mota	18	1.00	3–0	0	0	4	0	0	18.0	10	2	2	2	5	19	68	0	0	0	1
Darren Oliver	45	3.44	4–1	0	0	10	0	0	81.0	70	33	31	13	21	60	333	1	3	0	2
Henry Owens	3	9.00	0–0	0	0	1	0	0	4.0	4	4	4	0	4	2	19	0	0	0	0
Mike Pelfrey	4	5.48	2–1	0	4	0	0	0	21.1	25	14	13	1	12	13	99	2	3	0	0
Oliver Perez	7	6.38	1–3	0	7	0	1	1	36.2	41	26	26	7	17	41	165	1	3	0	0
Royce Ring	11	2.13	0–0	0	0	2	0	0	12.2	7	3	3	2	3	8	48	0	0	0	0
Duaner Sanchez	49	2.60	5–1	0	0	15	0	0	55.1	43	19	16	3	24	44	229	1	4	0	6
Alay Soler	8	6.00	2–3	0	8	0	1	1	45.0	50	33	30	7	21	23	208	3	1	0	1
Steve Trachsel	30	4.97	15–8	0	30	0	1	0	164.2	185	94	91	23	78	79	736	4	4	0	1
Billy Wagner	70	2.24	3–2	40	0	59	0	0	72.1	59	22	18	7	21	94	297	2	4	0	1
Dave Williams	6	5.59	3–1	0	5	1	0	0	29.0	39	18	18	5	4	16	126	1	2	0	1
Victor Zambrano	5	6.75	1–2	0	5	0	0	0	21.1	25	16	16	5	11	15	97	1	0	0	0
TOTAL	162	4.14	97–65	43	162	157	5	12	1461.1	1402	731	673	180	527	1161	6240	37	62	5	39

2007

NATIONAL LEAGUE EAST

Team	W	L	PCT	GB	AVG	ERA
Phillies	89	73	.549	—	.274	4.73
Mets	88	74	.543	1.0	.275	4.26
Braves	84	78	.519	5.0	.275	4.11
Nationals	73	89	.451	16.0	.256	4.58
Marlins	71	91	.438	18.0	.267	4.94

NL WILD-CARD

Team	W	L	PCT	GB	AVG	ERA
Rockies	90	73	.552	—	.280	4.32
Padres	89	74	.546	1.0	.251	3.70
Mets	88	74	.543	1.5	.275	4.26
Braves	84	78	.519	5.5	.275	4.11
Brewers	83	79	.512	6.5	.262	4.41

It took a team effort for the 2006 Mets to run away with the NL East title. A similar team effort was needed for the 2007 Mets to manufacture one of the greatest late-season collapses in major league history. The Mets went 10–2 between August 31 and September 12 to move seven games ahead of the second-place Phillies, and wasn't Jimmy Rollins looking pretty silly after declaring in spring training that the Phils were the team to beat in the division?

Rollins would have the last laugh as the Phillies stormed back to take the NL East on the final day of the season. The Philadelphia shortstop also came away with the NL MVP award, one of the few postseason honors to elude the Mets.

The Mets began the season with a convincing three-game sweep of the Cardinals, the team that derailed New York's World Series plans the previous October. The Mets outscored the Redbirds 20–2 in the sweep before opening a three-game series in Atlanta with an 11–1 rout of the Braves.

But it wasn't until May 16 when the Mets began to build a decent lead. New York was five games up after a crazy 12th-inning comeback against ex-Met Armando Benitez in a win over the Giants on May 29. However, the lead never grew larger until August 24 as the Mets played just one game over .500 for nearly three months.

Although the Mets never relinquished the division lead, there was a disturbing way in which they were grinding through the schedule. Some days, the pitching was dreadful. On other days, the fielding was suspect or the hitting was unproductive. Whatever it was, the Mets seemed to lack the killer instinct they displayed a year earlier despite some solid performances on the mound and at the plate.

John Maine and Oliver Perez were two of the biggest question marks as the Mets approached the season. Both had shown an ability to become big-game hurlers, demonstrated by the way they handled themselves during the 2006 postseason. Maine and Perez showed the playoffs were no fluke as they got off to terrific starts while giving the Mets the strikeout pitchers they sorely needed while Pedro Martinez was recovering from rotator cuff surgery.

Maine was outstanding during the first half of the year, going 10–4 with a 2.71 ERA. With David Wright, Carlos Beltrán, and Jose Reyes already slated to go to the All-Star Game as starters, it seemed Maine had earned the right to join them in the Midsummer Classic. But Maine was not selected to the team, and he began a swoon that compounded the Mets' summer struggles. He went 3–4 with a 5.94 ERA over his first nine starts after the break, including a rain-shortened one-hitter on July 29.

Perez was downright nasty when he wasn't downright puzzling. In five of his first 17 starts, he tossed at least seven innings while allowing fewer than two runs. But he also had a penchant for imploding during a single inning that made the difference in a game. Still, he was 9–6 with a 3.00 ERA in his first 17 starts, allowing just 85 hits in 109 innings.

Tom Glavine was on a mission for his 300th victory as he started the season 10 wins shy of the milestone. Glavine was in the midst of a six-game winning streak when he picked up win No. 300 against the Cubs August 5. But he seemed miscast as a Met while picking up the historic win, much in the same manner Tom Seaver appeared as he earned his 300th career victory while wearing a White Sox uniform in 1985.

Orlando Hernandez was solid as a No. 4 starter when he wasn't battling injuries. El Duque had nine starts in which he held opponents under two runs over six innings, but he also yielded at least six runs in four other starts.

Hernandez had been a suitable fifth starter in 2006, something the Mets never found in '07. Mike Pelfrey became the first Mets pitcher to begin a season 0–7 as a starter since Anthony Young went 0–8 in his first 10 starts of 1993. Jorge Sosa went 6–1 with a 2.64 ERA in his first seven starts of the season, but he followed that by going 1–5 with a 7.00 ERA in his next seven to earn a spot in the bullpen.

Chan Ho Park, Brian Lawrence, Dave Williams, and Jason Vargas were given chances to become the fifth starter, but the job never was filled to satisfaction following Sosa's stint.

The lineup remained solid, although it lacked the intimidation it emanated in 2006. Left fielder Moises Alou was the newcomer after general manager Omar Minaya signed him to a one-year contract with a team option. Alou, who turned 41 in July, was hitting .312 when he was sidelined by a calf injury in mid-May, causing him to miss 67 consecutive games. But Alou hit .353 after coming off the disabled list, compiling a 30-game hitting streak in which he batted .403 (48–119).

Wright became the third Met to enter the 30–30 club as he crushed 30 homers while stealing 34 bases. Wright also set a team record by getting a hit in 26 straight games bridging the 2006 and '07 seasons, a streak that was broken by Alou later in the 2007 season. The 25-year-old Wright also became the first Mets third baseman to win a Gold Glove.

Carlos Beltrán failed to match his stats from 2006, but he still led the team with 33 homers and 112 RBIs. Beltrán hit .276 despite playing on a pair of sore knees that eventually required off-season surgery.

Reyes seemed to have two seasons. The young shortstop batted .319 with four homers, 16 doubles, 39 steals, and 34 RBIs in the Mets' first 77 games. Reyes eventually broke Roger Cedeno's team record for stolen bases in a season, but he swiped just eight bags in his last 34 games. Reyes also hit only .247 after June 29, including a paltry .197 in the Mets final 32 games.

Delgado and Paul Lo Duca also saw their numbers drop. Delgado, who underwent elbow surgery after the 2006 season, finished third on the team with 24 homers and 87 RBIs. But he hit just .258 and had trouble laying off a steady diet of outside sliders that led to one of the worst offensive seasons of his career.

Lo Duca was dubbed "Captain Red Ass" by his teammates in 2006 for his volatile approach to the game, often annoying umpires and opposing pitchers alike. He finished seventh in the league with a .318 average in 2006, but that number dropped to .272 as he battled numerous injuries.

Shawn Green never emerged as the threat the Mets had hoped he'd be in 2007. Ironically, he'd be one of the team's better hitters in September, batting .397 with 10 RBIs in 63 at-bats while sharing time in right field with Lastings Milledge.

Jose Valentin also was a disappointment due to injuries. Valentin, who batted .271 with 18 homers and 62 RBIs as a minor league invite in 2006, slid to .241 with three homers and 18 RBIs in 51 games before suffering a broken shin in July.

Endy Chavez was another Met who spent a large portion of the season on the DL. Chavez was batting .292 when he tore a hamstring while trying to beat out a double-play grounder against the Phillies on June 6. He didn't play again until mid-August.

Minaya continued to fill holes as the injuries mounted. He already had Damion Easley, another spring training invite who became an integral part of the Mets' depth. Easley was given plenty of at-bats following injuries to Alou and Valentin, and he responded by hitting .280 with 10 homers and 26 RBIs in just 193 at-bats before suffering what would become a season-ending ankle injury during a game at Washington in August.

Ruben Gotay's bat was dependable off the bench while he batted .295 with four homers and 24 RBIs in 190 at-bats. Milledge and Carlos Gomez were given playing time in the outfield, and both contributed to victories.

When Valentin was deemed out for the season, Minaya acquired second baseman Luis Castillo from the Twins for a pair of minor leaguers. Castillo served as a solid No. 2 hitter when his knees allowed him to play without pain.

The Mets also played the entire season without Duaner Sanchez due to another shoulder injury, one that required surgery in late March. Sanchez's absence created a roster spot for rookie submarine hurler Joe Smith less than a year after he was drafted.

Smith was spectacular at the start of the season, allowing no runs over 15⅔ innings in his first 17 appearances.

He set a team record for the most consecutive scoreless appearances at the start of a career, a streak that also tied for the fifth longest in Mets history. (Billy Wagner would pitch scoreless ball in 20 consecutive outings later in the season).

Smith couldn't sustain his success into the summer, and he eventually was sent to New Orleans to fine tune his repertoire. With Smith in the minors—and both Scott Schoeneweis and Aaron Sele ineffective—the burden fell on Aaron Heilman and Pedro Feliciano to keep the damage at a minimum in the late innings before Wagner entered from the bullpen. Jorge Sosa was sent to the pen to give Heilman and Feliciano a break. But Guillermo Mota was absolutely horrible following a strong finish in 2006. Mets fans saved their loudest and longest boos for Mota, who returned to the active roster in May after serving a 50-game suspension for violating the major league steroids policy.

Heilman had another solid season despite losing his last four decisions. Feliciano continued to duplicate his 2006 numbers until September.

In a way, the return of Pedro Martinez made things worse for the bullpen. Just 11 months removed from rotator cuff surgery, Martinez would be kept on a fairly strict pitch count, making it probable manager Willie Randolph would be dipping into his bullpen by the sixth inning of Pedro's starts.

Martinez made his season debut on Labor Day and continued to pitch well through the rest of the year. But he didn't venture into the seventh inning in any of his five starts until September 29, when he suffered his only loss of the season.

The Mets had a seven-game lead and a magic number of 11 following a win over the Braves on September 12. The Phillies had closed to within two games by sweeping a four-game series from the Mets at Philadelphia in late August. But Philly proceeded to lose seven of its next 12 and appeared to be out of the division title chase with 17 games remaining. But the Phillies' mini-slide only set up one of the most dramatic comebacks, or collapses, depending on your perspective.

The Mets went 5–12 the rest of the season while the Phillies closed the campaign 13–4 to snatch the division title. The Mets compiled a 5.96 ERA during their swoon as Glavine, Maine, and Perez were unpredictable each time they took the mound. A bunion problem took Orlando Hernandez out of action for over two weeks in September before he worked out of the bullpen in his last three appearances. Once again, El Duque was sidelined when the Mets needed him most, forcing Pelfrey, Phil Humber, and Lawrence to make a combined four starts down the stretch. The overtaxed bullpen was running on fumes, and the team's fielding was pathetic at times. Scott Schoeneweis and Aaron Sele proved to be two of the Mets' best relievers down the stretch.

It was galling the way the Washington Nationals manhandled the Mets, winning five of six while scoring 57 runs. The Nats had gone 4–8 in their first 12 meetings with the Mets this season.

The Mets averaged 5.76 runs during their final 17 games, but the hitting was paltry at times. They managed just three hits in a 3–0 loss to the Cardinals, which put the Mets into a first-place tie with the Phillies heading into the season's final weekend. New York ended the year by collecting five hits versus the Marlins, with two of those hits coming after the first inning. The Mets mustered little offense after Florida exploded for seven runs in the first inning against Tom Glavine and the bullpen.

2007 Mets Statistics

Hitting	G	AB	R	H	2B	3B	HR	RBI	BB	SO	BA	OBP	SLG	SB	CS	GDP	HP	SH	SF	IBB
Sandy Alomar	8	22	1	3	1	0	0	0	0	3	.136	.136	.182	0	0	0	0	0	0	0
Moises Alou	87	328	51	112	19	1	13	49	27	30	.341	.392	.524	3	0	13	2	0	3	5
Chip Ambres	3	3	0	1	0	0	0	1	0	1	.333	.333	.333	0	0	0	0	0	0	0
Marlon Anderson	43	69	14	22	7	0	3	25	5	12	.319	.355	.551	3	1	2	0	1	2	1
Carlos Beltrán	144	554	93	153	33	3	33	112	69	111	.276	.353	.525	23	2	8	2	1	10	10
Luis Castillo	50	199	37	59	8	2	1	20	24	17	.296	.371	.372	10	2	2	0	7	1	0
Ramon Castro	52	144	24	41	6	0	11	31	10	39	.285	.331	.556	0	0	1	1	0	2	0
Endy Chavez	71	150	20	43	7	2	1	17	9	16	.287	.325	.380	5	2	5	0	5	1	0
Jeff Conine	21	41	2	8	2	0	0	5	7	8	.195	.306	.244	0	0	1	0	1	1	2
Carlos Delgado	139	538	71	139	30	0	24	87	52	118	.258	.333	.448	4	0	12	11	0	6	8
Mike Difelice	16	40	1	10	2	1	0	5	2	12	.250	.311	.350	0	0	2	2	2	1	0
Damion Easley	76	193	24	54	6	0	10	26	19	35	.280	.358	.466	0	1	2	5	0	1	1
Julio Franco	40	50	7	10	0	0	1	8	10	13	.200	.328	.260	2	1	1	0	0	1	0
Carlos Gomez	58	125	14	29	3	0	2	12	8	27	.232	.288	.304	12	3	0	3	0	3	2
Ruben Gotay	98	190	25	56	12	0	4	24	16	42	.295	.351	.421	3	3	2	1	3	1	1
Shawn Green	130	446	62	130	30	1	10	46	37	62	.291	.352	.430	11	1	14	5	1	1	4
Anderson Hernandez	4	3	1	1	0	0	0	0	0	1	.333	.333	.333	0	0	0	0	0	0	0
Ben Johnson	9	27	2	5	1	0	0	1	2	11	.185	.233	.222	0	0	0	0	0	1	0
Ricky Ledee	17	36	6	8	3	0	1	6	5	10	.222	.310	.389	1	0	0	0	1	1	1
Paul Lo Duca	119	445	46	121	18	1	9	54	24	33	.272	.311	.378	2	0	18	6	3	10	4
Lastings Milledge	59	184	27	50	9	1	7	29	13	42	.272	.341	.446	3	2	5	7	1	1	2
David Newhan	56	74	9	15	1	1	1	6	8	19	.203	.289	.284	2	0	1	1	0	0	0
Jose Reyes	160	681	119	191	36	12	12	57	77	78	.280	.354	.421	78	21	6	1	5	1	13
Jose Valentin	51	166	18	40	11	1	3	18	15	28	.241	.302	.373	2	1	5	0	1	1	4
David Wright	160	604	113	196	42	1	30	107	94	115	.325	.416	.546	34	5	14	6	0	7	6
Pitchers																				
Tom Glavine	33	56	3	12	1	0	0	4	6	5	.214	.286	.232	0	0	0	0	12	1	0
Orlando Hernandez	27	48	1	8	2	0	0	3	0	18	.167	.167	.208	2	0	0	0	6	0	0
Philip Humber	3	1	0	0	0	0	0	0	0	0	.000	.000	.000	0	0	0	0	1	0	0
Brian Lawrence	6	12	1	3	0	0	0	3	0	4	.250	.250	.250	0	0	0	0	0	0	0
John Maine	33	55	4	6	0	0	1	3	5	28	.109	.194	.164	0	0	0	1	14	1	0
Pedro Martinez	5	9	1	1	1	0	0	0	0	6	.111	.111	.222	0	0	0	0	2	0	0
Guillermo Mota	50	1	0	0	0	0	0	0	0	0	.000	.000	.000	0	0	0	0	0	0	0
Chan Ho Park	1	1	0	0	0	0	0	0	0	1	.000	.000	.000	0	0	0	0	0	0	0
Mike Pelfrey	15	21	1	2	1	0	0	0	1	9	.095	.136	.143	0	0	0	0	6	0	0
Oliver Perez	27	56	6	9	0	0	0	1	0	15	.161	.161	.161	0	1	0	0	6	0	0
Aaron Sele	31	4	0	0	0	0	0	0	1	1	.000	.200	.000	0	0	0	0	1	0	0
Joe Smith	52	1	0	0	0	0	0	0	0	1	.000	.000	.000	0	0	0	0	0	0	0
Jorge Sosa	41	25	0	5	2	0	0	1	3	9	.200	.286	.280	0	0	0	0	2	0	0
Jason Vargas	2	2	0	0	0	0	0	0	0	0	.000	.000	.000	0	0	0	0	1	0	0
Dave Williams	2	1	0	0	0	0	0	0	0	1	.000	.000	.000	0	0	0	0	0	0	0
TOTAL	162	5605	804	1543	294	27	177	761	549	981	.275	.342	.432	200	46	114	54	77	58	64

Pitching	G	ERA	W–L	SV	GS	GF	CG	SHO	IP	H	R	ER	HR	BB	SO	BFP	WP	HBP	BK	IBB
Jon Adkins	1	0.00	0–0	0	0	0	0	0	1.0	0	0	0	0	0	0	3	0	0	0	0
Ambiorix Burgos	17	3.42	1–0	0	0	5	0	0	23.2	17	10	9	3	9	19	98	2	2	0	0
Willie Collazo	6	6.35	0–0	0	0	1	0	0	5.2	7	4	4	0	5	0	27	0	0	0	1
Pedro Feliciano	78	3.09	2–2	2	0	12	0	0	64.0	64	26	22	3	31	61	275	1	5	1	4
Tom Glavine	34	4.45	13–8	0	34	0	1	1	200.1	219	102	99	23	64	89	855	2	4	0	2
Aaron Heilman	81	3.03	7–7	1	0	28	0	0	86.0	72	36	29	8	20	63	352	2	5	0	1
Orlando Hernandez	27	3.72	9–5	0	24	0	0	0	147.2	109	64	61	23	64	128	608	2	5	0	4
Philip Humber	3	7.71	0–0	0	1	2	0	0	7.0	9	6	6	1	2	2	32	0	0	0	0
Brian Lawrence	6	6.83	1–2	0	6	0	0	0	29.0	43	22	22	4	13	18	139	1	1	0	1
John Maine	32	3.91	15–10	0	32	0	1	1	191.0	168	90	83	23	75	180	810	2	5	0	3
Pedro Martinez	5	2.57	3–1	0	5	0	0	0	28.0	33	11	8	0	7	32	128	1	2	0	1
Guillermo Mota	52	5.76	2–2	0	0	10	0	0	59.1	63	39	38	8	18	47	261	2	2	0	2
Carlos Muniz	2	7.71	0–0	0	0	1	0	0	2.1	1	2	2	0	2	2	10	0	0	0	0
Chan Ho Park	1	15.75	0–1	0	1	0	0	0	4.0	6	7	7	2	2	4	20	1	0	0	0
Mike Pelfrey	15	5.57	3–8	0	13	0	0	0	72.2	85	47	45	6	39	45	342	3	9	0	1
Oliver Perez	29	3.56	15–10	0	29	0	0	0	177.0	153	90	70	22	79	174	765	6	7	0	1
Scott Schoeneweis	70	5.03	0–2	2	0	17	0	0	59.0	62	36	33	8	28	41	265	3	3	1	5
Aaron Sele	34	5.37	3–2	0	0	10	0	0	53.2	78	34	32	5	21	29	250	0	2	0	2
Joe Smith	54	3.45	3–2	0	0	14	0	0	44.1	48	18	17	3	21	45	205	2	7	0	4
Jorge Sosa	42	4.47	9–8	0	14	2	0	0	112.2	109	58	56	10	41	69	481	9	0	0	2
Lino Urdaneta	2	9.00	0–0	0	0	0	0	0	1.0	2	1	1	1	0	1	0	0	0	0	0

Pitching	G	ERA	W–L	SV	GS	GF	CG	SHO	IP	H	R	ER	HR	BB	SO	BFP	WP	HBP	BK	IBB
Jason Vargas	2	12.19	0–1	0	2	0	0	0	10.1	17	14	14	4	2	4	51	1	0	1	1
Billy Wagner	66	2.63	2–2	34	0	57	0	0	68.1	55	22	20	6	22	80	282	4	2	0	4
Dave Williams	2	22.85	0–1	0	1	1	0	0	4.1	12	11	11	2	5	2	29	1	0	0	1
TOTAL	162	4.26	88–74	39	162	160	2	2	1452.1	1415	750	687	165	570	1134	6293	36	61	3	40

2008

NL EAST

TEAM	W	L	PCT	GB	BA	ERA
Phillies	92	70	.568	—	.255	3.89
Mets	89	73	.549	3.0	.266	4.07
Marlins	84	77	.522	7.5	.254	4.44
Braves	72	90	.444	20.5	.270	4.47
Nationals	59	102	.366	32.5	.251	4.66

WILD-CARD

TEAM	W	L	PCT	GB
Brewers	90	72	.556	—
Mets	89	73	.549	1.0
Astros	86	75	.534	3.5
Cardinals	86	76	.531	4.0
Marlins	85	77	.522	5.0

The season is best summed up in the title of a song performed by noted chanteuse Britney Spears, who warbled, "Oops, I did it again." The chorus of the song is even more fitting once you get to the words, "I played with your heart, got lost in the game."

Certainly there was no way the Mets could produce a second straight late-season meltdown. The odds had to be in the Mets' favor after they grabbed a 3½-game lead with 17 to play, one year after blowing a seven-game lead with 17 remaining.

Then again, Mets owner Fred Wilpon had always held this fascination with the Brooklyn Dodgers, going so far as to replicate the best parts of Ebbets Field in his new ballpark in Queens. It should be noted that the Dodgers lost back-to-back pennants on the final day of the regular season, falling to the 1950 Phillies and 1951 Giants. Once the Mets' 2008 season was over, Wilpon had replicated another part of Dodgers lore.

Mets fans who were in shock after the 2007 season were bordering between bitter and pissed following the second collapse. Hey, this stuff used to happen to other teams, not the Mets. Remember how the Cubs faded in 1969, allowing the Mets to turn a 9½-game deficit into an eight-game victory in the NL East race? Remember how nobody wanted to take the division in 1973 until the Mets won 29 of their final 42 games to steal the crown?

Yes, the Mets were eliminated from the division race in the final week of the season five times between 1984 and '90. But the franchise had never blown a division or wild-card lead in the final week of a season until 1998, when they lost their last five games to miss forcing a three-way playoff for a wild-card berth by one victory. The 2008 campaign marked the third time in 11 seasons that the Mets coughed up a playoff berth in the final week. The black cat that strolled up and down the Cubs' dugout at Shea

in September 1969 must have had kittens whose offspring were living in the Mets' clubhouse, the manager's office, the bullpen, and the equipment room.

It was a lousy way to say good-bye to Shea Stadium, a venue that was considered state of the art when it opened in 1964. Yes, the old girl was victimized by sheer neglect in the 1970s and could never receive the type of makeover that allowed Busch Stadium or Angels Stadium to remain baseball shrines well into their fourth decade of existence. Shea might have been considered a dump by some in 2008, but it was our dump. It was a dump that housed two World Series champions, four pennant winners, and 14 playoff series. The memories included Tom Seaver's "Imperfect Game" against the Cubs in July 1969, Tommie Agee's two great catches in Game 3 of the '69 World Series, and Ron Swoboda's circus catch a day later. The longest victory in National League history was played at Shea in 1974, nine years before Rusty Staub broke or tied several pinch-hitting records there. There were walk-off hits in the postseason by Lenny Dykstra, Gary Carter, and Todd Pratt, and a huge walk-off error by Bill Buckner.

The Mets entered the final day of the schedule tied with the Brewers as New York prepared for their last regular-season game at Shea Stadium. The karma at Shea shouldn't have been any better as Oliver Perez warmed up on the mound. Mets fans are usually boisterous with a sprinkling of arrogance and cockiness whenever their team is on the cusp of great accomplishment. Instead, there was an unsettling aura of apprehension as the crowd seemed to anticipate that another disappointing three hours of baseball was on the horizon.

It wasn't just the stigma of 2007 that turned Mets fans into a jaded bunch. The 2008 squad took a long time to reach its peak, costing manager Willie Randolph his job in mid-June. New York opened the year 10–6 before dropping 28 of its next 49 games to fall 7½ games off the pace. Mike Pelfrey was 2–6 with a 5.33 ERA in his first nine starts. Perez carried a 4.98 ERA into July, and Pedro Martinez worked just 3⅓ innings during the first two months of the season after suffering an injury in his first start.

Newcomer Johan Santana and Maine anchored the rotation during the first two months but owned a combined record of just 15–13 despite a 3.40 earned run average.

The Martinez injury caused the Mets to audition Nelson Figueroa, Claudio Vargas, and Brian Stokes as fifth starters, all of whom pitched themselves out of favor by the end of June.

With the exception of Santana, none of the Mets starters went deep into games during the first three months. It was taking Pelfrey, Maine, and Perez an abnormal amount of pitches to get through five innings, causing action in the bullpen before most games had become official. Martinez was good for about five or six innings after he came off the disabled list, further taxing a relief corps that was questionable heading into the season.

Thanks to the heavy workload levied on Aaron Heilman, Pedro Feliciano, Scott Schoeneweis, and Joe Smith, the Mets became only the third team in modern major league history to have four relievers with at least 73 appearances. If you add Duaner Sanchez's body of work, the Mets were the fourth club to have five relievers appear in at least 66 games.

Schoenweis was the lone setup man to have a better year in 2008 than in '07. Heilman (5.21 ERA) had his worst season as a Mets reliever, and Feliciano recorded a 4.85 ERA after May 6.

The offense wasn't too bad during the first two months despite a slow-starting Carlos Delgado, an inconsistent Jose Reyes, and a nonexistent Moises Alou. The Mets averaged 7½ runners left on base through 54 games, but they also hit .256 with 50 homers and 244 RBIs while averaging 4.8 runs per game. Newcomers Ryan Church and Brian Schneider helped bolster the Mets' attack while Reyes, Delgado, David Wright, and Carlos Beltrán struggled to generate any consistent offense.

Beltrán and Delgado were the biggest mysteries. Beltrán batted just .256 with four homers in the Mets' first 48 games while being outperformed by Church, who carried a .309 average into June. Delgado appeared to be lost at the plate following off-season surgeries on his wrist and elbow, hitting .229 with only 35 RBIs in his first 75 games.

The Mets were struggling to play .500 ball as the calendar flipped to June. There were rumblings in the tabloids that Reyes, Beltrán, and Delgado weren't exactly thrilled to be playing for Randolph. All three denied any problems with their manager, but their overall performances suggested otherwise, and the team continued to play listless ball heading into an interleague series at Anaheim.

Randolph managed just as he played: with a low-key style and an expectation that the superstars would live up to their press clippings. He had stayed above the fray during his days with the "Bronx Zoo" Yankees, carefully choosing his words in postgame interviews while his older teammates popped off. It was Randolph's professional demeanor as a player and coach that got him a job as Mets manager in the first place, which made it all the more surprising when he decided to utter some very candid words during the Mets' sluggish start.

Randolph opened the season on the hot seat after the team's September free fall in 2007. His in-game strategy was scrutinized by the media, which made for a few contentious postgame sessions with the writers and broadcasters. He made the mistake of voicing his displeasure concerning his treatment by the media, particularly with the way SNY, the Mets' cable/satellite network, was depicting him in the dugout.

"Is it racial?" Randolph asked a reporter for the *Bergen Record* in May. "Huh? It smells a little bit.... I don't know how to put my finger on it, but I think there's something there."

Randolph immediately issued an apology after the story broke. Had the Mets been 10 games over .500 and kicking butt the way they did in 2006, nothing would have come of the *Record* story. But for the next four weeks, unfairly or not, Randolph was a dead man walking as long as the team had a losing record.

The guillotine finally came down with one very awkward swoop in June. Team management reportedly had decided to dismiss Randolph following a doubleheader split with the Rangers at Shea on June 15. But Randolph boarded the team plane for Anaheim and managed the club to a 9–6 win over the Angels in the series opener the next night. After the game, Randolph arrived at his hotel room around midnight—3 am in the east—and was told by general manager Omar Minaya that he was being let go.

The decision was a media disaster that turned Randolph into a sympathetic figure. Why did they allow him to fly across the country when his future was already decided? Were several Mets dogging it while Randolph played out his remaining days at the helm? And why did the Mets wait so long to give him a contract extension after he managed the team within one victory of the 2006 World Series?

Regardless, bench coach Jerry Manuel was named interim manager for the rest of the season. He lost his first game 6–1 to the Angels but made an immediate impression by pulling Reyes a few minutes into the game following his leadoff single. Reyes didn't appear to hustle down the line and was lifted in favor of pinch-runner Damion Easley, leading to an animated dugout discussion between Reyes and Manuel. The new skipper had drawn a line in the sand, and the players responded after the loss.

It's not that Manuel was a ball-breaker. He displayed the same low-key demeanor as Randolph but slowly began to see results, although the Mets continued to play .500 ball before they hit Yankee Stadium for a makeup game June 27.

Delgado had been a rally-killer before the Mets stepped off the team bus in the Bronx, striking out 63 times in the team's first 75 games. He had gone five games without an RBI and went hitless in his first two at-bats against the Yankees before beginning a season-ending stretch that had Mets fans chanting "M-V-P" whenever he stepped up to the plate.

Delgado hit a tiebreaking, two-run double in the fifth after the Mets squandered a 3–1 lead. He launched a grand slam the following inning and capped his Bronx bashing with a three-run blast that put the Mets ahead 15–5 in the eighth inning of a 15–6 victory. The nine RBIs broke the club record of eight set by Dave Kingman in 1976.

Delgado went 1-for-13 over the next four games but hit .313 with 24 homers, 70 RBIs, and 57 runs scored in his final 79 games. He was baseball's most productive hitter

Mike Pelfrey. Photo courtesy of David Ferry

Pelfrey was a huge part of the winning streak, getting the decision in a pair of 7–0 victories. He won seven straight decisions from June 16 through July 25 and was 10–3 with a 2.86 during a 15-start stretch through September 5.

Santana was even better as he lived up to expectations after the Mets acquired him from the Twins for four players. But the Mets seemed disinterested in generating offense for the lefty, who went 0–4 during a six-start span in June and July despite a 2.48 ERA.

Santana was incredibly good over the final three months, going 9–0 with eight no-decisions and a 2.09 ERA. He and Pelfrey propped a up a rotation that would have been better if Maine and Perez was able to duplicate their 2007 seasons.

Perez struck out 180 in 194 innings and was 10–7 with a 4.22 ERA. The lefty compiled a 3.56 ERA over the final three months but won just four times in his last 17 starts while pitching more than seven innings just once during that span.

Maine made just three starts after July 28 and missed the final month of the season with a shoulder injury. His absence put more pressure on Martinez to round into form, but the three-time Cy Young Award winner never got his ERA under 4.96 and went 0–3 with a 7.77 ERA in four starts during September.

The shaky rotation kept the relievers busy, but the patchwork bullpen was doing well enough over the first four months to put the game in the hands of Billy Wagner.

Wagner got off to a sensational start, allowing no earned runs while recording nine saves in his first 17 appearances. His ERA was a tidy 0.36 until June 8, when he began a string of three straight blown saves.

Wagner closed July by converting eight straight save chances to help the Mets go 18–8 for the month. But he felt a pop in his elbow July 29 and made one appearance four days later before he was placed on the disabled list. Wagner further damaged the elbow while throwing a simulated game in August. The Mets scheduled him for Tommy John surgery, ending his season and putting the team's playoff chances in serious jeopardy.

Wagner's departure didn't stop the Mets from going 18–11 in August, giving them a one-game lead heading into September. The lead grew to three games by September 3 and was up to 3½ games over the Phillies following a 13–10 win over the Nationals a week later. Luis Ayala took over the closer's role and did well in his first few outings after being acquired from Washington on August 17.

The Mets had a magic number of 14 with just 17 games to play. The remaining schedule had six games against the Braves, four against the Nationals, and four with the Cubs before concluding with a three-game set with the Marlins at Shea. The Cubs were about to wrap up the NL Central title, but the other three teams were a combined 50 games under .500 as the schedule appeared to tilt in the Mets' favor. That's when the bullpen went tilt.

over the second half and might have won MVP honors if the Mets reached the playoffs.

Alou was shelved for the season around the time Delgado turned into Lou Gehrig. Angel Pagan was the starting left fielder on Opening Day and played well until he dove into the stands for a foul ball at Dodger Stadium, leading to a shoulder injury that ended his season. But Fernando Tatis was an excellent alternative in left before the Mets recalled infielder Daniel Murphy from Triple A New Orleans to serve as the left-handed part of the left-field platoon. Alou wasn't missed over the final three months as Tatis and Murphy combined to hit .302 with 13 homers and 64 RBIs in 404 at-bats. Tatis earned Comeback Player of the Year honors as the Mets' most valuable utility player.

The Mets were still treading below .500 following a July 4 loss at Philadelphia, which left New York 42–44 but only 5½ games behind the East-leading Phillies. The Mets didn't lose again until after the All-Star break, forging a 10-game winning streak that put them in a first-place tie by July 17.

Every move made by Manuel became the wrong one as the relievers suddenly couldn't get anyone out. The team ERA over the final 19 games was 4.98, with the bullpen doing its part by allowing 30 percent of inherited runners to score.

The Mets began the 17-game stretch by dropping two of three to Atlanta and splitting a four-game set in Washington before the Braves took two of three from New York in Atlanta. When they left Georgia, the Mets were 1½ games behind the surging Phillies heading into the final week of the season.

New York managed to split its series with the Cubs, but the Brewers swept a series against the Pirates to pull even with the Mets for the wild-card with three games left. One day later, the Brewers had control of the wild-card after the Mets played a lethargic 6–1 loss to Florida.

Santana came through with an outstanding three-hit shutout on the penultimate day of the regular season, just as Maine had in 2007. Milwaukee lost to the Cubs that afternoon, leaving the Brewers and Mets tied for the wild-card. By now, the wild-card was the Mets' only shot at a playoff appearance after the Phillies wrapped up the division on Saturday.

Perez was given the task of extended the Mets' season. Ollie was terrific over the first five innings, holding the Marlins to no runs and one hit. However, Scott Olsen tossed two-hit ball over the first five innings as the Mets looked like they had another week left in the season. A sense of urgency was missing.

The Marlins chased Perez in the sixth while taking a 2–0 lead, but Beltrán smacked a two-run homer to knot the score in the bottom half. The Mets managed just one more hit the rest of the way.

Schoeneweis entered in the eighth inning with the game still tied 2–2. Three pitches later, Wes Helms cracked a solo homer to put the Marlins ahead to stay. And it took six pitches for Ayala to serve up a solo shot to Dan Uggla one batter later.

Meanwhile, Ryan Braun was hitting a two-run homer in the eighth inning to give the Brewers a 3–1 lead against the Cubs. There was joy at Miller Park and disbelief at Shea. The heartbreak was complete after the Mets lost 4–2 and the Brewers won 3–1.

The loss completely ruined what should have been a joyous sendoff for Shea. The Mets managed to get Dwight Gooden and Dave Kingman to appear at the festivities. The guests included George Theodore, who made Mets fans laugh in the 1970s with his gangly arms and loping stride. Unfortunately, no one felt like laughing this time.

2008 Mets Statistics

Hitting	G	AB	R	H	2B	3B	HR	RBI	BB	SO	BA	OBP	SLG	SB	CS	GDP	HP	SH	SF	IBB
Chris Aguila	8	12	0	2	0	0	0	0	2	4	.167	.286	.167	0	0	1	0	1	0	0
Moises Alou	15	49	4	17	2	0	0	9	2	4	.347	.389	.388	1	1	1	2	0	1	0
Marlon Anderson	87	138	16	29	6	0	1	10	9	27	.210	.255	.275	2	1	2	0	2	2	0
Carlos Beltrán	161	606	116	172	40	5	27	112	92	96	.284	.376	.500	25	3	11	1	1	6	13
Robinson Cancel	27	49	5	12	2	0	1	5	3	6	.245	.288	.347	1	2	0	0	1	0	0
Raul Casanova	20	55	5	15	2	0	1	6	6	10	.273	.344	.364	0	0	1	0	0	0	0
Luis Castillo	87	298	46	73	7	1	3	28	50	35	.245	.355	.305	17	2	13	2	7	2	2
Ramon Castro	52	143	15	35	7	0	7	24	13	34	.245	.312	.441	0	0	2	1	0	0	2
Endy Chavez	133	270	30	72	10	2	1	12	17	22	.267	.308	.330	6	1	6	0	9	2	3
Ryan Church	90	319	54	88	14	1	12	49	33	83	.276	.346	.439	2	3	9	3	1	3	3
Brady Clark	7	8	0	2	0	0	0	1	1	2	.250	.400	.250	1	0	1	1	1	0	0
Carlos Delgado	159	598	96	162	32	1	38	115	72	124	.271	.353	.518	1	1	16	8	0	8	19
Damion Easley	113	316	33	85	10	2	6	44	19	38	.269	.322	.370	0	0	15	7	2	3	0
Nick Evans	50	109	18	28	10	0	2	9	7	24	.257	.303	.404	0	0	1	1	0	2	2
Ramon Martinez	7	16	0	4	3	0	0	3	2	3	.250	.333	.438	0	0	1	0	0	0	0
Gustavo Molina	2	7	0	1	0	0	0	0	1	1	.143	.250	.143	0	0	0	0	0	0	0
Daniel Murphy	49	131	24	41	9	3	2	17	18	28	.313	.397	.473	0	2	4	1	0	1	1
Trot Nixon	11	35	2	6	1	0	1	1	6	9	.171	.293	.286	1	0	0	0	0	0	1
Abraham Nunez	2	2	0	0	0	0	0	0	0	0	.000	.000	.000	0	0	0	0	0	0	0
Angel Pagan	31	91	12	25	7	1	0	13	11	18	.275	.346	.374	4	0	0	0	1	2	0
Andy Phillips	4	5	1	1	0	0	0	0	0	0	.200	.200	.200	0	0	1	0	0	0	0
Argenis Reyes	49	110	13	24	0	0	1	3	4	20	.218	.259	.245	2	0	2	2	5	0	0
Jose Reyes	159	688	113	204	37	19	16	68	66	82	.297	.358	.475	56	15	9	1	5	3	8
Brian Schneider	110	335	30	86	10	0	9	38	42	53	.257	.339	.367	0	0	11	1	4	2	9
Fernando Tatis	92	273	33	81	16	1	11	47	29	59	.297	.369	.484	3	0	7	3	0	1	3
David Wright	160	626	115	189	42	2	33	124	94	118	.302	.390	.534	15	5	15	4	0	11	5
Pitchers																				
Tony Armas	3	3	0	0	0	0	0	0	0	0	.000	.000	.000	0	0	0	0	0	0	0
Nelson Figueroa	16	12	0	1	0	0	0	0	2	6	.083	.214	.083	0	0	0	0	1	0	0
Aaron Heilman	75	1	0	0	0	0	0	0	0	0	.000	.000	.000	0	0	0	0	0	0	0
Brandon Knight	4	3	0	0	0	0	0	0	0	2	.000	.000	.000	0	0	0	0	1	0	0
John Maine	26	46	3	5	0	0	0	3	6	23	.109	.212	.109	0	0	0	0	5	0	0
Pedro Martinez	20	39	3	6	1	0	0	4	0	15	.154	.154	.179	0	0	0	0	7	0	0
Jon Niese	3	6	0	1	0	0	0	0	0	4	.167	.167	.167	0	0	0	0	0	0	0
Mike Pelfrey	30	59	4	5	0	0	0	2	4	18	.085	.156	.085	0	0	0	1	8	0	0
Oliver Perez	32	56	2	6	1	0	0	3	4	23	.107	.167	.125	1	0	0	0	7	0	0
Duaner Sanchez	64	0	0	0	0	0	0	0	0					0	0	0	0	1	0	0
Johan Santana	32	78	5	11	5	0	0	1	3	24	.141	.173	.205	0	0	0	0	2	0	0

Hitting (continued)	G	AB	R	H	2B	3B	HR	RBI	BB	SO	BA	OBP	SLG	SB	CS	GDP	HP	SH	SF	IBB
Scott Schoeneweis	71	1	0	0	0	0	0	0	0	0	.000	.000	.000	0	0	0	0	0	0	0
Joe Smith	80	1	0	0	0	0	0	0	0	1	.000	.000	.000	0	0	0	0	0	0	0
Jorge Sosa	20	1	0	0	0	0	0	0	1	1	.000	.500	.000	0	0	0	0	0	0	0
Brian Stokes	24	3	0	2	0	0	0	0	0	1	.667	.667	.667	0	0	0	0	0	0	0
Claudio Vargas	10	8	1	0	0	0	0	0	0	6	.000	.000	.000	0	0	0	0	1	0	0
TOTAL	162	5606	799	1491	274	38	172	751	619	1024	.266	.340	.420	138	36	129	39	73	49	71

Pitching	G	ERA	W–L	SV	GS	GF	CG	SHO	IP	H	R	ER	HR	BB	SO	BFP	WP	HBP	BK	IBB
Tony Armas	3	7.56	1–0	0	1	1	0	0	8.3	11	7	7	2	1	6	37	1	0	0	0
Luis Ayala	19	5.50	1–2	9	0	13	0	0	18.0	23	12	11	3	2	14	78	0	0	0	0
Pedro Feliciano	86	4.05	3–4	2	0	14	0	0	53.3	57	24	24	7	26	50	237	2	3	0	8
Nelson Figueroa	16	4.57	3–3	0	6	2	0	0	45.3	48	26	23	3	26	36	211	0	2	0	1
Aaron Heilman	78	5.21	3–8	3	0	23	0	0	76.0	75	48	44	10	46	80	356	2	9	0	8
Brandon Knight	4	5.25	1–0	0	2	0	0	0	12.0	14	7	7	0	7	10	57	0	2	0	0
Eddie Kunz	4	13.50	0–0	0	0	0	0	0	2.7	5	4	4	1	1	1	14	2	1	0	0
John Maine	25	4.18	10–8	0	25	0	0	0	140.0	122	70	65	16	67	122	608	10	4	0	2
Pedro Martinez	20	5.61	5–6	0	20	0	0	0	109.0	127	70	68	19	44	87	493	2	6	1	3
Carlos Muniz	18	5.40	1–1	0	0	8	0	0	23.3	24	14	14	4	7	16	100	2	2	0	0
Jon Niese	3	7.07	1–1	0	3	0	0	0	14.0	20	11	11	2	8	11	69	0	0	0	0
Bobby Parnell	6	5.40	0–0	0	0	3	0	0	5.0	3	3	3	0	2	3	19	1	0	0	0
Mike Pelfrey	32	3.72	13–11	0	32	0	2	0	200.7	209	86	83	12	64	110	851	2	13	0	1
Oliver Perez	34	4.22	10–7	0	34	0	0	0	194.0	167	100	91	24	105	180	847	9	11	1	4
Ricardo Rincon	8	4.50	0–0	0	0	1	0	0	4.0	4	2	2	1	1	3	16	1	0	0	0
Duaner Sanchez	66	4.32	5–1	0	0	14	0	0	58.3	54	28	28	6	23	44	254	2	3	0	3
Johan Santana	34	2.53	16–7	0	34	0	3	2	234.3	206	74	66	23	63	206	964	9	4	2	5
Scott Schoeneweis	73	3.34	2–6	1	0	12	0	0	56.7	55	23	21	7	23	34	243	3	4	0	6
Joe Smith	82	3.55	6–3	0	0	12	0	0	63.3	51	28	25	4	31	52	271	1	4	0	4
Jorge Sosa	20	7.06	4–1	0	0	8	0	0	21.7	30	23	17	4	11	12	107	2	0	0	4
Brian Stokes	24	3.51	1–0	1	1	5	0	0	33.3	35	13	13	5	8	26	138	1	0	0	3
Claudio Vargas	11	4.62	3–2	0	4	2	0	0	37.0	33	20	19	4	11	20	150	1	2	0	0
Billy Wagner	45	2.30	0–1	27	0	34	0	0	47.0	32	17	12	4	10	52	184	2	0	0	0
Matt Wise	8	6.43	0–1	0	0	5	0	0	7.0	10	5	5	2	3	6	34	0	0	0	1
TOTAL	162	4.07	89–73	43	162	157	5	12	1464.3	1415	715	663	163	590	1181	6338	55	70	4	53

2009

NL EAST							
TEAM	W	L	PCT	GB		BA	ERA
Phillies	93	69	.574	—		.258	4.16
Marlins	87	75	.537	6.0		.268	4.29
Braves	86	76	.531	7.0		.263	3.57
Mets	70	92	.432	23.0		.270	4.45
Nationals	59	103	.364	34.0		.258	5.00

The best thing you can say about the Mets' 2009 season is that they didn't blow a playoff berth down the stretch for a third straight year. September was devoid of yips, bullpen meltdowns, and regrettable fielding miscues that plagued the previous two seasons. Thanks to a plethora of injuries, no one noticed the poor play in September once the last eight weeks of the season were rendered meaningless.

The Mets began the season with reliever Billy Wagner, outfielder Angel Pagan, and newly acquired starting pitcher Tim Redding on the disabled list, and the number of injuries reached ridiculous proportions by the end of July. Pagan and Redding weren't activated until mid-May, when catcher Brian Schneider, first baseman Carlos Delgado, and lefty Oliver Perez were sidelined. Schneider and Perez battled injuries the rest of the season, and Delgado didn't play another game after May 10.

For the 2009 Mets, D.L. could have stood for "dumb luck" as the ballclub saw its depth vanish at the speed of a Bobby Parnell fastball. Delgado and utility infielder Alex Cora landed on the disabled list May 16, 10 days before they were joined by shortstop Jose Reyes and outfielder Ryan Church. The Mets were just past the quarter mark of the season and already had two starting pitchers, their former closer, their starting catcher, half their starting infield, and their starting right fielder on the D.L. Add Cora and Pagan to the mix, and it was nine players already on the disabled list. At this rate, the Mets were going to look an awful lot like the Buffalo Bisons by the end of the year…which was exactly what happened.

For every player who was activated, another one took his place on the disabled list. Setup man J.J. Putz and starter John Maine were put on the shelf during the first two weeks of June. Putz sat out the rest of the season, and Maine didn't pitch again until September.

By the end of June, Carlos Beltrán had joined the swelling ranks of banged-up Mets. Beltrán's bone bruise on his right knee now left the team without its starting center fielder, first baseman, and shortstop. But thanks to a slow start by the Phillies, the Mets were just 1½ games out of first place on June 27, the last time they were over .500. After that, New York rode the express train to Suckville.

In keeping with what seemed to be team policy, the Mets were rather vague about the extent of the injuries to their top players. They insisted Delgado was day-to-day until he was transferred to the 60-day disabled list. Reyes had tendinitis behind his right calf and was going to be as good as new with a little rest. Ditto Beltrán's knee problem was portrayed as nothing serious. But Reyes experienced setbacks every time he appeared to be days away from returning, and Beltrán's bone bruise became a 2½-month absence.

The injuries never stopped. Guys who weren't expected to be with the team to begin with—Ramon Martinez, Fernando Nieve, and Fernando Martinez—put their names on the disabled list within weeks of their recall from the minors.

The injury gods stung the Mets in August as third baseman David Wright (concussion) and staff ace Johan Santana (elbow) joined the battered ranks. Wright tried to talk his way out of deactivation, but the team wasn't going to take a chance with their best available player after seeing Church try unsuccessfully to play through numerous concussions in 2008. Santana underwent surgery in late August, a no-brainer decision with the Mets out of contention.

Maine made a few token starts in September to prove his shoulder was sound. But Santana, Perez, and Jonathan Niese (hamstring) were unable to pitch, leaving the Mets with a late-season rotation of Maine, Mike Pelfrey, Nelson Figueroa, Pat Misch, and Redding. Livan Hernandez had long since been released by New York after an underwhelming stint in the rotation. Pelfrey wound up being the lone Met to make more than 25 starts in what became a frustrating season for the franchise.

This wasn't the way the Mets planned to christen their new ballpark. Citi Field officially opened on April 13 with Pelfrey on the mound against the Padres. In an ominous sign, Pelfrey surrendered a homer to Jody Gerut on the third pitch of the game before the Mets dropped a 6–5 decision.

There were some big moments during Year 1 of the new ballpark. Gary Sheffield, signed by the Mets before Opening Day after being cut loose by the Tigers in spring training, belted his 500th career home run to tie a game the Mets would eventually win 5–4 against the Brewers on April 17. Santana earned a 1–0 victory the next day and combined again with new closer Francisco Rodriguez for another 1–0 win over the Phillies on May 6.

But on the downside, Phillies second baseman Eric Bruntlett turned a game-ending, unassisted triple play August 23. It seemed only fitting for a Phillie to pull off the most memorable individual performance by the opposition at Citi Field since Phils hurler Jim Bunning tossed a perfect game during the Mets' first season at Shea Stadium.

Injuries were a reasonable excuse for the Mets' poor showing in 2009. However, the club didn't exactly play crisp baseball while at full strength. The Mets opened the season 10–13 before winning 18 of their next 26 games. They went 11–3 at Citi Field during that hot streak while climbing to the top of the NL East. But that stretch also included a three-game sweep at the hands of the Dodgers, highlighted by Church failing to step on third base as he was scoring what should have been the tiebreaking run in extra innings. The Mets wrapped up that loss by committing two of their five errors in the final inning, including a wild throw that brought home the winning run.

There were throws to the wrong base, poor base-running decisions, shaky middle relief, and scores of men stranded in scoring position, yet the Mets found themselves in first place shortly after Memorial Day.

One of the more pleasant early season surprises was Sheffield, who was deemed washed up by the Tigers before going 2-for-18 (.111) in his first 11 games—four starts—as a Met. The 41-year-old Sheffield was the team's top hitter in May, batting .348 with a .482 on-base percentage, four homers, four doubles, 15 RBIs, and 21 runs scored in 25 games. The Mets went 18–7 in those games and were hitting for a high enough average to overcome any deficiencies in the field or on the mound.

Beltrán also sizzled during April and May, hitting safely in 41 of his first 44 games to produce a .367 average with six homers, 15 doubles, 31 RBIs, and 31 runs scored. He owned a .467 on-base average through May 25 before the sore knee forced him and his .336 batting average to the sidelines on June 21.

Wright also swung a hot stick during the first two months and carried a .333 average into June. But Wright—like every other member of the Mets—was having trouble adjusting to the cavernous power alleys at Citi Field. Wright crushed a three-run homer in his second at-bat at the new park but hit just two more at home through July 30.

The spacious dimensions put a double whammy on Daniel Murphy, who was entering his first full season in the majors after impressing the front office following his 2008 recall. Murphy played all but four games of his minor league career as an infielder before the Mets made him their starting left fielder in the middle of '08. Murphy was at best a marginal outfielder at Shea Stadium, taking circuitous routes to balls without completely embarrassing himself. But he looked extremely uncomfortable in left at Citi Field despite working hard in spring training to improve his defense. Mets fans began to hold their breath any time an opposing batter sent a liner to left.

Murphy hit well enough early in the season to keep his starting job, recording a .320 average with 11 RBIs and 15 runs scored in his first 22 games. But his defensive misadventures eventually seemed to affect his hitting as he batted just .149 in 31 games from May 9 through June 14. Manager Jerry Manuel eventually put Murphy at first base when Delgado began to miss games. Murphy hit .282 from June 17 through the end of the season and led the Mets in home runs—with just 12. It was the lowest home run total ever for a Mets team leader in a full season.

But at least Murphy played in a club-high 155 games, including 124 starts. Other than Wright and Luis Castillo, no other Mets started more than 80 games.

The other corner outfield position was a mess as well. Church was expected to man right field as the club reported to spring training before Manuel said the job was up for grabs. Church hit well that spring and batted .280 in 67 games without fully convincing Manuel that he should be the everyday right fielder. Church's .332 on-base percentage and .375 slugging average did nothing to change Manuel's mind, and Church was traded to the Braves for fellow right fielder and slumping slugger Jeff Francoeur.

Castillo had a bounce back year of sorts, hitting .302 after posting a very disappointing .245 average in 87 games during 2008. Castillo came to camp in much better shape and finished second on the team with 20 stolen bases, but his .346 slugging average was sixth-worst in the majors among players who qualified for the batting title.

Whatever problems Francoeur had at the plate with the Braves vanished as soon as he became a Met. He hit .311 with 10 homers and 41 RBIs in 75 games despite tearing a left thumb ligament while making a diving catch against the Rockies on August 23. Francoeur's defense made him a fan favorite, as did his willingness to play out a lost season with a damaged thumb. He enhanced his popularity by driving in 19 runs in his first 21 games.

The biggest free-agent signing was closer Francisco Rodriguez, who set a major league record with 62 saves for the 2008 Angels. Rodriguez recorded 35 saves in 2009 and tied for the league lead with 66 games finished in his 70 appearances. But his 3–6 record, seven blown saves, and 3.71 ERA were underwhelming.

Hernandez and Redding were huge disappointments after signing with the Mets before the season. Hernandez didn't miss a start but went 7–8 with a 5.47 ERA before the Mets cut him in August. Redding wasn't much better, going 3–6 with a 5.10 ERA.

Perez was a complete bust after signing a three-year, $36 million contract as a free agent. General manager Omar Minaya hoped Perez would revert to his form of 2007, when he went 15–10 with a 3.56 ERA and 174 strikeouts in 177 innings. Instead Ollie spent much of 2009 on the disabled list and recorded a 6.82 ERA in 14 starts.

Pelfrey failed to build on his strong 2008 season, going 10–12 with a 5.03 earned run average in a team-high 31 starts. "Big Pelf" went 3–8 in his final 14 starts while being outpitched by the likes of Misch and Figueroa.

Santana was solid despite his sore elbow. A notoriously slow starter, Santana opened the campaign by going 7–2 with a 1.77 ERA in his first 10 starts before pitching to a 6.19 ERA in June. Had the Mets been playing for something late in the season, Johan probably would have tabled surgery until after the season. Instead, he was just another Met to work himself onto the disabled list.

The question in October was how to plot the following season. The Mets needed another starting pitcher, a first baseman, and a left fielder with some pop in his bat. But after owner Fred Wilpon's involvement in the Bernie Madoff Ponzi scheme—the media was led to believe the family lost hundreds of millions—speculation of the team's financial woes led many to believe they wouldn't be a major player in the free-agent market.

The Mets were outbid for John Lackey, the only stud among free-agent pitchers. Instead, they made a very attractive offer to Jason Bay and stood firm as other teams declined to give the outfielder a significantly better deal. Bay would be the new left fielder in 2010 as fans hoped he could supply the power that was nonexistent at Citi Field.

2009 Mets Statistics

Hitting	G	AB	R	H	2B	3B	HR	RBI	SB	CS	BB	SO	BA	OBP	SLG	TB	GDP	HP	SH	SF	IBB
Marlon Anderson	4	4	0	0	0	0	0	0	0	0	0	1	.000	.000	.000	0	0	0	0	0	0
Carlos Beltran	81	308	50	100	22	1	10	48	11	1	47	43	.325	.415	.500	154	9	1	0	1	10
Angel Berroa	14	27	4	4	1	0	0	2	0	0	3	6	.148	.233	.185	5	1	0	1	0	1
Emil Brown	3	5	0	1	0	0	0	0	0	0	1	0	.200	.333	.200	1	1	0	0	0	0
Robinson Cancel	1	1	0	0	0	0	0	0	0	0	0	0	.000	.000	.000	0	0	0	0	0	0
Luis Castillo	142	486	77	147	12	3	1	40	20	6	69	58	.302	.387	.346	168	15	1	19	5	3
Ramon Castro	26	79	5	20	5	0	3	13	0	0	8	16	.253	.322	.430	34	3	0	0	0	1
Ryan Church	67	232	26	65	16	0	2	22	6	2	17	36	.280	.332	.375	87	7	2	2	2	4
Alex Cora	82	271	31	68	11	1	1	18	8	3	25	28	.251	.320	.310	84	2	3	8	1	1
Carlos Delgado	26	94	15	28	7	1	4	23	0	0	12	20	.298	.393	.521	49	3	4	0	2	0
Nick Evans	30	65	5	15	5	1	1	7	0	0	4	20	.231	.275	.385	25	4	0	0	0	0
Jeff Francoeur	75	289	40	90	20	2	10	41	1	3	11	46	.311	.338	.498	144	3	3	0	5	3
Andy Green	4	4	0	1	0	0	0	0	0	0	1	1	.250	.400	.250	1	0	0	0	0	0
Anderson Hernandez	46	135	14	34	6	2	2	14	2	2	13	22	.252	.315	.370	50	4	0	0	1	1
Fernando Martinez	29	91	11	16	6	0	1	8	2	0	5	14	.176	.242	.275	25	0	3	1	0	0
Ramon Martinez	12	42	1	7	2	0	0	4	1	0	1	9	.167	.182	.214	9	1	0	1	0	0
Pat Misch	22	13	0	0	0	0	0	0	0	0	2	5	.000	.133	.000	0	1	0	2	0	0
Daniel Murphy	155	508	60	135	38	4	12	63	4	2	38	69	.266	.313	.427	217	13	0	4	6	4
Angel Pagan	88	343	54	105	22	11	6	32	14	7	25	56	.306	.350	.487	167	3	0	5	3	2
Jeremy Reed	126	161	9	39	6	2	0	9	0	3	14	36	.242	.301	.304	49	4	0	1	1	1
Argenis Reyes	9	17	0	2	0	0	0	0	1	0	1	4	.118	.167	.118	2	0	0	0	0	0
Jose Reyes	36	147	18	41	7	2	2	15	11	2	18	19	.279	.355	.395	58	2	0	0	1	1
Omir Santos	96	281	28	73	14	1	7	40	0	0	15	44	.260	.296	.391	110	9	2	2	6	1
Brian Schneider	59	170	11	37	11	0	3	24	0	0	18	21	.218	.292	.335	57	5	1	2	3	1
Gary Sheffield	100	268	44	74	13	2	10	43	2	1	40	46	.276	.372	.451	121	10	2	0	2	3
Cory Sullivan	64	136	17	34	2	5	2	15	7	1	19	22	.250	.338	.382	52	5	0	0	2	1
Fernando Tatis	125	340	42	96	21	4	8	48	4	1	22	54	.282	.339	.438	149	13	9	4	4	3

Hitting (continued)	G	AB	R	H	2B	3B	HR	RBI	SB	CS	BB	SO	BA	OBP	SLG	TB	GDP	HP	SH	SF	IBB
Josh Thole	17	53	2	17	2	1	0	9	1	0	4	5	.321	.356	.396	21	1	0	0	2	0
David Wright	144	535	88	164	39	3	10	72	27	9	74	140	.307	.390	.447	239	16	3	0	6	8
Pitchers																					
Pedro Feliciano	88	0	0	0	0	0	0	0	0	0	1	0	.000	1.000	.000	0	0	0	0	0	0
Nelson Figueroa	16	22	1	3	0	1	0	3	0	0	1	8	.136	.174	.227	5	0	0	2	0	0
Sean Green	79	1	0	0	0	0	0	0	0	0	0	1	.000	.000	.000	0	0	0	0	0	0
Livan Hernandez	24	40	0	5	0	0	0	0	0	0	1	4	.125	.146	.125	5	2	0	8	0	0
John Maine	16	27	0	4	0	0	0	2	0	0	0	11	.148	.148	.148	4	0	0	2	0	0
Jonathon Niese	5	8	0	1	0	0	0	0	0	0	0	3	.125	.125	.125	1	0	0	1	0	0
Fernando Nieve	8	9	0	3	0	0	0	1	0	0	0	3	.333	.333	.333	3	0	0	0	0	0
Bobby Parnell	68	8	1	1	0	0	0	0	0	0	0	3	.125	.125	.125	1	0	0	4	0	0
Mike Pelfrey	31	52	4	5	1	0	0	4	0	0	2	12	.096	.143	.115	6	1	1	5	1	0
Oliver Perez	14	22	1	6	0	0	0	0	0	0	1	7	.273	.304	.273	6	0	0	1	0	0
Tim Redding	30	29	0	2	0	0	0	0	0	0	0	9	.069	.069	.069	2	0	0	3	0	0
Johan Santana	25	42	1	7	3	0	0	4	0	0	5	14	.067	.255	.238	10	0	0	10	0	0
Ken Takahashi	28	2	0	0	0	0	0	0	0	0	0	2	.000	.000	.000	0	0	0	0	0	0
Wilson Valdez	41	86	11	22	3	2	0	7	0	1	8	10	.256	.326	.337	29	6	1	0	0	0
No PA for Broadway, Dessens, Fossum, O'Day, Putz, Rodriguez, Stokes, Stoner, Switzer and Wagner																					
TOTALS	162	5453	671	1472	295	49	95	631	122	44	526	928	.270	.335	.394	2150	144	36	88	55	49

Mets Pitching	G	ERA	W-L	SV	GS	GF	CG	SHO	IP	H	R	ER	HR	BB	SO	BF	WP	HBP	BK	WHIP
Mike Pelfrey	31	5.03	10-12	0	31	0	0	0	184.1	213	112	103	18	66	107	824	1	7	6	1.514
Johan Santana	25	3.13	13-9	0	25	0	0	0	166.2	156	67	58	20	46	146	701	1	3	0	1.212
Livan Hernandez	23	5.47	7-8	0	23	0	1	0	135	164	83	82	16	51	75	593	1	1	0	1.593
Tim Redding	30	5.10	3-6	0	17	2	0	0	120	122	72	68	18	50	76	525	4	2	0	1.433
John Maine	15	4.43	7-6	0	15	0	0	0	81.1	67	42	40	8	38	55	349	5	4	0	1.291
Oliver Perez	14	6.82	3-4	0	14	0	0	0	66	69	51	50	12	58	62	324	2	4	0	1.924
Francisco Rodriguez	70	3.71	3-6	35	0	66	0	0	68	51	34	28	7	38	73	295	1	1	0	1.309
Bobby Parnell	68	5.30	4-8	1	8	14	0	0	88.1	101	56	52	8	46	74	413	6	4	1	1.664
Brian Stokes	69	3.97	2-4	0	0	19	0	0	70.1	72	33	31	6	38	45	316	1	2	0	1.564
Sean Green	79	4.52	1-4	1	0	19	0	0	69.2	64	37	35	5	36	54	316	8	9	1	1.435
Pedro Feliciano	88	3.03	6-4	0	0	11	0	0	59.1	51	25	20	7	18	59	242	2	0	1	1.163
Nelson Figueroa	16	4.09	3-8	0	10	2	1	1	70.1	80	33	32	8	24	59	320	1	9	0	1.479
Pat Misch	22	4.12	3-4	0	7	0	1	1	59	62	27	27	9	19	23	251	1	2	0	1.373
Fernando Nieve	8	2.95	3-3	0	7	1	0	0	36.2	36	13	12	4	19	23	161	2	1	0	1.500
Elmer Dessens	28	3.31	0-0	0	0	8	0	0	32.2	24	12	12	5	10	14	130	1	2	0	1.041
J.J. Putz	29	5.22	1-4	2	0	6	0	0	29.1	29	18	17	1	19	19	135	1	0	0	1.636
Ken Takahashi	28	2.96	0-1	0	0	5	0	0	27.1	23	9	9	2	14	23	116	2	2	1	1.354
Jonathon Niese	5	4.21	1-1	0	5	0	0	0	25.2	27	12	12	1	9	18	110	1	0	0	1.403
Lance Broadway	8	6.75	0-0	0	0	3	0	0	14.2	19	11	11	0	6	9	67	0	0	0	1.705
Tobi Stoner	4	4.00	0-0	0	0	1	0	0	9	9	4	4	2	3	5	36	0	0	0	1.333
Casey Fossum	3	2.25	0-0	0	0	0	0	0	4	4	1	1	0	4	3	19	0	0	0	2.000
Jon Switzer	4	8.10	0-0	0	0	1	0	0	3.1	4	3	3	1	2	3	17	0	1	0	1.800
Darren O'Day	4	0.00	0-0	0	0	1	0	0	3	5	2	0	0	1	2	17	0	1	0	2.000
Billy Wagner	2	0.00	0-0	0	0	0	0	0	2	0	0	0	0	1	4	7	0	0	0	0.500
TOTALS	162	4.45	70-92	39	162	159	3	2	1426	1452	757	705	158	616	1031	6284	41	55	10	1.450

2010

NL EAST

TEAM	W	L	PCT	GB	BA	ERA
Phillies	97	65	.599	—	.260	3.68
Braves	91	71	.562	6.0	.258	3.57
Marlins	80	82	.494	17.0	.254	4.09
Mets	79	83	.488	18.0	.249	3.70
Nationals	69	93	.426	28.0	.250	4.13

Mets finish 12.0 games behind Braves for wild-card

The Mets spent a second consecutive September showcasing their prospects instead of battling for a playoff berth, which made you miss the good ol' days when they blew postseason berths on the final day of the season. The Mets took a seemingly encouraging season and mangled it by losing eight of 13 just before the All-Star break and opening the second half with a 2–9 road trip. They went 9–17 in July despite a decent team ERA of 3.43. The offense went south that month, compiling a .227 average and averaging 3.4 runs.

Just to be certain there would be no second-half comeback, the Mets opened August by losing four of five before posting a 12–16 mark for the month, leaving the Mets nine games out of a playoff berth with 30 games to play.

The pitching was pretty good throughout the season, compiling a 3.70 ERA with a rag-tag rotation that was pieced together on the fly by general manager Omar Minaya and manager Jerry Manuel. Journeyman knuckleballer R.A. Dickey and Japanese product Hisanori Takahashi were arguably the team's most consistent pitchers after each were signed to minor league contracts over the winter. Mike Pelfrey had a bounceback season, opening and ending the year strong before finishing with a career-high 15 wins. Johan Santana missed most of September following shoulder surgery after making 12 starts in which he pitched at least seven innings and allowed fewer than two runs. Even rookie Jonathon Niese looked good for 2½ months after coming off the disabled list June 5, going 7–3 with a 2.70 ERA in 15 starts before hitting a wall at the end of August.

Dickey and Niese helped Mets fans forget the injured John Maine and the deplorable Oliver Perez. Dickey became the first hurler to begin his Mets career with six straight wins, but the team's sporadic offense prevented him from winning more than three of his 12 starts during July and August despite a 2.30 ERA.

Takahashi was Mr. All-Everything on the Mets staff, starting 12 games and collecting eight saves when he wasn't serving as a middle reliever. Takahashi finished the year as the closer following Francisco Rodriguez's thumb injury.

Rodriguez provided the Mets with their most embarrassing moment of the season, punching the father of his girlfriend after blowing a lead against Colorado on August 11. He tore a ligament in his right thumb during the fight and was placed on the disqualified list before undergoing surgery.

Maine made his last start May 20, when he was pulled after facing just one hitter in Washington. Manuel made the quick hook after Maine failed to break 80 mph on any of his pitches.

Perez was just plain bad while pocketing $12 million in the second year of a three-year contract, going 0–3 with a 5.94 ERA in seven starts before he was banished to the bullpen. Perez continued to struggle as a reliever before the Mets asked him to go to the minors. Perez refused, angering many of his teammates while taking up a valuable roster spot. Manuel countered by declining to use his uncooperative lefty.

The Mets got around the issue by putting him on the disabled list after discovering a minor injury. Perez now had no choice but to accept a minor league rehab stint in July and was buried in the bullpen during the second half.

The Mets opened the season by dropping eight of 12 with the help of Maine, Perez, and an offense that hit .224 while averaging four runs and 8.2 men left on base. The lineup experienced a revival when first baseman Ike Davis was recalled from Buffalo. Davis helped the Mets follow their 4–8 start with a 9–1 home stand that included three-game sweeps of the Braves and Dodgers.

The Mets also helped themselves by going 13–5 versus the American League, highlighted by consecutive three-game road sweeps against the lowly Orioles and Indians. They hit a robust .323 while outscoring the Birds and Tribe 40–20. New York had a 9–18 road mark before reaching Baltimore.

By the time the Mets completed a 4–2 home stand against the Tigers and Twins on June 27, they were 11 games over .500 and within a half-game of the first-place Braves. They were hitting .260 with a .327 on-base percentage, and the team ERA was 3.68. Only three other National League teams had allowed fewer runs than New York at that stage of the season.

The season began to unravel with a 3–4 road trip through Miami and Washington, which was followed by a 2–4 home stand versus the Reds and Atlanta. The Mets had swept the Braves rather handily early, and another sweep would have put them in a first-place tie with Atlanta at the All-Star break. Instead, they were four games back and about to carve out one of the worst road trips in team history.

The Mets began the second half in San Francisco, where they dropped the first three games before getting a gift in the finale. The Giants appeared to score the winning run in the bottom of the ninth after Rodriguez blew a 3–1 lead in the inning, but Travis Ishikawa was incorrectly called out at the plate on a fielder's choice before the Mets rallied in the 10th.

The trip continued with an embarrassing 13–2 loss against the last-place Diamondbacks before Arizona completed a sweep with a 14-inning win. It was on to Los Angeles, where the Dodgers took three of four while holding the Mets to seven runs. New York was now 50–49 and 7½ games off the NL East lead. The latest trek also left the Mets with a pitiful 13–31 road record against National League opponents.

The travel log during the 11-game western swing was brutal. They were shut out four times and went 1–4 in one-run games. They hit .196 with a .301 slugging average while scoring 2.1 runs a game during the trip. The staff compiled a 3.67 ERA despite losses of 13–2 and 8–4. Worst of all, the Mets lost outfielder Jason Bay to a concussion that cost him the rest of the season.

Bay was the team's biggest free-agent pickup during the off-season but never put together one of his patented hot streaks. He was coming off career highs of 36 homers and 119 RBIs for the 2009 Red Sox before signing a four-year package with New York.

Bay was one of the underachievers during the 2–9 road trip, hitting .205 with no homers and three RBIs. Wright hit .182 with three RBIs on the trip before going 2-for-35 to open August. Reyes missed the San Francisco series before scoring in just one of the last seven games of the trip. Pagan was one of the more productive Mets regulars on the trip, homering twice and driving in four runs but hitting .220 after entering the second half with a .315 average. Davis hit three homers and drove in six runs on the trip while batting .196 with 16 strikeouts in 46 at-bats.

The most disappointing part of the road trip was the debut of Carlos Beltrán, who was wearing a heavy knee brace following off-season surgery. Beltrán could be forgiven for a rusty bat as he hit .167 with one RBI in 36 at-bats. But he was a shell of his former Gold Glove self in center field, misplaying several balls that would have been automatic outs two years earlier.

Jeff Francoeur was another rally-killer in the lineup, going 3-for-18 on the trip to lower his season average to .248. Beltrán's arrival caused Manuel to turn Francoeur into a part-time player, and the right fielder hit .140 in 31 games after the All-Star break.

Like Beltrán, Luis Castillo played himself out of the starting lineup and spent most of the final month on the bench. Castillo had only 106 at-bats and made just 27 starts after coming off the disabled list in mid-July.

Mets fans turned their attention to the development of Ruben Tejada, Lucas Duda, Josh Thole, and Dillon Gee, all of whom showed flashes of potential. Tejada displayed an excellent glove at second and short, but he also went 5-for-73 (.068) from July 1 through August 26 when he wasn't spending a few weeks in the minors. Duda compiled a .030 average in his first 13 games, going 1-for-33 before finding his stroke. The left fielder hit .414 with three homers and 10 RBIs in his next 11 games. Thole hit .324 in his first 31 games and .238 in his next 38.

Gee was impressive after going 13–8 with a hefty 4.96 ERA for the Bisons. He picked up a victory in his major league debut and was 2–1 with a 2.00 ERA through his first four starts as a Met.

The Mets clinched their second consecutive losing season before their final series and drew fewer than 2.6 million at Citi Field, two years after drawing more than four million their final season at Shea Stadium.

Manuel and Minaya were let go the day after the season ended. COO Jeff Wilpon insisted that day that ownership never denied Minaya any resources it would have taken to win a playoff berth and said the new GM would have full autonomy. Wilpon also said Minaya had full autonomy, refuting columns that said otherwise.

Wilpon said he would be open-minded as he interviewed new candidates, be they veteran GMs or another team's front-office personnel with a vision. He also admitted that there was too much misspent money over the previous two years.

Wilpon had been installed as chief operating officer in August 2002, when his father, Fred, completed a buyout of co-owner Nelson Doubleday. By the end of 2010, the Mets had dismissed four managers and three general managers, built one stadium, won one division title, blown two other postseason berths, and compiled a 663–687 record since August 2002, all while remaining among the league leaders in team payroll.

2010 Mets Statistics

Hitting	G	AB	R	H	2B	3B	HR	RBI	SB	CS	BB	SO	BA	OBP	SLG	TB	GDP	HP	SH	SF	IBB
Joaquin Arias	22	30	5	6	1	0	0	4	0	0	2	6	.200	.250	.233	7	0	0	1	0	0
Rod Barajas	74	249	30	56	11	0	12	34	0	0	8	39	.225	.263	.414	103	4	6	1	3	3
Jason Bay	95	348	48	90	20	6	6	47	10	0	44	91	.259	.347	.402	140	7	5	0	4	3
Carlos Beltrán	64	220	21	56	11	3	7	27	3	1	30	39	.255	.341	.768	94	4	1	0	4	5
Henry Blanco	50	130	10	28	5	0	2	8	1	0	11	26	.215	.271	.571	39	1	0	0	3	2
Chris Carter	100	167	15	44	9	0	4	24	1	2	12	17	.263	.317	.706	65	2	1	0	0	0
Luis Castillo	86	247	28	58	4	2	0	17	8	3	39	25	.235	.337	.604	66	6	0	11	2	1
Frank Catalanotto	25	25	2	4	1	0	0	1	0	0	1	5	.160	.192	.392	5	0	0	0	0	0
Alex Cora	62	169	14	35	6	3	0	20	4	1	10	16	.207	.265	.543	47	4	4	2	2	1
Ike Davis	147	523	73	138	33	1	19	71	3	2	72	138	.264	.351	.791	230	13	1	0	5	6
Lucas Duda	29	84	11	17	6	0	4	13	0	0	6	22	.202	.261	.678	35	2	1	0	1	0
Nick Evans	20	36	5	11	3	0	1	5	0	0	1	10	.306	.324	.797	17	1	0	0	0	0
Jesus Feliciano	54	108	12	25	4	1	0	3	1	0	6	12	.231	.276	.563	31	3	1	3	1	0
Jeff Francoeur	124	401	43	95	16	2	11	54	8	2	29	76	.237	.293	.662	148	7	7	0	10	8
Luis Hernandez	17	44	4	11	1	0	2	6	1	0	2	7	.250	.298	.707	18	1	1	0	0	0
Mike Hessman	32	55	6	7	2	1	1	6	0	0	8	23	.127	.262	.516	14	2	2	0	0	1
Mike Jacobs	7	24	1	5	1	0	1	2	0	0	3	7	.208	.296	.671	9	0	0	1	0	0
Fernando Martinez	7	18	1	3	0	0	0	2	0	1	1	5	.167	.273	.439	3	0	2	0	1	0
Gary Matthews	36	58	9	11	3	0	0	1	1	0	6	24	.190	.266	.507	14	1	0	1	0	1
Jenrry Mejia	30	3	1	1	0	0	0	0	0	0	0	1	.333	.333	.667	1	0	0	0	0	0
Pat Misch	12	8	0	1	0	0	0	0	0	0	0	4	.125	.125	.250	1	0	0	1	0	0
Mike Nickeas	5	10	0	2	0	0	0	0	0	0	0	5	.200	.200	.400	2	1	0	0	0	0
Angel Pagan	151	579	80	168	31	7	11	69	37	9	44	97	.290	.340	.765	246	9	1	6	3	5
Jose Reyes	133	563	83	159	29	10	11	54	30	10	31	63	.282	.321	.749	241	8	2	4	3	4
Fernando Tatis	41	65	6	12	4	0	2	6	0	0	6	19	.185	.254	.592	22	1	0	1	0	0
Ruben Tejada	78	216	28	46	12	0	1	15	2	2	22	38	.213	.305	.588	61	2	8	6	3	3
Josh Thole	73	202	17	56	7	1	3	17	1	0	24	25	.277	.357	.723	74	8	1	0	0	1
Justin Turner	4	8	1	1	1	0	0	0	0	0	1	0	.125	.222	.472	2	0	0	0	0	0
David Wright	157	587	87	166	36	3	29	103	19	11	69	161	.283	.354	.856	295	12	2	0	12	9
Pitchers																					
A. Dickey	25	51	7	13	2	0	0	5	0	0	3	8	.255	.296	.590	15	0	0	7	0	0
Dillon Gee	5	12	0	2	1	0	0	1	0	0	8	8	.167	.167	.417	3	0	0	0	0	0
John Maine	10	10	0	0	0	0	0	0	0	0	0	6	.000	.000	.000	0	0	0	4	0	0
Jonathon Niese	30	53	3	10	2	0	0	4	0	0	8	27	.189	.295	.521	12	0	0	5	0	0
Fernando Nieve	39	2	0	0	0	0	0	0	0	0	0	0	.000	.000	.000	0	0	0	0	0	0
Bobby Parnell	41	1	0	0	0	0	0	0	0	0	0	0	.000	.000	.000	0	0	0	0	0	0
Mike Pelfrey	32	62	2	7	0	0	0	3	0	0	2	13	.113	.141	.254	7	2	0	6	0	0
Oliver Perez	17	9	0	1	0	0	0	1	0	0	1	4	.111	.200	.311	1	0	0	1	0	0
Johan Santana	27	62	2	11	3	0	1	1	0	0	0	22	.177	.177	.452	17	0	0	5	0	0
Hisanori Takahashi	51	16	0	1	0	0	0	0	0	0	0	3	.063	.063	.125	1	0	0	4	0	0
Raul Valdes	36	10	1	4	1	0	0	1	0	0	0	3	.400	.400	.900	5	0	0	4	0	0
Totals	162	5465	656	1361	266	40	128	625	130	44	502	1095	.249	.314	.697	2091	101	46	74	57	53

Pitching	G	ERA	W–L	SV	GS	GF	CG	SHO	IP	H	R	ER	HR	BB	SO	BFP	WP	HBP	BK	WHIP
Manny Acosta	41	2.95	3–2	1	0	12	0	0	39.2	30	13	13	4	18	42	157	3	0	0	1.210
Elmer Dessens	53	2.30	4–2	0	0	6	0	0	47.0	41	14	12	4	16	16	194	0	3	0	1.213

Pitching (continued)	G	ERA	W–L	SV	GS	GF	CG	SHO	IP	H	R	ER	HR	BB	SO	BFP	WP	HBP	BK	WHIP
R.A. Dickey	27	2.84	11–9	0	26	0	2	1	174.1	165	62	55	13	42	104	713	11	4	0	1.187
Pedro Feliciano	92	3.30	3–6	0	0	16	0	0	62.2	66	24	23	1	30	56	280	1	6	0	1.532
Dillon Gee	5	2.18	2–2	0	5	0	0	0	33.0	25	10	8	2	15	17	136	0	0	0	1.212
Sean Green	11	3.86	0–0	0	0	0	0	0	9.1	7	6	4	1	8	12	48	0	4	0	1.607
Ryota Igarashi	34	7.12	1–1	0	0	11	0	0	30.1	29	24	24	4	18	25	135	3	0	0	1.549
John Maine	9	6.13	1–3	0	9	0	0	0	39.2	47	29	27	8	25	39	190	3	2	0	1.815
Jenrry Mejia	33	4.62	0–4	0	3	8	0	0	39.0	46	21	20	3	20	22	183	7	3	0	1.692
Pat Misch	12	3.82	0–4	0	6	2	0	0	37.2	43	20	16	4	4	23	159	0	1	0	1.248
Jonathon Niese	30	4.20	9–10	0	30	0	2	1	173.2	192	97	81	20	62	148	770	5	9	0	1.463
Fernando Nieve	40	6.00	2–4	0	0	9	0	0	42.0	37	28	28	10	22	38	185	2	2	0	1.405
Bobby Parnell	41	2.83	0–1	0	0	10	0	0	35.0	41	13	11	1	8	33	149	0	0	0	1.400
Mike Pelfrey	34	3.66	15–9	1	33	1	0	0	204.0	213	88	83	12	68	113	870	1	6	1	1.377
Oliver Perez	17	6.80	0–5	0	7	4	0	0	46.1	54	37	35	9	42	37	234	4	4	0	2.072
Francisco Rodriguez	53	2.20	4–2	25	0	46	0	0	57.1	45	14	14	3	21	67	236	3	2	1	1.151
Johan Santana	29	2.98	11–9	0	29	0	4	2	199.0	179	67	66	16	55	144	817	2	2	2	1.176
Tobi Stoner	1	3.86	0–1	0	0	0	0	0	2.1	3	1	1	0	1	0	11	0	0	0	1.714
Hisanori Takahashi	53	3.61	10–6	8	12	21	0	0	122.0	116	51	49	13	43	114	516	1	0	1	1.303
Raul Valdes	38	4.91	3–3	1	1	8	0	0	58.2	59	33	32	7	27	56	262	2	4	0	1.466
Totals	**162**	**3.70**	**79–83**	**36**	**162**	**154**	**8**	**4**	**1453.0**	**1438**	**652**	**597**	**135**	**545**	**1106**	**6245**	**48**	**52**	**5**	**1.365**

2011

NL EAST						
TEAM	W	L	PCT	GB	BA	ERA
Phillies	102	60	.630	—	.253	3.02
Braves	89	73	.549	13.0	.243	3.48
Nationals	80	81	.497	21.5	.242	3.58
Mets	77	85	.475	25.0	.264	4.19
Marlins	72	90	.444	30.0	.247	3.95

Mets finish 13.0 games behind Cardinals for wild-card

There was little reason for Mets fans to think the club would be a contender as training camp opened in February 2011, thanks to fallout from the Bernie Madoff Ponzi scheme. Ownership was bracing for a long, litigious nightmare as Irving Picard, the trustee for the thousands of people burned by Madoff, focused his recovery act on Fred Wilpon and Saul Katz. Picard believed Wilpon and Katz had profited from Madoff's 30-plus year scam to the tune of $500 million to $1 billion, and was prepared to recover every penny.

The Mets also hired a new general manager and manager in the off-season, picking Sandy Alderson to run the front office and putting Terry Collins in the dugout. Alderson had done a masterful job with the small-market Athletics of the 1980s, making shrewd trades, landing key free agents, and cultivating a productive farm system as the club won three straight AL pennants and a World Series from 1988 through 1990. Alderson was hired by the Mets from the commissioner's office to revive an underachieving farm system and turn the team into a more cost-efficient enterprise following the free-spending days of former GM Omar Minaya.

With the team's financial situation in question, Alderson's job was to rebuild the Mets while paring down payroll. The team lost two of its best relievers—Pedro Feliciano and Hisanori Takahashi—to free agency, although their departures became positives on the Mets' organizational ledger sheet once Takahashi lost his effectiveness with the 2011 Angels and Feliciano sat out the season with an injury.

Alderson went to the free-agent market and searched through the rummage bin, coming away with pitchers Chris Young, Chris Capuano, Tim Byrdak, Taylor Buchholz, Blaine Boyer, and Jason Isringhausen. All six had injury issues and appeared to be hunch bets as the team reported to camp. Alderson also inked utilitymen Willie Harris and Scott Hairston to contracts, while trimming payroll to the satisfaction of ownership.

Collins was known as a manager with a short shelf life before he came to the Mets. He quickly wore out his welcome in previous managerial stints with the Angels and Astros, leaving some to wonder how the Mets would respond to his personality. Any doubts were soon dashed as he handled a potential dicey situation concerning center field. He left it up to Carlos Beltrán to decide whether he should retain the position or move to right field in favor of Angel Pagan, who had become a much better center fielder than Beltrán by the summer of 2010. Beltrán agreed to move to right and was thankful Collins allowed him to be part of the decision, thus diffusing a potential powder keg.

There was also the matter of Jose Reyes' contract. He was due to become a free agent after the season and hoped to stay with the Mets, but the team's financial situation appeared to make it doubtful he would stay.

The Mets looked like a .500 team as they played out the exhibition season, which only made their 5–13 start to the regular season so unacceptable. It was during that start when Wilpon gave an in-depth interview with *New Yorker Magazine* to discuss the club's financial solvency and its on-field performance. Wilpon already was seeking a minor investor in the team, which had been a distraction since spring training.

The Mets ran off a six-game winning streak in late April and hovered around .500 over the next 3½ months. Collins had them playing with more enthusiasm than they had shown under Randolph and Manuel, albeit with a suspect pitching staff and a starting lineup that would continue to lose key players over the course of the season.

Jason Bay. Photo courtesy of David Ferry

Young looked like a potential ace of the staff until his cranky shoulder caused him to miss the last five months of the season. David Wright injured his back during an early season game and continued to play a few more weeks until he was diagnosed with a stress fracture. Ike Davis suffered what became a season-ending ankle injury when he collided with Wright on a popup in front of the mound at Colorado in mid-May. Thus, it could be argued that Davis may not have been injured had Wright's stress fracture been detected beforehand.

The Mets also lost Pagan for a month and continued to wait for Mike Pelfrey to perform as he had in 2010. Jason Bay battled deep slumps and remained the poster child for Minaya's free-spending ways after Alderson dispatched the equally disappointing Oliver Perez, Luis Castillo, and their hefty contracts during spring training. The Mets also were without ace Johan Santana, who missed the entire season due to a major shoulder injury.

By June, the infield often consisted of Daniel Murphy,

Justin Turner, and Lucas Duda, neither of whom was projected before the season to play vital roles with the team. Buchholz and Boyer were gone by then, leaving the bullpen in the hands of Francisco Rodriguez, Isringhausen, Rule 5 pickup Pedro Beato, Byrdak, Bobby Parnell, and many others.

And yet the Mets kept winning. Rookie Dillon Gee set a team rookie record by starting the season 7–0. Turner, Murphy and Duda contributed to the offense, as did Josh Thole and free-agent pickup Ronny Paulino.

But for the most part, the team was being carried by Reyes and Beltrán, both of whom were scheduled for free agency at the end of the season. Beltrán was by far the best power-hitter on the team in the absence of Wright and Davis, while also mastering the art of playing right field at quirky Citi Field. He was making a solid case for the Mets to re-sign him rather than send him to a contender in a trade deadline deal.

The Mets were sticking close to .500 when the Wilpon article hit the stands. Much of the piece dealt with his personal finances, but a few of his quotes were dedicated to trashing his own ballclub.

Wilpon called himself "a schmuck" for signing Beltrán to a seven-year, $119 million contract in the winter of 2005. Wilpon also said Reyes wasn't worth "Carl Crawford money," eluding to the seven-year, $142 million contract Crawford signed with the Red Sox over the winter. Wright also received a slap as Wilpon said he was a nice guy and very good, but not a superstar.

The timing of the article couldn't have been worse as Beltrán and Reyes had been carrying the team for weeks since the 5–13 start. Beltrán was leading the club in almost every power category, and Reyes was topping the majors in batting when the article was released.

Beltrán's production was overshadowed by Reyes, who was enjoying his finest major league season through the first four months. Reyes already had 15 triples and 30 stolen bases through June and was leading the National League with a .355 average by July 19. Mets fans were screaming for the team to re-sign Reyes to a contract.

The Mets continued to prosper even as Reyes spent 17 days on the disabled list in early July. Ruben Tejada took over at short for Reyes and anchored an infield that had Turner at second and Murphy at first. Wright came back after the All-Star break and immediately put together a 10-game hitting streak in which he hit .455 with two homers and 12 RBIs after hitting only .226 before landing on the disabled list. Pagan and Bay contributed big hits in July as the Mets found themselves within striking distance of the Braves for the wild-card.

The Mets were doing it with their "Buffalo" lineup. Tejada, Turner, and Duda were receiving significant playing time after opening the year with the Bisons. Ironically, much of the Mets' depth came courtesy of Minaya, who did a much better job acquiring role players than signing veteran free agents during his six-year run as GM.

The bullpen was altered when Alderson traded Rodriguez to the Brewers, a deal announced immediately after the All-Star game. The move shortened the bullpen and turned Isringhausen into the closer after opening the season at Triple A Buffalo.

The Mets dropped three of four after the Rodriguez trade before taking eight of 11 to move a season-high four games over .500. They swept a four-game set in Cincinnati for the first time in club history despite dealing Beltrán to the Giants before the series was over. The Reds series gave fans hope the club could stay in the wild-card race. A few players envisioned a playoff scenario in which the Mets face Beltrán's Giants in the division series.

But the Mets played themselves out of contention by dropping five straight following the sweep of the Reds. Reyes hit .314 in his first seven games after coming off the disabled list on July 19 but posted a .209 average in the next 11 games before heading back to the DL due to another hamstring issue.

Wright slumped, Bay sputtered, and the pitching staff stumbled as the Mets went 5–16 from July 30 through August 22. The loss of Rodriguez screwed up a delicate balance in the bullpen as Isringhausen and the set-up men continued to falter once the starters gave up their customary three runs in six innings.

Before the All-Star break, the bullpen had done a nice job of masking the shortcomings of the rotation. August was another story as the relievers were hammered with regularity. By August 22, Tim Byrdak was the lone receiver on the entire active roster with an ERA under 3.72.

The final blow came the last week of August. David Einhorn's bid to purchase a minority interest in the team fell apart, prompting fans to wonder and worry about the Mets' financial strategy as another off-season approached.

Reyes became the first Met to win a batting title, but it was anybody's guess as to whether he would defend that crown while in a Mets uniform. Months later, Reyes was a Miami Marlin.

2011 Mets Statistics

Hitting	G	AB	R	H	2B	3B	HR	RBI	SB	CS	BB	SO	BA	OBP	SLG	TB	GDP	HP	SH	SF	IBB
Mike Baxter	22	34	6	8	2	1	1	4	0	0	5	9	.235	.350	.441	15	1	1	0	0	0
Jason Bay	123	444	59	109	19	1	12	57	11	1	56	109	.245	.329	.374	166	8	2	1	6	3
Carlos Beltrán	98	353	61	102	30	2	15	66	3	0	60	61	.289	.391	.513	181	9	2	0	4	6
Ike Davis	36	129	20	39	8	1	7	25	0	0	17	31	.302	.383	.543	70	5	1	0	2	3
Lucas Duda	100	301	38	88	21	3	10	50	1	0	33	57	.292	.370	.482	145	5	7	1	5	3
Brad Emaus	14	37	2	6	0	0	0	1	0	0	4	9	.162	.262	.162	6	3	1	0	0	1
Nick Evans	59	176	26	45	10	2	4	25	0	1	15	48	.256	.314	.403	71	6	1	0	2	0
Scott Hairston	79	132	20	31	8	1	7	24	1	1	11	34	.235	.303	.470	62	2	2	0	0	2
Willie Harris	126	240	36	59	11	0	2	23	5	4	36	62	.246	.351	.317	76	6	4	1	2	3
Chin-lung Hu	22	20	2	1	0	0	0	1	1	0	1	11	.050	.091	.050	1	0	0	1	1	0
Fernando Martinez	11	22	3	5	2	0	1	2	0	0	1	7	.227	.261	.455	10	0	0	0	0	0
Daniel Murphy	109	391	49	125	28	2	6	49	5	5	24	42	.320	.362	.448	175	14	3	3	2	2
Mike Nickeas	21	53	4	10	1	0	1	6	0	1	4	11	.189	.246	.264	14	1	0	2	0	0
Angel Pagan	123	478	68	125	24	4	7	56	32	7	44	62	.262	.322	.372	178	4	1	4	5	4
Valentino Pascucci	10	11	1	3	0	0	1	2	0	0	0	3	.273	.273	.545	6	0	0	0	0	0
Ronny Paulino	78	228	19	61	13	0	2	19	0	0	15	38	.268	.312	.351	80	9	1	1	3	3
Jason Pridie	101	208	28	48	11	3	4	20	7	1	24	64	.231	.309	.370	77	2	0	3	1	2
Jose Reyes	126	537	101	181	31	16	7	44	39	7	43	41	.337	.384	.493	265	5	0	2	4	9
Josh Satin	15	25	3	5	1	0	0	2	0	0	1	11	.200	.259	.240	6	1	1	0	0	0
Ruben Tejada	96	328	31	93	15	1	0	36	5	1	35	50	.284	.360	.335	110	6	6	4	3	3
Josh Thole	114	340	22	91	17	0	3	40	0	2	38	47	.268	.345	.344	117	8	4	1	3	6
Justin Turner	117	435	49	113	30	0	4	51	7	2	39	59	.260	.334	.356	155	9	10	2	1	2
David Wright	102	389	60	99	23	1	14	61	13	2	52	97	.254	.345	.427	166	5	3	0	3	4
Pitchers																					
Miguel Batista	9	6	1	0	0	0	0	0	0	0	0	2	.000	.000	.000	0	0	0	2	0	0
Taylor Buchholz	22	2	0	0	0	0	0	0	0	0	0	0	.000	.000	.000	0	0	0	0	0	0
Chris Capuano	34	56	2	4	2	0	0	0	0	0	0	33	.071	.071	.107	6	1	0	6	0	0
D.J. Carrasco	38	0	0	0	0	0	0	0	0	0	0	0				0	0	0	1	0	0
R.A. Dickey	31	59	0	8	0	0	0	2	0	0	1	11	.136	.150	.136	8	1	0	9	0	0
Dillon Gee	29	46	3	5	0	0	0	4	0	0	2	22	.109	.160	.109	5	1	1	8	1	0
Jonathon Niese	28	49	1	3	0	1	0	1	0	0	4	33	.061	.132	.102	5	0	0	7	0	0
Mike Pelfrey	31	55	1	6	2	0	0	4	0	0	4	14	.109	.169	.145	8	0	0	4	0	0
Francisco Rodriguez	39	1	0	0	0	0	0	0	0	0	0	1	.000	.000	.000	0	0	0	0	0	0
Chris Schwinden	4	6	1	1	0	0	0	0	0	0	1	2	.167	.286	.167	1	0	0	0	0	0
Josh Stinson	14	0	0	0	0	0	0	0	0	0	1	0		1.000		0	0	0	0	0	0
Chris Young	4	9	1	3	0	0	0	2	0	0	0	4	.333	.333	.333	3	0	0	2	0	0
TOTAL	162	5600	718	1477	309	39	108	676	130	35	571	1085	.264	.335	.391	2188	112	51	65	48	56

Pitching	G	ERA	W–L	SV	GS	GF	CG	SHO	IP	H	R	ER	HR	BB	SO	BFP	WP	HBP	BK	WHIP
Manny Acosta	44	3.45	4–1	4	0	15	0	0	47.0	50	21	18	6	15	46	204	0	2	0	1.383
Miguel Batista	9	2.64	2–0	0	4	0	1	1	30.2	22	9	9	0	14	15	125	1	2	0	1.174
Pedro Beato	60	4.30	2–1	0	0	7	0	0	67.0	59	41	32	5	27	39	283	1	4	0	1.284
Blaine Boyer	5	10.80	0–2	1	0	3	0	0	6.2	13	8	8	2	1	1	33	0	1	0	2.100
Taylor Buchholz	23	3.12	1–1	0	0	8	0	0	26.0	22	10	9	5	7	26	107	0	1	0	1.115
Tim Byrdak	72	3.82	2–1	1	0	10	0	0	37.2	34	20	16	3	19	47	168	1	1	0	1.407
Chris Capuano	33	4.55	11–12	0	31	0	1	1	186.0	198	99	94	27	53	168	802	4	5	0	1.349
D.J. Carrasco	42	6.02	1–3	0	1	15	0	0	49.1	67	35	33	7	16	27	225	3	6	1	1.682
R.A Dickey	33	3.28	8–13	0	32	0	1	0	208.2	202	85	76	18	54	134	876	9	9	1	1.227
Dillon Gee	30	4.43	13–6	0	27	1	1	0	160.2	150	85	79	18	71	114	706	6	14	1	1.376
Danny Herrera	16	1.13	0–1	0	0	2	0	0	8.0	7	1	1	0	2	5	33	1	0	1	1.125
Ryota Igarashi	45	4.66	4–1	0	0	9	0	0	38.2	43	20	20	2	28	42	190	3	4	0	1.836
Jason Isringhausen	53	4.05	3–3	7	0	15	0	0	46.2	36	23	21	6	24	44	200	1	1	0	1.286
Pat Misch	6	10.29	1–0	0	0	2	0	0	7.0	11	8	8	1	4	5	37	0	1	0	2.143
Jonathon Niese	27	4.40	11–11	0	26	0	0	0	157.1	178	88	77	14	44	138	694	3	5	0	1.411
Mike O'Connor	9	2.70	0–1	0	0	2	0	0	6.2	5	2	2	0	3	8	29	0	1	0	1.200
Bobby Parnell	60	3.64	4–6	6	0	23	0	0	59.1	60	29	24	4	27	64	268	8	2	1	1.466
Mike Pelfrey	34	4.74	7–13	0	33	0	2	0	193.2	220	111	102	21	65	105	860	2	7	2	1.472
Francisco Rodriguez	42	3.16	2–2	23	0	34	0	0	42.2	44	15	15	3	16	46	187	2	2	0	1.406
Chris Schwinden	4	4.71	0–2	0	4	0	0	0	21.0	23	13	11	1	6	17	95	1	1	0	1.381
Josh Stinson	14	6.92	0–2	1	0	3	0	0	13.0	14	10	10	1	7	8	57	0	0	0	1.615
Dale Thayer	11	3.48	0–3	0	0	7	0	0	10.1	12	4	4	0	0	5	42	0	0	0	1.161
Chris Young	4	1.88	1–0	0	4	0	0	0	24.0	12	5	5	3	11	22	95	0	1	0	0.958
TOTAL	162	4.19	77–85	43	162	156	6	2	1448.0	1482	742	674	147	514	1126	6316	46	70	7	1.378

Player Profiles

Tommie Agee

Outfielder	Batted right, threw right
Born: 8/9/42	Magnolia, Alabama
Died: 1/22/01	New York, New York
Height: 5'11"	Weight: 195 #20

Tommie Agee Mets Career

YEAR	GP	AB	R	H	2B	3B	HR	RBI	K	BB	SB	AVG	SLG	OBP
1968	132	368	30	80	12	3	5	17	103	15	13	.217	.307	.255
1969	149	565	97	153	23	4	26	76	137	59	12	.271	.464	.342
1970	153	636	107	182	30	7	24	75	156	55	31	.286	.469	.344
1971	113	425	58	121	19	0	14	50	85	50	28	.285	.428	.362
1972	114	422	52	96	23	0	13	47	92	53	8	.227	.374	.317
TOTAL	661	2416	344	632	107	14	82	265	572	232	92	.262	.419	.329

ML Career

YEARS	GP	AB	R	H	2B	3B	HR	RBI	K	BB	SB	AVG	SLG	OBP
62–73	1129	3912	558	999	170	27	130	433	918	342	167	.255	.412	.320

Never has a Met gone from "hated" to "hero" in a shorter period as did Tommie Agee. He was one of the least popular Mets in the fans' eyes during the 1968 season but became a World Series hero a year later.

Tommie Lee Agee originally was signed by the Indians as an amateur free agent before the 1961 season. He was a highly regarded athlete after playing baseball at Grambling. The Indians shelled out quite a bit of dough to get him, although Ed Kranepool says Agee told him he let them off easy.

"He got an $80,000 bonus," Kranepool recalled shortly after Agee passed away, "but he said he could always have gotten more."

With help from his father, Agee was handling his own negotiations by phone.

"Tommie thought he could get a hundred thousand," Kranepool continued. When it got up to $80,000, his father said, 'Sign now!'"[1]

Former teammate Mudcat Grant remembered the first time he laid eyes on Agee during spring training in 1962.

"He wore a red tie, a red belt, red socks, and a white seersucker suit that was two sizes too big for him. His parents had obviously bought it for him and figured he'd grow into it.

"That moment in the clubhouse was the first time I ever saw Tommie," Grant said. "I said, 'C'mere, I got to talk to you.' I did for him what Larry Doby had done for me when I joined the Indians, and looked something like that. I got him a different tie, a different belt, and different socks."[2]

Grant also got him to ditch the suit.

Agee was in the majors a year later, making his debut September 14 at Minnesota. His first big-league hit came four days later against the Athletics in Kansas City as he went 1-for-4 in his first start.

Agee played parts of three seasons with the Indians but appeared in just 31 games for the big club, hitting .170 with one homer and five RBIs in 53 at-bats. But he showed promise with Triple A Portland in 1964, slugging 20 homers and stealing 35 bases while batting .272.

In an effort to right a previous wrong, the Indians reacquired the popular Rocky Colavito from the Athletics in a three-team, eight-player trade with the White Sox in January 1965. The White Sox acquired Agee and Tommy John in the swap, demonstrating why the Indians went 41 years between postseason appearances.

Agee actually looked like a bust after hitting only .226 with eight homers and 33 RBI for Triple A Indianapolis in 1965. But he made the White Sox's Opening Day roster in 1966 and played in a career-high 160 games, batting .273 while providing 22 homers, 86 RBIs, and 44 stolen bases. He finished third in the American League in steals, fourth with 172 hits, and seventh with 57 extra-base hits. Agee made the 1966 All-Star team and won the AL Rookie of the Year award in a landslide.

Agee earned his second All-Star berth in 1967, hitting 10 homers with 35 RBIs by the break. But the slick-fielding outfielder batted only .218 with four homers the rest of the way to finish with a disappointing .234 average. He was playing for a new manager, Eddie Stanky, who refused to coddle his players when they might need a kind word.

"I felt under pressure at all times," Agee once said of Stanky. "He was very difficult to play for. There was a lot of tension on that team."[3]

Gil Hodges was named the Mets manager after the 1967 season after five years in the Washington Senators' dugout. He had watched Agee up close and liked his ability to hit with power, steal bases, and cover ground in center field. Hodges convinced Mets management that Agee was what the team had been missing in center field. General manager Johnny Murphy acquired Agee and infielder Al Weis in a December 1967 deal that jettisoned Tommy Davis and Jack Fisher to the White Sox.

"In Agee, we've gotten a young player who has an outstanding glove and range, exceptional speed, and good power," said Hodges after the deal was completed.[4]

Agee realized he needed to make a good first appearance as a Met after failing to produce in 1967. He felt he

---

Catcher Jerry Grote embraces pitcher Jerry Koosman after winning the 1969 World Series. At left is teammate Ed Charles.

was a prime reason why the White Sox failed to beat out the Red Sox for the AL pennant.

"I just had a bad year," said Agee after accepting a $25,000 contract from the Mets before the 1968 season. "I felt that if I had hit a little better, the White Sox could have won the pennant. I was surprised I was traded, though. And I was surprised the Mets gave up Davis and Fisher. They gave a lot, but I feel that if they wanted me that badly, I'm more determined than ever to produce."[5]

Davis batted .268 with 50 RBIs for the '68 White Sox while Fisher recorded a 2.99 ERA in 180⅔ innings. Agee endured a miserable season, hitting only .217 with five home runs and 17 RBIs in 368 at-bats. Only Zoilo Versalles and Hal Lanier compiled a worse batting average among National League hitters with more than 360 at-bats.

Agee's struggles as a Met began immediately. He was beaned in the head by Bob Gibson during his first spring training at-bat on March 9.

"I told him, 'Watch out for Gibson, he's going to introduce himself to you,'" Ed Charles told the *New York Times* shortly after Agee died. "Sure enough, first pitch, bam, right in the head. You could hear it all over the ballpark. Thank God it hit him flush on the helmet."[6]

"I think it hit me below the batting helmet, right on my head," said Agee after being released from the hospital. "I didn't lose sight of the ball. It was thrown behind me, and I just couldn't get out of the way.

"Chances are it did not hit him below the helmet," Mets team physician Dr. Peter LaMotte shortly after the beaning. "If so, it would have knocked him out. I'll say this; if you have to get hit on the head, that's probably the best place. I guess that's why God made the skull so thick there."[7]

Agee recovered from the beaning and was in the Mets' Opening Day lineup a month later. He started the season by going 5-for-16 with five runs scored in the first four games, then went 0–10 in a 24-inning loss to Houston on April 15, 1968. He would stretch that hitless streak to 0-for-34, tying a team record before finally singling on May 1, to prompt a lengthy standing ovation at Shea Stadium.

"These people were wonderful, warm, marvelous," said an appreciative Agee after the game. "I had to do something for them."

Agee was hitting .174 with three homers and 10 RBIs by the All-Star break. He was losing playing time to Don Bosch, the Mets' previous "Center Fielder of the Future" who hit .140 in 93 at-bats the previous season.

Fans impatient for a winner eventually took out their frustrations on the newcomer. "It got so bad [that season], they'd see me poke my head out of the dugout and they'd boo me back in," said Agee during an interview for the Mets' 25th anniversary video.[8]

Agee seemed to press at home, batting .165 at Shea compared to a .263 mark on the road. He managed to put together a team-high 12-game hitting streak in September but failed to drive in a run during that stretch.

Hodges still had faith in Agee despite the presence of Amos Otis as the Mets assembled for 1969 spring training. Like Agee, Otis was a center fielder from the Mobile, Alabama, area. He hit .286 with 15 homers, 71 RBIs, and 21 stolen bases for Triple A Jacksonville in 1968.

But Otis had played all four infield positions during the '68 Instructional League as Hodges hoped Otis could fill another pressing need for the Mets: third base. Agee remained in center and became the catalyst of a light-hitting offense that would generate enough runs to support one of the league's best pitching staffs.

It helped that Agee knew Hodges had his back. Hodges could be tough on players who showed a lack of hustle or were unable to stay in game shape. But he continued to encourage his center fielder and always had time to speak with Agee. By the following spring, Agee was in a good frame of mind.

"I wanted to explode when the season ended," Agee recalled during the first week of the 1969 campaign. "The Mets sent me to Florida to work on my hitting, but after one week I told them I just had to get away. So I took two dozen baseballs, went home to Mobile, and spent the winter thinking.

"Every day, Cleon Jones and I would go out in a little boat and fish and talk about hitting. Then, in the afternoons, Tommy Aaron of the Atlanta Braves would come over and we'd go out to a playground and hit those two dozen baseballs around. And this spring in Florida, every time I'd bat, Cleon would tell me what I was doing wrong."[9]

Agee emerged as one of the team's top hitters in 1969, leading the team with 26 homers, 97 runs scored, and 76 RBIs while finishing second with 12 stolen bases. He smacked seven homers in his first 22 games, topping his total for all of 1968. His first home run of the season is considered the longest in the history of Shea Stadium as he drilled a pitch into the upper deck in left field during the third game of the year against the Expos.

Agee also had 15 RBIs at that point and was batting .297, 193 points higher than his 1968 average through 22 games.

He did some of his best hitting between June 22 and September 8, recording a .289 average with 17 homers and 46 RBIs in 76 games. The final game of that stretch was one of the turning points of the entire 1969 season.

The first-place Cubs were in free-fall, going 7–11 to see their lead trimmed to 2½ games over the Mets heading into a crucial two-game series at Shea Stadium that began September 8. Agee led off the bottom of the first against Bill Hands, who decided it might be a good idea to put Agee on his ass with an inside pitch in an effort to intimidate the Mets. Agee grounded out in the at-bat, but Jerry Koosman responded by drilling Cubs third baseman Ron Santo with a pitch.

The message was clear that the Mets wouldn't be intimidated, especially after Agee crushed a two-run homer in his next at-bat to put the Mets ahead 2–0 in the third. The Cubs knotted the score in the sixth before

Agee immediately fueled another rally. He slapped a ball to right field for a base hit and forced the issue by charging toward second base. Agee slid in under the tag for a leadoff double before scoring the go-ahead run on Wayne Garrett's single. Koosman struck out six over the final three innings while preserving a 3–2 victory, shaving another game off the Cubs' lead.

The Mets mauled the Cubs the next night before sweeping a doubleheader from the Expos a day later to move into first place. New York never relinquished the division lead, finishing eight games ahead of the Cubs. Agee didn't hit another homer after September 8, but he had given the team a push that allowed the Mets to go 15–5 in his last 20 games.

Agee rediscovered his power in the postseason, hitting two homers while batting .357 with four RBIs in the Mets' three-game sweep of the Braves in the first-ever NLCS. He hit only .167 in the World Series against the Orioles but put together one of the greatest all-around performances in postseason history during Game 3 at Shea.

Agee belted a leadoff homer in the bottom of the first to put the Mets ahead to stay, but the blast was an afterthought following his two incredible catches. New York had a 3–0 lead with two on and two out in the third when Elrod Hendricks drilled a fly ball to deep center. Agee sprinted toward the ball before making a sensational catch at the wall for the final out. He managed to hang onto the ball despite hitting the fence at almost full-speed.

"I haven't hit a ball that well to left field in two years," said the lefty-hitting Hendricks after Game 3. "I didn't think it would be caught. He was shading me to right-center. He ran a hell of a long ways.

"I didn't see him catch it. I was just thinking about going for three. I was a short way from second and I figured I had a standup triple. But then I look up and I see the white of the ball in his glove so I figured he still might drop it. Then he holds his glove up and I just said, 'Damn.'"[10]

Mets starter Gary Gentry retired the first two batters in the seventh before issuing three consecutive walks to load the bases, prompting Hodges to call for Nolan Ryan from the bullpen. Paul Blair sent a Ryan pitch to the gap in right-center, a sinking liner that appeared to be a sure hit. But Agee raced toward the ball and made a diving grab on the warning track to end the threat. Agee had produced a run with a homer and also saved five runs with his glove, helping the Mets take a 2–1 lead in the series.

"I thought I might get it without diving, but the wind dropped the ball straight down, and I had to hit the dirt," said Agee after the game.

Blair was still frustrated by the catch a few minutes after the Mets completed their Game 3 win. "If the ball drops, I might have an inside-the-park home run. I was just a step away from second base when he caught it," he said.[11]

Orioles manager Earl Weaver was very impressed by Agee's defense but equally dismayed by his team's failure to cash in on a pair of well-hit balls.

Tommie Agee at the 1987 Old Timers Day. Photo courtesy of David Ferry

"There have been center fielders in our league who have made one catch like he did," said an impressed Orioles manager Earl Weaver after the game. "But there wasn't anyone who came up with two in one game this year.

"You have to figure if Agee's got a sore leg or an ingrown toenail that hurts or he pulls a muscle in the first game, we've got five runs. And five runs isn't bad."[12]

The Mets won the next two games to finish off the Birds. Weis received the Babe Ruth Award as the World Series MVP, and Donn Clendenon came away with a car after he was named the best player in the Fall Classic by *Sport Magazine*. But Agee's heroics in Game 3 put the Mets in control of the series.

The World Series hangover seemed to elude Agee in 1970 while the Mets finished six games off the division lead. He led the team with a .286 average, 182 hits, 24 homers, 107 runs, and 31 steals while winning his second Gold Glove. Agee also had one of the more unproductive 20-game hitting streaks in major league history between April 16 and May 9, hitting .288 with three homers and nine RBIs. He scored 16 times during the streak but was taken out of the starting lineup by Hodges for a three-game stretch at the end of April.

Agee put together a better stretch a month later, batting .360 with nine home runs, 18 RBIs, and 20 runs in 17 games. He was named the NL Player of the Month for June, hitting .364 with 11 homers, 30 RBIs, and a .745 slugging percentage. The 11 home runs set a Mets team record for a single month.

Agee later strung together a 19-game hitting streak, but he also went 37 games without a homer between July 12 and August 20, collecting only nine RBIs in the process.

Agee ended the year on a nine-game hitting streak, but the Mets had played themselves out of the division race by then. He also appeared in 153 games, his most action in three seasons as a Met. He wouldn't come close to that figure in his final two years with the Mets as various injuries limited his availability.

Agee began to have left knee problems in 1970, suffering cartilage damage while sliding into home August 22. He damaged his right knee June 6, 1971, during an attempted steal. He missed eight games in May after bruising his ribs while trying to steal home. The right knee injury would force him on the disabled list in June and hamper him the rest of the season. Still, Agee managed to share the team lead with 28 steals and 14 homers while batting .285 in 1971.

Agee continued to be mired by injuries in 1972 as knee problems were joined by hamstring issues. The Mets picked up Willie Mays in May as part of a wonderful public relations gesture, but it also was supposed to give manager Yogi Berra another option if Agee missed significant action. Unfortunately, injuries to several players left Mays overworked and just as gimpy as Agee by the end of the season.

Agee's .227 batting average was his lowest in four years, as were his 13 homers, 47 RBIs, 52 runs, and 96 hits. He stole only eight bases in '72 and hadn't hit a triple since 1970. Agee also committed 11 errors, two years after winning a Gold Glove.

Trading Agee would leave the Mets without an everyday center fielder, but general manager Bob Scheffing dealt him anyway and got little in return. Agee was sent to Houston for Rich Chiles, who hit just .120 (3-for-25) in eight games for the 1973 Mets.

"I guess you'd have to say we were dissatisfied with Agee's playing," general manager Bob Scheffing said after making the trade at the winter meetings in Honolulu. Scheffing also suggested that the deal was designed to break up Agee and Jones, who also had a subpar season.[13]

Agee had his own problems in '73. In a bit of irony, Agee was now playing for Leo Durocher, who as Cubs manager in 1969 thought Agee could be intimidated by a brushback pitch. By now, Agee was having trouble with most pitches, batting .235 with eight homers and 15 RBIs in 83 games before he was dealt to the Cardinals on August 18. Agee appeared washed up at age 31.

The Cards were battling the Mets and three other clubs for the NL East title when the Redbirds arrived at Shea Stadium for a big two-game series. Agee went 1-for-4 with two strikeouts in the series opener as Jon Matlack pitched the Mets to their fifth straight win, giving them a two-game lead over the third-place Cardinals with seven games

remaining. Agee put the Cardinals ahead in the second game September 23, blasting a two-run homer off George Stone in the top of the first. The Mets eventually built a 5–2 lead, but Agee represented the potential tying run at the plate in the eighth inning following a pair of one-out walks issued by Tug McGraw. Agee ended the threat by hitting into an inning-ending double play before McGraw closed out a 5–2 win that kept the Mets a half-game ahead of the second-place Pirates.

Agee's two-run blast represented his final major league RBI. He was traded to the Dodgers in December and was released before the start of the 1974 season, ending his career.

Agee had several business ventures in New York during and after his playing days. He and teammate Cleon Jones were proprietors of Outfielder's Lounge on Astoria Boulevard near Shea Stadium during the early1970s. Agee later worked several jobs in recreation and worked for a title insurance company. He would become part of the Mets family again in the 1990s, representing the team at various functions.

Agee was leaving a midtown Manhattan office building the morning of January 22, 2001, when he suffered a heart attack. He died at Bellevue hospital at age 58.

"I'm devastated," said former teammate Ed Charles to the *New York Times* following Agee's death. "This is going to hurt. When Jackie Robinson passed, I had this reaction. I just cracked up. That's how I am today. Got to talk about it. Got to get it out. Such a generous guy. Nice guy. He'd do whatever he could for people. I thought he'd be around forever."

"We were close. We enjoyed each other's company in 1969 and after that. It was a good time.

"We were friends for life. We didn't have to go out every night to know we were there for each other. Our families were close. We knew he had heart trouble, but we figured the medicine would hold him until he could get an implant or something. We didn't expect this."[14]

"Tommie Agee was all about people," said Mets promotions director James Plummer at the time of Agee's death. "His smile lit up a room. On the day he died, he was making plans to help John Franco's charity bowling tournament for the March of Dimes. That was Tommie Agee."[15]

ML debut	Indians @ Twins, 9/14/62
Mets debut	@ Giants, 4/10/68
1st ML hit	RBI single vs. Dan Pfister, @ A's , 9/18/62 (with Indians)
1st Mets hit	single vs. Juan Marichal, @ Giants, 4/10/68
1st ML homer	solo shot vs. Art Fowler, Angels, 9/22/63 (with Indians)
1st Mets homer	solo homer vs. Phil Regan, @ Cubs, 5/10/68
1st ML RBI	RBI single vs. Dan Pfister, @ A's, 9/18/62 (with Indians)
1st Mets RBI	solo homer vs. Phil Regan, @ Cubs, 5/10/68
Most hits, ML/Mets game	5, @ Pirates, 8/8/70

Most homers, ML/Mets game   2, 8 times, all with Mets
Most RBI, ML game   5, vs. Orioles, 9/2/66 (with
                                 White Sox)
Most RBI, Mets game   4, 5 times
Acquired: Traded by the White Sox with Al Weis for Tommy Davis,
          Jack Fisher, Billy Wynne, and Dick Booker
          12/15/67.
Deleted: Traded to the Astros for Rich Chiles and Buddy Harris
          11/27/72.
AL All-Star, 1966, 1967
AL Rookie of the Year, 1966
NL Gold Glove, 1970

Edgardo Alfonzo

Infielder   Bats right, throws right
Born: 11/8/73   St. Teresa, Venezuela
Height: 5'11"   Weight: 185   #13

Edgardo Alfonzo Mets Career

YEAR	GP	AB	R	H	2B	3B	HR	RBI	K	BB	SB	AVG	SLG	OBP
1995	101	335	26	93	13	5	4	41	37	12	1	.278	.382	.301
1996	123	368	36	96	15	2	4	40	56	25	2	.261	.345	.304
1997	151	518	84	163	27	2	10	72	56	63	11	.315	.432	.391
1998	144	557	94	155	28	2	18	78	77	65	8	.278	.427	.355
1999	158	628	123	191	41	1	27	108	85	85	9	.304	.502	.385
2000	150	544	109	176	40	2	25	94	70	95	3	.324	.542	.425
2001	124	457	64	111	22	0	17	49	62	51	5	.243	.403	.322
2002	135	490	78	151	26	0	16	56	55	62	6	.308	.459	.391
TOTAL	1086	3897	614	1136	212	14	120	538	498	458	45	.292	.445	.367

ML Career

YEARS	GP	AB	R	H	2B	3B	HR	RBI	K	BB	SB	AVG	SLG	OBP
95-06	1506	5385	777	1532	282	18	146	744	617	596	53	.284	.425	.357

Edgardo Alfonzo was a fan favorite and a manager's dream during his time with the Mets. He played at a Gold Glove level at third base and continued to be among the National League's top-fielding infielders after he was asked to move over to second. He had four seasons in which he batted .300 with at least 502 plate appearances, more than any other Met before David Wright matched the mark in 2008.

Alfonzo came up huge in big spots, played hurt when needed, and rarely took a play off. Alfonzo likely would have been among the top five in almost all offense categories on the team's all-time list if his career hadn't been short-circuited by a back injury. He played the game with dignity and left the Mets in classy style, taking out a full-page ad in the local newspapers to thank the fans for their support.

He quickly became one of the Mets' top prospects after they signed him as an amateur free agent in February 1991. He hit .293 or better in each of his first four minor league seasons before joining the Mets in 1995, making the jump from Double A after batting .293 with 15 homers and 75 RBIs for Binghamton.

Alfonzo made his big-league debut in the Mets' 1995 season opener at Colorado on April 26. He collected his first hit and RBI on May 2 at Montreal before going 5-for-9 with four RBIs and his first home run in a three-game series at Cincinnati. Alfonzo hit a wall by mid-May, going 6-for-46 (.130) with no RBIs in a 13-game stretch. He pulled out of the slump by recording two hits in four of his next five games and batted .294 for the month of June. He batted .297 in July and raised his season average to .276 when he landed on the disabled list in August with a herniated disc. He batted .296 in September to finish with a .278 mark, second only to Steve Henderson on the Mets' single-season list for rookies with at least 340 at-bats.

Alfonzo played 123 games for the 1996 squad but still hadn't shown the extra-base power that would make him a serious offensive threat. He hit four homers for the second straight year and finished with 40 RBIs and a .261 average. Alfonzo actually put up Rey Ordonez–type numbers through mid-August, batting .226 with two homers and 23 RBIs in 234 at-bats. But he regained his stroke for the final seven weeks, collecting at least two hits in 12 of his last 44 games while batting .321 in 134 at-bats.

Alfonzo took off in 1997, finishing with team highs in batting (.315) and hits (163) while helping the Mets challenge for the NL wild-card. He strung together an 18-game hitting streak, going 29-for-70 (.414) during that span. His batting average was up to .335 after he went 4-for-6 with two RBIs against the Orioles on August 30. However, he failed to maintain his offense, hitting .230 with only six RBIs in his final 28 games. He received National League MVP consideration despite his subpar finish and was second to Ken Caminiti in Gold Glove voting.

Alfonzo's power numbers went up in 1998 as he set then–personal marks with 17 homers, 78 RBIs, and 28 doubles while scoring a team-high 94 runs. He also had 44 multi-hit games, including five straight in late August. But he ended the year hitting .278, 38 points below his 1997 output. Alfonzo batted only .257 in September after manager Bobby Valentine decided to keep him at the No. 2 spot in the lineup. But he managed to do his best hitting in the clutch, batting .359 with 57 RBIs in 175 at-bats with runners on base.

The Mets bolstered their lineup by signing Robin Ventura and Rickey Henderson after getting Mike Piazza in a 1998 midseason pickup. The top of the Mets lineup now had Henderson, Alfonzo, John Olerud, Piazza, and Ventura, arguably the best top five in team history to that point. But the addition of Ventura meant Alfonzo had to move to second base, where he had played for much of 1995 and '96.

With Alfonzo, Ventura, Ordonez, and Olerud starting almost every day, the Mets shattered the major league record for fewest errors by an infield (43). Alfonzo made a smooth transition to second, committing only five miscues for a .993 fielding percentage.

Fonzie won the NL Silver Slugger award for second sackers, ending the year with a .304 average while topping career highs with 27 homers, 108 RBIs, and 41 doubles. His RBI total was rather remarkable as he spent most of

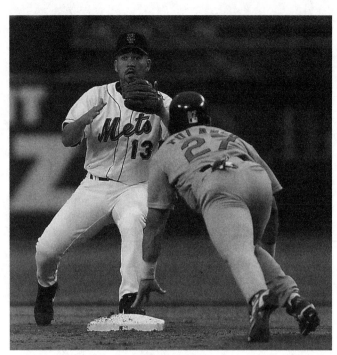

Edgardo Alfonzo

the year hitting second in the lineup. He sizzled in July, batting .385 with 11 doubles, four homers, and 20 RBIs in 109 at-bats. But his best game of the season—and his career—was still a few weeks away.

The Mets were just 3½ games behind the East-leading Braves when they arrived at the Astrodome on August 30. Alfonzo put on the greatest single-game performance in team history, going 6-for-6 with three home runs, five RBIs, and six runs scored as the Mets clobbered the Astros 17–1. He hit a solo homer in the first, a single in the second, a two-run homer in the fourth, and a solo shot in the sixth. Alfonzo set a team mark for hits and runs scored in a game when he delivered an RBI single in the ninth before scoring on Shawon Dunston's two-run single. He finished one triple shy of the cycle while outhitting the Astros 6–5.

The Mets were taking another stab at a playoff berth in September after ending 1998 on a five-game losing streak that left them one game off the wild-card lead. The Mets dropped six straight to fall two games off the pace with three to play. Alfonzo helped the Mets force a one-game playoff for the wild-card by going 4-for-12 in a three-game sweep of the Pirates. He delivered a one-out single in the bottom of the ninth of the finale before Mike Piazza scored the winning run on a wild pitch.

The Mets headed to Cincinnati for a playoff game to determine the wild-card champion. Alfonzo put the Mets ahead to stay just two batters into the game, belting a two-run homer to center before adding an RBI double in the fifth. The Mets beat the Reds 5–0 to earn a meeting with the Diamondbacks in the NLDS. Alfonzo was just getting hot.

He led the Mets to victory in their first postseason game since 1988, an 8–4 triumph at Arizona on October 5, 1999. He became the third National League player to homer in

his first postseason at-bat, then became the first player in major league history to hit a grand slam in his playoff debut. Alfonzo snapped a 4–4 tie with a two-out, bases-loaded blast off Bobby Chouinard.

Alfonzo also homered in the fourth inning of Game 4 to give the Mets a brief lead. With New York trailing 3–2 in the eighth, Alfonzo worked out a leadoff walk before scoring the tying run to force extra innings. The Mets wrapped up the series when Todd Pratt homered in the 10th inning.

Alfonzo led the Mets with three homers in the series and tied Olerud for the team lead with six RBIs. He got off to a terrific start in the NLCS versus the Braves, collecting three doubles while going 2-for-4 in each of the first two games. He doubled home a run to get the Mets within 4–3 in the eighth inning of Game 2, but the Braves held on to take a 2–0 lead in the series.

Alfonzo was silenced the rest of the way, going 2-for-19 with no RBIs and nine strikeouts, finishing with a .222 average for the series as the Mets lost in six games.

Alfonzo and the Mets would reach greater highs in 2000. He was named to the NL All-Star game for the first and only time of his career, going 0-for-2 in the contest. He was among the top 10 in batting most of the season before finishing tied with Piazza for 10th overall. Alfonzo also led the Mets with 40 doubles, 176 hits, and 95 walks while finishing second on the club with 25 homers and 94 RBIs. He finished second to Pokey Reese in the Gold Glove balloting despite finishing with a .985 fielding average compared to Reese's .980 mark.

The Mets challenged the Braves for the NL East crown until the final week of the season before winning the wild-card with ease. It gave Alfonzo another chance to showcase his talent on the big stage of the playoffs, and he immediately came out slashing.

Alfonzo hit safely in each game of the NLDS and NLCS. He ran his postseason hitting streak to a team-record 13 games dating to 1999 before he was stopped by the Yankees in Game 3 of the World Series.

He blasted a two-run homer to put the Mets ahead 4–1 in the ninth inning of Game 2 at San Francisco. Instead of being a game-clinching blast, it only served to prolong the game after J.T. Snow crushed a three-run homer off Armando Benitez in the bottom of the ninth. The Mets won the game in extra innings and didn't lose again until Game 3 of the NLCS. Alfonzo contributed with the following:

1. A game-tying double in the eighth inning of Game 3 of the NLDS before Benny Agbayani won it with a homer in the 13th.
2. A two-run double that gave the Mets a four-run lead in a 4–0 victory in the Game 4 clincher against the Giants, giving Bobby Jones a comfortable lead as he threw a one-hitter.
3. An RBI single that snapped a 3–3 tie in the eighth inning of Game 2 of the NLCS at St. Louis. The Mets blew the lead before winning.

4. An RBI single that sparked a four-run first in the Mets' 10–6 win over the Cardinals in Game 4 of the NLCS. The Redbirds blasted the Mets in Game 3 and were ahead 2–0 before Alfonzo's hit.

5. An RBI single that ignited a three-run first before the Mets completed a 7–0 victory in the Game 5 clincher.

6. A tiebreaking single that gave the Mets a 3–2 lead in the seventh inning of Game 1 of the World Series against the Yankees. The lead stood up until Benitez blew the save in the ninth inning of a 4–3, 13-inning loss.

Alfonzo was hitting .333 (15–45) with 10 RBIs in the 2000 postseason before taking the collar in Game 3 of the Fall Classic. He ended the Series with 17 career postseason RBIs, setting a team record. But an achy back would limit his effectiveness during his last two years as a Met.

He reached a pair of milestones in 2001, collecting his 900th career hit and 100th home run. Alfonzo also had a 15-game hitting streak and tied a then–Mets record by homering in four straight games. But he spent two weeks on the disabled list in June and ended the year batting only .243 with 17 homers and 49 RBIs.

Alfonzo had a much better year at the plate in 2002, hitting .308 while providing 16 homers and 56 RBIs. But the numbers were well short of his stats from 1997 through 2000, leaving the Mets with a tough decision to make.

Alfonzo, Piazza, Al Leiter, and John Franco were the most popular Mets at that point, but the team had sunk to last place at 72–90 in Alfonzo's final year of his contract. With concerns for his back and sagging production, the Mets allowed him to become a free agent at the end of the 2002 season. Fonzie signed with the Giants, who were just a few weeks removed from a World Series appearance.

He hit only .259 for the Giants in the 2003 regular season, but his bat woke up in the playoffs. He was 9-for-17 (.529) with four doubles, five RBIs, and three runs scored in the NLDS against the Marlins. Alfonzo accounted for half the team's 16 runs in the series, but the Giants lost in four games before Florida went on to win the World Series.

Alfonzo had a good year in 2004, hitting .289 with 11 homers and 77 RBIs in 139 games. But he played just 109 games in '05 while batting .277 with a career-low two homers.

The Giants traded Alfonzo down the coast to the Angels but was released in May 2006 after hitting only .100 in limited duty. He hooked on with the Blue Jays in May but was released four weeks later, forcing him to prove his worth with Bridgeport of the independent Atlantic League. With nothing to lose, the Mets signed Alfonzo off the Bridgeport roster in July. The organization assigned him to Triple A New Orleans to find out what he had left, but Alfonzo failed to earn a call-up, hitting .241 with three homers and 19 RBIs.

Alfonzo refused to quit after '06. He spent two years with the Long Island Ducks of the Atlantic League, hitting .329 with eight homers and 27 RBIs in 59 games in 2008 after recording a .266 average with 56 RBIs in 105 games the previous season. Fonzie was playing on a team that included ex-Mets Carl Everett, Richard Hidalgo, Vic Darensbourg, and Alay Soler. But Central Islip was as close as they would get to the majors.

He finished the '08 campaign in the Mexican League, hitting 280 in 55 games for Quintana Roo before an unsuccessful 21-game run with the Yomiuri Giants in 2009. He finally ended his career at age 36 after hitting only .154 in 78 at-bats for Newark of the Atlantic League in 2010.

ML/Mets debut	@ Rockies, 4/26/95
1st ML/Mets hit	RBI double vs. Jeff Fassero, @ Expos, 5/2/95
1st ML/Mets homer	2-run homer vs. Matt Grott, @ Reds, 5/6/95
1st ML/Mets RBI	RBI double vs. Jeff Fassero, @ Expos, 5/2/95
Most hits, ML/Mets game	6, @ Astros, 8/30/99
Most homers, ML/Mets game	3, @ Astros, 8/30/99
Most RBI, ML/Mets game	6, @ Astros, 8/30/99
Acquired: Signed as an amateur free agent, 2/19/91.	
Deleted: Signed with the Giants, 12/15/02.	

Carlos Beltrán

Outfielder	Bats both, throws right
Born: 4/17/77	Manati, Puerto Rico
Height: 6'1"	Weight: 190 #15

Carlos Beltrán Mets Career

YEAR	GP	AB	R	H	2B	3B	HR	RBI	K	BB	SB	AVG	SLG	OBP
2005	151	582	83	155	34	2	16	78	96	56	17	.266	.414	.330
2006	140	510	127	140	38	1	41	116	99	95	18	.275	.594	.388
2007	144	554	93	1153	33	33	33	112	111	69	23	.276	.525	.353
2008	161	606	116	172	40	5	27	112	96	92	25	.284	.500	.376
2009	81	308	50	100	22	1	10	48	43	47	11	.325	.500	.415
2010	64	220	21	56	11	3	7	27	39	30	3	.255	.427	.341
2011	98	353	61	102	30	2	15	66	61	60	3	.289	.513	.391
TOTAL	839	3133	551	878	208	17	149	559	545	449	100	.280	.500	.369

ML Career

YEARS	GP	AB	R	H	2B	3B	HR	RBI	K	BB	SB	AVG	SLG	OBP
98-11	1768	6767	1184	1917	390	73	302	1146	1213	831	293	.283	.496	.361

How does a player average 34 home runs and 113 RBIs, win two Silver Sluggers and three Gold Gloves over a three-year period and leave you wanting more? When he is miscast as the savior of a ballclub that is coming off three straight losing seasons.

Carlos Beltrán is arguably the greatest center fielder in Mets history and the only outfielder on the team to capture more than one Gold Glove and record three straight 100+ RBI seasons. He played through pain and contributed numerous walk-off hits during his time with the Mets. He was a leader by example, although his detractors will say Beltrán wasn't vocal enough on a team in desperate need of a leader.

He was passive by nature. How many players can average 31 homers and 102 RBIs and say they are comfortable hitting in the two-hole? Beltrán hit the hell out of the ball and made the highlight reels with his glove, but the soft-spoken Puerto Rican never craved the spotlight.

Beltrán signed what was then the richest contract in Mets history, a seven-year, $119 million package in December 2004 that seemed like a bargain four seasons into the deal. He became a Met shortly after hitting .435 with eight homers and 14 RBIs for the Astros in 12 games during the 2004 postseason. It was one of the greatest performances in MLB postseason history and escalated Beltrán's considerable value on the free-agent market.

Newly installed Mets general manager Omar Minaya was given the green light to spend money if it meant a winning season in 2005. Minaya began the makeover by inking free-agent pitcher Pedro Martinez to a four-year, $56 million contract. Beltrán was signed a few weeks later, giving Minaya's Mets instant credibility.

"I'm proud to be a part of the new Mets," Beltrán said at his introductory news conference. "I call it the new Mets because this organization is going in the right direction, the direction of winning.

"I expect a lot from myself. What I will do is what I have done my whole career: have fun."[16]

Martinez quickly became a hero at Shea, leading the staff in most categories. Beltrán struggled through numerous injuries and hit only .266 with 16 homers and 78 RBIs, numbers that were dwarfed by left fielder Cliff Floyd and third baseman David Wright. Cranky Mets fans were calling Beltrán "the next George Foster." They would eat their words a year later as Beltrán put together the finest season ever by a Mets outfielder.

Mets fans booed Beltrán incessantly in 2005 and were at full volume when he opened the 2006 season 0-for-9. Beltrán ended the slump with a two-run homer that gave the Mets an 8–5 lead against the Nationals April 6. The fickle faithful at Shea demanded Beltrán give a curtain call for his effort. Beltrán initially didn't want to oblige, ticked off over the shabby treatment he had received in his first 164 games as a Met. He finally came out of the dugout and doffed his cap at the urging of teammate Julio Franco before completing a four-RBI night.

Beltrán seemed more comfortable as a Met following the two-run blast. He pounded the hated Braves during a three-game series in early May, homering in each game while driving in four runs. Two weeks later, he crushed a three-run homer in the first inning of a 7–6 win after the Yankees grabbed a 4–0 lead in their first at-bat. Four days later, Phillies reliever Ryan Madson tossed seven shutout innings of relief before Beltrán launched a walk-off homer in the 16th inning to complete a 9–8 victory.

He sizzled in early June, batting .471 with four homers and 16 RBIs in eight games, driving home runs in each contest. Beltrán was now batting .300 with 18 home runs and 53 ribbies in 55 games. Mets fans got off his back, especially with the team about to run away with the NL East title.

Beltrán set career highs in 2006 with 41 homers and 116 RBIs while batting .275. He made the NL All-Star team, won his first Silver Slugger, captured his first Gold Glove, and finished fourth in the MVP voting. The Mets won their first division title in 18 years, 12 games ahead of the Phils.

The team swept the Dodgers in the division series before Beltrán delivered three homers and four RBIs against the Cardinals in the NLCS. New York dropped two of the first three games of the championship series and was in desperate need of a victory in Game 4. Beltrán came through by going 3-for-3 with a pair of solo homers and four RBIs in a 12–5 rout at Busch Stadium.

Beltrán got the Mets off to a good start in Game 7 by hitting a two-out double in the first before scoring on David Wright's single to make it 1–0. But the Mets trailed 3–1 in the bottom of the ninth following a two-run homer by Yadier Molina.

Jose Valentin and Endy Chavez opened the final inning with singles off Adam Wainwright, who quickly retired Floyd and Jose Reyes. Paul Lo Duca worked out a two-out walk to put the potential tying run on second base.

Up stepped Beltrán, who had torched the Cardinals during the 2004 NLCS and was hitting .308 with eight runs scored in this series. He took a called strike and fouled off the second pitch against the rookie reliever to fall into an 0–2 hole.

A base hit would likely tie the game, and a double would have given Beltrán instant membership into the Mets Hall of Fame. Wainwright threw a curveball that started off high and outside before finding its way across the strike zone. He had frozen Beltrán, who looked at strike three to end the series.

Devastated Mets fans looking for a scapegoat focused on Beltrán despite his overall play in the series. What they had neglected to remember was that Floyd had struck out looking three batters earlier when he also represented the winning run. Minaya had no problem coming to the defense of Beltrán.

"People who say you have to swing at that are people who never played the game, who never stood in the batter's box and faced a 90-plus-miles-per-hour fastball, then had the guy throw a curve," Minaya said.[17]

Mets fans spent the winter also wondering what might have been if Aaron Heilman hadn't thrown a gopher ball to Molina in the ninth or Beltrán had been able to protect the plate on a knee-buckling curveball. But the simple truth is that the mighty Mets lineup managed only two hits after the first inning of Game 7, none between the second and eighth. It took a brilliant catch by Endy Chavez just to keep the game tied 1–1 in the sixth inning.

Beltrán spent the next few weeks pondering the final out of the season. As the Mets reported to camp the following winter, he was asked to recount the final pitch of the 2006 season. Although Beltrán was burdened with the blame for the team's inability to reach the World Series, not enough credit was given to Wainwright for throwing a perfect pitch. Beltrán had no trouble heaping praise on Wainwright.

"The last pitch was a pitch, maybe this year, even if I feel good at the plate, I don't think I can hit that pitch," Beltrán said in February 2007. "That's how nasty that pitch was. It was a pitch on the outside corner for a strike. I mean, I saw it, but I couldn't do anything with it."[18]

There was no reason to think the Mets wouldn't successfully defend the NL East crown in 2007. The core group was returning from a squad that held a double-digit lead after June 22. Beltrán did his part in '07, pacing the squad with 33 homers and 112 RBIs while hitting .276. He created 172 of the team's 804 runs and helped them carry a seven-game lead into the final 17 games of the season.

Beltrán batted only .246 over those last 17 contests but provided five homers, 17 RBIs, and 13 runs. He manufactured 25 of the Mets' 98 runs during that stretch, but New York won only two games in which he had at least one RBI. The Mets dropped the division title to the Phillies on the last day of the season, thanks to some atrocious pitching over the final 2½ weeks. Minaya remedied the starting pitching problem by acquiring Johan Santana from the Twins before 2008 camp.

Phillies shortstop Jimmy Rollins boldly declared at the start of 2007 that his club was the team to beat. Beltrán issued a similar declaration in spring training 2008, marking the first time he had created bulletin board material for another ballclub.

"Without Santana," Beltrán began, "we felt as a team that we had a chance to win in our division. With him now, I have no doubt that we're going to win in our division. So this year, to Jimmy Rollins, we are the team to beat."[19]

The Mets got off to a lousy start in '08, leading to the dismissal of manager Willie Randolph. The knock on Randolph was that he failed to light a fire under a team that had frittered away a very winnable playoff berth the year before. There also was speculation that the Latino players had tuned out Randolph, leaving Beltrán and Delgado to answer questions about Willie's departure. But Beltrán was holding up his end at the time of the firing, hitting .277 with 10 homers and 48 RBIs in 69 games. He delivered two homers and three RBIs in Randolph's final game as manager.

Beltrán played well the rest of the year, hitting .289 with 17 home runs and 64 runs batted in. Beltrán and the Mets, who trailed the first-place Phillies by 7½ games on June 13, pulled into a tie for the division lead July 17 by virtue of a 10-game winning streak. New York led the NL East by 3½ games with "the dreaded" 17 games to play after Beltrán went 3-for-5 with two RBIs and two runs scored in Washington on September 10.

Again, no blame could be thrown at the feet of Beltrán after he batted .306 with four homers, 10 RBIs, and 11 runs scored in the final 17 contests. He delivered a game-winning single in the bottom of the ninth to give the Mets a 7–6 comeback win over the Cubs September 25, keeping the team a game behind the Phillies. But the Mets' horrendous bullpen allowed the Phillies to surge past them in

Carlos Beltrán. Photo courtesy of David Ferry

the final week before the Brewers overtook New York for the wild-card on the final day of the season. Beltrán's two-run homer in the finale provided the only scoring for the Mets in a 4–2 loss to the Marlins.

The 2009 season was a disaster for the Mets and Beltrán, who hit exceptionally well when healthy but managed to play just half their games. He became the first Mets everyday player to own a .400 average through the first 25 games of the season, thanks to a 16-game hitting streak in which he batted .443 with a .534 on-base percentage, three homers, and 11 RBIs in 61 at-bats from April 17 through May 5. Beltrán went hitless May 5 before he immediately embarked on an 11-game hit streak that gave him a .378 average through May 17.

He hit safely in 14 of his 16 games in June before experiencing pain in the back of his knee. By the time he was placed on the disabled list on June 22, he was hitting .336 and the Mets were just two games off the NL East lead at 34–33. New York was out of the race by the time he returned 2½ months later.

The injury was originally diagnosed as a bone bruise of his right knee and nothing more serious than that. But the pain never went away as Beltrán's day-to-day status became week-to-week. The knees had become a persistent problem for him ever since he joined the Mets. He underwent arthroscopic surgery on both knees after the 2007 season and managed to play a full season in 2008 despite soreness.

He returned to the lineup despite being at less than 100 percent, and it showed at the plate and on the field. Beltrán wasn't covering the outfield in the manner that allowed him to win Gold Gloves each of the previous three seasons. Although his .284 batting average in September matched his figure for all of 2008, he hit only two doubles and two homers in 19 games that month. Beltrán ended the year with a .325 average, 10 homers, and 48 RBIs in the Mets' first losing season since 2004.

The right knee continued to bother him through the off-season while the Mets hoped the pain would go away without surgery. Beltrán sought an outside opinion on the injury and was told he needed arthroscopic surgery to clean out the arthritic area in the knee. Beltrán told the Mets he would undergo the procedure in mid-January, although it led to media speculation the Mets were unaware he had opted for surgery before it occurred. He was annoyed the team was intimating he had surgery without the Mets knowing about it.

Days following the procedure and the ensuing brouhaha, Minaya explained that Beltrán indeed had told him about his pending surgery, but that Minaya asked him to go through the Mets' team of doctors first before having the operation. Minaya said he was okay with the surgery as long as Beltrán "followed the protocol."

"Everything is fine," Minaya said. "Listen, we have no problems with Carlos Beltrán. I have no problem with him, and ownership has no problem. We love him. The only issue was with the process, not the player."[20]

"I don't have hard feelings," said Beltrán after reporting to camp in February to continue his rehab work. "It just took me a while because I am a human being and I'm a person that has feelings.

"It took me like a week to forget about everything and focus on what is important for me," he said. "What is important for me right now is to be with the team, being ready and being able to play."[21]

The procedure meant Beltrán would not be available for training camp, although the original timetable called for him to be ready by May. May turned into July without Beltrán facing a major league pitch.

"It wasn't like I wanted to have the operation," Beltrán said nearly a year after returning to the active roster. "But when I met with the doctor in New York, the team doctor, he told me there was nothing he could do for me. The team doctor is saying there is nothing he can do for you. I was thinking: 'Well, that's the end of my career? I'm not going to play baseball anymore?'

"No, no. Come on, man. For a bone bruise? I'm not going to be able to play this game anymore? I wasn't going to give up. I felt that I needed to search for the best doctor in the world, and [agent Scott Boras] was able to find the doctors, and thank God I feel good.

"I wasn't going to do microfracture because microfracture is 12 months of rehab, and you don't know what you are going to get," Beltrán said. "I wanted to get scoped and be safe. If the scope doesn't work, then we move on to the next one."[22]

Unlike 2009, the Mets survived without Beltrán as Angel Pagan was displaying brilliance at the plate and in center field during the first half. The team opened the year 48–41, putting it within a game of the wild-card as All-Star break approached. The Mets were also looking forward to having Beltrán back when the team returned from the break.

Beltrán made his season debut in the opener of an 11-game road trip that opened the second half of the Mets' season.

"Even though I didn't cry, it was emotional for me," said Beltrán of his return to the lineup. "I know everything is going to be normal," he said, "but always the first day it's a tough assignment and the adrenaline is high. But tomorrow is going to be okay."[23]

He hit safely in his first four games before going 1-for-20 in his next six contests. Beltrán also was struggling on defense while playing with a cumbersome, heavy brace on his surgically repaired knee.

The Mets went 2–9 on the western swing and found themselves under .500 by August 6. Beltrán, offering little in the way of offense or solid defense, was hitting .185 with just one home run and seven RBIs in 24 games through August 11 before crafting a six-game hitting streak. The streak was too little, too late after the Mets had already fallen out of serious playoff contention. But it also sparked a season-ending 40-game stretch in which he batted .295 with six home runs, seven doubles, and 20 RBIs, typical Beltrán numbers for a quarter-season. He ended the year with a .255 average, seven homers, and 27 RBIs in 64 games.

The Mets made a managerial decision following their second straight losing campaign, hiring Terry Collins to replace Jerry Manuel. Collins was immediately faced with a tough decision involving center field after Pagan flourished and Beltrán struggled at the position in 2010.

Pagan had certainly earned the job, but Beltrán was the one with the Gold Gloves and more experience. Collins, believing it would be a slap to a former All-Star by moving him to right field against Beltrán's wishes, asked him to make the decision on his own. It took Beltrán only a few days to ascertain the team was better off with Pagan in center, a selfless choice that was lauded by the media and the ballclub.

"In my heart, I still feel that I can play center field," said Beltrán, "but at the same time, this is not about Carlos, this is about the team. In order for me to play center field, I need more time."[24]

A relieved Collins had handled his first potential brushfire with aplomb while gaining tremendous respect from his players for the manner in which the situation was handled.

He praised Beltrán's decision after the two met to discuss the matter, calling their conversation the most professional he'd ever had with a baseball player.

Beltrán and the Mets started slowly in 2011. He batted .244 in his first 14 games before the Mets soon dropped to 5–13. But Beltrán began to heat up in mid-April, embarking on an eight-game hitting streak before entering May with a .281 average. Though he had only three homers in April—two coming against the Nationals April 9—he also produced eight doubles and was displaying much better movement in the outfield.

Any doubts concerning his power were erased May 12 in Colorado as he became the eighth Met to homer three times in a game, and the first since Reyes in 2006. Beltrán hit two-run shots in the first, seventh, and ninth innings to set a career high for homers in a 9–5 win over the Rockies.

"It kind of feels like your first homer in the big leagues when you do something like that," he said after the game. "It's going to be a day I never will forget.

"I feel like a little kid, honestly," he said. "I never smile a lot, but I was smiling, I was happy. It felt great."[25]

The three-homer game gave Beltrán a .295 average and a .590 slugging percentage. He was consistent over the next two months as his average never dropped below .279. He was at his most productive in June, driving in 26 runs and scoring 18 times in 27 games as the Mets went 16–11 in those contests to work their way back into post-season contention.

With the Mets battling for a playoff berth, the big question was whether GM Sandy Alderson would move free-agents-to-be Beltrán and Reyes at the trade deadline. Doing so would make it appear the Mets weren't interested in winning, although logic dictated they did not have the players to make a playoff run.

Closer Francisco Rodriguez, who was in line to earn an automatic $17 million option for 2012 if he stayed in New York, was the first to go. He was sent to Milwaukee minutes after Beltrán had gone 1-for-2 with a run scored in the All-Star game, his sixth career selection to the Midsummer Classic. Rodriguez's departure shortened the bullpen, but the Mets continued to win while Beltrán continued to hit.

Beltrán was still being shopped around as the trade deadline neared, although Alderson made it known he wanted fair market value for his right fielder and wasn't about to make a move just to dump salary. As the Mets stayed above .500 and other clubs became more desperate, Beltrán's trade value rose.

Beltrán was a catalyst in the Mets' 8–6 win at Cincinnati July 26, going 1-for-3 with two walks, an RBI, and three runs scored. He was an ex-Met hours later, sent to San Francisco for the Giants' top minor league pitching prospect, Zack Wheeler.

"For me, personally, it's a sad day because I love Carlos," said teammate and friend R.A. Dickey. "He's a very complete individual, not only on the field, but off. That's a valuable piece that we're losing and it's kind of sad."[26]

The Giants were desperate for another bat as they were being challenged by Arizona for the NL West title. They owned a four-game lead after Beltrán went 0-for-4 in his Giants debut, a 4–1 triumph at Philadelphia.

Beltrán hit .244 with no homers and two RBIs in his first 11 games with the Giants before a wrist injury forced him onto the disabled list until August 23. By the time he returned to the starting lineup on August 24, the Giants were two games behind the Diamondbacks.

San Francisco continued its fade despite Beltrán , who batted .355 with eight doubles, seven homers, 16 RBIs, and 13 runs scored in his final 32 games. His productivity couldn't quell a free-fall that saw the Giants drop as many as nine games back before finishing eight behind the Diamondbacks.

The trade to the Giants happened 12 years after Beltrán was named the American League Rookie of the Year, and 16 years after he was taken by the Royals in the second round of the draft. He had a career-high 194 hits for the 1999 Royals while batting .293 with 22 homers and 108 RBIs. It began a 10-year stretch in which Beltrán drove in more than 100 runs eight times.

He ran into a little trouble with the Royals in 2000 after spending almost a month on the disabled list with a deep bruise on his right knee. He was suspended by the team August 3 for refusing to report to the team's rehab facility in Florida. He remained on the suspended list until August 18 and was recalled two weeks later before finishing the season with career lows of seven homers, 44 RBIs, and a .247 average in 98 games.

Beltrán rebounded in 2001, hitting .306 with 24 homers and 101 RBIs. He was one of the AL's best outfielders, finishing second in the majors with 14 assists and pacing the circuit with six double plays started. Beltrán also was hard to throw out on the base paths, stealing 31 bases in 32 attempts. He swiped 33 consecutive bases dating to 1999 before he was thrown out August 10.

Beltrán continued to excel as a five-tool player in 2002, batting .273 with 29 homers, 105 RBIs, 35 stolen bases, and 12 outfield assists. He remained the hitting star on a mediocre ballclub in 2003, becoming the first switch-hitter and the 11th player overall to hit .300, belt at least 25 homers, and steal 40 bases in one year. He finished '03 with a career-best .307 average, 26 home runs, and 100 ribbies.

He entered his walk-year in 2004, and the Royals needed to get off to a good start to even think about signing him to a long-term deal. He was hitting .278 with 15 homers and 51 RBIs in his first 69 games, but the Royals were just 28–41 when they decided to ship him to the Astros in a three-team trade with the A's.

Beltrán got off to a so-so start with Houston, batting .235 with 13 homers, 27 RBIs, and 12 stolen bases in his first 44 games. But he sizzled over the next 22 games as the Astros went 19–3 while Beltrán provided 10 home runs, 23 RBIs, and a .346 average. Houston captured the wild-card in large part to Beltrán's offense. What followed in the postseason was truly outstanding.

In his first playoff game, Beltrán was 2-for-3 with a two-run homer and three runs scored as the Astros hammered the Braves 9–3. Two games later, Beltrán smacked another two-run homer and scored twice as Houston took a 2–1 series lead. The Braves forced a fifth game, but that only allowed Beltrán to belt a pair of solo homers while going 4-for-5 with five RBIs and three runs scored to lead the Astros to their first-ever playoff series victory. He hit .455 with four homers and nine RBIs in 22 at-bats for the series.

Beltrán didn't cool off in the NLCS until Game 7, when he went 0-for-3 with a walk and a run scored. He hit .456 with four home runs, five RBIs, and 11 runs scored in the first six games of the series.

Overall in the playoffs, Beltrán had at least two hits and scored two or more runs in seven of the 12 games. He set a major league record by homering in five consecutive postseason contests, doing it from Game 5 of the NLDS to Game 4 of the NLCS. The streak helped him become the second player ever to belt eight home runs in a single postseason. His 21 runs scored broke a major league play-off mark, as well.

Beltrán said all the right things during the playoffs, letting everyone know he truly wanted to stay with the Astros but was open to other ideas. It appeared he might actually remain in Houston until the Mets ponied up more dough following the signing of Martinez. Beltrán inked the largest contract in team history to date, although his agent reportedly gave the Yankees one more chance to top the bid. The Yankees declined, putting Beltrán in Queens long enough to reach the playoffs again.

ML debut	Royals vs. A's, 9/14/98
Mets debut	@ Reds, 4/4/05
1st ML hit	single vs. Buddy Groom, A's, 9/14/98 (with Royals)
1st Mets hit	2-run homer vs. Paul Wilson, @ Reds, 4/4/05
1st ML homer	solo homer vs. Jaime Navarro, @ White Sox, 4/10/99 (with Royals)
1st Mets homer	2-run homer vs. Paul Wilson, @ Reds, 4/4/05
1st ML RBI	RBI triple vs. Jim Poole, @ Indians, 9/19/98
1st Mets RBI	2-run homer vs. Paul Wilson, @ Reds, 4/4/05
Most hits, ML game	4, 20 times, 8 times with Mets
Most homers, ML/Mets game	3, @ Rockies, 5/12/11
Most RBI, ML game	6, 4 times, 3 times with Royals
Most RBI, Mets game	6, @ Rockies, 5/12/11

Acquired: Signed as a free agent 1/13/05.
Deleted: Traded to the Giants with cash for Zack Wheeler, 7/27/11.
AL Rookie of the Year: 1999
NL All-Star, 2004, 2005, 2006, 2007, 2011
NL Gold Glove: 2006, 2007, 2008
NL Silver Slugger: 2006, 2007

Hubie Brooks

Infielder, Outfielder Bats right, throws right
Born: 9/24/56   Los Angeles, California
Height: 6'0"   Weight: 200   #39, #7

Hubie Brooks Mets Career

YEAR	GP	AB	R	H	2B	3B	HR	RBI	K	BB	SB	AVG	SLG	OBP
1980	24	81	8	25	2	1	1	10	9	5	1	.309	.395	.364
1981	98	358	34	110	21	2	4	38	65	23	9	.307	.411	.345
1982	126	457	40	114	21	2	2	40	76	28	6	.249	.317	.297
1983	150	586	53	147	18	4	5	58	96	24	6	.251	.321	.284
1984	153	561	61	159	23	2	16	73	79	48	6	.283	.417	.341
1991	103	357	48	85	11	1	16	50	62	44	3	.238	.409	.324
TOTAL	654	2400	244	640	96	12	44	269	387	172	31	.267	.372	.318

ML Career

YEARS	GP	AB	R	H	2B	3B	HR	RBI	K	BB	SB	AVG	SLG	OBP
80-94	1645	5974	656	1608	290	31	149	824	1005	387	64	.269	.403	.315

Joe McDonald is one of the more maligned general managers in Mets history. The team hit rock-bottom during his watch after the farm system was allowed to stagnate under previous GM Bob Scheffing. McDonald also never landed a big free agent because the Mets never allowed him to spend any significant money, not that many free agents were willing to play for one of baseball's bottom feeders.

However, McDonald revived the minor league operations by drafting Mookie Wilson, Wally Backman, Mike Scott, Neil Allen, and Tim Leary.

One of McDonald's best moves was taking Hubie Brooks with the third overall pick in the 1978 draft, although Kirk Gibson was still on the board when the Tigers took him at No. 12.

Brooks and Wilson became the poster kids on the new-look Mets. They hustled, smiled, and played good baseball, something that had been an infrequent happenstance at Shea for too many years. Brooks eventually became the best clutch hitter on a ballclub in dire need of a two-out hit.

Hubert Brooks Jr. was sent to Double A Jackson immediately after signing his first pro contract, but he hit only .216 with three homers and 16 RBIs in 153 at-bats after lighting up pitchers at Arizona State. He found his groove in 1979, hitting a team-high .305 for Jackson without displaying the power that would make him one of the National League's top-hitting infielders in the 1980s.

Brooks also played a few games in '79 for Tidewater before hitting .297 in 113 games for the 1980 Tides. He spent most of 1980 as the Tides' right fielder but would settle in at third base when the Mets recalled him in September.

The Los Angeles–born Brooks quickly showed he could hit major league pitching, batting .309 with a homer and 10 RBIs in 81 at-bats for the '80 Mets. He collected his first big-league hit off Rick Wise September 6 and cracked his first home run against Jim Otten October 4. Brooks had eight multi-hit games in 23 starts to secure the starting third base position for the 1981 season.

Brooks showed his premiere was no fluke by batting .307 in 1981, eighth-highest in the National League and the best by a Met since Cleon Jones hit .319 in 1971. He led the Mets in average, hits (110) and doubles (21) while finishing second to Dave Kingman with 38 RBIs during the strike-shortened season. Brooks finished third in the NL Rookie of the Year balloting and was the league's player of the week for September 14 through September 20. He remained a work-in-progress with the glove, finishing the season with 21 errors in 278 chances. Brooks tied a major league mark for third basemen by committing three errors in an inning May 10, a day after he made a huge defensive stop to preserve a victory.

A hamstring injury was a reason for his sub-par 1982 season. He batted .256 in his first 23 games despite hitting streaks of seven and eight games. Brooks brought his average up to .276 with a double June 1, but he pulled his left hamstring running out the base hit. The injury eventually landed him on the disabled list for the first time and caused him to miss 34 of 45 games from June 2 to July 22.

He hit three doubles August 6 to begin a 22-game stretch in which he hit .349 to lift his average to .276. He batted only .171 in his final 32 games, including a season-ending 1-for-24 slide that left him with a .249 mark.

Brooks had an odd year in 1983, batting just .251 overall but leading the league with a .354 average (51-for-144) with runners in scoring position. He hit .279 in the first half of the season but only .219 in the second, leaving some within the organization that he didn't have a good enough stick to overcome his fielding flaw. The Mets even tried him at second base for a few innings in September, but the team didn't have a better option at third.

Brooks now owned a .267 average with only 12 homers, 62 doubles, and 146 RBIs since being recalled in September 1980. He had the fewest home runs among National League third sackers with at least 1,000 at-bats from 1981 to 1983. He also had the second-fewest RBIs and the third-fewest doubles during that span. Brooks wasn't flashing much speed, and his 66 errors at third was an appalling figure.

He finally put it all together in 1984…and made himself trade bait in the process. Brooks set then-career highs with 159 hits, 23 doubles, 16 homers, 73 RBIs, and 48 walks while hitting .283. He set a team record by hitting safely in 24 straight games from May 1 to June 1, batting .398 in the process. His season average was at .323 by June 22, when he already had nine home runs to double his career home run production.

Brooks had helped the Mets stay in contention for the NL East crown by hitting .295 through August 28, when general manager Frank Cashen acquired third baseman Ray Knight from the Astros. Manager Davey Johnson asked Brooks to shift to shortstop to give Knight regular playing time, but the move backfired as Knight struggled while Brooks looked uncomfortable defensively at short. Hubie hit only .223 as a shortstop and compiled a .209 mark after September 1.

The trial run at shortstop served as a showcase for other major league GMs. The Mets seemed pretty set at six positions but were now lacking at third base and catcher. Cashen and the Expos opened discussions about a trade that would send Gary Carter to the Mets, but the All-Star catcher wouldn't come cheap. New York sent four players to the Expos for Carter, with Brooks being the most polished of the four players.

Brooks wasn't the league's smoothest shortstop in 1985, but he was the most productive at the plate. He won the first of his two Silver Slugger awards after batting .269 with 13 homers, 34 doubles, and a career-high 100 RBIs. He would have been a significant upgrade from what the Mets had at third and short in '85, but he was hardly missed as Carter hit .281 with 32 homers and 100 RBIs.

An All-Star berth finally came to Brooks in 1986. He was named the NL Player of the Month for May after hitting .341 with seven homers and 24 RBIs in 23 games. Hubie had an even higher batting average for June, posting a .354 mark to lift his season total to .336. He battled a sore hand much of the season but owned a .340 average on August 1 when he tried to avoid a Roger McDowell pitch at Shea Stadium. Brooks landed on his left thumb, tearing ligaments and causing him to undergo season-ending surgery two days later. He was approaching the finest season by an NL shortstop since Ernie Banks in 1960 before the injury. Brooks won his second straight Silver Slugger by finishing with a .340 average, 14 homers, and 58 RBIs in 80 games.

Brooks was ready by Opening Day 1987, but he was back on the DL just three days into the season after an errant pitch left him with a fractured right wrist. He was back in the lineup by May 25 and owned a .305 average after going 5-for-5 with a two-run homer and six RBIs against the Phillies June 12. He was named to the All-Star Game for the second consecutive season a few weeks later, but his trip to the Midsummer Classic was soon followed by a 20-for-129 (.155) slump that dipped his average to .241 by August 29. Brooks salvaged the season by tying a team record with 29 RBIs in September. He finished the year leading all NL shortstops with 14 homers, and his 72 RBIs were second only to Ozzie Smith of the Cardinals.

Hubie's fielding never came close to rivaling Smith's, so the Expos decided to convert him into an outfielder, moving him back to a position he played for Tidewater in 1980. The move paid off in 1988 as he hit a career-high 20 homers, drove in 90 runs, and hit .279 in 151 games. He became a free agent in 1989 after producing 14 homers and 70 RBIs.

Brooks signed with his hometown team, accepting a three-year contract with the Dodgers. He hit .266 with 20 homers, 91 RBIs, and a career-high 74 runs in his only year with the team.

Hubie Brooks (right) with Ray Knight (left)

The Dodgers moved him back to the Mets in a trade that brought Bob Ojeda to L.A. Brooks was returning just as Vince Coleman was coming and Darryl Strawberry was going.

A series of injuries killed the Mets' postseason hopes in 1991. Brooks went down for the season August 18 because of a pinched nerve in his neck. He still managed to hit 16 homers in 357 at-bats while playing right field. But his return to New York lasted only until the Mets traded him to the Angels for Dave Gallagher in December 1991.

Brooks spent his last three seasons in the American League, playing for the Angels and Royals before he was released by Kansas City in July 1994.

ML/Mets debut	@ Padres, 9/4/80
1st ML/Mets hit	single vs. Rick Wise, @ Padres, 9/6/80
1st ML/Mets homer	solo homer vs. Jim Otten, @ Cardinals, 10/4/80
1st ML/Mets RBI	RBI single vs. Mike Krukow, Cubs, 9/12/80
Most hits, ML game	5, 3 times
Most hits, Mets game	5, @ Cardinals, 6/28/83
Most homers, ML game	2, twice
Most homers, Mets game	2, @ Braves, 6/20/91
Most RBI, ML game	6, Expos vs. Phillies, 6/12/87
Most RBI, Mets game	4, 7 times

Acquired: Selected by the Mets in the first round (3rd overall) in the June 1978 draft.

Deleted: Traded to the Expos with Mike Fitzgerald, Floyd Youmans and Herm Winningham for Gary Carter, 12/10/84.

Gary Carter

Catcher	Batted right, threw right
Born: 4/8/54	Culver City, California
Died: 2/16/12	Weight: 210 #8
Height: 6'2"	

Gary Carter Mets Career

YEAR	GP	AB	R	H	2B	3B	HR	RBI	K	BB	SB	AVG	SLG	OBP
1985	149	555	83	156	17	1	32	100	46	69	1	.281	.488	.365
1986	132	490	81	125	14	2	24	105	63	62	1	.255	.439	.337
1987	139	523	55	123	18	2	20	83	73	42	0	.235	.392	.290
1988	130	455	39	110	16	2	11	46	52	34	0	.242	.358	.301
1989	50	153	14	28	8	0	2	15	15	12	0	.183	.275	.241
TOTAL	600	2176	272	542	73	7	89	349	249	219	2	.249	.412	.319

ML Career

YEARS	GP	AB	R	H	2B	3B	HR	RBI	K	BB	SB	AVG	SLG	OBP
74-92	2295	7971	1025	2092	371	31	324	1225	997	848	39	.262	.439	.335

There are just three players in Mets history who helped the club win a World Series and later earned induction into the Baseball Hall of Fame: Tom Seaver, Nolan Ryan, and Gary Carter. Of the three, Carter may be the least appreciated.

Seaver and Ryan were voted into the Hall in their first year of eligibility, each named on 98.8 percent of the ballots. Carter had to wait six years of eligibility to gain entry into Cooperstown, as if the voters had forgotten he batted .274 while averaging 25 home runs and 89 RBIs from 1977 to 1986. He ranked ninth in the majors in home runs and eighth in RBIs during that period despite playing the game's most physically challenging position.

He reached baseball's pinnacle by winning a World Series with the 1986 Mets, but his numerous offensive accomplishments with the team were eventually dwarfed by Mike Piazza, diminishing Carter's stature among younger Mets fans. But there's no forgetting Carter's arrival in New York was a signal the franchise was serious about winning a championship. Carter was an incredibly important part of their '86 title run, nurturing a young pitching staff and serving as one of the team's top power hitters. He was part of an outstanding squad that included several players who appeared headed for Cooperstown. Carter was the only one who made it, although much of his Hall of Fame résumé was built up during his days with the Montreal Expos.

Gary Edmund Carter was born in Culver City, California, and lived in the state until he was drafted by the Expos. He graduated from Sunny Hills High School in Fullerton, where his scholastic ability equaled his athletic prowess. Carter won 11 letters and was named Sunny Hills' Athlete of the Year as a senior after captaining the baseball, football, and basketball teams through two seasons. But he was also a member of the National Honor Society from 1968 to 1972 and graduated among the top 50 in a class of more than 2,000.

Carter had the perfect family life in his preteens. His father, Jim, coached him in Little League. His older brother, Gordy, was a budding athlete who was drafted by the Angels in the second round of the 1968 draft. His mother, Inge, kept the household balanced amid numerous ballgames and school events.

Inge was diagnosed with leukemia in 1965 and died shortly after Gary's 12th birthday, leaving the three males to forge a tighter bond. Gary immersed himself in sports and kept up his grades while tending to his additional household responsibilities.

"For a time, I thought football would be my future," Carter wrote in his 1987 book, *Dream Season*. "I was high school All-American as a sophomore and as a junior. I loved the emotion of the game, that feeling of proving yourself. I couldn't play my senior year because of a knee injury, but more than 100 big colleges offered me scholarships."[27]

Carter eventually signed a letter of intent to play football at UCLA before the Expos altered those plans by selecting him in the third round of the June 1972 draft. He signed with Montreal five days after his high school graduation and was assigned to Cocoa of the Florida Rookie League.

Carter finished the 1972 season with West Palm Beach of the Florida State League, where he hit .320 with a .460 on-base percentage in 63 plate appearances over 20 games.

Playing for the Expos at the time was a great way to advance through the minors if a player had any semblance of talent. The franchise won 70 or more games in three of its first four years in existence but did so with a veteran crew until the Expos acquired Ken Singleton, Mike Jorgensen, and Tim Foli for the popular Rusty Staub in the spring of 1972. Carter was immediately pegged as a top prospect and was assigned to Double A Quebec less than a year out of high school. He didn't disappoint, hitting .253 in 439 at-bats but walking 63 times while producing 15 homers, 16 doubles, 68 RBIs, and 65 runs scored in 130 games for the Carnavals at age 19. He capped the year by playing a few games at Triple A Peninsula, hitting .280 over 25 at-bats. After the season, Carter emerged as the MVP of the Caribbean World Series by helping Caguas of the Puerto Rican League win the championship.

He opened the 1974 season in the Triple A International League and continued to display outstanding power for his age, finishing second to Jim Rice on the circuit with 23 home runs and 83 RBIs. Carter also hit .268 and recorded a .354 on-base percentage while leading all league catchers with 114 games, 794 putouts, 65 assists, 15 double plays, and a .990 fielding percentage. He was named the top prospect at Triple A and earned his first major league promotion after helping Memphis win the South Division title.

Carter made his major league debut against the Mets on September 16, going 0–4 against Randy Sterling and Tug McGraw in a 3–2 loss. It would be Sterling's only major league victory and McGraw's final save as a Met. One day later, Carter collected his first major league hit with a single off Jon Matlack as a pinch-hitter in Game 1 of

a doubleheader, fueling a two-run seventh that led Montreal to a 3–2 win. He followed that by going 1-for-2 with a run scored off Tom Seaver to aid a 4–0 victory.

Carter had two hits in four of his next five games to finish with a .407 average in 27 at-bats. He produced his first three major league RBIs in an 11–2 rout of the Cubs in Game 2 of a doubleheader on September 25, and belted his first career home run off Hall-of-Famer Steve Carlton to lead a 3–1 win over the Phillies in his final game of the season.

Carter entered 1975 having proven he could hit major league pitching. The problem for the Expos was finding him a place to play. Catcher Barry Foote performed well at the plate in 1974, causing Carter to open the '75 campaign as Montreal's starting right fielder.

Carter still had a football mentality on the diamond. Behind the plate, he eschewed the safer swipe tag for bone-jarring collisions. In the outfield, Carter treated fences like blocking sleds, running into them as if he figured they'd give first. It was a theory that prevailed until he lost a battle with the bricks and ivy at Wrigley Field, knocking himself silly after running into the wall. In some respects, Carter may have prolonged his career by becoming the Expos' full-time catcher in June 1976.

He already had established himself as a major league hitter and immediately showed his trial run in September 1974 was no fluke, going 3-for-4 with an RBI single and a three-run homer in the Expos' 1975 season opener. He was now hitting .452 with 10 RBIs through his first 10 major league games.

He had three more multi-hit games in April 1975, giving him a .300 average through 21 contests before a seven-game slump knocked his average down to .213 by May 7. He belted his second homer of the season on May 12, beginning a 47-game stretch in which he batted .333 with seven home runs, 29 RBIs, and 15 runs scored through July 1. Coincidentally, Carter started hitting the same day he made his first start at catcher.

The hot streak raised his batting average back to .300 and earned him a berth on the National League's All-Star roster…as an outfielder. He took over for Pete Rose in left field before the bottom of the ninth inning of the Midsummer Classic and grabbed a fly ball hit by Rod Carew for the final out as the NL beat the AL 6–3 at Milwaukee.

Carter continued to see more action in right field than catcher until passing a slumping Foote on the depth chart in September. He hit safely in 11 of his last 12 games and finished with a .270 average, 20 doubles, 17 home runs, and 68 RBIs. Although those numbers are modest compared to Carter's eventual standards, he led the team in runs batted in and was second to Mike Jorgensen in home runs and slugging. Carter picked up nine of 24 votes for NL Rookie of the Year but finished second to San Francisco pitcher John Montefusco in the balloting.

Montreal ended up fifth in the NL East at 77–85 in '75, a two-win decline over its previous two seasons. The

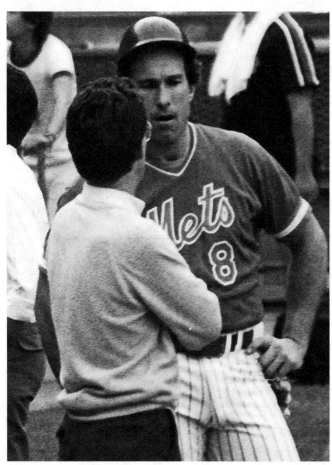

Gary Carter. Photo courtesy of David Ferry

regression led the Expos to fire Gene Mauch, their original manager. Montreal quickly demonstrated that Mauch wasn't the problem, going 43–85 under Karl Kuehl and finishing the season with a major league-worst 55–107 mark.

Carter's inactivity in 1976 led to the team's dismal record. He broke his left thumb in an outfield collision at Jarry Park on May 6 and broke a bone in his right hand while catching on September 19. The injuries limited Carter to 91 games as he hit only .219 with six home runs and 38 RBIs. However, he was promoted to starting catcher when Foote was traded on June 15, a move that allowed the Expos to utilize their young stable of outfielders.

Ellis Valentine was Montreal's starting center fielder for most of 1975 and was joined on the major league roster by fellow outfielders Warren Cromartie and Andre Dawson in September 1976. Carter and the outfield trio would help the Expos pass the Mets in the 1977 standings under first-year manager Dick Williams while playing their first season at Olympic Stadium.

Carter was the leader of the team's offense in '77, pacing the team with 31 home runs, a .356 on-base percentage, a .525 slugging average, and an .881 OPS. He also was second to veteran Tony Perez with 84 RBIs while ending up third with a .284 batting average.

Carter displayed superb defense in his first full season as a major league catcher, recording a .990 fielding percentage and throwing out 33 percent of his 168 base runners. Only Duffy Dyer had a higher fielding percentage among National League catchers.

Carter appeared in 157 games for the 1978 Expos but was unable to duplicate his '77 stats, hitting .255 with 20 home runs and 72 RBIs. He still managed to lead the team with 62 walks and 128 runs produced but failed to crack the top two in any other major offensive category. However, he threw out 42 percent of his potential base-stealers, committed just one passed ball and recorded a .989 fielding average to rank among the top four in each category among NL catchers. Carter now had a reputation as a tremendous two-way backstop just as Johnny Bench was beginning his decline.

Carter and Bench were among five catchers named to the NL All-Star team in 1979, with Bob Boone serving as the starter. Carter replaced Boone in the fifth inning of the Midsummer Classic in Seattle and poked an RBI single in his first at-bat to tie the game 5–5 before participating in one of the greatest defensive plays in All-Star history.

The American League had runners on first and second with two out in the eighth when Graig Nettles laced a single to right fielder Dave Parker, who grabbed the ball on one hop and fired a strike to Carter with a hard-charging Brian Downing heading to the plate. Carter grabbed the perfect throw and blocked the plate before tagging Downing for the final out of the inning.

"He knocked him off the plate!" yelled NBC broadcaster and former catcher Joe Garagiola as he described the play. "What a tag by Carter! A tremendous play by Carter! Oh, baby! What a play!"

Parker made one of the greatest tosses in All-Star Game history, but Garagiola couldn't get over the way Carter handled the throw while keeping himself in position to prevent Downing from scoring.

A play like that on national television only enhanced Carter's reputation as a defensive standout, especially after the NL won the game 7–6. It didn't hurt that he led the league in putouts and assists by a catcher while throwing out 46.8 percent of his base-stealers.

Carter also did a little hitting in 1979, batting .283 with 22 home runs, 26 doubles, 75 RBIs, and 76 runs scored. He ranked second on the team with a .338 on-base percentage and a .485 slugging average while handling a pitching staff that was first in the NL with a 3.14 ERA.

It was a breakthrough year for the Expos, who posted their first winning season at 95–65 and spent 81 days atop the NL East. Montreal led the division by as many as 6½ games and was in first place heading into the final week of the season before losing five of its last seven to finish two games behind the Pirates.

The division race spiked attendance in Montreal as the Expos finished fourth in the league with more than 2.1 million, almost tripling the Mets' turnstile count in '79.

The near-miss also led to high expectations as the Expos opened the 1980 season.

Carter won the first of his three straight Gold Glove awards in 1980, made the NL All-Star team again and drove in over 100 runs for the first time in his career. He topped the Expos with 29 home runs while providing 25 doubles, 101 ribbies, 76 runs scored, and a .264 batting average. Montreal again challenged for the NL East crown, leading the division for almost half the season before falling into a first-place tie with the Phils heading into a season-ending three-game set with Philadelphia in Montreal. The Phils wrapped up a playoff berth by winning the first two games as Carter went 0-for-7 in a pair of one-run losses.

The Expos finally earned a postseason bid in 1981 with help from a players strike. The work stoppage shut down major league ballparks for 50 days and caused commissioner Bowie Kuhn to declare a split season, with the winner of each half earning a spot in MLB's first-ever division series.

The Phillies were declared the first-half winner after compiling a 34–21 record before the strike went into effect in June 11. Montreal was 4½ games back after opening the season a disappointing 30–25 behind an inconsistent Carter, who hit .299 over his first 20 games before recording a .207 average in his 30 games before the strike.

The second half represented a clean slate for the Expos while the Phillies played lackluster ball, knowing they had already locked up a postseason berth. Carter was terrific in his first 16 games after the strike, homering five times and driving in 20 runs during August. He started every game after August 22 and produced 18 RBIs in Montreal's final 34 games to help them win the second-half title at 30–23, setting up a playoff meeting with the Phils and putting Carter in the postseason for the first time.

Carter hit an RBI double in his first playoff at-bat as the Expos knocked off the Phillies 3–1 in the NLDS opener. He powered Montreal to a 3–1 victory in Game 2, smacking a two-run homer to put the Expos ahead 3–0 in the third inning.

The Phils won the next two games despite Carter, who went 5-for-8 with one homer, two doubles, and three RBIs. But the Expos advanced as Carter went 1-for-4 in the deciding fifth game while handling Steve Rogers' six-hitter in a 3–0 shutout at Philadelphia.

Carter was the hitting star in the series, leading the Expos with a .421 average, eight hits, two homers, three doubles, and six RBIs. He produced seven of Montreal's 16 runs while compiling an .895 slugging average and handling a staff that posted a 2.05 ERA.

The Expos had home field advantage for the best-of-five NLCS against the Dodgers. Carter hit safely in all five games, again topping Montreal with a .438 average, seven hits, and three runs scored.

He went 1-for-3 with a walk in the decisive fifth game while the rest of the Expos managed just two hits. Carter called a nice game for Rogers, who limited the Dodgers to six hits in a complete-game victory. Unfortunately for the Expos, Rogers' sixth hit allowed was the difference in the series as Rick Monday slammed a two-out homer in the top of the ninth to put the Dodgers ahead 2–1.

The Expos' season hung in the balance as Carter stepped to the plate with two out in the bottom of the ninth against Fernando Valenzuela. Carter ran the count to 3–2 before walking, and Larry Parrish followed with a base-on-balls to put the potential series-winning run on base. But Bob Welch relieved Valenzuela and got Jerry White to hit a grounder to second, leaving the Expos 270 feet away from a World Series berth.

The playoff run helped turn Montreal into a rabid baseball city, but it would be the team's only postseason appearance before the franchise was relocated to Washington in 2005. For the record, Carter is the Expos' all-time postseason leader in batting (.429), one-base percentage (.488), slugging (.714), hits (15), homers (2), doubles (4), and RBIs (6). He hit safely in all 10 games, another Montreal playoff record.

The Expos posted winning records over the next two seasons without coming close to another playoff berth despite Carter, who had become the best catcher in the majors. Carter won the Silver Slugger for the second straight year after hitting .293 with 27 homers and 93 RBIs in 1982. He was an All-Star for the fifth straight time in 1983 before finishing with a .270 average, 17 home runs, 79 RBIs, and a career-high 37 doubles.

Carter's best offensive season with the Expos was his last as he set career highs with 175 hits, a .294 average, and a league-leading 106 RBIs while hitting 27 home runs and 32 doubles in 1984. He also appeared in a career-high 159 games and ruined the Mets' home opener by hitting a grand slam off Ron Darling in a 10–0 win for the Expos.

But the Expos ended the '84 season in fifth place at 78–83 despite Carter's heroics. It was the first time in five years that Montreal had posted a losing record, which led to a lot of finger-pointing. Pete Rose opened the season with the Expos and later said he had never been on a team that accepted losing so well. A large portion of Montreal's 1981 playoff roster was still with the ballclub in '84, causing management to wonder what was going wrong.

Part of the problem regarded team chemistry. Carter had become one of Montreal's most popular athletes, putting him in the same breath as Canadiens stars Guy Lafleur and Larry Robinson. Carter was the go-to guy when the media needed a quote, either in English or French. He had taken the effort to enroll in a French Berlitz course and became fluent in Quebec's two primary languages while a majority of his teammates loathed the thought of even answering a question in English. Carter reaped the benefits of his hard work by garnering several endorsement deals and becoming a media darling.

Some of it may have been self-serving on Carter's part as he tapped into new territory by becoming a bilingual spokesman in a Canadian province that greatly appreciated it. But many within the Expos clubhouse resented his popularity and his accessibility with the media, pinning him with the nicknames "Camera Carter" and "Teeth."

Through his final days, Carter spoke highly of the ex-teammates who belittled him behind his back. What he couldn't understand was how Expos management decided he was the reason behind the club's ambivalent play since the '81 NLCS.

Meanwhile, the Mets finally got off the mat in 1984 and finished 90–72, the second-best record in team history at the time. They led the NL East by 4½ games in late July before finishing second to the Cubs in a season that became a renaissance at Shea Stadium. The Mets had an outstanding group of young pitchers in Dwight Gooden, Ron Darling, Sid Fernandez, Walt Terrell, Bruce Berenyi, and closer Jesse Orosco. The lineup included Keith Hernandez, Darryl Strawberry, Mookie Wilson, Hubie Brooks, Wally Backman, and George Foster.

The '84 Mets set several team records for offense but were in need of another potent bat that could match up with the Cubs' lineup. Rookie Mike Fitzgerald was the No. 1 catcher behind the plate and did an admirable job handling the pitching staff, but he also brought up the rear in many offensive categories by hitting .242 with two homers and 33 RBIs.

Mets general manager Frank Cashen went to the winter meetings intent on finding another lethal bat to secure a playoff berth. The Expos were ready to part with Carter and let Cashen know he was available at the right price. Cashen knew Carter would solve his two biggest problems and moved quickly to broker a deal.

Carter was acquired by the Mets on December 10, 1984, a trade that is among Cashen's very best as a general manager. Cashen shipped Brooks and Fitzgerald to Montreal, along with prospects Floyd Youmans and Herm Winningham. It was a very heavy price to pay as Brooks had just tied the team-record hitting streak while Youmans and Winningham were considered among the Mets' two best players in the minors. But the trade also demonstrated the Mets were ready to win a pennant in 1985, thus turning the team into the No. 1 baseball attraction in New York.

With the Mets, Carter was allowed to blend in on a ballclub that was desperate for his type of talent. Several Mets weren't huge fans of Carter's perceived personality before the trade, but they loved him as a hitter and grew to like him as a person. They now understood that his zeal for the game was genuine, and appreciated that he was another player who could absorb the ever-growing stream of media in the clubhouse. Yes, he managed to land a national television commercial for Ivory Soap before his first at-bat as a Met. But whereas the Expos chafed at the media attention bestowed on Carter, the Mets couldn't care less if he became co-host of *The Today Show* and the MC of *Wheel of Fortune* since they also knew he might be the final piece of a championship puzzle.

The Mets' 1985 training camp was a three-ring media circus only 12 months after the team was starving for any positive publicity. Gooden was featured on *60 Minutes,* while other segments of the national media jumped on the bandwagon. Before the Mets embarked for New York, *Sports Illustrated* had George Plimpton pen a fictional piece on Mets prospect Sidd Finch, a highly eccentric pitcher who was well educated, played the French horn, and could throw 130 mph. The Finch piece was published in the April 1 edition of the magazine and was meant as an April Fool's joke, but Plimpton's straight-faced prose and the accompanying photos—through the cooperation of the Mets—had many readers believing Finch was a real person.

While Finch was fictitious, Carter's season debut with his new team was storybook. The Mets hosted the Cardinals on a bitterly cold afternoon that was unseasonable even by Opening Day standards. Carter was hit by a Joaquin Andujar pitch in his first at-bat but remained in the game, hitting a double and helping Dwight Gooden labor through six-plus innings before the Mets' young ace left with a 5–2 lead. The Redbirds chipped away against reliever Doug Sisk and tied the game in the ninth before the Mets left the bases loaded in the bottom half for the second straight inning to extend the game.

It was still 5–5 when Carter came to the plate with one out in the bottom of the 10th. Neil Allen struck out Hernandez for the first out before hanging a breaking ball that Carter swatted into the St. Louis bullpen. One game into his Mets career and Carter already was a New York hero, just as the team had hoped.

Carter hit safely in his next five games and was batting .325 through 11 contests before his average dropped to .231 by May 3. He hit a two-run homer in a 14–2 loss to the Reds on May 4, launched a tiebreaking grand slam in the eighth inning of a 5–3 victory versus the Braves on May 7, and smacked a three-run double in a 5–0 shutout of the Phillies three days later. But another slump ensued, trimming his average to .226 through his first 33 games as a Met.

His inconsistent start was quickly forgotten after he hit .336 with a .412 on-base percentage, six homers, 16 RBIs, and 19 runs scored during a 32-game stretch from May 22 through June 26. He had 11 multi-hit games during that span, including a pair of four-hit performances and a three-hit game. However, the Mets went just 15–17 in those 32 games, spending much of that time without an injured Strawberry. Many of Carter's teammates battled deep slumps that allowed the Cardinals to climb back into the race despite a 14–17 start.

St. Louis had been a "win with speed" ballclub since 1981 and took that philosophy to new heights by promoting outfielder Vince Coleman in mid-April. The Cards went 5-for-5 in stolen base attempts against Carter in a win over the Mets on April 23, three days after Coleman's promotion. St. Louis later stole six bases against Carter in a doubleheader split on June 9 and finished the season 27-for-33 (81.8 percent) versus the new Mets catcher, although the pitching staff deserved a lot of blame for its inability to keep the Cardinals close to the bag. Of the New York starters, only Ron Darling had a better-than-average pickoff move. Carter helped his own cause by picking off a pair of Cardinals during the season.

Although Carter had trouble with the St. Louis speedsters, he also threw out 45 of 117 runners (38.5 percent) against the rest of the National League while compiling the circuit's second-best fielding percentage among catchers at .992.

Carter was voted to the National League starting lineup in the All-Star Game for the fifth straight year, although he was unable to play due to a right knee injury that would require off-season surgery. The knee problem cropped up nine days after he collected five hits in one of the wildest games in Mets history, a 19-inning, 16–13 victory in Atlanta on July 4.

A pair of lengthy rain delays already had turned the Mets-Braves game into a marathon by the ninth inning. Carter delivered a pair of RBI singles during the first four innings to help the Mets take a 7–4 lead. But New York needed a run-scoring single by Lenny Dykstra in the ninth to send the game into extra innings, turning it into a classic.

The Mets blew leads in the 13th and 18th innings as the Braves countered with home runs in each comeback, including the only major league blast by pitcher Rick Camp. Carter led off the top of the 19th with his fifth hit of the game, igniting a five-run rally to make it 16–11. It was the first five-hit game for Carter, who tied his career high with the Giants five years later.

But New York still had trouble putting away the Braves. Terry Harper laced a two-run single with two out in the 19th, six innings after his two-run homer prolonged the silliness. The game finally ended when Darling fanned Camp, completing the Mets' longest victory since a 19-inning clash with the Dodgers in 1973. The five-hit game raised Carter's average to .278, but it would be almost two months before he cracked the .280 barrier.

Carter opened August by driving in 13 runs in 11 games before collecting just one RBI in his next 11 contests. He owned a .268 average with 17 homers and 62 RBIs through 115 games as the Mets headed into a four-game series in San Francisco at the end of August. That's when Carter began to carry the team on his back.

The Mets were three games behind the Cardinals when they opened the Giants series. Carter homered in each of his three games at San Francisco while going 5-for-12 as New York split four games to pull within two games of St. Louis before heading to San Diego.

The Mets were without Hernandez for the start of the Padres series while he testified in the Pittsburgh drug trial, putting the onus on Carter, Strawberry, and Foster to produce. Carter put together one of the greatest series in team history, collecting three hits in each game while providing five homers, 10 RBIs, and eight runs scored. He went 3-for-5 with an RBI and two runs scored as the Mets took the opener 12–4 to close within one game of the NL East lead. One day later, Carter tied a team record by slamming three homers while driving in six runs in an 8–3 rout. He capped the series by homering twice to become the first Met to sock five round-trippers over consecutive games as New York rolled to a 9–2 win.

The Mets followed the San Diego sweep by taking two of three in Los Angeles as Carter collected hits in each game, including a home run in a 14-inning victory in the series finale. In a make-or-break road trip, Carter had hits in all nine of his games and provided a .474 average with nine homers, 15 RBIs, and 13 runs scored. The Mets went 7–3 on the road trip, putting them in position to take control of the NL East race as they returned home to host the Cardinals.

New York grabbed the division lead by winning two of three from St. Louis, but the Cardinals moved back on top while the Mets won eight of their next 13 games. Carter was superb during the 13-game stretch, hitting .360 with five home runs, 18 RBIs, and eight runs scored. But the Mets continued to lose ground, falling four games back heading into a series finale in Pittsburgh on the next-to-last Sunday of the season.

The Mets split the first two games against the Pirates despite little help from Carter, who went 1-for-9 with an RBI and a run scored. Carter was 0-for-2 with two walks in his first four plate appearances of the getaway game, and New York trailed 7–6 in the ninth until Howard Johnson launched a homer off Cecilio Guante.

Hernandez hit a one-out single against Larry McWilliams in the 10th, giving Carter another opportunity to be the hero in a late-season game. Carter was just 1-for-11 in the series before clubbing a two-run blast to lead a 9–7 victory. The outcome, coupled with the Cardinals' loss in Montreal, brought New York within three games of St. Louis heading into a three-game series at Busch Stadium.

A sweep would leave the Mets and Cardinals tied with three games remaining. Carter doubled in the opener, but the game remained scoreless until Strawberry rocketed a Ken Dayley pitch off the stadium clock in the 11th inning to lead a 1–0 victory. Carter came through in Game 2, lacing an RBI single in the first inning to put the Mets ahead to stay in a 5–2 victory that cut the deficit to one game. Carter also had a hit in the third game, but the Cardinals claimed a 4–2 win to move two games ahead of New York with three to play. St. Louis clinched the division when the Mets lost 8–3 to the Expos in the next-to-last game of the year.

Carter earned NL Player of the Month honors in September/October for hitting .320 with 13 homers, 36 RBIs, and 24 runs scored in 32 games. The strong finish gave him a .281 average with 32 home runs and 100 RBIs, allowing Carter to join Frank Thomas and Dave Kingman as the only Mets to hit at least 30 homers in a season. Rusty

Staub was the only other Met with a 100-RBI season until Carter became the first player in team history with at least 30 homers and 100 ribbies.

Carter's outstanding climax couldn't hide the Mets' roster weaknesses. The team was lacking a fifth starter and a productive right-handed hitter at second base, deficiencies that were evident during the Mets' series with the Redbirds in September. General manager Frank Cashen, who had brought Carter to Queens, moved quickly to remedy the situation by acquiring lefty pitcher Bob Ojeda from the Red Sox and second baseman Tim Teufel from Minnesota. Both deals cost the Mets nothing more than prospects and gave the team confidence heading into 1986.

Manager Davey Johnson loved his roster as the team assembled for 1986 spring training. He declared in camp that the Mets would dominate the division, a seemingly boastful prediction after his ballclub finished three games behind the Cards and went 8–10 against them in the season series. But as Hall-of-Fame Cardinals pitcher Dizzy Dean said, it ain't braggin' if you can do it. And the Mets did it.

None of the Mets' non-platoon players had a "career" year in 1986. They didn't have to. The starting pitching was superb following the off-season acquisition of Ojeda. Teufel served as the right handed-hitting answer to Backman's left-handed production at second, thus deepening the lineup. Like the Carter acquisition, they were two trades in which Cashen didn't give up any important pieces of his major league roster to improve the ballclub.

The bench was strong, the bullpen was stronger, and the defense was crisp enough to support the pitchers. The question was whether Carter and the pitchers could stop the Cardinals from hitting well enough to repeat as NL champs.

The answer was demonstrated during a four-game series at St. Louis from April 24 through April 27. The Mets had a half-game lead over the Cardinals at 7–3 entering the series and were riding a five-game winning streak. But the Cards grabbed a 3–0 lead in the sixth inning of the series opener and were two outs from taking over first place despite Carter's RBI single in the eighth.

Howard Johnson came through with the Mets' first huge hit of the season, a two-run blast that knotted the score 4–4 in the ninth. One inning later, Foster's RBI single led a 5–4 victory that allowed the Mets to stay atop the division.

Carter went 0-for-2 in Game 2, but he also walked three times and scored twice as the Mets blew out the Redbirds 9–0. A 4–3 victory followed as Carter laced an RBI double and scored on Danny Heep's single in a four-run first. The Mets completed the sweep with a 5–3 triumph as Carter scored again while handling Ojeda's first complete-game win as a Met.

The Cardinals went 6-for-7 in stolen base attempts during the series, but they also hit only .191 with an equally meager .220 on-base percentage while being outscored

23–10. Although there were still five months remaining in the season, the Cardinals were 4½ games off the pace and would get no closer than that the rest of the way.

The Mets carried an 11-game winning streak and a five-game division lead into May after Carter and Strawberry hit two-run homers in an 8–1 pounding of the Braves in Atlanta. Carter finished the month with a .281 average, three home runs, 19 RBIs, and 14 runs scored to help the Mets go 13–3. His most productive game in April came in the Phillies' home opener as he went 3-for-5 with a two-run homer, five RBIs, and three runs scored to lead a 9–7 victory.

The Mets were spectacular the rest of the season and celebrated some of their best home performances by making curtain calls. A homer was worth a curtain call. Seven shutout innings? Ditto. A check-swing base hit to the opposite field in the bottom of the ninth? Same thing. The Mets took more curtain calls than Pavarotti, and why not? Pavarotti wasn't drawing 40,000 fans on nights when he was performing.

The curtain calls helped the Mets become baseball's most hated team in '86. Carter would accentuate his curtain calls with a violent fist-pump that only made him more loathed among his NL brethren. However, he managed to avoid starting any of the four benches-clearing incidents involving the Mets during the season, although one of the best fights of the year caused him to play another position.

The Mets were playing the Reds right after the All-Star break when third baseman Ray Knight became involved in shoving match with Eric Davis. Knight threw the first punch before 49 players and every coach became involved in the melee. Knight was tossed from the game, leaving the Mets without a third baseman since Howard Johnson had already replaced shortstop Rafael Santana in a double switch in the top of the ninth.

Carter wound up coming out from behind the plate to take over at third, a position he hadn't played since 1975. He was flawless at the hot corner, handling a sacrifice bunt on his first chance and participating in a snappy 3-5-4 double play to snuff out a potential winning rally in the bottom of the 12th.

Carter experienced a few ups and downs during the season as he continued to absorb physical punishment behind the plate. He batted just .222 in 78 games from April 27 through August 4, a span of over half the season. Yet he still managed to hit 15 homers, drive in 60, and score 47 as the Mets played .667 ball in those 78 games. Even when he was bad, he was good.

He appeared to be snapping out of his so-called slump in early August, producing a seven-game hitting streak in which he batted .357 with two homers and 11 RBIs to raise his average to .248 by August 11. Five days later, Carter thought his season was over.

Manager Davey Johnson gave Hernandez a day off against the Cardinals and asked Carter to play first base. He opened the game by making a nice play on a grounder by leadoff hitter Ozzie Smith and was involved in all three outs during the top of the third. But he injured his thumb while making a diving stop on a grounder by Mike LaValliere in the top of the third, leaving him with a partially tore thumb ligament that put him on the disabled list. Carter initially feared the thumb was broken and was relieved by the prognosis.

The injury should have given the rest of the NL East a chance to pare down their deficit on the Mets. But New York already had a 16-game lead over the second-place Expos at the time of the injury before going 11–3 during Carter's absence.

Carter returned on September 1, going 2-for-3 with an RBI and two runs scored in a 5–2 win over the Giants. He also drove in runs in each of the next four games, giving him 94 RBIs with 26 games remaining. But Carter finally hit an RBI drought, collecting just four in his next 21 games to leave him at 98 with four games remaining.

Carter hit the century mark on October 2, belting a three-run homer and driving in four during an 8–2 win over his old team. The blast came off Youmans, the pitching prospect who was packaged in the deal for Carter. It also made him the first Met in team history to drive in at least 100 runs in two seasons.

Carter tied Staub's single-season team record for RBI by launching a three-run homer in the first inning of a 9–0 rout of the Pirates, the next-to-last game of the regular season. The home run extended his hitting streak to 13 games, tying his career high set in 1979.

Carter sat out the last three innings and didn't play in the season finale as manager Davey Johnson tried to rest him for the playoffs. The time off was a reward for a job well done as Carter finished with a .255 average, 24 home runs, and 105 RBIs in 132 games to help the Mets set a team record with 108 victories. He capped the year by hitting .373 with 10 RBIs in his final 13 games, so there was no reason to believe he'd have any trouble against Houston in the National League Championship Series.

But Houston had been tough on Carter during the regular season. He homered twice in 11 games but hit just .190 in 42 at-bats. He was even worse against Mike Scott, going 1-for-12 in three games. As luck would have it, Scott was the Game 1 pitcher in the NLCS.

Scott blanked the Mets 1–0 as Carter went 0-for-4 with three strikeouts. The Mets were convinced that Scott was scuffing the ball and began to accumulate a collection of balls that landed in the dugout during the game. Most had an odd marking that appeared to be man-made. Carter was among the more accusatory Mets when Scott's name came up in postgame interviews.

Carter doubled home a run in Game 2 as the Mets evened the series with a 5–1 victory at Houston. The two-bagger would be his only hit until the 12th inning of Game 5, when he was given a chance to put the Mets ahead three games to two in the series.

Backman led off the 12th inning of the fifth game with a single and moved to second on an errant pickoff throw by Charlie Kerfeld while Hernandez was at the plate. Manager Hal Lanier elected to have Hernandez walked intentional to bring the struggling Carter to the plate. Hernandez turned to Carter after ball four and gave him a fist-pump as encouragement before trotting off to first.

Carter came to the plate in an 0-for-15 slump that left him 1-for-21 in the series. Most of the Mets were having trouble against Houston's pitching staff, but Carter's slump was grabbing the attention. A double play would have ended the rally and put Carter in line to set an NLCS record for hitting futility.

The at-bat was a 12-pitch battle as Kerfeld threw gas while running the count to 3–2. Carter fouled off several pitches before finally hitting a grounder through the infield, placing it in between second baseman Bill Doran and shortstop Dickie Thon. The ball continued into center field without much speed, allowing Backman to race around third with the winning run to give the Mets a 2–1 victory. Carter had lifted his series average to .091 while providing the Mets' second walk-off hit of the series.

In many respects, Game 6 was Game 7 for the Mets. A loss in Houston would force the Mets to face Scott, who already had recorded two complete-game victories while striking out 19 in 18 innings. Worse, he had gotten into the heads of the Mets like no other pitcher since John Tudor in 1985. But first, the Mets had to deal with lefty Bob Knepper.

Carter did little against Knepper, hitting three fly balls in as many at-bats through the first seven innings. Knepper was doing his best to stay in front after he was staked to a 3–0 lead in the first inning.

Knepper carried a two-hit shutout into the ninth, causing Mets announcer Bob Murphy to remind fans that Scott loomed on the horizon unless New York could generate a comeback. Dykstra led off the inning with a triple and was singled home by Wilson before Hernandez hit an RBI double to make it 3–2. Houston was now two outs from a stretching the series, but the Mets were on the verge of a tie game with Carter coming to the plate.

Carter and Strawberry drew consecutive 3–2 walks off closer Dave Smith to load the bases. Knight followed with a sacrifice fly to bring home Hernandez with the tying run and momentarily push back the thought of another game against Scott.

Carter also walked in the 11th but was stranded as the game continued. In the 14th, Carter led off with a single and moved to third on a walk and a bunt before Backman singled him home to give the Mets their first lead off the day. But Billy Hatcher turned an already long game into a marathon by homering off Jesse Orosco to send the game into the 15th.

Carter singled in the 15th, giving him two hits in the game after collecting just two hits in the first five games of the season. But he was erased on the basepaths, keeping the game tied until the Mets erupted for three runs in the 16th to take a 7–4 lead.

It was now time for the Astros to begin their own rally. Orosco was pitching on fumes as the Astros scored twice on a walk and three singles, sending Kevin Bass to the plate with the potential winning run on first. Carter, Orosco and Hernandez huddled together on the mound before Jesse fanned Kevin Bass to end the series, putting the Mets in the World Series for the first time in 17 years.

Carter ended the series with a .148 average, making him one of six Mets regulars to hit less than .250. But Carter also handled a staff that compiled a 2.29 ERA and a 1.048 WHIP, allowing just 49 hits in 63 innings.

The Red Sox were the Mets' next opponents. Once again, the Mets were the heavy favorites. And once again, they were tested within every inch of their fiber to fend off an upset.

Carter went 1-for-4 in each of the first two games, including an RBI single in the second contest, but New York lost each time and headed for Boston following a 9–3 pounding at Shea Stadium. Davey Johnson sensed his club was still weary from the grueling Astros series and decided to give his team a day off rather than force his players to take batting practice a little over 24 hours before Game 3. Carter and his wife, Sandy, spent most of the day in his hotel room enjoying the respite from October baseball.

Johnson was criticized by some for the move after the Mets collected just three runs and 12 hits in the first two games. No team appeared to need batting practice more than the Mets, who were now hitting .192 with just three home runs in the postseason.

But Johnson was proven right when the Mets began to attack Red Sox starter Oil Can Boyd in the first inning of Game 3. Dykstra homered on Boyd's third pitch of the evening before Carter provided the Mets' fourth straight hit, an RBI double off the Green Monster. Carter almost ran the Mets out of the rally when he and Hernandez wound up on third base simultaneously following a grounder by Knight. But Carter managed to get back to second and Hernandez remained on third just before Danny Heep's single scored both runners to make it 4–0.

Carter later slapped a two-run single to give the Mets a 6–1 lead in the sixth. That was more than enough runs for Ojeda, who held his old team to a run and five hits in seven innings of a 7–1 victory.

Carter was the hitting star in a 6–2 win in Game 4, going 3-for-4 with a pair of home runs. The game was scoreless until he bashed a two-run shot in the fourth inning, two batters before Knight singled home Strawberry. Dykstra added a two-run shot in the seventh, and Carter followed with a solo blast the following inning. The Mets now had back-to-back victories by a combined 13–3 margin after skipping BP between games two and three.

But Bruce Hurst shut down the Mets in Game 5 to lead a 4–2 win, putting the Red Sox within one victory of their first World Series title in 68 years. Carter went 0-for-4 to snap a six-game hitting streak that began with his walk-off single in Game 5 of the NLCS.

The Mets hosted Game 6 and quickly fell behind 2–0 against Roger Clemens, who held them hitless until Knight rapped an RBI single in the fifth following Strawberry's walk and steal. New York tied the game on a double-play grounder later in the inning, but the twin killing snuffed out the rally.

Boston pulled ahead 3–2 on an RBI grounder in the seventh following an error by Knight at third, but Carter came through again with a sacrifice fly to even in the score in the eighth. The sac-fly gave Carter eight RBI in the series and allowed the Mets to stave off elimination the first time.

New York had a great chance to win it in the ninth after putting runners on first and second with nobody and Howard Johnson at the plate. Johnson, who had laid down just one successful sacrifice bunt during the regular season, failed on two attempts against Calvin Schiraldi before striking out. Even with Knight on second, a base hit likely would have scored the winning run. Lee Mazzilli and Dykstra followed with fly balls to deep left to end the inning when a successful bunt attempt by HoJo would have allowed the Mets to win in regulation. Instead, the Mets and Red Sox partook in one of the most exciting 10th innings in baseball history.

Boston was whooping it up in the dugout after Dave Henderson homered on Rick Aguilera's second pitch of the inning. Aguilera fanned the next two hitters but allowed a double to Wade Boggs and an RBI single by Marty Barrett to make it 5–3.

Carter was due to hit third in the bottom of the 10th, giving him a chance to be the hero if Backman and Hernandez could get on base. Backman and Hernandez hit fly balls, putting Carter in position to make the final out in the series.

Carter kept the series alive by lacing a 2–1 pitch to left for a single, putting a little life into a Shea crowd that had gone numb from Boston's two-run 10th. Kevin Mitchell, who was on the phone with an airline trying to book a flight home during Carter's at-bat, was summoned by Johnson to hit for Aguilera. Mitchell poked a single to left, putting runners on first and second and heightening the excitement in the stands.

Knight was the next hitter and quickly fell behind 0–2 before lining an opposite-field single that landed both shallow and softly enough to score Carter and move Mitchell to third, allowing Wilson to provide the heroics and prompting Red Sox manager John McNamara to bring in reliever Bob Stanley.

Wilson and the Mets were down to their last strike before Stanley uncorked a pitch that was headed toward Wilson's feet. Wilson somersaulted over the ball as it skipped past the glove of catcher Rich Gedman and rolled toward the backstop. Mitchell sailed home with the tying run, 17 pitches and four batters after the Red Sox were on the verge of celebrating.

Wilson continued to stay alive at the plate by fouling off pitches before hitting a dribbler toward first baseman Bill

Buckner, who was allowed to remain in the game despite a pair of bad ankles that forced him to wear high-tops on the field.

Knight never stopped running as the ball skidded underneath Buckner's glove and into right field to cap an improbable in an amazing season. The Mets had momentum on their side following an incredible 6–5 victory. Best of all, they were scheduled to face Hurst, who won the first and fifth games of the series. Boyd was slated to go for the Bosox after being lit up by the Mets in Game 3.

And then it rained. Game 7 had to be pushed back a day, allowing McNamara to use Hurst on short rest. Hurst allowed just one hit while shutting out the Mets over the first five innings as the Red Sox grabbed a 3–0 lead. But Hurst tired in the sixth, loading the bases before Hernandez stroked a two-run single to left-center to put runners on first and third with one out and Carter coming up.

Carter delivered again, hitting a grounder to deep second to score Backman with the tying run. Once again, Carter helped the Mets get off the mat.

Carter ended the seventh inning with another ground-ball out, but not before the Mets scored three times to take a 6–3 lead. It was 8–5 Mets when Carter caught the final pitch of the series, a swinging strike by Barrett from Orosco to give the Mets their second World Series.

Carter also came away with postseason accolades, winning the Silver Slugger for the fifth time in six seasons and finishing third in the MVP voting. It would be his final Silver Slugger and the last time he picked up an MVP vote.

The Mets made two significant moves after winning the title, both of which took some of the heart and toughness out of the ballclub. Mitchell was sent to the Padres in a multiplayer deal for outfielder Kevin McReynolds, and Knight was allowed to sign with the Tigers after winning the World Series MVP award. The losses of Knight and Mitchell weren't necessarily felt at the plate in 1987, but the pair was missed in the clubhouse.

The Mets had other problems that led to a slow start in '87. Gooden opened the season on the restricted list after testing positive for cocaine, leaving the Mets without their ace for the first 60 days. Ojeda, Aguilera, and newcomer David Cone landed on the DL in May and would miss much of the season. Fernandez missed a couple of starts with a knee injury before occupying the disabled list with a shoulder ailment.

Carter had his own injury issues. He underwent knee surgery for the third time in three off-seasons with the Mets and finally started to show the results of over 1,500 games behind the plate. At age 33, the "Kid" was no longer a kid.

He hit .308 with three homers and 12 RBIs in his first 13 games of 1987 before batting just .143 with five ribbies in his next 32 contests. The Mets sputtered out of the gate and were 9½ games behind the first-place Cardinals heading into the All-Star break.

Carter was again named to the NL starting lineup in the Midsummer Classic, preventing him from taking a few days off. But there was no way he was going to pass up an opportunity to play after being voted in by Mets fans.

Carter's batting average never moved past .246 after the break before he settled for a .235 mark with 20 home runs and 83 RBIs. He managed to start 132 games behind the plate despite the balky knee and cracked the 20-homer plateau for the fourth straight year and the ninth time in his career. But his batting average, on-base percentage and slugging average were his lowest since his injury-filled 1976 season.

The Mets still managed to get back in the race as Carter collected 22 RBIs in 27 games from July 1 through August 7. He later drove in 10 runs in a nine-game span in late August while the Mets crept closer to the division lead. But their playoff hopes all but evaporated when they blew a 4–1 lead in the ninth inning of a 6–4, 10-inning loss to St. Louis at Shea Stadium on September 11. The Cards also won the next day and finished three games ahead of New York in what was a very unsatisfying season for the Mets. The team set several club records for offense but was unable to overcome the bloated number of injuries to the pitching staff and a substandard effort from the bullpen.

Cashen shipped Orosco to the Dodgers but otherwise declined to make any major changes to the team before 1988 training camp in the hope the rotation could remain healthy. Gooden, Darling, Ojeda, Fernandez, and Aguilera all had bounce-back seasons, and Cone pitched like the ace in a rotation that was the best in the National League once again.

The Mets appeared ready to dominate the division race again by starting off 38–17 to take a seven-game lead by June 6. The pitching was crisp, and the hitting was sound until the weather got hot.

Carter blazed in his first 17 games of the season, hitting .339 with a .449 on-base percentage, seven home runs, and 14 RBIs through April 26. His average dropped to .274 until he went 2-for-3 with a three-run homer and four RBIs at San Diego on May 16. Carter's blast off Padres hurler Greg Booker was his 278th as a catcher and the 299th of his career, putting him on the verge of joining Johnny Bench, Yogi Berra, and Carlton Fisk as the only backstops to homer 300 times. Fortunately for Carter and the Mets, they didn't ask Bench and Berra to follow him around while he chased the 300-home run plateau.

Carter raised his average to .295 on May 21 but remained stuck on 299 home runs. He was still at 299 by the end of May…and the end of June…and the end of July.

Carter went 64 games without a homer from May 17 to August 9 while hitting .237 with a .290 slugging average and only 15 RBIs. The Mets played .500 ball during that span, allowing the upstart Pirates to work their way into the division race.

The Mets' slump wasn't all Carter's fault. Hernandez and Howard Johnson were struggling, and McReynolds experienced a long power outage as the team averaged just 3.9 runs a game during Carter's home run drought.

Carter finally reached the milestone with a solo shot off Al Nipper in the second inning of a 9–6 win at Wrigley Field on August 11. It was Nipper who served up the first of Carter's two home runs in Game 4 of the 1986 World Series.

Carter also homered three days later before hitting just one over his final 31 regular season games. He batted only .215 with seven RBIs during that season-ending stretch to finish with a .242 average, 11 homers, and 46 ribbies in 503 plate appearances.

Carter's late-season skid didn't stop the Mets from winning the NL East with ease. They began to pull away in late August and finished 15 games ahead of the Pirates with the third 100-win season in team history, putting Carter in the postseason for the third time in his career.

The Dodgers hosted New York in the first two games of the NLCS and sent Orel Hershiser to the mound against Gooden in a terrific pitching matchup. Hershiser opened September by throwing five consecutive shutouts and tossed 10 scoreless innings in his final start of the regular season. He pitched at least nine innings in his last nine starts and continued his incredible pace by carrying a five-hit shutout and a 2–0 lead into the ninth inning of Game 1 of the NLCS before the Mets finally nailed him for an earned run.

Gregg Jefferies led off the ninth with a single before Strawberry doubled him home to chase Hershiser. McReynolds followed with a walk against Jay Howell before Howard Johnson grounded out, leaving the Mets one out from a loss with Carter heading to the plate.

Howell got two quick strikes before Carter produced his second hit of the night, a two-run double to put the Mets ahead 3–2. Randy Myers tossed a scoreless ninth to complete the comeback win.

But the series quickly unraveled from there. Carter went 0-for-4 in Game 2 as the Dodgers chased Cone while grabbing a 5–0 lead in the second inning of a 6–3 victory. The Mets regained control of the series with a sloppy 8–4 win at Shea Stadium, and carried a 4–2 lead into the ninth inning of Game 4 before Mike Scioscia's two-run homer off Gooden knotted the score. Kirk Gibson added a solo shot in the 12th inning before the Mets wasted a bases-loaded opportunity to lose 5–4.

The Dodgers clobbered the Mets 7–4 in Game 5 to take a 3–2 series lead back to Los Angeles, hours after New York was three outs away from going up three games to one. The Mets fought back to force a seventh game, but Hershiser tossed a complete-game shutout to eliminate New York.

Carter was 6-for-20 in the first five games of the series before going hitless in seven at-bats the rest of the way to end up with a .222 average and four RBIs. He underwent another knee surgery shortly after the Dodgers beat the A's in the World Series. By now, the only personal mark he was chasing was most knee surgeries by a pro athlete as he approached the numbers compiled by Joe Namath and Bobby Orr.

Carter got off to a terrible start in 1989, as did Hernandez. Both spent over two months on the disabled list, leaving the Mets without any vocal leadership as the team struggled to keep pace with the first-place Cubs.

Carter looked finished as a player once he was placed on the DL in May. He started just 22 of the Mets' first 30 games, hitting a woeful .114 with one home run and five RBIs in 79 at-bats. Base runners were stealing at will against Carter, who was now hearing boos at Shea Stadium on a regular basis. It was a lousy way for an 11-time All-Star to be treated, particularly after all he had done for the franchise.

Carter was unwilling to allow his season—or his career—to end so poorly, especially in the final year of his contract. He still loved to play the game despite the hours he was spending in the trainer's room. Both knees would be wrapped from near the top of his thigh to the middle of his calf, giving him a mummified appearance before he donned his uniform. His teammates grew to admire and appreciate all that was entailed in getting Carter onto the field, something that was lost on fans who were watching their team underachieve.

Carter returned July 25 and went 1-for-12 with no RBIs the rest of the month, lowering his average to .110. Cashen tried to salvage the season by acquiring reigning AL Cy Young winner Frank Viola from the Twins at the July 31 trade deadline. But unlike his acquisitions of Carter, Ojeda, and Teufel, this one cost the Mets dearly as they parted with Aguilera and prospect Kevin Tapani, both of whom helped Minnesota win the 1991 World Series.

Carter started only seven games in August as Davey Johnson tried to save him for a possible playoff run. But Carter also began to hit again, going 4-for-4 with two doubles at Philadelphia on August 9 before producing a pair of two-hit games later that month. He hit .370 with a .519 slugging average in limited playing time in August. He also singled in his first September at-bat before immediately going into an 0-for-11 skid through the middle of the month.

The Mets already were hinting that Carter and Hernandez would not be offered contracts for 1990. The team was in third place and 5½ games off the division lead with 14 games remaining when Mets fans began to lighten up on Carter, realizing he could be playing his final days with the ballclub.

Carter's last home run as a Met was a three-run blast that put them ahead to stay in a 5–2 win at Chicago on September 19, but the Cubs' magic number was seven with 12 games remaining. His last great game at Shea occurred against the Expos on September 23, a 13–6 rout of his former club. Carter went 3-for-5, drove in five runs, and scored twice to lead the victory while receiving a warm ovation before each at-bat.

The Mets played their final home game of the season on September 27, a 5–3 loss to the Phillies. Davey Johnson allowed Carter to receive one more standing ovation by using him as a pinch-hitter leading off the bottom of the ninth against Jeff Parrott. Carter took the first pitch for a ball before lining a double down the left-field line, igniting another ovation that continued as he was taken out for a pinch-runner.

Carter was a starter in his final game as a Met, going 0–5 at Pittsburgh on September 30 to end up with a .183 average, two home runs, and 15 RBIs in 50 games. He remained optimistic the Mets might want to keep him around in 1990.

"I would like to be able to finish my career here," Carter said a day before his final at-bat at Shea. "I've said that all along. I have no idea what they've decided, but I guess they've made up their minds already. Not playing much this year has been the most frustrating part. I didn't get much of a chance to show what I could do, and now a decision has already been made. But that's business. Whatever they decide I'll have to accept."[28]

Carter and Hernandez learned a few days later that the Mets had no interest in re-signing them. The two received word in a meeting with Cashen, who told the media the Mets were truly blessed to acquire people of their class. Carter demonstrated that class after the meeting.

"This ballclub is going through a transition," he said. "They are going with younger players. They have made some changes already, and will make more.

"But one door closes, and another will open. The good Lord has a plan for me. I can still play this game, and I know there'll be an opportunity out there. But these have been five great years. I heard the cheers and I heard the boos, and I like the cheers a lot more. Maybe I'll hear more of them."[29]

Carter played three more seasons as a backup catcher, one each with the Giants and Dodgers before ending his career with the 1992 Expos. He averaged 64 starts behind the plate during those three years, batting .238 with 20 home runs and 82 RBIs in 777 at-bats.

Carter retired as one of the most prolific offensive catchers in baseball history. He was also among the best defensive catchers in the game from 1974 through 1983 until the rigors of the position took a toll on his body. But he was named on only 42.3 percent of the Hall of Fame ballots in his first year of eligibility in 1998, and had to wait until 2003 before he was inducted. He already was a member of the Mets' Hall of Fame, receiving that honor in 2001.

Carter stayed in baseball since retiring as a player. He was named one of the original broadcasters of the expansion Florida Marlins in 1993, spending four years behind a mic before returning to the Mets as a roving catching instructor.

Carter became manager of the Mets' Gulf Coast team in 2005, leading it to a 37–16 record while mentoring Josh Thole. Carter also managed Orange County of the independent Golden League in 2008 and returned to Long Island as skipper of the Ducks in 2009. He guided the Ducks to a 74–66 mark and a berth in the Atlantic League Championship series for Bud Harrelson's club before taking his expertise to the college level.

Carter became head coach at Palm Beach Atlantic since 2010, allowing him to stay close to home year-round. Carter had lived in the area since he and Sandy got married in February 1975.

Gary and Sandy raised three children, daughters Christy and Kimmy, and son D.J. Christy and Kimmy appeared with Carter in his 1985 Ivory Soap commercial. Kimmy is head softball coach at Palm Beach Atlantic while her husband, Kyle Bloemers, is the school's assistant athletic director for compliance and marketing.

Carter's charity work was almost unparalleled by baseball standards. He was named sports chairman of the Leukemia Society of America in 1985 and earned the Joan Payson award for humanitarian service by the New York chapter of the Baseball Writers Association of American that year.

He later established the Gary Carter Foundation, which raises money for the education of school children in some of the economically challenged areas of Florida. The foundation's mission is to accelerate a child's reading skills through the GCF "Upgrades" and "All-Star Reader" programs, thus helping them pursue a secondary education. Carter holds numerous events for the foundation, but fans can also contribute to the cause by purchasing Carter memorabilia through the foundation's website.

Carter had just completed his second season as PBA's head coach when he announced in May 2011 that four tumors were discovered on his brain. Doctors at Duke University's brain tumor center said the location of the tumors made it difficult to remove through surgery, causing Carter to battle it through radiation.

But the cancer was very aggressive and had generated more tumors by Christmas. Carter met with his Palm Beach Atlantic team one final time on February 2, 2012, taking the field on a golf cart after the cancer robbed him of his ability to walk without peril. Two weeks later, Carter passed away at age 57.

ML debut	Expos vs. Mets, 9/16/74
Mets debut	vs. Cardinals, 4/9/85
1st ML hit	single vs. Jon Matlack, Mets, 9/18/74 (with Expos)
1st Mets hit	double vs. Ken Dayley, Cardinals, 4/9/85
1st ML homer	solo HR vs. Steve Carlton, Phillies, 9/28/74 (with Expos)
1st Mets homer	solo HR vs. Neil Allen, Cardinals, 4/9/85
1st ML RBI	sac-fly vs. Herb Hutson, @ Cubs, 9/24/74 (with Expos)
1st Mets RBI	solo HR vs. Neil Allen, Cardinals, 4/9/85
Most hits, ML game	5, Mets @ Braves, 7/4/85; Giants vs. Cubs, 7/7/90
Most homers, ML game	3, Expos vs. Pirates, 4/20/77; Mets @ Padres, 9/3/85
Most RBI, ML/Mets game	7, vs. Braves, 7/11/86
Acquired:	Traded by the Expos for Hubie Brooks, Mike Fitzgerald, Herm Winningham and Floyd Youmans.

Deleted: Released 11/14/89. Signed by the Giants 1/19/90.
Inducted Into Baseball Hall of Fame, 2003
NL All-Star, 1975, 1979, 1980, 1981, 1982, 1983, 1984, 1985, 1986, 1987, 1988
NL Silver Slugger, 1981, 1982, 1984, 1985, 1986
NL Gold Glove, 1980, 1981, 1982
NL RBI Leader, 1984

Donn Clendenon

First Baseman	Batted right, threw right	
Born: 7/15/35	Neosho, Missouri	
Died: 9/17/05	Sioux Falls, South Dakota	
Height: 6'4"	Weight: 210	#22

Donn Clendenon Mets Career

YEAR	GP	AB	R	H	2B	3B	HR	RBI	K	BB	SB	AVG	SLG	OBP
1969	72	202	31	51	5	0	12	37	62	19	3	.252	.455	.321
1970	121	396	65	114	18	3	22	97	91	39	4	.288	.515	.348
1971	88	263	29	65	10	0	11	37	78	21	1	.247	.411	.302
TOTAL	281	861	125	230	33	3	45	171	231	79	8	.267	.469	.328

ML Career

YEARS	GP	AB	R	H	2B	3B	HR	RBI	K	BB	SB	AVG	SLG	OBP
61-72	1362	4648	594	1273	192	57	159	682	1140	379	90	.274	.442	.328

The 1969 Mets were a few days removed from an 11-game winning streak when they made what is still considered the greatest trade-deadline deal in team history. As Leonard Koppett wrote in the *New York Times* on June 14, the Mets were "four games over .500, too far behind the Chicago Cubs to think seriously about first place, but well-positioned to make a season-long fight for second."[30]

The pitching wasn't a problem, and the defense was sound. But the starting lineup screamed out for a capable cleanup hitter who could actually put some fear in opposing pitchers. Tommie Agee was their top power threat, but he spent most of the season as the leadoff hitter. Cleon Jones hit a mere eight home runs while serving as the cleanup hitter for 56 of the Mets' first 57 games prior to the trade deadline.

The Mets also had a pair of seven-game streaks in which they failed to homer, and were averaging 3.8 runs per game before general manager Johnny Murphy was able to pry Donn Alvin Clendenon away from the expansion Expos.

"I went to Montreal, worked my way into shape and on June 15, they called me and asked if I'd come to New York. I said, 'Most definitely!'

"By that time, I was hitting okay. My timing was down, my hands had gotten the calluses, my feet were in shape.

"I think the first 16 to 18 games I played over there with the New York Mets I drove in the winning run or the tying run in 16 to 18 games."

There were both positives and negatives to Clendenon's game before he joined the Mets. He averaged 21 homers and 97 RBIs while hitting .300 from 1965 to 1966. Clendenon also finished sixth in the NL with 87 RBIs in

1968, when runs were at a premium. But his average was just .252 from the start of 1967 until the time he donned a Mets uniform. He also led the league in strikeouts twice and wasn't among the better glove men in the National League.

Clendenon made news earlier in '69 by refusing to report to the Astros after being traded by Montreal in January. Clendenon had spent his entire career with the Pirates until he was selected by the Expos in the October 1968 expansion draft. Clendenon even announced his retirement before training camp, saying he would not play for the Astros. It was nothing against Houston.

"I didn't want to play south of the border," Clendenon told Maury Allen in his book *After the Miracle*. "I had some personal problems at the time. My father was ill and soon passed. I had entered law school at Duquesne in Pittsburgh and didn't want to leave there. When they traded me to Houston—this was before a player had any say in a trade—I said some terrible things about Houston. I was going into law, and that was it. Then Bowie Kuhn got in the middle of it."[31]

Kuhn was in his first year as baseball commissioner when the Clendenon matter fell into his lap. Clendenon had no interest in playing for the Astros and even took a job with Scripto Pen in Atlanta. Kuhn eventually forged a compromise that put Clendenon back in a major league uniform.

The Expos kept Clendenon and reworked the trade on Opening Day, sending Jack Billingham and Skip Guinn to Houston. Clendenon didn't play for Montreal until April 19, less than two months before he became a New York Met.

Mets pitchers were understandably excited about the pickup after they were involved in 21 one-run contests in the 55 games prior to the trade.

"We never really had a legitimate home run hitter on the Mets until Clendenon came in," said Jerry Koosman in December 2008. "When he arrived, all of us pitchers felt good about that. Now, all of a sudden we have a guy that could turn the game around with one swing of the bat. So he hit some long balls for us that certainly helped us out that year, especially in the World Series.

"It was fun to watch him take batting practice because of the power he had. He hit a ton of home runs in batting practice, which made us all feel good."

Clendenon instantly became one of the most popular players in the clubhouse. He was an equal opportunity needler, razzing everyone regardless of color or age. He also took his share of abuse, especially when he would have himself paged in airports just to feel important.

"The Mets needed somebody to pound the ball," said Clendenon. "That was my job. I also kept the team loose. I got on everybody, black and white. I kept the guys free of pressure. No matter what happened that day, there was always the next day. I learned that with some good Pittsburgh teams.

"I would get to the clubhouse early and kid around with the guys. The coaches were important on that team—Yogi, Eddie Yost, Rube Walker, Joe Pignatano—and they were always there early. One of the reasons there were no racial problems was because they wouldn't allow it.

"Gus Mauch, the trainer, was always in early. I would get a rubdown from him and while he was working on me, I'd say, 'Are these the hands that rubbed Mantle and Ford and DiMaggio? Now they are rubbing this beautiful black body.' Everybody would laugh."[32]

The Mets felt his impact as an offensive threat almost immediately. He provided the go-ahead single in a 5–1 win against St. Louis June 22 and drove in three runs in a win over the Pirates June 29 before catching fire in July. He put together a six-game run in which he batted .385 with a homer, 11 RBIs, and five runs scored. That stretch included a go-ahead, three-run homer at Pittsburgh July 6, one game before he delivered a pinch-hit double and scored the tying run in a three-run ninth that lifted the Mets over the Cubs 4–3.

"I became somewhat of a leader on the field and off the field," he said. "It was just amazing to see these kids who didn't realize exactly the impact of what they were doing. But they knew they could beat anybody. How they would gel and come together as a team, it was remarkable. I think we epitomized teamwork that year.

"I think we had the youngest, greatest pitching staff at the time. We had pretty good hitters. All they needed was someone to drive in runs consistently for them. Fortunately, I filled that bill, and I think other guys could have filled that bill for them, too, if they had picked them up.

"But good pitching, good defense, and timely hitting, you've got a shot at it."

New York, which had fallen 9½ games behind the Cubs in mid-August, was just four games back after Clendenon slammed a tiebreaking solo homer off Gaylord Perry in the 10th inning of a 3–2 win at San Francisco. The blast was part of a West Coast trip in which Clendenon hit .393 with five homers, eight RBIs, and seven runs scored in only seven games. But the Mets were still five games back when they returned to New York.

The Mets opened their first September home stand by taking three of four from the Phillies, putting them just 2½ games behind Chicago heading into a two-game set with the reeling Cubs at Shea. Clendenon smacked a two-run homer in Game 2 of the Cubs series to help the Mets pull within a half-game of the division lead. New York climbed into first place one day later with a double-header sweep of the Expos and never trailed the rest of the season.

The Missouri-born Clendenon played a big role in the Mets' division clincher by launching a three-run homer in a five-run first that chased Cardinals starter Steve Carlton. Clendenon capped the scoring in the 6–0 victory by belting a solo shot in the fifth.

"When we got 'Clink,' he was one of those guys that could carry a team on his back for a week," said pitcher

Best RBI/At-Bat Percentage as a Met, Single Season, Minimum 90 RBI

Player	Year	RBI	AB	PCT
Donn Clendenon	1970	97	396	.2449
Mike Piazza	2000	113	482	.2344
Mike Piazza	1999	124	534	.2322
Carlos Beltran	2006	116	510	.2275
Carlos Delgado	2006	114	524	.2176
Gary Carter	1986	105	490	.2143

Jim McAndrew in 2008. "And when you have good pitching like we did, that's the difference between being a contender and being an also-ran. You don't lose 1–0 or 2–1. You win 3–2, 2–1, 1–0."

Clendenon hit nine of his 12 Mets homers over his final 28 games. He also ended up with 37 RBIs in 202 at-bats as a Met while serving as a potent platoon partner with Ed Kranepool. Twelve of Clendenon's 51 hits as a Met put the team ahead.

The Mets took on the Braves in the first National League Championship Series. Clendenon never got off the bench as Atlanta used three right-handed starters during New York's three-game sweep. But the Orioles, armed with lefty starters Mike Cuellar and Dave McNally, gave Clendenon plenty of opportunity to play in the Fall Classic. The right-handed hitter came away with the World Series MVP after leading the Mets with three home runs, four RBIs, and four extra-base hits.

"There is no most valuable player on this team," Clendenon said receiving the award. "We've got lots of them."[33]

Clendenon wasn't happy with the way the team performed during a 4–1 loss to the Orioles in the series opener. He looked around the field, dugout, and clubhouse, and saw a team that looked a little intimidated by World Series experience. Clendenon felt it was time for an attitude adjustment.

"Seaver was really tight," said Clendenon. "He was not loose. He was not throwing. I called a meeting after the game and we talked it over—just the players.

"I told them, 'Look, we can beat these guys. They think they're a dynasty. That's bullshit. We've got better pitching. You saw Seaver couldn't have blackened your eye if he hit you with that fastball in your eye. We can beat these guys.'

"The next [game], Koosman came out. I hit a home run to start it. Koosman just shut the door, and it was downhill all the way."

The Mets were held to one run in the first 12 innings of the World Series before Clendenon crushed a solo homer to the opposite field off Dave McNally in the fourth inning of Game 2. New York came away with a 2–1 victory after scoring the tiebreaking run with two out in the ninth.

Clendenon also went deep in Game 4, giving the Mets another early 1–0 lead. Again, New York won by scratching out a tiebreaking run in its final at-bat.

Looking to clinch their first championship, the Mets spotted the Orioles a 3–0 lead on home runs by McNally and Frank Robinson off Koosman in the top of the third. Koosman allowed just one more hit the rest of the way while the Mets chipped away at their deficit.

Naturally, it was Clendenon who sparked the comeback with a two-run blast in the sixth after Jones was hit by a pitch leading off the inning. Al Weis tied it with a solo shot in the seventh, an inning before Ron Swoboda singled home the go-ahead run and scored an insurance tally to cap a 5–3 victory and a World Series title.

"I think that Baltimore had a great team, but I think what happened was we outplayed them, we outhustled them and we had more determination. We wanted it. We were hungrier," Clendenon said.

He had as many home runs as Baltimore in the series and had more hits than every Oriole other than Boog Powell. He was among the busiest Mets after the season, appearing with his teammates on *The Ed Sullivan Show* and later co-starring in a Las Vegas act fronted by comedian Phil Foster. Koosman, Jones, Kranepool, and Agee were part if the show, as were Tom Seaver and Art Shamsky.

Some of the comedy went like this:

"Donn Clendenon, how did you feel when you were traded to the Mets," asked Foster.

"It was my first experience with a minority group," was Clendenon's reply.[34]

Okay, it wasn't Seinfeld, or even Carrot Top. But Clendenon and his teammates each came away with $10,000 for their effort.

Many Mets spent the winter of 1970 living off the World Series crown, which left several players a little less hungry heading into spring training. Clendenon was the exception, putting together his final exceptional season after hitting only .139 in 36 spring-training at-bats.

The Mets won their season opener 5–3 in Pittsburgh on Clendenon's pinch-hit, two-run single with two out in the bottom of the 11th. It was the first time the Mets had ever won on Opening Day.

One game later, Clendenon singled as a pinch-hitter with two out in the ninth before the Mets stranded the tying run on second in a 2–1 loss to the Pirates.

He had two hits and scored twice in his first start April 12, and delivered a three-run homer and four RBIs in a 10–2 rout of the Phillies April 19. He opened May by going 2-for-4 with a two-run single in a 2–1 win against the Padres, jumpstarting a month in which he batted .310 with three homers, eight RBIs, and 11 runs scored in 20 games.

Meanwhile, Kranepool was hitting just .118 and in an 0-for-17 skid when he was demoted to Triple A Tidewater June 24. But instead of giving the first base position to Clendenon on a full-time basis, manager Gil Hodges put him in a platoon with Art Shamsky through August 11.

Platooning didn't slow down Clendenon, who hit .344 with seven homers and 28 RBIs in 33 games during June and July. His most productive game of the season came July 28 as he was 2-for-3 with two homers and what was then a team-record seven RBIs in a 12–2 pounding of the Giants, giving him a .326 average for the season. The seven ribbies remained a club mark until Dave Kingman drove in eight against the Dodgers in June 1976.

Clendenon capped the year by hitting safely in 10 of 12 games, but the Mets fell short of repeating as NL East champs. He set a team record with 97 RBIs, topping the old mark of 94 set by Frank Thomas in 1962. Clendenon continued to hold the record until Rusty Staub drove in 105 in 1975.

Clendenon also finished with 22 home runs, his highest total since 1966. His .288 average was his best in four years, and his RBI output was one off his career high set in '66. He received MVP consideration, finishing 13th in the balloting at age 35.

Clendenon got off to a nice start in 1971, producing three-hit games in four of his first 18 starts. He was batting .293 with five homers and 11 RBIs in 82 at-bats through May 22 before his production suddenly stopped. Clendenon went 1-for-33 during a 12-game stretch from May 23 through June 15, dropping his average to .217. The Mets were tied for first when the drought began and were 3½ games back when it ended.

Clendenon came through with a few big hits the rest of the season. He ripped a walk-off home run in the 15th inning of a 6–5 win over the Phillies June 19 and went 2-for-4 with a two-run single and a two-run homer in a 9–2 laugher against the Dodgers August 28. Clendenon also belted a two-run homer and had three ribbies as the Mets broke a team record for runs in a 20–6 thrashing of the Braves in Atlanta in early August.

Clendenon batted .280 with 18 RBIs over his final 35 games, including 22 starts. But he provided just four home runs in that season-ending stretch, striking out an alarming 38 times in 100 at-bats.

He played just 88 games, his fewest since his rookie season in 1962. Clendenon ended up with 11 homers, 37 RBIs, and a .247 average, all far below his 1970 totals.

Clendenon was the victim of a numbers game by the end of 1971. Kranepool rebounded from his poor 1970 season by batting .280 and tying for the team lead with 14 home runs. Mike Jorgensen homered five times in 45 games and emerged as a slick-fielding first baseman. The Mets also had first baseman-outfielder John Milner waiting in the wings, making Clendenon the odd man out. Clendenon was released October 28, ending his 2½-year run as a Met with a .267 average, 45 home runs, and 171 RBIs. Tommie Agee was the only Met to hit more home runs (64) from 1969 through 1971, doing it in 765 more at-bats.

The Cardinals signed Clendenon a few weeks after he was let go by New York. He opened the 1972 campaign by going 0-for-18 and never got his batting average above

Donn Clendenon (right) is greeted by his teamates after his two-run homer in the sixth inning of Game 5 of the 1969 World Series.

.200 before he was released August 7. Clendenon's final home run was a tiebreaking solo shot off Dave Roberts in the eighth inning of a 3–2 win at Houston July 17. His last base hit was a single off Philadelphia's Steve Carlton August 5.

Clendenon ended up with a lifetime .274 average, 159 home runs, and 682 RBIs in a 13-season major league career. He accumulated 1,015 strikeouts from 1962 through 1970, second only to Lou Brock among National Leaguers during that period. Overall, it was a pretty good career considering he wasn't too interested in playing baseball until he was almost a teenager.

Clendenon was the salutatorian of his graduation class at Booker T. Washington in Atlanta after earning All-State recognition in three sports as a senior. He attended nearby Morehouse College, where he earned 12 sports letters in baseball, football, and basketball. He also received degrees in mathematics and physical education, demonstrating that his scholastic skills were equal to his athletic ability.

He became a teacher in Atlanta after college and was pursued by the Cleveland Browns, New York Knicks, and Harlem Globetrotters. The Pirates were also interested in Clendenon, who grew to love baseball through his stepfather, Nish Williams, a one-time Negro League player. Clendenon could have inked pro contracts and made quick money with the Browns, Knicks, or Globetrotters. But he chose to sign in 1957 with the Pirates, who were three years away from a championship and five years removed from a 42–112 season.

Clendenon had ulterior motives for choosing the Pirates. He felt a baseball career could be a springboard for bigger things in life.

"Baseball always was an avocation to me," Clendenon said nearly two decades after leading the Mets to a World Series title. "I knew I was using it to establish myself in the law later on. That's what I really wanted to do."[35]

He began to display his power stroke after hitting .254 with only six homers and 27 extra-base hits in Class D during the 1957 season. He spent the next two years in Grand Forks and Idaho Falls, which may have influenced his appreciation for small-town living after his playing days. He eventually settled in Sioux Falls upon his retirement from baseball.

Clendenon was productive in '58, batting .265 and collecting 43 extra-base hits for Grand Forks. He was virtually unstoppable the following year, belting 17 homers and 15 triples while batting .358 for Idaho Falls and Wilson.

Clendenon continued to maul minor league hurlers in 1959, although he was still in Class A ball after four pro seasons. He was the MVP of the South Atlantic League, batting .335 with 28 homers, 17 triples, 109 RBIs, and 92 runs scored in 137 games for Savannah in 1960.

Elevated to Triple A in 1961, Clendenon recorded a .290 average, 22 home runs, and 82 RBIs to earn a September call-up with Pittsburgh.

He was 26 when he went 0-for-3 with a walk in his major league debut as the Pirates' starting left fielder September 22 in Philadelphia. Clendenon was 5-for-11 with three runs scored while starting in right the next two games, slapping a double off John Buzhardt for his first major league hit in five at-bats.

Clendenon collected his first two RBIs September 30 against the Reds while going 4-for-5 with three runs scored. He ended his trial run with a .314 average and a .400 on-base percentage in 40 plate appearances over nine games.

Pro basketball teams continued to show interest in Clendenon. He was offered a tryout with the Pittsburgh Rens of the American Basketball League in 1961 and could have become a two-sport star.

Clendenon opened the '62 season with the Pirates and hit safely in his first three games. He belted his first big league homer off Billy O'Dell of the Giants in his fifth game of the season on May 1 but otherwise played sparingly for Pittsburgh over the first three months.

Manager Danny Murtaugh had used Clendenon almost exclusively in the outfield before making him a semi-regular first baseman. Clendenon carried a .239 average into August before supplanting Dick Stuart at first base. Clendenon batted .331 with five homers, 22 RBIs, and 23 runs scored in his final 45 games to finish with a .302 average. He ripped his first career grand slam August 11 against Dave Gerard of the Cubs, and drove in at least four runs on three occasions over the last two months of the season.

Cubs second baseman Ken Hubbs was named the NL Rookie of the Year, picking up 19 of 20 votes. Clendenon prevented Hubbs from winning the award unanimously, capturing the remaining vote after hitting .302 in 80 games.

Clendenon flashed some speed in 1963, swiping a career-high 22 bases to pace the Pirates after stealing a team-high 16 the previous year. Clendenon also led the '63 Bucs with 28 doubles and was second to Roberto Clemente with 155 hits, 15 home runs, 57 RBIs, and 65 runs scored while batting .275. But Clendenon had a league-high 136 strikeouts compared to just 38 walks.

Clendenon remained Pittsburgh's starting first baseman through 1968, although he did play two innings at third in 1965. He had a breakout year in 1965, batting .301 with 32 doubles, 14 home runs and 96 RBIs while becoming the second Pirate to play an entire 162-game schedule. He had a .328 average with 51 RBIs and 54 runs scored by the All-Star break but was not selected to play in the Midsummer Classic. The snub didn't stop him from putting together an 11-game hitting streak (.422) from July 5 through July 16, which raised his average to .333.

Clendenon doubled his home run total in 1966, hitting 28 while driving in 98 runs despite a slow start. He was batting just .250 with three homers and 19 RBIs in 41 games before producing 10 multi-hit games in June. His season average was over .300 by July 27 and stayed there for most of the final weeks of the season.

The Pirates found themselves in a tight race for the National League pennant. They were just one game behind the first-place Dodgers after Clendenon provided the team's lone RBI in a 4–3 loss at St. Louis. He did his best to put the Bucs over the top, blasting seven homers and driving in 17 runs over their final 18 games. But the Pirates went just 9–9 down the stretch and capped the year by losing three straight to the Giants in Pittsburgh to finish third overall, three games behind Los Angeles. Clendenon ended up with a .299 average and a career-best .520 slugging percentage.

Clendenon failed to keep up that pace in 1967, playing 131 games and hitting .249 with 13 home runs in 1967 before pacing the NL with 163 strikeouts in '68. He was sixth in the NL with a team-high 87 RBIs, and ranked third on the Bucs with 17 home runs.

But the Pirates finished just 80–82 in 1968, two years after challenging for a World Series berth. The team had established an outstanding farm system that included Al Oliver, Manny Sanguillen, and Richie Hebner. The Pirates felt Oliver was ready to take over at first base, which prompted them to deal the 33-year-old Clendenon.

Oliver hit well in 1969, but Clendenon helped the Mets finish 12 games ahead of Pittsburgh. Clendenon accumulated 12 of his 51 RBIs against the Pirates.

Clendenon established his law practice after he was let go by the Cardinals in August 1972. He received his law degree at Duquesne in 1978, passed the bar in Pennsylvania, and first worked in Pittsburgh before moving to Columbus, Ohio, to become a sports agent. He eventually settled in Sioux Falls, where he joined a law firm in 1987.

Clendenon didn't want to leave baseball altogether.

"I wanted to be a general manager," Clendenon told Maury Allen in *After the Miracle*. "I thought the Mets would hire me. They never did. I can't tell you why. You'll have to ask them."[36]

Clendenon was an infrequent visitor to Shea Stadium after he retired. He returned in 1979 as the Mets celebrated the 10-year anniversary of their first World Series championship. But the Old Timer's celebration was the only time he came back to Shea for almost two decades. Even as the Mets morphed into World Series winners in the mid-1980s, Clendenon was among the few members of the original title team who declined to take a bow. However, he still had a passion for the sport and missed the competition.

"You know what I enjoyed most about baseball? I enjoyed hitting under pressure," Clendenon said some 20 years after collecting his World Series MVP award. "That was the most fun, to get up there against Ferguson Jenkins or Bob Gibson or one of those really great pitchers and getting a base hit against them. That was satisfying. I don't think I'll do anything as satisfying again."[37]

Clendenon's reputation was tarnished when he pleaded guilty in 1988 to a charge of cocaine possession in Minnehaha County, South Dakota. He received a seven-day prison sentence, was placed on probation for two years, and ordered to perform community service. His conviction was expunged following his probation.

"What I did was kind of stupid on my part," admitted Clendenon. "No one ever said I was brilliant."[38]

He began to complain of fatigue during his drug rehabilitation, which led to a physical examination. Clendenon was diagnosed with leukemia, the same disease that killed his father and grandfather.

Clendenon moved to Sioux Falls after completing his drug rehabilitation in Utah. He enrolled at the

University of South Dakota and became a certified addiction counselor after a four-year internship, all while fighting off leukemia.

"Aftercare is where it's at," Clendenon said in 2000. "Making sure these guys get to meetings—not with other ballplayers but with other addicts, other drunks. I had to have a sponsor whose behind I couldn't whip; someone who would get in my face and tell me I was wrong, someone who would be at my house if I didn't show up in a meeting."[39]

Clendenon continued to counsel addicts and kept up with the law while continuing to fight off leukemia. He beat the disease for the better part of two decades.

"Every day I wake up is a blessing," he told *New York Times* columnist William C. Rhoden in 2000, five years before his death. "I have chronic lymphocytic leukemia. I will die from it or a side effect of it. It's going to eventually take me, I know. But I keep fighting."[40]

Clendenon attended Agee's funeral in 2001 and was still alive when former Mets teammates Cal Koonce and Tug McGraw passed away. Clendenon died in 2005, leaving his wife, Anne, sons, Donn and Val, and daughter, Donna.

It is impossible to think of 1969 without recalling Clendenon. The Mets won on pitching and defense that season, but it was a veteran first baseman who injected fear into the offense.

"Probably the most phenomenal year of my career," Clendenon told Kansas City broadcaster Greg Echlin. "I had retired from baseball, had no spring training, went to Montreal for five weeks and was traded to New York at the trade deadline.

"Joining the club, the club was 11½ games out, and to come on and win it by eight was just phenomenal."

ML debut	Pirates @ Phillies, 9/22/61
Mets debut	@ Phillies, 6/17/69
1st ML hit	double vs. John Buzhardt, @ Phillies, 9/23/61 (with Pirates)
1st Mets hit	single vs. Grant Jackson, @ Phillies, 6/17/69
1st ML homer	solo HR vs. Billy O'Dell, @ Giants, 5/1/62
1st Mets homer	3-run HR vs. Churck Hartenstein, @ Pirates, 7/6/69
1st ML RBI	RBI single vs. Ken Hunt, Reds, 9/30/61 (with Pirates)
1st Mets RBI	RBI single vs. Steve Carlton, Cardinals, 6/22/69
Most hits, ML game	4, 10 times, 9 times with Pirates
Most hits, Mets game	3, 16 times
Most homers, ML game	2, 8 times, 4 times with Mets and Pirates
Most RBI, ML/Mets game	7, vs. Giants, 7/28/70

Acquired: Traded by the Expos for Steve Renko, Kevin Collins, Bill Carden and Dave Colon, 6/15/69.

Deleted: Released 10/28/71. Signed by the Cardinals, 12/9/71.

David Cone

Pitcher	Bats left, throws right
Born: 1/2/63	Kansas City, Missouri
Height: 6'1"	Weight: 190 #44, #17, #16

David Cone Mets Career

YEAR	GP/GS	IP	H	R	ER	K	BB	W–L	SV	ERA
1987	21/13	99.1	87	46	41	68	44	5–6	1	3.71
1988	35/28	231.1	178	67	57	213	80	20–3	0	2.22
1989	34/33	219.2	183	92	86	190	74	14–8	0	3.52
1990	31/30	211.2	177	84	76	233	65	14–10	0	3.23
1991	34/34	232.2	204	95	85	241	73	14–14	0	3.29
1992	27/27	196.2	162	75	63	214	82	13–7	0	2.88
2003	5/4	18.0	20	13	13	13	13	1–3	0	6.50
Total	187/169	1209.1	1011	472	421	1172	431	81–51	1	3.13

Mets Career/Batting

GP	AB	R	H	2B	3B	HR	RBI	K	BB	SB	AVG
188	399	26	62	8	0	0	20	87	16	0	.155

ML Career

YEAR	GP/GS	IP	H	R	ER	K	BB	W–L	SV	ERA
86-03	450/419	2898.2	2504	1222	1115	2668	1137	194–126	1	3.46

It looked like a minor trade at the time, but it was one of the best steals in team history.

The Mets shipped backup catcher Ed Hearn to the Royals for David Cone in March 1987, a deal which seemed a little odd when it was completed. Hearn had performed well as Gary Carter's understudy in 1986 and became a bit of a cult hero after the Mets went 11–3 while Carter was on the disabled in August. Cone was joining a team that already possessed a deep rotation and a solid bullpen. But the deal made more sense when Major League Baseball announced it was giving Dwight Gooden a 60-day suspension for a failed drug test, a punishment that made Cone the Mets' No. 5 starter.

Cone was the losing pitcher in his first Mets appearance, allowing Ken Griffey's tiebreaking single in the ninth after tossing two scoreless innings of relief. He made three more relief appearances before manager Davey Johnson needed a fifth starter April 27. Cone was hammered in that start, surrendering 10 runs—seven earned—in five innings of an 11–1 loss to the Astros.

Cone showed his potential in his third start, firing a four-hitter in a 6–2 win at Cincinnati May 12 for his first major league victory. The win began a string in which he went 2–0 with a 2.96 ERA in four starts, but it would be 2½ months before he made his next appearance. Cone broke his right index finger when he was hit in the hand by an Atlee Hamaker pitch during a bunt attempt in San Francisco. He worked two shaky innings of relief in his first game following the injury before going 3–4 with a 2.50 ERA over 50⅓ innings in his final 10 appearances, including seven starts.

Cone also opened the 1988 season by pitching out of the bullpen, going 2–0 with a 3.63 ERA in 17⅓ innings. But an injury to fifth starter Rick Aguilera eventually gave

David Cone

Cone an opportunity to make his first start of the season May 3. The Kansas City, Missouri, native proceeded to toss his first major league shutout, scattering eight hits in an 8–0 shutout of the Braves. He also won his next four starts, leaving him 5–0 with a 0.72 ERA since joining the rotation.

Cone had gone from middle relief to No. 2 starter in a two-month span. He was 9–2 with a 2.52 ERA by the All-Star break, and he only got better in the second half. Cone closed out the season by going 11–1 with a 1.92 ERA, allowing just 92 hits while striking out 115 in 117 innings. He became the fourth Met to post a 20-win season, and finished second in the league in strikeouts and earned run average. He finished third in the Cy Young Award balloting, behind only Orel Hershiser of the Dodgers and Cincinnati's Danny Jackson. He also was 10th in the NL MVP voting.

Cone suddenly was the stud of the Mets' rotation after posting the sixth-best winning percentage of any 20-game winner in major league history at that point. He was also working for the *New York Post* as a guest columnist by the time the Mets opened the NLCS against the Dodgers. Unfortunately, his readership included Dodgers manager Tommy Lasorda, who fired up his team by highlighting Cone's published opinion that the Dodgers had an ordinary lineup and a shaky bullpen. Cone was thumped in Game 2 of the series, yielding five runs and five hits in just two innings. But with the Mets on the brink of elimination

in Game 6, he responded by throwing a five-hitter in a 5–1 victory. That was the last time Cone pitched for the Mets in a postseason game. He was employed by the Yankees the next time the Mets made the playoffs 11 years later.

Cone continued to pitch well over the next three seasons, leading the National League in strikeouts in 1990 and '91. He also paced the league with a 3.58 strikeout-to-walk ratio in 1990, and was tied for seventh in the NL with 14 wins in 1990. He went 42–32 during that span, winning 14 games each season while providing a few memorable mental flameouts.

There was a play in Atlanta in which Cone went to cover first base on a grounder. The runner was called safe at first on a close play, allowing the Braves to score a run. Cone spent the next few seconds arguing the call with the first base umpire while a second run was crossing home plate.

Cone also had a dugout confrontation with manager Bud Harrelson in Cincinnati during the 1991 season.

Cone tested the salary arbitration process in the winter of 1992 and came away with a reported $4.25 million contract for the season, a raise of $1.9 million. Mets management wasn't pleased with the arbitration verdict, especially with Cone on the verge of free agency.

Armed with a nice pay raise, Cone tossed shutouts in four of his first 10 starts while going 5–2 with a 2.06 ERA and 79 strikeouts in 78⅔ innings. He was putting together his best year since 1988, throwing five shutouts by July 17 and earning a trip to the All-Star game for the first time in four years.

But the Mets were sputtering despite the off-season acquisitions of Bret Saberhagen, Bobby Bonilla, Eddie Murray, and Willie Randolph. The team was expected to unseat the Pirates as NL East champions, but the Mets were two games under .500 after Cone beat the Cubs 4–2 August 2 to improve to 13–4. New York lost 12 of its next 13 to play itself out of the division race, leaving Cone's future with the team in question less than three months from free agency.

The Mets decided to shed payroll, and they started with Cone. He was shipped to the Blue Jays for Jeff Kent and Ryan Thompson as Toronto tried to win its first World Series. Cone went 4–3 with a 2.65 ERA in seven starts for the Jays to help them wrap up the AL East crown.

Cone won a pivotal Game 2 of the ALCS in Toronto after the A's took the opener. He was the losing pitcher in Game 5 before the Blue Jays wrapped up the pennant two days later. Cone also started Games 2 and 6 of the World Series, leaving the Game 6 clincher with a 2–1 lead before Dave Winfield's two-run double in the 11th gave Toronto its first title.

But Toronto was as interested in re-signing Cone as the Mets were in August. He was back in his hometown after the Royals inked him to a free-agent contract. Cone was perceived as a bad signing in 1993 after he went 11–14 with a 3.33 ERA. But he won the American League Cy Young Award during the strike-shortened 1994 season, going 16–5 with a 2.94 ERA while helping the Royals finish with the league's fifth-best record at 64–51.

The Blue Jays reacquired Cone just before the beginning of the 1995 season in an effort to claim a third straight World Series crown. He pitched well in his return to Toronto, compiling a 3.38 ERA and a 9–6 mark in 17 games. However, the Blue Jays were mired in last place in the AL East when they decided to send him to the Yankees an a salary dump.

Cone helped the Yanks nail down a 1995 wild-card berth by going 9–2 with a 3.82 ERA in 13 starts. He finished fourth in the Cy Young Award voting and began a 5½-year run with the Bombers. Cone experienced a scare after opening 1996 4–1 with a 2.08 ERA in six starts. He was diagnosed with an aneurysm in his pitching shoulder and underwent surgery in May, causing him to miss the next four months. He returned September 2 in Oakland, tossing seven no-hit innings but leaving the game after 85 pitches. Cone also went seven innings in his next two starts and helped the Yanks nail down their first division title in 15 years.

Cone was selected to the 1997 All-Star team, won 20 games a year later, and pitched a perfect game in 1999. He won four World Series with the Yankees and appeared in one series game against the Mets in 2000.

But Cone endured a terrible 2000 season, finishing 4–14 with a 6.91 ERA, by far his worst year in the majors. That didn't stop the Red Sox from signing him to a free-agent contract before the 2001 season. He went 9–7 with a 4.31 ERA in his lone year with Boston, going undefeated between May 23 and August 11 while helping the team stay in the playoff race despite the loss of Pedro Martinez to a torn rotator cuff.

The Red Sox refused to offer him salary arbitration after the season, and Cone sat out all of 2002 after failing to hook on with another team. But one of his old teams needed pitching help as it approached 2003.

Cone made a brief return to the Mets and turned back the clock in his first start of '03. He faced the Expos while braving temperatures in the 30s on April 4, but the weather didn't stop him from allowing just two hits over five innings of a 3–0 shutout. Cone left the bases loaded by striking out Vladimir Guerrero to end the third. He received a standing ovation from an appreciative audience that hoped the 40-year-old Cone could elude Father Time.

But Cone was done by the end of May, going 0–3 with a 9.00 ERA in his final 13 innings. He retired due to a chronic hip injury, leaving the game with five All-Star Game selections and four top-five finishes in the Cy Young balloting.

ML debut	Royals vs. Twins, 6/8/86 (1 IP, 3 H, 1 ER, 0 K, 0 BB)
Mets debut	vs. Braves, 4/11/87 (3 IP, 3 H, 1 ER, 2 K, 1 BB)
First ML strikeout	Danny Tartabull, Mariners, 6/11/86 (with Royals)
First Mets strikeout	Ken Oberkfell, Braves, 4/11/87
First ML/Mets win	@ Reds, 5/12/87
First ML/Mets save	@ Cardinals, 10/3/87

Most strikeouts, ML/Mets game	19, @ Phillies, 10/6/91
Low-hit ML CG	0, Yankees vs. Expos, 7/18/99 (perfect game)
Low-hit Mets CG	1, vs. Padres, 8/29/88; vs. Cardinals, 9/20/91
Acquired:	Traded by the Royals with Chris Jelic for Ed Hearn, Rick Anderson and Mauro Gozzo, 3/27/87.
Deleted:	Traded to the Blue Jays for Jeff Kent and a player to be named (Ryan Thompson), 8/27/92.
Re-acquired:	signed as a free agent, 2/13/03.
Deleted:	Retired, 5/30/05.

AL Cy Young Award, 1994
NL All-Star, 1988, 1992
AL All-Star, 1994, 1997, 1999
NL strikeout leader, 1990, 1991
NL walks leader, 1992
Tied for National League lead in shutouts (5), 1992

Roger Craig

Pitcher	Bats right, throws right
Born: 2/17/30	Durham, North Carolina
Height: 6'4"	Weight: 191 #38, #13

Roger Craig Mets Career

YEAR	GP/GS	IP	H	R	ER	K	BB	W–L	SV	ERA
1962	42/33	233.1	261	133	117	118	70	10–24	3	4.51
1963	46/31	236.0	249	117	99	108	58	5–22	2	3.78
Total	88/64	469.1	510	250	216	226	128	15–46	5	4.14

Mets Career/Batting

GP	AB	R	H	2B	3B	HR	RBI	K	BB	SB	AVG
88	145	1	10	0	0	0	2	72	9	0	.069

ML Career

YEAR	GP/GS	IP	H	R	ER	K	BB	W–L	SV	ERA
55-66	368/186	1536.1	1528	763	653	803	522	74–98	19	3.83

No player is more synonymous with the 1962 Mets than Roger Craig as he unintentionally helped mold the team's reputation as lovable losers. Craig pitched his heart out during his two years with the franchise, yet his 15–46 record led to the team's legendary status. The Mets went 6–8 during games in which he worked at least eight full innings during '62, and 7–16 when he went seven frames or more. Leave him in for at least seven innings in 1963, and the Mets were 7–15, with Craig absorbing 14 of those defeats.

Craig's wry humor allowed him to endure his time with the Mets and gain the affection of his teammates. He managed to keep the losses in perspective knowing the talent level of the ballclub. Put his stats in a different light and you'll find the Mets went 26–62 in the games he pitched for the Mets, a .295 winning percentage. They posted a .278 winning percentage in the other contests.

Roger Lee Craig was born in Durham, North Carolina, and attended North Carolina State on a basketball scholarship. He spent one year as a guard under head coach Everett Case before the Dodgers made him an offer to play baseball in 1950.

Craig was a solid long reliever and spot starter for the Dodgers upon breaking into the majors in 1955. He was 49–38 with a 3.73 ERA in seven seasons as a Dodger, including an 11–5 mark and a 2.06 ERA for the 1959 World Series team.

Craig struggled in 1961, one year after breaking his shoulder. He pitched in what was a career-high 40 games for the '61 squad but was only 5–6 with a 6.15 ERA in 112⅔ innings. The Dodgers left him exposed in the expansion draft, and the Mets snapped him up as one of their $75,000 selections.

Before heading to the Mets, Craig had never started more than 17 games except in 1956, when he made 32 starts and went 12–11 with a 3.71 ERA in 35 appearances. Craig was considered the ace of the staff that season, although he was still a work in progress as he reported to training camp.

"Roy Campanella worked hard with me last year," Craig said in a 1956 interview. "But until this spring I was still a thrower. Carl Erskine, a real pitcher, gave me the tip that worked like magic.

"After watching me labor to get the ball over the plate one day, Erskine asked me if I was aiming for the center of the plate, trying to throw a perfect strike. I admitted I was and asked him if that wasn't the aim of all pitchers.

"He told me he threw to spots and suggested I give it a try. So I now try to forget the plate is there. I set the spot where I am supposed to pitch the batter, high, low, outside, or inside. Of course, these spots are mostly in the strike zone and it's amazing how many balls go over the plate when it's no longer a mental hazard."[41]

The Mets had very little in the form of experienced starting pitching when they opened their inaugural spring training in 1962. Craig had the most when the Mets broke camp and was named the opening-day starter for the Mets' first-ever game April 11 at St. Louis, but only after scheduled starter Sherman Jones injured his eye while lighting a cigarette.

"We had one of the finest relief pitchers in the National League, Roger Craig, as a starter," said teammate Rod Kanehl. "He would have set all kinds of relief records had he been able to be used as a reliever. Roger was a good five-inning pitcher, had a good pick-off move, and he had a good sinker/slider. He could come in and get a ground ball, and boom, it's over. He was perfect for relief. But we had to use him as a starter."[42]

Craig immediately put his stamp on the '62 Mets by allowing five runs and eight hits in only three innings of an 11–4 loss to the Cardinals in the opener. He began the game by getting Curt Flood to fly out before allowing three straight singles, including Stan Musial's RBI hit that plated the first run scored against the Mets. One batter later, Craig committed the first balk in team history to bring home another run before Ken Boyer hit an RBI grounder.

Craig looked out of place in his first four starts, going 0–3 with an 11.68 ERA while averaging just over three innings. His first win as a Met came as a reliever as he tossed three scoreless frames in an 8–6 win over the Phillies April 28, one day after lasting just one inning as a starter versus Philly.

Craig didn't get his first win as a starter until June 10, when he pitched into the ninth inning of a 2–1 triumph at Wrigley Field. His first winning streak didn't come until August 4 through August 8, and he won three straight in September after falling to 7–23.

Craig enjoyed some success pitching in the Polo Grounds in 1962. He was 8–9 with a 3.74 ERA at the "Horseshoe," but 2–15 with a 5.16 ERA outside New York. But he and lefty Al Jackson were the two most dependable pitchers on the '62 squad, combining for 18 of the Mets' 40 victories. Craig either led or tied for the team lead in wins, starts, innings, complete games, and strikeouts, and helped his cause by picking off 13 runners. But as teammate Rod Kanehl intimated, Craig's record as a starter would have been a lot better if a second Roger Craig was around to relieve him.

"I lost 24 games my first year, and people sent me rabbits foots," Craig said almost 30 years later as he managed the Giants. "They sent me all these good-luck charms. And the fans were really behind me, and I look back and all those things—the adversity, the losing—really helped me in my teaching and to associate and relating to losses, a guy going 0-for-10 or maybe losing three in a row as a pitcher. It helps me a lot in relating to my players."

Craig's 10–24 overall mark in 1962 overshadows his good work as a reliever that season. He was 4–2 with a 0.87 ERA and three saves in 10⅓ innings in nine games out of the bullpen. Yes, Craig had a win, a loss or a save in all nine of his games as a reliever.

"I lost 24 games my first year with the Mets," Craig said a few years later. "You've got to be a pretty good pitcher to lose that many. What manager is going to let you go out there that often?"[43]

He passed his positive outlook onto Jackson, who went 8–20 before compiling a very respectable 13–17 mark for a club that won just 51 games in 1963.

"I lost 20 games that first year, and Craig told me it takes a hell of a pitcher to lose 20 games. I was thinking to myself, 'What the heck are you talking about?' I just lost 20 games, and I thought my life would just pass away. You know, after I thought about it, Craig was right, because if you're not pitching good, you're not going to [be in position to] lose 20 games. We just had a poor club."[44]

Craig got off to a nice start in 1963, posting a 2–2 mark with one save and a 3.07 ERA in six games, including one relief appearance. He wouldn't record another victory until August 9, becoming the year's first 20-game loser before there was a 20-game winner. Loss No. 20 came on August 4, 25 days before Sandy Koufax of the Dodgers won his 20th.

"Well, I reached 20 before Koufax did," Craig mused at the ridiculousness of his season.[45]

Craig posted a fairly respectable 4.16 ERA over 132 innings between May 4 and August 4. But he endured 18 consecutive losses during that span, beginning the streak by allowing five homers and nine runs over 4⅓ innings of a 17–4 loss to the Giants.

No other pitcher in National League history had dropped 18 straight decisions in a single season since Clifton Curtis with the 1910 Boston Braves. Craig was on the cusp of breaking the mark as he prepared to face the Cubs August 9.

Craig was vocal in the clubhouse before heading to the bullpen for what many figured would be his 19th consecutive loss. He went over the usual game situations, then told his teammates, "Seriously, fellows, I would like to win this game."[46]

Craig's losing streak featured ridiculous losses and a few games the Mets actually won. There were nine games during the skid in which he pitched at least eight innings and allowed two earned runs or fewer.

"Roger was a great competitor and a savvy pitcher," said batterymate Norm Sherry. "He would pitch great games for us and we couldn't score runs and we'd make errors. But he could handle all that. That's why he was such a good manager."[47]

Craig's losing streak ended in dramatic fashion. He went the distance on an eight-hitter but lost the lead when Billy Williams led off the eighth with a triple and scored the tiebreaking run on Ron Santo's sacrifice fly. But Craig finally received a long-awaited victory when Jim Hickman belted a grand slam with two outs in the bottom of the ninth for a 5–2 win.

Someone had the audacity to ask Craig if there was a small part of him that wanted to see the streak continue.

"Oh, gosh, no," Craig replied. "If I ever do that I'll quit this game. I'd try to keep myself in the right frame of mind. It wasn't easy, but I'd try."[48]

Craig paced the '63 team with 14 complete games and lowered his ERA to 3.78. But he finished just 5–22, still the worst winning percentage of any 20-game loser in team history.

"Sometimes I think that the worst thing that could happen to me would be to win," he said kiddingly at a luncheon a few days after ending his losing streak. "Then I wouldn't be a celebrity any more and the writers wouldn't interview me."[49]

Although he continued to put on a brave front in the clubhouse, Craig admitted the losing gnawed at him. Fortunately, his wife, Carolyn, was a great confidant during the darker days of the '63 campaign.

"When I'm on the road and I lose, I call her and tell her about it. I hear guys say all the time that you should leave the game in the clubhouse, but that's a lot of bunk.

"I discuss the game with Carolyn. She always asks me about my arm—I had all that trouble in 1959, you know. She never worried about my getting beat. Just about my arm. We talk a while, and then I forget it."[50]

Roger Craig warms up before a game against the Chicago Cubs at New York's Polo Grounds in 1963. He is wearing No. 13, although his regular number was No. 38.

Mercifully, the Mets traded Craig to the Cardinals after the 1963 season, allowing him to pitch for a championship team. He went 7–9 with a 3.25 ERA in 166 innings during the 1964 regular season before picking up a victory in Game 4 of the World Series, tossing scoreless ball over 4⅔ innings while the Cards erased a 3–0 deficit in a 4–3 win over the Yankees.

Craig spent the following season with the Reds before ending his major league career with the 1966 Phillies. He finished with a respectable 61–52 mark while pitching for teams not named the Mets. His Mets teammates respected both his toughness and demeanor.

"Roger was our best pitcher," said infielder Al Moran. "It seemed as though every game he pitched, he was in the ballgame. We just didn't have the hitting, the speed or the defense."

"You would never know he was in a losing streak," Duke Carmel added. "He just came out every day and did what he could."

"He never looked back, and he never felt sorry for himself," said Galen Cisco.[51]

Craig enjoyed great success as a major league pitching coach and manager. He was the first Padres skipper to lead the franchise to a winning record, going 84–78 for a 1978 squad that included Cy Young winner Gaylord Perry. Eleven years later, he became the first Giants manager to guide the franchise to the World Series since Alvin Dark in 1962. But the 1989 World Series was marred by an earthquake in the Bay Area just before Game 3 at Candlestick

Park, and the Giants waited two weeks to resume the series before the A's eventually completed a four-game sweep.

Craig went 738–737 as a manager, leading the Giants to two division titles while creating the catch-phrase "Hum Baby." He was hired by San Francisco in 1985 after tutoring the Tigers' hurlers to a runaway pennant and a World Series title. Craig had planned to retire after the '85 campaign but was coaxed out of that notion by the Giants.

He is also given credit for prolonging Mike Scott's major league career. Scott was close to being released by the Astros when he learned the splitter from the fellow former Met. Many felt Scott augmented his splitter with a scuff-ball while beating the Mets twice in the 1986 NLCS. In fact, Craig called him on it during a game between the Astros and Giants. Regardless, Scott was just one example of pitchers who became better under Craig's guidance.

"God bless Roger Craig," Scott told UPI reporter Milton Richman in 1986. "Roger was great. We went over to Grossmont Junior College in San Diego, and after watching me throw, he said my mechanics were fine.

"Then he said, 'Today we're going to talk about the pitch.' He meant the split-fingered fastball and he gave me three things to remember. He said first I had to make sure I threw it over the top. Second, I had to throw it exactly like a fastball, and third, if I wanted to control the pitch better, I had to put my fingers closer together on the ball."

"It's really not very hard to learn," said Craig. "When I was still pitching, guys like Elroy Face, Lindy McDaniel, and Diego Segui threw the pitch, and it was called a fork-ball. Some people say I discovered the split-fingered fast-ball. I don't know if I did. I just discovered a better way to teach it."[52]

ML debut	Dodgers vs. Reds, 7/17/55 (9 IP, 3 H, 1 ER, 6 K, 5 BB)
Mets debut	@ Cardinals, 4/11/62 (3 IP, 8 H, 5 ER, 1 K, 0 BB)
First ML strikeout	Gus Bell, Reds, 7/17/55 (with Dodgers)
First Mets strikeout	Gene Oliver, @ Cardinals, 4/11/62
First ML win	vs. Reds, 7/17/55
First Mets win	vs. Phillies, 4/28/62
First ML save	vs. Pirates, 9/4/55 (with Dodgers)
First Mets save	@ Phillies, 5/6/62
Most strikeouts, ML game	11, Dodgers @ Reds, 7/28/55
Most strikeouts, Mets game	8, @ Braves, 5/18/62; vs. Cubs, 5/28/63; vs. Cubs, 8/9/63
Low-hit ML CG	2, Dodgers @ Braves, 6/5/56; Dodgers @ Cubs, 7/16/56
Los-hit Mets CG	4, @ Cubs, 7/4/63; @ Astros, 7/27/63
Acquired:	Selected in the expansion draft, 10/10/61.
Deleted:	Traded to the Cardinals for George Altman and Bill Wakefield, 11/4/63.

Ron Darling

Pitcher	Bats right, throws right	
Born: 8/19/60	Honolulu, Hawaii	
Height: 6'3"	Weight: 195	#44, #12, #15

Ron Darling Mets Career

YEAR	GP/GS	IP	H	R	ER	K	BB	W–L	SV	ERA
1983	5/5	35.1	31	11	11	23	17	1–3	0	2.80
1984	33/33	205.2	179	97	87	136	104	12–9	0	3.81
1985	36/35	248.0	214	93	80	167	114	16–6	0	2.90
1986	34/34	237.0	203	84	74	184	81	15–6	0	2.81
1987	32/32	207.2	183	111	99	167	96	12–8	0	4.29
1988	34/34	240.2	218	97	87	161	60	17–9	0	3.25
1989	33/33	217.1	214	100	85	153	70	14–14	0	3.52
1990	33/18	126.0	135	73	63	99	44	7–9	0	4.50
1991	17/17	102.1	96	50	44	58	28	5–6	0	3.87
Total	257/241	1620.0	1473	716	630	1148	614	99–70	0	3.50

Mets Career/Batting

GP	AB	R	H	2B	3B	HR	RBI	K	BB	SB	AVG
272	519	39	75	20	2	2	19	173	15	1	.145

ML Career

YEAR	GP/GS	IP	H	R	ER	K	BB	W–L	SV	ERA
83–95	382/364	2360.1	2244	1139	1016	1590	906	136–116	0	3.87

One of Frank Cashen's first bold moves as the Mets' general manager was shipping the popular Lee Mazzilli to the Rangers for a pair of pitching prospects before the 1982 season. The trade also became Cashen's first steal.

Walt Terrell and Ron Darling were the young hurlers acquired for Mazzilli. Terrell pitched well for the Mets before he was dealt to the Tigers after the 1984 season for Howard Johnson. Darling stayed around long enough to help the Mets win one World Series and two division titles while emerging as one of the top pitchers in the starting rotation.

Darling had made a name for himself at Yale, where he was 25–8 with a 2.00 ERA and 256 strikeouts in 274 innings. In 1981 he tossed an 11-inning no-hitter in the NCAA tournament but lost 1–0 to Frank Viola and St. John's. He was taken ninth overall by the Rangers in the June draft and placed in Double A, where he went 4–4 with a 4.44 ERA with Tulsa in his only pro season with the Rangers.

The Mets put Darling in Triple A after acquiring him, and his Tidewater numbers were just 17–18 with a 3.88 ERA in two seasons. But he displayed a heavy fastball and an ability to work out of jams, earning himself a promotion when the rosters expanded in September 1983.

The Mets already had showcased some of their top minor league hurlers in 1983 by the time Darling took the mound September 6 against the Phillies at Shea Stadium. The Hawaiian stood above the rest of the prospects after his five-start stint, tossing a "quality" start in each game.

Darling's first major league start was a heartbreaker as he allowed only a run and five hits in 6 1/3 innings. With Mike Schmidt at the plate and Joe Morgan on base, Darling balked twice to let in the game's first run in a 2–0 loss.

Darling was 0–3 in his first four starts despite a 3.08 ERA. He finally earned his first big league win in his first complete game, tossing a seven-hitter in a 4–2 decision over the Pirates September 28.

Darling found himself pitching for his Tidewater skipper by 1984. Davey Johnson was promoted to manager before the season, and the new bench boss gave the younger Mets plenty of opportunities to perform at the major league level. Darling was part of a rotation that now included Dwight Gooden and Terrell, both of whom pitched for Johnson the previous season. The trio pitched so well that Cashen was able to release veterans Mike Torrez and Craig Swan.

Darling pitched 205⅔ innings in 1984, but Johnson usually had him on a short leash as Darling nibbled his way to 104 walks, by far the most on the team that season. With a strong bullpen, Johnson didn't hesitate to lift Darling at the first sign of trouble in the late innings.

Darling picked up a victory in the Mets' second game of the season, giving up two hits in six scoreless innings at Cincinnati. He also got to pitch the home opener but was lifted shortly after allowing Gary Carter's grand slam in the fourth inning of a 10–0 loss to the Expos.

Darling surrendered six runs over five innings in his next start, but he was 10–3 with a 3.34 ERA following a four-hit shutout of the Reds on July 6. But that was the last time he threw more than eight innings the rest of the season; he was 2–6 with a 4.32 ERA in his final 16 starts, but that didn't stop him from finishing fifth in the Rookie of the Year balloting.

Darling was a National League All-Star just a year later as he emerged as the Mets' No. 2 pitcher behind Gooden. He had another strong start in 1985, going 10–2 with two shutouts and a 2.62 ERA through mid-July. Darling won six consecutive starts between August 19 and September 15 to help the Mets stay in the division race.

The Mets were three games behind the first-place Cardinals with six games remaining when Darling opened a three-game series at St. Louis. He was brilliant in a pressure situation, allowing four hits in nine shutout innings before Darryl Strawberry belted a long homer in the 11th to win it 1–0. The Mets failed to catch the Cardinals at the end of 1985, and Darling finished just two walks shy of Nolan Ryan's single-season team record. But Darling finished seventh in the National League in strikeouts and was ninth in ERA despite topping the league in bases on balls.

Darling cut his walk total by 33 in 1986 while helping the Mets win their first World Series title in 17 years. He got off to a shaky start, going 1–0 with a 6.75 ERA in his first four starts, but the Mets won each of those games.

Darling proceeded to win his next five starts and was 11–3 with a 2.62 ERA following a six-hit shutout of the Cubs on July 29. Darling compiled a 1.97 ERA over 127⅔ innings between his fifth and 21st start. Manager Davey Johnson didn't let Darling pitch as deep into games over the final two months of the season, giving his staff time to

recharge for the inevitable postseason run. Darling had six no-decisions in his final 12 starts, but he lost just two of those games. The Mets went 26–8 in the 34 games he started.

Darling finished fifth in the NL Cy Young balloting, behind teammate Bob Ojeda. However, Darling was just fourth on the team in victories, in part to his team-high 13 no-decisions.

Darling's first postseason game was a bit rocky, but the Mets won anyway. He fell behind in Game 3 of the NLCS 4–0 by the second inning before holding the Astros scoreless on one hit over his last three frames. Darling had given the Mets time to stage a rally and beat the Astros 6–5 on Len Dykstra's two-run homer in the bottom of the ninth.

Darling joined Jon Matlack as the only Mets hurlers to start three games in the same World Series. Like Matlack's effort in 1973, an error by a second baseman contributed to Darling's 1–0 loss to the Red Sox in the series opener. Darling struck out eight and limited the Bosox to three hits in seven innings, but Tim Teufel let a grounder go through his legs in the seventh inning, allowing Jim Rice to score the game's lone run.

Darling's lone postseason victory came in Game 4 against Boston as he allowed four hits and six walks in seven shutout innings. He had now gone 17 consecutive postseason innings without allowing an earned run.

Johnson sent Darling to the mound for Game 7, but the right-hander was pulled in the fourth inning with the Red Sox leading 3–0. Dwight Evans and Rich Gedman opened the second inning with consecutive homers before Wade Boggs added an RBI single later in the inning. But the Mets scored eight runs in their final three at-bats to win the game and the series.

Darling's popularity soared that season. His good looks graced the cover of *GQ* and his personality landed him appearances on TV shows ranging from *Good Morning America* to *Sesame Street*. But Darling just tried to be "one of the guys" in the clubhouse, and he cringed whenever he was called "Mr. Perfect," a nickname given to him by Gary Carter.

Being one of the guys also caused him to spend a few hours in jail. He, Bob Ojeda, Rick Aguilera, Darryl Strawberry, and Teufel went to a Houston nightclub after a game to celebrate the birth of Teufel's son, Shawn. Strawberry left the bar a few minutes later after surveying the clientele and deciding that out-of-town ballplayers could become the target for trouble there. The other four were there at closing time, just long enough to be roughed up by off-duty police moonlighting as bouncers and security. The four players were arrested and released early in the morning, giving the tabloids enough back page fodder for the remainder of the weekend. Ironically, the four players weren't among the team's true party animals that season.

The Mets' starting rotation had gotten better in each of Darling's first three seasons. Dwight Gooden was the crown jewel on the staff, but Darling, Ojeda, and Sid Fernandez

Ron Darling records his first career shutout on June 15, 1984, against the St. Louis Cardinals.

could have been No. 1 starters on almost every other team. Darling seemed to thrive in the situation, knowing that if he had a bad outing, the other three would make sure a losing streak wouldn't ensue.

But Darling's importance to the team grew after Gooden received a 60-day suspension for a positive drug test. The punishment left the Mets without their marquee pitcher for the start of the 1987 season and put more pressure on Darling to succeed. He was now the No. 2 starter, and he'd soon emerged as the top guy when Bob Ojeda was placed on the disabled list with an elbow injury. Darling was 2–4 with a 5.58 ERA in 12 starts during Gooden's absence. Once Gooden returned, Darling went 10–4 with a 3.62 ERA the rest of the season, a stretch that included victories in six consecutive starts between July 22 and August 16. He helped the Mets move back into the division race as the Mets won 11 of his final 14 starts.

Darling was the starting pitcher in the opener of a three-game set with the Cardinals at Shea Stadium in September, a series that could have vaulted the Mets into first place with a sweep. Darling was magnificent over six innings, limiting the Cardinals to one hit in six innings while New York built a 4–1 lead. But he tore thumb ligaments while trying to make a diving grab of Vince Coleman's bunt-single, the only hit off Darling. Every Mets starter had been on the disabled or suspended list by the time Darling attempted that grab. The injury caused Darling to miss the rest of the season and contributed to the Mets' swoon.

Darling and the rest of the rotation were back in form in 1988, leading the Mets to their third 100-win season. Darling earned a career-high 17 victories, including a six-hitter in the Mets' NL East clincher against the Phillies on September 22. He also set a career-best with four shutouts, two coming in his first four starts of the season. He ended the season by going 5–0 with one shutout in his last eight starts.

Darling pitched pretty well under raw, rainy conditions in Game 3 of the NLCS against the Dodgers, giving up two earned runs in six innings of an 8–4 victory. But his next postseason outing was a disaster as he surrendered six runs in one-plus inning of a 6–0 loss to the Dodgers. Orel Hershiser tossed a five-hitter to put L.A. into the World Series after most baseball fans expected the Mets to waltz into a meeting with the A's.

In 1989 Darling joined Tom Seaver as the only Mets to win at least 10 games in at least six straight seasons. He also became the first Mets pitcher since Seaver in 1972 to homer in two consecutive starts. Darling also received a postseason honor, becoming the first Mets pitcher to win a Gold Glove.

Darling got off to an exceptionally poor start in '89, opening 0–3 with an 8.20 in his first four outings. He was just 4–5 with a 4.64 ERA by June 18 before finally settling in. Darling's season also included a four-start winning streak in which he posted a 1.07 ERA in 33⅔ innings. But he finished the season just 14–14 despite a 3.52 ERA and had become the No. 4 pitcher on the team with the arrival of Frank Viola.

Darling found himself challenging Ojeda for starts in 1990 as the two vied to become Davey Johnson's No. 5 starter, behind Viola, Gooden, David Cone, and Sid Fernandez. It was an odd situation to place a veteran who was just one year removed from a 17-win season. He was the fifth starter out of spring training, but the competition helped neither Darling nor Ojeda as the two were consistently shuttled in and out of the rotation, depending on which one faltered.

Darling was pulled from the rotation for a month after allowing five runs in a three-inning stint at San Francisco May 15. He was a starter in seven consecutive appearances between July 21 and August 21 but never found a rhythm. By now it seemed Darling and Ojeda were constantly auditioning for new manager Bud Harrelson, who had his team in the division title hunt but couldn't figure out what to do with the back end of his rotation.

Darling's seven-start streak was followed by seven straight appearances out of the bullpen. He won his final two starts in late September to finish 7–9 with a 4.50 ERA. Darling underwent surgery after the season to have bone chips removed from his right elbow.

Ojeda was traded to the Dodgers on December 15, making Darling a full-time starter once again heading into the 1991 season. But he averaged just six innings in his 17 starts as a Met that year, and had just two outings of more than seven innings.

With the Mets in desperate need of a setup man, Darling was sent to the Expos for Tim Burke around the All-Star break. Darling made just three starts for Montreal before joining the Athletics at the '91 non-waiver trade deadline. He went 3–0 in his first four Oakland starts before going 0–7 with a 5.40 ERA the rest of the way.

Darling was looking like a washed-up pitcher heading into the 1992 season, and he didn't change anyone's mind by opening the year 1–2 with a 5.45 earned run average. The four-start stretch in which he carried a no-hitter into the eighth inning against the Royals before former teammate Keith Miller led off with an infield single.

Darling had won just once in 14 starts dating to last August, but manager Tony La Russa and pitching coach Dave Duncan kept him in the rotation. Their patience was rewarded as Darling finished second to Mike Moore on the team in wins, innings pitched, and starts. Darling went 15–10 with a 3.86 ERA, tossing three shutouts between May 24 and July 24. He also started Game 3 of the ALCS, allowing two earned runs over six innings of a 7–5 loss to the Blue Jays.

Darling pitched three more seasons with the A's but went just 19–27 with a 5.17 ERA. He was released on August 21, 1995, about a month shy of completing a three-year, $7.5 million contract. It was time for Darling to find another line of work.

He worked his way into television, serving as a color analyst for the A's and appearing regularly on *The Best Damn Sports Show* before working his way back east. He did some work on YES Network before he was hired as the first TV color commentator of the Washington Nationals. Darling didn't offer much in the way of analysis during his one year with the Nats, primarily because he was partnered with a play-by-play man, Mel Proctor, who rarely drew Darling into an in-game conversation. Darling looked and sounded uncomfortable during his one year in Washington. But his career began to take off when he rejoined the Mets while working with Gary Cohen and ex-teammate Keith Hernandez on fledgling SNY. Viewers were treated to a baseball education, with a ballgame thrown in. The three immediate clicked and became the Mets' best broadcasting trio since Lindsey Nelson, Ralph Kiner, and Bob Murphy.

ML/Mets debut   vs. Phillies, 9/6/83 (6.1 IP, 5 H, 1 ER, 6 K, 1 BB)
First ML/Mets strikeout   Joe Morgan, Phillies, 9/6/83
First ML/Mets win   @ Pirates, 9/28/83
First ML save
Most strikeouts, ML/Mets game   12, vs. Dodgers, 8/29/84; vs. Dodgers, 5/27/86
Low-hit ML CG   2, 3 times, all with A's in 1992
Low-hit Mets CG   3, vs. Reds, 5/8/88
Acquired: Traded by the Rangers with Walt Terrell for Lee Mazzilli, 4/1/82.
Deleted: Traded to the Expos with Mike Thomas for Tim Burke, 7/15/91.
NL All-Star, 1985
NL Gold Glove, 1989

Carlos Delgado

First Baseman	Bats left, throws right
Born: 6/25/72	Aguadilla, Puerto Rico
Height: 6'3"	Weight: 240 #21

Carlos Delgado Mets Career

YEAR	GP	AB	R	H	2B	3B	HR	RBI	K	BB	SB	AVG	SLG	OBP
2006	144	524	89	139	30	2	38	114	120	74	0	.265	.548	.361
2007	139	538	71	139	30	0	24	87	118	52	4	.258	.448	.333
2008	159	598	96	162	32	1	38	115	124	72	1	.271	.518	.353
2009	26	94	15	28	7	1	4	23	20	12	0	.298	.521	.393
TOTAL	468	1754	271	468	99	4	104	339	382	210	5	.267	.506	.351

ML Career

YEARS	GP	AB	R	H	2B	3B	HR	RBI	K	BB	SB	AVG	SLG	OBP
93-09	2035	8657	1241	2038	483	18	473	1512	1745	1109	14	.280	.546	.383

Hockey Hall of Famer Herb Brooks was in his first season as the New York Rangers' head coach when he met the media after a tough victory at Madison Square Garden. His first postgame comment concerned the impatient New York fans.

"Boo…Yea…Boo…Yea…Boo," Brooks griped as he marveled at the fickleness of a crowd that was jeering the power play while imploring the team to win. The architect of the 1980 Miracle on Ice soon learned that New York wasn't Minnesota, 15 years before Carlos Delgado was reminded that New York isn't Toronto.

Carlos Delgado. Photo courtesy of David Ferry

Carlos Juan (Hernandez) Delgado was on the fast track to the Hall of Fame when he became a Met in November 2005. He had spent nine full seasons with the Blue Jays and one year with the Marlins upon his arrival at Shea Stadium. From 1996 to 2005, Delgado was seventh in the majors with 357 homers, fourth with 1,138 RBIs, and third with 750 extra-base hits (despite only 14 triples) while hitting .288.

Delgado was a two-time All-Star and a three-time Silver Slugger once he donned a Mets uniform. He had a fantastic inaugural season as a Met in 2006 and was one of the league's top hitters in the last four months of 2008. In between, he found out how tough Mets fans can be.

Delgado opened his Mets career by having one of the best-hitting Aprils in team history, ripping a team record-tying nine homers, driving in 20 runs, and hitting .298 while playing all 24 games that month. His first Mets homer was a two-run shot in his second game, putting them ahead 4–0 in the third inning before the Nationals came away with an extra-inning victory. The blast triggered an 11-game hitting streak in which Delgado batted .400 with five homers, 14 RBI, and 10 runs scored.

Delgado also drove in 26 runs in August, 14 coming during a seven-day span that saw him bat .480 in a seven-game winning streak. He reached the 100-RBI mark with a

two-run shot off John Smoltz on September 6 before joining Howard Johnson, Todd Hundley, and Beltran as the first Mets with 35 homers, 30 doubles, and 110 RBIs.

The first baseman usually saved his best games of 2006 for the road. He clobbered National League pitchers in their own ballparks, hitting .304 with 20 homers and 59 RBIs. At Shea, Delgado provided 18 homers and 55 RBIs but batted only .226 with a .487 slugging average, 121 points lower than his road slugging percentage.

By the time the 2006 regular season was over, Delgado was tied for 41st on the all-time list with 407 homers and 89th with 1,287 RBIs. But of the 40 players above him on the home run list, Ernie Banks was the only one without a postseason at-bat until Delgado helped the Mets win the 2006 NL East title.

Delgado was the Mets' best hitter in the '06 playoffs, batting .351 with four homers and 11 RBIs. He homered in his second postseason at-bat while going 4-for-5 with two RBIs and two runs scored in the Mets' Game 1 victory over the Dodgers in the NLDS. The home run made him only the second Met (Edgardo Alfonzo) to go deep in his first postseason contest with the team.

The Aguadilla, Puerto Rico, product established a team record for RBIs in an NLCS by driving home nine against the Cardinals. With the Mets trailing the Cardinals 2–1 in the series, Delgado hit a tiebreaking, three-run homer and matched a team mark with five ribbies in a 12–5 rout of the Redbirds at St. Louis after homering twice in Game 2.

Delgado had a .448 on-base percentage and an .821 slugging average in the NLCS, but the Mets lost the series in seven games to end their expected run to the World Series.

Everything seemed to go right for Delgado in 2006. The opposite was true in '07. The Mets entered 2007 as the favorites to win the NL East as long as Delgado could come back from separate surgeries on his right wrist and right elbow, which were performed one week apart right after the NLCS.

The Mets got off to a good start despite Delgado, who spent the first three months of the season trying to push his batting average above .230. He had just one homer and seven extra-base hits in his first 30 games, fueling speculation that he wasn't fully recovered from his off-season surgeries. But he squelched that talk by batting .270 with 11 homers and 27 RBIs in 41 games from May 26 to July 13. Delgado also had two walk-off RBIs in a three-game series against the Cubs in mid-May before ripping a game-ending homer off Armando Benitez to beat the Giants on May 26.

Delgado's 2007 batting average never rose above .267 after April 9, but that didn't stop the Mets from winning. They continued to win for a while after he strained his right hip flexor September 4, causing him to miss 14 games. New York took five of its first seven contests without Delgado, putting them seven games ahead of the second-place Phillies with just 17 games remaining. By the time he returned, the Mets' lead had shrunk to 1½ games heading toward the final 10 games of the year.

Delgado batted .297 with seven ribbies upon his return, and the Mets won their first three games with him back in the lineup. But the Phillies continued to win while the Mets closed the season 1–6 to miss the postseason by one game. Delgado broke his left hand when hit by a Dontrelle Willis pitch in the season finale, causing the slugger to spend another off-season rehabbing an injury.

The late-season collapse left Mets fans bitter and shell-shocked. It didn't help that the team went 20–27 from April 20 to June 10 to fall to 30–33 for the year, causing many of the Shea faithful to look for a scapegoat. They settled on Delgado, who owned a .242 average with nine homers and 32 RBIs by the time manager Willie Randolph was fired on June 17.

Delgado looked uninspired on the field while his bat appeared slow. There were reports of friction between Delgado and Randolph, although the first baseman strongly denied he had any problems with his skipper.

Delgado's average had slipped to .228 when he put together one of the finest single-game batting performances in Mets history. He set a team record by collecting nine RBIs in a 15–6 rout at Yankee Stadium on June 27, delivering a two-run double, a grand slam, and a three-run

blast to break Dave Kingman's 32-year-old mark of eight ribbies.

Delgado's assault on the Yankees began a season-ending stretch that saw him hit .308 while providing 27 homers and 80 RBIs in 84 games. He went 5-for-5 with three RBIs in an 11–1 pounding of the Braves on August 21, fours days before furnishing two homers and six RBIs versus the Astros.

Chants of "M-V-P! M-V-P!" bellowed throughout Shea whenever Delgado came through with one of his many go-ahead hits. The fans were appreciative of his ability to seemingly carry the team on his back as the Mets went from 7½ games back on June 10 to 3½ games ahead exactly three months later. Delgado and the rest of the Mets' offense managed to overshadow a horrible bullpen that would eventually become an albatross.

Delgado kept hitting while the Mets went 7–10 down the stretch, batting .324 with three homers and 11 RBIs. He might have received serious MVP consideration had the Mets made the postseason, but they were eliminated from the playoffs on the last day of the season for the second straight year. He was ninth in the balloting after finishing the season with a .271 average, 38 home runs, and 115 runs batted in.

Delgado was 30th on the all-time home run list with 469 as the 2009 season began. He averaged 33 homers and 105 RBIs in his first three seasons with the team, numbers that rivaled his statistics in his nine full seasons with the Blue Jays.

He was just three months past his 16th birthday when Toronto signed him as an amateur free agent in 1988. Delgado played sparingly for St. Catherines of the rookie New York–Penn League in 1989 before he was named the team's most valuable player a year later. He displayed his power for Single A Myrtle Beach in 1991, hitting .286 with 18 home runs and 70 RBIs to earn a brief call-up with Triple A Syracuse.

Delgado was the Florida State League MVP for Dunedin in 1992, leading the circuit with 30 homers and 100 RBIs while finishing second with a .324 average. He moved up to Double A the following season, taking Southern League MVP honors after pacing the league with 25 homers, 102 RBIs, 102 walks, 28 doubles, and 102 hits.

The Blue Jays took notice, recalling him after the league playoffs. Delgado walked in his major league debut October 1 at Baltimore.

Delgado cracked Toronto's season-opening roster in 1994 as a left fielder and crushed a two-run homer off Dennis Cook on Opening Day. He looked like a shoo-in for AL Rookie of the Year honors after his first 14 games, hitting .275 with eight home runs and 18 RBIs. But he was back in the minors by June 8 after batting only .177 with one homer in 29 games following his hot start.

Delgado also split the 1995 season between the Jays and Syracuse before finding a permanent spot on the big league roster in 1996. He was third on the team with 25 homers and 92 RBIs while seeing most of his playing time at designated hitter. But he also appeared in 27 games at first base and was showing enough ability to make John Olerud expendable. The Jays traded Olerud to New York after the season, thus marking the first time Delgado helped the Mets.

Delgado reached the 30-home run plateau for the first time in 1997, and received MVP consideration after hitting .292 with 38 homers and 115 RBIs for the 1998 Blue Jays. He became the sixth player in Toronto history to homer three times in a game, going deep against three different pitchers in a loss to the Rangers on August 4, 1998.

Delgado also nicked the Rangers for three homers August 6, 1999, while becoming the third player in Toronto history to hit at least 30 round-trippers in three consecutive seasons. He played every inning of every game until September 22, when he suffered a non-displaced fracture of his left tibia after fouling a ball off his leg.

He won his first Silver Slugger in '99, finishing with a .272 average, a career-high 44 home runs and 134 RBIs. Delgado followed that by earning his first All-Star berth in 2000 and finishing fourth in the American League with a .344 batting average. He also paced the league with 57 doubles, was second with a .470 on-base percentage and a .664 slugging percentage, and fourth with 137 RBIs.

Delgado was one of the American League's most feared hitters from 1998 through 2003, compiling the fourth-most homers (237), the third-most RBIs (137), and the second-most doubles (242). He finished second to Alex Rodriguez in the 2003 MVP balloting after batting .302 with 42 homers and a career-high 145 RBIs.

But the Blue Jays finished in third place in each of those six seasons despite Delgado's hitting prowess. Toronto also had become a "small market" team after drawing more than 4,000,000 fans a season between 1991 and 1993. The club left Delgado hanging as he entered his walk year in 2004, unsure whether it was a financially sound move to sign him to a long-term deal.

Delgado hit 30 homers for the eighth consecutive season in 2004, finishing with 32, 99 RBIs, and a .269 average despite missing 33 games with a strained rib cage. The Blue Jays let him walk after finishing last in the AL East with a 67–94 record.

Delgado also caused a stir in 2004 by declining to stay on the field when "God Bless America" was played at various ballparks during the height of the U.S.-Iraq war. He boldly was protesting the war during a time in which nationalism already had reached a fever pitch.

"I'm not trying to get anyone mad. This is my personal feeling," he said. "I don't want to draw attention to myself or go out of my way to protest. If I make the last out of the seventh inning, I'll stand there. But I'd rather be in the dugout."[53]

By 2004, Yankee Stadium was the only ballpark in which "God Bless America" was played during the seventh-inning stretch of every game. Delgado's stance hit the papers a few days before the Jays opened a July series in the Bronx. On the day the series began, the *New York Times* ran a column in which he said, "It takes a man to stand up for what he believes. I am not pro-war; I'm anti-war. I'm for peace."

Delgado was jeered before every at-bat for exercising his beliefs. Two years later, he was among the most popular players among New York baseball fans.

The Mets were among several teams to make a strong pitch for Delgado following the 2004 season. He would have been among the first free-agent signings by Omar Minaya, who became the general manager in September 2004. But negotiations fizzled as Delgado reportedly grew to resent Minaya's special assistant Tony Bernazard for placing too much emphasis on their shared Puerto Rican heritage. Delgado rejected a reported four-year, $52 million contract from the Mets and went to Florida.

Spurned by Delgado, the Mets landed free agents Pedro Martinez and Carlos Beltran. Delgado had one of his better seasons for the Marlins in 2005, batting .302 with 33 homers and 115 RBIs. But Florida finished with the NL's second-worst attendance despite an 83–79 record, leading management to shed contracts. Delgado's was one of the first to go.

Minaya finally acquired Delgado in November 2005, sending first baseman Mike Jacobs and pitcher Yusmeiro Petit to the Marlins for the slugger. The deal cooled the Mets' pursuit of outfielder Manny Ramirez, who was being dangled by the Red Sox.

Delgado had to make a few adjustments after coming to the Mets. He made his peace with Bernazard and agreed to stay on the field for "God Bless America" during those rare times it was played in ballparks. Delgado became the most productive first baseman in team history, dwarfing numbers amassed by Keith Hernandez, Dave Kingman, and Ed Kranepool.

ML debut	Blue Jays @ Orioles, 10/1/93
Mets debut	vs. Nationals, 4/3/06
First ML hit	single vs. Jack McDowell, White Sox, 4/4/94 (with Blue Jays)
First Mets hit	2-run HR vs. John Patterson, Nationals, 4/5/06
First ML homer	2-run HR vs. Dennis Cook, White Sox, 4/4/94 (with Blue Jays)
First Mets homer	2-run HR vs. John Patterson, Nationals, 4/5/06
First ML RBI	2-run HR vs. Dennis Cook, White Sox, 4/4/94 (with Blue Jays)
First Mets RBI	2-run HR vs. John Patterson, Nationals, 4/5/06
Most hits, ML game	5, twice, including Jays @ Mariners, 5/7/98
Most hits, Mets game	5, vs. Braves, 8/21/08
Most homers, ML game	4, Blue Jays vs. Devil Rays, 9/25/93
Most homers, Mets game	2, 12 times
Most RBI, ML/Mets game	9, @ Yankees, 6/27/08
Acquired: Traded by the Marlins for Mike Jacobs, Usmeiro Petit and Grant Psomas, 11/24/05.	
Deleted: Became a free agent, 11/5/09	

Lenny Dykstra

Outfielder   Bats left, throws left
Born: 2/10/63   Santa Ana, California
Height: 5'10"   Weight: 160   #4

Lenny Dykstra Mets Career

YEAR	GP	AB	R	H	2B	3B	HR	RBI	K	BB	SB	AVG	SLG	OBP
1985	83	236	40	60	9	3	1	19	24	30	15	.254	.331	.338
1986	147	431	77	127	27	7	8	45	55	58	31	.295	.445	.377
1987	132	431	86	123	37	3	10	43	67	40	27	.285	.455	.352
1988	126	429	57	116	19	3	8	33	43	30	30	.270	.385	.321
1989	56	159	27	43	12	1	3	13	15	23	13	.270	.415	.362
TOTAL	544	1686	287	469	104	17	30	153	204	181	116	.278	.413	.350

ML Career

YEARS	GP	AB	R	H	2B	3B	HR	RBI	K	BB	SB	AVG	SLG	OBP
85-96	1278	4559	802	1298	281	43	81	404	503	640	285	.285	.419	.375

He was multimillionaire who had spent the better part of his life crashing into walls and cashing in on Wall Street. He could read a stock prospectus as well as he read a pitcher's pick-off move to first base. And then he crashed to earth harder than he slammed into any outfield wall during his days with the Mets and Phillies. On the 25th anniversary of the Mets winning the 1986 World Series, Lenny Dykstra was spending time in jail on dozens of charges.

"Overachieving" and "reckless" are two words that could describe his major league career. He seemed to play every inning of every game in a dirty uniform before going head-first into the financial industry. Few scouts expected him to be a power hitter in baseball, yet he hit 81 homers and 405 extra-base hits during his 12-year major league career, although the Mitchell report indicates modern chemistry likely helped him reach the fences. He later surprised numerous teammates with his ability to net large sums of money through his investments. And just like his baseball career, his financial wizardry came to a screeching halt through a series of bad decisions.

At first glance, Leonard Kyle Dykstra seemed an overachiever once he reached the majors. He made his Mets debut in 1985, only four years after being taken in the 13th round of the draft. Dykstra's game was all speed and daring in the minors as he played exceptional defense in the outfield while stealing 250 bases in 306 chances during his first three pro seasons. He hit .291 with 77 steals for Shelby of the Single A South Atlantic League in 1982, finishing second in the league in steals and walks (95) while posting the third-best on-base percentage at .425. He dwarfed those numbers a year later.

A good nickname for him would have been the "Santa Ana Wind." The Santa Ana, California, native was the 1983 MVP of the Carolina League, leading the circuit with a .358 average and setting a league record with 105 stolen bases. He also paced the league with 136 games, 132 runs, 14 triples, 107 walks, and 188 hits while providing eight homers and 88 RBIs. Dykstra was responsible for 212 of the team's 786 runs and posted an outstanding .472 on-base percentage.

Sent to Double A Jackson in 1984, Dykstra stole 53 bases and hit .275 with 38 extra-base hits and 52 RBIs in 131 games. He paced the league with a team-record 100 runs scored and led all league outfielders with a .992 fielding percentage.

The 1985 Mets entered the season with a starting outfield of George Foster, Mookie Wilson, and Darryl Strawberry, forcing Dykstra to start the year with Triple A Tidewater. But he was called up to the Mets in May after infielder Ron Gardenhire was placed on the disabled list. Dykstra was sensational in his major league debut, going 2-for-5 with a two-run homer off Mario Soto in a 9–4 win at Cincinnati. He hit .417 (5-for-12) with three RBIs in the three-game series with the Reds, but he was returned to Tidewater to make room for pitcher Sid Fernandez.

Dykstra was recalled two more times in 1985 and played all 19 innings of the Mets' 16–13 win at Atlanta on July 3 and 4, going 3-for-9 with two RBIs. He hit .310 for the Tides and .254 for the Mets before finding a regular spot on the Mets' roster for the next 3½ seasons.

Dykstra became a fan favorite for his fearless play in the outfield, which earned him the nickname "Nails." No wall was too hard or too high, and turf burns seemed a badge of honor to Dykstra. More than one New York columnist compared Dykstra to Pete Reiser, another local favorite who had a habit of crashing into walls at Ebbets Field. Unlike Reiser, Dykstra didn't miss much playing time until his seventh major league season.

Dykstra became an important piece of the Mets' 1986 title run once Mookie Wilson suffered an eye injury during spring training. He started 17 of the Mets' first 23 games and compiled a .301 average with nine stolen bases and 16 runs scored by the time Wilson returned to the lineup May 9.

Dykstra shared center field with Wilson until Foster was released in July, allowing manager Davey Johnson to give Wilson playing time in left field. Dykstra never let up, finishing the year with a .295 average, eight homers, 27 doubles, 45 RBIs, 31 stolen bases, and 77 runs while usually hitting at the top of the order.

Dykstra and Wally Backman were the catalysts in the 1986 lineup. The pair combined for 144 of the team's 783 runs and 44 of the Mets' 118 stolen bases. A typical Mets victory in 1986 opened with runners on first and third as Dykstra and Backman set the table for Keith Hernandez, Gary Carter, and Darryl Strawberry.

The Mets won the 1986 NL East title with ease before embarking on a grueling six-game NLCS against the Astros. Dykstra put the Mets in the driver's seat by belting a walk-off, two-run homer in Game 3 to give the Mets a 2–1 series lead.

Dykstra also ignited the most important rally of the NLCS. The Mets trailed Houston 3–0 in Game 6 and were three outs away from facing Mike Scott when the lefty-hitting Dykstra led off the ninth with a pinch-hit triple off lefty Bob Knepper, who entered the inning with a two-hitter. The Mets tied the game with a three-run ninth and won the pennant with a 7–6 victory in 16 innings. Dykstra provided the eventual game-winning hit, an RBI single that put New York ahead 7–4 in the top of the 16th and left him with a .304 average in 23 at-bats in the series.

After winning their first NL pennant in 13 years the Mets dropped the first two games of the World Series against the Red Sox at Shea Stadium. The team flew into Boston before Johnson told his players to blow off the traditional between-games workout, leaving many scribes to wonder how the Mets could afford to miss the extra batting practice. Johnson felt his team was playing a little tight after surviving an exhausting six-game series against the Astros. He was second-guessed for the strategy until Dykstra led off Game 3 with a homer to right off Oil Can Boyd, igniting a four-run first that led the Mets to a 7–1 victory.

Dykstra also came through in Game 4, belting a two-run homer that put the Mets ahead 5–0 in a 6–2 victory that tied the series at two games apiece. In Game 7 Dykstra delivered a pinch-hit single and scored the Mets' fifth run in the seventh inning of an 8–5 win. He hit .296 (8-for-27) with three RBIs and four runs scored in the series to finish with a .300 average for the 1986 postseason.

Mets general manager Frank Cashen acquired the power-hitting, slick-fielding Kevin McReynolds to play left field in 1987, putting Dykstra and Wilson in a platoon role in center. Dykstra and Wilson weren't particularly thrilled to share center since both felt like they had earned a starting role with the team. Dykstra wasn't shy about voicing his displeasure, telling the media what was on his mind while wondering what it took to get the job on a permanent basis. He hit .326 with six homers, 11 doubles, and 17 RBIs in 141 at-bats while starting 32 of the team's first 53 games of 1987. But Wilson earned his share of the playing time by batting .313 in 128 at-bats during that same span. The platoon would continue for another two years.

Johnson managed to give each of his center fielders more than ample playing time as Dykstra appeared in 132 games while Wilson saw action in 124. Dykstra delivered 10 homers and 43 RBIs, and Wilson contributed nine home runs and 35 ribbies. Dykstra also had a 27–21 edge in stolen bases, but Wilson kept his average at a slightly more consistent level before finishing at .299, 14 points higher than Dykstra.

Neither player was able to help the Mets reach the 1987 postseason. The Mets set numerous offensive records that season, but a ridiculous amount of injuries to the pitching staff damaged the team's hopes of a second straight playoff berth.

The Mets returned to the postseason in 1988 as Dykstra paced the team with 30 stolen bases while contributing a .270 average, eight homers, and 33 RBIs. Wilson had fewer at-bats but produced the same number of homers, 41 RBIs, and a .296 average. Dykstra continued to grouse about his playing time, even suggesting that he'd be more

than willing to accept a trade. Even Wilson, who rarely said a negative word about the ballclub, was publicly unhappy with his situation. But the two never carried their frustration onto the field except to use it as a motivational tool.

Dykstra was the better of the two outfielders during the 1988 NLCS as Wilson hit only .154 with one RBI. Dykstra batted .429 in the seven-game series, with all three of his RBIs coming on a three-run homer in Game 5 after the Dodgers had taken a 6–0 lead. He went 2-for-5 and scored twice a day later as the Mets won in L.A. to force a Game 7. Dykstra also had one of the Mets' five hits off Orel Hershiser as the Dodgers' ace went the distance in a 6–0 victory.

The two-headed monster remained in center as the Mets began 1989. New York got off to a slow start, opening 34–31 while Dykstra was hitting .270. He went 1-for-3 with a double on June 18 at Philadelphia before learning after the game that he had been traded to the team in the other dugout.

It was Frank Cashen's worst deal as general manager of the Mets. He sent Dykstra, reliever Roger McDowell and a player to be named (Tom Edens) to the Phillies for Juan Samuel, a natural second baseman who was in his first full season as an outfielder. Samuel also had the option of demanding a trade after the season if he didn't like playing in New York. Mets fans helped him make that decision, often booing Samuel while he hit .228 with three homers and 28 RBIs in 86 games.

Meanwhile, Dykstra got off to a scorching start as a Phillie, hitting 6-for-13 with two RBIs and seven runs scored in his first series for his new team. He returned to Shea the weekend after the trade and went 2-for-11 in the Mets' three-game sweep of the Phillies.

Dykstra had his own struggles in Philadelphia, hitting just .181 in his final 63 games after lifting his average to .286 by July 22. But he rebounded in 1990, earning his first All-Star berth and finishing ninth in the NL MVP balloting while hitting a career-high .325 with nine homers, 35 doubles, 106 runs, and 33 stolen bases. He paced the team in runs, hits, average, doubles, walks, and stolen bases.

Dykstra was happy to be a Phillie at the start of 1991 spring training. He was lucky to be alive by early May. He and Darren Daulton were coming home from a bachelor party for teammate John Kruk when Dykstra slammed his car into two trees on the morning of May 6. Dykstra missed the next 61 games with broken ribs, a busted cheekbone, and a fractured collarbone. Police said both players initially declined medical attention before they were taken to a police station, where both began to complain of pain. Initial tests showed Dykstra's blood-alcohol level was higher than the legal .10 percent at the time of the accident.

Dykstra batted .429 in eight games following his return from the disabled list. The Phillies went 25–13 once Dykstra was activated, but his season ended when he refractured the collarbone while running into the outfield wall at Cincinnati. He finished the year with a .297 average and led the club with 24 steals despite playing just 63 games.

Injuries continued to plague Dykstra in 1992. He broke a small bone his left arm when hit by a Greg Maddux pitch on Opening Day, causing him to miss 15 games. He later missed 18 days with a strained right hamstring after compiling a 14-game hitting streak.

Dykstra's average sunk to .148 on May 9 before he hit .330 in his next 72 games. But his season ended when he broke his left hand diving into first base at Shea on August 15, leaving him with a .301 average that included a .368 mark with runners in scoring position.

Phillies fans already held Dykstra in high regard before he led the team to its first National League pennant in 10 years. Dykstra won his only Silver Slugger and finished second to Barry Bonds in the MVP voting after topping the Phillies with 143 runs, 194 hits, 44 doubles, 129 walks, and 37 stolen bases. The 143 runs was the most in the National League since Chuck Klein's 152 for the 1932 Phillies. He became the third NL player since 1958 to reach base 300 times, doing it in a major league–record 773 plate appearances. Dykstra also hit .305 with 19 homers and 66 RBIs while posting a .482 slugging percentage.

Dykstra continued his assault in the postseason, batting .285 with a pair of solo homers in the NLCS against the Braves. The series was tied at two games apiece until Dykstra launched a game-winning homer in the 10th inning to beat the Braves 4–3 in Atlanta. He also scored twice in the Phillies' series-ending victory in Game 6.

He likely would have been the 1993 World Series MVP had the Phils managed to beat the Blue Jays. He torched the Blue Jays over six games, hitting .348 with four homers, eight RBIs, nine runs scored, and a .500 on-base percentage. Dykstra went 3-for-5 with two homers and four RBIs in Game 4, helping Philly grab a 14–9 lead before the Blue Jays scored six times in the eighth to pull out a 15–14 victory. Two games later, Dykstra belted a three-run homer in a five-run seventh that put the Phillies ahead 6–5. The lead held up until Joe Carter smashed a series-ending three-run homer in the bottom of the ninth to give Toronto an 8–6 victory in Game 6.

Dykstra was an All-Star in 1994 and '95, but a back injury allowed him to play just 146 games in those seasons. He batted only .261 over 40 games in 1996 before announcing his retirement.

It was a shame that Dykstra played in only two World Series since he played his best on the biggest stage. He owns a .700 career slugging percentage in 13 Fall Classic games, including a .913 mark in 1993. Dykstra hit .321 with 10 homers, 19 RBIs, and a .661 slugging average in 32 postseason contests.

Dykstra had become a businessman before retiring as a major leaguer. He opened his first Lenny Dykstra Car Wash in Corona, California, in December 1993, catering to his clientele with a customer-friendly waiting area that rivaled most hotel lobbies. He and his brother, Kevin, placed the string of car washes in areas that would allow customers to shop or dine while their cars were given attention.

Lenny Dykstra celebrates as he rounds the bases after hitting the game-winning, two-run home run in Game 3 of the 1986 NLCS against the Houston Astros.

The car washes were an immediate financial success that allowed Dykstra to walk away from baseball without his hat in hand. But a former investment partner tarnished Dykstra's name in a 2005 lawsuit in which he sought to regain interest in the car wash business.

Dykstra gained and lost fortunes in real estate and the stock market. According to *Fortune*, Dykstra had $20 million invested in real estate and another $1 million in mutual funds when he retired. The mutual funds climbed to $1.7 million before tanking to $400,000 in 2002, causing him to fire his investment advisor and learn the market himself. He turned his $400 grand into millions within four years, but he filed for bankruptcy in 2009, claiming he owed more than $31 million and had only $50,000 in assets.

Things only got worse in 2011. Dykstra was arrested in April on a charge of embezzling from a bankruptcy estate. Federal prosecutors claimed he hid, sold, or destroyed more than $400,000 worth of items from his $18.5 million mansion without permission of a bankruptcy trustee. He was indicted in May on 13 counts.

He began to serve jail time in early June on grand theft auto and drug possession charges after allegedly using phony information to lease a car from a Southern California auto dealership. Police said they found cocaine, ecstasy, and steroids in his vehicle when he was arrested in April. He pleaded not guilty in mid-June to 25 counts in connection with the grand theft and drug possession charges and was ordered to stand trial.

The charges kept piling up in 2011, when in late August he was charged with exposing himself to women he met on Craigslist. He allegedly exposed himself to women who responded to ads in which he sought personal assistants or housekeepers. Dykstra remained in jail from his grand theft and drug charges and pleaded not guilty to the indecent exposure charges in September.

Dykstra wasn't the first player from the 1986 Mets to run afoul of the law. But unlike Strawberry and Dwight Gooden, there wasn't the groundswell of sympathy given to Dykstra.

In March 2012 he received a three-year sentence for his grand theft auto charge.

ML/Mets debut	@ Reds, 5/3/85
1st ML/Mets hit	2-run HR vs. Mario Soto, @ Reds, 5/3/85
1st ML/Mets homer	2-run HR vs. Mario Soto, @ Reds, 5/3/85
1st ML/Mets RBI	2-run HR vs. Mario Soto, @ Reds, 5/3/85
Most hits, ML game	4, 16 times, 10 times with Phillies
Most hits, Mets game	4, 6 times
Most homers, ML game	2, twice, including Phils vs. Cubs, 9/9/93
Most homers, Mets game	2, vs. Dodgers, 5/23/87
Most RBI, ML game 5, Phillies vs. Cubs, 9/9/93	
Most RBI, Mets game	4, vs. Braves, 7/20/87; @ Expos, 9/16/87

Acquired: Selected in the 13th round of the 1981 draft.
Deleted: Traded to the Phillies with Roger McDowell for Juan Samuel, 6/18/89.

Sid Fernandez

Pitcher	Bats left, throws left
Born: 10/12/62	Honolulu, Hawaii
Height: 6′1″	Weight: 230 #50

Sid Fernandez Mets Career

YEAR	GP/GS	IP	H	R	ER	K	BB	W–L	SV	ERA
1984	15/15	90.0	74	40	35	62	34	6–6	0	3.50
1985	26/26	170.1	108	56	53	180	80	9–9	0	2.80
1986	32/31	204.1	161	82	80	200	91	16–6	1	3.52
1987	28/27	156.0	130	75	66	134	67	12–8	0	3.81
1988	31/31	187.0	127	69	63	189	70	12–10	0	3.03
1989	35/32	219.1	157	73	69	198	75	14–5	0	2.83
1990	30/30	179.1	130	79	69	181	67	9–14	0	3.46
1991	8/8	44.0	36	18	14	31	9	1–3	0	2.86
1992	32/32	214.2	162	67	65	193	67	14–11	0	2.73
1993	18/18	119.2	82	42	39	81	36	5–6	0	2.93
Total	255/250	1584.2	1167	601	553	1449	596	98–78	1	3.14

Mets Career/Batting

GP	AB	R	H	2B	3B	HR	RBI	K	BB	SB	AVG
255	495	27	94	14	2	1	31	183	12	1	.190

ML Career

YEAR	GP/GS	IP	H	R	ER	K	BB	W–L	SV	ERA
83–97	307/300	1866.2	1421	749	696	1743	715	114–96	1	3.36

A good fastball and a deceptive release made Sid Fernandez one of the best strikeout pitchers of his day. The lefty would hide the ball in his motion before it would suddenly appear, giving batters little time to distinguish between his moving fastball and swooping curve. He was a major contributor to the Mets' success during the mid- to late '80s, although his value was often overlooked by the presence of Dwight Gooden, Ron Darling, and Bob Ojeda, and later, David Cone, Frank Viola, and Bret Saberhagen. If the Mets were the Beatles, Fernandez was Ringo Starr.

Fernandez was part of Frank Cashen's "stolen" rotation in 1986. Cashen had drafted Gooden with the fifth pick in the 1982 draft after Shawon Dunston, Augie Schmidt, Jimmy Jones, and Bryan Oelkers were taken with the first four selections. The Mets' GM also fleeced general managers while bringing Darling, Ojeda, and Fernandez into the fold via trades.

Cashen and his scouting staff were so high on Fernandez he sent valuable utility player Bob Bailor and one of his top setup men, Carlos Diaz, to the Dodgers to get him after the 1983 season. Fernandez opened 1984 with Tidewater and didn't make his Mets debut until July 16, when he held the Astros to two runs in seven innings to get the win in a 13–3 laugher. Fernandez also won his next two starts, and was 4–1 with a 2.20 ERA in his first seven games before hitting a wall. He didn't win another game until September 21, when the Mets had already played themselves out of contention for the NL East crown. However, Fernandez's overall body of work appeared to make him a certain starter when the Mets broke camp in 1985.

But the third Hawaiian-born player to pitch for the Mets (Carlos Diaz and Ron Darling were the first two) played himself off the Opening-Day roster by going 0–4 with an 8.38 ERA in spring training. He was recalled in May after posting a 4–1 mark with a 2.04 ERA for Triple A Tidewater.

Fernandez kept his Mets ERA below 2.84 the entire 1985 season. He was outstanding in his first start, walking six but allowing just one hit in six innings of a 4–0 shutout of the Phillies May 11. But he had been recalled around the time Darryl Strawberry was injured, and the Mets stopped hitting for about a month. Fernandez followed his season-opening win by going 0–4 despite a 2.79 ERA in his next six starts. He allowed just three hits in his first 13 innings but was just 1–1.

The Mets scored only 32 runs in Fernandez's first 13 starts of 1985. They finally broke out with a 16–4 win over the Astros July 27, but Fernandez had to settle for a no-decision after leaving the game with a 4–1 lead in the seventh. He put together one of his best starts late in the season, striking out nine in a two-hitter against Philadelphia that kept the Mets three games behind the first-place Cardinals with 11 games remaining. He ended the year ranked second on the team with 180 strikeouts and third with a 2.80 ERA, but his record was only 9–9.

Fernandez had opened his Mets career with a pair of .500 seasons, but that just proved to be a teaser as he would go 54–29 over the next four years, beginning with his career-high 16-win season for the 1986 champs. "El Sid" was the Mets' best pitcher during the first half of '86. He was 12–2 with a 2.67 ERA after tossing a two-hit shutout against the Braves July 11, which gave him a seven-start winning streak. Fernandez also made his first of two All-Star Game appearances, allowing two walks but striking out three in a scoreless eighth.

Fernandez faltered after his 11–0 shutout of the Braves July 11, going 3–3 with a 5.63 ERA in his next 11 starts. But he put it together after realizing he was no longer a shoo-in to start a playoff game. Gooden, Ojeda, and Darling had earned postseason starts, and by now the question was whether manager Davey Johnson would use four starters in the playoffs. Sid tied Gooden for the team lead with 200 strikeouts and finished with the best strikeouts/innings pitched ratio.

Fernandez did his best to persuade Johnson by compiling a 2.25 ERA in his final 24 innings, earning himself a starting nod in Game 4 of the NLCS. He gave up only three hits in six innings against the Astros, but one of the hits was a two-run homer by Alan Ashby in a 3–1 loss to Mike Scott, evening the series at two games apiece.

Johnson elected to go with a three-man rotation in the World Series, and the decision didn't have a positive impact until Game 7. Fernandez pitched poorly in Game 2 and was overpowering in Game 5. He saved his best for the clincher, holding the Red Sox hitless and striking out four in 2⅓ innings while giving the Mets a chance to crawl back from a 3–0 deficit created by starter Ron Darling. The Mets still trailed 3–0 when Fernandez threw his final pitch, but the game was tied 3–3 by the time Roger McDowell replaced him to start the seventh. Fernandez finished with a 1.35 ERA in the series, blanking the Red Sox in his last two outings.

Most of the 1987 Mets stumbled out of the gate, but Fernandez was an exception. He was the National League Pitcher of the Month for April after opening the year 4–1 with a 2.18 ERA. Fernandez was 8–2 with a 2.17 ERA following a 10–2 rout at Pittsburgh June 11, but the victory put the Mets only two games over .500 and 6½ games behind the division-leading Cardinals. The strong start earned Fernandez another All-Star nod, and he made the Mets proud by picking up the save in a 2–0, 13-inning win over the American League.

But Fernandez was having physical problems. He sprained his knee in a game against the Giants May 15, and spent much of the last two months battling a sore shoulder. He went just 4–6 with a 5.67 ERA after June 12 and was unavailable for the Mets' big series against the Cardinals at Shea in early September.

Fernandez tried things in reverse in 1988. He suffered his injury (hamstring) early in the year and was just 2–5 with a 4.50 ERA following a loss to the Dodgers on June 1. But he was outstanding the rest of the way, posting a 10–5 mark and a 2.47 ERA.

Sid Fernandez

Fernandez continued to be the fourth banana in the Mets' postseason rotation. Gooden, Cone, and Darling started the first three games of the NLCS against the Dodgers, and Gooden went back to the mound on his normal four day's rest in Game 4, only to blow a 4–2 lead when Mike Scioscia blasted a two-run homer in the ninth before L.A. tied the series at two games apiece.

Fernandez finally got a start in Game 5 with a chance to give the Mets the upper hand in the series, but he was pitching on nine days rest. He never found a rhythm and was chased in the fifth after Kirk Gibson's three-run homer put the Dodgers ahead 6–0. The Mets dropped that pivotal game and lost the series in seven games.

The Mets spent the second half of the 1989 season without Gooden due to a shoulder injury, putting pressure on the rest of the rotation. The Mets faded out of the playoff picture in August despite the acquisition of Frank Viola from the Twins just before the trade deadline. But Fernandez arguably had his best season, going 14–5 with a 2.83 ERA. He paced the team in wins, ERA and 198 strikeouts but received little attention due to the team's 87–75 record. Fernandez was the Mets' top starter after June 20, going 10–3 with a 2.55 ERA. He also set a team record for left-handed hurlers by striking out 16 against the Braves on July 14.

Fernandez arguably was every bit as good in 1990 as he had been in '89. He held opponents to a league-low .200 batting average, averaged 9.1 strikeouts per nine innings and was fifth in the NL with 181 Ks. He made 11 starts in which he allowed fewer than two runs while throwing at least six innings, but he still failed to win three of those games. He also went 0–3 with two no-decisions in five games in which have gave up only two runs in at least six innings. Of his 16 games with under three runs allowed,

Fernandez went only 8–5. He also had a 13-start stretch from June 20 to September 4 in which posted a 2.88 ERA in 81⅓ innings, but his record was just 5–6. The Mets went 11–19 in his starts as Fernandez posted a losing record for the first time in his seven major league seasons.

The 1991 season was almost a complete wash for Fernandez after he was hit by a line drive in spring training. He suffered a broken wrist that postponed his season debut until July 19, when he allowed just one run and three hits over six innings against the Dodgers. Fernandez was hit hard in his next start before compiling a 2.25 ERA over 32 innings in his next six games. But he didn't get his first win of the year until August 21 and missed the final month due to a left knee problem that required surgery.

Weight was a sensitive issue for Fernandez during his career. He always pitched with a few extra pounds, but his knee surgery put more pressure on him to drop a few waist sizes. Fernandez did his part by checking into a diet center before the 1992 season, a year after he was embarrassingly portrayed on the back cover of the *New York Post*. He showed up about 20 pounds overweight for the start of 1991 spring training and was doing extra running to shed his girth. Manager Bud Harrelson gave reporters a progress report on Fernandez's weight, saying his pitcher continued to carry a few extra pounds but was working to correct the problem. When told by beat writers that Harrelson had commented on his progress, Fernandez took offense to his weight being a continuing concern and went on a profanity-laced diatribe against his skipper without fully understanding what Harrelson said: "They treat me like a f–king dog here. I'm sick and tired of it."

That was enough fodder for the *Post* to put a cartoon caricature of Fernandez on the back page, with the pitcher sitting inside a dog house that had "El Sid" written on the front. Fernandez was more than a little peeved over the *Post*'s rendition of him.

Fernandez proved to be one of the Mets' very few bright spots in 1992, leading the team in ERA, wins, and innings pitched while finishing fourth in the NL in strikeouts. His pitching was rather ghastly during his first three starts (0–2, 8.49 ERA), but he was 14–9 with a 2.39 ERA the rest of the season while several other Mets were putting their stamp on a very poor season.

Fernandez spent his final season as a Met playing on one of the worst teams in franchise history. He had to settle for a no-decision against the Giants April 20 despite limiting them to a run and three hits with 14 strikeouts in eight innings. Fernandez allowed 17 hits in 9⅓ innings over his next two starts before he was sidelined for three months by a torn cartilage in his right knee. He compiled a 2.56 ERA after returning from knee surgery, but his record was only 4–6. His final win as a Met came October 2 at Florida, holding the Marlins to a run and just two hits in seven innings.

The Mets had completed their worst season since 1965 when they allowed Fernandez to become a free agent. By then, Fernandez, Gooden, and Howard Johnson were the last remaining members of the Mets' 1986 team.

Fernandez signed with the Orioles, who weren't paying attention to the fact that they were acquiring a fly-ball pitching to perform in a ballpark with extremely short power alleys. He surrendered 36 homers in just 145⅓ innings during his 1½ seasons with the Birds before he was released in July 1995. But he was the National League pitcher of the month in August after going 5–0 with a 2.68 ERA and 54 strikeouts in just 43⅔ innings for the Phillies.

Fernandez went 9–7 with a 3.38 ERA for the Phillies in 1995 and 1996 and was the team's Opening-Day starter in '96. However, he made only 22 starts during his 15 months with the team as the knee injuries had taken their toll. He signed with the Astros in December 1996 but managed to make only one start due to an elbow injury that forced him to retire in August.

Fernandez moved back to Hawaii, but baseball wasn't completely out of his system. He signed a minor league contract with the 2001 Yankees and was given an invitation to spring training. Fernandez made one start for the Yankees' Triple A team in Columbus before retiring again.

Fernandez continues to give back to his native Hawaii. He and his wife, Noelani, created the Sid Fernandez Foundation, which gives four $5,000 scholarships each year to students from his old high school.

Fernandez kept opponents to a .204 average as a Met, still a team record for pitchers with more than 750 career innings with the franchise. His 8.23 strikeouts per nine innings are second only to David Cone for Mets hurlers with at least 525 innings.

ML debut	Dodgers vs. Astros, 9/20/83 (3 IP, 2 H, 1 ER, 5 K, 1 BB)
Mets debut	@ Astros, 7/16/84 (7 IP, 8 H, 2 ER, 6 K, 0 BB)
First ML strikeout	Jerry Mumphrey, Astros, 9/20/83 (with Dodgers)
First Mets strikeout	Phil Garner, Astros, 7/16/84
First ML/Mets win	vs. Astros, 7/16/84
Most strikeouts, ML/Mets game	16, @ Braves, 7/14/89
Low-hit Mets CG	2, 5 times
Acquired:	Traded by the Dodgers with Ross Jones for Carlos Diaz and Bob Bailor, 12/8/83.
Deleted:	Became a free agent 10/25/93. Signed by the Orioles 11/22/93.

John Franco

Pitcher   Bats left, throws left
Born: 9/17/60   Brooklyn, New York
Height: 5'10"   Weight: 185   #31, #45

John Franco Mets Career

YEAR	GP/GS	IP	H	R	ER	K	BB	W–L	SV	ERA
1990	55/0	67.2	66	22	19	56	21	5–3	33	2.53
1991	52/0	55.1	61	27	18	45	18	5–9	30	2.93
1992	31/0	33.0	24	6	6	20	11	6–2	15	1.64
1993	35/0	36.1	46	24	21	29	19	4–3	10	5.20
1994	47/0	50.0	47	20	15	42	19	1–4	30	2.70
1995	48/0	51.2	48	17	14	41	17	5–3	29	2.44
1996	51/0	54.0	54	15	11	48	21	4–3	28	1.83
1997	59/0	60.0	49	18	17	53	20	5–3	36	2.55
1998	61/0	64.2	66	28	26	59	29	0–8	38	3.62
1999	46/0	40.2	40	14	13	41	19	0–2	19	2.88
2000	62/0	55.2	46	24	21	56	26	5–4	4	3.40
2001	58/0	53.1	55	25	24	50	19	6–2	2	4.05
2002	Injured, did not play									
2003	38/0	34.1	35	11	10	16	13	0–3	2	2.62
2004	52/0	46.0	46	28	27	36	24	2–7	0	5.28
Total	695/0	702.2	683	279	242	592	276	48–56	276	3.10

Mets Career/Batting

GP	AB	R	H	2B	3B	HR	RBI	K	BB	SB	AVG
677	15	0	0	0	0	0	0	9	0	0	.000

ML Career

YEAR	GP/GS	IP	H	R	ER	K	BB	W–L	SV	ERA
84–05	1119/0	1245.2	1166	466	400	975	495	90–87	424	2.89

Being a major league closer is often an over glorified yet thankless job. You are expected to convert a save because that's your sole reason for earning a major league paycheck. Blow a save, and you're a bum.

It was hard to stay angry at John Franco, who was Mr. Met—without the oversized baseball head—during his 15 seasons with the team. He was a Brooklynite who relied on guts, brains, and location instead of an overpowering fastball. Before Franco came to the Mets, Jesse Orosco was the team's all-time saves leader with 107. Franco obliterated the franchise record by recording 276, with all but eight coming in his first decade with the team.

But Franco somehow is one of the most underappreciated Mets in team history. He had been acquired for Randy Myers, who had a much better arm but lacked the intangibles to escape jams on days when he didn't have his best stuff. Franco occasionally turned a one-inning save into an adventure as he stayed away from a batter's strength, pitching carefully to a power hitter instead of challenging him. Most of his blown saves were the result of a bloop hit to the opposite field instead of a three-run blast into the upper deck. Franco averaged only one homer for every 13 appearances as a Met.

Franco began his Mets career 1–0 with eight saves and a 1.84 ERA in his first 12 games in 1990. He converted 17 straight save opportunities from July 4 to September 25, a stretch that began with saves in nine straight appearances. He pulled Mets fans to his side during a May 6 game in

which he had walked two batters in the 11th before balking home the tiebreaking run. Franco went face-to-face with plate umpire Doug Harvey following the questionable balk call, but the reliever wasn't ejected. The Mets won the game on a three-run homer by Kevin McReynolds.

The former Lafayette High standout was selected to the All-Star Game for the fourth and final time in his career. Franco worked a perfect ninth, leaving him perfect in 1⅔ innings of All-Star Game competition.

Franco already had 31 saves by September 1, when he helped the Mets climb into first place. But he picked a horrible time to go through an unfortunate stretch, going 1–3 with two saves, three blown saves and a 6.00 ERA in his last nine appearances. He didn't allow a single homer during the skid, but he surrendered numerous bloop singles and seeing-eye grounders, something that would become a Franco trademark when Lady Luck was blowing on some other guy's dice.

Franco led the league with a team-record 33 saves in 1990 and won his second Fireman of the Year award in the process. Myers finished second in both categories, but the ex-Met won a World Series with the Reds while Franco watched the postseason on television. It would be seven years before the Mets had another winning season.

Thus, Franco has the distinction of being the closer on more losing teams than any other pitcher in Mets history. The 1991 Mets went 77–84 despite Franco's 30 saves, third-most in the NL.

He was putting together one of his best seasons ever in 1992, but the year was pockmarked by two stints on the disabled list due to a sore elbow. The injury also led to friction between Franco and his new manager, Jeff Torborg. Franco was trying to pitch through pain in June and didn't want the opposition to know he was hurting. A save situation came up in which Torborg elected to call on someone other than Franco, who had worked the previous game. When pressed for a reason why he didn't use Franco, Torborg could have said he didn't want to pitch him in back-to-back games at that juncture of the season. Instead, Torborg revealed during his daily "show" on WFAN that Franco was bothered by a barking elbow and couldn't pitch. The public disclosure of the injury infuriated Franco and permanently damaged his relationship with Torborg. Franco also wound up on the disabled list for the first time in his career, missing all of July and September before he eventually underwent surgery to repair a torn flexor tendon in the elbow. He still posted a 1.64 ERA despite the injury, and finished 10th in the league with 15 saves.

Franco pitched sparingly at the start of 1993, making just two April appearances while recovering from the elbow surgery. He was DL'd again in April due to elbow soreness, and appeared to be fully recovered after he was activated. Franco was 2–0 with one save and a 0.75 ERA in 13 appearances between May 13 and June 27. But he was shelved again in August, this time because of a strained ribcage. He was rocked upon his return, posting a 10.45 ERA in 11 games while blowing four of his six save opportunities.

There was now speculation that Franco's days as a closer were numbered after being placed on the disabled list four times in two years. He silenced his detractors in 1994, leading the league with 30 saves despite a strike that wiped out the last seven weeks of the season. He converted 13 of 14 save opportunities over his last 17 outings, allowing him to overtake Jesse Orosco as the Mets' all-time saves leader. He also became baseball's all-time saves leader among left-handed pitchers.

Like the Mets, Franco got off to a slow start in 1995. He blew four of his first 10 save situations and was 2–1 with a 3.52 ERA by June 6. He appeared in only 14 of the Mets' first 38 games, mainly because there were few save opportunities. But he became very busy down the stretch after the Mets recalled highly touted prospects Bill Pulsipher and Jason Isringhausen. The Mets were 35–57 on August 5 before posting a league-best 34–18 mark the rest of the year. Franco played a major role in the turnaround, converting 17 of his 18 save opportunities while recording a 2.12 ERA over his final 20 games.

Any hopes of a winning record in 1996 were dashed by Pulsipher, Isringhausen, and rookie Paul Wilson, who were either injured or ineffective the entire season. Franco put together another outstanding year despite the Mets dearth of starting pitching, earning 28 saves and a 1.83 ERA. But he had been the Mets' chief closer in six straight losing seasons. Ron Taylor (1967–1968) and Skip Lockwood (1977–1978) were the only other Mets pitchers to lead the team in saves during more than one losing season. Although Franco had been toiling for mediocre teams, he was voted the top lefty reliever in the majors between 1976 and 1996 in a poll conducted by Rolaids, the sponsor of the season-ending relief award.

Franco was now the elder statesman on the team and a very popular figure among the media. He had a good relationship with the beat writers, often kidding them that he'd talk to his friends "Vito" and "Nunzio" if they wrote anything bad about him. There was no reason for the writers to turn on Franco, who was arguably the only valuable commodity on the pitching staff heading into the 1997 season. Franco was about to get some help.

Manager Bobby Valentine, in his first full season at the helm, somehow weaved together a decent starting rotation that was anchored by Mark Clark, Dave Mlicki, Rick Reed, and Bobby Jones. The Mets put together their first winning season since 1990 and challenged the eventual World Series champions, the Marlins, for the NL wild-card berth. With a better rotation and deeper bullpen, Franco was able to break his team record by recording 36 saves while compiling a 2.55 ERA. He blew just four saves and helped the Mets go 49–10 in the games he pitched. He also became the all-time saves leader for National League pitchers with 359. But Franco had to miss the last two

John Franco. Photo courtesy of David Ferry

weeks of the season due to a strained muscle on his left side.

The Mets challenged for the 1998 wild-card, and Franco was on the mound at the end of many of their 88 wins. He eclipsed his single-season saves mark by recording 37, which moved him into second place on the all-time saves list. Franco also became the Mets' all-time leader in games pitched, passing Hall of Famer Tom Seaver. He opened 1998 by allowing no runs and only two hits and two walks over eight innings in his first seven appearances, recording five straight saves in the process. He was untouchable between August 15 and September 14, picking up 13 saves and pitching scoreless ball over 13⅓ innings. His team-record 38th save came September 19 against Florida, which put the Mets in a tie with the Cubs for the wild-card lead. But he made just one more appearance in the final six games as the Mets ended the year on a five-game losing streak that left them one game off the wild-card lead.

By now, Franco had become a sympathetic figure. He had been one of the National League's best closers since 1985 and led the Mets in saves in each season with the team. He was second on baseball's all-time list with 397 saves and had compiled a 2.64 ERA in 832 games. But Franco still hadn't thrown a single pitch in the postseason. The closest he had come to a World Series was when he helped St. John's reach the regional finals of the College World Series.

Franco was 38 on Opening Day 1999. He had dutifully worn an orange T-shirt from the New York Department of Sanitation as a tribute to his father, who had provided for his children by working tirelessly on the trucks. Jim Franco died of a heart attack while driving his truck in 1987, 14 months after John Franco's mother, Mary, passed away from ovarian cancer.

People were rooting for Franco to finally get a chance to pitch a meaningful game in October. The Mets finally cooperated with a rollercoaster ride to the postseason, but the lefty had been supplanted as the closer by then.

Franco opened 1999 by converting his first 14 save opportunities and compiling a 1.74 ERA before he finally blew a win against the Reds on June 2. He had converted 19 of 20 save chances when he was placed on the disabled list with a sprained flexor tendon on the middle finger of his throwing hand. He was activated September 4, but there was a new closer on the team by then.

Armando Benitez, acquired from the Orioles in a three-team deal in December 1998, went 3–0 with 13 saves and a 2.92 ERA during Franco's absence. Benitez possessed an intimidating fastball and a "you can't hit this" mentality. Benitez had struck out 107 in just 66⅔ innings in his first 66 games as a Met. His overpowering stuff had prompted the Mets to change closers for the first time in nine years, leaving Franco as the setup man for Benitez.

But the bullpen shuffle didn't stop the Mets from another September collapse that saw them drop seven straight and eight of nine to fall two games off the wild-card lead with three games remaining. Franco put the team's postseason chances in further jeopardy by blowing a lead October 1 against the Pirates, allowing an infield single to Warren Morris with the bases loaded. But the Mets won the game on Robin Ventura's RBI single in the bottom of the 11th before capturing the wild-card in a one-game playoff with the Reds three days later. Franco was finally in a major league postseason.

Franco was the winning pitcher when the Mets closed out the NLDS against the Diamondbacks. He worked a perfect 10th inning in Game 4 before Todd Pratt won it with a series-clinching homer. Franco also worked 1⅓ innings of scoreless relief in the Mets' memorable Game 5 win over the Braves as the team extended the series on Robin Ventura's "grand slam single" in the 15th inning. But staked to a one-run lead in Game 6, he gave up a run in the eighth inning before the Mets lost the series on Kenny Rogers' bases-loaded walk to Andruw Jones. Franco posted a 1.42 ERA in the 1999 playoffs, allowing only one run in 6⅓ innings.

Franco remained a setup man in 2000 as the Mets won the wild-card for the second straight year and reached the World Series for the first time since 1986. He picked up four saves, but any shot of him catching Lee Smith as the all-time saves leader was long gone.

He had a hand in a pivotal Game 2 win in the 2000 NLDS against the Giants. Benitez had blown a 4–1 lead in the ninth by serving up a three-run homer to J.T. Snow. The Mets scratched out a run in the tenth before Benitez opened the bottom half by allowing a leadoff single, sending Valentine to the mound to replace his current closer with the former one. Franco got the save by getting Barry Bonds to look at strike three with the potential tying run on first. Franco also struck out Bonds to end the ninth inning of Game 3 before Benny Agbayani won it with a homer in the 13th.

Franco was the pitcher of record in the Mets' only 2000 World Series win, working a perfect eighth in Game 3 before Agbayani delivered a tiebreaking double. He also got the final out in the ninth inning of Game 5, but only after Al Leiter allowed the tiebreaking and insurance runs in the Yankees' series-clinching win.

Franco and the Mets had high hopes in 2001, but the team was an abysmal 54–68 and 13½ games out of first place following a loss to the Dodgers on August 17. He had 14 holds at that point, and he also had two saves, two blown saves, and an uncharacteristic 3.42 ERA.

The Mets went on a hot streak, winning 17 of 22 to pull within eight games of the Braves the morning of September 11, the day of the terrorist attacks on New York City. The season was shut down for a week while the city and country tried to cope with the loss of thousands of lives in the attacks on the World Trade Center and Pentagon. Franco and the Mets decided to honor the fallen heroes by wearing caps of the NYPD, FDNY, Port Authority, and EMS in their return to the diamond September 17. Fittingly, Franco got the victory in the Mets' first game back in Pittsburgh.

The Mets finally resumed their home schedule with an emotional game against the Braves four days later. Franco was charged with the go-ahead run in the eighth when Armando Benitez gave up an RBI double to Brian Jordan, but Mike Piazza won it with a two-run homer in the bottom of the eighth.

The Mets were three outs from climbing within three games of the division lead September 29 when Benitez took the mound in Atlanta with a 5–1 lead. But Benitez gave up three runs before he was replaced by Franco, who served up a two-out, walk-off grand slam to Jordan that effectively ended the Mets' postseason hopes.

Franco was now a 41-year-old pitcher entering 2002, and the years of beating hitters on guts and guile had taken their toll. He missed the entire year after undergoing Tommy John surgery, a procedure that would have prompted many pitchers to retire at that age. Franco was back on a major league mound May 30, 2003, but he was again part of a team that had little chance of reaching the postseason. He was 0–2 with a 3.68 ERA before he finally picked up a save July 21. He nailed down his 424th and final save by getting the final out in a 3–2 win August 24 against the Dodgers, the team that originally signed him 22 years earlier.

Franco didn't record a save in 2004 as he endured the worst season of his career. His last major league victory came July 3 against the Yankees, getting the final out in the top of the ninth before Kaz Matsui scored on a fielder's choice to win it.

Franco tried to extend his career with the 2005 Astros but was released July 2 after going 0–1 with a 7.20 ERA in 15 innings. He was a 44-year-old reliever at the time of his release, leaving the game with 90 wins and 424 saves in 1,119 games.

ML debut	Reds @ Braves, 4/24/84 (1 IP, 2 H, 1 ER, 1 K, 2 BB)
Mets debut	vs. Pirates, 4/11/90 (1.1 IP, 1 H, 0 ER, 1 K, 0 BB)
First ML strikeout	Steve Bedrosian, @ Braves, 4/24/84 (with Reds)
First Mets strikeout	Jay Bell, Pirates, 4/11/90
First ML win	vs. Astros, 5/1/84 (with Reds)
First Mets win	vs. Astros, 5/6/90
First ML save	vs. Giants, 4/29/84 (with Reds)
First Mets save	vs. Pirates, 4/11/90
Most strikeouts, ML/Mets game	5, vs. Braves, 6/11/96
Acquired:	Traded by the Reds with Don Brown for Randy Myers, 12/6/89.
Deleted:	Became a free agent 11/1/04. Signed by the Astros, 1/23/05.

Dwight Gooden

Pitcher	Bats right, throws right
Born: 11/16/64	Tampa, Florida
Height: 6′3″	Weight: 210 #16

Dwight Gooden Mets Career

YEAR	GP/GS	IP	H	R	ER	K	BB	W–L	SV	ERA
1984	31/31	218.0	161	72	63	276	73	17–9	0	2.60
1985	35/35	276.2	198	51	47	268	69	24–4	0	1.53
1986	33/33	250.0	197	92	79	200	80	17–6	0	2.84
1987	25/25	179.2	162	68	64	148	53	15–7	0	3.21
1988	34/34	248.1	242	98	88	175	57	18–9	0	3.19
1989	19/17	118.1	93	42	38	101	47	9–4	1	2.89
1990	34/34	232.2	229	106	99	223	70	19–7	0	3.83
1991	27/27	190.0	185	80	76	150	56	13–7	0	3.60
1992	31/31	206.0	197	93	84	145	70	10–13	0	3.67
1993	29/29	208.2	188	89	80	149	61	12–15	0	3.45
1994	7/7	41.1	46	32	29	40	15	3–4	0	6.31
TOTAL	305/303	2169.2	1898	823	747	1875	651	157–85	1	3.10

Mets Career/Batting

GP	AB	R	H	2B	3B	HR	RBI	K	BB	SB	AVG
309	730	59	144	15	5	7	65	131	13	1	.197

ML Career

YEAR	GP/GS	IP	H	R	ER	K	BB	W–L	SV	ERA
84–00	430/410	2800.2	2564	1198	1091	2293	954	194–112	3	3.51

As depicted on CBS's *60 Minutes* in 1985, Dwight Gooden had stern parents and a level head that made him the poster child for everything good in America. He seemed to make all the right choices while growing up in the Tampa, Florida, area, avoiding temptation due to the guidance of a strong family that kept him away from the drug scene in a rather shady neighborhood.

To this day, Gooden comes off in interviews as very affable, smiling and laughing while answering questions he's heard at least a dozen times that week. He is gracious. He is quiet. He is introspective. Most of all, he is not the same person who continued to find trouble during and after his career. It can be puzzling to understand how the Dwight Gooden seen on the mound and in the clubhouse could be the same person whose personal life is pockmarked by indiscretions.

Gooden already was the darling of the New York sports media by the end of 1984. In a multi-storied ad painted on a building near the Lincoln Tunnel, his 6′3″ frame could be seen in full contortion on the mound, his left leg almost touching his chin a split second before firing a fastball.

Gooden followed 1984 by putting together one of the greatest years in National League history. In 1985 he was the Mets' first 20-game winner since Tom Seaver, and owner of the majors' lowest ERA since Bob Gibson's remarkable 1.12 mark in 1968. He could be seen pitching in Bruce Springsteen's 1985 video "Glory Days," a song that has somehow become synonymous with baseball despite its theme of living in the past. Ironically, there were times when Gooden lived off his reputation for the final 15 years of his career.

There are many Mets who are perceived as disappointments, players whose sole indiscretion was an inability to hit a curve or harness their pitches. Had Dwight Eugene Gooden been a .500 pitcher over his first two major league seasons, the remainder of his career would have been more than acceptable. His indiscretion was to perform like a certain Hall of Famer before a 1991 shoulder injury and his ensuing drug battle turned him into merely an above-average pitcher.

Gooden was expected to be a first-round pick in the 1982 draft after striking out 130 in just 74 innings during his senior year at Hillsborough High School in Tampa. The Padres took Jimmy Jones with the third overall pick, and fellow pitcher Bryan Oelkers was chosen fourth by the Twins, leaving Gooden available when the Mets chose fifth. The selection looked very good as Gooden pitched well in his first pro season, going a combined 4–5 with a 2.73 ERA and 84 strikeouts in 79 innings for Kingsport and Little Falls. That was only a glimpse of what was to come.

Gooden struck out an incredible 300 in 191 innings while going 19–4 with a 2.50 ERA for Single A Lynchburg in 1983. He set a Carolina League record for strikeouts and also led the circuit in wins, ERA, and shutouts (6). Gooden was so impressive that Tidewater manager Davey Johnson asked to place him on his roster for the Triple A World Series. He went 1–1 in the series, earning a complete-game, 4–2 win over Denver. It capped a season in which he won two league championships, was named the MVP of the Carolina League, and recognized as the Minor League Player of the Year.

Johnson was hired as the Mets' manager in the winter of 1984, and his plan was to bring some of his best players with him. One such player was Gooden, but general manager Frank Cashen didn't want to rush his 19-year-old phenom after watching his previous phenom, Tim Leary, suffer a major injury in his first major league start. Johnson wouldn't back down in his insistence that Gooden be part of his 1984 Opening Day roster, especially after the hurler recording a 3.00 ERA in 18 innings during spring training. Cashen finally relented, and Gooden and the Mets became one of the best stories of the season.

"It was a lot of fun," Gooden described that spring training during a July 2011 interview with New York sportscaster Mike Mancuso. "I pitched good, and I give Davey a lot of credit for giving me the opportunity to make the team.

"I got the opportunity to play for Davey in '83. He called me up to Tidewater for the Triple A World Series. He told me that, wherever he managed the following year, I would go on his team.

"I was in spring training with the Mets as a non-roster player, I know I pitched pretty good but wasn't sure because the front office kept saying to the media that they were going to send me back to Double A, maybe Triple A. But Davey always told me, 'Don't worry about them. I'll get you in.'

"I remember the last day of camp, the fifth inning that day, Davey told me, 'You made the team.' The feeling I had in making that call to my dad and mom letting them know I made the team was just a dream come true."

Gooden won his major league debut April 7 in Houston, allowing a run and three hits in five innings as the Mets' No. 4 starter. Any Mets fan who ignored the club during spring training now believed the kid could lead the franchise to its first winning season in eight years. Meanwhile, the kid needed a few innings before he calmed down during his debut.

"Oh, man, I've never been so nervous in my life. It was a situation I wanted to be in the big leagues. I had my parents in the stands, just a year and a-half removed from high school. My legs just couldn't stop shaking.

"I remember in the Astrodome, just a great feeling trying to calm down. It probably took about 20 minutes before it sunk in that I was actually pitching."

He struck 10 in both his fourth and fifth starts of the year, giving him 36 in his first 27⅓ innings. But he was just 2–2 with a 4.85 ERA after surrendering eight runs in 2⅓ innings of a 10–1 loss to the Astros on May 6.

The rest of his season was incredible, beginning with an 11-strikeout, four-hit shutout at Los Angeles May 11. He reeled off a seven-game winning streak from August 11 to September 12, capping that stretch with back-to-back shutouts. He struck out 16 batters in two consecutive starts in late September after firing the 14th one-hitter in team history September 7 against the Cubs. But it took him about a half-season before he realized he could become a very special pitcher.

"Probably not until around the All-Star break," he said. "The first game, I pitched good and got the win. My dad asked me after the game, 'What do you think?' And I said, 'I probably should win a lot of games.'

"My second start was at Wrigley Field and I got knocked out in like the third inning. Then, I started thinking I wasn't ready.

"I think it was right around the All-Star break when I thought I could be pretty successful here."

He wowed a national television audience by striking out the side in his first All-Star inning, fanning Lance Parrish, Chet Lemon, and Alvin Davis in succession. His season only continued to get better.

The end result was a record-setting rookie season in which he led the majors with 11.39 strikeouts and 6.65 hits per nine innings while pacing the NL with 276 strikeouts. He broke Herb Score's record for strikeouts by a rookie and was the youngest player to appear in an All-Star Game before he became the youngest player ever to win a Rookie of the Year award.

"That was awesome," Gooden said about the rookie nod, "because I lived the dream making the big league club, and I never dreamed of any awards or anything like that. Once I was named Rookie of the Year, I felt it was a tremendous honor. You only have one shot of winning Rookie of the Year, and that made it that much more special."

Gooden had helped make Shea Stadium fun again. The Mets had spent the previous seven seasons struggling to draw 1 million fans at home. They drew 416,635 in Gooden's 16 starts alone, an average of 26,039. Gooden's strikeouts led to the "K Corner," where two fans would keep track of his punchouts.

Gooden and Darryl Strawberry became two of the most popular players on the 1984 squad. Both were young, good-looking players whose potential appeared limitless in '84. They also happened to be two of the best African American players produced by a franchise that before then was not known for its ability to cultivate minority players through the farm system. Strawberry served as an older brother for Gooden early on, and the two have become synonymous with each other ever since.

"Darryl kind of took me under his wing," said Gooden. "Really, from spring training, 1984, once I made the club, when we'd be on the road, he'd always come by and say, 'Hey Doc, you wanna go out to eat?'

"He'd constantly talk to me about confidence and what to look for, things to avoid. He was always very supportive, and our relationship now couldn't be any better.

"We've been through a lot of similarities with the off-field stuff and family stuff. We try to lean on each other when times are tough."

Gooden only got better in 1985, leading the majors with 24 wins, 268 strikeouts, and a 1.53 ERA. He became the first pitcher since Sandy Koufax in 1966 to lead the majors in the "Triple Crown" pitching categories. He shattered the team record for ERA and set a new mark with eight shutouts. He finished second in the majors in strikeouts and was topped only by teammate Sid Fernandez among all big league hurlers for hits allowed per nine innings.

Gooden also established a team record for a single season by winning 14 straight decisions, going unbeaten between May 25 and August 25. He became the youngest pitcher to become a 20-game winner, improving to 20–3 with a 9–3 win at San Diego on August 25.

"That year was like being in a groove," Gooden recalled over a quarter-century later. "Every game I was feeling locked in. I took the experience I got from my rookie year into the next season. That experience helped, and having Gary Carter as my catcher full time after throwing to him in the All-Star Game the year before gave me a world of confidence. It just felt like every game I was going to win."

The Mets were fighting the Cardinals for the NL East title in the final month of the season. Gooden did his part by allowing no earned runs over a 49-inning stretch from August 31 to October 2. His record in his final six starts was 4–0 with a 0.34 ERA, winning his last four starts.

Gooden became the youngest player ever to win a Cy Young Award, and only the ninth to win one unanimously. He was now 41–13 with a 2.00 ERA and 544 strikeouts in 494 innings over his first two seasons. The only criticism that could be levied against Gooden was his inability to stop runners from stealing bases on those occasions when he actually put a man on first. Pitching coach Mel Stottlemyre also wanted Gooden to economize his game by throwing fewer pitches, which also meant a reduction in strikeouts.

Gooden had another All-Star season while anchoring the majors' best pitching rotation in 1986. He went 17–6 with a 2.84 ERA and 200 strikeouts in 250 innings, but he wasn't as dominant as he was a year earlier. Gooden opened the season 5–0 with two shutouts and a microscopic 1.04 in his first six starts, which left him 23–1 with a 1.32 ERA since May 25, 1985. He pitched well the rest of 1986 but wasn't giving the performances to which fans had grown accustomed. From May 11 to August 11 he went just 7–4 with a 4.00 ERA in 17 starts, averaging nearly one homer allowed per nine innings. Stottlemyre had asked him to rely more on his fielders and less on his strikeouts, but something didn't seem quite right. Gooden allowed four or more earned runs in nine of his 33 starts. He made just one start in 1985 in which he gave up more than three runs.

Gooden erased any doubts by making two outstanding starts in the NLCS against the Astros, yielding just two earned runs in 17 innings while matched up against Mike Scott and Nolan Ryan. But the "What's wrong with Doc?" questions resurfaced during the World Series as he went 0–2 with an 8.00 ERA versus the Red Sox. The Mets' only

other loss of the series was Ron Darling's 1–0 heartbreaker in the opener.

"The postseason was great," Gooden said. "I remember facing Mike Scott the first game in Houston. He beat me 1–0. I gave up the home run to Glenn Davis in the bottom of the second, and that run stood up.

"My next start was at Shea Stadium against Nolan. I went 10 innings, pitched good and got a no-decision in that one.

"When I faced the Red Sox, it was one of those situations where maybe the innings caught up to me at the end. I just didn't have it, so I was kind of down because I didn't feel I contributed, but the players picked me up and we won it."

The Mets were honored with a tickertape parade along the Canyon of Heroes a day after winning Game 7, but Gooden overslept and missed the celebration.

Gooden's absence at City Hall only fueled rumors that had surfaced a few months earlier. While the Mets were rolling through the regular season, there were whispers that at least one player on the team was using cocaine. Gooden was one of several players suspected, but nothing was substantiated during the year. Besides, his public persona strongly suggested he wasn't the type.

His pattern of erratic behavior began after the 1985 season, when he missed a few public appearances. He angered Johnson by missing a spring training start due to a mysterious car accident, but the pitcher apologized while the team chalked it up to youthful indiscretion. However, another warning sign came when he, his sister, and his girlfriend were involved in a heated argument with a rental car clerk at LaGuardia Airport.

Gooden did nothing after the 1986 season to quash talk that *he* was the player on drugs. He was charged with resisting arrest and assaulting an officer during a brawl with Florida police following a traffic stop. The rumors were rampant by now, and Gooden announced he would undergo drug testing in an effort to end the stories.

Gooden had a poor spring training in 1987, posting a 7.31 ERA in 16 innings. His on-field performance only augmented the accusations before the Mets finally took him up on his offer to be randomly tested for drugs. Gooden tested positive for cocaine and was suspended by commissioner Peter Ueberroth for the first 60 days of the '87 season, putting more pressure on Bob Ojeda, Ron Darling, and Sid Fernandez to win while the Mets waited for their prodigal son to return.

The Mets were just 25–25 when Gooden was activated from the suspended list. Worse, Ojeda, Fernandez, Rick Aguilera, and David Cone all suffered injuries during Gooden's absence, and Darling was 2–4 with a 5.58 ERA over the first months. Journeyman Terry Leach emerged as the most dependable arm in the rotation, and he didn't make his first start of the year until May 22.

It was a contrite Gooden who finally made his season debut June 5 against the Pirates at Shea. He received a warm ovation from an "all-is-forgiven" crowd of more than 51,000 before holding the Bucs to a run and four hits in 6⅓ innings of a 5–1 victory.

Gooden was 9–3 with a 2.56 ERA after holding the Phillies to a run and six hits while striking out 11 in eight innings on August 4. He was actually pitching better than he did in 1986, and the scrutiny diminished as he again became the ace of the staff based on merit, not reputation.

Gooden had won four consecutive starts heading into a crucial game against the Cardinals September 12. The Mets had fallen 2½ games behind the first-place Redbirds following a devastating loss to St. Louis the previous day. Gooden responded to the challenge by giving up five runs in the first inning of an 8–1 loss to the Cards.

The Mets were back within 2½ games of the Cardinals when Gooden took the mound September 26 against the fifth-place Pirates. He left the mound trailing 5–1 in an 8–2 loss that crippled the team's postseason hopes.

Gooden and the Mets were in survival mode September 30 at Philadelphia, where he gave up three early runs but finished with 10 strikeouts and six hits allowed in nine innings. The game was tied 3–3 in the 10th until Luis Aguayo belted a one-out homer off Jesse Orosco to give the Phillies a victory and allow the Cards to clinch at least a tie for the NL East title.

The Mets finished second, but Gooden, despite a poor September, appeared to have worked out his off-field problems while reestablishing himself as the ace of the staff. He was fifth in the Cy Young voting after finishing seventh the previous year.

Gooden was part of a division champion again in 1988 as the Mets stormed through the final six weeks of the season to win the NL East by 15 games. He fired shutouts in three of his first 10 starts to match his total for all of 1987. Gooden was 8–0 with a 2.77 ERA after firing a four-hitter in a 4–0 win at Los Angeles on May 21, a victory that gave the Mets a 29–11 mark and a 4½-game lead over the Pirates. He won just five of his next 15 starts, going 5–6 and recording a 3.57 ERA while allowing more than one hit per inning, uncharacteristic numbers for Gooden. But he still managed to earn a spot on the NL All-Star team, taking the loss in a 2–1 game against the AL. It was fourth time he was picked to the Midsummer Classic—and the last.

Gooden and the Mets got hot late in the season. He was 5–2 with a 2.24 ERA in eight starts between August 16 and September 23, helping the Mets pull away from the Pirates. He had a chance for his second 20-win season before taking the loss in his final two starts.

Gooden was the Game 1 starter in the NLCS against the Dodgers as Mets followers wondered which Dwight Gooden would be on the mound—the guy who was fantastic in the 1986 NLCS or the person who was blasted by the Red Sox in the World Series? He was dynamite in his first 15 innings of the series, but the other 3⅓ innings contributed to the Mets' surprising loss to the Dodgers.

Dwight Gooden. Photo courtesy of David Ferry

Gooden appeared headed for a loss in the series opener despite holding L.A. to two runs and just four hits while striking out 10 in seven innings. Orel Hershiser was shutting out the Mets on five hits heading into the ninth inning, but New York chased Hershiser in the ninth while scoring three times to beat the Dodgers 3–2. Gooden had pitched well but was still seeking his first postseason victory by the end of the night.

He returned to the mound for Game 4 with a chance to put the Mets up 3–1 in the series. He was three outs away from getting his elusive playoff win after carrying a three-hitter and a 4–2 lead into the ninth. He opened the ninth by walking John Shelby before serving up a game-tying, two-run homer to Mike Scioscia, who had belted just three home runs the entire regular season. Gooden picked up another no-decision, but this time the Dodgers rallied to beat the Mets and square the series at two games apiece.

"That was probably one of the worst pitches of my career," Gooden said of the gopher ball. "One that I'd like to have back. I walked Shelby on four pitches to lead off that inning. And give Scioscia credit. Being a catcher, he probably figured that with me being a fastball pitcher, I was gonna try to get ahead. He jumped on it and hit it.

"Looking back on it, it probably changed the series."

There was speculation Gooden might start Game 7 on three days' rest, but manager Davey Johnson elected to go with Ron Darling, who had won the division clincher two weeks earlier and had one World Series win to his credit. The second-guessers were in full voice when Darling allowed a two-run single by Steve Sax that put the Dodgers ahead 4–0.

Gooden allowed two inherited runners to score in the second, thanks to a throwing error by Wally Backman. Otherwise, Doc held the Dodgers to one hit over three shutout innings before leaving what was a lost cause the way Hershiser was blowing away the Mets. Hershiser wrapped up the pennant for the Dodgers by tossing a five-hitter, putting an unexpectedly sudden end to the Mets' season.

Gooden also experienced a sudden end to his 1989 season. His strikeouts were up and his ERA was down as he opened the year 9–2 with a 2.56 earned run average and 7.7 Ks per nine innings. But he spent the month of June struggling to throw more than six innings per starts. He had to be taken out of a game after allowing three runs in two innings versus the Reds on July 1. He was diagnosed with his first pitching injury a day later, a small tear in the back of his shoulder. Gooden wouldn't pitch again until September 13 and would make just one more appearance the rest of the year.

He already had built an outstanding résumé heading into 1990. He became the third-youngest pitcher in the modern era to win 100 games, improving to 100–37 with a 5–3 triumph over the Expos June 19. Only Whitey Ford had reached 100 wins with fewer losses than Gooden.

The Mets had hoped Gooden and newcomer Frank Viola would anchor an outstanding rotation that included Cone and Fernandez, with Darling and Ojeda shuttling back and forth as the fifth starter. Gooden and Viola accounted for 39 of the Mets' 91 wins as the team battled the Pirates for the NL East crown before fading in mid September. Gooden finished 19–7 while averaging 8.6 strikeouts per nine innings, his best since 1985. But he also had the team's second-worst ERA for pitchers with at least 12 starts, a career-high 3.83 mark. He didn't get his ERA under 4.00 until July 22, and it rose to 4.39 on August 19 before he closed the season 6–1 with a 2.43 ERA in his last nine starts. Gooden won eight straight decisions heading into his final outing of the year but fell short of 20 wins by yielding eight runs over 4⅓ innings of a 9–4 loss at Pittsburgh on October 2, one day before Viola picked up his 20th win in the season finale.

The Mets had retooled in 1991, leaving Gooden as one of just six players from the 1986 team still on the Opening-Day roster. Doc was off the active roster by September 3 due to a shoulder injury that might have been prevented. He tossed a complete game April 13 against the Expos, allowing just seven hits and strikeout out 14. But he went the distance while throwing 147 pitches on a raw day at Shea, a rather high number for the sixth game of the season.

Gooden initially showed no effects from the high pitch count over his next six starts, compiling a 2.49 ERA. His ERA was 9.27 in his next four outings as the Mets began to tumble out of contention for the division title. The four-game slide was followed by a 10-game stretch in which he was 6–1 with a 2.28 ERA, including five shutout innings in a victory over the Cardinals on August 22. That would be his final start of the year.

Gooden originally was placed on the disabled list with inflammation in his shoulder. Two weeks after his final game of the season, he underwent arthroscopic surgery to repair a partial tear of the rotator cuff. It would be the last time he won more than 13 games or struck out 150 batters in a season.

Manager Bud Harrelson took plenty of heat for leaving Gooden out in the cold during the early season complete game against the Expos. Harrelson was entering his first full season as manager, and Gooden chalks up his skipper's decision to inexperience but stops short of blaming him for the injury.

"I pitched the whole game. It was kind of drizzling out and I threw like 150-something pitches. I never really bounced back from that. I was never the same after that.

"I really can't blame that, but I do think it had something to do with it."

Gooden made a quick recovery and was the starting pitcher for the Mets' 1992 home opener following a four-game road trip. Considering the surgery, he pitched very well in '92 but would never be the same dominant hurler again. Doctor K had been replaced by mild-mannered Dwight Eugene Gooden, who would lean on his nine seasons of major league experience to get batters out.

Gooden was now pitching for an underachieving team that would lose 193 games from 1992 through 1993. Ojeda, Darling, and Aguilera were long gone, Cone was dealt to Toronto in 1992, and Fernandez spent much of the '93 season on the DL. The Mets had gone from first to worst in seven years, making Gooden's 22–28 record between 1992 and '93 almost heroic.

Fans stopped talking about his pitching and focused on his hitting. He batted .200 with two homers and nine RBIs in 1993 after winning the Silver Slugger award as the NL's top hitting pitcher with a .264 mark the previous year.

The '93 Mets were just trying to avoid a 100-loss season when Gooden sat out the final month with shoulder soreness. The shoulder had become a persistent problem, but another recurring nightmare was about to end his Mets career.

Gooden opened 1994 3–4 with a ridiculous 6.31 ERA. He hadn't pitched this poorly since spring training 1987, just before he was suspended for violating baseball's substance abuse policy. Four days after surrendering nine runs in 5⅓ innings against the Pirates on June 24, he received his second suspension for testing positive for cocaine. He earned his third suspension while serving his second, only this time, it cost him the 1995 season.

Gooden was a free agent when the Yankees signed him just before the team reported for spring training in 1996. It began his warm relationship with owner George Steinbrenner.

"I can't thank George enough for the things he's done for me," he said. "After the '94 season when the Mets wanted to cut ties, I still wanted to play in New York. My heart was always in New York, and George gave me the opportunity to continue my career there.

"After I retired, the things he did for me and my family.... I'll always remember George."

He earned a spot on the starting rotation but struggled in the first month of the season. Gooden also was pitching while his father, Dan, was in ill health. The elder Gooden had a heart problem and had been using a kidney dialysis machine for a decade when he learned he needed open-heart surgery.

Dan Gooden was slated for heart surgery May 15, 1996. Dwight Gooden was 1–3 with a 5.67 ERA and showing no signs of improvement when he took the mound a day before his father was to undergo surgery. In an improbable performance given the circumstances, Dwight threw his only no-hitter, walking six and striking out five in a 2–0 win over the Mariners. He was carried off the field by his teammates, something he had never experienced during his overpowering days with the Mets. The win was part of an 15-game stretch in which he went 10–2 with a 3.41 ERA.

Gooden was reunited with Strawberry and Cone as the Yankees won their first World Series since 1978. But Gooden pitched himself off the postseason rotation by going 1–2 with a 9.23 ERA in his final nine starts.

Gooden had another so-so year in 1997, going 9–5 with a 4.91 ERA. But he earned a start in Game 4 of the ALDS, allowing a run and five hits in 5⅔ innings of the Yankees' 3–2 win over the Indians. He had helped the Yanks force a fifth game in a series they would lose, but he remained winless for his career in the postseason.

The Indians must have liked what they saw out of Gooden in the playoffs, signing him for the 1998 season. He went 8–6 while dropping his ERA to 3.76, his best since 1993. He helped the Tribe win their fourth straight AL Central title, but his team was a prohibitive underdog heading into the ALCS against a Yankee team that set a league record with 114 wins in the regular season.

Gooden faced his old team in Game 4 after the Indians took a 2–1 lead in the series. He gave up a first-inning homer to Paul O'Neill and left the game trailing 3–0 in a 4–0 loss. The Yankees didn't lose another game the rest of the postseason.

Gooden endured his worst season in 1999, going just 3–4 with a 6.26 ERA in 26 games, including 22 starts. The Indians allowed him to become a free agent, and it was two months until he signed a free-agent contract with the Astros. He made just one start for the Astros, allowing four runs in four innings before he was sold to his hometown Devil Rays, where he was 2–3 with a 6.63. He was released May 25.

Once again, Gooden was a man without a team. He was scheduled to make $500,000 in 2000, seven years after earning nearly $6 million in his final full season with the Mets.

The Yankees gave him another chance by signing him June 11. He made two minor league rehab starts before he was recalled by the team July 8, when Gooden's career came full circle. He was asked to pitch Game 1 of a duel-stadium doubleheader against the Mets, the first time two major league teams would play a "twin bill" in different ballparks in almost 100 years. Mets fans were heading to Shea Stadium hoping their former idol would fall flat on his face. But Gooden picked up the victory in a 4–2 decision over the Mets, allowing two runs in five innings.

Gooden actually pitched pretty well in his first four starts with the 2000 Yankees, going 3–0 with a 1.90 ERA. But 13 of his final 14 major league appearances came out of the bullpen, including his last victory, when he worked 5⅓ innings of two-run relief in a 10–5 win over the Royals September 5. His last loss came in his final start as he was touched for five runs in 2⅔ innings against the Tigers September 25.

Gooden burst onto the major league scene like a bolt of lightning, yet left quietly. There hasn't been a "Dwight Gooden Day," and nobody expects the Mets to retire his No. 16 anytime soon.

But Gooden continued to make news in his first few years after retiring. He was hired by the Yankees to serve as an instructor at the Yankees' 2002 spring training. Gooden had stayed clean upon his retirement, and Steinbrenner cited his former pitcher's good behavior as a reason to put him on the spring training staff and the team's special advisory board in Tampa. But one day after Steinbrenner called him a successful reclamation project, Gooden was arrested and charged with driving under the influence and doing it on a suspended license. The reclamation project was told to stay away from camp for the rest of spring training. The charge was reduced, but it wouldn't be the last time he was in the company of Florida's finest.

There were several scrapes with the law from 2003 to 2006 to further tarnish his reputation. Today, he continues his efforts to remain sober while concentrating on his primary duties as proud father.

"I'm definitely enjoying myself," Gooden explained. "Things are great. I've got seven kids. My oldest son, he's into music so he's got his music career started, and I support him. My two daughters, they're in college down in Tampa. And I have 14- and 16-year-old boys that are in high school. One's playing basketball, and the other is [playing] baseball and football.

"Now it's about me being there to support them because they followed me through my baseball time."

Gooden was in high demand in New York in 2011. He made an appearance at Citi Field in July, two weeks after donning a Yankees jersey for Old Timers' Day. The dual role might lead some to wonder where his allegiance lies.

"Always a Met," Gooden said without hesitation. "I'll always be a Met at heart, no doubt about it. I mean, I loved my time with the Yankees. No disrespect to the Yankees, but I'm definitely a Met."

ML debut	@ Astros, 4/7/84 (5 IP, 3 H, 1 ER, 5 K, 2 BB)
First ML strikeout	Dickie Thon, @ Astros, 4/7/84
First ML win	@ Astros, 4/7/84
First ML save	@ Cubs, 9/19/89
Most K's, ML/Mets game	16, vs. Pirates, 9/12/84; @ Phils, 9/17/84; vs. Giants, 8/20/85
Low-hit ML CG	0, Yankees vs. Mariners, 5/14/96
Low-hit Mets CG	1, vs. Cubs, 9/7/84

Acquired: Selected in the 1st round (5th overall) of the 1982 draft.
Deleted: Became a free agent, 10/24/94. Signed by the Yankees 2/20/96.

Led NL in wins, 1985
Led NL in ERA, 1985
Led NL in strikeouts, 1984, 1985
Led NL in innings pitched, 1985
Led NL in complete games (16), 1985
NL Rookie of the Year, 1984
NL Cy Young Award , 1985
NL All-Star, 1984, 1985, 1986, 1988

Jerry Grote

Catcher, Third Baseman, Outfielder　　　Bats right, throws right
Born: 10/6/42　　　San Antonio, Texas
Height: 5'10"　　　Weight: 185　　　#15

Jerry Grote Mets Career

YEAR	GP	AB	R	H	2B	3B	HR	RBI	K	BB	SB	AVG	SLG	OBP
1966	120	317	26	75	12	2	3	31	81	40	4	.237	.315	.327
1967	120	344	25	67	8	0	4	23	65	14	2	.195	.253	.226
1968	124	404	29	114	18	0	3	31	81	44	1	.282	.349	.357
1969	113	365	38	92	12	3	6	40	59	32	2	.252	.351	.313
1970	126	415	38	106	14	1	2	34	39	36	2	.255	.308	.313
1971	125	403	35	109	25	0	2	35	47	40	1	.270	.347	.339
1972	64	205	15	43	5	1	3	21	27	26	1	.210	.288	.304
1973	84	285	17	73	10	2	1	32	23	13	0	.256	.316	.290
1974	97	319	25	82	8	1	5	36	33	33	0	.257	.335	.326
1975	119	386	28	114	14	5	2	39	23	38	0	.295	.373	.357
1976	101	323	30	88	14	2	4	28	19	38	1	.272	.365	.350
1977	42	115	8	31	3	1	0	7	12	9	0	.270	.313	.333
TOTAL	1235	3881	314	994	143	18	35	357	509	363	14	.256	.329	.321

ML Career

YEARS	GP	AB	R	H	2B	3B	HR	RBI	K	BB	SB	AVG	SLG	OBP
63-81	1421	4339	352	1092	160	22	39	404	600	399	15	.252	.325	.316

The Mets had stockpiled several outstanding pitching prospects by the start of 1966 spring training, including Nolan Ryan, Jerry Koosman, and Tug McGraw. What the team lacked was an everyday catcher who could handle a young staff and show an ability to contribute on offense at an acceptable level.

The Mets already had gone through 14 catchers in their first four years of existence before finding a young prospect on a team full of youthful backstops. The Astros made Jerry Grote available after using four other catchers in 1965, sending the young Texan to the Mets for pitcher Tom Parsons and cash. The trade eventually became the first steal in Mets history, although it didn't receive much fanfare at its conception.

Grote was very happy to get out of Houston, even if it meant playing farther away from his native San Antonio, where he was a superb high school pitcher-catcher, won a state cross-country title, and was proficient in the mile.

"I was glad to come over to the Mets from Houston," said Grote in Maury Allen's book, *After the Miracle*. "I knew that team would never win. They had too many old players and they had no defense. It was different with the Mets. You could see the young talent. We had strong pitching and strong defense, and in 1969 I thought we were a lot like the 1965 Dodgers."[54]

"Jerry Grote was an important pickup," said former Mets general manager Bing Devine, who was assistant to president George Weiss at the time of the deal. "We were impressed with the way he caught and the way he ran a ball game. He didn't knock down the fences and make a big impression as a power hitter, but he could really catch and handle a pitcher, call a game and throw. When we got him, I don't think anyone else had a big opinion of him."[55]

There were reasons for the low expectations. Although he already was showing promise as an outstanding defensive catcher, Grote hit only .181 in 100 games for the Colt 45s in 1964 before spending the following year at Triple A Oklahoma City, where he batted .265 with 11 homers and 47 RBIs. He was a lifetime .182 hitter in 303 major league at-bats by the time he joined the Mets.

Grote also had a cocksure attitude befitting a stereotypical Texan. He demanded a pitcher's utmost attention and respect regardless of a hurler's previous major league experience. His on-field demeanor would chafe many of Houston's veteran pitchers as Grote made it known he was in charge of calling the game and didn't like to be second-guessed, even at age 21.

Grote was rarely second-guessed in his first year as a Met as he gained knowledge of National League hitters, making him a perfect fit for a pitching-oriented organization that was cultivating a host of talented young arms by the mid- to late 1960s. He could intimidate young pitchers on the field and befriend them off it. To this day, Mets pitchers praise Grote's handling of the staff and marvel at the minutia he could keep in his head.

Mets lefty Jon Matlack said in Peter Golenbock's book *Amazin'* that Grote was, "Quiet off the field, fun, a totally normal nice guy. Put the uniform on him, and he was totally different. He'd turn into an animal."

"I roomed with Grote for a little while. He had a tremendous mind for the game. He never entered into a late-inning problem without having as much knowledge as anybody could have. He would come out to the mound, and you might have first and second and one out, and whoever you were facing, he'd relay to you exactly what had happened the previous at-bats, pitch by pitch by pitch, exactly where the guy hit the ball and he'd sit and look at you. 'What do you want to do?' I'd say to him, 'You're putting down the fingers. Let's go get him.'

"Grotes was very quick on the uptake. He did most of the noticing about guys shifting their feet in the batter's box, any little thing that might help us. If a batter tried to peek back and try to see where he was setting up, I can remember on more than one occasion when he'd lean out from behind the plate and say to me, 'If this son of a bitch looks back here one more time, hit him in the head.' He was a tough player.

"Grote used to scare me to death when I'd be pitching to him, because if I bounced the ball with nobody on base, he was just as liable to knock me off the mound as not. But if there was somebody on base, he'd block it, snag it, do something to catch it, and just flip it back to you, no big deal."[56]

Grote also was able to instill confidence in a rookie pitcher by showing little fear or respect for the opposition. Bill Denehy was a rookie with the Mets in 1967, Grote's second season with the team.

"The first time we played the Giants, we were going over the lineup before the game," recalled Denehy. "We got to [Willie] Mays last, and since I was a rookie and had never pitched against these guys, I basically was listening to how we would pitch him and how we would defense him.

"I remember Jerry Grote stood up in the meeting and said, 'Fuck Willie Mays! He's not the toughest guy in the world. The first pitch, we're going to throw right at his fucking head, knock his ass down and see if he can hit from there!'"

Grote certainly was gaining the respect of the Mets staff in his first season with the team, even if he wasn't scaring opposing pitchers. He put together a nine-game hitting streak (11-for-25, .440) that raised his average to .292 on June 25. But he had just six RBIs by then and didn't hit his first home run as a Met until June 29. Grote batted only .204 in his final 201 at-bats to end up with a .237 average, three home runs and 31 RBIs in 120 games.

The Mets also had their most successful season to date in 1966 as the pitching staff featured a mixed bag of over-the-hill veterans, middle-of-the-road journeymen, and up-and-coming prospects. The team had three pitchers reach double-digits in victories in the same season for the first time in club history. The Mets went 43–59 (.467) in games started by Grote, 22–36 (.379) when he didn't.

Mets manager Wes Westrum—a former catcher himself—marveled at Grote's defensive ability.

"He was about the finest young receiver I have ever seen," crowed Westrum.[57]

Mets pitchers tolerated his abrasive on-field personality and his teammates got used to his red-ass nature. But Westrum grew weary of Grote in 1967 and was often publicly critical of the young receiver. The manager saw in Grote a player with a tremendous arm, good speed but a questionable concentration level. Westrum also wasn't crazy about the way Grote could rip into his pitchers on the mound, nor was he thrilled about Grote's incessant bitching with plate umpires. Things between Westrum and Grote came to a head during a game in Los Angeles on July 27, 1967.

According to George Vecsey's book, *Joy in Mudville* and baseball-reference.com Westrum used all three of his available catchers in the seventh inning with the Mets trailing the Dodgers. Starting catcher John Sullivan hit an RBI single to make it 3–2 before Grote pinch-ran for him. Pinch-hitter and No. 3 catcher Greg Goossen struck out with the tying run on third before Grote took over behind the plate in the bottom of the inning.

It took just a few pitches before Grote was complaining to plate ump Bill Jackowski about his calls on balls and strikes. Reliever Hal Reniff walked two in the inning but got out of a bases-loaded jam without allowing a run. Grote, still seething over Jackowski's calls, heaved a towel from the dugout after the inning and was ejected by third base umpire Harry Wendelstedt, leaving the Mets without a catcher.

The game went into extra innings with outfielder Tommie Reynolds serving as the emergency catcher. Reynolds did okay until he was charged with a passed ball that allowed the winning run to score in the bottom of the 11th.

Now it was Westrum's turn to seethe. He fined Grote $100 and let the writers know about it before benching him for the next game. Grote was furious the fine was made public.

Grote also couldn't have been too happy with his season. He was batting just .194 following the Dodgers game and finished the year hitting .195 with four homers, 12 extra-base hits, and 23 RBIs. Grote's batting average for 1967 remains the second-lowest single-season total by any Met with at least 350 plate appearances.

A new manager was in place by October 1967 as Gil Hodges returned to the Mets following a 4½-year run as the Senators' skipper. For players like Grote and Cleon Jones—another occupant of Westrum's doghouse—Hodges represented a new start.

Hodges knew a little bit about catching, having played the position for the Dodgers in the minors before switching to first base. He also knew how to handle young players with short fuses and helped turn Grote into an All-Star catcher within a few months.

Grote and Hodges had at least one thing in common; they detested the perception of the Mets as lovable losers and were ready to change the atmosphere within the organization. Hodges recognized the team's wealth of young pitchers and saw promise in Grote when Westrum saw disappointment.

If Grote needed tips on how to handle a pitching staff, he had to look no further than Mets coaches Yogi Berra, Rube Walker, and Joe Pignatano, all former major league catchers. Hodges knew Grote had the tools to become a great defensive catcher and concentrated on adjusting Grote's swing once the team reported to spring training in 1968.

"Gil changed me completely as a hitter," Grote said in *After the Miracle*. "I used to be way down on the bat and swung hard on every pitch. That was the way I was told to hit. Gil got me up on the bat and told me all I had to do was make contact, keep the ball in play, use the whole field. I started doing it that way and it worked. After that I gave up trying to pull everything. I would hit an occasional long ball, but I was most often just trying to punch the ball through the middle."[58]

The adjustments turned Grote into one of the team's top hitters in 1968. He finished second to Jones on the Mets in batting (.281), hits (114), and doubles (18) while posting a team-high .357 on-base percentage. He had a 10-game hitting streak (.461 in 38 at-bats) from May 7 through May 17 to lift his season batting average 44 points to .343. He was 10-for-16 (.625) against the Cubs in a four-game series during the streak and hit .482 against Chicago for the season.

Grote also batted .556 (10-for-18) in seven games from July 6 through July 14, a stretch that included a starting assignment in the All-Star Game. Playing ahead of Johnny Bench and Tom Haller in the Midsummer Classic at Houston, Grote went 0-for-2 and was lifted from the game before Mets teammates Tom Seaver and Jerry Koosman took their turns on the mound. Seaver struck out five in two innings, and Koosman fanned Carl Yastrzemski to earn the save in a 1–0 victory for the National League.

It marked the first time the Mets had three All-Star representatives in the same year, and it showcased the team's greatest strength. Seaver won 16 games for the second straight year and Koosman was 19–12. Most important, Seaver and Koosman were not intimidated by Grote's high standards for pitchers at a time when a few other young Mets hurlers welcomed the sight of J.C. Martin behind the plate.

Grote also solidified his reputation as an outstanding defensive catcher in 1968, nailing 30 of his 69 base-stealers (43 percent) and committing just one passed ball in 105 innings. By the end of the season, Cardinals speedster and one-time major league career stolen base leader Lou Brock called Grote the "toughest catcher to steal on."

The Mets finished out of the cellar in 1968 for the second time in their seven seasons and set a team record with 73 wins through outstanding pitching and solid defense. When the team reported for spring training in 1969 following a brief work stoppage, Hodges predicted the team could win 85 games. Grote went one step better.

"Only Grote seemed to know," remarked Tom Seaver. "He said repeatedly that spring that we could win, we were good enough to compete with anybody, we had the best team in the league. I thought we could be a .500 team."[59]

The expansion Expos were part of the newly formed National League East in 1969, which gave the Mets a pretty good chance to finish out of the cellar for the second straight season. But in their first game as baseball's first Canadian team, the Expos beat the Mets 11–10 at Shea Stadium on April 8. Grote did his part on offense, going 2-for-3 with two walks, an RBI, and three runs scored, but he also saw the bullpen surrender seven runs in four innings after Seaver was reached for four runs in five frames. To make matters worse, reliever Dan McGinn homered and ex-Met Don Shaw picked up the victory.

Grote went 2-for-4 with two RBIs in a 9–5 win the following day and provided three hits and four RBIs in an 11–3 rout of the Cardinals April 20.

Grote's training camp assessment of the team was looking ridiculous after the Mets lost to the expansion Padres 3–2 at Shea Stadium May 27 to fall to 18–23. New York already was nine games behind the first-place Cubs but only 3½ games out of second when the Mets embarked on a team-record 11-game winning streak. Grote started 10 of those 11 victories while hitting .278 in the process to raise his season average to .238. The winning streak vaulted the Mets into second place but allowed them to shave just two games off their deficit with the Cubs.

Hodges set up a consistent platoon system at first, second, third, and right, and made sure Grote wasn't overworked behind the plate. With J.C. Martin and Duffy Dyer at his disposal, Hodges gave Grote what amounted to one day off for every five days played. The time off allowed Grote to recover from nagging leg and hand injuries during the course of the year. Meanwhile, Cubs manager Leo Durocher rarely gave his regulars a day off, a strategy that showed up over the final seven weeks of the season.

Grote's durability was tested when he caught all 15 innings of a 1–0 win over the Dodgers on June 4 after going the distance in a pair of 11-inning games earlier in the season. He was the starting catcher when Tom Seaver tossed his one-hitter against the Cubs at Shea on July 9 as the Mets entered the midway point of the season 47–34. But his batting average was just .229 in the first half just a year after compiling a .291 average through the Mets' first 81 games of 1968.

The offensive production coming from Grote was representative of the Mets' hitting at that point. New York had a .243 team average in the first half and was winning games with outstanding pitching, a byproduct of Grote's work. Of the 15 pitchers used by the Mets that season, 10 had pitched in two seasons or fewer entering 1969, putting more responsibility on Grote to call a good game while maintaining a good relationship with his hurlers. The team ERA was 3.13 following Seaver's one-hitter and 3.42 by the end of July. But Mets hurlers combined for a ridiculous 2.31 earned run average over the final two months of the season, holding opponents to a .212 batting average and

Jerry Grote (15). Photo courtesy of Oscar W. Gabriel

tossing 10 shutouts in 63 games. Grote started 39 of those games while hitting above his 1968 pace, recording a .307 average with four home runs, 16 RBIs, and 23 runs scored. He manufactured 36 of the team's 237 runs (15 percent) and compiled 12 multi-hit games while the Mets went 32–10 in the games he played during August and September. New York was 9–3 in the 12 games Grote provided at least two hits.

Among his key performances down the stretch, Grote:

- Smacked a walk-off homer leading off the bottom of the 11th in a 6–5 win over the Braves August 3.
- Poked a tiebreaking RBI single in the seventh inning of a 2–1 victory against the Padres August 16.
- Ended a 3–2 win over the Dodgers with an RBI double in the bottom of the ninth August 23, a three-game series in which Grote was 6-for-8 with three RBIs and two runs scored in two games.
- Went 4-for-12 with two home runs, three ribbies, and four runs scored during a three-game set with the Phillies at Shea in early September, a series that put the Mets just 2½ games behind the Cubs heading into a two-game clash at Shea.

The Mets clinched their first playoff appearance on September 24 as Grote went 2-for-4 with a double while catching Gary Gentry's four-hit shutout of the Cardinals.

Grote finished the year hitting .252 with career highs of six home runs and 40 RBIs.

Grote and the Mets headed to the first-ever NL championship series as underdogs against the Braves, who had one of the league's best lineups and a solid pitching staff. The Mets batted .327 in the three-game sweep of Atlanta, outscoring the Braves 24–15 while Grote hit .167 (2-for-12) with an RBI and three runs scored in the series. Grote caught every inning of the NLCS and would do the same in the World Series against the Orioles. Grote was 4-for-19 (.211) in the Fall Classic but contributed two crucial at-bats in the series.

The Mets dropped the first game of the World Series and were tied 1–1 in the ninth inning of Game 2 when Grote poked a two-out single in the ninth to put runners on first and third. The hit allowed Ed Charles to produce the tiebreaking single in a 2–1 victory.

Grote also helped the Mets score an insurance run in the clinching Game 5 win over the Birds. Two batters after Ron Swoboda's tiebreaking double in the bottom of the eighth, Grote hit a smash that Boog Powell mishandled at first base, allowing Swoboda to score the insurance run.

Minutes later, Koosman jumped into Grote's arms after the Mets won the World Series. The Orioles, who were among the top three in the American League with a .265 average, 175 homers, and 779 runs scored during the regular season, hit only .146 in the World Series while Grote again caught every inning. Baltimore scored just five times over the final four games.

The Mets were the favorites to win the NL East in 1970, quite a turnaround for a ballclub that averaged over 100 losses in its first seven seasons. Grote had a good year at the plate by his standards, hitting .255 with 34 RBIs while scoring a career-high 38 runs for the second straight year. But the Mets never distanced themselves from the division contenders and finished a disappointing six games behind the Pirates after owning a share of first place in September.

The 1971 Mets got off to the best start in team history at that point, relying in pitching to forge a 21–10 record and a 2½-game lead by May 15. Grote landed on the cover of *Sports Illustrated* on June 21 and said the Mets were hungrier than they were in 1970.

"This spring there was no doubt that we were a more dedicated club than we were when we got to St. Petersburg the year before," he said. "When the pitchers and catchers arrived in camp we really went at things and there was a closeness that had to help us. We were thinking together about the job we had to do."[60]

The '71 Mets had the NL's best pitching staff, leading the league with a 2.99 ERA and 1157 strikeouts. With Grote behind the plate the opposition hit only .227 against the Mets and scored 400 runs in 122 games. Hodges gave Grote much credit for the team's mound success and was pleased by the way his No. 1 catcher had matured under his watch.

"I hesitate to imagine where the New York Mets would have been the last few years without Jerry," Hodges said.

"He is invaluable to us. He is intent and intense and he fights to get everything he can. He is durable and not afraid to play with injuries. Because of that he allows us to carry two catchers instead of three.

"When I came to the Mets I got a run-through on the players, and I did not like some of the things I heard about Jerry. He had a habit of getting into too many arguments with umpires and getting on some of the older players on the club."[61]

Seaver parroted Hodges's assessment of Grote in the same *Sports Illustrated* article, saying Grote was, "An excellent catcher now. In his earlier days his temper used to get away from him and he sometimes forgot that his primary job was to call a good game and become a catcher we could respect. In addition, he has reached that point where he gets the big hit when it's needed."[62]

Unfortunately, the Mets succumbed to the dreaded *Sports Illustrated* "cover jinx" soon after Grote graced the front of the magazine. The team went 9–20 in July and 12–17 in August to destroy any momentum generated from a 45–29 start. New York eventually fell under .500 and finished 13½ games behind the first-place Pirates at 83–79 while Grote hit .270 with a career-high and team-leading 25 doubles, two home runs, and 34 RBIs in 125 games. He paced all NL catchers in putouts for the second straight year, but a chest injury suffered in July hampered his throwing as Grote nailed 26 percent of his base runners, his worst single-season percentage to date. Grote entered the year having thrown out a remarkable 44 percent of his 423 base-runners heading into 1971, including a .565 mark in 1969. He went back over 50 percent again in 1972 despite bone chips in his throwing elbow.

The Mets got off to an unbelievable start in 1972, reeling off a team record-tying 11-game winning streak that left them 25–7 and six games ahead of Pittsburgh by May 21. The lineup now included Rusty Staub, Jim Fregosi, and Willie Mays, who was acquired from the Giants just before Mother's Day. New York hit .254 and averaged 4.2 runs while compiling a 2.91 ERA during the first 32 games as they threatened to run away with the division.

One of the team's top pitchers at the start of the season was Matlack, who became the Mets' first rookie to begin a season 6–0. Even he had to prove he could stand up to Grote and be his own man.

"He was extremely intimidating," Matlack said almost four decades after winning NL Rookie of the Year honors. "I can't remember what sequence of events or how long it went, but the beginning of '72, anytime I was pitching, anytime I bounced a ball and nobody was on base, he would just about clean me off the mound throwing the ball back at me and make some kind of gruff remark regarding it. It was just pushy and sort of picking on me, I assume like you would treat a rookie.

"I finally had my fill of it, and he came out to the mound at one point in some game. I don't recall when it was, sometime four or five weeks into my activity in the rotation. He had a habit of propping the mask on his head and he comes strutting out there and was gonna say something. I met him at the bottom of the mound and said, 'Look, I've had enough of this. I'm pitching. You're catching. Now, get back behind the plate and let's go to work.'

"He started laughing, and I was sort of stunned. He said, 'I've been waiting six weeks for that,' and went back to the plate.

"The whole thing that I thought was like rookie initiation was him trying to get me to take charge."

But a ridiculous number of injuries left the Mets with a skeletal lineup that pushed them out of playoff contention by mid-July. Grote, Staub, Mays, Cleon Jones, Tommie Agee, John Milner, Bud Harrelson, and Jim Fregosi all missed significant playing time, making Ed Kranepool the team leader in games played with only 122 by season's end. Things got so bad that Grote was asked to start in right field on July 12 before starting two straight games at third base in late August.

Grote and Jim Beauchamp were the lone Mets to hit two homers in a game that year. Grote went deep twice and drove in four runs against the Phillies May 19 to raise his average to .266. But Grote hit only .175 in 40 contests following his two-homer game and was able to start just six games at catcher after July 29 because of his elbow problem. He finally underwent surgery in mid-September and was ready for the start of spring training.

Grote and the Mets battled injuries again in 1973, although his 84 appearances represented a 20-game improvement over 1972. Grote also hit .256 compared to his .210 mark in 1972 and drove in 32 runs, 11 more than his previous total.

Mets Hitters in August/September 1969

	HR	RBI	R	AVG
Jerry Grote	4	16	23	.307
J.C. Martin	0	3	1	.147
Duffy Dyer	2	8	3	.254
Tommie Agee	10	28	42	.266
Cleon Jones	1	17	23	.324
Ron Swoboda	6	30	20	.232
Art Shamsky	6	22	18	.267
Rod Gaspar	0	5	5	.222
Ed Kranepool	2	5	6	.234
Donn Clendenon	10	20	22	.250
Ken Boswell	0	12	11	.366
Al Weis	0	6	3	.212
Bud Harrelson	0	12	19	.246
Ed Charles	1	4	7	.227
Wayne Garrett	0	14	12	.165

The Mets played two months without Grote, who broke his right arm when hit by a Ramon Hernandez pitch against the Pirates on May 11. He returned to the active roster on July 11 but broke his right pinkie after taking a foul tip off the hand four days later.

Mays, Milner, Jones, Harrelson, and George Theodore all spent time on the DL while Grote was sidelined, the prime reason why the Mets were last in the NL East at 53–65 following Grote's first career grand slam in a 7–0 shutout of the Padres on August 15. Three days later, the Mets finally had their entire starting lineup intact after Harrelson was activated.

In Harrelson's first game back, Grote went 4-for-5 in a 12–1 clobbering of the Reds, a victory that left New York 54–66 and 6½ games out of first. The rout ignited a season-ending 29–13 stretch that put the Mets in the postseason for the second time in five seasons. Grote started 38 of those 42 games, batting .297 with 14 RBIs and seven runs scored. The stretch included his tiebreaking bunt-single in the eighth inning of a 4–3 triumph over the Cubs on September 16, which left the Mets in fourth place but just 2½-games off the lead. They moved into first place five days later and won nine of their final 11 games to finish 1½ games ahead of the second-place Cardinals. The Mets didn't clinch the crown until the day after the scheduled end of the season, beating the Cubs 6–4 in Game 1 of a twin bill before the nightcap was rained out. Grote provided a two-run single that put New York ahead 3–0 in fourth inning of the clincher.

The NLCS against the Reds featured the league's top offensive catcher and the best defensive backstop. Johnny Bench was in the midst of capturing 10 consecutive Gold Gloves, but even he felt Grote was the better defensive player. Bench once said that if he and Grote were teammates, Bench would be a third baseman.

Grote again handled every inning of the Mets' five-game series win over Cincinnati, including a 12-inning assignment in a 2–1 loss in Game 4. The Reds scored just eight times in 39 innings while Mets pitchers posted a 1.33 ERA against the NL's best offensive ballclub. Grote provided a key hit in the series, a two-run single that gave the Mets a 4–0 lead in the ninth inning of a 5–0 triumph at Cincinnati, evening the series at a game apiece. Although he was just 4-for-19 (.211) in the series, Grote had more hits than every member of the Reds except Bench and Pete Rose. Hall of Famers Joe Morgan and Tony Perez were a combined 4-for-42 (.095).

The Mets faced the A's in the World Series, putting New York in another tough matchup against an offensive juggernaut. The A's were second in the majors with 758 runs scored and third with 128 stolen bases during the regular season, adding pressure on Grote and Mets pitchers to keep the bases clear.

The Mets took a 3–2 lead in the series by winning two of three games at Shea Stadium. The entire A's lineup outhit Grote just 8–4 while the Mets were winning Games 4 and 5. Grote hit .267 (8-for-30) with two runs scored and again played every inning of every game. He had a three-hit night in Game 4 after catching a total of 23 innings in the previous two contests.

But the Athletics captured the final two games of the series in Oakland to repeat as World Series champs. It represented the final hurrah before the Mets morphed into mediocrity for the next decade.

Grote's postseason durability was impressive considering his position. He was the lone Met to appear in all 188 innings of the team's first four postseason series, although Jones and Harrelson were close with 187 innings.

The Mets didn't come close to repeating as NL East champs in 1974, finishing fifth with a 71–91 record as injuries to Seaver and Tug McGraw destroyed any shot of New York contending for the title. Grote also suffered myriad injuries and missed the final five weeks with ligament damage in his right hand. But Grote was selected to the All-Star Game for the second and final time of his career, backing up Bench and entering the game in the ninth inning of a 7–2 victory.

Grote was enjoying a nice offensive spurt heading into the '74 Midsummer Classic, hitting .316 in 53 games from May 7 through July 21 to lift his average from .200 to .287. Only Kranepool (.370) and Don Hahn (.288) had a higher batting average among Mets heading into the break.

Grote continued to get dinged up while New York continued its free-fall from the division race. He decided to rest his damaged hand after hitting only .121 in 58 at-bats during August.

The 1975 season was among Grote's best in the majors. He appeared in 119 games after failing to play more than 97 in any of the three previous years. Grote also threw out 35 percent of his runners and recorded a league-best .995 field percentage in 765 chances while Ron Hodges and rookie John Stearns served as his backups.

Grote delivered at the plate in '75, hitting a career-high .295, tying a career high with 114 hits and falling one RBI short of his career best of 40. He was the fourth-toughest National League to strike out, fanning once every 18.6 at-bats.

Seaver won his third Cy Young Award, Rusty Staub set a team record with 105 RBIs, and Mike Vail matched Jones' club mark with a 23-game hitting streak. Despite Grote's contributions, the Mets played themselves out of playoff contention shortly after Labor Day and went 24–26 once Roy McMillan replaced Berra as manager in early August.

The Mets continued to walk the treadmill of indifference in 1976, finishing third for the fifth time in seven years. Grote had another good season when healthy, hitting .272 in 101 games. It marked the first time he had batted over .270 in consecutive seasons as he remained one of the few players left from the Mets' glory days. By the end of 1976, Grote, Kranepool, Harrelson, Seaver, and Koosman were the lone Mets remaining from their '69 club.

The franchise did little to keep pace with the Pirates and Phillies in the NL East. The Phils, laughingstocks when the Mets won the 1969 title, captured their second straight division flag in 1977. The Pirates weren't far behind, but the Mets were bringing up the rear on Memorial Day.

Grote batted .270 in just 42 games as a Met in '77 as he lost playing time to Stearns while the team tried to create evidence of a productive farm system. Team chairman M. Donald Grant and general manager Joe McDonald gutted the team at the June 15 deadline, sending Seaver to the Reds and top slugger Dave Kingman to the Padres. Grote found himself handling a starting rotation of Koosman, Jon Matlack, Craig Swan, Pat Zachry, and Nino Espinosa.

Swan was among the younger pitchers on the team and eventually grew to like having Grote call his games.

"He could be trouble if you didn't do what he said," Swan said. "He wanted you to throw the pitches he called. He made it very simple.

"I would shake him off now and then, and he would shake his head back at me. If a guy hit a home run, he wouldn't let you hear the end of it.

"Actually, we got along great. He was only testy on the field."[63]

The Mets were playing out the string when they did Grote a favor by sending him to the Dodgers on August 31, allowing him to be available for the postseason. Grote hit .259 in 27 at-bats as Steve Yeager's backup before appearing in the NLCS and World Series.

Grote remained a Dodgers backup in 1978 and saw action in the championship series and Fall Classic. He hit .271 in 40 at-bats during the regular season and was granted free agency in November.

He sat out the next two seasons and hooked up with the Royals in the spring of 1981. He was productive in very limited duty with Kansas City, hitting .304 in 56 at-bats over 22 games. Although he handled 93 chances without an error behind the plate, Grote threw out only four of 18 base-stealers (22 percent) and was released on September 1, preventing him from appearing in another postseason.

The Dodgers signed Grote on September 8 and used him in just two games after they already wrapped up a playoff spot by virtue of their first-half NL West title in a strike year. Grote was released October 14 at age 39, two weeks before the Dodgers won their first World Series in 16 years.

Grote wanted to remain in the game as a coach or manager and was finally hired by the Tigers before the 1985 season. He managed at both Single A Lakeland and Double A Birmingham before he was let go after the '85 season.

The Mets gave Grote their highest honor by inducting him into the team's Hall of Fame in 1992. When he left the Mets 15 years earlier, he was among the top five on the team's all-time list in games played (1,235), at-bats

(3,881), hits (994), doubles (143), RBIs (357), total bases (1,278), and extra-base hits (196).

Grote remains a fixture at the Mets' fantasy camps and says his knees and arm have held up long after retirement.

ML debut	Colt 45s vs. Phillies, 9/21/63
Mets debut	vs. Braves, 4/15/66
1st ML hit	single vs. Al Jackson, Mets, 9/27/63 (with Colt 45s)
1st Mets hit	single vs. Billy O'Dell, @ Braves, 4/24/66
1st ML homer	solo homer vs. Lew Burdette, @ Cubs, 6/26/64
1st Mets homer	solo homer vs. Bob Buhl, Phillies, 6/29/66
1st ML RBI	sac-fly vs. Dallas Green, Phillies, 9/21/63 (with Colt 45s)
1st Mets RBI	RBI single vs. Don Lee, Astros, 5/10/66
Most hits, ML/Mets game	4, 5 times
Most homers, ML/Mets game	2, @ Phillies, 5/19/72
Most RBI, ML game	7, Royals vs. Mariners, 6/3/81
Most RBI, Mets game	4, 4 times
Acquired:	Traded by the Astros for a player to be named (Tom Parsons) and cash, 10/19/65.
Deleted:	Traded to the Dodgers for two players to be named (Dan Smith and Randy Rogers), 8/31/77.

Bud Harrelson

Shortstop	Bats both, throws right	
Born: 6/6/44	Niles, California	
Height: 5'11"	Weight: 160	#3

Bud Harrelson Mets Career

YEAR	GP	AB	R	H	2B	3B	HR	RBI	K	BB	SB	AVG	SLG	OBP
1965	19	37	3	4	1	1	0	0	11	2	0	.108	.189	.154
1966	33	99	20	22	2	4	0	4	23	13	7	.222	.323	.313
1967	151	540	59	137	16	4	1	28	64	48	12	.254	.304	.317
1968	111	402	38	88	7	3	0	14	68	29	4	.219	.251	.273
1969	123	395	42	98	11	6	0	24	54	54	1	.248	.306	.341
1970	157	564	72	137	18	8	1	42	74	95	23	.243	.309	.351
1971	142	547	55	138	16	6	0	32	59	53	28	.252	.303	.319
1972	115	418	54	90	10	4	1	24	57	58	12	.215	.266	.313
1973	106	356	35	92	12	3	0	20	49	48	5	.258	.309	.348
1974	106	331	48	75	10	0	1	13	39	71	9	.227	.266	.366
1975	34	73	5	16	2	0	0	3	13	12	0	.219	.247	.329
1976	118	359	34	84	12	4	1	26	56	63	9	.234	.298	.351
1977	107	269	25	48	6	2	1	12	28	27	5	.178	.227	.255
TOTAL	1322	4390	490	1029	123	45	6	242	595	573	115	.234	.287	.324

ML Career

YEAR	GP	AB	R	H	2B	3B	HR	RBI	K	BB	SB	AVG	SLG	OBP
65-80	1533	4744	539	1120	136	45	7	267	653	633	127	.236	.288	.327

Look at the back of a Bud Harrelson baseball card and you'll find little to make you believe he was among the two most indispensable non-pitchers on the Mets during their first two pennant-winning teams. Topps listed him as 5'11" and anywhere from 150-155 pounds, although he was closer to 140 near the end of a typical season. He batted only .234 in his 13 seasons with the Mets, never hitting higher than .258 in any year. He averaged one home run every two seasons, leading to a .287 slugging average that was 37 points lower than his on-base percentage. Of the

26 National League players who had at least 5,000 plate appearances from 1965 through 1977, none had a lower batting average during that span than Harrelson.

But there's not a single pitcher on the 1970s Mets who wanted anyone other than Harrelson at shortstop. He was the glue of the infield, blessed with outstanding range, a strong arm, and a quick release. Harrelson was the first Mets infielder to win a Gold Glove and the team's first non-pitcher to be selected to consecutive All-Star Games. He also finished fourth among National Leaguers in stolen bases one year after winding up second in sacrifice hits.

Mets fans too young to see Harrelson play may have trouble appreciating his contributions, but longtime followers of the team will argue the ballclub never had as valuable a shortstop until Jose Reyes broke in over a quarter-century after Harrelson played his last game for the franchise.

Consider the impact Harrelson had on the starting lineup from 1968 through 1974. The Mets went 575–552 in 1127 games for a .510 winning percentage. They were 441–373 (.542) when Harrelson was in the lineup, 134–179 (.428) without him.

The only other non-platoon player with the Mets through that period was Cleon Jones, the best hitter produced by the Mets' farm system prior to their 1969 championship run. Jones hit .291 during that period, finishing among the top 10 National League hitters in 1969 and 1971. But the Mets could only muster a .517 winning percentage in his 813 starts as opposed to a .475 mark when he didn't. Even when Jones challenged for batting titles in '69 and '71, the Mets went 145–116 (.556) in his starts compared to a 145–108 (.573) record with Harrelson in the lineup. Jones also hit 53 points higher than Harrelson from 1968 through 1974, augmenting Harrelson's value to the team.

Derrel McKinley Harrelson was born in Niles, California, a town situated between San Francisco and San Jose. He attended Sunset High School in Hayward, California, before earning a basketball scholarship at San Francisco State. Harrelson showed leadership skills at Sunset, captaining the baseball, football, and basketball teams as a senior.

The Mets already were tracking Harrelson when he enrolled in college and signed him on June 7, 1963, after his freshman season. He was assigned to Salinas of the Class A California League in the summer of 1963, allowing him to stay close to home.

Harrelson didn't hit much at Salinas, recording a .229 average in 36 games in '63 before batting .231 there the following year. But he manufactured runs at the plate while demonstrating eye-popping range that made him one of the team's best young prospects heading into 1965.

Moved up to Triple A Buffalo in 1965, Harrelson was on the East Coast for the first time in his life but continued to impress Mets management by hitting .251 in 131 games. He made a whopping 31 errors at short after committing 34 miscues for Salinas in 1964, but there was no denying he had the defensive tools to become an outstanding major league shortstop.

Harrelson was called up after the completion of the '65 Triple A season. He made his debut as a pinch-runner against the Astros on September 2 and had his first major league at-bat three days later, replacing Roy McMillan in the second inning before going 0-for-2 versus the Cardinals.

Harrelson was 0-for-8 in the majors before slapping a single off Cubs pitcher Bob Hendley in the first inning of an 8–6 win on September 19. He collected three more hits the rest of the season but often looked overmatched, batting .108 with 11 strikeouts in 37 at-bats.

The Mets opened the 1966 season with Harrelson at Triple A Jacksonville, where he was teammates with fellow Northern Californian Tom Seaver for the first time as a professional. Harrelson hit just .221 for the Suns and committed 28 errors despite his raw defensive ability. Recalled again in mid-August, the Mets asked McMillan to serve as a mentor for the 22-year-old prospect.

McMillan was a magnificent fielder throughout his major league career, winning the first three NL Gold Gloves for shortstops after the award was instituted in 1957. He was a two-time All-Star and, like Harrelson, wasn't especially scary at the plate. A shoulder injury sidelined McMillan over the final few weeks of the 1966 season, but there was still hope he would return in '67.

McMillan could have balked after being given the task of grooming Harrelson as his replacement. Instead, he taught him the finer points of fielding over the next 18 months.

"I liked Harrelson right away, too," McMillan said. "He'd listen and try to do what you taught him. He already had good hands, good range and a real feel for the double play, so mostly it was just a case of experience.

"One thing I did correct, though, was the way he threw the ball from deep shortstop. He wasn't getting set before firing and neither was he getting his body into his throws. But he adjusted almost immediately."[64]

Harrelson was recalled in '66 to replace McMillan on the active roster. Unlike his 1965 trial run with the Mets, Harrelson showed comfort at the plate and on the field. He committed just one error in 29 games at shortstop, and hit .222 in 99 at-bats over 33 games overall. Just as impressive as his fielding was his running as he legged out four triples and seven stolen bases.

McMillan reported to spring training in 1967 and reinjured his shoulder, forcing him to announce his retirement in early May. Harrelson already had become the starting shortstop and displayed continued growth as a hitter, recording a .254 average with a .317 on-base percentage, 28 RBIs, 59 runs scored, and 12 stolen bases. He tied Jones for the team lead in steals (12) and was second to Tommy Davis with 59 runs scored.

Harrelson was among the Mets' three best hitters from May 27 through July 29, compiling a .321 average with a

.367 on-base percentage and 32 runs scored in 62 games to raise his season average to .291. But the rigors of playing his first full major league season caused the wiry infielder to wear down by late July. His average stood at .270 as late as August 28 before plummeting.

Any offense from Harrelson was still considered a bonus as long as he continued to develop as a fielder. But his glovework was on the wrong side of passable in the early going. He committed 11 errors in his first 20 games of '67 and finished with 32 for the season, leading to 23 unearned runs. But he made just five throwing errors while continuing to work with McMillan on his footwork and glove placement. Harrelson was second among NL shortstops in putouts and third in assists, proving he had the makings of an outstanding shortstop.

The Mets regressed for the second time in three years, finishing last at 61–101 after setting a club record with 66 victories in 1966. The 1967 season ranked as the second-best in Mets history at the time, although it wasn't enough for management to keep Wes Westrum as manager. There had been significant improvements made to the roster, most coming from within the farm system. The greatest homegrown talent was Seaver, who became the team's first NL Rookie of the Year after going 16–13 with a 2.76 ERA and 170 strikeouts in '67.

Seaver didn't find the team's losing culture the least bit funny. Neither did the Mets' new skipper. Gil Hodges was hired as manager on October 11, 1967, after nearly five full seasons running the Senators. Hodges never got Washington out of the American League's second division, but his work with the team was deemed remarkable by a local media that eventually inducted him into RFK Stadium's Wall of Fame.

Hodges already was beloved by Mets fans from his days as a dangerous slugger with the Dodgers. He was an original member of the 1962 Mets, an inept ballclub that created the franchise image as lovable losers. Hodges eventually changed that image but used the 1968 season to evaluate the players he had in the organization.

Hodges subjected his players to constant weigh-ins to better monitor the condition of his ballclub. In Harrelson's case, the problem was trying to stay above 150 throughout the season.

The 1968 team took giant steps toward respectability through pitching and defense. The Mets ranked fourth in staff ERA and were second in strikeouts, shutouts, and saves. New York also was fourth in fielding percentage and fewest errors, erasing the team's reputation for shoddy defense.

But the Mets were dead last in batting average, on-base percentage, and slugging. The Dodgers were the only club to score fewer runs than the Mets, who were shut out 22 times and set a major league record by striking out 1,203 times. New York averaged just 2.90 runs per game, negating the virtues of a pitching staff that was second in the NL with 3.06 runs allowed per game.

Harrelson was a major reason for the team's upgraded defensive showing, raising his fielding average from .958 in 1967 to .972. Harrelson hit only .219 in 111 games while playing through right knee pain that eventually led to the removal of torn cartilage. He drove in just 14 runs, scored 38, and stole only four bases in nine attempts. But he still managed to manufacture more runs (52) than Tommie Agee (42), the Mets' new center fielder who endured a miserable season.

The Mets set a team record with 73 wins in their first season under Hodges but didn't escape the cellar for good until September 11 and didn't clinch ninth place until the next-to-last game of the season.

New York finished the campaign without Hodges, who suffered a heart attack during the final week of the season. The players already had begun to buy into Hodges' program, and many saw him as a surrogate father. Harrelson was among those who believed his manager was something special.

Hodges was deemed fit to manage in 1969 after spending the winter in St. Petersburg. His players also enjoyed some unexpected free time in St. Pete as the start of training camp was postponed by a work stoppage. Several Mets worked out on their own and continued to bond as a ballclub before camps opened.

But it was the same old Mets at the start of 1969. They absorbed an 11–10 loss to the expansion Expos at Shea Stadium in the season opener before winning the next two games to climb above .500 for the second time in team history. But they suffered a three-game sweep by the Cardinals at Shea the next series and were eight games out of first place at 9–14 by May 3.

The Mets touched .500 again on May 21, only to lose the next five games to drop to 18–23, nine games behind the streaking, first-place Cubs.

Meanwhile, Harrelson was producing at the plate and on the field. He owned a .296 average after delivering a walk-off single in the 11th inning of a 1–0 win over the expansion Padres on May 29, a hit that also ignited an 11-game winning streak that vaulted the Mets back into the NL East race, albeit seven games behind Chicago by June 10. They won six games by one run during the streak and capped the stretch by scoring nine times in a win over the Giants.

Harrelson's season was put on hold by the US Military, which required his services as a reservist from June 25 through July 11. He said good-bye to his teammates after hitting an RBI triple in a 2–1 win over the Phillies, helping Seaver improve to 11–3.

New York dropped its first four games without Harrelson before winning nine of the last 11. Harrelson had to watch on television as Seaver carried a perfect game into the ninth inning of a 4–0 win over the Cubs on July 9, putting the Mets within 3½ games of Chicago at 47–34. The Mets had managed to creep closer while Hodges filled the shortstop position with Al Weis, who owned a .198 average following Seaver's one-hitter.

Harrelson didn't start again until July 19 as Hodges continued to use Weis at short. That decision paid dividends as Weis homered on consecutive days to lead the Mets to wins over the Cubs at Wrigley Field. Weis entered the series with just four home runs in 1,329 major league at-bats, an indication the Mets were in for a very special season.

Back in the lineup on July 20, Harrelson hit .249 the rest of the season but accumulated half of his 24 RBIs. His offensive contributions included a game-tying sacrifice fly that forced extra innings in a 7–6 win at Atlanta on August 3, and a two-run triple that snapped a scoreless tie in the seventh inning of a 3–2 victory over the Padres on August 17. But his biggest hit of the season might have been a walk-off single off Bob Gibson in the 11th inning of a 3–2 win over the Cardinals on September 23, giving the Mets an opportunity to clinch their first NL East title at Shea the following night.

New York was playing its final home game of the regular season when Harrelson came to the plate to lead off the bottom of the first against Steve Carlton on September 24. Harrelson promptly singled and went to second on a walk to Agee before Donn Clendenon launched a three-run homer. Two batters later, Ed Charles ripped a two-run homer to put the Mets ahead 5–0, ending Carlton's night and sending New York to a 6–0, playoff-clinching victory.

Harrelson finished the regular season hitting .248 with 24 RBIs, 42 runs scored, and six triples in 123 games. He also was third on the team with 54 walks and fifth with a .341 on-base percentage.

Harrelson and the Mets took on the Braves in the first-ever National League Championship Series. The Mets were believed to have a slight edge in pitching, but the Braves were given a decisive edge on offense with a lineup that featured Hall of Famers Hank Aaron and Orlando Cepeda, along with Tony Gonzalez and Rico Carty. Atlanta hammered Mets Seaver, Koosman, and Gentry, but Aaron was the lone Brave to finish with more RBIs than Harrelson in the series.

Harrelson was part of two rallies as the Mets took the opener 9–5 in Atlanta. He laced a two-run triple to give the Mets a brief 4–3 lead in the fourth before the Braves moved back in front. New York went ahead for good with a five-run eighth as Harrelson was walked intentionally with two out before scoring on pinch-hitter J.C. Martin's bases-clearing double.

Harrelson also contributed to the Mets' 11–6 rout in Game 2, poking an RBI double in the third and scoring later in the inning to make it 6–0. He went 0-for-3 in Game 3, but the Mets completed a sweep by downing the Braves 7–4 at Shea for their first pennant.

The Mets were also big underdogs as they faced the Orioles in the World Series. Harrelson went just 3-for-17 in the series but reached base in each of the first four games. He scored his lone run of the Fall Classic in Game 3, coming home on Gentry's RBI double to put the Mets ahead 2–0 in a 5–0 shutout of the Birds.

Harrelson was flawless in the field as New York completed its miracle run by dispatching the Orioles in five games. Of all the players in Baltimore's mighty lineup, only Boog Powell had more hits (5) than Harrelson as Mets pitchers held the Orioles to a .146 cumulative average.

The Mets were the favorites to repeat as NL champs in 1970, just two seasons after their ninth-place showing. It was an outstanding year for Harrelson, who set career highs in games played (157), runs (72), doubles (18), triples (8), RBIs (42), and walks (95). He became a base-stealer again, swiping 23 after entering the year with just 24 for his career. Harrelson stole home twice in 1970 and had three steals in a game against the Dodgers on April 26.

He broke a team record for walks in a season and tied Ed Kranepool's club mark with eight sacrifice flies. Harrelson also smacked the Mets' first home run of the season on April 17 against the Phillies, just his second career round-tripper and his first since an inside-the-park homer against the Pirates in Pittsburgh on August 17, 1967.

With a glove, Harrelson led all NL shortstops with 305 putouts and was fifth with 401 assists. He went 54 consecutive games without an error from June 24 through August 19, tying Don Kessinger's major league record for shortstops. He played 157 of 162 games, matching his mentor McMillan for the most by a Met in one season.

Harrelson received his first All-Star nod and was 2-for-3 with two runs scored at Cincinnati. He scored the National League's first run on a double-play grounder in the seventh and contributed to a three-run ninth that sent the game to extra innings.

The American League led 4–1 until Giants catcher Dick Dietz homered leading off the bottom of the ninth. Harrelson immediately followed with his second single of the game before Astros second baseman Joe Morgan singled him to second. Harrelson came home on Giants first baseman Willie McCovey's single, and Morgan scored the tying run via a sac-fly by Pirates right fielder Roberto Clemente. The NL eventually won it on an RBI single by ex-Met Jim Hickman in the 12th inning as Pete Rose barreled into catcher Ray Fosse to score. That was the final time Harrelson played on a national stage the rest of the year.

The Mets plodded through the season, never floating too high above the .500 mark. But none of the other NL East clubs made a charge through the first five months, allowing the Mets to grab a piece of first-place at 75–67 on September 9. New York spent one more day in a first-place tie before losing 12 of their final 19 games to finish 83–79, six games behind the Pirates. The 1970 season lacked the clutch hits and walk-off wins that highlighted the Mets' World Series run.

The Mets got off to a fast start in 1971, winning 21 of their first 31 ballgames. They owned a share of the division lead on June 9 but played themselves out of contention by going 13–31 from July 1 through August 15, a stretch reminiscent of Harrelson's early days with the team.

Only three Mets truly stood out in 1971. Jones finished seventh in the National League with a .319 average, tied for the club lead in homers, and paced the Mets in RBIs. Seaver had what some consider his best major league season, going 20–10 with career highs of 289 strikeouts and a 1.76 ERA.

Harrelson was the only other Met to have a season worth talking about. He was voted into the NL starting lineup for the All-Star game at Detroit before going 0-for-2. He also became the Mets' second Gold Glove winner, one year after Agee claimed one for his work in center field. Harrelson committed only 16 errors and had 441 assists while compiling a .978 fielding average in 140 games at short.

Bud put together another strong start at the plate. He crafted a 13-game hitting streak (.400 in 55 AB) from April 30 through May 15, giving him a .339 average through 31 games. He was hitting .303 after compiling an 11-game hitting streak from May 26 through June 9. Harrelson owned a .278 average as late as August 8 before finishing with a .252 mark with six triples, 32 RBIs, and 55 runs scored.

Harrelson tied Agee for the team lead with a career-high 28 stolen bases in 35 attempts. He also tied for second in walks with just 53, leading to a .319 on-base percentage that was 32 points below his 1970 mark.

The Mets finished 83–79 for the second straight year and entered the 1971–1972 off-season with serious holes in the lineup. Three players shared the club lead with just 14 home runs, and Jones was the top run producer with only 69 RBIs. The dearth of offense led manager Gil Hodges and general manager Bob Scheffing to construct two blockbuster deals before the 1972 season opener, neither of which is considered a great move by the Mets.

Scheffing was blasted in the tabloids after coming away with nothing at the winter meetings. A few days later, he sent Nolan Ryan, Leroy Stanton, Don Rose, and Francisco Estrada to the Angels for shortstop Jim Fregosi, whom the Mets planned to shift to third base. Ryan had a lousy second half in 1971, but Fregosi was coming off his worst offensive season.

The second major trade was announced after the players went on strike just before the start of the 1972 campaign. The Mets picked up Rusty Staub from the Expos for outfielder Ken Singleton, infielder Tim Foli, and first baseman/outfielder Mike Jorgensen, three of New York's brightest young players. Unlike Fregosi, Staub had a strong season in 1971 and possessed the power that was sorely needed by the Mets. Theoretically, the additions potentially gave the team its best lineup in history if Fregosi could have a bounceback year.

Hodges never got to see Staub in a Mets uniform. He was stricken with his second heart attack in 3½ years, killing him two days shy of his 48th birthday. It left a huge vacuum in leadership that altered the team's progress for the next decade.

The Mets replaced Hodges with first base coach Yogi Berra, who was very popular with the players yet did not have Gil's disciplinary presence. Hodges had become more withdrawn in 1971 but still had the utmost respect within the clubhouse. In contrast, Berra scared no one and was not a stickler for weigh-ins as long as his players showed up for work.

But Berra had the Mets streaking toward the quarter mark of the season behind a rejuvenated lineup and a starting rotation that now included rookies Jon Matlack and Buzz Capra. New York owned a 25–7 record and a six-game lead after completing a four-game sweep at Philadelphia on May 21. The roster now included Willie Mays, who hit a game-winning homer in his Mets debut against the Giants on Mother's Day and was expected to platoon in center and at first base.

Meanwhile, Harrelson was playing splendid defense but sputtered at the plate. He went 3-for-4 with an RBI in a 2–0 win over the Cubs on April 20, and provided a solo homer and two RBIs to lead a 7–4 win at San Francisco on May 1. But his average dropped from .288 on May 1 to .228 by the end of the month before falling near the Mendoza line in early July.

Harrelson's hitting was the least of the Mets problems as they entered the second half. Staub, Jones, Agee, Mays, Fregosi, Grote, and rookie John Milner all missed major chunks of the season due to injuries that turned the roster into Tidewater North. Harrelson strained his back in July and spent most of August on the disabled list while the Mets played with a patchwork lineup. Things got so bad that Grote and fellow catcher Duffy Dyer saw action in the outfield. The Mets were out of playoff contention after going 19–30 from July 16 through September 7.

Harrelson led the Mets with just 12 stolen bases and is credited in the 1973 Mets media guide with six game-winning hits. But he hit only .215 in 115 games as the Mets ended up a very disappointing 83–73.

Harrelson had a new double play partner by December 1972. The Mets acquired second baseman Felix Millan and pitcher George Stone from the Braves for Gentry and reliever Danny Frisella, by far the best trade in Scheffing's tenure as the Mets' GM. The trade gave the Mets the best double-play combo in their young history as Harrelson and Millan each had Gold Gloves to their credit.

Harrelson had a very strange start to the season as a hitter, collecting two hits in three straight games during the first week before a 4-for-42 slump dropped his average to .177 by the end of April. He opened May with a 3-for-3 performance, igniting a 19-game stretch that saw Harrelson bat .338 with seven RBIs and eight runs scored. His season average was a lofty .268 on June 4 when Reds catcher Bill Plummer barreled into Harrelson on a play at second, breaking Bud's left hand and keeping him out of action for five weeks.

Harrelson was just the latest Met to be sidelined as the team began to sink under the weight of an ever-growing disabled list. Milner, Grote, Mays, and Jones already had spent time on the DL when Harrelson was added. With

Grote, Jones, and Harrelson out of action, the Mets dropped 15 of their last 25 games in June and went 2–5 to open July before Jones and Harrelson were activated. On the day Jones returned, backup left fielder George Theodore dislocated his hip in an outfield collision that caused him to miss the next two months.

Harrelson was activated on July 8 and lasted until August 1, one day after he suffered a fractured sternum during a rundown play involving burly Pirates catcher Manny Sanguillen. The latest injury kept him off the field until August 18. The Mets went 7–9 during his latest absence and sat in the NL East basement at 53–66 when Harrelson reappeared in a 12–1 rout of the Reds.

Harrelson went 3-for-19 in his first eight games following his August return. The Mets split those eight games, keeping them in last place at 58–70 by August 26. But New York was only 6½ games out of first place as the front-running Pirates and Cardinals failed to take control of what was now a six-team race for the division crown. The disabled list was finally in the Mets' favor as everyone except Theodore was healthy enough to contribute to an improbable run toward a division crown.

Harrelson began a 10-game hitting streak on August 29, batting .361 as the Mets won seven times. He ended the streak with an 0-for-4 effort on September 7, but he also walked three times and scored what proved to be the deciding run in a 4–2, 15-inning win over the Expos. The Mets were fourth in the NL East after the victory, four games out of first despite a 68–73 record. Two days later, Harrelson drove in a run and scored another in a 3–0 win at Montreal, which cut the Mets' deficit to three games with 19 to play.

Harrelson hit safely in seven straight while compiling a .483 on-base percentage from September 13 through September 19, hiking his season average up to .261. Most important, the Mets went 5–2 during the streak to pull within 1½ games of the first-place Pirates.

The Mets took over the division lead by winning four straight from the Pirates from September 18 through September 21. The streak began with the Mets scoring five times in the ninth inning to turn a 4–1 deficit into a 6–5 victory.

Two days later, the Pirates had the potential go-ahead run on first with two out in the top of the 13th when Dave Augustine hit a drive that appeared destined for the Pittsburgh bullpen. But the ball bounced off the top of the left-field wall and into the waiting hands of Jones, who threw a strike to Wayne Garrett. Garrett, playing shortstop in place of Harrelson, sent the relay to rookie catcher Ron Hodges, who applied a tag as Richie Zisk bowled him over. Hodges held onto the ball and calmly rolled it back to the mound before delivering the game-winning single in the bottom half of the inning.

The two stunning victories had the Mets within a half-game of the Pirates and showed New York was a team of destiny once again. One day after the "Ball-off-the-Wall" game, the Mets blasted the Pirates 10–2 to take over first

Bud Harrelson leaps out of the way of a pitch during a 1977 game.
Photo courtesy of Oscar W. Gabriel

place for good. Harrelson delivered an RBI single that put the Mets ahead 6–2 in the third, beginning a six-game hitting streak that pushed his season average to .262.

There were still five teams still alive for the NL East crown heading into the final weekend of the season, with the Mets sitting one game ahead of Pittsburgh and 2½ in front of St. Louis heading into a four-game set at Wrigley Field. The Mets and Cubs were rained out on Friday and Saturday, forcing the two teams to play doubleheaders on Sunday and Monday. The Pirates lost both of their games as the Mets waited out the rain, giving New York a 1½-game lead over the Cardinals. All the Mets had to do was sweep the Sunday twin bill to claim their second division title.

Harrelson supplied one of the Mets' eight hits in the opener while Jon Matlack went the distance on a nifty five-hitter, but the Cubs scored the game's lone run to deny the Mets a Sunday celebration. The loss also allowed the Redbirds to temporarily move within a half-game of the division lead, pending the outcome of Game 2.

The Mets won the nightcap 9–2 to clinch no worse than a tie for the division championship. But the split also forced New York to make up their two remaining games with a twin bill at Chicago on Monday—the day after the scheduled end of the season—while the Pirates played a makeup game against the Padres.

The Mets grabbed a 5–0 lead through a steady drizzle in Game 1 as Seaver tried to earn his 19th win of the season. But Seaver was not sharp, allowing two hits in both the third and fourth innings before surrendering two runs on four singles in the fifth. Harrelson led off the top of the sixth with a double and moved to third on a bunt-single by Seaver, but the Cubs erased Harrelson at the plate on a fielder's choice before Millan hit into an inning-ending double play to keep the score 5–2.

Rick Monday's two-run homer with nobody out in the bottom of the seventh chased Seaver and got the Cubs within 6–4. Tug McGraw followed with three shutout innings, allowing just one hit while striking out four as the Mets celebrated their second playoff berth in five seasons.

The Mets again headed into the postseason as decided underdogs as they prepared to face the Reds, who captured the NL West with ease after winning pennants in 1970 and 1972. Seaver was the hardluck loser in the opener, striking out 13 in a complete-game six-hitter but allowing late-inning homers by Pete Rose and Johnny Bench to fall 2–1. Harrelson scored the Mets' lone run, working out a second-inning walk before Seaver doubled him home.

Jon Matlack beat the Reds 5–0 on a two-hitter to even the series at a game apiece. Staub's fourth-inning blast accounted for the only run until the Mets scored four times in the ninth, capped by Harrelson's RBI single.

Harrelson was 1-for-6 (.167) through the first two games of the series, and the Reds were 8-for-57 (.140). Harrelson made light of the situation by saying the Big Red Machine was hitting a lot like him. It was meant as a self-deprecating comment on his offensive shortcomings, but a few Reds didn't see it that way. Rose, who didn't need a reason to play the game hard, now had extra incentive as the series headed to Shea Stadium.

But the Mets were the club that appeared motivated in Game 3 as Rusty Staub hit a pair of homers while driving in four runs in his first two at-bats to stake New York to a 6–0 lead by the third inning. It was 9–2 when Rose hit a single off Koosman with one out in the fifth, but Rose was erased after Milner turned into a 3-6-3 double play to end the inning.

Rose slid hard into Harrelson in an effort to break up the double play. Harrelson responded by shoving Rose, sparking a benches-clearing melee that almost caused the Mets to forfeit the game. It took several minutes for the umpires to restore order as several scrums broke out near second base, although no one was ejected. Once the field was cleared, Rose took his position in left field and was greeted by a barrage of garbage—including liquor bottles—tossed from the stands. Mets fans continued to litter left field with debris despite the warnings from the PA announcer. The chaos was quelled after Berra, Mays, and several other Mets strolled out to left field to plea for a return to sanity.

Harrelson lost the fight to Rose on a decision before the Mets completed a 9–2 victory and wrapped up the pennant two days later. Harrelson batted a meager .167 in 18 at-bats during the series, but Rose and Bench were the only Reds to muster more hits.

The Mets started the World Series in Oakland and promptly lost the opener for the third straight series.

Mets Record With/Without Harrelson in Starting Lineup

Year	With	Without	%Diff
1965	3–6 (.333)	47–106 (.307)	+.026
1966	9–16 (.360)	52–79 (.397)	−.037
1967	54–90 (.375)	7–11 (.389)	−.014
1968	49–50 (.495)	24–39 (.381)	+.114
1969	72–43 (.626)	28–19 (.596)	+.030
1970	81–74 (.523)	2–5 (.286)	+.237
1971	73–65 (.529)	10–14 (.417)	+.112
1972	63–50 (.558)	20–23 (.465)	+.123
1973	59–43 (.578)	23–36 (.399)	+.179
1974	44–48 (.478)	27–43 (.386)	+.092
1975	8–15 (.348)	74–65 (.532)	−.184
1976	59–54 (.522)	27–22 (.551)	−.029
1977	33–51 (.393)	31–47 (.397)	−.004
Total	**607–605 (.501)**	**372–509 (.422)**	**+.079**

Game 2 was a wild affair as the Mets and A's went into extra innings before New York won 10–7 in 12 innings. Harrelson sparked a four-run 12th with a leadoff double before scoring the tiebreaking run on Mays' last major league hit.

Harrelson went 3-for-6 with an RBI in Game 2, but Mets fans may best remember the run he didn't score that afternoon. He opened the 10th inning with a single and moved to second on McGraw's sacrifice before an error by first baseman Gene Tenace put Harrelson on third with one out. Millan followed with a short fly to Joe Rudi, one of the AL's top defensive left fielders. Harrelson broke for the plate after the catch, daring Rudi to make a perfect throw to catcher Ray Fosse. The throw was a shade toward the first base side, but Fosse grabbed the toss before attempting a swipe-tag on Harrelson. Plate umpire Augie Donatelli raised his thumb to call Harrelson out, putting the Mets in a state of apoplexy. Mays, standing on his knees with arms raised to the heavens, pleaded with Donatelli to change the call. Harrelson insisted Fosse never applied the tag, and Berra took up the argument while calling Donatelli's decision, "A Goddamn joke." All was forgiven after the Mets scored four times in the 12th, thanks in part to two errors by A's backup second baseman Mike Andrews.

The Mets won two of the next three games at Shea behind some outstanding pitching and offensive heroics from Staub. But the A's won Game 6 in Oakland before wrapping up the series with a 5–2 victory.

The 1973 Fall Classic was arguably Harrelson's best display in a postseason series. He played errorless ball and went 6-for-24 with a .379 on-base percentage. It was his last appearance in the postseason as the Mets sputtered over the next decade. By the time New York made another playoff appearance, Harrelson was the team's third-base coach.

The Mets were beset with injuries again in 1974, only this time the pitchers were afflicted. Seaver went 11–11 while battling sciatica, and McGraw and Stone were hampered by shoulder problems as the Mets finished 71–91, their worst season since 1967. Harrelson homered for the first time in two years but hit only .227 after compiling a career-best .258 mark in 1973. Harrelson's 1974 medical chart included a strained left groin, a bruised finger, a fractured right hand, a sprained right knee, and a another groin strain, all limiting him to 106 games for the second straight year. He became the first Met to steal 100 bases in his career, and joined Kranepool and Jones as the only Mets to appear in 1,000 games at that point in team history. But the milestones didn't erase the fact that the Mets were an aging club that continued to waste strong pitching performance by trotting out an inferior lineup.

The Pirates captured their fourth division title in five years in 1974, while the Phillies and Expos showed marked improvement. Mets GM Joe McDonald tried to close the gap by acquiring third baseman and 1971 NL MVP Joe Torre in October 1974 before purchasing Giants slugger Dave Kingman before 1975 spring training. McDonald also acquired a new center fielder in December 1974, getting Del Unser from the Phils in a six-player swap that sent McGraw to Philadelphia.

The bolstered lineup did not include Harrelson for most of the 1975 season. He tried to play with a damaged right knee that prevented him from batting left-handed, but the injury robbed him of his natural range and dropped his batting average to .204 by the time he underwent surgery on May 31.

The Mets played the next three months with a shortstop platoon of Jack Heidemann and Mike Phillips while sticking close to .500. Harrelson was still on the disabled list when the Mets dropped five straight in early August, costing Berra his job and putting McMillan in charge of the team the remainder of the season.

The Mets' playoff hopes seemed to improve when Harrelson returned to the lineup on Labor Day. He went 1-for-1 with two walks to support Seaver, who picked up his 20th win of the year by pitching a 3–0 shutout over the Pirates to pull New York within four games of the division lead with 26 games to play. But Harrelson started just five more games as the Mets played themselves out of contention before settling for an 82–80 record, 10½ games out of first.

The Mets improved slightly in 1976 as Harrelson hit .234 with 26 RBIs while appearing in 118 games, his most since 1971. But Harrelson was no longer a vacuum at short, committing 20 errors and turning just 48 double plays. His .962 fielding percentage was his lowest in at least 100 games since 1967, a stat that became problematic for a team that had the division's worst offense. Koosman (21) and Matlack (17) set career highs for victories, but Seaver

went just 14–11 as the Mets finished 86–76, 15 games behind the division-winning Phillies.

Harrelson was 33 when he opened the 1977 season, and the Mets had done nothing to find a prospect that he could groom for the future the way McMillan had prepared Harrelson for his long major league career. Poor trades, bad drafts and an aversion to participate in the first-ever major league free-agent draft led to the Mets' death knell in '77.

Harrelson already had seen McGraw and Staub leave the Mets via bad trades in previous seasons. McDonald and board chairman M. Donald Grant, who was controlling the purse strings, did absolutely nothing to improve the roster before 1977 training camp. The Mets got one year older and a lot worse amid clubhouse bickering.

The Mets opened the season 15–30, leading second-year manager Joe Frazier to be replaced by Torre. The team showed signs of life in its two weeks under Torre but remained firmly entrenched in the NL East cellar.

Seaver and Kingman each wanted new contracts, but the club's performance and Grant's meddling prevented that from happening. Seaver finally demanded a trade and was sent to the Reds on June 15, the same night Kingman was shipped to San Diego. A bad team got worse, and Harrelson often had a front-row seat in the dugout when he wasn't trying to prevent the likes of Jackson Todd, Lee Roy Jackson, Nino Espinosa, Craig Swan, and Pat Zachry from losing games. Koosman followed his 21-win season with 20 losses, and Jon Matlack went 7–15 as New York fell to 64–98.

Harrelson made only six errors in 98 games at short for a .984 fielding percentage, but the knee problems severely diminished his range and prompted Torre to use the newly acquired Doug Flynn at short after he was acquired in the Seaver deal. Harrelson did little at the plate, batting .178 with nine extra-base hits, 12 RBIs, and 25 runs scored in 269 at-bats.

Koosman, Grote, Kranepool, Matlack, Millan, Milner, and Harrelson were the last remaining members of the 1973 Mets following the Seaver trade. Grote was traded to the Dodgers three months later, Millan signed with Taiyo Whales of the Japanese League after the season, and Matlack and Milner were traded in December. That left Harrelson, Koosman, and Kranepool still on the roster as the team entered 1978 spring training.

Harrelson was the next to go, sent to the Phillies during the '78 exhibition season. The Mets came away with nothing more than Fred Andrews, who never played an inning for New York. Although it was another salary dump, it allowed Harrelson to compete for a division title in 1978.

Harrelson played behind Larry Bowa in 1978 and saw action at second for the first time in his major league career. Bud hit .214 in 71 games, starting 16 times at second and six at short under Phils manager Danny Ozark.

He appeared to settle in as a utilityman for the Phillies in 1979, hitting .282 in 53 games while seeing action at short, second and—for the first time—third base and left field. But his versatility didn't prevent the Phils from missing the playoffs for the first time in four years, and he was released before the 1980 season.

Harrelson extended his career by signing with the Rangers in May 1980, putting him in the American League for the first time. He had a strong year offensively for Texas, batting .272 with a .373 on-base percentage, one home run, and nine RBIs in 87 games. But he committed 17 errors while sharing shortstop with Pepe Frias as the Rangers finished 76–85. Texas granted him free agency after the season, and Harrelson retired at age 36.

He gravitated back toward the Mets, who were under new ownership by January 1980. He served as first-base coach under manager George Bamberger in 1982 and became the team's color analyst on Sports Channel in 1983 before being named manager of the Mets' NY–Penn League affiliate at Little Falls after the season. Harrelson led Little Falls to a 44–31 record and a league title to merit a promotion to the club's South Atlantic League affiliate at Columbia. He continued to win as a minor league skipper, going 23–13 for Columbia before donning a Mets uniform again.

Third-base coach Bobby Valentine left the club in May 1985 to become manager of the Rangers, prompting the Mets to promote Harrelson to manager Davey Johnson's staff. Harrelson won another World Series ring as a coach with the 1986 Mets and was still at third base when the team captured the 1988 NL East crown.

Harrelson replaced Johnson as manager in May 1990 with the team two games under .500. He promptly lost four of his first five games before the Mets put themselves back into contention. New York tied a club record by reeling off an 11-game winning streak in June, part of a stretch in which the Mets went 25–4 to climb within one game of the division lead.

The Mets topped the division by Labor Day but finished four games behind the first-place Pirates at 91–71. Harrelson went 72–49 to earn another season as skipper.

The Mets opened strong in 1991 but stumbled though July and August due in part to injuries and a fractious clubhouse. Harrelson became the fall guy for the team's problems and was let go during the final week of the season after players complained that he had lost the clubhouse.

The Mets honored Harrelson by inducting him into their Hall of Fame in 1986. He remained on the team's top-10 list in games played, at-bats, runs scored, hits, doubles, triples, stolen bases, and total bases as he took over for Johnson as manager. Harrelson augmented his popularity while managing the team in 1990, only to be run out of town by an underachieving ballclub the following year.

He became a minor league owner in the 1990s, purchasing part of the Wilmington Blue Rocks of the Carolina League. He returned to his New York roots by buying part of the Long Island Ducks, where he remained part-owner and third-base coach of the independent Atlantic League franchise through 2012.

ML/Mets debut	vs. Astros, 9/2/65
First ML/Mets hit	single vs. Bob Hendley, @ Cubs, 9/19/65
First ML/Mets homer	solo HR vs. Juan Pizzaro, @ Pirates, 8/17/67
First ML/Mets RBI	RBI triple vs. Clay Carroll, @ Braves, 8/28/66
Most hits, ML/Mets game	4, 6 times
Most homers, ML game	1, 7 times
Most homers, Mets game	1, 6 times
Most RBI, ML/Mets game	3, 6 times

Acquired: Signed as an amateur free agent, 6/7/63.
Deleted: Traded to the Phillies for Fred Andrews and cash, 3/24/78.

Keith Hernandez

First Baseman	Bats left, throws left	
Born: 10/20/53	San Francisco, California	
Height: 6′0″	Weight: 195	#17

Keith Hernandez Mets Career

YEAR	GP	AB	R	H	2B	3B	HR	RBI	K	BB	SB	AVG	SLG	OBP
1983	95	320	43	98	8	3	9	37	42	64	8	.306	.434	.424
1984	154	550	83	171	31	0	15	94	89	97	2	.311	.449	.409
1985	158	593	87	183	34	4	10	91	59	77	3	.309	.430	.384
1986	149	551	94	171	34	1	13	83	69	94	2	.310	.446	.413
1987	154	587	87	170	28	2	18	89	104	81	0	.290	.436	.377
1988	95	348	43	96	16	0	11	55	57	31	2	.276	.417	.333
1989	75	215	18	50	8	0	4	19	39	27	0	.233	.326	.324
TOTAL	880	3164	455	939	159	10	80	468	459	471	17	.297	.429	.387

ML Career

YEAR	GP	AB	R	H	2B	3B	HR	RBI	K	BB	SB	AVG	SLG	OBP
74-90	2088	7370	1124	2182	426	60	162	1071	1012	1070	98	.296	.436	.384

The 1977 to 1983 seasons are among the darkest stretches in Mets history. The club already had bottomed out when it jettisoned Tom Seaver and Dave Kingman in June 1977, and began to show incremental improvement only after Mookie Wilson, Hubie Brooks, and Wally Backman were recalled 39 months later. General manager Frank Cashen took Darryl Strawberry with the first pick in the 1980, but the outfielder from Southern California wouldn't be ready to play in the majors for another three years. Cashen brought in outfielder George Foster in a February 1982 trade with the Reds and reacquired Seaver in the winter of '83, but the Mets continued to keep their winning percentage around .400 while battling the Cubs for the NL East cellar.

The farm system was looking better than it had in a decade through the work of Cashen, scouting director Joe McIlvaine, and director of minor league operations Steve Schryver. But fans continued to wait for prospects to mature while the team played in front of small gatherings at Shea Stadium. Seaver's better efforts were wasted, and Foster was struggling to resemble the hitter who won the NL MVP award six years earlier. Strawberry's promotion in May failed to spike attendance.

The team's culture began to change on June 15, 1983, as Cashen laid another plank on the foundation of the Mets by acquiring 1979 co-MVP Keith Hernandez from the Cardinals for closer Neil Allen and prospect Rick Ownbey. The trade gave the ballclub a legitimate RBI threat and a defensive wizard who could settle an infield full of unpolished gloves and erratic arms.

Mets fans cheered when news of the trade broke following a 4–3 win over the Cubs. Hernandez cried, and who could blame him. He was leaving the defending World Series champs and the only franchise he had known. To Hernandez, the Mets had been a guaranteed series win since '77 whenever St. Louis visited Queens. The Redbirds had Tom Herr, George Hendrick, Willie McGee, Lonnie Smith, and Andy Van Slyke in their lineup on most nights while the Mets boasted the likes of Ron Hodges, Jose Oquendo, and Brian Giles.

"Welcome to the Stems," Seaver said as Hernandez entered the clubhouse for the first time. Seaver was referring to "Mets" spelled backward in obvious derision of the team's situation. Hernandez didn't need to be reminded the Mets stunk at the time. New York dropped its first four games against Hernandez's Redbirds in 1983, leaving the Mets 6–16 versus St. Louis since the start of the previous season.

Hernandez said all the right things when meeting the media for the first time in pinstripes. But he wasn't happy. He thought about quitting after the trade and was convinced to stick it out knowing that—as a player with more than five years of service and in the midst of a long-term contract—he could demand a trade after the season. Heck, the Mets couldn't even give him his No. 37 he had worn with the Cardinals since 1976. That number had been retired by the Mets in 1965 to honor manager Casey Stengel. So Hernandez accepted No. 17, one less than the number he wore when he broke in with the Cardinals.

If Hernandez detested his plight, he didn't show it on the field. He became an instant leader on the team while knowing there was a good possibility he'd be playing for someone else in 1984. Most of all, he gave the Mets a sense of professionalism that had been lacking since 1977.

It didn't hurt that he hit a little bit, too. Hernandez batted .443 with a .514 on-base percentage and nine RBIs in his first 16 games as a Met, delivering at least two hits in 10 of those contests. Ironically, he made his Mets home debut in a doubleheader against the Cardinals on June 20, going 4-for-8 with a homer and three RBIs. He played all six games in the series, helping the Mets take four of six.

Hernandez hit .306 and recorded a .424 on-base percentage for the 1983 Mets, reaching base in 77 of his 89 starts. But it was his fielding that caused jaws to drop at Shea as Mets fans had never seen such outstanding defensive play at first base by a member of the home team.

The Mets went 39–50 (.438) in his starts compared to a 29–44 (.397) record without him in the 1983 lineup. The pitching also got better over the course of the year as Walt Terrell and Ron Darling, the two right-handers acquired in the April 1982 Lee Mazzilli trade, demonstrated they could handle National League hitters. Strawberry became the third Met to win NL Rookie of the Year honors, and the lefty-righty combo of Jesse Orosco and Doug Sisk gave

the team a solid bullpen. Now all Cashen had to do was convince Hernandez the team truly was on the upswing, a tough sell considering the team's last-place finish at 68–94.

Hernandez turned 30 following the season and could have gone to any contender, which would have set Cashen's rebuilding effort. But he decided to stay after learning more about a farm system that had Dwight Gooden, Len Dykstra, and Wally Backman waiting in the wings.

The Mets opened 1984 with an 8–1 loss at Cincinnati and were crushed in their home opener 10–0 by the Expos. They were also clobbered by scores of 11–2, 12–2, and 12–5 in their first 15 games yet managed to win nine times in that period and owned a share of the NL East by the end of April. What caused even greater optimism was their ability to win while Hernandez drove in just five runs in 20 games during the first month of the season.

Mets fans held their breath hoping the surprisingly good start wasn't an aberration. The Mets were 15–8 following a win over the Astros on May 4, the first time they had been seven games over .500 this late in a season since the end of 1976. Backman and Kelvin Chapman formed an excellent lefty-right tandem at second base, Strawberry was showing more confidence at the plate, Foster looked revitalized, and Gooden emerged as the ace of the pitching staff by his third start. They were displaying a winning attitude and looked nothing like the team that dropped 14 of its last 24 games in '83.

And then the Mets followed the 15–8 start by losing 15 of their next 23 games to fall back to .500, causing the Shea faithful to wonder if the team could contend. Cashen also noticed the fall-off and tinkered with the roster, releasing veteran pitchers Dick Tidrow, Mike Torrez, and longtime Met Craig Swan in favor of younger hurlers from the farm system.

The changes placed more emphasis on Hernandez as the leader of a team that had a lot of raw talent. One-half of the regular lineup—Mike Fitzgerald, Jose Oquendo, Darryl Strawberry, and Backman/Chapman—had yet to play a full major league season. Gooden and fellow rookie Ron Darling settled in as the team's top two pitchers, and the stable of setup men included youngsters Brent Gaff and Tom Gorman.

Hernandez served as on-field wet nurse and den mother to the pitching staff with the rookie Fitzgerald behind the plate. Hernandez made numerous trips to the mound to clear a pitcher's head, and gave them a fist-pump once they recorded a huge out. His contributions were extremely impressive considering he rarely had to serve in that capacity with the Cardinals and had been portrayed by St. Louis manager Whitey Herzog as a slightly disconnected teammate.

Hernandez had been portrayed as a player with a poor attitude as early as high school. He was a three-sport star at Capuchino High School in the San Francisco suburb of San Bruno, earning All-League in baseball, football, and basketball. He was the starting quarterback in football and a guard on the basketball team when he wasn't hitting .500 to set a Peninsula High School League record.

But he sat out his senior season of baseball in a dispute with his coach, an ill-timed demonstration that caused colleges and pro scouts to reassess Hernandez as a player. He waited until the 42nd round of the June 1971 draft before the Cardinals selected him.

Hernandez didn't play his first pro game until 1972 yet was at Triple A by the end of the year. He split 1973 between Double A Arkansas and Triple A Tulsa, where he batted .333 in 31 games.

He played a full season for Tulsa in 1974 and hit .351, topping all American Association players with at least 50 games played before he was recalled by the Cardinals in late August.

He made his major league debut at age 20 near his hometown, going 1-for-2 with two walks and an RBI at San Francisco. His first hit was an RBI single off Mike Caldwell, and the game was a sign of things to come—eventually.

Hernandez made the Cardinals' season-opening roster in 1975 but was hitting just .203 when he was sent back to Tulsa in early June. Recalled in September, he batted .350 in 22 games the rest of the way and never played another minor league game for the Cards.

He hit .290 from 1976 to 1977 and won his first Gold Glove in 1978. But his .255 average in '78 was stunning after he batted .291 with 41 doubles and 91 RBIs the previous year. The Cardinals had become non-contenders during Hernandez's first three full seasons with the club, making 1979 a pivotal year for his career.

Hernandez was sensational in 1979, leading the National League with a .344 average, 48 doubles, and 116 runs scored while providing 11 homers, 11 triples, and 105 RBIs. He captured another Gold Glove and was selected to the NL All-Star team for the first time as he carried a .325 average into the break.

Hernandez batted .367 with 48 RBIs in 75 games after the break, but the Cardinals finished 12 games out of first as Willie Stargell led the Pirates to the NL East title and an eventual World Series crown. Hernandez's strong finish put him in contention for the Most Valuable Player Award.

The '79 MVP voting was among the most debated in baseball history. Stargell's .281 average was a whopping 63 points below Hernandez's mark. Stargell smacked 21 more homers than Hernandez, but Keith finished with 19 more extra-base hits and 24 more RBIs. Hernandez also was a far superior first baseman and appeared in 161 compared to Stargell's 126.

The MVP vote was a split decision as Hernandez and Stargell shared the award. The balloting raised the argument as to whether the award should go to the league's best player or the person who most helped his team reach the postseason. But if you factor in sabermetrics, Hernandez's 7.2 Wins Above Replacement dwarfed Stargell's 2.3 that season. Hernandez may not have led the Cards to the playoffs, but he was statistically more valuable to the Red-

birds than Stargell was to the Pirates.

Hernandez compiled another strong season in 1980, hitting .321 with 16 homers, 99 RBIs, and league-highs of 111 runs and a .408 on-base percentage. Hernandez had a .360 average by May 28, but the Cardinals owned the NL's worst record. The team's struggles eventually led to the hiring of Whitey Herzog as manager, a move that helped them win the World Series just two years later.

Hernandez was consistent for Herzog from 1981 to 1982, hitting .306 during the strike-shortened '81 campaign before compiling a .299 average with 33 doubles, 94 RBIs, and career-highs of 100 walks and 19 stolen bases in '82. Hernandez possessed a swing perfectly suited for Busch Stadium, making him the linchpin in a lineup that included a good mix of veterans (Darrell Porter and George Hendrick) and youngsters (Tom Herr and Willie McGee). St. Louis reached the postseason for the first time since 1968 and handled the Braves and Brewers to claim the team's first championship in 15 years. Hernandez was a beast during the final three games of the World Series, going 7-for-12 with one homer, eight RBIs, and four runs scored.

The Cardinals won 10 of their first 15 games in 1983 but never separated themselves from the rest of the NL East. Herzog wasn't happy with the makeup of a ballclub that dropped nine of 14 before he pulled off a blockbuster deal.

Hernandez was off to an okay start in '83, hitting .284 with 15 doubles in 55 games. But Herzog had a problem with Hernandez's preparation before games and was unhappy with reports of his off-field indiscretions. Hernandez always spent time doing crossword problems in the clubhouse and never demonstrated the rah-rah attitude desired by his manager. There were rumors the Cardinals were ready to deal Hernandez to the Astros for Ray Knight and Vern Ruhle in early June, a trade that would have greatly altered the Mets' 1984 roster. Herzog was still trying to deal Hernandez when Cashen called to inquire about the Cardinals' interest in closer Neil Allen, whose recent erratic pitching and behavior had alarmed the Mets. Cashen also asked Herzog about the availability of Hernandez, and a deal was constructed about an hour before the trade deadline.

How did Hernandez handle the news of the trade?

"I cried in the shower," he admitted. "My agent rushed to the rescue. I wanted to know, if I retire, how much money would I have. He said not enough. I still wasn't going to report. He literally packed my bags and then cajoled me onto the plane to Montreal, where the Mets were playing in four hours.[65]

"In 1983, it wasn't easy being the Mets. You could read a losing team a mile away—on the field, in the dugout, everywhere. The players are listless; they care about what's happening (blood tells), but they're either numbed into lethargy or, as a kind of defensive mechanism, pretend they don't care. That was the Mets team—expecting to lose. Riding to Shea on the St. Louis team bus in 1980, we Cardinals burst into laughter the first time we saw the new publicity slogan mounted atop the stadium: The Magic is Back.

"The Mets deserved and received no respect, and here I was, coming over from the world champions to a team with four last-place finishes in six years, and the other two next-to-last. Banished. Shipped to the Siberia of baseball."[66]

Siberia became Mecca by the summer of 1984. Hernandez hit .368 with four homers and 18 RBIs in 22 games from June 5 through June 29 before the Mets won 11 of their first 12 games in July. Fernandez and trade deadline acquisition Bruce Berenyi bolstered the back end of the rotation as the team took over the division lead. The Mets went 36–14 from June 3 through July 27, and were a season-high 4½ games ahead of the Cubs following a win over Chicago in a series opener at Shea in late July. Brooks put together a team-record 24-game hitting streak in that span while Gooden solidified his status as the top candidate for NL Rookie of the Year.

But the Cubs eventually passed the Mets in the standings, taking the last three games of that four-game set in July before sweeping a four-game series in early August. The Mets dropped 13 of 16 after grabbing their largest division lead of the season, and finished 6½ games back.

Hernandez ended the year with a .311 average, 15 homers, 94 RBIs, and a .409 on-base average. He also finished second to Cubs second baseman Ryne Sandberg for NL MVP honors, a voting that would have been different if New York had claimed the division title.

The Mets assembled for 1985 camp amid a media frenzy. Gary Carter was acquired from the Expos for Brooks, Fitzgerald and two prospects, giving the team another bat alongside Hernandez, Strawberry, Foster, and newcomers Ray Knight and Howard Johnson. Gooden was the subject of a *60 Minutes* profile, and *Sports Illustrated* published a George Plimpton piece about a Mets pitching prospect named Sidd Finch, which was the center of their April 1 edition. The Cubs might have been the defending NL East champs, but the Mets were hogging the spotlight as they hosted the Cardinals in the 1985 season opener.

The 1985 season was an emotional roller coaster for the Mets, and Hernandez occupied the front car. It wasn't enough that Hernandez served as the on-field motivational coach, No. 3 hitter, and glue of the infield. He was also dealing with a contentious divorce proceeding and the prospect of testifying in the trial of Curtis Strong, a clubhouse caterer who was accused of supplying cocaine to major league players.

The Mets opened the year 5–0 for the first time in club history and dropped the Cubs out of contention by sweeping a three-game set at Shea in mid-June. But New York also struggled after Strawberry tore a thumb ligament May 11, absorbing a 26–7 beating in Philadelphia and ending June on a five-game losing streak that pushed them into fourth place, five games behind the Cardinals.

Hernandez hit .323 with 12 RBIs through the Mets' first 16 games before enduring a nine-week slump in which he hit only .229 in 58 games, dragging his season average to .251 as he prepared to face the Braves in a wild July 4 game in Atlanta.

"I'm in a dark forest. I'm killing this team," Hernandez told the media after hitting .220 with no homers and seven RBIs in June. The Mets went 11–18 that month to fall five games behind the first-place Cardinals.

No one knew his batting stance better than his father. Juan Hernandez had a satellite dish that allowed him to watch every Mets game from his suburban San Francisco home. Juan was a good ballplayer in his own right and had played with Stan Musial while the two were serving in the Navy during World War II. Juan educated Keith in the finer points of baseball, although Keith says his father never pressured him to become a major league player.

But Juan could dissect his son's hitting and often called him to lend advice. Juan was concerned that the divorce proceedings could be affecting him on the diamond, but he also picked up on Keith's hand movement and didn't see a normal rhythm to his swing. Mets videographer Joe Fitzgerald also saw a difference and gathered tapes that compared the hot and cold Hernandez to back Juan's theory.

On July 4, Hernandez got hotter than a firecracker. He doubled and scored in the first inning, hit a two-run triple in his third at-bat and homered in the eighth inning to put the Mets ahead 7–4. The Braves surged ahead with a four-run eighth, but the Mets tied it in the ninth before Hernandez became the fourth player in team history to hit for the cycle, delivering a single in the 12th inning. He finished 4-for-10 as the Mets beat Atlanta 16–13 in 19 innings, a rain-soaked game that didn't end until almost 4:00 AM. Although he went hitless in his last three at-bats, the game was a turning point in his season.

Hernandez hit .356 with six homers, 22 doubles, 60 RBIs, and 57 runs scored over his final 84 games. The Mets went 57–27 in those games and finished with eight more victories than they accumulated in 1984. But his former team stood between the Mets and a playoff berth heading into the final week of the season.

The Cardinals owned a three-game lead as they began a three-game series with the visiting Mets on October 1. Hernandez went 2-for-9 without producing a run in the first two games, but New York won both times to put itself in position to grab a share of first place with a sweep.

Hernandez did everything in his power to force a tie, going 5-for-5 with two RBIs in the finale and representing the tying run in the ninth. However, Danny Cox out-pitched Rick Aguilera as the Cardinals prevailed 4–3 to take a two-game lead with three to play.

Hernandez also went 3-for-3 with two RBIs in the Mets' next game against the Expos, giving him hits in eight straight at-bats. New York won the game 9–4 but was eliminated by St. Louis the following day.

The second-half streak was a testament to his will as a player. Hernandez was scheduled to testify in the Curtis Strong trial in late August, forcing him to leave the team for a few days during a West Coast trip. His testimony confirmed that he had used cocaine for three years while with the Cardinals, an admission that prompted New York columnist Dick Young to urge fans to boo Hernandez when he came to the plate for the first time at Shea after his court appearance. Instead, Hernandez received a standing ovation before hitting a game-tying single in the first inning of a 5–4 win over the Cardinals.

He finished the season with a .309 average, 10 home runs, 34 doubles, 94 RBIs, and 87 runs scored. Carter hit 32 homers and drove in 100 runs, and Strawberry homered 29 times despite missing six weeks. Gooden won the NL Cy Young Award after going 24–4 with a 1.53 ERA, but the team's 98–64 record was considered a disappointment. It didn't take long for Cashen to complete the puzzle.

Bob Ojeda was acquired from the Red Sox for next-to-nothing in terms of the Mets' 25-man roster. Ditto Tim Teufel, who was picked up from the Twins to serve as the right-handed bat to complement Backman at second base. Cashen had solved two roster flaws, causing Johnson to boast during spring training that the Mets would dominate in 1986.

Johnson's prediction was correct as the Mets won a team-record 108 games and finished 21½ games ahead of the second-place Phillies. New York held a five-game lead by the end of April and was up by 10 games by mid-June before cruising to its first playoff berth in 13 years.

What was amazing was the manner in which the Mets overwhelmed the rest of the league as none of their marquee players had career years. Foster never got on track before he was released in early August. Carter tied a club record with 105 RBIs but hit only .255. Strawberry belted 27 homers in 136 games after hitting 29 in just 111 contests in '85. Gooden finished with seven fewer wins, five more losses, and allowed 1.3 more runs per nine innings than his Cy Young Award–winning performance the previous year.

Hernandez remained an absolute thief at first base, but his offensive numbers were rather unspectacular by his lofty standards. He finished fifth in the NL with a .310 average, although that was only the fourth-best total of his major league career. Hernandez drove in 83 runs after collecting over 90 RBIs each of the previous two seasons. However, he also led the league with 94 walks and was second with a .413 on-base percentage, which allowed him to pace the team with 94 runs scored.

Hernandez, Carter, Strawberry, and Foster didn't carry the Mets' offense, but they didn't have to. Dykstra and Backman served as exceptional table-setters at the top of the lineup, Knight bounced back from two straight mediocre years to hit .298, Wilson made a smooth transition to left field following Foster's departure, and Teufel

Keith Hernandez runs the bases after hitting a two-run home run in Game 2 of the 1988 NLCS against the Dodgers.

was the perfect complement to Backman at second. And then there was rookie Kevin Mitchell, who started at six different positions by July and hit .368 over the first three months.

The pitching was fabulous. Ojeda, Gooden, Fernandez, Darling, and Roger McDowell all had at least 10 wins by the All-Star break while McDowell and Orosco shared closer duties. The only drawback to the season was its length as the Mets took all of the suspense out of the division race by mid-May.

Hernandez received numerous honors for his regular season accomplishments. He finished fourth in the MVP balloting, was selected the starting NL first baseman in the All-Star Game, and grabbed his ninth consecutive Gold Glove. None of that would matter come October unless the Mets won the World Series.

As easy as the regular season was for the Mets, the postseason was just as difficult. New York opened the NLCS by losing to the Astros 1–0 as Mike Scott struck out 14 in a five-hitter. Hernandez had one of the five hits, but he also struck out three times while questioning the legality of Scott's split-finger fastball.

The Mets were still seeking their first run of the series until Carter poked an RBI double off Nolan Ryan in the fourth inning of the second game. Hernandez singled and scored in the fourth before lacing a two-run triple that put the Mets ahead 5–0 an inning later.

Hernandez went 2-for-3 in Game 2 and had two hits in Game 3, giving him a .455 average for the series until he went hitless in four at-bats versus Scott in a 3–1 loss the next night.

Scott had a decided psychological advantage on the Mets, who began to collect baseballs they fouled off against the Houston ace. The players contended that virtually all of the balls had the same scuffmark, fueling their belief that Scott was an unabashed cheater. Worse, the series was tied at two games apiece, giving Scott an opportunity to pitch Game 7 unless the Mets could sweep the next two.

The Mets won Game 5 2–1 in 12 innings as Carter supplied the game-winning single after Hernandez was intentionally walked with Backman on second base. But the prospect of facing Scott once again loomed large as the Mets trailed Houston 3–0 in the top of the ninth in Game 6.

The boxscore shows Hernandez went 1-for-7 in the sixth game, but his base hit was among the biggest of the afternoon. Bob Knepper carried a two-hitter into the ninth before Dykstra hit a leadoff triple and scored on Wilson's single. A grounder by Mitchell left the Mets two outs from Game 7, but it also put Wilson in scoring position for Hernandez. Hernandez hit Knepper's final pitch of the afternoon for an RBI double, three batters before he scored the tying run on a sacrifice fly. The Mets went on to beat the Astros 7–6 in 16 innings, thus avoiding Scott and putting them in the World Series against the Red Sox.

But instead of Scott, the Mets had to deal with Bruce Hurst. The Red Sox's top lefty won the first and fifth games of the Fall Classic while silencing Hernandez (1-for-7) and fellow lefty Strawberry (1-for-6). Hurst's second victory gave Boston a three-games-to-two lead in the series with Roger Clemens scheduled to start the next game.

Game 6 went into extra innings tied 3–3 before the Red Sox scored twice in the 10th. The Mets had the heart of the order coming up in the bottom half, although they were without Strawberry due to a three-way switch in the top of the ninth. Once again, it was the unsung heroes of the 1986 Mets who allowed them to pull off a stunning win.

Backman, who had jumpstarted so many rallies during the regular season and playoffs, lifted a fly ball to left-center. A base hit would have brought up Hernandez with an opportunity to tie the game against Calvin Schiraldi, a Mets washout in 1985 who had become the Red Sox's closer. Hernandez ran the count to 2–1 before drilling a rope to left-center, but the ball was caught at the warning track to put the Mets within one out of elimination.

Hernandez jogged to the dugout, went down the tunnel, and continued into the clubhouse before popping open a Budweiser in the office of trainer Steve Garland. Hernandez was resigned to watching the final out on television rather than witnessing the Red Sox's pending celebration first-hand. He wasn't the only Met in the clubhouse as Carter came to the plate with two out and nobody on.

Carter lined a single to short to keep the series alive, causing Davey Johnson to call on Mitchell to pinch-hit for pitcher Rick Aguilera. The problem was, Mitchell was in the clubhouse and on the phone with a travel agent as he attempted to book a flight back home. Mitchell hiked up his uniform trousers and raced to the on-deck circle before stroking another single to put runners on first and third.

The Mets in Garland's office were thinking about heading back to the dugout with the tying run on base. Hernandez convinced them otherwise, believing their presence in the clubhouse was bringing the team good karma. And so they stayed. And so the rally continued.

Knight lifted a humpback liner over the head of second baseman Marty Barrett to send home Carter and put Mitchell at third. Out went Schiraldi and in came Bob Stanley to face Wilson. Never known as a patient hitter, Wilson went into a defensive mode after Stanley got two strikes on him. Stanley tried to go inside on Wilson when the ball headed toward the feet of the Mets outfielder. Always an agile runner, Wilson managed to avoid the ball as it bounded past catcher Rich Gedman and headed toward the backstop, allowing Mitchell to score the tying run while moving Knight to second.

The wild pitch also meant Hernandez might have to play first base after downing a few ounces of Anheuser-Busch's finest, but he never retreated to the dugout for fear the rally might end. He watched as Wilson took a few defensive swings against Stanley just to stay alive at the plate before hitting a slow roller to first baseman Bill Buckner.

When weighing Wilson's blazing speed and Buckner's positioning far behind the first-base bag, there was a chance Mookie would beat it out for an infield single. Instead, Buckner lifted his glove and came up empty as the ball rolled into right field, allowing Knight to score the winning run in one of the most dramatic elimination comebacks in World Series history.

Oil Can Boyd was scheduled to start Game 7 for the Red Sox until rain caused a one-day postponement. The rainout allowed Boston skipper John McNamara to replace Boyd with Hurst, a move that looked exceptional when the Red Sox grabbed an early 3–0 lead off Darling.

Hurst took a shutout into the sixth before the Mets loaded the bases with one out, bringing up Hernandez. Keith flied out in his first two at-bats of the night, leaving him 1-for-9 versus Hurst until he lashed a two-run single to jumpstart the Mets' rally. Carter added a game-tying grounder later in the inning, and Knight put the Mets ahead to stay with a leadoff homer in the seventh before Hernandez added a sacrifice fly for the eventual winning margin. The Mets scored eight times in their final three at-bats to win it 8–5, touching off a wild celebration that lasted into the wee hours of the morning.

The Mets were scheduled to be feted with a parade up the Canyon of Heroes the following afternoon. Hernandez overslept and was still in his apartment about 15 minutes before the festivities were scheduled to begin. He raced down to lower Manhattan and came face-to-face with a fence that stood between him and his more punctual teammates. Fans recognized their hero and gave him a boost over the fence, allowing him to participate in the fun.

The Mets were prohibitive favorites to repeat as World Series champs in 1987. Hernandez took his customary spot at first base for the start of the All-Star Game and came away with his 10th Gold Glove after the season. He also hit a career-high 18 homers while batting .290 with 89 RBIs.

Strawberry and Howard Johnson each joined the 30/30 club, becoming the first Mets to homer 30 times and steal 30 bases. Newcomer Kevin McReynolds chipped in 29 homers and 95 RBIs to help the Mets set several club records for offense.

But the first three months of the season were an absolute nightmare as the Mets struggled to stay above .500 while losing starting pitchers at an alarming rate. The bullpen suddenly made a habit out of blowing late-inning leads at a time when journeyman Terry Leach became the de facto ace of the rotation. The clubhouse became a battleground as players began to complain about Strawberry's habit of begging out of games due to minor ailments. Meanwhile, Hernandez hit .400 over his last 20 games of May and followed that with a .253 average in June.

The Mets were eight games out of first at 42–38 after being swept in a three-game set at Cincinnati, and the deficit would grow to double-digits within a few days. The once-cocky clubhouse had become a cauldron for bitching and finger-pointing as the Mets saw the Cardinals, Expos, and Cubs above them in the division standings.

Suddenly, the Mets became the hottest team in baseball. They went 36–19 from July 10 through September 9 as Hernandez hit .304 with 11 homers and 52 RBIs. New York was now within 1½ games of the division lead heading into a three-game series with the first-place Cardinals at Shea Stadium.

Hernandez went 2-for-4 with an RBI and a run scored as the Mets carried a 4–1 lead into the ninth inning of the series opener. Hernandez's performance raised his average to .304 and gave New York a chance to climb within a half-game of first place. But the Cardinals pulled out a 6–4 victory as Terry Pendleton slammed a game-tying, two-run homer with two out off McDowell before St. Louis plated two in the 10th to complete the comeback. The loss was the beginning of the end for the 1987 Mets, who split their next 20 games and were eliminated before taking the field for their last regular season series in St. Louis. Hernandez drove in 13 runs over his final 18 games but batted only .192 with 14 strikeouts in 73 at-bats.

Hernandez was only 34 as he entered 1988. He had played 14 major league seasons and 1,875 games without suffering a significant injury. Steve Garvey was the only other major leaguer to appear in more than 1,700 games at first base from 1975 to 1987, and Hernandez had him beat by 13 (1,861). Hernandez also had appeared in a team-high 615 games from 1984-87, 67 more than the runner up—and eight years younger—Strawberry.

Hernandez had one of his familiar cold starts in 1988, hitting .158 with only four RBIs while playing 15 of the Mets' first 16 games. However, the Mets went 11–5 in that span while the Cardinals dropped 12 of their first 16 to fall into last place.

The Mets began to pull away from the rest of the pack once Hernandez got hot. He homered twice while driving in a career-high seven runs in a 13–4 laugher in Atlanta on April 26, igniting a 27-game stretch in which he hit .410 with a .487 on-base percentage, five homers, 28 RBIs, and 21 runs scored through May 27. The Mets won 20 of those 27 games and were 34–15 for the season, tying their record pace through 49 games in 1986. They led the NL East by 4½ games over the upstart Pirates by the end of the May.

The lead was seven games following a 6–2 win at St. Louis, but the Mets ended the game without Hernandez. He pulled his right hamstring while running the bases and had to be placed on the disabled list for the first time in his career.

Hernandez returned to action by June 22 but re-injured the hamstring the following day and went back on the DL, this time until August 5. The Mets went 19–19 during second absence, allowing the Bucs to put a slight scare into New York. Pittsburgh got within two games of first place by July 27 before the Mets took the first three games of a four-game set against the Pirates at Shea Stadium.

Hernandez returned to help the Mets take three of four in Pittsburgh the first weekend of August, contributing a double and a two-run homer in his first game off the DL before finishing 5-for-13 over the last three games of the series. That brought his average up to .303, but it was the final time his season average was above .298 the rest of the year.

Hernandez hit only .210 with four homers and 13 RBIs in his next 34 games. He missed 10 days after re-injuring the hamstring on September 12, returning just in time to help the Mets clinch the NL East crown on September 22 against the Phillies.

Hernandez was hitting only .269 as the Mets prepared for their final two series. He was guaranteed his first sub-.297 season since 1978, but that was chalked up to his hamstring issues. Davey Johnson gave him time to prepare for the NLCS against the Dodgers, and Hernandez responded by going 6-for-13 in his final four games to end up with a .276 average, 11 homers, and 55 RBIs in 95 games.

The Mets again were prohibitive favorites to win the NL pennant as they traveled to Los Angeles for the first two games of the championship series. But New York was staring at a possible 2–0 loss to the Dodgers in the opener as

Hernandez stepped to the plate against Orel Hershiser in the top of the ninth.

Hernandez hit a slow grounder to first baseman Tracy Woodson, good enough to put leadoff hitter Gregg Jefferies into scoring position. Strawberry followed with an RBI double to make it 2–1, but he remained at second with two out until Carter delivered a two-run double to send the Mets to a 3–2 victory.

Hernandez went 1-for-4 in the opener and 2-for-3 with a two-run homer and three RBI in Game 2, but the Dodgers coasted to a 6–3 win in the second game to even the series at a game apiece.

Game 3 was one of the sloppiest in Mets postseason history as the two teams played through a steady rain following a one-day postponement. Hernandez contributed to the silliness on two occasions, the first of which was a throwing error on a bunt to allow the Dodgers to score an unearned run in the first inning. He almost took the Mets out of a productive sixth inning by slipping on the slick turf while rounding third, allowing Dodgers third baseman Jeff Hamilton to tag him out. But the Mets scored twice in the inning to tie the game, and finally went ahead for good during a five-run, two-out rally in which Hernandez walked with the bases loaded. Hernandez reached base four times in the Game 3 victory, going 1-for-2 with three walks as the Mets won 8–4.

He had another productive game the following night, going 2-for-5 with a walk to raise his series average to .444 and extend his postseason hitting streak to seven games dating to the 1986 World Series. Hernandez started the Mets' first scoring rally, leading off the fourth with a single before Strawberry and McReynolds hit back-to-back homers to put New York ahead 3–2.

It was a 4–2 game after McReynolds doubled and scored on Carter's triple in the sixth, and the lead held up until Dodgers catcher Mike Scioscia crushed a two-run homer off Gooden in the top of the ninth.

The game was still 4–4 when Kirk Gibson homered off McDowell with two out in the 12th, but the Mets threatened in the bottom half against a pair of former teammates. Tim Leary gave up consecutive singles to open the frame before Hernandez came to the plate against Orosco with one out. Hernandez loaded the bases by walking on a 3-2 pitch, sending up Strawberry with a chance to win it with a single. But the game ended seven pitches later as Strawberry popped up versus Orosco before center fielder John Shelby made a catch at the shoetops to deny McReynolds a possible game-winning hit off Hershiser. The 5–4 loss tied the NLCS at two games apiece after the Mets were within three outs of a 4–2 win and a 3–1 series lead.

The rest of the series led to an incomplete season for the Mets. Hernandez hit an RBI single that capped the scoring in a 5–1 victory in Game 6. But the Dodgers, who had dropped 10 of 11 to the Mets in the regular season, won the seventh game to advance to the World Series. Hernandez was 1-for-12 over the final three games to end the

series with a .269 average and a .406 on-base percentage.

The 1988 season signified a slight changing of the guard as the Mets were able to win the division without top-quality production from Hernandez and Carter. Strawberry drove in 101 runs and homered 39 times for the second straight year. McReynolds, the quiet outfielder acquired in a December 1986 trade for Mitchell, added 27 homers and 99 ribbies. But the biggest revelation was Jefferies, who hit .321 after being recalled in late August and posted a .333 average during the NLCS.

This set up a new dynamic in the clubhouse as the Mets reported for 1989 training camp. Management saw Jefferies as a future superstar and felt comfortable enough with his infield defense to trade the popular Backman to the Twins after the 1988 season. The front office also believed Jefferies would be the type of clutch hitter Hernandez had been during his first 4½ seasons with the Mets. Unfortunately, the players had loved Backman and grew to loathe Jefferies, who was granted special treatment by the powers that be and became a clubhouse pain in the butt.

Strawberry was feeling his oats after becoming the first Met to hit 30 homers and drive in 100 runs in back-to-back seasons. Hernandez had long prodded Strawberry to perform better, often using "unnamed" quotes in the papers to get his point across. Hernandez felt his handling of Strawberry was for the betterment of the Mets, and a majority of their teammates would agree. But Strawberry had grown to resent the innuendo in the media, especially when some of it was coming without confirmed attribution.

Strawberry's frustrations came to a head during the team photo shoot in spring training. He was unhappy with his contract—which had two years remaining—and threatened to walk out of camp the day before unless the Mets agreed to renegotiate. Hernandez and Gooden were among several high-profile Mets to tell the media Strawberry should just keep quiet and live up to his end of the contract. Hernandez blamed Strawberry's agent for giving him bad advice.

Players were being moved into position for the team photo when Strawberry approached Hernandez, now the team captain since 1987.

"Why did you say those things about me?" Strawberry demanded to know.

"I'm tired of your baby stuff," Hernandez fired back.

"I've been tired of yours for years," Strawberry responded moments before grazing Hernandez with a back-handed swipe to the cheek.

Gooden and reliever Randy Myers separated the two combatants before Hernandez and Strawberry worked things out in the office of Dr. Alan Lans, the team psychologist. One day later, Strawberry was seen on the back page of the tabloids, planting a kiss in the face of Hernandez.

Unfortunately for the Mets, Strawberry and Hernandez also picked 1989 to have their worst seasons with the team. "Straw" hit only .225 and hit 29 home runs, 10 fewer than in the previous two years. In Hernandez's case, his season was marred by another major injury.

Hernandez never put everything together in '89. He batted .208 in his first 13 games before recording a .333 average with two homers and nine RBIs in a 19-game span from April 22 to May 17. But seven of those RBIs came in two games, and he was averaging one strikeout per contest during that span.

Hernandez went 2-for-3 against the Dodgers on May 17, the fourth time in six games he had collected at least two hits. Hernandez was on first base in the fifth inning when Strawberry hit a grounder to shortstop Dave Anderson, who stepped on second before his relay throw drilled Hernandez in the right knee. Hernandez played the next two innings and came out of the game to have his knee examined. It was determined Anderson's throw left Hernandez with a broken kneecap, putting him out of action for eight weeks.

Carter already was on the DL due to knee surgery and didn't return until after Hernandez was activated. With Strawberry and Jefferies struggling, the Mets still managed to go 25–23 while Hernandez and Carter remained sidelined. That left the team 46–39 when Hernandez came back, but only 2½ games behind the East-leading Cubs.

Hernandez delivered an RBI single in his second at-bat after being activated. But he didn't start a game between July 19 and August 9, going 2-for-8 as a pinch-hitter. Davey Johnson hoped the rest would help rejuvenate Hernandez for a possible playoff push, but the layoff didn't help as he hit only .184 with three RBIs in 14 starts from August 27 to September 20 while the Mets continued to lose ground on the Cubs.

It was now evident that Hernandez wasn't going to be asked back in 1990. Davey Johnson recognized that possibility and used him as a pinch-hitter in the Mets' final home game. Mets fans gave Hernandez a standing ovation before and after he was retired on a line drive to left field, a putout that left him with a .233 average, four homers, and 19 RBIs in 75 games.

Hernandez and Carter were told shortly after the season that they weren't in the Mets' future plans, turning them into free agents. Ironically, Carter went to Hernandez's hometown by signing a one-year deal with the Giants. Hernandez wound up in Cleveland, playing for a ballclub that had managed to escape any semblance of playoff pressure during the previous 35 years.

Hernandez was brought in to provide the same type of leadership he exhibited with the 1983 Mets. The Indians had a few talented hitters and also had Orosco in their bullpen as a middle reliever. But the pitching was threadbare and the fielding bordered on hapless.

The signing backfired for Hernandez and the Indians. He appeared in each of Cleveland's first 20 games but hit just .200 in the process before receiving more days off. He was still batting .200 when he left a game on May 26 due to a torn calf muscle, putting him on the disabled list for

the third straight year. Hernandez returned on June 17, playing two innings and going 1-for-1 with a double and a run scored before reinjuring the calf.

Hernandez came back on July 12 but hurt his calf again a few days later to earn another trip to the disabled list. He didn't play the rest of the season but remained in the team's plans for 1991, although the Indians didn't know Hernandez had played his final major league game.

A back injury prevented Hernandez from returning to the majors. He underwent surgery and retired with 11 Gold Gloves, two Silver Sluggers, and five All-Star berths. But it would be more than a decade before Mets fans saw Hernandez again on a regular basis.

One year after retiring, Hernandez resurfaced on national television by playing himself on *Seinfeld*. Jerry Seinfeld, Larry David, and Larry Levin co-wrote an episode titled "The Boyfriend" in which Hernandez dates Elaine Benes and asks Seinfeld to help him move. Sensing he has developed a man-crush on the former Mets star, Seinfeld decides he can't help Hernandez move and allows Kramer to pitch in with the relocation. The episode is among the most popular in the history of the sitcom and earned Hernandez a place in the series finale.

Hernandez wrote his second book, *Pure Baseball: Pitch by Pitch for the Advanced Fan*, in 1994. Co-authored by Mike Bryan, who collaborated with Hernandez on the 1986 book, *If at First*, *Pure Baseball* concentrates on one generic major league game to give fans a keen understanding of how Hernandez breaks down strategy between pitchers, hitters, and managers.

Hernandez also appeared in an episode of *Law and Order* and again played himself in the Albert Brooks movie *The Scout* in 1994. But other than a few token appearances at Shea, there was a detachment between Hernandez and the fans who loved him.

Hernandez returned to the Mets' fold in 2002 as a part-time commentator on television broadcasts. When the team created SNY in 2006, he was teamed with Gary Cohen and Darling to form what has become one of the most respected broadcasting partnerships in Major League Baseball.

First ML game	Cardinals @ Giants, 8/30/74
First Mets game	@ Expos, 6/17/83
First ML hit	RBI single vs. Mike Caldwell, @ Giants, 8/30/74 (with Cardinals)
First Mets hit	single vs. Charlie Lea, @ Expos, 6/17/83
First ML homer	2-run HR vs. Doug Rau, @ Dodgers, 5/24/75 (with Cardinals)
First Mets homer	2-run HR vs. John Stuper, Cardinals, 6/20/83
First ML RBI	RBI single vs. Mike Caldwell, @ Giants, 8/30/74 (with Cardinals)
First Mets RBI	RBI single vs. Jeff Reardon, @ Expos, 6/18/83
Most hits, ML game	5, 4 times
Most hits, Mets game	5, @ Expos, 8/8/85; @ Padres, 9/2/85; @ Cardinals, 10/3/85

Most homers, ML game	2, 3 times
Most homers, Mets game	2, @ Cubs, 6/10/87; @ Braves, 4/26/88
Most RBI, ML/Mets game	7, @ Braves, 4/26/88

Acquired: Traded by the Cardinals for Neil Allen and Rick Ownbey, 6/15/83.

Deleted: Became a free agent, 11/13/89. Signed by the Indians, 12/7/89.

NL MVP, 1979 (co-MVP with Willie Stargell)

NL All-Star, 1979, 1980, 1984, 1986, 1987

Silver Slugger, 1980, 1984

Gold Gloves, 1978, 1979, 1980, 1981, 1982, 1983, 1984, 1985, 1986, 1987, 1988

NL Batting Leader, 1979

NL On-base% Leader, 1980

NL Doubles Leader, 1979

NL Runs Scored Leader, 1979, 1980

NL Walks Leader, 1986

Jay Hook

Pitcher	Bats left, throws right
Born: 11/18/36	Waukegan, Illinois
Height: 6'2"	Weight: 185 #47

Jay Hook Mets Career

YEAR	GP/GS	IP	H	R	ER	K	BB	W–L	SV	ERA
1962	37/34	213.2	230	137	115	113	71	8–19	0	4.84
1963	41/20	152.2	168	104	93	89	53	4–14	1	5.48
1964	3/2	9.2	17	10	10	5	7	0–1	0	9.31
Total	81/56	376.0	415	251	218	207	131	12–34	1	5.22

Mets Career/Batting

GP	AB	R	H	2B	3B	HR	RBI	K	BB	SB	AVG
85	110	10	23	1	0	0	6	38	10	0	.209

ML Career

YEAR	GP/GS	IP	H	R	ER	K	BB	W–L	SV	ERA
57–64	160/112	752.2	808	482	437	394	275	29–62	1	5.23

Many former major leaguers have gone on to forge productive careers. Jay Hook can be best described as a successful businessman who happens to be a former major leaguer.

Hook is a man with many hats. He wore a Mets cap for just three years before leaving baseball for a series of highly successful positions with major corporations. The Illinois native and current Michigan resident also has helped build minds and heal bodies, all while raising four children with his wife, Joan.

Hook was a bonus baby when he signed with the Reds in 1957. He was just 20 when he made his major league debut, holding the Cardinals hitless over 2⅓ innings September 3, 1957. His two other 1957 appearances were starts, including five hitless innings against the Braves September 29.

Injuries and illness plagued him in three of his next four seasons, the exception being 1960, when he set career highs with 11 wins, 222 innings pitched, and a 4.50 ERA. The Reds made Hook available in the expansion draft after he battled the mumps while going 1–3 with a 7.76 ERA in 62⅔ innings in 1961. The Mets took him as one of their four $125,000 selections.

"My wife and I were driving home," he said. "We had a little sports car, a little Austin Healey, and we were driving that back because I went back to grad school every winter. We were somewhere around Indianapolis, and we heard on the radio we had been traded.

"I really didn't have any strong feelings about it because I knew I was on that [expansion] list. You hated to move from a pennant contender, but at the same time, New York…that was kind of exciting at the time. Moving to a great city.

"And so it was with a little bit of mixed emotions that I had. I didn't have a lot of negative feelings, but it was unsure.

"We had physicals near the end of the year. I received a call from the Mets right away, and they wanted me to go to Mayo or Johns Hopkins because in the tests that were taken, the blood count was still kind of out of whack because of the infection.

"I was with the Reds the whole time [I was recovering from the mumps]. They didn't put me on the disabled list. But I wondered why I still felt so weak. [The tests] kind of explained it."

In baseball circles, Hook will always be remembered as the first winning pitcher in Mets history. The Mets had started the 1962 season 0–9 before the mechanical engineering graduate from Northwestern pitched a five-hitter in a 9–1 win over the Pirates at Forbes Field April 23. Casey Stengel lavished the right-hander with praise, although it was slightly left-handed.

"He has as much stuff as any pitcher in baseball," crowed Stengel, before taking a slight swipe at Hook. "But he won't brush them back. If he pitched like Sal Maglie, nobody would beat him."

Stengel allowed Hook to have his moment. "Don't take my picture," Stengel told the photographers. "Take the picture of the boy that wins one. Come back and see me when we win 26 straight."[67]

Hook's victory also had his manager thinking about the team's prospects for the remainder of 1962. "Ninety-nine more wins and we got the pennant," joked Stengel.[68]

Ask Hook what he recalls about that victory, and he'll tell you that, "I remember I got one or two hits! In fact, I think I drove in a run or two."

Hook provided a two-run single during a four-run second that put the Mets ahead 6–0. He made the lead stand up in the historic victory.

"After the game, Casey wanted me to talk to the writers a lot, and by the time I had finished, everyone had showered and the ballpark had run out of hot water.

"So I ended up jumping in the whirlpool. And then we had to catch a plane."

Hook almost pitched New York to victory April 17, taking a shutout into the sixth inning of his Mets debut before Norm Larker hit a two-run homer that put the Colts ahead 2–0. Hook gave up just the two runs and six hits in eight innings, leaving with a 2–1 deficit before Gus Bell homered with two outs in the bottom of the ninth to force extra innings. But Don Buddin launched a three-run homer off Herb Moford to keep the Mets winless.

Hook owned a 1.59 ERA in 17 innings following his first victory. But his next 14 appearances were spotty as he went 3–8 with a 7.60 ERA, yielding 75 hits in 58 innings. Hook began to lower his ERA by throwing back-to-back complete game victories, beating the Colts 13–2 on June 23 and the Dodgers 10–4 on June 29. By now he was the Mets' wins leader with six despite a 5.46 ERA. The Mets scored at least six runs in seven of his first 16 starts, giving Hook a luxury not granted to the rest of the rotation.

Hook had a 7–9 record following a 5–3 win over the Giants July 15. He was the first Met to beat the Dodgers, and the first to knock off both the Giants and Dodgers. Hook also collected three of his first seven wins over the Cubs, becoming the first Met to beat any team three times.

He actually pitched better following his July 15 victory over the Giants, compiling a 4.08 ERA in his final 106 innings while throwing six complete games. However, he went just 1–10 in those 15 starts as the Mets rode the bullet train to 120 losses.

Hook never thought during spring training that the Mets could possibly set a modern major league record for losses. He felt he was surrounded by talented teammates that spring, although most were a bit long in the tooth.

"It was great experience," he said, "because there were so many people on the roster who had been real stars. You look at that and think, man, maybe we do have a chance. But as we proved, it was short-lived."

And how! The Mets opened 3–16 before winning nine of 12 to move out of the NL cellar. But the team embarked on a 17-game losing streak that left them 12–36 and on pace for a record-setting year. The Mets lost by one or two runs in 10 of Hook's 19 losses. Of those 19 losses:

1. Hook tossed seven complete games.
2. Hook made eight starts in which he pitched at least eight innings and allowed fewer than three runs.

"I guess toward the second half of the season I was getting very angry after every game," he said. "I realized I had to reign in my emotions if I was going to stay mentally active because I hated to lose. There were games when you think you should have won and you didn't get run support. And then there were games when you got knocked out in the second or third inning.

"Probably my biggest weakness was the inconsistency of pitching, and I don't know what to attribute that to. Some days I'd really have it, and other days—I don't know if it was not enough mental focus or whatever."

Hook felt he had an idea that could help his team avoid prolonged slumps. He was far ahead of his time as his solution is now practiced in a different form by major leaguers every day.

"I was doing research at Northwestern University in the field called magnetohydrodynamics, but it was really mechanical engineering. I was doing work in really high-speed photography, and this was before video cameras. I tried to talk the club into doing films of batters and pitchers. I couldn't talk them into it, but I thought we could take fairly high-speed pictures of players when they were going good, and make a file copy of that. And when they got into a slump or weren't effective pitching, take other pictures."

Instead of self-coaching, the Mets relied on the wit and wisdom of Stengel, who said the Mets came up with ways to lose he didn't know existed. Stengel wasn't loved by every member of the Mets, but he and his wife, Edna, were held in very high regard by Hook and his family.

"We had two kids at the time," Hook said, "and they were maybe three and four years old. In spring training, my wife would always dress the kids up and we would go out for supper, sometimes at cafeterias down in St. Petersburg.

"A number of times we went to places where Casey and Edna were. Casey came over and was talking to our kids, and our kids were polite. So whenever Casey and Edna would see us, they would come over and take the kids or talk to them.

"When we were in New York, if there was a press luncheon or something, we'd take our kids. Casey would come and grab them and take them up to the head table or the podium, and Joan and I would sit in the back.

"Casey knew our family and knew our kids, so they were like a third set of grandparents. It was terrific, and we had a wonderful attitude toward Casey because of the way he treated our children."

Hook almost blew his relationship with Stengel before the Mets played their first home game. The pitcher used the wrong approach to aid himself and a few of his teammates in acquiring in-season housing, but the situation was quickly resolved.

"I was elected the player rep for the Mets," he said, "and I interfaced with Casey a little. I started off a little sideways with the club. When we returned to New York, there were 40 to 50 percent of the players who were well versed in baseball and moving around, and a number of them had been in the New York market before.

"But there were a number of us who had never lived in New York. I asked Ralph Kiner and Bob Murphy if they would announce that some of the players were looking for places to live for their families. I screwed up because I should have gone to the club and said, 'This is what I want to do,' but I didn't.

"So they make the announcement, and people started calling the park. The operators weren't really geared to take down information, and so they didn't.

"I went into Casey and told him what I had done. 'But I want you to know that if I don't have a place for my family to live, when we go on the road, I'm not going.' Just to call attention to the problem.

"Of course he hit the ceiling. 'Don't tell me I'm going to have problems with you and your family!'"

Housing became the least of the Mets' problems. They went through 17 pitchers and 28 position players—including seven catchers—in an attempt to avoid history. The moves couldn't stop the team from finishing 18 games behind the Cubs—for ninth place! The scenario was surprising to Hook and his teammates.

"That's one of the neat things about baseball," he remembered, "and I share this with people when I talk with them; it's a new game every day, and even though we lost so many games, I guess I never thought that we didn't have a chance tomorrow. So you always play like that.

"And we really had some big-name players, the Richie Ashburn's, and the Gil Hodges's, that group of players. I guess I look at it and say I'm sorry we lost so many games and I wish I had been a better pitcher."

Hook, Al Jackson, and Roger Craig were back to anchor the Mets' rotation in 1963 after the trio combined to go 26–63 in the team's inaugural season. The Mets shaved nearly a full run off the team ERA, but Hook was the lone returning starter whose earned run average rose in 1963. The team also had more trouble scoring runs and failed to give Hook the offensive support that helped him win eight games in '62.

Hook went 0–4 in his first five starts of 1963 before going the distance on a four-hitter in a 4–2 win over the Phillies May 8. He also tossed a two-hitter in a 2–1 win over the Cubs May 30, but the gem still left him with a 5.43 ERA.

Hook was 3–10 with a hefty 6.45 ERA when Stengel decided to put him in the bullpen for the next seven weeks. He was allowed to start five games after August 25 but was still unable to provide the type of pitching needed for a club that finished last in the league in hitting (.219) and ninth in slugging (.315), homers (96), and runs (501).

The Mets moved into Shea Stadium in 1964, but Hook never got a chance to pitch there. He started twice while making three appearances on the road, surrendering 10 earned runs before the Mets sent him to the Braves for Roy McMillan on May 8.

"When I was traded to Milwaukee, they wanted to send me to Denver. I told them I would go there, but I only needed three weeks to have five years in the major leagues," Hook said.

"And so they committed to bringing me back in September, no matter what. [With Denver] I tore up my knee trying to take out this shortstop on a double play, and so I couldn't pitch any more. But they brought me back to Milwaukee and I was with the Braves for the last five weeks.

"I saw Casey Stengel at the '68 World Series in Detroit. He said, 'Why'd you get out of baseball?' I told him I tore

Jay Hook

up my knee trying to take out a shortstop on a double play. He asked, 'How'd you get to first?'

"I think the first seven years Joan and I were married, we moved 22 times. But it was being in Evanston, Illinois, during the winter, going to school, then we'd go to spring training for a couple of months. Next, we'd be wherever we were going to be for the summer. So it was doing a lot of moving around.

"At the end of the '64 season I looked at my career and said, 'Yeah, I made the major leagues but I'm just a mediocre pitcher, so I better start working on the next career.'"

Hook had little trouble finding another job. He received a master's degree in thermodynamics during his playing career before he was hired by Chrysler, working in product planning.

"It was really a fun job," he said, "because I was working on vehicles that were two, three, four years out. The product planners would work with styling and manufacturing, finance and marketing on what would happen to vehicles three to four years from now.

"When *Motor Trend* or *Road and Track* would want to be writing about the new vehicles, we would build production cars, cars that would be finished in the spring for a fall release. They wouldn't be built on the regular production lines but they would be examples of what we'd be producing.

"At that time, the 426 Hemi engine was a big deal, and it was a hot vehicle. When we would have these pre-production cars out at the proving grounds, we'd always have a few of these hot vehicles out there.

"These writers loved that, and it was a little nerve-wracking because all of the writers thought they were Barney Oldfield! You'd drive with them and they'd go up a hill and want all four wheels off the ground for a photographer.

"But it was a lot of fun because we were messing around with a lot of hardware."

Hook had hoped to take a job with Chrysler in Europe, but it was blocked by his immediate boss who didn't want to lose him. He had been with Chrysler for four years when he received an overture from another company.

"We had been active in the Methodist church and I was singing in the choir," Hook remembered. "There was a guy there that worked for Rockwell International, and he was putting together a product planning department. He knew I had that background, so he kept talking to me, and I helped him with the organization.

"After he interviewed a number of people, he said, 'Jay, how about coming over to Rockwell and heading up the product planning department?'

"If Chrysler had talked to me about what plans they had for me, I may not have made the move. But they hadn't. They blocked the European thing, our kids were little and I thought it would have been great to have some international experience. So I ended up going to Rockwell.

"Later, [Rockwell] gave me the marketing staff, along with the product planning. I later became a vice president managing some divisions for them."

Jay had the forging, casting, and mass transit divisions for Rockwell at one point. He was doing plenty of traveling for the company while continuing to make contact with some important people, which led to a memorable cab ride.

"The guy that was heading Pullman Standard at that time was Jim McDivitt, who was one of the astronauts. I was in New York for a meeting and McDivitt came in from Chicago. We went down to get a cab, and there was McDivitt and I and two other guys. They got in the back seat and I in the front seat.

"McDivitt says to the cabbie, 'You're not going to believe this, but the guy next to you in the front seat pitched the first game the Mets ever won.'

"Then I said, 'Cabbie, you're not going to believe this, but the guy that was just talking in the back seat was an astronaut and one of the first guys to go around the moon.'

"When we got out to pay, the cabbie said to me, 'You guys have got to be kidding me.' Can you imagine that cabbie going back to the barn talking to the cab drivers and telling them [who he picked up]?"

Hook was later hired by Masco in 1978 as a group president who reported to the president of the company. When he got there, they gave him five companies to run. By the time he left in the early 1990s, 20 companies were reporting to him. But Hook wasn't ready to retire.

"I decided I wanted to have a third career," he said. "I'd had a sports career and a successful business career.

"I had been asked to do some things for Northwestern University, and I was on the board of a seminary which was also on the campus. I knew I wasn't going to be president of Masco, so I thought it would be a good time to start this other career, which I call a service career.

"I became a professor for nine years and headed up an MBA program for manufacturing management at Northwestern. It's successful and called the Triple-M program.

"It is half-taught by the professors in McCormick Engineering and half by the Kellogg Business School. It's been a great success and a forerunner to many other programs at Northwestern where you integrate schools, which isn't easy to do.

"We started a program called 'Engineering First' where freshmen in the curriculum become excited about engineering. Instead of having them take just basic courses, we involve them in engineering-related things right from the start."

He and Joan eventually moved to a farm in Northern Michigan.

"I cut a little hay. It's a place that's user-friendly for grandchildren."

Jay and Joan have 13 grandchildren. He stays very active by doing things that are important to him.

"When we moved to the farm, I thought there were three things in which I wanted to be involved. One was the church, and I've been very active with the Methodist church in the state of Michigan. Second is health care, and I'm on the investment committee at the hospital. Third is education, and I still serve on the advisory board at the seminary, at Garrett Evangelical, the Methodist church in the state and the local church. Also, I remain on an advisory board at Northwestern University, and the foundation board at NMC Community College.

"When you don't want to be paid for something, boy, there are a lot of things you can do," Hook says with a hearty laugh.

"It doesn't take a lot of time, but you stay active. I tell my grandkids I'm just a local farmer."

ML debut	Reds vs. Cardinals, 9/3/57 (2.1 IP, 0 H, 0 ER, 2 K, 2 BB)
Mets debut	vs. Colt 45s, 4/17/62 (8 IP, 6 H, 2 ER, 5 K, 1 BB)
First ML strikeout	Eddie Kasko, Cardinals, 9/3/57 (with Reds)
First Mets strikeout	Roman Mejias, Colt 45s, 4/17/62
First ML win	@ Cubs, 7/18/59 (with Reds)
First Mets win	@ Pirates, 4/23/62
First ML/Mets save	vs. Colt 45s, 7/15/63
Most strikeouts, ML game	10, 3 times, including Reds vs. Dodgers, 5/18/60
Most Strikeouts, Mets game	10, vs. Pirates, 7/19/62; vs. Phillies, 5/8/63
Low-hit ML CG	2, Reds @ Braves, 9/20/60; Mets vs. Cubs, 5/30/63

Acquired: Selected in the expansion draft, 10/10/61.
Deleted: Traded to the Braves with a player to be named (Adrian Garrett) for Roy McMillan, 5/8/64.

Todd Hundley

Catcher, Outfielder   Bats both, throws right
Born: 5/27/69   Martinsville, Virginia
Height: 5'11"   Weight: 185   #49, #9

Todd Hundley Mets Career

YEAR	GP	AB	R	H	2B	3B	HR	RBI	K	BB	SB	AVG	SLG	OBP
1990	36	67	8	14	6	0	0	2	18	6	0	.209	.299	.274
1991	21	60	5	8	0	1	1	7	14	6	0	.133	.217	.221
1992	123	358	32	75	17	0	7	32	76	19	3	.209	.316	.256
1993	130	417	40	95	17	2	11	53	62	23	1	.228	.357	.269
1994	91	291	45	69	10	1	16	42	73	25	2	.237	.443	.303
1995	90	275	39	77	11	0	15	51	64	42	1	.280	.484	.382
1996	153	540	85	140	32	1	41	112	146	79	1	.259	.550	.356
1997	132	417	78	114	21	2	30	86	116	83	2	.273	.549	.394
1998	53	124	8	20	4	0	3	12	55	16	1	.161	.266	.261
TOTAL	829	2549	340	612	118	7	124	397	624	299	11	.240	.438	.323

ML Career

YEAR	GP	AB	R	H	2B	3B	HR	RBI	K	BB	SB	AVG	SLG	OBP
90–03	1225	3769	495	883	167	7	202	599	988	453	14	.234	.443	.320

It often takes a while for a ballplayer to match his advanced billing. Mets fans waited patiently for Todd Hundley to live up to the team's hype machine, watching his batting average languish below .240 in each of his first five major league seasons. Although his defense met expectations, Hundley continued to tease the Shea faithful with his sporadic hitting until 1994.

Almost magically, Hundley became one of the team's top run producers from 1995 to 1997. He collected 112 RBIs in 1996 while setting a major league record for home runs by a catcher. But a damaged elbow put him on the shelf at the start of 1998 and prompted the Mets to get Mike Piazza, thus leaving Hundley as the lone link between Gary Carter and Piazza behind the plate.

Hundley's legacy should be more than a bridge between Hall of Fame catchers, but the elbow injury, coupled with his inclusion in the Mitchell Report on performance-enhancing drugs, makes some Mets fans question the value of his exceptional three-year run as one of the greatest backstops in team history. It didn't help Hundley's stature that he performed well while the Mets were non-contenders.

Todd Randolph Hundley was born in Martinsville, Virginia, and grew up in Palatine, Illinois, a Chicago suburb. He graduated from William Fremd High School, where he hit .404 as a junior and .367 as a senior while developing into one of the top catching prospects in the 1987 draft.

The Mets took him in the second round with the 39th overall selection, hoping he could emerge as the heir apparent to Carter.

"I was just blown away," Hundley said about being taken by the Mets. "I mean, here I am, just out of high school, and the reigning World Series champs take me? It was awesome."[69]

Mets fans were well familiar with the Hundley name. His father, Randy, was a 1969 NL All-Star, two years after win-

ning a Gold Glove. Randy Hundley hit over .250 just twice in a full major league season, and he tried to break up Tom Seaver's perfect game bid in July 1969 with a bunt attempt leading off the ninth inning. He was an iron man as catchers go, averaging 148 games started from 1966 to 1969.

Randy said in a 1992 interview for *Mets Magazine* that it wasn't long before Todd took an interest in sports.

"Two years old," the elder Hundley said of his son. "He had a ball in his hand constantly, and a whiffle bat. He played a lot. That's all he wanted to do. I have a great picture of him, from spring training, carrying one of my mitts. He was still in diapers for crying out loud. It's the neatest picture, I think. Kind of typifies him."[70]

Todd was projected as a fine defensive player and a better hitter than his father, but it took him three minor league seasons before he demonstrated he could handle a bat. Assigned to Little Falls of the rookie NY–Penn League after the draft, Hundley hit only .146 in 34 games to earn another season with the team. He didn't do much better in 1988, recording a .188 average with two homers, eight doubles, and 18 RBIs in 52 games before receiving a one-game look at Single A St. Lucie.

The Mets gave him a slight promotion in 1989, sending him to Columbia of the low A South Atlantic League. Hundley made an impression in the first inning of the season opener by participating in a 2-4-2 triple play, handling a strikeout and nailing a runner at second base before applying a tag at the plate to get .

Hundley also began to produce at the plate, logging 31 multi-hit games while hitting .269 with 11 home runs, 23 doubles, and 66 RBIs. He had a five-RBI game against Asheville a few days after playing in the South Atlantic League All-Star Game.

He also excelled behind the plate, throwing out 11 straight runners in May and nailing 47 of his 126 runners (37 percent) for the season. His progress couldn't have come at a better time for the Mets.

Carter spent most of '89 on the disabled list and hit only .183 over 50 games in the final year of his contract. The Mets granted him free agency and hoped a three-man contingent of Mackey Sasser, Orlando Mercado, and Barry Lyons could hold down the position in 1990 while Hundley continued his minor league apprenticeship. Hundley opened the year at Double A Jackson and was recalled three times by the Mets.

The first promotion occurred on May 18. Put into the starting lineup by manager Davey Johnson, Hundley went 1-for-4 with a fourth-inning double off Padres starter Bruce Hurst. Not bad for a kid who originally thought he had been traded the night before.

Clint Hurdle was managing Jackson and asked Hundley to come into his office to let him know of the promotion.

"[He] sat me down and asked if I wanted a beer," Hundley said, "then, I definitely knew something was up. He said to me, 'Well, you're going to San Diego,' and right away I'm thinking, 'Oh great, they traded me.'

"So I said, 'Well, who did they get for me?' And Clint was confused. 'You're going to San Diego because that's where the Mets are.'

"I knew that both Orlando Mercado and Barry Lyons were hurt. And Davey's telling me about Frank Viola, how easy he is to catch and all, and I just broke in, 'Are you saying I'm catching?' And he says, 'Well, yeah.' I just left. I needed to think about that one.

"My first at-bat, Bruce Hurst struck me out on three pitchers—just zip, zip, zip, thank you very much and good-bye. My next at-bat, I doubled down the line, and Kevin Elster got thrown out at the plate.

"I remember I was too scared to even see how many people were in the stadium that night. Finally, by about the eighth inning, I looked around—it was maybe 40,000 people. I was floored."[71]

He started six more games the rest of the month and was sent down after going 0-for-19 following his double.

Recalled again in July, Hundley went hitless in his first three at-bats before lining a tiebreaking, RBI double off Rob Dibble in a 10–3 rout of the Reds. Hundley went 2-for-3 with an RBI and two-runs scored in his next game and went 7-for-27 (.259) for the month before he was sent back to Jackson.

Hundley showed little power at Jackson, hitting just one home run and 15 extra-base hits in 81 games. But he also batted .265 and threw out 48 percent of his 87 base-runners to top all Texas League backstops and earn another recall in late August.

He spent the rest of the year serving primarily as a defensive replacement when newly acquired Charlie O'Brien was lifted for a pinch-hitter in the late innings. Hundley's average as a Met dropped to .151 by August 26 before he finished 6-for-14 (.429) to end up at .209. He had the honor of throwing down signals in Frank Viola's 20th win of the season.

The Mets shipped Hundley to Triple A Tidewater at the start of 1991 and resisted the temptation of recalling him until after the International League season. Hundley hit .375 in 16 at-bats during the exhibition season and grew into a power hitter with the Tides, smacking 14 home runs and 24 doubles while compiling a .273 average with 66 RBIs. He was named to the midseason International League All-Star team and played in the Triple A All-Star Game. Hundley was named the league's fourth-best prospect in a vote of managers by Baseball America after pacing the Tides in homers and RBIs.

The Mets already had played themselves out of playoff contention by the time Hundley was recalled on September 4. He saw plenty of action down the stretch, starting 17 of his 21 games and handling 96 chances without an error. He belted his first big league homer on September 26 against the Pirates, a pinch-hit blast off Bill Landrum in the 14th inning. Hundley supplied a two-run triple the next day but hit only .133 over 60 at-bats in his latest major league stint.

Hundley's first full major league season came in 1992 as an underachieving Mets squad finished fifth in the six-team NL East despite the additions of Bobby Bonilla, Eddie Murray, and Bret Saberhagen. Hundley continued to live up to his reputation as an outstanding defensive catcher, committing only three errors in 751 chances for a .996 fielding percentage that set a team record for catchers. Hundley also was behind the plate for 12 of the Mets' 13 shutouts and didn't record an error until his 38th game of the season. Mainly, he was just trying to blend in without putting added pressure on himself.

"I think that's the biggest thing, try to not do too much," Hundley said during spring training. "I know I'm not going to be the hero of the team and I'm not trying to be. I need to play my game and not try and be somebody else."

"He's got to get the confidence of those guys," his father said about Hundley's relationship with a veteran pitching staff. "And that's not an easy job because they're pretty set in their ways. He needs to learn how they think. He's got to be a babysitter at times, but tough occasionally, know the psyche of the pitcher, always be thinking three pitches ahead. It may not be easy for awhile, but if the pitchers hang on and bear with him, I think they'll enjoy pitching to him."[72]

Hundley also had his moments with a bat. He hit .400 during a seven-game hitting streak from July 22 through August 2, homered in back-to-back starts in April, and provided a pair of three-RBI games during June. He finished the year with seven homers and 32 RBIs in 123 games but hit only .209, the fifth-lowest total in the majors for players with at least 375 plate appearances.

Although Hundley was handed the starting job out of spring training, he wound up sitting a lot during the first half of the season as new manager and former catcher Jeff Torborg tried to keep Sasser and O'Brien sharp. Hundley didn't appreciate the inactivity at first.

"I learned not to fight the situation," Hundley said the following spring. "The first half, I was just fighting the situation. I wasn't getting the playing time I expected, and I was just fighting it. I was frustrated all the time.

"The second half, I took on the attitude that this was the way it was going to be. I was going to deal with it the best way I could, and the way to do that was to put up numbers."[73]

Hundley remained the No. 1 catcher in 1993 as the Mets went 59–103, the fifth-worst record in team history. He remained a solid defensive catcher and showed improvement at the plate, hitting 11 homers and 17 doubles while finishing fourth on the team with 53 RBIs. His slugging average rose 41 points to .357, but his .269 on-base percentage was second-worst among major leaguers with at least 430 plate appearances, while his .228 average was fifth-worst.

The Mets now wondered if they had developed another strong-fielding, weak-hitting catcher in the Jerry Grote/

Duffy Dyer mold, although Grote's .256 average as a Met was comparing very favorably to Hundley's .213 mark at this stage of his career.

The 1994 season was a turning point for Hundley, who was among the team's most dangerous hitters over the first four weeks. Hundley owned a .351 average with eight home runs and 15 RBIs through his first 19 contests, capping that stretch by smacking a pair of solo homers in a 7–4 win over the Dodgers on May 1. But just as Mets fans thought he had gotten over the hump, Hundley batted .149 over his next 33 games to drop his season average to .225 before his season took another upturn.

Facing the Marlins on June 18, Hundley became only the fourth Met in team history to homer from both sides of the plate in the same game. He crushed a three-run homer in the third inning before his seventh-inning blast allowed him to join Lee Mazzilli, Howard Johnson, and Bobby Bonilla in the Mets' switching-hitting power annals. The display ignited a 27-game stretch in which Hundley hit .272 with six homers, 13 RBIs, and 16 runs scored. The Mets went 15–12 in those games and surprisingly flirted with the .500 mark the rest of the season.

The season came to an abrupt halt in mid-August as a strike eventually caused the cancellation of the remainder of the season. Hundley ended up with a .237 average and was third on the team with 16 home runs and a .443 slugging average. He also hiked his on-base percentage above the .300 mark for the first time in his career, and was sixth among all NL catchers with a 32.8 success rate against base-stealers.

The Mets finished 55–58 after general manager Joe McIlvaine shed the roster of several high-priced, low-reward malcontents. The team was now in the midst of a youth movement, and the 25-year-old Hundley was being counted on to take the Mets and its young pitching staff to a level of prosperity not seen by the franchise in five years. But the team continued to experience growing pains through the first three months of 1995.

Hundley opened the season in grand style, becoming the second Met in team history—and the first since Richie Hebner in 1979—to collect four hits and drive in four runs on Opening Day. He provided his RBI on one swing, ripping a grand slam off Bill Swift to erase the Rockies' 5–1 lead in Colorado. But the Mets blew one-run leads in the ninth, 13th, and 14th innings as Dante Bichette launched a three-run homer in the bottom of the 14th to give the Rockies a victory in their first game at Coors Field.

Hundley also provided a go-ahead, two-run double to lead the Mets to a 10–8 win over the Cardinals in the home opener on April 26 before delivering a tiebreaking grand slam in the 10th inning of a 5–1 win at Montreal on May 4. He had a .300 average with four homers and 17 RBIs while appearing in each of the Mets' first 23 games, 18 as a starter.

Hundley's average dipped to .237 after going 0-for-3 in 7–3 loss June 17 against the Astros at Shea, which gave the Mets an 18–30 record that put them 12½ games out of first place. It was also the first major league start by Bill Pulsipher, who was among the most coveted arms in the farm system.

The season began to turn after the loss. Hundley went 2-for-3 with a three-run homer and four RBIs in a 10–4 rout of the Astros, beginning a season-ending stretch in which he batted .311 with 11 homers and 32 ribbies in 51 games. He went on the disabled list on July 24 with a sprained wrist that kept him out of action for five weeks. Shortly before he went on the DL, the Mets recalled pitcher Jason Isringhausen from Triple A Norfolk, another one of the team's young pitching gems.

Hundley had added responsibility when he was activated. His hitting was reaching new heights and his defense remained stellar, but he was being asked to mentor two highly touted prospects that weren't much younger than he was.

Pulsipher and Isringhausen flourished the rest of the way, although Pulsipher had to be shut down in mid-September. The two combined to go 14–9 with a 3.44 ERA in 31 starts, helping the Mets post the National League's second-best record after the All-Star break at 44–31 en route to an encouraging 69–75 record.

Hundley finished the season with a .280 average with 15 home runs and 51 RBIs. He also became more patient at the plate, walking 42 times for a team-high .382 on-base percentage. Hundley courteously deflected praise for his improved stats toward Tom McCraw, his longtime hitting coach.

"I've been with him five years now," Hundley said after the season. "Eight if you count the minors. And he's so good at helping you relax. He knows everybody's strength and weaknesses, and works within that. He doesn't make you do what you're not capable of.

"And all along, he just wanted me to be patient, wait for my pitch. At times, I just couldn't do it. But it started working for me [in 1995] and it's just snowballed."[74]

The Mets added former first-round pick Paul Wilson to the rotation by the 1996 season opener, giving the team a starting staff that included four homegrown hurlers. Expectations were high during spring training, especially after McIlvaine acquired center fielder Lance Johnson and left fielder Bernard Gilkey in the off-season. Mets fans also watched Edgardo Alfonzo, Butch Huskey, Jeff Kent, Rico Brogna, and Carl Everett develop into potent hitters during the last two seasons, giving hope the team could challenge for a playoff berth if the young pitchers came through.

Hundley put up spectacular numbers in what is considered among the most potent lineups in club history. His 41st and final home run came on September 14 against Atlanta's Greg Maddux, breaking Roy Campanella's 43-year-old record for catchers. It came six days after Hundley topped Darryl Strawberry's club mark of 39 home runs.

Todd Hundley

Hundley's 41 home runs also set a National League record for switch hitters, beating the old mark of 38 set by Howard Johnson with the 1991 Mets. Mickey Mantle had been the only switch-hitter in major league history to belt 40 homers in a season until Hundley and Ken Caminiti did it in '96. Unfortunately, Hundley and Caminiti would be linked in another form years later.

Hundley and Bernard Gilkey became the first Mets teammates to drive in 100 runs in the same season. A hefty number of their RBI opportunities were provided by Lance Johnson, who shattered club records and led the National League with 21 triples and 227 hits. They were also the second set of Mets teammates to belt more than 30 home runs apiece, joining Howard Johnson and Strawberry in 1987.

Hundley was selected to the NL All-Star team for the first time in his career. But the Mets were a disappointing

41–46 when he made the trip, thanks to a shaky rotation and mediocre defense.

Pulsipher appeared in four games during the exhibition season before undergoing Tommy John surgery in April, ending his season and effectively killing his career. Isringhausen and Wilson were nothing short of terrible all year, combining for an 11–26 record and a 5.05 ERA. Bobby Jones, Mark Clark, and Pete Harnisch became the team's most dependable pitchers despite their combined 1.30 WHIP.

The staff also had trouble keeping runners close to the bag, which dropped Hundley's success rate against base-stealers to 25 percent in 98 attempts. Hundley committed 10 passed balls while joining his father as one of the first 18 players in major league history to catch at least 150 games.

He received NL MVP consideration despite the team's 71–91 record. He finished fourth in the league with 41 home runs and ninth with 79 walks, almost doubling his career high for base-on-balls. He ended up third on the team with a .356 on-base percentage and was second to Gilkey with a .550 slugging mark.

Hundley was now being compared to other great New York catchers: Grote, Carter, Campanella, Yogi Berra, Bill Dickey, Elston Howard, and Thurman Munson.

"To be included in that elite group would be something very special, but I'm not there yet," Hundley said after the season. "The [home run] record gives me a chance because it's something that sets me apart. I can't even put into words what it feels like to be part of major league history. But until I can produce like that over several years, I don't think I can be compared to those guys.

"I could feel the [fans] pushing me for the record. They knew how tired and worn out I was by the end of the season, but they wanted me to get it. They pulled me through.

"I'm telling you, to be part of major league history was an incredible feeling. But to be part of New York history… I don't know if it gets any better than that.

"When I finish my playing, I'd love for people to look back on my career and say I belong in that group with Yogi and Roy and Thurman. But to do that, I've got to win the World Series. That's something else all those other guys did. If I have to play 20 years to do it, that's what I have to do."[75]

"I like the kid," said Berra. "I like to watch him play. I like the fact that he goes out there everyday. And he's obviously got a lot of power. His father never hit the ball that far. It's tough catching every day and being a good hitter, too. Especially doing it year after year. You've got to be strong. But this kid is. He had a great year. He's definitely headed the right way."[76]

The Mets had a new manager by the end of the season. Hundley had flourished under no-nonsense skipper Dallas Green, who could be highly critical of young players. Green chased a young Jeromy Burnitz out of New York and said publicly that Wilson and Isringhausen had no business being in the majors while they struggled in 1996. Green's candor and the team's poor record led to his dismissal in August 1996, elevating Bobby Valentine to manager. Once Valentine was hired, Hundley hit .196 with just three home runs and 12 RBIs in his final 29 games of '96.

Valentine was considered a more positive influence on a rebuilding team than Green, but he also used the media to play head games with his players. Valentine was the master of the off-handed comment, causing writers and broadcasters to head back to the player in question to assess Valentine's opinion. Hundley was part of this strategy by the middle of 1997 while the team was enjoying a renaissance.

Hundley hit only .152 in his first 14 games of '97 before catching fire. He batted .414 with seven homers, 25 RBIs, and 19 runs scored in 19 games from April 19 through May 9, arguably his greatest stretch as a major league hitter.

His season average soared to .300 by the time he clubbed a go-ahead, three-run homer in the eighth inning of a 10–7 victory in Atlanta on July 10. The blast helped the Mets take three of four from the Braves and came a few days after Hundley made his second and final All-Star appearance.

The Mets owned the wild-card lead at 51–39 after the Atlanta series, 1½ games ahead of the Expos despite limited production from Gilkey and Johnson. Gilkey was in the midst of a deep slump and Johnson was hitting about 70 points below his .330 average of 1996. With Hundley behind the plate, the Mets' pitching was surprisingly good while Pulsipher, Isringhausen, and Wilson contributed nothing.

Hundley had a big game in a 10–1 pounding of the Reds on July 20, going 4-for-4 with two homers and five RBIs to raise his average to .301. It was part of a streak in which the Mets won seven straight games played by Hundley to pull within 5½ games of the NL East lead.

But the Marlins eventually caught the Mets for the wild-card and were charging hard with a veteran lineup that was more productive than New York's starting eight. Gilkey continued to slump, and Johnson turned himself into trade bait by the end of July.

Instead of lighting a fire under Gilkey or Johnson, Valentine opted to throw criticism toward his catcher by telling the media he thought Hundley was spending too much time out on the town and needed to get more sleep.

"He's a nocturnal person," Valentine told the media in August. "He needs more rest. He has a really tough time getting to sleep after games. I heard one night he stayed out until 4 o'clock in the morning before he was ready to go sleep. Tough duty. It'll wear on you a lot.

"He's not out running around. I've had curfews, he's been in. Not asleep. I'm not dictating anybody's lifestyle. What world-class athletes do is take care of their bodies, because the body is the machine they drive to win or lose the race. It's evident Todd hasn't had a full night's sleep."[77]

The slight may have also been designed to wake up the rest of the Mets' younger players, but it left Hundley to quell rumors that his supposed night-owl lifestyle was hurting the ballclub. Hundley and Valentine were never chummy after that.

The Mets went just 29–31 after July 27 to finish behind the Marlins for the wild-card. Gilkey continued to hit poorly, and Johnson was jettisoned to the Cubs with Clark on August 8 in a deal that brought center fielder Brian McRae and relievers Mel Rojas and Turk Wendell to New York. The trade was designed to bolster the bullpen, but it only served to help New York fall out of the race.

Hundley helped prop up the Mets' lagging postseason hopes by going 5-for-7 with two homers and seven RBIs in the first two games of a late August series with the Padres at Shea. Hundley tied the first game with a two-run homer in the bottom of the ninth and belted a grand slam in the seventh inning of Game 2 to lead New York to victories each time.

But Hundley was playing with a damaged elbow that diminished his effectiveness behind the plate. He went 11-for-25 during his first seven games of September before starting just two games the rest of the season. Hundley still hit 30 homers and drove in 86 runs despite the injury and finished the year with a .273 average and a team-best .549 slugging average in 132 games. He also set career highs with 83 walks and a .394 on-base percentage, finishing second to John Olerud on the team in both categories to help the Mets end up 88–74.

Hundley's elbow injury became intolerable by September 9, when he started and left after just two innings. He had been playing with a stretched ligament in the elbow for about five years and developed bone chips due to the unstable ligament. Hundley tried to continue playing until the Mets were eliminated from the postseason race, but his contributions consisted of a few pinch-hitting appearance and one start. Once the Mets were eliminated, Hundley went to see Dr. James Andrews and was told he needed ligament replacement surgery. The best case scenario had Hundley returning to the lineup by the 1998 All-Star break, although there was little chance of him being healthy enough to catch at all that season.

"The main thing now is to not rush back," Hundley said immediately after the surgery. "That's where I could screw everything up. I want to do this as a one-time deal and not have a Jay Payton–type scenario. Seven to 12 months is the average, and a year is definitely a possibility. It could be that, or three years, if I try and come back too quickly.

"I'm sure they're going to have to do something," Hundley continued as he discussed the Mets' possibility of getting another catcher. "If they do that, hopefully, that catcher will help us win a bunch of games and then I can step in and win a bunch of games."[78]

Hundley was willing to be patient after watching Payton try to return from ligament replacement surgery too soon, forcing him to undergo a second procedure within a year. Plus, Hundley had every reason to believe he'd have a job waiting for him once he was healthy. He was arguably the second-best catcher in the National League, behind only Mike Piazza.

The Mets even told him not to worry about his job status. The plan was to find a new No. 1 catcher for '98 and slide Hundley behind the plate once he was ready. Besides, what were the Mets going to do…acquire Piazza? That appeared to be a pipe dream that even the most optimistic Mets fan couldn't fathom.

Hundley continued his rehab while the Mets looked for catching solutions during spring training. The team went into the season with a tandem of Tim Spehr and Alberto Castillo behind the plate. Spehr went 2-for-5 as the Opening-Day catcher and collected hits in two of the next three games before a 3-for-37 skid dropped his average to .137. Castillo singled home the lone run as a pinch-hitter in the Mets' 14-inning triumph over the Phillies in the season opener but went hitless in his first five starts. Castillo was a good-luck charm of sorts as the Mets went 14–8 in his first 22 starts, but his offensive production was sporadic.

The Mets won 13 of their first 20 games despite a punchless offense that sorely missed Hundley. They averaged a healthy 4.6 runs in that span but hit only .248 with 11 homers before the team's fortunes began to sour. New York batted .239 while averaging 3.8 runs over the next 23 games, leading to a 10–13 mark that put the team back in the thick of mediocrity while Hundley amped up his hitting regimen.

It was during the skid when the Dodgers, unable to work out a contract extension with Piazza during spring training, sent him to the Marlins with Todd Zeile for Bonilla, Charles Johnson, Gary Sheffield, Jim Eisenreich, and Manuel Barrios. It was an odd acquisition by the Marlins considering they were in the midst of a fire sale that deleted most of the players that led them to the World Series. There was little doubt Piazza would be dealt before the trade deadline.

The New York media—WFAN's Mike and the Mad Dog in particular—began to wonder what it would take for the Mets to get Piazza since it was obvious he was only a Florida rental. Mets general manager Steve Phillips continued to deny the Mets had any interest in Piazza, saying they were prepared to make do until Hundley was able to play again.

"I'd have the best platoon catching tandem in the history of baseball," Phillips joked when asked about Piazza on May 15, the day after the Marlins acquired the All-Star. "But I don't see a fit for us. For me to give up chips to get a player for the rest of this year who duplicates—when healthy—one of our strengths, it really doesn't make sense to do anything like that."

"I'm ready to go," Hundley added as he prepared to continue his rehab in Florida. "But I also have to face the realities of it and be smart about it. I feel like I can swing at a ball coming at me, though."[79]

Hundley continued to bust his butt in rehab and spoke of catching again in midseason, but his optimism turned to anger as reports of the Mets' interest in Piazza began to multiply.

"I'll see you next year," Hundley said when asked what he'd do if Piazza joined the team. "Let him catch the rest of the year. I'll come back next year.

"If you can make a deal like that one, it's like getting Barry Bonds; it's like Griffey Jr. Why should I even take a chance of coming back? If we can get that type of player, why even risk it? Let him have it. He can be a free agent next year and get $10 or $15 million. I'll see you next year.

"Basically, all it boils down to is I'm trying to get back for the team. I don't want to risk myself and my career. Every doctor I spoke to and everyone who's had this says take a year off. I haven't taken the year off."[80]

Hundley faced live pitching again for the first time on May 21. One day later, the Mets landed Piazza after dropping to the bottom of the National League in homers and slugging average. Piazza arrived at Shea Stadium a day after Hundley reported to St. Lucie to continue his rehab. Both said all the right things, but they also reiterated they wanted to remain behind the plate.

Hundley's future with the Mets was now murky but hardly over. The team still had to complete the task of re-signing Piazza, who was scheduled for free agency after the season. If he walked, Hundley would be catching for the Mets again in 1999. Even if Piazza signed, Hundley might stay if he or Piazza would be willing to change positions.

Hundley opened his minor league rehab assignment by going 0-for-2 with two walks as an outfielder for the Gulf Coast Mets before playing nine more games in the outfield for St. Lucie. Several Mets couldn't wait for his return.

"We've been missing something," John Franco said the day before Hundley was activated. "And now we have our leader back. He's been our leader on the field when he was catching every day. And when he was fine, nobody had the kind of presence like Todd does. His presence should help us immediately, even if it might not make a couple of guys happy because of playing time."[81]

The Mets hoped Hundley could take over in left field for Gilkey, whose hitting woes hadn't waned. Hundley received a very warm ovation at Shea as his name was announced in the starting lineup for his major league season debut on July 11. He singled in four trips to the plate before coming out of the game for defensive purposes after seven innings and no putouts in an 8–4 win against Montreal. He went 0-for-2 the next game before delivering a two-run single in a 4–2 loss to the Braves the following day. He continued to look good at the plate on July 16, producing his first two-hit game to raise his average to .286. But he looked far from comfortable in left field, where trips toward the outfield wall or down the foul line were adventurous. As outfielders go, Hundley looked like an All-Star catcher.

By early August his performance at the plate was almost as fruitless as his attempts at catching line drives. Hundley went 2-for-31 (.065) from July 22 through August 3, and he was still looking for his first home run of the season until he launched a two-run shot to break a 2–2 tie in the third inning of a 4–2 triumph at St. Louis on August 10. He went 5-for-7 over a two-game stretch August 6 and August 7 before beginning a deep batting slump. Hundley hit only .109 while striking out 28 times in his final 46 at-bats that month.

Valentine had seen enough by the time Hundley's average sunk to .162 on August 27. Hundley was placed on the disabled list due to elbow irritation before starting another rehab stint at Norfolk, where he caught three games before returning to the Mets.

Hundley was back behind the plate on September 13 in Montreal and caught 10 innings at Houston two days later before delivering his biggest pinch-hit of the season, a solo homer in the 11th inning to beat the Astros 4–3. The blast left New York within a half-game of the Cubs for the wild-card lead. But Hundley went 0-for-5 with three strikeouts off the bench the rest of the season, and the Mets lost their last five games to end up one win short of forcing a three-way tie for the wild-card.

Hundley finished with a .161 average, three home runs, 12 RBIs, and 55 strikeouts in 124 at-bats over 53 games. He proved he wasn't cut out for the outfield, which meant his days as a Met were over unless Piazza went elsewhere. Piazza signed a seven-year, $92 million contract by the end of October, and Hundley was traded to the Dodgers on December 1.

The Hundley trade worked out very well for both parties. The Mets received Roger Cedeno and Charles Johnson, who was immediately shipped to Baltimore for Armando Benitez. Cedeno and Benitez were key contributors in 1999 as the Mets reached the playoffs for the first time in 11 years.

The Dodgers gave Hundley a chance to prove himself as a catcher again. He caught 108 times in '99 and hit .207 with 24 home runs, 55 RBIs, and 49 runs scored. Hundley's .436 slugging average was 170 points higher than his 1998 mark, but his 107 stolen bases allowed were second-most in the National League.

He took another positive step in 2000, hitting 24 home runs for the second straight season while batting .284 with 70 RBIs in 90 games. He set a career high with a .579 slugging average and had his batting average over .300 as late as September 13, numbers that helped his bargaining position after the Dodgers granted him free agency.

Hundley decided to follow in his father's footsteps by signing a four-year, $23.5 million package with the Cubs in December 2000. But he hit poorly during his two seasons in Chicago, recording a .199 average with 28 home runs, 66 RBIs, and 169 strikeouts in 512 at-bats while battling a bad back. He averaged just 85 games for the Cubs before they sent him back to the Dodgers in December 2002.

Hundley began his second stint in L.A. by collecting eight RBIs in his first 12 games, including a pinch-hit,

three-run homer in a 4–3 victory against the Padres on April 17. But he sat out nearly four consecutive months due to back pain and was relegated to pinch-hitting duties in September, hitting another three-run homer but otherwise going 0-for-7 to finish with a .182 average in 33 at-bats.

Hundley's career arc was at its apex from 1995 to 1997 as he batted .269 with a .535 slugging average, 86 home runs, and 249 RBIs. He hit only .219 with 35 home runs in his first five seasons, and .217 with 81 home runs over his final six years before retiring after the 2003 campaign.

There are numerous power hitters who have constructed similar arcs in their careers. However, Hundley's great three-year run was tarnished when he was named in the December 2007 Mitchell Report on performance-enhancing drug use in baseball. Former Mets clubhouse attendant Kirk Radomski told investigators he sold Hundley steroids and testosterone three or four times beginning in 1996.

Without the steroid implications, Hundley would be remembered by Mets fans as one of the few reasons to come to Shea in the early to mid-1990s. It was fun to watch him blossom as a hitter at a time the team was wending its way back toward contention. Fans agonized with him as he tried unsuccessfully to master left field, taking one for the team when all he wanted to do was catch.

And just as they did for the New York returns of Carter and Piazza, fans gave Hundley a standing ovation before his first Shea Stadium at-bat as a former Met.

First ML/Mets game @ Padres, 5/18/90
First ML/Mets hit double vs. Bruce Hurst, @ Padres, 5/18/90
First ML/Mets homer solo HR vs. Bill Landrum, Pirates, 9/26/91
First ML/Mets RBI RBI double vs. Rob Dibble, @ Reds, 7/12/90
Most hits, ML/Mets game 4, 6 times
Most homers, ML game 2, 16 times, 4 times with Dodgers and Cubs
Most homers, Mets game 2, 8 times
Most RBI, ML/Mets game 7, @ Giants, 6/18/96
Acquired: Selected in the second round of the 1987 draft.
Deleted: Traded to the Dodgers with Arnold Gooch for Roger Cedeno and Charles Johnson, 12/1/98.
NL All-Star, 1996, 1997

Ron Hunt

Infielder   Bats right, throws right
Born: 2/23/41   St. Louis, Missouri
Height: 6′0″   Weight: 186   #33

Ron Hunt Mets Career

YEAR	GP	AB	R	H	2B	3B	HR	RBI	K	BB	SB	AVG	SLG	OBP
1963	143	533	64	145	28	4	10	42	50	40	5	.272	.396	.334
1964	127	475	59	144	19	6	6	42	30	29	6	.303	.406	.357
1965	57	196	21	47	12	1	1	10	19	14	2	.240	.327	.309
1966	132	479	63	138	19	2	3	33	34	41	8	.288	.355	.356
TOTAL	459	1683	207	474	78	13	20	127	133	124	21	.282	.379	.344

ML Career

YEAR	GP	AB	R	H	2B	3B	HR	RBI	K	BB	SB	AVG	SLG	OBP
63-74	1483	5235	745	1429	223	23	39	370	382	555	65	.273	.347	.368

The 1962 Mets roster included a who's who of one-time great National Leaguers trying to prolong their careers. The team featured Gil Hodges, Richie Ashburn, Frank Thomas, Gus Bell, and Charlie Neal, who combined for 21 All-Star appearances before joining New York's newest National League franchise. The quintet also averaged 34 years of age and contributed to the team's 40–120 record, the worst in modern major league history.

Mets fans came out to watch the former stars while hoping the day would come when the team would acquire a ballplayer that would represent the future. Ed Kranepool debuted for the Mets in September at age 17 but appeared to be a few years away from making an impact in the National League. One month later, the franchise acquired its first young star as Ron Hunt made the team out of 1963 training camp and remained the Mets' best player until he was traded.

Hunt had been toiling in the Braves system since he signed with the ballclub at age 18 in 1959. He batted .295 with 16 home runs for Cedar Rapids of the Class B Three-I League in 1961 and carved out a .309 average for Austin of the Double A Texas League the following season. He earned All-Star honors at second base in 1962 but was buried in an organization that had a strong middle infield at the major league level. The Braves also had Denis Menke and Sparky Anderson playing second for Triple A Toronto.

"I signed with the Milwaukee Braves organization," Hunt began in a September 2011 interview, "and they had a three-year option on me. Jackie and I got married September 16, 1961. That was the happiest day of my life… that's what she tells me to tell everybody!

"In 1962, we went to Louisville, Kentucky, as a Triple A player. I was cut Opening Day and told I was going to Austin, Texas. Now, we weren't making a lot of money, and now I've gotta go home to the trailer we had just rented and tell her we were packing up and going to Austin, Texas.

"We get to Austin around 2:00 or 3:00 PM, and a guy comes out and says, 'Are you Hunt? We're going to put you on a plane for Amarillo, and we'll take care of your wife.' I was gone for two weeks and they didn't take care of my wife. One of the guys' wives—Linda Holmes—that I had played with in the past came to the ballpark, took her and found her an apartment.

"I got off the plane, went to the ballpark, and Jimmy Brown from the old 'Gas House Gang' was the manager. He said, 'You tired.?' I said, 'Yes sir.' He said, 'Do you want to play?' I said, 'Hell yeah, I didn't come here to piss around. I want to play.'

"So I wound up playing, and Solly Hemus was sent out there by the Mets and Mr. Weiss to see me play. I had a pretty good game, a pretty good year, and he put in a word for me, so they purchased my contract to become a Met."

The Braves willingly sold Hunt to the Mets during the 1962 World Series rather than lose him in the minor league draft. The acquisition of Hunt came at the urging of Mets coach Solly Hemus, who watched the young middle infielder while on a scouting assignment.

"I saw the way he hustled and the way he worked hard," Hemus recalled three years later. "You knew they wouldn't scare him out of the big leagues."[82]

Little did Hemus or the Mets know that they had acquired their first young star.

To give you an indication of how highly regarded Hunt was heading into 1963 spring training, he didn't merit a bio in the first edition of the Mets' Yearbook. But he became team owner Joan Payson's favorite player in short time and emerged as the team MVP in a season-ending poll of Mets fans.

Hunt played winter ball before reporting to his first Mets training camp in 1963. Although the Mets committed a ridiculous 39 errors at second base in '62, Hunt found himself very low on the positional depth chart before making the club out of spring training.

"I guess I was No. 7 of seven second basemen," recalled Hunt, "But the winter ball was outstanding because I played 'little ball,' hit behind the runner, bunt, squeeze, drag bunt, sacrifice fly. I had guys down there like Paul Waner, Eddie Stanky, Solly Hemus, Cookie Lavagetto, and then of course, Casey. You bust your ass for Casey and he never forgot you."

Hunt eventually earned the distinction of being the all-time major league leader in hit-by-pitches. He spent his 12-year major league career sacrificing his body at the plate and on the infield, a virtue that also caused him to spend time on the disabled list as a Met. He left his mark in New York as the Mets' first starter in an All-Star game and the team's first player to hit over .300 and qualify for a batting title. But he is best remembered by longtime Mets fans for his non-stop hustle and aw-shucks demeanor, never serving as a self-promoter despite statistics that often dwarfed those of his teammates.

Ronald Kenneth Hunt was born in St. Louis and grew up in Overland, Missouri, where he attended Ritenour High School and lettered in baseball, football, and basketball. He quarterbacked the football team and was an All-Suburban selection in 1958, but his passion was baseball.

"I came from a split home and never lived with my dad," said Hunt. "My Grandpa and Grandma Gronemeyer kind of raised me while my mom worked. He got me started in baseball. He taught me how to throw the ball and hit the ball in the alleys and cobblestone streets of North St. Louis. I hit and he shagged.

"Lee Engert was my high school coach. When I was in grade school at age 13, he put together a little basketball thing after school. That's how I was introduced to him.

"When I was in junior high, to play varsity as a freshman, we had to either walk or take a regular bus to the high school to play. I made the freshman team, me and a buddy by the name of Larry Goodman."

Another influence was Tiny Tipton, a coach who asked Hunt if he'd like to play for the Hudson Beavers, a club made up of players older than Hunt.

Dick Keeley helped Hunt land a contract. He was a scout for the Braves and had envisioned Hunt as a second baseman. The problem was, Bill Wessler already was the starting second baseman on Hunt's team, and a good one at that. Wessler willingly gave up his position to Hunt, who impressed Keeley enough to land a contract with the Braves.

"Buddy Ailsworth was an assistant Legion coach who helped me negotiate my contract with the major league scout because I didn't know what we were doing," Hunt laughed.

Hunt was just 22 when he reported to Mets camp in 1963. He put his scrappiness on display during the exhibition season and made an impression on manager Casey Stengel, who spent much of 1962 trying to convince team president George Weiss to bring him younger talent. Hunt stood out in camp, providing a productive bat while constantly peeling off a dirty uniform after each game. Better still, Hunt could actually field the ball with consistency while demonstrating better-than-average range. Stengel recognized a "gamer" when he saw one, especially after Hunt showed a willingness to play hurt in an exhibition game.

"I had just twisted my ankle," said Hunt. "I was on the bench. This was before we broke camp in '63. I had a pretty bad ankle. I was working it out, working it out. And the sonuvabitch was just throbbing like hell.

"I was sitting on the bench and had it propped up. Casey comes down the bench and he said, 'Can you play?' I said, 'Yeah.' So he goes along on his way.

"Three or four innings go by and he comes over and says, 'Can you hit?' I said, 'Yeah.'

"He said, 'Okay, I'll tell you what. The pitcher leads off the next inning. I want you to pinch-hit. You go up there, you get on base, I'll get you a pinch-runner.' I said, 'Okay.'

"So I went up. And by God, I dribbled one up the middle for a base hit. I got down to first base. He called time, got me a pinch-runner.

"I got back to the bench. My leg was just throbbing like a sonuvabitch. I sit down and prop my leg up. And here he comes, walking down the bench. I looked up at him. He looked down at me and he winked. And kept walking.

"And that was it. Whether that prompted me breaking camp with the club on the major league roster as a bullpen catcher or not, I don't know. But I'd venture to say it didn't hurt."[83]

It took a few games before Hunt was able to pry himself off the bench. Another young newcomer, Larry Burright, hit just .190 in 21 at-bats while starting the Mets' first six games at second base. Hunt didn't see any action in those games as the Mets remained winless, prompting him to ask Stengel for a meeting.

"I ran across Casey in Connie Mack Stadium in Philadelphia, and I said, 'Casey? Ron Hunt, No. 33.' The reason you'd say it that way is because Casey knew everybody by number, not by name. He was asked why one time, and he said, 'Because the numbers are always here. The names change.'

"I said, 'Can I talk to you?' and he said 'Sure, kid.' I said, 'I'd like to play. The guy you've got playing second base now isn't doing a very good job offensively and defensively, and maybe this would be a good time to see if I can play here or not.' He said, 'Son, you want to play that bad? Okay, you play tomorrow.' And that's how I got my start."

Stengel was impressed with the kid's nerve and put him in the starting lineup for the first time April 16 at Cincinnati. Hunt and Duke Snider provided the lone offensive highlights for the Mets as they dropped a 7–4 decision to the Reds. Hitting second in the lineup, Hunt walked in his first at-bat before lining a single off Jim Maloney in the fourth inning for his first major league hit. He reached on a run-scoring error in the fifth and came home on Jim Hickman's double before Snider's two-run blast capped a four-run rally that got the Mets within 6–4. Hunt said he finished the game 4-for-4 while playing errorless ball at second, although baseball-reference.com notes he was 2-for-3.

He went 0-for-4 the next game as the Mets lost 5–0 at Cincinnati to fall to 0–8 heading into a four-game set at the Polo Grounds against the Braves, Hunt's former team. Mets fans didn't get a chance to see Hunt play in the team's first homestand and were hoping the club wouldn't match its 0–9 start of 1962. Hunt failed to impress the home crowd in his first at-bat, grounding into an inning-ending double play in the first inning. But he had them cheering by the end of the day.

Hunt singled in the third and laced an RBI triple that put the Mets ahead 3–0 in the fourth. Meanwhile, Roger Craig carried a four-hit shutout into the eighth until Len Gabrielson hit a leadoff single and scored on Hank Aaron's two-run homer. Don Dillard added an RBI double to knot the score in the eighth.

Tracy Stallard relieved Craig and got out of the inning by getting Joe Torre to pop up to Hunt. But Stallard issued a bases-loaded walk to Eddie Mathews in the ninth to give the Braves their first lead, putting the Mets within three outs of their second straight 0–9 start.

Choo Choo Coleman led off the bottom of the ninth with a single, and Hickman doubled him to third with one out, putting the winning run in scoring position with Hunt at the plate. Hunt capped his three-hit, three-RBI game with a game-ending, two-run double to become the Mets' first hero of the season.

Payson showed her appreciation by sending a floral bouquet to Hunt and his wife, Jackie, at their Manhattan apartment after the game. Unfortunately, Hunt spent the next several hours dealing with an allergic reaction to the flowers.

"I had trouble breathing most all my life," said Hunt. "I had hay fever, took shots and everything. But I got over it, and we thanked Mrs. Payson personally for the gesture."

The Mets completed a four-game sweep of his ex-team as Hunt went 1-for-8 with an RBI and three walks in the final three games. He hit .280 while playing every inning of an ensuing six-game road trip to solidify his spot as the team's new second baseman.

Hunt was playing well enough for Stengel and Weiss to decide their rookie second baseman deserved a raise.

"You want to know how much I made as a rookie?" Hunt asked. "Seven thousand dollars. That was the rookie salary. Casey called me in the office about a month into the season and he said, 'Son, you need a raise.' I said, 'Yes, sir.' He said, 'How's $500 sound?' I said, 'Is that $500 a month?' He said, 'No! That's 500 a year.' So I called my wife and she said, 'We'll take it!'"[84]

Hunt received folk hero status at the Polo Grounds for his rough-and-tumble style. He was by far the most exciting player on a team that compiled a .219 batting average and finished 51–111. He endeared himself to fans with his belly-flop slides and daring base-running. He stole home against the Dodgers by kicking the ball out of catcher Doug Camilli's mitt, and had no aversion to bunting for a base hit with two strikes. Best of all, Hunt was trying to inject some spirit into an offense that had no life. Mets fans eventually grew to cherish him once they knew him.

"Let me tell you about the first Met fan I ran across," Hunt said. "I'm coming down the steps out there in center field at the Polo Grounds. I'm about halfway down the steps when this young voice yelled out , '33!' I looked up, and I'm looking in the eyes of a 12-year-old kid thinking maybe he wants my autograph. And he says, 'Whose reject are you?'"

New Yorkers have always appreciated a player who hustled, and no one hustled more than Ron Hunt. That allowed him to become the most popular player on the '63 Mets.

"They taught me I.O.U.s," Hunt said of the Mets fans. "Make sure you're clean and green on the I.O.U.s.

"The fans were regular Joe Blow fans, just like me. They were the old Giants and Dodgers fans, and when those teams left town, we inherited a lot of the fans. They stuck with us even though we didn't play the best ball in the world. And we didn't have too many suits in the stands. It was mostly working class, and I guess that's why they looked at me because I had to work hard for what I got and what I did.

"Duke Snider took me under his wing and gave me a chance to learn from a veteran. A couple of other guys on the team had the same opportunity but chose not to do it. But Duke taught me the mental aspect of the game and the dos and don'ts. Then I went out and tried them, and I guess that's why Duke kind of helped me that year. I never forgot it."

Despite his nonstop motor and incredible on-field intensity, at least one teammate thought Hunt had the facial features of someone trying to stay awake. Unlike the modern-day David Wrights and Jose Reyes, Hunt rarely smiled on the field and didn't feel fraternizing with opponents was part of his job description.

"I used to call him Nap-Time," said Mets pitcher Roger Craig in 1965. "He's got those sleepy eyelids. He looks like he is always about to fall off for an hour's nap.

"That's until he gets on the field. Then he doesn't miss a thing."[85]

Hunt reeled off a 12-game hitting streak and reached base in 17 consecutive games. He was hitting .314 with a .395 on-base percentage by May 17 before a 13-for-78 slump from May 22 to June 12 dropped his average to .251. But unlike numerous wannabe Mets prospects, Hunt bounced back to hit .284 with seven home runs, 28 RBIs, and 45 runs scored in his final 90 games to finishing with a .272 average, a .351 on-base percentage, 10 homers, 28 doubles, 42 ribbies, and 64 runs scored. Hunt led the team in batting, runs, hits, and doubles while becoming the first Met under age 25 to appear in more than 140 games. He was also hit by a pitch for the first time on April 21 by Claude Raymond of the Braves. Ironically, the two were teammates with the Expos when Hunt set what was the major league record for hit-by-pitches in a season eight years later.

Hunt lost the NL Rookie of the Year award to another scrappy, hustling second baseman. Pete Rose collected 17 of 20 first-place votes while Hunt claimed two and Phillies pitcher Ray Culp captured the other. Hunt had to settle for runner-up status despite providing more homers and RBIs than Rose while hitting only one point lower than the eventual all-time hit king.

"I wouldn't trade my experience for Pete's because of the upbringing I got in New York by the fans and Duke Snider, Casey Stengel, Solly Hemus, Eddie Stanky, and Paul Waner," Hunt said. "I might not have ever met them with another team. And they're the ones who took a liking to me."

Hemus was in attendance when Ron and Jackie held a 50th anniversary party in Missouri in September 2011.

"I went up to Solly and asked him, 'What brought me to your attention?' He said, 'Because you played the way I did.'

"The Mets on the field treated me good. Off the field, the fans treated me really good."

Hunt was already earning the admiration of opposing players and managers for his hard-nosed style.

"He's a tough kid," said Phillies skipper Gene Mauch. "Somebody might punch him in the nose, but before he's through he might make $40,000 or $50,000 for a long time. It might be worth a few socks."[86]

Hunt's salary wasn't close to those figures in 1963, causing him and Jackie to scrimp on living arrangements as he established himself in the majors.

"We had to stay over in New Jersey because we couldn't afford everything in New York," Hunt recalled. "We were only making $7,000 living in Manhattan, so we had to look for places that Jackie and I could afford, and then we worked for a living during the winter when we came home to Missouri.

"We stayed in Fort Lee, New Jersey, and then we stayed in Maspeth in a basement apartment with the Piazza family. He cut my hair a couple of times and said, 'By the way, we have a basement apartment that we'd like to rent out to you.' So the next morning, all the kids in the neighborhood came knocking on the door and asked, 'Can Ronnie come out and play catch?'"

The 1964 campaign would be Hunt's finest in the majors. He hit .477 with a .521 on-base percentage during a season-high 11-game hitting streak from June 9 through June 19, putting him among the league leaders in batting at .338 by the end of the streak. Hunt batted .350 for the month and carried a .324 average into July, but the Mets spent most of the first three months trying to stay ahead of their wretched 1962 pace. However, Hunt's opponents took notice of his fine hitting and gritty play, naming him to the starting lineup for the All-Star Game at Shea Stadium.

"I guess Casey had a big thing to do with that," Hunt said of his starting nod. "I think we were in Pittsburgh when the stats came out, and I was leading Bill Mazeroski. Casey said, 'If they don't vote this kid as the best All-Star second baseman in the league this year, they're stupid because he is having one helluva year.'

"And then they asked me about Mazeroski, and I said Mazeroski is an idol just like Red Schoendienst is an idol and Alvin Dark was an idol. These were guys I looked up to because of the way they played. I told them, 'As far as I'm concerned, I'm having a better year than he is and I should be the second baseman.'"

Hunt received a standing ovation at the Midsummer Classic as he stepped to the plate for the first time leading off the bottom of the third. He singled off Dean Chance but was stranded at second to end the inning, keeping the AL ahead 1–0. Hunt grounded out in the fifth inning and struck out in the seventh before the American League carried a 4–3 lead into the bottom of the ninth.

Hunt was due to bat fifth in the ninth inning, which would have given him a chance to play the hero in front of his fans. Willie Mays opened the frame with a walk against Dick Radatz, stole second, and scored the tying run on Orlando Cepeda's single. Cepeda moved into scoring position on a throwing error by first baseman Joe Pepitone, and Ken Boyer popped out before AL skipper Al Lopez elected to walk Johnny Edwards intentionally to set up a potential meeting between Radatz and Hunt.

Hunt never got a chance to face Radatz as manager Walter Alston sent up Hank Aaron as a pinch-hitter. Aaron struck out for the second out before Johnny Callison's three-run blast gave the NL a 7–4 victory. For Hunt, it was

Ron Hunt made an appearance at the Shea Stadium finale, September 28, 2008. Photo courtesy of Oscar W. Gabriel

a rare opportunity to celebrate a victory after the Mets opened the season winning just 21 of the 76 games in which he appeared.

Hunt cooled off a bit the rest of July but kept his batting average above .300 the rest of the season. He was hitting .309 until he was injured during a 6–5 win over the Dodgers on September 4, causing him to miss 15 games. He returned to the lineup on September 23 and went 0-for-9 in three games before sitting out the last eight games.

A great example of Hunt's determination occurred during a 1964 game against the Braves. He was on third base when Frank Thomas grounded to third with one out. Hunt waited for the Braves to start a potential inning-ending double play before breaking for the plate.

Second baseman Frank Bolling saw Hunt heading home and threw to catcher Ed Bailey, beating Hunt by about 30 feet. Rather than give up on the play, the 185-

pound Hunt leveled the 210-pound Bailey, sending both players through the air.

Bailey countered by throwing a punch at Hunt, sparking a benches-clearing incident that led to Menke slamming Stengel to the ground after the 73-year-old manager climbed onto his back.

"Oh, my God," thought Menke, "I've killed Casey Stengel."[87] Menke picked up Stengel and apologized.

"The pile broke up, and the fight was over," Rod Kanehl remembered. "Bobby Bragen was the Milwaukee manager. The writers came in and said, 'Bragan says you're just a bunch of pop-offs and showboats and you can't play ball so you have to fight instead.' They asked me about it, and I said, 'You don't see any blood in this locker room, do you? Go over and check their locker room.'"[88]

No one was more appreciative of Hunt's will to win than his skipper.

"Sure, he took a chance," Stengel said about Hunt's base running. "Sure, he ran into the catcher. What did you want him to do, get tagged like a goddamn fairy? We got enough guys on the team who'll tippy-toe up to the catcher and say, 'Oooh, pardon me, I'm out.'"[89]

Hunt finished with a .303 average, three points higher than teammate Joe Christopher. Hunt finished second to Christopher on the club in hits (144), doubles (19), runs scored (59), on-base percentage (.359), and slugging (.406) as New York finished 53–109, only a two-win improvement over 1963.

It would be another 32 years before the Mets had a pair of teammates hit .300 or better in the same season while qualifying for a batting title. Hunt's average remained a club record until Cleon Jones batted .340 in 1969.

Hunt's fielding percentage improved in 1964, one year after he led all NL second basemen with 26 errors in 144 games. He committed just 12 miscues in 109 games in '64 and turned a higher rate of double plays. Hunt received a 10th-place vote in the MVP balloting to finish in a tie for 25th. The lone vote made him the first player from a National League expansion team to receive any MVP consideration.

Hunt continued to play the game with reckless abandon in 1965, and his style finally cost him significant playing time. He injured a finger playing handball in the winter of 1965 and was unable to make his season debut until April 30, when he went 1-for-3 and scored the Mets' lone run in a 6–1 loss to the Reds. Hunt went 7-for-13 with two hit-by-pitches in his first four games, proving the finger was no longer a problem.

The Mets were hosting the Cardinals on May 11 when Hunt was involved in a collision with second baseman Phil Gagliano in the fifth inning. Hunt was trying to grab a ground ball when Gagliano plowed into him, causing a severely separated shoulder that sickened his manager and the team doctor.

"The bone was out of the shoulder," said Stengel after the game. "You wish he wouldn't play so hard to get hurt, but that's what he is, a tough player."

"I had to hold my thumb on the bone to keep it from cracking through the skin," added Dr. Peter LaMotte.[90]

There was a good chance Hunt would be lost for the season after such a gruesome injury. Instead, he was back by August 2, playing with the Mets in an exhibition game against Double A Williamsport, and was on the active roster three days later. New York went 25–57 without Hunt en route to a 50–112 record, the second-worst in team history.

The injury occurred just as the Mets were giving many of their younger players a chance to shine. A 20-year-old Kranepool was the Mets' lone All-Star representative, and a 21-year-old Ron Swoboda set a team rookie record with 19 home runs. Tug McGraw and Bud Harrelson also made their major league debuts in 1965, but the club really missed Hunt's spark during a nearly three-month stretch that saw Stengel step down as manager due to a broken hip.

Meanwhile, the Mets' grounds crew worked hard to get Hunt into shape.

"They shagged for me," said Hunt. "They pitched to me. In fact, Weiss sent a message to them that they couldn't do that anymore. I went up to see Mr. Weiss and said, 'I'm trying to get in shape and get back in the game, and these guys are trying to help me. And you're telling me they can't help me at all? How the hell am I going to get back in shape?'

"He sent a message back to them saying, 'It's okay to help Hunt out but you get your damn work done, too.'"

It was another case where the "little man" was befriending Hunt. He recognized the help of the grounds crew especially Pete Flynn and a guy he nicknamed "Bubbles."

Hunt appeared in only 57 games the entire season, batting .240 with 12 doubles and 21 runs scored. Kranepool and Swoboda cooled off considerably in the second half, McGraw lost seven of his nine decisions, and Harrelson did little to persuade new manager Wes Westrum to make him the starting shortstop over veteran Roy McMillan. But the Mets held firm on their new philosophy to bring in young talent in the spring of 1966, giving Cleon Jones a chance to become the starting center fielder.

It took a while for Hunt to get into a hitting groove in 1966. He batted only .220 through his first 14 games before producing seven multi-hit games in his next eight contests, batting a robust .471 during that span to hike his average up to .321.

Hunt opened a series at San Francisco in late May by going 6-for-6 with a walk, two hit-by-pitches and two runs scored in the first two games to lift his season average to .347. He was 3-for-3 in the second game of the series, supplying a two-run single in the fifth and a tiebreaking, three-run homer in the eighth to lead the Mets to a 7–5 victory. The outcome gave New York a 12–14 record and put them within 6½ games of the first-place Giants, lofty heights for a team that averaged 113 losses in its first four seasons.

Hunt was named to the National League All-Star team for the second time in three years, making him the first Met to go to the Midsummer Classic on two occasions. Hunt replaced Jim Lefebvre in the sixth inning and went 0-for-1 with a sacrifice as the NL pulled out a 2–1 victory in 10 innings. Hunt's bunt in the bottom of the 10th moved Tim McCarver to second before Maury Wills singled home McCarver with the winning run.

The Mets finished out of the cellar for the first time in club history, ending up ninth with a 66–95 record. Hunt was the offensive catalyst, leading the Mets with a .288 average, a .356 on-base percentage and 138 hits while finishing second with 63 runs scored, and 19 doubles. Hunt also paced the team with 11 hit-by-pitches, marking the third time in four seasons he reached double-digits in that category. Forty-five years later, Hunt said he didn't feel any great sense of vindication by coming back from a tough injury.

"I never thought about it," Hunt said. "I just did my job, and my job was to play the best I could and keep the job that I was given and earned. And you did that by maybe shortening the swing or shortening the arm swing at second because of the injury. You just did it.

"I took over the position [in '63] from a guy who wasn't having a good start to the season, and I didn't want to give it up. I just went out there and busted my ass."

Weiss stepped down as the team's de facto general manager after the 1966 season, leaving Bing Devine to mold the roster over the winter. One of Devine's first moves was getting rid of the Mets' most popular player.

Hunt and Jim Hickman were sent to the Dodgers for Tommy Davis and Derrell Griffith on November 29, 1966. Davis was a two-time All-Star and a two-time NL batting champ, but the trade was not welcomed by Mets fans that had made Hunt the face of the franchise. Davis was two years older than Hunt and was just two seasons removed from a serious ankle injury that robbed him of his exceptional speed. The deal also left the Mets with a second base platoon of Eddie Bressoud and Chuck Hiller. The problem was, the Mets neglected to tell Hunt of the trade.

"Dick Young got a hold of me," Hunt said. "He was the one who told me I was traded. The Mets front office didn't even bother to call me. I get a call from Dick Young asking, 'What do you think of the trade?' I said, 'I don't know a damn thing about a trade. What are you talking about?' He told me I was traded to the Dodgers for Tommy Davis, and I said, 'Well, this is a helluva way to find out. Why the hell are you calling me for and not the Mets?' I thought that was pretty horseshit.

"I approached Mrs. Payson when I came into town later. She was sitting down, and I went over to her, took my hat off as a courtesy and said, 'Mrs. Payson? Ron Hunt. I thought it was pretty bad that you all would trade me and not even bother to call me after the four years I put down here one way or the other.' She said she didn't know and was sorry."

Hunt had every reason to be elated with the trade. The Dodgers were coming off a National League pennant after winning the World Series in 1963 and '65. Los Angeles was also a combined 150½ games better than the Mets since Hunt broke in with New York in 1963.

But Hunt was not happy about leaving New York. The quiet man from Missouri had developed roots in Queens and hoped to be around when the Mets finally became contenders. As it was, the trade failed to elevate the Mets' progress as they finished 61–101 despite Davis, who led the Mets in batting, homers, and RBIs. Through Young's column in the *Daily News*, Hunt was able to thank Mets fans for their support.

"To my friends in New York: I want to thank you for all the happiness you have given my family and me," Hunt began. "Everything I have or hope to have, I owe to the most wonderful people in the world—the New York fans.

"It wasn't my desire to leave the Mets. I came up with the Mets, and I wanted to be a part of the ballclub and give the Met fans a winning team that they deserve.

"My thanks to the Mets' front office for giving me the first opportunity to play, especially Solly Hemus and Casey Stengel. And by no means least, thanks to the sportswriters and announcers of New York for their helping hand. Without it, no one would have known about me in the first place. I sure hate to leave nice people. C'mon out. I'll see you at Shea when the Dodgers come to town."[91]

Hunt had an okay season with the Dodgers, hitting .263 with a .344 on-base percentage, three homers, 33 RBIs, and a team-high 10 hit-by pitches. But his average represented a 25-point drop over 1966, and he failed to crack the team's top three in any offensive category. However, he struck out just 24 times in 442 plate appearances to remain one of the league's toughest players to fan.

The Dodgers finished a very disappointing 73–89 in 1967 and moved quickly to alter the roster. The Dodgers dealt Hunt just before the start of 1968 spring training, sending him and middle infielder Nate Oliver to the Giants for catcher Tom Haller and a minor leaguer. The trade did nothing to move the Dodgers back into contention, but it helped San Francisco finish second each of the next two seasons.

Hunt was durable in 1968 despite continuing to sacrifice his body at the plate. He appeared in 148 games and scored 79 runs, both career highs at that point. Although his batting average was a pedestrian .250, his on-base percentage was .371 as he walked a career-high 78 times and led the league with 25 hit-by-pitches. It was the first of seven straight seasons in which Hunt paced the league in hit-by-pitches, accumulating 192 of his 243 HBPs during that span.

One of Hunt's biggest hits of the season was a solo homer in the first inning against the Cardinals on September 17. It was the only run scored in Gaylord Perry's no-hitter.

"I hit it off Robert Gibson," said Hunt.

Hunt had two more strong years with the Giants and received MVP consideration in 1969. He batted .262 with a .361 on-base percentage in '69 and hit .281 with a .394 OBP the following season. Hunt also was hit by 51 pitches over those two seasons while providing 40 doubles, 82 RBIs, and 142 runs scored.

The Giants finished a distant third to the Reds in 1970 and were ready to unleash a new keystone combo. Chris Speier was the shortstop-in-waiting, and second baseman Tito Fuentes was biding his time as a utilityman in '70. The Giants cleared out second base for Fuentes by sending Hunt to the Expos for Dave McDonald on December 30.

The deal initially seemed to put Hunt back in expansion hell as the Expos prepared for their third major league season. It didn't take Hunt long to become one of Montreal's favorite players, just as he was with the expansion Mets.

Hunt managed to play a career-high 152 games for the 1971 Expos despite setting a major league record with 50 hit-by-pitches. His desire to disregard his body led to a .402 on-base percentage, topped only by Mays, Joe Torre, and Aaron among National Leaguers that season. Hunt also hit .279 and established career highs with 89 runs and a .759 OPS while helping the Expos climb out of the cellar.

The hit-by-pitch total was staggering. Hunt was plunked once per 12.76 plate appearances yet sat out only 10 games the entire season. To put his HBP total in perspective, the next seven players among the NL season leaders combined for only 49, with teammate Rusty Staub finishing second in the league with just nine. Hunt credited an ex-Met for his career-altering decision to crowd the plate.

"Gil Hodges was there in spring training in '63," Hunt began, "and he was talking to one of the other veterans about his philosophy on hitting. It was to the effect that he had trouble with the outside two inches of the plate, but the rest of the plate was his.

"With San Francisco, it was kind of cold out there to play, so you wore extra clothing, which kind of hindered your swing and being loose. So I was a little tighter. I choked up on the bat a little bit more and was having trouble getting around, so I moved a little bit away from the plate and had trouble with that.

"So I crowded that plate and thought, 'If that worked for Gil Hodges with the outside of the plate, why wouldn't it work for me with the inside of the plate.' So I crowded the plate, bloused my uniform, choked up on the bat and worked in front of a mirror. In 12 years, I never got called for getting hit on purpose. So, the first two inside inches of the plate was theirs if they could hit it. The rest of the plate was mine, and if they didn't hit the two inches, they hit me.

"I remember Casey saying years before that if you get hit by a pitch and it leads to the winning run, you get $50 or a suit of clothes. And his tailor was pretty horseshit, so we took the money. But that's how I started taking the

pitches and getting on base. Even though I wasn't a speedster, with the idea of my leading off, the other ballplayers could see a lot of pitches, how they were throwing and why they would hit me and put me on the base. Especially with the Giants, where you had guys like Bobby Bonds, Willie Mays, Willie McCovey, Jim Ray Hart, and Jim Davenport coming up behind me."

The Expos produced another losing season in 1972 as Hunt batted .253 with a league-high 26 hit-by-pitches in 129 games. But the ballclub was closer to respectability as Ken Singleton, Tim Foli, and Mike Jorgensen became major contributors after coming to Montreal from the Mets for Rusty Staub. The team took another step in 1973 after promoting highly touted pitching prospect Steve Rogers from the minors.

An injury limited Hunt to 113 games in 1973, his fewest since 1967. But he provided an offensive spark for the Expos that season, hitting .309 with 24 HBPs and career-highs of 10 stolen bases and a .418 on-base percentage.

The Expos hovered near the .500 mark most of the season, which was good enough to stay in contention for the division title. Hunt appeared in 100 of the Expos' first 103 games through July, hitting .305 with a .420 on-base percentage and 57 runs scored.

Hunt continued his solid hitting into the first week of August. He went 3-for-3 with a walk while scoring the only runs in a 2–0 victory over the Cardinals on August 2, and provided a pair of two-hit games in a three-game sweep of the Cubs the next series. But Hunt suffered a knee injury while trying to score against the Giants on August 8, putting him out of commission the rest of the month and leaving the Expos without their top hitter for average. Montreal immediately felt his loss by losing their next seven games against lefty hurlers.

The Expos were still in the thick of the division race when Hunt returned to poke a pinch-hit double in a 12–0 rout of Philadelphia on September 2. The victory gave the Expos a 65–70 record but put them within 3½ games of the NL East lead.

Hunt and the Expos hosted the Mets in a three-game set at Montreal. Hunt went 3-for-7 in the series to lift his average to .309, but he also suffered a season-ending knee injury in the finale while trying to avoid an outfield collision. Hunt underwent surgery to repair torn cartilage, diminishing Montreal's offense for the stretch run. He received a top-10 vote in the MVP balloting after the season.

Without Hunt, the Expos split their last 20 games to finish 79–83, 3½ games behind the division-winning Mets. Many Montreal fans feel the team would have been a division champion in only its fifth season had Hunt been able to play more than 13 of the Expos' final 58 games.

"If you start thinking about winning and losing, you're probably going to lose a lot more than you win," Hunt said of the '73 Expos' ability to sneak up on the rest of the NL East. "You just go out there and play the game, and you've just got to take one game at a time. I think that's what we did, and everything was clicking for us.

"And then I slid into a catcher. I had a chance of running the guy over in San Francisco or sliding into him. I'd seen the ball right in the glove and tried to slide. I hit his knee, and I guess I stuck him with my spikes. When he rolled, he broke my knee.

"I tried to come back with therapy, wrapping and some of those cortisone shots, but that didn't work."

The '73 season was one of several in which Hunt had a chance to earn a postseason berth. The Giants also continued while Hunt was in San Francisco but didn't make the playoffs until the year after he left the ballclub.

"That's the only thing I missed in my 12 years; not getting a chance to play in the postseason to see if my ass would get as tight as some of the others," said Hunt.

The Expos failed to improve in 1974 and were out of postseason contention by late summer despite Hunt, who hit .268 with a .375 on-base percentage while serving as the team's leadoff hitter and third baseman. He put together a 10-game hitting streak in June and batted .435 in 10 games from June 23 through July 1 to raise his average to .280.

The Cardinals were the only team in line to battle the Pirates for the NL East championship by September. The Redbirds tried to fortify their pennant push by claiming Hunt off waivers on September 5, giving the team a dependable utility player with a high on-base percentage. But the Expos, like the 1966 Mets, weren't very forthright in telling Hunt of their plans to move him.

"I was sitting on the bench during a Cardinal game in St. Louis, and the score is 3–2 Cardinals. I had a chance to pinch-hit in the seventh inning and didn't. I had a chance to pinch-hit in the ninth inning and didn't," Hunt remembered.

"So I waited on the bench until everybody cleared, and I went over to Gene Mauch and said, 'What's going on?' He said, 'I don't know.'

"I walk into the clubhouse and all of my stuff's already packed."

The move gave Hunt the opportunity to play close to home for the first time in his career. He delivered a pinch-hit in extra innings for the Cardinals against the Pirates on September 17 but went 4-for-23 with St. Louis to end up with a .263 average for the season. Hunt claimed his seventh straight hit-by-pitch title with 16, marking the 11th time in 12 seasons he was plunked at least 10 times.

"I went to spring training with the Cardinals in '75," Hunt recalled. "They wanted me to be the backup to Ted Sizemore, and I said I had no problem with that. But then they wanted me to take a salary cut, and I said, 'No, we ain't doing that.' In those days, when you're busting your ass to make a living, I could make that much and be home. So they didn't want to do anything [with the contract], and I quit.

"And then they tried to screw me out of my severance pay. The general manager of the Cardinals at that time was Bing Devine. He called me in and said, 'We're going to let you go if you want to hook up with another team. We're going to give you four or five thousand dollars.'

"I said, 'I don't think that's right. I'll come back tomorrow.' So I called [union chief] Marvin Miller, and he said, 'Oh, no, they owe you $10,000.'

"I walked in the next day, and Devine already had the check. I said, 'You're trying to screw me, aren't you?' So I left…and left them a $19 motel bill.

"Like I said about the I.O.U.s, you try not to forget them and you don't want to owe.

"I got a call from Hank Aaron saying he wanted me to manage in the minors in Johnson City, Tennessee. I said, 'Hank, is that a bus league?' He said, 'Sort of,' and I said, 'Sort of, my ass. It either is or it isn't. I ain't going back to no bus league.'

"I think the Orioles called me and Oakland called me. Oakland wanted me to be the backup to a new second baseman they had."

The A's wanted Hunt to go to the minors, but he felt he would be of more value staying in the majors and helping the rookie get over the rough patches.

"They didn't want to do that, and I told them I wasn't going back to the minors. So that was it," he said.

"My wife and I had been together since I was 15, and we were both getting a little pissed off about the way some of the things were being handled. And I thought I was owed a little more respect than that."

Hunt continues to lend his baseball expertise to fledgling players. He began a baseball camp on his sprawling property in Missouri, designing a facility comparable to those on many college campuses. He did it for his love and respect for the game as he tried to further the careers of young players.

"I no longer have the camps, but I do clinics," Hunt said. "The Mets—when Nelson Doubleday was there—allowed me to use Shea Stadium to help me raise money and didn't charge me a lot. When this other guy [Fred Wilpon], took over, hell, he wanted $50,000 when all I made was about $12,000.

"I travel and do clinics for free, but with the fundraisers and everything that I used to have, I don't have anymore, so I have to charge them for room and board and expenses. And I travel wherever they want me to go as long as they pay the freight. But I don't make anything.

"It's called the Ron Hunt Eagles Baseball Association. We had a baseball program for 18 years in which I recruited ballplayers. I had a friend by the name of Bob Hopps who organized clinics in East Brunswick, New Jersey, for New York kids as payback for the fans. And then I organized clinics and camps for the Montreal Expos—who were very good to us off the field—up there for fans that I needed to pay back, I thought.

"I did it for 18 years, and [the players] came out here and lived with us. We had 24 kids from out of state and out of country, and we had about the same amount locally.

We built an infield on our front yard—we've got 110 acres here. We use Barn 2, which is where I have a working farm with cattle. We used Barn 2 and put lights there so we can take indoor batting practice. We raised pretty close to $100,000 to build a ballfield in what is now called Lake St. Louis, and we gave the ballpark back to them when we were done.

"We probably got about 98 percent of our kids into college with some kind of scholarship help. And also, coaches that came in here from college, I allowed them to use my name as a reference for any college that they wanted to get a job with. I'd have them call me, and I'd be more than happy to tell them what I thought of their coaching abilities.

"We had two kids per position and eight pitchers, and in the 18 years that we ran the program—we stopped in about 2003, I think—we didn't piss one arm away. We didn't allow them to throw sliders. We didn't allow them to throw the curveball unless they threw it correctly. We counted pitches and we just asked the pitchers point blank from Day One, 'What do you think your best pitch is?' One of them said 'the slider' and another said 'curveball.' I said, 'No, your best pitch is a strike. Your second best pitch is location, and then if you can change speeds with location, you're in pretty good shape. And then if you want to throw the curveball, fine, but you've got to throw it correctly, and you're not going to overuse it."

Hunt said he received a lot of help from longtime Mets executive Bob Mandt, an original member of the team's front office who died in October 2010. "He helped me organize a fundraiser with Ray Lammie, who was a member of the fantasy campers. Without Lammie, my fundraisers wouldn't have been as great.

"He put together a fundraiser for me at KeySpan Park in Brooklyn. Ray passed away a couple of years ago, so my fundraisers kind of went to hell because he was organizing it and getting players. After Ray passed, I learned how many times he contributed to the fundraisers without telling me about it."

Hunt also credited the old-time Mets fans for prolonging the success of his camp.

"The ones before 'suits.' Those are the ones that I got to know on and off the field. We made most of our friends off the field. In fact, when Jackie and I had our 50th wedding anniversary, we had a shindig here in which 10 people came from different states."

Hunt's courtship with Jackie began with the same hustle and smarts he displayed on major league diamonds. Their relationship led to three children and three grandchildren.

"I used to ride a bike over to my buddy's house, leave the bike and tell her, 'I just walked five miles to date you.'"

Hunt left the game with a major league-leading 243 hit-by-pitches, 45 more than then runner-up Frank Robinson. His single-season record of 50 HBPs remains a major league record, 15 more than runner-up Don Baylor. But

Baylor eventually surpassed Hunt's all-time mark before Craig Biggio retired with a major league-record 285.

There is a push to get Hunt inducted into the Mets Hall of Fame, an honor that appears to be long overdo considering his accomplishments during the early days of the ballclub. Never a politician, Hunt isn't overly concerned about the possibility of being inducted since he already knows his place in history and realizes how much he was appreciated by the fans.

"I just figured if I was worthy of it in the minds of whoever is voting for it, then I should have it," Hunt said. "If not, I'm not worried about it. I played the game clean. I never used any dope. I was never on pot. I never did steroids.

"In the beginning of the Mets, just because we didn't win a pennant didn't mean we didn't bust our ass. Besides that, those people need to say 'thank you' to those fans that came out and paid to watch us play, because they wouldn't have had the money to take those kids they kept in the minors and bring them up when they were ready.

"If they want to do anything, they can invite me back to sit in the stands with the fans and say 'hi' to the regular fans.

"The fun that we had there, I wouldn't trade for anything."

The appreciation fans had for Hunt grew from watching him play hard. He was the team's singular ray of hope in 1963, and remained the franchise's only two-time All-Star until Tom Seaver in 1967 and '68. Hunt said all he was trying to do was make an honest living.

"I went through life thinking that if I don't do the job, then somebody is going to do it for me, so why don't I do it well. If they like me, they like me. If they don't, they don't. If I show off and pout and dog it, they have a reason not to play me. I tried not to give them that reason."

First ML game	@ Reds, 4/16/63
First ML hit	single vs. Jim Maloney, @ Reds, 4/16/63
First ML homer	solo HR vs. Bob Buhl, @ Cubs, 4/24/63
First ML RBI	RBI triple vs. Bob Shaw, Braves, 4/19/63
Most hits, ML game	4, 13 times, 4 times with Giants and Expos
Most hits, Mets game	4, @ Reds, 6/14/63; @ Cubs, 5/26/64; @ Braves, 6/28/64
Most homers, ML game	1, 39 times
Most homers, Mets game	1, 20 times
Most RBI, ML game	6, Giants @ Reds, 4/18/70
Most RBI, Mets game	5, @ Giants, 5/20/66

Acquired: Sold by the Braves, 10/11/62.

Deleted: Traded to the Dodgers with Jim Hickman for Tommy Davis and Derrell Griffith, 11/29/66.

NL All-Star, 1964, 1966

NL Hit by Pitcher Leader, 1968, 1969, 1970, 1971, 1972, 1973, 1974

Al Jackson

Pitcher   Bats left, throws left
Born: 12/25/35   Waco, Texas
Height: 5'10"   Weight: 160   #15, #38

Al Jackson Mets Career

YEAR	GP/GS	IP	H	R	ER	K	BB	W–L	SV	ERA
1962	36/33	231.1	244	132	113	118	78	8–20	0	4.40
1963	37/34	227.0	237	128	100	142	84	13–17	1	3.96
1964	40/31	213.1	229	115	101	112	60	11–16	1	4.26
1965	37/31	205.1	217	111	99	120	61	8–20	1	4.34
1968	25/9	92.2	88	42	38	59	17	3–7	3	3.69
1969	9/0	11.0	18	13	13	10	4	0–0	0	10.64
Total	184/138	980.2	1033	541	464	561	304	43–80	6	4.26

Mets Career/Batting

GP	AB	R	H	2B	3B	HR	RBI	K	BB	SB	AVG
235	313	26	46	9	1	1	14	108	7	0	.147

ML Career

YEAR	GP/GS	IP	H	R	ER	K	BB	W–L	SV	ERA
59–69	302/184	1389.1	1449	725	614	738	407	67–99	10	3.98

No one has represented the Mets with more class and humor than Alvin Neill Jackson, who has been with the organization for the better part of the last 50 years. He was the team's best hurler during the early days of the franchise and has served tirelessly as a pitching coach and minor league instructor in the Mets system. Jackson also has been selected to travel to Australia and Ghana on behalf of the Mets as the team utilized his ability to sell baseball and put smiles on the faces of those he meets. He has been part "Pitching Guru" and part "Good Humor Man" while contributing as a team ambassador.

It would have been interesting to see how Jackson's major league career might have panned out if the Mets hadn't selected him from the Pirates in the 1961 expansion draft. The little lefty from Waco, Texas, led all National League pitchers with 73 losses from 1962 to 1965. The Pirates averaged 84 wins during that span while the Mets averaged 48.5. Jackson managed to post a .421 winning percentage from 1963 to 1964 while the Mets were winning just 32 percent of their games.

He was New York's most dependable starter during the team's first four years, leading the Mets in wins and strikeouts three times during that span. And he was 24–19 with a 3.30 ERA while pitching for major league teams other than the Mets.

The Mets brought him back in 1968, a time when the team was about to shed its laughingstock image. But he was dealt to the Reds three months and three days before New York beat the Orioles to win the 1969 World Series. Instead of celebrating with the Mets, Jackson had to settle for being the best pitcher on one of the worst expansion teams in major league history.

Jackson also couldn't get a break with the Pirates despite four consecutive outstanding minor league seasons, beginning with his 18–9, 2.07 ERA campaign with Lincoln

of the Single A Western League in 1958. He followed that by going 18–9 with a 2.33 ERA for Triple A Columbus in 1959, when he also made his major league debut May 3 against the Cardinals. He appeared in eight games for the Pirates that year, compiling a 6.50 ERA in 18 innings.

Jackson didn't pitch for the Pirates again until 1961, going 1–0 with a 3.42 ERA in 24 innings. He picked up his first big league win September 30 against the Reds, tossing a complete-game 11-hitter in an 11–6 victory. Jackson managed to stay in that game after serving up a three-run homer by Leo Cardenas in a five-run seventh.

He went 12–7 with a 2.89 ERA for Columbus in 1961 before the Pirates exposed him in the expansion draft. He had spent the previous year preparing for the possibility of becoming available in the draft.

"I kind of realized that something was going to happen," recalled Jackson in 2008. "The previous year I had gone in there [to the team office] the last day of the season to talk to Joe Brown, the general manager of the Pittsburgh Pirates at the time. I wanted to know what my future was with the organization because I kind of was a basketball—up and down.

"I thought I was ready to go to the big leagues, but there were very few chances with that ballclub that I was going to the big leagues. I kind of asked him what my future was, and at that point I think he said, 'I think you can make any major league team.' So from that, I just took it that I was gone!

"I knew the expansion was coming up. I didn't think too much about it, but I was really, really wanting to play for Pittsburgh. I had come up through that organization six, seven years, so I was kind of wondering if I would ever make that ballclub."

Jackson was one of the Mets' $75,000 draft picks in October 1961, giving him a great chance to finally crack a major league rotation.

Jackson began his Mets career by going 0–2 with an 8.31 ERA in four games—including two starts—before pitching the team's first shutout on April 29 at the Polo Grounds. He scattered eight hits in an 8–0 shutout of the Phillies, giving the Mets their first winning streak.

Jackson later threw the first one-hitter in Mets history, striking out nine in a 2–0 win over the Colt 45s on June 22. But the no-hitter was broken up by Joey Amalfitano just two batters into the game.

"He bunted a lot, so we played him in to bunt and he hits the ball right by my third baseman [Felix Mantilla]," he said. "It might have ticked off his glove. That was the only base hit I gave up that night.

"But the defense played one hell of a ballgame. They got me out of some jams making such good plays. But I guess that's what happens when you're flirting with no-hitters sometimes.

"I never thought about [the no-hitter] because I had given up the base hit. During those times, no-hitters were far from my mind. I was just trying to win any way I could."

It was one of his four shutouts that year, the only complete-game shutouts thrown by the Mets that year. He also tossed a 15-inning complete game August 14 against the Phillies, allowing only six hits but losing 3–1.

"I'm going on and going on and going on, and in the 13th Charlie Neal leads off with a triple. We're at home, so I figure, 'Hey, we're going to score this run, the game's over.' They turn around, we don't score, and now I've got to try to pick it up again. They asked me to come out of the game, and I said, 'No, I'm not coming out of this game.'

"I'm worse than dead tired [at that point]. I'm dead. But it was in me not to quit. I wanted to win that game so bad and I wind up losing it."

The Phillies finally broke the 1–1 tie, scoring twice after Marv Throneberry let a grounder go through his legs. It was one of many tough losses for Jackson that season.

"All of them were aggravating. First of all, I had never been with a losing club before. To go through 120 games losing for the season, I don't know why I didn't have ulcers," he recalled with a chuckle. "It was hard to win ballgames."

Jackson led the team in ERA (4.40), and tied for the club lead with 118 strikeouts. The Mets earned 11 of their 40 victories in games pitched by Jackson.

Jackson also had the pleasure of playing for manager Casey Stengel that season and felt the skipper helped him prepare for games.

"He'd talk about 'making them play your game. You know your game better than you know theirs, so make them play your game.'

"I remember that starting pitchers, on the first day of a series, he would have them conduct a meeting and say what they were going to do. The first time I had the chance to do this, I'm telling them what I was going to do to different batters, 'I'm going to pitch them this way, that way.'

"When it was over, he called me into his office and said, 'Don't you ever do that again. Never tell people how you're going to pitch anybody because I could trade some of these people the next day. Just tell people where to play. That will make you do the things you are capable of doing.'

"He was just so different, it was unreal."

Jackson got off to a terrific start in 1963. He was 4–3 with a 2.54 ERA after holding the Dodgers to two runs in 11 innings of a 4–2, 13-inning loss May 19. He was just 6–14 with a 4.70 earned run average following an 8–0 loss to the Braves August 2. But he was outstanding the rest of the year, going 7–3 with a 2.49 ERA and five complete games in his last 11 outings, including 10 starts. The Mets were 16–21 in games he pitched, 35–90 when he didn't. Jackson also paced the team with 13 wins, a club record that would stand until Tom Seaver went 16–13 in 1967. Of the four expansion teams, only Houston's Turk Farrell had more victories (14) than Jackson that year.

"In '63, I thought I pitched so well that year. I really learned how to pitch. I learned how to pitch before that, but it had really come together in '63.

"We only won 51 games that year, but then I won the 49th, the 50th and the 51st. I won the last three games!"

Jackson was indeed the pitcher of record in the Mets' final three wins of '63. But the Mets also dropped 14 games during that season-ending stretch.

Jackson tossed two shutouts in his first 18 games of 1964, but his record was only 3–10 with a 4.55 ERA by June 23. He pitched well after that, going 8–6 with a 4.03 ERA in 118⅓ innings.

Jackson actually got a chance to pitch in a pennant race, although it was in a spoiler's role. He tossed a five-hit shutout against the first-place Cardinals on the final Friday of the season, preventing the Redbirds from clinching their first NL pennant in 18 years.

"I was supposed to pitch Thursday night in Milwaukee, and after Thursday there was only three days left. But the old man [Stengel] came to me and said, 'They think we're going to lay down to these guys. Why don't you pitch on Friday night.'

"I thought I was just going to pitch that game [against the Braves] and go home. But when they said I'd pitch Friday night I said, 'Okay, I have no problem with that.'

"We get to town and they have 'Welcome Yankees' or something like that. I guess they thought they were going to kick our butts."

The Yankees were going to be the American League representative in the upcoming World Series. Cardinals fans expected their team to waltz away with the NL pennant sometime during the team's three-game series against the visiting Mets.

"Friday night we're taking BP. All the writers are there, and I think I could have mentioned, 'I just might pitch a no-hitter tonight.' I was really kidding around. I never kidded around like that before, I usually was pretty serious. I had my butt kicked a few times so I'm not usually out there boasting," laughed Jackson.

"That was probably one of my better games pitching that year. Against Gibson, I beat him 1–0."

Jackson's gem only delayed the coronation. St. Louis celebrated the next day following a 15–5 rout of the Mets.

Once again, the 1964 Mets had more success when Jackson was on the mound. New York was 43–70 in games he pitched over the franchise's first three seasons compared to a 101–260 mark when he didn't. He also pitched seven of the Mets' first 19 shutouts.

Jackson endured his second 20-loss season in 1965 despite leading the team with a 4.34 ERA, three shutouts, and 120 strikeouts. He ended the season by going 6–11 with a 3.53 ERA in 132⅔ innings for a team that dropped 112 games.

Jackson finally got an opportunity to play for a contender when the Mets sent him to the Cardinals in a trade that brought 1964 NL MVP Ken Boyer to New York. He was the Cards' second-best pitcher in 1966, posting a 2.51 ERA and a 13–15 record. Jackson was sixth in the league in ERA and ninth with 11 complete games, but he never felt that season was one of vindication since he thought he had already become a solid pitcher.

"I knew that I had become a pretty decent pitcher. I wasn't a flame-thrower or a power pitcher, but I was effective with what I had. I wasn't afraid of any hitter at any time. It was just a lack of runs [with the Mets]."

Jackson opened 1967 in the Cardinals' rotation and was pulled after starting off 3–2 with a 5.44 ERA in his first eight games. He fired his second career one-hitter April 25 against the Astros but made only three starts after May 29. Jackson compiled a 3.02 ERA in his final 31 games.

Jackson was back with the Mets in 1968, pitching on a staff that now included Tom Seaver, Jerry Koosman, and Nolan Ryan. He made nine starts and posted a 2.52 ERA with three saves in 35 2/3 innings out of the bullpen. Jackson also opened the '69 season with New York but was sold to the Reds in July after giving up at least two runs in five of his nine relief outings.

Jackson still had a rooting interest in the Mets during the summer of '69, even while he toiled for another team.

"Oh, yeah, no doubt about it. It seemed I'd spent my whole life with them. I was kind of embedded. I dream blue!

"Once you were around with that organization for a few years, you're really embedded. You're really part of the family."

Jackson was a winner in his final major league game, tossing 3⅔ scoreless innings against the Astros on September 26. He went to spring training with the 1970 Reds and was released April 13, ending his major league career.

Although saddled with a 67–99 career record, Jackson never regretted spending a majority of that time with the bumbling Mets.

"I thought I probably would have won more ballgames with a better ballclub. But I take pride in the club that I play on, regardless of what it is. I was just trying to win the next game."

Jackson stayed in the game as a minor league coach with the Mets and was reunited with original Met Don Zimmer, serving as Boston's pitching coach from 1977 to 1979. He also spent three years on the Orioles' coaching staff from 1989 to 1991 and was the Mets' bullpen coach during their back-to-back playoff appearances in 1999 and 2000. He remains with the team as a spring training instructor.

"I work with the pitchers and do the fundamentals. I tend to look toward the younger pitchers because I get a chance to see them in the summer [while living in St. Lucie]. I make a trip to Triple A and Double A and see the prospects. I have a few words to say about it."

Jackson has been responsible for molding some of the best pitching talent in team history. Ron Darling gives Jackson much credit for turning him into a major league prospect.

Al Jackson warms up before a 1962 game at Shea Stadium.

"He wanted to do a lot of things," said Jackson about Darling. "I remember him coming to me. When I first got him his confidence was at zero. He had great stuff, but his confidence was at zero, so that kind of nullifies his stuff.

"He was wondering one day if we were going to go over the hitters. I told him 'When you start throwing strikes, we'll go over the hitters. Until then, forget about it. Let's take it one step at a time.'

"We had a 100-pitch count at the time. Not only him, but there were a couple of guys where I told them I wasn't getting what I need—and they're not getting what they need—because they're not throwing strikes. I said, 'We're going to a four-man rotation. You're going to pitch every four days instead of five. You're going to be on the mound every other day.'"

Jackson would have Darling and the rest of the starters throw a side session one day after a start. Following another off-day, the hurlers would return to make another start.

"We did that for about five weeks, and those 100 pitches started to turn into seven, eight innings. Now, we're starting to arrive. [I told them], 'You're going to be too tired for any waste. You have no waste.'

"It happened to me. I think what turned me into a pitcher with control was because I pitched every four days.

"I thought I'd try it [as a pitching coach]. Nobody in the organization said no, so we did that."

"That's what turned Darling's season around. Before the season was over, he was in the big leagues."

Jackson also has been the face of the Mets on overseas trips, including a trek to Ghana in 2007.

"That was a most exciting trip in the most different place. It's not the most fabulous place, but people were there, and it seemed they were hungry for baseball. And there were kids there with some talent.

"To look at the fields they play on, there was no way we would play on it.

"My wife went on the trip. She doesn't miss any trips."

In fact, Nadine Jackson has encouraged her husband to make the journeys abroad.

"I remember one time the Mets asked me to go to Australia. Somebody had told me Australia was like 13, 14 hours from L.A. I said, 'I don't want to go that far.'

"So when they asked me to go I said, 'I don't think so.' When I came home, I told my wife, 'Can you believe they asked me to go to Australia? That's so far.'

"She gave me the phone. 'Call them back and tell them you're going!' So I got talked into that one.

"When [Mets general manager Omar Minaya] called and asked me to go to Africa, she was sitting in front of me. I told Omar, 'Well, I don't think I want a divorce. I think I'll go.'"

Jackson has collected some great memories during his nearly five decades with the Mets. He left the team the first time as the all-time leader in most pitching categories. He has mentored numerous minor leaguers who went on to log important innings for the Mets. But Jackson can't isolate just one or two memories that stand out.

"It's hard to figure just one thing," he said. "I think you have to ball it up as a group. The years that I spent there, as a player, coach, whatever, it was a great ride. An outstanding ride. And I really haven't finished yet."

ML debut	Pirates vs. Cardinals, 5/3/59 (2 IP, 3 H, 1 ER, 2 K, 0 BB)
Mets debut	vs. Pirates, 4/14/62 (7 IP, 9 H, 6 ER, 5 K, 4 BB)
First ML strikeout	Joe Cunningham, Cardinals, 5/3/59 (with Pirates)
First Mets strikeout	Bill Virdon, Pirates, 4/14/62
First ML win	vs. Reds, 9/30/61 (with Pirates)
First Mets win	vs. Phillies, 4/29/62
First ML/Mets save	vs. Phillies, 6/23/63
Most strikeouts, ML/Mets game	11, vs. Phillies, 5/4/65
Low-hit ML CG	1, twice, including Cardinals @ Astros, 4/25/67
Low-hit Mets CG	1, vs. Colts, 6/22/62

Acquired: Selected in the expansion draft, 10/10/61.
Deleted: Traded to the Cardinals with Charley Smith for Ken Boyer, 10/20/65.
Reacquired: Traded by the Cardinals 10/13/67 as the player to be named in a 7/16/67 deal that sent Jack Lamabe to St. Louis.
Deleted: Sold to the Reds, 7/13/69.

Howard Johnson

Third Baseman, Short Stop, Outfielder
Bats both, throws right
Born: 11/29/60   Clearwater, Florida
Height: 5'10"   Weight: 175   #20, #44

Howard Johnson Mets Career

YEAR	GP	AB	R	H	2B	3B	HR	RBI	K	BB	SB	AVG	SLG	OBP
1985	126	389	38	94	18	4	11	46	78	34	6	.242	.393	.300
1986	88	220	30	54	14	0	10	39	64	31	8	.245	.445	.341
1987	157	554	93	147	22	1	36	99	113	83	32	.265	.504	.364
1988	148	495	85	114	21	1	24	68	104	86	23	.230	.422	.343
1989	153	571	104	164	41	3	36	101	126	77	41	.287	.559	.369
1990	154	590	89	144	37	3	23	90	100	69	34	.244	.434	.319
1991	156	564	108	146	34	4	38	117	120	78	30	.259	.535	.342
1992	100	350	48	78	19	0	7	43	79	55	22	.223	.337	.329
1993	72	235	32	56	8	2	7	26	43	43	6	.238	.379	.354
TOTAL	1154	3968	627	997	214	18	192	629	827	556	202	.251	.459	.341

ML Career

YEAR	GP	AB	R	H	2B	3B	HR	RBI	K	BB	SB	AVG	SLG	OBP
82-95	1531	4940	760	1229	247	22	228	760	1053	692	231	.249	.446	.340

If ever there were a Rodney Dangerfield among the list of Mets All-Stars, it would be Howard Michael Johnson. Cardinals manager Whitey Herzog showed him no respect by accusing Johnson of corking his bats after he opened 1987 on a hot streak. Mets fans grumbled when HoJo followed his best seasons with mediocre ones. Management constantly tried to find new position for the third baseman, whose fielding skills never quite matched his prowess at the plate.

But Johnson laughed off Herzog's accusations, dealt with the boo-birds, and willingly tried to learn new positions if it meant the team had a chance to be better, even if it also meant a few personal embarrassing moments. He was a very good ballplayer, a better teammate and an even better person during his nine years with the Mets.

His stats show he was the first player in Mets history to lead the National League in homers and RBI in the same season (1991). He was the third Met to hit more than 30 homers in three different seasons, and the third to post a pair of 100-RBI years. If Johnson had any major fault, it was that his best seasons came on some of the Mets' more disappointing ballclubs during the Frank Cashen/Al Harazin era.

It took Johnson just three years to reach the majors after being selected by the Tigers with the 12th overall pick in the 1979 draft, shortly after he graduated from Clearwater High School in Florida and attended St. Petersburg Junior College.

The Tigers assigned him to Lakeland of the Single A Florida State upon his signing. He struggled in his first minor league season, hitting .235 with three homers, 18 extra-base hits, 49 RBIs, and 85 strikeouts in 456 at-bats. But he found his stroke in 1980, making the FSL All-Star team and finishing the year with a .285 average, 10 home runs, 28 doubles, 69 RBIs, and 31 stolen bases. Johnson also led all league third basemen with a .966 fielding percentage.

Moved up to Double A Birmingham in 1981, Johnson delivered 22 homers, 28 doubles, and 19 steals while hitting .266. He opened 1982 with Triple A Evansville but was recalled by the Tigers May 13, one day before making his major league debut in Toronto.

Johnson singled and scored in his first game and belted his first big-league home run April 28 against Minnesota's Pete Redfern. But he was returned to Evansville after hitting .188 in 12 games, including seven starts.

The Tigers brought him back in June to play one game and recalled him again August 13. Johnson spent the rest of the season with Detroit and put together a torrid stretch in which he batted .520 (13-for-25) during a six-game hitting streak. He later hit safely in 11 straight games and ended the major league portion of his season with a .316 average in 54 games.

The Tigers put him on the 1983 Opening Day roster, but Johnson began the season in a 4-for-31 slump. He was farmed out May 27 after going 2-for-4 with a homer and two runs scored in his final big-league game of the year. He fractured his right index finger in a Triple A game June 1, and broke it again 3½ weeks later before undergoing corrective surgery that cost him the rest of the season.

Johnson was the Tigers' Opening-Day third baseman in 1984, providing two hits, a double, and an RBI in an 8–1 rout of the Twins. He owned a .296 average by May 26 after collecting two more hits and a ribbie in a loss that left the Tigers 35–7. He followed that with an eight-game hitting streak (.520 in 25 at-bats) that pushed his average to .333 by June 13. Johnson batted .305 for the month of June before his stats began to take a tumble.

The Tigers coasted to the AL East title despite Johnson's .219 average in 66 games over the final three months of the regular season. He ended up hitting .248 for the season with 12 homers and 50 RBIs in 116 games, belting a grand slam and five three-run homers along the way. But he spent most of the postseason on the bench as manager Sparky Anderson was reluctant to use his young third baseman in a pressure situation. HoJo didn't play in the three-game sweep of the Royals in the ALCS and had just one at-bat in the World Series win over the Padres, which gave Detroit its first championship since the '68 Tigers.

Johnson was shipped to the Mets in December 1984 for pitcher Walt Terrell in what appeared on the surface to be a strange deal. New York had acquired veteran third baseman and two-time All-Star Ray Knight during the '84 season, prompting the team to shift Hubie Brooks to shortstop before sending him to the Expos in the Gary Carter trade. The Tigers didn't appear to be lacking for hurlers after leading the AL with a 3.49 ERA that season, and they were getting what was arguably the Mets' No. 4 pitcher.

Anderson was both Johnson's biggest publicist and harshest critic during HoJo's time in Detroit. Sparky, who had seen George Foster, Ken Griffey Junior, and Dan Driessen become talented young hitters with the Reds, had no problem touting Johnson as a potential star. But when the Tigers made the postseason for the first time in 12 years, Anderson wasn't sure Johnson could perform on the big stage.

The Mets also were seeking their first playoff appearance in 12 years when they reported for 1985 spring training. The switch-hitting Johnson showed much more power from the left side in '84 and was expected to compliment Knight as a lefty-righty tandem at the hot corner. Both played below expectations in 1985 as the two combined to bat .232 with 17 home runs and 82 RBIs.

Johnson was the starting third baseman in the 1985 opener, working out a bases-loaded walk in the first inning and going 1-for-4 in a game Carter won with a 10th-inning home run. But Howard promptly followed that with an 0-for-14 skid that contributed to his .127 average through May 5. After the opener, Johnson didn't crack the .200 barrier until July 4, when he went 3-for-5 with four runs scored in the Mets' memorable, 16–13, 19-inning win in Atlanta. He gave the Mets a 10–8 lead with a two-run blast in the top of the 13th.

July was a productive time for Johnson as he hit .324 (24-for-74) with four homers and 15 RBIs in his first 21 games of the month to lift his average to .230. Following the July 4 marathon, he batted .277 with nine home runs and 35 ribbies to finish the year at .242.

The Mets and Cardinals were tied for the division lead when the two squads opened a three-game series at Shea Stadium on September 10. In the opener, Johnson capped a five-run first with a grand slam before the Mets hung on to beat the Redbirds 5–4. Two days later, he doubled home a run to give New York a 4–0 lead in a game the Mets would win 7–6 in the bottom of the ninth, putting them in first place.

Johnson had come through in the team's first crucial series of September. He also fared well in the Mets' three-game set in St. Louis later that month, going 4-for-10 with an RBI. However, the Mets dropped the finale of the Cardinals series at Busch Stadium to fall two games back with three remaining before St. Louis wrapped up the division two days later.

Johnson's late-season surge (a .309 average in 68 at-bats from September 10 through October 3) seemed to belie Anderson's opinion that he was shaky when the games really meant something. It also got the Mets fans off his back after he endured some torturous moments early in 1985,

Howard Johnson (left) and outfielder Clint Hurdle prep for batting practice. Photo courtesy of David Ferry

right side of the plate while taking some pressure off the switch-hitting Johnson, who batted only .156 in 77 at-bats as a right-handed stick.

Johnson avoided duplicating his ugly start from 1985, hitting .343 with a homer and six RBIs in his first 13 games through May 3. He also supplied what many consider the most important hit of the regular season, a blast that showed the Mets weren't intimidated by the big, bad Cardinals.

The Mets entered an April 24 game in St. Louis on a five-game winning streak that gave them a 7–3 record, a half-game ahead of the Redbirds. The Cards were two outs away from a 4–2 victory that would have given them the division lead until Johnson launched a two-run homer off closer Todd Worrell to force extra innings. The Mets won it in 10 and swept the four game series to take a four-game lead after just 14 games. The sweep was part of a stretch during which they won 13 consecutive games played by Johnson.

The Mets were without Johnson for three weeks in June after he broke his arm in an outfield collision with Lenny Dykstra. When he returned June 23, Johnson promptly posted his first career two-homer game in a loss to the Expos.

The Mets already were on cruise control by the time Johnson was activated, 10 games ahead of the Expos and a whopping 17½ games in front of the Cards. A rejuvenated Knight batted .362 during the first 12 games Johnson missed and finished the season with a .298 average, 80 points higher than his 1985 total.

Johnson helped the Mets pad their lead in July with a pair of big three-run hits. The Mets, fresh off three straight losses in Houston, were tied 3–3 with the Reds in the 14th inning when Johnson unloaded a three-run homer to lead a 6–3 win at Cincinnati July 22. Six days later, Hojo provided a three-run double in the first inning of a 9–2 rout of the Cubs.

Johnson eventually tailed off, but it was hardly noticed with the Mets enjoying a 20-game lead by August 23. He hit only .233 over the final three months to finish with a .245 average, 10 homers, and 39 ribbies.

Knight was the starting third baseman by the time the Mets opened the NLCS against the Astros. Johnson cracked the starting lineup for just one game in the postseason, going 0-for-4 in a Game 2 loss to the Red Sox in the World Series.

The inactivity didn't prevent him from being the subject of some second-guessing by the media in Game 6. The Mets had a chance to win it in the bottom of the ninth after putting runners on first and second with nobody out in a 3–3 game. Pinch-hitting for shortstop Kevin Elster in an obvious bunting situation, Johnson was asked by Davey Johnson to move both runners into scoring position after recording just two sacrifices in 671 plate appearances during his first two seasons as a Met. Johnson failed to lay down a bunt and struck out before Lee Mazzilli and Lenny

including the day he tied a team record with three errors in a 7–6 win over the Braves July 18. Despite his early season woes, Johnson still set then personal records with 94 hits, 18 doubles, and four triples.

The Mets were on a mission heading into 1986. Manager Davey Johnson proclaimed in spring training that the Mets would dominate the rest of the National League, a statement buoyed by confidence after the team picked up lefty pitcher Bob Ojeda and second baseman Tim Teufel, which solved two problems that plagued the Mets down the stretch in 1985.

The Mets also had versatile rookie Kevin Mitchell, who played six positions in 1986 and saw action at third. Teufel and Mitchell gave the team more of a presence from the

Dykstra hit fly balls that would have scored a runner on third.

Not knowing his mic was open, NBC broadcaster Vin Scully could be heard questioning the strategy to have Johnson attempt the bunt. But the failed bunt set up one of the wildest innings in World Series history.

Had Johnson advanced the runners, there might not have been a 10th inning, which would have meant no dramatic comeback, no run-scoring wild pitch, no E3 on the game's final play.

The Mets claimed their second World Series title two days later with an 8–5 win over the Red Sox. Johnson never got off the bench in Game 7 and finished the postseason 0-for-7 in four games.

The Mets made several off-season moves that made Johnson a starter in 1987. They dealt potential third sacker Kevin Mitchell to the Padres and failed to reach a contract agreement with Knight, allowing Knight to sign with the Orioles in February. Johnson entered spring training as the only true candidate for the starting job.

Nineteen-eighty-seven was one of disappointment for the Mets, but it was a career-changing season for Johnson. He and Darryl Strawberry became the first players in Mets history to hit 30 homers and steal 30 bases in the same season. Strawberry had fallen just short of the 30-30 club in each of his previous three years, averaging 27 home runs and 27 steals. But Johnson had never hit more than 12 homers or swiped over 10 bags until '87, when he belted 36 round-trippers and stole 32 bases while hitting .265 with 99 RBIs.

Many major leaguers increased their home run totals in 1987 as MLB tried to diffuse reports that the baseball was juiced—wrapped tighter than usual to produce an increased number of longballs. Not everyone was buying the company line that the ball was the same as ever, and not everyone believed Howard Johnson had the ability to slam 30 home runs.

Nobody said a peep when Strawberry socked 39 homers, 10 over his previous career high. Newcomer Kevin McReynolds hit a career-high 29, and Hernandez belted a career-best 18. But Johnson's power surge was unexpected and, according to at least one opposing manager, unbelievable. He began the season with just three round-trippers and 12 RBIs in 19 games during April. Johnson smacked five homers and drove in 13 runs during an eight-game streak in May. Two months later, he hit seven home runs in a 13-game span, four coming during the last three games of a four-game set at Houston. He had 20 by the All-Star break, already eight more than his previous career high.

Herzog had seen enough after Johnson homered for the second time in two games against the Cardinals during a late July series. Herzog tried to have the bat confiscated following the first home run, but the batboy already had taken the wood to the bat rack. The Cards' skipper was faster the next day, asking plate umpire Joe West to confiscate the bat following the second blast. Johnson was vin-

dicated when the bat checked out, but Herzog remained convinced Johnson was cheating.

"He looks like Babe Ruth up there, and I know he ain't that good," said Herzog, according to the New York Times. "I know the bat is corked. I tried to get it last night, but the batboy got it before it hit the ground. I wish I had a hatchet."

On August 6, HoJo socked a second-inning homer against the Cubs and had his bat quickly confiscated by plate umpire John Kibler. Davey Johnson, saying he was playing "tit for tat," asked that Andre Dawson's bat be confiscated following the first of his two home runs in the game. Howard Johnson joked after the bat was cleared through X-ray.

"Now we'll learn the effect of X-rays on wood," cracked the red-hot third baseman, as reported in Sports Illustrated.

A day later, reliever and team prankster Roger McDowell, Johnson's partner in "hotfoot," sauntered through the clubhouse equipped with a carpenter's belt that carried sandpaper, emery boards, cork and a saw.

But Herzog didn't think bat-corking was a laughing matter. "I say if they challenge a bat and it is corked, then suspend the player for life. I'm waiting for some pitcher to get killed because some guy uses a corked bat," he said in an August 17, 1987, SI article.

Johnson was the Mets' most lethal hitter in a powerful lineup during the summer. He crushed 19 homers and had 48 RBIs while hitting .310 in 57 games from July 1 through September 2. The Mets were 6½ games behind the division-leading Cardinals when he began his charge. Nine weeks later, they were hosting the Redbirds with a chance to take over first place with a sweep.

But the Mets dropped two of three to the Cardinals and were eliminated from the title chase with three games left in the season. The Mets averaged 5.4 runs in September and October but went only 18–13. Johnson posted a .178 average with two home runs and 10 RBIs in 20 games after September 3.

Pitching, the team's strong suit in 1986, had become the team's Achilles' heel a year later. Co-closer Jesse Orosco had his worst season as a Met, and all five members of the starting rotation were sidelined either by injury of suspension. For a change, the Mets relied on their offense to keep the team afloat, finishing first in the league in batting average (.268) and runs scored (823) while blasting the second-most home runs (192).

General manager Frank Cashen elected to keep most of the core group intact, dealing only Orosco after the season. The lineup remained the same at the start of 1988, which meant Johnson was back as the everyday third baseman.

This was heady stuff for the Mets back then. Johnson joined Hubie Brooks as the only Mets third basemen to start four straight opening days. The team returned to the postseason in '88 despite Johnson, who hit .230 with 24 home runs, 68 RBIs, and 23 stolen bases. He never got on a hot stretch, compiling a season-best hitting streak of just six games and never hitting higher than .281 in a single month. Johnson also struggled from the right side of the plate, batting .183 in 143 at-bats.

As he did in 1986, Johnson provided one of the biggest home runs of the season. The second-place Pirates had closed within 4½ games of the Mets heading into a three-game series at Three Rivers Stadium. The Bucs split the first two games and had a 7–6 lead with two out in the ninth when Johnson blasted a 1–2 pitch from Jim Gott over the left-field wall to force extra innings. Two innings later, McDowell doubled and scored on McReynolds' single to give the Mets an 8–7 win and a 5½-game lead.

The Mets didn't add a major offensive contributor until late August, when Cashen felt prospect Gregg Jefferies was ready for the majors. The problem was, Jefferies was a natural third baseman on a team that could have used more pop at shortstop or second.

Ever the good teammate, Johnson willingly slid over to shortstop to accommodate Jefferies, who sparked the team's late-season push to the NL East title by hitting .321 in 29 games. Meanwhile, Johnson failed to homer in his final 17 games while recording a dismal .148 average. Things got worse for HoJo in the postseason.

The Mets hit only .242 while the pitching faltered during the seven-game loss to the Dodgers. Johnson bore the brunt of the criticism by going 1-for-18 (.056) with six strikeouts, although he scored twice during the Mets' 8–4 win over Los Angeles in Game 3. Davey Johnson benched Johnson in favor of shortstop Kevin Elster in Game 7 before using HoJo as a pinch-hitter with two out in the ninth inning of a 6–0 game. The series ended with Johnson looking at strike three.

Johnson's single in Game 5 was his lone hit of the series, and the only base hit he'd collect in postseason play. HoJo never appeared in a playoff game after '88, finishing with a miserable .038 average for his postseason career.

Jefferies was expected to be in the lineup for 1989, but the question was where. Cashen provided the answer by dealing second baseman Wally Backman to the Twins at the 1988 winter meetings and giving the position to Jefferies, keeping Johnson at third base. On paper, the Mets had a better lineup than they had in '88, but the team chemistry was compromised and the ballclub slogged through a very disappointing 1989 season.

Jefferies showed limited ability as a second baseman and failed to produce as he had the previous September. Hernandez and Carter provided little offense and battled injuries as they played out the final year of their contracts. McReynolds appeared to have reached a plateau as a player, and the Mets dealt three outfielders while making Juan Samuel their starting center fielder.

The only scary hitters in the lineup were Johnson, Strawberry, and McReynolds, who had his worst season since 1985. The trio hit 87 of the team's league-high 147 home runs and supplied 263 of 633 RBIs. But Strawberry hit just .225 as the club finished seventh in the league in batting average.

Johnson made the first of his two All-Star appearances in 1989 before setting or matching career highs in almost every major offensive category. He went 3-for-4 with a solo homer and three RBIs in the Mets' Opening-Day win over the Cardinals on April 3, clubbed a walk-off homer in the 10th inning of a 3–2 win against the Reds on May 3, and smacked a two-run shot one game later in a 2–1 victory against Houston.

Johnson was sensational in June, homering in three straight games and four of five early in the month before socking a pair of two-run blasts June 19. For the month, HoJo batted .340 with 11 home runs, 24 RBIs, eight doubles, and six stolen bases in 25 games.

Johnson stayed close to .300 through September 2 before settling for a career-high .289 average that helped him end up fifth in the MVP voting. He also set personal bests with a team-leading 104 runs, 41 doubles, 101 RBIs, 41 stolen bases, and a .559 slugging average. Johnson would surpass his home run, RBI, and runs scored totals two years later, when he also finished fifth in the MVP balloting.

Johnson saw a lot of action at shortstop in 1990, starting a career-high 63 games there and opening 89 games at third. His 1990 stats would have been more than acceptable during his first five major league seasons, but his numbers were disappointing compared to 1989 and '87.

One of his better stretches of 1990 came during the Mets' 11-game winning streak in late June. HoJo hit safely in 10 straight games for a .316 average that pushed his season total to .236.

Johnson also hit .417 during a six-game batting streak that pushed his average to .253 by August 20. It was the first time his average was that high since May 26, but it never got any higher the rest of the year as Johnson finished with a .244 average, 23 home runs, and 90 RBIs.

An odd-number year brought out the best in Johnson once again. He was named to the NL All-Star team and finished with career-highs of 38 home runs, 117 RBIs, and 108 runs while hitting .259. He did it despite starting 60 games somewhere other than his customary third-base position. Johnson opened the season as the starting shortstop and ended it as the right fielder, which led to the Mets thinking they found their newest center fielder.

Johnson was one of the very few bright spots in an otherwise disappointing 1991 season. New York was 48–34 and only 2½ games out of first place by July 12, when Johnson already had provided 20 home runs and 64 RBIs for the season. Johnson continued to hammer the ball, but the Mets went just 29–50 the rest of the way to post their first losing season since 1983.

Johnson's 117 RBIs set a team record that would stand until Robin Ventura drove in 120 in 1999. Johnson also broke a team mark with 108 runs scored, and he became the first Met to have at least 30 homers and 30 stolen bases in three different seasons. But over the next four years,

HoJo would accumulate only 31 home runs and 131 RBIs as he battled several injuries before retiring in 1995.

The slide began in 1992 after the Mets acquired right fielder Bobby Bonilla, second baseman Willie Randolph, first baseman Eddie Murray, and pitcher Bret Saberhagen. The Mets were the favorite to win the NL East despite their 77–84 mark the previous season, but they never held a piece of first place after Opening Day and fell out of the race by dropping 12 of 13 games in early August. The slide began after Johnson fractured his right wrist July 28, causing him to miss the rest of the season.

Johnson was New York's starting center fielder for the first three months, a position he had played a total of zero times since becoming a Met.

"Going to center was a lot harder than I thought it would be," Johnson said to the *New York Times* in 1994. "There was a lot more wear and tear physically. You have to cover a lot of ground; there's a lot of running. It took its toll on me.

"I didn't want to back down from it because I thought if I kept at it, I could overcome it. It was definitely hard, but I never asked to come out."

He actually played better than expected, or at least better than Keith Miller had when the Mets tried to turn him into the starting center fielder in 1990. It was another instance in which Johnson was willing to change positions without worrying about possible embarrassment. He made only three errors in 82 starts in center but totaled only two assists as he tried to play through shoulder and knee pain.

With his season already short-circuited by the wrist injury, Johnson underwent surgery on his left shoulder and had both knees cleaned out on August 25. It was hoped the early procedures would allow him to do what he did best: destroy National League hurlers in an off-numbered year. However, another wave of physical setbacks ruined those expectations and earned Johnson a ticket out of New York.

Johnson was back at third base when the Mets began play in '93, but he hit only five home runs and drove in 22 runs in his first 51 games before a viral infection landed him on the disabled list by mid-June, causing him to miss three weeks. He had a few early season highlights, reaching base safely in eight straight plate appearances and passing Ed Kranepool for second on the Mets' all-time RBI list.

Two days after being activated, Johnson swiped his 200th career base while going 2-for-3 with a homer, two RBIs, and three runs scored in a loss to the Giants July 4. Eighteen days later, HoJo played his final game as a Met.

Batting second on July 22, Johnson singled in the first inning against Kevin Gross of the Dodgers before attempting to steal second. In a double indignity, Johnson (1) was thrown out by Mike Piazza and (2) suffered a broken thumb on the play, ending his season and Mets career.

By the end of '93, Johnson was second on the Mets' all-time list in home runs (192), RBIs (629), stolen bases (202), extra-base hits (429), runs (627), and doubles (214). He also was among the top 10 in total bases (1,823), games played (1,154), at-bats (3.968), and hits (997).

Johnson took his game to Colorado after the 1993 season, signing a free-agent contract to play for the Rockies in their second season. There were 184 home runs hit at Mile High Stadium in '93, demonstrating that it might be the right venue for Johnson to revive his career at age 33. Another 120 were hit there in 1994, but HoJo only accounted for only three. Johnson hit .278 in Denver that year, but his season totals of 10 home runs, 40 RBIs, and a .211 average in 93 games suggested that he was nearing the end of the line as a major league player.

The Rockies allowed him to become a free agent after the 1994 season. He signed with the Cubs near the start of the 1995 season and went 2-for-4 in his first game with his former rival April 30. Johnson went another four weeks before getting another hit in a Chicago uniform, suffering through an 0-for-21 slump that ended with a two-run blast against Florida. He homered again in that game but immediately entered an 0-for-21 skid that dropped his season average to .100 in 50 at-bats by June 10. However, he continued to get the occasional start and lasted the entire season as the Cubs battled for the NL wild-card.

Johnson ripped a walk-off, two-run homer to beat the Dodgers 2–0 on June 16, and he torched L.A. again August 14 with a game-tying single in the ninth inning of an 11-inning win at Dodger Stadium. With the Cubs down 9–7 in the eighth inning and facing elimination on September 28, Johnson hit an RBI single and scored on a double before Chicago won 12–11 in 11 innings. The Cubs won again the following day before they were eliminated from the wild-card race in the next-to-last game of the season.

In what now appears to have been a nice gesture, Cubs manager Jim Riggleman had Johnson start at third base in the season finale. HoJo had opened Chicago's previous nine games at third, hitting .310 with nine runs scored before going 3-for-4 with two RBIs in what would be his final game in the majors on October 1, 1995, against the Astros.

Johnson eventually returned to the Mets two years later as part of their professional scouting staff. He remained in that capacity until 2001, when he was hired as hitting coach of the Brooklyn Cyclones for their inaugural season as the Mets' NY–Penn League affiliate. Promoted to manager in 2002, Johnson guided the Cyclones to a 38–38 record before returning as a minor league hitting coach for Single A St. Lucie in '03.

Johnson climbed the minor league ladder as a hitting coach, working with Double A Binghamton's players in 2004 and spending the next two years at Triple A Norfolk. He returned to the majors in 2007 as the Mets' first-base coach and became the team's hitting coach when Rick Down was dismissed on July 12. Johnson continued to mentor the team's hitters in 2010 before the coaching staff was overhauled upon the arrival of new manager Terry Collins.

Johnson and his wife, Kim, have two daughters and one son. Their son, Glen, was a chip off the old block, becoming a switch-hitting shortstop and earning a scholarship at Jacksonville University.

ML debut	Tigers @ Blue Jays, 4/14/82
Mets debut	vs. Cardinals, 4/9/85
1st ML hit	single vs. Jim Clancy, @ Blue Jays, 4/14/82 (with Tigers)
1st Mets hit	single vs. Neil Allen, Cardinals, 4/9/85
1st ML homer	solo homer vs. Pete Redfern, @ Twins, 4/28/82 (with Tigers)
1st Mets homer	solo homer vs. Steve Bedrosian, Braves, 5/7/85
1st ML RBI	solo homer vs. Pete Redfern, @ Twins, 4/28/82 (with Tigers)
1st Mets RBI	bases-loaded walk vs. Joaquin Andujar, Cardinals, 4/9/85
Most hits, ML/Mets game	5, @ Cubs, 9/8/88
Most homers, ML game	2, 6 times
Most homers, Mets game	2, 5 times
Most RBI, ML/Mets game	5, @ Cubs, 6/13/90; @ Expos, 4/19/92

Acquired: Traded by the Tigers for Walt Terrell, 12/7/84.
Deleted: Became a free agent, 10/26/93. Signed by the Rockies, 11/19/93.

Cleon Jones

Outfielder, First Baseman   Bats right, throws left
Born: 8/4/42   Mobile, Alabama
Height: 6'0"   Weight: 190   #34, #12, #21

Cleon Jones Mets Career

YEAR	GP	AB	R	H	2B	3B	HR	RBI	K	BB	SB	AVG	SLG	OBP
1963	6	15	1	2	0	0	0	1	4	0	0	.133	.133	.133
1965	30	74	2	11	1	0	1	9	23	2	1	.149	.203	.171
1966	139	495	74	136	16	4	8	57	62	30	16	.275	.372	.318
1967	129	411	46	101	10	5	5	30	57	19	12	.246	.331	.282
1968	147	509	63	151	29	4	14	55	98	31	23	.297	.452	.341
1969	137	483	92	164	25	4	12	75	60	64	16	.340	.482	.422
1970	134	506	71	140	25	8	10	63	87	57	12	.277	.417	.352
1971	136	505	63	161	24	6	14	69	87	53	6	.319	.473	.382
1972	106	375	39	92	15	1	5	52	83	30	1	.245	.331	.305
1973	92	339	48	88	13	0	11	48	51	28	1	.260	.395	.315
1974	124	461	62	130	23	1	13	60	79	38	3	.282	.421	.343
1975	21	50	2	12	1	0	0	2	6	3	0	.240	.260	.283
TOTAL	1201	4223	563	1188	182	33	93	521	697	355	91	.281	.406	.340

ML Career

YEAR	GP	AB	R	H	2B	3B	HR	RBI	K	BB	SB	AVG	SLG	OBP
63–76	1213	4263	565	1196	183	33	93	524	702	360	91	.281	.404	.339

There was a man on first with two out when Orioles second baseman Davey Johnson hit the final pitch of the 1969 World Series. The future Mets manager sent a deep fly toward left field, the only place where a sensational catch wasn't made at Shea Stadium during the series.

Center fielder Tommie Agee had executed a pair of remarkable catches to rob the Orioles of at least five runs in the Mets' 5–0 victory in Game 3. One day later, right fielder Ron Swoboda sprawled to the turf to end Brooks Robinson's threat of a potential game-winning hit in the ninth inning of a 2–1, 10-inning win.

But with the Mets one out away from winning the World Series, the ball found its way toward Cleon Jones, the team's best hitter during the regular season. Jones took a few steps back and made a routine catch before his right knee hit the turf in a genuflect, a fitting end to a miraculous season.

Some 40 years later, Jones' catch can be seen on replay as many times as Agee's two grabs or Swoboda's circus catch. It was fitting that the final putout of the World Series should be made by Jones. After all, he was one of the biggest reasons why they got there in the first place.

The Mets weren't known as an organization that developed hitters prior to 1969. Pitchers Tom Seaver, Jerry Koosman, Nolan Ryan, Tug McGraw, and Gary Gentry had come through the system, and a host of talented arms would reach the majors via the farm system within months.

Prior to 1969, the Mets had developed Jones, Swoboda, Ed Kranepool…and little else as the team relied on its ability to win 2–1 games. By the end of the season, Jones was the first homegrown Met to hit over .300, finishing with a .340 mark on a championship ballclub that had a .242 team average.

Jones was an exceptional high school athlete in Mobile, Alabama, excelling in baseball and football while playing with Tommie Agee. The two were outstanding players on the gridiron and the diamond.

"In high school, Cleon was the better football player but I was the better baseball player," Agee told the *New York Times* in 1969. He was a halfback and I was the wide receiver. On one play—the 949 option—he'd run wide and could either keep going or find me. One season we made eight or nine touchdowns on it.

"Cleon was something. He had to throw the ball, all I had to do was catch it and run. And he even scored 24 touchdowns in three years."

Jones actually set a state record by scoring 26 touchdowns his senior year to earn a football scholarship. According to Maury Allen's *After the Miracle*, he once said that, "When I was playing I could throw a football 60 yards in the air and then run downfield and catch it."

Jones caught the Mets' interest in high school before attending Alabama A&M, where, according to the Mets' 1975 media guide, he scored 17 touchdowns in two seasons. New York signed him to his first pro contract on July 5, 1962, 30 days shy of his 20th birthday. But he didn't play his first minor league game until 1963, when he batted .360 in 14 games for Auburn of the NY–Penn League and .305 during a 49-game run with Raleigh of the Single A Carolina League.

The second-year Mets gave him his first look at major league pitching in September 1963, just 14 months after signing him. Jones was 0-for-7 before poking a single off Bobby Bolin of the Giants September 22. He also hit an RBI grounder in that game, three days before singling against Sandy Koufax to finish 2-for-15 in his first stint as a Met.

The Mets were slightly more patient with Jones the next two years. He spent all of 1964 with Triple A Buffalo, hitting .278 with 16 home runs, 70 RBIs, and team highs of 22 doubles, 139 hits, and 96 runs scored. Jones was placed on the 1965 Mets Opening Day roster, along with fellow rookies Ron Swoboda and Tug McGraw. Jones hit a two-run single in the ninth inning of a 4–3 loss to the Astros in his second game of the season and went 2-for-4 in his seventh to help Warren Spahn pick up his first win as a Met. But he had more strikeouts (13) than hits (5) in his first 13 games of the season and was demoted in early May after hitting .156.

Jones paced the 1965 Bisons with 122 hits and 61 runs in 123 games before getting another look-see from the Mets in September. He belted his first major league homer September 22 against Pittsburgh's Bob Friend but went 6-for-42 for the month to end the year with a .149 average as a Met.

Jones made the Mets out of spring training again in 1966 and homered in the season opener against the Braves. He hit .345 in April and owned a .290 average with four homers, 32 RBIs, 38 runs scored, and eight stolen bases at the midway point of the season. He had become the team's everyday center fielder and was receiving attention as a possible Rookie of the Year candidate as the Mets headed into September. Jones finished the year with a team-record 16 stolen bases, was second in batting (.275) and hits (136), and tied for second with 57 RBIs. He was tied for fourth in the rookie balloting, receiving one of 20 first-place votes after helping the Mets finish out of the cellar for the first time in club history.

Jones and the Mets regressed in 1967 as the team lost more than 100 games for the fifth time in six years. He led the team with a .385 average during the Grapefruit League season but opened the regular campaign 0-for-18 and possessed a .140 average heading into June. Jones hit .292 over the next three months and went on a 13-game hitting streak in mid-August but contributed only two home runs and 13 extra-base hits during that 80-game stretch. He ended the year with a .246 average, five home runs, and 30 RBIs in 129 games.

Gil Hodges became the manager following the 1967 season and reunited Jones and Agee. Hodges thought Jones' high school buddy would be a productive center fielder in New York, which meant Jones would be shifted to left field. Agee suffered through a miserable season in 1968, but Jones was the Mets' best hitter as the team finished with a team-record 73 wins.

Jones broke his team record for stolen bases by swiping 23 in 35 attempts. He also finished sixth in the league with a .297 average and paced the Mets with 63 runs, 151 hits, and 29 doubles.

Jones struggled early in '68, posting a .223 average over the first two months. But he opened June on an 11-game hitting streak and hit .343 with six homers, 18 RBIs, and 18 runs scored for the month. He hit .429 in his final 10 games, solidifying his place as the best hitter in the lineup and the best offensive threat ever produced by the franchise at that point.

However, Jones was top dog on an offense full of puppies. The Mets were dead last in the National League with a .228 batting average and next-to-last with 473 runs scored. Meanwhile, the team finished fourth with a 2.72 ERA and second with 1,014 strikeouts, 17 shutouts, and 499 runs allowed.

Unlike previous off-seasons, the Mets declined to upgrade the offense. Hodges and general manager Johnny Murphy tried to acquire Joe Torre from the Braves, but the asking price was steep. And so the Mets entered 1969 with cannons on the mound and a pop-gun offense. Fortunately, the squad was loaded with talented young arms that could win almost any game if staked to three runs. The offense complied.

The Mets finished ninth in the league with 632 runs scored, but it was almost a run a game better than they scored in 1968, the difference between ninth place and a World Championship. Agee and Art Shamsky had bounce-back seasons, and Jones received protection as the No. 3 hitter in the lineup when the Mets acquired Donn Clendenon on June 15.

Jones was hitting at a torrid pace well before Clendenon became a Met, opening the season 11-for-21 (.524) with a homer, six RBIs, and five runs scored in the first five games. His average stood at .432 by May 1 and hovered around the .400 mark until the third week in May. The second month of the season also included his first career grand slam, a blast off future teammate of the Braves May 10.

Jones needed just 78 games to collect his first 100 hits of the year, reaching the milestone in clutch fashion July 8 against the Cubs. The Mets trailed 3–1 in the ninth until Jones hit a two-run double off Ferguson Jenkins. One batter later, Jones scored on Ed Kranepool's single, giving the Mets an unexpected win after Jenkins carried a one-hitter into the final inning.

Jones was named the starting left fielder for the '69 All-Star Game in Washington. He flourished in his only Midsummer Classic experience, going 2-for-4 with two runs scored as the National League coasted to a 9–3 win.

Jones owned a .346 average after hitting a double in his first at-bat in Game 2 of a twin bill against the Astros July 30. But in the third inning with the Mets already trailing 6–0 following a 16–3 loss in the opener, Jones seemed to take a casual route toward Johnny Edwards' base hit to left, turning it into an RBI double.

Hodges, who had seen his team play lethargic in back-to-back losses, didn't think Jones had hustled on the Edwards hit and was ready to make a statement to his young team. The skipper ambled out of the dugout and continued to walk past the pitcher's mound toward shortstop Bud Harrelson.

"I pointed to myself and I said, 'Me?'" Harrelson recalled years later to the *New York Times*. "He shook his head. He said, 'Not you,' and he kept walking right past me and out into left field."

Harrelson followed his manager until Hodges reached Jones. "Gil asked Cleon if he was okay," Harrelson said. "Cleon said, 'My leg's a little tight.' Gil said, 'Okay, come with me.' And off they went."

"I had a bad leg. Gil knew that," said Jones in *After the Miracle*. "He asked me about it before the game. He came out there and told me to follow him in. He said if I was too hurt to run, I was too hurt to play. Sure, I was embarrassed. Gil was tough. He did everything with a purpose. We had words after the game. Nobody likes that. I didn't hold a grudge. Gil was my man. He knew what was going on around that team. I don't think we could have won without him."

The Mets were about to fall 5½ games behind the NL East–leading Cubs when Hodges made an example of Jones. The move sent a message to the team that, if they were going to win the division, they had to do it in butt-busting fashion.

Jones was benched for the next two games and was used only as a pinch-hitter the following two days. He hit .371 in 12 games after Hodges pulled him in the Astros game, but the Mets continued to stumble and were 9½ games in back of Chicago following an 8–3 loss in Houston August 13.

The Mets immediately began a late charge, shaving five games off the Cubs' lead by August 31 while Jones hit .365 during his final 17 games of the month. Various injuries allowed him to play just 12 games in September, but he still contributed as he challenged for NL batting title.

The Mets were within a half-game of the Cubs after Jones walked and scored on Ken Boswell's two-run double in the first inning of a 7–1 rout of Chicago September 9. The Cubs lost again the next day to the Phillies, meaning the Mets could take over first place by percentage points if they earned at least a split of the Expos in a doubleheader at Shea.

New York was tied 2–2 in the 12th inning of the opener when Jones laced a two-out single. He moved to second on a walk to Rod Gaspar before Ken Boswell singled home Jones to put the Mets in first place for the first time in team history.

The lead continued to grow, giving Hodges a chance to rest his leading hitter. Jones had his average up to .347 on September 11, just three points from taking over the batting crown. But he went 5-for-25 the rest of the season to finish third in the batting race at a team-record .340, behind only Roberto Clemente and Pete Rose.

The extra rest seemed to recharge Jones in time for the first-ever NLCS against the Braves. The Mets trailed the series opener 5–4 until he slapped an RBI single to spark a five-run seventh in a 9–5 win.

In Game 2 Jones was 3-for-5 with a homer, three RBIs, and two runs scored. After the Mets blew most of a 9–1

lead, Jones launched a two-run homer in the seventh inning to cap the scoring in an 11–6 win.

Jones capped his first-ever playoff series by going 2-for-4 as the Mets completed a three-game sweep of the Braves, 7–4. He doubled and scored in a three-run fifth that put New York ahead 6–4 before Nolan Ryan completed an outstanding seven-inning relief performance.

Jones was 6-for-14 (.429) with a homer, four RBIs, and four runs scored in the series. He also had a .786 slugging average that was third-best on the team behind Agee and Boswell.

Next up for the Mets were the Orioles, who won 109 games during the regular season before sweeping the Twins in the ALCS. Baltimore was expected to roll over the youngsters from Queens, especially after the Birds beat Tom Seaver 4–1 in the opener.

Jones did not have a great series, going just 3-for-19 with no RBIs and two runs scored. But his third hit was huge. The Mets were tied 3–3 in the bottom of the eighth in Game 5 when Jones led off with a double. Two batters later, he scampered home with the tiebreaking run on Swoboda's double before an error led to the fifth run in a 5–3, series-clinching victory. Jones capped his greatest season in the majors by scoring the winning run in the World Series.

The Mets trailed the clincher 3–0 after Jerry Koosman surrendered homers to pitcher Dave McNally and Frank Robinson in the third inning. It remained 3–0 when Jones headed to the plate in the sixth inning.

McNally threw a pitch that bounced in the batter's box before landing in the Mets' dugout. Jones tried to explain to plate umpire Lou DiMuro that the ball hit him on the foot before heading out of play. DiMuro wasn't buying Jones' argument until Hodges came out of the dugout with the baseball. He showed the DiMuro a smudge of shoe polish on the ball, enough evidence to award Jones first base.

Earlier in the sixth, Orioles slugger Frank Robinson tried to convince DiMuro that he was hit by a pitch that was ruled a foul ball. Robinson went so far as to head back to the dugout to receive treatment on the area where he was supposedly hit. After several minutes, Robinson returned to the plate and struck out.

But the "Shoe Polish Incident" sparked the Mets' comeback. Jones was on first when Clendenon drilled his third homer of the season to get New York within 3–2. One inning later, light-hitting Al Weis tied the game with a blast to left-center.

After the game, Hodges was asked if he would hold onto the shoe polish ball as a souvenir.

"I wouldn't keep a thing like that," Hodges told the *New York Times* in jest. "First thing you know, one of you fellows would say that it wasn't shoe polish and we'd have a controversy. This way you have to take our word for it."

Back in Mobile after the postseason, Jones and Agee were the guests of honor at a parade. One of their biggest

Cleon Jones (21) races for the plate with the Mets' go-ahead run as Braves catcher Bob Didier searches for the ball (near Jones' left foot) after a bad throw from first in the eighth inning of the National League playoff game, October 4, 1969. Jones put the Mets ahead to stay, and the Mets scored three more in the inning to beat the Braves 9–5.

supporters was a very proud Curtis Horton, who was the high school baseball coach for both players.

"There are not too many coaches who have two boys on a major league club, period," said Curtis Horton, who coached Jones and Tommie Agee in high school, according to the *New York Times.* "And it's really something when you have two on the same team in a World Series."

Jones and Agee had a special kinship and helped motivate the other. They roomed together on the road and provided the bulk of the team's offense.

"We're pretty close. We have a couple of differences. Cleon likes wine and I like Scotch. He likes to fish and I like to hunt. He likes the blues, I like rock 'n' roll. He tries to get to sleep before me at night, because he says I snore and I'll keep him awake. He gets up first, too, and gets the record-player going."

Jones and the rest of the Mets lapped up the fruits of victory, leaving the team a little less hungry heading into

1970. The team didn't stray too far from first place, leading the division a total of 29 days and never falling more than five games back until the final day of the season. But the Mets had to settle for third place at 83–79 after owning a share of the lead on September 14.

Jones was among the bigger disappointments, hitting into what was a team-record 26 double plays and battling injuries. He was relegated to two pinch-hitting appearances from June 24 to July 16 due to pulled hamstring and groin muscles. His average was .237 by August 6, 103 points lower than his record-breaking average the previous season.

He hiked his average to .251 by August 23 before embarking on a 23-game hitting streak, a team record that would stand until Mike Vail tied it in 1975 and Hubie Brooks broke it in 1984. Jones hit .408 and recorded a .592 slugging average during the streak, providing 11 extra-base hits, 16 RBIs, and 20 runs scored. However, the Mets won just 12 of those 23 games and continued to plod through the rest of the year without duplicating their 38–11 finish from 1969. Jones finished second on the team with 140 hits and 25 doubles, but his .277 average was underwhelming after he emerged as one of the league's top hitters 12 months earlier.

"When we won the World Series in 1969, I woke up every morning pinching myself, asking is it real," said Jones to the *Times* after signing his 1971 contract. "When we didn't win it this year, I realized how real it had been.

"People ask me all the time, what happened? Well, in my own case, I didn't concentrate this year the way I should have. You're in the game to win and to make money, but it can't be a seven-month thing. It has to be a 12-month thing. I just didn't pay the price."

The Mets appeared to have gotten over their World Series hangover by opening the 1971 season 21–10, giving them a 2½-game lead by May 15. They were only two games back before enduring a 9–20 July that took them out of the race and left players to seek individual achievements.

For Jones, that meant reestablishing himself as one of the National League's top hitters. While the rest of the Mets were failing to generate much offense, Jones hit .356 with seven homers and 36 RBIs in July and August to give him a .329 average heading into the final month. He finished seventh in the league with a .319 average, 44 points below Joe Torre's NL-high. Jones led the team in hits (161) and RBIs (69), tied for the team lead with 14 home runs and was second with 24 doubles. It was the first and only time Jones was tops among Mets in home runs.

The 1972 season was excruciating in many respects. Armed with newly acquired Rusty Staub and fortified by the acquisition of Willie Mays in May, the Mets charged out to a 25–7 mark that put them six games ahead in the division. Jones did his part by batting .300 with 13 RBIs and 11 runs scored in those first 32 games.

But one by one, the Mets lost players due to injury. Staub broke his hand, Agee dealt with hamstring issues, Harrelson developed a bad back, Grote tried to play through elbow chips, rookie John Milner battled groin and neck problems, Gary Gentry had arm trouble, and Father Time finally caught up to Mays. Jones was among the infirmed, sidelined by an elbow injury that occurred while playing first base. He led the team with just 58 RBIs while playing 106 games, his least amount of action since 1965. Jones also hit only five home runs and batted .245, his worst production since becoming a regular.

He wasn't the only Mobile product to have a lousy year with the Mets. Agee battling hamstring issues and hit only .227 in 114 games before he was practically given away to the Astros after the season. The Agee trade left the Mets with Hahn and Mays as a center field platoon heading into the 1973 season, and may have left a wakeup call for their left fielder.

Jones was 30 years old when the Mets reported to spring training in 1973. He was outstanding during the exhibition season, hitting .321 with two home runs and a team-high 11 RBIs in 18 games. He continued his hot hitting into the season opener, going 3-for-3 with two blasts and three ribbies off Steve Carlton to support Tom Seaver in a 3–0 shutout of the Phillies. But his average was only .243 when he injured his right knee and forearm making a diving catch against Glenn Beckert in a 7–0 loss to the Cubs April 19. He didn't play again until May 11, when he began a six-game hitting streak that included 10 hits and 11 runs scored in 29 at-bats. But Jones left the team in San Francisco May 29 and headed back to New York to have his right arm placed in a cast. He didn't play again until July 7, the day George Theodore broke his hip in an outfield collision with Hahn.

Jones was one of seven Mets to land on the DL by July 8, along with John Milner, Willie Mays, Jerry Grote, Bud Harrelson, Jerry May, and George Theodore. The starting pitching managed to hold up, but the lineup was suspect at times, leading to a 32–49 record from May 1 to July 31.

The Mets weren't getting much production out of Jones during the early summer as he tried to play through his aches and pains. He became the first player to collect 1,000 hits as a Met when he doubled against Pittsburgh on August 2. The milestone hit sparked a 15-game stretch in which he batted .321 in 56 at-bats to raise his average to .274. However, the Mets went just 7–8 in that span leaving them last in the NL East at 53–66 on August 17, 7½ games behind the Cardinals.

Harrelson was activated a day later, which finally put the Mets at full strength for the first time since April 28. The Mets went a league-best 29–13 following Harrelson's return, with Jones hitting six home runs and driving in 17 runs in his final 14 games despite a .235 average.

The RBI streak began with a two-run single off Fergie Jenkins in the first inning of a 5–1 win over the Cubs on September 15. Six days later, Jones put the Mets ahead with a two-run double in the first inning of a 10–2 rout of the Pirates, which gave New York sole possession of the division lead for the first time all season.

Jones also had two RBIs in a 5–2 win over the Cardinals on September 23, the Mets' sixth consecutive win. When the Mets held Willie Mays Night on September 25, Jones had two RBIs in a 2–1 win over the Expos, providing the tiebreaking, solo homer in the sixth inning. And when the Mets clinched the division crown the day after the season was scheduled to end, Jones put New York ahead to stay with a solo homer before finishing with two RBIs in a 6–4 victory.

His greatest contribution to the stretch drive occurred during a three-game sweep of the Pirates at Shea as he delivered eight RBIs and began one of the strangest defensive plays in team annals.

Jones had an RBI in the series opener, but his game highlight came on defense in the 13th inning. In one of the most memorable—and bizarre—plays in clubs history, Dave Augustine drilled a Ray Sadecki pitch for what at first appeared to be a sure home run to left. Jones headed toward the warning track when the ball hit the top of the fence and caromed right back to him as Richie Zisk headed toward third base. Jones threw a strike to Wayne Garrett, who fired a perfect relay throw to catcher Ron Hodges to nail Zisk at the plate, preserving a 3–3 tie before the Mets won 4–3 in the bottom of the 13th.

A day later, Jones belted a two-run homer and a three-run shot in a 7–3 win over the Bucs. Jones put the game out of reach with his three-run blast in the eighth to cap the scoring.

Jones capped the series with his go-ahead, two-run double that helped the Mets move into first place for good.

The veteran outfielder had gained a lot of respect from his teammates, particularly from a rookie outfielder who received playing time while Jones was injured early in the season.

"Cleon Jones—if his knee is sound—he was the best hitter in baseball, I think," said George Theodore to the *New York Times* in 2008. "He had a great September, but he was also hitting off of one knee. A lot of people didn't realize that left knee that you push against, he couldn't do it.

"I guess in '69 when he hit .340, he was capable of doing that every year."

The Mets took on the Reds in the NLCS and dropped the first game 2-1 before pulling out their second pennant in five seasons. Jones was 6-for-20 (.300) with two doubles, three RBIs, and three runs scored in the series.

With the Mets clinging to a 1–0 lead in Game 2, Jones spanked an RBI double to ignite a four-run ninth, supporting Jon Matlack's two-hitter in a 5–0 win. He went 2-for-3 in a 9–2 rout of the Reds a day later and factored into the Mets' 7–2 victory in the Game 5 clincher. With the final game knotted 2–2, Jones doubled home Garrett to trigger a four-run fifth, giving Tom Seaver more than enough runs for his final career playoff victory.

Jones hit .286 in the World Series, but the Mets blew a three-games-to-two lead and lost to the A's in seven. His lone home run and RBI came in a 10–7, 12-inning victory in Game 2.

Jones accumulated a nice body of work in four postseason series, batting .284 (23-for-81) with two homers, eight RBIs, and 14 runs scored in 20 games. Many publications predicted the Mets would repeat as NL East champions in 1974, but injuries to Seaver, Tug McGraw, and George Stone led to a fifth-place finish at 71–91, the team's worst mark in seven years.

The Mets prepared for the '74 season by going 11–13 during an exhibition season that included a slight altercation between longtime teammates Jones and Harrelson. Both players downplayed the incident, as did their teammates.

"Nothing to it," said Jones.

"Just one of those things," added Ed Kranepool to the *Times*. "We've been in the sun too long. Only one punch

has been landed in all the time I've been with this club, and I knocked out [Tim] Foli with it." Kranepool decked Foli in 1971.

Jones played with an injured knee for most of the 1974 season, but it didn't stop him from putting together his best regular season in three years. He hit a team-best .282 with 13 homers, a team-high 23 doubles, 60 RBIs, and 62 runs scored in 124 games, missing much of September due to torn cartilage in his left knee.

When the '74 season ended, Jones was the team's all-time leader in runs (561), hits (1,176), doubles (181), home runs (93), RBIs (519), extra bases (307), and total bases (1,702). He also was second in games (1,180), at-bats (4,173), and triples (33), and third with 91 stolen bases.

Torn knee cartilage was serious business in the mid-1970s. Jones underwent surgery October 11 and was able to play just two games the following spring training. The Mets went north without him, putting him in extended spring training to continue rehabilitation on the knee. The assignment led to an embarrassing moment in team history.

Jones was still in Florida when he was cited for indecent exposure in the spring. Police found him in a comprising position with a woman in a van. The woman was not his wife, a public relations shocker to those fans who revered Jones.

His wife, Angela, was featured in many Mets yearbooks under sections involving team wives. Daughter Anja once escorted Casey Stengel to the field during an Old Timer's Day introduction. The incident in Florida was enough of an embarrassment to the Jones family and could have been kept quiet by the team. The charge was quickly dropped and could have been spun as a misunderstanding. Instead, the Mets, trying to purvey their squeaky-clean image to the public, staged a news conference in which Cleon, flanked by his wife, apologized for the episode. It was one of the team's bigger PR blunders and led to friction between Jones and Mets brass, particularly board chairman M. Donald Grant.

Jones eventually made his season debut May 27 against the Dodgers, poking a single as a pinch-hitter before going 3-for-3 with an RBI double versus the Padres four days later. He owned a .385 through his first 10 games but never started back-to-back games for manager Yogi Berra, who let him stagnate on the bench.

In fairness to Berra, the roster had changed since Jones went under the knife the previous October. Newcomer Dave Kingman, who was hitting homers at a team-record pace, had supplanted Jones as the left fielder when he wasn't playing first base. Milner and Ed Kranepool were hitting well while serving as the first-base platoon, giving Jones little opportunity to play.

Berra put Jones in the starting lineup in Game 1 of a doubleheader July 11 against the Reds and used him in a pinch-hitting role during the nightcap. Jones didn't play again for another week, when he lined out to short as a pinch-hitter in the seventh inning of a 4–3 loss to the Braves.

Berra asked Jones to take over in left field after the at-bat with the Mets trailing 3–1. Jones, unhappy with his recent role with the team, refused to take the field in the top of the eighth. Berra ripped into Jones, ordered him back to the clubhouse, and drew a line in the sand. He went to Grant and general manager Joe McDonald, demanding Jones be cut from the team for insubordination.

The Mets suspended Jones the next day and let him twist before releasing him from his contract a week later. Days after his final game, Jones admitted that frustration over playing time led to his refusal to follow Berra's orders.

"I've been teed off for weeks," he told the *New York Times*. "What happened last night was the last straw. What would be my first choice? To play left field for the Mets, regularly, but it won't happen.

"I can't help them with my butt on the bench. I'm ready to play, my knee is okay. I've been ready to play for weeks. I'm a winning ballplayer. We won two pennants since I've been here, and I had a hand in both of them. Now they're trying to tell me I'm not good enough to play for this club?

"All they do is use me to pinch-hit with nobody on base, things like that."

By many accounts, Berra already had lost many members of the team with his relaxed approach to discipline. Hodges used to run a daily weigh-in to make sure his players were in top shape. But Berra, who took over as manager following Hodges' death in April 1972, didn't keep diligent tabs on the team's "growth" chart. Some players cited Jones as one of the biggest offenders.

"With Cleon, Yogi was trying to make the point that Cleon had put on a couple of pounds and he thought he should be in better shape," said Jerry Koosman in Peter Golenbock's book *'Amazin*. "That's what Yogi was getting at. Hodges had ruled the club with an iron hand, had weigh-ins all the time, and Yogi didn't and consequently even though we were adults, some of us stretched the rules a little bit, and Yogi let it go by."

Jones initially sought to fight the suspension through arbitration, but the Mets lifted the ban while placing him on irrevocable waivers July 27, ending his Mets career.

The *New York Times* printed the official statement: "Having exhausted all avenues in an attempt to reconcile this problem, we are offering Cleon Jones his unconditional release. We see nothing to be gained in going through the arbitration procedure. Regardless of the result, the problem would not be resolved. We have no desire to hurt anyone. The suspension is being lifted, and Cleon will be paid in full. We feel another club will sign him, and we wish him well."

Nearly six years later, Jones acknowledged that his days as a Met might have been numbered following the Florida incident, particularly with the way the team handled the matter.

"That incident in Florida greased the slides for me as a player with the Mets," said Jones to the *Times* after return-

ing to the team in a minor league capacity. "I didn't feel I did anything wrong, but Mr. Grant was set in his ways, and I guess he felt it was his duty to do something about it. I just wanted to get it over with. I never was mad with Grant.

"Anyhow, it was all downhill…. Everything got out of hand. I was playing hurt, and the team was losing. Then I had that altercation with Yogi. I don't think he was trying to hurt me, but somebody had to be the fall guy, and it was me. It was just a bad situation.

"Life is full of complexities. You just try to go from day to day. I don't look back on those old problems very much anymore. I try to dwell on positive things."

But he almost finished out the season at Shea anyway. He was in negotiations with the Yankees, who were sharing Shea while Yankee Stadium was being renovated. But talks eventually stalled, keeping him off a major league diamond the rest of the season.

"The issue is whether we'll give him a bonus for signing, said Yankees president Gabe Paul to the *New York Times* in August. "Salary isn't the problem, but the bonus is. Maybe we set a precedent with Catfish Hunter [whom the Yankees signed as a free agent before the season], but not everybody is Catfish Hunter. We'd like very much to get Jones if we can settle the bonus matter."

Jones never signed with the Yankees and had to wait until the winter of 1976 before netting a contract with the White Sox. It was a bit ironic that Jones went to the team that employed Agee when he won the 1966 AL Rookie of the Year Award.

But Chicago dropped Jones in May 1976. He went 6-for-12 during a three-game segment to bring his average up to .267 by April 28 before an 0-for-10 skid dropped him to .200, leading to his release.

Jones struggled financially immediately after his playing career ended before regaining his footing. He eventually returned to the Mets organization as a minor league hitting instructor in 1981.

ML/Mets debut	vs. Colt 45s, 9/14/63
1st ML/Mets hit	single vs. Bobby Bolin, @ Giants, 9/22/63
1st ML/Mets homer	solo ohomer vs. Bob Friend, @ Pirates, 9/25/95
1st ML/Mets RBI	RBI grounder vs. Bob Garibaldi, @ Giants, 9/22/63
Most hits, ML/Mets game	4, @ Pirates, 8/17/67; @ Phils, 7/6/68; @ Reds, 8/18/74
Most homers, ML/Mets game	2, vs. Phillies, 4/6/73; vs. Pirates, 9/19/73
Most RBI, ML/Mets game	5, 4 times

Acquired: Signed as an amateur free agent before the 1963 season.
Deleted: Released, 7/27/75. Signed by the White Sox 4/3/76.

Dave Kingman

First baseman, Outfielder, Third Baseman
Bats right, throws right
Born: 12/21/48   Pendleton, Oregon
Height: 6′6″   Weight: 215   #26

Dave Kingman Mets Career

YEAR	GP	AB	R	H	2B	3B	HR	RBI	K	BB	SB	AVG	SLG	OBP
1975	134	502	65	116	22	1	36	88	153	34	7	.231	.494	.284
1976	123	474	70	113	14	1	37	86	135	28	7	.238	.506	.286
1977	58	211	22	44	7	0	9	28	66	13	3	.209	.370	.263
1981	100	353	40	78	11	3	22	59	105	55	6	.221	.456	.326
1982	149	535	80	109	9	1	37	99	156	59	4	.204	.432	.285
1983	100	248	25	49	7	0	13	29	57	22	2	.198	.383	.265
TOTAL	664	2323	302	509	70	6	154	389	672	211	29	.219	.453	.287

ML Career

YEAR	GP	AB	R	H	2B	3B	HR	RBI	K	BB	SB	AVG	SLG	OBP
71-86	1941	6677	901	1575	240	25	442	1210	1816	608	85	.236	.478	.302

Before Darryl Strawberry arrived at Shea Stadium, there was just one player in Mets history who could make a fan adjust the timing of his trip to the bathroom or concession stands. No one wanted to miss a Dave Kingman at-bat during his first two seasons with the Mets for fear of missing the longest home run ever hit. His homers seemed effortless as Kingman could use his quick wrists, 6′6″ frame, and uppercut to flick a ball over the auxiliary scoreboard in left field.

To appreciate Kingman was to understand the team's home run history prior to his arrival in 1975. Frank Thomas held the Mets record for round-trippers with 34, doing it in their inaugural season. Over the next 12 years, Tommie Agee, Donn Clendenon, and John Milner would be the only Mets to hit more than 20 home runs in a season, and Agee and Clendenon were gone by the time Kingman showed up for spring training at Huggins-Stengel Field in 1975.

David Arthur Kingman already had built a well-earned reputation as a power hitter by the time the Mets bought him from the Giants for $150,000 on February 28, 1975. He crushed 29 homers and drove in 83 runs for the 1972 Giants before smacking 42 home runs the next two seasons. His career average stood at just .224, he struck out once per 2.94 at-bats and his fielding was a bit unsettling, but his raw power was exactly what the Mets needed to complement Milner, Rusty Staub, Wayne Garrett, and Felix Millan in the '75 lineup. Although his fielding was a bit suspect, he possessed a laser arm that also made him a potential major league prospect as a pitcher during his days at Southern Cal.

An old Giants teammate was awaiting Kingman at St. Petersburg and was willing to help the young slugger cut down on his strikeouts.

"It's a mental problem," said Willie Mays, two years removed from his last spring training as an active player. "He's trying to hit home runs every time so he chases bad pitches, especially high ones. In San Francisco he was unhappy, so they couldn't get through to him. But I can talk to him, and I will."

"I take a big cut at the ball," Kingman said of his approach at the plate. "It's the type of hitter I am, so I'll strike out a lot. Yes, I expect there'll be a lot of pressure on me in New York, too, but nothing is handed to you."[92]

Instead of Mays, it was another former NL batting champ who helped Kingman with his swing. Mays wanted to eliminate Kingman's uppercut, but Mets hitting coach Phil Cavaretta focused on his strengths after trying that spring to stop Kingman from dropping his right shoulder when he swung.

"We had tried to get him to make contact more often to lessen his strikeouts but he couldn't cope with it," said Cavaretta the following season. "It's not his makeup. So we let him be himself. He appreciated that. In the past some people had told him to make so many changes that it just messed up his natural power."

"Phil was very patient with me," Kingman said in 1976. "He didn't try to shorten my swing. He let me be me. I'll always take my big cut. But he helped me become more selective in the pitches I swing at, more patient in waiting for my pitch."[93]

Kingman was one of many good-hitting outfielders let go by the Giants in the early 1970s. The team also developed and dispatched George Foster, Garry Maddox, and Gary Matthews without getting much in return. Kingman wasted little time impressing Mets fans, launching a mammoth home run off Yankees free agent Catfish Hunter in a spring training game that was televised back to New York. He added another blast that night for good measure.

"He hit some like that off me in Arizona," remarked Hunter after the game. "If he had hit that one in Arizona, it would've gone another hundred feet.

"If you're going to give them up, there's no need to give up a cheap one."

The winning pitcher in that 3–0 victory also marveled at Kingman's power.

"That first one was just incredible, absolutely incredible," said Tom Seaver. He didn't even swing that hard. I think he's beginning to realize that if he tried to hit it that hard, he couldn't. The only other ball I can remember seeing hit like that was Reggie Jackson's homer in the All-Star game in Detroit. You just flinch and say, 'Thank God he didn't hit it back through the box.'"[94]

Kingman went deep on Opening Day, belting a game-tying home run off Steve Carlton in the fourth inning of a 2–1 win over the Phillies. He also homered in the third and fourth games of the season and had four long balls in his first 10 games with the team. His power made Mets fans ignore the fact that he also struck out in 13 of his first 15 games with the team.

Kingman's average stood at .219 with 11 homers and 29 RBIs through June, but he earned Player of the Month honors in July by hitting .322 with 13 homers and 31 RBIs

Dave Kingman (26) slaps a ball into the outfield during a 1976 game.
Photo courtesy of Oscar W. Gabriel

in 31 games. He single-handedly helped the Mets win a 10–9 game against the Astros July 20, homering twice and driving in six runs.

"My mistake in San Francisco was that I listened to too many people rather than rely on my own instincts," Kingman explained after the game. "It takes a long time to learn that some days will be bad and some good, and that each day is new. This was one of those days when everything went right."[95]

The 13 homers in July topped Agee's team record of 11 for a single month. Kingman also hit .386 during a 10-game hitting streak that ended August 2.

Kingman showed a willingness to play where needed, appearing in 71 games in the outfield, 58 at first, and 12 at third. He spent much of the last two weeks of the season as

the starting third baseman, allowing Mike Vail an opportunity to run his hitting streak to 23 games to tie Cleon Jones' team record.

Kingman matched Thomas' single-season team record for home runs with a solo shot in a 7–0 win at Pittsburgh September 11, one of his seven homers belted at Three Rivers Stadium that season. He went 3-for-28 with 10 strikeouts in his next six games before breaking the Mets' home run mark in grand fashion, launching a walk-off, two-run blast in the bottom of the ninth to beat the Cubs 7–5.

"That was a hard one to get," Kingman remarked after the game. "I don't know why, but I haven't been swinging the bat too well since tying the club record. Now I can forget all about records and go back to the frame of mind I was in before I began thinking about home runs."[96]

Kingman ended the year with a team-high 36 home runs and was second to Staub with 88 RBIs. He also paced the Mets in stolen bases with seven and was fourth in hits despite a .231 average.

Mets general manager Joe McDonald inexplicably dealt Staub to the Tigers after the season, leaving Kingman with little protection in the lineup for 1976. New York was seventh in the league with 615 runs scored and eighth with 560 RBIs in '76.

Staub's departure made Kingman a one-man wrecking crew and the only scary member of the Mets' lineup. He opened the season by going 0-for-7 in his first two games before producing a seven-game stretch in which he hit .323 with seven homers, 15 RBIs, and eight runs scored. He won two games for the Mets during that span, belting a go-ahead, three-run homer in the ninth inning of a 10–8 win at Chicago April 15 and launching a three-run blast in a 3–0 win over the Braves April 28.

"I ended up spring training shaky," said Kingman after swatting his seventh home run of the year on April 19. "I wasn't hitting the ball well, I wasn't comfortable. But last week I suddenly felt comfortable. It just happened. I can't explain why. And when I'm comfortable, I'm snapping the bat. That's the secret—bat speed. I've got good wrists and forearms, and being tall, I think I get a little more leverage than the other guys. But bat speed is the most important thing, that and playing everyday. I always had the confidence that the ability was there. I just wanted the opportunity to play every day and the Mets gave it to me.[97]

Kingman also hit well that May, delivering eight homers, 18 RBIs, and 15 runs scored. He had two homers and five ribbies in a 6–2 win over the Padres May 7 and went 4-for-5 with two homers and three RBIs in a 6–3 victory Atlanta five days later.

Kingman's most productive game as a Met came on June 4 in Los Angeles. Jim Hickman had been the lone Met to belt three home runs in a game until Kingman went deep three times on consecutive pitches while driving in eight runs in an 11–0 rout of the Dodgers. The eight ribbies remained a team record until Carlos Delgado broke it with nine against the Yankees in 2008.

Kingman duplicated his three-homer, eight-RBI feat against the Dodgers two years later, which prompted a famous, profanity-laced tirade from Los Angeles manager Tom Lasorda.

Kingman homered the next day and owned a .234 average with a league-high 30 homers and 69 RBIs in 86 games by the All-Star break. He was chasing Mike Schmidt for the NL home run title while fielding questions concerning the possibility of breaking Roger Maris' single-season record.

"That's pretty far-fetched," Kingman said a few weeks into the season. "That's a record set by another ballplayer in another ballpark in another time. I don't make predictions. I have 'em inside me but I don't talk about 'em. I'd like to lead the league but so would Mike Schmidt."[98]

He opened the second half by hitting a go-ahead, two-run homer in a 3–1 win over the Astros before belting a solo shot three days later.

Kingman had 32 homers in 90 games and was challenging the one-year record until July 19, when he dove for a sinking liner hit by Braves pitcher Phil Niekro. Kingman's thumb bent back in his glove as he landed on the turf, leaving him with torn ligaments that would keep him out of action until August 27. The home run record was safe, but he still had a shot at becoming the first Met to win a home run title.

Without Kingman, the Mets hit six home runs and scored 105 runs in 33 games between July 20 and August 25, going 16–17 and killing any possible chance to get back into the NL East race.

The Pendleton, Oregon, native had a good September, batting .263 with five home runs, 14 RBIs, and 14 runs scored. But Mike Schmidt came away with the home run crown by hitting 38, one more than Kingman in 37 more games. Kingman topped the team with 86 RBIs and 70 runs scored despite missing six weeks to help the Mets finish with 86 wins, their best regular season since 1969.

Full-fledged free agency hit baseball at the end of the 1976 season, giving the Mets ample opportunity to immediately bolster the lineup. Lee Mazzilli and John Stearns were the only true prospects in the farm system at the time, and a spending spree was the only way the Mets could challenge the Phillies and Pirates for NL East supremacy. But team chairman M. Donald Grant refused to dole out any big contracts and was prepared to rebuild through a minor league operation that was barren. Grant and general manager Joe McDonald also declined to make any significant trades in the off-season, leaving Kingman unprotected in the lineup once again.

It might have been fun to see how Kingman performed amid a lineup of productive hitters. He could have been more selective at the plate, knowing another experienced bat was capable of driving in runs. But he was a one-man offense heading into 1977, the feature act in what would become a very bad show.

Kingman also felt that if he was the team's primary source of offense, he should be paid accordingly. He was in the final year of his contract and was angling for a multiyear pact that was on par with the money handed out to the first wave of free agents.

Tom Seaver's contract was the absolute ceiling for the Mets in 1977, and their best pitcher was scheduled to make $225,000 that year. The Mets did not want to begin a salary battle with their entire roster by offering Kingman a contract worth more than Seaver's income. But Kingman also knew how much other sluggers had been given through free agency and felt his contract request was reasonable.

"My only demands are in line with the dollar figures given to other players on other clubs," Kingman said in spring training after watching several free agents accepted deals far exceeding $1 million. "The Mets adhere to a policy of trying to remain in their own league on salaries. Tom Seaver is the best pitcher in baseball, and if he was in my position today, he would get considerably more this year than he got last year—more than anybody, and way over Catfish Hunter.

"I look around and see the dollar figures of other players and I ask, why? Why should I play for the old figures the Mets are imposing. Rusty Staub tried for something extra and was traded. Tom Seaver may leave this club in two years if the Mets do not upgrade their policies. He got a very good contract last year – good at the time. But the game of baseball has changed completely since then. It's supply and demand.

"I don't want to leave New York, unless I have to. No, I'm not threatening to play out my option. I am as conscious of the New York fan as this so-called family is. I leave it to the New York fan [as to] who's in the right. I want a six-year contract or a one-year contract, nothing in between. You sell yourself for six years, you're giving away your prime years. But they're treating you like in the Dark Ages."

Seaver concurred, knowing his teammate wanted to eclipse his current salary.

"The club is negotiating as if the reserve clause is still in effect," said Seaver, who was trying to renegotiate his own deal. "Sooner or later, they're going to have to come to the realization that the salary structure has changed. They don't want to face reality. Five years ago, the players told the owners to reach an equitable settlement. But the owners gambled and lost."[99]

Kingman made $90,000 in 1976 while finishing second in the NL in home runs. He rejected a reported $200,000 contract in the spring of 1977 as he sought, according to the *New York Times*, twice that amount plus a bonus. Legendary *New York Times* columnist Red Smith wrote during spring training that it was time the Mets recognized that a new pay scale had been created throughout Major League Baseball.

It can be a disruption to have one player grousing about his contract. But when your two best players are unhappy with their compensation, chaos ensues. And the 1977 Mets front office was more than willing to make the worst of a bad situation.

In Seaver's case, Grant funneled his thoughts into the head of *Daily News* columnist Dick Young, who wrote scathing prose depicting Seaver as a selfish bum before dragging the pitcher's family into the criticism. But with Kingman, the team went public by disclosing to the media his supposed contract demands. McDonald went a step further by belittling Kingman's value.

"We offered Kingman $200,000 a year for two, three, four or five years," McDonald began in a news conference after Kingman held court. "He wants $2 million, including a bonus. If he is insisting on a trade, we'll try to accommodate him. But in no way will we let him make his own trade.

"Other clubs are not that interested. Dave hits home runs, but he also strikes out a lot. And we found that he does not rank very high in production. For example, in pressure situations late in games where you're three runs behind with men on base, Mike Schmidt of Philadelphia knocks in a run 42 percent of the time, Steve Garvey of Los Angeles 36 percent of the time, and Kingman only 18 percent."[100]

In truth, Kingman in 1976 hit .282 with six homers and 12 RBIs in 85 at-bats during the seventh inning or later with his team tied, ahead by one or the tying run at least on deck. Schmidt batted .282 with seven homers and 22 RBIs in the same 85 at-bats during those situations while playing on a ballclub with a much better lineup. Garvey also benefited from a better group of hitters surrounding him as he compiled a .339 average with three homers and 17 RBIs in 118 at-bats in games that were "late and close."

McDonald's news conference prompted Kingman to fire an immediate salvo.

"Grant forced me to play out my option," Kingman said. "He wants to put the blame on me, the way he did on Tom Seaver. I wanted to leave the door open, but Grant slammed it. I'd like to play in New York, but now it's impossible. I cherish everything about the Mets except M. Donald Grant and his mismanagement."[101]

Kingman's public derision of Grant came after he launched a tiebreaking, two-run homer in the seventh inning of a 3–1 win over the Reds. It was his sixth home run of the '77 exhibition season, although the blast raised his batting average to a mere .200. The date of that game: April Fool's Day.

The Mets were screwing with Kingman's head in another way. They wanted him to hit more to right field, a theory that was supposed to raise his batting average and RBI production. But it was a difficult challenge for Kingman, whose natural swing sent balls deep into the left-field sky and created a 360-foot jog around the bases. Asking Kingman to hit to right was like asking Monet to paint with his toes.

After two years most Mets fans accepted Kingman for what he was, a prodigious home run hitter whose strikeouts and errors could be just as game-changing as his blasts. But the game was becoming slightly less enjoyable for Kingman as he played out his contract while dealing with the mounting pressure of being the only legitimate slugger on the team.

"The pressure of this game can really drive you up a tree," Kingman said during the Mets' first homestand of 1977. "I can't think of any other way to make a living: baseball is the only thing that I excel at, but I don't think people know how hard it is to get to the big leagues. They don't understand the pressures of having to do this job.

"Sure, I hear the fans boo, and I know that the overwhelming majority of them would give anything to wear this uniform. But they don't know that if you can't do the job, you're gone. You try putting that into words. They don't know what it's like. They don't know what I'm like. All they know is what they read.

"I enjoy being with people. I just wanna be like the next guy. Sometimes I wish I could play a musical instrument, or sing. I sit back in awe of someone who can really sing well—just plain sing.

"You know," he continued with a small laugh, "I've never booed a singer."[102]

Kingman got off to a fine start in '77, hitting safely in 14 of 17 games during April and posting a .294 average with six home runs and 18 RBIs. His strikeouts were down and his on-base percentage was up, but the Mets still compiled a losing record for the month. He smashed a pair of three-run homers in a 9–2 win over the Padres April 29, which gave the Mets a 7–9 record.

The Mets hit bottom in May, going 8–21 and changing managers on Memorial Day. Kingman contributed to the plunge by hitting .151 with two home runs, six runs scored, and 26 strikeouts in 22 games.

Kingman normally had a lousy relationship with the media. He had been burned by a 1976 *Sports Illustrated* article that compared him with Mike Schmidt of the Phillies. The piece lauded Schmidt's fielding and solid batting average while portraying Kingman as a buffoonish slugger who did little else. And he was in no mood to make friends with the press while the Mets continued their descent into the basement.

Seaver, who was going through similar contract squabbles with management, had most of the writers in his corner and continued to pitch well despite the team's record. Those same writers showed no compassion for Kingman due to their adversarial relationship, allowing him to bear the brunt of the blame for the Mets' collapse. However, Seaver publicly remained a sympathetic voice and beat the drum for Kingman through the media.

"I can kid Dave, and he'll smile," Seaver said. "I'll walk by and call him a 'militant' or an 'ingrate,' and Dave will smile. It takes a special psyche to deal with all this garbage the club's giving him, but Dave's strong. As soon as he hits a couple of homers in front of everybody, the Mets will realize that they've made a mistake, and maybe they'll start treating him as a human being."[103]

Kingman's struggles at the plate continued through the first two weeks of June as he hit .193 with one home run and 21 strikeouts in 14 games. Three-fourths of his run production came on a three-run homer off Philadelphia's Jim Kaat in a 3–2 victory on June 5. They were his last home run and RBI as a Met until 1981.

Grant decided to rid himself of his top two players—and biggest headaches—at the June 15 trade deadline. Seaver had worked out a deal with owner Lorinda de Roulet but rescinded after Young wrote a column saying Nancy Seaver was jealous of Ruth Ryan because her husband, Nolan, was making far more money. Seaver requested a trade and was moved to Cincinnati for pitcher Pat Zachry and three prospects.

With Seaver's departure sending shockwaves through New York, Kingman's exit became an afterthought. He was shipped to the Padres for Bobby Valentine and Paul Seibert, neither of which would be with the Mets when Kingman put together his finest major league season in 1979.

Kingman managed to play for one team in all four major league divisions in 1977. He spent two productive months with the Padres, hitting .238 with 11 homers and 38 RBIs in 56 games before he was moved to the Angels, who sent him to the Yankees within two weeks.

The Yankees picked up Kingman primarily for a three-game series at Boston's Fenway Park, where they hoped he could do damage to the Green Monster. He homered in each of his first three games with New York, including a pinch-hit blast at Fenway September 19. Kingman batted .250 with four home runs and seven RBIs in eight games for the Yanks but was unable to play in the postseason because he was acquired after the September 1 cutoff date.

"We were teammates on the Angels for about 10 days," said reliever Dyar Millar, who also became Kingman's teammate with the 1981 Mets. "We had a nice lunch one day, then parted and said: 'See you at the ballpark.' When I got there, his locker was cleaned out. He'd been traded to the Yankees after lunch."[104]

Kingman was able to hit 26 homers and drive in 78 runs despite the constant address changes, but his .444 slugging percentage was his lowest since his final season with the Giants.

The Yankees, who didn't have room for another designated hitter and weren't interested in giving him a bonus, allowed Kingman to become a free agent. The American League seemed well suited for Kingman, whose defense made him a liability at most positions. But he returned to the National League, signing a deal with the Cubs that allowed the avid boater to enjoy Lake Michigan.

Kingman and Wrigley Field were a perfect match. Since 1973, Kingman had been a .336 hitter with 18 homers and 43 RBIs in 125 at-bats there. Give him a full season at the Friendly Confines, and Kingman seemed capable of 36 homers and 86 RBIs without playing a single road game in 1978. Those numbers led to speculation he could become the majors' single-season home run champ.

"It's flattering to hear that talk," said Kingman during 1978 training camp. "It's part of what I'm paid for. I'll say this, the possibility is there. But beyond that, I'm not going to elaborate.

"It's a ballpark conducive to hitting," he added about Wrigley Field. "It's hard to put into words. You don't have to hit it good at Wrigley Field to hit it out of there. And it's not that I was hitting against Cub pitching. I'm just comfortable there."[105]

He was part of a lineup that led the National League with a .264 average in 1978 and was fifth with 664 runs scored. The Cubbies managed to hit only 72 home runs the entire season, but Kingman was responsible for 28 while hitting .266 with 79 RBIs. He also cut down on his strikeouts, fanning 111 times in 448 plate appearances.

The 1979 Cubs challenged for the NL East title in the first 3½ months of the season, riding Kingman's bat to a 50–39 start that left them 1½ games out of first by July 21. Kingman was responsible for much of the offense, hitting .292 with 29 homers and 70 RBIs during that span to earn his second trip to the All-Star Game.

He hammered his old team in late July at Shea Stadium, going 6-for-8 with five homers and six RBIs in the first two games of a series against the Mets to raise his average to an uncharacteristic .303. He opened August with nine RBIs in the first four games and already had tied his career high of 37 home runs by August 4.

Kingman leveled off the rest of the year but still led the league with career-highs of 48 home runs, a .613 slugging average and a .956 OPS while setting personal bests with a .288 average and 115 RBIs. He finished 11th in the MVP voting for a team that went 80–82, the first time he had received any votes for the award since 1976. He blasted Mets pitching that year, belting nine home runs and driving in 20 runs while posting a .364 average in 66 at-bats.

Kingman opened 1980 by winning NL Player of the Month honors for April, batting .346 with six home runs and 16 RBIs. But he injured his shoulder May 8 and made two trips to the disabled list, causing him to appear in just 81 games the entire season. He still finished with a .277 average, 18 home runs, and 57 ribbies, but was fined by the team for missing a game while making a personal appearance. He was on the disabled list at the time, but the game he missed happened to be "Dave Kingman T-Shirt Day."

Kingman seemed to have found a home in Chicago. He owned a .278 average with 94 homers and 251 RBIs in 345 games over three seasons with the Cubs while limiting his strikeouts to just one per four at-bats. But the Cubs didn't come any closer to earning a playoff berth with Kingman than they had in 32 previous seasons without him. Kingman was a day away from reporting to camp with the 1981 Cubs when he learned his spring training destination would be Florida and not Arizona. Mets general manager Frank Cashen brought back the team's most prolific home run hitter in exchange for Steve Henderson.

Kingman was rejoining the Mets in the same condition they were in when he left. They had just completed their fourth straight losing season and had little drawing power outside of matinee idol Lee Mazzilli. One positive was that the ballclub was much younger than it was in 1977 and was ready to put rookies Mookie Wilson and Hubie Brooks into the lineup on an everyday basis. But the Mets also gave up one of their top hitters to get Kingman.

The slugger made a peace offering to the media upon reporting to St. Petersburg, handing out expensive pens and telling the writers he hoped they'd write nice things about him. He was looking for a fresh start in old surroundings and made an effort to get along with the scribes in '81.

Kingman was rather introspective as he met with the beat writers after reporting to camp, discussing his personality and how baseball fit in with his life.

"I am a recluse," Kingman started off while trying to explain his demeanor. "By nature, I'm private. I never liked the front row. Notoriety does not come easily to me. I've even dated girls who made that complaint—that I don't talk enough.

"Everybody's hot and cold, I guess. Everybody has his moments. When I have my sullen times, I want to be left alone. If you call that moody, okay.

"Baseball is a job to me, not an obsession. I'm not after publicity in New York. I will fight it as I have done in the past. I don't want to compete with anybody for the man-about-town title. I'm not a night person. You won't catch me out late. I'm an early riser, up at seven every morning, preparing myself in several ways for my job.

"I'm like an actor. I want to perform. But, if an actor went to the theater and performed before empty seats, it would be boring. I'll create some excitement on the field. Criticize me for what I do on the field. When I leave the field, leave me alone."[106]

Kingman then condensed those thoughts into five words. "I'm not moody. I'm private."

In a bit of irony, Cashen gave Kingman a five-year contract, the same length he had requested from the Mets in 1977. He had an ally in the front office this time, although Cashen admitted to some apprehension in bringing Kingman back to New York.

"I was concerned," Cashen said before Kingman handed out chrome fountain pens to the media and lending his self-evaluation. "The first morning, we had breakfast, Kingman and Joe Torre and I. You know, I was concerned he would resume fighting with the press. I suggested that maybe bygones should be bygones. But I never expected that he'd respond by starting a honeymoon with everybody. If I'd known that, I would have saved myself an ulcer."[107]

"Sky King" started off slowly in 1981, going 3-for-19 in his first seven games before launching his first home run of the season. His average was at .200 until May 25, when he began a seven-game stretch in which he batted .375 with six home runs, 13 RBIs and eight runs scored. That was part of a 22-game span that bore nine homers, 18 RBIs, and a .269 average just before a strike wiped out the next two months of the season.

Once the strike ended, Kingman batted .319 with five homers and 14 RBIs to help the Mets open the second half 7–5 following a 17–34 mark in the first half. He went the next 22 games without a round-tripper before launching a three-run blast that helped New York stay within striking distance of the second-half title.

Kingman finished tied for third in the National League with 22 homers and 10th with 59 RBIs despite a .221 average that included a .188 mark in his final 38 games. He also managed to walk a career-high 55 times to lift his on-base percentage to a respectable .326, by far his highest as a Met.

Cashen got Kingman some protection in 1982, sending three players to the Reds for power-hitting outfielder George Foster. The lineup looked much better on paper, especially if Ellis Valentine, acquired in May 1981, could revert to form. Brooks was coming off a .307 season, Wilson batted .271 in '81, and Rusty Staub posted a .317 average in part-time duty. But Valentine and Foster combined for only 21 homers and 118 RBIs, again leaving the onus on Kingman to produce runs.

Kingman had a feast-or-famine season in 1982, blasting 37 of the Mets' 97 home runs while driving in 99 runs, six shy of Staub's then-Mets record. He was the first Met to lead the league in home runs and came within 11 RBIs of pacing the circuit in that category. His 80 runs scored was his second-best single-season total. But Kingman topped the league by striking out a career-high 156 times. He also hit only .204, which remains the lowest single-season average for a Met who qualified for the batting title. It marked the first time the NL Cy Young Award winner had a higher batting average than the home run champion as Steve Carlton ended the year with a .218 average.

The Mets still hadn't shown any improvement in the standings. They played over .500 ball during the first two months of the season, but a 15-game losing streak in August led to a last-place finish and a 65–97 record.

Mets fans were growing impatient with Cashen's rebuilding program and took aim at Foster and Kingman when the 1983 team got off to a 10–20 start despite the return of Tom Seaver. Kingman hit six home runs and drove in 13 runs while scoring 11 times during the first 30 games, but he heard plenty of boos due to his .188 average and 23 strikeouts. He hit for average in early June, batting .303 during an eight-game hitting streak that was capped by his game-winning two-run homer in the 17th inning against the Expos June 10.

Darryl Strawberry had been added to the lineup by then, and George Foster was hitting for power again. But the Mets were still missing an on-field leader who could hit for average, drive in some runs, and lead a young ballclub.

Five days after Kingman's game-winning blast, Cashen acquired first baseman Keith Hernandez from the Cardinals in one of the best deals in team history. The trade also meant the end of Kingman as the Mets' everyday first baseman. The proud slugger started just six games the rest of the season, none after July 28. He had only 57 at-bats following Hernandez's arrival, hitting .175 with a homer and six RBIs. His last home run as a Met came July 2, a two-shot shot as a pinch-hitter in a 6–5 loss at Philadelphia.

Kingman headed back to the Bay Area in 1984, signing with the A's as a designated hitter. Once again, he found Mecca after leaving the Mets, hitting 35 homers and collecting a career-high 118 RBIs while batting .268 for the '84 Athletics. He spent three years with Oakland, averaging 33 home runs and 101 RBIs before his contract was up at the end of 1986.

Kingman remained a man without a team at the start of 1987. He finally signed a minor league deal with the Giants in July at age 38 and reported to Triple A Phoenix. Kingman played 20 games for the Firebirds and retired after hitting .203 with two home runs in 59 at-bats.

He eventually collected his final major league check in 1995, almost 8½ years after his last major league game. An arbitrator ruled Major League Baseball was guilty of collusion during the 1986–1987 free-agent signing period as owners tried to harness contracts by tendering minimal offers. Kingman was awarded $648,000 on a lost-job claim for 1987, plus interest for a total of $829,849.54.

Kingman remained the Mets' all-time home run leader with 154 until Strawberry broke the mark in 1988. Kingman was warmly received by Mets fans as he was introduced at the closing of Shea Stadium in 2008, when he was ranked fourth on the team's all-time list.

ML debut	Giants vs. Pirates, 7/30/71
Mets debut	vs. Phillies, 4/8/75
1st ML hit	RBI double vs. Nelson Briles, Pirates, 7/31/71 (with Giants)
1st Mets hit	solo homer vs. Steve Carlton, Phillies, 4/8/75
1st ML homer	grand slam vs. Dave Giusti, Pirates, 7/31/71 (with Giants)
1st Mets homer	solo homer vs. Steve Carlton, Phillies, 4/8/75
1st ML RBI	RBI double vs. Nelson Briles, Pirates, 7/31/71 (with Giants)
1st Mets RBI	solo homer vs. Steve Carlton, Phillies, 4/8/75
Most hits, ML game	4, 9 times, 4 times with Cubs
Most hits, Mets game	4, 4 times
Most homers, ML game	3, 5 times, 3 times with Cubs
Most homers, Mets game	3, @ Dodgers, 6/4/76
Most RBI, ML game	8, 3 times
Most RBI, Mets game	8, @ Dodgers, 6/4/76

Acquired: Sold by the Giants for $150,000, 2/28/75.

Deleted: Traded to the Padres for Bobby Valentine and Paul Siebert, 6/15/77.

Reacquired: Traded by the Cubs for Steve Henderson and cash, 2/28/81.

Deleted: Released 1/28/84. Signed by the A's 3/29/84.

Jerry Koosman

Pitcher
Born: 12/23/42
Height: 6'2"

Bats right, throws left
Appleton, Minnesota
Weight: 208   #36

Jerry Koosman Mets Career

YEAR	GP/GS	IP	H	R	ER	K	BB	W–L	SV	ERA
1967	9/3	22.1	22	17	15	11	19	0–2	0	6.04
1968	35/34	263.2	221	72	61	178	69	19–12	0	2.08
1969	32/32	241.0	187	66	61	180	68	17–9	0	2.28
1970	30/29	212.0	189	87	74	118	71	12–7	0	3.14
1971	26/24	165.2	160	66	56	96	51	6–11	0	3.04
1972	34/24	163.0	155	81	75	147	52	11–12	1	4.14
1973	35/35	263.0	234	93	83	156	76	14–15	0	2.84
1974	35/35	265.0	258	113	99	188	85	15–11	0	3.36
1975	36/34	239.2	234	106	91	173	98	14–13	2	3.42
1976	34/32	247.1	205	81	74	200	66	21–10	0	2.69
1977	32/32	226.2	195	102	88	192	81	8–20	0	3.49
1978	38/32	235.1	221	110	98	160	84	3–15	2	3.75
Total	376/346	2544.2	2281	994	875	1799	820	140–137	5	3.09

Mets Career/Batting

GP	AB	R	H	2B	3B	HR	RBI	K	BB	SB	AVG
376	807	33	98	12	1	2	39	386	31	1	.121

ML Career

YEAR	GP/GS	IP	H	R	ER	K	BB	W–L	SV	ERA
67–85	612/527	3839.1	3635	1608	1433	2556	1198	222–209	17	3.06

Jerry Koosman is the common thread that connects several "firsts" in Mets history. He was on the mound for the team's first-ever home-opener victory, World Series win, and Fall Classic clincher. The southpaw also was the winning hurler in the "Pete Rose–Bud Harrelson" playoff game, and the pitcher of record when the Mets took a three games to two lead over the A's in the 1973 World Series.

Although his body of work is more than impressive, Jerome Martin Koosman spent most of his Mets career working in Tom Seaver's shadow, or at least that was the case until the postseason. The Mets have never had a better October pitcher than the lefty from Appleton, Minnesota. He made five postseason starts, and the Mets won them all. But there were numerous ways Koosman almost didn't pitch for the New York Mets.

Koosman was difficult to scout in Minnesota, primarily because his high school didn't have a team. Instead, he started playing semipro ball on Sunday afternoons when he was 13. He also played a year of American Legion ball at age 15 and continued to throw in semipro games until he went into the service. He enrolled at the University of Minnesota at Morris, but the first-year college didn't have a baseball team. Koosman later transferred to the State School of Science in Lofton, North Dakota, but was ineligible to pitch. Although he eventually caught the eye of Mets scout Red Murff, Koosman still didn't have a proper stage to showcase his talent.

He was drafted into the army in 1962 and eventually stationed in Grafton, Illinois, at a spot where there wasn't enough flat land to form a baseball diamond.

Koosman came home on leave and asked his dentist—the commanding major general of the Minnesota National Guard—if he could do anything to get him transferred. The dentist wasn't sure he could pull that off, so Koosman took matters into his own hands, taking the OCS test in the hopes of becoming a warrant officer and training in helicopters in Texas. He passed the test and was transferred to Fort Bliss to continue training and play baseball.

Still, facing other soldiers wasn't exactly comparable to pitching against the USC Trojans. But his catcher was the son of a Shea Stadium usher. Legend has it that the catcher told his father about this pitching talent who was worthy of a look-see by the Mets.

"Well, that's one of the stories, and it is true," remembered Koosman in a December 2008 interview. "John Lucchese was my catcher, and his dad was an usher at Shea Stadium. My catcher told his dad that he had a good pitcher down there and the Mets ought to send a scout down to see me.

"Prior to that, Red Murff had already scouted me. But then the Mets called him and he scouted me a second time because of that letter.

"The Mets liked the story of the catcher, so they never really promoted the other story that Murff had already seen me."

Murff signed him to a contract in 1964. The Mets thought they were getting a 21-year-old hurler, but Koosman admitted years later that he had fibbed about his age.

"That's when I was in the service. There were a couple, three scouts that were down watching us work out. Our manager, Pete Peters—this was in El Paso, Texas—lined us all up on the baseball field down the baseline, asking our names and how old we were.

"There was a guy named Ron Taylor, a right-handed starter to my left. They asked him how old he was and he says, 'Twenty-two.' The scout shakes his head and says, 'Geez, you're a little old because it takes four years in the minor leagues. You'd be 26, 27 before you get to the big leagues.' At that time, they're thinking when you're 30, you're over the hill so they wouldn't get their money back out of you.

"I was also 22 at the time, so when he comes to me, I told him I was 21. He didn't say anything negative about it.

"So I said I was born in 1943, not 1942. I don't know if that helped or not, but I got signed."

Another Koosman story claimed he was almost released while in the minors, but was saved by an outstanding loan he owed the Mets.

"In 1966 I went to Atlanta to work for the Georgia Power Company after Christmas. I got a grunt job as a lineman's helper so I could stay in great shape and do a lot of exercising for spring training.

"Gerry Wild was a good friend of mine who played with me at Greenville in '65. Jerry Johnson was also a good friend who played there, as well.

"I had a new car, so the three of us decided we were going to drive to spring training together. Since Gerry was from that area and it was raining the first day, we let him drive.

"We're going through Athens, Georgia, and the light had turned yellow, so he kicked it. The light turned red before we got to the intersection, another car was timing it and hit us broadside, totaling my car.

"So now, how do we get to spring training? None of us had any money to afford a bus ticket, so we talked it over to decide who's going to call [Director of Minor League Operations] Joe McDonald and borrow the money. Out of all of us, I was 7–11 the year before and I had the best record! So I was voted to call McDonald.

"I called him, and he wired me $50 for the three of us to get to spring training. While we were waiting, I was looking at a car dealer and I called my dad. He said, 'Geez, you need a car anyway.' He financially helped me out, and I bought another car there. So we ended up driving down there anyway.

"When it came down to the time when they wanted to release me, McDonald claimed that he said, 'Well, we can't release him yet because he still owes the Mets $50!

"So that's another story that evidently the Mets wanted to use for PR."

They allegedly wanted to keep him in the organization long enough to pay off the bill, and he began to flourish once veteran pitcher Frank Lary showed him a new pitch.

"In spring training 1966 he taught me the slider. Certainly, there's more than one way to throw the slider, but he taught me a way so I wouldn't hurt my elbow, as he explained it.

"It just worked instantly for me. I remember throwing a few pitches, and I just had a smile on my face. I said, 'Well, nobody can hit this pitch.' And he said, 'If you throw it right, you are correct.'

"Then [the Mets] had a meeting on who they were going to release. My name came up, and Lary says, 'Geez, don't release him. I just taught him the slider and he has a helluva slider.'

"So Clyde McCullough said, 'Hell, I'll take him north with me to Auburn.

"Later, when I'm going to Auburn, I overslept and missed the bus to the airport that morning. So I talked to Bill Virdon—who had the Double A club at Williamsport—and asked if I could ride with him up there and then fly up.

"They landed in Syracuse and then I took a bus or something to Auburn, 20 miles away. I got in that night a little later than the Auburn team.

"I was on Clyde's 'black list.' For a month he didn't pitch me and just made me work out extra hard. They got in a jam—they were short of pitchers—and he had to use me in relief. Of course, I was strong and blew everybody away.

"Then I got a start because somebody couldn't pitch. I wound up in the starting rotation and leading the league in some categories.

Koosman Highlights

Low-Hit Complete Games

Date	Team	Hits/Score
8/27/69	@ Padres	2 (4–1)
9/20/70	Pirates	2 (4–1)
9/11/76	Cardinals	2 (4–1)
9/4/79*	Royals	2 (5–1)

Strikeouts

Date	Team	Total/Score
5/28/69	Padres	15 (1–0)
6/23/80*	Royals	15 (4–1)

* with Twins

"I went on and had a great year at Auburn. One thing the slider did for me was that in every sacrifice situation, I threw the slider and I never gave up a sacrifice bunt that year."

Armed with the slider, Koosman had a sensational year for Auburn in 1966, leading the NY–Penn League with a 1.38 ERA while going 12–7 with 174 strikeouts in 170 innings. He was in the majors a few months later, earning a spot on the 1967 Opening Day roster and making his Mets debut with 2⅔ innings of hitless relief in a 5–1 loss to the Phillies April 14, the third game of the season.

"We were in Philadelphia, at Connie Mack Stadium, and I was in the bullpen. Harvey Haddix was the pitching coach and Wes Westrum was the manager.

"Westrum got up Ralph Terry and myself. Of course, I was nervous and was throwing hard, getting ready quick… just 'get the ball, throw it, get the ball, throw it.'

"I was throwing so hard and a little bit wild that Haddix—rather than stand outside the bullpen—went back behind the screen. He was afraid to be out there!

"He's making motions toward me, and I'm thinking he's asking me if I was all right or ready. I kind of shook my head 'yes,' but what he was trying to tell me was that I was in the game, and he was afraid to come out from behind the screen because I was throwing so fast.

"So the umpire had to walk all the way out there and tap me on the shoulder to say, 'Son, you're in the game.'

"And then I pitched 2⅔ hitless innings."

Koosman made four more relief appearances and had a 4.82 ERA in 9⅓ innings when he was sent down to Triple A Jacksonville in May.

"After the first month they cut three of us because, at the time, you went north with 28 guys and after 30 days you had to cut three people. So they cut myself, Greg Goossen and Ralph Terry.

"I went to Triple A Jacksonville, finished the season there and was called back up the last month."

He posted a 2.43 ERA with an 11–10 record and 183 strikeouts in 173 innings for the Suns. His WHIP was an impressive 1.03, earning him a September call-up.

Koosman made three starts in the final two weeks of the 1967 season, going 0–2 with an 8.18 ERA in just 11 innings. But he was named to the 1968 starting rotation by new manager Gil Hodges, who assigned him the task of pitching the second game of the season. Koosman proved he belonged by beating the Dodgers at Los Angeles April 11, his first big league victory.

"I pitched against the Giants in Palm Springs as my last spring training start. It was the first time I faced Willie Mays, and it was just awesome.

"Then we go to Frisco, and that's when Martin Luther King was assassinated, so the game I was supposed to pitch was canceled.

"I was moved back, pitched the first game in L.A. and shut them out 4–0 on four singles. Hodges was pretty happy because he beat Walter Alston. It was Gil's first year back in the league, and he had a lot of respect for Walter."

Koosman also started the home opener April 17 against the Giants, and it didn't look like he'd last long.

"There was a base hit, an error and then I walked Willie McCovey, so the bases are loaded with nobody out and Willie Mays coming up. Just looking at Willie, he couldn't wait to get in there, bases loaded, nobody out, facing a left-hander. He's going to eat me up.

"I remember a year or two before Clyde McCullough told me, 'Son, whenever you're in trouble, reach back for old No. 1.' So I did. I struck out Willie on fastballs.

"Jim Ray Hart was up next and I popped him up to Jerry Grote on a fastball. Then I struck out Jack Hiatt and went on to win 3–0."

He gave up just six more hits the rest of the way while striking out 10. Koosman had joined Bob Shaw and Jack Fisher as the only pitchers to throw back-to-back shutouts as a Met. Koosman also opened his third start with three shutout innings, giving him 21 straight to open the season.

"My third game was against Houston, and I'm sticking the bat up their butts, too. In the fourth inning, there was a runner on first with Bob Aspromonte up. I threw him a good fastball down and away, and he hit a double to left-center. It was just a great pitch that he hit off me, and it scored the run.

"I win the game 3–1, but that one pitch cost me a shutout."

Koosman also tossed consecutive shutouts in July 1968, a month after Seaver did it. The second shutout string left Koosman with a 14–5 record and a 1.76 ERA, six shutouts, and 11 complete games in 21 starts. He already had shattered the team record for shutouts and was three wins away from topping Seaver's club mark with two months still left in the season.

"I had another game that summer against Bob Bolin of the Giants. We went 12 innings against each other and the score was nothing-nothing. That was another I was close to getting."

Koosman collecting his 16th victory August 14, matching Seaver's team record with a complete-game seven-hitter in a 4–1 decision over the Dodgers August 14.

He broke the win mark September 7 at Pittsburgh. Koosman would have become the Mets' first 20-game winning had he won three of his last four starts, but he split his final four games to end the year 19–12 with a team-record 2.08 ERA. His shot at 20 wins ended his next-to-last start of the year September 24 in Atlanta, the night Hodges suffered his first heart attack.

"I got knocked out that game. I was taken out in the sixth inning and I think I had given up six runs by then. It was one of the worst starts I ever had. Whether it was because Gil was on my mind or it was too hot, I don't know what happened.

"I went in the clubhouse and Gil was laying on the trainer's table, just really red in the face. I said, 'Gosh, Gilly, are you all right?' He says, 'Yeah, I'll be all right.'

"I left him alone to rest, but I had no idea he had a heart attack or thought he was ill.

"I hope he didn't have the heart attack because of me since I wasn't doing very well on the mound that night!"

Koosman won the Mets' final game of the season, firing a three-hitter against the Phillies at Shea Stadium. One of those hits still bothered him 40 years later.

"I was going after my 19th win. I had gone quite a while without getting a 'W.'

"It was in the sixth inning when Gene Mauch pinch-hit Johnny Callison against me. I remember saying to myself, "God is this guy [Mauch] nuts? They pinch-hit a left-hander against me?'

"I was taught not only to get left-handers out, but to embarrass them so bad that they wouldn't want to hit off me again because I would just bury left-handers.

"By God, he hit a solo home run off me and I won that game 3–1. But it was another game where that one pitch— I don't know what happened there—ruined another shutout that I should have had."

He finished a close second to Reds catcher Johnny Bench in the NL Rookie of the Year voting, losing by a 10½ to 9½ margin.

"I was told that Seaver had won it the year before and some of the writers didn't think it was right to make it two in a row for the Mets. Jim Enright in Chicago felt that Bench and I were both deserving of it so he split his vote. It was the first time in history that a writer split his vote."

According to the 1969 Mets Media Guide Koosman almost burned himself out of baseball months later. His left hand was scalded by popcorn butter sauce in a kitchen accident shortly after New Year's Day. He put up mediocre numbers in spring training of 1969, allowing eight runs and 12 hits in eight innings. He also struggled in his first two starts of the regular season, going 0–2 with an 8.68 ERA in 9⅓ innings. He followed the slow start by tossing 13⅓ scoreless innings, including a five-hit shutout against the Pirates April 23.

Jerry Koosman at first base in 1977. Photo courtesy of Oscar W. Gabriel

Koosman gave up just two hits in 4⅓ scoreless innings in his next start April 29 versus the Expos, but it would be a while before he retired another batter.

"I had two strikes on John Bateman, so I was going to bust him inside with a good fastball, which I did. And then my arm went numb!"

"I wasted time on the mound trying to wait for the numbness to go away. Being I was taking too much time, Jerry Grote came out and wanted to know what was wrong because I was a fast worker. I said, 'Grotes, my arm went numb.'

"So he looks in the dugout and motions to Gil Hodges. Gil comes out there with trainer Tom McKenna and they took me to the clubhouse. By the time I got there my arm was fine.

"[McKenna] moved my arm around different ways and nothing was wrong with it, so I just thought we'd jumped the gun. They wanted to be cautious with me, so they sent me back to New York the next day and was examined by Dr. Lamotte, our team physician. He couldn't find anything wrong, so I got on a plane and flew to Chicago to join the club there.

"It was my second day to throw, so I went out on the sideline and couldn't get a ball to home plate, my arm hurt so bad.

"We go up to the trainer's room and Gil Hodges, [GM] John Murphy and the trainers are there. I'm laying on my stomach on the trainer's table and they're trying to figure out what the heck is wrong. I told them that my shoulder hurt deep down in the joint area.

"I recall John Murphy saying, 'Geez, you know I remember when I was pitching for the Yankees and my shoulder felt the same way, but the pain wasn't in there.'

"I was laying on the trainer's table with my arms out forward. He said, 'Mine hurt right here.' He stuck his finger in there and I came right off the table.

"They found out that my teres minor muscle had knotted up. The only way to help that out was to milk it…pressure on the thumbs and just press it, milk it.

"I did that for a month and it hurt so bad, tears would come to my eyes every day until it would get numb and I couldn't feel it. Finally, they milked it out smooth and I was able to come back and still throw well again."

Koosman was outstanding immediately upon his return, going 4–2 with a 0.60 ERA while allowing only 35 hits in 60 innings over seven starts. He set a team record with 15 strikeouts in holding the Padres to four hits over 10 innings of a 1–0, 11-inning win, a game that started the Mets on a team-record 11-game winning streak.

Seaver ended the 1969 season by winning 10 straight decisions, but Koosman wasn't far behind. Koosman went 8–1 with a 2.35 ERA and seven complete games in his final 11 starts to help the Mets close the season with 38 victories in their final 49 games.

The Mets had whittled a 9½-game deficit to 2½ games within a month before Koosman was asked to start the opener of an incredibly important two-game series against the first-place Cubs. He was opposed by Bill Hands, who tried to intimidate the Mets by brushing back Tommie Agee leading off the bottom of the first. Nothing needed to be said to Koosman as he took the mound for the top of the second. He opened the frame by drilling Ron Santo on the wrist, sending a message to the Cubs that the bullying tactics weren't going to work.

Koosman knew payback was in order "once Hands knocked Agee down. My theory always was not to necessarily get the next hitter, but get the best hitter. I figured if I got their best hitter, that would stop the knockdown contest.

"It just so happened that I got them out 1-2-3 in the first inning and Hands threw at Agee with the first pitch. The leadoff hitter in the second inning was Ron Santo, so I just went after him.

"When I came up to the plate, Hands tried to drill me. I remember hollering at him, 'You pussy, you don't throw the ball hard enough to hurt anybody!' I didn't mind getting drilled, because I could get out of the way of his fastball."

Agee later hit a two-run homer and scored the tiebreaking run to support Koosman's 13-strikeout, seven-hit victory. The Cubs were now officially spooked, and the Mets blew them out the next night to pull within a half-game of first. The win also started Koosman on a five-start winning streak that included back-to-back shutouts at Pittsburgh and Montreal.

Not known as a hitter at that point, Koosman drove in the only run in his victory over the Pirates, less than three hours before Don Cardwell had the lone RBI in a 1–0 victory that gave the Mets a doubleheader sweep and a 4½-game lead over the Cubs with eight games remaining.

"I was a good bunter, but I was overmatched when it came to swinging the bat. We didn't get any batting practice then. You'd hit every fifth day, and your pitches in the cage were mostly bunting.

"Gil's theory was he didn't want us pitchers on the bases wasting our energy. There were times when Gil told me, 'Go up there and strike out!' And it's tough striking out looking good, you know?

"But he'd only tell us that when we were winning and had the game in concrete already."

Koosman was a terrible hitter when he came up to the majors, going 17-for-247 (.069) from 1967 through 1970. But he became a contributor at the plate midway through his career, compiling a .193 average (47-for-243) with 17 RBIs and 30 sacrifices between 1974 and '76. He also finished fourth in the NL in sacrifices and was second in the league in 1984.

Koosman tossed his sixth and final shutout of 1969 on September 26 at Philadelphia, two days after the Mets clinched the NL East title. He had proven he was more than ready for the postseason.

The Mets entered the NLCS with a reputation as a great-pitching, soft-hitting team. But they opened the series with a 9–5 victory over the Braves before staking Koosman to an 8–0 lead by the fourth inning of Game 2. Koosman gave up a fourth-inning run and was chased in the fifth after giving up a three-run homer to Hank Aaron and a two-run single by Clete Boyer. But Ron Taylor worked out of the fifth-inning jam as he and Tug McGraw combined to toss 4⅓ shutout innings in an 11–6 win that put the Mets up 2–0 in the series.

"Atlanta was never a good park for us to pitch in. It was always hot down there. I remember winning a game there 1–0 on a Sunday afternoon and it was so ungodly hot.

"Atlanta had the short fences and a can-of-corn fly ball could go out of that ballpark. We just never had good luck in that park and I really don't know why.

"They had a good club at that time.

"I remember it was supposed to be a pitching duel against the Braves, but it wound up being a hitter's duel, which was quite rare for us."

The Mets were NL champs a day later, earning the right to face the mighty Orioles in the World Series.

The Birds demonstrated their awesome attack by reaching Seaver for four runs and six hits in five innings of a 4–1 victory in the series opener. Koosman had to pitch well for the Mets to avoid an 0–2 hole heading to Shea Stadium. Koosman delivered again.

"My goal that day was to pitch a no-hitter—a perfect game—and get a hit every time up to bat. I had the [no-hitter] going into the seventh. I shook Grote off on a fastball to Paul Blair and threw him a curveball that he hit for a base hit between third and short. He stole second on the next pitch, which caught me off guard. I wasn't ready for it. And then Brooks Robinson got a base hit up the middle that scored Blair.

Koosman retired his next six batters while Al Weis poked an RBI single that put the Mets ahead 2–1 in the ninth inning.

"They were going to pinch-hit for me, but since Al Weis got that hit, Gil let me hit because I would be facing Boog Powell, the left-hander. I didn't get Boog Powell out, so they took me out and brought in Ron Taylor for the last out. He got them out on a smash to Ed Charles. Glider made a helluva catch just getting to the ball, and then a lollipop throw to first."

New York won the next two games, putting Koosman on the mound to possibly close out the series.

Koosman opened Game 5 with two scoreless innings before Mark Belanger led off the third with a single and pitcher Dave McNally followed with a two-run homer. Three batters later, Frank Robinson took Koosman deep to make it 3–0.

"There was a bunting situation with McNally, and in all our bunting situations we were taught to throw high, hard fastballs that, hopefully, they'd pop up. Instead, he swings away and hits a home run. We were all shell-shocked.

"I was very perturbed. I got them out [to end the inning], and I was mad. I couldn't wait to go up and hit off McNally because I was going to do the same thing to him. I hit a line drive off the wall in left field. I didn't get it up in the air enough or I would have had a home run off of him. But I led off with a double and was left stranded on second base."

Koosman allowed just one hit the rest of the way while the Mets chipped away against McNally and the Baltimore bullpen. Donn Clendenon hit a two-run blast in the sixth, and Weis added a seventh-inning homer that tied the game 3–3. With Eddie Watt on the mound, the Mets scored twice on a pair of doubles and an error to carry a 5–3 lead into the ninth inning.

Koosman opened the ninth inning by walking Frank Robinson before retiring the next three batters in order, ending the series by getting future Mets manager Davey Johnson to hit a deep fly to Cleon Jones.

Weis and Clendenon received MVP awards for the series, but Koosman deserved plenty of credit by going 2–0 with a 2.04 ERA in 17⅔ innings.

Koosman and the Miracle Mets were the toast of baseball, winning their first World Series just eight seasons after setting a modern major league record with 120 losses. But the Mets finished in third place over the next two seasons in part because of injuries to their top left-hander.

Koosman pitched well over the first two months of the 1970 season, going 2–3 with a 2.57 ERA in 66⅔ innings. But he left a game May 22 with a forearm injury and was struck on the mouth by a Gary Gentry line drive during batting practice, preventing him from making another start until June 20. Koosman labored through the rest of the season, pitching to a 10–4 mark and a 3.41 ERA. He tied for the team lead with seven wins after the All-Star break, but he struck out only 73 in his final 145⅓ innings, an indication that his arm was not sound despite the amount of work.

The arm woes continued in 1971 as he missed two starts in June before sitting out between July 6 and August 14. Again, his ERA was a respectable 3.04, but he logged only 96 strikeouts in 165⅔ innings while going 6–11. He was 10 starts into the '71 season when another injury developed.

"I don't remember what year it was, but I was pitching in Frisco. There was a cold wind blowing on my back the whole game, and I pitched 11 innings. I tore the rhomboid muscles between my shoulder blade and backbone.

"That really slowed me down for about three years, until the adhesions broke loose and I got my fastball back."

Koosman also got off to a rocky start in 1972, compiling a 10.57 ERA while losing his first three decisions. He was relegated to the bullpen, but the demotion seemed to help as Koosman went 2–0 without allowing a run in 12⅔ innings over seven outings. Manager Yogi Berra put him back in the rotation, and Koosman went 4–0 with a 1.54 ERA in his first six starts after the promotion. Most important, "Kooz" allowed only 30 hits while striking out 48 in 46⅔ innings. Koosman pitched shutout ball in his first two July starts, holding the Expos and Padres to nine hits in 19 innings. He experienced another dovetail after that, compiling a 6.14 ERA while going 2–7 in his next nine starts. The erratic performances led to a 4.14 ERA, his worst in any full season as a Met. He wasn't even the top lefty in the rotation, losing that honor to Jon Matlack, the NL Rookie of the Year. But Koosman's turnaround was about to begin.

Koosman threw a four-hit shutout against the Braves April 29, 1973 giving him a 4–0 record and a 1.06 ERA in his first four starts of the year. He was 5–0 following an 8–1 win over the Braves May 9 before the Mets suddenly stopped scoring runs for him. New York provided only 12 runs in his next six starts while he went 0–5 with a 3.74 ERA. Another five-game losing streak began in late July, giving Koosman an 8–14 record despite a 3.47 ERA.

Injuries ravaged the Mets' starting lineup in the summer of 1973. Cleon Jones, Jerry Grote, Willie Mays, and Bud Harrelson were on the disabled list on June, and Harrelson made two trips to the DL before August. But Koosman began to win again as the regulars returned, leading to an improbable charge to the National League pennant.

Koosman ended his second five-game losing streak of the year with a five-hitter in a 2–1 win over the Reds August 19. The outcome left the Mets in last place at 55–66, 6½ games off the NL East lead. It also started a season-ending stretch in which Koosman went 6–1 with a 1.30 ERA in 76⅓ innings over his final 10 starts. Seaver deservedly won the NL Cy Young Award that season, but Koosman was the Mets' best pitcher down the stretch. He set a club record by tossing 31⅔ shutout innings between August 19 and September 7 to lead the Mets back into playoff contention despite a sub.500 record.

"I blew that [scoreless streak] up in Montreal. I don't know what inning it was but I gave up a run. I know that wore on me for a while there because of my selection of pitches. I was certainly trying to extend that streak."

Mays gave his "Say Good-bye to America" speech just before Koosman threw his first pitch against the Expos on September 25. Koosman allowed no earned runs while pitching into the seventh inning of a 2–1 victory that put the Mets 1½ games ahead of the second-place Pirates with five games left.

The Mets dropped their next two games and were in danger of losing their stranglehold on the division lead until Koosman came through in his final start of the regular season, holding the Cubs to two unearned runs in a complete-game six-hitter won by the Mets 9–2. New York clinched the division title a day later as Seaver beat the Cubs.

The Mets split the first two games of the NLCS at Cincinnati, giving Koosman a chance to put New York in control of the series. He delivered once again by going the distance, striking out nine and scattering eight hits in a 9–2 rout of the Reds in Game 3. Koosman gave up a pair of runs in the third inning, but only after Rusty Staub's three-run homer put the Mets ahead 6–0.

Game 3 is best remembered for the Rose-Harrelson melee at second base.

"Buddy Harrelson and I talked about that in New York while signing autographs [in November 2008]. Somehow, it came up and Buddy claims that he had said something about the Reds. Rose took it out on him.

"As I recall, the first time up I threw Rose a slow curveball and he popped it up in the infield. When he got back to the dugout he said, 'Throw the ball you big dumb f–kin' donkey!' That's what a lot of hitters say when they want fastballs. I didn't look in the dugout but I heard him say it and said to myself, 'Wait 'til the next time up.'

"Well, the next time up I tried to drill him four times and missed, so he goes to first on a walk and then took it out on Buddy Harrelson. All this time, I thought maybe I just added to the feud that was going on between those two. I thought I had caused that!"

Koosman was heading back to the dugout after getting Joe Morgan to hit into an inning-ending double play. Rose made a hard slide into Harrelson in an effort to break up the twin-killing. Harrelson took exception to the slide and Rose pushed back before the brawl began.

"I thought I got out there fairly quick, but in looking at the film, I don't know how so many guys beat me to the pile. I was probably about the fifth, sixth guy in there, but I was probably one of the closest guys to the pile. I imagine the second baseman, third baseman and first baseman all beat me to it.

"I guess I didn't see it right away. I turned and watched the throw to second, then I must have looked some other place before I looked back there again.

It might have been a good thing for the Reds that Koosman was a little slow getting to the fracas. He had a reputation among his teammates as being a very powerful person.

"Kooz was as country strong as they get," remembered teammate Jim McAndrew. "He was not only a good pitcher, he was a great pitcher. Seaver used to comment, 'I hope he never finds out how strong he really is.' He just had brute strength as far as his upper body is concerned."

In his book, *Miracle in New York*, Clendenon remembered an unintentional feat of strength by Koosman during batting practice in 1969.

"I was swinging my 40-ounce bat, my heaviest bat, to loosen up. The pitchers were still up, and as I was getting ready for batting practice, I looked around to see if anyone was close and saw no one. So I swung my big bat fairly hard. Just as I started my swing, Jerry Koosman was walking back to take an extra swing and he walked up right behind me. As I swung, my bat hit him right across the chest. Jerry didn't even flinch and said, 'Is that as hard as you can swing, Sonny?' I was amazed I hadn't killed or injured him."[108]

Growing up in Minnesota gave Koosman the opportunity to build his body through hard work.

"I was born and reared on a farm and all I knew was hard labor, from picking up rocks to hauling bales to shoveling ear corn into a corn sheller, cleaning out steer sheds, and cleaning barns. It was always heavy labor.

"When I was pitching coach for the Mets in 1991 and 1992 in the minors, I remember one year I got my pitchers together toward the end of the season and asked them, 'Okay, now what are you guys going to do this winter to prepare yourselves for next spring?' One was going to be working at Burger King, and another was going to go to the gym. I said, 'God, don't you guys have a grain elevator or something where you can get a job and throw feedsacks, get some hard labor in?' They looked at my like I was an idiot!"

The Mets wrapped up the NLCS in five games, and Koosman was the starting pitcher in Game 2 of the 1973 World Series, a memorable contest in which the Mets blew a 6–3 lead before scoring four times in the 10th to beat the A's 10–7. But Koosman had showered long before the final out was made, allowing three runs and six hits in just 2⅓ innings.

Koosman was substantially better in Game 5, holding the A's to three hits in 6⅓ innings before McGraw finished up a 2–0 shutout that got the Mets within one victory of

Koosman Milestones

Strikeouts

1st	April 14, 1967 @ Phillies	(Chris Short)
500th	April 23, 1971 @ Cubs	(Ron Santo)
1,000th	July 20, 1974 @ Padres	(Dave Winfield)
1,500th	May 22, 1977 @ Reds	(Bill Plummer)
2,000th	June 3, 1980 vs. Red Sox*	(Dwight Evans)
2,500th	April 12, 1985 @ Astros&	(Mike Scott)

Wins

1st	April 11, 1968 @ Los Angeles	4-0
50th	May 9, 1971 vs. Cardinals	9-5
100th	June 24, 1975 vs. Cardinals	9-5
150th	July 4, 1979 vs. Mariners*	7-2
200th	August 19, 1983 @ Rangers#	6-1

* With Twins # With White Sox & With Phillies

winning their second World Series. But Oakland prevailed in seven games, beating Seaver and Matlack for the Athletics' second straight title.

"We were all pretty confident we were going to win one game out there. But we lost the two games, and it was just a shocker to us."

Koosman and Matlack had good seasons in 1974. Koosman paced the Mets in wins while going 15–11 with a then career-high 188 strikeouts and a 3.36 ERA in 265 innings. Matlack was arguably the best pitcher on the staff, recording a team-best 2.41 ERA and seven shutouts. But the injury bug continued to bite the Mets, and it affected the pitching staff. Seaver battled a sciatica problem while going 11–11 with a 3.20 ERA, his worst season as a Met to date. McGraw recorded only four saves and was 6–11 with a 4.16 ERA. Without major contributions from Seaver and McGraw, the Mets finished just 71–91, their worst season since 1967. Koosman was 4–0 with a 2.03 ERA in his first seven starts of '74. But when he lost, he usually deserved it as he allowed at least five runs in six of his 11 losses.

Koosman had a wildly inconsistent season in 1975, giving up at least five runs in 10 of his 34 starts. But the Mets had a sniff of the division title in early September, and Koosman helped the cause by going 4–2 with a 2.50 ERA in his final eight starts to finish the year 14–13. He had reached the 14-win plateau for the fifth time in his eight seasons, but his walks spiked to a career-high 98.

Koosman put it all together in 1976, finishing second to San Diego's Randy Jones in the Cy Young balloting. He opened the year 6–1 with a 2.77 ERA, but a five-game losing streak dropped him to 6–6 with a 4.36 ERA by June 21. He was outstanding after that, going 15–4 with three shutouts, 15 complete games, and a 1.79 ERA in 20 games, including 19 starts. Koosman gave up only two runs in

three of those four losses as he was victimized by the same poor run support that led to Seaver finishing the year just 14–11.

Koosman became the second 20-game winner in Mets history when he beat the Cardinals 4–1 September 16, striking out a season-high 13 in a four-hitter. He could have easily had 23 wins, pitching complete-game losses in two of his final three starts.

"My dad died during spring training. My dad and I were very close, and there was a peace about me. I felt like his presence was with me constantly.

"My concentration that year was the best it had ever been. I was never able to get back into that depth of concentration again. Every feeling of my body and my motion, I knew if I threw something a little bit rushed or a little bit wrong, I felt it right away, and I corrected it on the next pitch.

"My physical awareness of every pitch I threw stood right out. My concentration was so good I didn't even hear the fans. Everything was silent."

But Koosman was a runner-up for a postseason award for the second time in eight years. Jones claimed the 1976 Cy Young, receiving more first-place votes (15–7) and points (96–69) than Koosman.

"The Padres were well aware of Randy going after the Cy Young Award because they pitched him every three days quite a bit so he could get more starts and more wins. Of course the Mets wouldn't alter the rotation, and I was pitching every fifth day. So he got more starts than me.

"Although I struck out more and our ERAs were very close—I was 21–10 and Randy was 22–14—he got more starts."

Koosman, Matlack, Seaver, and Mickey Lolich formed arguably the best starting rotation in 1976. Matlack won a career-high 17 games and posted a 2.95 ERA to finish sixth in the Cy Young voting. Seaver led the NL with 235 strikeouts and was third with a 2.59 ERA. Lolich had to settle for an 8–13 mark despite a 3.22 ERA.

The quartet went 60–44 for a team that finished just 86–76. Great pitching was often wasted by poor hitting, especially when the Mets hit just six homers while Dave Kingman missed six weeks with a thumb injury.

The Mets had a great chance to bolster their 1977 lineup through the first full year of free agency. Instead, they wasted their talented arms by sitting on their hands, coming away with nothing of significance when several talented hitters were available. The farm system was unproductive and the budget was tight, leading to a dramatic free fall in 1977.

The Mets settled into last place early in 1977 under managers Joe Frazier and Joe Torre despite their exceptional rotation. Koosman had compiled a 2.82 ERA by June 13 but was just 5–6. Two days later, the "Tom and Jerry" show was broken up as the Mets sent the disgruntled Seaver to the Reds.

Koosman never put together a winning streak in 1977 despite his 3.49 ERA. He was 8–11 after allowing a run and only two hits in a 4–1 win over the Padres on July 29. Koosman ended the season with nine consecutive losses to join a handful of hurlers to follow a 20-win season with 20 losses. The Mets scored just 22 runs in 10 games during his season-ending skid.

"I remember the last game in '77. Torre called me into the office the day before and said, 'You know, Kooz, I'm not going to start you tomorrow?' I asked 'Why not?' He says, 'Because I don't want you to lose 20.' I said, 'You're looking at it all wrong. I'm gonna win that game!'

"Well, I went out there and lost it. I lost No. 20."

Things only got worse in 1978. Koosman was the only starter remaining from the 1976 rotation as Matlack was sent to Texas in a multiplayer deal. Matlack followed his 7–15 season in '77 by going 15–13 with a 2.27 ERA for the Rangers. Seaver was 16–14 with a 2.88 ERA for the Reds, including a no-hitter on June 16. Koosman was 2–8 with a 4.03 ERA at the time of Seaver's no-hitter.

"I know [in 1976] we had equal to a Double A ballclub. We couldn't score any runs, we couldn't throw anybody out, guys were going from first-to-third, second-to-home on us.

"And '77 was the same way. My chest hurt just from going out there, pitching my butt off and not getting anything for it.

"I believe in '78, they scored 26 runs for me all year because I kept track of everything I did. The next year when I pitched for the Twins I had 26 runs scored for me the first two games. That's when Roy Smalley made the comment that I need touchdowns to win."

It was evident by Koosman's record that pitching for the Mets wasn't fun anymore when you've already had the experience of playing on two pennant winners and one World Series club. Craig Swan won the NL ERA title in 1978, and Pat Zachry made the All-Star team by virtue of his 10 victories over the first three months. But Koosman looked frustrated on the mound as he labored through a career-worst 3–15 campaign. He picked up his final win as a Met by outpitching Seaver in Cincinnati on July 13. Koosman went 0–6 in his final 13 starts despite a 3.42 ERA. The Mets scored two runs or fewer in seven of those starts, including a seven-game stretch in which they totaled nine runs.

Koosman spent the last two weeks pitching out of the bullpen, saving two games in five appearances. He was an ex-Met by December.

"I forced a trade. I felt it was going to take a long time for the Mets to rebuild, and I didn't want to go through all that at that stage of my career. I wanted to be with a winning club. I remember saying if I was going to play for a losing club, I could just as well play for one at home, and the Twins weren't winning at the time.

"They had 10 teams they could trade me to because I was a 10-and-5 guy. It took so long for them to do it that when they still hadn't traded me, I just narrowed it to one team. I said, 'Trade me to the Twins or I'm going to retire.' I was ready to retire and do an air-freight business.

"They didn't call my bluff. They traded me to the Twins, which was a good trade for the Mets because they got Jesse Orosco as one of the players.

"So I went to the Twins and I won 20 in 1979."

Koosman flourished in his new but familiar surroundings, finishing sixth in the AL Cy Young voting with a 20–13 record and a 3.38 ERA for the 1979 Twins. He had sandwiched 20-win seasons around a two-year period that saw him go 11–35.

Koosman was 16–13 with a 4.03 ERA for the Twins in 1980 and spent the second half of the following season in the bullpen.

"In '81 we went on strike for six weeks. When we came back, manager Billy Gardner decided he was going to use the starters in relief, 'And pitch you more often to get your arms back in shape.'

"One week he brought me in five times. I saved five games in one week. The last game I pitched in relief was in Milwaukee. I came in with the bases loaded, nobody out and got 'em out with any runs scoring. I got into the dugout and couldn't lift my left arm to take my cap off."

Koosman was wearing a different cap soon after as the Twins shipped him to the White Sox on August 30. The Chisox had become his third team, just as the White Sox became Seaver's third ballclub three years later.

"Because of my success in relief, the White Sox noted that and wanted me as a relief pitcher. So that's when negotiations started to get me down there as a relief pitcher.

"Down there, Tony La Russa used me as a starter, long man, short man, everything. I never really had a steady job and never did too much there.

"If you're a reliever, they get you up five times to bring you in the ballgame without putting you in. Then the sixth time, you're half worn-out by then.

"A manager has a tough job to do running a ballclub and knowing every position. But how many times do you get a guy up in the bullpen, don't use him, and then by the time you finally put him in, he's already pitched a game down there?"

Koosman put together back-to-back 11–7 seasons for the White Sox and was traded to the Phillies before spring training, 1984. Back in the National League, the 41-year-old Koosman enjoyed one final good season by recording a 3.27 ERA and a 14–15 record in 224 innings. He started 18 games for the 1985 Phillies but was released in December after going 6–4 with a 4.62 ERA. The release came days shy of his 43rd birthday.

"It was good to be back in the National League with Steve Carlton, an old friend of mine. There was Gus Hoeffling, the strength coach.

"I was in as good shape as I'd ever been. We just had some bad luck there. [General manager and manager] Paul Owens said I should have won 22 to 25 games in '84. There were five games thrown away on throwing errors, so I won 14 games that year. I could have won 21, anyway.

"In '85 I hurt me knee working out, so they drained it. Two days later it filled up again, they drained it again, and finally they said I needed an operation.

"I had arthroscopic surgery on it and worked hard for a month, but I was too macho. I came back too early—after a month—and my knee gradually got weaker out there pitching.

"I didn't give it enough time. The doctor told me I had to give it six weeks and I was back in four. I just worked it too hard, didn't let it heal.

"I remember the last pitch I threw in the big leagues, my knee was caving in beneath me and I threw a lollipop pitch to the catcher so I wouldn't balk. I was back in the disabled list and retired that winter.

"I was still throwing 89 to 92 mph, but my knee hadn't completely healed in January. [Cardinals manager] Whitey Herzog wanted me to be the second starter behind [Joaquin] Andujar, and the White Sox wanted me back as a left-handed reliever. But I still had a sharp pain in my knee and didn't want to stick them with a bad knee.

"I sent them both copies of the operation, which were on videotape. The Phillies had videotaped it. They both said, 'Your knee is better than a lot of knees we have on the club.'

"But I decided at the end of January I wanted to hang it up and spend time with my family. Also, I didn't think my knee was ready.

"Come March, my knee was fine. I really wish I had played a couple more years.

"And now I've got a steel knee. [In 2006] I had to have it replaced because it was so bad I had to walk sideways or backwards with the pain."

Koosman tried to stay in baseball following his playing career. He returned to Minnesota and was asked to jump-start a country-wide league that would aid the development of young talent.

"I was hired by a small company here to start a new amateur baseball league for 16 to 19 year olds who would play against each other in the summer time when school was out. There would be 102 teams in the United States. I had all professional and college coaching for them, along with pro umpires.

"It was arranged according to population. For example, Minnesota would have one team, it would be all the best kids in the country and they'd play each other all summer long. I had Jim Kaat as the commissioner, and it was really going to be a wonderful league, called 'America's Best.'

"When I had it set up and ready to go I needed a sponsor. I went to Oscar Mayer to see if they were interested in sponsoring us. And they were. They asked if the big leagues had endorsed it and I said I hadn't asked them yet. They said, 'You get the big leagues to endorse it and we'll sponsor it.'

"So I went to some of the owners, and they thought it was a great idea, too. They took it to the owners' meeting and it was voted down. They said they wouldn't endorse it the first year but would the second if it went down okay.

"Since they wouldn't endorse it, I couldn't get the money and we closed it down. But it would have showcased all the top talent around the United States for college drafting, scholarships, and pro ball.

"I told them if all the owners stuck $50,000 into it, we could play the season. But they didn't want to invest, and $50 grand wasn't a lot of money to a big-league club in '88 or '89."

The league never got off the ground, leaving him available to return to pro ball as a coach. The Mets brought him back to handle their minor league hurlers at a time when the franchise didn't have many top-flight prospects.

"Frank Cashen and Buddy Harrelson called and wanted me to come back and work with their young pitchers. I did that in '90 and '91, coaching in Pittsfield, Massachusetts, and Columbia, South Carolina. I did really well with my pitching staff, although I didn't really have any prospects except one.

"Steve Phillips was the minor league director then. He had different ways he thought I should work my pitchers to get them in shape. He didn't agree with a lot of stuff I was doing, so I just decided it wasn't for me.

"When I was going to talk to him to tell him I wasn't coming back, he beat me to the punch and said he wasn't going to ask me back.

"That's how that ended up, although my pitching staff led the league each year."

Koosman had enough of baseball following his two-year stint in the Mets' farm system. He became involved in an engineering company in Phoenix that handled several government contracts. But he says the work dried up when President Clinton scaled back the military budget by closing bases and canceling contracts.

"One of the things we still had going at the time was the technology to make a soft-serve ice cream machine that was self-cleaning. Instead of tearing it apart and cleaning it, we could clean it automatically.

"We developed that, and I ended up buying my partner out because he was doing things that I certainly didn't agree with. I moved the company from Phoenix to Wisconsin. I was invited into a building of other engineers.

"I was retired in Florida at the time, so I had to sell the house there, and my wife and I moved up to Wisconsin. I continued on [the self-cleaning soft ice cream machines] and have it very close but haven't finished yet. I've had bad luck the last two years [2007–2008]. Of the two engineers I hired to finish it up, one got very ill and the other took a job with 3M and is too busy to get at it. So it's just dormant at this time.

"It's patented and everything, but I just haven't gotten it out the door. I guess I probably need to make some calls and get in touch with the right people to finish it up, license it or sell it."

The move from Florida to Wisconsin put stress on his marriage. Koosman had been with his wife, Lavonne, since his early days with the Mets.

"Originally, she didn't want to move to Florida, but she did and she loved it. Then, she didn't want to move back to Wisconsin, but we had to. Things just kind of went south and finally one day she said, 'I don't want to be married anymore.'

"We ended up getting divorced in 2003."

Jerry and Lavonne have three children, all of whom are doing well.

"I have a son, my oldest, who lives in Bozeman, Montana. He's got two kids and works for a company that does in-depth credit checks.

"My next son lives five miles from me. He's got two kids and flies for Northwest. My daughter is in Florida, and she sells medical supplies."

Koosman remains a fixture in the Mets family, appearing at card shows with the rest of his former teammates when time permits. He also received one of the loudest ovations after the final game at Shea Stadium, applause that was much deserved following his exceptional 12-season run with the Mets.

ML/Mets debut	@ Phillies, 4/14/67 (2.2 IP, 0 H, 0 ER, 2 K, 2 BB)
First ML/Mets strikeout	Chris Short, @ Phillies, 4/14/67
First ML/Mets win	@ Dodgers, 4/11/68
First ML/Mets save	@ Cubs, 5/24/72
Most strikeouts, ML game	15, twice, including Twins vs. Royals, 6/23/80
Most strikeouts, Mets game	15, vs. Padres, 5/28/69
Low-hit ML CG	2, 4 times
Low-hit Mets CG	2, @ Padres, 8/27/70; vs. Pirates, 9/20/70; @ Cards, 9/11/76
Acquired:	Signed as an amateur free agent, 8/27/64.
Deleted:	Traded to the Twins for a player to be named (Jesse Orosco) and Greg Field, 12/8/78.

NL All-Star, 1968, 1969

Ed Kranepool

First Baseman, Outfielder   Bats left, throws left
Born: 11/8/44   Bronx, New York
Height: 6'3"   Weight: 205   #21, #7

Ed Kranepool Mets/ML Career

YEAR	GP	AB	R	H	2B	3B	HR	RBI	K	BB	SB	AVG	SLG	OBP
1962	3	6	0	1	1	0	0	0	1	0	0	.167	.333	.167
1963	86	273	22	57	12	2	2	14	50	18	4	.209	.289	.256
1964	119	420	47	108	19	4	10	45	50	32	0	.257	.393	.310
1965	153	525	44	133	24	4	10	53	71	39	1	.253	.371	.303
1966	146	464	51	118	15	2	16	57	66	41	1	.254	.399	.316
1967	141	469	37	126	17	1	10	54	51	37	0	.269	.373	.321
1968	127	373	29	86	13	1	3	20	39	19	0	.231	.295	.271
1969	112	353	36	84	9	2	11	49	32	37	3	.238	.368	.307
1970	43	47	2	8	0	0	0	3	2	5	0	.170	.170	.250
1971	122	421	61	118	20	4	14	58	33	38	0	.280	.447	.340
1972	122	327	28	88	15	1	8	34	35	34	1	.269	.394	.336
1973	100	284	28	68	12	2	1	35	28	30	1	.239	.306	.310
1974	94	217	20	65	11	1	4	24	14	18	1	.300	.415	.350
1975	106	325	42	105	16	0	4	43	21	27	1	.323	.409	.370
1976	123	415	47	121	17	1	10	49	38	35	1	.292	.410	.344
1977	108	281	28	79	17	0	10	40	20	23	1	.281	.448	.330
1978	66	81	7	17	2	0	3	19	12	8	0	.210	.346	.280
1979	82	155	7	36	5	0	2	17	18	13	0	.232	.303	.287
TOTAL	1853	5436	536	1418	225	25	118	614	581	454	15	.261	.377	.316

Mets president George Weiss had two goals in mind when he formed the team's first organizational roster in the winter of 1962. One was to bring in players with name recognition, drawing cards who could fill the dilapidated Polo Grounds. The other was to build a competent farm system as soon as possible so those aging veterans taken in the expansion draft could be replaced. Ed Kranepool was part of both goals, a high school sensation from the Bronx who was wearing a Mets uniform just a few weeks after signing his first contract.

There is no question Kranepool was rushed to the majors, but Weiss and the Mets felt a few days in the majors in 1962 might help the first baseman-outfielder contribute to the '63 team.

Edward Emil Kranepool was only 17 when he received an $85,000 bonus to sign with the Mets on June 27, 1962. He was a standout hitter at James Monroe High School, breaking Hall of Famer Hank Greenberg's team home run record with 21 and gaining the attention of major league scouts. The 6'3" Kranepool also set several school basketball records and received numerous scholarships to play hoops at the college level. The Mets outworked and outbid the colleges and other major league teams to retain his services.

Kranepool moved up the Mets' organization in a hurry, playing just 20 games with Auburn of the NY–Penn League and only seven contests with the Tigers' South-Atlantic League team in Knoxville before joining the Syracuse Chiefs for 14 Triple A games. He hit .351 with 18 RBIs for Auburn and posted a .278 average at Knoxville before batting .209 with the Chiefs.

He was still only 17 years old and had only 41 professional games under his belt when Weiss brought him up in September. Kranepool made his debut at the Polo Grounds on September 22, hitting a grounder to second after replacing Gil Hodges at first. Kranepool made his first start the next day and went 0-for-3 before hitting a double off Don Elston of the Cubs. He played a week later and finished 1-for-6 as a Met that season, giving him a .295 average for four different teams in his first year. At 17 years and 318 days of age, "The Krane" remains the youngest player ever to appear in a Mets game.

It might have made sense to keep the Mets' top prospect in the minors for the entire 1963 season following his whirlwind introduction to professional baseball. Instead, Kranepool was the Mets' starting first baseman in the season opener against the Cardinals. He won a roster spot after an impressive spring training that included a three-homer game against the Orioles in Portsmouth, Virginia. Two of those home runs came off Hall of Famer Robin Roberts before he went deep against Stu Miller, an All-Star the previous season.

Kranepool went 0-for-4 in the 1963 opener but entered May with a .300 average and four extra-base hits in 12 games. His first major league home run came April 19 against Bob Shaw, who became a teammate of Kranepool's in 1966.

He spent the next nine weeks batting only .164 with a homer, eight doubles, and eight RBIs in 56 games before he was sent to Triple A Buffalo in early July. Kranepool hit well for the Bisons in 53 games, smashing five home runs and driving in 33 runs while batting .310 in 203 at-bats. He also showed power in the alleys by collecting eight triples and seven doubles. He returned to the Mets in September, hitting .274 in 18 games to finish with a .209 average.

Kranepool opened 1964 with the Mets and was farmed out to Buffalo by mid-May after posting a .139 average. He lit up International League pitching in 15 games, batting .352 with three homers and seven RBIs before he was recalled May 31, one day after playing all 18 innings of a doubleheader.

It became a memorable weekend for Kranepool, who broke out of an 0-for-16 slump as a major leaguer by lining a second-inning single against Juan Marichal in Game 1 of a twin bill against the Giants on May 31. He went 1-for-4 in the opener before going the distance in the Mets' 23-inning loss to the Giants in the nightcap. New York trailed 6–1 in the sixth until Kranepool hit an RBI triple to spark a comeback. He went 3-for-10 in the game and was 4-for-14 in the doubleheader to bring his average up to .180. Kranepool also made the final putout in the Mets' second-ever triple play, which snuffed out a Giants rally in the 14th.

Kranepool had played 49 innings over two days following the Mets' 8–6 marathon loss to the Giants. But the doubleheader began a 13-game hitting streak in which he batted .345 with 11 RBIs. He never saw the minors again until 1970 and finished the year batting .257 with 10 home runs and 45 RBIs. Still a teenager, Kranepool was third on

the team with 108 hits and four triples, tied for second with 19 doubles and fourth in homers despite playing only 109 games.

The Mets still had several veterans by 1965, including 44-year-old Warren Spahn and 40-year-old Yogi Berra. But the farm system was finally bearing fruit as Ron Swoboda, Cleon Jones, Tug McGraw, Kevin Collins, Greg Goossen, and Jim Bethke all saw significant action. Bethke replaced Kranepool as the youngest player on the Mets roster before the 18-year-old Collins made his debut September 1.

Kranepool opened the '65 season on a 12-game hitting streak in which he batted .457 with three homers and 12 RBIs. He had a .365 average by May 15 and was hitting .341 as late as June 9, earning a trip to the All-Star Game as the Mets' lone representative. But an 0-for-31 strike dragged his average down to .291 by June 20, and he hit only 207 in his last 107 games of the season to end the year with a .253 average. Still he led the Mets in batting, hits and doubles as a 20-year-old.

The Mets and their fan base were hoping for a little more from Kranepool after 1965. He had shown glimpses of potential stardom, putting together several double-digit hitting streaks and playing solid, yet unspectacular, defense at first base and the corner outfield positions. Kranepool was a fulltime starter in 1966 and '67 but seemed to be on a treadmill since 1964, churning out near-identical numbers each season. He paced the '66 Mets with 16 homers and was among the top four on the team in virtually every positive offensive category from 1966 to 1967. But his career highs at that point were 16 home runs, 57 RBIs, and a .269 average, hardly the numbers of a budding All-Star. He had 469 at-bats in 1967 and never had more than 421 in a season the remainder of his career.

Gil Hodges, the man Kranepool replaced in his major league debut, became Mets manager in 1968. Kranepool started 97 games at first that season and produced his lowest numbers since 1963, hitting .231 with three home runs, 13 doubles, and 20 RBIs. He went 84 at-bats before collecting his first two RBIs of the season and didn't homer until his 158th at-bat. Kranepool had a 34-game stretch in which he batted .330 from May 30 to July 14, but he also provided only one home run and seven RBIs in that span. A growing concern within the organization was that Kranepool would never become more than he was by the end of 1968.

However, Kranepool was one of the better Mets hitters in the first few weeks of 1969, hitting .324 with three home runs, 16 RBIs, and nine runs scored through May 4. But the team went just 9–13 in his first 22 games and was 18–23 through the quarter mark of the season before catching fire. He hit .385 while playing seven games during a team-record 11-game winning streak that began in late May, but his average was down to .256 when Kranepool was suddenly forced into a platoon role.

General manager Johnny Murphy picked up slugging first baseman Donn Clendenon at the June 15 trade deadline. The right-handed hitting Clendenon gave the Mets a power boost and played a big part in the team's second-half surge toward its first playoff berth. Kranepool's average continued to nose-dive, but he was producing timely hits with regularity.

The Mets opened a huge three-game series against Ferguson Jenkins and the Cubs July 8. Jenkins carried a one-hitter into the ninth, the lone hit courtesy of Kranepool's fifth-inning homer. New York trailed 3–1 until Cleon Jones knotted the score with a two-run double. Kranepool ended the game with a base hit that scored Jones and put the Mets within 4½ games of the first-place Cubs.

Kranepool's body of work the rest of the season included a tiebreaking double in the eighth inning of a 4–3 win over the Expos July 13 and an RBI single and a solo homer in a 2–0 win against Montreal September 18, allowing the Mets to pad their division lead. He finished the season with eight game-winning RBIs and became the Mets' all-time home run leader with 62, eclipsing Jim Hickman's 60. Kranepool ended the year with a .238 average, 11 home runs, and 49 RBIs, significantly better numbers than he produced in 1968.

The Mets finished the regular season 100–62, eight games ahead of the Cubs and seven games better than the Braves, the team New York faced in the first-ever National League Championship Series.

Atlanta started right-handers Phil Niekro, Ron Reed, and Pat Jarvis in the first three games of the NLCS, which put Kranepool in the starting lineup for all three games. Kranepool hit .250 in 12 at-bats, including an RBI single that jumpstarted the Mets in an 11–6 victory over the Braves in Game 2. He scored twice in the Mets' series-opening, 9–5 victory and recorded the final putout as New York completed a three-game sweep of Atlanta.

The Mets were heavy underdogs heading into the World Series against the Orioles, who came within the 1954 Indians' AL record for victories in a season. Baltimore also had lefty starters Mike Cuellar and Dave McNally, giving Clendenon a chance to start the games they pitched while Kranepool awaited Jim Palmer in Game 3.

The Mets split the first two games before pounding Palmer in a 5–0 victory in Game 3. Kranepool capped the win by slamming a solo homer off reliever Dave Leonhard, his lone career postseason homer. Clendenon was named the MVP of the series after providing three homers and four RBI, which meant Mets first basemen accounted for four of the team's six home runs and five of New York's 13 RBIs.

Clendenon was the team's top run producer in 1970, but many other Mets came up flat as the team finished six games behind the division-winning Pirates after leading the race in September.

It didn't help that Kranepool's relationship with Hodges was often icy. He and close friend Ron Swoboda were two

Ed Kranepool. Photo courtesy of Oscar W. Gabriel

of the team's most outspoken Mets and weren't afraid to voice their opinion on the team, even if it meant showing up Hodges. Kranepool and Hodges had a heated discussion that eventually involved Swoboda the night before Gil had his first heart attack in Setepmber 1968.

Kranepool spent a larger portion of the year following the Mets from the Tidewater, Virginia, area after being sent to Triple A June 24. He owned a .118 average with no homers and one RBI in 34 at-bats before heading to the Tides. Clendenon had taken over at first base and set a then-team record with 97 RBIs, giving Kranepool little chance to play.

Kranepool wasn't happy about his limited playing time but made the most of his demotion, hitting .310 with seven homers and 45 RBIs in just 47 games before returning to the Mets. He had only 13 at-bats following his call-up but hit .308 and delivered a big RBI single off Bob Gibson in the 11th inning of a 4–3 victory at St. Louis September 1. He ended the year with a .170 average in just 47 at-bats, his smallest body of work since 1962.

Clendenon struggled in 1971, allowing Kranepool to reclaim the first-base position in an otherwise disappointing season for the Mets. Krane usually batted fourth or fifth in the lineup and finished the year tied for the team lead with 14 home runs and second with 58 RBIs while batting .280, a career high figure at that point. But a sputtering lineup coupled with inconsistent pitching led to an 83–79 record despite a 30–18 start.

Clendenon was released in October, which would have meant even more at-bats for Kranepool in 1972. But rookie first baseman-outfielder John Milner wowed the front office in spring training, capturing the Johnny Murphy Award as the team's best player in spring training. First baseman Jim Beauchamp was picked up from the Cardinals before the season, and Willie Mays was acquired in May. Add Cleon Jones' 20-game stint at first and Kranepool was down to 83 starts at the position. But Kranepool was among the more durable players on a team that was ravaged by injury. Kranepool was one of just five Mets to appear in at least 110 games that season. Of those five, he and Wayne Garrett were the only ones to avoid the disabled list.

Kranepool led the 1972 Mets with 122 games played and batted .269 with eight home runs and 34 RBIs. He hit a two-run homer and had three RBIs in a 4–0 win over the Pirates on Opening Day, but his batting average was just .204 on July 22 until he hit .326 with 20 RBIs over his final 60 games.

Kranepool, Mays, Beauchamp, and Milner saw the bulk of the action at first base in 1973, with Milner establishing himself as the starter early in the season. Kranepool started 42 games at first and 31 games in the outfield but hit only .239 with one home run and 35 at-bats. He wasn't in the starting lineup for any of the Mets' final 14 games while they took over first place and won the division the day after the season was scheduled to end. But he provided a huge RBI single in a three-run 10th that pulled the Mets out of last place on August 31.

Kranepool wasn't expected to play much in the postseason, and he kept his fanny glued to the bench while the Mets and Reds split the first four games of the NLCS. But Rusty Staub suffered a separated shoulder in Game 4 and was unable to play in the Game 5 clincher, forcing manager Yogi Berra to move Milner from first base to the outfield. That also meant Kranepool starting at first base in the Mets' biggest game since the 1969 World Series.

The Mets had two runners in scoring position in the bottom of the first when Kranepool strode to the plate with two out. He had accumulated just four at-bats since September 15 and hadn't faced major league pitching in seven days before he slapped a two-run single to give the Mets a 2–0 lead in a 7–2 win over the Reds. He was 1-for-2 in the game to lift his postseason average to .278 before he went 0-for-3 as a pinch-hitter in the Mets' seven-game loss to Oakland in the World Series.

Kranepool was just 2-for-16 as a pinch-hitter during the 1973 regular season and owned a .189 career average in 206 at-bats in games he did not start. With Milner slated

to start at first base in '74 while Staub and Cleon Jones patrolled the corner outfield spots, there wasn't much reason to expect Kranepool to improve on his 1973 statistics. But Kranepool was one of the better stories on a team that went 71–91 a year after coming within one victory of its second World Series title.

Kranepool tied Philadelphia's Tony Taylor for the National League lead with 17 pinch-hits, breaking Chuck Hiller's team record of 16. Kranepool was lethal off the bench, hitting .486 as a pinch-hitter and .432 as a reserve to end the season with a .300 average, 20 points above his previous career high. He went 5-for-5 with a walk as a pinch-hitter during a six-game stretch in July and accounted for a .614 slugging average in pinch-hit duties the entire season.

The 29-year-old Kranepool managed to transform his game when his roster spot was on the line. He owned a .400 batting average on July 16 primarily because of his newfound pinch-hitting prowess, although that average was bolstered by a two-game stretch in which he went 6-for-11 with a homer and four RBIs during consecutive starts at Wrigley Field in late June.

It took 13 seasons, but Kranepool had finally found a niche as pinch-hitter par excellence.

He continued his incredible pinch-hitting stroke into 1975, going 8-for-20 to give him a 25-for-55 mark (.455) over two seasons. He also hit extremely well as a starter, providing a .318 average with four home runs and 40 RBIs in 82 games to finish with a career-high .323 mark in '75.

Fans that had blamed Kranepool for the team's early failures were now in his corner, sending chants of "Ed-die! Ed-die! Ed-die!" throughout Shea anytime he came off the bench to pinch-hit. It was a far cry from the day when a fan at the Polo Grounds showed up with a banner that asked, "Is Ed Kranepool over the hill?"

Kranepool's average stood at .376 on June 13, 1975, thanks in part to a 14-game span in which he was 23-for-46 with nine RBIs and 10 runs scored after Milner landed on the DL with a hamstring injury. He later put together an 18-game hitting streak in which he batted .441 to put his average at .360 on August 5. His final average was marred by a season-ending 8-for-45 slump that began August 23 with the Mets just four games off the division lead.

Kranepool's career was on a treadmill again, except this time it was for his consistent contribution. He was a very good hitter on a marginally offensive ballclub, and new manager Joe Frazier rewarded him by giving him 415 at-bats in 1976, more than he had since the '71 season.

Kranepool played left field and first base while hitting .292 with 10 home runs, 49 RBIs, and seven game-winning ribbies. He crashed into an outfield fence August 4, leaving him with a left elbow injury that caused him to miss nearly three weeks. He batted .330 in 94 at-bats after returning to the lineup August 24 to end the year on a high note.

Kranepool became the team's all-time home run leader again in 1976 and reached the 100-homer plateau with a go-ahead, two-run homer in a 9–8 win August 3. He also became No. 1 on the team in RBI, base hits, and extra-base hits, putting him on top of the team's all-time list in eight difference categories.

Kranepool was now 29-for-65 (.446) as a pinch-hitter since 1974 but was needed on the field more in '76 following injuries to right fielder Mike Vail and left fielder-first baseman Dave Kingman. That fact that he had become one of the team's top offensive players again was a credit to him, and also an indictment on the Mets' lineup and the team's farm system. The team hadn't gotten any younger since the 1973 pennant and was eight games under .500 in three seasons since taking the A's to a seventh game in the Fall Classic.

Kranepool remained one of the team's top offensive contributors in 1977, when the bottom completely dropped out of the organization. He was playing on a last-place team for the first time in 10 years as he saw many of his teammates from the '73 club leave for better situations. When the 1977 came to a close, Kranepool, Koosman, Milner, and Bud Harrelson were the only players remaining from the last playoff team. Milner and Harrelson were gone before the 1978 opener, and Koosman was mercifully traded to the Twins after the '78 season.

The team's free fall did nothing to diminish Kranepool's productivity in 1977 as he hit .281 with 10 homers and 40 RBIs in just 281 at-bats during a season in which Lee Mazzilli, John Stearns, and Steve Henderson had emerged as the focal points of the offense.

Kranepool paced the NL with a .448 average as a pinch-hitter, going 13-for-29 with a homer and 14 ribbies. Six of his pinch-hit RBIs won or tied games, including a game-tying two-run homer and a walk-off, two-run double over the last five weeks.

Willie Montanez became the Mets' starting first baseman in 1978, and Henderson was patrolling left, leaving Kranepool to start just nine games that year. Kranepool failed to get his average above .250 after July 15 and settled for a .210 mark in only 66 games, his fewest appearances since 1970. But he was 15-for-50 (.300) as a pinch-hitter and hit three home runs in that capacity to tie a team record set by Ed Charles in 1968. Kranepool now owned an outstanding .396 batting average (57-for-144) as a pinch-hitter since 1974. His 96 career pinch-hits stood ninth on baseball's all-time list as he approached the 1979 campaign, his 18th in the majors.

Now 34 years of age, Kranepool played more in '79 than he did the previous year, starting 33 of his 82 games and hitting .232 with two home runs and 17 runs batted in 155 at-bats. He had his best month in August, batting .304 with seven RBIs in 56 at-bats before posting a .200 average in 50 September at-bats.

The pinch-hit magic that he possessed for five seasons suddenly disappeared. Kranepool had a decent .262 on-base average as a pinch-hitter but went just 6-for-37 in that capacity to claim a .162 batting average. He doubled off the bench during a 4–2 victory in the season finale, a win that prevented the Mets from reaching the century mark in losses for the first time in 12 years.

Changes were afoot at Shea after the season. The de Roulet family was entertaining offers after announcing in November 1979 that the Mets would be sold by year's end. With the sale looming, the team declined to re-sign any of its free agents not otherwise deemed vital for the club's rebuilding. That meant Kranepool was shown the door November 1, less than three weeks before his 35th birthday.

But Kranepool almost remained with the Mets—as board chairman or team president. He became part of a potential ownership group headed by Robert Abplanalp, a close friend of Richard Nixon who had gotten to know Kranepool over the years. Abplanalp made his money with Precision Valve Corporation after inventing the first workable aerosol valve that could be mass-produced cheaply.

Abplanalp was on the short list of potential owners, a group that included former Ambassador to Cuba Earl Smith, ex-major league manager Herman Franks, Nelson Doubleday, and Fred Wilpon. Kranepool would become the Mets' operating head if Abplanalp was successful in purchasing the team.

Kranepool's participation in the Abplanalp group made it the odds-on favorite to get the Mets. But Wilpon, who had been trying to purchase the team since Joan Payson died in 1975, joined forces with Doubleday to put together the winning bid. They agreed to pay what was then a major league record, $21.3 million for a ballclub that had finished in last place three years running. They also made Kranepool a Mets outsider for the second time in a month.

Kranepool found no takers as he tried to hook up with another ballclub. He wasn't about to become a hanger-on with the Mets, whose new front office had no room for the longest-running act in team history. Fortunately, he was well prepared for life after baseball.

Kranepool had become a licensed stock broker long before the Mets won their first World Series. He also had various business interests that allowed him to rub elbows with the likes of Abplanalp and other well-vested people.

ML/Mets debut	vs. Cubs, 9/22/62
1st ML/Mets hit	double vs. Don Elston, Cubs, 9/23/62
1st ML/Mets homer	solo homer vs. Bob Shaw, Braves, 4/19/63
1st ML/Mets RBI	solo homer vs. Bob Shaw, Braves, 4/19/63
Most hits, ML/Mets game	4, 6 times
Most homers, ML/Mets game	2, 6 times
Most RBI, ML/Mets game	4, 5 times
Acquired: Signed as an amateur free agent, 6/27/62.	
Deleted: Became a free agent, 11/1/79.	

Al Leiter

Pitcher   Bats left, throws left
Born: 10/23/65   Toms River, New Jersey
Height: 6'3"   Weight: 215   #22

Al Leiter Mets Career

YEAR	GP/GS	IP	H	R	ER	K	BB	W–L	SV	ERA
1998	28/28	193	151	55	53	174	71	17–6	0	2.47
1999	32/32	213	209	107	100	162	93	13–12	0	4.23
2000	31/31	208	176	84	74	200	76	16–8	0	3.20
2001	29/29	187⅓	178	81	69	142	46	11–11	0	3.31
2002	33/33	204⅓	194	99	79	172	89	13–13	0	3.48
2003	30/30	180.2	176	83	80	139	94	15–9	0	3.99
2004	30/30	173.2	138	65	62	117	97	10–8	0	3.21
Total	213/213	1360	1222	574	517	1106	546	95–67	0	3.42

Mets Career/Batting

GP	AB	R	H	2B	3B	HR	RBI	K	BB	SB	AVG
198	394	10	33	7	1	0	14	208	28	0	.084

ML Career

YEAR	GP/GS	IP	H	R	ER	K	BB	W–L	SV	ERA
87–95	419/382	2391	2152	1101	1010	1974	1163	162–132	2	3.80

One team's fire sale is another team's gain. Al Leiter and the Florida Marlins had just won the 1997 World Series in only their fifth year of existence, shattering the Mets' major league record for fastest expansion team to win a championship. But the Marlins drew poorly until the playoffs, and the ballclub was at odds with Miami-Dade County and the state over funding for a ballpark. Owner Wayne Huizenga began to pare down payroll immediately after the Series, allowing all of his free agents to go elsewhere while ordering other stars to be traded for prospects. It appeared Leiter was going to spend the 1998 season on a rebuilding team before the Marlins shipped him to the Mets for four prospects, including A.J. Burnett.

The Mets, who finished just five games behind the Marlins for the NL wild-card, hoped the trade would put them over the top and into the playoffs for the first time in 10 years. Leiter did his best to get them there, setting career highs with 17 victories and a 2.47 ERA while recording 174 strikeouts, the second-best total of his career. He lent credibility to a rotation that included Rick Reed, Bobby Jones, Masato Yoshii, and several others who took turns as the No. 5 starter.

Leiter was outstanding over the first 2½ months of the season, going 9–3 with two shutouts and a 1.60 ERA. He earned his first Mets victory April 7 at Wrigley Field, holding the Cubs to an earned run and six hits in five innings. The lefty became the first Met in five years to toss two shutouts in the same season when he beat the Expos on a five-hitter June 16 at Montreal. The two shutouts came as Leiter was winning six consecutive starts between May 23 and June 21. But the streak ended June 26, when Leiter partially tore the patellar tendon in his left knee during a loss to the Yankees. The injury robbed Leiter of a chance to pitch in an All-Star Game for the second time in his career.

Leiter was out until July 18, when he allowed only two hits in six shutout innings at Philadelphia. He was excellent down the stretch, winning seven of his final nine starts while recording a 2.71 ERA. Leiter beat the Marlins 5–0 September 20, allowing five hits while striking out nine in eight innings. The victory gave the Mets a one-game lead over the Cubs in the wild-card race with five games remaining, but New York didn't win another game the rest of the way. Leiter was tagged with a 4–0 loss on the next-to-last day of the season.

Leiter's 17 wins in 1998 were the most by a Met since Frank Viola won 20 in 1990. Leiter finished third in the NL in ERA, seventh in strikeouts, and third in winning percentage to finish sixth in the Cy Young voting.

Leiter's stats declined in 1999, but the season had a much happier ending. He got off to a terrible start, opening 2–5 with a 6.39 ERA while continuing to battle knee pain. However, Leiter returned to his 1998 form after taking 11 days off between starts. He was the NL Pitcher of the Month in June, winning all five of his starts while compiling a 2.62 ERA. His first start of the month came with the Mets on an eight-game losing streak that dropped them under .500 and led to the removal of pitching coach Bob Apodaca. Leiter was asked to end the streak, and he did it with a superb seven-inning performance against the Yankees on June 6, allowing only four hits in a 7–2 victory. The win ignited a stretch in which the Mets won 15 of 18 to move back into the playoff picture.

Leiter spent July and August pitching at a win-one, lose-one pace before he dropped three consecutive starts in September.

The Mets were counted out of the wild-card hunt after dropping seven straight in late September. The skid ended when Leiter outpitched Greg Maddux in a 9–2 rout of the Braves, but it left the Mets 1½ games off the wild-card lead with four to play. The deficit grew to two games when the Mets lost the rubber game against Atlanta. Only a sweep against Pittsburgh and a collapse by the Reds and Astros would get the Mets into the playoffs. The Pirates, Reds and Astros responded in kind.

Leiter wasn't available for the Pittsburgh series at Shea, but the Mets completed a thrilling sweep to force a one-game playoff at Cincinnati for the wild-card. Pitching on his normal four days' rest, Leiter tossed a two-hit shutout in a 5–0 win over the Reds to get the Mets into the postseason for an NLDS against the Diamondbacks.

The one-game playoff meant Leiter wouldn't pitch until Game 4, but the Mets took two of the first three to give him a chance to win the clincher. Leiter left the game leading 2–1 with two on and two outs in the eighth before Armando Benitez gave up Jay Bell's two-run double. The Mets won the game—and the series—when Todd Pratt homered in the 10th inning.

The Mets now had to face the Braves in the NLCS, with Leiter pitching Game 3 at Shea. Leiter was every bit as good against the Braves as he was versus the Reds 11 days earlier, allowing just three hits in seven innings. But his throwing error led to a first-inning run that gave the Braves a 1–0 victory and a 3–0 lead in the series.

The Mets pulled out the next two games in their final at-bat, including Robin Ventura's grand-slam single. Leiter was asked to extend the series to a seventh game when he took the mound at Turner Field for Game 6. Just 25 pitches later, Leiter was walking off the mound after surrendering four runs on just two hits without retiring a batter. He loaded the bases by hitting two batters and walking another, and was lifted after Eddie Perez hit a two-run single. A fifth run was charged to Leiter when Brian Hunter hit a sacrifice fly against Pat Mahomes.

The Mets erased the five-run deficit and had leads of 8–7 and 9–8 in the late innings before the Braves won the game in 11 innings 10–9. Leiter had pitched like an ace in his previous four starts before his early wildness in Game 6 contributed to the Mets' loss.

The Mets had never been to the postseason in back-to-back seasons before 2000. Leiter helped them get there by going 16–8 with a 3.20 ERA and a career-high 200 strikeouts. He was pitching pain-free after undergoing left knee surgery the previous October and was 10–1 with a 3.04 ERA after a seven-inning, 12-strikeout performance in a 9–1 pounding of the Braves July 1. Leiter also had a pair of 12-strikeout performances in August before tossing his lone shutout of the season, a five-hitter against the Phillies September 10. The Mets went 21–10 in his 31 starts and won the wild-card by a comfortable eight-game margin over the Dodgers. New York was in the hunt for the NL East crown heading into the final week of the year, but the Braves clinched the division at Shea with a 7–1 win over Leiter September 26. One day later, the Mets wrapped up their second straight postseason appearance and ended the regular season on a five-game winning streak heading into the NLDS against the Giants.

Mike Hampton was hit hard in Game 1 at San Francisco, putting pressure on Leiter to stop the Mets from falling behind 2–0 in the series. The Mets led 4–1 before Leiter gave up a leadoff double to Barry Bonds in the bottom of the ninth. Manager Bobby Valentine lifted Leiter after 126 pitches, but the move backfired when J.T. Snow launched a game-tying three-run homer off Benitez. Benitez was credited with the victory when the Mets rallied in the 10th for a 5–4 win.

Leiter also was the Game 2 starter in the NLCS against the Cardinals, working a day after Mike Hampton led the Mets to a 6–2 victory in the opener. Leiter left the game with a 5–3 lead after striking out nine in seven innings. The bullpen robbed Leiter of another playoff win, allowing two runs in the eighth before the Mets pulled out a 6–5 win.

The Mets clinched the pennant when Hampton tossed a three-hitter in a 7–0 pounding of the Cards in Game 5. The short series gave Leiter an opportunity to start the World Series opener at Yankee Stadium. Leiter was terrific

in Game 1, blanking the Yankees until David Justice broke a scoreless tie with a two-run double. Leiter tossed a scoreless seventh and left the game with a 3–2 lead after scattering five hits. John Franco protected the lead, but Armando Benitez loaded the bases with one out in the ninth before giving up Chuck Knoblauch's game-tying sacrifice fly. The Mets lost in 12 innings 4–3.

Leiter put together a courageous effort in Game 5 as the Mets needed a victory to extend the Series. Leiter carried a five-hitter into the ninth with the game tied 2–2. He opened the inning by fanning Tino Martinez and Paul O'Neill before Jorge Posada worked out a nine-pitch walk. Leiter had thrown 138 pitches by the time he walked Posada, but Valentine decided to keep him in rather than go with Benitez or Franco. Pitch No. 141 was a single by Scott Brosius. Pitch No. 142 was an RBI single by Luis Sojo that actually scored two runs because of outfielder Jay Payton's throwing error. Leiter received a warm ovation as he left the mound following Sojo's hit. The Series ended when Mike Piazza lifted a fly ball that was caught by Bernie Williams in deep center.

Leiter struck out nine in the Game 5 loss, relying on his cutter to get the big outs. Leiter referred to the cutter as "the gift" because he felt it was the only reason he was in the majors.

Leiter had another gift in 2001: pinpoint control. He averaged about four walks per nine innings until 2000, when he trimmed it to a walk every three innings. In 2001 he was walking just 2.2 batters per nine innings and made three starts in which he worked at least seven innings without issuing a free pass.

But Leiter got off to a shaky start in 2001 despite his new-found control, going 0–3 with a 5.87 ERA in his first four games. But the ERA was down to 3.25 by July 17, when he tossed seven shutout innings in a 1–0 win over the Blue Jays. Leiter was just 7–10 with a 3.44 ERA following a 2–1 loss to the Padres, which also dropped the Mets 12 games under .500 and 13½ games out of first place. However, Leiter and the Mets suddenly got red hot after that as he won four consecutive starts while pitching to a 2.48 ERA. The Mets were still four games under .500 following his fourth straight win, but they were making a charge on the Braves.

Leiter didn't pitch again for another 12 days because of the terrorist attacks on Manhattan and Washington. The layoff didn't stop his momentum as he picked up a no-decision after allowing only one run in seven innings of a 4–1 win at Pittsburgh September 17.

Leiter also picked up no-decisions in his next two starts despite allowing only one run over eight innings each time. Both of those games were losses to the Braves, including an 8–5 loss in which the Braves scored seven runs in the ninth off Benitez and Franco after Leiter limited them to four hits. The shocking loss dropped the Mets five games out of first with seven to play.

Leiter finished the year just 11–11, his lowest win total since 1997. But he had no decisions in six starts in which

Al Leiter. Photo courtesy of David Ferry

he allowed fewer than two runs. It was more of the same in 2002 as Leiter went 13–13 despite a 3.48 ERA. He was excellent through mid May, going 5–2 with a 1.74 ERA. But the Mets had trouble scoring runs or keeping leads on most days he was on the mound. They were held to two runs or fewer 14 times in his 33 starts. Leiter also had five no-decisions when giving up no more than one run.

Leiter received ample run support in 2003, helping him finish the year 15–9 despite a 3.99 ERA. His control problems resurfaced as he averaged 4.7 walks per nine innings, more than doubling his 2001 average.

A Leiter start was becoming excrutiating to watch. His cutter was now being fouled off instead of missed completely, leading to more walks, a higher pitch count, and fewer innings. He walked at least five in eight of his 30 starts and lasted more than six innings just 10 times. But Leiter also allowed only 138 hits in 173⅔ innings, one of the best ratios for his career.

Leiter beat the Cubs 3–2 September 26 with what was becoming a typical Leiter performance: six innings, two runs, two hits, five walks, and five strikeouts in 110 pitches. He had nine no-decisions in games he allowed fewer than three runs while pitching for a team that finished under .500 for the third straight year. He compiled a 3.21 ERA,

his lowest since 2000. But new general manager Omar Minaya declined to pick up the $10.2 million option on Leiter's contract for 2005.

According to a December 9, 2004, article in the *New York Times*, Leiter was offered a one-year deal worth $4 million guaranteed, with another $3 million in reachable incentives. He liked the deal and was prepared to sign on November 16, the first day he was eligible for free agency. But he told the *Times* he declined the offer after Minaya called and gave him a November 19 deadline to accept the contract. Little did Leiter know at the time that Minaya was about to spend big money on free agents Pedro Martinez and Carlos Beltrán.

Leiter passed on the offer and instead signed a one-year deal with the Marlins worth a guaranteed $7 million. Leiter went on WFAN's Steve Summers show to say he felt Minaya had demonstrated he didn't want the now 39-year-old hurler on the team. It sparked a he-said/he-said episode that augmented Leiter's ugly divorce from the Mets.

Leiter was back with the Marlins, eight years after helping them win their first championship. He had pitched a no-hitter for the ballclub and was 27–21 with a 3.51 ERA in two seasons with the team. But his return to the team was unsuccessful as he went 3–7 with a 6.64 ERA and 60 walks in 80 innings. The Marlins designated him for assignment in July and shipped him back to the Yankees, the team that drafted Leiter in the second round of the 1984 draft.

Leiter turned back the clock in his first game back with the Bombers, allowing only one run and three hits while striking out eight in 6⅓ innings of a 5–3 win at Fenway Park. He later went 3–0 with a 3.10 ERA during a five-start sequence in August, but he was tagged for six runs in ⅔ of an inning against Oakland September 2 before pitching out of the bullpen the rest of the way.

Leiter finally picked up a playoff victory in 2005, 12 years after getting credit for a win against the Phillies in Game 1 of the World Series. He retired two batters in the seventh inning of Game 4 of the NLDS against the Angels before the Yankees scored twice in the bottom of the seventh to pull out a 3–2 win and extend the series.

Leiter signed with the Yankees in January 2006 before he retired during spring training. He remained with the team as a broadcaster on the YES Network and also joined the fledgling MLB Network in January 2009.

ML debut	Yankees vs. Brewers, 9/15/87 (6 IP, 4 H, 1 ER, 8 K, 4 BB)
Mets debut	vs. Phillies, 4/2/98 (6 IP, 7 H, 3 ER, 4 K, 1 BB)
First ML strikeout	Mike Felder, Brewers, 9/15/87 (with Yankees)
First Mets strikeout	Scott Rolen, Phillies, 4/2/98
First ML win	vs. Brewers, 9/15/87
First Mets win	@ Cubs, 4/7/98
First ML save	@ Orioles, 6/28/93 (with Blue Jays)
Most strikeouts, ML/Mets game	15, @ Cubs, 8/1/99
Low-hit ML CG	0, Marlins vs. Rockies, 5/11/96
Low-hit Mets CG	2, @ Reds, 10/4/99; @ Expos, 4/18/02

Acquired: Traded by the Marlins with Ralph Millard for A.J. Burnett, Jesus Sanchez and Robert Stratton, 2/6/98.
Deleted: Became a free agent, 11/11/04. Signed by the Marlins, 12/8/04.

Jon Matlack

Pitcher	Bats left, throws left
Born: 1/19/50	West Chester, Pennsylvania
Height: 6′3″	Weight: 205 #35, 32

Jon Matlack Mets Career

YEAR	GP/GS	IP	H	R	ER	K	BB	W–L	SV	ERA
1971	7/6	37	31	18	17	24	15	0–3	0	4.14
1972	34/32	244	215	79	63	169	71	15–10	0	2.32
1973	34/34	242	210	93	86	204	99	14–16	0	3.20
1974	34/34	265⅓	221	82	71	195	76	13–15	0	2.41
1975	33/32	228⅔	224	105	86	154	58	16–12	0	3.39
1976	35/35	262	236	94	86	153	57	17–10	0	2.95
1977	26/26	169	175	86	79	123	43	7–15	0	4.21
Total	203/199	1448	1312	557	488	1023	419	82–81	0	3.03

Mets Career/Batting

GP	AB	R	H	2B	3B	HR	RBI	K	BB	SB	AVG
204	441	32	57	3	0	0	23	217	57	0	.129

ML Career

YEAR	GP/GS	IP	H	R	ER	K	BB	W–L	SV	ERA
71–83	361/318	2363	2276	970	835	1516	638	125–126	3	3.18

Jon Matlack would have been the ace of most major league pitching staffs from 1972 to 1976. During that time he averaged 15 victories, 248 innings, and 175 strikeouts while compiling a 2.84 ERA, fourth best in the National League. Also in that span, Matlack was seventh in the NL with 75 wins, fifth with 1,242 innings, fourth with 876 strikeouts, and second with 23 shutouts.

Matlack may have been overshadowed by Tom Seaver and Jerry Koosman, although he was just as important to the ballclub and enjoyed a stretch of three straight postseason starts that is unparalleled among Mets hurlers. No team had a better trio of starters from the early to mid-'70s than the Mets. He became a permanent member of the rotation in '72, four years after Koosman and five seasons following Seaver's major league debut. Although his achievements are curiously overlooked more than 30 years later due to Koosman's and Seaver's involvement with the 1969 championship club, Mets fans who remember the handsome lefty from West Chester, Pennsylvania, will tell you the team's decline would have begun years earlier had he pitched elsewhere. He also had one of the coolest middle names in Mets history.

Jonathan Trumpbour Matlack began to gain the attention of scouts while pitching for West Chester High School. As an eventual fourth-overall pick by the Mets in the June 1967 draft, he was obviously on many teams' radars but oblivious to the attention.

"The attention of scouts I think came my junior year of high school, but I'm not positive," Matlack recalled in a June 2011 interview. "I kept noticing guys with clipboards and stopwatches behind the backstop at our games. I finally asked Charlie Perrone, who was the coach of the high school team, 'What are all those guys doing back there?' He said 'They're scouts.' I had no idea what a scout was, so I asked, 'What's a scout?' And so he explained to me what a scout's job was, and my next question was, 'Well, why are they here?' And he said, 'Well, they're watching some of our players.' And I said, 'Oh, really? Who?'

"And it was me and a catcher named Bobby Owens, and I think there were a couple of other guys of interest on our ballclub my junior year. So that was my first indication that there might be interest in my ability to play."

With Matlack serving as ace of the Warriors' staff, West Chester won 40 straight games in the Ches-Mont League from 1965 to 1967. The Mets, whose longest winning streak from 1962 to 1967 was seven, grabbed Matlack one year after his battery-mate, Owens, was selected by the Cubs in the third round.

"I was just excited," Matlack said of being chosen by the Mets. "It really didn't matter to me at that time who would have picked me. It was just getting an opportunity to play professionally, and having it be fairly close to home was even more exciting."

John Matlack. Photo courtesy of Oscar W. Gabriel

"Potentionally another Koosman" was the way Matlack was described in an organizational assessment, according to the 1971 Mets media guide. He began to live up to his potential in 1968, going 13–6 with a 2.76 ERA in 173 innings for Raleigh-Durham of the Class A Carolina League. He jumped two levels to Triple A Tidewater in 1969, going 14–7 that season and 12–11 in 1970, although his ERA was a mediocre 4.14. He was recalled by the Mets September 1970 but didn't get into a game while the Mets battled the Pirates and Cubs for the NL East title.

Matlack opened the 1971 season with the Tides and was recalled July 7 following an injury to Koosman. The promotion came a few weeks after he came within five outs of a perfect game against Charleston.

Matlack was solid in his big-league debut July 11, picking up a no-decision in a 5–3 loss after allowing two runs and six hits in seven innings. He remembers "being nervous because it was the second game of a doubleheader, and I think the clubhouse guy was going to bill me for the carpet I wore out walking around in the clubhouse before the game started.

"I pitched fairly credibly, and I thought I had a chance to win because it was right close to the All-Star break. If I recall correctly, Seaver was not going to get another start, and they ended up using him in relief.

"I had given up a homer to [Tony] Perez early, and they had pinch-hit for me later in the ballgame. I think we took the lead based on whoever pinch-hit for me. Seaver came in to relieve and I had a lead at the time, so I'm in the clubhouse with Seaver caddying for me, thinking I've got my first win. And he gave up another home run to Perez, and we ended up losing the game."

Ed Kranepool pinch-hit for Matlack and drew a walk with the Mets trailing 2–1 in the eighth before Tommie Agee hit an RBI single and scored on Donn Clendenon's double to make it 3–2. Seaver relieved Tug McGraw with one out in the eighth and surrendered a three-run blast by Perez, causing Matlack to wait nine more months for his first big-league win. Matlack made four more starts and was returned to Tidewater in early August after going 0–3 with a 5.14 ERA.

"I think it was more an adjustment to understanding the difference between a quality pitch in Triple A and a quality pitch in the big leagues," Matlack said of his first major league experience. "There was a difference, and when I got outside of that zone, hitters would make you pay for it. So it was learning to make that subtle adjustment and stay away from mistakes because that's where guys make their living."

He was back with the Mets in September and held the Pirates to a run and five hits in eight innings of his lone start following his second recall of the season. It was a nice way to end the year, although he wasn't sure that start was a springboard for his outstanding 1972 campaign.

"It may have been. I honestly don't know. I just know that having the opportunity to be up there was a step in the right direction. I went to Puerto Rico that winter, and that was another stepping stone that helped me understand higher-caliber competition and the things I needed to do to compete against higher-caliber competition.

"Coming into spring training I had played nonstop through the winter, so I was in good shape and raring to go. And I think that also gave me a step up because it wasn't like I was coming back after a winter of nothing. I had been playing and was fairly sharp. I think that helped, as well."

Matlack had shown the potential to handle big-league batters in 1971 and proved it a year later by becoming the second Met to win the National League Rookie of the Year award. But he wasn't sure where he fit into manager Yogi Berra's plans when the team broke camp in 1972.

"I think I was the bottom of the heap," Matlack said of his place on the staff in April. "And nobody really ever told me that I had made the staff. Because of off-days, we were going with four starters early and I would be in the bullpen until the fifth spot was needed.

"I think they were looking for ways to keep me going, so there were opportunities to pitch out of the bullpen."

He picked up his first major league win on April 23, tossing four shutout innings of relief against the Cubs. He entered the game trailing 2–1 and retired the side in order in his first inning of work. Back-to-back homers by Cleon Jones and Jim Fregosi put the Mets ahead 4–2 in the bottom half before Matlack struck out Billy North, Rick Monday, and Billy Williams in succession in the sixth. Matlack also capped the scoring in an 8–2 victory by slapping an RBI single in the eighth inning.

"That was a day when Gentry had started the game, we were behind, and ultimately came back to win. Whether that outing had anything to do with it, or whether it was the timing the schedule produced for a circumstance where you needed a fifth starter that got me in there, I really don't know."

Matlack was brilliant in his first start five days later, tossing a six-hitter in a 6–1 win at Los Angeles April 28. He was 6–0 with a 1.95 ERA after firing a three-hit shutout against the Phillies May 30. No other Mets rookie in club history opened a season 6–0 until Dillon Gee in 2011. But with the Mets ravaged by injuries and skidding out of the division lead, the lefty went 2–5 with a 3.86 ERA in his next seven starts.

Matlack had a great support group as he progressed in 1972. There was Seaver as the staff ace, Jerry Koosman and Ray Sadecki as the veteran lefties, and Jerry Grote behind the plate.

"They were unbelievably helpful. I roomed with Grote a little bit. I roomed with Sadecki some, a little bit less than Grote. Grote and I roomed together a couple of years. My locker was between Seaver and Koosman, and they were of tremendous help, all of them.

"Koozy, being left-handed and just a little quirky, was also my bridge partner, so we played cards together and talked a lot of shop. Tommy was the consummate professional who offered pearls of wisdom as he deemed necessary. A lot of times, they were timely and just helped me along the way. It was just a great circumstance to come up in."

Matlack was outstanding over the final 2½ months to secure the Rookie of the Year award, going 7–5 with a 2.03 earned run average in his final 18 starts. He ended up 15–10 with a 2.32 ERA to easily outdistance Giants catcher Dave Rader as the league's top rookie.

"There was some mention of it in late August and early September," Matlack said of his chances of securing the award. "A writer would mention it from time to time, and I really wasn't too aware of what it was all about. Subsequently, I became the Rookie of the Year and was contacted about it. And it was something that was nice, but still, I didn't have the depth of it.

"It probably wasn't until after I was done playing—and people started talking about it and comparing you to other people who had won the award, and people who were signature hunters who had bats that just had rookies of the year on them, or something that they had designed that was signatures of all rookies of the year—that I realized that it was pretty special."

Matlack's rookie season is also fondly remembered in Pittsburgh. He became the answer to a trivia question as he gave up Roberto Clemente's 3,000th and final major league hit in the fourth inning of a 5–0 loss at Three Rivers Stadium on September 30. The game followed back-to-back starts in which he tossed five-hitters without allowing an earned run, including a 1–0 shutout win over the Phillies. People quickly forgot those two gems after he served up Clemente's milestone hit. Even Matlack admits he didn't know Clemente was about to join an exclusive club.

"I'm reminded about it frequently," Matlack said nearly four decades later. "It gives me almost instant credibility with the Latin players who are aware of it. They hear my name and, upon meeting me, they'll take a step back and say, 'Oh, you the guy…Clemente!'

"I had no idea. I was a rookie struggling on a day I'm trying to win another ballgame. I was behind. I had walked too many guys. I was having trouble finding the plate that day.

"I had thrown this guy five or six consecutive fastballs, had a 2–2 count, and was gonna try to backdoor a breaking ball and hopefully surprise him. I'm ticked off when I threw the ball because I realize that the pitch is not gonna quite make the strike zone. It's gonna stay away. And I'm sort of upset because I know as it comes out of my hand that I've got a 3–2 count to deal with…or at least so I thought.

"He took that big stride like he always did, kept his hands back and somehow that thing looked enticing to him. He went out and hit the living daylights out of it—a line drive that one-hopped the center-field wall—and I'm like, 'Damn, how'd he ever hit that?'

"The place goes crazy, and I'm waiting to get the ball back because we've got a game to play. The umpire's giving him the ball at second base, and I'm going, 'What in the hell is this about?' And about that time, I'm noticing the scoreboard say '3,000,' and then the light bulb finally went off in my dumb head that this guy just got his 3,000th hit. No wonder there's a big hoopla about that."

Mets fans wanted to see how Matlack would respond after snagging baseball's top rookie honor. Seaver got off to a 2–5 start a year after winning the 1967 Rookie of the Year award. Matlack also opened the 1973 season with a 2–5 record in his first seven starts, but his 4.96 ERA was a bit alarming. Most important, Matlack was lucky to be alive following his seventh start.

He was nursing a lead in the seventh inning against the Braves May 8 when Marty Perez scorched a line drive that ricocheted off Matlack's head and landed in the Mets' dugout. When the date May 8, 1973 was mentioned, Matlack quickly uttered one word—headache.

"I remember it like it was yesterday," Matlack recalled. "I'm in a tight ballgame, a 3–2 lead in the seventh inning and it's starting to rain. It's misting and getting a little sloppy out there, and I've got the bases loaded, two outs, Perez is at the plate. I threw him a 2–2 curveball that is not a strike, but he offers and I think we're gonna get a call on the swing. The home plate umpire doesn't call it, so we appeal and the first-base umpire doesn't call it. So now I'm 3–2 with the bases loaded and a one-run lead.

"I know I've got to make a good pitch, and in an attempt to throw a quality fastball I think I tried to put too much into it, overthrew it, landed too hard on the mound and my head jolted as I released the ball. And I lost sight of it as it went to the plate.

"And I can still see him swing the bat. I can still hear the crack of the bat hitting the ball, but I don't pick up the baseball until it's—I don't know—15 feet away. I barely got my bare hand in front of it before it hit me. It was like somebody set off a flash cube off in my head.

"My mouth hurt instantly. I thought I got hit in the mouth. I lay down on the mound and I'm reaching for what's left of my teeth. Grote's out there and he grabs my hand. He won't let my do anything. He says, 'Just wait for the trainer.' And I'm still thinking I got hit in the mouth, but I can see something from the top corner of my eye, and I realize, 'Oh my God, that's my forehead.' It had swollen enough that I could see it. It's at that point that I realize I've been hit in the head, and I have the sensation that I'm really weak. My head is sore, but not terribly so, and I just feel weak."

His wife Dee was in the stands and immediately thought the worst.

"In an effort to keep me dry, the people taking me off the field covered me up with a tarpolin. She thought that because I had been covered up—you see these TV shows where when somebody's dead they just cover 'em up—her initial reaction was, 'Oh my God, he must be dead.' So she comes flying down to the clubhouse and trying to figure out what's going on, and they let her in to reassure her that I'm okay.

"They cut my uniform off me and are going to put me in an ambulance to the hospital. They undressed me on the stretcher on the training table. I'm down to a pair of shorts and a jockstrap, and they're going to put me in an ambulance and send me down to Roosevelt Hospital in Manhattan."

The rest of Matlack's evening was like a magical mystery tour full of blunders as he tried to receive treatment for a head injury.

"I've got an ice bag I'm supposed to hold on my head, and the guys driving the ambulance—with all the traffic in the parking lot—can't find the way out to get on the Grand Central Parkway. So I'm looking through the window in the back of the ambulance, hollering the directions at these guys to help them out of the parking lot! They finally got out of the parking lot, and I lay back down and put the ice bag on my head.

"We get down to the hospital and it's been raining. There have been accidents, so there's a backup. They horse me out of the ambulance—still in the rain, in my shorts, getting wet—and we go into the emergency room. There's a guy on a gurney that's full-size next to me in the hall, and I think he was drunk. He's trying to get off his gurney and damn near goes falling on me because I'm on the lower one. It was a comedy of errors.

"They finally get me into an intensive care room, and when the shift changes, there are people who are getting off their shift and heard that I'm there, and they're wandering in looking for autographs! I mean, it was really an interesting scenario.

"I get released three days later, having many tests and them deciding I've got a crack in my forehead. They send me home, and there's a [TV] crew waiting for me up at my house in Katonah that want to put an eye patch on me and put me in a wheelchair to make it look more sensational because I don't look like I have anything wrong. I don't even have a brush burn or a bruise or anything. It was sort of crazy."

Matlack suffered a linear fracture of the frontal bone but was back on the mound just 11 days later, working six shutout innings against the Pirates.

"I was a nervous wreck," Matlack said of his return to the mound. "I knew one thing: I wanted to get back out there. But I wasn't sure how I was going to react to balls hit in my direction. I didn't really have any balls hit at me, but I had numerous balls hit to second and short, so they were in my general direction, and I became very happily aware that I wasn't flinching, I wasn't blinking. Everything seemed to be normal except that I had to wear this funny band over my forehead and one of Seaver's hats because it was the only one big enough to go over all that stuff. It kept moving around as I was throwing pitches, and I was constantly having to adjust it, but I was tickled to death to be able to get back out there and play."

Matlack seemed to be afflicted with the dreaded sophomore jinx by June 4, when he lost to the Reds to drop his record to 2–8 with a 4.63 earned run average. He pitched in bad luck at times, losing by the thinnest of margins and receiving no run support when he was at his best. But he also had four starts during that span in which he allowed at least five runs.

"Trying to figure out what you needed to do to be consistent, I honestly don't know that I can attribute anything that would make any sense to it. I think I got to trying to do more than I needed to. Looking back at it I think there were times when I may have taken teams for granted when that was a mistake. I think it was more a process of learning the game, what I was about…the things I needed to do to give that consistent effort.

But he was exceptional the rest of the way, going 12–8 with a 2.62 earned run average while factoring in the Mets' improbable charge to the NL East title.

The Mets were in last place at 52–64, 7½ games off the division lead after Matlack blew a 2–1 lead in the ninth inning of a 3–2 loss to the lowly Padres August 13. He proceeded to win his next five decisions, recording a 3.21 ERA in eight starts along the way to help the Mets move back into contention. Matlack authored a four-hitter in a 2–0 shutout of the Cardinals September 22, giving the Mets a one-game lead and putting them over the .500 mark for the first time since May 26.

With New York City's huge budget deficit, crumbling infrastructure, and ongoing mayoral race, the Mets were the hot story just two months after even the Shea faithful had left them for dead.

"I don't know if anybody believed or didn't believe at that point," Matlack said of the feeling in the clubhouse by the end of July. "What I did know was that we had a scrappy bunch of guys that, on a night at Shea when a ball could have skipped off the top of the fence and been a home run, it hit right on the point of the fence to the outfielder, and a relay throw cut a runner down at the plate that was an important run."

The "ball-off-the-wall" play came in the 13th inning of a victory against the Pirates, shortly before the Mets took over the division lead. Cleon Jones corralled the ball and fired a throw to shortstop Wayne Garrett, who nailed Richie Zisk at the plate while catcher Ron Hodges withstood a jarring collision. Hodges singled home the winning run in the bottom half.

"We went on at that point to play really solid baseball," said Matlack. "And it was done with a mix-and-match of different guys' efforts to put together a pretty good stretch of wins. Ultimately, in that year I think every team had a time at first place in the division. We just took ours at the end of it. It was a crazy, up-and-down year, and we were able to put together a stretch of quality play when it mattered."

He followed his late-season shutout of the Redbirds with a complete-game five-hitter against the Cubs September 30, but the Mets lost 1–0 to extend the season by one day before they eventually clinched at Wrigley Field.

Matlack arguably pitched the most important game of the Mets' 1973 postseason. New York lost 2–1 to the Reds in the opener of the NLCS, with Seaver striking out 13 but allowing solo homers in each of the last two innings. It was up to Matlack to prevent the Mets from falling behind 2–0 in the series.

"I charted the day before when Tommy pitched and we got beat 2–1. Two solo homers. Bench and Rose each hit one. And I'm looking at that game chart and going, 'How in the hell do you do any better than this?' and thinking I've got my work cut out for me the next day.

"And all I'm trying to do was what it took at-bat to at-bat to make quality pitches, get outs and keep us in the ballgame, and it was a very close ballgame until the [ninth]."

Matlack's performance in Game 2 was among the five best in Mets postseason history. He tossed a two-hitter in a 5–0 win at Cincinnati, allowing only a pair of singles by Andy Kosko. Matlack spent most of the game protecting a 1–0 lead created by a Rusty Staub homer until the Mets scored four times in the ninth to take control.

"Gullett was pitching for Cincinnati, and Rusty said before the game, 'He tips his pitches. I'm gonna get one today. You keep him close.' And I'm thinking, 'Okay, that's good. I hope it's early.'

And it was. Staub homered off Gullett in the fourth inning, and Matlack faced just four batters over the minimum to pitch the first complete-game shutout in Mets playoff history.

The Mets needed Seaver to wrap up the NLCS in five games, which meant Matlack would start the opener of the World Series against the heavy-hitting A's. He shut down the Oakland lineup on three hits in six innings, but an error by second baseman Felix Millan allowed the Athletics to score two unearned runs in the third inning of a 2–1 victory.

The A's had a 2–1 Series lead when Matlack took the mound for Game 4. An error by Wayne Garrett led to an unearned run in the third inning, but Staub went 4-for-4 with two homers and five RBIs to power the Mets to a 6–1 victory that evened the Series.

Matlack had now pitched three straight postseason games without allowing an earned run in 23 innings. The Reds and A's, two of the best hitting teams in baseball that season, nicked Matlack for a grand total of eight hits. The Mets hoped their baffling lefty wouldn't be needed to pitch another game after they grabbed a 3–2 Series lead against Oakland. But Seaver, pitching on three days' rest in a questionable move by manager Yogi Berra, lost 3–1 in Game 6 to force a seventh game. Berra gave the ball to Matlack for the clincher as the Mets sought their second championship in five seasons. But Matlack, also throwing on three days' rest, was lifted while the A's were scoring four runs in the third inning of a 5–2 victory. The Mets fell one win short of the title, but Matlack was a big reason why they got that far.

Matlack had no problem with Berra's decision to go with Seaver on short rest instead of relying on lefty George Stone to close out the Series, but it was still a stinging loss.

"You can flip a coin," Matlack said of Berra's strategy. "You can look at it 100 different ways. I don't know if there was a right or a wrong to it.

"I think guys in Yogi's position make the right decision if they run with their gut, and they are the guys who are in the trenches and know the personalities. It's far better to make a decision based on that information than to make it based on some set of statistics.

"I'm not sure on what he based his decision, but in playing for Yogi I know one thing: he did very little to disrupt what was going on.

"Looking at that Series, we could've—should've—won all of the first six games. The real Oakland ballclub I don't think showed up until Game 7. It was just one of those things where for whatever reason—circumstances, fate, nerves, I don't know—our guys didn't take advantage of that circumstance when the A's were in a lull, and it did not pan out. It was a wonderful experience, and I wouldn't trade it for anything. I was really sort of amazed that when it was over, the disappointment that I felt and probably a handful of other guys. But there were a whole lot of guys that felt a lot of relief that it was over."

Matlack was the Mets' best starting pitcher in 1974, finishing first in the league with seven shutouts, third with a 2.41 ERA, and fourth with 195 strikeouts. But the team never competed for the division title as injuries caused many of their regulars to miss significant playing time for the third straight year.

Matlack and Koosman were the only players on the Mets to enjoy "typical" seasons. Matlack finished second to Koosman on the team with 13 victories and began a streak of three straight All-Star berths. He had a 9–5 record and a 2.55 earned run average by the time he worked a scoreless inning against the American League All-Stars at Pittsburgh July 23. Matlack recorded a sparkling 2.22 ERA while pitching four shutouts in the second half of the season, yet won just four of his final 15 starts to finish the year 13–15. He refuses to call it a frustrating season.

"My job was to go out there on a given day when it was my assignment to start and keep our team in the ballgame as long as they left me in the ballgame. I did that. I did that for all but three starts. In 35 or 36 starts I think I gave up more than three runs three times. In my mind, I'm doing what I'm supposed to do.

"I didn't realize until these people that are good with numbers and statistics put a bunch of stuff together years later. The Elias Sports bureau and all that kind of stuff were showing that if I had pitched for Cincinnati or Oakland that year, just based on average runs scored, I would have been 33–3.

"I do know there was a bunch of ballgames that were very close. I think it was eight times that I got beat allowing less than three runs.

"But at the time you're going through it—close but no cigar, goddamn if we had just got that hit or I hadn't given up that run—you looked at it [as frustrating]. But I never thought about it like I was getting gypped or should have got more wins. We had an opportunity to win every one of those games, but for whatever reason, we didn't win a lot of 'em."

The 1974 season also included Matlack's second one-hitter. He allowed a third-inning single to John Curtis in a 4–0 shutout of the Cardinals on June 29, one year after one-hitting the Astros.

Matlack went 16–12 with a 3.39 ERA in 1975, his first winning season since '72. He won five consecutive starts from May 12 to June 2, and added a six-start winning streak in the second half of the season. Matlack had a shot at his first 20-win season following a six-hitter against the Dodgers August 29, which left him 16–8 for the season. But the Mets scored only 14 runs in his final six starts while Matlack went 0–4 with a 4.04 earned run average.

Matlack also made his second All-Star appearance that season, tossing two shutout innings and striking out four in the National League's 6–3 win. He bailed out the senior circuit after Seaver served up a game-tying, three-run homer to Carl Yastrzemski in the sixth inning. Matlack and Bill Madlock came away with co-MVP honors for the game, marking the first time a Met had received the award.

The Mets had one of the NL's worst offenses again in 1976, but it didn't stop Matlack from opening 10–2 with a 2.62 ERA. He pitched shutouts in two of his first three starts and had four whitewashes by the time he arrived in Philadelphia for his third consecutive All-Star Game. But Matlack went 35 days before finally picking up his 11th victory despite compiling a 3.05 ERA during the winless skid. He ended the season with a career-high 17 wins and a 2.95 earned run average.

The Mets' offense was hardly a juggernaut, finishing among the bottom three in most categories. That was nothing new for Matlack, Seaver, and Koosman, who helped the team finish 86–76.

"It was challenging," chuckled Matlack. "I don't know if you look at it as difficult. When I got into the Met organization, the pitching was where it was built. Pitching and defense. The mindset of anybody who walked out there was to put zeros on the board. That was your goal every inning, every out, every day that you worked. That's what everybody strove to do. It was, 'Be as stingy as you can be.' It wasn't like, 'I can't give up any runs if I'm gonna win.' It was, 'I don't want to give up any runs even if we get nine runs.'"

The Mets finally went belly-up in 1977 after cornering the market in mediocrity for three years. Matlack, Seaver, and Koosman were the only reasons the franchise didn't take a severe nosedive several years earlier. But by '77, Seaver was pitching with a lousy contract, Koosman was pitching in bad luck, and Matlack was pitching with a sore shoulder.

"I realized that things weren't quite right when I'm trying like hell to throw the ball hard and it doesn't seem to be going anywhere. I think I'm making good pitches and guys are squaring them up, not necessarily because of location but because they're just not getting there with the same zip.

"We go into Atlanta and I sat down at the counter at the hotel to get a bite to eat. [Pitching coach] Rube Walker was there, and a few other people. They came around with the glasses of water and slapped them on the counter. I reached down to lift that glass of ice water off the counter, and in order to get it up, had to set my elbow on the table and use my biceps. I looked at Rube and said, 'Rube, we've got a problem. I can't even pick up this glass of water.'

"I really had no pain. I just sort of felt 'dishraggy.' They checked me out and found this strain, supposed muscle weakness, imbalance from front to back, and I got put on a pretty strict regimen of exercises—most of them manual—with the trainer or Dr. Parkes, depending on who was around."

Matlack somehow managed to throw three shutouts despite the shoulder injury, which limited him to 26 starts and contributed to his 7–15 record and 4.21 ERA. He tossed back-to-back shutouts early in the season, silencing the Dodgers on seven hits May 13 and scattering five hits against the Giants five days later. But Matlack went just 4–11 with a 4.64 earned run average the rest of the season, missing most of September due to injury. He earned a victory in his final start as a Met September 30, allowing two runs in 5⅔ innings at St. Louis. It was his first win since July 27.

Matlack was determined to come back from the shoulder ailment and help the Mets enter Year 2 of their rebuilding phase. The medical staff gave him a series of exercises to do during the winter months.

"It was really my first attempt at weights in my pro career, with Nautilus equipment. Once I got the strength balanced and back, I never had another problem with the shoulder."

Matlack was back in form by the start of 1978 spring training, but his rejuvenated shoulder was now underneath a different uniform. The Mets handled Matlack in the same manner they treated McGraw's shoulder problem three years earlier, trading him instead of gambling on his ability to bounce back from the injury. He was dealt to the Rangers in a four-team deal that brought Willie Montanez to the Mets December 8, 1977. Several newspaper accounts made it appear Matlack had requested a trade, but he said over 30 years later that wasn't the case.

"I get a little bent out of shape because I never demanded a trade. And I remember thinking at the time, 'Where do these guys get off twisting things around to make it sound like this?'

"What was frustrating to me was there was not an apparent effort to help the offense. We had good defense. We had good pitching. And there was no real attempt to bolster the club offensively. My comments were made in that direction, that I would like to see some offensive help and was hoping the club would do something along those lines.

"I had no desire to leave New York. I had no plans to become a free agent or any of that nonsense. That was the farthest thing from my mind. I wanted to see the club be made competitive. However they came out in the paper, that's how my comments were intended."

Matlack immediately made the trade look bad, just as McGraw did when he was shipped to the Phillies. Matlack immediately became the ace of a Rangers staff that included Ferguson Jenkins, finishing second on the team with 15 wins and leading the club with 33 starts, 18 complete games, 270 innings, and a 2.27 ERA. He also tied Jenkins for the club lead with 157 strikeouts and was second to Yankees ace Ron Guidry among American League hurlers in ERA. Matlack was fifth in the league with a 1.12 WHIP, fourth with 1.7 walks per nine innings, and fourth in complete games.

"To be back on the field, able to compete, feeling 100 percent healthy was phenomenal," Matlack said. "I worked hard over the winter to gain the ability to do that and was very pleased with the results. I pitched effectively all year long. I probably could have won a lot more ballgames, but it just didn't pan out that way. But I was very pleased with the effort.

"And it wasn't as if, 'Well, I'll show you guys' or any of that nonsense. There was a rude awakening when I got

traded that this is really a business, and people make decisions for a lot of reasons. You may not understand all of them, but you do become like a piece of equipment because they can pretty much send your contract and you go with it within the rules and regulations of the game whenever they want to. That was a little bit of a jolt for me."

Matlack made only 13 starts in 1979, going 5–4 with a 4.13 ERA through July 1 before undergoing bone chip surgery. He was the Rangers' Opening Day starter in 1980 but was restricted due to the surgery. However, he still managed to pitch 234⅔ innings and go 10–10 with a 3.68 ERA.

The 1981 season was marred by a contentious strike that wiped out two months of the schedule, leading to a split season. Matlack was a member of the union negotiating committee, which he feels put him "in the doghouse with management for the role I played in the strike."

Matlack suddenly found himself working out of the bullpen by the start of 1982, and remained a spot-starter and long reliever until he was released following the 1983 campaign.

Matlack became an active pitcher again in 1989, going 10–2 for the St. Petersburg Pelicans of the short-lived Senior Professional Baseball Association before becoming a successful pitching coach.

Matlack's first stop as a minor league coach was with the Padres in a short-season league in 1988. He remained with the organization until after the 1992 campaign, when a new ownership group cleaned house. That was followed by a two-year stint in the White Sox organization and a one-year return to San Diego before following Padres GM Randy Smith to Detroit.

He was the Tigers' pitching coach in 1996 before settling in as the organization's minor league pitching coordinator. He oversaw the development of Justin Verlander among other talented Detroit pitchers, and remained with the ballclub until he was told in August 2011 that the team was making a change. He got the usual "we're going in a different direction" speech from Tigers assistant GM Al Avila.

Jon and Dee have three children, and the grandchild count was seven by the middle of 2011. His oldest daughter, Kristin, lives near her parents in Magnolia, north of Houston. Jennifer resides in Allen, north of Dallas. Daniel lives in New Jersey and works in Manhattan.

There's a growing Texas twang to Matlack's accent these days. "My home base is Houston, Texas. I still own property in New York that is for sale [as of June 2011], but in today's market, who knows when it will sell?

"My wife had a job opportunity and actually wanted to be closer to our kids and grandkids. We do have a daughter and a couple of grandkids that live in the north side of Houston. We have settled about 38–40 miles from Houston since August 2010. For right now, that is home. She's working and is happy doing what she's doing. I'm close to an airport, so I can do what I do. I get home as often as I can…it's usually two weeks out and 4–5 days at home, so it's not too bad."

ML/Mets debut @ Reds, 7/11/71 (7 IP, 6 H, 2 ER, 1 K, 0 BB)
First ML/Mets strikeout Lee May, @ Reds, 7/11/71
First ML/Mets win vs. Cubs, 4/23/72
First ML save @ Angels, 7/1/78 (with Rangers)
Most strikeouts, ML/Mets game 12, vs. Giants, 5/8/74
Low-hit ML/Mets CG 1, vs. Astros, 7/10/73; vs. Cardinals, 6/29/74
Acquired: Selected in the 1st round (4th overall) of the 1967 draft.
Deleted: Traded to the Rangers in a four-team deal with the Braves and Pirates 12/8/77. The Mets also sent John Milner to the Pirates and received Willie Montanez from the Braves, and Tom Grieve and a player to be named (Ken Henderson) from the Rangers.
NL Rookie of the Year, 1972
NL All-Star, 1974, 1975, 1976
NL All-Star Game Co-MVP, 1975
NL Shutouts Leader, 1974 (7), 1976 (6)

Lee Mazzilli

Outfielder, First Baseman Bats both, throws right
Born: 3/25/55 New York, New York
Height: 6′1″ Weight: 185 #12, 16, 13

Lee Mazzilli Mets Career

YEAR	GP	AB	R	H	2B	3B	HR	RBI	K	BB	SB	AVG	SLG	OBP
1976	24	77	9	15	2	0	2	7	14	4	5	.195	.299	.323
1977	159	537	66	134	24	3	6	46	72	72	22	.250	.339	.339
1978	148	542	78	148	28	5	16	61	82	69	20	.273	.432	.353
1979	158	597	78	181	34	4	15	79	74	93	34	.303	.449	.395
1980	152	578	82	162	31	4	16	76	92	82	41	.280	.431	.370
1981	95	324	36	74	14	5	6	34	53	46	17	.228	.358	.324
1986	39	58	10	16	3	0	2	7	11	12	1	.276	.431	.417
1987	88	124	26	38	8	1	3	24	14	21	5	.306	.460	.399
1988	68	116	9	17	2	0	0	12	16	12	4	.147	.164	.227
1989	48	60	10	11	2	0	2	7	19	17	3	.183	.317	.364
TOTAL	979	3013	404	796	148	22	68	353	443	438	152	.264	.396	.357

ML Career

YEAR	GP	AB	R	H	2B	3B	HR	RBI	K	BB	SB	AVG	SLG	OBP
76–89	1475	4124	571	1068	191	24	93	460	627	642	197	.259	.385	.359

It's not easy being the lone major league prospect on a pretty bad ballclub, especially in a big city with little patience. Expectations become inflated due to the organization's desperation to win games and retain a fan base. Pressure is placed squarely on the player to perform to such expectations and deliver the ballclub from evil—or at least get them out of the cellar.

When those expectations are not met, fans are apt to deem the prospect an underachiever or a failure, regardless of his inherent ability. His teammates receive a free pass for their shortcomings, but the face of the franchise is not given such leeway.

Compound the fact that the player is performing in his city of birth, one can appreciate how difficult it was for Lee Mazzilli to excel during his first stint as a Met.

Flip the calendar ahead almost 10 years from the day of his major league debut. Mazzilli had just been released by the last-place Pirates and was a man without a team. The Mets, seeking a reserve outfielder to complement Mookie Wilson, Len Dykstra, and Darryl Strawberry, re-signed their former phenom and gave him a chance to play for a winner. This time, expectations were low and production was high, allowing the prodigal son to return home in a positive environment.

Son of a former professional welterweight boxer, Mazzilli already was an accomplished athlete before concentrating on baseball. He won eight national championships as a speed-skater from 1965 to 1972, capturing the St. Louis Silver Skates title three straight years, beginning in '65. The switch-hitting Mazzilli is also ambidextrous but threw only right-handed in pro ball.

Taken with the Mets' first pick in the June 1973 draft, Lee Louis Mazzilli played just three minor league seasons before making his big-league debut in September 1976. He batted .269 with 11 homers, 48 RBIs, and 46 stolen bases as a minor league rookie for Anderson of the Western Carolinas League in 1974. He continued to excel as a speed merchant the following year, swiping seven bags during a seven-inning game for Visalia of the Class A California League against San Jose June 7. He contributed 49 steals for the season while batting .281 with 13 home runs, 52 RBIs, and 103 runs scored.

Mazzilli made his Shea Stadium debut directly from Jackson of the Double A Texas League after batting .292 with 91 runs scored and league highs of 28 stolen bases and 111 walks in 1976. He was one of the most highly touted offensive players in team history on the basis of his .280 average, 36 home runs, 55 doubles, 143 RBIs, and 123 steals in three minor league seasons.

The Abraham Lincoln High School product poked a tapper back to the mound as a pinch-hitter in his first big-league at-bat September 7, one day before crushing a three-run homer off the bench in an 11–5 win over the Cubs. Twelve days later, Mazzilli belted a two-run, walk-off homer to beat the Pirates 5–4.

Mazzilli batted .435 in 23 at-bats over six games from September 17 to 22, further demonstrating his readiness as a major leaguer. But a season-ending 3-for-33 skid (.091) left him with a .195 average as a Met.

Mazzilli didn't quite feel he was a sure thing as he reported to 1977 spring training. The Mets really didn't have a viable alternative in center field, making him a near-lock to be on the Opening Day roster. Mazzilli had his doubts.

"He was very nervous, very scared about making the club," said Mets equipment manager Charlie Samuels three years later. "He kept asking me, 'What do you hear?' Like he thought I knew something."[109]

The team didn't initially intend to make Mazzilli their marquee player for 1977. They still had veterans Dave Kingman, Bud Harrelson, Felix Millan, John Milner, and Ed Kranepool in the lineup, plus Tom Seaver and Jerry Koosman at the top of the rotation. Mazzilli and fellow rookie Roy Staiger were supposed to fly under the radar while they acclimated themselves to major league pitching. But Kingman and Seaver were traded June 15, Millan suffered a season-ending shoulder injury August 12, Harrelson hit .178 for the season and Kranepool started just 71 games due to his stellar pinch-hitting ability.

The Mets' roster woes led to their first last-place finish in 10 years and put more focus on Mazzilli, who looked overmatched at times during the first five months of the season. "Maz" put together a 10-game hitting streak from April 29 to May 8 to lift his average to .264 before hitting a meager .197 in 208 at-bats over his next 66 games. He batted .293 with three home runs and 19 RBIs over his final 33 games to end up with a .250 average, six homers, 24 doubles, 46 ribbies, and 22 stolen bases. Mazzilli finished second in hits (134), doubles, steals, and walks (72) for a team that was last among NL teams in batting, homers, and runs scored. It wasn't a bad first season, especially for a kid playing a few miles from home. However, he admitted he pressed a bit early in the year.

"When you're a rookie and you're trying to impress management so they won't send you back to the minors, you have a tendency to hurry things too much," said Mazzilli in 1979. You get a little impatient and maybe go for some balls you should leave alone.

"But after you get established, you can set your own pace. I'm a better hitter than when I came up, but a batting title is not my thing right now. My thing is getting on base and scoring runs."[110]

The team used its overhauled 1977 roster as a marketing tool, using the slogan "Bring Your Kids to See Our Kids" by mid August. There were suggestions the slogan could have been rewritten to "Bring Your Kids to Beat Our Kids" after the Mets went 39–63 following the departures of Seaver and Kingman. By season's end, the lineup featured Mazzilli, veteran Lenny Randle and former Reds youngsters Steve Henderson, Joel Youngblood, and Doug Flynn. Henderson finished second in the NL Rookie of the Year balloting, but the Mets didn't have enough Steve Hendersons to field a competitive starting lineup. Add to that an unproductive farm system, and the Mets were doomed for the remainder of Mazzilli's first stay with the team.

The Mets still believed Mazzilli could become a star as they headed into 1978, but any comparisons to the great New York center fielders of the past were silenced. Mazzilli wasn't making anyone forget Willie, Mickey, and the Duke—or even Tommie Agee, for that matter. Mazzilli had exceptional range and speed for a center fielder, but his arm strength and power at the plate appeared very ordinary by the 1978 opener.

That didn't stop the Mets from making Mazzilli the focal point of their marketing, taking advantage of his good looks and Brooklyn roots in an attempt to drum up ticket sales. Henderson was virtually ignored in the ad campaigns despite outperforming Mazzilli in batting, homers, RBIs, and runs scored while playing 60 fewer games in 1977. Some Mets fans took note of the slight and began to resent Mazzilli as an undeserving poster boy, especially after the team held "Lee Mazzilli Poster Day" in 1978. However, Henderson never sought the attention and couldn't care less if he was part of any promotional campaign, leaving Mazzilli as a logical—if not overenthusiastic—choice.

"I like anonymity," Mazzilli said in 1980. "I like to go home and relax. The times I go out, do my thing, if people see me, fine. I can do that every day of the week, be in all the papers, the scandal, this and that.… Pretty soon you can't walk anywhere without people bothering you. I'm sure Reggie [Jackson] goes through that all the time. It's flattering at times, sure, but I'm sure Reggie likes his peace of mind, too."[111]

The gap between Mazzilli and Henderson closed in '78 as Lee hit a team-high .273 with 16 home runs, 28 doubles, 61 RBIs, 20 stolen bases, and 78 runs scored. Mazzilli doubled home an insurance run in an Opening Day victory and belted a two-run homer in the eighth inning of the next game to spark a 6–5 comeback win. He had hitting streaks of nine and 10 games during May and was hitting .315 after going 4-for-5 with three runs scored in a win over the Dodgers June 5.

Mazzilli contributed eight homers and 25 RBIs over his next 65 games but hit only .204 in 221 at-bats during that span, dropping his season average to .259 by August 22. He closed the year by posting a .347 average with four round-trippers and 13 ribbies over 98 at-bats in 26 games.

General manager Joe McDonald was given little opportunity to improve the major league roster after the team's second straight last-place finish, even after owner Lorinda de Roulet replaced the tight-fisted M. Donald Grant as board chairman. Randle's contract was erased from the books when he was released before the 1979 season, leaving a core lineup of Mazzilli, Henderson, Flynn, Willie Montanez, and John Stearns. Youngblood became more of a presence on the roster during the season, while Kranepool was phased out and eventually released.

Mazzilli was the best of the bunch in 1979, earning his lone All-Star berth as the Mets' only representative. He led the National League to a 7–6 victory in Seattle after entering the game in the eighth inning. He smacked a game-tying solo homer leading off the eighth before working a tiebreaking, bases-loaded walk with two out in the ninth. But Mazzilli was edged out for the MVP award by right fielder Dave Parker, who drove in a run and made a tremendous throw to nail Brian Downing at the plate to end the eighth.

Although the Mets were required to have one All-Star representative, Mazzilli earned the nod on his own merit. He had a .354 average through June 4 and was at .320 by the All-Star break. Mazzilli put together a 12-game hitting streak during May and also had five consecutive multi-hit games before finishing with a .379 average for the month. But the Mets were unable to take advantage of Mazzilli's hot bat, going 8–18 for the month and landing in sole possession of the basement May 7.

Lee Mazzilli slides into home plate to score against the St. Louis Cardinals in a March 1977 game.

Mazzilli experienced a batting drought for more than a quarter of the season, hitting .229 with 19 RBIs in 44 games before embarking on a career-best 19-game hitting streak on August 27, hitting .429 but providing no home runs and only seven RBIs. The Mets went just 4–15 during the streak and needed to win their last six games just to avoid their first 100-loss season in 12 years. Mazzilli socked a three-run homer in the penultimate game of the season, putting New York ahead 5–0 in an 8–7 win at St. Louis.

Mazzilli's .303 average ranked 10th in the National League and was fourth-best in Mets history at the time. His 34 stolen bases and 93 walks were second-most on the franchise's single-season list. He also tied Richie Hebner for the club lead with 79 RBIs and was second to Youngblood with 15 homers.

Manager Joe Torre wasn't too concerned about Mazzilli's power numbers so long as the fellow Brooklynite continued to hit for average.

"He still uses the whole field to drop the ball in safely, only now he's learning to hit home runs," Torre said in 1979. "I wouldn't want him to think long ball all the time, because he really doesn't have that kind of power. But if the situation is right, I like to see him go for it. This kid can beat you in a lot of ways, and he's improved his average all four years he's been in the league."[112]

Torre began to experiment with Mazzilli at first base in mid-September, giving him 15 starts at the position. The move was designed to keep Mazzilli's bat in the lineup while putting the strong-armed Youngblood in center. Youngblood was second among National Leaguers with 18 outfield assists in 1979, giving the strategy credence.

Torre continued to use Mazzilli at first through the first two months of the 1980 campaign without much success. Mazzilli had a .375 on-base percentage through June 1 but was batting just .243 with no home runs and 13 RBIs in 42 games before returning to center field.

Mazzilli possessed a .234 average when he began an 18-game hitting streak June 18. He batted .368 with a .442 on-base percentage, six home runs, and 12 RBIs during the streak, including homers in four consecutive games. But unlike his 19-game streak of 1979, the Mets went 11–7 to worm their way into the NL East hunt. New York was in fourth place at 39–40 at the end of the streak, 4½ games out of first despite a 9–18 start to the season.

Mazzilli and several teammates were tough to miss if you rode a bus or train through the city. The Mets embarked on an ad campaign with the slogan "The Magic Is Back," using the faces of individual players who gave their reasons why fans should head to Shea. Mazzilli's 4' x 8' subway platform poster was sold at the Shea Stadium concession stands for $10, five times the price of the team yearbook.

The campaign was mocked at the start of the year but began to build up steam as the team continued its improbable playoff push into mid-August. The Mets were contending with strong fielding, timely hitting, and a solid bullpen. They went 47–39 with a 3.42 ERA from May 14 to August 13 and were in position to make things interesting with the Phillies heading to Shea for a five-game series. But the Phils blitzed the Mets in a sweep, beginning the team's downfall. New York also had lost Flynn, Stearns, and Craig Swan to injury by the end of August, contributing to another losing season.

Mazzilli was the lone Met to hit more than 10 home runs in 1980, and the only one from the Opening Day roster with more than eight. He accounted for 26 percent of the Mets' 61 home runs despite failing to go deep until June 6. Mazzilli also paced the club with 152 games played, 162 hits, 82 runs, 31 doubles, 76 RBIs, 41 stolen bases, 82 walks, a .370 on-base percentage and a .431 slugging average. Four seasons after becoming the face of the franchise, Mazzilli had earned the role.

But the Mets were no closer to contention than they were in his first full season. The farm system had begun to draft well in 1977, picking up Hubie Brooks, Wally Backman, and Mookie Wilson before using the first pick in the 1980 draft to select Darryl Strawberry. Brooks, Backman, and Wilson were called up late in 1980 and became starters the following year. The Mets also reacquired Dave Kingman from the Cubs for Henderson, and re-signed Rusty Staub in the winter of '81. But the pitching remained unimpressive.

With a new supporting cast, Mazzilli played through his worst season as a Met to date. He homered in the season opener but hit only .163 with three RBIs in his first 24 games, ending that stretch without driving in a run for 12 straight games.

Mazzilli's offense began to pick up just before the players went on strike in mid-June, causing a two-month work stoppage and leading to a split season. The strike gave the Mets a chance to forget about their 17–34 start and concentrate on salvaging the second half.

With a clean slate, the Mets were able to stay in contention for a playoff berth well into September. Mazzilli hit .265 over his final 17 games of August to lift his average to .221. He was hitting .237 after back-to-back three-hit games September 9 to 11, but he settled for a .228 mark with six homers and 34 RBIs in just 95 games. Mazzilli still managed to finish second on the team in home runs, stolen bases (17), doubles (14), and walks (46).

The Mets went 24–28 in the second half to end up 41–62, their fifth straight losing season. That allowed Mazzilli,

Stearns, and Swan to become the first Mets to spend five consecutive full years on the team's major league roster without playing on a winning ballclub. Ed Kranepool was part of seven straight losing seasons but spent at least part of those first three years in the minors.

Mazzilli reported to 1982 spring training as the Mets' starting center fielder. He left Florida as a member of the Texas Rangers, traded for pitching prospects Ron Darling and Walt Terrell before the regular-season opener. General manager Frank Cashen felt Wilson was more than capable of playing center field, leaving Mazzilli as an unnecessary commodity. What the Mets truly needed was young pitching, and both Darling and Terrell eventually landed on the major league roster in 1983. Although the trade was ripped by a majority of Mets fans at the time, it proved to be Cashen's first fleecing since taking over in 1980.

"It was a trade that was widely criticized in New York," said Frank Cashen in Peter Golenbock's book *Amazin'*, "because the Italian Stallion was the closest thing we had to a superstar at the time, and to give him up for two guys who never played in the major leagues, no matter how much you tell them about promise, it doesn't cut it. New York is a different town to have to work in than any other club. New York is a now town. What are you going to do for me today? The whole star system, Broadway, that's what the city is, and I had to do some things I had to do, even if they were unpopular, and trading Lee Mazzilli was one of them."[113]

"We had Mookie Wilson waiting in the wings," remembered assistant general manager Lou Gorman. "Wilson had outstanding speed and range. He could move into center field and become an outstanding performer at that position. With Wilson ready we could move Mazzilli, particularly if we could add some depth to our pitching staff."[114]

Mazzilli didn't spend much time in Texas. He got off to a terrific start, recording a .310 average with two homers and nine RBIs while hitting safely in 12 of his first 15 games. He also had a five-game hitting streak from May 13 to 17. But in between, Mazzilli struggled through an 0-for-27 skid and later landed on the disabled list from May 20 to June 29 after battling shoulder and wrist problems.

Mazzilli was batting just .241 when he was brought back to New York August 8, going to the Yankees for Bucky Dent.

Mazzilli looked rejuvenated upon his return to the Big Apple, hitting safely in his first five games with the Yanks before finishing the month of August with a .324 average, four home runs, and 11 RBIs in 20 games in pinstripes. But he posted a .185 average in 54 September at-bats to end up with a .251 mark, 10 homers, and 34 RBIs in 95 games.

The Pirates became Mazzilli's fourth team in nine months when he was dealt by the Yankees in December 1982. He spent the next 3½ years as a reserve outfielder/ first baseman for Pittsburgh, never starting more than 71 games in a season. He went 16-for-56 (.286) as a pinch-hitter in 1985, finishing second to Thad Bosley among all National Leaguers in pinch-hits. But he started just 15 games and logged just 117 at-bats the entire season.

Mazzilli accidentally helped the Mets win a game June 6, 1984. The Bucs and Mets were tied 1–1 in the ninth when he led off with a walk, stole second, and moved to third on a grounder. Jason Thompson followed with a fly ball to center, allowing Mazzilli to score the winning run. However, Mets manager Davey Johnson screamed for catcher Mike Fitzgerald to throw the ball to third after seeing Mazzilli leave third base prior to Mookie Wilson's catch. Fitzgerald made the toss to Brooks at third before umpire Doug Harvey called Mazzilli out, sending the game into extra innings before the Mets won it on a wild pitch in the 13th inning.

Mazzilli remained the Pirates' top pinch-hitting threat as they opened the 1986 season against the Mets. He hit .294 in 15 starts for the Bucs but was just 5-for-37 (.135) with three RBIs as a pinch-hitter before he was released July 23.

The Mets were already rolling through their '86 schedule and carried a double-digit lead into the All-Star break. They had no weaknesses except in left field, where George Foster was showing signs of slowing down. Foster began to grumble as his playing time was taken by Wilson, Kevin Mitchell, and Danny Heep, all of whom were hitting better than the former National League MVP.

The Mets added another outfielder August 1, bringing back Mazzilli by giving him a minor league contract and a chance to make the ballclub. He played six games for Triple A Tidewater and was recalled August 7, the same day Foster was placed on waivers for the purpose of releasing him. Mazzilli appeared to be a nice fit for the Mets. He could play all three outfield positions, spell Keith Hernandez at first base and serve as another potent bat off the bench.

Mazzilli went 0-for-3 but also scored three times and walked twice in his first four games as a Met. He ended an 0-for-7 skid by belting a two-run homer in the ninth inning of his fifth game, three days before homering again. He ended up with a .276 average in 58 at-bats as a Met, including a 3-for-3 game in the regular-season finale.

Mazzilli made the Mets' playoff roster, putting him in the postseason for the first time in 11 major league seasons. He was one of Mike Scott's 14 strikeout victims in Game 1 of the NLCS at Houston before producing a pinch-single in the third game.

Mazzilli provided crucial pinch-hits in the sixth and seventh games of the World Series against Boston. The Mets trailed 3–2 in the eighth inning of Game 6 when he poked a leadoff single before scoring the tying run on Gary Carter's sac-fly. Two days later, the Mets were down 3–0 in the sixth as Mazzilli pinch-hit for Sid Fernandez. Mazzilli sparked the game-tying rally with a single and scored on Hernandez's two-run single. The Mets completed an 8–5

comeback win to capture their second World Series title.

Mazzilli continued to flourish as a utility player for the 1987 Mets, starting just 15 games but hitting .306 overall with three homers, eight doubles, and 24 RBIs in 124 at-bats. He was terrific as a pinch-hitter, batting .309 (17-for-55) with two home runs and 11 RBIs. His 17 pinch-hits tied Montreal's Wallace Johnson for the major league lead and helped him land a two-year contract in December.

Mazzilli's best day of the season was June 7 in a doubleheader against the Pirates. He had three RBIs in the opener, including a game-winning, two-run double in the bottom of the 10th. Mazzilli followed that with a three-run homer and a two-run single in the nightcap to finish the day with eight RBIs, one-third of his season output.

Mazzilli also became a more vocal teammate in the clubhouse, calling out Darryl Strawberry for his penchant for allowing minor injuries and/or illnesses to keep him out of the lineup. It's not often a No. 5 outfielder has the stones to publicly criticize a team's top slugger, but the Mets took off almost immediately after Mazzilli's comments.

The Mets missed the playoffs in 1987 but returned as NL East champions the following season without a lot of help from Mazzilli. He had a pair of two-RBI games and just one multi-hit game before finishing the year with a .147 average, no home runs, and 12 RBIs. Mazzilli batted .233 (7-for-30) with eight RBIs as a pinch-hitter, but just .103 in 15 games as a starter.

Mazzilli almost helped the Mets win the pivotal fourth game of the Championship Series against the Dodgers at Shea. Los Angeles took the lead on Kirk Gibson's two-out solo homer in the top of the 12th before Mackey Sasser and Mazzilli laced singles to start the bottom half. The Mets filled the bases with one out, making Mazzilli the potential winning run on second. But Jesse Orosco got Darryl Strawberry on a pop-up to second before Kevin McReynolds hit a sinking liner that was caught by center fielder John Shelby at his shoe tops, allowing the Dodgers to earn a 5–4 win that knotted the series at two games apiece.

Maz went 0-for-1 the next afternoon and was hit by a pitch with two out to prolong the ninth inning of Game 7 before the Mets were beaten in Los Angeles. His postseason batting average now stood at .333 in 12 at-bats.

Mazzilli was just 34 when he opened the 1989 season, his last in the majors. He beat the Phillies with a three-run homer as a pinch-hitter in the eighth inning of a 4–2 triumph April 19 and didn't produce another hit until June 5. Mazzilli was 0-for-16 with seven walks and two runs scored in 18 games during the hitless skid before going 2-for-2 with a solo homer off the bench.

Mazzilli went 7-for-21 with a solo homer and three RBIs in 10 games from June 5 to 23, but his playing time never increased. He and Wilson had become the spare outfielders after center fielder Juan Samuel was acquired from Philadelphia for Lenny Dykstra and Roger McDowell June 18. Both Mazzilli and Wilson griped about playing time and asked for a trade. Both went to the Blue Jays July 31, Wilson through a trade and Mazzilli via the waiver wire. The moves allowed them to compete in the 1989 postseason.

Mazzilli had a smashing debut as a Jay, going 3-for-3 with a solo homer, two RBIs, and two walks in an 8–0 rout of the Royals August 2. He also homered August 9 and again August 18 before adding one more September 9. He closed with a pinch-hit single September 29 against Baltimore, the final regular-season at-bat of his career.

Mazzilli started the first two games of the Championship Series against the A's, the first time he had ever been in the starting lineup for a postseason game. But he went 0-for-7 over the two games and finished 0-for-8 in the series, leaving him with a career .200 average in the postseason.

Mazzilli dabbled in a bit of everything after retiring as a player. He tried acting, starring as Tony in the off-Broadway show *Tony 'n' Tina's Wedding* in 1992. He moved on to television, hosting a sports show on what is now WNYW in New York. The station was the one-time employer of Dani Folquet, an on-air reporter who became Dani Mazzilli when the two got married in 1984. They had a daughter, Jenna, in 1988 before Dani gave birth to twins, Lacey and L.J., in 1990. The young family was a big reason why Mazzilli spent seven years away from baseball and remained close to home.

The baseball itch got to Mazzilli in 1997. He became manager of the Yankees' Florida State League affiliate at Tampa and led them to the 1998 championship series in his second year at the helm. Mazzilli moved up to Double A Norwich in 1999 and led the Navigators to the Eastern League final before becoming the Yankees' first base/outfield coach under his former teammate and manager, Joe Torre.

Mazzilli remained in the Yankees dugout for four years before he was named manager of the Orioles in November 2003. He didn't do badly in his first stint as skipper, going 129–140 for a team that lacked much pitching or defense. The Birds were 51–56 in 2005 when he was dismissed in July 2005. Baltimore went 70–92 the following season.

He returned to the Mets fold in December 2006, hired as the lead studio analyst for SportsNet New York, the team's cable network. Mazzilli spent two years at SNY before he was replaced by former teammate Bob Ojeda before the 2009 season.

First ML/Mets game @ Cubs, 9/7/76
First ML/Mets hit   3-run HR vs. Darold Knowles, @ Cubs, 9/8/76
First ML/Mets homer   3-run HR vs. Darold Knowles, @ Cubs, 9/8/76
First ML/Mets RBI   3-run HR vs. Darold Knowles, @ Cubs, 9/8/76
Most hits, ML/Mets game   4, 8 times
Most homers, ML/Mets game   2, @ Dodgers, 9/3/78; @ Cubs, 6/30/79; vs. Cards, 7/13/80
Most RBIs, ML/Mets game   5, vs. Cubs, 9/14/80; vs. Pirates, 6/7/87

Acquired: Selected in the first round (14th overall) of the June 1973 draft.
Deleted: Traded to the Rangers for Walt Terrell and Ron Darling, 4/1/82.
Reacquired: Signed as a free agent, 8/3/86.
Deleted: Selected off waivers by the Blue Jays, 7/31/89.
NL All-Star, 1979

Roger McDowell

Pitcher   Bats right, throws right
Born: 12/21/60   Cincinnati, Ohio
Height: 6'1"   Weight: 185   #42

Roger McDowell Mets Career

YEAR	GP/GS	IP	H	R	ER	K	BB	W–L	SV	ERA
1985	62/2	127⅓	108	43	40	60	37	6-5	17	2.83
1986	75/0	128	107	48	43	65	42	14-9	22	3.02
1987	56/0	88⅔	95	41	41	32	28	7-5	25	4.16
1988	62/0	89	80	31	26	46	31	5-5	16	2.63
1989	25/0	35⅓	34	21	13	15	16	1-5	4	3.31
Total	280/2	468⅓	424	184	163	228	154	33-29	84	3.13

Mets Career/Batting

GP	AB	R	H	2B	3B	HR	RBI	K	BB	SB	AVG
281	61	4	15	5	0	0	6	21	3	0	.246

ML Career

YEAR	GP/GS	IP	H	R	ER	K	BB	W–L	SV	ERA
85–96	723/2	1050	1045	454	385	524	410	70-70	159	3.30

There probably isn't a Mets fan alive who rooted for the ballclub in 1986 and thought Roger McDowell would be a major league pitching coach one day, serving as a reminder that there's more to a ballplayer than meets the eye.

On the mound, McDowell was a consummate professional who remains the Mets' single-season leader in victories by a reliever. He was always prepared to take the mound in a tight spot and came through for the Mets more often than not. His work in Game 6 of the 1986 National League Championship Series alone was among the very best relief efforts in team history and should balance out any memory of an unfortunate gopher ball surrendered during the 1987 stretch run or 1988 postseason.

McDowell had the perfect makeup for a reliever, willing to enter the fire and douse the flames. He also exhibited traits similar to those of another Mets reliever, Tug McGraw. Both were exuberant pitchers with impish grins, but while McGraw could demonstrate extreme intensity on the mound, McDowell often appeared as if nothing phased him. McDowell chewed gum on the mound and often blew bubbles in between—and even during—pitches. The gum was also part of his bag of tricks as it helped him create what became his specialty as a Met: the hotfoot.

He delighted in administering the hotfoot to teammates and coaches, first-base coach Bill Robinson in particular. But the hotfoot was just one of his many ways to break the tension on those exceptional Mets teams of the 1980s.

Show up for batting practice, and you might see McDowell wearing roller skates as he fielded grounders. Walk near his locker, and you would come across his collection of fright masks and rubber spiders. But there was no denying he was all business as he came out of the bullpen to provide outstanding relief pitching during his 4½ seasons with the Mets.

Roger Alan McDowell was born and raised in Cincinnati, playing ball for Colerain High School before attending Bowling Green. He won all-league honors as a pitcher in both high school and college before the Mets selected him in the third round of the June 1982 draft.

McDowell showed potential as a minor league rookie by going 8–4 with a 2.97 ERA for Shelby of the rookie South Atlantic League and Lynchburg of the Class A Carolina League, starting 11 of his 12 games. Moved up to Double A Jackson in 1983, he finished second in the Texas League with nine complete games and 172 innings, but was 11–12 with a bloated 4.86 ERA while pitching with a sore right elbow that required surgery in January 1984. The elbow procedure was expected to keep McDowell sidelined the entire 1984 season, but he was back on the mound for Jackson August 23 before tossing shutout ball in his first five innings.

McDowell wasn't much of a strikeout pitcher before the injury, fanning 178 in 273 innings during his first two pro seasons. Following surgery, McDowell had a little more jump and movement on his pitches as the ball now tailed away from the strike zone. He fanned eight in 7⅓ innings during the 1984 regular season before his relief work in the postseason helped Jackson win the Texas League championship.

Mets general manager Frank Cashen placed him on the 40-man roster for 1985 spring training, although McDowell initially appeared to be a longshot to make the club out of camp. He still hadn't thrown a pitch in Triple A and was just 13 months removed from elbow surgery when he reported to St. Petersburg. But McDowell had one of the best camps among Mets hurlers, leading all relievers with 23⅔ innings pitched and recording a 2.28 ERA with 17 strikeouts in eight appearances to earn a spot on the Opening Day roster. Davey Johnson put him in the bullpen before giving him a chance to show his stuff as a starting pitcher.

"I remember the first two days of the '85 season," McDowell told Denver broadcaster Bruce Morton 25 years later. "Gary Carter, who the Mets had just traded for, was an integral part of the first two wins. It was huge from the standpoint of Gary coming over and contributing right off the bat to that club."

The Mets began the year by sweeping a two-game series from the Cardinals at Shea Stadium, winning both games in extra innings. Carter ended the opener with a 10th-inning homer, two days before McDowell picked up the victory against the Cards in his major league debut on April 11.

"I don't know who pitched before me, I just remember Jack Clark was the first hitter and grounded out to short. Terry Pendleton was the second hitter, and I struck him out. Then Darrell Porter hit a ground ball to second base for the third out, and we won it in the bottom of the inning.

"I remember the hitters and I remember my inning, but other than that, it was just very exciting."

Actually, McDowell fanned Pendleton for the third out after getting Porter on a grounder to second. He pitched a perfect 11th in his lone inning of work before Keith Hernandez and Carter opened the bottom half with singles. Danny Heep won it by working out a bases-loaded walk against former Mets closer Neil Allen, making McDowell the ninth pitcher in team history to win his big-league debut.

McDowell was also the winner in his second appearance two days later, tossing two shutout innings of relief to beat the Reds, his favorite team growing up. When he returned to his native Cincinnati in May, he was a member of the starting rotation.

An injury to Bruce Berenyi prompted Johnson to try McDowell as a starter against the Pirates April 28. The rookie left the game with a 4–2 lead in the sixth before Calvin Schiraldi allowed a game-tying homer later in the inning. Neither team scored again until first baseman Jason Thompson's error in the bottom of the 18th gave the Mets a 5–4 victory.

McDowell's next start was against the Reds at Riverfront Stadium. "It was a Saturday *Game of the Week* back when baseball was only on once a week," McDowell recalled. "It was Tony Kubek and Joe Garagiola. It was a very exciting day for me and my family, as well. My dad was there. My mom was there, my brothers and sisters. So it was pretty neat to have my first start in the big leagues be in Cincinnati."

McDowell left the game trailing 3–2 with the bases loaded in the sixth before Doug Sisk surrendered a grand slam to Nick Esasky, tacking on three more earned runs to McDowell's stats. Ironically, it was the bullpen that destroyed McDowell's ERA as a starting pitcher.

"After those two starts they decided that my best role was in the bullpen, and that's were I stayed the rest of my career."

Schiraldi and Sisk may have done the Mets a favor by making McDowell's stats appear unimpressive as a starter. McDowell headed back to the bullpen and allowed just one earned run over 27⅓ innings in his next 10 appearances, going 3–0 with three saves in the process. The Mets now had a two-headed monster in closing situations as the right-handed McDowell was the perfect complement to lefty Jesse Orosco. McDowell was 4–4 with 17 saves and a 2.29 ERA over his final 55 appearances, averaging two innings per outing. He ended his rookie season 6–5 with a 2.83 ERA and 17 saves in 62 games.

McDowell and Orosco combined for 34 saves in 1985, but the Mets finished three games behind the division-winning Cardinals. New York added Bob Ojeda to the starting rotation in the fall of '85 as they tried to earn their first playoff berth in 13 years. With McDowell and Orosco at their disposal, the Mets built a double-digit lead before the All-Star break and clinched the NL East title by September 17.

The bullpen was a huge factor in the team's success. McDowell led the Mets with 22 saves, one more than Orosco as the two combined to earn wins or saves in 65 of the team's 108 victories. Although the Mets seemed loaded with talent heading into the season, McDowell still felt he had to prove himself to secure a spot in the pen.

"I had just completed my first full year, so going into the '86 spring training, I still didn't feel I had established myself enough to consider that I warranted a spot in the bullpen. That being said, you had Gary Carter on the team, and Keith Hernandez, Ray Knight and Mookie Wilson. George Foster was still on the team. You had a whole group of veteran guys, and I'm a 22-year-old kid. I'm going to keep my mouth shut and just go out and try to make the team.

"I think we had a good team just from the standpoint of 1984, the year before I got there, when the Mets were in contention with the Cubs until the last stage of the season. In '85 we were all the way in contention until the last weekend of the season. We felt we had a good club with the starting pitching and the bullpen, the offense and the defense, especially up the middle with Rafael Santana and Wally Backman, Mookie and Lenny Dykstra in center and Gary behind the plate. We thought we had a good ballclub but we still had to go out and play the game."

Johnson was masterful in knowing when to use McDowell and Orosco. Orosco had been the Mets' top closer from 1982 to 1984, winning 13 games on a 1983 squad that lost 95 games. Given the circumstances of dual closers, McDowell and Orosco could have squawked about their role since both were worthy of taking over the closer's role outright. Instead, they bought into the strategy developed by Johnson and pitching coach Mel Stottlemyre.

"I really enjoyed it. I really learned a lot. Each one of us had our teams, and I matched up well against some teams. More likely than not, they were the teams that had the right-handed hitting lineups: the Cincinnati Reds, the San Diego Padres at the time, the Dodgers, and the Cubs. Those were kind of my teams that I would finish the games. With Jesse, he had the rest of them.

"Davey had the luxury of matching up, and we had two other guys down there along with Rick Aguilera. We had Tom Gorman and Doug Sisk. There was Eddie Lynch, who was very instrumental in my development both as a pitcher and a player. Bruce Berenyi as well. They were veteran guys in the bullpen. They shared their thoughts and experiences in how to deal with the successes and failures of being in the bullpen. I had never been in a bullpen until I was in the major leagues, so it was something I had to learn on the fly."

Roger McDowell (center) clowns around during the second game of the 1988 NLCS.

McDowell managed to win 14 games in 1986, breaking Orosco's team record for relievers set only three years earlier. Ten of those victories came in games in which the Mets were trailing or tied when he entered. Three wins were registered following blown saves, and another occurred after he allowed a tiebreaking run in the ninth inning. McDowell acknowledged 24 years later that he was in the right place at the right time for many of his victories.

"I got lucky," McDowell said with a chuckle. "More than anything, we had a very talented pitching staff that kept us in games into the late innings. I just had the good fortune of sometimes I'd blow games and end up getting the win. Sometimes I'd be in tie games and get the win.

"It's funny because that year I started off 7–0, so my last 16 decisions I was 7–9. It started out good and didn't end so well, but Jesse and I combined for 43 saves out of the bullpen."

McDowell and Orosco weren't the first lefty-righty relief tandem to share late-inning duties with the Mets. Danny Frisella and Tug McGraw were No. 1 and 1A for Gil Hodges in 1971, combining for 20 saves and 19 victories in 201⅔ innings. Like McGraw and Frisella, McDowell and Orosco were comfortable sharing the closer's role while developing a strong kinship.

"I became real good friends with Jesse and have stayed good friends," said McDowell. "There was no animosity.

We pulled for each other, and I think that was a big part of that success.

"He's a very caring individual and very competitive. To hold the games-pitched record and to be one of very few players to play in four decades is a credit to the maintenance of his health, his durability and the fact that he was left-handed. Jesse was a great teammate, a great competitor and a guy you always wanted in a foxhole with you."

Orosco would also avail himself when McDowell needed help pulling off one of his most memorable pregame stunts. The Mets were on the road in 1986 when McDowell masterminded his great "handstand" caper. He wore a jersey top as pants and put the uniform pants over his head, making it look like he was doing a handstand. McDowell once said he used a pair of Rusty Staub's old uniform pants so his head wouldn't get "scrunched" up.

"That was kind of my idea. That was in L.A. I had gone to the mask store that day, and for some reason I had seen something on TV regarding the Mardi Gras and had seen people who looked like they were walking upside down. That's where I got the idea from.

"Jesse helped me with putting everything on. I walked down to the dugout, and Bill Robinson said I need to go on the field. This is Dodger Stadium…this is a place where you don't screw around. This is a sanctuary, Dodger Stadium. I stepped out of the dugout, they put it on the big scoreboard and the rest is history."

The handstand was a one-time deal, but the hotfoot was a recurring site at Shea Stadium in 1986. So adept was McDowell at the hotfoot that he and Howard Johnson once co-hosted a TV spot called "The Wonderful World of Hotfoot," which was featured in the team's 1986 video.

McDowell's system was rather elaborate. Rather than just sticking a book of matches to the shoes of a player or coach, McDowell wrapped the matches around a cigarette and used the cigarette as a timing device. McDowell would light the "fuse" from underneath the dugout bench, giving his target ample time to walk onto the field before the matches would ignite and laughter would ensue.

McDowell's saves ratio was probably higher than his hotfoot ratio, but his teammates finally got their revenge by taking a pair of Roger's shoes, placing them on the warning track in front of the Mets dugout and burning them. Even McDowell had to appreciate the prank.

"I just always had fun. I enjoy the game. I love to come to the ballpark. And I love collecting masks and going into different mask stores. L.A. and Hollywood were the best. Obviously they have things other than masks in those stores, and you get some ideas here and there. [It was] just something to break up the monotony of the season and have some fun because I always enjoy coming to the ballpark. Still, to this day, it's the greatest office. I still love coming here, and that hasn't changed from those days."

McDowell could make light of almost any situation, no matter how dark. Ron Darling, Bob Ojeda, Rick Aguilera, and Tim Teufel were arrested the morning of July 19, 1986, following an incident at a Houston nightclub, a situation created by a mix of overly imbibed ballplayers and overly enthusiastic off-duty police serving as bouncers. The four players were held overnight in a local jail before they were released. When they reached the clubhouse, McDowell had already run several strips of trainers tape in front of each locker of the offending teammate, making each cubicle look like a jail cell. The Mets owned a 12½-game lead in the NL East at the time of the arrests, and were 15½ games up by the end of July.

It was gallows humor for a juggernaut that put together one of the greatest regular seasons in National League history. Only two NL teams won more games than the 1986 Mets, who finished 108–54 with an outstanding bullpen, a great rotation, solid defense, timely hitting, and a roster full of players who would not accept defeat.

The Mets played hard both on and off the field. They were involved in four on-field brawls in 1986, two started by Ray Knight and one involving first-base coach Bill Robinson. They completely trashed a charter plane after clinching the National League pennant in Houston in one of several incidents that has grown hair with age. McDowell declined to confirm the Mets' reputation as hard partyers, although he acknowledged the '86 club was a hard-nosed crew on the field.

"There are some stories that over the years may be embellished somewhat, maybe blown up to more than lifelike proportions. We were just a ballclub that played the game hard on the field. We came to the ballpark and expected to win every day. We had guys that had that ability. Kevin Mitchell was the fourth infielder and your fourth outfielder. Rick Aguilera was a swing guy and part-time starter. These guys go on to have great big-league careers. We were lucky and fortunate enough to have people—not only on an everyday basis but the quality of the individual backing up when the regulars needed a day off—who would have been starters for any other team."

The 1986 season was a cakewalk for the Mets, but the postseason was anything but. They were beaten twice by Astros ace Mike Scott during the NLCS and were scheduled to face him in Game 7, which made Game 6 so crucial. The Mets led the series three games to two but trailed 3–0 in the ninth inning before rallying to tie the game.

Johnson called on McDowell to pitch the bottom of the ninth and kept him on the mound through the 13th inning. McDowell put together one of the greatest relief performances in Mets playoff history, rivaling the work performed by Nolan Ryan in the 1969 postseason. McDowell faced the minimum 15 batters during his five innings of work, allowing no runs and just one single. But the Mets didn't score until the top of the 14th and didn't win the pennant until the 16th, when the Astros scored twice off Orosco before he fanned Kevin Bass to end the 4:42 marathon.

"We went into that game knowing how pivotal it was." McDowell remembered. "We were up a game, and if we lose Game 6, we're going to face Mike Scott again. He had already won two games, and even after the fact, he was the MVP of the championship series. It was a great testament to what he did for the Houston Astro ballclub. Mentally, he was in everybody's head as far as the New York Mets. Everybody thought he was scuffing the baseball. When you're out there on the mound and you're beating a team mentally, that's half the battle.

"We knew we were gonna have to win that game, and it didn't look very good. Bob Knepper pitched a terrific game and Bobby Ojeda pitched for us. We were down 3–0, and then Lenny leads off the ninth with a triple in the right-center-field gap. It was like a little jumpstart, and we ended up tying the game with very clutch hitting against a very good closer in Dave Smith.

"I got to pitch the ninth through 13th innings. Houston wasn't one of my teams during the course of the season. I don't know how many years *USA Today* had been out, but it was relatively new. I remember going into the series they had a little box rating the guys who did well against the other teams and those who didn't. I didn't do so well against the Astros during the regular season. I think I was 0–3 with about a 12.00 ERA. Take all that stuff into account, and it's not looking too promising for our team when I come into the game in the bottom of the ninth.

"There were a lot of really, really good defensive plays in the five innings I was in there. I was fortunate to keep them shut out for five innings, and Jesse winds up getting the win. Obviously, it's a game you never forget in a ballpark, an atmosphere, and a setting…it was really, really a loud crowd. And it was fun. A lot of fun."

McDowell ran his postseason shutout streak to 11⅓ innings before allowing two runs in the eighth inning of a 6–2 win over the Red Sox in Game 4 of the World Series. Boston won the fifth game to take a 3–2 lead in the series and led 5–3 in the 10th inning of Game 6 before the Mets staged a miraculous rally to force a seventh game.

New York also trailed 3–0 in Game 7 when the bullpen helped lead the team to its second championship. McDowell was the winning pitcher in the clincher, working a scoreless seventh to keep the game tied 3–3 before Ray Knight's leadoff homer in the bottom half sparked a three-run rally in an 8–5 win.

The Mets entered 1987 as the prohibitive favorites to repeat as World Series champs, but a string of misfortune snuffed out any chance at a division title. McDowell was among the unfortunate, missing the season opener following surgery.

The Mets were in fourth place as late as June 23 and were 10 games out on July 22 before getting hot. Orosco was the only pitcher of significance on the roster who did not miss any part of the season due to injury or suspension, and he suffered his worst season as a Met. McDowell

still has trouble understanding how the Mets were unable to win a second straight division title despite the problems with the pitching staff.

"I don't know. I started off the year with hernia surgery. We were ready to break camp in St. Petersburg and I had to undergo hernia surgery and missed six or eight weeks. That was the year Doc [Gooden] went into rehab to start the season.

"Maybe all the stars didn't line up as well as they did the previous year."

The stars appeared to be aligned when the Mets took the field for the start of a three-game series against the first-place Cardinals September 11. A series sweep would put New York 1½ games ahead of St. Louis, which wasn't a far-fetched thought since the Mets had shaved nine games off the Cardinals' lead in seven weeks.

Homers by Darryl Strawberry and Mookie Wilson helped the Mets build a 4–0 lead by the second inning. It was 4–1 after Darling completed a six-inning, one-hit performance.

Rookie Randy Myers tossed a scoreless seventh before McDowell worked out of a first-and-third situation by getting the speedy Vince Coleman to hit into a double play to end the eighth.

McDowell was within one out of collecting a save in a 4–1 victory when Willie McGee hit an RBI single. Moments later, Terry Pendleton crushed a game-tying, two-run homer off McDowell to send the game into extra innings. Orosco gave up two runs in the 10th before the Cardinals completed a 6–4 victory, which derailed any momentum the Mets had gathered since late July. By the time the Mets arrived in St. Louis for a season-ending three-game series, the Cardinals had clinched the division.

McDowell picked up a career-high 25 saves in 1987, but he also blew seven save chances and finished with a 4.16 ERA. Orosco was worse, compiling a 4.44 earned run average while going 3–9 with 16 saves in 22 chances.

The Mets had a new lefty-righty bullpen combo by the 1988 season opener. Orosco was sent to the Dodgers, where he would win another World Series ring at the Mets' expense. Myers took over as the Mets' lefty closer and combined with McDowell for 42 saves as the team won the NL East by 15 games over the Pirates. McDowell rebounded from his inconsistent 1987 campaign, going 5–5 with a 2.63 ERA and 16 saves in a team-high 62 appearances.

The Mets had a two-games-to-one lead over the Dodgers in the NLCS until McDowell put the capper on a very disappointing night in Game 4 at Shea. Gooden blew a 4–2 lead in the ninth when Mike Scioscia hit a two-run homer, and the Mets had the winning run on second with two out in the 11th before Howard Johnson fouled out. McDowell retired the final hitter in the top of the 11th and got the first two outs in the 12th before Kirk Gibson belted a tie-breaking homer. McDowell was hung with the loss when the Mets wasted a one-out, bases-loaded opportunity in the bottom of the 12th. New York dropped the series in seven games after taking 10 of 11 from the Dodgers during the regular season.

McDowell got off to a nice start in 1989, picking up saves in four straight appearances from April 20 to May 1. His earned run average was 0.79 after he collected a save in a 3–1 triumph over the Braves May 1, but he went 1–5 with one blown save and a 4.50 ERA over his next 18 games. Myers eventually became the full-time closer, and McDowell and outfielder Dykstra were traded to the Phillies for Juan Samuel June 18. The deal didn't come as a complete shock to McDowell, a move that is among the very worst in Mets history.

"I don't want to say I was somewhat surprised because I had not been pitching well. I did not pitch well in spring training and was not pitching well during the season. It didn't come as a surprise, but it did come as a heartbreaker because of the guys I had grown up with and played the game with for four years. Now I have to go on the other side. But I guess the opportunity for me to go and pitch late in games again for the Philadelphia Phillies—and Lenny to get the opportunity to play on an everyday basis—was kind of like the carrot in front of our noses. You've been pitching in the big leagues for four years now, and it's like, 'We're not sure you can do it anymore.' So it was kind of like a little bit of a shove to kick you into gear and get back to being competitive again."

McDowell immediately became the Phillies' closer and went 3–3 with 19 saves and a microscopic 1.11 ERA in 44 appearances the rest of the year. Dykstra helped the Phils win the 1993 pennant before a back injury caused him to retire after 11 major league seasons. Samuel hit .228 for the Mets and demanded a trade following the '89 season.

The trade began a career-ending eight-year span in which McDowell pitched for the Phillies, Dodgers, Rangers, and Orioles. He led the National League with 60 games finished for the 1990 Phils but was 6–8 with 22 saves and a 3.86 ERA for a fourth-place ballclub. McDowell went 12–17 with 44 saves and a 2.90 ERA during his time with the Phils before heading to the Dodgers in the middle of the 1991 season.

The Dodgers kept him through the 1994 strike season. McDowell collected 14 saves for the 1992 Dodgers but spent his last two years in Los Angeles as a set-up man for Jim Gott in 1993 and Todd Worrell in '94.

His 1995 season was with the Rangers as McDowell was 7–4 with four saves and a 4.02 ERA in his first year as an American Leaguer. He was part of the Orioles' 1996 AL wild-card team, going 1–1 with four saves and a 4.25 ERA in 41 appearances though August 14 before he was placed on the disabled list with a shoulder injury that required surgery. McDowell signed a minor league contract with the White Sox after the 1996 season but failed to make the '97 roster, ending his career at age 35.

The Dodgers hired him as a minor league pitching coach in 2002. He mentored prospects at Class A South Georgia from 2002 to 2003 before spending the next two years handling the pitchers at Triple A Las Vegas. One year later, McDowell was replacing one of the most respected pitching coaches in major league history.

The Dodgers didn't have many pitching prospects at Triple A from 2004 to 2005. Las Vegas compiled a 5.45 ERA in '04 and a league-worst 6.21 ERA the following season. But those stats were of little concern to the Braves as they sought a replacement for Leo Mazzone, who left the organization after guiding the Atlanta staff to 14 consecutive playoff berths, five pennants, and one World Series. The Braves were always among the top five in staff ERA during that stretch, which made his departure that much more noticeable.

Atlanta interviewed several coaching prospects before hiring McDowell, who impressed general manager John Schuerholz and assistant GM Frank Wren before he was added to manager Bobby Cox's staff. The hiring came at a time when the Braves were in transition following their record streak of postseason appearances. Tom Glavine and Greg Maddux were gone by 2006, John Smoltz was 39, and the rest of the rotation consisted of journeymen, leading to Atlanta's first losing season since 1990. But through shrewd trades and an excellent farm system, McDowell had plenty to work with as the Braves challenged the Phillies for the 2010 NL East crown. Any comparisons between McDowell and Mazzone were minimal five years after he became pitching coach, although he admitted it wasn't easy to replace a man who coached six Cy Young Award winners.

"I don't want to say it wasn't difficult, but I believed in what type of individual I am and what type of pitching coach I am. Hopefully, the pitchers that I have on my staff can get together with me and forge a bond, a relationship and a trust, and we can go through a season and make adjustments that need to be made.

"I was comfortable in my own skin and very happy and lucky to get the opportunity here. Mr. Schuerholz, Bobby, and Frank Wren believed in my ability to do my job. When I became a coach, it was no different from when I was in the minor leagues trying to become a player in the major leagues. It's what I wanted to do, and so I had to learn my craft. I went down to the minor leagues and got very fortunate. I was a coach in the minor leagues for four years and got this opportunity. I'm very humbled by it."

ML/Mets debut	vs. Cardinals, 4/11/85 (1 IP, 0 H, 0 ER, 1 K, 0 BB)
First ML/Mets strikeout	Terry Pendleton, Cardinals, 4/11/85
First ML/Mets win	vs. Cardinals, 4/11/85
First ML/Mets save	vs. Phillies, 5/11/85
Most strikeouts, ML game	5, Mets @ Dodgers, 6/23/85; Rangers @ Twins, 8/28/95

Acquired: Selected in the 3rd round of the 1982 draft.

Deleted: Traded to the Phillies with Lenny Dykstra and a player to be named (Tom Edens) for Juan Samuel, 6/18/89.

Tug McGraw

Pitcher	Bats right, throws left
Born: 3/30/44	Martinez, California
Died: 1/5/04	Brentwood, Tennessee
Height: 6'0"	Weight: 185 #45

Tug McGraw Mets Career

YEAR	GP/GS	IP	H	R	ER	K	BB	W–L	SV	ERA
1965	37/9	97.2	88	47	36	57	48	2–7	1	3.32
1966	15/12	62.1	72	38	37	34	25	2–9	0	5.54
1967	4/4	17.1	13	16	15	18	13	0–3	0	7.79
1969	42/4	100.1	89	31	25	92	47	9–3	12	2.24
1970	57/0	90.2	77	40	33	81	49	4–6	10	3.28
1971	51/1	111	73	22	21	109	41	11–4	8	1.70
1972	54/0	106	71	26	20	92	40	8–6	27	1.70
1973	60/2	118.2	106	53	51	81	55	5–6	25	3.86
1974	41/4	88.2	96	43	41	54	32	6–11	3	4.16
Total	361/36	792.2	685	316	279	618	350	47–55	85	3.17

Mets Career/Batting

GP	AB	R	H	2B	3B	HR	RBI	K	BB	SB	AVG
363	157	12	27	6	0	1	15	43	8	0	.172

ML Career

YEAR	GP/GS	IP	H	R	ER	K	BB	W–L	SV	ERA
65–84	824/39	1514.2	1318	597	528	1109	582	96–92	180	3.14

Relief pitchers usually have a love-hate relationship with the fans. It's the nature of the job, as you are expected to close out two-run victories but are vilified when you don't.

Thus, it's rare when a reliever can become a folk hero with two franchises, particularly two ballclubs in the same division. But a glove-thumping, screwball-throwing Irishman was able to accomplish that.

Mets fans claim Tug McGraw as their own. He won his first World Series ring with the 1969 team and was the catalyst for the "Ya Gotta Believe" team in 1973.

"His being left-handed never hurt," said former Mets teammate Bob Apodaca, "seeing things from a different perspective, always looking at the positives. [He was] a comical person, always looking to have fun. But when he crossed the lines, he was dead serious, and another man that was extremely prepared.

"We would split a lot of the games my rookie year in '74. He had some injury problems that particular year. Just watching the way he handled things, the way he handled stress, the way he handled being down in the bullpen, knowing the phone was going to ring and that it was going to be his name called to get up.

"You learn so much just by watching, and if you pay attention, you pick up little things. Those are the things that I got from Tug—just his professionalism and his anticipation of handling stressful situations and how he did it."

Phillies fans embraced McGraw, who recorded the final out in the first World Series ever won by the franchise. McGraw also stayed in the Philly area after retiring as a player, doing local television work and even co-creating his own cartoon strip.

"He was very competitive, obviously," said Phillies teammate Larry Bowa. "He did a great job of closing games for us. But he coined that 'Yes We Can,' with the Phillies. He was one of those guys that didn't let anything bother him. If he blew a save on Monday, on Tuesday, you wouldn't know he blew a save. He had that kind of personality, and he could pitch every day. He didn't just get one-inning saves. He'd give you three innings, 2⅔. He loved to pitch, loved to compete, and had a lot of fun playing baseball."

But McGraw cut his teeth with the Mets while cutting hair in the process. The Californian was signed as an amateur free agent in 1964, a few months after his brother, Hank, was inked by the Mets. Hank McGraw persuaded Mets officials to give his baby brother a look, but the older McGraw was supposed to be the sibling that broke into the majors first.

Tug made Hank look like an excellent talent evaluator as he went 5–2 with a 1.53 ERA in 47 innings for Cocoa of the Florida Rookie League immediately after signing with the Mets. McGraw tossed a seven-inning no-hitter against Houston's rookie team in his first professional start and was promoted to Auburn of the New York–Penn League for the final few weeks of the minor league season.

McGraw, Ron Swoboda, Jim Bethke, and Danny Napoleon each made the Mets out of spring training. Actually, they had to be on the Opening Day roster or else the Mets risked losing them in the first-year draft. New York had lost outfielder Paul Blair to the Orioles in that draft a year earlier, forcing the Mets to bring up some of their best prospects before they were ready.

Manager Casey Stengel used McGraw almost exclusively out of the bullpen before the 'Ol' Perfessor' stepped down at the end of July. McGraw made his big-league debut April 18 at Shea Stadium against the Giants, retiring the only two batters he faced while stranding the bases loaded in the eighth inning. McGraw fanned the first hitter he faced, Hall of Famer Orlando Cepeda.

"His bat looked like the biggest bat I'd ever seen in my life," said McGraw almost a decade later. "It looked like a telephone pole, and he was a helluva hitter, anyway. So I was unbelievably nervous, my knees shaking, all kinds of anxiety, all butterflies in my stomach, as nervous as you can be.

"Chris Cannizzaro was our catcher, and I remember the first pitch I threw was a curveball for a strike. We worked the count to 2–2, and then I threw him a slow curveball that he looked at for strike three. No shit. I jumped up in the air and started walking around like we'd just won the World Series or something. My mind was streaking all over the place, thinking that only the year before I'd been in college trying to strike out guys—or getting smoked by guys—and here I was in the big leagues striking out Cepeda. It was super, and I was acting like a crazy man out there, and I still had to get one guy out to end the inning."[115]

McGraw had a 2.79 ERA in his first 9⅔ major league innings after tossing a scoreless ninth to earn his first career save May 24 against the Phillies. He made his first major league start July 28 at Wrigley Field but lasted only 2/3 of an inning, giving up three runs and five hits, including Billy Williams' two-run homer.

McGraw didn't start again until August 22, when he earned his first major league win by going the distance on a seven-hitter in a 4–2 win over the Cubs. His next start turned him into an instant folk hero as he became the first Met to beat Sandy Koufax. He allowed only two runs while pitching into the eighth inning of a 5–2 victory.

"It was unreal, beating Koufax," McGraw said in his book, *Screwball*. "Because it was my second straight win and he was Koufax, he was the the the best, he'd won the Cy Young Award and 25 games and everything."[116]

McGraw tossed a complete game in his next start but absorbed a loss in a 3–2 setback against the Astros. It began a season-ending streak in which McGraw went 0–5 in six starts despite a 3.49 earned run average. The string of tough losses left him 2–7 with a 3.32 ERA for the season.

Big things were now expected from McGraw, who had become one of the team's first legitimate home-grown pitching prospects. But a winter hitch in the Marine Corps followed an elbow injury that stunted his progress. McGraw was 2–9 with a 5.37 ERA in 15 games, including 12 starts.

McGraw spent most of 1967 with Jacksonville, where he regained his effectiveness through a new "out" pitch. According to McGraw's book *Ya Gotta Believe*, teammate Ralph Terry told him he had long tried to develop a screwball and showed him the grip in the instructional league after the '66 season.

"The next day we were warming up at the ballpark and I tried Terry's grip for a screwball. It worked. In the pepper game the next day, whoa, there it was. I stuck with it, and the next thing I knew, I had my pitch."[117]

McGraw said it took a while before his backstops felt comfortable calling for his new pitch. Not many pitchers at that point in major league history were known for an outstanding screwball, and there were doubts a kid with a 4–19 record in his first three seasons could throw the pitch with any effectiveness.

"At first the catchers didn't want to call for the screwball in tough spots where I was behind the hitters in the count," said McGraw in 1974. "They'd only go to it when I was ahead of the hitter in safe situations. I guess they didn't know if I could control the pitch. They had to build up their own confidence, too, and later they'd take a chance with it for a strikeout or a double play. It was a slow thing, nothing overnight."[118]

He led the International League with a 1.98 ERA in 1967 and was third with 161 strikeouts, finishing 22 behind league leader Jerry Koosman. He struck out 14 in back-to-back starts, breaking Tom Seaver's single-game team record for Ks.

McGraw was recalled in September and was promptly hammered in his four starts, going 0–3 with a 7.94 earned

run average. He struck out 10 while allowing only three hits in six-plus innings against the Astros September 27, but a three-run homer by future teammate Bob Aspromonte erased Houston's 2–1 deficit and sent McGraw to the showers.

McGraw had gained a reputation as a free spirit during his four years with the organization. He was a licensed barber and would give haircuts to teammates and coaches when asked. Mets TV producer Joe Gallagher even arranged to have Tug give a haircut to broadcaster Ralph Kiner on the air.

But the team's climate changed in October 1967, when Gil Hodges was hired as the team's third full-time manager. Hodges was a former marine himself with a no-nonsense style that seemed to contradict McGraw's. Hodges saw untapped talent in McGraw but didn't feel he was ready to make the major league team in 1968. Tom Seaver, Jerry Koosman, Nolan Ryan, and Dick Selma had passed him on the depth chart, and Jim McAndrew was just a few months away from making his Mets debut. Hodges decided he needed a season's worth of seasoning. McGraw spent all of 1968 pitching for Jacksonville, going 9–9 with 10 complete games and a 3.42 ERA in 166 innings. Seaver won 16 games for the second straight year. Koosman set a team record with 19 victories and finished second to Reds catcher Johnny Bench in the NL Rookie of the Year voting. Ryan set a team record by fanning 14 in a game. McAndrew displayed poise while compiling a 2.28 earned run average following his recall in July. And Gary Gentry went 13–12 with a 3.42 ERA in his first season for Jacksonville. With a surplus of pitching talent, the Mets exposed McGraw in the October 1968 expansion draft and didn't pull him after the Padres and Expos had made their first few selections. The Mets were ready to receive nothing for McGraw before they finally protected him later in the draft.

McGraw reported to spring training and struck out 18 while allowing just nine hits in 17⅔ innings. He made the ballclub after his one-year exile, but he would be working out of the Mets' bullpen. Hodges felt McGraw could be the lefty to complement veteran right-hander Ron Taylor out of the pen. McGraw would continue to pitch out of major league bullpens until 1984.

McGraw was outstanding in his first relief effort of the season, picking up the Mets' first victory by holding the Expos to a run and five hits with seven strikeouts in 6⅓ innings April 9. Hodges gave him a start in Game 2 of a doubleheader against the Cubs May 4, two days after McGraw worked a scoreless inning of relief. McGraw pitched the Mets to a 3–2 victory, striking out eight in a nine-hitter that lowered his ERA to 1.61 in his first 22⅓ innings of the year.

McGraw also started his next three games due to an injury to Koosman, but Tug was tagged for 10 earned runs in 11⅔ innings before spending the rest of the year in the pen.

McGraw saved five games in a seven-outing stretch from May 31 to June 20. His string of saves coincided with the

Mets' first 11-game winning streak in team history. McGraw worked two scoreless innings against Houston July 31 and didn't allow a run until August 31. He pitched 20⅔ consecutive scoreless innings during that stretch while the Mets climbed back into the division title hunt. From July 2 through the end of the regular season, McGraw was 5–2 with seven saves and a 0.73 ERA in 49⅓ innings!

Tug was the winning pitcher the night before the Mets clinched the NL East title, pitching four shutout innings before Bud Harrelson won the game with an RBI single in the bottom of the 11th. Hodges' decision to turn McGraw into a reliever was a big reason why the Mets made the playoffs in only their eighth season.

Fittingly, Taylor saved Game 1 of the NLCS against the Braves, and McGraw picked up the save in Game 2. McGraw didn't get into a World Series game against the Orioles, who were heavy on right-handed hitting. But Tug was doused in champagne for the third time in less than a month after the Mets took out the Birds in five games. Better yet, McGraw had arrived as a solid reliever and wouldn't make another trip to the minors.

Neither McGraw nor Taylor could duplicate their 1969 success the following years. McGraw was 4–6 with 10 saves and a 3.28 ERA, a jump of more than one run from his previous earned run average. He opened the year by allowing no earned runs in 10 innings over his first six appearances, but his ERA climbed as high as 5.20 by June 7. Tug seemed to give up two or three runs every fourth appearance while the Mets themselves were struggling to find the consistency that propelled them into the 1969 playoffs. He worked five innings of relief to pick up a victory September 8 against the Expos, which put the Mets within just a half-game of the division lead. He recorded a 1.27 earned run average in his final 10 appearances, but New York went 9–13 to close the season six games behind the first-place Pirates.

Meanwhile, Danny Frisella had emerged as the No. 3 option for Hodges out of the pen. Like McGraw, Frisella originally came up to the majors as a starter before switching over to relief. The two would enjoy a great year in 1971, although the Mets would finish 83–79 for the second straight year.

McGraw and Frisella combined for 19 victories and 20 saves in '71 while posting ERAs under 2.00. Seaver won the National League ERA title with a career-best 1.76 mark, but McGraw's 1.70 earned run average was the best among Mets pitchers with at least 100 innings. McGraw won a career-best 11 games and struck out 109 batters in 111 innings.

"He didn't save many games for me," Koosman said with a laugh. "He never had good luck behind me. As close friends as we were, I think he tried too hard. I remember I'd come into the clubhouse, and he'd ask, 'Hey Kooz, are you pitching today?' I'd say 'Yup,' and he'd say, 'Me, too.' So I would try my best not to let him in a ballgame. He'd come in and screw it up."

McGraw became the Mets' primary closer in 1972, posting a 1.70 ERA and recording a team-record 27 saves, smashing Taylor's record of 13. Tug also picked up the victory in his first All-Star Game appearance, tossing the final two innings of a 4–3, 10-inning win. He struck out four in the game, including future Hall of Famers Reggie Jackson and Carlton Fisk.

McGraw finished second in the NL with 27 saves and fifth with 54 appearances, but the Mets were ready to break up one of their primary assets. Frisella was traded with Gary Gentry to the Braves for lefty George Stone and Gold Glove second baseman Felix Millan, who was acquired to give the Mets better range up the middle. General manager Bob Scheffing gambled that his team needed only one top-flight closer in the pen and was willing to deal Frisella to shore up the infield. That gamble blew up in his face for about 4½ months.

McGraw actually got off to a nice start in 1973, converting his first five save opportunities while pitching to a 1.35 ERA in his first 13⅓ innings. But he blew back-to-back save chances in a series against Houston in early May, surrendering six runs while retiring only one batter in the second appearance.

"We had a 4–1 lead late in the [second] game when they called to the bullpen and said my favorite words: 'Get McGraw ready.'

"When I got in, though, I wasn't ready. I walked the first batter, and then the second. I couldn't believe it. I buckled down and struck Lee May out, but then promptly walked the next two, forcing in a run. I was reeling at this point, and by the end of the inning four runs had scored off of me and we were en route to a 9–5 loss. The performance rocked me."[119]

From May 4 to July 7 McGraw was 0–4 with six saves, seven blown saves and a ridiculous 8.00 ERA. Manager Yogi Berra tried newly acquired Phil Hennigan to close out games without much success, leaving the bullpen in shambles. Harry Parker, who opened the season in the rotation, was now Berra's cross-your-fingers guy in the ninth inning. Things got so bad for McGraw that Berra had him pitch the final two innings of a game the Mets already were trailing 7–1.

"There was a game up in Montreal, early in July," recalled McGraw. "I came into it when we were playing catch-up ball in a close game. That is, the game was close until I got into it. They got seven runs off me in less than one inning. I gave up a grand slam to Bob Bailey. I think Tim Foli hit a double off me after that. Then John Boccabella hit a home run. I walked a couple of guys, and before somebody else got the side out, I had given up seven big ones.

"Well, that was probably as low as you could go in a slump. I felt it couldn't get any worse, but I still didn't know what was wrong. I'd been playing professional ball for 10 years, and I'd been playing ball since I was seven. And standing on the mound up in Montreal, I didn't have

Tug McGraw in August 1980. Photo courtesy of David Ferry

any feel for the baseball at all. I didn't have any idea how to throw the baseball. It was as though I'd never played before in my entire life. I just felt like dropping to my knees and saying, 'Shit, I don't know what to do. Don't know what to do. Cannot hack it anymore.'"[120]

The Mets were in the cellar by midseason, thanks in large part to the team's terrible bullpen. McGraw, the happy-go-luckiest guy in the clubhouse, had lost all confidence in himself.

During his slump, McGraw met with Joe Badamo, who was an insurance salesman, a motivational speaker, and a friend of Hodges before Gil passed away.

"I needed Joe that day; I needed help getting my confidence back. I had just forgotten how to pitch—at least, how to pitch well.

"Joe kept saying, 'You've got to believe in yourself.' If I didn't believe, I could never do it. I had to stop worrying, start thinking positively. 'You gotta believe, Tug.'[121]

Board chairman M. Donald Grant wanted to meet with his boys to give them a pep talk, as if a rah-rah speech was going to light a spark in the team. Actually, his talk eventually became the rallying point for the rest of the season.

Grant gave a rambling speech in which he said he understood the core of the lineup had been decimated by injury. He told the ballclub that it could turn around the season if it just believed in itself, just as Badamo had told

McGraw. McGraw responded by jumping out of his chair, grabbing teammates and shouting, "Ya Gotta Believe!!!"

He said years later that his meeting with Badamo left him feeling good as he headed to the ballpark. McGraw was jovial as he got dressed and headed to the outfield for batting practice. He wanted to spread his newfound attitude on the rest of his team.

"The next thing you know," said McGraw, "we had a group of pitchers in the outfield and I was giving a big sermon on how you gotta believe. Saying you gotta believe, not just in your mind but in your heart, and you gotta believe you want to win and believe you can win, and that kind of stuff.

"It was a joke, you know. We were all laughing about it. It wasn't meant to be serious, just something new, something different in the middle of a slump. Instead of acting sulky all the time, you can come out and act normal, be crazy, be flaky. What the hell, we were buried in the cellar at the time, everybody was down, and I was just having a good time screwing around having a good time that day. But the fans caught on to it.

"After batting practice, we got into the clubhouse, and it was announced that Donald Grant, the chairman of the board of directors, wanted to have a meeting with us. He came down and wanted to give us a pep talk. When guys are in the middle of a slump and still in last place, though, pep talks don't go over too good. But Grant came down, anyway, and gave us a real good talk. He said look, I know a lot of guys have been hurt, and Grote's been out, Buddy's been out, Cleon's feet have been hurting him, George Theodore's out, Staub's been hurting and all that. But he wanted us to know the front office was aware we weren't a last-place ballclub. They knew our main horses were out of action, and they considered us a big family, and when somebody was hurt, it hurt them as much as it hurt us, so to speak.

"And he said I believe that when you guys get healthy, there'll still be time left for you to get healthy on the field and win this thing.

"Well, damned if that didn't hit me, because I was sitting there still thinking, 'I gotta believe. I gotta believe in myself'—and he came out and snuck that 'we gotta believe' in on us. He threw that at us, and I sort of caught it…and as soon as the meeting was over, I started running around the clubhouse to each locker hollering at guys, 'Do you believe?' and 'You gotta believe.' And grabbing guys by the hair and pulling their heads up and yelling, 'You gotta believe.' And everybody thought I was crazy.

"Some of the guys were laughing, and some were afraid to laugh because they thought I was mimicking Mr. Grant, and some of them were laughing because they thought I was mimicking him. They thought it was a riot that I'd be stupid enough to mimic the chairman of the board while he was still in the clubhouse. On his way out, he walked into the trainer's room, where he heard me, and he asked Bob Scheffing, our general manager, 'Do you think McGraw was trying to mock me?'

"Scheffing said no, he didn't think I was. But I kept it up after Grant had gone."[122]

Grant stormed out of the clubhouse before retreating to his office. Ed Kranepool, McGraw's road roomie at the time, told the struggling reliever he better go up to Grant's office and ask for mercy.

"So I stood in front of his desk. I said, 'Let me start off with an apology. I didn't realize how offensive I was being. I thought the gotta believe as a real positive thing and I didn't see how you'd be offended by it.'

"He said, 'Well, I was, and the only thing that will keep you here is if we start winning some ballgames.' And he wasn't laughing. He meant business."[123]

Berra tried to change McGraw's fortunes by having him start two games in July, giving him the innings he needed while using him in no-pressure situations. McGraw was blasted in his first start, surrendering six earned runs and 10 hits in 6⅓ at Atlanta July 17, a little over a year after he picked up his All-Star victory in the same ballpark. In the team's best comeback of the year, the Mets scored seven times in the ninth inning to beat the Braves 8–7, preventing McGraw from falling to 0–5.

Tug fared much better in his second start, although the Mets lost to the Expos 5–2. McGraw allowed a run and four hits over 5⅔ innings before leaving the game with a 2–1 lead. Let somebody else blow the save.

McGraw returned to the bullpen and pitched six shutout innings while picking up two saves in three appearances since his start against Montreal. But he was the loser in his next two outings, giving a walk-off hit in San Francisco before yielding five runs in the 16th inning of an 8–3 loss to the Reds August 20. The Cincinnati setback left the Mets last in the NL East at 55–67, seven games behind the first-place Cardinals. The Mets would go 27–12 the rest of the way, and McGraw would lead the charge.

Mets fans weren't believing anything by mid-August. The team stunk, and the *New York Post* ran a mail-in poll asking fans who was to blame for the team's dismal performance. The *Post* didn't include players, but it did include Grant, Berra, and Scheffing.

McGraw finally picked up his first win August 22 against the Dodgers, pitching two shutout innings before Millan and John Milner hit RBI singles in the bottom of the ninth to give the Mets a 4–3 win. Before the game, McGraw's record stood at 0–6 with a 5.45 ERA and 13 saves in 20 chances. He was incredible the rest of the season, picking up either a win or a save in 17 of his last 19 games. McGraw went 5–0 with 12 saves and a 0.88 earned run average.

McGraw picked up his biggest save September 23 against the Cardinals in front of nearly 52,000 at Shea. He issued back-to-back walks with one out in the eighth to bring the potential tying run to the plate. The hitter was former teammate Tommie Agee, who hit a two-run homer off George Stone earlier in the game. McGraw got Agee to bounce into an inning-ending double play before working in and out of a two-on, two-out jam in the ninth.

The win allowed the Mets to stay a half-game ahead of the second-place Pirates with one week left in the season. "Ya Gotta Believe" had become the city's rallying cry as the Mets tried to reach the postseason for the second time in history.

McGraw also picked up the save on "Willie Mays Night" and was on the mound when the Mets clinched the division title October 1 at Wrigley Field. Seaver had just served up a two-run homer to Rick Monday to pull the Cubs within 6–4 with nobody out in the seventh. McGraw replaced Seaver and proceeded to allow one hit in three shutout innings, ending the game by getting Glenn Beckert to pop into an unassisted double play.

"We piled into the little old locker room at the top of the rickety flight of stairs in Wrigley Field, and all hell broke loose in a restrained sort of way. It was slightly restrained because, even though we had just come back from the dead and won the Eastern championship, we were supposed to play the second game of the doubleheader to complete the schedule.

"But the umpires decided it was too wet to play the second game. So we stopped being restrained and poured it on, hollering and screaming and wondering what all the people who'd counted us out of the human race a couple of months earlier must have been thinking. They tell me that I jumped on one of our equipment trunks with a bottle of champagne and kept screeching, 'You Gotta Believe!' with all the guys yelling back at me.

"A couple of hours later, they managed to round us up and we boarded our bus for O'Hare Field. We flew back to New York in the rain, still hooting and hollering. I got hold of the microphone in the back of the plane and that the stewardesses used to tell people to fasten their seatbelts and I went into one of my acts, announcing screwball awards in a history-making voice.

"You know, dumb-ass things like 'Workhorse of the Year Award' to Bob Apodaca, for throwing eight pitches against the Pittsburgh Pirates. 'Poison Pen Award' to one or two of the writers for giving up in July. 'Executive of the Year Award' to Bob Scheffing, for trading Nolan Ryan to the California Angels.

"It was pretty good fun until Jerry Koosman grabbed the mike from me and did his *Hogan's Heroes* bit, the way they gave the orders of the day in the Nazi POW camps. 'The starting pitchers on the Mets baseball team,' he said, 'give their Bullpen of the Year Award to Tug McGraw—because we would've won by 25 games if he hadn't screwed up all those games early in the season.'"[124]

McGraw didn't pitch in the 1973 NLCS against the Reds until Game 4. Seaver, Jon Matlack, and Koosman had tossed complete games while the Mets were taking a 2–1 lead in the series. Tug entered Game 4 two batters after Tony Perez had tied the contest 1–1 with a homer off George Stone. McGraw tossed 4⅓ innings of shutout relief before Pete Rose eventually won it with a homer off Parker in the 12th inning.

Shea Stadium was about to burst as McGraw relieved Seaver in the ninth inning of Game 5 with the Mets ahead 7–2. New York was a decisive underdog in the series after finishing the regular season 82–79, the worst record for a playoff team at the time. McGraw entered with the bases loaded and one out before retiring Joe Morgan and Dan Driessen to end the series.

McGraw made the final putout at first base, then sprinted for dear life toward the dugout as Mets fans swarmed the field in a very scary assembly.

"I was like a linebacker breaking tackles, elbowing and shoving the guys who were trying to make souvenirs of my hat, my glove, the ball, and my uniform. After the fans poured on the field, they started to take the place apart.

"It was a mob scene; the police had no control. Then again, they were probably just as ecstatic as our fans were."[125]

The Mets split the first two games in Oakland, with Mc-Graw getting the victory in a sloppy 10–7, 12-inning win over the A's in Game 2. He blew the save in the ninth inning but managed to pitch six innings of relief, allowing four runs. McGraw also hit a bunt single and scored the deciding run in the Mets' four-run 12th. But he needed Stone to get the final three outs to close the victory.

McGraw made four other appearances in the Series, shutting out the A's in 7⅓ innings. He picked up the save in Game 5, working the final 2⅔ innings of a 2–0 shutout that gave the Mets a 3–2 lead in the Series.

But the Mets dropped the final two games of the Series in Oakland, ending their improbable run.

McGraw was the toast of the town despite the Series loss. Eastern Airlines started using "Ya Gotta Believe" for its TV commercials in 1974 and gave McGraw $5,000 for the privilege. Otherwise, McGraw was flying low in 1974.

McGraw got off to another terrible start, giving up a game-winning, two-run homer to Mike Schmidt in the 1974 season opener at Philadelphia. Tug gave up at least a run in each of his first six appearances and had a 9.00 ERA when he was placed on the disabled list with a shoulder injury. But the beatings continued after he was activated.

McGraw had a 6.35 earned run average and had cashed in on just two of his first five save opportunities by mid-season. Mets optimists hoped he would pull off a similar comeback that led the team to its second World Series, but the shoulder wouldn't allow it.

Berra even put McGraw back into the rotation in late August with the team 10 games out of first place. McGraw picked up a victory in his first start and tossed a five-hit shutout in the second before allowing four runs in eight innings of a 6–4 loss to the Expos.

He picked up his 85th and final save as a Met September 16, 1974, against the Expos, tossing two-hit ball over 3⅓ shutout innings. His final appearance as a Met came in a start against Pittsburgh September 28, when he was charged with six earned runs in 4⅓ innings.

McGraw was 6–11 with a 4.16 ERA with the '74 Mets, allowing more than one hit per inning for the first time since 1966. He spent time on the disabled list and asked the team to discover the root of his shoulder problem. McGraw said the Mets only prescribed pain-killers and felt his late-season starts were only a ploy to showcase his durability.

The Phillies, perennial also-rans or worse since their choke job in September 1964, were interested in McGraw. The Mets and Phils engineered a blockbuster trade that sent McGraw and outfielders Don Hahn and Dave Schneck to Philly for reliever Mac Scarce, outfielder Del Unser, and catching prospect John Stearns. According to McGraw in his book, *Ya Gotta Believe*, the Phillies were unaware of his shoulder problem when he reported to spring training. Surgery was performed on St. Patrick's Day as a large cyst was removed from the shoulder. The procedure allowed McGraw to extend his career by 10 years and become a Philadelphia legend in the process.

"Everything I own has 'Mets' stamped on it," McGraw said after coming to the realization he was joining another organization. "Everything I have I owe to the Mets. Sure, I figured that I'd be traded sometime in the next two years because I'm an eight-year man now, and in two more years I'd have them over a barrel—you know, I could veto a trade then. But this I never expected."[126]

Tug didn't make his Phillies debut until April 26, 1975, against the Pirates. He notched his first win as a Phillie a week later against the Pirates, one day after notching his first save for the team. McGraw didn't face the Mets until June 29 at Shea Stadium, tossing seven scoreless innings of relief to help the Phils sweep a doubleheader. He pitched three perfect innings to earn the save in the opening, then blanked the Mets on one hit in four innings to get the win. But the Mets got their revenge a week later in Philadelphia as Dave Kingman and Jerry Grote homered in a three-run ninth to pull out a 4–3 win.

McGraw made the All-Star team for the second time and ended the '75 campaign 9–6 with 14 saves and a 2.98 ERA. He tied Gene Garber for the team lead in saves and fifth in victories while dispelling thoughts that he was finished as a pitcher.

The Phillies became the class of the NL East in 1976, winning the first of three straight division titles. McGraw went 22–16 with 29 saves and a 2.77 ERA during the three-year title run as he shared the closer's role with Gene Garber and Ron Reed.

The 1979 season was a downer for McGraw and the Phillies. The Phils were prohibitive favorites to win their fourth straight division crown after signing Pete Rose to a free-agent contract. But the team finished fourth at 84–78 after averaging 98 wins the previous three years. Tug went 4–3 with 16 saves in 18 chances while appearing in a career-high 65 games. But his earned run average swelled to 5.16, a full run higher than his final number in his final year as a Met.

McGraw rebounded in 1980 while helping the Phillies win their first World Series title, going 5–4 with 20 saves and a career-best 1.46 ERA. The Phils were tied for first with the Expos after McGraw blew a save in a 2–1 loss to the Giants September 2. He didn't allow an earned run after that, going 5–0 with five saves in 26 innings over 15 games. The late-season scoreless streak helped him finish fifth in the Cy Young balloting.

The Phillies had never won a single postseason series during their 98-season history until they beat the Astros in five games to take the NLCS. McGraw was the losing pitcher in Game 3, allowing a run in the 11th inning to put Houston ahead 2–1 in the series. But he nailed down his second save of the series in Game 4 before the Phillies earned their first World Series berth in 30 years.

McGraw factored in three of the Phillies' four wins against the Royals, picking up a win and two saves. He worked three shutout innings of relief to get the victory in Game 5, ending the game by fanning Jose Cardenal with the bases loaded. Two days later, he picked up the save in the Game 6 clincher. Tug made things interesting in the final inning of the Series, loading the bases with one out before Frank White hit a popup in foul territory. The ball glanced off the glove of catcher Bob Boone, which seemed for a moment to give White a reprieve. But Rose, who had trailed the play, lunged after the ball and speared it for the second out. McGraw pounded his glove over his heart after Rose's catch, then closed out the win by striking out Willie Wilson.

The Phillies reached the playoffs again in 1981, winning the first half of the strike-shortened season. The strike led to the first division series in major league history as the Phils took on the Expos, the second-half champs. The Phillies had coasted in the second half after they were given a playoff berth in August. The malaise continued with back-to-back losses to open the postseason, but the Phillies stayed alive by taking Game 3 before McGraw earned his final postseason victory with three shutout innings of relief to even the series. Steve Rogers outpitched Steve Carlton in the decisive Game 5 to end the Phillies' season. It was the last time McGraw would pitch in a postseason.

McGraw spent three more seasons with the Phillies but was used primarily as a setup man. He picked up his 180th and final career save August 2, 1982, against the Expos and finished his career by making 80 appearances without a save. He announced his retirement on Valentine's Day, 1985, almost 20 years after making his major league debut.

McGraw stayed in Philadelphia and served as a baseball reporter for WPVI. He hung onto his Phillies roots but would receive thunderous ovations when he was introduced at Mets old-timers' games. He was inducted into the Mets Hall of Fame in 1993, the seventh player so honored.

McGraw's induction came a few years after Tim McGraw had burst onto the country music scene. In 1966, before he married his wife, Phyllis, Tug had become friendly with a woman named Betty while he was pitching for Jacksonville. A year later, Betty had tried to inform

him that he had fathered a boy, but McGraw refused to believe it and asked Mets farm director Johnny Murphy for help. According to his book, *Ya Gotta Believe*, it was decided that he would deny he was the father. But he also knew it was a possibility and told Phyllis as much before they got married.

Tim McGraw was 11 years old when he finally met his natural father. They kept in touch the first year, but Tug admittedly remained distant for about five years until Betty tried to claim child support. Tug still wasn't fully sure he could be the father until he saw 17-year-old Tim. It took one glance for Tug to realize he didn't need a paternity test to prove Tim was his son.

Tug and Phyllis already had two children, Mark and Cari, when Tim became a fixture in McGraw's life. But Tug and Phyllis separated shortly after his final major league season. The divorce was finalized in 1987, four years before he married his second wife, Diane. The McGraws moved to Orlando and later California before Tug returned to Philadelphia, this time with his fourth child and third son, Matthew. But the marriage ended in 2001, and a series of bad business moves left him broke. He moved into a house with former teammate Larry Christenson for a few months before a Phillies minority owner offered him a room at one of his low-budget motels.

"Here I was, a 58-year-old former world champion baseball player—at one time the highest-paid relief pitcher in the game of baseball—and I was homeless, penniless, and living in a budget motel with my former colleagues feeling sorry for me. Although I know I hadn't hit rock bottom, I didn't want to see what the bottom looked like."[127]

Tim McGraw was now one of the hottest performers in country music, perennial Grammy winner, and CMA recipient. Tim continued to check in on his father, either while he was on the road or in Nashville. But Tug refused to let his son know how bad things were.

Tug got a break in 2002 when former teammate and Phils manager Larry Bowa asked him to work with pitchers in spring training. He would get $30,000 for the spring while getting his foot back in the game.

McGraw was invited back to work with the Phillies at Clearwater in 2003. He continued to serve as pitching mentor but was experiencing several health issues. He was suddenly unable to complete easy tasks and finally checked himself into a local hospital. He was there a few hours before an MRI showed two masses in his head. The doctor initially told McGraw he had three weeks to live, saying the masses in the brain signaled that there probably was more cancer in his body.

Tim McGraw was scheduled to perform in Orlando when he learned of the diagnosis. This time, Tug couldn't BS his son about his current state. Tim would continue with his concert tour through Florida, making his scheduled appearance at night before returning to Tampa to handle his father's affairs. Phyllis, Mark, Cari, and Matthew were at Tug's bedside while the once unflappable pitcher was pondering his own mortality. Hank was there, as well, and would serve as McGraw's "nurse" after Tug underwent surgery.

Tim and his wife, Faith Hill, worked their connections and had Tug admitted to the H. Lee Moffitt Center in Tampa. After six hours of surgery, McGraw was told the surgery had removed 99.9 percent of the tumor.

Less than four months later, McGraw made an appearance at Veterans Stadium to pull off a "countdown" number to signify how many games the Phillies had left in the venue before heading to Citizens Bank Park in 2004. Later in July, he was at Shea Stadium as the Mets honored the 30th anniversary of the "Ya Gotta Believe" team. McGraw and John Franco rode out of the bullpen in the old cart used by relievers during McGraw's days at Shea. Tug received a standing ovation before heading to the mound, where he threw a pitch to former teammate Jerry Grote.

Tim McGraw had spared no expense during the ordeal, insisting on the best possible treatment for his dad. He was juggling a career and a family, something his father had trouble doing both during and after his major league career.

But the cancer had already returned and was more progressive. A second surgery was performed at Duke Medical Center just a few days after his Shea Stadium appearance. But, after a few weeks of aggressive treatment, the cancer continued to grow.

McGraw went back to Duke in December for another MRI. This time, he was told the treatment was working and the tumors were shrinking. He received that news December 8, less than a month before he died at age 59.

Mets and Phillies fans have been at odds for the better part of five decades. But the common thread was their love and appreciation of McGraw through his brightest and darkest moments. He helped both teams win their first championships and was part of improbable pennant runs, the 1973 Mets and 1983 Phillies.

But McGraw showed his best side when he was at his lowest point in life. Sometimes, stats don't fully measure a pitcher's value.

"He was one of my best friends. We talked constantly up until he got sick and was in the hospital. Tug was the kind of guy that was always up," remembered Koosman. "The only time I ever saw Tug down was when the Mets were trading him, because he didn't want to leave the Mets. They traded him because he had a lump in his back that they thought was possibly more than a cyst, something they'd have to operate on and really hurt his pitching career. That's why they traded him, and it turned out it was nothing.

"Of course, later I get traded to Philly and there we are in spring training. We were the last two guys in the clubhouse, we're showering together and I said, 'Tug, if we had known we were going to last this long we probably should have taken better care of ourselves.'

"Tug was a very positive person. He never thought negative about any situation in baseball, he knew he could handle it. He loved the stage. He loved every time he was brought into the game. He was a great rooter, even in the bullpen. He started a contest with all the relief pitchers on points: if you did this or that, you got so many points. And they competed amongst each other. He was very, very good for a ballclub."

ML/Mets debut   vs. Giants, 4/18/65 (2/3 IP, 0 H, 0 ER, 1 K, 0 BB)
First ML/Mets strikeout   Orlando Cepeda, Giants, 4/18/65
First ML/Mets win   vs. Cardinals, 8/22/65
First ML/Mets save @ Phillies, 5/24/65
Most strikeouts, ML/Mets game   10, vs. Astros, 9/22/67
Low-hit ML/Mets CG   2, @ Phillies, 8/21/66
Acquired: Signed as an amateur free agent, 6/12/64.
Deleted: Traded to the Phillies with Don Hahn and Dave Schneck for Del Unser, John Stearns, and Mac Scarce, 12/3/74.
NL All-Star, 1972, 1975

Felix Millan

Second Baseman   Bats right, throws right
Born: 8/21/43   Yabucoa, Puerto Rico
Height: 5'11"   Weight: 172   #16, 17

Felix Millan Mets Career

YEAR	GP	AB	R	H	2B	3B	HR	RBI	K	BB	SB	AVG	SLG	OBP
1973	153	638	82	185	23	4	3	37	22	35	2	.290	.353	.332
1974	136	518	50	139	15	2	1	33	14	31	5	.268	.311	.317
1975	162	676	81	191	37	2	1	56	28	36	1	.283	.348	.329
1976	139	531	55	150	25	2	1	35	19	41	2	.282	.343	.341
1977	91	314	40	78	11	2	2	21	9	18	1	.248	.315	.294
TOTAL	681	2677	308	743	111	12	8	182	92	161	11	.278	.337	.326

ML Career

YEAR	GP	AB	R	H	2B	3B	HR	RBI	K	BB	SB	AVG	SLG	OBP
66–77	1480	5791	699	1617	229	38	22	403	242	318	67	.279	.343	.322

Before 1973, Cleon Jones and Tommie Agee were the only players in Mets history to hit over .260 for the ballclub in at least 2,000 career at-bats. Jones, Ron Hunt, Joe Christopher, and Tommy Davis were the lone Mets to hit .300 or better in a season and qualify for a batting title, another indication that offense never was the team's strong suit in its first 11 years of existence.

The Mets' historically mediocre lineup made Felix Millan's contributions to the team that much more appreciated. He was the only Met to hit over .280 in three different seasons during the 1970s, and the second Met ever to do it in consecutive years.

Millan's durability and bat control also made him a fan favorite. He was the first Met to play 162 games in a season, and the hardest to strike out. He stepped into the batter's box 2,954 times as a Met and fanned just 92, an average of once per 32.1 plate appearances.

Felix Bernardo Millan was acquired in Bob Scheffing's finest trade as general manager of the Mets, and one of the biggest all-time heists in club history. New York would not have won the National League pennant without pulling off the deal, although the swap was full of question marks from the start.

The Mets picked up Millan and left-hander George Stone from the Braves on November 2, 1972, for pitchers Gary Gentry and Danny Frisella. Millan, Stone, and Gentry were coming off their worst major league seasons to date, and Frisella recorded his worst winning percentage and ERA since 1968. But the Mets needed a steady second baseman after Ken Boswell's batting average slumped to .211 over 100 games in 1972. Millan hit only .257 in '72 and failed to earn a spot on the National League All-Star team for the first time in four years. But he also captured his second career Gold Glove, making him an upgrade over the dependable yet limited Boswell.

"I was glad that I got traded from Atlanta to New York because I knew I was coming to a Latin American market," Millan said nearly three decades after his final game with the Mets. "Everybody likes baseball here. I was happy to come because I love to play baseball and I knew I was going to give it 100 percent. Ever since I played for the Mets, my life changed. Atlanta was nice, but it's not like New York. I love to come see the kids here."[128]

Mets manager Yogi Berra liked the deal. "Now we've got a second baseman who can play every day. Millan can fit right into the batting order. He's a good No. 2 hitter. He doesn't strike out very often, and he's a good man to play hit-and-run. He's steady the infield."[129]

Millan gave the Mets a legitimate No. 2 hitter for the first time in team history. The Mets didn't steal a lot of bases under Berra, but Millan allowed the Mets to use the hit-and-run with more frequency than most teams, giving Rusty Staub and John Milner more opportunities to hit with runners in scoring position.

The pitchers were looking forward to having Millan behind them.

"A really good double play combination means I won't have to throw as many screwballs," said Tug McGraw following the trade. "A lot of times if I don't feel too sure of the double play combination behind me, I go for the strikeout. But now I'm able to go to the curveball to get the batter to hit it on the ground, and save a lot of wear and tear on my arm."[130]

The difference at the top of the order was clearly evident during Millan's first spring training as a Met's No. 2 hitter. He led the 1973 exhibition squad with 22 hits and 10 runs scored while batting .344 in 62 at-bats. Leadoff hitter Bud Harrelson also sparkled at the plate, hitting an uncharacteristic .314 with five RBIs and nine runs scored in 17 games. If the Mets could sustain this type of attack deep into the regular season, they would certainly challenge for the National League East title. But Harrelson got hurt early in the season, as did Jerry Grote, John Milner, Willie Mays, and Cleon Jones. The injuries destroyed the Mets' balance and paved a direct route to the division cellar, a position they'd occupy most of the summer.

TOUGHEST METS TO STRIKE OUT
(minimum 2,000 at-bats)

	Player	AB	K	AB/K
1.	Felix Millan	2677	92	29.1
2.	Doug Flynn	2137	158	13.5
3.	Rusty Staub	2571	204	12.6
4.	Ken Boswell	2116	207	10.2

One of the few constants in the lineup during the first half of '73 was Millan, though Felix got off to a lousy start as a Met. He doubled and scored on Opening Day and went 2-for-3 with an RBI and two runs scored in the third game. But he hit only .125 with no RBIs in 64 at-bats the rest of the month and entered May with a .158 average.

Millan began May with a 13-game hitting streak, batting .409 with 11 runs scored to lift his season average to .275. He was hitting .300 for the year after going 4-for-4 with an RBI and two runs scored in a 10–2 rout of San Diego June 16.

He put together a season-high 18-game hitting streak from July 13 to August 1, compiling a .413 average with 12 runs scored. But the Mets went just 9–9 during the streak to stay in last place, now 10½ games behind the first-place Cardinals.

The Mets finally had their Opening Day lineup available again when Harrelson came off the DL August 18. New York was still in last place at the time, but now just 7½ games off the pace. Millan was arguably the team's best hitter following Harrelson's return, batting .306 with 14 RBIs and 21 runs scored in the Mets' final 42 games. He had at least two hits in 14 of the last 28 games, helping New York go 20–8 to win the NL East by 1½ games over the Cards.

Millan ended the regular season with a .290 average, set a team record with 185 hits and led the Mets with 82 runs. He was the NL Player of the Week for June 11–17, going 14-for-25 (.560). Millan also was the National League's toughest man to strikeout, fanning 22 times in 638 at-bats (one K in every 31.77 at-bats)

He was outstanding with the glove, committing just nine errors (.989) and turning 99 double plays despite spending much of the year without Harrelson as his double-play partner. Millan received MVP consideration for the first time, finishing tied for 16th in the voting.

Millan's strong hitting continued into the NLCS against the Reds. He went 0-for-3 in a series-opening loss and was 0-for-3 in Game 2 before poking a single to spark a four-run ninth in a 5–0 victory that left the series tied heading to Shea Stadium. He added an RBI single and scored twice in a 9–2 rout of the Reds in Game 3.

Felix Millan takes a swing in a 1978 game. Photo courtesy of Oscar W. Gabriel

Millan came close to providing the series-winning hit, lashing a run-scoring single to put the Mets ahead 1–0 in Game 4. The lead held up until Tony Perez hit a solo homer in the seventh, which allowed Pete Rose to furnish the tiebreaking blast in the 12th. The Mets had just three hits in the game, two by Millan.

The Mets beat the Reds 7–2 in the fifth and deciding game. Millan started the game's first rally with a one-out single in the first before scoring on Ed Kranepool's two-run single. Cincinnati eventually knotted the score before Millan bunted and reached base on a fielder's choice to put runners on first and third with nobody out in the fifth. Three hits and four runs later, the Mets had a 6–2 lead as Millan scored the second run of the rally on a single by Willie Mays.

Millan hit .316 with two RBIs and five runs scored in the series, collecting all six of his hits in his final 13 at-bats. He stretched his postseason hitting streak to five games by lacing a triple in the fifth inning of the World Series opener in Oakland. But the sure-handed Millan also made a huge error that led to two unearned runs in the 2–1 loss to the A's.

The game was scoreless with two out in the bottom of the third when pitcher Ken Holtzman hit a double off starting pitcher Jon Matlack. Speedy Bert Campaneris followed with a grounder that went straight toward Millan for a certain third out. Mets fans watched in horror as the ball went right through the legs of Millan for a run-scoring error, allowing Holtzman to score. Campaneris promptly stole second on a botched pickoff and came home on Joe Rudi's single to put Oakland ahead 2–0.

Millan didn't hide after the game, accepting full blame for his flub. "I just missed it. I was waiting for the hop and it just didn't take the hop. I didn't get down for the ball. I've made errors before, but never one so important. Jon pitched a beautiful game. He told me, 'Don't worry about it, we'll get some runs,' but we only got one."

"Felix can't be perfect," said Matlack after the game. "I'm not perfect. I wish they'd hit the ball to Felix all the time. As soon as Campaneris hit the ball to Felix, I thought, 'That's great, we're out of the inning.' I wasn't even backing up the play. But he missed it, that's all. I missed the pickoff play after that."[131]

History was repeated in Game 1 of the 1986 World Series as Mets second baseman Tim Teufel misplayed a grounder to allow the lone run to score at Boston. Minutes after the miscue, NBC Sports, which was televising the game, showed video of Millan's error.

Millan went 0-for-6 in Game 2, but the Mets won 10–7 in 12 innings to even the Series. New York jumped out to a 2–0 lead in the first inning of Game 3 at Shea as Millan singled and scored the second run on a wild pitch. But the Mets stranded two runners in the inning and finished the game with 14 runners left on base in a 3–2, 10-inning loss to the A's.

The Mets eventually dropped the Series in seven games after taking a three-games-to-two lead. Millan hit safely in five of those games but hit only .188 in 32 at-bats, giving him a .254 lifetime average in 63 postseason at-bats. He never got into another playoff game.

But the Mets got the better of the Braves in the Millan trade. Stone led the National League with an .800 winning percentage, going 12–3 and winning his last eight decisions as the No. 4 starter. Gentry tried to pitch with a severe shoulder injury and threw just 26 innings after the '73 season.

New York was considered the favorite to win the 1974 NL East title based on their outstanding pitching and defense. But pitchers Tom Seaver and Tug McGraw battled injuries all season while the Mets' offense managed to hit worse than it did in 1973. Rusty Staub recorded his lowest batting average since 1965, and Wayne Garrett failed to build on his strong '73 season.

Millan hit only .268 with 50 runs scored in 136 games, missing 13 games with a chipped bone in his hand and another seven due to a nose infection. But Millan broke his own team record with 24 sacrifices and set a club record for regulars with just 14 strikeouts, fanning once per 41.78 plate appearances.

The Mets ended up 71–91 before embarking on an 18-game series against Japanese teams in October. Many players weren't thrilled about the trip, but Millan, John Milner, and newcomer Joe Torre appeared in every game. Millan even flexed his limited muscles during the series, belting three homers and providing eight extra-base hits, nine RBIs, and 13 runs scored.

Millan felt it was very important for him to have a bounce-back season, if only to demonstrate he hadn't lost a step. He helped himself at the plate by switching to a lighter bat.

"I wanted to prove to myself that I could do it age the age of 32," Millan said about playing all 162 games in 1975.

"I decided to switch from a 37-ounce bat to a 34-ounce Joe Torre model. It was a concession of age. I found I was not getting around on the ball with the heavier bat."[132]

The 1975 season was Millan's best as a Met statistically. He became the first Met to play every game in a season, a feat that wasn't accomplished again until John Olerud played a full 1999 season. Millan remains the only Met to start all 162 games in a season, sitting out just nine innings.

He got off to a slow start in '75, hitting .247 in 42 games through June 2 before recording a .305 average over his next 28 games. Millan later produced a 19-game hitting streak from July 5 to 26, batting .425 with six RBIs and 11 runs scored. He also hit safely in 13 straight games from August 25 to September 7 to raise his batting average to .300 before settling for a .283 mark. But the Mets went a combined 17–15 during his two lengthy hitting streaks and otherwise played .500 ball the rest of the season.

It was a record-setting season for the Mets offensively. Dave Kingman topped Frank Thomas' home run mark by hitting 36 while Staub was driving in 105 runs to break Donn Clendenon's team record. Millan bested his own team mark by collecting a career-high 191 hits and also set a club record with 37 doubles. He also finished third on the team with 56 RBIs, a lofty number for a No. 2 hitter. Only 32 other players in the majors had driven in more runs from the No. 2 hole in the lineup from 1954 to 1975.

Millan was the toughest man to strike out in the majors for the third straight year, fanning once per 26.54 plate appearances. He now had 64 strikeouts over 2,027 plate appearances as a Met (31.67). His ability to make contact overshadowed his 102 walks over the same period, the 18th fewest among all major leaguers with at least 1,500 plate appearances during that span.

Millan deserved to take the winter off after playing a full slate. Instead, he played for Caguas in the Puerto Rico Winter League, just as he had for several seasons.

"Because I love this game," Millan said matter-of-factly before the 1976 season. "I can never pay back what I owe to baseball. It has given me enjoyment, the respect of my people, security for my family and comfort. Is there more a man can want?"[133]

Millan had three four-hit games in 1975, all coming during a one-week span in late July. The first time helped Joe Torre tie an unwanted major league record.

The Mets were hosting the Astros July 21 when Millan singled in the first, third, sixth and eighth innings of what would become a 6–2 loss. Each time Millan reached base, Torre proceeded to erase him with a double-play grounder. No one had hit four double-play grounders in 36 years, and no one has done it since. Torre took the dubious honor with good humor and has even embellished the story.

"I'd like to thank Felix Millan for making all of this possible," Torre remarked after the game.[134]

Millan now says Torre has put his own spin in his account of the record-tying performance.

"He says the last ball he hit was against the fence and I waited on first base just to set the record," Millan recalled jokingly. "I always tried to break up double plays but I couldn't do it. I'm really sorry for Joe, but I'm making him famous like he did to me."[135]

Torre was just in his first year with the Mets in 1975, but he already had a long history with Millan. Torre was

TOUGHEST METS TO STRIKE OUT IN A SINGLE SEASON (minimum 450 at-bats)

	Player	AB	K	AB/K	Year
1.	Felix Millan	518	14	37.0	1974
2.	Felix Millan	638	22	29.0	1973
3.	Felix Millan	531	19	27.9	1976
4.	Felix Millan	676	28	24.1	1975
5.	Lance Johnson	682	40	17.1	1996

the Braves' starting catcher when Millan made his major league debut in 1966. Felix didn't become a regular with Atlanta until 1968, when his hitting and fielding made him an integral part of the Braves' powerful lineup. Millan kept his average around the .300 mark throughout the season and became the glue of the infield, which made a positive impression on Torre.

"It's amazing," said Torre that season. "Kit's only a rookie, but it seems like every rally we have, he's either starting it, in the middle of it, or putting the finishing touch to it."

Millan originally was signed by the Kansas City Athletics before the 1964 season. He played ball in his native Yabucoa, Puerto Rico, where his father worked in a sugar cane factory. Millan's baseball ability gave his family of five brothers and three sisters an opportunity to bring more money into the household. He also hit as if his family depended on every at-bat, recording a .291 average with 35 RBIs and 48 runs scored in 95 games for Daytona Beach of the Florida State League.

But the A's organization had been a poor judge of talent since winning three straight American League pennants from 1929 to 1931, spending most of the next 37 years in the second division. The Athletics allowed the 21-year-old Millan go to the Braves in the November 1964 first-year draft.

Millan hit .302 in 1965 and was at Double A Austin of the Texas League by the end of the year. It was then that he decided to choke up on the bat, leaving about one-third of his lumber to rest underneath his hands.

"I couldn't hit home runs," Millan said 40 years later. "I was a small guy, skinny, and I could run fast. I had a manager, Hub Kittle, who took me every day at 3:00 o'clock in the afternoon to teach me how to hit that way. He had me hitting second. I liked it there because I could advance the runner, get my base hits, and hit .300. I figured, 'I'd love to hit 25 home runs' but my build was not that way. For me it was, get on base and score some runs. And bunting helped me a lot."[136]

Millan opened the 1966 season with Austin but was with the Braves by June. He made his major league debut June 2, singling in his first at-bat against Bob Bolin of the Giants. Five days later, Millan went 4-for-5 with two runs scored in an 11–6 win over the Mets at Shea Stadium.

Millan's batting average with the Braves never dropped below .259 the rest of the season, but his playing time diminished after June 21. He went a month without an at-bat and was eventually sent back to the minors before receiving another recall.

Millan finished with a .275 average in 91 at-bats for the Braves in 1966 before he hit .235 in 41 games the following game. He headed into 1967 determined to make the Opening Day roster as the team's starting second baseman.

"Before I left Puerto Rico last spring," Millan said in the summer of 1968, "I tell my father that I will be the most hustlingest ballplayer in camp. I hustle all the time. I do not believe I have the job won at all, even though everyone say I do. But now I want to keep it. The crowds, the big ones, they use to scare me. But now I love to play before the big crowds."[137]

Millan made the most of his first full major league campaign, finishing second on the team with a .289 average, and third with 22 doubles on a club that had Hank Aaron, Torre, and Felipe Alou. Braves manager Luman Harris was comparing Millan with the game's best second basemen.

"He's the type player that you never realize is around until the game is over," Harris said during the season. "Then you look up and he's got two hits, an RBI, a stolen base, and he's been in on two double plays.

"Millan is going to replace Bill Mazeroski as the best second baseman in this league, and I don't mean that as a knock against Maz. But Maz is 31 years old and Felix already has as much range as Maz ever had.

"The most fantastic thing about him is his quickness. I can name you about five balls hit to him this year that took bad hops at the last possible second. His hands were down there to field the ball—and then suddenly he was jumping in the air, catching the ball above his head."[138]

Millan earned his first All-Star berth and Gold Glove in 1969 while helping the Braves win the NL West, their first playoff berth in 11 years. He embarked on a 13-game hitting streak shortly before the All-Star break and continued to flash range at second. Opposing managers were even gushing over the play of the Atlanta infielder.

"Everything there is to do, he does well," said Preston Gomez, who was managing the Padres at the time. "Millan has the best range of anybody in the league, and he goes back on pop flies better than anybody.

"He moves the ball around and he hits it sharp. He's one of the best hit-and-run men in the league and he's a very good bunter."[139]

"He is the closest thing to a perfect ballplayer that I've ever seen," said Harris during his team's run toward the 1969 NL West crown. "I'll tell you one thing; we wouldn't be where we are without Felix Millan."[140]

The Braves were in a dogfight for the division crown in August as five teams were within 3½ games of the lead. Atlanta was in fourth place following a 2–0 loss to the Dodgers September 8 before winning 17 of their final 21 to capture the flag by three games over the Giants.

The Mets were the Braves' opponents in the first-ever National League Championship Series. The Mets were considered underdogs despite winning seven more games during the regular season and taking eight of 12 from Atlanta. Millan was among the more productive Braves in the series, going 4-for-12 with three walks for a .467 on-base percentage. But he was unable to score or drive in a run as Atlanta fell to the Mets in three straight.

Millan also was an All-Star in each of his next two seasons. He batted a career-high .310 with 25 doubles and a career-high 16 stolen bases in 1970 before pounding out a .289 average the following season. Millan became the first Atlanta player to produce a six-hit game, doing it July 6, 1970, against the Giants. That feat wouldn't be duplicated by another Brave for 37 years.

Millan also recorded just 15 errors in each of those seasons and turned 120 double plays in 1971. But the Braves were regressing, finishing 76–86 following their division title run before a third-place finish at 82–80 in 1971. The franchise recorded a 70–84 record during the strike-shortened 1972 season, ending the year with Eddie Mathews as manager after Lum Harris was let go in late July. Millan won his second and final Gold Glove in 1972, but his slumping bat—coupled with the Braves' dire need for more pitching—led to his departure.

Millan already was among the top 10 in several Mets hitting categories after just three years with the team. He added 55 more runs scored, 25 doubles, and 35 RBIs to his career totals in 1976. He set a personal best with 41 walks while compiling a .282 average and .341 on-base percentage. Millan also ran his consecutive games streak to 192 games until a shoulder injury forced him out of the lineup May 12. The shoulder problem led to his batting average falling to .230 by mid June.

He finally got hot again in August, hitting .390 for the month to raise his average to .276. The month also included an 11-game hitting streak in which Millan batted .444 with seven multi-hit games. He added another 11-game hitting streak (.392) in September and was hovering around the .290 mark before going 1-for-12 in the final three-game series of the year.

The Mets had one of the National League's oldest rosters by the end of 1976. They had five regulars over age 30, and the average age of the starting rotation was 30, as well. Outside of outfielder Lee Mazzilli, the Mets had no prospects in the minors as they headed to 1977 spring training.

The Mets got off to a miserable start, putting the team in last place by May 3. Second-year manager Joe Frazier was fired on Memorial Day and replaced by Torre, who had trouble assembling a healthy, productive infield. General manager Joe McDonald finally acquired some hitting help, but it cost the Mets Dave Kingman and Tom Seaver. New York fell into the cellar for good July 2 and finished last for the first time in 10 years at 64–98.

Millan wasn't around to finish the season. He was hitting .248 in his 91st game of the year when he was asked to enter Game 2 of an August 12 doubleheader at Pittsburgh as a defensive replacement in the sixth inning.

Mario Mendoza hit a grounder to shortstop Doug Flynn, who flipped to Millan as a hard-charging Ed Ott was trying to break up a possible inning-ending double play. Ott barreled into Millan, who took exception to the contact by trying to massage Ott's face with the baseball. Ott picked up the diminutive Millan and threw him to the infield, causing Millan's right shoulder to separate. The injury caused Millan to miss the rest of the season, his last in the majors. But he held little animosity toward Ott, even hours after the incident.

"It's funny," Millan said almost 30 years later. "After the thing with Ed Ott—after the game we went out and talked to each other. It wasn't nothing personal. He tried to break the double play. I wasn't outside the line. Things happen, but after the game everything was fine."[141]

The shoulder damage occurred just four months after the opening of the Felix Millan Little League on the Lower East Side of Manhattan. The league flourished in 1978, but Millan wasn't around to oversee its growth.

Millan left North America to play baseball in Japan, signing with the Taiyo Whales and playing for them from 1978 until his retirement in 1980.

Millan eventually returned to the Mets organization and was head of Latin American player development in the 1990s. He was a roving instructor in the minors when he wasn't filling in as a translator or handling visas and passports.

Millan was thankful for his 17 years as a professional baseball player.

"I think I had more good things than negative things and I enjoyed every moment of playing baseball in the United States and in Puerto Rico. I thank God for giving me the ability to play baseball and the knowledge to teach these young kids."[142]

When he's not coaching, Millan spends these days in Florida with his wife, Mercy. The two raised one son and one daughter. Meanwhile, the Felix Millan Little League continues to produce young talent in New York City.

First ML game	Braves vs. Giants, 6/2/66
First Mets game	vs. Phillies, 4/6/73
First ML hit	single vs. Bobby Bolin, Giants, 6/2/66 (with Braves)
First Mets hit	double vs. Steve Carlton, Phillies, 4/6/73
First ML homer	solo HR vs. Sammy Ellis, @ Reds, 9/28/67 (with Braves)
First Mets homer	solo HR vs. Tom Bradley, Giants, 6/13/73
First ML RBI	RBI FC vs. Don Dennis, Cardinals, 6/5/66 (with Braves)

First Mets RBI   RBI triple vs. Reggie Cleveland, @ Cardinals, 4/11/73

Most hits, ML game	6, Braves vs. Giants, 7/6/70
Most hits, Mets game	4, 9 times
Most homers, ML game	1, 22 times
Most homers, Mets game	1, 8 times
Most RBIs, ML game	5, Braves vs. Astros, 9/20/72
Most RBIs, Mets game	4, vs. Cubs, 7/2/75; @ Cubs, 7/26/75

Acquired: Traded by the Braves with George Stone for Danny Frisella and Gary Gentry, 11/2/72.

Deleted: Signed by the Taiyo Whales (Japan) after the 1977 season.

NL All-Star, 1969, 1970, 1971

NL Gold Glove, 1969, 1972

Rey Ordóñez

Shortstop	Bats right, throws right
Born: 11/11/71	Havana, Cuba
Height: 5'9"	Weight: 160 #0, 10

Rey Ordóñez Mets Career

YEAR	GP	AB	R	H	2B	3B	HR	RBI	K	BB	SB	AVG	SLG	OBP
1996	151	502	51	129	12	4	1	30	53	22	1	.257	.303	.289
1997	120	356	35	77	5	3	1	33	36	18	11	.216	.256	.255
1998	153	505	46	124	20	2	1	42	60	23	3	.246	.299	.278
1999	154	520	49	134	24	2	1	60	59	49	8	.258	.317	.319
2000	45	133	10	25	5	0	0	9	16	17	0	.188	.226	.278
2001	149	461	31	114	24	4	3	44	43	34	3	.247	.336	.299
2002	144	460	53	117	25	2	1	42	46	24	2	.254	.324	.292
TOTAL	916	2937	275	720	115	17	8	260	313	187	28	.245	.304	.290

ML Career

YEARS	GP	AB	R	H	2B	3B	HR	RBI	K	BB	SB	AVG	SLG	OBP
96–04	973	3115	291	767	129	17	12	287	339	191	28	.246	.310	.289

Any Mets fan who watched Rey Ordóñez likely has two vivid memories of the Gold Glove shortstop.

The first would be of Ordóñez back-handing a grounder between short and third, taking it on the short hop and—sometimes from his knees—firing to first to nail the runner by a step. It was a play that occurred time and again over his seven years with the team, and damned if he didn't make it look routine within his first two seasons.

The second would be of him at the plate with at least one runner in scoring position and two out in a close game, taking a 2–2 fastball and sending it high into the air before the opposing second baseman snagged it to kill a rally.

Great as he was defensively, Reinaldo (Pereira) Ordóñez never received the love and appreciation given to Bud Harrelson despite being Harrelson's superior with the glove and at the plate. Playing on teams with good hitting in 1999 and 2000, Ordóñez had plenty more opportunities to drive in runs than did Harrelson on the Mets' popgun offenses of the early 1970s. Rey could make 2–3 outstanding plays at short in a game, but fans would call WFAN on the overnight to discuss his inability to drive home the tiebreaking run in the eighth inning of a 4–3 loss.

Ordóñez compiled a .199 average in 156 at-bats with a runner on third and two out and was a lifetime .187 hitter with two strikes. But he left the majors with a .379 average in 162 at-bats with a man on third and less than two out. Ordóñez also was the first Mets shortstop to drive in 60 runs in a season, and only the third with 25 doubles.

Defense was why Ordóñez was signed by the Mets in the first place. He was a wizard at short in his native Cuba and blew away major league scouts with his glove while playing in the independent Northern League immediately after his defection in 1993. Four years after leaving Cuba, Ordóñez garnered the first of three straight Gold Glove awards and eventually set a major league record for most consecutive errorless games as a shortstop.

Ordóñez was with the Cuban national team in Buffalo for the University Games when he defected July 7, 1993, leaving his wife and infant son back home. He was the second Cuban player in history to defect to the United States, two years after pitcher René Arocha. Ordóñez said through an interpreter in a 1994 *New York Times* interview that baseball wasn't his prime reason for leaving his homeland.

"I defected in search of freedom, because there is no such thing as freedom in Cuba. It's tough to get away from the personal freedom thing. It's always being checked on by government officials. Everywhere you go, you have to stay in touch with those officials."[143]

Ordóñez figured it would be a matter of months before he saw his wife and son again. He and his wife, Lisa Maria, divorced shortly before he defected in hopes it would make it easier for her to eventually obtain a U.S. visa that would reunite the family. Her father, who had defected from Cuba in the 1980s, arranged for Ordóñez to be met in Buffalo by a family friend and whisked away to freedom. She told the *New York Times* in 1999 she encouraged Ordóñez to defect but added her husband left Cuba feeling unsure he could pull off the defection.

"There is no food for my son to eat in Cuba," Ordóñez told the *New York Times* shortly after his defection. "I felt making $118 a month, which I get playing baseball, there was little I could do. I can do more for them by being here."[144]

Ordóñez went from the Cuban nationals to the St. Paul Saints, hitting .283 with seven RBIs and 10 runs scored in 15 games. Saints owner Marvin Goldklang said it didn't take long for Ordóñez to impress the coaches.

"During his first workout with the staff, it took 75 grounders before they could get him to miss one," said Goldklang, who also was a minority owner of the Yankees at the time. "Several scouts told me he would have been a first- or second-round pick in the Rule IV draft if he had been eligible. And one scout told me he's better defensively than any shortstop in the American League."[145]

Ordóñez was one of several players to flee Cuba in 1993. Major League Baseball decided to parcel out the defectors by holding a weighted lottery based on the teams' records in '93. Since the Mets stumbled through a 59-win season, they chose first and selected Ordóñez.

The Mets assigned Ordóñez to Class A St. Lucie for the start of the 1994 season. Ordóñez didn't stay there long, earning a promotion to Double A Binghamton after hitting .309 with 21 doubles, 11 stolen bases, 40 RBIs, and 47 runs scored in 79 games. He earned a trip to the Florida State League all-star game and was third in the circuit in hitting at the time of his recall.

Ordóñez batted .262 in 48 games for Binghamton and ended up with a .291 average, 31 doubles, 60 RBIs, and 69 runs scored for the year. He received a Doubleday Award as the MVP at St. Lucie after showing the potential to become a highly productive major league shortstop.

Norfolk was Ordóñez's next stop. He led the Triple A team in games and at-bats, and tied for the team lead with 21 doubles, but his average sunk to .214. However, Ordóñez also hit .289 with runners in scoring position and .308 (16-for-52) with runners in scoring position and two out.

He continued to play exceptional defense, leading all International League shortstops with 646 total chances and turning 88 double plays.

There were also personal changes in Ordóñez's life. His divorce stuck after Lisa Maria was denied a visa in 1994. Ordóñez soon remarried and became a father for the second time when his new wife, Gloryanne, gave birth to a daughter, Sonia, in August 1995. Meanwhile, Rey's son remained in Cuba.

José Vizcaíno was the Mets' starting shortstop in 1995, hitting .287 and committing just 10 errors (.984) in 135 games. When the Mets opened the '96 season, Vizcaíno had been moved over to second base to make room for Ordóñez, who made the team after hitting .254 in 22 exhibition games.

Ordóñez immediately drew comparisons to Harrelson and Kevin Elster, the Mets' best defensive shortstops at this point in club history. Ordóñez had unbelievable range and a quick release, allowing him to turn sure hits into outs. Like most shortstops, Rey rushed some plays and occasionally made ill-advised throws that led to his career-high 27 errors.

Ordóñez made an impression in the season opener against the Cardinals April 1. With the Mets trailing 6–3 in the seventh, Ordóñez dropped to his knees to take a low relay throw from left fielder Bernard Gilkey while Royce Clayton made the turn at third. Ordóñez pivoted and fired a 150-foot heave to the plate to nail Clayton. Moments later, he provided a single in a four-run rally that gave the Mets a 7–6 victory.

"The kid is on his knees with the ball," said St. Louis manager Tony LaRussa. "We've got a guy halfway home and I figured that's seven."[146]

Mets skipper Dallas Green was equally impressed. "When you throw somebody out from your knees on a relay, you're doing something special. He's got great feet, a great arm. His instincts are tremendous. He's special."[147]

Not many in the Mets organization expected Ordóñez to hit like he did in April. He ended the month on a 14-game hitting streak that began with a 4-for-5 outing at Colorado April 14. Ordóñez added six more multi-hit games to the streak, giving him a .354 average heading into May. He continued to hit well until June, when a month-long 13-for-84 drought (.155) trimmed his average from .312 to .260. He finished the year with a .257 average, still well above expectations at the start of the season. His first home run came September 19 at Philadelphia, beginning a four-year stretch in which he belted his lone home run of the season in the final month.

Surprisingly, his defense became cause for concern as the season wore on. Ordóñez continued to make the tough plays, but the routine ones became the toughest. He cost the Mets a couple of victories but committed just three errors over the final five weeks.

"He has had a lot of peaks and valleys this year," said Green shortly before he was fired in late August. "He started out with a great peak offensively and defensively, getting the accolades and all the ESPN highlights. But reality set in when things started going downhill. But we've had a couple of good talks and he has righted himself after those talks. I feel comfortable he's going to be fine."[148]

Green was spot on in his assessment. Ordóñez claimed his first Gold Glove in 1997, committing only nine errors in 535 chances to lead all shortstops with a .983 fielding percentage. He remained rock steady on the field despite a broken left hand that kept him out of action from June 2 to July 11.

Ordóñez continued to backhand balls hit toward third base, sinking to his knees before rising and throwing in one motion. It was a highly unorthodox way to play balls hit to the left of short, but his exceptional balance and fast release kept base hits and errors to a minimum. He also improved under the tutelage of coach Cookie Rojas, who implored Ordóñez to know the speed of the base runners.

"You heard he made a lot of errors," said teammate and first baseman John Olerud in 1997. "And you figure he might be a little wild. But he's been right there almost every time; I haven't had to dig many throws out of the dirt."[149]

Offensively, Ordóñez was a disappointment. He went 2-for-3 with a solo homer and three RBIs September 2, and 2-for-4 with a ribbie a day later to put his season average at .237. He wouldn't get another hit until September 19, going 0-for-37 to set a team hitless-streak record for nonpitchers. Ordóñez's average never climbed above .250 after July 20 as he finished with a .216 mark for the Mets, who finished with a winning record for the first time in seven years.

Valentine felt it was time Ordóñez started to contribute at the plate. The skipper often pinch-hit for Ordóñez in the late innings of a close ballgame in 1997, but those days were over as the team changed calendars.

Ordóñez hit a game-ending grounder with the potential tying run on third in an 8–7 loss to the Cubs at Wrigley Field. It would have been a typical situation to pinch hit for Ordóñez in '97, but Valentine felt it time for Ordóñez to become more responsible at the plate.

Two days later, Ordóñez delivered a two-out, tiebreaking single in the ninth inning to give the Mets a 2–1 win at Milwaukee. One reason the Mets were in position to win was his diving stop that turned a potential RBI single into an inning-ending double-play grounder.

"Rey becoming a complete player that we can count on all-around, that's one of our goals," Valentine said after giving Ordóñez a chance to win the game.[150]

"If Bobby feels like that, it gives me confidence," Ordóñez said through an interpreter. "I feel a lot more confident knowing I'll be getting four at-bats instead of being pinch-hit for, like in the past."[151]

However, his production in '98 was sporadic. He put together an 11-game hitting streak in early April and hit .400 (24-for-60) over his final 19 games of July. But from April 21 to July 4, Ordóñez hit only .216 in 63 games.

Once again, Ordóñez waited until September before hitting his lone homer of the year. He hit a two-run blast September 15 at Houston and added an RBI double that gave the Mets a brief lead in the 11th before the Astros won 6–5 in 12 innings.

New York led the wild-card by one game over the Cubs with five games left in the season. The Mets proceeded to lose all five games while Ordóñez went 2-for-16 with one RBI. He ended the year batting .246 with 42 RBIs and 46 runs scored. One promising stat was his .286 average from the seventh to ninth innings of games. But the fans were getting a little impatient with Ordóñez, who committed 17 errors after making just nine in 1997.

Ordóñez quieted his naysayers in 1999 by hitting .258 with 60 RBIs, 49 runs scored, and 24 doubles. He was fifth on the team in runs batted in and sixth in doubles as the Mets earned their first postseason berth in 11 years.

But the year wasn't without a few struggles. Ordóñez was benched for a game in April after throwing a fit when his name was left off the starting lineup. But he caught fire later in the month, embarking on a 47-game segment in which he hit .344 to lift his average from .170 to .303 by June 22. The stretch included a 9–6 win over the Cardinals as Ordóñez delivered three hits, drove in a pair of runs, and scored twice from second on infield grounders.

The average was at .292 July 1 before he went just 10-for-76 over his next 22 games. His season mark was down to .249 until he launched his first career grand slam in an 11–1 rout of the Phillies September 18. For the fourth straight year, Ordóñez waited until September to smack his lone home run.

The season also included a brawl with teammate Luis Lopez on the team bus at San Diego in early September. The fight left Ordóñez with a bruise under his left eye and a gash that required six stitches.

The Mets also had to scrap to reach the postseason after blowing the wild-card lead during the final week of the season. They were two games out with three remaining before Ordóñez went 4-for-10 in a three-game sweep of the Pirates, putting the Mets in a one-game playoff with the Reds. New York reached the division series by posting a 5–0 victory at Cincinnati.

Ordóñez hit well in his first postseason series, going 4-for-14 (.286) with two RBIs against the Diamondbacks. He laid down a squeeze bunt in the series opener and slapped an RBI single that put the Mets ahead to stay in a 9–2 rout of Arizona in Game 3.

The Mets hit poorly in the championship series yet almost became the first team in major league history to force a Game 7 after dropping the first three contests. Mike Piazza batted just .167, Robin Ventura hit .120, and Rickey Henderson compiled a .174 mark. But no one hit worse than Ordóñez, who closed the series on an 0-for-16 skid to finish 1-for-24 (.042) against the Braves. It was a tough way to end what was his most productive season in the majors.

Shortly after the postseason, Ordóñez received his third and final Gold Glove after recording just four errors in 640 chances. His .994 fielding percentage was a National League record for shortstops and just .002 below the major league mark held by Cal Ripken. Ordóñez also played errorless ball over the final 100 games of the season to set a record for shortstops.

The Mets avoided salary arbitration with Ordóñez by signing him to a four-year contract in January 2000. The contract did not include a no-trade clause as the team continued its interest in Mariners shortstop Alex Rodriguez. Despite his flashy glove and timely hits in 1999, the Mets continued to look for a better option at short.

"They've been talking about that ever since I've been on the team," Ordóñez said through his wife and interpreter. "It's never happened. I just hope I can stay in New York."[152]

The Mets had to look for another shortstop eight weeks into the 2000 season. Ordóñez was hitting only .188 when he broke his arm while covering second base, causing him to miss the rest of the season. The Mets tried Kurt Abbott and Melvin Mora at short for a few weeks, but both were defensive liabilities. Desperate for a glove man to stick between Ventura and Edgardo Alfonzo, general manager Steve Phillips sent Mora to the Orioles for Mike Bordick, the best fielding shortstop in the American League at the time.

But Bordick was a rental and would return to the Orioles through free agency the following winter. Mora went on to have an excellent career with the O's, landing on two AL All-Star teams and twice hitting 27 homers in a season.

The broken arm had done considerable damage to the Mets. They managed to win the National League pennant without Ordóñez but could have used Mora in the outfield over the next few years.

Rey Ordonez makes a dive to throw out a player during a 1996 game.

Al Leiter lamented the fact that Ordóñez wasn't around for the postseason. Leiter gave up the World Series–winning hit to Luis Sojo in the ninth inning of Game 5.

"The fact that Rey's the best shortstop out there, there might have been an opportunity for him to knock the ball down," said Leiter the following winter. "Whether that saves a run or not, we'll never know. But maybe."[153]

Ordóñez entered 2001 spring training wanting to improve his offense. His defense hadn't tarnished after the injury, but his bat was as anemic as ever.

"We're not crippled by whatever his offensive production is," Phillips said, "but we're better if he's better."[154]

Ordóñez agreed, saying he needed to make changes in his hitting approach. Rey played 149 games in 2001 and posted a .336 slugging percentage, his career high as a Met. He also belted three home runs, almost matching his career output up to then. But his .247 batting average and .299 on-base percentage left management wanting more. Only four other National Leaguers posted a lower on-base percentage while qualifying for the batting title.

Ordóñez got hot in mid-August, around the time the Mets began to climb up the NL East standings. He batted .330 with two homers, 15 RBIs, and 16 runs scored from

August 16 to September 19, helping the Mets go 20–6 and pull within 5½ games of the first-place Braves. But he cooled off once the Mets returned to Shea following the September 11 attacks, which caused a nine-day disruption to the season.

The Mets' 40-man roster featured 19 new players after Phillips finished dealing during the winter of 2002. Ordóñez remained on the team after hitting .280 in the second half, but he didn't take his roster spot for granted. He worked hard during the offseason, adding weight training to a regimen that included the usual hitting, running, and throwing.

"It's a big difference coming into spring training in shape," said Ordóñez, now 29 years old. "This was my first year I worked real hard in the off-season. Before I was stupid. I understand to hit I have to work hard and be a little stronger. It's not like you're hitting 20, 25 home runs, but you never know."[155]

The extra training had its pluses and minuses in 2002. Ordóñez set career highs with 25 doubles and 53 runs scored while hitting .254, well above his career average. But his on-base percentage slipped to .292, the fifth worst among National Leaguers with at least 475 at-bats. More important, his bulkier frame may have led to his more limited range at shortstop. Ordóñez still displayed a flashy glove, but with fewer jaw-dropping plays. He committed 19 errors, the most since his rookie season.

The Mets were at a crossroads in the fall of 2002. They finished in the NL East cellar for the first time in six years, causing Phillips to overhaul the roster once again. This time, Ordóñez was one of the first to go.

New York shipped Ordóñez to the Devil Rays after agreeing to pick up $4.5 million of his $6.5 million salary. The Mets received Russ Johnson and Josh Pressley, neither of whom ever played for New York.

The Ordóñez deal was made possible by the rapid progession of José Reyes, who made his major league debut for the Mets June 10, 2003, one month after Ordóñez played his final game for Tampa Bay.

Rey got off to a fantastic start with the Devil Rays, producing 11 multi-hit games and batting .316 while starting the team's first 34 contests. He had three home runs by April 18 to tie his career high with 146 games left on the schedule. But his season ended May 8, when he tore a ligament in his left knee.

Ordóñez was granted free agency in October before signing with the Padres in January 2004. The Padres hoped Ordóñez would keep the shortstop position warm for Khalil Greene, who was almost ready to play in the majors every day. But Ordóñez left training before the end of the exhibition season.

"He was playing very, very well for us, but he looked at his competition and saw it the way we did," said Padres general manager Kevin Towers in May 2004. "He figured for the first time in his career he wasn't going to win the job, so rather than get released, he thought the best way to handle it was to jump ship and leave."[156]

Ordóñez resurfaced with the Cubs May 18, six days after he was officially released by the Padres. The Cubs got little out of Ordóñez, who hit .164 in 23 games and failed to display much defensive skill.

The year wasn't a total loss for Ordóñez. He became a U.S. citizen in August 2004, 11 years after his defection. But he also put his major league career on hold for two years before signing a minor league contract with the Mariners in November 2006.

Ordóñez almost made it to Opening Day. He was on the Mariners' original 25-man roster but was reassigned to the minor league camp after the team acquired Jason Ellison from the Giants. Saying he was too old for the minors, Ordóñez, then 35, asked to be released in an effort to hook up with another major league team. It never happened.

ML/Mets debut	vs. Cardinals, 4/1/96
1st ML/Mets hit	single vs. Rick Honeycutt, Cardinals, 4/1/96
1st ML/Mets homer	solo homer vs. Rich Hunter, @ Phillies, 9/19/96
1st ML/Mets RBI	fielder's choice/E6 vs. Alan Benes, Cardinals, 4/4/96
Most hits, ML/Mets game	4, 8 times
Most homers, ML game	1, 12 times
Most homers, Mets game	1, 8 times
Most RBIs, ML game	4, 4 times
Most RBIs, Mets game	4, vs. Phils, 9/18/99; @ Marlins, 5/31/02; vs. Astros, 7/31/02

Acquired: Signed as an amateur free agent, 10/29/93.
Deleted: Traded to the Devil Rays for two players to be named (Russ Johnson and Josh Pressley), 12/15/02.
NL Gold Glove, 1997, 1998, 1999

Jesse Orosco

Pitcher	Bats right, throws left
Born: 4/21/57	Santa Barbara, California
Height: 6'2"	Weight: 185 #61, 47

Jesse Orosco Mets Career

YEAR	GP/GS	IP	H	R	ER	K	BB	W-L	SV	ERA
1979	18/2	35	33	20	19	22	22	1–2	0	4.89
1981	8/0	17.1	13	4	3	18	6	0–1	1	1.56
1982	54/2	109.1	92	37	33	89	40	4–10	4	2.72
1983	62/0	110	76	27	18	84	38	13–7	17	1.47
1984	60/0	87	58	29	25	85	34	10–6	31	2.59
1985	54/0	79	66	26	24	68	34	8–6	17	2.73
1986	58/0	81	64	23	21	62	35	8–6	21	2.33
1987	58/0	77	78	41	38	78	31	3–9	16	4.44
Total	372/4	595.2	480	207	181	506	240	47–47	107	2.73

Mets Career/Batting

GP	AB	R	H	2B	3B	HR	RBI	K	BB	SB	AVG
372	56	2	10	0	0	0	4	23	6	0	.179

ML Career

YEAR	GP/GS	IP	H	R	ER	K	BB	W-L	SV	ERA
79–03	1252/4	1295	1055	512	455	1179	581	87–80	144	3.16

Jesse Orosco's lengthy major league career took him full circle. He was drafted and signed by the Twins in 1978 but didn't pitch for them until 25 years later. In between, he was a Met, a Dodger, an Indian, a Brewer, an Oriole, a Cardinal, a Dodger again, a Padre, and a Yankee before coming to the Twin Cities for his final major league season in 2003.

The Mets were in the process of purging the last remaining players from their 1973 pennant-winning team when they acquired Orosco from the Twins for Jerry Koosman. He made the 1979 Mets out of spring training and retired the only batter he faced in a 10–6 win at Wrigley Field on Opening Day. He pitched well in his first six appearances, allowing just four hits and three walks over eight innings while posting a 1.13 ERA. But he went 0–2 with a 6.87 ERA over his next 10 relief outings, beginning with his first major league loss May 5 at San Francisco. He made two starts in June (0–0, 4.15 ERA in 8⅔ innings) before spending the rest of the '79 season as a starter for Triple A Tidewater.

Orosco was with Double A Jackson for all of 1980, starting just one of his 37 games and picking up three saves while going 4–4 with a 3.68 ERA. He was a spot starter for the 1981 Tides, where he was 9–5 with a 3.31 ERA. He was recalled by the Mets that September, 27 months after his last major league appearance. Orosco looked like a potential closer as he struck out 18 in 17⅓ innings while allowing just three earned runs. The Cubs nicked him for three runs in the Mets' 10–9 loss September 24. His first big-league save came September 18, when he held the Cardinals to four hits while striking out four over three shutout innings. Orosco's September audition was the start of a record-setting career as a reliever.

Orosco continued to strike out batters at a decent rate in 1982, his first full season in the majors. His 89:40 strikeout-to-walk ratio was exceptional for a rookie, and two of his 10 losses were as a starter. He emerged as the team's top set-up man, although he entered just 23 games when the Mets were tied or leading. His first save of the season didn't come until July 21, when he tossed four shutout innings of a 6–2 win over the Giants. The Mets won just 15 of the 54 games in which Orosco pitched, but he contributed four wins, five holds, and four saves.

Neil Allen remained the Mets' closer at the start of the 1983 season, but Orosco took over the role by the end of April and was selected to the All-Star Game. Orosco set a team record with 13 relief victories and recorded a team-high 17 saves to become the only Mets pitcher to lead the team in both categories for the same season. Just as impressive was his 1.47 ERA, 1.04 WHIP, and three homers allowed in 110 innings. Orosco finished third in the NL Cy Young Award voting and received MVP consideration.

Orosco pitched four hitless innings to win two games in a series against the Reds in May. He trumped that by winning both ends of a July 31 doubleheader against the Pirates, pitching a total of four innings and earning the victory in the 12th inning each time. It was the second occasion Orosco had pitched at least two innings while appearing in both ends on a twin bill.

For the 1983 season, Orosco allowed just 10 of his 37 inherited runners to score, and he never let his ERA climb above 1.62 after April 15. He won nine straight decisions, falling one shy of Tom Seaver's then–team record. His season ended with a save and two losses in his last three appearances before he was shut down for the final two weeks due to elbow stiffness.

Orosco continued his exceptional pitching in 1984, only this time he was working for a postseason contender. He pitched scoreless ball over 12 innings of his first seven outings, picking up the win or the save each time. He saved both ends of a doubleheader twice during the year and worked at least two innings in 25 of his 60 appearances. Orosco saved 31 games, smashing Tug McGraw's team record of 27 set in 1972. The mark would stand until John Franco picked up 33 saves in 1990.

Orosco had just two appearances that would be considered embarrassing. He surrendered four runs in the eighth inning of a 10–6 loss to the Astros May 5 and was rocked for five runs in an inning versus the Cardinals September 11. But the Mets were winners in 48 of the 60 games he pitched as the team seriously challenged for the NL East

title for the first time in 11 years. Orosco was rewarded for his efforts with another All-Star Game selection.

Orosco's save total dropped back down to 17 in 1985, but he now had help in the bullpen. Rookie Roger McDowell carried some of the load, tying for the team lead with 17 saves while appearing in a team-high 62 games. Together, they went 14–11 with a 2.79 ERA as the Mets won 98 games, then the second-best mark in team history.

Orosco continued to make a habit of killing rallies, allowing just nine of 46 inherited runners to score. Between 1983 and '85, Orosco had entered games with a total of 119 inherited runners. Just 30 crossed the plate. He blew eight saves in 1985 and was credited with the victory in four of them.

Orosco finally showed some cracks during a huge three-game series against the Cardinals at Shea Stadium in September. He served up a leadoff homer to Cesar Cedeno in the 10th inning of a heartbreaking 1–0 loss September 11, which left the two teams in a tie for first. Orosco also gave up a game-tying homer to Willie McGee in the ninth inning a day later before getting the win on a Keith Hernandez single in the bottom of the ninth.

Orosco earned the victory in one of the most memorable games of the season. He pitched in and out of a two-on, two-out jam in the bottom of the 10th at St. Louis before Darryl Strawberry launched a clock-breaking solo homer in the 11th. Orosco sealed the win with a scoreless 11th that gave the Mets a chance to grab a share of first place by the time they left St. Louis. (The Mets split the next two games of the series to fall two games back.)

Manager Davey Johnson continued to trot out his two-headed monster of Orosco and McDowell during the 1986 season as the two combined for 43 saves in the Mets' team-record 108 victories. Orosco picked up 21 saves but also blew eight leads in what became a pressure-free regular season. Orosco's most memorable appearance of the season came in a game in which he didn't record a decision or save. He entered in the 10th inning of a tie game at Cincinnati before allowing a one-out single to Pete Rose. Pinch-runner Eric Davis stole second and third, but his slide on the second steal irritated third baseman Ray Knight. Knight threw a punch that led to the best Mets-Reds brawl since the Pete Rose–Bud Harrelson fracas in the 1973 playoffs. Knight was thrown out of the game and replaced by catcher Gary Carter. After a strikeout, Roger McDowell replaced Orosco, who moved into right field to replace Kevin Mitchell! Orosco and McDowell would take turns between the mound and the outfield, depending on who was at the plate. Orosco even caught a fly ball hit by Tony Perez before the Mets eventually won it in the 14th inning on Howard Johnson's three-run homer.

Orosco finished 8–6 for the second straight year while lowering his ERA to 2.33, his best since 1983. He had won 44 games as a reliever to break the Mets' all-time record previously held by Tug McGraw. Orosco would tack on three more victories during the 1986 NLCS.

Jesse Orosco (47) shouts as he greets first baseman Keith Hernandez after a Mets win over the St. Louis Cardinals on October 1, 1985.

Orosco entered in the eighth inning of Game 3 with the Mets trailing the Astros 5–4. One inning later, he came away with his first postseason victory when Len Dykstra hit a two-run homer off Dave Smith in the bottom of the ninth.

Orosco also worked the 11th and 12th innings of Game 5 before Gary Carter's RBI single in the bottom of the 12th gave the Mets a 2–1 win. Then came Game 6, when Orosco finally allowed a run for the first time in the series. The Mets had taken a 4–3 lead in the top of the 14th, but the Astros tied the game on Billy Hatcher's homer in the bottom of the inning. Two innings later, Orosco was asked to protect a 7–4 lead. Orosco allowed RBI singles by Hatcher and Glenn Davis before striking out Kevin Bass to end the game and the series.

Astros pitcher and former Met Mike Scott walked away with MVP honors for the series, but Orosco accounted for three-fourths of the Mets wins.

Orosco was just as good in the World Series, and his bat contributed to the Game 7 victory. He picked up the save in Game 4 as the Mets knotted the Series at two games apiece. He also worked a scoreless eighth in the Mets' incredible Game 6 win over the Red Sox.

Orosco was put in an incredible pressure situation in Game 7. Roger McDowell had just surrendered a two-run double by Dwight Evans to get the Red Sox to within a run at 6–5. Orosco entered the game with the tying run at second and nobody out before retiring the last three batters in order to end the threat. The eighth inning is somewhat lost in Mets lore since the team scored twice in the eighth to go ahead 8–5. But Orosco killed any momentum the Bosox might have had after the Mets turned a 3–0 deficit into a 6–3 lead.

Orosco came to the plate in the bottom of the eighth with a runner on second and the Mets leading 7–5. He padded the lead with an RBI single, then tossed a perfect ninth to end the Series. In a repeat of the final out in the NLCS, Orosco threw his glove into the air after fanning Marty Barrett for the final out.

Orosco could have been the World Series MVP after firing 5⅔ scoreless innings in four games. But Ray Knight came away with the honor after producing clutch hits in Games 6 and 7, including the go-ahead homer in the final game.

The Mets hoisted their World Series flag before the season opener April 7 against Pittsburgh. Orosco picked up the save in the opener, and worked two innings for the save in the Mets' next game. Little did he know it at the time, but the lefty was about to have his worst season as a Met.

Orosco suddenly had a penchant for serving up homers in big spots, and the longball would doom the 1987 Mets as they finished three games behind the Cardinals. It wasn't just the fact that Orosco was feeding the gopher, but rather who was hitting them. On April 18 at St. Louis, he entered in the bottom of the ninth with the Mets ahead 8–7. The lead evaporated when Orosco gave up Tom Pagnozzi's first major league hit, an RBI single with one out. Orosco issued a two-out walk to Ozzie Smith before Tommy Herr zapped him for a walkoff grand slam. Herr had belted all of 16 homers in 3,200 career at-bats before sending the Cardinals' fans home happy.

Three months later, Orosco was asked to protect another one-run lead against the Astros. But rookie Gerald Young knotted the score with an RBI single in his 61st big-league at-bat before Billy Hatcher smacked a three-run homer to put the Astros up 5–2. Yes, the same Billy Hatcher who nicked Orosco for a game-tying solo homer in the 14th inning of Game 6 of the NLCS.

There are two homers that seemed to bury the Mets in September. One was Terry Pendleton's game-tying, two-run blow off McDowell in the ninth inning of a 6–4, 10-inning loss to the Cardinals after the Mets carried a one-hitter into the inning. Orosco followed McDowell by allowing two runs in the 10th to absorb the loss.

The last of Orosco's game-ending home run pitches allowed the Redbirds to clinch at least a tie for the NL East title. The Mets and Phillies were tied 3–3 with one out in the bottom of the 10th when Luis Aguayo stepped into the batter's box with a .205 average and 11 homers for the season. He walked out of the batter's box hitting .209 with 12 homers and slamming a solo shot off Orosco at the Vet.

Orosco never got his 1987 ERA below 4.40 after April 14. He allowed just six of his 25 inherited runners to score (24 percent), but 41 of his own 109 base runners were able to circle the bases (38 percent).

The man who had nasty stuff and a world of confidence suddenly appeared vulnerable. The Mets decided it was a good time to part with Orosco, sending him to the Dodgers in a three-team, eight-player deal with the Athletics.

Orosco would save only 39 games the rest of his career, only eight more than his career high in 1984. But he did it while pitching 16 more seasons and setting a major league record for appearances by a pitcher.

Ironically, Orosco faced the Mets in the playoffs during his first year with the Dodgers. He surrendered two runs without retiring a batter while the Mets were scoring five times in the bottom of the eighth to pull out an 8–4 victory in Game 3. Orosco almost blew Game 4 after Kirk Gibson homered off Roger McDowell to put the Dodgers ahead 5–4. Orosco walked his first batter, Keith Hernandez, to load the bases with one out, then went 3–0 to Darryl Strawberry before manager Tommy Lasorda raced to the mound to give his reliever a pep-talk/butt-kicking. Strawberry popped out to second for the second out before Orel Hershiser retired Kevin McReynolds, thanks to a game-saving grab by center fielder John Shelby.

Lasorda didn't use Orosco in the '88 World Series, and he was allowed to join the Indians via free agency.

Orosco was a Met again for about three months prior to the 2000 season. He was dealt by the Orioles for Chuck McElroy in December 1999, and later sent by the Mets to the Cardinals for Joe McEwing.

Orosco also was reacquired by the Dodgers before spending his final season with the Padres, Yankees, and Twins. He topped Hoyt Wilhelm's all-time mark of 1,070 games by 182 (1,252) before finally retiring following the 2003 season. He threw his final pitch at age 46.

ML/Mets debut   @ Cubs, 4/5/79 (1/3 IP, 0 H, 0 ER, 0 K, 0 BB)
First ML/Mets strikeout   Greg Luzinski, @ Phillies,
                                     4/20/79
First ML/Mets win   vs. Phillies, 4/22/79
First ML/Mets save vs. Cardinals, 9/18/81
Most strikeouts, ML game   5, 12 times, 8 times with Mets
Acquired: Traded by the Twins 2/7/79 as the player to be named in a
         deal that also sent Greg Field to the Mets for Jerry
         Koosman, 12/8/78.
Deleted: Traded to the Dodgers in a three-team deal with the Athletics.
         The Mets also received Kevin Tapani and Wally
         Whitehurst from the Athletics, and Jack Savage
         from the Dodgers. The Athletics received Bob
         Welch and Matt Young from the Dodgers. The
         Dodgers received Orosco from the Mets, and
         Alfredo Griffin and Jay Howell from the Athletics,
         12/11/87.

NL All-Star, 1983, 1984

Mike Piazza

Catcher, First Baseman   Bats right, throws right
Born: 9/4/68   Norristown, Pennsylvania
Height: 6'3"   Weight: 197   #31

Mike Piazza Mets Career

YEAR	GP	AB	R	H	2B	3B	HR	RBI	K	BB	SB	AVG	SLG	OBP
1998	109	394	67	137	33	0	23	76	53	47	1	.348	.607	.417
1999	141	534	100	162	25	0	40	124	70	51	2	.303	.575	.361
2000	136	482	90	156	26	0	38	113	69	58	4	.324	.614	.398
2001	141	503	81	151	29	0	36	94	87	67	0	.300	.573	.384
2002	135	478	69	134	23	2	33	98	82	57	0	.280	.544	.359
2003	68	234	37	67	13	0	11	34	40	35	0	.286	.483	.377
2004	129	455	47	121	21	0	20	54	78	68	0	.266	.444	.362
2005	113	398	41	100	23	0	19	62	67	41	0	.251	.452	.326
TOTAL	972	3478	532	1028	193	2	220	655	546	424	7	.296	.542	.373

ML Career

YEAR	GP	AB	R	H	2B	3B	HR	RBI	K	BB	SB	AVG	SLG	OBP
92–07	1912	6911	1048	2127	344	8	427	1335	1113	759	17	.308	.545	.377

There is no doubt Mike Piazza is among the five most popular players in Mets history. When healthy, Piazza was the team's most devastating hitter since Darryl Strawberry and its best drawing card. Fans at Shea would delay a trip to the concession stands or bathrooms if a potential Piazza at-bat drew near.

Nobody wanted to miss the game-altering ability he demonstrated with a three-run homer to cap a 10-run eighth against the Braves, or his game-winning, two-run homer in the Mets' first home game after the 9/11 attacks. Piazza also could dominate in long stretches, such as the 15-game RBI streak he put together in 2000.

When Piazza left the Mets in 2005, he was No. 1 on the team's all-time list with a .542 slugging average, second with 220 home runs and 655 RBIs, third with a .297 batting average and 415 extra-base hits, and fourth with 193 doubles and a .393 on-base percentage.

No one was better during his first 3½ seasons with the ballclub, although it took a few months before Mets fans warmed up to the 12-time All-Star. Piazza didn't hit his first Met homer until his eighth game and belted only five in his first 43 contests. Although he hit .331 with 14 doubles during those 43 games, he drove in just 17 runs as the Mets went only 21–22.

Fans expected a whole lot more and began to boo every time he failed to produce with a runner on base. After two months on the team, he was receiving the same treatment normally reserved at the time for Rey Ordóñez. Whether it was his pending free agency or the pressures of playing on a new team, Piazza looked like he was pressing whenever he came to the plate with men on base.

Piazza was coming off his finest season when he began discussions on a contract extension with the Dodgers in the winter of 1998. Unable to reach an agreement, the Dodgers shopped him around until they found a taker on May 14. The Marlins, looking to unload the contracts of Charles Johnson, Bobby Bonilla, and Gary Sheffield, sent the trio and two others to Los Angeles for Piazza and Todd Zeile. Eight days later, Piazza was a Met in a deal that turned prospects Preston Wilson and Ed Yarnall into Marlins.

The acquisition of Piazza was done through a media smokescreen. Some within the organization admitted anonymously that the team was looking to get the All-Star. But general manager Steve Phillips said otherwise while reminding all who would listen that he already had a good catcher in Todd Hundley, who was coming off major elbow surgery and had yet to make his 1998 season debut.

"I'd have the best platoon catching tandem in the history of baseball," said Phillips a few days before the trade. "But I don't see a fit for us. For me to give up chips to get a player for the rest of this year who duplicates—when healthy—one of our strengths, it really doesn't make sense to do anything like that."[157]

"We've got arguably one of the top three catchers in baseball ourselves," Phillips added in reference to Hundley, who wasn't expected back until after the All-Star break. With the team battling for a playoff berth, there was no time to wait for Hundley.

Talk of Piazza coming to the Mets didn't sit well with Hundley, who hinted he might take the entire season off to rehabilitate his elbow if Piazza returned.

"If you can make a deal like that one, it's like getting Barry Bonds; it's like Griffey Jr. Why should I even take the chance of coming back? If we can get that type of player, why even risk it? Let him have it. He can be a free agent next year and get $10 million or $15 million. I'll see you next year."[158]

Getting Piazza seemed a no-brainer on WFAN as Mets fans called into the radio station seething over the team's supposed disinterest in the slugger. Mike Francesa and Chris Russo used their show to implore the Mets to make the deal—any deal—for Piazza. Mets co-owner Fred Wilpon went on the station to diffuse the criticism, saying the team had four offers on the table for a star player. While Wilpon was in full spin control, co-owner Nelson Doubleday was urging Phillips to strike a deal for Piazza.[159]

Wilpon declined to mention the names of those players during a Thursday interview. By Friday, Piazza was a Met and Phillips was singing a different tune.

"I'm ecstatic to be able to acquire an offensive force that instantly adds credibility to our lineup," gushed Phillips just days after saying Piazza wasn't a good fit.[160]

In many ways, Mets fans, and not Phillips, brought Piazza to New York.

Piazza made an effort to avoid stepping on Hundley's toes immediately after the trade, mentioning the logjam at catcher and saying he'd do whatever asked to help the team. But he also recognized the transition may not go smoothly.

"I know the media in New York is bigger than in Los Angeles, so it's not going to be easy. I'm definitely not Superman, so I just want to try to get in there and help the team as much as possible and contribute and just kind of settle down a little bit."[161]

The Mets ranked last in the National League in home runs and slugging percentage at the time of the trade, and were next to last in runs scored. Closer John Franco was so appreciative of Piazza's presence that he gave up his jersey No. 31 for Piazza and switched to No. 45, Tug McGraw's old number.

Any contributions from Piazza would be a blessing, and he came through in his first game May 23 against the Brewers at Shea by hitting an RBI double and catching Al Leiter's four-hitter in a 3–0 victory. The Mets drew close to 33,000 for the game, which at the time was their third-largest crowd of the season. Walk-up ticket sales were noticed by Franco as he tried to make his way to the ballpark.

"I got stuck in traffic," Franco said. "First time in a long time I got stuck in traffic coming in here."[162]

In addition to surrendering his number to Piazza, Franco also had the guest bedroom in his new house waiting for his new catcher, who needed a place to stay until the Mets went on the road following their weekend series with the Brewers.

"I've known Mike a long time," Franco said. "He's perfect for this city. He's young, single, a billboard kind of guy. Fifth Avenue is going to eat him up. He'll find out that if you're a favorite in New York, the fans will go crazy. It's going to be like when Reggie Jackson came to the Yankees. He's a marquee guy.

"This is what it was like in the '80s when the Mets were getting Carter and Hernandez and Strawberry and Gooden. He's a big bopper, a fan favorite, a good guy."[163]

The Mets sold out the series finale and clobbered the Brewers to complete a three-game sweep. Piazza eventually stretched his team-opening hitting streak to nine games, going 15-for-39 (.385) with four RBIs, seven runs scored, and a .515 slugging average. The Mets won their first seven games with Piazza behind the plate and appeared poised to make their first serious pursuit of a playoff berth since 1990.

But the boo-birds were flying over Shea by mid-July. Piazza hit only .268 with one homer during a 12-game period, with the Mets losing eight times, leading to impatience in Queens. New York was 14½ off the NL East lead and 4½ games behind the wild-card leaders heading into July 18, when Piazza hit two home runs in a 7–0 rout of the Phillies. It touched off a season-ending 66-game period that saw him bat .359 with 18 homers, 19 doubles, 59 RBIs, and 39 runs scored.

But it still took a while before he started to hit in the clutch. He had a .227 batting average with runners in scoring position as a Met after going 1-for-4 in a loss to the Pirates on July 20. He lined out with the bases loaded in his first at-bat that game and struck out in his last two, prompting a cascade of boos as he made his way back to the dugout.

"I understand the situation," Piazza said after the game. "I don't question their reaction at all. I'm just very frustrated right now. I'm trying to do my best. But I'm definitely disappointed with my performance. And it compounds it that we're not playing well as a team."

"It's not the most productive .330," Piazza remarked about his batting average as a Met at that point. "I'll be the first to say that. I'm not really ripping the cover off the ball. I know I'm not hitting the way I should hit. And so it's easy to say I'm hitting .330. But I don't feel like I'm contributing. And I'm my own worst critic."[164]

The clutch hits started to come by the end of July and continued the rest of the season. He hit .378 in September and homered six times during his first 15 games of the month. The Mets eventually took over the wild-card lead and had a magic number of five over the Cubs and three over the Giants heading into New York's final five games.

Piazza was 7-for-20 in the last week of the season, but the Mets went 0–5 to finish one game behind the Cubs and Giants for the wild-card. It was an unsettling way to end the year considering Piazza was brought in to secure a playoff berth, although he was hardly at fault for the collapse.

Piazza had made it clear over the summer that he wanted to test the free-agent market after the season. Some within his inner circle reportedly suggested the booing he heard during the summer might dissuade him from staying in New York. There were reports as early as August saying he wasn't coming back after the season. By then, the Mets and Piazza already had agreed negotiations wouldn't resume until after the regular season.

Piazza already had turned down a six-year, $84 million offer from the Dodgers earlier in the year, leading to speculation the Mets would have to pony up a seven-figure contract to keep him. But negotiations began to appear in the Mets' favor when Piazza didn't immediately file for free agency after the World Series. Days after the Series, Piazza put his signature on a seven-year, $91 million contract to the delight of Doubleday, who was previously being portrayed as a silent partner in the Mets hierarchy before nudging Phillips to get him.

"This tells the fans that we appreciate the fact that they came back to watch us play after we acquired Mike," said Doubleday in September. "They wanted a marquee player, we needed a marquee player, and we got them a marquee player."[165]

Doubleday recognized "marquee." Without Piazza, the Mets drew an average of 18,112 fans in their first 24 home games of 1998. Once he came on board, attendance nearly doubled to 34,589. Doubleday figured the acquisition meant an additional $22 million in revenue for the Mets.

Piazza knew the contract meant a bigger bulls-eye on his chest protector. But the booing in 1998 allowed him to adapt to baseball in New York, where even a Hall of Fame catcher is only as good as his last at-bat.

"When I looked inside, I realized this is where I wanted to be," Piazza said after the contract was signed. "When you're not successful here, it's tough. But when you win here, it's twice as good as anyplace else. And if I happen to be so fortunate to go in the Hall of Fame, it's definitely going to be in a Mets uniform.

"When I realized what had transpired with the Dodgers, I knew that no matter where I went, it would have been the same. And I just felt I might as well get booed by the best. Going somewhere else—with no offense to any other place—would be a letdown. When you come here, you get infected by the attitude. And you always know where you stand."[166]

The signing also seemed to change the team philosophy on payroll constraint. Hours after the Piazza deal, Leiter accepted a free-agent contract worth $32 million over four years. Six weeks later, the Mets inked third baseman Robin Ventura to a three-year, $23 million contract and soon signed all-time stolen base leader Rickey Henderson. On the day the Mets landed Ventura, they also picked up speedy outfielder Roger Cedeno and catcher Charles Johnson from the Dodgers for Hundley, who was no longer needed once Piazza was signed. Through Johnson, the Mets were able to get reliever Armando Benitez from the Orioles.

But the focus was on Piazza as the Mets arrived for the start of spring training. He had the good looks, the gaudy stats, and the huge contract. All he had to do was guide the team to its first postseason berth in over a decade while showing leadership skills.

"I've never really turned away from a challenge in my career," Piazza said during camp. "You can't ever be afraid to do something. The Mets went a long way to acquire me. I just wanted to give it a shot and fulfill their expectations. I believe in leadership. And I definitely believe I'm a leader. But I believe I lead by example. I've never been anybody who reacts to somebody who is waving the flag."[167]

The Mets entered 1999 with considerably more talent than they had at the end of '98. Their station-to-station style of offense was eradicated by Henderson and Cedeno, as the Mets stole 150 bases in 1999 compared to a league-low 62 the previous season. With Piazza and Ventura serving as the power source, New York's home run total rose from 136 to 181. Benitez eventually took over as the closer, leaving Franco to serve as the top set-up man for a bullpen that now included Turk Wendell and Dennis Cook. One wonders if the Mets would have made such roster moves had Piazza signed elsewhere.

Piazza opened 1999 by hitting .385 with two homers and nine RBIs in six games, missing two weeks between the fifth and six games due to a sprained MCL in his right knee. His average was down to .273 until he homered in four straight games from May 17 to 21, going 10-for-16 with six RBIs and six runs scored during that streak, while raising his average to .327.

Piazza embarked on a career-high 24-game hitting streak four days later, batting .353 with eight homers, 10 doubles, 18 RBIs, and 18 runs. The streak was a great opportunity for self-promotion, but Piazza would have none of that as he continued to downplay his torrid stretch.

When asked about the possibility of breaking Benito Santiago's record hitting streak for catchers, Piazza pointed out that Santiago did it as a rookie. When the streak reached 24 games, tying the club record set by Hubie Brooks, Piazza compared it to Pete Rose's league-record 44-game streak. What mattered to Piazza was getting the Mets into the playoffs.

"To me, a hitting streak is not really one of those things that you worry about," said Piazza when he tied Brooks' mark. "I haven't done that at any point in my career. It's kind of cool. It's a nice little footnote. Let's just say if it ends tonight. I won't have any problem getting to sleep."[168]

Oddly, the Mets went on a season-high eight-game losing streak during that stretch to fall one game under .500 at 27–28 following a loss to the Yankees on June 5.

"This is disappointing," Piazza said after loss No. 8. "It's really tough. We didn't play a bad game; we just keep making the same one or two mistakes that keep hurting us. That's what happens when you're losing."[169]

The Mets placed utility man Bobby Bonilla and outfielder Brian McRae on irrevocable waivers and "reassigned" three coaches—including hitting coach Tom Robson—once the losing streak reached eight games. The players now had no excuses for their faulty performances, and manager Bobby Valentine put his own head on the chopping block by saying he should by fired unless the team showed significant improvement over the next 55 games.

The losing streak ended in the Bronx as Piazza blasted a two-run homer off Roger Clemens to put the Mets ahead 6–0 in the third inning of a 7–2 win over the Yankees. The victory opened a 55-game stretch in which the Mets went 40–15 to move into the NL East lead, 1½ games ahead of Atlanta. Piazza's average was at .311 by the end of the hot stretch, demonstrating the lineup was deep enough to support the pitching staff when Piazza didn't contribute as much. In fact, Piazza was just 16-for-77 with runners in scoring position by July 3.

Piazza hit "only" .298 over his final 47 games, but he also delivered 17 homers, 47 RBIs, 36 runs, and a .380 on-base average while striking out just 19 times in 167 at-bats. Although the Braves eventually passed the Mets in the division race, New York had a strong hold on the wild-card lead heading into the final two weeks of the season. Piazza homered in an 8–6 win over the Phillies on Sunday, September 19, as the Mets stayed within a game of Atlanta while building a four-game lead over the Reds for the wild-card with 12 games to play.

"We had a tough finish last year," Piazza said two days earlier. "We didn't get into the playoffs. But I still feel that it's a little different situation this year. You got different guys—everyone trying to turn the page on what happened last year."[170]

The Mets didn't win again for 1½ weeks, dropping seven straight to fall 1½ games behind the Astros for the wild-card. Piazza homered twice and drove in five runs during the skid but hit only .222.

"I'm at a loss for words," he said after the sixth consecutive loss. "I don't want to say it, but it can't get much worse. I think everyone is stunned."[171]

New York ended the slide with a 9–2 rout of the Braves on September 29, only to lose to Atlanta the following day. It was eerily similar to the team's 1998 collapse, only this time they still had a few games in which to make up the difference. Unbelievably, Piazza was supremely confident in his teammates and the club's ability to sneak into the playoffs.

"As far as I'm concerned, with these guys here, if we're in the same position next year, I'll take it," Piazza said. "If we're in the same position the year after that, I'll take it. I hope we're always in a position to get to the postseason."[172]

The Mets trailed the Reds and Astros by two games heading into a three-game series at Shea Stadium against the Pirates, who had their eyes on finishing over .500 for the first time in seven years. Anything less than a sweep would likely kill the Mets' chances to make the playoffs, and the Bucs hadn't been swept in a three-game series since July 2–4. The likelihood of the Mets playing themselves into the postseason appeared so slight that just 29,528 attended the series opener.

The Mets carried a 2–0 lead into the eighth inning of Game 1, thanks to homers by Piazza and Ventura, along with Kenny Rogers' three-hit pitching over seven frames. But the Pirates scratched out a pair of runs in the eighth to force extra innings.

The Mets put runners on second and third with two out in the 11th before Pittsburgh manager Gene Lamont elected to walk Piazza intentionally to bring up Ventura in a lefty-lefty maneuver. Ventura ended the game with a walk-off single that brought some life back into the clubhouse. The Reds and Astros lost that night, dropping New York's deficit to one game.

Piazza was behind the plate the next night as Rick Reed fired a three-hitter in a 7–0 rout of the Pirates. Piazza capped the scoring with a two-run blast in a five-run eighth, around the time the Reds completed a loss at Milwaukee. The Mets and Reds were now tied for the wild-card with one game left, causing fans to pack Shea for the regular-season finale as New York tried to earn its first playoff berth in 11 years.

The Mets fell behind on Kevin Young's RBI single just four batters into the game. The Pirates managed just two more hits the rest of the afternoon, giving the Mets an opportunity to tie the game on Darryl Hamilton's fourth-inning double.

It remained 1–1 when Bobby Bonilla opened the bottom of the ninth with a weak tapper to first base. But Melvin Mora and Edgardo Alfonzo followed with consecutive singles to put runners on first and third with one out and John Olerud heading to the plate. Lamont had Olerud walked intentionally to send up Piazza, who had grounded into a league-high 27 double plays. Lamont also replaced lefty reliever Greg Hansell with right-hander Brad Clontz, who uncorked a wild pitch on his first delivery to Piazza. Piazza raised his hands and celebrated with his teammates as Mora scooted home from third to give New York a 2–1 victory.

But the Mets still didn't know whether they had clinched a playoff berth. The Reds-Brewers game was delayed several hours and didn't begin until most of the Mets had left Shea. The Reds eventually rolled to an easy victory to set up a one-game wild-card playoff with the Mets at Cincinnati.

The Reds pitched carefully to Piazza, who walked three times in five at-bats while going 0-for-2. But Alfonzo launched a two-run homer in the first and Leiter tossed a two-hitter as the Mets won 5–0, putting Piazza in the postseason for the first time in three years.

"You've got to enjoy this because very few players have this opportunity," Piazza said after the playoff. "I've been in a few, and we haven't done so great. I guess we don't have too much time to enjoy it, but we'll enjoy it while we can."[173]

The Mets immediately got on a plane to Phoenix to take on the Diamondbacks in the division series the following night. Game 1 was a microcosm of the Mets' regular season as they blew a three-run lead before winning 8–4 on Alfonzo's grand slam in the ninth. Piazza singled in each of the first two games to stretch his postseason hitting streak to six games. But he also took another foul tip off his thumb in Game 2, leaving him sorer than usual. X-rays were negative, but Piazza experienced an adverse reaction to a cortisone injection, making the thumb too stiff and swollen for him to play the rest of the series.

The injury left catching duties in the hands of backup Todd Pratt, who was coming off his best major league season to date. Pratt went 0-for-2 in the third game, but he also walked twice and scored once as the Mets blasted the Diamondbacks 9–2 to take a 2–1 series lead.

Pratt also started Game 4 after Piazza was deemed unable to play. Pratt was hitless in his first four at-bats of the afternoon, leaving him 0-for-8 lifetime in the postseason as he stepped to the plate in the bottom of the 10th with the score tied 3–3. Pratt ended the series with a Piazza-like clout, launching a walk-off homer to put the Mets into the NLCS against the Braves.

"I kept telling Todd, 'Just hang in there, you can hit these guys,'" Piazza said after the game. "And he did."[174]

The Mets dropped the first three games of the championship series as Piazza went 2-for-11. He drove in a run in the opener and had two of the Mets' seven hits in a 1–0 loss in Game 3.

The Mets staved off elimination by capturing the next two games despite Piazza, who was 1-for-9 with five strikeouts to drop his average for the postseason to .172. Piazza was still bothered by swelling and soreness in his left hand but continued to stay in the lineup.

He also was hitless in his first two at-bats of Game 6 before helping New York erase a huge deficit. Atlanta led 5–0

Mike Piazza. Photo courtesy of Oscar W. Gabriel

into the sixth until Piazza hit a sacrifice fly and Hamilton followed with a two-run single to make it 5–3. The Braves seemed to ice the victory by scoring twice in the bottom half, but the Mets still weren't ready to die.

Henderson and Olerud delivered run-scoring hits in the seventh to make it 7–5 as Piazza prepared to face John Smoltz. Piazza picked that time to belt his first postseason homer since his first playoff game four years earlier, a game-tying, two-run blast to deep right field.

Piazza was taken out of the game with the score tied 8–8 in the bottom of the ninth. The Mets went ahead 9–8 on Pratt's sac-fly in the 10th and came within two outs of becoming the first team in major league history to force a seventh game after dropping the first three contests. But the Braves tied it in the 10th and won it on a bases-loaded walk in the 11th.

Banged up after seven months of jarring collisions and foul tips off his bare hand, Piazza deserved praise for playing through pain. But the most painful sight concerning Piazza was his .167 average in the NLCS. He had ended a 12-game postseason homerless streak with his blast in Game 6, but there were growing whispers that Piazza was becoming another superstar who could not meet expectations in October. The criticism came after he set a team record with 124 RBIs and became the first catcher ever to post a pair of 40-homer seasons, finishing seventh among all National Leaguers in both categories. Piazza also received MVP consideration, earned a berth on the NL All-Star team, and won the Silver Slugger, all for the seventh time in as many full seasons.

He also completed the trifecta in 2000, finishing third in the MVP race and getting the starting nod in the All-Star Game. But Piazza was unable to play in the midsummer classic after being beaned by Yankees pitcher Roger Clemens in Game 2 of a day-night, two-stadium doubleheader on July 8.

Piazza went 3-for-4 with a grand slam in his previous meeting versus Clemens on June 9, leaving him 7-for-12 (.583) with a double, three homers, and nine RBIs against the seven-time Cy Young Award winner. One month later, Clemens felt it was time for retribution.

Piazza led off the bottom of the second and took a strike on the first pitch. Clemens' next delivery was a high fastball that tailed toward Piazza's head. Piazza had no time to react as the ball crashed into his helmet, leaving him motionless on the ground for several seconds before he stood up two minutes later. Piazza was helped back to the clubhouse and was diagnosed with a concussion. Clemens stayed in the game and won 4–2 before the Mets ripped the Rocket in their clubhouse for what they felt was a bush-league move.

"He busted him right in his face, man," Lenny Harris said. "For a guy with the experience he has, a pitcher with great control, that's not good for the game. If you want to hit someone, you hit him from the head down, not in the face. The guy's got a bright career ahead of him and a ball hits him in his face, it could end his career.[175]

"It seemed to me like if Clemens was concerned, he should have walked up to Mike and asked him if he was all right. He just stood there. That was bad."

"I think it was bull," added Valentine. "I think it was terrible. I hope someday he'll pitch in a National League park where we play against him."[176]

Clemens insisted it was a pitch that got away, and Yankees manager Joe Torre said he would have been shocked if his ace was throwing at Piazza intentionally.

"I wasn't trying to hit him in the head," Clemens said the day after the beaning. "I was trying to crowd him, pitch him inside. The guy's hit me well, and I was trying to make an adjustment, but the adjustment I was trying to make wasn't to hit the guy in the head."[177]

Piazza wasn't buying Clemens' argument. "I thought it was definitely intentional," Piazza said. "I could respect the fact that he's throwing inside. I could respect the fact of getting hit, getting hit in the ribs or the body. I know that's part of the game. I accept that and I don't have any problem with that. But I feel there's a difference between that and almost ending my career. He's got no remorse. I'm kind of flattered, in a weird way, because he's trying to tell me the only way to get me out is to try to hurt me."

"I really can't say I have respect for him right now," Piazza said. "Roger has very good control. I think he only walked one guy during the game. If the shoe fits, that's the way it is. I wish I could remember him as a great pitcher, as a Cy Young Award winner. But I know I can't do that."[178]

Besides the beaning, Piazza and the Mets went through the remainder of the regular season without the constant drama that punctuated 1999. They opened the year by splitting a pair of games against the Cubs in Tokyo before dropping five of their next seven to fall to 3–6. The Mets quickly righted the ship, winning 11 of their next 12 to move into a first-place tie, and challenged the Braves for the division title until the final week of the season before allowing Atlanta to clinch at Shea with five games remaining.

Unlike 1998 and '99, the Mets stormed to the finish line and won the wild-card by eight games over the Dodgers. New York headed into the playoffs on a five-game winning streak, two years after a season-ending five-game skid cost them a wild-card berth.

Meanwhile, Piazza had another outstanding season as he led the team with 38 homers, 113 RBIs, and a .614 slugging average. He tied Alfonzo for the club lead with a .324 batting average, 10th best in the league.

Piazza also posted the NL's best fielding percentage among catchers at .997, the first time he had cracked the top 10 since 1994. Piazza critics loved to hammer the fact that he threw out only 23 percent of his base stealers, but those detractors were missing the big picture.

Piazza called an exceptional game, asking his batterymates to pitch to their strengths. With a speedy runner on first, many catchers might ask for a fastball to reduce the odds of the runner stealing second. But on a pitching staff that featured Al Leiter's cut fastball and Mike Hampton's changeup, Piazza never hesitated to call for their best pitch in order to retire the batter.

Piazza was also adroit at blocking pitches. He led the NL with 12 passed balls in both 1995 and '96 and was among the top five, five times from 1993 to 1999. But Piazza was charged with just three passed balls in 2000 while handling Leiter's unpredictable cutter and Hampton's heavy fastball. Piazza's work helped the Mets finish third in the league in ERA and second in strikeouts. But once the calendar was flipped to October, Mets fans hoped Piazza would also show improvement at the plate in the postseason.

The Giants were the Mets' opponents in the NLDS. Piazza hammered San Francisco pitching during the regular season, hitting .467 with two homers, two doubles, and four RBIs in five games. In fact, Piazza was a career .329 hitter with eight homers, 17 RBIs, and 18 runs scored in 24 games versus New York's potential NL playoff opponents, giving hope he would finally have a monster postseason.

The Mets beat the Giants in four games despite little offensive help from Piazza, who went 3-for-14 without driving in a run. He was now a .211 career hitter in the postseason with two homers, seven RBIs, four runs, and 17 strikeouts in 71 at-bats over 18 games. He was on the losing end of his two division series with the Dodgers, but the Mets had found a way to win two of their first three playoff rounds with Piazza behind the plate. The next two series were quite different for Piazza.

The Mets traveled to St. Louis for the first two games of the NLCS. The Cardinals won one more game than the Mets during the regular season but lost the season series 6–3 as Piazza batted .348 with two homers and four RBIs.

Timo Perez opened Game 1 with a double and moved to third on a wild pitch before Alfonzo was walked, putting runners at the corners with Piazza coming up. Piazza swung at the first pitch from Darryl Kile and slammed it down the left-field line for a double to drive in Perez and put the Mets ahead to stay. The Mets' dugout was ecstatic, particularly coach John Stearns.

"The monster's out of the cage!!!! The Monster's out of the cage!!!!" wailed Stearns, who sensed the magnitude of the base hit.

Piazza finished 2-for-4 as the Mets dumped the Redbirds 6–2. It was only his fourth multi-hit performance in 19 playoff games, but it sent a message to St. Louis manager Tony La Russa and his pitching staff. Piazza was walked five times—three times intentionally—over the next four games, yet he stayed in a midseason hitting groove.

Piazza walked three times in Game 2 but also hit a solo homer in a 6–5 victory. He was involved in three rallies during Game 4, belting another solo homer and scoring three times as the Mets won 10–6 to get within one victory of their first World Series in 14 years.

Game 5 was a 7–0 rout by the Mets as Hampton tossed a three-hitter to clinch series MVP honors. Piazza supported Hampton with one hit and two runs scored to end the series hitting .412 with a .545 on-base percentage, two homers, and four RBIs despite the Cardinals' attempt to pitch him carefully. Most impressive was Piazza's ability to either score or collect an RBI in the first inning of each of the Mets' four victories. He also hit safely in all five games.

No one was happier about Piazza's performance than Phillips, the same Phillips who claimed in 1998 that the Mets were ready to ride out Hundley's injury rather than acquire Piazza.

"When we got Mike Piazza, it gave our organization credibility," said Phillips. "We went from being a nice little team on the field and in people's perception to a real contender.

"He was booed and had negative press for the first time in his career. But when you work and persevere, the reward is that much higher, and as I look back now, there was no better player we could have got."[179]

Next up for the Mets were the Yankees in the first Subway Series since 1956. It also meant another meeting between Piazza and Clemens, although that didn't occur until Game 2.

The Mets lost the opener in a heartbreaker 4–3 in 12 innings as Piazza went 1-for-5 to stretch his hitting streak to six games. He was the third batter up in Game 2 when Clemens sparked another incident between the two players.

Clemens looked especially pumped up at the start of the game, fanning Perez and Alfonzo before the count went 1–2 on Piazza. Mike didn't swing at the first three pitches and was jammed on the fourth, breaking his bat as the ball rolled into foul territory on the first-base side. The barrel of the bat sailed in the direction of Clemens, who grabbed the wood with his bare hand and fired it in the direction of Piazza running down the line. Piazza stopped dead in his tracks, turned to Clemens, and asked, "What's your problem?" Piazza took a few steps toward Clemens as both benches emptied while plate umpire Charlie Reliford got in between the two potential combatants. Clemens appeared

to explain to Piazza that he thought the bat was the ball. It had been well over a century since baseball rules stated that you could retire a runner on a grounder by hitting him with the baseball, so that excuse was ridiculous.

Order was restored after a few minutes, and Piazza grounded out to second to end the inning. The next 7½ innings were even uglier for the Mets as the Yankees built a 6–0 lead. Clemens dominated the Mets, allowing two hits while striking out nine over eight innings, causing Mets fans to gnash their teeth at the thought of him beating the Mets for the second time in two starts.

The Mets rallied once Clemens left. Piazza ended the shutout with a two-run blast off Jeff Nelson, and Jay Payton's three-run bomb against Mariano Rivera suddenly got the Mets within 6–5 before Kurt Abbott struck out to end the game.

The Yankees had a two-games-to-none lead by the end of the night, but the media attention revolved around the latest Piazza-Clemens flap.

Clemens now had a new story; he didn't notice Piazza was near the area where he threw the bat and was just trying to clear the area. He told Reliford as much during the confrontation and was sticking to that account.

"There was no intent," said Clemens, who added he was surprised Piazza had run down the line. "I was running extremely high. I had to go and calm down. I was extremely fired up. I had to calm down and stay focused."[180]

"I went out to confront him about it and, obviously, he chose to—whatever his excuse was," said Piazza. "As far as demanding an apology, an apology is only as good as where the source is coming from. So I really couldn't care less about an apology or anything else. It was a stupid situation. What can you say?"[181]

Back at Shea, the Mets made it two games to one in the Series by scoring twice in the eighth to win 5–3. The Yankees held a 2–1 lead until Piazza, who went 1-for-4, led off the bottom of the sixth with a ground-rule double before scoring on Todd Zeile's double.

Piazza hit a two-run homer in the third inning of Game 4, but it came after the Yankees built a 3–0 lead. Neither team scored after Piazza's blast, giving the Bombers a three-games-to-one advantage.

Game 5 came down to a productive ninth inning by the Yankees against a weary pitcher. The Mets grabbed a 2–1 lead in the second inning, but the Yanks knotted the score on Derek Jeter's solo shot off Al Leiter in the sixth. Leiter was still on the mound in the ninth, striking out the first two hitters before the Yankees rallied to score twice on his 142nd pitch.

Piazza was the Mets' last hope in the bottom of the ninth. Benny Agbayani walked with one out and moved to second on defensive indifference before Alfonzo skied to right to move Agbayani to third and bring up Piazza.

"He came up with a man on base, down by two," Phillips said after the game. "It seems to me that's supposed to be part of the script."[182]

Piazza's Stats Compared to Hall of Fame Catchers with 100 HRs

Name	GP	HR	XB	RBI	BA	OBP	SLG
Mike Piazza	1912	427	779	1335	.307	.377	.545
Johnny Bench	2158	389	794	1376	.267	.342	.476
Carlton Fisk	2499	376	844	1330	.269	.341	.457
Yogi Berra	2120	358	728	1430	.285	.348	.482
Gary Carter	2295	324	726	1225	.262	.335	.439
Roy Campanella	1215	242	438	856	.276	.360	.500
Gabby Hartnett	1990	236	696	1179	.297	.370	.489
Bill Dickey	1789	202	617	1209	.313	.382	.486
Ernie Lombardi	1853	190	494	990	.306	.358	.460
Mickey Cochrane	1482	119	516	832	.320	.419	.478

Rivera threw a strike on the first pitch before Piazza launched a fly ball to deep left-center. Had Piazza gotten all of it, the ball would have sailed into the bleachers in left-center. Instead, Piazza got under the ball just enough to turn it into a deep fly ball that center fielder Bernie Williams grabbed for the final out.

Piazza finished his lone Fall Classic batting .273 with a pair of two-run homers while stretching his postseason hitting streak to 10 games. The monster was indeed out of the cage, but it would be another six years before it had a chance to roam again in the playoffs as the Mets failed to reach the postseason during the remainder of his seven-year contract.

Piazza spent the rest of the winter pondering the what-ifs. Aside from just missing a game-tying home run, Piazza might have prevented the Yankees' two-run ninth in Game 5 had he been in front of the plate instead of behind it following Luis Sojo's tiebreaking single. As it was, Payton's throw hit runner Bernie Williams at the plate, allowing a second run to score on the play.

"Maybe I could have got a little bit better hop," Piazza said while discussing the go-ahead play a few months later. "It's timing, it's a crapshoot. Sorry, those things happen. You roll the dice and it came up snake eyes."

"The minute you start to feel so depressed, you kind of feel, 'Hey, we have a lot to be proud of,'" Piazza said about the 2000 season. "And the minute you say we have a lot to be proud of, you start to get depressed. You're in this sort of limbo."[183]

Hampton became a one-year rental as he bolted New York for a free-agent contract with the Rockies after the 2000 season. The Mets briefly courted free-agent shortstop Alex Rodriguez before determining his price tag was too rich. Gary Sheffield was also on the Mets' radar, but Phillips was unwilling to part with the Dodgers' unrea-

sonable asking price of either Piazza or Alfonzo. Phillips instead picked up free-agent pitchers Kevin Appier and Steve Trachsel, and gambled on Payton and Perez to show continued improvement at the plate.

Piazza reached a few milestones during 2001, recording his 1,500th hit, 300th home run, 900th RBI, and 200th double. He became the 12th player in major league history to have at least seven straight seasons with at least 30 homers, reaching the plateau with his 300th blast as a catcher. Piazza also was named to the NL All-Star team for the ninth straight year and picked up his ninth Silver Slugger, finishing with a .300 average, 36 homers, and 94 RBIs.

But the Mets spent most of the year struggling to stay near the .500 mark. Piazza batted only .269 through New York's first 81 games while Alfonzo hit just .251. Other than newcomers Desi Relaford and Tsuyoshi Shinjo, the rest of the Mets' lineup sputtered through the first three months while the rotation and bullpen were wildly inconsistent. The Mets dropped 10 games under .500 by May 19 and played .500 ball over the next two months, prompting Phillips to deal Pratt and relievers Turk Wendell and Dennis Cook before the July trade deadline.

New York's mediocre performance continued despite Piazza's .386 average, .491 on-base percentage, seven homers, and 20 RBIs in 27 games from June 24 to August 2. Alfonzo continued to struggle while Ventura completely bottomed out, hitting .132 with two homers and seven RBIs from June 27 to August 16. None of the Mets outfielders had cracked double digits in home runs, and Relaford was the only player other than Piazza to be flirting with a .300 average. The Mets were 54–68 and 13½ games out of first place by August 17 following their seventh consecutive loss.

And then the Mets suddenly started to win again, taking seven of their next eight and 11 of 14 to climb within 7½ games of the East-leading Braves by September 1. They also won six straight from September 3 to 8 but were still eight games out with 18 to play following a 4–2 loss at Florida on September 9.

The Mets went from Miami to Pittsburgh for a three-game set with the lowly Pirates, an opportunity for New York to come home above .500 for the first time since the third game of the year. The team was several hours from heading to PNC Park for batting practice when planes crashed into both main towers of the World Trade Center, killing thousands and leaving New Yorkers in a state of grief, anger and disbelief. Major League Baseball put the season on hold for a week to give the nation time to heal from the terrorist attacks on New York and the Pentagon. The Mets returned home and pitched in with the relief efforts, as the parking lot at Shea was used as a staging area. They were scheduled to resume the season at home against the Pirates, but MLB shifted the series to Pittsburgh to give the city a few more days to make preparations to heighten security at Shea Stadium.

The layoff didn't slow down the Mets, who swept three games from the Bucs by a combined 20–8 margin while the Braves were getting swept. The Mets honored the fallen members of the NYPD, FDNY, EMT, and Port Authority by wearing caps from each entity during the series. Piazza went 3-for-10 with a pair of homers, four RBIs, and three runs scored over the last two games of the series to help New York get within five games of Atlanta.

Baseball finally returned to New York on September 21, with the Braves serving as the Mets' opponent. Atlanta won the previous day to move 5½ games ahead of New York.

"It's okay to cry," Piazza said before the game. "It's okay to let your guard down a little and feel sad, because you should. It's going to take a lot longer than this to heal. I don't know if we'll ever really heal as a country. I know we'll have to move on."[184]

The crowd of 41,235 was understandably subdued for most of the game following an emotional pregame ceremony that ended with the Mets and Braves hugging and shaking hands. The Mets trailed 1–0 in the fourth before Piazza doubled and scored on Shinjo's sacrifice fly. It remained 1–1 until Brian Jordan laced an RBI double with two out in the eighth, but the Mets had Piazza due to hit in the bottom half.

Matt Lawton opened the half-inning by grounding out to short before Alfonzo worked out a nine-pitch walk, making Piazza the potential go-ahead run at the plate against Steve Karsay. Two pitches later, Piazza launched one of the most memorable home runs of his career, a majestic blast that hit a scaffolding of cameras well beyond center field. Piazza's third extra-base hit of the evening made Shea Stadium a fun place again, allowing fans to temporarily forget about the previous 10 days in New York.

"I'm just so happy I was able to come through in that situation and give people something to cheer about," Piazza said afterward. "That's what they came out here for, to be diverted a little from their losses and their sorrow."[185]

"This is really tough to put in perspective. New York has been so strong throughout all of this. I met some kids today who lost their fathers. All I know is that this has brought so much good in people, so much positive energy. I'm just proud that I can be a part of it."[186]

The Mets hung on for a 3–2 win and clobbered the Braves the next day to pull within 3½ games with 12 left in the season. Atlanta took the getaway game as Piazza went 1-for-5 to end up 6-for-12 in the emotionally exhausting series.

New York swept the next series in Montreal to inch closer to the division lead despite an injury to Piazza in the first inning of the second game. Piazza didn't start Game 3 of the series, but he provided a game-breaking, three-run double as a pinch-hitter in the ninth inning as the Mets outscored the Expos 12–6.

The Mets headed to Atlanta, where another sweep would leave them tied with the Braves heading into a series against the Pirates and Expos. New York had gone an astonishing 24–6 since mid-August to put itself in position to pull off the franchise's greatest late-season comeback since the 1973 squad went from worst to first over the final five weeks.

The Braves took the opener 5–3 and grabbed an early 1–0 lead the following afternoon, but Piazza came through with a three-run double in the third before scoring on a wild pitch. The Mets tacked on another run and were one out from a 5–2 victory when Marcus Giles hit a two-run double off Armando Benitez. Jordan won it by launching a grand slam on an 0–2 pitch from Franco, effectively ending the Mets' chances to reach the postseason for a third straight year.

"It's a shame, because you come so far," Piazza said after the loss reduced the Mets' magic number for elimination to three with seven games left. "Without saying it's completely over, obviously you just can't lose a game like this when you're in the situation we're in. You just can't. We've had a couple in the last couple of weeks that were tough."[187]

The Mets won the next day as Piazza went 4-for-5 with a solo homer, giving him a .348 average with nine round-trippers and 26 RBIs in 31 games since the team began its turnaround. New York returned home four games out with six to play before losing four times to finish 82–80.

Phillips pulled off a pair of blockbuster trades after the season, landing former AL MVP Mo Vaughn and future Hall of Famer Roberto Alomar. Both moves backfired as the Mets finished 75–86 to fall into the division cellar for the first time since 1996.

Piazza homered 33 times and increased his RBI total from 94 to 98 to earn his 10th and final Silver Slugger. But he scored just 69 runs and hit .280, the first time he had ever batted below .300 since his brief call-up in 1992. He recorded a .188 average with two homers during a 19-game stretch in May, and only .194 in 28 games from July 28 to August 31. Although he hit .338 with nine homers and 22 RBIs in September, many speculated Piazza's 10 seasons behind the plate had taken some life out of his bat.

But there was one record Piazza wanted to hunt down before he even considered a position change. He became the National League all-time home run leader for catchers on August 17 against the Dodgers, passing Johnny Bench with his 328th. The blast left him 24 away from breaking Carlton Fisk's major league home run mark for catchers, a figure he was expected to reach by August 2003. Instead, he missed three months of the season and hit only 11 homers in 68 games.

Piazza got off to an excellent start in '03, hitting .336 with seven homers and 15 RBIs in his first 31 games. His RBI production was on the puny side only because the rest of the lineup struggled to get on base.

But his season was derailed by a grade 3 sprain of his right groin while batting in San Francisco May 16. He didn't play again until August 13, when the Mets already had stumbled their way out of playoff contention.

Piazza went 3-for-5 with a two-run homer and five RBIs in his first game off the disabled list. He continued to hit well over the next two weeks and had 14 RBIs in 11 games following his return. Although he ended the season on an eight-game hitting streak, Piazza still hit only .207 over his final 25 games to finish with a .286 average, 11 home runs, and 34 RBIs in 68 games.

Piazza went over the 1,000 RBI plateau with a three-run homer in Atlanta in late August. One month later, he was donning a first baseman's mitt in a game for the first time in a decade. Vance Wilson saw the bulk of the action behind the plate during Piazza's absence while No. 3 catcher Jason Phillips flourished playing first base. Phillips received Rookie of the Year consideration and kept his average around .300 most of the season before settling at .298.

Mets management thought now was a good time for Piazza to be transformed into a first baseman. His throwing arm had eroded as he absorbed the punishment that comes with the position. Phillips wasn't a significant upgrade over Piazza defensively, but he was eight years younger and appeared ready to take over as catcher on a regular basis.

Piazza worked out at first base during training camp but never managed to grasp the rudimentary skills. His footwork was sloppy and his reaction time was slow while he appeared to miss his time behind the plate despite the physical abuse.

The Mets allowed him to start the season behind the plate as he continued to chase Fisk's home run record. Piazza homered in an Opening Day win over the Braves and went 5-for-5 with two homers and four RBIs the next night before finishing the series 8-for-15. Piazza was now within two home runs of breaking Fisk's mark.

He didn't homer again until April 27 as he fittingly tied the mark in Los Angeles. The record finally fell on May 5 as Piazza went deep off Giants pitcher Jerome Williams at Shea Stadium.

"I'm really excited and really proud," Piazza said after his blast helped the Mets win. "I'm blessed. I've lived a dream. Everything from here on in is icing."[188]

He became the Mets' No. 1 first baseman the following week, and he said all the right things even if he knew in his heart he still belonged at catcher.

"I'm so happy with the way the situation has worked out," Piazza said of his pending move to first base after breaking Fisk's record. "I'm enjoying learning the position and I feel I'm getting better at it. Right now, it's still a day-by-day situation. But I know it's important that I develop at first base as I get into my late thirties."[189]

Piazza's footwork was no better at Shea than it was at St. Lucie. He spent the rest of the season shuttling between his old and new positions while Phillips hit poorly and the Mets spiraled out of the postseason races by early August. Even the arrival of David Wright and the return of José Reyes couldn't stop the Mets from recording their third straight losing season.

The Mets acquired Gold Glove first baseman Doug Mientkiewicz before the Mets reported for 2005 training camp, spelling the end of Piazza's days at the position. The ballclub now hoped a move back to catcher would reignite Piazza's bat after he hit only .268 with 20 homers and 54 RBIs in 129 games.

New general manager Omar Minaya improved the club before 2005 by signing free agents Carlos Beltrán and Pedro Martinez. Beltrán was coming off a tremendous postseason that inflated his asking price in negotiations. Martinez was the top pitcher on the free-agent market after helping the Red Sox win their first World Series title in 86 years. That Minaya was able to sign both players was a signal the team was ready to contend in the final season of Piazza's contract.

One of the bigger question marks entering the season was Piazza. Would he be the hitter that batted .273 with 31 homers and 88 RBIs over the previous two years, or the guy who socked 33 homers and drove in 98 runs in 2002? The Mets would have settled for something in between as they worked themselves into wild-card contention by mid-August.

Piazza was optimistic before the start of training camp yet knew he likely wouldn't have one of his typical years. "My body feels good," Piazza said in late January. "I still feel like I can be productive. Maybe not the way I was 10 years ago. I realize it will be very tough to live up to those standards. But I'm sort of at peace with who I am. And this year, I know what my job is."[190]

Piazza had a clear view of the future and recognized this could be his final year with the Mets. With a bolstered offense and a starting rotation that now included Martinez, Tom Glavine, Steve Trachsel, Kris Benson, and Victor Zambrano, Piazza hoped to go out on a high note.

"In a way it's a long road," he said after reporting for spring training. "I kind of see the end of that road, and after that it doesn't really matter. I want it to be a good sort of last lap, so to speak. I want it to be positive, hopefully with us in the playoffs."[191]

Mike played the role of elder statesman to perfection in spring training, mentoring Reyes and enjoying his chance to catch Martinez. Piazza also told new manager Willie Randolph he'd be willing to play a few games at first base, although Randolph never asked him to discard his catcher's mask during the regular season.

Piazza never got into one of his torrid hitting streaks in 2005. He batted only .242 over the first two months before posting a .314 average in June. But he provided only three homers and nine RBIs that month and owned a .260 average with nine home runs and 36 RBIs by the All-Star break. His lasting popularity earned him a starting berth on the NL All-Star team for the final time in his career.

There was an 11-day period in July when Piazza had three games in which he homered and drove in three runs. He had a big night at the plate against the Brewers on August 4, hitting a two-run homer and producing three hits and five RBIs. But he managed to play just 23 games after the Brewers contest, hitting .178 with five homers and nine RBIs. He suffered a hairline fracture of his left wrist in mid-August, causing him to miss 24 games.

Piazza's bat speed through the strike zone had diminished. But instead of trying lighter wood, he seemed resigned to the fact he wasn't the same hitter at 36 that he was at 32.

"I'm stubborn," Piazza said in September when asked about the possibility of dropping bat weight after spending his entire career hitting with 32-ounce lumber. "My ego isn't allowing me to."[192]

"I compare it to a new car," Piazza added when discussing the regression of his game. "When you get a new car, the power windows go up quick—it's quicker and you get more response. And then when it gets older, little things start to break. Things fall off. Our bodies are machines. You have to be pragmatic. You have to be realistic."[193]

The Mets were just 60–58 when the broken wrist forced Piazza out of the lineup. The team proceeded to win eight of its next 10 games without Piazza to pull within a half-game of the wild-card lead. The Mets hit .267 with 14 homers and 55 RBIs while averaging 5.9 runs per game during that stretch, and the pitching staff posted a sparkling 2.08 ERA. They were winning games with Wright, Reyes, Cliff Floyd, and a minor league first baseman named Mike Jacobs, who went 7-for-13 with four homers and 13 RBIs in his first four games. It was now evident the Mets could win without Piazza, although they quickly learned they weren't good enough to make the playoffs. Piazza returned September 10 while the Mets were in the midst of a 3–15 skid that took them out of the wild-card race and put them four games under .500.

Piazza hit only .188 in 11 games from September 18 to October 1, but the Mets still won 10 times to clinch their first winning season since 2001. Piazza contributed a pair of homers and three RBIs in a 6–5 win over the Nationals on September 25, but the Mets trailed 5–4 until Wright and Jacobs sandwiched solo homers around Piazza's foul pop to first.

Wright and Floyd combined for 63 homers and 200 RBIs. Reyes led the NL with 17 triples and 60 stolen bases, and Jacobs crushed 11 home runs in only 30 games. Beltrán was considered a major disappointment in his first season with the Mets, as nagging injuries limited him to a .266 average with 16 homers, 34 doubles and 78 RBIs. However, Beltrán's substandard season was better than Piazza's, as the 36-year-old catcher hit only .251 with 19 homers, 23 doubles, and 62 RBIs.

By the end of the season, it was evident the Mets likely would have a new starting catcher in 2006, prompting fans to will Piazza to greatness as the team closed out the year with a three-game set with the Rockies at Shea Stadium. Piazza was received warmly before each of his eight at-bats and was given one final standing ovation as he came up in the sixth inning of the season finale. In an appreciative

gesture by Randolph, Piazza was allowed to warm up reliever Shingo Takatsu in the eighth inning before he was lifted for backup catcher Mike Difelice, allowing Piazza to hear the full throats of Mets fans one more time.

"I'm humbled," Piazza said of the ovations after the game. "Genuinely humbled. I just feel like part of the family. I tried to be a role model for the organization and do the best I could. I'm kind of exhaling now because it's taken a lot out of me. This was such a huge part of my life. It will always be a big part of my life, with the fans and the great times and the tough times. You can't describe the emotion of leaving this ballpark some nights where I actually was walking on air, and other nights where I just wanted to crawl under a rock and never come out. It brought out every ounce of emotion. I'm just going to exhale. This was an amazing day for me."[194]

Piazza was granted free agency after the World Series. The Mets found a new catcher in early December, acquiring another ex-Dodger and -Marlin—Paul Lo Duca—for two prospects. Piazza went unsigned until he landed a one-year deal with the Padres on February 3, putting him back in Southern California.

The Padres weren't quite sure what they had when they signed Piazza, just as the Dodgers didn't know he would become a tremendous hitter when they took him in the 62nd round of the 1988 draft. The Dodgers selected him in part as a favor to manager Tommy Lasorda, who was very friendly with the Piazza family and was godfather to Mike's brother, Tom.

Piazza grew up in the affluent Philadelphia suburb of Norristown and graduated from Phoenixville High School. He continued to work hard at his hitting in high school after failing to make the varsity his sophomore season. Piazza's father, Vince, had a successful car dealership and possessed the resources to set up a batting cage in the yard. Vince also had the type of connections to get Hall of Fame slugger Ted Williams to look at his teenage son.

Williams was doing a card show in the area when a friend of the Piazzas told the former Red Sox great of a talented 16-year-old hitter in the area. Williams traveled to the Piazza home and came away highly impressed with Mike's hitting ability.

"Mike hits it harder than I did when I was 16," Williams said in a video shot by the Piazza family during his visit. "I never saw anybody who looked better at that age."[195]

Piazza owned a copy of Williams' book, *The Science of Hitting*. Williams left after writing this inscription in the book: "To Mike, follow this book. As good as you look now, I'll be asking you for tickets."[196]

Piazza made the high school varsity as a junior and was named the MVP of his league as a senior. He also took American Legion MVP honors before enrolling at Miami-Dade North Community College. He hit well at Miami-Dade after being bypassed by the major colleges, and quickly became an outstanding minor league hitter after going unnoticed in the draft.

Piazza was in his third pro season when he batted .277 with 29 homers and 80 RBIs for Bakersfield of the Class A California League in 1991 to earn circuit All-Star honors for the second time. He was in the majors by 1992 after hitting a combined .350 with 23 homers and 90 RBIs for Double A San Antonio and Triple A Albuquerque.

He made his major league debut with the Dodgers against the Cubs on September 1, 1992, going 3-for-3 with a double and a walk in four plate appearances. He launched his first big-league homer 11 days later, a three-run shot off Steve Reed while catching Pedro Astacio's six-hitter in a 7–0 win over the Giants. Piazza finished the year hitting .232 with one homer and seven RBIs in 69 at-bats to earn the job as the Dodgers' No. 1 catcher for the next five years.

The 62nd-round pick became the ninth unanimous selection as NL Rookie of the Year in 1993 after hitting .318 with 35 homers and 112 RBIs. The home run total was a rookie record for catchers and third most behind Wally Berger and Frank Robinson among all position players. He also claimed his first Silver Slugger and All-Star appearance before finishing ninth in the NL MVP balloting.

Piazza was among the NL's greatest hitters during the rest of his stay with the Dodgers. He hit .337 with a .401 on-base percentage, 167 home runs, and 526 RBIs from 1993 to 1997, stats worthy of a long-term contract as he reported for training camp in '98.

But the Dodgers had failed to win a playoff series during Piazza's stay with the team. He rejected a multi-year offer during training camp as the Dodgers hoped he could be signed at a "hometown" discount. The only National Leaguer with a higher average than Piazza's from 1993 to 1997 was Tony Gwynn, and Gwynn's 48 home runs were 121 fewer than Piazza's.

Piazza was willing to play out his contract and test the free-agent market, prompting the Dodgers to trade him to the Marlins in May 1998. The Marlins had no interest in signing Piazza to a big contract and immediately put him on the block, allowing the Mets to get him before Memorial Day.

Eight years later, Piazza was just trying to prolong his career as he donned a Padres uniform. He helped San Diego win the NL West at 88–74 as he tied for second on the Padres with 22 homers while hitting .268 with 68 RBIs.

The Padres made their only 2006 visit to Shea Stadium in early August. Piazza received a hero's welcome in the opener of the three-game set before going 1-for-4 in a 3–2 loss to the Mets.

Game 2 of the series pitted Piazza and the Padres against Martinez as New York tried to expand its enormous lead in the NL East race. The Mets had a 4–0 lead in the fourth inning when Piazza launched a homer to right-center off Martinez to earn a smattering of applause from the Shea diehards.

Two innings later, Piazza homered again off Martinez to get the Padres within 4–2. This time, the boos almost outweighed the cheers from fans who wanted their team to nail down the victory.

Piazza came up again in the eighth with the tying run on first and Aaron Heilman on the mound for the Mets. The time for sentimentality had finally expired as fans implored Heilman to retire the SOB. Piazza almost wrecked a certain Mets win, belting a drive to deep center before Beltrán flagged it down to keep the game 4–2. Fans at Shea were able to appreciate Piazza's performance only after the Mets nailed down a 4–2 victory. It was the last time Piazza stepped to the plate at Shea Stadium.

Piazza sat out the series finale and had a chance to return to Shea in 2007, this time with the Oakland Athletics. But Piazza was on the disabled list when the A's were swept by the Mets in June.

The Athletics signed Piazza after the 2006 season with plans to use him as their top designated hitter and a backup catcher. Piazza never caught an inning for the A's and finished 2007 with a .275 average, eight homers and 44 RBIs in 83 games.

Piazza was 39 when he quietly announced his retirement in 2008. He left the game with a .308 average, 427 home runs, and 1,335 RBIs over 16 seasons. It only seemed a matter of time before the Hall of Fame opened its doors to the 62nd-round pick that had shattered virtually every major offensive category among catchers.

First ML game	Dodgers @ Cubs, 9/1/92
First Mets game	vs. Brewers, 5/23/98
First ML hit	double vs. Mike Harkey, @ Cubs, 9/1/92 (with Dodgers)
First Mets hit	RBI double vs. Jeff Juden, Brewers, 5/23/98
First ML homer	3-run HR vs. Steve Reed, Giants, 9/12/92 (with Dodgers)
First Mets homer	solo HR vs. Jason Schmidt, @ Pirates, 6/1/98
First ML RBI	3-run HR vs. Steve Reed, Giants, 9/12/92 (with Dodgers)
First Mets RBI	RBI double vs. Jeff Juden, Brewers, 5/23/98
Most hits, ML/Mets game	5, @ Pirates, 4/14/00; @ Braves, 4/7/04
Most homers, ML game	3, Dodgers @ Rockies, 6/29/96
Most homers, Mets game	2, 17 times
Most RBIs, ML game	7, Dodgers @ Phillies, 8/27/95
Most RBIs, Mets game	6, @ Diamondbacks, 4/30/02; @ Phillies, 7/3/02

Acquired: Traded by the Marlins for Preston Wilson, Ed Yarnall and Geoff Geotz, 5/22/98.

Deleted: Became a free agent, 10/28/05. Signed by the Padres, 2/3/06.

NL Rookie of the Year, 1993

All-Star Game MVP, 1996

NL All-Star, 1993, 1994, 1995, 1996, 1997, 1998, 1999, 2000, 2001, 2002, 2004, 2005

NL Silver Slugger, 1993, 1994, 1995, 1996, 1997, 1998, 1999, 2000, 2001, 2002

Rick Reed

Pitcher   Bats right, throws right
Born: 8/16/64   Huntington, West Virginia
Height: 6'0"   Weight: 205   #35

Rick Reed Mets Career

YEAR	GP/GS	IP	H	R	ER	K	BB	W–L	SV	ERA
1997	33/31	208.1	186	76	67	113	31	13–9	0	2.89
1998	31/31	212.1	208	84	82	153	29	16–11	0	3.48
1999	26/26	149.1	163	77	76	104	47	11–5	0	4.58
2000	30/30	184	192	90	84	121	34	11–5	0	4.11
2001	20/20	134.2	119	53	52	99	17	8–6	0	3.48
Total	140/138	888.2	868	380	361	590	158	59–36	0	3.66

Mets Career/Batting

GP	AB	R	H	2B	3B	HR	RBI	K	BB	SB	AVG
134	255	22	44	8	0	2	21	79	9	0	.173

ML Career

YEAR	GP/GS	IP	H	R	ER	K	BB	W–L	SV	ERA
88–03	273/245	1545.2	1601	748	692	970	285	93–76	1	4.03

Rick Reed

Rick Reed certainly can be called a late bloomer. His major league record stood at 4–7 with a 5.08 ERA after spending parts of eight seasons with the Pirates, Royals, Rangers, and Reds. Reed's baseball career was in such jeopardy that he agreed to cross the picket line and pitch for the Reds' replacement team during spring training, 1995. The Mets signed him after the 1995 season, but he spent all of 1996 with Triple A Norfolk, going 8–10 with a 3.16 ERA.

Reed was 32 when he finally cracked the Mets' roster in 1997. He proceeded to give the team five solid seasons and emerge as a front-of-the-rotation hurler.

Reed was a big reason why the Mets were wild-card contenders in 1997, just a year after the team went 71–91. The West Virginia native was outstanding between Opening Day and June 1, going 4–2 with a 1.81 ERA in 74⅔ innings. He went the distance in his first win as a Met, a seven-hitter in a 6–2 decision over the Reds April 22.

Reed won six straight decisions between June 23 and August 4, compiling a 3.02 ERA during a span that began with a complete-game win over the Braves. His record stood at 10–4 with a 2.77 following that stretch, which included 18 consecutive scoreless innings. He compiled a 3.19 ERA the rest of the season but won just three of his last eight decisions.

Reed had proved he belonged in the majors, 11 years after making his pro debut. He finished sixth in the National League with a 2.89 ERA and was second with just 1.3 walks per nine innings. Reed also worked at least six innings in 28 of his 31 starts.

Reed's ERA rose by more than a half-run in 1998, but the Mets finally gave him solid run support with the acquisition of Mike Piazza. Reed finished tied for 10th in the National League with a career-high 16 victories, tied his personal best of 18 consecutive scoreless innings and was named to the NL All-Star team for the first time.

Reed flirted with perfection twice in 1998. He retired the first 20 Devil Rays June 8 at Shea Stadium before Wade Boggs doubled to end the perfect-game bid. Reed settled for his fifth career complete game and third shutout. Reed also carried a perfect game into the seventh inning against the Marlins 11 days later. Edgar Renteria ended it with a one-out single before Florida rallied for a 3–2 win.

Reed continued to display durability, pitching at least seven innings in 19 of his 31 starts in 1998. He had gone at least six innings in 55 of his first 62 starts as a Met while leading the club in innings pitched in 1997 and '98.

Reed helped the Mets end their 11-year postseason drought in 1999 by finishing sixth in the NL with a .688 winning percentage. He went six or more innings in 17 of his 26 starts but was beginning to break down. He was placed on the disabled list in April because of a slightly torn calf muscle, and returned to the DL in late summer with a strained middle finger on his pitching hand. He had won a career-high seven straight decisions between June 15 and August 2 before landing on the disabled list the second time.

Reed was the Mets' good luck charm down the stretch in 1999 as the team won 12 of his final 17 starts. He capped his regular season by tossing a three-hit shutout in a 7–0 win over the Pirates October 3, which kept the Mets mathematically alive in the wild-card race.

Reed also pitched well in his two 1999 postseason starts. He was the winning pitcher in the Mets' 9–2 rout of the Diamondbacks in Game 3 of the Division Series, allowing two runs and four hits in six innings. Reed also helped the Mets avoid a four-game sweep against the Braves in the NLCS, giving up two runs and three hits over seven-plus innings of a no-decision before John Olerud hit a two-run single in the eighth to put the Mets ahead. Reed carried a one-hit shutout into the eighth but was lifted after giving up back-to-back homers to Brian Jordan and Ryan Klesko.

Reed was bothered by various injuries in 2000, but they didn't stop him from posting his second straight 11–5 record, tying him for sixth in the NL in winning percentage. Reed spent 17 days on the disabled list after breaking a bone in his left wrist. He already had been injured by a comebacker once that season before Andruw Jones tagged him on the wrist by a line drive.

Reed didn't miss a start following his stint on the DL, going 7–3 with a 3.47 ERA in 15 games. The Mets won 16 of his last 22 starts and were 21–9 in games started by Reed in 2000.

Reed also was showing an ability to handle a bat. He hit .204 and finished second in the league with 14 sacrifice bunts in 2000, one season after batting .244. He also shares the Mets record for doubles by a pitcher in one season, hitting five in 1997.

Reed continued his string of solid postseason performances by allowing two runs and seven hits in six innings against the Giants in Game 3 of the 2000 NLDS. The Mets rallied to tie the game in the eighth before Benny Agbayani won it with a solo homer in the 13th.

Reed was shelled in Game 3 of the NLCS against the Cardinals, yielding four earned runs and eight hits in 3⅓ innings of the Mets' only loss of the series. But he bounced back in Game 3 of the World Series, giving up two runs in six innings before the Mets scored twice in the eighth to beat the Yankees 4–2.

Reed opened the 2001 season by throwing consecutive complete games, allowing just three runs and seven hits but going 1–1. He was 6–2 with a 2.49 ERA after shutting out the Phillies on a four-hitter June 5. By that time, Reed had walked just eight in 90⅓ innings.

Reed improved to 7–2 by beating the Orioles 10–3 June 12. He was selected to the 2001 All-Star Game, the second time he had received such an honor. But he faltered during a stretch in which he went 1–4 with a 5.63 in seven starts from June 17 to July 26, his final games as a Met.

The Mets were nine games under .500 and 11½ games out of first when Reed made his last start with the team.

Needing another bat in their lineup, the Mets sent Reed to the Twins for outfielder Matt Lawton July 30.

Reed made 12 starts for the 2001 Twins but was just 4–6 with a 5.19 ERA. He rebounded in 2002, going 15–7 with a 3.78 ERA in 188 innings for the Twins. But he was able to pitch just 135 innings a year later, losing 12 of his 18 decisions and posting a 5.07 ERA.

The Twins granted him free agency after the 2003 season. Reed returned to his original team, signing a minor league deal with the Pirates in 2004. But he failed to make the team out of spring training and retired at age 39, ending an 18-year pro career.

ML debut	Pirates vs. Mets, 8/8/88 (8 IP, 3 H, 0 ER, 4 K, 1 BB)
Mets debut	@ Giants, 4/5/97 (7 IP, 3 H, 0 ER, 5 K, 2 BB)
First ML strikeout	Wally Backman, Mets, 8/8/88 (with Pirates)
First Mets strikeout	José Vizcaino, @ Giants, 4/5/97
First ML win	vs. Mets, 8/8/88
First Mets win	vs. Reds, 4/22/97
First ML save	@ Cardinals, 6/13/90 (with Pirates)
Most strikeouts, ML/Mets game	12, vs. Pirates, 10/2/99
Low-hit ML CG	3, 5 times
Low-hit Mets CG	3, vs. Rays, 6/8/98; vs. Pirates, 10/2/99; @ Braves, 4/5/01

Acquired: Signed as a free agent, 11/7/95.
Deleted: Traded to the Twins for Matt Lawton, 7/30/01.

José Reyes

Shortstop, Second Baseman   Bats both, throws right
Born: 6/11/83   Villa Gonzalez, Dominican Republic
Height: 6′0″   Weight: 160   #7

José Reyes Mets Career

YEAR	GP	AB	R	H	2B	3B	HR	RBI	K	BB	SB	AVG	SLG	OBP
2003	69	274	47	84	12	4	5	32	36	13	13	.307	.434	.334
2004	53	220	33	56	16	2	2	14	31	5	19	.255	.373	.271
2005	161	696	99	190	24	17	7	58	78	27	60	.273	.386	.300
2006	153	647	122	194	30	17	19	81	81	53	64	.300	.487	.354
2007	160	681	119	191	36	12	12	57	78	77	78	.280	.421	.354
2008	159	688	113	204	37	19	16	68	82	66	56	.297	.475	.358
2009	36	147	18	41	7	2	2	15	19	18	11	.279	.395	.355
2010	133	563	83	159	29	10	11	54	63	31	30	.282	.428	.321
2011	126	537	101	181	31	16	7	44	41	43	39	.337	.493	.384
TOTAL	1050	4453	735	1300	222	99	81	423	509	333	370	.292	.441	.341

Darryl Strawberry was one of the very few homegrown Mets position players who could force you to postpone a trip to the bathroom or the concession stands when he was at the plate for fear of missing the greatest home run ever hit. You could hear the buzz throughout Shea Stadium when he was about to take his turn at bat, be it in the uniform of the Mets, Dodgers, or Yankees.

José Reyes took it a step further, keeping fans in their seats for an entire inning. If he led off with a single, you'd wait for him to steal second and/or third. If he tripled, there was always the chance he could swipe home. Although it was exciting to watch Strawberry crush a homer off the scoreboard in right-center at Shea—or off the

Mets Leadoff Hitters—Average Stats Per Game
(minimum 200 career games)

Player	GP	R	H	TOB	XB	RBI	BA	OBP	SLG	OPS
José Reyes	945	.735	1.27	1.64	.398	.410	.294	.344	.447	.791
Mookie Wilson	697	.654	1.18	1.53	.304	.349	.281	.334	.399	.723
Bud Harrelson	521	.422	0.88	1.42	.132	.171	.228	.312	.274	.585
Lenny Dykstra	385	.647	1.11	1.57	.348	.351	.278	.343	.412	.755
Tommie Agee	351	.638	1.16	1.61	.399	.504	.277	.336	.461	.797
Vince Coleman	220	.650	1.07	1.53	.232	.286	.271	.338	.357	.695
Lee Mazzilli	214	.603	1.08	1.65	.369	.388	.291	.376	.460	.836
Lance Johnson	214	.720	1.40	1.75	.341	.416	.327	.370	.457	.827
Roger Cedeno	209	.646	1.10	1.53	.273	.278	.277	.277	.378	.715
Wayne Garrett	206	.553	0.94	1.64	.248	.344	.245	.245	.355	.704
Lenny Randle	200	.540	1.07	1.64	.245	.220	.271	.271	.361	.718

clock at Busch Stadium—it was equally thrilling to see Reyes turn a blooper in the alley into a three-base hit.

But, as in the case with Strawberry, Reyes put up exceptional numbers in certain offensive categories but always kept some fans wondering if he could do a little bit more. He has led the National League in stolen bases three times and either led or tied for the league lead in triples on four occasions.. He's also paced the circuit in hits once and earned four selections to the All-Star Game. He ranked fifth on the team's all-time list with a .292 career batting average among Mets with at least 2,000 plate appearances through 2011, yet he was only 16th in on-base percentage. His detractors would say Reyes was only a marginal leadoff hitter based on his ability to get on base, thanks to just 333 walks in 4,453 at-bats. However, the accompanying statistical chart of Mets leadoff hitters demonstrates that Reyes can be considered the best leadoff hitter in team history and that his on-base percentage doesn't take away from his power, speed, and game-altering ability. Of the 11 Mets who have batted leadoff in at least 200 games, Reyes—based on a per-game average—ranks first in hits and runs scored; second in batting, extra-base hits, and RBI; tied for second in total bases; third in on-base percentage; tied for third in times on base; fourth in slugging and OPS; and tied for fourth in on-base percentage.

Like Strawberry's 1986 Mets, the 2006 squad was loathed throughout most of the National League, especially within the NL East. Reyes sparked some of that animosity with his numerous celebratory handshakes that might have been better left for the dugout. He also annoyed opponents with his fist-pumping or hand-clapping whenever he delivered an extra-base hit or swiped a bag. Some felt Reyes was showing up his opponents with his exuberance, but it was just his way of enjoying the game. And few Mets over the last quarter-century have appeared to love playing the game as much as the Dominican shortstop.

José Bernabe Reyes was only two months past his 16th birthday when he signed with the Mets as an amateur free agent in August 1999. He caught the attention of Dominican scouts while playing for Felix de Leon High School, and was a member of the team only because his actual high school—Liceo Delia Reyes—didn't have a baseball program.

Eddy Toledo was the Mets scout who noticed Reyes and convinced the team to sign him. Toledo said he just had a hunch the kid could play in the majors one day.

"How do they say in English what they paint above saints?" Toledo asked *New York Times* in 2003. "A halo? I saw something like that, something special. He didn't have an arm. He couldn't run. He didn't have a bat. But he looked like a player.

"With José, it's like he was born to play baseball. His love of the game. He's a special one. It's possible I'll never find another one like that before I retire."[197]

Reyes began his pro career in 2000, hitting .250 with 10 stolen bases in 49 games for Kingsport of the rookie Appalachian League. He soon developed into one of the Mets' better prospects by hitting .307 with 15 triples and 30 steals in 108 games for Class A Capital City in 2001.

The Mets promoted him twice in 2002, putting him at St. Lucie of the Class A Florida State League before he ended the year at Double A Binghamton. Reyes stole 58 bases and poked 19 triples in 134 games while batting .288 to earn the Mets' Sterling Organizational Player of the Year award. He also was named *USA Today*'s Minor League Player of the Year and took MVP honors in the

Futures All-Star Game. However, the Mets were not prepared to rush their speedy prospect.

"The conservative approach—and the right approach from our philosophy—would be for him to spend at least part of the year in Triple A, and let's see where he develops from there," said Mets assistant GM Jim Duquette during 2003 spring training. "If he plays well, if he forces his way to the big leagues, then we'll deal with that. Every time we've challenged him, he's risen and actually excelled. That's what's been exciting for us."[198]

Reyes was just 19 when he opened 2003 at Triple A Norfolk. The Mets had hoped to give him a full year with the Tides, but those plans were scuttled due to a combination of his accelerated development and an injury to season-opening shortstop Rey Sanchez.

Sanchez did not get off to a good start, hitting .225 in 38 games before landing on the disabled list for the second time that season. Manager Art Howe used Joe McEwing at short for a few games during Sanchez's absences, but the versatile McEwing did not display great range at the position.

Meanwhile, Reyes already had stolen an International League–leading 26 bases through 42 games at Norfolk and was the organization's best defensive shortstop when the Mets decided to promote him on June 10 following Sanchez's injury.

"We expect José to go back to Norfolk when Rey returns," said general manager Steve Phillips in a statement before Reyes' big-league debut.[199]

Reyes went 2-for-4 with a double and two runs scored in his debut June 10 as the Mets lost to the Rangers 9–7. After the game, Reyes called his debut "another great moment in my life."[200]

Reyes went 1-for-16 over his next four games before torching the Angels in Anaheim during the series finale, going 3-for-4 with a grand slam, five RBIs, and his first stolen base.

"That's another great moment in my life," said Reyes of the grand slam, echoing what he said following his major league debut.[201]

Reyes already had 11 RBIs through nine big-league games and drove in at least three runs in four contests from June 15 to July 1. But his batting average was an anemic .200 and his on-base percentage was only .211 through his first 25 major league contests. Reyes was also just 1-for-3 in stolen-base attempts at that point before his bat and legs got going.

"I feel good and I feel comfortable," Reyes said with confidence heading into July. "I've learned a lot. I go out and enjoy the game."[202]

Reyes collected three hits in back-to-back games against the Phillies on July 12 and 13 before hitting .421 during a nine-game hitting streak from July 19 to 27. He went 0-for-8 in his next two games but followed that with a 17-game hitting streak in which he batted .425 with a .462 on-base percentage and 18 runs scored from July 30 to August 18.

The streak was the second-longest by a Mets rookie at the time, topped only by Mike Vail's 23-game stretch in 1975. It also lifted his batting average to .317.

Reyes set a Mets rookie mark for hits in a month with 39 in August, but he also sprained his left ankle on August 31 and spent the rest of the season on the disabled list, finishing with a .307 average, 21 extra-base hits, 32 RBIs, and 47 runs scored in 67 games.

Just as encouraging were his base-running and defensive stats through his final two months. He was successful on 12 of his final 13 stolen-base attempts to finish second among NL rookies with 13. He also played errorless ball over his final 35 games after making nine miscues in his first 34 contests.

Mets fans were anticipating what Reyes could do over a full season. He was everything the team's PR machine said he was during his half season in New York, ranking among the top 10 in most rookie offensive categories despite his limited at-bats. The Mets had become an aging ballclub before Reyes broke into the majors, with former All-Stars Mo Vaughn, Roberto Alomar, and Mike Piazza failing to produce as expected in 2003. Reyes represented a fresh start on a team that was about to unveil another blue-chip prospect in 2004.

But Reyes also opened training camp at a new position. The Mets had signed Japanese All-Star shortstop Kaz Matsui to a three-year contract during the 2003–2004 offseason and wanted Reyes to slide over to second base. The Mets' new keystone combination didn't play together until June 19 and started just 42 games due to injuries to both players.

Reyes was the first to land on the disabled list, straining his hamstring during spring training. The Mets initially thought he might be ready by the first or second week of the regular season, but the injury lingered while the team tried to alter his running style. Reyes experienced several setbacks during his extended spring training and minor league rehabs before finally making his season debut in mid-June.

"If I go there at 70 percent and get hurt again, maybe I miss the whole year," he said. "I don't want to do that. They don't want to do that. It's my future and my career. I don't do anything else. I just play baseball."[203]

Reyes got off to another sluggish start, hitting only .119 in his first 10 games and .195 over his first 19. However, he was handling second base better than Matsui was playing short, fueling sentiment that Reyes should be returned to his natural position.

Reyes started to sizzle at the plate on July 7, starting an 18-game stretch in which he batted .358 with eight doubles, six RBIs, and 12 runs scored to hike his average to a season-high .270. He was 11-for-11 in stole-base attempts during that span, but he still hadn't tripled since his first game of the season. He finally legged out a triple on August 10 but was diagnosed with a stress fracture in his left leg three days later, keeping him out of action until September 24.

Meanwhile, Matsui had been a tremendous disappointment at shortstop when healthy. Although he showed excellent range, Matsui appeared to have trouble adjusting to the all-dirt infields in the majors after years of handling bounces off artificial surfaces in Japan. He also didn't have Reyes' arm and was unable to spark the offense, hitting in the .260s with little power.

The Mets were about to begin a season-ending series against the Expos when Reyes and Matsui switched positions, a decision that occurred the day after Omar Minaya was introduced as the Mets' new general manager. Minaya now had Reyes and rookie David Wright on the left side of his infield, and the cornerstones of the team's rebuilding program. Wright had been given a half-season to prove his worth, and the third baseman responded by hitting .293 with 14 homers and 40 RBIs in 69 games. Reyes showed flashes of his 2003 form before finishing with a .255 average and 19 stolen bases in 21 attempts over 53 games. They were now being counted on to bolster a lineup that already had Piazza, Cliff Floyd, and Mike Cameron, and would include Carlos Beltrán by January 2005.

Minaya also signed three-time Cy Young Award winner Pedro Martinez to a four-year package in the winter of 2004, making him the ace of a staff that had Tom Glavine, Steve Trachsel and Jae Seo. The Mets had a new manager in Willie Randolph, leading to high expectations entering 2005 training camp.

One of the Mets' major question marks entering 2005 was whether Reyes could last a full season. He had missed 109 games in '04 due to the hamstring injury and the stress fracture. Reyes would sit out only 15 games over the next four seasons.

With Wright at the hot corner, the Mets became the first team in modern National League history to have a shortstop and third baseman appear in at least 150 games in the same season before their 22nd birthdays. Wright batted .306, homered 27 times, and became the first Met to drive in over 100 runs in his first full major league season.

Reyes became the first Met to lead the NL in stolen bases, swiping 60 in 75 attempts. He was the second Met to top the circuit in triples, hitting 17 nine years after Lance Johnson led the league with a team record 21. Reyes also paced the league in at-bats and plate appearances while hitting .273 with seven homers, 17 doubles, 58 RBIs, and 99 runs scored in his first full major league campaign.

Reyes was outstanding defensively after regaining his natural position, participating in 105 double plays with Matsui and Miguel Cairo as his double-play partners. Reyes committed 18 errors but came up with several outstanding gems while showing more range and confidence than Matsui.

Among Randolph's biggest responsibilities in 2005 were to show Matsui the finer points of second base while molding Reyes into a smarter, more mature player. In Matsui's case, the educational process occurred on the field during batting practice each day. As for Reyes, he and Randolph would have chats in the manager's office as Willie tried to learn more of his shortstop's thought process.

"I have him come in here and I just say: 'What's up? What's going on?'" said Randolph. "I'm looking to get him to open up about how he feels. The best way to get through to young players is to get them to talk. I like young guys to initiate conversation, and right now, he doesn't initiate. He's not as open as I'd like. But he will be. Hopefully we're going to be together for a long time."

"I feel a lot more comfortable having someone like Willie who will talk to me about baseball and explain things to me that I don't know," said Reyes. "He tells me about how the game is supposed to be played, about how to do this and do that. I know I have things to work on."[204]

His fielding was a bit more consistent than his batting. He had a .300 average through the first 10 games but was down to .258 before constructing a 20-game hitting streak from July 17 to August 7. Reyes batted .374 with 19 runs scored and 11 stolen bases during the streak to help the Mets go 12–8. He owned a .280 average by the end of the streak but hit only .257 with 29 runs scored in his final 51 games as the Mets finished out of the playoff picture for the fifth straight year after flirting with the wild-card just before Labor Day.

Another knock on Reyes at this point was his ability to draw walks. His .300 on-base percentage was only sixth on the team as he walked just 27 times in 733 plate appearances, or once every 27 trips to the plate. Only Colorado's Neifi Perez had a worse on-base percentage among National Leaguers who hit at least .265 and qualified for the batting title.

But at least Reyes was back to being Reyes. He was enjoying baseball as he did before the hamstring injury—and Matsui's arrival—had turned him into a gimpy second baseman in 2004. Reyes had long abandoned the Mets' idea of changing his running style to lessen the possibility of injuries.

"I just run one way now, my old way," Reyes said in 2005. "Last year was tough for me. It's just like old times for me at shortstop. Since I was a little kid, I always played shortstop, since I was eight years old."[205]

Minaya bolstered the 2006 lineup by acquiring catcher Paul Lo Duca and first baseman Carlos Delgado from the Marlins. Lo Duca was the prototypical No. 2 hitter and helped Reyes increase his stolen-base and runs-scored totals. Delgado was there to drive in Reyes if Beltrán hadn't already done so.

Reyes led the NL in triples (17) and steals (64) for the second straight year while making significant improvement in other categories. He almost doubled his walk total (53) from 2005 despite 30 fewer plate appearances. But it took a while for his bat to heat up.

Reyes was hitting just .231 through 18 games despite an eight-game hitting streak from April 5 to 14. He had a .250 batting average and a .312 on-base percentage through May 31 before taking off.

José Reyes against the Phillies in August 2006. Photo courtesy of David Ferry

Reyes hit .373 with 28 runs scored in 25 games during June to help the Mets pad their lead in the NL East race. He was so hot in June that he became the second Met ever to take back-to-back NL Player of the Week honors, and the ninth to hit for the cycle. Reyes accomplished the cycle on June 21 against the Reds, going homer-double-triple-single.

While the Mets were running away with the division, Minaya was working hard to lock Reyes into a long-term deal, one that would keep him with the team long after he was free-agent eligible. By August, Reyes accepted a four-year, $23.25 million contract that included an $11 million option for 2011.

It appeared to be a win-win as Reyes now had a lengthy deal that wasn't going to break the Mets. But the contract looked small after Wright agreed to a six-year, $55 million package with a club option for 2013 just three days later. Reyes never said anything over the next five seasons about the disparity of the contracts.

Mets fans liked what they were seeing out of Reyes and voted him onto the National League starting lineup for the All-Star Game. Reyes had to miss the game because of an injury suffered the day before the All-Star break.

Reyes hit .300 both before and after the All-Star break to help the Mets win their first division title in 18 years. He reached base safely in 30 of his final 35 contests, including 18 straight from August 22 to September 11. The streak included his first three-homer game August 15 at Philadelphia, making him the first player in team history to homer three times in a game and also hit for the cycle in the same year. The thrill of his three–home run game was muted by the Mets' lopsided loss to the Phillies that night.

"I can't get too excited because we lost," said Reyes of his team record-tying feat before focusing on the rest of the series. "We have to forget about it. We have two more games here. We have to keep our heads up."[206]

He later added his first career inside-the-park homer September 7 against the Dodgers.

Reyes finished the season ranked fourth in the NL with 122 runs, eighth with 194 hits and ninth with 56 multi-hit games. He also became the first player in history with at least 122 runs scored, 194 hits, 19 homers, and 64 stolen bases in a season.

Reyes did it while hitting in front of one of the greatest lineups in Mets history. He was among five Mets with at least 30 doubles, and one of five with at least 18 home runs. Reyes was fourth on the club with 81 RBIs despite hitting in the leadoff spot, another indication of the Mets' balanced lineup.

New York won the NL East with ease at 97–65, 12 games ahead of the Phillies. But the team also made some enemies along the way with their exuberant on-field celebrations during games. If Reyes scored on a home run, he was at the plate to administer one of his various hand/fist/elbow/forearm exchanges. Reyes was branded a hot dog by some teams that didn't appreciate his enthusiasm. It was reminiscent of 1986, when the Mets became baseball's most despised teams for their curtain calls following home runs.

The '06 Mets really didn't care what other players thought of them. They were now the National League's best team heading into the postseason, and the favorites to reach the World Series. However, the club's showmanship would come to haunt them in 2007 as every NL club had extra incentive to pound them into submission.

The Mets swept the Dodgers in the 2006 NLDS by a combined 19–11 margin, although New York trailed in the middle innings of the first and third games. Reyes went just 2-for-12 in the series but still managed to account for five of the 19 runs. He walked and scored the tiebreaking run in the seventh inning of Game 1 and had the first and last RBI in the Mets' 4–1 victory in Game 2. After the Mets blew a 4–0 lead in Game 3, Reyes sparked a three-run sixth with a game-tying single before scoring on Beltrán's base hit to put New York ahead 7–5 in a series-clinching 9–5 victory.

Reyes had a pair of three-hit games in the NLCS against the Cardinals while stringing together a five-game hit streak. He was 3-for-4 with an RBI and two runs scored in a 9–6 loss in Game 2 before collecting one hit in three of the next contests. He extended the streak by hitting a leadoff homer off Chris Carpenter and scoring twice in the Mets' 4–2 victory in Game 6, which stretched the series to the limit.

"He's our igniter, offensively and defensively—especially on offense," Wright said. "As he goes, we go. That's the ultimate shot of energy, when your leadoff guy goes deep against a Cy Young winner."

"My teammates told me today, I have to get on base," Reyes said. "Every time I get on base, something good is going to happen. I just was able to get on base a lot, and the most important thing about it is we won."[207]

The Mets produced just four hits in Game 7 and fell an extra-base hit short of advancing to the World Series. New York took a 1–0 lead on Wright's RBI single in the bottom of the first and didn't get another hit until the ninth, a half-inning after Yadier Molina's two-run homer put the Cardinals ahead 3–1.

José Valentin and Endy Chavez singled to open the bottom of the ninth before Floyd struck out as a pinch-hitter, bringing up Reyes as the potential series-winning run. Reyes stroked a liner to center to end his 0-for-5 night, dropping his average for the series to .281 and leaving the Mets one out from elimination.

Lo Duca followed Reyes' liner by walking to load the bases, giving Beltrán an opportunity to be the hero. But Beltrán struck out looking to end the Mets' season a few games sooner than expected.

The Mets made just one major change to their division title–winning lineup, allowing Floyd to leave via free agency and replacing him with Moises Alou. The lineup was otherwise left intact as the Mets headed into 2007 training camp as the favorites to repeat as division champs despite issues to the rotation.

Reyes continued to improve as a hitter during the first half of 2007, compiling a .307 average with nine triples, 46 stolen bases and 61 runs scored in 86 games through the All-Star break. He also became a much more patient hitter at the plate, walking 47 times by the break for a .387 on-base percentage. Reyes was muzzling critics who felt he'd be only a marginal leadoff hitter at best if he didn't stop chasing balls out of the strike zone.

The Mets began to sputter in June, and a 4–0 loss to the Astros on July 7 left them 14–20 in their last 34 games. Reyes failed to run out a grounder that hugged the foul line in the eighth inning of the Houston contest, three games after showing no hustle out of the box following another ground ball. The second lapse prompted Randolph to yank him from the game.

"That should never have happened," Reyes said. "I know what I did was wrong. I didn't want to look like an idiot. I'm sure people watching were surprised. I usually never try to slow down."

"I only have two rules, two simple basic rules: be on time and play hard," Randolph said after the game. "I watch things. Sometimes I let things go if it's not something that's habit forming. But if I see it begin to be somewhat of a pattern, you'll sit next to me. I'm not going to change that. That's the way I've always been.

"When you're not playing well, you have to get after it; when you're not playing well and you don't put out like you should, it makes you look worse. I don't have a problem with winning or losing games. But win or lose, if you lose you're going to play the game hard. If you don't, it makes what you guys see look worse or what I see look worse."[08]

Reyes, Wright, and Beltrán were plugging along at their 2006 pace, but the rest of the lineup was inconsistent. Alou and Valentin missed huge chunks of playing time, Delgado's power numbers dropped, Shawn Green lost his home run stroke, and Lo Duca kept his average around the .270 mark for much of the season after finishing among the league leaders in 2006. The inconsistent hitting prevented the Mets from running away from the rest of the NL East, but it didn't stop them from sitting atop the division for over four consecutive months.

Reyes was hitting .308 after going 3-for-5 with three runs scored against the Braves on August 9. His average remained above .300 as the Mets carried a seven-game lead into a four-game set at Philadelphia at the end of August. New York lost all four games as Reyes went 1-for-15 with three walks and only one run scored.

The Phillies series began a season-ending stretch in which Reyes hit only .197 with nine RBIs and 20 runs scored in 32 games. The Mets still managed to push the division lead back to seven games with 17 remaining heading into a series against the Phillies at Shea. Reyes hit safely in all three games, but the Phils completed another sweep to draw closer to the division lead.

The Phillies had extra incentive to make a late-season push; they passionately hated the Mets and didn't appreciate Reyes' theatrics or that of a few of his teammates. Neither did the Marlins or Nationals, both of which did the Phils a favor by going 8–6 versus New York over the final 2½ weeks despite their woeful records.

Reyes had a big game against the Nats at Shea on September 25, going 3-for-5 with two homers and four RBIs. He crushed a three-run blast in the ninth inning, four batters before Alou laced a three-run double. But the Mets trailed 10–3 when the inning began and left the tying run on third as Washington completed an agonizing 10–9 win over New York.

The Mets still had a two-game edge over the Phils before losing four of their next five games to finish one game behind Philadelphia. Reyes provided little offense in those five games, going 2-for-23 with one walk and one run scored.

He started hearing boos from the crowd at Shea Stadium down the stretch. It was the first time fans had shown impatience with Reyes, who said he understood their displeasure.

"They wanted me to do good, so that's why they booed me," Reyes said.[209]

Reyes hit only .251 after the break to end up with a .280 average, 12 triples, 57 RBIs, and 119 runs, all drop-offs from 2006. But he also doubled 36 times and shattered a team record with 78 stolen bases, 12 more than Roger Cedeno's previous mark set in 1999. Although his batting average slipped 20 points, his on-base percentage was .357 for the second straight year as he finished with a career-high 78 walks.

Mets management tried after the season to tone down the team's on-field acts of elation. Lastings Milledge, who helped sparked a benches-clearing incident during the next-to-last game of the season, was sent to the Nationals for right fielder Ryan Church and catcher Brian Schneider. Manager Willie Randolph also asked Reyes to stifle his celebrations, suggesting he save them for the dugout.

Reyes had been the most enthusiastic player on the ballclub since his recall four years earlier, making him the darling of Mets fans who serenaded his name whenever he came through in a key situation. Reyes wasn't trying to annoy the members of the other dugout, and his *joie de vivre* helped the Mets stay loose. But ask a member of the Phillies which Mets annoyed him the most, and Reyes and Milledge were on a very short list.

Randolph's request seemed to make sense since there was no reason to antagonize another team, especially one that just lapped you in the final 2½ weeks of the previous season. But it also seemed to take some of the starch from Reyes' overall game, especially during the first month of 2008.

Reyes began the season with eight multi-hit games in the Mets' 26 contests during April, but he honed a meager .250 average in the process. He had only six steals for the month, putting him on pace for 37 for the season.

He appeared to break out of his funk on May 2, going 4-for-5 with a double, two triples, and three runs scored in a 7–2 win over the Diamondbacks. Reyes didn't hit another triple the rest of the month, but he batted .316 with five homers, 15 RBIs, and 20 runs scored in 28 games while lifting his season average to .285.

Meanwhile, the Mets were having trouble staying above .500, and looked lethargic just a few months after manufacturing one of the greatest late-season fades in major league history. Reyes did his best to prop up the offense in early June, hitting .290 with seven stolen bases and 12 runs in the Mets' first 14 games that month. But New York was just 33–35 heading into a series at Anaheim in mid-June, sparking speculation that Randolph would be let go.

Reyes opened the road trip by going 2-for-4 with two doubles and three runs scored in a 9–6 win over the Angels. Hours later, Reyes learned he had a new manager.

Bench coach Jerry Manuel took over amid rumors that several members of the Mets had stopped hustling for Randolph. Manuel immediately made a statement by benching Reyes in the first inning of his first game as skipper.

Reyes led off with a single but didn't sprint toward first with his normal gait. Manuel came out of the dugout and pulled him from the game, which led Mets broadcasters to wonder if Reyes' hustle down the line prompted the decision. After the Mets lost 6–1, Manuel insisted he was worried Reyes had a nagging injury that might get worse with extended playing time. Eventually, Manuel divulged his plan for sparking his stagnant club.

"As soon as they come off the field, I tell them what to expect," Manuel said. "You need to address those. I really believe that our team plays good for five, six innings, then all of a sudden, where's the focus and intensity?"

"It's the first game, the first inning," Beltrán said. "People are thinking, let's see how he reacts to Reyes's behavior. It's not a big deal, but you watch."[210]

The two continued their conversation in the runway between the dugout and clubhouse. By the third inning, Reyes and Manuel were calmly sitting next to each other. Message sent. Message received, as Reyes was 3-for-5 with three runs scored in an extra-inning win at Anaheim to raise his average to .297.

The Mets finally got hot toward the end of June and took over the NL East lead the day after the All-Star break. Reyes was among the catalysts, hitting .326 with a .392 on-base percentage, nine RBIs, and 12 runs scored in 21 games from June 27 to July 20. The Mets went 14–7 during that span, which included a 10-game winning streak that catapulted them to the top of the division.

Reyes kept producing in late July, hitting a three-run homer in a 6–3 win over the Phillies and going 4-for-8 with a solo shot in an extra-inning loss to the Cardinals.

The rivalry between the Mets and Phillies only intensified that month, with Reyes serving as lightning rod. The

Phils were plenty steamed after Reyes provided a theatrical display following his go-ahead, three-run blast off reliever Ryan Madson in late July. He pointed to the sky milliseconds after the ball made contact with his bat, and continued in that pose as he reached second. Even before he sat down in the dugout, it was the usual array of fist-pumps and hand gestures that was making him one of the least-liked opponents in the league.

The Phillies had said little about Reyes and the Mets' celebratory display before that night. They unloaded the following morning.

"Do I think he's a hot dog?" manager Charlie Manuel was asked. "He's got some polish on him. Cockiness is good if it's handled right and to a certain degree. He's a very talented player; he could be one of the best players in baseball. But at the same time, he's got a lot of growing up to do."

"That's the way that team is. They're going to do that," said Madson before admitting that his team loathed the Mets.[211]

The war was on, as if nobody recognized the Phillies' hatred for the Mets before the game. What Reyes had done was akin to going to the zoo and poking a stick at a lion. A few weeks after he ticked off the Phillies, Reyes received on-air criticism from Mets broadcaster Keith Hernandez, who knew a thing or two about on-field demeanor. Reyes displayed immaturity by throwing his glove to the ground following a throwing error during a Sunday game against the Yankees. The gesture evoked memories of shortstop Tanner Boyle in the 1976 movie *The Bad News Bears*, except Boyle got a free pass because he was only 12.

Hernandez took Reyes to task after the play, intimating that it was time the Mets stopped tolerating his immaturity and turned him into an adult. The comments led to a verbal confrontation between Reyes and Hernandez on a team flight to St. Louis after the game, although the exchange never came close to becoming violent.

Reyes was just as good in August as he batted .317 with 10 extra-base hits and 20 runs scored in 28 games to help the Mets go 18–11 for the month. New York carried a one-game lead into September and increased it to 3½ games with 17 games left after Reyes went 1-for-3 with two runs in a 13–10 win over the Nationals. Reyes continued to produce, but the Mets' bullpen imploded down the stretch while the team eliminated itself from the division race before the final game of the season. On the day the Mets said good-bye to Shea Stadium, they fell to the Marlins 4–2 to lose the wild-card by a game to the Brewers.

Reyes had at least two hits in six of the Mets' final 17 games and finished with a .297 average. He led the league with a career-high 204 hits and 19 triples while collecting a career-best 72 extra-base hits. Reyes also passed Mookie Wilson as the Mets' all-time leader in triples and stolen bases while making his contract extension look like slave wages for a two-time All-Star shortstop. The only statistical downside was his 56 stolen bases as he abdicated his NL throne to Willy Taveras.

Injuries destroyed the Mets' playoff chances in 2009, none more crucial than Reyes' right leg problem. He opened the year by hitting .279 with 11 multi-hit games in his first 36 contests, recording a .350 on-percentage and setting a pace for a career-high 80 walks.

Reyes reeled off a 12-game hitting streak in April and started the Mets' first 33 games, hitting .286 after going 3-for-5 with three doubles and a walk in a loss at Atlanta. But he started just once in the next six contests before leaving a May 20 game at Los Angeles with a right calf injury. Reyes didn't play another inning the rest of the season.

The leg problem originally wasn't deemed to be too serious, just as his injury during 2004 spring training wasn't expected to keep him out of action for any significant amount of time. But he never began a rehab assignment until September, long after the Mets had played themselves out of playoff contention. The team had hoped Reyes might make a September return until he tore his right hamstring, putting him on the shelf for good.

No one was more frustrated with the latest hamstring injury than Reyes. By September, he was still hoping to play a few games just to gain some confidence heading into 2010. He also began to hear speculation he was either jaking it or too afraid to test the leg.

"I don't know why people sometimes think I don't want to be on the field," Reyes said. "I live for baseball, I always play baseball since I was little. I don't do nothing at my house, just watch TV and spend time with my family. But I love to be on the field. So that's my main goal, like I said. If I'm ready the last week of the season, then I'm going to play the last week of the season."

"I've been working so hard you guys don't know."[212]

He underwent surgery in October to rectify the original injury as scar tissue was removed from the accessory hamstring tendon around his right knee. Reyes went to camp with the Mets and was soon diagnosed with a thyroid condition that led him to miss the entire 2010 exhibition season and the first series of the regular season.

Reyes made his '10 season debut in the fifth game but failed to give the offense an immediate lift, batting .154 with two RBIs and two runs scored in his first eight games while the Mets dropped to 4–8. The offense began to click only after Ike Davis was recalled from Triple A Buffalo to take over at first base prior to the start of a 10-game homestand. With Davis in the lineup, the Mets went 9–1 on the homestand and won the opener of a six-game road trip to move into first place by the end of April.

New York continued to win despite minimal production from Reyes, whose batting average was down to .211 after he went 0-for-4 in the opener of a series against the Yankees at Citi Field on May 21. Reyes began a nine-game hitting streak the next afternoon, batting .462 with nine RBIs, three stolen bases, and nine runs scored through the rest of the month to bring his average up to .259 and perk up his enthusiasm.

"I missed all those things I do now; I missed them last year," Reyes said. "Now I can do everything I did before—hit a triple, steal a base, diving. I missed the game last year. I know when I get going, everybody gets going. Hopefully, it can continue to be like that."[213]

Reyes put together a 12-game hitting streak (.438) from June 8 to 19, went hitless on June 20 and was 9-for-16 over the next four games, leaving him with a .288 average, six triples, six homers, 31 RBIs, 50 runs scored, and 19 stolen bases through his first 68 games. The Mets climbed to within a half-game of the NL East lead by June 27 in large part due to the top of the order. Reyes and Angel Pagan had become a better 1-2 threat than Reyes and Lo Duca had been in 2006, especially with Pagan hitting well over .300 and stealing more bases than Reyes. All was well at Citi Field.

The Mets began to sputter two weeks before the All-Star Game and accelerated their freefall with a 2–9 road trip that left them near the .500 mark again. Reyes was one of the few positives during a western swing in which the Mets stopped hitting. He sat out the first four games of the trip in San Francisco due to a sore right oblique that he aggravated during the final series before the break. He showed he was in peak form after returning to the lineup, reeling off another 12-game hitting streak from July 19 to 31.

But the rest of the Mets' offense struggled while Reyes flourished. Reyes hit .333 in his first 12 games after the break, but the other Mets batted a combined .196 through the end of July despite Beltrán's return to the lineup. Beltrán, Wright, Pagan, and Jeff Francoeur endured deep batting slumps. Jason Bay was out of action due to a concussion suffered near the end of the team's forgettable July road trip, an injury that would force him to miss the final two months. The catching tandem of Rod Barajas and Henry Blanco produced just seven RBIs during June and July. Second baseman Luis Castillo was battling injuries and still hadn't found his hitting stroke. By the time the Mets absorbed a 14–1 loss to the lowly Diamondbacks at Citi Field on August 1, they were just 53–52 and 6½ games out of first place.

Reyes hit .302 in 23 games during August, but the Mets went 10–13 in those contests to fall out of contention. He scored only 13 times and worked out just three walks the entire month as New York slipped into fourth place in the East and out of postseason contention.

The Mets dropped 10 of their final 15 games to finish 79–83, their second straight losing season. Reyes compiled a .256 average for the month and finished at .282 with 11 homers, 10 triples, 54 RBIs, and 83 runs scored in 133 games, all respectable season-ending numbers considering the amount of rust he had to shed in April. He also had more walks (31) than stolen bases (30) for the third straight year, although both stats were among the more disappointing aspects of his season. Only five other National Leaguers eligible for the batting title walked fewer times than Reyes, and his stolen-base total was tied for seventh. Pagan finished with seven more steals, marking the first time Reyes had failed to lead the Mets in stolen bases during a full season.

Manuel and Minaya were let go the day after the 2010 season finale. Manuel was replaced by Terry Collins, who had a reputation as a no-nonsense, high-demand skipper during his days in Houston and Anaheim. Sandy Alderson took over as general manager and brought in former GMs J.P. Ricciardi and Paul DePodesta as his top lieutenants, signaling a significant change of direction as the Mets tried to shake off their four-year malaise. The franchise was just 326–322 since their last playoff berth, including a 149–175 mark since the start of 2009.

One of Alderson's first moves was picking up the fifth-year option on Reyes' contract as the Mets weren't ready to give the starting shortstop job to Ruben Tejada. Reyes showed up at camp in great shape and was in the season-opening lineup as the team embarked on its 50th season. He went 0-for-4 in the opener before batting .344 with one homer, six RBIs, nine runs scored, and five stolen bases during an ensuing 13-game hitting streak. The José Reyes salary push was on, although the team went just 4–9 during his hit streak.

His batting average never dipped below .300 after April 19, and he was able to start the Mets' first 52 games while contributing heavily in their victories. He tripled twice in a win over the Dodgers May 6 and was 4-for-5 with two triples in a 9–5 rout of the Phillies May 29.

Reyes was everything Mets fans had always hoped in May, hitting .364 with a .421 on-base percentage, 11 stolen bases, 10 RBIs, 18 runs scored, nine doubles, and six triples. He also became the focal point of the team's offense after Ike Davis and David Wright landed on the disabled list that month.

Reyes and Beltrán were heading up an everyday lineup that included a host of players who either spent much of 2010 in Buffalo (Justin Turner, Daniel Murphy, and Tejada) or signed minor league contracts before training camp (Scott Hairston and Willie Harris). The starting rotation and the bullpen were wildly inconsistent during the first two months, Jason Bay was floating in and out of slumps, and Angel Pagan spent time on the DL. Yet the Mets were hovering near .500 after Reyes batted .462 during a 12-game hitting streak from May 24 to June 8.

Reyes continued his stellar hitting in June, recording a .385 average with 11 stolen bases, 15 RBIs, 29 runs scored, seven triples, and five doubles for the month. He already had 15 triples by June 30, putting him on pace to become only the second player in modern major league history to triple at least 30 times in a season.

Alderson took note of Reyes' spectacular start and attempted to negotiate a contract as the season reached the halfway point. Reyes also saw his stats and realized he didn't want to mess up a good thing as he moved closer to free agency. Reyes announced in June that any further contract talks would have to occur after the season.

"I don't want any distractions on my mind, I just want to play baseball," Reyes said. "Nothing has changed. I want to stay here. I want to be a New York Met my whole career. But right now I just want to play baseball."[214]

Reyes' stance was not a shock, although it began to scare Mets fans who didn't want to lose him. Support for Reyes at Citi Field became more fervent than ever as fans made signs urging the club to re-sign him. They also demonstrated Reyes' popularity by electing him into the National League starting lineup for the All-Star Game. It would be the fourth time he had been chosen to play in the midsummer classic, but also the third time he couldn't play due to injury.

Reyes singled in the first inning of a July 2 game against the Yankees and attempted to steal second when he felt a twinge in his left hamstring and scooted back to first. He was taken out of the game in the second inning and went on the disabled list the following day. Reyes had a major league–leading .354 average at the time of the injury.

Reyes returned to the lineup July 19 and hit only .256 in 18 games before the hamstring pushed him back onto the DL. He embarked on a 14-game hit streak immediately after his return, although he hit only .298 during the streak to drop his average to .329 following an 0-for-4 performance against the Nationals September 12.

Brewers outfielder Ryan Braun and Dodgers outfielder Matt Kemp had closed the gap on Reyes, turning the batting race into a three-horse field. By early September, Reyes was saying publicly that a batting title, while a nice achievement, wouldn't determine whether he had a successful season. That didn't stop his teammates from realizing it would be quite an accomplishment for Reyes and the ballclub.

"If it happens, I mean, it's great, because not too many people have the opportunity to win a batting title in the big leagues," Reyes said.

"I know it would mean a lot for him," said Wright. "And I think it would mean a lot to us as an organization."[215]

Reyes hit safely in his final eight games, posting a .433 average in 30 at-bats. But the batting championship was up for grabs heading into the final game of the season. Reyes opened the bottom of the first in the last game by bunting for a base hit, giving him a .337 average compared to Braun's .334.

And then Reyes pulled himself out of the game, confident that he had secured the title. Since it was a meaningless game in a third straight losing season for the Mets, Reyes wasn't putting the team in jeopardy by taking the rest of the day off. However, many fans at Citi Field weren't happy to see the early exit, and members of the media chastised him for taking the "easy way out" when Braun still had a chance to win the batting crown. Reyes and Collins had to answer the criticism after the game.

"I know it's kind of tough," Reyes said of the fans' reaction after he left the game. "I wanted to stay in the game. But they have to understand, too, what's going on. They have to feel happy about it if I win the batting title. I do it for the team and for the fans, too.

"A lot of people told me, 'You shouldn't play today.' I said: 'No, I want to play. I want to be there. I want to be there for the fans. They can see me.' Because I don't know if next year I'm going to be here."

"I understand," Collins said of the disappointment displayed by some fans following Reyes' departure. "I heard some comments from the stands. I don't blame them. People pay a good price to come to these games. You got to understand that I ask these players to do a lot…we've worked hard to get their respect this year, and they deserve ours."[216]

Collins choked up while addressing the issue during his postgame news conference. It was obvious he had grown particularly close to Reyes and had appreciated the effort given by his often undermanned roster throughout the course of the season. Reyes had completed an exceptional season, and Collins knew it. He also knew there was a chance he would be losing his offensive catalyst within a few months.

First ML/Mets game @ Rangers, 6/10/03
First ML/Mets hit   single vs. John Thomson, @ Rangers, 6/10/03
First ML/Mets homer   grand slam vs. Jerrod Washburn, @ Angels, 6/15/03
First ML/Mets RBI   RBI grounder vs. Jay Powell, @ Rangers, 6/12/03
Most hits, ML/Mets game   5, vs. Braves, 5/5/06
Most homers, ML/Mets game   3, @ Phillies, 8/15/06
Most RBIs, ML/Mets game   5, @ Angels, 6/15/03
Acquired: Signed as an amateur free agent, 8/16/99.
NL All-Star, 2006, 2007, 2010, 2011
NL Batting Champion, 2011
NL Hits Leader, 2008
NL Stolen Base Leader, 2005, 2006, 2007
NL Triples Leader, 2005, 2006, 2008
NL At-Bats Leader, 2005, 2008

Johan Santana

Pitcher Bats left, throws left
Born: 3/13/79 Tovar Merida, Venezuela
Height: 6'0" Weight: 210 #57

Johan Santana Mets Career

YEAR	GP/GS	IP	H	R	ER	K	BB	W–L	SV	ERA
2008	34/34	234.1	206	74	66	206	63	16–7	0	2.53
2009	25/25	166.2	156	67	58	146	46	13–9	0	3.13
2010	29/29	199	179	67	66	144	55	11–9	0	2.98
2011	Injured, did not pitch									
TOTAL	88/88	600	541	208	190	496	164	40–25	0	2.85

Mets Career/Batting

GP	AB	R	H	2B	3B	HR	RBI	K	BB	SB	AVG
88	182	8	29	11	0	1	6	60	8	0	.159

ML Career

YEAR	GP/GS	IP	H	R	ER	K	BB	W–L	SV	ERA
00–10	339/263	1908.2	1609	708	658	1877	528	133–69	1	3.10

There was a large contingent of Mets fans who believed the franchise had become a bit star-crossed by the end of its first decade of the 21st century. That opinion intensified as fans watched the Mets lose postseason berths on the final day of consecutive seasons after they left the potential winning run on base in Game 7 of the 2006 NLCS. The late-season failures were followed by an injury-ravaged 2009 season and a 2010 campaign in which several key players underachieved during the second half.

Johan Santana was supposed to be the solution to the Mets' problems when he was acquired in what quickly became a lopsided trade with the Twins before the start of 2008 spring training. His résumé already included two Cy Young Awards, three AL strikeout titles, and two ERA crowns before he threw his first pitch with the Mets. He became the fourth American Leaguer since 1945 to win pitching's Triple Crown when he won 19 games, struck out 245, and compiled a 2.77 ERA with Minnesota in 2006.

But even a pitcher of Santana's immense talent somehow got sucked into the team's string of bad luck. He would have been a 20-game winner in 2008 had the Mets provided him with a few more runs, and the wasted performances were the difference between an NL East title and the Mets' second-place finish.

Santana had offseason surgery in 2008 and was unable to finish the next two seasons due to other physical maladies. The ailments didn't prevent Santana from compiling the National League's third-best ERA and third-best WHIP among pitchers with at least 600 innings from 2008 to 2010. However, his 40 victories were only tied for eighth among NL hurlers during that span, thanks primarily to lousy run support. There were 43 starts in which he tossed at least seven innings and gave up two runs or fewer, and he won just 24 of those games. Of all major league pitchers who threw between 11–15 games of at least eight innings with fewer than two runs scored between 2008 and 2010, Santana had the fewest victories with seven in 12 starts. Comparatively, Phillies lefty Jamie Moyer was able to win eight starts in which he allowed at least four runs in six innings or fewer, another gnawing difference between the Phils and Mets during that period. It was difficult for a Mets fan to accept that too many of Santana's best performances were being wasted, especially when there was a significant talent drop-off between Santana and the rest of the rotation.

It was also tough to accept a season without Santana. He underwent shoulder surgery in September 2010 and missed the following season after there was hope he would return after the All-Star break.

However, there was a time when general managers weren't sure Santana would ever become a productive pitcher in the majors. The Astros allowed him to be taken by Florida in the December 1999 Rule V draft, and the Marlins turned around and sent him to the Twins the same day for a minor league pitching prospect. Imagine the Astros with a rotation of Roger Clemens, Roy Oswalt, Andy Pettitte, and Santana in the 2005 World Series.

Johan Alexander Santana was signed by Houston as a 16-year-old amateur free agent out of Tovar Merida, Venezuela, in 1995. Santana graduated from Liceo Jose Nucete Sardi High School, where he excelled in baseball and soccer before spending four undistinguished seasons in the Astros' chain.

Santana broke into pro ball as a reliever for the Astros' Dominican team in 1996, going 4–3 with three saves and a 2.70 ERA while striking out 51 and allowing 26 hits in 40 innings. He pitched sparingly in 1997 and spent most of '98 at Auburn of the New York–Penn League, going 7–5 with a 4.26 earned run average and 88 strikeouts in 86⅔ innings. Moved up to Michigan in 1999, Santana was named to the Class A Midwest League all-star game before finishing 8–8 with a 4.66 ERA.

The Marlins claimed the 20-year-old lefty with a Rule V pick and tried to parlay the selection into something sweeter later that day. Santana was a lifetime 19–21 pitcher with a 4.77 ERA and 325 strikeouts in 334 innings when he was dealt to the Twins for Jared Camp, who already had advanced to Triple A and allowed just one earned run while striking out 14 in 10⅔ innings for Buffalo of the International League in 1999 after opening the season in A ball.

"He was one of those prearranged Rule V deals," said Twins general manager Terry Ryan. "They wanted a guy whom we took, and they gave us Santana. A lot of people pinpointed Camp. A lot of people wanted him because he had a good arm and showed it in the Arizona Fall League."[217]

The Marlins projected Camp as a tough right-hander out of the bullpen and were more than willing to take a chance on a pitcher four years older than Santana. Camp never reached the majors, and the Twins watched Santana develop into one of the American League's very best pitchers.

"Houston has some of the best players coming out of the country, and they trade everyone," said White Sox manager Ozzie Guillen in 2005 of the Twins' ability to get Santana before sending him to the Twins. "I don't know what's the reason to trade all those kids. Houston had Santana and Garcia and Abreu. They are pretty loaded."[218]

It took a while for Santana to become a key part of Minnesota's rotation. He spent all of 2000 on the Twins' major league roster and remained a spot starter until 2004, when he claimed his first AL Cy Young Award.

Santana made his big-league debut in a mop-up role, tossing a scoreless ninth in a 7–0 loss to the Devil Rays in the 2000 season opener on April 3. He was a starter in his next three appearances, holding the Royals to a run and five hits over five innings of a no-decision on April 7 before yielding 13 earned runs over seven innings in losses to the hard-hitting Red Sox and Rangers in his next two starts to move back into the pen.

Santana picked up his first major league triumph as a reliever while beating his original team, limiting the Astros to a run and three hits over five innings at Houston to

Johan Santana. Photo courtesy of David Ferry

lower his ERA to 7.22 in 33⅔ innings. But he was hit hard the rest of the way and finished the year 2–3 with a 6.49 ERA in 30 games, including five starts.

The 2001 season included a two-month stay on the disabled list due to a partial tear of the flexor muscle in his left elbow. He opened the season in the bullpen and pitched well enough to make three starts just before the All-Star break until the elbow injury caused the Twins to put him on the shelf in July. He didn't pitch again until late September and finished 1–0 with a 4.74 ERA and 28 strikeouts in 43⅔ innings.

The Twins remained patient with the lefty but sent him to Triple A Edmonton to begin 2002. Santana finally emerged as a strikeout pitcher, fanning 16 for the Trappers against New Orleans on April 29 and going 5–2 with 75 Ks in 48⅔ innings to earn another promotion on May 31.

Santana was pounded the day of his recall, allowing four runs over 5⅓ innings of relief against the Angels. But he also struck out six while tossing 91 pitches to earn another chance to pitch in the Twins' rotation.

He was among the AL's top starters in June 2002, going 3–1 with a 1.88 ERA while holding opponents to a .198 average. Santana struck out 37 in 28⅔ innings and didn't allow more than two runs in any of his five starts that month.

Santana continued to enjoy success as a starter the rest of the season but was often used out of the bullpen during the second half as the Twins won the AL Central, their first playoff berth since 1991. Santana ended up 8–6 with a 2.99 ERA and a team-high 137 strikeouts in just 108⅓ innings. But he struggled out of the pen during the postseason, yielding six runs in 6⅓ innings.

Twins manager Ron Gardenhire opened 2003 with a starting rotation of Brad Radke, Joe Mays, Kyle Lohse, and ex-Mets Rick Reed and Kenny Rogers, making Santana a late-inning reliever once again. Santana received three starts during the first three months, winning all three and allowing only two runs and nine hits in 18 innings. Overall, he was 4–1 with a 2.43 earned run average through July 5, striking out 71 in 63 innings and holding opponents to a .203 batting average.

Mays pitched poorly during the first four months due to an elbow problem that required Tommy John surgery in September. He was dropped from the rotation in early July, paving the way for Santana to become the Twins' best pitcher over the next 4½ years.

Santana was banged around in three of his four starts during July, going 0–2 and compiling a 5.18 earned run average in 24⅓ innings. A subsequent injury to Reed gave

Gardenhire no choice but to keep Santana in the rotation, a predicament that led Minnesota to its second consecutive division crown as Santana emerged as a pitching stud.

Santana was named the AL Pitcher of the Month for August after going 5–0 with a 1.07 ERA, 0.952 WHIP, and 44 strikeouts in 42 innings over six starts. He tossed 20⅔ consecutive scoreless innings from August 8 to 19 and struck out 10 in back-to-back appearances.

Santana was pounded by the Rangers in his first start of September but received a no-decision despite surrendering seven runs and eight hits in four innings. He rebounded quite nicely, winning his next three starts for an eight-game winning streak that left him 12–3 with a 3.17 ERA heading into his final regular-season appearance. Santana tuned up for the playoffs by throwing five shutout innings to lower his ERA to 3.07.

The Twins honored him with the Joseph W. Haynes Award as the team's pitcher of the year, and the Charles O. Johnson Award as the club's most improved player. Santana also set a team record and led the AL with an .800 winning percentage and finished eighth in the league with 169 strikeouts despite making only 18 starts in his 45 appearances.

Santana helped the Twins take Game 1 of the ALDS against the Yankees in the Bronx, allowing three hits over four shutout innings in his first career playoff start and leaving with Minnesota ahead 1–0. The Twins dropped the next two games before Santana went back to the mound on short rest. Santana allowed just one hit over the first 3⅓ innings before the Yankees chased him during a six-run fourth. The Yankees completed an 8–1 victory to advance to the ALCS, but Santana would fare much better against the Yankees the following October.

The Twins went to 2004 training camp with a goal to reach the postseason for a team-record third straight year, but the rotation was thinner after Reed retired after the 2003 season and Rogers accepted a free-agent contract with the Rangers. That put a little more pressure on Santana to perform as he did during the final two months of '03.

Santana won his first American League Cy Young Award after going 20–6 with 265 strikeouts and a 2.61 ERA. He led the circuit in strikeouts, strikeouts per nine innings, ERA, and WHIP. Santana also allowed only 156 hits in 228 innings and came within one victory of winning pitching's Triple Crown.

However, the season couldn't have gotten off to a more disappointing start for Santana and the Twins. He went 2–4 with a 5.50 earned run average in his first 12 starts, allowing 76 hits in 68⅔ innings. Santana allowed at least four runs in half those starts while recording a 1.442 WHIP.

Ironically, his fortunes began to turn in a start against the Mets on June 9 at the Metrodome. Santana fanned 10 and allowed just one run and six hits in seven innings before the Twins completed a 5–3 victory.

The win over the Mets began a season-ending 22-start stretch in which Santana went 18–2 with a 1.36 ERA, a

.148 batting average against, and a 0.696 WHIP in 159⅓ innings. He allowed only 80 hits, struck out 204 and held opponents to a .203 slugging average, allowing him to become the first player to be a unanimous selection for the Cy Young Award after failing to earn a berth in the All-Star Game. Santana capped the regular season by winning his final 13 decisions.

The Twins won the AL Central crown with ease, leading by 13½ games by mid-September and finishing nine games ahead in a relatively weak division. Minnesota won 24 of Santana's 34 starts en route to 92 victories.

Minnesota had to face the Yankees again in the division series, with Santana getting the assignment in Game 1. Santana didn't have his best stuff in the opener, allowing nine hits and striking out five in seven innings. But he threw 63 of his 93 pitches for strikes and led a 2–0 victory in the Bronx.

The Yankees captured the next two games to put Santana in a must-win situation as he took the mound for Game 4 at Minneapolis. Santana did all he could to extend the Twins' season, allowing a run and five hits while fanning seven in five innings. He left the game with a 5–1 lead, but the Yankees rallied against the Twins' bullpen and closed out the series with a 6–5 victory. Santana compiled a 0.75 ERA for the series despite a 1.500 WHIP.

Santana finally earned his first All-Star nod in 2005, opening the year 7–2 with a 3.31 ERA in 13 starts through June 8. He compiled a 5.91 ERA while going 0–3 in five starts prior to the All-Star break but was 9–2 with a 1.59 ERA over his final 15 starts to end up 16–7 with a 2.87 ERA and a league-high 237 strikeouts. However, the Twins' string of playoff appearances ended at three as they finished third in the AL Central at 83–79.

Santana won the AL's Triple Crown for pitchers in 2006 and joined Roger Clemens and Pedro Martinez as the only hurlers to be unanimously chosen as the AL Cy Young Award winner in two seasons. Santana got off to another slow start, losing his first three decisions and maintaining an ERA over 3.00 until June 8. But he won his first three starts in May and went 5–0 with a 1.05 ERA in six starts during June to earn AL Pitcher of the Month honors again. Santana was 9–5 with a 2.95 ERA as he made his second consecutive trip to the All-Star Game.

But the Twins were 11 games out of first when they returned from the break. Santana pushed them over the top by going 10–1 with a 2.54 ERA and 107 strikeouts in 102⅔ innings in the second half. Minnesota won 13 of his last 15 starts and captured its fourth division crown in five years with a 96–66 record, the fourth-best record since the team moved from Washington in 1961. Santana was the league leader in wins (19), ERA (2.77), strikeouts (245), innings pitched (233.2), and WHIP (0.997).

The Twins were able to avoid the Yankees in the division series, instead squaring off against the A's. Santana pitched the series opener again and allowed just two runs over eight innings, but the Twins trailed 2–1 when he left before absorbing a 3–2 loss to Oakland. It was the final postseason game thrown by Santana as the A's completed a three-game sweep to add to Minnesota's recent playoff frustration.

The Twins missed the postseason in 2007 as Santana went 15–13 with a 3.33 ERA. He led the AL with a 1.073 WHIP but failed to win at least one of the league's Triple Crown categories for the first time since becoming a regular member of Minnesota's rotation. Santana had more strikeouts (235) than hits allowed (183) for the sixth consecutive season, but he couldn't prevent Minnesota from finishing 79–83.

The Twins under general manager Terry Ryan had become one of baseball's most successful small-market teams despite constant roster upheaval. The franchise couldn't afford to re-sign its top players at market value and had to rebuild from within as the Twins' stars migrated to other franchises.

The pitching staff had been completely overhauled since Santana became a permanent part of the rotation in August 2003. Deft drafting and shrewd trades allowed the Twins to remain well-stocked with young arms. By the end of 2007, Santana was the team's latest star to be dangled as trade bait as he entered the final year of his contract.

Ryan didn't want to lose Santana without receiving what he felt was fair compensation, which prompted the big-market sharks to circle the Twin Cities. Santana was the most desirable hurler available in the fall of 2007, although he wasn't set to become a free agent until after the 2008 season.

The Yankees and Red Sox were considered the front-runners to acquire Santana during the winter meetings. Both clubs had enough young talent to pull off a swap as the media quickly turned the Santana sweepstakes into a two-team race.

As for the Mets, they had serious interest in Santana after their starting pitching led a late-season meltdown that cost them the NL East title. But the Mets' minor league system was threadbare compared to that of the Yankees and Red Sox. It was highly doubtful that the Mets could come away with Santana as long as the Yanks and Bosox had a surplus of prospects.

However, Santana remained property of the Twins at the conclusion of the winter meetings. Boston was willing to part with either outfielder Jacoby Ellsbury or pitcher Jon Lester in a package, but they balked when Ryan asked for both.

The Yankees offered the Twins a trade that included pitcher Phil Hughes and outfielder Melky Cabrera, but Ryan also wanted another one of the Bombers' top prospects. The Yankees balked.

Ryan played chicken with the Red Sox and Yankees, figuring their intense desire to beat the other to Santana would create a more palatable offer for Minnesota. Instead, the two richest teams in the American League folded their cards and hoped they could forge a better deal during the 2008 season knowing the Twins didn't want to lose Santana for nothing more than draft picks.

Meanwhile, Minaya remained in touch with Ryan through the fourth week of January 2008. Three of the Mets' top prospects were outfielder Carlos Gomez and pitchers Philip Humber and Kevin Mulvey. Gomez played for the Mets in 2007 and was projected as one of the team's starters by the end of the decade. Humber made one start in September, and Mulvey was the team's top hurler in the low minors. The Mets also had Deolis Guerra, who compiled a 2.20 ERA in 17 starts for Class A Hagerstown in 2006. Minaya let the Twins know that all four could be had for Santana, provided the Mets were able to sign Santana to a long-term contract.

Minaya's perseverance paid off as he stole Santana from under the noses of the Red Sox and Yankees. The Twins agreed to accept Gomez, Humber, Mulvey, and Guerra, and gave the Mets a 72-hour window to sign Santana to a deal.

"Johan, believe me, he loved Minnesota, and if everything had been equal, he would have stayed," Gardenhire said. "But, really, there was a huge difference where we were and were able to do and what this club was able to do. That's hard to compete with."[219]

Negotiations went a few minutes past the deadline before New York had a new ace in the fold, at a record price of $137.5 over six years plus a seventh-year option. Once the dust settled, many scouts felt the Mets gave the Twins an inferior offer to those made by the Red Sox and Yankees.

Regardless, the Mets now had the best pitcher in the National League East after finishing one victory shy of a playoff berth. New York's projected top three starters in 2008 combined for 45 wins the previous year. The Phillies' best three starters compiled only 39 victories en route to a division title in 2007. The Santana trade turned the Mets into preseason favorites to capture the NL East in their final year at Shea Stadium.

"This team will have everything it takes to go all the way to make it happen," Santana said at his introductory news conference. "New York is the capital of the world, a great baseball city, and I'm looking forward to that. I know exactly what it takes to do my job. And I'm going to help any way I can."[220]

Armed with a huge contract and high expectations, the last thing Santana wanted to do was get off to another slow start with a new team in an impatient city. He bucked a career-long trend by pitching better in the first half of 2007 (10–6, 2.75 ERA) than the second half (5–7, 4.04 ERA). But from 2004 to 2006, he was 23–16 with a 3.56 ERA before the All-Star break, and 32–3 with a 1.78 ERA after.

"I was excited to get him," David Wright said. "There's a lot of anticipation. You're talking about the coveted prize of the off-season in baseball."[221]

Although the Yankees were outbid for Santana's services, at least two of their players were glad to see him out of the American League. Jason Giambi and Derek Jeter had seen enough of his change-up.

"The thing that makes his change-up so tough is how he controls it," Giambi said. "He doesn't bounce it. It just comes to the plate like a fastball and falls off. You can't guess with him He's too smart. He'll see that. Then he'll throw three fastballs down the middle."

"He's as good as anyone in the game at doing that," added Jeter. "A lot of pitchers slow their motion down on a change-up. If you watch it, you can see it. But he doesn't do that."[222]

Santana won the 2008 season opener, holding the Marlins to two runs and three hits while striking out eight over seven innings of a 7–2 win at Florida. He no-hit the Marlins until Josh Willingham belted a two-out, two-run homer in the fourth, a half-inning after the Mets erupted for six runs to break a scoreless tie.

"I'm here trying to do my job and at the same time trying to please a lot of people," Santana said following the game. "I'm very happy to be part of this team, and it's always nice and good when you see that you get those kinds of ovations by the fans. I'm very excited. I'm just going to keep doing my job and keep people happy and clapping."[223]

Santana absorbed a loss to the Braves in his next start despite allowing only one run in seven innings. It was the first of nine games in which the Mets scored two runs or fewer with Santana on the mound.

The Mets didn't have much trouble scoring runs for the other starters while saving some of their worst offensive performances for Santana. In his seven losses and 11 no-decisions, Santana had eight starts in which he pitched at least seven innings and allowed three earned runs or fewer. The Mets scored just 12 times in his seven losses.

Santana pitched well in the first half, recording a 2.84 ERA and 114 strikeouts in 126⅔ innings over 19 starts. He went 0–4 in his last five starts in June and was just 8–7 heading into the All-Star break. Santana went six consecutive starts without a victory from June 6 to July 4 despite a 2.48 earned run average, an indication of the team's poor run support for their new ace.

Santana didn't lose another game after June 28, going 9–0 with a 2.09 ERA in 17 starts. He beat the Phillies twice during an 11-day span over the final month of the season, the second of which prevented New York from falling into a first-place tie with Philadelphia with 19 games to play.

The Mets expanded their lead over the Phillies to 3½ games with 17 remaining before the Phils overtook New York during the final week. The Mets were one game behind the Brewers for the wild-card with two games to play as Santana took the mound for his final start of the regular season against the Marlins on September 27.

Santana was superb in a 2–0 victory that allowed the Mets to pull into a tie with Milwaukee. He worked out of a bases-loaded jam in the fifth, the only inning in which he put more than one runner on base. He struck out nine and went the distance for his second shutout since mid-August.

"I'm speechless," reliever Scott Schoeneweis said. "He's incredible, superhuman…. A machine, a relentless machine. If anyone's worth $150 million when it comes to being an athlete, well, you can finish the sentence."

"That's the way I felt today," said Santana. "I saw those guys swinging and swinging and putting the ball in play, so I had a pretty good chance. It's tough to say at what point I knew I would have the whole game, but I felt from the very beginning that I would have a very good chance to go the whole game."

"He's always good," José Reyes added. "But today, he was amazing."[224]

Santana went 4–0 with a 1.83 earned run average in September to finish 16–7 with a 2.53 ERA and 206 strikeouts in 234⅓ innings. He was responsible for three of the Mets' final five wins, but it wasn't enough for the team to avoid its second straight agonizing finish. The bullpen imploded down the stretch and surrendered two homers in the season finale, a 4–2 loss to Florida that left the Mets one game behind the wild-card-winning Brewers.

Santana's September performances earned more appreciation after it was revealed he was pitching with a torn meniscus in his left knee. He underwent surgery a few days after his final start and was ready for spring training.

"I had been icing it for the last two months," Santana said two months after his superb outing against Florida. "The last four starts is when I felt it got worse, when it was really tough for me to bend my knee. But that game, I was so into it that I didn't feel anything, to be honest. As soon as the game was over, though, I ran back to the training room and got some ice and tape and started to feel some relief."[225]

Santana was the NL ERA champ in '08 and also led the circuit in innings pitched and was second in strikeouts. But the Mets hit poorly in too many of his starts, which hurt them over the long haul. Minaya tried to remedy that problem by giving the bullpen a makeover, acquiring Francisco Rodriguez, J.J. Putz, and Sean Green during the December 2008 winter meetings. That didn't stop the Mets from finding another way to waste Santana's best efforts.

Santana was in top form during the first two months of 2009, going 7–2 with a 1.77 ERA in 10 starts. He was the Mets' season-opening starter for the second straight year, allowing a run and three hits while striking out seven over 5⅔ innings to lead a 2–1 win over the Reds in frigid Cincinnati. He followed that by striking out 13 over seven innings against the Marlins, but he was victimized by an error that brought in two unearned runs in a 2–1 loss.

Santana didn't allow an earned run in four of his first seven starts and already had 86 strikeouts in 66 innings heading into June. One of his best early outings was in a 1–0 victory over the Brewers at Citi Field as he limited the Brewers to five hits while striking out seven in seven innings. It was one of those performances that had teammates gushing.

"When it's like today and runs are scarce, he doesn't allow contact—or at least he makes it difficult for them to make good contact," Wright said. "He senses when we have a tough offensive matchup or when the other guy's throwing the ball well, which is what happened today. Johan always matches him. He has that sixth sense. I really believe that.

"Ideally, we'd get one for Johan every time he pitches, and that would be enough, and we'd save the rest of the runs for everybody else. But we know that's not going to happen. We know we have to do a better job of repaying the favor because he's always the one bailing us out."

"That's what I'm here for," Santana said. "I know that every time I go out there it's going to be very important. And every time I'm out there, I try to make it very special."[226]

Santana was also a bit more boisterous in his second year with the team. He allowed himself to have fun, telling jokes and doing numerous impressions, including a spot-on version of Mets vice president of public relations Jay Horwitz.

"When you get here, you're new, you don't know the guys around here, no one knows what to expect," Santana said in 2009. "I'm talking about the personal side, not the baseball. I was taking the time to get to know each guy around here. When you are the pitcher that everyone's expecting a lot from, all I wanted to do was to make sure that I made everyone else feel comfortable.

"It's not like I'm different or that they have to talk to me differently. I'm very serious when I get on the mound, for sure, but at the same time, I'm just one more human being in the clubhouse and I like to have fun."

"He comes in here with a smile on his face and he leaves with a smile on his face," said teammate Ryan Church. "He loves what he does, he loves being in here, and we love being around him. That excitement, that joy, that passion—it rubs off on people."[227]

There was little funny about the season itself. The Mets were beset by a ridiculous number of injuries throughout the year. They lost José Reyes and Carlos Delgado to season-ending injuries in May and were without Carlos Beltrán in July and August. New York's disabled list also included David Wright, Brian Schneider, John Maine, Oliver Perez and Putz, leaving manager Jerry Manuel with an active roster more befitting a Triple A team.

Santana's name eventually showed up on the disabled list. He pitched through late August but was not his usual dominant self, going 6–7 with a 4.05 ERA and just 60 strikeouts in 100⅔ innings over his final 15 starts. He managed to throw at least seven innings in 10 of those starts but was doing so without his normal repertoire. Santana lost a few miles on his fastball, which made his off-speed pitches less effective.

The Mets played themselves out of the playoff picture by the end of July despite Santana, who posted a 1.82 ERA

in five starts that month. He continued to pitch through August until the Mets, with little to play for over the final six weeks, shut him down. Santana underwent surgery to remove bone fragments from his left elbow on September 1, leaving him 13–9 with a 3.13 earned run average for the year.

The Mets entered 2010 as playoff contenders despite their 70–92 mark in 2009. Preseason prognosticators weighed Santana's dominance as a reason to believe the team could rebound from its worst season in six years. Since 2004, Santana had led the majors with 99 wins, 1,335 strikeouts, a 2.86 ERA, and a .219 opponents' batting average.

Santana displayed that dominance in the season opener, picking up the victory in a 7–1 rout of the Marlins after allowing a run and four hits in six innings. He was roughed up by the Nationals in his next start before tossing seven shutout frames in a 20-inning, 2–1 win at St. Louis on April 17.

Santana pitched shutout ball in consecutive starts at Milwaukee on May 28 and at San Diego on June 2. However, the Mets lost both games and were just 6–6 in his first 12 outings despite his 2.76 earned run average. He struggled the rest of June, going 1–3 with a 5.96 ERA in four starts. But the Mets were within a half-game of the NL East lead as they entered the final week of the month.

He opened July by going 3–0 with an 0.71 ERA in five starts, including a three-hit shutout in a memorable outing against the Reds on July 5. Santana helped his own cause by drilling his first major league home run, capping a 12-pitch at-bat to put the Mets ahead to stay in the third inning of a 3–0 victory.

Santana displayed his grittiness in a no-decision against the Cardinals on July 28. He was torched for six runs as the Cards sent 12 men to the plate in the top of the first. Santana threw 38 pitches while allowing eight hits in the opening frame, but he held St. Louis to one run over the next 4⅔ innings, giving the Mets a chance to tie the game in the eighth before losing in extra innings.

Santana was outstanding at times in 2010. He had 14 starts in which he pitched at least seven innings and held opponents under three runs. Santana threw two shutouts and tossed scoreless ball in nine of his 29 starts.

Meanwhile, the Mets looked like postseason contenders as they entered the All-Star break, sporting a 48–40 record that put them second in the NL East, four games behind the Braves. But they opened the second half by going 2–9 on a West Coast road trip and fell under .500 by August 6.

Santana tried to prop up the Mets' playoff chances in August by tossing a four-hit shutout versus the Rockies after holding the Phillies scoreless over 7⅓ innings of a 1–0 victory in his previous start. But New York lost Santana's final three starts of August and were just trying to salvage a .500 season as he took the mound in Atlanta on September 2.

Santana limited the Braves to a run and three hits over five innings of a 3–1 victory to improve to 11–9 with a 2.98 ERA. He capped the outing by striking out Omar Infante with the potential tying run on second before leaving the game with what the Mets called tightness in his upper left chest. Santana downplayed the injury after the game, intimating he could have gone out to pitch the sixth before pitching coach Dan Warthan opted to err on the side of caution. Warthan made the right move.

Santana threw in a bullpen session a few days later and said he was fine as he tried to convince management that he could finish the season. But a subsequent MRI revealed a tear of the interior capsule in his left shoulder, preventing him from finishing a season for the second straight year. Santana ended up 11–9 with a 2.98 ERA before the Mets completed their second consecutive losing campaign.

Santana's 2011 season consisted of a series of encouraging signs and subtle setbacks. Even as late as May the Mets felt he was about six to eight weeks away from pitching for them again, although there was no true way to establish a timetable for his return. Only a few pitchers have undergone the procedure, and none truly returned to their previous form. The Mets were not about to take any chances on their $137 million star hurler.

"I'm not going to go out and do something crazy," he said as the rest of the staff was preparing for spring training. "We're going to go one step at a time. I'm feeling good, and then we'll go from there.

"I know they talk about Jorge Posada having the same surgery a few years back and he's out there playing. I was told last year when everything happened that it's a rare type of injury that you don't see out there very often, but it is out there.

"When you get your arm all cleaned up and fixed, there's always a question mark. You never know, time will tell. But if everything goes right and I feel good, I'm going to continue playing as much as I can."[228]

His minor league rehab was pushed back after he felt discomfort in the shoulder while throwing off a mound in July, and it wasn't until August when he finally pitched in a minor league game. Assigned to Class A St. Lucie, Santana made two starts, worked five innings, and allowed one run and five hits while striking out five. The small body of work and the Mets' record by mid-September gave them no reason to put him on the major league roster.

Santana played heavily in the Mets' plans as they shaped the 2012 roster. His absence left the team without a stopper, but it also allowed the Mets to gauge how other pitchers had progressed or regressed. The Mets' rotation recorded a 4.12 ERA and averaged just six innings per start, further demonstrating just how valuable Santana would be in 2012.

ML debut	Twins vs. Devil Rays, 4/3/00 (1 IP, 1 H, 0 ER, 1 K, 0 BB)
Mets debut	@ Marlins, 3/31/08 (7 IP, 3 H, 2 ER, 8 K, 2 BB)
First ML strikeout	José Canseco, Devil Rays, 4/3/00 (with Twins)
First Mets strikeout	Hanley Ramirez, @ Marlins, 3/31/08
First ML win	@ Astros, 6/6/00 (with Twins)
First Mets win	@ Marlins, 3/31/08
First ML save	@ Tigers, 7/19/02 (with Twins)
Most strikeouts, ML game	17, Twins vs. Rangers, 8/19/07
Most strikeouts, Mets game	13, @ Marlins, 4/12/09
Low-hit ML CG	3, 5 times
Low-hit Mets CG	3, @ Pirates, 8/17/08; vs. Marlins, 9/27/08; vs. Reds, 7/6/10

Acquired: Traded by the Twins for Carlos Gomez, Phil Humber, Kevin Mulvey, and Deolis Guerra, 2/2/08.

AL Cy Young Award, 2004, 2006
AL Gold Glove, 2007
AL All-Star, 2005, 2006, 2007
NL All-Star, 2009
AL ERA Leader, 2004, 2006.
NL ERA Leader, 2008.
AL Strikeout Leader, 2004, 2005, 2006

Tom Seaver

Pitcher	Bats right, throws right
Born: 11/17/44	Fresno, California
Height: 6'1"	Weight: 205 #41

Tom Seaver Mets Career

YEAR	GP/GS	IP	H	R	ER	K	BB	W–L	SV	ERA
1967	35/34	251	224	85	77	170	78	16–13	0	2.76
1968	36/35	277.2	224	73	68	205	48	16–12	1	2.20
1969	36/35	273.1	202	75	67	208	82	25–7	0	2.21
1970	37/36	290.2	230	103	91	283	83	18–12	0	2.82
1971	36/35	286.1	210	61	56	289	61	20–10	0	1.76
1972	35/35	262	215	92	85	249	77	21–12	0	2.92
1973	36/36	290	219	74	67	251	64	19–10	0	2.08
1974	32/32	236	199	89	84	201	75	11–11	0	3.20
1975	36/36	28.1	217	81	74	243	88	22–9	0	2.38
1976	35/34	271	211	83	78	235	77	14–11	0	2.59
1977	13/13	96	79	33	32	72	28	7–3	0	3.00
1983	34/34	231	201	104	91	135	86	9–14	0	3.55
TOTAL	401/395	3045.2	2431	953	870	2541	847	198–124	1	2.57

Mets Career/Batting

GP	AB	R	H	2B	3B	HR	RBI	K	BB	SB	AVG
420	975	70	146	17	5	6	60	355	80	4	.150

ML Career

YEAR	GP/GS	IP	H	R	ER	K	BB	W–L	SV	ERA
67–86	656/647	4782.2	3971	1674	1521	3640	1390	311–205	1	2.86

The Franchise. It was a nickname placed on Tom Seaver almost from the moment he threw his first major league pitch. He altered the perception of the Mets, changed the philosophy of the organization, and helped turn the franchise into a champion within 3½ years after being acquired in a special lottery. The nickname is apropos.

Imagine the Mets without Seaver. Imagine the club without those four 20-win seasons, three Cy Young Awards, three ERA titles, and five strikeout crowns. Imagine someone other than Seaver guiding the team to the 1969 World Series and 1973 NL pennant. Eventually, someone within the organization imagined the franchise would be better off without "the Franchise," a notion that placed the team into an abyss for seven seasons until a new pitching phenom made his way onto the roster in 1984, one year after Seaver's one-year return.

As a pitcher, Seaver had mechanics that should be taught to every high school pitcher. Study the video and watch how his legs produce a large portion of the energy that made his fastball so lethal. He said he adopted those mechanics as a scrawny teenager to get more velocity on his pitches. Take note of the way his right knee touches the mound as he throws a pitch, paying particular attention to the location of his arm, elbow, and shoulder when his knee hits the turf. Compare the delivery of his fastball and slider, and try to determine when you notice a difference in the break.

As a teammate, Seaver changed the climate in the clubhouse once he joined the club in 1967. He was no-nonsense on the mound, at the plate, and in the dugout. He was respectful of his veteran teammates and never resorted to the glare pitchers often use when someone makes an error behind him. But when there was down time in the clubhouse, Seaver could be the chief cut-up or an encouraging teammate.

As the face of the franchise, Seaver was a go-to guy for the media as he gave thoughtful answers without resorting to the baseball book of clichés. He could speak for hours without ever embarrassing himself or the ballclub, all while giving frank assessments of himself and the Mets.

There are 17 pitchers in major league history who have recorded more wins than Seaver. Fourteen pitchers since 1901 have thrown at least 3,000 innings and recorded a lower ERA. Five pitchers have struck out more hitters. Seven pitchers have a better WHIP. But of the 7,586 players who threw a major league pitch between 1901 and 2010, none can top Seaver's combination of 311 victories, 3,640 strikeouts, 2.86 ERA, and 1.121 WHIP. For that, he earned his other nickname: "Tom Terrific."

George Thomas Seaver was born and raised in Fresno, California. His father, Charles, was an excellent golfer who won several amateur championships in California and was undefeated as a member of the 1932 U.S. Walker Cup team, 30 years before he and Mike Fetchick won the Bing Crosby Pro-Am.

"On the golf course, he was a real perfectionist," said Seaver about his father. "Even in Sunday play with my mom and myself. If he shot a 74, he'd recap every stroke and say he shanked that ball or pulled another into a trap. Baseball is to me what golf was to him."[229]

His mother, Betty, was a pretty fair golfer in her own right and, according to Seaver, could outperform her husband on the putting green. As a kid, Tom would often have his mother read him the book, *The Little Engine That Could*, a tale that could serve as a parable for the Mets' 1969 season.

His brother, Charles, was six years older than Tom and an excellent swimmer at Fresno High and the University of California. Oldest sister Katie was a good swimmer and volleyball player at Stanford, and another sister, Carol, was a phys-ed major at UCLA.

"Our family was always competitive," Seaver said in 1969. "Even when my father was working around the house, he wanted perfection, and he tried to instill that striving in us, too. I learned a real respect for the value of work, not as a means—not just for the money it can bring you—but for the pleasure of doing something as well as you can, as near perfectly as you can."[230]

Seaver was high school teammates with Dick Selma and Wade Blasingame, both of whom reached the majors and were a year older than Tom. Selma was a flame-thrower who was signed by the Mets during the team's infancy. But at the time, Seaver was a self-described junk-baller who went 6–5 as a senior, his only year on the varsity.

"I threw a slip pitch and a slider and a sinker," Seaver said in his book, *The Perfect Game*. "I even tried throwing a knuckler. I just wasn't strong enough to throw a real fastball.

"I did manage to make the All-City baseball squad as the third pitcher, mostly because there wasn't anyone else to choose. When the professional scouts came around looking over the local talent, some of the other kids got good offers. I didn't even get conversation; not one scout approached me."[231]

Seaver pitched American Legion ball the summer of his high school graduation and took a job with a packing company. A stint in the Marine Corps began to appeal to Seaver following six months in the packing plant.

He was 5′11″ and 165 pounds when he enlisted, and 6′1″ and 195 pounds after completing his hitch. Stories of his increased height and weight vary with each telling, but you get the idea.

He entered Fresno City College in the fall of 1963 with hopes of parlaying his time there into a baseball scholarship at Southern Cal. Seaver wanted to attend Southern Cal out of high school but said he didn't want his father to pay for it after sending Tom's brother and sisters to college.

Seaver went 11–2 and was the MVP of the City College team in 1964, but that earned only a lukewarm response from Trojans baseball coach Rod Dedeaux. There were a limited number of scholarships available, and Dedeaux still didn't know if Seaver could handle top-level competition.

Dedeaux's reluctance prompted Seaver to pitch that summer for the Alaska Goldpanners, a team that included future major leaguers Graig Nettles, Rick Monday, Curt Motton, and Gary Sutherland. Seaver spent most of the summer as a back-end rotation man and a reliever before the team competed in the National Baseball Congress tournament in August.

The Goldpanners were playing their fourth game of the tournament when Seaver was asked to protect a 2–0 lead with the bases loaded in the fifth. He proceeded to walk the first two hitters and surrender a single that made it 3–2 before getting out of the inning. In the sixth, Seaver came to the plate with the bases loaded and hit a grand slam to put the Goldpanners ahead to stay. He won the game, was named to the NBC tournament all-star team, and earned his scholarship to USC.

Seaver enrolled in the pre-dental program not knowing if he had the ability to become a major leaguer. But his 10–2 record for the Trojans as a sophomore caused the Dodgers to take him in the 10th round of the June 1965 draft. However, the Dodgers blanched when Seaver mentioned an asking price of $50,000, allowing him to remain an amateur. His amateur status came into question the following winter.

Seaver spent another summer in Alaska and pitched in the NBC semifinals against the Wichita Dreamliners, a team that included former Mets Charlie Neal and Rod Kanehl. Seaver was beaten 6–3 but left an impression on the opposition. Kanehl told him he'd be a major league pitcher some day.

The Dodgers' negotiating rights to Seaver lapsed a few days after New Year's Day 1966, making him available in the January draft. The Braves took him in the secondary phase of the draft and had to race the clock to sign him before the Trojans' season began. Atlanta's selection of Seaver came two picks after the Mets chose outfielder James Taylor of SMU.

Major League Baseball rules at the time prohibited college draft picks from signing contracts once their team began its season. The Braves negotiated quickly and surpassed Seaver's hopes of a $50,000 deal, signing him to a $51,500 package that included a $40,000 bonus and money to pay for college. The Braves also planned to bring him to training camp and send him to Richmond of the Triple A International League once the season began.

The contract was signed on February 24, after the Trojans played a pair of exhibition games in which Seaver did not appear. The school went to the office of Baseball Commissioner William Eckert and protested the signing, asking that it be nullified since USC had begun its season, albeit with exhibition games. Eckert sided with the school, which was a relief to the Trojans until the NCAA stepped in and stripped Seaver of his eligibility for signing a pro contract.

The two decisions left Seaver without a team. He never received a dime from the Braves, but the NCAA took a hard line on the contract and barred him from college ball. The Seaver family threatened litigation until Eckert came up with a compromise: he fined the Richmond Braves and barred the parent club from signing him for three years. However, he made Seaver available in a special draft in which any team could participate if it was willing to match Atlanta's offer.

Nelson Burbrink, the Mets' amateur scout in California, was very high on Seaver. Burbrink liked Seaver's pitching repertoire and was very impressed with the kid's demeanor on the mound. Once Seaver was put on the block, Burbrink strongly recommended to minor league secretary Joe McDonald and director Bing Devine that the Mets sign him.

Neither Devine nor McDonald had seen Seaver pitch, but they had the utmost respect for Burbrink's judgment. It was McDonald's job to coordinate the entire scouting and minor league departments and keep track of all potential prospects. Devine was team president George Weiss' right-hand man and a highly-respected talent evaluator from his days as general manager of the Cardinals. It was up to Devine and McDonald to convince Weiss that Seaver was a worthwhile investment.

Weiss was not known for reckless spending and saw Seaver as a high-risk signing. Devine and McDonald spent several weeks wearing Weiss down, reciting Burbrink's assessment of Seaver and reminding Weiss that the Fresno product could be the type of pitcher the team long coveted. Finally, Weiss threw up his hands and told Devine to add the Mets to the special draft.

Devine and McDonald were feeling pretty good about their selling job until only two other teams, the Phillies and Indians, decided to participate in the Seaver sweepstakes. Their elation with Weiss' decision had turned to worry after 16 other major league teams decided Seaver wasn't worth $51,500.

The Seaver lottery was handled in the commissioner's office on April 2, which prevented Seaver from participating in spring training. Seaver and his parents were on the phone with assistant commissioner Lee MacPhail as the draft was held. MacPhail provided play-by-play as he told Seaver that his services were now officially property of the New York Mets.

Devine and McDonald had concurring feelings of jubilation and trepidation after learning the Mets now owned Seaver. What if this guy didn't pan out, like so many other highly touted, early Mets prospects? Fortunately, they also knew that Weiss was scheduled to step down at the end of the season.

"I was glad to hear that the Mets had been picked," Seaver said. "I was glad mostly because I knew they offered the fastest possible path to the major leagues. They'd finished in 10th place in each of the first four years of their existence, and if any club needed young pitching, it was the Mets."[232]

Many prospects will buy a car or a house when they receive their first contract. In Seaver's case, his most extravagant purchase was an engagement ring for his long-time girlfriend, Nancy McIntyre. He proposed the day he signed, with plans to get married after the season.

Seaver went to the Mets' minor league camp and was assigned to the team's Triple A affiliate at Jacksonville. He hit a two-run double and beat Rochester 4–2 in his first start before tossing a two-hit shutout in his next appearance. In New York, Devine and McDonald were breathing a sigh of relief after Seaver compiled a 1.04 ERA while striking out 20 in his first 17⅔ innings.

"Seaver has a 35-year-old head on top of a 21-year-old body," said Jacksonville manager Solly Hemus. "Usually, we get a 35-year-old body attached to a 21-year-old head."

Even his teammates were impressed. Bill Denehy was part of the Suns' 1966 staff, and was one of the Mets' top prospects before eventually joining Seaver on the 1967 Mets roster.

"When I saw him first in '66 he was a little older than I was and much more mature than I was," recalled Denehy 43 years later. "He was more in command of his pitches and his presence on the mound. He had pitched at USC and had done his military stint. He was already married, so mature-wise, he was in much better shape than I was.

"As far as his stuff, his control and command, he had an excellent fastball, his slider I think was his second-best pitch, and he could move the ball around a little bit.

"I was definitely impressed with Tom. I thought he was going to be a definite, bona fide major league pitcher, but at that point in time I don't think any of us knew what our futures might turn out to be."

After winning his first two starts Seaver went 10–12 the rest of the season but led the Suns with 12 victories and 188 strikeouts. Of the 21 pitchers used by Jacksonville that season, 20 pitched in the majors before or after 1966. Only Larry Miller bettered Seaver's 3.13 ERA among Suns pitchers with at least 100 innings. Orioles prospect Tom Phoebus was the lone International League pitcher with more strikeouts than Seaver.

"I knew he was going to be good," recalled Suns teammate Craig Anderson 45 years later. "I liked his approach to the game. He was serious. He was competitive and he didn't let things bother him. He was 12–12 that year, but he pitched pretty consistent baseball.

"I didn't know he was going to be a Hall of Famer, but I knew he had the tools to be a good pitcher in the big leagues. He took it from there, and just got better and better."

But Seaver wasn't entirely happy at the start of the season. He was 3,000 miles away from his fiancée and missed her companionship, leading him to mail her an airline ticket with a request that they get married immediately. They celebrated their 46th anniversary in 2012.

The 1967 Mets reported to spring training after vacating the NL cellar for the first time in team history. The farm system was finally beginning to bear fruit as Cleon Jones and Bud Harrelson had impressive seasons with the big club the year before. But the Mets' reputation as a pitching organization had yet to take shape as Seaver tried to win a spot on the major league roster. Selma and Tug McGraw were hard throwers who lacked Seaver's maturity. Nolan Ryan and Jerry Koosman were in the mix for a spot on the staff but were destined to spend most of 1967 in the minors.

The Mets thought enough of Seaver to give him a relatively low uniform number when he got to camp. He saw the No. 41 hanging in his locker and continued to wear it the rest of his career. Twenty-one years later, the Mets retired the jersey.

But Seaver still hadn't faced a major league team as he took the mound for the first time during the exhibition season. He quickly showed he was ready for the big leagues, displaying poise while mowing down the opposition. Seaver looked like a cinch to make the big club until the Tigers torched him for nine runs before manager Wes Westrum lifted the beleaguered hurler in the fourth inning.

"I was really embarrassed that Westrum took me out," Seaver said of the shellacking. "How often do you ever see a pitcher taken out in the middle of an inning in an exhibition game? I said to myself, 'That's it. We're going back to Jacksonville and the minors.'

"I got a drink of water in the dugout and felt the tears building up in my eyes. The newspapermen covering the Mets had been writing that I had a chance to make the team. Then I had gone out there, and nothing went right. The feeling of the tears was getting stronger so I got a towel, wet it, sat down and put it over my head. I didn't want to be seen and didn't care to see anything.

"Suddenly I felt a strong hand patting me gently on my back. I heard something mumbled. I think it was, 'Stick in there,' or something like that. I looked up; the hand and voice belonged to Yogi Berra.

"I can remember thinking, 'What in the world is Yogi Berra doing coming over to talk to me?' It was a warm scene for me inside. It helped me a little bit.

"Looking back, I supposed it meant to me that I had sort of a friend on the staff—somebody who thought enough of my ability to try to cheer me up when I was depressed."[233]

Westrum judged the Tigers beating as a mere aberration and decided to bring Seaver north with the rest of the team. The pitching rotation remained in question as the team prepared to host the Pirates on Opening Day, although newly acquired Don Cardwell was slated to start against the team that had just traded him. In addition to Seaver, Westrum had veterans Jack Fisher and Bob Shaw at his disposal. Both Fisher and Shaw won 11 games for the Mets in 1966, making Seaver the logical No. 4 starter in the rotation. But Westrum declined to name his second-game starter until after the opener.

Cardwell pitched well against the Pirates, allowing three runs and six hits while striking out nine in eight innings. But the Mets committed five errors and allowed three runs in the ninth to lose 6–3. As the Mets trudged back to the clubhouse, Westrum decided the future was now and announced that Seaver would pitch the second game.

Seaver made his major league debut on April 13 in front of 5,005 fans at Shea. He immediately put himself in trouble by giving up a leadoff double to Matty Alou but worked out of a first-and-third situation by fanning Donn Clendenon to end the inning. He also struck out Bill Mazeroski and Gene Alley to start the second, and didn't allow a run until Roberto Clemente's RBI single in the third.

Seaver surrendered a fourth-inning run following a walk and a hit batsman to put his major league ERA at 4.91 before blanking the Pirates the rest of the way.

It was a 2–2 tie in the sixth when Seaver put runners on first and second, causing Westrum to visit the mound.

"I was very tired," Seaver said. "I had pitched as hard as I could and I was done. He asked me how I felt, and I said he ought to get a fresh arm in the game. It wouldn't have made much sense to try to talk myself into staying in.

"The emotion had drained me along with the physical output. Then we won the game and I was one of the happiest persons right then. I'd done well for myself and I'd helped the Mets win.

"You know, I don't have a single thing as a souvenir from that game. I wish I had the lineup card with my name on it and Wes Westrum's signature on the bottom, but you don't think of that at the time. Maybe that's because you don't want to appear too young."[234]

The pitching line on Seaver in his first game: 5⅔ innings, 2 runs, 6 hits, 8 strikeouts, and 4 walks. Pinch-hitter Chuck Hiller's RBI double in the eighth allowed Chuck Estrada to come away with the victory in a 3–2 decision.

Seaver picked up his first big league win in his next start one week later, also at Shea Stadium. A small gathering of 5,379 watched him allow one run and eight hits with no walks in 7⅓ innings as the Mets beat the Cubs 6–1. The lone blemish was his 0-for-2 performance at the plate after he went 1-for-1 with a walk in his debut.

Fittingly, Bud Harrelson secured Seaver's first victory with a two-run single in the eighth to cap the scoring. The two Californians eventually became inseparable while spending the next decade with the franchise. Harrelson emerged as a slick-fielding but light-hitting shortstop, and the glue of the Mets' infield. But also hit about 30 points higher than his career batting average whenever Seaver was on the mound.

Seaver tossed his first complete game in his next appearance, allowing an unearned run and four hits over 10 innings in a 2–1 win at Wrigley Field on April 25. Seaver opened the 10th with a single and scored on Al Luplow's two-out hit. He had a shutout until Harrelson committed a two-out error in the ninth to bring him the lone run.

"After the game," said Seaver, "I'm ecstatic, but Buddy Harrelson is sitting in front of his locker in tears. 'I cost you your shutout,' he was crying. Those are beautiful memories you don't forget. Buddy was like a brother to me. We went out for dinner that night and we didn't come right home. We were just a couple of puppies."[235]

Not only could Seaver pitch, but he was factoring in rallies. The batting average eventually dipped below .200, but he was 8–5 with a 2.65 ERA when he made his first All-Star appearance for the National League. It marked the first time a Mets pitcher had been invited to the midsummer classic, and Seaver didn't disappoint.

The All-Star Game was 1–1 until Tony Perez homered against Catfish Hunter in the top of the 15th. Seaver saved the victory for Don Drysdale, giving up a one-out walk to eventual AL MVP Carl Yastrzemski before fanning Ken Berry to end the game.

"As I walked in from the bullpen in the 15th inning, I looked around at all the stars on the field and was awed. But the moment I got on the mound, I felt I belonged. I deserved to be there. I pitched a scoreless inning to get the save. I walked Carl Yastrzemski on four pitches—all of them on purpose. He was the only one they had left who could hurt me, and I wasn't going to let him."[236]

Seaver stumbled in his first three starts after the All-Star break before going 6–5 with a 1.98 ERA in his final 13 appearances. He set team records with 16 victories, 170 strikeouts, and a 2.76 earned run average to become the first Met to win the NL Rookie of the Year Award. Seaver picked up 11 of 20 first-place votes while fellow pitchers Dick Hughes of the Cardinals and Gary Nolan of the Reds claimed the others.

Seaver gave some credit for his success to a one-time 20-game winner and a three-time All-Star who was part of manager Wes Westrum's coaching staff in 1967.

"Our pitching coach, Harvey Haddix, worked with me on my curve, slider, and change-up. He helped me improve the curve 100 percent. He taught me to release the ball away from my body so that my hand speed would be quicker and I'd increase the velocity of the ball's rotation."[237]

Seaver's season failed to stop the Mets from losing 100 games for the fifth time in six seasons. Mets fans who embraced the team's role as lovable losers in 1962 were growing tired of the act as attendance dropped by almost 400,000 from 1966. The losing wasn't as frustrating for the fan base as the team's inability to sustain any visible improvement. The difference in victories between the 1963 and '67 teams was just 10, and the Mets' record regressed between 1964 and '65 and from 1966 to '67.

No one was unhappier with the culture than Seaver, who was the team's only pitcher under 24 to win more than four games in '67. The reinforcements would come the following spring.

"There was an aura of defeatism, and I refused to accept it," said Seaver. "Maybe some of the others started to feel how I felt because I noticed that the team seemed to play better behind me than it did for any other pitchers."[238]

"I have an awful lot of enthusiasm when I go out there," he said, "and fellows like Harrelson and Ron Swoboda do, too. The young guys don't know what it's been like to lose and lose, and we expect to win.

"I guess anyone who has been with a club for a long, long time can kind of accept defeat, but we have enough fresh blood to compete with confidence."[239]

The Mets' top three pitchers of 1966 were Fisher, Shaw, and Dennis Ribant. All three were gone once Devine and Johnny Murphy engineered a December 1967 trade that sent Fisher and Tommy Davis to the White Sox for Tommie Agee and Al Weis. Devine stepped down to reclaim his old GM job with the Cardinals, putting the organization in the hands of Murphy. Those moves occurred after Gil Hodges was hired as the Mets' third manager.

Hodges was the exact brand of manager the Mets needed to guide a squad that was about to become considerably younger. He was strict yet patient, allowing the kids to make mistakes so long as they were quickly corrected. He was a father figure in pinstripes, scolding players in private yet patient enough to listen to their personal problems if they really needed to talk. Most important, Hodges was a great teacher for a ballclub that needed a quick education in winning.

Cardwell was the only starting pitcher over 25 when the Mets broke camp in '68. Hodges and Murphy deemed Jerry Koosman and Nolan Ryan ready to join a rotation that included Seaver, Cardwell, and Selma. The positive results were immediate as the Mets finished fourth in the league with a 2.72 ERA, second with 1,014 strikeouts, and first with 1,250 hits allowed. The staff was also aided by a defense that allowed only 50 unearned runs after surrendering 78 in 1967.

Koosman won 19 games, set a club record with a 2.08 ERA and came within a half-vote of sharing the NL Rookie of the Year Award with Reds catcher Johnny Bench. Ryan averaged five walks per nine innings but also surrendered just 93 hits while fanning 133 in 134 innings. Selma and rookie Jim McAndrew combined for a 13–17 record, but they also teamed for a 2.60 ERA and 214 hits allowed in 249⅓ innings. The newcomers were so strong that Hodges and Murphy were allowed to keep Tug McGraw in the minors the entire season to work on his conversion as a relief pitcher. The future suddenly looked extremely bright for Mets hurlers, especially after they bought into the teachings of their new pitching coach.

"The first time I saw Rube Walker at our training camp in 1968, I was skeptical," Seaver recalled of his new pitching guru. "I'd never met a pitching coach who hadn't pitched himself. Rube had been a catcher, mostly with the Dodgers behind Roy Campanella. But he quickly convinced me. He had spent his whole life studying pitchers.

"Rube knew how to condition his pitchers, knew how to pace them, and he treated them all as individuals. He never insisted that all of the pitchers use the same motion, the same style; he let them use whatever was best for them. He was, like Gil, always calm, always reasonable. He never got mad at anyone except an umpire once in a while.

"The better I got to know Rube, the more I liked him. I found him one of the funniest men I'd ever met, quietly funny, with his little North Carolina phrases. Once, on a miserably hot day in St. Louis, Rube walked over to me in the locker room and said, 'I'll tell you how hot it is. I saw a dog chasing a cat this morning, and they were both walking.'

"Another time, he watched me warm up, and he wasn't pleased with the way I was throwing. 'Seaver,' he said, 'you got as much chance today as a one-legged man in a butt-kicking contest.'"[240]

Seaver didn't allow himself to be completely satisfied with his 1967 performance and quickly went about improving himself physically. Although his 176 strikeouts in '67 was a team record, he still didn't consider himself a power pitcher and wanted to join that exclusive group. Being the ballclub's top hurler wasn't enough.

"I realized I had to use the bigger muscles in my body to get maximum energy for my delivery," Seaver said 10 years later. "Power would have to come from my legs and back. So I started lifting weights and doing exercises that would build up those muscles."[241]

Seaver pitched through all kinds of bad luck during the first two months of the 1968 campaign. He posted a 1.91 ERA and kept opponents under three earned runs in each of his 11 starts. But his record was a meager 2–5 as the Mets scored a total of 19 runs for him.

Seaver posted the same 1.91 ERA in June but managed to go 5–0 with three shutouts as the Mets scored 20 times in his games. The streak put Seaver back in the All-Star Game for the second straight year, and he lowered his earned run average to 1.79 by July 23.

He finished the year 16–12 with a 2.20 ERA and a team record 205 strikeouts, starting a major league–record string of nine straight seasons in which he fanned at least 200 batters. His WHIP was 0.978 by the end of the season, yet the Mets managed to go just 18–18 in his 36 starts thanks to a Punch-and-Judy lineup that finished last in the league in batting, on-base percentage, and slugging.

The Mets set a team record with 73 wins on the strength of pitching and defense. It was a 12-win bump over 1967, the team's biggest jump since a 16-win climb from 1965 to 1966. The improvement was also reflected in the attendance as the Mets drew more than 200,000 over 1967 and finished second in the league at 1,717,657.

But the offense didn't get any better in the off-season. The winter meetings came and went without the Mets making a single move. Murphy had a chance to acquire slugging catcher Joe Torre from the Braves during 1969 training camp but balked at Atlanta's asking price of Jerry Grote and Ryan.

Fortunately, the pitchers already had developed mental calluses created by the offensive malaise of '68. To a man, the staff knew it had to allow fewer than four runs a game to have any chance to win. Seaver made it his job to let the other young hurlers know their responsibility was keeping the club in the ballgame, and let the chips fall where they may.

"He was mature beyond his years," said McAndrew of Seaver in 2009. "And he was supportive, too. In '68, when I'd lose those 1–0 games, he was the guy who would help me out even though he might have been younger than me. He was much more mature and much older in that respect.

"He'd sit down with you after a game, and if you'd lose 1–0, he'd just smile at you and say, 'Look at their lineup and ours. Who do you think pitched the best game?'"

There was one positive in the Mets' favor as the team reported for camp in 1969. The Montreal Expos and San Diego Padres came into the National League as expansion clubs, giving the Mets 30 opportunities to beat up on inferior talent. There was no reason to believe the Mets couldn't win 20 of those games, putting them almost one quarter of the way toward a .500 campaign.

Hodges came into camp saying he thought the Mets could win 85 games, a prediction that was scoffed at by the media. A group of Mets had already dissected the team's chances and also felt Hodges' assessment was off base. But those players were actually more positive than their manager as they entertained thoughts of reaching the playoffs.

"During training camp in the spring of 1969, Bud Harrelson, Jerry Grote, Nolan Ryan, and I often went fishing at night. We brought along coffee and beer and doughnuts, and, while we fished, we talked about almost everything, including baseball. 'You know,' one of us said early in training camp, 'we can win our division if we play up to our potential.' The other three of us didn't disagree.

"We didn't talk that way too loudly because we knew if the sportswriters heard us, they'd scoff, and if the average fan heard us, he'd laugh, and if the oddsmakers in Las Vegas heard us, they'd ignore us. They had already decided that the odds against the New York Mets winning the Eastern Division championship of the National League were 100-to-1.

"But the four of us—Harrelson, Grote, Ryan, and me—and just about everyone else on our ballclub didn't really care what the oddsmakers said, didn't care if the sportswriters scoffed, and the fans laughed. We wanted to win. We felt we could win.

"Often during spring training, Jerry Grote and I stood on the lawn of my rented home in St. Petersburg and analyzed our chances, and we decided that we could actually win, provided Nolan Ryan fulfilled his promises a pitcher, provided Ron Swoboda and Ed Kranepool fulfilled their promise as hitters, provided Tommie Agee regained his batting eye."[242]

Filled with giddy thoughts of finishing over .500 and winning the NL East, the Mets opened the 1969 season by hosting the expansion Expos. Hodges sent Seaver to the mound with the Mets trying to earn the first season-opening victory in club histoy. Seaver wasn't at his best, yielding four runs—two earned—on six hits and three walks in five innings. He even allowed Expos pitcher Dan McGinn to touch him for a solo homer, but Agee's three-run double in the second and a three-run fourth gave New York a 6–4 lead. Seaver left the game with a chance to pick up the victory before the Expos scored the next seven runs in what became an 11–10 loss for the Mets.

Same old Mets, thought the fans, and that mantra continued as the team got off to an 18–23 start. Seaver opened 6–2 with a 1.96 ERA, one shutout, and five complete games

before surrendering five runs in four innings in a loss to the Astros in the team's 40th game. The Mets also lost the next day before embarking on the first 11-game winning streak in club history, which allowed the franchise to reach new heights. The Mets had never before been more than one game over .500 at any time during their first seven seasons. The streak gave them a 29–23 record, but they remained seven games behind the sizzling Cubs following the 11th consecutive victory on June 10. Five days later, Murphy finally pulled the trigger on a deal that brought veteran first baseman and right-handed slugger Donn Clendenon from the Expos.

The Mets continued to chip away at the Cubs' lead with help from Seaver. He went 5–0 in June and pitched the Mets to an 11–6 win over the Pirates on July 4. Five days later, the Mets had a six-game winning streak and were within 4½ games of the Cubs when Seaver took the mound to face Chicago at Shea Stadium.

Seaver experienced tightness in his pitching shoulder as he warmed up in the bullpen, and he still didn't feel right as he retired the Cubs in succession in the top of the first. But he fanned Ron Santo, Ernie Banks, and Al Spangler in order in the second, giving him five strikeouts after two innings.

Seaver laced an RBI single in the bottom of the second before working a perfect third to maintain a 3–0 lead. The shoulder problems he experienced in the bullpen were long gone as he continued to mow down the Cubs in order during the fourth, fifth, and sixth innings.

Don Kessinger and Glenn Beckert opened the seventh with fly-ball outs, marking the first time the Cubs had sent a ball out of the infield since the first batter in the fifth inning. Seaver retired the next hitter to get out of the seventh with a perfect game still intact.

Santo began the eighth by swatting a lazy fly ball to Agee in center before Seaver fanned Banks and Spangler. Twenty-four up, twenty-four down.

The 25th man was Randy Hundley, who tried to bunt his way on leading off the ninth and sent a tapper back to the mound. Seaver gobbled up the grounder and threw to first to maintain the perfect game.

The next man up was rookie center fielder Jim Qualls, who was starting a day after center fielder Don Young committed two big miscues during a three-run ninth that allowed the Mets to win 4–3. Qualls was a .234 hitter in 47 career at-bats after hitting a fly ball to right and a grounder to first in his first two at-bats that night. In a Cubs starting lineup that included three future Hall of Famers and seven All-Stars, Qualls was deserving of his place as the No. 8 hitter on the team.

"Before the game Gil Hodges asked us if we knew anything about him," Seaver said of Qualls. "Bobby Pfeil, our second baseman that night, remembered him from the minors five years before.

"We decided to throw him hard stuff. I had gotten him out twice. The first pitch to him was a fastball, thigh-high

Tom Seaver pitches in a 1983 game. Photo courtesy of Oscar W. Gabriel

on the outside half of the plate. I was working for a place of my own on the list of perfect games. There had been only eight of them in 70 years of baseball."[243]

The ninth did not come on July 9, 1969. Qualls deposited a clean single into left-center field, beyond the reach of Jones, Agee, or Weis. Seaver walked off the mound, lifted his cap above his head and used his left arm to wipe the sweat off his face as the crowd of over 50,000 began to applaud his effort. Seaver acknowledged the ovation with a tip of his cap before retiring pinch-hitter Willie Smith and Kessinger to complete his one-hitter. It remains the closest a Mets pitcher has come to a perfect game as the ballclub continues to seek its first no-hitter.

"It was a disappointing moment," Seaver said of the Qualls hit. "I know Nancy cried in the stands behind the plate. But I felt as if somebody had opened a spout in my foot and the joy all went out of me. I got the last two Cubs in kind of a fog."[244]

Seaver assessed his performance 20 years later: "Conceivably, it might be the best game I ever pitched, considering the pennant race, the 54,000 fans in the stands. The hitters were doing everything I wanted. I think I made two mistakes in the game. One of them was to Qualls. I didn't know much about him as a hitter. I had never seen him before that night."[245]

Seaver refers to it as his "imperfect game," but it showed the Mets were not at all intimidated by the mighty Cubs. The Mets went into Chicago the following week and took two of three, sweeping a doubleheader to pull within four games of the division lead.

Seaver was selected to his third consecutive All-Star Game that month and was 15–7 with a 2.66 ERA by August 5. But the Mets went just 15–17 following Seaver's bid for a perfect game, putting the club in third place and 9½ games behind Chicago with 49 games to play.

Seaver quelled the skid by pitching into the eighth inning of a 5–3 win over the Braves in sweltering Atlanta on August 9. The victory began a season-ending stretch in which he went 10–0 with a 1.34 ERA, three shutouts, eight complete games, and a .263 slugging average against in 11 starts.

The Mets rode Seaver's arm to a 38–11 record in their last 49 games, winning some in ridiculous fashion. Cardwell and Koosman drove in the only runs in a doubleheader sweep at Pittsburgh on September 12, three days before Swoboda nullified Steve Carlton's major league–record 19-strikeout performance by belting a pair of two-run homers in a 4–3 win at St. Louis. Meanwhile the Cubs dropped 27 of their final 45 games to finish eight games behind the Mets, a 17½-game turnaround from mid-August. New York finished eight games ahead of Chicago at 100–62, a 27-game improvement over 1968.

Some members of the Mets look at the Clendenon trade as the point when they thought they could win the division. Others point to the pair of 1–0 victories in the September twin bill at Forbes Field. Seaver said he got pennant fever while the team was nearing the end of its 11-game winning streak in June.

"At different times during the season, the players jumped on the bandwagon. For me, it was a game we were playing against the Dodgers at Shea Stadium. It was a 1–1 game, and we had a single up the middle. Dodgers center fielder Willie Davis had a clear shot at the runner at home plate, but the ball went under his glove, and he couldn't make a throw. We had won another one-run ballgame, and at that juncture, I said, 'We're going to win this thing.'"[246]

It didn't hurt that Hodges was pushing all the right buttons. "We were managed by an infallible genius in the final six weeks of the season," said Seaver. "Every move Gil made worked. If he lifted a starter, the relief pitcher was brilliant. If he decided to stick with a starter who seemed to be tiring, the man revived. If he let a weak hitter bat in a critical situation, the man came through with a hit. If he called on a pinch-hitter, the man delivered. Gil seemed to have absolute faith in his own judgment, his own methods, and we came to share it. He could do no wrong. If he had decided one day to have me pinch-hit for Cleon Jones, I would have hit a homer. No doubt about it."[247]

The NL East title meant a meeting with the Braves in the first-ever National League Championship Series. Atlanta had a far superior lineup and a strong front end of the rotation. The prognosticators felt the Braves needed to score runs against the Mets' starters to secure a spot in the World Series.

And the Braves had their way with Seaver, Koosman, and rookie Gary Gentry as the trio was tagged for 13 earned runs in 13⅔ innings. Seaver opened the series in Atlanta and was reached for eight hits and three walks in seven innings. He blew a pair of leads, served up homers to Hank Aaron and Tony Gonzalez, and was trailing 5–4 before the Mets erupted for five runs in the top of the eighth to beat the Braves 9–5.

Koosman was chased in the fifth inning the next afternoon after blowing much of a 9–1 lead. Gentry was lifted with the bases loaded in the third inning of Game 3. But the Mets' unheralded offense outperformed the Braves' attack in winning those games 11–6 and 7–4 to complete a three-game sweep. New York averaged nine runs in the series after scoring 3.9 runs a game during the regular season. The Mets were now National League champs and headed for the World Series against Baltimore.

The Orioles had an even deeper attack than the Braves. Again, Seaver was slated to start the opener. And again, Seaver showed up without his best stuff. This time, a calf injury was partially to blame as Seaver hurt himself while

shagging flies in the outfield before Game 2 of the Atlanta series.

"I couldn't run the next day—Monday—or Tuesday or Wednesday. I ran a little on Thursday, gingerly, not risking further injury, then again on Friday, but only a little.

"On Saturday, I pitched the opening game of the World Series, and in the fourth inning, because I had run so little all week, my legs began to tire. My pitches started to drop out of the strike zone; instead of throwing low strikes, I threw low balls. I lost my good stuff. With two men out and no one on base, I gave up a walk, four hits and three runs."[248]

Seaver also had to deal with the first firestorm of his major league career. He had always been one to carefully choose his words until he agreed to sign a petition against the Vietnam War. The petition was to be part of an ad that said, "If the Mets can win the World Series, then we can get out of Vietnam." United Press International ran a story before the ad came out, quoting Seaver as saying, "I think it's perfectly ridiculous what we're doing about the Vietnam situation. It's absurd. When the Series is over, I'm going to have a talk with Ted Kennedy, convey some of my ideas to him and then take an ad in the paper. I feel very strongly about this."[249]

But the ad was the work of the anti-war Moratorium Day committee and was not funded by Seaver. The UPI story led to some embarrassment, although Seaver admitted to signing the petition.

"I didn't hesitate. I said I'd sign the ad. I'd done a lot of thinking about the war, and I felt that it was wrong, that it wasn't helping the United States, that it was damaging our national image without adding much to our national security. I wasn't opposed to all wars. I wasn't a confirmed pacifist. But I did feel that this particular war was wrong."[250]

Fortunately, a bulk of the Mets fan base was made up of 20-somethings just like Seaver, most of whom shared his views on the war. If anything, he had cultivated a new group of fans. But there was still a World Series to win.

Don Buford was the first Oriole to face Seaver in the opener. He also became the first Oriole to score, lifting a home run to right field. Seaver didn't allow another run until the Birds nicked him for three in the fourth inning to go ahead 4–0. Meanwhile Orioles pitcher Mike Cuellar was holding the Mets' attack in check and completed a six-hitter in a 4–1 victory. Seaver's ERA through his first two postseason games was a very uncharacteristic 6.75.

Koosman helped the Mets knot the Series the next afternoon, carrying a no-hitter into the seventh and pitching into the ninth inning of a 2–1 victory. When the Series resumed at Shea, Gentry and Ryan combined to blank the Orioles 5–0 behind two sensational catches by Agee. Seaver pitched the next afternoon.

The Mets had a 2–1 lead in the Series when the Mets took the field for Game 4. Harrelson fired bullets to Clendenon before the opening pitch. Agee played catch with Jones and Swoboda in the outfield. But Grote had yet to get into his catching crouch as NBC broadcaster Curt Gowdy discussed a brief delay to the start of the game. That delay was caused by Seaver's urgent need to go to the bathroom before taking the mound.

The game began better than the opener as Seaver fanned Buford to get things going. Paul Blair followed with a base hit but was still on first when Seaver struck out Boog Powell to end the inning.

Clendenon homered in the second to put the Mets on top, and Seaver worked out of a one-out, first-and-third jam in the third inning to maintain the lead.

Seaver didn't allow another hit until Frank Robinson and Powell slapped consecutive one-out singles in the ninth to put the tying run on third. Next up was Brooks Robinson, who went with the pitch and sent a drive toward right-center field.

Swoboda was patrolling right field that afternoon and did not have a reputation as a great fielder. It was Swoboda who ran awkwardly toward Buford's leadoff drive in Game 1 before making an off-balance lunge at the eventual home run. His body slid down the right-field wall as if he were Wile E. Coyote in a Warner Brothers cartoon.

This time, Swoboda got a great jump and sped straight for the ball. The safe move would have been to grab it on the hop and prevent Powell from chugging over to third on an RBI single. But Swoboda wasn't interested in conceding a run. He dove for the ball, snared it in his glove and made a 360-degree tumble before firing home in an attempt to nail Frank Robinson at the plate. It remains one of the greatest catches in World Series history. But had he missed the ball, Seaver could have fallen behind by at least 2–1.

Seaver got out of the inning by getting Elrod Hendricks to fly out to Swoboda before the Mets left the potential winning run in scoring position to force extra innings. It was still 1–1 after Seaver stranded runners on first and third in the top of the 10th.

Seaver gave up just a run and six hits in 10 innings of work but was staring at a possible no-decision unless the Mets could score in the bottom half. He was due to bat third in the inning, and a trip to the plate seemed out of the question if the Mets could put a runner in scoring position.

Grote led off the inning with a double off Dick Hall and was replaced by pinch runner Rod Gaspar. Orioles manager Earl Weaver elected to walk the light-hitting Weis intentionally, forcing Hodges to pinch-hit for Seaver.

J.C. Martin was sent to the plate with a chance to win the game. Martin laid down a bunt, which had some wondering why Hodges hadn't just sent up Seaver in a bunting situation.

The bunt was perfect. Reliever Pete Richert had no chance to throw out Gaspar or Weis, and Martin was more than halfway down the line when Richert tossed the ball to Powell. It never got there as the throw glanced off Martin's arm and dribbled toward second base, allowing Gaspar to

score the winning run. Seaver had his first World Series win, and the Mets were now one victory away from their first championship.

"It was great to win a 10-inning game, but the difference was the next day when Kooz pitched and won the fifth and clinching game. The Koosman game was much more important from a team-winning effort. When you're pitching, there is a continual flow of emotions. My game was important to me only because it made what happened the next day possible."[251]

Koosman spotted the Birds a 3–0 lead on homers by pitcher Dave McNally and Frank Robinson in the third inning. It remained a three-run deficit until Clendenon crushed a two-run homer in the sixth and Weis added a solo blast an inning later. The Mets scored twice in the eighth before Koosman completed a 5–3 victory that touched off the third celebration at Shea Stadium in 22 days.

Seaver came away with the first of his three Cy Young Awards after finishing the regular season 25–7 with 2.21 ERA. He also received the Hickok Belt as the professional athlete of the year, and was named the *Sports Illustrated* Sportsman of the Year.

The Mets sang on *The Ed Sullivan Show.* A few performed with comedian Phil Foster in a Las Vegas revue. They gave speeches on the rubber chicken circuit, signed thousands of autographs, and reveled in an amazing season. When they got to spring training, there were 11 other teams preparing to beat the crap out of the upstart Mets. Unfortunately, the Mets were still living off their championship as they headed toward the season opener.

The 1970 season began positively as the Mets won on Opening Day for the first time in club history. Seaver worked the first eight innings before Ron Taylor picked up the win in a 5–3 decision at Pittsburgh.

Seaver won each of his next six starts to run his regular-season winning streak to 16 since August 1969. He tied Carlton's single-game strikeout record by fanning 19 Padres in a 2–1 win on April 22, capping the gem by whiffing his final 10 hitters to set a big-league record for consecutive strikeouts.

"I happened to be throwing the ball extremely well," Seaver said of that outing. "I had it all, power and precision. I used just fastballs and sliders. The circumstances were right for me. It was an overcast day, and it was difficult for the batters to see. Plus, it was a close game, so the pressure was on all the way."[252]

Seaver finally lost on May 11 despite striking out 12 in a complete game. One start later, he fanned 15 in his second career one-hitter, losing the no-no when Phillies catcher Mike Compton singled in the third inning.

Seaver lost his next four starts before tossing seven consecutive complete-game victories, giving him a 14–5 record with a 2.41 ERA and 177 strikeouts in 172 innings. His WHIP was a ridiculous 0.941 by virtue of just 117 hits allowed.

But the Mets were chugging along at a .500 pace. Agee was duplicating his 1969 stats, Clendenon was on pace to set a club record for RBIs, and Ken Boswell was putting himself in the record book for consecutive errorless games at second base. But Koosman, Ryan, and Gentry were wildly inconsistent, making McAndrew the second-most dependable starter during the first half.

Yet the Mets remained in the race despite never climbing more than 10 games over .500 after July 9. Pittsburgh and Chicago failed to run away from the rest of the pack, allowing the Mets to entertain thoughts of a second straight playoff berth.

The Mets were 70–64 and within a half-game of the division lead when Seaver struck out 11 while going the distance in a 7–3 win over the Cardinals on September 2. The victory left Seaver with an 18–10 mark and made him a cinch to win 20 games with five to six starts remaining.

Seaver finished the season with 283 strikeouts, setting a National League record for right-handed pitchers. He also paced the league with a 2.82 ERA and finished among the top five in victories. But he closed the season with the worst five-game stretch of his young career, going 0–2 with a 5.16 ERA and 46 base runners allowed in 29⅔ innings. The Mets made a slow fade out of the race and finished third at 83–79, six games behind the Pirates.

He was unfairly made the scapegoat by some in the media. Seaver won only one of his final 10 starts, resulting in a 2–8 record for the Mets in those games. But he was only part of the problem as the Mets failed to come up with the timely hitting and shut-down pitching that allowed them to rip the NL East crown from the Cubs in 1969.

The Mets seemed to put that disappointing season behind them by opening 1971 30–18 with a 2.50 ERA behind the strong pitching of Seaver and Ryan. The two combined to go 13–3 with a 1.76 ERA and 148 strikeouts in 148⅔ innings during the Mets' first 48 games, putting the club within a half-game of first place by June 4.

But it quickly became a summer to forget as the Mets went 28–42 from June 5 to August 15, including a hideous 6–20 mark in July. Ryan's ERA soared over the last four months, Koosman battled an aching shoulder, McAndrew couldn't buy a win, and Gentry remained the same enigmatic .500 pitcher he was in 1969 and '70. The pitching woes were a bad mix for a team that didn't have a player who hit more than 14 homers for the season.

The Mets were playing for pride over the final month, none more so than Seaver. He was sensational over his final 12 starts, going 9–2 with a 0.93 ERA and 112 strikeouts in 107 innings. Seaver surrendered just 58 hits over that span to record a .162 batting average against.

His penultimate start of the season provided his third one-hitter in three years, a 3–1 win over the Pirates. He retired his first 18 batters until Dave Cash walked and Vic Davalillo singled. The outcome left Seaver with a 19–10 record and 276 strikeouts with four games left in the season.

Hodges allowed Seaver to pitch what was now a meaningless season finale on three days' rest. But the game was anything but meaningless for Seaver as he tossed a complete game in a 6–1 win over the Cardinals, giving him 20 wins for the year while clinching the National League ERA and strikeout totals with career bests. His 0.946 WHIP for the season was also a career high, as were his 6.7 hits per nine innings and 9.1 strikeouts per nine innings.

"I thought it was the best year of my career," said Seaver in 1988. "I had an earned run average of 1.76, I led the league with 289 strikeouts, had 61 walks, and threw four shutouts. In 28 starts, I allowed two earned runs or less. In 32 starts, I allowed three or less. But I had to win that final day of the season to get 20 wins. Despite everything else I accomplished that year, I still had to win on the last day of the season for 20. I got it with a seven-hitter against the Cardinals, striking out 13."[253]

Ryan was traded after the season, packaged with three prospects for infielder Jim Fregosi as the Mets tried to bolster a lackluster offense. General manager Bob Scheffing also pulled off a trade with the Expos before the season began, landing slugging right-fielder Rusty Staub for three players.

The Staub trade was announced a few days after the Mets' world was rocked by the death of Hodges, who succumbed to his second heart attack in 3½ years. Hodges had just finished a round of golf with his coaches on what became an off-day after the Major League Players Association called its first strike the weekend before the season opener. He was replaced by Berra, the man who gave Seaver words of encouragement following the rookie's final exhibition start in 1967.

Seaver entered 1972 as the ace of a staff that now had Koosman, Gentry, and rookies Buzz Capra and Jon Matlack in the rotation. McAndrew and Ray Sadecki were being counted on to round out the starting five in case the rookies faltered.

The pitching was outstanding over the first few weeks as the Mets won 25 of their first 32 games to take a six-game lead in the National League East. They acquired Willie Mays while the team was in the midst of a team record–tying 11-game winning streak. Matlack was unbeaten through his first six decisions, Capra looked like a veteran in his first five outings, and Gentry appeared poised to have a breakout season.

But a slew of injuries crippled the team by the first week of June. Staub missed the better part of three months with a broken bone in his hand. Agee, Jones, Mays, Grote, and rookie John Milner shuttled in and out of the lineup due to various injuries. New York again played itself out of contention by midsummer and needed to win nine of its last 12 just to finish 10 games over .500.

Seaver was outstanding once again, although he wasn't the same dominant pitcher he was in '71. He went 21–12, made the All-Star team for the sixth time in as many seasons, and finished second in the league with 249 strikeouts.

But his 2.92 ERA was his highest since reaching the majors, and his 1.115 WHIP was his worst since 1967.

Mets fans had gotten spoiled and were surprised by the reduced strikeouts and inflated ERA. However, he also became just the eighth pitcher in modern National League history to record at least 21 wins, 249 strikeouts, and an ERA at 2.92 or better. Not bad for a perceived off-year.

Gentry was the latest Mets starter to be dispatched as Scheffing sought a better lineup during the 1972 winter meetings. Gentry and reliever Danny Frisella were jettisoned to the Braves for second baseman Felix Millan and George Stone. Millan was expected to prolong rallies as the No. 2 hitter, but Stone was penciled in as a fifth starter at best, making the trade initially appear as another hit on the pitching staff. The only other trade of significance involved Agee, as he was sent to the Astros following a poor season.

The rest of the lineup was the same, as management felt there was no way the club could run into another rash of injuries. But the disabled list began to grow the moment the Mets opened the season. Jones, Milner, Grote, Harrelson, and Mays landed on the DL by June 1, leaving it up to the pitchers to keep the Mets in the race.

The rotation eventually became a solid foursome as Seaver, Koosman, Matlack, and Stone kept the Mets in games. Unfortunately, they occasionally had to leave the outcome of a game in the hands of Tug McGraw, who got off to a nice start before enduring a miserable three-month slump that pushed the Mets into the NL East cellar by June 25 despite winning 19 of their first 34 games.

Seaver was fantastic over the first four months, going 12–5 with a 1.96 ERA. He allowed two runs or fewer in three of those five losses and had four no-decisions in which he held opponents under three runs. With that in mind, it's conceivable he could have been 19–2 heading into August.

Matlack and Koosman were pitching well enough to lose, combining for a 15–25 record despite a 3.41 ERA. McAndrew was ineffective, and Stone was putting too many leads in the hands of a shaky bullpen as the Mets carried a 44–57 record into August.

The lineup was at full strength by mid-August once Harrelson completed his second stint on the disabled list, but the Mets continued to waste solid pitching. Seaver compiled a 0.99 ERA in 63⅓ innings over seven starts in August, tossing two shutouts and allowing no more than two runs in any appearance. But the Mets went just 3–4 in those appearances and were 61–71 after Seaver absorbed a complete-game, 1–0 loss in 10 innings at St. Louis on August 30. Seaver was now 15–8 with a 1.71 ERA for the season.

Fortunately for the Mets, they were only 6½ games out of first place following the loss and came back to win the next two games before settling for a four-game split with the Cardinals. That was followed by three-games-out-of-four series wins against the Expos and Phillies, and a pair of three-game series victories against the Phils and Cubs. The Mets now stood at 73–76 heading into a two-game set against the first-place Pirates in Pittsburgh.

The Bucs blasted the Mets 10–3 in the opener as Seaver surrendered more than three earned runs for the first time since June 8. Pittsburgh was ready to pull the plug on the Mets' season the next night, coming within two outs of a 4–1 victory until New York erupted for five runs in the ninth to eke out a 6–5 win and pull within 2½ games of first place.

In a scheduling quirk, the two teams opened a three-game set at Shea the next night. Stone pitched the Mets to a 7–3 victory in the opener before the "Ball-off-the-Wall" play helped New York beat the Pirates 4–3 in 13 innings in Game 2. Seaver was on the mound in the finale with a chance to pitch the Mets into first place, an improbable situation only four weeks earlier.

Seaver went the distance on a five-hitter after being lit up by the Pirates earlier in the week. Jones and Grote each hit two-run doubles in the first inning before homers by Milner, Garrett, and Staub led to a 10–2 rout, putting the Mets atop the division.

The Mets stretched their winning streak to seven games and led the division heading into a doubleheader at Chicago on the final day of the season. A sweep would clinch the NL East and allow the Mets to avoid a makeup doubleheader the following day. But Matlack lost a heartbreaker in the opener 1–0 before New York settled for a split, keeping the Pirates and Cardinals alive as the Mets' season was extended by one day.

Just 1,918 showed up on a drizzling, dreary afternoon at Wrigley Field to watch Seaver try to wrap up the title. Seaver allowed five hits through the first four innings, but the Mets provided him with a 5–0 lead by the time he took the mound in the bottom of the fifth. The run support was welcomed as Seaver gutted out 8⅓ innings while allowing four runs and a season-high 11 hits. McGraw got the final two outs in a 6–4 victory as the Mets won the division despite an 82–79 record, then the worst mark for a postseason club in history.

The Mets had five days off before opening the NLCS at Cincinnati, allowing Seaver to pitch Game 1. It was arguably Seaver's best postseason performance as he allowed only six hits while striking out 13 in a complete game. He even drove in the Mets' lone run with a two-out double in the second to score Harrelson, then protected the 1–0 lead for the next five innings.

Seaver opened the eighth by fanning Hal King, leaving him five outs from victory until Pete Rose smacked a solo homer to tie it. The Reds walked off the field in the ninth with a 2–1 win after Johnny Bench homered.

The Mets won the next two games behind the stellar pitching of Matlack and Koosman before a gem by George Stone was wasted in a 2–1, 13-inning loss in Game 4, forcing a fifth and final game and sending Seaver back to the mound.

TOM SEAVER LIFETIME vs. HALL OF FAMERS (minimum 50 AB)

Name	AB	H	HR	RBI	AVG	OBP	SLG
Lou Brock	152	38	1	9	.250	.274	.362
Willie Stargell	130	31	8	20	.238	.301	.546
Joe Morgan	109	32	5	11	.294	.415	.505
Tony Perez	119	25	3	19	.210	.240	.361
Mike Schmidt	85	16	2	5	.188	.317	.294
Johnny Bench	84	15	2	8	.179	.271	.333
Billy Williams	85	21	1	11	.247	.305	.353
Hank Aaron	82	18	5	10	.220	.290	.476
Willie McCovey	77	20	6	16	.260	.376	.584
Dave Winfield	73	18	3	12	.247	.304	.397
Ron Santo	68	17	5	10	.250	.354.	.518
Gary Carter	64	12	1	4	.188	.268	.234
Roberto Clemente	62	15	2	6	.242	.277	.355
Andre Dawson	58	13	1	12	.224	.266	.414
TOTAL	1,248	291	45	153	.233	.300	.413

Seaver wasn't as sharp in the clincher as he was in the opener, but he didn't have to be. He gave up an RBI single to Tony Perez to knot the score 2–2 in the fifth before the Mets erupted for four runs in the bottom half to take control. Seaver pitched into the ninth but loaded the bases with a single and two walks before McGraw recorded the final two outs to finish off the Reds.

The Mets' inability to win Game 4 of the NLCS prevented Seaver from pitching either of the first two games of the World Series in Oakland. New York still came away with a split and had Seaver on the mound when the Series shifted to Shea Stadium.

Seaver struck out 12 and allowed seven hits in eight innings while pitching on five days' rest. He was staked to a 2–0 lead in the first on a homer by Jones and a run-scoring wild pitch, and it remained 2–0 until Sal Bando and Gene Tenace each doubled in the sixth. Oakland eventually tied the game in the eighth as Bert Campaneris singled, stole second, and scored on Joe Rudi's single. The Mets threatened in the ninth before Campaneris manufactured another run in the 11th to give the A's a 3–2 win.

The Mets won the next two games to take a 3–2 lead in the series. It was now up to Berra to decide whether to bypass Stone and go with Seaver on short rest in Game 6. Stone ended the regular season on an eight-game winning streak and was brilliant in Game 4 of the NLCS before earning a save in the second game of the Fall Classic.

Berra decided to go for the kill, putting his ace on the mound for Game 6. But Seaver received little run support for the third time in the postseason as Oakland pulled out a 3–1 victory. Seaver allowed two runs in seven innings, but the Mets didn't score until the top of the eighth.

The loss now meant Berra had to start Matlack on short rest for Game 7. Matlack had pitched three postseason games without allowing an earned run in 23 innings, but he was chased in the fourth inning as Oakland earned a 5–2 victory to win the Series.

Seaver captured his second Cy Young Award by ending the year 19–10 and leading the league with 251 strikeouts, a 2.08 ERA, and 18 complete games. Only Ron Bryant's 24 wins with San Francisco prevented Seaver from claiming pitching's Triple Crown.

Scheffing did nothing to improve the club after the '73 season, again banking on the hunch the Mets couldn't possibly run into a spate of injuries for the third straight year. But the maladies continued into 1974, leading to a 71–91 record and a fifth-place finish. This time, Seaver was among those battling injuries.

Seaver developed sciatica during the first half of the season and tried to pitch through agonizing pain. For a pitcher whose power came from his legs and hips, it was about the worst injury he could have suffered. He was 3–6 with a 3.89 ERA when he fired three-hit ball over five shutout innings against the Phillies on June 21, exactly 10 years after Phils ace Jim Bunning tossed a perfect game against the Mets. But Seaver had to pull himself from the game and didn't pitch again for 11 days, marking the first time in his major league career that he had gone more than six days between starts during the regular season.

He won his next two starts by tossing shutout ball but was shut down for 19 days due to his now-worrisome condition. He came back to fire a four-hit shutout against the Astros to improve to 4–0 with a 0.00 ERA in 26⅓ innings over four starts. But he was pummeled in his next outing July 31, allowing seven runs in 4⅓ innings before yielding seven runs over 13 innings in his next two appearances.

There were flashes of the old Seaver, like the 10⅔ innings he threw in a 2–1 loss at Houston on August 19, and the shutout he pitched against the Astros 10 days later. But he generally had trouble working past the seventh inning, and his strikeouts-per-nine-innings was down to 7.15 heading into his final four starts.

Not that his problems radically altered the Mets' season. The offense was meager and the bullpen was unreliable when Bob Apodaca was in the rotation. McGraw battled a shoulder problem that limited him to just three saves in nine chances. Unlike 1973, there was no playoff push after August 15.

Seaver continued to press on despite playing for nothing more than pride. He struck out 11 in a four-hit shutout against the Cubs September 13 but failed to pitch more than six innings in his next two appearances. He was pulled from a start after six innings versus the Phillies on September 25, which left him 11–10 with a 3.25 ERA. Seaver still had pain in his back, butt, and leg, causing the Mets to discuss shutting him down for the final eight games of the season.

Seaver had begun the year with a chance to become the first pitcher in National League history to record 200 or more strikeouts in seven consecutive years. That goal appeared out of reach with Seaver at 187 heading into the final week of the season. Seaver still wanted to go for the mark and reportedly received a little help from the man who eventually ran him out of town.

According to the team's 1975 media guide, Mets board chairman M. Donald Grant suggested to team physician James Parkes that Seaver pay a visit to Dr. Kenneth Riland, a noted osteopath whose patients included Vice President Nelson Rockefeller. Seaver underwent two therapy sessions over a five-day period before deeming himself ready to make one more start October 1 against the Phillies.

The Phils were the National League's most-improved ballclub and had a lineup featuring Mike Schmidt, Greg Luzinski, Willie Montanez, Dave Cash, and Del Unser. They were also one of the toughest teams to strike out, making Seaver's goal that much harder as he took the mound.

The Phillies had Seaver's chief nemesis on the bench. Tommy Hutton finished his career with a .248 average and never had more than 381 at-bats in any season. But he owned Seaver, compiling a .320 average a .438 on-base percentage, a .545 slugging average, three homers, and 15 RBIs in 62 at-bats. Seaver accounted for 13.6 percent of Hutton's major league home runs and 8 percent of his 186 RBIs.

"I can't explain why I had success hitting against Seaver," said Hutton. "I just seemed to be able to guess right with him. If I guessed fastball, I got it. If I guessed change-up, I got that. It was just luck, and I feel honored to have had such good luck hitting against such a great pitcher. He was a class guy who mastered his position."[254]

Hutton also had his way with Bob Gibson and Juan Marichal, hitting a combined .322 versus the two Hall of Famers. However, he managed just two RBIs in 59 at-bats against them.   .

Even without Hutton in the lineup, Seaver trailed 2–0 just four batters into the game, allowing a pair of singles and a two-run double before shutting out Philadelphia the rest of the way. He had eight strikeouts through six innings, but a 2–1 deficit made it possible that Berra would replace him with a pinch-hitter.

Seaver was due to bat third in the bottom of the seventh after fanning Luzinski, Unser, and Jay Johnstone in succession to run his strikeout total to 11. Berra allowed Seaver to hit after Bruce Boisclair and Ron Hodges were retired in order by Phils starter Jim Lonborg.

Seaver still had 11 strikeouts as he entered the ninth inning, having failed to fan anyone in the eighth. Still two shy of the mark, Seaver opened the ninth by striking out Schmidt and Montanez to reach the 200 mark. He capped the inning by fanning Mike Anderson, putting him at 201 strikeouts.

But the Mets failed to score after the fifth, leaving Seaver with an 11–11 record and a 3.20 ERA. He deemed his final start a breakthrough in his battle with sciatica, and he felt good enough to accompany the Mets on a series of exhibition games in Japan. Seaver made five starts and struck out 28 in 29 innings against Japanese hitters.

Seaver was back in form in 1975, winning his third and final NL Cy Young Award based on a 22–9 record, 243 strikeouts, and 2.38 earned run average. He paced the league in wins and strikeouts, and was third in ERA, but the Mets' shot at a division crown was stymied by a weak back end of the rotation and a bullpen that was downright horrible over the first two months. The Mets suddenly found themselves short of quality pitching depth after years of trading their surplus of arms for hitters.

Berra was fired in early August following a five-game losing streak that put New York 9½ games out of first. The Mets made a brief charge in late August under interim skipper Roy McMillan and were only four games back after Seaver picked up his 20th victory with a four-hit shutout of the Pirates on Labor Day. He also reached 200 strikeouts in that game to become the first in major league history to reach the plateau in eight straight seasons. Walter Johnson and Rube Waddell were the only other pitchers with seven consecutive 200-strikeout seasons at that point in baseball history.

"I'm very happy to have it," Seaver said of the strikeout record after the game. "The two guys you pass aren't too shabby. But I don't know yet how it will shape up in my mind—I'll have to go back and do some reading into baseball history.

"Considering everything, though, this might be my biggest day—the 20th game, the 200 strikeouts, and shutting out the Pirates in a pennant race."[255]

But the Mets played themselves into a third-place finish at 82–80 by losing 16 of their final 26 games. McMillan stepped down and was replaced by longtime Mets minor league skipper Joe Frazier.

Nineteen-seventy-five was also the year arbitrator Peter Seitz ruled against baseball's reserve clause, deciding the codicil as written didn't automatically bind players to their current ballclubs in perpetuity. The judgment allowed pitchers Dave McNally and Andy Messersmith to sign with other clubs and set up baseball's first free-agent system. McNally retired after the season, but Messersmith signed a three-year, $1 million contract with the Braves after making $90,000 with the 1975 Dodgers. Messersmith, a very good pitcher but a notch below Seaver's talent, was now making almost double what Seaver was due to earn in 1976.

Seaver saw the pending free-agent market as an opportunity to at least gauge the Mets' interest in renegotiating his contract. Given his résumé and stature with the ballclub, it didn't seem like a bad idea for the Mets to keep their top pitcher happy. A multiyear package would have been a win-win for both sides; Seaver would be better compensated for his efforts, and the Mets would lock up the face of the franchise for a few years while other clubs spent big money to obtain the services of star pitchers.

But Grant was a visionary. He envisioned the Mets were playing in the 1940s and that free agency would be nothing more than a fad. Grant was highly insulted that Seaver would be so ungrateful to ask for a new deal before his current one had run out. But Grant did his bidding through the media and McDonald, who was now in his second year as the Mets' general manager.

Daily News columnist Dick Young toed the company line, writing that Seaver was an ingrate as Grant stood in the background. Seaver had to state his case to McDonald, a loyal company man who had been with the organization since 1962. Grant stayed out of the line of fire, although it's believed he was feeding information to Young for his *Daily News* column.

Seaver and McDonald were arguing about the contract in spring training when McDonald mentioned/threatened that he already had a deal in place that would send Seaver elsewhere. It was reported that McDonald had negotiated a trade that would ship Seaver to the Dodgers for pitcher Don Sutton, although McDonald denied in 2011 that such a deal was firmly in place. Seaver called McDonald's bluff, telling him to "make the bleeping deal." But McDonald didn't have the heart.

Seaver finally accepted a new contract with a bump in pay, but the package would be dwarfed by the deals handed to free agents after the 1976 season. Seaver truly gave the Mets the hometown discount after a hard stance during training camp.

"I'm just glad it's all over," Seaver said after the package was hammered out in the groundskeeper's office at Fort Lauderdale Stadium. "It's been a very trying six weeks. I found it very difficult to concentrate on pitching in my last two starts. I don't think there's any doubt that it'll help our entire ballclub knowing this situation is over."[256]

Seaver finished 1976 with 235 strikeouts to lead the league for the fifth and final time and extend his string of seasons with at least 200 Ks to nine. He also finished third in the National League with a 2.59 ERA, tossed five shutouts for the third straight year, and went the distance 13 times.

He would have had more complete games had the Mets' offense provided him with three runs or more in 17 of his 35 starts. There was a 10-start stretch from July 17 to September 3 in which the Mets scored just 17 times for Seaver. The feeble run support led to a 14–11 record, ranking him third on the team in victories.

The Mets ended up third in the NL East for the fifth time in seven years, but their 86–76 record actually represented the second-best at that point in club history. Seaver, Koosman, and Matlack combined to go 52–32 while the rest of the staff was 34–44. The offense was anemic, especially while slugger Dave Kingman missed six weeks with a thumb injury.

The first free-agent market opened for business after the 1976 World Series. The Mets, in desperate need for a couple of bats, declined to make Reggie Jackson an offer and made only token attempts to sign center fielder Gary Matthews. The Mets came away with zilch, instead relying on rookies Lee Mazzilli and Roy Staiger to provide an offensive spark in 1977.

"How can you not even try?" Seaver wondered about the team's free-agent stance during his second day of spring training. "We traded our center fielder last year. How can a team that depends so much on pitching trade its center fielder without a replacement? And who knows how long this pitching staff can keep holding up?"[257]

Meanwhile, several pitchers hit the jackpot through free agency, while other clubs reworked contracts with their existing star pitchers. Seaver was now among the lowest-paid 20-game winners when he reported to 1977 training camp, and Kingman was similarly unhappy with his contract. For Seaver, the Mets were no longer the same happy family they appeared to be just two years earlier, and they were now giving Kingman a hard time in contract negotiations.

"It's different. For the first time, I feel much of the joy has gone. I still have professional pride, but the larger feeling for the club is gone. Not for the other players—I still feel the same relationship with the players. And there's been no change with the fans—I received many letters of support. But there is a big change in my relations with the front office.

"They put out all those statements last year about what an ingrate I was and about how fragile my career might become because of injuries. But it was clear that the same pitcher they were knocking in public would become their big man, overnight, if I signed and behaved.

"I did sign, but I still resent the way they mishandled my case. There's no question of my loyalty. There should be no issue of loyalty in Dave Kingman's contract dispute, either—he's only been with the club two years. Players should be reasonable, but I feel that I'm for Kingman all the way."

"Do I sit around and sulk every day?" Seaver asked. "Just every other day. I have no loss of feeling for the owners, Mrs. De Roulet, or the others. But I think it was mishandled by Grant and McDonald. It's got to the point where I'm not enjoying the start of spring training as I should. Things between us are different. The relationships have changed."[258]

At this point Seaver didn't seem to care if 20 pitchers made more money than he did through free agency. He was just tired of watching teams like the Phillies pass the Mets in terms of competitive balance. Throw the Pirates into the equation, and the Mets had little shot of making the 1977 playoffs unless their division rivals stumbled through 162 games as they did four years earlier.

Most galling was that the Mets appeared to have the

resources to improve the ballclub through the free-agent highway, yet were fumbling for loose change in their pockets while the rest of baseball beat them to the toll plaza.

McDonald publicly stated early in spring training that the team was banking on its top three starters to win the division. That didn't stop Grant from mentioning during camp that several teams were interested in acquiring Seaver, which would have disrupted the team's imbalanced house of cards.

"We're not trying to trade Tom Seaver," Grant said. "We have had some requests from other teams, from people asking if we were disgusted enough by his recent statements. So there have been some conversations.

"We replied: What are you offering? But nobody has come up with nearly enough. But we have no desire to trade him unless it's so indicated by Seaver himself."[259]

Again, Grant was turning the screws to make it appear Seaver wanted out while ignoring the crux of the problem. Meanwhile, the club continued to bat down reports of a trade during spring training. It was becoming a rerun of 1976 spring training.

The start of the season was a disaster. Neither Mazzilli nor Staiger distinguished themselves as major league hitters during the first two months as the Mets played so poorly that Frazier was replaced by Joe Torre on Memorial Day. Kingman hit well over the first three weeks before entering a severe batting slump that created a black hole on offense. Grote, Harrelson, and Millan had reached their mid- to late thirties and were playing like it.

The one positive was Seaver, who went 4–0 with a 1.52 ERA in five starts during April before getting hit hard in May. Speculation grew that he was unhappy with his contract, although that was no reason for his stretch of poor performances. Seaver was more disgusted with the team's position in the NL East cellar.

"When you think that just a few months ago, with our pitching, management could really have helped us. They had a golden opportunity—and they did nothing."[260]

Grant was adamant Seaver would not work out another deal before his current one ran out. McDonald was no help, either, trying to play the role of good soldier while his ballclub was fighting to climb out of the cellar.

June 15 was the trade deadline that season, and it was anyone's guess as to whether Seaver's contract situation would lead to a deal. Seaver struck out 10 in a five-hit shutout against the Reds on June 7, then went the distance on a five-hitter in a 3–1 win over the Astros five days later and three days before the trade deadline.

Many on the Mets treated the Houston victory as Seaver's last stand, figuring he was going elsewhere. Seaver received a big hug from catcher John Stearns after the final out, an embrace so tight it appeared the players knew it was Seaver's last game in a Mets uniform.

After the game, Seaver didn't want to talk about his future with the team, and Torre still expected him to be on the mound for him on June 17. But Torre and McDonald acknowledged the possibility of a trade was very strong.

"The clubs are talking," said Torre following the victory. "That's all I can tell you. So far, what's been offered is far from equal. I do think Tom is happier than he was before."

"We're talking to clubs as we have been," McDonald said. "There's no trade until it's consummated. I guess he's like we are. We aren't that at ease. He obviously isn't and hasn't been. Nor are we, because he's on record as saying he wants to be traded."[261]

Rumors of Seaver's departure continued when he finally did an end-around on Grant and McDonald by negotiating directly with team owner Lorinda de Roulet. The two hammered out the parameters of a long-term contract that would keep Seaver in a Mets uniform. De Roulet was happy. Seaver was happy.

The *Daily News* published a Dick Young column the day of the trade deadline. This time, Young dragged Seaver's wife, Nancy, into it by saying she was jealous of Nolan Ryan's spouse because Nolan was making more dough with the Angels. That was the last straw.

"That all started because of Dick Young in the paper writing bad stuff about Tom and Nancy, and Nolan and Ruth Ryan," said Jerry Koosman more than three decades later. "Not that Nolan and Ruth were there anymore, but he had been writing some stuff that I know made Seaver mad. It just snowballed, and Seaver finally got tired of being in New York and listening to stuff from the writers, especially Young.

"There were some hurt feelings there, and you know the trade was going to happen. Seaver had had enough of it and wanted to go.

"It was a black day for the Mets when they traded him."

Seaver contacted Mets public relations director Herb Weissman and told him to get in touch with de Roulet to tell her the deal was off. Seaver knew Young's column had to have been spoon-fed by Grant, although it's unclear whether Grant knew Seaver already had a contract agreement in place.

McDonald had been working on a deal with the Reds and completed it a few minutes before the midnight deadline, sending Seaver to the Reds for pitcher Pat Zachry, infielder Doug Flynn, and outfield prospects Steve Henderson and Dan Norman. McDonald also shipped Kingman to the Padres for reliever Paul Seibert and utilityman Bobby Valentine, and traded infielder Mike Phillips to the Cardinals for utilityman Joel Youngblood. The three deals have become known in Mets lore as "The Midnight Massacre."

Seaver broke down as he met the media at Shea following the trade. He certainly didn't look like someone who truly wanted to leave the Mets, but it was also very evident he couldn't play for Grant.

"My loyalty was used against me, and I was called an ingrate," he said. "I saw years being thrown out of the window because my loyalty was attacked after all those years. But if I was guilty of anything at that point, I was guilty of being extremely naïve.

"I don't know if I really want to ride back through the history of all this, but it all goes back to my signing my contract last year. Things were said then and written in the press, mainly by Dick Young. My loyalty was attacked. Then a couple of days ago, I was talking to the club and there was a little discussion about the possibility of a new contract. They didn't want to renegotiate, and I can understand that. But my proposal was to play the next two years under my current contract and talk to them about the three years after that: 1979, 1980, and 1981.

"But the next day, Dick Young dragged my wife and family into it, and I couldn't take that. I called the Mets and said, 'That's it, it's all over.' This alliance or whatever it is—this alliance between Young and the chairman of the board—is stacked against me. As far as the fans go, I've given them a great number of thrills, and they've been equally returned. The ovation I got the other night…"

That's when the situation truly hit him. Eleven seasons with the same team. Almost 200 victories. Three Cy Young Awards. Two pennants and one World Series.

"Come on, George," Seaver said to himself as he tried to continue. But he was unable to speak. Instead, he wrote out the remainder of his thoughts and handed it to another newsman.

"And the ovation I got the other night after passing Sandy Koufax," Seaver penned about moving ahead of the Dodgers great for 13th on the all-time strikeout list, "that will be one of the most memorable and warm moments in my life."[262]

The trade allowed Seaver to post his fifth and final 20-win season, finishing 21–6 with a 2.58 ERA. He tossed a three-hit shutout against Montreal in his Reds debut and went 13–1 with a 2.11 ERA in his final 16 starts.

The great stretch run included his return to Shea Stadium on Sunday, August 21. He received a hero's welcome before pitching a six-hitter with 11 strikeouts in a 5–1 win over the punchless Mets. The Mets drew 46,265 for the game, the team's season-high for a home game.

Seaver continued to enjoy great success with Cincinnati. He tossed his lone no-hitter on June 16, 1978, against the Cardinals before helping the Reds win the 1979 NL West title. Seaver was also sensational during the 1981 strike season, leading the league in wins and finishing 14–2 with a 2.54 ERA. But his days as a dominating strikeout artist appeared to be over as Seaver fanned only 319 in 549⅓ innings from 1979 to 1981.

He finished second to Dodgers rookie Fernando Valenzuela in the 1981 NL Cy Young Award voting before enduring an injury-plagued 1982 season. He opened the campaign by battling the flu and developed a thigh injury before missing much of the second half to a shoulder problem. It marked the first time Seaver had suffered an upper-body injury.

Seaver ended up 5–13 with a 5.50 ERA in 1982, not a

good sign for a 38-year-old pitcher. It gave the Reds reason to dangle him in a trade, especially with the club rebuilding after failing to win a postseason game since acquiring Seaver.

It was time for the Mets to right a wrong. From a franchise standpoint, the 1977 Seaver trade wasn't a horrible move. The Mets weren't going to contend for a playoff berth with or without Seaver, and the deal brought the club a very good pitcher when healthy, a Gold Glove second baseman, and an outfielder who remains the Mets' career leader in batting average. But the Seaver trade was also public relations nightmare that triggered the mass exodus of Matlack, Koosman, Grote, Harrelson, and Milner.

Mets general manager Frank Cashen brought back Seaver in December 1982, shipping pitcher Charlie Puleo and two prospects to the Reds as compensation. Seaver was happy to return but gave no guarantees he would pitch like he had during his first stint with the club.

"I don't know what the public will remember or expect," he said during his re-introductory news conference. "I'm not going to go out next season with a sign saying, 'It's 1983 and I'm 38 years old.'

"When I pitch, I'll still have to get Pete Rose and Mike Schmidt out. No promises have been made to me, and no directions given to me. They want me to come back here and be Tom Seaver.

"I'm not around to pick up a paycheck. If I can't pitch, I don't expect to be paid. After next year, if they don't want me to pitch, I don't get paid. I didn't ask for a guaranteed contract, and I don't want one.

"I've been booed here, and I've been cheered here. And, when I was booed, I richly deserved it. The scene has been set. Now, I've got to go out and do it."[263]

It was a fantastic move from a public relations standpoint, as Mets fans welcomed the prodigal son back to New York. It was also something Cashen had in mind as far back as 1981.

"I just feel that there are some players who deserve to finish their careers where they are remembered for their greatness," said Cashen nearly two years before making the deal. "A Jim Palmer should finish his career in Baltimore. Brooks Robinson should not and did not play for anyone but the Orioles. Bob Gibson deserved to play his entire career with St. Louis. There are players of that ilk who deserve it. Tom Seaver is one."[264]

The Mets' major league roster was about as crummy as when Seaver left. The 1983 Mets included former Seaver teammates Staub, Kingman, and George Foster, who had came to the Mets from the Reds the previous season. However, the pitching staff lacked depth, and the bulk of the prospects were a year away.

But for one chilly afternoon in April, all was perfect at Shea Stadium. Seaver, with his warmup jacket hanging from his right arm, strode from the bullpen to a thunderous ovation. It was as if he never left. Mayor Ed Koch and 46,687 paying customers attended Seaver's return against Steve

AWARDS AS A MET

NL Rookie of the Year	1967
NL Cy Young	1969, 1973, 1975
NL All-Star	1967–1973, 1975–1978, 1981

LEAGUE LEADER AS A MET

Wins	1969, 1975
Strikeouts	1970, 1971, 1973, 1975, 1976
ERA	1970, 1971, 1973

Carlton and the Phillies on Opening Day.

Seaver began the game by fanning Pete Rose and struck out four others while pitching three-hit ball over six shutout innings. He felt a twinge in his thigh muscle during the sixth inning, prompting his departure. But the Mets failed to score while he was on the mound, allowing Doug Sisk to win his major league debut.

"It was a very emotional day. I have a lot of memories here. It was great to be back, but so emotional that I still felt it for two innings."[265]

"It's just a step. I've always said that one game doesn't get you in a slump and one game doesn't get you out of a slump. Pitching six innings does not make me confident I am physically able to pitch. I have to pitch more."[266]

Seaver was the ace of what was a rather unimpressive rotation until Walt Terrell and Ron Darling were recalled from Triple A Tidewater, showcasing two of the talented arms in the organization.

The Mets secured the bottom of the NL East standings by May despite Seaver, who lost five of his first eight decisions while compiling a 2.71 ERA.

Seaver finished the year strong, posting a 1.50 ERA over 24 innings in his last four starts to finish 9–14 with team highs of 135 strikeouts, a 3.55 ERA and a 1.242 WHIP. But it was a sad commentary on the franchise when he remained the top pitcher on the Mets six years after he was jettisoned to Cincinnati.

Seaver was 39 and held the second-richest contract on the club when Cashen exposed him in the free-agent compensation draft. Cashen figured teams would shy away from Seaver's age and large salary, thus allowing him to protect a prospect while keeping Seaver in the fold. But the White Sox, fresh off an AL West title, saw Seaver as the perfect compliment to their young rotation. Seaver went to Chicago, leaving the Shea faithful to wonder if Cashen really knew what he was doing.

Seaver continued to defy Father Time. The White Sox got a pitcher who went 31–22 with a 3.56 ERA in two seasons with the team. Seaver also claimed his 300th career victory in a Chicago uniform, doing it in New York at Yankee Stadium on August 4, 1985.

"It was like I was levitating on the mound," Seaver said

after tossing 145 pitches that afternoon. "I hadn't felt like that since 1969 when I was going for a perfect game against the Cubs. Just like then, this was a constant emotional drain."

"The rules say I've got to be in the clubhouse," said White Sox manager Tony LaRussa, who was ejected during the game. "But I wasn't gonna miss this game. I watched it from the runway. This is Seaver going for 300, for history. I had to be there.

"We've learned one thing in the year and a half that he's been with us, and it's that he's dead honest with the game on the line. He wants the club to have the best chance to win. He was asked if he had enough to finish it, and both times he said yes."

"That's pretty exciting," said Carlton Fisk, who caught the game. "How many guys have ever won 300 games? How many have won 300 in the modern era?"[267]

The milestone victory left Seaver 12–8 with a 2.92 ERA for the year. But on that day, Dwight Gooden allowed no earned runs in a five-hitter as the Mets beat the Cubs 4–1 at Wrigley Field. It caused some to reflect on what might have happened had Seaver been retained by the Mets in 1984. The thought of Seaver and Gooden on the same team was pondered by Mets fans, but there is a very strong possibility Gooden wouldn't have been on the major league roster in 1984 had Seaver been around. As it was, Seaver picked up his milestone win on a day Gooden improved to 17–3 with a 1.57 ERA for the season.

Seaver finished the 1985 season 16–11 with a 3.17 ERA. They were his most victories since 1979, and his best ERA since 1981, an exceptional achievement for a pitcher about to reach his 41st birthday. There was no reason to believe he couldn't pitch past his 45th birthday.

The White Sox had played themselves out of the 1986 playoff chase when they decided to send Seaver to the Red Sox on June 29, giving him a chance to participate in the postseason. Boston had Roger Clemens, Bruce Hurst, and Oil Can Boyd in their rotation, making Seaver the perfect addition to a rotation of young pitchers as the Red Sox tried to nail down the AL East crown.

Seaver made 16 starts for Boston, going 5–7 with a 3.80 ERA until a knee injury caused him to miss the last two weeks of the regular season and the entire postseason. The knee problem short-circuited the possibility of Seaver pitching against his old team in the World Series.

The Red Sox beat the Angels in the ALCS to earn the right to face the Mets in the Fall Classic. Had Seaver been healthy, there was the chance he would have started Game 4 instead of Al Nipper. Instead, the Mets teed off on Nipper in the fourth game to tie the Series before beating the Red Sox in a memorable seven-game battle.

Seaver turned 42 three weeks after the World Series and five days after he was granted free agency. He was ready to retire and enjoy life with Nancy and his daughters unless a team in New York or Boston was interested in signing him. Training camp came and went without an offer, and his agent announced in May that Seaver was "essentially retired." That was before an old flame came calling.

The 1987 Mets found themselves short of quality pitchers two months into the season. Starters Bob Ojeda, Rick Aguilera, and David Cone were on the shelf; Sid Fernandez had a balky knee; and Dwight Gooden was just a few days removed from a suspension. The situation left the Mets relying on the likes of Don Schulze and John Mitchell to round out the rotation as the club fell further behind the first-place Cardinals.

Cashen got on the phone with Seaver and coaxed him into a no-strings-attached deal to see if he had anything left. Seaver hadn't faced a major league hitter for nine months, so it was a "let's see what you've got" proposition that he accepted.

"I was looking for a time and place to announce my retirement," said Seaver, "when the Mets said they were interested. It was quite a surprise. Physically, I feel terrific. I started throwing at home when we started talking seriously and I feel good, but the proof is in the pudding. Today is the fifth time I'll be throwing, and Monday will be the sixth. The seventh will probably be on Thursday."[268]

Cashen put him through an extended spring training that consisted of an exhibition game between the Mets and Tidewater Tides and simulated games against minor league hitters. It took about two weeks before Seaver and Cashen concluded he was done. Seaver was now a former major league pitcher and ready to start the next phase of his life.

The Mets retired his uniform No. 41 and inducted him into their Hall of Fame in 1988. Cooperstown was next as Seaver was elected in 1992 after receiving a record 98.84 percent of the votes in his first year of eligibility. He also spent time as a New York Yankees broadcaster before returning to the Mets as their television color analyst. Seaver remained behind the Mets mike from 1999 until the end of 2005, when the Mets launched SNY.

Seaver is back in Northern California, where he has turned a hobby into a vocation. He had a passion for fine wine during his days as Staub's teammate, and became an enologist. Seaver purchased 116 acres on Diamond Mountain in Calistoga in 1998. He planted his first 2.5 acres of cabernet grapes in 2000 and added another acre of vines eight years later.

GTS Vineyards is a thriving winery in Calistoga. He chose to use his initials for the company name rather than bank on his reputation as a Hall of Fame pitcher, allowing the product to stand on its own merit. Nancy put together the sales and marketing operation of the vineyards from scratch, and their niece, Karen, serves as business manager.

The vineyard's inaugural vintage of Cabernet Sauvignon was produced in 2005 and released in 2008. Selections include "Cabernet GTS" and "GTS Nancy's Fancy." After years of being compared to Koufax, Drysdale, Gibson, and Marichal, Seaver is now being judged favorably with the best vintners of Napa Valley.

ML/Mets debut   vs. Pirates, 4/13/67 (5⅓ IP, 6 H, 2 ER, 8 K, 4 BB)

First ML/Mets strikeout	Donn Clendenon, Pirates, 4/13/67
First ML/Mets win	vs. Cubs, 4/20/67
First ML /Mets save	@ Phillies, 7/7/68
Most strikeouts, ML/Mets game	19, vs. Padres, 4/22/70
Low-hit ML CG	0, Reds vs. Cardinals, 6/16/78
Low-hit Mets CG	1, 5 times

Acquired: Signed as an amateur free agent 4/6/66 following a special lottery involving Phillies and Indians.

Deleted: Traded to Reds for Doug Flynn, Pat Zachry, Steve Henderson, and Dan Norman, 6/15/77.

Reacquired: Traded by Reds for Charlie Puleo, Lloyd McClendon, and Jason Felice, 12/16/82.

Deleted: Selected by the White Sox as a free-agent compensation pick.

Inducted into the Baseball Hall of Fame, 1992

Rusty Staub

Outfielder, First Baseman   Bats left, throws right
Born: 4/1/44   New Orleans, Louisiana
Height: 6'2"   Weight: 200   #4, 10

Rusty Staub Mets Career

YEAR	GP	AB	R	H	2B	3B	HR	RBI	K	BB	SB	AVG	SLG	OBP
1972	66	239	32	70	11	0	9	38	13	31	0	.293	.452	.372
1973	152	585	77	163	36	1	15	76	52	74	1	.279	.421	.361
1974	151	561	65	145	22	2	19	78	39	77	2	.258	.406	.347
1975	155	574	93	162	30	4	19	105	55	77	2	.282	.448	.371
1981	70	161	9	51	9	0	5	21	12	22	1	.317	.466	.398
1982	112	219	11	53	9	0	3	27	10	24	0	.242	.324	.309
1983	104	115	5	34	6	0	3	28	10	14	0	.296	.426	.371
1984	78	72	2	19	4	0	1	18	9	4	0	.264	.361	.291
1985	54	45	2	12	3	0	1	8	4	10	0	.267	.400	.400
TOTAL	942	2571	296	709	130	7	75	399	204	333	0	.276	.419	.359

ML Career

YEAR	GP	AB	R	H	2B	3B	HR	RBI	K	BB	SB	AVG	SLG	OBP
63–85	2951	9720	1189	2716	499	47	292	1466	888	1255	47	.279	.431	.362

Rusty Staub wore several hats during his major league career, and he wore many hats after playing his last game. He was a Colt .45, an Astro, an Expo, a Met, a Tiger, and a Ranger. He was the first player to collect 500 hits for four different major league teams, and retired with more than 2,700 hits. Staub was so popular in Montreal and New York that he had two tours of duty with both clubs. He became the Expos' first true star and received the nickname "Le Grand Orange" in appreciation for his red hair and ability to hit .300 for an expansion team.

Staub later evolved into one of the most successful pinch-hitters in Mets history, about a decade after helping New York win the 1973 National League pennant as their top everyday player.

His popularity remained just as strong a quarter-century since he hung up his spikes. He spent a few years in the Mets' broadcast booth and opened two highly acclaimed restaurants in Manhattan during the 1980s. But his humanitarian efforts following the 9/11 attacks on the World Trade Center made him more important to the city than he was during his days in pinstripes.

You won't find Staub's name among the Mets' top 10 lists in any major offensive categories other than pinch-hitting, stats he compiled after becoming a part-time player. That shouldn't diminish the fact that he was the offensive catalyst on the team's charge to the 1973 pennant, one year after his injury derailed the Mets' playoff hopes.

Daniel Joseph Staub first came to the Mets when the team and its fans were in mourning following the death of manager Gil Hodges. Hodges and general manager Bob Scheffing spent much of the 1971 offseason negotiating with the Expos to bring Staub to New York and continued to work on the trade through the exhibition season.

The Mets mustered very little offense while finishing in a third-place tie at 83–79 the previous season. Three players tied for the team lead with a mere 14 homers, and Cleon Jones paced the team in RBIs with just 69. The Mets hit only .249 as a team despite having five players bat .270 or better in at least 400 at-bats. The offense failed to support a pitching staff that led the National League with a 2.99 ERA and 1,157 strikeouts while compiling a 1.198 WHIP.

Hodges and Scheffing had hoped to find a slugger at the 1971 winter meetings but came away empty-handed. They continued to negotiate with the Expos for Staub, but Montreal's asking price was steep. Expos general manager John McHale wanted players who could contribute immediately and continued to inquire about Ken Singleton, Mike Jorgensen, Tim Foli, and Jon Matlack. If the Mets were to make a trade for Staub, they had to prepare to part with their top young talent.

The Mets went to training camp without Staub and played their preseason games before the first players' strike in major league history began the weekend before the season opener. With nothing else to do, Hodges and his coaches spent Sunday playing golf before making dinner plans. As they left the golf course, Hodges suffered a massive heart attack and died two days shy of his 48th birthday.

The Mets conducted business as usual despite the loss of their field leader. They made two major announcements the day of Hodges' funeral, the first of which was to introduce Yogi Berra as the new Mets manager. The second bombshell was the confirmation of a deal that sent Staub to the Mets for Singleton, Foli, and Jorgensen.

Staub immediately became the Mets' best offensive threat, but the ballclub had to sit through a 10-day strike before the big redhead made his debut at Shea Stadium against the Pirates on April 15. Expectations were high as Staub went to the plate for the first time as a Met.

During the Expos' first three years in existence (1969–1971), Staub led the team with a .296 average, 78 homers, 508 hits, 83 doubles, and 270 RBIs. He also demonstrated decent speed by pacing the club with 18 triples and 24 stolen bases. Meanwhile, no Met had more than 465 hits, 64 home runs, 74 doubles, or 207 RBIs from 1969 to 1971. Bud Harrelson had more triples and stolen bases than

Staub but hit only .248. Cleon Jones recorded a .311 average during that span while producing just 36 home runs.

As the Mets' cleanup hitter on Opening Day, Staub poked a leadoff single off Dock Ellis in the second inning before scoring the game's first run on a double by Jim Fregosi. With Tom Seaver and Tug McGraw combining on a five-hitter, the Mets beat Pittsburgh 4–0.

The Mets went 8–4 in April as Staub batted .298 in 47 at-bats. He had a trio of three-hit games that month and hit his first homer as a Met off Fred Norman at San Diego in a 4–3 victory April 27. Staub's presence in the lineup allowed No. 3 hitter Tommie Agee to see better pitches while giving Jones a greater opportunity to drive in runs in the five hole. Jones was hitting .333 as the Mets entered the month of May, proving Staub was having a trickle-down effect on the rest of the lineup.

The Mets bolstered their offense by getting Willie Mays from the Giants in May. Mays provided the theatrics in his Mets debut, hitting a solo homer to break a 4–4 tie in a 5–4 win over his former team on Mother's Day, May 14. But Mays' heroics were set up by Staub, who crushed a grand slam off Sam McDowell in the first inning following three straight walks.

The Mets swept the Giants that weekend to ignite an 11-game winning streak that tied the team record set in 1969. Staub batted .364 with three homers, nine RBIs, and seven runs scored during the last nine games of the streak. The Mets finally lost 2–1 at Wrigley Field as Staub went 4-for-4 with a game-tying single to raise his average to .310.

The winning streak gave the Mets a 25–7 record, putting them a whopping six games ahead of the second-place Pirates in the NL East. Agee was batting .289, Staub was at .287, Jones owned a .300 average, and Fregosi was hitting .279 as the No. 6 hitter. Seaver already had seven wins, rookie Jon Matlack was 5–0, and the team ERA was 2.91. The team was poised to settle the NL East race by Independence Day until an errant pitch by Atlanta's George Stone altered the Mets' season.

The Mets breezed through a 5–2 win over the Braves June 3 at Shea Stadium, leaving New York five games ahead of the second-place Pirates. Seaver improved to 8–2 with help from Tug McGraw's eighth save. But with the Mets leading 4–1 in the bottom of the seventh, Staub was plunked on the right wrist by Stone to begin another rally. Staub completed the game and hit a two-run homer off Jim Nash in a 2-for-4 performance the following afternoon. He had a three-hit game June 8 and drove in two runs the next day while continuing to play every inning of every game despite stiffness in his right hand.

Staub homered twice and had eight RBIs in 13 games after being hit by Stone, but the soreness finally caused him to be taken out of a June 18 game at Cincinnati. The Mets still owned the NL's best record following a 2–1 win over the Reds, a half-game ahead of the Pirates. But Staub wouldn't see another pitch for a full month.

The Mets prescribed rest for Staub's injury before he

was inserted into the lineup July 18 against the Dodgers. He drove in New York's only run in a 2–1 setback at Los Angeles, a loss that left the Mets five games behind the NL East–leading Pirates. One day later, the Mets learned that Staub had a broken hamate bone that forced him onto the disabled list.

The season was a bust after that. Agee, Jones, Harrelson, and Mays were bogged down by injuries, leaving the Mets with a rag-tag lineup. Berra had to use catchers Jerry Grote and Duffy Dyer in the outfield, and he gave Lute Barnes and Dave Schneck their major league debuts during a road trip through California. By the time Staub was ready to come off the DL, the Mets were 14½ games behind Pittsburgh with 17 games remaining. New York went 36–47 in the three months they were without Staub, killing the possibility of another division title. Staub hit .350 in 20 at-bats in his first six games back from the disabled list and finished with a .293 average, nine homers, and 38 RBIs in 66 games.

The Mets made two significant moves to the lineup in the fall of 1972, shipping Agee to the Astros for Rich Chiles and acquiring second baseman Felix Millan from Atlanta. In a bit of irony for Staub, the Mets also received Stone from the Braves while sending pitchers Gary Gentry and Danny Frisella to Atlanta.

Millan gave the Mets an outstanding glove man at second base and a solid No. 2 hitter to set the table for Staub. Millan and Staub were the only Mets to appear in at least 150 games in 1973 as the injury bug continued to bite the team.

Staub went 3-for-4 with a pair of solo homers against the Astros April 25 but hit just .159 with four RBIs in 20 games for the month. The Mets still managed to go 12–8 in April, giving them the division lead until a host of injuries crippled the lineup. Mays and Milner spent much of May on the DL before Jones, Harrelson, and Grote were sidelined in June. The Mets were in last place by June 29, 12 games off the pace.

Millan had become a table-setter on a team with few utensils, hitting .272 over the first three months of the season. The only other positive force in a moribund lineup was Staub, who batted .328 with 29 RBIs and 24 runs scored in 51 games from May 2 to June 30.

The Mets were written off by the media before the All-Star break, and with good reason. The pitching was solid, as Seaver, Koosman, Matlack, and Stone helped them record a 3.44 ERA over the first three months despite a horrible bullpen. But the Mets hauled a .239 average into July and continued to wait for their injured players to round into form. Grote and Harrelson remained on the DL by July 1, and Fregosi was sent to the Rangers July 11 after failing to provide any offense.

The losing continued well into August. Staub, Millan, and Wayne Garrett were the only Mets regulars to avoid a trip to the disabled list. The Mets occupied the NL East cellar at 52–65 following a 9–0 loss at San Diego August

14. The only positive sign came from the "games behind" column in the standings, which showed the Mets only 8½ games out of first. They were actually closer to their division lead than the Giants, who sat 9½ games behind the Reds despite a 64–53 record. San Francisco would have had a 1½-game lead had they been in the NL East.

Staub kept his average hovering between .270 and .280 most of the summer despite getting few pitches to drive. He was also dealing with sore knuckles after being hit by a Ramon Hernandez pitch May 11. However, Staub hit only .235 with 10 RBIs in a 31-game stretch just before the Mets returned to full strength around the fourth week of August.

The Mets began their charge up the standings on August 27 as Staub belted a grand slam to give them a 5–2 lead in a 6–5 win over the Padres. New York remained in last place at 59–70 following the game, but only 6½ games out of first. The win ignited a season-ending stretch in which the Mets went 23–9. Only the Expos played better than .500 ball in the NL East after August 27.

The Padres victory was the beginning of a season-ending hot streak for Staub, who batted .321 with five homers, 21 RBIs, and 24 runs scored in the Mets' final 33 games. He ended the regular season on a 15-game hitting streak that included a two-run homer in a 10–2 pounding of the Pirates September 21, a victory that put the Mets into first place to stay.

"We were in last place, but no one took control of our division, and then all of a sudden we started winning every series," said Staub. "It was nothing momentous, nothing extraordinary. It was just a bounce here, a break there, and our pitching came around. You play all these days right now so that in September you have an opportunity to get hot and win."[269]

Five teams were still alive in the division race heading into the final weekend of the season, with the Mets holding a one-game lead heading into a four-game set against the Cubs in Chicago. Two straight days of rain pushed back the series opener to Sunday. The Mets were now scheduled to end the season with back-to-back doubleheaders.

As luck would have it, the Mets actually increased their lead to 1½ games without playing, which meant a sweep of Sunday's doubleheader would give them the division crown. But the Mets dropped the opener 1–0, with Staub going 1-for-4 while making the last out of an inning three times with a runner on base. The three-day layoff may have thrown off Staub's timing, but he was back in form during the second game.

The Mets clinched at least a tie for the NL East title by crushing the Cubs 9–2 in Game 2. Staub scored the game's first run on Jones' two-run single in the first inning before finishing the day with three hits and three RBIs. Staub put an exclamation point on the rout by hitting a two-run double in the ninth before scoring on Wayne Garrett's single.

The second twinbill was scheduled for Monday,

October 1, the day after the regular season. A victory in either game would give the Mets the division. Staub grounded out in his first at-bat of Game 1 before going 4-for-4 with two runs scored and an RBI the rest of the way. His RBI single in the fifth inning put the Mets ahead 4–0 in a 6–4 win that touched off a celebration in the clubhouse. Game 2 was now unnecessary and unplayed as rain caused the nightcap to be canceled.

In his first opportunity to play for a postseason berth, Staub went 7-for-10 with four RBIs and four runs scored in the final two regular-season games, leaving him with a .279 average, 15 homers, and a team-high 76 runs batted in. He also established a club mark with 36 doubles, breaking the previous record of 32 set by Tommy Davis in 1967. The record lasted until Millan hit 37 two years later.

The Mets were not given much hope to beat the Reds in the NLCS, and their chances appeared to diminish after Cincinnati took the opener 2–1 at Riverfront Stadium. Staub went 0-for-2 with two walks in Game 1 and flied out in the first inning of the second game before launching a solo homer in the fourth to put the Mets ahead to stay. He later walked and scored in a four-run ninth that gave the Mets a 5–0 lead before Matlack completed a two-hit shutout.

Staub starred in the Mets' 9–2 pounding of the Reds at Shea in Game 3, hitting a solo homer in the first inning to put New York ahead for good before adding a three-run blast to make it 6–0 in the second inning. He was now 3-for-7 with three homers, five RBIs, and four runs scored in the series, helping New York pull within one victory of the World Series.

The Mets were tied 1–1 in the 11th inning of the fourth game when Dan Driessen belted a drive to right with runners on first and third and two out. It appeared to be a sure two-run double until Staub made a spectacular catch before crashing hard into the outfield wall. Staub finished the game, which the Reds won 2–1 in 12 innings to send the series to the limit. But Staub separated his right shoulder while making the Driessen catch, forcing him to miss Game 5.

"Driessen had hit a ball off Tug McGraw in the gap in right center," Staub recalled one year after retiring. "There are times when you know that if you are going to catch the ball, you're going to hit the wall. I just decided I would try to make the catch. I did, and I partially separated my shoulder on the play. It almost cost me playing in the World Series that year."[270]

Evern without Staub, the Mets hammered the Reds 7–2 to win their second National League pennant and earn the right to face the A's in the World Series. The question now was whether Staub would be able to participate in the Fall Classic.

"It didn't look as though I'd play in the Series. In fact, I was used as a decoy in the first game against the Oakland A's. But I talked Yogi Berra into letting me play after that, and he did. I played in all seven games, went 11-for-26, in-

cluding 4-for-4 in the fourth game, hit .423, and felt closer than ever to the people in the seats."[271]

Staub sat out the opener, which the Athletics won in Oakland 2–1. He returned to the lineup for Game 2, going 1-for-5 while his damaged shoulder forced him to throw underhand after catching balls to right. He was taken out in the ninth inning of what became a 10–7 win in extra innings, evening the Series.

The Mets dropped Game 3 at Shea as Staub went 2-for-4 with a double while showing no signs of his severe shoulder injury. One day later, Rusty put together one of the greatest batting performances in Mets postseason history.

The Mets needed a victory to avoid falling behind 3–1 in the Series. Staub did his part by going 4-for-4 with a homer and five RBIs in a 6–1 rout of the Athletics to even the Series. He set the tone by crushing a three-run homer in the first inning following singles by Garrett and Millan. Three innings later, Staub laced a two-run single to cap the scoring.

The Mets took Game 5 2–0 to take a 3–2 Series lead over Oakland. The A's captured the last two games to win their second straight World Series title, with Staub going 3-for-8 with an RBI.

"It's really something to be proud of," said Staub after assessing the season. "To be able to come back from last place in our division, like we did, then win the playoffs and get to the seventh game, I'm really proud of what we did."[272]

Staub hit safely in the final six games of the Series to finish with a .423 average versus Oakland and a .341 mark in the postseason. He went 10-for-21 (.476) with six RBIs in the final five games despite the achy shoulder.

The Mets made no significant roster moves in the off-season despite a pedestrian 82–79 record during the regular season. The prevailing thought was that the Mets wouldn't endure a third straight season with a ridiculous number of injuries. Scheffing guessed wrong.

Grote and Harrelson sat out a total of 121 games, and Seaver and Tug McGraw were less than 100 percent. The only Mets to play more than 137 games were Staub and Garrett, and they combined to hit just .242.

Staub experienced his worst season since 1965, batting .258 with 19 homers, 22 doubles, and 78 RBIs. He had little protection in an offense that hit only .235 for the season. Without a healthy Seaver and McGraw, the Mets finished fifth in the NL East at 71–91, their worst season since 1967.

New general manager Joe McDonald bolstered the offense in the offseason, getting Joe Torre and Del Unser before acquiring Dave Kingman a few weeks before the start of training camp. On paper, the Mets entered the 1975 campaign with their best lineup in team history, giving Staub some much-needed protection. However, Staub wasn't certain he'd be on the squad following the '74 campaign. He knew there were concerns about his weight and whether it was hampering his productivity.

"I don't want to be traded," Staub said after the season.

"I want to play for the Mets and I want the Mets fans to see the kind of year Rusty Staub can really have. I agree I have had some problems with my weight. After the 1973 season, I let myself get away. But it wasn't my weight that was a problem. When I pulled a hamstring in July, it wasn't because I was out of shape. It was because of the soft infield. I stepped in a hole rounding first and I pulled up lame. Ask anybody who ran or played on that infield, and they'll tell what shape the infield was in."[273]

The Mets broke several club hitting records in '75, including a .256 team average and 217 doubles. Kingman belted 36 homers to top Frank Thomas' club mark of 34, and Staub became the Mets' single-season leader in RBIs with 105 while batting .282 with 19 homers and 30 doubles.

"Having people in front of you get on base is the secret of making 100 RBIs, said Staub in praise of his teammates. "With Del Unser, Millan, and Mike Vail batting first, second, and third and having super years, I'm having my best one, too."[274]

On the pitching side, Seaver went 22–9 to double his win total of 1974. But the acquisitions of Torre and Unser cost the Mets relievers McGraw and Ray Sadecki, which led to numerous blown ballgames during the first two months of the season before McDonald acquired Skip Lockwood and Ken Sanders.

Staub had a 10-game hitting streak in July and batted .330 for the month. He also hit .330 over the final month, including a 5-for-6 performance with one RBI against the Phillies September 20. The RBI made him the first Met ever to go over the century mark for a single season.

But a rookie outfielder began to hog the spotlight as the Mets concluded an 82–80 season. Mike Vail was recalled by the Mets in mid-August after leading the International League in hitting for Tidewater. Vail went 3-for-11 in his first four games before embarking on a 23-game hitting streak that tied Jones' club record. He had a .352 average at the end of the streak and finished the year with a .302 average.

Mets fans entered the offseason picturing an outfield of Vail, Unser, and Staub in 1976. The trio combined to bat .290 while giving Kingman plenty of RBI opportunities. For once, the Mets wouldn't have to rely solely on pitching to contend for a division title.

Instead of keeping that outfield intact, the Mets went the cheap route. Staub was just 31 years old as he concluded the 1975 season, and his 105 RBIs showed he wasn't slowing down. But he earned a reported $110,000 in '75 while Vail was due to make slightly more than the league minimum in 1976. Rather than keep Staub, the Mets sent him to the Tigers in December for veteran pitcher Mickey Lolich and outfield prospect Billy Baldwin. Lolich was coming off a 12–18 season and went 8–13 in his lone season as a Met.

The trade is considered as one of the worst in Mets history. Lolich retired after the 1976 season, and Baldwin wasn't given much playing time as a Met. Worse, Vail suffered a severe ankle injury in the winter of 1976 and never became the hitter the Mets had projected. New York managed to go 86–76 despite one of the National League's most inept lineups. Meanwhile, Staub flourished in Detroit, hitting .299 with 15 homers and 96 RBIs in '76 while earning an All-Star berth for the first time since his days as an Expo. The midsummer nod came more than 13 years after his major league debut.

Staub began his professional career in 1962 after signing with the Houston Colt .45s the previous September. The Colts scooped him up after the New Orleans native was named the Louisiana Scholastic Athlete of the Year.

The Colts and Mets selected from the same group of "over-the-hill" talent and unproven prospects in the October 1961 expansion. The Colts did a little better job finding young talent through other sources, and landed a star-in-waiting when they inked Staub.

"The pickings were lean and thin, older players and not-so-premium premium players," said Tal Smith, who was the farm director of the Colt .45s and later became the Astros' president. "There was a lot more excitement about signing Rusty Staub as a 17-year-old free agent than about anyone on the expansion list."[275]

Staub's passion for baseball was created early. He played Little League, Babe Ruth League, American Legion ball, high school ball, and also honed his skills in the New Orleans Recreation Department. He recalled in 1968 that he attended just one professional game growing up, watching the New Orleans Pelicans of the Southern Association. Staub and his brother, Chuck, were too busy playing baseball to watch someone else do it.

"All I knew from the time I was a little boy was studying and baseball," Staub said in 1968.[276]

He was 18 when he batted .293 with 23 homers, 20 doubles, and 93 RBIs in 140 games for Class B Durham, finishing second in the Carolina League in ribbies and round-trippers. Staub was in the majors a year later, an example of why Houston was so far ahead of the Mets during their first six years in existence. The 1963 Colt .45s roster also included Joe Morgan, Jimmy Wynn, and Jerry Grote, all of whom were 21 or younger.

"I was a 19-year-old rookie then hoping for a chance to stay in the major leagues for a few years," Staub said. "I didn't know what the future might hold for me. Coming into that season I had had two years of instructional league ball. I went to spring training that season hoping I could impress someone, but I had very little hopes of ever making it to the major league club at that time.

"With about two weeks left in spring training, some of the veterans, on our trip to Las Vegas, decided to have a good time, and I wound up playing. I got three hits that day, two hits the next day, and three the day after that. All of a sudden, I was hitting about .420 when spring training ended and they decided that not only was I going to make the big-league club but I was going to play right field.

"It was a little bit odd for me because I had come up

as a first baseman and I didn't even own an outfielder's glove. I borrowed one from someone, and that's how I got started."[277]

Colts manager Grady Hatton says Staub more than earned his way onto the Opening Day roster: "The reason Rusty stayed with us the first year was that he was the best hitter in camp that spring."[278]

Staub made his major league debut April 9 against the Giants in Houston, going 1-for-3 with an RBI single off Jack Sanford. Staub hit safely in 19 of his first 23 starts and owned a .268 average after going 3-for-4 with two RBIs in a 4–1 win over the Cubs May 10. He struggled over the next 4½ months, hitting .206 with six homers and 30 RBIs in 120 games to drop his average to .216. But he ended the season by going 6-for-13 with four RBIs and three runs scored in a three-game series against the Mets to finish with a .224 average, six homers, and 45 RBIs.

Rusty opened the 1964 season by batting .202 through July 3 before he was sent to the minors for a two-month stint in the Triple A American Association, where he hit .314 with 20 homers and 45 RBIs in just 71 games for Oklahoma City. Staub was recalled in September and never played another game in the minors.

Opposing pitchers weren't the only obstacles for Staub during his first two years in Houston. The ballclub played its home games at Colt Stadium, an outdoor facility that seemed to double as a sauna in July and August.

"There was no place to hide," Staub said of the heat. "The dugout roof had tar on it. Everything was metallic. I remember Ernie Banks, whom I dearly love, always used to say, 'Let's play two.' I remember one day they carried him out on a stretcher in the first game of a doubleheader."[279]

And if the heat didn't get you, the insects would. The area around Colt Stadium was a more popular flight pattern than Shea Stadium ever was.

"Everybody talks about their size," said Staub. "Sure, they were huge, but size was not the problem. Quantity—that was the problem. We kept mosquito repellent in the dugout, and we'd spray ourselves before we went on the field."[280]

Staub and his teammates had a new ballpark by 1965, moving into the Astrodome and becoming the first ballclub to play in an indoor stadium. The club now had an opportunity to play all of its home games in 72-degree temperatures, thanks to an efficient air-conditioning system. But there were a few minor details that had to be worked out.

"It was awesome," Staub said 20 years later. "Everybody was excited by the Mercury astronauts down the road at the space center. The team had changed its name that winter from the Colt .45s to the Astros. Then we played five games in three days against the Yankees and Orioles, and I'll never forget how they made Mantle the leadoff batter in the opening game Friday night. He lined a single to center field. The next time, he hit a home run.

"I played right field for the Astros, and I'd seen the As-

Rusty Staub at the Shea Stadium finale in 2008.
Photo courtesy of Oscar W. Gabriel

trodome take shape. The club had invited me and Bob Lillis to escort season-ticket buyers to their new locations during the winter. But opening night was awesome.

"The only problem was, when we played the Orioles the next afternoon, you couldn't see the ball against the plastic roof when the sun was out. They coated it when we took our first road trip, then coated it heavier. Then the grass died. They sprayed it green for a while, but finally had to install artificial turf."[281]

Staub got progressively better over the next three years, hitting .256 in 1965 and .280 the following year before breaking out in '67. Staub earned his first All-Star selection in 1967 and hit a career-high .333, had a league-best 44 doubles, with 10 homers, 74 RBIs, and 71 runs scored.

The Astrodome was a tough venue for any power hitter, and it led Staub to become a stroke hitter. Jimmy Wynn was the lone Astro to hit more than 12 home runs during the first four seasons of the Astrodome. Staub was third on the list with 10, hitting 33 home runs on the road from 1965 to 1968. He was one of the first three hitters to hit a ball on top of the right-field stands at Pittsburgh's Forbes Field, an example of his power. But the balls didn't fly out of Houston, causing Staub to concentrate on contact.

"I want to become a hitting machine," said Staub in

1968. "Do everything the same way every time. That way, I'll never have a slump."

Staub's batting average slipped to .291 in 1968 to finish ninth among all National Leaguers in the "Year of the Pitcher" after ending up fifth in '67. Staub also was selected to the NL All-Star team again and provided 37 doubles and 72 RBIs. But the Astros finished last for the first time in club history despite a team record–tying 72 wins.

It was in Houston where Staub gained a reputation as a culinary wizard.

He was exposed to fine dining by his parents, both of whom were excellent cooks. He learned to handle himself in the kitchen and often entertained his teammates during his early days with the Colts and Astros. He gained a reputation as an excellent cook after hosting a Christmas dinner party in 1967, making all of the food himself.

"From that point on, I was more than just a jock," he said. "People would invite me out to restaurants for dinner, then take me back to meet the chef. Pretty soon I was being invited to help out in the restaurant kitchens."[282]

Houston had a 474–658 record through its first seven seasons, which compares very favorably to the Mets' 394–737 mark in the same span. But unlike the Mets at Shea, attendance at the Astrodome had dropped significantly since baseball's first indoor venue opened in 1965. The Astros drew 1.32 million in '68, a decrease of close to 800,000 fans from 1965. Mets attendance held steady during their first five years at Shea, and the team drew about 450,000 more fans than Houston in 1968.

The Astros decided to make a major trade in January 1969, sending Staub to the expansion Expos for slugging first baseman Donn Clendenon and outfielder Jesus Alou. The deal hit a snag when Clendenon refused to report to the Astros, but commissioner Bowie Kuhn stepped in and brokered a deal that sent Jack Billingham to Houston as a substitute for Clendenon. It proved to be a bad deal for the Astros, who made an even bigger blunder by shipping Morgan and Billingham to the Reds after the 1971 season.

Staub immediately became Montreal's most popular athlete not named Jean Beliveau, hitting .302 with 29 home runs and 79 RBIs in 1969. He was the first player to belt 25 homers and hit .300 in an expansion team's first season. Staub paced the club in batting, homers, on-base percentage (.426), runs scored (89), hits (166), and walks (110), and was tied for second in RBIs and doubles (26). He also opened the season by going 2-for-3 with three walks, a solo homer, two RBIs, and two runs scored in an 11–10 win over the Mets.

Expos fans also bestowed a new nickname on Staub, who quickly became the people's choice. Staub wrote in a 1986 article for the *New York Times* that he had answered to the nicknames "Orange" or "Big Orange" at times while a member of the Astros. It evolved into "Le Grand Orange" in his early days with the Expos.

"The name wasn't formalized for the public until one

day when we were playing in Los Angeles. I hit a home run and made a pretty good catch when Willie Crawford hit a pea against the fence. The next day in the newspapers, I was 'Le Grand Orange.' And in both English and French papers, it stayed that way."[283]

Staub improved his run production in 1970, setting career highs with 30 homers and 98 runs scored, seven triples, 12 stolen bases, and 112 walks while hitting .274. He had another strong year in '71, hitting .311 with 19 homers and 97 ribbies as the Expos climbed out of the cellar at 71–91. But the franchise was seeking an infusion of young talent that could take the team to the next level as they approached the 1972 season.

The Staub-to-the-Mets trade is viewed by some as a great maneuver for the Expos, who received three everyday players in Singleton, Foli, and Jorgensen. However, Foli would have remained a utility player with the 1972 Mets, and Jorgensen would have been a platoon player at first base and the outfield, although both were sorely missed when New York was hit by a tsunami of injuries. Singleton had a great year in 1973 but otherwise never hit his stride until he was traded to the Orioles. Thus, the trade should be viewed as a wash considering Staub's contributions to the Mets' 1973 pennant run.

Staub made another return trip to Montreal in 1979, dealt by the Tigers for a player to be named July 20. The Expos had become one of the top teams in the NL East and battled the Pirates down to the wire for a playoff berth.

Staub had a nice 3½-year run in Detroit, hitting .277 with 70 homers and 358 RBIs in 549 games. He drove in a career-best 121 runs for the 1978 Tigers but was slumping when he was sent back to Montreal. Staub also had lost most of his speed in Detroit and was spending more time as a designated hitter before returning to Canada.

Staub's second stint with the Expos was short as he hit .267 with three homers and 14 RBIs in 38 games. He started just 19 of Montreal's final 62 games in 1979 due to the fast artificial surface at Olympic Stadium and the presence of outfielders Andre Dawson, Ellis Valentine, and Warren Cromartie. The Expos also had Tony Perez at first base, giving Staub little opportunity to play regularly.

Staub became a DH again after the Expos dealt him to the Rangers in March 1980. He batted .300 for the first time since 1971, drove in 55 runs and scored 42 in 109 games for Texas before becoming a free agent after the '80 season.

It seemed logical for Staub to sign with another American League team, where he could garner more at-bats as a DH. Instead, he became one of the National League's most prolific pinch-hitters of the early '80s after accepting an opportunity to play for the Mets again.

The Mets' glory days were long behind them when Staub resurfaced in Flushing. The club went 261–388 from 1977 to 1980, a record comparable to his time with the expansion Colts/Astros. But general manager Frank Cashen sought to fill seats at Shea and reacquired both

Staub and Kingman while waiting for his ripening farm system to reap the benefits of high draft picks.

"These are talented young people," Staub said of the roster and the team's farm system, "but they need mature people who've been around to pat them on the back and prod them. They have to learn how to win. Learning to play is one thing; learning to win is another. That's part of what being a veteran is about, that and showing by example."[284]

Staub understood he didn't have the luxury of cracking the lineup as a designated hitter. He also realized he'd have to watch his diet and maintain his weight, which had increased since his previous stint as a Met.

"I realized a long time ago that I'd have to work harder. I'm not gifted with speed. Some people have been better athletes than me, like the Mayses and Clementes.

"I also have to watch my diet constantly. In the winter, if I eat more than one and a half meals a day, I'm going to gain weight. If I do, I'm going to blow up. And if I do that, the baseball career's going to be gone.

"The trouble is, there's not much food that I don't like. I'm very big for bread, pastries, pastas, all the things I can't afford to eat. But I want to play baseball when I'm 40, so I make the choice. It's that simple: I think I have another contract to sign in this game."[285]

Staub hit .311 with five home runs and 15 RBIs in his 40 games as a starter. Staub hit a solo homer as the starting first baseman in the season opener to help New York beat the Cubs 2–0. He later went 10-for-21 (.476) during a five-game hitting streak in April and owned a .315 season average when the 61-day players strike began in mid-June.

Staub was the everyday first baseman until May 12, when he was forced into a reserve role due to a left foot injury that kept him from starting for about a month. He finished the year strong, batting .476 with two homers, five doubles, and six RBIs in 14 games to help the Mets stay within striking distance of the second-half division chase until the last week of the season. Staub homered twice in a 2–2 tie with the Cubs October 1, his first multihomer game in eight years.

Staub excelled as a pinch-hitter in '81, going 9-for-24 (.375) with a .476 on-base average and six RBIs. It began a five-year stretch in which he was the best pinch-hitter in the majors. But it was a few weeks into the 1982 season before he truly started to produce in that role at a ridiculously consistent basis.

The Mets acquired left fielder George Foster before the '82 campaign, which meant Kingman had to move to first base in place of Staub. Rusty delivered an RBI single as a pinch-hitter in a season-opening win at Philadelphia before going 1-for-13 his next 13 times off the bench. His batting average for the season stood at just .095 in 21 at-bats until he crushed a walk-off, solo homer as a pinch-hitter to beat the Giants 7–6 on May 9. The blast began a season-ending run in which Staub went 10-for-43 with seven walks and 12 RBIs in a pinch-hitting role.

Staub managed to start 45 games and ended the year with a .242 average, three homers, 27 RBIs, and 24 walks in 250 plate appearances. The Mets finished last for the first time in three seasons and occupied the cellar at the end of 1983, when Staub enjoyed his finest year as a pinch-hitting specialist.

Given the Mets' record and quality of their pitching staff, Staub had plenty of opportunities to come off the bench in '83. He set a major league record with 81 pinch-hit appearances and tied a big league mark with 25 pinch-hit RBIs. Staub also collected 24 pinch-hits, one shy of the major league record. Eight of those hits came in consecutive pinch-hitting appearances, matching the big-league mark set by Dave Philley in 1958.

Staub was one shy of the record when he faced Ron Reed, a pitcher with whom he was well familiar. Reed broke in with the Braves in 1966, three years after Staub made his major league debut.

Staub took an 0–1 slider and deposited it into right-center to tie Philley's record. In a gesture of true sportsmanship, Reed called for the ball from umpire Billy Williams and walked toward first base before handing the ball to Staub while a crowd of over 37,000 continued to give Rusty a standing ovation.

"It was great to get it and great that people got so excited," Staub said after the game. "But it's yesterday's news now.

"I don't think I've mastered pinch-hitting. You try to work on a good approach, that's all. And, anyway, you're only as good as your last at-bat, and your next at-bat."[286]

The pinch-hitting streak began with a two-run double against the Expos June 11 and included a walk-off single versus the Cubs June 14, and a solo homer off Expos hurler Steve Rogers. He was named the NL Player of the Week ending June 19 after going 7-for-8 with a homer and two RBIs.

Staub hit three of the Mets' 12 pinch-hit homers in 1983 and shattered Ed Kranepool's single-season team records for pinch-hits and pinch-hit RBIs. He capped his bench heroics with a two-run double in the bottom of the ninth to beat the Expos 5–4 October 2.

Staub started just 10 games all year and posted a .372 on-base average off the bench. He finished the season with three home runs, 28 ribbies, and a .296 average, including a .294 average as a starter.

The Mets finally gave Staub a chance to produce for a winning ballclub in 1984. New York had compiled seven straight losing seasons, a streak that began the year after Staub was shipped off to the Tigers. But the additions of Keith Hernandez, Ron Darling, and Walt Terrell, along with the emergence of home-grown talent Darryl Strawberry, Dwight Gooden, Mookie Wilson, Hubie Brooks, and Wally Backman, turned the Mets into contenders. Staub started just one game the entire year, going 1-for-4 August 1 to end a season-opening streak of 52 consecutive games as a pinch-hitter.

Staub was 7-for-21 with six RBIs in his first 24 plate appearances off the bench through the first two months of the '84 season. He hit a game-tying double in the eighth inning of a 2–1, 11-inning win at Montreal April 25 and stroked an RBI single four days later to help the Mets move into first place for the first time that late in a non-strike season since 1976. The media began to compare the team to Staub's 1973 squad, although he quickly tried to put that argument to rest.

"Don't talk to me about 1973," he said in late June. "At this point, we're playing better than in '73. We were awful most of '73 until August. We had a lot of injuries. Buddy Harrelson was hurt, Jerry Grote was hurt. Then we were awesome."[287]

He carried a .357 average into July before the magic suddenly left his bat. Staub hit .171 from July 1 to September 18 before he went 3-for-4 with a homer and four RBIs in his last four trips to the plate that season. Staub won back-to-back games for the Mets against the Phillies in late September, stroking a tiebreaking, two-run double off Tug McGraw in the eighth inning of a 7–5 victory September 24 and crushing a walk-off, two-run homer to cap a four-run ninth in a 6–4 triumph. The blast allowed Staub to join Ty Cobb as the only players to homer before their 20th birthday and after their 40th. He finished the year leading the National League in pinch-hits (18) and pinch-hit RBIs (18) for the second straight year, prompting the Mets to bring him back for his ninth season in New York. No one was happier about his return than Mets broadcaster Tim McCarver and manager Davey Johnson, each of whom had tremendous respect for Staub's plate savvy.

"There were only a handful of hitters I ever caught behind who seemed to be one pitch ahead of me," McCarver said of Staub. "[Keith] Hernandez was one, Ron Santo, too. Rusty, definitely. He could break down what a pitcher and catcher were thinking."

"He had his area of the plate," Johnson said, "and he could wait for his pitch. If he didn't get it, he could still go with the pitch with two strikes. That's commanding the strike zone."[288]

The bat remained quick, but his feet were anything but. He was the heaviest player on the Mets, a fact not lost on teammate Roger McDowell. Once Staub retired, McDowell got the idea to go out on the field at Dodger Stadium while pretending to do a handstand. He wore a Mets uniform upside down, wearing his jersey as pants and donning pants over his upper body to give the impression he was walking on his hands. McDowell said he chose Staub's old uniform pants, giving him more room for his head.

"I don't deny that my body is not the most beautiful in the world now," he says. "But thank God they don't pay me for how I look."[289]

The 1985 season was his last in the majors. Staub opened the year by going 1-for-5 as a pinch-hitter in the Mets' first 16 games before he finally had to play the field in a crazy 18-inning win over the Pirates April 28 at Shea Stadium.

Staub entered the game in right field as part of a double-switch in the 12th inning of a 4–4 tie, and doubled in his first at-bat to put runners on second and third with nobody out. It was the Mets' first hit since Strawberry's grand slam in the bottom of the first inning, but the Mets left the bases loaded to extend the game.

Among the most memorable moments from that game was the sight of Staub constantly switching positions with outfielder Clint Hurdle. Manager Davey Johnson played the percentages and tried to keep Rusty out of the corner outfield slot where he thought the Pirates might hit the ball. But in the top of the 18th, Pittsburgh had a runner on first with two out when Staub made a game-saving catch of Doug Frobel's looping fly ball to right, grabbing the ball at his shoe-tops while on the dead run.

"It was a great catch," said Pirates manager Chuck Tanner. "If this was a World Series, they'd be talking about it for 30 years."[290]

The Mets finally won the game when Hurdle's ground ball to first skipped underneath the glove of first baseman Jason Thompson in the bottom of the 18th.

Staub should have been the hero in a game against the Expos June 22. The Mets trailed 2–0 with two on and two out in the bottom of the seventh when Johnson asked Staub to pinch-hit for rookie Lenny Dykstra. Staub crushed a pitch from Jeff Reardon down the right-field line, but the ball went foul at the last moment. One swing later, Staub slammed a three-run homer to right to put the Mets ahead 3–2, but New York eventually lost the game in extra innings. It was Staub's 292nd and final major league home run.

Staub never started a game in 1985 and ended the year batting .267 with one home run and eight RBIs. The Mets tried unsuccessfully to convince him to play another season, but he didn't think his 42-year-old body could play another season. Upon his retirement, Staub ranked 32nd on the all-time hit list with 2,716, five behind Lou Gehrig.

Staub spent the rest of the decade splitting his time between his restaurants and the Mets' broadcast booth. He opened Rusty's on Third Avenue in 1977 and Rusty's on Fifth 12 years later, allowing patrons to sample both his cuisine and his taste in wines. One of the house specialty dishes was his baby back ribs.

He immediately became a Mets broadcaster following his retirement and was behind the mike for the Mets' 1986 World Series season and their run to the 1988 NL East crown. He remained in the booth through 1995.

Staub established the New York Police and Fire Widows' and Children's Benefit Fund in 1985. According to its website, the Benefit Fund immediately delivers a check to the family of a "first responder" who dies in the line of duty, and provides ongoing assistance through financial and emotional support. The fund gained added praise for its work and support following the 9/11 attacks. For Staub, the fund was a natural transition from baseball.

"I had an uncle, Marvin Mortin, a motorcycle police officer, killed in the line of duty," Staub said. "I remember the anguish. In the late '50s, you can imagine what the benefits were for families.

"In 1985, I read about a fireman's death, leaving a wife and three children. I said to myself instead of just saying, 'Geez, that's awful,' get off your fat butt and do something. We put on a picnic."

"We have a lot of corporate help, keeping overhead down in both programs," he said. "As soon as a fireman's name goes on the Wall of Valor, we deliver a check for $25,000 the very next day, then a yearly benefit.

"We have a dinner every year at Gracie Mansion, and people who suffered losses years ago hug you and cry on your shoulder, and it's hard for me not to cry."[291]

The Benefit Fund says 90 percent of every dollar donated goes directly to the families and includes members of the Port Authority and Emergency Medical Services, which made Staub an even bigger hero today than he ever was in a baseball uniform.

Staub still remains among the most popular Mets ever and makes numerous appearances at Citi Field through the Benefit Fund. He said the bond he and the fans had cultivated made it even tougher to end his playing days with the Mets.

"I can't tell you how much their support, through the good times and the bad times, has meant for me. They've cheered my name—'Rusty, Rusty, Rusty'—on innumerable occasions, and I think the one thing I'll miss most is being able to grab my bat and go to home plate while they're chanting, and try to get a hit.

"I would never trade in the memories and good times I had in New York for anything, and I'm just glad I turned to baseball for my career."[292]

First ML game	Colt 45s vs. Giants, 4/9/63
First Mets game	vs. Pirates, 4/15/72
First ML hit	RBI single vs. Jack Sanford, Giants, 4/9/63
First Mets hit	single vs. Dock Ellis, Pirates, 4/15/72
First ML homer	2-run HR vs. Don Drysdale, Dodgers, 6/3/63
First Mets homer	solo HR vs. Fred Norman, @ Padres, 4/27/72
First ML RBI	RBI single vs. Jack Sanford, Giants, 4/9/63
First Mets RBI	solo HR vs. Fred Norman, @ Padres, 4/27/72
Most hits, ML game	5, Expos @ Reds, 5/30/70; Mets @ Dodgers, 5/24/73; Mets vs. Phillies, 9/20/75
Most homers, ML game	2, 12 times, 5 times with Expos
Most homers, Mets game	2, 4 times
Most RBIs, ML game	6, Astros vs. Giants, 5/6/68
Most RBIs, Mets game	5, @ Braves, 7/18/73
Acquired: Traded by the Expos for Ken Singleton, Tim Foli, and Mike Jorgensen, 4/5/72.
Deleted: Traded to the Tigers with Bill Laxton for Mickey Lolich and Billy Baldwin, 12/12/75.
Reacquired: Signed as a free agent, 12/16/80.
Deleted: Retired after the 1985 season.
NL All-Star, 1967, 1968, 1969, 1970, 1971

AL All-Star, 1976
NL Doubles Leader, 1967

John Stearns

Catcher, Infielder, Outfielder   Bats right, throws right
Born: 8/21/51   Denver, Colorado
Height: 6'0"   Weight: 185   #16, 12

John Stearns Mets Career

YEAR	GP	AB	R	H	2B	3B	HR	RBI	K	BB	SB	AVG	SLG	OBP
1975	59	169	25	32	5	1	3	10	15	17	4	.189	.284	.268
1976	32	103	13	27	6	0	2	10	11	16	1	.262	.379	.364
1977	139	431	52	108	25	1	12	55	76	77	9	.251	.397	.370
1978	143	477	65	126	24	1	15	73	57	70	25	.264	.413	.364
1979	155	538	58	131	29	2	9	66	57	52	15	.243	.355	.312
1980	91	319	42	91	25	1	0	45	24	33	7	.285	.370	.346
1981	80	273	25	74	12	1	1	24	17	24	12	.271	.333	.329
1982	98	352	46	103	25	3	4	28	35	30	17	.293	.415	.349
1983	4	0	2	0	0	0	0	0	0	0	0	—	—	—
1984	8	17	6	3	1	0	0	1	2	4	1	.176	.235	.333
TOTAL	809	2679	334	695	152	10	46	312	294	323	91	.259	.375	.341

ML Career

YEAR	GP	AB	R	H	2B	3B	HR	RBI	K	BB	SB	AVG	SLG	OBP
74–84	809	2681	334	696	152	10	46	312	294	323	91	.260	.375	.341

There were days during his Mets career when it appeared John Stearns had forgotten which sport he had chosen for his vocation. He was a hard-hitting defensive back and a soft-handed catcher while attending college at the University of Colorado. Stearns sometimes played baseball as if trapped in a football player's body, seeming to enjoy the most violent collisions at home plate.

Stearns spent most of his major league career with some pretty bad Mets teams, playing in front of a few thousand people at Shea Stadium. It didn't matter how many fans were in attendance; Stearns played all out and relished the numerous jarring hits. He survived the constant contact, but his career was shortened by a nagging elbow problem that first surfaced in 1982 and pushed him out of baseball two years later. By then, he was among the top 10 in several offensive categories on the Mets' all-time lists.

John Hardin Stearns was born in Denver, where he played baseball, football, and basketball at Thomas Jefferson High School. He won Denver Prep League batting titles as a junior and senior, hitting .420 as a shortstop in 1968 before posting a .532 mark as a catcher. Stearns spurned an offer from the Athletics, who chose him in the 13th round of the June 1969 draft before he decided to attend college.

Stearns enrolled at Colorado and became a two-sport star for the Buffaloes. As a football player, he went to four Bowl Games, was an All–Big 8 selection at safety, and left the Buffs as their all-time leader with 16 interceptions. But his football talent was dwarfed by his baseball prowess. Stearns hit .413 in each of his last two years at Colorado and led all NCAA Division I-A players with 15 home runs and an .819 slugging average as a senior in 1973.

The Buffalo Bills selected him in the 17th round of the NFL draft in the hopes he might want to abandon baseball. However, Stearns was a blue-chip major league prospect and was taken second overall by the Phillies in the June 1973 major league draft, just behind Texas high school pitching phenom David Clyde.

The Phils initially assigned Stearns to Reading of the Double A Eastern League while Clyde was making his major league debut right out of high school. Stearns hit only .241 with three homers and 24 RBIs in 67 games, but he also walked 46 times in just over 200 plate appearances.

Stearns split the 1974 campaign between Class A Rocky Mount and Triple A Toledo before joining the Phillies in September. He batted .343 in 62 games in the Carolina League and .266 in 77 contests as an International League catcher. Stearns made his major league debut September 22 versus the Expos, going 1-for-2 with a single in his first at-bat against Mike Torrez. He spent the rest of the year on the bench as the Phils finished with 80 victories for the first time since 1967.

Stearns emerged as one of the top minor league catching prospects after just two years of pro ball, but the Phillies already felt they had a solid starting catcher in Bob Boone. That made Stearns expendable as the Phils sought a quality closer at the December 1974 winter meetings.

Tug McGraw had just come off his worst season as a Mets reliever when new general manager Joe McDonald dangled the lefty at the meetings. McDonald was also seeking an eventual replacement for Jerry Grote, who turned 32 that fall and hadn't played more than 97 games since 1971.

The Mets eventually sent McGraw and outfielders Don Hahn and Dave Schneck to the Phillies for Stearns, center fielder Del Unser, and reliever Mac Scarce. Hahn, Schneck, Unser, and Scarce were all sent elsewhere by August 1976, making it a McGraw-for-Stearns swap as the two teams found much different levels of success by the end of the decade. With McGraw, the Phillies captured three straight NL East titles from 1976 to 1978 before winning the 1980 World Series. It was a great trade for the Phillies as McGraw became a fan favorite. Meanwhile, there was nothing Stearns could do to reverse the Mets' misfortunes during that period.

Stearns made the Mets out of 1975 spring training and earned the John J. Murphy Award as the club's best rookie during the exhibition season. He earned the honor by hitting .308 with two homers and five RBIs in 15 games while battling Ron Hodges and Gerry Moses for the backup catcher's job. Best of all, Stearns displayed a bit of Grote's tenacious playing style while being groomed as the heir apparent.

Grote had his last great year for the Mets in 1975, hitting .295 and remaining healthy enough to play 119 games. Stearns didn't see any action until the sixth game of the season and appeared in only 59 games the entire year, making 46 starts. He went 1-for-3 in his first game as a Met on April 16, hitting a double off John Denny of the Cardinals.

Stearns went 4-for-15 (.267) in his first five starts and opened June by going 5-for-16 (.313) during a four-game hitting streak before rust took over his bat. His batting average fell below .200 for good July 6, and he ended the year with a .189 average, three homers, and 10 RBIs in 169 at-bats. He flashed his defensive potential by recording a .994 fielding percentage and throwing out 37 percent of his base runners.

Stearns made the 1976 Mets Opening Day roster despite batting .176 in eight games during the exhibition season. He was optioned to Triple A Tidewater in mid-May after opening the regular season 1-for-15 in six games. But Stearns responded to the demotion by carving out his best minor league season, hitting .310 with 10 homers, 17 doubles, 45 RBIs, and 11 stolen bases in 102 games for Triple A Tidewater before rejoining the Mets in September.

Grote suffered a pulled ribcage muscle August 27, giving Stearns plenty of time to show he could perform in the majors. Stearns took advantage of the opportunity by hitting .262 with two home runs, six doubles, and 10 RBIs in 32 games. He hit a game-tying homer in a 7–6 win over the Pirates September 19 and batted .295 for the month. Stearns also had a four-game stretch in which he went 11-for-17 (.647) with a homer, three RBIs, and seven runs scored from September 6 to 10. The Mets won all four games and finished 16–10 in games started by Stearns that month. It now appeared the Mets had a viable replacement for Grote, especially after Stearns nailed 54 percent of his base runners.

The 1976 Mets posted what was then the second-best record in team history, going 86–76 but finishing 15 games behind the Phillies. The pitching remained solid as Tom Seaver, Jerry Koosman, and Jon Matlack anchored a staff that included Mickey Lolich and a bullpen led by Skip Lockwood and Bob Apodaca. But the lineup featured Grote, Felix Millan, Bud Harrelson, and Ed Kranepool, all of whom were at least 31 years old. The Mets ranked just fifth in home runs despite Dave Kingman, who finished second in the National League with a team-record 37. The team hit only six homers in 36 games while Kingman was sidelined with a thumb injury.

The team was in dire need of an offensive infusion heading into the 1977 season, but McDonald and team chairman M. Donald Grant decided to stand pat, ignore the first-ever free-agent market, and wait for Stearns and fellow youngsters Lee Mazzilli, Roy Staiger, Bruce Boisclair, and Mike Vail to flourish. That strategy led to the Mets becoming the cesspool of the National League, finishing last or next-to-last in each season from 1977 to 1983.

There was no reason to think the Mets wouldn't compile a winning record as they headed into 1977. Stearns and Boisclair hit well the previous season, and Vail tied a club record with a 23-game hitting streak in 1975 before a severe ankle injury cost him much of '76. The Mets still

John Stearns crawls for the base as Cincinnati Reds third baseman Pete Rose fights to keep control of the ball in his mitt during a 1978 game.

had Seaver, Koosman, Matlack, Kingman, and John Milner. Joe Torre and Ed Kranepool were coming off .300 seasons. The key components of a strong bullpen were returning, as well, and the Mets had youngsters Stearns and Mazzilli ready to play key roles in 1977. Although they didn't appear equipped to challenge the Phillies for the division title, many scribes projected them to win at least 85 to 90 games based on a strong pitching staff and highly touted newcomers.

Those projections became nothing more than wishful thinking as the Mets lost over 90 games for the first time in 10 years. They began the year 9–9 before dropping 21 of their next 27, leading the Mets to fire manager Joe Frazier May 31 and replace him with Joe Torre.

Seaver and Kingman were embroiled in contract disputes before they were jettisoned at the June 15 trade deadline. Matlack battled a sore arm, and Koosman was healthy enough to lose 20 games a year after winning 21. Bud Harrelson batted a career-low .178 and newcomer Doug Flynn hit .191 after coming to the Mets in the Seaver deal.

Stearns was among the few Mets who lived up to expectations in '77, pacing the team with 25 doubles, tying for the club lead with 12 homers and finishing third with 55 RBIs while batting .251. He got hot the day of the Seaver trade, starting a 15-game hitting streak in which he batted .449 with three homers, nine RBIs, and nine runs scored. Stearns was also the starting catcher when Seaver picked up his final victory before heading to the Reds. One month later, Stearns represented the Mets in the All-Star Game,

catching the ninth inning of the National League's 7–5 win over the American League at Yankee Stadium.

Stearns carried a .313 average into July as he caught the bulk of the games while Grote watched from the bench. The Mets were confident enough in Stearns to send Grote to the Dodgers in another salary dump late in the season. Stearns struggled at the plate following his 15-game hitting streak, batting .192 with two homers and 22 RBIs over his final 74 games. He also made 15 errors in 127 games behind the plate but threw out 37 percent of his would-be base stealers.

The Mets made no significant improvements to the ballclub in 1978 or '79, leading to two more last-place finishes. McDonald and board chairman M. Donald Grant continued their housecleaning by trading Matlack and Milner in a four-team swap that brought Willie Montanez, Tom Grieve, and Ken Henderson to New York in December 1977. The Mets also traded Harrelson just before the 1978 season and shipped Koosman to the Twins in the fall of '78, leaving Kranepool as the lone player remaining from their 1973 pennant-winning team.

Stearns was a big fish in a small pond over the next three years, giving the Mets some of their few highlights in an otherwise dreary period. He stole 25 bases in '78 to tie Johnny Kling's National League record for catchers set in 1902. Stearns also hit .264 with 24 doubles while setting career highs with 15 homers and 73 RBIs in 143 games during the 1978 campaign.

He established career highs in 1979 with 29 doubles and 155 games played, and earned his second berth on the National League All-Star team. But he ended the year batting .243 with nine homers and 66 RBIs, all drop-offs from 1978. Stearns also stole 15 bases but was caught 15 times as Torre played small ball to squeeze out as many runs as possible from his Punch-and-Judy offense. With a thin rotation, a suspect bullpen, and weak lineup, the Mets finished 63–99 and needed a season-ending six-game winning streak just to avoid their 100th loss. It marked the last time Stearns played more than 98 games in a single season.

Stearns played for new owners in 1980. Nelson Doubleday and Fred Wilpon purchased the Mets from the De Roulet family before the season for $21 million, a major league record at the time. The sale came well after the best free agents were taken during the off-season, leaving the Mets with little hope for a turnaround in 1980.

Stearns, Mazzilli, Joel Youngblood, and Steve Henderson represented the heart of the Mets' lineup as they entered the campaign. The rotation consisted of Craig Swan, Pat Zachry, and several journeymen who tried to avoid turning the season into another mockery.

The Mets sputtered out of the gate as expected despite Stearns, who opened the year by batting .321 with 13 RBIs and 15 runs scored in the team's first 28 games. Stearns was unable to prevent the Mets from losing 18 of their first 27 games, putting the club 8½ games out of first by mid-May.

But a funny thing happened to the Mets over the next three months. Torre managed to the team's strong suit and had them playing aggressive baseball while recognizing the team had little power but good contact hitters. His patchwork rotation was fortified by a decent bullpen that included late-inning relievers Neil Allen and Jeff Reardon. Mazzilli moved back to center field in late May after a failed experiment at first base. The acquisition of right fielder Claudell Washington gave the team an established hitter to go with Stearns, Mazzilli, Henderson, Mazzilli, speedster Frank Taveras, and an improved Doug Flynn.

The Mets started to play decent baseball after their 9–18 start. Although they never put together a winning streak longer than four games, the Mets began to chip away at their deficit while Stearns handled an overachieving pitching staff. The team went 47–39 from May 14 to August 13, batting .274 with 42 homers. The pitching staff compiled a 3.42 ERA despite striking out just 500 in 799⅔ innings and inducing only 45 double-play grounders during that period.

Stearns was among the major contributors during the team's ascension to contention, hitting .270 with a .340 on-base percentage, 35 RBIs, and 29 runs scored from May 13 through late July. He was selected to the All-Star Game for the third time in four years and saw some action at first base after Mazzilli returned to center. But Stearns was also the first Mets regular to suffer a season-ending injury, breaking the tip of his right index finger on a foul tip July

26. He underwent season-ending surgery August 11, two days before the Mets beat the Pirates to pull within one game of .500 and 7½ games of first place.

New York went a major league-worst 11–38 down the stretch, beginning with a five-game sweep at the hands of the Phillies at Shea Stadium August 14 to 17. The Mets settled for a fifth-place finish at 67–95, the first time they avoided the cellar since 1976.

Stearns also had a knack for torturing other team mascots. The Mets were in Atlanta one day when Chief Nockahoma wrapped up his pregame dance near the visiting dugout before racing to his teepee beyond the left-field fence. He wasn't speedy enough to elude Stearns, the former defensive back who made a diving tackle of the mascot.

Another time, the Mets were in Philadelphia when the Phillie Phanatic made the mistake of performing too close to Stearns. The Phanatic ended his routine by sticking his tongue out at Stearns before the catcher playfully punched him in the snout. The Phanatic went down in a heap, although it was merely a pratfall that entertained the fans at Veterans Stadium. Those were two of the more memorable moments for the Mets during the Stearns era.

The Mets reacquired Kingman and Rusty Staub after the 1980 season and also added former Cy Young winner Randy Jones and outfielder Ellis Valentine. But the Mets were just 17–34 before the '81 strike split the season into two halves. Stearns batted .267 in the first half and .275 in the second to finish with a .271 average. He also ended a 365 at-bat homerless drought dating to 1979 by smacking a go-ahead, two-run shot off Steve Carlton in the eighth inning of a 5–4 win over the Phillies September 16. The Mets stayed in the second-half race until the final week of the season before finishing 4½ games behind the Expos.

The Mets added another big bat in 1982, getting George Foster from the Reds. New York opened strong, going 27–21 to occupy second place, 3½ games out of first heading into June. Stearns owned a .327 average with 14 RBIs and 27 runs scored by June 1 to help the Mets become the surprise team of the National League East. But a weak rotation and an injury to Allen led to another last-place finish at 65–97.

It was a career-altering season for Stearns, who set personal highs by hitting .293 with a .415 slugging average while hitting 25 doubles and stealing 17 bases. He began to experience elbow pain in June and didn't start another game that season after August 16. Stearns landed on the disabled list August 20 with what the team called muscular tendinitis of the inner aspect of the right elbow. The Mets placed his elbow in a cast and hoped the pain would subside without surgery.

Stearns had just one at-bat during the 1983 exhibition season while rehabbing the elbow. Activated April 12, he was slated to play that night before experiencing more discomfort in the elbow. He went back on the DL three days later and underwent surgery June 10. He had just 17 at-bats the rest of his career, all in 1984.

Stearns had another surgery in October 1983 and didn't start another game until the final weekend of 1984. The injury couldn't have come at a worse time for Stearns as the Mets finally had become legitimate playoff contenders in '84.

The Mets were eliminated from the NL East during the final week of the 1984 campaign before manager Davey Johnson allowed Stearns to start the final two games. Stearns went 2-for-10 during a season-ending series at Montreal to end the year with a .176 average. Stearns' final at-bat was an RBI single off Bill Gullickson in the season finale September 30.

Stearns hooked up with the Reds after he was granted free agency in November 1984. Assigned to Triple A Denver, he hit .264 in 72 games for the Bears in 1985 before ending his playing career at age 33.

With his fiery demeanor and a catcher's knowledge of the game, Stearns eventually became a scout, a minor league manager and a major league coach. He was hired as an advance scout with the Brewers in 1987. From there, he was employed by the Astros, Yankees, Reds, and Blue Jays before returning to the Mets as catching coach in November 1999. It was Stearns who uttered the phrase, "The monster's out of the cage," when Mike Piazza began to heat up against the Cardinals in the 2000 NLCS.

Stearns was elevated to third-base coach in 2001 before returning to the minors as the Mets' Double A manager at Binghamton. He went 63–78 in the Eastern League in 2003, and 72–72 as Norfolk's manager the following season before spending 2004 as the Mets' minor league catching instructor.

He switched organizations in 2006, hired by Washington as manager of the Nationals' Double A affiliate at Harrisburg before running the organization's Triple A Columbus franchise for a season. He was back at Harrisburg for the 2008 and 2009 seasons.

First ML game	Phillies @ Expos, 9/22/74
First Mets game	@ Cardinals, 4/16/75
First ML hit	single vs. Mike Torrez, @ Expos, 9/22/74
First Mets hit	double vs. John Denny, @ Cardinals, 4/16/75
First ML/Mets homer	solo HR vs. Ray Burris, @ Cubs, 4/30/75
First ML/Mets RBI	RBI single vs. Rick Reuschel, Cubs, 4/20/75
Most hits, ML/Mets game	4, 5 times
Most homers, ML/Mets game	1, 46 times
Most RBIs, ML/Mets game	4, @ Expos, 6/1/77; vs. Astros, 6/19/77; vs. Astros, 7/20/78
Acquired:	Traded by the Phillies with Del Unser and Mac Scarce for Tug McGraw, Don Hahn and Dave Schneck, 12/8/74.
Deleted:	Became a free agent 11/8/84.

Darryl Strawberry

Outfielder	Bats left, throws left
Born: 3/12/62	Los Angeles, California
Height: 6'6"	Weight: 200 #18

Darryl Strawberry Mets Career

YEAR	GP	AB	R	H	2B	3B	HR	RBI	K	BB	SB	AVG	SLG	OBP
1983	122	420	63	108	15	7	26	74	128	47	19	.257	.512	.336
1984	147	522	75	131	27	4	26	97	131	75	27	.251	.467	.343
1985	111	393	78	109	15	4	29	79	96	73	26	.277	.557	.389
1986	136	475	76	123	27	5	27	93	141	72	28	.259	.507	.358
1987	154	532	108	151	32	5	39	104	122	97	36	.284	.583	.398
1988	153	543	101	146	27	3	39	101	127	85	29	.269	.545	.366
1989	134	476	69	107	26	1	29	77	105	61	11	.225	.466	.312
1990	152	542	92	150	18	1	37	108	110	70	15	.277	.518	.361
TOTAL	1109	3903	662	1025	187	30	252	733	960	580	191	.263	.520	.359

ML Career

YEAR	GP	AB	R	H	2B	3B	HR	RBI	K	BB	SB	AVG	SLG	OBP
83–99	1583	5418	898	1401	256	38	35	1000	1352	816	221	.259	.505	.357

Expectations often turn the legacy of a productive major leaguer into one of disappointment. The expectations will overshadow a player's body of work, regardless of his place in major league history.

Consider for a moment that only eight players in major league history have hit 335 homers, driven in 1,000 runs, stolen 221 bases, and compiled a .505 slugging percentage. Darryl Strawberry is one of the eight, producing those numbers over 17 major league seasons. He's on a list that includes Hank Aaron, Willie Mays, Barry Bonds, and Sammy Sosa, fine company indeed.

However, Strawberry is the first to tell you he never lived up to the huge expectations placed on him even before he played professional baseball.

The hype began at Crenshaw High in Los Angeles, where his coach was comparing him to one of the greatest hitters ever.

"I asked Darryl, 'Do you know who Ted Williams is?'" said Crenshaw coach Brooks Hurst while Strawberry was his top player. "He said, 'Well…' and kind of hesitated. I said, 'Well, there's a little generation gap here. But you're going to be a black Ted Williams, because you hit just like Ted.'"[293]

Hurst wasn't the only one awed by Strawberry's talent. Strawberry was the consensus No. 1 prospect in the 1980 draft, and the Mets were lucky enough to have stunk just enough the previous year to garner the top pick. The Mets had never before developed a player with the potential to hit 40 homers, drive in more than 100 runs, steal 30 bases, and hit .280 or better, sending the New York hype machine into full throttle as Strawberry began his career.

When healthy, motivated, and focused, Strawberry could carry the Mets' offense for weeks at a time. But there were too many instances in which baseball was secondary in his life, leading to unfulfilled expectations when he had the talent to emerge as one of the game's most feared hitters. If Strawberry was the greatest hitting prospect ever to be drafted by the Mets, he can also be considered one of the bigger disappointments. He twice hit 39 homers as a Met, drove in more than 100 runs in three seasons with the team and stole more than 25 bases in four consecutive years. But for longtime Mets followers, there is always the nagging thought that he was talented enough to put together seasons of 40 homers, 40 steals, and 120 RBIs without breaking a sweat.

Darryl Eugene Strawberry was born and raised in Los Angeles, excelling in baseball and basketball at Crenshaw High while receiving scholarship offers in both sports. He helped Crenshaw win the city basketball championship but decided to concentrate on baseball while following in his older brothers' footsteps. Michael Strawberry played two seasons in the low minors for the Angels, and Ronnie went on to play college baseball. Darryl also had two sisters, making it a five-sibling brood under the care and guidance of their mother, Ruby. Darryl's father, Henry, remained a fixture in the household until he decided to leave rather than adhere to Ruby's demand that he stop gambling. Darryl was 13 when his parents split up.

The Strawberry brothers used sports as an outlet, and it didn't take long for Darryl to become the family's most accomplished athlete. He was hounded by major league scouts and college recruiters by his junior year of high school, and he abandoned plans for college once it was evident he would be the first pick in the 1980 draft.

It was the Mets' first draft under new general manager Frank Cashen, who inherited a team that needed to win its last six games just to avoid 100 losses in 1979. The ballclub drew a pitiful 788,905 during the '79 season, by far the lowest attendance figure in team history at that point.

The Mets drafted quite well during Joe McDonald's last three years as GM, but the kids still weren't ready while most of the current major leaguers had worn out their welcome in New York. The Yankees outdrew the Mets by more than a 3-to-1 margin in 1979. The Rangers reached the Stanley Cup finals in '79, one year before the Islanders won the first of their four straight Cups. The Jets had improved to the point *Sports Illustrated* picked them to win the '81 Super Bowl. With the Yankees, Rangers, Isles, and Jets performing well, the Mets were now an afterthought in New York just over a decade after owning the city. The team desperately needed a superstar.

Seven of the Mets' first 10 selections in the June 1980 draft reached the majors, including all three of their first-round picks. But Strawberry was the player Mets fans followed as they trolled through the *Sporting News* for information about the team's farm system.

The Mets had hoped Strawberry might be ready for the majors by 1984. Cashen had no plans to rush his prized prospect, who signed six weeks after the draft and began his minor league career by stroking a single in his first at-bat for Kingsport of the rookie Appalachian League. Strawberry ended the abbreviated season hitting .268 with five homers, 27 RBIs, and five stolen bases in 44 games.

Moved up to Class A Lynchburg in 1981, Strawberry stole 31 bases and hit 13 homers while collecting 22 doubles, 78 RBIs, and 84 runs scored in 123 games. But his .255 average and 105 strikeouts in 420 at-bats demonstrated why Cashen wanted to be patient with his 19-year-old prodigy.

Strawberry wrecked Cashen's plans by winning the Double A Texas League MVP award in 1982, leading the circuit with 34 homers, 101 runs scored, and a .604 slugging average for Jackson. He also tied for second in the league with 45 stolen bases and was third with 97 RBIs while hitting a solid .283.

Strawberry was promoted to Triple A Tidewater following the Texas League playoffs and went 5-for-20 with a homer and four runs scored for the Tides. He came to New York after the International League playoffs, but only to receive one of the Doubleday Awards as co-MVP of the Jackson Mets.

The Mets were concluding their sixth consecutive losing season when Strawberry came north to accept his award. The team flirted with an NL East title through mid-August 1980, finished just 4½ games out of first during the second-half strike season in 1981 and posted a 27–21 record to start the 1982 campaign. But the Mets finished a combined 173–254 from 1980 to 1982 after going 193–293 over the previous three seasons. Things didn't get any better at the start of 1983.

Strawberry went to camp with the '83 Mets and hit .306 with four homers and eight RBIs in 36 at-bats during the exhibition season. He tied George Foster for the team lead in home runs and was among the club leaders in extra-base hits, RBIs, and runs scored. Cashen again resisted the urge to rush Strawberry, sending him to Tidewater with thoughts of keeping him there the rest of the season.

Tom Seaver's return to the Mets allowed them to draw nearly 47,000 for his season-opening start at Shea Stadium. One game later, the Mets played in front of only 5,730 as they remained unbeaten. But the team quickly reeled off losing streaks of six, five, and four games, leading to a 6–15 record by May 4.

Meanwhile, Strawberry was torturing Triple A hurlers. He hit three homers and drove in 13 runs while striking out 18 times in 57 at-bats over 16 games for the Tides. Strawberry also raised eyebrows by hitting .333, swiping seven bases, and scoring 12 times.

Cashen decided to roll the dice with the Mets on pace for a 46–116 record. He brought up Strawberry to start in right field against the visiting Reds on May 6, one game after the Mets slogged their way through a 4–3 loss to Houston in front of 5,511 fans at Shea. In fact, the three-game series with the Astros attracted just 15,719, which might have factored into Cashen's decision to promote Strawberry.

Strawberry's debut outdrew the Houston series by 203 fans on a warm Friday night. He went hitless in four at-bats and struck out three times, but the second of his two walks ignited a game-winning rally.

Strawberry worked out a two-out walk in the bottom of the 13th and demonstrated his speed—and guts—by stealing second. Mike Jorgensen also walked to send up Foster, who ended the game with a three-run homer for a 7–4 Mets win. Strawberry had scored the winning run in his first game as a Met, giving the Shea faithful a brief bit of joy.

Strawberry was also 0-for-4 in the next game, and 3-for-26 as a Met when he faced Pirates reliever Lee Tunnell in the fifth inning at Pittsburgh on May 16. Strawberry picked that at-bat to launch his first major league home run, a two-run poke that put New York ahead 7–1 in an 11–4 victory.

Strawberry homered the next game and went deep again two days later, part of a four-game stretch in which he was 6-for-18 with three homers, seven RBIs, and four runs scored. That was followed by a 5-for-45 skid that dropped his average to .161 through 24 games.

The slump had Mets fans wondering if they were watching the next Ted Williams or the next Don Bosch. Like Strawberry, Bosch was a highly-touted outfield prospect when he came to the Mets in December 1966 before hitting .157 with three homers in 204 at-bats. Strawberry quelled the comparisons to Bosch by going 8-for-23 in his next four games through June 13 to lift his average to the Mendoza Line. Two days later, Cashen acquired Keith Hernandez in a trade with the Cardinals.

Strawberry helped Hernandez beat his old team on June 22, slamming a three-run homer and driving in four runs in a 6–4 victory at Shea. That started a season-ending stretch in which Strawberry batted .290 with 23 homers, 11 doubles, 62 RBIs, 12 steals, and 51 runs scored in 88 games. He became the first Mets non-pitcher to win the NL Rookie of the Year Award, ending the season with a .257 average, 26 homers, and 74 RBIs.

Strawberry and the Mets were still viewed as a work in progress as they reported to 1984 spring training under new manager Davey Johnson, who was Strawberry's skipper at Tidewater in '83. Johnson had firsthand knowledge of the Mets' farm system, having managed at several levels while mentally separating the prospects from the suspects. Johnson fought to have Dwight Gooden put on the season-opening roster and envisioned the positives in having Wally Backman platoon with Kelvin Chapman at second base. Johnson also started his catcher from Tidewater, picking rookie Mike Fitzgerald to handle a staff that included youngsters Ron Darling and Walt Terrell. The new ingredients led to a startling turnaround as the Mets challenged for the NL East title in 1984.

There was also another startling transformation on the Mets: the emergence of talented, young, black players. Gooden, Strawberry, Mookie Wilson, and Hubie Brooks were all under 28, products of the team's farm system, and among the most important players on the roster. When the quartet started against the Astros on April 7, it marked the first time the Mets had three homegrown

African American position players on the field while another homegrown African American was on the mound.

As the youngsters of the group, Gooden and Strawberry naturally gravitated toward each other while the media billed them as best buddies. Gooden was the ace of the staff and Strawberry became the most feared power hitter on the team. Together, they helped the Mets carry a 4½-game division lead into late July before the Cubs eventually passed them.

The 1984 season marked the first time Strawberry led the team in home runs, RBIs, and slugging, blasting 26 balls over the wall, driving in 97, and posting a .467 slugging mark. He also finished second on the team in runs scored (75) and walks (75), and was third with 27 doubles, 27 stolen bases, and a .343 on-base percentage. But his .251 average was the lowest among Mets who qualified for the batting title.

Dave Kingman was the only Met to hit more homers or RBIs than Strawberry in his first two seasons with the team at that point in club history. But Kingman already had established himself as an all-or-nothing power hitter and produced more strikeouts (288) than hits (229) when he came to the Mets. Conversely, Strawberry demonstrated an ability to harness his swing as a young major leaguer, spraying singles to the opposite field when the need arose. There was still hope he could cut down on his strikeouts and become a consistent .280 hitter.

Strawberry came close to doing that in 1985, hitting .277 despite a forgettable first three months of the season. He went 4-for-28 without an RBI during a nine-game stretch that ended with Strawberry landing on the disabled list after tearing a thumb ligament on May 11. He returned on June 28 and proceeded to go 1-for-12 with no RBIs while his average dropped to .200 by July 1.

Strawberry wasn't the only Met struggling at the plate. Hernandez battled to keep his average above .250, newcomer Howard Johnson was hitting .191, and Backman stopped producing as a right-handed batter, all of which made the Mets susceptible to left-handed pitching. But the Mets, buoyed by great starting pitching from Gooden, Darling, and rookies Rick Aguilera and Roger McDowell, prevented the Cardinals from taking a sizeable lead in the NL East in '85.

Strawberry was arguably the Mets' best hitter over the final three months, hitting .306 with a .425 on-base percentage, a .611 slugging mark, 23 homers, 67 RBIs, and 61 runs scored in 83 games. The second-half stretch included a two-homer, seven-RBI game against the Braves on July 20, and a three-homer assault at Wrigley Field on August 5. But one of the more memorable blasts of his career occurred during the final week of the season.

The Mets were three games behind the Cardinals with six games left when the two teams opened a three-game set in St. Louis. Darling tossed shutout ball for nine innings in Game 1, but the Mets failed to score during John Tudor's 10 innings.

finishing just three behind Carter's team-leading home run total despite his lengthy absence. Strawberry also paced the club with a .557 slugging average, a 90-point increase over 1984.

Strawberry's 1986 season wasn't as good, but that didn't stop the Mets from dominating the National League. In fact, none of the Mets' other marquee players—Hernandez, Carter, Foster, and Gooden—had career years. However, there was a different hero every day as the Mets rolled to a 108–54 record to capture the division by a whopping 21½ games.

Strawberry had a strong April, capping the month with a 5-for-5 performance in a rout of the Braves. He hit .313 with 14 RBIs in 16 games that month as the Mets went 13–3.

The Mets continued to pad their lead despite an inconsistent Strawberry. He hit only .167 from May 3 to 24 before hitting a robust .398 with six homers, 10 doubles, 19 RBIs, and 21 runs scored in his next 26 games. The hot streak included a July 3 victory in which he homered twice and had four RBIs, including a game-tying, two-run blast in the 10th inning just before Ray Knight went deep to beat the Astros.

Strawberry owned a .299 average with a .400 on-base percentage, a .567 slugging average, 12 homers, and 44 RBIs through 63 games. He homered 15 times while driving in 49 runs the rest of the way, but his .223 average in his final 73 games was puzzling.

The Mets seemed poised to overpower the Astros in the NLCS. New York led the league with a .263 average, a .339 on-base percentage, a .401 slugging mark, and 783 runs scored. In addition, the Mets finished third with 148 home runs and had three players with at least 25 stolen bases. The Mets also had the deepest pitching staff in the majors as they entered the postseason as prohibitive favorites to win it all.

Houston managed to silence the Mets' offense, holding it to a .189 average in the six-game series. Strawberry hit only .227 while striking out 12 times in 22 at-bats, but he also paced the club with two homers and five RBIs while finishing second to Backman with four runs scored.

Strawberry's two homers were game-savers. The Mets trailed 4–1 in the sixth inning of Game 3 until he ripped a three-run homer off lefty Bob Knepper. New York eventually won it on Lenny Dykstra's two-run shot in the bottom of the ninth to take a 2–1 series lead.

Two days later, Strawberry socked a game-tying, solo homer in the fourth inning off Nolan Ryan, who allowed only one other hit through nine innings. Once again, Strawberry's blast eventually allowed the Mets to win again in their final at-bat to grab a three-games-to-two lead.

The Mets finally won the series' decisive Game 6 in Houston, 7–6 in 16 innings. Strawberry scored a go-ahead run on Backman's single in the 13th, but the Astros extended the game on Billy Hatcher's homer in the bottom half.

Darryl Strawberry. Photo courtesy of David Ferry

Ken Dayley replaced Tudor and opened the 11th by fanning Hernandez and Gary Carter before Strawberry took his turn against the left-hander. Strawberry was 0-for-4 with two strikeouts before crushing a Dayley delivery deep into the night. The ball slammed off the scoreboard clock, drawing comparisons to Roy Hobbs' blast at Wrigley Field in the movie, *The Natural*. It provided the game's lone run as the Mets pulled within two games of the Redbirds.

The Mets also won the next day but failed to complete the sweep, putting them two games back with three remaining. The Cardinals clinched two days later, and the Mets had to settle for a second straight runner-up finish despite a 98–64 record.

Strawberry hit 29 homers and drove in 79 runs while appearing in only 111 games due to the thumb injury,

Strawberry also ignited the game-winning, three-run rally with a leadoff double before coming to the plate on Knight's single. The Mets tacked on two more runs and then held on for a 7–6 win to earn a meeting with the Red Sox in the Fall Classic.

Boston's rotation featured lefty Bruce Hurst, who struck out Strawberry three times in seven at-bats while winning the first and fifth games of the series. Red Sox fans hardly took pity on Strawberry, serenading him with chants of, "DAAAAAAAAAAA-RYLLLLLLL, DAAAAAAAAAAA-RYLLLLLLL," during Game 5 after he made the final out in the sixth and eighth innings. The boisterous assault was meant as derision, but Mets fans eventually turned it into a positive.

Boston carried a 3–2 Series lead back to New York and led 2–0 in Game 6 until Strawberry walked and scored during a two-run fifth. Strawberry had a chance to be the hero in the bottom of the eighth as he headed to the plate with two runners on following Carter's game-tying sac fly. Strawberry hit a drive to center that was caught by Dave Henderson for the final out, keeping the score tied 3–3. It was his final at-bat of the night.

Lee Mazzilli opened the eighth-inning rally with a single as a pinch-hitter for reliever Jesse Orosco. Since Strawberry made the last out—and with a new pitcher entering the game for the Mets—Davey Johnson elected to pull a double-switch and replace Strawberry with Mazzilli in right field.

The strategy ticked off Strawberry, who went straight to the clubhouse and left Shea Stadium before the game ended. He couldn't understand how a player of his importance could be pulled in the late innings with a World Series crown at stake.

The Mets eventually won the game 6–5 with a three-run 10th capped by first baseman Bill Buckner's error. It was one of the most incredible finishes in World Series history and allowed the Mets to extend their season, but Strawberry wasn't around to see the rally. The media noticed his absence after the game and wrote inches of copy about it once Game 7 was postponed a day because of rain.

Having patched things up with Johnson, Strawberry was back in the starting lineup against Hurst for the seventh game and was hitless in his first three at-bats. But the Mets rallied from a 3–0 deficit and took a 4–3 lead on Knight's homer in the seventh.

It was 6–5 when Strawberry led off the eighth with a titanic blast off Al Nipper to give the Mets breathing room. He took his time chugging around the bases, a move that prompted Nipper to drill him with a pitch in spring training the following March. But as he made his approach toward home plate he was serenaded by chants of, "DAAAAAAAAAAA-RYLLLLLLL, DAAAAAAAAAAA-RYLLLLLLL," from the appreciative crowd at Shea. It was his only RBI of the Series. The Mets celebrated an 8–5 victory a few minutes later, giving them their second World Series title.

The team appeared poised to begin a dynasty, and Strawberry seemed ready to take his game to another level. The lineup was bolstered by the acquisition of left fielder Kevin McReynolds, whose 26 homers and 96 RBIs in 1986 were comparable to Strawberry's 27 home runs and 93 ribbies. But the Mets never won another pennant with Strawberry on the team, posting one division title and three second-place finishes in four years.

Strawberry should have been able to spend the winter of '87 celebrating his contributions to one of the greatest teams in major league history, a ballclub that was as cocky as they come. Cashen took away some of the team's heart by sending Kevin Mitchell to the Padres for McReynolds and allowing Knight to sign a free-agent deal with the Tigers. The club's perception was that Mitchell, a tough-as-nails kid from a rough section of San Diego, was a bad influence on Strawberry and Gooden. Mitchell, Strawberry, and Gooden were the only African American players on the playoff roster under age 25, and the three spent a bit of time together before and after games. As the ballclub would soon learn, Strawberry and Gooden managed to get into trouble without Mitchell's help.

Strawberry's personal life was already spiraling out of control before Mitchell was jettisoned. His marriage to his first wife, Lisa, was built on mistrust and a host of bad decisions by both. Lisa was left with a broken nose following an altercation with Darryl in Houston during the NLCS. Another off-season altercation prompted Lisa to take their son, D.J., and head to her mother's home. She filed for a separation weeks later.

Darryl and Lisa were a match made in hell. She was a headstrong woman who took advantage of the lifestyle afforded the wife of a star baseball player, spending lavishly without any notion of a budget. Darryl did his part to ruin the marriage by staying out late and coming home either drunk or high. Darryl's misconduct was the by-product of playing for a high-profile ballclub that was revered in the world's biggest city.

If Strawberry's personal life was going to be a problem in 1987, he didn't show it during the first four weeks of the season. He homered in each of the first three games while opening the campaign on a 10-game hitting streak. By May 2, Strawberry was hitting .325 with a .687 slugging average, seven homers, 21 RBIs through 22 games. Most encouraging was his 14 strikeouts in his first 83 at-bats after he whiffed 18 times in 45 at-bats during the postseason.

Strawberry appeared ready to perform at the lofty expectations placed on him in high school. He had surpassed Carter and Hernandez as the most dangerous hitter on the team early in the season, as did McReynolds and Howard Johnson.

Strawberry continued to hit homers at a prodigious pace, crushing 13 in 50 games from May 3 to June 28. He also logged a .384 on-base percentage during that span, but his .232 batting average and 26 RBIs demonstrated he wasn't taking full advantage of his plate appearances. The

Mets went just 26–24 in those 50 games and were watching the Cardinals run away with the division title.

The Mets needed all the offense they could muster heading into July. Gooden was just rounding into form after being suspended for the first 60 days of the season following a positive drug test. Sid Fernandez, Bob Ojeda, Aguilera, and David Cone all missed starts or landed on the disabled list during the first three months, making journeyman side-armer Terry Leach the de facto ace of the staff after he opened the season 7–0. The pitching situation was grim enough to prompt Cashen to talk Tom Seaver into a possible return to the Mets, but that plan was scuttled when the greatest pitcher in team history struggled against minor leaguers.

Strawberry went 2-for-5 in an 8–7 loss to the Cardinals on June 29, lifting his season average to .268. He begged out of the next game of the series, citing the flu. However, he was well enough to cut tracks for a rap album hours before batting practice. His absence infuriated many of his teammates, many of whom called out Strawberry for his cavalier attitude toward the team.

Strawberry was on pace to appear in 160 games that season before taking himself out of the lineup for an important game against the division leader. With a suspect rotation, coupled with a 7½-game difference between the Mets and the Cardinals, his teammates recognized the need for Strawberry to perform at a higher level for the club to have any chance to overtake the Redbirds. Backman and Lee Mazzilli ripped Strawberry in the press for his absence, and Strawberry countered by saying he was going to "punch that redneck [Backman] in the face."

Strawberry sat out the last two games of the series while the Mets pulled out victories. But the team fell 10½ games behind St. Louis eight days later and was 44–40 just days before the All-Star break.

Strawberry went 2-for-14 in the first five games after the break before demonstrating his exceptional talent. He was outstanding over his final 65 games, hitting .305 with a .404 on-base percentage, 18 homers, 52 RBIs, 56 runs scored, and 21 stolen bases.

The Mets pulled themselves back into the division race and had a chance to take over first place as they hosted St. Louis for a three-game scrum from September 11 to 13. The series began one game after Strawberry went 3-for-5 with two homers, four RBIs, and three runs scored in an 11–5 rout of the Phillies.

Strawberry put a charge into the series opener against St. Louis by ripping a two-run homer to put the Mets ahead 3–0 in the first inning. But New York blew a 4–1 lead in the ninth and lost 6–4 in 10 innings. The two teams split the last two games, allowing the Cardinals to leave New York with a 2½-game lead. St. Louis eventually clinched the division the night before they hosted the Mets in the final series of the regular season.

It was Strawberry's finest season statistically, but it wasn't enough to get the Mets into the playoffs for a sec-

ond straight year. He set career highs with 154 games played, 108 runs scored, 151 hits, 32 doubles, 39 homers, 104 RBIs, 36 stolen bases, 97 walks, a .398 on-base percentage, and a .583 slugging average. He and Howard Johnson also became the first Mets with 30 homers and 30 steals in the same season as the two emerged as a lethal tandem from the left side of the plate. Strawberry, Johnson, and McReynolds accounted for 104 of the Mets' 192 homers, 298 of the team's 771 RBIs, and 82 of the club's 159 steals.

The 1988 Mets resembled the 1986 version though the first 2½ months of the season, recording a 45–24 record that gave them a 7½-game lead. Strawberry twice went deep while the Mets set a team-record with six homers on Opening Day, leading to a 10–6 rout of the Expos in Montreal. He homered in his first at-bat of the season, six innings before his second blast hit the roof at Olympic Stadium.

Strawberry left Montreal after going 8-for-12 with three homers, four RBIs, and five runs scored. He owned a .361 average by the end of April, and was batting .284 with 21 homers and 55 RBIs before heading to his fifth consecutive All-Star appearance. He opened the second half hitting .370 with three homers and nine runs scored in seven games before becoming part of a team-wide hitting slump that allowed the upstart Pirates to work themselves into playoff contention.

Strawberry's final numbers were comparable to his 1987 season: a .269 average with 39 homers, 101 RBIs, and 101 runs scored. He homered nine times and drove in 19 runs in his last 25 games as the Mets shook off the Pirates and coasted to their second division title in three years.

The Mets opened the NLCS in Los Angeles against the Dodgers, who went 1–10 against the Mets during the regular season. The Dodgers' lineup paled in comparison to the Mets, the back end of the rotation was suspect, and the bullpen was unheralded. But Los Angeles had Orel Hershiser and Kirk Gibson, two players who helped derail the Mets' trip to the World Series.

Strawberry fared better in the series than he did in the 1986 playoffs, hitting .300 with one home run, six RBIs, and five runs scored. He doubled home the Mets' first run off Hershiser in the ninth inning of a 3–2 victory in the opener, and went 3-for-5 with three RBIs in a Game 3 win that gave New York a two-games-to-one lead.

Strawberry also ignited the Mets' offense in Game 4, launching a game-tying, two-run homer in the fourth inning before McReynolds added a go-ahead blast just two pitches later. It was 4–2 in the ninth until Gooden served up a game-tying, two-run shot to Mike Scioscia, three innings before Gibson's first homer of the series gave Los Angeles a 5–4 victory and a split of the first four games.

Gibson also homered the next afternoon before Cone stymied the Dodgers to send the series to a seventh game. Strawberry contributed to the Mets' 5–1 victory in Game 6, going 1-for-2 with two walks and two runs scored. But Hershiser, who picked up the save in Game 4, mowed down the Mets in the seventh game 6–0 to put L.A. in the World Series. Strawberry went 0-for-4 in the clincher and was 3-for-17 in the final four games after going 6-for-13 in the first three.

It was not a happy camp as the Mets reported to Port St. Lucie in February 1989. The team was still feeling the sting of failure after falling to the Dodgers in the playoffs, and Strawberry was unhappy with his contract. He had two years left on his deal and was threatening to leave camp unless the Mets offered him a healthier paycheck. Hernandez was among the most vocal Mets to come out against Strawberry's contract stance, saying Strawberry was getting bad advice from his agent and should honor the remainder of the deal.

Soon after Hernandez's comments were published, the Mets gathered for a team photo when the photographer tried to put Strawberry next to Hernandez.

"I ain't sitting next to no backstabber," Strawberry mumbled before confronting Hernandez. The two exchanged words before Strawberry took a swing at the team captain, leading to a public relations disaster as photographers clicked away while teammates tried to separate the pair. One day later, they actually kissed and made up on camera before resuming training camp.

But Strawberry and Hernandez contributed to what became a lackluster season. Hernandez missed almost 2½ months due to injury and hit just .233 in 75 games. Strawberry made the All-Star team again but hit only .225 with 29 homers and 77 RBIs in 134 games as the Mets finished 87–75, six games behind the division-winning Cubs.

Hernandez and Carter were let go after the season, leaving a leadership vacuum in the clubhouse. It was an opportunity for Strawberry to become the face of the Mets while earning his coveted contract extension. Instead, Strawberry embarrassed the team before spring training.

Strawberry was arrested and charged with assault with a deadly weapon in yet another altercation with his wife, Lisa. This time, he agreed to enter Smithers Center for alcohol rehabilitation in February 1990. It was the same facility that housed Gooden during his 1987 battle with cocaine, adding another link between the two players.

Fresh out of rehab, Strawberry went 8-for-21 with two homers and seven RBIs in eight games during an exhibition season truncated by a lockout. When the games counted, Strawberry opened the season by hitting just .230 with five home runs and 16 RBIs. At this pace, he was looking at a 20-homer, 64-RBI season that would certainly guarantee him a ticket out of New York.

Strawberry went 5-for-8 with two homers and three RBIs in his next two games, but the Mets' record was just 20–22 through 42 games as they watched the first-place Pirates put distance between themselves and New York. Management responded to the sluggish start by firing Davey Johnson on May 28 and replacing him with coach Bud Harrelson, who Strawberry considered a confidant in tough times.

It took Strawberry and the Mets a little over a week to alter their course under Harrelson. Strawberry went on an 18-game hitting streak from June 8 to 29, hitting .412 with a .500 on-base percentage, an .853 slugging mark, nine homers, 24 RBIs, and 16 runs scored. The streak began with a three-game sweep of the Pirates as Strawberry went 5-for-11 with four homers and eight RBIs. He also hammered the Bucs during a two-game split in Pittsburgh a week later, homering twice and driving in five runs while reaching base six times in 10 plate appearances.

The Mets went 16–2 during the hitting streak to move into a first-place tie on the strength of a team record–tying 11 straight wins.

Strawberry and his agent continued attempts to hammer out a multiyear contract with the Mets. The hitting streak was nearing an end when Strawberry received great news from 3,000 miles away; the Athletics signed slugger Jose Canseco to a five-year, $23.5 million contract extension in late June.

If anything, Canseco's deal gave Strawberry a financial measuring stick. Strawberry was a much better outfielder despite his occasional defensive lapses, and Canseco had missed most of 1989 due to injury. Canseco's offensive stats from 1986 to 1989 (.268 with 123 homers, 411 RBIs, and 76 stolen bases) were comparable to Strawberry's (.260, 134 homers, 375 RBIs, 104 steals).

Strawberry continued his contract drive into July in the hopes he'd have a new deal before the season ended. He was named to the NL All-Star team for the seventh straight year and was hitting .307 three days after the break. For the first time in his career, Strawberry was consistently playing to the lofty expectations placed on him during his days at Crenshaw High.

Best of all, Strawberry seemed happy. He was playing his most inspired defense since his 1985 thumb injury and had become a vocal leader in the clubhouse. The Mets were challenging for a postseason berth, doing it while Strawberry was out from under the imposing shadow cast by Hernandez and Carter.

But the Mets weren't willing to spend "Canseco Money" on Strawberry, offering him a reported three-year package worth $9.2 million in July. The deal represented a sizeable increase from the $1.8 million he had averaged during the six-year pact he signed before the 1985 season, but it was moderate compared to the money other sluggers were making at the time. Strawberry flatly rejected the deal, and the two sides broke off negotiations in mid-July.

"I'm going to have to file for free agency," Strawberry said after contract talks ended. "They are backing off on contract negotiations. Nothing can be accomplished. They wanted to give me a three-year deal, and I'm not interested in a three-year deal."

"I'm happy in New York," Strawberry maintained. "I've been here for seven years. I want to be here for five more years. I just enjoy it here. It's a real letdown knowing it had to come to this point."[294]

Strawberry went 2-for-4 with a homer the day he announced negotiations had been tabled. His average stood at .307 with 23 homers and 58 RBIs through 79 games, putting him on pace for his first 40-homer season and a team record–shattering 116 RBIs. The Mets could only hope he'd continue his contract drive by displaying the same passionate play that made fans forgot his mediocre 1989 season.

Strawberry put together a devastating five-game stretch through Labor Day, going 10-for-20 with two homers, 10 RBIs, and nine runs scored. The Mets won all five games to cap a seven-game winning streak that put them atop the NL East, a half-game ahead of the Pirates.

But the Mets had become susceptible to left-handed pitching over the course of the season and faced a steady diet of southpaws during the stretch run. The Pirates, a half-game ahead of the Mets heading into a three-game series in Pittsburgh on September 5 and 6, started lefties Zane Smith, Neal Heaton, and Randy Tomlin. Strawberry homered in the series but went 1-for-9 as the Mets were swept by a combined 12–3 score.

The Mets pulled off a two-game sweep of Pittsburgh at Shea the following week as Strawberry supplied a titanic three-run blast off right-hander Doug Drabek to wipe out a 2–0 deficit in a 6–3 victory that clawed New York within 1½ games of first. But the Mets dropped six of their next seven to kill any shot at a division crown.

Strawberry provided 14 homers and 50 RBIs while delivering numerous key hits after contract talks broke off. However, his .244 average, .316 on-base percentage and .447 slugging average during that span contributed to the Mets' inability to nail down a playoff berth.

The Mets allowed Strawberry to become a free agent and declined to make him an offer that would keep him in New York. The Dodgers wasted little time bringing Strawberry back home, signing him to a five-year package worth $20.25 million on November 8. One month later, the Mets replaced Strawberry with free-agent outfielder Vince Coleman, who would become an even bigger disappointment than Strawberry ever was in Queens.

Strawberry gave the Dodgers one good season, hitting .265 with 28 homers and 99 RBIs. Although it wasn't as productive as the .277 average, 37 homers and career-high 108 RBIs he furnished in 1990, he did it despite a damaged shoulder that caused him to miss significant chunks of time over the first half of the season.

Strawberry appeared in 139 games for the '91 Dodgers, his fewest since 1986. He played in just 136 games over the next four seasons and was released by both the Dodgers and Giants without completing his contract.

A back injury caused him to miss 119 games in 1992 and eventually led to surgery to repair a herniated disk in September. He tried to return near the start of the '93 campaign, but recurring back pain limited him to 32 games and a .140 average. He was looking like a broken-down player as he approached 1994 training camp.

Strawberry's life in Los Angeles was just as stormy as it had been in New York. His last two seasons with the Mets included a paternity suit in April 1989, one month before Lisa Strawberry filed for divorce. A 1990 blood test backed the paternity suit as proof he had fathered a child with Lisa Clayton.

The pattern of poor behavior continued with the Dodgers even after he had become a born-again Christian. He was arrested in September 1993 for allegedly striking his then live-in girlfriend, Charisse Simons, who would become his wife. Police declined to press charges, but the federal government wasn't as forgiving on another matter. In March 1994 the IRS and U.S. Attorney's Office began an investigation into allegations he failed to report more than $300,000 received from autograph and memorabilia shows. The inquiry began shortly after he signed off on a costly divorce to Lisa. That's when Strawberry hit rock bottom. Again.

Strawberry was chronically late for batting practice during the Dodgers' 1994 exhibition season. He admittedly was back to boozing and using cocaine to the point where he failed to show up for a preseason game against the Angels in Anaheim on April 3. He was finally located around midnight, but not before wire reports said he was missing. Longtime followers of Strawberry had a pretty good idea of what happened, and many feared the worst until he resurfaced and checked into the Betty Ford Clinic five days later.

Strawberry completed his rehab program within a few weeks and was promptly released by the Dodgers despite their monetary obligation to him. The organization—manager Tommy Lasorda, the players, the coaches, and the front office—was exasperated, exhausted, and elated to see him go. Lasorda even offered a quote that summed up his grave disappointment in Strawberry. When asked if Strawberry was a "dog" as a player, Lasorda countered by saying, "He's not a dog. A dog is loyal and runs after balls!"

Strawberry was a man without a team by May 28, but he also felt fortunate to be sober again while in the midst of a strengthening relationship with Charisse. Their son, Jordan, was born a little more than two weeks before Strawberry went AWOL for the Angels game. With a new family member to support, he went back to work after signing with the Giants in June 1994.

Strawberry showed the back wasn't a problem anymore as he hit .345 with four homers and 16 RBIs in 16 games from July 14 to 31 after collecting just one hit in his first 11 at-bats with San Francisco. But he hit only .077 with one RBI in his next 26 at-bats, dropping his season average to .239 in 29 games before the players went on strike in mid-August, eventually leading to the cancellation of the remaining regular-season games and the playoffs.

Strawberry suddenly had no income. He was also worrying about his 55-year-old mother, who was diagnosed with breast cancer and refused to undergo radiation treatments. He dealt with the tough times by going back to his old vices: alcohol and drugs.

Strawberry failed a drug test in January 1995 and was released the next month. When the strike was eventually settled in March, he was still unemployed and remained so for three months until he landed another gig in New York.

Yankees owner George Steinbrenner, who collected several former Mets All-Stars in the mid-1990s, signed Strawberry after he completed his drug suspension and while he was under house arrest following his guilty plea for federal tax evasion. Steinbrenner talked about players deserving second chances and saw Strawberry as a reclamation project worth pursuing.

"We are supportive of Darryl and we shall do everything possible to help him meet the challenge ahead," said Steinbrenner. "At the same time, we feel confident Darryl will do the absolute best for us."[295]

Strawberry was recalled in early August and hit .276 with three homers and 13 RBIs in 32 games to begin a five-year stint as a part-time player for the Yankees. He helped the 1995 team reach the postseason for the first time in 14 years but was unsigned as training camp began the following winter.

Ruby Strawberry lost her battle with breast cancer in February 1996, putting Darryl in a state of depression. A few weeks earlier, the agent who resurrected Strawberry's career, Bill Goodstein, died of a heart attack. But instead of finding friendship in his old demons, Strawberry resisted temptation before charting the course for his 1996 season.

Strawberry went to the bottom rung of professional baseball, signing with the St. Paul Saints of the independent Northern League. The Yankees didn't have room for him on their roster at the start of 1996 training camp, but a spot eventually became available after he hit .435 with 18 homers in 29 games for the Saints.

Strawberry was back with the Yanks by the first week of July. He went 0-for-10 in his first three games before going 2-for-4 with two homers and four RBIs in Game 2 of a doubleheader against Baltimore on July 13. Four weeks after his Bombers debut, Strawberry blasted three homers in a 9–2 rout of the White Sox in the Bronx.

His 1996 regular season consisted of 63 games, a .262 average, 11 homers, 13 doubles, 36 RBIs, and 35 runs scored. Prorate that into a full 162-game season and Strawberry was on pace for 28 homers, 33 doubles, 92 RBIs, and 90 runs scored, a rather typical season for him.

Strawberry earned a spot on the playoff roster and helped the Yankees win their first World Series since 1981. He went just 0-for-5 in two games during the division series against Texas before producing arguably his finest playoff series ever. Strawberry lit up Baltimore pitching for three homers and five RBIs while going 5-for-12 in four games during the ALCS. He starred in the Yankees' 8–1 victory in Game 4, crushing two homers and driving in three runs at Baltimore. One day later, his solo homer capped a six-run third that led to a 6–4 victory and the AL pennant.

335 HRs, 1,000 RBIs, 221 SBs, and a .505 SLG

PLAYER	HR	RBI	SB	SLG
Barry Bonds	762	1,996	514	.607
Hank Aaron	755	2,297	240	.555
Willie Mays	660	1,903	338	.557
Alex Rodriguez*	613	1,831	301	.571
Sammy Sosa	609	1,667	234	.534
Gary Sheffield	509	1,676	253	.514
Larry Walker	383	1,311	230	.565
Darryl Strawberry	335	1,000	221	.505

* Through 2010

The Yankees beat the Braves in the Fall Classic as Strawberry went 3-for-16 with a .350 on-base percentage. He was a champion again on October 26, one day shy of the 10th anniversary of the Mets' Game 7 win over the Red Sox.

Strawberry went to 1997 training camp virtually guaranteed to make the Yankees. He was their starting left fielder in the first three games despite suffering a knee injury during spring training. The balky knee landed him on the disabled list by mid-April, followed by knee surgery in June. He hit just .107 in 29 at-bats the entire season and became a free agent again at age 35.

Steinbrenner showed faith in Strawberry by re-signing him for 1998. Strawberry rewarded the Yankees' owner by playing inspired baseball at times, hitting .247 with a .542 slugging average, 24 homers, and 57 RBIs in 295 at-bats over 101 games.

But he spent much of the summer battling a stomach ailment that caused his appetite to disappear. He lost weight and tried to quell the pain by downing Maalox before games, but he'd feel the same by the end of the night.

The Yankees put together a record-setting regular season, winning 114 games to break Cleveland's mark of 111 set during a 154-game season in 1954. Strawberry went 2-for-2 in a rout of the Devil Rays in the regular-season finale on September 27 before finally deciding to have his stomach examined by a doctor.

He was initially diagnosed with diverticulitis shortly before the Yankees opened the division series against the Rangers. A subsequent CAT scan revealed a growth in his colon, causing him to miss a second straight game and leading to a follow-up colonoscopy that showed a potentially malignant tumor that was blocking his colon. The Yankees flew to Texas while Strawberry prepared for cancer surgery. Steinbrenner stayed in New York to be with Darryl and Charisse at Columbia Presbyterian Hospital.

The four-hour surgery was followed by two weeks in the hospital. He didn't see most of his teammates until the World Series parade, shortly after the Yankees swept the Padres for their second title in three years.

Strawberry was reminded of how much he was appreciated in New York. He received thousands of cards and letters while hospitalized, well wishes from many people who might have booed him on occasion in Queens or the Bronx. In the eyes of Mets and Yankees fans, Strawberry could be both frustrating and disappointing to watch at times. But there was something about him that would make a fan forgive and forget, and not just because of his ability to belt a three-run homer. Whereas Mays, Aaron, DiMaggio, and Musial were legendary, Strawberry appeared vulnerable at times, causing fans to root for him regardless of his latest indiscretion.

Strawberry needed more surgery in January after scar tissue materialized, causing another blockage in his intestine. The procedure put him behind the rest of the Yankees in camp and led management to keep him in Tampa while the team opened the season. It was a blow to Strawberry, who worked very hard to be ready for the opener and was still without a contract when the exhibition season began.

Strawberry handled the situation poorly. While on rehab, he went to a Tampa bar and took his first drink in four years before purchasing cocaine later that night. He left the bar and headed toward a seedy section of Tampa, where he tried to score more cocaine from a woman who thought his inquiry also meant sex. The woman was an undercover police officer posing as a prostitute. She claimed Strawberry offered her money for sex, a charge he denied. The situation landed him in jail overnight before he pleaded no contest to cocaine possession.

Commissioner Bud Selig handed Strawberry a 120-day suspension that effectively killed his season. But Steinbrenner remained a loyal friend, keeping Strawberry on the team long enough to enjoy a few more weeks as a Yankee.

Strawberry played well in his truncated season, batting .327 with a .500 on-base percentage, three homers, five doubles, and six RBIs in just 49 at-bats. He also helped the Yankees win their second straight World Series, going 5-for-15 with two homers in the postseason. Strawberry hit a second-inning single off John Smoltz in Game 4 of the World Series before the Yankees completed a sweep. It was his final major league hit.

Strawberry failed a drug test in January 2000 and was suspended for the entire season. Steinbrenner remained publicly supportive of Strawberry's problems, but this time he cut ties before spring training.

Any possibility of another comeback ended when his cancer returned. He underwent another procedure in New York, this time to remove part of his kidney. Doctors prescribed Ambien, Percodan, and Vicodin to help him get through the pain, but it only led to another addiction and another brush with the law.

With his system full of prescription drugs, Strawberry went for a drive and wrecked his car without realizing it. A police officer pulled him over, called for backup, and arrested him. The upshot was that Strawberry's probation was extended another 18 months.

He checked into another rehab facility, all while dealing with chemotherapy and five months under house arrest. Strawberry snapped again, walking out of the facility and seeking a drug-using acquaintance. He went missing for several days before turning himself into authorities.

Strawberry was admitted to a hospital psychiatric ward and placed on suicide watch before being sentenced to another rehab facility, where he spent 10 months before being kicked out for having relations with a female participant.

The latest incident led to another court date. He spent a month in prison before being given the option of spending one year in a lockdown treatment facility followed by five years' probation, or an 18-month jail term. Despondent over his situation and unwilling to handle another treatment facility, he opted for prison. He was transferred to the Gainesville Correctional Institution by May 2002 and served 11 months, walking out at age 41.

His baseball career was over and his second marriage was failing. Charisse filed for divorce while Strawberry tried to get his life back in order. He did it by staying clean and reacquainting himself with God, two things which led him to his third wife.

Strawberry and Tracy Boulware began dating after they met at a Narcotics Anonymous recovery convention. Tracy also had fought addiction but had been clean for a year before they were introduced. Strawberry was still battling his addiction and relapsed at times during their courtship before she guided him toward sobriety—by moving from Florida to Missouri. She told him to get clean and showed him how to do it, serving as both a comforting friend and a strict counselor.

Strawberry appears to have his life back in order. He married Tracy and is back in good graces with the Mets. He received one of the loudest ovations when he was introduced as part of the team's 20th anniversary celebration of the 1986 championship club, proving Mets fans were still willing to forgive and forget. He spent time as an analyst during Mets broadcasts on SNY, giving frank assessments on the state of the team.

There are some who wonder when Strawberry will take another drink, have another snort, or appear on another police blotter. But there hasn't been a ripple of controversy since his third marriage as he tries to teach others through lectures and charities of the demons that have conquered him time and again. For this period, Strawberry is exceeding expectations.

First ML game	vs. Reds, 5/6/83
First ML hit	RBI single vs. Ben Hayes, Reds, 5/8/83
First ML homer	2-run HR vs. Lee Tunnell, @ Pirates, 5/16/83
First ML RBI	RBI single vs. Ben Hayes, Reds, 5/8/83

Most hits, ML/Mets game	5, @ Braves, 4/30/86
Most homers, ML game	3, Mets @ Cubs, 8/5/85; Yankees vs. White Sox, 8/6/96
Most RBIs, ML game	7, Mets vs. Braves, 7/20/85; Dodgers vs. Padres, 8/21/91

Acquired: Selected in the first round (1st overall) of the 1980 draft.
Deleted: Became a free agent, 11/5/90. Signed by the Dodgers, 11/8/90.
NL Rookie of the Year, 1983
NL All-Star, 1984, 1985, 1986, 1987, 1988, 1989, 1990, 1991
NL Silver Slugger, 1988, 1990
NL Home Run Leader, 1988
NL Slugging Leader, 1988
NL OPS Leader (.908), 1988

Craig Swan

Pitcher	Bats right, throws right
Born: 11/30/50	Van Nuys, California
Height: 6'3"	Weight: 215 #27

Craig Swan Mets Career

YEAR	GP/GS	IP	H	R	ER	K	BB	W–L	SV	ERA
1973	3/1	8.1	16	9	8	4	2	0–1	0	8.64
1974	7/5	30.1	28	19	15	10	21	1–3	0	4.45
1975	6/6	31	38	22	22	19	13	1–3	0	6.39
1976	23/22	132.1	129	64	52	89	44	6–9	0	3.54
1977	26/24	146.2	153	76	69	71	56	9–10	0	4.23
1978	29/28	207.1	164	62	56	125	58	9–6	0	2.43
1979	35/35	251.1	241	102	92	145	57	14–13	0	3.29
1980	21/21	128.1	117	59	51	79	30	5–9	0	3.58
1981	5/3	13.2	10	6	5	9	1	0–2	0	3.29
1982	37/21	166.1	165	70	62	67	37	11–7	1	3.35
1983	27/18	96.1	112	63	59	43	42	2–8	0	5.51
1984	10/0	18.2	18	17	17	10	7	1–0	0	8.20
Total	229/184	1230.2	1191	569	508	671	368	59–71	2	3.72

Mets Career/Batting

GP	AB	R	H	2B	3B	HR	RBI	K	BB	SB	AVG
229	358	18	54	3	0	1	18	131	24	0	.151

ML Career

YEAR	GP/GS	IP	H	R	ER	K	BB	W–L	SV	ERA
73–84	231/185	1235.2	1199	575	514	673	368	59–72	2	3.74

The Mets became known as a pitching franchise after cultivating the careers of Tom Seaver, Jerry Koosman, Nolan Ryan, Gary Gentry, and Jon Matlack in the late 1960s and early '70s. The collection of exceptional arms was strong enough to allow the Mets to send Ryan and other talented young hurlers to other ballclubs.

Craig Swan was supposed to lead a second wave of young Mets pitching prospects into the major leagues during the mid 1970s. That group included Nino Espinosa, Randy Sterling, Randy Tate, and Hank Webb, all of whom put together strong statistics at Triple A. But Espinosa had his best seasons in Philadelphia, Sterling's big-league career never took off, Tate spent just one year in the majors, and Webb flamed out after showing promise in 1975.

Swan had the longest career of the five, spending all or part of 12 seasons with the Mets and often serving as the ace of the staff. The Mets thought enough of Swan to give him a five-year contract before the 1980 campaign, but injuries permitted him to throw just 423⅓ innings from the time he inked the contract to the time the Mets released him one month into the fifth year of the deal.

However, his shoulder problems allowed him to make a natural transition to another career: rolfing. He continues to perform the procedure on patients nearly 30 years after his first experience with rolfing.

"No doubt, I found my profession through my injuries," Swan said in a September 2011 interview. "And it was just by accident, too, because nobody in professional baseball had heard of rolfing at that point.

"I was recovering from the rotator cuff tear in 1980, and Dr. Parkes, the team physician, didn't want to do the old surgery because they didn't have arthroscopic surgery perfected yet, and they had to open up the whole shoulder. What he told me was that guys come back to lead fairly normal lives, but nobody had recovered from that to pitch. Ever. He said we were going to try something new, which was to do nothing for nine months. And in the nine months I waited, I found rolfing. And now I've gotten to help thousands of people with this kind of unique therapy that Dr. Rolf created."

The shoulder remains a mystery to surgeons nearly four decades since Tommy John had a ligament grafted from his right wrist to his left elbow. It took Nationals prospect Stephen Strasburg about 11 months to return to the majors after undergoing Tommy John surgery. But Mets lefty Johan Santana was unable to pitch more than a few minor league innings for the 2011 Mets following major shoulder surgery in September 2010.

Rolfing seemed to buy Swan a couple more years in the majors, but it became his profession too soon because of other injuries related to the shoulder.

"I coached for 17 years in Connecticut after I was done with baseball," Swan began, "and there were so many pitchers we would lose before they got to age 12. I don't know if the shoulder was made to do it, but we keep doing it."

Former Swan teammate Mike Marshall has since developed a revolutionary pitching motion designed to relieve stress on the shoulder and elbow. Swan fully appreciates Marshall's theories on mechanics but believes it will never catch on in the majors.

"They're not going to go for that so much," Swan said of major league coaches and executives. "It's so against what everybody else had learned. Plus, the way he makes the pitchers step, it's just so much learning to try to throw the screwball that Mike did, and not everybody can do that."

"It was the same thing that they tried to do with me when I got up to Shea. They tried to switch me to Seaver's style because he uses his legs more than I did. And I couldn't do it. I had done it the other way for 20 years."

The comparisons between Swan and Seaver were very easy to make. Both grew up in California, attended Pac-8 schools and had legs like tree trunks. Seaver gained a tremendous amount of his pitching power from his lower body, and the Mets felt the same could happen with Swan. Swan was never able to duplicate Seaver's mechanics, but he did manage to soak up plenty of knowledge.

"We were big and strong, we both threw real hard and we threw to spots," Swan said. "And we did have similar styles. Our breaking pitches weren't that good, and we relied on a fastball that we spotted in the strike zone.

"Seaver was one person [I'd study] because our styles were the same. If we got a chance to sit next to each other and watch somebody else pitch, or if I watched him pitch, I would just learn a lot about the hitters either watching him throw or actually talking about it in the dugout.

"That was very helpful to me because I didn't have any trick pitches. I had to get by with a fastball-slider, so I needed to know exactly what the hitters couldn't hit. It took me a couple of years to do that. Things fell together, and I had some decent years."

Craig Steven Swan had a brilliant college career at Arizona State, leaving Tempe as the all-time leader in wins (47), strikeouts (459), and innings pitched (457). The Mets took Swan in the third round of the 1972 draft after he was 16–1 with 154 strikeouts in 143 innings as a senior with the Sun Devils. Like Seaver, Swan pitched semipro ball in Alaska for three years.

The Cardinals were the first team to select Swan in the draft, taking him in the 23rd round out of high school in June 1968. Swan elected to attend college for four years, giving the Mets a chance to get him.

Swan was assigned to Double A Memphis right after the '72 draft and went 7–3 with a 2.24 ERA, 81 strikeouts, and 26 strikeouts in 108 innings over 14 starts. He was at Triple A Tidewater by 1973, posting a 7–5 record and a 2.34 earned run average in 100 innings despite appendicitis that led to peritonitis.

"I had a couple of attacks when I was a junior and senior in college," Swan said of his former appendix, "and they were able to not do the surgery so I could continue with the baseball season. By the time they got in there [to operate], I had gangrene because of the other two attacks, and I had some infection in there.

"And so I missed two months down in Tidewater, and then got to pitch [my major league debut]. But I didn't pitch that much that season."

Swan owned a 14–8 record and a 2.29 ERA through his first two pro seasons. His strikeout-to-walk ratio was better than 3-to-1, another reason for the Mets to promote him to the majors in September 1973.

He made his big-league debut on Labor Day following back-to-back shutouts with the Tides. He was thrust into Game 2 of a September 3 doubleheader against the Phillies at Shea after Jerry Koosman had outpitched Steve Carlton 6–0 in the opener.

Swan was roughed up by the Phils, allowing four earned runs over 4⅓ innings and leaving the game trailing 5–2 after the Mets had given him a 3–1 lead in the first inning.

"I remember my knees shaking," Swan said of his debut. "I remember I'd never seen so many people in one place in my life. And it was the second day that I had been in New York City. And so it was pretty overwhelming for me.

"I didn't do very well. I gave up four runs in four innings, but once the game got started, I lost all the nervousness and just got down to pitching, which happened every time I pitched anyway. I was hoping people could not see my knees shaking as I stood on the mound before the first pitch."

Two relief appearances followed, leaving him with an 8.64 ERA in his first stint as a Met.

The Mets still thought highly of Swan, as did several teams. New York balked at a proposed trade for Jimmy Wynn after the Astros insisted Swan be included in the deal.

Swan struggled mightily in 1974, going 2–3 with a 4.73 ERA for the Tides and 1–3 with a 4.45 ERA for the Mets. Swan picked up his first major league win at Wrigley Field May 11, holding the Cubs to four hits over six shutout innings of a 6–3 decision. He was eventually shut down September 10 after the Mets learned he had a stress fracture of his right elbow.

"I came out throwing and made the team as the fifth starter in '74. But I didn't get to pitch for six weeks because, back then, with off-days and rainouts, they would always skip over the fifth starter because Seaver would start again. So I didn't pitch for six weeks.

"When I came out after six weeks of not pitching, my mechanics were so bad that within a month I broke my elbow. But they didn't know it was broken until the end of the year.

"I got sent down to Tidewater and pitched with it broken. They had it X-rayed before I went down and brought me back up for some reason in September. I got X-rayed again, and then they could see the break. They overlapped the old X-ray on the new X-ray, and they could see the break because it was so small. But I had pitched with it for a couple of months.

"I thought that was the end of my career because when you have an injury that they can't find, you really get scared. That was the scariest time in my career because I thought I was done…at 24.

"I had the weirdest injuries when I was with the Mets. I even had boils on my armpits," Swan said with a hearty laugh as he recalled his medical history with the team.

The Mets didn't baby Swan in 1975 as he led the International League with 13 complete games, set a Tides record with a seven-game winning streak, and posted a 2.24 ERA. He was lit up at the major league level, going 1–3 with a 6.39 ERA. But Swan felt very satisfied about the season.

"Especially in 1974 with the elbow," said Swan. "It was like I was back. I was able to get going again in trying to stick in the big leagues. It was very satisfying.

"Just the year before, I thought I was done. I got my real estate license in Arizona. I was ready to sell land in Arizona at 24 years old."

The Mets worked Swan hard in 1975 despite his medical history. He remained the team's top pitching prospect and threw 177 innings for the Tides, second only to Sterling's 179 innings. Swan's work helped Tidewater win the Governor's Cup as International League champions under manager Joe Frazier, who was promoted to Mets skipper the following year.

"I was doing so well down at Tidewater that he would not let me throw on the side, which was two days after you started a game. He wouldn't let me throw on the side until the end of a game because he might use me in relief that day. And I got two saves besides the wins I got that year. You wouldn't see that today!"

Swan went north with the Mets out of spring training in 1976 and was superb in his third start, striking out 11 in a complete-game shutout of the Braves April 28. He pitched into the eighth inning of a 4–2 win over the Reds in his next outing before losing his next five starts. He allowed no earned runs over seven innings but took the loss in a 5–1 setback at San Diego on June 7. However, that game began a stretch in which he posted a 2.51 ERA over his final 15 appearances, including 14 starts. Swan had earned his spot in the rotation and finished the year 6–9 with a 3.54 earned run average. He was the youngster on a rotation that featured Seaver, Koosman, Matlack, and Mickey Lolich.

"I enjoyed being around those guys," Swan said 35 years later. "I learned a lot. My pitching style was a lot like Seaver's, and then Koosman would help me with my mechanics. It was really nice having those guys around."

But the starting five was quickly altered, beginning in the winter of 1977. Lolich opted to retire rather than spend another year in New York. Seaver was the next to go, banished to the Reds on June 15, 1977, following a dispute with management.

"By '77 we had free agency established. When they got rid of Tom, that's what the clubs were doing because Tom was our player rep, and he was bringing back the information from [union chief] Marvin Miller for us so we could learn what was going on.

"What happened back then was a lot of the club owners resented the player reps. I think that's probably the reason Tom got traded more than anything. He was our player rep and he was very strong-minded when it came to the union. We would sit with Marvin Miller and Tom for hours about that, and it's probably why the union is still the strongest."

Swan spent the next six seasons being the best pitcher on a bad team. That is to say, he was the Mets' ace when he was healthy. Swan managed to pitch more than 166 innings just twice during that span, doing it in 1978 and '79. He led the National League with a 2.43 ERA in '78 but won just nine times that season as the Mets scored three runs or fewer in 13 of his 28 starts.

"I think I only had one bad game that season. Out in L.A., I gave up some runs against the Dodgers in a couple of innings. But other than that, every start was pretty solid.

Craig Swann. Photo courtesy of David Ferry

"One of the funnier things was I was hoping for losses because, being in New York, my relatives who were all in California would read the newspaper, but if you didn't have enough decisions, you weren't included in the ERA leaders.

"So here I was 1–5 at the All-Star break with a 2.50 ERA…that had to be some kind of record. Luckily, I had a pretty good second half, too, and won eight games.

"I was really competing with a guy named Steve Rogers of the Expos. He and I were trading the lead back and forth through September. I couldn't exactly remember what happened, but Steve started working for the players' association years ago. I was calling to get some information, and he picked up. I said, 'Steve, how are you doing?' and we talked.

"I said, 'In '78, what happened to you?' I remember I had to go out and pitch against the Cardinals, and if I gave up less than two runs in seven or eight innings, I knew I was going to win it. But I didn't remember what happened to Steve.

"So when I got to talk to him, he said he had injured himself and couldn't finish the last two weeks. So he could have won it if I pitched poorly against the Cardinals."

Swan set career highs of 14 wins and 145 strikeouts in 1979, accounting for 22 percent of the Mets' 63 wins. He became the second pitcher in club history to win at least 14 games while the club finished with at least 90 losses. Although his ERA climbed nearly one run to 3.29, it can be argued that Swan pitched better in 1979 than he did while capturing the ERA crown.

"I certainly won more games, but I don't think I pitched as well as in '78," Swan opined. "It was just that I was getting more run support. I was pitching pretty well and keeping us in the games, but I seem to remember getting more run support, so I got more victories.

"I didn't know about the 90 losses and winning 14 games. I did know that the year before, when I won nine games, somebody told me I was the second pitcher in the history of baseball to win the ERA title and not win 10 games."

Although he was now the ace of the staff, Swan was also given an even greater responsibility in the bullpen. The Mets had a tomato garden in the home bullpen at Shea Stadium, the handiwork of bullpen coach Joe Pignatano. Swan watched the master gardener and eventually expanded the crops.

"Piggy had about eight tomato plants out there," said Swan. "He started teaching me how to garden around '77 or '78. By the time '80 rolled around, I was taking a Rototiller in there, and I had not eight tomato plants, but 20, plus every other vegetable. The garden was 50 feet long and 10 feet wide. I had green beans growing on the plexiglass.

"And I loved when fans came out and would sit there in the stands at the loge level, and I would explain what vegetable this was and what vegetable that was.

"I enjoyed doing the gardening more than watching the baseball because, as a starting pitcher, you watch four out of five games your entire career, and it gets a little old.

"I did enjoy that, and I still garden today because of Joe Pignatano."

A series of injuries would plague Swan over the next five years, just as soon as he signed the most lucrative contract in Mets history following the 1979 campaign. The length of the deal was both unprecedented in Mets circles and a testament to the team's belief he would be their ace for a long time.

Swan was outstanding at times in 1980, starting the season 5–6 with a 2.60 ERA in his first 17 starts. He went the distance in four of those starts and didn't allow more than four runs in any. That stretch included a three-hit shutout of the Braves on May 25 and a 10-inning, 6–2 win over the Dodgers on June 11. But he was sidelined from July 17 to August 15 with a sore shoulder, and shut down for good after August 21. Swan was diagnosed August 22 with a slightly torn rotator cuff that wouldn't require surgery.

Swan said he began to experience shoulder pain around the middle of 1980.

"I think I was 5–2 before the shoulder went," remembered Swan. "It was so devastating to me that I kind of lost my mind there for a while. I just signed a five-year contract and felt so guilty about having this guaranteed money and now I've torn my rotator cuff. I certainly wasn't going to give the money back, but I definitely had some bad feelings about that.

"Luckily, I got to come back and pitch a little bit more in '82. I did okay, but I never threw as hard as before the rotator cuff tear."

Swan went through a rigorous rolfing program during the winter of 1981, a regimen that would influence his next career. He was pitching for the Mets again by April 19, but he broke a rib in his next start when he was struck in the back by a throw from catcher Ron Hodges on a steal attempt.

A players' strike cost him nearly two months of the season, but the shoulder pain returned when he pitched in an exhibition game against the Blue Jays as a tuneup for the second half of the season.

Swan wouldn't pitch again until October 1, when he declared his shoulder pain-free after throwing 4⅓ innings against the Cubs.

Swan bounced back to have a strong season in 1982, leading the team with 11 wins and a 3.35 ERA. But his strikeouts were down to 67 over 166⅓ innings.

"I was always a pretty good spot pitcher, so I just had to do that better," Swan said of his reduced velocity. "I just had to hit my spots and not make mistakes. I pitched with Randy Jones and saw Tommy John, and they could do it."

A year later, he was 2–8 with a 5.51 ERA while often pitching out of the bullpen for interim manager Frank Howard. During spring training of 1983, Swan felt a pop in his right arm.

"I felt something in my triceps throwing a pitch in spring training against the White Sox in Sarasota," Swan said. "It made my arm kind of twinge. It really didn't hurt, but it made my arm go numb. The next pitch went against the backstop. I missed the catcher altogether.

"I struggled with that injury, which didn't really hurt me, but I could only throw 35–45 pitches at top velocity. And what they would note is the radar gun would go from 90 mph down to 80.

"I didn't do very well with that injury that season, and I didn't tell anybody, either, because I had just recovered from the rotator cuff and was feeling kind of guilty about that…being hurt all the time. So I just kept pitching the best I could. But they got me out of there soon enough because I wasn't doing very well."

Swan began the 1984 season with the Mets, but there was no tread on the tires. Swan came in to relieve a game against the Phillies April 21 with the Mets trailing 4–2 in the fifth. He served up a three-run homer to Glenn Wilson in a five-run fifth, and left the game after surrendering eight runs in three innings. He followed that with 4⅔ shutout innings in his next three appearances but was tagged for three runs in two innings against the Reds May 7. Swan was released by the Mets two days later, about five months short of fulfilling his five-year contract. The timing couldn't have been worse.

"They were starting to get some good ballplayers back," said Swan of the resurgent Mets, who were about to post their first winning season in eight years. "It was nice to see that. But I knew the arm wasn't going to let me [pitch]. I knew I was in trouble there. I was hanging on by a thread.

"It was frustrating in that I was hurt again. Little did I know that they were going to turn into the team that they did. They were showing signs of it when Davey Johnson came over.

"I went with the Angels, and the same thing was happening. I'd throw my 45 pitches and could feel this tingling down my arm. Again, it didn't hurt, but I would lose strength.

"The Angels sent me off to a surgeon in Houston. He opened up my arm and said I had torn the covering, this fascial tissue that forms the end of the muscle. I had torn it at the middle of the triceps, and this scar tissue grouped over a nerve, so when I used the muscle, the scar tissue would grind on the nerve and make my arm go dead.

"And it's interesting because as a rolfer, that's the tissue we mainly work on. It was kind of ironic that the tissue in the body that finished me in baseball is what I've been working on for 25 years in other people's bodies."

Swan earned a degree at the Rolf Institute in 1986. Rolfing deals with manipulation and lengthening of the tendons that cover muscles, thus alleviating pain that would otherwise lead to surgery. One might think a ballclub like the Mets would utilize his services, especially from one of their own.

"I've only had a couple of guys come here, and it was back in the early '90s when Steve Garland was the trainer. He sent Vince Coleman up here with his back issue. Bret Saberhagen was already getting rolfed by a rolfer in Kansas City.

"I did work with the team for a while, and they were loving it. But then the trainer said that if Dr. Altchek okayed the rolfing, the club would pay for it. So I worked down there for about a month and submitted the bills for the players I had worked on, and Al Harazin came down and said, 'We're not paying for this.' I said, 'Okay, I was misinformed then. I can't do it for free. It's too hard.'

"So I worked a couple of months with the Mets. I had a full practice up here, and it was almost too much for me to go down there and work with the team. Some of the players wanted to get the work done after the game, so it was a long day.

"I think there should be a rolfer on each staff, but what happened was, I noticed there was a little competition because the players actually wanted to come and see me, and I think the trainers and doctors didn't feel so good about that, like I was taking their boys or something. So I just kind of faded away.

"I enjoy working on athletes and things like that, but I also like working on everyday people just as much."

Swan remarried after his playing career ended…and he also ended up remarrying his second wife. "It's a little confusing, I'm sure," Swan says with a big laugh. Her name is Kelly, and we've been together off and on for 20 years, mostly on.

"The first wife gave me the boot after baseball because I was home too much. And that happens with baseball players. As soon as the husband stops traveling, the wife's not use to that."

Swan has two children from his first marriage. His daughter lives in Dayton, Ohio, with their three grandchildren. His son, Mark, is part of his very successful rolfing practice in Old Greenwich, Connecticut.

"The people can see all they want if they go to greenwichrolfing.com. I've had a website for a couple of years now. I've got a couple of videos on there with Dr. Rolf explaining the work, our theories and what we do.

"My son, who's been getting the work done on his body since he was six years old, pitched at Dartmouth and got his degree there. He tried the business world for two years and absolutely hated it. After that, he was at the Rolf Institute when he was 26. He's been working with me in this office for about five years, and it's been wonderful."

ML/Mets debut	vs. Phillies, 9/3/73 (4⅓ IP, 9 H, 4 ER, 2 K, 2 BB)
First ML/Mets strikeout	Bill Robinson, Phillies, 9/3/73
First ML/Mets win	@ Cubs, 5/11/74
First ML/Mets save	@ Dodgers, 7/18/82
Most strikeouts, ML/Mets game	13, vs. Phillies, 7/4/78
Low-hit ML/Mets CG	2, vs. Giants, 4/25/79; vs. Braves, 6/15/79

Acquired: Selected in the 3rd round of the 1972 draft.
Deleted: Released, 5/9/84. Signed by the Angels 5/23/84.
League Leader as a Met — ERA, 1978

Ron Swoboda

Outfielder, First Baseman   Bats right, throws right
Born: 6/30/44   Baltimore, Maryland
Height: 6'2"   Weight: 205   #14, 4

Ron Swoboda Mets Career

YEAR	GP	AB	R	H	2B	3B	HR	RBI	K	BB	SB	AVG	SLG	OBP
1965	135	399	52	91	15	3	19	50	102	33	2	.228	.424	.291
1966	112	342	34	76	9	4	8	50	76	31	4	.222	.342	.296
1967	134	449	47	126	17	3	13	53	96	41	3	.281	.419	.340
1968	132	450	46	109	14	6	11	59	113	52	8	.242	.373	.325
1969	109	327	38	77	10	2	9	52	90	43	1	.235	.361	.326
1970	115	245	29	57	8	2	9	40	72	40	2	.233	.392	.340
TOTAL	737	2212	246	536	73	20	69	304	549	240	20	.242	.387	.319

ML Career

YEAR	GP	AB	R	H	2B	3B	HR	RBI	K	BB	SB	AVG	SLG	OBP
65–73	928	2581	285	624	87	24	73	344	647	299	20	.242	.379	.324

Ask Ron Swoboda about team chemistry on the 1969 Mets and he'll also tell you about his friendship with a New York poet before mentioning his appreciation for French impressionism. He'll bring up Hunter S. Thompson when discussing his method for writing sports scripts. He's a lover of live music, enjoys museums, and is a patron of New Orleans artists. He's done freelance writing for *New Orleans Magazine*, creating such non-sports articles as "A Walk through the Garden of Sculptures," and also detailing the lives and works of local musicians.

All of this may come as a surprise to longtime Mets fans who remember him from his playing days. Swoboda had the physique of Li'l Abner, possessing broad shoulders the front office hoped would carry the club into the 1970s. He received the nickname "Rocky" by virtue of his inconsistent fielding during his early days with the team. He battled manager Gil Hodges at times, groused about playing time, and struck out a little too often. The overall package could give a fan the impression he was just another jock. In truth, he was—and is—quite the opposite.

Ronald Alan Swoboda was born in Baltimore and grew up in nearby Sparrows Point, where he was a three-sport athlete in baseball, football, and soccer. He played third base and the outfield for the high school team, in a league that played only a handful of games each season. The brevity of the schedule prompted him to find other outlets in which to improve his game.

It was in the summer leagues where Swoboda truly honed his skills, through the help of coaches like Sterling "Sheriff" Fowble. Fowble coached 14–16 age-group sandlot teams for nearly five decades and was recognized as one of Baltimore's finest youth baseball instructors. His list of players includes Hall of Famer Al Kaline and major leaguers Dave Boswell, Jim Spencer, and Phil Linz.

"I was 15 going on 16 when I first played for him," recalled Swoboda in a July 2011 interview. "I had played down in Baltimore County for teams that just didn't play that kind of competition. If you were going to progress, you needed someone where you were going to play better baseball.

"He recruited me. He saw me playing and asked if I wanted to come play for him. I didn't search him out. I didn't know who he was. He had seen me playing in some games and asked me if I wanted to try out. I didn't know what it was, but I thought, 'Well, this sounds like a good thing,' so I went and tried out.

"I didn't set the world on fire. I was probably one of the last—if not the last—contracts he [gave out] that year. In other words, you signed a contract to play for him. It's amateur stuff, but it kept you from jumping to somebody else. It meant you were playing for the team.

"You knew from the get-go that this was a pretty good team, and they had a history of excellence, and you were going to get tested a little bit. The first year there was a bit of a struggle because I was a third baseman who really wasn't a very good third baseman. I played behind a guy named Dave Pivec, who was a football player out of Patterson High School. He played for the Rams, played in Canada, went to Notre Dame. I got to play a little bit.

"The next year, Sheriff switched me to the outfield after the season had started, and I was pretty indignant about it.

It felt like a demotion. You're the starting third baseman one day, and the next day some kid comes in and he's playing third base. He had good hands and was a good third baseman, plain and simple. But I went into the outfield feeling like I'd just gotten demoted.

"A guy hit a ball over my head the first game. I ran this thing down, got it back in as fast as I could to the relay guy, and I think we threw him out at third base. It was the first play where I really got to do something, and it was like, 'Hey, man, that was cool. Maybe there's something to this.'

"I had a lot to learn about playing the outfield, and Sheriff's style was he yelled at you. It got your attention. I never took it as a negative. I took it as, 'Hey, listen up!' When you missed the cut-off man, he yelled at you. When you screwed it up, you heard about it. It wasn't like he yelled at you during the game, but he was enthusiastic and he got excited about it.

"If you were playing for him, you felt special. You felt like this was how you were going to learn to play baseball. This was the best baseball you could play in the city of Baltimore.

"I played for him, and I played for Walter Youse. There was also a year there when I played for the Dolphin Club. It wasn't a bad team. They weren't bad people. It's just that they weren't as good as Walter Youse's team. They played in that same 16–19 league. I got warned that this Walter Youse was this horrible guy who didn't care about you. I heard all kinds of propaganda about the guy. I played for him the next year, had a great time, and learned more baseball.

"Again, this was some of the best baseball you could play in the city of Baltimore. If I don't play for Sheriff Fowble, if I don't play for Walter Youse, I don't get to play professional baseball. I think it's as simple as that."

Swoboda's confidence level wavered in his late teens. He was giving his all to become a more refined baseball player, but he also had doubts his hard work would lead to a pro career. Swoboda's solution was to just work even harder.

"I just didn't think I was doing it. Some guy from Towson High School was throwing curveballs and getting me out. I remember going to the outfield after striking out or popping up or doing something awful. I stood in the outfield and, geez, tears came and I'm crying out there, upset because I had put a lot into this, and it looked to me like it wasn't going anywhere. It looked to me like it was over, and I was pretty upset about it.

"But that summer, I played for Walter Youse. I think we played more than 90 ballgames in the summer, and we played every day.

"It's like that thing Malcolm Gladwell talks about in *Outliers*. Bill Gates and those guys got on computers, and the computers spoke to them, and they just put a tremendous amount of hours into it. The Beatles were just another band from Liverpool before they got the gig in Scotland for a couple of months and they played six to eight hours a day or something crazy like that, where they were forced to play a lot. That sort of a regimen tells you the two most important things you need to learn, and that is, 'Can you play?' and 'Do you want to play?'

"It was such a regimen. We had a guy who could come out and throw us curveballs, so you'd have batting practice against curveballs. There ain't anything like that, where this guy could throw you some curveballs to the point where, when you saw one in a game, you'd seen one before. You had some familiarity with the animal. So I think that it put me ahead of the game as an amateur.

"We went to Johnstown for the AAABA tournament out there, and I had a real good tournament. A couple of scouts said something to me there, and I said, 'Well, I'm going back to the University of Maryland.' That was really where I was headed, except Sheriff Fowble, who was what they call the 'bird dog' scout, was a part-time scout for the Mets. He said, 'We want to talk to you, me and a guy named Wid Matthews.'

"They came into our home, sat me down, and said, 'Look, we're going to make an offer to you. We don't know if this offer's gonna be there tomorrow.' You know, they put a little pressure on me, and we weren't businesspeople. They gave me a piece of paper, and the piece of paper had $35,000 written on it. My mom and dad made about $13,500 with both of them working.

"So they had just offered me a whole lot of money, and I felt like I could do a few things with that money. And I did. I bought myself a car, bought my brother a car, I paid off what was left on my folks' house, I went back to college and paid a little bit of that, spent it on gas and insurance and picking up my own expenses from that point in time. I pretty much ate it all up, didn't do any investing with it, and moved on."

The Mets were in a bit of a rush to develop young talent when they signed Swoboda in September 1963. The team was in the process of completing a 111-loss season just a year after setting a modern major league record with 120 losses. Swoboda and a few other top prospects were invited to a pre–spring training camp in an effort to further evaluate the farm system.

"Casey Stengel and some of the big-league coaches wanted to take a look at the young players in 1964. I still hadn't played a minor league game and still got to go to spring training. I got to go to this pre–spring training camp and did pretty well, and then they invited me to regular spring training. So for a couple of weeks there, I was at regular spring training playing against everybody else.

"I ran into Gus Triandos, who had played for the Baltimore Orioles and had been traded to the Phillies. He gave me a trophy one time at a baseball dinner I went to. I think it was for Sheriff's team. And he had worked at Fox Chevrolet where my dad was a service salesman, and so I knew him. My dad had invited him to dinner one night, and he was really a great guy.

"We're out there on the field and here's Gus Triandos, and I got up to him and introduced myself. He couldn't have been nicer. He said, 'You sure know how to make a guy feel old!' I know how he feels now.

"I think he called me a fastball. He didn't tell me it was coming, but I think he got me a couple of fastballs off of Dallas Green, who was pitching for the Phillies. And I hit one over the center-field wall, which was about 380 feet at Al Lang Field."

By the end of camp, Swoboda was known as a guy who could "break a few windows." Unfortunately, he actually did it with his arm, not his bat. Swoboda possessed a very strong arm but had to work on charging balls without sailing his throws over the heads of cut-off men. One such throw soared completely over the playing field before creating a loud crash.

"Somebody was hitting me some balls and I was playing catch with Carlton Willey, trying to hit the cut-off man. I let one fly and it went up over his head and hit a glass panel on a door to Casey Stengel's office. There were three horizontal panels of glass to the door, and my throw went right through the middle one.

"It was opaque, and you could sort of see this figure walking down. He didn't open the door right away. He looked through the hole! And I thought, 'Well, this isn't good.'

"He opened the door and just said, 'Goddammit, throw the ball away from the clubhouse!' And I thought, 'That's good advice.'"

According to the 1965 Mets Yearbook, he hit .300 in Florida before the team resisted the urge to bring him north. But they still hastened his development by having him bypass rookie ball and Class A altogether.

"They sent me out to Buffalo," said Swoboda. "I opened my first season with the Buffalo Bisons. That was the Mets' Triple A team. So I go to my first big-league spring training and got sent out to Buffalo. I finished up spring training with Buffalo.

"My first game was in Richmond against the Yankees. I think I went 2-for-5 with a home run my first game. The next day, Mel Stottlemyre was pitching for them and he struck me out four times. He had a pretty good sinker-slider or sinker-curveball thing going. It was pretty good stuff, and I'd never seen anything like that before. I thought I hit every one one of 'em, and I didn't, you know what I mean? I saw 'em all pretty good, but I didn't hit 'em."

Double A pitchers weren't much of a problem for Swoboda, who hit .276 with a .348 on-base percentage, 14 home runs, 21 doubles, 61 RBIs, and 65 runs scored in 117 games. He finished second among all Eastern League players in home runs, one behind teammate Bobby Sanders while playing in 21 fewer games. Oddly, Sanders never played another game after 1964.

Swoboda also showed his good and bad side as a fielder in the Eastern League, recording 12 outfield assists and committing 11 errors.

Ron Swoboda drives a ball down the left-field line for a double that scores Cleon Jones from second to put the Mets ahead for the first time in the eighth inning of Game 5 of the 1969 World Series.

Swoboda fared well in the International League, batting .242 with three homers and 11 RBIs in 22 games while adding two more assists and three errors to his season totals. Buffalo finished a surprising third in the league at 80–69 behind a roster filled with Mets who had already washed out at the major league level. Of the 45 players who saw action with the '64 Bisons, only Swoboda, Ed Kranepool, Cleon Jones, and Dick Selma received any significant playing time with the Mets after 1964. Nineteen of those 45 players were at least 27 years old, another indication the Mets did not have many youngsters ready for the majors.

The Mets also had to prove to their fan base that there was actual talent in the farm system. The best under-24 players on the major league ballclub by the end of 1964 were Ron Hunt and Kranepool, and Hunt was actually a product of the Braves' minor league chain. Kranepool was just 20 at the start of 1965, but fans at Shea already had unfurled a banner asking, "Is Ed Kranepool Over the Hill?"

Swoboda made the 1965 Mets out of spring training, as did three other prospects who, like Swoboda, had just one year of pro ball under their belt. Swoboda believes he, Tug McGraw, Jim Bethke, and Danny Napoleon landed on the major league roster due in large part to a previous error committed by the front office. None of the four was polished.

"That was a complete lark based upon Paul Blair," Swoboda said of making the roster. "They lost Paul Blair after the 1962 season. In 1964 he was playing with the Orioles.

"They didn't protect him the way you were supposed to back in those days, before the draft. They had a rule in Major League Baseball called the First-Year Rule, meaning if you have played one year of organized professional baseball, you were subject to being drafted by any other team for a certain amount of money. What it did was keep the wealthy teams from buying up all the amateur talent with bonuses.

"The Mets just screwed up and did not protect Paul Blair. There were two ways to protect you. One was to designate you as the player they could send out, and the other was to keep you in the big leagues. And they didn't do that.

So they kept four of us—me, Tug McGraw, Jim Bethke, and Danny Napoleon—in the big leagues. My thinking was that it was an overreaction to losing Paul Blair, who in my opinion was the best center fielder of his era. I don't think there was anybody better than him."

Swoboda appeared as a pinch-hitter in the 1965 season opener, lining out to second against Hall of Famer Don Drysdale in the sixth inning. Swoboda smacked his first major league homer the next game, a solo shot off Turk

Farrell as a pinch-hitter in the bottom of the 11th to ignite a three-run rally before the Mets lost 7–6.

Stengel finally started Swoboda in the sixth game of the season, and showed enough confidence in the rookie's defensive ability to put him in center field. Swoboda homered in his first at-bat against Gaylord Perry and finished 1-for-4 before sitting out the next two games.

Swoboda continued to hit well through the first week of May. He socked another pinch-hit homer in the ninth inning at San Francisco on April 23, triggering a rally that saw the Mets turn an 8–4 deficit into a 9–8, 11-inning victory. Two days later, he produced an RBI double and a two-run homer while the Mets were building a 4–0 lead in a 4–3 triumph over the Giants on April 25. He also smacked a game-tying solo shot off Sammy Ellis in Cincinnati on May 1 before winning a game all by himself one week later, ripping a three-run homer and a solo shot in a 4–2 triumph against the Braves.

Swoboda's first two-homer game gave him a .320 average with seven round-trippers, 14 RBIs, 10 runs scored, and nine strikeouts in just 50 at-bats through his first 18 games. His slugging average was an outstanding .780 as Mets fans cheered their newest star.

Swoboda continued his torrid pace for the next 2½ weeks. He hit .423 during a seven-game hitting streak from May 15 to 21 and went 3-for-8 with three RBIs in a two-game set against the Cubs in late May. Swoboda was hitting .298 with a .375 on-base percentage, 11 homers, 28 RBIs, and 20 runs scored in 37 games by the time the Cubs left Shea Stadium.

It was among the greatest starts by a rookie in major league history. Swoboda was averaging a Ruthian one home run per 10.36 at-bats while recording a .698 slugging average. He became the everyday center fielder by April 25 and compensated for his 28 strikeouts by walking 14 times.

Swoboda had become a staple in the outfield just a few years after Willie Mays, Mickey Mantle, and Duke Snider were the mainstays at center field in Gotham. All three eventually were elected to the Hall of Fame, but none came close to duplicating Swoboda's first 37 games in the majors. Mantle had more RBIs and runs scored in his first 37 games, although he did it with 35 more at-bats. Mays compiled a higher on-base percentage through 37 games. Otherwise, Swoboda had them all beat.

It's not as if Swoboda was facing inferior pitching during those 37 games. He came to the plate against Hall of Famers Drysdale, Perry, Juan Marichal, Jim Bunning, and Bob Gibson, along with 20-game winners Joey Jay, Jack Sanford, Claude Osteen, and Jim Maloney.

And Swoboda was enjoying his off days, taking in the sights and sounds of the neighboring boroughs.

"Me and Tug McGraw, we would get on the No. 7 train, ride downtown, look at the buildings, and walk around. One day we went into town and talked our way into the audience of the Johnny Carson show. They let us in. We didn't know anything about what it took to get in the audience, but we bullshitted our way in there.

"We didn't have a clue about the city. There was one of the special cops, Freddie Amadeo, I think his name was. He lived in Brooklyn, and he'd invite us over to his house to have a big Italian meal on Sunday nights after the game, and it was fabulous. And we'd go over to Coney Island and ride the Cyclone or get in the batting cages. It was cool.

"We'd go downstairs in Freddie's house, and his club basement was a shrine to the Brooklyn Dodgers. He had all these pictures and framed newspaper clippings from when he followed them as a kid. I remember one time Tug turned to me and he said, 'Do you think we'll ever be on anybody's wall like this?' And with my usual prescience, I said, 'I don't know.'

"Now you're 67 years old and people still pay money to get your autograph and want to tell you all the sparkle you put in their life by things you did on the ball diamond when all you were trying to do was keep yourself in the big leagues, just trying to stay around as long as you could.

"It's wonderful, and it gets better as you get older—the fact that people still come out and tell you how much enjoyment they got out of watching you play."

Swoboda was an early favorite to win the 1965 NL Rookie of the Year Award before the Mets faced Bob Veale in a 6–1 loss to the Pirates at Shea Stadium on May 28. Swoboda went 0-for-4 with two strikeouts to drop his average to .288. It was the start of a season-ending stretch in which Swoboda hit only .200 with eight homers and 22 RBIs in 98 games, compiling more strikeouts (76) than hits (57) while walking only 19 times. Kranepool wound up representing the Mets in the All-Star Game, and he also slumped badly in the second half as the Mets finished 50–112.

Swoboda and Kranepool combined to hit only .210 with seven homers and 29 RBIs in 428 at-bats after the All-Star break, leaving Mets fans to wonder again if the franchise had any legitimate prospects in the system. Yogi Berra served as the team's first-base/hitting coach but was unable to pass along any tips to snap the two players out of their slumps.

"I didn't know anything about what I was doing," Swoboda admitted. "I had no clue. I'm not sure I ever had any clue about hitting when I was playing. I don't think I had any real awareness of what made my swing and how to deconstruct it. I had no idea of the technique of swinging a bat.

"Yogi tried, for sure. I make a joke when I say Yogi said about hitting, 'Well, if you can't hit it, don't swing at it.'

"'What about two strikes, Yogi?' I'd ask. 'Well, then you have to swing at it,' he'd say. And you're like, 'Well, I'm glad you cleared that one up.'

"There weren't a lot of hitting coaches around back then. I had trouble with the breaking ball, the slider. Galen Cisco got me out there a little bit. The coaches had him throwing me sliders. It seemed to make my swing longer because you're trying to slow your swing up. Without thinking about it, you're trying to hit the ball to right field, and I really didn't know how to hit the ball to right field. So you made your swing longer, which was counterproductive in terms of getting to the ball quicker, and I forgot how to hit. I couldn't make it happen."

Swoboda finished the season with a team-best 19 home runs, a Mets rookie record that stood until Darryl Strawberry belted 26 in 1983. Swoboda also was third on the club with 50 RBIs and second with 52 runs scored, but his .228 average was a disappointment considering his excellent start. Any serious comparisons between Swoboda and "Willie, Mickey, and the Duke" had ended.

Cleon Jones was the starting center fielder in 1966, which pushed Swoboda to the left side of the outfield for most of the season. Jones finished fourth in the NL Rookie of the Year balloting after hitting .276 with eight homers and 57 RBIs, evidence that the Mets did indeed have talent in the minors.

Meanwhile, Swoboda's playing time was reduced a bit as the Mets went 66–95, the first time the franchise had avoided 109 losses. Swoboda got off to a slow start and never compiled a batting streak longer than four games. He was batting .188 before hitting a three-run homer and a two-run triple in Game 1 of a doubleheader at Philadelphia on July 4. Swoboda finished with 50 RBIs for the second straight year but batted only .222 with eight homers and 21 extra-base hits in 112 games.

New general manager Bing Devine made several moves following the 1966 season, two of which involved starting outfielders. The first sent Hunt and original Met Jim Hickman to the Dodgers for outfielder Tommy Davis, one week before the Mets acquired outfielder Don Bosch and pitcher Don Cardwell from the Pirates for Gary Kolb and Dennis Ribant. Bosch was hailed as the team's center fielder for the next decade, which meant moving Jones to right field and putting Swoboda in a platoon with Kranepool at first base.

The revamped outfield lasted 23 games altogether, long enough for Bosch to hit himself out of the lineup. Swoboda was back in right field by May 12 despite a slow start at the plate.

Swoboda started just 10 of the Mets' first 23 games, hitting .171 in 35 at-bats before starting in right field for the first time at St. Louis. He responded by going 3-for-5 and scoring twice in a 7–5 loss before collecting two hits the next game. Swoboda was hitting .260 by the time the Mets returned home a few days later.

Swoboda was one of the Mets' best hitters for average over the final two months. He opened August on a seven-game hitting streak and hit .362 with three home runs and 16 RBIs in 94 at-bats that month. His average stood at a career-high .281 with 13 home runs and 53 RBIs in 449 at-bats by the end of the season. The year included a 10-game hitting streak and featured several outstanding defensive plays in right. He had eight assists in 108 games in the outfield, but he also committed nine errors after leading

all National League left fielders in fielding percentage in 1966.

"I went to winter ball after the '66 season," Swoboda said. "I went down to Puerto Rico and started off great guns there, but then I got so homesick. I didn't have a real good season there as it turned out, but when I got back and went to spring training, I got going good in '67 and had a very good year.

"In truth, I really didn't hit .281. I had five bunt base hits that year. Nobody thinks about that, but if you add up what it was worth in points, it was worth 15 points. It's more like I hit .266 and I bunted .281."

The Mets rewarded him with a healthy pay hike. He accepted a one-year contract that was worth four times what he made his rookie season.

"I walked in there with Johnny Murphy to start negotiating a contract. I think I might have been making $14,000–$15,000, and I think Murphy offered me $28,000. I said, 'Mr. Murphy, you know if I could get $30,000, it would be the difference in me living in a nicer apartment. And, I like a nice round number.'

"He said, 'If I give you the $30,000, are you going to give us the same kind of effort?' I said, 'Of course! I only play one way, and you're not gonna make me rich.'

"But it seemed to me like an awful lot of money when I walked out of his office based on what I had been making. I made $7,500 my rookie year, and that included a $1,500 big-league bonus. And I was living off of that in New York. In fact, I was saving money. I lived within my means. I was a waif. I was a naif. I was this kid."

The Mets were impressed with Swoboda's maturity and ability to hit to right field. Whatever disappointment they felt in 1966 was wiped out after he hit .291 with 12 home runs and 48 RBIs in his final 107 games of '67.

But the Mets returned to the National League cellar, finishing 61–101 to prompt a managerial change. Westrum was told in late September that he would be replaced, causing him to leave with 11 games left in the season. The Mets hired Gil Hodges as their skipper during the 1967 World Series, beginning an oil-and-vinegar relationship between the former Dodgers great and Swoboda.

"I got on his nerves," admitted Swoboda. "We didn't have an easy relationship, and I blame my immaturity. We kind of got on one another's nerves. I don't know what it was. It was something there that I should have just shut up and listened to him, but I just couldn't pull it off.

"He never asked you to do anything that wasn't what you ought to be doing. He didn't want you to be doing anything but get better and play better and do good. He was the manager making the decisions, but there was something about [the situation]. We just grated on each other.

"He knew so much baseball, and if I could've just shut up, done what I was supposed to do, and kept it zipped up, I would have been fine. But I was emotional, and he wasn't emotional. He had been through World War II. I don't know how much anybody knows about that. He was a marine in the island campaigns. I even asked Gilly, his kid, if he even talked about it. He said, 'He sat me down one time, told me a couple of things and said that's the way we're going to leave it.'"

There were no problems between the two at the start of the 1968 season as Swoboda started the first 44 games. He continued to hit the ball to all fields and emerged as a better defensive option than newly acquired Art Shamsky in right. Swoboda opened the season by going 2-for-4 with an RBI single and a three-run homer, putting the Mets ahead 4–0 by the third inning in San Francisco. It was 4–2 with one out in the bottom of the ninth until Jim Ray Hart stroked an RBI single and Jesus Alou followed with a two-run double to give the Giants a 5–4 win. New manager, same old Mets.

Swoboda also hit safely in his next four games and ended the month with a .267 average, seven home runs, 16 RBIs, and 12 runs scored in 16 games. He became the second player in Mets history to homer in four consecutive games, doing it from April 19 to 21 to tie Larry Elliot's team record. Swoboda's strong start earned him the cover of *Sports Illustrated*'s May 6 issue, making him the first Met other than Stengel to receive the honor.

Swoboda had a .275 average by mid-May, but his production dropped significantly the rest of the season. He drove in six runs during a season-high nine-game hitting streak in July and had 10 home runs and 46 RBIs through 90 games by the end of the month. But other than a one-homer, five-RBI game against the Giants on August 20, Swoboda failed to provide the same production he contributed over the first four months and finished with a .242 average and team highs of 59 RBIs, 52 walks, and 113 strikeouts. Although his batting average represented a 39-point drop over 1967, it was 14 points higher than the Mets' team mark in the "Year of the Pitcher." Only three other Mets with at least 350 at-bats had had a better average than Swoboda.

Pitching allowed the Mets to finish out of the cellar at 73–89. They compiled the fourth-best ERA in the National League at 2.72 and were second with 17 shutouts, 32 saves and 1,014 strikeouts. The fielding was strong up the middle, although Agee was terrible at the plate in his first season as the Mets' center fielder.

The 1969 lineup looked a lot like it did at the end of '68, although Hodges had hoped to turn rookie Amos Otis into a third baseman before going with a platoon of newly acquired Wayne Garrett and Ed Charles. Hodges also had a lefty-right tandem at second with Al Weis and Ken Boswell before the platooning affected Swoboda.

Rookie Rod Gaspar was the Mets' starting right fielder for the first 10 games while Swoboda split time with Jones in left. Swoboda returned to right field on April 19 and started there for 16 of the next 18 games before Hodges utilized a starting outfield of Jones, Otis, and Agee for four straight games in May.

The outfield situation became clearer by mid-May, but the solution continued to cut into Swoboda's playing time. Shamsky was activated on May 15 after recovering from a back injury suffered during camp. Shamsky and Swoboda became a lefty-righty platoon, with the lefty-hitting Shamsky seeing the bulk of the action in right while Swoboda received playing time in place of Jones. Swoboda started just 17 games in left from May 15 to August 20 before emerging as the everyday starter in right field for the team's stretch drive.

"That drove me crazy," Swoboda said of platooning, "and I told Gaspar that. I understand what Gil was doing, and Gaspar was a pretty good player and a damned good defensive player. He could hit a little bit, too.

"But it drove me crazy that he put him in there as a defensive replacement for me, and I worked my ass off trying to get him to not do that. I finally did, and it was one little battle I won."

The sporadic starts didn't bother Swoboda at the plate early on. He batted .364 in his first 11 games and carried a .320 average into May before tailing off. Swoboda hit only .158 with two homers and eight RBIs in 32 games from May 1 to July 4, but the Mets went 20–12 in those games to work themselves back into the NL East race.

New York was 18–23 and nine games behind the Cubs before a team-record 11-game winning streak from May 28 to June 10. The Mets continued to inch nearer the Cubs, cutting the deficit to 3½ games following Tom Seaver's one-hitter versus Chicago on July 9.

Swoboda never got his batting average above .251 after May, but he provided key hits for a popgun offense that was bolstered by the acquisition of Donn Clendenon on June 15. Swoboda worked out a game-winning, bases-loaded walk to beat the Giants on June 1, hit an RBI single to ignite a five-run comeback in a win over the Pirates on July 6, singled home the go-ahead run in a 9–7 win against the Expos and went 3-for-4 with an RBI and two runs scored in a 10-inning triumph at Montreal on July 20.

The Mets started to sag in late July and fell into third place, 9½ games behind the Cubs by August 13. That's when Swoboda began to raise his production, driving in 13 runs in his final 11 games of the month. He supplied two RBIs in four of those 11 games, and drove in four runs—including a go-ahead, three-run double—in a 7–4 comeback win over the Dodgers on August 24.

The Mets continued to chip away at Chicago's lead and finally moved ahead of the Cubs with a doubleheader sweep of the Expos on September 11. Swoboda helped keep the Mets in first place the rest of the way, winning two games with his bat down the stretch.

Two days after climbing into first, the Mets were locked in a 1–1 tie in the eighth inning at Pittsburgh when Swoboda unloaded a grand slam off reliever Chuck Hartenstein. Two days later, Swoboda allowed New York to pull out an improbable win against a record-setting pitcher.

Steve Carlton baffled the Mets in St. Louis on September 15, becoming the first pitcher in major league history to strike out 19 hitters in a nine-inning game. Swoboda atoned for a first-inning strikeout by smacking a go-ahead, two-run blast in the fourth. But the Cardinals scratched out a pair of runs to go ahead 3–2 the following inning before Swoboda became Carlton's 13th strikeout in the sixth.

Carlton got out of a bases-loaded jam in the seventh by fanning Amos Otis to preserve the Cardinals' lead. But the Mets surged back on top an inning later as Agee led off with a single and scored on Swoboda's second two-run blast of the night. Swoboda's first multi-homer game since May 8, 1965, allowed the Mets to surge 4½ games in front of Chicago with 15 to play.

The Mets were now another great story in what was a very memorable year in U.S. history. The decade is a tumultuous timeline that begins with the Vietnam War and the election of John F. Kennedy as President. Kennedy was assassinated 79 days after Swoboda signed his first contract, and the war in Southeast Asia escalated under President Lyndon Johnson while a social war grew in America. Johnson pushed through the Civil Rights Act in 1964 but was unable to abate urban unrest despite his Great Society. Riots led to fires that burned down urban communities from Newark to Watts, and the anger reached its zenith following the assassination of Dr. Martin Luther King in April 1968. Robert F. Kennedy was killed two months later, leaving Americans to wonder what the hell was happening to the country.

And then came the 1969 Mets, whose roster was a compilation of people from all walks of life. Ed Charles, a 36-year-old African American third baseman who spent his first 10 pro seasons in the minors as he "waited his turn," lockered near 33-year-old Don Cardwell, a crew-cut Caucasian from North Carolina. White Texans Jerry Grote, Ken Boswell, and Nolan Ryan hung out with Black Alabamans Tommie Agee and Cleon Jones. The anchors of the bullpen were 24-year-old Californian Tug McGraw and 31-year-old Ontario native Ron Taylor. The manager and coaches hailed from Indiana, St. Louis, Brooklyn, and North Carolina. In many respects, the Mets clubhouse was the Great Society.

"Those were the '60s," said Swoboda. "And there was this incredible social experiment going on…free love, the flower generation, anti–Vietnam War and the great economy as a result of the war industry, a man landing on the moon, and Woodstock. It was just an interesting time.

"The liberal capital of America is New York, and we were exposed to a lot of different things."

The success of the Mets allowed players to walk in different circles. Pearl Bailey was a huge fan and would head to Shea when she was in town. Jackie and Ari Onassis would take in a ballgame or two with Caroline and John. Jones and Agee were invited to barbecues thrown by Louie Armstrong. Swoboda also branched out following a chance meeting with a wordsmith.

"A real good friend of mine was a poet named Joel Oppenheimer, a wonderful fan. We met at some kind of panel discussion on educational TV. I was well-coifed, short back then, and an athlete. And in walks this long-haired hippie poet who's pretty much an alcoholic but a different kind of alcoholic. I never saw Joel Oppenheimer drunk back then. He drank by the clock, always kept a little bit of it in him. But he was never under the influence, and he told me it served its purpose. And he smoked, and his fingernails were getting a little black, and he's killing himself with alcohol and cigarettes, but he was in every other way an urbane, gentle, man, a scholar. I'd never met a scholar before.

"And he was a huge baseball fan. His father was a Giants fan and he became a Mets fan. He believed in the advocacy of the position you were in when you watched the game. You must remain there to keep the good vibe going. You didn't get up and change your seat or anything if things were going good. You did it if things when things were going bad.

"But he used to play these games going through the baseball encyclopedia and getting all of these Jewish baseball All-Star teams, a baseball team full of guys whose names were colors, guys who were Polish. He just had fun with it.

"We became pretty good friends. He lived in Westbeth on the West Side in an apartment building that was rent-controlled for artists of various sorts. We visited him there quite a bit.

"Later on in his life he became the poet-in-residence at New England College up in Henniker, New Hampshire. That's where he died.

"I didn't know what to do with his poetry. To my uninformed ears it was reasonably profane and full of references to male and female organs used in very creative ways, double-backed beasts and other allusions to sexual acts. I didn't know what to make of it, frankly.

"Later on, after I had read a little bit and tried to write a little bit—I have books of his stuff that dazzle me—we talked about how he learned poetry at Black Mountain College, which was an educational experiment outside of Asheville, North Carolina. That was where he met a guy by the name of Butler, who gave him the best idea of what you needed to be a poet. He didn't try to tell him how to write poetry, he told him what he needed to be a poet. What you needed to know was everything else. You need to fill in the blanks, and off he went."

Swoboda continued to expand his awareness in other forms of expression. If he found something of interest, it was consumed with the same passion he had for baseball.

"A neighbor who cared about art had this big book of impressionist art on the coffee table. I just happened to flip through it one day while having a beer, looked at it, and went, 'Wow, that's pretty interesting.' And I went out and got myself one of those books just like hers and started a love affair with art that's really centered around the impressionists. I just sort of parachuted into the middle of French Impressionism and spread out to a few things;

a little bit of the salon stuff that was going on around the same time. A little bit of Postimpressionism. Early 20th-century guys.

"I have collected a few books on it and visited a fair amount of it here and in Paris. Really, the most wonderful place I can go to is my art books."

The 1969 Mets continued to create their own work of art and clinched their first playoff berth on September 24 as Swoboda walked and scored in a 6–0 shutout of the Cardinals. He ended the regular season hitting .235 with a .326 on-base percentage, nine homers, 52 RBIs, and 38 runs scored in 327 at-bats, finishing third on the team in RBIs and fourth in walks despite his part-time status.

The right-field platoon was a major reason for the Mets' success. Swoboda and Shamsky combined for 23 home runs and 99 RBIs in 630 at-bats over 209 appearances. Meanwhile, Agee led the team with 76 RBIs while Jones managed just 75 despite a .340 average.

The platoon continued into the first-ever National League Championship Series, which was bad news for Swoboda. The Braves went with three right-handers during the series, putting Swoboda on the bench in favor of Shamsky. Swoboda never got in a game as Shamsky recorded a team-high .538 average in 13 at-bats to help the Mets sweep Atlanta.

Swoboda's first World Series game was played in his hometown as the Mets traveled to Baltimore for the first two contests. He was inserted into the starting lineup against lefty Mike Cuellar in the opener and provided one of the Mets' six hits, but Swoboda's first play was forgettable.

Don Buford opened the bottom of the first by hitting a deep fly ball toward Swoboda, who moved awkwardly toward the fence. Swoboda jumped for the ball but was a couple of feet from the fence, leaving him unable to brace his fall. The ball sailed over the fence to give the Orioles a lead while Swoboda tried to gather himself.

"It should have never gotten over the wall. I misplayed it as badly as you could misplay it. I was nervous, frozen. I looked like a mechanical man going back on the ball. There was no smoothness. I never really connected with it.

"That little nine-year-old kid who really didn't know how to play baseball but was just beginning is in there with you. And his eyes are as big as saucers, and you've got to get him to calm down a little bit.

"I think the immensity of a World Series, I hadn't gotten loose into it yet, and I hadn't bought into the idea that there we were. And here comes a pretty tough play, and I misplayed it—let it get over the wall."

It was the only run of the inning, and it left Swoboda pretty ticked off.

"I was barking that I should have caught it, and Ed Kranepool came by and said something pretty pointy about, 'Shut the fuck up and get the next one.' And it was the right thing to say. It was like, get off of that, go out and get the other ones.

"I loosened up a little bit, and the rest of the World Series was pretty good."

The Orioles added three runs in the fourth and coasted to a 4–1 victory. Swoboda walked during the Mets' lone scoring rally in the seventh and singled leading off the ninth before Cuellar shut the door.

The Mets got even in Game 2 as Jerry Koosman and Ron Taylor combined for a two-hitter in a 2–1 victory. Swoboda started against lefty Dave McNally and went 0-for-4, leaving him 1-for-7 through two games. Swoboda went 5-for-8 the rest of the way to finish with a team-high six hits despite sitting out the Mets' 5–0 win over Jim Palmer and the Birds in Game 3.

October 15, 1969, would become the second-greatest day of Swoboda's career, and not because he became the first Met to collect three hits in a World Series game. The Mets carried a two-games-to-one Series lead into the afternoon and had Seaver on the mound against Cuellar.

Seaver had a three-hit shutout and a 1–0 lead after Blair led off the ninth with a fly ball to Swoboda. But Frank Robinson and Boog Powell followed with consecutive singles to put the tying run on third base with one out and Brooks Robinson at the plate.

Robinson hit a sinking liner that, at first glance, appeared to be a certain base hit. Swoboda took off at the crack of the bat and made a perfect route toward the ball before diving, his entire body stretched horizontally. The ball was just a few inches from landing when Swoboda snared it as he hit the ground, completing the Mets' third tremendous outfield catch in two days. The play was breathtaking on television as Swoboda doesn't appear on screen until the last second as the camera keys in on the expected landing spot of the ball. He also had the presence of mind to get up quickly and toss a throw to the plate, but it was too late to prevent Frank Robinson from scoring the tying run.

It was an amazing catch, and also a very risky one. The safe play would have been for Swoboda to play it on the hop and prevent Powell from moving over to third. If he doesn't make the diving grab, the ball rolls to the wall and Powell scores standing up with the go-ahead run while Brooks Robinson chugs into third. Swoboda's bit of daring made the catch even more remarkable.

"I just didn't see any other alternative at the time," Swoboda said of his decision to dive for the ball. "I broke when the ball was hit.

"I had worked very hard with Eddie Yost on taking balls off the bat. What he'd hit me were line drives. Some of them ended up ground balls, but basically he was hitting it hard right at me. That was our little practice—five or 10 minutes of line drives or ground balls, catching them on the right foot and turning the right way, reading it from about 150 feet away. That's how I practiced in the outfield, and it made me better, made me comfortable on line drives. I read the ball off the bat quicker, better, more accurately.

"I took the best route that I thought I could take to get to that ball. Brooksie hit it pretty hard.

"If you see where I went to get it, if I take a deeper angle, it might get by me, anyway. Take a deeper angle and it's gonna take longer to get there. That thing never had much altitude. You might end up with a bad hop. There's no guarantee that I would get to it if I take a deeper angle.

"I just went for it, and there wasn't a whole lot of thinking about it. It was reflex, and I had worked on my reflexes and I did read the ball pretty well off the bat and I did get a good jump on the ball. I think probably because conventional wisdom was that I wasn't all that much out there in right field, I felt I was a pretty damn good right fielder after all the work I put into it. And I played with confidence out there.

"Look, I missed the first ball that came to me because I was so freakin' nervous I'm lucky I didn't break something, I was so tight. But after that I loosened up and played. I was a pretty good right fielder and I did work at getting good jumps on the ball. And I got a good jump on that one, and the only thing I could see was to keep going and try for the catch.

"I thought it was going to beat me. I did for the longest time. There was no way you could feel like you were gonna catch that ball."

"Only Swoboda would make that catch, I'm telling you right now," said Gaspar. "Only he would have attempted to make that catch because of his personality. That was the greatest outfield play I've ever seen. No doubt. Better than Willie Mays or any of the other guys because Mays was supposed to make those catches. [Jim] Edmonds is supposed to make those catches. Swoboda wasn't supposed to make those catches, and he made that catch, and I'm telling you it was the best play I've ever seen by an outfielder."

But the inning wasn't over. Elrod Hendricks, who was similarly robbed of a run-scoring, extra-base hit by one of Agee's two incredible catches the day before, lined out to Swoboda to keep the game tied 1–1. Swoboda had three putouts in the inning and received a standing ovation as he jogged back to the dugout.

Swoboda followed his circus catch by collecting his third hit of the day, putting runners on first and third with two out in the bottom of the ninth. But the game went into the 10th inning before Seaver worked out of a first-and-third jam to keep it 1–1. The Mets won it in the bottom of the 10th as pinch-hitter J.C. Martin laid down a bunt in an effort to move Gaspar to third base with Agee due up next. Reliever Pete Richert retrieved the bunt and made a toss to first that hit Martin on the elbow, allowing Gaspar to score the winning run to put the Mets up 3–1 in the series.

It was just the latest implausible victory in the Mets' improbable charge to the championship. Seaver went the distance on a six-hitter, Swoboda made a sensational catch, and the game ended with a throwing error on a bunt play. One day earlier, Agee's two circus catches saved at least five runs in a 5–0 shutout. Two games earlier, Jerry

Koosman carried a no-hitter into the seventh before the Mets scratched out a 2–1 victory.

But it appeared the Series was heading back to Baltimore after the Orioles carried a 3–0 lead into the bottom of the sixth in Game 5. McNally socked a two-run homer off Koosman in the top of the third before Frank Robinson's mammoth blast gave the O's a three-run cushion later in the inning.

The Mets eventually tied the game as Clendenon launched a two-run homer in the sixth before Al Weis hit a solo shot an inning later.

Koosman worked a perfect eighth before Jones came through again with a leadoff double in the bottom half. Clendenon failed to move Jones to third, grounding out to Brooks Robinson to put the game in the hands of Swoboda with one out and reliever Eddie Watt on the mound.

Watt was a tough right-handed sidearmer who held right-handed batters to a .140 average during the 1969 regular season. Hodges didn't even consider lifting Swoboda for Shamsky, allowing Swoboda to provide the game-winning hit of the World Series. Swoboda hit a flair down the left-field line, about 100 feet past the third-base bag. Buford, who'd made Swoboda look silly with his home run in the opener, got a late break on the ball before trapping it. Jones immediately sensed that Buford was having trouble with the ball and circled third before scoring on Swoboda's double. Swoboda later scored from second on an error by Powell, giving the Mets a 5–3 lead that would hold up as Koosman completed a five-hitter. The series ended when Jones grabbed Davey Johnson's fly ball to the warning track, leading Mets fans to tear up the field for the third time in 22 days.

Swoboda hit .400 in 15 at-bats and performed one of the greatest catches in World Series history. But Clendenon received the *Sport Magazine* MVP after hitting three homers, and Weis was given the Babe Ruth Award for leading the team with a .455 average and socking the game-tying home run in Game 5.

"I think so much happened that seemed so natural and easy because we weren't trying to make anything happen. We were just trying to play the best we could play. We didn't have any responsibility back in '69. We got on this incredible role with a great pitching staff, and the addition of Donn Clendenon—which was the key piece in the puzzle.

"There were some arm problems that straightened out for Koosman, Gentry, and McAndrew. And this collection of arms got on a role, and you just felt like we came out of the weeds. We were flopping around .500 the first half of the season, thinking, 'Well, it looks like we're gonna be a little better. If we'd been .500 it would have still been the best year we'd ever had. Eighty-one wins would have been quite a step forward, but we did a little better than that.

"The synergy and the implausibility of all the pieces coming together the way they did when they did, all of that staggers my imagination. I can't explain it."

The celebration continued through the winter, although some might say the hangover lasted through the summer of 1970. Swoboda and the Mets were honored with a ticker-tape parade up the Canyon of Heroes the day after the series. They appeared on *The Ed Sullivan Show*, singing "Ya Gotta Have Heart." Some performed in a Las Vegas lounge act with comedian Phil Foster, making more money during their two-week run on the Strip than a rookie earned in 1969. They were guests of honor on the Rubber Chicken Circuit, getting a few hundred bucks here and there to regale fans with tales of a wonderful season.

Swoboda passed on the easy money he could have made performing in Vegas, instead heading to the Far East.

"I went to Vietnam for my second USO tour," said Swoboda "I had done it in '68. In '69, we're still there, and I was not a supporter of the war, but I was a supporter of the soldiers, most of whom were drafted. The implications of that are different from today, where all of the people in the military now joined the National Guard of their own volition, or they joined the regular Army of their own volition. What's happened to them after that is activation and lots of tours in dangerous places.

"Back then, most of the guys were drafted, and there were 50-some-thousand people killed in that war. My point was, it's an unpopular war, but these guys, a lot of them didn't choose to be there. It was chosen for them.

"So I thought it would be a neat thing to do, and I was curious to see what it looked like, what the place looked like. It's a big chunk of history there. I didn't want to be in the service, I don't want to be carrying an M-16, I can tell you that. But I did want to see it, and I wanted to see if we could make people feel like we didn't hate them because they got drafted."

The 1970 season began with the Mets winning their opener for the first time in club history as Swoboda scored the tiebreaking run in the 11th inning of a 5–3 triumph in Pittsburgh. But it was evident early on that the Mets didn't have the same spark that catapulted them to greatness the previous year. Kranepool got off to a terrible start and was banished to the minors in late June, leaving Swoboda without one of his closest pals on the team. Swoboda crawled into Hodges' doghouse by butting into an argument between Hodges and Kranepool after a game.

Swoboda also wasn't thrilled with his playing time, which was trimmed again in 1970 as he now battled Shamsky, newly acquired Dave Marshall, and rookie Ken Singleton for right-field duty.

Swoboda got off to a nice start, making 21 starts while appearing in 38 of the Mets' first 42 games. He went 2-for-4 with four RBIs in a 5–1 win over the Cardinals on May 26, leaving him with a .284 average with 16 ribbies for the season. Swoboda ended the month by going 4-for-11 with two homers, five RBIs and four runs scored in a doubleheader sweep of the Astros, which gave him 17 RBIs in his last 15 games.

Swoboda vs. Willie Mays, Mickey Mantle, and Duke Snider after 37 ML Games

Player (Yr)	AB	AVG	OBP	SLG	HR	RBI	R
Swoboda ('65)	114	.298	.375	.698	11	28	20
Mays ('51)	139	.288	.381	.532	7	27	20
Mantle ('51)	149	.289	.353	.443	4	31	29
Snider ('47)	74	.243	.282	.311	0	5	6

However, Swoboda's bat was silent in June as he hit .116 in 43 at-bats over 18 games without delivering an RBI. The slump dropped his average to .222 and prompted the Mets to recall Singleton when they farmed out Kranepool on June 24.

Swoboda rebounded in July, going 2-for-2 in his first game of the month and batting .414 with five home runs, 10 RBIs, and 10 runs scored in 17 games, including eight starts. The Mets won 11 of the 17 games to keep pace with the Pirates and Cubs in a very tight NL East race.

But Swoboda started just eight games in August and ended the month in a 3-for-24 slump. It became a 3-for-49 skid after Swoboda went hitless in his first 15 at-bats in September. Singleton and Shamsky became the new platoon in right as Swoboda started just three of the Mets' final 27 games. Swoboda ended up hitting .233 with nine homers, 40 RBIs, and 29 runs scored in what was then a career-low 245 at-bats.

The Mets had a share of first place in mid-September but dropped 10 of their final 15 games to finish six games out of first. It was a very winnable division considering the Pirates won only 89 games to reach the postseason for the first time in a decade. But the Mets never won more than four straight games after July 9 and settled for a third-place finish at 83–79.

Swoboda wasn't happy after the season. He was still among the younger Mets at age 26, but he had seen his plate appearances fall from 508 in 1968 to 289 in 1970. Never a shrinking violet, Swoboda told the media he would love to be traded if it meant playing for another club on a regular basis.

"You know, I was frustrated with myself and frustrated with the team. And I said some of the stupidest shit I've ever heard uttered in baseball. Just stupid shit.

"When I look at it now—I've got some of those clippings—you just cringe when you read it and go, 'What were you thinking?' It's just emotions. Your emotions get out there in front of your brain.

"First off, I wasn't good at anything I wasn't emotionally involved in. If it didn't appeal to my emotions, it didn't matter to me much. If I wasn't emotionally engaged, I wouldn't be any good at it."

The off-season came and went with Swoboda still a Met despite his deteriorating relationship with Hodges. Swoboda reported to spring training and hit .243 with one homer, eight RBIs, and four runs scored in 14 games during the exhibition season.

The Mets were a week away from opening the regular season when Swoboda received his wish and was traded. But general manager Bob Scheffing sent Swoboda to the Siberia of the National League, dealing him to the Expos for good-field, no-hit outfielder Don Hahn.

Swoboda was with Montreal less than three months. He hit .253 in 75 at-bats over 39 games for the Expos but produced no homers and only six RBIs. Swoboda didn't play until he laced an RBI triple as a pinch-hitter in Montreal's fourth game of the season.

The Yankees brought him back to New York at the end of June, sending Ron Woods to the Expos in a strong public relations move. The Yankees were the No. 2 team in New York and drew just 1.1 million in 1970, more than 1.6 million below the Mets' figure. What better way to boost attendance than to grab a hero from the Mets' past? But the deal did little to turn Swoboda into an everyday player.

Swoboda began his Yankees career by delivering an RBI single in four at-bats while starting in left field on June 25. He went 13-for-36 (.361) while compiling a .461 average and six RBIs in his first 11 games following the trade. A five-game hitting streak raised his season average to .272 by September 17, but the Yankees were just playing for pride after falling hopelessly behind the first-place Orioles by June. The Bombers finished a mediocre 82–80 despite a lineup that featured Thurman Munson, Roy White, and Bobby Murcer.

Although Swoboda was back in New York, he was in no better position than he was with the Mets. He was still battling for playing time, starting just 41 games for the Bombers as outfielders Murcer, White, and Felipe Alou each received over 500 plate appearances. Worst of all, the Yankees were in a division with the mighty Orioles while the Mets battled the very catchable Pirates.

Things didn't get any better for Swoboda at the beginning of 1972. He started just three of the Yankees' first 72 games while serving as the team's top right-handed pinch-hitter. He went 0-for-6 with three walks in June as a pinch-hitter without persuading manager Ralph Houk to put him in the lineup.

He appeared to turn around his season by slugging a pinch-hit homer against the Angels on July 10 before going 2-for-4 with an RBI as a starter the next game. But his average was down to .209 after going 0-for-3 in Game 1 of a twin bill in Boston on August 2.

Swoboda hit well the rest of the month, making 10 starts and hitting .317 in 41 at-bats. He had back-to-back three-hit games in early August to lift his average to .262, but he started just five of the Yankees' final 60 games and

finished with a .248 average, one home run and 12 RBIs in 133 at-bats. He was unable to deliver consistently as a pinch-hitter, going 4-for-26 with one homer and two RBIs the entire season.

Swoboda entered 1973 as the Yankees' fifth outfielder and top right-handed designated hitter. But he went 0-for-8 in his first two games as a DH and hauled an .056 average into May before starting only four games the rest of the season. He had become the 25th man on the roster by the fourth week of the season and went 0-for-10 from May 8 to August 2. His average was down to .069 before he went 1-for-2 in back-to-back games in early August.

Swoboda poked his final major league homer on September 12, ruining a shutout bid by Boston's Rogelio Moret in the Bronx. It was also Swoboda's final hit in the majors as he went 0-for-6 the rest of the way before he was released after the season.

He was able to stay visible in New York a few more years. WCBS-TV, recognizing his popularity and strong communication skills, hired him as a weekend sports anchor in 1974. The station already had done well with an ex–major leaguer as Jim Bouton enjoyed a successful run as its sportscaster.

"I was contacted by a guy named Eric Ober, who was the assistant news director at WCBS. They wanted to talk to me. I went in there and they asked if I had any interest. This was after I was released by the Atlanta Braves in the spring of 1974.

"I was interested, and it was crazy that they gave me a little bit of instruction, a little bit of this and a little bit of that. They just pushed me in the cart, and off I went. It was pretty clunky and pretty bumpy and not a graceful segue.

"That news room I was in with Jim Jensen and Dave Marash…Rolland Smith and Dave Marash were the 11:00 PM news anchors in the news room, which was a new concept. And the reporters there: John Tesh, J.J. Gonzalez, Chris Borgen. Lynn Scherr was there. Linda Ellerbe was a reporter there. They had some mondo talent there."

Swoboda was a polished broadcaster by the winter of 1976, but he also wondered if he could still play in the majors after a two-year absence. The Mets gave him an invitation to spring training, but it was evident he had lost a step or two. Swoboda returned to WCBS after training camp before working in Milwaukee and Phoenix. He was between stations when WCBS asked him to make a cameo as their on-site reporter for the Mets' 1986 playoff run.

"I had not had my contract renewed out in Phoenix, and I was making some inroads into coming back to New Orleans. I had not signed anything. Didn't have anything concrete in the works, but I got a call from WCBS to come back and freelance for them covering the Mets during the playoffs and World Series.

"In '86, it was wonderful. I just did pieces and live shots, and it was incredible. And I did some pretty good stuff. It was inspiring as hell because it was some of the most compelling baseball I'd ever seen. The National League

Championship Series—holy shit, was that great baseball. And then the World Series…it was magical.

"A year and a-half later they offered me a job backing up Warner Wolf. I really wanted to do it, but nobody else wanted me to do it. My wife didn't want me to go back there. Part of me didn't want to bounce around. They only offer you those 13-week deals. Part of me wanted to go back and do a little better job of it because you felt like, 'I'd like to go back there and look more like a sportscaster than I did before. Nobody thought that was very smart, and so I stayed right here in New Orleans with no huge regret, really."

Swoboda was a TV sports anchor in New Orleans for two decades and still takes a turn behind the mike, serving as the TV color analyst for the New Orleans Zephyrs and handling SEC games for Cox Sports.

"The last 10 years I've really tried hard to learn a lot of baseball. You learn a lot by just being around it, but I've really tried to spend more time talking to coaches and managers, especially at the Triple A level. In college baseball, those guys are pretty sharp."

Swoboda was a frequent contributor to *New Orleans Magazine* until 2005, using the style he had honed for television. He came to the conclusion that it took a sharp ear to create quality material.

"When you're in television, you're writing your own copy and you try to write lively stuff to say. Write to your own voice, and it helps give you a voice. You sound it out through your own ears. You try to make it sound like something somebody would actually say. It's much easier to do it that way if you write it that way.

"I heard Hunter S. Thompson say one time that he really does filter it through his own sense of speech so that it has a voice, like your delayed auditory feedback. I think it's the best advice you can give anybody. It won't come out right away, but if you keep doing it and keep practicing the process, if you have any alacrity with the language, it'll start coming out because you need to hear it. It should dance a little bit. It should have a little rhythm. The only way you can get to that is to run it through your speech center."

Swoboda remains happily married to Cecilia, whose face appears in several Mets yearbooks. Cecilia received her undergraduate degree from the University of Maryland and became a speech pathologist following her master's studies at Hofstra while Ron was playing for the Mets.

"She works with closed-skull injuries and stroke victims as it would affect speech mechanism. She's been doing that a long time. I always try to enunciate correctly because she's good at it, she's been doing it a long time, and if I can't say it, somebody might say, 'She's doing you a lot of good!'"

Ron and Cecilia raised two boys, R.J. and Brian, and both are doing well. Swoboda's father continues to live on the same property he owned when he and his wife raised Ron. The original home burned down and was replaced by a new structure.

Swoboda's mother passed away in Maryland in 2006, shortly after Hurricane Katrina. He spent several weeks with his parents following the hurricane, allowing him to procure his mom's recipe for Maryland Crab Soup, which he lovingly considers a legacy.

"My oldest son lives here with his two daughters," said Swoboda. "He is a craft beer guy for a distributor. Over the last few years he's become the craft beer guru at this distributorship, helping them put together a bunch of brands and stuff. He just loves it.

"My youngest son works for a company that does landscaping. He has two daughters, and he and his wife live out in Stewartstown, Pennsylvania.

"The crazy thing is we got $19,000 as our winning share from the '69 World Series. I used it almost to the penny to buy unimproved land out in Shawsville, Maryland. My youngest son lives about nine miles from the property. He goes up there and does a little shooting, a little camping. There's a neat little creek that runs through there. It's beautiful.

"I sold a little lumber off it a couple of times. It's red oak, black oak, white oak. I sold some of the oak off—very selective cuts. It helps you pay the taxes. My youngest son really loves being up there, and I'm glad that we can keep it."

Ron and Cecilia continue to collect artwork from local artists. He says he can describe what he was thinking and feeling as he acquired each item.

"It's like my granddaughter asked me: 'Granddad, why is everything a story?' I told her, 'It's a story because that's how I remember it.' These things all connect. To have something in your house that you really like to look at, that was made by people that you know and care about, it's pretty cool.

"I've got a painting on my wall here. It's done by a guy who's been sort of a local phenomenon named James Michalopoulos. He does these fronts of New Orleans houses, and they look as if you took a picture of a house with a fisheye lens and then paint it. He does a lot of palette-knife techniques of the fronts of houses. And the lighting on this picture right here coming from the window of our patio is really interesting. It's amazing what it looks like. I look at this painting a lot. It's a big one. It's probably the painting I spent the most money on. When my wife and I moved into this house we wanted to buy one of his paintings because it's a New Orleans home, and he did wonderful studies on New Orleans houses. He has a wonderful technique with a palette knife, a wonderful feel for his paint and his colors.

"We spent all afternoon trying to decide what we were going to walk out of there with, and the one we did we've loved every day since we did it. And that's like 13 to 14 years ago."

First ML/Mets game vs. Dodgers, 4/12/65
First ML/Mets hit   solo HR vs. Turk Farrell, Astros, 4/14/65
First ML/Mets homer   solo HR vs. Turk Farrell, Astros, 4/14/65
First ML/Mets RBI   solo HR vs. Turk Farrell, Astros, 4/14/65

Most hits, ML game 4, Mets @ Phillies, 8/15/67; Yankees @ Red Sox, 7/5/71

Most homers, ML/Mets game	2, vs. Braves, 5/8/65; @ Cardinals, 9/15/69; vs. Astros, 5/31/70
Most RBIs, ML/Mets game	5, @ Phillies, 7/4/66; vs. Giants, 8/20/68; vs. Astros, 5/31/70

Acquired: Signed as an amateur free agent, 9/3/63.
Deleted: Traded to the Expos with Rich Hacker for Don Hahn, 3/31/71.

Frank Thomas

Outfielder, First Baseman, Third Baseman
Bats right, throws right
Born: 6/11/29   Pittsburgh, Pennsylvania
Height: 6′3″   Weight: 205   #25

Frank Thomas Mets Career

YEAR	GP	AB	R	H	2B	3B	HR	RBI	K	BB	SB	AVG	SLG	OBP
1962	156	571	69	152	23	3	34	94	95	48	2	.266	.496	.329
1963	126	420	34	109	9	1	15	60	48	33	0	.260	.393	.317
1964	60	197	19	50	6	1	3	19	29	10	1	.254	.340	.295
TOTAL	342	1188	122	311	38	5	52	173	172	91	3	.262	.434	.319

ML Career

YEAR	GP	AB	R	H	2B	3B	HR	RBI	K	BB	SB	AVG	SLG	OBP
51–66	1766	6285	792	1671	262	31	286	962	894	484	15	.266	.454	.320

Mets president George Weiss wasn't pleased when he received the list of players available in the 1961 expansion draft. The National League had rigged the setup after watching the Angels and Senators come away with a few good players in the 1960 AL expansion draft. The senior circuit did a better job protecting its existing teams by trimming the number of players available on the major league roster while allowing teams to hide their best young prospects in the minors.

Once the draft was over, Weiss still sought a legitimate power threat that was young enough to play every day. Eighteen days after the draft, Weiss managed to acquire Frank Joseph Thomas from the Braves for cash and a player to be named.

The Braves protected Thomas from the draft after he hit .284 with 25 home runs and 67 RBIs in 124 games in 1961. He was an established power hitter, belting at least 21 home runs in eight of his first nine full seasons. Thomas also was a three-time All-Star who finished fourth in the MVP voting in 1958, his final year with the Pirates.

Considering the dearth of talent on the Mets' 1962 spring training roster, it's a wonder Weiss managed to pry Thomas from the Braves. But it proved to be his best post-expansion draft acquisition and gave the Mets a foundation at the plate. The deal also gave Thomas a chance to play for manager Casey Stengel, who was hired by the Mets after winning 10 pennants in 12 seasons with the Yankees.

"I had a great year for him, so I was in the field most of the time," said Thomas in a July 2009 interview.

"I always said he probably forgot more baseball than I'll ever know. I enjoyed playing for him. I just think if you were playing for him and you were doing good, he'd just let you play."

The Mets were absolutely horrible their first season, establishing a modern major league record of 120 losses. But can you imagine how bad the team would have been if Thomas hadn't been dealt by the Braves?

"I thought we had the nucleus of a pretty good ballclub. If you look at the record, we lost 51 games by one run in the seventh, eighth, and ninth innings. We scored a lot of runs.

"We didn't have any pitching. We didn't have any closers like they have today, and if we would have had that, we would have been right up in the thick of the pennant race."

Thomas was one of the few constants in the 1962 lineup, batting either fourth or fifth in each of his 145 starts. No Met was in the starting lineup more than Thomas, who became indispensable once a majority of the team's expansion draft picks proved they weren't going to contribute.

Thomas was the first Met to homer in the Polo Grounds, the first to homer twice in a game, and the first with a double-digit hitting streak. He was also the first Met to collect more than four RBIs when he clipped the Phillies for six on August 1.

"The Polo Grounds was a good park for me because I was strictly a pull hitter."

Thomas, Richie Ashburn, and Felix Mantilla were the most dependable Mets hitters in '62. Thomas appeared in the team's first 64 games and produced an early season 11-game hitting streak before getting hot again in mid-May. He hit safely in 18 consecutive games beginning on May 12, providing five homers, 16 RBIs, and 11 extra-base hits in the process. The Mets actually went 7–2 during the first nine games of the streak before embarking on a 17-game skid that remains a team record. The hot stretch raised his average to .326 by June 3 and allowed him to stay around the .300 mark until early August.

Lost in the silliness of the season was Thomas homering twice in three straight contests, doing it in the first three games of August. Naturally, the Mets lost all three games. But he produced one of his more memorable home runs in the second game of a doubleheader the following day, August 4, against the Reds.

"That 14th inning against Cincinnati. The first game, I just missed a home run to right field, which I usually don't do—hit to right field. I just got one off the end of the bat, and it just missed. That would have set an all-time record because I hit six home runs over three consecutive games. The next game, I hit one in the 14th inning to win the ballgame."

Thomas hit a dry spell beginning August 22, going 7-for-55 (.127) with just one home run in 18 games. He broke out on September 14 while damaging the Reds' pennant hopes again, going 3-for-4 with four RBIs in a 10–9 win that dropped Cincinnati six games off the pace.

The Mets wasted most of Thomas' best offensive performances, losing all five games in which he homered twice and going 8–17 when he belted at least one home run. New York also lost Thomas' six-RBI game and was 2–7 when he produced at least two extra-base hits.

The media had a great time writing about the Mets' exploits that season. But Thomas felt the writers often went overboard in their criticism of the ballclub without giving the players a fair shake.

"Things happen on the field," Thomas once told a scribe. "The ball can take a bad hop, the ball can hit the edge of the grass and come up one way. You see it from a different angle when you're up in that press box, and you really don't know what you're talking about half the time.

"I've been called a fatalist by one of the writers in New York because I was reading a thing with [Norman] Vincent Peale. We were in Chicago, and I had just hit a home run to win the ballgame.

"He says, 'Oh, you're reading about positive thinking?' I looked at the writer and said, 'You know, it's easy to write something nice about somebody who's going good. Have you ever tried to write something nice about somebody who's going bad?' He didn't know what to say."

Thomas ended the season leading the Mets in homers (34), RBIs (94), doubles (23), hits (152), runs scored (69), and slugging (.496). His home run output remained a team record until Dave Kingman belted 36 in 1975. His RBI record fell when Donn Clendenon drove in 97 in 1970.

But Thomas still holds the major league record for most home runs by a player on a first-year team. He owned the expansion record for most RBIs until Andres Galarraga and Charlie Hayes drove in 98 apiece for the 1993 Rockies.

Thomas was a notch above his teammates when it came to power hitting, but he occasionally fit right in as a fielder. He had 14 outfield assists but also committed four errors in 10 games at third base. However, on a team of defensively challenged players, Thomas was among the better glove men.

Thomas was charged with two errors at third in the fourth inning of a game against the Cardinals July 8, helping St. Louis score five times to take a 9–0 lead. Thomas was vociferously booed following the second miscue and heard it from the fans as he exited the field. When he reached the dugout, Marvelous Marv Throneberry came over to him and asked, "What are you trying to do, steal my fans?"

Thomas seemed to handle the losing better than most Mets. He and Ashburn were the only 30-something Mets to come close to producing their typical offensive numbers, and Ashburn was so disgusted with the losing that he retired at season's end rather than endure another year of embarrassment. Thomas' background made him better suited to find the silver lining.

Thomas spent three years in a seminary of the Carmelite Order before giving pro baseball a shot. The Pittsburgh

native signed with the hometown Pirates in 1947 and began his career at the lowest minor league level before quickly climbing up the chain. Thomas hit .295 with 14 homers, 39 doubles, and 132 RBIs in 138 games for Tallahassee of the Class D Georgia-Florida League in 1948, and combined to bat .319 with 14 round-trippers and 87 RBIs in three minor league stops a year later.

Thomas displayed a potent bat and also impressed teammates with another feat; catching fastballs bare-handed during batting and fielding practice.

"I did it as a dare when I was in Waco, Texas, in 1949.

"First of all, when I was a kid, mom and dad could not afford a glove. I played fast-pitch softball and I played shortstop. I got used to catching balls like that.

"In Waco, we had a pitcher named Bill Pierro, who was from Brooklyn. He was in the outfield with two other pitchers, popping off, saying how hard he can throw, and I said, 'I'll catch your fastball bare-handed.' He said, 'Like heck you will!'

"I said, 'Okay, let's draw a line 60'6", but first of all I want you to go to the bullpen and warm up.' He said, 'You can't catch it after I've warmed up.'

"We draw the line, and I caught three. He said, 'I'm not warm,' and I said, 'I knew you would say that. We'll go down to the bullpen and warm up.'

"He went down to the bullpen to warm up, he came back and I caught five more. He didn't know what to say. So I deflated his ego."

Pierro went 18–11 with a 2.96 ERA that season and pitched for the Pirates in 1950.

"When I was with the Mets, Richie Ashburn and I were warming up, and Willie Mays came down. Richie said, 'Hey, Willie, wanna make a quick hundred?' And he says, 'Yeah, what do I have to do?' He said, 'I'll bet you Thomas can catch your fastball bare-handed.' Mays said, 'Like heck he can!'

"So we went down by the dugout, and I thought he was ready. I dropped the glove and I caught it. He went over to Richie and said, 'Let's make it a $10 bet!'

"I never did get paid! Every time I see him, he says, 'Look at all the publicity you got out of it!'"

Thomas continued to hit well in the minors and was recalled by August 1951 after batting .289 with 23 homers and 85 RBIs for Double A New Orleans. The Pirates gave him a 39-game run and watched him bat a respectable .264 with two home runs and 16 RBIs.

He played most of 1952 with New Orleans, hitting .303 with 35 home runs and 131 RBIs to finally secure a spot on Pittsburgh's roster. He also played six games for the Bucs that season but batted just 2-for-21 (.095).

The 1952 Pirates were dreadful, finishing 42–112 to earn the right to be called one of the worst teams in major league history. Ten years later, Thomas was able to claim he was part of two of the worst teams in the sport.

"When I was with the Mets, it got to a point where we'd go to the ballpark and wonder how we were gonna lose today because we lost every which way you want to think about.

"It was the same way with the Pirates. When you have a losing ballclub, what else can you think?

"But ballplayers have so much pride about themselves. They really don't look at it that way because every day is a fresh start. You can get beat 15–0 today, and tomorrow you start all over again as a fresh slate.

"You take football. They play one day a week. If they lose, they brood over it for a whole six days before they play their next game."

Ralph Kiner was one of the few reasons to attend a game at Forbes Field between 1946 and '52. He either led or tied for the league lead in homers each season, hitting more than 50 twice and averaging 42 during that run. Kiner was traded to the Cubs in June 1953 in part because of Thomas' ability to hit the long ball at spacious Forbes Field. The team took out "Greenberg Gardens" in left field shortly after Thomas became a Pirates mainstay.

"If they had left the "Gardens" up for me like they did for Ralph Kiner, I would have hit a lot more home runs. But they moved the fence out 30 feet. You had 365 feet down the line in left, a 25-foot scoreboard, 406 in left-center and 457 in dead center.

"You're supposed to hit more home runs in your home ballpark than you are on the road. In 1958, when I hit 35 home runs, I hit nine at Forbes Field and 26 on the road. That's the proof of the pudding right there.

"I hit 30 home runs and drove in 102 runs as a center fielder, which is still a record as a first-year man," Thomas remembered of his 1953 season. "It's never been broken since 1953. It's a long time to hold a record.

"I still hold a record in Pittsburgh as a third baseman with 35 home runs, and I was the first player to hit the fourth home run in succession when I was with the Braves."

Thomas led the 1953 Pirates in homers and RBIs while compiling a .255 average. He became the second Pirate ever to reach the 30–home run plateau, and hit at least 23 in each of the next four years. He was selected to the 1958 All-Star Game before finishing the year with a .281 average and career highs of 35 home runs and 109 RBIs. It was the third All-Star nod in five years for Thomas, who helped the Pirates finish with their best record since 1944.

But there were times when playing in his native Pittsburgh had its drawbacks.

"It's always a problem playing in your hometown. I was born only about a five- to 10-minute walk from Forbes Field, so I used to walk to the ballpark. I'd go past all the bars that they had—I don't drink—and they'd say, 'What, are you too hot for us, or too big?' Stuff like that.

"So you stop in, you have a Coke, a 7-Up or something like that, and if you go to the ballpark and make an error, somebody would yell at you, 'We saw you at the bar. Why don't you just spend more time at the bar!' So you were damned if you do and damned if you don't."

"But that's the way life is in your hometown. They expected the impossible of you. Every time you come up, you're supposed to hit a home run if you're a home run hitter. And if you're a run producer, you're supposed to drive in every man in scoring position. But it doesn't happen that way because, as statistics prove, you're going to drive in only one out of every seven."

The Bucs won the 1960 World Series in a shocker over the mighty Yankees, but Thomas wasn't around to enjoy it. Thomas was dealt to the Reds in 1959 and shipped to the Cubs a year later after hitting just .225 with 12 homers and 47 RBIs.

"When I was traded from Pittsburgh for [Don] Hoak, [Harvey] Haddix, and [Smoky] Burgess after the '58 season, they got three major league players and there were three other major league players that went with me: Whammy Douglas, [Jim] Pendleton, and Johnny Powers. But I was the only one that was playing regularly, whereas the three players the Pirates got, they were regular players.

"That's my claim to fame. I helped the Pirates win the pennant in 1960 with those three guys!"

After missing the Pirates' 1960 title run, Thomas also missed the Reds' charge to the 1961 pennant. He opened the '61 season with the Cubs and was traded to Milwaukee, where he hit .284 with 25 homers and 67 RBIs.

Thomas didn't mind heading to the expansion Mets, but he felt he was duped by Braves general manager John McHale.

"When I talked to him in September, before I signed my contract I said, 'I'm going to ask you one thing before we do anything; what are your intentions for me come 1962?' He says, 'You're gonna be my starting left fielder.' And I said, 'If that's the case, then bring out whatever contract you want me to sign, and I'll sign it. I'm doing that because you give me a chance to play regularly again. But if you have any intentions of trading me, please, do not sign me. Let me deal with the club you're going to trade me to.'

"I went home in September, and that November, I was up in the Poconos hunting with my friends, and my wife called and said, 'You just got sold to the Mets.'

Thomas wasn't upset about heading to New York, but he wasn't pleased by the way it played out.

"I'm never disappointed in going anywhere. The only thing that disappointed me is people lied to me, and that was the thing that bothered me more than anything else."

The manner in which Thomas became a Met is part of the team lore. He was traded by the Braves with a player to be named for a player to be named. Thomas was in the Opening Day lineup with Gus Bell and shared the same outfield with Bell for the first six weeks of the season. But Weiss still hadn't completed the deal with the Mets 31 games into the season. Finally, Weiss sent Bell to the Braves on May 21 and also received Rick Herrscher in return to complete the deal. In effect, the Mets swapped members of their first-ever starting lineup for each other.

Weiss remained one of baseball's busiest executives through the end of 1962 and into '63. Thomas, Charlie Neal, and Roger Craig were the only players to be in the Mets' first two Opening Day lineups as Weiss tried to solve the team's pitching and fielding problems. The Mets cut their ERA by nearly one run but committed the same amount of errors (210) while generating very little offense. The team batting average dropped 21 points to .219, the home run total plunged from 139 to 96, and the Mets scored 116 fewer runs than in 1962. Thomas led the team with just 60 RBIs and belted 15 home runs, fewer than half as many as he hit the previous season. The 1963 lineup also included Duke Snider, as the two usually traded off serving as the cleanup hitter. But there was no reason to pitch to either player when the rest of the roster hardly posed a threat.

The Mets left the decaying Polo Grounds for Shea Stadium after the 1963 season. Most players were happy to leave the Giants' old ballpark for a state-of-the-art facility in Queens. But Thomas had a valid reason for wanting to stay in Upper Manhattan.

The Polo Grounds had the perfect dimensions for a pull hitter. The left-field fence was a mere 279 feet from home plate, but the upper deck was only 250 feet from the point of contact. Thomas hit 43 home runs in 188 games at the Polo Grounds, compared to the 45 he smacked in 422 games at Pittsburgh's Forbes Field. Of all visiting players, only Stan Musial hit more home runs in "The Horseshoe" during the Giants' last five seasons in New York.

The short porch was a tantalizing target for a right-handed hitter like Thomas, and there was further enticement to hit the ball down the line. A boat was given to the player who hit the Howard Clothes sign the most times during the season.

"They had a boat on both the left- and right-field walls. If you hit it on the fly you got so many points, if you hit it on the bounce you got so many points, and if you hit it on the ground you got so many points.

"This one particular day I kept pulling the ball, and Casey told me, 'If you want to be a sailor, join the Navy!'"

Although he didn't mind playing there, Shea Stadium was not tailored to Thomas' hitting style, and his power numbers took a hit in 1964. He didn't homer at the new ballpark until May 10 and went another two months before hitting another. Thomas ripped a game-winning two-run homer as a pinch-hitter against Curt Simmons July 9 to give the Mets a 4–3 victory over the Cardinals. It was his final homer as a Met, but not his final blast at Shea that year. He smacked a two-run homer that put the Phillies ahead 6–2 in the seventh inning of a 6–4 win over New York on August 9.

Thomas hit .298 in 34 games at Shea in 1964 but produced only eight extra-base hits in 114 at-bats. After batting .254 overall in his first 60 games of the season, he was dealt to the Phils for Wayne Graham and Gary Kroll in August.

Frank Thomas with his former manager, Casey Stengel, just after he was traded to the Phillies in 1964.

The trade finally gave Thomas a chance to play for a pennant contender. He opened the Phillies portion of his career by recording a .337 average with four home runs, 18 RBIs, eight doubles, and 14 runs scored in 23 games. The Phillies went 16–7 in those contests to turn a tenuous 2½-game lead into a six-game cushion by August 29.

Philadelphia still had a six-game lead when Thomas broke a thumb September 8, an injury that led mightily to the team's free-fall.

"What was ironic about the whole thing was it was a makeup game. I dove into second base and my hand went underneath the bag and hit the pin. It was like a boxer's break.

"I got two more hits, even with a broken thumb. I'd come into the dugout and put it in ice right away, and the next time I hit I could swing the bat."

Thomas was still caring for the thumb when he returned to the Warwick Hotel, his temporary home after the trade.

"After the game was over, I told the busboy to bring me up one of those large cans and fill it up with ice. I put my hand in it all night.

"When I woke up, it was all warm and my hand was all puffed up. I called the trainer and he said, 'Get to the hospital.' I went to the hospital, they took X-rays and they said, 'Yeah, you have a hairline fracture.' I said to the doctor, 'Don't tell anybody. Come to the ballpark, give me a

Most Home Runs by a Player on a First-Year Team

Player	Team	HR	Year
Frank Thomas	Mets	34	1962
Rusty Staub	Expos	29	1969
Leon Wagner	Angels	28	1961
Leroy Stanton	Mariners	27	1977
Ken Hunt	Angels	25	1961
Don Mincher	Pilots	25	1969
Charlie Hayes	Rockies	25	1993
Nate Colbert	Padres	24	1969

little shot of novocaine so I still have feeling in my fingers where I can grip the ball.' I told him I have the World Series handed to me and I have all winter to heal. And he wouldn't do it. He put a cast on it and that was it."

The thumb kept him out of the lineup for 2½ weeks. The Phillies lost their fifth in a row upon his return, slicing their lead to 1½ games over the Reds.

The Phils also lost the next four games that Thomas played to fall out of first. It was part of a monumental collapse that led to a third-place finish after the Phillies led by 6½ games with 12 to play.

One loss sticks out most in Thomas' memory.

"When the kid from Cincinnati [Chico Ruiz] stole home with Mahaffey pitching. We lost the game 1–0, and he steals home with [Frank] Robinson hitting. That's one game that really stuck out the whole year."

Phils manager Gene Mauch takes plenty of blame for the meltdown, but Thomas says he understood Mauch's strategy of shortening the rotation and using the regulars almost exclusively.

"He was trying to win the pennant and then give everybody a rest. He could have pitched [Jack] Baldschun. He could have pitched [Dallas] Green. He could have pitched [Art] Mahaffey. He could have pitched [Ed] Roebuck. He tried to do the best he could, and it didn't work out.

"After [Jim] Bunning and [Chris] Short got four days' rest, they came back and beat the Cincinnati Reds the last two games of the season, but it was too late."

"Things like that always happen, and right away the media is going to clamp down on [Mauch], and that's what they've done."

Thomas hit .294 with seven homers and 26 RBIs in 39 games for the Phils that season but was unable to cash a World Series check. Once again, Thomas was the victim of bad timing. Within a few months, he was an ex-Phillie.

Thomas was 36 when he opened the 1965 season with the Phillies. He got off to a so-so start, hitting .260 with a

homer and seven RBIs in 35 games before he was involved in a confrontration with Richie Allen, the team's young hitting star.

The Phillies were in the middle of batting practice when Thomas and Allen got into a fight on the field.

"Mauch put me in to pinch-hit the night before with runners on first and third and one out. I tried to bunt to put the winning run in scoring position and bring the tying run in, but I eventually struck out.

"The next day, I'm taking BP with the extra men. I bunted down first base, and Richie yelled, 'That's 24 hours too late!'

"And I said, 'What, are you getting like Muhammad Clay, always running at the mouth?'"

According to Thomas, he went back to the batting cage and leaned over to get a handful of dirt. Thomas said when he turned around, Allen sucker-punched him.

"I bit my tongue and was spitting blood. I didn't know what I was doing after that."

Thomas smacked Allen with his bat before the two were finally separated. The Phillies quickly decided that Allen and Thomas couldn't coexist. Mauch told Thomas he was being cut shortly after Frank contributed a big hit.

"I hit a home run [as a pinch-hitter in the eighth inning] to tie the ballgame up that night. I played the last two innings, and we lost the ballgame. I saw him [Mauch] when I was shaving, and he took me upstairs and said, 'We put you on irrevocable waivers, which means a club's gonna claim you, but we can't take you back.'

"My words to him were, 'I think you're being very unfair to me in that respect,' and his answer was, 'You're 35, and [Allen's] 26.'

"I called [general manager John] Quinn, because Quinn always liked me. He told me, 'I have to stick by my manager.' I told him there are two sides to every story, and he should hear my side, but he wouldn't listen."

The Phils sold him to the Astros later that month. He spent six weeks with Houston before returning to Milwaukee, where he finished the season with a .220 average, four home runs, and 17 RBIs in 73 games.

Thomas was released by the Braves before the start of the 1966 season. He signed with the Cubs in May but was let go three weeks later after going 0-for-5 as a pinch-hitter.

Thomas returned to Pittsburgh and had little trouble adjusting to life after baseball.

"I went to work for ICM School of Business. I went around to the high schools talking education to kids. I used to make 35 presentations a week.

"When I first went with them, I said, 'If you're going to hire me as a ballplayer, I don't want to work for you. I'll make a name for myself in this. You just let me do what I want to do.'

"So I went to 300 high schools, talked to the guidance counselors, and I would ask them after they listened to my presentation, 'Do you think you'd have a teacher that would like a period off?'

"My last year with them I was probably going to about 120 high schools because I couldn't go to any more.

"I did that for 18 years. Never missed a day. I retired when I was 55 years old in 1984, and I've been retired ever since."

"It was starting to bother my throat, making all those presentations. You never think that you have little muscles in your throat, but you do. I said it was time for a young kid to get up at 4:00 AM, go out, and drive 200 miles and make seven presentations."

Thomas met his wife, Dolores, in 1949 and married her two years later. They've been together ever since, producing a large family.

"We had eight kids, seven living and one deceased. We have 12 grandkids, three step-grandkids, two step-great grandkids, and one great grandkid on our side. So, Christmas is expensive!

"My wife loves Pittsburgh. Ten of the 12 grandkids are here in Pittsburgh. She's not about to move.

"I hate the winters, but I really don't have to go out in it unless I have to go to the store. Usually, the main roads are open, so I don't mind it that much. I just don't like the ice in that respect."

When the weather is good, Thomas can be seen on the golf course, playing a full schedule of events during the year.

"I shoot in the 80s," Thomas said in 2009. "I shot my age last year—79—so now I'm 80 and can shoot 80 now!"

"I play a lot of charity scrambles, and you meet a lot of nice people that way. It's a lot of fun."

Thomas also has spent years collecting baseball cards. A fire in 1991 wiped out his collection, but fans who learned of the loss began to send him cards in an effort to replenish his compilation.

He is still on the lookout for several All-Star cards from the coveted 1952 Topps set, although he can always look at a three-time All-Star every time he shaves.

ML debut	Pirates vs. Cubs, 8/17/51
Mets debut	@ Cardinals, 4/11/62
1st ML hit	double vs. Cubs, 8/17/51
1st Mets hit	solo homer vs. Tom Sturdivant, Pirates, 4/13/62
1st ML homer	2-run HR vs. George Spencer, @ Giants, 8/30/51
1st Mets homer	solo homer vs. Tom Sturdivant, Pirates, 4/13/62
1st ML RBI	vs. Cubs, 8/17/51
1st Mets RBI	sac-fly vs. Larry Jackson, @ Cardinals, 4/11/62
Most hits, ML game 4, 13 times	
Most hits, Mets game	4, vs. Cubs, 6/26/63
Most homers, ML game	3, Pirates @ Reds, 8/16/58
Most homers, Mets game	2, 5 times, all in 1962
Most RBIs, ML game	Pirates @ Giants, 6/11/58
Most RBIs, Mets game	6, vs. Phillies, 8/1/62

Acquired: Traded by the Braves with a player to be named (Rick Herrscher) for a player to be named (Gus Bell) and cash, 11/28/61.

Deleted: Traded to the Phillies for Wayne Graham, Gary Kroll, and cash, 8/7/64.

Marv Throneberry

First Baseman	Batted left, threw left
Born: 9/2/33	Collierville, Tennessee
Died: 6/23/94	Fisherville, Tennessee
Height: 6'1"	Weight: 195 #2

Marv Throneberry Mets Career

YEAR	GP	AB	R	H	2B	3B	HR	RBI	K	BB	SB	AVG	SLG	OBP
1962	116	357	29	87	11	3	16	49	83	34	1	.244	.426	.306
1963	14	14	0	2	1	0	0	1	5	1	0	.143	.214	.200
TOTAL	130	371	29	89	12	3	16	50	88	35	1	.240	.418	.302

ML Career

YEAR	GP	AB	R	H	2B	3B	HR	RBI	K	BB	SB	AVG	SLG	OBP
55–63	480	1186	143	281	37	8	53	170	295	130	3	.237	.416	.311

As his monogram will attest, Marvin Eugene Throneberry was born to be a Met.

Throneberry may not have given the 1962 team its identity as bumbling ballplayers, but he certainly augmented it. He didn't commit all 210 of the Mets' errors in their inaugural season, but he manufactured some of the more memorable miscues. When Mets fans waited for the other shoe to drop during a tight ballgame, Throneberry was usually the man holding the brown loafers.

But the Mets were damn lucky to have Throneberry on the team as he usually delivered excitement in myriad situations.

Many are under the assumption that Throneberry was an original Met, but that wasn't the case. The team was horrible even before he got there, opening the '62 season with nine straight losses and owning a 5–16 record upon his arrival. The lousy start was a big reason Marvelous Marv became a Met in the first place.

It took team president George Weiss less than a month before realizing his blueprint for success was being kicked away or overthrown. Weiss used the expansion draft to acquire ballplayers that were well known by New York fans and—with few exceptions—he came away with a host of aging veterans whose best days were behind them.

Weiss quickly sought to alter the roster after the Mets dropped their first nine games, still a record for an expansion team. Ironically, the first player he took in the expansion draft—catcher Hobie Landrith—was one of the first to go despite a .289 average in 45 at-bats. Landrith was the player to be named in a May 9 trade with the Orioles for Throneberry, a player with whom Weiss was very familiar.

Throneberry originally was signed by the Yankees before the 1952 season, Weiss' fifth as the Bombers' general manager. Throneberry immediately showed promise in the minors, hitting .276 with 16 home runs and 69 RBIs for Class B Quincy of the Three-Eye League in 1952 before he was given a few games at Triple A Kansas City later that season. He remained at Quincy for most of 1953, recording a .286 average with 30 homers, seven triples, and 85 RBIs.

Marv Throneberry reaches high for a wild throw as Cardinals pitcher Bob Gibson reaches first safely in a 1962 game at the Polo grounds.

Throneberry was one of the Yankees' top minor league prospects from 1954 to 1957, belting 139 homers and driving in 472 runs in 609 games. He pounded American Association pitching in 1956, leading the league with 42 homers and 145 RBIs while hitting .315 with 31 doubles for Denver. A year later, Throneberry accounted for 40 of the Bears' home runs and 124 RBIs.

Comparisons were being drawn between Throneberry and Mickey Mantle. Both hit for power and possessed good speed early in their careers, but the Yankees discounted Throneberry's home run numbers due to the rarified air in Denver. However, there was no denying that he was their top power-hitting prospect in the minors.

He made his major league debut September 25, 1955, at Fenway Park, going 2-for-2 with a two-run double and a sacrifice fly while playing against his brother, Faye. But Throneberry wouldn't appear in another major league game until 1958, when he hit seven homers and drove in 19 runs while hitting .227 in 150 at-bats during the regular season before going 0-for-1 in the World Series.

Throneberry appeared in 80 games for the 1959 Yankees, delivering a .250 average, eight home runs, and 22

RBIs. However, he was having a tough time cracking the everyday lineup and hit only 3-for-33 (.091) off the bench, including a 1-for-15 mark as a pinch-hitter.

In those days the Yankees did a lot of trading with the Kansas City A's, who were described by many as the Yankees' other Triple A team. Marv joined the Athletics in December 1959, traded with veterans Hank Bauer, Don Larsen, and Norm Siebern for three players, including Roger Maris.

Throneberry seemed like a lock to garner regular playing time with the A's, who had just finished seventh in the eight-team American League in 1959. But he started just two of his first 18 games of 1960 while batting .125 with no homers and one RBI before earning more playing time as the season progressed.

Throneberry's average climbed to .333 after he batted .429 (12-for-28) with four homers and 10 RBIs in an 11-game sequence from May 22 to June 3. Another cold spell followed before he hit .317 with four homers and 22 RBIs after July 28 to finish with a .250 average. He was third on the team with 11 homers and fifth with 41 RBIs despite only 234 at-bats.

He split the 1961 season between the A's and O's, going to Baltimore in June for Gene Stephens. Throneberry banged out 11 homers for the second straight season, but he hit only .226 in 96 games. He stumbled out of the gate with the Birds in 1962, going 0-for-9 in nine games before falling into the Mets' laps.

The Mets were hoping Throneberry could spell Gil Hodges at first base while serving as a dependable pinch-hitter. At the time of the trade, there was no reason to believe his fielding would be problematic. He had committed only 15 errors in 1,604 career chances (.991) at first base before the trade and was a capable outfielder.

But something happened as he donned his new blue pinstripes. Throneberry was flawless defensively in his first game as a Met and was on the back end of two double plays. But he was charged with an error on a botched pick-off play in his second game and booted a grounder for a two-run error in his fourth start. The legend of Marvelous Marv Throneberry was off and running.

Throneberry also wasn't doing much at the plate, hitting .186 with no RBIs in his first 43 at-bats as a Met. At this point, Marv had produced more runs for the other team than he had with the Mets, and the fans let him know it. He was the first Met to truly absorb the wrath of fans wishing the team could just play .333 ball. In this stage of his Mets career, the errors weren't funny, and the hitting was frustrating to both himself and the paying customer.

The boo-birds were taking aim at Throneberry, although they would give him a break if another Met made an error. Frank Thomas heard it from the fans after misfiring on two throws from third base. After the inning was over, Throneberry came over to Thomas and asked, "What are you trying to do, steal my fans?"[296]

Throneberry finally broke out of his hitting slump June 9, collecting three hits and lifting a sacrifice fly in an 11–6 win over the Cubs. He also had three hits in a loss to the Colt .45s five days later and finally raised his season average to .250 by ripping a pair of solo homers August 2 against Philadelphia, his only multi-homer game as a Met.

The two-homer game came a few days after one of his many misadventures in the field. The Mets and Cardinals were tied 5–5 in the eighth inning at St. Louis on July 29 when Ken Boyer hit a two-run single with the bases loaded, putting Stan Musial on third base. One batter later, Boyer tried to steal second but was caught in a rundown with Throneberry and second baseman Charlie Neal. Throneberry was so intent on nailing Boyer that he didn't notice Musial breaking for home. Throneberry finally got a glimpse of Musial as the Hall of Famer was about to score, then threw to shortstop Rod Kanehl to nail Boyer at second. The Cards now had a 6–3 lead, which made the Mets' two-run ninth nothing more than a nice try.

Sometimes Throneberry could make two mistakes in the same inning, as he did during the opener of a double-header against the Cubs at the Polo Grounds June 17.

Cubs right fielder Don Landrum led off the game with a walk and tried to steal second before he was caught in a rundown. Landrum was in the base path as he ran back to first, but Throneberry collided with him without possessing the ball. Landrum was awarded second base due to interference, went to third on a grounder, and scored on Ron Santo's two-run triple before Lou Brock launched a homer into the center-field bleachers some 460 feet away.

Four unearned runs were charged to Al Jackson that inning because of the interference call on Throneberry, but Marv seemed to redeem himself by lacing a two-run triple in the bottom of the first. With Throneberry standing on third, the Cubs made an appeal play to first base, believing he missed the bag. Umpire Dusty Boggess called him out, prompting manager Casey Stengel to come out of the dugout to argue the call.

There are several retold versions of what happened next, but whether it was first-base coach Cookie Lavagetto or Boggess who told Stengel, the fact remained that Throneberry missed second base as well.

"Well, I know he touched third because he's standing on it," Stengel told Boggess before retreating for the dugout.

Throneberry was credited with two RBIs on the play but was 0-for-5 with two strikeouts in an 8–7 loss.

The fielding faux pas had some wondering what happened to the hot-shot Yankee prospect.

"When he came up to the Yankees he found he couldn't break in," said Ralph Houk during his first stint as the team's manager. "He was bucking Skowron, Siebern, and others all those years, and I guess he got discouraged—also older, and he didn't get to play as much. He must have lost his coordination gradually because of not playing regularly."[297]

On at least two occasions, Marv handled a grounder with a runner breaking for the plate before throwing home too late to get the out. In one game against the Cardinals, he dropped a two-out pop-up in foul territory with a runner on third in a tie game, only to have the batter single on the next pitch to drive in the winning run.

Throneberry's on-field exploits often had the media heading for his locker stall after the game. Marv generally was good-natured in answering questions concerning the latest bizarre play surrounding the first baseman. Sometimes, Throneberry would have Richie Ashburn, who lockered next to him, answer the questions on his behalf.

"The writers would come in, and Ashburn would tell them, 'Throneberry says, "Blah, blah, blah, blah,"'" recalled Rod Kanehl in Peter Golenbock's book, *Amazin'*. "And they would quote Throneberry. But it was Ashburn's glibness that put the words in Throneberry's mouth. And it was Ashburn who schooled him on the fact, 'Accept the notoriety, good or bad.' I roomed with him. Marv didn't take it badly. He was a celebrity, he liked his celebrity, and he got along with it. He signed autographs. Mentally, he was in great shape."[298]

"I don't mind if they get on me," said Throneberry in August. "But when they start calling me stupid, that's different."[299]

Throneberry demonstrated his sense of humor hadn't waned when he spoke with teammate Jay Hook before a doubleheader against the Cardinals July 7. Throneberry was hitting .230 with two homers and 14 RBIs in 43 games as a Met as he struck up a conversation with the starting pitcher.

"He said, 'Hook, you're an engineer, right?'" recalled Hook in 2008. "And I said, 'Yeah.' And he said, 'Engineers can print real good, can't they?' And I said, 'Yeah, I took drafting, and I can print pretty good.'

"So he went above his locker and he took [his nameplate] out, turned it over and he got me a pen. He said, 'Write, "Marvelous Marv."' So I wrote, 'Marvelous Marv,' and he put it above his locker. All the writers came in after the game, and there's this 'Marvelous Marv' above his locker.

"He named himself, really. I was the conduit by which it got visualized.

"The next day in the papers, it was 'Marvelous Marv' did whatever he did."

What Throneberry did was smack a pinch-hit, two-run homer in the bottom of the ninth to beat the Cardinals 5–4 in the first game before going 2-for-4 with a solo blast in the nightcap. Throneberry had doubled his home run total as a Met in one afternoon, and the "Marvelous Marv" nameplate gave the scribes something else to write.

Teammate Frank Thomas felt the press went a bit overboard in their portrayal of Throneberry.

"The media gets onto something, and they just continue to ride the train in that respect," Thomas said. "That's what they did with him.

"The media is really something, and I can say that now because I'm out of the game and I really don't care what they would say about me."

Throneberry was a good fit for New York and grew to accept the bustling city. He was more than happy to share his nuances with the many players who shuttled on and off the 1962 roster.

"Marv Throneberry was from Springfield or Joplin, Missouri," Mets teammate Larry Foss recalled. "And he's telling me, a hick from Kansas, how to walk down Fifth Avenue because I was a gentleman and I'd let people pass.

"'Hey, do this,' Marv said. And he was bumping into people, and they didn't even turn around thinking he was rude. That was my roommate, Marvelous Marv."

The mood of the fans toward Throneberry went from exasperated to sympathetic around the second week of August, which coincided with the Mets' elimination from the pennant race. A Marv Throneberry Fan Club had been started, and its members could be seen at the Polo Grounds. Four of those members even created T-shirts, each with one letter of Throneberry's name. They would spell out M-A-R-V—or V-R-A-M—depending on which angle you saw them.

They also carried a banner that read, "Cranberry, Strawberry, We Love Throneberry!"

The spectators at the Polo Grounds had finally taken Throneberry to their bosoms, and he repaid them with a few more heroics at the plate. Marv wasn't in the starting lineup when the Mets took on the Pirates in Game 2 of a doubleheader on August 21. Coach Solly Hemus was tossed from the game in the fifth inning and replaced by Gene Woodling. When Woodling had to be used as a pinch-hitter, Stengel asked Throneberry to take over as the first-base coach. Throneberry received a warm ovation as he took the field in the bottom of the seventh, a complete turnaround from the constant booing he heard just a few weeks earlier.

The Mets trailed 4-1 in the bottom of the ninth before putting the first two runners on base. Charlie Neal whiffed for the first out, and Felix Mantilla followed with an RBI single, but Frank Thomas hit a fly ball to center for the second out.

Stengel already had used four pinch-hitters when he told Throneberry to grab a bat and face Roy Face, much to the delight of the few hundred fans still left in the park. The game ended when Throneberry blasted a three-run homer to right-center, completing a four-run rally that gave the Mets a 5–4 victory. Throneberry touched every base and sent the Mets to their 31st victory in 126 games.

His last big game as a Met came in an 8–2 rout of the Reds on September 16. He tied the game 2–2 with an RBI single in the first inning, hit a solo homer in the third, and worked a bases-loaded walk an inning later. The 2-for-3 game raised his Mets average to .251, but the home run off Sammy Ellis would be his last in the majors.

Throneberry went 3-for-23 (.130) the rest of the season to end the year with a .244 average, 16 home runs, and 49 RBIs for the Mets. He finished the club's inaugural season ranked second on the team in homers and slugging percentage (.426), and fourth in RBIs.

Throneberry also was presented with a $6,000 luxury cruiser before the team's final home game of the season. He had earned the prize by hitting the Howard Clothes sign on the right-field fence more times than any other player. The clothing chain also presented Ashburn with a boat that day for being voted the team MVP by the sportswriters.

The following day, a legal advisor for Major League Baseball told Throneberry he had to declare the boat on his taxes as income since he earned it through a feat of skill, whereas Ashburn dodged taxes because his boat was an award.

To make matters worse, Throneberry and Ashburn had little use for water vessels. When Ashburn asked Throneberry what he'd do with the boat, Marvelous Marv replied, "Search me. I live in Colliersville, Tennessee. The nearest water is the Wolf River about eight miles from my house. And it's too big for my bathtub. How about you?"

Ashburn faced the same dilemma. "You think you got trouble…I live on a prairie in Nebraska!"[300]

Paying taxes on a useless boat seemed a perfect way to end 1962, and it bemused Throneberry.

"I don't think I'll ever forget this season," Throneberry said once it was all over. "I win a boat but it costs me money. I think I'll go home and try to forget the whole year. Make like it never happened."[301]

Throneberry wasn't taxed for receiving the Ben Epstein "Good Guy Award" as the player most cooperative with the media during 1962.

"I think that was because most of the sportswriters knew that they had stretched the truth quite a bit," recalled Dixie Throneberry, Marv's widow, in an interview for Janet Paskin's book *Tales from the New York Mets*. "And they decided to give him the award because he was a good guy about it. There's so much myth mixed in with the truth, I don't think he got the appreciation he should have gotten."[302]

It was the least the writers could do for allowing Throneberry to inspire some of their better quips. Jimmy Breslin came up with the line, "Having Throneberry play for your team was like having Willie Sutton work for your bank!"

At the awards banquet, he good-naturedly told the audience he was a little afraid to come up to accept the award for fear he might drop it.

"He was a character, laid back and quiet," remembered teammate Craig Anderson in 2011. "The players sort of took to him when he got there. He got this 'Marvelous Marv' nickname, and that just got it going. He started to have all these screwed-up plays happen to him. Of course, the writers really started to gloss over his screwups, and he'd hit a home run here and there. He got to be very popular through posters and through the press. But he was very laid back and didn't make any big deal about it.

"The players around him, like Ashburn and Kanehl, made him a star. Somebody started calling him 'Marvelous Marv,' and then they decided they'd put that name on his locker. Jay Hook made the nameplate for Marv, and he said Marv came up to him and said, 'I don't know how to spell all these words. You write this.' I think Ashburn was the instigator behind all that.

"And now here's this name out there, and he starts making errors and screwing up on plays. And everybody loved him for it. He took it seriously. He wasn't a jokester.

"And then he gets a Miller commercial later on, and there was probably more money made there than he made in baseball."

He received the honor as he was in the middle of negotiating his 1963 contract. He was unhappy with Weiss' offer and headed to Florida at his own expense to see if he could get a few more dollars from the team president.

According to Ralph Kiner's book, *Kiner's Corner*, Throneberry made his case for a larger contract by reminding Weiss' assistant, Johnny Murphy, that, "I brought some people in."

"You also drove some away," countered Murphy.[303]

"I think he brought fans in that year," said Anderson. "The people were so happy to have National League baseball back, we could do no wrong even though we were lousy."

The holdout cost him valuable at-bats in spring training, leaving him unprepared for the season. The Mets also had another first baseman after acquiring Tim Harkness from the Dodgers.

Throneberry struck out as a pinch-hitter in the 1963 season opener and went 0-for-3 in his lone start April 11 at Milwaukee. He poked an RBI single against the Braves four days later and doubled as a pinch-hitter against Milwaukee at the Polo Grounds April 21, his final hit in the majors.

Throneberry was just 2-for-14 when he was sent to the minors for "conditioning purposes" in early May.

"I may be back sooner than a lot of people think," said Throneberry after learning of the demotion. "I'm going to leave my name up there above the locker room."[304]

"I hope he hits 25 or 50 home runs down there so I can pull him back quick," Stengel said.[305]

He hit 16 homers and drove in 44 runs for Triple A Buffalo following his demotion, but his .176 batting average kept him in the minors the rest of the year. He opened 1964 with the Bisons and went 1-for-12 in eight games before retiring at age 30.

Throneberry returned to Tennessee, where he lived until his death in 1994. He became a salesman and worked in public relations after leaving baseball, but he returned to the spotlight when the Miller Brewing Company asked if he might be interested in starring in a commercial.

Miller Lite was introduced by the brewery in the mid-1970s with the help of several humorous television ads featuring former athletes. Throneberry's turn came in 1983,

saying in his commercial, "If I do for Lite what I did for baseball, I'm afraid their sales will go down." He did a few more Miller Lite commercials, giving the line, "I still don't know why they asked me to do this commercial."

Although he turned self-deprecation into a cottage industry, Throneberry was proud of his playing career.

"Hey, I really wasn't that bad a ballplayer," he said in 1982. "I always thought I was a good ballplayer. I played in the major leagues 11 years. There are millions of ballplayers in this country not good enough to make the majors."

Throneberry was 60 when he died of cancer in June 1994, leaving his wife Dixie, daughters Gail, Sandra, and Laurie, sons Gil and Jody, 10 grandchildren, and four great-grandchildren. Sadly, the Mets failed to recognize his passing with a uniform patch or any other reminder of Throneberry's importance to the franchise's early days.

ML debut	Yankees @ Red Sox, 9/25/55
Mets debut	vs. Braves, 5/11/62
1st ML hit	2-run double vs. Frank Baumann, @ Red Sox, 9/25/55 (with Yankees)
1st Mets hit	single vs. Bob Shaw, Braves, 5/11/62
1st ML homer	vs. Bill Fischer, @ White Sox, 5/20/58 (with Yankees)
1st Mets homer	solo homer vs. Bob Bruce, @ Colt 45s, 6/14/62
1st ML RBI	sac-fly vs. Frank Sullivan, @ Red Sox, 9/25/55 (with Yankees)
1st Mets RBI	RBI single vs. Bob Buhl, @ Cubs, 6/9/62
Most hits, ML game	3, 13 times
Most hits, Mets game	3, @ Cubs, 6/9/62; @ Colt 45s, 6/14/62
Most homers, ML game	2, Orioles @ A's, 6/27/61; Mets vs. Phillies, 8/2/62
Most RBIs, ML game	5, vs. White Sox, 4/29/61 (with A's)
Most RBIs, Mets game	3, @ Reds, 8/10/62; vs. Pirates, 8/21/62; vs. Reds, 9/16/62

Acquired: Traded by the Orioles for a player to be named (Hobie Landrith) and cash, 5/9/62.

Robin Ventura

Third Baseman, First Baseman   Bats left, throws right
Born: 7/14/67   Santa Maria, California
Height: 6'1"   Weight: 198   #4

Robin Ventura Mets Career

YEAR	GP	AB	R	H	2B	3B	HR	RBI	K	BB	SB	AVG	SLG	OBP
1999	161	588	88	177	38	0	32	120	109	74	1	.301	.529	.379
2000	141	469	61	109	23	0	24	84	91	75	3	.232	.439	.338
2001	142	456	70	108	20	1	21	61	101	88	2	.237	.419	.359
TOTAL	444	1513	219	394	81	1	77	265	301	237	6	.260	.468	.360

ML Career

YEARS	GP	AB	R	H	2B	3B	HR	RBI	K	BB	SB	AVG	SLG	OBP
89–04	2079	7064	1006	1885	338	14	294	1182	1179	1075	24	.267	.444	.362

There were so many great moments during Robin Ventura's rather brief Mets career. He captured a Gold Glove in 1999 while anchoring an infield that set a major league record for fewest errors in a season. He became the first player to hit a grand slam in both ends of a doubleheader. He delivered a walk-off single in the 11th inning against the Pirates October 1, 1999, helping the Mets crawl out of a two-game hole on the final weekend of the season to win the NL wild-card. And there was the "grand slam single," one of the oddest occurrences in major league postseason history, a hit that kept the Mets alive in the 1999 NLCS.

Ventura's first season as a Met was so good that the Shea faithful gave him a relatively free pass on what would become a pretty mediocre final two seasons with the team. Ventura was brought to New York to get the team over the hump after a dreadful collapse in the final week of the 1998 season. He did that and more while playing on a bad left knee and with a sore right shoulder, proving that New York isn't always a "what have you done for us lately?" town.

Third base had generally been a problematic position for the Mets before Ventura got there. Wayne Garrett patrolled the position for the better part of 7½ seasons while management continued to look for a replacement. Howard Johnson compiled three of the best offensive seasons in team history while playing third, but his fielding was never exceptional.

The Mets actually had an outstanding third baseman before Ventura joined the team. Edgardo Alfonzo had emerged as an excellent glove man and a solid offensive contributor. But Ventura's presence led to a position switch for Alfonzo, who should have won at least one Gold Glove at second base.

Ventura had delivered consistently good numbers with the White Sox from 1990 to 1998, hitting as many as 34 homers and 105 RBIs and batting .295. He already owned five Gold Gloves by the time the Mets signed him to a free-agent contract in December 1998.

The Southern Californian enjoyed arguably his best major league season with the 1999 Mets. He was part of an infield that included Alfonzo, Rey Ordóñez, and John Olerud, a collection of gloves that made the 1986 Mets infield look like the Bad News Bears—and Keith Hernandez. Ventura batted .375 (15-for-40) with two home runs, 11 RBIs, three doubles, and four runs scored during a season-opening 10-game hitting streak. He capped his first month as a Met with a 3-for-4, one-homer, three-RBI game against the Giants to put his average at .298.

Ventura hit only .237 in May, but his month included five homers, 21 RBIs, and a very special doubleheader against the Brewers May 20. He hit a grand slam in the first game and added another in the nightcap to become the only major leaguer to belt grand slams in each end of a twin bill. Ventura added another bases-loaded blast August against San Francisco to join John Milner (1976) as the only other Met to hit three grand slams in a single season.

His fielding was every bit as good as his hitting during the first two months. He and Alfonzo possessed great range, allowing Ordóñez to play within his position without forcing plays. The Mets' starting infield graced the cover of *Sports Illustrated* later that season, touted as the best ever assembled.

To appreciate Ventura was to appreciate the Mets' history of free-agent signings. With the exception of Brett Butler in 1995, each of the team's high-profile free-agent signees had lousy first seasons with the Mets, a trend that would continue with Mo Vaughn and Roberto Alomar in 2002. Ventura was more than living up to the reputation he developed during his years with the White Sox. He hit a ridiculous .529 (9-for-17) with the bases loaded, .556 (5-for-9) with runners on second and third and .338 (54-for-160) with seven homers and 86 RBIs with men in scoring position.

Ventura sizzled from June 1 to September 6, hitting .345 with 21 homers, 21 doubles, 71 RBIs, and 53 runs scored in 85 games. He was named the National League Player of the Week ending August 1 and finished the year with 120 RBIs, breaking Darryl Strawberry's team record of 108 among left-handed hitters.

The Mets came very close to duplicating their September collapse of 1998, falling two games off the wild-card lead with three games remaining after owning a four-game lead over the Reds with two weeks left. Ventura helped the Mets stay afloat by hitting 6-for-16 with a homer and four RBIs in the final four games, including the playoff contest at Cincinnati. He hit a solo homer and the game-ending single in a 3–2 win over the Pirates October 1, which began the Mets' playoff surge. He collected two hits the next night and delivered base hits in each of the next two games.

Ventura was now in the playoffs for the first time since 1993, when he batted just .200 with a homer and five RBIs against the Blue Jays. He hit only .154 in the 1999 postseason with no home runs and two RBIs in 39 at-bats. Teammate Todd Pratt robbed him of a homer and three ribbies, but no one seemed to care after the fact.

Ventura opened the NLCS against the Braves by going 0-for-16 before poking a single in the 11th inning of Game 5. Four innings later, he provided one of the more memorable blasts in postseason history.

The Mets trailed 3–2 and were one out from elimination when Pratt worked a bases-loaded walk to keep the team's season alive. Up stepped Ventura, who sent a ball over the wall in right-center at Shea for what should have been a grand slam. He was nearing the second-base bag when Pratt grabbed him in a bearhug, causing Ventura to pass him on the base lines. Ventura also never touched second and was credited with a single after many Mets fans shut off their sets thinking it was a 7–3 victory for New York. Regardless, the hit sent the series back to Atlanta, where the Mets absorbed an agonizing loss that ended their season.

Ventura hit only .120 in the NLCS before undergoing surgery on his left knee and right shoulder in the fall. Although he was ready for the start of 2000 spring training, Ventura was unable to duplicate his 1999 regular season. He never got his batting average above .262 and finished with a .232 average, 24 home runs, and 84 RBIs. That included a two-game stretch in mid-April in which he drove in 10 runs and smacked his 14th career grand slam, which tied him with Ken Griffey Jr. for the most among active players at the time.

Ventura finished the regular season by batting .320 with three homers, 13 RBIs, and nine runs scored in his final 16 games, giving hope that he'd have a better postseason than he did the previous year.

Although Ventura hit just .167 in 48 at-bats during the playoffs and World Series, he also came through with several clutch hits. He smacked a two-run homer to support Bobby Jones in a one-hit shutout against the Giants in the Game 4 clincher in the NLDS. He had three RBIs as the Mets earned a 10–6 victory over the Cardinals in Game 4 of the NLCS, one hit after providing an RBI single during a three-run first that helped the Mets close out the series. His lone World Series home run came in the only Mets victory in the World Series against the Yankees. He finished the 2000 postseason with eight RBIs in 14 games.

Ventura got off to a nice start in 2001, batting .304 with five homers, 14 RBIs, and 15 runs scored in 29 games. He won the season opener with a pair of two-run homers, including a blast in the 10th inning against the Braves. His 15th grand slam gave the Mets a 7–5 comeback win over the Astros May 1. Ventura also drove in 14 runs and scored 10 times while the Mets were going 20–4 from August 18 to September 27 to get back into the NL East race. He reached the 20-homer mark for the eighth time but ended the year hitting only .237 with 21 homers 20 doubles and 61 RBIs.

Ventura was 34 years old by the end of the 2001 season and 12 years removed from his major league debut with the White Sox. His Gold Glove ability had turned to silver while his bat speed slowed down. Mets general manager Steve Phillips, smart enough to sign Ventura as a free agent three years earlier, sent the third baseman to the Yankees for David Justice in December 2001. Justice never played a game for the Mets, and Ventura enjoyed one final hurrah after replacing Scott Brosius at third for the Yankees.

Ventura hit 27 home runs and drove in 93 runs as the Yanks reached the postseason for the eighth straight season. He was one of the team's better hitters during the ALDS loss to the Angels, hitting .286 (4-for-14) with four RBIs against the eventual World Series champs.

He was back in California after opening 2003 with the Yankees. Ventura compiled a .251 average with nine homers and 42 RBIs in 117 games before the Bombers sent him to the Dodgers, where he would end his playing career. He was a role player during his 1½ seasons with Los Angeles, hitting .234 with 10 homers and 41 RBIs in 261

Robin Ventura at the Shea Stadium finale ceremony in 2008.
Photo courtesy of David Ferry

at-bats before retiring after the 2004 season, 16 years after he was taken by the White Sox with the 10th overall pick in the draft.

In retrospect, it's very surprising that Ventura wasn't taken earlier in the 1988 draft. Three of the nine players taken ahead of him never reached the majors, and only three of those nine appeared in an All-Star Game. He received both the Golden Spikes Award and Dick Howser Trophy as college baseball's top player that season after hitting .391 with 26 home runs and 96 RBIs for Oklahoma State. Ventura reeled off a 58-game hitting streak as a sophomore in 1987 before helping the Cowboys reach the College World Series for the second straight year. He was *Baseball America*'s College Player of the Year in '87 following a .428 average, 21 homers, and 110 RBIs. He was Oklahoma State's all-time hits leader by the time he left school and would be named the College Player of the Decade by *Baseball America*.

It didn't take long for Ventura to reach the majors. He made his pro debut with the 1989 Birmingham Barons of the Double A Southern League, hitting .278 with 67 RBIs and 93 walks in 454 at-bats before the White Sox promoted him in September.

Ventura hit .178 in 45 at-bats for the White Sox in '89 and posted a .249 with five home runs and 54 RBIs in 493 at-bats a year later. He hit his stride in 1991, collecting his first Gold Glove and finishing with 23 homers, 100 RBIs, and a .284 average. Only Frank Thomas had more homers, runs batted in, hits, and doubles than Ventura among Chicago's second-place roster. But it was his fielding that turned heads.

Ventura's prowess at the plate in college overshadowed his glove work. It's not often that a second-year player receives a Gold Glove, and he also won the award the next two years before ending his career with six. He also drove in 287 runs while collecting Gold Gloves in three straight seasons.

Ventura and Thomas were the White Sox's version of "Batman and Robin" from 1991 to 1996, combining to hit 354 homers and drive in 1,261 runs. Ventura averaged 23 home runs and 94 RBIs while batting .282. He reached the 100 RBI mark twice in that span and smacked a career-high 34 home runs in 1996.

Perhaps Ventura's most embarrassing moment came in 1993, when he charged the mound after Nolan Ryan threw a pitch near his head. The 46-year-old Ryan handled himself well, putting Ventura into a headlock and pummeling the back of his head.

The White Sox were in the middle of their 1997 spring training when Ventura suffered his first major injury, a compound fracture and a dislocation of his right ankle while sliding into home plate March 21. The injury landed him on the disabled list for the first time and kept him out of action until July 24.

The gruesome injury didn't stop Ventura from hitting .377 with three homers, 10 RBIs, and 14 runs scored in his first 20 games of the season. He was hitting .305 by September 8 before a .164 mark in his final 16 games left him with a .262 average, tying his worst since 1990.

Ventura appeared fully recovered by the start of 1998 and set a career high with four triples while providing 21 homers and 91 RBIs in 161 games. He also hit a pair of walk-off home runs and came away with his fifth and final American League Gold Glove. Only Brooks Robinson (16) and Buddy Bell (six) had won more among AL third-sackers.

Ventura became a free agent at the end of the 1998 season. The White Sox wanted to keep him in the fold, but the Mets were the more aggressive pursuer after successfully re-signing Piazza to a contract. Ventura spent most of his Mets career hitting fifth behind Piazza in a lineup that set then–team records with a .279 average, 853 runs, 297 doubles, and 814 RBIs.

Ventura provided one of the funnier moments in Mets history. The team was in a rain delay at Yankee Stadium in 2000 when he decided to kill time while entertaining the water-logged fans. He donned Piazza's jersey top and affixed a faux Fu Manchu mustache to his face to look more like the real deal.

Ventura stepped up to the plate and flashed Piazza's signature "I'm ready" sign to an imaginary home plate umpire before using his teammate's swing to hit a phantom homer. Ventura rounded the bases/tarp before completing his journey with a bellyflop that appeared to start halfway down the third-base line. It was another reason why Mets fans had a soft spot for Ventura while he struggled at times during his last two seasons with the team.

Upon his retirement, only five other players had more career grand slams than Ventura's 16.

Ventura gave television a try after his playing career, serving as a part-time analyst for the White Sox in 2005. He has also worked as a color analyst for ESPN, broadcasting the Little League World Series, among other baseball events.

He settled back in Southern California with his wife Stephanie, daughters Rachel, Madison, and Grace, and son Jack. He planned to stay there until the White Sox brought him back in June 2011 as a special advisor to director of player development Buddy Bell.

The White Sox sought a manager after failing to work out a contract extension with Ozzie Guillen near the end of the 2011 campaign. The ballclub pulled off a surprise by hiring Ventura, who had no previous managerial or coaching experience at any professional level.

ML debut	White Sox @ Orioles, 9/12/89
Mets debut	@ Marlins, 4/5/99
1st ML hit	RBI single vs. Ben McDonald, @ O's, 9/12/89 (with White Sox)
1st Mets hit	single vs. Vic Darensbourg, @ Marlins, 4/5/99
1st ML homer	solo homer vs. Roger Clemens, Red Sox, 4/18/90)
1st Mets homer	solo homer vs. Mike Thurman, @ Expos, 4/9/99
1st ML RBI	RBI single vs. Ben McDonald, @ O's, 9/12/89 (with White Sox)
1st Mets RBI	sac-fly vs. Alex Fernandez, @ Marlins, 4/5/99
Most hits, ML game	5, @ Brewers, 6/29/95; @ Twins, 9/23/95 (both with White Sox)
Most hits, Mets game	4, @ Cubs, 7/31/99; @ Brewers, 8/3/99
Most homers, ML game	2, 21 times, 15 times with White Sox
Most homers, Mets game	2, 5 times
Most RBIs, ML game	8, @ Rangers, 9/4/95 (with White Sox)
Most RBIs, Mets game	6, @ Marlins, 6/28/99; @ Cubs, 7/31/99; @ Pirates, 4/16/00

Acquired: Signed as a free agent, 12/1/98.
Deleted: Traded to the Yankees for David Justice, 12/7/01.

Mookie Wilson

Outfielder   Bats both, throws right
Born: 2/9/56   Bamberg, South Carolina
Height: 5'10"   Weight: 170   #1

Mookie Wilson Mets Career

YEAR	GP	AB	R	H	2B	3B	HR	RBI	K	BB	SB	AVG	SLG	OBP
1980	27	105	16	26	5	3	0	4	19	12	7	.248	.352	.325
1981	92	328	49	89	8	8	3	14	59	20	24	.271	.372	.317
1982	159	639	90	178	25	9	5	55	102	32	58	.279	.369	.314
1983	152	638	91	176	25	6	7	51	103	18	54	.276	.367	.300
1984	154	587	88	162	28	10	10	54	90	26	46	.276	.409	.308
1985	93	337	56	93	16	8	6	26	52	28	24	.276	.424	.331
1986	123	381	61	110	17	5	9	45	72	32	25	.289	.430	.345
1987	124	385	58	115	19	7	9	34	85	35	21	.299	.455	.359
1988	112	378	61	112	17	5	8	41	63	27	15	.296	.431	.345
1989	80	249	22	51	10	1	3	18	47	10	7	.205	.289	.237
TOTAL	1116	4027	592	1112	170	62	60	342	692	240	281	.276	.394	.318

ML Career

YEAR	GP	AB	R	H	2B	3B	HR	RBI	K	BB	SB	AVG	SLG	OBP
80–91	1403	5094	731	1397	227	71	67	438	866	282	327	.274	.386	.314

If one is putting together a 25-man roster of the all-time greatest Mets, that person might be hard-pressed to place Mookie Wilson in the starting lineup. Put together a team of most popular Mets, and William Hayward Wilson is a starting outfielder without question.

Wilson played the game of baseball with the same enthusiasm for every at-bat, every inning, every game, every season. His obvious love and respect for the game allowed fans to overlook his so-so on-base percentage and lower-than-average arm strength. Mets fans were appreciative of the way he played each game and respected the fact that he rarely complained when he eventually had to share his position with Lenny Dykstra.

Plus, it didn't hurt that he provided the most memorable at-bat in Mets history.

The Mets were mediocre and on their way to becoming downright crappy when they drafted Wilson in the second round of the 1977 draft. It was one of many strong draft picks by general manager Joe McDonald, who otherwise served as the team scapegoat while the penny-pinching front office prevented him from making significant improvements to the ballclub.

The Mets liked what they saw during Wilson's two years at the University of South Carolina. He landed on several All-America teams and hit .357 for the Gamecocks in 1977 with eight home runs, 33 stolen bases, and 33 RBIs. He signed with the Mets shortly after helping South Carolina finish second in the College World Series as a sophomore.

Wilson displayed modest power and hellacious speed as he apprenticed in the minors from 1977 to 1980. He hit .290 for Low A Wausau in '77 and continued to produce after making the jump to Double A Jackson a year later. He paced the Texas League with 15 triples and was fifth with 38 stolen bases in 1978, all while batting .292

with 72 RBIs and 72 runs scored in 132 games. His most memorable moment at Double A came June 22 as he married his wife, Rosa, at home plate prior to the game. The two have been together ever since.

Wilson spent the next two years with Triple A Tidewater and continued to manufacture runs with his speed. He was second in the International League with 49 steals and 84 runs scored, tied for second with 10 triples and fourth with 141 hits while batting .267 in 1979.

Frank Cashen could have been tempted to put Wilson on his 1980 Opening Day roster after the Bamberg, South Carolina, product hit .267 in spring training. But Cashen wanted to give Wilson and fellow prospect Hubie Brooks another year at Triple A before letting them loose on major league pitching. Besides, the Mets were years away from contention, so there was no reason to rush the top prospects.

Wilson gave switch-hitting a try for the first time during spring training in 1980 to take advantage of his exceptional speed. The natural right-hander was an instant success from the left side, hitting .298 in 436 at-bats for the Tides compared to .278 in 79 at-bats as a righty. The extra year in the minors didn't hurt Wilson as he led the International League with 195 hits while finishing sixth with a .295 average. He also stole 50 bags and scored 92 runs, both minor league career highs.

Wilson made his Mets debut September 2 against the Dodgers and continued to hit better from the left side, posting a .274 mark compared to a .143 average from the right. He opened his major league career 1-for-14 before finishing a homer shy of the cycle at San Diego September 6. He had another three-hit game five days later and went 4-for-5 with a triple and three runs scored against the Cubs September 14. The four-hit game was part of a seven-game hitting streak in which Wilson raised his average from .209 to .296. His was up to .313 by September 23 following back-to-back two-hit games.

More impressive was that Wilson was playing with a fractured right pinky that bothered him while batting right-handed. He tailed off the final 10 games of the season, going 1-for-25 in seven starts to finish with a .248 average and a .325 on-base percentage in his first major league action.

Brooks hit .309 in 81 at-bats during his September recall, giving the Mets a pair of proven rookie hitters heading into 1981. This was a rare occurrence for the Mets, who had developed several outstanding pitchers but usually came up empty or miscalculated on their hitting prospects. John Milner, Lee Mazzilli, and Steve Henderson were the only Mets between 1970 and 1980 to log at least 350 at-bats in their first full major league seasons, and only Henderson hit over .250 in his rookie year. By 1981, Ron Hunt (.272 in 1963), Cleon Jones (.275 in 1966), and Henderson (.297 in 1977) were the only Mets rookies with at least 350 at-bats to record a batting average higher than .250, and Henderson went straight to the Mets from the Reds in the 1977 Tom Seaver trade. Wilson and Brooks were expected to end that drought in 1981, but a players' strike kept both players under 360 at-bats.

The Mets had never before produced a prospect like Wilson, who could swipe bases with regularity, hit for average, and chew up ground in the outfield. Jones was a more polished hitter as a rookie, but Wilson had a base-stealer's mentality and lived to rattle a pitcher from the base paths. He ranked eighth among all National Leaguers with 24 stolen bases in 1981 and hit a very respectable .271 following a slow start. Wilson owned a .203 average on May 24 before embarking on a 21-game tear in which he batted .405 (34-for-84) with 12 stolen bases and 19 runs scored. His average stood at .290 after he went 4-for-6 with a walk-off, two-run homer and three RBIs in a 7–6 win over the Cardinals September 20. But nagging ankle and knee injuries led to a season-ending 4-for-36 slump, leaving Brooks as the first Met to hit .300 and qualify for the batting title in his rookie season.

But at least Wilson and Brooks proved there was talent on the farm. Cashen made a blockbuster deal in the winter of 1982 to improve the lineup, getting George Foster from the Reds without losing any of the team's top prospects. Cashen also hired a new manager, replacing Joe Torre with George Bamberger after the 1981 season.

The 1982 Mets also relied more on their homegrown talent as Ron Gardenhire became the everyday shortstop while Wally Backman and Brian Giles shared second. The farm system now accounted for half the starting lineup, along with starting pitchers Craig Swan and Mike Scott, and closer Neil Allen. Cashen was prepared to sink or swim with his prospects, and the Mets treaded water for much of the first half, winning 34 of their first 64 games. Wilson did his part by hitting .293 with 21 stolen bases, 25 RBIs, and 34 runs scored as the team's starting center fielder and leadoff hitter.

But the '82 team hit the skids as soon as the opposition got their third looks at the starting rotation. Allen missed most of the final four months, and the team ended August on a 15-game losing streak to fall 30 games under .500. But Wilson still produced in the second half, providing a pair of four-hit games and eight games with at least three hits to end the year with a .279 average. He obliterated the team record for stolen bases, finishing with 58 to top Frank Taveras' mark of 42 set in 1979. Wilson also put together a pair of 13-game hitting streaks and hit nine triples, matching Charlie Neal's team mark set in the Mets' first season.

The only major flaw in Wilson's offensive game was selectivity at the plate. He walked just 32 times in 677 plate appearances in 1982, or once every 21.2 times up. He also struck out 102 times and posted a .314 on-base percentage, ranking 52nd among 65 National Leaguers who qualified for the batting title that season. But there was no denying Wilson was the most exciting player on the team.

The Mets were a vastly improved team by the end of 1983, although their 68–94 record was only three wins better than 1982. Tom Seaver was reacquired before the season, Darryl Strawberry was recalled in May, Keith Hernandez was stolen from the Cardinals in June, and Ron Darling made his major league debut in September.

And Wilson remained the model of consistency, hitting .276 with seven home runs, 51 RBIs, and team highs of 24 doubles, 176 hits, and 54 stolen bases. Wilson also recorded just 18 walks and 103 strikeouts in 663 plate appearances, and his .300 on-base percentage was fifth-worst in the National League among those eligible for the batting title. Brooks owned the league's worst on-base percentage, and teammate George Foster had the third-worst.

But Wilson could win games with his bat and legs as proven by an exceptional doubleheader against the Pirates July 31. In Game 1, he went 3-for-5 and tied the game with an RBI single in the eighth before the Mets beat the Bucs 7–6 in 12 innings. Hours later, Wilson led off the 12th inning with a single, moved to second on a sacrifice, and scored from second on a forceout to give the Mets a 1–0 victory and a doubleheader sweep. Wilson's daring dash allowed Jesse Orosco to win both ends of the twin bill.

The Mets made another managerial change in October 1983, and this one affected Wilson. Davey Johnson was a mathematical whiz who used computer printouts and good old baseball horse sense to write out his lineup. He noticed Wilson's on-base percentage and thought his center fielder might be better suited as the No. 6 hitter in the lineup. With Wilson's speed and batting average, he had a chance to provide a spark near the bottom of the order by creating rallies that wouldn't otherwise occur. Not many first-year managers would have the guts to take a 50-plus base-stealer and place him sixth in the lineup, but Johnson had enough daring to make it happen.

The decision paid dividends of sorts as Wilson hit .287 with 12 steals and 12 runs scored in the Mets' first 38 games of the season. The problem was that the new leadoff hitters—Wally Backman and Ron Gardenhire—were making Wilson's previous on-base percentage look pretty good.

Wilson spent most of the final four months hitting from the No. 1 or 2 spots as Johnson tried to find tablesetters for Hernandez, Foster, and Strawberry. Once he was moved back to the top of the order, Wilson hit .306 with four home runs, 10 RBIs, and 16 runs scored in 25 games. Wilson also failed to work a single base-on-balls during that span, but the Mets were in first place by one game over the Phillies by the end of that run.

Wilson also put together a 15-game hitting streak from June 8 to 23, batting .328 during that span. The Mets won 11 of those 15 games to stay atop the NL East, but the team would fall to second while Mookie struggled at the plate. He hit only .237 from July 12 to September 15, scoring 38 times but recording 45 strikeouts in 61 games. The slump included a miserable four-game series in which he was 1-for-17 with six strikeouts against the Padres.

Mookie hit .349 over his final 15 games to end the year with a .276 average for the second straight year. He also had 10 triples to break the mark he shared with Neal. And Wilson remained the team's best defensive center fielder since Tommie Agee, covering plenty of landscape while playing in between Foster and Strawberry. Having Wilson out there was like employing a fourth outfielder as he allowed Foster to concentrate on the left side of the field.

The Mets had more outfield depth in 1985 as Lenny Dykstra was recalled in May while Wilson tried to recover from a sore shoulder. Dykstra was Wilson's equal as a center fielder and almost as adept as a base runner. Dykstra's production gave Wilson a few extra days to recover from the right shoulder pain, but the soreness returned in June.

Injury rehabilitation was something new to Wilson, who played in all but 21 games the previous three seasons. He was placed on the disabled list July 1 after his shoulder failed to come around with rest, the first time he had landed on the DL as a major leaguer. Wilson underwent shoulder surgery July 3 and didn't play again until September 1, allowing Dykstra an opportunity to gain valuable playing time that would come in handy a year later.

Wilson was back in time to help the Mets stay with the Cardinals in the NL East race. He went 3-for-5 and scored three times September 12 against the Cardinals, including the winning run in the bottom of the ninth of a 7–6 victory that gave the Mets a one-game lead with 24 games remaining. That began a five-game stretch that saw Wilson collect three hits in four of those contests. He hit .307 in September to raise his average from .260 to .276. It was the third straight year he finished with a .276 average, and his 24 stolen bases allowed him to take over the team's all-time lead.

Wilson underwent another shoulder procedure in October and spent the winter rehabilitating the injury. Many within the organization blamed coach Frank Howard for Mookie's shoulder woes. Howard felt Wilson could improve his arm strength through constant long tossing, and the shoulder began to hurt a few weeks after he began the throwing drills.

The Mets were slight favorites to win the NL East when they reported to spring training in February 1986. But a spring training injury to Wilson had some wondering if the Mets had enough outfield depth to overcome his absence.

This injury was scary. Wilson was participating in a rundown drill when he was hit in the face by a throw from Rafael Santana, breaking his glasses. Mookie had to be carted off the field and needed 21 stitches to close a cut around his right eye. He was unable to play until May 9.

Dykstra was now the everyday center fielder and earned the right to stay there by hitting .301 with nine stolen bases and 15 runs scored while Wilson recovered.

Manager Davey Johnson now had two starting center fielders and two leadoff hitters once Wilson rejoined the team. With Foster playing left and Strawberry in right,

Mookie Wilson. Photo courtesy of David Ferry

there would be little chance for Wilson and Dykstra to be in the lineup at the same time. Both center fielders were making a strong case that they should be playing every day. Fortunately for them, Foster went into a deep slump that led to his benching, and he was released after claiming racism had played a part in his demotion.

Even after Foster was let go, there still wasn't enough room to play both Wilson and Dykstra on an everyday basis. Strawberry was a fixture in right, Danny Heep played well once he took over for Foster, Kevin Mitchell's bat and versatility garnered him playing time, and Mazzilli was reacquired when Foster was jettisoned.

Johnson somehow managed to appease all six of his outfielders and played Wilson in left and center while Dykstra started about five of every seven games. Mazzilli and Heep were often used as pinch-hitters and Mitchell continued his tour of the Mets' infield and outfield. There was strength in numbers, particularly on the bench. And the extra talent was kept happy by the team's record pace. The Mets clinched their first NL East title in 13 years on September 17 against the Cubs and ended up with a club-record 108 wins.

Wilson was getting enough at-bats to continue his consistent hitting through early September. His average stood at .302 after he went 2-for-5 against the Phillies September 15. He remained in contention for his first .300 season until he went 3-for-23 in his final seven games to finish with a .289 mark.

The Mets faced the Astros in the NLCS, which guaranteed that Wilson would start at least two games. Houston had lefty Bob Knepper scheduled to start the third and sixth game of the series, which put Wilson in center over the lefty-hitting Dykstra. But Wilson was in the starting lineup each game, playing left field when Mike Scott or Nolan Ryan was on the mound.

Wilson actually had more at-bats than Dykstra in the NLCS but hit a meager 3-for-26 (.115) with two runs scored, one RBI, and seven strikeouts. The duo ignited the most important rally of the season at the time, contributing back-to-back hits to start the ninth inning of Game 6 before the Mets won the pennant in extra innings.

Knepper carried a two-hit shutout and a 3–0 lead into the ninth inning of Game 6. A Houston victory meant the Mets would have to face Mike Scott in Game 7, a hideous proposition considering Scott had held New York to eight hits in posting a pair of complete-game victories.

The Mets didn't see Scott again until 1987. Dykstra led off the ninth with a triple and scored on Wilson's single three pitches later. It was a nifty piece of hitting by Wilson, who fell behind 0–2 in the count before slapping a dying quail over the head of second baseman Bill Doran.

Wilson scored the Mets' second run on Keith Hernandez's double before Ray Knight knotted the score with a sacrifice fly.

The game went into the 16th inning before the Mets scored three times to take a 7–4 lead. The Astros scored twice in the bottom half before Jesse Orosco struck out Kevin Bass to wrap up the Mets' third pennant.

The nail-biting NLCS seemed like just another playoff series by the time Game 6 of the World Series was over. And much of the excitement was generated by one single at-bat in the 10th inning, courtesy of Wilson.

The Red Sox scored twice in the 10th to take a 5–3 lead, putting them within three outs of their first World Series title in 68 years. Wally Backman and Keith Hernandez were retired on fly balls to left-center to start the bottom half of the inning before Gary Carter, Kevin Mitchell, and Ray Knight hit consecutive singles to get the Mets within 5–4.

Mitchell was on third and Knight occupied first when Wilson strode to the plate with a chance to be a hero or a goat. Red Sox reliever Bob Stanley had just replaced closer Calvin Schiraldi when Wilson went to the plate. Stanley quickly got two strikes on Mookie before Wilson stayed alive by fouling off four pitches. The eighth pitch of the at-bat came close to hitting Wilson in the leg, which would have loaded the bases for Howard Johnson. Instead, Wilson jackknifed to get out of the way as the pitch sailed wide of Rich Gedman's catcher's mitt, allowing Mitchell to

score the tying run. Knight moved up to second base on the play before Wilson put the capper on the most memorable at-bat in team history.

Wilson handled a tough pitch and sent it skidding down the first-base line in the direction of Bill Buckner, who was playing semi-deep behind the bag. Buckner bent down and came up empty as the ball continued to roll into short-right field. Knight scored from second to end the most improbable comeback in postseason history.

But the Mets still had a Game 7 to play, and all the momentum they had gathered was muted when rain caused the clincher to be postponed one day. The Bosox jumped out to an early 3–0 lead and managed to keep it until the sixth, when Wilson again contributed to an important rally.

Mazzilli and Wilson hit one-out singles before a walk to Tim Teufel loaded the bases for Hernandez. Two pitches later, Hernandez lined a two-run single before Carter knotted the score with a grounder.

The Mets scored three times in the seventh and twice in the eighth with Wilson reaching base during both rallies. New York completed an 8–5 victory when Orosco fanned Marty Barrett, earning the Mets a trip through the Canyon of Heroes the next day.

Wilson scored three runs in the Series and finished with a .267 average and a .321 on-base percentage. He reached base five times during the final two games and tied for the team lead with three stolen bases in the Series.

Cashen failed to clear up the logjam in the outfield during the off-season. In fact, he muddled it by acquiring left fielder Kevin McReynolds in a deal that sent Mitchell to the Padres. The trade meant Wilson and Dykstra would be sharing center field, much to the chagrin of both players.

The center-field situation was among the many sidebars of a disappointing 1987 season. McReynolds put together an outstanding season but lacked the clubhouse chemistry provided by Mitchell and Knight, who was not re-signed after 1986. Strawberry ticked off his teammates with his habitual lateness and his lame excuses for begging out of ballgames. Dwight Gooden's drug suspension caused him to miss the first two months, and the rest of the rotation would wind up on the disabled list at some point during the year.

Neither Dykstra nor Wilson were thrilled about their platoon status, but each handled it differently. Wilson usually said the right things to the press and continued to produce as if he were unphased by his limited at-bats. Dykstra did enough popping off for both of them, publicly wondering why his talent was being wasted.

Johnson juggled his lineup so that Wilson played in 124 games, just eight fewer than Dykstra. Together, they hit .292 with 19 home runs, 77 RBIs, 144 runs scored, and 48 stolen bases in 816 at-bats. Wilson set career highs with a .299 average, a .359 on-base percentage, and a .455 slugging average. He compiled a .375 average in April and was hitting .345 by the end of May despite his job-share. His average didn't dip below .300 until July 19, and he owned a .302 mark after hitting a huge three-run homer against the Phillies September 9.

Despite all the injuries and off-field problems, the Mets had a chance to grab the division lead when they hosted a three-game series against the Cardinals in mid-September. Wilson belted a solo homer that put the Mets ahead 4–1 in the series opener September 11. The score remained 4–1 with two outs in the ninth until Willie Mc-Gee sliced an RBI single and Terry Pendleton followed with a two-run blast. St. Louis won the game 6–4 in extra innings and hammered Gooden in the second game before the Mets salvaged the finale to get within 2½ games of first. But the pennant race seemed to end the moment Pendleton hit a shot that sailed over Wilson's head and over the wall.

The Mets headed into 1988 determined to erase the disappointment of the previous season. New York owned a 5½-game lead and a 30–11 record by May 22, and Wilson compiled a .289 while appearing in 25 of those games. The pitching remained strong over the next three months, but the hitting was stagnant as the Mets played .500 ball long enough for the Pirates to enter the division race. Wilson contributed to the offensive funk by batting an uncharacteristic .192 with seven RBIs, five steals, and 12 runs scored in 41 games from May 24 to August 1. He didn't look sharp at the plate again until he put together a 10-game hitting streak in which he batted .480 from August 6 to 16. What was impressive about the streak was that Wilson started just four of those games.

The Mets finally shook off the Pirates by late August and won the division by 15 games. Wilson contributed mightily to the stretch run, hitting .385 with five homers, 13 extra-base hits, 22 RBIs, and 30 runs scored in his final 46 games. He had a season average of .302 after going 3-for-4 with a two-run homer, four RBIs, and three runs scored in a 14–1 pounding of the Cardinals September 24. But he missed the .300 mark once again, settling for a .296 after going 2-for-14 in his final four games.

The Mets returned to their midseason hitting malaise when they faced the Dodgers in the NLCS. They won two of the first three games but needed a great pitching effort from David Cone to force a seventh game. Wilson provided the tiebreaking single in a five-run eighth that sent the Mets to an 8–4 victory in Game 3. But Wilson didn't play again after going 0-for-4 in Game 4, which left him 2-for-13 (.154) for the series. The Mets dropped Game 7 6–0 to Orel Hershiser and the Dodgers.

Wilson was the Mets' all-time leader in stolen bases (274), runs (570), and triples (61) when the 1989 season began. He also was third on the team's career list with 1,061 hits, 160 doubles, and a .284 average. But Wilson's frustrations over playing time continued to grow, especially after the Mets pulled off one of the worst trades in club history. Dykstra was sent to Philadelphia, where he would

finally get a chance to accumulate 500 at-bats every season. In return, the Mets received Juan Samuel, who would start in center over Wilson.

Samuel played poorly but continued to start almost every day as Wilson stewed on the bench. Mookie, who was hitting a career-low .205 in part-time duty, finally asked for a trade with the team out of the pennant race by late July. The Mets did him a favor by shipping him to the Blue Jays, who would capture the AL East with the help of their new 33-year-old center fielder.

But Wilson's season-long slump dragged on into his first 10 games with Toronto as he batted .150 in 40 at-bats, dropping his average to .197. But the slump was halted by a 14-game hitting streak in which he batted .462 with 10 RBIs, 15 runs scored, and nine stolen bases. Mookie was back to being Mookie as he hit .298 in two months with the Jays to help them earn an ALCS meeting with the heavily favored A's. Wilson even received AL MVP consideration for his effort.

Toronto dropped the best-of-seven in five games as Wilson hit .263 with two runs batted in and two runs scored. He went 2-for-4 with an RBI and a run scored in the Jays' lone win of the series, a Game 3 verdict over Oakland at Toronto.

Wilson stole 23 bases in 1990, his best single-season output since 1986. He also reached 600 plate appearances for the first time in six years, ending up with a .265 average, 51 RBIs, and 81 runs scored while playing center and left. But his number of games played dropped from 147 in 1990 to 86 in '91 as he hit only .241 and compiled a .277 on-base percentage.

The Blue Jays elected not to sign him to a contract once his two-year package expired in October 1991. Wilson decided to retire at age 35, just one season before the Jays won their first World Series.

Mookie would return to the Mets in several capacities over the next two decades. He rejoined the club in December 1993 as a member of the Community Outreach Program and a roving minor league outfield instructor. Wilson was elevated to first-base/outfield coach of the Mets under manager Bobby Valentine in October 1996 and remained there until the end of Valentine's run in 2002. Wilson also became a recording artist while a Mets coach, writing 11 gospel songs that were released as a CD in 2000. He and Rosa wrote songs for a second CD that was released a year later.

Wilson was reassigned as manager of the Mets' Appalachian affiliate at Kingsport following the 2002 season. He spent two seasons there and skippered the 2005 Brooklyn Cyclones.

Mookie was back in a Mets uniform by 2011, hired as manager Terry Collins' first-base coach.

The Mets inducted him into their Hall of Fame in 1996, 10 years after he gave them the most amazing at-bat in team history. He remains among the Mets' all-time leaders in most offensive categories.

First ML/Mets game @ Dodgers, 9/2/80
First ML/Mets hit   single vs. John Curtis, @ Padres, 9/4/80
First ML/Mets homer   solo HR vs. Nino Espinosa,
                                       @ Phillies, 6/2/81
First ML/Mets RBI   RBI grounder vs. Bobby Castillo, @ Dodgers,
                     9/2/80
Most hits, ML/Mets game   5, @ Padres, 5/23/86
Most homers, ML/Mets game   2, @ Phillies, 4/10/88
Most RBIs, ML game   4, 5 times, 4 times with Mets
Acquired: Selected in the 2nd round of the 1977 draft.
Deleted: Traded to the Blue Jays for Jeff Musselman and Mike Brady,
         7/31/89.

David Wright

Third Baseman   Bats right, throws right
Born: 12/20/82   Norfolk, Virginia
Height: 6'0"   Weight: 200   #5

David Wright ML/Mets Career

YEAR	GP	AB	R	H	2B	3B	HR	RBI	K	BB	SB	AVG	SLG	OBP
2004	69	263	41	77	17	1	14	40	40	14	6	.293	.525	.332
2005	160	575	99	176	42	1	27	102	113	72	17	.306	.523	.388
2006	154	582	96	181	40	5	26	116	113	66	20	.311	.531	.381
2007	160	604	113	196	42	1	30	107	115	94	34	.325	.546	.416
2008	160	626	115	189	42	2	33	124	118	94	15	.302	.534	.390
2009	144	535	88	164	39	3	10	72	140	74	27	.307	.447	.390
2010	157	587	87	166	36	3	29	103	161	69	19	.283	.503	.354
2011	102	389	60	99	23	1	14	61	97	52	13	.254	.427	.345
TOTAL	1106	4161	699	1248	281	17	183	725	897	535	151	.300	.508	.380

The Mets' farm system has produced few power hitters and even fewer quality third basemen, which should make David Wright among the most appreciated players in franchise history. Wright made a quick climb up the organizational ladder and eventually became the first home-grown Met to hit over .300 with at least 30 homers and 100 RBIs in a season. He also was the first Mets non–first baseman to win at least two Gold Gloves, and the third Met to join the 30-30 club. No one in club history has had more 100 RBI seasons, 35 double seasons, or .300 average seasons.

Wright has also been among the most congenial players in club history, doing so without any ulterior motives. He continues to sign autographs with the same appreciation he displayed when he was a rookie, as if he remembers what it was like to be a fan in Norfolk trying to collect a minor league player's scribble on a baseball. He's always been among the most accessible players for media interviews, patiently and politely answering questions even during the most difficult parts of the season.

He's a natural for commercials, flashing an engaging smile that always appears genuine. He carries that same persona during batting practice and warm-ups, sharing a chuckle with teammates while demonstrating that baseball is a boy's game played by men.

Mets fans devoured Wright's personality during his first few seasons, appreciating his outstanding production and positive demeanor when the franchise was climbing back toward respectability in 2005 and '06. They loved the night at San Diego in the 2005 season when he made a bare-handed, over-the-shoulder catch of a blooper in short-left field. They reveled in his ability to collect two-strike hits. They marveled at his maturity. He was the closest thing the Mets had to Derek Jeter, which in time became a blessing and a curse.

Wright emerged as the most popular Met in 2005 with just 69 major league games under his belt. He carried that distinction into 2006 as the team won its first division title since 1988. But he also remained the face of the franchise as it blew playoff berths in 2007 and '08. He heard boos for the first time in 2007, less than three years removed from his major league debut.

Wright gave diplomatic answers after each tough loss, never pointing fingers or heaving criticism toward his teammates. He remained the voice of reason in the clubhouse while fans clamored for him to light a fire under the team, the way Hernandez, Backman, or Dykstra used to. Blasting teammates was never Wright's style, which led some fans to believe he lacked leadership qualities to rescue the club from an abyss in tough times. Instead, Wright led by example as he usually had an ample amount of infield clay on his jersey by the third inning.

But criticism of Wright began to surface following the team's September 2008 meltdown. If he was the supposed front man for the franchise, and the franchise had just blown consecutive playoff berths, then through guilt by association, Wright was at fault. Fans would call the sports talk stations wondering why Wright was so friendly to the opposition, players who wanted to bury the Mets every night. Wright also never lost his cool when Mets followers felt the team needed a clubhouse leader who could inspire.

And then there was the Mets' move to Citi Field in 2009. Wright hit 62 home runs at Shea Stadium during his first four full seasons in the majors, including 21 in 2008. Although he was the all-time home run leader at Citi Field through 2011, Wright hit only 22 in the first three years of the new park.

The Mets stopped blowing playoff races primarily because they weren't good enough to compete. They had yet to produce a winning season since leaving Shea, causing Wright to accept criticism for the team's losing. With his power numbers down and his strikeouts and errors up, Wright was hearing more negative comments than ever about his play. Even team ower Fred Wilpon said in a *New Yorker* article that Wright was "a really good kid. A very good player. Not a superstar." When asked to comment on Wilpon's quote, Wright did what he's always done during his time in New York. He took the high road and continued to bust his butt on the field.

David Allen Wright was born in Norfolk, Virginia, and became a Mets fan by watching the team's Triple A squad at Tidewater.

"My dad used to take my brothers and I out there when I was relatively young," Wright told New York broadcaster Mike Mancuso in a September 2011 interview. "I've got some great baseball memories of Harbor Park. I was fortunate that my dad being a police officer in Norfolk, he knew some of the officers could earn some extra money doing security at the ballpark, so I always got some foul balls and got to shake a couple of players' hands, so that was fun for me."

He attended Hickory High School in nearby Chesapeake, where he hit .438 with 13 home runs and 90 RBIs in four seasons with the varsity. He earned All-State honors from 1999 to 2001, and was named the Gatorade Virginia High School Player of the Year in 2001 after batting .538 with six homers and 19 RBIs as a senior in 2001.

There is a strong possibility the Mets wouldn't have landed Wright if they hadn't lost Mike Hampton to free agency in the fall of 2000. The Mets received Colorado's first-round selection and were given a supplemental first-round pick as compensation for Hampton, who inked a six-year, $120 million contract with the Rockies.

New York used its first selection—18th overall—to take Notre Dame pitcher Aaron Heilman, then watched as Mike Fontenot, Bobby Crosby, Jeremy Bonderman, and 16 other players came off the draft board before the Mets took Wright with the 38th pick.

"Draft day was actually pretty crazy," Wright remembered 10 years later. "I liked to think I was a pretty good student, and I actually had a couple of exams I had to take the morning of draft day, before the draft became a big event on TV like it is now.

"I went to class in the morning, took my exams, and came home at the end of the first round. The Mets picked me between the first and the second rounds, so I was there at home with my family, some friends, and some coaches. It was pretty surreal."

The Mets assigned him to Kingsport of the rookie Appalachian League, where he immediately showed promise by hitting .300 with four homers, seven doubles, 17 RBIs, and nine stolen bases in 36 games.

Promoted to Columbia of the South Atlantic League in 2002, Wright drove in 93 runs, scored 85 times, and stole 21 bases to earn team co-MVP honors with Justin Huber. *Baseball America* named him the league's 10th best big-league prospect after he finished third on the circuit in RBIs and fourth in runs scored.

The Mets tried to be patient with Wright, moving him up a level to St. Lucie of the Class A Florida State League in 2003. But he became the Mets' top minor league prospect by the end of the year, leading the FSL with 39 doubles and 75 RBIs while hitting .270 with a team-high 15 home runs. Wright batted .342 after July 8 and received the organization's Sterling Award as the top player at St. Lucie.

Wright opened 2004 at Double A Binghamton but didn't stay very long. He hit .363 with 10 homers, 27 doubles, 40 RBIs, and 44 runs scored in 60 games before heading to Triple A Norfolk on June 14. He was in New York five weeks later after recording a .298 average with eight homers and 17 RBIs in 31 games for the Tides.

Wright's promotion to the majors came at a time when the front office thought it had a shot at earning a playoff berth. The Mets had a lineup featuring sluggers Mike Piazza, Cliff Floyd, Richard Hidalgo, and Mike Cameron. José Reyes was back in action after rehabbing an injury, giving the Mets speed at the top of the order. Flanked by a strong group of hitters, Wright was able to ease into major league life without feeling like a savior.

"I was lucky, too, that I went to spring training with the team earlier that year, so I got to know a lot of the guys from there, and they really welcomed me with open arms," Wright said. "It could have been a tricky situation with Ty Wigginton, who was the third baseman. But he was really great to me coming up. So was Joe McEwing and Cliff Floyd. It was a huge veteran group, and they could have really made me an outsider, but they welcomed me, took me out to dinner, took really good care of me. I felt comfortable there, and I think that translated into me being comfortable on the field."

Wright made his debut at Shea Stadium on July 21 against the Expos. His arrival was highly anticipated due to his minor league stats, but he showed none of the pressure that normally accompanies such high expectations.

You could tell there was something different about the kid the moment he walked onto the field for batting practice. He exchanged laughs with Floyd and Hidalgo near the batting cage and looked confident as he took his swings and gobbled up grounders. Watching Wright assimilate with the rest of the Mets evoked memories of Gregg Jefferies, another well-hyped prospect who quickly alienated his teammates. Wright obviously was mature beyond his 21 years. Now if he could only hit.

Wright went 0-for-4 in his major league debut as the Mets beat the Expos to pull within three games of the division lead despite a 47–47 record. He doubled in his second at-bat the next afternoon before finishing the day 2-for-4 and scoring the game's first run in a 4–1 loss to the Expos.

His first home run came off John Patterson, a solo shot in an ugly 19–10 loss at Montreal on July 26. He also doubled twice in the series finale but was hitting only .216 with two RBIs in 10 games as the Mets entered August.

However, the Mets were confident enough in Wright to trade Wigginton to the Pirates in a deal that brought Kris Benson to New York. Wright immediately went on a tear that lasted the rest of the season.

Wright hit safely in his first three games of August before going 3-for-6 with two doubles, a three-run homer and six RBIs in an 11–6 rout of the Brewers. He batted .303 with six homers and 19 RBIs for the month, producing nine multi-hit games while usually hitting sixth in the lineup. He posted his first four-hit game on August 21, going 4-for-6 with three doubles and three runs scored in an 11–9 win over the Giants.

David Wright. Photo courtesy of David Ferry

Wright got off to a slow start at the plate in 2005, hitting only .220 with seven RBIs through his first 15 games. However, he also owned a .361 on-base percentage through that point of the season while hitting anywhere from fifth through seventh in the lineup.

The Mets began the year with five straight losses before Wright smacked a two-run homer in the eighth inning of a 6–1 triumph in Atlanta, sparking a six-game winning streak. He belted a grand slam during the streak, and was batting .304 and riding a nine-game hitting streak by May 1.

Wright remained very consistent the rest of the season, hitting safely in a season-high 15 games from July 10 to 28 to run his average to .299. His average fluctuated between .299 and .316 the rest of the season and remained above .300 after August 11.

Meanwhile, Beltrán battled injuries and couldn't come close to duplicating his numbers from 2004. Piazza showed wear and tear from over a decade behind the plate and endured his worst year as a Met. Cameron missed the last 1½ months of the season after suffering multiple facial fractures in a hideous outfield collision with Beltrán in San Diego. Second baseman Hideki Matsui hit below expectations and missed over one-third of the season due to a knee injury.

The Mets' key offensive components were Wright, Floyd, and Reyes as the trio helped the ballclub stay in the wild-card hunt until the second week of September. Wright was the top run producer, tying Reyes for the team lead with 99 runs scored and finishing first with 102 RBIs. Wright also paced the Mets with 42 doubles and 72 walks while ending up second to Floyd with 27 home runs. He finished two doubles shy of Bernard Gilkey's then single-season record set nine years earlier.

Wright was eighth in the league with a .306 average, making him the sixth homegrown Met in club history to hit .300 or better for the team. He ranked among the NL's top 10 in doubles, hits, extra-base hits, RBIs, and total bases, lofty stats for a guy playing in his first full major league season. Randolph demonstrated confidence in his third baseman by hitting him no lower than fifth in the lineup after mid-July.

The lineup was completely overhauled during the 2005–2006 offseason. Wright, Reyes, Floyd, and Beltrán remained key components in the batting order as the Mets said good-bye to Piazza, Cameron, and first baseman Mike Jacobs, a late-season call-up who hit .310 with 11 homers in just 100 at-bats.

Minaya replaced Piazza with Lo Duca, who was acquired from the Marlins for two prospects, including Gaby Hernandez. Jacobs was packaged in another deal with the Marlins, a blockbuster that made Carlos Delgado the new first baseman. Nady took over for Cameron in right, giving the Mets a very balanced attack from both sides of the plate. The Mets also signed utilityman Jose Valentin as injury insurance, a pickup that proved crucial after Matsui got off to a poor start in 2006.

But the Mets went just 11–17 for the month, to sink near the bottom of the NL East standings, making September interesting only to fans who continued to track the progress of the Mets' new third baseman. Wright continued to hit well, producing his first two-homer game on September 2 against the Marlins and collecting four hits in a 13-inning loss to the Phillies on September 11. He batted .396 with five homers and 12 RBIs during the first 14 games of the month and finished the season with a .293 average, 14 home runs, and 40 RBIs in 69 games.

The Mets ended the year 71–91, 25 games behind the division-winning Braves. Omar Minaya was hired as general manager during the last week of the season, and Willie Randolph replaced Art Howe as manager in November.

Minaya immediately bolstered the club by signing free agents Carlos Beltrán and pitcher Pedro Martinez, giving the Mets a potentially lethal lineup while enhancing a starting rotation in need of an ace. Beltrán's arrival let Randolph keep Wright near the bottom of the lineup, allowing Wright to continue his rapid maturity as a major league hitter without placing any additional pressure to perform.

Armed with the switch-hitting Valentin, Reyes, and Beltrán, the Mets could field a lineup of six right-handed hitters against southpaw starters or start five lefty hitters versus right-handers. That gave New York the National League's best starting eight, a lineup that featured power and speed. The Mets rode the offense to their first division title in 18 years, pulling out countless wins in their final at-bat and maintaining a double-digit lead in the NL East race over their final 91 games.

Wright was in the middle of the production, hitting third through fifth in an order that produced three .300 hitters, three players with at least 114 RBIs, and three players with 38 doubles or more. He led the team with a .311 average, tied for first with 116 RBIs, and paced the club with 40 doubles.

Wright was voted onto the National League starting lineup for the All-Star Game after hitting .324 with 18 homers, 20 doubles, and 66 RBIs through the Mets' first 81 games. He hit .469 with three homers and 12 RBIs during a season-opening nine-game hitting streak and batted .372 with 42 ribbies in a 44-game stretch from May 4 to June 22. He had 74 RBIs by the All-Star break to set a franchise record before finishing second to Ryan Howard in the All-Star Home Run Derby.

Wright became the 14th player to homer in his first career All-Star at-bat and finished the game 1-for-3. But he experienced a power slump after the midsummer classic, hitting just two while batting .257 in his first 40 games following the break, and only two in 25 games in September. Mets followers began to wonder if Wright's participation in the Home Run Derby had altered his swing or approach at the plate. But he also ended the year on a 12-game hitting streak, which seemed to bode well for the Mets heading into the postseason.

Wright hit safely in each game of the Mets' sweep of the Dodgers in the Division Series, going 4-for-12 with two doubles and four RBIs. He had three RBIs in the opener, hitting a two-run double and an RBI double as the Mets took a 6–5 victory.

The Cardinals managed to silence Wright in the NLCS, limiting him to a .160 average and two RBIs in 25 at-bats. He went 0-for-10 to open the series before slamming a tie-breaking solo homer in Game 4 to ignite a 12–5 rout in St. Louis. Wright also gave the Mets a 1–0 lead in Game 7 with an RBI single in the bottom of the first. The lead held up for just one inning, and St. Louis went ahead for good on Yadier Molina's two-run blast in the top of the ninth before the Mets left the bases loaded to end the series.

"It's tough to call it a disappointment," Wright said as he assessed the 2006 season five years later. "Obviously, it's a disappointment when you don't win the World Series, but we still had a tremendous season. We got banged up with some of our starting pitching right before the playoffs, but to this day it's my finest baseball moment, playing in those playoffs, experiencing playoff baseball in New York. When I look back on it, I don't think of it as a disappointment

or a negative. I look back on it, and it makes me smile and brings back some great memories."

The playoffs didn't diminish what Wright had done during the regular season. Colorado's Garrett Atkins was the only other National Leaguer to hit at least .310 with 25 homers, 116 RBIs, 95 runs scored, 40 doubles, and 70 extra-base hits. Besides, whatever problems Wright had in the postseason could be fixed by the time the Mets prepared for the 2007 playoffs. Or at least that was the plan.

There was nothing wrong with Wright's hitting overall in 2007 as he improved on every major offensive category except RBIs, leading the team in batting (.325), on-base percentage (.416), and slugging (.546). He became the Mets' third member of the 30-30 club, setting then-career highs with 30 homers and 34 stolen bases.

"I'd like to do it again," Wright said of joining the 30-30 club. "It was kind of in the middle of one of those disappointing Septembers, so I don't think I got to experience it the way I would have liked. I would have liked to do it on the way to winning another National League East or getting into the playoffs. Unfortunately, that didn't happen.

"That's the kind of player I want to be, the kind of player that can do it all. You'd like to be the best at everything. You want to do everything in the game exceptionally well, and I think the 30-30 club sort of exemplifies that."

As a run-producer, Wright became the first player in team history to drive in over 100 runs in three consecutive seasons. He and Reyes also were the first players in club history to score at least 95 runs in three consecutive seasons. Wright created 190 of the Mets' 804 runs (23.6 percent) and was fifth in the majors with 33 go-ahead RBIs.

Wright's speed and power made him the only major leaguer in 2007 to have at least 30 homers, 100 RBIs, 100 runs scored, and 12 stolen bases. He also was one of just four players to record three hitting streaks of at least 14 games that season.

Wright opened 2007 by hitting safely in 14 straight games but didn't homer until his 25th contest. His batting average was just .244 by the end of April, but that didn't prevent the Mets from going 15–9 for the month.

Wright homered eight times in May and became the 11th Met to go deep in at least four straight games (June 7–10), giving him 12 in 36 games after hitting just two in his previous 49 games dating to 2006. The power surge scuttled talk that his participation in the 2006 Home Run Derby had ruined him for life.

Wright clubbed only four homers in July, but he also hit .333 with 22 RBIs in 27 games. Problem was, Beltrán was the only other Met who was driving in runs on a consistent basis as New York went 13–14 in July to cut their division lead to three games over the Phillies, but the team remained atop the NL overall standings despite a mediocre 59–47 record.

The Mets opened August by winning 14 of 22 games to expand their lead. Wright was outstanding during that stretch, hitting .403 with a .529 on-base percentage, five homers, 18 RBIs, and 25 runs scored. The hot streak helped the Mets move seven games ahead of the Phillies, who were struggling to stay over .500. But New York dropped the next five games, including four straight to the Phillies to tighten the division race.

The Mets stretched the lead back to seven games by mid-September. Wright helped the cause by homering four times in his first 10 games that month, and hit two more during an ensuing three-game series with the Phillies at Shea. But Philadelphia still managed to complete a three-game sweep in New York to slice the Mets' lead to 3½ games with 14 remaining.

New York still had reason to feel confident despite the sweep, and they had a game in hand thanks to a rescheduled game against the Cardinals. If the Mets split their last 14 games, the Phillies would have to win 10 of their last 14 to force a one-game playoff for the NL East title. Thirteen of the Mets' final 14 games were against the Marlins and Nationals, who had no motivation other than their intense dislike for the Mets.

The Fish and Nats viewed Wright as an okay guy who never wasted an opportunity to engage their players in conversation anytime they reached third base. But the Marlins and Nationals had developed a deep disdain for Reyes and Lastings Milledge, whose on-field celebrations were perceived as over-the-top. Although the two clubs already were eliminated from postseason contention, they wanted nothing more than to make sure the Mets also had their butts on their living room couch when the playoffs began.

The Nationals and Marlins failed to completely silence Wright, who had begun a season-ending 17-game hitting streak during the Phillies' sweep in New York. Wright sizzled over the final 14 games, hitting .426 with seven doubles, nine RBIs, and 13 runs scored. Unfortunately for the Mets, he and Moises Alou were the only players swinging hot bats down the stretch as New York dropped five of six against lowly Washington and went 4–4 in eight other games.

Wright went 3-for-4 with an RBI and three runs scored in a 13–0 rout of the Marlins, which put New York in a tie with the Phillies heading into the season finale. But by the time Wright poked his next hit, Florida already had a 7–1 lead en route to an 8–1 drubbing that ended the Mets' season. The Phillies took five of seven versus Washington down the stretch and captured an improbable division crown by slamming the Nats 6–1 in the finale.

Wright still managed to collect a few postseason honors. He won a Gold Glove for the first time and picked up his first Silver Slugger in an otherwise demoralizing season for the Mets. As a franchise previously known for its incredible stretch runs in 1969 and 1973, the Mets were now lumped in with the 1951 Dodgers, 1964 Phillies, 1978 Red Sox, and 1995 Angels as teams with the greatest late-season collapses in major league history.

The Mets said all the right things as they reported to 2008 training camp. The meltdown supposedly was be-

hind them, as were the spotty starting pitching and inconsistent run production. The club had parted with Lo Duca, who had served as the unofficial team captain and chief clubhouse instigator the previous two years. Lo Duca's work with the media in 2006 made him the go-to guy after games, but the clubhouse now needed a vocal leader who could carry the team on his shoulders and become the face of the franchise.

That was something that seemingly didn't interest Beltrán or Delgado. Reyes was chatty with the press during wins but leaned on baseball clichés and wasn't perceived to be up to the challenge of being a team leader. With Lo Duca gone, the media began to lean heavily on Wright to be the new voice of the clubhouse. However, Wright didn't have the type of personality to play what *New York Daily News* columnist Mike Lupica referred to in his 1988 book *Wait 'Til Next Year* as the "he said…what do you say?" game with the media, as Hernandez had during the Mets' glory days of the mid-1980s. Wright wasn't about to throw a teammate under the bus and always spoke positively of the Mets' fortunes, no matter the circumstances.

Randolph tried to guide his players through choppy waters through the first two months of the '08 campaign. The Mets added two-time AL Cy Young Award winner Johan Santana to the rotation, but John Maine and Oliver Perez were wildly inconsistent and Pedro Martinez spent most of April and May on the disabled list. Even worse, Beltrán and Delgado got off to slow starts and were rumored to be very unhappy with Randolph at the helm.

Ever the professional, Wright stayed above the fray and publicly supported his manager while the Mets carried a sub-.500 record into June. Wright began the season by hitting .344 with 19 RBIs in 16 games, driving in three runs in two of the Mets' first three contests and collecting five ribbies in a 6–0 win over the Nationals on April 15. Wright also backed up his Gold Glove status by opening the year with 27 consecutive errorless games.

But the Mets were receiving minimal support from the other "core" members of the lineup. Reyes hit .285 with seven homers, five triples, 17 stolen bases, and 34 runs in 52 games through the first two months but was off his game at short. Randolph was also trying to get Reyes to minimize his celebrations when his signature vivacity was part of his game.

Beltrán hit only .204 with just two stolen bases through his first 27 games, and Delgado owned a .215 average by May 28 and was showing little enthusiasm around the first-base bag. Delgado's defensive prowess never made Mets fans forget the Gold Glove–winning Hernandez, but at least he displayed full effort in 2006 and helped Wright pick up a Gold Glove in '07. By June of 2008, Delgado was showing an aversion to getting his uniform dirty.

The rampant displays of disinterested performances made fans appreciate Wright that much more. He continued to exhibit nonstop hustle while the rest of the core group didn't exactly draw comparisons to Pete

Rose. However, Wright couldn't stop the Mets from falling under .500 in June, nor could he prevent Randolph from losing his job.

Jerry Manuel became interim manager on June 17 and made a statement just moments after the opening pitch that night in Anaheim. José Reyes led off with a single but failed to bust it down the line before Manuel told him to take the rest of the night off. The two had a short yet animated conversation before the Mets completed a 6–1 loss to the Angels. Manuel insisted he pulled Reyes from the game out of concern for another possible injury, saying something had to be physically wrong with his shortstop if he didn't go top speed to first base. Reyes looked a helluva lot faster the next night. Beltrán began to hit, and Delgado started to dive after grounders.

Wright's batting average began a slow ascent after Manuel was hired. He hit .392 with four homers, 13 RBIs, and nine runs scored in his first 14 games under Manuel, but the Mets split those games and remained under .500 after dropping the opener of a four-game series in Philadelphia on July 4. Thirteen days and 10 straight wins later, New York was in first place at 52–44 after Wright hit a game-tying, two-run homer in the ninth inning of a 10–8 comeback win at Cincinnati immediately after the All-Star break. Wright furnished a pair of four-RBI games during the winning streak, although he wasn't hitting with his usual consistency.

Wright got red hot in August, hitting .365 with 11 RBIs during a 12-game hitting streak in which the Mets won eight times. He closed the month by going 6-for-14 with two homers, three RBIs, and three runs scored in a three-game series at Florida.

The Mets won six of eight to open September, giving them a 3½-game lead over the Phillies with 17 to play. That stretch was capped by a two-game sweep of the Nationals in which Wright was 6-for-8 with one home run, four RBIs, and four runs scored. New York scored 23 runs during the sweep but proceeded to collect just 13 runs in dropping four of their next five games to fall a half-game behind the Phillies with 12 games left on the schedule. The Mets were also feeling pressure from the Brewers, who closed the gap in the wild-card race.

The Mets won their next two games despite Wright, who was 0-for-10 with no walks and three strikeouts. He hit safely in his next nine games, batting .500 with two homers, 10 RBIs, and eight runs scored in 36 at-bats. But the Mets were eliminated from the NL East race and were tied with the Brewers for the wild-card with one game to play after Wright ran the hitting streak to nine games. The Marlins again stood between the Mets and a possible playoff berth. And again, the Marlins sent the Mets home for the winter.

Wright went 0-for-4 as New York collected only four hits in a 4–2 loss to Florida in the final game at Shea. The Brewers got the job done by winning their regular-season finale to avoid a one-game playoff with the Mets.

"It's frustrating and really disappointing when you play such good baseball for 85–90 percent of the year and you just can't close it at the end," Wright said of the team's finishes in 2007 and '08. "I think those are opportunities that we missed, and you never get a chance to go back in history and redo that, which I think everybody would like to."

"Hopefully we have more opportunities on the horizon and we can learn from those mistakes because I think it makes you stronger as a person and a baseball player to deal with some of the failures that we've dealt with, and we know we've had our fair share. The old saying is that what doesn't kill you makes you stronger, so hopefully, moving forward, we can use that as a learning tool."

It was another strong season statistically for Wright, who hit .302 while setting career highs in homers (33), RBIs (124), and runs (115). He matched personal bests with 42 doubles and 94 walks but stole only 15 bases, his lowest total since his first pro season.

Wright came away with a Gold Glove and a Silver Slugger for the second straight year, and was second in the NL in runs batted in and hits. He also tied Piazza's team record for RBIs in a season and was now among the top 10 Mets in most career statistical categories.

The Mets bid good-bye to Shea and moved into Citi Field in April 2009. The new ballpark had asymmetrical outfield dimensions, with fences a few feet closer to those at Shea in many cases. Although the outfield walls were four to eight feet higher throughout most of the new park, no one had any idea just how tough it would be for the Mets to homer during their first season at Citi Field. Nor did anyone know that a ridiculous number of Mets were about to wind up on the disabled list.

Wright was affected by the new venue, hitting .298 with just five homers and 25 RBIs in 70 games there as opposed to a .331 average with 21 homers and 68 RBIs in Shea's final season. But Citi Field didn't stop Wright from hitting .324 with 44 RBIs and 20 stolen bases in 86 games prior to the All-Star break. He initially didn't show any disdain for hitting at Citi Field, providing the Mets' first hit in the new ballpark with a double before adding a three-run homer later in the opener.

The injuries began to hit the 2009 Mets almost from the start of the season. Delgado and Reyes suffered what amounted to season-ending injuries by May, and Beltrán began a 2½-month stay on the DL in June. The Mets also lost right fielder Ryan Church and catcher Brian Schneider during the first two months, often leaving Wright as the only reliable hitter in the lineup.

Wright tried to carry the offense on his own, which led him to become more impatient at the plate. His walk total fell off in 2009, and he struck out in 22.6 percent of his plate appearances compared to 16.1 percent the previous year. Hitting at cavernous Citi Field wasn't helping his stride, either.

The Mets got Wright some lineup protection by acquiring Jeff Francoeur from the Braves for Church on July 10.

The trade proved to be too little, too late as injuries continued to derail the team's playoff hopes. Wright found himself on the DL for the first time in his career by the middle of August.

Wright's average was .324 as he stepped in to face Giants starter Matt Cain on August 15. Cain quickly got ahead in the count 0–2 before uncorking a tailing, rising fastball that took a path toward Wright's helmet. Wright had no chance to get out of the way, and lay motionless in the batter's box for several seconds before he began to stir. He was taken out of the game and placed on the disabled list for the first time in his career two days later.

The Mets were 54–62 before the beaning, and 59–72 when he returned. Wright had three hits and three RBIs in his third game back, and went 3-for-5 with two homers, six RBIs, and three runs scored in a 10–9 win at Philadelphia on September 12. But he hit only .239 with an equally uncharacteristic .289 on-base percentage for the month to end up with a .307 average.

Wright finished with 39 doubles and 27 stolen bases but hit only 10 homers while driving in 72 runs, ending his string of four straight seasons with at least 26 home runs and 102 runs batted in. He also lost the Gold Glove and Silver Slugger awards to fellow Norfolk-area native Ryan Zimmerman of the Nationals.

The Mets had several concerns as they headed into 2010 training camp, one of which involved Wright's significant home run drop-off. The club hit a major league–low 95 home runs, 30 fewer than the next-to-last Pirates and 77 fewer than the Mets hit at pitcher-friendly Shea Stadium in 2008. Wright was the focus of the power drop only because he was the lone deep threat on the team to play anything close to a full season for the 2009 Mets.

Wright looked like his old self in his first at-bat of 2010, smacking a two-run homer in the first inning to put the Mets ahead to stay in a season-opening win over the Marlins at Citi Field on April 5. But he didn't hit another home run in Queens until June 5 versus Florida, ending a streak of 28 home games and 120 plate appearances without one. He provided 39 RBIs and scored 28 times overall through June 5 before catching fire at the start of a three-game sweep in Baltimore. Wright hit .406 with 11 doubles, 24 RBIs, and 22 runs scored in 24 games from June 11 to July 6. The hot streak allowed him to enter the All-Star break with a .314 average, 14 home runs, 25 doubles, 65 RBIs, and 52 runs scored. The Mets headed into the break in second place in the NL East, four games behind the Braves and within one game of the wild-card.

Wright and Pagan were the team's most consistent hitters in the first half and compensated for the absence of Beltrán, who missed the first half recovering from knee surgery. Francoeur cooled off after a season-opening 10-game hitting streak, Reyes was putting together what was for him an average season, Luis Castillo had reverted to his unproductive 2008 batting form, and newcomer Jason Bay hit only .265 with six home runs after setting career

highs with 36 homers and 119 RBIs for the Red Sox in 2009.

Add the fact that Oliver Perez and John Maine were no longer part of the rotation, and you had a situation that reeked of trouble. But Wright and Pagan were among the league leaders in hitting at the break despite the lineup woes, helping the Mets carry a 48–40 record into the All-Star break. There was still hope New York could grab a postseason berth as long as Wright and Pagan kept hitting, but their bats went stone cold once the Mets began what became a miserable 2–9 road trip to start the second half.

Pagan stumbled through the first few games of the trip after moving from center field to right to make room for Beltrán. Beltrán went 5-for-16 in his first four games but was hitting .167 in 36 at-bats by the end of the trip. Pagan batted only .220 during the West Coast swing as the Mets were shut out four times in 11 games.

Wright contributed little during the trip, hitting .182 with a .224 on-base percentage and 14 strikeouts in the 11 games. He delivered just one RBI base hit, a solo homer in a 4–3, extra-inning win over the Giants July 18.

Wright's strikeouts were beginning to unsettle Mets fans. Of the 33 major leaguers who hit at least 100 home runs from 2005 to 2008, he was the 20th toughest player to strike out. But he fanned 14 times for every home run hit in 2009 and was among the league leaders in strikeouts by the midway point of 2010. When he whiffed four times in four plate appearances during a 6–2 loss to the Rockies on August 11, Wright already had 125 strikeouts through 111 games and was on pace to shatter the team record of 156 set by Tommie Agee in 1970 and matched by Dave Kingman in 1982.

Wright saw his batting average drop below .300 for good on August 3 while the Mets struggled to stay over the .500 mark. He finished with a .283 average, his worst since a .270 mark for St. Lucie in 2003. His average was dragged down by a 59-game stretch in which he hit only .234 from July 10 to September 18. The Mets dropped 36 of those games and were out of contention by Labor Day.

Wright also broke a team record with 161 strikeouts and recorded just four of his 19 stolen bases in the second half. On the plus side, he jacked out 29 homers, laced 36 doubles, and drove in 103 runs. But that meant little to Mets fans who watched their ballclub post a losing record for the fifth time in nine seasons.

The Mets did little to improve the team in the winter of 2011 and opened the season with serious question marks in the rotation and the bullpen. There was another host of injuries that diluted the potency of the starting lineup. This time, Wright was among the missing.

Wright hit .308 while starting the first 13 games of 2011, but the Mets won just four of those games. He went 0-for-18 in his next five games, and his average was down to .226 when he was placed on the disabled list in mid-May due to a sore back. He started 39 of the team's first 40 games despite the injury, but his slumping bat was enough evidence to conclude a couple of weeks off could do him wonders.

The Mets eventually learned Wright had a stress fracture in his back, causing him to sit out until July 22. The team managed to go 30–28 while Wright and teammate Ike Davis were out of action.

Wright sizzled upon his return, batting .455 with two homers and 12 RBIs during a 10-game hitting streak from July 22 to 31. The hot stretch included nine hits, six RBIs, and five runs scored during the Mets' first-ever four-game sweep of Cincinnati, which put the team within three games of the wild-card lead.

The Mets also won the next night in Washington before posting the National League's fourth-worst record the rest of the way to end up 77–85. Wright put up strong power numbers over his final 53 games, producing six homers and 12 doubles while driving in 31 runs. But he also had more strikeouts (49) than hits (46) and batted just .231 over the final two months to finish with a .254 average, 14 home runs, and 61 RBIs. It marked the first time Wright had a lower batting average than the team's overall figure.

The club had a major decision to make after the season, one involving Reyes. He became the first Met to win a batting championship, compiling a .337 mark, 83 points higher than Wright's. Reyes did it in the final year of his contract and was among the most coveted players on the 2011 free-agent market. There was a chance Reyes and Wright, the Mets' answer to Butch and Sundance, would be broken up. That was a scenario that didn't please Wright when he spoke of their relationship in September 2011, seven years after they became teammates for the first time.

"I would say we are as close to being 'baseball brothers' as can be," said Wright. "I think that we've been through some trying times. We've had some good times together here. The biggest thing is we've grown up together. We've matured together. We've made our fair share of mistakes. But it's a great relationship, and hopefully, we'll be teammates for a long time to come."

Ever the optimist, Wright evaluated the team's future in the waning days of 2011 and liked what he saw. He was also hopeful the team could turn Citi Field into a more hitter-friendly facility, one that would take advantage of his power to right-center.

"You ask any hitter, and his answer is the hitter wants the ballpark to be a little more hitter-friendly. So I'm excited about that [prospect].

"It's always frustrating to hit a ball good and not be rewarded for it. That being said, I've had three years now in the new ballpark, so I know what to expect going into the season. Like any other hitter, I'm really excited about the changes that could be made because a lot of my strengths are alley-to-alley. Those are some of the bigger changes that they are talking about making."

"I'm excited about some of the young talent we have. Obviously, Sandy and the front office have their finger on the pulse of this team. They understand not only about the ballpark, but the personnel. They've brought in some real good people and real good players. I really like the direction this organization is headed in. And hopefully, I'm here for a long time to experience the good, some of the bad times, and some of the ugly times. I wouldn't have it any other way. Hopefully, there are some good days to come."

Wright lost "Brother" Reyes, who signed with the Marlins after the season. The Mets brought in the fences at Citi Field during the winter of 2012. But with Reyes elsewhere, the Mets hoped Wright, Davis, Jason Bay, and Daniel Murphy could take advantage of the new outfield dimensions. As 2012 training camp approached, the Mets seemed no better than they were prior to Wright's big-league debut.

First ML/Mets game vs. Expos, 7/21/04
First ML/Mets hit   double vs. Zach Day, Expos, 7/22/04
First ML/Mets homer   solo HR vs. John Patterson, @ Expos, 7/26/04
First ML/Mets RBI   solo HR vs. John Patterson, @ Expos, 7/26/04
Most hits, ML/ Mets game   4, 15 times
Most homers, ML/Mets game   2, 17 times
Most RBIs, ML/Mets game   6, 8/5/04 @ Brewers, 8/10/05 @ Padres, 9/12/09 @ Phillies
Acquired: Selected in the 1st round (38th overall) in the 2001 draft.
NL All-Star, 2006, 2007, 2008, 2009, 2010
NL Gold Glove, 2007, 2008
NL Silver Slugger, 2007, 2008

The Strategists

George Bamberger   1982–1983

Born: August 1, 1923   Staten Island, NY
Died: April 4, 2004   North Redington Beach, FL
Named Manager: 10/20/81
Resigned: 6/3/83

George Bamberger Mets Managerial Record

YEAR	GMS	W	L	PCT	POS.
1982	162	65	97	.401	6th, NL East
1983	46	16	30	.348	6th, NL East
Total	208	81	127	.389	

Major League Totals

YEARS	GMS	W	L	PCT
1978–1986	936	458	478	.489

George Bamberger was a tremendous pitching coach with the Orioles during their AL pennant run of 1969 to 1971. The O's had four 20-game winners in 1971 and boasted 18 20-game winners while he mentored the staff between 1968 and 1977.

Bamberger also was the first manager to have a winning season with the Milwaukee Brewers, averaging 94 victories in 1978 and '79, his first two years with the team. But he suffered a heart attack that required surgery in March 1980. He returned to the team in June, leading the Brew Crew to a 47–45 mark the rest of the season. He relinquished the job after the season but was coaxed back into a major league dugout by Mets general manager Frank Cashen, who was his GM at Baltimore.

There was hope Bamberger would mold the Mets' collection of young and/or underachieving arms into a solid staff. What the Mets and Bamberger didn't know at the time was that their top pitchers of the 1980s had yet to enter the farm system.

With a lineup that included Mets home-growns Mookie Wilson and Hubie Brooks, slugger Dave Kingman and the newly acquired George Foster from the Reds, expectations were rising when Bamberger took over. But Bamberger's own expectations were realistic, if not discouraging.

"He started off in spring training with a meeting in which he said, 'Boys, if we can play .500 ball, I'll be happy,'" recalled Ron Gardenhire, a Mets infielder who would became a solid manager with the Twins. "Any time you start off like that you get the feeling right away that, geez, he doesn't look to win. He looks for a .500 season. I thought that was bad."[1]

The '82 Mets weren't bad at the start, sitting 24–18 and 1½ games off the NL East lead on May 24. They were only three games back on June 20 before they dropped 16 of their next 20 to fall completely out of the race.

Bamberger would watch his Mets lose 15 straight in August, two off the team record. After avoiding the NL East cellar in 1980 and '81, the Mets hit rock bottom in 1982 with a 65–97 mark.

Bamberger had Tom Seaver in his rotation in 1983, and he would welcome rookie Darryl Strawberry to the team in May, but the losing continued. The Mets dropped eight of nine to fall to 16–30 on June 2. Bamberger had tried to resign twice before, only to be talked out of it by general manager Frank Cashen. Having failed to lure Earl Weaver out of retirement, Cashen accepted Bamberger's third resignation attempt and gave the job to bench coach Frank Howard on an interim basis.

Bamberger would return as the Brewers' skipper in 1985, going 142–171 in two seasons at the helm.

Yogi Berra   1972–1975

Born: May 12, 1925   St. Louis, MO
Named Manager: 4/6/72
Dismissed: 8/6/75
NL East Title, 1973
NL Pennant, 1973

Yogi Berra Mets Managerial Record

YEAR	GMS	W	L	PCT	POS.
1972	156	83	73	.532	3rd, NL East
1973	161	82	79	.509	1st, NL East
1974	162	71	91	.438	5th, NL East
1975	109	56	53	.514	3rd, NL East
Total	588	292	296	.497	

Major League Totals

YEARS	GMS	W	L	PCT
1964–1985	930	484	444	.522

Record includes 2 ties in 1964

Yogi Berra joined the Mets' coaching staff for the 1965 season, months after he was fired by the Yankees despite leading them to an American League pennant and a 7th game against the Cardinals in the 1964 World Series. Berra coached under managers Casey Stengel, Wes Westrum, and Gil Hodges from 1965 to 1971. He was the lone holdover from Westrum's staff when Hodges took over in 1968.

Manager Casey Stengel throws plastic baseballs to the crowds gathered during his welcome parade in 1962. As the new team's public face, Stengel was hired to create fans and sell tickets.

Berra was introduced as the team's manager on April 6, 1972, hours after Hodges was laid to rest following his second heart attack in 3½ years. At the same news conference, the Mets also announced the acquisition of Rusty Staub from the Expos for Ken Singleton, Tim Foli, and Mike Jorgensen.

The '72 season didn't start until April 15 because of the first players' strike in major league history. The delay didn't stop the Mets from starting the year 25–7, which gave them a six-game lead on May 21. The Mets also had acquired Willie Mays earlier that month, and rookie Jon Matlack was 6–0 with a 1.95 ERA entering June.

But injuries ravaged the Mets that season. Rusty Staub was hit on the right hand by a George Stone pitch in Atlanta on June 3. Staub continued to play for another two weeks before the pain became unbearable. He sat out a month and returned for one game before doctors determined he had a broken hamate bone.

Injuries held Jerry Grote to 64 games. Tommie Agee batted just .227 while battling hamstring issues. Bud Harrelson and Cleon Jones also missed chunks of time, and Jim Fregosi never hit consistently after he broke his thumb in spring training.

The starting pitching was pretty solid once again, with Tom Seaver, Jerry Koosman, Jon Matlack, and Jim McAndrew combining to go 58–42. But the bench lacked depth after the Mets made the Staub trade, leading to a disappointing 83–73 record. They went 57–66 after May 21.

Berra and the Mets went into the 1973 season with basically the same roster they had in '72, with one exception. They had acquired slick-fielding second baseman Felix Millan and lefty George Stone from the Braves for pitchers Gary Gentry and Dan Frisella, one of the greatest steals in team history.

But the injury bug continued. Harrelson, Jones, Grote, and John Milner were out of the lineup a combined 237 games, leaving Berra with a patchwork lineup that continued to waste solid pitching efforts. The team was 12 games under .500 in mid-July, while the crosstown Yankees were challenging for the AL East crown. The pressure was on Berra to win, and win immediately.

Berra was being compared unfavorably to Hodges, the man he replaced just a year earlier. While Hodges appeared to have the respect of most players, Berra's crew was wondering if he had the mettle to win the close ones.

"In baseball, you hear guys horsing around, asking questions like, 'What's the difference between Hodges and Berra,'" said Tug McGraw. "And some joker can always get a laugh by answering 'six innings.' In the third, Gil was thinking about what he was going to do in the sixth. In the sixth, Yogi was thinking about what he should have done in the third."[2]

McGraw had his own problems in 1973. He had become the lead arsonist for a lousy bullpen in which the best weapon had become rookie Harry Parker. Tug's record stood at 0–4 with a 5.85 ERA and five blown saves when Berra

gave him a pair of starts in July. Although McGraw was hammered in the first start, he held the Expos to an earned run over 5⅔ innings in the next. After that, Berra saw McGraw go 5–2 with 14 saves and a 1.65 ERA.

But Berra was in serious danger of losing his job. Mets chairman Donald Grant reportedly was ready to fire Berra with the team seemingly out of the pennant race. The New York Post ran a poll asking who should be fired: Berra, GM Bob Scheffing, or Grant. Mets fans overwhelmingly threw their support toward Berra, feeling the other two were at fault for the team's struggles.

Suddenly, the regulars seemed to get healthy all at once. The Mets were backing solid pitching with timely hits. The team finally moved into fifth on August 29 after two months in the basement. Fourth place was theirs on September 5. They were in fourth on the morning of September 18, 3½ games off the division lead. Four days later, they led the NL East and never looked back, winning their second division crown in five seasons.

The Mets upset the Big Red Machine in the NLCS, then took the Athletics to seven games before losing the World Series.

But Berra was criticized for his handling of the rotation in the World Series. With the Mets up 3–2 in the series, many felt Berra should go with Stone in Game 6 at Oakland. Instead, he went with Seaver on three day's rest before giving the ball to Matlack in Game 7. Seaver failed to close it out, and Matlack was hammered in the early innings, leaving the Mets just short of their second championship.

The start of the 1974 season looked eerily similar to '73, with injuries hammering the Mets. Tom Seaver was bogged down by sciatica, and McGraw couldn't shake a shoulder problem. The Mets were 11 games under .500 on August 16, about the same place they found themselves in '73. But they also were 8½ games out of first and with little chance to repeat as long as McGraw and Seaver were struggling. The team finished fifth at 71–91, its worst season since 1967.

Berra had a healthy Seaver to start the 1975 season. But he also began the year with a suspect bullpen that didn't include McGraw, who was jettisoned to the Phillies in a multiplayer deal.

The Mets stayed around the .500 mark but weren't close to sniffing first place. They were 10½ games out by mid-July when an incident occurred that would lead to Berra's dismissal.

Berra used Cleon Jones as a pinch-hitter on July 18 against the Braves and was ready to put him in the outfield to start the eighth inning with the Mets down 3–1. Jones, who had lost his starting left field job to Dave Kingman due to a knee injury that was slow to heal, showed up his manager by refusing to take the outfield. Berra told Jones to take off his uniform and later insisted he apologize to the team. Berra wanted Jones suspended, but Donald Grant initially refused before Jones was released a week later.

Manager Yogi Berra (left) greets the newest member of the 1975 Mets, slugger Joe Torre, as general manager Joe McDonald looks on. Torre would later become manager himself, from 1977 to 1981.

Despite the release, it was evident that Berra had lost control of the team.

"Yogi ran a looser ship," Koosman said 35 years after the team's improbable march to the NL pennant. "He wasn't as strict as Gil. Unfortunately, some guys took advantage of that. They didn't keep their weight down as they should have, they probably weren't in the best shape they could have been. They probably didn't follow curfew as well as they should have. There was always a little stretching of the rules here and there when you run too loose a ship, and it kind of gets away from you.

"Yogi was a good baseball man a very honest individual and a great person. It's just that he went about it in a little different way [than Hodges]."

Following the power struggle, the Mets gave Berra about two weeks to right the ship. But after the Mets lost a doubleheader at Shea to the Expos by identical 7–0 scores, Berra was out.

Several players acknowledge that the Mets could have won multiple division titles under Berra if the team had stayed healthy. But the weight of the standings—and the shadow of Hodges—proved to be Berra's undoing. Matlack, one of Berra's more self-motivated players, was among the Mets who had no problem with his skipper's handling of the ballclub.

"Yogi was easy to play for," said Matlack. "He was hard to understand when he came to the mound, but he was easy to play for. He only did stuff that seemed to help what was going on and never really got in our way. He was one of those managers that [said], 'Here are the bats and balls, guys, go play some ball today and let's win.'"

Matlack felt Berra wouldn't have been any more effective as a skipper had he been the disciplinarian Hodges was: "I don't know if that would have made a lot of difference. I think Yogi was Yogi. I think that type of manager is absolutely fine. I have no issues with Yogi or the way he ran the game or the ballclub."

"He was a players' manager," adds Bob Apodaca. "Very relaxed. Very few rules. Just be on time, play your butt off and be prepared. He was an easy man to play for and very likable. If you couldn't play for him you couldn't play for anybody. Yogi was a delight to be around."

Berra would manage again in 1984, taking the Yankees to an 87–75 record. But owner George Steinbrenner pulled the trigger on Berra just 16 games into the '85 season, firing the popular Yankee with the team 6–10.

Berra's feud with Steinbrenner would last over a decade. All was forgiven after the two talked during a dedication for the Yogi Berra Museum, which is a great venue for all baseball fans living near—or visiting—the Montclair, New Jersey, area.

Terry Collins   2011—present

Born: May 27, 1949 Midland, Michigan
Named Manager: 11/23/10

Terry Collins Mets Managerial Record

YEAR	GMS	W	L	PCT	POS.
2011	162	77	85	.475	4th, NL East

Major League Totals

YEARS	GMS	W	L	PCT
1994–2011	1040	521	519	.501

News that the Mets had hired Terry Collins as manager for the 2011 and 2012 seasons didn't create an immediate groundswell of optimism among the team's fan base. If the franchise was to give the job to a "recycled" manager, fans wanted to see Bobby Valentine return to the post after leaving the club with the second-highest win total among managers. However, Valentine wasn't even considered for the position as new general manager Sandy Alderson settled on Collins, Wally Backman, Bob Melvin, and Chip Hale as his four finalists. Of the four, Backman was the people's choice due to his fiery personality and winning pedigree as a Met.

The Mets had losing records their previous two years under Jerry Manuel, a manager whose personnel was ravaged by injuries. Manuel was self-deprecating and remained easy-going with the media no matter what the situation, which earned him the respect of his players but didn't always lead to positive results.

The difference between Collins and Manuel was evident the moment Collins was stepped to the podium for his introductory news conference at Citi Field in November 2010. Collins could say in 10 seconds what it took a minute for Manuel to convey. Collins was right to the point, speaking in sound bytes and showing tremendous optimism.

Collins had player-relations issues during his sometimes stormy three-year stints as manager of both the Astros and Angels. There were reports he had alienated the top players on both ballclubs and resigned as the Angels' skipper following a near mutiny. In both cases, Collins was replaced by a manager who would lead those teams to the postseason.

Questions were raised during his first Mets news conference about his relationship with previous players. He seemed to answer every question with complete honesty, saying he had mellowed in the 11 years since his last day as a manager.

"I'm not the evil devil that a lot of people have made me out to be," Collins said.[3]

Collins also was candid about his previous failings as a manager, saying it taught him to be more accessible to players.

"Losing brings negativism into the clubhouse, and I did a bad job managing the clubhouse," Collins admitted about the end of his Angels days when Mo Vaughn led a player coup. "Not question about it. I'm accountable for that. I was the manager of that team, and I should have done a better job of staying on top of it. I didn't. I learned from it. It will never happen…. I will guarantee it will not happen here.

"That was a huge learning experience. My patience over the years has changed. I'm a lot more patient. I know that's a word you don't like to use too much in New York because that's why you don't use the word 'rebuilding' because I don't think you can rebuild in New York. You've got to go forward."[4]

He also was forthright during an interview with WFAN's Mike Francesa a few minutes after the news conference, discussing everything from his managerial shortcomings and his arrest for driving under the influence in 2002. When asked about reports that Astros stars Craig Biggio and Jeff Bagwell were unhappy with his work in Houston, Collins said he hadn't heard such stories and said he had nothing but respect for the two ballplayers. Collins really did seem like a changed man ready to take on the challenge of reviving the Mets.

It's not that Collins was unsuccessful running the Houston dugout. The Astros finished second in each of his three years at the helm recording a 224–197 record from 1994 to 1996. The '94 Astros were 66–49 and within a half-game of the Reds for the NL Central lead when players went on strike in mid-August, leading to the cancellation of the postseason. Back in business in 1995, Houston finished one game behind the Rockies for the wild-card at 76–68. Collins was let go following a tumultuous 1996 campaign in which the Astros went 82–80, six games behind the NL Central–leading Cardinals. With Collins out of the way, the Astros won the next three division crowns under Larry Dierker.

Collins didn't have to wait long to get another managing gig, hired by the Angels in the fall of 1996. The Halos finished second in their first year under Collins at 84–78 and challenged for the 1998 AL West crown at 85–77 before winding up three games behind the Rangers. But his style began to grate on his players as the Angels went into a free-fall in their first season with slugger Mo Vaughn in the lineup. Vaughn had played for easy-going skippers in Boston and was unhappy with his new bench boss, leading to acrimony that couldn't be quelled while the Angels were going 25–55 in their final 80 games under Collins. The team was 31 games under .500 and 28 games out of first when Collins stepped down in early September. It would be another decade before Collins was rehired as a major league manager.

Mike Scioscia eventually replaced Collins in Anaheim and led them to their first World Series championship within three seasons, doing it with a completely overhauled pitching staff and the absence of Vaughn.

Collins served in various baseball capacities before he was named Mets manager. He was a Cubs advance scout in 2000 and a third base coach with the Devil Rays in 2001 before spending the next five years in the Dodgers organization, serving as a field coordinator from 2002 to 2004 before a two-year run as their director of player development.

Collins went from the NL West to the Far East, managing the Orix Buffaloes of the Japanese Pacific League from 2007 to 2008 before becoming the Mets' field coordinator in 2009. His initial position with the Mets allowed him to familiarize himself with some of the prospects that would be given a chance to compete for major league jobs in the winter of 2011.

Collins had a potential problem on his hands the moment position players began to report for his first training camp as Mets manager. Carlos Beltrán had long been the team's center fielder until a knee injury robbed him of some agility. Angel Pagan played a very capable center field while subbing for Beltran in 2010, much better than Beltran's work in the second half. It was obvious to most Mets observers who should be the center fielder in 2011. It was probably obvious to Collins as well until he made a decision that won over his players. He allowed Beltran to determine whether he could outperform Pagan in center. After two weeks, Beltran agreed to abdicate the position while thanking Collins for allowing him to go out on his own terms.

"Giving me the confidence and being so honest with me, I think that's why we handled this thing so professionally," Beltrán said of Collins. "He gave me the opportunity of choosing, [but] I've never been a selfish player in my career. Based on the condition of the knee, it's better that Pagan handle center field."

"You're hoping and praying it goes like this," Collins said. "You're hoping your star walks in and says, 'This is what's best for this team at this particular moment, and you'll have no problem with me, now let's get ready to play.' That's what you are hoping for. But you've got to get ready for them to say, 'No, I'm the center fielder here.'"[5]

Collins was hailed in the press for the way he handled it. His players also appreciated it and quickly bought into Collins' way of treating players like men. The players noted a strong emphasis on repetition and discipline, two components that seemed lost on the Mets at times in 2010.

The next tough task was cobbling together a rotation and a bullpen from the spare parts Alderson had collected on the cheap. The back end of the rotation featured Chris Young and Chris Capuano, each of whom were once star pitchers before injuries turned them into projects. Of the bullpen candidates, closer Francisco Rodriguez, enigmatic Bobby Parnell, and 2010 disappointment Ryota Igarashi were the lone holdovers from the previous season.

The Mets suffered a rare season-opening loss on their way to a 4–11 start, which tied for the third-worst 15-game start in club history. Other than Young, the rotation was pretty brutal when the bullpen wasn't pitching the Mets out of ballgames. A few more clutch hits or strong defensive plays might have been the difference between 4–11 and 8–7.

Manager Terry Collins poses at Citi Field just after taking a new post with the Mets, November 2010.

Nothing was going right, yet Collins refused to blow a fuse in public. He continued to say his ballclub was better than its 4–11 record and would turn things around very soon. His positive reinforcement was welcomed in the clubhouse and appeared to be quite a contrast from his reputation with the Astros and Angels.

The Mets made matters worse by dropping the first two games of a home series against the lowly Astros to fall to 5–13 before winning six in a row. New York played .500 ball over the next few games before Collins finally chose a time to go ballistic.

The Mets held a 2–0 lead against Pittsburgh June 1 before allowing nine runs over the seventh and eight innings. Bad pitches and indifferent defense allowed the Bucs to prolong rallies as the Mets dropped to 25–30. Collins used his postgame news conference to extol the virtues of Pirates outfielder Andrew McCutcheon while trashing his team's ability to play fundamental baseball.

"I don't know how to describe [the seventh inning]," he said. "I'm sick of trying to describe seventh innings. I'll tell you what, Andrew McCutchen plays the game right. That son of a bitch runs down there 3.9, 4.0 flat, and you better catch it and execute it. He gets a ground ball to third base and beats it out. That's how you play, and that's how we've got to start playing.

"I'm running out of ideas here. You know, do we play hard? Absolutely. That's not the issue. The issue is not effort. It's about execution. We need to add on points when we get the lead. I'm not looking for home runs. I'm looking for quality at bats. We can't make careless mistakes, but we do. We give up at bats. We can't do that. We don't have that kind of team.

"Make no mistake about it, I truly believe in the players we have. I don't care where they started the season. I don't care. I don't care who were All-Stars, who weren't All-Stars, this is a team thing; it's not one guy, it's not two guys; it's a team thing. I sit up here every night trying to figure out what can we do to get us over the top. Should we hit and run more? Well, who do you have up there? You have guys up there you shouldn't hit and run with. Should we bunt more? Well, if we don't get bunts down, then you're putting them in situations to fail. Guys are pitching good, but we get in situations where when guys need to make a pitch they don't make the pitch. I don't have the answers. I'm searching. I'm wringing the rag dry, coming in here, having to look at you guys looking at me like I'm a stinking fool. I told these guys, 'We're good enough, but we have to play the game right.' We just can't continue to make foolish mistakes.

"They're big-league players. They should be able to do it. They should be able to do it! I don't know if it's not anticipating the play. I'm not in their minds. But, it's how you play the game. This is a team thing. And, I'm not just pointing the finger at the players. I told the coaches, 'We've got to do a better job, we've got to take responsibility for this.' I'm the manager. It comes back on my shoulders.

"In that seventh inning, those were my players I put out there, who I believe in. So, therefore, maybe I need to make some adjustments. And, by God, they'll be made. I don't know it comes with finding different players. But, they'll be made. Something's going to be changing."

Manuel had never flogged the entire ballclub in public, nor had Willie Randolph. Art Howe knew what kind of team he had and declined to make a bad situation worse. Bobby Valentine would tweak certain players through the media in an effort to get a point across. But it had been 15 years since a Mets skipper—Dallas Green—had given the ballclub such a public scolding.

Once the diatribe was over, reporters spent the next 24 hours getting the players' take on Collins. To a man, they were in agreement that Collins was dead on in his criticism. A few of the Mets veterans from Randolph's days said it was a long time coming for the ballclub.

The Mets won the next afternoon to begin a stretch in which they went 20–12 to climb back into wild-card contention. By the time they swept a four-game series in Cincinnati for the first time ever and followed it with a series-opening win at Washington, the Mets were a season-high four games over .500 at 55–51 and 3½ games off the wild-card lead despite trading Rodriguez and Beltrán in July.

Collins put them in contention by milking great production out of Reyes, Justin Turner, Daniel Murphy, Ruben Tejada, Lucas Duda, and Ronny Paulino while Ike Da-

vis was sidelined with a season-ending ankle injury. Wright, who hit only .226 before sitting out nearly two months with a stress fracture in his back, compiled a 10-game hitting streak upon his return and was carrying the offense by late July. Pagan was flashing his 2010 form and Jason Bay was constantly showing signs of breaking out of what would become a two-year slump.

But the pitching just wasn't very consistent. Mike Pelfrey struggled as the de facto staff ace as the Mets went the entire season without Johan Santana. Jonathon Niese was erratic, Dillon Gee was mediocre after mid-June, and Capuano seemed to hit a wall in the fifth inning of every other start. The only consistent starter was R.A. Dickey, for whom the Mets simply declined to score runs.

Once Rodriguez was dealt during the All-Star Game, Jason Isringhausen took over the closer's role long enough to pick up his 300th save. After that, Bobby Parnell faltered as the closer, and Manny Acosta often pitched in bad luck in that capacity after two months of wonderful service as a set-up man.

The Mets were long out of the playoff race by September, and it was a wonder Collins kept them in contention as long as he did. He could deal with the fact the team wasn't going to play October baseball, but he was not about to tolerate sloppy baseball. He challenged his team again following another substandard performance in September.

"The perception I have right now?" Collins began. "We folded it up. And I won't stand for that. You want to see me be intense? You guys are going to see it. I don't play that game.

"Our fans should be upset. I don't blame them a bit. No energy, none at all, on the field. This is not the way we played all year long."

In some respects it was a miracle Collins to steer the Mets away from a 90-loss season. Although there were tough stretches in April, August, and September, he never lost the ballclub. They played hard despite missing numerous key components and finished 77–85.

The season brought the Mets their first batting champion as Jose Reyes finished with a .337 average, seven points ahead of Milwaukee's Ryan Braun. Collins took some heat after the season finale for allowing Reyes to pull himself from the game following a bunt single in the bottom of the first. During his defense of Reyes, Collins also revealed just how proud he was of his ballclub.

"I understand," Collins said of the scattered jeers from the stands after Reyes headed to the dugout. "I heard some comments from the stands. I don't blame them. People pay a good price to come to these games. You got to understand that I ask these players to do a lot."

And then Collins choked up, much like a father would watching his overachieving son graduate high school with a "C" average. It took Collins several moments before he composed himself and finished his thought.

"We've worked hard to get their respect this year, and they deserve ours."

It was obvious Collins had the utmost respect for his team following 162 games. It was also apparent that the Mets loved playing for Collins.

Collins was rewarded for his effort as the Mets picked up the 2013 option on his contract the day before the season ended. Now he had to hope to manage a healthy club with a better pitching staff in 2012.

Mike Cubbage   1991

Born: July 21, 1950 Charlottesville, VA
Named Interim Manager: 9/29/91
Returned to coaching staff following the 1991 season

Mike Cubbage Managerial Record

YEAR	GMS	W	L	PCT	POS.
1991	7	3	4	.429	5th, NL East

Mike Cubbage skippered the Mets for the final week of a very disappointing 1991 season. The Mets had sunk to fifth place in the NL East just a year after challenging the Pirates for the division title. They played fairly well through mid-June of '91, then sputtered for the next two months while Bud Harrelson lost control of the team.

The Mets won their first game under Cubbage, 4–3 over the Phillies, but lost four of the last six.

Cubbage had an excellent managerial record in the Mets farm system, going 539–376 and finishing no worse than second between 1983 and '89. But he was never given serious consideration to take over the big club in 1992. Despite his minor league resume, Cubbage hasn't managed in the majors since his seven-game stint with the '91 Mets.

Joe Frazier   1976–1977

Born: October 6, 1922   Liberty NC
Named Manager: 10/3/75
Dismissed: 5/31/77

Joe Frazier Mets Managerial Record

YEAR	GMS	W	L	PCT	POS.
1976	162	86	76	.531	3rd, NL East
1977	45	15	30	.333	6th, NL East
Total	207	101	106	.488	

Major League Totals

YEARS	GMS	W	L	PCT
1976–1977	207	101	106	.488

When you look at the Mets during Joe Frazier's stint as manager, one thing comes to mind; it wasn't his fault. Frazier became the skipper for a franchise that had virtually nothing in the farm system and would ignore the free agent market until Nelson Doubleday and Fred Wilpon purchased the team before the 1980 season.

The Mets hired from within when they sought a permanent replacement for Yogi Berra after the 1975 season, selecting Frazier, a longtime minor league skipper and former major league outfielder. Many Mets scribes were expecting the team to hire a veteran major league skipper for the 1976 season. But the job went to Frazier, who spent 10 minor league seasons as a manager, winning five pennants, including four with the Mets. He was named the minor league manager of the year in 1975 after guiding the Tidewater Tides to an 86–55 record and the International League championship.

Frazier took over a team that had been 18 games under .500 while Yogi Berra and Roy McMillan ran the team during the 1974 and '75 seasons. Frazier guided the 1976 Mets to an 86–76 record, the second-best mark in team history at the time. He did it with an offense that was bereft of power while Dave Kingman spent five weeks on the disabled list with a torn ligament in his left thumb.

Jerry Koosman cracked the 20-win mark for the first time in 1976, and Jon Matlack was 17–10 with a 2.95 ERA. But Tom Seaver received little offensive support while going 14–11 with a 2.59 ERA, pitching for a team that hit just .246 with 102 homers.

Koosman especially liked pitching for Frazier: "Joe Frazier worked well with me. In 1976 I went out and won 21 games for him because he left me in there. He didn't jerk me out for a pinch-hitter like Yogi did. The Mets had a tough time scoring runs, so a lot of times if there was a runner in scoring position in a close game, Yogi felt 'we have to get that run now.' When Frazier came in, he handed me the ball and said, 'You know what you have to do, take care of it.'"[6]

Unfortunately for Frazier, a solid rotation (Seaver, Koosman, Matlack, Mickey Lolich, and Craig Swan) couldn't compensate for an offense that hit just six homers in 33 games while Kingman was sidelined. The Mets finished 15 games behind the Phillies in the NL East despite a 10-game winning streak in early summer.

The Mets needed a productive bat and another starter when they headed to the 1976 winter meetings. They came away with neither, thanks in part to the emergence of M. Donald Grant, who took over the team following the death of original owner Joan Payson in September 1975.

Frazier recognized what he had on his roster and continued to tinker with a patchwork lineup that included Kingman and little else. Rookie Lee Mazzilli was supposed to be a can't-miss prospect heading into the 1977 season, but the rest of the offense consisted of aging veterans Bud Harrelson, Felix Millan, and Jerry Grote, plus an inexperienced Roy Staiger at third base. The inability to acquire a hitter, combined with a lack of talent in the farm system, spelled sudden doom for the '77 Mets. Tack on Tom Seaver's contract squabble and you had a team that would stumble to a 15–30 record under Frazier before he was dismissed in May 1977.

The Mets started the '77 season 6–5 before losing 25 of their final 34 under Frazier. They scored more than three runs just four times during that 34-game stretch while Seaver's beef with management continued to grow.

Frazier was fired after the Mets dropped a doubleheader to the Expos at Shea Stadium. Joe Torre replaced Frazier and proceeded to win seven of his first eight games at the helm. But the seeds of infertility had been planted, and Frazier would become the first of four managers to come and go before the team finally achieved respectability in 1984.

Dallas Green — 1993–1996

Born: August 4, 1934   Newport, Delaware
Named Manager: 5/19/93
Dismissed: 8/26/96

Dallas Green Mets Managerial Record

YEAR	GMS	W	L	PCT	POS.
1993	124	46	78	.371	7th, NL East
1994	113	55	58	.487	3rd, NL East
1995	144	69	75	.479	2nd, NL East
1996	131	59	72	.450	4th, NL East
Total	512	229	283	.447	

Major League Totals

YEAR	GMS	W	L	PCT
1979–1996	932	454	478	.487

The Mets needed a skipper who could clamp down on what had become the most incorrigible group of players in team history, someone who could weed out the bad actors while finding the patience to help develop some of the younger players on the team. In other words, they needed the Anti-Torborg.

The Mets had become the most expensive group of cellar-dwellers when Dallas Green took over for Jeff Torborg on May 19, 1993. The team was just a few weeks into what would become the Mets' worst season since 1965. Things didn't get a whole lot better under Green, who dealt with two firecracker-tossing incidents (Vince Coleman and Bret Saberhagen) and one bleach-throwing embarrassment (Saberhagen).

Quite often, a team will raise its performance level under a new skipper. But the couldn't-be-bothered Mets went 9–27 in their first 36 games under Green before finally winning two in a row at the end of June. Green, who had been with the Mets' front office in 1991 and worked as a National League scout in 1992 and the beginning of '93, was evaluating talent from the dugout. Every veteran was put on notice, and each prospect was given enough leash to either run with the big dogs or hang himself.

"Every clubhouse has some mavericks and they have their idiosyncrasies," Green said 17 years after taking over for Torborg. "New York obviously is a place that's really difficult for the players because everything is dissected, and every word and every action is backpage news kind of stuff. When I came in we weren't very friendly with the press. We weren't very friendly with the media and really weren't

very friendly with the fans. My attempt was to change that as quickly as I could.

"We didn't have a great ballclub. I thought we could have played better, but we just didn't get that job done. Eventually, we just didn't have enough manpower. Most of those guys were older, veteran-type guys that had been through the wars. Doc Gooden was part of that and got nailed one more time for his fourth or fifth drug thing [in 1994]. We lost him for most of the rest of the year. Stuff like that kept popping up and it was difficult to get the older guys to understand that we needed everybody on our side—fans and media—to get ourselves on track and play the kind of baseball we needed to play. I had a helluva time selling that, obviously."

Many of the younger players flourished under Green. Jeff Kent looked like a legitimate hitter in 1993, a few months after being acquired from the Blue Jays in the David Cone trade. Kent had his troubles with the glove but batted .270 with 21 homers and 80 RBI in '93. He hit well over .280 for Green and would eventually become an MVP.

Todd Hundley's career progressed during Green's time in the dugout, and Rico Brogna emerged as a solid first baseman as a Met after bouncing around the minors. Youngster Bobby Jones became a vital part of the Mets' rotation under Green, earning Rookie of the Year consideration in 1994 before being named to the NL All-Star team three years later.

But many of the team's pitching "prospects" in the mid-1990s failed to flourish under Green, often through no fault of the manager. Bill Pulsipher and Jason Isringhausen displayed much potential when they were recalled during the 1995 season, and Paul Wilson was projected as a No. 1 pitcher for the Mets. But the three were abject failures in 1996, either due to injury or ineffectiveness.

"They kind of hurt those kids right from the beginning," remembered Green. All winter they had all three of those guys on *Sporting News*, every TV show, and all the back pages of the papers about how great they were gonna be, and they were pretty good. We had a good look at Pulsipher and Isringhausen, and we thought that they were going to hold up and be all right. We didn't know much about Wilson other than he was a No. 1 draft choice and hadn't had a lot of success at the minor league level.

"I tried to caution that everybody has a learning process he has to go through to be a major league pitcher, and these kids were kind of rushed. We rushed them, and they weren't able to handle—on and off the field—the responsibilities of being a major league guy."

You can't discount the Mets' improvement under Green in 1994. The rotation was younger, and Eddie Murray and Vince Coleman were replaced by hungrier players who kept the team close to .500 all season before the players' strike. Saberhagen stayed out of trouble and finished 14–4 with a 2.74 ERA and a ridiculous 13 walks in 177⅓ innings. The Mets were 55–58 when the

'94 strike was called, leaving them two shy of their 1993 win total despite playing 49 fewer games.

"They were the kind of baseball players I like," Green said. "I like game-situation guys. I like gamers, and we had a few of those. We didn't have enough of them, but we had a few. We mixed in some veterans that kept us going pretty good."

The Mets stumbled through the first half of the 1995 season under Green until Pulsipher and Isringhausen were recalled that summer. The Mets were 35–57 following a loss in August 5, leaving them 24 games off the NL East lead. New York posted the National League's best record after that, going 34–18 while giving Mets fans hope that a contender was on the horizon.

But upon further review, it was a miracle the Mets could play so well at the end of 1995. Jose Vizcaino was the starting shortstop, and the outfield consisted of the aging Brett Butler, journeyman Joe Orsulak, the troubled Carl Everett, malcontent Bobby Bonilla, and the disappointing Ryan Thompson. However, rookie Edgardo Alfonzo finished the year batting .278 after a slow start, providing proof there was legitimate hitting talent in the farm system.

The Mets were ready to unveil the third part of "Generation K" in 1996 as Wilson earned a spot on the rotation to join Pulsipher and Isringhausen. But Pulsipher missed the entire season following elbow surgery, and Isringhausen and Wilson were hit hard most of the season.

There were several team hitting records set by the Mets in 1996. Newcomer Lance Johnson batted .333 and broke team marks with 227 hits and 21 triples. Todd Hundley set a National League record for catchers with 41 homers, and Bernard Gilkey hit .317 with 30 homers while tying Howard Johnson's team record of 117 RBIs.

But Green wasn't around to see the end of the 1996 season. He was dismissed and replaced by Bobby Valentine, a former Mets coach and minor league skipper who had been coveted by the organization.

"My coaching staff and I went through a hell of a lot of adversity in that time we were there," said Green. "It started with changing some of the coaching staff and bringing a staff in that I liked and trusted. I had some good people and we worked very, very hard to try to change the atmosphere and playing of the Mets. But we ran into a strike year. We ended up having to go through spring training with the replacement players. It was just a terrible, terrible time for all of baseball, not just the Mets. We never were able to right the ship."

Green knew a bit about righting ships. He spent two years managing in the Phillies' minor league system after retiring as a player in 1967. He later joined the team's front office as assistant farm director before becoming director of minor leagues and scouting when Paul Owens was hired as general manager in June 1972. The Phils went from NL East doormats to division champs within four years as Owens made shrewd deals while Green bolstered the farm system and suggested trades.

The Phillies reached the playoffs in 1976, ending a 26-year-long postseason drought. They repeated as NL East champs in 1977 and '78 under manager Danny Ozark but were unable to reach the World Series.

The team got off to a disappointing start in 1979 and struggled to play .500 ball. Players were comfortable with Ozark, but comfort seemed to evolve into lethargy. The Phils were two games under .500 when Owens dismissed Ozark and named Green his manager in late August.

"I never had any aspirations to be a manager," Green said. "I was really training myself—and Paul Owens was kind of training me—to become general manager. He felt when he was ready to step down, I would be a logical heir apparent because I was born and raised a Phillie. That was my goal, but I felt at the time—and Paul did, too—that we just needed somebody that knew the minor league system very well, knew the team inside and out and knew what he was trying to accomplish. What he was trying to accomplish the last 30 days of that season after Danny Ozark got fired was to really find out if this was the beginning of the end of that team, or whether they really wanted to play some championship baseball and get back some of the glory they had in '76, '77, and '78.

"I went down there with the implied job of finding out who wanted to play for the Phillies and who didn't, and what changes we had to make over the winter time to get back on track, or whether Paul really had to start dismantling that team and put together another one."

The Phillies finished the '79 season 19–11 under Green to end up with 84 wins, six fewer than in 1978.

Green remained in the dugout in 1980 to the chagrin of many players. The Phillies dealt with injuries to closer Tug McGraw and slugger Greg Luzinski during the first three months and were just 35–32 following a double-header loss to the Mets at Philadelphia on June 28. They picked up the pace for a few games, winning nine of 12 to take a one-game lead in the division. But a six-game losing streak left them 47–44 by July 23.

"Nobody really liked me coming in and being manager in 1980 because they really loved Danny and they thought I was there to do something different. Right from the very beginning we had a lot of controversy with the players and myself, and we lost 10 days of spring training because of a players' strike. So I lost the training part [of camp] and an important part of putting a team together.

"We had several different things happening during the season that we had to overcome, including injuries. We lost Tug until July. We lost Bull when he hurt his knee again. We had to keep battling, and the players kept battling me. I kept trying to get the message across that we had a game plan and we were gonna stick to the game plan, and that they weren't going to run the asylum, I was.

"It wasn't until the 161st game that we woke up and figured it all out."

The Phillies were 57–53 as they headed into a five-game set against the surprising Mets at Shea in mid-August.

New York was hovering around the .500 mark and just 2½ games behind the third-place Phillies before Green and his team caught fire. The Phils swept the five-game set by a combined 36–11 margin to begin a season-ending stretch in which they went 34–18 to claim their fourth division title in five years.

But the division race wasn't decided until the final weekend. The Phillies and Expos were tied for first as the two teams prepared for a three-game clash in Montreal. Philadelphia won the opener and was tied 4–4 in the 10th until Mike Schmidt smashed a two-run homer to clinch the NL East crown.

Green felt the tight division race helped the Phillies in the postseason. "I think it made all the difference in the world," he said. "That team had adversity and overcame it right from the very beginning."

The Phillies pulled out a thrilling win against Houston in the NLCS to reach the World Series for the first time since 1950. Philadelphia claimed its first championship by beating the Royals in six games.

Green stayed on as manager in 1981 and had the Phillies in first place when a two-month players' strike began in June. They were guaranteed a playoff berth after the strike was settled as commissioner Bowie Kuhn decided the season would be split into two halves, with the division winner of each half competing in a best-of-five NLDS.

The Expos captured the second half while the Phils played to a 25–27 mark. Montreal had momentum on its side and pulled out a five-game series win over Philadelphia.

Green could have stayed on as the Phillies' skipper in 1982, but another challenge presented itself. The Cubs were coming off back-to-back last-place seasons when they began to pursue Green to take over as general manager. Although he hated to leave the Phils, Green realized the offer was too good to pass up.

"The Carpenter family sold the Phillies in spring training of '81. It kind of took us all aback and we weren't sure what was going to happen to the ballclub. It was the strike year, and we ended up losing half the season. We didn't repeat, so it kind of looked like the beginning of the end of that team.

"But that really wasn't the 'decision' part of it. I could have stayed with the Phillies and wanted to stay when Mr. Giles and his group came in. But they wanted me to continue to manage. They weren't ready for me to become the general manager.

"The offer that the Cubs made was just too enticing. I was really going to have the opportunity to take over a team that nobody respected, nobody in baseball thought was very good, and do my own thing out there. That was really the thought process that changed my mind.

"Paul Owens was really the guy that said, 'Dallas, it's a wonderful opportunity and you should really take it. Even though the Phillies want you to stay and I want you to stay, you really should take this opportunity to go out on your own.'"

One of Green's first moves was to fleece the Phillies. His knowledge of the farm system allowed him to get Ryne Sandberg while swapping Larry Bowa for fellow shortstop Ivan DeJesus in January 1982. Sandberg became a Hall of Fame second baseman but was considered by some reporters as just a throw-in in the deal.

"I knew Ryne from the minor leagues because I was director of minor leagues and scouting for the Phillies for 10 years. I knew his athletic ability and knew what he was going to be able to do. He had two years in a row of outstanding Triple A performance and it was really time for him to move to the big leagues, but the Phillies weren't going to be able to play him at all. They had a shortstop, a second baseman, a third baseman and a center fielder, and those were the four positions I thought Ryan was going to be able to play.

"Because of my contacts here in Philadelphia I knew they were in a squabble with Larry Bowa on a contract problem. I knew I had one of the only shortstops that was going to fill the bill in DeJesus, so I just kept hanging on, hanging on, hanging on. We just told them if we were gonna make a deal, I was in a position to build inventory and I could play Ryne Sandberg and they couldn't. They were gonna send him back to Triple A. They finally relented because they knew they had to get that shortstop."

The Cubs finished fifth in each of Green's first two seasons as GM despite Sandberg and Bowa, but they found themselves in contention in 1984 when Green picked up Rick Sutcliffe from the Indians in June.

"That was a deal that sent a future Hall of Famer to Cleveland in Joe Carter, along with Mel Hall. I got Sutcliffe and a kid named George Frazier out in the bullpen, and a left-handed hitting backup catcher [Ron Hassey]. I kind of filled three holes that we had, and Sutcliffe went on to have a Cy Young year and led us to the championship."

It took a while after the Sutcliffe deal before the Cubs took off. They were 4½ games behind the division-leading Mets on July 27 before going 40–22 the rest of the way to finish 6½ games ahead of New York. Sutcliffe captured the NL Cy Young, and Sandberg was named MVP after leading the Cubbies to their first playoff berth in 39 years.

Chicago won the first two games of the NLCS against San Diego to get within one victory of the World Series before the Padres rallied to take the next three games and the pennant. The Cubs wouldn't make the playoffs again until 1989, two years after Green left the club. However, Green was still on board when the team acquired Greg Maddux, Rafael Palmeiro, Shawon Dunston, and Mark Grace.

"We didn't have a timetable," Green said of his blueprint for the Cubs. "We didn't have a five-year plan that people think we should have had. I told them from the very beginning I wanted to win as soon as I could.

"What we didn't realize was that we really won too quick. We got there in '81, our first season was '82 and we win the whole thing in '84. In '85 we started having breakdowns physically and didn't play very good in '85 and '86.

"Gordon Goldsberry did a tremendous job in setting up the minor league system and revamping the scouting and development system, but the kids weren't ready. Maddux, Grace, Palmeiro, and Dunston—all those kids that he had drafted and signed—they weren't quite ready for the big leagues yet. As a result, when we had the breakdowns, we didn't have the manpower to back it up and we took our lumps. But we left them in pretty darned good shape."

The Cubs won the 1989 NL East title under Don Zimmer, clinching it about a month after Green was dismissed as manager of the Yankees. Green opened the season in the Yankees' dugout and was replaced by Bucky Dent after going 56–65. The Yankees finished in the AL East cellar the following year.

Green returned to the Phillies' front office after his reign as manager of the Mets. He has served as senior advisor to the general manager since 1998, working with Ed Wade, Pat Gillick, and Ruben Amaro.

"I came back to Philadelphia with Eddie Wade's blessing and encouragement. I enjoyed working for him. I worked with Pat Gillick in the same role. It's just a role that fits a guy that has over 50 years in professional baseball. At my age, it's kind of the thing to do. I can vent. I can say exactly what I want to say, and if people want to take the advice, they can take it. If they don't they throw it away.

"I go to all the home games, I see a lot of the minor league kids and I still see the development process of baseball. I love the job. It's a perfect job for an older guy like me."

Green was inducted into the team's Wall of Fame in 2006, 51 years after signing his first pro contract with the Phillies. Although he went just 20–22 as a major league pitcher, Green received due recognition for becoming the fourth rookie manager ever to lead a team to a World Series title, and the first skipper to win one with the Phillies.

"Those honors come as a result of winning in 1980 as much as anything, along with longevity with the ballclub. I signed with them as a kid, and all but 15 years of my baseball career have been with Philadelphia. It was a great, great honor. I was then, and still am, very proud of the fact that my plaque is up on that wall."

Bud Harrelson   1990–1991

Born: June 6, 1944 Niles, Calif.
Named Manager: 5/29/90
Dismissed: 9/29/91

Bud Harrelson Mets Managerial Career					
YEAR	GMS	W	L	PCT	POS
1990	120	71	49	.592	2nd, NL East
1991	154	74	80	.481	5th, NL East
Total	274	145	129	.529	

Few players in Mets history were as popular as Bud Harrelson, the diminutive shortstop and two-time National League All-Star. Harrelson never hit higher than .258 in any season with the Mets, but his glovework was sorely missed by the staff when he sat out games due to injury.

Harrelson was part of the Mets' purge of 1977 and 1978, going to the Phillies for a player (Fred Andrews) who appeared in just 16 major league games, none with New York. But Harrelson returned to the Mets organization in 1981, working as a broadcaster, coach, and minor league manager. He became the third base coach when Bobby Valentine left to manage the Texas Rangers during the 1985 season.

Harrelson remained on the Mets' staff under Davey Johnson, often serving as the man who would listen to players gripe about their manager. He had bonded with most of the players, and his status as a Met-for-life made the front office feel comfortable.

There was tremendous pressure on Johnson to win the 1990 NL East title after a lackluster 1989 season that saw the Mets win 87 games following a 100–60 campaign. But the Mets stumbled out of the gate in '90, falling into fourth place with a 20–22 record when Johnson was replaced by Harrelson on May 28.

The Mets didn't play any better in their first five games under Harrelson, losing four to drop 8½ games off the pace. But the team suddenly got hot on June 8, winning 18 of its next 20—and 23 of 26—to pull within a half-game of the Pirates.

Harrelson seemed the perfect manager for the team. By 1990, Johnson expected his players to act and play like professionals. But the roster had changed dramatically in 1990 as the Mets acquired younger players while veterans Keith Hernandez, Gary Carter, Mookie Wilson, and Lee Mazzilli were either released or traded during and after the '89 season. Harrelson had earned the confidence of his younger club and was getting a tremendous season out of Darryl Strawberry while the outfielder was going through contentious contract negotiations.

However, Strawberry thought his relationship with Harrelson changed after the Mets broke off contract talks in July. Management felt Strawberry wasn't worth the five-year, $23.5 million package Jose Canseco had just signed. Harrelson toed the company line, and Strawberry felt betrayed. The outfielder was hitting an uncharacteristic .307 by July 6. He continued to produce over the final three months, but his average was just .248 in his final 78 games.

Still, Harrelson had the Mets in first place between July 26 and August 5, and the team was 22 games over .500 following a Labor Day rout of the Cardinals. But the Mets suddenly had trouble hitting left-handed pitching. New York went 5–13 in games started by lefties from August 20 through the end of the season. The biggest embarrassment came in a doubleheader loss at Shea Stadium on September 20, when rookie southpaws Brian Barnes and Chris Nabholz helped the Expos win. Nabholz tossed a one-hit shutout in the nightcap.

The Mets fell short of the NL East title, but Harrelson already had earned a contract for the 1991 season. He came close to becoming the first Mets manager to have a pair of 20-game winners in the same season. Frank Viola picked up his 20th win during the final series, but Dwight Gooden had to settle for 19 victories just a year after he missed over two months due to shoulder pain.

The Mets retooled following the 1990, acquiring free agent Vince Coleman while allowing Strawberry to sign with the Dodgers after low-balling him in free agency. With Gooden, Viola, and David Cone, the staff appeared to be good enough to challenge for a third division title in six seasons. But an early season decision by Harrelson robbed the Mets of pitching depth.

Gooden was on the mound during a raw, damp day against the Expos April 13, five days after he pitched eight innings in winning the season opener. Gooden went the distance on a seven-hitter while striking out 14 in a 5–3 win over Dennis Martinez. Gooden also threw 149 pitches under adverse weather conditions in what was only the sixth game of the season. The outing left Gooden with a very sore shoulder that would require surgery in August.

Harrelson also had a very public argument with David Cone that could be seen by television viewers. Cone had shaken off a pitchout call and confronted Harrelson about the decision when he got to the dugout. Harrelson poked his finger into Cone and appeared to shove his hurler before they were separated. They downplayed the confrontation after the game, but it was becoming clear Harrelson's authority was waning.

This never happened to the Mets under Gil Hodges, and that was part of the problem.

Hodges was the quiet leader on the Brooklyn Dodgers, and he cast a very large shadow at Shea after becoming the Mets' manager in 1968. One of his All-Star players was Harrelson, who had a picture of Hodges on his office wall behind his desk when he became the skipper. Comparisons between the two were made when the Mets went on that incredible streak under Harrelson in 1990. Those comparisons grew louder by the middle of the 1991 season, for all the wrong reasons.

Hodges worked well with the media, many of whom may had been intimated by his physical stature and popularity among New York baseball fans. The wiry Harrelson had referred to the media as "the enemy" and bristled at any criticism of his managing skills.

Harrelson also got little out of Coleman, who was expected to give the Mets their first true leadoff hitter since, well, Harrelson. But hamstring issues and a hatred for the Mets' infield dirt at Shea led to Coleman's first disappointing season in the majors.

Despite all the squabbling, the Mets were just 2½ games out of first place after taking the first three games of a four-game series against the Padres at Shea in mid-July. They were 49–35 at that point, but went 28–49 the rest of the season.

Harrelson wasn't around for the season finale. He was dismissed and replaced by Mike Cubbage with seven games left in the season.

Just like Willie Mays misjudging fly balls in Oakland during the 1973 World Series, Bud Harrelson's managerial stint somewhat tarnished his reputation in New York baseball lore. He was a two-time All-Star who made life easier for one of the National League's top pitching staffs in the 1960s and '70s. Harrelson was a media favorite as a player, but the constant grilling from the manager's office gave writers and broadcasters reason to dismiss Harrelson as a Hodges wanna-be who couldn't. The funny thing is that Harrelson had the second-best winning percentage of any Mets manager when he was shown the door.

Gil Hodges   1968–1972

Born: April 4, 1924 Princeton, Indiana
Died: April 2, 1972 West Palm Beach, Florida
Became Manager: 10/11/67
Died 4/2/72
NL East Title, 1969
NL Pennant, 1969
World Series, 1969

Gil Hodges Mets Managerial Record

YEAR	GMS	W	L	PCT	POS.
1968	162	73	89	.451	9th, NL
1969	162	100	62	.617	1st, NL East
1970	162	83	79	.512	3rd, NL East
1971	162	83	79	.512	3rd, NL East
Total	648	339	309	.523	

Major League Totals

YEARS	GMS	W	L	PCT
1963–1971	1414	660	753	.467

Most great leaders are either feared or loved. Gil Hodges happened to be both in the eyes of many of his former players, most of whom speak of him with reverence nearly four decades after his death.

It's no mistake the Mets' fortunes turned when the team worked out a deal with the Senators to bring Hodges back to New York following the 1967 season. Hodges was an original Met, but bad knees put a premature end to a career that should have earned him a plaque at Cooperstown.

Hodges became a major league manager without the usual prerequisite stint in the minors. He already had shown solid leadership skills as a player, serving as the heart and soul of the great Brooklyn Dodgers teams of the 1950s.

Hodges is one of few skippers to be traded twice. He took over as Washington's manager in May 1963 after being acquired from the Mets for Jim Piersall, less than three weeks after Hodges collected his final major league RBI. Hodges spent the next 4½ seasons turning the expansion Nats into a hard-working but mediocre ballclub, which was a drastic improvement from the sometimes horrible baseball being played in the nation's capital since their last pennant in 1933. His work was so lauded in D.C. that he was inducted into the Wall of Heroes at RFK Stadium.

Although his credentials as a player and a manager were impressive, it was his demeanor that is best remembered by those who were around him during his days as Mets manager.

"He was one of those guys who made you believe in yourself," said Jim McAndrew. "He was an anomaly as far as managers are concerned, whether it be in business or anyplace. He committed to you in spring training and made boys act like men because he'd tell you, 'I believe in you, and if you believe in me, it's your responsibility to perform like I believe in you.'

"He gave you the self-confidence necessary if you weren't a confident person to begin with.

"He didn't support you with a rah-rah pat on the back. In our generation, the fathers made eye contact with you and didn't have to say anything. It was the eye contact as far as approval or disapproval.

"He had that management skill. Every once in a while, like a father trying to raise a teenager, he'd have to pull people behind closed doors and say, 'Here's the way it is, this is what I think, and you better get there or else we're going to have problems.'

"He was special in any walk of life. He was a special man, and I was fortunate to have crossed paths with him during my life."

"He was just a legend," said Pam Frisella, wife of reliever Danny Frisella. "He was so soft-spoken. When he spoke he didn't have to yell. You just knew he knew what he was doing. I think you just had the confidence in him as a human being and as a manager.

"He just had a gentleness about him…certainly not as a player. I don't know if a player would say that. There weren't that many people that I felt that way about, but he certainly was."

Hodges was a Brooklynite despite his Indiana roots. He married a Brooklyn girl, Joan Lombardi, and raised his family on Bedford Avenue. The locals bowled at Gil Hodges Lanes when they weren't watching their kids play baseball at Gil Hodges Field. He never sold his Brooklyn home.

The Mets decided to bring Hodges back to the borough, but he didn't come cheap. The Senators didn't want to lose their manager, but they finally relented after getting pitcher Bill Denehy and $100,000 from the Mets.

The Mets already were showing improvement when Hodges took over. Bud Harrelson, Cleon Jones, Ron Swoboda, and Ed Kranepool were homegrown players and mainstays in the lineup. Tom Seaver was coming off his Rookie of the Year campaign, and the Mets had Jerry Koosman, Nolan Ryan, Gary Gentry, and Tug McGraw waiting in the wings.

"When he came to the team, he began to define everybody's role," remembered reliever Ron Taylor. "My role

First baseman Gil Hodges shows off his Mets contract after signing with the team in 1962. He would become its manager just six years later.

was as his right-handed closer. Tug McGraw was going to become the left-handed closer. We knew what he expected of us and what our jobs were."

"He also brought a winning attitude to the clubhouse. That's nothing against Wes Westrum. He did a fine job."

Hodges used the 1968 season as a period of instruction and observation. He wanted to see how his players responded to tough situations rather than pulling them out at the first sign of trouble. If Koosman loaded the bases in the eighth, Hodges often let him work out of the jam. Was Cleon Jones having trouble with certain right-handers? Hodges gave him the at-bats to prove he could deliver. The strategy seemed to give players confidence to the point where catcher Jerry Grote thought in the winter of 1969 his team could make the playoffs.

Although Hodges took chances with his nubile talent, the Mets still finished with a team-record 73 wins in '68. Koosman won 19 games and finished a vote shy of beating Johnny Bench for the NL Rookie of the Year award. Seaver won 16 games for the second straight year while lowering his ERA by a half-run. Grote batted a career-high .282, one year after compiling a .195 average. Jones hit .297, and Ken Boswell batted .261 and landed on the Topps All-Rookie team. His players quickly learned they were playing for a special skipper

"Gil was just an amazing person," recalled Koosman 40 years later. "He's a gentleman's gentleman. He knew baseball inside out and was always at least two or three steps ahead of the opposing manager. He knew his ballplayers completely, what they could do and couldn't do. And he never put any of us in an embarrassing situation that we couldn't handle.

"He knew what it took to win and he made sure that each of us understood that. We were to do our jobs, and our jobs only.

"It takes a lot of weight off your shoulders knowing that all you had to do is take care of yourself and not worry about the next guy because when you're a team out there, you *do* worry about the next guy. And you want everybody to be successful.

"He taught you that your job is to know where everybody's playing and why, and then do your job.

"If there were any problems at the ballpark, he didn't want them to carry over to your private life at home. Even if he fined you, he fined you in cash because he didn't want your wife to see a canceled check and ask what that was for, what did you do to get fined. And then he gave the money to his Little League club in Brooklyn.

"He ran a tight ship and certainly one in which he treated everyone the same. There were no stars on his ballclub."

Hodges had used the 1968 season as a springboard to '69, particularly when it came to his handling of Tommie Agee and Tug McGraw.

Agee was coming off a disappointing 1967 season when the Mets acquired him from the White Sox, one year after he was named the AL Rookie of the Year. Agee went 0-for-10 in a 24-inning loss at the Astrodome, triggering an 0-for-34 skid that tied a team record. Agee spent most of the season hitting under .200 and lost playing time to Don Bosch in center. But Hodges saw Agee bat .400 over his final 10 games, raising his average to .217.

McGraw didn't make the Mets in 1968 after spending parts of three seasons with the team as a spot starter. Hodges felt McGraw was better suited as a reliever if he could develop another pitch, and the lefty spent a year in Jacksonville honing a screwball that would allow him to pitch in the majors through 1984.

Hodges planted the seeds for the 1969 season, but he almost didn't see them bloom from the dugout. The Mets were playing out the string in Atlanta on September 24 when he felt a pain in his chest. He had pitched pregame batting practice as usual but left the dugout early in the game to lie down. Trainer Tom McKenna sent Hodges to a hospital, where it was determined the 44-year-old skipper had suffered a heart attack.

Hodges spent a month in the hospital before heading to Florida to recuperate. He was able to resume his managerial career after being told to quit smoking and watch his diet.

Hodges was back with the team as it reported to camp in St. Petersburg for the 1969 season. He had shed a few pounds and given up the smokes, but there was another significant change. Hodges had seen enough of his team to feel it was ready to erase its bumbling image. He even predicted in spring training that his club would win 85 games, a 12-game improvement from the team's high-water mark. The nurturing Hodges became a bit more of a taskmaster as he saw the potential in his team. By now, he knew what his team could or couldn't do, and he was ready to crack the whip when needed.

"We were so organized because he ran it like a business, and he was the boss," remembered Rod Gaspar. "As the saying goes, he was the chief and we were the Indians. Whatever he said went. We knew it and respected him big time. He was the best manager I ever played for obviously, and as many people have said, he should be in the Hall of Fame both as a player and a manager."

Hodges watched his team lose to the expansion Expos in the 1969 season opener before the Mets eventually improved to 18–18 on May 21, the first time the team was at .500 so late in a year. A five-game losing streak followed, but the Mets were off and running after winning a team-record 11 straight. The pitching was solid, the defense was flawless, and the hitting was timely, if not scary, during the winning streak. Hodges' prediction of an 85-win season didn't look ridiculous at that point, but the Mets were going to have to overtake a red-hot Cubs team to extend their season.

The Mets whittled the Cubs' lead down to 3½ games with Seaver's one-hitter against the Cubs on July 9, but the deficit grew to 9½ games following an 8–2 loss at Houston on August 13. New York had played sub-.500 ball for the better part of a month, and Hodges wasn't about to tolerate that kind of record.

Hodges showed he meant business during a doubleheader loss in which the Mets were outscored 27–8 by the Astros on July 30. He simmered while Houston was scoring 10 times in the third inning of the nightcap. Gentry was chased during the third before Nolan Ryan gave up an RBI double to Johnny Edwards. Hodges came out of the dugout following the Edwards hit, but it wasn't to lift Ryan. Hodges felt Cleon Jones had loafed while retrieving Edward's base hit to left. The manager walked past Ryan and Harrelson before reaching Jones. Hodges escorted his .346 hitter off the field and didn't start him again until August 4. Hodges had made his point. If the Mets were going to lose the division, they would do it playing their best baseball.

The Cubs appeared to have an insurmountable lead by mid-August, when the Cardinals had become their closest pursuers. That's when the Mets began a charge that saw them go 38–11 the rest of the year while the Cubs limped home at 18–27.

Hodges had a fresh lineup down the stretch while Leo Durocher, his former Brooklyn skipper, had used the same players almost every day. Five of the Cubs' eight regulars played at least 151 games. Jones and Agee were the lone Mets to appear in more than 124 contests, and they were providing the offensive spark that propelled them to the division lead.

It took the Mets less than a month before they turned their 9½-game deficit into a one-game lead following a doubleheader sweep of the Expos. They were "Ya Gotta Believe" before McGraw had coined the phrase, posting six shutouts and holding opponents under three runs in 17 of 28 contests. New York also pulled off a pair of 1–0 victories at Pittsburgh, a doubleheader sweep in which pitchers Don Cardwell and Koosman drove in the lone runs.

The NL East title was theirs after Gentry went the distance and Donn Clendenon homered twice in a 6–0 win over the Cardinals on September 24.

Hodges continued his platooning to perfection in the playoffs. Ron Swoboda and Donn Clendenon never got off the bench during the NLCS as the Braves went with three right-handed starters during the sweep. Instead, Swoboda watched fellow right-fielder Art Shamsky hit .538 in the three-game sweep. Kranepool batted .250 while Clendenon awaited his turn at first base.

Swoboda and Clendenon would become two of the heroes in the World Series win over the Orioles. All Swoboda did was bat .400, deliver the tiebreaking double in the clincher, and provide one of the greatest catches in World Series history. Clendenon walked off with *Sport Magazine*'s MVP award for the series after belting three homers while posting a .357 average.

The Mets had gone from ninth place in 1968 to a World Series championship a year later, all while exceeding Hodges' preseason win prediction by 15 games, 22 including the postseason.

A four-month long celebration began the moment Davey Johnson's fly ball nestled into Jones' glove in deep left field. The Mets could be seen singing "You Gotta Have Heart" on *The Ed Sullivan Show*. They were singing Christmas carols at Radio City Music Hall. They were part of comedian/actor Phil Foster's Las Vegas act, some of them making as much money as they did during the '69 regular season.

The Mets were the favorites to repeat as NL East champions. Hodges would work with a 1970 roster that was virtually identical to the championship team. New York stayed close to first place the entire season, but the timely hits were fewer, the outstanding pitching starts were rarer, and the clutch victories were at a premium. Tommie Agee duplicated his solid 1969 season, Donn Clendenon set a team record with 97 RBIs, and Cleon Jones broke a club mark with a 23-game hitting streak. However Jones saw his overall production drop as his batting average slipped 63 points from '69.

The pitching often was mystifying. Seaver was working on his second straight Cy Young Award until he won just once in his last 10 starts. Various injuries limited Koosman to 12 wins, and Gentry was unable to take the next step despite well-above-average stuff. The three combined to win 16 fewer games than they accumulated in 1969.

And they weren't getting much help from the back end of the rotation. Ryan continued to frustrate Mets management with an outstanding fastball but little command. He set a team record with 97 walks while going 7–11.

Jim McAndrew posted a 3.56 ERA but finished 10–14. Newcomer Ray Sadecki pitched well over his 19 starts but went just 1–2 after July 8.

One of Hodges' biggest failures of the season was Joe Foy, the Mets' latest third-base acquisition. Foy had a reputation as a carouser off the field and a bad actor in the clubhouse. But Hodges was confident he could rein in the 27-year-old New Yorker, leaning on general manager Johnny Murphy to ship Amos Otis to the Royals for Foy.

But Foy remained incorrigible while hitting a meager .236 and setting career-lows with six homers and 37 RBIs. He showed up at the ballpark in a hung-over state, although alcohol may have had nothing to do with it. Hodges decided to teach him a lesson by keeping him in the lineup despite his condition. But Foy could barely move as line drives and grounders whizzed by him. Hodges finally took him out of the game for fear Foy might get himself killed. Foy was dropped at the end of the season.

Still, the Mets remained a rather close group. Hodges and the organization also realized long road trips interrupted a player's family life, so the team did something about it.

"The thing Gil liked was the wives going on the road," Pam Frisella said. "It was a diversion. It kept [the players] from probably staying out too late. Everything was 'team.' Team plane, team bus, team everything. And the wives were always welcome.

"I think he was smart enough to know that if the wives went, the guys wouldn't stay out all night."

For whatever reason, the Mets couldn't recapture the magic that defined the 1969 season. Things only got worse in '71.

The Mets actually got off to their best start to date and were tied for first place at 32–20 on June 9. But New York endured a horrendous summer, going 21–37 in July and August to play itself out of the race.

Hodges continued to play the prospects in an effort to recapture the glory of '69. With Swoboda jettisoned to Montreal and Art Shamsky struggling, Ken Singleton became the starting right fielder while displaying flashes of his bright future. Tim Foli saw action in 97 games, most of them at third base after newcomer Bob Aspromonte played himself out of the position.

But Ryan continued his enigmatic pitching, eclipsing his 97 walks of 1970 by issuing a ridiculous 116 free passes. Ryan was 8–4 with a 2.05 ERA after tossing seven shutout innings against the Pirates June 30. He went 2–10 with a 6.94 ERA the rest of the season, contributing mightily to the Mets' second straight 83–79 season.

Hodges was losing patience in his still-young ballclub. Some players complained that Hodges had become more distant and was less of a father-figure than he had been.

Worse, he was smoking again, three years after he was told to swear off cigarettes following his heart attack.

"Watch the cigarettes," warned Joan Hodges before her husband left New York for spring training in February of 1972. But Hodges had three pressing concerns as he headed to Florida.

The Mets had shipped Ryan to the Angels for shortstop Jim Fregosi, who was expected to become the team's latest third baseman of the future. Hodges spent plenty of time hitting fungos at Fregosi as he prepared for the exhibition season. One of those hits left Fregosi with a broken thumb, causing him to miss the start of exhibition play.

Hodges and general manager Bob Scheffing were working on a deal for a bonafide, experienced hitter to pencil into the lineup. The two wanted outfielder Rusty Staub and spent March working on a package with the Expos. Without a deal in place, the Mets would open the season with pretty much the same underwhelming lineup they displayed the previous two years.

Hodges also wasn't sure the season would begin on time. The first major league work stoppage was looming as the season opener drew near. Players voted to strike on the final weekend of spring training, leaving Hodges and his coaching staff with little to do.

Hodges and his coaches decided to play a round of golf on Sunday, April 2. They had just made dinner plans when they began to disperse. Hodges turned away, then collapsed onto the walkway. He had suffered his second heart attack, this one fatal.

The Mets had lost their leader, and the funeral reunited the striking players for the worst possible reason. Astonishingly, the team overshadowed the service by making two major announcements later in the day. The Mets named Yogi Berra to replace Hodges, and they also had completed a deal to bring Staub to Shea Stadium.

Berra ran a lax clubhouse compared to Hodges, and the results began to show up in the trainer's room. The Mets' list of injured players reached ridiculous proportions in 1972 and 1973, and players took advantage of Berra's easygoing approach. Weigh-ins were a thing of the past, allowing certain players to play beyond their ideal girth.

The Mets won a pennant 18 months after Hodges died. But the team often would miss his regimented style that prevented things from getting out of hand in the clubhouse.

Frank Howard 1983

Born: August 8, 1936 Columbus, OH
Named Interim Manager: 6/3/83
Returned to coaching staff following the 1983 season

Frank Howard Mets Managerial Record

YEAR	GMS	W	L	PCT	POS.
1983	116	52	64	.448	6th, NL East

Major League Totals

YEARS	GMS	W	L	PCT
1981–1983	226	93	133	.412

Frank Howard took over on June 3, 1983, as the Mets were showing signs of life. Darryl Strawberry had made his major league debut 29 days earlier, Keith Hernandez would be acquired on June 15, and Walt Terrell and Ron Darling would be part of the staff by the end of the season.

The Mets needed a closer after sending Neil Allen to the Cardinals for Hernandez. Howard gave the job to Jesse Orosco, who went 9–5 with 13 saves and a 1.55 ERA after inheriting the job.

Strawberry also emerged as a potential star under Howard, although batting coach Jim Frey received most of the credit for working with the 21-year-old outfielder.

But the Mets never climbed out of the NL East cellar despite the infusion of talent. They had just one winning road trip under Howard (4–2 in August) and went 30–30 at home.

Howard would serve as a caretaker manager, returning to the coaching staff when Davey Johnson was hired before the '84 season.

Art Howe 2003–2004

Born: December 15, 1946 Pittsburgh, Pennsylvania
Named Manager: 10/28/02
Dismissed: 10/4/04

Art Howe Managerial Record

YEAR	GMS	W	L	PCT	POS.
2003	161	66	95	.410	5th, NL East
2004	162	71	91	.438	4th, NL East
Total	323	137	186	.424	

Major League Totals

YEARS	GMS	W	L	PCT
1989–2004	2266	1129	1137	.498

Art Howe had his greatest managerial success with the low-budget Athletics from 2000 to 2002. He captured two division titles during that three-year span and collected 205 wins over his final two seasons with the team. Yet, the A's were more than willing to part with Howe in part due to his failure to win a postseason series. The perception within the Oakland front office was that bench coach Ken Macha deserved more than ample credit for the team's strong run, and pitching coach Rick Peterson was the one who molded Tim Hudson, Mark Mulder, and Barry Zito into stud hurlers.

Howe still had a year remaining on his A's contract when the team gave him permission to seek other offers. It seemed rather odd that a manager who had averaged 99 wins over his last three seasons would be allowed to walk away. That didn't stop the Mets from quickly snatching Howe from the Athletics just 3½ weeks after firing Bobby Valentine. Howe was given a four-year contract by the

Mets, who also had a chance to hire Lou Piniella.

Howe took over a team that finished a very disappointing 75–86 under Valentine in 2002. The Mets were expected to be serious contenders after acquiring former All-Stars Roberto Alomar and Mo Vaughn prior to the '02 campaign. Both players wound up compiling their worst major league stats since becoming everyday players.

General manager Steve Phillips spent more of Fred Wilpon's money after hiring Howe, signing free agents Tom Glavine and Cliff Floyd to multiyear contracts.

The Mets now had a starting lineup that included five current and former All-Stars (Mike Piazza, Vaughn, Alomar, Floyd, and Jeromy Burnitz), and two other former All-Stars (Jay Bell and Tony Clark) off the bench. The front end of the rotation had past and present All-Stars in Glavine, Al Leiter, and Steve Trachsel. Phillips had just signed Graeme Lloyd and Mike Stanton to join a bullpen that included Armando Benitez, John Franco, and David Weathers.

Highly touted prospect Jae Seo had made the ballclub out of spring training, and former first-round pick Aaron Heilman was waiting in the wings.

Howe also welcomed David Cone into camp as the former Met looked to prolong his career. Cone had a good spring training and earned a spot in the rotation.

On paper, the Mets were a roto-nerd's dream, and Phillips had stockpiled the ballclub like a rotisserie owner in a free-agent league. The Mets now had the second-highest payroll in the majors at $116.9 million, about $32 million behind the Yankees. It was up to Howe to use a fresh approach to get the maximum out of his high-priced roster or else Phillips was a goner. Three and a-half months into the season, Phillips was a goner.

Piazza got off to an exceptional start, hitting .336 with seven homers and 15 RBIs in his first 31 games. But he tore his right groin muscle during a game at San Francisco May 16, keeping him out of action about three months.

At least Piazza lasted longer than Vaughn, who played his final major league game May 2. Vaughn and the Mets had hoped rest would solve his arthritic knee condition, but he limped out of the majors after hitting .190 with three homers in 27 games in 2003.

Cone's departure may have been the saddest as Mets fans were rooting for the prodigal son. The game-time temperature was 37 degrees when he made his season debut, but he still managed to strike out five while holding the Expos to two hits in five shutout innings of a 4–0 win, the last of his 194 major league victories. Cone was hammered in his next four outings before calling it a career.

Alomar continued to prove his best days were behind him. Roger Cedeno was a bust in his return to the Mets. And Floyd managed to play through August 18 despite a bone spur in his Achilles' tendon.

Floyd stayed on the active roster two months after Phillips was fired. The Mets were last in the NL East at 28–35 when Phillips was replaced by Jim Duquette.

Adding to the misery was Glavine, who had his worst season since 1988. The lefty went 9–14 with a 4.52 ERA, a year after winning 18 games while compiling a 2.96 ERA with the Braves. Glavine set the tone for the entire season when he was rocked for five runs and eight hits over 3⅔ innings of a 15–2 loss to the Cubs on Opening Day.

It was evident that Arthur Henry Howe Jr. had picked a bad time to change jobs. By the end of the season, rookies Ty Wiggington and Jason Phillips had become his most dependable players as the Mets played out a 66–95 season, the team's worst since 1993.

But there was hope in the form of Jose Reyes, who made his major league debut June 10, a day shy of his 20th birthday. Reyes went 2-for-4 with an RBI and two runs scored in his first game, five days before belting a grand slam against the Angels. He managed to drive in 19 runs in his first 25 games despite a .209 average. But he was terrific the rest of the way, hitting .355 while stealing 12 bases in his final 44 games.

It was hard to blame Howe for the Mets' fortunes in 2003. You couldn't fault his managerial skills since most of his established players were injured or well past their expiration date. Howe was buried on WFAN, either for bringing in a reliever too early or going with his starter too long. But it is tough to juggle a pitching staff when the starters are gassed in the sixth before the bullpen throws gas on the situation.

Newly crowned general manager Duquette made a pair of big moves following the 2003 campaign, inking free agent outfielder Mike Cameron and signing Japanese standout Kazuo Matsui.

Cameron gave the Mets a Gold Glove in center field, and Matsui was brought in to play shortstop. But there was just one little problem—the Mets already had a shortstop in Reyes, who was asked to play second base.

Reyes wasn't the only Met who had to learn a new position in spring training. The team was hoping Piazza would make a smooth transition from catcher to first base, which was like asking George W. Bush to captain a debate team. As a catcher, Piazza was one hell of a hitter. As a first baseman, he was one hell of a catcher.

Howe was expected to start two players out of position, along with a "rookie" shortstop in Matsui, a second-year third baseman in Wigginton, and a second-year catcher in Phillips.

This is how Howe was rewarded. Wigginton hit .285 but lost his starting job to some rookie named David Wright before "Wiggy" was traded. Matsui homered in his first major league at-bat and hit .272 while rarely displaying the Gold Glove reputation he earned on the artificial surfaces in Japan. Piazza played first base with the agility of Nureyev: Rupert Nureyev. And Reyes spent the first 2½ months of the season on the disabled list with a nagging hamstring injury.

Yet, the Mets were in the division hunt by July 15 thanks to a slow start by the Braves. New York often rode the heroics of Richard Hidalgo, who was acquired from the Astros for Weathers and pitcher Jeremy Griffiths in June. Hidalgo could carry the Mets on his back for a week, as he did when he homered in five straight games. But he was colder more often than he was hot, finishing the year batting only .228 as a Met.

Glavine was 7–3 with a 2.03 ERA in June before losing his next five starts. Al Leiter compiled a 3.21 ERA but taxed the bullpen with his inability to pitch into the eighth.

The Mets were under .500 in late July, but they were within striking distance of the division lead when Duquette made two major trades, one of which would haunt the franchise. Duquette sent Wigginton to the Pirates in a deal that brought pitcher Kris Benson to the Mets. The team also acquired enigmatic hurler Victor Zambrano from the Devil Rays for the Mets' top pitching prospect, lefty Scott Kazmir.

Benson seemed to follow one great outing with a poor one. Zambrano won his first two starts but was shut down after August 17.

Howe and the Mets also counted on catcher Jason Phillips to duplicate his .298 average from 2003. The sure-handed but slow-footed catcher was the man who replaced Piazza behind the plate. He ended the season hitting just .218 and didn't provide much of a defensive upgrade over Piazza.

Once again, Howe was vilified on talk radio for some of his questionable strategy. But for the second straight season, he never got a chance to skipper a healthy team with a deep rotation or a solid bullpen.

Howe was told before the end of the 2004 season that he wouldn't be coming back. The Mets' lackluster end to the campaign also ended Duquette's run as GM.

The team brought back two former Mets employees to right the ship in 2005. Howe was replaced by Willie Randolph, the Mets' starting second baseman in 1992. Omar Minaya took over for Duquette after previously serving as the team's assistant GM.

Howe had experienced both ends of the baseball spectrum over the past five years. He had great success with the cash-conscious A's before suffering with the free-spending Mets. Anyone who questions the schism between big- and small-market franchises should talk to Howe. He got the best out of one tight-fisted organization and saw few positive results from a team willing to spend.

Davey Johnson   1984–1990

Born: January 30, 1943   Orlando, Florida
Named Manager: 10/13/84
Dismissed 5/29/90
NL East Title, 1986, 1988
NL Pennant, 1986
World Series, 1986

Davey Johnson Managerial Record

YEAR	GMS	W	L	PCT	POS.
1984	162	90	72	.556	2nd, NL East
1985	162	98	64	.605	2nd, NL East
1986	162	108	54	.667	1st, NL East
1987	162	92	70	.568	2nd, NL East
1988	160	100	60	.625	1st, NL East
1989	162	87	75	.537	2nd, NL East
1990	44	20	22	.476	2nd, NL East
Total	1012	595	417	.588	

Major League Totals

YEARS	GMS	W	L	PCT
1984–2000	2039	1148	888	.564

The Washington Nationals were suddenly in need of a manager when Jim Riggleman abruptly resigned 75 games into the 2011 season. John McLaren was named interim skipper for a weekend series while the front office negotiated with Davey Johnson, who was serving as a special advisor to general manager Mike Rizzo.

Johnson was 68 and had not managed a major league club since 2000. But the challenge conjured up memories of his first season with the Mets in 1984. Like the 2011 Nats, the '84 Mets were rebuilding through a farm system that had been partially cultivated by Johnson. The comparisons between the two jobs were obvious as Johnson finished out the 2011 campaign.

"It was a similar situation in that I knew the minor league system," Johnson told Washington broadcaster Craig Heist in a September 2011 interview, "but not as good as I knew it with the Mets because I had managed two years in the Mets' minor league system, and I roved one year. I didn't manage in the Nationals' organization, but I had been following them off and on for five years. In two spring trainings, I was with the big club and at the minor league camp getting to know everybody there. Both situations were with teams coming from last place and trying to make a move.

"I remember my first year with the Mets, one of the conversations I had with general manager Frank Cashen was that, 'I've got a number of veterans on this ballclub and will give them every opportunity to succeed, but I really like some of the younger players better.' So I broke camp with the veterans, and I think about six weeks into the season I was allowed to release the veterans, like Torrez and Swan. We called up some people I liked from the minor league system.

"Coming in [with the Nationals] during the middle of the year—kind of unexpectedly—I definitely wasn't as well-prepared as I was managing the Tidewater club, winning the Triple A World Series [in 1983] and stepping in as manager of the big club. The main difference has been learning the competition and helping establish young players, which I had a hand in at New York because we had young pitchers and young position players.

"But by and large it was a great similarity in that in both situations, I knew the system and knew a lot of the talent."

Mets general manager Frank Cashen finally had a nice collection of young talent by the end of the 1983 season.

Who better to manage the team than his most successful minor league skipper?

David Allen Johnson won a Texas League title with the Jackson Mets in 1981 and rallied the Tidewater Tides to the Governor's Cup Championship and a Triple A World Series triumph two years later. In between, he served as a roving infield instructor for the Mets but seemed more than ready to manage at the highest level.

Johnson and Cashen had known each other for close to two decades. Cashen joined the Orioles' front office in 1966, Johnson's rookie season with the Birds. Cashen was also the general manager when Johnson was traded by the O's to the Braves following the 1972 season.

Cashen decided the 41-year-old Johnson would be his skipper for the 1984 season.

"Our club is ready to make a move in the National League, and Johnson can be the catalyst," said Cashen as he introduced his new manager.

Johnson was the perfect choice because he got a first-hand look at most of the team's prospects and could help shape the roster. Cashen still had the final say in player personnel decisions but was willing to bend when Johnson insisted certain players had to be part of his ballclub.

One of those players was Wally Backman, who failed to impress Mets brass despite hitting .273 in his first 423 major league at-bats. He was toiling in Tidewater in 1983 and ticked off at the organization when Johnson pulled him aside and assured him he'd be playing for the Mets if Johnson ever became the manager. Backman and Kelvin Chapman, who played briefly for the Mets in 1979 but didn't merit a bio page in the team's 1984 press guide, became the second-base platoon.

"I always liked guys that I consider 'foxhole guys' and had a good role," Johnson said of his 1984 through 1986 clubs. "The Wally Backmans and the Lenny Dykstras were going to constantly pay attention and were going to battle you to get on base. And I took those guys over guys who had more talent but couldn't fill the roles that I was looking for.

"With Keith Hernandez, Darryl Strawberry, Gary Carter, and Howard Johnson, I had plenty of run-producers. So the table-setters were very important."

The Mets entered the 1984 exhibition season with a penciled-in rotation of Mike Torrez, Walt Terrell, Ron Darling, and Tim Leary, with Ed Lynch slotted as the No. 5 guy. But Johnson also had a 19-year-old prospect with an ungodly fastball and a breaking ball rarely seen from a teenager. The kid had helped Tidewater win the Triple A title a few months earlier after striking out 300 batters in 191 innings for Single A Lynchburg during the regular season. Cashen wanted his star prospect to spend another year in the minors, but Johnson insisted the prospect was ready for the majors right now. Johnson won out, and Dwight Gooden became the Mets' top starter and the 1984 Rookie of the Year.

"There were several things I had to overcome," Johnson said of Gooden's promotion. "No. 1, [three years] before

that, Tim Leary was called up from Jackson, Mississippi, and made the club. He pitched in Chicago in freezing weather and hurt his shoulder. So I told Frank that was not going to happen, that I wouldn't take that chance with Dwight and that I would take care of him. I told him, 'Just keep an open mind going into spring training' because I knew he could handle every level.

"I fought for him to go to A-ball. They didn't think that at 18 he could handle A-ball, but I said, 'No problem,' and he handled that very easily. And then I had him in Triple A that year, and he won two games in the Triple A World Series.

"Frank kept an open mind, and I got my wish. Dwight made the club."

Johnson said he knew Gooden would be a special pitcher after watching him throw for about five minutes shortly after he was drafted.

"I had him when he broke in at 17 down at Kingsport. I had him on that team with Randy Myers and Floyd Youmans, and Dwight was so far ahead of them it wasn't even funny. He had great command.

"I made sure there wasn't a reoccurrence of the previous year because Dwight's first start was in Houston in 70 degree weather. I only let him go five innings and he won that game. And the rest is kind of history."

First baseman Keith Hernandez was entering his first full season with the Mets, and George Foster was about to begin the third year of a five-year contract as the team's left fielder. Otherwise, Johnson was using homegrown talent to fill out his lineup card. Mike Fitzgerald did the bulk of the catching, Backman and Chapman shared second, Ron Gardenhire and Jose Oquendo would platoon at short, and Hubie Brooks patrolled third. Foster was joined in the outfield by Mookie Wilson and Darryl Strawberry, who had just won the NL Rookie of the Year award.

Most baseball writers predicted the 1984 Mets would struggle to finish close to the .500 mark. But those scribes probably weren't expecting the pitching to finish second in the NL in strikeouts and saves, third in shutouts and fifth in hits allowed.

"We had a lot of holes," Johnson acknowledged 27 years later. "We weren't very good offensively. We had very young pitching, and my bullpen was half put together.

"I thought we had a good year because we got outscored by 18 runs yet we were 18 games over .500."

Johnson's Mets opened the '84 campaign by ending a nine-game winning streak in season openers. They were mauled by the Reds 8–1 in Cincinnati on Opening Day and dropped their home opener 10–0 to the Expos. The first 26 games of the season also included losses of 11–2, 12–2, 12–5, 8–3, 10–6, 10–1, and 11–2. Yet, they were tied for first place at 15–11, thanks to winning streaks of six, five and three games. The Mets hadn't owned a piece of first place this late in the season since 1976, and fans started to take notice. A box seat ticket had been easy to get for a decade, but by mid-summer, a spot in the upper deck could be expected if one waited until game day to purchase a seat.

Gooden was lit up in three of his first 13 starts, but he was 6–3 with a 2.61 ERA by June 16. Darling also was hit hard in several starts before winning seven consecutive outings, giving him a 10–3 record. Terrell was 5–6 despite a 3.06 ERA in his first 13 starts. And the bullpen featured Doug Sisk, Tom Gorman, and Brent Gaff as setup men for Jesse Orosco, giving the Mets their deepest relief corps in eight years.

But Johnson desperately needed more pitching help as the staff surrendered at least six runs in 15 of the Mets' first 55 games. Torrez, Craig Swan, and Dick Tidrow were released early in the season, and reinforcements were on the way. Cashen improved the starting rotation by acquiring Bruce Berenyi on June 15, a month before recalling rookie Sid Fernandez from Tidewater. Berenyi and Fernandez combined for 15 wins over the final 3½ months, and Johnson and pitching coach Mel Stottlemyre were credited for their ability to nurture a young group of hurlers.

"The biggest job a manager has is managing a pitching staff," said Johnson. "I was always curious about how every manager I ever played for handled a pitching staff, and I watched the effects of that handling on the staff. I tried to pick up what were the good things and what were the things I didn't like about the handling of a pitching staff.

"And then you put in your personal feelings about how you want to run a pitching staff. But I think the most important job for any manager is handling the pitchers. The starting pitchers are one thing, but the bullpen is paramount—being able to handle the bullpen, set it up right, and have it functioning at its maximum without wearing it out is the only way you're going to win."

The infusion of pitching helped the Mets to take a 4½ game division lead at 59–37 on July 27 following Gooden's 2–1 win over the second-place Cubs. One month earlier, Hubie Brooks had set a team record with a 24-game hitting streak. Pennant fever was spreading throughout the five boroughs, northern New Jersey, southern Connecticut, and beyond.

As exciting as the Mets had become, the Cubs literally had an ace in the hole. Rick Sutcliffe almost singlehandedly prevented Johnson from becoming the Mets' first rookie skipper to make the playoffs. Sutcliffe went 16–1 with a 2.69 ERA after the Cubbies acquired him from Cleveland. He won all four of his starts against the Mets, the difference between New York finishing two games ahead or six games behind in the NL East.

The Mets were playing meaningful September baseball for the first time in 11 years, thanks in part to Johnson's leadership. Gooden opened a crucial series against the Cubs at Shea by firing a one-hitter in a 10–0 rout September 7. A three-game sweep would have put the Mets within four games of the first-place Cubs, but Sutcliffe wrecked those plans with a shutout the next day.

New York was 9½ games behind the Cubs following a loss at Wrigley Field on September 15. Instead of their first division title since 1973, the Mets had to settle for the second-best record in team history at 90–72. Johnson certainly appeared to be the right choice for the job.

Johnson earned a mathematics degree from Trinity University in San Antonio and was one of the first managers to use a computer to analyze statistical data. But he spent most of the 1984 season—and the rest of his major league managerial career—playing hunches, figuring he had more baseball acumen than his hard drive. Relievers like Brent Gaff and Tom Gorman enjoyed their finest major league seasons in 1984.

"I thought he was outstanding," said Ed Lynch. "I never saw a manager handle young pitchers as good as he did. The ultimate compliment you can give a manager is when you're sitting in the bullpen and the phone rings, everyone down there knows who the guy is who's going to get up. He had a plan and he was going to stick with it. Now, he had some good pitchers, and he's not going to go out there and manage the way he did if Dwight Gooden doesn't go out and pitch into the eighth inning every night like he did as a 19-year old. But the way he handled Dwight and the way he handled the young guys, the way he communicated with me.… I was like the staff-saver, pitch those five innings in a 10–0 game and I would go in and just mop it up and two days later do it again. And I didn't care. I just wanted to pitch."

Even his computer knew the Mets needed another productive bat in their lineup heading into 1985, along with an experienced catcher to handle the team's young pitchers. Cashen found both in one player, getting Gary Carter from the Expos in a deal that included Brooks, Fitzgerald, and two prospects of little consequence.

The Mets appeared ready to challenge the Cubs in 1985. New York was in first place on June 5 before a 2–9 stretch dropped them to fourth heading into a four-game series with the Northsiders at Shea in mid-June. The Mets responded with a four-game sweep that seemed to take the Cubs out of the race. The problem was, there was a new Beast in the East.

The Cardinals, with rookie speed demon Vince Coleman, were atop the division. They had Joaquin Andujar, John Tudor, and Danny Cox at the top of the rotation. With apologies to Dwight Gooden, who would win the 1985 NL Cy Young Award in a waltz, the Cardinals had a deeper starting staff than did New York.

Cashen had spent the off-season building a team that was better than the Cubs. Having accomplished that, he also had a starting catcher and a pitching staff that had trouble preventing Coleman, Willie McGee, Ozzie Smith, and Tommy Herr from swiping bags at will. Even Andy Van Slyke finished the year with 34 steals. The Redbirds ended the season with just 87 homers, but the Mets weren't ready to handle the team's 314 thefts.

Gooden was the marquee player for the Mets in 1985, going 24–4 with 268 strikeouts and a team-record 1.53 ERA. He was unbeaten for nearly three months of the season, going 14–0 with a 1.72 ERA between May 30 and August 25. Down the stretch, Gooden was 4–0 with a 0.34 ERA in his final six starts, allowing no earned runs over a five-start stretch that covered 44 innings.

Carter was every bit the offensive player the Mets had hoped, leading the team with 32 homers and 100 RBIs while batting .281. He won the season opener with a 10th-inning homer, and belted five home runs during a two-game stretch at San Diego while Hernandez was completing his testimony during the Pittsburgh cocaine trial.

It was a very difficult season for Hernandez both on and off the field, but Johnson never wavered in his support for the Gold Glove first baseman. Hernandez was in the middle of divorce proceedings while the Pittsburgh trial hung over his head. A former Phillies caterer, Curtis Strong, was accused of trafficking cocaine to several prominent major leaguers, one of which was Hernandez. During his testimony, Hernandez admitted to using cocaine for three years between 1980 and 1982 but said he had been clean since then, calling coke "a demon in me."

On the field, Hernandez managed to finish the year hitting .309 with 91 RBIs despite batting only .226 with 19 RBIs in 55 games from May 3 to July 3. He ended that slump by hitting for the cycle in a 19-inning victory in Atlanta that had to have Johnson searching for the Rolaids. The Mets tied the game in the ninth, then blew a two-run lead in the 13th and a one-run lead in the 18th before scoring five times in the 19th for a 16–13 victory.

Strawberry was back in the lineup by then after missing seven weeks with a torn ligament in his right thumb. Danny Heep had played admirably in right during Strawberry's absence, but the Mets posted a losing record while Straw recovered.

Johnson had dealt with a slumping Hernandez and an injured Strawberry during the first half of the 1985 season. But he had no answer for the team's shortcomings in the rotation. Berenyi landed on the disabled list early in the season with a partially torn rotator cuff, elevating Lynch to the No. 4 spot while making rookie Rick Aguilera his fifth starter. Pitching depth hurt the Mets in September and October when they could have used an experienced fifth starter after Lynch developed back spasms in September.

The rotation was bolstered in the winter of 1986 as Cashen acquired Bob Ojeda from the Red Sox. The soft-tossing lefty could neutralize the Cardinals' bats while chewing up innings. He would also become the Mets' most consistent starter in 1986.

The Mets also brought in second baseman Tim Teufel to spell Backman at second when opponents went with lefty starters. Blessed with a deep rotation, a dependable bullpen, and an outstanding starting lineup, Johnson was pretty confident entering spring training in 1986.

"We won't just win the division, we'll dominate," crowed Johnson at St. Petersburg early in camp. He realized he had a packed roster that also included rookie Kevin Mitchell, who made the 1986 team out of spring training.

"I felt like from '84 we got better," Johnson said over a quarter-century after the Mets' last title team. "We picked up Gary Carter for Hubie Brooks and Mike Fitzgerald. Then we traded Walt Terrell for Howard Johnson. We helped our offense immensely there. We picked up Ray Knight and Tim Teufel. My bullpen was a lot stronger. My starters had more experience, and I liked my offense. I felt like we had no holes.

"I told them in the spring we'd gone from miraculously winning 90 in '84 to winning 98 games and getting beat out by the Cardinals. And I said, 'Not only are we going to win, we're going to dominate.' I truly believed it.

"A pretty good sign was at the end of April when Whitey Herzog said, 'Nobody's catching them.'"

The Mets opened the 1986 season with back-to-back wins before dropping three straight. An 11-game winning streak followed, putting the Mets on cruise control.

The Cubs got off to a poor start, and the Mets took control of the division by sweeping a four-game series in St. Louis at the end of April. The *New York Post* began to display a magic number for the Mets by mid-July as the team did what Johnson predicted, dominate the race.

The Mets wrapped up the 1986 division title by September 17, the fastest clinching in team history. They torched the National League with a club-record 108 wins. Only the Phillies, who swept a three-game series at the Vet in mid-September to delay the clincher, posted a winning record against New York for the season.

One of the turning points came April 21 (yes, that early), when the right-handed-hitting Ray Knight came up to hit against righty Cecilio Guante with the Mets trailing 4–2 in the eighth. Knight expected Johnson to lift him in favor of fellow third baseman Howard Johnson in a lefty-righty switch. Knight stayed in the game and responded with a two-run blast before the Mets won it in the bottom of the ninth.

Knight, who hit .218 the previous season, realized his manager had confidence in him. Knight finished the year batting .298 and was named the MVP of the World Series.

The Mets appeared to be the bullies of the league until the postseason, when they ran into former Met Mike Scott and the Astros in the NLCS. But New York's last three wins of the series came in dramatic fashion. Dykstra, who didn't start Game 3, hit a walk-off two-run homer in the ninth to give the Mets a 2–1 lead in the series. Two days after Scott went the distance on a three-hitter, Gary Carter, hitting .048 in the series, delivered the game-winning single in extra innings to get the Mets within one victory of the World Series.

Game 6 became one of the greatest postseason dramas in major league history. The Astros took a 3–0 lead into the ninth when Johnson asked Dykstra to pinch-hit for Ojeda leading off the inning. Dykstra's triple off lefty Bob Knepper sparked a game-tying, three-run rally before the Mets won it in 16 innings for their first pennant in 13 years.

The Mets held an excessive celebration on the team's charter back to New York, prompting United Airlines to send the team a hefty bill for damage done to the plane. An agitated Cashen met with the players and told them they would have to pay the cost of the repairs. In a show of defiance, Johnson ripped up the bill in front of his players after Cashen left, furthering stamping his reputation as a player's manager.

The Mets dropped the first two games of the World Series to the Red Sox before heading to Boston. The Mets were required by Major League Baseball to go through batting practice at Fenway Park the day before Game 3. Instead, Johnson gave his team the day off and garnered the club a hefty fine. But the time off seemed to help as the Mets dominated the Red Sox in Games 3 and 4 before Boston took Game 5 to move within a victory of their first World Series title in 68 years.

With Game 6 tied 3–3 in the ninth, Johnson asked pinch-hitter Howard Johnson, who hadn't laid down a sacrifice all season, to bunt with runners on first and second with nobody out. Howard Johnson put down two meager bunt attempts before finally striking out. A successful bunt would have put runners on second and third, which would have allowed Lee Mazzilli's fly ball to win the game. Instead, the game went into extra innings.

Aguilera got three outs in the ninth before faltering. The Red Sox took a 4–3 lead when Dave Henderson hit a leadoff homer off Aguilera in the 10th, and Marty Barrett followed with an RBI single that seemed to give Boston an insurmountable 5–3 lead. However, Boston manager John McNamara trumped Howard Johnson's bunting gaffe in the ninth by allowing former Met Calvin Schiraldi to start the 10th while keeping the immobile Bill Buckner at first base. The bottom half of the inning started innocently enough as Backman and Hernandez flew out, putting the Red Sox within one out of a championship.

Carter kept the series alive with a single and went to second on Kevin Mitchell's base hit before Knight's single got the Mets within 5–4. McNamara continued his string of bad hunches by having Bob Stanley relieve Schiraldi, the former Mets prospect who appeared to be a three-run homer waiting to happen.

Wilson provided the most memorable at-bat in team history as he tried to avoid making the final out of the season. He skipped over a wild pitch that also eluded the glove of Rich Gedman, allowing Mitchell to score the tying run. Knight now represented the winning run at second, and Howard Johnson's failed bunt attempt in the ninth was a distant memory.

Wilson continued to foul off pitches before sending a slow roller down the first-base line. Knight was sprinting toward third when the ball approached Buckner. Buckner let the ball go underneath his glove for an error, allowing Knight to score just a few minutes after the Mets' scoreboard was congratulating Bruce Hurst for winning the World Series MVP.

"One of my mottos that I live by is you can never take anything for granted in the game of baseball," Johnson said of the 10th inning. "Whether you have a nine-run lead, you never take it for granted that you've won the game. My fear is always when I have a lead, I'll lose it. You make all your moves based on the possible moves at that time.

"When you win 108 games, you're not taking anything for granted, and I certainly didn't take it for granted that the game was over, although I did look over at the bench on the Red Sox side, and everybody was on the top step waiting to celebrate on the field.

"Even though we're two runs down, two strikes, two outs, we got three straight hits, a wild pitch, a ground ball to Buckner. Game over. But once the wild pitch came had tied the score, I knew the game was over. We were gonna win it some way.

"It was just like that in Game 7. I knew that three runs down in Game 7, we were going to win that game."

The Mets wound up winning Game 7 despite falling behind 3–0. Strawberry, who left the clubhouse before the Game 6 victory and felt he had been betrayed by Johnson for lifting him from that game, furnished a key home run that helped the Mets wrap up the series. But it was Knight, the man Johnson let hit in that April 21 game, who provided the tie-breaking homer in the seventh inning.

Johnson also made a smart move by bringing in Fernandez for Darling, who had yielded three runs over 3⅔ innings. Fernandez tossed hitless ball over the next 2⅓ frames, giving the Mets time to tie the game.

The Mets were prohibitive favorites heading into the 1987 season, so much so that Johnson didn't have to tell the media how good his team would be. But there was a little concern about Gooden, who had displayed some erratic behavior in the off-season after pitching poorly in the World Series. Gooden overslept and missed the World Series parade, although many Mets had trouble arriving on time for the festivities. Gooden and his fiancée also were involved in a headline-grabbing altercation with a rental-car employee a few weeks later. He didn't throw particularly well during the exhibition season, but the worst news would come just before the start of the '87 campaign.

Johnson lost his ace when Gooden was suspended for testing positive for cocaine. Gooden was forced to miss the first 60 days of the season, leaving Ojeda to start the opener and indicating the '87 season wouldn't be a smooth ride for New York.

"We had some signs in spring training when Dwight came in and had to go into rehab for two months," Johnson said. "That was a big shocker. And before we left spring training, Roger McDowell suffered a hernia.

"During the course of that year, four more of my starting pitchers were out for at least two months with injuries. Yet we still had a chance until Darling had a no-hitter going against the Cardinals when we were 1½ games back. I think it was the seventh or eighth inning when he jammed his thumb fielding a topper between the mound and first, and he was out for the year.

"And then McDowell gave up a two-run homer to Terry Pendleton, and that was about it. We ended up winning 93 games.

"I compared it with the Cubs in '84. They had two injuries to their pitching staff in '85, and they didn't win 80 games. I had my top six guys out two months and we wound up winning 93. I thought it was a pretty good year."

Ojeda spent 3½ months on the disabled list due to an injured left elbow. Fernandez missed a start due to a sprained knee before spending 18 days in August on the DL with a shoulder injury. Rick Aguilera was lost for almost three months because of a sprained elbow ligament. Darling tore ligaments in his right thumb while making a diving catch on a pop fly September 11, causing him to miss the rest of the season. Even new acquisition David Cone sat out 2½ months after breaking his finger during a bunt attempt in late May.

Johnson was forced to use journeymen Jeff Innis, Don Schulze, and Tom Edens in his rotation. Things got so bad the Mets asked Tom Seaver to make a comeback attempt early in the season, but the Hall of Famer showed little during his minor league stint.

Team harmony came into question, with Strawberry at the center of the storm. Strawberry was showing up late for batting practice and begged out of one start because of the flu, hours after cutting a rap recording. Backman and Lee Mazzilli were two of the more vocal Mets showing their displeasure with Straberry's antics. Knight could have served as a calming influence in the clubhouse, but Cashen decided not to sign the World Series MVP, allowing him to go to the Tigers.

Hernandez had his own problems, opening the season hitting .255 through May sixth. From May 1 through June 9, Hernandez batted .303 but drove in just 11 runs in 33 games.

Kevin McReynolds was acquired from the Padres in a deal that sent Mitchell to his native San Diego. McReynolds failed to display the bravado possessed by his teammates and was usually the first player to exit the ballpark following a game.

Despite the injuries, bickering, and slumps, Johnson had his Mets winning again by the end of August. They took eight of 11 heading into a crucial series against the first-place Cardinals at Shea, and they were one out from a 4–1 victory that would have pushed them within a half-game of the division lead. But Roger McDowell gave up an RBI single to McGee before Terry Pendleton launched a game-tying two-run blast to center. The Cards scored twice in the 10th off Jesse Orosco to win it, giving them a 2½-game lead over the Mets. New York still had 22 games remaining, but the Pendleton blast served as a springboard for the Redbirds, who never led by less than 1½ games the rest of the way.

Johnson was questioned for a move he made during a September 30 game at Philadelphia. Gooden had struck out 10 while holding the Phillies to six hits in nine innings.

Manager Davey Johnson speaks with reporters before Game 1 of the 1986 World Series.

When the game went to the 10th, Johnson felt Gooden had done enough and put the ball in the hands of Orosco, whose final season as a Met included a few miserable performances. This would be one of those bad outings as Orosco served up a one-out homer to Luis Aguayo that allowed the Cardinals to clinch at least a tie for the NL East title.

The Mets rebounded nicely in 1988, starting off 38–17 to move seven games ahead of the second-place Pirates. McReynolds and Strawberry carried the Mets' offense for the first five months before Johnson had another hot bat in his lineup.

The Mets recalled infielder Gregg Jefferies, who hit .321 in 29 games but caused a few problems in the clubhouse, not all his doing. Jefferies was taking at-bats from Backman, who was hitting over .300 for the second time in three seasons. The rookie had been the club's crown jewel in the farm system and was treated as such, which led to resentment from his new teammates. Jefferies didn't help himself with a sometimes abrasive, selfish personality. But there was no question he could hit, one reason why the Mets went 20–7 down the stretch in games he started.

Shortly before Jefferies' arrival, the Mets completed a 78-game stretch in which they were two games under .500. The surprising Pirates got within 1½ games of the Mets, but New York always seemed to win when it mattered.

The pitching was back in form, and Johnson had another weapon in his arsenal. Cone went 20–3 and led the club with 212 strikeouts and a 2.22 ERA. Gooden won 18 games, Darling had 17 victories, and Ojeda posted a 2.88 ERA while going 10–13. Randy Myers and Roger McDowell combined for 42 saves as Johnson once again had an effective bullpen.

But a changing of the guard was emerging at Shea. Both Hernandez and Carter missed huge chunks of time due to injuries, allowing Dave Magadan and Mackey Sasser to receive increased playing time. Johnson still had Wilson and Dykstra in center field, but neither was happy with his platoon role.

The Mets pulled away after August 21, going 29–8 to turn a 3½-game lead into a 15-game cushion at season's end. New York clinched the division title September 22, but the celebration was dampened by Ojeda, who almost severed the upper portion of his left middle finger while at home a day earlier. Ojeda was done for the season, and his career was in doubt.

Ojeda aside, the Mets entered the NLCS very healthy and were a mortal lock to reach the World Series. Their opponent was the Dodgers, who dropped 10 of 11 games against the Mets during the regular season.

The Mets used a ninth-inning rally to take the series opener, but Cone, who was serving as a guest columnist for the *New York Post* during the postseason, insinuated after the game that the Dodgers' lineup didn't pose much of a threat. L.A. responded in Game 2 by reaching Cone for five runs in the first two innings of a 6–3 victory over the Mets.

New York rebounded by winning a sloppy third game, and they enjoyed a 4–2 lead in the ninth inning of Game 4 until Gooden served up a game-tying blast to Mike Scioscia. Kirk Gibson put the Dodgers ahead with a homer off McDowell before Orel Hershier picked up the save by working out of a bases-loaded jam in the 12th. Hershiser previously had silenced the Mets' bats over the first eight innings of Game 1.

Gibson also homered in Game 5 to put the Dodgers ahead 3–2 in the series. Cone rebounded from his Game 2 debacle to fire a five-hitter in Game 6, but Hershiser was brilliant in the deciding seventh game, sending the Mets home much earlier than expected.

"I thought we had a good chance to go back to the World Series," Johnson began, "and the Scioscia home run kind of ruined that. We had some other things that went against us."

The 1989 season was a nightmare for Johnson, who lost Gooden to a shoulder injury and went most of the year without Hernandez and Carter, who were aging rapidly.

Jefferies got off to a terrible start, but Johnson continued to start him every day. Cashen had handed Jefferies the starting second base job by dealing Backman to the Twins after the 1988 season. Not only was Jefferies struggling at the plate, he was lousy at second.

"I knew at some point that Carter and Hernandez were going to be finished and that we needed to make a spot for Jefferies in the everyday lineup and use his bat," said Johnson. "When we moved him to second base, I knew it was going to be a project because he had never played second base before and we had depth at third.

"Before I could establish him, we went through one full year, which was tough. And then they let me go in '90.

"There were a lot of guys who didn't like Jefferies' personality. I was trying to work through that, and if he had started to hit .330 and doing the things he was capable of doing—things he eventually did in St. Louis—he would have been accepted."

The Wilson-Dykstra situation was solved when Dykstra was shipped to the Phillies with McDowell for Juan Samuel, who was asked to play center field after years as the Phils' second baseman. Samuel became the starter, and Wilson saw even less playing time before he was dealt to the Blue Jays. Other players were now ticked off at Johnson for treating Jefferies with kid gloves. Some suspected Johnson wasn't calling the shots when it came to the rookie, figuring their manager was being manipulated by Cashen.

By now, Johnson's relationship with Cashen seemed a bit strained. The skipper complained that Cashen no longer alerted him on possible player moves, and Cashen was annoyed by Johnson's disinterest in reigning in players when they needed discipline. Johnson continues to receive high praise from his '86 players for the way he handled the roster both on and off the field. He remained a laissez-faire skipper in 1989, treating his players like men. But with a 21-win difference between the 1986 and 1989 clubs, the front office wanted more discipline.

Cashen also decided the team was playing too much golf on the road and ordered his players to stop traveling with their clubs. Johnson told his ballclub the golf ban was B.S. but asked the players to keep their clubs under wraps.

The Mets never made a serious challenge for the division title despite acquiring reigning AL Cy Young Award winner Frank Viola from the Twins at the July 31 trade deadline. Viola joined the team right after the Mets had been swept in a three-game set at Wrigley, which put New York six games behind the first-place Cubs. The Mets got within 1½ games in late-August before going 18–20 the rest of the way.

Johnson appeared to be on a short leash as the 1990 season approached. There were several reports within the New York media that intimated Cashen wanted to fire Johnson after the 1989 season. Instead, Johnson entered his seventh season as the team's manager, but he'd do it without a few of his coaches. First-base/hitting coach Bill Robinson and third base coach Sam Perlozzo were shown the door, allowing Bud Harrelson to move up the coaching depth chart by the time the '90 season began. Harrelson had been a good soldier for the Mets following his playing days and remained a popular figure among Mets fans.

Johnson had what appeared to be a solid rotation with Viola, Gooden, Cone, Darling, and Fernandez heading into 1990. But after Samuel requested a trade, the Mets left the center-field job in the incapable hands of Keith Miller, who was a nice infielder off Johnson's bench but hardly an everyday outfielder.

The Mets opened the season with an ugly 12–3 loss to the Pirates, who also took the rubber match of the series. New York didn't put together a winning streak until late-April, when they won five straight to improve to 9–7. The Mets were in fourth place at 20–22 when management decided a change was needed. Johnson, who by now was the longest-serving manager in team history, was dismissed and replaced by Harrelson.

The breakup was acrimonious. Johnson was not allowed to meet with his team one final time, receiving the same bum's rush given to many of his better ballplayers. He never returned to Shea Stadium again, even bowing out of the team's 20th anniversary celebration of the 1986 championship.

Johnson was back in a major league dugout in 1993, taking over for Tony Perez as Reds manager. He was let go by Cincinnati owner Marge Schott after the 1995 season despite leading the club to its second straight NL Central title.

The Orioles immediately scooped up Johnson and put him in their dugout in 1996. Baltimore won the wild-card in '96 and captured the AL East the following year while reaching the ALCS both times. But that wasn't good enough for owner Peter Angelos, who dismissed Johnson just hours after he was named AL Manager of the Year.

Whatever troubles Johnson may have had with Cashen, they paled in comparison to his time under the meddling thumbs of Schott and Angelos.

"I just kind of burns you out because you want to do well for the organization and the ownership," said Johnson. "That's who you work for. And I wasn't able to please them. In both cases, it had nothing to do with baseball."

Lost on Schott and Angelos was Johnson's ability to adapt his managerial style to his available talent. The Reds won their back-to-back division crowns through team speed and exceptional defense while the Orioles made their consecutive playoff appearances with an arsenal of veteran power hitters. Johnson managed to the team's strength each time.

"Every team is different," said Johnson. "You can't have one style of managing fit all teams. Certainly, Cincinnati was different from Baltimore.

"In Cincinnati, we were a running team based on speed with Deion Sanders, Reggie Sanders, and Barry Larkin. It was a fun team to manage.

"We had to struggle through a strike year. We were winning the division my first full year there. There were some improvements we had to make my first year there in replacing Tony Perez. But we beat Houston by about

10 full games in my first full year there, beat the Dodgers and then lost to the Braves in the championship series. We couldn't get by Maddux and Glavine. Then I was fired there, Ray Knight was hired, and I went to Baltimore.

"It was tough being in the same division as the Yankees. The Orioles were more of a home run-hitting team. It was a strikeout or a home run feast or famine, so we didn't run as much. We couldn't hit-and-run or steal. We played more for the 'Earl Weaver big inning.' We won the wild card my first year there, and then we went wire-to-wire in '97 to win the pennant. I thought we were making progress, but then I couldn't please the owner."

Johnson's success with both the Reds and Orioles is augmented by the success of those franchises once he left. By the start of 2012, the Reds have made just one postseason appearance since Johnson was let go, and they haven't won a playoff game since his last season there. The Orioles were even more pitiful than the Reds following Johnson's departure, recording 14 consecutive losing seasons under seven different managers.

Johnson was hired to manage the Dodgers after sitting out the 1998 season. The franchise still had a great reputation for building from within, cultivating numerous rookies of the year while usually staying in contention every season since leaving Brooklyn. Johnson got there when the farm system hit a dry patch, leading to an imbalanced roster when he took over in 1999.

"The tough part of that decision," he said of taking the Dodgers job, "was I thought the minor league system was in better shape. I assumed it was the 'Dodgers' minor league system, but their minor leagues were in shambles when I arrived. We had a team basically put together as a right-handed hitting team and a right-handed pitching team. When we had to compete with a couple of clubs loaded with left-handed hitters and pitchers...it was a tough, uphill battle there."

Johnson tried to persuade Randy Johnson to sign with the Dodgers after his half-season with the Astros. Johnson eventually signed with the Diamondbacks, and the Dodgers overpaid for Kevin Brown after the bulk of the free-agent pitching talent had signed with other clubs. With Brown as the staff ace, the Dodgers went 163–161 without making the postseason. Johnson was replaced by Jim Tracy after an 86–76 finish in 2000.

Many people within baseball's inner circle were surprised when Johnson accepted the challenge of taking over the Nationals, who were still seeking their first winning season since moving to Washington in 2005. Ten major league seasons had passed since Johnson was last in a major league dugout, and he appeared to be quite comfortable living in Florida while sharing his wisdom with Rizzo and the rest of the Nationals' brass from afar. But for Johnson, the opportunity to don a big-league uniform again seemed to make sense.

"There were several reasons," Johnson said in 2011. "No. 1, when you look at the organization and you know the front office—from Rizzo and all his staff, all the scouts he's accumulated—and you know the quality of those people, you know that ownership has got to be on the ball. I met part of the ownership in Mark Lerner and liked him, so I felt that part of the equation was fine.

"Was I up for the challenge? I like challenges, but I like the organization from top to bottom. My wife was okay with me going back fulltime…that was a big concern. And seeing as though I spent most of my upbringing following the Nationals or being an Oriole, I was very comfortable with the city and the surroundings. When I looked at it, I thought I was the best person to do the interim job. I felt like I was the most qualified and best candidate they could pick.

"I felt like the club was a little bit in turmoil once the manager [Jim Riggleman] resigned. The first thing it needed was more stability, and I felt I could bring that in a fairly short time. And I like the makeup on the ballclub. There were some imbalances in the roster, but I felt I was fully capable of helping tweak that eventually, and getting it more to my liking."

Washington baseball fans got a glimpse of Johnson's managerial acumen toward the end of 2011 as the Nats swept four-game series in New York and Philadelphia. Prospects Tom Milone and Brad Peacock pitched well in the rotation while rookie reliever Henry Rodriguez displayed more confidence as a late-innings reliever. The Nats were beginning to resemble the 1984 Mets, a good sign for the team's future.

Johnson remains the most successful manager in Mets history. No skipper has led the Mets to six straight winning seasons as Johnson did from 1984 to 1989. His .588 winning percentage continues to top the all-time list, and he's the only manager other than Bobby Valentine to guide the club to two playoff appearances.

"I enjoyed my time there," Johnson said of his days in the Mets dugout. "I spent three years in the minor leagues and I was there almost into my 10th year with the club. I was kind of thinking that I would be there a while, and that I had helped not only get continuity at the major league level but also at the minor league level. But nobody's ever willing to take a step back to take a step forward in New York.

"I thought my time there was cut a little short, but that's just baseball.

"It's great to manage a winner anywhere, but with New York, it was a joyride there. The fans were great from Day One. We had an exciting first year, a more exciting second year, and an off-the-charts third year. And it was only fitting that we won the way we did. We gave everybody hope to never give up. In life, there's always a chance. That's a memory that will always stay with me."

Jerry Manuel   2008–2010

Born: December 23, 1953   Hahira, Georgia
Named Interim Manager: 6/17/08
Dismissed: 10/4/10

Jerry Manuel Managerial Record

YEAR	GMS	W	L	PCT	POS.
2008	93	55	38	.591	2
2009	162	70	92	.432	4
2010	162	79	83	.488	4
Total	417	204	213	.489	

Major League Totals

YEAR	GMS	W	L	PCT
1998–2010	1388	704	684	.507

The Mets were nine months removed from their 2007 meltdown and three months from the next collapse when Mets COO Jeff Wilpon decided Willie Randolph needed to be replaced. Dumping Randolph meant firing the manager with the second-best winning percentage in team history, bested only by Davey Johnson. But there was a growing contingent of Mets that appeared to have stopped playing hard for Randolph.

Bench coach Jerry Manuel had a great relationship with the players and often served as a buffer when a long reliever or a middle infielder had a beef with Randolph. Players grew to respect and—most of all—trust Manuel, which made him the logical choice as interim manager until a permanent successor could be found.

Unlike Randolph, Manuel already had previous experience as a major league skipper before taking over the Mets' dugout. He managed the White Sox from 1998 to 2003, going 500–471 and earned AL Manager of the Year honors by leading the team to the AL Central title in 2000.

Manuel was part of Randolph's original coaching staff in 2005 and felt rather uneasy about replacing him, especially in the manner the Mets turned the decision into a public-relations blunder. Randolph was fired around 3:00 am eastern time after the team played the first game of a western swing. The media wondered why Randolph wasn't let go after the Mets had completed a homestand one day earlier, saying it was cruel to let him get on the team plane to California if Wilpon already had made up his mind about the dismissal. Manuel had wanted another crack at managing in the majors, but not under these circumstances.

However, Manuel was very confident that he could turn around a team that was 34–35 when he took over on June 17, 2008.

"I think that hopefully they have respect for me in the clubhouse, and I have a respect for the players," Manuel said after the promotion. "With that being said, I think we have a foundation there so we can really grow and get us back on track."[7]

Manuel was a welcome change for several players, most notably Carlos Delgado and Carlos Beltrán. Randolph was a stoic person as a player and remained so as a manager, rarely showing much emotion in the dugout and carefully choosing his spots to argue with an umpire. Randolph also delegated authority and allowed Manuel to mediate any problems a player might have with his manager. In other words, Randolph stayed to himself and was not the touchy-feely guy that Manuel personified.

Manuel had no trouble jawing with umps to protect his players, something that was not in Randolph's DNA. Manuel kept his door open and had good communication with a large percentage of his players. He would laugh in the dugout, celebrate with his men following a good play, and serve as a father figure to some players.

The media loved his demeanor during postgame news conferences. Manuel was self-deprecating and didn't become antagonistic when a writer or broadcaster called him out on a managerial decision that backfired.

It took a while for the hiring to bear fruit. The Mets dropped his managerial debut 6–1 to the Angels and didn't climb over the .500 mark for good until July 7, when New York won the third game of what would become a 10-game winning streak. The Mets were tied for first at 52–44 by the end of the streak.

The Mets sizzled in July and August, compiling a 36–19 record that helped them take a three-game lead by September 3. Delgado had returned his 2006 hitting form, Beltrán was playing inspired defensive baseball and Jose Reyes was demonstrating the game-breaking skills that made him one of baseball's most feared leadoff hitters despite his relatively low on-base percentage.

The Mets as a whole were playing smarter baseball, paying attention to detail while keeping their intensity at a high level. They hit .282 with 73 homers and 294 RBIs while averaging 5.4 runs per game from July 1 to September 3.

The Mets were winning despite the absence of closer Billy Wagner, who didn't pitch after August 2 due to an inflamed elbow that eventually required Tommy John surgery. Wagner's injury threw off the Mets' delicate ecosystem within the bullpen. The relief corps in 2008 wasn't exactly the league's most reliable even with a healthy Wagner. Finding another closer amid a bullpen full of underachievers was a task that Manuel never completed, and the situation brought down the rest of the relievers, most of whom were overworked due to the rotation's inability to consistently pitch deep into games.

It became commonplace for Manuel to use four to five relievers per game in an effort to close out a tight victory. He tried to create the best matchups late in games and would use a hurler for just one batter if he thought that pitcher would have trouble retiring the next hitter.

After a while, a high number of Manuel's moves—most of which seemed logical in that particular instance—backfired at the worst times. Five different pitchers blew saves during an 11-day stretch in September. Five games were lost by the bullpen after September 12, some in horrific fashion.

The bullpen was the primary culprit as the Mets blew a 3½-game lead over the final 17 games and finished three games behind the NL East champion Phillies and one game in back of the Brewers for the wild card. The Phillies went on to win the World Series, doing it with a solid bullpen and a rotation led by Cole Hamels.

"Obviously, that was the thing we were lacking," Manuel said of the team's pitching. "It was part of the issues we were dealing with coming down the stretch. We've got enough to compete, I think. But with Philadelphia winning the World Series, that intensifies the rivalry."[8]

Manuel finished the season 55–38 (.591), one percentage point behind Bud Harrelson for the best record by an interim manager in team history. The players battled for Manuel to the very end of the season, but the pitching problems were never corrected.

The front office recognized Manuel's assets to the team and gave him a two-year contract after the season.

"Jerry did a very good job taking over the club midseason," said general manager Omar Minaya in a statement, "and we believe that he is the right person to manage our team and lead us to the postseason."[9]

Players liked the fact he was up front with them and very communicative. Brian Schneider was one of his strongest supporters during his two-year stay in New York and felt Manuel never tried to B.S. his players.

"Jerry's a very smart man," said Schneider during the 2009 season. "He'll never just blurt anything out for the sake of blurting it out. He'll always let you know what he's thinking, and as a player that's a good thing. You always like to know where you stand."[10]

The lineup remained virtually intact heading into 2009. The bullpen was overhauled, but the rotation was no better that it was at the end of '08, with Livan Hernandez replacing Pedro Martinez. The Mets dropped nine of their first 15 games and were just 10–13 before winning seven straight and 11 of 13 to move into first place at 21–15, 1½ games ahead of the Phillies. However, the team was running, throwing and fielding itself out of too many wins, a small problem that became an epidemic by the end of June.

The Mets appeared to take a 3–2 lead in the 11th inning of a May 18 game in Los Angeles after Angel Pagan doubled home Ryan Church. Problem was, Church missed third base and was called out to end the inning, erasing the go-ahead run before the Dodgers scored in the bottom half to win it. That was a game in which the Mets committed five errors, two in the 11th inning alone.

And there was a game in which the Mets were one out away from an 8–7 victory over the Yankees in the Bronx before closer Francisco Rodriguez got Alex Rodriguez to hit a popup to second with the potential winning run on first. Luis Castillo took several steps toward the ball before it glance off his glove for a walk-off error.

There were numerous mental lapses by Pagan on the base paths and in the outfield. Castillo had a habit of

Jerry Manuel

bunting runners over to third following leadoff doubles, which often snuffed out rallies instead of enhancing them. Mike Pelfrey balked himself to a loss in San Francisco after the Mets took the first three games of the series. Rookie Fernando Martinez failed to run out a popup before the ball landed to the turf, an example of unbelievable lack of hustle for a player in his first week as a major leaguer.

The mental mistakes eventually gave way to devastating injuries. Of the Mets' nine starters in the season opener, seven landed on the disabled list and three were out of action at least three months. Mike Pelfrey was the only member of the original 2009 starting rotation to stay on the active roster the entire season, and he regressed from 2008.

The injuries led to Manuel using 53 players, one off the team record set in 1967. Manuel also used 11 different starting pitchers and 13 relievers over the course of what truly was an agonizing season for the team. The Mets finished fourth in the NL East at 70–92, thanks mainly to a deplorable 40–72 mark from May 30 to September 30. Manuel hated the team's performance but used humor in admitting the losses were getting to him.

"Now that they're mounting, I feel like I've got this big thing hanging with me every day," Manuel said during the final week of a lost season. "Even though I'm trying to get rid of it, it's like he's trying to be my friend or something, and I really don't want him to be my friend."[11]

Humor could be Manuel's safety valve, and it helped him continue a strong relationship with his players and the media. He could take a tense situation and put it in its proper place through levity.

"It's very important," he said of his ability to handle pressure through humor. "I go back to my hero. Gandhi was said to have a great sense of humor. I read that one time he met Charlie Chaplin, and he had Chaplin in stitches."

Manuel's appreciation of Gandhi blossomed through his love of Dr. Martin Luther King Jr. An avid reader of King's legacy, Manuel took notice of a photograph of King reading a book that contained "Gandhi" on the cover, before learning more about the Indian leader. Manuel also admires Tolstoy, and there aren't too many managers well versed in the works and lives of those three men.

"They move men," Manuel said while he was still the Mets' bench coach. "I always wanted to move men, to take them to a level that they've never seen before. Let's see how far you can go is how I feel."[12]

Gandhi and King carried heavy burdens while leading millions through some of the most turbulent times during the last century. By comparison, Manuel felt it was much easier to handle 25 to 40 men while handling his toughest critics in New York and Chicago. He had little trouble absorbing blame, deflecting praise and admitting he can be even better as a leader.

"I would rather the emphasis—when the team struggles—be on me, and on them when we're playing well," Manuel said following the 2008 season. "I don't have a problem with where we are right now. It gives me an opportunity to prove myself over a period of time."[13]

Although the depleted Mets played boneheaded baseball at times, they continued to hustle for Manuel through the end of the season. The best example of that was Castillo, who begged the team for a second chance after performing so poorly during his injury-filled 2008 season. Castillo raised his average 57 points to .302, including a .359 mark in 65 games from July 5 to September 22, when the games didn't mean very much.

The front office gave Manuel a free pass for the season since he wasn't the cause of the injuries. However, he also knew the team would have to get off to a fast start in 2010 for him to have any shot of returning for 2011.

The Mets opened the season with newcomer Jason Bay in left field and recent addition Jeff Francoeur in right. It was hoped the two could improve a lineup that finished last in the majors with 95 home runs and had yet to figure out cavernous Citi Field. Instead, they became two of the team's major disappointments at the plate, although Bay quickly grew to appreciate Manuel's positive spin on any situation.

"He's by far the most positive guy I've ever played for," Bay said three months into the season, "and I don't care if you're playing Little League or major league baseball, positivity goes a long way. It tends to be contagious. That's no slight to anybody else. That's just, given the market, the uncertainties, the ups and downs we've gone through.

"He's never wavered on his stance of being positive and standing behind guys. I know it's easy to get caught up in certain things, but he hasn't. He's really been the same guy to us, from spring training until now, and I understand how difficult that is, and I respect that."[14]

While the Mets picked up Bay as a free agent, they failed to improve the rotation during the fall and winter. Ace Johan Santana was recovering from off-season surgery for the second straight season, and No. 2 starter Pelfrey was hoping to correct the problems that led to his 5.03 ERA in 2009. The rest of the starting staff was projected to be comprised of the brittle and enigmatic John Maine and Oliver Perez, the team's best starters in 2007 but major question marks three years later. Rounding out the rotation was rookie Jonathon Niese, who emerged as a capable lefty.

Maine didn't pitch after May 20, six days after Perez was pulled from the rotation due to ineffectiveness. Santana was shelved in September before undergoing surgery that month. Niese spent time on the DL before pitching very well for about three months.

Newcomers Hisanori Takahashi and knuckleballer R.A. Dickey became two of the most valuable members of a staff that pitched much better than in 2009. Manuel had Takahashi open the year as a middle reliever and put him in the rotation following Maine's injury before turning him into the closer once Francisco Rodriguez punched his way onto the disabled list in August. Manuel's handling of Takahashi turned the Japanese import into one of the team's better stories of 2010.

Dickey was effective after being recalled from Buffalo and remained that way the rest of the year, although Manuel refrained from lavishing praise on him until around the All-Star break. It just didn't make sense that a 35-year-old reclamation project would emerge as the team's most consistent starter. Then again, the entire season didn't seem to make sense.

Manuel was on the hot seat after the Mets got off to a 4–8 start, but the players remained in his corner.

"He's our leader," Pelfrey said. "If someone has to lose their job because of how we're performing, that's unfortunate."[15]

Things began to change April 19, when first baseman Ike Davis was promoted from Buffalo after a spectacular spring training. Davis lit a fire under a stagnant offense and the Mets won 10 of their next 11 games while looking like a playoff contender.

Pagan eventually became the team's starting center fielder after sharing the job with Gary Matthews Jr. for the first two weeks of the season. Pagan played outstanding defense and was the team's most consistent hitter while avoiding the type of miscues that had Manuel shaking his head in 2009.

The Mets were 43–32 and within a half-game of the first-place Braves after Niese pitched superbly in a 6–0 shutout of the Twins June 27. Manuel was being touted as a manager of the year candidate for putting the team in contention despite a rag-tag rotation, a disappointing offense and the absence of Beltran.

But the Mets were four games back by the All-Star break at 48–40 before opening the second half with an abysmal 2–9 road trip. Beltran was ineffective at the plate and looked hesitant and slow in center while wearing a heavy knee brace. Wright went through a deep slump in July. Bay went on the disabled list with a season-ending concussion shortly after the All-Star break. Catchers Rod Barajas and Henry Blanco were providing little offense. Francoeur never hit consistently after April. Davis was fishing at pitches out of the strike zone. Castillo played himself out of a starting job, and his replacement, Ruben Tejada, hit .068 in his first 28 games after July 1.

The Mets never climbed higher than one game over .500 after July 31 and fell 10 games out of first by August 15. By Labor Day, the media began to assume Manuel would not be back in 2011, but the players continued to work hard for him despite their place in the standings. Manuel's biggest responsibility down the stretch was preparing the younger Mets to take the next step, even with the chance Manuel wouldn't be with the club in 2011. Prospects Josh Thole, Lucas Duda, Nick Evans, Dillon Gee, and Ruben Tejada received ample playing time to prove themselves as the Mets went 9–10 over the last three weeks to finish 79–83.

The ax fell the day after the season as Manuel and Minaya were told they wouldn't be needed in 2011.

Roy McMillan 1975

Born: July 17, 1929   Bonham, Texas
Died: November 2, 1997   Bonham, Texas
Named Interim Manager: 8/6/75
Returned to coaching staff at the end of the 1975 season

Roy McMillan Mets Managerial Record

YEAR	GMS	W	L	PCT	POS.
1975	50	26	27	.491	3rd, NL East

Major League Totals

YEAR	GMS	W	L	PCT
1972–1975	55	27	28	.491

Roy McMillan was a three-time Gold Glove winner and a two-time All-Star for the Milwaukee Braves. He ended his playing career with the Mets and would remain in the organization until 1970, when he began a three-year stint as a Milwaukee Brewers coach. He managed the 1969 Jackson Mets to the Texas League title after taking over late in the season.

McMillan was back with the Mets in 1973 as the first-base coach and remained there until he replaced Yogi Berra as manager on August 6, 1975.

The Mets had just lost five in a row and were 56–53 when McMillan became manager. He earned a rain-soaked 9–6 win over the Expos in his first game as skipper.

The Mets got within four games of the division lead by reeling off five straight wins during a late-August road trip in San Diego and Los Angeles. But the Mets would continue to fade out of the playoff picture in September, losing 10 of 12 between August 30 and September 10.

During McMillan's stint as manager, Rusty Staub set a team record with 105 RBIs, Dave Kingman topped the team mark with 36 homers, Mike Vail embarked on a franchise record-tying 23-game hitting streak, and Tom Seaver would secure his third Cy Young Award by finishing 22–9 with a 2.38 ERA. But McMillan had failed to spark a long winning streak that would put the Mets back into serious postseason contention.

The Mets had another manager in mind for the 1976 season. According to the 1976 Mets press guide, McMillan said, "[Joe] Frazier was the only man seriously considered for the job."

McMillan was back as the Mets' first base coach under Frazier in 1976. He was off the coaching staff a year later.

Salty Parker   1967

Born: July 8, 1912   East St. Louis, Illinois
Died: July 27, 1992 Houston, Texas

Salty Parker Mets Managerial Record					
YEAR	GMS	W	L	PCT	POS.
1967	11	4	7	.364	10th, NL

Major League Totals				
YEAR	GMS	W	L	PCT
1967–1972	13	5	8	.417

S alty Parker was the definition of "interim manager." He finished out the 1967 season for the Mets after Wes Westrum resigned with 11 games remaining. But he was never given any serious consideration to take over the team once management felt it could grab Gil Hodges from the Washington Senators.

Parker was a baseball lifer. He played in the minors between 1930 and 1954, serving as a player/coach during his final seasons. His major league playing career consisted of 11 games for the 1936 Tigers, batting .280 with four RBIs in 25 at-bats.

Parker's only season on the Mets' coaching staff was in 1967. Westrum had guided the team to a club-record 66 victories in 1966, but the Mets took a step back in '67 and were about to finish 10th for the fifth time in six seasons when the team decided Westrum wouldn't return in 1968. Westrum opted to resign rather than finish the season, giving Parker a chance to manage for the first time at the major league level.

Parker took over for the start of a four-game series against the Astros. The Mets dropped the first game 8–0 but earned a split of the series. That series included a three-hit shutout victory by Tom Seaver on September 23, the 16th and final win of his Rookie of the Year season.

The Mets dropped the series finale against the Astros to start a five-game losing streak. The skid ended with back-

to-back victories at Los Angeles, including Bill Graham's only major league win. The Mets ended the season with a four-game split of the Dodgers to finish 4–7 under Parker.

Parker wasn't part of Gil Hodges' staff in 1968. He joined the Astros' coaching crew and served two games as the team's interim manager in between Harry Walker's dismissal and Leo Durocher's hiring in 1972.

Willie Randolph   2005–2008

Born: July 6, 1954   Holly Hill, South Carolina
Named Manager: 11/4/04
Dismissed: 6/17/08
NL East Title, 2006

Willie Randolph Mets Managerial Record					
YEAR	GMS	W	L	PCT	POS.
2005	162	83	79	.512	3rd, NL East
2006	162	97	65	.599	1st, NL East
2007	162	88	74	.543	2nd, NL East
2008	69	34	35	.493	3rd, NL East
Total	555	302	253	.544	

T he Mets had just completed their third-straight losing season when newly minted general manager Omar Minaya began to interview five candidates for the vacant manager's position. Two of the potential successors to Art Howe—Jim Riggleman and Terry Collins—were former big league managers who had led their teams to the National League playoffs. Carlos Tosca was the third ex-manager on the short list after compiling a .500 record in parts of three seasons with the low-budget Blue Jays. A fourth candidate was Rudy Jaramillo, a highly-respected hitting coach for the Rangers when Minaya worked for the club.

The fifth man in contention for the job was Willie Randolph, who had interviewed for the Mets job in 2002 before then general manager Steve Phillips settled on Howe. In fact, Randolph had interviewed for several other managerial positions before meeting with the Mets for a second time two years later.

Randolph couldn't have been a more perfect fit for the Mets at the time. The team needed a skipper with a proven record as a winner. As a player, Randolph was the quiet man on the "Bronx Zoo" Yankees and eventually became part of Joe Torre's coaching staff while the Bombers won four championships in five years. Randolph also had Mets ties, having rooted for the team as a kid before ending his major league career with the franchise.

Once the Mets settled on Randolph, he displayed as much relief as elation after failing to land other managing positions.

"When you spill your heart and soul to general managers, it does take a lot out of you," Randolph said of his numerous interviews. "But I never really gave up hope. A lot of those interviews came down to a person you felt comfortable with. I feel very comfortable here. I think this is where I should be. I think it's where I belong."[16]

"I learned a lot from working with Joe Torre," Randolph said before he was hired. "You take a little bit from everyone and form your own identity and own style. I'm a winner. I know about winning, and that's what you have to rely on."

Randolph also had faith in the Mets' front office. Minaya was supposedly given total control by owner Fred Wilpon and COO Jeff Wilpon after the team foundered under previous GMs Phillips and Jim Duquette. Randolph felt he and Minaya would provide a winning combination.

"The problems they've had here in the past I'm not concerned about," Randolph said as the Mets were still deciding on a skipper. "I feel real comfortable and sure they're committed to turning this around and winning."[17]

"Willie Randolph, for me, is a New Yorker," Minaya said. "And managing in New York is not only about baseball. It's about understanding the New York fan base, the media and the beat of the city. Us New Yorkers have an edge."[18]

Minaya was so confident in his decision to hire Randolph that he put his own butt on the chopping block: "A lot of his success will depend on the job I do. I've got to give him the right players."[19]

Two of the most highly sought free agents that fall were Carlos Beltrán and Pedro Martinez. Both of were outstanding in the 2004 postseason, and both were exactly what the Mets needed to merit instant credibility within the New York sports landscape. Minaya secured both players, agreeing to give Martinez a four-year contract and outbidding the Yankees for Beltrán.

Both turned in terrific Mets debuts during the 2005 season opener. Beltrán slammed a two-run homer and had three RBIs to back Martinez, who allowed just three hits while striking out 12 in six innings. But the bullpen blew a 6–3 lead as the Mets lost to the Reds on back-to-back homers in the bottom of the ninth. The opener served as a precursor for the remainder of the season.

The Mets also dropped the second game before the Reds completed a sweep the next day. It was on to Atlanta, where the Mets lost the first two games of the series. Randolph was now 0–5, marking the first time the Mets had dropped their opening five games under a new manager since Casey Stengel's 1962 squad opened 0–9. The skid ended when Martinez fired a two-hitter to beat the Braves 6–1 and spark a six-game winning streak.

The Mets never strayed far from the .500 mark during the first four months of 2005 despite an offense that appeared to be lethal on paper. Randolph used his bench to near perfection as Marlon Anderson, Chris Woodward, and Ramon Castro came through with numerous big hits. Every major offensive category was led by Cliff Floyd, David Wright, or Jose Reyes, a trio that accounted for 473 of the Mets' 722 runs by the end of the season.

But injuries caused second baseman Kaz Matsui to miss nearly half the season. Catcher Mike Piazza spent much of the year trying to keep his average above .260. Slick-fielding first baseman Doug Mientkiewicz failed to provide much offense when healthy. Mike Cameron slugged .477 but drove in just 39 runs in 308 at-bats before suffering a season-ending facial injury in a collision with Beltrán at San Diego in early August.

The biggest disappointment was Beltrán, who hit 38 homers and stole 42 bases for the Royals and Astros in 2004 before hitting .435 with eight home runs in 12 post-season games. Projected as the greatest five-tool player in Mets history when he was signed in January, Beltrán was beset with injuries that limited his power and speed.

Randolph was also saddled with an incomplete bullpen. Roberto Hernandez was marvelous as the eighth-inning set-up man during the first half. The rookie manager did a wonderful job utilizing Aaron Heilman, who opened the year as a starter before becoming a lights-out reliever in the second half. But Randolph had no other viable resources as he tried to get the game in the hands of closer Braden Looper.

Looper served up the back-to-back homers in the season opener and never showed consistency at any point of the season. It was later learned that Looper was hiding a shoulder injury and continued to pitch in pain through the second half.

Randolph still had the Mets in the playoff hunt despite their issues. Martinez had his best season as a Met, and Tom Glavine posted a non-losing record for the first time since joining the team in 2003. Jae Seo emerged as a capable starter and finished the year 9–2 with a 2.59 ERA. The three helped the Mets go 14–6 from August 5 through August 26, putting the team in the wild-card chase after languishing in last place in the NL East at the beginning of the month.

The Mets beat the Phillies 6–4 on August 30, leaving them just a half-game off the wild-card lead despite a pedestrian 69–62 record. But the victory was part of a stretch in which the Mets went 3–15 to play themselves out of playoff contention.

The club continued to play hard for Randolph over the final two weeks, winning 10 of 13 to finish 83–79. It was the Mets' first winning season since an 82–80 mark in 2001, but it was short of their 89–73 Pythagorean projection in a year when 89 wins would have earned the Mets a tie for the wild-card. However, the season gave management reason to believe the Mets were only a couple players away from reaching the playoffs again.

The Mets actually had holes to fill in the infield and outfield, behind the plate, in the rotation, and in the bullpen. The only true untouchables at this point were Wright, Reyes, Floyd, Beltrán, Martinez, and Glavine. Kaz Matsui was an untouchable because of his contract after two disappointing seasons. Minaya revamped the lineup and brought in a new group of relievers, addressing the problems that sabotaged the team late in the season.

Cameron, Mientkiewicz, Mike Jacobs, and Piazza were replaced by Xavier Nady, Carlos Delgado, and Paul Lo Duca. Minaya also issued a minor league contract to veteran Jose

Willie Randolph

Valentin, who could spell Floyd in left and serve as second base insurance if Matsui faltered again. Endy Chavez was another player whose transaction flew under the radar but became vital as the 2006 season progressed.

Duaner Sanchez, Chad Bradford, and Darren Oliver were brought in to join Heilman as setup men for new closer Billy Wagner, who was the team's biggest prize in the 2005–2006 free-agent market. Minaya also brought back Pedro Feliciano, who pitched overseas in 2005 after playing parts of the previous three seasons in New York. The sextet soon represented one of the deepest pens in team history, an essential commodity for a ballclub that entered 2006 with a thin rotation.

Glavine, Martinez, and Trachsel represented a pretty strong front end of the rotation, with Victor Zambrano serving as the "cross-your-fingers" fourth starter. But the team entered camp without a sure No. 5 starter after Minaya sent Kris Benson to the Orioles for prospect John Maine and reliever Jorge Julio. Heilman was given a chance to win the job before Randolph and pitching coach Rick Peterson settled on rookie Brian Bannister as the fifth starter.

Those plans were quickly scuttled when Zambrano and Bannister both got hurt in April. Rookie Alay Soler and

veteran Jose Lima washed out as starters, and Maine spent most of the first three months at Triple A Norfolk. Minaya came through again by acquiring Orlando Hernandez from the Diamondbacks for an ineffective Julio.

Randolph did a wonderful job keeping the Mets on autopilot the entire regular season. He used the bullpen to perfection, winning most situational battles with a relief corps that combined to go 32–15 with 43 saves and a 3.28 ERA compared to a 65–50 mark and a 4.67 ERA from the rotation. The starters compiled a much better record once Hernandez arrived, but an effective bullpen made Randolph's job much easier, although it can be said that Randolph made the bullpen look good by using his relievers to their strength.

The lineup was so good that Randolph's only major responsibility was deciding when to give his starters a rest. When Nady underwent an appendectomy, Chavez replaced him in right field and actually hit for a higher average while displaying a superior glove. Valentin became the everyday second baseman and was a valuable component of the Mets' offense. Maine joined the rotation for good when Martinez suffered a strained right calf, going 6–2 with a 3.33 with his final 12 regular season starts.

The Mets entered the All-Star break with a 12-game lead in the NL East. The bullpen and lineup were sensational, the starters had become solid and the fielding was tight. The offense benefited from a tremendous balance of speed and power. Thanks to the switch-hitting Reyes, Beltrán, and Valentin, Randolph could start six productive left-handed hitters against right-handed starters, and six right-handers versus lefties.

New York was 22 games over .500 and 13½ games ahead in the division when the first crisis hit. Sanchez separated his shoulder in a car accident near Miami while trying to chase down a late-night meal the morning of July 31, hours before the non-waiver trade deadline. The injury left Minaya desperate for another reliever when he really needed another starting pitcher. Minaya was forced to ship Nady to the Pirates for former Met Roberto Hernandez, but he also got enigmatic lefty Oliver Perez in the deal.

The trade toppled Randolph's lineup balance, although that didn't stop the Mets from winning 14 of 18 from August 5 through August 24. The lead was 14½ games by the end of the streak, at which time the Mets had the lefty-hitting Shawn Green in right field.

Crisis No. 2 occurred as the Mets were trying to nail down their first division crown in 18 years. Martinez was hit hard in two starts following his calf injury and was diagnosed with a torn rotator cuff September 29, ending his season. The injury gave the Mets no time to find a formidable replacement, although Perez was beginning to show signs of effectiveness before Martinez went down.

There was a clubhouse crisis days after the Mets wrapped up a playoff berth. Rookie Lastings Milledge was perceived by some teammates as having a rather cavalier attitude and not respecting the game. He showed up late for batting practice and talked a lot of smack on a ballclub full of trash-talkers. Players grumbled about Milledge's clubhouse demeanor until a sign was placed in Milledge's locker that read, "Know Your Place, Rook!" The Mets now had their first controversy of the season.

Crisis No. 4 came as the Mets were preparing to take on the Dodgers in the division series. Hernandez had been scheduled to pitch the opener until he injured his calf while jogging in the outfield the day before. That forced Randolph to open the series with Maine, who had won a total of eight major league games at that point in his career.

The Mets encountered a fifth crisis while they were completing a sweep of the Dodgers. Floyd had to take himself out of the clincher after reinjuring his strained Achilles' while scoring in the third inning of a 9–6 victory at Los Angeles. Randolph opted to keep Floyd on the NLCS roster against the Cardinals knowing Chavez could replace him in left if necessary. Chavez took over for Floyd in the third inning of the opener and started the rest of the series.

Randolph managed the playoffs in the same manner he guided the club during the regular season, a sign he had complete faith in what each member of the team could do in a certain situation. Unfortunately, the Mets fell one extra-base hit short of advancing to the World Series.

The Mets far exceeded preseason expectations by winning the NL East in a walk, but they had become World Series favorites by the time they clinched the division. The loss to the Cardinals in Game 7 left a bad taste, especially in the manner they dropped the game. Light-hitting Yadier Molina put St. Louis ahead with a two-run homer in the ninth, and Beltrán struck out with the bases loaded to end it. It was just as agonizing a conclusion as the end of the 1988 season, when the Mets were considered a lock to face the A's in the Fall Classic before losing to the Dodgers in the NLCS.

Randolph handled almost every crisis positively. Hernandez was effective in late-innings situations, although he was not Sanchez's equal at that point in his career. Green hit .300 in 30 at-bats during the postseason. Maine grew up during the playoffs and pitched a gem that forced the NLCS to a seventh game, and Perez picked up a victory in Game 4 of the championship series before pitching admirably in Game 7.

Randolph also left his players alone during the season. There was little need for team meetings with the Mets holding a 12-game lead by June 28. Lo Duca kept the clubhouse loose with his incessant needling, and his teammates gave it right back. But the Milledge incident was a bit worrisome, as were some of the moves the Mets didn't make in the winter of 2007.

Minaya didn't seek a frontline starting pitcher despite knowing Martinez wasn't expected to pitch again until September. He also let Bradford and Oliver leave via free agency figuring Guillermo Mota, Ambiorix Burgos, Scott Schoeneweis, and Aaron Sele would be ample replacements. Floyd became a free agent and was replaced by

Moises Alou, the talented yet oft-injured outfielder who was nearing his 40th birthday.

The 2007 Mets opened the season 4–0 and owned a 4½-game lead heading into June before suffering their first prolonged slump in almost two years. They dropped 13 of 16 from June 3 through June 20 without relinquishing the division lead. In fact, the Mets spent nearly 4½ consecutive months in first place and owned a seven-game lead with 17 to play despite numerous injuries and individual slumps.

Alou hit .341 and reeled off a team-record 30-game hitting streak but appeared in just 87 games. Lo Duca's .272 average for the season was 46 points below 2006. Delgado battled injuries and produced 24 homers and 87 RBIs after delivering 38 round-trippers and 114 ribbies the previous year. Valentin suffered a knee injury that kept him from playing the last three months, leaving the Mets without a regular second baseman until Luis Castillo was acquired in late July. Green batted .291, but his 10 homers and 46 RBIs ranked last or next to last among all National Leaguers with at least 100 games in right field.

The bullpen was in shambles. Mota, Schoeneweis, and Sele combined to go 5–6 with two saves and a 5.42 ERA in 156 appearances. Burgos was sent to the minors by the end of May, and Feliciano and Heilman weren't the shutdown relievers they were in '06. Rookie Joe Smith was outstanding over the first two months, posting a 1.37 ERA with eight holds in as many chances before pitching to a 6.50 ERA in his final 25 appearances.

The staff's bright spot was the pitching of Maine and Perez, each of whom went 15–10 and finished among the league's top 10 in strikeouts. Glavine won games despite a relatively high ERA and became the first pitcher to pick up his 300th victory in a Mets uniform when he beat the Cubs in August.

Martinez returned earlier than expected and was 2–0 with a 1.69 ERA and 17 strikeouts in 16 innings over his first three starts. Ironically, it was his third start that began the Mets' swoon, although he left the September 15 game against the Phillies with a 3–1 lead after allowing a run and five hits while striking out nine in six innings.

The Mets appeared to be a lock for another playoff berth as they entered the final three weeks of the season. They were swept in a four-game series at Philadelphia in late August, putting the Phils within two games of the Mets with 29 games left. New York shook off the sweep by winning 10 of their next 12 to open a seven-game cushion that gave them a magic number of 11 with 17 games remaining.

Randolph and the Mets were turning the race into a runaway despite a lackluster bullpen and an offense that was sluggish at times. Once they concluded a three-game series against the Phillies at Shea, 13 of the last 14 games were to be played against the Nationals and Marlins, two teams battling for the NL East basement.

The Nats were up to the challenge, taking five of six from the Mets while outscoring New York 57–39. By the time the Marlins came to Shea for a season-ending three-game series, the Mets' division lead had vanished. Florida pushed the Mets into second place for the first time since May 15 by downing Perez 7–4. Maine was outstanding in the second game of the series, striking out 14 and taking a no-hitter into the eighth as the Mets cruised to a hostile 13–0 rout that included a benches-clearing incident, leaving the Marlins very ticked off heading into the season finale. The Phillies fell to the Nationals, giving the Mets a share of the NL East lead with one game remaining. All New York had to do was win the finale to clinch at least a tie for the division crown, setting up a winner-take-all against Philadelphia.

Glavine picked this game to toss perhaps the worst game of his fantastic career. He allowed seven runs while retiring just one batter as the Mets went down 8–1, allowing the Phillies to win the East with a victory against the Nationals.

"I thought they were a little uncomfortable with the spiral," Randolph said of the ballclub. "Because you've never experienced that, we can't assume that a player is going to get himself back in the right direction."[20]

Pitching was to blame for the late-season meltdown, although Randolph took plenty of heat for the collapse. Nearly every one of his bullpen decisions in 2006 worked like magic, but the results were different the following year. Minaya had said after hiring Randolph that it was the responsibility of the general manager to get him the necessary players to reach the playoffs. In retrospect, the players failed Minaya and Randolph, but Randolph was the one who received the most criticism after the season. Randolph never received proper credit for his use of the bullpen in 2006, but he took the heat when the relievers stunk in September 2007.

"I've always been associated with winning, and it hurts deep down inside, really hurts, to be associated with this type of collapse," Randolph said after the season. "That's not how we play the game, and there's no way in the world that I thought we would be in this position right now talking about this; I thought we'd be preparing for the postseason. But it's a cruel lesson in life and baseball. Make your bed and you live in it. We definitely set us up for this disappointment."[21]

The Mets announced two days after the season that Randolph would be retained. It would be a few months before they really let him twist in the wind.

Meanwhile, Minaya did nothing to improve the bullpen during the off-season as he counted on Schoeneweis, Feliciano, Heilmann, and Sanchez to have bounce back years. Only Schoeneweis did. Sanchez missed all of 2007 following surgery and did not exactly stay true to the rehab regimen laid out for him, showing up out of shape and with an unexpected drop in velocity and movement. Matt Wise was acquired before camp but suffered an early season injury and missed the last five months. Sanchez was released before the end of the season.

Minaya picked up outfielder Ryan Church and Brian Schneider from the Nationals for Milledge, thus settling three areas of concern. Church replaced Green, who retired after the '07 season. Schneider took over for Lo Duca, whose leadership came into question following the team's late-season stumble. And despite all of Milledge's potential, he had worn out his welcome with his habitual tardiness and on-field celebrations that were considered "over the top" by many of his teammates and most of the opposition.

Milledge and Reyes put a target on the backs of the Mets with their machinations and gyrations while celebrating great plays. They team was despised by the rest of the division and motivated the sputtering Marlins and Nationals to knock them out of the postseason. The 1986 Mets were similarly loathed by their opponents, but the team had the wherewithal to ignore the hatred.

Minaya wasn't able to land another starting pitcher until a little more than two weeks before the start of spring training, and he was rewarded for his patience. The Mets were battling the Red Sox and Yankees for the services of two-time Cy Young Award winner Johan Santana, who was being dangled by the Twins. Both the Red Sox and Yanks had the pitching talent to make a deal, but both teams balked at Minnesota's asking price. Santana was in the walk year of his contract, and the Twins didn't want to risk losing him without receiving a fair amount of prospects in return. They said yes to the Mets' offer of outfielder Carlos Gomez and pitchers Philip Humber, Kevin Mulvey, and Deolis Guerra, giving the Mets a projected rotation of Santana, Martinez, Maine, Perez, and Orlando Hernandez. Glavine was allowed to return to the Braves.

The Mets came to St. Lucie with high hopes and limped out of camp with more question marks. Alou, Hernandez, and backup catcher Ramon Castro opened the regular season on the disabled list, and it remained unclear if the team had shaken off the disappointment of 2007. Alou was replaced by Angel Pagan, who had rejoined the Mets in January. Mike Pelfrey was asked to serve as the No. 5 starter in place of Hernandez after going 3–8 with a 5.57 ERA in 2007.

The Mets were 22–19 and within a game of first place by May 18. Church and Schneider were very pleasant surprises on offense, but Beltran hit only .200 in April and had five home runs during the first two months. Delgado batted .357 in the first seven games before recording a .190 average with seven homers and 37 strikeouts over his next 42 starts. Reyes hit .246 in his first 32 games and was not demonstrating his usual zeal for the game. Wright had 11 homers and 40 RBIs by the end of May but was reluctant to assume the role of team leader in the clubhouse.

Although the Mets had several All-Stars on their roster, most seemed satisfied to play the role of co-star while waiting for someone else to serve as team leader. They had become a passive ballclub while playing for a passive manager, a bad mix for a club that was in the same division as the Phillies. The Mets were the Phillies' equal in terms of talent, but the Phils had an air of confidence the Mets lacked. Their leaders were vocal and cocky while their manager, Charlie Manuel, played his dumb-like-a-fox persona to perfection.

The Mets moved three games over .500 in mid-May by sweeping a rain-abbreviated two-game series in the Bronx before going 1–6 the remainder of the road trip. They opened a four-game series at San Diego with three straight 2–1 losses before the Padres completed the sweep. The Mets had a 30–32 record when they returned to Shea, and promptly lost the first game of the homestand.

Many of the losses could be described as bizarre or ugly. The bullpen blew leads at an alarming rate while the offense failed to produce with runners in scoring position. The unflappable Randolph just rolled with it.

"We've had some of the most bizarre endings that I've ever had in my life. You can't even make it up," he said.[22]

The media wondered how long Randolph could keep his job while the Mets continued to play mediocre baseball. It was the prime topic of discussion during postgame interviews amid reports that Reyes, Beltrán, and Delgado weren't happy with their manager. Minaya continued to back his skipper.

"The reality at the end of the day is that he's our manager," Minaya said in mid-June. "He's got my support. He has ownership's support. I believe that we're working hard, that he's going to be able to turn our team around. The frustrating part of it is that we've lost a lot of close games. It's not that we're being blown out. It's close games. That happens in championship seasons."

Randolph finally demonstrated some frustration with the way he felt he was being treated in the media and spoke candidly to *Bergen Record* writer Ian O'Connor in May without realizing his comments might be published. Randolph told O'Connor he wasn't pleased with the way SNY cameras portrayed him during and after games.

"Is it racial?" Randolph asked O'Connor. "Huh? It smells a little bit.

"I don't know how to put my finger on it, but I think there's something there."[23]

Randolph spent the next few days apologizing for playing the race card. All would be forgiven if the Mets could string together an eight-game winning streak. Instead, they continued with their inconsistent effort while Randolph had to answer for his lack of animation in the dugout.

"I think I'm always the calmest under pressure," Randolph said. "I've always felt that way. I was brought up that way. That's the way I grew up. I tend to be probably more focused and intense when I'm doing well because I want to continue to do that. I'm probably pushing the hammer more when I'm doing well than when things aren't going well, because I know when things aren't going the way they're supposed to go, you can't overreact. As the leader of this ballclub, I don't want my players to feel that kind of pressure."[24]

However, Randolph also knew the front office was growing impatient with the team's performance. The Mets took two of three from the Rangers in another series plagued by inconsistent starting pitching, an unreliable bullpen and an inability to drive in runners in scoring position. When the Mets completed the series, Randolph asked Minaya to relieve him of his duties if ownership felt it was necessary.

"I said: 'Omar, do this now. If you're going to do this, do this now. I know you've got a lot of pressure on you, but if I'm not the guy to lead this team, then don't let me get on this plane.' I did say that to him."[25]

"Guys, we've been going day to day," Minaya said before the Mets left for Anaheim. "It's fair to say that Willie's our manager and, as I said before, those situations are always under evaluation, and I'm always evaluating those situations."[26]

Randolph made the trip to Anaheim and managed them to a 9–6 win over the Angels. He hoped it was the start of a successful road trip that would push the focus back on his players.

"We spend so much time talking about all this extracurricular stuff, man, and it's like, this team just needs to focus on playing winning baseball. That's the way we started out in spring training, and that should be the main focus here. It's unfortunate, but that's the way it should be."

Hours later, Minaya met with Randolph and told him he was dismissed. Randolph said he thought the meeting was about his staff.

"I thought he was talking about whacking a couple of my coaches," Randolph said after returning to his New Jersey home. "That's why I was stunned; I didn't think it was going to happen. At the time, I felt the way he was talking to me, that I was pretty secure for the time being.

"I felt all along this team would play better and we would eventually get into the season and really do well. In my mind, this all happened way, way too early."[27]

The Mets were skewered for their handling of the firing. Why do it at the beginning of a West Coast road trip? Why do it in the middle of the night after most of the team's traveling media party had gone to bed? And who actually made the decision to allow Randolph to get on the plane? Minaya maintained it was his decision despite his public backing of Randolph just 24 hours earlier. Even Randolph wasn't certain the firing was Minaya's idea.

"I have my doubts," Randolph said two days later. "Let's just leave it at that. I have my doubts."[28]

Randolph spent the next two years as bench coach under Brewers manager Ken Macha. By the end of 2010 he was hoping to get another shot at managing in the majors again.

"The past two years, I'm glad I did it because I think it's really helped me with my growth. I've learned a lot. Not just Xs and Os, but seeing the game from a different perspective because when you're a manager, you're in a certain bowl. But when you're a bench coach, you're managing per se, but you're seeing the game from a different perspective."[29]

The Brewers opened the final week of the 2010 season playing the Mets at Citi Field. By then, Minaya's job security was in serious jeopardy following two straight losing seasons. Randolph took the high road by speaking glowingly of his former boss, still able to muster some class a little more than two years after their messy divorce.

"Omar and I will always have a certain bond together. I'm eternally grateful for him for giving me the opportunity going through what I went through for years. I know his family, and Omar's really a solid baseball man. Anytime this kind of stuff is going around people that you know and like, you're concerned for them or you hope it works out for them. Omar, and I've told him this before, I'm always rooting for him."[30]

Randolph and Minaya will forever be linked in Mets lore as architects of the 2006 division title and the meltdown that followed. Randolph left the franchise with the second-best winning percentage among managers.

Casey Stengel   1962–1965

Born: July 30, 1890 Kansas City, Missouri
Died: September 29, 1975   Glendale, California
Named Manager: 10/17/61
Temporarily stepped down 7/25/65 due to broken hip
Resigned: 8/29/65

Casey Stengel Mets Managerial Record

YEAR	GMS	W	L	PCT.	POS.
1962	160	40	120	.250	10th, NL
1963	162	51	111	.315	10th, NL
1964	162	53	109	.327	10th, NL
1965	95	31	64	.326	10th, NL
Total	579	175	404	.302	

Major League Totals

YEARS	GMS	W	L	PCT
1938–1965	3766	1905	1842	.508

The Mets officially became a National League franchise on October 17, 1960. One day later, the Yankees announced that Charles Dillon "Casey" Stengel would not be back as their manager. Within two weeks, George Weiss was replaced as the Yankees' general manager, accepting a retirement deal that would keep him on team payroll as an advisor.

Stengel had been asked to retire following a 12-season stint in which he won 10 pennants and seven World Series. He had been hired by Weiss following a 1948 season in which the Bombers had the audacity to finish in third place in Weiss' first season as GM.

The Stengel hiring was met by quizzical looks and/or hearty laughter, particularly in Boston, Stengel's second major league managerial stop.

Before Weiss had hired him, Stengel was known as a clown who failed to get his teams out of the first division during eight-plus seasons as manager of the Dodgers and Braves.

Stengel fit in perfectly with the Dodgers, a franchise that had won just two pennants—none after 1920—prior to his hiring. He broke into the majors with the 1912 Dodgers, the year before Ebbets Field opened. He gained a reputation as a bit of a "dandy" who enjoyed nice clothes but didn't always have the available funds to pay for them. At least one shopkeeper placed in his storefront window a bounced check signed by Stengel, making it rather ironic that Stengel would become the vice-president of Glendale National Bank in California.

Stengel actually was a pretty good ballplayer, hitting .284 in 4,288 at-bats. He went 4-for-4 in his first big league game and became adept at playing the tricky caroms off the Ebbets Field outfield wall.

Stengel was dealt in 1918 to the Pirates and played sparingly in his first season with the team. A year later, he was still with the Pirates and getting some rough treatment from the fans at Ebbets Field when he decided to give them something to remember.

Stengel had gotten his hands on a small bird and brought it to the dugout. He later stepped to the plate amid a chorus of jeers, then turned around and acknowledged the fans. As he tipped his cap toward the crowd, the bird appeared on Stengel's head before flying away. Fans began to laugh at the stunt, forgetting for a moment why they were booing him in the first place. Stengel had the last laugh as he became the first player to get a positive response after giving fans "the bird."

The zaniness resumed when Stengel became the Dodgers' manager in 1934, but it wasn't a solo act. The team often found creative ways to lose games, something Stengel would witness some 30 years later.

Stengel's Dodgers finished sixth, fifth, and seventh in his three years as skipper, hardly impressive numbers. But with the Great Depression at its height, the Dodgers finished third, fourth, and third in attendance.

The turnstiles were moving, but the team was losing both on the field and on the ledger sheet. Stengel was fired and replaced by Burleigh Grimes, who won five fewer games in his first season than Stengel did in his last.

Stengel was back in the majors in 1938, guiding the Boston Braves to a 77–75 record and a fifth-place finish. The Braves ended up 12 games out of first but didn't crack the first division after the 49th game of the season.

Stengel never won more than 65 games during any of the next four-plus seasons, leading to his dismissal. Things got so bad that the Boston writers named a local cab driver as their Sportsman of the Year. The cabbie had accidentally run over Stengel, breaking his leg.

The Braves actually were showing improvement in 1943 when Stengel was dismissed in mid-August. At the time, his career record as a major league manager was 534–742, numbers that won't get you into Cooperstown.

It would be six years before Stengel resurfaced as a major league skipper, and he'd do it with the most storied franchise in the game's history. Stengel had just led the

Oakland Oaks to the PCL title in 1948 when Weiss went shopping for a manager for the Yankees. Bucky Harris was let go just a year after winning the 1947 World Series, creating a job opening for the 58-year-old Stengel.

The Yankees hadn't won fewer than 77 games since 1925. Stengel hadn't won more than 77 games as a skipper, making the hiring even more curious.

Before the announcement, Stengel's greatest achievement in Yankee Stadium was hitting a game-winning inside-the-park homer in the 1923 World Series despite arriving at home without a shoe. Seventeen years after the hiring, Stengel would be enshrined at Cooperstown.

Stengel's first season with the Yanks was a huge struggle. He spent most of the year without Joe DiMaggio, who was battling bone spurs in his heel. Many other Yankees were either banged up or at the end of their careers, forcing Stengel to platoon at several positions. The only Yankee with more than 447 at-bats was Phil Rizzuto, who claimed he was belittled by Stengel during a 1935 tryout with the Dodgers. Rizzuto said Stengel told him the only way he'd make a living was by getting a shoe-shine box.

The Yankees trailed the Red Sox by one game with two to play in the '49 season before wrapping up the American League pennant with back-to-back victories. A World Series title followed. And another. And another. And another. And another.

Stengel had guided the Yankees to five World Series in his first five years as manager. No other team had won more than four straight before the rubber-faced, large-eared Stengel reached the Bronx.

Stengel seemed to have a gift for knowing when to start a player, sit a player, start a pitcher, or bring in a reliever. He gained a reputation as a push-button manager given the wealth of talent on the Yankees. He had used the same managing strategy with the Dodgers and Braves, except now he had the "buttons." He credited his former manager John McGraw for his style of platooning, keeping players fresh and putting them in situations in which Stengel thought they would excel.

Many of the Yankees under Stengel were veterans who were unaccustomed to sharing playing time. But the skipper knew they'd be more productive with a little rest, and he figured his disgruntled ballplayers wouldn't be too unhappy when they went to the bank to cash their World Series checks. Things became so obnoxiously successful for the Yankees that players would plan their family budget based on a World Series appearance. Weiss even used it in contract talks, reminding a player there was postseason money to go along with his salary.

Stengel didn't give any of his players preferential treatment, which rankled his biggest superstar. Joe DiMaggio had become accustomed to star treatment from his managers and expected the same from Stengel.

Stengel understood DiMaggio's importance in the Yankees' stratosphere in 1949, which is why he was put in the lineup every day upon his return from injury. But Stengel witnessed a slower bat and slower feet from DiMaggio in 1950 and 1951, causing the manager to limit the outfielder's playing time. Stengel tried to play DiMaggio at first base, which his star player took as a public humiliation given his body of work as a center fielder.

To Stengel's fortune, DiMaggio was leaving just as Mickey Mantle was emerging. Mantle was brought up to the Yanks in 1951, DiMaggio's final season. The Mick played right field and was wearing No. 6 when he broke in, as the Yankees figured, the line of greatness that started with the No. 3 Ruth and continued with No. 4 Gehrig and No. 5 DiMaggio. But Mantle got off to a shaky start in '51 and was sent to the minors. He was handed No. 7 upon his recall.

DiMaggio recognized Mantle was the heir apparent in center field, but the veteran wanted to go out on his own terms. Stengel didn't show him the door, but he seemed to hold it for him.

Stengel felt his trick to managing was simple. He thought there would be five guys who love him and five guys who hate him. The trick, he'd say, was keeping the five guys who hated him away from the 15 who weren't sure. He managed to keep his players relatively happy.

Weiss actually rebuilt the Yankees twice during Stengel's reign, but the wins kept coming. The Yankees followed their fifth straight World Series title with a 103-win season in 1954. But they finished eight games behind the Indians, who set an American League record with 111 victories.

Stengel had the Yankees back in the Series in 1955, only to lose a seven-game set to the Dodgers. The Yanks returned the favor a year later, beating the Dodgers in a seven-game series that featured the first perfect game in postseason play.

Staked to a 6–0 lead in Game 2 of the 1956 series, Don Larsen couldn't get out of the second inning. The Dodgers and Yankees eventually split the first four games, and there was a question as to who would start Game 5 for the Yanks. Stengel went with Larsen, who needed just 97 pitches to toss a perfect game.

For Game 7, Stengel chose Johnny Kucks to go against Dodgers standout Don Newcombe. Kucks hadn't started a game in the series, but he tossed a three-hit shutout to give Stengel his sixth World Series title.

The Yankees also won pennants in 1957 and '58, but the World Series opponent each time was the Braves. Milwaukee beat the Bombers the first time and had a three-games-to-one lead in the second when the Yanks took the last three games for their seventh championship under Stengel.

The Yankees finished third in 1959 before capturing their 10th and final pennant under Stengel in 1960. New York absolutely dominated the series against the Pirates on paper, earning their three victories by scores of 16–3, 10–0, and 12–0. They erased a 9–7 deficit in the ninth inning of Game 7, but Bill Mazeroski's homer in the bottom of the ninth gave the Pirates the title.

Four days after the Game 7 loss, Stengel was 70 years old and out of baseball. The Yankees had forced him out but tried to make it seem like Stengel had agreed to retire. During the news conference to announce his removal, Stengel made it clear that "my services are no longer required." When asked about an Associated Press report that said he had resigned, Stengel replied, "What does the United Press say?" He was hinting that UPI got it right by saying he was fired.

"I'll never make the mistake of turning 70 again," quipped Stengel.

Stengel headed back to California, where he was prepared to enjoy a lifetime as a bank executive. He had struck it rich in a couple of non-baseball investments.

A few months later, Weiss had been named president of the Mets after the team drove through a loophole in his Yankees contract. Weiss' settlement with the Yankees stated he'd be paid by the team as long as he didn't become the general manager of any other major league team during his five-year deal as an "advisor." The Mets sidestepped that clause and named him team president, never giving him the title of general manager. Thus, Weiss was able to run the Mets while taking money from the Yankees.

Weiss needed a manager for his expansion team, and he looked no further than Stengel. But his old skipper was enjoying life in California and wasn't too responsive to Weiss' early overtures. Weiss kept calling, Stengel kept pondering, and the cat-and-mouse game continued for months.

Finally, the Mets had their first major signing. Days before the 1961 World Series, the Mets announced that Stengel would manage the team in '62.

Mets pitcher Larry Foss felt Stengel was a logical choice to become the team's first manager.

"Casey Stengel came to the Mets as a draw for the New York fans because everyone knew Casey, whether you were a Yankee fan or what," Foss said. "I think they all kind of appreciated Casey for the way he got let out so Ralph Houk could come in and get that job because Ralph was getting a little antsy and they were going to lose him, so Casey went."

Stengel was excited, telling the press, "It's a great honor for me to be joining the Knickerbockers." He had gotten the team's name wrong, but he would make up for that gaffe over the next few months.

Stengel was expected to win championships after being hired by the Yankees. As manager of the Mets, the expectations were considerably lower. He was hired to sell tickets, sell tickets, and sell tickets. Stengel did his job with aplomb, appearing on a float at the 1961 Macy's Thanksgiving Day Parade and showing up at any available rubber-chicken banquet. The 71-year-old Stengel was back in business and instilling life into the fledgling team. He honored every media request and became the front man for what would become a very bad act.

The Mets and Houston Colt 45s participated in the expansion draft a day after the World Series ended. As a sign of things to come, the Mets lost the coin flip and had to choose second.

New York's first pick was Giants catcher Hobie Landrith, who had just 71 major league at-bats in 1961. Stengel told the media it was a logical choice: "You gotta have a catcher or else you'll have a lot of passed balls."

The expansion draft was a farce for the two new teams. The National League had made sure every original team would keep its top prospects and everyday players, allowing the Mets and Colts to pick from the bottom of the heap. Both teams wondered if they could bypass the $2 million expansion draft fee and just go with their own prospects. But the new teams were subject to the expansion rules that allowed the old teams to fill their wallets while losing marginal talent.

The Mets and Colts hit the draft with different philosophies. The Colts went with slightly younger players who had some tread on their tires and could fill holes until the farm system flourished. Houston never had a major league team and could afford that luxury. Weiss felt he had to fill his roster with "name" players, regardless of their current ability. He grabbed plenty of Dodgers, a couple of Giants and several former All-Stars. By the spring of 1962, the Mets had Gil Hodges, Charlie Neal, Frank Thomas, Richie Ashburn, and Gus Bell, all former All-Stars past their prime. What Weiss didn't have was a capable pitching staff, not that one was available.

In a perfect world, Stengel would have been able to use Roger Craig in long relief, a job in which Craig excelled while with the Dodgers. Craig finished tied for second on the 1962 Mets with 42 appearances and 34 games started. He was a valuable five-inning pitcher in an era when most starters went at least seven frames. With Craig in the bullpen, the Mets certainly would have avoided the modern-day record for losses in a season. But Stengel needed him in a rotation that had Al Jackson, Jay Hook, and little else.

Jackson was the closest thing the Mets had to a young prospect in 1962. Just 26 on Opening Day, the lefty had pitched in only 11 major league games before joining the Mets. He would quickly learn to appreciate Stengel.

"I found that he was such a unique individual, a unique type of manager," Jackson said. "I can understand why they called him 'The Ol' Perfessor,' because he taught all the time.

"What was so unique to me about him was that I had been around a lot of other managers, and a lot of other managers would say what they would do after it happened. Casey would say what he would do before it happened. I thought that was a great teaching tool.

"Very seldom did he talk to you face-to-face. He would walk up and down the dugout and just start talking about the game. One day he was talking about, 'If I was a left-handed pitcher, I would do this, I would do this, I would do this.' Then, I looked around and I was the only one there. That's the type of guy—the uniqueness—he was."

Hook was a year younger than Jackson but had already appeared in 79 big league games when he was drafted by the Mets.

Stengel spent the spring of '62 selling his Mets to writers, broadcasters, fans, and businessmen. Countless hours were spent trying to convince the masses the Mets would be competitive. Stengel did a nice job as the team drew more than 922,000, a paltry figure today but better than four other National League teams in 1962. The attendance figure was nearly 300,000 better than what the Giants drew in 1957, and a little more than 100,000 less than the Dodgers' total gathering in their final year at Ebbets Field.

"Many people will ask me if there is anything from baseball that helped me get ahead in business," said Hook, who had an extremely successful career after baseball. "I'd tell them the lessons I learned from Casey Stengel.

"He was very customer-oriented. He knew he didn't have a great team and realized it was a new franchise. He knew there were a lot of Brooklyn fans and Giant fans that felt alienated because the teams moved out of town.

"He knew that the vehicle to get to those people was the newspapers. At that time, I don't know how many newspapers there were, but there had to be at least three in New York. He would make sure that he made the newsman's job easy. He knew that they had to have a story that day and had to fill their column. He would call them into his office after the game—get them a beer or something else to drink—and he would sit and talk with them for 20 minutes or a half-hour after the game.

"He was what I call 'customer-focused.' I think that was really helpful for the Mets because I think that first year we drew almost as many fans as the Yankees. They were winners and we were dismal losers."

Fans were treated to a plethora of creative ways to lose a ballgame. The '62 Mets opened with nine straight losses and didn't earn their first home win until April 28, their eighth game at the Polo Grounds. They dropped 16 of their first 19 before the unspeakable happened: they began to win consistently.

New York took nine of its next 12, including a pair of doubleheader sweeps against the Braves. They went 8–1 in games decided by two runs of fewer in that span. And then reality set in.

They were 12–19 following a twin bill sweep in Milwaukee May 20. The Mets didn't win again until June 8, dropping 17 straight to set what remains a team record. It took them 74 games to reach the 20-win mark, and another 85 before they won their next 20.

Stengel watched the club commit 210 errors that led to an outrageous 147 unearned runs. By the end of the year, the Mets had four pitchers with at least 17 losses, led by Craig's 24 setbacks. Of the 17 pitchers used, Ken Mackenzie was the only one with a winning record.

The Mets finished last with a .240 batting average, but they also were sixth with 139 homers and fifth with 40 triples. They had just enough offense to score runs, which gave them the ability to blow leads.

Thomas hit 34 homers and drove in 94 runs. The home run total was a team record that stood until 1975, and his RBI output remained a team-high for seven more seasons.

Ashburn hit .306 in 475 plate appearances, Felix Mantilla batted .275, and Charlie Neal collected nine triples for a team record that would stand for nearly two decades.

Stengel also had three former Yankees on his bench, none named Mantle, Maris, or Berra. Gene Woodling was a valuable bench player after serving in the same capacity for Stengel's Yankees from 1949 to 1954. Rod Kanehl was finally given a shot at the major league level after a decade in the minors, mostly in the Yankee chain. Kanehl first impressed Stengel during one 1954 spring training, when he leapt over an outfield fence to retrieve a ball.

And then there was Marvin Eugene Throneberry, who spent parts of three major league seasons with the Yankees under Stengel before drifting to Kansas City and Baltimore. Throneberry hit 15 homers in 344 at-bats for the Bombers but couldn't crack the everyday lineup. He was receiving even less playing time in Baltimore when the Mets acquired him for Landrith.

Throneberry set career highs in every major hitting category except runs scored in 1962. His fielding was just as offensive, as his glove cost the team more leads than he gave the Mets with his bat. He fit right in.

Throneberry was among several former Yankees to see action with the new ballclub that year. Stengel often wished he had other players from his days in the Bronx.

"I was sitting in the bullpen down the right-field line in the old Polo Grounds," recalled Larry Foss in 2011. "Sitting out there was Red Ruffing, our pitching coach. The telephone rings. Ruffing answers it, talks for about three to four seconds, hangs it up, turns to us, and says, 'Guys, you're not going to believe who the old man just asked for. He asked for Johnny Blanchard to come up to pinch-hit.' And Blanchard was still with the Yankees! That actually happened!"

Stengel had better luck managing the media as he intentionally shielded his players by bringing attention to himself. He gave time to everyone but had a particularly strong relationship with the beat writers. He wasn't a fan of magazine scribes because, he felt, they would use stale quotes and twist them to get their own point across, not Stengel's. He was at his best on camera, where his use of tangents and stories were on display so fans could better understand the Stengel mystique.

Whitey Herzog was in the front office when he took note of Stengel's media savvy: "Casey said to me one time, 'When you're going to get interviewed and they say they want to ask you for two minutes or two questions, just talk until your time's up. That way, they can't ask you as much and you can't get in trouble.' He'd talk until his time was up, and then you couldn't ask him any more."

Writers could have blasted the team's performances, and many took the liberty of chronicling the team's misfortunes with some of the best prose ever given a last-place club. Stengel fed the writers, the writers fed the fans and the fans were able to appreciate the worst team in modern baseball history. At least one player intimated that Stengel's relationship with the press was warmer than that with his players.

"He was not a person that you got close to," pitcher Craig Anderson said. "I don't know if the older players were a little closer, but the younger ones were not. He was sort of aloof as a manager but he was in the papers all over the place. To the press and the media, he was the star player.... He liked them around. He liked to talk to them about baseball, and they were able to create and write a lot of stories about us. As bad a team as we were, they were never short on writing stories because of him. So he was really good for the game in that respect. He was also good for us because he was able to buffer us from the press. Nowadays, they hound the guys when things are going pretty bad.

"As far as managing goes, I really had a hard time figuring him out. I think that was a consensus among players, that that's just the way he was. I played with a lot of managers and would know what they'd think and when they were going to bring you into a game. I had trouble figuring out when Stengel was going to put me in.

"But I know how good he was for the game, and he drew people to the ballpark. He was a legend in his own time…funny. And he did know the game, too, but sometimes when he tried to communicate it, we didn't quite understand what he was saying, and I'm sure the writers had the same problem at times.

"I have to say that I really enjoyed being around the man that year. Of course, he sent me down the next year, so I wasn't happy with that."

A few scribes wondered how Stengel could stomach the poor display of baseball. Others felt the game was passing him by and that Casey wasn't as sharp as he had been with the Bombers.

"Everybody said, 'Stengel's getting senile,'" Foss said almost five decades later. "Bullshit! He wasn't senile, he was bored to death. I mean, geez, I don't know how he made it to the ballpark."

Stengel had cultivated a strong fan base, and he even supported its "mischievous" ways. Homemade banners had begun to sprout up at the Polo Grounds, something rarely seen in major league parks. At first, the Mets did their best to confiscate the banners, saying they were blocking the view of those gathered to actually watch the Mets stumble through an 8–4 loss. Stengel became one of the organization's first proponents of the artwork and admitted in a television interview that he was distracted by them.

"Why, they're the most amazing fans that I've ever seen in baseball," Stengel said as he began one of his more famous media diatribes. "I've been in World Series games since 1916. I've been with enormous crowds in stadiums. I've played before 96,000. But the Mets, I'll have to say they stick by you. They stick by you in the hotels. They're on the streets. They're carrying placards. They're going through the place. You find them out in right field, and four innings later, if you get a base hit, they'll be over on the left-field line. They make up wonderful placards. The placards are terrific. I even have to stop and look at them. I think I've made 15 mistakes this year reading the plac-ards instead of watching the pitcher or watching the hitter to take my men out.

"And then they have that effeminate appeal, too, the Mets have. Our players look into the stands and have a graceful walk when they go up to the plate. And if they get a home run, they know that they come in there and everybody bows to 'em and pats 'em on the back."

Stengel had helped make it fun to watch a team lose 120 games. But one of the questions was whether he was actually watching the entire game. There were reports that he occasionally would snooze in the dugout, but those stories only enhanced his legend.

"They say Casey would fall asleep during games," said Ashburn on the video *The Lighter Side of the Mets.* "I personally never saw him do it, but I wouldn't have blamed him a bit if he had."

One of Stengel's best on-field moments that season actually came in an exhibition game. The Mets and Yankees were meeting for the first time March 22, and Stengel wasn't about to lose to his old team. He also knew what it would mean to the team's stature if he pulled out a victory.

The Mets hung on for a 4–3 victory at Huggins Field, a win that was played up in the New York papers. The team had shown it could beat the big boys, even if the big boys weren't playing at their top level.

Writers weren't the only ones who would be leave bewildered following a meeting with Stengel. Don Zimmer had just broken out of a slump when Stengel sidled next to the third baseman.

"I think I got a hit in the first game, a hit the second game, and then I think I went 0-for-38," Zimmer said in 1989. "I got another scratch hit, and Casey finally called me in, and he was trying to explain about how I'll like the center field fence and I'd like this and that. I didn't know what he was talking about, so finally I said, 'Case, what are you talking about?' And he said, 'Oh, we just traded you to the Cincinnati Reds.'"

Joe Pignatano was one of the Mets' midseason pickups in 1962. He had been a third-string catcher for the Dodgers and spent time in Kansas City before the Mets picked him up from San Francisco in June.

"I sat on the bench, just gathering my thoughts because I knew I was at the end of my career," Pignatano recalled of his first day with the team. "And Casey came and sat beside me, and we chatted for about an hour.

"And along came Jack Lang, who welcomed me to the club, and with that, he asked Casey who was going to catch today. And Casey said, 'Well, that Pignatano fella if he ever gets here.' That was my indoctrination to the Mets."

You can't blame Stengel if he had trouble remembering his players' names. The Mets had 45 different players on team payroll in 1962, and their dismal record led to quite a turnover in 1963 as Weiss tried to replace his older, washed up players with younger, washed up players.

Bob G. Miller remembers a pair of Stengel quips from the '62 season.

"One time he came to the mound and said, 'How do you feel?'" Miller remembered. "I said, 'Geez, skip, I feel pretty good. I'm not tired.' And he said, 'Well, you may not be tired, but your outfielders are!'

"One other thing about Casey—and everyone on the bench just about flipped. It was a close ballgame. I think the score was tied in the eighth or ninth inning. Casey was looking out at the Dodgers bullpen and he said, 'Who's that warming up in the Dodgers bullpen? I wish he'd turn around. I can only see his number.'"

"It was fun to be on the bench with him," added 1962 Met Rick Herrscher. "You'd come out to the ballpark and you'd see 13 sportswriters around him on the field. Of course, I'd try to get close enough to listen to the double-talk. He was a showman, obviously."

Stengel's coaching staff in 1962 was a who's who of baseball talent. Hall-of-Famer Red Ruffing served as Casey's pitching coach.

"Ruffing was a nice man, but he was just a figurehead coach," Craig Anderson said. "I liked him and he liked me, and he put me in games. The teaching element is what's been a big plus in the game now. I think there's a much higher level of teaching going on at all levels of baseball now. Back then you had a lot of 'name' coaches, people who played the game really well and then became coaches.

"I wish he'd said, 'Hey, come over here, I want to show you something that might help.' I was too young to realize I should have picked his brain.

"Cookie Lavagetto was there, but I think he was more of a teaching coach. Red Kress was just a coach who did a lot of the training stuff.

"Solly Hemus tried to help Casey run that team. He was an ex-manager, and so was Cookie, so I guess they both talked to Stengel quite a bit. And Cookie was a good guy. They knew the game, too."

Ruffing wasn't the only Hall of Famer on Stengel's original Mets staff. Stengel also had Rogers Hornsby, one of the greatest hitters of his era.

"He wasn't there all the time," pitcher Craig Anderson recalled of Hornsby. "I don't remember him traveling with us all the time. But I'll tell you what; he wasn't afraid to tell you what a great hitter he was, and there was nobody better than him. And he was a great hitter, so what are you going to say?

"One day we were having a pregame conference on how to pitch the other players. We're sitting there, and the coaches started going up and down their lineup. They were talking, 'Throw him in, throw him out, throw him low, throw him high.' And Hornsby on every hitter would say, 'This guy can't…just throw the ball down the middle, he can't hit.'"

Weiss did a nice job improving the pitching staff during the winter of 1963, adding Carl Willey and Tracy Stallard to a rotation that still included Craig and Jackson. The team ERA dropped by almost a full run, although it remained the worst in the National League.

Stengel had another future Hall of Famer in his outfield for 1963. Duke Snider was purchased from the Dodgers,

Fastest Mets Managers

50 wins	83 games	Bud Harrelson (50–33)
50 losses	69 games	Casey Stengel (19–50)
100 wins	174 games	Bud Harrelson (100–74)
100 losses	134 games	Casey Stengel (34–100)
200 wins	339 games	Davey Johnson (200–139)
200 losses	280 games	Casey Stengel (79–200–1)
250 wins	314 games	Davey Johnson (150–164)
250 losses	347 games	Casey Stengel (96–250–1)
300 wins	492 games	Davey Johnson (300–192)
300 losses	427 games	Casey Stengel (126–300–1)
400 wins	666 games	Davey Johnson (400–266)
400 losses	575 games	Casey Stengel (173–400–2)
500 wins	829 games	Davey Johnson (500–329)

months after Ashburn retired. Unlike DiMaggio in 1951, Snider didn't chafe over playing time and had gotten used to playing the corner outfield positions after years in center.

Stengel also had a revamped infield. Charlie Neal was the lone holdover, although he moved over from second to third base. Al Moran was the new shortstop, and Tim Harkness was at first.

The new second baseman practically had to beg Stengel for a chance to play. Rookie Ron Hunt was logging plenty of time as the Mets' bullpen catcher when he finally told his manager he was better than any other second baseman on the team. Stengel must have liked the kid's brashness because Hunt was in the lineup the next day. Hunt didn't play an inning of the Mets' first six games, but he became a mainstay after going 5-for-12 with three RBIs in his first three starts.

The pitching was better in '63, but the hitting was horrible and the fielding was still abysmal. The Mets batted .219 with 96 homers, far off their totals from '62. At least the Mets were able to keep pace in the errors department, logging 210 for the second straight year, including 139 from the infielders. And they did it without Marv Throneberry for most of the season. Throneberry got off to a terrible start following some testy contract negotiations with Weiss. Marvelous Marv opened the season going 2-for-14 before he was sent to Triple A Buffalo in May, never to be seen in a Mets uniform again.

The Mets also said good-bye to Hodges, allowing him to become the Senators' manager. In return, the Mets picked up Jimmy Piersall, who would try to compete with Stengel for laughs.

Piersall was batting just .210 as a Met when he hit his lone homer for the team, which also happened to be the 100th of his career. He had told teammates beforehand that he would make it a memorable milestone blast, and he certainly delivered by backpedaling around the bases to the delight of more than 19,000 at the Polo Grounds that afternoon. The move may have reminded longtime fans of the day Stengel came to the plate with a bird underneath his cap, but the manager didn't appear to be impressed. Piersall went 3-for-5 that game before going on a 4-for-38 slide that earned him his release a month after his homer.

"Stengel must have felt there was room for only one clown on the team," said Ed Kranepool, who was fighting to stay in the majors.

Stengel tried to show patience with his younger players, although he seemed more comfortable playing the veterans. Two of his under-thirties were Harkness and outfielder-first baseman Duke Carmel, who had shown promise at the minor league level but still hadn't delivered in the bigs. Both eventually were stamped by Stengel as troublemakers, and he'd make them pay.

Stengel continued to get a free pass from most of those covering the Mets. But Howard Cosell was a major critic of Stengel and would use his daily spot on WABC radio to put together a case against the manager. By 1964, Harkness was more than willing to oblige, giving Cosell ammunition to verbally assail Stengel.

Harkness had 375 at-bats in 1963 and came through with a few walk-off hits, including a memorable grand slam in extra innings. But he was buried on the bench a year later after going public with his negative critique of Stengel.

At least Harkness remained in the majors. Stengel stuck it to Carmel for a comment he made at a party throw by Joan Payson during 1964 spring training. According to Ron Swoboda in Peter Golenbock's book, *Amazin'*, Stengel was addressing his team, telling his players not to spend all the money they make and to save for down the road.

"He told us, 'When you're going out after a game, don't go out with five guys, go out with two or three. If you go out with five guys, by the time everyone buys back, you're drunk.'"

That's when Carmel picked a bad time to make a funny comment.

"I've seen you out with 10 guys," quipped Carmel, according to Swoboda. Carmel was met by a dead stare from Stengel. Almost instantly, Carmel was sent to the minors and would never get another chance to play for the Mets. The team had just two players hit more than 11 homers during the '64 season. Meanwhile, Carmel was clobbering International League pitching, ripping 35 homers and driving in 99 runs while hitting .271. But he never got a recall and would resurface in the majors with the Yankees a year later.

Stengel had made his point: Show him up and you're a goner. Criticize him, and you're a goner. It was hard enough for Stengel to manage a team that averaged 115 losses in its first three seasons. He didn't need any splintering of the clubhouse. Besides, the team was going to lose with or without Carmel and Harkness.

One of the new faces in 1964 was rookie Bill Wakefield, a pitcher who quickly got on Stengel's good side.

"Casey was terrific to me and I have absolutely no complaints. I was just thrilled to be in the big leagues," Wakefield said. "Casey is a very loyal guy to his old friends, and he had some dear old friends in Kansas City that he knew from high school days or when he spent a lot of time there. The Yankees would come into town, and he would spend time there. These guys were big baseball fans and reported back to Casey over the years about young players who played in Kansas City.

"I think Casey still had his memory of wanting to be a dentist. He wanted to practice dentistry, but all the equipment was set up for right-handed people, so he couldn't become a dentist. So he kind of thought, 'Well, this guy, Wakefield, his dad's a doctor, he's from Kansas City, so he must be a pretty good kid.'

"In terms of the baseball aspect of it, with the Yankees, Casey had all the talent in the world. He was more of a game manager. With the Mets, there's no question he knew that if you win 40 games a year, you've got to do something more than just manage the players. He was always good with a quote. He always loved 'my writers.' His role was a little bit different with the Mets.

"I always thought he was a good motivator. He had a wonderful way where if he wanted to give you a jab, he wouldn't really direct it toward you. We'd have a clubhouse meeting and he'd say, 'Listen guys, this is a West Coast tour now. This is not set up as a honeymoon trip, and it's not set up to meet girlfriends.' At which point several guys knew exactly what he was talking about.

"He had a good way of getting his point across by making references. I always admired that and would think, 'Psychologically, this guy really knows how to motivate you.' Without really criticizing you, he'd get his point across."

Later on in 1964 the Mets acquired infielder Wayne Graham, who went on to become a tremendously successful head baseball coach at Rice University. Back then, he was just hoping to receive a little playing time.

The Houston native had been with the club about seven weeks when the team traveled to his home town to face the Colts in a three-game. Graham didn't start the first two games of the series, going 0-for-1 as a pinch-hitter and serving as a defensive replacement in the other game.

"Wayne was from Houston," recalled Wakefield, "and he and I were talking when he said, 'I'd sure like to play. My family's coming out.' So I told him to go up and talk to Casey.

"So Wayne goes up and says, 'Casey, my family's gonna be here. Any chance of me playing?' And Casey kind of said, 'What's your name again?'

"Wayne tells him his name, and Casey says, 'Okay, Wayne, you're starting at third base tonight.' So Wayne got to play, went 0-for-3, and never started again.

"Casey was pretty good about giving a guy a chance."

The Mets got older and younger at the same time in

1965. Warren Spahn and Yogi Berra were acquired in the off-season to serve as player/coaches. Spahn was expected to mentor a young pitching staff that was about to include Dick Selma and Tug McGraw. Berra would get nine at-bats before calling it a career, spending the rest of the season as the first base-hitting coach for fledgling players like Swoboda and Kranepool.

Meanwhile, Spahn seemed more interested in prolonging his own career than that of others. The younger pitchers groused over the lack of attention they were receiving from the winningest lefty in major league history. Spahn lost his last eight decisions and was released in mid-July, both as a pitcher and pitching coach.

The Mets also would have a new manager shortly after Spahn's departure. It was old-timer's day weekend at Shea, and Stengel was serving as host of the festivities. The Mets had invited many of Stengel's former teammates and players, giving the 75-year-old manager opportunity to relive better days.

Stengel was holding court at Toots Shor's when he stopped to go to the bathroom. He slipped on wet tile and fell to the surface before rejoining his audience. But he felt pain in the hip and decided to call it a night, taking a cab back home. He tried to sleep, but the pain had become excruciating. Stengel went to the hospital, where it was determined he had broken the hip.

The team was now in the hands of Wes Westrum, who became interim manager over Berra. Stengel and the Mets expected their original skipper to be back for the 1966 season. But a few weeks later it became evident that Stengel wouldn't be physically able to stay in the dugout. The team announced his retirement in early September but kept him on staff as a vice-president and goodwill ambassador.

Stengel made appearances for the team over the next decade, showing up at every Old Timer's Day. But he looked frail when introduced at the 1975 Old Timer's gala. He was fighting cancer, and it wasn't long before the man who coined the phrase "Amazin' Mets" would pass away that year at age 85, leaving the team without three of their most important original members. Five days earlier, Payson had passed away at 72. Weiss died in 1972, as well.

Jeff Torborg   1992–1993

Born: November 26, 1941   Plainfield, New Jersey
Named Manager: 10/11/91
Dismissed: 5/19/93

Jeff Torborg Mets Managerial Record

YEAR	GMS	W	L	PCT	POS.
1992	162	72	90	.444	5th, NL East
1993	38	13	25	.342	7th, NL East
Total	200	85	115	.425	

Major League Totals

YEAR	GMS	W	L	PCT
1977–2003	1352	634	718	.469

Jeff Torborg was an excellent defensive catcher who caught no-hitters by Sandy Koufax and Nolan Ryan. He eventually became a solid major league coach and a serviceable baseball broadcaster. But as a big-league skipper, Torborg continued to be in the wrong place at the wrong time.

Torborg's first stint as a major league manager was as a 35-year-old with the 1977 Indians, who hadn't won a pennant in 23 years and wouldn't win another until 1995. He spent parts of three seasons with the Tribe while compiling a .436 winning percentage.

Torborg was the White Sox's manager between 1989 and '91. Torborg finished last in his first season but led the Chisox to a pair of second-place showings before leaving. The White Sox won the AL West two years later.

Torborg also was dismissed in 2003 after going 16–22 to start his second season with the Marlins. Florida beat the Yankees in the World Series that October.

Eleven years earlier, the Mets figured they had a solid replacement for Bud Harrelson when they hired Torborg to manage the 1992 team. Torborg had averaged 91 wins with the South-Siders during his final two years there. The Mets had bolstered their pitching staff by acquiring Bret Saberhagen, and Bobby Bonilla had just signed the richest free-agent contract in major league history. It was a match made in heaven, right? In a way, it was.

Torborg's first job during 1992 spring training was to quell the firestorm created when a woman accused several Mets of sexually assaulting her. A wave of paranoia struck the usually media-friendly Mets clubhouse, prompting players to boycott writers and broadcasters for a few days. The players may have had a right to protest the coverage from the page-six media, but they were taking it out on people who were there to cover their on-field exploits. Right from the start, it appeared the inmates were running the asylum.

Torborg was handed a pretty talented roster as the Mets spared no expense to assure themselves a division title. They were the favorites to win the National League East in 1992 despite the Pirates' two-year stranglehold on the title. But a large collection of those players were misfits and malcontents who had trouble dealing with the pressure of playing for a mediocre team in New York.

"Barry Bonds was pretty easy to deal with, but Bobby Bonilla was impossible," said a Pirates front-office staffer after Bonilla was signed by the Mets. "Bonds cooperates when we need him to do an appearance or show up at a clinic. Bonilla was a lot tougher, even though he was portrayed as the 'good guy' on the team compared to Bonds. Bonilla is a phony, and they'll find that out in a hurry."

Bonilla wasn't Torborg's only headache. Vince Coleman was coming off his worst major league season, hitting .255 and stealing 37 bases in only 72 games just a year after batting .292 with 77 steals for the Cardinals. Dwight Gooden had undergone shoulder surgery the year before, rookie Todd Hundley did the bulk of the catching for an experienced rotation, aging Willie Randolph was the starting second baseman, and hitless wonder Dick Schofield was at short.

Davey Johnson handed down just one team rule while managing the Mets: show up ready to play. Wanna get hammered after the game and play 36 holes of golf the next day? Fine, so long as you are ready to take your position for the first pitch that night.

Torborg had a shorter leash. He banned alcohol on team flights, which went over about as well as a three-hour delay at LAX. The new skipper also announced that his wife would be accompanying him on road trips, and that the Mets would extend similar invitations to the wives and girlfriends of players and coaches for certain trips. He put the team on notice that the days of off-field embarrassments were over. Instead, the Mets saved their more embarrassing moments for the ballpark.

Torborg had constant meetings, gathering his position players for hitters confabs and going over the opposing lineup with the pitchers. This was cutting into the players' free time, and the meetings weren't appreciated despite their scouting value.

Dwight Gooden was one player who didn't seem to mind the meetings, according to Peter Golenbock's book *Amazin'*.

"I thought Jeff did a good job," said Gooden. "He was the most prepared and organized man I ever played for. He was the first manager to have hitters' and pitchers' meetings; the opposing team was thoroughly scouted, and before each series, we went over the strengths and weaknesses. So what was wrong with preparation?"

Absolutely nothing, but Gooden was one of very few who bought into the preparation. Most of his teammates couldn't be bothered, and the apathy swelled as the team began to lose in 1992.

The Mets won their season opener 4–2 in 10 innings at St. Louis on Bonilla's second homer of the night. The Mets dropped six of their next seven but immediately went 12–3, giving them a 14–9 record by May 1. They were just 27–24 following a win over San Francisco June 2, leaving them just a half-game out of first place. Just 2½ weeks later, the Mets were eight games off the pace as the clubhouse sniping grew. Players didn't like the way Torborg handled a game, and to hell with all these stupid rules.

By then, it was evident some of Torborg's most important players weren't quite grasping the team concept. After Bonilla was charged with an error in right field during a game, he got on the dugout phone at the end of the inning. An emergency call? No, he was trying to get in touch with PR director Jay Horwitz to see how and why he was charged with an error. All this after Bonilla had just contributed to the Cubs' seven-run first inning!

Bonilla tried to fib his way through the incident, saying he called his old buddy Horwitz to see how he was feeling. Bonilla said he didn't get to see Horwitz before the game (just show up at batting practice and you'll find that Horwitz is Mr. Ubiquitous) and wanted to know how Horwitz was dealing with his bad cold. The story became the company line, except nobody was believing it.

New York already had been getting to Bonilla, months after he told the media at his first news conference with the Mets that, "You're not going to be able to wipe the smile off my face." Bonilla could be seen wearing earplugs in the outfield during one game. The fans had been riding him hard, due in part to his .130 average at Shea over the first seven weeks of the season. Bonilla claimed he was just taking the advice of hitting Tom McCraw by wearing ear plugs at the plate, and didn't want to take them out because they had to be fitted just right. The writers weren't buying the explanation after being B.S'd a few times already by baseball's richest player.

One of the final public embarrassments of the season came in September, when Coleman was thrown out of a game for arguing a checked-swing third strike. Torborg raced out of the dugout to protect his player from a possible suspension. He tried to lead Coleman back to the dugout. The outfielder shoved him back in a display of defiance and rage. When Torborg demanded an apology, Coleman demanded Torborg do something physically impossible. Coleman was given a two-game suspension.

That incident occurred about two months after Torborg was entangled in a similar situation with Bonilla, who had been tossed from a game for arguing after taking his time stepping into the batter's box following a called strike. Home plate umpire Harry Wendelstedt ordered Steve Avery to throw a pitch while Bonilla lollygagged. Bonilla went face-to-face with Wendelstedt, prompting Torborg to come out of the dugout. Instead of taking up his player's argument, Torborg went after Bonilla, shouting at him to get his head in the game.

Torborg often didn't need any help to create PR snafus. Part of his contract called for him to do a daily report for WFAN. Sometimes, he broke big news about his players, although some of that information was supposed to be kept within the confines of the clubhouse.

When asked why he didn't use closer John Franco at the end of a game the Mets would lose in the ninth, Torborg explained that Franco had a sore elbow. Torborg could have recited his rule that he wouldn't use his closer for more than an inning or in a tie game. Instead, he threw Franco under the bus, enraging the fiery Brooklynite and ruining whatever player-manager relationship the two might have had.

Franco eventually underwent elbow surgery by late September. Saberhagen missed the better part of two months due to a finger injury. Gooden endured his first losing season, and Cone was sent to the Blue Jays at the trade deadline after the Mets decided they wouldn't, or couldn't, resign him at season's end.

The Mets had turned into a disaster that is best chronicled in *The Worst Team Money Can Buy*, by Bob Klapisch and John Harper. By the end of the season, the players didn't want to play, the writers didn't want to write, and the fans didn't want to watch.

After years of back-page headlines and on-field exploits, the Mets had created an air of disinterest during Torborg's first year as manager. And it only got worse in 1993.

Coleman, Bonilla, and Eddie Murray were back for another season of fun and merriment. Bonilla and Murray put up pretty solid numbers in 1993, and the Mets' offense received a boost from Jeff Kent in his first full season with the team. But the pitching was downright horrendous despite the presence of Gooden and Bret Saberhagen. No Mets pitcher made more than 29 starts, and Franco appeared in just 35 games due to a tender elbow, a strained rib cage muscle and a cut on his left thumb.

Not that any of that mattered to Torborg by the end of the season. The Mets got out of the gate with an 8–7 record, thanks in part to a 4–1 mark against the expansion Rockies. But the Mets won just five of their next 23 games, leading to Torborg's dismissal.

Dallas Green would guide the club to a 46–78 mark the rest of the way, completing the Mets' worst season since 1965.

Joe Torre   1977–1981

Born: July 18, 1940 Brooklyn, N.Y.
Named Manager: 5/31/77
Dismissed: 10/4/81

Joe Torre Mets Managerial Record

YEAR	GMS	W	L	PCT	POS.
1977	117	49	68	.419	6th, NL East
1978	162	66	96	.407	6th, NL East
1979	162	63	99	.389	6th, NL East
1980	162	67	95	.414	5th, NL East
1981	103	41	62	.398	5th, NL East
Total	706	286	420	.405	

Major League Totals

YEARS	GMS	W	L	PCT
1977–2010	4329	2326	1997	.538

Joe Torre was in the unenviable position of inheriting a ballclub that had deteriorated and was about to get worse. Torre didn't pay attention to the negatives, looking at it as an opportunity to become a manager at the big-league level, and doing it while overlapping his playing career.

He was enjoying a bounce-back season for the Mets in 1976, hitting .300 while platooning at first and third base. He learned that he was being shopped around by the Mets but let them know he would like to remain with the organization past his playing career.

"In '76 general manager Joe McDonald came up to me and asked 'How would you like to go to the Yankees?' I said, 'Well, I've never been on a pennant winner, but just in the event that you change managers down the road, as long as I'm going to be considered, then fine. But I want to let you know that I'd like an opportunity—in the event you make a change in the next couple of years—to be considered.'

"I don't know why I wasn't traded to the Yankees. Whether they couldn't get together on a player or what I said had an impact."

Torre's veteran leadership was appreciated by more than a few Mets. Former teammate Leon Brown said Torre always loved to talk baseball with anyone and used the chats as a learning experience for both parties.

"I learned so much baseball—that I didn't know—from Joe Torre. He gave a lot of information, and he'd asked, 'Why did you think that' every time we had a disagreement about something," Brown said.

"He was the kind of guy that said, 'Be honest.' And when we disagreed on something, he wanted to know why. And I've seen him use a lot of the strategies that we talked about in his baseball. He did listen, and that's why he is where he is today.

"We'd sit there and we dissected games. At least he did, and I'd listen most of the time. Every now and then he'd ask me a question. We didn't always agree. He was the veteran and I had to learn from him. And I did."

The Mets were in the market for a manager less than a year after Torre spelled out his desires to McDonald. New York already was 10½ games out of first place by May 11, 1977, and would climb out of the basement for just one day after that. The Mets began speaking with Torre about taking over while Joe Frazier was still running the team.

"We're playing an exhibition game in Tidewater," Torre said. "During the early part of the game—I was shaving because you try to get in and out of those small clubhouses so the guys who weren't playing could get that stuff out of the way—my general manager walked in and said 'How would you like to manage this team?'

"I wind up going the next day to meet with M. Donald Grant in New York City. We agreed that I would be the next manager. The only thing is, they didn't know at the time when they were going to make that move. It was probably four, five, six days later that they officially made the decision."

Torre was more than happy to take over for Frazier, although he was saddled with a roster of underachieving kids and disgruntled prospects. He was also in charge of players who were his teammates just a day earlier, but Torre didn't believe the transition was difficult.

"I was still the senior citizen over there [as a player]. A lot of players looked to me as the older guy, the more experienced guy. So the transition of being a manager was a little unusual, but there was some kind of separation based on my experience."

Less than three weeks into the job, Torre saw the Mets trade Tom Seaver and Dave Kingman, leaving the team without its Hall of Fame pitcher and top run producer.

"That was a difficult time. I took over the 31st of May and then June 15 we're trading Seaver and we're trading Kingman and Mike Phillips. There was a lot of crap that went on, but the fact of the matter is I was still excited about getting this opportunity to manage at the big league level. Unfortunately, [losing key players] happens. When it comes down to players who are unhappy, something has to be done about it, and Tom Seaver, unfortunately, had to be moved out of town to Cincinnati."

The Mets actually performed well once Torre took over for Frazier, winning seven of their first eight to get within nine games of .500. Ironically, Seaver beat Pat Zachry 8–0 on June 7 to give the Mets a 22–31 record.

Torre actually remained on the active roster until June 18, making him the National League's first player/manager since Solly Hemus with St. Louis in 1959. He put himself into two games as a pinch-hitter, going 0-for-1 with a walk.

A week after the Seaver trade, the Mets began a 2–15 stretch that left them 21½ games out of first place by July 8, killing any shot at a .500 season. Yet, Torre was feeling a rebirth in baseball by running the ballclub after spending the previous two-plus seasons as a platoon player.

"Anytime you get your first manager job—you go from being a part-time player and all of a sudden you're a manager—it's like being a regular player again. It was exciting for me to get that opportunity in my hometown like that."

Although the Mets were terrible at that point, they continued to play hard for Torre. Unfortunately, "hard-working, but lousy" would be the pattern for the Mets under Torre until his dismissal at the end of the 1981 season.

It didn't matter who managed the Mets in the late '70s and early '80s. They were going to stink as long as the de Roulets allowed Grant to control the purse strings. The Yankees signed Reggie Jackson during the winter of 1977. The Mets signed nobody that winter and wouldn't pick up a free agent of any significance during Grant's Reign of Error. The Yankees signed Tommy John, Luis Tiant, and Goose Gossage. The Mets countered with contracts for Wayne Twitchell and Tom Hausman.

"I remember Joe was still learning how to handle pitchers," said Jerry Koosman, "when to take them out, when to leave them in, etc. It's a tough thing to learn if you've never been a pitcher.

"I also remember that year Joe pinch-hit for me at least one time, maybe two when the game was 0–0 and we had a runner on second with two outs. He told me, 'I've got to take advantage of scoring every run we can because we're not scoring runs.' I said, 'Geez, at least give me a chance to throw a shutout. You call the bullpen and the bullpen is always good for three or four runs. Let me throw a shutout.'

"He was more of a hitters' manager starting out, and the bullpen couldn't save any games for me. We just didn't have a very good ballclub then."

Torre did what he could with what little he had, although he gave everyone a chance to prove they belonged. He also had his players putting out maximum effort despite their record.

"I always feel you try to control what you can, and that's playing hard and working hard and doing all that stuff. If it's not good enough to win, it's not good enough to win, but we were going to do everything we could to try to be as good a club as we could be, do the things we could do and try to do them well."

"Torre handled the players well," remembered Craig Swan in the book *Amazin'*. "He used what he had. There are only so many things you can do during a ball game, and it seemed he did those things."

And it seemed the players liked working for Torre. The 1979 Mets were in danger of losing 100 games for the first time in 12 years, falling to 57–99 with a loss to the Cubs in Game 1 of a doubleheader. They managed to keep their loss total in double-digits.

"I was proud of the fact that we were trying not to lose 100 games and I think we had to win the last five or six in a row not to lose 100 that one year.

"Different teams, you have different carrots you have to dangle for yourself."

The Mets had nine players from their 1973 NL pennant team on the roster when Torre took over for Frazier in '77. All were gone by the start of the 1980 season, yet Torre's team actually played very good ball for a three-month stretch in 1980 and was still alive in the 1981 second-half race until the final week.

The 1980 Mets opened 9–18, putting them 8½ games off the pace by mid-May. They won 10 of their next 14 and were in fourth place less than a month later. The climb continued, and the Mets were 42–42 and just four games out of first place on July 15. They continued to play around .500 and were 7½ games back when they opened a five-game series against the Phillies at Shea in mid-August. A sweep would have had Mets fans thinking about a division title. Instead, the Mets were swept by a combined 40–12 score, jumpstarting a stretch in which they dropped 25 of 28.

"We had some players who we lost [due to injury]. We always knew that we were relying on the people we had. We didn't have a lot of depth, but you do as well as you can. If it's not good enough, so be it. You try to make adjustments from there."

Torre was on the hot seat by the start of the 1981 season. Frank Cashen was entering his second season as general manager and wanted to see some improvement after using the previous season as an evaluation tool. The players did nothing to save Torre's job in the first half of the '81 campaign, starting off 17–34 before the players strike. The strike shaved 59 games off the schedule, which was a blessing in itself. Once the strike was settled, commissioner Bowie Kuhn gave the Mets new life by cutting the season into halves and giving playoff berths to the division winners of each half.

The Mets started the second half 6–2 but failed to win more than two straight for about a month after that. They finally strung together a four-game winning streak that put them 20–20, just 2½ games off the division lead with 12 to play. But the Mets closed the season by losing eight of 12 to finish the second half in fourth place. Anything short of a postseason berth wasn't going to be enough for Cashen to retain Torre. The team announced during the season finale that Torre wouldn't be back.

"He obviously didn't have the weapons or the arsenal

he had later with the Yankees, but he was a tough task-master then," recalled Ed Lynch, who pitched for Torre from 1980 to 1981. "It was a different world in '81 than the world that Joe came back into in '96.

"Obviously, when you have the caliber of player he inherited with the Yankees, it was a lot different than the caliber of player he inherited when he took over with the Mets in '77.

"He was tough, but he taught me a lot. The thing that meant most to me was, the day he got fired, I went into his office. I remember he was getting dressed, and I went in and said, 'Joe, I just wanted to thank you for the opportunity that you gave me.' And he says, 'You know what? You're a tough son of a bitch.' And I said, 'Joe, that's the highest compliment anyone can give you.' Because I pitched in '81 with a bad arm and I knew I might not get a second opportunity, so I went out there and pitched with basically a very, very sore elbow. I think he appreciated that and that meant the world to me. And I have the utmost respect for Joe."

Torre was quickly hired as the Braves' skipper for 1982. The '82 Braves won their first 13 games of the season and captured the NL West for the first time since 1969.

Torre later managed the Cardinals and became one of the most successful managers in Yankees history, winning four World Series and six pennants while reaching the postseason in each of his 12 seasons in pinstripes. Torre became the Dodgers' skipper in November 2007 after refusing a one-year contract to remain with the Yanks. He guided the Dodgers to consecutive NL West titles while extending his string of consecutive playoff appearances to 14, tying Bobby Cox of Atlanta.

Torre had the Dodgers in contention for a third-straight playoff berth in 2010 until injuries to several key players pushed them out of the races. He announced in late September that he was stepping down after the season. Although he was now 70 years old, Torre didn't rule out a possible return to someone's dugout.

Bobby Valentine　　　1996–2002

Born: May 13, 1950　　Stamford, Connecticut
Named Manager: 8/26/96
Dismissed: 10/1/02
NL Wild Card, 1999, 2000　　NL Pennant, 2000

Bobby Valentine Managerial Record

YEAR	GMS	W	L	PCT	POS.
1996	31	12	19	.387	4th, NL East
1997	162	88	74	.543	3rd, NL East
1998	162	88	74	.543	2nd, NL East
1999	163	97	66	.595	2nd, NL East
2000	162	94	68	.580	2nd, NL East
2001	162	82	80	.506	3rd, NL East
2002	161	75	86	.466	5th, NL East
Total	1003	536	467	.534	

Major League Totals

YEAR	GMS	W	L	PCT
1985–2002	2189	1117	1072	.510

The Mets hadn't had much success since they fired the somewhat cocky, occasionally outspoken Davey Johnson, who was a player's manager while leading the team to two postseasons in the mid- to late '80s. The Mets' fortunes began to turn in 1996, when they hired the somewhat cocky, occasionally outspoken Bobby Valentine, who was a player's manager while leading the team to two postseasons.

Johnson played the latter portion of his career in Japan. Valentine has spent two stints as a manager in the Japanese Leagues. The two also shared the same Mets dugout for a little over a season, with Valentine serving as Johnson's third-base coach before being hired as manager of the Texas Rangers in 1985.

Valentine began the 1996 managing the Tidewater Tides after leading the Chiba Lotte Marines to a team-record second-place finish the previous year. He was let go by the Marines following the '95 season, reportedly because he had become more popular than the general manager.

The Mets were languishing in fourth place, 13 games under .500 and 23 games behind the first-place Braves when Valentine replaced Dallas Green in late August. New York had high hopes after posting the National League's best record over the final 52 games of 1995. The Mets had put together one of the best-hitting clubs in franchise history, but the projected plan of having Paul Wilson, Jason Isringhausen, and Bill Pulsipher win 15 games apiece never came to fruition.

Green's firing was not the decision of general manager Joe Mcilvaine. That edict came down from team co-owner Fred Wilpon, who made the decision shortly after Green said of Pulsipher, Wilson and Isringhausen, "They don't belong in the big leagues. That may sound harsh and negative, but what have they done to get here?"

What Pulsipher and Isringhausen had done was prevent Green from getting fired after the 1995 season. Wilpon gave him a stay of execution after the Mets' strong finish. But Pulsipher underwent major elbow surgery in April. Isringhausen pitched ineffectively before undergoing shoulder and elbow procedures. Wilson had surgery to repair a torn labrum in his right shoulder after the season.

Green was a rigid disciplinarian who could intimidate with a firm handshake or an angry stare, whereas Valentine used psychological warfare to get his point across. Valentine often went through the media to spark a player, whether it was a left-handed compliment or a flat-out criticism.

The Mets actually played worse under Valentine than they did for Green in '96, but the team was more relaxed as it tried to complete a lost season.

Valentine spent those 31 games more as an observer, and he watched Lance Johnson and Todd Hundley complete record-breaking seasons. Johnson shattered team marks with 21 triples and 230 hits, and Hundley became the single-season leader with 41 homers, then a major league record for catchers.

But the rotation was in shambles, leaving Mark Clark and Bobby Jones as Valentine's most dependable starters by season's end.

McIlvaine come up empty at the winter meetings, prompting Valentine to intimate that the team needed to be more aggressive in the free agent market. Valentine wanted another hitter in front of Hundley, along with some bullpen help. McIlvaine came through in January by stealing first baseman John Olerud from Toronto. Olerud had led the American League in hitting at .363 in 1993, but his average had spiraled each subsequent year, bottoming out at .274 in 1996.

Valentine came out of 1997 spring training with a pitching staff primarily consisting of journeymen and cast-offs featuring Armando Reynoso, Brian Bohanon, Pete Harnisch, Dave Mlicki, and a former replacement player named Rick Reed. The assemblage of hurlers didn't exactly cause Mets fans to save money for postseason tickets, but Valentine got plenty of mileage out of most of them eventually.

The Mets opened the season 8–14 before winning 23 of their next 32. They shuttled between third and fourth place before moving into a tie for second on July 24, a spot they occupied for four days before staying in third the rest of the season.

You could forget about a set lineup with Valentine at the helm, at least in '97. He had 10 players who would appear in at least 112 games, and the batting order would shuffle according to who was hot, who was cold, and who was pitching. What Valentine did was give his core group of players plenty of at-bats, while displaying confidence in each of them.

Valentine had the Mets in the wild-card chase throughout the second half of the season despite sub-par performances from three of his most important hitters. Bernard Gilkey batted just .197 with six homers and 28 RBIs in his first 60 games, one year after hitting .317 with 30 homers, 117 RBIs, and a team-record 44 doubles. Hundley's production also dropped as he battled a sore elbow, and second baseman Carlos Baerga hardly resembled the player who averaged 19 homers and more than 90 RBIs while batting over .300 in each of his final four full seasons with the Indians.

Valentine chose Hundley to take the heat, intimating to the media that his catcher wasn't getting enough sleep, which fueled speculation that Hundley's carousing had led to his falloff.

Valentine also had problems with pitcher Pete Harnisch, who was hospitalized for depression during the season. Before Harnisch was diagnosed, he had a meeting with Valentine in which he felt his skipper insinuated the right-hander was afraid to pitch.

Things escalated in late August, when Harnisch verbally assaulted Valentine at a Baltimore hotel before telling WFAN, "There's not really a guy on this team that respects Bobby Valentine." The manager quickly received the backing of Gilkey, Butch Huskey, and Carl Everett. Even Hundley chipped in, saying, "I respect Bobby and his staff." Harnisch was dealt to Milwaukee by early September.

Valentine had won a turf battle in the clubhouse. He also was working with a new general manager after McIlvaine was replaced by Steve Phillips in July. Valentine had grown frustrated when asking the front office for reinforcements, only to find out McIlvaine was scouting his own minor league prospects.

Phillips hoped he had bolstered the Mets' postseason chances by working out a deal that sent Johnson, Clark, and Manny Alexander to the Cubs for Brian McRae, Turk Wendell, and Mel Rojas on August 8. But Wendell pitched spotty at best, Rojas was an arsonist at times, and McRae's bat didn't match up to Johnson's.

The Mets finished the 1997 season 88-74, five games off the wild-card lead. Reed was the surprise of the staff, going 13–9 with a 2.89 ERA in his first full season in the majors. Jones made the National League All-Star team before finishing with 15 wins, the most by a Mets hurler since Frank Viola won 20 games and Dwight Gooden won 19 in 1990. The performances of Reed and Jones seemed to contradict Harnisch's charge that Valentine and pitching coach Bob Apodaca were a joke.

Valentine also received valuable production from Olerud, who batted .294 with 22 homers and a team-high 102 RBIs. Olerud's new manager let him play his game after Blue Jays skipper Cito Gaston had asked him to hit with more power. Olerud didn't have the home run stroke, and his average suffered in Toronto. Chalk one up to Valentine, who still desired another power hitter when the 1998 season opened.

Phillips bolstered the rotation in the off-season, getting Al Leiter from the Marlins for A.J. Burnett and two other prospects. Leiter thus became the first dependable lefty starter at Valentine's disposal and would serve as the team's ace for most of his stay with the Mets.

Leiter opened the season pitching to Alberto Castillo, who had inherited the catching chores while Hundley recovered from elbow and shoulder surgery. Hundley was expected to be out until mid-June.

Masato Yoshii was signed from Japan and thrust into the rotation. Valentine was familiar with Yoshii, having managed against him in the Japanese Central League.

The Mets entered the 1998 season with a good, but not great, lineup. Edgardo Alfonzo was coming off a breakout season in which he batted .315 with 72 RBIs. But without Hundley, Valentine had to hope Gilkey and Baerga could regain their power stroke while McRae continued to produce extra-base hits.

Olerud seemed poised to break Cleon Jones' team-record .340 average, compiling a .343 mark by May 21. Alfonzo was batting just .239 by May 21, and he and Olerud had combined for only seven homers from what is supposed to be the power positions of the infield.

In fact, the Mets had belted just 25 homers in their first 43 games when the front office finally gave Valentine a power threat. Having successfully pried Leiter from the Marlins, the team went back to Florida to solve their power deficiency. Just a few days after being acquired by the Marlins, Mike Piazza was sent to the Mets in a package that included outfielder Preston Wilson. The home run problem was solved, but another situation emerged.

Before Piazza's arrival, the plan was for Hundley to be given time to recover from his surgeries before reclaiming his starting job behind the plate. Days before the Piazza deal, Phillips said publicly the Mets weren't looking to acquire the All-Star catcher and expected to have Hundley handling the pitchers in 1999. It's not certain if Phillips had just fibbed or that owner Fred Wilpon had engineered the trade. Either way, Valentine now had a ticked-off Hundley who would soon prove he was as good an outfielder as Piazza was a first baseman.

Hurt feelings aside, the Mets had a playoff berth to clinch. The Braves were in the process of running away with the NL East title, but New York was within 1½ games of the wild-card-leading Cubs when Piazza made his Mets debut May 23. He hit an RBI double in his first game as a Met, a 3–0 win over the Brewers.

But Valentine had to wait a while before enjoying Piazza's power stroke. Piazza hit a torrid .331 in his first 43 games as a Met, but that included just five homers and 17 RBIs. Some impatient Mets fans started booing him for his inability to produce game-breaking hits while the team stayed in the playoff race. The Mets played a game under .500 during that span, but the team got hot once he found his power stroke.

On July 29 Piazza began a 48-game stretch in which he batted .364 with 16 homers and 49 RBIs. The Mets went 31–20 during that span, leaving them just a ½-game behind the wild-card-leading Cubs. At the same time, Olerud hit .366 with 10 homers and 36 RBIs. Alfonzo, who had hit 18 career homers entering the season, already had 17 with 76 RBIs by mid-September.

By the time Leiter picked up his 17th victory of the season on September 20, the Mets held a one-game lead over the Cubs and a magic number of five for winning the wild-card. The Cubs went just 3-3 the rest of the season, taking three games off that magic number. But the Mets ended the year with a five-game losing streak when just one victory would have forced a three-way tie with the Cubs and Giants.

The Cubs and Giants lost their regular season finales, which would have given the Mets a chance to extend their season. Valentine has asked Hideo Nomo to start the season finale in Atlanta and halt the team's losing streak. But Nomo, who seemed to alternate one decent start with one horrible outing, declined to make that start, forcing Valentine to go with Armando Reynoso in the most important game of his major league managerial career.

Nomo eventually threw four brilliant innings of three-hit shutout ball, but it came after Reynoso was torched for five runs in less than two innings. The Cubs and Giants played a one-game playoff at Wrigley Field, hours after the Mets had put their clubhouse belongings in garbage bags and bade farewell to Shea until next season.

Hundley, who batted .161 in 134 at-bats and made five errors in 34 games as a left fielder, was sent to the Dodgers, Piazza original team. Hundley was replaced by 40-year-old Rickey Henderson, who hit only .236 in his latest return to the Athletics in '98.

The Hundley trade was part of a very successful three-team swap in which the Mets received outfielder Roger Cedeno from the Dodgers and Armanto Benitez from the Orioles.

The Mets also traded one headache for another, sending the unproductive Rojas to the Dodgers for Bobby Bonilla.

New York had to alter its infield after signing free-agent Robin Ventura, the power-hitting, slick-fielding third baseman. Ventura's presence sent Alfonzo to second base, where he continued to play exceptional defense.

But the biggest signing of the 1998–1999 off-season was Piazza, who accepted a seven-year contract rather than test the free-agent market.

Valentine had a retooled roster when he reported to St. Lucie in February 1999. Cedeno and Henderson would give him much more speed after the Mets finished last in the National League with 62 steals in 1998. The infield consisted of potential Gold Glovers in Olerud, Alfonzo, Ventura, and shortstop Rey Ordonez, who already had won Gold Gloves the last two years.

The outfield arms were not the greatest, but Henderson, McRae, and Cedeno would make up for that by covering a lot of ground.

Benitez represented another setup man for Franco, who also had Wendell and Dennis Cook working the late innings.

Phillips seemed to have assembled a vastly improved roster, but you wouldn't know it by the team's 27–28 start. The Mets were scoring plenty of runs, but the team ERA was a dismal 4.87 through 55 games. Leiter and Reed had seen a spike in their earned run averages, and Jones was trying to rediscover his All-Star form of 1997.

In the first power-play move involving Phillips and Valentine, Bob Apodaca was dismissed as pitching coach and replaced by Dave Wallace. Bullpen coach Randy Niemann also was reassigned, as was hitting coach Tom Robson. The firings served as a reminder to Valentine that he didn't have final say in personnel decisions. Phillips had done a nice job adding depth to the lineup and bench. It was up to Valentine to get the team out of its slump. That Apodaca, Niemann, and Robson were let go in the middle of a series with the Yankees was not lost on Valentine. But the skipper defiantly said, "I'm not worried about my job. I believe that if in the next 55 games we're not better, I shouldn't be the manager."

The Mets turned it on after that, winning 40 of those 55 games to jump back into the division race. But they did

Mets Managers' Records After:

	50 Gms	100 Gms	200 Gms	250 Gms	300 Gms	400 Gms	500 Gms	600 Gms
Casey Stengel	13–37	26–74	56–143–1	69–180–1	84–215–1	113–285–2	150–348–2	
Wes Westrum	14–36	32–67–1	76–123–1	93–156–1	112–187–1			
Gil Hodges	23–27	47–53	91–109	124–126	154–146	213–187	263–237	314–286
Yogi Berra	33–17	55–45	104–96	125–125	152–148	201–199	246–254	
Roy McMillan	24–26							
Joe Frazier	24–26	51–49	100–100					
Joe Torre	23–27	42–58	84–116	102–148	123–177	166–233–1	205–294–1	244–355–1
George Bamberger	27–23	44–56	80–120					
Frank Howard	19–31	45–55						
Davey Johnson	27–23	59–41	113–87	141–109	174–126	242–158	304–196	361–239
Bud Harrelson	34–16	61–39	117–83	135–115				
Jeff Torborg	26–24	49–51	85–115					
Dallas Green	14–36	34–66	79–121	106–144	124–176	177–223	226–274	
Bobby Valentine	19–31	49–51	105–95	133–117	157–143	213–187	277–223	332–268
Art Howe	22–28	42–58	85–115	111–139	127–173			
Willie Randolph	26–24	51–49	107–93	135–115	169–131	223–177	276–224	
Jerry Manuel	29–21	58–42	106–94	122–128	147–153			
Terry Collins	23–27	50–50						

so without Valentine for a two-game stretch after he was suspended for a comical incident during an extra-inning win over Toronto at Shea on June 9.

Valentine was ejected during the game for arguing a close call. He dutifully traipsed to the clubhouse to watch the rest of the game on television. But this was before HD, and Valentine wanted a clear image of the action.

In the bottom of the 12th, a man wearing a Mets T-shirt, sunglasses (this was a night game), and a phony mustache was seen in the Mets' dugout. It was Valentine, who was caught on camera. The commissioner's office levied a suspension and a fine, causing him to miss part of a subsequent road trip. The Mets won both games without Valentine.

The Mets lowered their ERA to 4.14 in their first 69 games under Wallace, going a torrid 49–20 in the process. It was the team's best sustained period since 1988, and it put the Mets into a first-place tie with the Braves at 75–48.

But the pitching was a very small part of the team's surge. The Mets' infield defense was among the best ever assembled as Olerud, Alfonzo, Ordonez, and Ventura combined for just 27 errors the entire season. Ordonez and Ventura each won Gold Gloves at the end of the season, and Alfonzo was more than deserving after posting a .993 field percentage (five errors in 712 chances) while playing a new position. The Mets had streaks of 38, 21, 17, and 13 games in which they didn't allow an unearned run.

Valentine also utilized the team's speed to its full capacity. The Mets stole only 62 bases in 1998. Cedeno topped that by himself a year later, swiping a team-record 66 bags while Henderson added 37 thefts. New York ended up with 150 steals, nine short of the club mark.

The Mets were battling the Braves for the division lead in late July when Phillips acquired starter pitcher Kenny Rogers, relievers Chuck McElroy and Billy Taylor, outfielder Darryl Hamilton and utilityman Shawon Dunston. New York went ahead by as many as two games over the second-place Braves while putting together a five-game winning streak at the beginning of August. Later that month, the Mets won 12 of 16 but actually lost ground on Atlanta.

Valentine seemed to have the Mets on cruise control at the start of September. They opened the month 12–5 to climb 34 games over .500 for the first time since 1988. The stretch left New York with the second-best record in the league, just a game behind the Braves and four games ahead of the Reds for the wild card. Fans began to focus on a potential division title with a playoff spot practically locked up.

But suddenly the Mets couldn't hit the ball, leading to a seven-game losing streak that was reminiscent of the team's season-ending five-game skid the previous year. New York batted just .215 with 15 runs and 12 extra-base hits during the slide.

The bats awoke while Leiter pitched the Mets to a 9–2 victory in Atlanta, but the Braves took the rubber game of the series, leaving New York two games behind the Reds and Astros for the wild-card lead with three games remaining. Cincinnati and Houston also were tied for first in the NL Central. The Mets could at least force a one-game playoff with a sweep of the Pirates, provided the Reds or Astros dropped two of their final three games.

The Pirates were about to complete their seventh consecutive losing season. However, the Reds and Astros were also wrapping up their schedule versus sub-.500 ballclubs.

A postseason berth—and Valentine's job—lay in the balance as Kenny Rogers took the mound for Game 1 versus the Pirates. Unlike the old days when Mets fans would cling to hope with the team so close to a playoff spot, just 29,528 bothered to come to the game, figuring there was no way the Reds or Astros were about to lose their final series.

But a mini-miracle was about to unfold. The Mets won the series opener in 11 innings, then slaughtered the Bucs in Game 2 in front of about 18,000 empty seats. Meanwhile, the Reds dropped the first two games of their series, leaving the Mets and Cincinnati in a tie for the wild-card heading into the final day of the season.

Shea was packed for the season finale as Orel Hershiser tried to pitch the Mets into the playoffs. Hershiser and the bullpen had combined to hold the Bucs to three hits while every one of Valentine's pitching moves worked out. But the game was tied 1–1 in the bottom of the ninth when Melvin Mora, hitting .133 on the season, singled with one out.

Mora had entered the game as a defensive replacement for Henderson. Valentine still had Shawon Dunston on the bench, but he elected to use the rookie who spent the previous year playing in China.

Alfonzo followed with a single to put runners on first and third. Olerud was walked intentionally to load the bases before Mora scampered home with the winning run after reliever Brad Clontz threw a wild pitch to Piazza.

The Reds managed to win their final game following a lengthy rain delay, setting up a one-game playoff in Cincinnati. Valentine had Leiter pitching on his regular fifth day, and the lefty put the Mets into the postseason with a two-hit shutout of the Reds.

It's one thing to have brains, and another to possess a talented bullpen. Valentine had both and he worked them to perfection in the NLDS against the Diamondbacks. The relievers threw 3 1/3 shutout innings of one-hit relief in the opener, keeping the game tied long enough for Edgardo Alfonzo to hit a grand slam in the ninth.

A pair of lopsided games followed, the Diamondbacks easily winning Game 2 and the Mets blasting Arizona in Game 3 before Valentine asked his new closer, Benitez, to bail out Leiter in the eighth inning with a 2–1 lead in Game 4.

Benitez had taken the closer's role after Franco was placed on the DL July 3. Benitez had been fantastic at the position, but he surrendered a go-ahead two-run double to Jay Bell before Cedeno lifted a fly ball to tie the game in the bottom half.

Benitez was perfect in the ninth, as was John Franco an inning later. Franco got the victory, and the Mets advanced to the NLCS, when backup catcher Todd Pratt belted a homer over the center-field wall in the 10th.

Pratt started the last two games following a thumb injury to Piazza. The Mets scored 13 runs with Piazza out of the lineup.

New York began a series against the hated Braves around the time a lengthy *Sports Illustrated* article about Valentine hit the stands. In it, he questioned the intelligence of some of his players and discussed the purge of his coaching staff. The timing of the article couldn't have been worse for Valentine, who saw his team drop the first three games of the NLCS with a rather underwhelming offense.

The Mets stayed alive when John Olerud's two-run single in the eighth gave them a 3–2 win in Game 4. That set up an incredible 15-inning game that made baseball fans recall New York's 16-inning epic against Houston.

Valentine went through nine pitchers and had Game 3 starter Rick Reed warming up in the bullpen. The Braves went ahead on Keith Lockhart's RBI triple in the 15th, but Todd Pratt worked out a bases-loaded walk before Robin Ventura hit a grand-slam single to end it. Ventura had homered but was only credited with a single after a jubilant Pratt went to bearhug the game's hero, thus crossing the basepaths with Ventura.

Another miracle seemed possible despite the fact that no team had ever come back from a 3–0 deficit in a major league postseason series. But Valentine had his ace on the mound, just long enough for Leiter to yield five runs in the bottom of the first.

The Mets eventually tied the game 7–7 before blowing one-run leads in both the eighth and 10th innings. John Franco and Armando Benitez had wasted those leads, and Valentine was down to Rogers at the start of the 11th.

Rogers had pitched poorly in playoff starts against the Diamondbacks and Braves, and he ended the Mets' season by walking Andruw Jones with the bases loaded.

Later on, it was reported that the little-used Bonilla spent the last three innings of the game playing cards with Henderson, who was lifted in the eighth inning after going 2-for-5 with an RBI and a run scored. Several Mets were outraged that the two would retreat to the clubhouse during a do-or-die game. The card game distracted the minds of those who had spent most of the last two years second-guessing Valentine's game strategy.

The *Sports Illustrated* article and the Rogers collapse had blown over by the time Valentine assembled the Mets for spring training. The regular season would begin in Japan, where Valentine remained popular with local fans.

Valentine was a fantastic goodwill ambassador for the team and major league baseball while the Mets prepared for a two-game trip to Tokyo. He was able to address the media in Japanese, which endeared him even more to the locals.

Valentine selected newly acquired Mike Hampton as his opening-day starter, but the lefty issued nine walks in losing to the Cubs.

The Mets had sent Cedeno and Octavio Dotel to the Astros for Hampton, who was expected to solidify the rotation. Hampton pitched poorly in his first four starts before going 14–7 with a 2.80 ERA the rest of the way.

Valentine also had to deal with Henderson, who by now was covering more ground on a card table than he could in left field. Henderson also got off to a bad start at the plate while angling for a contract extension. The all-time stolen base leader eventually was released, leaving the left-field position open for Benny Agbayani.

The Mets also had to deal with the loss of Ordonez, who broke his arm while covering second base on a stolen base attempt in the first inning of a game May 29. Valentine inserted the versatile Mora at short, but the results were often catastrophic.

With Mora at short and newly acquired Todd Zeile at first, the Mets' infield defense was considerably weaker than it had been in 1999. Phillips fixed that by getting slick-fielding Mike Bordick from the Orioles for Mora, a wonderful short-term move that had long-term ramifications.

But it would be a highly successful season for Valentine and the Mets. Hampton added depth to the rotation, Bordick solidified the infield, and rookie Jay Payton and new right fielder Derek Bell gave the Mets more power.

Valentine also had a deeper bench after pinch-hitter deluxe Lenny Harris returned to the team. Ventura's average dropped 69 points, but the outfielders picked up the offensive slack.

The Mets stayed away from the ridiculous highs and lows that defined 1999. They had a good grasp on the wild-card over the summer while preventing the Braves from running away with the division. Atlanta clinched the NL East at Shea on September 27, but the Mets wrapped up the wild-card with a win over the Braves a day later. Valentine became the first Mets manager to lead the franchise to the postseason in back-to-back years.

Hampton opened the NLDS the way he began the season, by pitching horribly. The Giants took the series opener and forced extra innings in Game 2 when Benitez served up a three-run homer to J.T. Snow in the ninth. But Franco closed out a 10-inning victory by getting Barry Bonds on a called third strike.

The Mets went ahead 2–1 in the series on Benny Agbayani's solo blast in the 12th before Bobby Jones put together a superb performance in the Game 4 clincher. Jones, who posted a 5.06 ERA during the regular season, threw a one-hit shutout and came within a Jeff Kent double of joining Don Larsen as the only pitchers to throw a no-hitter in postseason play.

The NLCS offered little drama after Hampton tossed seven shutout innings in the opener. Piazza, who had been criticized in the past for underperforming in the postseason, hit .412 with two homers and four RBIs.

But the key to the series was Timo Perez, a little-used outfielder who took over in right when Bell suffered a high ankle sprain in Game 1 of the NLDS. Perez scored eight of the Mets' 31 runs in the NLCS while hitting .304.

Once again, a Valentine hunch worked. He could have pressed Hamilton of Bubba Trammell into service following Bell's injury, but the manager wanted them as pinch-hitters.

The series ended when Hampton tossed a three-hitter in a 7–0 shutout of the Cardinals in Game 5. The Mets had won their first pennant in 14 years. They now waited for the Yankees to wrap up their ALCS with Seattle before preparing for the first Subway Series since 1956.

The Mets were overmatched, winning just one game in a tight five-game series while the Bombers captured their 26th World Series title. But it wouldn't be a postseason series loss without some criticism directed at Valentine, particularly after the Game 5 clincher.

Leiter had pitched well over eight innings, allowing five hits and two walks while striking out seven. He rarely pitched into the ninth that year and had two complete games to his credit during the regular season. Although Leiter's pitch count was high, Valentine elected to have him work the ninth, when he would be facing the teeth of the Yankees' power in a 2–2 game.

There was no second-guessing after Leiter fanned Tino Martinez and Paul O'Neill to start the ninth. Jorge Posada kept the inning alive with a walk before Scott Brosius singled to put runners on first and second.

Leiter was now desperate for an out, breathing hard as he tried to retire the light-hitting Luis Sojo. On his 142nd and final pitch of the night, Leiter got Sojo to hit a soft grounder that took several hops as it reached the infield dirt. But the ball eluded a diving Kurt Abbott, allowing Posada to score the tiebreaking run. Brosius scampered home when Jay Payton's throw to the plate bounced off a sliding Posada and into foul territory.

Leiter was now out of the game, and the Mets were out of time.

There was little reason to feel Valentine wouldn't have his team contending for a 2001 playoff berth. However, it took five months before the Mets took a serious stab at their third consecutive postseason appearance.

Hampton fled the Mets for a free-agent contract with the Rockies, saying he liked the school system and family atmosphere in Denver. Jones was allowed to become a free agent despite his one-hitter against the Giants in the postseason. Jones had struggled during the 2000 regular season and would enjoy little success with the '01 Padres.

The Mets filled the rotation by landing Kevin Appier and Steve Trachsel, a pair of innings eaters who could give the bullpen a break.

There were few changes to the lineup, although Ordonez was healthy again and Perez had earned a platoon role in the outfield.

The Mets signed outfielder Tsuyoshi Shinjo, one of the first two Japanese position players to become an everyday player in the majors. The other was Ichiro Suzuki, who also was beginning his first major league season. Suzuki was the American League MVP and Rookie of the Year. Shinjo didn't have a bad season, batting .268 with 10 homers and 56 RBIs in 400 at-bats.

The 2001 season was a major struggle for Valentine as he watched Ventura and Alfonzo battle injuries while hitting far below their expected numbers. Ventura finished second on the team with just 21 homers while hitting a meager .237 with 101 strikeouts. Alfonzo saw his batting average drop 81 points to .243 while his RBI total fell by nearly 50 percent.

Just three Mets hit more than 10 homers in 2001 as the team finished 15th in the league with 147.

Appier pitched well from start to finish, but Trachsel was dreadful in his first eight starts. He was sent to the minors after serving up four homers in the third inning of a 6–1 loss to the Padres, which left his record 1–6 with an 8.24 ERA.

The bullpen, the backbone of the staff the previous two seasons, was downright ordinary and inconsistent. Of their top five relievers, only Wendell had an ERA below 3.77, and he would implode after being traded to the Phillies in July.

The pen had made Valentine look like a genius at times during the two-year postseason run. Now, he could never be sure what to expect after handing the ball to one of his relievers.

The rotation was supposed to be the big question mark entering the 2001 campaign. Instead, it became the team's strength, which didn't bode well for the Mets.

The Mets opened the season by taking two of three from the Braves in Atlanta. That would be the last time New York was over the .500 mark until September 19. The Mets were a season-worst 14 games under .500 as late as August 17 and they were 13½ games out of first a day later.

Things got so bad that Phillips had started to build for the future in July, dealing Wendell and Cook to the Phillies for Bruce Chen and a minor leaguer, four days after sending Pratt to the Phils for fellow catcher Gary Bennett.

Highly touted prospect Alex Escobar made his major league debut May 8 but soon showed he wasn't ready to face major league pitching.

The Mets continued to wallow through a dismal season, spending most of the summer trying to stay out of last place. And then all of a sudden, the magic was back.

The turnaround began with a 5–4 comeback win at Los Angeles August 19 as Alfonzo tied the game with a single before Agbayani hit a sacrifice fly for the final run. Piazza drove in two runs after entering day with just 67 RBIs in the Mets' first 123 games.

The win began a stretch in which New York won seven of eight. A two-game skid followed, putting the Mets 10½ games out of first with 30 remaining.

The Mets captured nine of their next 10 before losing to the Marlins on September 9. They were two games under .500 and eight games off the pace.

The Mets wouldn't play another game for eight days while baseball took a backseat to life itself. They were scheduled to begin a series in Pittsburgh September 11, but the attacks on the World Trade Center and Pentagon that morning caused a suspension to the major league and NFL seasons.

Even those who didn't like Valentine at this point had to admire the way he immersed himself into the relief effort. He spent countless hours at the staging area in the Shea Stadium parking lot, doing some of his best managing that season while loading goods onto trucks and organizing workers. When looking back on the days following the attack, no one in baseball did more to help the cause than the former three-sport standout from Stamford, Connecticut.

The Mets were supposed to resume the season at Shea against the Pirates. But with Shea still being used as a staging area, the series was switched to Pittsburgh, where the Mets resumed their winning ways.

The team finally returned home from the Steel City following a three-game sweep that pushed the Mets over the .500 mark and within five games of the first-place Braves. The opponent would be those same Braves, beginning with an extraordinary pregame ceremony to honor those lost in the attacks. In a show of national unity, the Mets and Braves exchanged hugs and handshakes after lining up on the foul lines before the game.

The Mets continued to wear hats from the NYFD, NYPD, EMS, and Port Authority Police in recognition of their service. It was supposed to be a one-time deal in Pittsburgh, but the team was allowed to wear the hats the remainder of the season.

By the seventh inning, Mets fans were starting to smile as a sense of normalcy began to envelop the ballpark. Liza Minellli hugged and kissed Payton following her seventh-inning rendition of "New York, New York." Piazza provided Minelli's encore, belting a go-ahead two-run homer in the eighth to send the Mets to a 3–2 win over the Braves.

The emotional win was followed by a 7–3 triumph over the Braves, which put the Mets within 3½ games of the Braves with 12 remaining. A city in mourning had reason to rejoice as the team appeared poised to pull off a comeback not seen since the 1973 club.

The Mets lost the series finale but followed it with a three-game sweep at Montreal. They were five games over .500 and within three games of the Braves heading into a three-game set in Atlanta. A sweep would leave them tied for first place. Season ticket and partial plan holders began to receive invoices for playoff tickets.

The Mets lost the series opener to Tom Glavine, but there was still time to catch the Braves. The next day, New

York carried a 5–1 lead into the ninth, thanks in part to Piazza's three-run double. Valentine asked Benitez to close out the victory in a non-save situation, and what could be better than pitching with a four-run lead?

Benitez never got the final out, surrendering an RBI single and a two-run double before leaving the game leading 5–4.

On came John Franco, the Mets' former closer who had proven during the last two postseasons that he could get the big outs in crucial situations. Franco immediately walked the .214-hitting Wes Helms before serving up a walk-off grand slam to Andruw Jones.

The Mets won the series finale, but the bubble had burst. New York ended the season by dropping five of seven to the Pirates and Expos, two teams that would finish the year in last place.

At least the Mets had given their fans some excitement during the worst period in New York City history. They also had something on which to build heading into 2002.

Phillips fortified the '02 lineup by getting former and current American League All-Stars Roberto Alomar and Mo Vaughn in trades. Phillips also reacquired Cedeno and Jeromy Burnitz to play the corner outfield positions. The only significant loss was Appier, who sent to the Angels in the Vaughn deal. Appier got to taste champagne after helping Anaheim win the World Series. Vaughn got to hear the wrath of boos as he struggled through knee pain while enduring his worst full major league season to date.

Through good seasons and bad, Mets fans often singled out one player in which to voice their displeasure. Richie Hebner, Dave Kingman, Doug Sisk, and Gregg Jefferies had been singled out to bear the brunt of their team's misfortunes. But the faithful could choose from several players in '02, as Vaughn, Alomar, Burnitz, Cedeno, and Trachsel served as vocal whipping boys at Shea. Newcomer Shawn Estes heard his share of boos while failing to display the form that earned him 15 wins only two years earlier.

In addition to Estes, the rotation also included Jeff D'Amico and Pedro Astacio, two pitchers whose best days were behind them. Trachsel became the Mets' second-most dependable pitcher on a staff that hardly resembled the Seaver-Koosman-Matlack collection.

Dave Weathers and Scott Strickland were brought in to fortify the bullpen, but there was little opportunity to pitch meaningful innings after the Mets played themselves out of playoff contention by late June.

The team actually owned a share of first place on May 29 despite a pedestrian 28–25 record. The Braves would soon leave the Mets in their dust, expanding their lead over New York to double-digits by the end of June.

Alomar, coming off a .336 season, batted a meager .266 and left his Gold Glove in Cleveland. Cedeno, still the team's single-season record holder with 66 stolen bases, swiped just 25 bags while struggling to stay over the .250 mark. Piazza hit 33 homers with 98 RBIs but batted only .288. Alfonzo lifted his average to .308 but drove in just

56 runs. Burnitz finished the year with 32 more strikeouts than hits. And Vaughn, the man brought in to revive the team's offense, drove in 72 runs and led the Mets with 145 strikeouts.

Phillips had assembled a rotisserie team without checking the expiration date of his acquisitions. That left Valentine with a gun and no bullets as everything he did to revive the ballclub seemed to end in a strikeout or a 6-4-3 double play.

There also was a virus on the team. Alomar had a penchant for sliding into first base on a close play at the bag. The move caught on with Cedeno and Ordonez, although adding speed during a slide would have defied the laws of physics.

Valentine publicly said he didn't like the headfirst slides into first, but they continued throughout the season. They became a talking point on WFAN, but the Mets never slid into first place the second half of the season. Instead, the team went 6–21 in August, reeling off 12 straight losses that put them 23 games behind the Braves. The Mets never got closer than six games under .500 the rest of the way.

Valentine prepared for an end-of-the-season meeting with Phillips and Fred Wilpon, presuming they would discuss moves needed to improve the ballclub. Valentine reportedly spent the start of the meeting giving his take on the ballclub and what was needed to become a contender again. But instead of beginning preparations for his seventh full season as the Mets' skipper, Valentine got whacked. He was fired and replaced by Art Howe, who had a worse time trying to bring respectability to the dugout.

Valentine went back to Japan to manage the Marines, enjoying life on the east side of the planet instead of the east side of Manhattan. Some fans had lobbied the Mets to bring back Valentine following Howe's dismissal at the end of 2004. But he stayed in Japan while another former infielder was given the job.

107–202

Wes Westrum   1965–1967

Born: November 28, 1922   Clearbrook, Minnesota
Died: May 28, 2002   Clearbrook, Minnesota
Named Interim Manager: 7/25/65
Resigned: 9/21/67

Wes Westrum Managerial Career

YEAR	GMS	W	L	PCT	POS.
1965	67	19	48	.284	10th, NL
1966	161	66	95	.407	9th, NL
1967	151	57	94	.377	10th, NL
Total	379	142	237	.374	

Major League Totals

YEARS	GMS	W	L	PCT
1965–1975	627	260	366	.415

To many Mets fans, Wes Westrum was little more than the bridge between Casey Stengel and Gil Hodges, losing a majority of the 374 games he managed. But he was in charge of molding the ballclub as it went through a youth infusion. The Mets finally had their own prospects and didn't have to rely on castoffs to fill the roster. The Mets had stunk with over-the-hill veterans; they were now prepared to stink with their own players.

Westrum became the skipper after Casey Stengel broke his hip during a party following Old Timer's Day in July 1965. Team president George Weiss allowed Stengel to name his temporary successor as both figured the Ol' Perfessor would be back for the 1966 season. To the surprise of many, Stengel selected Westrum over Yogi Berra, whom he called his "assistant manager" during their days with the Yankees.

Berra had managed the Yanks to a pennant the previous year but was fired, allowing him to become a player/coach with the Mets. Westrum had never been a big-league skipper before but had a reputation as a heady baseball man who had been the New York Giants' catcher when they won the 1951 pennant and 1954 World Series. In between, he had been a two-time All-Star, which was quite an achievement considering he batted .220 and .224 in those seasons. He was a great defensive receiver and a terrific handler of pitchers, earning a reputation as a sharp baseball mind.

Westrum was following Stengel, which was like Marcel Marceau following Frank Sinatra as the headliner at the MGM Grand. Stengel could fill a writer's notebook with quotes and have radio guys scrambling for more tape. Often, a two-minute interview with Casey consisted of one question.

Westrum would give good answers, but without the flare of his predecessor. He occasionally handed the media a malaprop, calling a tight game "a real cliff-dweller." He unintentionally created a catchphrase during his days with the Mets. After a rough loss, he often would say, "Oh, my God, wasn't that awful?" Since there were many rough losses, as soon as he'd say, "Oh, my God," the scribes would mouth "wasn't that awful."

The media would have to work harder to get a lively quote out of Westrum. But the climate had changed at Shea. One of Stengel's primary jobs was to sell tickets and keep the Mets on the back page. Westrum's sole responsibility was to win ballgames.

Westrum didn't do a lot of winning in 1965. The team actually had a worse winning percentage under Westrum than it did with Stengel in the dugout.

A few weeks after Stengel's fall, Westrum was given the job on a permanent basis. Stengel learned his hip would never allow him to manage again. Thus, it was up to Westrum to turn the fledgling Mets into a respectable ballclub, no miracles expected.

Westrum actually is an important part of Mets history when you consider Tom Seaver, Bud Harrelson, Jerry Grote, Ken Boswell, Jerry Koosman, Nolan Ryan, Don Cardwell, Ron Taylor, Danny Frisella, and Dick Selma all made their major league and/or Mets debut under Westrum. Ron Swoboda was playing his first major league season, and Cleon Jones had just 47 big league at-bats and was toiling in the minors when Westrum was hired.

There was a new mindset at Huggins-Stengel field when the Mets arrived for spring training in 1966. The team was ready to sink or swim with its prospects, although veteran Ken Boyer was brought in from the Cardinals to solidify the infield. Grote was the new catcher, having been acquired from the Astros for pitcher Tom Parsons. Kranepool patrolled first base, Ron Hunt was at second, and American League veteran Eddie Bressoud got the bulk of the playing time at short. Jones emerged as an everyday outfielder, spending most of his time in center.

But the pitching primarily consisted of journeymen. Of the 19 hurlers who appeared in a 1966 Mets game, only Tug McGraw, Selma, Ryan, Dick Rusteck, and Larry Bearnarth had started their careers with the franchise.

Jack Fisher and Dennis Ribant headed into the season as the Mets' top starters before Bob Shaw and Bob Friend were added in June. Fisher, Ribant, and Shaw each won 11 games and were a collective 33–33. The 16 other pitchers combined for the remaining 33 wins that season.

Coincidentally, three players on the '66 team (Harrelson, Roy McMillan, and Dallas Green) became future Mets managers. Seven players (Grote, Harrelson, Kranepool, Swoboda, Jones, McGraw, and Ryan) would be sipping champagne at Shea three years later.

Westrum was a practitioner of positive reinforcement. He posted motivational signs throughout the clubhouse in an effort to shed the team's losing image. His methods seemed to be working as the team spent the season avoiding the cellar.

Some of the kids started to play well. Grote hit .237 after failing to get a major league at-bat with Houston the previous year. The Mets picked up Grote figuring Westrum's wealth of catching knowledge would rub off on the San Antonio native. But it would be a couple more years before Grote emerged as a refined handler of pitchers.

Jones finished second to Ron Hunt on the team in hitting, batting .275 in his first full major league season. Jones also led the club with 16 stolen bases and 74 runs scored.

But Swoboda and Kranepool seemed to stagnate in '66. Swoboda had set a team-record for left-handed hitters with 19 homers in 1965, many of them coming in the first half of that season. The Baltimore-bred Swoboda smacked just eight in '66 while batting a meager .222.

Kranepool was continuing to put up mediocre numbers following his 1965 All-Star Game invitation. Kranepool was batting .287 at the '65 All-Star break before finishing the year at .253. He followed that with a .254 season that included a team-high 16 homers and 57 RBIs.

McGraw and Selma were considered the team's top pitching prospects at the major league level, but neither distinguished himself. McGraw had the worst winning percentage of any Mets pitcher with at least one victory, going 2–9 with a 5.34 ERA. Selma saw spot duty with the team, finishing the year 4–6 with a 4.24 ERA in 80⅔ innings.

Yet, the Mets avoided the cellar for the first time in team history. Ironically, it was Leo Durocher, Westrum's former skipper with the Giants, who guided the Cubs to a last-place finish in 1966.

There certainly was reason to celebrate the Mets' "lofty" perch in the standings. Across town, the Yankees had won four more games than the Mets but finished in the American League basement for the first time since 1912. Furthermore, the Mets outdrew the Yankees by more than 800,000 fans.

There was no denying the Mets were playing a better brand of baseball. These guys could catch the ball, throw to the right base and generally avoid the comical miscues that plagued the franchise in its first four seasons.

But the Mets' improvement was minor. They still finished behind the Astros, their National League expansion brethren. Jones and Grote had earned their places in the starting lineup, but Kranepool and Swoboda hadn't improved, and the pitching was only slightly better than it was in 1965.

Worse, the Mets had lost their identity. They were no longer the lovable losers who could erase a 6–1 deficit before blowing the game on a throwing error. But at least they pushed the turnstiles, drawing nearly 200,000 more fans than they did in 1964, their inaugural season at Shea.

There were few changes made to the roster as the 1967 season drew near. Tommy Davis was acquired from the Dodgers to play left field, which initially moved Swoboda to first base. Harrelson became the regular shortstop, and free-agent pickup Ed Charles eventually supplanted Boyer at third.

The Mets also acquired Don Bosch from the Pirates to become the center fielder of the future. The Mets had built up Bosch as the next Willie Mays, but Jones spent the bulk of the season in center while Bosch hit just .161.

Fortunately, the Mets also landed pitcher Don Cardwell in the deal that brought them Bosch. Cardwell hit one homer and drove in three runs while batting .158. Bosch finished the year with no homers and two ribbies.

Harrelson got off to a lousy start in 1967 but continued to display great range at short. He made just nine of his 32 errors during the second half of the season while finishing the year hitting .254.

Harrelson was the second-best rookie on the Mets that year. The top honor went to a pitcher who was a member of the USC Trojans a year earlier.

George Thomas Seaver had an eye-opening year for Triple A Jacksonville in 1966, going 12–12 with a 3.13 ERA. He was having a good spring training until the Tigers lit him up in his final exhibition outing. But the Mets were so impressed with Seaver that they brought him North and had him start their second game of the season.

Little did he know at the time, but Westrum finally had an ace in the rotation. Seaver, who didn't care for the Mets' losing reputation, went 16–13 with a 2.76 ERA and 170 strikeouts in a team-high 251 innings.

Seaver was everything the Mets were not at that point. He absolutely hated to lose and wanted his teammates to feel likewise. Seaver was the Mets' lone representative to the All-Star Game and would win the National League Rookie of the Year Award.

But much of the Mets' homegrown talent had regressed under Westrum in 1967. Swoboda hiked his average up to .281 which will forever be his career high. Swoboda also belted 13 homers and drove in 53 runs, better-than-average numbers when compared to his teammates.

Kranepool hit a career-best .269, although his home run total dropped from 16 to 10. Grote's average slumped to .195, and Jones dropped to .246 with five homers and 30 RBI.

New general manager Bing Devine continued to shuffle the roster in an effort to keep the team out of the cellar. The Mets used a team-record 54 players, including a major league-record 27 pitchers in 1967. Boswell, Koosman, Frisella, and Amos Otis made their big-league debuts, but Westrum wasn't able to avoid another last-place finish.

"We didn't play too well," Bob Johnson recalled of the '67 season, "and he said to me one time in the dugout as we're throwing the ball around and booting it, 'Bobby, isn't it a shame that grown men get paid to play like that?'

"He was the nicest guy and was really low-key."

The Mets fell into the cellar for good on August 22, all while Westrum was trying to get a contract extension. Attendance dropped by nearly 400,000 despite Seaver's terrific season, giving another reason for a managerial change.

Westrum was told in mid-September that he wouldn't be retained as manager. Rather than finish out the season, he resigned with 11 games remaining, leaving the team in the hands of coach Salty Parker.

Westrum got another chance to manage in 1974 with the Giants, replacing Charlie Fox in midseason. The Giants finished fifth in '74 and third in '75 under Westrum, going a combined 118–129. That would be his final stint as a major league manager.

The General Managers

Sandy Alderson 2010–present

Born: 11/22/47   Seattle, Washington
Named General Manager: 10/29/10

The Mets went outside the organization to find a general manager when Nelson Doubleday and minority investor Fred Wilpon initially bought the team in January 1980. Prior to that, the club had hired GM's—Bing Devine, Johnny Murphy, Bob Scheffing, and Joe McDonald—with previous connections to the team.

Doubleday and Wilpon saw the state of the Mets in the winter of 1980 and asked Major League Baseball to help them find a front office leader, which led to Frank Cashen's successful run at the position.

Some 30 years later, and without Doubleday as partner, Wilpon again turned to the offices of Major League Baseball to find a new general manager. The club went 79–83 in 2010 despite the second-highest payroll in the majors, and the minor league system was believed to be in shambles. In an impatient market like New York, Wilpon and co-owner Saul Katz were under pressure to find a capable man to turn around the organization after five years under Omar Minaya.

Sandy Alderson, who had been a highly successful GM, was working in the commissioner's office when the search began. Alderson turned the A's into a mini-dynasty in the 1980s, winning three straight pennants and a World Series. He also helped the Padres become contenders a few years before going to work for Commissioner Bud Selig.

In many respects, Alderson was the anti-Minaya. He built a contender in Oakland through a strong farm system, excellent trades, and an occasional free-agent pickup without breaking the bank. His Oakland ballclub was the first major league franchise to win three straight pennants since the A's of 1972 through 1974.

News of Alderson's appointment was greeted with relief by Mets fans. With few exceptions, the team's best prospects at the time rested in the low minors, while the major league team had several ugly contracts still on the books.

It was evident from the moment of Alderson's introductory news conference that things were going to be different. There would be no quick fix as Alderson said team payroll would be slashed to a more palatable rate, about $40 million to $60 million less than in 2010. That meant grabbing free agents on the cheap and relying on a new group of talent evaluators to form the roster. Alderson hired two former general managers—J.P. Ricciardi and Paul DePodesta—to help him sift through the rubble while assistant GM John Ricco was kept on the staff to lend his appraisals of the current prospects.

It was around Thanksgiving 2010 when the Mets' financial woes became public. Irving Picard, serving as a trustee to those bilked in the Bernard Madoff Ponzi scheme, sued Fred Wilpon and Katz, claiming they knew Madoff's investment strategy wasn't legitimate. Picard portrayed the Mets' owners as co-conspirators in the scheme, a charge Wilpon and Katz immediately and vehemently denied. Wilpon and Katz invested a ton of money before Madoff's house of cards was leveled, which made them appear as sympathetic figures after they admitted in early 2009 to losing hundreds of millions through Madoff.

However, Picard argued that Wilpon and Katz also netted a good sum of cash before the collapse and was looking to recoup that money for redistribution for the poor souls who lost their life savings. Picard wanted at least $500 million from the Mets, which was more than half the value of the franchise.

Wilpon and Katz maintained their innocence but also knew they were in a money pinch after two unsuccessful seasons at Citi Field. Mets attendance went from 4,042,045 in their final year at Shea Stadium to 2,559,738 in their second year at the new venue. Sponsors were fleeing the ballclub, creating another revenue vacuum by the end of 2010.

The Mets took out a loan through the MLB to quell their financial straits. Finally, Wilpon and Katz announced they would seek another investor to prop up the team's rather unstable economic situation. By now, the team looked just as bad on the ledger sheet as it did in the box scores.

All of this made Alderson's job that much tougher as he remained prudent in player decisions. Hisanori Takahashi, arguably the Mets' best pitcher in 2010, was allowed to enter free agency after the team was unable to work out a contract. That was perceived as a big blow to the Mets' pitching staff until he compiled a 6.59 ERA in his first 15 appearances with the Angels.

The Mets also had a projected starting rotation of Mike Pelfrey, R.A. Dickey, Jonathon Niese, and who-knows-what as they approached Christmas. Alderson eventually inked Chris Young and Chris Capuano, both of whom were once among the National League's top hurlers before injuries turned them into reclamation projects. Alderson also picked up reliever Pedro Beato and second baseman Brad Emaus through the Rule V draft, another indication the team was going to be built on educated hunches.

The Mets management family attends Game 2 of the 1969 National League playoffs. From left: Charles Payson, general manager John Murphy, chairman M. Donald Grant, and owner Joan Payson.

Alderson filled the bullpen depth with Jason Isringhausen, Tim Byrdak, Blaine Boyer, Taylor Buchholz, and D.J. Carrasco. None of the five was considered a "sure thing," making the Mets' corps of relievers an even bigger question mark than the starting rotation.

As the Mets entered 2011 training camp, the most ridiculous contracts still on the books belonged to second baseman Luis Castillo and pitcher Oliver Perez. Castillo, who hit .235 and showed limited range in 86 games in 2010, was due to make $6 million. Perez was owed twice that sum in 2011 after going 0–5 with a 6.80 ERA in 46⅓ innings the year before. Neither player got through the exhibition season as Alderson cut both within days of each other. The moves satisfied a fan base tired of seeing both players, but the Mets still went into the season opener without a bona fide second baseman or an imposing left-handed reliever.

Alderson's best off-season move may have been the hiring of Terry Collins as manager. Collins was selected over a group that included Mets third base coach Chip Hale, Brooklyn Cyclones manager Wally Backman, and former major league skipper Bob Melvin. Collins had been a successful manager in the majors but hadn't been in a big league dugout for about a decade. His intensity as a skipper helped him turn the Angels and Astros into contenders but also created near-mutinies at both stops.

Willie Harris was signed by Sandy Alderson before training camp in 2011 and provided key hits during the season. Photo courtesy of David Ferry

But Collins was praised for running a wonderful camp in the winter of 2011. Players liked Collins for his positive outlook, attention to detail, and ability to call out players without embarrassing them. The media liked his straightforward assessment of players.

The problem was, the Mets also entered the season well behind the rest of the NL East in terms of talent and prospects. The Phillies had the best starting pitching in the majors, and the Braves and Marlins possessed better overall pitching. The Nationals appeared to be at least a year away from assembling a forbidding rotation, but they had also formed an infield defense that was vastly improved.

Nothing seemed to go right for the Mets in their first 18 games of 2011 as they lost 13 times and demonstrated the pitching staff would not be very good. Young initially appeared to be the best man in the rotation, but it took just two starts before his shoulder began to act up. Pelfrey struggled as the de facto staff ace, Niese was erratic, Capuano had trouble getting out of the fifth inning, and Dickey was unable to maintain the same brilliant control that made him such a good pitcher in 2010.

Emaus won the starting second base job but was returned to the Blue Jays before the end of April. He lasted longer than Boyer, who was designated for assignment after losing twice during the first week of the season.

The Mets followed their 5–13 start with a six-game winning streak and remained within a few above and below .500 through early September despite numerous key injuries. Staff ace Johan Santana never threw a major league pitch, Ike Davis didn't play after mid-May because of an ankle injury, David Wright missed two months due to a stress fracture in his back, and eventual NL batting champ Jose Reyes had two stints on the disabled list.

These types of injuries had ruined the Mets the previous two seasons. This club was a little tougher, demonstrating it could win with infielders Justin Turner, Daniel Murphy, and Ruben Tejada playing almost every day. Dillon Gee was recalled in late April and became the first Met to start a season 7–0. Niese looked very good at times, and Dickey rediscovered his effective knuckler.

Although Turner, Murphy, Tejada, Gee, Niese, and Dickey were all products of the Minaya regime, many of Alderson's signings kept the Mets afloat for the first four months. Isringhausen served as a solid set-up man for closer Francisco Rodriguez. Byrdak flourished following a rather nightmarish first few weeks as the Mets' lefty setup man. Ronny Paulino became the catcher of choice for a couple of Mets starters and carried a .320 batting average into the All-Star break.

The Mets also got a lot of mileage out of Willie Harris and Scott Hairston, a pair of utility players signed by Alderson before training camp. Both provided key hits during the season, with Hairston belting three pinch-hit home runs.

Alderson had to address several contract issues as the Mets headed to the All-Star break within striking distance of the wild-card. Rodriguez was on pace to earn an automatic $17 million contract option for 2012 if he finished 55 games. Given the team's financial state, that option was not an option. Beltran and Reyes were in the final year of their contracts and were performing beyond expectations, each earning berths in the All-Star Game. But with the Mets floating among the wild-card contenders, Alderson had the unenviable task of deciding whether to push on for a playoff berth or deal his closer and two best position players for prospects in an effort to rebuild the franchise. Two of the ugliest seven-letter words in New York are "pothole" and "rebuild," making Alderson's decisions even tougher as impatient Mets fans didn't want to face the prospect of several more losing seasons.

Alderson shipped Rodriguez to Milwaukee in a deal that was announced minutes after the All-Star Game. The trade was an obvious salary dump as Rodriguez fetched only two players to be named yet kept the Mets' spending options open for 2012.

The Mets managed to win without K-Rod as Jason Isringhausen assumed the closer's role and quickly picked up seven saves to reach 300 for his career. As the team stayed around the .500 mark in late July, Alderson said he would not deal Beltran or Reyes unless he received what he considered equal value in return. Alderson's public stance may have increased the quality of offers for Beltran amid tight races for all eight playoff berths in July.

The Giants, looking to shake themselves from the second-place Diamondbacks in the NL West, were in need of an offensive boost and focused on Beltran. Alderson held off on a trade until the Giants included Zack Wheeler, their top minor league pitching prospect, in the deal. The trade was completed July 28, just as the Mets were about to record a four-game sweep in Cincinnati for the first time in club history.

With Beltran gone, Alderson announced to the relief of the fan base that Reyes would be a Met the remainder of the year. Mets fans could deal with the losses of Rodriguez and Beltran, but they implored the team to re-sign Reyes, who was at the height of his popularity.

Reyes became the first Met ever to win a National League batting title, but his battle with Milwaukee's Ryan Braun and Matt Kemp of the Dodgers was the only late-season drama offered by the Mets. The pitching remained suspect as the team fell out of contention by early August.

However, Capuano emerged as one of Alderson's better "Wal-Mart" purchases, leading the team with 168 strikeouts and topping all starters with a 3.17 strikeout-to-walk ratio. Byrdak served as one of the team's top set-up men and Beato survived a rookie season in which he took his lumps and never cowered.

The Mets finished 77–85 in Alderson's first season as their architect, a two-win drop off from 2010. However, Alderson also demonstrated he could still turn a modest budget and a patchwork of prospects and discarded free agents into a ballclub that gave Mets fans probably more positive memories than they experienced in 2009 or 2010.

Bing Devine   1966–1967

Born: 3/1/16   St. Louis, Missouri
Died: 1/27/07   St. Louis, Missouri
Named General Manager: 11/14/66
Resigned: 12/5/67

The 1964 Cardinals were mired in fifth place by mid-August of Bing Devine's eighth season as general manager, causing owner Gussie Busch to decide it was time to clean house. They did not look anything like a pennant contender despite the work of Devine, who acquired future Hall-of-Fame outfielder Lou Brock from the Cubs for pitcher Ernie Broglio in a multiplayer swap.

The Brock trade initially appeared to be a great swap... for the Cubs. Broglio was one year removed from an 18–8 season, and Brock was an underachieving speedster who batted .257 and succeeded on only 69 percent of his 72 stolen base attempts during his four seasons in Chicago.

Brock caught fire immediately after donning a Cardinals uniform. Broglio went 7–19 the rest of his career before retiring in 1966. But the fleecing wasn't enough to save Devine's job. Busch fired him on August 17 with the team sitting nine games behind the first-place Phillies.

Eight weeks later, the Cardinals celebrated their first World Series championship in 18 years. Devine already had his next job, hired by the Mets as the heir apparent to president George Weiss. The problem was, Weiss had no timetable for his retirement.

"I don't think George Weiss was involved in my hiring," Devine said. "When I came, he was there, and it was supposed to be his last year. It was indicated to me they didn't want to kick George Weiss out arbitrarily. He had devoted so much to the Yankees and then to the Mets, so they wanted to do it properly and on a reasonable schedule he could live with."[1]

Devine spent his first two seasons with the Mets looking at amateur players while assessing young talent on other minor league rosters. He would evaluate each Mets scout's first-round pick in his territory and formulate his own ranking.

"George Weiss wanted me to go out and check them all and put them all together and see if I could come up with a plan of who should be number one, two, and three. Since then, I've always jokingly said, 'I think George wanted to get me out of his hair, and that was an easy way to do it,' but I'm not sure if that was true. It may have come into play, but who knows."[2]

That left Devine in charge of formulating the Mets' strategy for the first-ever major league draft in June 1965. Four of the Mets' first 12 picks in that draft appeared in at least one game for the 1969 World Series club.

Devine was instrumental in the hiring of Whitey Herzog as third-base coach for the 1966 season. Herzog lasted only one year at the position before attempting to join the Kansas City A's to be closer to home. Devine got wind of Herzog's pending defection, raised his salary, and hired him as his special assistant. Herzog was named director of player personnel at the end of 1967, another decision that led to the team's championship run in 1969.

Devine was also the point man for the June 1966 draft. He had a chance to select a college outfielder who eventually became a Hall of Famer and beat the Mets in the 1973 World Series. Instead, the Mets selected a catcher who never made it past Triple A.

"We had the first choice in the draft," Devine said nearly four decades later. "And it was between Reggie Jackson and a high school catcher by the name of Steve Chilcott. We took the catcher, and there are a lot of things that go into it. We felt we were really short on catching in the organization at the minor league level at the time, and we needed catchers on the big league club, so we kind of made up our minds as we went through the draft to get a catcher, and Chilcott was the best of the lot."[3]

He came away unimpressed after traveling to Alvin, Texas, to watch a young fireballer named Nolan Ryan. According to Devine, Ryan gave up a lot of hits when he wasn't walking the ballpark.

But Ryan came highly recommended by Red Murff, a Mets scout who had earned Devine's trust. Murff explained to Devine that Ryan just had a bad game and was a hell of a lot better than he had demonstrated. Devine told Murff that if he wanted to write a glowing scouting report on Ryan, he wouldn't refute it. Ryan was taken by the Mets in the 12th round of the 1965 draft, one round after Jim McAndrew was chosen by New York.

Months later, Devine recommended the acquisition of catcher Jerry Grote from the Astros for Tom Parsons and cash. What was considered a lightly regarded trade at the time helped catapult the Mets to respectability as Grote eventually became a forceful presence for a young pitching staff. Devine called it one of his first important deals, and it demonstrated he had a strong working relationship with Weiss. Devine said he always checked with Weiss on potential trades. Weiss had the utmost regard for Devine's scouting ability, although sometimes it took a bit of arm-twisting to prod Weiss into signing off on a deal.

"The guy I was closest to there was Joe McDonald, who went on to become general manager with the Cardinals when Whitey Herzog was manager in the '80s," Devine said. "Joe and I got in cahoots to manipulate George Weiss and get things done."[4]

One of their manipulations helped the Mets keep Jerry Koosman. Weiss was told by several members of the farm system that Koosman wasn't a prospect. According to his book, *The Memoirs of Bing Devine*, Devine said that Koosman owed the team about $500. Devine also knew Weiss hated to get rid of players who owed money to the team, and Weiss wanted that cash.

"Joe McDonald said, 'I'll keep putting it out to George that Koosman still owes us money and that we better keep him till we get all of it back.' So that's what Joe did. George never did trade Koosman, and he ended up winning 17 games for the Mets in '69 and two more when they won the World Series against Baltimore."[5]

Devine had to do quite a selling job to convince Weiss that Southern Cal pitcher Tom Seaver was worth acquiring in a special lottery. Seaver initially signed with the Braves in January 1966, but the deal was finalized after the Trojans began their exhibition season. Major League Baseball voided the contract since the Braves violated a rule prohibiting major league teams from signing college players during the season. The NCAA barred Seaver from pitching for USC, leaving him without a team until the Seaver family threatened to sue MLB. Commissioner Spike Eckert decided to hold a special lottery for any team willing to match Seaver's contract, which was reported to be anywhere from $40,000 to $55,000.

"Joe McDonald and I had trouble convincing George Weiss that we should go into the drawing. George said, 'We don't have proof he's worth that kind of money.' Remember, $40,000 back then was like $4 million now," Devine said in 2004.

"But I thought: if you're losing 100 games a year and competing for attention in New York with the Yankees, you'd better do something. So Joe McDonald and I talked George into it a day or two before the drawing.

"We theorized that George finally gave in because we had been talking about Seaver by using so many facts and figures. George probably thought, 'If he's that good, then 12 of 15 teams will be in the pool…and our chances will be slim of getting him anyway.'

"But George didn't know that our chances were one in three! The only three clubs in the pool were the Mets, Philadelphia and Cleveland.

"I can remember getting the call from Lee MacPhail, who was an executive in the commissioner's office. I took the call, and he told me, "You've got Seaver.'

"Forty years later, the whole thing is indelible in my mind.

"I remember thinking, 'Great!'

"And then, 'Uh-oh, Joe and I are in trouble.'

"But when we told George, he just shrugged his shoulders, as if to say, 'So be it.'

"Even though we were paying Seaver a lot of money, we actually gave him a little bonus when we won his rights. We liked him, and we wanted him happy because he wasn't going to the team of his choice.

"And he was worth it."[6]

Seaver remains the greatest player ever produced by the Mets, winning three Cy Young Awards from 1969 to 1975 and helping the team capture one World Series and two pennants.

"I didn't know all of that would happen when Joe McDonald and I convinced George Weiss to go after him. I hadn't even seen Seaver pitch before that drawing, but our scouts really liked him. And I'd learned from Frank Lane that if you don't do anything, you'll never do anything wrong...but you'll never do anything right, either."[7]

Lane made an impression on Devine in many ways while Bing served as Lane's top lieutenant with the Cardinals. Known as "Trader Lane" during his days as GM of the Cardinals and Indians, he reveled in manufacturing multiplayer deals and constantly shuffled his roster to attain maximum results. Unfortunately, Lane never won a pennant as general manager and was vilified in Cleveland for sending popular slugger Rocky Colavito to the Tigers for singles hitter Harvey Kuenn, a deal that contributed greatly to the Indians' downward spiral that kept the franchise dormant into the mid-1990s.

Devine showed during his lone season as Mets GM that he had a little bit of Lane in him. The Mets set a record by using 54 players and tied another by sending 27 pitchers to the mound in 1967 as Devine made—by his count—54 trades during his 12-month reign. That was the year Seaver made his major league debut and instantly became the ace of the pitching staff, winning 16 games. Unfortunately, Seaver's win total represented 26 percent of the Mets' victories as the team lost more than 100 games for the fifth time in six seasons.

The Mets' best hitter in '67 was Tommy Davis, acquired by Devine from the Dodgers for Jim Hickman and Ron Hunt in November 1966. Davis led the team with a .302 average, 16 homers, and 76 RBIs in his lone season with the Mets.

Devine presided over several more important drafts. Ken Singleton was selected in the first round of the January 1967 draft, less than six months after the Mets grabbed Jon Matlack in the first round and later landed Rod Gaspar and Gary Gentry in the June Secondary Phase.

Players continued to come and go after the June draft. Over a 9½-week period from June 10 through August 15, Devine acquired Nick Willhite, Bob Hendley, Dennis Bennett, Hal Reniff, Phil Linz, Bill Southworth, Cal Koonce, and Joe Grzenda while jettisoning Jack Hamilton, Rob Gardner, John Stephenson, Al Luplow, Al Yates, Chuck Hiller, Jack Lamabe, Ken Boyer, Sandy Alomar, Bob Shaw, and Hawk Taylor. That's 19 players changing hands in those 66 days, not counting the three bodies that came and went as "players to be named."

Devine sought a new manager after the season. Wes Westrum left in mid-September after being told he wouldn't be back in 1968. Many within the Mets' hierarchy thought Gil Hodges would be the perfect skipper for the team, a notion Devine admits he never initially considered. But Hodges was still working for the Senators and had made great strides in improving a ballclub that was almost as bad as the Mets. The Senators weren't willing to lose Hodges without compensation, so Devine had to pull off another trade to get his manager. Washington came away with Bill Denehy and $100,000 for the man who led the Mets to the 1969 World Series.

"The guy who really keyed that, who was very important in getting agreement from Washington on the deal was Johnny Murphy, who worked for me. I knew that Murphy and George Selkirk, the Washington general manager, had once been roommates playing on the Yankees, and that's why I put Johnny Murphy in the position of talking to Washington. Incidentally, I knew George Selkirk well, though I did not get involved in that deal talking to him personally.

"Hodges was outstanding, and the ownership—the people who knew him and liked him, they were right. Give the ownership a plus for that."[8]

Getting Davis the previous November gave Devine a major piece in what became his final trade proposal with the Mets. He agreed to send Davis, Jack Fisher, Billy Wynne, and Buddy Booker to the White Sox for Tommie Agee and Al Weis on December 15. Agee hit poorly the first four months of 1968, and Weis served as a backup to Bud Harrelson and Ken Boswell. A year later, Agee was one of the Mets' World Series heroes and Weis provided one of the most important home runs in the team's postseason history.

But Devine wasn't around for the completion of that trade. He continued to make his home in St. Louis during his time with the Mets, commuting back and forth from New York during the off-season. Devine jumped at the opportunity to cut his commute.

Stan Musial stepped down as the Cardinals' general manager following their 1967 World Series win. The vacancy allowed Devine to rejoin the Cardinals, where he remained the GM through 1978.

Devine said Mets board chairman M. Donald Grant tried to persuade him to stay in New York by offering him a small piece of the team. Devine told him the offer was generous but not enough to turn down a chance to return to St. Louis, his family, and his old team.

Murphy took over for Devine and finalized the Agee trade. The Mets, armed with a flourishing farm system through the work of Devine, Murphy, McDonald, and Herzog, went 73–89 in 1968 before winning the World Series the following autumn.

"I had no idea the Mets would win the World Series two years later," Devine said about leaving in 1967. "I'm not trying to pat myself on the back. But the big deal for Agee on December 15, 1967, was the only deal they made until the middle of June in '69. That's when Johnny Murphy acquired Donn Clendenon, a platoon first baseman from Montreal.

"It's really kind of unbelievable: he's the only player who came in after I left until they won the World Series. So I left the Mets in pretty good shape."[9]

Jim Duquette   2003–2004

Born: 5/4/66
Named General Manager: 6/12/03
Reassigned to Sr. VP of Baseball Operations: 9/30/04

The Mets became National League champions in 2000 through shrewd trades and successful signings. Less than three years later, they were the most expensive last-place team in Major League Baseball as attempts to bolster the roster through a free-spending policy severely backfired.

Roberto Alomar and Mo Vaughn were complete busts in a Mets uniform after being acquired before the 2002 season. Closer Armando Benitez stopped saving his worst outings for pressure situations, putting the capper on a chronically faltering bullpen. Mike Piazza was breaking down, leaving virtual no one capable of carrying the team's offense.

Jim Duquette was put in charge of cleaning up the mess, taking over as interim general manager when Steve Phillips was dismissed on June 12, 2003. Duquette had been climbing the organizational ladder since being hired as an assistant to the Mets' minor league and scouting departments in 1991.

Duquette's responsibilities with the Mets were vast. He was named director of player personnel in October 1997 and promoted to assistant GM one year later. Duquette handled everything from contract negotiations, salary arbitration cases, player personnel moves, and staff recommendations. He was well-versed in the workings of the organization and well-trusted by an ownership group that now wanted him to kick the bums to the curb.

There was no reason to believe the Mets could suddenly storm their way back into contention when Duquette was thrust into the GM's role. His primary goal during the summer of 2003 was to recycle a collection of underachieving, high-priced players into a bunch of prospects that could help the Mets down the road.

It took Duquette a little over two weeks before he completed his first sell-off, sending Alomar to the White Sox for Royce Ring, Edwin Almonte, and Andrew Salvo. Ring was one of Chicago's brighter pitching prospects and projected to be part of the Mets' bullpen within two to three years.

Two weeks later, he jettisoned outfielder Jeromy Burnitz to the Dodgers for Victor Diaz, Kole Strayhorn, and Joselo Diaz before shipping Benitez to the Yankees for three prospects. Duquette capped the month of July by sending reliever Graeme Lloyd and shortstop Rey Sanchez to other clubs.

Duquette received praise for managing to restock a farm system criticized for its failure to provide relief when the Mets were struggling at the major league level. The team ate salary on most of the deals, but Duquette managed to give the franchise a fresh look after just seven weeks on the job.

The deals had no positive impact at the major league level as the Mets finished in the NL East basement for the second straight year. However, the trades also demonstrated Duquette's working knowledge of other farm systems while also clearing the decks for another free-agent splash. He was rewarded for his efforts when the Mets named him the permanent general manager on October 28.

Duquette opened the Mets' checkbook for the first time on December 10, signing Japanese shortstop Kaz Matsui to a three-year contract worth about $8 million annually. Matsui was one of the most popular players in Japan, displaying exceptional power, outstanding speed, and an exceptional glove at shortstop. But signing Matsui meant a position change for Jose Reyes, who lived up to his hype after breaking into the majors in May 2003.

Another free agent, Mike Cameron, was signed by Duquette as the solution to the team's problems in center field. Cameron represented the first Mets center fielder to display both power and outstanding defense since Tommie Agee some 30 years earlier.

The Mets opened 2004 training camp amid tepid optimism and numerous question marks. The feeling was that they could contend if:

1. Piazza could master first base and revert to the hitter who was good for 30 homers and 100 RBIs.
2. Reyes could learn the intricacies of second base.
3. Matsui could hit and field in Queens as he had in Japan.
4. Catcher Jason Phillips could duplicate his .298 average from his rookie year in 2003.
5. Third baseman Ty Wigginton could produce over a full season without wearing down as he did in 2003.
6. Cameron and Cliff Floyd could combine for 50 homers and 180 RBIs.
7. Ex-Yankees Shane Spencer and Karim Garcia could provide consistent offense while serving as the right field platoon.
8. Al Leiter, Tom Glavine, Steve Trachsel, and Jae Seo could pitch deep into games, thus taking some heat off a suspect collection of middle relievers.
9. New closer Braden Looper could perform better than old closer Benitez.

Almost none of that happened. Piazza's footwork at first base resembled Herman Munster at a sock hop. Reyes spent the first three months on the disabled list with a leg injury, and Matsui's combination of power, speed, and defense never saw the light of day at Shea. Phillips hit 80 points below his 2003 average and eventually switched positions with Piazza. Spencer and Garcia opened strong but were both ex-Mets by the second week of August. The starting rotation didn't pitch deep enough to avoid the overexposure and overwork of the setup men that were taking saves away from a very effective Looper.

And yet the Mets still found themselves on the periphery of contention as they headed toward the July trade deadline. Duquette picked up outfielder Richard Hidalgo from the Astros for David Weathers and Jeremy Griffiths on June 17, a deal which provided a huge jolt to the lineup. Always a streaky hitter, Hidalgo was terrific over his first two months with the team and opened July by homering in a team-record five straight games. Reyes began to round into form following months of inactivity, and Duquette added another bat by promoting third baseman David Wright from Triple A Norfolk.

The Mets were just 49–52 as they approached the trade deadline, but they were only six games off the NL East lead after closing within one game of first place on July 15. The Braves kept the Mets in the division race by playing mediocre ball over the first 3½ months, creating an air of vulnerability that prompted Duquette to become a buyer at the deadline.

Hoping a pair of starting pitchers could put the Mets in a playoff race, Duquette engineered trades with the going-nowhere Pirates and Devil Rays. He picked up former first overall pick Kris Benson from the Pirates, along with infield prospect Jeff Keppinger for Wigginton and prospects Matt Peterson and Jose Bautista. Wigginton had become expendable following Wright's arrival, so Duquette was essentially getting Benson for three players who weren't vital to the Mets' short-term plans. Bautista eventually became a 50-home run hitter for the 2010 Blue Jays, but that was long after the Pirates lost patience in his development.

Although Benson never lived up to his pre-draft projections as an eventual staff ace on a contending team, the trade wasn't bad. Unfortunately, Duquette made another trade the same day, one that looked horrible two years later.

Starting pitcher Victor Zambrano and reliever Bartolome Fortunato were picked up from the Devil Rays for a pair of prospects. Zambrano had been an enigmatic pitcher during his 3½ years with Tampa Bay, possessing an excellent fastball without the stones to throw it consistently for strikes. He led the American League in walks in 2003 and was averaging nearly seven free passes per nine innings in 2004 before heading to New York.

Mets pitching coach Rick Peterson was supremely confident he could turn Zambrano into a stud pitcher. That's exactly what Duquette was envisioning when he sent Scott Kazmir—the Mets' best pitching prospect in a decade—to the Devil Rays.

Zambrano suffered a season-ending injury three starts into his Mets career, went 7–12 with a 4.17 ERA in 2005, and started off 1–2 with a 6.75 earned run average for the 2006 team before spending the last five months of the regular season on the disabled list.

Kazmir quickly became the Rays' top pitcher, going 33–26 with a 3.52 ERA and 576 strikeouts in 532⅓ innings from 2005 through 2007 before helping Tampa Bay reach the 2008 World Series following 10 consecutive losing seasons.

Critics of the trade compared it to the Mets' Nolan Ryan–for–Jim Fregosi trade with the Angels in December 1971. Kazmir's presence on a major league mound continued to haunt Mets officials until he developed arm problems in 2009.

Neither Benson nor Zambrano could prevent the two-month free fall that had the Mets battling the Expos to stay out of the NL East cellar. Matsui, one of the iron men in the Japanese leagues, missed most of the second half with a back injury that left a vacuum at the top of the lineup. Hidalgo's bat went cold in August and was still forming ice crystals until the season finale. Piazza's offense continued to decline and the middle relievers were wildly inconsistent while many of the September call-ups showed they weren't of major league timbre.

The Mets' play on the field down the stretch did nothing to improve Duquette's standing with ownership. It also didn't help that a highly regarded former Mets executive was interested in returning to the team.

Omar Minaya was completing a three-year run as GM of the Expos and had a strong reputation as an assessor of young talent. He worked with Duquette in the Mets' front office from 1997 until he was asked to take over the Expos once Major League Baseball took over the franchise in 2002.

Minaya immediately had the Expos in playoff contention, making a series of moves in an effort to both reach the postseason and keep the franchise in Quebec. The Expos posted consecutive 83–79 seasons from 2002 to 2003 despite a Wal-Mart shopper's budget. But the team also finished with the NL's worst attendance both years, figures that only got worse when the Expos got off to a poor start in 2004.

Reports of the team's move to Washington grew rampant after the '04 All-Star break, prompting Minaya to investigate other opportunities. The Mets jumped at the chance to have Minaya take over the club after the 2004 season, which meant a demotion for Duquette despite a glorified title.

Duquette was named the Mets' senior vice president of baseball operations on September 30, 2004, but the position had no teeth. Most of his recommendations had to be approved by Minaya, putting him in the same position he was in during the last year of the Phillips regime. He stuck it out before taking a similar job with the Orioles in 2006.

Al Harazin 1991–1993

Named general manager 9/27/91
Resigned 6/22/93

The Mets had completed a very successful yet somewhat underachieving period when Al Harazin was promoted to replace Frank Cashen as general manager on September 27, 1991. Harazin took over just as the Mets were completing their first losing season in eight years and immediately vowed to turn the team into contenders before making several moves that made the Mets look like the team to beat in the National League East.

Harazin had a strong background in baseball business operations. Armed with an honors degree from Northwestern University and a law degree from the University of Michigan, Harazin handled the Orioles' business affairs from 1974 until he was hired by Cashen after the 1980 season to become a Mets vice president.

Harazin's forte was contracts, putting him on the money side of baseball operations. His early responsibilities with the Mets were handling radio and television, marketing, advertising, public relations, promotions, and scoreboard operations. He was there to channel as much money as possible into the organization while maintaining high standards in each department. Diamond Vision became part of the Mets' outfield landscape in 1982, feeding stats and videos to Mets fans at Shea while becoming a rich source of advertising and sponsorship income for the ballclub.

Harazin received a promotion after the 1984 season, becoming VP of baseball operations under Cashen while staying on the money side of the organization. His new responsibilities focused on the negotiation of major league player contracts, putting him closer to the baseball end of the organization.

Harazin was elevated to senior VP in 1985 and handled the design and construction of the Mets' spring training complex in Port St. Lucie, Florida, which opened in 1988. By now, Harazin was a high-ranking executive for one of the most respected baseball organizations as the Mets finished either first or second from 1984 through 1990 while winning one World Series and two division titles. Cashen was a master at delegating responsibility, evaluating the strengths of his front office with the same success rate in which he handled the major league roster. Harazin continued to negotiate contracts through the help of VP of baseball operations Joe McIlvaine, scouting director Roland Johnson, and minor league operations director Gerry Hunsicker.

Cashen was nearing his 69th birthday as he entered his 12th season as GM in 1991. The logical candidate to replace him was McIlvaine, who helped evolve a rather moribund farm system into a fertile production line while suggesting several trades that allowed Cashen to turn the Mets into champions. But McIlvaine left the Mets to become general manager of the Padres after the 1990 season rather than wait a year to take over for Cashen.

Through a series of bad trades and signings, the Mets plummeted into fifth place in 1991, one season after losing the NL East title to the Pirates during the final week. The front office was restructured after the season as Cashen gave up his GM duties to become COO and senior vice president.

Harazin took the GM title, and Hunsicker was promoted from director to VP of baseball operations. The two absorbed many of Cashen's previous responsibilities, making it difficult for organizational outsiders to determine who was actually in charge of the ballclub. Hunsicker had been involved in player development since 1988 and was now responsible for contract negotiations, turning him into the point man for player agents.

Owners Nelson Doubleday and Fred Wilpon weren't happy with the team's decline and told Harazin to use whatever means possible to make the Mets important again. Harazin was allowed to significantly increase player payroll as the Mets sought a quick fix to their problems.

"I don't think there is any question we are going to have to make major changes," Harazin said after being introduced as the sixth general manager. "My priority is to prove to Mets fans that 1991 was an aberration and that what the Mets are all about is winning more games than any team in baseball as we did in 1984 to 1990. I intend to explore all avenues in improving the club. We can't afford to ignore free agency.

"My message to Mets fans is: don't despair. The Mets will field a team next April 6 in St. Louis that will be interesting and exciting, a pennant-contending club."[10]

One of Harazin's first orders of business was to hire Jeff Torborg as manager. Torborg was a no-nonsense skipper who stressed fundamentals and preparation, which was somewhat of a departure from the days of Davey Johnson and Bud Harrelson. Torborg was following two skippers who treated their players like men and didn't care about their social lives or preparation as long as they were ready once they crossed the lines.

Next, Harazin signed Eddie Murray to a $7.5 million, two-year contract that was viewed as excessive by many beat writers. Murray had baseball's highest RBI total from 1982 to 1991, but his defense continued to decline while his batting average dropped 70 points to .260 in 1991. The signing also altered the Mets' defense as Dave Magadan was moved back to third base while Howard Johnson was entrusted with the center field position.

Right fielder Bobby Bonilla was the best player available on the free-agent market and was courted by Harazin until the White Sox emerged as the front-runner for his services. The White Sox had seen Bonilla blossom since trading him to the Pirates, and were prepared to outbid everyone else for his services. But talks between the White Sox and Bonilla stalled, putting the Mets back in the running as they got into a bidding war with the Angels and Phillies. The Angels offered Bonilla a five-year deal worth $27.5 million, and the Phillies made only a slightly better offer than their original proposal before Bonilla's camp heard from Harazin.

According to the *New York Times*, the Mets' original offer to Bonilla was for $25 million over five years, although the final season wasn't guaranteed. Once he learned of the Angels' negotiations, Harazin bumped up the Mets' offer to a very complicated five-year package worth a major league–record $29.5 million. Through deferments and annuities, Bonilla remained on team payroll well after his retirement.

The signing was praised by the local press. Mets beat writer Joe Sexton wrote in the *New York Times* that Harazin had radically altered the direction of the team:

"He has quickly and decisively unburdened himself of the organization's traditional reluctance to sign free agents to long-term, multimillion-dollar deals.

"Bonilla may not be a colossal talent, but his acquisition registers an enormous impact on the Mets, the shifts that result likely to be felt in everything from the club's public perception to its daily lineup. For Bonilla is both an engaging personality—his charisma can infect a clubhouse, his unaffected self-confidence can defuse the pressures of performance—and an intriguing offensive force."[11]

Harazin managed to pick up first prize in the free-agent sweepstakes while filling a void created when right fielder Darryl Strawberry was low-balled by the Mets in their 1990 contract negotiations. Harazin also had managed to weaken the Pirates, the Mets' chief rivals at the time.

Harazin then set his sights on improving the starting rotation. Nine days after signing Bonilla, the Mets acquired two-time AL Cy Young Award winner Bret Saberhagen and utilityman Bill Pecota from the Royals for left fielder Kevin McReynolds, second baseman Gregg Jefferies, and utilityman Keith Miller. The trade allowed Vince Coleman to move back to left field after a disappointing first season as the Mets center fielder. Jefferies was replaced by veteran Willie Randolph, giving the Mets a past or present All-Star at first base, second base, and all three outfield positions. Each of the Mets' top four starting pitchers—Saberhagen, Dwight Gooden, Sid Fernandez, and David Cone—had been selected to All-Star Games, as had closer John Franco.

"I was concerned about the perception of the people who buy our tickets," Harazin said after revamping the roster in December. "I felt the perception after last season was not only that the Mets weren't a very good club, but also that we weren't a very interesting team. I made up a wish list in early October of what I wanted to accomplish and was fortunate enough by mid-December to be able to cross almost everything off that list."[12]

On the surface, the Mets appeared loaded as they headed to training camp. There were questions concerning the age and defense of the team, both of which would come back to haunt the club by the end of July. But everything looked rosy after Bonilla hit a pair of homers—including the go-ahead, two-run blast in the 11th inning—to lead the Mets to a 4–2 win over the Cardinals at Busch Stadium. Cone allowed two runs and five hits while striking out nine in eight innings before winning pitcher Jeff Innis and Franco each worked one scoreless frame.

But Harazin's grand scheme was undermined by a collection of players that either underachieved or spent much of the season on the disabled list. Bonilla, now the highest-paid player in the majors, hit a paltry .249 with 19 homers and 70 RBIs. He showed deficiencies in right field and finished tied for 125th among all big leaguers with a 1.5 Wins Above Replacement.

Bonilla also became a public relations nightmare. He once used the dugout phone during a game to call the press box to complain about an error he had received during the first inning. As the boo-birds grew louder at Shea, he wore ear plugs in right field and explained that he used them to better concentrate at the plate. He was also nasty to the media after telling them during his introductory news conference that they'd be unable to wipe the smile off his face.

Bonilla was only part of the problem. Johnson quickly showed he wasn't a center fielder before missing over a third of the season due to injury. Coleman continued to bitch about the slow infield dirt at Shea and appeared in just 71 games due to leg problems. Randolph started more games at second than the Mets originally had planned before the 37-year-old infielder suffered an injury that kept him out for nearly two months. Saberhagen started just 15 games, missing most of four months due to a mysterious finger injury that had him listed as day-to-day in the Mets press notes for several weeks. Franco appeared in only 31 games, and Gooden posted the first losing season of his career while compiling the worst ERA among the starting pitchers.

Adding to the misery, starting catcher Todd Hundley hit only .209, while Dick Schofield recorded a .205 average after being acquired by Harazin as the Mets' starting shortstop early in the season.

Yet the Mets were just four games out off the NL East lead as late as July 29 despite a 49–52 record. Two weeks later, they were 12½ games back after losing a 16-inning game to the first-place Pirates. Suddenly, the Mets' aggressive pursuit of excellence turned into a sell-off.

Cone, arguably the team's best pitcher through the first five months, was dealt to the Blue Jays for Jeff Kent and a player to be named who became Ryan Thompson. Cone was leading the National League in strikeouts and owned a 13–7 record with a 2.88 ERA before helping Toronto win its first World Series.

Cone was eligible for free agency in the fall of 1992 after beating the Mets in salary arbitration in February. Cone was expected to command a huge contract after the season, and the Mets never bothered to feel him out despite his insistence he could be re-signed at a hometown discount.

The Cone trade signified that the Mets had shifted from their free-spending policy, which severely hamstrung Harazin in his ability to improve the club before the 1993 season. The team already owned several bad contracts and wasn't about to throw more money into the equation.

There was no way Harazin could have predicted the rash of injuries that beset the team in '92, nor could he expect Bonilla to play so far below expectations. Much of the season could be attributed to bad luck, although there was one major signing in which Harazin was roasted by the fans and media.

Torborg appeared to be in over his head the moment he entered the Mets' dugout. He tried to ban alcohol on team buses and flights, and wanted to allow player wives and girlfriends to travel with the team on road trips. Both edicts were swatted down by the players, who were prepared to sneak booze onto team flights and didn't want their better halves to be privy to the tawdriness that occasionally accompanied road trips.

He was unable to handle Coleman and Bonilla, two headstrong players whose on-field tantrums embarrassed Torborg. Torborg also mishandled a few appearances on WFAN by divulging information that was supposed to be kept under wraps.

But Harazin was in no position to change managers or aggressively seek a quick fix after the Mets finished 72–90 in 1992. Doubleday and Wilpon refused to throw good money after bad, and a languishing farm system left Harazin with no options to improve the club.

Harazin still managed to pull off one major deal, getting four-time All-Star and four-time Gold Glove shortstop Tony Fernandez from the Padres in October. But like most of Harazin's moves, it backfired as Fernandez hit .225 and made six errors in 48 games before he was traded to the Blue Jays in June.

The 1993 Mets opened the season by sweeping a two-game set from the expansion Rockies, and were 6–4 through 10 games before falling into last place for good on April 29. Harazin fired Torborg in May and replaced him with Dallas Green, but the team remained on pace for its first 100-loss season in 26 years when Harazin resigned in June and was replaced by Joe McIlvaine, who left the Padres for a chance to rebuild the Mets.

Harazin's legacy with the Mets is proof that a spending spree won't necessarily buy you a division title. But the ownership's decision to tighten the purse strings gave Harazin no opportunity to correct his mistakes. He had no resources available from a farm system that was built primarily through Hunsicker and McIlvaine. Ironically, Hunsicker and McIlvaine were on team payroll as the Mets headed into 1994.

Joe McDonald   1974–1980

Born: 7/5/29   Staten Island, New York
Named General Manager: 10/1/74
Reassigned as VP, Baseball Operations: 2/21/80

The rise of Joe McDonald through the Mets system was a testament to his diligence and perseverance. He helped stockpile, develop, and administrate a farm system that allowed the franchise to become World Series champions in just eight seasons. He was a big cog in a front-office machine that included George Weiss, Johnny Murphy, Bing Devine, Whitey Herzog, and Bob Scheffing during the Mets' first 15 years of existence.

McDonald's impressive results led to his appointment as general manager on October 1, 1974. The Mets posted winning records in each of his first two seasons as GM before the process of building a ballclub was altered greatly in 1976 by free agency. McDonald hoped to augment the farm system by participating in the first free-agent market, but Chairman of the Board M. Donald Grant scuttled that notion. The crowning blow came when Grant had his contract dispute with Tom Seaver, followed by Dave Kingman's departure.

The Mets occupied the NL East cellar during McDonald's last three years as general manager. However he laid a positive foundation for the team's future by scouting and drafting a host of players who would play key roles in the team's 1986 championship, four years after McDonald won a World Series as the Cardinals' general manager.

McDonald was born on Staten Island in 1929 and grew up four miles from Ebbets Field. His father worked at the Dodgers' ballpark and got him a job there before Joe completed high school. McDonald was grateful for the opportunity "in that particular era, to be able to see these players as a kid that I was, when few had the benefit of doing so because of no television.

"There I sat," McDonald continued in a July 2011 interview. "And I never cheered. And I looked and was absorbing all of these players. To see Musial. To see Medwick and the bat control he had. To see Warren Spahn, who was my favorite pitcher from the left side. All of this was an incredible experience that I had, which, which would prove to be so invaluable later. For that, I'll always be grateful.

"Baseball was in my genes and in my blood."

The Dodgers left Ebbets Field in 1957 and were replaced by the expansion Mets five years later. McDonald landed a job with the new ballclub and began working for the Mets the day of their first-ever game.

After the season, he was moved into the minor league department, where he was an assistant to Wid Matthews. Gradually, and taking on more responsibility, he headed up the scouting and minor league departments by 1965.

"In 1965 I had the dubious distinction of conducting the first ever free-agent draft," McDonald said. "That was an experience. We didn't know what we were doing. When I say 'we,' I'm meaning myself and my peers within other organizations. Should we have a list? Should we have an alphabetical list, which I was smart enough to consider because, as the players were drafted in rapid order and fashion, you had to check the alphabetical to make sure you scratched the name from the other [list]. It was that primitive. It was pioneer stuff. And I'm in charge? I'm just a kid! The duty was huge, and I enjoyed it and enveloped it. But quite frankly, it was pressurized because we didn't know quite how to go about it.

"And of course I made the inevitable first-round mistake. We drafted Les Rohr, and he petered out at Double A, which is the way things happen. There's no assurance a first-round pick is going to make it.

"But I might say that I was also fortunate in that we picked Nolan Ryan in the 12th round."

Ryan wasn't on the radar of many teams despite his outstanding fastball. In fact, Ryan had a poor outing in front of a Mets contingent of Bing Devine and scout Red Murff, who had tailed Ryan for almost two years. Devine urged Murff to write up his scouting report on Ryan as Murff saw fit before it was taken for consideration prior to the draft.

"I didn't see him until he reported to Marion, Virginia, in the Appalachian League," McDonald said of Ryan. "He may have grown tired during the tail end of his high school season. That, and the fact he had not physically matured are the only feasible reasons why he was a late pick. The arm action, delivery, and curveball was there to begin with. The explosive fastball would follow with maturation.

"Why he waited that long before he was picked…because he was a good-looking kid. You could project that he was going to grow into something. He was very slender. He wasn't fully matured physically."

McDonald did quite well in the inaugural major league draft. In addition to Ryan, the Mets landed Ken Boswell in the fourth round, Jim McAndrew in the 11th, and Steve Renko in the 24th. Boswell and McAndrew were key players on the 1969 World Series winners and remained with the Mets when they won the 1973 NL pennant. Renko was packaged in a deal that sent Donn Clendenon to the Mets in June 1969, a trade that put the team over the top that season.

McDonald and Devine also had to convince team president George Weiss to enter a special lottery for the rights to a junior pitcher from Southern Cal: Tom Seaver. Weiss initially was against the gamble, believing that no college kid was worth the money the Mets would have to pay Seaver. McDonald said it was a very rare occasion when they had to run a potential signing through Weiss, but the Seaver lottery was one of those instances.

"It wasn't easy," said McDonald of the selling job he and Devine accomplished, "on this signing, because there was so much notoriety attached to it, we did have to get George's consent to match it.

"We matched the Braves, which was a caveat placed by the commissioner that we were willing—as were Cleveland and Philadelphia—to match the Braves' contract.

"Was it a stroke of luck? Yes, in that we beat out the other two clubs. What about all the other clubs who did not evaluate Tom as we did? Not enough credit is given to Nelson Burbrink and the scouts who liked Tom's potential. And it's very true that I have to give credit to our scouts who liked Tom's potential."

McDonald was working for Devine once George Weiss stepped down after the 1966 season. The two already had a strong professional relationship and continued to acquire exceptional young talent through the four 1967 drafts. The Mets landed Ken Singleton with their first pick in the January draft, took Jon Matlack with the fourth overall selection in the June draft, and snared both Rod Gaspar and Gary Gentry with two of their first three picks in the June secondary draft.

"Joe McDonald had started in the Mets' organization with some office job, and by the time I got there in '64 he was a low-level guy in the minor league department," said Devine. "When I left in '67, he was really my right-hand man, the assistant to the president and general manager. He had a great work ethic. It always comes back to work ethic with people I admire, and I admired Joe.

"When I first got to New York, he was a great contact for me. He was one of those guys who knew where the bodies were buried. He'd tip me off on certain people—and certain directions to go or not to go.

"He was very trustworthy. He was willing to take a stand, which was very important to me. He'd give you an opinion and he wouldn't back down, no matter what you thought about it. And he was very perceptive. He was right about Koosman and he was right about Seaver. It's one thing to have an opinion and stick to it, but that's not much good if your opinion is misguided."[13]

McDonald and Devine weren't the only one-two combination in what was an exceptionally talented Mets front office. McDonald and Herzog formed a tandem that worked very autonomously and efficiently. So much so that Whitey would later bring McDonald to St. Louis to take over as GM of the Cardinals, who became World Series champions in 1982.

Herzog not only had management skills, he was an outstanding talent evaluator. The fact that Herzog/McDonald helped in the development of more than half of the 1969 roster is a testament to their success. Of the 35 players on the 1969 Mets, 20 were either drafted or signed as amateur free agents by the team. How many championship ballclubs can claim 57 percent of their players were homegrown talent?

"It's pretty impressive considering we started in '62 with a pretty poor team," McDonald said. "And to go where we did in seven years, and to do it with half the roster [from the farm]. To me, that's the self-satisfaction that Whitey and I received, as well as Scheff, John Murphy, and everybody who was aboard.

"When you look at the pitching staff, Seaver, Koosman, Gentry, McGraw, McAndrew, and then go around with Duffy Dyer and Kranepool, Boswell, Harrelson, Swoboda, and Cleon…add it all up and it's a pretty incredible thing.

"When I tell you Whitey was a good evaluator, he was the cross-checker for the New York Mets when we chose Jon Matlack. And I don't think that many clubs would have picked Matlack that early. This man could tell talent.

"We had a fantastic working relationship. It was a wonderful relationship, and it still is.

"These were my most enjoyable years, the satisfaction of signing a player and seeing him make the necessary sacrifices to succeed, and then to have that player emerge into a major league player is so rewarding. This was when I really enjoyed my stay with the Mets.

"We did our thing. Would you believe I never had a budget? I never had to go to the general manager or ownership and say, 'This is what I want to give Timmy Foli,' for example. I had full authority. Would they know [about the contracts]? Of course. But I didn't have to tell them in advance. I just went back and forth with the scout who was in the field signing the player.

"Agents weren't on the scene then, so it was the scout who actually signed the player. It wasn't the general manager and it wasn't ownership, which it's become, where an agent wants to talk to the owner. He doesn't even want to talk to the general manager. The evolving process has deprived scouts of the pride they experienced in signing their players.

"The climate was very different, to say the least. And that's where I enjoyed it. And I didn't low-ball anybody. I was always fair, and that's why we got them signed."

Herzog left the organization to become manager of the Rangers in 1973 after seeing numerous Mets prospects—Amos Otis, Singleton, Foli, Ryan—dealt away. One year later, McDonald was promoted to general manager as Scheffing's hand-picked successor.

"It wasn't like I was interviewed," said McDonald. "It wasn't like I asked for the position. It was Bob Scheffing—God bless him—who was a great man and recommended me to Don Grant. And Don Grant didn't call me or interview me or any of that."

The Mets were coming off a 71–91 campaign when McDonald was promoted to GM, just a year after winning the National League pennant. McDonald wasted little time retooling the major league roster, getting corner infielder

Joe Torre from the Cardinals for pitcher Ray Sadecki on October 13.

His next major trade was a bit more difficult from both a professional and personal level. The Mets were in need of a productive center fielder and a young catcher as McDonald headed to the December 1974 winter meetings. The Phillies had both in Del Unser and John Stearns, but they wanted Tug McGraw in return. Reliever Mac Scarce was sent to the Mets to balance out the loss of McGraw. Outfielders Dave Schneck and Don Hahn joined McGraw in Philly.

McDonald had been close to McGraw, who had just completed his 11th season with the organization and was coming off a poor season caused by a shoulder ailment. McDonald hated to part with his closer but also knew he had to improve the team.

"The deal was made at 1:00 am," McDonald remembered almost four decades later. "It was 2:00 am when I called him. It was cold. It was not how you would want it. But you've got to understand, when you make a trade, you can't sit on it. It has to be done, and it's not ideal that you couldn't go face-to-face.

"I was very emotional over it because he had been one of my top bobos. I can remember him in Cocoa, Florida, in '64. Tug came to me and said, 'Could I borrow $10?' I said, 'What for?' He said, 'I want to buy a dog.' Right away, I knew that this was a crazy left-hander.

"He called me lefty because I was left-handed. I wrote his check left-handed. We had that kind of an affinity where we'd call each other 'Lefty.'

"And I gave him the $10, by the way, but I never got it back.

"So for me to trade this guy, whom I had so much respect and affection for, was very difficult. It was very, very emotional."

McDonald continued to revamp the ballclub. He acquired slugging outfielder/first baseman Dave Kingman, "whom I stole for $50,000 from Horace Stoneham. I made the deal with Horace himself. I never talked to anybody else but Horace, the owner of the San Francisco Giants.

"I had a good relationship with Dave."

Kingman enjoyed wood-working and asked McDonald if the Mets would pay for the shipping of his lathing equipment.

"I said sure, I'll take that. My goodness, I figured it would maybe be $500. It turned out to be $7,000," said McDonald with a hearty laugh.

The moving bill was a bargain after Kingman set a club record with 36 home runs while driving in 88 runs in 1975. Unser played as McDonald had hoped, recording a .294 average and 13 outfield assists. Rusty Staub drove in 105 runs to establish a team record. Seaver won his third Cy Young Award and combined with Koosman and Matlack to post a 52–34 record.

McDonald also did a tremendous job turning a very suspect bullpen into one of the team's strong suits. He acquired veteran Ken Sanders from the Angels for catcher

Ike Hampton before the season opener, and purchased Skip Lockwood from the A's in late July. Both Sanders and Lockwood opened the year in the minors before teaming with Bob Apodaca to form a deep pen from August 1975 through September 1976.

McDonald admits Lockwood fell into his lap. "It's Sunday afternoon," McDonald begins, "I'm at home, and Charlie Finley calls me."

Finley was inquiring about another Mets player when McDonald began to quiz him on Lockwood, who was toiling for Oakland's Triple A team at Tucson.

"My scouts are why I had success. And Harry Minor—it might have been the day before—saw Skip pitch, and he said to me, 'He's worth a shot if you ever get around to it.'

"And I said to Charlie Finley, 'Well, what about that Skip Lockwood?' And he said, 'I won't put the gun to your head.' And I said, 'Okay, what's it going to take?'

"My recollection was $25,000. I said, 'Deal.'

Other than the bullpen, the biggest surprise of the year was furnished by Mike Vail, who was recalled in August after leading the International League in hitting. McDonald insisted the Cardinals include him in a minor deal that also sent infielder Jack Heidemann to New York for utilityman Ted Martinez in December 1974. Vail tied a Mets record by hitting safely in 23 straight games near the end of '75 and finished with a .302 average in 162 at-bats.

But the Mets continued to get one year older as they finished third in the NL East at 82–80. Torre did not hit well and showed diminished range at third base, while Bud Harrelson missed most of the season with a knee injury that required surgery. Although the team's record represented an 11-game improvement over 1974, the Mets played themselves out of playoff contention by mid-September despite Vail's outstanding hitting.

Manager Yogi Berra was dismissed in early August following a five-game skid that pushed the Mets 9½ games behind the first-place Pirates. The firing came less than three weeks after Cleon Jones was released following his refusal to play left field after a pinch-hitting appearance. The Mets briefly perked up under interim skipper Roy McMillan and were within four games of first by Labor Day before fizzling.

McDonald named a new manager in October 1975, picking Joe Frazier to the post as McMillan returned to coaching. Frazier had never managed in the majors before, but he had led his minor league teams to league championships in each of the previous three seasons and had first-hand knowledge of the Mets' top minor league prospects. McDonald and Grant were highly supportive of the appointment and continued to recite Frazier's 242–173 and three minor league titles from 1972 to 1974 during his introductory news conference.

"Joe Frazier's got all the qualifications you'd want," said McDonald. "He wins. Frazier was the only man seriously considered for the job."

Grant's power base never changed once team owner Joan Payson died in August 1975 and the franchise was handed down to her daughter, Lorinda de Roulet. Although her mother was an ardent baseball fan, de Roulet was a baseball neophyte who knew little about the sport and proved that by giving Grant free rein to meddle in baseball operations. She also put her daughters on the board of directors, and the two siblings knew even less about baseball, according to a source familiar with the machinations of the front office in 1975.

McDonald entered the 1975 winter meetings knowing he had one too many outfielders and needed another starting pitcher. Of Vail, Staub, Kingman, Unser, and John Milner, Staub was the oldest by only one year but was drawing the highest salary. However, he was the best overall hitter on the team after batting .282 and smashing the club RBI record. Unser's .294 average came with only 30 extra-base hits. Kingman's 36 homers were accompanied by a team-low .231 average and a team-high 153 strikeouts. Vail's major league resume consisted of 38 games.

Staub was so certain he was on his way out of New York that he declined to pick up the lease on his New York apartment. But Mets fans held out hope Staub would remain with the team until he was sent to the Tigers at the winter meetings for three-time All-Star lefty Mickey Lolich and outfield prospect Billy Baldwin. Staub was 31 and coming off his best year as a Met. Lolich was 34 and coming off an 18-loss season following an AL-high 21 losses in 1974.

"We needed pitching," said McDonald, "and I had seen Mickey pitch of course, and he was one helluva pitcher. We needed a good, starting left-handed pitcher."

Vail, groomed to take over for Staub in right field, dislocated his ankle during a pickup basketball game in 1975 and missed most of the '76 season before compiling mediocre numbers for a less-than-mediocre 1977 team. He was gone by the start of the '78 season.

"I was shocked," McDonald said while describing how he learned of Vail's injury. "It was a Sunday afternoon and I got the call from the doctor in Norfolk. When he told me of the ankle injury, he said it was a dislocation, and I said, 'Good, it's not broken.' And he told me it was worse.

"This kid was going to be a good hitter, a really good hitter. That was extremely disappointing."

Seaver almost didn't throw a pitch for the Mets in '76. He went to camp seeking a long-term deal for money commensurate to what the first wave of free-agent pitchers were going to receive that fall. Seaver wanted to stay in New York and was willing to accept a hometown discount. But Grant chose to ignore Seaver's request to negotiate since a contract was already in place.

McDonald admits he had talked to the Dodgers about a deal involving Seaver and Don Sutton, although he adds there was nothing concrete.

"There was a conversation," McDonald said. "Was it in depth and would come to fruition? No. It was just one of those things, but it was discussed.

"It must have been the other side who talked about it—or the agent because Sutton had an agent—because I never did.

"It was only because I was under orders because I knew where Grant was coming from. Otherwise, I would have never had that conversation. I was getting a reading, and I was realizing that it was an untenable situation between two men."

Seaver's problems with Grant were just beginning, and it was an example of how much influence Grant planned to wield on personnel decisions. McDonald said he still had complete control of the farm system and was allowed to make trades as he wished.

"I didn't have a tight relationship with Grant in my prior positions because he never showed that much interest in the minor leagues," said McDonald. "I did have a strong relationship with [board member and vice president] Herb Walker because Herbie loved the minors and he loved coming to spring training. He took an interest in the minor leagues. He loved Whitey, and we'd have a ball.

"He'd only come in for a few days, maybe a week. Don Grant never did any of that…and that's okay. But to say that I had a strong relationship with Don Grant, that's absolutely wrong."

The Mets had an excellent pitching staff heading into 1976, but their popgun offense became a peashooter attack when Kingman tore ligaments in his left thumb right after the All-Star break, causing him to miss six weeks. The injury prompted McDonald to orchestrate what quickly became a disastrous deal as Unser and Wayne Garrett went to the Expos for Pepe Mangual and Jim Dwyer. Mangual hit just .186 in 41 games and eventually lost the starting center field job to rookie Lee Mazzilli, another Mets prospect rushed to the majors. Mazzilli was now the future of the Mets primarily because he was their only decent hitting prospect.

The Mets still finished 86–76 in McDonald's second year as GM despite Kingman's injury. The record was the second-best in team history at the time, although it was 15 games worse than the NL East-winning Phillies. With the first free agent draft around the corner, there was reason to believe McDonald could sign enough hitting to win another 10 games and contend in 1977.

McDonald wanted to improve the Mets through free agency, but the process only gave the team another chance to pass on Reggie Jackson. If Jackson's contract demands were too rich for the Mets, they could have gone after Gary Matthews or Joe Rudi. The Mets could have landed Bobby Grich to add more pop among the infielders.

Instead, Grant showed no interest in buying players, which turned McDonald into a casual observer of the free-agent process. McDonald made an offer to Matthews but was badly outbid by Ted Turner of the Braves, one of several owners who spent lavishly during the first few years of free agency. Jackson signed with the Yankees for $2.7 million while the Mets' top slugger, Kingman, was re-signed to playing for a paltry $200,000 in 1977. Grant's hard-line stance on free agency prevented a frustrated McDonald from making any significant improvements for 1977.

"I'll take the heat," McDonald said of his trades. "If I made bad deals, that's me. I didn't have money to work with. The one thing Don Grant wasn't in favor of doing is giving a lot of money to free agents. As you know, [free agency] is all part of it now. It's very hard to just do it with a farm system. The farm system is absolutely vital. Large-market clubs, able and willing to spend, have an indisputable advantage to succeed.

"Look at the number of free agents.…I don't know who I ever signed as a free agent. I tried to sign Pete Rose. I tried to sign a lot of players. But I couldn't stand up to the other clubs' offers. Therefore, we had a mediocre series of years."

The money thrown around in the free-agent market made the Mets' contracts minimal by comparison. Kingman and Seaver entered '77 training camp wanting deals comparable to those doled out to the free agent class of '76. Seaver, a four-time 20-game winner, a three-time ERA champ and a five-time strikeout king, was now making about one-third what Jackson was raking in with the Yankees.

Kingman got off to a decent start but was struggling mightily by the end of April as the Mets sunk to the NL East basement. Seaver won seven of his first 10 decisions and was back as the ace of the staff despite an everyday lineup that had trouble hitting or catching the ball. By June it was evident Kingman's days as a Met were numbered with his average hovering around .200.

"Shortly before the trading deadline, Dave and I had lunch in Queens, and he gave me his desired terms and salary request. When I relayed the proposal to Grant, that spelled the end of Kingman."

Seaver still held out hope that he could forge a new contract with the Mets, and said he went over the head of McDonald to broker a deal. Seaver said he met with de Roulet to see if they could come to a happy compromise. De Roulet didn't know squat about baseball, but she understood Seaver's importance to the franchise. According to Seaver, the two worked out a package worth a total of $700,000 for the 1978 and '79 seasons, putting him in line with the richest players. And then Grant got in the way.

New York Daily News writer Dick Young wrote a column condemning the greediness of Seaver while dragging his wife, Nancy, into the equation. Young wrote that Nancy Seaver was jealous of Ruth Ryan, Nolan's wife, because the former Met was making more money than the current Met.

Seaver felt it was obvious Grant had fed Young a spoonful of crap before creating the column. Whether Grant knew Seaver may have already worked out a contract with de Roulet is not certain. But when Young's column hit the newsstands on June 15—the old trade deadline—Seaver said he told de Roulet the deal was off and demanded he be dealt to another team. It also caused McDonald to swing a trade that was distasteful to both McDonald and the Mets' fan base.

"Let's put this in capital letters…I DID NOT WANT TO TRADE TOM SEAVER!" McDonald said. "I didn't want to do it. And I had been negotiating successfully all those contracts up to the Seaver contract issue. This was, plain and simple, a case where Don Grant and Tom were in an immovable position. There was no hope. It was out of my hands, and it became an ownership decision.

"The day of the trade, there was a board of directors meeting. I was not on the board, and therefore, I was not in attendance when the ultimate decision to make the trade was made. It was in an apartment on Park Avenue where Grant stayed in the city. And I was not allowed to be in that room when this took place, when this was discussed.

"Therefore, even though the stigma's there—people always want to throw it up to me, I'm the guy who traded Seaver, I was the general manager and my name will forever be linked to the trade—it's unfair to the extent that I didn't want to make the deal.

"I was precluded from talking any more about it. It became an issue between two people. And then with Herbie Walker and Mrs. De Roulet and Mr. Payson present and in the board of directors meeting, the decision was made.

"Again, I'll take heat any time it's thrown my way, but I refuse to take the blame for trading Tom Seaver."

The Mets received outfielders Steve Henderson and Dan Norman, pitcher Pat Zachry and infielder Doug Flynn for Seaver. McDonald also shipped the disgruntled Kingman to the Padres for reliever Paul Siebert and utilityman Bobby Valentine the same night as the Seaver deal to complete what became known among Mets fans as the "Midnight Massacre." McDonald also acquired utilityman Joel Youngblood from the Cardinals for Mike Phillips on June 15, a swap that in time became the bright spot on an otherwise gloomy day.

Infielder Lenny Randle was one of McDonald's best pickups of the season. Randle was exiled by the Rangers at the end of April after punching his manager during spring training. Randle flourished once he received a second chance from McDonald, hitting .304 with a team-high 78 runs scored.

McDonald also had to switch managers on Memorial Day as Frazier was replaced by Torre, who briefly served as player-manager before submitting his retirement papers. The Mets won seven of their first eight under Torre before going 46–68 the rest of the way to end up in the cellar for the first time in 10 years.

McDonald continued to purge the roster by packaging Matlack and Milner in a four-team trade with the Pirates, Braves, and Rangers in December before shipping Harrelson to the Phillies during 1978 spring training. Koosman was sent away to Minnesota after the 1978 season, leaving Kranepool as the only player left from the 1973 pennant-winning team until he was released in October 1979. Trading Koosman was another tough call by McDonald, but the deal had a very positive result a few years later as Jesse Orosco, acquired in the trade, flourished out of the Mets bullpen.

"I loved Jerry," said McDonald. "He and I were tight. But then, in all sincerity, he said, 'Joe if you don't trade me to Minnesota, I'm quitting.' Now that might have been all talk, but I believed him.

"I'm in Hawaii for the winter meetings and I'm trying to extract some talent for Jerry, who still had a lot left in the tank, I felt. I finally went over some heads and got to the owner, Mr. Griffith. I forget some of the names of the players that were handed to me.

"And here's where good scouting comes into play. Dave Madison, an old Yankees pitcher, was my scout in the instructional league just prior to the trade. He saw Jesse pitch at Huggins-Stengel Field for the Minnesota Twins. So when I picked up the phone in Hawaii and talked to Mr. Griffith, I said, 'How about Jesse Orosco?' He said, 'Oh, you can have him.' We hang up the phone. The deal is made.

"So under duress—which I was—I managed to get a player, and that was Jesse."

The de Roulet clan announced during the 1979 season that the team was for sale, which further prevented McDonald from sprucing up the roster. The Mets won their last six games just to avoid their first 100-loss season in 12 years, and the team drew a franchise-worst 788,905 fans to finish last in the league in both attendance and victories.

The team was sold to publishing magnate Nelson Doubleday and real estate developer Fred Wilpon for $21 million, then a record price for a major league franchise and a shocking figure considering the depth of the franchise. The new owners reassigned McDonald to vice president of baseball operations after hiring Frank Cashen to serve as their new GM.

"I really liked Frank and I still talk to Cashen," McDonald said in 2011. "I'll pick up the phone every three or four months and we'll chat."

Cashen recognized McDonald's scouting ability and put it to good use. The club had the first pick in the June 1980 draft following a third consecutive last-place finish.

"Roger Youngwood, a terrific evaluator, had followed Darryl Strawberry and had a very strong report on him," said McDonald.

The front office was divided on whether to take Strawberry or Billy Beane with the first selection. Cashen asked

McDonald to head to Los Angeles to watch Strawberry play in a game at Dodger Stadium. Strawberry's stock rose when he smacked what McDonald described as a 425-foot homer to right-center. The swing immediately reminded McDonald of one of the greatest hitters in history.

"What I saw was Ted Williams…immediately," McDonald said. "I studied Ted's swing like so many other people. It's hard to duplicate it. But Darryl Strawberry should have been, could have been, one of the greatest hitters in our game. And I could see the incredible potential when I saw the swing. And I wasn't wrong. This time, I had it right. In many cases I don't, and that's the way it is when you're judging amateur ballplayers."

Cashen took Strawberry with the No. 1 pick and used one of his two first-round sandwich picks to grab Beane.

"He was brilliant," McDonald said of Cashen. "He got both. That's a fantastic story."

Strawberry was now part of a farm system that also included Hubie Brooks, Mookie Wilson, Wally Backman, Orosco, Mike Scott, and Ed Lynch, all of whom were acquired by McDonald. Things were looking up in the organization just as McDonald was preparing to rejoin Herzog in St. Louis.

McDonald took over for Herzog as the Cardinals' GM shortly after the 1982 season opener, allowing Herzog to concentrate on his managerial duties. The Cardinals captured the NL East, knocked off the Braves in the championship series, and took out the Brewers to win their first World Series since 1967.

McDonald stayed on for two more seasons in St. Louis and joined the Tigers in 1987, serving as GM from 1991 to 1992. He was still scouting in 2011 at age 82, working as a consultant for the Red Sox while living in Florida.

Omar Minaya   2004–2010

Born: 11/10/58   Dominican Republic
Named General Manager: 9/29/04
Dismissed: 10/4/10

New York has always been a "what have you done for me lately" kind of town. No one knows that more than Omar Minaya, who was Prince of the City in 2006 and run out of town four years later.

There are only three general managers in club history to build a playoff team in their second full season: Johnny Murphy, Steve Phillips, and Minaya. But while Murphy flew under the radar by choosing to build through the farm system, Minaya made one headline-grabbing acquisition after another while exponentially increasing team payroll.

Minaya's time as Mets GM can be sliced into three parts, with each segment representing a gradual decline. He had the Midas touch during his first two years, landing some of the most desirable free-agent talent and obtaining key players through trades while also signing several reclamation projects that factored into the Mets' 2006 playoff run. Segment 2 featured one poorly handled managerial switch and a pair of September collapses caused by several key injuries and a suspect bullpen. The final segment was marred by a plethora of injuries, bad contracts, and a farm system unable to compensate for the unsightly performances at the major league level.

Minaya was treated like the prodigal son when he was hired as general manager of the Mets on September 30, 2004. He served as assistant GM and senior assistant GM under Steve Phillips from September 1997 until he left the organization to become general manager of the Expos in February 2002. He spent three seasons trying to keep the Expos in Montreal, making numerous trades to improve the ballclub and rekindle local interest in the franchise. Most of Minaya's early deals in Montreal were built for short-term success as he tried to turn a 68-win team into a playoff contender. He put together 83-win teams in his first two years at the helm before Major League Baseball, which took control of the franchise before Minaya's arrival, put the clamps on any spending in 2004.

The Expos' 233–253 record under Minaya from 2002 to 2004 was better than the Mets' 212–272 mark during the same period. With the Expos poised for a move to Washington, Minaya left the club to take over the Mets.

Minaya's daring as a general manager was one reason the Mets were interested in bringing him back to Queens. He also had a reputation as an outstanding international scout dating to his time with the Rangers as he helped the team sign Sammy Sosa and Fernando Tatis. Outside of shortstop Jose Reyes—who was scouted by Minaya—the Mets didn't have a strong representation of Latino ballplayers at any level when Minaya was asked by team owner Fred Wilpon to revive the franchise. Wilpon allowed Minaya to be as creative as possible in overhauling the roster and gave his new GM access to his checkbook. Wilpon wanted to see improvement at the minor league level, but he also sought a quick fix at Shea. Minaya complied by acquiring the two most desirable free agents in the 2004–2005 free-agent market.

First, Minaya had to find a manager. Willie Randolph was one of the most respected baseball men in New York since his rookie season in 1976, yet had been passed over for numerous managerial vacancies before interviewing with the Mets for the second time in three years. Randolph finally got a chance to run a club as Minaya made him the first black manager of a New York baseball team, the first major decision by the first Latino GM in New York sports history.

Next came the roster. Pedro Martinez had just helped the Red Sox win their first World Series in 86 years and owned three Cy Young Awards. Carlos Beltran's stock rose dramatically after he hit .455 with eight homers and 14 RBI in 14 games for the Astros during the postseason. They were the crown jewels on the free-agent market and expected to command large contracts.

The Mets weren't given much of a chance to sign either player after finishing fourth in the NL East in 2004.

Martinez was expected to re-sign with the Red Sox, and Beltrán appeared poised to sign with a contender that had big pockets. Neither player appeared willing to hook up with a rebuilding club, but Minaya managed to acquire both players by offering the best contracts available.

The Red Sox looked at Martinez's age, size, and number of innings pitched and saw a ticking time bomb. They initially offered him a three-year package while balking on a fourth year. Martinez had averaged 225 innings from 1996 to 2000 but threw just 719 innings over the next four years. He was coming off a career-worst 3.90 ERA after leading his league in that category five times in the previous seven years.

Martinez craved a fourth year on his contract and felt slighted the Red Sox refused to extend their deal, causing him to shop his wares elsewhere. Most baseball executives figured Martinez was posturing and would eventually accept Boston's offer until Minaya came in with a four-year package worth about $14 million per season. The contract was signed on December 17, giving Minaya his first major acquisition.

Next on the Mets' free-agent radar was Blue Jays first baseman Carlos Delgado, who averaged 36 homers and 114 RBIs while hitting .286 from 1996 to 2004. Minaya and assistant GM Tony Bernazard went hard after the Puerto Rican slugger, selling him on the Latino slant within the front office and the roster. But Delgado was more interested in winning a World Series and signed with a Marlins club that was one year removed from a championship.

Delgado's snub put Minaya in the Beltran sweepstakes. The Mets made the outfielder an offer he couldn't refuse—a seven-year package worth about $17 million per season, but his agent double-checked with the Yankees just to make sure he couldn't pry another few bucks out of George Steinbrenner.

Minaya spent $175 million of Wilpon's money to acquire the two players, one of whom would actually play just once every fifth day. It was the same type of gamble former GM Steve Phillips made when he traded for second baseman Roberto Alomar and Mo Vaughn three years earlier, two reasons why Phillips was yakking on ESPN instead of working in Queens. However, the signings of Martinez and Beltrán were essential in putting the Mets back near the top of the New York sports landscape. For a franchise eyeing instant success, Minaya couldn't do much better than snaring the best free agents.

But Minaya also displayed his talent as a baseball scout by filling out the rest of the roster. He signed Gold Glove first baseman Doug Mientkiewicz after losing the bidding on Delgado, grabbed infielders Miguel Cairo and Chris Woodward as insurance for Jose Reyes and Kaz Matsui, inked utilityman and pinch-hitter Marlon Anderson, acquired Ramon Castro as the backup catcher to Piazza, and added Roberto Hernandez to a bullpen in need of another middle reliever. Those moves alone made the Mets better than the 2004 version, but Martinez and Beltrán put some excitement into the franchise as the team prepared for its first series in Cincinnati.

Paul Lo Duca filled general manager Omar Minaya's need for a catcher and also became a productive hitter.
Photo courtesy of Oscar W. Gabriel

The Mets opened 2005 on a five-game losing streak, followed that by winning six in a row and never got higher than eight games over .500 the rest of the season. Martinez won 15 games with a 2.82 ERA and 208 strikeouts to move into exclusive company among Mets hurlers. Only Tom Seaver, Jerry Koosman, Dwight Gooden, and David Cone had posted seasons with at least 15 wins, 200 strikeouts, and an ERA better than 2.85.

Nagging injuries prevented Beltrán from having the same success as Martinez in '05. Beltran managed to avoid the disabled list but hit a very disappointing .266 with 17 homers and 78 RBIs while incurring the wrath of fans at Shea Stadium.

Mike Piazza was an even bigger drag on the offense as he played out the final season of his seven-year deal, recording a .251 average with 19 homers and 61 RBIs. Mike Cameron's home run numbers sagged before he missed the last 48 games following a horrible outfield collision with Beltrán. Closer Braden Looper pitched through shoulder pain and wasn't nearly as effective as he was in

2004. Matsui matched his substandard numbers from 2004 and appeared in a little more than half the team's games. Mientkiewicz also had injury issues and didn't provide much offense after April.

Yet the Mets were within a half-game of the wild-card as Labor Day approached. Cliff Floyd, David Wright, and Reyes became the heart of the lineup and combined to score 283 of the team's 722 runs. Hernandez and Aaron Heilman fortified the bullpen, and Jae Seo eventually became a valuable fifth starter. Anderson, Woodward, Castro, and Jose Offerman did a nice job off the bench, giving the Mets a strong quartet of pinch-hitters.

But the team's subtle deficiencies became glaring weaknesses down the stretch. The Mets played themselves out of the race by dropping 15 of 18 before an 11–3 finish left them 83–79. The September slump tarnished the season but didn't stop the Mets from finishing 12 games better than 2004.

Minaya filled several holes in 2005, but more existed as he began to form his 2006 roster. Piazza was not going to be re-signed, creating a need for both a catcher and a power hitter. Looper was let go after the season, leaving the Mets without a closer for a bullpen that was erratic at best in '05. Rookie first baseman Mike Jacobs flourished over the final six weeks of 2005, but there was a noticeable hole in his swing. Cameron had agreed to move from center to right field following the Beltran signing but wasn't entirely happy at his new position. And Matsui had become undependable after appearing in just 221 of 324 games since signing in the winter of 2004. That left Minaya seeking a catcher, a closer, a few middle relievers, and a backup second baseman, all while hoping his lineup could provide enough offense for a thin rotation.

The catcher became Paul Lo Duca, who lacked Piazza's power but was a more productive hitter by now. Minaya finally landed Delgado, taking advantage of the same Marlins fire sale that allowed Lo Duca to fall into his lap. Getting Lo Duca and Delgado cost the Mets only Jacobs and prospect Gaby Sanchez, who didn't become a regular for the Marlins until 2010.

Minaya filled the closer's role by using Wilpon's money to get free agent Billy Wagner, who appeared to be a long shot to join the Mets before he agreed to a four-year deal. Minaya also found another right fielder by sending Cameron to the Padres for Xavier Nady in what initially appeared to be a risky move given Nady's limited major league experience.

Lo Duca, Delgado, Wagner, and Nady helped the Mets become serious contenders, but it was Minaya's minor moves that turned the team into NL East champions. The bullpen was completely overhauled through a series of trades, signings, and minor league invitations. Minaya sent Seo and a pitching prospect to the Dodgers for Duaner Sanchez in January, a trade that was talked about as one of the greatest deals in team history until Sanchez went out for a bite to eat in Florida. Free agent sidearmer Chad Bradford was signed to a one-year deal before New Year's Eve, Darren Oliver accepted a minor league contract and

an invitation to spring training, and Pedro Feliciano was re-signed after training camp opened in February. Wagner, Heilman, Sanchez, Bradford, Feliciano, and Oliver represented the National League's deepest bullpen in 2006, and one of the best in Mets history.

Minaya also made two other off-season moves that paid off handsomely by October, signing outfielder Endy Chavez and utilityman Jose Valentin to minor league contracts. Chavez had been a disappointment as a major leaguer, and Valentin was believed to be washed up at age 35 before reporting to Mets camp. Neither player was expected to contribute much to the 2006 club if they were fortunate enough to make the team. Instead, they played major roles in what would become the last great season at Shea Stadium.

And there was the trade that sent Kris Benson to Baltimore. Minaya gave up a bona fide fourth starter for two of the Orioles' better pitching prospects—reliever Jorge Julio and starter John Maine. Julio was the main guy in the deal, blessed with an outstanding fastball and projected as a late-innings set-up man. Maine was thought of as nice insurance in case the Mets ran into rotation problems at the major league level.

The 2006 Mets busted out of the gate with eight wins in their first nine games. They owned a 9½-game lead by mid-June and cruised to the team's easiest division title since 1986, all while the team overcame injuries through Minaya's shrewd leadership. The bullpen and deep bench allowed Randolph to look like a genius in the late innings, as did a lineup that was second to none in Mets history.

The regular season was not devoid of drama. Early injuries to starting pitchers Victor Zambrano and rookie Brian Bannister left the Mets with a rotation of Martinez, Tom Glavine, Steve Trachsel, and whoever was healthy. Alay Soler looked great in his first three starts before pitching himself out of the rotation. Mike Pelfrey was called up in July but quickly demonstrated he wasn't ready.

Once again, Minaya had the answer to the Mets rotation. He replaced Zambrano with veteran Orlando Hernandez, who was struggling with the Diamondbacks before coming to the Mets in early May for Julio. Hernandez pitched well after the deal, but he was also indirectly responsible for Minaya and Randolph finding a fifth starter.

Hernandez had a minor injury before he was scheduled to face the Astros at Shea the night of July 21. It rained that afternoon, prompting Randolph to push back Hernandez's start one day and replace him with Maine, who had enjoyed only marginal success during his first two call-ups that season. Maine was brilliant as an emergency starter against Houston, tossing a four-hitter in a 7–0 victory that put him in the rotation for good.

The Mets' second baseman that night was Valentin, who put them ahead with a grand slam in the second inning. Valentin had taken over the position two months earlier and had already become one of the key components to a formidable lineup.

Comparisons between Minaya's 2006 Mets and general manager Frank Cashen's 1986 squad started around June as the team began to run away with the NL East crown. The Mets' '86 lineup featured an impressive display of power and speed but lacked the pizzazz of the '06 version. Beltrán was on his way to a 40-homer season, a plateau never reached by any member of the 1986 Mets. Beltran, Delgado, and Wright combined for 105 home runs and 346 RBIs while the '86 Mets triumvirate of Darryl Strawberry, Gary Carter, and Keith Hernandez provided 64 home runs and 281 runs batted in.

Lenny Dykstra and Wally Backman were the table-setters for the 1986 Mets as they combined to hit over .300 with 44 stolen bases. Reyes stole 64 bases by himself in '06 and scored 122 runs compared to the 144 produced by Dykstra and Backman.

But the rest of the positive comparisons favored the 1986 Mets, who had much better starting pitching. Dwight Gooden, Bob Ojeda, Ron Darling, Sid Fernandez, and Rick Aguilera were far superior to Martinez, Glavine, Trachsel, Hernandez, and Maine. And in an era when starting pitchers went at least seven innings, Jesse Orosco, Roger McDowell, and Doug Sisk were enough to lead the Mets to victory. By 2006, Randolph often had to navigate his way through four relievers before nailing down a victory.

With an exceptionally balanced lineup and a shutdown pen, Minaya only had to seek a starting pitcher as the July 31 trade deadline approached. The rotation was the only cause for concern, although Maine appeared to be a revelation as the No. 5 starter.

But Minaya's wish-list was radically altered a few hours before the trade deadline. The Mets had a day off on July 30 before starting a three-game series in Florida. Sanchez, who had become Radolph's eighth-inning man, decided to leave the team hotel with some friends to look for a late-night/early morning meal. The vehicle carrying the Sanchez party was involved in a serious accident, leaving the right-hander with a separated shoulder that was diagnosed as a season-ending injury.

Judging by the estimated time of the Sanchez injury, Minaya had about 13 hours to come up with another reliever instead of dealing from strength to land a starter. It's anyone's guess as to how much the cab accident altered the 2006 season and the Mets' short-range success. Minaya filled the hole in the bullpen by reacquiring Hernandez from the Pirates, but he did so while parting with Nady, throwing off the balance of a lineup that had been able to alternate lefty-righty through the pitcher's spot.

Minaya also came away with a struggling lefty starter who had worn out his welcome in Pittsburgh. Oliver Perez was banished to the minors after opening the season 2–10 with a 6.63 ERA just two years after recording a 12–10 record with a 2.98 ERA and 239 strikeouts in 196 innings.

The trade left the Mets without a veteran right fielder. Lastings Milledge saw the bulk of the action in right during August, but Minaya was skeptical the rookie was mature enough to handle the responsibility, especially after Milledge continued to show up minutes before batting practice while irritating his teammates with his clubhouse demeanor.

Minaya used the waiver trade deadline to pick up right fielder Shawn Green for Double A pitcher Evan MacLane. The 33-year-old Green was a three-time 40-home run hitter and a one-time Gold Glover, although those days were long behind him despite his relatively young age. Green remained an imposing figure at the plate, but his presence in the lineup left the Mets a bit top-heavy with left-handed hitters.

The Sanchez injury hit the Mets very hard as the team was trying to wrap up the NL East title. Martinez missed most of August due to injury and was roughed up in two starts in mid-September before he was diagnosed with a torn rotator cuff, putting him on the shelf for 11 months. The injury left the Mets with a potential playoff rotation of Glavine, Hernandez, and Trachsel, which seemed formidable enough to get the team to the World Series.

Hernandez was named the Game 1 starter of the NLDS against the Dodgers but never got to the mound. He suffered a torn calf muscle jogging in the outfield the day before the series opener and didn't pitch again that season. Randolph had no other choice but to start Maine in Game 1.

Maine came through with a gritty performance in Game 1 before the bullpen pitched the last 4 1/3 innings of a win against Los Angeles at Shea. Glavine was superb the next night, but Trachsel was hammered in Game 3 before the Mets completed a three-game sweep.

The NLCS was settled by many of Minaya's acquisitions. Delgado was outstanding in a seven-game series against the Cardinals, hitting .304 with three homers and nine RBIs. Valentin was second on the club with five RBIs, and Beltrán batted .296 with three homers and four ribbies.

But the Mets trailed the series 3–2 and faced the prospect of using Maine to start Game 6 and Perez in a potential seventh game. Maine exhibited a virtuoso effort, allowing two hits over 5 1/3 innings before leaving the game with a 2–0 lead. Maine got the victory in a 4–2 decision that forced a seventh game at Shea Stadium.

Perez was almost as good in his second career playoff start, holding the Cardinals to a run and four hits in six innings before leaving a 1–1 tie. He was bailed out by Chavez, who made an incredible leaping catch at the left-field wall to rob Scott Rolen of a two-run homer in the sixth.

But the Mets' capable bullpen was anything but in the series. Wagner was hammered in a Game 2 loss and allowed a pair of runs in the ninth inning of Game 6 before closing out the victory. Heilman pitched well until surrendering a tiebreaking, two-run homer to Yadier Molina in the ninth inning of Game 7, putting the Mets three outs from elimination.

The Mets had pulled out numerous comeback wins in their final at-bat during the regular season and appeared poised to snatch the series from the Cardinals after loading the bases with two out in the bottom of the ninth. Valentin and Chavez opened the inning with singles, and Lo Duca kept the Mets alive with a two-out walk, sending up Beltrán as the potential hero against rookie Adam Wainwright. Wainwright fanned Beltrán on three pitches, putting St. Louis in a World Series they eventually won in five games against a Tigers team that stopped hitting at the worst time.

Minaya deserves plenty of credit for the Mets' success in 2006. Ask any Mets fan at the start of the year if they would accept a division title and a Game 7 loss in the NLCS, and they would have said yes. Minaya constantly tinkered with the roster during the year and came up with numerous stopgaps to keep the team from foundering. Delgado, Chavez, Valentin, Maine, and Perez helped the Mets get within one victory of the World Series.

And Minaya did it in a season in which the Yankees finished with the same record before they were swept by the Tigers in the division series. Minaya now had a chance to turn the Mets into the most significant baseball team in New York, something that his recent predecessors—Al Harazin, Joe McIlvaine, Steve Phillips, and Jim Duquette—had failed to do.

The 2006 bullpen had been created by a number of one-year contracts and hunches, most of which worked in Minaya's favor. But it also meant that pitchers like Bradford, Oliver, and Feliciano were free agents after the season, and all three had performed well enough to demand hefty raises. Bradford and Oliver were allowed to sign elsewhere, further throwing off a bullpen ecosystem that was hampered when Sanchez was injured. Minaya replaced Bradford and Oliver with veterans Scott Schoeneweis and Aaron Sele while also picking up flame-thrower Ambiroix Burgos.

Minaya was unable to do anything to improve the rotation. He allowed Trachsel to become a free agent and dealt Bannister to the Royals for Burgos, leaving the team with a projected rotation of Glavine, Hernandez, Maine, Perez, and a big question mark at No. 5. Jason Schmidt and Barry Zito were the top pitchers on the free-agent market, and Minaya was wise to steer clear of both as neither pitched well in 2007.

Minaya also allowed Floyd to become a free agent and replaced him with 40-year-old Moises Alou, who was a much better hitter than Floyd when healthy. But Alou appeared in just 98 games for the 2006 Giants after playing in only 123 contests the previous year.

The Mets, with a history rich in pitching, were ready to rely on their outstanding lineup for the second straight year. No National League team appeared to have a better lineup than the Mets' order of Reyes, Lo Duca, Beltran, Delgado, Wright, Alou, Green, and Valentin.

Maine and Perez became the top pitchers in the 2007 rotation while staying among the league leaders in wins and strikeouts. Glavine picked up his 300th career win and put together a few performances reminiscent of his days with the Braves.

The lineup continued to produce despite a series of problems. Delgado, Alou, and Valentin landed on the disabled list at least once during the season and combined to play in just 277 games. Chavez was off to a great start before tearing a hamstring, causing him to miss three months. Lo Duca was unable to duplicate his production at the plate, and Green never regained his power stroke. But the offense was bolstered by a strong bench that now included Damion Easley and Ruben Gotay, two more bargain-basement acquisitions that led Mets fans to believe Minaya was a damn genius.

The starting rotation was thin, the bullpen was overworked, and the lineup was slightly patchwork as the Mets headed into September. But the team owned a seven-game lead over second-place Philadelphia with 17 games heading into a three-game set with the Phillies at Shea. If the Mets took two of three versus Philly, the lead would be 7½ games with a magic number of just six with 14 games left.

But the Phillies exposed all the Mets' weaknesses, hammering the starters and the bullpen while out-performing the lineup in a three-game sweep that pulled them within 3½ games of first place. New York followed that by going 4–3 versus the lowly Marlins and Nationals while the Phillies continued to win, dropping the deficit to 2½ games heading into the final week.

The last week was a miserable combination of pitching and hitting for the Mets. They were outscored 32–19 at home by the Nationals in an ugly sweep that trimmed their lead to one game. When they finally received a good pitching performance, the offense folded in a 3–0 loss to the Cardinals in a makeup game that allowed the Phillies to grab a share of the division lead heading into the final series of the year. The Mets finished up at home against the Marlins while the Phillies hosted the Nationals.

The Mets put forth a pathetic display of defense, pitching and hitting in a 7–4 loss to the Marlins in the series opener, putting them one game back with two to play. Maine sparked the Mets in Game 2, carrying a no-hitter into the eighth inning and finishing with 14 strikeouts as New York blew out Florida 13–0 while the Phils were losing to the Nats.

All the Mets had to do in the finale was beat the Marlins on the final day to clinch at least a tie for the division lead and set up a one-game playoff. Wins by the Mets and Phillies would cause the possibility of a ridiculous four-way tie with the Padres and Rockies for three playoff berths, creating a scheduling nightmare for major league baseball.

Glavine was the starter in the season finale. He had allowed 10 runs in 10 innings over his previous two starts but was in line to become the 11th pitcher in major league history to have a 15-win season after his 41st birthday. A win against the Marlins would set up a possible play-in game featuring Martinez, who pitched well in September and was still the best big-game pitcher in the rotation.

Glavine snuffed out all hope by surrendering seven runs in the first inning of an 8–1 loss. Meanwhile 44-year-old Phillies lefty Jamie Moyer allowed no earned runs over 5⅓ innings as the Phillies beat the Nats 6–1 to win the division and keep the Mets out of the playoffs.

It was a shocking climax to a season in which the Mets managed to maintain control without a perfect roster. But the last two weeks showed the team needed a better rotation, a deeper bullpen, and a more dependable lineup.

Minaya tackled the lineup first, allowing Lo Duca and Green to become free agents while replacing them with catcher Brian Schneider and outfielder Ryan Church, who were acquired from the Nationals for Milledge. However, Minaya sat on the sidelines while the Red Sox and Yankees tried to pry Johan Santana from the Twins.

Santana still had one year left on his Minnesota contract but was being shopped around by the ballclub. The Yanks and Bosox put together packages that were rejected by Twins general manager Terry Ryan, who appeared willing to wait until the middle of 2008 to extract the best deal possible for his top pitcher. The Yankees and Red Sox eventually pulled their deals off the table, leading many to believe Santana would pitch for the Twins in 2008.

Minaya continued to negotiate with Ryan, offering him what few top prospects the Mets still had in their system. At the time, the Mets' farm system was criticized for its dearth of prospects while the major league roster teetered on the brink of excellence. It was believed that Minaya didn't have the personnel that could persuade Ryan to send a two-time AL Cy Young Award winner to the Mets. But Minaya sensed the Twins' willingness to part with Santana and brokered a trade that sent four prospects to Minnesota for the new ace of the Mets' staff.

It was an incredible acquisition by Minaya based on the team's talent pool at the minor league level. He didn't part with a single player expected to be a contributor to the 2008 team.

Santana gave the Mets a potentially strong rotation. However, the bullpen problems were not addressed as the overworked trio of Heilman, Schoeneweis, and Feliciano were asked to get the Mets into the ninth inning with a lead.

Minaya also reacquired outfielder Angel Pagan from the Cubs in January as outfield insurance in case Alou got hurt. Alou eventually developed a hernia problem during spring training, setting up an outfield of Beltrán flanked by newcomers Pagan and Church.

The revamped outfield was the least of the Mets' problems as they trudged through the quarter-mark of the 2008 season. Pagan and Church got off to strong starts while displaying excellent defense for a pitching staff looking for fly-ball outs. Santana was outstanding in April and remained so through the rest of the season.

But the Mets opened the campaign by playing lethargic ball after blowing a very winnable division title in 2007. Alou spent the first month on the DL and Delgado struggled at the plate following elbow and wrist surgeries. Reyes, the high-energy leadoff hitter, was wildly inconsistent through May as Randolph tried to quell his on-field celebrations. Martinez strained a hamstring in his first start of the year, leaving a huge void in the rotation. It all led to a slow start that put Randolph's head on the chopping block as the calendar was flipped to June.

Minaya's first hire as general manager was Randolph, and he continued to back his manager while the team slid under the .500 mark. Reports surfaced that the Latino connection of Delgado, Beltrán, and Reyes weren't happy with the way Randolph was handling the ballclub. Coincidentally, Delgado and Reyes got off to slow starts while demonstrating that Randolph may have lost the clubhouse in his fourth season on the job.

The Mets were scheduled to fly to the west coast following a home series against the Rangers. Minaya remained adamant before the Texas scrum that Randolph's job was not in immediate danger. Things looked even better for Randolph after the Mets took two of three from the Rangers before boarding a plane for California.

The Mets won the series opener against the Angels to move within a game of .500. Randolph conducted his postgame media chat and headed to the team hotel for a much-needed night of sleep following the cross-country flight.

It was around midnight—3:00 am in New York—when Randolph received a knock on the door. It was Minaya telling him he was making a managerial change. Randolph was out after posting the second-best winning percentage of any Mets manager.

The media were critical of the timing. Why make Randolph travel to the West Coast if he was going to be fired after the first game of the trip? Why was it done after the Mets had just won three of four? Why was it done long after the last deadline for New York newspapers?

With the Wilpons still in New York, Minaya had to answer to the charges of what was becoming a public relations disaster. Minaya placed the blame squarely on his shoulders, saying he didn't make the decision until the morning after the team left for Anaheim. He swept away any criticism that was piling up at the feet at the Wilpons and bore the brunt of criticism, although few were buying the notion the decision to fire Randolph was entirely Minaya's.

The Mets were just 40–42 as they entered July, a small miracle considering the shape of the pitching staff. Some of Santana's best starts were wasted either by poor run support or shaky middle relief. Maine and Perez looked okay for the first three months but didn't perform with the same dominance they exhibited in 2007. Pelfrey lost six consecutive starts before going 3–0 with a 3.52 ERA in five starts during June.

The Mets' biggest free-agent pickup in the winter of 2005 was now the worst starter on the staff 3½ years later. Martinez looked very good in September 2007 after returning from rotator cuff surgery, and appeared in top form the following March. But he was injured in the team's second game of the regular season and remained on the disabled list for two months while Randolph tried to get by with Nelson Figueroa and Claudio Vargas as fifth starters.

Martinez was pounded with regularity for about six weeks after his return, compiling a 6.51 ERA in seven starts while failing to pitch more than six innings. When

Martinez finally began to show glimpses of his old self, another injury put him on the shelf another 2½ weeks.

The Mets finally got hot the first weekend in July after alternating wins and losses since June 24. They reeled off a 10-game winning streak bolstered by strong starting pitching, a good bullpen, and a rejuvenated lineup. Delgado, Wright, Reyes, and Beltrán took over the offense, mashing the ball while the team averaged 6.4 runs during the winning streak.

The Mets climbed into a first-place tie right after the All-Star break and took a two-game lead on July 25 after moving nine games over .500 for the first time all year. A four-game skid soon followed before the Mets won 13 of 16 from August 7 to August 22 to move 2½ games ahead of the Phillies. They were doing it with rookie Daniel Murphy playing out of position in left field and 38-year-old Damion Easley at second base while Alou nursed another injury and Castillo failed to produce at the plate. Tatis, another Minaya find who had played just 28 major league games between 2004 and 2007, was coming up with big hits in key situations while playing right field in place of Church, who was battling concussion-like symptoms.

But there were bullpen concerns as the Mets headed into September. Sanchez returned to pitch in 2008 but was not the same pitcher he was two years earlier. Heilman, Schoeneweis, Feliciano, and Joe Smith were appearing in an inordinate amount of games as the rotation was unable to pitch deep into games. Wagner was hampered by an elbow problem that was considered a day-to-day proposition for about four weeks.

The bullpen started to collapse the moment Wagner walked off the mound following a truncated mound session in early September. He was diagnosed with a torn ligament that ended his season and left the Mets without a closer.

Interim skipper Jerry Manuel formed a bullpen by committee, but Wagner's absence now meant Heilman, Schoeneweis, Feliciano, and Smith had to cover another inning. Minaya acquired reliever Luis Ayala, who was cut by the last-place Nationals earlier in the season but was nudged into the closer's role after a few strong outings with the Mets.

The Mets continued to score enough runs to hide the pitching problems. They opened a 3½-game lead over the Phils with 17 left and also owned a better record than the Brewers in case their playoff fate rested on a wild-card berth.

The lead evaporated within six days as the Mets scored on 13 runs while going 1–4. They scored 57 runs over their next nine games but won just five times as the bullpen continued to implode. New York was one game off the division lead and tied with the Brewers for the wild-card with three to play as they prepared for a three-game series with the Marlins. One year earlier, the Mets were tied for the NL East and wild-card leads heading into a three-game scrum with Florida before blowing a playoff berth. The latest situation left Mets fans a bit fatalistic as they bade farewell to Shea Stadium.

The final weekend was nearly identical to the end of 2007 as the Mets looked lackadaisical in dropping the series opener. Santana, pitching on a bad knee that would require surgery after the season, fired a three-hitter as the Mets pulled out a 2–0 victory on Saturday. Meanwhile, the Phillies won the first two games of their series with the Nationals to clinch the division, but the Mets were still tied with the Brewers for the wild-card heading into the final game at Shea Stadium.

Perez gave the Mets 5⅓ gritty innings in the finale, blanking the Marlins until John Baker hit an RBI single to put Florida ahead in the sixth. Smith entered with the bases loaded later that inning and promptly walked a batter to make it 2–0, but Beltran ripped a two-run homer in the bottom of the sixth to knot the score.

The bullpen reared its ugly head again in the eighth as Schoeneweis served up a tiebreaking solo homer to Wes Helms before Dan Uggla went deep against Ayala two batters later. The Mets stranded the potential tying run on first in the bottom half and failed to register a hit in the ninth to secure a 4–2 loss while the Brewers were winning 3–1 to capture the wild-card. For the second straight year, the Mets were shut out of the postseason on the final day.

Minaya let Martinez and Alou walk after the season, declining to sign either free agent. Alou set a club record by hitting safely in 30 straight games toward the end of 2007 and finished the year with a .341 average before hitting .347 in 2008. But Alou appeared in only 102 games and missed 222 during his frustrating two-year stay with the Mets.

Martinez might be considered a free-agent bust by those who look at his limited contributions over the final 2½ years of his contract. He averaged just eight wins during his four-year stay in New York and left as a broken-down hurler before temporarily reviving his career with the Phillies.

But Martinez was also the acquisition that put everything in place for a 2006 division title run. Without Pedro, Minaya probably didn't have a chance to sign Beltran and may not have had reason to acquire Delgado, Lo Duca, and Wagner the following winter. Minaya might have relied on a farm system that had produced Wright, Reyes, and Pelfrey before petering out again.

Minaya's top concern heading into the December 2008 winter meetings was revamping a tired bullpen, but other pitching problems created a chicken-or-the-egg situation. Sure the relievers were ineffective down the stretch, but it was due to a rotation that failed to consistently chew up innings. By reconfiguring the pen without addressing the rotation, Minaya ran the risk of burning up his relievers again by the end of August. The problem was, the supply of free-agent starting pitchers with high pedigrees came with a huge price tag, and the Mets already were among the top three teams in terms of payroll.

Minaya reconfigured the bullpen and received praise for his effort. He left the winter meetings with free-agent closer Francisco Rodriguez, who had just set a major league record with 62 saves for the '08 Angels. Minaya also crafted a complicated three-team, 12-player deal that brought in Sean Green and J.J. Putz. Gone in the trade were Heilman and Smith, along with Chavez and several prospects.

But the rotation was no better in 2009. Minaya gobbled up Tim Redding before spring training and signed Livan Hernandez after Redding was injured during training camp. Santana was fully recovered from knee surgery and Pelfrey was being counted on after going 11–3 with a 2.96 ERA from May 31 through September 8, 2008. Minaya made an unsuccessful pitch for free agent Derek Lowe and wound up re-signing Perez to a three-year, $36 million deal. Maine was penciled in as the No. 4 starter, ahead of Hernandez as the 2009 season began.

The only other major change to the Mets was the home field. The team moved into Citi Field, a beautiful facility with all the amenities the Mets had sought for about two decades. National League clubs soon learned it was a pitcher's haven, although the Mets failed to fully take advantage and finished with the NL's fifth-worst ERA. Opposing pitchers enjoyed themselves in the Mets' new playpen, holding the occupants to 49 home runs and 4.23 runs per game despite a .274 average.

The Mets had problems scoring runs all season, finishing 12th in the league while compiling an NL-high .270 average. The arrival of veteran slugger Gary Sheffield couldn't prevent them from hitting a major league-low 95 homers or recording the league's fifth-worst slugging percentage. The Mets had five players—Sheffield, Wright, Beltran, Delgado, and Tatis—with 30-homer seasons on their résumés prior to the season. That quintet banged out only 42 for all of 2009, neither of whom hit more than 10.

Yet the Mets were looking pretty decent by mid-May, winning 11 of 14 to take over the division lead at 21–15, 1½ games ahead of the Phils. Sheffield was making valuable contributions as Minaya's latest reclamation project after being dumped by the Tigers at the end of spring training. Church appeared to be fully recovered mentally and physically from the string of concussions that short-circuited his 2008 season. Even Luis Castillo was hitting for average following one of the worst seasons of his career. The only real early season disappointment was Murphy, who was handed the starting left field job out of spring training after hitting over .300 in 2008. Murphy turned nearly every fly ball into an adventure, prolonging innings with each misstep. He was eventually replaced by Sheffield, who at 41 was unable to handle the rigors of an everyday outfielder.

By the end of May, the Mets were having trouble winning games or keeping players on the field. Wagner and Angel Pagan opened the season on the disabled list and were joined by Schneider on April 17. Perez was the first starting pitcher to go on the disabled list after a poor April. Pagan was activated May 16, the same day Delgado landed on the DL with a hip injury that ended his career. The Mets' slide down the NL standings began the day after Delgado was deactivated and the day after newcomer Joey Cora was DL'd because of a torn thumb ligament.

Reyes and Church appeared on the DL May 26. Church was activated June 7, but Reyes remained sidelined through the end of the season with a calf injury that bog-gled the team's medical staff. When Putz was placed on the disabled list June 5, the Mets were still in decent shape at 29–24. But the team began to struggle once Maine and Beltrán were put on the DL later in June.

Minaya seemed to have enough insurance at Triple A Buffalo after signing numerous major leaguers to minor league contracts, just as he had by inking Marlon Anderson, Valentin, Woodward, Castro, Feliciano, Hernandez, Oliver, and Bradford from 2004 through 2006. But that magic had waned as the new infusion of veteran talent from the minors was unable to prop up a debilitated big-league roster.

The disabled list included Maine, Perez, Putz, Reyes, Beltrán, and Delgado when the Mets sunk under .500 for good on June 29. Minaya found a new right fielder on July 10, getting Jeff Francoeur from the Braves for Church. Francoeur immediately became the team's best clutch hitter in a lineup that now featured Wright, Sheffield, Castillo, and Pagan, but there was virtually no production coming from the bottom three in the lineup.

The losses mounted, as did the frustration and the injuries. Sheffield was put on the DL against his wishes with the team 10½ games off the pace by late July. Wright suffered a concussion when he was hit by a Matt Cain pitch August 15. Even rookie call-up Jonathan Niese tore his hamstring while on the mound in early August, ending his season.

The Mets finally provided some good news on the injury front by activating Wagner on August 20. Wagner stuck around long enough to be traded to the Red Sox five days later, the same day Santana underwent season-ending surgery to remove bone chips from his pitching elbow.

Four-fifths of the Mets' projected season-opening rotation—Santana, Maine, Perez, and Redding—had been DL'd by late August. The lone holdout was Pelfrey, who was having a miserable season. The rotation by Labor Day consisted of Pelfrey, rookie Bobby Parnell and journeymen Nelson Figueroa, Pat Misch, and Redding.

Two-thirds of the season-opening lineup—Schneider, Delgado, Reyes, Wright, Beltrán, and Santana—made appearances on the disabled list at one time or another in 2009. Putz, the projected set-up man to Rodriguez, didn't pitch after June 4.

Manuel used 53 different players in 2009, one off the club record set during Bing Devine's wheeler-dealer days of 1967. Of the 53 players, 19 made at least one trip to the disabled list. The injuries contributed to a nosedive that led to a 70–92 finish following an 89–73 season. The 19-win drop-off represented the team's worst decline since 1990 to 1991. The Nationals were the only thing standing in the way of the Mets' first last-place finish since 2003.

The organization was an absolute mess heading into the 2009–2010 off-season. The Mets' top two minor league teams—Buffalo and Binghamton—went a combined 115–176 in '09, giving Minaya's growing legion of detractors ammunition to demonstrate the farm system had gone to hell under his watch. Minaya had to dismiss VP of player development Tony Bernazard at midseason for challenging the manhood of the Binghamton Mets. Buffalo's ownership wanted assurances the Bisons were going to be competitive in 2010 after sporting the worst record in the International League in their first year as a Mets affiliate.

The financial state of the Mets came into question before the 2009 season began. Wilpon and co-owner Saul Katz had made a fortune investing much capital through Bernard Madoff for nearly three decades. The staggering profits helped fund Citi Field and keep Mets payroll among the highest in the majors since 1999.

But Madoff was indicted before the '09 season opener for running a Ponzi scheme that bilked his investors out of billions. Mets management initially gave the impression that Wilpon and Katz had lost a huge chunk of cash but were still solvent enough to field a highly competitive ballclub in 2010. Yet Minaya laid low at the winter meetings and didn't make a significant player acquisition until January 5, when he signed free-agent outfielder and former Mets farmhand Jason Bay to a four-year, $64 million contract. Minaya also inked Japanese pitchers Hisanori Takahashi and Ryota Igarashi to bolster the bullpen.

Bay had a power stroke that appeared able to penetrate the outfield seats at Citi Field. Most of Bay's home runs with the Red Sox landed near the left-field pole at Fenway, and the left-field line was among the more forgiving places for a slugger at Citi Field. With Beltrán and Francoeur covering the rest of the outfield, Mets fans tried to remember the last time the team had a more formidable trio. By spring training, the Mets were wondering how they'd spend half the season without Beltrán in center.

Beltrán managed to play the final month of 2009, but his knee problem wasn't getting any better as training camp approached. He sought an outside opinion about the knee and was told he needed surgery after the Mets' medical team determined he could avoid a procedure.

Beltrán eventually opted to have the knee surgically repaired. It became another PR nightmare for the Mets, who originally made it appear he had the operation before consulting the team until Beltrán issued a statement saying management was aware of his decision before the procedure took place.

Minaya filled the void in center by acquiring Gary Matthews Jr. from the Angels for Brian Stokes, one of the Mets' better pitchers in 2009. The plan was to have Matthews share the position with Pagan, who hit well and showed great range in the outfield in '09 but was prone to silly decisions that led to a few losses.

Matthews was quickly let go by the Mets as Pagan turned into one of the team's best players, flashing great range in center while keeping his average near .300 all season. He was a big reason why the Mets were 48–41 by the All-Star break while the wait for Beltrán continued.

Wright's power returned, as did Pelfrey's effectiveness. Reyes rejoined the team the first weekend of the season and took a while to find his stroke before rounding into form. The bullpen, projected to be an ongoing problem all season, turned into the team's greatest strengths through the help of Takahashi.

The rotation was in shambles by early May. Maine was lifted from a game against the Nationals after failing to crack 82 mph on the radar through two batters, and Perez was getting lit up when he wasn't walking the ballpark.

Niese joined the rotation and drew comparisons to Jon Matlack as he put together a stretch in which he was 7–3 with a 2.70 ERA in 15 starts from June 5 to August 21. If he was the Mets' second-best pitcher during that period, then a journeyman right-hander was No. 1.

R.A. Dickey had one foot out of major league baseball when Minaya signed him to a minor league contract before 2010 spring training. Little was expected of Dickey, who entered the year 22–28 with a 5.43 ERA as a major leaguer and opened the season in Buffalo.

Dickey had been working on a hard knuckler in an effort to regain his footing in the majors. The pitch was effective in May, but fans and the media kept waiting for his magic to wear off. It never did as Dickey finished first on the team with a 2.84 ERA and tied for second with 11 wins.

Takahashi was another great find, making the team out of spring training and becoming the top middle reliever until his services were needed in the rotation. As first-year Mets go, Takahashi was everything Bay was not.

Bay hit just six home runs by the All-Star break after swatting 36 for the Red Sox the previous year. He was almost as bad as Francoeur, who hit around .200 after opening the year on a sizzling 10-game hitting streak. The two created a black hole in the middle of the lineup through mid-July.

Wright was among the league leaders in RBI by the end of June and formed a nice quartet with Pagan, Reyes, and rookie first baseman Ike Davis, who captured the hearts of fans with outstanding defense and incredible power. But the foursome also contributed to a July to forget.

The Mets opened the second half with Beltrán finally back in the lineup and promptly went 2–9 on an 11-game road trip. They hit a measly .196 with a .302 slugging percentage despite a three-game series against the pitching-starved Diamondbacks. The road trip also cost the Mets Bay, who suffered a concussion serious enough to sideline him the rest of the season.

Two weeks later, Rodriguez got into a scrap with the father of his girlfriend after a loss to the Rockies at Citi Field. Rodriguez broke his thumb during the fracas and was done for the year, leaving the Mets without Minaya's top free-agent signings from the previous two winters.

The team played itself out of playoff contention by mid-August, which allowed the media to start a Minaya death watch. The team's payroll was estimated at around $140 million dollars, second only to the Yankees. The Mets were getting little bang for their buck, especially while attendance at Citi Field was dropping at an alarming rate.

The team's record wasn't the only reason to portray Minaya as a goner. The minor league system had developed Niese and Davis under Minaya's watch but had been otherwise incapable of helping the Mets since 2009. Minaya had also signed Castillo to a four-year, $24 million package after 2007 and gave Perez a three-year deal worth $36 million prior to 2009. Both contracts hung like an albatross of failure.

Another contract under scrutiny belonged to Santana, who pitched well when healthy but had spent each of his first two off-seasons as a Met recovering from surgery. Santana always managed to come back in top form and was pitching well in 2010 until he walked off the mound following a five-inning performance at Atlanta in early September.

Mets fans and media initially were given the usual "day-to-day" prognosis on Santana until it was determined he needed major shoulder surgery that threatened his 2011 season, leaving the team with another high-salaried player incapable of helping the ballclub.

The Mets finished 2010 in the same manner they limped home in '09, and it finally cost Minaya his job. Fittingly, the Mets dropped their season finale on a bases-loaded walk by Perez, a signature finish to a second straight underperforming year for the ballclub.

Minaya and Manuel were let go the day after the season ended. The Wilpons let it be known how frustrated they were over the last four seasons and vowed to make it up to Mets fans. But their "I feel your pain" posture was followed by major belt-tightening as the Mets continued to use one-half of Minaya's blueprint for success. New GM Sandy Alderson combed the market for discount pitching and off-the-rack hitting without diving into the free-agent pool.

The highlights of the Minaya regime included a quick rebuilding of the major league roster, a division title, and two late-season folds followed by two depressing seasons. The contracts given to Castillo, Perez, Santana, Rodriguez, and Bay were among the lowlights when he left, as was the condition of the farm system.

John Murphy   1968–1970

Born: 7/14/08   New York, New York
Died: 1/14/70   New York, New York
Named General Manager: 12/27/67
Died while GM: 1/14/70

Although the notion might be considered blasphemous, the Mets had a Holy Trinity in 1969. The father was manager Gil Hodges, who led them to an improbable division title before beating the heavily favored Orioles in the World Series. The son was Tom Seaver, a 25-game winner who went the distance in the Mets' 10-inning victory over the Orioles in Game 4.

The holy spirit would be Johnny Murphy, the affable general manager who saw his team win a championship in his second year on the job but didn't live long enough to watch them try for a repeat.

Some might say Murphy was at the right place at the right time as the Mets evolved into champions. He was surrounded by outstanding baseball men who allowed him to inherit a rich farm system that included some of the finest young arms in the game.

But Murphy was also the right man at the right time. He patiently allowed his fledgling ballclub to develop in 1968, making no major roster moves while his prospects learned on the fly. Once the Mets proved to be contenders in 1969, Murphy engineered an in-season trade that put the team over the top.

John Joseph Murphy was a well-known figure in New York baseball long before joining the Mets' front office. He was an outstanding reliever and spot starter with the Yankees from 1932 to 1946, recording a 93–53 record and leading the American League four times in saves, an unofficial statistic at the time. The Yankees won each of the six World Series in which he pitched as Murphy recorded a 1.10 ERA in 16⅓ innings. He went 2–0 in the postseason and was the winning pitcher in Game 4 of the 1941 World Series, a 7–4 contest in which the Yankees scored four times in the ninth after Dodgers catcher Mickey Owen failed to handle Hugh Casey's strikeout pitch with two out.

Murphy's Yankees career began in 1929 after the native New Yorker graduated from Fordham. He was New York savvy, allowing him to prosper in tight spots on the mound under manager Joe McCarthy.

Murphy finished his playing career with the 1947 Red Sox and became the team's supervisor of New England scouting operations the following winter. He was promoted to director of player personnel in 1948 and was Boston's farm director through the 1960 season.

He jumped at a chance to return home when Mets president George Weiss offered him a job as chief scout for the incubating franchise in the spring of 1961. Murphy combed the major and minor leagues for potential talent in which to stockpile the Mets for the October expansion draft. But the National League set up draft rules that made it difficult for the team to acquire many players with a future in baseball, rendering the majority of Murphy's scouting reports useless.

The hard work was noticed by Weiss, who quickly made Murphy his consigliore. Murphy continued to handle scouting and was given the duty of handling some contract negotiations.

The Mets were having a hard time re-signing Throneberry following his memorable 1962 season. Throneberry finished second on the team with 16 home runs and a .406 slugging average. He also committed 17 errors at first base, many of which cost the Mets ballgames while elevating him to legendary status in both the Mets' annals and his own mind. No player was booed more consistently than "Marvelous Marv" until August, when fans began to take pity on him and appreciate him on his own merit. Throneberry was a cult hero over the final two months, a feeling that was fresh on his mind as he sat down with Murphy for contract discussions.

"People came to the park to holler at me, just like Mantle and Maris," Throneberry remarked as he tried to squeeze a few more dollars out of Murphy. "I drew people, too."

"You drove some away, too," countered Murphy.

"I took a lot of abuse," remembered Throneberry.

"You brought most of it on yourself," replied Murphy.

"I played in the most games of my career," stated Throneberry without realizing he had become the straight man in a comical negotiation session.

"But you didn't play well in any of them," was Murphy's punch line.[14]

Murphy had a big ol' Irish heart until it came time to handle a contract. When it came down to money, Mr. Softee often became a hard-liner.

Joe Christopher was arguably the Mets' best hitter in 1964, topping the club with 76 RBIs and 26 doubles, and finishing second with a .300 average and 16 homers. Murphy and Christopher went back and forth with contract figures following the season before the Mets decided to set the ceiling at $17,000. Negotiations dragged on for several more days until Christopher and the Mets settled on $17,500. Murphy made Christopher work hard for each of those 500 dollars.

Murphy was a vice president by the time he hammered out Christopher's contract. He remained a VP when Weiss stepped down and was replaced by Devine following the 1966 season.

Devine already had spent two seasons in the Mets organization and developed a strong working relationship with Whitey Herzog and Joe McDonald. The three were primarily responsible for shaping the farm system and formulating draft picks.

With Devine in charge, Murphy became the buffer between the GM and Chairman of the Board M. Donald Grant. Team owner Joan Payson spent much of her summer months away from New York and relied on Grant to oversee the operation. Grant saw himself as a baseball expert and would sometimes clash with Herzog on player personnel decisions. Part of Murphy's job was to assure Grant that Devine, McDonald, and Herzog were doing a fine job running the organization. Murphy and Grant had their fractious moments, but Grant also had confidence in Murphy's recommendations. Murphy allowed Devine, Herzog, and McDonald to do their jobs without harmful interference.

The Mets were in the transactions agate of newspaper sports sections quite often in 1967 as Devine bought, sold, and traded his way to a 61–101 record without parting with any of the Mets' top prospects. Most general managers are at their busiest during the off-season before playing the cards they are dealt. Not Devine, who gave Mets fans reason to buy a scorecard. During one seven-week period at midseason, Devine acquired or deleted 19 players in an effort to maintain a competitive roster without messing up the farm system.

Devine also hired manager Gil Hodges after the 1967 season and was working on a major trade when the Cardinals asked him to return to the team in his old role as general manager. Devine's family remained in St. Louis during his time with the Mets, so a move back to Missouri

was a no-brainer. That left the Mets without a general manager for most of December.

Murphy handled the job while ownership discussed a successor. Meanwhile, a potential deal with the White Sox remained on the table, a swap that went a long way in helping the Mets win the 1969 World Series. Murphy sent veterans Tommy Davis and Jack Fisher, along with Billy Wynne and Buddy Booker, to Chicago. Coming to the Mets were outfielder Tommie Agee and utility infielder Al Weis. Devine laid the groundwork on the deal, but Murphy was the one who had to sign off on what was a fairly risky proposition.

Agee was the 1966 AL Rookie of the Year but slumped badly in virtually every offensive category the following summer. Davis was the Mets' best hitter in 1967, outperforming Agee in batting, homers, and RBI.

But the Mets were in desperate need of a center fielder with range in the outfield and pop in his bat. Cleon Jones saw the bulk of the action in center for the '67 Mets after Don Bosch played himself out of the role. But Jones was not a prototypical center fielder and lacked the range Agee possessed. Hodges, who had seen Agee play while managing the Senators, recommended to Murphy that the deal be completed.

Murphy was named general manager on December 29, 1967, and didn't acquire another player until shortly before the season opener, when he signed free-agent infielder Phil Linz. Like Devine, Murphy had complete faith in the work being done by Herzog and McDonald.

"John was a fine man," Herzog recalled in Peter Golenbock's 2002 book *Amazin'*. "But his nickname was 'Grandma'—he just couldn't seem to make a decision. That was fine with me, since I moved in to make all the tough ones for him. All Murphy really cared about were the bonus babies and the big pitchers. He let me run the organization pretty much as I wanted.

"One morning in spring training I released about $400,000 worth of bonus babies without bothering to check with him.

"'Oh my God,' John said when I told him what I'd done. 'Tell me you didn't really do that.'

"'Yeah, John,' I said. 'I can't look at them any more. We're better off getting them out of here. They're just taking up space. We've got to get this organization moving. If any of them ever makes the big leagues, you can have my job.' None of them ever did."[15]

The 1968 season marked a change of strategy within the organization. No longer were the Mets depending on other clubs to fill out their roster as 19 of the 34 players to appear in a game for the team that year were either drafted or signed as amateur free agents. The average age of the ballclub was 25.9 years, and none of the pitchers was older than 32. The 34 players used were a mark of stability after 54 players wore the pinstripes in 1967.

The Mets opened 1968 with prospects Jerry Koosman and Nolan Ryan in the rotation. Koosman set team records with 19 victories and a 2.08 ERA, and was among the

Mets' three representatives in the '68 All-Star Game. Ryan broke the club mark for strikeouts in a game and averaged a team-high 8.9 strikeouts per nine innings.

Jim McAndrew was recalled in midseason and carved out a 2.28 ERA in 79⅓ innings. Veteran Don Cardwell and Mets farmhand Dick Selma also posted earned run averages under three as the team finished fourth in the league with a 2.72 ERA.

Tom Seaver had another outstanding season after winning the NL Rookie of the Year award in 1967, finishing 16–12 with a 2.20 ERA and a team-record 205 strikeouts. Seaver stood head and shoulders above the rest of the rotation as the team opened the 1968 season. By September, he was being pushed by Koosman and Ryan.

Perhaps the best pitching move of the season was Hodges' decision to leave Tug McGraw in the minors the entire season with Murphy's blessing. McGraw had shown occasional flashes of brilliance in the majors after being recalled in 1965, but he was a two-pitch pitcher in a three-pitch league before he began to tinker with a screwball. Hodges watched him during 1968 training camp and determined McGraw could become a serviceable part of the organization if he perfected his scroogie and learned to pitch out of the bullpen. That decision paid dividends over the next five years.

The 1968 season has long been branded the "Year of the Pitcher," but a few Mets hitters offered some highlights. Jones hit .297 with 14 homers and 29 doubles as the everyday left fielder. Catcher Jerry Grote hit .282 and was named to the NL All-Star team for the first time. Second baseman Ken Boswell was chosen to the Topps All-Rookie team after hitting .261 in 75 games, and shortstop Bud Harrelson was the glue of the infield.

Third baseman Ed Charles was the team's oldest player at 35 after re-signing with the club before the season. Charles hit .276 and paced the team with 15 homers despite appearing in just 117 games. "The Glider" was also third with 53 RBIs and provided outstanding leadership in the clubhouse.

The Agee-Weis acquisition was looking pretty good until a 24-inning, 1–0 loss at Houston on April 15. Agee went 0-for-10 in the marathon and also went hitless in his next 24 at-bats to drive his average down to .100 by May 1. Weis ended that game by allowing a ground ball to go through his legs at shortstop.

Many potential rallies were sabotaged by Agee during the first four months. His batting average was just .165 as late as July 23 and remained under .200 until September 18. Things got so bad that Hodges sat Agee in favor of Bosch, the Mets' biggest disappointment of 1967.

The Mets finished dead last in the National League with a .228 batting average, a .281 on-base percentage and a .315 slugging average, yet the season was still considered a sign of progress. Buoyed by an outstanding pitching staff, the Mets managed to escape the cellar for only the second time in team history and finished with a team-record 73 wins. It marked the first time the Mets had finished ahead

of the Astros, their 1962 expansion brethren. But with another expansion draft coming up in October 1968, there was a chance the Mets' farm system would lose a few valuable pieces as Murphy huddled with Herzog and McDonald to determine who should be exposed.

The Mets lost just one pitcher of note in the draft as Selma went to the Padres before being traded to the Cubs. McGraw was left unprotected long after Murphy could have pulled him back, but neither the Padres nor the Expos were interested before the Mets decided to keep him.

Another pitcher dangled in the draft was Don Shaw, who somehow had become one of Grant's favorites. Shaw, who allowed one run in 12 innings at the major league level in 1968, remained available until the Expos grabbed him in the 20th round. When Grant heard of the selection, he gasped and said, "Not my Donnie Shaw!"

McGraw stayed. Shaw went. That decision was indirectly responsible for two pennants and one World Series, showing Murphy and his staff knew talent.

With the expansion draft out of the way, Murphy was a casual observer during the winter meetings. He picked up infielder Wayne Garrett in the Rule V draft, acquired pitcher Jack DiLauro from the Tigers in December and sold catcher Greg Goosen to the expansion Seattle Pilots before training camp.

The start of camp was delayed a few days by the first union job action in major league history. The demands of the players were small and included money for their likeness on baseball cards and other MLB marketing endeavors. One of the union's more vocal player representatives was Braves slugger Joe Torre, who was in full support of newly minted Major League Baseball Players Association head Marvin Miller. The Braves perceived Torre's involvement as treason and shopped him around during the exhibition season. One of the suitors for Torre was Murphy, who traded numerous phone calls with Atlanta GM Paul Richards.

Torre was 28 and a career .294 hitter with 142 home runs and five All-Star appearances, making him a tantalizing acquisition for Murphy and Hodges. Once the Braves let it be known that they insisted on a package that included Ryan and Grote, Murphy told them to have a nice day and went into the season with a ballclub rife with pitching a devoid of consistent hitting. Murphy put rookie flamethrower Gary Gentry on the Opening-Day roster, along with rookies Rod Gaspar and Duffy Dyer.

The Mets' young talent was another year older as the team opened the season against the Expos. Optimism was high that the Mets would finally win a season opener for the first time, but the expansion Expos took advantage of bad pitching and sloppy play to beat the Mets at Shea Stadium.

Murphy watched as the Mets dropped 23 of their first 41 games to fall nine games behind the first-place Cubs following a 3–2 loss to the expansion Padres on May 27. What followed made the "Amazing Mets" truly amazing.

Backed up outstanding pitching and clutch hitting the Mets reeled off an 11-game winning streak in which they outscored their opponents 43–22. They pulled out a 1–0 win at Los Angeles in 15 innings on June 4 to tie the previous club mark of seven straight wins before sweeping three from the Padres.

The streak ended with a 7–2 loss at San Francisco on June 11. Four days later, Murphy pulled off a trade that led to the Mets' first championship, getting first baseman Donn Clendenon from the Expos for prospects Steve Renko, Kevin Collins, Dave Colon, and Jay Carden.

Clendenon represented the power hitter the Mets had lacked since Ron Swoboda hit 19 homers as a rookie in 1965. Three years earlier, Clendenon set career highs with 28 homers, 98 RBIs, and a .520 slugging average while batting .299.

The Mets became Clendenon's fourth team in eight months. He was acquired by the Expos from the Pirates in the October 1968 expansion draft and went to the Astros two months later. But Clendenon balked at the move to Houston, refusing to report and threatening to retire before Commissioner Bowie Kuhn asked the Astros and Expos to reconfigure the deal to keep Clendenon in Montreal. Clendenon remained in limbo until the day of the Expos' season opener.

The trade also marked the first time in club history the Mets had acquired an established veteran for players cultivated through the team's farm system. Finally, other teams wanted the Mets' young talent.

Clendenon was more than just a perfect fit in the Mets' lineup. He was a settling influence in the clubhouse, bringing the team closer together with his sharp wit, self deprecation, and years of experience. He picked on all the young Mets, regardless of age, race, or background. Clendenon felt it was his job to keep his new teammates loose while also reminding them of the task at hand: a playoff berth.

Hodges used the right-handed Clendenon in a platoon with the lefty-hitting Kranepool. Clendenon hit only .160 in his first 25 at-bats with the Mets before reeling off a six-game hitting streak in which he was 10-for-26 with one home run and 11 RBIs. He capped that streak by stroking a double as a pinch-hitter in the ninth inning and scoring the tying run in a 4–3 win over the Cubs July 8, putting New York within 4½ games of Chicago for the NL East lead.

Clendenon recorded a .266 average with 12 home runs and 33 RBIs in his final 177 at-bats while constantly providing key hits, turning Murphy's first solely engineered trade into a doozy.

But the Mets began to regress following Seaver's one-hitter against the Cubs on July 9, going 15–17 to fall into third place, 9½ games behind the Cubs. There were moments in early August when Murphy had every right to press the panic button. But with the trade deadline long passed, Murphy had no choice but to rely on the veterans and home-grown talent he helped put together. By the time the waiver-trade deadline arrived, the Mets had turned themselves around and were pecking at the clicking heels of the Cubs.

The Mets took over first place for the first time in club history by sweeping a doubleheader from the Expos on September 10, exactly four weeks after they were 9½ games off the pace. They continued to expand the lead through outstanding pitching, crisp fielding, and timely hitting before clinching the NL East on September 24. Torre, the hitter the Mets sought during spring training, made the final out that secured the division crown.

The Mets won 38 of their final 49 games to finish 100–62, eight games ahead of the Cubs. No other team won more than 29 games after August 13, and only the Orioles had a better record among all major league clubs by the end of the season.

Yet the Mets weren't counted on to go far in the postseason. The Braves won the NL West by virtue of an outstanding lineup and a strong front end of the rotation. The Mets had the better pitching but were no match for an Atlanta wrecking crew featuring future Hall-of-Famers Hank Aaron and Orlando Cepeda.

Seaver was hit hard by the Braves in Game 1, Koosman was chased during the fifth inning of Game 2 and Gentry failed to get out of the third inning of the third game. That didn't stop the Mets from sweeping the series by a combined 27–15. Jones, who finished third in the NL with a .340 batting average during the regular season, went 6-for-14 with a home run and four RBIs. Jones, Agee, Boswell, Art Shamsky, and Garrett combined to bat .409 with six home runs and 17 RBIs. Atlanta's quintet of Aaron, Cepeda, Tony Gonzalez, Rico Carty, and Felix Millan contributed a .361 average with five home runs and 12 RBIs.

The Orioles also won their pennant in a sweep, setting up what appeared to be a World Series mismatch on paper. Baltimore's top three pitchers were Mike Cuellar, Dave McNally, and Jim Palmer, who were every bit as good as Seaver, Koosman, and Gentry in '69. The Birds had a far superior lineup that was expected to handle New York's youthful array of arms. And when Don Buford homered against Seaver leading off the first inning of Game 1, the rout appeared to be on. Baltimore cruised to a 4–1 victory as Cuellar went the distance on a six-hitter.

The World Series opener also marked the first postseason game for Clendenon, who remained on the bench during the NLCS as the Braves used a trio of right-handed starters. Clendenon went 2-for-4 versus Cuellar and would provide just three more hits the rest of the series. But the three hits were home runs as he helped the Mets win Games 2, 4, and 5.

Clendenon's first two blasts gave the Mets early leads in 2–1 victories. He jumpstarted his team in Game 5, ripping a two-run homer in the sixth inning after the Orioles took a 3–0 lead. Three innings later, Clendenon was jumping on the backs of Grote, Koosman, and Charles while the team celebrated a 5–3 victory and its first World Series title.

Murphy's young pitching staff limited the mighty Birds to just five runs over the final four games of the series while three of his acquisitions—Agee, Weis, and Clendenon—provided the highlights. Agee homered leading off the first inning of Game 3 before making two spectacular catches that saved at least five runs in a 5–0 shutout. Weis, who hit just six career home runs heading into the series, belting the game-tying blast in the seventh inning of Game 5. Clendenon was named the World Series MVP after hitting .357 with team-highs of three home runs, four RBIs, and four runs scored.

Murphy's track record as a trader was sparse by October 1969, but the two trades he did finalize were essential to the team's championship. He went into December prepared to part with members of his talented farm system to acquire veteran help.

Murphy pulled off another shrewd move on December 12, getting veteran pitcher and former 20-game winner Ray Sadecki from the Giants, along with outfielder Dave Marshall. All it cost the Mets was outfielder Jim Gosger and Bob Heise, two players who combined to hit .237 the rest of their careers. Sadecki was an integral part of the Mets' charge to the 1973 pennant. Chalk up another steal for "Fordham Johnny."

But another trade preceded the Sadecki-Marshall trade and was influenced by Hodges. Charles was released after the '69 season, and Garrett hit only .218 with one home run for the title team, leading the Mets to believe they needed another third baseman to improve the lineup. Hodges had managed in the American League against Joe Foy, a player possessing a potent bat and a checkered past. Foy had carved out a reputation as a hard partier who could be very tough to manage, but Hodges saw too much offensive potential to worry about his shortcomings.

Foy hit .262 with 11 homers and 71 RBIs for the 1969 Royals, which would have made him one of the Mets' top hitters that season. Hodges and Murphy, armed with enough young talent to pry away a veteran player from a fledgling ballclub, were prepared to send two prospects to Kansas City for Foy. This deal now shows up on everybody's short list of worst trades in Mets history.

The Mets parted with Bob Johnson, who compiled a 3.07 ERA in 214 innings for the 1970 Royals before helping the Pirates win the 1971 World Series. Murphy also jettisoned Amos Otis, a top minor league prospect who failed to hit much for the 1969 Mets.

Hodges had tried unsuccessfully to convert Otis into a third baseman before the 1969 season. Otis had become very comfortable as a center fielder in the minors, but the Mets already had a starting center fielder in Agee. That made Otis expendable, allowing Murphy to engineer the team's most harmful trade of the decade.

Foy lasted just one season as a Met, hitting .236 in 99 games and constantly testing the patience of Hodges. Otis went to five All-Star Games as a member of the Royals from 1970 to 1976, won three Gold Gloves, and finished among the top four in MVP voting on two occasions. Mets fans would lament his departure long after Agee was traded to Houston after the 1972 season. But the team's fortunes took an immediate turn for the worse when Murphy suffered a heart attack on December 30, 15 days after the Sadecki trade and one day before his 38th wedding anni-

versary. He and his wife, Betty, held hands in the intensive care unit at Roosevelt Hospital on their anniversary as the calendar flipped to a new decade.

Murphy was just 61 when he suffered a second heart attack on January 14. This time, it was massive and fatal. His death left the organization with the same type of void he managed to fill just over two years earlier. This time, that void remained for a decade.

The key part of Murphy's legacy was his ability to prevent Grant from meddling in player personnel decisions. Grant had his pet players and would try to influence moves involving the major league roster and the farm system. His evaluations would irritate Herzog, who turned a good farm system into a great one while constantly butting heads with Grant. If Herzog felt Murphy had a tough time making decisions, he and Mets fans should also be thankful that Murphy would intervene whenever Grant was ready to fire his uppity farm director.

Bob Scheffing took over after Murphy died, and the buffer between Grant and the Mets' true braintrust died with it. Through Scheffing and Payson, Grant was allowed to wield more power while showing all the foresight of a 1940s baseball GM. The Mets reeled off four straight winning seasons after Murphy's passing, but the heart of the ballclub—the farm system—was soon bereft of talent.

Steve Phillips   1997–2003

Born: 5/18/63
Named General Manager: 7/16/97
Dismissed: 6/12/03

The Mets enjoyed some great moments while Steve Phillips ran the front office. They challenged for the wildcard during his first two Septembers at the position before making the postseason in consecutive years for the first time in club history. The Mets almost pulled off an amazing run toward a division title in 2001 before several disappointing, high-priced deals eventually led to his departure in 2003.

Stephen Francis Phillips played baseball, basketball, and football while attending DeLaSalle Collegiate in Detroit. As a football player, he set a single-season school record with 1,257 rushing yards and twice led the school to the Catholic League championship game. Phillips also had his baseball uniform No. 7 retired.

Phillips planned to play college football for Northwestern coach Dennis Green before the Mets selected him in the fifth round of the 1981 draft. Phillips accepted the Mets' $42,000 contract offer and hit .281 with four homers and 10 RBIs in 89 at-bats for Kingsport that year.

He didn't climb above Single A until 1986 and went to the Tigers organization after batting .218 in 87 games for Double A Jackson in '87. He hit .254 in 22 games for Detroit's Double A club at Glens Falls before ending his playing career with a .250 average in 618 minor league games.

Phillips continued his education while playing in the

minors, attending Lawrence Institute of Technology and Wayne State University before receiving his B.S. in psychology from the University of Michigan in 1989.

The Mets hired him in January 1990 as their administrative assistant of scouting and minor league operations. He became the team's minor league director in September 1991 and was promoted to assistant general manager in December 1995. The Mets were named the Minor League Organization of the Year by *Baseball America* in 1995.

Phillips spent the next 19 months as the No. 2 man under general manager Joe McIlvaine. The Mets suddenly became contenders in 1997 despite a 4–10 start, pushing 10 games over .500 by June 23 and carrying a 48–38 record into the All-Star break. But co-owner Fred Wilpon wasn't happy with the day-to-day operations of the front office and decided to dismiss McIlvaine, who was in the final year of his contract. McIlvaine was a baseball wonk who loved nothing more than scouting a prospect but was slow to make major moves at the major league level. Wilpon questioned McIlvaine's skill set and said there were certain parts of the job that he neglected. McIlvaine was not big on media interaction, whereas Phillips was very comfortable discussing the organization with reporters.

Also, Phillips was often the point man in the office while McIlvaine took a first-hand look at his minor league talent. Wilpon chose Phillips to take over in July.

"There is no question about it, that being the point person for the organization, making the decisions and discussing the decisions, I think is a vital aspect of the job, and a skill that is necessary to do it," Phillips said a few days after taking over as GM.

"Joe has the skill. He is very articulate in interviews. He just didn't care for that aspect of the job as much."[16]

Phillips quickly demonstrated his tenacity, making numerous waiver claims that blocked other teams from making deals. He also spent the latter part of July crafting a multiplayer deal with Cubs GM and former Met Ed Lynch. Phillips was unable to complete the deal by the July 31 deadline, but he continued to speak with Lynch until the two were able to agree on a six-player swap eight days after the deadline. Phillips picked outfielder Brian McRae and relievers Turk Wendell and Mel Rojas from Chicago for outfielder Lance Johnson and two players to be named, who turned out to be starting pitcher Mark Clark and infielder Manny Alexander. Although Wendell would emerge as a valuable member of the bullpen, neither he nor Rojas was able to solve the Mets' late-innings problems as the team finished 88–74, four games off the wild-card lead. Still, it was the most excitement created at Shea Stadium since 1990 and allowed Phillips to dip into his farm system to acquire players who could make an immediate impact in '98.

Phillips again addressed the bullpen in the off-season, acquiring lefty Dennis Cook and right-hander John Hudek in December. He added another starting pitcher by signing Japanese product Masato Yoshii in January. But the biggest off-season move came days before training camp

as Al Leiter was acquired from Florida with Ralph Milliard for A.J. Burnett, Jesus Sanchez, and Robert Stratton.

Leiter represented the ace the Mets sorely needed in 1997, but he wasn't going to do much to improve the team's power problems. The Mets hit 153 home runs in '97, just two off the league average. However, the team was looking at the prospect of playing the first three to four months without catcher Todd Hundley, who paced the team with 30 home runs the previous year and had banged out 71 since 1996. Phillips was unable to land another heavy hitter in the off-season despite the urging of Valentine, who thought the club had just about everything else to win the wild-card.

Valentine's assessment was spot on as the Mets hit only 12 home runs while opening the 1998 season 14–14. They were wasting too many strong outings by Leiter, Yoshii, Rick Reed, and Bobby Jones while their .240 team batting average prevented many big rallies.

The Mets were still hanging around .500 when catcher Mike Piazza was dealt by the Dodgers to the Marlins after failing to work out a long-term contract with Los Angeles. It was obvious the Marlins, who had just gutted payroll after winning the '97 World Series, did not plan to keep Piazza very long.

Members of the Mets media saw Piazza as the solution to the team's power woes, although Phillips continued to state publicly that Piazza wasn't a good fit for the team since Hundley was set to return in late June or early July. What the Mets needed were productive corner outfielders, not a second All-Star catcher.

The Mets were 23–20 after homering twice in a 6–1 win over the Reds on May 21. One day later, Piazza was a member of the Mets after being acquired from the Marlins for three of New York's top prospects, including outfielder Preston Wilson. It was a surprising move considering Phillips and Wilpon had continued to insist they could live without Piazza. Their stance changed when co-owner Nelson Doubleday, who rarely meddled in player personnel matters, urged Phillips to acquire him regardless of Hundley's pending status. Once Piazza was in the fold, Phillips hinted more deals could be coming.

"I think we were in that rebuilding stage for several years," he said. "But we got to that point of winning 88 games, to where you're on the brink of doing it. You have to shift from being a team that's rebuilding to a team that has to make that effort to get to the next level.

"A couple of people have said that to me, 'I guess you're looking to go for it this year.' I said, 'Yeah, we want to win this year.'"[17]

The deal allowed John Olerud to concentrate more on his on-base percentage and less on his power numbers after he belted 22 home runs in 1997, two off his career high. Piazza's presence also took pressure off Edgardo Alfonzo, Butch Huskey, and McRae, but it also caused Hundley to feel betrayed after being assured he'd be the starting catcher once he was healthy enough to return.

Piazza started off slowly as a Met yet finished with a .348 average, a .607 slugging average, 23 homers, 33 doubles, and 76 RBIs in 109 games. Olerud established both career high and team records by batting .354 with a .447 on-base percentage, all while driving in 93 runs and belting 22 homers for the second straight year. Leiter pitched as hoped, going 17–6 with a 2.47 ERA and 174 strikeouts in 193 innings. Cook and Wendell served as outstanding setup men for closer John Franco, who earned 38 saves.

But the season ended poorly. The Mets led the wild-card heading into the final week of the season before dropping their final five games to end up one game back. The team faltered in virtually every aspect of the game during the collapse, causing Phillips to retool once again. He had two new starting outfielders, a starting third baseman, and a new eighth-inning reliever by the time the Mets reported to camp. But he almost lost his job in the process.

Phillips received a short leave of absence in November 1998 after admitting to an affair with a Mets minor league employee. Ownership remained in his corner after Phillips was forthright when approached about the affair.

"Rather than make up a story of where I was, I thought it was important to tell the truth," Phillips said after returning to work. "I needed to make my family situation a priority and be home to deal with the problems I caused.

"And in those last two weeks, we've started the process. I'm not back up here with my collar buttoned down and my tie in place saying that everything is back in order. This is going to be a lengthy process. And I don't know what the ultimate result will be."[18]

"We do not believe that his admission of a consensual relationship of short-lived duration with a woman is reason to say that he cannot carry out his responsibilities with the Mets," Wilpon said a few days before Phillips rejoined the team.[19]

Phillips engineered two steals on the same day at the winter meetings, fleecing the Dodgers and Orioles. First, he shipped Hundley and pitching prospect Arnold Gooch to Los Angeles for outfielder Roger Cedeno and catcher Charles Johnson. He immediately flipped Johnson, sending him to Baltimore straight up for reliever Armando Benitez. One day later, Phillips signed Gold Glove third baseman Robin Ventura to a free-agent contract, allowing Edgardo Alfonzo to be moved to second. Two weeks later, outfielder Rickey Henderson was under contract with the Mets. Phillips had acquired Cedeno, Benitez, Ventura, and Henderson within 15 days while giving up just one player—Hundley—from his big-league roster.

The Mets now had another potential 30-home-run hitter in Ventura to go with Piazza. Ventura also solidified the infield defense, giving the Mets four potential Gold Glovers in the infield. Henderson and Cedeno added speed to the Mets' arsenal after the ballclub finished dead last in the league with 62 stolen bases in 1998. Benitez represented the intimidating flamethrower the team had lacked since Randy Myers was traded to the Reds for Franco in the fall of 1989.

Phillips wasn't done. He signed free agent Pat Mahomes on December 21, a deal that wasn't fully appreciated until he went 8–0 in 39 relief appearances in 1999. Another underappreciated pickup was Orel Hershiser, who was signed as a free agent about a week before the opener.

The lineup was awesome entering the season and only got better when outfielder Darryl Hamilton was acquired in a trade-deadline swap from Colorado. Piazza, Alfonzo, Ventura, Henderson, and Cedeno each hit over .300 and qualified for the batting title, an exceptional accomplishment for a franchise that had never produced more than two .300 hitters in the same season.

Cedeno shattered a club record with 66 stolen bases, four more than the Mets managed to swipe the previous year. The 40-year-old Henderson was good for 37 steals and became the first Met over age 32 to hit over .300.

The Mets set a record for fewest infield errors in a single season as Ventura, Alfonzo, Olerud, and Rey Ordonez combined for just 27. Ventura and Ordonez came away with Gold Gloves, and Alfonzo was a deserving candidate.

Hershiser finished second on the team with 179 innings pitched and tied Leiter for the club lead with 13 victories. Hershiser's presence became crucial when Bobby Jones went down with a season-ending back injury.

Benitez was sensational during the first half and took over as closer when Franco went on the disabled list early that summer. Benitez was so good in his new role to force Valentine to keep him as closer even after Franco returned.

The Mets also had three players—Piazza, Ventura, and Alfonzo—hit 27 or more home runs in 1999. The only previous time the Mets had three players swat that many homers was 1987, when Darryl Strawberry, Kevin McReynolds, and Howard Johnson combined to hit 104.

Phillips had built a power-hitting team that recorded a high batting average and displayed excellent speed. The infield defense was second to none, while Cedeno's range in center and right field saved the team several runs. The bullpen, crafted almost entirely from Phillips acquisitions, was among the best in baseball and covered up deficiencies in the rotation. And the Mets almost blew a playoff berth anyway.

The club opened pretty strong until an eight-game losing streak left the Mets 27–28 through 55 games and prompted Phillips to fire pitching coach Bob Apodaca, bullpen coach Randy Niemann, and hitting coach Tom Robson before a series finale at Yankee Stadium. Valentine fumed over the dismissals and said he should be the next to go if the team didn't play markedly better over the next 55 games.

"In my view, we are underachieving as a team," Phillips said immediately after the dismissals. "Our starting pitching has struggled for a good part of the year, and recently our entire pitching staff. We weren't getting the job done. A third of the way through the season we had to make a decision to get the ship righted and get back on track to where we want to be."

"On the hitting side, we are doing some things very well. We lead the league in on-base percentage. But we are eighth in runs scored and we lead all of baseball in runners left on base. We're getting them on, but we're not getting them in."[20]

Fifty-five games and 40 victories later, the Mets were leading the wild-card and challenging the Braves for the division crown.

Phillips continued to tinker with the roster before the trade deadline, getting Kenny Rogers for highly touted prospect Terrence Long and Leo Vazquez. Rogers was the lefty starter the Mets sorely needed as the team entered the stretch run, causing Phillips to part with one of his blue-chip prospects.

Hamilton and reliever Chuck McElroy were sent by the Rockies to the Mets for McRae, reliever Rigo Beltran, and a prospect July 31. The swap represented one of Phillips' best deadline deals and gave the Mets another .300 hitter.

"He's not afraid to make a deal, and that's big," Leiter said the following winter. "A lot of G.M.'s are afraid to pull the trigger, because it's their neck on the line."[21]

Veteran shortstop Shawon Dunston was also picked up at the deadline for Craig Paquette, another trade that produced a high yield. But the third deadline pickup became a short- and long-term disaster as Phillips dealt reliever Greg McMichael and disappointing former phenom Jason Isringhausen to the A's for reliever Billy Taylor. Of the many trades Phillips engineered during his six years as GM, the Isringhausen transaction was among his worst as the "Izzy" became an elite closer in Oakland while Taylor fizzled in his two months as a Met.

Rogers solidified the rotation, Hamilton improved the outfield, and Dunston provided depth at several positions. The trio helped the Mets stay atop the wild-card standings and create a scare in Atlanta over the next seven weeks.

New York was one game behind the Braves and four games ahead of the Reds for the wild card following the Mets' 8–6 win over the Phillies September 19. They owned the second-best winning percentage in all of baseball at 92–58, 1½ games better than the other team in New York. Eight games and seven losses later, the Mets were two games behind the Astros and Reds for the wild-card with just three games to play. They had somehow managed to duplicate the same late-season swoon that cost them the 1998 wild-card, although they still had one weekend to avoid a collapse.

The Mets closed out the regular season with a series against the Pirates at Shea Stadium. Fans were so certain the team would complete the meltdown that only 29,548 bothered to attend a 3–2, 11-inning victory that was decided on Ventura's bases-loaded hit. The Mets drew under 37,000 the next night as Reed pitched a three-hitter in a 7–0 victory that left them tied with Cincinnati for the wild-card heading into the final day.

The regular season finale had Phillips' fingerprints all over it. Hershiser allowed just two hits in 5⅓ innings before Cook, Mahomes, Wendell, and Benitez combined to pitch 3⅔ shutout innings of one-hit relief while striking out five. But the game remained tied heading into the bottom of the ninth until Melvin Mora, a minor leaguer signing by Phillips in 1998, hit a one-out single to spark the winning rally. Mora moved to third on Alfonzo's base hit and scored the winning run on a wild pitch to give the Mets at least a tie for the wild-card, pending the outcome of the Reds' rain-delayed game at Milwaukee.

Once the Reds won their game, the Mets traveled to Cincinnati for a one-game playoff the following day. Leiter fired a two-hitter and Henderson homered as the Mets won 5–0 to take the wild-card and earn a meeting with Arizona.

The Mets won the division series in four games as Todd Pratt ended it with a solo homer in extra innings. The Braves grabbed a three-games-to-none lead in the NLCS before the Mets took the next two games by storming back from one-run deficits in their final at-bat. The Mets trailed 3–2 in the 15th inning of Game 5 until Pratt worked out a bases-loaded walk with two out and Ventura followed with his "Grand Slam Single."

Game 6 was another exciting game as the Mets grabbed an 8–7 lead in the eighth after trailing 5–0 and 7–3. But the Braves tied it in the eighth and 10th innings before winning it on Rogers' bases-loaded walk to Andruw Jones in the 11th. New York had come within two outs of becoming the first team in big league history to force a seventh game after dropping the first three.

"As dramatic as everything was for us to get to that point, and for a bases-loaded walk to end the season, it wasn't right." Phillips said the following spring. "At that point it was, 'Okay, what's the plan, Steve?'"[22]

The final loss also came with some controversy. Henderson and Bobby Bonilla, who was reacquired by the Mets from the Dodgers for Mel Rojas in a mutual salary dump in December 1998, were accused of playing cards in the clubhouse while the Mets rallied. Bonilla, who battled knee problems while hitting .160 in 60 games, was released in January while Henderson was put on a short leash. Henderson's .315 average in 1999 allowed Phillips and the Mets to be a bit more tolerant of his alleged indiscretions.

Phillips had to face the possibility of losing one of his top players for the first time as GM when Olerud filed for free agency after the season. Olerud had his heart set on returning to his native Washington and inked a deal with the Mariners, creating a huge void at first.

"We are a work-the-count kind of offense," Phillips said following Olerud's defection. "We take pitchers deep into the count, so we focus on pitches per plate appearance, which translates into on-base percentage, which translates into runs scored.

"John was an on-base percentage guy. He drove in 96 with two guys in front of him with over .400 on-base averages. He walked 125 times. One of the things I think is that even without John, we're going to have a significant number of guys on base, and that a guy who swings more will drive in more runs. So we've changed our offense a little that way, but without letting the opposing pitcher off the hook by letting him do less work."[23]

Rogers also became a free agent after pitching poorly in the postseason. Phillips allowed him to ink a deal with the Rangers, leaving a void in the rotation.

Phillips found a new first baseman by inking free-agent Todd Zeile, who had played only a handful of games at the position before 2000 but was a player who showed a willingness to adapt to any situation. Zeile was inked December 16, one week before Phillips completed a blockbuster trade with Houston.

Lefty Mike Hampton went 22–4 with the '99 Astros but was about to enter the final year of his contract. Another 20-win season would make it financially impossible for the Astros to re-sign him, causing the team to shop him around at the winter meetings. Phillips gave Mets fans an early Christmas present by getting Hampton and outfielder Derek Bell for Cedeno, talented prospect Octavio Dotel, and a minor leaguer.

Phillips also made two moves that appeared insignificant when they were completed in March. He picked up minor league outfielder Timo Perez and acquired utility-man Joe McEwing from the Cardinals for Jesse Orosco, who was acquired by Phillips before camp. McEwing quickly became the Mets' supersub, but Perez's impact wasn't felt until September.

Olerud and Rogers were the only major losses suffered by the Mets during the off-season. The team entered 2000 as a playoff favorite before Phillips had to deal with a few question marks. Henderson spent the spring angling for a new contract and was released in May after hitting .219 in 31 games, turning the Mets into a station-to-station offense once again. Hampton experienced control problems in his first three starts, but Bell's bat was making the Cedeno deal look pretty good through the first month of the year.

The Mets, who had avoided a major injury in 1999, finally had one in May 2000 as Ordonez broke his arm against the Dodgers, keeping him out the rest of the season. Mora replaced Ordonez but was unable to play well defensively, causing Phillips to find another shortstop at the July trade deadline.

Other than Henderson and Ordonez, the Mets were able to avoid the drama that made 1999 a turbulent season. Jay Payton became the new center fielder following an injury to Hamilton and hit well enough to finish third in the Rookie of the Year balloting. Benny Agbayani made the Mets forget about Henderson in left field, and the streaky-hitting Bell was able to carry the club from time to time.

But it was apparent Mora wasn't an everyday shortstop, causing Phillips to make a deal that was a perfect short-term remedy but a disastrous long-term move. Mora was dealt to the Orioles for Mike Bordick, a Gold Glove-caliber shortstop who could produce at the plate when his knees weren't bothering him. Bordick was also slated for free agency after the season and was expected to return to the Orioles.

Steve Phillips signed first baseman Todd Zeile during the 1999–2000 off-season. Photo courtesy of David Ferry

Bordick's acquisition came after Phillips had a deal in place that would have brought All-Star shortstop Barry Larkin to New York. Larkin nixed the deal as a five-and-10 man and remained with the Reds.

The Mets created distance between themselves and the rest of the wild-card contenders following the Bordick trade. They stayed in the NL East race until the final week of the season and captured the wild-card with relative ease, making Phillips the first GM in club history to build back-to-back postseason teams.

The Perez deal also paid off handsomely in the fall as he provided a spark in September to earn his way onto the postseason roster as a spare outfielder. Once Bell suffered a severe ankle injury in Game 1 of the National League Division Series in San Francisco, Perez became the right fielder.

The Mets dispatched the Giants in four games before facing the Cardinals in the Championship Series, where Hampton and Perez led the way. Hampton was named the MVP of the NLCS after going 2–0 while tossing shutout ball in 16 innings. Perez was a major disruption to the

Cards, batting .304 and setting an NLCS record with eight runs scored as the Mets prevailed in five games to set up the first Subway Series in 44 years.

Piazza also had an outstanding NLCS, hitting .412 with two homers, four RBIs, and seven runs scored after entering the series with a .211 lifetime average in the postseason. Phillips said Piazza was the one who changed the culture of the franchise.

"When we got Mike Piazza, it gave our organization credibility," Phillips said. "We went from being a nice little team on the field and in people's perception to a real contender.

"He was booed and had negative press for the first time in his career. But when you work and persevere, the reward is that much higher, and as I look back now, there was no better player we could have got.

"In the last three years, we've gone from being a team that was usually on the no-trade clause list to one that players have wanted to play for. Al Leiter stayed. Robin Ventura wanted to come. Todd Zeile."[24]

The Mets lost the World Series in five games but played valiantly every night. They dropped a one-run decision in extra innings in the opener and scored five times in the ninth inning of Game 2 before losing by a run. The Mets pulled within 2–1 in the series by taking the third game 4–2 before losing 3–2 the following night. The Yankees closed out the series by scoring twice in the ninth off Leiter to beat the Mets 4–2.

The successful season came as Phillips and Valentine were working on the final year of their contracts. Both were rewarded with multiyear deals, allowing them to continue a strong working relationship. The two admitting to butting heads at times, but the results had been positive since the two were paired together. As an accomplished ballroom dancer, Valentine knew when to lead and when to follow.

"Steve and I are going to demonstrate not only to the outside world, but to those within our organization, that this is the ultimate team effort, that we are going to put forth an effort that will rival those who locked hands and climbed mountains and put the flag on the top of mountains during wars," Valentine said after receiving his extension. "This is going to be the real thing. Not that it wasn't before, but we've learned what's right and wrong from many experiences that we've had, good and bad. And what's right is to be together."

"I think the one thing we've both had to deal with is forgiveness," Phillips said. "There's been times when either one of us has felt offended by the other, by something said or something done. If you're going to make things work, you've got to move forward and do what's in the best interests of the organization. You've got to get over it sometimes."[25]

Hampton and Bordick were crucial to the Mets' late-season success, and neither showed much interest in staying with the team past 2000. Hampton inked a huge deal with the Rockies and Bordick returned to Baltimore, keeping Phillips very busy in the off-season.

Although Ordonez was expected to be 100 percent in 2001, the Mets had eyes on another free-agent shortstop. Alex Rodriguez had played out his contract with the Mariners and was the most sought-after player on the market. Phillips and the Mets entered into aggressive negotiations with A-Rod once the free-agent signing period began before backing off, claiming Rodriguez was making demands that would be divisive to the team. The negotiations irritated Rodriguez's agent, Scott Boras, who only a year early was calling Phillips a model general manager.

"I think Steve has a dynamic about him that is really important to the Mets," Boras says. "He's experienced in three ways. First, he has pursued the big deal and landed it, and he has the confidence to do it again. Second, he has dealt with New York, professionally and personally, and has come out on top. Third, he knows what he's doing; he's credible."[26]

Phillips was still hopeful he could reach a deal with Rodriguez and Boras, but he also had to explain why the Mets were suddenly disinterested in landing baseball's top player at the time. The contract demands made by Rodriguez and Boras were far more than what was given to Piazza, the Mets' star player since 1998.

"The way it was explained to me was those things, that structure that was necessary to manage him, is necessary to manage him," Phillips said of Rodriguez's request for his own office at Shea Stadium and several personal assistants. "He's been managed for the last couple of years. The structure they have in place with the office and staff is necessary to handle his life off the field and on the field and allow him to be able to perform.

"For the last two years he has functioned as a managed athlete. Because he's evolved into an international icon and earning $15 to $20 million off the field, those other demands take a lot of attention, and without that structure he wouldn't be able to succeed."[27]

Surmising that the managed athlete was unmanageable, Phillips had Ordonez back at short for the 2001 opener after Rodriguez took a 10-year contract with the Rangers.

Phillips accepted quantity over quality after losing Hampton, signing free agents Kevin Appier and Steve Trachsel to join the rotation. Both were innings-eaters who enjoyed success in big game situations, but neither matched what Hampton had given the Mets in 2000.

The Mets also signed Japanese outfielder Tsuyoshi Shinjo and picked up Desi Relaford to bolster the bench. Shinjo was a highly stylized player who occasionally sported orange hair and accessorized with extra-large orange wrist bands. Relaford plugged holes at several positions and actually was more valuable to the Mets than Shinjo. Both were strong yet inexpensive signings by Phillips.

Appier showed guts on the mound and became a fan favorite by staying in an early season game against the Marlins after being drilled on the cheek by a pitch. But Trachsel started off poorly and was sent to the minors for a rehab assignment after giving up four homers in the third inning of a 15–3 drubbing by the Padres on May 17.

Pitching was the least of the Mets' problems during the first four months of the 2001 season. Ventura stopped hitting for power, Alfonzo stopped hitting for average, and Perez stopped hitting altogether. Shinjo, Relaford, and Shinjo were often the catalysts of the offense, causing pitchers to throw carefully to Piazza.

As the trade deadline approached, the Mets were sellers instead of buyers with the team seemingly out of the playoff hunt. Phillips moved to bolster the team for the future, sending Wendell, Cook, and Pratt to the Phillies in two separate deals while acquiring lefty pitcher Bruce Chen and backup catcher Gary Bennett. Phillips also released Hamilton, whose ankle problem limited his production just two years after he provided a huge spark to the offense.

Reed was the next to go, sent to Minnesota July 30 for outfielder Matt Lawton, whose brother had been a Mets prospect. Reed's departure appeared to be the final blow to whatever chance the Mets had to work themselves back in the division race.

With their eye on next season, the Mets fell to 54–68 and 13 ½ games off the NL East pace by August 17, a frustrating turn of events considering the Braves weren't playing too well, either. Despite the salary dumps and reconfigured bullpen, the Mets suddenly went on an unexpected hot streak that vaulted them back into contention. They won 10 of their last 13 games in August and opened September by winning seven of nine before heading to Pittsburgh for a three-game set. Hours before the series with the Pirates was to begin on September 11, terrorists had flown planes into the Twin Towers, leaving thousands either dead or missing. The attacks led Major League Baseball to suspend the season for eight days as Valentine and the rest of the Mets worked at a staging area in the parking lot of Shea Stadium.

New York City was in need of a lift after the attacks, and Phillips' team provided it by sweeping the Pirates before returning to Shea just five games out of first place heading into a series with the Braves. The Mets were the first major league team to play in New York and invited hundreds of first responders and other members of the city's fire, police, Port Authority, and EMT departments.

Piazza put a positive charge into the night by drilling a two-run homer to lead the Mets to a 3–2 win over the Braves. The Mets also won the next day to get within 3½ games of Atlanta before dropping the series finale.

A three-game sweep of the Expos in Montreal followed the emotional Atlanta series, putting the Mets within three games of the Braves heading into a weekend set at Turner Field. But the Mets dropped the opener and blew a 5–1 lead in the ninth inning of the next game to play themselves out of the race. Still, their 82–80 record was quite an accomplishment, considering the team's record in mid-August.

Wilpon had a strong working relationship with Phillips heading into the off-season and believed he was shrewd enough to turn the team into serious challengers for another playoff berth. Although the Mets' budget for players in 2002 was around $95 million, Wilpon said he wouldn't mind going over that figure if it meant another pennant.

"We have a 100 percent track record there," Wilpon said, referring to the times Phillips has asked for special permission to make a move. "We've said yes every time. Over four or five years, there have been several times; more than two.

"Someone said to me, 'You're not going to get any free agents.' I said, 'That's not entirely what Steve said.' Steve said we will more likely be getting our significant changes through the trade route because of the nature of our team. But he didn't preclude us from the free-agent market."[28]

Phillips spent the off-season trying to improve virtually every aspect of the ballclub. Ventura was traded to the Yankees for David Justice, who remained a Met for three days. Justice was shuttled to the A's for pitchers Mark Guthrie and Tyler Yates, two days before starting pitcher Shawn Estes was acquired from the Giants for Shinjo and Relaford.

The Mets pulled off the biggest blockbuster deal of the winter meetings as Phillips picked up 12-time All-Star and 10-time Gold Glove second baseman Roberto Alomar from Cleveland, along with pitcher Mike Bacsik and a prospect for Jerrod Riggan, Alex Escobar, Matt Lawton, Billy Traber, and Earl Snyder. The deal was completely unexpected after Indians GM Marc Shapiro said two weeks earlier that Alomar wasn't going anywhere.

"To have thought that we would be able to manage the payroll and get a No. 3 hitter that can get on base, slug, steal bases, and play defense at a Gold Glove caliber as Alomar can—I wouldn't have thought it was possible," Phillips said. "So we're obviously very, very happy about the deal."[29]

The Alomar deal represented the Mets' "win now" mentality after their impressive late-season showing. Traber was New York's top pitching prospect and Escobar represented the best outfield talent. Alomar hit .336 with 20 homers and 100 RBIs while giving absolutely no indication he was about to reach the downside of his career.

Phillips padded the lineup two weeks later, landing slugger Mo Vaughn from the Angels for Appier. Vaughn missed all of 2001 due to injury after hitting .272 with 36 homers and 117 RBIs for Anaheim in 2000. Like Alomar, Vaughn was in his early thirties and appeared to have several good years left in his ever-expanding body.

Phillips also added two new outfielders as the Mets reacquired Cedeno and Jeromy Burnitz, who had become a dangerous slugger with the Brewers. Burnitz was packaged in a January 21 deal that sent starting pitcher Jeff D'Amico to Milwaukee for Alex Ochoa, Lenny Harris, and Glendon Rusch. Ochoa and two other players were picked up from the Rockies the same day for Agbayani and Zeile.

The Mets entered the season with a starting rotation of Leiter, Trachsel, D'Amico, Estes, and free-agent signee

Pedro Astacio. The bullpen now had Guthrie and veteran David Weathers as setup men for Armando Benitez. And when the Mets lost Franco to Tommy John surgery, Phillips picked up Scott Strickland from the Expos.

The new rotation, revamped bullpen, and bolstered lineup made the Mets appear ready to make another post-season appearance. Instead, the acquisitions provided a bad mix of starting pitchers who had seen better days, former All-Stars who suddenly lost their hitting stroke, and speedsters who refused to run. Even worse for Phillips and the Mets, they had increased team payroll dramatically to seize an opportunity to finally finish ahead of the Braves. By season's end, they also finished behind the Phillies, Marlins, and Expos in a season that conjured up memories of the Mets' miserable 1992 season.

The Mets actually had an 18–11 record and a one-game lead despite an offense that scored three runs or fewer 16 times during that stretch. They owned a share of first place as late as May 29, but their free fall had already begun.

Phillips remained certain the team would snap out of its malaise since the lineup was just too good to perform this poorly.

"We're going to hit better, no question about it," Phillips said in June as the Mets slid into fourth place. "I think everybody's 40 or 50 points below their career averages right now. We're just in one of those group slumps."[30]

The slumping Mets prompted Wilpon to issue the dreaded vote of confidence, all while making promises that were eventually broken.

"Steve and Bobby will actively complete their contracts with the New York Mets, and hopefully will be here longer than their contracts," Wilpon told the *New York Times* in reference to Phillips and Valentine. "They will complete their contracts."[31]

The Braves left them in the dust and were 10½ games ahead of New York by the end of June. The margin reached 20 games by August 14 and topped out at 27½ games by the penultimate day of the season.

Most of the newcomers were somewhere in between disappointing and dreadful. Vaughn made roughly $12 million for hitting .259 with 26 homers, 18 doubles, and 72 RBIs, statistics that were much lower than his norm. Alomar's .266 average, 11 homers, and 53 RBIs came at a cost of about $8 million. Alomar stole only 16 bases after averaging 30 the previous 10 years, and his glovework at second deteriorated in direct proportion to his offense. Burnitz cashed paychecks totaling over $7 million before taxes, compensation for his .215 average, 19 home runs, 54 RBIs, and 135 strikeouts in 479 at-bats. Cedeno looked nothing like the player that hit .313 with 66 stolen bases, finishing 2002 with a .260 average and 25 steals. Cedeno's $2.375 million salary was five times more than in 1999 and was about to double in 2003.

The bullpen fared pretty well despite the loss of Franco as Weathers and Guthrie each had ERAs under 3.00. But Estes and D'Amico never showed any consistency and combined to go 10–19 with a 4.75 ERA in 52 starts.

There were other contributing factors to the Mets' 75–86 finish, but there was little Phillips could do in the way of acquiring new offensive talent. Vaughn, Alomar, and Burnitz each had at least one more year remaining on his contract and were slated to cost the Mets a combined $37.3 million dollars in 2003. That didn't stop Phillips attempting to spend his way out of the team's mess.

Cliff Floyd was inked to a free-agent deal, about 2½ months after Phillips fired Valentine. Floyd and Valentine had feuded for years, making it doubtful the outfielder would have ever considered the Mets as long as Bobby V. was in the dugout. Now all the Mets had to do was hope Floyd didn't flame out like so many other recent pickups.

In Phillips' defense, there was no way he could have predicted the deterioration of Alomar, Burnitz, and Cedeno. Vaughn was a gamble given his hefty salary and recent injury problems. But the starting rotation pretty much performed to expectations, prompting Phillips to seek another stud pitcher.

Phillips managed to pry free-agent lefty Tom Glavine from the Braves, giving him a four-year package worth more than $42 million. Mike Stanton left the Yankees for Mets money. Phillips also brought back Shinjo and signed lefty reliever Graeme Lloyd, right-hander Dan Wheeler, infielder Jay Bell, and first baseman Tony Clark. Another interesting acquisition was David Cone, who was back with the team 11 years after the Mets jettisoned him to the Blue Jays.

Phillips had a new manager in place when the Mets reported for 2003 spring training, hiring former A's skipper Art Howe. It was the first managerial hire by Phillips, who took over as GM 10 months after Valentine entered the Mets dugout in 1996.

The new faces led to the same result, only worse. Vaughn appeared in just 27 games before landing on the DL for good with a degenerative hip condition that ended his career. Alomar showed no physical maladies yet continued to hit around .260, more than 40 points behind his lifetime average. Burnitz's bat showed great improvement, although he and Cedeno were shifted around in the outfield. Cedeno ran even less frequently than in 2002 and failed to cover ample ground when Floyd and Burnitz were flanked next to him in the outfield.

The bullpen faltered as Benitez, Weathers, Stanton, Lloyd, Wheeler, and Pedro Feliciano all had ERAs over 3.00 and developed a propensity to blow late-inning leads. Howe used 20 different pitchers out of the bullpen and often had his fingers crossed when even his better setup men were brought in with runners on base.

The Mets actually turned Glavine into a losing pitcher for the first time since his early days with the Braves. Glavine occasionally fell victim to limited offense or an incendiary bullpen, although many of his struggles were self-inflicted as he went 9–14 with a 4.52 ERA.

The lone bright spot among the newcomers was Floyd, who hit .290 with 18 homers, 25 doubles, and 68 RBIs in

108 games before he was shelved in August due to heel surgery. Phillips was gone long before Floyd was placed on the disabled list.

The Mets looked at their exorbitant payroll, dwindling attendance, and poor record when they dismissed Phillips in June and replaced him with assistant Jim Duquette. Wilpon set forth a new blueprint for success after the team managed to duplicate the moves that turned them into expensive failures only a decade earlier.

"There are no quick fixes in this game and we must bring people from our minor leagues, we must scout them better, we must develop them better, and we must have a pipeline to the major league club," Wilpon said. "That's important for this club and perhaps for any club. We're going to work on that and stress that."[32]

It took Duquette about a month to shed several high-salaried players, but it took another GM—Omar Minaya—to turn the team into a legitimate contender again.

Phillips landed on his feet as a broadcaster and soon became one of ESPN's top analysts, working in the studio and at the ballgames. For many fans, he was a nice change of pace after years of listening to Joe Morgan. Phillips offered outstanding commentary and rarely held back on criticism when he deemed it necessary.

But his television career was short-circuited in 2009 by another affair, this time with an ESPN office assistant who began to harass Phillips' wife. Phillips was suspended after the situation became tabloid fodder.

"I am deeply sorry that I have put my family and colleagues through this," Phillips said in a statement released by ESPN. "It is a personal matter that I will not comment on further."[33]

Phillips checked himself into a counseling program in Mississippi and was fired by the network. He returned to broadcasting in 2010, serving as a baseball insider on the *Mike Francesa Show* on WFAN before becoming part of Chris Russo's broadcast team on Sirius XM. By October 2011 he was co-host of the *Gary and Phillips in the Morning Show* on Mad Dog Radio.

"To have the chance to do a national daily radio show, in drive time, on a top-notch channel like Mad Dog Radio, is one of the more thrilling opportunities of my career," Phillips said.[34]

Steve Phillips was back on top just 12 months after an embarrassing fall.

Bob Scheffing   1970–1974

Born: 8/11/13   Overland, Missouri
Died: 10/26/85   Phoenix, Arizona
Named General Manager: 1/19/70
Resigned: 10/1/74

The Mets had four winning seasons in the five years Bob Scheffing was general manager, including their improbable 1973 pennant run. He was the only Mets GM to post winning seasons in each of his first four full years at the post until Steve Phillips did it from 1998 to 2001.

But the Scheffing era is best remembered by one horrendous trade, underachievement at the major league level, a ridiculous number of player injuries, and a farm system that was going to seed during his watch. The injuries certainly were beyond his control and torpedoed what was shaping up to be a marvelous playoff run in 1972. However, the bulk of the team's fortunes from 1970 to 1974 rest edsquarely on his shoulders as the Mets went from defending champs to fifth-place finishers.

Robert Boden Scheffing was a respected baseball man before joining the Mets in 1966. He was a minor league manager at age 24 before enjoying an eight-year career as a major league catcher who hit .300 for the 1948 Cubs. His big-league playing career was interrupted by a three-year hitch in the Navy during World War II, preventing him from playing for the Cubs in the 1945 World Series.

Scheffing ended his playing career in 1951 and spent the next two years as a coach for the St. Louis Browns before joining the Cubs' staff in 1954. He took over as manager of the Cubs' Pacific Coast League team in 1955, leading it to a third-place finish before winning the 1956 title by 16 games.

Cubs owner Phil Wrigley hired him to manage his team in 1956. The '57 Cubs finished last in Scheffing's rookie season as a major league skipper before going 146–162 over the next two years, marking the first time since 1946 and 1947 that the Cubs had gone two straight years without finishing last or next-to-last.

But Scheffing was let go after the 1959 season and spent the next year coaching on Charley Dressen's staff at Milwaukee before he was hired to manage in Detroit. Scheffing's 1961 Tigers put a scare into the mighty Yankees, pulling within 1½ games of first place on August 31 before an eight-game losing streak took them out of contention.

The '61 Tigers finished with 101 victories, the team's best showing since the '34 Bengals won 101 games and the pennant. Scheffing led Detroit to an 85–76 mark in 1962 but was fired after opening 24–36 the following season.

Scheffing remained in the Tigers organization through 1965, working as a broadcaster in 1964 before becoming a scout the next year. He was seeking more responsibility by the winter of 1966, and he used a rather unique way to fish for a new job.

Scheffing's association with the Mets began with a Christmas card. He sent season's greetings to several manager league general managers, along with a note stating his interest in a new challenge. Bing Devine was the Mets' front office official who received Scheffing's card and passed it along to team president George Weiss.

Devine was in St. Louis with his family for the Christmas holiday. So was Scheffing, who was visiting his mother when he received a call from Devine. The two met at the lunch counter of a local supermarket, had a couple of hotdogs, and discussed an opening in the Mets' front office.

When they left the grocery store, Scheffing was the Mets' new director of player development.

The Mets soon became one of baseball's most admired farm systems as the team drafted and signed several pitchers who became team mainstays well into the 1970s. Scheffing quickly saw the level of pitching talent and recommended to his minor league managers that their pitchers work every fifth day rather than the normal four days during that era. With the abundance of young arms in the system, it allowed more hurlers to showcase their wares while protecting their arms.

Scheffing also had two outstanding baseball men at his side: Whitey Herzog and Joe McDonald. Herzog regularly visited each minor league team and had the best handle on determining who were the prospects and suspects. McDonald kept Herzog's assessments in order as director of minor league operations, and their work led to a team breakthrough in 1968. Nine of the team's 14 pitchers that season were home-grown Mets, as were 10 of the 20 position players.

Johnny Murphy shuffled the deck after replacing Devine as GM following the 1967 season, elevating Herzog to director of player personnel while reassigning Scheffing to special assignments. Scheffing was now a jack of all trades, tending to the Mets prospects while monitoring players from other teams. His evaluations were partly responsible for the Mets acquiring Tommie Agee, Al Weis, Ray Sadecki, and Wayne Garrett. Between Scheffing, Murphy, Herzog, and McDonald, the Mets had cultivated enough talent to win the World Series in only their eighth year of existence.

Murphy held Scheffing in high esteem. According to the Mets' 1970 media guide, Murphy said in November 1969 that "if anything ever happens to me, Bob Scheffing is my man for the job." Two months later, Murphy suffered two major heart attacks 15 days apart and died in January 1970 at age 61.

The Mets didn't have an assistant general manager in those days, which put Scheffing, Herzog, and McDonald in the mix to replace Murphy under difficult circumstances. All three were worthy of the job despite having different strengths. Herzog knew the farm system better than anyone, and McDonald was the administrative brains that put everything in place.

Scheffing's involvement in the farm system had been downsized since 1968, but his role in "special assignments" made him aware of the talent possessed by other organizations. He had a successful run as manager of two major league teams and owned a longer major league résumé than Herzog and McDonald. Murphy's suggestion that Scheffing was his heir apparent seemed to go a long way in the decision by the Mets' board of directors to name Scheffing as the team's new general manager in January 19, 1970. No one was more pleased than Devine.

"You've come a helluva long way from that supermarket," Devine told Scheffing.

Scheffing's hiring also came with a shift of responsibilities at the top. Board chairman M. Donald Grant and VP James Thompson absorbed more duties on the business side, allowing Scheffing to concentrate on the roster while giving Grant a stronger voice in player personnel.

The Mets' roster was pretty much set when Scheffing took over. Pitcher Ray Sadecki and outfielder Dave Marshall were acquired from the Giants for Jim Gosger and Bob Heise, giving the Mets more depth at both positions. The team's only other major off-season trade occurred on December 3, when Murphy acquired third baseman Joe Foy from the Royals for outfielder Amos Otis and pitcher Bob Johnson. Within months, that trade was recognized as the worst in team history. Sadly, Scheffing managed to top that two years later.

There was little reason for Scheffing to break up the roster of a defending champion. His first deal sent third-string catcher J.C. Martin to the Cubs for backstop Randy Bobb a few days before the 1970 season opener. Outside of Ken Singleton's promotion from Triple A, Scheffing didn't make any other moves until he sold Don Cardwell and Cal Koonce four days apart in early June.

The Mets stayed close to first place the entire season without making the type of charge that allowed them to overtake the Cubs in 1969. Scheffing picked up a couple of veteran pitchers in September, getting former Cy Young Award winner Dean Chance from the Indians and trading Rod Gaspar to the Padres for reliever Ron Herbel. The deals failed to ignite the Mets as they finished third at 83–79, six games behind the division-winning Pirates.

Scheffing made only token changes to the Mets' roster in the off-season after the club finished with 17 fewer wins than it amassed in 1969. He found a new third baseman, picking up Bob Aspromonte from the Braves for Herbel after allowing Foy to go to the Senators. Scheffing also sent Ron Swoboda to the Expos for fellow outfielder Don Hahn just before the season opener.

The Mets got off to a terrific start in 1971, winning 21 of their first 31 games to take a 2½-game lead by May 15. Tom Seaver was on his way to a 20-win season, and Nolan Ryan opened the campaign 8–4 with a 2.05 ERA in 14 appearances. Cleon Jones bounced back from a disappointing 1970 season and was among the league leaders in hitting.

But the team began to stumble amid injuries to Agee and Koosman. The Mets took themselves out of contention by going 9–20 in July, leading to a second straight 83–79 season. Art Shamsky and Donn Clendenon—playoff heroes two years earlier—combined to hit .226 with 16 homers and 55 RBIs. Weis was released in May after going hitless in 14 plate appearances, and Aspromote wound up with a .225 average despite a hot start.

Part of the problem was the Mets' faith in the farm system. Singleton became the everyday right fielder and hit .245 with 13 homers, Mike Jorgensen demonstrated power and exceptional defense at first base, and Tim Foli provided a win-at-all-costs mentality as he played second, third, and short.

But the Mets had forgotten that it took a big trade in June 1969 to turn them into legitimate threats. Murphy gave up four prospects—Steve Renko, Kevin Collins, Dave Colon, and Bill Carden—to get Clendenon from the Expos. Scheffing never pulled off such a trade during his first two seasons as general manager. After two straight third-place finishes, Scheffing was under the gun to change the Mets' fortunes.

The beat writers watched in disbelief as Scheffing did nothing to improve the ballclub at the November-December winter meetings. No one on the Mets hit 15 homers in 1971 as Jones and Bud Harrelson were the only players to appear in more than 125 games. There were token appearances by Mets prospects Jon Matlack and John Milner, but their presence did nothing to change the team's fortunes. Singleton looked like a keeper, and Foli and Jorgensen seemed like nice utility players. But Ryan and Gary Gentry appeared to have plateaued as the Mets tried to rely on pitching to make the 1971 playoffs.

The Mets needed hitting, and every beat writer and fan knew it. Scheffing, Grant, and manager Gil Hodges were skewered for the team's inability to bolster the offense at the winter meetings. Scheffing bore most of the criticism after doing little to give the Mets a lineup that wouldn't waste a pitching staff that had finished first in the National League in ERA and strikeouts.

And the Mets had a plethora of pitching talent at the ready. Seaver, Jerry Koosman, Gentry, and Ryan made up the front of the rotation, with Jim McAndrew and Sadecki serving as spot starters. Matlack made a few starts in 1971 when Koosman was hurt, and Buzz Capra was ready for the majors after going 13–3 with a 2.19 ERA for Triple A Tidewater. That left eight starters at the Mets' disposal, a curious embarrassment of riches for a team in dire need of a power hitter.

Seaver was untouchable. Koosman had shoulder issues. Gentry had developed into a .500 pitcher. McAndrew struggled in 1971. Sadecki had become very valuable as a No. 5 starter and a long reliever. Matlack and Capra had a combined 42 major league innings under their belts and were a risk to any team willing to trade an experienced, productive hitter.

And then there was Ryan, who possessed the scariest fastball among the octet but still hadn't harnessed his control. Ryan followed his outstanding start in '71 by going 2–9 with a 7.62 ERA in 52 innings over the final 2½ months. The Mets were beginning to wonder what they had in the flamethrower from Alvin, Texas, who had teased the front office and coaches with his incredible stuff since becoming a regular member of the roster in 1968. However, the Mets felt they could get more in a trade for Ryan than if they dangled Gentry, McAndrew, Matlack, and/or Capra.

The question was what the Mets could get for Ryan. Several available hitters were already moved during the winter meetings, including Frank Robinson, Dick Allen, John Mayberry, Lee May, Joe Morgan, Cesar Geronimo,

and Rick Monday. What the Mets sought was a power-hitting third baseman, and none of the players involved in the 15 trades at the winter meetings fit that description. The closest player to meet the Mets' criteria was a veteran shortstop being shopped by the Angels.

Jim Fregosi was a six-time All-Star, a one-time Gold Glove shortstop, and the primary reason why the Angels challenged for the AL pennant in just their seventh season. He batted as high as .290 in a full season (1967), slugged 22 homers in 1970, poked 32 doubles in 1966, and led the AL in triples with 13 in 1968. However, Fregosi endured his worst year as an Angel in 1971 and hadn't played a single major league inning at third base. That didn't stop Scheffing and Hodges from believing he could handle third base and regain his batting stroke. The Mets also looked at his .268 average and 115 homers in 11 seasons with the Angels and felt he still had an upside at age 30.

It took a future Hall-of-Fame pitcher and three prospects to pry a slumping Fregosi from the Angels' hands. Five days after the winter meetings, Ryan, outfielder Leroy Stanton, pitcher Don Rose, and catcher Francisco Estrada were traded to California, giving the Mets their newest starting third baseman.

Ryan's 939 strikeouts in 840 innings as a Met were offset by a 29–38 record, 344 walks, and a 3.58 ERA. He averaged 6.8 walks per nine innings over his last two years in New York, and his 1.495 WHIP during that span was far worse than Seaver's 1.012, McAndrew's 1.143, McGraw's 1.190, Frisella's 1.209, Sadecki's 1.222, Koosman's 1.247, and Gentry's 1.251.

Fregosi's presence would have allowed Garrett to serve as the utility infielder. Garrett's on-base percentage was among the best on the team, giving Hodges a chance to use him at second and short on days when he sought a little more offense.

Scheffing wasn't done tinkering with the roster. He and Hodges spent part of spring training holding discussions with the Expos about Montreal outfielder Rusty Staub, a player whose bat seemed to be a perfect fit for the Mets. Staub had better power than anyone on the Mets' spring training roster and was a proven RBI man. At the time, he also had decent speed for a slugger and was a very good fielder who at age 28 was just coming into his prime.

The Mets again were prepared to part with prospects—lots of them. The Mets were offered up Singleton, who hit 13 homers in just 298 at-bats as a platoon right fielder in 1971. Singleton compiled a .374 on-base percentage to compensate for his .245 average, and his 64 strikeouts in 366 plate appearances demonstrated his plate awareness.

Hodges badly wanted Staub, and the Expos wanted something more than Singleton. Hodges and Scheffing gave up Foli and Jorgensen, each of whom were good role-players at the time but could hardly be considered untouchables.

The Staub trade was announced hours after Hodges was laid to rest. The manager was stricken by his second heart attack in 3½ years and died the Sunday before the scheduled start of the season. The Mets assembled a news conference after the funeral to announce the Staub deal and introduce Yogi Berra as the successor to Hodges. The timing of the majors announcements were questioned by writers who felt the team wasn't giving Hodges much respect.

A 10-day strike by the Major League Players Association pushed back the season a few days but didn't dampen the enthusiasm of Mets fans giddy about the prospects of witnessing a much-improved lineup that potentially featured a great mix of speed and power.

Scheffing was looking like a genius while the Mets opened 25–7, setting a team record for best 32-game start. Staub and Fregosi hit well and contributed heavily to a team-record 11-game winning streak that put the Mets six games ahead of the Pirates as the season approached the quarter mark.

Scheffing also added Willie Mays at the behest of team owner Joan Payson, acquiring the Giants center fielder from the Giants for pitcher Charlie Williams and $50,000. Mays starred in his first game as a Met, slamming a tie-breaking homer against his former team to break a 4–4 tie in a 5–4 win on Mother's Day, four innings after Staub hit a grand slam.

Rookie John Milner was looking good as Jorgensen's replacement, Teddy Martinez was doing his best Foli impression, and Staub was outhitting Singleton, all of which made the Expos deal look very good through 32 games. Ryan wasn't missed while Matlack opened the season 6–0 with a 1.87 ERA in his first eight starts and Fregosi batted .306 in his first 26 games as a Met. It didn't matter that the Mets were getting minimal contributions from Agee and Jones.

The season began to change once Staub was plunked on the hand by a pitch in Atlanta. The Mets were five games ahead when Staub got hurt, and a half-game in front when he made a brief return. By the time the Mets figured out seven weeks later that he had a broken bone in his hand, they were 5½ games out of first and sinking fast.

Staub was just part of an ever-growing list of injured Mets. Agee and Jones sat out a combined 92 games, Harrelson missed 41 games, Fregosi appeared in only 101 games, and Grote made just 60 starts. Mays at age 41 was forced to play almost every day until his knees and shoulder gave out in early August. Milner's production plummeted following a collision with Harrelson in July. With Singleton, Foli, Jorgensen, and Stanton now on other rosters, Scheffing had few legitimate replacements.

The limited resources caused Berra to be very creative with his lineup. Both Grote and Duffy Dyer moved from behind the plate to the outfield. Jones saw action at first base, and Agee appeared in left field for the first time as a Met. Fregosi played innings at shortstop and first base when he was healthy enough to contribute. Kranepool was the lone Met to appear in more than 117 games, and

Harrelson and Agee were the only players to show up on Berra's starting lineup for over 100 games.

On the mound, Seaver was his usual outstanding self and Matlack put together a season worthy of becoming the second Met to win the NL Rookie of the Year Award. McAndrew had his best year as a Met while serving as the No. 4 starter. But Koosman and Gentry battled injuries all season, and Capra developed a blister problem that limited his effectiveness after April. The pitching-rich Mets suddenly had a thin rotation after Seaver, Matlack, and McAndrew. Meanwhile, Ryan began to live up to his promise as he led the American League with 329 strikeouts and nine shutouts while going 19–16 with a 2.28 ERA.

Scheffing's two most significant trades since becoming the Mets' general manager had blown up in his face. The team earned run average ranked just fifth in the National League at 3.26. Seaver, Matlack, McAndrew, and lefty closer Tug McGraw combined for a 2.54 ERA in 772 2/3 innings. The rest of the staff pitched to a 4.14 ERA, with Koosman and Gentry each posting earned run averages over four for the first time.

Fregosi's production was such that Wayne Garrett saw the bulk of the action at third base over the final two months. Fregosi hit only .232 with five homers and 32 RBIs in 101 games while Stanton recorded a .251 average with 12 homers in 127 games. Forget about Ryan—Stanton alone was making the Fregosi trade look bad.

In Montreal, Singleton hit 14 homers and Jorgensen added 13, which would have placed them second and tied for third on the Mets. Singleton also hit .274 in 585 plate appearances, which would have led the Mets since no player on the New York roster qualified for a batting title.

The Mets somehow finished 83–73 in their first year under Berra despite allowing 50 more runs than they scored. They were 10 games out of first by August 16 and went 58–66 following their blistering start, leading to their third-consecutive third-place finish.

The Ryan trade wasn't the only reason for Scheffing to feel heat heading into the 1972 winter meetings. Three straight mediocre seasons began to affect the bottom line as attendance slid from 2.7 million in 1970 to 2.1 million in 1972. The Mets remained the NL's top draw in '72, but a 22 percent slip over a three-year period was noticeable.

Scheffing still had an excess of pitching as he began to bargain at the winter meetings. One of his first moves was to break up the Mobile tandem of Jones and Agee, shipping the latter to the Astros for Rich Chiles and Buddy Harris. The prevailing feeling within the Mets front office was that Jones and Agee weren't a good influence on each other, making the Agee trade addition by subtraction.

Scheffing also had other needs. He sought out the Braves, who let it be known that second baseman Felix Millan could be had for a couple of arms. Atlanta wanted Gentry and Frisella, who had experienced a disappointing 1972 season after he and McGraw formed the best lefty-right bullpen in the National League the previous two years. Scheffing got the Braves to include lefty George Stone, the pitcher who short-circuited Staub's season—and the Mets' pennant push—with his errant toss the previous June.

The swap remains one of the finest in team history. Millan quickly became the best No. 2 hitter the Mets ever had while playing second base better than his predecessors. Stone emerged as the No. 4 starter in 1973, leading the league with an .800 winning percentage while going 12–3 with a 2.80 ERA. Gentry started just 14 games in two-plus seasons with the Braves before his release in May 1975. Frisella recorded a 4.67 ERA in 87 innings for Atlanta and was dealt to San Diego after the 1974 season.

Scheffing also received another dividend from an October 1971 trade that brought Jim Beauchamp from the Cardinals to the Mets. One of the throw-ins coming to New York was Harry Parker, who made the Mets out of 1973 training camp and eventually became a vital part of the bullpen that season. However, one of the players who went to St. Louis was pitching prospect Jim Bibby, who eventually became a two-time 19-game winner and led the NL in winning percentage in 1979 and '80.

With Millan and Harrelson, the Mets had their best defensive double-play combo ever while the two served as the top two hitters in the batting order. Unfortunately, the two didn't play together much from June 5 to August 18 as Harrelson spent a majority of that time on the disabled list.

Once again, the Mets had to deal with a variety of injuries. Mays, Grote, and Milner landed on the DL by May 13. Jones and Harrelson were sidelined in June, and Grote didn't return to the active roster until July 11. Harrelson made a return trip to the DL on August 3, leaving with the Mets without their All-Star shortstop for almost seven weeks of the summer.

Unlike 1972, the Mets didn't get off to a great start before the injuries. The '73 version was 17–15 after 32 games, an eight-game deficit over the previous year. By the time the Mets lost a 10-inning game to Cincinnati on August 17, they were nestled in last place at 53–66 and wasting another Cy Young–worthy season from Seaver. "Tom Terrific" was on pace for a 20-win season despite the collection of hitters supporting him. Koosman and Matlack were a combined 17–29 by mid-August as they received virtually no run support.

Things were already looking ugly by July. Fregosi got off to another slow start before Scheffing finally gave up, selling him and his .234 average to the Rangers on July 11. The deal came four days before Ryan tossed his second no-hitter of the season, leading to further criticism of Scheffing's stewardship.

What was killing the Mets' season was one of their healthy veterans. Closer Tug McGraw was an All-Star in 1972 before finishing the year with a 1.70 ERA for the second straight season. He set a team record with 27 saves in '72 to earn the responsibility of finishing victories for the Mets once Frisella departed.

McGraw was absolutely horrible from May 4 through July 7, blowing seven of 13 save opportunities while going 0–4 with an 8.00 ERA in 37 innings. He pitched to a .424 on-base percentage in that stretch as he allowed 15 of his 30 inherited runners to score.

Berra eventually put McGraw in the rotation in an effort to correct his flaws. Tug was torched for six runs in six innings versus Atlanta in his first start before holding the Expos to a run over 5⅔ innings on July 30. He converted his first two save opportunities in August but lost his next two decisions to fall to 0–6 with a hefty 5.45 ERA by August 20.

The Mets were so bad by midsummer that the *New York Post* decided to conduct a poll asking fans to choose whether Scheffing, Berra, or Grant should be fired. Berra received the most sympathy from voters who overwhelmingly pinned the blame on the others.

Meanwhile, New York's other team was mounting a postseason push. The Yankees of Bobby Murcer, Roy White, Mel Stottlemyre, Fritz Peterson, and Sparky Lyle were showing a lot more life than the Mets. Fans were flocking to the Bronx to get a glimpse of the club as it played its final season before the renovation of Yankee Stadium. The Bombers were tied for first at 60–50 by August 1 to further siphon fans from the Mets. By August 19 the Yankees were three games out of first while the Mets were 55–66.

Bad as the Mets were, they stood just 6½ games off the division lead when Harrelson returned to shortstop on August 18. Harrelson's activation marked the first time the Mets had their season-opening lineup intact since April 27. With Harrelson back, the Mets hit .262 and averaged four runs a game the rest of the way while the pitching staff posted a 2.62 ERA. McGraw was back in top form, and the rotation was so good that Seaver was actually the fourth-most successful hurler down the stretch while Matlack, Koosman, and Stone piled up wins. Koosman set a team record with 31 consecutive scoreless innings and Matlack was 7–2 with a 2.66 ERA after July 30. Stone didn't lose a game over the final two months while opposing managers saved their aces for matchups against Seaver.

The Mets vacated the cellar for good on August 31, moved into fourth on September 5, took over second on September 20, and grabbed the division lead a day later despite a 77–77 record. New York was 22–11 in its first 33 games after Harrelson came back, but the offense was being highlighted by Staub, Jones, and Garrett, who was supposed to be replaced by Fregosi 21 months earlier.

New York actually won the division title a day later than scheduled. Five teams were still alive heading into the final weekend, and the Cardinals and Pirates were in the hunt after the Mets split a pair at Wrigley Field on the final scheduled day of the campaign. A pair of rainouts during the Cubs series led to another twin bill the day after the scheduled end of the season. The Mets finally clinched with a 6–4 win in Game 1 before the second game was canceled by rain.

The Mets continued the hot streak by winning their second pennant, holding the mighty Reds lineup to eight runs in a five-game NLCS. They took a 3–2 lead in the World Series against the A's as Staub went 8-for-18 with a homer and five RBIs despite a separated shoulder.

But in a much-criticized move, Berra elected to go with Tom Seaver on short rest in Game 6 rather than Stone, who was outstanding in Game 4 against the Reds after winning his last eight decisions during the regular season. Seaver lost the sixth game 3–1 before a tired Matlack was hit hard while making his third start of the season. Oakland's 5–2 victory in Game 7 left the Mets one game short of another championship.

The September division charge gave Scheffing and Berra another season at the controls while also providing the franchise a false sense of superiority. Scheffing made no alterations to the major league roster other than to send McAndrew to the Padres. Yes, it was a roster that had just won a National League pennant, but it was virtually the same group that finished 13½ games out of first place the year before. Scheffing was happy to go into training camp with light-hitting Don Hahn as the starting center fielder. He didn't mind having third base patrolled by Garrett after the team spent three straight years trying to replace him. He had faith in Grote, Harrelson, and Jones, who had missed a total of 405 games since 1972.

Scheffing made just one other move before the 1974 season opener, selling Capra to Atlanta on March 26. All Capra did was go 16–8 with a league-best 2.28 ERA and a league-low 6.8 hits allowed per nine innings for the '74 Braves.

Opening Day in Philadelphia was a harbinger. Seaver struggled at times over seven innings, allowing three runs and seven hits before leaving with a 4–3 lead. McGraw struck out two in a perfect eighth before serving up a two-run, walk-off homer to Mike Schmidt in the bottom of the ninth.

Seaver spent the rest of the year battling sciatica and went 11–11 with a 3.20 ERA, the first time his earned run average had been over three. McGraw tried to pitch through a shoulder problem while duplicating his first four months of 1973. Their physical ailments left the Mets without an ace or a closer.

Stone was shelved by a shoulder injury early in the season, leaving Koosman and Matlack as the Mets' only consistent starters. Koosman was the only non-reliever to post a winning record, going 15–11 with a 3.36 ERA. Matlack's 2.41 ERA was bolstered by seven shutouts, yet he finished just 13–15 as the Mets refused to score runs for him.

The injury bug bit the Mets again as Grote, Harrelson, and Jones sat out 159 games. Staub led the team with 19 homers and 78 RBIs but hit only .258, his lowest average since 1965. The team's best on-base percentage among players in at least 97 games was Harrelson's .366, but he also batted only .227 and scored 48 runs.

Between McGraw's worrisome pitching and the latest rash of injuries, 1974 was looking a lot like '73 as the Mets fell into last place on June 16 yet were just seven games out of first heading into August. But there was no "Ya Gotta Believe," as the Mets continued to stumble. They finished fifth at 71–91, the team's worst showing since 1967.

The Mets' first major move of the '74 off-season was to allow Scheffing to step down. The team went 402–401 during his tenure, captured a pennant, and experienced an unfathomable amount of injuries. He engineered one incredibly bad trade, one exceptionally good one, and another that can at best be considered a wash given Singleton's excellent career with the Expos and Orioles.

George Weiss   1961–1966

Born: 6/23/84   New Haven, Connecticut
Died: 8/13/72   Greenwich, Connecticut
Named President: 3/14/61
Stepped Down to Become Director: 11/14/66

It is still hard to evaluate the job done by George Weiss as the first president of the Mets. Quiet by nature, Weiss helped give the Mets their identity by hiring Casey Stengel as his manager and bringing back several ex-Brooklyn Dodgers and New York Giants to round out his original roster. He also hired Johnny Murphy and Bing Devine, two men crucial to the formation of the 1969 Mets. In fact, Weiss did most of the club's original hiring, assembling the scouting department, the front-office staff, and the stadium employees. However, the expansion draft proved a total disaster, and it took nearly a half-decade before the farm system began to produce competent major league players.

Getting Stengel was a stroke of genius on Weiss' part as Casey was the team's greatest asset in terms of marketing and public relations. As general manager of the Yankees, Weiss hired Stengel to manage the team for the 1949 season, and the pair won 10 pennants and seven World Series in 12 seasons before the two were let go by owner Dan Topping following the 1960 World Series.

Mets owner Joan Payson originally sought Branch Rickey to serve as the team's first general manager. Rickey built National League dynasties with the Cardinals and Dodgers, and was among the organizers of the Continental League until major league owners agreed to place teams in four of the eight cities targeted by the fledgling circuit. New York received a franchise through the persistence of Rickey and Bill Shea, and it was Shea who suggested to Payson that Rickey was the perfect candidate to mold the franchise. But the 80-year-old Rickey put himself out of the running by asking for full autonomy and a $5 million budget to start up the franchise. That was even too rich for the very rich Payson, who then turned her interest toward Weiss.

Weiss was still in the employ of the Yankees but had little to do with the day-to-day operations of the ballclub in 1961. He spent much of his first year of forced semire-tirement at home, which prompted a great line from his wife, Hazel, when asked about finally having her husband around the house.

"When I married George it was for better or worse, but not for lunch," replied Mrs. Weiss. "He just has to get a job. In baseball or not, but a job."[35]

Weiss was the first major hire by the Mets, although it took a bit of semantics for him to be allowed to join the club. He still had four years left on a five-year contract as an "advisor" with the Yankees that would be voided if he signed on to serve as general manager for another franchise. The Mets did an end-around by hiring him as team president, thus allowing him to still draw a check from the Yankees.

"He is in the clear as far as the Yankees are concerned," said Topping after Weiss left for the Mets. "Whether he is in the clear under the rules of baseball is for someone else to decide."[36]

The irony in the Weiss hiring was that, as GM of the Yankees, he was very public about his opposition of a sta-dium built by the City of New York for a possible National League franchise. He pointed out the expense for the pro-posed ballpark, the unfairness of having taxpayers foot the bill and the location—off the Grand Central Parkway in a Queens swamp. Once he was introduced as Mets presi-dent, Weiss immediately changed his tune and trumpeted the ballpark proposal as a positive for the city and the team.

As president, Weiss still had all the responsibilities of a general manager, including a task of naming the Mets' first manager. Weiss had to press hard to convince Stengel to return to baseball. The Ol' Perfessor was reluctant to come back and was more than happy to be living in Glen-dale, California, where he was serving as a bank vice presi-dent. Weiss eventually wore down Stengel and introduced his new skipper before the end of the 1961 regular season.

Hiring Stengel was an easy decision. Selecting a team from the 1961 expansion draft was not. The Mets and Houston Colt .45s had to choose from a list of broken-down players and unproven prospects, a group so incon-sequential at the time that Colts GM Paul Richards threat-ened to bypass the draft entirely. The American League had held a similar draft for the Washington Senators and Los Angeles Angels one year earlier and watched as the '61 Halos won 70 games with a nice mix of youngsters and veterans. The National League was not about to let its new clubs get their hands on many serviceable players, which left Weiss and Richards angry as they prepared for the draft.

There was no reason to question Weiss' acumen as an assessor of talent. He managed to "rebuild" the Yankees three times during his reign without finishing any lower than third in the American League, and he left the club capable enough to win two World Series and four pen-nants in the four years after he left.

Weiss felt fans would be more inclined to head to the Polo Grounds if he used the expansion draft to acquire players who were well known to New York fans. He grabbed several former All-Stars and numerous players with roots to New York National League baseball. The expansion draft picks included ex-Dodgers Gil Hodges, Roger Craig, Char-lie Neal, and Don Zimmer, former Giants Hobie Landrith and Ray Daviault, and one-time All-Stars Richie Ashburn and Gus Bell. The draft would have been very beneficial to the Mets had it been held in 1957 instead of 1961 as most of these players were well past their prime.

Richards was less interested in choosing name players knowing, Houston was just happy to have a team. Through the draft he assembled a ballclub that managed to finish eighth in the 10-team National League with 64 wins in 1962, six games ahead of the established Cubs. The Colts, playing in a much smaller market than New York, drew just as many people at gnat-infested Colts Stadium than the Mets attracted at the dilapidated Polo Grounds. But the Colts also played colorless, forgettable baseball in their first season while the Mets turned losing into an ab-solute art form.

Weiss' best expansion-draft pick was Al Jackson, a lefty from the Pirates' minor league chain. Weiss later acquired Frank Thomas from the Braves for cash and a player to be named. It is hard to imagine just how bad the Mets would have been without those two players.

The Mets opened the 1962 season with nine straight losses before winning 12 of their next 22 to surge into seventh place. But things fell apart once the team made its first trip to Houston for a series against their expan-sion brothers. A series of flight delays prevented the Mets from getting into their Houston hotel until around 5:00 AM. The Mets proceeded to lose that night, and the 16 en-suing games, as well, to fall to 12–36 and 24 games out of first place by June 6.

Weiss scrambled to find reinforcements, but many GMs were reluctant to help out after being fleeced by Weiss so many times during his Yankees days. One of his in-sea-son pickups was Marv Throneberry, who personified the team's futility with his atrocious fielding. Throneberry fin-ished second to Thomas on the team with 16 homers, but he also committed 17 errors at first base and was booed unmercifully at the Polo Grounds before becoming a cult hero in August.

Weiss jettisoned many of his expansion picks before the season ended. The problem was, too many remained as the Mets set a modern major league record with 120 loss-es. Jackson lost 20 games and posted a 4.40 ERA, but he also threw the team's only four complete-game shutouts, tossed the first one-hitter in club history, and tied Craig for the team lead with 118 strikeouts. Thomas ended up with 34 homers and 94 RBIs, team records that would stand until the 1970s. But the duo couldn't compensate for the team's league-high 5.04 ERA, a league-worst 204 errors and a league-low .240 batting average.

The '62 Mets may have made news for all the wrong reasons, but at least they made news. They finished with 24 fewer wins than the Colt .45's and would continue to finish behind Houston in the standings until 1968. But the Mets had managed to steal the affections of New York baseball fans in '62 with their uncanny ability to constantly snare defeat from the jaws of victory. As bad as they were, they still managed to cut into the Yankees attendance figure despite the Bombers' charge toward their third straight pennant.

If Weiss formed his roster to boost attendance, then he accomplished his mission. The Giants drew just 653,923 in their final year at the Polo Grounds, nearly 300,000 less than the 1962 Mets. However, Weiss also may have retarded the team's growth through the draft and his ensuing in-season acquisitions.

Weiss spent the 1962–1963 off-season shoring up the club's defense while building a younger foundation. Ed Kranepool factored into the Mets' 1963 plans after being signed as a 17-year-old outfielder/first baseman out of James Monroe High School in the Bronx the previous June. The Mets also inked outfield prospect Cleon Jones before the 1963 season and reached contract terms with shortstop Bud Harrelson in June 1963.

But Weiss and the Mets made a huge mistake by leaving Paul Blair unprotected in the 1962 first-year draft, allowing the Orioles to claim the speedy outfield prospect. Blair helped the Birds win World Series in 1966 and 1970 while claiming eight Gold Gloves in center field. The loss of Blair would alter the way the Mets handled their future prospects, sometimes to the detriment of the player. It also created a void in center until Tommie Agee was acquired after the 1967 season.

The 1963 Mets were only slightly better than the original squad. Weiss traded for pitcher Carl Willey, who tossed four shutouts and crafted a 3.10 ERA, over a run per game less than Jackson's team-best ERA in 1962. Jackson was brilliant at times, going 13–17 on a team that finished 51–111. Craig also dropped his earned run average considerably but managed to lose 18 straight decisions en route to a 5–22 season.

Veteran hurler Tracy Stallard was added to the mix and contributed a 6–17 record and a 4.71 ERA while Jay Hook went 4–14 with a 5.48 earned run average. The Mets still shaved nearly a full run off the team ERA despite Stallard and Hook, but the ballclub still finished last in team ERA and committed 210 errors for the second straight year despite Weiss' attempt to shore up the defense. Worse, the club hit a league-worst .219, giving the Mets opportunities to blow leads of 2–1 instead of 5–4.

Nineteen-sixty-four almost mirrored '63 as the Mets hit poorly while winning just 53 games. The team had now averaged 48 in its first three seasons while the Colts amassed 65 wins per season. The Angels already had posted two winning seasons in their first four years in existence. Even the Senators had managed to avoid the cellar twice in

their first three years while averaging 11 more victories than the Mets.

The only thing new about the '64 Mets was the stadium. Aside from Ed Kranepool, the team still hadn't produced any young talent able to demonstrate a modicum of ability to compete in the majors. The Mets' top four starting pitchers averaged 27 years of age, as did the rest of the ballclub. They were the youngest of the four expansion teams as Weiss had discarded all but Jackson, Jim Hickman, and Chris Cannizzaro from his group of 22 expansion draft players by the end of the 1964 season.

Weiss' best acquisition in the fall of 1964 may have been Devine, who had been forced out as general manager of the Cardinals six weeks before they won the World Series. Devine was hired by Weiss as assistant to the president with the promise he'd be the team's next president once Weiss stepped down. In the interim, Devine was expected to assess major league talent in other organizations and oversee a farm system that was about to bear fruit.

A youth movement emerged in 1965 as the Mets headed north with youngsters Tug McGraw, Ron Swoboda, Jim Bethke, and Danny Napoleon. Swoboda hit 16 home runs by the All-Star break, and McGraw became the first Mets pitcher to beat Sandy Koufax. But the quartet eventually proved they had been rushed to the majors and would need time to become consistent contributors.

And the Mets couldn't continue their tortoise-like pace of improvement, finishing 50–112 for their worst showing since 1962. Stengel was forced to step down as manager after breaking his hip in a fall during his 75th birthday celebration in late July, putting the team in the hands of Wes Westrum. Westrum was rehired for 1966 despite a 19–48 record after replacing Stengel.

Devine learned before the end of 1965 that he'd have to wait another year before occupying Weiss' office. Weiss decided to stay on another year, which also gave Devine another season to evaluate other team's young talent while keeping an eye on his own minor league prospects. With Murphy serving as assistant to the president, Devine as director, Bob Scheffing in charge of minor league operations, and Whitey Herzog serving as a minor league instructor/coordinator, the Mets were finally about to show significant improvement. Weiss' underlings were responsible for the acquisition of catcher Jerry Grote from Houston in October 1965, four months after the Mets selected Nolan Ryan, Ken Boswell, and Jim McAndrew in the first-ever major league draft.

Grote became the No. 1 catcher in 1966 while Mets fans also got to watch Cleon Jones, Bud Harrelson, Swoboda, and Kranepool on an everyday basis. Devine was instrumental in the Mets picking up veteran third baseman Ken Boyer from St. Louis and pitcher Bob Shaw from the Giants.

Jones hit .275 as a rookie in 1966, Harrelson became a sure-handed shortstop under the guidance of veteran Roy McMillan, Kranepool banged out a career-high 16 homers, and Grote showed at age 23 that he was a strong leader behind the plate. Ryan was recalled near the end of the season, giving Mets fans their first glimpse of his blazing fastball.

With Shaw among their 11-game winners, the Mets finished 66–95, the first time they hadn't lost at least 109 games. They also managed to escape the cellar for the first time while giving hope they were on their way to respectability.

Tom Seaver eventually helped put the Mets over the top, but he came very close to pitching for another team. The USC product was taken in the first round of the January 1966 draft and signed a contract in February while the Trojans were playing the exhibition portion of their 1966 schedule.

Neither Seaver nor the Braves saw anything wrong with him signing a deal before Southern Cal began its regular season. But the contract was voided by Major League Baseball because it was finalized after the Trojans had begun their season. Then the NCAA stepped in and declared Seaver ineligible for college ball because he had signed a professional contract, leaving him without an outlet for which to perform.

The Seaver family threatened both MLB and the NCAA with litigation until baseball commissioner William Eckert ruled that Seaver's services would be available via a special lottery to any team willing to match the Braves' $50,000 bonus.

Weiss was dead set against giving an unproven college pitcher that much money. He saw it as a risky investment, but Devine felt it was a chance for the Mets to have a talented pitcher fall into their laps. Mets scout Nelson Burbrink had monitored Seaver's progress in college and felt he was an exceptional talent, but it took a persistent sales pitch by Devine to persuade Weiss to enter the lottery. Seaver never would have been a Met if Weiss hadn't been convinced he was worth the money.

The Mets had another crucial decision to make a few weeks after winning the Seaver sweepstakes. The most impressive hitter available in the June 1966 draft was an Arizona State product named Reggie Jackson. No one was hitting the ball harder in college than Jackson, a tremendous athlete who also played football and basketball in high school.

But Jackson also had shown he was his own man and occasionally clashed with coach Bobby Winkles. Jackson already had a high opinion of himself and enjoyed his status as BMOC at Tempe. Had he been a white kid, he might have been portrayed as confident, but being of mixed race

during the civil rights movement of the 1960s didn't help his odds with the scouts.

The Mets had the first pick in the draft, putting them in position to take the future Hall of Famer for a team desperate for a power hitter. Instead, they passed on Jackson and selected high school catcher Steve Chilcott, who never got past Triple A before a back problem forced him to retire in 1972 at age 23. The A's grabbed Jackson with the second pick and won the World Series a few months after Chilcott played his final professional game.

Devine falls on the sword for the selection of Chilcott, a backstop selected by a team that believed at the time it was weak at the position after Grote opened the season hitting .215 through May 31. In Peter Golenbock's book *Amazin'*, Devine remembers the day he and Stengel went to see Chilcott collect six hits in eight at-bats during a doubleheader.

"I do recall that Chilcott hit well," Devine said about the scouting trip. "We had to leave before the second game was over to get back to the ballgame in Los Angeles [where the Mets were facing the Dodgers]. I got in the car and I said to Casey, 'All right, you've seen him. We have to make a decision. What do you think of Chilcott?' He said, 'He got six out of eight, didn't he? That's all I need to know.'

"That didn't push me over the line, but I had a lot of help. A lot of people agreed, 'take the catcher, period.'"[37]

Although the Mets managed to avoid 100 losses in 1966, they remained the worst of the four expansion clubs. The Angels reached 80 wins for the third time in six seasons, the Senators went 71–88 in their third year under Hodges and the Astros claimed 72 victories. But at least the Mets had closed the gap on the Yankees, who fell into the American League cellar following a 70–92 season.

Weiss finally stepped down as team president after the 1966 season but remained with the club as a director until his death in August 1972. Devine lasted just one season as team president before the Cardinals rehired him as GM in the fall of 1967. Through Weiss' group of baseball braintrust—Murphy, Devine, Scheffing, and Herzog—the Mets won the World Series two years later.

As a player evaluator, Weiss has to take his share of the blame for the Mets' poor record during his five seasons a club president. However, he demonstrated an outstanding ability to align himself with strong baseball men and a willingness to listen to his minions when there were disagreements in player personnel matters. He left the club in very good hands when he gave up his role as president.

The Postseason

1969 NLCS: Mets vs. Atlanta Braves

METS WIN SERIES 3–0

The Mets won seven more games than the Braves during the regular season, went 8–4 versus Atlanta, allowed 90 fewer runs, and had a better run differential. But many were picking the Braves to win the first-ever NLCS based on their potent lineup and the Mets' inexperience.

"We've made some believers," Mets manager Gil Hodges said before the series. "Now we'll have to make some more."[1]

Atlanta's attack featured Henry Aaron (44 home runs), Orlando Cepeda (88 RBIs), and Rico Carty (.342). The Braves outslugged the Mets in most individual offensive categories during the regular season and were capable of assaulting a team, as they did in a 15–3 pounding of the Mets that year.

The Braves were able to flex their muscles in the NLCS against Mets starters Tom Seaver, Jerry Koosman, and Gary Gentry. The trio allowed 13 earned runs and 20 hits in 13⅔ innings. However, Mets relievers Nolan Ryan, Ron Taylor,

and Tug McGraw were outstanding, holding the Braves to two earned runs and seven hits in 13⅓ innings (1.35 ERA).

Hank Aaron homered in each game of the series, but the rest of the Braves managed just two more in the Mets' sweep.

Meanwhile, the Mets were able to crush almost anyone the Braves sent to the mound, scoring 27 runs in the series after averaging 3.9 runs per regular-season game. Atlanta starters were tagged for 14 earned runs in only 14 innings.

"Everyone said it was going to be a pitching-duel series, and it turned out to be the opposite," quipped Koosman. "It was a hitters' duel."[2]

Art Shamsky hit .538 for the series (7-for-13), and Tommie Agee and Ken Boswell each homered twice.

The sweep certainly impressed Atlanta general manager Paul Richards. "We ought to send the Mets to Vietnam. They'd end the war in three days."[3]

GAME 1, October 4, Atlanta: Mets 9, Braves 5

Tom Seaver certainly isn't at his best in his first career postseason outing, but the Mets' offense more than makes up for Seaver's shortcomings. The Mets give Seaver a 2–0 lead, but Tony Gonzalez and Hank Aaron hit back-to-back RBI doubles in the third inning to push the Braves ahead 3–2.

Bud Harrelson laces a two-run triple in the fourth to put the Mets back in front for one inning. Tony Gonzalez leads off the fifth with a homer before Hank Aaron's solo shot off Seaver gives the Braves a 5–4 edge later in the inning.

The Mets take control with a five-run eighth off Phil Niekro. Wayne Garrett leads off with a double and scores on

a Cleon Jones single. Jones later steals third on a pickoff attempt and scores the go-ahead run on first baseman Orlando Cepedo's throwing error. Niekro gets the next two batters before J.C. Martin—pinch-hitting for Seaver—delivers a two-run single. Gonzalez lets Martin's hit skip by him in center field, allowing the fifth and final run of the inning.

Ron Taylor works a perfect eighth but puts runners on second and third with two outs in the ninth. Taylor closes out the Mets' first postseason win by getting Cepeda to pop out to Ken Boswell at second.

GAME 2, October 5, Atlanta: Mets 11, Braves 6

Tommie Agee has a hand in four rallies as the Mets leave Fulton County Stadium with a 2–0 lead in the series. Agee leads off the game with a single and scores on Ed Kranepool's single, putting the Mets ahead to stay. Agee pads the Mets' lead with a two-run homer in the second

and is intentionally walked with two outs in the third before Wayne Garrett's run-scoring single makes it 6–0.

The Mets close the scoring when Agee walks and scores on Cleon Jones' two-run blast in the seventh. Jones contributes three hits and three RBIs.

Ray Knight raises his arms after hitting a go-ahead home run in the seventh inning of Game 7 of the 1986 World Series against the Boston Red Sox. The Mets beat the Sox 8–5 to complete a 4–3 Series victory and become world champs for the second time.

Ken Boswell also belts a two-run homer and Art Shamsky adds three hits, including an RBI single.

Jerry Koosman is cruising until the Braves get their third looks at him. The lefty has the bases empty with two outs in the fifth when Felix Millan singles, Tony Gonzalez walks, and Hank Aaron launches a three-run homer. Two more Braves reach base before Clete Boyer hits a two-run single that chased Koosman.

Ron Taylor and Tug McGraw combine to hold the Braves to two hits over 4-1/3 shutout innings, allowing the Mets to increase their lead.

The Mets now head to Shea after scoring 20 runs on 23 hits at the Launching Pad.

GAME 3, October 6, New York: Mets 7, Braves 4

For the second time in 12 days, the Mets give their fans a reason to tear up the field. The Mets complete a three-game sweep of the Braves for their first National League pennant and a berth in the World Series against Baltimore.

Manager Gil Hodges usually had Gary Gentry on a short leash, and today is no different. With no outs and two on in the third, Hodges lifts the rookie right-hander right after Rico Carty belts a long foul ball into the left-field seats. Nolan Ryan follows and is sensational over seven innings of relief despite allowing Orlando Cepeda's two-run homer in the fifth, which gives the Braves a brief 4–3 lead. The Alvin, Texas, fireballer enters the game after Hank Aaron's double puts runners on second and third with nobody out. Ryan sandwiches an intentional walk with a pair of strikeouts before getting Bob Didier to fly out, ending the inning without a Brave crossing home. Ryan retires seven straight following Cepeda's homer and doesn't allow a runner past second the rest of the way.

The light-hitting Ryan, a career .110 hitter (8-for-73) at this point, sparks the Mets' three-run fifth with a leadoff single before scoring on Wayne Garrett's go-ahead, two-run homer. Ken Boswell adds an RBI single later in the fifth to make it 6–4.

Boswell has three hits and three RBIs, finishing the series with a team-high five ribbies.

Bedlam breaks out at Shea after Tony Gonzalez taps out to third baseman Wayne Garrett for the final out of the series.

"We felt we were pretty lucky to win that series, because we had never scored those kinds of runs," Koosman said. "I mean, we just felt God was with us. We couldn't do anything wrong. We couldn't lose a game."[4]

Game 1, October 4, Fulton County Stadium
METS 9, BRAVES 5

METS	AB	R	H	BI	BRAVES	AB	R	H	BI
Agee cf	5	0	0	0	Millan 2b	5	1	2	0
Garrett 3b	4	1	2	0	Gonzalez cf	5	2	2	2
Jones lf	5	1	1	1	HAaron rf	5	1	2	2
Shamsky rf	4	1	3	0	Carty lf	3	1	1	0
Weis pr-2b	0	0	0	0	Lum lf	1	0	1	0
Boswell 2b	3	2	0	0	Cepeda 1b	4	0	1	0
Gaspar rf	0	0	0	0	Boyer 3b	1	0	0	1
Kranepool 1b	4	2	1	0	Didier c	4	0	0	0
Grote c	3	1	1	1	Garrido ss	4	0	1	0
Harrelson ss	3	1	1	2	Niekro p	3	0	0	0
Seaver p	3	0	0	0	Aspromonte ph	1	0	0	0
Martin ph	1	0	1	2	Upshaw p	0	0	0	0
Taylor p	0	0	0	0					
Totals	35	9	10	6	Totals	36	5	10	5

Mets	020	200	050	9	10	1
Braves	012	010	100	5	10	2

METS	IP	H	R	ER	BB	SO
Seaver (W, 1–0)	7	8	5	5	3	2
Taylor (S, 1)	2.0	2	0	0	0	2
Total	9	10	5	5	3	4

BRAVES	IP	H	R	ER	BB	SO
Niekro (L, 0–1)	8.0	9	9	4	4	4
Upshaw	1	1	0	0	0	1
Totals	9	10	9	4	4	5

E—Boswell (1), Cepeda (1), Gonzalez (1); DP—Mets 0, Braves 2; 2B—Carty (1), Millan (1), Gonzalez (1), HAaron (1), Garrett (1), Lum (1); 3B—Harrelson; HR—Gonzalez (1), HAaron (1); SB—Cepeda (1), Jones (1); SF—Boyer; Time—2:37. ATT—50,122.

Game 2, October 5, Fulton County Stadium
METS 11, BRAVES 6

METS	AB	R	H	BI	BRAVES	AB	R	H	BI
Agee cf	4	3	2	2	Millan 2b	2	1	2	0
Garrett 3b	5	1	2	1	Gonzalez cf	4	1	1	0
Jones lf	5	2	3	3	HAaron rf	5	1	1	3
Shamsky rf	5	1	3	1	Carty lf	4	2	1	0
Gaspar pr-rf	0	0	0	0	Cepeda 1b	4	1	2	1
Boswell 2b	5	1	1	2	Boyer 3b	4	0	1	2
McGraw p	0	0	0	0	Didier c	4	0	0	0
Kranepool 1b	4	0	1	1	Garrido ss	4	0	1	0
Grote c	5	1	0	0	Reed p	0	0	0	0
Harrelson ss	5	1	1	1	Doyle p	0	0	0	0
Koosman p	2	1	0	0	Pappas p	1	0	0	0
Taylor	0	0	0	0	TAaron ph	1	0	0	0
Martin ph	1	0	0	0	Britton p	0	0	0	0
Weis 2b	1	0	0	0	Upshaw p	1	0	0	0
Aspromonte ph	1	0	0	0					
Neibauer p	0	0	0	0					
Totals	42	11	13	11	Totals	35	6	9	6

Mets	132	210	200	11	13	1
Braves	000	150	000	6	9	3

METS	IP	H	R	ER	BB	SO
Koosman	4-2/3	7	6	6	4	5
Taylor (W, 1–0)	1-1/3	1	0	0	0	2
McGraw (S, 1)	3	1	0	0	1	1
Total	9	9	6	6	5	8

BRAVES	IP	H	R	ER	BB	SO
Reed (L, 0–1)	1-2/3	5	4	4	3	3
Doyle	1	2	2	0	1	3
Pappas	2-1/3	4	3	3	0	4
Britton	1/3	0	0	0	1	0
Upshaw	2-2/3	2	2	2	1	1
Neibauer	1	0	0	0	0	0
Totals	9	13	11	9	6	11

E—Harrelson (1), Cepeda (2), Gonzalez (2), Boyer; DP—Mets 2, Braves 1; 2B—Jones (1), Harrelson (1), Garrett (1), Carty (2), Cepeda (1); HR—Agee (1), Boswell (1), HAaron (2); SB—Agee 2 (2), Garrett (1), Jones (2); Time—3:10; ATT—50,270.

Game 3, October 6, Shea Stadium
METS 7, BRAVES 4

BRAVES	AB	R	H	BI	METS	AB	R	H	BI
Millan 2b	5	0	0	0	Agee cf	5	1	3	2
Gonzalez cf	5	1	2	0	Garrett 3b	4	1	1	2
HAaron rf	4	1	2	2	Jones lf	4	1	2	0
Carty lf	3	1	1	0	Shamsky rf	4	1	1	0
Cepeda 1b	3	1	2	2	Gaspar pr-rf	0	0	0	0
Boyer 3b	4	0	0	0	Boswell 2b	4	1	3	3
Didier c	3	0	0	0	Weis 2b	0	0	0	0
Lum ph	1	0	1	0	Kranepool 1b	4	0	1	0
Jackson ss	0	0	0	0	Grote c	4	1	1	0
Garrido ss	2	0	0	0	Harrelson ss	3	0	0	0
Alou ph	1	0	0	0	Gentry p	0	0	0	0
Tillman c	0	0	0	0	Ryan p	4	1	2	0
Jarvis p	2	0	0	0					
Stone p	1	0	0	0					
Upshaw p	0	0	0	0					
Aspromonte ph	1	0	0	0					
Totals	35	4	8	4	Totals	36	7	14	7

Braves	200	020	000	4	8	1	
Mets	001	231	00X	7	14	0	

BRAVES	IP	H	R	ER	BB	SO
Jarvis (L, 0–1)	4-1/3	10	6	6	0	6
Stone	1	2	1	1	0	0
Upshaw	2-2/3	2	0	0	0	2
Totals	8	14	7	7	0	8

METS	IP	H	R	ER	BB	SO
Gentry	2	5	2	2	1	1
Ryan (W, 1–0)	7	3	2	2	2	7
Totals	9	8	4	4	3	8

E—Millan; DP—Braves 1, Mets 0; 2B—HAaron (2), Cepeda (2), Agee (1), Kranepool (1), Jones (2), Grote (1); HR—HAaron (3), Agee (2), Boswell (2), Cepeda (1), Garrett (1); S—Harrelson; Time—2:24; ATT—53,195.

1969 NLCS Statistics

COMPOSITE LINESCORE

	123	456	789	R	H	E
Mets	153	641	250	27	37	2
Braves	212	180	100	15	27	6

METS HITTING

Player	BA	G	AB	R	H
Tommie Agee	.357	3	14	4	5
Ken Boswell	.333	3	12	3	4
Wayne Garrett	.385	3	13	3	5
Rod Gaspar	—	3	0	0	0
Gary Gentry	—	1	0	0	0
Jerry Grote	.167	3	12	3	2
Bud Harrelson	.182	3	11	2	2
Cleon Jones	.429	3	14	4	6
Jerry Koosman	.000	1	2	1	0
Ed Kranepool	.250	3	12	2	3
J.C. Martin	.500	2	2	0	1
Tug McGraw	—	1	0	0	0
Nolan Ryan	.500	1	4	1	2
Tom Seaver	.000	1	3	0	0
Art Shamsky	.538	3	13	3	7
Ron Taylor	—	2	0	0	0
Al Weis	.000	3	1	1	0
Total	.327	3	113	27	37

2B—Garrett 2, Jones 2, Agee, Grote, Harrelson, Kranepool; 3B—Harrelson; HR—Agee 2, Boswell 2, Garrett, Jones; RBI—Boswell 5, Agee 4, Jones 4, Garrett 3, Harrelson 3, Martin 2, Grote, Kranepool, Shamsky; SB—Agee 2, Jones 2, Garrett.

BRAVES HITTING

Player	BA	G	AB	R	H
Hank Aaron	.357	3	14	3	5
Tommie Aaron	.000	1	1	0	0
Felipe Alou	.000	1	1	0	0
Bob Aspromonte	.000	3	3	0	0
Clete Boyer	.111	3	9	0	1
Jim Britton	—	1	0	0	0
Rico Carty	.300	3	10	4	3
Orlando Cepeda	.455	3	11	2	5
Bob Didier	.000	3	11	0	0
Paul Doyle	—	1	0	0	0
Gil Garrido	.200	3	10	0	2
Tony Gonzalez	.357	3	14	4	5
Sonny Jackson	—	1	0	0	0
Pat Jarvis	.000	1	2	0	0
Mike Lum	1.000	2	2	0	2
Felix Millan	.333	3	12	2	4
Gary Neibauer	—	1	0	0	0
Phil Niekro	.000	1	3	0	0
Milt Pappas	.000	1	1	0	0
Ron Reed	—	1	0	0	0
George Stone	.000	1	1	0	0
Bob Tillman	—	1	0	0	0
Cecil Upshaw	.000	3	1	0	0
Total	.258	3	106	15	27

2B—HAaron 2, Carty 2, Cepeda 2, Gonzalez, Lum, Millan; 3B—None; HR—HAaron 3, Cepeda, Gonzalez; RBI—HAaron 7, Boyer 3, Cepeda 3, Gonzalez 2; SB—Cepeda.

METS PITCHING

Player	G	ERA	W–L	SV	IP	H	ER	BB	SO
Nolan Ryan	1	2.57	1–0	0	7	3	2	2	7
Tom Seaver	1	6.43	1–0	0	7	8	5	3	2
Jerry Koosman	1	11.57	0–0	0	4-2/3	7	6	4	5
Ron Taylor	2	0.00	1–0	1	3-1/3	3	0	0	4
Tug McGraw	1	0.00	0–0	1	3	1	0	1	1
Gary Gentry	1	9.00	0–0	0	2	5	2	1	1
Total	3	5.00	3–0	2	27	27	15	11	20

BRAVES PITCHING

Player	G	ERA	W–L	SV	IP	H	ER	BB	SO
Phil Niekro	1	4.50	0–1	0	8	9	4	4	4
Cecil Upshaw	3	2.84	0–0	0	6-1/3	5	2	1	4
Pat Jarvis	1	12.46	0–1	0	4-1/3	10	6	0	6
Milt Pappas	1	11.57	0–0	0	2-1/3	4	3	0	4
Ron Reed	1	21.60	0–1	0	1-2/3	5	4	3	3
Paul Doyle	1	0.00	0–0	0	1	2	0	1	3
Gary Neibauer	1	0.00	0–0	0	1	0	0	1	0
George Stone	1	9.00	0–0	0	1	2	1	0	1
Jim Britton	1	0.00	0–0	0	1/3	0	0	1	0
Total	3	6.92	0–3	0	26	37	20	10	25

1969 World Series: Mets vs. Baltimore Orioles

METS WIN SERIES 4–1

After New York swept the Braves 3–0 in the NLCS, outfielder Rod Gaspar had predicted his Mets would pull off a four-game sweep of the Orioles. The proclamation incensed Frank Robinson, the head of the Orioles' "Kangaroo Court."

"Bring on Ron Gaspar," uttered Robinson.

Teammate Merv Rettenmund was quick to correct. "Not Ron. That's Rod, stupid."

"Okay, bring on Rod Stupid," replied the future Hall of Famer who was displaying the confidence many in the Orioles clubhouse possessed heading into the Series.

Okay, so the Birds weren't familiar with the Mets' fifth outfielder. Maybe they'd know who platooned at third base for the NL champs.

"No idea," said Robinson.[5]

"Couldn't tell you," admitted Brooks Robinson.

The O's were prohibitive favorites to take the Series after winning 112 games, including a three-game sweep of the Twins in the first American League Championship Series. When asked if he considered the Mets a team of destiny, Orioles scout and former major league GM Frank Lane quipped, "Indeed I do. I believe they are destined to be beaten easily by the Orioles.[6]

Orioles third starter Jim Palmer didn't believe they took the Mets lightly, although he admits his team was extremely talented with the likes of Don Buford, Boog Powell, Baul Blair, Frank Robinson, Brooks Robinson, Mike Cuellar, and Dave McNally

"Everybody thinks that just because you win 109 games…there's such a big difference between being confident and knowing what it takes to win," Palmer said 42 years later. "Obviously, that was probably the best club I played on. Buford was a great leadoff hitter. Blair hit 26 home runs and had 25 going into September. He did not have a good September. Frank was Frank, even though he had that collision in '67 with Al Weis, and maybe his vision wasn't as good. Boog was a year from being the Most Valuable Player. We had a great platoon with Hendricks and Etchebarren behind the plate. I had been hurt a little bit that year early on but was well…it was just a matter of having one leg shorter than the other. Cuellar and McNally were terrific. It was Mike's first year in the American League, and they both won 20 games, so we had a real good ballclub.

"I think anybody back then knew that anybody can win a short series, which is what a World Series is. We had learned that lesson in the first round of the playoffs where we won (Game 1). Boog hit a two-out homer off Jim Perry to tie it up and then we won it on a bunt in the 12th. And then McNally beat Dave Boswell 1–0. I got the laugher up in Minnesota. We were well aware that it doesn't matter how good a team we were, when you play good teams—and the Twins had a nice team that year—anything can happen.

"I don't think it was one team being overconfident. I think in a short series against a very good ballclub, they played better."

The Mets were given some simple advice from manager Gil Hodges before the Series.

"He said, 'You guys don't have to be anything but what you've been,'" recalled Ron Swoboda. "He was saying, you don't have to play any better than you've been playing, so don't try to be better, just play the game. And by then, we knew that."[7]

And that's exactly what they did. The Mets averaged only three runs and seven hits in the Series, yet they never had to make a return trip to Baltimore following Game 2. Meanwhile, New York's pitching staff held the powerful Orioles to a .146 average and just four extra-base hits. The Birds managed only five runs and 17 hits in their four losses.

You had to appreciate Hodges' skills as a platoon manager to understand the team's success during the 1969 season. Lefty hitters Ken Boswell, Art Shamsky, and Ed Kranepool started each of the three NLCS games. Boswell batted .333 with a team-high five RBIs, Shamsky hit a team-leading .538, and Kranepool had a hit in each game against the Braves. But they saw little action in the World Series as Hodges elected to start their right-handed counterparts with the Orioles throwing lefty starters in four of the five games.

The moves worked to perfection. Al Weis hit a team-high .455 with a homer and three RBIs while replacing Boswell at second base. Ron Swoboda started the four games thrown by Baltimore lefties, hitting .400 with the Series-winning RBI double as Shamsky's replacement in right. Donn Clendenon took over at first base for Kranepool, hitting .357 with a Series-high three homers and four RBIs. When Kranepool started Game 3 against the right-handed Jim Palmer, he homered to give the Mets a five-run cushion.

The Mets' starting pitchers allowed just two multiple-run innings during the entire World Series, and none in Games 2, 3, and 4. New York hitters produced just three multi-run innings, but two came after the Orioles grabbed a 3–0 lead in Game 5.

GAME 1, October 11, Baltimore: Orioles 4, Mets 1

It took the Orioles just two pitches before they owned a 1–0 lead against Tom Seaver. Don Buford belted a fly ball that went beyond the reach of Ron Swoboda and over the fence in right field.

"I look at the film now, and I look like a mechanical man going after the ball," says Swoboda. "I turned the wrong way, I stutter-stepped, drifted back to the fence, and I jumped late…I let the damn thing get over the fence."

Seaver didn't allow a hit over the next two innings, but the Orioles took control with a three-run fourth. Mark Belanger and Mike Cuellar delivered RBI singles before Buford's run-scoring double made it 4–0.

Cuellar had a two-hit shutout heading into the seventh until the Mets loaded the bases with two singles and a walk. Al Weis lifted a sacrifice fly to drive in Donn Clendenon, but the rally died when pinch-hitter Rod Gaspar grounded out to third.

The Mets sent the tying run to the plate in the ninth after Ron Swoboda singled and Al Weis walked. Cuellar completed his six-hitter by retiring pinch-hitter Art Shamsky on a grounder to second.

The Mets averaged 12 hits a game in the NLCS but managed just five singles and a double versus Cuellar. Meanwhile, Seaver's postseason ERA stood at 6.75 in two starts.

"Buford did what Buford did, and we knew Tom Seaver was a terrific pitcher," said Palmer. "What was he, 25–7? We knew the Mets were good. We knew they had a veteran team. We knew they had surprised a lot of people—the Miracle Mets and whatever. But our scouting reports told us they were good."

GAME 2, October 12, Baltimore: Mets 2, Orioles 1

Jerry Koosman bounced back nicely after he was torched for six runs and seven hits over 4-2/3 innings against the Braves in the NLCS. Koosman carried a no-hitter into the seventh against the Orioles and was staked to a 1–0 lead when Donn Clendenon homered off Dave McNally in the fourth. Paul Blair ended the no-hit bid with a leadoff single in the seventh before stealing second and scoring on Brooks Robinson's game-tying single.

McNally carried a three-hitter into the ninth and quickly retired the first two hitters of the inning. Ed Charles and Jerry Grote followed with back-to-back singles before Al Weis singled home Charles.

It was up to Koosman to protect the 2–1 lead. He opened the ninth by retiring Don Buford and Paul Blair, but Frank Robinson and Boog Powell walked to prolong the game. Ron Taylor relieved Koosman and retired Brooks Robinson on a grounder to third to end the game.

The Mets had earned a road split against the best team in the majors during the regular season. The first three hitters in the Mets' lineup went 2-for-22 at Baltimore, but light-hitting Al Weis had driven in two of the Mets' three runs from the eight-hole.

"If you go back to Game 2," Palmer begins, "Koosman beats McNally 2–1, and we hit rockets all over the ballpark. But a lot of times, good defense, good pitching, sometimes you don't get breaks.

"If you were there, you would have said, 'Boy, we hit a lot of balls hard.' But again, that's baseball."

Following the split, the Mets were batting a "robust" .188. Not to worry, because the mighty Birds were hitting .136.

GAME 3, October 14, New York: Mets 5, Orioles 0

In NHL terms, center fielder Tommie Agee was a +6 in this game. He led off the bottom of the first with a homer before saving five runs with two of the finest catches in World Series history.

The Mets held a 3–0 lead in the fourth inning when the Orioles put runners on first and third. With two outs, Elrod Hendricks belted a shot toward the 396-foot mark in center field. Agee raced onto the warning track and backhanded the deep fly before hitting the wall.

Agee bailed out Nolan Ryan with two outs in the seventh after Gary Gentry walked the bases loaded. Paul Blair hit a sinking liner to right-center that appeared to be good for three runs. But Agee sprinted to the ball and made a diving catch on the warning track for the final out.

Gary Gentry pitched well in his lone career postseason victory, lasting 6-2/3 innings and leaving with a 5–0 lead. He also hit a two-run double that put the Mets ahead 3–0 in the fourth.

Nolan Ryan picked up the save but loaded the bases in the ninth inning before striking out Blair to end the game.

Ed Kranepool's solo homer in the sixth gave the Mets a five-run cushion. Jerry Grote doubled home the Mets' other run.

The Mets held the Orioles to just five runs and 16 hits over the first three games of the Series. New York managed just six hits in each contest but led the Series 2–1.

GAME 4, October 15, New York: Mets 2, Orioles 1 (10 innings)

If luck had been on the Orioles' side, they would have walked away with a 2–1, nine-inning win to tie the Series. Problem was, Lady Luck wasn't residing in Baltimore at that moment.

Ten tremendous innings pitched, one sensational catch, and a screwball play allowed the Mets to come away with the victory.

The pitching came from Tom Seaver, who struggled in the Mets' Game 1 loss in Baltimore. Seaver had runners on second and third with two outs in the third before getting out of the jam. He continued to protect a 1–0 lead until the ninth, when back-to-back singles put runners on first and third with one out.

The game-saving catch came from an unlikely source. Brooks Robinson sent a sinking liner to the gap in right-center, where right fielder Ron Swoboda made a back-handed, diving catch with his body parallel to the turf. Swoboda rolled over once and had the presence to quickly get the ball back to the infield. Although Frank Robinson scored on the play, Boog Powell had to stay at first base.

"The play that Swoboda made was not the right play," said Palmer in 2011. "'Big Lady' should have just let the ball drop in front of him. The ball could have easily gone by him for a double or triple, although Brooks had hit it, so it wasn't going to be a triple.

"Agee did what he was supposed to do. Swoboda, you know, he made a great play. I love Ronnie. I see him every year at the BAT dinner, but at the end of the day, it's probably an ill-advised play that turned out smelling like roses."

After Jerry Grote led off the bottom of the 10th with a double, manager Gil Hodges sent J.C. Martin to pinch-hit for Seaver. Martin laid down a bunt that was fielded by Pete Richert. The reliever spun around and nailed Martin on the left wrist, sending the ball toward second base. Pinch runner Rod Gaspar sprinted home with the winning run to put the Mets ahead 3–1 in the Series.

The Orioles felt Martin was out of the base path when he was struck by the ball, but plate umpire Shag Crawford ruled otherwise. The call gnawed at the Birds for months.

"We went up to Cumberland Valley for the umpire banquet," Palmer remembered. "And Eddie Watt was there, and Shag Crawford lived up in that area. Somebody said, 'Due to a death in the family, Shag Crawford couldn't be here tonight.' Eddie Watt got up and said, 'Obviously, one of the Mets died.' And Eddie wasn't known for his sense of humor."

GAME 5, October 16, New York: Mets 5, Orioles 3

Things did not look good for the Mets after the Orioles belted a pair of third-inning homers off Jerry Koosman to take a 3–0 lead. But the lefty from Minnesota would surrender just one hit the rest of the way, allowing the Mets to chip away against Dave McNally and Eddie Watt.

McNally got the Birds on the board with a two-run homer that scored Mark Belanger. Koosman retired the next two batters before Frank Robinson collected his only extra-base hit of the series, a solo shot that gave the Orioles a three-run cushion.

Koosman led off the bottom of the third with a double but was stranded. The Mets would leave five runners on base over the first five innings, but their fortunes would change with the help of some shoe polish.

McNally threw inside to Cleon Jones leading off the sixth. Jones thought he was hit on the foot by the pitch, but umpire Lou DiMuro ruled the ball never hit Jones before it bounced into the Mets' dugout.

Out came manager Gil Hodges with evidence that would persuade DiMuro to change his mind. Hodges showed DiMuro a ball that had a smudge of shoe polish, clear evidence that Jones was indeed hit by the pitch.

"After the ball bounced, it came into our dugout," said Koosman years later. "The ball came to me, and Gil told me to brush it against my shoe, and I did, and he came

Jerry Koosman throws a pitch during Game 5 of the 1969 World Series.

over and got the ball from me and took it out there and showed [DiMuro]."[8]

Just a half-inning earlier, Frank Robinson claimed he was hit on the thigh by a Koosman pitch, and even went to the runway of the Orioles' dugout to receive treatment.

But DiMuro felt the ball ticked off Robinson's bat and called the pitch a strike. Robinson would strike out.

With Jones on first base, Donn Clendenon crushed his third homer of the series to get the Mets within 3–2.

One inning later, Al Weis, who had hit two homers during the 1969 regular season, and 10 for his career at that point, tied the game with a blast to left.

Jones would start the winning rally in the eighth with a leadoff double. Donn Clendenon grounded out, but Ron Swoboda put the Mets in front with an RBI double. Swoboda later scored the insurance run when Boog Powell and Eddie Watt made errors on Jerry Grote's grounder to first.

Koosman was nervous as he warmed up for the ninth. He immediately walked Frank Robinson before Powell hit into a force-out.

Koosman retired Brooks Robinson for the second out before Davey Johnson stepped to the plate. Johnson would become the second future Mets manager to make the final out in a clincher (Joe Torre grounded into an game-ending double play as the Mets clinched the NL East). Johnson lifted a fly ball that nestled into the glove of a kneeling Jones in left before bedlam broke out at Shea for the third time in 22 days.

Fans immediately stormed the field, grabbing anything that wasn't—and was—nailed down. Swoboda would call it the most appropriate loss of institutional control he can ever recall.[9]

Koosman quickly went from jubilation to preservation. "I just turned around, and here comes Grote, and I jumped on him. I just was so elated, and here come the fans. They came right through the cops, and my mind immediately went from celebration to running for your life!"[10]

Clendenon was named *Sport Magazine*'s World Series MVP. Al Weis was named the MVP by the BBWAA.

New York City would hold its third tickertape parade of the year, this time to celebrate the Mets' unlikely World Series victory. It came three months after the Apollo 11 astronauts were the city's guests of honor, and nine months after the Jets won Super Bowl III.

Palmer can recite all the strange occurrences in the Series more than four decades later, but he acknowledges the Mets earned the championship.

"I gave up the only home run I ever gave up to a leadoff guy in Game 3 [Agee]," said Palmer. "Swoboda made all the great catches. Same thing with Tommie Agee."

"If you go back to all the plays, all the umpiring plays, the ball in the dugout off the shoe of Cleon Jones, etc., etc., five games can end in a hurry."

"They believed that they could beat anybody, and they did."

Game 1, October 11 at Baltimore
ORIOLES 4, METS 1

METS	AB	R	H	BI	ORIOLES	AB	R	H	BI
Agee cf	4	0	0	0	Buford lf	4	1	2	2
Harrelson ss	3	0	1	0	Blair cf	3	0	0	0
Jones lf	4	0	1	0	F.Robinson rf	4	0	0	0
Clendenon 1b	4	1	2	0	Powell 1b	4	0	1	0
Swoboda rf	3	0	1	0	B.Robinson	4	0	0	0
Charles 3b	4	0	0	0	Hendricks c	3	1	1	0
Grote c	4	0	1	0	Johnson 2b	2	1	0	0
Weis 2b	1	0	0	1	Belanger ss	3	1	1	1
Seaver p	1	0	0	0	Cuellar p	3	0	1	1
Dyer ph	1	0	0	0					
Cardwell p	0	0	0	0					
Gaspar ph	1	0	0	0					
Taylor p	0	0	0	0					
Shamsky ph	1	0	0	0					
Totals	31	1	6	1	Totals	30	4	6	4

Mets	000	000	100	1	6	1	
Orioles	100	300	00X	4	6	0	

METS	IP	H	R	ER	BB	SO
Seaver (L, 0–1)	5	6	4	4	1	3
Cardwell	1	0	0	0	0	0
Taylor	2	0	0	0	1	3
Totals	8	6	4	4	2	6

ORIOLES	IP	H	R	ER	BB	SO
Cuellar (W, 1–0)	9	6	1	1	4	8

E—Weis; DP—Mets 0, Orioles 1; 2B—Clendenon, Buford; HR—Buford (1); SF—Weis; Time—2:13; Attendance—50,429.

Game 2, October 12 at Baltimore
METS 2, ORIOLES 1

METS	AB	R	H	BI	ORIOLES	AB	R	H	BI
Agee cf	4	0	0	0	Buford lf	4	0	0	0
Harrelson ss	3	0	0	0	Blair cf	4	1	1	0
Jones lf	4	0	0	0	FRobinson rf	3	0	0	0
Clendenon	3	1	1	1	Rettenmund pr	0	0	0	0
Swoboda rf	4	0	0	0	Powell 1b	3	0	0	0
Charles 3b	4	1	2	0	BRobinson 3b	4	0	1	1
Grote c	4	0	1	0	Johnson 2b	2	0	0	0
Weis 2b	3	0	2	1	Etchebarren c	3	0	0	0
Koosman p	4	0	0	0	Belanger ss	3	0	0	0
Taylor p	0	0	0	0	McNally p	3	0	0	0
Totals	33	2	6	2	Totals	29	1	2	1

Mets	000	100	001	2	6	0	
Orioles	000	000	100	1	2	0	

METS	IP	H	R	ER	BB	SO
Koosman (W, 1–0)	8-2/3	2	1	1	3	4
Taylor (S, 1)	1/3	0	0	0	0	0
Totals	9	2	1	1	3	4

ORIOLES	IP	H	R	ER	BB	SO
McNally (L, 0–1)	9	6	2	2	3	7

2B—Charles; HR—Clendenon (1); SB—Blair (1); Time—2:20; Attendance—50,850.

Game 3, October 14 at New York
METS 5, ORIOLES 0

ORIOLES	AB	R	H	BI	METS	AB	R	H	BI
Buford lf	3	0	0	0	Agee cf	3	1	1	1
Blair cf	5	0	0	0	Garrett 3b	1	0	0	0
FRobinson rf	2	0	1	0	Jones lf	4	0	0	0
Powell 1b	4	0	2	0	Shamsky rf	4	0	0	0
BRobinson 3b	4	0	0	0	Weis 2b	0	0	0	0
Hendricks c	4	0	0	0	Boswell 2b	3	1	1	0
Johnson 2b	4	0	0	0	Gaspar rf	1	0	0	0
Belanger ss	2	0	0	0	Kranepool 1b	4	1	1	1
Palmer p	2	0	0	0	Grote c	3	1	1	1
May ph	0	0	0	0	Harrelson ss	3	1	1	0
Leonhard p	0	0	0	0	Gentry p	3	0	1	2
Dalrymple ph	1	0	1	0	Ryan p	0	0	0	0
Salmon pr	0	0	0	0					
Totals	31	0	4	0	Totals	29	5	6	5

Orioles	000	000	000	0	4	1	
Mets	001	231	00X	5	6	0	

ORIOLES	IP	H	R	ER	BB	SO
Palmer (L, 0–1)	6	5	4	4	4	5
Leonhard	2	1	1	1	1	1
Totals	8	6	5	5	5	6

METS	IP	H	R	ER	BB	SO
Gentry (W, 1–0)	6-2/3	3	0	0	4	5
Ryan (S,1)	2-1/3	1	0	0	2	3
Totals	9	4	0	0	6	8

E—Palmer; 2B—Grote (1), Gentry (1); HR—Agee (1), Kranepool (1); S—Garrett; Time—2:23; Attendance—56,335.

Game 4, October 15 at New York
METS 2, ORIOLES 1 (10)

ORIOLES	AB	R	H	BI	METS	AB	R	H	BI
Buford lf	5	0	0	0	Agee cf	4	0	1	0
Blair cf	4	0	1	0	Harrelson ss	4	0	1	0
FRobinson rf	4	1	1	0	Jones lf	4	0	1	0
Powell 1b	4	0	1	0	Clendenon 1b	4	1	1	1
BRobinson 3b	3	0	0	1	Swoboda rf	4	0	3	0
Hendricks c	3	0	0	0	Charles 3b	3	0	0	0
Johnson 2b	4	0	0	0	Shamsky ph	1	0	0	0
Belanger ss	4	0	1	0	Garrett 3b	0	0	0	0
Cuellar p	2	0	1	0	Grote c	4	0	1	0
May ph	1	0	0	0	Gaspar pr	0	1	0	0
Watt p	0	0	0	0	Weis 2b	3	0	2	0
Dalrymple ph	1	0	1	0	Seaver p	3	0	0	0
Hall p	0	0	0	0	Martin ph	0	0	0	0
Richert p	0	0	0	0					
Totals	34	1	6	1	Totals	34	2	10	1

Orioles	000	000	001	0	1	6	1
Mets	010	000	000	1	2	10	1

ORIOLES	IP	H	R	ER	BB	SO
Cuellar	7	7	1	1	0	5
Watt	2	2	0	0	0	2
Hall (L, 0–1)	0	1	1	0	0	0
Rickert	0	0	0	0	0	0
Totals	9	10	2	1	1	7

METS	IP	H	R	ER	BB	SO
Seaver (W, 1–1)	10	6	1	1	2	6

E—Garrett (1), Richert (1); DP—Orioles, 3; 2B—Grote (2); HR—Clendenon (2); SF—BRobinson; S—Martin; Time—2:33; Attendance—57,367.

Game 5, October 16 at New York
METS 5, ORIOLES 3

ORIOLES	AB	R	H	BI	METS	AB	R	H	BI
Buford lf	4	0	0	0	Agee cf	3	0	1	0
Blair cf	4	0	0	0	Harrelson ss	4	0	0	0
FRobinson rf	3	1	1	1	Jones lf	3	2	1	0
Powell 1b	4	0	1	0	Clendenon 1b	3	1	1	2
Salmon pr	0	0	0	0	Swoboda	4	1	2	1
BRobinson 3b	4	0	0	0	Charles 3b	4	0	0	0
Johnson 2b	4	0	1	0	Grote c	4	0	0	0
Etchebarren c	3	0	0	0	Weis 2b	4	1	1	1
Belanger ss	3	1	0	0	Koosman	3	0	1	0
McNally p	2	1	1	2					
Motton ph	1	0	0	0					
Watt p	0	0	0	0					
Totals	32	3	5	3	Totals	32	5	7	4

Orioles	003	000	000	3	5	2	
Mets	000	002	12X	5	7	0	

ORIOLES	IP	H	R	ER	BB	SO
McNally	7	5	3	3	2	6
Watt (L, 0–1)	1.0	2	2	1	0	1
Totals	8	7	4	4	2	7

METS	IP	H	R	ER	BB	SO
Koosman (W, 2–0)	9	5	3	3	1	5

E—Watt, Powell; 2B—Swoboda (1), Koosman (1), Jones (1); HR—Robinson (1), McNally (1), Clendenon (3), Weis (1); SB—Agee (1); Time—2:14; Attendance—57,397.

1969 World Series Statistics

COMPOSITE LINESCORE

	123	456	789	10	R		H	E
Mets	130	103	231	1	15		35	2
Orioles	103	300	101	0	9		23	4

METS HITTING

Player	BA	G	AB	R	H
Tommie Agee	.167	5	18	1	3
Ken Boswell	.333	1	3	1	1
Don Cardwell	—	1	0	0	0
Ed Charles	.133	4	15	1	2
Donn Clendenon	.357	4	14	4	5
Duffy Dyer	.000	1	1	0	0
Wayne Garrett	.000	2	1	0	0
Rod Gaspar	.000	3	2	1	0
Gary Gentry	.333	1	3	0	1
Jerry Grote	.211	5	19	1	4
Bud Harrelson	.176	5	17	1	3
Cleon Jones	.158	5	19	2	3
Jerry Koosman	.143	2	7	0	1
Ed Kranepool	.250	1	4	1	1
J.C. Martin	—	1	0	0	0
Nolan Ryan	—	1	0	0	0
Tom Seaver	.000	2	4	0	0
Art Shamsky	.000	3	6	0	0
Ron Swoboda	.400	4	15	1	6
Ron Taylor	—	2	0	0	0
Al Weis	.455	5	11	1	5
Total	.220	5	159	15	35

2B—Grote 2, Charles, Clendenon, Gentry, Jones, Koosman, Swoboda; 3B—None; HR—Clendenon 3, Agee, Weis, Kranepool: RBI—Clendenon 4, Weis 3, Gentry 2, Agee, Grote, Kranepool, Swoboda; SB—Agee.

ORIOLES HITTING

Player	BA	G	AB	R	H
Mark Belanger	.200	5	15	2	3
Paul Blair	.100	5	20	1	2
Dun Buford	.100	5	20	1	2
Mike Cuellar	.400	2	5	0	2
Clay Dalrymple	1.000	2	2	0	2
Andy Etchebarren	.000	2	6	0	0
Dick Hall	—	1	0	0	0
Elrod Hendricks	.100	3	10	1	1
Dave Johnson	.063	5	16	1	1
Dave Leonhard	—	1	0	0	0
Dave May	.000	2	1	0	0
Dave McNally	.200	2	5	1	1
Curt Motton	.000	1	1	0	0
Jim Palmer	.000	1	2	0	0
Boog Powell	.263	5	19	0	5
Merv Rettenmund	—	1	0	0	0
Pete Richert	—	1	0	0	0
Brooks Robinson	.053	5	19	0	1
Frank Robinson	.188	5	16	2	3
Chico Salmon	—	2	0	0	0
Eddie Watt	—	2	0	0	0
Total	.146	5	157	9	23

2B—Buford; 3B—None; HR—Buford, McNally, Robinson; RBI—Buford 2, McNally 2, BRobinson 2, Belanger, Cuellar, FRobinson; SB—Blair.

METS PITCHING

Player	G	ERA	W–L	SV	IP	H	ER	BB	SO
Jerry Koosman	2	2.04	2–0	0	17-2/3	7	4	4	9
Tom Seaver	2	3.00	1–1	0	15	12	5	3	9
Gary Gentry	1	0.00	1–0	0	6-2/3	3	0	5	4
Nolan Ryan	1	0.00	0–0	1	2-1/3	1	0	2	3
Ron Taylor	2	0.00	0–0	1	2-1/3	0	0	1	3
Don Cardwell	1	0.00	0–0	0	1	0	0	0	0
Total	5	1.80	4–1	1	45	23	9	15	28

ORIOLES PITCHING

Player	G	ERA	W–L	SV	IP	H	ER	BB	SO
Mike Cuellar	2	1.12	1–0	0	16	13	2	4	13
Dave McNally	2	2.81	0–1	0	16	11	5	5	13
Jim Palmer	1	6.00	0–1	0	6	5	4	4	5
Eddie Watt	2	3.00	0–1	0	3	4	1	0	3
Dave Leonhard	1	4.50	0–0	0	2	1	1	1	1
Dick Hall	1	—	0–1	0	0	1	0	1	0
Pete Richert	1	—	0–0	0	0	0	0	0	0
Total	5	2.72	1–4	0	43	35	13	15	35

1973 NLCS: Mets vs. Cincinnati Reds

METS WIN SERIES 3–2

The "Ya Gotta Believe" Mets had five days to prepare for the Reds after clinching the NL East the day after the regular season was scheduled to end. The extra rest allowed Tom Seaver to start back-to-back games and gave the team time to recharge after their improbable stretch run. That was the good news.

The bad news was they were facing the Reds, who had claimed their second straight NL West title by hammering opposing pitching staffs. The Reds were among the top six in every offensive category and finished second with 741 runs, 133 more than the Mets accumulated during the regular season.

Joe Morgan, Tony Perez, and Johnny Bench each hit 25 or more homers, Perez and Pete Rose batted over .300, and Bench and Perez each drove in more than 100 runs. The Mets had no regulars with more than 23 homers, 76 RBIs, or a .290 average. Perez and Morgan arguably were the Reds' most dangerous hitters. Perez was second on the team with a .314 average, first with 27 homers, and second with 101 RBIs. Morgan was second in the NL with 67 stolen bases and sixth with 63 extra-base hits, doing it while batting .290 with 26 homers and 82 RBIs.

The Mets completely muzzled the two future Hall of Famers while keeping Bench in check. Perez and Morgan combined to hit .095 (4-for-42) with one homer and three RBIs. Bench went 3-for-4 with the game-winning homer in Game 1 of the series. He batted .133 (2-for-15) the rest of the way.

To show how feeble Perez and Morgan were at the plate, the Mets' entire pitching staff went 4-for-14 (.286) with two RBIs and two runs scored. Seaver and Jerry Koosman produced as many hits for the Mets as Perez and Morgan did for the Reds.

Rusty Staub had a huge series in his first postseason experience. He hit only .200 but belted three homers, scored four times, and had five RBIs before a shoulder injury caused him to miss Game 5. Even with Staub out of the lineup, his replacements accounted for three ribbies in the clincher. Ed Kranepool delivered a two-run single in his first series at-bat after being penciled into the lineup following Staub's injury. Willie Mays delivered an RBI single as a pinch-hitter for Kranepool during the Mets' pivotal four-run fifth in Game 5.

The Mets were the better clutch hitters during the series, batting a sizzling .471 (16-for-34) with runners in scoring position as opposed to the Reds' 2-for-28 mark (.071).

The most memorable incident of the series may have been the Bud Harrelson–Pete Rose fight in Game 3. Rose slide hard into Harrelson at second base in a futile attempt to break up a double play. Rose sprung to his feet and promptly received a shove from the diminutive shortstop.

"I was trying to knock him into left field," chirped Rose. "I play hard, not dirty…I might even slide harder tomorrow, if it's possible."

According to the book *Amazin' Met Memories*, Harrelson thought the slide was excessive. "I though he hit me with his elbow on the left side of my head intentionally…I didn't like what he did, and he didn't like what I said."

The Rose-Harrelson fracas was just round one. Both bullpens got into the mix once they reached the infield. Reds reliever Pedro Borbon quickly threw a punch at Buzz Capra to give the brawl more staying power. Players eventually retrieved their caps as order was being restored. Borbon accidentally grabbed a Mets cap and placed it on his head. After realizing his fashion *faux pas*, Borbon grabbed the cap, put it in his mouth, and bit a huge chunk out of the bill.

Years later, according to the book *Amazin'*, Jerry Koosman said Harrelson made a statement by standing up to Rose. "Maybe we didn't have the strength Cincinnati had, but we weren't going to back down, and that's what Buddy was proving. 'I'm half your size, but tell you what, I'm not going to take it.'"

The Reds showed very little fight for most of the series. Although Bench and Rose provided game-winning homers, Cincinnati hit just .186 and never scored more than two runs in any game.

GAME 1, October 6, Cincinnati: Reds 2, Mets 1

Tom Seaver certainly did enough to win the series opener. He doubled home the Mets' only run, struck out 13 and held the Reds to six hits in a complete game. But a pair of solo homers allowed the home team to come away with a victory.

The Mets took a 1–0 lead in the second inning when Bud Harrelson walked and scored on Seaver's two-bagger.

New York would not get another hit after Seaver put the Mets ahead. Seaver gave up leadoff hits in the fourth, fifth and seventh innings but continued to throw a shutout. The 1–0 lead stood up until the bottom of the eighth, when Pete Rose hit a one-out homer.

Rusty Staub led off the ninth with a walk but never advanced past first, giving the Reds a chance to win it in regulation. Johnny Bench sent the Reds' faithful home with a victory by belting a game-winning homer with one out in the bottom of the ninth.

Bench had three of the Reds' six hits, and two of their four extra bases.

GAME 2, October 7, Cincinnati: Mets 5, Reds 0

Andy Kosco stood between Jon Matlack and a no-hitter as the Mets evened the series. Kosco reached base three times with a pair of singles and a walk. But the rest of the Reds' lineup went 0-for-25 against the Mets' lefty, who tossed the team's first complete game in an NLCS game.

Rusty Staub snapped a scoreless tie with a solo blast in the fourth, the first of his four homers during the 1973 postseason. Staub also walked and scored in the Mets' four-run ninth.

Don Gullett and Clay Carroll combined to two-hit the Mets until the ninth, but New York finally broke through against future Met Tom Hall and Game 1 winner Pedro Borbon. Cleon Jones doubled the Mets' lead with an RBI single before scoring on Jerry Grote's two-run single. Bud Harrelson capped the scoring with an RBI single.

Matlack ended the game by retiring three future Hall of Famers, getting Joe Morgan and Tony Perez to fly out before fanning Johnny Bench for the last of his nine strikeouts.

Manager Yogi Berra still hadn't dipped into his bullpen as Tom Seaver and Matlack combined to hold the Reds to two runs and eight hits at Riverfront Stadium.

GAME 3, October 8, New York: Mets 9, Reds 2

It began as a routine, inning-ending double play and evolved into the most memorable brawl in major league postseason history.

The Mets already were ahead 9–2 in the fifth when Pete Rose was retired on Joe Morgan's 3-6-3 double-play grounder. Rose made a hard slide and quickly popped up to his feet. Bud Harrelson took exception to the takeout slide and shoved Rose before the two started to go at one another.

The benches and bullpens emptied before order was finally restored on the field. It took a little longer for order to be restored in the stands.

Fans threw bottles and other garbage at Rose when he took his position in left field in the bottom of the fifth.

Reds manager Sparky Anderson eventually pulled his team off the field. The Mets were in danger of forfeiting the game to the Reds when Yogi Berra, Willie Mays and other Mets went out to left and pleaded with the fans to behave themselves. The fans relented, allowing Jerry Koosman to complete an eight-hitter.

Rusty Staub put the Mets ahead to stay with a solo homer in the bottom of the first before adding a three-run blast that capped a five-run second.

Koosman went 2-for-4, scored on Staub's second homer and added an RBI single to his cause.

Dennis Menke homered for the Reds, who've managed just four runs and 16 hits in the series thus far.

GAME 4, October 9, New York: Reds 2, Mets 1 (12 innings)

Mets fans had a new reason to boo Pete Rose after he hit a solo homer off Harry Parker in the top of the 12th to extend the series to a fifth game.

The Mets didn't score after Felix Millan hit an RBI single with two outs in the bottom of the third. Millan also led off the ninth with a single but never advanced, putting the Mets in extra innings for the second time in their postseason history.

George Stone, who won his last eight decisions of the regular season, blanked the Reds until Tony Perez belted a long homer with one out in the seventh. Stone was re-placed by Tug McGraw after issuing a two-out walk later in the inning.

Stone faced just two batters over the minimum but received little support.

Millan's run-scoring single was the lone hit allowed by Fred Norman. The Reds' bullpen followed with seven scoreless innings and retired the last 12 Mets in order.

Rusty Staub made a sensational grab of Rose's fly ball to end the sixth but came away with a slightly separated shoulder when he slammed into the wall in right field. He would be forced to miss Game 5.

GAME 5, October 10, New York: Mets 7, Reds 2

With Rusty Staub out with a partially separated shoulder, manager Yogi Berra was forced to move Cleon Jones to right field and play Ed Kranepool in left. The move paid immediate dividends as Kranepool, who didn't play in the first four games of the series, came through with a two-run single in the bottom of the first.

Tom Seaver worked out of a bases-loaded jam in the first inning but eventually gave up the 2–0 lead. Dan Driessen hit a sacrifice fly in the third, two innings before Tony Perez knotted the score with an RBI single.

But the Mets took control of the game by scoring four times in the fifth on two doubles, a pair of singles and a walk. New York got a break when third baseman Dan Driessen failed to tag out Wayne Garrett at third on Felix Millan's bunt. Cleon Jones followed with the tiebreaking double before Willie Mays pinch-hit for Kranepool. Mays hit a chopper that bounced about 30 feet into the air near home plate. Reds reliever Clay Carroll was unable to throw to the plate in time to get Felix Millan, giving Mays his only hit of the series.

Don Hahn followed with a run-scoring fielder's choice before Bud Harrelson's single drove in Mays for the fourth run of the inning.

Jones added an insurance run with a single that scored Seaver in the sixth.

Pitching on three day's rest, Seaver was two outs from a complete-game six-hitter before tiring. Larry Stahl singled and Seaver walked Hal King and Pete Rose in consecutive at-bats to load the bases. Tug McGraw came in to retire Joe Morgan on a popup to short before Dan Driessen hit a series-ending grounder to first.

The win allowed Yogi Berra to join Joe McCarthy as the only managers to win pennants in both leagues. Ironically, Reds skipper Sparky Anderson would become the first skipper to win World Series in both leagues (Reds, '75 and '76, Tigers, '84).

As they did three times in 1969, Mets fans stormed the field, tore up the turf and grabbed the bases. This time, it had the look of mob rule that angered people on both sides. A disgusted Seaver said, "those people don't care anything about baseball, or that we won. It's just an excuse to them to go tear something up."

Anderson concurred. "I never thought I'd see anything like this in America. Then again, who says New York is America?"

"I was there," said Kash Beauchamp, who was in the stands watching his father, Jim. I think part of the problem was half the people there were stoned!"

Game 1, October 6 at Cincinnati
REDS 2, METS 1

METS	AB	R	H	BI	REDS	AB	R	H	BI
Garrett 3b	4	0	1	0	Rose lf	4	1	1	1
Millan 2b	3	0	0	0	Morgan 2b	4	0	0	0
Staub rf	2	0	0	0	Driessen 3b	4	0	1	0
Milner 1b	3	0	1	0	Perez 1b	4	0	0	0
Jones lf	4	0	0	0	Bench c	4	1	3	1
Grote c	4	0	0	0	Griffey cf	2	0	0	0
Hahn cf	3	0	0	0	Geronimo rf	3	0	1	0
Harrelson ss	2	1	0	0	Chaney ss	2	0	0	0
Seaver p	3	0	1	1	Stahl ph	1	0	0	0
Crosby ss	0	0	0	0					
Billingham p	1	0	0	0					
King ph	1	0	0	0					
Hall p	0	0	0	0					
Borbon p	0	0	0	0					
Totals	28	1	3	1	Totals	30	2	6	2

Mets	010 000 000	1	3	0
Reds	000 000 011	2	6	0

METS	IP	H	R	ER	BB	SO
Seaver (L, 0–1)	8.1	6	2	2	0	13

REDS	IP	H	R	ER	BB	SO
Billingham	8.0	3	1	1	3	6
Hall	0.0	0	0	0	1	0
Borbon (W, 1–0)	1	0	0	0	0	0
TOTAL	9	3	1	1	4	6

DP—Mets 0, Reds 1; 2B—Seaver (1), Bench (1), Driessen (1); HR—Rose (1), Bench (1); SH—Millan, Billingham; Time—2:00; ATT—53,431.

Game 2, October 7 at Cincinnati
METS 5, REDS 0

METS	AB	R	H	BI	REDS	AB	R	H	BI
Garrett 3b	5	0	0	0	Rose lf	4	0	0	0
Millan 2b	4	1	1	0	Morgan 2b	4	0	0	0
Staub rf	3	2	1	1	Perez 1b	4	0	0	0
Jones lf	3	1	1	1	Bench c	4	0	0	0
Milner 1b	3	1	0	0	Kosco rf	2	0	2	0
Grote c	4	0	1	2	Driessen 3b	3	0	0	0
Hahn cf	3	0	2	0	Geronimo cf	3	0	0	0
Harrelson ss	4	0	1	1	Chaney ss	0	0	0	0
Matlack p	2	0	0	0	Armbrister ph	1	0	0	0
					Hall p	0	0	0	0
					Borbon p	0	0	0	0
					Gullett p	0	0	0	0
					Gagliano ph	1	0	0	0
					Carroll p	0	0	0	0
					Menke ph-ss	1	0	0	0
Totals	31	5	7	5	Totals	27	0	2	0

Mets	000 100 004	5	7	0
Reds	000 000 000	0	2	0

METS	IP	H	R	ER	BB	SO
Matlack (W, 1–0)	9	2	0	0	3	9

REDS	IP	H	R	ER	BB	SO
Gullett (L, 0–1)	5	2	1	1	2	3
Carolll	3	0	0	0	1	2
Hall	1/3	2	4	4	2	0
Borbon	2/3	3	0	0	0	1
TOTAL	9	7	5	5	5	6

DP—Mets 0, Reds 1; HR—Staub (1); S—Matlack, Gullett; Time—2:19; ATT—54,041

Game 3, October 8 at New York
METS 9, REDS 2

REDS	AB	R	H	BI	METS	AB	R	H	BI
Rose lf	4	0	2	0	Garrett 3b	4	0	0	1
Morgan 2b	4	0	1	1	Millan 2b	3	2	1	1
Perez 1b	4	0	0	0	Staub rf	5	2	2	4
Bench c	4	0	1	0	Jones lf	3	1	2	0
Kosco rf	4	0	0	0	Milner 1b	4	0	1	1
Armbrister cf	4	0	1	0	Grote c	3	2	1	0
Menke 3b	4	1	1	1	Hahn cf	4	1	2	0
Chaney ss	3	0	0	0	Harrelson ss	4	0	0	0
Gagliano ph	1	0	0	0	Koosman p	4	0	2	1
Grimsley p	0	0	0	0					
Hall p	0	0	0	0					
Stahl ph	1	1	1	0					
Tomlin p	0	0	0	0					
Nelson p	1	0	0	0					
King ph	1	0	1	0					
Borbon p	0	0	0	0					
Totals	35	2	8	2	Totals	34	9	11	8

Reds	002 000 000	2	8	1
Mets	151 200 00X	9	11	1

REDS	IP	H	R	ER	BB	SO
Grimsley (L, 0–1)	1-2/3	5	5	5	1	2
Hall	1/3	1	1	1	1	1
Tomlin	1-2/3	5	3	3	1	1
Nelson	2-1/3	0	0	0	1	0
Borbon	2	0	0	0	0	2
Totals	8	11	9	9	4	6

METS	IP	H	R	ER	BB	SO
Koosman (W, 1–0)	9	8	2	2	0	9

E—Kosco (1), Garrett (1); DP—Mets 1, Reds 0; 2B—Bench (2), Jones (1); HR—Staub, 2 (3), Menke (1); SF—Garrett; Time—2:48; ATT—53,967.

Game 4, October 9 at New York
REDS 2, METS 1

REDS	AB	R	H	BI	METS	AB	R	H	BI
Rose lf	5	1	3	1	Garrett 3b	5	0	0	0
Morgan 2b	4	0	0	0	Millan 2b	5	0	2	1
Perez 1b	6	1	1	0	Staub rf	5	0	0	0
Bench c	4	0	1	0	Jones lf	5	0	0	0
Kosco rf	4	0	1	0	Milner 1b	4	0	0	0
Menke 3b	4	0	1	0	Grote c	4	0	1	0
Geronimo cf	5	0	0	0	Hahn cf	3	1	0	0
Chaney ss	2	0	0	0	Harrelson ss	4	0	0	0
Armbrister ph	1	0	0	0	Stone p	1	0	0	0
Crosby ss	1	0	1	0	McGraw p	1	0	0	0
Driessen pr-3b	1	0	0	0	Boswell ph	1	0	0	0
Norman p	1	0	0	0	Parker	0	0	0	0
Stahl ph	1	0	0	0					
Gullett p	1	0	0	0					
Gagliano ph	1	0	0	0					
Carroll p	0	0	0	0					
Griffey ph	1	0	0	0					
Borbon p	0	0	0	0					
Totals	42	2	8	2	Totals	38	1	3	1

Reds	000	000	001	001	2	8	0
Mets	001	000	000	000	1	3	1

REDS	IP	H	R	ER	BB	SO
Norman	5	1	1	1	3	3
Gullett	4	2	0	0	0	3
Carroll (W, 1–0)	2	0	0	0	0	0
Borbon (S, 1)	1	0	0	0	0	0
Totals	12	3	1	1	3	6

METS	IP	H	R	ER	BB	S
Stone	6-2/3	3	1	1	2	4
McGraw	4-1/3	4	0	0	3	3
Parker (L, 0–1)	1.0	1	1	1	0	0
Totals	12	8	2	2	5	7

E—McGraw (1); LOB—Reds 10, Mets 4; DP—Mets 2, Reds 1; HR—Perez (1), Rose (2); S—Morgan; WP—McGraw (1); Time—3:07; ATT—50,786.

Game 5, October 10 at New York
METS 7, REDS 2

REDS	AB	R	H	BI	METS	AB	R	H	BI
Rose lf	4	1	2	0	Garrett 3b	5	1	1	0
Morgan 2b	4	1	1	0	Millan 2b	4	2	2	0
Driessen 3b	4	0	1	1	Jones rf-lf	5	1	3	2
Perez 1b	4	0	1	1	Milner 1b	3	1	1	0
Bench c	3	0	0	0	Kranepool lf	2	0	1	2
Griffey cf	4	0	1	0	Mays ph-cf	3	1	1	1
Geronimo rf	4	0	0	0	Grote c	4	0	1	0
Chaney ss	2	0	0	0	Hahn cf-rf	4	0	0	1
Stahl ph	1	0	1	0	Harrelson ss	4	0	2	1
Billingham p	2	0	0	0	Seaver p	3	1	1	0
Gullett p	0	0	0	0	McGraw p	0	0	0	0
Carroll p	0	0	0	0					
Crosby ph	1	0	0	0					
Grimsley p	0	0	0	0					
King ph	0	0	0	0					
Totals	33	2	7	2	Totals	37	7	13	7

Reds	001	010	000	2	7	1
Mets	200	041	00X	7	13	1

REDS	IP	H	R	ER	BB	SO
Billingham (L 1–1)	4.0	6	5	5	1	3
Gullett	0.0	0	1	1	1	0
Carroll	2.0	5	1	1	0	0
Grimsley	2.0	2	0	0	1	1
Total	8.0	13	7	7	3	4

METS	IP	H	R	ER	BB	SO
Seaver (W, 1–1)	8.1	7	2	1	5	4
McGraw (S, 1)	2/3	0	0	0	0	0
Total	9.0	7	2	1	5	4

E—Jones, Driessen; 2B—Morgan (1), Griffey (1), Rose (1), Jones (2), Garrett (1), Seaver (2); SB—Driessen (1). WP—Seaver. Time—2:40. ATT—50,323.

1973 NLCS Statistics

COMPOSITE LINESCORE

Mets	362	341	004	000	23		37	4
Reds	003	010	111	001	8		31	2

METS HITTING

Player	BA	G	AB	R	H
Ken Boswell	.000	1	1	0	0
Wayne Garrett	.087	5	23	1	2
Jerry Grote	.211	5	19	2	4
Don Hahn	.235	5	17	2	4
Bud Harrelson	.167	5	18	1	3
Cleon Jones	.300	5	20	3	6
Jerry Koosman	.500	1	4	1	2
Ed Kranepool	.500	1	2	0	1
Jon Matlack	.000	1	2	0	0
Willie Mays	.333	1	3	1	1
Tug McGraw	.000	2	1	0	0
Felix Millan	.316	5	19	5	6
John Milner	.176	5	17	2	3
Harry Parker	—	1	0	0	0
Tom Seaver	333	2	6	1	2
Rusty Staub	.200	4	15	4	3
George Stone	.000	1	1	0	0
Total	.220	5	168	23	37

2B—Jones 2, Seaver 2, Garrett; 3B—None; HR—Staub 3; RBI—Staub 5, Jones 3, Grote 2, Harrelson 2, Kranepool 2, Millan 2, Garrett, Hahn, Koosman, Mays, Milner, Seaver; SB—None.

REDS HITTING

Player	BA	G	AB	R	H
Ed Armbrister	.167	3	6	0	1
Johnny Bench	.263	5	19	1	5
Jack Billingham	.000	2	3	0	0
Pedro Borbon	—	4	0	0	0
Clay Carroll	—	3	0	0	0
Darrell Chaney	.000	5	9	0	0
Ed Crosby	.500	3	2	0	1
Dan Driessen	.167	4	12	0	2
Phil Gagliano	.000	3	3	0	0
Cesar Geronimo	.067	4	5	0	1
Ken Griffey	.143	3	7	0	1
Ross Grimsley	—	2	0	0	0
Don Gullett	.000	3	1	0	0
Tom Hall	—	3	0	0	0
Hal King	.500	3	2	0	1
Andy Kosco	.300	3	10	0	3
Dennis Menke	.222	3	9	1	2
Joe Morgan	.100	5	20	1	2
Roger Nelson	.000	1	1	0	0
Fred Norman	.000	1	1	0	0
Tony Perez	.091	5	22	1	2
Pete Rose	.381	5	21	3	8
Larry Stahl	.500	4	4	1	2
Dave Tomlin	—	1	0	0	0
Total	.186	5	167	8	31

2B—Bench 2, Driessen, Griffey, Morgan, Rose; 3B—None; HR—Rose 2, Bench, Menke, Perez; RBI—Perez 2, Rose 2, Bench, Driessen, Menke, Morgan; SB—None.

METS PITCHING

Player	G	ERA	W–L	SV	IP	H	ER	BB	SO
Tom Seaver	2	1.62	1–1	0	16-2/3	13	3	5	17
Jerry Koosman	1	2.00	1–0	0	9	8	2	0	9
Jon Matlack	1	0.00	1–0	0	9	2	0	3	9
George Stone	1	1.35	0–0	0	6-2/3	3	1	2	4
Tug McGraw	2	0.00	0–0	1	5	4	0	3	3
Harry Parker	1	9.00	0–1	0	1	1	1	0	0
Total	5	1.33	3–2	1	47-1/3	31	7	13	42

REDS PITCHING

Player	G	ERA	W–L	SV	IP	H	ER	BB	SO
Jack Billingham	2	4.50	0–1	0	12	9	6	4	9
Don Gullett	3	2.00	0–1	0	9	4	2	3	6
Clay Carroll	3	1.29	1–0	0	7	5	1	1	2
Fred Norman	1	1.80	0–0	0	5	1	1	3	3
Pedro Borbon	4	1.93	1–0	1	4-2/3	3	1	1	3
Ross Grimsley	2	12.27	0–1	0	3-2/3	7	5	2	3
Roger Nelson	1	0.00	0–0	0	2-1/3	0	0	1	0
Dave Tomlin	1	16.20	0–0	0	1-2/3	5	3	1	1
Tom Hall	3	54.00	0–0	0	2/3	3	4	3	1
Total	5	4.50	2–3	0	46	37	23	19	28

1973 World Series: Mets vs. Oakland Athletics

ATHLETICS WIN SERIES 4–3

Tug McGraw makes his third appearance in as many games as he delivers a pitch in the ninth inning of Game 3 of the 1973 World Series against the Oakland A's in New York. McGraw pitched two scoreless innings, but the Mets lost 3–2 in 11 innings.

The World Series almost seemed anticlimactic considering the way the Mets had reached the Fall Classic. Ravaged by injuries, left for dead in July, and occupying the NL East cellar on August 30, the Mets managed to win the division before beating the mighty Reds in a five-game NLCS.

Again, the Mets appeared overmatched offensively in a postseason series. The A's scored 150 more runs during the regular season, belted 63 more homers, and hit 14 points higher than the Mets. Oakland also had a pitching staff that was the Mets' equal. Both had future Hall of Fame starting pitchers (Tom Seaver and Catfish Hunter) and All-Star hurlers (Jon Matlack, Jerry Koosman, Tug McGraw, Ken Holtzman, Vida Blue, Rollie Fingers).

The Mets staff did its part by silencing the Athletics' potent attack, holding it to a .212 average and just two homers, none during the first six games of the Series. But the Mets' glovemen faltered at the worst times, leading to one loss and contributing to another. Two-time Gold Glove second baseman Felix Millan misplayed a potential inning-ending grounder, allowing two unearned runs to score in a 2–1 loss in the Series opener. And Jerry Grote's passed ball in Game 3 set up Bert Campaneris' game-winning single in Game 3. The Mets made 10 errors and allowed five unearned runs in the Series, three with Matlack on the mound.

Rusty Staub's shoulder injury didn't prevent the Mets' right fielder from being the most productive player in the Series. He led all regulars in batting (.423) and hits (11) while tying Reggie Jackson for most RBIs (6).

But the Mets had trouble retiring Campaneris and Jackson, who combined to hit .300 (18-for-60) in the Series while their teammates batted a combined .182.

Campy hit the grounder that was booted by Millan in Game 1. The Oakland shortstop also scored the tying run and singled home the winning run in Game 3 before adding the tiebreaking, two-run homer in Game 7.

Jackson put Game 7 out of reach with a two-run blast that gave the A's a 4–0 lead, one day after lacing a pair of RBI doubles to help Oakland extend the Series.

It would be 13 years before the Mets would reach the postseason again. Seaver, McGraw, Grote, John Milner, and Duffy Dyer would appear in other postseasons, but Matlack, Koosman, and Staub wouldn't play another meaningful October game.

Ken Boswell tied a World Series record with three pinch-hits. Darold Knowles came out of the Oakland bullpen to appear in all seven games, setting a World Series mark.

GAME 1, October 13, Oakland: A's 2, Mets 1

Normally surehanded Felix Millan was wearing the goat horns after this one despite hitting the first triple in Mets World Series history. Millan's error at second base led to two unearned runs as the Mets lost Game 1 of a postseason series for the third time in four tries.

The A's had nobody on and two outs in the bottom of the third after Dick Green was thrown out trying to steal second base. Winning pitcher Ken Holtzman kept the inning alive with a double off hardluck loser Jon Matlack. Bert Campaneris followed with what should have been an inning-ending grounder to second. But Millan let the ball scoot through his legs, allowing Holtzman to score the game's first run. Campy promptly stole second before Joe Rudi's single made it 2–0 Oakland.

Millan won a Gold Glove the previous year and committed just nine errors during the 1973 regular season, one more than his 1972 total.

The Mets got a run back in the fourth when John Milner poked an RBI single following a Cleon Jones double. Wayne Garrett possibly cost the Mets a run in the fifth when he bunted into a double play. Millan followed with a triple before Willie Mays hit an inning-ending fly ball to right.

The Mets hit leadoff singles in the sixth and seventh innings off reliever Rollie Fingers but failed to score, allowing the A's to take the opener. Darold Knowles got the final two outs for the save.

Matlack pitched well enough to win, allowing no earned runs and three hits in six innings.

GAME 2, October 14, Oakland: Mets 10, A's 7 (12 innings)

Until Game 6 of the 1986 World Series, this was the craziest Fall Classic contest in Mets history. It set a World Series record for the longest game (4:13), featured the final hit of Willie Mays' career, and included five Oakland errors, two committed by the soon-to-be-infamous Mike Andrews at second base in the Mets' four-run 10th.

The Mets scored four times in the sixth inning to take their first lead of the Series. Don Hahn and Bud Harrelson hit back-to-back RBI singles before a throwing error by reliever Darold Knowles allowed two more runs. Following the error, the Mets had runners on second and third with one out but could not score.

The A's forced extra innings when Tug McGraw surrendered back-to-back RBI singles by Reggie Jackson and Gene Tenace with two outs in the ninth. McGraw tossed six innings of relief and delivered a bunt single that helped fuel a four-run 12th.

The Mets thought they had gone ahead 7–6 in the 10th inning. Bud Harrelson led off the inning with a single and advanced to third on a bunt and an error. Felix Millan followed with a fly ball to left that appeared deep enough to score Harrelson. But Joe Rudi fired the ball to the plate, where catcher Ray Fosse made a sweeping tag to nail Harrelson, who insisted Fosse's glove never touched him. Willie Mays pleaded on his knees for home plate umpire Augie Donatelli to change his call. Replays were inconclusive, but Donatelli's decision allowed for an entertaining 12th inning.

Harrelson led off the 12th with a double and moved to third on McGraw's bunt-single. Two outs followed before Mays delivered an RBI single that put the Mets ahead to stay. It would be his final major league hit.

Mays also helped prolong the game with two fielding miscues, 19 years after making one of the greatest catches in World Series history. He lost two fly balls in the sun, one in the ninth and another in the 12th. It would be his last game as an outfielder.

The Mets scored two more runs in the 12th when Andrews couldn't handle John Milner's grounder to second. Andrews also provided New York's fourth and final run of the inning when he threw away Jerry Grote's ground ball.

McGraw eventually ran out of gas, leaving the game with runners on first and third and nobody out in the bottom of the 12th. George Stone immediately gave up Jesus Alou's RBI single before getting the final three outs for his first and only postseason save.

Controversy swirled around the A's between Games 2 and 3, when owner Charlie Finley attempted to put Andrews on the disabled list. Finley ordered a medical evaluation and even convinced Andrews to sign a statement saying he was injured as Finley tried to replace the veteran with rookie infielder Manny Trillo on the roster (Oakland had tried to talk the Mets into allowing Trillo to be activated before the Series). The ploy seemed to unify the A's and contributed to manager Dick Williams' announcement to the team before Game 3 that he would step down at the end of the Series.

Finley's roster maneuver was thwarted by commissioner Bowie Kuhn, who reinstated Andrews and fined the team $7,000. Andrews received a standing ovation at Shea Stadium when he came up as a pinch-hitter in the eighth inning of Game 4.

GAME 3, October 16, New York: A's 3, Mets 2 (11 innings)

Bert Campaneris was the linchpin in the victory, scoring the tying run and providing an RBI single in the 11th to give the A's a 2–1 Series lead.

Wayne Garrett was 1-for-11 in the Series before belting a leadoff homer in the bottom of the first. Felix Millan and Rusty Staub followed with singles, and Millan scampered home on a wild pitch to put the Mets ahead 2–0. Later in the first, the Mets had runners on first and second with one out following first baseman Gene Tenace's error on John Milner's grounder. But the Mets wouldn't score another run the rest of the game.

Tom Seaver carried a four-hit shutout into the sixth and struck out the side during the second and fifth innings. Seaver eventually was nicked for a run when Sal Bando and Tenace doubled in the sixth.

Seaver still had a 2–1 lead until the eighth, when Campaneris led off with a single and stole second before scoring on Joe Rudi's single.

Tug McGraw worked out of a two-on, nobody out jam in the ninth, and Rusty Staub hit a ground-rule double in the bottom of the ninth to give the Mets a chance to win in regulation. But John Milner hit a fly ball to right for the final out of the inning.

Campaneris put the A's ahead with a run-scoring single in the eleventh after a passed ball by Jerry Grote put Ted Kubiak at second base. The Mets tried to rally in the bottom of the inning when Wayne Garrett led off with a single and was bunted to second. Paul Lindblad picked up the save by getting Rusty Staub to fly out before Cleon Jones grounded out to Campaneris at short.

GAME 4, October 17, New York: Mets 6, A's 1

Rusty Staub set a Mets record for most hits and RBIs in a World Series game, going 4-for-4 with five ribbies to help New York even the series at two games apiece.

The Mets got all the runs they would need just three batters into the game, when Staub deposited a Ken Holtzman pitch over the wall in left-center for a three-run homer following singles by Wayne Garrett and Felix Millan. The Mets would tack on three more runs in the fourth, with Staub hitting a two-run single to cap the rally.

Jon Matlack was outstanding for the third consecutive postseason start, holding the A's to an unearned run and

three hits over eight innings. The A's scored their lone run in the fourth, when Sal Bando reached on Garrett's error and moved to third on a single before scoring on Gene Tenace's RBI grounder.

Matlack had allowed no earned runs and just eight hits over 23 innings in three career postseason starts at this point. Only errors by Felix Millan and Garrett got between Matlack and a lengthy shutout streak.

Holtzman lasted just one-third of an inning, charged with three runs and four hits. He would bounce back to win Game 7 of the Series.

GAME 5, October 18, New York: Mets 2, A's 0

The Mets got another outstanding pitching performance and took a 3–2 lead in the series by stifling the A's. Jerry Koosman made up for his poor performance in Game 2 by holding Oakland to three hits and four walks over 6-1/3 innings. Koosman sailed through the Athletics' lineup until the seventh, when Gene Tenace led off with a walk and moved to third on Ray Fosse's one-out double. Fosse's two-bagger ended Koosman's night.

It was up to Tug McGraw to get out of the jam and protect a 2–0 lead. McGraw walked Deron Johnson to load the

bases before Angel Mangual popped out. Tug ended the threat by getting Bert Campaneris to look at strike three.

The Mets opened the scoring in the second when Cleon Jones led off with a double and John Milner singled him home. Don Hahn added an RBI triple with two outs in the sixth to make it 2–0.

At this point the Mets' ERA in the Series was 1.65. If you take away the stats from Game 2, the Mets had allowed a total of two earned runs in 37 innings (0.49).

GAME 6, October 20, Oakland: A's 3, Mets 1

Manager Yogi Berra had a big decision to make as the team flew to Oakland. He could start George Stone for Game 6 or elect to use Tom Seaver on short rest. Stone led the National League in winning percentage during the regular season (.800) and pitched very well in Game 4 of the NLCS. Seaver would win the Cy Young Award after pacing the NL with 251 strikeouts and a 2.08 ERA while going 19–10.

Seaver wasn't bad on three days' rest during the regular season, posting a 3.35 ERA in six starts, including a pair of two-earned-runs/nine-inning efforts. He also pitched into the ninth inning of Game 5 of the NLCS following a three-day breather, allowing two runs and seven hits. But his ERA was a stingy 1.86 in games with four or more days of rest.

Stone hadn't lost since July 8 against Atlanta, going 8–0 with five no-decisions. Lefty hitters went 14-for-72 (.194) against the southpaw, which might have neutralized Reggie Jackson.

"He pitched super all season and deserved a shot," remembered Tug McGraw. "But Yogi went with Seaver. The club stopped hitting anyway" (*Amazin'*, Golenbock, p. 315).

There was the "what if?" factor to consider. What if the Mets lost Game 6 with Stone on the mound? Berra would have Seaver pitching Game 7 on full rest. What if the Mets lost Game 6 with Seaver on the mound? Berra would have to go with Jon Matlack on three days' rest, something Matlack did in a Game 4 victory.

The problem wasn't that Seaver didn't pitch well in Game 6, but that Catfish Hunter was the better pitcher that afternoon. Seaver held the A's to a pair of runs and six hits while striking out six in seven innings. He allowed a pair of RBI doubles to Reggie Jackson over the first three innings but gave up only two hits over his final four frames. Ken Boswell pinch-hit for Seaver in the top of the eighth and delivered the first of three straight singles by the Mets. Felix Millan got the Mets within 2–1 with an RBI single that put the tying run on third with one out. But Darold Knowles fanned Rusty Staub for the second out, and Rollie Fingers got Cleon Jones on a fly ball to center to end the eighth-inning threat.

The A's added an unearned run in the eighth when Jackson singled and went to third on Don Hahn's error in center. Jesus Alou lifted a sac fly that capped the scoring.

Hunter carried a three-hit shutout into the eighth before Knowles and Fingers closed out the victory.

"I asked the other guys, and they all said [Hunter] had nothing," said Wayne Garrett in the book *The Amazing Mets*. "We were loose. We were confident. We thought we had 'em. Maybe we were trying too hard to win it in six. Maybe we were pressing."

The loss meant Jon Matlack would take the mound for Game 7, one year removed from winning NL Rookie of the Year honors.

GAME 7, October 21, Oakland: A's 5, Mets 2

Until now, Jon Matlack had been phenomenal during the postseason, allowing no earned runs and just eight hits in 23 innings. He won two of his three starts and allowed a pair of unearned runs in the Game 1 loss to the A's.

It took three games, but the Athletics finally figured out the lefty from West Chester, Pennsylvania, who is one of the most underrated pitchers in Mets history. Matlack wouldn't get out of the third inning, allowing four earned runs on four hits and a walk to raise his career postseason ERA to 1.40. He would never get another chance to pitch in a postseason game.

Matlack retired seven of the first eight batters he faced in Game 7 before winning pitcher Ken Holtzman doubled off him for the second time in the series. Bert Campaneris and Reggie Jackson followed with two-run homers later in the third, sending Matlack to the showers.

Campaneris later scored on Joe Rudi's fifth-inning single to give the A's a five-run cushion. At that point, fans of the "Ya Gotta Believe" Mets stopped believing.

Rusty Staub chased Holtzman with an RBI double that put the Mets on the board in the sixth. Gene Tenace booted Ed Kranepool's potential series-ending grounder, allowing a run to score while sending the possible tying run at the plate. But Darold Knowles got Wayne Garrett to hit a weak popup to short, giving the A's their second straight World Series title.

Holtzman should be credited for bouncing back from a miserable performance in Game 4, when he was chased during the Mets' three-run first inning. He went 2–1 in the Series, pitching against Matlack each time. Although Matlack had the better ERA in the three games (2.16 to 4.22), Holtzman was the one fitted for a World Series ring.

Game 1, October 13 at Oakland
A's 2, METS 1

METS	AB	R	H	BI	A's	AB	R	H	BI
Garrett 3b	5	0	0	0	Campaneris ss	4	1	1	0
Millan 2b	4	0	1	0	Rudi lf	3	0	1	1
Mays cf	4	0	1	0	Bando 3b	3	0	1	0
Jones lf	4	1	2	0	Jackson cf-rf	3	0	0	0
Milner 1b	4	0	2	1	Tenace 1b	3	0	0	0
Grote	4	0	0	0	Alou rf	3	0	0	0
Hahn rf	2	0	0	0	Davalillo cf	0	0	0	0
Kranepool ph	1	0	0	0	Fosse c	3	0	0	0
Harrelson ss	2	0	0	0	Green 2b	2	0	0	0
Hodges ph	0	0	0	0	Holtzman p	1	1	1	0
Martinez pr	0	0	0	0	Mangual ph	1	0	0	0
Matlack p	0	0	0	0	Fingers p	1	0	0	0
Boswell ph	1	0	1	0	Knowles p	0	0	0	0
McGraw p	0	0	0	0					
Staub ph	0	0	0	0					
Beauchamp ph	1	0	0	0					
Totals	32	1	7	1	Totals	26	2	4	1

Mets	000	100	000	1	7	2	
A's	002	000	00X	2	4	0	

METS	IP	H	R	ER	BB	SO
Matlack (L, 0–1)	6	3	2	0	2	3
McGraw	2	1	0	0	1	1
Totals	8	4	2	0	3	4

A's	IP	H	R	ER	BB	SO
Holtzman (W, 1–0)	5	4	1	1	3	2
Fingers	3-1/3	3	0	0	1	3
Knowles (S, 1)	2/3	0	0	0	0	0
Totals	9	7	1	1	4	5

E—Millan, Mays; DP—Mets 0, A's 2; 2B—Holtzman, Jones; 3B—Millan; SB—Campaneris; S—Matlack, Rudi; Time—2:26; Attendance—46,021.

Game 2, October 14 at Oakland
METS 10, A's 7 (12)

METS	AB	R	H	BI	A's	AB	R	H	BI
Garrett 3b	6	1	1	1	Campaneris ss	6	2	1	0
Millan 2b	6	0	0	0	Rudi lf	5	1	2	1
Staub rf	5	0	1	0	Bando 3b	5	2	1	1
Mays pr-cf	2	1	1	1	Jackson cf	6	1	4	2
Jones lf	5	3	3	1	Tenace 1b	3	0	1	1
Milner 1b	6	1	2	0	Alou rf	6	0	3	2
Grote c	6	1	2	0	Fosse c	5	0	0	0
Hahn cf-rf	7	1	1	1	Green 2b	2	0	0	0
Harrelson ss	6	1	3	1	Mangual ph	1	0	0	0
Koosman p	1	0	0	0	Kubiak 2b	0	0	0	0
Sadecki p	0	0	0	0	Andrews 2b	2	0	0	0
Theodore ph	1	0	0	0	Blue p	2	0	0	0
Parker p	0	0	0	0	Pina p	0	0	0	0
Kranepool ph	0	0	0	0	Knowles p	0	0	0	0
Beauchamp ph	1	0	0	0	Conigliaro ph	1	0	0	0
McGraw p	2	1	1	0	Odom p	0	0	0	0
Stone p	0	0	0	0	Johnson ph	1	0	0	0
					Lewis pr	0	1	1	0
					Fingers p	1	0	0	0
					Lindblad p	0	0	0	0
					Davalillo ph	1	0	0	0
Totals	54	10	15	5	Totals	47	7	13	7

Mets	011	004	000	004	10	15	1
A's	210	000	102	001	7	13	5

METS	IP	H	R	ER	BB	SO
Koosman	2-1/3	6	3	3	3	4
Sadecki	1-2/3	0	0	0	0	3
Parker	1	1	0	0	0	0
McGraw (W, 1–0)	6	5	4	4	3	8
Stone (S, 1)	1	1	0	0	1	0
Totals	12	13	7	7	7	15

A's	IP	H	R	ER	BB	SO
Blue	5-1/3	4	4	4	2	4
Pina	0	2	2	0	0	0
Knowles	1-2/3	1	0	0	2	2
Odom	2	2	0	0	0	2
Fingers (L, 0–1)	2-2/3	6	4	1	0	2
Lindblad	1/3	0	0	0	0	0
Totals	12	15	10	5	4	10

E—Koosman, Bando, Tenace, Andres (2), Knowles; DP—Mets 1, A's 1; 2B—Rudi, Alou, Jackson, Johnson, Harrelson; 3B—Bando, Campaneris, Jackson; HR—Jones (1), Garrett (1); SB—Campaneris (2); S—McGraw; Time—4:13; Attendance—49,151.

Game 3, October 16 at New York
A's 3, METS 2 (1)

A's	AB	R	H	BI
Campaneris ss	6	1	3	1
Rudi lf	5	0	2	1
Bando 3b	4	1	2	0
Jackson rf	5	0	0	0
Tenace 1b	3	0	1	1
Davalillo cf-1b	5	0	1	0
Fosse c	2	0	0	0
Borque ph-1b	2	0	1	0
Lewis pr	0	0	0	0
Lindblad p	1	0	0	0
Fingers p	0	0	0	0
Green 2b	2	0	0	0
Alou ph	1	0	0	0
Kubiak 2b	1	1	0	0
Hunter p	2	0	0	0
Johnson ph	1	0	0	0
Knowles p	0	0	0	0
Mangual ph	2	0	0	0
Totals	42	3	10	3

METS	AB	R	H	BI
Garrett 3b	4	1	2	1
Millan 2b	5	1	2	0
Staub rf	6	0	2	0
Jones lf	5	0	0	0
Milner 1b	3	0	1	0
Grote c	5	0	0	0
Hahn cf	5	0	1	0
Harrelson ss	5	0	2	0
Seaver p	3	0	0	0
Beauchamp ph	1	0	0	0
Sadecki p	0	0	0	0
McGraw p	0	0	0	0
Mays ph	1	0	0	0
Parker p	0	0	0	0
Totals	43	2	10	1

A's	000	001	010	01	3	10	1
Mets	002	000	00X	00	2	10	2

A's	IP	H	R	ER	BB	SO
Hunter	6	7	2	2	3	5
Knowles	2	0	0	0	1	0
Lindblad (W, 1–0)	2	3	0	0	1	0
Fingers (S, 1)	1	0	0	0	0	0
Totals	11	10	2	2	5	5

METS	IP	H	R	ER	BB	SO
Seaver	8	7	2	2	1	12
Sadecki	0	1	0	0	0	0
McGraw	2	1	0	0	1	1
Parker (L, 0–1)	1	1	1	0	1	1
Totals	9	10	3	2	3	14

E—Hunter, Millan (2); 2B—Rudi, Hahn, Bando, Tenace Staub; HR—Garrett; SB—Campaneris (3); S—Bando, Millan; Time—3:15; Attendance—56,617.

Game 4, October 17 at New York
METS 6, A's 1

A's	AB	R	H	BI
Campaneris ss	4	0	0	0
Rudi lf	4	0	1	0
Bando 3b	3	1	0	0
Jackson cf	4	0	1	0
Tenace 1b	3	0	1	1
Alou rf	4	0	0	0
Fosse c	4	0	1	0
Green 2b	1	0	0	0
Mangual ph	1	0	0	0
Kubiak 2b	1	0	0	0
Johnson ph	1	0	1	0
Holtzman p	0	0	0	0
Odom p	1	0	0	0
Knowles p	0	0	0	0
Conigliaro ph	1	0	0	0
Pina p	0	0	0	0
Andrews ph	1	0	0	0
Lindblad p	0	0	0	0
Davalillo ph	0	0	0	0
Totals	33	1	5	1

METS	AB	R	H	BI
Garrett 3b	4	2	1	0
Millan 2b	5	1	1	0
Staub rf	4	1	4	5
Jones lf	3	0	1	0
Theodore lf	1	0	0	0
Milner 1b	3	0	0	0
Grote c	4	0	3	0
Hahn cf	4	1	1	0
Harrelson ss	2	1	1	0
Matlack p	3	0	1	0
Sadecki p	0	0	0	0
Totals	33	6	13	5

A's	000	100	000	1	5	1
Mets	300	300	00x	6	13	1

A's	IP	H	R	ER	BB	SO
Holtzman (L, 1–1)	1/3	4	3	3	1	0
Odom	2-2/3	3	2	2	2	0
Knowles	1	1	1	0	1	1
Pina	3	4	0	0	2	0
Lindblad	1	1	0	0	0	1
Totals	8	6	5	13	6	2

METS	IP	H	R	ER	BB	SO
Matlack (W, 1–1)	8	2	1	1	2	5
Sadecki (S, 1)	1	1	0	0	1	2
Totals	9	1	1	5	3	7

E—Green, Garrett; DP—A's 4, Mets 0; HR—Staub (1); Time—2:41; Attendance—54,817.

Game 5, October 18 at New York
METS 2, A's 0

A's	AB	R	H	BI	METS	AB	R	H	BI
Campaneris ss	3	0	1	0	Garrett 3b	3	0	0	0
Rudi lf	4	0	0	0	Millan 2b	4	0	0	0
Bando 3b	3	0	1	0	Staub rf	3	0	1	0
Jackson cf	3	0	0	0	Jones lf	4	1	2	0
Tenace 1b	1	0	0	0	Milner 1b	4	0	2	1
Odom p	0	0	0	0	Grote c	3	1	1	0
Bourque ph	0	0	0	0	Hahn cf	4	0	1	1
Alou rf	4	0	0	0	Harrelson ss	2	0	0	0
Fosse c	4	0	1	0	Koosman p	3	0	0	0
Green 2b	2	0	0	0	McGraw p	1	0	0	0
Johnson ph	0	0	0	0					
Lewis pr	0	0	0	0					
Kubiak 2b	1	0	0	0					
Blue p	2	0	0	0					
Knowles p	0	0	0	0					
Mangual ph	1	0	0	0					
Fingers p	0	0	0	0					
Conigliaro ph	1	0	0	0					
Totals	29	0	3	0	Totals	31	2	7	2

A's	000	000	000	0	3	1
Mets	010	001	00x	2	7	1

A's	IP	H	R	ER	BB	SO
Blue (L, 0–1)	5-2/3	6	2	2	1	4
Knowles	1/3	0	0	0	1	1
Fingers	2	1	0	0	2	1
Totals	8	7	2	2	4	6

METS	IP	H	R	ER	BB	SO
Koosman (W, 1–0)	6.1	3	0	0	4	4
McGraw (S, 1)	2-2/3	0	0	0	3	3
Totals	9	3	0	0	7	7

E—Campaneris, Garrett; DP—A's 0, Mets 1; 2B—Jones, Fosse; 3B—Hahn; S—Grote; Time—2:39; Attendance—54,817.

Game 6, October 20 at Oakland
A's 3, METS 1

METS	AB	R	H	BI	A's	AB	R	H	BI
Garrett 3b	3	0	1	0	Campaneris ss	4	0	0	0
Millan 2b	4	0	1	1	Rudi lf	3	1	1	0
Staub rf	4	0	1	0	Bando 3b	4	1	1	0
Jones lf	4	0	0	0	Jackson rf-cf	4	1	3	2
Milner 1b	4	0	1	0	Tenace c-1b	3	0	0	0
Grote c	4	0	1	0	Davalillo cf	2	0	0	0
Hahn cf	3	0	0	0	Alou ph-cf	0	0	0	1
Kranepool ph	1	0	0	0	Johnson 1b	4	0	1	0
Harrelson ss	3	0	0	0	Fosse c	0	0	0	0
Seaver p	2	0	0	0	Green 2b	3	0	1	0
Boswell ph	1	1	1	0	Hunter p	3	0	0	0
McGraw p	0	0	0	0	Knowles p	0	0	0	0
					Fingers p	0	0	0	0
Totals	33	1	6	1	Totals	30	3	7	3

Mets	000	000	010	1	6	2
A's	101	000	01X	3	7	0

METS	IP	H	R	ER	BB	SO
Seaver (L, 0–1)	7	6	2	2	2	6
McGraw	1	1	1	0	1	1
Totals	8	7	3	2	3	7

A's	IP	H	R	ER	BB	SO
Hunter (W, 1–0)	7-1/3	4	1	1	1	1
Knowles	1/3	2	0	0	0	1
Fingers (S, 2)	1-1/3	0	0	0	0	0
Totals	9	6	1	1	1	2

E—Garrett, Hahn; DP—Mets 1, A's 0; 2B—Jackson 2; SF—Alou; Time—2:07. Attendance—49,333.

Game 7, October 21 at Oakland
A's 5, METS 2

METS	AB	R	H	BI	A's	AB	R	H	BI
Garrett 3b	5	0	0	0	Campaneris ss	4	2	3	2
Millan 2b	4	1	1	0	Rudi lf	3	1	2	1
Staub rf	4	0	2	1	Bando 3b	4	0	0	0
Jones lf	3	0	0	0	Jackson cf-rf	4	1	1	2
Milner 1b	3	1	0	0	Tenace c-1b	3	0	0	0
Grote c	4	0	1	0	Alou rf	1	0	0	0
Hahn cf	4	0	3	0	Davalillo cf	3	0	0	0
Harrelson ss	4	0	0	0	Johnson 1b	3	0	0	0
Matlack p	1	0	0	0	Fosse	1	0	1	0
Parker p	0	0	0	0	Green 2b	4	0	0	0
Beauchamp ph	1	0	0	0	Holtzman p	2	1	1	0
Sadecki p	0	0	0	0	Fingers p	1	0	1	0
Boswell ph	1	0	1	0	Knowles p	0	0	0	0
Stone p	0	0	0	0					
Kranepool ph	1	0	0	0					
Martinez ph	0	0	0	0					
Totals	35	2	8	1	Totals	33	5	9	5

Mets	000	001	001	2	8		1
A's	004	010	00X	5	9		1

METS	IP	H	R	ER	BB	SO
Matlack (L, 0–1)	2-2/3	4	4	4	1	3
Parker	1-1/3	0	0	0	1	1
Sadecki	2	2	1	1	0	1
Stone	2	3	0	0	0	3
Totals	8	9	5	5	2	8

A's	IP	H	R	ER	BB	SO
Holtzman (W, 2–1)	5-1/3	5	1	1	1	4
Fingers	3-1/3	3	1	0	1	2
Knowles (S, 2)	1/3	0	0	0	0	0
Totals	9	8	2	1	2	6

E—Jones, Tenace; DP—Mets 0, A's 1; 2B—Holtzman, Millan, Staub; HR—Campaneris (1), Jackson (1); Time—2:37; Attendance—49,333.

1973 World Series Statistics

COMPOSITE LINESCORE

Mets	521	406	011	004		24	66	10
A's	317	111	122	011		21	51	9

METS HITTING

Player	BA	G	AB	R	H
Jim Beauchamp	.000	4	4	0	0
Ken Boswell	1.000	3	3	1	3
Wayne Garrett	.167	7	30	4	5
Jerry Grote	.267	7	30	2	8
Don Hahn	.241	7	29	2	7
Bud Harrelson	.250	7	24	2	6
Ron Hodges	—	1	0	0	0
Cleon Jones	.286	7	28	5	8
Jerry Koosman	.000	2	4	0	0
Ed Kranepool	.000	4	3	0	0
Ted Martinez	—	2	0	0	0
Jon Matlack	.250	3	4	0	1
Willie Mays	.286	3	7	1	2
Tug McGraw	.333	5	3	1	1
Felix Millan	.188	7	32	3	6
John Milner	.296	7	27	2	8
Harry Parker	—	3	0	0	0
Ray Sadecki	—	4	0	0	0
Tom Seaver	.000	2	5	0	0
Rusty Staub	.423	7	26	1	11
George Stone	—	2	0	0	0
George Theodore	.000	2	2	0	0
Total	.253	7	261	24	66

2B—Staub 2, Jones 2, Hahn, Harrelson, Millan; 3B—Hahn, Millan; HR—Garrett 2, Jones, Staub; RBI—Staub 6, Garrett 2, Hahn 2, Milner 2, Harrelson, Jones, Mays, Millan; SB—None.

A's HITTING

Player	BA	G	AB	R	H
Jesus Alou	.158	7	19	0	3
Mike Andrews	.000	2	3	0	0
Sal Bando	.231	7	26	5	6
Vida Blue	.000	2	4	0	0
Pat Bourque	.500	2	2	0	1
Bert Campaneris	.290	7	31	6	9
Billy Conigliaro	.000	3	3	0	0
Vic Davalillo	.091	6	11	0	1
Rollie Fingers	.333	6	3	0	1
Ray Fosse	.158	7	19	0	3
Dick Green	.063	7	16	0	1
Ken Holtzman	.667	3	3	2	2
Catfish Hunter	.000	2	5	0	0
Reggie Jackson	.310	7	29	3	9
Deron Johnson	.300	6	10	0	3
Darrold Knowles	—	7	0	0	0
Ted Kubiak	.000	4	3	1	0
Allan Lewis	—	3	0	1	0
Paul Lindblad	.000	3	1	0	0
Angel Mangual	.000	5	6	0	0
John Odom	.000	3	1	0	0
Horacio Pina	—	2	0	0	0
Joe Rudi	.333	7	27	3	9
Gene Tenace	.158	7	19	0	3
Total	.212	7	241	21	51

2B—Jackson 3, Holtzman 2, Rudi 2, Alou, Bando, Fosse, Johnson, Tenace; 3B—Bando, Campaneris, Jackson; HR—Campaneris, Jackson; RBI—Jackson 6, Rudi 4, Alou 3, Campaneris 3, Tenace 3, Bando; SB—Campaneris 3.

METS PITCHING

Player	G	ERA	W–L	SV	IP	H	ER	BB	SO
Jon Matlack	3	2.16	1–2	0	16-2/3	10	4	5	11
Tom Seaver	2	2.40	0–1	0	15	13	4	3	18
Tug McGraw	5	2.63	1–0	1	13-2/3	8	4	9	14
Jerry Koosman	2	3.12	1–0	0	8-2/3	9	3	7	8
Ray Sadecki	4	1.93	0–0	1	4-2/3	5	1	1	6
Harry Parker	3	0.00	0–1	0	3-1/3	2	0	2	2
George Stone	2	0.00	0–0	1	3	4	0	1	3
Total	7	2.22	3–4	3	65	51	16	28	62

A's PITCHING

Player	G	ERA	W–L	SV	IP	H	ER	BB	SO
Rollie Fingers	6	0.66	0–1	2	13-2/3	13	1	4	8
Catfish Hunter	2	2.02	1–0	0	13-1/3	10	3	4	6
Vida Blue	2	4.91	0–1	0	11	11	6	3	8
Ken Holtzman	3	4.22	2–1	0	10-2/3	13	5	5	6
Darold Knowles	7	0.00	0–0	2	6-1/3	5	0	5	5
John Odom	2	3.86	0–0	0	4-2/3	2	2	2	2
Paul Lindblad	3	0.00	1–0	0	3-1/3	1	0	1	1
Horacio Pina	2	0.00	0–0	0	3	0	0	2	0
Total	7	2.32	4–3	0	66.0	35	17	26	36

1986 NLCS: Mets vs. Houston Astros

METS WIN SERIES 4–2

On a short list of great postseason series, the 1986 NLCS gets much consideration. The Mets were prohibitive favorites to win their first playoff series in 13 years after steamrolling through the regular-season schedule. They set a team record with 108 wins and ended the schedule with 11 victories in their last 13 games. They hadn't played a meaningful game since September 17, when they beat the Cubs 4–2 to clinch the NL East title. The early clinching allowed manager Davey Johnson to rest his regulars down the stretch, but even his "B" lineup averaged almost seven runs over the last five games.

Darryl Strawberry watches his fifth-inning home run against the Houston Astros sail just fair in Game 5 of the 1986 NLCS.

The Mets went 31–13 in their final 44 contests, including a four-game skid that prevented them from clinching even earlier than they did.

At first glance, the Astros didn't seem to pose much of a threat to the Mets' juggernaut. They won 12 fewer games than New York, hit eight points lower than the Mets' league-leading .263 average, and finished second to Davey Johnson's squad with a 3.15 ERA. But Houston won 29 of its final 44 games to win the NL West by 10 games. That paled in comparison to the Mets' 21½-game cushion at the end of the season, but the Astros had gained confidence after taking over the division lead on July 21.

At this point, baseball alternated home-field advantage between the East and West divisions in the LCS every year. It was the Mets' turn to host a possible four games if the series went seven, but the NFL forced the Mets to open on the road. The Astros caught a break because the Houston Oilers had a scheduled home game at the Astrodome against the Chicago Bears on Sunday, October 12, which was the scheduled date of Game 4 in the NLCS. The Astrodome was unavailable, giving the Astros home-field advantage in the Series. Oilers fans got to watch their team lose its fifth straight game since a season-opening victory.

The Mets' run to the 1973 World Series had caused the Jets to play their first six games on the road that year. But the Astros apparently lacked the same kind of pull.

The Mets didn't have much luck in their last regular-season trip to the dome, dropping three straight in somewhat agonizing fashion after clobbering the Astros 13–2 in the series opener. During that weekend, Ron Darling, Tim Teufel, Rick Aguilera, and Bob Ojeda were arrested outside a Houston bar following an altercation with off-duty police who were moonlighting as bouncers.

And so the Mets were opening the NLCS in a city that was the site of some of their worst moments of the season. Their misery was compounded by two former Mets, one who would start Game 1 and another who taught that hurler a trick pitch.

Mike Scott had an undistinguished career as a Met before being shipped to the Astros for Danny Heep. Scott wasn't doing much in a Houston uniform until original Met Roger Craig showed him how to throw a splitter. Scott emerged as the ace on an Astros staff that already included Nolan Ryan, throwing a no-hitter in the Astros' division clincher.

Scott's splitter was fluttering in Games 1 and 4 of the series, the only victories by the Astros. He tossed a pair of complete games, allowing just eight hits while striking out 19. The Mets thought he was scuffing the ball during the series opener, and they decided to retrieve balls thrown by

Scott during Game 4. New York sent more than a dozen baseballs to the commissioner's office as proof Scott was cheating his way to victory. The Mets got no satisfaction from Bowie Kuhn, which meant Scott would be allowed to pitch a Game 7 if the series went that far.

Scott was playing mind games, with more than a few Mets, especially Gary Carter. The Mets catcher was 0-for-8 with four strikeouts against Scott, which contributed to his 1-for-21 start in the series.

Scott wasn't the only Astros pitcher to give the Mets fits. Bob Knepper took a shutout into the sixth inning of Game 4 and carried a 3–0 lead into the ninth inning of Game 6, one day after Nolan Ryan held New York to two hits over nine innings. But the Mets managed to win all three games in their final at-bat.

The hitting and starting pitching was evenly matched in the series; it was the bullpen that was the difference for the Mets. Jesse Orosco, Roger McDowell, Rick Aguilera, and Doug Sisk combined for a 1.29 ERA in 21 innings. Orosco gave up all three runs, but he also was the winning pitcher in three of the four Mets victories. Meanwhile, the Mets had their way with the Houston bullpen, which posted a 4.19 ERA. With runs at a premium—the two teams combined for 38 in the six games—the Mets' relievers had a huge role in winning the series.

There were timely hits by the Mets. Dykstra's two-run homer off Dave Smith in the bottom of the ninth won Game 3. Carter singled home the winning run in the 12th inning of Game 5 after collecting just one hit in his previous 21 at-bats. The Mets also scored three times in the 16th inning of the Game 6 clincher before Jesse Orosco struck out Kevin Bass with the tying run on second to end the series.

GAME 1, October 8, Houston: Astros 1, Mets 0

Dwight Gooden got his postseason career off to a fine start, holding the Astros to a run and seven hits while striking out five in seven innings. But Mike Scott was almost unhittable as he struck out 14 in a five-hit shutout that gave the Astros their only series lead.

Keith Hernandez and Gary Carter each fanned three times against Scott, who also whiffed Darryl Strawberry and Ray Knight two times apiece. Scott had the Mets looking foolish at times while throwing a splitter that seemed to defy physics. Most splitters will make a sudden drop within 10 feet of the batter. Scott's was magical as he could make it tail up or veer to either side.

Gooden fell behind in the second when he served up a homer to Glenn Davis, the Astros' top hitter during the regular season. Gooden later give up three straight one-out singles in the fourth before Scott hit into an inning-ending double play to keep the game 1–0.

The Astros had just one hit over their final five at-bats, but they already had generated enough offense to take the opener.

The Mets' best late-inning threat came when pinch-hitter Danny Heep and Lenny Dykstra hit consecutive one-out singles in the eighth. Scott got out of the inning unscathed by fanning Wally Backman and Keith Hernandez.

Darryl Strawberry represented the potential tying run in the ninth when he stole second following his one-out single. Strawberry was still standing on second when Knight struck out to end the game.

GAME 2, October 9, Houston: Mets 5, Astros 1

It looked like the Mets' hitting woes were going to extend into Game 2 after Nolan Ryan retired his first 10 batters in order. Was another ex-Met going to lead the Astros to a second straight victory? The answer was "no" after the Mets tagged Ryan for five runs and seven hits in his final two innings of work.

Ryan already had fanned five in a scoreless game before Wally Backman and Keith Hernandez nicked him for back-to-back one-out singles in the fourth. Gary Carter drove in the Mets' first run of the NLCS with a double, the only hit in his first 21 at-bats of the series. Darryl Strawberry scored Hernandez with a sacrifice fly that put the Mets ahead 2–0.

Things got better for the Mets in the fifth as they tallied three times on four hits, capped by a two-run triple by Hernandez that made it 5–0. Hernandez, Backman, and Lenny Dykstra each had two hits at the top of the order and combined to score four of the five runs.

The other run was scored by Bob Ojeda, who tiptoed in and out of trouble while tossing a 10-hitter, the last complete game to be thrown by a Mets pitcher in the postseason until David Cone beat the Dodgers in Game 6 two years later.

The second inning of this game is often overlooked when recalling the series, but it was one that was vitally important to the Mets' psyche. Kevin Bass hit a one-out double and moved to third when Jose Cruz singled. The Mets hadn't scored in the first 11 innings of the series and appeared baffled against Ryan, so a rally here could have given the Astros great momentum. But Ojeda got out of the jam by throwing out Bass at the plate on a fielder's choice for the second out before striking out Dickie Thon to keep the game scoreless.

Ojeda also stranded runners on second and third in the fifth to preserve a 5–0 lead. He didn't allow a run until Phil Garner's RBI single in the seventh.

GAME 3, October 11, New York: Mets 6, Astros 5

The is where the series gets exciting as the Mets pull off the first of their two walk-off victories, thanks to the first of Lenny Dykstra's 10 career postseason homers.

Ron Darling allowed just one hit over his final three innings of work, but the Astros already had a 4–0 lead by the time Darling hit the showers. Bill Doran's two-run homer to center gave Houston a four-run advantage in the second inning, just 10 batters through the Astros' lineup.

Meanwhile, Bob Knepper cruised through the first five innings, allowing only four hits and staying out of trouble. Knepper weathered a mini-storm in the fourth when the Mets put runners on first and second with two outs, getting Ray Knight to fly out.

But the Mets were starting to put decent wood on the ball after getting their second looks at the lefty. Knepper got through the first three innings with six ground-ball outs, two strikeouts and a fly ball. New York was making louder outs over the next two frames before finally erupting in the sixth.

The Mets still trailed 4–0 when Kevin Mitchell and Keith Hernandez opened the sixth with singles. Craig Reynolds booted Gary Carter's grounder to score Mitchell with the Mets' first run. One batter later, Darryl Strawberry knotted the score with a three-run blast that landed just above the auxiliary scoreboard in right field.

It took the Mets a half-inning to fall behind again. Ray Knight's throwing error at third set up Denny Walling's tiebreaking grounder that put the Astros up 5–4.

Houston still had the lead when Dave Smith entered in the bottom of the ninth to get a three-out save. He retired just one batter.

Wally Backman led off the inning with a drag bunt down the first-base line. Glenn Davis grabbed the grounder in plenty of time, but Backman eluded the tag. Replays showed Backman could have been called for running out of the baseline, and manager Hal Lanier briefly argued with umpire Dutch Rennert to no avail.

Houston's second gaffe of the inning came when Alan Ashby's passed ball allowed Backman to scoot over to second. Smith retired pinch-hitter Danny Heep on a fly ball to center, preventing Backman from moving over to third.

Backman had no trouble scoring from second after Dykstra hit a fly ball down the right-field line. It barely had enough distance to go over the wall, but it was good for a two-run homer that gave the Mets a 2–1 lead in the series.

The Mets' bullpen was solid after Darling scuffled. Rick Aguilera and Jesse Orosco each allowed no earned runs and one hit in two innings, with Orosco picking up the first of his three wins of the NLCS.

GAME 4, October 12, New York: Astros 3, Mets 1

The Mets had to face Mike Scott once again while Davey Johnson used his fourth starter of the series. Sid Fernandez took the ball and held the Astros to just three hits in six innings. Unfortunately, two of those hits went over the wall.

Fernandez was victimized by the Mets' postseason layout of the auxiliary box seats along the lines, which cut the room in foul territory. El Sid gave up a leadoff single to Glenn Davis in the second before striking out Kevin Bass and Jose Cruz. Fernandez almost got out of the inning when Alan Ashby hit a pop-foul down the third-base line. Ray Knight gave chase but ran out of room as the ball landed in the temporary seats. Ashby took advantage of his second chance by launching a two-run homer to left, putting the Astros ahead 2–0.

That was enough offense for Scott, who already had gotten into the Mets' collective heads. Scott fanned only five after recording 14 Ks in the series opener, but he was just as tough to hit.

By now, the Mets were certain Scott was cheating. They began to gather evidence by collecting balls throw by Scott that had gone out of play without landing in the seats. Keith Hernandez, who was 0-for-8 in the series against Scott, was shown on TV holding one of the balls for closer examination. He gave a pronounced nod of the head, as if to tell viewers the ball was scuffed.

Dickie Thon gave the Astros an insurance run by smacking a solo shot off Fernandez in the fifth. Scott did the rest, holding the Mets to just a Ray Knight single over the first seven innings.

The Mets finally manufactured their first run off Scott when Mookie Wilson led off the eighth with a single before moving from first to third on a grounder. Wilson came home on Danny Heep's sacrifice fly to get the Mets within two runs.

Scott completed a three-hitter by getting Gary Carter to fly out with a runner on third, evening the series at two games apiece.

GAME 5, October 14, New York: Mets 2, Astros 1 (12 innings)

Dwight Gooden had arguably the best fastball of any Mets pitcher since Nolan Ryan. The two finally squared off after the game was postponed a day because of rain.

The game was still scoreless after the Mets received a break in the top of the second. Kevin Bass and Jose Cruz led off the inning with singles to put runners on first and third. Gooden fanned Alan Ashby for the first out before getting Craig Reynolds to hit into a double play. But replays showed Reynolds beat the throw to first, which would have allowed Bass to score the game's first run. Instead, the Astros had to wait until the fifth to take a 1–0 lead.

Ashby led off the fifth with a double and scored on Bill Doran's grounder, which seemed like enough offense the way Ryan was pitching. The 39-year-old Ryan had retired his first 13 batters in order, recording two strikeouts in each of the first four innings. Darryl Strawberry ended the perfect game with a long homer that tied the score, his second game-tying blast of the series.

Ryan lasted nine innings, holding the Mets to just two hits while striking out 12. Gooden went an inning longer, scattering nine hits and working out of a mini-jam in the 10th.

Jesse Orosco followed with two perfect innings of relief, and Charlie Kerfeld retired his first seven batters in order after replacing Ryan. Kerfeld finally made the mistake of giving up a base hit to Wally Backman, who would again help manufacture a victory.

Kerfeld was paying close attention to the speedy Backman, who swiped 13 bases in 20 attempts during the regular season after averaging 31 steals the previous two years. Kerfeld eventually uncorked an errant pickoff throw that skipped past Glenn Davis, putting Backman on second.

Keith Hernandez was walked intentionally to set up a potential inning-ending double play with the slumping Gary Carter at the plate. Carter was just 1-for-21 in the series and hitless since delivering an RBI double in the fourth inning of Game 2. The catcher came through with a single to center that scored Backman, putting the Mets up 3–2 in the series.

The Mets somehow had control of the series despite collecting only 32 hits in the first five games. New York already had wasted fine starts by Dwight Gooden in Game 1 and Sid Fernandez in Game 4. Now, they were on a mission to close out the series without having to face Mike Scott.

GAME 6, October 16, Houston: Mets 7, Astros 6 (16 innings)

The Astrodome was filled with over 45,000 delirious Astros fans after Jose Cruz hit a single to left off Bob Ojeda to give Houston a 3–0 lead in the bottom of the first. Phil Garner's RBI double put the Astros ahead, and Glenn Davis added a run-scoring single before Cruz almost raised the roof on the "Eighth Wonder of the World."

The Mets were in deep trouble. They had been held under three runs in three of the first five games in the series, twice by Mike Scott, who was the scheduled pitcher in Game 7. Scott already had thrown two complete games, holding New York to a run and eight hits while striking out 19.

Ojeda was great over the next four innings, allowing just one hit before Rick Aguilera came on to throw three innings of one-hit relief.

But the Mets were doing nothing against Bob Knepper, who had unraveled in the sixth inning of Game 3. Knepper carried a two-hit shutout into the ninth and hadn't allowed a runner past second base before manager Davey Johnson sent up the lefty-hitting Lenny Dykstra to hit against the lefty-throwing Knepper leading off the ninth. Johnson's strategy worked as Dykstra lined a triple to center before scoring on Mookie Wilson's bloop single that was just out of the reach of second baseman Bill Doran. The Mets finally had broken through against Knepper, but they still needed two more runs for it to matter.

Kevin Mitchell hit a grounder to third for the first out, but Keith Hernandez followed with a long double that scored Wilson and chased Knepper.

It was now up to closer Dave Smith to send the series to a seventh game. The Astros' bullpen hadn't come through with a big out in the series before now, and Smith wasn't about to end that streak. He walked Gary Carter and Darryl Strawberry to load the bases before Ray Knight lifted a sacrifice fly to tie the game.

The Mets left the bases loaded to end the top of the ninth, and Roger McDowell got three straight outs in the bottom of the inning. That's when the fun started.

McDowell tossed five shutout innings of one-hit relief to keep the Mets in the game. Kevin Bass nicked him for a single in the 12th but was thrown out by Carter on an attempted steal.

The Mets didn't get a hit between the 10th and 13th innings, but Carter came through again with a leadoff single to start the 14th. Darryl Strawberry walked, and Ray Knight laid down a bunt that put runners on second and third with one out.

Wally Backman delivered his third clutch hit of the series, poking an RBI single that scored Carter. The Mets now had runners on second and third with one out after Bass made a poor throw to the plate. But New York wasted a chance to tack on insurance runs, leaving Jesse Orosco to protect a one-run lead.

Orosco and the Mets were two outs from a pennant after Bill Doran struck out swinging. Up stepped Billy Hatcher, who picked a perfect time to collect his first RBI of the series. Hatcher drove a pitch that hit the foul pole before slowly sliding down the netting and onto the field. The homer would have been meaningless if Howard Johnson or Mookie Wilson could have delivered base hits in the top of the inning. Instead, the game dragged into the 15th inning.

Orosco worked a perfect 15th to set the stage for a memorable ending to the NLCS. Aurilio Lopez was still in the game after yielding the go-ahead run in the 14th. Darryl Strawberry opened the 16th with a double and scored on Ray Knight's single, giving the Mets the lead for the second time in extra innings.

Jeff Calhoun, who hadn't pitched in the series, was brought in to prevent any further scoring. One walk and two wild pitches later, the Mets had an insurance run. But it was Dykstra's RBI single off Calhoun that scored the eventual series-winning run.

Orosco was running on fumes as he entered the bottom of the 16th. Doug Sisk was available, but there was no way Johnson was going to trust anyone but his best lefty reliever. Orosco opened the inning by striking out Craig Reynolds before giving up a walk and a single. Hatcher delivered again for the Astros with an RBI single, and Glenn Davis poked another run-scoring single with two outs. Houston was just a base hit away from tying the game once again as Bass stepped to the plate. Bass hadn't driven in a run in the series despite tying for the team lead with seven hits. Orosco prepared to face Bass following a mound meeting with Hernandez and Carter. Hernandez says he told Carter, "If you call anything but a slider, we're fighting," a charge Carter denies. Orosco stuck with his slider long enough to strike out Bass on a 3–2 pitch, ending the marathon game and one of the most intense playoff series in major league history.

Game 1, October 8 at Houston
ASTROS 1, METS 0

METS	AB	R	H	BI		Astros	AB	R	H	BI
Dykstra cf	3	0	1	0		Hatcher cf	3	0	0	0
Backman 2b	4	0	0	0		Doran 2b	4	0	0	0
Hernandez 1b	4	0	1	0		Walling 3b	4	0	0	0
Carter c	4	0	0	0		Davis 1b	4	1	1	1
Strawberry rf	4	0	1	0		Bass rf	4	0	2	0
Wilson lf	4	0	0	0		Cruz lf	4	0	1	0
Knight 3b	4	0	0	0		Ashby c	1	0	1	0
Santana ss	2	0	1	0		Reynolds ss	3	0	2	0
Mazzilli ph	1	0	0	0		Thon ss	0	0	0	0
Orosco p	0	0	0	0		Scott p	3	0	0	0
Gooden p	2	0	0	0						
Heep ph	1	0	1	0						
Elster pr-ss	0	0	0	0						
Totals	33	0	5	0			30	1	7	1

Mets	000 000 000	0	5	0	
Astros	010 000 00x	1	7	1	

METS	IP	H	R	ER	BB	SO
Gooden (L, 0–1)	7	7	1	1	3	5
Orosco	1	0	0	0	0	1
Totals	8	7	1	1	3	6

ASTROS	IP	H	R	ER	BB	SO
Scott (W, 1–0)	9	5	0	0	1	14

LOB—Mets 7, Astros 8; E—Reynolds (1); 2B—Bass (1); HR—Davis (1); SB—Strawberry (1), Dykstra (1), Bass (1), Hatcher (1); Time—2:56; ATT—44,131.

Game 2, October 9 at Houston
METS 5, ASTROS 1

METS	AB	R	H	BI		ASTROS	AB	R	H	BI
Dykstra cf	5	1	2	0		Hatcher cf	5	1	1	0
Backman 2b	5	2	2	1		Doran 2b	4	0	1	0
Hernandez 1b	3	1	2	2		Garner 3b	3	0	1	1
Carter c	5	0	1	1		Davis 1b	4	0	1	0
Strawberry rf	3	0	0	1		Bass rf	3	0	2	0
Wilson lf	4	0	1	0		Cruz lf	4	0	1	0
Knight 3b	3	0	1	0		Ashby c	4	0	0	0
Santana ss	4	0	1	0		Thon ss	4	0	2	0
Ojeda p	4	1	0	0		Ryan p	1	0	0	0
						Pankovitz ph	1	0	0	0
						Andersen p	0	0	0	0
						Puhl ph	1	0	1	0
						Lopez p	0	0	0	0
						Kerfeld p	0	0	0	0
						Lopes ph	1	0	0	0
Totals	36	5	10	5			35	1	10	1

Mets	000 230 000	5	10	0	
Astros	000 000 100	1	10	2	

METS	IP	H	R	ER	BB	SO
Ojeda (W, 1–0)	9	10	1	1	2	5

ASTROS	IP	H	R	ER	BB	SO
Ryan (L, 0–1)	5	7	5	5	0	5
Andersen	2	1	0	0	1	2
Lopez	1-1/3	2	0	0	2	1
Kerfeld	2/3	0	0	0	0	0
Total	9	10	5	5	3	8

LOB—Mets 8, Astros 9; E—Davis, Hatcher; 2B—Carter (1), Dykstra (1), Bass (2); 3B—Hernandez (1); IBB—Hernandez 2, Knight; SF—Strawberry; SB—Wilson (1); Time—2:40; ATT—44,391.

Game 3, October 11 at New York
METS 6, ASTROS 5

ASTROS	AB	R	H	BI	METS	AB	R	H	BI
Doran 2b	4	2	2	2	Wilson cf-lf	4	0	0	0
Hatcher cf	3	1	2	0	Mitchell lf	4	1	2	0
Walling 3b	5	1	1	2	Orosco p	0	0	0	0
Davis 1b	3	0	1	0	Hernandez 1b	4	1	2	0
Bass rf	3	0	0	0	Carter c	4	1	0	0
Cruz lf	3	0	1	1	Strawberry rf	4	1	2	3
Ashby c	4	0	0	0	Knight 3b	4	0	1	0
Reynolds ss	2	1	1	0	Teufel 2b	3	0	0	0
Lopes ph	1	0	0	0	Backman 2b 1	1	1	1	0
Kerfeld p	0	0	0	0	Santana ss	3	0	0	0
Smith p	0	0	0	0	Heep ph	1	0	0	0
Knepper p	3	0	0	0	Darling p	1	0	0	0
Thon ss	1	0	0	0	Mazzilli ph	1	0	1	0
					Aguilera p	0	0	0	0
					Dykstra ph-cf 2	1	1	1	2
Totals	32	5	8	5	Totals	36	6	10	5

Astros	220	000	100	5	8	1	
Mets	000	004	002	6	10	1	

ASTROS	IP	H	R	ER	BB	SO
Knepper	7	8	4	3	0	3
Kerfeld	1	0	0	0	0	1
Smith (L, 0–1)	1/3	2	2	2	0	0
Total	8-1/3	10	6	5	0	4

METS	IP	H	R	ER	BB	SO
Darling	5	6	4	4	2	5
Aguilera	2	1	1	0	2	1
Orosco (W, 1–0)	2	1	0	0	1	2
Total	9	8	5	4	5	8

LOB—Astros 7, Mets 5; E—Knight (1), Reynolds (2); PB—Ashby 2; WP—Darling; HR—Strawberry (1), Dykstra (1), Doran (1); HBP—Davis; SH—Hatcher; SB—Hatcher 2 (3), Bass (2); Time—2:55; ATT—55,052.

Game 4, October 12 at New York
ASTROS 3, METS 1

ASTROS	AB	R	H	BI	METS	AB	R	H	BI
Doran 2b	4	0	0	0	Dykstra cf	4	0	1	0
Hatcher cf	4	0	0	0	Backman 2b	4	0	0	0
Garner 3b	3	0	0	0	Hernandez 1b	4	0	0	0
Walling ph-3b	1	0	1	0	Carter c	4	0	0	0
Davis 1b	3	1	1	0	Strawberry rf	3	0	0	0
Bass rf	3	0	0	0	Wilson lf	3	1	1	0
Cruz lf	4	0	0	0	Knight 3b	3	0	0	0
Ashby c	3	1	1	2	Santana ss	2	0	0	0
Thon ss	3	1	1	1	Heep ph	0	0	0	1
Scott p	3	0	0	0	Sisk p	0	0	0	0
					Fernandez p	1	0	0	0
					Mazzilli ph	1	0	0	0
					McDowell p	0	0	0	0
					Johnson ph	1	0	0	0
					Elster ss	0	0	0	0
Totals	31	3	4	3	Totals	30	1	3	1

Astros	020	010	000	3	4	1	
Mets	000	000	010	1	3	0	

ASTROS	IP	H	R	ER	BB	SO
Scott (W, 2-0)	9.0	3	1	1	0	5

METS	IP	H	R	ER	BB	SO
Fernandez (L,0-1)	6.0	3	3	3	1	5
McDowell	2.0	0	0	0	0	1
Sisk	1.0	1	0	0	1	0
Total	9.0	4	3	3	2	6

LOB—Astros 3, Mets 3; E—Scott; 2B—Walling (1); HR—Ashby (1) Thon (1); SF—Heep (1); SB—Backman (1); Time—2:23; ATT—55,038

Game 5, October 14 at New York
METS 2, ASTROS 1 (12)

ASTROS BI	AB	R	H	BI	METS	AB	R	H	
Doran 2b	4	0	1	1	Dykstra cf	5	0	0	0
Hatcher cf	3	0	1	0	Backman 2b	5	1	1	0
Walling 3b	5	0	1	0	Hernandez 1b	4	0	1	0
Davis 1b	5	0	0	0	Carter c	5	0	1	1
Bass rf	5	0	2	0	Strawberry rf	3	1	1	1
Cruz lf	5	0	1	0	Wilson lf	4	0	0	0
Ashby c	5	1	1	0	Orosco p	0	0	0	0
Reynolds ss	4	0	1	0	Knight 3b	4	0	0	0
Thon ph-ss	1	0	0	0	Santana ss	3	0	0	0
Ryan p	3	0	0	0	Mazzilli ph	1	0	0	0
Puhl ph	1	0	1	0	Elster ss	0	0	0	0
Kerfeld p	0	0	0	0	Gooden p	3	0	0	0
Heep lf	1	0	0	0					
Totals	41	1	9	1	Totals	38	2	4	2

Astros	000	010	000	000	1	9	1
Mets	000	010	000	001	2	4	0

ASTROS	IP	H	R	ER	BB	SO
Ryan	9	2	1	1	1	12
Kerfeld (L, 0-1)	2-1/3	2	1	1	1	3
Total	11-1/3	4	2	2	2	15

METS	IP	H	R	ER	BB	SO
Gooden	10	9	1	1	2	4
Orosco (W, 2-0)	2	0	0	0	0	2
Total	12	9	1	1	2	6

LOB—Astros 7, Mets 4; E—Kerfeld; 2B—Ashby (1); HR—Strawberry (2); IBB—Hernandez; SH—Hatcher; SB—Doran (1), Puhl (1); CS—Bass; Time—3:45; ATT—54,986.

Game 6, October 16 at Houston
METS 7, ASTROS 6 (16)

METS	AB	R	H	BI	ASTROS	AB	R	H	BI
Wilson cf-lf	7	1	1	1	Doran 2b	7	1	2	0
Mitchell lf	4	0	0	0	Hatcher cf	7	2	3	2
Elster ss	3	0	0	0	Garner 3b	3	1	1	1
Hernandez 1b	7	1	1	1	Walling ph-3b	4	0	0	0
Carter c	5	0	2	0	Davis 1b	7	1	3	2
Strawberry rf	5	2	1	0	Bass rf	6	0	1	0
Knight 3b	6	1	1	2	Cruz lf	6	0	1	1
Teufel 2b	3	0	1	0	Ashby c	6	0	0	0
Backman ph-2b	2	1	1	1	Thon ss	3	0	0	0
Santana ss	3	0	1	0	Reynolds ph-ss	3	0	0	0
Heep ph	1	0	0	0	Knepper p	2	0	0	0
McDowell p	1	0	0	0	Smith p	0	0	0	0
Johnson ph	1	0	0	0	Puhl ph	1	0	0	0
Orosco p	0	0	0	0	Andersen p	0	0	0	0
Ojeda p	1	0	0	0	Pankovitz ph	1	0	0	0
Mazzilli ph	1	0	0	0	Lopez p	0	0	0	0
Aguilera p	0	0	0	0	Calhoun p	0	0	0	0
Dykstra ph-cf	4	1	2	1	Lopes ph	0	1	0	0
Totals	54	7	11	6		56	6	11	6

Mets	000	000	003	000	010	3	7	11	0
Astros	300	000	000	000	010	2	6	11	1

METS	IP	H	R	ER	BB	SO
Ojeda	5	5	3	3	2	1
Aguilera	3	1	0	0	0	1
McDowell	5	1	0	0	0	2
Orosco (W, 3–0)	3	4	3	3	1	5
Total	16	11	6	6	3	9

ASTROS	IP	H	R	ER	BB	SO
Knepper	8-1/3	5	3	3	1	6
Smith	1-2/3	0	0	0	3	2
Andersen	3	0	0	0	1	1
Lopez (L, 0–1)	2	5	3	3	2	2
Calhoun	1	1	1	1	1	0
Total	16	11	7	7	8	11

LOB—Mets 9, Astros 5; E—Bass; WP—Calhoun 2; 2B—Hernandez (1), Strawberry (1), Davis (1), Garner (1); 3B—Dykstra (1); HR—Hatcher (1); IBB—Backman, Dykstra; SH—Orosco; SF—Knight; SB—Doran (2); CS—Bass 2; Time—4:42; ATT—45,718.

1986 NLCS Statistics

COMPOSITE LINESCORE

Mets	000	244	015	001	010	3	21	43	1
Astros	550	020	200	000	010	2	17	49	7

METS BATTING

Player	BA	G	AB	R	H
Rick Aguilera	—	2	0	0	0
Wally Backman	.238	6	21	5	5
Gary Carter	.148	6	27	1	4
Ron Darling	.000	1	1	0	0
Lenny Dykstra	.304	6	23	3	7
Kevin Elster	.000	4	3	0	0
Sid Fernandez	.000	1	1	0	0
Dwight Gooden	.000	2	5	0	0
Danny Heep	.250	5	4	0	1
Keith Hernandez	.269	6	26	3	7
Howard Johnson	.000	2	2	0	0
Ray Knight	.167	6	24	1	4
Lee Mazzilli	.200	5	5	0	1
Roger McDowell	.000	2	1	0	0
Kevin Mitchell	.250	2	8	1	2
Bob Ojeda	.000	2	5	1	0
Jesse Orosco	—	4	0	0	0
Rafael Santana	.176	6	17	0	3
Doug Sisk	—	1	0	0	0
Darryl Strawberry	.227	6	22	4	5
Tim Teufel	.167	2	6	0	1
Mookie Wilson	.115	6	26	2	3
Totals	.189	6	227	21	43

2B—Carter, Dykstra, Hernandez, Strawberry; 3B—Dykstra, Hernandez; HR—Strawberry 2, Dykstra; RBI—Strawberry 5, Dykstra 3, Hernandez 3, Backman 2, Carter 2, Knight 2, Heep, Wilson; SB—Backman, Dykstra, Strawberry, Wilson.

ASTROS BATTING

Player	BA	G	AB	R	H
Larry Andersen	—	2	0	0	0
Alan Ashby	.130	6	23	2	3
Kevin Bass	.292	6	24	6	7
Jeff Calhoun	—	1	0	0	0
Jose Cruz	.192	6	26	0	5
Glenn Davis	.269	6	26	3	7
Bill Doran	.222	6	27	3	6
Phil Garner	.222	3	9	1	2
Billy Hatcher	.280	6	25	4	7
Charlie Kerfeld	—	3	0	0	0
Bob Knepper	.000	2	5	0	0
Davey Lopes	.000	3	2	1	0
Aurelio Lopez	—	2	0	0	0
Jim Pankovits	.000	2	2	0	0
Terry Puhl	.667	3	3	0	2
Craig Reynolds	.333	4	12	1	4
Nolan Ryan	.000	2	4	0	0
Mike Scott	.000	2	6	0	0
Dave Smith	—	2	0	0	0
Dickie Thon	.250	6	12	1	3
Denny Walling	.158	5	19	1	3
Total	.218	6	225	17	49

2B—Bass 2, Ashby, Davis, Garner, Walling; 3B—None; HR—Ashby, Davis, Doran, Hatcher, Thon; RBI—Davis 3, Doran 3, Ashby 2, Cruz 2, Garner 2, Hatcher 2, Walling 2, Thon; SB—Hatcher 3, Bass 2, Doran, Puhl.

METS PITCHING

Player	G	ERA	W–L	SV	IP	H	ER	BB	SO
Rick Aguilera	2	0.00	0–0	0	5	2	0	2	2
Ron Darling	1	7.20	0–0	0	5	6	4	2	5
Sid Fernandez	1	4.50	0–1	0	6	3	3	1	4
Dwight Gooden	2	1.06	0–1	0	17	16	2	5	9
Rog. McDowell	2	0.00	0–0	0	7	1	0	0	3
Bob Ojeda	2	2.57	1–0	0	14	15	4	4	6
Jesse Orosco	4	3.38	3–0	0	8	5	3	2	10
Doug Sisk	1	0.00	0–0	0	1	1	0	1	0
Total	6	2.29	4–2	0	63	49	16	17	40

ASTROS PITCHING

Player	G	ERA	W–L	SV	IP	H	ER	BB	SO
Larry Andersen	2	0.00	0–0	0	5	1	0	2	3
Jeff Calhoun	1	9.00	0–0	0	1	1	1	1	0
Charlie Kerfeld	3	2.25	0–1	0	4	2	1	1	4
Bob Knepper	2	3.52	0–0	0	15-1/3	13	6	1	9
Aurelio Lopez	2	8.10	0–1	0	3-1/3	7	3	4	2
Nolan Ryan	2	3.86	0–1	0	14	9	6	1	17
Mike Scott	2	0.50	2–0	0	18	8	1	1	19
Dave Smith	2	9.00	0–1	0	2	2	2	3	2
Total	6	2.87	2–4	0	62-2/3	43	20	14	57

1986 World Series: Mets vs. Boston Red Sox

METS WIN SERIES 4–3

It is tough to write objectively about the 1986 World Series if you were—or are—a fan of either participating team. The Mets fan revels in the absurdity of the comeback, trailing 5–3 in Game 6 and down to the last out with nobody on base and the champagne on ice in the Boston clubhouse…. The Red Sox fan shudders at the fiendishness of the collapse, the 10th-inning meltdown in Game 6 and the blown 3–0 lead in Game 7.

The cynic might describe each game thusly:

Game 1—Decided on an error.
Game 2—Both starters stunk before the game really got out of hand.
Game 3—Pretty much decided seven batters into the game.
Game 4—Pretty much decided seven innings into the game.
Game 5—Mets' ace stumbled again, Red Sox's No. 2 hurler shuts door.
Game 6—Decided on a wild pitch *and* an error.
Game 7—Losing team blew a three-run lead, winning team almost blew a three-run lead.

The Series included two homers on fly balls that popped out of the mitt of the right fielder, poorly executed bunts by both hitters and fielders, questionable decision-making by both managers, and the overall silliness of the last two Series games. The first run of the Series came home on an error; the last run scored on a base hit by a relief pitcher. A player who hit .218 the previous year was named the World Series MVP, one game after his error almost cost his team the title.

Yet the 1986 World Series is considered a classic by many, right up there with the 1952, 1975, 1991, and 2001 Fall Classics. The Mookie Wilson at-bat in Game 6 is one of the wildest five to 10 minutes of baseball and summed up the resiliency of the Mets during the 1986 postseason. New York earned three walk-off wins after the regular season, two against Houston and one versus the Red Sox.

The Mets weren't battle-tested in the regular season. They won 108 games and finished 21-1/2 games ahead of the second-place Phillies. For some Mets, pressure during the regular season meant trying to wrap up a home victory within 2-1/2 hours so they could spend even more time at Finn McCool's, their favorite watering hole. That's why the drama of the NLCS and World Series is so appreciated by Mets fans.

The Mets were expected to handle the Red Sox despite Boston's formidable lineup and the presence of Roger Clemens, who was coming off a near-duplication of Dwight Gooden's 1985 regular season. New York had the edge in team speed, owned a deeper rotation, and possessed a better bullpen. Both teams were coming off gut-wrenching games in the LCS. The Mets needed a pair of walk-off wins and a 16-inning victory to dispose of the Astros. The Red Sox were an out away from elimination in Game 5 of the ALCS before knocking out the Angels in seven games.

The Mets had a bit of trouble scoring off Bob Knepper in the NLCS. The lefty had a rather ordinary 3.52 ERA in the series, but he kept New York scoreless in 14 of the 15-2/3 innings he pitched. The Red Sox had their own "Bob Knepper" as they sent out lefty Bruce Hurst to pitch games 1, 5, and 7. Hurst combined on a shutout in the opener, tossed a complete game in Game 5, and carried a 3–0 lead into the sixth inning of the seventh game. Hurst almost single-handedly wrecked the Mets' victory parade before wilting in the late innings of his final start.

Dwight's Gooden's ERA in the Series speaks for itself. He was rocked in Game 2 and never found a rhythm in Game 5, losing both contests. Gooden also was the subject of the first questionable managerial decision in the Series.

New York already had dropped the opener and was down 4–2 with two outs and two runners on in the fourth inning of Game 2 when Gooden's turn at bat came up. Mets manager Davey Johnson, figuring Gooden would eventually solve the Red Sox, let his ace come to the plate. Gooden grounded out to end the threat before serving up a two-run homer to Dwight Evans in the fifth. Gooden ended the fifth by striking out the last three batters, but the game was decided by then.

If the Mets hadn't won Game 6, many would have blamed it on one of Johnson's decisions in the bottom of the ninth with the score tied 3–3. Ray Knight led off with a walk and beat the throw to second on Mookie Wilson's bunt, putting runners on first and second. It was light-hitting Kevin Elster's turn to hit, but Johnson instead sent Howard Johnson to the plate. The move seemed to signal that Howard Johnson, who had just one sacrifice bunt all year—none since July 26—would be hitting away to win the game. Instead Johnson put down two miserable bunt attempts before striking out. The Mets still had runners on first and second, which made Lee Mazzilli's ensuing fly ball to left field meaningless. Worse, it meant Johnson would play shortstop in the 10th inning instead of the sure-handed Elster.

But Davey Johnson didn't commit the most questionable managerial decisions in the Series. That honor went to Red Sox skipper John McNamara for allowing the gimpy Bill Buckner to go out to first base for the bottom of the 10th in Game 6 when he had Dave Stapleton available.

Some have ripped McNamara for using Calvin Schiraldi, and then Bob Stanley to try to close out the World Series win. McNamara also was skewered for asking Schiraldi to pitch the seventh inning of Game 7, when Schiraldi served up Ray Knight's go-ahead homer. But it's not like McNamara had a lot of bullpen options. Schiraldi, the former Met who was dealt in the Bob Ojeda trade the previous December, emerged as the closer almost by default. It was Schiraldi's job to protect a 5–3 lead in the 10th inning of Game 6, and he didn't.

Oil Can Boyd could have been asked to pitch the seventh inning of Game 7, but the volatile right-hander unraveled during his Game 3 start and was emotionally devastated after being passed over to start the seventh game due to a rainout the previous day. That left McNamara to call on Schiraldi.

The Mets appeared to play the first two games of the series with a Houston hangover. New York managed just four hits in the opener and lost the game on an error in the seventh inning, wasting a great outing by Ron Darling. Gooden was brutal in Game 2, but the Mets' bullpen was no better in the 9–3 loss at Shea.

The Mets now had an 0–2 deficit heading into three games at Fenway Park. The Red Sox had won their previous five playoff games and were about to face former teammate Bob Ojeda in Game 3. This is when Davey Johnson made one of his best decisions of the Series.

Both teams are required by major league rules to practice the day before games 3 and 6 or else pay a stiff fine. Johnson thought the fine was worth it, giving his team an extra day to relax and recharge for the rest of the Series.

It took just a few batters to realize the Mets were back to their confident selves. They scored four runs off Boyd in the first inning of Game 3, thanks in part to a botched rundown by the Red Sox. Dykstra led off the game with a homer and finished the night 4-for-5 with two runs scored. Ojeda was outstanding over seven innings, combining with Roger McDowell on a five-hitter.

The Mets needed a few more innings to get the offense going in Game 4, although Darling did his part by keeping the game scoreless before New York broke through with a three-run fourth. Gary Carter snapped the scoreless tie with a two-run homer before adding a long blast over the Green Monster in the eighth inning. Len Dykstra also smacked a two-run shot while Darling and the bullpen limited the Red Sox to seven hits in a 6–2 victory.

The Mets scored 13 runs on 25 hits in the first two games at Fenway after managing just three runs and 12 hits in the two games at Shea. New York also had Gooden going in Game 5, and there was no way Hurst was expected to shut down the Mets in back-to-back starts.

But Hurst helped the Red Sox take a 3–2 lead in the Series, tossing a 10-hitter and blanking the Mets until the eighth in a 4–2 victory. Gooden was tagged for four runs and nine hits in four-plus innings, leaving the game after allowing three straight hits to start the fifth.

Darryl Strawberry was having a miserable time at this stage of the Series. He was batting just .222 (4-for-18) with six strikeouts, no homers, and zero RBIs. Red Sox fans gave him a hard time at Fenway, serenading him with chants of "DAAAAAA-RYLLLLLL" in the late innings of Game 5.

The Fenway faithful had some fun at the expense of the Mets, and why not? The Sox were up 3–2 in the Series with Roger Clemens on the mound for Game 6 at Shea. That's when the Mets received some unsolicited support from one of their own fans. Michael Sergio has since become an Emmy Award–winning director and a critically acclaimed screenwriter. Before that, he was best known for his role as the man who rocked Shea Stadium in Game 6.

The ballpark was surprisingly quiet in the first inning, considering the importance of the game. Two days earlier, Mets fans had expected Gooden to revert to form and help the team carry a 3–2 lead into the contest. But with the Mets now on the brink of elimination, fans were cautiously optimistic Ojeda could outpitch Clemens and force a seventh game.

The word "cautious" didn't seem to be in Sergio's vocabulary, at least not when he pulled off one of the greatest stunts in World Series history. Ojeda was trying to complete the opening inning when a low-flying object appeared from the horizon past the outfield fence. It was Sergio, who had parachuted into Shea and made a perfect landing on the first-base side of the infield. He had a homemade "Let's Go Mets" banner tied to the chute to signify why a person would perform such a crazy stunt.

Sergio was quickly grabbed by guards and police before he was escorted into the Mets' dugout and out of the ballpark for booking. Game 7 starter Ron Darling gave him a thumbs-up, but starting second baseman Wally Backman said Sergio, "scared the shit out of me. I was kind of standing there, and everybody was screaming and yelling, and the next thing I knew, this guy came right over my head. He landed, and the police got him. With the level of intensity out there, I think he relaxed us because it became a joke."[11]

If the Mets were relaxed, there weren't showing it. They fell behind 2–0 and didn't get a hit until the fifth, when they tied it with a two-run rally. Boston regained the lead in the seventh, but the Mets knotted it again in the eighth and had a chance to win it in the ninth after putting the first two runners on base. However, the game went into the 10th, which has become one of the more memorable innings in baseball history. Down 5–3 with two outs and nobody on in the bottom of the inning, the Mets strung together three straight hits before a wild pitch and an error forced a Game 7.

Thanks to a rainout, the Mets were facing Hurst once again instead of Boyd, whose first-inning meltdown in Game 3 helped New York get back in the Series. Hurst blanked the Mets for the first five innings, and the Red Sox enjoyed a 3–0 lead.

Historically, the Bosox were in a bad place. They were up 3–0 in the sixth inning in Game 7 of the 1975 World Series, only to lose 4–3 to the Reds. Eleven years later, the Mets used the sixth inning to tie the game and chase Hurst before Ray Knight hit a go-ahead homer to spark a three-run seventh. Boston scrambled back with a pair of runs in the eighth to cut the Mets' lead to 6–5, but Strawberry led off the bottom of the eighth with a homer before reliever Jesse Orosco delivered an RBI single for the final run.

Orosco completed the Series in the same manner he finished the NLCS, striking out the final hitter. The Mets were now the champions for the first time in 17 years following a pair of epic playoff series.

GAME 1, October 18, New York: Red Sox 1, Mets 0

The Series opener was eerily similar to Game 1 of the 1973 World Series; a lefty starter shut down the Mets while the opposition won on an error by the second baseman.

Bruce Hurst limited the Mets to four hits—all singles—and four walks over eight shutout innings of a 1–0 victory. Hurst got into a mini-jam when Keith Hernandez led off the sixth with a walk and Gary Carter followed with a single, putting runners on first and second with nobody out. But the threat was stopped when Ray Knight grounded into a double play after Darryl Strawberry was caught looking at strike three.

Mets starter Ron Darling was equally impressive through his first six frames, limiting the Red Sox to three hits while striking out seven. But he gave up the lone run in the seventh without surrendering a hit, thanks in part to his own wildness.

Jim Rice worked a leadoff walk before Darling uncorked a wild pitch that put the Red Sox's left fielder on second. Darling redeemed himself by getting Dwight Evans to bounce back to the mound while keeping Rice at second.

Rich Gedman followed with a grounder right at second baseman Tim Teufel, who was starting instead of Wally Backman due to the lefty-throwing Hurst. Teufel let the ball skip past his glove and into right-center field, allowing Rice to score from second. Because of Darling's errant pitch and Teufel's miscue, the Red Sox had manufactured a run instead of an inning-ending double play. That was enough offense the way the Mets were hitting Hurst.

Teufel tried to redeem himself with a leadoff single in the bottom of the seventh, but pinch-runner Backman never got past second before the inning was over. Hurst got three flyball outs in the eighth, and ex-Met Calvin Schiraldi closed out Boston's first World Series victory since Carlton Fisk's homer in Game 6 of the 1975 Fall Classic.

Teufel went 2-for-3, but the rest of the team went 2-for-26.

GAME 2, October 19, New York: Red Sox 9, Mets 3

An expected pitcher's duel turned out to be a lopsided win for the Red Sox despite an ineffective Roger Clemens. Dwight Gooden was terrible, Rick Aguilera was lousy, and Sid Fernandez was horrible as the Red Sox banged out 18 hits.

Gooden didn't possess his overpowering fastball and had trouble locating his curve, which spelled trouble in the third inning. He actually didn't allow a hit until Wade Boggs laced an RBI double in the third, which began a string of three straight run-scoring hits. Marty Barrett and Bill Buckner followed with run-scoring singles to put the Red Sox up 3–0.

It was Clemens' turn to stumble in the bottom of the third. Gooden laid down a bunt single that put runners on first and second with nobody out. Lenny Dykstra bunted the runners over before Wally Backman singled home Rafael Santana. Gooden scored on Keith Hernandez's grounder to make it 3–2 Boston.

It's always interesting to see how a pitcher will fare an inning after running the bases. In Gooden's case, it wasn't good. Dave Henderson led off the fourth with a homer to double the Red Sox's lead.

The Mets threatened against Clemens in the bottom of the fourth. Santana hit a two-out single to put runners on first and second with the pitcher's spot coming up. Instead of pinch-hitting for Gooden, manager Davey Johnson allowed his pitcher to hit for himself. Gooden responded by grounding out to Buckner at first to end the inning.

Gooden struck out three straight to end the top of the fifth, but only after surrendering a two-run blast to Dwight Evans that put the Bosox up 6–2. Gooden's night was over, charged with five earned runs and eight hits in five innings. Clemens wouldn't be around much longer, either.

Hernandez singled off second baseman Barrett's glove in the bottom of the fifth to put runners on first and third with one out. Rather than let his ace get out of the jam with a four-run lead, manager John McNamara made his first questionable move of the Series by lifting Clemens in favor of Steve Crawford. Gary Carter made McNamara pay for the decision by delivering an RBI single to get the Mets within 6–3. But the Mets' scoring ended right there. The inning could have been bigger if Evans didn't make a great diving catch on Lenny Dykstra's leadoff fly to right.

Henderson and Spike Owen hit consecutive RBI singles in the seventh off Rick Aguilera to make it 8–3 before Wade Boggs doubled home a run against Sid Fernandez in the ninth.

The Mets would head to Fenway Park down 2–0 in the Series. Few teams have won a World Series after dropping the first two games at home.

The Mets also became the third team to go the first two games of a World Series without an extra-base hit, joining the 1926 Yankees and 1939 Reds. Neither the Yanks nor the Reds won those Series.

GAME 3, October 21, Boston: Mets 7, Red Sox 1

Bob Ojeda helped the Mets avoid a 2–0 deficit in the NLCS. Manager Davey Johnson was now asking Ojeda to prevent the team from falling behind 3–0 in the World Series.

Ojeda was pitching against the team that couldn't get rid of him fast enough the previous winter. Ojeda spent 1985 shuttling between the rotation and the pen while the Red Sox tried to figure out if he was better suited for relief work. Ojeda was vocal about his displeasure with the situation, and the Bosox were ready to dump him after fellow lefty Bruce Hurst had emerged as a keeper.

With the prospect of facing his former teammates at their ballpark in a must-win game, Ojeda was outstanding over seven innings, giving up a run and five hits while using his "dead-fish" hook to strike out six hitters. Just as important, the Mets' bats woke up.

Lenny Dykstra put the Mets ahead just three pitches after PA announcer Sherm Feller announced him as the leadoff hitter, depositing an Oil Can Boyd pitch past the Pesky Pole in right field. It was the Mets' first extra-base hit of the series, and the first time they held a lead. They weren't done.

Wally Backman and Keith Hernandez followed with singles before Gary Carter laced an RBI double, the Mets' fourth straight hit to start the game.

Darryl Strawberry struck out for the first out, and Ray Knight hit a grounder to third that provided one of the funnier moments in the Series. Third baseman Wade Boggs threw home to get Hernandez at the plate, but the Mets first baseman got caught in a rundown before returning safely to third. Problem was, Carter already had headed toward third and was a dead duck. Carter started to retreat back to second base and appeared to be a sure out until shortstop Spike Owen, worried that Hernandez might break for the plate, faked a throw home. Owen's move gave Carter time to get back to second safely, loading the bases with one man out.

Danny Heep took advantage of the extra man on base by lacing a two-run single that made it 4–0. Just seven batters into the game, the Mets had scored more runs than they had in Games 1 and 2.

Dykstra went 4-for-5 and Carter drove in three runs, but the rest of the game belonged to Ojeda. The Red Sox didn't score after Marty Barrett's RBI single in the third. Ojeda stranded a runner in scoring position in the second, third, fifth, and sixth innings to keep it a 4–1 game.

Carter expanded the lead with a two-run single in the seventh before Knight's RBI double made it 7–1 in the eighth. Roger McDowell followed with two perfect innings of relief to secure the win.

GAME 4, October 22, Boston: Mets 6, Red Sox 2

Gary Carter hit four postseason home runs during his major league career, two coming in the 1981 NLDS against the Phillies. The other two were belted in this game, helping the Mets even the Series at two games apiece.

Carter had driven in four of the Mets' first 10 runs against the Red Sox while proving his .148 average in the NLCS was a complete aberration. Now it was time for him to flex his muscles.

Game 4 was scoreless until the fourth, when Wally Backman led off with a single and moved to second on a grounder. Up stepped Carter, who hadn't homered in 64 postseason at-bats since a blast in Game 4 of the 1981 NLDS. To this point the Mets hadn't lifted a ball in the air against Red Sox starter Al Nipper, who had recorded nine ground-ball outs and a strikeout while giving up a pair of ground-ball singles. Carter ended that stretch with a two-run shot that easily cleared the Green Monster in left.

Darryl Strawberry continued the rally with a double before Danny Heep singled him home. Both hits were line drives, showing the Mets had solved Nipper after only one look at him.

Carter also tagged Nipper for an opposite-field double leading off the sixth but was stranded by Nipper, who was working his final inning.

The box score shows that Mets starter Ron Darling allowed no runs and only four hits in seven innings against the Red Sox, but he labored through most of it. He issued a pair of two-out walks to load the bases in the bottom of the first before Dwight Evans grounded out to end the inning. Darling also gave up a leadoff double in the second and put runners on first and third with two outs in the fifth but still kept the Bosox off the scoreboard. Darling caught a break in the sixth when Rich Gedman hit a two-out single that moved Evans over to third. But

Gedman decided to test Mookie Wilson's arm in left and was nailed at second base for the final out. Darling still had a 3–0 lead.

Lenny Dykstra padded the Mets' lead with a two-out, two-run homer to right that bounced off the glove of Evans and into the bullpen. Dykstra now had three postseason homers after hitting just eight during the regular season.

Carter made it 6–0 in the seventh, crushing a long homer that soared over the netting above the Monster. It was Carter's third hit of the night, giving him a .412 average in the first four games of the Series.

Darling walked two more in the seventh before getting out of the inning with the shutout intact. Manager Davey Johnson gave the ball to Roger McDowell for the final two innings.

It took McDowell three batters to ruin the shutout. Jim Rice led off with a double, and Evans singled him home with one out. Dave Henderson lifted a sacrifice fly for Boston's second run before McDowell retired the final four Red Sox to finish a 6–2 victory.

GAME 5, October 23, Boston: Red Sox 4, Mets 2

The Mets had been spoiled by Dwight Gooden during his three years with the team. In an era where "quality starts" (3 earned runs in 6 innings) was becoming a legitimate statistic, Gooden was pure quality. Only twice during his career had he posted back-to-back starts that weren't "quality." He allowed more than three runs just once in his 35 starts of 1985.

There was no reason to believe Gooden couldn't bounce back from his miserable performance in Game 2. And after scoring 13 runs in their last two games, there was confidence the Mets would solve Bruce Hurst in their second meeting against him. But Gooden was bad, Hurst was outstanding, and the Red Sox were up 3–2 in the Series following a 4–2 win.

Gooden put four consecutive runners on base in the bottom of the first without allowing a run, thanks to his pickoff of Marty Barrett at first base. Gooden hit Don Baylor to fill the bases with two outs before Dwight Evans hit a fly ball to left to end the inning.

Gooden wasn't as lucky in the second and third innings. Dave Henderson hit a one-out triple in the second

and scored on Spike Owens' sacrifice fly, putting the Red Sox ahead to stay. One inning later, Dwight Evans singled home Bill Buckner, who had reached base on shortstop Rafael Santana's error.

Gooden was pulled in the fifth after giving up three straight hits to start the inning. Jim Rice tripled, and Don Baylor poked an RBI single before Dwight Evans singled to end Gooden's night. Henderson made it 4–0 with an RBI double off Sid Fernandez, who retired his next 10 batters.

Meanwhile, the Mets were doing nothing against Hurst, who blanked the Mets until Tim Teufel's solo homer in the eighth. New York had a great opportunity to tie the game 2–2 in the top of the fifth, putting runners on second and third with one out. Hurst ended the threat by striking out Lenny Dykstra before Teufel grounded out.

Hurst went the distance on a 10-hitter, throwing 130 pitches in what was expected to be his final appearance of the Series. Thanks to a rainout between Games 6 and 7, the Mets would have to face him one more time.

GAME 6, October 25, New York: Mets 6, Red Sox 5 (10 innings)

This can hardly be considered one of the best-played games in World Series history, but it's at or near the top of the list when it comes to dramatic finishes. The Red Sox, one strike away from their first championship in 68 years, let the title sail by a catcher's mitt and skid underneath a first baseman's glove. The Mets were able to rally their way to a seventh game while first baseman Keith Hernandez sat in the trainer's room sipping a Budweiser.

The Red Sox didn't just blow one lead in the potential clincher: They coughed up three. They led 2–0 heading into the fifth inning and were up by a run in the bottom of the eighth. Both times the Mets came out of the inning with a tie.

Bob Ojeda was asked to do what he had already accomplished three times in this postseason, only this time the season hung in the balance. The Mets never trailed during the games in which Ojeda took the mound follow-

ing a loss. Ojeda's performance in this game was gritty as he struggled over the first two innings before settling down.

The top of the first was interrupted by a parachutist who landed on the infield, but the delay didn't stop the Red Sox from taking an early lead. Wade Boggs led off the game with a single and later scored on a double by Dwight Evans. Marty Barrett provided the Red Sox's third hit of the second inning, driving in Spike Owen to make it 2–0.

A two-run lead was looking good as long as Roger Clemens was mowing down the Mets. He struck out two batters in each of the first three innings and had a no-hitter until the fifth, when Darryl Strawberry poked an RBI single that got the Mets within a run. Mookie Wilson followed with a base hit to put runners on first and third with nobody out. New York tied the game on Danny Heep's double-play grounder before Clemens got out of the inning.

The Mets had a chance to grab their first lead since Game 4 during the sixth inning. Wally Backman and Keith Hernandez hit back-to-back one-out singles, but Backman was standing on third when the last out was made.

World Series MVP Ray Knight almost was the goat of the series. Knight threw high on a grounder by Jim Rice to give the Red Sox a first-and-third situation with one out in the seventh. The Mets almost pulled off an inning-ending double play, but Dwight Evans beat Kevin Elster's relay throw, allowing Marty Barrett to score the tiebreaking run.

Pinch-hitter Lee Mazzilli led off the bottom of the eighth with a single before Lenny Dykstra reached base on a fielder's choice that put Mazzilli on second. Backman laid down a perfect bunt to move both runners into scoring position, and Hernandez was walked to load the bases with one out. Carter picked up his eighth RBI of the Series with a sacrifice fly that once again tied the game. Dykstra moved to third on the play but was stranded when Darryl Strawberry hit a fly ball to end the inning.

That's when Davey Johnson made a double-switch that angered Strawberry and left the Mets without their top power threat. Mazzilli, who had pinch-hit for reliever Jesse Orosco, replaced Strawberry in right field. Rick Aguilera came in to relieve Orosco, and Strawberry went to the clubhouse to pout. As it was, Mazzilli almost had a chance to win the game in the ninth.

Aguilera faced the minimum in the ninth before the Mets went back to work against their former teammate, Schiraldi. Ray Knight worked out a leadoff walk and beat a throw to second on Mookie Wilson's bunt attempt, putting the winning run in scoring position. But the potential rally began to unravel when Davey Johnson asked Howard Johnson to bunt the runners over. Johnson missed the first bunt attempt and fouled off the second before finally striking out.

Mazzilli followed with a deep fly to left that would have scored Knight if Johnson had bunted successfully. Instead, the runners stayed put before Dykstra lifted another fly ball to end the inning.

Next to Doug Sisk, Aguilera had seen the least amount of work among Mets hurlers during the Series. As much as Sisk was booed during the season, Mets fans probably were wishing he was on the mound after Aguilera served up a tiebreaking homer to Dave Henderson leading off the 10th. Things got worse when Wade Boggs laced a two-out double and scored on Marty Barrett's single, putting the Red Sox ahead 5–3.

Schiraldi, who became the Red Sox's closer during the second half of the season, was asked to close out the World Series. He already had given up one lead, but he was looking good after getting Backman and Hernandez to fly out. The Red Sox were one out away from their elusive sixth championship, and then one strike away with Gary Carter at the plate. Carter extended the game with a single, leaving Kevin Mitchell to keep the rally alive.

Mitchell had spent part of the half-inning trying to make arrangements to fly back to San Diego. He was in the clubhouse when told he would have to hit if Carter got on base. Mitchell grabbed his pants, minus a protective cup, hustled to the on-deck circle, and headed to the plate hoping he wouldn't be the final out of the Series. He wasn't.

Mitchell lined a single in almost the same spot Carter's hit had landed. The Mets still trailed by two, but they had the tying run on base. At least the team was going down with a fight.

Knight lined another single to score Carter, pulling the Mets within 5–4 and chasing Schiraldi from the mound. In came Bob Stanley and up stepped Wilson as the two helped orchestrate the most memorable at-bat in Mets history.

Wilson's theory to hitting was "Thou shalt not pass without offering." He was not about to work a walk and put the pressure on Howard Johnson, who already had botched a huge at-bat just one inning earlier. Wilson came up hacking until he saw a pitch he couldn't hit and Rich Gedman couldn't catch. Stanley uncorked a pitch that broke inside on Wilson, who managed to skip over the errant toss. Gedman didn't come close to grabbing the throw, allowing Mitchell to score the tying run.

The Mets were left for dead just four batters earlier. With the Sox only an out away from victory, a message flashed briefly on the jumbotron congratulating Bruce Hurst for winning the series MVP award. Now, the Mets had tied the game for the third time and could win it if Wilson delivered a single. Wilson fouled off several pitches but never got the single he wanted. But the Mets won the game anyway.

Wilson hit a slow dribbler down the first-base line in the direct path of Bill Buckner. Dave Stapleton was usually patrolling first base in late-game situations for the Red Sox because of Buckner's bad ankles, which had limited his mobility. McNamara kept Buckner in the game, and the move helped the Mets win the Series.

Buckner, playing rather deep behind the first-base bag, let the ball come to him instead of charging it on his gimpy ankles. Buckner bent down to grab the ball before…

"And a ground ball…trickling…gets by Buckner!!!! Rounding third is Knight, and the Mets will win the ballgame. The Mets win!!! They *win*!!!!!!!," yelled Mets announcer Bob Murphy.

"A little roller up the first-base line…behind the bag… it gets through Buckner!!! Here comes Knight, and the Mets win it!" cried Vin Scully on NBC.

The Mets had pulled games out of their butts during the NLCS, but nothing like this. They had trumped their three-run comeback in the ninth inning of Game 6 against the Astros, doing it after two outs and nobody on base.

GAME 7, October 27, New York: Mets 8, Red Sox 5

The Game 6 comeback almost made the deciding game seem anticlimactic. Millions of sports fans think the Mets won the World Series on Buckner's error, just like millions believe Mike Eruzione's goal against the Soviets gave the United States the 1980 Olympic gold medal in hockey. But there was still a Game 7 left to play, and Mother Nature apparently was no fan of the Mets.

Rain had caused the game to be postponed a day, which allowed Red Sox manager John McNamara to change his starting pitchers. Oil Can Boyd, hit hard during the Mets' 7–1 victory in Game 3, was the scheduled starter in the clincher. But the rainout let McNamara switch to Bruce Hurst, who shut down the Mets in Games 1 and 5. The plan worked to perfection…for 5-1/3 innings.

Mets skipper Davey Johnson countered with Ron Darling, a hard-luck loser in Game 1 and an impressive winner in the fourth game. Darling had limited Boston to 13 hits in 14 innings without allowing an earned run. He had suffered just two losses at Shea Stadium the entire season and was a much, much better risk than Dwight Gooden on three days' rest.

Darling's night ended in the fourth inning. Dwight Evans and Rich Gedman hit back-to-back homers to start the second before Wade Boggs added an RBI double that put the Bosox up 3–0 later in the inning. Darling was about to face Boggs with a runner on second and two outs in the fourth when Johnson made the quick hook, replacing Darling with Sid Fernandez. It proved to be one of Johnson's best managerial decisions of the entire Series.

Fernandez walked Boggs before retiring the next seven Red Sox in order, four by strikeout. El Sid almost appeared to be pitching with a chip on his shoulder after becoming the odd starter out in the World Series rotation. Fernandez was the winning pitcher for the Mets in the clincher, even though he didn't get credit for the victory.

The Hawaiian held the Red Sox at bay while the Mets hitters tried to figure out Hurst. The Boston southpaw was lights out once again as he carried a one-hitter into the bottom of the sixth. Ray Knight was the Mets' lone base runner over the first five innings, poking a two-out single in the second.

Hurst opened the sixth by getting a ground-ball out before the Mets struck in the same cobra-like fashion they displayed in the ninth inning of Game 6 of the NLDS, when they were almost as desperate for runs.

Pinch-hitter Lee Mazzilli and Mookie Wilson hit consecutive singles before Tim Teufel walked to load the bases. That brought up Hernandez, who was just 5-for-24 in the Series, 1-for-9 against Hurst. Hernandez broke

through with a two-run single before Gary Carter hit an RBI grounder one batter later to knot the score at 3–3. For the third time in the postseason, the Mets had tied a game in which they trailed by at least three runs. They erased deficits of 4–0 and 3–0 in victories over the Astros in the NLCS. A third such comeback would mean a championship.

Hurst was gassed by the end of the sixth, just four days after tossing a complete-game victory over the Mets. McNamara decided to replace Hurst with Calvin Schiraldi, who had helped blow Game 6 by surrendering three straight singles in the 10th inning.

Chants of "Caaaaalllll-vin, Caaaaalllll-vin!" cascaded through the stadium as Mets fans gave Schiraldi the same treatment Darryl Strawberry received in Game 5 at Fenway. Ray Knight cut through the air of hostility by crushing a leadoff homer in the seventh to put the Mets ahead.

Things only got worse for the former Met. Pinch-hitter Lenny Dykstra followed Knight's blast with a single before moving to second on a wild pitch. Rafael Santana singled home Dykstra and moved to second on Roger McDowell's bunt, which ended Schiraldi's outing after just 1/3 inning.

Another ex-Met, Joe Sambito, loaded the bases with an intentional walk and a walk before Hernandez came through again, this time with a sacrifice fly. The Mets now had a 6–3 lead and were six outs from their second World Series crown. They were on Easy Street, right? Wrong.

Entering his second inning of work, McDowell gave up back-to-back singles leading off the eighth before Dwight Evans laced a two-run double to put the Red Sox with 6–5. That prompted Johnson to take out McDowell in favor of Jesse Orosco, who by now was used to this kind of postseason pressure. Boston didn't get another base runner the rest of the way.

The Mets' late-inning assault resumed when Darryl Strawberry ripped a long leadoff homer off Al Nipper, who seethed while the outfielder made a deliberate trip around the bases. Nipper would exact his revenge by drilling Strawberry with a pitch in spring training. Too little, too late.

Orosco plated the Mets' eighth run with a high chopper that got through the infield for a single that scored Knight. New York had scored eight times in its final three at-bats after managing just eight runs in their previous 25 innings.

Eight was enough for Orosco, who capped his perfect night of work by striking out Marty Barrett to end the Series. The Mets had an 8–5 victory and their first World Series title since 1969.

Game 1, October 18 at New York
RED SOX 1, METS 0

RED SOX	AB	R	H	BI	METS	AB	R	H	BI
Boggs 3b	4	0	0	0	Wilson lf	4	0	1	0
Barrett 2b	4	0	1	0	McDowell p	0	0	0	0
Buckner 1b	4	0	1	0	Dykstra cf	3	0	0	0
Stapleton 1b	0	0	0	0	Hernandez 1b	3	0	0	0
Rice lf	2	1	1	0	Carter c	4	0	1	0
Evans rf	3	0	0	0	Strawberry rf	2	0	0	0
Gedman c	4	0	0	0	Knight 3b	3	0	0	0
Henderson cf	4	0	2	0	Teufel 2b	3	0	2	0
Owen ss	2	0	0	0	Backman 2b	1	0	0	0
Hurst p	3	0	0	0	Santana ss	2	0	0	0
Greenwell ph	1	0	0	0	Heep ph	1	0	0	0
Schiraldi p	0	0	0	0	Darling p	2	0	0	0
					Mitchell lf	1	0	0	0
Totals	31	1	5	0		29	0	4	0

Red Sox	000	000	100	1	5	0	
Mets	000	000	000	0	4	1	

RED SOX	IP	H	R	ER	BB	SO
Hurst (W, 1–0)	8	4	0	0	4	8
Schiraldi (S 1)	1	0	0	0	1	1
Total	9	4	0	0	5	9

METS	IP	H	R	ER	BB	SO
Darling (L, 0–1)	7	3	1	0	3	8
McDowell	2	2	0	0	2	0
Total	9	5	1	0	5	8

LOB—Red Sox 8, Mets 8; E—Teufel (1); WP—Darling 2; IBB—Barrett; SH—Santana; SB—Wilson (1), Strawberry (1); Time—2:59; ATT—55,076.

Game 2, October 19 at New York
RED SOX 9, METS 3

RED SOX	AB	R	H	BI	METS	AB	R	H	BI
Boggs 3b	5	1	2	2	Dykstra cf	3	0	1	0
Barrett 2b	5	0	2	1	Backman 2b	3	1	2	1
Buckner 1b	5	0	2	1	Hernandez 1b	4	0	1	1
Stapleton 1b	1	0	0	0	Carter c	4	0	1	1
Rice lf	6	2	3	0	Strawberry rf	4	0	0	0
Evans rf	4	2	2	2	Heep lf	2	0	0	0
Gedman c	5	0	1	0	Aguilera p	0	0	0	0
Henderson cf	5	2	3	2	Orosco p	0	0	0	0
Owen ss	4	1	3	1	Mazzilli ph	1	0	0	0
Romero ss	0	0	0	0	Fernandez p	0	0	0	0
Clemens p	1	1	0	0	Sisk p	0	0	0	0
Crawford p	1	0	0	0	Johnson 3b	4	0	0	0
Greenwell ph	1	0	0	0	Santana ss	4	1	2	0
Stanley p	1	0	0	0	Gooden p	2	1	1	0
					Wilson lf	2	0	0	0
Totals	44	9	18	9		33	3	8	3

Red Sox	003	120	201	9	18	0	
Mets	002	010	000	3	8	1	

RED SOX	IP	H	R	ER	BB	SO
Clemens	4-1/3	5	3	3	4	3
Crawford (W, 1–0)	1-2/3	1	0	0	0	2
Stanley (S, 1)	3	2	0	0	1	3
Total	9	8	3	3	5	8

METS	IP	H	R	ER	BB	SO
Gooden (L, 0–1)	5	8	6	5	2	6
Aguilera	1	5	2	2	1	1
Orosco	2	2	0	0	0	3
Fernandez	1/3	3	1	1	0	1
Sisk	2/3	0	0	0	1	1
Total	9	18	9	8	4	12

LOB—Red Sox 13, Mets 9; E—Hernandez (1); 2B—Boggs 2; HR—Henderson, Evans; SH—Dykstra, Clemens; CS—Backman (1); Time—3:36; ATT—55,063.

Game 3, October 21 at Boston
METS 7, RED SOX 1

METS	AB	R	H	BI	RED SOX	AB	R	H	BI
Dykstra cf	5	2	4	1	Boggs 3b	3	0	1	0
Backman 2b	5	1	1	0	Barrett 2b	4	0	2	1
Hernandez 1b	4	1	2	0	Buckner 1b	4	0	0	0
Carter c	5	1	2	3	Rice lf	3	0	0	0
Strawberry rf	4	1	1	0	Baylor dh	4	0	1	0
Knight 3b	4	0	1	1	Evans rf	4	0	0	0
Heep dh	3	0	1	2	Gedman c	4	0	0	0
Mitchell ph	0	0	0	0	Henderson cf	2	1	1	0
Mazzilli ph	1	0	0	0	Owen ss	3	0	0	0
Wilson lf	4	0	0	0	Boyd p	0	0	0	0
Santana ss	4	1	1	0	Sambito p	0	0	0	0
Ojeda p	0	0	0	0	Stanley p	0	0	0	0
McDowell p	0	0	0	0					
Totals	39	7	13	7		31	1	5	1

Mets	400	000	210	7	13	0
Red Sox	001	000	000	1	5	0

METS	IP	H	R	ER	BB	SO
Ojeda (W, 1–0)	7	5	1	1	3	6
McDowell	2	0	0	0	0	0
Total	9	5	1	1	3	6

RED SOX	IP	H	R	ER	BB	SO
Boyd (L, 0–1)	7	9	6	6	1	3
Sambito	0	2	1	1	0	0
Stanley	2	2	0	0	0	1
Total	9	13	7	7	1	4

LOB—Mets 6, Red Sox 6; PB—Gedman; WP—Ojeda, Sambito; 2B—Knight (1), Carter (1), Baylor (1); HR—Lenny Dykstra (1); Time—2:58; ATT—33,595.

Game 4, October 22 at Boston
METS 6, RED SOX 2

METS	AB	R	H	BI	RED SOX	AB	R	H	BI
Dykstra cf	5	1	1	2	Boggs 3b	5	0	0	0
Backman 2b	4	1	2	0	Barrett 2b	4	0	2	0
Hernandez 1b	3	0	0	0	Buckner 1b	5	0	0	0
Carter c	4	2	3	3	Rice lf	4	1	1	0
Strawberry rf	4	1	2	0	Baylor dh	3	0	0	0
Knight 3b	4	0	2	1	Evans rf	3	1	1	1
Heep dh	4	0	0	0	Gedman c	4	0	3	0
Wilson lf	4	1	2	0	Henderson cf	3	0	0	1
Santana ss	4	0	0	0	Owen ss	1	0	0	0
Darling p	0	0	0	0	Greenwell ph	0	0	0	0
McDowell p	0	0	0	0	Romero ss	0	0	0	0
Orosco p	0	0	0	0	Nipper p	0	0	0	0
					Crawford p	0	0	0	0
					Stanley p	0	0	0	0
Totals	36	6	12	6		32	2	7	2

Mets	000	300	210	6	12	0
Red Sox	000	000	020	2	7	1

METS	IP	H	R	ER	BB	SO
Darling (W, 1–1)	7	4	0	0	6	4
McDowell	2/3	3	2	2	1	0
Orosco (S, 1)	1-1/3	0	0	0	0	1
Total	9	7	2	2	7	5

RED SOX	IP	H	R	ER	BB	SO
Nipper (L, 0–1)	6	7	3	3	1	2
Crawford	2	4	3	3	0	2
Stanley	1	1	0	0	0	0
Total	9	12	6	6	1	4

LOB—Mets 4, Red Sox 11; E—Gedman 2B—Strawberry (1), Carter (2), Gedman, Barrett (1), Rice (1); HR—Carter 2 (2), Dykstra (2); SF—Henderson; SB—Wilson 2 (3), Backman (1); CS: Strawberry (1); Time—3:22; ATT—33,920.

Game 5, October 23 at Boston
RED SOX 4, METS 2

METS	AB	R	H	BI	RED SOX	AB	R	H	BI
Dykstra cf	5	0	1	0	Boggs 3b	5	0	2	0
Teufel 2b	4	1	2	1	Barrett 2b	4	0	2	0
Hernandez 1b	4	0	1	0	Buckner 1b	5	1	1	0
Carter c	4	0	0	0	Stapleton 1b	0	0	0	0
Strawberry rf	4	0	1	0	Rice lf	3	1	2	0
Knight 3b	4	0	1	0	Baylor dh	3	1	1	1
Mitchell dh	4	0	1	0	Evans rf	4	0	2	1
Wilson lf	4	1	2	0	Gedman c	4	0	0	0
Santana ss	2	0	1	1	Henderson cf	4	1	2	1
Gooden p	0	0	0	0	Owen ss	3	0	0	1
Fernandez p	0	0	0	0	Hurst p	0	0	0	0
Totals	35	2	10	2		35	4	12	4

Mets	000	000	011	2	10	1
Red Sox	011	020	00x	4	12	0

METS	IP	H	R	ER	BB	SO
Gooden (L, 0–2)	4	9	4	3	2	3
Fernandez	4	3	0	0	0	5

RED SOX	IP	H	R	ER	BB	SO
Hurst (W, 2–0)	9	10	2	2	1	6

LOB—Mets 8, Red Sox 11; E—Santana (1); 2B—Wilson (1), Teufel (1), Henderson (1), Barrett (1); 3B—Henderson (1), Rice (1); HR—Teufel (1); SH—Santana; SF—Owen; Time—3:09; Att—34,010.

Game 6, October 25 at New York
METS 6, RED SOX 5 (10)

RED SOX	AB	R	H	BI		METS	AB	R	H	BI
Boggs 3b	5	2	3	0		Dykstra cf	4	0	0	0
Barrett 2b	4	1	3	2		Backman 2b	4	0	1	0
Buckner 1b	5	0	0	0		Hernandez 1b	4	0	1	0
Rice lf	5	0	0	0		Carter c	4	1	1	1
Evans rf	4	0	1	2		Strawberry rf	2	1	0	0
Gedman c	5	0	1	0		Aguilera p	0	0	0	0
Henderson cf	5	1	2	1		Mitchell ph	1	1	1	
Owen ss	4	1	3	0		Knight 3b	4	2	2	2
Clemens p	3	0	0	0		Wilson lf	5	0	1	0
Greenwell ph	1	0	0	0		Santana ss	1	0	0	0
Schiraldi p	1	0	0	0		Heep ph	1	0	0	0
Stanley p	0	0	0	0		Elster ss	1	0	0	0
Johnson ph-ss	1	0	0	0						
Ojeda p	2	0	0	0						
McDowell p	0	0	0	0						
Orosco p	0	0	0	0						
Mazzilli ph-rf	2	1	1	0						
Totals	42	5	13	5			36	6	8	3

Red Sox	110	000	100	2	5		13	3
Mets	000	020	010	3	6		8	2

RED SOX	IP	H	R	ER	BB	SO
Clemens	7	4	2	1	2	8
Schiraldi (L, 0–1)	2-2/3	4	4	3	2	1
Stanley	0	0	0	0	0	0
Total	9-2/3	8	6	4	4	9

METS	IP	H	R	ER	BB	SO
Ojeda	6	8	2	2	2	3
McDowell	1-2/3	2	1	0	3	1
Orosco	1/3	0	0	0	0	0
Aguilera (W, 1–0)	2	3	2	2	0	3
Total	10	13	5	4	5	7

LOB—Red Sox 14, Mets 8; E—Knight (1), Elster (1), Buckner (1), Gedman (2), Evans (1); WP—Stanley; 2B—Boggs, Evans; HR—Henderson; IBB—Hernandez, Boggs; SH—Backman, Dykstra, Owen; SF—Carter; SB—Strawberry 2 (3); Time—4:02; ATT—55,078.

Game 7, October 27 at New York
METS 8, RED SOX 5

RED SOX	AB	R	H	BI		METS	AB	R	H	BI
Boggs 3b	4	0	1	1		Wilson cf-lf	3	1	1	0
Barrett 2b	5	0	1	0		Teufel 2b	2	0	0	0
Buckner 1b	4	1	2	0		Backman pr-2b	1	1	0	0
Rice lf	4	1	2	0		Hernandez 1b	4	0	1	3
Evans rf	4	1	2	3		Carter c	4	0	0	1
Gedman c	4	1	1	1		Strawberry rf	4	1	1	1
Henderson cf	2	1	0	0		Knight 3b	4	2	3	1
Owen ss	3	0	0	0		Mitchell lf	2	0	0	0
Baylor ph	1	0	0	0		Dykstra ph-cf	2	1	1	0
Nipper p	0	0	0	0		Santana ss	3	1	1	1
Crawford p	0	0	0	0		Darling p	1	0	0	0
Hurst p	0	0	0	0		Fernandez p	0	0	0	0
Armas ph	1	0	0	0		Mazzilli ph	1	1	1	0
Schiraldi p	0	0	0	0		McDowell p	0	0	0	0
Sambito p	0	0	0	0		Orosco p	1	0	1	1
Stanley p	0	0	0	0						
Romero ss	1	0	0	0						
Totals	33	5	9	5			32	8	10	8

Red Sox	030	000	020	5	9	0
Mets	000	003	32x	8	10	0

RED SOX	IP	H	R	ER	BB	SO
Hurst	6	4	3	3	1	3
Schiraldi (L, 0–2)	1/3	3	3	3	0	0
Sambito	1/3	0	0	0	2	0
Stanley	1/3	0	0	0	0	0
Nipper	1	3	2	2	1	0
Crawford	2/3	0	0	0	0	0
Total	9	10	8	8	4	3

METS	IP	H	R	ER	BB	SO
Darling	3-2/3	6	3	3	1	0
Fernandez	2-1/3	0	0	0	1	4
McDowell (W, 1–0)	1	3	2	2	0	1
Orosco (S, 2)	2	0	0	0	0	2
Total	9	9	5	5	2	7

LOB—Red Sox 6, Mets 7; WP—Schiraldi; 2B—Evans (2); HR—Strawberry (1), Knight (1), Gedman (1), Evans (2); IBB—Wilson, Santana; HBP—Wilson; SH—McDowell, Hurst 2; SF—Hernandez; Time—3:11; ATT—55,032.

1986 World Series Statistics

Composite Linescore

Mets	402	333	761	3	32	65	5
Red Sox	155	140	441	2	27	69	4

METS BATTING

Player	BA	G	AB	R	H
Rick Aguilera	—	2	0	0	0
Wally Backman	.333	6	18	4	6
Gary Carter	.276	7	29	4	8
Ron Darling	.000	3	3	0	0
Lenny Dykstra	.296	7	27	4	8
Kevin Elster	.000	1	1	0	0
Sid Fernandez	—	3	0	0	0
Dwight Gooden	.500	2	2	1	1
Danny Heep	.091	5	11	0	1
Keith Hernandez	.231	7	26	1	6
Howard Johnson	.000	2	5	0	0
Ray Knight	.391	6	23	4	9
Lee Mazzilli	.400	4	5	2	2
Roger McDowell	—	5	0	0	0
Kevin Mitchell	.250	5	8	1	2
Bob Ojeda	.000	2	2	0	0
Jesse Orosco	1.000	4	1	0	1
Rafael Santana	.250	7	20	3	5
Doug Sisk	—	1	0	0	0
Darryl Strawberry	.208	7	24	4	5
Tim Teufel	.444	3	9	1	4
Mookie Wilson	.269	7	26	3	7
Total	.271	7	240	32	65

2B—Carter 2, Knight, Strawberry, Teufel, Wilson; 3B—None; HR—Carter 2, Dykstra 2, Knight, Strawberry, Teufel; RBI—Carter 9, Knight 5, Hernandez 4, Dykstra 3, Heep 2, Santana 2, Backman, Orosco, Strawberry, Teufel; SB—Strawberry 3, Wilson 3, Backman.

RED SOX BATTING

Player	BA	G	AB	R	H
Tony Armas	.000	1	1	0	0
Marty Barrett	.433	7	30	1	13
Don Baylor	.182	4	11	1	2
Wade Boggs	.290	7	31	3	9
Oil Can Boyd	—	1	0	0	0
Bill Buckner	.188	7	32	2	6
Roger Clemens	.000	2	4	1	0
Steve Crawford	.000	3	1	0	0
Dwight Evans	.308	7	26	4	8
Rich Gedman	.200	7	30	1	6
Mike Greenwell	.000	4	3	0	0
Dave Henderson	.400	7	25	6	10
Bruce Hurst	.000	3	3	0	0
Al Nipper	—	2	0	0	0
Spike Owen	.300	7	20	2	6
Jim Rice	.333	7	27	6	9
Ed Romero	.000	3	1	0	0
Joe Sambito	.000	2	0	0	0
Calvin Schiraldi	.000	3	1	0	0
Bob Stanley	.000	5	1	0	0
Dave Stapleton	.000	3	1	0	0
Total	.278	7	248	27	69

2B—Boggs 3, Barrett 2, Evans 2, Baylor, Gedman, Henderson, Rice; 3B—Henderson, Rice; HR—Evans 2, Henderson 2, Gedman; RBI—Evans 9, Henderson 5, Barrett 4, Boggs 3, Owen 2, Baylor, Buckner, Gedman; SB—None.

METS PITCHING

Player	G	ERA	W–L	SV	IP	H	ER	BB	SO
Rick Aguilera	2	12.00	1–0	0	3	8	4	1	4
Ron Darling	3	1.53	1–1	0	17-2/3	13	3	10	12
Sid Fernandez	3	1.35	0–0	0	6-2/3	6	1	1	10
Dwight Gooden	2	8.00	0–2	0	9	17	8	4	9
Rog. McDowell	5	4.91	1–0	0	7-1/3	10	4	6	2
Bob Ojeda	2	2.08	1–0	0	13	13	3	5	9
Jesse Orosco	4	0.00	0–0	2	5-2/3	2	0	0	6
Doug Sisk	1	0.00	0–0	0	2/3	0	0	1	1
Total	7	3.29	4–3	2	63	69	23	28	53

RED SOX PITCHING

Player	G	ERA	W–L	SV	IP	H	ER	BB	SO
Oil Can Boyd	1	7.71	0–1	0	7	9	6	1	3
Roger Clemens	2	3.18	0–0	0	11-1/3	9	4	6	11
Steve Crawford	3	6.23	1–0	0	4-1/3	5	3	0	4
Bruce Hurst	3	1.96	2–0	0	23	18	5	6	17
Al Nipper	2	7.11	0–1	0	6-1/3	10	5	2	2
Joe Sambito	2	27.00	0–0	0	1/3	2	1	2	0
Calvin Schiraldi	3	13.50	0–2	1	4	7	6	3	2
Bob Stanley	5	0.00	0–0	1	6-1/3	5	0	1	4
Total	7	4.31	3–4	2	62-2/3	65	30	21	43

1988 NLCS: Mets vs. Los Angeles Dodgers

DODGERS WIN SERIES 4–3

There are two postseason series that gnaw on the soul of a Mets fan. Watching Carlos Beltran strike out looking with the bases loaded in the bottom of the ninth to end Game 7 of the 2006 NLCS might be the worst moment in team history. Games 4, 5, and 7 of the 1988 NLCS rank right up there as well.

Before the series began the question wasn't whether the Mets would beat the Dodgers, but rather in how many games. New York didn't have a starting pitcher as hot as Orel Hershiser, but there was little else to worry about. The Mets had a deep rotation, a better bullpen, a more powerful lineup and a deeper bench. They demonstrated that by taking 10 of 11 from the Dodgers during the regular season.

The Mets weren't as scary as they were two years earlier, but the lineup was a helluva lot better than the Dodgers' starting eight. Kirk Gibson was LA's most imposing hitter, and he accounted for only 76 RBIs during the regular season. Gibson belted 25 homers and Mike Marshall added 20, but just one other Dodger had more than eight. Gibson was the lone Dodgers regular to hit over .277. Aside from Gibson, Marshall and Steve Sax, the Dodgers featured journeyman players named Mickey Hatcher, John Shelby, Franklin Stubbs, Jeff Hamilton, Alfredo Griffin, Mike Davis and Dave Anderson. It was the least-imposing collection of hitters ever allowed to compete in the NLCS since the 1973 Mets, which should have been a warning sign in itself.

The strength of the Dodgers was starting pitching, which was traditionally the case. Hershiser would be the unanimous winner of the NL Cy Young Award after going 23–8 with a 2.26 ERA in 267 innings. He was 16–7 with a 3.02 ERA by mid-August before throwing six shutouts, eight complete games and one 10-inning outing. He pitched to a 0.44 ERA in his last nine starts and ended the season by breaking Don Drysdale's major league record for consecutive scoreless innings.

Tim Belcher was named the NL Rookie of the Year after going 12–6 with a 2.91 ERA. Former Met Tim Leary also compiled a 2.91 earned run average while going 17–11, his best season in the majors. The Dodgers also had John Tudor as their No. 4 starter, a lefty who gave the Mets fits during his days with the Cardinals.

The closing chores were shared by Jay Howell, Alejandro Pena and ex-Met Jesse Orosco, who combined for 42 saves and a 2.16 ERA in 212 innings. But there was a reason why none of them became the team's sole closer.

The standings show the Mets won the NL East by a very comfortable 15 games over the Pirates, but the season was a struggle at times. New York opened the season 32–14 before playing just two games over .500 between May 29 and August 13. However, they were able to push away the surging Pirates by taking three of four from the Bucs in consecutive series during late July and early August.

The pitching was outstanding the entire season, finishing first or second in every category except innings pitched. The biggest surprise was David Cone, who had gone 5–6 with a 3.71 ERA in 1987 after the Mets acquired him from Kansas City. Cone finished third in the Cy Young voting in '88 after going 20–3 with a 2.22 ERA and 213 strikeouts.

Dwight Gooden was an 18-game winner, Ron Darling won a career-high 17 and Bob Ojeda compiled a 2.88 ERA. The bullpen now featured Randy Myers and Roger McDowell after Orosco was jettisoned to the Dodgers following the 1987 season. Myers went 7–3 with 26 saves and a 1.72 ERA while striking out 69 in 68 innings. McDowell picked up 16 saves and compiled a 2.63 ERA.

Darryl Strawberry, Kevin McReynolds, Lenny Dykstra, Mookie Wilson and Wally Backman put up their usual solid numbers, but Howard Johnson regressed after hitting 36 homers and driving in 99 runs in 1987. Gary Carter hit only .242 with 11 homers while playing in pain most of the season. Keith Hernandez tore his hamstring June 23, causing him to miss 37 games. Hernandez hit only .247 with 20 RBIs in 41 games after returning to the lineup.

The Mets' offense received a boost when Gregg Jefferies was called up from Triple A Tidewater in late August. Jefferies batted .397 in his first 17 games, producing at least three hits in six of those contests.

The Mets were loaded heading into the series, although one key piece was missing. Ojeda nearly severed the tip of a finger on his pitching hand in a household accident, leaving him unavailable for the NLCS and putting his career in jeopardy. Ojeda had been a terrific teammate since joining the ballclub in 1986 and gave the Mets depth in the rotation. But with just four starting pitchers needed in the series, the very capable Sid Fernandez would slide in as the No. 4 man. Fernandez again averaged over a strikeout an inning while going 12–10 with a 3.03 ERA.

The Dodgers were supposed to be a speed bump in the Mets' path to a World Series rematch against either the Athletics or Red Sox, who were vying for the AL pennant. The Mets thought they took a major step toward another World Series berth by rallying in the ninth inning against Hershiser and the Dodgers' bullpen in Game 1. LA took Game 2 by roughing up David Cone, but the series-opening victory gave the Mets a chance to clinch the pennant at Shea if they swept their three home games.

Game 3 was a poorly played game that was won by the Mets, giving them a 2–1 lead. New York was three outs away from taking a 3–1 series lead until Mike Scioscia tied Game 4 with a two-run homer before Kirk Gibson's blast won it in extra innings.

New York trailed the series for the first time after the Dodgers put together a convincing victory in Game 5, leaving the Mets' fate in the hands of Cone. But a complete-game victory by Cone set up a seventh game, which only allowed Hershiser to shut out the Mets on five hits in a 6–0 victory.

The much-maligned Dodgers offense hit just .214 with three homers and 30 RBIs the entire series, but the team picked its spots in which to produce. Gibson drove in six runs despite just four hits, delivering the game-winning homer in Game 4 and the deciding three-run blast in Game 5.

Dykstra batted .429 and Jefferies hit .333 while Darryl Strawberry had his finest postseason to date, hitting .300 with a homer and a team-high six RBIs. But Johnson dragged down the Mets' attack by going 1-for-18 with six strikeouts. Carter went 5-for-16 with three RBIs in the first four games, including the game-winning double in the opener. But he went 1-for-11 the rest of the way.

GAME 1, October 4, Los Angeles: Mets 3, Dodgers 2

The Mets were shut out in Game 1 of both the NLCS and World Series in 1986. It looked like more of the same as they stepped to the plate to face Orel Hershiser in the ninth inning with the Dodgers leading 2–0.

Hershiser ended the regular season by throwing 59 consecutive shutout innings, breaking the major league record set by former Dodger Don Drysdale. The scoreless streak included five shutouts and a final game in which he scattered four hits in 10 scoreless innings. He faced the Mets one start before his record streak, pitching a seven-hitter but losing 2–1 on August 24 at Shea.

Hershiser carried a five-hit shutout into the ninth inning of this game, stranding a runner on third twice in the process. Gregg Jefferies led off the ninth with a single and moved to second when Keith Hernandez hit a grounder that was too slow for first baseman Tracy Woodson to start a double play. Darryl Strawberry drove in Jefferies by lining a double to right-center, which also chased Hershiser from the mound.

Jay Howell immediately walked Kevin McReynolds before fanning Howard Johnson for the second out of the inning. It was up to Gary Carter to prolong the game, something he managed to do in Game 6 of the 1986 World Series. Carter delivered again, stroking a two-run double to center to put the Mets ahead 3–2.

Randy Myers stayed in the game for his second inning of work, and the hard-throwing lefty retired the side in order to pick up the victory in his first postseason appearance. Myers entered the game after Gooden gave up two runs and four hits while striking out 10 in seven innings.

Gooden was the pitcher the Mets had in the '86 NLCS, not the struggling hurler who allowed eight earned runs in as many innings during the World Series. But it appeared Gooden would be pinned with a tough loss after Alfredo Griffin hit an RBI single to put the Dodgers ahead 2–0 in the seventh.

Jefferies finished with three hits as he appeared to break out of his two-week slump. The rookie infielder hit .389 in his first 24 games following his August call-up before a season-ending 7-for-37 slide drove his final average down to .321. Jefferies would be the Mets' second-best hitter of the NLCS.

GAME 2, October 5, Los Angeles: Dodgers 6, Mets 3

David Cone has said he would have become a journalist if he hadn't been taken by the Royals in the third round of the 1981 draft. The New York Post gave him a chance to "write" his own column during the NLCS, and he wasted little time putting both feet in his mouth.

He criticized Dodgers reliever Jay Howell and belittled Orel Hershiser's performance after the series opener. Cone questioned Howell's pitching repertoire and wondered how he could possibly throw a curveball to Gary Carter with two outs and two on in the ninth (Carter laced a go-ahead two-run double). Cone also said Hershiser was "lucky" and Dwight Gooden was better in the opener.

Ever the motivator, Dodgers manager Tommy Lasorda used Cone's printed comments to his advantage, firing up a team that managed just four hits in Game 1. It took the Dodgers just two innings to collect five hits off Cone in Game 2, racing out of a 5–0 lead that sent the Mets' right-hander to the showers.

Mike Marshall hit RBI singles in each of the first two innings off Cone, who lasted just 14 batters. The Dodgers already were up 1–0 when they scored four times in the second, highlighted by Mickey Hatcher's two-run double.

Rick Aguilera, Terry Leach and Roger McDowell combined to hold the Dodgers to a pair of hits over six innings, but LA already had more than enough runs to even the series.

The Mets got within 5–2 when Keith Hernandez smacked his first postseason homer since Game 6 of the 1982 World Series, a two-run blast off Tim Belcher in the fourth inning. Hernandez also hit an RBI single with one out in the ninth to chase Belcher.

Jesse Orosco replaced Belcher and quickly surrendered a single to Darryl Strawberry, prompting Lasorda to bring in Alejandro Pena. Pena walked Howard Johnson to load the bases with two outs before Gary Carter ended the game with a fly ball to right.

GAME 3, October 8, New York: Mets 8, Dodgers 4

You would be hard pressed to recall a postseason game that was played any worse. Shea Stadium was completely waterlogged following a rainstorm that caused the game to be pushed back a day. The rain continued during the game, and temperatures stayed in the 40s while the two teams took 3:44 to complete 8-1/2 innings.

The rainout allowed Tommy Lasorda to send Orel Hershiser back to the mound against Ron Darling, who had won the NL East clincher against the Phillies. Darling matched Hershiser's performance, although both pitchers labored through most of the game.

The Dodgers led 3–0 by the third inning, thanks to Mike Scioscia's RBI single and a pair of run-scoring grounders. Darling helped the Dodgers' cause by issuing back-to-back walks to open a two-run second.

The Mets began to chip away when Hershiser struck out Mookie Wilson on a wild pitch that allowed Wilson to reach first base. Gregg Jefferies singled Wilson to second before Darryl Strawberry hit a double to right that scored Mookie.

The poor field conditions began to truly impact the game in the bottom of the sixth with the Dodgers ahead 3–1. Keith Hernandez led off with a single before Strawberry hit a single that was bobbled by left fielder Kirk Gibson. Hernandez tried to move over to third base, but the muddy infield caused him to lose his footing before he reached the bag, making him the first out of the inning.

Third baseman Jeff Hamilton then committed the Dodgers' second error of the inning, making a wild throw on Kevin McReynolds' grounder. Howard Johnson made the second out of the inning before Gary Carter and Wally Backman delivered consecutive RBI singles to knot the score.

Roger McDowell retired his first five hitters after replacing Darling to start the seventh. But McDowell suddenly lost his control after opening the eighth with back-to-back strikeouts. Scioscia and Hamilton singled before McDowell walked Mike Davis and Mike Sharperson to force in the go-ahead run.

Jay Howell relieved Hershiser to start the eighth inning, but he was out of the game after five pitches. Manager Davey Johnson and several Mets felt Howell had been doctoring the ball during the series. First base coach Bill Robinson watched as Howell continued to grab at the strings of his glove. Robinson relayed his information to Johnson, who called time and asked plate umpire Joe West to inspect Howell's glove. Howell was ejected from the game when West found pine tar on the mitt, allowing the Mets to feast on the rest of the Dodgers' bullpen.

Alejandro Pena completed Howell's walk of McReynolds before Howard Johnson laid down another failed sacrifice bunt (see Game 6, 1986 World Series). McReynolds was nailed at second on the bunt, but Johnson made up for the gaffe by stealing second before scoring on Wally Backman's game-tying double with two outs. Dykstra prolonged the inning with a walk before Jesse Orosco entered the game.

Mookie Wilson greeted his ex-teammate by hitting the go-ahead single before Jefferies was hit by a pitch to load the bases. Hernandez made it 6–4 by working out a bases-loaded walk that ended Orosco's afternoon.

Strawberry capped the five-run eighth with a bloop single that scored Wilson and Elster, giving the Mets their largest postseason lead since Game 4 of the 1986 World Series.

David Cone worked the ninth to close out a sloppy victory that gave the Mets a 2–1 lead.

GAME 4, October 9, New York: Dodgers 5, Mets 4 (12 innings)

By now the Mets had played 36 playoff games in their history without ever blowing a lead in the ninth inning of a loss. The only time they had coughed up a lead in the ninth was Game 4 of the 1969 World Series, which they eventually won 2–1 in 10 innings. They had earned 10 of their 23 postseason victories by scoring the winning run in their final at-bat. This time the tables were turned.

Dwight Gooden was in complete control heading into the ninth inning with a 4–2 lead. He had given up just one hit since John Shelby delivered a two-run single in the top of the first, but his pitch count was around 120 as he opened the ninth.

An overly critical/knee-jerk observer could say manager Davey Johnson should have replaced Gooden with lefty closer Randy Myers with Shelby and Mike Scioscia due up as the first two hitters. The switch-hitting Shelby already had two hits against Gooden and batted just .238 against lefties during the regular season. The lefty-hitting Mike Scioscia hit .244 with no homers versus lefties in 1988. But these Dodgers weren't exactly Murderer's Row, and Dwight Gooden was, well, Dwight Gooden.

Gooden pitched carefully to Shelby before walking him on four pitches, which made Scioscia the potential tying run at the plate. Scioscia had been 3-for-17 with no homers and 1 RBI against Gooden in 1988, including a 1-for-3 mark in Game 1. Catcher Gary Carter looked for Gooden to get ahead in the count immediately.

"I knew (Scioscia) was notorious for liking to take the first pitch. We always knew when he was taking and you could just lay it in there, and he wasn't going to swing. All I was thinking about was trying to get ahead of him. With the first pitch, we were trying to hit the outside corner, not trying to throw one right down the middle."[12]

Gooden caught too much of the plate and Scioscia uncharacteristically pounced, sending the pitch over the wall in right-center to tie the game 4–4. The game went into extra innings after the Mets were three outs away from taking a 3–1 lead in the series.

Myers worked a perfect 10th and made a nice throw to second on a bunt attempt to quell a Dodger rally in the 11th. The Mets put runners on first and second in the bottom of the 11th before Howard Johnson popped up to third to end the inning. Johnson would have won the game with his first career postseason RBI. Instead, he ended his career without ever driving in a run in the playoffs or World Series.

Roger McDowell quickly got two outs after relieving Myers to start the 12th. Up stepped Kirk Gibson, who untied the game with the first of his memorable homers in the 1988 postseason.

The Mets now trailed 5–4 in the bottom of the 12th but were facing an ex-Met, just as they had in Game 6 of the 1986 World Series. Tim Leary opened the inning by surrendering singles to Mackey Sasser and pinch-hitter Lee Mazzilli to put runners on first and second with nobody out. Leary left after getting Gregg Jefferies to pop out.

In came another former Met as Dodgers manager Tommy Lasorda called on Jesse Orosco to finish the game. Orosco promptly walked Keith Hernandez to load the bases before going 3–0 to Darryl Strawberry. Out came Lasorda, who was rather animated while telling Orosco to throw a friggin' strike. Strawberry got under a pitch and popped up to second, getting Orosco off the hook.

Lasorda made one final trip to the mound, this time to bring in Orel Hershiser, the Dodgers' ace who had pitched seven innings the previous day. His job was to retire Kevin McReynolds, who had crushed a tiebreaking solo homer in the fourth.

McReynolds almost won it with a blooper to center, which would have made him an untouchable "Met-for-Life" in the eyes of the Shea faithful. But Shelby made a shoestring catch to preserve the Dodgers' victory, tying the series at two games apiece.

Scioscia's homer wrecked what would have been the Mets' third comeback win of the series. The Dodgers led 2–0 until Darryl Strawberry and McReynolds ripped back-to-back homers to put the Mets ahead 3–2 in the fourth. McReynolds also scored an insurance run on Carter's sixth-inning triple before the law of averages finally caught up with the Mets.

GAME 5, October 10, New York: Dodgers 7, Mets 4

The Mets had hoped to bounce back following their agonizing loss in Game 4. The team headed into the game with a 10–2 lifetime record in postseason games following a loss, dropping only Game 7 of the 1973 World Series and Game 2 of the 1986 World Series. History was on their side. Kirk Gibson, Rick Dempsey and Tim Belcher were not.

Sid Fernandez, making his first postseason start since Game 4 of the 1986 NLCS, limited the Dodgers to one hit over the first three innings of his first outing in nine days. Less than two innings later, the Mets were staring at a six-run deficit after Gibson crushed a three-run homer with nobody out, ending Fernandez's day.

Fernandez had retired Gibson leading off the fourth before giving up a single and a walk. Dempsey followed with a two-run double before scoring on Alfredo Griffin's two-bagger.

Gibson's second homer of the series gave Belcher a 6–0 lead in the fifth. The Mets were hitting Belcher pretty hard but had only one single to show for it.

Howard Johnson poked a one-out single in the fifth, his only hit of the series. Wally Backman singled one batter later before Lenny Dykstra slammed a three-run homer to cut the Dodgers' lead in half.

Dykstra also doubled and scored on Gregg Jefferies' single in the eighth to make it 6–4, which led Dodgers manager Tommy Lasorda to dip into his bullpen. Ricky Horton fanned Keith Hernandez but gave up a single to Darryl Strawberry to put runners on first and second. Kevin McReynolds hit a grounder to the left side of the infield off Brian Holton, but the ball hit Jefferies as he was running to third, keeping runners on first and second with two outs. Holton retired Gary Carter on a fly ball to end the Mets' last threat of the game.

Mike Marshall added an RBI triple in the ninth to cap the scoring. The Mets went quietly against Holton in the ninth before hopping on a plane to Los Angeles trailing the series three games to two.

The unheralded Holton, who had three saves in 109 relief appearances before the game, had helped the Dodgers take control of the series by getting the final five outs. Maybe the Dodgers were a team of destiny.

GAME 6, October 11, Los Angeles: Mets 5, Dodgers 1

Kevin McReynolds hauled a .150 average into this game while David Cone hauled the memory of his terrible performance in Game 2. Both players had a major hand in forcing a Game 7.

Cone was fantastic in becoming the first Mets pitcher to throw a complete game in the postseason since Bob Ojeda in Game 2 of the 1986 NLCS. Tom Seaver was the previous Mets right-hander to go the distance in a playoff game, doing it in a Game 1 loss at Cincinnati in 1973.

But Cone looked very shaky at the start, sandwiching a wild pitch around two walks to put runners on first and second with Kirk Gibson strolling to the plate with nobody out in the first. Cone settled down after grabbing Gibson's bunt-popup for the first out, getting Mike Marshall to fly to left before striking out John Shelby for the final out of the inning.

Cone gave up just one hit over the next four innings before finally allowing a run in the fifth, but the Mets already had a 4–0 lead entering the inning.

First baseman Mickey Hatcher's error allowed Lenny Dykstra to get on base leading off the game. Wally Backman singled Dykstra to third and McReynolds hit a sacrifice fly that put the Mets ahead to stay. Kevin Elster's double made it 2–0 in the third before McReynolds ripped a two-run homer for a 4–0 lead in the top of the fifth.

Cone retired the first two batters in the bottom of the fifth before giving up a single to reliever Brian Holton and a walk to Steve Sax. Hatcher's RBI single got the Dodgers within three runs before Keith Hernandez laced an RBI single in the top of the sixth to restore the Mets' four-run cushion.

Cone retired 12 straight batters following Hatcher's run-scoring hit. But Mike Scioscia and Jeff Hamilton kept the game going with two-out singles in the bottom of the ninth before Mike Davis flied out to end the game.

The great news was that the Mets had stretched the series to the limit. The bad news was that they would have to face Orel Hershiser once again.

GAME 7, October 12, Los Angeles: Dodgers 6, Mets 0

Ron Darling already had picked up a victory in the Mets' division clincher less than a month earlier, tossing a six-hitter in a 3–1 win over the Phillies. A Game 7 certainly holds more weight, but Darling had pitched in tough situations before. Besides, Dwight Gooden could give the Mets 3 to 5 innings on two days rest if Darling faltered.

Darling lasted just 10 batters, and by the time Gooden came to the rescue, the Dodgers had a 4–0 lead with nobody out in the second inning. It was 6–0 after Gooden faced his first four batters, which was more than enough offense for Orel Hershiser on this night.

Hershiser opened with a scoreless first after working out of a two-on, two-out jam. Darling began his night by allowing a single and a double before Kirk Gibson hit a sacrifice fly to produce the only run the Dodgers would really need.

Darling failed to retire any of the five batters he faced in the second, allowing three straight singles before Mike Scioscia scored on Gregg Jefferies' error at third. Steve Sax followed with a two-run single that put the Dodgers ahead 4–0 and sent Darling to the showers. LA tacked on two more runs on second baseman Wally Backman's throwing error and John Shelby's sacrifice fly.

Dodgers manager Tommy Lasorda was so confident in the outcome that he took out Gibson to start the top of the fourth. Gibson was battling knee and hamstring problems that would limit him to one at-bat in the World Series, albeit the biggest at-bat of the entire season.

The Mets managed one hit in each of the first four innings against Hershiser. They would get one more hit the rest of the way, ending the series when pinch-hitter Howard Johnson struck out looking.

Game 1, October 4 at LA
METS 3, DODGERS 2

Mets	AB	R	H	BI	Dodgers	AB	R	H	BI
Wilson cf	4	0	1	0	Sax 2b	3	1	1	0
Myers p	0	0	0	0	Stubbs 1b	3	0	0	0
Jefferies 3b	4	1	3	0	Woodson ph-1b	1	0	0	0
Hernandez 1b	4	0	1	0	Gibson lf	4	0	0	0
Strawberry rf	4	1	1	1	Howell p	0	0	0	0
McReynolds lf	3	1	0	0	Marshall rf	4	0	1	1
Johnson ss	4	0	0	0	Shelby cf	4	0	0	0
Elster ss	0	0	0	0	Scioscia c	3	1	1	0
Carter c	4	0	2	2	Dempsey ph	1	0	0	0
Backman 2b	3	0	0	0	Hamilton 3b	3	0	0	0
Gooden p	2	0	0	0	Griffin ss	3	0	1	1
Dykstra ph-cf	0	0	0	0	Hershiser p	2	0	0	0
					Gonzalez lf	0	0	0	0
Totals	32	3	8	3		31	2	4	2

Mets	000	000	003	3	8	1
Dodgers	100	000	100	2	4	0

METS	IP	H	R	ER	BB	SO
Gooden	7	4	2	2	1	10
Myers (W, 1–0)	2	0	0	0	0	0
Total	9	4	2	2	1	10

DODGERS	IP	H	R	ER	BB	SO
Hershiser	8-1/3	7	2	2	1	6
Howell (L, 0–1)	2/3	1	1	1	1	1
Total	9	8	3	3	2	7

LOB—Mets 5, Dodgers 4; E—Backman (1); DP—Mets 0, Dodgers 2—2B—Strawberry (1), Carter (1), Scioscia (1); HBP—Sax; SH—Backman; SB—Steve Sax; Time—2:45; ATT—55,582.

Game 2, October 5 at LA
DODGERS 6, METS 3

Mets	AB	R	H	BI	Dodgers	AB	R	H	BI
Dykstra cf	3	1	1	0	Sax 2b	5	1	1	1
Jefferies 3b	3	1	1	0	Hatcher 1b	3	2	1	2
Hernandez 1b	3	1	2	3	Gibson lf	2	0	0	0
Strawberry rf	4	0	2	0	Marshall rf	4	1	3	2
McReynolds lf	4	0	0	0	Shelby cf	4	0	0	0
Johnson ss	3	0	0	0	Scioscia c	4	0	1	0
Carter c	4	0	0	0	Hamilton 3b	1	1	0	0
Backman 2b	3	0	0	0	Griffin ss	4	0	0	1
Cone p	0	0	0	0	Belcher p	4	1	1	0
Sasser ph	1	0	0	0	Orosco p	0	0	0	0
Aguilera p	1	0	0	0	Peña p	0	0	0	0
Leach p	0	0	0	0					
Wilson ph	1	0	0	0					
McDowell p	0	0	0	0					
Totals	30	3	6	3		31	6	7	6

Mets	000	200	001	3	6	0
Dodgers	140	010	00x	6	7	0

METS	IP	H	R	ER	BB	SO
Cone (L, 0–1)	2	5	5	5	2	2
Aguilera	3	2	1	1	2	0
Leach	2	0	0	0	1	2
McDowell	1	0	0	0	0	1
Total	8	7	6	6	5	5

DODGERS	IP	H	R	ER	BB	SO
Belcher (W, 1–0)	8-1/3	5	3	3	3	10
Orosco	0	1	0	0	0	0
Peña (S, 1)	2/3	0	0	0	1	0
Total	9	6	3	3	3	10

LOB—Mets 4, Dodgers 7; DP—Mets 0, Dodgers 2; 2B—Dykstra (1), Jefferies (1), Hatcher; HR—Hernandez (1); HBP—Hamilton; SB—Gibson (1); CS—Strawberry (1); Time—3:10; ATT—55.780.

Game 3, October 8 at New York
METS 8, DODGERS 4

Dodgers	AB	R	H	BI	Mets	AB	R	H	BI
Sax 2b	5	1	1	0	Wilson cf	4	2	1	1
Hatcher 1b	4	0	1	0	Cone p	0	0	0	0
Woodson 1b	1	0	0	0	Jefferies 3b	3	0	1	0
Gibson lf	5	0	1	1	Elster pr-ss	0	1	0	0
Marshall rf	4	1	0	0	Hernandez 1b	2	0	1	1
Shelby cf	2	1	1	0	Strawberry rf	5	1	3	3
Scioscia c	4	0	2	0	McReynolds lf	4	0	0	0
Gonzalez ph	0	1	0	0	Johnson ss-3b	4	2	0	0
Dempsey c	0	0	0	0	Carter c	4	0	1	1
Hamilton 3b	3	0	1	1	Backman 2b	4	1	2	2
Griffin ss	3	0	0	0	Darling p	2	0	0	0
Davis ph	0	0	0	0	Magadan ph	1	0	0	0
Howell p	0	0	0	0	McDowell p	0	0	0	0
Peña p	0	0	0	0	Myers p	0	0	0	0
Orosco p	0	0	0	0	Dykstra ph-cf	0	1	0	0
Horton p	0	0	0	0					
Hershiser p	3	0	0	0					
Heep ph	0	0	0	0					
Sharperson ph-ss	0	0	0	1					
Totals	34	4	7	3		33	8	9	8

Dodgers	021	000	010	4	7	2
Mets	001	002	05x	8	9	2

DODGERS	IP	H	R	ER	BB	SO
Hershiser	7	6	3	1	4	4
Howell	0	0	1	1	1	0
Peña (L, 0–1)	2/3	1	2	2	1	0
Orosco	0	1	2	2	1	0
Horton	1/3	1	0	0	0	0
Total	8	9	8	6	7	4

METS	IP	H	R	ER	BB	SO
Darling	6	5	3	2	4	5
McDowell	1-2/3	2	1	1	1	3
Myers (W, 2–0)	1/3	0	0	0	1	0
Cone	1	0	0	0	0	1
Total	9	7	4	3	6	9

LOB—Dodgers 9, Mets; E—Hernandez (1), McDowell (1), Hamilton (1), Gibson (1); DP—Dodgers 1, Mets 0; WP—Hershiser; 2B—Backman (1), Strawberry (2); IBB—Hernandez; HBP—Jefferies; SB—Johnson (1), Sax (2), Shelby (1); Time—3:44; ATT—44,672.

Game 4, October 9 at New York
DODGERS 5, METS 4 (12)

Dodgers	AB	R	H	BI	Mets	AB	R	H	BI
Sax 2b	5	1	1	0	Wilson cf	4	0	0	0
Hatcher 1b	4	1	0	0	McDowell p	0	0	0	0
Peña p	0	0	0	0	Mazzilli ph	1	0	1	0
Stubbs ph	1	0	0	0	Jefferies 3b	5	0	0	0
Leary p	0	0	0	0	Hernandez 1b	5	1	2	0
Orosco p	0	0	0	0	Strawberry rf	6	1	1	2
Hershiser p	0	0	0	0	McReynolds lf	5	2	2	1
Gibson lf	6	1	1	1	Carter c	4	0	2	1
Marshall rf	5	0	0	0	Myers p	0	0	0	0
Shelby cf	4	1	2	2	Dykstra cf	1	0	0	0
Scioscia c	4	1	1	2	Teufel 2b	3	0	0	0
Dempsey ph-c	0	0	0	0	Backman 2b	1	0	0	0
Hamilton 3b	4	0	0	0	Elster ss	2	0	0	0
Sharperson ph-3b	1	0	0	0	Johnson ph-ss	2	0	0	0
Griffin ss	4	0	1	0	Gooden p	3	0	1	0
Tudor p	2	0	0	0	Sasser c	2	0	1	0
Holton p	0	0	0	0	Darling pr	0	0	0	0
Heep ph	0	0	0	0					
Horton p	0	0	0	0					
Davis p	0	0	0	0					
Woodson ph-1b	2	0	1	0					
Totals	42	5	7	5		44	4	10	4

Dodgers	200	000	002	001	5	7	1
Mets	000	301	000	000	4	10	2

DODGERS	IP	H	R	ER	BB	SO
Tudor	5	8	4	4	1	1
Holton	1	0	0	0	1	1
Horton	2	0	0	0	0	1
Peña (W, 1–1)	3	0	0	0	3	1
Leary	1/3	2	0	0	0	0
Orosco	1/3	0	0	0	1	0
Hershiser (S, 1)	1/3	0	0	0	0	0
Total	12	10	4	4	6	4

METS	IP	H	R	ER	BB	SO
Gooden	8	5	4	4	5	9
Myers	2-1/3	1	0	0	1	0
McDowell (L, 0–1)	1-1/3	1	1	1	0	1
Total	12	7	5	5	6	10

LOB—Dodgers 8, Mets 10; E—Elster 2 (2), Hatcher; DP—Dodgers 1, Mets 1; WP—Gooden 2; 2B—McReynolds (1); 3B—Carter (1); HR—Strawberry (1), McReynolds (1), Scioscia (1), Gibson (1); SH—Griffin; SB—McReynolds (1), Sax 3 (5), Shelby (2); CS—Wilson (1); Time—4:29; ATT—54,014.

Game 5, October 10 at New York
DODGERS 7, METS 4

Dodgers	AB	R	H	BI	Mets	AB	R	H	BI
Sax 2b	5	1	1	0	Dykstra cf	3	2	2	3
Hatcher 1b	3	1	1	0	Jefferies 3b	4	0	2	1
Stubbs ph-1b	2	0	0	0	Hernandez 1b	4	0	0	0
Gibson lf	5	1	2	3	Strawberry rf	4	0	1	0
Gonzalez pr-lf	0	1	0	0	McReynolds lf	4	0	1	0
Marshall rf	5	1	3	1	Carter c	4	0	1	0
Shelby cf	3	1	1	0	Johnson ss	4	1	1	0
Dempsey c	4	1	2	2	Backman 2b	4	1	1	0
Davis ph	1	0	0	0	Fernandez p	1	0	0	0
Scioscia c	0	0	0	0	Leach p	0	0	0	0
Hamilton 3b	4	0	1	0	Magadan ph	1	0	0	0
Griffin ss	4	0	1	1	Aguilera p	0	0	0	0
Belcher p	4	0	0	0	Sasser ph	1	0	0	0
Horton p	0	0	0	0	McDowell p	0	0	0	0
Holton p	0	0	0	0	Mazzilli ph	1	0	0	0
Totals	40	7	12	7		35	4	9	4

Dodgers	000	330	001	7	12	0
Mets	000	030	010	4	9	1

DODGERS	IP	H	R	ER	BB	SO
Belcher (W, 1-0)	7	7	4	4	1	6
Horton	1/3	1	0	0	0	1
Holton (S, 1)	1-2/3	1	0	0	0	1
Total	9	9	4	4	1	8

METS	IP	H	R	ER	BB	SO
Fernandez (L, 0-1)	4	7	6	6	1	5
Leach	1	1	0	0	0	1
Aguilera	2	1	0	0	0	3
McDowell	2	3	1	1	1	0
Total	9	12	7	7	2	9

LOB—Dodgers 8, Mets 5; E—Johnson (1); 2B—Dykstra (2), Dempsey 2 (2), Marshall (1), Griffin (1); 3B—Marshall (1); HR—Dykstra (1), Gibson (2); SB—Gibson (2); Time—3:07; ATT—52.069.

Game 6, October 11 at LA
METS 5, DODGERS 1

Mets	AB	R	H	BI	Dodgers	AB	R	H	BI
Dykstra cf	4	2	2	0	Sax 2b	2	0	0	0
Backman 2b	4	0	2	0	Hatcher 1b	3	0	1	1
Hernandez 1b	5	0	1	1	Gibson lf	4	0	0	0
Strawberry rf	3	2	1	0	Gonzalez lf	0	0	0	0
McReynolds lf	4	1	4	3	Marshall rf	4	0	0	0
Jefferies 3b	4	0	0	0	Shelby cf	4	0	0	0
Carter c	4	0	0	0	Scioscia c	4	0	1	0
Elster ss	3	0	1	1	Hamilton 3b	4	0	2	0
Cone p	4	0	0	0	Griffin ss	3	0	0	0
					Davis ph	1	0	0	0
					Leary p	1	0	0	0
					Holton p	1	1	1	0
					Horton p	0	0	0	0
					Heep ph	1	0	0	0
					Orosco p	0	0	0	0
Totals	35	5	11	5		32	1	5	1

Mets	101	021	000	5	11	0
Dodgers	000	010	000	1	5	2

METS	IP	H	R	ER	BB	SO
Cone (W, 1-1)	9	5	1	1	3	6

DODGERS	IP	H	R	ER	BB	SO
Tim Leary (L, 1-1)	4	6	4	3	3	3
Brian Holton	1-1/3	1	1	1	0	0
Ricky Horton	1-2/3	2	0	0	2	1
Jesse Orosco	2	2	0	0	1	0
Total	9	11	5	4	6	4

LOB—Mets 13, Dodgers 7; E—Hamilton (2), Hatcher (2); DP—Mets 0, Dodgers 2; PB—Scioscia; WP—Cone; 2B—Dykstra (3), Elster (1), McReynolds (2); HR—McReynolds (2); IBB—Elster; HBP—Dykstra; SH—Backman, Cone; SF—McReynolds; SB—Backman (1), Hernandez (1), McReynolds (2); Time—3:16; ATT—55,885.

Game 7, October 12 at LA
DODGERS 6, METS 0

Mets	AB	R	H	BI	Dodgers	AB	R	H	BI
Dykstra cf	3	0	1	0	Sax 2b	5	2	3	2
Backman 2b	3	0	1	0	Hatcher 1b-lf	4	0	1	0
Hernandez 1b	3	0	0	0	Gonzalez lf	0	0	0	0
Strawberry rf	4	0	0	0	Gibson lf	0	0	0	1
McReynolds lf	4	0	0	0	Stubbs 1b	2	0	2	0
Jefferies 3b	4	0	2	0	Marshall rf	4	0	0	1
Carter c	3	0	0	0	Shelby cf	3	0	0	1
Aguilera p	0	0	0	0	Scioscia c	3	1	2	0
Mazzilli ph	0	0	0	0	Hamilton 3b	4	1	1	0
Elster ss	3	0	1	0	Hershiser p	4	1	0	1
Johnson ph	1	0	0	0					
Darling p	1	0	0	0					
Gooden p	0	0	0	0					
Magadan ph	1	0	0	0					
Leach p	0	0	0	0					
Sasser c	1	0	0	0					
Totals	31	0	5	0		33	6	10	6

Mets	000	000	000	0	5	2	
Dodgers	150	000	00x	6	10	0	

METS	IP	H	R	ER	BB	SO
Darling (L, 0–1)	1	6	6	4	0	2
Gooden	3	1	0	0	2	1
Leach	2	3	0	0	0	1
Aguilera	2	0	0	0	0	1
Total	8	10	6	4	2	5

DODGERS	IP	H	R	ER	BB	SO
Hershiser (W, 1–0)	9	5	0	0	2	5

LOB—Mets 8, Dodgers 7; E—Backman (2), Jefferies—DP—Mets1, Dodgers 1; WP—Hershiser; 2B—Jefferies (2), Hatcher; HBP—Mazzilli, Dykstra; SF—Shelby, Gibson; SB—Mazzilli (1); Time—2:51; ATT—55,693.

1988 NLCS Statistics

COMPOSITE LINESCORE

Mets	102	554	064	000	27	58	8
Dodgers	5(11)1	350	113	001	31	52	5

METS BATTING

Player	BA	G	AB	R	H
Rick Aguilera	.000	3	1	0	0
Wally Backman	.273	7	22	2	6
Gary Carter	.222	7	27	0	6
David Cone	.000	3	4	0	0
Ron Darling	.000	3	3	0	0
Lenny Dykstra	.429	7	14	6	6
Kevin Elster	.250	5	8	1	2
Sid Fernandez	.000	1	1	0	0
Dwight Gooden	.200	3	5	0	1
Keith Hernandez	.269	7	26	2	7
Gregg Jefferies	.333	7	27	2	9
Howard Johnson	.056	6	18	3	1
Terry Leach	—	3	0	0	0
Dave Magadan	.000	3	3	0	0
Lee Mazzilli	.500	3	2	0	1
Roger McDowell	—	4	0	0	0
Kevin McReynolds	.250	7	28	4	7
Randy Myers	—	3	0	0	0
Mackey Sasser	.200	4	5	0	1
Darryl Strawberry	.300	7	30	5	9
Tim Teufel	.000	1	3	0	0
Mookie Wilson	.154	4	13	2	2
Total	.242	7	240	27	58

2B—Dykstra 3, Jefferies 2, McReynolds 2, Strawberry 2, Backman ,Carter, Elster; 3B—Carter; HR—McReynolds 2, Dykstra, Hernandez, Strawberry; RBI—Strawberry 6, Hernandez 5, Carter 4, McReynolds 4, Dykstra 3, Backman 2, Elster, Jefferies, Wilson; SB—McReynolds 2, Backman, Hernandez, Johnson, Mazzilli.

DODGERS BATTING

Player	BA	G	AB	R	H
Tim Belcher	.125	2	8	1	1
Mike Davis	.000	4	2	0	0
Rick Dempsey	.400	4	5	1	2
Kirk Gibson	.154	7	26	2	4
Jose Gonzalez	—	5	0	2	0
Alfredo Griffin	.160	7	25	1	4
Jeff Hamilton	.217	7	23	2	5
Mickey Hatcher	.238	6	21	4	5
Danny Heep	.000	3	1	0	0
Orel Hershiser	.000	4	9	1	0
Brian Holton	1.000	3	1	1	1
Ricky Horton	—	4	0	0	0
Jay Howell	—	2	0	0	0
Tim Leary	—	2	1	0	0
Mike Marshall	.233	7	30	3	7
Jesse Orosco	—	4	0	0	0
Alejandro Pena	—	3	0	0	0
Steve Sax	.267	7	30	7	8
Mike Scioscia	.364	7	22	3	8
Mike Sharperson	.000	2	1	0	0
John Shelby	.167	7	24	3	4
Franklin Stubbs	.250	4	8	0	2
John Tudor	.000	1	2	0	0
Tracy Woodson	.250	3	4	0	1
Total	.214	7	243	31	52

2B—Dempsey 2, Hatcher 2, Griffin, Marshall, Scioscia; 3B—Marshall; HR—Gibson 2, Scioscia; RBI—Gibson 6, Marshall 5, Griffin 3, Hatcher 3, Sax 3, Shelby 3, Dempsey 2, Scioscia 2, Hamilton, Hershiser, Sharperson; SB—Sax 5, Gibson 2, Shelby 2.

METS PITCHING

Player	G	ERA	W–L	SV	IP	H	ER	BB	SO
Rick Aguilera	3	1.29	0–0	0	7	3	1	2	4
David Cone	3	4.50	1–1	0	12	10	6	5	9
Ron Darling	2	7.71	0–1	0	7	11	6	4	7
Sid Fernandez	1	13.50	0–1	0	4	7	6	1	5
Dwight Gooden	3	2.95	0–0	0	18-1/3	10	6	8	20
Terry Leach	3	0.00	0–0	0	5	4	0	1	4
Rog. McDowell	4	4.50	0–1	0	6	6	3	2	5
Randy Myers	3	0.00	2–0	0	4-2/3	1	0	2	0
Total	7	3.94	3–4	0	64	52	28	25	54

DODGERSPITCHING

Player	G	ERA	W–L	SV	IP	H	ER	BB	SO
Tim Belcher	2	4.11	2–0	0	15-1/3	12	7	4	16
Orel Hershiser	4	1.09	1–0	1	24-2/3	18	3	7	15
Brian Holton	3	2.25	0–0	1	4	2	1	1	2
Ricky Horton	4	0.00	0–0	0	4-1/3	4	0	2	3
Jay Howell	2	27.00	0–1	0	2/3	1	2	2	1
Tim Leary	2	6.23	0–1	0	4-1/3	8	3	3	3
Jesse Orosco	4	7.71	0–0	0	2-1/3	4	2	3	0
Alejandro Pena	3	4.15	1–1	1	4-1/3	1	2	5	1
John Tudor	1	7.20	0–0	0	5	8	4	1	1
Total	7	3.32	4–3	3	65	58	24	28	42

1999 NLDS: Mets vs. Arizona Diamondbacks

METS WIN SERIES 3–1

The Mets were more than prepared for postseason pressure despite an 11-year absence in the playoffs. Trailing the NL wild card by two games with three to play, the Mets swept the Pirates in a season-ending three-game series to force a winner-take-all game at Cincinnati for a playoff berth. The Mets jumped out to an early lead against the Reds before Al Leiter completed a gem that put the team in the NLDS.

The Mets now faced the how-the-hell-did-they-make-the-playoffs-in-just-two-seasons Arizona Diamondbacks, who won the NL West with 100 victories after going 65–97 in their first year of existence.

The Diamondbacks went 7–2 against the Mets in the regular season, averaging more than eight runs in the seven victories. Arizona swept a three-game set at Shea, outscoring the Mets 20–9 while triggering an eight-game losing streak for New York. Former Met Armando Reynoso and Omar Daal each beat New York twice during the season.

The D'Backs became almost instant contenders by acquiring a few high-priced veterans who still had a few productive years left in them. Starters Matt Williams and Jay Bell were holdovers from the 1998 team, as were Damian Miller and Travis Lee. Steve Finley, Luis Gonzalez and Tony Womack were added in the winter of 1999 before rookie Erubial Durazo was recalled in late July to provide a spark down the stretch.

Arizona's biggest free-agent pickup before the 1999 season was Randy Johnson, who had won 39 games and struck out 620 over the past two years. The Big Unit fanned 364 in just 271⅔ innings for the '99 Diamondbacks, anchoring a rotation that was competent up top but not very deep. A solid bullpen helped Arizona finish second in the league with a 3.77 ERA despite playing in hitter-friendly Bank One Ballpark.

The Mets didn't have a single starting pitcher with more than 13 wins or an ERA under 4.00. Al Leiter was the best of the lot, going 13–12 with a 4.23 ERA, one year after posting a 17–6 mark and a 2.47 earned run average. Orel

Hershiser was a valuable addition after being released by the Indians in spring training. The 40-year-old Hershiser also won 13 games and was second on the staff in innings pitched.

The Mets' 1999 infield is considered one of the greatest collection of gloves ever assembled. Shortstop Rey Ordonez made just four errors while Edgardo Alfonzo accounted for only five at second base. John Olerud and Robin Ventura each had only nine miscues as the starting quartet combined to average just one error every six games.

It also didn't hurt that the infield could hit a bit. Olerud, Alfonzo and Ventura combined for 78 of the Mets' 181 homers and drove in 314 runs. Ordonez finished fifth on the team with 60 RBIs while hitting out of the eighth spot in the lineup. Olerud set a team record with 125 walks, which accounted for his .427 on-base percentage.

The offense centered around catcher Mike Piazza, who was terrific in his first full season with the team. Piazza belted 40 homers with 124 homers while batting .303.

The Diamondbacks also had to contend with the Mets' speed. Roger Cedeno hit .313 with a team-record 66 stolen bases, and Rickey Henderson batted .315 with 37 swipes.

The two teams looked pretty even offensively, and the Mets faced the prospect of batting against Johnson twice in the series. But New York was able to hit Johnson and muzzle the Arizona batters, two keys to the series.

Alfonzo accounted for nine of the Mets' 22 runs despite hitting only .250. Alfonzo homered twice and had five RBIs in his first career postseason game. Rickey Henderson batted .400 with five runs and six stolen bases while continuing to put pressure on the Diamondbacks' staff.

But it took a backup catcher to get the Mets into the NLCS. Todd Pratt started the last two games due to Mike Piazza's sore thumb, leaving New York without its top offensive weapon. Pratt went 0-for-7 before ending the series with a solo blast to dead-center off Matt Mantei, making him only the fourth person in major league history to end a series with a home run.

GAME 1, October 5, Phoenix: Mets 8, Diamondbacks 4

Edgardo Alfonzo was one of the most important players on the Mets' road to respectability, and the team's longest-tenured starting infielder. It only seemed fair he was the one to make the biggest impact in the Mets' first postseason game since 1988.

Alfonzo joined exclusive company by becoming the third player in National League history to homer in his

first postseason at-bat, going deep with one out in the opening inning against Randy Johnson to get the Mets off to a good start. Alfonzo's second homer of the night would be the game-winner.

The first-inning blast helped the Mets build a 4–1 lead. John Olerud made it 3–0 with a two-run homer in the third before Rey Ordonez laid down a suicide squeeze an inning later, scoring Robin Ventura to put the Mets ahead 4–1.

The Mets had no days off heading into the game, which meant No. 5 starter Masato Yoshii had to pitch the opener after manager Bobby Valentine used his top four pitchers to keep the team in the wild-card race. Yoshii pitched admirably over the first five innings, allowing two runs and four hits while keeping the Mets in front. He retired five straight batters after Erubiel Durazo belted a solo shot with one out in the fourth to get the Diamondbacks within 4–2. Valentine tried to squeeze another inning out of his starter, but Yoshii was lifted one batter after Luis Gonzalez tied the game with a two-run homer.

Dennis Cook, Turk Wendell and Armando Benitez were outstanding in relief, facing the minimum 11 batters and allowing just one hit. They gave the Mets just enough time to stage a ninth-inning rally that would give them an edge in the series.

Johnson was looking very strong heading into the ninth. The Big Unit struck out the last two batters in the top of the eighth and hadn't allowed a hit since the fourth. But Johnson was gone after giving up two hits and a walk to load the bases with one out.

Reliever Bobby Chouinard got Rickey Henderson to hit a grounder that third baseman Matt Williams threw to the plate for the second out. Up stepped Alfonzo, who gave the Mets an 8–4 lead while becoming the first player in major league history to hit a grand slam in his first post-season game. The first grand slam in Mets playoffs history gave Alfonzo five RBIs, tying Rusty Staub's team mark set in Game 4 of the 1973 World Series.

Benitez tossed a perfect ninth to close out the victory, allowing the Mets to wrestle home-field advantage from the Diamondbacks. It also marked only the third time in eight playoff series the Mets had taken a series opener in the postseason.

GAME 2, October 6, Phoenix: Diamondbacks 7, Mets 1

Kenny Rogers hadn't been known as a "money" pitcher before he got to the Mets, giving up 11 earned runs in seven innings over four playoff appearances, including three starts. His entire postseason experience had come with the 1996 Yankees, pitching past the third inning in just one of his three starts.

But Rogers had pitched exceptionally well for the Mets after being acquired from the A's in late July. When the Mets were on the brink of elimination, the lefty struck out 10 while giving up two runs and five hits in seven-plus innings against the Pirates to help New York stay in the race. It seemed at the time that any problems Rogers had about pitching for a New York team were over. Unfortunately, it was business as usual by the time he was lifted in the fifth inning of this game.

The Mets grabbed a 1–0 lead in the third when John Olerud hit an RBI grounder. The bottom of the third began innocently enough as Rogers retired the first two hitters. But he loaded the bases with a pair of singles and a hit batsman before issuing a game-tying walk to Greg Colbrunn, one innings after Colbrunn hit a leadoff double.

Steve Finley's two-run single put the Diamondbacks ahead to stay later in the third, but Rogers appeared to have collected himself by striking out the final two hitters in a perfect fourth.

The game got out of hand after Rogers left with a runner on first and one out in the fifth. Pat Mahomes gave up a single to Matt Williams and got Colbrunn to strike out before Finley came through again, lacing a two-run double that put the D-Backs ahead 5–1.

Finley also worked out a bases-loaded walk against Octavio Dotel before Turner Ward's run-scoring grounder made it 7–1.

Arizona starter Todd Stottlemyre put at least one runner on base in each inning he worked. The Mets had a great opportunity to score in the fourth after Robin Ventura led off with a walk and Darryl Hamilton reached on an error. But Ventura was picked off second by catcher Kelly Stinnett before Roger Cedeno hit into an inning-ending double play.

GAME 3, October 8, New York: Mets 9, Diamondbacks 2

Bobby Valentine's starting lineup was missing its most productive bat, but that didn't stop the Mets from putting together their most lopsided postseason victory since a 9–2 rout of the Reds in Game 3 of the 1973 NLCS. Mike Piazza had to sit out because of a sore thumb on his catching hand, which put Todd Pratt behind the plate to handle starting pitcher Rick Reed. Nobody noticed Piazza's absence after the Mets erupted for six runs in the sixth to take a seven-run lead.

Pratt extended the Mets' first rally by working out a two-

out walk, allowing Rey Ordonez to stroke an RBI single that put New York ahead 1–0 in the second inning. It was 3–0 an inning later after John Olerud hit an RBI single and scored on Robin Ventura's grounder.

The Mets loaded the bases in the fourth but couldn't score, which looked big after pinch-hitter Turner Ward belted a two-run homer to get the Diamondbacks within 3–2 in the fifth. But the Diamondbacks managed just one hit the rest of the way.

New York broke it open in the sixth, thanks again to

a little help from Pratt. He led off the inning with a walk and scored on Rickey Henderson's single. John Olerud followed with a two-run single and Roger Cedeno singled to make it 7–2 before Darryl Hamilton capped the six-run assault with a two-run single.

Arizona went down quietly after that, mustering just one hit versus the Mets' bullpen over the final three innings.

Reed was excellent in his first postseason appearance, holding the Diamondbacks to four hits in six innings. But the difference in the Mets' two victories had been the bullpen, which threw two-hit ball over 6-2/3 shutout innings while the Diamondbacks relievers yielded seven runs in 4-2/3.

GAME 4, October 9, New York: Mets 4, Diamondbacks 3 (10 innings)

The Mets had to play a second straight game without Mike Piazza, which allowed his backup to deliver one of the most memorable hits in team history. Todd Pratt had a very productive regular season as the team's No. 2 catcher, hitting three homers in 140 at-bats while setting then career highs with 21 RBIs and a .293 average. But all that was overshadowed by his walk-off homer that put the Mets into the NLCS.

Al Leiter was on the mound for New York for the first time since his two-hit shutout against the Reds in the one-game wild-card playoff. Leiter was superb once again, holding the Diamondbacks to three hits over 7 2/3 and leaving the game tied 1–1.

Edgardo Alonzo gave Leiter a lead with his third homer of the series, a solo shot leading off the fourth. But Greg Colbrunn evened the score with a one-out blast off Leiter in the fifth, which also ended Leiter's no-hit bid.

The Mets regained the lead in the sixth as Benny Agbayani laced an RBI double following singles by Rickey Henderson and John Olerud. Agbayani's hit put runners on second and third with one out, but the Mets failed to produce an insurance run.

Leiter followed with a scoreless seventh and retired the first two hitters in the eighth before pinch-hitter Turner Ward walked and Tony Womack singled, prompting manager Bobby Valentine to replace his ace with Armando Benitez. The Mets' new closer quickly gave away the lead when Jay Bell hit a two-run double that put the Diamondbacks ahead 3–2. Benitez also surrendered a single to Matt Williams, but Melvin Mora, a defensive replacement for Henderson, threw out Bell at the plate for the final out of the inning.

The Mets retied the game in the bottom of the eighth without a hit. Alfonzo led off with a walk before Tony Womack, who entered that game as a defensive replacement for ex-Met Bernard Gilkey in right field, dropped Olerud's fly ball to put runners on second and third with nobody out. Roger Cedeno knotted the score with a sacrifice fly that brought home Alfonzo.

New York had a chance to take the lead later in the inning, but Rey Ordonez struck out with the bases loaded to end the eighth.

Benitez worked a perfect ninth and John Franco did the same in the 10th, keeping the game 3–3.

Matt Mantei opened the bottom of the 10th by retiring Robin Ventura before Pratt hit a fly ball to deep center. Steve Finley, who would win his third Gold Glove in four seasons, drifted back toward the ball and appeared to have it lined up as he approached the outfield wall. He timed his jump perfectly and reached over the wall before bringing his glove back into the field of play. Pratt rounded first but made an abrupt stop as he waiting to see whether Finley had made the catch. Finley had nothing but air in his glove. Pratt had delivered the series-winning homer that put the Mets into the NLCS. He became another unlikely candidate to lead the team to a postseason victory, recalled Leiter.

"I think of Ron Swoboda, who certainly wasn't a great player, but what people will forever remember him for is the catch he made in right field with Tom Seaver on the mound. He's a hero. But if you look at his career numbers, he doesn't have hero numbers. That's refreshing. Here's Swoboda, one of the heroes of '69, and you think of Todd Pratt in '99, and albeit we didn't get into the World Series, (Pratt) was a hero."[13]

Game 1, October 5 at Phoenix
METS 8, DIAMONDBACKS 4

Mets	AB	R	H	BI	DBACKS	AB	R	H	BI
Henderson lf	3	2	0	0	Womack rf	4	1	1	0
Benitez p	0	0	0	0	Bell 2b	3	1	1	1
Alfonzo 2b	5	2	2	5	Gonzalez lf	3	1	2	2
Olerud 1b	5	1	3	2	Williams 3b	4	0	0	0
Piazza c	5	0	1	0	Durazo 1b	4	1	1	1
Agbayani rf	4	0	0	0	Finley cf	3	0	1	0
Wendell p	0	0	0	0	Frias ss	4	0	0	0
Hamilton cf	0	0	0	0	Stinnett c	3	0	0	0
Ventura 3b	4	1	2	0	Johnson p	3	0	1	0
Dunston cf	3	0	1	0	Chouinard p	0	0	0	0
Cook p	0	0	0	0					
Cedeno rf	1	0	0	0					
Ordonez ss	3	1	1	1					
Yoshii p 2	0	0	0	0					
Mora cf-lf	1	1	0	0					
Totals	36	8	10	8		31	4	7	4

Mets	102	100	004	8	10	0
Diamondbacks	001	102	000	4	7	0

METS	IP	H	R	ER	BB	SO
Yoshii	5-1/3	6	4	4	0	3
Cook	1-2/3	1	0	0	1	1
Wendell (W, 1–0)	1	0	0	0	1	0
Benitez	1	0	0	0	0	0
Total	9	7	4	4	2	4

DIAMONDBACKS	IP	H	R	ER	BB	SO
Johnson (L, 0–1)	8-1/3	8	7	7	3	11
Chouinard	2/3	2	1	1	0	0
Total	9	10	8	8	3	11

LOB—Mets 5, Diamondbacks 3; DP—Mets 2, Diamondbacks 0; 2B—Ventura (1), Gonzalez (1), Johnson (1); 3B—Womack (1); HR—Alfonzo 2 (2), Olerud (1), Durazo (1), Gonzalez (1); SH—Ordonez; SF—Bell; SB—Henderson 2 (2); Time—2:53; ATT—49,584.

Game 2, October 6 at Phoenix
DIAMONDBACKS 7, METS 1

Mets	AB	R	H	BI	DBACKS	AB	R	H	BI
Henderson lf	3	1	2	0	Womack ss-rf	5	0	0	0
Alfonzo 2b	4	0	0	0	Bell 2b	5	2	2	0
Olerud 1b	3	0	0	1	Gonzalez lf	1	2	0	0
Piazza c	4	0	1	0	Williams 3b	4	3	3	0
Ventura 3b	2	0	0	0	Colbrunn 1b	2	0	1	1
Hamilton cf	2	0	0	0	Finley cf	3	0	2	5
Agbayani ph-rf	1	0	0	0	Gilkey rf	3	0	0	0
Cedeno rf-cf	3	0	1	0	Ward ph	1	0	0	1
Dunston ph	1	0	0	0	Swindell p	0	0	0	0
Ordonez ss	4	0	1	0	Stinnett c	4	0	1	0
Rogers p	2	0	0	0	Stottlemyre p	3	0	0	0
Mahomes p	0	0	0	0	Olson p	0	0	0	0
Bonilla ph	1	0	0	0	Frias ss	1	0	0	0
Dotel p	0	0	0	0					
JFranco p	0	0	0	0					
Pratt ph	1	0	0	0					
Totals	31	1	5	1		32	7	9	7

Mets	001	000	000	1	5	0
Diamondbacks	003	020	20x	7	9	1

METS	IP	H	R	ER	BB	SO
Rogers (L, 0–1)	4-1/3	5	4	4	2	6
Mahomes	1-2/3	3	1	1	0	1
Dotel	1/3	1	2	2	2	0
Franco	1-2/3	0	0	0	0	1
Total	8	9	7	7	4	8

DIAMONDBACKS	IP	H	R	ER	BB	SO
Stottlemyre (W, 1–0)	6-2/3	4	1	1	5	6
Olson	1/3	0	0	0	0	0
Swindell	2	1	0	0	0	1
Total	9	5	1	1	5	6

LOB—Mets 8, Diamondbacks 7; E—Bell (1); DP—Mets 1 Diamondbacks 1; 2B—Ordonez (1), Williams (1), Finley (1), Colbrunn (1); HBP—Colbrunn, Gonzalez; SB—Henderson 3 (5), Ordonez (1); Time—3:13; ATT—49,328.

Game 3, October 8 at New York
METS 9, DIAMONDBACKS 2

DBACKS	AB	R	H	BI	METS	AB	R	H	BI
Womack rf	4	0	0	0	Henderson lf	5	1	3	1
Bell 2b	4	0	0	0	Mora lf	0	0	0	0
Gonzalez lf	3	0	0	0	Alfonzo 2b	3	2	1	0
Williams 3b	4	0	2	0	Olerud 1b	4	2	2	3
Durazo 1b	3	0	0	0	Agbayani rf	2	1	2	0
Finley cf	3	0	1	0	Cedeno ph-rf	2	1	1	1
Fox ss	3	0	0	0	Ventura 3b	4	0	0	1
Plesac p	0	0	0	0	Dunston cf	2	0	0	0
Chouinard p	0	0	0	0	Hamilton ph-cf	3	0	1	2
Swindell p	0	0	0	0	Pratt c	2	1	0	0
Harris ph	1	0	0	0	Ordonez ss	3	0	1	1
Stinnett c	3	1	1	0	Reed p	1	0	0	0
Daal p	1	0	0	0	Bonilla ph	0	1	0	0
Ward ph	1	1	1	2	Wendell p	1	0	0	0
Holmes p	0	0	0	0	JFranco p	0	0	0	0
Frias ss	1	0	0	0	Hershiser p	0	0	0	0
Totals	31	2	5	2		32	9	11	9

Diamondbacks	000	020	000	2	5	3
Mets	012	006	00x	9	11	0

D'BACKS	IP	H	R	ER	BB	SO
Daal (L, 0–1)	4	6	3	3	3	4
Holmes	1-1/3	1	4	4	3	0
Plesac	1/3	3	2	2	0	0
Chouinard	1-1/3	1	0	0	0	1
Swindell	1	0	0	0	2	0
Total	8	11	9	9	8	5

METS	IP	H	R	ER	BB	SO
Reed (W, 1–0)	6	4	2	2	3	2
Wendell	1	0	0	0	1	0
Franco	1	1	0	0	0	0
Hershiser	1	0	0	0	0	1
Total	9	5	2	2	4	3

LOB—Diamondbacks 6, Mets 9; E—Daal (1), Womack (1), Fox (1); DP—Diamondbacks 1, Mets 1; WP—Reed; 2B—Alfonzo (1), Stinnett (1); HR—Ward (1); IBB—Alfonzo; SH—Ordonez, Reed; SB—Henderson (6), Cedeno (1); Time—3:05; ATT—56,180.

Game 4, October 9 at New York
METS 4, DIAMONDBACKS 3 (10)

DBACKS	AB	R	H	BI	METS	AB	R	H	BI
Womack ss-rf	5	1	1	0	Henderson lf	4	1	1	0
Bell 2b	2	0	1	2	Mora lf	0	0	0	0
Gonzalez lf	3	0	0	0	Alfonzo 2b	4	2	1	1
Williams 3b	4	0	1	0	Olerud 1b	4	0	2	0
Mantei p	0	0	0	0	Agbayani rf	3	0	1	1
Colbrunn 1b	3	1	1	1	Cedeno rf	1	0	0	1
Finley cf	4	0	1	0	Ventura 3b	4	0	1	0
Gilkey rf	3	0	0	0	Pratt c	5	1	1	1
Frias ss	1	0	0	0	Hamilton cf	3	0	0	0
Stinnett c	4	0	0	0	Ordonez ss	4	0	1	0
Anderson p	2	0	0	0	Leiter p	3	0	0	0
Ward ph	0	1	0	0	Benitez p	0	0	0	0
Olson p	0	0	0	0	Franco ph	0	0	0	0
Swindell p	0	0	0	0	Dunston pr	0	0	0	0
Harris 3b	1	0	0	0	JFranco p	0	0	0	0
Totals	32	3	5	3		35	4	8	4

Diamondbacks	000	010	020	0	3	5	1
Mets	000	101	010	1	4	8	0

DIAMONDBACKS	IP	H	R	ER	BB	SO
Anderson	7	7	2	2	0	4
Olson	0	0	1	0	1	0
Swindell	1/3	0	0	0	1	0
Mantei (L, 0–1)	2	1	1	1	3	1
Total	9-1/3	8	4	3	5	5

METS	IP	H	R	ER	BB	SO
Leiter	7-2/3	3	3	3	3	4
Benitez	1-1/3	2	0	0	1	2
Franco (W,1–0)	1	0	0	0	0	1
Total	10	5	3	3	4	7

LOB—Diamondbacks 4, Mets 10; E—Womack (2); DP—Diamondbacks 1, Mets 0; 2B—Agbayani (1), Ventura (2), Bell (1); HR—Alfonzo (3), Pratt (1), Colbrunn (1); IBB—Olerud, Ventura, Gonzalez; HBP—Bell; SH—Mora; SF—Cedeno; CS—Bell; Time—3:23; ATT—56,177.

1999 NLDS Statistics

COMPOSITE LINESCORE

Mets	115	207	014	1	22	34	0
D'Backs	004	152	220	0	16	26	5

METS BATTING

Player	BA	G	AB	R	H
Benny Agbayani	.300	4	10	1	3
Edgardo Alfonzo	.250	4	16	6	4
Armando Benitez	—	2	0	0	0
Bobby Bonilla	.000	2	1	1	0
Roger Cedeno	.286	4	7	1	2
Dennis Cook	—	1	0	0	0
Octavio Dotel	—	1	0	0	0
Shawon Dunston	.167	4	6	0	1
John Franco	—	3	0	0	0
Matt Franco	1.000	1	0	0	0
Darryl Hamilton	.125	4	8	0	1
Rickey Henderson	.400	4	15	5	6
Orel Hershiser	—	1	0	0	0
Al Leiter	.000	1	3	0	0
Pat Mahomes	—	1	0	0	0
Melvin Mora	.000	3	1	1	0
John Olerud	.438	4	16	3	7
Rey Ordonez	.286	4	14	1	4
Mike Piazza	.222	2	9	0	2
Todd Pratt	.125	3	8	2	1
Rick Reed	.000	1	1	0	0
Kenny Rogers	.000	1	2	0	0
Robin Ventura	.214	4	14	1	3
Turk Wendell	.000	2	1	0	0
Masato Yoshii	.000	1	2	0	0
Total	.254	4	134	22	34

2B—Ventura 2, Agbayani, Alfonzo, Ordonez; 3B—None; HR—Alfonzo 3, Olerud, Pratt; RBI—Alfonzo 6, Olerud 6, Cedeno 2, Hamilton 2, Ordonez 2, Agbayani, Henderson, Pratt, Ventura; SB—Henderson 6, Cedeno, Ordonez.

DIAMONDBACKS BATTING

Player	BA	G	AB	R	H
Brian Anderson	.000	1	2	0	0
Jay Bell	.286	4	14	3	4
Bobby Chouinard	—	2	0	0	0
Greg Colbrunn	.400	2	5	1	2
Omar Daal	.000	1	1	0	0
Erubiel Durazo	.143	2	7	1	1
Steve Finley	.385	4	13	0	5
Andy Fox	.000	1	3	0	0
Hanley Frias	.000	4	7	0	0
Bernard Gilkey	.000	2	6	0	0
Luis Gonzalez	.200	4	10	3	2
Lenny Harris	.000	2	2	0	0
Darren Holmes	—	1	0	0	0
Randy Johnson	.333	1	3	0	1
Matt Mantei	—	1	0	0	0
Gregg Olson	—	2	0	0	0
Dan Plesac	—	1	0	0	0
Kelly Stinnett	.143	4	14	1	2
Todd Stottlemyre	.000	1	3	0	0
Greg Swindell	—	3	0	0	0
Turner Ward	.500	3	2	2	1
Matt Williams	.375	4	16	3	6
Tony Womack	.111	4	18	2	2
Total	.206	4	126	16	26

2B—Bell, Colbrunn, Finley, Gonzalez, Johnson, Stinnett, Williams; 3B—Womack; HR—Colbrunn, Durazo, Gonzalez, Ward; RBI—Finley 5, Bell 3, Ward 3, Colbrunn 2, Gonzalez 2, Durazo; SB—None.

METS PITCHING

Player	G	ERA	W–L	SV	IP	H	ER	BB	SO
Arman. Benitez	2	0.00	0–0	0	2-1/3	2	0	1	2
Dennis Cook	1	0.00	0–0	0	1-2/3	1	0	1	1
Octavio Dotel	1	54.00	0–0	0	1/3	1	2	2	0
John Franco	3	0.00	1–0	0	3-2/3	1	0	0	2
Orel Hershiser	1	0.00	0–0	0	1	0	0	0	1
Al Leiter	1	3.52	0–0	0	7-2/3	3	3	3	4
Pat Mahomes	1	5.40	0–0	0	1-2/3	3	1	0	1
Rick Reed	1	3.00	1–0	0	6	4	2	3	2
Kenny Rogers	1	8.31	0–1	0	4-1/3	5	4	2	6
Turk Wendell	2	0.00	1–0	0	2	0	0	2	0
Masato Yoshii	1	6.75	0–0	0	5-1/3	6	4	0	3
Total	4	4.00	3–1	0	36	26	16	14	22

DIAMONDBACKS PITCHING

Player	G	ERA	W–L	SV	IP	H	ER	BB	SO
Brian Anderson	1	2.57	0–0	0	7	7	2	0	4
Bob Chouinard	2	4.50	0–0	0	2	3	1	0	1
Omar Daal	1	6.75	0–1	0	4	6	3	3	4
Darren Holmes	1	27.00	0–0	0	1-1/3	1	4	3	0
Randy Johnson	1	7.56	0–1	0	8-1/3	8	7	3	11
Matt Mantei	1	4.50	0–1	0	2	1	1	3	1
Gregg Olson	2	0.00	0–0	0	1/3	0	0	1	0
Dan Plesac	1	54.00	0–0	0	1/3	3	2	0	0
Todd Stottlemyre	1	1.35	1–0	0	6-2/3	4	1	5	6
Greg Swindell	3	0.00	0–0	0	3-1/3	1	0	3	1
Total	4	5.35	1–3	0	35-1/3	34	21	21	28

1999 NLCS: Mets vs. Atlanta Braves

BRAVES WIN SERIES 4–2

The Mets' reward for knocking off the Diamondbacks in the NLDS was a chance to play the Atlanta Braves, a team that had won the season series 9–3 in each of the previous two years. New York never trailed Atlanta by more than six games until September 26 and led the division as late as August 18. But the Braves had the best starting rotation in baseball and could silence the Mets' bats almost at will. Greg Maddux, Tom Glavine and John Smoltz won Cy Young Awards in the 1990s, and Kevin Millwood finished third in the Cy Young balloting in 1999.

The lineups were evenly matched in nearly every department. The Mets hit 13 points higher (.279) but scored only 13 more runs. The Braves hit 16 more homers and stole just two fewer bases.

The Mets had the better bullpen, although Terry Mulholland and Mike Remlinger did a terrific job as setup men for John Rocker, who finished with 38 saves.

The first two games went as expected. Maddux outpitched Masato Yoshii in the opener and Kevin Millwood was better than Kenny Rogers in Game 2. Future teammates Al Leiter and Tom Glavine hooked up in a pitchers' duel, but an unearned run in the first inning was the difference in a 1–0 game that gave the Braves a 3–0 lead in the series.

The Mets had played better when desperate during the season. They went 15–3 after an eight-game losing streak dropped them to 27–28. The Mets also won their last four games during the season when just one loss meant another disappointing finish. And faced with the prospect of taking on Randy Johnson in a Game 5 at Phoenix, the Mets settled the NLDS with a walk-off homer by backup catcher Todd Pratt in extra innings.

The Mets were four outs from elimination in Game 4 when John Olerud hit a two-run single to extend the series. Down 3–2 in the 15th inning of Game 5, Pratt walked with the bases loaded before Robin Ventura "singled" over the wall in right-center to force a sixth game. The Mets also fell behind 5–0 and 7–3 in Game 6 before eventually taking an 8–7 lead in the eighth inning. But the jig was up when the Braves tied the game in the eighth and 10th innings before winning the series on a bases-loaded walk in the bottom of the 11th.

Eddie Perez, who became Atlanta's starting catcher following a season-ending injury to Javy Lopez, won named the series MVP after going 10-for-20 with two homers and five RBIs.

There were many heroes and villains in the NLCS, but nobody gets more heat about his performance than Kenny Rogers, who was a huge reason why the Mets made the playoffs. Rogers unraveled in the sixth inning of Game 2, blowing a 2–0 lead by serving up a pair of two-run homers. Rogers also ended the series by walking Andruw Jones with the bases loaded, which supposedly proved he can't pitch in a big spot. Seven years later, who went 2–0 without allowing an earned run over 23 innings for the Tigers in the postseason.

A pair of ensuing stories kept the series fresh long after it ended. It was revealed that Rickey Henderson and Bobby Bonilla were involved in a card game while the Mets were in extra innings against the Braves in Game 6. Both players were out of the game at that point, but they showed no interest in the outcome. A few weeks later, Sports Illustrated did a profile on John Rocker in which the Braves closer made racist and homophobic remarks about New York and its baseball fans, which originally earned him a 28-day suspension for the start of the 2000 season. The suspension was eventually cut to 14 days, and Rocker made an uncomfortable apology during a news conference at Shea Stadium when the Braves made their first trip to New York in 2000.

GAME 1, October 12, Atlanta: Braves 4, Mets 2

Masato Yoshii and the Mets' bullpen combined to hold the Braves' 3 through 6 hitters 0-for-10, but Atlanta got production from the top and bottom of the lineup. It took the Braves just two batters before they took the lead on Bret Boone's RBI single following a single and a stolen base by Gerald Williams. Williams also snapped a 1–1 tie with an RBI single in the fifth before Eddie Perez added a solo homer an inning later to make it 3–1. Walt Weiss drove in the Braves' fourth run with his third hit of the game, an eighth-inning single for a 4–1 lead. Perez and Williams each provided two of the Braves' eight hits as the Mets dropped to 3–6 in series openers.

Greg Maddux did a nice job muzzling the Mets, holding them to a run and five hits in seven innings. Maddux blanked New York after Mike Piazza's RBI grounder in the fourth, one inning after Yoshii killed a rally.

Roger Cedeno led off the third with a double and raced to third when Gerald Williams bobbled the hit in left. Rey Ordonez hit a little nubber in front of the plate for the first out before Yoshii attempted a suicide squeeze. Yoshii missed the bunt, making Cedeno a dead duck when he arrived at the plate.

Yoshii was lifted with two outs in the fifth, charged with two runs on five hits.

The Mets left a runner on third in the eighth when John Olerud struck out against John Rocker to end the inning. Todd Pratt delivered an RBI single off Rocker in the ninth to make it 4–2, but the lefty closer retired Ordonez to end the game.

Cedeno and Edgardo Alfonzo each had two hits and provided the Mets' only extra-base hits, three doubles. The rest of the starting lineup managed just one hit, a single by Olerud.

GAME 2, October 13, Atlanta: Braves 4, Mets 3

Kenny Rogers had never pitched into the sixth inning of a postseason start before this game. Manager Bobby Valentine should have settled for five innings.

Rogers somehow managed to hold the Braves scoreless over the first five frames despite yielding six hits and a pair of walks. Mike Piazza helped out the lefty by throwing out two base runners, and the Mets turned two double plays while forging a 2–0 lead.

Rogers retired the leadoff batter in the sixth before going walk-homer-single-homer to earn a trip to the Mets' clubhouse. Eddie Perez chased Rogers with a tiebreaking two-run homer, two batters after Brian Jordan smacked a two-run shot.

Edgardo Alfonzo came through with an RBI double in the eighth that pushed the Mets within 4–3 with one man out. Braves manager Bobby Cox replaced starter Kevin Milwood with John Rocker, who fanned John Olerud and Robin Ventura in between a two-out walk to Mike Piazza. In a sign of things to come, John Smoltz worked a perfect ninth for his first major league save.

Melvin Mora was the center of the Mets' offense, launching a solo homer that made it 2–0 in the fifth before scoring on Alfonzo's third double of the series. Roger Cedeno singled home the game's first run in the second.

GAME 3, October 15, New York: Braves 1, Mets 0

The Mets hadn't committed two errors in an inning the entire season until now, and it led to the game's lone run.

Al Leiter opened the game by walking Gerald Williams before Bret Boone hit a slow roller back to the mound. Leiter grabbed the ball in plenty of time to get Boone at first, but he hesitated his throw before pulling John Olerud off the bag. With runners on first and second and one out manager Bobby Cox called for a double-steal that worked out probably better than he planned. Mike Piazza's throw to second sailed into center field, allowing Williams to score. The only run of the game had been manufactured by zero hits, a walk and two miscues.

Leiter got out of the inning when the Mets turned a double play on Brian Jordan's fly ball, which Darryl Hamilton threw to the plate to nail Boone. Piazza made a nice play hanging onto the ball after Boone barreled into him.

First inning aside, the Mets played solid defense behind Leiter, who allowed just three hits in seven innings. Rickey Henderson threw out Chipper Jones and Eddie Perez trying to stretch leadoff singles into doubles. Perez also had an infield single in the second but was erased on a double-play liner that was speared by Robin Ventura at third.

Meanwhile, Braves starter Tom Glavine worked out of trouble in a pair of innings while preserving the shutout. The Mets put runners on first and third in both the second and fourth innings before their weakest hitters

(Leiter and Rey Ordonez) made the final out. Glavine gave up seven hits and struck out eight over seven innings while staying ahead in the count most of the game.

Mike Remlinger tossed a scoreless eighth before John Rocker was greeted with boos and bottles as he entered to start the bottom of the ninth. Mets fans didn't fully appreciate Rocker's grandstanding sprints from the bullpen, nor did they like his animation on the mound. Most of all, the Shea brethren hated the fact that nobody on the Mets could hit him.

The Mets put the tying run on base for the final time when shortstop Walt Weiss booted Benny Agbayani's leadoff grounder in the ninth. Todd Pratt struck out pinch-hitting for Robin Ventura, who was hitless in the series at that point. Rocker also retired the last two hitters for his second save of the series before running to the safety of the dugout.

Leiter had an otherwise outstanding performance but remained winless lifetime in postseason play. "Seven innings and three hits, I'll take that for the rest of my career," said the lefty. But Leiter's best effort couldn't stop the Mets from falling behind 3–0 in a postseason series for the first time.

"We've looked at some pretty bleak situations before," said Olerud, who had just seen his team pull out a wild-card berth two weeks earlier.

GAME 4, October 16, New York: Mets 3, Braves 2

The Mets held Atlanta to only three hits for the second straight game. This time, they put together just enough offense to win.

As good as Al Leiter was in the Game 3 loss, Rick Reed was even better as he limited the Braves to one hit over the first seven innings. Reed walked nobody and faced the minimum 21 batters heading into the eighth, retiring the side in order six times. Bret Boone hit a one-out single in the fourth but was erased by Mike Piazza on an attempted steal.

The Mets managed just one hit off John Smoltz until John Olerud hit a two-out homer to open the scoring in the sixth, ending a 15-inning scoreless drought for New York. Olerud's blast appeared to be ample scoring for the Mets to extend the series.

But the Braves drew within six outs of wrapping up the series when Brian Jordan and Ryan Klesko hit back-to-back homers to start the eighth, ending Reed's night. The right-hander received a nice ovation from Mets fans who might have thought the series was about to end. But a loudmouth pitcher and a future loudmouth manager helped New York extend the NLCS.

Smoltz gave up a leadoff single to Roger Cedeno in the eighth and was lifted after Rey Ordonez popped up a bunt attempt for the first out of the inning. Mike Remlinger struck out Benny Agbayani for the second out before the Mets flashed their speed.

Cedeno stole second while Melvin Mora was in the process of working out a walk, which prompted Braves manager Bobby Cox to bring in lefty John Rocker to pitch to the left-handed Olerud, who struck out against Rocker in the ninth inning of Game 2. Olerud also had been 0-for-9 with five strikeouts against Rocker in his career.

In a daring move, Mets skipper Bobby Valentine called for a double-steal to put the potential go-ahead run on second. Cedeno barely beat the throw to third to keep the rally alive.

This was when one of Cox's moves finally backfired like a '72 Pinto. He brought in Rocker as part of a double-switch in which he replaced shortstop Walt Weiss with Ozzie Guillen. Olerud found the new guy, hitting a grounder that glanced off Guillen's glove for a two-run single that put the Mets ahead 3–2. With Weiss' range and glove at short, the ball likely would have been gobbled up for the final out of the inning. Instead, the Mets had finally scored while Rocker was on the mound, giving the Braves' closer another opportunity to act stupid.

Rocker heard it from the fans after getting the final out of the inning. Instead of ignoring the hecklers, Rocker looked up and flashed a three-oh with his fingers to signify that the Braves were still ahead 3–0 in the series.

Armando Benitez closed out the victory by getting Keith Lockhart to strike out. The Mets had new life and were about to play one of the more memorable games in team history.

Even sweeter was that the Mets had rallied against Rocker. Before the series he wondered what it would take to shut up Mets fans, saying, "I don't mind 98% of the fans, it's the 2% that cause me to hate them."

Olerud declined to trash Rocker, only to say, "To come back and get the win and get a couple of runs off Rocker, who we really haven't done much against, is a big win for us." The first baseman didn't want to get drawn into a pissing match with Rocker, but winning pitcher Turk Wendell was more candid.

"It was very pleasurable. I think he got what was coming to him," crowed the reliever.

Wendell also stirred his own internal controversy after the game. Rickey Henderson headed to left field to start the eighth inning but was pulled in favor of Mora. Henderson felt embarrassed by the move, and Valentine fell on the sword by saying he had forgotten to tell him he would make a switch to start the inning. Henderson breezed by Valentine in the dugout following the move and continued to the clubhouse before leaving the ballpark without speaking to reporters. Wendell intimated that Henderson was a quitter and questioned the work habits of the all-time leading base-stealer.

"If he doesn't respect me, then tough luck," said Henderson of Wendell. "He should be happy he's in this position. He wouldn't be here if not for me."

GAME 5, October 17, New York: Mets 4, Braves 3 (15 innings)

Robin Ventura's lifetime statistics show him with three homers and 19 RBIs in the postseason. He would have four home runs and 22 RBIs if a teammate hadn't cross his path, but at least Ventura knows he hit a grand-slam single to win a playoff game.

Ventura's walk-off hit was just another odd play in a game that was played through a steady drizzle over 5:46, which set a record for the longest contest in postseason history. It capped an inning in which the Mets fell behind before extending the series once again.

The Mets were shut out over 13 consecutive scoreless innings in between John Olerud's homer and Todd Pratt's bases-loaded walk. Olerud's two-run blast opened the scoring with one out in the bottom of the first. Braves starter Greg Maddux scattered five hits over the next six innings and pitched out of trouble in the second and sixth.

Maddux gave up a leadoff double to Darryl Hamilton in the second, but the Mets outfielder was stranded at third. Later, first baseman Ryan Klesko made two errors that put runners on second and third with one out, but Maddux wiggled out of the jam by getting Rey Ordonez to ground into an inning-ending double play.

The Braves had tied the game by the time Maddux completed his seven innings of work. Mets starter Masato Yoshii allowed just one hit until the fourth, when Bret Boone and Chipper Jones opened the inning with back-to-back doubles before Brian Jordan delivered the game-tying single. Yoshii was lifted after walking the next batter, putting Orel Hershiser in the game with runners on first and second and nobody out.

Yoshii was starting only because manager Bobby Valentine felt Hershiser would do a better job out of the bullpen. Hershiser showed his skipper was right by striking out Andruw Jones and red-hot Eddie Perez before Walt Weiss grounded out to end the inning. Hershiser struck out five while holding the Braves to one hit over 3 1/3 innings, leaving the game after hitting Boone with a pitch.

Valentine used four pitchers in the seventh while Atlanta loaded the bases without a hit. Pat Mahomes ended the threat by getting Andruw Jones to fly out.

John Franco stranded a runner in scoring position in the eighth, and Armando Benitez did the same in the tenth before Kenny Rogers tossed two shutout innings of relief.

But the Mets were doing little against the Braves' pen. John Olerud greeted Terry Mulholland with a leadoff single in the eighth, but that would be the Mets' last hit until Robin Ventura's two-out single in the 12th.

Rookie Octavio Dotel became the ninth pitched used by Valentine when the right-hander began the 13th inning. Dotel almost became the losing pitcher when Keith Lockhart hit a two-out single and tried to score on Chipper Jones' double to right. But rookie Melvin Mora, who was making a habit out of providing big plays in the series, threw out Lockhart at the plate to end the inning.

Lockhart got his revenge in the 15th by lacing a two-out triple that scored Walt Weiss, who had singled and stolen second. It was now up to Kevin McGlinchy to close out the pennant for Atlanta. McGlinchy recorded the last two outs in the 14th but retired only one hitter after that.

Shawon Dunston led off the bottom of the 15th with a 12-pitch at-bat. He singled and stole second before pinch-hitter Matt Franco walked. Franco batted for Dotel, which left Rick Reed and scheduled Game 6 starter Al Leiter as Valentine's only available pitchers. Reed was in the bullpen warming up, just a few hours after throwing 7+ innings.

Edgaro Alfonzo bunted the runners over before Olerud was walked intentionally, putting Todd Pratt at the plate with the bases loaded. Pratt walked on five pitches to tie the game once again, eight days after he provided the series-winning homer against the Diamondbacks.

Next up was Ventura, whose 12th-inning single ended his series-opening 0-for-17 skid. Ventura hit a drive that cleared the wall in right-center, a grand slam that gave the Mets a 7–3 victory. But Ventura never got a chance to circle the bases. Pratt stepped in front of Ventura while giving the Mets' latest hero a bearhug, thus passing Ventura on the base paths. Instead of a grand slam, Ventura was only credited with a single, but the hit still extended the NLCS.

Ventura didn't seem to mind having the grand slam reduced to a single. "As long as I touched first base, we won, so that's good enough for me."

The Mets had become only the second team in postseason history to force a sixth game after dropping the first three. They were about to follow one crazy game with yet another.

Rocker got in a parting shot at Mets fans knowing he wouldn't be returning to Shea until next year. "A majority of the Mets fans aren't human," said Rocker just days after claiming he had a problem with just 2% of them. "The bottom line is 80% of Mets fans are Neanderthal." Fans scraped their knuckles on the blacktop as they headed for the parking lot or subway, not knowing if they'd be back at Shea again this year.

GAME 6, October 19, Atlanta: Braves 10, Mets 9 (11)

"Everything you've done in the past, they'll forget about and remember this."
—*Kenny Rogers*

Rogers is the one who is blamed for the Mets losing this game and the series. The revisionists fail to remember that starting pitcher Al Leiter surrendered five runs without retiring a batter, John Franco blew a one-run lead in the eighth and Armando Benitez did the same in the 10th. Sure, it would have been nice if Rogers could have gotten Andruw Jones to take his bat off his shoulders during the final at-bat of the series, getting the Braves outfielder to hit into an inning-ending double play instead of walking with the bases loaded. But it took 1/3 of the Mets' pitching staff to lose this, not just Rogers.

Leiter, who pitched so brilliantly during a 1–0 loss in Game 3, couldn't find the plate in the bottom of the first. He was pitching on three days' rest for only the second time in his career, and the first time in five years. Leiter hit two of the first three batters he faced and was down 1–0 after Gerald Williams stole third and came home on the first of Mike Piazza's two throwing errors in the game.

Brian Jordan followed with an RBI single and Eddie Perez added a two-run single that chased Leiter.

One of the most unappreciated parts of the game was the work by reliever Pat Mahomes, who gave up just one hit over four shutout innings after replacing Leiter. Mahomes prevented the game from getting out of reach, although a 5–0 lead looked pretty safe while Braves starter Kevin Millwood was shutting out the Mets over the first five innings.

The Mets got back in the game by collecting five straight hits to start the sixth. Mike Piazza hit a sacrifice fly before Darryl Hamilton's two-run single got New York within 5–3. But pinch-hitter Jose Hernandez delivered a two-run single off Dennis Cook with two outs to make it 7–3 after Turk Wendell loaded the bases.

It took just five batters before the Mets knotted the score against John Smoltz in the seventh. Pinch-hitter Matt Franco and Rickey Henderson opened the inning with back-to-back doubles before John Olerud singled to make it 7–5. Mike Piazza, who at this point had just one home run and five RBIs in 55 career postseason at-bats, took a Smoltz delivery over the wall in right-center to knot the score. It marked the first time in Mets history they had tied a postseason game after trailing by more than four runs.

Orel Hershiser worked a perfect seventh to keep the score tied, allowing Melvin Mora to lace the go-ahead single in the eighth. But pinch-runner Otis Nixon stole second and continued to third on Piazza's second bad throw of the night before scoring on Brian Hunter's RBI single.

Todd Pratt almost was the hero again, hitting a sacrifice fly to put New York ahead 9–8. It came off John Rocket,

who had been involved in a minor car crash the day before. The Mets had a chance to add an insurance run, but Edgardo Alfonzo struck out to end the inning after Melvin Mora had stolen third base.

But Benitez couldn't hold the lead after working a scoreless ninth. Andruw Jones led off the bottom of the tenth with a single and Ryan Klesko walked before pinch-hitter Ozzie Guillen hit the game-tying single. Mora made a huge play on the hit, throwing out Klesko at third base for the second out of the inning. Jorge Fabregas followed with a fly to left to end the inning.

The Mets went down 1-2-3 against Russ Springer in the 11th, leaving it up to Kenny Rogers to prolong the Mets' season. It took Rogers three pitches before he was in trouble. Gerald Williams led off with a double and was bunted over to third, prompting manager Bobby Valentine to ask Rogers to walk Chipper Jones and Brian Jordan intentionally to load the bases. Andruw Jones worked a full count before taking a pitch high and outside for ball four, ending the series.

Valentine yelled "Oh NO!" as the pitch missed the strike zone. Jones said he was going to wait out Rogers until he saw a strike. Jones' patience put the Braves in the World Series for the fifth time since 1991.

John Franco, the elder statesman on the pitching staff, realized how hard the Mets tried to become the first time in major league history to force a Game 7 after dropping the first three contests. "I think every guy in this room should be proud of the way we handled ourselves. Valentine made similar remarks, saying his team was a champion without the trophy.

Game 1, October 12 at Atlanta
BRAVES 4, METS 2

Mets	AB	R	H	BI	Braves	AB	R	H	BI
Henderson lf	4	0	0	0	Williams lf	5	1	2	1
Alfonzo 2b	4	1	2	0	Boone 2b	4	0	1	1
Olerud 1b	4	0	1	0	CJones 3b	1	0	0	0
Piazza c	4	0	0	1	Jordan rf	3	0	0	0
Ventura 3b	3	0	0	0	Klesko 1b	3	0	0	0
Hamilton cf	3	0	0	0	Battle ph-1b	1	0	0	0
Dunston ph	1	1	0	0	Remlinger p	0	0	0	0
Cedeno rf	3	0	2	0	Rocker p	0	0	0	0
Pratt ph	1	0	1	1	AJones cf	3	1	0	0
Ordonez ss	4	0	0	0	Perez c	3	1	2	1
Yoshii p	2	0	0	0	Weiss ss	4	1	3	1
Mahomes p	0	0	0	0	Maddux p	2	0	0	0
Cook p	0	0	0	0	Hunter 1b	1	0	0	0
MFranco ph	0	0	0	0					
Mora ph	0	0	0	0					
Wendell p	0	0	0	0					
Totals	33	2	6	2		30	4	8	4

Mets	000	100	001	2	6	2
Braves	100	011	01x	4	8	2

METS	IP	H	R	ER	BB	SO
Yoshii (L, 0–1)	4-2/3	5	2	2	2	1
Mahomes	1-1/3	2	1	1	0	1
Cook	1	0	0	0	2	1
Wendell	1	1	1	1	1	2
Total	8	8	4	4	5	5

BRAVES	IP	H	R	ER	BB	SO
Maddux (W, 1–0)	7	5	1	1	1	2
Remlinger	2/3	0	0	0	1	0
Rocker (S, 1)	1-1/3	1	1	0	0	2
Total	9	6	2	1	2	4

E—Henderson (1), Olerud (1), Williams (1), CJones (1); WP—Rocker; 2B—Alfonzo 2 (2), Cedeno (1), Perez (1), Weiss (1); HR—Perez; IBB—CJones, Jordan; SH—Maddux, Perez; SB—Williams, CJones, Weiss; CS—Cedeno (1); Time—3:09; ATT—44,172.

Game 2, October 13 at Atlanta
BRAVES 4, METS 3

Mets	AB	R	H	BI	Braves	AB	R	H	BI
Henderson lf	2	0	0	0	Williams lf	4	0	1	0
Mora lf	2	2	1	1	Boone 2b	4	0	1	0
Alfonzo 2b	4	0	2	1	CJones 3b	2	1	0	0
Olerud 1b	4	0	0	0	Jordan rf	4	1	1	2
Piazza c	3	0	0	0	AJones cf	4	1	3	0
Ventura 3b	3	1	0	0	Perez c	4	1	2	2
Hamilton cf	3	0	1	0	Hunter 1b	3	0	0	0
Dunston ph	1	0	0	0	Weiss ss	3	0	1	0
Cedeo rf	4	0	1	1	Millwood p	2	0	0	0
Ordonez ss	3	0	0	0	Rocker p	0	0	0	0
Bonilla ph	1	0	0	0	Smoltz p	0	0	0	0
Rogers p	1	0	0	0					
Wendell p	0	0	0	0					
MFranco ph	1	0	0	0					
Benitez p	0	0	0	0					
Totals	32	3	5	3		30	4	9	4

Mets	000	010	010	3	5	1
Braves	000	004	00x	4	9	1

METS	IP	H	R	ER	BB	SO
Rogers (L, 0–1)	5-1/3	9	4	4	3	1
Wendell	1-2/3	0	0	0	1	1
Benitez	1	0	0	0	0	2
Total	8	9	4	4	4	4

BRAVES	IP	H	R	ER	BB	SO
Millwood (W, 1–0)	7-1/3	5	3	2	1	4
Rocker	2/3	0	0	0	1	2
Smoltz (S, 1)	1	0	0	0	0	1
Total	9	5	3	2	2	7

E—Alfonzo (1), CJones (2); DP—Mets 2, Braves 0; 2B—Alfonzo (3); HR—Mora (1), Jordan (1), Perez (2); IBB—Piazza; SH—Rogers; CS—Williams (1), AJones (1); Time—2:42; ATT—44.624.

Game 3, October 15 at New York
BRAVES 1, METS 0

Braves	AB	R	H	BI	Mets	AB	R	H	BI
Williams lf	3	1	0	0	Henderson lf	4	0	1	0
Boone 2b	4	0	0	0	Olerud 1b	3	0	1	0
CJones 3b	4	0	1	0	Alfonzo 2b	4	0	0	0
Jordan rf	4	0	0	0	Piazza c	4	0	2	0
AJones cf	3	0	0	0	Agbayani rf	4	0	0	0
Perez c	3	0	2	0	Ventura 3b	3	0	0	0
Hunter 1b	2	0	0	0	Pratt ph	1	0	0	0
Weiss ss	2	0	0	0	Mora cf	4	0	2	0
Glavine p	2	0	0	0	Ordonez ss	4	0	1	0
Remlinger p	0	0	0	0	Leiter p	2	0	0	0
Rocker p	0	0	0	0	Dunston ph	1	0	0	0
					JFranco p	0	0	0	0
					Benitez p	0	0	0	0
Totals	27	1	3	0		34	0	7	0

Braves	100	000	000	1	3	1
Mets	000	000	000	0	7	2

BRAVES	IP	H	R	ER	BB	SO
Glavine (W, 1–0)	7	7	0	0	1	8
Remlinger	1	0	0	0	0	1
Rocker (S,2)	1	0	0	0	0	1
Total	9	7	0	0	1	10

METS	IP	H	R	ER	BB	SO
Leiter (L, 0–1)	7	3	1	0	3	5
Franco	1/3	0	0	0	1	0
Benitez	1-2/3	0	0	0	0	3
Total	9	3	1	0	4	8

E—Piazza (1), Weiss (1); DP—Braves 1, Mets 2; WP—Glavine. SH—Glavine; SB—Williams, Boone; CS—Dunston (1); Time—3:04; ATT—55,911.

Game 4, October 16 at New York
METS 3, BRAVES 2

Braves	AB	R	H	BI	Mets	AB	R	H	BI
Williams lf	4	0	0	0	Henderson lf	3	0	0	0
Boone 2b	3	0	1	0	Mora lf	0	1	0	0
Lockhart ph	1	0	0	0	Olerud 1b	4	1	2	3
CJones 3b	3	0	0	0	Alfonzo 2b	4	0	0	0
Jordan rf	3	1	1	1	Piazza c	3	0	0	0
Klesko 1b	3	1	1	1	Ventura 3b	3	0	0	0
Hunter 1b	0	0	0	0	Hamilton cf	3	0	0	0
AJones cf	3	0	0	0	Cedeno rf	3	1	3	0
Perez c	3	0	0	0	Ordonez ss	3	0	0	0
Weiss ss	3	0	0	0	Reed p	2	0	0	0
Rocker p	0	0	0	0	Wendell p	0	0	0	0
Smoltz p	2	0	0	0	MFranco ph	0	0	0	0
Remlinger p	0	0	0	0	Agbayani ph	1	0	0	0
Guillen ss	1	0	0	0	Benitez p	0	0	0	0
Totals	28	2	3	2		29	3	5	3

Braves	000	000	020	2	3	0
Mets	000	001	02x	3	5	0

BRAVES	IP	H	R	ER	BB	SO
Smoltz	7-1/3	4	2	2	0	7
Remlinger (L, 0–1)	1/3	0	1	1	1	1
Rocker	1/3	1	0	0	0	1
Total	8	5	3	3	1	9

METS	IP	H	R	ER	BB	SO
Reed	7	3	2	2	0	5
Wendell (W, 1–0)	1	0	0	0	0	0
Benitez (Save, 1)	1	0	0	0	0	1
Total	9	3	2	2	0	6

HR—Olerud (1), Jordan (2), Klesko (1). SB—Cedeno 2 (2), Mora (1). CS—Boone; Time—2:20; ATT—55,872.

Game 5, October 17 at New York
METS 4, BRAVES 3 (15)

Braves	AB	R	H	BI	Mets	AB	R	H	BI
Williams lf	7	0	1	0	Henderson lf	5	1	1	0
Boone 2b	3	1	1	0	Rogers p	0	0	0	0
Nixon pr	0	0	0	0	Bonilla ph	1	0	0	0
Lockhart 2b	4	0	2	1	Dotel p	0	0	0	0
CJones 3b	6	1	3	1	MFranco ph	0	0	0	0
Jordan rf	7	0	2	1	Cedeno pr	0	1	0	0
Klesko 1b	2	0	0	0	Alfonzo 2b	6	0	1	0
Hunter ph-1b	3	0	0	0	Olerud 1b	6	1	2	2
AJones cf	5	0	0	0	Piazza c	6	0	1	0
Perez c	4	0	2	0	Pratt c	0	0	0	1
Battle pr	0	0	0	0	Ventura 3b	7	0	2	1
Myers c	1	0	0	0	Mora rf-cf-rf	6	0	1	0
Weiss ss	6	1	2	0	Hamilton cf	3	0	2	0
Maddux p	3	0	0	0	Agbayani ph-rf-lf	1	0	0	0
Hernandez ph	1	0	0	0	Ordonez ss	6	0	0	0
Mulholland p	0	0	0	0	Yoshii p	1	0	0	0
Guillen ph	1	0	0	0	Hershiser p	1	0	0	0
Remlinger p	0	0	0	0	Wendell p	0	0	0	0
Springer p	0	0	0	0	Cook p	0	0	0	0
Fabregas ph	1	0	0	0	Mahomes p	1	0	0	0
Rocker p	0	0	0	0	JFranco p	0	0	0	0
McGlinchy p	1	0	0	0	Benitez p	0	0	0	0
					Dunston ph-cf	3	1	1	0
Totals	55	3	13	3		53	4	11	4

Braves	000	200	000	000	001	3	13	2
Mets	200	000	000	000	002	4	11	1

BRAVES	IP	H	R	ER	BB	SO
Maddux	7	7	2	2	0	5
Mulholland	2	1	0	0	0	2
Remlinger	2	1	0	0	0	2
Springer	1	0	0	0	1	1
Rocker	1-1/3	0	0	0	0	2
McGlinchy (L, 0–1)	1	2	2	2	4	1
Total	14-1/3	11	4	4	5	13

METS	IP	H	R	ER	BB	SO
Yoshii	3	4	2	2	1	3
Hershiser	3-1/3	1	0	0	3	5
Wendell	1/3	0	0	0	1	1
Cook	0	0	0	0	0	0
Mahomes	1	1	0	0	2	1
Franco	1-1/3	1	0	0	0	2
Benitez	1	1	0	0	0	1
Rogers	2	1	0	0	1	1
Dotel (W, 1–0)	3	4	1	1	2	5
Total	15	13	3	3	12	19

E—John Olerud (1), Ryan Klesko 2; DP—Braves 2, Mets 2; 2B—Hamilton (1), CJones 2, Williams, Perez, Weiss, Boone; 3B—Keith Lockhart; HR—John Olerud (2); IBB—Olerud, CJones 2, Williams, Jordan, Perez; HBP—Boone; SH—Alfonzo, AJones; SB—Agbayani (1), Dunston (1), Nixon, Weiss, Battle; CS—Ryan Klesko; Time—5:46; ATT—55,723.

Game 6, October 19 at Atlanta
BRAVES 10, METS 9 (11)

Mets	AB	R	H	BI	Braves	AB	R	H	BI
Henderson lf	5	1	2	1	Williams lf	5	2	1	0
JFranco p	0	0	0	0	Boone 2b	4	1	0	0
Pratt c	0	0	0	1	CJones 3b	3	1	1	1
Alfonzo 2b	5	1	1	0	Jordan rf	4	1	1	1
Olerud 1b	6	2	2	1	AJones cf	5	3	2	1
Piazza c	4	1	1	3	Perez c	3	0	2	2
Benitez p	0	0	0	0	Nixon pr	0	1	0	0
Dunston ph	1	0	0	0	Myers c	1	0	0	0
Rogers p	0	0	0	0	Hunter 1b	1	1	1	2
Ventura 3b	6	1	1	0	Klesko ph-1b	0	0	0	0
Hamilton cf	5	0	3	2	Weiss ss	3	0	0	0
Cedeno rf	2	0	0	0	Guillen ph-ss	1	0	1	1
Agbayani ph-rf-lf	1	2	1	0	Millwood p	2	0	0	0
Ordonez ss	4	0	0	0	Mulholland p	0	0	0	0
Leiter p	0	0	0	0	Lockhart ph	0	0	0	0
Mahomes p	1	0	0	0	Hernandez ph	1	0	1	2
Bonilla ph	1	0	1	0	Smoltz p	0	0	0	0
Wendell p	0	0	0	0	Remlinger p	0	0	0	0
Cook p	0	0	0	0	Battle ph	1	0	0	0
Franco ph	1	1	1	1	Rocker p	0	0	0	0
Hershiser p	0	0	0	0	Fabregas ph	1	0	0	0
Mora ph-rf	2	0	2	1	Springer p	0	0	0	0
Totals	44	9	15	9		35	10	10	9

Mets	000	003	410	10	9	15	2
Braves	500	002	010	11	10	10	1

METS	IP	H	R	ER	BB	SO
Leiter	0	2	5	5	1	0
Mahomes	4	1	0	0	1	1
Wendell	1-2/3	1	2	2	1	1
Cook	1/3	1	0	0	0	0
Hershiser	1	0	0	0	0	0
Franco	1	2	1	1	0	1
Benitez	2	2	1	1	2	2
Rogers (L, 0–2)	1/3	1	1	1	3	0
Total	10-1/3	10	10	10	8	5

BRAVES	IP	H	R	ER	BB	SO
Millwood	5-1/3	8	3	3	0	5
Mulholland	2/3	0	0	0	1	0
Smoltz	1/3	4	4	4	0	0
Remlinger	1-2/3	2	1	1	1	0
Rocker	2	1	1	0	1	1
Springer (W, 1–0)	1	0	0	0	0	0
Total	11	15	9	8	3	6

E—Piazza 2 (3), Hunter; DP—Mets 2, Braves 1; 2B—Alfonzo (4), Franco (1), Henderson (1), Ventura (1), Williams; HR—Piazza (1); IBB—CJones, Jordan, Hunter; HBP—Williams, CJones, Jordan; SH—Ordonez, Perez, Weiss, Boone; SF—Pratt, Piazza, Hunter; SB—Henderson (1), Mora (2), CJones 2 (3), Williams (3), Nixon (2), Boone (2), Hunter (1); CS—Benny Agbayani (1); Time—4:25; ATT—52,335.

1999 NLCS Statistics

COMPOSITE LINESCORE

Mets	210	114	441	100	002	—	21 49 8
Braves	700	217	040	110	001	—	24 46 7

METS BATTING

Player	BA	G	AB	R	H
Benny Agbayani	.143	47	2	1	
Edgardo Alfonzo	.222	6	27	2	6
Armando Benitez	—	5	0	0	0
Bobby Bonilla	.333	3	3	0	1
Roger Cedeno	.500	5	12	2	6
Dennis Cook	—	3	0	0	0
Octavio Dotel	—	1	0	0	0
Shawon Dunston	.143	5	7	2	1
John Franco	—	3	0	0	0
Matt Franco	.500	5	2	1	1
Darryl Hamilton	.353	5	17	0	6
Rickey Henderson	.174	6	23	2	4
Orel Hershiser	.000	2	1	0	0
Al Leiter	.000	2	2	0	0
Pat Mahomes	.000	3	2	0	0
Melvin Mora	.429	6	14	3	6
John Olerud	.296	6	27	4	8
Rey Ordonez	.042	6	24	0	1
Mike Piazza	.167	6	24	1	4
Todd Pratt	.500	4	2	0	1
Rick Reed	.000	1	2	0	0
Kenny Rogers	.000	3	1	0	0
Robin Ventura	.120	6	25	2	3
Turk Wendell	—	5	0	0	0
Masato Yoshii	.000	2	3	0	0
Total	.218	6	225	21	49

2B—Alfonzo 4, Cedeno, MFranco, Hamilton, Henderson, Ventura; 3B—None; HR—Olerud 2, Mora, Piazza; RBI—Olerud 6, Piazza 4, Pratt 3, Hamilton 2, Mora 2, Alfonzo, Cedeno, Henderson, Ventura; SB—Cedeno 2, Mora 2, Agbayani, Dunston, Henderson.

BRAVES BATTING

Player	BA	G	AB	R	H
Howard Battle	.000	3	2	0	0
Bret Boone	.182	6	22	2	4
Jorge Fabregas	.000	2	2	0	0
Tom Glavine	.000	1	2	0	0
Ozzie Guillen	.333	3	3	0	1
Jose Hernandez	.500	2	2	0	1
Brian Hunter	.100	6	10	1	1
Andruw Jones	.217	6	23	5	5
Chipper Jones	.263	6	19	3	5
Brian Jordan	.200	6	25	3	5
Ryan Klesko	.125	4	8	1	1
Keith Lockhart	.400	3	5	0	2
Greg Maddux	.000	2	5	0	0
Kevin McGlinchy	.000	1	1	0	0
Kevin Millwood	.000	2	4	0	0
Terry Mulholland	—	2	0	0	0
Greg Myers	.000	2	2	0	0
Otis Nixon	.000	2	0	1	0
Eddie Perez	.500	6	20	2	10
Mike Remlinger	.000	5	0	0	0
John Rocker	.000	6	0	0	0
John Smoltz	.000	3	2	0	0
Russ Springer	.000	2	0	0	0
Walt Weiss	.286	6	21	2	6
Gerald Williams	.179	6	28	4	5
Total	.223	6	206	24	46

2B—CJones 2, Perez 2, Weiss 2, Williams 2, Boone; 3B—Lockhart; HR—Jordan 2, Perez 2, Klesko; RBI—Jordan 5, Perez 5, Hernandez 2, Hunter 2, Boone, Guillen, AJones, CJones, Klesko, Lockhart, Weiss, Williams; SB—CJones 3, Williams 3, Boone 2, Nixon 2, Weiss 2, Battle, Hunter.

METS PITCHING

Player	G	ERA	W–L	SV	IP	H	ER	BB	SO
Arman. Benitez	5	1.35	0–0	1	6-2/3	3	1	2	9
Dennis Cook	3	0.00	0–0	0	1-1/3	1	0	2	1
Octavio Dotel	1	3.00	1–0	0	3	4	1	2	5
John Franco	3	3.38	0–0	0	2-2/3	3	1	1	3
Orel Hershiser	2	0.00	0–0	0	4-1/3	1	0	3	5
Al Leiter	2	6.43	0–1	0	7	5	5	4	5
Pat Mahomes	3	1.42	0–0	0	6-1/3	4	1	3	3
Rick Reed	1	2.57	0–0	0	7	3	2	0	5
Kenny Rogers	3	5.87	0–2	0	7-2/3	11	5	7	2
Turk Wendell	5	4.76	1–0	0	5-2/3	2	3	4	5
Masato Yoshii	2	4.70	0–1	0	7-2/3	9	4	3	4
Total	6	3.49	2–4	1	59-1/3	46	23	31	47

BRAVES PITCHING

Player	G	ERA	W–L	SV	IP	H	ER	BB	SO
Tom Glavine	1	0.00	1–0	0	7	7	0	1	8
Greg Maddux	2	1.93	1–0	0	14	12	3	1	7
Kev. McGlinchy	1	18.00	0–1	0	1	2	2	4	1
Kevin Millwood	2	3.55	1–0	0	12-2/3	13	5	1	9
Ter. Mulholland	2	0.00	0–0	0	2-2/3	1	0	1	2
Mike Remlinger	5	3.18	0–1	0	5-2/3	3	2	3	4
John Rocker	6	0.00	0–0	2	6-2/3	3	0	2	9
John Smoltz	3	6.23	0–0	1	8-2/3	8	6	0	8
Russ Springer	2	0.00	1–0	0	2	0	0	1	1
Total	6	2.69	4–2	3	60-1/3	49	18	14	49

2000 NLDS: Mets vs. San Francisco Giants

METS WIN SERIES 3–1

You wouldn't have expected Timo Perez, Benny Agbayani and Bobby Jones to emerge as the stars in a series that featured Mike Piazza, Robin Ventura, National League MVP Jeff Kent and MVP runnerup Barry Bonds.

Perez spent the previous four seasons in Asia and didn't play in the majors until September 1. He was expected to come off the bench as a pinch-hitter and a defensive replacement in the playoffs after starting just nine games the final month of the season. But right fielder Derek Bell injured his ankle in the third inning of the series opener, leaving the Mets to sink or swim with Perez the rest of the series. Perez was superb in right field while batting .294 with three RBIs and two runs scored in the series.

Agbayani had a knack for delivering key home runs, including a tiebreaking grand slam in the 10th inning of the Mets' second game of the season against the Cubs in Tokyo. Mired in a 6-for-37 slump that began the final week of the regular season, Agbayani ended the second-longest playoff contest in team history with a homer in the 13th inning of Game 3.

Jones was spectacular in his postseason debut, becoming the first pitcher to throw a one-hit shutout in the postseason since Boston's Jim Lonborg in 1967. It didn't hurt that the gem came in the Mets' series-clinching victory in Game 4.

The Mets won the series despite hitting just .210. Mike Piazza, Robin Ventura, Jay Payton and Mike Bordick were a drag on the starting lineup until Ventura belted a tiebreaking two-run homer in Game 4. Agbayani and Edgardo Alfonzo were the only Mets to bat over .214 while starting each game of the NLDS.

But the Giants' offense was muzzled by the Mets' pinching staff. Ellis Burks and J.T. Snow each hit three-run homers and combined for seven of the team's 11 RBIs. But San Francisco was blanked over the final 18 innings of the series following a two-run rally in the fourth inning of Game 3.

Bonds ended the series 0-for-10 to slide his average down to .176. His career postseason average was now .196 with one homer and six RBIs in 97 at-bats.

Kent hit 6-for-16 (.375) with an RBI, and Snow batted .400 with four ribbies. The rest of the Giants hit .167 with one homer and six RBIs.

The Mets had an edge in the bullpen during the series, although Benitez served up a game-tying three-run homer to Snow in the ninth inning of Game 2. With the exception of Snow's blast, the Mets' relievers combined for 11-2/3 shutout innings. Meanwhile, Giants relievers lost twice and allowed five runs and 14 hits in 19 innings.

The series began in San Francisco, where the Giants swept a four-game series from New York by a combined 32–11 at the beginning of May. The Mets took three of four from San Francisco at Shea in August, dropping the finale 11–1.

The Giants scored 118 more runs than the Mets while hitting .15 higher during the regular season. New York finished third in ERA, just ahead of San Francisco. But the Mets were the team that came up with the clutch hits throughout the NLDS, allowing them to earn a meeting with a former division rival.

GAME 1, October 4, San Francisco: Giants 5, Mets 1

Mike Hampton had only one bad inning, but one was enough while Livan Hernandez was handling the Mets. Hampton opened the bottom of the third by retiring the first two hitters on grounders before Bill Mueller flared a single to left to keep and Barry Bonds tripled him home. Two batters later, Ellis Burks launched a three-run homer that put the Giants ahead 5–1.

In a way, the Bonds triple helped the Mets win the National League pennant. Right fielder Derek Bell suffered a high ankle sprain on the play and was replaced by Darryl Hamilton just before Burks' homer. Timo Perez started

the next 13 games in right field and was the catalyst in the Mets' NLDS and NLCS wins.

Hernandez was masterful while pitching into the eighth inning, blanking the Mets after Jay Payton hit a sacrifice fly in the top of the third. Hernandez was lifted from the game with two outs and the bases loaded in the eighth. But Felix Rodriguez ended the threat by striking out Hamilton.

Mike Piazza and Robin Ventura were a combined 0-for-7 for the Mets, who dropped to 3–7 in playoff series openers.

GAME 2, October 5, San Francisco: Mets 5, Giants 4

This game is an example of why Al Leiter never won a postseason game with the Mets (for further evidence, see Game 3 of the 1999 NLCS and Game 2 of the 2000 NLCS). Leiter carried a four-hitter and a 4–1 lead into the ninth but was replaced by closer Armando Benitez after Barry Bonds led off with a double. Three batters later, Benitez served up a game-tying three-run homer to pinch-hitter J.T. Snow before poaching the victory.

The Mets used a two-out rally in the 10th to regain the lead. Darryl Hamilton lined a double before scoring on Jay Payton's single, giving Benitez another chance to close out the win.

But Benitez was pulled in favor of John Franco after Armando Rios led off the bottom of the 10th with a single. Rios was bunted over to second before shortstop Mike Bordick threw him out at third on a fielder's choice.

That left it up to Bonds, who still wasn't known as a clutch postseason player. He represented the winning run at the plate, but the crafty Franco got him looking to end the game, evening the series 1–1.

"Coming back to win in the 10th shows we're strong enough mentally not to ever give up," Leiter said after accepting a tough no-decision. "That was a huge momentum shift, both ways, in a matter of moments."

Hamilton was a little more enthusiastic about the victory. "It was pretty incredible. The fact that we were up three runs, to lose it in the ninth, but to come back.... I think our mindset obviously changed and we felt very positive after that."

The Mets seemed to be in control when Edgaro Alfonzo hit a two-run homer in the ninth to make it 4–1. Timo Perez drove in the first two runs with a second-inning single. Perez went 3-for-5 with a run scored in his first postseason start.

"He's very positive when he goes out there and plays," Hamilton said of his outfield partner. "He knows that when he goes out there that he can make something happen to help this ballclub win."

GAME 3, October 7, New York: Mets 3, Giants 2 (13 innings)

For the second time in five playoff games the Mets were involved in a battle that lasted more than five hours. Benny Agbayani, who was 0-for-5 in the game and 2-for-10 in the series, ended the marathon with a one-out homer in the bottom of the 13th.

"It's a great feeling to be the man," said Agbayani after belting the Mets' third walkoff homer in postseason history. "We're one of those teams that never say die. We know anything can happen.

"It's just a great feeling to go out there and hit a home run in the big dance, in the playoffs."

It was the third time Agbayani had earned heavy high-light-show recognition during the year. The first was his grand slam against the Cubs in Tokyo, sending the Mets to their first win of the year. The second came against the Giants in August, when he lost track of the number of outs. Agbayani caught Marvin Benard's sacrifice fly and, thinking it was the third out, gave it to a kid in the stands along the leftfield line while Ellis Burks was scoring from second on the play. This homer was a lot sweeter than his mental gaffe. "I guess I won't be remembered just for that anymore," laughed the outfielder.

Agbayani came through after winning pitcher Rick White worked in and out of a two-on, two-out jam in the top of the 13th. Barry Bonds stranded runners on first and second by popping up to end the half-inning, two days af-

ter striking out looking against John Franco for the final out in Game 2.

"If you read his track record, he hasn't done very good in the postseason," White told the media following the game. "So that's all I was thinking about, was just don't make a mistake here."

The Mets had to rally after Bobby Estalella and Marvin Benard hit RBI singles off Rick Reed in the fourth inning.

Russ Ortiz was still working on a no-hitter when Mike Bordick led off the bottom of the sixth with a walk. The no-hitter was gone after Darryl Hamilton singled, and the shutout ended when new fan favorite Timo Perez singled to make it 2–1 with runners on first and second with nobody out. But the Mets didn't tie the game until Edgardo Alfonzo hit a two-out, RBI double in the eighth off Robb Nen, who hadn't blown a save since July 2.

The Mets stranded two runners in the ninth and left the bases loaded in the 11th before Agbayani gave the Mets a 2–1 lead in the series. Agbayani was partly responsible for the missed opportunity in the 11th, failing to get down a bunt attempt with runners on first and second with nobody out before flying out

The Mets' bullpen was outstanding, limiting the Giants to four hits in seven shutout innings. It would be four days before manager Bobby Valentine would need his bullpen again.

GAME 4, October 8, New York: Mets 4, Giants 0

Bobby Jones struggled during the regular season, winning 11 games but posting a 5.06 ERA in 154-2/3 innings. He earned a spot in the postseason rotation by going 3–1 with a 3.54 earned run average in his last four regular-season starts. He would reward manager Bobby Valentine's faith in him by tossing the finest game in Mets postseason history.

"If he needed vindication, I'm glad he got it," Valentine said after Jones became the first pitcher to throw a one-hit shutout in the postseason since Jim Lonborg in the 1967 World Series. "People like to look at the speed gun and say he's not an upper-echelon pitcher. But it's what he does with that 84 mph fastball that torments people."

Jones guided the Mets to a series-clinching victory while becoming only the third pitcher in major league postseason history to throw a one-hit shutout. The only base runners he allowed came in the fifth inning, when Jeff Kent led off with a double and Jones walked J.T. Snow and Doug Mirabelli to load the bases. But the inning ended when pitcher Mark

Gardner popped up to second to keep the Mets ahead 2–0.

Jones retired his final 13 batters and ended the series by getting Barry Bonds to line out to center. Bonds went hitless in his final 10 at-bats in the series, making the Giants' final out in their three losses.

"I just felt I could throw the ball wherever I wanted to. I had confidence in all of my pitches," said Jones.

Robin Ventura entered the game 1-for-11 with no homers or RBIs in the series, but he gave the Mets a quick 2–0 lead in the first inning with a two-run homer following a two-out walk to Mike Piazza. Edgardo Alfonzo doubled the lead with a two-run double that chased Gardner in the fifth.

That was more than enough offense for Jones, who had never pitched in a postseason game before helping the Mets advance to the NLCS against the Cardinals. Game 2 starter Al Leiter was especially happy for his teammate.

"To go out and pitch the best game of his life and dismiss all the critics who thought this was a bad decision," said Leiter, "he went out and nailed it."

Game 1, October 4 at San Francisco
GIANTS 5, METS 1

Mets	AB	R	H	BI	Giants	AB	R	H	BI
Agbayani lf	3	0	1	0	Benard cf	4	0	0	0
Cook p	0	0	0	0	Davis ph	1	0	0	0
White p	0	0	0	0	Nen p	0	0	0	0
McEwing lf	0	0	0	0	Mueller 3b	5	2	2	0
Harris ph	1	0	0	0	Bonds lf	3	1	2	1
Payton cf	3	0	0	1	Kent 2b	3	1	1	1
Alfonzo 2b	4	0	1	0	Burks rf	3	1	1	3
Piazza c	3	0	0	0	Aurilia ss	4	0	2	0
Ventura 3b	4	0	0	0	Snow 1b	3	0	1	0
Zeile 1b	3	0	1	0	Estalella c	4	0	0	0
Bell rf	1	0	0	0	Hernandez p	3	0	0	0
Hamilton rf-lf	2	0	0	0	Rodriguez p	0	0	0	0
Rusch p	0	0	0	0	Crespo ph	1	0	1	0
Bordick ss	3	1	1	0	Murray cf	0	0	0	0
Hampton p	2	0	1	0					
Wendell p	0	0	0	0					
Perez ph-rf	2	0	0	0					
Totals	31	1	5	1		34	5	10	5

Mets	001	000	000	1	5	0
Giants	104	000	00x	5	10	0

METS	IP	H	R	ER	BB	SO
Hampton (L, 0–1)	5-1/3	6	5	5	3	2
Wendell	2/3	0	0	0	0	2
Cook	2/3	0	0	0	1	1
White	2/3	4	0	0	0	0
Rusch	2/3	0	0	0	0	2
Total	8	10	5	5	4	7

GIANTS	IP	H	R	ER	BB	SO
Hernandez (W, 1–0)	7-2/3	5	1	1	5	5
Rodriguez	1/3	0	0	0	0	1
Nen	1	0	0	0	0	0
Total	9	5	1	1	5	6

2B—Zeile (1), Mueller (1), Aurilia (1); 3B—Bonds (1); HR—Burks (1 ; IBB—Snow; SF—Payton; SB—Bonds (1); Time—3:06; ATT—40,430.

Game 2, October 5 at San Francisco
METS 5, GIANTS 4 (10)

Mets	AB	R	H	BI	Giants	AB	R	H	BI
Perez rf	5	1	3	2	Murray cf	4	0	1	0
Alfonzo 2b	5	1	1	2	Benard ph	0	0	0	0
Piazza c	4	0	2	0	Mueller 3b	5	0	1	0
Zeile 1b	5	0	0	0	Bonds lf	5	1	1	0
Ventura 3b	3	0	0	0	Kent 1b-2b	4	2	2	0
Agbayani lf	2	0	1	0	Burks rf	3	0	1	1
McEwing pr-lf	0	0	0	0	Martinez 2b	3	0	0	0
Hamilton ph-lf	1	1	1	0	Snow ph-1b	1	1	1	3
Payton cf	5	1	1	1	Aurilia ss	4	0	0	0
Bordick ss	4	1	1	0	Estalella c	4	0	0	0
Leiter p	4	0	0	0	Estes p	0	0	0	0
Benitez p	0	0	0	0	Rueter p	0	0	0	0
Franco p	0	0	0	0	Henry p	0	0	0	0
					Crespo ph	1	0	0	0
					Rodriguez p	0	0	0	0
					Rios ph	1	0	1	0
Totals	38	5	10	5		35	4	8	4

Mets	020	000	002 1	5	10	0
Giants	010	000	003 0	4	8	0

METS	IP	H	R	ER	BB	SO
Leiter	8	5	2	2	3	6
Benitez (W, 1–0)	1	3	2	2	0	0
Franco (S, 1)	1	0	0	0	0	1
Total	10	8	4	4	3	7

GIANTS	IP	H	R	ER	BB	SO
Estes	3	3	2	2	3	3
Rueter	4-1/3	3	0	0	1	1
Henry	2/3	0	0	0	1	0
Rodriguez (L, 0–1)	2	4	3	3	0	3
Total	10	10	5	5	5	7

DP—Mets 1, Giants 2; 2B—Piazza (1), Hamilton (1), Burks (1), Bonds (1); HR—Alfonzo (1), Snow (1); HBP—Ventura; SH—Benard; SB—Kent; Time—3:41; ATT—40,430.

Game 3, October 7 at New York
METS 3, GIANTS 2 (13)

Giants	AB	R	H	BI	Mets	AB	R	H	BI
Benard cf-rf	6	0	1	1	Perez rf	6	0	1	1
Mueller 3b	6	0	2	0	Alfonzo 2b	5	0	2	1
Bonds lf	5	0	0	0	Piazza c	4	0	1	0
Kent 2b	6	0	2	0	McEwing pr-3b	1	0	1	0
Burks rf	4	1	1	0	Ventura 3b-1b	5	0	1	0
Fultz p	0	0	0	0	Agbayani lf	6	1	1	1
Snow 1b	4	0	2	0	Payton cf	5	0	1	0
Aurilia ss	4	0	0	0	Zeile 1b	3	0	0	0
Nen p	0	0	0	0	White p	0	0	0	0
Rios ph	1	0	0	0	Bordick ss	2	1	0	0
Mirabelli c	1	0	0	0	Benitez p	0	0	0	0
Estalella c	4	1	1	1	Pratt ph-c	1	0	0	0
Crespo ph	1	0	0	0	Reed p	1	0	0	0
Rodriguez p	0	0	0	0	Hamilton ph	1	0	1	0
Murray cf	1	0	0	0	Cook p	0	0	0	0
Ortiz p	3	0	0	0	Wendell p	0	0	0	0
Embree p	0	0	0	0	Harris ph	1	1	0	0
Henry p	0	0	0	0	Franco p	0	0	0	0
Martinez ss	3	0	2	0	Abbott ss	2	0	0	0
Totals	49	2	11	2		43	3	9	3

Giants	000	200	000	000	0	2	11	0
Mets	000	001	010	000	1	3	9	0

GIANTS	IP	H	R	ER	BB	SO
Ortiz	5-1/3	2	1	1	4	4
Embree	2/3	0	0	0	0	0
Henry	1-2/3	0	1	1	0	1
Nen	1-1/3	2	0	0	1	3
Rodriguez	2	2	0	0	1	2
Fultz (L, 0–1)	1-1/3	3	1	1	0	0
Total	12-1/3 9	3	3	6	10	

METS	IP	H	R	ER	BB	SO
Reed	6	7	2	2	2	6
Cook	2/3	0	0	0	1	0
Wendell	1-1/3	0	0	0	1	3
Franco	1	1	0	0	0	1
Benitez	2	1	0	0	1	3
White (W, 1–0)	2	2	0	0	2	4
Total	13	11	2	2	7	17

DP—Mets 0, Giants 2; 2B—Alfonzo (1), Mueller (2); HR—Agbayani (1); IBB—Piazza, Snow, Bonds; HBP—Bordick; SH—Mueller; SB—Payton (1), Harris (1); CS—Alfonzo (1); Time—5:22; ATT—56,270.

Game 4, October 8 at New York
METS 4, GIANTS 0

Giants	AB	R	H	BI	Mets	AB	R	H	BI
Benard cf	4	0	0	0	Perez rf	4	1	1	0
Mueller 3b	4	0	0	0	Alfonzo 2b	4	0	1	2
Bonds lf	4	0	0	0	Piazza c	3	1	0	0
Kent 2b	3	0	1	0	Ventura 3b	2	1	1	2
Burks rf	3	0	0	0	Agbayani lf	4	0	2	0
Snow 1b	2	0	0	0	McEwing pr-lf	0	0	0	0
Aurilia ss	3	0	0	0	Payton cf	4	0	1	0
Mirabelli c	1	0	0	0	Zeile 1b	3	0	0	0
Crespo ph	1	0	0	0	Bordick ss	3	0	0	0
Estalella c	0	0	0	0	Jones p	4	1	0	0
Gardner p	2	0	0	0					
Henry p	0	0	0	0					
Embree p	0	0	0	0					
Davis ph	1	0	0	0					
Del Toro p	0	0	0	0					

Giants	000	000	000	0	1	1	
Mets	200	020	00x	4	6	0	

GIANTS	IP	H	R	ER	BB	SO
Gardner (L, 0–1)	4-1/3	4	4	4	2	5
Henry	1-2/3	1	0	0	2	0
Embree	1	0	0	0	0	0
Del Toro	1	1	0	0	0	2
Total	8	6	4	4	4	7

METS	IP	H	R	ER	BB	SO
Jones (W, 1–0)	9	1	0	0	2	5

E—Aurilia; WP—Gardner; 2B—Alfonzo (2), Agbayani (1), Perez (1), Kent (1); HR—Ventura (1); IBB—Ventura; HBP—Bordick; SB—Perez (1); CS—Payton (1); Time—2:48; ATT—52,888.

2000 NLDS Statistics

COMPOSITE LINESCORE

Mets	221	021	012	100	1	13 30 0
Giants	114	200	003	000	0	11 30 1

METS BATTING

Player	BA	G	AB	R	H
Kurt Abbott	.000	1	2	0	0
Benny Agbayani	.333	4	15	1	5
Edgardo Alfonzo	.278	4	18	1	5
Derek Bell	.000	1	1	0	0
Armando Benitez	—	2	0	0	0
Mike Bordick	.167	4	12	3	2
Dennis Cook	—	2	0	0	0
John Franco	—	2	0	0	0
Darryl Hamilton	.500	3	4	1	2
Mike Hampton	.500	1	2	0	1
Lenny Harris	.000	2	2	1	0
Bobby Jones	.000	1	4	1	0
Al Leiter	.000	1	4	0	0
Joe McEwing	1.000	4	1	0	1
Jay Payton	.176	4	17	1	3
Timo Perez	.294	4	17	2	5
Mike Piazza	.214	4	14	1	3
Todd Pratt	.000	1	1	0	0
Rick Reed	.000	1	1	0	0
Glendon Rusch	—	1	0	0	0
Robin Ventura	.143	4	14	1	2
Turk Wendell	—	2	0	0	0
Rick White	—	2	0	0	0
Todd Zeile	.071	4	14	0	1
Total	.210	4	143	13	30

2B—Alfonzo 2, Agbayani, Hamilton, Perez, Piazza, Zeile; 3B—None; HR—Agbayani, Alfonzo, Ventura; RBI—Alfonzo 5, Perez 3, Payton 2, Ventura 2, Agbayani; SB—Harris, Payton, Perez.

GIANTS BATTING

Player	BA	G	AB	R	H
Rich Aurilia	.133	4	15	0	2
Marvin Benard	.133	4	14	0	1
Barry Bonds	.176	4	17	2	3
Ellis Burks	.412	4	13	2	3
Felipe Crespo	.250	4	4	0	1
Russ Davis	.000	2	2	0	0
Miguel del Toro	—	1	0	0	0
Alan Embree	—	2	0	0	0
Bobby Estalella	.083	4	12	1	1
Shawn Estes	.000	1	0	0	0
Aaron Fultz	—	1	0	0	0
Mark Gardner	.000	1	2	0	0
Doug Henry	—	3	0	0	0
Livan Hernandez	.000	1	3	0	0
Jeff Kent	.375	4	16	3	6
Ramon Martinez	.333	2	6	0	2
Doug Mirabelli	.000	2	2	0	0
Bill Mueller	.250	4	20	2	5
Calvin Murray	.200	3	5	0	1
Robb Nen	—	2	0	0	0
Russ Ortiz	.000	1	3	0	0
Armando Rios	.500	2	2	0	1
Felix Rodriguez	—	3	0	0	0
Kirk Rueter	.000	1	0	0	0
J.T. Snow	.400	4	10	1	4
Total	.205	4	146	11	30

2B—Mueller 2, Aurilia, Bonds, Burks, Kent; 3B—Bonds; HR—Burks, Snow; RBI—Burks 4, Snow 3, Benard, Bonds, Estalella, Kent; SB—Bonds, Kent.

METS PITCHING

Player	G	ERA	W–L	SV	IP	H	ER	BB	SO
Armando Benitez	2	6.00	1–0	0	3	4	2	1	3
Dennis Cook	2	0.00	0–0	0	1-1/3	0	0	2	1
John Franco	2	0.00	0–0	1	2	1	0	0	2
Mike Hampton	1	8.44	0–1	0	5-1/3	6	5	3	2
Bobby Jones	1	0.00	1–0	0	9	1	0	2	5
Al Leiter	1	2.25	0–0	0	8	5	2	3	6
Rick Reed	1	3.00	0–0	0	6	7	2	2	6
Glendon Rusch	1	0.00	0–0	0	2/3	0	0	0	2
Turk Wendell	2	0.00	0–0	0	2	0	0	1	5
Rick White	2	0.00	1–0	0	2-2/3	6	0	2	4
Total	4	2.48	3–1	1	40	30	11	16	36

GIANTS PITCHING

Player	G	ERA	W–L	SV	IP	H	ER	BB	SO
Miguel del Toro	1	0.00	0–0	0	1	1	0	0	2
Alan Embree	2	0.00	0–0	0	1-2/3	0	0	0	0
Shawn Estes	1	6.00	0–0	0	3	3	2	3	3
Aaron Fultz	1	6.75	0–1	0	1-1/3	3	1	0	0
Mark Gardner	1	8.31	0–1	0	4-1/3	4	4	2	5
Doug Henry	3	2.25	0–0	0	4	1	1	3	1
Liv. Hernandez	1	1.17	1–0	0	7-2/3	5	1	5	5
Robb Nen	2	0.00	0–0	0	2-1/3	2	0	1	3
Russ Ortiz	1	1.69	0–0	0	5-1/3	2	1	4	4
Felix Rodriguez	3	6.23	0–1	0	4-1/3	6	3	1	6
Kirk Rueter	1	0.00	0–0	0	4-1/3	3	0	1	1
Total	4	2.97	1–3	0	39-1/3	30	13	20	30

2000 NLCS: Mets vs. St. Louis Cardinals

METS WIN SERIES 4–1

The Mets were able to snatch up their fourth National League pennant while the organization exacted some revenge on the team that nosed them out of NL East titles in 1985 and '87. But the Cardinals looked pretty scary heading into Game 1 of the NLCS.

Even without a healthy Mark McGwire the Cardinals were able to blast the Braves out of the postseason in a three-game sweep. Jim Edmonds spearheaded the rout by hitting .571 with two homers and seven RBIs for the Redbirds, who scored 24 runs in the three games. The Cardinals held the Braves to a .189 average while allowing only one homer and nine runs. They were just continuing a pattern that saw them go 26–11 after August 23. The late-season stretch also included a three-game sweep of the Mets at St. Louis the beginning of September.

But the Mets had swept a three-game set from the Cards at Busch Stadium in late May before doing it again in New York two months later. The Cardinals were the only NL playoff team to post a losing record against New York.

New York entered the NLCS off a four-game series win over the Giants, who had the league's best regular-season record. By now, the Mets were looking like a ballclub worthy of playing for the World Series title, and proved that against St. Louis with three convincing victories and a ninth-inning rally in the other win.

The Cardinals got off to great starts versus the Braves in the NLDS, scoring a total of 10 runs in the first inning of the three games. The Mets were the team that started off strong in the championship series, producing 11 runs in the opening inning, including seven in the first inning of the final two games.

Mike Piazza had the best postseason series of his career, hitting .412 with two homers and four RBIs while scoring seven times. Edgardo Alfonzo also swung a lethal bat, posting a .444 average with four ribbies and five runs scored. And Todd Zeile stuck it to one of his former teams, setting a Mets NLCS record with eight RBIs while batting .368.

But the stars of the series were Timo Perez and Mike Hampton as the Mets captured their first pennant since 1986. Perez had at least one hit in each game of the series and tied an NLCS mark with eight runs scored. Five of those runs came while the Mets were outscoring the Cardinals 17–6 in the final two games of the series. Hampton was the series MVP and shutting out the Redbirds in each of his two starts. He capped the series with a three-hitter after tossing seven innings in a series-opening win.

Outside of Hampton the Mets' pitching was shaky in the series. If you take away Hampton's 16 shutout innings, the Mets posted a 5.58 ERA. But that was still better than the Cardinals' 5.86 team ERA, which included an 8.06 mark by their starting hurlers.

GAME 1, October 11, St. Louis: Mets 6, Cardinals 2

Mike Hampton was pinned with the Mets' only loss of the NLDS, surrendering five runs in 5-1/3 innings of Game 1. He made up for that poor performance by blanking the Cardinals over seven innings in the NLCS opener while outpitching former teammate Darryl Kile.

The Mets led before Kile retired a batter. Timo Perez opened the game with a double and scored on Mike Piazza's two-base hit before Robin Ventura lifted a sacrifice fly that put New York ahead 2–0.

Mets fans must have thought they were in for a very long night when Hampton walked Will Clark to load the bases with two outs in the bottom half of the first. But Hampton preserved the two-run lead by getting Carlos Hernandez to ground out.

Hampton worked just one perfect inning and continued to put himself in mini-jams without cracking. St. Louis had a runner on second with one out in the third and fifth innings, then put a runner at third in the sixth and seventh. But the lefty continued to get the big outs while the Mets expanded their lead. Hampton sparked the Mets'

fifth-inning rally with a one-out single before scoring from second on Edgardo Alfonzo's single that made it 3–0.

Hampton put nine men on base during his seven innings but extended the Mets' shutout streak, which reached 26 innings when John Franco worked a scoreless eighth.

"I just wanted a quality start that puts the team in position to win," Hampton said after the game. "It was one of those games where every pitch had a meaning behind it. You're focused on every pitch trying to execute it."

New York doubled its lead with a pair of ninth-inning homers. Former Cardinal Todd Zeile led off with a blast against Mike James, who also served up a two-run homer to Jay Payton. James angered the Mets by hitting Mike Bordick with a pitch following Payton's blast before Jason Christiansen got the last three outs of the inning.

The Mets were deprived of a second straight shutout when shortstop Kurt Abbott threw away a potential game-ending ground ball. Ray Lankford scored on the error and Jim Edmonds added an RBI grounder before Armando Benitez retired Eric Davis on a grounder to third.

GAME 2, October 12, St. Louis: Mets 6, Cardinals 5

The Mets were able to go up 2–0 in the series by scoring an unearned run in the ninth after blowing a pair of two-run leads. The Cardinals rallied for two runs in the eighth, preventing Al Leiter from picking up his elusive first postseason victory.

Edgardo Alfonzo and Todd Zeile delivered RBI singles with two outs in the eighth to put the Mets ahead 5–3. But the Redbirds answered back by scoring twice in the eighth off the New York bullpen after Leiter concluded his work. Carlos Hernandez scored on a wild pitch by John Franco to make it 5–4, and J.D. Drew knotted the game with a two-out double off Turk Wendell. Mark McGwire was walked intentionally before Wendell fanned Craig Paquette to end the rally.

The Mets wasted little time regaining the lead. Robin Ventura led off the ninth with a grounder that was booted by first baseman Will Clark. Benny Agbayani bunted Ventura over to second before Jay Payton hit an RBI single that gave the Mets their third lead of the game.

The Mets had bent twice without breaking, a sign they were going to reach the World Series for the first time in 14 years. "We know what it takes to win," said Alfonzo following the contest. "The one thing we just set our mind to, to never give up, just keep fighting until the end. One more time, we proved it."

Cardinals starter Rick Ankiel couldn't get out of the first inning, walking three and throwing a wild pitch. Zeile hit a sacrifice fly and Agbayani added an RBI double that put the Mets up 2–0 and ended Ankiel's night. Mike Piazza launched an opposite-field homer that made it 3–1 in the third.

The Mets had a great opportunity to add runs in the fourth. Alfonzo lined a two-out triple and Piazza was walked intentionally before Zeile worked out a free pass to load the bases. Robin Ventura grounded out to end the threat when the Mets had a chance to put away the game.

The lead vanished when Leiter surrendered RBI doubles by Edgar Renteria and Fernando Tatis in the bottom of the fifth. Leiter appeared to settle in after losing the lead, retiring his final seven batters to keep the game deadlocked. But he was lifted for a pinch-hitter in the Mets' two-run eighth after throwing 125 pitches and striking out nine.

Benitez closed out the victory, and the Mets headed home with a 2–0 lead in the series. It marked the first time they had taken the first two games of a playoff round since the 1969 NLCS.

Piazza knew the Mets hadn't won anything yet. "We can't let up. We just have to keep going. We are happy about this win but we aren't done by any means at all. Hopefully, we will come out aggressive at home."

GAME 3, October 14, New York: Cardinals 8, Mets 2

Rick Reed had just one poor outing in his five postseason starts as a Met. This was it.

Reed failed to get out of the fourth inning, leaving the game after Edgar Renteria's RBI single gave the Cardinals a 5–1 lead. Jim Edmonds put the Cardinals ahead just three batters into the game, doubling home a pair of runs following a single and an error. Reed also gave up a single to Will Clark to put runners on first and third with nobody out in the first. The Mets' starter regrouped in time to strike out Ray Lankford, Fernando Tatis and J.D. Drew to

end the inning. But Lankford and Tatis drove in runs in the third to make it 4–1.

The Mets were held to seven singles and no RBIs, scoring their two runs on double-play grounders that killed potentially big rallies. St. Louis allowed just two hits after scoring three times in the fifth to take an 8–2 lead.

Andy Benes limited the Mets to six hits and three walks over eight innings, striking out the side in the seventh inning. Dave Veres also fanned three straight to end the game after Mike James put two runners on.

GAME 4, October 15, New York: Mets 10, Cardinals 6

The Mets won easily by getting outstanding production from the top six hitters in the lineup. Robin Ventura and Todd Zeile supplied two-run doubles while the Mets were building a 7–2 lead in the first two innings. Benny Agbayani added an RBI double and a run-scoring single during the early uprising, and Edgardo Alfonzo chipped in an RBI double that opened the scoring.

The Mets began the bottom of the first with four straight doubles to take a 3–0 lead. Agbayani resumed the doubles parade after Zeile grounded out. The Mets doubled five

times during the rally, setting a postseason record for two-base hits in an inning.

Each of the first six hitters in the Mets' lineup doubled off Darryl Kile, who was rocked for seven runs and eight hits in three innings.

Ventura had three RBIs, and Piazza and Timo Perez each scored three times in the Mets' highest postseason run production since Game 2 of the 1973 World Series. Piazza also hit a solo homer in the fourth to put the Mets ahead 8–3.

Bobby Jones, who pitched a one-hit shutout in the NLDS clincher a week earlier, gave most of the lead back before he was lifted in the fifth inning ahead 8–4. Jim Edmonds nicked him for a two-run homer in the first inning, and Will Clark added a third-inning blast before the Cardinals scored three times in the fifth to close within 8–6.

The score remained 8–6 until Mike Timlin and Tatis had trouble throwing the ball in the sixth. Mike Bordick scored on Tatis' second error of the inning after Timlin walked Bordick and hit Alfonzo. Ventura's fly ball scored Perez to make it 10–6 later in the inning.

Glendon Rusch allowed two inherited runners to score but was otherwise excellent, tossing three shutout innings to keep the Mets ahead. "Those are the three huge innings," said manager Bobby Valentine of Rusch's performance. "I mean, we don't win the game without that kind of performance, I don't think."

John Franco put two runners on with two outs in the eighth, and Armando Benitez faced a two-on, nobody out situation in the ninth. But the Cards failed to score in the late innings, allowing the Mets to escape with a 3–1 lead in the series. The Mets now wanted to close out the series on their home turf.

"We don't want to go back to St. Louis, Piazza said. "We have our guy (Mike Hampton) on the mound that has pitched great for us...We want to take care of it tomorrow and hopefully come out and score runs and win the game."

GAME 5, October 16, New York: Mets 7, Cardinals 0

Mike Hampton topped his performance in the series opener while helping the Mets wrap up their fourth National League pennant. Hampton was named the NLCS Most Valuable Player after tossing a three-hitter that included eight strikeouts and just one walk. He allowed just one base runner after the fourth inning and retired his last 11 batters.

"(Hampton) did everything anybody could hope he could do in the biggest game of his life and mine, too," said Bobby Valentine, who was finally in the World Series after 1,885 games as a big league manager

The game was virtually decided five batters into the bottom of the first. Timo Perez led off with a single and stole second before advancing to third on a throwing error by catcher Carlos Hernandez. Edgardo Alfonzo and Robin Ventura wrapped RBI singles around Mike Piazza's walk before Todd Zeile finally made the first out of the half-inning, an RBI grounder.

The three-run first allowed Hampton to relax. "That settled me down," said the Mets' latest postseason hero. "My emotions were running high. I was really pumped up for this."

Cardinals starter Pat Hentgen stuck around long enough for Zeile to chase him with a three-run double in the fourth. "I just wanted to hit it hard," said Zeile. "I didn't care where it went."

Mike Timlin and Britt Reames followed with 2-1/3 shutout innings of relief, but the game and the series were over.

The game took on a disturbingly comical note when Rick Ankiel took the mound in the seventh inning. Ankiel walked two of the four batters he faced and threw a pair of wild pitches with Alfonzo at the plate, allowing the seventh and final run to score. Manager Tony LaRussa mercifully took Ankiel out of the game before the young lefty could endure any more embarrassment.

Tempers flared when Jay Payton was hit on the head by a Dave Veres pitch in the eighth inning. Both benches emptied but no punches were thrown.

Hampton closed out the victory by getting pinch-hitter Rick Wilkins to hit a fly ball to short center. Perez half-ran, half-hopped after the ball before snagging it for the final out.

"I felt very happy and very secure because the last out was in my hands," Perez said with assistant GM Omar Minaya serving as his interpreter. "The last out was in my control...I was just jumping for joy."

The Mets still didn't know who they would be playing in the World Series. The Mariners had forced a sixth game of the ALCS by pounding the Yankees the previous day.

"I'd love to see a Subway Series, said Zeile. "I have unfinished business with the Yankees as far as I'm concerned. They've eliminated me the other three times I've had a chance to be in the postseason."

Piazza had a great perspective on the pennant. "You feel like a rock star playing in a town like this. But now I can appreciate it twice as much.

"It's like graduation day, only better. We've put in so much work, and the results are finally there."

Game 1, October 11 at St. Louis
METS 6, CARDINALS 2

Mets	AB	R	H	BI	Cardinals	AB	R	H	BI
Perez rf	5	1	1	0	Vina 2b	4	0	1	0
Alfonzo 2b	3	1	1	1	Renteria ss	5	1	1	0
Piazza c	4	0	2	1	Edmonds cf	5	0	2	0
Ventura 3b	2	0	0	1	Davis rf	5	0	1	0
Zeile 1b	4	1	1	1	Clark 1b	3	0	1	0
Agbayani lf	4	0	1	0	Hernandez c	4	0	1	0
McEwing pr-lf	0	1	0	0	Marrero pr-c	0	0	0	0
Payton cf	4	1	1	2	Drew lf	3	0	0	0
Bordick ss	3	0	0	0	Dunston ph-lf	1	0	0	0
Abbott pr-ss	0	0	0	0	Polanco 3b	3	0	1	0
Hampton p	3	1	1	0	James p	0	0	0	0
JFranco p	0	0	0	0	Christiansen p	0	0	0	0
Hamilton ph	0	0	0	0	Lankford ph	1	1	1	0
Trammell ph	1	0	0	0	Kile p	1	0	0	0
Benitez p	0	0	0	0	Tatis ph-3b	2	0	0	0
Totals	33	6	8	6		37	2	9	0

Mets	200	010	003	6	8	3	
Cardinals	000	000	002	2	9	0	

METS	IP	H	R	ER	BB	SO
Hampton (W, 1–0)	7	6	0	0	3	4
Franco	1	1	0	0	0	1
Benitez	1	2	2	0	0	0
Total	9	9	2	0	3	5

CARDINALS	IP	H	R	ER	BB	SO
Kile (L, 0–1)	7	5	3	3	2	1
James	1	3	3	3	0	0
Christiansen	1	0	0	0	0	1
Total	9	8	6	6	2	2

E—Perez (1), Agbayani (1), Abbott (1); DP—Mets 0, Cardinals 1; WP—Hampton; 2B—Piazza (1), Perez (1), Clark (1), Lankford (1); HR—Payton (1), Zeile (1); HBP—Bordick; SF—Ventura; Time—3:08; ATT—52,255.

Game 2, October 12 at St. Louis
METS 6, CARDINALS 5

Mets	AB	R	H	BI	Cardinals	AB	R	H	BI
Perez rf	5	1	1	0	Vina 2b	5	1	1	0
Alfonzo 2b	3	2	2	1	Renteria ss	5	1	3	1
Piazza c	2	2	1	1	Edmonds cf	4	0	0	0
Zeile 1b	3	0	2	2	Tatis 3b	3	0	1	1
JFranco p	0	0	0	0	Morris p	0	0	0	0
Wendell p	0	0	0	0	Hernandez c	1	1	0	0
Benitez p	0	0	0	0	Clark 1b	4	1	2	0
Ventura 3b	4	0	1	0	Dunston rf-lf	3	1	1	0
McEwing pr-3b	0	1	0	0	Lankford lf	3	0	1	0
Agbayani lf	4	0	1	1	Polanco ph	0	0	0	0
Payton cf	4	0	1	1	Drew ph-rf	1	0	1	1
Abbott ss	3	0	0	0	Marrero c	3	0	1	1
MFranco ph-1b	2	0	0	0	Veres p	0	0	0	0
Leiter p	3	0	0	0	McGwire ph	0	0	0	0
Hamilton ph	1	0	0	0	Kile pr	0	0	0	0
Bordick ss	1	0	0	0	Timlin p	0	0	0	0
					Ankiel p	0	0	0	0
					Reames p	1	0	0	0
					Davis ph	0	0	0	0
					Paquette 3b	2	0	0	0
Totals	35	6	9	6		36	5	10	4

Mets	201	000	021	6	9	0	
Cardinals	010	020	020	5	10	3	

METS	IP	H	R	ER	BB	SO
Leiter	7	8	3	3	0	9
Franco	2/3	1	2	2	1	0
Wendell (W, 1–0)	1/3	1	0	0	1	1
Benitez (S, 1)	1	0	0	0	1	1
Total	9	10	5	5	3	11

CARDINALS	IP	H	R	ER	BB	SO
Ankiel	2/3	1	2	2	3	1
Reames	4-1/3	3	1	1	3	6
Morris	2-2/3	3	2	2	2	2
Veres	1/3	1	0	0	0	0
Timlin (L, 0–1)	1	1	1	0	0	0
Total	9	9	6	6	8	9

E—Vina (1), Edmonds (1), Clark (1); PB—Marrero; WP—Franco; 2B—Agbayani (1), Zeile (1), Dunston (1), Clark (2), Renteria (1), Tatis (1), Drew (1); 3B—Alfonzo (1); HR—Piazza (1); IBB—Piazza 2, McGwire; SH—Agbayani, Dunston; SF—Zeile; SB—Renteria 3; Time—3:59; ATT—52,250.

Game 3, October 14 at New York
CARDINALS 8, METS 2

Cardinals	AB	R	H	BI	Mets	AB	R	H	BI
Vina 2b	5	1	2	1	Perez rf	4	1	1	0
Renteria ss	4	2	2	2	Alfonzo 2b	4	0	2	0
Edmonds cf	5	0	1	2	Piazza c	4	0	1	0
Clark 1b	3	1	2	0	Ventura 3b	3	1	0	0
Lankford lf	2	0	1	1	Zeile 1b	4	0	2	0
McGwire ph	1	0	0	0	Agbayani lf	3	0	1	0
Paquette lf	2	0	1	0	Payton cf	3	0	0	0
Tatis 3b	3	1	1	1	Bordick ss	2	0	0	0
Drew rf	5	1	2	0	MFranco ph	1	0	0	0
Hernandez c	5	1	1	1	Reed p	1	0	0	0
Benes p	3	1	1	0	Rusch p	0	0	0	0
Wilkins ph	1	0	0	0	Hamilton ph	1	0	0	0
James p	0	0	0	0	White p	0	0	0	0
Veres p	0	0	0	0	Harris ph	1	0	0	0
					Cook p	0	0	0	0
					Wendell p	0	0	0	0
					Trammell ph	1	0	0	0
Totals	39	8	14	8		32	2	7	0

Cardinals	202	130	000	8	14	0
Mets	100	100	000	2	7	1

CARDINALS	IP	H	R	ER	BB	SO
Benes (W, 1–0)	8	6	2	2	3	5
James	0	1	0	0	1	0
Veres	1	0	0	0	0	3
Total	9	7	2	2	4	8

METS	IP	H	R	ER	BB	SO
Reed (L, 0–1)	3-1/3	8	5	4	1	4
Rusch	2/3	0	0	0	0	1
White	3	5	3	3	1	1
Cook	1	1	0	0	0	2
Wendell	1	0	0	0	0	1
Total	9	14	8	7	2	9

E—Ventura (1); DP—Cardinals 2, Mets 0; 2B—Edmonds (1), Tatis (2); HBP—Clark; SH—Benes, Renteria; SF—Tatis; Time—3:33; ATT—55,693.

Game 4, October 15 at New York
METS 10, CARDINALS 8

Cardinals	AB	R	H	BI	Mets	AB	R	H	BI
Vina 2b	5	1	1	0	Perez rf	4	3	2	0
Renteria ss	3	0	0	1	Alfonzo 2b	4	1	1	1
Edmonds cf	5	1	2	3	Piazza c	3	3	2	2
Clark 1b	4	1	1	1	Ventura 3b	2	2	1	3
Lankford lf	3	0	1	0	Zeile 1b	4	0	1	2
Tatis 3b	4	0	1	0	Agbayani lf	4	0	2	2
Drew rf	3	1	1	0	McEwing lf	0	0	0	0
Paquette ph-rf	1	0	0	0	Payton cf	4	0	0	0
Hernandez c	4	1	2	0	Bordick ss	3	1	0	0
Marrero pr	0	0	0	0	Jones p	2	0	0	0
Kile p	1	0	0	0	Rusch p	0	0	0	0
James p	0	0	0	0	JFranco p	0	0	0	0
Davis ph	1	1	1	1	Harris ph	0	0	0	0
Timlin p	0	0	0	0	Trammell ph	1	0	0	0
Dunston ph	1	0	1	0	Benitez p	0	0	0	0
Morris p	0	0	0	0					
Christiansen p	0	0	0	0					
Polanco ph	0	0	0	0					
Totals	35	6	11	6		31	10	9	10

Cardinals	200	130	000	6	11	2
Mets	430	102	00x	10	9	0

CARDINALS	IP	H	R	ER	BB	SO
Kile (L, 0–2)	3	8	7	7	3	2
James	1	1	1	1	0	0
Timlin	2	0	2	0	1	0
Morris	1	0	0	0	0	0
Christiansen	1	0	0	0	0	0
Total	8	9	10	8	4	2

METS	IP	H	R	ER	BB	SO
Jones	4	6	6	6	0	2
Rusch (W, 1–0)	3	3	0	0	0	2
Franco	1	1	0	0	1	1
Benitez	1	1	0	0	1	1
Total	9	11	6	6	2	6

E—Tatis 2 (2); DP—Cardinals 0, Mets 1; 2B—Alfonzo (1), Agbayani (2), Piazza (2), Ventura (1), Zeile (2), Perez (2), Vina (1), Davis (1); HR—Piazza (2), Clark (1), Edmonds (1); IBB—Piazza; HBP—Alfonzo; SH—Rusch, Renteria; SF—Ventura, Renteria; SB—Perez (1); CS—Perez (1); Time—3:14; ATT—55.665.

Game 5, October 16 at New York
METS 7, CARDINALS 0

Cardinals	AB	R	H	BI	Mets	AB	R	H	BI
Vina 2b	4	0	1	0	Perez rf-cf	5	2	2	0
Polanco 3b	2	0	0	0	Alfonzo 2b	4	1	2	1
Paquette ph	1	0	0	0	Piazza c	4	2	1	0
Edmonds cf	3	0	0	0	Ventura 3b	3	1	1	1
McGwire ph	1	0	0	0	Zeile 1b	4	0	1	3
Davis rf	3	0	0	0	Agbayani lf	2	0	1	0
Drew rf	0	0	0	0	Payton cf	4	0	1	0
Wilkins ph	1	0	0	0	McEwing pr-rf	0	0	0	0
Clark 1b	3	0	1	0	Bordick ss	4	1	1	0
Renteria ss	3	0	0	0	Hampton p	3	0	0	0
Lankford lf	3	0	0	0					
Hernandez c	2	0	0	0					
Marrero c	1	0	0	0					
Hentgen p	1	0	1	0					
Timlin p	0	0	0	0					
Tatis ph	1	0	0	0					
Reames p	0	0	0	0					
Ankiel p	0	0	0	0					
James p	0	0	0	0					
Dunston ph	1	0	0	0					
Veres p	0	0	0	0					
Totals	30	0	3	0		33	7	10	5

Cardinals	000	000	000	0	3	2	
Mets	300	300	10x	7	10	0	

CARDINALS	IP	H	R	ER	BB	SO
Hentgen (L, 0–1)	3-2/3	7	6	6	5	2
Timlin	1/3	0	0	0	1	0
Reames	2	2	0	0	1	0
Ankiel	2/3	0	1	1	2	1
James	1/3	0	0	0	0	0
Veres	1	1	0	0	0	0
Total	8	10	7	7	9	3

METS	IP	H	R	ER	BB	SO
Hampton (W, 2–0)	9	3	0	0	1	8

E—Clark (2), Hernandez (1); WP—Ankiel 2; 2B—Piazza (3), Zeile (3); HBP—Payton; SH—Hampton; SB—Perez (2); Time—3:17; ATT—55,695.

2000 NLCS Statistics

COMPOSITE LINESCORE
Mets	(12)31	512	124	31	43	4
Cardinals	412	280	022	21	47	7

METS BATTING
Player	BA	G	AB	R	H
Kurt Abbott	.000	2	3	0	0
Benny Agbayani	.353	5	17	0	6
Edgardo Alfonzo	.444	5	18	5	8
Armando Benitez	—	3	0	0	0
Mike Bordick	.077	5	13	2	1
Dennis Cook	—	1	0	0	0
John Franco	—	3	0	0	0
Matt Franco	.000	2	3	0	0
Darryl Hamilton	.000	3	2	0	0
Mike Hampton	.167	2	6	1	1
Lenny Harris	.000	2	1	0	0
Bobby Jones	.000	1	2	0	0
Al Leiter	.000	1	3	0	0
Joe McEwing	.000	4	0	2	0
Jay Payton	.158	5	19	1	3
Timo Perez	.304	5	23	8	7
Mike Piazza	.412	5	17	7	7
Rick Reed	.000	1	1	0	0
Glendon Rusch	—	2	0	0	0
Bubba Trammell	.000	3	3	0	0
Robin Ventura	.214	5	14	4	3
Turk Wendell	—	2	0	0	0
Rick White	—	1	0	0	0
Todd Zeile	.368	5	19	1	7
Total	.262	5	164	31	43

2B—Piazza 3, Zeile 3, Agbayani 2, Perez 2, Alfonzo, Ventura; 3B—Alfonzo; HR—Piazza 2, Payton, Zeile; RBI—Zeile 8, Ventura 5, Alfonzo 4, Piazza 4, Agbayani 3, Payton 3; SB—Perez 2.

CARDINALS BATTING
Player	BA	G	AB	R	H
Rick Ankiel	—	2	0	0	0
Andy Benes	.333	1	3	1	1
Jason Christiansen	—	2	0	0	0
Will Clark	.412	5	17	3	7
Eric Davis	.200	4	10	1	2
J.D. Drew	.333	5	12	2	4
Shawon Dunston	.333	4	6	1	2
Jim Edmonds	.227	5	22	1	5
Pat Hentgen	1.000	1	1	0	1
Carlos Hernandez	.250	5	16	3	4
Mike James	—	4	0	0	0
Darryl Kile	.000	3	2	0	0
Ray Lankford	.333	5	12	1	4
Eli Marrero	.000	4	4	0	0
Mark McGwire	.000	3	2	0	0
Matt Morris	—	2	0	0	0
Craig Paquette	.167	4	6	0	1
Placido Polanco	.200	4	5	0	1
Britt Reames	.000	2	1	0	0
Edgar Renteria	.300	5	20	4	6
Fernando Tatis	.231	5	13	1	3
Mike Timlin	—	3	0	0	0
Dave Veres	—	3	0	0	0
Fernando Vina	.261	5	23	3	6
Rick Wilkins	.000	2	2	0	0
Total	.266	5	177	21	47

2B—Clark 2, Tatis 2, Davis, Drew, Dunston, Edmonds, Lankford, Renteria, Vina; 3B—None; HR—Clark, Edmonds; RBI—Edmonds 6, Renteria 4, Tatis 2, Clark, Davis, Drew, Hernandez, Lankford, Marrero, Vina; SB—Renteria 3.

METS PITCHING
Player	G	ERA	W–L	SV	IP	H	ER	BB	SO
Arman. Benitez	3	0.00	0–0	1	3	3	0	2	2
Dennis Cook	1	0.00	0–0	0	1	1	0	0	2
John Franco	3	6.75	0–0	0	2-2/3	3	2	2	2
Mike Hampton	2	0.00	2–0	0	16	9	0	4	12
Bobby Jones	1	13.50	0–0	0	4	6	6	0	2
Al Leiter	1	3.86	0–0	0	7	8	3	0	9
Rick Reed	1	10.80	0–1	0	3-1/3	8	4	1	4
Glendon Rusch	2	0.00	1–0	0	3-2/3	3	0	0	3
Turk Wendell	2	0.00	1–0	0	1-1/3	1	0	1	2
Rick White	1	9.00	0–0	0	3	5	3	1	1
Total	5	3.60	4–1	1	45	47	18	11	39

CARDINALS PITCHING
Player	G	ERA	W–L	SV	IP	H	ER	BB	SO
Rick Ankiel	2	20.25	0–0	0	1-1/3	1	3	5	2
Andy Benes	1	2.25	1–0	0	8	6	2	3	5
J. Christiansen	2	0.00	0–0	0	2	0	0	0	1
Pat Hentgen	1	14.73	0–1	0	3-2/3	7	6	5	2
Mike James	4	15.43	0–0	0	2-1/3	5	4	1	0
Darryl Kile	2	9.00	0–2	0	10	13	10	5	3
Matt Morris	2	4.91	0–0	0	3-2/3	3	2	2	2
Britt Reames	2	1.42	0–0	0	6-1/3	5	1	4	6
Mike Timlin	3	0.00	0–1	0	3-1/3	1	0	2	0
Dave Veres	3	0.00	0–0	0	2-1/3	2	0	0	3
Total	5	5.86	1–4	0	43	43	28	27	24

2000 World Series: Mets vs. New York Yankees

YANKEES WIN SERIES 4–1

Mike Piazza hits a broken-bat foul ball against Yankees starter Roger Clemens during the first inning of Game 2 of the 2000 World Series at Yankee Stadium. Clemens threw the head of the broken bat toward Piazza, causing a flare-up of their long-smoldering feud.

This was the 14th "Subway Series," the first in 44 years and the 11th that would wind up in the Yankees' favor. All five games were decided by two runs or fewer, including an opener that was settled in extra innings after the Mets blew a lead in the ninth.

There are so many "what-ifs" to this Series. What if Timo Perez had been running full steam when Todd Zeile hit a double off the top of the left-field wall in the sixth inning of Game 1? What if Zeile's hit cleared the fence, giving starter Al Leiter a 2–0 lead? What if Armando Benitez hadn't unraveled in the ninth inning of the opener? What if Mike Hampton had shown his pennant-winning form in Game 2, when the Yankees hit him hard over six innings? What if Leiter had been pulled to start the ninth inning of Game 5? What if Derek Jeter had never been born? What if the Pirates had hung onto Luis Sojo?

What-ifs are for losers, and the Mets lost the Series to a team that won seven fewer games during the regular season. The Yankees simply got more clutch hits while outpitching the Mets. Although the Yankees had a tremendous lineup, their grunt players provided some of the biggest hits of the Series. Former Met Jose Vizcaino capped a 4-for-6 night by delivering the walk-off single in Game 1 (Vizcaino went 0-for-9 the rest of the Series). Scott Brosius homered in Game 2 before his sac-fly put the Yanks ahead 5–0 in the seventh. Brosius and Luis Sojo drove in runs following Jeter's leadoff homer to give the Yankees a 3–0 lead in a 3–2 victory in the fourth game, one day before Sojo would deliver the Series-winning hit.

The Mets pitched to a very respectable 3.47 ERA in the Series, but the Yankees' staff was better. The Yanks also shut down Timo Perez, who was the surprising hitting star in the NLCS. The scouts did a thorough job in finding Perez' weaknesses at the plate, and the outfielder went just 2-for-16 in the Series after collecting a hit in each of his eight starts during the NL playoffs.

GAME 1, October 21, Yankee Stadium: Yankees 4, Mets 3 (12 innings)

This was the quintessential "opportunity lost" for the Mets, who squandered two terrific scoring opportunities in regulation before losing in extra innings.

Al Leiter and Andy Pettitte were outstanding while pitching shutout ball over the first five innings. Leiter had limited the Yankees to a pair of second-inning singles while Pettitte held the Mets to three hits. Timo Perez provided the Mets' fourth hit off Pettitte when he led off the sixth with a single. Two outs followed before Todd Zeile hit a long fly to left field. Perez ran hard to second base but eased up as Zeile's hit appeared headed for the stands. But the ball hit the top edge of the wall before caroming back toward left fielder David Justice. Perez tried to turn on the speed as he rounded third, but shortstop Derek Jeter made a perfect throw to Jorge Posada, nailing Perez at the plate and keeping the game 0–0.

It didn't stay scoreless long after. Jose Vizcaino led off the bottom of the sixth with a single and moved to second on a one-out walk before Justice laced a two-run double to left field. Leiter left runners on second and third to end the inning, but the Yankees had a 2–0 lead.

The Mets finally got to Pettitte in the seventh, scoring three times to take a 3–2 lead. Benny Agbayani and Jay Payton poked one-out singles before Todd Pratt walked to load the bases. Pinch-hitter Bubba Trammell, who went 0-for-3 in the NLCS, tied the game with a two-run single and moved to second when Perez bunted for the second out. Edgardo Alfonzo put the Mets ahead with an infield single that scored Pratt.

Leiter left the game with a 3–2 lead after tossing seven strong innings. John Franco kept the Mets ahead by working a scoreless eighth before New York almost tacked on insurance runs against Mariano Rivera.

Rivera hit Pratt with a pitch before Kurt Abbott doubled to put runners on second and third with one out and the red-hot Perez at the plate. The Yankees had done their homework on Perez and knew which pitches he liked to chase. Perez was no match for Rivera's cutter, hitting a weak grounder to second before Alfonzo struck out to end the inning.

The Mets still owned a one-run lead and were two outs from victory when Paul O'Neill patiently worked out a 10-pitch walk against Armando Benitez, who seemed to deflate after losing O'Neill. Luis Polonia and Vizcaino singled to load the bases before Chuck Knoblauch hit a sacrifice fly that forced extra innings.

The Mets never put a runner on base following Abbott's ninth-inning double. Rivera was perfect in his second inning of work before Mike Stanton retired all six hitters he faced.

Turk Wendell, who had allowed one hit over 3-1/3 innings of the Mets' previous two playoff rounds, opened the bottom of the 12th by getting Bernie Williams to tap out to second. The Yankees quickly loaded the bases with a single, a double and an intentional walk before Wendell got Luis Sojo to hit a foul pop near the plate for the second out. But Vizcaino offered at the first pitch he saw from Wendell, lining a single to left that finally ended the game.

GAME 2, October 22, Yankee Stadium: Yankees 6, Mets 5

The Mets were facing Roger Clemens for the first time since the Rocket beaned Mike Piazza in the head with a purpose pitch July 8, leaving the catcher with a concussion that forced him to miss the All-Star Game. It didn't take long for the two to cross paths in another controversial play.

Piazza launched a grand slam off Clemens June 9 and ended his major league career batting .421 (8-for-19) with four homers and 10 RBIs against the seven-time Cy Young Award winner. In other words, Piazza owned Clemens.

Clemens made his statement in the first inning of Game 2. Timo Perez and Edgardo Alfonzo struck out to open the game before Piazza stepped up. The Mets' catcher shattered his bat while hitting a foul ball. The barrel of the bat bounced toward Clemens, who inexplicably picked up the wood and heaved it toward Piazza. Piazza stopped in his tracks, turned to Clemens and asked what his problem was. Clemens initially gave Piazza a non-answer before telling reporters after the game that he thought the bat was the ball. Either way, Piazza wasn't buying the story.

"When he threw the bat, I basically just walked out to see what his problem was," said Piazza after going 0-for-3 against Clemens. "I started asking him and he really had no response. It was bizzare, it was bizarre."

Clemens blamed his actions on the intensity of the moment. "Before I let go of the bat, I had no idea that Mike had ran. I told the plate umpire that there was no intent. Again, I was fired up, emotional, grabbed the bat to sling it toward our on-deck circle where our bat boys were at."

Piazza eventually grounded out to end the inning, sending Mike Hampton to the mound to begin his first World Series start. It was a disaster.

Hampton reverted to his NLDS form, becoming, the guy who surrendered five runs over 5-1/3 innings of the series opener in San Francisco, not the pitcher who tossed 16 shutout innings over two starts to win the NLCS Most Valuable Player Award. Hampton got the first two outs of the inning, but a pair of walks were followed by RBI singles by Tino Martinez and Jorge Posada.

Scott Brosius added a leadoff homer in the second before Paul O'Neill's RBI single made it 4–0 in the fifth.

The Yankees tacked on single runs in the seventh and eighth inning to make it 6–0, allowing Jeff Nelson to enter the ninth with a big cushion. The two extra runs were critical by the end of the game.

With Clemens out of the game, Piazza launched a two-run blast off Nelson to get the Mets within 6–2. At least they were going down with a fight. Robin Ventura followed with a single, forcing Yankees manager Joe Torre to bring in Mariano Rivera, who almost blew the game.

Rivera retired his first batter, but Benny Agbayani singled before a passed ball put runners in scoring position.

Lenny Harris hit a comebacker to Rivera, who nailed Ventura at the plate for the second out. That proved to be a big play after Jay Payton launched a three-run homer to pull the Mets within 6–5.

Kurt Abbott ended the game by striking out, giving the Yankees a 2–0 lead in the Series. The Bombers had jumped out to a six-run lead while Clemens was limiting the Mets to a pair of hits in eight innings. The Mets made a nice charge with a pair of homers in a five-run ninth. But the big topic was Clemens' recent brush with Piazza, which irritated Torre.

"Why would (Clemens) throw it at (Piazza)? So he could get thrown out of the second game of the World Series? Does that make any sense to anybody? Somebody answer me! You guys ask me questions. Somebody answer my question. Why would he do it? Because he's angry with him? That's the reason? He's angry so he screws 24 other people on his team."

It wouldn't have been the first time, Joe. Clemens was tossed from Game 4 of the 1990 ALCS for arguing balls and strikes with plate umpire Terry Cooney in the second inning following a walk to A's second baseman Willie Randolph. Clemens left the game trailing 1–0. Five pitches later, Mike Gallego laced a two-run double off Tom Bolton to give Oakland a 3–0 lead in a 3–1 win in the clincher. So much for Torre's "team-first" theory on Clemens.

Major League Baseball wasn't buying Clemens' explanation, either. MLB lord of discipline Frank Robinson fined Clemens $50,000 for "inappropriate" actions on the field.

The Mets had their own problems. Perez failed to get a hit for the first time in nine postseason starts. Hampton had pitched the Mets into an 0–2 hole, putting pressure on Rick Reed to bounce back from his poor outing in Game 3 of the NLCS.

"We have our work cut out for us," chirped Mets manager Bobby Valentine. "No one said it was going to be easy. I think they know it is not going to be easy. We're going to make it as tough as possible for them."

GAME 3, October 24, Shea Stadium: Mets 4, Yankees 2

Rick Reed gave the Mets exactly what they needed: an opportunity to win. Reed struck out eight over six solid innings, leaving the game for a pinch-hitter after Todd Zeile doubled home the tying run in the bottom of the sixth.

The sixth looked like one of those "uh-oh" innings for the Mets after Zeile's two-bagger put runners on second and third with nobody out. Benny Agbayani walked to load the bases before Orlando Hernandez struck out Jay Payton and Mike Bordick. The rally ended when Darryl Hamilton, pinch-hitting for Reed, hit into a force at second to keep the game tied 2–2.

The Mets had Hernandez on the ropes and let him escape. El Duque entered the game 8–0 with a 1.90 ERA in nine career postseason games, all starts. Hernandez worked a perfect seventh before recording his 12th strikeout of the game, fanning Robin Ventura leading off the eighth. Ventura went down on three pitches, six innings after opening the scoring with a solo homer.

Hernandez had retired seven straight since getting into the bases-loaded jam in the sixth. He didn't record another out the rest of the game.

Todd Zeile hit a single and scored the tiebreaking run when Benny Agbayani hit a liner that rolled to the wall in left-center for a double. El Duque was pulled after Jay Payton's single put runners on second and third.

Bubba Trammell supplied the insurance run with a sacrifice fly, and Armando Benitez supplied a scoreless ninth, retiring the last three batters following Chuck Knoblauch's leadoff single.

The Yankees had a chance to break it open in the fourth after Paul O'Neill's RBI triple gave them a 2–1 lead. Scott Brosius walked and Hernandez laid down a bunt that put runners on second and third with two out. But Reed ended the threat by fanning Jose Vizcaino, keeping the Mets within striking distance.

The Mets had handed El Duque his first postseason loss while getting outstanding pitching from Reed and the bullpen. They also handed the Yankees their first loss in 15 World Series games since Game 2 of the 1996 Fall Classic. More important, momentum seemed to swing toward their side.

GAME 4, October 25, Shea Stadium: Yankees 3, Mets 2

It took just one pitch for Derek Jeter and the Yankees to regain momentum in the Series. Jeter sent Bobby Jones' first offering over the wall in left field to put the Bombers ahead. Two innings later, the Yankee shortstop laced a leadoff triple and scored on Luis Sojo's groundout to make it 3–0.

But the three-run cushion shriveled to one when Mike Piazza ripped a homer to left in the third following a single by Timo Perez. It was the only run scored in the Series by Perez, who had just tied an NLCS record by scoring eight times against the Cardinals.

The Mets managed just three hits after Piazza's second homer of the Series, and didn't move a runner past first base the rest of the way as the Yankee relievers protected the lead. Yanks skipper Joe Torre pulled starter Denny Neagle with two out in the fifth just before Piazza got another look at the lefty. Former Met David Cone got Piazza on a short fly to right to end the inning.

Jeff Nelson, Mike Stanton and Mariano Rivera followed with four innings of two-hit relief to secure a victory that put the Yankees on the verge of their third straight World Series title.

"We're giving everything we have out there, and they're giving just a little extra," said Mets manager Bobby Valentine. "They scored an extra run tonight. We have a lot of hits saved up. Hopefully, over the next three games they'll all come out."

GAME 5, October 26, Shea Stadium: Yankees 4, Mets 2

Yankees infielder Luis Sojo had opened the season with the Pirates, who would go on to post the fourth-worst record in the National League. Six months later, the utility infielder produced a World Series–clinching hit.

Sojo poked an RBI single with two outs in the bottom of the ninth to send the Yankees to their 26th championship. The Yanks had put runners on first and second with two outs before Sojo hit a soft grounder that eluded shortstop Kurt Abbott and continued into center field, scoring Jorge Posada. Jay Payton's throw to the plate hit Posada and rolled into the Mets' dugout, allowing Scott Brosius to come home with the insurance run.

It was a tough way for Al Leiter to remain winless as a Met in the postseason. Leiter threw 142 pitches and opened the ninth inning by striking out Tino Martinez and Paul O'Neill. But a nine-pitch walk to Posada kept the inning alive before Brosius singled on Leiter's 142nd pitch.

Leiter actually contributed to a two-run second that gave the Mets a 2–1 lead. Bubba Trammell, who replaced the slumping Timo Perez in the starting lineup, worked out a one-out walk and moved to second on Jay Payton's single before Kurt Abbott's grounder put runners on second and third.

Leiter popped up a bunt attempt, but pitcher Andy Pettitte failed to come up with the ball, allowing Trammell to score the tying run. Benny Agbayani followed with an infield single that put the Mets ahead. The Mets had played the smallest of small-ball to take the lead, but the Yankees would knot the score with their second solo homer of the night.

Derek Jeter erased the Mets' lead with a blast in the sixth, four innings after Bernie Williams' solo shot gave the Yankees a brief 1–0 edge. The Mets threatened in the bottom of the sixth as Payton and Abbott hit back-to-back singles before Leiter bunted them into scoring position. But Pettitte retired Agbayani on a grounder to end both the inning and the Mets' final legitimate threat of the Series.

Agbayani gave the Mets one last hope by working out a one-out walk. He took second on defensive interference and moved to third on a fly ball, leaving Mike Piazza as the potential tying run at the plate with two outs against Mariano Rivera. Piazza took a home run cut but got under the pitch, sending a drive to deep center that Williams snared for the final out of the Series.

Mets manager Bobby Valentine was questioned for staying with Leiter deep into the ninth, but his pitcher appreciated the decision. "I was grateful he gave me the opportunity to win. Deep down I felt I could get that third out. It is the lowest of the lows after the highest of highs."

Game 1, October 21 at Yankee Stadium
YANKEES 4, METS 3 (12)

Mets	AB	R	H	BI	Yankees	AB	R	H	BI
Perez rf	6	0	1	0	Knoblauch dh	4	1	0	1
Alfonzo 2b	6	0	1	1	Jeter ss	4	1	1	0
Piazza dh	5	0	1	0	Justice lf	4	0	1	2
Zeile 1b	5	0	2	0	Bellinger pr-lf	0	0	0	0
Ventura 3b	5	0	0	0	Hill ph-lf	1	0	0	0
Agbayani lf	4	1	2	0	Williams cf	4	0	0	0
McEwing lf	1	0	0	0	Martinez 1b	6	1	2	0
Payton cf	5	1	1	0	Posada c	5	0	1	0
Pratt c	2	1	0	0	O'Neill rf	4	1	1	0
Bordick ss	1	0	0	0	Brosius 3b	3	0	1	0
Trammell ph	1	0	1	2	Polonia ph	1	0	1	0
Abbott ss	2	0	1	0	Sojo 3b	2	0	0	0
Leiter p	0	0	0	0	Vizcaino 2b	6	0	4	1
Franco p	0	0	0	0	Pettitte p	0	0	0	0
Benitez p	0	0	0	0	Nelson p	0	0	0	0
Cook p	0	0	0	0	Rivera p	0	0	0	0
Rusch p	0	0	0	0	Stanton p	0	0	0	0
Wendell p	0	0	0	0					
Totals	43	3	10	3		44	4	12	4

Mets	000	000	300	000	3	10	0
Yankees	000	002	001	001	4	12	0

METS	IP	H	R	ER	BB	SO
Leiter	7	5	2	2	3	7
Franco	1	1	0	0	0	0
Benitez	1	2	1	1	1	1
Cook	0	0	0	0	2	0
Rusch	1-2/3	1	0	0	2	0
Wendell (L, 0–1)	1	3	1	1	1	0
Total	11-2/3	12	4	4	9	8

YANKEES	IP	H	R	ER	BB	SO
Pettitte	6-2/3	8	3	3	1	4
Nelson	1-1/3	1	0	0	0	0
Rivera	2	1	0	0	0	3
Stanton (W, 1–0)	2	0	0	0	0	3
Total	12	10	3	3	1	10

LOB—Mets 8, Yankees 15; DP—Mets 1, Yankees 0; WP—Rusch 2; 2B—Agbayani (1), Zeile (1), Abbott (1), Posada (1), Justice (1); HBP—Pratt 2; SH—Bordick; SF—Knoblauch; IBB—Posada, Williams, O'Neill; CS—Piazza (1), Knoblauch (1); Time—4:51; ATT—55,913.

Game 2, October 22 at Yankee Stadium
YANKEES 6, METS 5

Mets	AB	R	H	BI	Yankees	AB	R	H	BI
Perez rf	4	0	0	0	Knoblauch dh	4	0	0	0
Alfonzo 2b	3	1	1	0	Jeter ss	5	1	3	0
Piazza c	4	1	1	2	Justice lf	3	1	0	0
Ventura 3b	4	0	1	0	Bellinger lf	0	0	0	0
Zeile 1b	4	0	2	0	Williams cf	3	1	0	0
Agbayani lf	4	1	1	0	Martinez 1b	5	1	3	2
Harris dh	4	1	0	0	Posada c	3	1	2	1
Payton cf	4	1	1	3	O'Neill rf	4	0	3	1
Bordick ss	2	0	0	0	Brosius 3b	3	1	1	2
Hamilton ph	1	0	0	0	Vizcaino 2b	4	0	0	0
Abbott ss	1	0	0	0	Clemens p	0	0	0	0
Hampton p	0	0	0	0	Nelson p	0	0	0	0
Rusch p	0	0	0	0	Rivera p	0	0	0	0
White p	0	0	0	0					
Cook p	0	0	0	0					
Totals	35	5	7	5		34	6	12	6

Mets	000	000	005	5	7	3	
Yankees	210	010	11x	6	12	1	

METS	IP	H	R	ER	BB	SO
Hampton (L, 0–1)	6	8	4	4	5	4
Rusch	1/3	2	1	1	0	0
White	1-1/3	1	1	1	1	1
Cook	1/3	1	0	0	0	0
Total	8	12	6	6	6	5

YANKEES	IP	H	R	ER	BB	SO
Clemens (W, 1–0)	8	2	0	0	0	9
Nelson	0	3	3	3	0	0
Rivera	1	2	2	2	0	1
Total	9	7	5	5	0	10

LOB—Mets 4, Yankees 1; E—Payton (1), Bordick (1), Perez (1), Clemens (1); PB—Posada WP—Clemens; 2B—Jeter 2 (1), O'Neill (1), Martinez (1); HR—Payton (1), Piazza (1), Brosius (1); HBP—Alfonzo, Justice; SF—Brosius; CS—Vizcaino; Time—3:30; ATT—56,059.

Game 3, October 24 at Shea Stadium
METS 4, YANKEES 2

Yankees	AB	R	H	BI	Mets	AB	R	H	BI
Vizcaino 2b	4	0	0	0	Perez rf	3	0	0	0
Polonia ph	1	0	0	0	Alfonzo 2b	4	0	0	0
Jeter ss	4	1	2	0	Piazza c	4	1	1	0
Justice lf	3	0	1	1	Ventura 3b	3	1	2	1
Williams cf	4	0	0	0	Zeile 1b	4	1	2	1
Martinez 1b	3	1	1	0	Agbayani lf	3	0	1	1
Posada c	4	0	0	0	McEwing pr-lf	0	1	0	0
O'Neill rf	4	0	3	1	Payton cf	4	0	1	0
Brosius 3b	2	0	0	0	Bordick ss	3	0	1	0
Hill ph	1	0	0	0	Harris ph	0	0	0	0
Sojo 3b	0	0	0	0	Trammell ph	0	0	0	1
Hernandez p	2	0	0	0	Benitez p	0	0	0	0
Stanton p	0	0	0	0	Reed p	1	0	1	0
Knoblauch ph	1	0	1	0	Hamilton ph	1	0	0	0
Abbott ph-ss	1	0	0	0	Wendell p	0	0	0	0
					Cook p	0	0	0	0
					JFranco p	0	0	0	0
Totals	33	2	8	2		31	4	9	4

Yankees	001	100	000	2	8	0	
Mets	010	001	02x	4	9	0	

YANKEES	IP	H	R	ER	BB	SO
Hernandez (L)	7-1/3	9	4	4	3	12
Stanton	2/3	0	0	0	0	1
Total	8	9	4	4	3	13

METS	IP	H	R	ER	BB	SO
Reed	6	6	2	2	1	8
Wendell	2/3	0	0	0	1	2
Cook	1/3	0	0	0	1	1
JFranco (W, 1–0)	1	1	0	0	0	0
Benitez (S, 1)	1	1	0	0	0	1
Total	9	8	2	2	3	12

LOB—Yankees 10, Mets 8; DP—Yankees 0, Mets 1; 2B—Agbayani (2), Piazza (1), Ventura (1), Zeile (2), O'Neill (2), Justice (2); 3B—O'Neill (2); HR—Ventura (1); HBP—Brosius, Justice; SH—Reed, Hernandez; SF—Trammell; Time—3:39; ATT—55,299.

Game 4, October 25 at Shea Stadium
YANKEES 3, METS 2

Yankees	AB	R	H	BI	Mets	AB	R	H	BI
Jeter ss	5	2	2	1	Perez rf	3	1	1	0
Sojo 2b	4	0	1	1	Abbott ph-ss	1	0	0	0
Justice lf	5	0	0	0	Alfonzo 2b	3	0	0	0
Bellinger lf	0	0	0	0	Piazza c	4	1	1	2
Williams cf	4	0	0	0	Zeile 1b	4	0	2	0
Martinez 1b	4	0	2	0	McEwing pr	0	0	0	0
O'Neill rf	4	1	2	0	Benitez p	0	0	0	0
Posada c	3	0	0	0	Ventura 3b	4	0	0	0
Brosius 3b	1	0	1	1	Agbayani lf	3	0	0	0
Neagle p	2	0	0	0	Payton cf	4	0	2	0
Cone p	0	0	0	0	Bordick ss	2	0	0	0
Canseco ph	1	0	0	0	Harris ph	0	0	0	0
Nelson p	0	0	0	0	JFranco p	0	0	0	0
Stanton p	0	0	0	0	MFranco 1b	1	0	0	0
Rivera p	1	0	0	0	Jones p	2	0	0	0
					Rusch p	0	0	0	0
					Hamilton ph	0	0	0	0
					Trammell ph-rf	1	0	0	0
Totals	34	3	8	3		32	2	6	2

Yankees	111	000	000	3	8	0	
Mets	002	000	000	2	6	1	

YANKEES	IP	H	R	ER	BB	SO
Neagle	4-2/3	4	2	2	2	3
Cone	1/3	0	0	0	0	0
Nelson (W, 1–0)	1-1/3	1	0	0	1	1
Stanton	2/3	0	0	0	0	2
Rivera (S, 1)	2	1	0	0	0	2
Total	9	6	2	2	3	8

METS	IP	H	R	ER	BB	SO
Jones (L, 0–1)	5	4	3	3	3	3
Rusch	2	3	0	0	0	2
JFranco	1	1	0	0	0	1
Benitez	1	0	0	0	1	0
Total	9	8	3	3	4	6

LOB—Yankees 9, Mets 6; E—Trammell (1); DP—Yankees 1, Mets 1; 3B—O'Neill (2), Jeter (1); HR—Piazza (2), Jeter (1); IBB—Brosius, Posada; SF—Brosius; SB—Sojo; Time—3:20; ATT—55,290.

Game 5, October 26 at Shea Stadium
YEANKEES 4, METS 2

Yankees	AB	R	H	BI		Mets	AB	R	H	BI
Vizcaino 2b	3	0	0	0		Agbayani lf	4	0	1	1
Knoblauch ph	1	0	0	0		Alfonzo 2b	5	0	1	0
Stanton p	0	0	0	0		Piazza c	5	0	2	0
Hill ph	1	0	0	0		Zeile 1b	3	0	0	0
Rivera p	0	0	0	0		Ventura 3b	4	0	0	0
Jeter ss	4	1	1	1		Trammell rf	3	1	1	0
Justice lf	4	0	1	0		Perez rf	0	0	0	0
Bellinger lf	0	0	0	0		Payton cf	4	1	2	0
Williams cf	3	1	2	1		Abbott ss	3	0	1	0
Martinez 1b	4	0	0	0		Leiter p	2	0	0	0
O'Neill rf	3	0	0	0		JFranco p	0	0	0	0
Posada c	3	1	1	0		Hamilton ph	1	0	0	0
Brosius 3b	4	1	1	0						
Pettitte p	3	0	0	0						
Sojo 2b	1	0	1	1						
Totals	34	4	7	3			34	2	8	1

Yankees	010	001	002	4	7	1	
Mets	020	000	000	2	8	1	

YANKEES	IP	H	R	ER	BB	SO
Pettitte	7	8	2	0	3	5
Stanton (W, 2–0)	1	0	0	0	0	1
Rivera (S, 1)	1	0	0	0	1	1
Total	9	8	2	0	3	7

METS	IP	H	R	ER	BB	SO
Leiter (L, 0–1)	8-2/3	7	4	3	3	9
JFranco	1/3	0	0	0	0	0
Total	9	7	4	3	3	9

LOB—Yankees 6, Mets 10; E—Payton (2), Pettitte (1); 2B—Piazza (2); HR—Jeter (2), Williams (1); IBB—Zeile; SH—Leiter; Time—3:32; ATT—55,292.

2000 World Series Statistics

COMPOSITE LINESCORE

Mets	032	001	325	000	—	16 40 5	
Yankees	332	113	113	001	—	19 47 2	

METS BATTING

Player	BA	G	AB	R	H
Kurt Abbott	.250	5	8	0	2
Benny Agbayani	.278	5	18	2	5
Edgardo Alfonzo	.143	5	21	1	3
Armando Benitez	—	3	0	0	0
Mike Bordick	.125	4	8	0	1
Dennis Cook	—	3	0	0	0
John Franco	—	4	0	0	0
Matt Franco	.000	1	1	0	0
Darryl Hamilton	.000	4	3	0	0
Mike Hampton	—	1	0	0	0
Lenny Harris	.000	3	4	1	0
Bobby Jones	.000	1	2	0	0
Al Leiter	.000	2	2	0	0
Joe McEwing	.000	3	1	1	0
Jay Payton	.333	5	21	3	7
Timo Perez	.125	5	16	1	2
Mike Piazza	.273	5	22	3	6
Todd Pratt	.000	1	2	1	0
Rick Reed	1.000	1	1	0	1
Glendon Rusch	—	3	0	0	0
Bubba Trammell	.400	4	5	1	2
Robin Ventura	.150	5	20	1	3
Turk Wendell	—	2	0	0	0
Rick White	—	1	0	0	0
Todd Zeile	.400	5	20	1	8
Total	.229	5	175	16	40

2B—Agbayani 2, Piazza 2, Zeile 2, Abbott, Ventura; 3B—None; HR—Piazza 2, Payton, Ventura; RBI—Piazza 4, Payton 3, Trammell 3, Agbayani 2, Alfonzo, Ventura, Zeile; SB—None.

YANKEES BATTING

Player	BA	G	AB	R	H
Clay Bellinger	—	4	0	0	0
Scott Brosius	.308	5	13	2	4
Jose Canseco	.000	1	1	0	0
Roger Clemens	—	1	0	0	0
David Cone	—	1	0	0	0
Orlando Hernandez	.000	1	2	0	0
Glenallen Hill	.000	3	3	0	0
Derek Jeter	.409	5	22	6	9
David Justice	.158	5	19	1	3
Chuck Knoblauch	.100	4	10	1	1
Tino Martinez	.364	5	22	3	8
Denny Neagle	.000	1	2	0	0
Jeff Nelson	—	3	0	0	0
Paul O'Neill	.474	5	19	2	9
Andy Pettitte	.000	2	3	0	0
Luis Polonia	.500	2	2	0	1
Jorge Posada	.222	5	18	2	4
Mariano Rivera	.000	4	1	0	0
Luis Sojo	.286	4	7	0	2
Mike Stanton	—	4	0	0	0
Jose Vizcaino	.235	4	17	0	4
Bernie Williams	.111	5	18	2	2
Total	.263	5	179	19	47

2B—Jeter 2, Justice 2, O'Neill 2, Martinez, Posada; 3B—O'Neill 2, Jeter; HR—Jeter 2, Brosius, Williams; RBI—Brosius 3, Justice 3, Jeter 2, Martinez 2, O'Neill 2, Sojo 2, Knoblauch, Posada, Vizcaino, Williams; SB—Sojo.

METS PITCHING

Player	G	ERA	W–L	SV	IP	H	ER	BB	SO
Arman. Benitez	3	3.00	0–0	1	3	3	1	2	2
Dennis Cook	3	0.00	0–0	0	2/3	1	0	3	1
John Franco	4	0.00	1–0	0	3-1/3	3	0	0	1
Mike Hampton	1	6.00	0–1	0	6	8	4	5	4
Bobby Jones	1	5.40	0–1	0	5	4	3	3	3
Al Leiter	2	2.87	0–1	0	15-2/3	12	5	6	16
Rick Reed	1	3.00	0–0	0	6	6	2	1	8
Glendon Rusch	3	2.25	0–0	0	4	6	1	2	2
Turk Wendell	2	5.40	0–1	0	1-2/3	3	1	2	2
Rick White	1	6.75	0–0	0	1-1/3	1	1	1	1
Total	5	3.47	1–4	1	46-2/3	47	18	25	40

YANKEES PITCHING

Player	G	ERA	W–L	SV	IP	H	ER	BB	SO
Roger Clemens	1	0.00	1–0	0	8	2	0	0	9
David Cone	1	0.00	0–0	0	1/3	0	0	0	0
Orl. Hernandez	1	4.91	0–1	0	7-1/3	9	4	3	12
Denny Neagle	1	3.86	0–0	0	4-2/3	4	2	2	3
Jeff Nelson	3	10.12	1–0	0	2-2/3	5	3	1	1
Andy Pettitte	2	1.98	0–0	0	13-2/3	16	3	4	9
Mariano Rivera	4	3.00	0–0	2	6	4	2	1	7
Mike Stanton	4	0.00	2–0	0	4-1/3	0	0	0	7
Total	5	2.68	4–1	2	47	40	14	11	48

2006 NLDS: Mets vs. Los Angeles Dodgers

METS WIN SERIES 3–0

The Mets entered a playoff series as prohibitive favorites for the first time since the 1988 NLCS, also against the Dodgers. That previous one didn't go too well for the Mets, who were beaten in a seven-game series after going 10–1 versus Los Angeles during the regular season.

New York took just four of seven from L.A. during the 2006 regular season en route to the National League's best record. No NL team had a winning record against the Mets, who were a combined 23–10 against the Dodgers and the rest of the West Division.

The Dodgers tied for the NL's second-best record but had to settle for the wild-card by virtue of their season series with the Padres, who were credited with the NL West title. That was a break for the Mets as the Padres had a slightly better top of the rotation.

Carlos Beltran, Carlos Delgado and David Wright combined for 105 home runs, 108 doubles and 346 RBIs. Wright, Paul Lo Duca and Jose Reyes hit over .300, and Reyes led the National League with 17 triples and 64 stolen bases.

The Dodgers didn't have a single player with more than 20 home runs or 100 RBIs. Nomar Garciaparra, J.D. Drew and Rafael Furcal accounted for 55 home runs and 256 RBIs. However, just one member of the Dodgers' postseason starting lineup hit under .282 during the regular season. The Mets had just three regulars with an average better than .282, and the team overall was just eighth in the NL with a .334 on-base percentage.

But the Mets went from prohibitive to slight favorites about 26 hours before the series was to begin. Scheduled Game 1 starter Orlando Hernandez injured his right calf while running in the outfield during a workout the afternoon before the series opener. The Mets declined to say if El Duque would be able to pitch again the rest of the postseason, but it was most certain he wouldn't face the Dodgers.

The injury left the Mets scrambling for a starter. Tom Glavine would have been the logical choice even before Hernandez got hurt, but manager Willie Randolph wisely declined to use his top lefty on three days' rest. Steve Trachsel had just rejoined the team after attending to a family matter on the West Coast and hadn't pitched since September 24, when he worked five innings against the Nationals. Oliver Perez worked the regular-season finale but wouldn't have been an option after a wildly inconsistent regular season.

Randolph settled on John Maine, who would be pitching on his normal four days' rest. Maine allowed just three runs over six innings of his final regular-season start, leaving him 6–5 with a 3.60 earned run average in 16 games,

including 15 starts. It was the first time he had started more than eight major league games in any season.

Hernandez went down a few days after Pedro Martinez was diagnosed with a left calf injury that caused him to miss the rest of the postseason. The Mets also learned Martinez had two tears in his right shoulder and would be out until the end of August 2007.

"The best thing we can do to make the absence of those guys less is to go out there and score a bunch of runs and take all the pressure off our pitcher," said Glavine, who pitched a masterpiece in Game 2, in the *New York Times*.

Cliff Floyd had his own injury problems. The left fielder received a cortisone injection on his sore left Achilles' tendon before the final series of the regular season and said he felt better. Carlos Delgado missed the last two regular-season games with a rib cage injury but otherwise felt fine.

The rest of the lineup was in good shape, and the team's mix of power and speed continued to be devastating in the series. The Mets belted 200 home runs during the season compared to the Dodgers' 153. New York led the league with 146 steals, 18 more than the Dodgers. However, the Dodgers led the league with a .276 average, 12 points higher than the Mets' mark.

Injuries to Martinez and Hernandez left the Dodgers with an edge in starting pitching. However, the Mets' bullpen compiled a 3.28 ERA in 542-2/3 innings, .84 earned runs lower than the Los Angeles relief corps. The Mets were expected to win the series out of the pen, sending out Chad Bradford, Darren Oliver, Pedro Feliciano, Roberto Hernandez and Aaron Heilman before going to closer Billy Wagner.

Although the series ended in a sweep, no Mets fan could feel completely comfortable until the 27th inning. New York blew a 4–1 lead in the opener and a 4–0 advantage in Game 3 before rallying against the Dodgers' bullpen each time. Glavine was the only Mets starter to work at least five innings, and the bullpen pitched to a 5.40 ERA while showing signs of overuse.

When the Mets needed a run, they relied on speed, power and a few well-placed hits to trigger a rally. Reyes and Endy Chavez helped the Mets bunt their way to victory in Game 2, one day after New York turned two homers and a pair of doubles in a series-opening win. The Mets wrapped up the sweep with a hitting clinic in Los Angeles, stringing together three consecutive RBI hits on two occasions. A good number of those hits were Texas Leaguers that sailed just out of the reach of the Dodger infielders.

Six different Mets had at least two RBIs in the series. Chavez, Delgado, Wright, Floyd and Lo Duca combined to bat .407 with two home runs, three doubles and 11 RBIs. Green was outstanding in the clincher, going 3-for-5 with two doubles and two RBIs.

Former Met Jeff Kent was the top hitter, recording a .615 average in 13 at-bats. But the Mets held Garciaparra, Furcal and Drew to a .182 mark in 33 at-bats

while the trio managed to make the final out in 12 of 27 innings.

The series seemed to exorcise memories of the Mets' disappointing showing against the Dodgers in the NLCS 18 years earlier. It also set up a meeting of former bitter division rivals.

GAME 1, October 4, New York: Mets 6, Dodgers 5

The Mets quickly experienced one of those moments in which destiny appeared to be on their side. Starter John Maine worked a perfect first inning before allowing singles to Jeff Kent and J.D. Drew to open the second.

Russell Martin followed with a base hit that bounced off the right-field wall and right at Shawn Green. Green took the ball on a hop and threw to second baseman Jose Valentin, who unleashed a perfect throw to the plate to get a slow-moving Kent for the first out.

Catcher Paul Lo Duca was showing the ball to plate umpire John Hirschbeck when Drew barreled toward the plate.

"When I showed him the ball, it was like he was telling me, 'You better watch out,' " Lo Duca said.[14]

Lo Duca twirled around and made a sweep tag to nail Drew and keep the game scoreless.

Maine allowed an RBI double to ex-Met Marlon Anderson before settling down again, allowing just a pair of singles before leaving with one out in the fifth. He surrendered six hits but just one run over 4⅓ innings, giving manager Willie Randolph he could have hoped as an emergency starter.

Carlos Delgado homered in his second career postseason at-bat to knot the game in the fourth inning, two batters before Cliff Floyd belts a solo shot. David Wright's two-run double in the sixth made it a 4–1 lead that looked pretty safe with Gulliermo Mota about to toss his second inning of work.

Mota had been lights out for the Mets during the regular season, and completed a perfect sixth inning by fanning Drew and Martin. But the Dodgers tied it in the seventh on Rafael Furcal's RBI single and Nomar Garciaparra's two-run double.

Delgado and Wright came through again in the bottom of the seventh to put the Mets back on top. Delgado singled home the tiebreaking run and Wright added an RBI double one pitch later.

Aaron Heilman tossed a perfect eighth before Billy Wagner gave up a pair of doubles in the ninth. Wagner picked up the save by fanning Garciaparra, allowing the Mets to improve to 5–8 in playoff series openers.

GAME 2, October 5, New York: Mets 4, Dodgers 1

The Mets put together their cleanest victory of the series as Tom Glavine pitched superbly over six shutout innings, allowing just four hits and two walks. Glavine didn't allow a hit until the fourth and stranded the potential tying run at third base to end the fifth. It was Glavine's 13th postseason victory and first since the 2001 NLDS.

"Glavine pitched in a situation where we were pressing for a win in New York, and he is the wrong guy to face when you are pressing," Dodgers second baseman Jeff Kent said in the *New York Times*. "He throws that changeup and fastball off the plate, and you get frustrated and swing at it, and we forced ourselves to swing at it."

The Mets played small ball most of the night, winning with six singles, two sacrifices and a double. Endy Chavez manufactured the game's first run in the bottom of the

third, leading off with a single and moving over to second on a wild pitch before taking third on a grounder. Jose Reyes followed with an RBI grounder that put the Mets ahead to stay.

Chavez also singled in the fifth before Paul Lo Duca's sac-fly drove in Jose Valentin with the second run.

The Mets managed to break it open in the sixth, loading the bases before pinch-hitter Julio Franco hit an RBI grounder to score David Wright. Reyes added an RBI single to make it 4–0.

The Dodgers were held to four hits until Aaron Heilman served up Wilston Betemit's eighth-inning homer. But Heilman and Billy Wagner combined to retire the Dodgers' final five hitters, leading the Mets one win away from their seventh trip to the NLCS.

GAME 3, October 7, Los Angeles: Mets 9, Dodgers 5

A pair of ex-Dodgers helped the Mets complete their first postseason sweep since the 1969 NLCS. Shawn Green and Paul Lo Duca drove in two runs apiece and combined

for five of the Mets' 14 hits. Green had RBI hits in each of the game's first two scoring rallies before his leadoff double sparked a three-run sixth.

The Mets hammered Greg Maddux in the first inning, collecting five straight singles following a one-out walk by Lo Duca. David Wright, Cliff Floyd and Green provided RBI singles during a nine-pitch sequence with two out to give New York a 3–0 lead. Green added an RBI double in the third to make it 4–0.

The lead vanished over the next two innings. Steve Trachsel was pulled after James Loney's two-run single got Los Angeles within 4–2 in the fourth. Carlos Beltran had trouble fielding Loney's hit, putting runners on second and third with one out. But Darren Oliver got out of the jamming by spearing Andre Ethier's liner before catching Wilson Betemit in a rundown to end the threat.

The Dodgers went ahead on the fifth on Jeff Kent's two-run blast off Oliver and Pedro Feliciano's two-out, bases-loaded walk to Loney. Feliciano was able to poach the victory, thanks to consecutive RBI singles by Jose Reyes, Lo Duca and Beltran in the sixth.

The Mets tacked on two more runs in the eighth as Lo Duca hit an RBI single and scored on a throwing error. Aaron Heilman maintained the 9–5 lead with a scoreless eighth before Wagner got the last three outs to cap the sweep.

"We didn't win with any monstrous home runs or anything like that," Mets closer Billy Wagner, who finished off the Dodgers in the ninth inning, said. "We played small-ball.

"A lot of the hits we got weren't hit hard, but they were in the right spot. And you have to have those in this league."[15]

The victory was dampened by Cliff Floyd's barking Achilles. He had to take himself out of the game in the third inning after hopping home from second on Green's double. Floyd had been 4-for-9 with a homer and two RBIs in the series.

Game 1, October 4 at New York
METS 6, DODGERS 5

Dodgers	AB	R	H	BI	Mets	AB	R	H	BI
Furcal ss	4	1	1	1	Reyes ss	4	1	0	0
Lofton cf	4	0	0	0	Lo Duca c	5	1	2	0
Martinez ph	1	0	1	1	Beltran cf	2	1	0	0
Repko pr	0	0	0	0	Delgado 1b	5	2	4	2
Garciaparra 1b	5	0	1	2	Wright 3b	4	0	2	3
Kent 2b	4	0	2	0	Floyd lf	3	1	1	1
Drew rf	4	0	1	0	Heilman p	0	0	0	0
Martin c	4	1	1	0	Wagner p	0	0	0	0
Anderson lf	4	1	2	1	Green rf	4	0	0	0
Betemit 3b	3	2	2	0	Valentin 2b	3	0	0	0
Lowe p	1	0	0	0	Maine p	1	0	0	0
Hendrickson p	0	0	0	0	Feliciano p	0	0	0	0
Lugo ph	1	0	0	0	Bradford p	0	0	0	0
Penny p	0	0	0	0	Tucker ph	1	0	0	0
Broxton p	0	0	0	0	Mota p	1	0	0	0
Saenz ph	1	0	0	0	Chavez lf	1	0	0	0
Totals	36	5	11	5		34	6	9	6

Dodgers	010	000	301	5	11	1
Mets	000	202	20x	6	9	1

DODGERS	IP	H	R	ER	BB	SO
Lowe	5-1/3	6	4	4	2	6
Hendrickson	2/3	0	0	0	0	1
Penny (L, 0–1)	1	2	2	2	2	1
Broxton	1	1	0	0	1	1
Total	8	9	6	6	5	9

METS	IP	H	R	ER	BB	SO
Maine	4-1/3	6	1	1	2	5
Feliciano	1/3	0	0	0	0	1
Bradford	1/3	0	0	0	0	0
Mota (W, 1–0)	2	3	3	3	0	4
Heilman	1	0	0	0	0	0
Wagner (S, 1)	1	2	1	1	0	2
Total	9	11	5	5	2	12

LOB—Dodgers 7, Mets 10; E—Valentin (1), Kent (1); DP—Dodgers 0, Mets 1 2B—Wright 2 (2), Anderson (1), Martinez (1), Garciaparra (1), Betemit (1); HR—Floyd (1), Delgado (1); IBB—Floyd, Betemit; HBP—Valentin; SH—Lowe; SB—Reyes (1), Furcal; Time—3:05; ATT—56,979.

Game 2, October 5 at New York
METS 4, DODGERS 1

Dodgers	AB	R	H	BI	Mets	AB	R	H	BI
Furcal ss	3	0	0	0	Reyes ss	3	0	1	2
Lofton cf	4	0	0	0	Lo Duca c	3	0	1	1
Garciaparra 1b	3	0	1	0	Beltran cf	3	0	0	0
Betemit 3b	1	1	1	1	Delgado 1b	4	0	1	0
Kent 2b-1b	4	0	2	0	Wright 3b	4	0	1	0
Drew rf	4	0	0	0	Floyd lf	4	1	1	0
Saito p	0	0	0	0	Valentin 2b	2	2	0	0
Martin c	3	0	0	0	Chavez rf	4	1	2	0
Anderson lf-rf	4	0	0	0	Glavine p	1	0	0	0
Lugo 3b-2b	3	0	1	0	Franco ph	1	0	1	1
Kuo p	2	0	0	0	Feliciano p	0	0	0	0
Tomko p	0	0	0	0	Heilman p	0	0	0	0
Hendrickson p	0	0	0	0	Wagner p	0	0	0	0
Martinez ph	1	0	0	0					
Billingsley p	0	0	0	0					
Ethier lf	0	0	0	0					
Totals	32	1	5	1		29	4	7	4

Dodgers	000	000	010	1	5	1
Mets	001	012	00x	4	7	0

DODGERS	IP	H	R	ER	BB	SO
Kuo (L, 0–1)	4-1/3	4	2	2	2	4
Tomko	2/3	2	2	0	1	0
Hendrickson	1	1	0	0	0	0
Billingsley	1	0	0	0	0	2
Saito	1	0	0	0	0	1
Total	8	7	4	2	3	7

METS	IP	H	R	ER	BB	SO
Glavine (W, 1–0)	6	4	0	0	2	2
Feliciano	1	0	0	0	1	1
Heilman	1	1	1	1	0	1
Wagner (S, 2)	1	0	0	0	0	0
Total	9	5	1	1	3	4

LOB—Dodgers 7, Mets 7; E—Tomko; WP—Kuo.; 2B—Lo Duca (1), Lugo (1); HR—Betemit (1); IBB—Reyes; SH—Glavine, Valentin; SF—Lo Duca; Time—2:57; ATT—57,029.

Game 3, October 7 at LA
METS 9, DODGERS 5

Mets	AB	R	H	BI	Dodgers	AB	R	H	BI
Reyes ss	5	1	1	1	Furcal ss	4	0	1	0
Lo Duca c	3	1	2	2	Lofton cf	5	0	1	0
Beltran cf	4	1	2	1	Anderson lf	5	1	2	0
Delgado 1b	5	1	1	0	Kent 2b	5	2	4	2
Wright 3b	4	1	1	1	Drew rf	5	1	1	0
Floyd lf	2	1	2	1	Martin c	5	1	3	0
Chavez lf	3	0	1	0	Betemit 3b	4	0	1	0
Green rf	5	1	3	2	Loney 1b	4	0	3	3
Valentin 2b	4	0	0	0	Maddux p	1	0	0	0
Trachsel p	2	0	0	0	Ethier ph	1	0	0	0
Oliver p	0	0	0	0	Hendrickson p	0	0	0	0
Bradford p	0	0	0	0	Garciaparra ph	1	0	0	0
Feliciano p	0	0	0	0	Broxton p	0	0	0	0
Tucker ph	0	1	0	0	Billingsley p	0	0	0	0
Mota p	0	0	0	0	Saenz ph	1	0	0	0
Woodward ph	1	1	1	0	Tomko p	0	0	0	0
Heilman p	0	0	0	0	Saito p	0	0	0	0
Franco ph	1	0	0	0	Martinez ph	1	0	0	0
Wagner p	0	0	0	0					
Totals	39	9	14	8		42	5	16	5

Mets	301	003	020	9	14	2
Dodgers	000	230	000	5	16	2

METS	IP	H	R	ER	BB	SO
Trachsel	3-1/3	6	2	2	1	2
Oliver	1-1/3	3	3	3	0	0
Bradford	0	1	0	0	1	0
Feliciano (W, 1–0)	1/3	0	0	0	1	0
Mota	2	3	0	0	0	1
Heilman	1	2	0	0	0	0
Wagner	1	1	0	0	0	2
Total	9	16	5	5	3	5

DODGERS	IP	H	R	ER	BB	SO
Maddux	4	7	4	4	2	0
Hendrickson	1	0	0	0	1	0
Broxton (L, 0–1)	1	4	3	3	1	2
Billingsley	1	1	0	0	0	1
Tomko	1/3	2	2	1	1	0
Saito	1-2/3	0	0	0	0	3
Total	9	14	9	8	5	6

LOB—Mets 9, Dodgers 13; E—Wright (1), Beltran (1), Betemit (1), Loney (1); DP—Mets 2, Dodgers 2; 2B—Green 2 (2), Woodward (1), Kent (1); HR—Kent (1); IBB—Valentin; HBP—Lo Duca, SB—Beltran (1), Furcal; CS—Reyes (1); Time—3:51; ATT—56,293.

2006 NLDS Statistics

COMPOSITE LINESCORE

Mets	302	217	220	16 30 3	
Dodgers	010	230	311	11 32 4	

METS BATTING

Player	BA	G	AB	R	H
Carlos Beltran	.222	3	9	2	2
Chad Bradford	—	2	0	0	0
Endy Chavez	.375	3	8	1	3
Carlos Delgado	.429	3	14	3	6
Pedro Feliciano	—	3	0	0	0
Cliff Floyd	.444	3	9	3	4
Julio Franco	—	2	2	0	0
Tom Glavine	000	1	1	0	0
Shawn Green	.333	2	9	1	3
Aaron Heilman	—	3	0	0	0
Paul Lo Duca	.455	3	11	2	5
John Maine	000	1	1	0	0
Guillermo Mota	000	2	1	0	0
Darren Oliver	—	1	0	0	0
Jose Reyes	.167	3	12	2	2
Steve Trachsel	000	1	2	0	0
Michael Tucker	000	2	1	1	0
Jose Valentin	000	3	9	2	0
Billy Wagner	—	3	0	0	0
Chris Woodward	1.000	1	1	1	1
David Wright	.333	3	12	1	4
Total	.294	3	102	19	30

2B—Green 2, Wright 2, Lo Duca, Woodward; 3B—None; HR—Delgado, Floyd; RBI—Wright 4, Lo Duca 3, Reyes 3, Delgado 2, Floyd 2, Green 2, Beltran, Franco; SB—Beltran, Reyes.

DODGERS BATTING

Player	BA	G	AB	R	H
Marlon Anderson	.308	3	13	2	4
Wilson Betemit	.500	3	8	3	4
Chad Billingsley	—	2	0	0	0
Jonathan Broxton	—	2	0	0	0
J.D. Drew	.154	3	13	1	2
Andre Ethier	.000	2	1	0	0
Rafael Furcal	.182	3	11	1	2
Nomar Garciaparra	.222	3	9	0	2
Mark Hendrickson	—	3	0	0	0
Jeff Kent	.615	3	13	2	8
Hong-Chih Kuo	000	2	0	0	0
Kenny Lofton	.077	3	13	0	1
James Loney	.750	1	4	0	3
Derek Lowe	000	1	1	0	0
Julio Lugo	.250	2	4	0	1
Greg Maddux	000	1	1	0	0
Russell Martin	.333	3	12	2	4
Ramon Martinez	.333	3	3	0	1
Brad Penny	—	1	0	0	0
Jason Repko	—	1	0	0	0
Olmedo Saenz	000	2	2	0	0
Takashi Saito	—	2	0	0	0
Brett Tomko	—	2	0	0	0
Total	.296	3	108	11	32

2B—Anderson, Betemit, Garciaparra, Kent, Lugo, Martinez; 3B—None; HR—Betemit, Kent; RBI—Loney 3, Garciaparra 2, Kent 2, Anderson, Betemit, Furcal, Martinez; SB—Furcal 2.

METS PITCHING

Player	G	ERA	W–L	SV	IP	H	ER	BB	SO
Chad Bradford	2	0.00	0–0	0	1/3	1	0	1	0
Pedro Feliciano	3	0.00	1–0	0	1-2/3	0	0	2	2
Tom Glavine	1	0.00	1–0	0	6	4	0	2	2
Aaron Heilman	3	3.00	0–0	0	3	3	1	0	1
John Maine	1	2.08	0–0	0	4-1/3	6	1	2	5
Guillermo Mota	2	6.75	1–0	0	4	6	3	0	5
Darren Oliver	1	20.25	0–0	0	1-1/3	3	3	0	0
Steve Trachsel	1	5.40	0–0	0	3-1/3	6	2	1	2
Billy Wagner	3	3.00	0–0	2	3	3	1	0	4
Total	3	3.67	3–0	2	27	32	11	8	21

DODGERS PITCHING

Player	G	ERA	W–L	SV	IP	H	ER	BB	SO
Chad Billingsley	2	0.00	0–0	0	2	1	0	0	3
Jon. Broxton	2	13.50	0–1	0	2	5	3	2	3
M. Hendrickson	3	0.00	0–0	0	2-2/3	1	0	1	1
Hong-Chih Kuo	1	4.15	0–1	0	4-1/3	4	2	2	4
Derek Lowe	1	6.75	0–0	0	5-1/3	6	4	2	6
Greg Maddux	1	9.00	0–0	0	4	7	4	2	0
Brad Penny	1	18.00	0–1	0	1	2	2	2	1
Takashi Saito	2	0.00	0–0	0	2-2/3	0	0	0	4
Brett Tomko	2	9.00	0–0	0	1	4	1	2	0
Total	3	5.76	0–3	0	25	30	16	13	22

2006 NLCS: Mets vs. St. Louis Cardinals

CARDINALS WIN SERIES 4–3

Left fielder Endy Chavez robs the St. Louis Cardinals' Scott Rolen of a home run in the top of the sixth inning of Game 7 of the 2006 NLCS at Shea Stadium. Chavez threw back to first and doubled off the Cardinals' Jim Edmonds to end the inning.

There was reason to believe the Cardinals were only a speed bump on the Mets' path to the World Series. The Mets took four of six from St. Louis during the regular season en route to 97 victories, 14 more than the Cardinals. New York had the division title well in hand by the All-Star break, whereas the Cardinals had to wait until the next-to-last day of the regular season to wrap up the NL Central crown.

The hitters were evenly matched. The Mets batted .264 with a .445 slugging average, 200 homers, 800 RBIs, and 564 extra-base hits during the regular season compared to the Cardinals' .269 batting average, .431 slugging, 184 homers, 745 RBIs, and 503 extra-base hits. But the Mets had questions concerning left fielder Cliff Floyd, who played the second half of the regular season with a sore Achilles' and strained the tendon during Game 3 of the division series.

"I'm not really confident right now," Floyd said in the *New York Times* the day before the NLCS began. "I'm not going to lie to you."

If you go by the "team with the best hitter" theory, the Cardinals had the edge with Albert Pujols. The first baseman hit 49 homers and drove in 137 runs while hitting .331, numbers that no Met could match. Pujols also batted .333 with a homer and three RBI in the Cardinals' NLDS win over the Diamondbacks, giving him a .336 average with 11 home runs lifetime in the postseason. Game 1 starter Tom Glavine said in the *New York Times* before the series the Mets didn't plan to be foolish when facing Pujols: "I can assure you we're not going to stand on the mound and just stupidly say, 'The better side of me wants to get him out and I have something to prove,' or something like that. That's not going to happen."

Theoretically, the big difference between the two teams was speed as the Mets led the National League with 146 stolen bases and hit 41 triples. The Cardinals were near the bottom of the league in three-baggers and steals, quite a change from the St. Louis clubs that tortured the Mets in the mid-1980s. However, the Cards had Yadier Molina and his outstanding arm behind plate to neutralize Reyes and Endy Chavez. Molina also did a little hitting in the series.

"José has to be patient," Mets first base coach Sandy Alomar said before the series. "We know Molina is one of the best, and he is going to make things difficult, but we think we can find some opportunities."

"I really think the key to this series is how he does against Reyes," Mets backup catcher Ramon Castro said of Molina in the *Times*. "Yadier is one of the best defensive catchers around. But, you know, I still like Reyes."

Neither team appeared to have an edge in starting pitching. Injuries to Pedro Martinez and Orlando Hernandez left the Mets scrambling for arms before the division series. The Cardinals had a postseason rotation of Jeff Weaver, Chris Carpenter, Jeff Suppan and Anthony Reyes, who combined for a 42-37. Mets starters Tom Glavine and Steve Trachsel each entered the playoffs with 15 victories, tying Carpenter for seventh best among National League hurlers.

The Mets seemed to have a huge advantage in the bullpen since Cardinals closer and ex-Met Jason Isringhausen was sidelined by injury. Billy Wagner compiled 40 saves with help from a relief corps that included Roberto Hernandez, Aaron Heilman, Pedro Feliciano, Chad Bradford, Darren Oliver, and Guillermo Mota. The Cardinals countered with Adam Wainwright, Randy Flores, Brad Thompson, Josh Kinney, Tyler Johnson, Josh Hancock, and Braden Looper in their bullpen, a septet that would have had trouble landing on the Mets' roster. Without Isringhausen, Wainwright was the lone Cardinals reliever in the series to record more than one save during the regular season. Overall, Mets relievers posted a 3.21 ERA in the NLCS while the Cardinals' pen was at 5.89.

But the pennant came down to the Cardinals' closer being much better than the Mets' closer. Wainwright picked up two saves and tossed three scoreless innings while Wagner was tagged for five runs in 2 2/3 innings. The Cardinals took away home field advantage from the Mets by scoring three times off Wagner in the ninth inning of Game 2. Wainwright secured the pennant for the Cardinals by stranding two runners in scoring position in a 4–2 victory in Game 5 before fanning Beltran with the bases loaded to end the series.

The Cardinals also had playoff experience on their side. They were playing in their third straight NLCS, having beaten the Astros in 2004 before falling to Houston the following autumn. Beltran and Floyd were the lone Mets position player to have experienced any significant postseason action before this series, and he almost single-handedly beat St. Louis in the '04 NLCS by hitting .417 with four homers and five RBIs.

Beltran was having a wonderful NLCS two years later until the season-ending strikeout. He hit a two-run homer in the series opener and went deep twice in a much-needed Game 5 victory. He owned a .308 average for the series before that final out.

Delgado also had a strong NLCS, tying Beltran for the team lead in home runs and pacing the club with three doubles and nine RBI while hitting .304. Shawn Green also hit .304, and Jose Reyes was an absolute pest while hitting .281 with five runs scored and two stolen bases.

But David Wright, Endy Chavez, and Paul Lo Duca combined to hit .185 in 81 at-bats after each hit .306 or better during the regular season. Chavez batted only .185 with one run scored but atoned for his offensive deficiencies by making one of the greatest catches in Mets postseason history. Lo Duca's .207 average included a big two-run single that put the Mets ahead 4-0 in the seventh inning of a 4-2 victory in Game 6. Wright homered in Game 4 but was 4-for-25 in the series.

The series evoked memories of the 1988 NLCS, when the Mets were also favored to beat the Dodgers after going 10–1 against Los Angeles during the regular season. Although the Cardinals didn't have an Orel Hershiser to baffle the Mets, they used their playoff experience to derail a Mets-Tigers World Series.

GAME 1, October 12, Shea Stadium: Mets 2, Cardinals 0

A three-game sweep of the Dodgers in the NLDS allowed manager Willie Randolph to start Tom Glavine in the opener. Glavine tied for the team lead with 15 victories and was brilliant in the Mets' Game 2 win over the Dodgers. The 40-year-old lefty also received an extra day of rest for this one after it was postponed by rain the previous night.

Glavine blanked the Cardinals on four hits over seven innings in a performance reminiscent of his days in Atlanta. His only rough patch came in the third inning, when he allowed back-to-back one-out singles to Yadier Molina and pitcher Jeff Weaver before getting David Eckstein to line into an inning-ending double play.

However, Weaver carried a one-hitter into the sixth and didn't look anything like the pitcher that couldn't perform in New York for the Yankees. He opened the sixth by retiring Glavine and Jose Reyes on grounders before Paul Lo Duca singled to keep the inning alive.

Next up was Carlos Beltran, who took the count to 2–2

before blasting a two-run homer to right-center. Carlos Delgado followed with a double before David Wright was walked intentionally, ending Weaver's night.

Glavine and the Mets' bullpen held Albert Pujols, Juan Encarnacion and Scott Rolen—the Cardinals' 3-4-5 hitters—hitless in 10 at-bats. Glavine ended his perfect first inning by fanning Pujols.

"I feel like I'm pitching as well as I have at any point in the year," said Glavine in the *New York Times*, who had now thrown 19 consecutive innings dating to the regular season.

The Cardinals were no-hit following Beltran's home run. Guillermo Mota allowed a two-out walk in the eighth inning, and Billy Wagner did the same in the ninth before Wagner got pinch-hitter Scott Spiezio to hit a soft pop-up to second, ending the game.

It was Wagner's third save in the Mets' first four games of the postseason. One game later, Spiezio and Wagner would experience opposite results.

GAME 2, October 13, Shea Stadium: Cardinals 9, Mets 6

Held in check by journeyman Jeff Weaver for the first five innings of the opener, the Mets teed off on Cards ace Chris Carpener during the first two innings of Game 2. Carlos Delgado's three-run blast in the first inning put the Mets ahead 3–0, and Jose Reyes made it 4–2 with an RBI double in the second. Both Mets rallies began with leadoff doubles by their speedsters—Reyes and Endy Chavez—but John Maine wasted little time blowing the lead.

Maine walked a tightrope in pitching into the fifth inning of the NLDS opener. He wasn't as fortunate this time as he pitched on nine days' rest, loading the bases on two walks and an error before getting Ronnie Belliard to pop up to Reyes for the first out. Yadier Molina followed with a two-run double to get the Cardinals within 3–2 before Maine retired the next two hitters.

One inning later, Maine surrendered a game-tying, two-run homer by Jim Edmonds before settling down. Manager Willie Randolph elected to lift Maine for a pinch-hitter in the bottom of the fourth, leaving the outcome in the hands of his battle-tested bullpen.

It remained 4–4 until Delgado launched another homer, a solo shot off Carpenter in the fifth. Reyes walked and scored on Paul Lo Duca's double an inning later, and the Mets carried a 6–4 lead into the seventh.

Guillermo Mota retired the first two hitters in the seventh before Albert Pujols singled and Jim Edmonds walked. Scott Spiezio knotted the score with a two-run triple that almost cleared the fence in right field.

The Mets had a great chance to retake the lead in the eighth as Reyes singled for his third hit of the night before Lo Duca walked with one out. But Beltran hit a double-

play grounder to second, ending the threat.

Randolph went with closer Billy Wagner in the ninth inning of a tie game. The lefty hadn't allowed a home run in a win of save situation since August 9, when he gave up a meaningless blast in a 4–3 win over the Padres. The streak ended nine pitches later as So Taguchi, who hit two home runs in 361 plate appearances during the regular season, smacked a leadoff homer to put the Cardinals ahead to stay. Pujols followed with a double and scored on Spiezio's two-base hit before Juan Encarnacion added an RBI single to close the scoring.

The difference in the game was the bullpens. Five Redbird relievers combined to blank the Mets on two hits over the final 3⅔ innings following Lo Duca's RBI double. The Mets' pen was roughed up, tagged for five runs and eight hits following Maine's four innings of work.

Randolph lamented the work of his relievers but felt confident they would bounce back.

"We made some bad pitches at the wrong time. Our bullpen's resilient. They're strong. At this time of year, everybody's ready to go. My guys love to pitch," he said in the *New York Times*.

Wagner said he'd have no trouble rebounding from his woeful performance. "I've played 10 years, blown 50 saves, saved 324. That's how you do it."

The Mets wanted to take a 2–0 lead into St. Louis, especially since the one-day postponement of Game 1 screwed with the rotation by forcing the two teams to play five straight days. That meant Glavine had to be pushed back to Game 5, forcing Randolph to start Oliver Perez in Game 4. Perez didn't pitch in the division series after going 3–13 with a 6.55 ERA during the regular season.

The Mets remained very optimistic heading into St. Louis, where they dropped two of three in what was a 3–6 road trip in May.

"We've had bigger challenges than this," said Randolph. "We just have to get that back tomorrow. We kind of let that one slip away."

GAME 3, October 14, Busch Stadium: Cardinals 5, Mets 0

The Mets had no trouble with the bullpen on this night after absorbing a cumulative beating in Game 2. Darren Oliver did the heavy lifting, giving the Mets six shutout innings of relief while holding the Cardinals to three hits.

Unfortunately, New York already trailed 5–0 by the time the lefty recorded his first out.

Steve Trachsel was brutal in the second-shortest postseason start in Mets history, allowing five runs on five hits and five walks in one-plus inning. He threw just 21 of his 43 pitches for strikes and was unable to string together two consecutive outs.

Eckstein singled on Trachsel's second pitch of the evening before he was picked off with Preston Wilson at the plate. Wilson worked out Trachsel's first walk, and Albert Pujols singled, but Jim Edmonds fouled out to David Wright for the second out, giving Trachsel a chance to wiggle out of the jam until Scott Spiezio laced a two-run triple to put the Cardinals ahead to stay. Spiezio now had five RBIs in his last three at-bats dating to Game 2.

Trachsel promptly loaded the bases on a pair of walks before fanning Yadier Molina to end the inning. But the beat-down resumed in the second inning as pitcher Jeff Suppan homered to left on an 0–2 pitch.

Trachsel again loaded the bases on two walks and a hit with nobody out following Suppan's homer. Manager Willie Randolph finally yanked Trachsel after watching his starter issue free passes to five of his first 12 batters.

Pitching coach Rick Peterson did his best Yogi Berra impression to sum up Trachsel's performance in the *New York Times*: "On this stage, any day you have a bad day it's a bad day to have a bad day."

In came Oliver, who followed Trachsel's wildness by uncorking a wild pitch to make it 4–0. A fifth run came on Jim Edmonds' grounder three pitches later before Oliver restored order.

Suppan was brilliant over eight innings, holding the Mets to three hits and a walk while whiffing four. His only moment of danger came when Jose Reyes tripled with two out in the third before Paul Lo Duca fanned to end the threat.

Oliver threw free and easy after pitching in and out of a second-and-third situation in the fifth. He retired his final seven hitters—six on grounders—before leaving the game for a pinch-hitter in the eighth.

The Mets were held hitless over the final four innings as they struggled at the plate for the second time in three games. Suppan cooled off Delgado and kept David Wright on ice as the pair went 0-for-3. Wright was now 0-for-9 with three walks in the series.

The biggest positive was Oliver, who gave his bullpen brethren a breather if just for one night. Randolph went through seven pitchers in Game 2 after making 14 pitching changes in the three-game sweep of the Dodgers.

"You cannot do this over 162 games," Peterson said in the *Times*. "But we are in the Champagne round now. We only need to do it for 11 games."

The Mets were now in danger of not bring the series back to Shea Stadium. The prospects of a Game 4 victory were somewhat unlikely with 3–13 Oliver Perez taking the mound. Randolph remained an optimist.

"We've been in tougher spots than this. We feel like we're in pretty good shape, even though we're down 2–1."

GAME 4, October 15, Busch Stadium: Mets 12, Cardinals 5

It wasn't a great performance by Oliver Perez. It wasn't even very good. But it was more than enough to help the Mets tie the series with the help of a reinvigorated offense.

Perez kept the damage to a minimum as he labored over 5⅔ innings, allowing five runs, nine hits, three homers, and three walks.

Making his first career postseason appearance, Perez worked out of a two-on, one-out situation in the first inning by getting Juan Encarnacion to hit into an inning-ending double play. He allowed a run and three hits in the second inning but was helped out by Endy Chavez's throw that nailed Ronnie Belliard at third following Yadier Molina's RBI single.

Encarnacion hit a game-tying triple in the third inning to tie the game 2–2, but the Mets had a 5–2 lead by the time Perez allowed another run.

The Mets belted four homers over the first seven innings after managing just three hits in eight innings against Jeff Suppan the night before. David Wright was 0-for-10 in the series before launching a solo homer in the third, two batters after Carlos Beltrán smacked the first of his two home runs.

It was a 2–2 game until Carlos Delgado drilled a three-run blast off reliever Brad Thompson in the top of the fifth. Light-hitting David Eckstein closed the gap with a solo blast in the bottom half, but the Mets erupted for six runs in the sixth to take command.

Delgado also ignited the sixth-inning assault with a two-run double before Shawn Green singled home Beltrán. Jose Valentin followed with a three-run double that gave the Mets an 11–3 lead, allowing Willie Randolph to stay with Perez a little longer than expected.

Perez gave Randolph reason to pull him by serving up gopher balls to Jim Edmonds and Molina in the sixth. Beltran's solo shot in the seventh capped the scoring.

Between the Mets' resurgent hitting and Perez's ability to pitch into the sixth, Randolph was allowed to rest Aaron Heilman and Billy Wagner for a second straight night, giving the Mets bullpen options for Game 5.

Beltran reached base five times, finishing 3-for-3 with two walks, two RBIs, and four runs scored after going 1-for-8 in the previous two games. Delgado's five RBIs were a Mets LCS record and tied a team mark for a postseason game. Valentin had two hits and three RBIs, and Wright was 1-for-4 to raise his postseason average to .200.

Delgado already had 11 RBIs in the series, one off the team record of 12 set by John Olerud in 1999. "I played twelve and a half years and never sniffed the playoffs," Delgado said in the *New York Times*. "This is what every athlete wants."

Unfortunately, Delgado's next RBI didn't come until April as the Cardinals pitched very carefully to the clean-up hitter with Wright scuffling in the No. 5 spot.

"Can't go to the same place to get him out," Tony La Russa said in the *Times* of Delgado's first four games. "You've got to mix it up, and if you've made a mistake like we've made, he punishes you."

The 12 runs broke a club postseason record of 11 that stood since Game 2 of the 1969 NLCS. The Mets had seven homers, seven doubles and a triple out of their 32 hits in the series. They were hitting .264 and averaging 5.57 runs per game since the postseason began. They hit only .247 while scoring nine times in three games the rest of the series.

GAME 5, October 17, 2006, Busch Stadium: Cardinals 4, Mets 2

The Mets finally received a break regarding their pitching staff when Game 5 was pushed back a day because of rain, allowing Tom Glavine to throw on his normal fifth day. Glavine had been terrific thus far in the postseason, going 2–0 while allowing no runs and eight hits in 13 innings over two starts.

His success in the series opener came from keeping the ball away from the Cardinals' top sluggers. He exhibited pin-point control in Game 1, just as he had in Game 2 of the division series.

The Mets almost gave Glavine a lead in the first inning, putting runners on first and third with two out before slumping David Wright struck out against Jeff Weaver to end the threat. Glavine gave up singles to the leadoff hitter in each of the first two innings without budging, then worked a perfect third inning to keep it scoreless.

The Mets broke through in the fourth as Jose Valentin lashed a two-run double to score Carlos Delgado and Shawn Green. Glavine had a chance to pad the lead before he grounded out to short to end the inning.

Glavine had retired seven straight after Preston Wilson opened the fourth by flying out to center. The veteran lefty now had a postseason shutout streak of 16⅓ innings, the best by a Met in the postseason since Mike Hampton tossed 17⅓ consecutive scoreless innings in 2000.

Up stepped Albert Pujols, who was 0-for-3 with a walk against Glavine in the series before smashing a home run on a 2–2 pitch, getting the Cards within 2–1. Glavine retired Juan Encarnacion on a pop-up for the second out before unraveling, yielding a walk and a single before Ronnie Belliard singled to tie the game.

It remained 2–2 until David Eckstein led off the bottom of the fifth with a single and scored on Wilson's double.

Glavine walked Pujols intentionally before leaving the game.

Reliever Chad Bradford promptly gave up a single to load the bases with nobody out before pitching out of the jam with Mets down only 3–2.

The Cardinals had all the runs they'd need as the Mets managed just three hits following Valentin's two-run double. New York threatened in the eighth off Josh Kinney, putting the tying run on second following back-to-back one-out hits by Carlos Delgado and David Wright. Randy Flores came in to retire Shawn Green before Adam Wainwright fanned Valentin.

Wright's double in the eighth was just his second hit in 17 at-bats in the series. Wright went four straight games without a hit during the regular season, but that skid came in the first month when such stats aren't as magnified.

"It's frustrating, but you can't sit here and feel sorry for yourself," Wright said to the *New York Times* after the game. "You have to take advantage of the opportunities you do get. They're pitching me well. All in all, I'm having some good at-bats, some bad at-bats, fighting off pitches. They're hitting their spots. To shut down this offense—it's just not me—you have to give credit to their pitching staff.

"Obviously it's magnified," he continued, "but as far as my confidence, I feel good up there. I want to be up there in big situations. I'm not scared going up there. I'm not timid. I'm just not producing the way I want to. I have to start doing that. Everybody has to do their part and right now I'm not doing my part."

The Cardinals were looking like one of those teams of destiny. They ran into such clubs during the 1985 and '87 World Series, taking a 3–1 series lead over the Royals and a 3–2 lead against the Twins before losing each time.

The Mets were the team of destiny in 1969 and received payback when the Dodgers came out of nowhere to beat them in the 1988 NLCS. A victory in Game 5 would make the Mets feel a bit more comfortable about having John Maine and, if necessary, Oliver Perez as their next two starters.

GAME 6, October 20, Shea Stadium: Mets 4, Cardinals 2

The Mets were five days shy of the 20th anniversary of their improbable comeback in Game 6 of the World Series when John Maine was asked to perform his own miracle. The rookie right-hander had failed to get out of the fifth inning in either of his two postseason starts and was now given the task of making sure the Mets extended their season by at least one more game.

Maine had trouble with his command at times, just as he had in the Mets' 9–6 loss in Game 2. He threw just 54 of his 98 pitches for strikes and walked four batters during his 5⅓ innings of work. But he also allowed just two hits and left to a standing ovation with the Mets leading 2–0 in the sixth.

Both hits were one-out singles in the first inning. He struck out Jim Edmonds on three pitches before plunking Juan Encarnacion to load the bases before Scott Rolen hit an inning-ending fly ball to right, allowing Maine to walk off the mound unscathed.

It took leadoff hitter Jose Reyes just three pitches to give Maine the lead for good. Reyes launched his first career postseason home run off Chris Carpenter, who had served up a three-run blast to Carlos Delgado in the first inning of Game 2.

"That's a huge lift to get the crowd in the game," said Paul Lo Duca in the *New York Times*. "Especially just after they left the bases loaded in the first inning. That's a huge momentum shift."

The Mets doubled their lead in the fourth on Shawn Green's RBI single. Maine followed with a perfect fifth, ending the frame by striking out Albert Pujols.

Maine walked the leadoff hitter in the sixth and was taken out after Juan Encarnacion hit a fly ball to left. Chad Bradford and Guillermo Mota followed, with each reliever getting the Cardinals to hit into inning-ending double plays to keep it 2–0.

Pinch-hitter Michael Tucker started what would be the Mets' final multi-run rally of the season, hitting a two-out single off Braden Looper and stealing second before going to third on a single by Jose Reyes. Reyes stole second, putting two runners in scoring position a few pitches before Paul Lo Duca drove them in with a single.

The Mets had a 4–0 lead when Billy Wagner replaced Aaron Heilman to start the ninth. Fans began to squirm as Wagner gave up a single and a double with nobody out, but the closer retired the next two hitters to get the Mets within one out of a seventh game. Pinch-hitter So Toguchi, who hit a tiebreaking solo homer off Wagner to spark a three-run ninth in Game 2, lined a 1–2 pitch to left for a two-run double. Wagner finally nailed down the victory by retiring Eckstein.

Maine's performance was trumpeted by Lo Duca and Tom Glavine, two team leaders who were averse to doling out high accolades.

"We saw the maturation of a kid that's going to be a good pitcher and you'll see him for a long time," Lo Duca said in the *Times*. "He grew a lot tonight."

"In Mets annals this will be looked at as one of the biggest games," Glavine chimed in. "For a guy at his position, his stage of his career, it was huge."

History was now on the Mets' side. Of the 11 previous teams to force a seventh game after trailing an LCS 3–2, eight went on to win the pennant. The '88 Mets were one of the three exceptions.

GAME 7, October 19, Shea Stadium: Cardinals 3, Mets 1

It would have been quite a story if a pitcher with a 3–13 record during the regular season could win a seventh game in an LCS. Oliver Perez was given the start over Steve Trachsel, who tied for the team lead with 15 victories but was hammered in his two postseason starts.

Perez came to the Mets July 31 as the throw-in in the Roberto Hernandez-for-Xavier Nady deal after reliever Duaner Sanchez separated his shoulder. Perez was one of the National League's best young pitchers in 2004, striking out 239 in 196 innings while going 12–10 with a 2.98 as a 22-year-old left for the lowly Pirates. Two years later, the Bucs sent him to the minors after he opened the season 2–10 with a 6.63 ERA.

Crash Davis of "Bull Durham" fame would have referred to Perez as a "million-dollar arm with a ten-cent head." On this night, the Mets witnessed the million-dollar arm with a lot of help from left fielder Endy Chavez.

Perez tossed a scoreless first before the Mets pushed across their only run of the night. Game 3 winner Jeff Suppan retired the first two Mets on grounders and allowed a double to Carlos Beltran before Carlos Delgado walked. David Wright, with just three hits in the first six games of the series, slapped an opposite field single to give the Mets their first run in nine innings against Suppan.

Perez quickly lost the lead, allowing a pair of singles that put runners on first and third before Ronnie

Belliard's suicide squeeze tied the game. From then on, it was an intense pitchers' duel until the ninth inning.

Suppan was almost as good as his eight-inning, three-hit performance in Game 3. The New York native pitched no-hit ball from the second through the seventh innings before leaving the game for a pinch-hitter. Although Suppan walked five, he threw strikes on 65 of his 104 pitches.

Perez was also cruising until the sixth, when he faced Scott Rolen with a runner on first and one out. Rolen was 0-for-2 in the game and 4-for-19 in the series before sending a fly ball toward the left-field bullpen.

Endy Chavez had become the Mets' starting left fielder only because Cliff Floyd was unable to play due to an inflamed Achilles' tendon. Chavez was a gifted defensive player who used his speed to his advantage.

Chavez broke toward the left-field wall immediately and was still sprinting as he reached the warning track. Without missing a stride, Chavez leaped above the fence and snagged the ball about a foot past the wall, robbing Rolen of a sure home run.

Veteran Jim Edmonds was also sure the ball was going out. He was between second and third base when Chavez pulled the ball out of the Cardinals bullpen. Chavez had the presence of mind after the catch to throw a perfect strike to cutoff man Jose Valentin before they doubled up Edmonds at first to end the inning.

Chavez's catch immediately conjured up memories of Tommie Agee's two sensational catches in Game 3 of the 1969 World Series, and Ron Swoboda's circus grab the following day. Unfortunately, the Mets failed to seize the karma as they loaded the bases without a hit in the bottom of the sixth without scoring. Chavez made the final out to snuff out the rally.

Chad Bradford followed Perez to the mound and pitched a perfect seventh inning before Aaron Heilman tossed a scoreless eighth. Heilman walked Albert Pujols with two out and nobody on base before getting Juan Encarnacion to swing at strike three.

Suppan's night was done after he retired the Mets in order in the eighth following a leadoff walk by Carlos Beltran. Heilman opened the ninth by fanning Edmonds before allowing a single to Rolen.

Yadier Molina was one of the least-feared hitters in the Cardinals lineup heading into the series but was 7-for-22 with a homer and four RBI as he came up to face Heilman with Rolen on base. One pitch later, the Cardinals had a 3–1 lead after Molina hit a drive to left that even Chavez couldn't track down.

The Mets now needed another Buckner-Wilson type miracle to advance to the World Series, and they had the bottom of the order facing Adam Wainwright to start the ninth. Valenin and Chavez singled to give the Mets runners on first and second with nobody out and Heilman scheduled to hit next. Manager Willie Randolph countered with Floyd, who had been to the plate just once since the series opener. Fans of "small ball" wanted to see Floyd bunt the

runners into scoring position, although the power hitter hadn't laid down a successful bunt since 1997. What Mets fans were hoping for was a Kirk Gibson-type at-bat, coming off the bench to hit a game-winning homer.

"I had one thing on my mind—send us to Detroit," Floyd said in the *New York Times*. "Unfortunately I didn't. Tip your cap to Wainwright. He made some good pitches."

Instead, Wainwright caught him looking at a 2–2 pitch for the first out before Reyes hit a scorching liner to center. With the Mets one out from extinction, Paul Lo Duca walked to load the bases and send up Beltrán, who had killed the Cardinals in the NLCS two years earlier.

Funny how a single at-bat can change the course of history. Beltrán was the most feared hitter on the Mets at that point, and Wainwright was a 25-year-old reliever in his first full season in the big leagues. The confrontation reeked of a mismatch until Wainwright worked the count to 0–2.

Beltrán froze on the third pitch, a nasty slider that caught the plate for strike three. The Mets now added another year to their World Series drought and would keep the streak alive with breathtaking collapses the next two years.

"We faced some good pitching," said Wright following the game. "This is the playoffs. We saw some good arms. Tip your cap to them. They deserved to win. They played tremendous baseball. They played the kind of winning baseball that I've watched on T.V. that wins playoff games—good pitching, good defense and they got some timely hits. We weren't able to do that. It's not what we didn't do; it's what they did."

"You feel like you've taken steps," Minaya said in the *Times*. "If you don't get to the World Series, then at least I feel we've taken steps to win the World Series. We are heading in the right direction."

Wainwright became a starter the following year, enjoying moderate success before an injury limited him to 20 games in 2008. He won 39 games over the next two seasons, becoming one of the league's best starters.

The called third strike is etched in memories of Mets fans as Buckner's error in 1986 is imprinted in the minds of Red Sox fans. Just as Buckner should not bear the entire burden of Boston's loss in the 1986, Beltrán's fate might have changed had Floyd provided a productive plate appearance three batters earlier.

Game 1, October 12 at New York
METS 2, CARDINALS 0

Cardinals	AB	R	H	BI	Mets	AB	R	H	BI
Eckstein ss	3	0	0	0	Reyes ss	4	0	0	0
Wilson lf	4	0	1	0	Lo Duca c	4	1	2	0
Pujols 1b	3	0	0	0	Beltran cf	4	1	1	2
Encarnacion rf	4	0	0	0	Delgado 1b	3	0	2	0
Rolen 3b	3	0	0	0	Wright 3b	3	0	0	0
Edmonds cf	3	0	1	0	Floyd lf	1	0	0	0
Spiezio ph	1	0	0	0	Chavez lf	3	0	0	0
Belliard 2b	3	0	0	0	Green rf	2	0	1	0
Molina c	1	0	1	0	Valentin 2b	3	0	0	0
Miles ph	1	0	0	0	Glavine p	2	0	0	0
Looper p	0	0	0	0	Franco ph	1	0	0	0
Weaver p	2	0	1	0	Mota p	0	0	0	0
Johnson p	0	0	0	0	Wagner p	0	0	0	0
Thompson p	0	0	0	0					
Rodriguez ph	1	0	0	0					
Bennett c	0	0	0	0					
Totals	29	0	4	0		30	2	6	2

Cardinals	000	000	000	0	4	0	
Mets	000	002	00x	2	6	0	

CARDINALS	IP	H	R	ER	BB	SO
Weaver (L, 0–1)	5.2	4	2	2	2	1
Johnson	1.0	0	0	0	1	2
Thompson	0.1	0	0	0	0	0
Looper	1.0	2	0	0	0	0
Total	8.0	6	2	2	3	3

METS	IP	H	R	ER	BB	SO
Glavine (W, 1–0)	7.0	4	0	0	2	2
Mota	1.0	0	0	0	1	1
Wagner (S, 1)	1.0	0	0	0	1	0
Total	9.0	4	0	0	4	3

LOB: Cardinals 6, Mets 7; DP: Cardinals 0, Mets 2; 2B: Delgado 2 (2); HR: Beltran (1); IBB: Wright; SB: Green (1); Time: 2:52; ATT: 56,311.

Game 2, October 13 at New York
CARDINALS 9, METS 6

Cardinals	AB	R	H	BI	Mets	AB	R	H	BI
Eckstein ss	4	0	0	0	Reyes ss	4	2	3	1
Duncan lf	4	0	0	0	Lo Duca c	3	0	1	1
Taguchi lf	1	1	1	1	Beltran cf	4	1	0	0
Pujols 1b	4	3	2	0	Delgado 1b	5	2	2	4
Edmonds cf	3	3	1	2	Wright 3b	3	0	0	0
Spiezio 3b	4	2	2	3	Green rf	4	0	1	0
Johnson p	0	0	0	0	Valentin 2b	4	0	1	0
Wainwright p	0	0	0	0	Chavez lf	4	1	1	0
Encarnacion rf	4	0	1	1	Maine p	0	0	0	0
Belliard 2b	5	0	0	0	Tucker ph	0	0	0	0
Molina c	5	0	3	2	Bradford p	0	0	0	0
Carpenter p	2	0	0	0	Feliciano p	0	0	0	0
Rodriguez ph	1	0	0	0	AH'rn'nd'z ph	1	0	0	0
Hancock p	0	0	0	0	Mota p	0	0	0	0
Flores p	0	0	0	0	Heilman p	0	0	0	0
Wilson ph	1	0	0	0	Franco ph	1	0	0	0
Kinney p	0	0	0	0	Wagner p	0	0	0	0
Rolen 3b	0	0	0	0	RHernandez p	0	0	0	0
Totals	38	9	10	9		33	6	9	6

Cardinals	022	000	203	9	10	1	
Mets	310	011	000	6	9	2	

CARDINALS	IP	H	R	ER	BB	SO
Carpenter	5.0	6	5	5	4	1
Hancock	0.1	1	1	1	1	1
Flores	1.2	1	0	0	0	0
Kinney (W, 1–0)	1.0	1	0	0	1	1
Johnson	0.1	0	0	0	0	1
Wainwright	0.2	0	0	0	0	0
Total	9.0	9	6	6	6	4

METS	IP	H	R	ER	BB	SO
Maine	4.0	2	4	3	5	3
Bradford	1.2	1	0	0	0	1
Feliciano	0.1	0	0	0	0	0
Mota	0.2	2	2	2	1	0
Heilman	1.1	1	0	0	0	1
Wagner (L, 0–1)	0.2	4	3	3	0	0
Hernandez	0.1	0	0	0	0	0
Total	9.0	10	9	8	6	5

LOB: Cardinals 8, Mets 9; E: Delgado (1), Lo Duca (1), Belliard (1); DP: Cardinals 2, Mets 0; WP: Heilman; 2B: Reyes (1), Lo Duca (1), Chavez (1), Pujols (1), Spiezio (1), Molina; 3B: Spiezio (1); HR: Delgado 2 (2), Edmonds (1), Taguchi (1); HBP: Tucker; SH: Lo Duca, Maine; SB: Eckstein; Time: 3:58; ATT: 56,349.

Game 3, October 14 at St. Louis
CARDINALS 5, METS 0

Mets	AB	R	H	BI	Cardinals	AB	R	H	BI
Reyes ss	4	0	1	0	Eckstein ss	4	1	1	0
Lo Duca c	4	0	0	0	Wilson rf	3	2	1	0
Beltran cf	4	0	1	0	Pujols 1b	3	1	2	0
Delgado 1b	3	0	0	0	Edmonds cf	4	0	0	1
Wright 3b	3	0	0	0	Spiezio lf	4	0	1	2
Green rf	2	0	0	0	Taguchi lf	0	0	0	0
Valentin 2b	3	0	1	0	Rolen 3b	3	0	1	0
Chavez lf	3	0	0	0	Belliard 2b	2	0	1	0
Trachsel p	0	0	0	0	Molina c	4	0	0	0
Oliver p	2	0	0	0	Suppan p	1	1	1	1
Tucker ph	1	0	0	0	Duncan ph	1	0	0	0
Hernandez p	0	0	0	0	Kinney p	0	0	0	0
Totals	29	0	3	0		29	5	8	4

Mets	000	000	000	0	3	0	
Cardinals	230	000	00x	5	8	0	

METS	IP	H	R	ER	BB	SO
Trachsel (L,0—1)	1.0	5	5	5	5	1
Oliver	6.0	3	0	0	1	3
Hernandez	1.0	0	0	0	0	0

CARDINALS	IP	H	R	ER	BB	SO
Suppan (W, 1°0)	8.0	3	0	0	1	4
Kinney	1.0	0	0	0	0	0

LOB: Mets 3, Cardinals 8; WP: Oliver 3B: Reyes (1), Spiezio (2); HR: Suppan (1); SH: Suppan 2; SB: Beltran (1); Time: 2:53; ATT: 47,053.

Game 4, October 15 at St. Louis
METS 12, CARDINALS 5

Mets	AB	R	H	BI	Cardinals	AB	R	H	BI
Reyes ss	6	1	1	0	Eckstein ss	3	1	2	1
Lo Duca c	6	2	1	0	Rodriguez ph	1	0	0	0
Beltran cf	3	4	3	2	Spiezio lf	3	1	0	0
Delgado 1b	4	2	2	5	Pujols 1b	4	0	0	0
Wright 3b	4	2	1	1	Encarnacion rf	4	0	1	1
Green rf	5	1	2	1	Rolen 3b	4	1	1	0
Valentin 2b	4	0	2	3	Edmonds cf	3	1	1	1
Chavez lf	5	0	1	0	Taguchi ph-cf	1	0	1	0
Perez p	3	0	0	0	Belliard 2b	4	0	2	0
Bradford p	0	0	0	0	Molina c	3	1	2	2
Feliciano p	0	0	0	0	Miles ph	1	0	1	0
Tucker ph	1	0	1	0	Reyes p	1	0	0	0
Mota p	0	0	0	0	Duncan ph	1	0	0	0
					Thompson p	0	0	0	0
					Flores p	0	0	0	0
					Hancock p	0	0	0	0
					Johnson p	0	0	0	0
					Wilson ph	1	0	0	0
					Looper p	0	0	0	0
					Bennett ph	1	0	0	0
Totals	41	12	14	12		35	5	11	5

Mets	002	036	100	12	14	1	
Cardinals	011	012	000	-5	11	1	

METS	IP	H	R	ER	BB	SO
Perez (W,1-0)	5.2	9	5	5	1	3
Bradford	1.1	0	0	0	0	0
Feliciano	1.0	1	0	0	0	1
Mota	1.0	1	0	0	0	1
Total	9.0	11	5	5	1	5

CARDINALS	IP	H	R	ER	BB	SO
Reyes	4.0	3	2	2	4	4
Thompson (L, 0–1)	0.1	3	3	2	0	1
Flores	0.2	1	0	0	0	1
Hancock	0.0	3	5	5	2	0
Johnson	1.0	2	1	1	0	2
Looper	3.0	2	1	1	0	1
Total	9.0	14	12	11	6	9

LOB: Mets 8, Cardinals 5; E: Delgado (2), Belliard (2); DP: Mets 3, Cardinals 1; WP: Feliciano; 2B: Delgado (3), Valentin (1); 3B: Encarnacion (1); HR: Beltran 2 (3), Wright (1), Delgado (3), Edmonds (1), Eckstein (1), Molina (1); HBP: Eckstein; SB: Belliard (1); Time: 3:31; ATT: 46,600.

Game 5, October 17 at St. Louis
CARDINALS 4, METS 2

Mets	AB	R	H	BI	Cardinals	AB	R	H	BI
Reyes ss	5	0	1	0	Eckstein ss	5	1	2	0
Lo Duca c	4	0	1	0	Wilson lf	5	0	1	1
Beltran cf	4	0	1	0	Pujols 1b	3	1	1	1
Delgado 1b	3	1	1	0	Encarnacion rf	3	0	1	0
Wright 3b	4	0	1	0	Rolen 3b	3	1	1	0
Green rf	4	1	1	0	Edmonds cf	3	0	1	0
Valentin 2b	3	0	1	2	Belliard 2b	4	0	1	1
Chavez lf	4	0	1	0	Wainwright p	0	0	0	0
Glavine p	2	0	0	0	Molina c	3	0	0	0
Bradford p	0	0	0	0	Weaver p	2	0	0	0
Feliciano p	0	0	0	0	Duncan ph	1	1	1	1
Tucker ph	1	0	0	0	Kinney p	0	0	0	0
RHernandez p	0	0	0	0	Flores p	0	0	0	0
Mota p	0	0	0	0	Miles 2b	1	0	1	0
Floyd ph	1	0	0	0					
Totals	35	2	8	2		33	4	10	4

Mets	000	200	000	2	8	0	
Cardinals	000	211	00x	4	10	0	

METS	IP	H	R	ER	BB	SO
Glavine (L,1–1)	4.0	7	3	3	3	2
Bradford	0.1	1	0	0	0	1
Feliciano	1.2	1	1	1	0	0
RHernandez	1.0	0	0	0	2	0
Mota	1.0	1	0	0	0	0
Total	8.0	10	4	4	5	3

CARDINALS	IP	H	R	ER	BB	SO
Weaver (W, 1–1)	6.0	6	2	2	2	1
Kinney	1.1	2	0	0	0	3
Flores	0.1	0	0	0	0	0
Wainwright (S, 1)	1.1	0	0	0	0	2
Total	9.0	8	2	2	2	6

LOB: Mets 8, Cardinals 10; DP: Mets 1, Cardinals 0; WP: Hernandez; 2B: Wright (1), Valentin (2), Chavez (2), Green (1), Wilson (1); 3B: Miles (1); HR: Pujols (1), Duncan (1); IBB: Edmonds, Pujols; SB: Eckstein; CS: Rolen; Time: 3:26; ATT: 46,496.

Game 6, October 18 at New York
METS 4, CARDINALS 2

Cardinals	AB	R	H	BI	Mets	AB	R	H	BI
Eckstein ss	4	0	0	0	Reyes ss	4	2	3	1
Spiezio lf	4	0	1	0	Lo Duca c	4	0	1	2
Pujols 1b	3	0	2	0	Beltran cf	4	1	1	0
Edmonds cf	3	0	0	0	Delgado 1b	4	0	0	0
Encarnacion rf	3	1	1	0	Wright 3b	4	0	1	0
Rolen 3b	4	1	1	0	Green rf	3	0	2	1
Belliard 2b	4	0	1	0	Valentin 2b	4	0	0	0
Molina c	3	0	0	0	Chavez lf	4	0	1	0
Carpenter p	2	0	0	0	Maine p	2	0	0	0
Duncan ph	1	0	0	0	Bradford p	0	0	0	0
Looper p	0	0	0	0	Mota p	0	0	0	0
Johnson p	0	0	0	0	Tucker ph	1	1	1	0
Taguchi ph	1	0	1	2	Heilman p	0	0	0	0
					Wagner p	0	0	0	0
Totals	32	2	7	2		34	4	10	4

Cardinals	000	000	002	2	7	1	
Mets	100	100	20x	4	10	0	

CARDINALS	IP	H	R	ER	BB	SO
Carpenter (L, 0–1)	6.0	7	2	2	0	4
Looper	0.2	3	2	2	0	0
Johnson	1.1	0	0	0	0	0
Total	8.0	10	4	4	0	4

METS	IP	H	R	ER	BB	SO
Maine (W,1–0)	5.1	2	0	0	4	5
Bradford	1.0	1	0	0	0	0
Mota	0.2	0	0	0	0	0
Heilman	1.0	1	0	0	0	1
Wagner	1.0	3	2	2	0	0
Total	9.0	7	2	2	4	6

LOB: Cardinals 8, Mets 7; E: Rolen (1); DP: Cardinals 1, Mets 2; 2B: Rolen (1), Taguchi (1); HR: Reyes (1); IBB: Pujols; HBP: Green, Encarnacion; SB: Reyes 2 (2), Tucker (1), Eckstein (3); Time: 2:56; ATT: 56,334.

Game 7, October 19 at New York
CARDINALS 3, METS 1

Cardinals	AB	R	H	BI	Mets	AB	R	H	BI
Eckstein ss	3	0	1	0	Reyes ss	5	0	0	0
Wilson lf	3	0	0	0	Lo Duca c	4	0	0	0
Spiezio ph	1	0	0	0	AHrnandz pr	0	0	0	0
Taguchi lf	0	0	0	0	Beltran cf	4	1	1	0
Pujols 1b	2	0	0	0	Delgado 1b	1	0	0	0
Encarnacion rf	4	0	0	0	Wright 3b	4	0	1	1
Edmonds cf	3	1	1	0	Green rf	3	0	0	0
Rolen 3b	4	1	1	0	Valentin 2b	3	0	1	0
Molina c	4	1	2	2	Chavez lf	4	0	1	0
Belliard 2b	3	0	1	1	Perez p	2	0	0	0
Suppan p	2	0	0	0	Bradford p	0	0	0	0
Flores p	0	0	0	0	Tucker ph	1	0	0	0
Rodriguez ph	1	0	0	0	Heilman p	0	0	0	0
Wainwright p	0	0	0	0	Floyd ph	1	0	0	0
Totals	30	3	6	3		32	1	4	1

Cardinals	010	000	002	3	6	1
Mets	100	000	000	1	4	1

CARDINALS	IP	H	R	ER	BB	SO
Suppan	7.0	2	1	1	5	2
Flores (W, 1–0)	1.0	0	0	0	0	2
Wainwright (S, 2)	1.0	2	0	0	1	2
Total	9.0	4	1	1	6	6

METS	IP	H	R	ER	BB	SO
Perez	6.0	4	1	1	2	4
Bradford	1.0	0	0	0	0	0
Heilman (L,0–1)	2.0	2	2	2	1	3
Total	9.0	6	3	3	3	7

LOB: Cardinals 6, Mets 11; E: Delgado (3), Rolen (2); DP: Cardinals 0, Mets 2; 2B: Beltran (1), Eckstein (1); HR: Molina (2); IBB: Green, Pujols 2; HBP: Valentin, Eckstein; SH: Suppan, Belliard; Time: 3:23; ATT: 56,357.

2006 NLCS STATISTICS

COMPOSITE LINESCORE

Mets	512	349	300	—	27 54 4
Cardinals	273	223	207	—	28 56 4

METS BATTING

Player	BA	G	AB	R	H
Carlos Beltran	.296	7	27	8	8
Chad Bradford	—	5	0	0	0
Endy Chavez	.185	7	27	1	5
Carlos Delgado	.304	7	23	5	7
Pedro Feliciano	—	3	0	0	0
Cliff Floyd	.000	3	3	0	0
Julio Franco	.000	2	2	0	0
Tom Glavine	.000	2	4	0	0
Shawn Green	.304	7	23	2	7
Aaron Heilman	—	3	0	0	0
Anderson Hernandez	.000	2	1	0	0
Roberto Hernandez	—	3	0	0	0
Paul Lo Duca	.207	7	29	3	6
John Maine	.000	2	2	0	0
Guillermo Mota	—	5	0	0	0
Darren Oliver	.000	1	2	0	0
Oliver Perez	.000	2	5	0	0
Jose Reyes	.281	7	32	5	9
Steve Trachsel	—	1	0	0	0
Michael Tucker	.400	6	5	1	2
Jose Valentin	.250	7	4	0	6
Billy Wagner	—	3	0	0	0
David Wright	.160	7	25	2	4
Total	.231	7	234	27	54

2B—Delgado 3, Chavez 2, Valentin 2, Beltran, Green, Lo Duca, Reyes, Wright; 3B—Reyes; HR—Beltran 3, Delgado 3, Reyes, Wright; RBI—Delgado 9, Valentin 5, Beltran 4, Lo Duca 3, Green 2, Reyes 2, Wright 2; SB—Reyes 2, Beltran, Green, Tucker.

CARDINALS BATTING

Player	BA	G	AB	R	H
Ron Belliard	.240	7	25	0	6
Gary Bennett	.000	2	1	0	0
Chris Carpenter	.000	2	4	0	0
Chris Duncan	.125	5	8	1	1
David Eckstein	.231	7	26	3	6
Jim Edmonds	.227	7	22	5	5
Juan Encarnacion	.182	6	22	1	4
Randy Flores	—	4	0	0	0
Josh Hancock	—	2	0	0	0
Tyler Johnson	—	4	0	0	0
Josh Kinney	—	3	0	0	0
Braden Looper	—	3	0	0	0
Aaron Miles	.667	3	3	0	2
Yadier Molina	.348	7	23	2	8
Albert Pujols	.318	7	22	5	7
Anthony Reyes	.000	1	1	0	0
John Rodriguez	.000	4	4	0	0
Scott Rolen	.238	7	21	4	5
Scott Spiezio	.235	6	17	3	4
Jeff Suppan	.333	2	3	1	1
So Taguchi	1.000	5	3	1	3
Brad Thompson	—	2	0	0	0
Adam Wainwright	—	3	0	0	0
Jeff Weaver	.250	2	4	0	1
Preston Wilson	.176	6	17	2	3
Total	.248	7	226	28	56

2B—Eckstein, Molina, Pujols, Rolen, Spiezio, Taguchi, Wilson; 3B—Spiezio 2, Encarnacion, Miles; HR—Edmonds 2, Molina 2, Duncan, Eckstein, Pujols, Suppan, Taguchi; RBI—Molina 6, Spiezio 5, Edmonds 4, Taguchi 3, Belliard 2, Encarnacion 2, Duncan, Eckstein, Pujols, Suppan, Wilson; SB—Eckstein 3, Belliard.

METS PITCHING

Player	G	ERA	W–L	SV	IP	H	ER	BB	SO
Oliver Perez	2	4.63	1–0	0	11-2/3	13	6	3	7
Tom Glavine	2	2.45	1–1	0	11	11	3	5	4
John Maine	2	2.89	1–0	0	9-1/3	4	3	9	8
Darren Oliver	1	0.00	0–0	0	6	3	0	1	3
Chad Bradford	5	0.00	0–0	0	5-1/3	3	0	0	2
Aaron Heilman	3	4.15	0–1	0	4-1/3	4	2	1	5
Guillermo Mota	5	4.15	0–0	0	4-1/3	4	2	2	2
Pedro Feliciano	3	3.00	0–0	0	3	2	1	0	1
Billy Wagner	3	16.88	0–1	1	2-2/3	7	5	1	0
Ro. Hernandez	3	0.00	0–0	0	2-1/3	0	0	2	0
Steve Trachsel	1	45.00	0–1	0	1	5	5	5	1
Total	7	3.98	3–4	1	61	56	27	29	33

CARDINALS PITCHING

Player	G	ERA	W–L	SV	IP	H	ER	BB	SO
Jeff Suppan	2	0.60	1–0	0	15	5	1	6	6
Jeff Weaver	2	3.09	1–1	0	11-2/3	10	4	4	2
Chr. Carpenter	2	5.73	0–1	0	11	13	7	4	5
Braden Looper	3	5.79	0–0	0	4-2/3	7	3	0	1
Anthony Reyes	1	4.50	0–0	0	4	3	2	4	4
Randy Flores	4	0.00	1–0	0	3-2/3	2	0	0	3
Tyler Johnson	4	2.45	0–0	0	3-2/3	2	1	1	5
Josh Kinney	3	0.00	1–0	0	3-1/3	3	0	1	4
Ad. Wainwright	3	0.00	0–0	2	3	2	0	1	4
Br. Thompson	2	27.00	0–1	0	2/3	3	2	0	1
Josh Hancock	2	162.00	0–0	0	1/3	4	6	3	1
Total	7	3.84	4–3	2	61	54	26	24	36

METS POSTSEASON RECORDS

NLDS Individual Batting Records

Games Played
Career   8   Benny Agbayani, Edgardo Alfonzo and Robin Ventura.

ABs
Game   6   Timo Perez and Benny Agbayani, 10/7/00 vs. Giants (13 innings).

Series   18   Edgardo Alfonzo, 2000 vs. Giants.

Career   34   Edgardo Alfonzo.

Runs
Game   2   done 7 times, last by Jose Valentin, 10/5/06 vs. Dodgers

Series   6   Edgardo Alfonzo, 1999 vs. Diamondbacks.

Career   7   Edgardo Alfonzo.

Hits
Game   4   Carlos Delgado, 10/4/06 vs. Dodgers.

Series   7   John Olerud, 1999 vs. Diamondbacks.

Career   9   Edgardo Alfonzo.

Doubles
Game   2   David Wright, 10/4/06 vs. Dodgers; Shawn Green, 10/7/06 @ Dodgers.

Series   2   4 times, last by David Wright and Shawn Green, 2006 vs. Dodgers.

Career   3   Edgardo Alfonzo

Triples
Game   No Met has tripled in the NLDS.

Homers
Game   2   Edgardo Alfonzo, 10/5/99 @ D'backs.

Series   3   Edgardo Alfonzo, 1999 vs. D'backs.

Career   4   Edgardo Alfonzo.

RBIs
Game   5   Edgardo Alfonzo, 10/5/99 @ D'backs.

Series   6   Edgardo Alfonzo and John Olerud, 1999 vs. D'backs.

Career   11   Edgardo Alfonzo.

Batting Average (Min. 10 PA)
Series   .455   Paul Lo Duca, 2006 vs. Dodgers

Career   .455   Paul Lo Duca

On-Base Percentage (Min. 10 PA)
Series   .526   John Olerud, 1999 vs. Diamondbacks

Career   .526   John Olerud

Slugging Average (Min. 10 PA)
Series   .875   Edgardo Alfonzo, 1999 vs. D'backs

Career   .706   Edgardo Alfonzo

Walks
Game   3   Carlos Beltran, 10/4/06 vs. Dodgers.

Series   5   Carlos Beltran, 2006 vs. Dodgers.

Career   8   Robin Ventura

Strikeouts
Game   3   Benny Agbayani, 10/5/99 @ D'backs Mike Piazza, 10/7/00 vs. Giants; Bobby Jones, 10/8/00 vs. Giants.

Series   5   Rey Ordonez, 1999 vs. Diamondbacks

Career   7   Mike Piazza

Stolen Bases
Game   3   Rickey Henderson, 10/6/99 @ D'backs.

Series   6   Rickey Henderson, 1999 vs. D'backs.

Career   6   Rickey Henderson.

NLDS Individual Pitching Records

Wins
Series   1   9 times

Career   1   9 times

Losses
Series   1   Kenny Rogers, 1999 vs. D'backs; Mike Hampton, 2000 vs. Giants.

Career   1   Kenny Rogers, Mike Hampton.

Saves
Series   2   Billy Wagner, 2006 vs. Dodgers.

Career   2   Billy Wagner.

ERA (Series Min. 5 IP, Career Min. 10 IP)
Series   0.00   Bobby Jones, 2000 vs. Giants (9 IP); Tom Glavine, 2006 vs. Dodgers.

Career   2.87   Al Leiter (15-2/3 IP)

Games
Series   3   John Franco, 1999 vs. Diamondbacks; P. Feliciano, A. Heilman and B. Wagner, 2006 vs. Dodgers.

Career   5   John Franco

Games Started
Series   1   11 times.

Career   2   Rick Reed and Al Leiter.

Complete Games

Series	1	Bobby Jones, 2000 vs. Giants
Career	1	Bobby Jones

Innings Pitched

Game	9	Bobby Jones, 10/8/00 vs. Giants.
Series	9	Bobby Jones, 2000 vs. Giants.
Career	15⅔	Al Leiter.

Runs

Game	5	Mike Hampton @ Giants, 10/4/00
Series	5	Mike Hampton, 2000 vs. Giants
Career		

Earned Runs

Game	5	Mike Hampton @ Giants, 10/4/00
Season	5	Mike Hampton, 2000 vs. Giants
Career	5	Al Leiter and Mike Hampton

Strikeouts

Game	6	3 times, last by Rick Reed, 10/7/00 vs. Giants.
Series	6	Kenny Rogers, 1999 vs. Diamondbacks Al Leiter and Rick Reed, 2000 vs. Giants.
Career	10	Al Leiter.

Walks

Game	3	4 times, last by Al Leiter, 10/5/00 @ Giants.
Series	3	4 times.
Career	6	Al Leiter

NLCS Individual Batting Records

Games Played

Career	13	Wally Backman, Gary Carter, Len Dykstra, Keith Hernandez, Darryl Strawberry.

ABs

Game	7	Keith Hernandez, 10/15/86 @ Astros; Mookie Wilson, 10/15/86 @ Astros; Robin Ventura, 10/17/99 vs. Braves.
Series	32	Jose Reyes, 2006 vs. Cardinals.
Career	54	Gary Carter.

Runs

Game	4	Carlos Beltran, 10/15/06 @ Cardinals.
Series	8	Timo Perez, 2000 vs. Cardinals Carlos Beltran, 2006 vs. Cardinals.
Career	9	Len Dykstra, Darryl Strawberry.

Hits

Game	4	Kevin McReynolds, 10/11/88 @ Dodgers.
Series	9	Gregg Jefferies and Darryl Strawberry, 1988 vs. Dodgers Jose Reyes, 2006 vs. Cardinals.
Career	14	Edgardo Alfonzo, Keith Hernandez, Darryl Strawberry.

Doubles

Game	2	Edgardo Alfonzo, 10/12/99 @ Braves. Carlos Delgado, 10/12/06 vs. Cardinals
Series	4	Edgardo Alfonzo, 1999 vs. Braves.
Career	5	Edgardo Alfonzo.

Triples

Game	1	6 times, last by Jose Reyes, 10/14/06 @ Cardinals.
Series	1	6 players, last Jose Reyes, 2006 vs. Cardinals.
Career	1	6 players.

Homers

Game	2	Rusty Staub, 10/8/73 vs. Reds Carlos Delgado, 10/13/06 vs. Cardinals Carlos Beltran, 10/15/06 @ Cardinals
Series	3	Rusty Staub, 1973 vs. Reds; Carlos Beltran and Carlos Delgado, 2006 vs. Cardinals.
Career	3	Mike Piazza, Rusty Staub, Darryl Strawberry, Carlos Beltran, Carlos Delgado.

RBIs

Game	5	Carlos Delgado, 10/15/06 @ Cardinals.
Series	9	Carlos Delgado, 2006 vs. Cardinals.
Career	11	Darryl Strawberry.

Batting Average (Min. 10 PA Series, 15 PA Career)

Series	.538	Art Shamsky, 1969 vs. Braves
Career	.429	Melvin Mora

On-Base % (Min. 10 PA Series, 15 PA Career)

Series	.600	Lenny Dykstra, 1988 vs. Dodgers.
Career	.500	Melvin Mora

Slugging Average (Min. 10 PA Series, 15 PA Career)

Series	.941	Mike Piazza, 2000 vs. Cardinals.
Career	.857	Tommie Agee

Walks

Game	3	4 times, last by Carlos Delgado, 10/19/06 vs. Cardinals.
Series	6	Robin Ventura, 2000 vs. Cardinals. Carlos Delgado, 2006 vs. Cardinals.
Career	9	Keith Hernandez.

Strikeouts

Game	3	5 times, last by Oliver Perez, 10/15/06 @ Cardinals.
Series	12	Darryl Strawberry, 1986 vs. Astros
Career	17	Darryl Strawberry

Stolen Bases

Game	2	Tommie Agee, 10/5/69 @ Braves Roger Cedeno, 10/16/99 vs. Braves; Jose Reyes, 10/18/06 vs. Cardinals.
Series	2	8 times, last Jose Reyes, 2006 vs. Cardinals.
Career	2	8 players.

NLCS Individual Pitching Records

Wins

Series	3	Jesse Orosco, 1986 vs. Astros.
Career	3	Jesse Orosco.

Losses

Series	2	Kenny Rogers, 1999 vs. Braves.
Career	2	Sid Fernandez and Kenny Rogers.

Saves

Series	1	3 times, last by Billy Wagner, 2006 vs. Cardinals.
Career	2	Armando Benitez.

ERA (Series Min. 7 IP, Career Min. 10 IP)

Series	0.00	Mike Hampton, 2000 vs. Cardinals (16 IP) Roger McDowell, 1986 vs. Astros (7 IP) Jon Matlack, 1973 vs. Reds (9 IP)
Career	0.00	Mike Hampton (16 IP).

Games

Series	5	Armando Benitez and Turk Wendell, 1999 vs. Braves; Chad Bradford and Guillermo Mota, 2006 vs. Cardinals.
Career	8	Armando Benitez.

Starts

Series	2	12 times, last by Tom Glavine, John Maine and Oliver Perez, 2006 vs. Cardinals.
Career	4	Dwight Gooden.

Complete Games

Series	1	6 times, last by Mike Hampton, 10/16/00 vs. Cardinals.
Career	1	6 times.

Innings

Game	10	Dwight Gooden, 10/14/86 vs. Astros.
Series	18⅓	Dwight Gooden, 1988 vs. Dodgers.
Career	35⅓	Dwight Gooden.

Runs

Game	6	4 times, last by Bobby Jones, 10/15/00 vs. Cardinals.
Series	9	Ron Darling, 1988 vs. Dodgers
Career	13	Ron Darling

Earned Runs

Game	6	3 times, last by Bobby Jones, 10/15/00 vs. Cardinals.
Series	6	7 times, last by Oliver Perez vs. Cardinals, 2006.
Career	10	Ron Darling

Strikeouts

Game	13	Tom Seaver 10/6/73 @ Reds.
Series	20	Dwight Gooden, 1988 vs. Dodgers.
Career	29	Dwight Gooden.

Walks

Game	5	4 times, last by Steve Trachsel, 10/14/06 @ Cardinals
Series	9	John Maine, 2006 vs. Cardinals
Career	13	Dwight Gooden

World Series Individual Batting Records

Games Played

Career	12	Jerry Grote, Bud Harrelson, Cleon Jones.

ABs

Game	7	Don Hahn, 10/14/73 @ Athletics.
Series	32	Felix Millan, 1973 vs. Athletics.
Career	49	Jerry Grote.

Runs

Game	3	Cleon Jones 10/14/73 @ Athletics.
Series	5	Cleon Jones, 1973 vs. Athletics.
Career	7	Cleon Jones.

Hits

Game	4	Rusty Staub, 10/17/73 vs. Athletics Len Dykstra 10/21/86 @ Red Sox.
Series	11	Rusty Staub, 1973 vs. Athletics.
Career	12	Jerry Grote.

Doubles

Game	1	done 29 times.
Series	2	7 times, last by B. Agbayani. T. Zeile and M. Piazza, 2000 vs. Yankees.
Career	3	Cleon Jones.

Triples

Game	1	Felix Millan, 10/13/73 @ Athletics; Don Hahn, 10/18/73 vs. Athletics.
Series	1	Don Hahn and Felix Millan, 1973 vs. Athletics.
Career	1	Don Hahn and Felix Millan.

Homers

Game	2	Gary Carter, 10/22/86 @ Red Sox.
Series	3	Donn Clendenon, 1969 vs. Orioles.
Career	3	Donn Clendenon.

RBIs

Game	5	Rusty Staub, 10/17/73 vs. Athletics.
Series	9	Gary Carter, 1986 vs. Red Sox.
Career	9	Gary Carter.

Batting Average (Min. 15 PA)

Series	.455	Al Weis, 1969 vs. Orioles
Career	.455	Al Weis

On-Base Percentage (Min. 15 PA)

Series	.563	Al Weis, 1969 vs. Orioles
Career	.563	Al Weis

Slugging Average (Min. 15 PA)

Series	1.071	Donn Clendenon, 1969 vs. Orioles
Career	1.071	Donn Clendenon

Walks

Game	2	9 times, last by Darryl Strawberry, 10/25/86 vs. Red Sox.
Series	5	Keith Hernandez, 1986 vs. Red Sox W.Garrett, B.Harrelson, J.Milner, 1973 vs. Athletics
Career	8	Bud Harrelson

Strikeouts

Game	4	Wayne Garrett, 10/14/73 @ Athletics.
Series	11	Wayne Garrett, 1973 vs. Athletics
Career	12	Wayne Garrett

Stolen Bases

Game	2	Mookie Wilson, 10/22/86 @ Red Sox; Darryl Strawberry, 10/25/86 vs. Red Sox.
Series	3	Darryl Strawberry and Mookie Wilson,1986 vs. Red Sox.
Career	3	Darryl Strawberry and Mookie Wilson.

World Series Individual Pitching Records

Wins

Series	2	Jerry Koosman, 1969 vs. Orioles
Career	3	Jerry Koosman.

Losses

Series	2	Jon Matlack, 1973 vs. Athletics; Dwight Gooden, 1986 vs. Red Sox.
Career	2	Jon Matlack, T. Seaver, Dwight Gooden.

Saves

Series	2	Jesse Orosco, 1986 vs. Red Sox.
Career	2	Jesse Orosco.

ERA (Series Min. 7 IP, Career Min. 14 IP)

Series	1.53	Ron Darling, 1986 vs. Red Sox (3 ER, 17⅔ IP).
Career	1.53	Ron Darling.

Games

Series	5	Tug McGraw, 1973 vs. Athletics Roger McDowell, 1986 vs. Red Sox.
Career	5	Tug McGraw and Roger McDowell.

Starts

Series	3	Jon Matlack, 1973 vs. Athletics Ron Darling, 1986 vs. Red Sox
Career	4	Jerry Koosman, Tom Seaver.

Complete Games

Series	1	Jerry Koosman, 1969 vs. Orioles; Tom Seaver, 1969 vs. Orioles.
Career	1	Jerry Koosman and Tom Seaver.

Innings

Game	10	Tom Seaver, 10/15/69 vs. Orioles.
Series	17⅔	Jerry Koosman, 1969 vs. Orioles Ron Darling, 1986 vs. Red Sox.
Career	30	Tom Seaver.

Runs

Game	6	Dwight Gooden, 10/19 vs. Red Sox
Series	10	Dwight Gooden, 1986 vs. Red Sox
Career	10	Dwight Gooden

Earned Runs

Game	5	Dwight Gooden, 10/19/86 vs. Red Sox
Series	8	Dwight Gooden, 1986
Career	9	Tom Seaver

Strikeouts

Game	12	Tom Seaver, 10/16/73 vs. Athletics
Series	18	Tom Seaver, 1973 vs. Athletics
Career	27	Tom Seaver

METS CAREER POSTSEASON LEADERS

Batting

Games
Edgardo Alfonzo	24
Robin Ventura	24
Benny Agbayani	22
Mike Piazza	22
7 players	20

ABs
Edgardo Alfonzo	100
Robin Ventura	87
Mike Piazza	86
Gary Carter	83
Cleon Jones	81

Hits
Edgardo Alfonzo	26
Cleon Jones	23
Mike Piazza	22
Lenny Dykstra	21
Benny Agbayani	20
Keith Hernandez	20

Doubles
Edgardo Alfonzo	8
Cleon Jones	7
Benny Agbayani	6
Mike Piazza	6
Todd Zeile	6

Triples
8 Players	1

HRs
Mike Piazza	5
Edgardo Alfonzo	4
Carlos Delgado	4
Len Dykstra	4
Rusty Staub	4
Darryl Strawberry	4

RBIs
Edgardo Alfonzo	17
Gary Carter	15
Keith Hernandez	12
John Olerud	12
Mike Piazza	12
Darryl Strawberry	12

Batting Average (Min. 20 PA)
Roger Cedeno	.421 (21 PA)
Ken Boswell	.421 (20 PA)
Carlos Delgado	.351 (43 PA)
John Olerud	.349 (48 PA)
Rusty Staub	.341 (46 PA)
Gregg Jefferies	.333 (32 PA)
Lenny Dykstra	.328 (76 PA)
Shawn Green	.313 (37 PA)
Todd Zeile	.302 (61 PA)
Benny Agbayani	.299 (82 PA)

On-Base % (Min. 20 PA)
Ken Boswell	.450 (20 PA)
Carlos Delgado	.442 (43 PA)
Gregg Jefferies	.438 (32 PA)
Roger Cedeno	.429 (21 PA)
Carlos Beltrán	.422 (45 PA)
Benny Agbayani	.420 (82 PA)
Lenny Dykstra	.419 (76 PA)
John Olerud	.417 (48 PA)
Rusty Staub	.413 (46 PA)
Shawn Green	.405 (37 PA)

Slugging Average (Min. 20 PA)
Carlos Delgado	.757 (43 PA)
Ken Boswell	.737 (20 PA)
Rusty Staub	.683 (46 PA)
Lenny Dykstra	.609 (76 PA)
Tommie Agee	.563 (36 PA)
John Olerud	.558 (48 PA)
Carlos Beltran	.556 (45 PA)
Kevin McReynolds	.536 (32 PA)
Mike Piazza	.500 (97 PA)
Edgardo Alfonzo	.480 (113 PA)

Walks
Robin Ventura	17
Benny Agbayani	14
Keith Hernandez	14
Edgardo Alfonzo	10
Bud Harrelson	10
John Milner	10
Mike Piazza	10

Strikeouts
Darryl Strawberry	23
Edgardo Alfonzo	19
Wayne Garrett	19
Mike Piazza	17
Mookie Wilson	15

Stolen Bases

Rickey Henderson	7
Mookie Wilson	4
Darryl Strawberry	4
5 players	3

Pitching

Wins

Jerry Koosman	4
Jesse Orosco	3
Tom Seaver	3
Turk Wendell	3
6 pitchers	2

Losses

Dwight Gooden	3
Kenny Rogers	3
Tom Seaver	3
6 pitchers	2

Saves

Armando Benitez	3
Billy Wagner	3
Jesse Orosco	2
6 pitchers	1

ERA (Min. 14 IP)

*Jon Matlack	1.40
*Tom Glavine	1.59
Tug McGraw	1.66
John Franco	1.88
Jesse Orosco	1.98
Armando Benitez	2.00
*Bob Ojeda	2.33
*Tom Seaver	2.85
*Mike Hampton	2.96
Rick Aguilera	3.00
Roger McDowell	3.10
*Dwight Gooden	3.25

= Starting Pitcher

Games

Armando Benitez	15
John Franco	15
Turk Wendell	13
Roger McDowell	11
Dennis Cook	10

Starts

Tom Seaver	7
Al Leiter	7
Jerry Koosman	6
Dwight Gooden	6
Ron Darling	6

Complete Games

Jerry Koosman	2
Tom Seaver	2
5 players	1

Innings Pitched

Tom Seaver	53⅔
Al Leiter	45⅓
Dwight Gooden	44⅓
Jerry Koosman	40
Ron Darling	29⅔

Strikeouts

Tom Seaver	46
Al Leiter	40
Dwight Gooden	38
Jerry Koosman	31
Rick Reed	25
Ron Darling	24

Mets Career Postseason Batting Statistics

KURT ABBOTT

	G	AB	R	H	2B	3B	HR	BI	BB	SO	BA	SB
2000 NLDS	1	2	0	0	0	0	0	0	0	1	.000	0
2000 NLCS	2	3	0	0	0	0	0	0	0	2	.000	0
2000 WS	5	8	0	2	1	0	0	0	1	3	.250	0
POST TOT	**8**	**13**	**0**	**2**	**1**	**0**	**0**	**0**	**1**	**6**	**.154**	**0**

BENNY AGBAYANI

	G	AB	R	H	2B	3B	HR	BI	BB	SO	BA	SB
1999 NLDS	4	10	1	3	1	0	0	1	0	3	.300	0
2000 NLDS	4	15	1	5	1	0	1	1	3	3	.333	0
NLDS TOT	8	25	2	8	2	0	1	2	3	6	.320	0
1999 NLCS	4	7	2	1	0	0	0	0	4	2	.143	1
2000 NLCS	5	17	0	6	2	0	0	3	4	0	.353	0
NLCS TOT	9	24	2	7	2	0	0	3	8	2	.292	1
2000 WS	5	18	2	5	2	0	0	2	3	6	.278	0
POST TOT	22	67	6	20	6	0	1	7	14	14	.299	1

TOMMIE AGEE

	G	AB	R	H	2B	3B	HR	BI	BB	SO	BA	SB
1969 NLCS	3	14	4	5	1	0	2	4	2	5	.357	1
1969 WS	5	18	1	3	0	0	1	1	2	5	.167	1
POST TOT	8	32	5	8	1	0	3	5	4	10	.250	2

RICK AGUILERA

	G	AB	R	H	2B	3B	HR	BI	BB	SO	BA	SB
1986 NLCS	2	0	0	0	0	0	0	0	0	0	—	0
1988 NLCS	3	1	0	0	0	0	0	0	0	1	.000	0
NLCS TOT	5	1	0	0	0	0	0	0	0	1	.000	0
1986 WS	2	0	0	0	0	0	0	0	0	0	—	0
POST TOT	7	1	0	0	0	0	0	0	0	1	.000	0

EDGARDO ALFONZO

	G	AB	R	H	2B	3B	HR	BI	BB	SO	BA	SB
1999 NLDS	4	16	6	4	1	0	3	6	3	2	.250	0
2000 NLDS	4	18	1	5	2	0	1	5	1	2	.278	0
NLDS TOT	8	34	7	9	3	0	4	11	4	4	.265	0
1999 NLCS	6	27	2	6	4	0	0	1	1	9	.222	0
2000 NLCS	5	18	5	8	1	1	0	4	4	1	.444	0
NLCS TOT	11	45	7	14	5	1	0	5	5	10	.311	0
2000 WS	5	21	1	3	0	0	0	1	1	5	.143	0
POST TOT	24	100	15	26	8	1	4	17	10	19	.260	0

WALLY BACKMAN

	G	AB	R	H	2B	3B	HR	BI	BB	SO	BA	SB
1986 NLCS	6	21	5	5	0	0	0	2	2	4	.238	1
1988 NLCS	7	22	2	6	1	0	0	2	2	5	.273	1
NLCS TOT	13	43	7	11	1	0	0	4	4	9	.256	2
1986 WS	6	18	4	6	0	0	0	1	3	2	.333	1
POST TOT	19	61	11	17	1	0	0	5	7	11	.279	3

JIM BEAUCHAMP

	G	AB	R	H	2B	3B	HR	BI	BB	SO	BA	SB
1973 NLCS		DID NOT PLAY										
1973 WS	4	4	0	0	0	0	0	0	0	1	.000	0

DEREK BELL

	G	AB	R	H	2B	3B	HR	BI	BB	SO	BA	SB
2000 NLDS	1	1	0	0	0	0	0	0	0	0	.000	0
2000 NLCS		INJURED, DID NOT PLAY										
2000 WS		INJURED, DID NOT PLAY										

CARLOS BELTRAN

	G	AB	R	H	2B	3B	HR	BI	BB	SO	BA	SB
2006 NLDS	3	9	2	2	0	0	0	1	5	2	.222	1
2006 NLCS	7	27	8	8	1	0	3	4	4	3	.296	1
POST TOT	10	36	10	10	1	0	3	5	9	5	.278	2

ARMANDO BENITEZ

	G	AB	R	H	2B	3B	HR	BI	BB	SO	BA	SB
1999 NLDS	2	0	0	0	0	0	0	0	0	0	—	0
2000 NLDS	2	0	0	0	0	0	0	0	0	0	—	0
NLDS TOT	4	0	0	0	0	0	0	0	0	0	—	0
1999 NLCS	5	0	0	0	0	0	0	0	0	0	—	0
2000 NLCS	3	0	0	0	0	0	0	0	0	0	—	0
NLCS TOT	8	0	0	0	0	0	0	0	0	0	—	0
2000 WS	3	0	0	0	0	0	0	0	0	0	—	0
POST TOT	11	0	0	0	0	0	0	0	0	0	—	0

BOBBY BONILLA

	G	AB	R	H	2B	3B	HR	BI	BB	SO	BA	SB
1999 NLDS	2	1	1	0	0	0	0	0	1	0	.000	0
1999 NLDS	3	3	0	1	0	0	0	0	0	2	.333	0
POST TOT	5	4	1	1	0	0	0	0	1	2	.250	0

MIKE BORDICK

	G	AB	R	H	2B	3B	HR	BI	BB	SO	BA	SB
2000 NLDS	4	12	3	2	0	0	0	0	3	4	.167	0
2000 NLCS	5	13	2	1	0	0	0	0	3	1	.077	0
2000 WS	4	8	0	1	0	0	0	0	0	3	.125	0
POST TOT	13	33	5	4	0	0	0	0	6	8	.121	0

KEN BOSWELL

	G	AB	R	H	2B	3B	HR	BI	BB	SO	BA	SB
1969 NLCS	3	12	3	4	0	0	2	5	1	5	.333	0
1973 NLCS	1	1	0	0	0	0	0	0	0	0	.000	0
NLCS TOT	4	13	3	4	0	0	2	5	1	5		0
1969 WS	1	3	1	1	0	0	0	0	0	0	.333	0
1973 WS	3	3	1	3	0	0	0	0	0	0	1.000	0
WS TOT	4	6	2	4	0	0	0	0	0	0	.667	0
POST TOT	8	19	5	8	0	0	2	5	1	5		0

CHAD BRADFORD

	G	AB	R	H	2B	3B	HR	BI	BB	SO	BA	SB
2006 NLDS	2	0	0	0	0	0	0	0	0	0	—	0
2007 NLCS	5	0	0	0	0	0	0	0	0	0	—	0
POST TOTAL	7	0	0	0	0	0	0	0	0	0	—	0

DON CARDWELL

	G	AB	R	H	2B	3B	HR	BI	BB	SO	BA	SB
1969 NLCS		DID NOT PLAY										
1969 WS	1	0	0	0	0	0	0	0	0	0	—	0

GARY CARTER

	G	AB	R	H	2B	3B	HR	BI	BB	SO	BA	SB
1986 NLCS	6	27	1	4	1	0	0	2	2	5	.148	0
1988 NLCS	7	27	0	6	1	1	0	4	1	3	.222	0
NLCS TOT	13	54	1	10	2	1	0	6	3	8	.185	0
1986 WS	7	29	4	8	2	0	2	9	0	4	.276	0
POST TOT	20	83	5	18	4	1	2	15	3	12	.217	0

ROGER CEDENO

	G	AB	R	H	2B	3B	HR	BI	BB	SO	BA	SB
1999 NLDS	4	7	1	2	0	0	0	2	1	1	.286	1
1999 NLCS	5	12	2	6	1	0	0	1	0	1	.500	2
POST TOT	9	19	3	8	1	0	0	3	1	2	.421	3

ED CHARLES

	G	AB	R	H	2B	3B	HR	BI	BB	SO	BA	SB
1969 NLCS		DID NOT PLAY										
1969 WS	4	15	1	2	1	0	0	0	0	2	.133	0

ENDY CHAVEZ

	G	AB	R	H	2B	3B	HR	BI	BB	SO	BA	SB
2006 NLDS	3	8	1	3	0	0	0	0	0	0	.375	0
2006 NLCS	7	27	1	5	2	0	0	0	0	1	.185	0
POST TOT	10	35	2	8	2	0	0	0	0	1	.228	0

DONN CLENDENON

	G	AB	R	H	2B	3B	HR	BI	BB	SO	BA	SB
1969 NLCS		DID NOT PLAY										
1969 WS	4	14	4	5	1	0	3	4	2	6	.357	0

DAVID CONE

	G	AB	R	H	2B	3B	HR	BI	BB	SO	BA	SB
1988 NLCS	3	4	0	0	0	0	0	0	0	0	.000	0

DENNIS COOK

	G	AB	R	H	2B	3B	HR	BI	BB	SO	BA	SB
1999 NLDS	1	0	0	0	0	0	0	0	0	0	—	0
2000 NLDS	2	0	0	0	0	0	0	0	0	0	—	0
NLDS TOT	3	0	0	0	0	0	0	0	0	0	—	0
1999 NLCS	3	0	0	0	0	0	0	0	0	0	—	0
2000 NLCS	1	0	0	0	0	0	0	0	0	0	—	0
NLCS TOT	4	0	0	0	0	0	0	0	0	0	—	0
2000 WS	3	0	0	0	0	0	0	0	0	0	—	0
POST TOT	10	0	0	0	0	0	0	0	0	0	—	0

RON DARLING

	G	AB	R	H	2B	3B	HR	BI	BB	SO	BA	SB
1986 NLCS	1	1	0	0	0	0	0	0	0	0	.000	0
1988 NLCS	3	3	0	0	0	0	0	0	0	2	.000	0
NLCS TOT	4	4	0	0	0	0	0	0	0	2	.000	0
1986 WS	3	3	0	0	0	0	0	0	0	1	.000	0
POST TOT	6	6	0	0	0	0	0	0	0	3	.000	0

CARLOS DELGADO

	G	AB	R	H	2B	3B	HR	BI	BB	SO	BA	SB
2006 NLDS	3	14	3	6	0	0	1	2	0	3	.429	0
2006 NLCS	7	23	5	7	3	0	3	9	6	3	.304	0
POST TOT	10	37	8	13	3	0	4	11	6	6	.351	0

OCTAVIO DOTEL

	G	AB	R	H	2B	3B	HR	BI	BB	SO	BA	SB
1999 NLDS	1	0	0	0	0	0	0	0	0	0	—	0
1999 NLCS	1	0	0	0	0	0	0	0	0	0	—	0
POST TOT	2	0	0	0	0	0	0	0	0	0	—	0

SHAWON DUNSTON

	G	AB	R	H	2B	3B	HR	BI	BB	SO	BA	SB
1999 NLDS	4	6	0	1	0	0	0	0	0	1	.167	0
1999 NLCS	5	7	2	1	0	0	0	0	0	2	.143	1
POST TOT	9	13	2	2	0	0	0	0	0	3	.154	1

DUFFY DYER

	G	AB	R	H	2B	3B	HR	BI	BB	SO	BA	SB
1969 NLCS		DID NOT PLAY										
1969 WS	1	1	0	0	0	0	0	0	0	0	.000	0

LEN DYKSTRA

	G	AB	R	H	2B	3B	HR	BI	BB	SO	BA	SB
1986 NLCS	6	23	3	7	1	1	1	3	2	4	.304	1
1988 NLCS	7	14	6	6	3	0	1	3	4	0	.429	0
NLCS TOT	13	37	9	13	4	1	2	6	6	4	.351	1
1986 WS	7	27	4	8	0	0	2	3	2	7	.296	0
POST TOT	20	64	13	21	4	1	4	9	8	11	.328	1

KEVIN ELSTER

	G	AB	R	H	2B	3B	HR	BI	BB	SO	BA	SB
1986 NLCS	4	3	0	0	0	0	0	0	0	1	.000	0
1988 NLCS	5	8	1	2	1	0	0	1	3	0	.250	0
NLCS TOT	9	11	1	2	1	0	0	1	3	1	.182	0
1986 WS	1	1	0	0	0	0	0	0	0	0	.000	0
POST TOT	10	12	1	2	1	0	0	1	3	1	.167	0

PEDRO FELICIANO

	G	AB	R	H	2B	3B	HR	BI	BB	SO	BA	SB
2006 NLDS	3	0	0	0	0	0	0	0	0	0	—	0
2006 NLCS	3	0	0	0	0	0	0	0	0	0	—	0
POST TOT	6	0	0	0	0	0	0	0	0	0	–	0

SID FERNANDEZ

	G	AB	R	H	2B	3B	HR	BI	BB	SO	BA	SB
1986 NLCS	1	1	0	0	0	0	0	0	0	0	.000	0
1988 NLCS	1	1	0	0	0	0	0	0	0	0	.000	0
NLCS TOT	2	2	0	0	0	0	0	0	0	0	.000	0
1986 WS	3	0	0	0	0	0	0	0	0	0	.000	0
POST TOT	5	2	0	0	0	0	0	0	0	0	.000	0

CLIFF FLOYD

	G	AB	R	H	2B	3B	HR	BI	BB	SO	BA	SB
2006 NLDS	3	9	3	4	0	0	1	2	1	2	.444	0
2006 NLCS	3	3	0	0	0	0	0	0	0	1	.000	0
POST TOT	6	12	3	4	0	0	1	2	1	3	.333	0

JOHN FRANCO

	G	AB	R	H	2B	3B	HR	BI	BB	SO	BA	SB
1999 NLDS	3	0	0	0	0	0	0	0	0	0	—	0
2000 NLDS	2	0	0	0	0	0	0	0	0	0	—	0
NLDS TOT	5	0	0	0	0	0	0	0	0	0	—	0
1999 NLCS	3	0	0	0	0	0	0	0	0	0	—	0
2000 NLCS	3	0	0	0	0	0	0	0	0	0	—	0
NLCS TOT	6	0	0	0	0	0	0	0	0	0	—	0
2000 WS	4	0	0	0	0	0	0	0	0	0	—	0
POST TOT	15	0	0	0	0	0	0	0	0	0	—	0

JULIO FRANCO

	G	AB	R	H	2B	3B	HR	BI	BB	SO	BA	SB
2006 NLDS	2	2	0	0	0	0	0	1	0	1	.000	0
2007 NLCS	2	2	0	0	0	0	0	0	0	2	.000	0
POST TOTAL	4	4	0	0	0	0	0	1	0	3	.000	0

MATT FRANCO

	G	AB	R	H	2B	3B	HR	BI	BB	SO	BA	SB
1999 NLDS	1	0	0	0	0	0	0	0	1	0	.000	0
2000 NLDS		DID NOT PLAY										
1999 NLCS	5	2	1	1	1	0	0	0	1	0	.500	0
2000 NLCS	2	3	0	0	0	0	0	0	0	1	.000	0
NLCS TOT	7	5	1	1	1	0	0	0	1	1	.200	0
2000 WS	1	1	0	0	0	0	0	0	0	1	.000	0
POST TOT	9	6	1	1	1	0	0	0	2	2	.167	0

WAYNE GARRETT

	G	AB	R	H	2B	3B	HR	BI	BB	SO	BA	SB
1969 NLCS	3	13	3	5	2	0	1	3	2	2	.385	1
1973 NLCS	5	23	1	2	1	0	0	1	0	5	.087	0
NLCS TOT	8	36	4	7	3	0	1	4	2	7	.194	1
1969 WS	2	1	0	0	0	0	0	0	2	1	.000	0
1973 WS	7	30	4	5	0	0	2	2	5	11	.167	0
W.S.TOTALS	9	31	4	5	0	0	2	2	7	12	.161	0
POST TOT	17	67	8	12	3	0	3	6	9	19	.179	1

ROD GASPAR

	G	AB	R	H	2B	3B	HR	BI	BB	SO	BA	SB
1969 NLCS	3	0	0	0	0	0	0	0	0	0	—	0
1969 WS	3	2	1	0	0	0	0	0	0	0	.000	0
POST TOTAL	6	2	1	0	0	0	0	0	0	0	.000	0

GARY GENTRY

	G	AB	R	H	2B	3B	HR	BI	BB	SO	BA	SB
1969 NLCS	1	0	0	0	0	0	0	0	0	0	—	0
1969 WS	1	3	0	1	1	0	0	2	0	2	.333	0
POST TOTAL	2	3	0	1	1	0	0	2	0	2	.333	0

TOM GLAVINE

	G	AB	R	H	2B	3B	HR	BI	BB	SO	BA	SB
2006 NLDS	1	1	0	0	0	0	0	0	0	0	.000	0
2006 NLCS	2	4	0	0	0	0	0	0	0	0	.000	0
POST TOT	3	5	0	0	0	0	0	0	0	0	.000	0

DWIGHT GOODEN

	G	AB	R	H	2B	3B	HR	BI	BB	SO	BA	SB
1986 NLCS	2	5	0	0	0	0	0	0	0	2	.000	0
1988 NLCS	3	5	0	1	0	0	0	0	0	2	.200	0
NLCS TOT	5	10	0	1	0	0	0	0	0	4	.100	0
1986 WS	2	2	1	1	0	0	0	0	0	0	.500	0
POST TOT	7	12	1	2	0	0	0	0	0	4	.167	0

SHAWN GREEN

	G	AB	R	H	2B	3B	HR	BI	BB	SO	BA	SB
2006 NLDS	2	9	1	3	2	0	0	2	0	2	.333	0
2006 NLCS	7	23	2	7	1	0	0	2	4	3	.304	1
POST TOT	9	32	3	10	3	0	0	4	4	5	.313	1

JERRY GROTE

	G	AB	R	H	2B	3B	HR	BI	BB	SO	BA	SB
1969 NLCS	3	12	3	2	1	0	0	1	1	4	.167	0
1973 NLCS	5	19	2	4	0	0	0	2	1	3	.211	0
NLCS TOT	8	31	5	6	1	0	0	3	2	7	.194	0
1969 WS	5	19	1	4	2	0	0	1	1	3	.211	0
1973 WS	7	30	2	8	0	0	0	0	0	1	.267	0
W.S. TOT	12	49	3	12	2	0	0	1	1	4	.245	0
POST TOT	20	80	8	18	3	0	0	4	3	11	.225	0

DON HAHN

	G	AB	R	H	2B	3B	HR	BI	BB	SO	BA	SB
1973 NLCS	5	17	2	4	0	0	0	1	2	4	.235	0
1973 WS	7	29	2	7	1	1	0	2	1	6	.241	0
POST TOT	12	46	4	11	1	1	0	3	3	10	.239	0

DARRYL HAMILTON

	G	AB	R	H	2B	3B	HR	BI	BB	SO	BA	SB
1999 NLDS	4	8	0	1	0	0	0	2	2	0	.125	0
2000 NLDS	3	4	1	2	1	0	0	0	1	1	.500	0
NLDS TOT	7	12	1	3	1	0	0	2	3	1	.250	0
1999 NLCS	5	17	0	6	1	0	0	2	0	4	.353	0
2000 NLCS	3	2	0	0	0	0	0	0	0	0	.000	0
NLCS TOT	8	19	0	6	1	0	0	2	0	4	.316	0
2000 WS	4	3	0	0	0	0	0	0	0	2	.000	0
POST TOT	19	34	1	9	2	0	0	4	3	7	.265	0

MIKE HAMPTON

	G	AB	R	H	2B	3B	HR	BI	BB	SO	BA	SB
2000 NLDS	1	2	0	1	0	0	0	0	0	1	.500	0
2000 NLCS	2	6	1	1	0	0	0	0	0	1	.167	0
2000 WS	1	0	0	0	0	0	0	0	0	0	—	0
POST TOT	4	8	1	2	0	0	0	0	0	2	.250	0

BUD HARRELSON

	G	AB	R	H	2B	3B	HR	BI	BB	SO	BA	SB
1969 NLCS	3	11	2	2	1	1	0	3	1	2	.182	0
1973 NLCS	5	18	1	3	0	0	0	2	1	1	.167	0
NLCS TOT	8	29	3	5	1	1	0	5	2	3	.172	0
1969 WS	5	17	1	3	0	0	0	0	3	4	.176	0
1973 WS	7	24	2	6	1	0	0	1	5	3	.250	0
W.S. TOT	12	41	3	9	1	0	0	1	8	7	.220	0
POST TOT	20	80	6	14	2	1	0	6	10	10	.175	0

LENNY HARRIS

	G	AB	R	H	2B	3B	HR	BI	BB	SO	BA	SB
2000 NLDS	2	2	1	0	0	0	0	0	0	0	.000	1
2000 NLCS	2	1	0	0	0	0	0	0	0	1	.000	0
2000 WS	3	4	1	0	0	0	0	0	1	1	.000	0
POST TOT	7	7	2	0	0	0	0	0	1	2	.000	1

DANNY HEEP

	G	AB	R	H	2B	3B	HR	BI	BB	SO	BA	SB
1986 NLCS	5	4	0	1	0	0	0	1	0	2	.250	0
1986 WS	5	11	0	1	0	0	0	2	1	1	.091	0
POST TOT	10	15	0	2	0	0	0	3	1	3	.133	0

AARON HEILMAN

	G	AB	R	H	2B	3B	HR	BI	BB	SO	BA	SB
2006 NLDS	3	0	0	0	0	0	0	0	0	0	—	0
2006 NLCS	3	0	0	0	0	0	0	0	0	0	—	0
POST TOT	6	0	0	0	0	0	0	0	0	0	—	0

RICKEY HENDERSON

	G	AB	R	H	2B	3B	HR	BI	BB	SO	BA	SB
1999 NLDS	4	15	5	6	0	0	0	1	3	1	.400	6
1999 NLCS	6	23	2	4	1	0	0	1	0	5	.174	1
POST TOT	10	38	7	10	1	0	0	2	3	6	.263	7

KEITH HERNANDEZ

	G	AB	R	H	2B	3B	HR	BI	BB	SO	BA	SB
1986 NLCS	6	26	3	7	1	1	0	3	3	6	.269	0
1988 NLCS	7	26	2	7	0	0	1	5	6	7	.269	0
NLCS TOT	13	52	5	14	1	1	1	8	9	13	.269	0
1986 WS	7	26	1	6	0	0	0	4	5	1	.231	0
POST TOT	20	78	6	20	1	1	1	12	14	14	.256	0

OREL HERSHISER

	G	AB	R	H	2B	3B	HR	BI	BB	SO	BA	SB
1999 NLDS	1	0	0	0	0	0	0	0	0	0	—	0
1999 NLCS	2	1	0	0	0	0	0	0	0	0	—	0
POST TOT	3	1	0	0	0	0	0	0	0	0	—	0

RON HODGES

	G	AB	R	H	2B	3B	HR	BI	BB	SO	BA	SB
1973 NLCS		DID NOT PLAY										
1973 WS	1	0	0	0	0	0	0	0	1	0	.000	0

GREGG JEFFERIES

	G	AB	R	H	2B	3B	HR	BI	BB	SO	BA	SB
1988 NLCS	7	27	2	9	2	0	0	1	4	0	.333	0

HOWARD JOHNSON

	G	AB	R	H	2B	3B	HR	BI	BB	SO	BA	SB
1986 NLCS	2	2	0	0	0	0	0	0	0	0	.000	0
1988 NLCS	6	18	3	1	0	0	0	0	1	6	.056	1
NLCS TOT	8	20	3	1	0	0	0	0	1	6	.050	1
1986 WS	2	5	0	0	0	0	0	0	0	2	.000	0
POST TOT	10	25	3	1	0	0	0	0	1	8	.040	1

BOBBY JONES

	G	AB	R	H	2B	3B	HR	BI	BB	SO	BA	SB
2000 NLDS	1	4	1	0	0	0	0	0	0	3	.000	0
2000 NLCS	1	2	0	0	0	0	0	0	0	1	.000	0
2000 WS	1	2	0	0	0	0	0	0	0	1	.000	0
POST TOT	3	8	1	0	0	0	0	0	0	5	.000	0

CLEON JONES

	G	AB	R	H	2B	3B	HR	BI	BB	SO	BA	SB
1969 NLCS	3	14	4	6	2	0	1	4	1	2	.429	2
1973 NLCS	5	20	3	6	2	0	0	3	2	4	.300	0
NLCS TOT	8	34	7	12	4	0	1	7	3	6	.353	2
1969 WS	5	19	2	3	1	0	0	0	0	1	.158	0
1973 WS	7	28	5	8	2	0	1	1	4	2	.286	0
W.S. TOT	12	47	7	11	3	0	1	1	4	3	.234	0
POST TOT	20	81	14	23	7	0	2	8	7	9	.284	2

RAY KNIGHT

	G	AB	R	H	2B	3B	HR	BI	BB	SO	BA	SB
1986 NLCS	6	24	1	4	0	0	0	2	1	5	.167	0
1986 WS	6	23	4	9	1	0	1	5	2	2	.391	0
POST TOT	12	47	5	13	1	0	1	7	3	7	.277	0

JERRY KOOSMAN

	G	AB	R	H	2B	3B	HR	BI	BB	SO	BA	SB
1969 NLCS	1	2	1	0	0	0	0	0	1	2	.000	0
1973 NLCS	1	4	1	2	0	0	0	1	1	1	.500	0
NLCS TOT	2	6	2	2	0	0	0	1	2	3	.333	0
1969 WS	2	7	0	1	1	0	0	0	0	4	.143	0
1973 WS	2	4	0	0	0	0	0	0	0	3	.000	0
W.S. TOT	4	11	0	1	1	0	0	0	0	7	.091	0
POST TOT	6	17	2	3	1	0	0	1	2	10	.176	0

ED KRANEPOOL

	G	AB	R	H	2B	3B	HR	BI	BB	SO	BA	SB
1969 NLCS	3	12	2	3	1	0	0	1	1	2	.250	0
1973 NLCS	1	2	0	1	0	0	0	2	0	0	.500	0
NLCS TOT	4	14	2	4	1	0	0	3	1	2	.286	0
1969 WS	1	4	1	1	0	0	1	1	0	0	.250	0
1973 WS	4	3	0	0	0	0	0	0	0	0	.000	0
W.S. TOT	5	7	1	1	0	0	1	1	0	0	.143	0
POST TOT	9	21	3	5	1	0	1	4	1	2	.238	0

TERRY LEACH

	G	AB	R	H	2B	3B	HR	BI	BB	SO	BA	SB
1988 NLCS	3	0	0	0	0	0	0	0	0	0	—	0

AL LEITER

	G	AB	R	H	2B	3B	HR	BI	BB	SO	BA	SB
1999 NLDS	1	3	0	0	0	0	0	0	0	2	.000	0
2000 NLDS	1	4	0	0	0	0	0	0	0	2	.000	0
NLCS TOT	2	7	0	0	0	0	0	0	0	4	.000	0
1999 NLCS	2	2	0	0	0	0	0	0	0	1	.000	0
2000 NLCS	1	3	0	0	0	0	0	0	0	2	.000	0
NLCS TOT	3	5	0	0	0	0	0	0	0	3	.000	0
2000 WS	2	2	0	0	0	0	0	0	0	0	.000	0
POST TOT	7	14	0	0	0	0	0	0	0	7	.000	0

PAUL LO DUCA

	G	AB	R	H	2B	3B	HR	BI	BB	SO	BA	SB
2006 NLDS	3	11	2	5	1	0	0	3	1	1	.455	0
2006 NLCS	7	29	3	6	1	0	0	3	2	2	.207	0
POST TOT	10	40	5	11	2	0	0	6	3	3	.275	0

DAVE MAGADAN

	G	AB	R	H	2B	3B	HR	BI	BB	SO	BA	SB
1988 NLCS	3	3	0	0	0	0	0	0	0	2	.000	0

PAT MAHOMES

	G	AB	R	H	2B	3B	HR	BI	BB	SO	BA	SB
1999 NLDS	1	0	0	0	0	0	0	0	0	0	—	0
1999 NLCS	3	2	0	0	0	0	0	0	0	2	.000	0
POST TOT	4	2	0	0	0	0	0	0	0	2	.000	0

JOHN MAINE

	G	AB	R	H	2B	3B	HR	BI	BB	SO	BA	SB
2006 NLDS	1	1	0	0	0	0	0	0	0	1	.000	0
2006 NLCS	2	2	0	0	0	0	0	0	0	2	.000	0
POST TOT	3	3	0	0	0	0	0	0	0	3	.000	0

J.C. MARTIN

	G	AB	R	H	2B	3B	HR	BI	BB	SO	BA	SB
1969 NLCS	2	2	0	1	0	0	0	2	0	0	.500	0
1969 WS	1	1	0	0	0	0	0	0	0	0	.000	0
POST TOT	3	3	0	1	0	0	0	2	0	0	.333	0

TED MARTINEZ

	G	AB	R	H	2B	3B	HR	BI	BB	SO	BA	SB
1973 NLCS		DID NOT PLAY										
1973 WS	2	0	0	0	0	0	0	0	0	0	.000	0

JON MATLACK

	G	AB	R	H	2B	3B	HR	BI	BB	SO	BA	SB
1973 NLCS	1	2	0	0	0	0	0	0	1	2	.000	0
1973 WS	3	4	0	1	0	0	0	0	2	1	.250	0
POST TOT	4	6	0	1	0	0	0	0	3	3	.167	0

WILLIE MAYS

	G	AB	R	H	2B	3B	HR	BI	BB	SO	BA	SB
1973 NLCS	1	3	1	1	0	0	0	1	0	0	.333	0
1973 WS	3	7	1	2	0	0	0	1	0	1	.286	0
POST TOT	3	10	2	3	0	0	0	2	0	1	.300	0

LEE MAZZILLI

	G	AB	R	H	2B	3B	HR	BI	BB	SO	BA	SB
1986 NLCS	5	5	0	1	0	0	0	0	0	3	.200	0
1988 NLCS	3	2	0	1	0	0	0	0	0	0	.500	1
NLCS TOT	8	7	0	2	0	0	0	0	0	3	.286	1
1986 WS	4	5	2	2	0	0	0	0	0	0	.400	0
POST TOT	12	12	2	4	0	0	0	0	0	3	.333	1

ROGER MCDOWELL

	G	AB	R	H	2B	3B	HR	BI	BB	SO	BA	SB
1986 NLCS	2	1	0	0	0	0	0	0	0	0	.000	0
1988 NLCS	4	0	0	0	0	0	0	0	0	0	—	0
NLCS TOT	6	1	0	0	0	0	0	0	0	0	—	0
1986 WS	5	0	0	0	0	0	0	0	0	0	—	0
POST TOT	11	1	0	0	0	0	0	0	0	0	.000	0

JOE McEWING

	G	AB	R	H	2B	3B	HR	BI	BB	SO	BA	SB
2000 NLDS	4	1	0	1	0	0	0	0	0	0	1.000	0
2000 NLCS	4	0	2	0	0	0	0	0	0	0	—	0
2000 WS	3	1	1	0	0	0	0	0	0	0	.000	0
POST TOT	11	2	3	1	0	0	0	0	0	0	.500	0

TUG MCGRAW

	G	AB	R	H	2B	3B	HR	BI	BB	SO	BA	SB
1969 NLCS	1	0	0	0	0	0	0	0	0	0	—	0
1973 NLCS	2	1	0	0	0	0	0	0	0	1	.000	0
NLCS TOT	3	1	0	0	0	0	0	0	0	1	.000	0
1969 WS		DID NOT PLAY										
1973 WS	5	3	1	1	0	0	0	0	0	1	.333	0
POST TOT	8	4	1	1	0	0	0	0	0	2	.250	0

KEVIN MCREYNOLDS

	G	AB	R	H	2B	3B	HR	BI	BB	SO	BA	SB
1988 NLCS	7	28	4	7	2	0	2	4	3	5	.250	2

FELIX MILLAN

	G	AB	R	H	2B	3B	HR	BI	BB	SO	BA	SB
1973 NLCS	5	19	5	6	0	0	0	2	2	1	.316	0
1973 WS	7	32	3	6	1	1	0	1	1	1	.188	0
POST TOT	12	51	8	12	1	1	0	3	3	2	.235	0

JOHN MILNER

	G	AB	R	H	2B	3B	HR	BI	BB	SO	BA	SB
1973 NLCS	5	17	2	3	0	0	0	1	5	3	.176	0
1973 WS	7	27	2	8	0	0	0	2	5	1	.296	0
POST TOT	12	44	4	11	0	0	0	3	10	4	.250	0

KEVIN MITCHELL

	G	AB	R	H	2B	3B	HR	BI	BB	SO	BA	SB
1986 NLCS	2	8	1	2	0	0	0	0	0	1	.250	0
1986 WS	5	8	1	2	0	0	0	0	0	3	.250	0
POST TOT	7	16	2	4	0	0	0	0	0	4	.250	0

MELVIN MORA

	G	AB	R	H	2B	3B	HR	BI	BB	SO	BA	SB
1999 NLDS	3	1	1	0	0	0	0	0	1	0	.000	0
1999 NLCS	6	14	3	6	0	0	1	2	2	2	.429	2
POST TOT	9	15	4	6	0	0	1	2	3	2	.400	2

GUILLERMO MOTA

	G	AB	R	H	2B	3B	HR	BI	BB	SO	BA	SB
2006 NLDS	2	1	0	0	0	0	0	0	0	0	.000	0
2006 NLCS	5	0	0	0	0	0	0	0	0	0	—	0
POST TOT	7	1	0	0	0	0	0	0	0	0	.000	0

RANDY MYERS

	G	AB	R	H	2B	3B	HR	BI	BB	SO	BA	SB
1988 NLCS	3	0	0	0	0	0	0	0	0	0	—	0

BOB OJEDA

	G	AB	R	H	2B	3B	HR	BI	BB	SO	BA	SB
1986 NLCS	2	5	1	0	0	0	0	0	0	0	.000	0
1988 NLCS		INJURED, DID NOT PLAY										
1986 WS	2	2	0	0	0	0	0	0	0	1	.000	0
POST TOT	4	7	1	0	0	0	0	0	0	1	.000	0

JOHN OLERUD

	G	AB	R	H	2B	3B	HR	BI	BB	SO	BA	SB
1999 NLDS	4	16	3	7	0	0	1	6	3	2	.438	0
1999 NLCS	6	27	4	8	0	0	2	6	2	3	.296	0
POST TOT	10	43	7	15	0	0	3	12	5	5	.349	0

DARREN OLIVER

	G	AB	R	H	2B	3B	HR	BI	BB	SO	BA	SB
2006 NLDS	1	0	0	0	0	0	0	0	0	0	—	0
2006 NLCS	1	2	0	0	0	0	0	0	0	2	.000	0
POST TOT	2	2	0	0	0	0	0	0	0	2	.000	0

REY ORDONEZ

	G	AB	R	H	2B	3B	HR	BI	BB	SO	BA	SB
1999 NLDS	4	14	1	4	1	0	0	2	0	5	.286	1
1999 NLCS	6	24	0	1	0	0	0	0	0	2	.042	0
POST TOT	10	38	1	5	1	0	0	2	0	7	.132	1

JESSE OROSCO

	G	AB	R	H	2B	3B	HR	BI	BB	SO	BA	SB
1986 NLCS	4	0	0	0	0	0	0	0	0	0	—	0
1986 WS	4	1	0	1	0	0	0	1	0	0	1.000	0
POST TOT	8	1	0	1	0	0	0	1	0	0	1.000	0

HARRY PARKER

	G	AB	R	H	2B	3B	HR	BI	BB	SO	BA	SB
1973 NLCS	1	0	0	0	0	0	0	0	0	0	—	0
1973 WS	3	0	0	0	0	0	0	0	0	0	—	0
POST TOT	4	0	0	0	0	0	0	0	0	0	—	0

JAY PAYTON

	G	AB	R	H	2B	3B	HR	BI	BB	SO	BA	SB
2000 NLDS	4	17	1	3	0	0	0	2	0	4	.176	1
2000 NLCS	5	19	1	3	0	0	1	3	2	5	.158	0
2000 WS	5	21	3	7	0	0	1	3	0	5	.333	0
POST TOT	14	57	5	13	0	0	2	6	2	14	.228	1

TIMO PEREZ

	G	AB	R	H	2B	3B	HR	BI	BB	SO	BA	SB
2000 NLDS	4	17	2	5	1	0	0	3	0	2	.294	1
2000 NLCS	5	23	8	7	2	0	0	0	1	3	.304	2
2000 WS	5	16	1	2	0	0	0	0	1	4	.125	0
POST TOT	14	56	11	14	3	0	0	3	2	9	.250	3

MIKE PIAZZA

	G	AB	R	H	2B	3B	HR	BI	BB	SO	BA	SB
1999 NLDS	2	9	0	2	0	0	0	0	0	4	.222	0
2000 NLDS	4	14	1	3	1	0	0	0	4	3	.214	0
NLDS TOT	6	23	1	5	1	0	0	0	4	7	.217	0
1999 NLCS	6	24	1	4	0	0	1	4	1	6	.167	0
2000 NLCS	5	17	7	7	2	0	0	0	1	3	.412	0
NLCS TOT	11	41	8	11	2	0	1	4	2	9	.268	0
2000 WS	5	22	3	6	2	0	2	4	0	4	.273	0
POST TOT	22	86	12	22	5	0	3	8	6	20	.256	0

TODD PRATT

	G	AB	R	H	2B	3B	HR	BI	BB	SO	BA	SB
1999 NLDS	3	8	2	1	0	0	1	1	2	1	.125	0
2000 NLDS	1	1	0	0	0	0	0	0	0	0	.000	0
NLDS TOT	4	9	2	1	0	0	1	1	2	1	.111	0
1999 NLCS	4	2	0	1	0	0	0	3	1	1	.500	0
2000 NLCS		DID NOT PLAY										
2000 WS	1	2	1	0	0	0	0	0	1	2	.000	0
POST TOT	9	13	3	2	0	0	1	4	4	4	.154	0

RICK REED

	G	AB	R	H	2B	3B	HR	BI	BB	SO	BA	SB
1999 NLDS	1	1	0	0	0	0	0	0	0	1	.000	0
2000 NLDS	1	1	0	0	0	0	0	0	0	0	.000	0
NLDS TOT	2	2	0	0	0	0	0	0	0	1	.000	0
1999 NLCS	1	2	0	0	0	0	0	0	0	0	.000	0
2000 NLCS	1	1	0	0	0	0	0	0	0	0	.000	0
NLCS TOT	2	3	0	0	0	0	0	0	0	0	.000	0
2000 WS	1	1	0	1	0	0	0	0	0	0	1.000	0
POST TOT	5	6	0	1	0	0	0	0	0	0	.167	0

JOSE REYES

	G	AB	R	H	2B	3B	HR	BI	BB	SO	BA	SB
2006 NLDS	3	12	2	2	0	0	0	3	2	2	.167	1
2006 NLCS	7	32	5	9	1	1	1	2	1	3	.281	2
POST TOT	10	44	7	11	1	1	1	5	3	5	.250	3

KENNY ROGERS

	G	AB	R	H	2B	3B	HR	BI	BB	SO	BA	SB
1999 NLDS	1	2	0	0	0	0	0	0	0	1	.000	0
1999 NLCS	3	1	0	0	0	0	0	0	0	1	.000	0
POST TOT	4	3	0	0	0	0	0	0	0	2	.000	0

GLENDON RUSCH

	G	AB	R	H	2B	3B	HR	BI	BB	SO	BA	SB
2000 NLDS	1	0	0	0	0	0	0	0	0	0	—	0
2000 NLCS	2	0	0	0	0	0	0	0	0	0	—	0
2000 WS	3	0	0	0	0	0	0	0	0	0	—	0
POST TOT	6	0	0	0	0	0	0	0	0	0	—	0

NOLAN RYAN

	G	AB	R	H	2B	3B	HR	BI	BB	SO	BA	SB
1969 NLCS	1	4	1	2	0	0	0	0	0	1	.500	0
1969 WS	1	0	0	0	0	0	0	0	0	0	—	0
POST TOT	2	4	1	2	0	0	0	0	0	1	.500	0

RAY SADECKI

	G	AB	R	H	2B	3B	HR	BI	BB	SO	BA	SB
1973 NLCS		DID NOT PLAY										
1973 WS	4	0	0	0	0	0	0	0	0	0	—	0
POST TOT	4	0	0	0	0	0	0	0	0	0	—	0

RAFAEL SANTANA

	G	AB	R	H	2B	3B	HR	BI	BB	SO	BA	SB
1986 NLCS	6	17	0	3	0	0	0	0	0	3	.176	0
1986 WS	7	20	3	5	0	0	0	2	2	5	.250	0
POST TOT	13	37	3	8	0	0	0	2	2	8	.216	0

MACKEY SASSER

	G	AB	R	H	2B	3B	HR	BI	BB	SO	BA	SB
1988 NLCS	4	5	0	1	0	0	0	0	0	1	.200	0

TOM SEAVER

	G	AB	R	H	2B	3B	HR	BI	BB	SO	BA	SB
1969 NLCS	1	3	0	0	0	0	0	0	0	0	.000	0
1973 NLCS	2	6	1	2	2	0	0	1	1	1	.333	0
NLCS TOT	3	9	1	2	2	0	0	1	1	1	.222	0
1969 WS	2	4	0	0	0	0	0	0	0	2	.000	0
1973 WS	2	5	0	0	0	0	0	0	0	2	.000	0
W.S. TOT	4	9	0	0	0	0	0	0	0	4	.000	0
POST TOT	7	18	1	2	2	0	0	1	1	5	.111	0

DOUG SISK

	G	AB	R	H	2B	3B	HR	BI	BB	SO	BA	SB
1986 NLCS	1	0	0	0	0	0	0	0	0	0	—	0
1986 WS	1	0	0	0	0	0	0	0	0	0	—	0
POST TOT	2	0	0	0	0	0	0	0	0	0	—	0

ART SHAMSKY

	G	AB	R	H	2B	3B	HR	BI	BB	SO	BA	SB
1969 NLCS	3	13	3	7	0	0	0	1	0	3	.538	0
1969 WS	3	6	0	0	0	0	0	0	0	0	.000	0
POST TOT	6	19	3	7	0	0	0	1	0	3	.368	0

RUSTY STAUB

	G	AB	R	H	2B	3B	HR	BI	BB	SO	BA	SB
1973 NLCS	4	15	4	3	0	0	3	5	3	2	.200	0
1973 WS	7	26	1	11	2	0	1	6	2	2	.423	0
POST TOT	11	41	5	14	2	0	4	11	5	4	.341	0

GEORGE STONE

	G	AB	R	H	2B	3B	HR	BI	BB	SO	BA	SB
1973 NLCS	1	1	0	0	0	0	0	0	0	1	1	.000	0
1973 WS	2	0	0	0	0	0	0	0	0	0	—	0
POST TOT	3	1	0	0	0	0	0	0	0	1	1	.000	0

DARRYL STRAWBERRY

	G	AB	R	H	2B	3B	HR	BI	BB	SO	BA	SB
1986 NLCS	6	22	4	5	1	0	2	5	3	12	.227	1
1988 NLCS	7	30	5	9	2	0	1	6	2	5	.300	0
NLCS TOT	13	52	9	14	3	0	3	11	5	17	.269	1
1986 WS	7	24	4	5	1	0	1	1	4	6	.208	3
POST TOT	20	76	13	19	4	0	4	12	9	23	.250	4

RON SWOBODA

	G	AB	R	H	2B	3B	HR	BI	BB	SO	BA	SB
1969 NLCS		DID NOT PLAY										
1969 WS	4	15	1	6	1	0	0	1	1	3	.400	0

RON TAYLOR

	G	AB	R	H	2B	3B	HR	BI	BB	SO	BA	SB
1969 NLCS	2	0	0	0	0	0	0	0	0	0	—	0
1969 WS	2	0	0	0	0	0	0	0	0	0	—	0
POST TOT	4	0	0	0	0	0	0	0	0	0	—	0

TIM TEUFEL

	G	AB	R	H	2B	3B	HR	BI	BB	SO	BA	SB
1986 NLCS	2	6	0	1	0	0	0	0	0	0	.167	0
1988 NLCS	1	3	0	0	0	0	0	0	0	1	.000	0
NLCS TOT	3	9	0	1	0	0	0	0	0	1	.111	0
1986 WS	3	9	1	4	1	0	1	1	1	2	.444	0
POST TOT	6	18	1	5	1	0	1	1	1	3	.278	0

GEORGE THEODORE

	G	AB	R	H	2B	3B	HR	BI	BB	SO	BA	SB
1973 NLCS		DID NOT PLAY										
1973 WS	2	2	0	0	0	0	0	0	0	0	.000	0

STEVE TRACHSEL

	G	AB	R	H	2B	3B	HR	BI	BB	SO	BA	SB
2006 NLDS	1	2	0	0	0	0	0	0	0	0	.000	0
2007 NLCS	1	0	0	0	0	0	0	0	0	0	—	0
POST TOT	2	2	0	0	0	0	0	0	0	0	.000	0

BUBBA TRAMMELL

	G	AB	R	H	2B	3B	HR	BI	BB	SO	BA	SB
2000 NLCS	3	3	0	0	0	0	0	0	0	2	.000	0
2000 WS	4	5	1	2	0	0	0	3	1	1	.400	0
POST TOT	7	8	1	2	0	0	0	3	1	3	.250	0

MICHAEL TUCKER

	G	AB	R	H	2B	3B	HR	BI	BB	SO	BA	SB
2006 NLDS	2	1	1	0	0	0	0	0	1	0	.000	0
2006 NLCS	6	5	1	2	0	0	0	0	0	1	.400	1
POST TOT	8	6	2	2	0	0	0	0	1	1	.333	1

JOSE VALENTIN

	G	AB	R	H	2B	3B	HR	BI	BB	SO	BA	SB
2006 NLDS	3	9	2	0	0	0	0	0	2	4	.000	0
2006 NLCS	7	24	0	6	2	0	0	5	2	5	.250	0
POST TOT	10	33	2	6	2	0	0	5	4	9	.182	0

ROBIN VENTURA

	G	AB	R	H	2B	3B	HR	BI	BB	SO	BA	SB
1999 NLDS	4	14	1	3	2	0	0	1	4	2	.214	0
2000 NLDS	4	14	1	2	0	0	1	2	4	1	.143	0
NLDS TOT	8	28	2	5	2	0	1	3	8	3	.179	0
1999 NLCS	6	25	2	3	1	0	0	1	2	5	.120	0
2000 NLCS	5	14	4	3	1	0	0	5	6	0	.214	0
NLCS TOT	11	39	6	6	2	0	0	6	8	5	.154	0
2000 WS	5	20	1	3	1	0	1	1	1	5	.150	0
POST TOT	24	87	9	14	5	0	2	10	17	13	.161	0

BILLY WAGNER

	G	AB	R	H	2B	3B	HR	BI	BB	SO	BA	SB
2006 NLDS	3	0	0	0	0	0	0	0	0	0	—	0
2006 NLCS	3	0	0	0	0	0	0	0	0	0	—	0
POST TOT												

AL WEIS

	G	AB	R	H	2B	3B	HR	BI	BB	SO	BA	SB
1969 NLCS	3	1	0	0	0	0	0	0	0	0	.000	0
1969 WS	5	11	1	5	0	0	1	3	4	2	.455	0
POST TOT	8	12	2	5	0	0	1	3	4	2	.417	0

TURK WENDELL

	G	AB	R	H	2B	3B	HR	BI	BB	SO	BA	SB
1999 NLDS	2	1	0	0	0	0	0	0	0	1	.000	0
2000 NLDS	2	0	0	0	0	0	0	0	0	0	—	0
NLDS TOT	4	1	0	0	0	0	0	0	0	0	.000	0
1999 NLCS	5	0	0	0	0	0	0	0	0	0	—	0
2000 NLCS	2	0	0	0	0	0	0	0	0	0	—	0
NLCS TOT	7	0	0	0	0	0	0	0	0	0	—	0
2000 WS	2	0	0	0	0	0	0	0	0	0	—	0
POST TOT	13	1	0	0	0	0	0	0	0	0	.000	0

RICK WHITE

	G	AB	R	H	2B	3B	HR	BI	BB	SO	BA	SB
2000 NLDS	2	0	0	0	0	0	0	0	0	0	—	0
2000 NLCS	1	0	0	0	0	0	0	0	0	0	—	0
2000 WS	1	0	0	0	0	0	0	0	0	0	—	0
POST TOT	4	0	0	0	0	0	0	0	0	0	—	0

MOOKIE WILSON

	G	AB	R	H	2B	3B	HR	BI	BB	SO	BA	SB
1986 NLCS	6	26	2	3	0	0	0	1	1	7	.115	1
1988 NLCS	4	13	2	2	0	0	0	1	2	2	.154	0
NLCS TOT	10	39	4	5	0	0	0	2	3	9	.128	1
1986 WS	7	26	3	7	1	0	0	0	1	6	.269	3
POST TOT	17	63	7	12	1	0	0	2	4	15	.179	4

CHRIS WOODWARD

	G	AB	R	H	2B	3B	HR	BI	BB	SO	BA	SB
2006 NLDS	1	1	1	1	1	0	0	0	0	0	.1000	0
2006 NLCS		DID NOT PLAY										

DAVID WRIGHT

	G	AB	R	H	2B	3B	HR	BI	BB	SO	BA	SB
2006 NLDS	3	12	1	4	2	0	0	4	1	4	.333	0
2006 NLCS	7	25	2	4	1	0	1	2	4	4	.160	0
POST TOT	10	37	3	8	3	0	1	6	5	8	.216	0

MASATO YOSHII

	G	AB	R	H	2B	3B	HR	BI	BB	SO	BA	SB
1999 NLDS	1	2	0	0	0	0	0	0	0	1	.000	0
1999 NLCS	2	3	0	0	0	0	0	0	0	2	.000	0
POST TOT	3	5	0	0	0	0	0	0	0	3	.000	0

TODD ZEILE

	G	AB	R	H	2B	3B	HR	BI	BB	SO	BA	SB
2000 NLDS	4	14	0	1	1	0	0	0	4	3	.071	0
2000 NLCS	5	19	1	7	3	0	1	8	2	4	.368	0
2000 WS	5	20	1	8	2	0	0	1	1	5	.400	0
POST TOT	14	53	2	16	6	0	1	9	7	12	.302	0

Mets Career Postseason Pitching Statistics

RICK AGUILERA

	G	ERA	W–L	SV	CG	IP	H	ER	BB	SO
1986 NLCS	2	0.00	0–0	0	0	5	2	0	2	2
1988 NLCS	3	1.29	0–0	0	0	7	3	1	2	4
NLCS TOT	5	0.75	0–0	0	0	12	5	1	4	6
1986 WS	2	12.00	1–0	0	0	3	8	4	1	4
POST TOT	7	3.00	1–0	0	0	15	13	5	5	10

ARMANDO BENITEZ

	G	ERA	W–L	SV	CG	IP	H	ER	BB	SO
1999 NLDS	2	0.00	0–0	0	0	2-1/3	2	0	1	2
2000 NLDS	2	6.00	1–0	0	0	3	4	2	1	3
NLDS TOT	4	3.38	1–0	0	0	5-1/3	6	2	2	5
1999 NLCS	5	1.35	0–0	1	0	6-2/3	3	1	2	9
2000 NLCS	3	0.00	0–0	1	0	3	3	0	2	2
NLCS TOT	8	0.93	0–0	2	0	9-2/3	6	1	4	11
2000 WS	3	3.00	0–0	1	0	3	3	1	2	2
POST TOT	15	2.00	1–0	3	0	18	15	4	8	18

CHAD BRADFORD

	G	ERA	W–L	SV	CG	IP	H	ER	BB	SO
2006 NLDS	2	0.00	0–0	0	0	1/3	1	0	1	0
2006 NLCS	5	0.00	0–0	0	0	5-1/3	3	0	0	2
POST TOT	7	0.00	0–0	0	0	5-2/3	4	0	1	2

DON CARDWELL

	G	ERA	W–L	SV	CG	IP	H	ER	BB	SO
1969 WS	1	0.00	0–0	0	0	1	0	0	0	0

DAVID CONE

	G	ERA	W–L	SV	CG	IP	H	ER	BB	SO
1988 NLCS	3	4.50	1–1	0	1	12	10	6	5	9

DENNIS COOK

	G	ERA	W–L	SV	CG	IP	H	ER	BB	SO
1999 NLDS	1	0.00	0–0	0	0	1-2/3	1	0	1	1
2000 NLDS	2	0.00	0–0	0	0	1-1/3	0	0	2	1
NLDS TOT	3	0.00	0–0	0	0	3	1	0	3	2
1999 NLCS	3	0.00	0–0	0	0	1-1/3	1	0	2	1
2000 NLCS	1	0.00	0–0	0	0	1	1	0	0	2
NLCS TOT	4	0.00	0–0	0	0	2-1/3	2	0	2	3
2000 WS	3	0.00	0–0	0	0	2/3	1	0	3	1
POST TOT	10	0.00	0–0	0	0	6	4	0	8	6

RON DARLING

	G	ERA	W–L	SV	CG	IP	H	ER	BB	SO
1986 NLCS	1	7.20	0–0	0	0	5	6	4	2	5
1988 NLCS	2	7.71	0–1	0	0	7	11	6	4	7
NLCS TOT	3	7.50	0–1	0	0	12	17	10	6	12
1986 WS	3	1.53	1–1	0	0	17-2/3	13	3	10	12
POST TOT	6	3.94	1–2	0	0	29-2/3	30	13	16	24

OCTAVIO DOTEL

	G	ERA	W–L	SV	CG	IP	H	ER	BB	SO
1999 NLDS	1	54.00	0–0	0	0	1/3	1	2	2	0
1999 NLCS	1	3.00	1–0	0	0	3	4	1	1	3
POST TOT	2	8.10	1–0	0	0	3-1/3	5	3	3	3

PEDRO FELICIANO

	G	ERA	W–L	SV	CG	IP	H	ER	BB	SO
2006 NLDS	3	0.00	1–0	0	0	1-2/3	0	0	2	2
2006 NLCS	3	3.00	0–0	0	0	3	2	1	0	1
POST TOT										

SID FERNANDEZ

	G	ERA	W–L	SV	CG	IP	H	ER	BB	SO
1986 NLCS	1	4.50	0–1	0	0	6	3	3	1	5
1988 NLCS	1	13.50	0–1	0	0	4	7	6	1	5
NLCS TOT	2	8.10	0–2	0	0	10	10	9	2	10
1986 WS	3	1.35	0–0	0	0	6-2/3	6	1	1	10
POST TOT	5	5.40	0–2	0	0	16-2/3	16	10	3	20

JOHN FRANCO

	G	ERA	W–L	SV	CG	IP	H	ER	BB	SO
1999 NLDS	3	0.00	1–0	0	0	3-2/3	1	0	0	2
2000 NLDS	2	0.00	0–0	1	0	2	1	0	0	2
NLDS TOT	5	0.00	1–0	1	0	5-2/3	2	0	0	4
1999 NLCS	3	3.38	0–0	0	0	2-2/3	3	1	1	3
2000 NLCS	3	6.75	0–0	0	0	2-2/3	3	2	2	2
NLCS TOT	6	5.44	0–0	0	0	5-1/3	6	3	3	5
2000 WS	4	0.00	1–0	0	0	3-1/3	3	0	0	1
POST TOT	15	1.88	2–0	1	0	14-1/3	11	3	3	10

GARY GENTRY

	G	ERA	W–L	SV	CG	IP	H	ER	BB	SO
1969 NLCS	1	9.00	0–0	0	0	2	5	2	1	1
1969 WS	1	0.00	1–0	0	0	6-2/3	3	0	5	4
POST TOT	2	2.08	1–0	0	0	8-2/3	8	2	6	5

TOM GLAVINE

	G	ERA	W–L	SV	CG	IP	H	ER	BB	SO
2006 NLDS	1	0.00	1–0	0	0	6	4	0	2	2
2006 NLCS	2	2.45	1–1	0	0	11	11	3	5	4
POST TOT	3	1.59	2–1	0	0	17	15	3	7	6

DWIGHT GOODEN

	G	ERA	W–L	SV	CG	IP	H	ER	BB	SO
1986 NLCS	2	1.06	0–1	0	0	17	16	2	5	9
1988 NLCS	3	2.95	0–0	0	0	18-1/3	10	6	8	20
NLCS TOT	5	2.04	0–1	0	0	35-1/3	26	8	13	29
1986 WS	2	8.00	0–2	0	0	9	17	8	4	9
POST TOT	7	3.25	0–3	0	0	44-1/3	43	16	17	38

MIKE HAMPTON

	G	ERA	W–L	SV	CG	IP	H	ER	BB	SO
2000 NLDS	1	8.44	0–1	0	0	5-1/3	6	5	3	2
2000 NLCS	2	0.00	2–0	0	1	16	9	0	4	12
2000 WS	1	6.00	0–1	0	0	6	8	4	5	4
POST TOT	4	2.96	2–2	0	1	27-1/3	23	9	12	18

AARON HEILMAN

	G	ERA	W–L	SV	CG	IP	H	ER	BB	SO
2006 NLDS	3	3.00	0–0	0	0	3	3	1	0	1
2006 NLCS	3	4.15	0–1	0	0	4-1/3	4	2	1	5
POST TOT										

ROBERTO HERNANDEZ

	G	ERA	W–L	SV	CG	IP	H	ER	BB	SO
2006 NLDS		DID NOT PLAY								
2006 NLCS	3	0.00	0–0	0	0	2-1/3	0	0	2	0

OREL HERSHISER

	G	ERA	W–L	SV	CG	IP	H	ER	BB	SO
1999 NLDS	1	0.00	0–0	0	0	1	0	0	0	1
1999 NLCS	2	0.00	0–0	0	0	4-1/3	1	0	3	5
POST TOT	3	0.00	0–0	0	0	5-1/3	1	0	3	6

BOBBY JONES

	G	ERA	W–L	SV	CG	IP	H	ER	BB	SO
2000 NLDS	1	0.00	1–0	0	1	9	1	0	2	5
2000 NLCS	1	13.50	0–0	0	0	4	6	6	0	2
2000 WS	1	5.40	0–1	0	0	5	4	3	3	3
POST TOT	3	4.50	1–1	0	1	18	11	9	5	10

JERRY KOOSMAN

	G	ERA	W–L	SV	CG	IP	H	ER	BB	SO
1969 NLCS	1	11.57	0–0	0	0	4-2/3	7	6	4	5
1973 NLCS	1	2.00	1–0	0	1	9	8	2	0	9
NLCS TOT	2	5.27	1–0	0	1	13-2/3	15	8	4	14
1969 WS	2	2.04	2–0	0	1	17-2/3	7	4	4	9
1973 WS	2	3.12	1–0	0	0	8-2/3	9	3	7	8
W.S. TOT	4	2.39	3–0	0	1	26-1/3	16	7	11	17
POST TOT	6	3.38	4–0	0	1	40	31	15	15	31

TERRY LEACH

	G	ERA	W–L	SV	CG	IP	H	ER	BB	SO
1988 NLCS	3	0.00	0–0	0	0	5	4	0	1	4

AL LEITER

	G	ERA	W–L	SV	CG	IP	H	ER	BB	SO
1999 NLDS	1	3.52	0–0	0	0	7-2/3	3	3	3	4
2000 NLDS	1	2.25	0–0	0	0	8	5	2	3	6
NLDS TOT	2	2.87	0–0	0	0	15-2/3	8	5	3	10
1999 NLCS	2	6.43	0–1	0	0	7	5	5	4	5
2000 NLCS	1	3.86	0–0	0	0	7	8	3	0	9
NLCS TOT	3	5.14	0–1	0	0	14	13	8	4	14
2000 WS	2	2.87	0–1	0	0	15.7	12	5	6	16
POST TOT	7	3.60	0–2	0	0	45	33	18	13	40

PAT MAHOMES

	G	ERA	W–L	SV	CG	IP	H	ER	BB	SO
1999 NLDS	1	5.40	0–0	0	0	1-2/3	3	1	0	1
1999 NLCS	3	1.42	0–0	0	0	6-1/3	4	1	3	3
POST TOT	4	2.25	0–0	0	0	8	7	2	3	3

JOHN MAINE

	G	ERA	W–L	SV	CG	IP	H	ER	BB	SO
2006 NLDS	1	2.08	0–0	0	0	4-1/3	6	1	2	5
206 NLCS	2	2.89	1–0	0	0	9-1/3	4	3	9	8
POST TOT										

JON MATLACK

	G	ERA	W–L	SV	CG	IP	H	ER	BB	SO
1973 NLCS	1	0.00	1–0	0	1	9	2	0	3	9
1973 WS	3	2.16	1–2	0	0	16-2/3	10	4	5	11
POST TOT	4	1.40	2–2	0	1	25-2/3	12	4	8	20

ROGER McDOWELL

	G	ERA	W–L	SV	CG	IP	H	ER	BB	SO
1986 NLCS	2	0.00	0–0	0	0	7	1	0	0	3
1988 NLCS	4	4.50	0–1	0	0	6	6	3	2	5
NLCS TOT	6	2.08	0–1	0	0	13	7	3	2	8
1986 WS	5	4.91	1–0	0	0	7-1/3	10	4	6	2
POST TOT	11	3.10	1–1	0	0	20-1/3	17	7	8	10

TUG McGRAW

	G	ERA	W–L	SV	CG	IP	H	ER	BB	SO
1969 NLCS	1	0.00	0–0	1	0	3	1	0	1	1
1973 NLCS	2	0.00	0–0	0	0	5	4	0	3	3
NLCS TOT	3	0.00	0–0	1	0	8	5	0	4	4
1969 WS		DID NOT PLAY								
1973 WS	5	2.63	1–0	1	0	13-2/3	8	4	9	14
POST TOT	8	1.66	1–0	2	0	21-2/3	13	4	13	18

GUILLERMO MOTA

	G	ERA	W–L	SV	CG	IP	H	ER	BB	SO
2006 NLDS	2	6.75	1–0	0	0	4	6	3	0	5
2000 NLCS	5	4.15	0–0	0	0	4-1/3	4	2	2	2
POST TOT	7	5.40	1–0	0	0	8-1/3	10	5	2	7

RANDY MYERS

	G	ERA	W–L	SV	CG	IP	H	ER	BB	SO
1988 NLCS	3	0.00	2–0	0	0	4-2/3	1	0	2	0

BOB OJEDA

	G	ERA	W–L	SV	CG	IP	H	ER	BB	SO
1986 NLCS	2	2.57	1–0	0	1	14	15	4	4	6
1988 NLCS		INJURED, DID NOT PLAY								
1986 WS	2	2.08	1–0	0	0	13	13	3	5	9
POST TOT	4	2.33	2–0	0	1	27	28	7	9	15

DARREN OLIVER

	G	ERA	W–L	SV	CG	IP	H	ER	BB	SO
2006 NLDS	1	20.25	0–0	0	0	1.3	3	3	0	0
2006 NLCS	1	0.00	0–0	0	0	6	3	0	1	3
POST TOT	2	3.95	0–0	0	0	7.3	6	3	1	3

JESSE OROSCO

	G	ERA	W–L	SV	CG	IP	H	ER	BB	SO
1986 NLCS	4	3.38	3–0	0	0	8	5	3	2	10
1986 WS	4	0.00	0–0	2	0	5-2/3	2	0	0	6
POST TOT	8	1.98	3–0	2	0	13-2/3	7	3	2	16

HARRY PARKER

	G	ERA	W–L	SV	CG	IP	H	ER	BB	SO
1973 NLCS	1	9.00	0–1	0	0	1	1	1	0	0
1973 WS	3	0.00	0–1	0	0	3-1/3	2	0	2	2
POST TOT	4	2.08	0–2	0	0	4-1/3	3	1	2	2

OLIVER PEREZ

	G	ERA	W–L	SV	CG	IP	H	ER	BB	SO
2006 NLDS		DID NOT PLAY								
2006 NLCS	2	4.63	1–0	0	0	11-2/3	13	6	3	7

RICK REED

	G	ERA	W–L	SV	CG	IP	H	ER	BB	SO
1999 NLDS	1	3.00	1–0	0	0	6	4	2	3	2
2000 NLDS	1	3.00	0–0	0	0	6	7	2	2	6
NLDS TOT	2	3.00	1–0	0	0	12	11	4	5	8
1999 NLCS	1	2.57	0–0	0	0	7	3	2	0	5
2000 NLCS	1	10.80	0–1	0	0	3-1/3	8	4	1	4
NLCS TOT	2	5.23	0–1	0	0	10-1/3	11	6	1	9
2000 WS	1	3.00	0–0	0	0	6	6	2	1	8
POST TOT	5	3.81	1–1	0	0	28-1/3	28	12	7	25

KENNY ROGERS

	G	ERA	W–L	SV	CG	IP	H	ER	BB	SO
1999 NLDS	1	8.31	0–1	0	0	4-1/3	5	4	2	6
1999 NLCS	3	5.87	0–2	0	0	7-1/3	11	5	7	2
POST TOT	4	6.94	0–3	0	0	11-2/3	16	9	9	8

GLENDON RUSCH

	G	ERA	W–L	SV	CG	IP	H	ER	BB	SO
2000 NLDS	1	0.00	0–0	0	0	2/3	0	0	0	2
2000 NLCS	2	0.00	1–0	0	0	3-2/3	3	0	0	3
2000 WS	3	2.25	0–0	0	0	4-1/3	6	1	2	2
POST TOT	6	1.04	1–0	0	0	8-2/3	9	1	2	7

NOLAN RYAN

	G	ERA	W–L	SV	CG	IP	H	ER	BB	SO
1969 NLCS	1	2.57	1–0	0	0	7	3	2	2	7
1969 WS	1	0.00	0–0	1	0	2-1/3	1	0	2	3
POST TOT	2	1.93	1–0	1	0	9-1/3	4	2	4	10

RAY SADECKI

	G	ERA	W–L	SV	CG	IP	H	ER	BB	SO
1973 WS	4	1.93	0–0	1	0	4-2/3	5	1	1	6

DOUG SISK

	G	ERA	W–L	SV	CG	IP	H	ER	BB	SO
1986 NLCS	1	0.00	0–0	0	0	1	1	0	1	0
1986 WS	1	0.00	0–0	0	0	2/3	0	0	1	1
POST TOT	2	0.00	0–0	0	0	1-2/3	1	0	2	1

TOM SEAVER

	G	ERA	W–L	SV	CG	IP	H	ER	BB	SO
1969 NLCS	1	6.75	1–0	0	0	7	8	5	3	2
1969 NLCS	2	1.62	1–1	0	1	16-2/3	13	3	5	17
NLCS TOT	3	3.04	2–1	0	1	23-2/3	21	8	8	19
1969 WS	2	3.00	1–1	0	1	15	12	5	3	9
1973 WS	2	2.40	0–1	0	0	15	13	4	3	18
W.S. TOT	4	2.70	1–2	0	1	30	25	9	6	27
POST TOT	7	2.85	3–3	0	2	53-2/3	46	17	14	46

GEORGE STONE

	G	ERA	W–L	SV	CG	IP	H	ER	BB	SO
1973 NLCS	1	1.35	0–0	0	0	6-2/3	3	1	2	4
1973 WS	2	0.00	0–0	1	0	3	4	0	1	3
POST TOT	3	0.93	0–0	1	0	9-2/3	7	1	3	7

RON TAYLOR

	G	ERA	W–L	SV	CG	IP	H	ER	BB	SO
1969 NLCS	2	0.00	1–0	1	0	3-1/3	3	0	0	4
1969 WS	2	0.00	0–0	1	0	2-1/3	0	0	1	3
POST TOT	4	0.00	1–0	2	0	5-2/3	3	0	1	7

STEVE TRACHSEL

	G	ERA	W–L	SV	CG	IP	H	ER	BB	SO
2006 NLDS	1	5.40	0–0	0	0	3-1/3	6	2	1	2
2006 NLCS	1	45.00	0–1	0	0	1	5	5	5	1
POST TOT	2	14.54	0–1	0	0	4-1/3	11	7	6	3

BILLY WAGNER

	G	ERA	W–L	SV	CG	IP	H	ER	BB	SO
2006 NLDS	3	3.00	0–0	2	0	3	3	1	0	4
2006 NLCS	3	16.88	0–1	1	0	2-1/3	7	5	1	0
POST TOT	6	10.13	0–1	3	0	5-1/3	10	6	1	5

TURK WENDELL

	G	ERA	W–L	SV	CG	IP	H	ER	BB	SO
1999 NLDS	2	0.00	1–0	0	0	2	0	0	2	0
2000 NLDS	2	0.00	0–0	0	0	2	0	0	1	5
NLDS TOT	4	0.00	1–0	0	0	4	0	0	3	5
1999 NLCS	5	4.76	1–0	0	0	5-2/3	2	3	4	5
2000 NLCS	2	0.00	1–0	0	0	1-1/3	1	0	1	2
NLCS TOT	7	3.86	2–0	0	0	7	3	3	5	7
2000 WS	2	5.40	0–1	0	0	1-2/3	3	1	2	2
POST TOT	13	2.84	3–1	0	0	12-2/3	6	4	10	14

RICK WHITE

	G	ERA	W–L	SV	CG	IP	H	ER	BB	SO
2000 NLDS	2	0.00	1–0	0	0	2-2/3	6	0	2	4
2000 NLCS	1	9.00	0–0	0	0	3	5	3	1	1
2000 WS	1	6.75	0–0	0	0	1-1/3	1	1	1	1
POST TOT	4	5.14	1–0	0	0	7	12	4	4	6

MASATO YOSHII

	G	ERA	W–L	SV	CG	IP	H	ER	BB	SO
1999 NLDS	1	6.75	0–0	0	0	5-1/3	6	4	0	3
1999 NLCS	2	4.70	0–1	0	0	7-2/3	9	4	3	4
POST TOT	3	5.54	0–1	0	0	13	15	8	3	7

6

SHEA STADIUM

GAME TIME BUDWEISER

Sheraton
HOTELS & RESORTS
sheraton.com

AMERICAN			CARDS	
INN	R	P		
NYY	27		22	SS
OAK	55		3	3B
LAA	40		5	1B
DET	38		15	CF
TOR	39		34	
CLE	34		47	RF
BAL	35		12	2B
CWS	34		99	LF
TB	11			
KC	40		4	C
TEX	37		30	P
MIN	52			
BOS	52			
SEA	45			

Armitron
AMERICA'S WATCH   12:23

METS		NATIONAL		
INN		INN	R	P
7	SS	CHI		38
3	1B	WAS		61
15	CF	CIN		39
30	LF	PHI		43
44	RF	MIL		53
5	3B	PIT		55
11	C	SF		50
25	2B	HOU		22
45	P	ARZ		55
		COL		16
		FLA		22
		SD		44
		ATL		32
		LA		45

UMPIRES
PL 82 49 2B
1B 31 61 3B
RF   LF

Champion MORTGAGE   VS.

CAP DAY

Mohegan Sun    BANCO POPULAR    HIP HEALTH PLAN OF NEW YORK

396   amtrak.com   371   GEICO   358

Mets Records and Category Leaders

METS SINGLE-GAME RECORDS

Individual/Hitting

Plate Appearances	12	Felix Millan vs. Cardinals, 9/11/74 John Milner vs. Cardinals, 9/11/74
At-Bats	11	Dave Schneck vs. Cardinals, 9/11/74
At-Bats, 0 Hits	10	Tommie Agee @ Astros, 4/15/68 Ron Swoboda @ Astros, 4/15/68 Wayne Garrett vs. Cardinals, 9/11/74
Runs	6	Edgardo Alfonzo @ Astros, 8/30/99
Hits	6	Edgardo Alfonzo @ Astros, 8/30/99
Doubles	3	26 times, last by Lucas Duda @ Rangers, 6/25/11
Triples	3	Doug Flynn @ Expos, 8/5/80
Home Runs	3	8 times
Extra-Base Hits	4	8 times, last by Edgardo Alfonzo @ Astros, 8/30/99
Total Bases	16	Edgardo Alfonzo @ Astros, 8/30/99
Times On Base	6	24 times, last by Jose Reyes vs. Giants, 5/3/11
RBI	9	Carlos Delgado @ Yankees, 6/27/08
Walks	5	Vince Coleman vs. Pirates, 8/10/92
Intentional Walks	3	Claudell Washington vs. Padres. 8/26/80 Vince Coleman vs. Pirates, 8/1/92 Todd Hundley @ Pirates, 6/28/97 David Wright vs. Yankees, 5/19/07 David Wright @ Braves, 7/18/09
Strikeouts	5	Ron Swoboda @ Astros, 4/15/68 Ron Swoboda vs. Cardinals, 6/22/69 Frank Taveras vs. Padres5/1/79 Dave Kingman vs. Astros, 5/28/82 Ryan Thompson vs. Cardinals, 9/29/93
Stolen Bases	4	Vince Coleman @ Cardinals, 6/26/92 Vince Coleman vs. Expos, 6/23/93 Roger Cedeno @ Phillies, 5/14/99 David Wright @ Giants, 5/14/09
Caught Stealing	3	Len Randle @ Expos, 4/15/78
Hit By Pitch	2	24 times last by Ruben Tejada vs. Marlins, 9/1/11
Sacrifice Bunts	3	Sid Fernandez vs. Astros, 7/24/87 Livan Hernandez @ Marlins, 4/11/09
Sacrifice Flies	2	24 times, last by Jeff Francoeur vs. Marlins, 8/24/10
Grounded-DP	4	Joe Torre vs. Astros, 7/21/75

Individual/Pitching

Innings Pitched	15	Al Jackson vs. Phillies, 8/14/62 Rob Gardner vs. Phillies, 10/2/65
Earned Runs	11	Orlando Hernandez @ Phillies, 8/15/06
Runs	11	Craig Anderson vs. Dodgers, 8/26/62 Jack Fisher @ Giants, 6/3/67 Orlando Hernandez @ Phillies, 8/15/06
Hits	15	Tom Seaver @ Phillies, 5/25/76
Walks	10	Mike Torrez @ Reds, 7/21/83

Shea Stadium as seen from the No. 7 train (top) and the scoreboard from inside the ballpark, as seen in 2005, three years before its final season.

Photos courtesy of Oscar W. Gabriel

Strikeouts	19	Tom Seaver vs. Padres, 4/22/70
		David Cone @ Phillies, 10/6/91
Fewest K's, CG	0	5 Times, last by Mike Torrez @ Cubs, 6/8/83
Home Runs	5	Roger Craig vs. Giants, 5/4/63
Wild Pitches	3	20 times
		last by Johan Santana @ DBacks, 5/4/08
Balks	3	Don Rowe @ Phillies, 4/22/63
		Mike Pelfrey @ Giants, 5/17/09
Stolen Bases	7	Tom Seaver vs. Reds, 8/10/74 (Duffy Dyer)
Pickoffs	2	20 times, last by Tom Glavine @ Cardinals, 8/6/04
Hit by Pitches	3	8 times, last by Oliver Perez vs. Marlins, 9/28/07

Team Hitting

Plate Appearances	103	vs. Cardinals, 9/11/74 (25 Inn.)
At-Bats	89	vs. Cardinals, 9/11/74 (25 Inn.)
Runs	23	@ Cubs, 8/16/87 (23–10)
Hits	28	@ Braves, 7/4/85 (16–13, 19 Inn.)
Hits, 9 Inn.	23	@ Cubs, 5/26/64 (19–1)
	23	@ Rockies, 4/29/00 (13–6)
Doubles	10	@ Expos, 9/27/01 (12–6)
Triples	4	vs. Cubs, 5/23/70 (8–14)
	4	vs. Padres, 7/6/79 (5–6)
Home Runs	7	@ Phillies, 4/19/05 (16–4)
Extra-Base Hits	13	@ Diamondbacks, 8/24/05 (18–4)
Total Bases	44	@ Diamondbacks, 8/24/05 (18–4)
Times On Base	40	@ Braves, 7/4/85 (16–13, 19 Inn.)
Times On Base, 9 Inn	34	@ Cubs, 6/12/90 (19–8)
RBI	22	@ Cubs, 8/16/87 (23–10)
Walks	16	@ Dodgers, 6/29/62 (10–4)
Intentional BBs	6	vs. Padres, 8/26/80 (18 Inn.)
Intentional BBs, 9 Inn.	5	@ Cubs, 7/17/95
Strikeouts	22	vs. Giants, 5/31/64 (6–8, 23 Inn.)
Strikeouts, 9 Inn.	19	@ Cardinals, 9/15/69 (4–3)
Stolen Bases	7	@ Giants, 5/14/09
Caught Stealing	4	3 times, last @ Pirates, 9/20/80

Hit By Pitch	3	24 times, last vs. Nationals, 4/9/11
Sacrifice Bunts	5	vs. Pirates, 8/10/92
		@ Colorado, 4/26/95
		@ Braves, 7/18/09
Sacrifice Flies	4	3 times, last @ Yankees, 6/24/05
Grounded-DP	6	@ Giants, 8/21/04, (11–9, 12 Inn.)
Ground-DP, 9 Inn	5	5 times, last @ Milwaukee, 8/6/02

Team/Pitching

Innings Pitched	25	vs. Cardinals, 9/11/74 (3–4)
Earned Runs	24	@ Phillies, 6/11/85 (7–26)
Runs	26	@ Phillies, 6/11/85 (7–26)
Hits	27	@ Phillies, 6/11/85 (7–26)
Walks	15	vs. Cubs, 9/16/72 (5–18)
Strikeouts	20	vs. Cubs, 8/1/99 (5–4, 13 Inn.)
Strikeouts, 9 Inn	19	vs. Padres, 4/22/70 (2–1)
		@ Phillies, 10/6/91 (7–0)
Fewest K's,	0	45 times, last @ Braves, 7/17/09 (1–7)
Home Runs	7	@ Cubs, 6/11/67 (10–18)
		@ Phillies, 9/8/88 (4–16)
Wild Pitches	4	6 times, last @ Rockies, 5/6/97 (11–12)
Balks	4	@ Phillies, 4/22/63 (6–8)
Stolen Bases	8	@ Braves, 7/16/88
Hit by Pitches	4	vs. Nationals, 4/6/06

Team/Miscellaneous

Lopsided Victory	18	@ Cubs, 5/26/64 (19–1)
Lopsided Loss	19	@ Phillies, 6/11/85 (26–7)
Lopsided Shutout Win	14–0	@ Cubs, 7/29/65
		@ Reds, 4/19/98
Lopsided Shutout Loss	16–0	vs. Braves, 7/2/99
Shortest Game	1:36	@ Braves, 4/27/73
Longest Game	7:23	vs. Giants, 5/31/64, 2nd GM
Longest Game, Inn.	25	vs. Cardinals, 9/11/74
Most Errors	7,	vs. Pirates, 8/1/96
Most Double Plays	5,	@ Cubs, 6/9/83
		vs. Marlins, 6/5/97
Biggest Comeback Win	8	@ Astros, 9/2/72
Biggest Blown Lead	8	@ Cubs, 4/19/80

METS SINGLE-SEASON RECORDS

Individual Hitting

Games	162	Felix Millan	1975
		John Olerud	1999
Plate Appearances	765	Jose Reyes	2007
At–Bats	696	Jose Reyes	2005
Average	.354	John Olerud	1998
On Base %	.447	John Olerud	1998
Slugging %	.614	Mike Piazza	2000
OPS	1.012	Mike Piazza	2000
Runs	127	Carlos Beltran	2006
Hits	227	Lance Johnson	1996
Doubles	44	Bernard Gilkey	1996
Triples	21	Lance Johnson	1996
Home Runs	41	Todd Hundley	1996
		Carlos Beltran	2006
Extra-Base Hits	80	Howard Johnson	1989
		Carlos Beltran	2006
Total Bases	334	David Wright	2008
Times On Base	309	John Olerud	1999
RBI	124	Mike Piazza	1999
		David Wright	2008
Walks	125	John Olerud	1999
Intentional Walks	25	Howard Johnson	1988
Strikeouts	161	David Wright	2010
Stolen Bases	78	Jose Reyes	2007
Caught Stealing	21	Len Randle	1977
		Jose Reyes	2007
Hit By Pitch	13	Ron Hunt	1963
		John Olerud	1997
Sacrifice Bunts	24	Felix Millan	1974
Sacrifice Flies	15	Gary Carter	1985
		Howard Johnson	1991
Grounded-DP	27	Mike Piazza	1999
Pinch-Hits	24	Rusty Staub	1983
Pinch-Hit Homers	4	Danny Heep	1983
		Mark Carreon	1989
Pinch-Hit RBI	25,	Rusty Staub	1983

Individual Pitching

Games	92	Pedro Feliciano	2010
Games Started	36	4 times, 3 by Tom Seaver	
Complete Games	21	Tom Seaver	1971
Shutouts	8	Dwight Gooden	1985
Wins	25	Tom Seaver	1969
Losses	24	Roger Craig	1962
		Jack Fisher	1965
Saves	43	Armando Benitez	2001
Innings Pitched	290.2	Tom Seaver	1970
Earned Runs	117	Roger Craig	1962
Lowest ERA*	1.53	Dwight Gooden	1985
Winning %	.870	David Cone (20–3)	1988

Pedro Feliciano hold the Mets single-season record for games played at the pitcher position with 92. Photo courtesy of David Ferry

Runs	137	Jay Hook	1962
Hits	261	Roger Craig	1962
Walks	116	Nolan Ryan	1971
Strikeouts	289	Tom Seaver	1971
Home Runs	35	Roger Craig	1962
Wild Pitches	18	Jack Hamilton	1966
Balks	10	David Cone	1988
Hit by Pitches	16	Pedro Astacio	2002

* = Among Qualifiers for season ERA title

Team Hitting

	TOTAL	YEAR
Games	164	1965
At-Bats	5,618	1996
Highest Average	.279	1999
Lowest Average	.219	1963
On Base %	.363	1999
Slugging %	.445	2006
Most Runs	853	1999

Fewest Runs	473	1968
Most Hits	1,553	1999
Fewest Hits&	1168	1963
Most Doubles	323	2006
Fewest Doubles&	156	1963
Most Triples	49	2009
Fewest Triples&	14	1999
Most Home Runs	200	2006
Fewest Home Runs&	61	1980
Extra-Base Hits	564	2006
Fewest Extra-Base Hits	284	1967
Total Bases	2,474	2006
Times On Base	2389	1999
RBI	814	1999
Walks	717	1999
Intentional Walks	88	1985
Most Strikeouts	1,202	1968
Fewest Strikeouts&	735	1974
Most Stolen Bases	200	2007
Fewest Stolen Bases	27	1973
Hit By Pitch	65	2001
Sacrifice Bunts	108	1973
Sacrifice Flies	59	1997
Grounded-DP	149	1999
Pinch-Hits	75	1993
Pinch-Hit Avg.	.363	1999

Team Pitching

	TOTAL	YEAR
Games	164	1965
Most Complete Games	53	1976
Fewest Complete Games&	2	2004, 2007
Most Shutouts	28	1969
Fewest Shutouts&	4	1962
Wins	108	1986
Losses	120	1962
Most Saves	51	1987
Fewest Saves&	10	1962
Most Earned Runs	801	1962
Fewest Earned Runs&	449	1968
Highest ERA	5.04	1962
Lowest ERA	2.72	1968
Most Runs	948	1962
Fewest Runs&	499	1968
Most Hits	1,577	1962
Fewest Hits&	1,217	1969
Most Walks	617	1999
Fewest Walks&	404	1988
Most Strikeouts	1,217	1990
Fewest Strikeouts&	717	1964,* 1983
Most Home Runs	192	1962
Fewest Home Runs&	78	1988

* = 162-game Schedule

METS OPPONENTS

SINGLE-GAME RECORDS

Individual Hitting

Plate Appearances	11	7 times, last by Bake McBride Ken Reitz, Ted Sizemore, Reggie Smith, and Joe Torre, Cardinals, 9/11/74
At-Bats	10	8 times, last by Terry Harper, Braves, 7/4/85
Most At-Bats, 0 Hits	9	Bob Aspromonte, Astros, 4/15/68 Manny Mota, Dodgers, 5/24/73 Tim Flannery, Padres, 8/26/80
Runs	4	51 times, last by Bryan LeHair, Cubs, 9/11/11
Hits	6	Willie Davis, Dodgers, 5/24/73 Bill Madlock, Cubs, 7/26/75 Skip Schumaker, Cardinals, 7/26/08
Doubles	4	Shannon Stewart, Blue Jays, 7/18/00
Triples	2	22 times, last by Nick Hundley, @ Padres, 8/16/11
Home Runs	3	12 times, twice by Willie McCovey last by Cody Ross, Marlins, 9/11/06
Extra-Base Hits	4	Willie Stargell, Pirates, 9/17/73 Shannon Stewart, Blue Jays, 7/18/00 Adam LaRoche, Braves, 9/15/09
Total Bases	14	Pete Rose, Reds, 4/29/78 (3 HRs, 2 singles)
Times On Base	6	19 times, last by Bryan Peterson, @ Marlins, 9/6/11
RBI	7	9 times, last by Cody Ross, Marlins, 9/11/06
Walks	5	Elrod Hendricks, Cubs, 9/16/72 Tim Foli, Expos, 9/7/73 Dale Murphy, Braves, 4/22/83 Ivan Rodriguez, Marlins, 4/8/03
Intentional Walks	3	Hank Aaron, Braves, 5/22/71 Ted Simmons, Cardinals, 9/30/77 Mike Matheny, Cardinals, 8/11/02 Carlos Delgado, Marlins, 9/22/05
Strikeouts	5	Delino DeShields, Expos, 9/17/91 Corey Patterson, Cubs, 9/19/02

Stolen Bases	4	Tim Raines, Expos, 10/2/83
		Vince Coleman, Cardinals,
		6/30/86
		Kevin Bass, Astros, 5/7/89
Caught Stealing	2	42 times
		last by Matt Lawton, Indians,
		6/15/04.
Hit By Pitch	3	Chase Utley, Phillies, 4/8/08
Sacrifice Bunts	4	Kris Benson, Pirates, 4/18/04
Sacrifice Flies	3	Candy Maldonado, Giants,
		8/29/87
Grounded-DP	3	Johnny Estrada, Phillies, 5/30/01

Team Hitting

Runs:	26	@ Phillies, 6/11/85
Hits:	27	@ Phillies, 6/11/85
Doubles:	10	@ Phillies, 6/11/85
Triples:	4	Pirates, 4/29/81
		@ Phillies, 9/19/84
Home Runs:	7	@ Cubs, 6/11/67
		@ Phillies, 9/8/98
RBI:	25	@ Phillies,6/11/85
Walks:	15	@ Cubs, 9/16/72
Strikeouts:	20	@ Cubs, 8/1/99
Stolen Bases:	8	@ Braves, 7/16/88

Individual Pitching

Innings Pitched	15	Chris Short, Phillies, 10/2/65
		(GM 2)
Earned Runs	10	Kevin Gross, Phillies, 8/5/87
		Drew Hall, Cubs, 8/16/87
		Brad Penny, Dodgers, 5/7/08
		Mitchell Boggs, Cardinals, 7/3/08
Runs	11	Mitchell Boggs, Cardinals, 7/3/08
Hits	16	Juan Marichal, Giants, 6/15/68
Walks	11	Sammy Ellis, Reds, 4/24/62
Strikeouts	19	Steve Carlton, Cardinals, 9/15/69
Fewest K's, CG	0	13 times, last by Tom Glavine,
		Braves, 6/15/93
Home Runs	5	Brett Tomko, Reds, 6/15/99
		Vicente Padilla, Phillies, 4/19/05
Wild Pitches	3	15 times, twice by J.R. Richard
		and Shawn Estes
		last by Zach Day, Expos, 9/19/03
Balks	3	Jim Gott, Pirates, 8/6/88
Stolen Bases	5	Charlie Puleo, Reds, 7/14/83
		Jaime Navarro, @ Cubs, 5/3/96
		Jake Peavy, Padres, 8/22/07
		Cole Hamels, 5/28/11
Pickoffs	2	13 times, twice by Randy Jones
		last by Mike Maroth, Cardinals,
		6/25/07
Hit by Pitches	3	6 times, last by Jamie Moyer,
		Phillies, 4/12/07

SINGLE-SEASON RECORDS

Batting Average (Minimum 45 at-bats)

Player	TM	AVG	Year
Rico Carty	MIL	.509 (29–57)	1964
Jim Davenport	SF	.500 (25–50)	1962
Matty Alou	PIT	.491 (27–55)	1967
Stan Musial	STL	.468 (22–47)	1962
Dave Collins	CIN	.468 (22–47)	1980
Jay Bell	PIT	.457 (21–46)	1993
Jeff Stone	PHI	.453 (24–53)	1984
Ron Fairly	LA	.450 (27–60)	1962
Pete Rose	PHI	.446 (29–65)	1979
Wes Parker	LA	.444 (20–45)	1970
Eric Yelding	HOU	.444 (20–45)	1990
Tony Gwynn	SD	.444 (20–45)	1993

Home Runs

Player	TM	HR	Year
Willie Stargell	PIT	10	1966
Richie Allen	PHI	10	1968
Hank Aaron	MIL	9	1962
Willie McCovey	SF	9	1963
Jim Ray Hart	SF	9	1966
Dave Kingman	CHI	9	1979
Willie Mays	SF	8	1962
Rico Carty	MIL	8	1964
Lee May	CIN	8	1968
Dave Kingman	CHI	8	1980
Ryan Howard	PHI	8	2006

RBI

Player	TM	BI	Year
Hank Aaron	MIL	28	1962
Rico Carty	MIL	27	1964
Dick Allen	PHI	25	1968
Ken Boyer	STL	23	1962
Frank Howard	LA	23	1962
Willie Mays	SF	23	1962
Deron Johnson	CIN	23	1965
Willie Stargell	PIT	23	1966
Ryne Sandberg	CHI	22	1990
Ryan Howard	PHI	21	2006

Doubles

Player	TM	2B	Year
Tim Wallach	MON	11	1985
Larry Parrish	MON	10	1979
Juan Samuel	PHI	10	1988
Marquis Grisson	MON	10	1992
Bobby Abreu	PHI	10	2002

Lou Brock	STL	9	1968
Paul O'Neill	CIN	9	1991
Brian McCann	ATL	9	2007
Martin Prado	ATL	9	2009
Gaby Sanchez	FLA	9	2010

Triples

Player	TM	3B	Year
Roberto Clemente	PIT	5	1965
Larry Bowa	PHI	5	1975
Neifi Perez	COL	5	1999
Tony Taylor	PHI	4	1963
Donn Clendenon	PIT	4	1965
Joe Morgan	HOU	4	1965
38 Players		3	

Stolen Bases

Player	TM	SB	Year
Tim Raines	MON	17	1983
Vince Coleman	STL	15	1987
Maury Wills	LA	14	1962
Vince Coleman	STL	14	1989
Von Hayes	PHI	12	1984
Juan Samuel	PHI	12	1984
Lou Brock	STL	11	1966
Davey Lopes	LA	11	1975
Ron LeFlore	MON	11	1980
Tim Raines	MON	11	1982
Vince Coleman	STL	11	1990
Tim Raines	MON	11	1990

Wins

Player	TM	W–L	Year
Jack Sanford	SF	5–0	1962
Jim Golden	HOU	5–0	1962
Bib Friend	PIT	5–0	1962
Jim Maloney	CIN	5–0	1963
Jim Bunning	PHI	5–0	1964
Don Drysdale	LA	5–0	1964
Bob Gibson	STL	5–0	1965
Juan Marichal	SF	5–0	1965
Gary Nolan	CIN	5–0	1967
Larry Christensen	PHI	5–0	1976
Don Drysdale	LA	5–1	1965

Strikeouts

Player	TM	SO	Year
Jim Maloney	CIN	53	1963
Steve Carlton	PHI	50	1982
Sandy Koufax	LA	48	1965
Steve Carlton	PHI	47	1972
Gary Nolan	CIN	47	1967

Bob Gibson	STL	46	1965
Ryan Dempster	FLA	43	2001
Jim Bunning	PHI	42	1965
Jim Maloney	CIN	42	1965
Jim Maloney	CIN	42	1966
Steve Carlton	STL	42	1969
Javier Vazquez	MON	42	2003

ERA
(Minimum 18 innings)

Player	TM	ERA	Year
Bob Friend	PIT	0.00 (26.1 IP)	1963
Ron Perranoski	LA	0.00 (18.1 IP)	1963
Bob Bruce	HOU	0.00 (19 IP)	1964
Vern Law	PIT	0.00 (27 IP)	1965
Tom Griffin	HOU	0.00 (25 IP)	1969
Phil Niekro	ATL	0.00 (18 IP)	1971
Don Sutton	LA	0.00 (18 IP)	1972
Claude Osteen	LA	0.00 (18 IP)	1972
Mario Soto	CIN	0.00 (18 IP)	1981
Juan Marichal	SF	0.20 (45 IP)	1965

CAREER HITTING RECORDS vs. METS

Batting Average
Minimum 200 At-Bats
At-Bat Total In Parenthesis

1.	Derek Jeter	.381	(320)
2.	Rico Carty	.380	(300)
3.	Tony Gwynn	.356	(739)
4.	Gene Richards	.355	(265)
5.	Todd Helton	.347	(331)
6.	Omar Infante	.345	(238)
7.	Matty Alou	.333	(513)
8.	Ken Griffey Sr.	.332	(358)
	Mark Grudzielanek	.332	(319)
10.	Tommy Davis	.331	(296)
11.	Clau. Washington	.330	(206)
12.	Greg Colbrunn	.325	(228)
13.	Tony Gonzalez	.323	(437)
14.	Gary Sheffield	.322	(475)
	Rondell White	.322	(227)
16.	Mike Easler	.321	(218)
17.	Roberto Clemente	.319	(656)
	Bob Watson	.319	(354)
19.	Chipper Jones	.318	(812)
20.	Bill White	.317	(416)
21.	Joe Torre	.316	(746)
	Mark Grace	.316	(618)
23.	Ted Simmons	.315	(635)
	Dave Winfield	.315	(305)
25.	Cristian Guzman	.314	(239)
26.	Ellis Valentine	.313	(278)
27.	Dick Groat	.312	(369)

28.	Vladimir Guerrero	.311	(360)
	Albert Pujols	.311	(280)
	Edgar Renteria	.311	(432)

On-Base Percentage (Minimum 225 Plate App.)
Plate App. In Parenthesis

1.	Rico Carty	.460	(347)
2.	Todd Helton	.446	(396)
3.	Ron Hunt	.435	(436)
	Derek Jeter	.435	(354)
5.	Gene Richards	.432	(303)
6.	Clau. Washington	.423	(241)
7.	Steve Ontiveros	.420	(255)
8.	Jim Gilliam	.419	(268)
9.	Eddie Mathews	.418	(368)
	Jason Thompson	.418	(299)

Slugging Average (Minimum 225 Plate App.)
Plate App. In Parenthesis

1.	Dave Kingman	.632	(295)
2.	Albert Pujols	.614	(321)
3.	Rico Carty	.607	(347)
4.	Willie McCovey	.597	(730)
5.	Willie Mays	.580	(624)
6.	Vladimir Guerrero	.578	(415)
	Clau. Washington	.578	(241)
7.	Todd Helton	.577	(396)
9.	Willie Stargell	.576	(938)
10.	Derek Jeter	.575	(354)

Home Runs

1.	Willie Stargell	60
2.	Mike Schmidt	49
3.	Chipper Jones	48
	Willie McCovey	48
5.	Hank Aaron	45
6.	Pat Burrell	42
7.	Willie Mays	39
8.	Barry Bonds	38
9.	Andre Dawson	36
10.	Billy Williams	34
11.	Dick Allen	33
12.	Dale Murphy	32
13.	Ryan Howard	31
14.	Tony Perez	30
	Gary Sheffield	30
	Joe Torre	30
17.	Andres Galarraga	28
	Sammy Sosa	28
	Jimmy Wynn	28
	Lee May	28
21.	Steve Garvey	27
	Ron Santo	27

	Johnny Bench	27
	Ryne Sandberg	27
25.	Ron Cey	26
	Gary Carter	26
	Andruw Jones	26
	Chase Utley	26

RBI

1.	Willie Stargell	182
2.	Mike Schmidt	162
3.	Chipper Jones	154
4.	Barry Bonds	140
5.	Andre Dawson	138
6.	Willie McCovey	134
7.	Hank Aaron	126
	Tim Wallach	126
9.	Ryne Sandberg	122
	Billy Williams	122
11.	Ron Santo	119
12.	Tony Perez	118
13.	Joe Torre	117
14.	Pete Rose	109
15.	Willie Mays	106
	Pat Burrell	106
17.	Lou Brock	105
	Ron Fairly	105
19.	Willie Davis	100
20.	Andres Galarraga	99
	Ted Simmons	99
22.	Rusty Staub	98
23.	Johnny Bench	96
	Ron Cey	96
	Greg Luzinski	96
	Dave Parker	96

Hits

1.	Pete Rose	396
2.	Lou Brock	289
3.	Tony Gwynn	263
4.	Chipper Jones	258
5.	Willie Davis	256
	Andre Dawson	256
7.	Larry Bowa	254
8.	Ryne Sandberg	248
9.	Willie Stargell	237
10.	Joe Torre	236
11.	Barry Bonds	232
	Mike Schmidt	232
13.	Billy Williams	230
14.	Tim Wallach	229
15.	Jimmy Rollins	211
16.	Roberto Clemente	209
17.	Ron Santo	207
18.	Hank Aaron	203

19.	Willie McGee	202
20.	Ted Simmons	200
21.	Mark Grace	195
	Don Kessinger	195
	Ozzie Smith	195
23.	Dave Parker	192
24.	Tony Perez	190

Doubles

1.	Pete Rose	64
2.	Lou Brock	55
3.	Barry Bonds	52
4.	Tony Gwynn	50
	Tim Wallach	50
6.	Andrew Dawson	48
7.	Willie Stargell	44
	Chipper Jones	44
9.	Roberto Clemente	43
10.	Bobby Abreu	42
	Andruw Jones	42
	Tony Perez	42

Triples

1.	Lou Brock	18
2.	Larry Bowa	14
3.	Roberto Clemente	12
	Pete Rose	12
5.	Delino DeShields	11
	Willie Mays	11
	Tony Perez	11
	Ron Santo	11
	Andy Van Slyke	11
10.	Donn Clendenon	10
	Willie Davis	10
	Tony Taylor	10
	Mitch Webster	10

Extra-Base Hits

1.	Willie Stargell	111
2.	Barry Bonds	99
3.	Chipper Jones	96
4.	Andre Dawson	93
	Mike Schmidt	93
6.	Pete Rose	87
7.	Willie McCovey	86
8.	Lou Brock	83
	Tony Perez	83
10.	Hank Aaron	80

Total Bases

1.	Pete Rose	517
2.	Willie Stargell	475

3.	Chipper Jones	454
4.	Mike Schmidt	431
5.	Andre Dawson	430
6.	Barry Bonds	416
7.	Lou Brock	410
8.	Billy Williams	381
9.	Ryne Sandberg	380
10.	Hank Aaron	376

Walks

1.	Mike Schmidt	169
2.	Joe Morgan	149
3.	Barry Bonds	148
4.	Chipper Jones	140
5.	Pete Rose	136
6.	Ron Santo	119
7.	Bobby Abreu	108
8.	Hank Aaron	107
9.	Bob Bailey	100
	Ozzie Smith	100
	Jimmy Wynn	100

Strikeouts

1.	Mike Schmidt	208
2.	Willie Stargell	206
3.	Lou Brock	191
4.	Andres Galarraga	176
5.	Andre Dawson	175
6.	Andruw Jones	153
7.	Pat Burrell	149
	Greg Luzinski	149
9.	Tim Wallach	142
10.	Ryne Sandberg	141

Stolen Bases

1.	Lou Brock	97
2.	Tim Raines	77
3.	Vince Coleman	64
4.	Joe Morgan	60
5.	Willie Davis	55
	Jimmy Rollins	55
7.	Maury Wills	54
8.	Omar Moreno	49
9.	Barry Bonds	46
	Brett Butler	46

CAREER PITCHING RECORDS vs. METS

Games

1.	Kent Tekulve	114
2.	Lee Smith	85
3.	Steve Carlton	76

4.	Gene Garber	75	
5.	Bruce Sutter	70	
	John Smoltz	70	
7.	Ron Reed	67	
	Phil Niekro	67	
9.	Greg Maddux	66	
10.	Steve Bedrosian	63	

Innings

1.	Steve Carlton	550.2
2.	Greg Maddux	428.1
3.	Phil Niekro	393.0
4.	Bob Gibson	385.0
5.	Juan Marichal	342.1
6.	Rick Reuschel	314.1
7.	Jerry Reuss	309.0
8.	John Smoltz	308.2
9.	Steve Rogers	283.0
10.	Don Sutton	278.2

Hits

1.	Steve Carlton	483
2.	Greg Maddux	392
3.	Phil Niekro	340
4.	Jerry Reuss	323
5.	Rick Reuschel	315
6.	Bob Gibson	306
7.	Juan Marichal	292
	John Smoltz	292
9.	Livan Hernandez	285
10.	Gaylord Perry	251

Earned Runs

1.	Steve Carlton	191
2.	Greg Maddux	160
3.	Phil Niekro	132
4.	Rick Reuschel	126
5.	Livan Hernandez	121
6.	John Smoltz	118
7.	Jerry Reuss	112
8.	Bob Gibson	110
9.	Bob Forsch	105
	Fergie Jenkins	105

ERA (Minimum 100 IP)
Innings Pitched in Parenthesis

1.	Sandy Koufax	1.44	(162.0)
2.	Bob Friend	1.61	(145.2)
3.	Gene Garber	1.69	(106.1)
	Alan Foster	1.76	(107.1)
5.	Jack Billingham	1.81	(134.1)
	J.R. Richard	1.90	(113.2)

7.	Claude Osteen	2.09	(228.1)
8.	Gary Nolan	2.09	(193.1)
9.	Juan Marichal	2.13	(342.1)
	Vern Law	2.13	(126.2)
11.	Pedro Martinez	2.21	(118.0)
12.	Danny Jackson	2.22	(117.1)
13.	Larry Jackson	2.24	(216.2)
14.	Zane Smith	2.26	(202.2)
	Don Drysdale	2.26	(262.1)
16.	Steve Avery	2.31	(136.1)
17.	Jack Sanford	2.32	(100.2)
18.	Bill Stoneman	2.37	(102.2)
19.	Ron Reed	2.39	(229.2)
20.	Tug McGraw	2.39	(101.2)

Best Winning Percentage (Min. 15 Decisions)
Record in Parenthesis

1.	Larry Jackson	.913	(21–2)
2.	Sandy Koufax	.895	(17–2)
3.	Bob Friend	.875	(14–2)
4.	Don Drysdale	.800	(24–6)
	Pedro Martinez	.800	(12–3)
6.	Juan Marichal	.765	(26–8)
	Darryl Kile	.765	(13–4)
8.	Mike Krukow	.759	(22–7)
9.	Gene Garber	.750	(12–4)
	Don Wilson	.750	(12–4)

Worst Winning Percentage (Min. 15 Decisions)
Record in Parenthesis

1.	Nelson Briles	.238	(5–16)
2.	Jose DeLeon	.250	(4–12)
3.	Brad Penny	.278	(5–13)
4.	Bill Singer	.294	(5–12)
5.	Ken Holtzman	.313	(5–11)
6.	Rick Reuschel	.359	(14–25)
7.	Tom Griffin	.400	(6–9)
	Mark Davis	.400	(6–9)
9.	Bryn Smith	.409	(9–13)
	Lee Smith	.409	(9–13)

Wins

1.	Greg Maddux	35
2.	Steve Carlton	30
3.	Bob Gibson	28
4.	Juan Marichal	26
5.	Phil Niekro	25
6.	Don Drysdale	24
7.	Mike Krukow	22
8.	Larry Jackson	21
	Burt Hooton	21
10.	Jim Maloney	19
11.	Jim Bunning	18

	John Smoltz	18
	Don Sutton	18
14.	Tom Glavine	17
	Fergie Jenkins	17
	Sandy Koufax	17
	Rick Wise	17
18.	John Denny	16
	Bob Knepper	16
	Claude Osteen	16

Losses

1.	Steve Carlton	36
2.	Rick Reuschel	25
3.	Jerry Reuss	21
4.	Greg Maddux	19
5.	Nelson Briles	16
	Livan Hernandez	16
7.	Bob Knepper	15
	Fergie Jenkins	15
	John Smoltz	15
10.	Burt Hooton	14
	Phil Niekro	14
	Bob Gibson	14
13.	Larry McWilliams	13
	Brad Penny	13
	Gaylord Perry	13
	Steve Rogers	13
	Bryn Smith	13
	Lee Smith	13
19.	8 Pitchers	12

Complete Games

1.	Bob Gibson	27
	Steve Carlton	27
3.	Juan Marichal	26
4.	Don Drysdale	18
5.	Phil Niekro	17
6.	Burt Hooton	14
	Fergie Jenkins	14
	Sandy Koufax	14
	Don Sutton	14
10.	Jim Bunning	13
	Greg Maddux	13
	Claude Osteen	13
	Jerry Reuss	13

Shutouts

1.	Juan Marichal	9
	Claude Osteen	9
3.	Jim Bunning	7
	Don Drysdale	7
5.	Larry Jackson	6
	Bob Knepper	6

7.	Burt Hooton	5
	Sandy Koufax	5
	Vern Law	5
10.	Steve Carlton	4
	John Denny	4
	Bob Gibson	4
	Bill Hands	4
	Jim Maloney	4
	Steve Rogers	4
	Tommie Sisk	4
	Bob Veale	4

Strikeouts

1.	Steve Carlton	464
2.	Bob Gibson	306
3.	Greg Maddux	291
4.	John Smoltz	280
5.	Phil Niekro	248
6.	Juan Marichal	241
7.	Jim Maloney	232
8.	Fergie Jenkins	222
9.	Gaylord Perry	201
10.	Don Sutton	201

Walks

1.	Steve Carlton	190
2.	Phil Niekro	145
3.	Bob Gibson	142
4.	Rick Reuschel	105
	Fern. Valenzuela	105
6.	Greg Maddux	103
7.	Jerry Reuss	97
	Steve Rogers	97
9.	Kevin Gross	89
10.	Jim Maloney	87

Saves

1.	Lee Smith	38
	Bruce Sutter	38
3.	Trevor Hoffman	33
4.	Rod Beck	24
	John Smoltz	24
6.	Tug McGraw	22
	Robb Nen	22
8.	Randy Myers	21
9.	Jeff Reardon	20
	Mariano Rivera	20

CATEGORY LEADERS

At Bats

YEAR-BY-YEAR AT-BAT LEADERS

1962
Frank Thomas	**571**
Charlie Neal	508
Felix Mantilla	466

1963
Ron Hunt	533
Jim Hickman	494
Frank Thomas	420

1964
Joe Christopher	543
Ron Hunt	475
Charley Smith	443

1965
Roy McMillan	528
Ed Kranepool	525
Charley Smith	499

1966
Ken Boyer	496
Cleon Jones	495
Ron Hunt	479

1967
Tommy Davis	**577**
Bud Harrelson	540
Ed Kranepool	469

1968
Cleon Jones	509
Ron Swoboda	450
Jerry Grote	404

1969
Tommie Agee	565
Cleon Jones	483
Wayne Garrett	400

1970
Tommie Age	**636**
Bud Harrelson	564
Cleon Jones	506

1971
Bud Harrelson	547
Cleon Jones	505
Tommie Agee	425

1972
Tommie Agee	422
Bud Harrelson	418
Cleon Jones	375

1973
Felix Millan	**638**
Rusty Staub	585
Wayne Garrett	504

1974
Rusty Staub	561
Wayne Garrett	522
Felix Millan	518

1975
Felix Millan	**676**
Rusty Staub	574
Del Unser	531

1976
Felix Millan	531
Dave Kingman	474
John Milner	415

1977
Lee Mazzilli	537
Lenny Randle	513
John Stearns	431

1978
Willie Montanez	609
Steve Henderson	587
Lee Mazzilli	542

1979
Frank Taveras	635
Lee Mazzilli	597
Joel Youngblood	590

1980
Lee Mazzilli	578
Frank Taveras	562
Joel Youngblood	514

1981
Hubie Brooks	358
Dave Kingman	353
Mookie Wilson	328

1982
Mookie Wilson	639
George Foster	550
Dave Kingman	535

1983
Mookie Wilson	638*
George Foster	601
Hubie Brooks	586

1984
Mookie Wilson	587
Hubie Brooks	561
Keith Hernandez	550

1985
Keith Hernandez	593
Gary Carter	555
Rafael Santana	529

1986
Keith Hernandez	551
Gary Carter	490
Ray Knight	486

1987
Kevin McReynolds	590
Keith Hernandez	587
Howard Johnson	554

1988
Kevin McReynolds	552
Darryl Strawberry	543
Howard Johnson	495

1989
Howard Johnson	571
Kevin McReynolds	545
Gregg Jefferies	508

1990
Gregg Jefferies	604
Howard Johnson	590
Darryl Strawberry	542

1991
Howard Johnson	564
Kevin McReynolds	522
Gregg Jefferies	486

1992
Eddie Murray	551
Bobby Bonilla	438
Dick Schofield	420

1993
Eddie Murray	610
Bobby Bonilla	502
Jeff Kent	496

1994
Jeff Kent	415
Jose Vizcaino	410
Bobby Bonilla	403

1995
Jose Vizcaino	509
Rico Brogna	495
Jeff Kent	472

1996
Lance Johnson	**682***
Bernard Gilkey	571
Todd Hundley	540

1997
John Olerud	524
Edgardo Alfonzo	518
Bernard Gilkey	518

1998
Edgar Alfonzo	557
John Olerud	557
Brian McRae	552

1999
Edgardo Alfonzo	628
Robin Ventura	588
John Olerud	581

2000
Derek Bell	546
Edgardo Alfonzo	544
Todd Zeile	544

2001
Todd Zeile	531
Mike Piazza	503
Rey Ordonez	461

2002
Roberto Alomar	590
Roger Cedeno	511
Edgardo Alfonzo	490

2003
Ty Wigginton	573
Roger Cedeno	484
Jason Phillips	403

2004
Mike Cameron	493
Kaz Matsui	460
Mike Piazza	455

2005
Jose Reyes	**696***
Carlos Beltran	582
David Wright	575

2006
Jose Reyes	647
David Wright	582
Carlos Delgado	524

2007
Jose Reyes	681
David Wright	604
Carlos Beltran	554

2008
Jose Reyes	688*
Dave Wright	626
Carlos Beltran	606

2009
David Weight	535
Daniel Murphy	508
Luis Castillo	486

2010
David Wright	587
Angel Pagan	579
Jose Reyes	563

2011
Jose Reyes	537
Angel Pagan	478
Jason Bay	444

Bold = Sets New Record
* = Led or tied for NL Lead

SINGLE SEASON AT-BAT LEADERS

	AB	PLAYER	YEAR
1.	696	Jose Reyes	2005
2.	688	Jose Reyes	2008
3.	682	Lance Johnson	1996
4.	681	Jose Reyes	2007
5.	676	Felix Millan	1975
6.	647	Jose Reyes	2006
7.	639	Mookie Wilson	1982
8.	638	Felix Millan	1973
		Mookie Wilson	1983
10.	636	Tommie Agee	1970
11.	635	Frank Taveras	1979
12.	628	Edgardo Alfonzo	1999
13	626	David Wright	2008
14.	610	Eddie Murray	1993
15.	609	Willie Montanez	1978
16.	606	Carlos Beltran	2008
17.	604	Gregg Jefferies	1990
		David Wright	2007
19.	601	George Foster	1983
20.	598	Carlos Delgado	2008
21.	597	Lee Mazzilli	1979
22.	593	Keith Hernandez	1985
23.	590	Roberto Alomar	2002
		Howard Johnson	1990
		Kevin McReynolds	1987
		Joel Youngblood	1979

CAREER AT-BATS LEADERS

	AB	PLAYER
1.	5,436	Ed Kranepool
2.	4,453	Jose Reyes
3.	4,390	Bud Harrelson
4.	4,223	Cleon Jones
5.	4,161	David Wright
6.	4,027	Mookie Wilson
7.	3,968	Howard Johnson
8.	3,903	Darryl Strawberry
9.	3,897	Edgardo Alfonzo
10.	3,881	Jerry Grote
11.	3,478	Mike Piazza
12.	3,164	Keith Hernandez
13.	3,133	Carlos Beltran
14.	3,013	Lee Mazzilli
15.	2,937	Rey Ordonez
16.	2,910	Kevin McReynolds
17.	2,817	Wayne Garrett
18.	2,679	John Stearns
19.	2,677	Felix Millan
20.	2,571	Rusty Staub
21.	2,549	Todd Hundley
22.	2,416	Tommie Agee
23.	2,400	Hubie Brooks
24.	2,389	George Foster
		John Milner

Batting Average

YEAR-BY-YEAR BATTING AVERAGE LEADERS
Minimum 502 Plate Appearances

1962
Felix Mantilla	**.275**
Frank Thomas	.266
Charlie Neal	.260
(Rich. Ashburn .306, 473 PA)	

1963
Ron Hunt	.272
Jim Hickman	.229
(Frank Thomas .260, 458 PA)	

1964
Ron Hunt	**.303**
Joe Christopher	.300

1965
Ed Kranepool	.253
Johnny Lewis	.245
Charley Smith	.244

1966
Ron Hunt	.288
Cleon Jones	.275
Ken Boyer	.266

1967
Tommy Davis	.302
Ed Kranepool	.269
Bud Harrelson	.254
(Ron Swoboda .281, 494 PA)	

1968
Cleon Jones	.297
Ron Swoboda	.242
(Jerry Grote .282, 454 PA)	

1969
Cleon Jones	**.340**
Tommie Agee	.271
(Art Shamsky .300, 349 PA)	

1970
Tommie Agee	.286
Cleon Jones	.277
Bud Harrelson	.243
(Art Shamsky .293, 458 PA)	

1971
Cleon Jones	.319
Bud Harrelson	.252
(Tommie Agee .285, 482 PA)	
(Ed Kranepool .280, 467 PA)	

1972
Strike Season, Min. 484 PA
(Rusty Staub .293, 277 PA)	
(Ed Kranepool .269, 368 PA)	
(Willie Mays .267 in 242 PA)	

1973
Felix Millan	.290
Rusty Staub	.279
Wayne Garrett	.256

1974
Cleon Jones	.282
Felix Millan	.268
Rusty Staub	.258

1975
Del Unser	.294
Felix Millan	.283
Rusty Staub	.282
(Ed Kranepool .323, 357 PA)	

1976
Felix Millan	.282
John Milner	.271
Dave Kingman	.238
(Joe Torre .310, 340 PA)	

1977
Lenny Randle	.304
Lee Mazzilli	.250
(S. Henderson .297, 398 PA)	

1978
Lee Mazzilli	.273
Steve Henderson	.266
John Stearns	.264

1979
Lee Mazzilli	.303
Joel Youngblood	.275
Richie Hebner	.268
(S. Henderson .306, 393 PA)	

1980
Steve Henderson	.290
Lee Mazzilli	.280
Frank Taveras	.279

1981
Strike Season, Min. 319 PA
Hubie Brooks	.307
Mookie Wilson	.271
Frank Taveras	.230

1982
Mookie Wilson	.279
George Foster	.247
Dave Kingman	.204
(John Stearns .293, 392 PA)	

1983
Mookie Wilson	.276
Hubie Brooks	.251
George Foster	.241
(K. Hernandez .306, 389 PA)	

1984
Keith Hernandez	.311
Hubie Brooks	.283
Mookie Wilson	.276
(Wally Backman .280, 499 PA)	

1985
Keith Hernandez	.309
Gary Carter	.281
Wally Backman	.273
(D. Strawberry .277, 470 PA)	

1986
Keith Hernandez	.310
Ray Knight	.298
Darryl Strawberry	.259
(Wally Backman .320, 440 PA)	
(Len Dykstra .295, 498 PA)	

1987
Keith Hernandez	.290
Darryl Strawberry	.284
Kevin McReynolds	.276
(Tim Teufel .308, 350 PA)	
(Mookie Wilson .299, 425 PA)	

1988
Kevin McReynolds	.288
Darryl Strawberry	.269
Howard Johnson	.230
(Wally Backman .303, 347 PA)	
(Mookie Wilson .296, 410 PA)	

1989

Howard Johnson	.287
Kevin McReynolds	.272
Gregg Jefferies	.258
(Dave Magadan .286, 429 PA)	

1990

Dave Magadan	.328
Gregg Jefferies	.283
Darryl Strawberry	.277
(Mackey Sasser .307, 288 PA)	

1991

Gregg Jefferies	.272
Howard Johnson	.259
Kevin McReynolds	.259
(Keith Miller .280, 304 PA)	

1992

Eddie Murray	.261
Bobby Bonilla	.249
(Chico Walker .308, 255 PA)	
(Dave Magadan .283, 379 PA)	

1993

Eddie Murray	.285
Jeff Kent	.270
Bobby Bonilla	.265
(Joe Orsulak .284, 441 PA)	

1994

Strike Season, Min. 350 PA

Jeff Kent	.292
Bobby Bonilla	.290
Jose Vizcaino	.256
(Rico Brogna .351, 138 PA)	

1995

Strike Season, Min. 446 PA

Rico Brogna	.289
Jose Vizcaino	.287
Jeff Kent	.278
(Bobby Bonilla .325, 351 PA)	
(Brett Butler .311, 418 PA)	

1996

Lance Johnson	.333
Bernard Gilkey	.317
Jose Vizcaino	.303

1997

Edgardo Alfonzo	.315
John Olerud	.294
Butch Huskey	.287

1998

John Olerud	**.354**
Edgardo Alfonzo	.278
Brian McRae	.264
(Mike Piazza .348, 446 PA)	

1999

Rickey Henderson	.315
Roger Cedeno	.313
Edgardo Alfonzo	.304

2000

Edgardo Alfonzo	.324
Mike Piazza	.324
Jay Payton	.291

2001

Mike Piazza	.300
Todd Zeile	.266
Rey Ordonez	.247
(Desi Relaford .302, 340 PA)	

2002

Edgardo Alfonzo	.308
Mike Piazza	.280
Roberto Alomar	.266
(Timo Perez .295, 481 PA)	

2003

Roger Cedeno	.267
Ty Wigginton	.255
(Jason Phillips .298, 453 PA)	

2004

Kaz Matsui	.272
Mike Piazza	.266
Mike Cameron	.231

2005

David Wright	.306
Cliff Floyd	.273
Jose Reyes	.273

2006

Paul Lo Duca	.318
David Wright	.311
Jose Reyes	.300

2007

David Wright	.325
Jose Reyes	.280
Carlos Delgado	.258
(Moises Alou .341 in 360 PA)	
(Shawn Green .290 in 490 PA)	

2008

David Wright	.302
Jose Reyes	.297
Carlos Beltran	.284

2009

David Wright	.307
Luis Castillo	.302
Daniel Murphy	.266
(Carlos Beltran .325, 357 PA)	
(Jeff Francoeur .311, 308 PA)	

2010

Angel Pagan	.290
David Wright	.283
Jose Reyes	.282

2011

Jose Reyes	.337*
Angel Pagan	.262
Jason Bay	.245

Bold = Sets New Team Record
* = Led or tied for NL Lead

SINGLE SEASON AVERAGE LEADERS

Minimum 502 Plate Appearances

	AVG	PLAYER	YEAR
1.	.354	John Olerud	1998
2.	.340	Cleon Jones	1969
3.	.337	Jose Reyes	2011
4.	.333	Lance Johnson	1996
5.	.328	Dave Magadan	1990
6.	.325	David Wright	2007
7.	.324	Edgardo Alfonzo	2000
		Mike Piazza	2000
9.	.319	Cleon Jones	1971
10.	.318	Paul Lo Duca	2006
11.	.317	Bernard Gilkey	1996
12.	.315	Edgardo Alfonzo	1997
		Rickey Henderson	1999
14.	.313	Roger Cedeno	1999
15.	.311	Keith Hernandez	1984
		David Wright	2006
17.	.310	Keith Hernandez	1986
18.	.309	Keith Hernandez	1985
19.	.308	Edgardo Alfonzo	2002
20.	.307	Hubie Brooks	1981
		David Wright	2009
22.	.306	David Wright	2005
23.	.304	Edgardo Alfonzo	1999
		Len Randle	1977
25.	.303	Ron Hunt	1964
		Lee Mazzilli	1979
		Mike Piazza	1999
		Jose Reyes	2007

Also

	.348	Mike Piazza, 446 PA, 1998
	.323	Ed Kranepool, 357 PA, 1975
	.320	Wally Backman, 440 PA, 1986

CAREER BATTING AVERAGE LEADERS

Minimum 2000 Plate Appearances

	AVG	PLAYER
1.	.315	John Olerud
2.	.300	David Wright
3.	.297	Keith Hernandez
4.	.296	Mike Piazza
5.	.292	Edgardo Alfonzo
		Dave Magadan
	.292	Jose Reyes
8.	.287	Steve Henderson
9.	.283	Wally Backman
10.	.281	Cleon Jones
11.	.280	Carlos Beltran
12.	.278	Felix Millan
13.	.276	Rusty Staub
		Mookie Wilson
15.	.274	Joel Youngblood
16.	.272	Kevin McReynolds
17.	.270	Bobby Bonilla
18.	.267	Hubie Brooks
		Carlos Delgado
20.	.264	Lee Mazzilli
21.	.263	Darryl Strawberry
22.	.262	Tommie Agee
23.	.261	Ed Kranepool
24.	.259	John Stearns
25.	.256	Jerry Grote

Complete Games

YEAR-BY-YEAR COMPLETE GAMES LEADERS

1962
Jay Hook	13
Roger Craig	13
Al Jackson	12

1963
Roger Craig	14
Al Jackson	11
Carl Willey	7

1964
Al Jackson	11
Tracy Stallard	11
Jack Fisher	8

1965
Jack Fisher	10
Al Jackson	7
Warren Spahn	5

1966
Jack Fisher	10
Dennis Ribant	10
Bob Shaw	7

1967
Tom Seaver	18
Jack Fisher	7
Don Cardwell	3
Bob Shaw	3

1968
Jerry Koosman	17
Tom Seaver	14
Don Cardwell	5

1969
Tom Seaver	*18*
Jerry Koosman	16
Gary Gentry	6

1970
Tom Seaver	19
Jim McAndrew	9
3 pitchers	5

1971
Tom Seaver	21
Gary Gentry	8

Ray Sadecki	5

1972
Tom Seaver	13
Jon Matlack	8
Jerry Koosman	4
Jim McAndrew	4

1973
Tom Seaver	18*
Jon Matlack	14
Jerry Koosman	12

1974
Jon Matlack	14
Jerry Koosman	13
Tom Seaver	12

1975
Tom Seaver	15
Jerry Koosman	11
Jon Matlack	8

1976
Jerry Koosman	17
Jon Matlack	16
Tom Seaver	13

1977
Nino Espinosa	7
Jerry Koosman	6
Jon Matlack	5
Tom Seaver	5

1978
Nino Espinosa	6
Craig Swan	5
Pat Zachry	5

1979
Craig Swan	10
6 pitchers	1

1980
Pat Zachry	7
Craig Swan	4
Mark Bomback	2

1981

Pete Falcone	3
Pat Zachry	3
Mike Scott	1

1982
Pete Falcone	3
4 pitchers	2

1983
Tom Seaver	5
Mike Torrez	5
Walt Terrell	4

1984
Dwight Gooden	7
Walt Terrell	3
Ron Darling	2

1985
Dwight Gooden	16*
Ed Lynch	6
Ron Darling	4

1986
Dwight Gooden	12
Bob Ojeda	7
Ron Darling	4

1987
Dwight Gooden	7
Sid Fernandez	3
Ron Darling	2

1988
Dwight Gooden	10
David Cone	8
Ron Darling	7

1989
David Cone	7
Sid Fernandez	6
Bob Ojeda	5

1990
Frank Viola	7
David Cone	6
Sid Fernandez	2
Dwight Gooden	2

1991
David Cone	5
Dwight Gooden	3
Frank Viola	3

1992
David Cone	7

Sid Fernandez	5
Dwight Gooden	3

1993
Dwight Gooden	7
Bret Saberhagen	4
Eric Hillman	3

1994
Bret Saberhagen	4
Jason Jacome	1
Bobby Jones	1
Pete Smith	1

1995
Bobby Jones	3
Bret Saberhagen	3
Bill Pulsipher	1

1996
Bobby Jones	3
Mark Clark	2
Pete Harnisch	2

1997
Bobby Jones	2
Rick Reed	2
3 pitchers	1

1998
Al Leiter	4
Rick Reed	2
3 pitchers	1

1999
Kenny Rogers	2
Al Leiter	1
Rick Reed	1
Masato Yoshii	1

2000
Mike Hampton	3
Al Leiter	2
Glendon Rusch	2
Jason Isringhausen	2

2001
Rick Reed	3
Kevin Appier	1
Glendon Rusch	1
Steve Trachsel	1

2002
Pedro Astacio	3
Al Leiter	2
3 pitchers	1

2003

Steve Trachsel	2
Al Leiter	1
23 pitchers	0

2004

Kris Benson	1
Tom Glavine	1
24 pitchers	0

2005

Pedro Martinez	4

Tom Glavine	2
Aaron Heilman	1
Jae Seo	1

2006

John Maine	1
Oliver Perez	1
Alay Soler	1
Steve Trachsel	1

2007

Tom Glavine	1
John Maine	1

(Neither CG went 9 Inn.)

2008

Johan Santana	3
Mike Pelfrey	2

2009

Nelson Figueroa	1
Livan Hernandez	1
Pat Misch	1

2010

Johan Santana	4

R.A. Dickey	2
Jonathon Niese	2

2011

Mike Pelfrey	2
Miguel Batista	1
R.A. Dickey	1
Chris Capuano	1
Dillon Gee	1

Bold = Sets Team Record
Ital. = Ties Team Record
*= Leads or Tied For NL

Single Season Complete Games Leaders

	CG	Player	Year
1.	21	Tom Seaver	1971
2.	19	Tom Seaver	1970
3.	18	Tom Seaver	1967, 1969, 1973
6.	17	Jerry Koosman	1968, 1976
8.	16	Dwight Gooden	1985
		Jerry Koosman	1969
		Jon Matlack	1976
11.	15	Tom Seaver	1975
12.	14	Roger Craig	1963
		Jon Matlack	1973, 1974
		Tom Seaver	1968
16.	13	Roger Craig	1962
		Jay Hook	1962
		Jerry Koosman	1974
		Tom Seaver	1972, 1976
21.	12	Dwight Gooden	1986
		Al Jackson	1962
		Jerry Koosman	1973
		Tom Seaver	1974
25.	11	Al Jackson	1963, 1964
		Jerry Koosman	1975
		Tracy Stallard	1964

Career Complete Games Leaders

	CG	Player
1.	171	Tom Seaver
2.	108	Jerry Koosman
3.	67	Dwight Gooden
4.	65	Jon Matlack
5.	41	Al Jackson
6.	35	Jack Fisher
7.	34	David Cone
8.	27	Roger Craig
9.	25	Ron Darling
		Craig Swan
11.	23	Sid Fernandez
12.	22	Gary Gentry
13.	20	Pat Zachry
14.	19	Jim McAndrew
15.	17	Bob Ojeda
16.	16	Jay Hook
		Tracy Stallard
18.	13	Nino Espinosa
		Nolan Ryan
		Ray Sadecki
21.	12	Don Cardwell
		Bret Saberhagen
		Frank Viola
24.	11	Dennis Ribant
25.	10	Bobby Jones
		Al Leiter
		Bob Shaw

Doubles

YEAR-BY-YEAR DOUBLES LEADERS

1962
Frank Thomas	23
Jim Hickman	18
Felix Mantilla	17

1963
Ron Hunt	28
Jim Hickman	21
3 Players	12

1964
Joe Christopher	26
Ed Kranepool	19
Ron Hunt	19

1965
Ed Kranepool	24
Charley Smith	20
Roy McMillan	19

1966
Ken Boyer	*28*
Ron Hunt	19
Cleon Jones	16

1967
Tommy Davis	32
Ed Kranepool	17
Ron Swoboda	17

1968
Cleon Jones	29
Jerry Grote	18
Ron Swoboda	14
Art Shamsky	14

1969
Cleon Jones	25
Tommie Agee	23
Ken Boswell	14

1970
Tommie Agee	30
Cleon Jones	25
Art Shamsky	19

1971
Jerry Grote	25
Cleon Jones	24
Ken Boswell	20
Ed Kranepool	20

1972
Tommie Agee	23
Duffy Dyer	17
3 Players	15

1973
Rusty Staub	36
Felix Millan	23
Wayne Garrett	20

1974
Cleon Jones	23
Rusty Staub	22
John Milner	19

1975
Felix Millan	37
Rusty Staub	30
Dave Kingman	22

1976
Felix Millan	25
John Milner	25
Ed Kranepool	17

1977
John Stearns	25
Lee Mazzilli	24
Lenny Randle	22

1978
Willie Montanez	32
Steve Henderson	30
Lee Mazzilli	28

1979
Joel Youngblood	*37*
Lee Mazzilli	34
John Stearns	29

1980
Lee Mazzilli	31
Frank Taveras	27
Joel Youngblood	26

1981
Hubie Brooks	21
Lee Mazzilli	14
Doug Flynn	12
John Stearns	12

1982
John Stearns	25
Mookie Wilson	25
George Foster	23

1983
Mookie Wilson	25
George Foster	19
Hubie Brooks	18

1984
Keith Hernandez	31
Mookie Wilson	28
Darryl Strawberry	27

1985
Keith Hernandez	34
Wally Backman	24
George Foster	24

1986
Keith Hernandez	34
Len Dykstra	27
Darryl Strawberry	27

1987
Len Dykstra	*37*
Kevin McReynolds	32
Darryl Strawberry	32

1988
Kevin McReynolds	30
Darryl Strawberry	27
Howard Johnson	21

1989
Howard Johnson	41
Gregg Jefferies	28
Darryl Strawberry	26

1990
Gregg Jefferies	40*
Howard Johnson	37
Dave Magadan	28

1991
Howard Johnson	34
Kevin McReynolds	32
Dave Magadan	23

1992
Eddie Murray	37
Bobby Bonilla	23
Howard Johnson	19

1993
Eddie Murray	28
Jeff Kent	24
Bobby Bonilla	21

1994
Bobby Bonilla	24
Jeff Kent	24
David Segui	17

1995
Rico Brogna	27
Bobby Bonilla	25
Jeff Kent	22

1996
Bernard Gilkey	**44**
Todd Hundley	32
Lance Johnson	31

1997
John Olerud	34
Bernard Gilkey	31
Carl Everett	28

1998
Brian McRae	36
John Olerud	36
Mike Piazza	33

1999
Edgardo Alfonzo	41
John Olerud	39
Robin Ventura	38

2000
Edgardo Alfonzo	40
Todd Zeile	36
Derek Bell	31

2001
Mike Piazza	29
Desi Relaford	27
Todd Zeile	25

2002
Timo Perez	27
Edgardo Alfonzo	26
Rey Ordonez	25

2003

Ty Wigginton	36
Roger Cedeno	25
Cliff Floyd	25
Jason Phillips	25

2004

Kaz Matsui	32
Mike Cameron	30
Cliff Floyd	26

2005

David Wright	42
Carlos Beltran	34
Jose Reyes	24

2006

David Wright	40
Paul Lo Duca	39
Carlos Beltran	38

2007

David Wright	42
Jose Reyes	36
Carlos Beltran	33

2008

David Wright	42
Carlos Beltran	40
Jose Reyes	37

2009

David Wright	39
Daniel Murphy	38
Carlos Beltran	22
Angel Pagan	22

2010

David Wright	36
Ike Davis	33
Angel Pagan	31

2011

Jose Reyes	31
Carlos Beltran	30
Justin Turner	30

Bold = Sets Team Record
Ital. = Tied team Record
*= Led or Tied For NL Lead

Single-Season Doubles Leaders

	2B	PLAYER	YEAR
1.	44	Bernard Gilkey	1996
2.	42	David Wright	2005, 2007, 2008
5.	41	Edgardo Alfonzo	1999
		Howard Johnson	1989
7.	40	Edgardo Alfonzo	2000
		Gregg Jefferies	1990
		David Wright	2006
		Carlos Beltran	2008
11.	39	Paul Lo Duca	2006
		John Olerud	1999
		David Wright	2009
14.	38	Carlos Beltran	2006
		Daniel Murphy	2009
		Robin Ventura	1999
17.	37	Lenny Dykstra	1987
		Howard Johnson	1990
		Felix Millan	1975
		Eddie Murray	1992
		Jose Reyes	2008
		Joel Youngblood	1979
23.	36	Brian McRae	1998
		John Olerud	1998
		Rusty Staub	1973
		Ty Wigginton	2003
		Todd Zeile	2000
		Jose Reyes	2007
		David Wright	2010

Career Doubles Leaders

	2B	PLAYER
1.	281	David Wright
2.	225	Ed Kranepool
6.	222	Jose Reyes
3.	214	Howard Johnson
4.	212	Edgardo Alfonzo
9.	208	Carlos Beltran
5.	193	Mike Piazza
7.	187	Darryl Strawberry
8.	182	Cleon Jones
10.	170	Mookie Wilson
11.	159	Keith Hernandez
12.	153	Kevin McReynolds
13.	152	John Stearns
14.	148	Lee Mazzilli
15.	143	Jerry Grote
16.	130	Rusty Staub
17.	123	Bud Harrelson
18.	118	Todd Hundley
19.	115	Rey Ordonez
20.	111	Felix Millan
21.	110	Dave Magadan
22.	109	John Olerud
23.	108	Joel Youngblood
24.	107	Tommie Agee
25.	104	Lenny Dykstra
25.	100	John Milner

Earned Runs

YEAR-BY-YEAR EARNED RUN LEADERS

1962
Roger Craig	117
Jay Hook	115
Al Jackson	113

1963
Al Jackson	100
Roger Craig	99
Tracy Stallard	81

1964
Jack Fisher	107*
Al Jackson	101
Tracy Stallard	95

1965
Jack Fisher	111*
Al Jackson	99
Warren Spahn	61

1966
Jack Fisher	94
Bob Shaw	73
Dennis Ribant	67

1967
Jack Fisher	115*
Tom Seaver	77
Don Cardwell	47
Bob Shaw	47

1968
Tom Seaver	68
Jerry Koosman	61
Don Cardwell	59

1969
Gary Gentry	89
Tom Seaver	67
Jerry Koosman	61

1970
Tom Seaver	91
Gary Gentry	77
Jerry Koosman	74

1971
Gary Gentry	73
Nolan Ryan	57
Jerry Koosman	56
Tom Seaver	56

1972
Tom Seaver	85
Jerry Koosman	75
Gary Gentry	73

1973
Jon Matlack	86
Jerry Koosman	83
Tom Seaver	67

1974
Jerry Koosman	99
Tom Seaver	84
Jon Matlack	71

1975
Jerry Koosman	91
Jon Matlack	86
Tom Seaver	74

1976
Jon Matlack	86
Tom Seaver	78
Jerry Koosman	74

1977
Jerry Koosman	88
Jon Matlack	79
Nino Espinosa	76

1978
Nino Espinosa	107*
Jerry Koosman	98
Mike Bruhert	71

1979
Craig Swan	92
Pete Falcone	85
Kevin Kobel	63

1980
Pete Falcone	79
Ray Burris	76
Mark Bomback	74

1981
Pat Zachry	64
Mike Scott	59
Greg Harris	34

1982
Charlie Puleo	85
Mike Scott	84
Pete Falcone	73

1983
Mike Torrez	108*
Tom Seaver	91
Ed Lynch	83

1984
Ron Darling	87
Walt Terrell	84
Dwight Gooden	73

1985
Ron Darling	80
Ed Lynch	73
Sid Fernandez	53

1986
Sid Fernandez	80
Dwight Gooden	79
Ron Darling	74

1987
Ron Darling	99
Sid Fernandez	66
Dwight Gooden	64

1988
Dwight Gooden	88
Ron Darling	87
Sid Fernandez	63

1989
David Cone	86
Ron Darling	85
Bob Ojeda	74

1990
Dwight Gooden	99
David Cone	76
Frank Viola	74

1991
Frank Viola	102
David Cone	85
Dwight Gooden	76

1992
Dwight Gooden	84
Sid Fernandez	65
David Cone	63

1993
Frank Tanana	91
Pete Schourek	85
Dwight Gooden	80

1994
Pete Smith	81
Bobby Jones	56
Bret Saberhagen	54

1995
Bobby Jones	91
Dave Mlicki	76
Bill Pulsipher	56

1996
Bobby Jones	96
Pete Harnisch	91
Jason Isringhausen	91

1997
Dave Mlicki	86
Bobby Jones	78
Mark Clark	67
Rick Reed	67

1998
Bobby Jones	88
Rick Reed	82
Masato Yoshii	75

1999
Al Leiter	100
Orel Hershiser	91
Masato Yoshii	85

2000
Bobby Jones	87
Glendon Rusch	85
Rick Reed	84

2001
Glendon Rusch	92
Steve Trachsel	86
Kevin Appier	82

2002
Pedro Astacio	102
Jeff D'Amico	80
Al Leiter	79

2003

Tom Glavine	92
Steve Trachsel	86
Al Leiter	80
Jae Seo	80

2004

Steve Trachsel	90
Tom Glavine	85
Jae Seo	64

2005

Tom Glavine	83
Kris Benson	80
Victor Zambrano	77

2006

Steve Trachsel	91
Tom Glavine	84
Pedro Martinez	66

2007

Tom Glavine	99
John Maine	83
Oliver Perez	70

2008

Oliver Perez	91
Mike Pelfrey	83
Pedro Martinez	68

2009

Mike Pelfrey	103
Livan Hernandez	83
Tim Redding	72

2010

Mike Pelfrey	83
Jonathon Niese	81
Johan Santana	66

2011

Mike Pelfrey	102
Chris Capuano	94
Dillon Gee	79

Bold = Sets Team Record
* = Leads or Tied NL

Single Season Earned Run Leaders

	ER	Player		Year
1.	117	Roger Craig		1962
2.	115	Jack Fisher		1967
		Jay Hook		1962
4.	113	Al Jackson		1962
5.	111	Jack Fisher		1965
6.	108	Mike Torrez		1983
7.	107	Nino Espinosa		1978
		Jack Fisher		1964
9.	103	Mike Pelfrey		2009
10.	102	Pedro Astacio		2002
		Frank Viola		1991
	97	Mike Pelfrey		2011
13.	101	Al Jackson		1964
14.	100	Al Jackson		1963
		Al Leiter		1999
16.	99	Roger Craig		1963
		Ron Darling		1987
		Dwight Gooden		1990
		Al Jackson		1965
		Jerry Koosman		1974
		Tom Glavine		2007
22.	98	Jerry Koosman		1978
23.	96	Bobby Jones		1996
24.	95	Tracy Stallard		1964
25.	94	Jack Fisher		1966
	94	Chris Capuano		2011

Career Earned Runs Leaders

	ER	Player
1.	875	Jerry Koosman
2.	870	Tom Seaver
3.	747	Dwight Gooden
4.	630	Ron Darling
5.	558	Bobby Jones
6.	553	Sid Fernandez
7.	517	Al Leiter
8.	508	Craig Swan
9.	488	Jon Matlack
10.	464	Al Jackson
11.	443	Tom Glavine
12.	435	Steve Trachsel
13.	429	Mike Pelfrey
14.	427	Jack Fisher
15.	421	David Cone
16.	361	Rick Reed
17.	312	Gary Gentry
18.	310	Ed Lynch
19.	299	Pat Zachry
20.	287	Jim McAndrew
21.	279	Tug McGraw
22.	272	Oliver Perez
23.	265	Bob Ojeda
24.	264	Pete Falcone
25.	251	John Maine

Earned Run Average

YEAR-BY-YEAR ERA LEADERS
Minimum 162 Innings

1962
Al Jackson	**4.40**
Roger Craig	4.51
Jay Hook	4.82

1963
Carl Willey	**3.10**
Roger Craig	3.78
Al Jackson	3.96

1964
Galen Cisco	3.62
Tracy Stallard	3.79
Jack Fisher	4.23

1965
Jack Fisher	3.94
Al Jackson	4.34
(Tug McGraw 3.32, 97.2 IP)	

1966
Dennis Ribant	3.20
Jack Fisher	3.68
Bob Shaw	3.92

1967
Tom Seaver	**2.76**
Jack Fisher	4.70

1968
Jerry Koosman	**2.08**
Tom Seaver	2.20
Dick Selma	2.76

1969
Tom Seaver	2.21
Jerry Koosman	2.28
Gary Gentry	3.43

1970
Tom Seaver	2.82*
Jerry Koosman	3.14
Jim McAndrew	3.56

1971
Tom Seaver	**1.76***
Ray Sadecki	2.92
Jerry Koosman	3.04
(Tug McGraw, 1.70, 111 IP)	

1972
Strike Season, Min. 156 IP
Jon Matlack	2.32
Jim McAndrew	2.80
Tom Seaver	2.92
(Tug McGraw 1.70, 106 IP)	

1973
Tom Seaver	2.08*
Jerry Koosman	2.84
Jon Matlack	3.20

1974
Jon Matlack	2.41
Tom Seaver	3.20
Jerry Koosman	3.36

1975
Tom Seaver	2.38
Jon Matlack	3.38
Jerry Koosman	3.42

1976
Tom Seaver	2.59
Jerry Koosman	2.69
Jon Matlack	2.95

1977
Nino Espinosa	3.42
Jerry Koosman	3.49
Jon Matlack	4.21

1978
Craig Swan	2.43*
Jerry Koosman	3.75
Nino Espinosa	4.73
(Pat Zachry 3.33, 138 IP)	

1979
Craig Swan	3.29
Pete Falcone	4.16
(Kevin Kobel 3.51, 161.2 IP)	

1980
Pat Zachry	3.01
Ray Burris	4.02
Mark Bomback	4.09

1981
Strike Season, Min. 103 IP
Mike Scott	3.90
Pat Zachry	4.14

1982
Craig Swan	3.35
Pete Falcone	3.84
Charlie Puleo	4.47
(Ed Lynch 3.55, 139.1 IP)	

1983
Tom Seaver	3.55
Ed Lynch	4.28
Mike Torrez	4.37
(Jesse Orosco 1.47, 110 IP)	

1984
Dwight Gooden	2.60
Walt Terrell	3.52
Ron Darling	3.81
(Doug Sisk 2.09, 77.2 IP)	

1985
Dwight Gooden	**1.53***
Sid Fernandez	2.80
Ron Darling	2.90

1986
Bob Ojeda	2.57
Ron Darling	2.81
Dwight Gooden	2.84

1987
Dwight Gooden	3.21
Sid Fernandez	3.81
Ron Darling	4.29
(Terry Leach 3.22, 131.3 IP)	

1988
David Cone	2.22
Bob Ojeda	2.88
Sid Fernandez	3.03

1989
Sid Fernandez	2.83
Bob Ojeda	3.47
David Cone	3.52
Ron Darling	3.52

1990
Frank Viola	2.67
David Cone	3.23
Sid Fernandez	3.46

1991
David Cone	3.29
Dwight Gooden	3.60
Frank Viola	3.97
(Jeff Innis 2.66, 84.2 IP)	

1992
Sid Fernandez	2.73
David Cone	2.88
Dwight Gooden	3.67

1993
Dwight Gooden	3.45
Frank Tanana	4.48
(Sid Fernandez 2.93, 119.2 IP)	

1994
Strike Year, Min. 113 IP
Bret Saberhagen	2.74
Bobby Jones	3.15
Pete Smith	5.15

1995
Strike Year, Min. 144 IP
Bobby Jones	4.19
Dave Mlicki	4.26
(Jason Isringhausen 2.81, 93 IP)	
(Bret Saberhagen 3.35, 110 IP)	

1996
Mark Clark	3.43
Pete Harnisch	4.21
Bobby Jones	4.42

1997
Rick Reed	2.89
Bobby Jones	3.63
Dave Mlicki	4.00

1998
Al Leiter	2.47
Rick Reed	3.48
Masato Yoshii	3.93

1999
Al Leiter	4.23
Masato Yoshii	4.40
Orel Hershiser	4.58

2000
Mike Hampton	3.14
Al Leiter	3.20
Glendon Rusch	4.01

2001

Al Leiter	3.31
Kevin Appier	3.57
Steve Trachsel	4.46
(Rick Reed 3.48, 134.2)	

2002

Steve Trachsel	3.37
Al Leiter	3.48
Pedro Astacio	4.79

2003

Steve Trachsel	3.78
Jae Seo	3.82
Al Leiter	3.99

2004

Al Leiter	3.21
Tom Glavine	3.60
Steve Trachsel	4.00

2005

Pedro Martinez	2.82
Tom Glavine	3.53
Kris Benson	4.13
(Jae Seo 2.59, 90.1 IP)	
(Aaron Heilman 3.17, 108 IP)	

2006

Tom Glavine	3.82
Steve Trachsel	4.97
(John Maine 3.60, 90 IP)	

2007

Oliver Perez	3.56
John Maine	3.91
Tom Glavine	4.45

2008

Johan Santana	2.53*
Mike Pelfrey	3.72
Oliver Perez	4.22

2009

Johan Santana	3.13
Mike Pelfrey	5.03

2010

R.A. Dickey	2.84
Johan Santana	2.98
Mike Pelfrey	3.66

2011

R.A. Dickey	3.28
Chris Capuano	4.55
Mike Pelfrey	4.74

Bold = Sets Team Record
* = Leads or Tied For NL

Single Season ERA Leaders

Minimum 162 Innings

	ERA	Player	Year
1.	1.53	Dwight Gooden	1985
2.	1.76	Tom Seaver	1971
3.	2.08	Jerry Koosman	1968
		Tom Seaver	1973
5.	2.20	Tom Seaver	1968
6.	2.21	Tom Seaver	1969
7.	2.22	David Cone	1988
8.	2.28	Jerry Koosman	1969
9.	2.32	Jon Matlack	1972
10.	2.38	Tom Seaver	1975
11.	2.41	Jon Matlack	1974
12.	2.43	Craig Swan	1978
13.	2.47	Al Leiter	1998
14	2.53	Johan Santana	2008
15.	2.57	Bob Ojeda	1986
16.	2.59	Tom Seaver	1976
17.	2.60	Dwight Gooden	1984
18.	2.67	Frank Viola	1990
19.	2.69	Jerry Koosman	1976
20.	2.73	Sid Fernandez	1992
21.	2.74	Bret Saberhagen	1994
22.	2.76	Tom Seaver	1967
		Dick Selma	1968
24.	2.80	Sid Fernandez	1985
25.	2.81	Ron Darling	1986

Career ERA Leaders

Minimum 500 Innings

	ERA	Player
1.	2.57	Tom Seaver
2.	2.73	Jesse Orosco
3.	2.85	Johan Santana
4.	3.03	Jon Matlack
5.	3.09	Jerry Koosman
6.	3.10	John Franco
		Dwight Gooden
8.	3.12	Bob Ojeda
9.	3.13	David Cone
10.	3.14	Sid Fernandez
11.	3.16	Bret Saberhagen
12.	3.17	Tug McGraw
13.	3.31	Frank Viola
14.	3.36	Ray Sadecki
15.	3.42	Al Leiter
16.	3.50	Ron Darling
17.	3.54	Jim McAndrew
18.	3.56	Gary Gentry
19.	3.58	Nolan Ryan
20.	3.63	Pat Zachry
21.	3.66	Rick Reed
22.	3.72	Craig Swan
23.	3.82	Ed Lynch
24.	3.91	Pete Falcone
25.	3.97	Tom Glavine

Games Pitched

YEAR-BY-YEAR GAMES PITCHED LEADERS

1962
Craig Anderson	50
Roger Craig	42
Ken Mackenzie	42

1963
Larry Bearnarth	58
Galen Cisco	51
Roger Craig	46

1964
Bill Wakefield	62
Larry Bearnarth	44
Willard Hunter	41

1965
Jack Fisher	43
Larry Bearnarth	40
Frank Lary	35

1966
Jack Hamilton	57
Rob Gardner	41
Dennis Ribant	39

1967
Ron Taylor	50
Don Shaw	40
Jack Fisher	39

1968
Ron Taylor	58
Cal Koonce	55
Tom Seaver	36

1969
Ron Taylor	59
Tug McGraw	42
Cal Koonce	40

1970
Tug McGraw	57
Ron Taylor	57
Tom Seaver	37

1971
Danny Frisella	53
Tug McGraw	51
Ron Taylor	45

1972
Tug McGraw	54
Danny Frisella	39
Tom Seaver	35

1973
Tug McGraw	60
Harry Parker	38
Tom Seaver	36

1974
Bob Miller	58
Tug McGraw	41
Bob Apodoca	35
Jerry Koosman	35

1975
Rick Baldwin	54
Bob Apodaca	46
Tom Seaver	36
Jerry Koosman	36

1976
Skip Lockwood	56
Bob Apodaca	43
Jon Matlack	35
Tom Seaver	35

1977
Skip Lockwood	63
Bob Apodaca	59
Bob Myrick	44

1978
Skip Lockwood	57
Dale Murray	53
Jerry Koosman	38

1979
Dale Murray	58
Neil Allen	50
Ed Glynn	46

1980
Jeff Reardon	61
Neil Allen	59
Tom Hausman	55

1981
Neil Allen	43
Pete Falcone	35
Ray Searage	26

1982
Jesse Orosco	54
Neil Allen	50
Ed Lynch	43

1983
Doug Sisk	67
Jesse Orosco	62
Carlos Diaz	54

1984
Jesse Orosco	60
Doug Sisk	50
Brent Gaff	47

1985
Roger McDowell	62
Jesse Orosco	54
Doug Sisk	42

1986
Roger McDowell	75
Jesse Orosco	58
Doug Sisk	41

1987
Jesse Orosco	58
Roger McDowell	56
Doug Sisk	55

1988
Roger McDowell	62
Randy Myers	55
Terry Leach	52

1989
Randy Myers	65
Don Aase	49
Rick Aguilera	36

1990
John Franco	55
Alejandro Pena	52
Bob Ojeda	38
Wally Whitehurst	38

1991
Jeff Innis	69
John Franco	52
Alejandro Pena	44

1992
Jeff Innis	76
Anthony Young	52
Wally Whitehurst	44

1993
Jeff Innis	67
Mike Maddux	58
Pete Schourek	41

1994
John Franco	47
Roger Mason	41
Josias Manzanillo	37

1995
Jerry Dipoto	58
Doug Henry	51
John Franco	48

1996
Doug Henry	58
Jerry Dipioto	57
John Franco	51
Dave Mlicki	51

1997
Greg McMichael	73
John Franco	59
Cory Lidle	54

1998
Dennis Cook	73
Turk Wendell	66
John Franco	61

1999
Turk Wendell	80
Armando Benitez	77
Dennis Cook	71

2000
Turk Wendell	77
Armando Benitez	76
Dennis Cook	68

2001
Armando Benitez	73
John Franco	58
Rick White	55

2002
Mark Guthrie	68
Scott Strickland	68
Armando Benitez	62

2003

David Weathers	77
Mike Stanton	50
Armando Benitez	45

2004

Mike Stanton	83
Braden Looper	71
Ricky Bottalico	60

2005

Roberto Hernandez	67
Braden Looper	60
Aaron Heilman	53

2006

Aaron Heilman	74
Chad Bradford	70
Billy Wagner	70

2007

Aaron Heilman	81
Pedro Feliciano	78
Scott Schoeneweis	70

2008

Pedro Feliciano	86*
Joe Smith	82
Aaron Heilman	78

2009

Pedro Feliciano	88*
Sean Green	79
Francisco Rodriguez	70

2010

Pedro Feliciano	92*
Hisanori Takahashi	53
Elmer Dessens	53
Frankc Rodriguez	53

2011

Tim Byrdak	72
Pedro Beato	60
Bobby Parnell	60

Bold = Sets Team Record
Ital. = Ties Team Record
*= Leads or Tied For NL

Single Season Games Pitched Leaders

	GP	Player	Year
1	92	Pedro Feliciano	2010
2.	88	Pedro Feliciano	2009
3.	86	Pedro Feliciano	2008
4.	83	Mike Stanton	2004
5.	82	Joe Smith	2008
6.	81	Aaron Heilman	2007
7.	80	Turk Wendell	1999
8.	79	Sean Green	2009
9.	78	Pedro Feliciano	2007
		Aaron Heilman	2008
11.	77	Armando Benitez	1999
		Dave Weathers	2003
		Turk Wendell	2000
14.	76	Armando Benitez	2000
		Jeff Innis	1992
16.	75	Roger McDowell	1986
17.	74	Aaron Heilman	2006
18.	73	Armando Benitez	2001
		Dennis Cook	1998
		Greg McMichael	1997
		Scott Schoeneweis	2008
22.	72	Tim Byrdak	2011
23.	71	Dennis Cook	1999
		Braden Looper	2004
		Dave Weathers	2002

Career Games Pitched Leaders

	GP	Player
1.	695	John Franco
2.	459	Pedro Feliciano
3.	401	Tom Seaver
4.	376	Jerry Koosman
5.	372	Jesse Orosco
6.	361	Tug McGraw
7.	333	Armando Benitez
8.	305	Dwight Gooden
	305	Aaron Heilman
10.	288	Jeff Innis
11.	285	Turk Wendell
12.	280	Roger McDowell
13.	269	Ron Taylor
14.	263	Doug Sisk
15.	257	Ron Darling
16.	255	Dennis Cook
		Sid Fernandez
18.	229	Craig Swan
19.	227	Skip Lockwood
20.	223	Neil Allen
21.	213	Al Leiter
22.	203	Jon Matlack
23.	193	Bobby Jones
24.	187	David Cone
25.	185	Randy Myers

Games Played

YEAR-BY-YEAR GAMES PLAYED LEADERS

1962
Frank Thomas	156
Felix Mantilla	141
Jim Hickman	140

1963
Jim Hickman	146
Ron Hunt	143
Duke Snider	129

1964
Joe Christopher	154
Jim Hickman	139
Jesse Gonder	131

1965
Roy McMillan	157
Ed Kranepool	153
Johnny Lewis	148
Joe Christopher	148

1966
Ed Kranepool	146
Cleon Jones	139
Ken Boyer	136

1967
Tommy Davis	154
Bud Harrelson	151
Ed Kranepool	141

1968
Cleon Jones	147
Tommie Agee	132
Ron Swoboda	132

1969
Tommie Agee	149
Cleon Jones	137
Wayne Garrett	124

1970
Bud Harrelson	157
Tommie Agee	153
Cleon Jones	134

1971
Bud Harrelson	142
Cleon Jones	136
Jerry Grote	125

1972
Ed Kranepool	122
John Milner	117
Bud Harrelson	115

1973
Felix Millan	153
Rusty Staub	152
Wayne Garrett	140

1974
Wayne Garrett	151
Rusty Staub	151
John Milner	137

1975
Felix Millan	162*
Rusty Staub	155
Del Unser	147

1976
Felix Millan	139
John Milner	127
Dave Kingman	123
Ed Kranepool	123

1977
Lee Mazzilli	159
John Stearns	139
Lenny Randle	136

1978
Willie Montanez	159
Steve Henderson	157
Doug Flynn	156

1979
Lee Mazzilli	158
Joel Youngblood	158
Doug Flynn	157

1980
Lee Mazzilli	152
Joel Youngblood	146
Steve Henderson	143

1981
Doug Flynn	105
Dave Kingman	100
Hubie Brooks	98

1982
Mookie Wilson	159
George Foster	151
Dave Kingman	149

1983
George Foster	157
Mookie Wilson	152
Hubie Brooks	150

1984
Keith Hernandez	154
Mookie Wilson	154
Hubie Brooks	153

1985
Keith Hernandez	158
Rafael Santana	154
Gary Carter	149

1986
Keith Hernandez	149
Len Dykstra	147
Rafael Santana	139

1987
Howard Johnson	157
Keith Hernandez	154
Darryl Strawberry	154

1988
Darryl Strawberry	153
Kevin Elster	149
Howard Johnson	148

1989
Howard Johnson	153
Kevin Elster	151
Kevin McReynolds	148

1990
Howard Johnson	154
Gregg Jefferies	153
Darryl Strawberry	152

1991
Howard Johnson	156
Kevin McReynolds	143
Daryl Boston	137

1992
Eddie Murray	156
Dick Schofield	142
Daryl Boston	130

1993
Eddie Murray	154
Jeff Kent	140
Bobby Bonilla	139

1994
Bobby Bonilla	108
Jeff Kent	107
Jose Vizcaino	103

1995
Jose Vizcaino	135
Rico Brogna	134
Jeff Kent	125

1996
Lance Johnson	160
Bernard Gilkey	153
Todd Hundley	153

1997
John Olerud	154
Edgardo Alfonzo	151
Bernard GIlkey	145

1998
John Olerud	160
Brian McRae	159
Rey Ordonez	153

1999
John Olerud	162*
Robin Ventura	161
Edgardo Alfonzo	158

2000
Todd Zeile	153
Edgardo Alfonzo	150
Jay Payton	149

2001
Todd Zeile	151
Rey Ordonez	149
Robin Ventura	142

2002
Jeromy Burnitz	154
Roberto Alomar	149
Roger Cedeno	149

2003
Ty Wigginton	156
Roger Cedeno	148
Timo Perez	127

2004

Mike Cameron	140
Todd Zeile	137
Eric Valent	130

2005

Jose Reyes	161
David Wright	160
Carlos Beltran	151

2006

David Wright	154
Jose Reyes	153
Carlos Delgado	144

2007

Jose Reyes	160
David Wright	160
Carlos Beltran	144

2008

Carlos Beltran	161
David Wright	160
Jose Reyes	159
Carlos Delgado	159

2009

Daniel Murphy	155
David Wright	144
Luis Castillo	142

2010

David Wright	157
Angel Pagan	151
Ike Davis	147

2011

Jose Reyes	126
Willie Harris	126
Angel Pagan	123

Bold = New Record
Ital = Matches Record
*= Led or tied NL

Single Season Games Leaders

	GP	PLAYER	YEAR
1.	162	Felix Millan	1975
		John Olerud	1999
3.	161	Carlos Beltran	2008
		Jose Reyes	2005
		Robin Ventura	1999
6.	160	Lance Johnson	1996
		John Olerud	1998
		David Wright	2005
		Jose Reyes	2007
		David Wright	2007, 2008
12.	159	Lee Mazzilli	1977
		Brian McRae	1998
		Willie Montanez	1978
		Mookie Wilson	1982
		Jose Reyes	2008
		Carlos Delgado	2008
18.	158	Edgardo Alfonzo	1999
		Keith Hernandez	1985
		Lee Mazzilli	1979
		Joel Youngblood	1979
22.	157	Doug Flynn	1979
		George Foster	1983
		Bud Harrelson	1970
		Steve Henderson	1978
		Howard Johnson	1987
		Roy McMillan	1965

Career Games Leaders

	GP	PLAYER
1.	1853	Ed Kranepool
2.	1322	Bud Harrelson
3.	1235	Jerry Grote
4.	1201	Cleon Jones
5.	1154	Howard Johnson
6.	1116	Mookie Wilson
7.	1109	Darryl Strawberry
8.	1106	David Wright
9.	1086	Edgardo Alfonzo
10.	1050	Jose Reyes
11.	979	Lee Mazzilli
12.	972	Mike Piazza
13.	942	Rusty Staub
14.	916	Rey Ordonez
15.	883	Wayne Garrett
16.	880	Keith Hernandez
	839	Carlos Beltran
18.	829	Todd Hundley
19.	809	John Stearns
20.	787	Kevin McReynolds
21.	765	Wally Backman
22.	741	John Milner
23.	737	Ron Swoboda
24.	701	Dave Magadan
25.	695	John Franco

Hits Allowed

YEAR-BY-YEAR HITS ALLOWED LEADERS

1962
Roger Craig	261
Al Jackson	244
Jay Hook	230

1963
Roger Craig	249
Al Jackson	237
Jay Hook	168

1964
Jack Fisher	256
Al Jackson	229
Tracy Stallard	213

1965
Jack Fisher	252
Al Jackson	217
Warren Spahn	140

1966
Jack Fisher	229
Dennis Ribant	184
Bob Shaw	171

1967
Jack Fisher	251
Tom Seaver	224
Don Cardwell	112

1968
Tom Seaver	224
Jerry Koosman	221
Don Cardwell	156

1969
Tom Seaver	202
Gary Gentry	192
Jerry Koosman	187

1970
Tom Seaver	230
Jerry Koosman	189
Jim McAndrew	166

1971
Tom Seaver	210
Gary Gentry	167
Jerry Koosman	160

1972
Jon Matlack	215
Tom Seaver	215
Jerry Koosman	155

1973
Jerry Koosman	234
Tom Seaver	219
Jon Matlack	210

1974
Jerry Koosman	258
Jon Matlack	221
Tom Seaver	199

1975
Jerry Koosman	234
Jon Matlack	224
Tom Seaver	217

1976
Jon Matlack	236
Tom Seaver	211
Jerry Koosman	205

1977
Jerry Koosman	195
Nino Espinosa	188
Jon Matlack	175

1978
Nino Espinosa	230
Jerry Koosman	221
Mike Bruhert	171

1979
Craig Swan	241
Pete Falcone	194
Kevin Kobel	169

1980
Mark Bomback	191
Ray Burris	181
Pete Falcone	163

1981
Pat Zachry	151
Mike Scott	130
Pete Falcone	84

1982
Mike Scott	185
Charlie Puleo	179
Craig Swan	165

1983
Mike Torrez	227
Ed Lynch	208
Tom Seaver	201

1984
Walt Terrell	232
Ron Darling	179
Dwight Gooden	161

1985
Ron Darling	214
Dwight Gooden	198
Ed Lynch	188

1986
Ron Darling	203
Dwight Gooden	197
Bob Ojeda	185

1987
Ron Darling	183
Dwight Gooden	162
Terry Leach	132

1988
Dwight Gooden	242
Ron Darling	218
David Cone	178

1989
Ron Darling	214
David Cone	183
Bob Ojeda	179

1990
Dwight Gooden	229
Frank Viola	227
David Cone	177

1991
Frank Viola	259*
David Cone	204
Dwight Gooden	185

1992
Dwight Gooden	197
David Cone	162
Sid Fernandez	162

1993
Frank Tanana	198
Dwight Gooden	188
Eric Hillman	173

1994
Bret Saberhagen	169
Bobby Jones	157
Pete Smith	145

1995
Bobby Jones	209
Dave Mlicki	160
Bill Pulsipher	122

1996
Bobby Jones	219
Mark Clark	217
Pete Harnisch	195

1997
Dave Mlicki	194
Rick Reed	186
Bobby Jones	177

1998
Rick Reed	208
Bobby Jones	192
Masato Yoshii	166

1999
Al Leiter	209
Orel Hershiser	175
Masato Yoshii	168

2000
Glendon Rusch	196
Mike Hampton	194
Al Leiter	192

2001
Glendon Rusch	216
Kevin Appier	181
Al Leiter	178

2002
Al Leiter	194
Pedro Astacio	192
Steve Trachsel	170

2003
Tom Glavine	205
Steve Trachsel	204
Jae Seo	193

2004

Tom Glavine	204
Steve Trachsel	203
Al Leiter	138

2005

Tom Glavine	227
Kris Benson	171
Victor Zambrano	170

2006

Tom Glavine	202
Steve Trachsel	185
Pedro Martinez	108

2007

Tom Glavine	219
John Maine	168
Oliver Perez	153

2008

Mike Pelfrey	209
Johan Santana	206
Oliver Perez	167

2009

Mike Pelfrey	213
Livan Hernandez	164
Johan Santana	156

2010

Mike Pelfrey	213
Jonathon Niese	192
Johan Santana	179

2011

Mike Pelfrey	220
R.A. Dickey	202
Chris Capuano	198

Bold = Team Record
Ital. = Ties Team Record
* = Leads or Tied For NL

Single Season Hits Allowed Leaders

	Hits	Player	YEAR
1.	261	Roger Craig	1962
2.	259	Frank Viola	1991
3.	258	Jerry Koosman	1974
4.	256	Jack Fisher	1964
5.	252	Jack Fisher	1965
6.	251	Jack Fisher	1967
7.	249	Roger Craig	1963
8.	244	Al Jackson	1962
9.	242	Dwight Gooden	1988
10.	241	Craig Swan	1979
11.	237	Al Jackson	1963
12.	236	Jon Matlack	1976
13.	234	Jerry Koosman	1973, 1975
15.	232	Walt Terrell	1984
16.	230	Nino Espinosa	1978
		Jay Hook	1962
		Tom Seaver	1970
19.	229	Jack Fisher	1966
		Dwight Gooden	1990
		Al Jackson	1964
22.	227	Tom Glavine	2005
		Mike Torrez	1983
		Frank Viola	1990
25.	224	Jon Matlack	1975
		Tom Seaver	1967, 1968

Career Hits Allowed Leaders

	HITS	Player
1.	2431	Tom Seaver
2.	2281	Jerry Koosman
3.	1898	Dwight Gooden
4.	1473	Ron Darling
5.	1312	Jon Matlack
6.	1255	Bobby Jones
7.	1222	Al Leiter
8.	1191	Craig Swan
9.	1167	Sid Fernandez
10.	1057	Tom Glavine
11.	1033	Al Jackson
12.	1011	David Cone
13.	988	Jack Fisher
14.	967	Steve Trachsel
15.	965	Mike Pelfrey
16.	868	Rick Reed
17.	815	Ed Lynch
18.	738	Pat Zachry
19.	690	Bob Ojeda
20.	685	Tug McGraw
21.	683	John Franco
22.	667	Gary Gentry
23.	664	Jim McAndrew
24.	600	Pete Falcone
25.	565	Ray Sadecki

Hits

YEAR-BY-YEAR HITS LEADERS

1962
Frank Thomas	152
Charlie Neal	132
Felix Mantilla	128

1963
Ron Hunt	145
Jim Hickman	113
Frank Thomas	109

1964
Joe Christopher	163
Ron Hunt	144
Ed Kranepool	108

1965
Ed Kranepool	133
Roy McMillan	128
Charley Smith	122

1966
Ron Hunt	138
Cleon Jones	136
Ken Boyer	132

1967
Tommy Davis	174
Bud Harrelson	137
Ed Kranepool	126
Ron Swoboda	126

1968
Cleon Jones	151
Jerry Grote	114
Ron Swoboda	109

1969
Cleon Jones	164
Tommie Agee	153
Ken Boswell	101

1970
Tommie Agee	182
Cleon Jones	140
Bud Harrelson	137

1971
Cleon Jones	161
Bud Harrelson	138
Tommie Agee	121

1972
Tommie Agee	96
Cleon Jones	92
Bud Harrelson	90

1973
Felix Millan	185
Rusty Staub	163
Wayne Garrett	129

1974
Rusty Staub	145
Felix Millan	139
Cleon Jones	130

1975
Felix Millan	191
Rusty Staub	162
Del Unser	156

1976
Felix Millan	150
Ed Kranepool	121
John Milner	120

1977
Len Randle	156
Lee Mazzilli	134
John Stearns	108

1978
Steve Henderson	156
Willie Montanez	156
Lee Mazzilli	148

1979
Lee Mazzilli	181
Frank Taveras	167
Joel Youngblood	162

1980
Lee Mazzilli	162
Frank Taveras	157
Steve Henderson	149

1981
Hubie Brooks	110
Mookie Wilson	89
Dave Kingman	78

1982
Mookie Wilson	178
George Foster	136
Hubie Brooks	114

1983
Mookie Wilson	176
Hubie Brooks	147
George Foster	145

1984
Keith Hernandez	171
Mookie Wilson	162
Hubie Brooks	159

1985
Keith Hernandez	183
Gary Garter	156
Wally Backman	142

1986
Keith Hernandez	171
Ray Knight	145
Len Dykstra	127

1987
Keith Hernandez	170
Kevin McReynolds	163
Darryl Strawberry	151

1988
Kevin McReynolds	159
Darryl Strawberry	146
Len Dykstra	116

1989
Howard Johnson	164
Kevin McReynolds	148
Gregg Jefferies	131

1990
Gregg Jefferies	171
Darryl Strawberry	150
Dave Magadan	148

1991
Howard Johnson	146
Kevin McReynolds	135
Gregg Jefferies	132

1992
Eddie Murray	144
Bobby Bonilla	109
Dave Magadan	91

1993
Eddie Murray	174
Jeff Kent	134
Bobby Bonilla	133

1994
Jeff Kent	121
Bobby Bonilla	117
Jose Vizcaino	105

1995
Jose Vizcaino	146
Rico Brogna	143
Jeff Kent	131

1996
Lance Johnson	227*
Bernard Gilkey	181
Todd Hundley	140

1997
Edgardo Alfonzo	163
John Olerud	154
Butch Huskey	135

1998
John Olerud	197
Edgardo Alfonzo	155
Brian McRae	146

1999
Edgardo Alfonzo	191
Robin Ventura	177
John Olerud	173

2000
Edgardo Alfonzo	176
Mike Piazza	156
Todd Zeile	146

2001
Mike Piazza	151
Todd Zeile	141
Rey Ordonez	114

2002
Roberto Alomar	157
Edgardo Alfonzo	151
Mike Piazza	134

2003
Ty Wigginton	146
Roger Cedeno	129
Jason Phillips	120

2004

Kaz Matsui	125
Mike Piazza	121
Mike Cameron	114

2005

Jose Reyes	190
David Wright	176
Carlos Beltran	155

2006

Jose Reyes	194
David Wright	181
Paul Lo Duca	163

2007

David Wright	196
Jose Reyes	191
Carlos Beltran	153

2008

Jose Reyes	204*
David Wright	189
Carlos Beltran	172

2009

David Wright	164
Luis Castillo	147
Daniel Murphy	135

2010

Angel Pagan	168
David Wright	166
Jose Reyes	159

2011

Jose Reyes	181
Angel Pagan	125
Daniel Murphy	125

Bold = Sets Team Record
Ital = Matches Team Record
*= Led or tied for NL

Single Season Hits Leaders

	HITS	PLAYER	YEAR
1.	227	Lance Johnson	1996
2.	204	Jose Reyes	2008
3.	197	John Olerud	1998
4.	196	David Wright	2007
5.	194	Jose Reyes	2006
6.	191	Edgardo Alfonzo	1999
		Felix Millan	1975
		Jose Reyes	2007
9.	190	Jose Reyes	2005
10.	189	David Wright	2008
11.	185	Felix Millan	1973
12.	183	Keith Hernandez	1985
13.	182	Tommie Agee	1970
14.	181	Bernard Gilkey	1996
		Lee Mazzilli	1979
		David Wright	2006
		Jose Reyes	2011
17.	178	Mookie Wilson	1982
18.	177	Robin Ventura	1999
19.	176	Edgardo Alfonzo	2000
		Mookie Wilson	1983
		David Wright	2005
22.	174	Tommy Davis	1967
		Eddie Murray	1993
24.	173	John Olerud	1999

Career Hits Leaders

	HITS	PLAYER
1.	1418	Ed Kranepool
2.	1300	Jose Reyes
3.	1248	David Wright
4.	1188	Cleon Jones
5.	1136	Edgardo Alfonzo
6.	1112	Mookie Wilson
7.	1029	Bud Harrelson
8.	1028	Mike Piazza
9.	1025	Darryl Strawberry
10.	997	Howard Johnson
11.	994	Jerry Grote
12.	939	Keith Hernandez
13.	878	Carlos Beltran
14.	796	Lee Mazzilli
15.	791	Kevin McReynolds
16.	743	Felix Millan
17.	720	Rey Ordonez
18.	709	Rusty Staub
19.	695	John Stearns
20.	670	Wally Backman
21.	667	Wayne Garrett
22.	640	Hubie Brooks
23.	632	Tommie Agee
24.	612	Todd Hundley
25.	610	Dave Magadan

Home Runs

YEAR-BY-YEAR HOME RUNS LEADERS

1962
Frank Thomas	34
Marv Throneberry	16
Jim Hickman	13

1963
Jim Hickman	17
Frank Thomas	15
Duke Snider	14

1964
Charley Smith	20
Joe Christopher	16
Jim Hickman	11

1965
Ron Swoboda	19
Charley Smith	16
Johnny Lewis	15
Jim Hickman	15

1966
Ed Kranepool	16
Ken Boyer	14
Ed Bressoud	10

1967
Tommy Davis	16
Jerry Buchek	14
Ron Swoboda	13

1968
Ed Charles	15
Cleon Jones	14
Art Shamsky	12

1969
Tommie Agee	26
Art Shamsky	14
Cleon Jones	12
Donn Clendenon	12

1970
Tommie Agee	24
Donn Clendenon	22
Wayne Garrett	12

1971
Tommie Agee	14
Ed Kranepool	14
Cleon Jones	14

1972
John Milner	17
Tommie Agee	13
Ken Boswell	9
Rusty Staub	9

1973
John Milner	23
Wayne Garrett	16
Rusty Staub	15

1974
John Milner	20
Rusty Staub	19
Wayne Garrett	13
Cleon Jones	13

1975
Dave Kingman	36
Rusty Staub	19
Del Unser	10

1976
Dave Kingman	37
John Milner	15
Ed Kranepool	10

1977
Steve Henderson	12
John Stearns	12
John Milner	12

1978
Willie Montanez	17
Lee Mazzilli	16
John Stearns	15

1979
Joel Youngblood	16
Lee Mazzilli	15
Richie Hebner	10

1980
Lee Mazzilli	16
Claudell Washington	10
Steve Henderson	8
Joel Youngblood	8

1981
Dave Kingman	22
Lee Mazzilli	6
Rusty Staub	5
Ellis Valentine	5

1982
Dave Kingman	37*
George Foster	13
Ellis Valentine	8

1983
George Foster	28
Darryl Strawberry	26
Dave Kingman	13

1984
Darryl Strawberry	26
George Foster	24
Hubie Brooks	16

1985
Gary Carter	32
Darryl Strawberry	29
George Foster	21

1986
Darryl Strawberry	27
Gary Carter	24
George Foster	13
Keith Hernandez	13

1987
Darryl Strawberry	39
Howard Johnson	36
Kevin McReynolds	29

1988
Darryl Strawberry	39*
Kevin McReynolds	27
Howard Johnson	24

1989
Howard Johnson	36
Darryl Strawberry	29
Kevin McReynolds	22

1990
Darryl Strawberry	37
Kevin McReynolds	24
Howard Johnson	23

1991
Howard Johnson	38*
Hubie Brooks	16
Kevin McReynolds	16

1992
Bobby Bonilla	19
Eddie Murray	16
Daryl Boston	11

1993
Bobby Bonilla	34
Eddie Murray	27
Jeff Kent	21

1994
Bobby Bonilla	20
Ryan Thompson	18
Todd Hundley	16

1995
Rico Brogna	22
Jeff Kent	20
Bobby Bonilla	18

1996
Todd Hundley	41
Bernard Gilkey	30
Butch Huskey	15

1997
Todd Hundley	30
Butch Huskey	24
John Olerud	22

1998
Mike Piazza	23
John Olerud	22
Brian McRae	21

1999
Mike Piazza	40
Robin Ventura	32
Edgar Alfonzo	27

2000
Mike Piazza	38
Edgardo Alfonzo	25
Robin Ventura	24

2001

Mike Piazza	36
Robin Ventura	21
Edgardo Alfonzo	17

2002

Mike Piazza	33
Mo Vaughn	26
Jeromy Burnitz	19

2003

Jeromy Burnitz	18
Cliff Floyd	18
Tony Clark	16

2004

Mike Cameron	30
Richard Hidalgo	21
Mike Piazza	20

2005

Cliff Floyd	34
David Wright	27
Mike Piazza	19

2006

Carlos Beltran	41
Carlos Delgardo	38
David Wright	26

2007

Carlos Beltran	33
David Wright	30
Carlos Delgado	24

2008

Carlos Delgado	38
David Wright	33
Carlos Beltran	27

2009

Daniel Murphy	12
Carlos Beltran	10
Jeff Francoeur	10
Gary Sheffield	10
David Wright	10

2010

David Wright	29
Ike Davis	19
Rod Barajas	12

2011

Carlos Beltran	15
David Wright	14
Jason Bay	12

Bold = Sets Team Record
Ital. = Tied Team Record
* = Led or Tied For NL

Single Season Home Run Leaders

	HR	PLAYER	YEAR
1.	41	Carlos Beltran	2006
		Todd Hundley	1996
3.	40	Mike Piazza	1999
4.	39	Darryl Strawberry	1987
		Darryl Strawberry	1988
6.	38	Carlos Delgado	2006, 2008
		Howard Johnson	1991
		Mike Piazza	2000
10.	37	Dave Kingman	1976
		Dave Kingman	1982
		Darryl Strawberry	1990
13.	36	Howard Johnson	1987
		Howard Johnson	1989
		Dave Kingman	1975
		Mike Piazza	2001
17.	34	Bobby Bonilla	1993
		Cliff Floyd	2005
		Frank Thomas	1962
20.	33	Mike Piazza	2002
		Carlos Beltran	2007
		David Wright	2008
23.	32	Gary Carter	1985
		Robin Ventura	1999
25.	30	Mike Cameron	2004
		Bernard Gilkey	1996
		Todd Hundley	1997
		David Wright	2007

Career Home Run Leaders

	HR	PLAYER
1.	252	Darryl Strawberry
2.	220	Mike Piazza
3.	192	Howard Johnson
4.	183	David Wright
5.	154	Dave Kingman
6.	149	Carlos Beltran
7.	124	Todd Hundley
8.	122	Kevin McReynolds
9.	120	Edgardo Alfonzo
10.	118	Ed Kranepool
11	104	Carlos Delgado
12.	99	George Foster
13.	95	Bobby Bonilla
14.	94	John Milner
15.	93	Cleon Jones
16.	89	Gary Carter
17.	82	Tommie Agee
18.	81	Cliff Floyd
		Jose Reyes
20.	80	Keith Hernandez
21.	77	Robin Ventura
22.	75	Rusty Staub
23.	69	Ron Swoboda
24.	68	Lee Mazzilli
25.	67	Jeff Kent

Inherited Runners

Year-by-Year Leaders
Minimum 20 Inherited Runners

Year	Pitcher	IR	RS	PCT
1962	Craig Anderson	29	4	.138
1963	Don Rowe	21	7	.333
1964	Willard Hunter	32	9	.281
1965	Gord Richardson	46	11	.239
1966	Rob Gardner	21	3	.143
1967	Don Shaw	37	9	.243
1968	Bill Short	42	3	.071
1969	Cal Koonce	22	4	.180
1970	Ron Taylor	54	18	.333
1971	Tug McGraw	23	3	.130
1972	Chuck Taylor	20	5	.250
1973	Phil Hennigan	25	4	.200
1974	Bob Miller	50	18	.360
1975	Bob Apodaca	37	14	.378
1976	Bob Apodaca	31	5	.161
1977	Bob Myrick	21	4	.190
1978	Paul Siebert	20	2	.100
1979	Dale Murray	31	6	.194
1980	Ed Glynn	28	9	.321
1981	Neil Allen	21	6	.286
1982	Jesse Orosco	48	12	.250
1983	Jesse Orosco	37	10	.270
1984	Doug Sisk	20	5	.250
1985	Jesse Orosco	46	9	.196
1986	Roger McDowell	32	4	.125
1987	Randy Myers	38	6	.158
1988	Roger McDowell	33	4	.121
1989	Randy Myers	54	10	.185
1990	Alejandro Pena	21	7	.333
1991	John Franco	25	8	.320
1992	Jeff Innis	50	15	.300
1993	Jeff Innis	34	9	.265
1994	Jo. Manzanillo	30	15	.500
1995	John Franco	21	5	.238
1996	Dave Mlicki	27	5	.185
1997	Greg McMichael	52	15	.288
1998	John Franco	20	3	.150
1999	Armando Benitez	30	6	.200
	Pat Mahomes	25	4	.200
2000	Turk Wendell	40	6	.150
2001	Dennis Cook	27	4	.148
2002	Mark Guthrie	37	6	.162
2003	Mike Stanton	20	5	.250
2004	Ricky Bottalico	33	8	.242
2005	Ro. Hernandez	29	5	.172
2006	Chad Bradford	53	10	.189
2007	Scott Schoeneweis	43	7	.163
2008	Joe Smith	63	11	.175
2009	Pedro Feliciano	54	10	.185
2010	Fernando Nieve	26	4	.154
2011	D.J. Carrasco	26	6	.231

Career Inherited Runners Leaders
40 or More Inherited Runners

	Pitcher	IR	RS	PCT
1.	Bill Short	42	3	.071
2.	Randy Myers	148	27	.182
3.	Chad Bradford	53	10	.189
4.	Don Shaw	46	9	.196
5.	Roberto Hernandez	44	9	.205
6.	Bob Myrick	46	10	.217
7.	Jesse Orosco	263	62	.236
8.	Tim Byrdak	67	16	.239
9.	Pedro Feliciano	303	74	.244
10.	Dennis Cook	192	47	.245
11.	Cal Koonce	81	20	.247
12.	Skip Lockwood	146	38	.260
13.	Turk Wendell	145	38	.262
14.	Gordie Richardson	57	15	.263
15.	Elmer Dessens	52	14	.269
16.	Scott Schoeneweis	89	24	.270
17.	Scott Strickland	44	12	.273
18.	Terry Leach	82	23	.280
	Eric Gunderson	50	14	.280
20.	Armando Benitez	99	28	.283
21.	Jeff Innis	179	51	.285
22.	Roger McDowell	143	44	.308
23.	Jorge Sosa	42	13	.310
	David Weathers	100	31	.310
	Willard Hunter	42	13	.310
	Brian Stokes	45	14	.311
27.	Joe Smith	114	36	.316
28.	Tug McGraw	219	70	.320
	Mike Maddux	50	16	.320
30.	John Franco	247	81	.328
31.	Ryota Igarashi	63	21	.333
32.	Ron Taylor	215	72	.335
33.	Bob Apodaca	118	40	.339
34.	Aaron Heilman	108	37	.343
35.	Doug Sisk	151	52	.344
36.	Carlos Diaz	43	15	.349
37.	Greg McMichael	80	28	.350
	Heath Bell	40	14	.350
39.	Ray Sadecki	82	29	.354

40.	Wally Whitehurst	70	25	.357
	Bob Miller	56	20	.357
42.	Dick Selma	53	19	.358
43.	Tom Hausman	50	18	.360
44.	Rick Baldwin	86	32	.372
45.	Jerry Dipoto	67	25	.373
46.	Neil Allen	144	54	.375
47.	Dale Murray	77	29	.377
48.	Harry Parker	62	24	.387
49.	Dyar Miller	49	19	.388
50.	Mike Stanton	72	28	.389
51.	Darrell Sutherland	41	16	.390
52.	Jack Hamilton	48	19	.396
53.	Ed Glynn	65	26	.400
54.	Bill Wakefield	42	17	.405
55.	Pat Mahomes	60	25	.417
56.	Larry Bearnarth	117	49	.419
	Doug Henry	43	18	.419
58.	Dwight Bernard	51	22	.431
59.	Galen Cisco	57	26	.439
60.	Danny Frisella	102	45	.441
61.	Dan Wheeler	51	23	.451
62.	Al Jackson	42	19	.452
63.	Sean Green	41	19	.463
64.	Ken Mackenzie	54	27	.500
	Josias Manzanillo	42	21	.500

100 or More Inherited Runners

	Pitcher	**IR**	**RS**	**PCT**
1.	Randy Myers	148	27	.182
2.	Jesse Orosco	263	62	.236
3.	Pedro Feliciano	303	74	.244
4.	Dennis Cook	192	47	.245
5.	Skip Lockwood	146	38	.260
6.	Turk Wendell	145	38	.262
7.	Jeff Innis	179	51	.285
8.	Roger McDowell	143	44	.308
9.	David Weathers	100	31	.310
10.	Joe Smith	114	36	.316
11.	Tug McGraw	219	70	.320
12.	John Franco	247	81	.328
13.	Ron Taylor	215	72	.335
14.	Bob Apodaca	118	40	.339
15.	Aaron Heilman	108	37	.343
16.	Doug Sisk	151	52	.344
17.	Neil Allen	144	54	.375
18.	Larry Bearnarth	117	49	.419
19.	Danny Frisella	102	45	.441

Innings Pitched

YEAR-BY-YEAR INNINGS PITCHED LEADERS

1962		**1972**	
Roger Craig	233.1	Tom Seaver	262.0
Al Jackson	231.1	Jon Matlack	244.0
Jay Hook	213.2	Gary Gentry	164.0

1963		**1973**	
Roger Craig	236.0	Tom Seaver	290.0
Al Jackson	227.0	Jerry Koosman	263.0
Carl Willey	183.0	Jon Matlack	242.0

1964		**1974**	
Jack Fisher	227.2	Jon Matlack	265.1
Tracy Stallard	225.2	Jerry Koosman	265.0
Al Jackson	213.1	Tom Seaver	236.0

1965		**1975**	
Jack Fisher	253.2	Tom Seaver	280.1
Al Jackson	205.1	Jerry Koosman	239.2
Warren Spahn	126.0	Jon Matlack	228.2

1966		**1976**	
Jack Fisher	230.0	Tom Seaver	271.0
Dennis Ribant	188.1	Jon Matlack	262.0
Bob Shaw	167.2	Jerry Koosman	247.1

1967		**1977**	
Tom Seaver	251.0	Jerry Koosman	226.2
Jack Fisher	220.1	Nino Espinosa	200.0
Don Cardwell	118.1	Jon Matlack	169.0

1968		**1978**	
Tom Seaver	277.2	Jerry Koosman	235.1
Jerry Koosman	263.2	Craig Swan	207.1
Don Cardwell	179.2	Nino Espinosa	203.2

1969		**1979**	
Tom Seaver	273.1	Craig Swan	251.1
Jerry Koosman	241.0	Pete Falcone	184.0
Gary Gentry	233.2	Kevin Kobel	161.2

1970		**1980**	
Tom Seaver	290.2	Ray Burris	170.1
Jerry Koosman	212.0	Pat Zachry	167.2
Gary Gentry	188.1	Mark Bomback	162.2

1971		**1981**	
Tom Seaver	286.1	Pat Zachry	139.0
Gary Gentry	203.1	Mike Scott	136.0
Jerry Koosman	165.2	Pete Falcone	95.1

1982		**1993**	
Pete Falcone	171.0	Dwight Gooden	208.2
Charlie Puleo	171.0	Frank Tanana	183.0
Craig Swan	166.1	Eric Hillman	145.0

1983		**1994**	
Tom Seaver	231.0	Bret Saberhagen	177.1
Mike Torrez	222.1	Bobby Jones	160.0
Ed Lynch	174.2	Pete Smith	131.1

1984		**1995**	
Dwight Gooden	218.0	Bobby Jones	195.2
Walt Terrell	215.0	Dave Mlicki	160.2
Ron Darling	205.2	Bill Pulsipher	126.2

1985		**1996**	
Dwight Gooden	276.2*	Mark Clark	212.1
Ron Darling	248.0	Bobby Jones	195.2
Ed Lynch	191.0	Pete Harnisch	194.2

1986		**1997**	
Dwight Gooden	250.0	Rick Reed	208.1
Ron Darling	237.0	Dave Mlicki	193.2
Bob Ojeda	217.1	Bobby Jones	193.1

1987		**1998**	
Ron Darling	207.2	Rick Reed	212.1
Dwight Gooden	179.2	Bobby Jones	195.1
Sid Fernandez	156.0	Al Leiter	193.0

1988		**1999**	
Dwight Gooden	248.1	Al Leiter	213.0
Ron Darling	240.2	Orel Hershiser	179.0
David Cone	231.1	Masato Yoshii	174.0

1989		**2000**	
David Cone	219.2	Mike Hampton	217.2
Sid Fernandez	219.1	Al Leiter	208.0
Ron Darling	217.1	Glendon Rusch	190.2

1990		**2001**	
Frank Viola	249.2*	Kevin Appier	207.2
Dwight Gooden	232.2	Al Leiter	187.1
David Cone	211.2	Glendon Rusch	179.0

1991		**2002**	
David Cone	232.2	Al Leiter	204.1
Frank Viola	231.1	Pedro Astacio	191.2
Dwight Gooden	190.0	Steve Trachsel	173.2

1992		**2003**	
Sid Fernandez	214.2	Steve Trachsel	204.2
Dwight Gooden	206.0	Jae Seo	188.1
David Cone	196.2	Tom Glavine	183.1

2004

Tom Glavine	212.1
Steve Trachsel	202.2
Al Leiter	173.2

2005

Pedro Martinez	217.0
Tom Glavine	211.1
Kris Benson	174.1

2006

Tom Glavine	198.0
Steve Trachsel	164.2
Pedro Martinez	132.2

2007

Tom Glavine	200.1
John Maine	191.0
Oliver Perez	177.0

2008

Johan Santana	234.1*
Mike Pelfrey	200.2
Oliver Perez	194.0

2009

Mike Pelfrey	184.1
Johan Santana	166.2
Livan Hernandez	135.0

2010

Mike Pelfrey	204.0
Johan Santana	199.0
R.A. Dickey	174.1

2011

R.A. Dickey	208.2
Mike Pelfrey	193.2
Chris Capuano	186.0

Bold = Sets Team Record
Ital. = Ties Team Record
* = Leads or Tied For NL

Single Season Innings Leaders

	IP	Player	Year
1.	290.2	Tom Seaver	1970
2.	290	Tom Seaver	1973
3.	286.1	Tom Seaver	1971
4.	280.1	Tom Seaver	1975
5.	277.2	Tom Seaver	1968
6.	276.2	Dwight Gooden	1985
7.	273.1	Tom Seaver	1969
8.	271	Tom Seaver	1976
9.	265.1	Jon Matlack	1974
10.	265	Jerry Koosman	1974
11.	263.2	Jerry Koosman	1968
12.	263	Jerry Koosman	1973
13.	262	Jon Matlack	1976
		Tom Seaver	1972
15.	253.2	Jack Fisher	1965
16.	251.1	Craig Swan	1979
17.	251	Tom Seaver	1967
18.	250	Dwight Gooden	1986
19.	249.2	Frank Viola	1990
20.	248.1	Dwight Gooden	1988
21.	248	Ron Darling	1985
22.	247.1	Jerry Koosman	1976
23.	244	Jon Matlack	1972
24.	242	Jon Matlack	1973
25.	241	Jerry Koosman	1969

Career Innings Pitched Leaders

	IP	Player
1.	3045.1	Tom Seaver
2.	2544.2	Jerry Koosman
3.	2169.2	Dwight Gooden
4.	1620.0	Ron Darling
5.	1584.2	Sid Fernandez
6.	1448.0	Jon Matlack
7.	1360.0	Al Leiter
8.	1230.2	Craig Swan
9.	1215.2	Bobby Jones
10.	1209.1	David Cone
11.	1005.1	Tom Glavine
12.	980.2	Al Jackson
13.	956.1	Steve Trachsel
14.	931.2	Jack Fisher
15.	888.2	Rick Reed
16	876.2	Mike Pelfrey
17.	792.2	Tug McGraw
18.	789.1	Gary Gentry
19.	764.0	Bob Ojeda
20.	741.2	Pat Zachry
21.	730.1	Ed Lynch
22.	729.2	Jim McAndrew
23.	702.2	John Franco
24.	607.2	Pete Falcone
25.	600.1	Ray Sadecki

Losses

YEAR-BY-YEAR LOSSES LEADERS

1962
Roger Craig	24*
Al Jackson	20
Jay Hook	19

1963
Roger Craig	22*
Tracy Stallard	17
Al Jackson	17

1964
Tracy Stallard	20*
Galen Cisco	19
Jack Fisher	10

1965
Jack Fisher	24*
Al Jackson	20
Warren Spahn	12

1966
Jack Fisher	14
Jack Hamilton	13
Bob Shaw	10

1967
Jack Fisher	18*
Tom Seaver	13
Don Cardwell	9
Bob Shaw	9

1968
Don Cardwell	13
Jerry Koosman	12
Tom Seaver	12

1969
Gary Gentry	12
Don Cardwell	10
Jerry Koosman	9

1970
Jim McAndrew	14
Tom Seaver	12
Nolan Ryan	11

1971
Nolan Ryan	14
Gary Gentry	11
Jerry Koosman	11

1972
Jerry Koosman	12
Tom Seaver	12
Gary Gentry	10
Jon Matlack	10

1973
Jon Matlack	16
Jerry Koosman	15
Tom Seaver	7

1974
Jon Matlack	15
Harry Parker	12
3 Pitchers	11

1975
Jerry Koosman	13
Randy Tate	13
Jon Matlack	12

1976
Mickey Lolich	13
Tom Seaver	11
Jerry Koosman	10
Jon Matlack	10

1977
Jerry Koosman	20*
Jon Matlack	15
Nino Espinosa	13

1978
Nino Espinosa	15
Jerry Koosman	15
Skip Lockwood	13

1979
Pete Falcone	14
Craig Swan	13
Neil Allen	10

1980
Ray Burris	13
Neil Allen	10
Pete Falcone	10
Pat Zachry	10

1981
Pat Zachry	14*
Mike Scott	10
Randy Jones	8

1982
Mike Scott	13
Pete Falcone	10
Randy Jones	10
Jesse Orosco	10

1983
Mike Torrez	17*
Tom Seaver	14
Ed Lynch	10

1984
Walt Terrell	12
Ron Darling	9
Dwight Gooden	9

1985
Sid Fernandez	9
Ed Lynch	8
Rick Aguilera	7

1986
Roger McDowell	9
Rick Aguilera	7
4 pitchers	6

1987
Jesse Orosco	9
Ron Darling	8
Sid Fernandez	8

1988
Bob Ojeda	13
Sid Fernandez	10
Ron Darling	9
Dwight Gooden	9

1989
Ron Darling	14
Bob Ojeda	11
David Cone	8

1990
Sid Fernandez	14
Frank Viola	12
David Cone	10

1991
Frank Viola	15
David Cone	14
Wally Whitehurst	12

1992
Anthony Young	14
Dwight Gooden	13
Sid Fernandez	11

1993
Anthony Young	16
Dwight Gooden	15
Frank Tanana	15

1994
Pete Smith	10
Bobby Jones	7
Mauro Gozzo	5
Mike Remlinger	5

1995
Bobby Jones	10
Pete Harnisch	8

1996
Jason Isringhausen	14
Pete Harnisch	12
Paul Wilson	12

1997
Dave Mlicki	12
Greg McMichael	10
Bobby Jones	9
Rick Reed	9

1998
Rick Reed	11
Bobby Jones	9
John Franco	8
Masato Yoshii	8

1999
Orel Hershiser	12
Al Leiter	12
Masato Yoshii	8

2000
Glendon Rusch	11
Mike Hampton	10
Al Leiter	8

2001

Steve Trachsel	13
Glendon Rusch	12
Al Leiter	10

2002

Al Leiter	13
Pedro Astacio	11
Steve Trachsel	11

2003

Tom Glavine	14
Jae Seo	12
Steve Trachsel	10

2004

Tom Glavine	14
Steve Trachsel	13
Jae Seo	10

2005

Tom Glavine	13
Victor Zambrano	12
Kris Benson	8
Pedro Martinez	8

2006

Pedro Martinez	8
Steve Trachsel	8
Tom Glavine	7
Orlando Hernandez	7

2007

John Maine	10
Oliver Perez	10

2008

Mike Pelfrey	11
John Maine	8
Aaron Heilman	8

2009

Mike Pelfrey	12
Johan Santana	9

2010

Jonathon Niese	10
R.A. Dickey	9
Mike Pelfrey	9
Johan Santana	9

2011

R.A. Dickey	13
Mike Pelfrey	13
Chris Capuano	12

Bold = Sets Team Record
Ital. = Ties Team Record
* = Leads or Tied For NL

Single Season Loss Leaders

	L	Player	Year
1.	24	Roger Craig	1962
		Jack Fisher	1965
3.	22	Roger Craig	1963
4.	20	Al Jackson	1962, 1965
		Jerry Koosman	1977
		Tracy Stallard	1964
8.	19	Galen Cisco	1964
		Jay Hook	1962
10.	18	Jack Fisher	1967
11.	17	Craig Anderson	1962
		Jack Fisher	1964
		Al Jackson	1963
		Tracy Stallard	1963
		Mike Torrez	1983
16.	16	Al Jackson	1964
		Jon Matlack	1973
		Anthony Young	1993
19.	15	Galen Cisco	1963
		Nino Espinosa	1978
		Dwight Gooden	1993
		Jerry Koosman	1973, 1978
		Jon Matlack	1974, 1977
		Frank Tanana	1993
		Frank Viola	1991

Career Loss Leaders

	L	Player
1.	137	Jerry Koosman
2.	124	Tom Seaver
3.	85	Dwight Gooden
4.	81	Jon Matlack
5.	80	Al Jackson
6.	78	Sid Fernandez
7.	73	Jack Fisher
8.	71	Craig Swan
9.	70	Ron Darling
10.	67	Al Leiter
11.	59	Steve Trachsel
12.	56	John Franco
		Bobby Jones
		Tom Glavine
15.	55	Tug McGraw
16.	54	Mike Pelfrey
17.	51	David Cone
18.	49	Jim McAndrew
19.	47	Jesse Orosco
20.	46	Roger Craig
		Pat Zachry
22.	43	Galen Cisco
23.	42	Gary Gentry
24.	40	Neil Allen
		Ed Lynch
		Bob Ojeda

On Base Percentage

YEAR-BY-YEAR OBP LEADERS
Minimum 502 Plate Appearances

1962
Charlie Neal	.330
Felix Mantilla	.330
Frank Thomas	.329
(Richie Ashburn .424, 473 PA)	

1963
Ron Hunt	.334
Jim Hickman	.299
(Duke Snider .345, 415 PA)	

1964
Joe Christopher	.360
Ron Hunt	.357

1965
Johnny Lewis	.331
Ed Kranepool	.303
Charley Smith	.273

1966
Ron Hunt	.356
Cleon Jones	.318
Ed Kranepool	.316

1967
Tommy Davis	.342
Ed Kranepool	.321
Bud Harrelson	.317
(Ron Swoboda .340, 494 PA)	

1968
Cleon Jones	.341
Ron Swoboda	.325
(Jerry Grote .357, 454 PA)	

1969
Cleon Jones	.422
Tommie Agee	.342
(Art Shamsky .375, 349 PA)	

1970
Cleon Jones	.352
Bud Harrelson	.351
Tommie Agee	.344
(Wayne Garrett .390, 454 PA)	

1971
Cleon Jones	.382
Bud Harrelson	.319
(Tommie Agee .362, 482 PA)	
(Ed Kranepool .340, 467 PA)	

1972
Strike Season, Min. 484 PA
(Wayne Garrett .374 in 377PA)	
(Rusty Staub .372, 277 PA)	
(John Milner .340, 423 PA)	

1973
Rusty Staub	.361
Wayne Garrett	.348
Felix Millan	.332

1974
Rusty Staub	.347
Cleon Jones	.343
John Milner	.337

1975
Rusty Staub	.371
Del Unser	.337
Felix Millan	.329
(Wayne Garrett 379, 328 PA)	

1976
John Milner	.362
Felix Millan	.341
Dave Kingman	.286
(Joe Torre .358, 340 AB)	

1977
Lenny Randle	.383
Lee Mazzilli	.340
(Steve Henderson .372, 398 PA)	

1978
John Stearns	.364
Lee Mazzilli	.353
Steve Henderson	.333
(Elliott Maddox .370, 469 PA)	

1979
Lee Mazzilli	.395
Richie Hebner	.354
Joel Youngblood	.346

1980
Lee Mazzilli	.370
Steve Henderson	.368
Joel Youngblood	.340

1981
Strike Season, Min. 319 PA
Hubie Brooks	.345
Dave Kingman	.326
Lee Mazzilli	.324

1982
Mookie Wilson	.314
George Foster	.309
Dave Kingman	.285
(Wally Backman .387, 312 PA)	

1983
Mookie Wilson	.300
George Foster	.289
Hubie Brooks	.284
(Keith Hernandez .424, 389 PA)	

1984
Keith Hernandez	.409
Darryl Strawberry	.343
Hubie Brooks	.341
(Wally Backman .360, 499 PA)	

1985
Keith Hernandez	.384
Gary Carter	.365
George Foster	.331
(Dar. Strawberry .389, 470 PA)	

1986
Keith Hernandez	.413
Darryl Strawberry	.358
Ray Knight	.351
(Len Dykstra .377, 498 PA)	
(Wally Backman .376, 440 PA)	

1987
Darryl Strawberry	.398
Keith Hernandez	.377
Howard Johnson	.364
(Tim Teufel .398, 350 PA)	

1988
Darryl Strawberry	.366
Howard Johnson	.343
Kevin McReynolds	.336
(Dave Magadan .393, 380 PA)	
(Wally Backman .388, 347 PA)	

1989
Howard Johnson	.369
Kevin McReynolds	.326
Gregg Jefferies	.314

1990
Dave Magadan	.417
Darryl Strawberry	.361
Kevin McReynolds	.353

1991
Dave Magadan	.378
Howard Johnson	.342
Kevin McReynolds	.322

1992
| Bobby Bonilla | .348 |
| Eddie Murray | .336 |

(Dave Magadan .390, 379 PA)

1993
Bobby Bonilla	.352
Eddie Murray	.325
Jeff Kent	.320

(Howard Johnson .354, 280 PA)

1994
Strike Season, Min, 350 PA
Bobby Bonilla	.374
Jeff Kent	.341
Jose Vizcaino	.310

(Rico Brogna .380, 138 PA)

1995
Strike Season, Min. 446 PA
Rico Brogna	.342
Jose Vizcaino	.332
Jeff Kent	.327

(Bobby Bonilla .385, 351 PA)
(Brett Butler .381, 418 PA)

1996
Bernard Gilkey	.393
Lance Johnson	.362
Todd Hundley	.356
Jose Vizcaino	.356

1997
John Olerud	.400
Todd Hundley	.394
Edgardo Alfonzo	.391

1998
John Olerud	.447
Brian McRae	.360
Edgardo Alfonzo	.355

(Mike Piazza .417, 446 PA)

1999
John Olerud	.427
Rickey Henderson	.423
Roger Cedeno	.396

2000
Edgardo Alfonzo	.425
Mike Piazza	.398
Todd Zeile	.356

(Benny Agbayani .391, 414 PA)

2001
Mike Piazza	.384
Todd Zeile	.359
Robin Ventura	.359

(Benny Agbayani .364, 339 PA)
(Desi Relaford .364, 340 PA)

2002
Edgardo Alfonzo	.391
Mike Piazza	.359
Mo Vaughn	.349

2003
| Roger Cedeno | .320 |
| Ty Wigginton | .318 |

(Cliff Floyd .376, 425 PA)

2004
Mike Piazza	.362
Kaz Matsui	.331
Mike Cameron	.319

2005
David Wright	.388
Cliff Floyd	.358
Carlos Beltran	.330

2006
Carlos Beltran	.388
David Wright	.381
Carlos Delgado	.361

2007
David Wright	.416
Jose Reyes	.354
Carlos Beltran	.353

(Moises Alou .392 in 360 PA)

2008
David Wright	.390
Carlos Beltran	.376
Jose Reyes	.358

2009
David Wright	.390
Luis Castillo	.387
Daniel Murphy	.313

(Carlos Beltran .415 in .357 PA)

2010
David Wright	.354
Ike Davis	.351
Jason Bay	.347

2011
Jose Reyes	.384
Jason Bay	.329
Angel Pagan	.322

Bold = Sets Team Record
Ital. = Ties Team Record
* = Leads or Tied For NL Lead

Single Season On Base Leaders
Minimum 502 Plate Appearances

	OBP	PLAYER	YEAR
1.	.447	John Olerud	1998
2.	.427	John Olerud	1999
3.	.425	Edgardo Alfonzo	2000
4.	.423	Rickey Henderson	1999
5.	.422	Cleon Jones	1969
6.	.417	Dave Magadan	1990
7.	.416	David Wright	2007
8.	.413	Keith Hernandez	1986
9.	.409	Keith Hernandez	1984
10.	.400	John Olerud	1997
11.	.398	Mike Piazza	2000
		Darryl Strawberry	1987
13.	.396	Roger Cedeno	1999
14.	.395	Lee Mazzilli	1979
15.	.394	Todd Hundley	1997
16.	.393	Bernard Gilkey	1996
17.	.391	Edgardo Alfonzo	1997, 2002
19.	.390	David Wright	2008, 2009
21.	.388	Carlos Beltran	2006
		David Wright	2005
23.	.387	Luis Castillo	2009
24.	.385	Edgardo Alfonzo	1999
25.	.384	Keith Hernandez	1985
		Mike Piazza	2001

Also

	.424	Richie Ashburn, 1962 (473 PA)
	.417	Mike Piazza, 1998 (446 PA)
	.393	Dave Magadan, 1988 (370 PA)
	.391	Benny Agbayani, 2000 (414 PA)

Career On Base Percentage Leaders
Minimum 2000 Plate Appearances

	OBP	Player
1.	.425	John Olerud
2.	.391	Dave Magadan
3.	.387	Keith Hernandez
4.	.380	David Wright
5.	.373	Mike Piazza
6.	.369	Carlos Beltran
7.	.367	Edgardo Alfonzo
8.	.360	Steve Henderson
9.	.359	Darryl Strawberry
10.	.358	Rusty Staub
11.	.357	Lee Mazzilli
12.	.356	Bobby Bonilla
13.	.353	Wally Backman
14.	.351	Carlos Delgado
15.	.348	Wayne Garrett
16.	.341	Howard Johnson
		John Stearns
18.	.340	Cleon Jones
	.340	Jose Reyes
20.	.339	John Milner
21.	.333	Joel Youngblood
22.	.331	Kevin McReynolds
23.	.329	Tommie Agee
24.	.326	Felix Millan
25.	.324	Bud Harrelson

Runs Batted In

YEAR-BY-YEAR RBI LEADERS

1962
Frank Thomas	94
Felix Mantilla	59
Charlie Neal	58

1963
Frank Thomas	60
Jim Hickman	51
Duke Snider	45

1964
Joe Christopher	76
Charley Smith	58
Jim Hickman	57

1965
Charley Smith	62
Ed Kranepool	53
Ron Swoboda	50

1966
Ken Boyer	61
Cleon Jones	57
Ed Kranepool	57

1967
Tommy Davis	73
Ed Kranepool	54
Ron Swoboda	53

1968
Ron Swoboda	59
Cleon Jones	55
Ed Charles	53

1969
Tommie Agee	76
Cleon Jones	75
Ron Swoboda	52

1970
Donn Clendenon	97
Tommie Agee	75
Cleon Jones	63

1971
Cleon Jones	69
Ed Kranepool	58
Tommie Agee	50

1972
Cleon Jones	52
Tommie Agee	47
John Milner	38
Rusty Staub	38

1973
Rusty Staub	76
John Milner	72
Wayne Garrett	58

1974
Rusty Staub	78
John Milner	63
Cleon Jones	60

1975
Rusty Staub	105
Dave Kingman	88
Felix Millan	56

1976
Dave Kingman	86
John Milner	78
Ed Kranepool	49

1977
Steve Henderson	65
John Milner	57
John Stearns	55

1978
Willie Montanez	96
John Stearns	73
Steve Henderson	65

1979
Richie Hebner	79
Lee Mazzilli	79
John Stearns	66

1980
Lee Mazzilli	76
Joel Youngblood	69
Steve Henderson	58

1981
Dave Kingman	59
Hubie Brooks	38
Lee Mazzilli	34

1982
Dave Kingman	99
George Foster	70
Mookie Wilson	55

1983
George Foster	90
Darryl Strawberry	74
Hubie Brooks	58

1984
Darryl Strawberry	97
Keith Hernandez	94
George Foster	86

1985
Gary Carter	100
Keith Hernandez	91
Darryl Strawberry	79

1986
Gary Carter	105
Darryl Strawberry	93
Keith Hernandez	83

1987
Darryl Strawberry	104
Howard Johnson	99
Kevin McReynolds	95

1988
Darryl Strawberry	101
Kevin McReynolds	99
Howard Johnson	68

1989
Howard Johnson	101
Kevin McReynolds	85
Darryl Strawberry	77

1990
Darryl Strawberry	108
Howard Johnson	90
Kevin McReynolds	82

1991
Howard Johnson	117*
Kevin McReynolds	74
Gregg Jefferies	62

1992
Eddie Murray	93
Bobby Bonilla	70
Howard Johnson	43

1993
Eddie Murray	100
Bobby Bonilla	87
Jeff Kent	80

1994
Jeff Kent	68
Bobby Bonilla	67
Ryan Thompson	59

1995
Rico Brogna	76
Jeff Kent	65
Jose Vizcaino	56

1996
Bernard Gilkey	117
Todd Hundley	112
Lance Johnson	69

1997
John Olerud	102
Todd Hundley	86
Butch Huskey	81

1998
John Olerud	93
Brian McRae	79
Edgardo Alfonzo	78

1999
Mike Piazza	124
Robin Ventura	120
Edgardo Alfonzo	108

2000
Mike Piazza	113
Edgardo Alfonzo	94
Robin Ventura	84

2001
Mike Piazza	94
Todd Zeile	62
Robin Ventura	61

2002
Mike Piazza	98
Mo Vaughn	72
Edgardo Alfonzo	56

2003
Ty Wigginton	71
Cliff Floyd	68
Jason Phillips	58

2004

Mike Cameron	76
Cliff Floyd	63
Mike Piazza	54

2005

David Wright	102
Cliff Floyd	98
Carlos Beltran	78

2006

Carlos Beltran	116
David Wright	116
Carlos Delgado	114

2007

Carlos Beltran	112
David Wright	107
Carlos Delgado	87

2008

David Wright	124
Carlos Delgado	115
Carlos Beltran	108

2009

David Wright	72
Daniel Murphy	63
Carlos Beltran	48

2010

David Wright	103
Ike Davis	71
Angel Pagan	69

2011

Carlos Beltran	66
David Wright	61
Jason Bay	57

Bold = SetsTeam Record
Ital. = Ties Team Record
*= Leads or Tied For NL

Single Season RBI Leaders

	RBI	PLAYER	YEAR
1.	124	Mike Piazza	1999
		David Wright	2008
3.	120	Robin Ventura	1999
4.	117	Bernard Gilkey	1996
		Howard Johnson	1991
6.	116	Carlos Beltran	2006
		David Wright	2006
8.	115	Carlos Delgado	2008
9.	114	Carlos Delgado	2006
10.	113	Mike Piazza	2000
11.	112	Todd Hundley	1996
		Carlos Beltran	2007
13.	108	Edgardo Alfonzo	1999
		Darryl Strawberry	1990
		Carlos Beltran	2008
16.	107	David Wright	2007
17.	105	Gary Carter	1986
		Rusty Staub	1975
19.	104	Darryl Strawberry	1987
20.	103	David Wright	2010
21.	102	John Olerud	1997
		David Wright	2005
23.	101	Howard Johnson	1989
		Darryl Strawberry	1988
25.	100	Gary Carter	1985
		Eddie Murray	1993

Career RBI Leaders

	RBI	PLAYER
1.	733	Darryl Strawberry
2.	725	David Wright
3.	655	Mike Piazza
4.	629	Howard Johnson
5.	614	Ed Kranepool
6.	559	Carlos Beltran
7.	538	Edgardo Alfonzo
8.	521	Cleon Jones
9.	468	Keith Hernandez
10.	456	Kevin McReynolds
11	423	Jose Reyes
12.	399	Rusty Staub
13.	397	Todd Hundley
14.	389	Dave Kingman
15.	361	George Foster
16.	357	Jerry Grote
17.	353	Lee Mazzilli
18.	349	Gary Carter
19.	342	Mookie Wilson
20.	339	Carlos Delgado
21.	338	John Milner
22.	312	John Stearns
23.	304	Ron Swoboda
24.	295	Bobby Bonilla
		Wayne Garrett

Runs Scored

YEAR-BY-YEAR RUNS SCORED LEADERS

1962
Frank Thomas	69
Charlie Neal	59
Hickman/Mantilla	54

1963
Ron Hunter	64
Jim Hickman	53
Duke Snider	44

1964
Joe Christopher	78
Ron Hunt	59
Altman/Hickman	48

1965
Johnny Lewis	64
Ron Swoboda	52
Charley Smith	49

1966
Cleon Jones	74
Ron Hunt	63
Ken Boyer	62

1967
Tommy Davis	72
Bud Harrelson	59
Ron Swoboda	47

1968
Cleon Jones	63
Ron Swoboda	46
Ed Charles	41

1969
Tommie Agee	97
Cleon Jones	92
Ken Boswell	48

1970
Tommie Agee	107
Wayne Garrett	74
Bud Harrelson	72

1971
Cleon Jones	63
Ed Kranepool	61
Tommie Agee	58

1972
Bud Harrelson	54
Tommie Agee	52
John Milner	52

1973
Felix Millan	82
Rusty Staub	77
Wayne Garrett	76

1974
John Milner	70
Rusty Staub	65
Cleon Jones	62

1975
Rusty Staub	93
Felix Millan	81
Dave Kingman	65
Del Unser	65

1976
Dave Kingman	70
John Milner	56
Felix Millan	55

1977
Len Randle	78
Steve Henderson	67
Lee Mazzilli	66

1978
Steve Henderson	83
Lee Mazzilli	78
Willie Montanez	66

1979
Joel Youngblood	90
Frank Taveras	89
Lee Mazzilli	78

1980
Lee Mazzilli	82
Steve Henderson	75
Frank Taveras	65

1981
Mookie Wilson	49
Dave Kingman	40
Lee Mazzilli	36

1982
Mookie Wilson	90
Dave Kingman	80
George Foster	64

1983
Mookie Wilson	91
George Foster	74
Darryl Strawberry	63

1984
Mookie Wilson	88
Keith Hernandez	83
Darryl Strawberry	75

1985
Keith Hernandez	87
Gary Carter	83
Darryl Strawberry	78

1986
Keith Hernandez	94
Gary Carter	81
Len Dykstra	77

1987
Darryl Strawberry	108
Howard Johnson	93
Keith Hernandez	87

1988
Darryl Strawberry	101
Howard Johnson	85
Kevin McReynolds	82

1989
Howard Johnson	104*
Kevin McReynolds	74
Gregg Jefferies	72

1990
Gregg Jefferies	96
Darryl Strawberry	92
Howard Johnson	89

1991
Howard Johnson	108
Kevin McReynolds	65
Gregg Jefferies	59

1992
Eddie Murray	64
Bobby Bonilla	62
Dick Schofield	52

1993
Bobby Bonilla	81
Eddie Murray	77
Jeff Kent	65

1994
Bobby Bonilla	60
Jeff Kent	53
Jose Vizcaino	47

1995
Rico Brogna	72
Jose Vizcaino	66
Jeff Kent	65

1996
Lance Johnson	117
Bernard Gilkey	108
Todd Hundley	85

1997
John Olerud	90
Bernard Gilkey	85
Edgardo Alfonzo	84

1998
Edgardo Alfonzo	94
John Olerud	91
Brian McRae	79

1999
Edgardo Alfonzo	123
John Olerud	107
Mike Piazza	100

2000
Edgardo Alfonzo	109
Mike Piazza	90
Derek Bell	87

2001
Mike Piazza	81
Robin Ventura	70
Todd Zeile	66

2002
Mike Piazza	69
Mo Vaughn	67
Jeromy Burnitz	65
Roger Cedeno	65

2003
Ty Wigginton	73
Roger Cedeno	70
Cliff Floyd	57

2004

Mike Cameron	76
Kaz Matsui	65
Cliff Floyd	55

2005

Jose Reyes	99
David Wright	99
Cliff Floyd	85

2006

Carlos Beltran	127
Jose Reyes	122
David Wright	96

2007

Jose Reyes	119
David Wright	113
Carlos Beltran	93

2008

Carlos Beltran	116
David Wright	115
Jose Reyes	113

2009

David Wright	88
Luis Castillo	77
Daniel Murphy	60

2010

David Wright	87
Jose Reyes	83
Angel Pagan	80

2011

Jose Reyes	101
Angel Pagan	68
Carlos Beltran	61

Bold = Team Record
Ital. = Ties Team Record
*= Leads or Tied For NL

Single Season Runs Leaders

	R	PLAYER	YEAR
1.	127	Carlos Beltran	2006
2.	123	Edgardo Alfonzo	1999
3.	122	Jose Reyes	2006
4.	119	Jose Reyes	2007
5.	117	Lance Johnson	1996
6.	116	Carlos Beltran	2008
7.	115	David Wright	2008
8.	113	David Wright	2007
		Jose Reyes	2008
10.	109	Edgardo Alfonzo	2000
11.	108	Bernard Gilkey	1996
		Howard Johnson	1991
		Darryl Strawberry	1987
14.	107	Tommie Agee	1970
		John Olerud	1999
16.	104	Howard Johnson	1989
17.	101	Darryl Strawberry	1988
	101	Jose Reyes	2011
19.	100	Mike Piazza	1999
20.	99	Jose Reyes	2005
		David Wright	2005
22.	97	Tommie Agee	1969
23.	96	Gregg Jefferies	1990
		David Wright	2006
25.	94	Edgardo Alfonzo	1998
		Keith Hernandez	1986

Career Runs Leaders

	R	PLAYER
1.	735	Jose Reyes
2.	699	David Wright
3.	662	Darryl Strawberry
4.	627	Howard Johnson
5.	614	Edgardo Alfonzo
6.	592	Mookie Wilson
7.	563	Cleon Jones
8.	551	Carlos Beltran
9.	536	Ed Kranepool
10.	532	Mike Piazza
11.	490	Bud Harrelson
12.	455	Keith Hernandez
13.	405	Kevin McReynolds
14.	404	Lee Mazzilli
15.	389	Wayne Garrett
16.	359	Wally Backman
17.	344	Tommie Agee
18.	340	Todd Hundley
19.	334	John Stearns
20.	315	John Milner
21.	314	Jerry Grote
22.	308	Felix Millan
23.	302	Dave Kingman
24.	296	Rusty Staub
25.	290	George Foster

Sacrifice Flies

YEAR-BY-YEAR SACRIFICE FLIES LEADERS

1962	Felix Mantilla	7	1980	Joel Youngblood	9	1999	Edgardo Alfonzo	9
1963	Ron Hunt	6	1981	Hubie Brooks	6	2000	Jay Payton	8
1964	Joe Christopher	6	1982	Ellis Valentine	7	2001	Edgardo Alfonzo	5
1965	Ed Kranepool	8	1983	Danny Heep	5		Desi Relaford	5
1966	Ken Boyer	7	1984	Keith Hernandez	9	2002	Rey Ordonez	4
1967	Ed Charles	6	1985	Keith Hernandez	10	2003	Timo Perez	9
1968	Ed Charles	4	1986	Gary Carter	15*	2004	Jason Phillips	5
	Art Shamsky	4	1987	Kevin McReynolds	8	2005	Carlos Beltran	6
1969	Wayne Garrett	5	1988	Darryl Strawberry	9	2006	Carlos Delgado	10*
	Art Shamsky	5	1989	Kevin Elster	8	2007	Carlos Beltran	10
1970	Bud Harrelson	8	1990	Dave Magadan	10		Paul LoDuca	10
1971	Cleon Jones	5	1991	Howard Johnson	15*	2008	David Wright	11*
1972	Rusty Staub	5	1992	Eddie Murray	8	2009	David Wright	6
1973	Cleon Jones	8	1993	Eddie Murray	9		Daniel Murphy	6
1974	Rusty Staub	7	1994	Joe Orsulak	7		Omir Santos	6
1975	Rusty Staub	9	1995	Joe Orsulak	6	2010	David Wright	12
1976	Mike Phillips	5	1996	Bernard Gilkey	8	2011	Jason Bay	6
1977	Ed Kranepool	5	1997	Bernard Gilkey	12*			
1978	Willie Montanez	9	1998	Carlos Baerga	7	* = Led NL or tied for NL		
1979	Richie Hebner	8		John Olerud	7			

Single Season Sac-Fly Leaders

	SF	Player	Year
1.	15	Howard Johnson	1991
		Gary Carter	1986
3.	12	Bernard Gilkey	1997
	12	David Wright	2010
5.	11	David Wright	2008
6.	10	6 Players	

Career Sac-Fly Leaders

	SF	Player
1.	58	Ed Kranepool
2.	53	David Wright
3.	50	Howard Johnson
4.	41	Cleon Jones
5.	40	Edgardo Alfonzo
6.	39	Darryl Strawberry
7.	38	Carlos Beltran
8.	37	Rusty Staub
9.	33	Kevin McReynolds
10.	31	Gary Carter, Keith Hernandez

Hit by Pitch

YEAR-BY-YEAR HIT BY PITCH LEADERS

Year	Player	HBP		Year	Player	HBP		Year	Player	HBP
1962	Frank Thomas	8		1980	Elliott Maddox	6*		1997	John Olerud	13
1963	Ron Hunt	13		1981	4 players	2		1998	Carlos Baerga	6
1964	Ron Hunt	11		1982	Hubie Brooks	5		1999	John Olerud	11
1965	Joe Christopher	6			Joel Youngblood	5		2000	Benny Agbayani	7
1966	Ron Hunt	11		1983	4 players	4		2001	Joe McEwing	10
1967	Ed Charles	7		1984	George Foster	6		2002	Jeromy Burnitz	10
	Tommy Davis	7		1985	Gary Carter	6			John Valentin	10
1968	Art Shamsky	7		1986	Gary Carter	6			Mo Vaughn	10
1969	Cleon Jones	7			Darryl Strawberry	6		2003	Jason Phillips	10
1970	Cleon Jones	5		1987	Howard Johnson	5		2004	Cliff Floyd	11
1971	Mike Jorgensen	3		1988	Gary Carter	7		2005	Cliff Floyd	11
	Ted Martinez	3			Darryl Strawberry	7		2006	Cliff Floyd	12
1972	Duffy Dyer	5		1989	Juan Samuel	10		2007	Carlos Delgado	11
	John Milner	5		1990	Gregg Jefferies	5		2008	Carlos Delgado	8
1973	Felix Millan	6		1991	Keith Miller	5		2009	Fernando Tatis	9
1974	Felix Millan	8		1992	Dick Schofield	5		2010	Ruben Tejada	8
1975	Felix Millan	12*		1993	Jeff Kent	8		2011	Justin Turner	10
1976	Felix Millan	7		1994	Fernando Vina	12*				
1977	John Stearns	7		1995	Jeff Kent	8		* = Led NL or tied		
1978	John Stearns	8		1996	Bernard Gilkey	4				
1979	Richie Hebner	8			Carl Everett	4				

Single Season HBP Leaders

	HBP	Player	Year
1.	13	John Olerud	1997
	13	Ron Hunt	1963
3.	12	Cliff Floyd	2006
		Fernando Vina	1994
		Felix Millan	1975
6.	11	Carlos Delgado	2007
		Cliff Floyd	2005
		Cliff Floyd	2004
		John Olerud	1999
		Ron Hunt	1966
		Ron Hunt	1964

Career Hit by Pitch Leaders

	HBP	Player
1.	41	Ron Hunt
2.	39	Cleon Jones
3.	37	Cliff Floyd
4.	36	Felix Millan
5.	33	Carlos Delgado
	33	David Wright
7.	29	Edgardo Alfonzo
8.	28	John Olerud
		Jeff Kent
10.	26	Darryl Strawberry

Sacrifice Hits

YEAR-BY-YEAR SACRIFICE HITS LEADERS

1962	Charlie Neal	9
1963	Ron Hunt	8
1964	Galen Cisco	6
	Roy McMillan	6
1965	Roy McMillan	16
1966	Ron Hunt	10
1967	Bud Harrelson	7
	Cleon Jones	7
1968	Ed Kranepool	10
1969	Rod Gaspar	7
	Gary Gentry	7
1970	Bud Harrelson	12
1971	Bud Harrelson	13
1972	Jim McAndrew	10
1973	Felix Millan	18
1974	Felix Millan	24
1975	Felix Millan	17
1976	Jerry Koosman	13
1977	Bruce Boisclair	7
	Nino Espinosa	7
	Bud Harrelson	7
1978	Tim Foli	12
1979	Frank Taveras	10
1980	Frank Taveras	10
1981	Doug Flynn	7
	John Stearns	7
1982	Ron Gardenhire	12
1983	Ed Lynch	11
1984	Dwight Gooden	10

1985	Wally Backman	14
1986	Wally Backman	14
1987	Ron Darling	10
	Sid Fernandez	10
1988	Wally Backman	9
	Ron Darling	9
	Dwight Gooden	9
1989	Sid Fernandez	10
1990	Dwight Gooden	14
1991	Frank Viola	10
1992	Dick Schofield	10
1993	Sid Fernandez	8
	Bret Saberhagen	8
1994	Bobby Jones	8
1995	Bobby Jones	18
1996	Mark Clark	10
	Pete Harnisch	10
1997	Rey Ordonez	14
1998	Rey Ordonez	15
1999	Al Leiter	11
	Rey Ordonez	11
2000	Rick Reed	14
2001	Rey Ordonez	7
2002	Timo Perez	10
2003	Steve Trachsel	11
2004	Steve Trachsel	11
2005	Miguel Cairo	12
2006	Endy Chavez	11
2007	John Maine	14
2008	Endy Chavez	9
2009	Luis Castillo	19
2010	Luis Castillo	11
2011	R.A. Dickey	9

= Led NL or tied

Single Season Sac Leaders

	SH	Player	Year
1.	24	Felix Millan	1974
2.	19	Luis Castillo	2009
3.	18	Bobby Jones	1995
		Felix Millan	1973
5.	17	Felix Millan	1975
6.	16	Roy McMillan	1965
7.	15	Rey Ordonez	1998
		Jerry Koosman	1973
9.	14	John Maine	2007
		Rick Reed	2000
		Rey Ordonez	1997
		Dwight Gooden	1990
		Wally Backman	1986
		Wally Backman	1985

Career Sacrifice Hits Leaders

	SH	Player
1.	85	Dwight Gooden
		Jerry Koosman
3.	77	Tom Seaver
		Bud Harrelson
5.	68	Felix Millan
6.	64	Rey Ordonez
		Sid Fernandez
		Ron Darling
9.	61	Bobby Jones
10.	60	Wally Backman

Saves

YEAR-BY-YEAR SAVES LEADERS

1962
Craig Anderson	4
Roger Craig	3
3 Pitchers	1

1963
Larry Bearnarth	4
Ken Mackenzie	3
Roger Craig	2

1964
Willard Hunter	5
Larry Bearnarth	3
Bill Wakefield	2

1965
Dennis Ribant	3
Dave Eilers	2
Gordie Richardson	2

1966
Jack Hamilton	13
Dennis Ribant	3
6 Pitchers	1

1967
Ron Taylor	8
Hal Reniff	4
Don Shaw	3

1968
Ron Taylor	13
Cal Koonce	11
Al Jackson	3

1969
Ron Taylor	13
Tug McGraw	12
Cal Koonce	7

1970
Ron Taylor	13
Tug McGraw	10
Jim McAndrew	2
Rich Folkers	2

1971
Danny Frisella	12
Tug McGraw	8
Ron Taylor	2

1972
Tug McGraw	27
Danny Frisella	9
Chuck Taylor	2

1973
Tug McGraw	25
Harry Parker	5
Buzz Capra	4

1974
Harry Parker	4
Bob Apodaca	3
Tug McGraw	3

1975
Bob Apodaca	13
Rick Baldwin	6
Ken Sanders	5

1976
Skip Lockwood	19
Bob Apodaca	5
Ken Sanders	1

1977
Skip Lockwood	20
Bob Apodaca	5
Bob Myrick	2

1978
Skip Lockwood	15
Dale Murray	5
Mardie Cornejo	3

1979
Skip Lockwood	9
Neil Allen	8
Ed Glynn	7

1980
Neil Allen	22
Jeff Reardon	6
5 pitchers	1

1981
Neil Allen	18
Jeff Reardon	2
4 pitchers	1

1982
Neil Allen	19
Jesse Orosco	4
Mike Scott	3

1983
Jesse Orosco	17
Doug Sisk	11
Neil Allen	2
Carlos Diaz	2

1984
Jesse Orosco	31
Doug Sisk	15
Ed Lynch	2

1985
Roger McDowell	17
Jesse Orosco	17
Doug Sisk	2

1986
Roger McDowell	22
Jesse Orosco	21
3 pitchers	1

1987
Roger McDowell	25
Jesse Orosco	16
Randy Myers	6

1988
Randy Myers	26
Roger McDowell	16
Terry Leach	3

1989
Randy Myers	24
Rick Aguilera	7
Roger McDowell	4

1990
John Franco	33*
Alejandro Pena	5
Wally Whitehurst	2

1991
John Franco	30
Alejandro Pena	4
Pete Schourek	2

1992
John Franco	15
Anthony Young	15
Lee Guetterman	2

1993
John Franco	10
Mike Maddux	5
Jeff Innis	3
Anthony Young	3

1994
John Franco	30*
Mike Maddux	2
Josias Manzanillo	2

1995
John Franco	29
Doug Henry	4
Jerry Dipoto	2

1996
John Franco	28
Doug Henry	9
Derek Wallace	3

1997
John Franco	36
Greg McMichael	7
Cory Lidle	2
Mel Rojas	2

1998
John Franco	38
Turk Wendell	4
Mel Rojas	2

1999
Armando Benitez	22
John Franco	19
Dennis Cook	3
Turk Wendell	3

2000
Armando Benitez	41
John Franco	4
Dennis Cook	2

2001
Armando Benitez	43
John Franco	2
Rick White	2

2002
Armando Benitez	33
Scott Strickland	2
Mark Guthrie	1

2003

Armando Benitez	21
David Weathers	7
Mike Stanton	5

2004

Braden Looper	29
Bartolome Fortunato	1
Orber Moreno	1

2005

Braden Looper	28
Aaron Heilman	5
Roberto Hernandez	4

2006

Billy Wagner	40
Chad Bradford	2
Jorge Julio	1

2007

Billy Wagner	34
Pedro Feliciano	2
Scott Schoeneweis	2

2008

Billy Wagner	27
Luis Ayala	9
Aaron Heilman	3

2009

Francisco Rodriguez	35
J.J. Putz	2
Bobby Parnell	1
Sean Green	1

2010

Francisco Rodriguez	25
Hisanori Takahashi	8
3 Pitchers	1

2011

Francisco Rodrguez	23
Jason Isringhausen	7
Bobby Parnell	6

Bold = Team Record
Ital. = Ties Team Record
* = Led league or tied

Single Season Saves Leaders

	SV	Player	Year
1.	43	Armando Benitez	2001
2.	41	Armando Benitez	2000
3.	40	Billy Wagner	2006
4.	38	John Franco	1998
5.	36	John Franco	1997
6.	35	Francisco Rodriguez	2009
7.	34	Billy Wagner	2007
8.	33	Armando Benitez	2002
		John Franco	1990
10.	31	Jesse Orosco	1984
11.	30	John Franco	1991, 1994
13.	29	John Franco	1995
		Braden Looper	2004
15.	28	John Franco	1996
		Braden Looper	2005
17.	27	Tug McGraw	1972
		Billy Wagner	2008
19.	26	Randy Myers	1988
20.	25	Roger McDowell	1987
		Tug McGraw	1973
		Francisco Rodriguez	2010
23.	24	Randy Myers	1989
24.	23	Francisco Rodriguez	2011
25.	22	Neil Allen	1980
		Armando Benitez	1999
		Roger McDowell	1986

Career Saves Leaders

	SV	Player
1.	276	John Franco
2.	160	Armando Benitez
3.	107	Jesse Orosco
4.	101	Billy Wagner
5.	86	Tug McGraw
6.	84	Roger McDowell
7.	83	Francisco Rodriguez
8.	69	Neil Allen
9.	65	Skip Lockwood
10.	57	Braden Looper
11.	56	Randy Myers
12.	49	Ron Taylor
13.	33	Doug Sisk
14.	26	Bob Apodaca
15.	24	Danny Frisella
16.	18	Cal Koonce
		Anthony Young
18.	14	Jack Hamilton
19.	13	Doug Henry
20.	11	Harry Parker
21.	10	Jeff Reardon
		Turk Wendell
23.	9	Dale Murray
		Alejandro Pena
		Aaron Heilman
		Luis Ayala

Shutouts

YEAR-BY-YEAR SHUTOUTS LEADERS

1962
Al Jackson	4
16 Pitchers	0

1963
Carl Willey	4
Grover Powell	1
11 pitchers	0

1964
Al Jackson	3
Galen Cisco	2
Tracy Stallard	2

1965
Al Jackson	3
Galen Cisco	1
Tom Parsons	1
Dick Selma	1

1966
Jack Fisher	2
Bob Shaw	2
4 pitchers	1

1967
Don Cardwell	3
Tom Seaver	2
3 pitchers	1

1968
Jerry Koosman	7
Tom Seaver	5
Dick Selma	3

1969
Jerry Koosman	6
Tom Seaver	5
Gary Gentry	3

1970
Jim McAndrew	3
Gary Gentry	2
Nolan Ryan	2
Tom Seaver	2

1971
Tom Seaver	4
Gary Gentry	3
Ray Sadecki	2

1972
Jon Matlack	4
Tom Seaver	3
Jerry Koosman	1

1973
Jerry Koosman	3
Jon Matlack	3
Tom Seaver	3

1974
Jon Matlack	7*
Tom Seaver	5
Tug McGraw	1
Ray Sadecki	1

1975
Tom Seaver	5
Jerry Koosman	4
Jon Matlack	3

1976
Jon Matlack	6*
Tom Seaver	5
Jerry Koosman	3

1977
Jon Matlack	3
Tom Seaver	3
4 pitchers	1

1978
Pat Zachry	2
Mike Bruhert	1
Nino Espinosa	1
Craig Swan	1

1979
Craig Swan	1
Pete Falcone	1
Kevin Kobel	1

1980
Pat Zachry	3
Mark Bomback	1
Mike Scott	1
Craig Swan	1

1981
Pete Falcone	1
18 pitchers	0

1982
Randy Jones	1
Terry Leach	1
Charlie Puleo	1

1983
Tom Seaver	2
Walt Terrell	2
Neil Allen	1

1984
Dwight Gooden	3
Ron Darling	2
Walt Terrell	1

1985
Dwight Gooden	8
Ron Darling	2
Terry Leach	1
Ed Lynch	1

1986
Ron Darling	2
Dwight Gooden	2
Bob Ojeda	2

1987
Dwight Gooden	3
Sid Fernandez	1
Terry Leach	1

1988
Bob Ojeda	5
David Cone	4
Ron Darling	4

1989
David Cone	2
Sid Fernandez	2
Bob Ojeda	2

1990
Frank Viola	3
David Cone	2
Sid Fernandez	1
Dwight Gooden	1

1991
David Cone	2
Dwight Gooden	1
Pete Schourek	1

1992
David Cone	5*
Sid Fernandez	2
Bret Saberhagen	1

1993
Dwight Gooden	2
Sid Fernandez	1
Eric Hillman	1
Bret Saberhagen	1

1994
Jason Jacome	1
Bobby Jones	1
17 pitchers	0

1995
Bobby Jones	1
21 pitchers	0

1996
Pete Harnisch	1
Jason Isringhausen	1
Bobby Jones	1

1997
Bobby Jones	1
Dave Mlicki	1
Armando Reynoso	1

1998
Al Leiter	2
Rick Reed	1
18 pitchers	0

1999
Al Leiter	1
Rick Reed	1
Kenny Rogers	1

2000
Mike Hampton	1
Al Leiter	1
18 pitchers	0

2001
Kevin Appier	1
Rick Reed	1
Steve Trachsel	1

2002
Al Leiter	2
4 pitchers	1

2003
Steve Trachsel	2
Al Leiter	1
23 pitchers	0

2004
Kris Benson	1
Tom Glavine	1
24 pitchers	0

2005
Tom Glavine	1
Aaron Heilman	1
Pedro Martinez	1

2006
John Maine	1
Oliver Perez	1
Alay Soler	1

2007
Tom Glavine	1**
John Maine	1**

2008
Johan Santana	2
23 pitchers	0

2009
Pat Misch	1
Nelson Figueroa	1

2010
Johan Santana	2
R.A. Dickey	1
Jonathon Niese	1

2011
Miguel Batista	1
Chris Capuano	1

Bold = SetsTeam Record
Ital. = Ties Team Record
* = Led league or tied
**= Did not shutout 9 inn.

Single Season Shutouts Leaders

	SHO	Player	Year
1.	8	Dwight Gooden	1985
2.	7	Jerry Koosman	1968
		Jon Matlack	1974
4.	6	Jerry Koosman	1969
		Jon Matlack	1976
6.	5	David Cone	1992
		Bob Ojeda	1988
		Tom Seaver	'68, '69, '74, '75, '76
13.	4	David Cone	1988
		Ron Darling	1988
		Al Jackson	1962
		Jerry Koosman	1975
		Jon Matlack	1972
		Tom Seaver	1971
		Carl Willey	1963
20.	3	Don Cardwell	1967
		Gary Gentry	'69, '71
		Dwight Gooden	'84, '87, '88
		Al Jackson	'64, '65
		Jerry Koosman	'73, '76
		Jon Matlack	'73, '75, 77
		Jim McAndrew	1970
		Tom Seaver	'72, '73, '77
		Dick Selma	1968
		Craig Swan	1979
		Frank Viola	1990
		Pat Zachry	1980

Career Shutouts Leaders

	SHO	Player
1.	44	Tom Seaver
2.	26	Jerry Koosman
		Jon Matlack
4.	23	Dwight Gooden
5.	15	David Cone
6.	10	Ron Darling
		Al Jackson
8.	9	Sid Fernandez
		Bob Ojeda
10.	8	Gary Gentry
11.	7	Al Leiter
		Craig Swan
13.	6	Jim McAndrew
		Pat Zachry
15.	4	Don Cardwell
		Jack Fisher
		Bobby Jones
		Johan Santana
		Dick Selma
		Steve Trachsel
		Frank Viola
		Carl Willey
23.	3	Galen Cisco
		Tom Glavine
		Terry Leach
		Rick Reed
		Ray Sadecki
		Bob Shaw
		Walt Terrell

Slugging Percentage

YEAR-BY-YEAR SLUGGING % LEADERS

Minimum 502 Plate Appearances Except Where Noted

1962
Frank Thomas	.496
Felix Mantilla	.399
Charlie Neal	.388

1963
Jim Hickman	.399
Ron Hunt	.396
(Duke Snider .401, 415 PA)	

1964
Joe Christopher	.466
Ron Hunt	.406

1965
Charley Smith	.393
Ed Kranepool	.371
Johnny Lewis	.384
(Ron Swoboda .424, 438 PA)	

1966
Ken Boyer	.415
Ed Kranepool	.399
Cleon Jones	.372

1967
Tommy Davis	.440
Ed Kranepool	.373
Bud Harrelson	.304
(Ron Swoboda .419, 494 PA)	

1968
Cleon Jones	.452
Ron Swoboda	.373

1969
Cleon Jones	.482
Tommie Agee	.464
(Art Shamsky .488, 349 PA)	

1970
Tommie Agee	.469
Cleon Jones	.417
Bud Harrelson	.309
(D. Clendenon .515, 443 PA)	
(Art Shamsky .432, 442 AB)	

1971
Cleon Jones	.473
Bud Harrelson	.303
(Ed Kranepool .447, 467 PA)	
(Tommie Agee .428, 482 PA)	

1972
Strike Season, Min. 484 PA
(Rusty Staub .452, 278 PA)	
(Willie Mays .446, 242 PA)	
(John Milner .423, 423 PA)	

1973
John Milner	.432
Rusty Staub	.421
Wayne Garrett	.403

1974
Cleon Jones	.421
John Milner	.408
Rusty Staub	.406

1975
Dave Kingman	.494
Rusty Staub	.448
Del Unser	.392

1976
Dave Kingman	.506
John Milner	.447
Felix Millan	.343
(Ed Kranepool .410, 455 PA)	

1977
Len Randle	.404
Lee Mazzilli	.339
(S. Henderson .480, 398 PA)	

1978
Lee Mazzilli	.432
John Stearns	.413
Steve Henderson	.399
(J. Youngblood .436, 285 PA)	

1979
Lee Mazzilli	.449
Joel Youngblood	.436
Richie Hebner	.393

1980
Lee Mazzilli	.431
Steve Henderson	.402
Joel Youngblood	.381

1981
Strike Season, Min. 319 PA
Dave Kingman	.456
Hubie Brooks	.411
Mookie Wilson	.372
(J. Youngblood .531, 161 PA)	

1982
Dave Kingman	.432
Mookie Wilson	.369
George Foster	.367

1983
George Foster	.419
Mookie Wilson	.367
Hubie Brooks	.321
(D. Strawberry .512, 473 PA)	
(K. Hernandez .434, 386 PA)	

1984
Darryl Strawberry	.467
Keith Hernandez	.449
George Foster	.443

1985
Gary Carter	.488
George Foster	.460
Keith Hernandez	.430
(D. Strawberry .557, 470 PA)	

1986
Darryl Strawberry	.507
Keith Hernandez	.446
Gary Carter	.439
(Len Dykstra .445, 498 PA)	

1987
Darryl Strawberry	.583
Howard Johnson	.504
Kevin McReynolds	.495
(Tim Teufel .545, 350 PA)	

1988
Darryl Strawberry	.545*
Kevin McReynolds	.496
Howard Johnson	.422
(M. Wilson .431, 410 PA)	

1989
Howard Johnson	.559
Darryl Strawberry	.466
Kevin McReynolds	.450

1990
Darryl Strawberry	.518
Dave Magadan	.457
Kevin McReynolds	.455

1991
Howard Johnson	.535
Kevin McReynolds	.416
Gregg Jefferies	.374

1992
Bobby Bonilla	.432
Eddie Murray	.423
(Daryl Boston .426, 334 PA)	

1993
Bobby Bonilla	.522
Eddie Murray	.467
Jeff Kent	.446
(J. Burnitz .475, 306 PA)	

1994
Strike Season, Min. 350 PA
Bobby Bonilla	.504
Jeff Kent	.475
Ryan Thompson	.434

1995
Strike Season, Min 446 PA
Rico Brogna	.485
Jeff Kent	.464
Jose Vizcaino	.365
(B. Bonilla .599, 351 PA)	
(T. Hundley .484, 326 PA)	

1996
Bernard Gilkey	.562
Todd Hundley	.550
Lance Johnson	.479

1997
Todd Hundley	.549
John Olerud	.489
Edgardo Alfonzo	.432

1998
John Olerud	.551
Brian McRae	.462
Edgardo Alfonzo	.427
(Mike Piazza .607, 446 PA)	

1999
Mike Piazza	.575
Robin Ventura	.529
Edgardo Alfonzo	.502

2000
Mike Piazza	.614
Edgardo Alfonzo	.542
Todd Zeile	.467
(B. Agbayani .480, 414 PA)	

2001
Mike Piazza	.573
Robin Ventura	.419
Edgardo Alfonzo	.403
(Desi Relaford .472, 340 PA)	

2002
Mike Piazza	.544
Edgardo Alfonzo	.459
Mo Vaughn	.456

2003
Ty Wigginton	.396
Roger Cedeno	.378
(Cliff Floyd .518, 425 PA)	
(Jason Phillips .442, 453 PA)	

2004
Mike Cameron	.479
Mike Piazza	.444
Kaz Matsui	.396

2005
David Wright	.523
Cliff Floyd	.505
Carlos Beltran	.414

2006
Carlos Beltran	.594
Carlos Delgado	.548
David Wright	.531

2007
David Wright	.546
Carlos Beltran	.525
Carlos Delgado	.448
(M. Alou .524 in 360 PA)	

2008
David Wright	.534
Carlos Delgado	.518
Carlos Beltran	.500

2009
David Wright	.447
Daniel Murphy	.427
Luis Castillo	.346
(C. Beltran .500 in 357 PA)	
(J. Francoeur .498 in 308 PA)	

2010
David Wright	.503
Ike Davis	.440
Jose Reyes	.438

2011
Jose Reyes	.493
Jason Bay	.374
Angel Pagan	.372

Bold = Sets Team Record
Ital. = Ties Team Record
* = Led NL or tied

Single Season Slugging Leaders

Minimum 502 Plate Appearances

	SL%	PLAYER	YEAR
1.	.614	Mike Piazza	2000
2.	.594	Carlos Beltran	2006
3.	.583	Darryl Strawberry	1987
4.	.575	Mike Piazza	1999
5.	.573	Mike Piazza	2001
6.	.562	Bernard Gilkey	1996
7.	.559	Howard Johnson	1989
8.	.551	John Olerud	1998
9.	.550	Todd Hundley	1996
10.	.549	Todd Hundley	1997
11.	.548	Carlos Delgado	2006
12.	.546	David Wright	2007
13.	.545	Darryl Strawberry	1988
14.	.544	Mike Piazza	2002
15.	.542	Edgardo Alfonzo	2000
16.	.535	Howard Johnson	1991
17	.534	David Wright	2008
17.	.531	David Wright	2006
18.	.529	Robin Ventura	1999
19.	.525	Carlos Beltran	2007
20.	.523	David Wright	2005
21.	.522	Bobby Bonilla	1993
22.	.518	Darryl Strawberry	1990
		Carlos Delgado	2008
23.	.507	Darryl Strawberry	1986
24.	.506	Dave Kingman	1976
25.	.505	Cliff Floyd	2005

Also

.607, Mike Piazza, 1998 (446 PA)

.557, Darryl Strawbery, 1995 (470 PA)

.525, Benny Agbayani, 1999 (314 PA)

.518, Cliff Floyd, 2003, (425 PA)

Career Slugging Percentage Leaders

Minimum 2000 Plate Appearances

	SL%	Player
1.	.542	Mike Piazza
2.	.520	Darryl Strawberry
3.	.508	David Wright
4.	.506	Carlos Delgado
5.	.501	John Olerud
6.	.500	Carlos Beltran
7.	.495	Bobby Bonilla
8.	.460	Kevin McReynolds
9.	.459	Howard Johnson
10.	.453	Dave Kingman
11.	.445	Edgardo Alfonzo
12.	.441	Jose Reyes
13.	.438	Todd Hundley
14.	.429	Keith Hernandez
15.	.423	Steve Henderson
16.	.422	George Foster
17.	.419	Tommie Agee
		Rusty Staub
19.	.415	John Milner
20.	.412	Gary Carter
21.	.410	Joel Youngblood
22.	.406	Cleon Jones
23.	.396	Lee Mazzilli
24.	.394	Mookie Wilson
25.	.392	Jim Hickman

Stolen Bases

YEAR-BY-YEAR STOLEN BASES LEADERS

1962
Richie Ashburn	12
Elio Chacon	12
Joe Christopher	11

1963
Rod Kanehl	6
Choo Choo Coleman	5
Ron Hunt	5

1964
Joe Christoper	6
Ron Hunt	6
Dick Smith	6

1965
Joe Christopher	4
Johnny Lewis	4
3 Players	3

1966
Cleon Jones	16
Ron Hunt	8
Bud Harrelson	7

1967
Bud Harrelson	12
Cleon Jones	12
Tommy Davis	9

1968
Cleon Jones	23
Tommie Agee	13
Ron Swoboda	8

1969
Cleon Jones	16
Tommie Agee	12
Rod Gaspar	7
Ken Boswell	7

1970
Tommie Agee	31
Bud Harrelson	23
Joe Foy	22

1971
Tommie Agee	28
Bud Harrelson	28
Cleon Jones	6
Ted Martinez	6

1972
Bud Harrelson	12
Tommie Agee	8
Ted Martinez	7

1973
Wayne Garrett	6
Bud Harrelson	5
Ted Martinez	3

1974
John Milner	10
Bud Harrelson	9
Felix Millan	5

1975
Dave Kingman	7
Gene Clines	4
John Stearns	4
Del Unser	4

1976
Bruce Boisclair	9
Bud Harrelson	9
3 players	7

1977
Lenny Randle	33
Lee Mazzilli	22
John Stearns	9

1978
John Stearns	25
Lee Mazzilli	20
Lenny Randle	14

1979
Frank Taveras	42
Lee Mazzilli	34
Joel Youngblood	18

1980
Lee Mazzilli	41
Frank Taveras	32
Steve Henderson	23

1981
Mookie Wilson	24
Lee Mazzilli	17
Frank Taveras	16

1982
Mookie Wilson	58
Bob Bailor	20
John Stearns	17

1983
Mookie Wilson	54
Darryl Strawberry	19
Bob Bailor	18

1984
Mookie Wilson	46
Wally Backman	32
Darryl Strawberry	27

1985
Wally Backman	30
Darryl Strawberry	26
Mookie Wilson	24

1986
Len Dykstra	31
Darryl Strawberry	28
Mookie Wilson	25

1987
Darryl Strawberry	36
Howard Johnson	32
Len Dykstra	27

1988
Len Dykstra	30
Darryl Strawberry	29
Howard Johnson	23

1989
Howard Johnson	41
Juan Samuel	31
Gregg Jefferies	21

1990
Howard Johnson	34
Daryl Boston	16
Keith Miller	15

1991
Vince Coleman	37
Howard Johnson	30
Gregg Jefferies	26

1992
Vince Coleman	24
Howard Johnson	22
Chico Walker	14

1993
Vince Coleman	38
Chico Walker	7
Tony Fernandez	6
Howard Johnson	6

1994
John Cangelosi	5
Joe Orsulak	4
Fernando Vina	3

1995
Brett Butler	21
Jose Vizcaino	8
Damon Buford	7

1996
Lance Johnson	50
Bernard Gilkey	17
Jose Vizcaino	9

1997
Carl Everett	17
Lance Johnson	15
3 players	11

1998
Brian McRae	20
Edgardo Alfonzo	8
Butch Huskey	7

1999
Roger Cedeno	66
Rickey Henderson	37
Edgardo Alfonzo	9

2000
Derek Bell	8
Lenny Harris	8
Melvin Mora	7

2001
Desi Relaford	13
Matt Lawton	10
Joe McEwing	8

2002

Roger Cedeno	25
Roberto Alomar	16
Jeromy Burnitz	10
Timo Perez	10

2003

Roger Cedeno	14
Jose Reyes	13
Ty Wigginton	12

2004

Mike Cameron	22
Jose Reyes	19
Kaz Matsui	14

2005

Jose Reyes	60*
Carlos Beltran	17
David Wright	17

2006

Jose Reyes	64*
David Wright	20
Carlos Beltran	18

2007

Jose Reyes	78*
David Wright	34
Carlos Beltran	23

2008

Jose Reyes	56
Carlos Beltran	25
Luis Castillo	17

2009

David Wright	27
Luis Castillo	20
Angel Pagan	14

2010

Angel Pagan	37
Jose Reyes	30
David Wright	19

2011

Jose Reyes	39
Angel Pagan	32
David Wright	13

Bold = Sets Team Record
Ital. = Ties Team Record
*= Led NL or tied

Single Season Steals Leaders

	SB	PLAYER	YEAR
1.	78	Jose Reyes	2007
2.	66	Roger Cedeno	1999
3.	64	Jose Reyes	2006
4.	60	Jose Reyes	2005
5.	58	Mookie Wilson	1982
6.	56	Jose Reyes	2008
7.	54	Mookie Wilson	1983
8.	50	Lance Johnson	1996
9.	46	Mookie Wilson	1984
10.	42	Frank Taveras	1979
11.	41	Howard Johnson	1989
		Lee Mazzilli	1980
13.	39	Jose Reyes	2011
14.	38	Vince Coleman	1993
15.	37	Vince Coleman	1991
		Rickey Henderson	1999
		Angel Pagan	2010
18.	36	Darryl Strawberry	1987
19.	34	Howard Johnson	1990
		Lee Mazzilli	1979
		David Wright	2007
22.	33	Len Randle	1977
23.	32	Wally Backman	1984
		Howard Johnson	1987
		Frank Taveras	1980
	32	Angel Pagan	2011

Career Stolen Bases Leaders

	SB	PLAYER
1.	370	Jose Reyes
2.	281	Mookie Wilson
3.	202	Howard Johnson
4.	191	Darryl Strawberry
5.	152	Lee Mazzilli
6.	151	David Wright
7.	116	Lenny Dykstra
8.	115	Bud Harrelson
9.	106	Wally Backman
10.	105	Roger Cedeno
11.	100	Carlos Beltran
12.	99	Vince Coleman
13.	92	Tommie Agee
14.	91	Cleon Jones
		John Stearns
16.	90	Frank Taveras
17.	87	Angel Pagan
18.	67	Kevin McReynolds
19.	65	Lance Johnson
20.	63	Gregg Jefferies
21.	55	Steve Henderson
	55	Luis Castillo
	55	Angel Pagan
24	47	Len Randle
25.	45	Edgardo Alfonzo
		Daryl Boston

Strikeouts (Hitters)

YEAR-BY-YEAR STRIKEOUT LEADERS

1962
Jim Hickman	96
Frank Thomas	95
Charlie Neal	90

1963
Jim Hickman	120
Tim Harkness	79
Duke Snider	74

1964
Charley Smith	101
Joe Christopher	92
Jim Hickman	90

1965
Charley Smith	123
Johnny Lewis	117
Ron Swoboda	102

1966
Ed Bressoud	107
Jerry Grote	81
Ron Swoboda	76

1967
Jerry Buchek	101
Ron Swoboda	96
Tommy Davis	71

1968
Ron Swoboda	113
Tommie Agee	103
Cleon Jones	98

1969
Tommie Agee	137
Ron Swoboda	90
Wayne Garrett	75

1970
Tommie Agee	156
Donn Clendenon	91
Cleon Jones	87

1971
Cleon Jones	87
Tommie Agee	84
Donn Clendenon	78

1972
Tommie Agee	92
Cleon Jones	83
John Milner	74

1973
John Milner	84
Wayne Garrett	74
Rusty Staub	52

1974
Wayne Garrett	96
Cleon Jones	79
John Milner	77

1975
Dave Kingman	153
Del Unser	76
Rusty Staub	55
Joe Torre	55

1976
Dave Kingman	135
Bud Harrelson	56
Bruce Boisclair	55

1977
Steve Henderson	79
John Stearns	76
Lee Mazzilli	72

1978
Steve Henderson	109
Willie Montanez	92
Lee Mazzilli	82

1979
Joel Youngblood	84
Lee Mazzilli	74
Frank Taveras	72

1980
Lee Mazzilli	92
Steve Henderson	90
Joel Youngblood	69

1981
Dave Kingman	105*
Hubie Brooks	65
Mookie Wilson	59

1982
Dave Kingman	156*
George Foster	123
Mookie Wilson	102

1983
Darryl Strawberry	128
George Foster	111
Mookie Wilson	103

1984
Darryl Strawberry	131
George Foster	122
Mookie Wilson	90

1985
Darryl Strawberry	96
George Foster	87
Howard Johnson	78

1986
Darryl Strawberry	141
Mookie Wilson	72
Keith Hernandez	69

1987
Darryl Strawberry	122
Howard Johnson	113
Keith Hernandez	104

1988
Darryl Strawberry	127
Howard Johnson	104
Mookie Wilson	63

1989
Howard Johnson	126
Darryl Strawberry	105
Kevin Elster	77

1990
Darryl Strawberry	110
Howard Johnson	100
Kevin McReynolds	61

1991
Howard Johnson	120
Hubie Brooks	62
Kevin Elster	53

1992
Dick Schofield	82
Howard Johnson	79
Todd Hundley	76

1993
Bobby Bonilla	96
Jeff Kent	88
Ryan Thompson	81

1994
Bobby Bonilla	101
Ryan Thompson	94
Jeff Kent	84

1995
Rico Brogna	111
Jeff Kent	89
Ryan Thompson	77

1996
Todd Hundley	146
Bernard Gilkey	125
Butch Huskey	77

1997
Todd Hundley	116
Bernard Gilkey	111
Carl Everett	102

1998
Brian McRae	90
Edgardo Alfonzo	77
John Olerud	73

1999
Robin Ventura	109
Roger Cedeno	100
Edgardo Alfonzo	85

2000
Derek Bell	125
Robin Ventura	91
Todd Zeile	85

2001
Todd Zeile	102
Robin Ventura	101
Mike Piazza	87

2002
Mo Vaughn	145
Jeromy Burnitez	135
Roger Cedeno	92

2003
Ty Wigginton	124
Roger Cedeno	86
Tony Clark	73

2004

Mike Cameron	143
Cliff Floyd	103
Kaz Matsui	97

2005

David Wright	113
Cliff Floyd	98
Carlos Beltran	96

2006

Carlos Delgado	120
David Wright	113
Carlos Beltran	99

2007

Carlos Delgado	118
David Wright	115
Carlos Beltran	111

2008

Carlos Delgado	124
David Wright	118
Carlos Beltran	96

2009

David Wright	140
Daniel Murphy	69
Luis Castillo	58

2010

David Wright	161
Ike Davis	138
Angel Pagan	97

2011

Jason Bay	109
David Wright	97
Jason Pridie	64

Bold = Sets Team Record
Ital. = Ties Team Record
*= Led NL or tied

Single Season Strikeouts Leaders

	SO	PLAYER	YEAR
1.	161	David Wright	2010
2.	156	Tommie Agee	1970
		Dave Kingman	1982
4.	153	Dave Kingman	1975
5.	146	Todd Hundley	1996
6.	145	Mo Vaughn	2002
7.	143	Mike Cameron	2004
8.	141	Darryl Strawberry	1986
9.	140	David Wright	2009
10.	138	Ike Davis	2010
11.	137	Tommie Agee	1969
12.	135	Jeromy Burnitz	2002
		Dave Kingman	1976
14.	131	Darryl Strawberry	1984
15.	128	Darryl Strawberry	1983
16.	127	Darryl Strawberry	1988
17.	126	Howard Johnson	1989
18.	125	Derek Bell	2000
		Bernard Gilkey	1996
20.	124	Ty Wigginton	2003
		Carlos Delgado	2008
22.	123	George Foster	1982
		Charley Smith	1965
24.	122	George Foster	1984
		Darryl Strawberry	1987

Career Strikeouts Leaders

	SO	PLAYER
1.	960	Darryl Strawberry
2.	897	David Wright
3.	827	Howard Johnson
4.	697	Cleon Jones
5.	692	Mookie Wilson
6.	672	Dave Kingman
7.	624	Todd Hundley
8.	595	Bud Harrelson
9.	581	Ed Kranepool
10.	572	Tommie Agee
11.	549	Ron Swoboda
12.	546	Mike Piazza
13.	545	Carlos Beltran
14.	509	Jerry Grote
	509	Jose Reyes
16.	498	Edgardo Alfonzo
17.	496	George Foster
18.	465	Wayne Garrett
19.	459	Keith Hernandez
20.	443	Lee Mazzilli
21.	416	Jim Hickman
22.	387	Hubie Brooks
23.	386	Jerry Koosman
24.	382	Carlos Delgado
25.	368	John Milner

Strikeouts (Pitchers)

YEAR-BY-YEAR STRIKEOUT LEADERS

1962
Roger Craig	118
Al Jackson	118
Jay Hook	113

1963
Al Jackson	142
Tracy Stallard	110
Roger Craig	108

1964
Tracy Stallard	118
Jack Fisher	115
Al Jackson	112

1965
Al Jackson	120
Jack Fisher	116
Gary Kroll	62

1966
Jack Fisher	127
Bob Shaw	104
Jack Hamilton	93

1967
Tom Seaver	170
Jack Fisher	117
Don Cardwell	71

1968
Tom Seaver	205
Jerry Koosman	178
Nolan Ryan	133

1969
Tom Seaver	208
Jerry Koosman	180
Gary Gentry	154

1970
Tom Seaver	283*
Gary Gentry	134
Nolan Ryan	125

1971
Tom Seaver	289*
Gary Gentry	155
Nolan Ryan	137

1972
Tom Seaver	249
Jon Matlack	169
Jerry Koosman	147

1973
Tom Seaver	251*
Jon Matlack	205
Jerry Koosman	156

1974
Tom Seaver	201
Jon Matlack	195
Jerry Koosman	188

1975
Tom Seaver	243*
Jerry Koosman	173
Jon Matlack	154

1976
Tom Seaver	235*
Jerry Koosman	200
Jon Matlack	153

1977
Jerry Koosman	192
Jon Matlack	123
Nino Espinosa	105

1978
Jerry Koosman	160
Craig Swan	125
Pat Zachry	78

1979
Craig Swan	145
Pete Falcone	113
Kevin Kobel	67

1980
Pete Falcone	109
Jeff Reardon	101
Pat Zachry	88

1981
Pat Zachry	76
Pete Falcone	56
Greg Harris	54
Mike Scott	54

1982
Pete Falcone	101
Charlie Puleo	98
Jesse Orosco	89

1983
Tom Seaver	135
Mike Torrez	94
Jesse Orosco	84

1984
Dwight Gooden	276*
Ron Darling	136
Walt Terrell	114

1985
Dwight Gooden	268*
Sid Fernandez	180
Ron Darling	167

1986
Sid Fernandez	200
Dwight Gooden	200
Ron Darling	184

1987
Ron Darling	167
Dwight Gooden	148
Sid Fernandez	134

1988
David Cone	213
Sid Fernandez	189
Dwight Gooden	175

1989
Sid Fernandez	198
David Cone	190
Ron Darling	153

1990
David Cone	233*
Dwight Gooden	223
Frank Viola	182

1991
David Cone	241*
Dwight Gooden	150
Frank Viola	132

1992
David Cone	214
Sid Fernandez	193
Dwight Gooden	145

1993
Dwight Gooden	149
Frank Tanana	104
Bret Saberhagen	93

1994
Bret Saberhagen	143
Bobby Jones	80
Pete Smith	62

1995
Bobby Jones	127
Dave Mlicki	123
Pete Harnisch	82

1996
Mark Clark	142
Bobby Jones	116
Pete Harnisch	114
Jason Isringhausen	114

1997
Dave Mlicki	157
Bobby Jones	125
Rick Reed	113

1998
Al Leiter	174
Rick Reed	153
Masato Yoshii	117

1999
Al Leiter	162
Armando Benitez	128
Masato Yoshii	105

2000
Al Leiter	200
Glendon Rusch	157
Mike Hampton	151

2001
Kevin Appier	172
Glendon Rusch	156
Steve Trachsel	144

2002
Al Leiter	172
Pedro Astacio	152
Steve Trachsel	105

2003
Al Leiter	139
Steve Trachsel	111
Jae Seo	110

2004

Al Leiter	117
Steve Trachsel	117
Tom Glavine	109

2005

Pedro Martinez	208
Victor Zambrano	112
Aaron Heilman	106

2006

Pedro Martinez	137
Tom Glavine	131
Orlando Hernandez	112

2007

John Maine	180
Oliver Perez	174
Orlando Hernandez	128

2008

Johan Santana	206
Oliver Perez	180
John Maine	122

2009

Johan Santana	146
Mike Pelfrey	107
Tim Redding	76

2010

Jonathon Niese	148
Johan Santana	144
Hisanori Takahashi	114

2011

Chris Capuano	168
Jonathon Niese	138
R.A. Dickey	134

Bold = Sets Team Record
Ital. = Ties Team Record
* = Led NL or tied

Single Season Strikeout Leaders

	SO	Player	Year
1.	289	Tom Seaver	1971
2.	283	Tom Seaver	1970
3.	276	Dwight Gooden	1984
4.	268	Dwight Gooden	1985
5.	251	Tom Seaver	1973
6.	249	Tom Seaver	1972
7.	243	Tom Seaver	1975
8.	241	David Cone	1991
9.	235	Tom Seaver	1976
10.	233	David Cone	1990
11.	223	Dwight Gooden	1990
12.	214	David Cone	1992
13.	213	David Cone	1988
14.	208	Pedro Martinez	2005
		Tom Seaver	1969
16	206	Johan Santana	2008
17.	205	Jon Matlack	1973
		Tom Seaver	1968
19	201	Tom Seaver	1974
20.	200	Sid Fernandez	1986
		Dwight Gooden	1986
		Jerry Koosman	1976
		Al Leiter	2000
24.	198	Sid Fernandez	1989
25.	195	Jon Matlack	1974

Career Strikeout Leaders

	SO	Player
1.	2541	Tom Seaver
2.	1875	Dwight Gooden
3.	1799	Jerry Koosman
4.	1449	Sid Fernandez
5.	1172	David Cone
6.	1148	Ron Darling
7.	1106	Al Leiter
8.	1023	Jon Matlack
9.	714	Bobby Jones
10.	671	Craig Swan
11.	618	Tug McGraw
12.	592	John Franco
13.	590	Rick Reed
14.	580	Steve Trachsel
15.	563	Gary Gentry
16.	561	Al Jackson
17.	516	Tom Glavine
18.	506	Jesse Orosco
19	496	Johan Santana
20.	494	Oliver Perez
21.	493	Nolan Ryan
	493	Mike Pelfrey
23.	475	Jack Fisher
24.	467	John Maine
25.	464	Pedro Martinez

Triples

YEAR-BY-YEAR TRIPLES LEADERS

1962
Charlie Neal	9
Felix Mantilla	4
4 players	3

1963
Jim Hickman	6
Ron Hunt	4
3 Players	3

1964
Joe Christopher	8
Ron Hunt	6
Ed Kranepool	4

1965
Ed Kranepool	4
4 Players	3

1966
Ed Bressoud	5
Cleon Jones	4
Ron Swoboda	4

1967
Cleon Jones	5
Bud Harrelson	4
Ron Swoboda	3
Bob Johnson	3

1968
Ron Swoboda	6
Cleon Jones	4
Art Shamsky	4

1969
Ken Boswell	7
Bud Harrelson	6
Tommie Agee	4
Cleon Jones	4

1970
Bud Harrelson	8
Cleon Jones	8
Tommie Agee	7

1971
Cleon Jones	6
Bud Harrelson	6
Ed Kranepool	4

1972
Ted Martinez	5
Jim Fregosi	4
Bud Harrelson	4

1973
Felix Millan	4
Wayne Garrett	3
Bud Harrelson	3
John Milner	3

1974
Ted Martinez	7
Wayne Garrett	3
Felix Millan	2
Rusty Staub	2

1975
Mike Phillips	7
Jerry Grote	5
Rusty Staub	4

1976
Mike Phillips	6
Bud Harrelson	4
John Milner	4

1977
Lenny Randle	7
Steve Henderson	6
Lee Mazzilli	3
John Milner	3

1978
Steve Henderson	9
Doug Flynn	8
Lenny Randle	8
Joel Youngblood	8

1979
Frank Taveras	9
Steve Henderson	8
Doug Flynn	5
Joel Youngblood	5

1980
Doug Flynn	8
Steve Henderson	8
Lee Mazzilli	4
Claudell Washington	4

1981
Mookie Wilson	8
Lee Mazzilli	5
Doug Flynn	4

1982
Mookie Wilson	9
Gary Rajsich	3
John Stearns	3

1983
Darryl Strawberry	7
Mookie Wilson	6
Hubie Brooks	4

1984
Mookie Wilson	10
Darryl Strawberry	4
3 players	2

1985
Mookie Wilson	8
Wally Backman	5
3 players	4

1986
Len Dykstra	7
Darryl Strawberry	5
Mookie Wilson	5

1987
Mookie Wilson	7
Kevin McReynolds	5
Darryl Strawberry	5

1988
Mookie Wilson	5
Len Dykstra	3
Darryl Strawberry	3

1989
Howard Johnson	3
Dave Magadan	3
Kevin McReynolds	3

1990
Dave Magdan	6
Gregg Jefferies	3
Howard Johnson	3

1991
Vince Coleman	5
Daryl Boston	5
Howard Johnson	5

1992
Kevin Bass	2
Daryl Boston	2
Eddie Murray	2
Dick Schofield	2

1993
Vince Coleman	8
Jeromy Burnitz	6
Joe Orsulak	4

1994
Jeff Kent	5
Jose Vizcaino	3
3 players	2

1995
Brett Butler	7
Edgardo Alfonzo	5
Jose Vizcaino	5

1996
Lance Johnson	21*
Jose Vizcaino	6
Rey Ordonez	4

1997
Lance Johnson	6
Manny Alexander	3
Carl Everett	3
Rey Ordonez	3

1998
Brian McRae	5
John Olerud	4
6 players	2

1999
Roger Cedeno	4
Benny Agbayani	3
Ray Ordonez	2

2000
Lenny Harris	3
Todd Zeile	3
Edgardo Alfonzo	2
Melvin Mora	2

2001
Rey Ordonez	4
Joe McEwing	3
Benny Agbayani	2

2002

Timo Perez	6
Roberto Alomar	4
Jay Payton	3

2003

Ty Wigginton	6
Roger Cedeno	4
Jose Reyes	4

2004

6 players	2

2005

Jose Reyes	17*
Kaz Matsui	4
Victor Diaz	3

2006

Jose Reyes	17*
Endy Chavez	5
David Wright	5

2007

Jose Reyes	12
Carlos Beltran	3
Luis Castillo	2
Endy Chavez	2

2008

Jose Reyes	19*
Carlos Beltran	5
Daniel Murphy	3

2009

Angel Pagan	11
Cory Sullivan	5
Daniel Murphy	4
Fernando Tatis	4

2010

Jose Reyes	10
Angel Pagan	7
Jason Bay	6

2011

Jose Reyes	16
Angel Pagan	4
Lucas Duda	3
Jason Pridie	3

*= Led NL or Tied
Ital. = Tied Team Record
Bold = Sets Team Record

Single Season Triples Leaders

	3B	PLAYER	YEAR
1.	21	Lance Johnson	1996
2.	19	Jose Reyes	2008
3.	17	Jose Reyes	2005, 2006
5.	16	Jose Reyes	2011
6.	12	Jose Reyes	2007
7.	11	Angel Pagan	2009
8.	10	Mookie Wilson	1984
		Jose Reyes	2010
10.	9	Steve Henderson	1978
		Charlie Neal	1962
		Frank Taveras	1979
		Mookie Wilson	1982
14.	8	Joe Christopher	1964
		Vince Coleman	1993
		Doug Flynn	1978, 1980
		Bud Harrelson	1970
		Steve Henderson	1979, 1980
		Cleon Jones	1970
		Len Randle	1978
		Mookie Wilson	1981, 1985
		Joel Youngblood	1978
		Mookie Wilson	1987

Career Triples Leaders

	3B	PLAYER
1.	99	Jose Reyes
2.	62	Mookie Wilson
3.	45	Bud Harrelson
4.	33	Cleon Jones
5.	31	Steve Henderson
6.	30	Darryl Strawberry
7.	27	Lance Johnson
8.	26	Doug Flynn
9.	25	Ed Kranepool
10.	23	Angel Pagan
11.	22	Lee Mazzilli
12.	20	Wayne Garrett
		Ron Swoboda
14.	18	Jerry Grote
		Howard Johnson
		Joel Youngblood
17.	17	Lenny Dykstra
		Rey Ordonez
19.		David Wright
		Carlos Beltran
21.	15	Ken Boswell
		Len Randle
23.	14	Tommie Agee
		Edgardo Alfonzo
		Wally Backman
		Joe Christopher
		Vince Coleman
		Ted Martinez
		Kevin McReynolds
		Mike Phillips
		Jose Vizcaino

Walks (Hitters)

YEAR-BY-YEAR WALKS LEADERS

1962
Richie Ashburn	81
Elio Chacon	76
Charlie Neal	56

1963
Duke Snider	56
Jim Hickman	44
Ron Hunt	40

1964
Joe Christopher	48
Jim Hickman	36
Ed Kranepool	32

1965
Johnny Lewis	59
Bobby Klaus	45
Ed Kranepool	39

1966
Ed Bressoud	47
Ron Hunt	41
Ed Kranepool	42

1967
Bud Harrelson	48
Ron Swoboda	41
Ed Kranepool	37

1968
Ron Swoboda	52
Jerry Grote	44
Cleon Jones	31

1969
Cleon Jones	64
Tommie Agee	59
Bud Harrelson	54

1970
Bud Harrelson	95
Wayne Garrett	81
Joe Foy	68

1971
Ken Singleton	61
Bud Harrelson	53
Cleon Jones	53

1972
Wayne Garrett	70
Bud Harrelson	58
Tommie Agee	53

1973
Rusty Staub	74
Wayne Garrett	72
John Milner	62

1974
Wayne Garrett	89
Rusty Staub	77
Bud Harrelson	71

1975
Rusty Staub	77
Wayne Garrett	50
Jerry Grote	38

1976
John Milner	65
Bud Harrelson	63
Wayne Garrett	52

1977
John Stearns	77
Lee Mazzilli	72
Lenny Randle	65

1978
Elliott Maddox	71
John Stearns	70
Lee Mazzilli	69

1979
Lee Mazzilli	93
Joel Youngblood	60
Richie Hebner	59

1980
Lee Mazzilli	82
Steve Henderson	62
Elliott Maddox	52
Joel Youngblood	52

1981
Dave Kingman	55
Lee Mazzilli	46
John Stearns	24

1982
Dave Kingman	59
George Foster	50
Wally Backman	49

1983
Keith Hernandez	64
Ron Hodges	49
Darryl Strawberry	47

1984
Keith Hernandez	97
Darryl Strawberry	75
Wally Backman	56

1985
Keith Hernandez	77
Darryl Strawberry	73
Gary Carter	69

1986
Keith Hernandez	94*
Darryl Strawberry	72
Gary Carter	62

1987
Darryl Strawberry	97
Howard Johnson	83
Keith Hernandez	81

1988
Howard Johnson	86
Darryl Strawberry	85
Dave Magadan	60

1989
Howard Johnson	77
Darryl Strawberry	61
Dave Magadan	49

1990
Dave Magadan	74
Kevin McReynolds	71
Darryl Strawberry	70

1991
Dave Magadan	83
Howard Johnson	78
Kevin McReynolds	49

1992
Bobby Bonilla	66
Eddie Murray	66
Dick Schofield	60

1993
Bobby Bonilla	72
Howard Johnson	43
Eddie Murray	40

1994
Bobby Bonilla	55
David Segui	33
Jose Vizcaino	33

1995
Brett Butler	43
Todd Hundley	42
Rico Brogna	39
Carl Everett	39

1996
Todd Hundley	79
Bernard Gilkey	73
Lance Johnson	33

1997
John Olerud	85
Todd Hundley	83
Bernard Gilkey	70

1998
John Olerud	96
Brian McRae	80
Edgardo Alfonzo	65

1999
John Olerud	125
Edgardo Alfonzo	85
Rickey Henderson	82

2000
Edgardo Alfonzo	95
Robin Ventura	75
Todd Zeile	74

2001
Robin Ventura	88
Todd Zeile	73
Mike Piazza	67

2002
Edgardo Alfonzo	62
Mo Vaughn	59
Jeromy Burnitz	58

2003
Cliff Floyd	51
Ty Wigginton	46
Jason Phillips	39

2004

Mike Piazza	68
Mike Cameron	57
Cliff Floyd	47

2005

David Wright	72
Cliff Floyd	63
Carlos Beltran	56

2006

Carlos Beltran	95
Carlos Delgado	74
David Wright	66

2007

David Wright	94
Jose Reyes	77
Carlos Beltran	69

2008

David Wright	94
Carlos Beltran	92
Carlos Delgado	72

2009

David Wright	74
Luis Castillo	69
Carlos Beltran	47

2010

Ike Davis	72
David Wright	69
Angel Pagan	44
Jason Bay	44

2011

Carlos Beltran	60
Jason Bay	56
David Wright	52

Bold = Team Record
Ital. = Ties Team Record
*= Lead NL or tied

Single Season Walks Leaders

	BB	PLAYER	YEAR
1.	125	John Olerud	1999
2.	97	Keith Hernandez	1984
		Darryl Strawberry	1987
4.	96	John Olerud	1998
5.	95	Edgardo Alfonzo	2000
		Carlos Beltran	2006
		Bud Harrelson	1970
8.	94	Keith Hernandez	1986
		David Wright	2007, 2008
11.	93	Lee Mazzilli	1979
	92	Carlos Beltran	2008
13.	89	Wayne Garrett	1974
14.	88	Robin Ventura	2001
15.	86	Howard Johnson	1988
16.	85	Edgardo Alfonzo	1999
		John Olerud	1997
		Darryl Strawberry	1988
19.	83	Todd Hundley	1997
		Howard Johnson	1987
		Dave Magadan	1991
22.	82	Rickey Henderson	1999
		Lee Mazzilli	1980
24.	81	Richie Ashburn	1962
		Wayne Garrett	1970
		Keith Hernandez	1987

Career Walks Leaders

	BB	PLAYER
1.	580	Darryl Strawberry
2.	573	Bud Harrelson
3.	556	Howard Johnson
4	535	David Wright
5.	482	Wayne Garrett
6.	471	Keith Hernandez
7.	458	Edgardo Alfonzo
8.	454	Ed Kranepool
9.	449	Carlos Beltran
10.	438	Lee Mazzilli
11.	424	Mike Piazza
12.	363	Jerry Grote
13.	355	Cleon Jones
14.	347	Dave Magadan
15.	338	John Milner
16.	333	Rusty Staub
	333	Jose Reyes
18.	323	John Stearns
19.	306	John Olerud
20.	299	Todd Hundley
21.	263	Kevin McReynolds
22.	260	Wally Backman
23.	243	Bobby Bonilla
24.	240	Ron Swoboda
		Mookie Wilson

Walks (Pitchers)

YEAR-BY-YEAR WALKS LEADERS

1962
Al Jackson	78
Jay Hook	71
Roger Craig	70

1963
Al Jackson	84
Tracy Stallard	77
Carl Willey	69

1964
Tracy Stallard	73
Bill Wakefield	61
Al Jackson	60

1965
Jack Fisher	68
Al Jackson	61
Galen Cisco	51

1966
Jack Hamilton	88
Rob Gardner	64
Jack Fisher	54

1967
Tom Seaver	78
Jack Fisher	64
Don Cardwell	39

1968
Nolan Ryan	75
Jerry Koosman	69
Dick Selma	54

1969
Tom Seaver	82
Gary Gentry	81
Jerry Koosman	68

1970
Nolan Ryan	97
Gary Gentry	86
Tom Seaver	83

1971
Nolan Ryan	116
Gary Gentry	82
Tom Seaver	61

1972
Tom Seaver	77
Gary Gentry	75
Jon Matlack	71

1973
Jon Matlack	99
Jerry Koosman	76
Tom Seaver	64

1974
Jerry Koosman	85
Jon Matlack	76
Tom Seaver	75

1975
Jerry Koosman	98
Tom Seaver	88
Randy Tate	86

1976
Tom Seaver	77
Jerry Koosman	66
Jon Matlack	57

1977
Jerry Koosman	81
Craig Swan	56
Nino Espinosa	55

1978
Jerry Koosman	84
Nino Espinosa	75
Pat Zachry	60

1979
Pete Falcone	76
Craig Swan	57
Wayne Twitchell	55

1980
John Pacella	59
Pete Falcone	58
Pat Zachry	58

1981
Pat Zachry	56
Randy Jones	38
Pete Falcone	36

1982
Charlie Puleo	90
Pete Falcone	71
Mike Scott	60

1983
Mike Torrez	113*
Tom Seaver	86
Doug Sisk	59

1984
Ron Darling	104
Walt Terrell	80
Dwight Gooden	73

1985
Ron Darling	114*
Sid Fernandez	80
Dwight Gooden	69

1986
Sid Fernandez	91
Ron Darling	81
Dwight Gooden	80

1987
Ron Darling	96
Sid Fernandez	67
Dwight Gooden	53

1988
David Cone	80
Sid Fernandez	70
Ron Darling	60

1989
Bob Ojeda	78
Sid Fernandez	75
Ron Darling	74

1990
Dwight Gooden	70
Sid Fernandez	67
David Cone	65

1991
David Cone	73
Dwight Gooden	56
Frank Viola	54

1992
David Cone	82*
Dwight Gooden	70
Sid Fernandez	67

1993
Dwight Gooden	61
Frank Tanana	48
Pete Schourek	45

1994
Bobby Jones	56
Pete Smith	42
Mike Remlinger	35

1995
Dave Mlicki	54
Bobby Jones	53
Bill Pulsipher	45

1996
Jason Isringhausen	73
Paul Wilson	71
Pete Harnisch	61

1997
Dave Mlicki	76
Bobby Jones	63
Mark Clark	47

1998
Al Leiter	71
Hideo Nomo	56
Bobby Jones	53
Masato Yoshii	53

1999
Al Leiter	93
Orel Hershiser	77
Masato Yoshii	58

2000
Mike Hampton	99
Al Leiter	76
Pat Mahomes	66

2001
Kevin Appier	64
Steve Trachsel	47
Al Leiter	46

2002
Al Leiter	69
Steve Trachsel	69
Shawn Estes	66

2003
Al Leiter	94
Tom Glavine	66
Steve Trachsel	65

2004

Al Leiter	97
Steve Trachsel	83
Tom Glavine	70

2005

Victor Zambrano	77
Tom Glavine	61
Kris Benson	49
Kaz Ishii	49

2006

Steve Trachsel	78
Tom Glavine	62
Orlando Hernandez	41

2007

Oliver Perez	79
John Maine	75
Tom Glavine	64
Orlando Hernandez	64

2008

Oliver Perez	105*
John Maine	67
Mike Pelfrey	64

2009

Mike Pelfry	66
Oliver Perez	58
Livan Hernandez	51

2010

Mike Pelfrey	68
Jonathon Niese	62
Johan Santana	55

2011

Dillon Gee	71
Mike Pelfrey	65
R.A. Dickey	54

Bold = Sets Team Record
Ital. = Ties Team Record
* = Led NL or tied

Single Season Walks Leaders

	BB	Player	Year
1.	116	Nolan Ryan	1971
2.	114	Ron Darling	1985
3.	113	Mike Torrez	1983
4.	105	Oliver Perez	2008
5.	104	Ron Darling	1984
6.	99	Mike Hampton	2000
		Jon Matlack	1973
8.	98	Jerry Koosman	1975
9.	97	Al Leiter	2004
		Nolan Ryan	1970
11.	96	Ron Darling	1987
12.	94	Al Leiter	2003
13.	93	Al Leiter	1999
14.	91	Sid Fernandez	1986
15.	90	Charlie Puleo	1982
16.	88	Jack Hamilton	1966
		Tom Seaver	1975
18.	86	Gary Gentry	1970
		Tom Seaver	1983
		Randy Tate	1975
21.	85	Jerry Koosman	1974
22.	84	Al Jackson	1963
		Jerry Koosman	1978
24.	83	Tom Seaver	1970
		Steve Trachsel	2004

Career Walks Leaders

	BB	Player
1.	847	Tom Seaver
2.	820	Jerry Koosman
3.	651	Dwight Gooden
4.	614	Ron Darling
5.	596	Sid Fernandez
6.	546	Al Leiter
7.	431	David Cone
8.	419	Jon Matlack
9.	368	Craig Swan
10.	354	Steve Trachsel
11.	353	Bobby Jones
12.	350	Tug McGraw
13.	344	Nolan Ryan
14.	324	Gary Gentry
15.	323	Tom Glavine
16.	314	Mike Pelfrey
17.	304	Al Jackson
18.	301	Oliver Perez
19.	300	Pat Zachry
20.	276	John Franco
21.	242	Jack Fisher
22.	241	Pete Falcone
23.	240	Jesse Orosco
24	238	John Maine
25.	213	Bob Ojeda

WHIP

YEAR-BY-YEAR WHIP LEADERS

Minimum 162 Innings Except Where Noted

1962
Al Jackson	1.39
Jay Hook	1.41
Roger Craig	1.42

1963
Carl Willey	1.19
Roger Craig	1.30
Al Jackson	1.41

1964
Galen Cisco	1.23
Tracy Stallard	1.27
Al Jackson	1.36

1965
Jack Fisher	1.26
Al Jackson	1.35

1966
Dennis Ribant	1.19
Jack Fisher	1.23
Bob Shaw	1.27

1967
Tom Seaver	1.20
Jack Fisher	1.43

1968
Tom Seaver	0.98
Jerry Koosman	1.10
Don Cardwell	1.14

1969
Tom Seaver	1.04
Jerry Koosman	1.06
Gary Gentry	1.17

1970
Tom Seaver	1.08
Jim McAndrew	1.11
Jerry Koosman	1.23

1971
Tom Seaver	0.95*
Ray Sadecki	1.12
Gary Gentry	1.23
(Tug McGraw 1.03, 111 IP)	

1972
Strike Season, Min. 156 IP
Jim McAndrew	1.06
Tom Seaver	1.12
Jon Matlack	1.17
(Tug McGraw 1.05, 106 IP)	

1973
Tom Seaver	0.98*
Jerry Koosman	1.18
Jon Matlack	1.28

1974
Jon Matlack	1.12
Tom Seaver	1.16
Jerry Koosman	1.29

1975
Tom Seaver	1.09
Jon Matlack	1.23
Jerry Koosman	1.39

1976
Tom Seaver	1.06
Jerry Koosman	1.10
Jon Matlack	1.12

1977
Nino Espinosa	1.22
Jerry Koosman	1.22
Jon Matlack	1.29
(S. Lockwood 1.14, 104 IP)	

1978
Craig Swan	1.07
Jerry Koosman	1.30
Nino Espinosa	1.50

1979
Craig Swan	1.19
Pete Falcone	1.47

1980
Pat Zachry	1.23
Ray Burris	1.38
Mark Bomback	1.48

1981
Strike Season, Min. 103 IP
Mike Scott	1.21
Pat Zachry	1.50

1982
Craig Swan	1.21
Pete Falcone	1.36
Charlie Puleo	1.57

1983
Tom Seaver	1.24
Ed Lynch	1.43
Mike Torrez	1.53
(Jesse Orosco 1.04, 110 IP)	

1984
Dwight Gooden	1.07*
Ron Darling	1.38
Walt Terrell	1.45

1985
Dwight Gooden	0.97
Sid Fernandez	1.10
Ed Lynch	1.13

1986
Bob Ojeda	1.09
Dwight Gooden	1.11
Ron Darling	1.20

1987
Dwight Gooden	1.20
Ron Darling	1.34

1988
Bob Ojeda	1.00
Sid Fernandez	1.05
David Cone	1.12

1989
Sid Fernandez	1.06
David Cone	1.17
Ron Darling	1.31

1990
Sid Fernandez	1.10
David Cone	1.14
Frank Viola	1.15

1991
David Cone	1.19
Dwight Gooden	1.27
Frank Viola	1.35

1992
Sid Fernandez	1.07
David Cone	1.24
Dwight Gooden	1.30

1993
Dwight Gooden	1.19
Frank Tanana	1.34
(S.Fernandez, 0.99, 120 IP)	
(B.Saberhagen 1.06, 139 IP)	

1994
Strike Year, Min. 113 IP
Bret Saberhagen	1.03
Bobby Jones	1.33
Pete Smith	1.42

1995
Strike Year, Min. 144 IP
Dave Mlicki	1.33
Bobby Jones	1.34
(B.Saberhagen 1.14, 110 IP)	

1996
Mark Clark	1.25
Pete Harnisch	1.32
Bobby Jones	1.35

1997
Rick Reed	1.04
Bobby Jones	1.24
Dave Mlicki	1.39

1998
Rick Reed	1.12
Al Leiter	1.15
Bobby Jones	1.25

1999
Masato Yoshii	1.30
Orel Hershiser	1.41
Al Leiter	1.42

2000
Al Leiter	1.21
Rick Reed	1.23
Glendon Rusch	1.26

2001
Kevin Appier	1.19
Al Leiter	1.20
Steve Trachsel	1.24
(Rick Reed 1.01, 135 IP)	

2002

Al Leiter	1.29
Pedro Astacio	1.33
Steve Trachsel	1.38

2003

Jae Seo	1.27
Steve Trachsel	1.31
Tom Glavine	1.48

2004

Tom Glavine	1.29
Al Leiter	1.35
Steve Trachsel	1.41

2005

Pedro Martinez	0.95*
Kris Benson	1.26
Tom Glavine	1.36

2006

Tom Glavine	1.33
Steve Trachsel	1.60
(P.Martinez, 1.11, 133 IP)	

2007

John Maine	1.27
Oliver Perez	1.31
Tom Glavine	1.41

2008

Johan Santana	1.15
Mike Pelfrey	1.36
Oliver Perez	1.40

2009

Johan Santana	1.21
Mike Pelfrey	1.51

2010

Johan Santana	1.15
R.A. Dickey	1.18
Mike Pelfrey	1.19

2011

R.A. Dickey	1.227
Chris Capuano	1.349
Dillon Gee	1.376

Bold = Sets Team Record
Ital. = Tied Team Record
*= Led NL or Tied

Single Season WHIP Leaders

Minimum 162 IP

	WHIP	PLAYER	YEAR
1.	0.946	Tom Seaver	1971
2.	0.949	Pedro Martinez	2005
3.	0.965	Dwight Gooden	1985
4.	0.976	Tom Seaver	1973
5.	0.980	Tom Seaver	1968
6.	1.004	Bob Ojeda	1988
7.	1.026	Bret Saberhagen	1994
8.	1.039	Tom Seaver	1969
9.	1.042	Rick Reed	1997
10.	1.053	Sid Fernandez	1988
11.	1.058	Sid Fernandez	1989
	1.058	Jerry Koosman	1969
13.	1.063	Tom Seaver	1976
14.	1.064	Jim McAndrew	1972
15.	1.067	Sid Fernandez	1992
16.	1.071	Craig Swan	1978
17.	1.073	Dwight Gooden	1984
18.	1.077	Tom Seaver	1970
19.	1.088	Tom Seaver	1975
20.	1.090	Bob Ojeda	1986
21.	1.096	Jerry Koosman	1976
22.	1.099	Sid Fernandez	1990
23.	1.100	Jerry Koosman	1968
24.	1.104	Sid Fernandez	1985
25.	1.107	Jim McAndrew	1970

Career WHIP Leaders

Minimum 500 IP

	WHIP	PLAYER
1.	1.076	Tom Seaver
2.	1.079	Bret Saberhagen
3.	1.113	Sid Fernandez
4.	1.155	Rick Reed
5.	1.175	Dwight Gooden
		Johan Santana
7.	1.182	Bob Ojeda
8.	1.184	Jim McAndrew
9.	1.192	David Cone
10.	1.195	Jon Matlack
11.	1.209	Jesse Orosco
12.	1.219	Jerry Koosman
13.	1.240	Frank Viola
14.	1.255	Gary Gentry
15.	1.267	Craig Swan
16.	1.284	Ray Sadecki
17.	1.288	Ron Darling
18.	1.300	Al Leiter
19.	1.306	Tud McGraw
20.	1.312	John Maine
21.	1.320	Jack Fisher
22.	1.323	Bobby Jones
23.	1.332	Ed Lynch
24.	1.363	Al Jackson
25.	1.365	John Franco

Winning Percentage

YEAR-BY-YEAR WINNING % LEADERS

Minimum 10 Decisions Except Where Noted

1962
Jay Hook (8-19)	.296
Roger Craig (10-24)	.294
Al Jackson (8-20)	.286
(Ken Mackenzie 5-4, .555)	

1963
Al Jackson (13-17)	.433
Carl Willey (9-14)	.391
Galen Cisco (7-15)	.318

1964
L. Bearnarth (5-5)	.500
Al Jackson (11-16)	.423
Jack Fisher (10-17)	.370

1965
Gary Kroll (6-6)	.500
Galen Cisco (4-8)	.333
Al Jackson (8-20)	.286

1966
Dennis Ribant (11-9)	.550
Bob Shaw (11-10)	.524
Jack Fisher (11-14)	.440

1967
Tom Seaver (16-13)	.552
Ron Taylor (4-6)	.400
Don Cardwell (5-9)	.357

1968
J. Koosman (19-12)	.613
Cal Koonce (6-4)	.600
Tom Seaver (16-12)	.571

1969
Tom Seaver (25-7)	.781
Tug McGraw (9-3)	.750
Ron Taylor (9-4)	.692

1970
Danny Frisella (8-3)	.727
Ray Sadecki (8-4)	.667
Tom Seaver	.600

1971
Tug McGraw (11-4)	.733*
Tom Seaver (20-10)	.667
Danny Frisella (8-5)	.615

1972
Tom Seaver (21-12)	.636
Jon Matlack (15-10)	.600
Tug McGraw (8-6)	.571

1973
George Stone (12-3)	.800*
Harry Parker (8-4)	.667
Tom Seaver (19-10)	.655

1974
J. Koosman (15-11)	.577
Tom Seaver (11-11)	.500
Ray Sadecki (8-8)	.500
Bob Apodaca (6-6)	.500

1975
Tom Seaver (22-9)	.710
Jon Matlack (16-12)	.571
Hank Webb (7-6)	.538

1976
J. Koosman (21-10)	.677
Jon Matlack (17-10)	.629
S. Lockwood (10-7)	.588

1977
Tom Seaver (7-3)	.700
Pat Zachry (7-6)	.538
Craig Swan	.474

1978
Pat Zachry (10-6)	.625
Dale Murray (8-5)	.615
Craig Swan (9-6)	.600

1979
Craig Swan (14-13)	.519
Kevin Kobel (6-8)	.429
Neil Allen (6-10)	.375

1980
M. Bomback (10-8)	.556
Tom Hausman (6-5)	.545
Jeff Reardon (8-7)	.533

1981
Strike Season, Min. 7 Dec.
Pete Falcone (5-3)	.625
Neil Allen (7-6)	.538
Ed Lynch (4-5)	.444

1982
Craig Swan (11-7)	.611
Charlie Puleo (9-9)	.500
Pete Falcone (8-10)	.444

1983
Jesse Orosco (13-7)	.650
Ed Lynch (8-8)	.500
Walt Terrell (10-10)	.500

1984
D. Gooden (17-9)	.654
Jesse Orosco (10-6)	.625
Bruce Berenyi (9-6)	.600

1985
D. Gooden (24-4)	.857
Ron Darling (16-6)	.727
Rick Aguilera (10-7)	.588

1986
Bob Ojeda (18-5)	.783*
D. Gooden (17-6)	.739
Sid Fernandez (16-6)	.727

1987
Terry Leach (11-1)	.917*
Rick Aguilera (11-3)	.786
D. Gooden (15-7)	.682

1988
David Cone (20-3)	.870*
Randy Myers (7-3)	.700
D. Gooden (18-9)	.667

1989
Sid Fernandez (14-5)	.737*
Dwight Gooden (9-4)	.692
David Cone (14-8)	.636
Randy Myers (7-4)	.636

1990
D. Gooden (19-7)	.731
Frank Viola (20-12)	.625
David Cone (14-10)	.583

1991
D. Gooden (13-7)	.650
David Cone (14-14)	.500
Frank Viola (13-15)	.464

1992
David Cone (13-7)	.650
S. Fernandez (14-11)	.560
D. Gooden (10-13)	.435

1993
B. Saberhagen (7-7)	.500
Sid Fernandez (5-6)	.455
D. Gooden (12-15)	.444

1994
Strike Year, Min. 7 Dec.
B. Saberhagen (14-4)	.778
Doug Linton (6-2)	.750
Bobby Jones (12-7)	.632

1995
Strike Year, Min. 9 Dec.
J. Isringhausen (9-2)	.818
Dave Mlicki (9-7)	.563
Bobby Jones (10-10)	.500
B. Saberhagen (5-5)	.500

1996
Bobby Jones (12-8)	.600
Mark Clark (14-11)	.560
Dave Mlicki (6-7)	.462

1997
Bobby Jones (15-9)	.625
Brian Bohanon (6-4)	.600
Rick Reed (13-9)	.591

1998
Al Leiter (17-6)	.739
A. Reynoso (7-3)	.700
Rick Reed (16-11)	.640

1999
Octavio Dotel (8-3)	.727
Rick Reed (11-5)	.688
Dennis Cook (10-5)	.667

2000

Rick Reed (11-5)	.688
Al Leiter (16-8)	.667
Bobby Jones (11-6)	.647

2001

Armando Benitez	.600
Rick Reed (8-6)	.571
Kevin Appier (11-10)	.524

2002

P. Astacio (12-11)	.522
Al Leiter (13-13)	.500
S. Trachsel (11-11)	.500

2003

Al Leiter (15-9)	.625
S. Trachsel (16-10)	.615
Jae Seo (9-12)	.429

2004

Al Leiter (10-8)	.555
S. Trachsel (12-13)	.480
Tom Glavine (11-14)	.440

2005

Jae Seo (8-2)	.800
P. Martinez (15-8)	.652
R. Hernandez (8-6)	.571

2006

Tom Glavine (15-7)	.682
Steve Trachsel (15-8)	.652
O. Hernandez (9-7)	.563

2007

O. Hernandez (9-5)	.643
Tom Glavine (13-8)	.619
John Maine (15-10)	.600
Oliver Perez (15-10)	.600

2008

Johan Santana (16-7)	.696
Oliver Perez (10-7)	.588
John Maine (10-8)	.556

2009

Pedro Feliciano (6-4)	.600
Johan Santana (13-9)	.591
John Maine (7-6)	.538

2010

Mike Pelfrey (15-9)	.625
His. Takahashi (10-6)	.625
R.A. Dickey (11-9)	.550
Johan Santana (11-9)	.550

2011

Dillon Gee	.684
Jonathon Niese	.500
Chris Capuano	.478

Bold = Sets Team Record
Ital. = Ties Team Record
* = Led NL or tied

Single Season Winning % Leaders

Minimum 10 Decisions

	W%	Player	Year
1.	.917 (11-1)	Terry Leach	1987
2.	.870 (20-3)	David Cone	1988
3.	.857 (24-4)	Dwight Gooden	1985
4.	.818 (9-2)	Jason Isringhausen	1995
5.	.800 (12-3)	George Stone	1973
	.800 (8-2)	Jae Seo	2005
7.	.786 (11-3)	Rick Aguilera	1987
8.	.783 (18-5)	Bob Ojeda	1986
9.	.781 (25-7)	Tom Seaver	1969
10.	.778 (14-4)	Bret Saberhagen	1994
11.	.750 (9-3)	Tug McGraw	1969
12.	.739 (17-6)	Al Leiter	1998
	.739 (17-6)	Dwight Gooden	1984
14.	.737 (14-5)	Sid Fernandez	1989
15.	.733 (11-4)	Tug McGraw	1971
16.	.731 (19-7)	Dwight Gooden	1990
17.	.727 (8-3)	Octavio Dotel	1999
	.727 (16-6)	Sid Fernandez	1986
	.727 (16-6)	Ron Darling	1985
	.727 (8-3)	Danny Frisella	1970
21.	.714 (15-6)	Ron Darling	1986
22.	.710 (22-9)	Tom Seaver	1975
23.	.700 (7-3)	Armando Reynoso	1998
	.700 (7-3)	Randy Myers	1988
	.700 (7-3)	Tom Seaver	1977

Career Winning % Leaders

Minimum 50 Decisions

	W%	Player	Record
1.	.649	Dwight Gooden	157-85
2.	.621	Rick Reed	59-36
3.	.615	Tom Seaver	198-124
	.615	Johan Santana	40-25
5.	.614	David Cone	81-51
6.	.586	Ron Darling	99-70
		Al Leiter	95-67
8.	.582	Pedro Martinez	32-23
9.	.580	Bret Saberhagen	29-21
10.	.578	Rick Aguilera	37-27
11.	.569	Bobby Jones	74-56
12.	.560	Bob Ojeda	51-40
13.	.557	Sid Fernandez	98-78
14.	.549	John Maine	39-32
15.	.545	Ray Sadecki	30-25
16.	.543	Frank Viola	38-32
17.	.532	Roger McDowell	33-29
18.	.528	Steve Trachsel	66-59
19.	.521	Tom Glavine	61-56
20.	.505	Jerry Koosman	140-137
21.	.503	Jon Matlack	82-81
22.	.500	Jesse Orosco	47-47
	.500	Oliver Perez	29-29
24.	.494	Gary Gentry	41-42
25.	.487	Ed Lynch	38-40

Wins

YEAR-BY-YEAR WINS LEADERS

1962
Roger Craig	10
Al Jackson	8
Jay Hook	8

1963
Al Jackson	13
Carl Willey	9
Galen Cisco	7

1964
Al Jackson	11
Tracy Stallard	10
Jack Fisher	10

1965
Jack Fisher	8
Al Jackson	8
Gary Kroll	6

1966
Jack Fisher	11
Dennis Ribant	11
Bob Shaw	11

1967
Tom Seaver	16
Jack Fisher	9
Don Cardwell	5

1968
Jerry Koosman	19
Tom Seaver	16
Dick Selma	9

1969
Tom Seaver	25*
Jerry Koosman	17
Gary Gentry	13

1970
Tom Seaver	18
Jerry Koosman	12
Jim McAndrew	10

1971
Tom Seaver	20
Gary Gentry	12
Tug McGraw	11

1972
Tom Seaver	21
Jon Matlack	15
Jerry Koosman	11
Jim McAndrew	11

1973
Tom Seaver	19
Jerry Koosman	14
Jon Matlack	14

1974
Jerry Koosman	15
Jon Matlack	13
Tom Seaver	11

1975
Tom Seaver	22*
Jon Matlack	16
Jerry Koosman	14

1976
Jerry Koosman	21
Jon Matlack	17
Tom Seaver	14

1977
Nino Espinosa	10
Craig Swan	9
Jerry Koosman	8

1978
Nino Espinosa	11
Pat Zachry	10
Craig Swan	9

1979
Craig Swan	14
Neil Allen	6
Pete Falcone	6
Kevin Kobel	6

1980
Mark Bomback	10
Jeff Reardon	8
3 pitchers	7

1981
Neil Allen	7
Pat Zachry	7
Pete Falcone	5
Mike Scott	5

1982
Craig Swan	11
Charlie Puleo	9
Pete Falcone	8

1983
Jesse Orosco	13
Ed Lynch	10
Mike Torrez	10

1984
Dwight Gooden	17
Ron Darling	12
Walt Terrell	11

1985
Dwight Gooden	24*
Ron Darling	16
Rick Aguilera	10
Ed Lynch	10

1986
Bob Ojeda	18
Dwight Gooden	17
Sid Fernandez	16

1987
Dwight Gooden	15
Ron Darling	12
Sid Fernandez	12

1988
David Cone	20
Dwight Gooden	18
Ron Darling	17

1989
David Cone	14
Ron Darling	14
Sid Fernandez	14

1990
Frank Viola	20
Dwight Gooden	19
David Cone	14

1991
David Cone	14
Dwight Gooden	13
Frank Viola	13

1992
Sid Fernandez	14
David Cone	13
Dwight Gooden	10

1993
Dwight Gooden	12
Bret Saberhagen	7
Frank Tanana	7

1994
Bret Saberhagen	14
Bobby Jones	12
Doug Linton	6

1995
Bobby Jones	10
Jason Isringhausen	9
Dave Mlicki	9

1996
Mark Clark	14
Bobby Jones	12
Pete Harnisch	8

1997
Bobby Jones	15
Rick Reed	13
Mark Clark	8
Dave Mlicki	8

1998
Al Leiter	17
Rick Reed	16
Bobby Jones	9

1999
Orel Hershiser	13
Al Leiter	13
Masato Yoshii	12

2000
Al Leiter	16
Mike Hampton	15
3 pitchers	11

2001
Kevin Appier	11
Al Leiter	11
Steve Trachsel	11

2002
Al Leiter	13
Pedro Astacio	12
Steve Trachsel	11

2003
Steve Trachsel	16
Al Leiter	15
Tom Glavine	9
Jae Seo	9

2004
Steve Trachsel	12
Tom Glavine	11
Al Leiter	10

2005
Pedro Martinez	15
Tom Glavine	13
Kris Benson	10

2006
Tom Glavine	15
Steve Trachsel	15
Orlando Hernandez	9
Pedro Martinez	9

2007
John Maine	15
Oliver Perez	15
Tom Glavine	13

2008
Johan Santana	16
Mike Pelfrey	13
Oliver Perez	10
John Maine	10

2009
Johan Santana	13
Mike Pelfrey	10
John Maine	7
Livan Hernandez	7

2010
Mike Pelfrey	15
R.A. Dickey	11
Johan Santana	11

2011
Dillon Gee	13
Jonathan Niese	11
Chris Capuano	11

Bold = Sets Team Record
Ital. = Ties Team Record
* = Led NL or tied

Single Season Wins Leaders

	W	Player	Year
1.	25	Tom Seaver	1969
2.	24	Dwight Gooden	1985
3.	22	Tom Seaver	1975
4.	21	Jerry Koosman	1976
		Tom Seaver	1972
6.	20	David Cone	1988
		Tom Seaver	1971
		Frank Viola	1990
9.	19	Dwight Gooden	1990
		Jerry Koosman	1968
		Tom Seaver	1973
12.	18	Dwight Gooden	1988
		Bob Ojeda	1986
		Tom Seaver	1970
15.	17	Ron Darling	1988
		Dwight Gooden	1984, 1986
		Jerry Koosman	1969
		Al Leiter	1998
		Jon Matlack	1976
21.	16	Ron Darling	1985
		Sid Fernandez	1986
		Al Leiter	2000
		Jon Matlack	1975
		Rick Reed	1998
		Tom Seaver	1967, 1968
		Steve Trachsel	2003
		Johan Santana	2008

Career Wins Leaders

	W	Player
1.	198	Tom Seaver
2.	157	Dwight Gooden
3.	140	Jerry Koosman
4.	99	Ron Darling
5.	98	Sid Fernandez
6.	95	Al Leiter
7.	82	Jon Matlack
8.	81	David Cone
9.	74	Bobby Jones
10.	66	Steve Trachsel
11.	61	Tom Glavine
12.	59	Rick Reed
		Craig Swan
14.	51	Bob Ojeda
	50	Mike Pelfrey
16.	48	John Franco
17.	47	Tug McGraw
		Jesse Orosco
19.	43	Al Jackson
20.	41	Gary Gentry
		Pat Zachry
22.	40	Johan Santana
23.	39	John Maine
24.	38	Jack Fisher
		Ed Lynch
		Frank Viola

Extra Base Hits

YEAR-BY-YEAR EXTRA BASE HITS LEADERS

1962
Frank Thomas	60
Charlie Neal	34
Jim Hickman	33

1963
Jim Hickman	44
Ron Hunt	42
Tim Harkness	25

1964
Joe Christopher	50
Ed Kranepool	33
Charley Smith	32

1965
Charley Smith	39
Ed Kranepool	38
Ron Swoboda	37

1966
Ken Boyer	44
Ed Kranepool	33
Ed Bressoud	30

1967
Tommy Davis	48
Ron Swoboda	33
Ed Kranepool	28

1968
Cleon Jones	47
Ron Swoboda	31
Art Shamsky	30

1969
Tommie Agee	53
Cleon Jones	41
Art Shamsky	26

1970
Tommie Agee	61
Donn Clendenon	43
Cleon Jones	43

1971
Cleon Jones	44
Ed Kranepool	38
Tommie Agee	33

1972
Tommie Agee	36
John Milner	31
Duffy Dyer	28

1973
Rusty Staub	52
Wayne Garrett	39
John Milner	38

1974
Rusty Staub	43
John Milner	39
Cleon Jones	37

1975
Dave Kingman	59
Rusty Staub	53
Felix Millan	40

1976
Dave Kingman	52
John Milner	44
Ed Kranepool	28
Felix Millan	28

1977
John Stearns	38
John Milner	35
Steve Henderson	34
Lenny Randle	34

1978
Steve Henderson	49
Lee Mazzilli	49
John Stearns	40

1979
Joel Youngblood	48
Lee Mazzilli	43
John Stearns	40

1980
Lee Mazzilli	51
Joel Youngblood	36
Steve Henderson	33

1981
Dave Kingman	36
Hubie Brooks	27
Lee Mazzilli	25

1982
Dave Kingman	47
Mookie Wilson	39
George Foster	38

1983
George Foster	49
Darryl Strawberry	48
Mookie Wilson	38

1984
Darryl Strawberry	57
Mookie Wilson	48
George Foster	47

1985
Gary Carter	50
Darryl Strawberry	48
Keith Hernandez	48

1986
Darryl Strawberry	59
Keith Hernandez	48
Len Dykstra	42

1987
Darryl Strawberry	76
Kevin McReynolds	67
Howard Johnson	59

1988
Darryl Strawberry	69
Kevin McReynolds	59
Howard Johnson	46

1989
Howard Johnson	80
Darryl Strawberry	56
Kevin McReynolds	50

1990
Howard Johnson	63
Gregg Jefferies	58
Darryl Strawberry	56

1991
Howard Johnson	76*
Kevin McReynolds	49
Gregg Jefferies	30

1992
Eddie Murray	55
Bobby Bonilla	42
Daryl Boston	27

1993
Bobby Bonilla	58
Eddie Murray	56
Jeff Kent	45

1994
Bobby Bonilla	45
Jeff Kent	43
Ryan Thompson	33

1995
Rico Brogna	51
Bobby Bonilla	47
Jeff Kent	45

1996
Bernard Gilkey	77
Todd Hundley	74
Lance Johnson	61

1997
John Olerud	57
Todd Hundley	53
Butch Huskey	52

1998
Brian McRae	62
John Olerud	62
Mike Piazza	56

1999
Robin Ventura	70
Edgardo Alfonzo	69
Mike Piazza	65

2000
Edgardo Alfonzo	67
Mike Piazza	64
Todd Zeile	61

2001
Mike Piazza	65
Robin Ventura	41
Edgardo Alfonzo	39

2002
Mike Piazza	58
Mo Vaughn	44
Edgardo Alfonzo	42

2003
Ty Wigginton	53
Cliff Floyd	45
3 players	36

2004
Mike Cameron	61
Cliff Floyd	44
Kaz Matsui	41
Mike Piazza	41

2005
David Wright	70
Cliff Floyd	58
Carlos Beltran	52

2006
Carlos Beltran	80
David Wright	71
Carlos Delgado	70

2007
David Wright	73
Carlos Beltran	69
Jose Reyes	60

2008
David Wright	77
Jose Reyes	72
Carlos Beltran	72

2009
Daniel Murphy	54
David Wright	52
Angel Pagan	39

2010
David Wright	68
Ike Davis	53
Jose Reyes	50

2011
Jose Reyes	54
Carlos Beltran	47
David Wright	38

Bold = Sets Team Record
Ital. = Ties Team Record
*= Led NL or tied

Single Season Extra Base Hits Leaders

	XB	PLAYERS	YEAR
1.	80	Carlos Beltran	2006
		Howard Johnson	1989
3.	77	Bernard Gilkey	1996
		David Wright	2008
5.	76	Howard Johnson	1991
		Darryl Strawberry	1987
7.	74	Todd Hundley	1996
8.	73	David Wright	2007
	72	Jose Reyes	2008
		Carlos Beltran	2008
11.	71	David Wright	2006
		Carlos Delgado	2008
13.	70	Carlos Delgado	2006
		Robin Ventura	1999
		David Wright	2005
16.	69	Edgardo Alfonzo	1999
		Darryl Strawberry	1988
		Carlos Beltran	2007
19.	68	David Wright	2010
20.	67	Edgardo Alfonzo	2000
21.	66	Kevin McReynolds	1987
		Jose Reyes	2006
23.	65	Mike Piazza	1999, 2001
25.	64	Mike Piazza	2000

Career Extra Base Hits Leaders

	XB	PLAYER
1.	481	David Wright
2.	469	Darryl Strawberry
3.	424	Howard Johnson
4.	415	Mike Piazza
5.	402	Jose Reyes
6.	374	Carlos Beltran
7.	368	Ed Kranepool
8.	346	Edgardo Alfonzo
9.	308	Cleon Jones
10.	292	Mookie Wilson
11.	289	Kevin McReynolds
12.	249	Keith Hernandez
		Todd Hundley
14.	238	Lee Mazzilli
15.	230	Dave Kingman
16.	212	Rusty Staub
17.	208	John Stearns
18.	207	Carlos Delgado
19.	206	John Milner
20.	203	Tommie Agee
21.	201	Bobby Bonilla
22.	200	George Foster
23.	196	Jerry Grote
24.	178	Cliff Floyd
25.	177	John Olerud

Notes

1. Year-by-Year Recaps

1   Peter Golenbock, *Amazin': The Miraculous History of New York's Most Beloved Baseball Team* (New York: St. Martin's Griffin, 2002), 132.

2   Maury Allen, *The Incredible Mets* (New York: Paperback Library, 1969), 39.

3   Golenbock, *Amazin'*, 118.

4   Allen, *The Incredible Mets*, 43.

5   Ibid., 42.

6   Golenbock, *Amazin',* 172.

7   Ibid., 232.

8   Ibid., 234.

9   Ibid., 330.

10   1981 Mets Information Guide, 2.

11   "Saberhagen Admits to 'Joke,'" *New York Times*, July 28, 1993.

12   "Flashback: Mets Fire Coaches During Subway Series," *New York Post*, June 8, 2008 (reprinted from June 6, 1999, article).

13   "Mets Pull Out of the Rodriguez Sweepstakes," *New York Times*, November 14, 2000.

14   "A-Rod regrets saying no to Mets, doesn't make same mistake with Yankees," *New York Daily News*, March 25, 2008.

2. Player Profiles

1   "BASEBALL; Friends And Family Bid Agee Farewell," *New York Times*, 1/27/01.

2   Ibid.

3   Maury Allen, *After the Miracle* (London: Franklin Watts, 1989), 188.

4   "Mets Get Agee for Davis and Fisher in Completing Trade With White Sox," *New York Times*, 12/16/67.

5   "Mets Award Agee Center Field And a Salary Raise to $25,000," *New York Times*, 1/26/68.

6   "Sports of The Times; Amazing Mets Lose Their Leadoff Man," *New York Times*, 1/23/01.

7   "Agee Hurt as Mets Bow," *New York Times*, 3/10/68.

8   New York National League Baseball Club, Mets Baseball: The 25th Season, "An *Amazin'* Era," 1986 Information Guide, 1986.

9   "Mets Top Expos 4-2, on Agee's 2 Homers," *New York Times*, 4/11/69.

10   "Palmer Calls Scouting Report on Gentry as Pitcher and Batter Misleading," *New York Times*, 10/15/69.

11   "Mets, Led By Agee, Beat Orioles 5–0; Lead 201 In Series," *New York Times*, 10/15/69.

12   "Palmer Calls Scouting Report on Gentry as Pitcher and Batter Misleading," *New York Times*, 10/15/69.

13   "Mets Send Agee to the Astros for Pair," *New York Times*, 11/28/72.

14   "Sports of The Times; Amazing Mets Lose Their Leadoff Man," *New York Times*, 1/23/01.

15   Mets 2001 Media Guide.

16   "Beltrán Brings Great Hope to 'New Mets'," *New York Times*, 1/12/05.

17   "Forget the Strikeout. Fans Need to Move On," *New York Times*, 10/21/06.

18   "Mets Are Packing Roster For the Early Bird Specials," *New York Times*, 2/20/07.

19   "Santana's Here, and Mets Are 'Team to Beat,'" *New York Times*, 2/17/08.

20   "Minaya Dials Back Mets' Ire on Beltrán," *New York Times*, 1/15/10.

21   "Beltrán Says His Feelings Have Healed," *New York Times*, 2/22/10.

22   "Beltrán's Knee Is Strong and So Are His Numbers," *New York Times*, 6/27/11.

23   "Beltrán Returns, Full of Emotion, as the Mets Fall," *New York Times*, 7/16/10.

24   "Beltrán Makes a Move the Mets Were Hoping For," *New York Times*, 2/28/11.

25   "With 3 Homers, Beltrán Fills Power Void Left by Davis," *New York Times*, 5/13/11.

26   "Beltrán All but Gone to the Giants," *New York Times*, 7/27/11.

27   Gary Carter with John Hough Jr., *A Dream Season* (New York: Harcourt, 1987), 38.

28   "Fernandez Remains a Hot Arm and Bat," *New York Times*, 9/27/89.

29   "Mets Say Farewell to Carter and Hernandez and to an Era," *New York Times*, 10/4/89.

30   "Mets Seek Trade Before Deadline to Bolster Attack," *New York Times*, June 15, 1969.

31   Allen, *After the Miracle*, 61.

32   Ibid., 70–71.

33   "Donn Clendenon, 70, MVP for the 1969 'Miracle Mets,'" *New York Times*, 9/19/05.

34   "As Vaudevillians, Mets find Bel Canto Tough to Hit," *New York Times*, 11/8/69.

35   Allen, *After the Miracle*, 61.

36   Ibid., 63.

37   Ibid., 65.

38   Ibid., 66.

39   "Sports of the Times; Compassion From One Who Knows," *New York Times*, 2/26/00.

40   Ibid.

41   "Thin Man Plus 20 Pounds," *Baseball Digest*, 9/56.

42   Peter Golenbock, *Amazin': the Miraculous History of New York's Most Beloved Baseball Team* (New York: St. Martin's Griffin, 2003), 132.

43   "They Said It," *Sports Illustrated*, 3/1/68.

44   Dan Zachofsky, *Idols of the Spring: Baseball Interviews about Preseason Training* (Jefferson, NC: McFarland, 2001), 170.

45   "He Reached 20 Before Koufax Did," *Baseball Digest*, 12/63.

46   Ibid.

47   William Ryczek, *The Amazin' Mets, 1962-69* (Jefferson, NC: McFarland, 2008), 60.

48   "He Reached 20 Before Koufax Did," *Baseball Digest*, 12/63.

49   Ibid.

50   Ibid.

51   Ryczek, *The Amazin' Mets*, 60–61.

52   "Roger Craig's Little Secret—the Pitch That Has Changed Baseball," UPI, 6/8/86.

53 "Delgado Makes a Stand by Taking a Seat," *New York Times*, 7/21/04.

54 Allen, *After the Miracle*, 111.

55 Peter Golenbock, *Amazin'*, 185.

56 Ibid., 288.

57 Allen, *After the Miracle*, 109

58 Ibid, p111.

59 Ibid, p234.

60 "Beware Of The Cliff Dwellers," *Sports Illustrated*, 6/21/71.

61 Ibid.

62 Ibid.

63 Peter Golenbock, *Amazin'*, 353.

64 "He's Their Kind of Ballplayer," *Christian Science Monitor* reprinted by the *Anchorage Daily News*, 10/21/73.

65 Keith Hernandez with Mike Bryan, *If at First: A Season with the Mets* (New York: McGraw-Hill, 1986), 12.

66 Hernandez, *If at First*, 11.

67 Jerry Mitchell, *The Amazin' Mets* (1974), 64.

68 Peter Golenbock, *Amazin'*, 117.

69 "A Family Tradition," New York Mets Official Scorecard, 1996.

70 "Home Grown and Catching On," Mets Magazine and Official Scorebook, 1992.

71 "A Family Tradition," New York Mets Official Scorecard, 1996.

72 Ibid.

73 "Todd Hundley: The Man Behind the Mask," *Mets Magazine* and Official Scorebook, 1993.

74 "A Family Tradition," New York Mets Official Scorecard, 1996.

75 "Heroes and Dreams," New York Mets Official Scorecard, 1997.

76 Ibid.

77 "Hum, Machiavelli: Valentine Irks Hundley," *New York Times*, 8/21/97.

78 "Hundley Plans Not to Rush His Return From Surgery," *New York Times*, 9/29/97.

79 "Mets Weigh Joining The Chase For Piazza," *New York Times*, 5/15/98.

80 "Speculation on Piazza Leaves Hundley Fuming," *New York Times*, 5/20/98.

81 "A Big Welcome Mat in the Outfield," *New York Times*, 7/11/98.

82 "Toughest Guy in the League," *Baseball Digest*, 10/65.

83 David Cataneo, Casey Stengel: Baseball's 'Old Professor,' (Nashville, TN: Cumberland House, 2003), 53.

84 "Where Are They Now?," *Baseball Digest*, 6/08.

85 "Toughest Guy in the League," *Baseball Digest*, 10/65.

86 Ibid.

87 Maury Allen, *The Incredible Mets* (New York: Paperback Library, 1969), 62.

88 Peter Golenbock, *Amazin'*, 156.

89 George Vecsey, *Joy in Mudville: Being a Complete Account of the Unparalleled History of the New York Mets from Their Most Perturbed Beginnings to Their Amazing Rise to Glory and Renown* (New York: McCall, 1970), 119.

90 "Toughest Guy in the League," *Baseball Digest*, 10/65.

91 "Young Ideas," *New York Daily News*, 11/30/66.

92 "Kingman Joins Mets at Camp," *New York Times*, 3/3/75.

93 "Dave Anderson; Those Kingman and Schmidt Home Runs," *New York Times*, 4/20/76.

94 "Seaver Wins, 3–0; Kingman Hits Pair," *New York Times*, 3/13/75.

95 "His 2d Homer, in 8th, Sinks Astros, 10-9," *New York Times*, 7/21/75.

96 "Mets Win on Kingman Clout," *New York Times*, 9/19/75.

97 "Dave Anderson; Those Kingman and Schmidt Home Runs," *New York Times*, 4/20/76.

98 "Dave Anderson; Those Kingman and Schmidt Home Runs," *New York Times*, 4/20/76.

99 "Kingman-Mets Gap Hardens: He Wants More Than Seaver," *New York Times*, 3/11/77.

100 "Mets Ready To Trade Kingman," *New York Times*, 4/2/77.

101 "Mets Ready To Trade Kingman," *New York Times*, 4/2/77.

102 "The Mets' Kingman: Slugger and Enigma," *New York Times*, 4/17/77.

103 "The Mets' Kingman: Slugger and Enigma," *New York Times*, 4/17/77.

104 "Kingman Prepares To Erase The Past," *New York Times*, 3/9/81.

105 "Dave Kingman Is 'Comfortable' Now," *New York Times*, 3/12/78.

106 "Kingman Prepares To Erase The Past," *New York Times*, 3/9/81.

107 "Kingman Prepares To Erase The Past," *New York Times*, 3/9/81

108 Donn Clendenon, *Miracle in New York* (Sioux Falls, SD: Penmarch, 1999), 110.

109 "Urban Centerfielder," *New York Magazine*, August 18, 1980.

110 "Lee Mazzilli: The Maturing of a Hitter," *Baseball Digest*, December, 1979.

111 "Urban Centerfielder," *New York Magazine*, August 18, 1980.

112 "Lee Mazzilli: The Maturing of a Hitter," *Baseball Digest*, December, 1979.

113 Golenbock, *Amazin'*, 369.

114 Lou Gorman, *High and Inside: My Life in the Front Offices of Baseball*, , 2008, 196.

115 Tug McGraw and Joseph Durso, *Screwball*, 1975, 97–98.

116 Ibid., 100.

117 Ya Gotta Believe, Tug McGraw with Don Yaeger, 2004, 76.

118 Screwball, 58.

119 Ya Gotta Believe, 123.

120 Screwball, 29–31.

121 Ya Gotta Believe, 130–131.

122 Screwball, 33–35.

123 Ya Gotta Believe, 134.

124 Screwball, 46–47.

125 Ya Gotta Believe, 145.

126 Screwball, ix.

127 Ya Gotta Believe, 255.

128 52 Weeks: Interviews with Champions!, Dave Hollander, 2006, 252.

129 "Mets Get Millan in Braves' Trade," *New York Times*, 11/2/72.

130 "Mr. Millan All Pro and No Con," New York Mets Program and Scorecard, 1973.

131 "Millan Bewails His Error, Saying Ball 'Didn't Hop,'" *New York Times*, 10/14/73.

132 "Millan Like in 'Me On Base," New York Mets Program and Scorecard, 1976.

133 Ibid.

134 The Yankee Years, Joe Torre and Tom Verducci, 2009, 4.

135 52 Weeks: Interviews with Champions!, 254.

136 Ibid.

137 "Felix Is One Sweet Ballplayer," *Sports Illustrated*, 7/22/68.

138 Ibid.

139 "Felix Millan—Close to the Perfect Player," *Baseball Digest*, October 1969.

140 Ibid.

141 52 Weeks: Interviews with Champions!, 254.

142 "Millan Had 12-Year Chokehold on Majors," Sarasota Herald-Tribune.

143   "Mets Sign Ordóñez, a Defector from Cuba," *New York Times*, 2/9/94.

144   "Cuban Players Defect, But Often with a Cost," *New York Times*, 4/25/99.

145   "Mets Sign Ordóñez," *New York Times*, 2/9/94.

146   "'O' Stands For Ordóñez Ovations," *New York Times*, 4/2/96.

147   Ibid.

148   "Again, Ordóñez's Errors Reap Bad Consequences," *New York Times*, 8/25/96.

149   "He Does It His Way, and It's Magnificent," *New York Times*, 12/5/97.

150   "Mets' Confidence Game: Ordóñez Delivers for Valentine." *New York Times*, 4/12/98.

151   Ibid.

152   "Mets sign Ordóñez to $19 Million Pact," *New York Times*, 1/26/00.

153   "Ordóñez Needs to Alter His Offensive Approach," *New York Times*, 2/28/01.

154   "Mets Trying To Bolster Ordóñez's Bat," *New York Times*, 3/26/01.

155   "Ordóñez Embraces New Role as a Hitter," *New York Times*, 2/26/02.

156   "New Talent and Smarts Put Padres in the Hunt," *New York Times*, 5/9/04.

157   "Mets Weigh Joining the Chase for Piazza," *New York Times*, 5/16/98.

158   "Speculation on Piazza Leaves Hundley Fuming," *New York Times*, 5/20/98.

159   "Doubleday Takes Wheel and Revs Up the Mets," *New York Times*, 5/31/98.

160   "Mets Get Piazza's Power at Bat and at the Gate," *New York Times*, 5/23/98.

161   Ibid.

162   "Piazza Swings a Bat and Suddenly It's the '80s," *New York Times*, 5/24/98.

163   "Will the Numbers Work Out for Piazza as He Shifts to New York?" *New York Times*, 5/24/98.

164   "Another Silent Night For Mets' Meek Bats," *New York Times*, 7/21/98.

165   "The Mets Agree to Make Piazza Baseball's Richest Player; Leiter Says He Is Close to a $32 Million Deal," *New York Times*, 10/25/98.

166   "Piazza, Risking Boos, Accepts Challenge with Mets," *New York Times*, 10/27/98.

167   "Piazza Embraces New York Challenge," *New York Times*, 4/5/99.

168   "Letting Hits Fall Where They May," *New York Times*, 6/23/99.

169   "Struggling to Move Beyond OK," *New York Times*, 6/5/99.

170   "First Things First; Mets Need to Win," *New York Times*, 9/18/99.

171   "Mets Trailing for Wild Card after 6 Days of Disaster," *New York Times*, 9/27/99.

172   "The Planets Might Just Be Aligned for This Team," *New York Times*, 10/2/99.

173   "The Mets Eliminate Cincinnati, the Doubts and the Frustration," *New York Times*, 10/5/99.

174   "More Mystical Success for Mets at Shea," *New York Times*, 10/10/99.

175   "Piazza Is Hurt; Mets Are Furious," *New York Times*, 7/9/00.

176   "A Strong Hint of 1986 Years Later," *New York Times*, 7/9/00.

177   "Another Chapter in the Turf Wars of New York," *New York Times*, 7/10/00.

178   "Groggy and Angry, Piazza Rips Clemens," *New York Times*, 7/10/00.

179   "The Man Who Made the Mets," *New York Times*, 10/17/00.

180   "Clemens at His Best, and Most Bizarre," *New York Times*, 10/23/00.

181   "Piazza Is Calm as Teammates Scorn Clemens," *New York Times*, 10/24/00.

182   "The Mets Lose Series, But Their Pride Is Intact," *New York Times*, 10/27/00.

183   "One Is Not the Loneliest Number," *New York Times*, 3/5/01.

184   "Emotional Return Home for Mets," *New York Times*, 9/21/01.

185   "Not Just Another Day on the Job," *New York Times*, 9/22/01.

186   "Business Is Anything but Usual," *New York Times*, 9/22/01.

187   "The Mets Run Out of Miracles," *New York Times*, 9/30/01.

188   "Piazza's Mighty Swat Breaks Fisk's Mark," *New York Times*, 5/6/04.

189   "Record Broken, First Base Looms Larger for Piazza," *New York Times*, 5/7/04.

190   "Piazza Does Not Rule Out Retiring After Season," *New York Times*, 1/25/05.

191   "Piazza Eager to Focus on Being Better Hitter," *New York Times*, 2/18/05.

192   "As Bodies Mull Retirement, Two Aging Baseball Stars Play On," *New York Times*, 9/28/05.

193   Ibid.

194   "For Piazza and Mets Fans, a Last Embrace Before Letting Go," *New York Times*, 10/3/05.

195   Nick Friedman, Mike Piazza, 2007, 27.

196   Ibid.

197   "Reyes Again Justifies a Scout's Act of Faith," *New York Times*, 8/29/03.

198   "Reyes Receives Little Chance to Show His Stuff in Debut," *New York Times*, 3/9/03.

199   "Reyes's Arrival Is Special Moment for the Mets," *New York Times*, 6/11/03.

200   Ibid.

201   "Trachsel Supports the Star Turn by Reyes with a One-Hitter," *New York Times*, 6/16/03.

202   "His Job Secure, Reyes Lifts the Mets," *New York Times*, 7/1/03.

203   "Reyes Finds the Going Is Lonely in St. Lucie," *New York Times*, 5/6/04.

204   "Mets' Manager and Mentor: Randolph Counsels Reyes," *New York Times*, 6/21/05.

205   "With Speed at Top, Mets Have New Energy," *New York Times*, 6/6/05.

206   "Reyes Hits Three Homers, But Hernández Falters," *New York Times*, 8/16/06.

207   "With Big Game, Reyes Shows Why He's an Igniter," *New York Times*, 10/19/06.

208   "A Message Is Delivered with the Benching of Reyes," *New York Times*, 7/8/07.

209   "Mets Complete Stunning Collapse," *New York Times*, 9/30/07.

210   "Manuel Stakes His Ground," *New York Times*, 6/19/08.

211   "A Celebration by Reyes Adds Heat to a Rivalry," *New York Times*, 7/25/08.

212   "While Jeter Chases History, Frustration Builds for Reyes," *New York Times*, 9/9/09.

213   "Mets' Reyes Has Mates on the Move," *New York Times*, 6/19/10.

214   "Reyes Postpones Contract Talks as Athletics Drop Mets," *New York Times*, 6/21/11.

215   "Reyes Has Something to Chase: The Mets' First Batting Crown," *New York Times*, 9/6/11.

216 "Reyes Hits, Then Sits and Eventually Celebrates," *New York Times*, 9/28/11.

217 "Some Minor League Machinations Gave Minnesota an Ace," *New York Times*, 9/12/04.

218 "Astros Sharing Their Wealth from Venezuela," *New York Times*, 10/26/05.

219 "The Ace Does Nothing to Quell Fears of His Decline," *New York Times*, 6/26/10.

220 "Santana Easily Navigates Bumper-to-Bumper Coverage," *New York Times*, 2/7/08.

221 "Pitches and Spirits Are Up in Santana's Debut," *New York Times*, 3/1/08.

222 "Santana's Change-up: Hitters Never See It Coming," *New York Times*, 3/3/08.

223 "Santana's Start Helps Mets Forget Finish," *New York Times*, 4/1/08.

224 "With Santana in Role of Ace, Mets Draw Even for Wild-Card," *New York Times*, 9/27/08.

225 "Santana Is on the Road to Recovery," *New York Times*, 12/6/08.

226 "Santana Is Brilliant, and the Mets Need Him to Be," *New York Times*, 4/10/09.

227 "Blending In; Standing Out: Entering Second Season with Mets, Santana Finds His Rhythm in Clubhouse," *New York Times*, 4/6/09.

228 "Santana's Return Is Still Months Away," *New York Times*, 2/17/11.

229 "Seaver: Cast in Mold of a Pro." New York Mets 1972 Program and Scorecard.

230 "Sportsman of the Year: Tom Seaver," *Sports Illustrated*, 12/22/69.

231 Tom Seaver with Dick Schaap, The Perfect Game, 1970, 19.

232 Ibid., 26.

233 Tom Seaver with Steve Jacobson, Baseball Is My Life, 1973, 6–7.

234 Ibid., 82–83.

235 "Tom Seaver Picks His 10 Most Memorable Games," *Baseball Digest*, 11/88.

236 Ibid.

237 "Tom Seaver: An *Amazin'* All-Star Rookie," Boys' Life, 5/68.

238 "Maybe It's Time to Break Up the Mets," *Sports Illustrated*, 9/22/69.

239 "Tom Seaver: An *Amazin'* All-Star Rookie."

240 The Perfect Game, 72.

241 "Tom Seaver and the Art of Power Pitching," Boys' Life, 9/77.

242 The Perfect Game, 41–43.

243 Baseball Is My Life," 101.

244 Ibid., 102.

245 "Tom Seaver Picks His 10 Most Memorable Games."

246 Tim McCarver with Jim Moskovitz and Danny Peary, Tim McCarver's Diamond Gems, 2008, 186.

247 The Perfect Game, 66.

248 Ibid., 86.

249 Ibid., 48.

250 Ibid., 50–51.

251 "Tom Seaver Picks His 10 Most Memorable Games."

252 Ibid.

253 Ibid.

254 Ibid.

255 "Seaver Gets Nos. 20 and 200 in 3–0 Victory Over Pirates," *New York Times*, 9/2/75.

256 "Mets, Seaver Agree to a Three-Year Contract," *New York Times*, 4/6/76.

257 "Mets Front Office Blasted by Seaver," *New York Times*, 2/27/77.

258 Ibid.

259 "Mets Report Some Teams Seek Seaver," *New York Times*, 3/16/77.

260 "Seaver Angry as Mets Are Defeated, 4–3," *New York Times*, 5/16/77.

261 "Seaver Seems Upset by Trade Talk After His 5-Hitter Defeats Astros," *New York Times*, 6/13/77.

262 "Seaver's Farewell Is Tearful and Bitter," *New York Times*, 6/17/77.

263 "Seaver Rejoins Mets with a Year Guaranteed," *New York Times*, 12/17/82.

264 "Tom Seaver Comes Home," New York Mets 1983 Official Scorebook.

265 "51,024 See Mets Win 2–0" *New York Times*, 4/6/83.

266 "Everything Under Control," *New York Times*, 4/6/83.

267 "300! Seaver Arrives Smoothly at Milestone," *New York Times*, 8/5/85.

268 "Seaver Feels 'Terrific' as He Returns to Shea," *New York Times*, 6/7/87.

269 "Whether Winning or Losing, Mets Find the Middle Ground," *New York Times*, 7/16/05.

270 "From Colt .45s to the Mets '86," *New York Times*, 7/13/86.

271 Ibid.

272 Jacob Kanarek, From First to Worst: The New York Mets, 1973–1977, 2008, 65.

273 Ibid., 94.

274 "Mets Win on Kingman Clout," *New York Times*, 9/19/75.

275 "ESPN on Mark to Last Pick for Expansion Draft," *New York Times*, 11/18/97.

276 "Rusty—Budding Bat King," *Baseball Digest*, 12/68.

277 "From Colt .45s to the Mets '86."

278 "Rusty—Budding Bat King."

279 "History With a Bite," *New York Times*, 10/8/86.

280 Ibid.

281 "Dome Anniversary," *New York Times*, 4/8/85.

282 "Wine Talk: A Voice of the Mets Has a Nose for Wine," *New York Times*, 8/1/90.

283 "From Colt .45s to the Mets '86."

284 "Staub Seeking Good New Days," *New York Times*, 4/18/81.

285 "Staub Battles Pounds to Fatten Bankroll," *New York Times*, 3/12/81.

286 "Staub a Master in Pinch," *New York Times*, 6/28/83.

287 "Shake Down the Memories," *New York Times*, 6/24/84.

288 "Staub Plans to Stay Retired," *New York Times*, 3/3/86.

289 "The Diet Secrets of Rusty Staub," *New York Times*, 6/30/85.

290 "Mets Recover from Marathon Game," *New York Times*, 4/30/85.

291 "For Rusty, It's All about Giving," *New York Post*, 6/14/04.

292 "From Colt .45s to the Mets '86."

293 "Next Pick: Strawberry," *Sports Illustrated*, 4/7/80.

294 "Mets Halt Contract Talks with Strawberry," Associated Press, 7/14/90.

295 "Please Check All Baggage: Yanks Sign Strawberry," *New York Times*, 6/20/95.

296 Jerry Mitchell, *The Amazing Mets*, 1974, 73.

297 Ibid., 110–111.

298 Golenbock, *Amazin'*, 2002, 134.

299 "With 'Marvelous,' Pay's the Thing," *New York Times*, August 12, 1962.

300 *The Amazing Mets*, 77.

301   Ibid.
302   Janet Paskin, *Tales from the New York Mets*, 2004, 173.
303   Ralph Kiner with Joe Gergen, *Kiner's Corner*, 1987, 52.
304   "Throneberry Is Sent to Buffalo, *New York Times*, 5/10/63.
305   Ibid.

3. The Strategists

1   Peter Golenbock, *Amazin': the Miraculous History of New York's Most Beloved Baseball Team* (New York: St. Martin's Griffin, 2003), 374.
2   Ibid., 300.
3   "Terry Collins Fever: Try Not to Catch It," *Wall Street Journal*, 11/24/10.
4   "Collins says he's learned from mistakes; expects Mets to compete next year," *New York Post*, 11/24/10.
5   "Beltran No Longer 'Center' of Attention For Mets," *New York Post*, 3/1/11.
6   Golenbock, *Amazin'*, 325.
7   "Mets New Manager Mixes Intellect With fire," *New York Times*, 6/19/08.
8   "Manuel Addresses Needs, Finding Humor in Mets' Flaws," *New York Times*, 11/10/08.
9   "Mets and Manuel Agree to Two-Year Contract," *New York Times*, 10/3/08.
10   "Mets' Manuel Is in Uniform as He Mixes and Matches," *New York Times*, June 17, 2009.
11   "Despite It All, Manuel Retains Passion for the Job," *New York Times*, 9/30/09.
12   "Mets Bench Coach Prefers Being Heard and Not Seen," *New York Times*, 2/24/07.
13   "Manuel Plans to Give Mets a Lesson in Selfless Baseball," *New York Times*, 10/4/08.
14   "Manuel's Positive Energy Ignites Mets," *New York Times*, 6/6/10.
15   "Pressed Together, Mets Feel The Heat," *New York Times*, 5/22/10.
16   "Mets and Randolph Launch a New Era," *New York Times*, 11/5/04.
17   "Randolph is Named to Lead the Mets," *New York Times*, 11/4/04.
18   "Mets and Randolph Launch a New Era," *New York Times*, 11/5/04.
19   "Now That Search is Over, the Hard Work Begins," *New York Times*, 11/5/04.
20   "Randolph Cites Reasons for the Mets' Collapse," *New York Times*, 10/3/07.
21   Ibid.
22   "Another Great Start, Another Bad Finish," *New York Times*, 6/13/08.
23   "Telling? Mets COO Wilpon declines comment on Randolph," ESPN.com, 5/22/08.
24   "Randolph Remains Seemingly Unfazed by Talk of Firing," *New York Times*, 6/15/08.
25   "Randolph Says He Paid Price for Minaya's Closure," *New York Times*, 6/19/08.
26   "A Split and Mixed Feelings for the Mets," *New York Times*, 6/16/08.
27   "Randolph: Move Was 'Too Early,'" Associated Press, 6/19/08.
28   "Randolph Says He Paid Price for Minaya's Closure," *New York Times*, 6/19/08.
29   "Randolph Hopes to Land Job as Manager This Winter," Associated Press, September 27, 2010.
30   "Willie Randolph 'rooting for' Omar Minaya, hopes for another managing gig while keeping eye on Mets," *New York Daily News*, 9/28/10.

4. The General Managers

1   Peter Golenbock, *Amazin': the Miraculous History of New York's Most Beloved Baseball Team* (New York: St. Martin's Griffin, 2003), 180.
2   Ibid., 181.
3   Ibid., 183.
4   Bing Devine with Tom Wheatley, *The Memoirs of Bing Devine* (Champaign, IL: Sports Publishing, 2004), 29.
5   Ibid., 30.
6   Ibid., 31.
7   Ibid., 32.
8   Golenbock, *Amazin'*, 193-4.
9   *Memoirs of Bing Devine*, 48.
10   Mets Information Guide, 1992, 7.
11   "Mets Sign Bonilla for $29 Million, Making Him Richest in Baseball," *New York Times*, 12/3/91.
12   Mets Information Guide, 1992, 7.
13   *Memoirs of Bing Devine*, 32
14   Golenbock, *Amazin'*, 139.
15   Ibid., 199.
16   "Phillips Succeeding His Mentor," *New York Times*, 7/17/97.
17   "More Trades Are Possible, Phillips Says," *New York Times*, 5/26/98.
18   "The Mets Return Phillips to General Manager's Job," *New York Times*, 11/17/98.
19   "The Mets Leave Options Open on General Manager," *New York Times*, 11/10/98.
20   "Mets Shake Up Staff, Dismissing 3 Coaches," *New York Times*, 6/6/99.
21   "Steve Phillips' Winter of Content," *New York Times*, 3/26/00.
22   Ibid.
23   Ibid.
24   "The Man Who Made The Mets," *New York Times*, 10/17/00.
25   "The Mets Re-Sign The Team of Valentine and Phillips," *New York Times*, 11/1/00.
26   "Steve Phillips' Winter of Content," *New York Times*, 3/26/00.
27   "Phillips and Mets Avoid Off-Season Shutout by Adding Appier to the Starting Rotation," *New York Times*, 12/11/00.
28   "Wilpon Might Increase Payroll," *New York Times*, 12/1/01.
29   "Mets Turn Alomar Into Crown Jewel Of Their Infield," *New York Times*, 12/12/01.
30   "Mets' Makeover Has Not Helped Their Offense," *New York Times*, 5/31/02.
31   "No Changes Expected In Mets' Leadership," *New York Times*, 6/20/02.
32   "Mets Tell Phillips: Enough is Enough," *New York Times*, 6/13/03.
33   "ESPN's Phillips Takes Leave After Report of an Affair," *New York Times*, 10/22/09.
34   "Steve Phillips Joins SIRIUS XM's All-Sports Mad Dog Radio Channel," prnewswire.com, 9/30/11.
35   Jerry Mitchell, *The Amazin' Mets* (1974), v.
36   Leonard Koppett, *The New York Mets* (New York: Collier Books,1974), 30.
37   Golenbock, *Amazin'*, 184.

5. The Postseasons

1   Leonard Koppett, *The New York Mets*, 1974, p. 231.
2   Golenbock, *Amazin'*, 241.
3   Ibid., 243.
4   *Ibid., 242.*

5 Vecsey, *Joy in Mudville*, 233.
6 Mitchell, *The Amazing Mets*, 210.
7 Golenbock, *Amazin'*, 244.
8 Ibid., 258.
9 Ibid., 260.
10 Ibid., 259–60.
11 Ibid.
12 Ibid., 522.
13 Ibid., 593.
14 "Pitching Parade Is a Winning Formula; A Base-Running Blunder Dooms the Dodgers," *New York Times*, October 5, 2006.
15 "Mets Clinch Berth in NLCS with Sweep of Dodgers," *USA Today*, October 8, 2006.

ACKNOWLEDGMENTS

I was blessed when I found an outstanding publisher almost the moment I sent out the original proposal for the book. Triumph Books Editorial Director Tom Bast took an immediate liking to the project and laid the foundation for the book. Don Gulbrandsen handled the editorial aspect and gave me plenty of room to create what I thought was an essential publication for any Mets fan.

I must give thanks to the public relations departments of the Diamondbacks, Phillies, Nationals, Braves, Pirates, Dodgers, Tigers, Rays, and Rangers, all of which were kind enough to give me access to their players, coaches, and front office personnel when needed. The Newark Bears, Winston-Salem Dash, and Potomac Nationals also granted me access to coaches who happened to be former Mets.

Most of the statistical information was provided by baseball-reference.com, by far the greatest Internet source for any fan of the sport. Two other terrific sources were Ultimatemets.com and MBTN.com, both of which were invaluable as I tried to locate players, comb through fan remembrances of the franchise, and get a handle on uniform numbers.

I also received tremendous help from several Associated Press Broadcasting stringers. Many of the interviews in this book were conducted by Bruce Morton, Mike Moriarty, Greg Echlin, Mike Mancuso, Mike Young, Ryan Leong, Gary McKillips, Craig Heist, and Ted Fleming. Their work was essential at a time when I thought the project was about to go up in flames due to clubhouse credential issues.

My Associated Press co-workers—John Schulz, Jim Militello, John Klobucar, Jack Briggs, Jim Bell, Marv Schneider, Oscar Gabriel, Dave Winslow, and Shelley Adler—were a source of encouragement and allowed me to prattle on about the project as they also took messages from former Mets returning my phone calls.

Guy Fletcher and Jamie Kempton, two journalists whom I hold in high regard, provided tremendous support and told me to push on with the project before I had found a great publisher. And when I drew closer to the deadline, Jackie Elfers provided great encouragment and support as she read countless bio samples. Everyone should have friends like Guy, Jamie, and Jackie, who along with Schulz, Winslow, Gabriel, Morton, and Mancuso lent their help in the final editing process.

The motivation for writing the book was fueled by Ken Gill, who practically dared me to do it following a lengthy, animated baseball argument at a local watering hole. Gill was a year away from becoming Father Kenneth Gill as this book went to press.

Most important, I thank the past and current players, coaches, and managers of the Mets for giving their time to conduct interviews. As luck would have it, the first interview was with Ron Swoboda, one of my favorite players as a kid. Ron gave me 90 minutes of his time in 2008 as we talked about the Mets, New Orleans, Baltimore, and the Giants' recent Super Bowl win over the Patriots. Minutes after I hung up with Swoboda, another Ron—Taylor—told funny stories of his admission into medical school. The two put me at ease and gave me the courage to cold-call many Mets of yesteryear.

Joe Christopher came to my home for an interview. Rod Gaspar spoke to me at length, then helped me arrange other interviews. Taylor, George Theodore, and Ed Hearn gave me early encouragement, telling me how much they liked the potential of the project.

Finally, thanks to my mother and father, Rosemary and David. Mom cultivated my passion for writing and was helpful in critiquing the early stages of the book. Dad gets credit for, among other things, taking me to my first Mets game as we watched Ken Singleton hit two homers to help Tom Seaver pick up his 20th victory on the final day of the 1971 season.

ABOUT THE AUTHOR

Dave Ferry has been with the Associated Press since 1992 after five years as Assistant Director of Public Relations for the Washington Capitals. He grew up in Nanuet, New York, and began his Mets obsession in 1971, chronicling each game in his grade school notebooks.

Ferry lives in Fairfax, Virginia, with his wife, Jacki, and daughter, Jane.

Total Mets is his first book.